AMERICAN
ART DIRECTORY

AMERICAN ART DIRECTORY

1976

Edited by JAQUES CATTELL PRESS

R. R. BOWKER COMPANY
A Xerox Education Company
New York & London

Published by R. R. Bowker Co. (A Xerox Education Company)
1180 Avenue of the Americas, New York, N.Y. 10036

International Standard Book Number: 0-8352-0858-3
International Standard Serial Number: 0065-6968
Library of Congress Catalog Card Number: 99-1016

Printed and bound in the United States of America

Contents

Preface

Entries for over 3300 art museums, art libraries, art associations, and art schools and studios, including universities and colleges with art departments and museums, in the United States, Canada, and abroad are geographically listed in this 46th edition of the *American Art Directory*.

There is an increase in all categories, with reports for over 1600 museums, libraries, and art associations in the United States, 150 in Canada, and 250 major museums abroad. The Art Schools section contains approximately 1200 schools in the United States, 50 in Canada, and 100 abroad.

In addition, there are sections listing children's and junior museums, state arts councils, directors and supervisors of art education in the school systems of the United States, art magazines, newspapers carrying art notes and their critics, scholarships and fellowships, open exhibitions, and traveling exhibitions with booking agencies.

Beginning with this edition, biennial revision has been scheduled to set publication simultaneously with *Who's Who in American Art,* the companion biographical compilation of people active in the art world in the United States, Canada, and Mexico.

The editors wish to thank the officers of the American Federation of Arts for their cooperation and encouragement. Recognition is given to the National Art Education Association for providing the survey of supervisors and directors of art education in state departments of education and public school systems, and to the Associated Councils of the Arts for their directory of state and provincial arts councils.

Without the cooperation of the art organizations in returning questionnaires with new or updated information, compilation of this directory would not have been possible. The editors have made a concerted effort to reproduce the material as accurately and completely as possible within the confines of format and scope. However, the publishers do not assume and hereby disclaim any liability to any party for any loss or damage caused by errors or omissions in the *American Art Directory,* whether such errors or omissions result from negligence, accident, or any other cause.

Criticisms or recommendations concerning the usefulness of this edition are invited. Correspondence should be directed to The Editors, *American Art Directory,* P.O. Box 25001, Tempe, Arizona 85282.

Anne Rhodes, *Administrative Managing Editor*
Fred Scott, *General Manager*
Jaques Cattell Press

Olga Weber, *Managing Editor, Directories—Editorial/Publisher Coordination*
R. R. Bowker Company

April 1976

AFA Committees

EXECUTIVE

Mrs. Jacob M. Kaplan, *Chairman*
Charles Benton
James Biddle
Mrs. Brooke Blake
Francis E. Brennan
J. Carter Brown
Arthur D. Emil
Irvin L. Levy
Thomas M. Messer
David A. Prager
Mrs. Judith Rothschild
Mrs. Otto L. Spaeth
John W. Straus
Dr. Evan H. Turner
Leonard C. Yaseen
Wilder Green, *Director (ex-officio)*

NATIONAL EXHIBITION

Mrs. Ruth Bowman
200 East 66 St., Apt. E-1904
New York, N.Y. 10021

Mr. J. Carter Brown *(Chairman)*
Director
National Gallery of Art
Constitution Ave. at Sixth St., N.W.
Washington, D.C. 20565
(202) 737-4215

Mr. Rand Castile
Director
Japan House Gallery
333 East 47 St.
New York, N.Y. 10017
(212) 832-1155

Mr. Charles Chetham
Director
Smith College Museum of Art
Northampton, Mass. 01060
(413) JU 4-2700

Mr. Richard D. Collins
President
Western States Arts Foundation
1430 Larimer Sq., Suite 200
Denver, Colo. 80202
(305) 571-1561

Mrs. Elaine Dee (Mrs. Leo J.)
Curator, Drawings and Prints
Cooper-Hewitt Museum of Design
9 East 90 St.
New York, N.Y. 10028
(212) 860-2011

Ms. Suzanne Delehanty
Director
Institute of Contemporary Art
University of Pennsylvania
34 & Walnut Sts.
Philadelphia, Pa. 19174
(215) 243-7108

Ms. Virginia Field
Associate Director
Asia House Gallery
112 East 64 St.
New York, N.Y. 10021
(212) PL 1-4210

Mr. Martin L. Friedman
Director
Walker Art Center
Vineland Place
Minneapolis, Minn. 55403
(612) 377-7500

Mr. Lloyd Goodrich
c/o Whitney Museum of American Art
945 Madison Ave.
New York, N.Y. 10021
(212) 249-4100

Mr. Walter Hopps
National Collection of Fine Arts
Eighth & G Sts., N.W.
Washington, D.C. 20560

Mr. George M. Irwin
428 Main St.
Quincy, Ill. 62031
(217) 224-2006

Ms. Una E. Johnson
341 West 24 St.
New York, N.Y. 10011

Mr. William R. Johnston
Assistant Director
Walters Art Gallery
Baltimore, Md. 21201
(301) SA 7-2075

Mrs. Alice M. Kaplan (Mrs. Jacob M.)
760 Park Ave.
New York, N.Y. 10021
(212) 628 1862

Mr. William S. Lieberman
Director, Dept. of Painting and Sculpture
Museum of Modern Art
11 West 53 St.
New York, N.Y. 10019
(212) 956-6100

What Is AFA?

The American Federation of Arts is a private, non-profit, educational organization, whose aim, as outlined in its charter, is to cultivate a greater knowledge and appreciation of historical and contemporary art throughout the United States and of American art abroad. This goal is accomplished, primarily, by the organization and circulation of exhibitions—often to areas not favored with large museums or permanent collections. In recent years, the federation has also been focusing on the development of an expanding film program.

AFA was founded in 1909 with the active encouragement of President Theodore Roosevelt and his secretary of state, Elihu Root. Its charter members included such eminent citizens as Honorable Robert Woods Bliss, William Merrit Chase, Charles L. Freer, Homer St. Gaudens, Henry Cabot Lodge, Andrew W. Mellon, and J. Pierpont Morgan.

The present board of trustees is unique in that it is equally composed of museum professionals and art patrons from across the country. This partnership makes of this board a potential forum of professionals and lay-members, whose concerns can include art issues of substantial and national relevance.

The federation is partially supported by a national membership comprised of both individuals and institutions. More than 400 chapter members—museums, art associations, university art galleries, schools, libraries, and corporations—contribute to and benefit from the programs sponsored by the American Federation of Arts. These include reduced exhibition fees, discounts on art books and magazines, a program providing magazine and book discounts to the members of AFA chapter organizations and many other benefits for both institutions and individuals. AFA also initiates and encourages the development of cooperative programs in the arts among institutions throughout the country.

The exhibitions of the American Federation of Arts program draw upon the rich collections of museums, galleries, corporations, and individuals throughout this country and abroad. The AFA exhibition program encourages lenders to share works of art of all periods with a larger public.

The professional staff of AFA, located in New York, initiates their programs by drawing upon the curatorial expertise of noted scholars. It administers all aspects of its exhibitions, including the selection, assembly, and preparation of works of art for travel, scheduling and continuous monitoring of each exhibition as it tours, and the production of accompanying publications and other educational materials or programs. A National Exhibition Committee lends its professional advice in reviewing proposed exhibition programs. This committee consists of museum directors and representatives of state arts councils.

Contributions to the American Federation of Arts are deductible for income tax purposes.

ART ORGANIZATIONS

ARRANGEMENT AND ABBREVIATIONS
KEY TO ART ORGANIZATIONS

ARRANGEMENT OF DATA

The sequence in which subdivisions of the AMERICAN ART DIREC-TORY are presented will be found in the Table of Contents.

National Organizations are followed by their chapters or branches with name of secretary.

In most cases, average attendance is the annual average for the past two calendar years unless otherwise noted.

Amount of dues is for the year unless otherwise noted.

ABBREVIATIONS AND SYMBOLS

Admin—Administration, Administrative
Adminr—Administrator
Admis—Admission
Adv—Advisory
AM—Morning
Ann—Annual
Approx—Approximate, Approximately
Asn—Association
Assoc—Associate
Asst—Assistant
Bldg—Building
c—circa
Chap—Chapter
Chmn—Chairman
Cl—Closed
Comt—Committee
Corresp—Corresponding
Cur—Curator
Dept—Department
Dir—Director
Dist—District
Div—Division
Ed—Editor

Educ—Education
Enrl—Enrollment
Ent—Entrance
Estab—Established
Exec—Executive
Exten—Extension
Fel(s)—Fellowship(s)
Fri—Friday
Gen—General
Hon—Honorary
Hr—Hour
Inc—Incorporated
Incl—Including
Jr—Junior
Lect—Lecture(s)
Lectr—Lecturer(s)
Librn—Librarian
Mem—Membership
Mgr—Manager
Mo—Monthly
Mon—Monday
Mss—Manuscripts
Nat—National
PM—Afternoon

Pres—President
Prin—Principal
Prog—Program
Pub—Public
Publ—Publication, Publish
Res—Residence, Resident
Sat—Saturday
Schol—Scholarship
Secy—Secretary
Soc—Society
Sr—Senior
Sun—Sunday
Supt—Superintendent
Supv—Supervisor
Thurs—Thursday
Treas—Treasurer
Tues—Tuesday
Tui—Tuition
TV—Television
Univ—University
V.Pres—Vice President
Wk—Week

Wed—Wednesday

Yr—Year(s)

✠Chapter of The American Federation of Arts

*No response to questionnaire
†Used in text to denote collections currently being enlarged.
‡Denotes accredited courses in Architecture.
§On leave of absence.

United States National and Regional Organizations

AMERICAN ABSTRACT ARTISTS
218 W. 20th St, New York, NY 10011.
Leo Rabkin, Pres.
Ruth Eckstein, Secy.
Esphyr Slobodkina, Treas.
Nick Kazak, Exhibition Chmn.
Estab. Nov, 1936, active 1937, to further cause; develop and educate through exhibitions and publications; financed by membership.
Quarterly meetings; mem. 60; dues $7.50.
Exhibitions held at Betty Parsons Gallery.
Activities: Traveling exhibitions organized and circulated.
Publications: Books and catalogs.

AMERICAN ARTISTS PROFESSIONAL LEAGUE, INC.
112 E. 19th St, New York, N.Y. 10003. Tel: (212) 475-6650
Frank C. Wright, Pres.
Mary Keim Tietze, Secy.
Estab. 1928 to advance the cause of fine arts in America, through the promotion of high standards of beauty, integrity and craftsmanship in painting, sculpture and the graphic arts; to emphasize the importance of order and coherent communication as prime requisites of works of art through exhibitions and publications; supported by membership.
Meetings monthly, Oct. - May; mem. 950; dues $15.
Exhibitions: Annually.
Activities: Broadcasts, telecasts; lectures open to the public, quite a few visiting lecturers per year; demonstrations, exhibitions; paintings, sculpture, graphics available to members, state chapters, etc, on consignment; classes for adults and children.
Publications: AAPL News Bulletin, irregularly.
Income: $8000-$10,000.
Attendance: Annual Show 20,000-30,000.

AMERICAN ASSOCIATION OF MUSEUMS
2333 Wisconsin Ave. N.W, Washington, DC 20007.
Tel: (202) 338-5300
Joseph Veach Noble, Pres.
Richard McLanathan, Dir.
Roberta H. Faul, Editor
Estab. 1906, inc. 1920, to promote the welfare and advancement of museums as educational institutions, as agencies of scientific and academic research, and as cultural centers of the community, to encourage interest and inquiries in the field of museology through meetings, reports, papers, discussions, and publications; to increase and diffuse knowledge of all matters relating to museums.
Activities: Answers a wide range of inquiries coming from both the museum field and the general public, provides a museum consultation service which advises museums on problems of operation and program development, and conducts an active international program. Publishes Museum News, 6 times per year. Subscription $12 a year. Official Museum Directory published 1961, 1967, 1971, 1973 and 1975.

AMERICAN ASSOCIATION OF UNIVERSITY WOMEN
2401 Virginia Ave. N.W, Washington, DC 20037.
Tel: (202) 785-7700
Helen B. Wolfe, Gen. Dir.
Estab. 1882 to unite alumnae of different institutions for the purpose of continuing their intellectual growth, furthering the advancement of women, and providing enlightened leadership. Mem. approx. 190,000. Biennial conventions.
Association's Educational Center has available guidance in a wide range of the arts, including studio painting, writing, music structure, acting, dance, development of environmental awareness and action. Awards for women in the creative arts are made annually to enable practicing artists to advance their careers in printmaking, photography, painting, sculpting and film-making.

Library: Small general reference library is maintained at the Educational Center.
Publications: The Journal, magazine, twice a year, Journal, newspaper, 5 times yearly, occasionally feature arts in education.

AMERICAN CERAMIC SOCIETY, INC.—DESIGN DIVISION
65 Ceramic Dr, Columbus, Ohio 43214. Tel: (614) 268-8645
Frank P. Reid, Exec. Dir.
Open weekdays 8:30 AM - 5 PM. Estab. 1899 to promote the arts, science and technology of ceramics. Ann. meeting Apr; Design Division mem. 22, General Society mem. 9400; dues $30, junior $15, student $6.
Library: Primarily journals in areas of science and technology; approx. 100 texts on art and history of ceramics.
Publications: Ceramic Abstracts, bimonthly; Journal, bimonthly; Ceramic Bulletin, monthly.

AMERICAN COUNCIL FOR THE ARTS IN EDUCATION
115 E. 92nd St, New York, NY 10028.
Eldon Winkler, Pres.
Robert Glidden, V.Pres.
Gerry J. Martin, Secy-Treas.
Estab. 1957, a federation of national organizations concerned with furthering the cause of all the arts in American education; financed by Foundation grants, Federal grants, membership, some income from contract research. Winter meeting Jan. or Feb; summer meeting June or July; 22 constituent societies; annual dues $25.

AMERICAN CRAFTS COUNCIL
44 W. 53rd St, New York, NY 10019. Tel: (212) 977-8989
Mrs. Vanderbilt Webb, Chmn. of Board
John L. Baringer, V.Chmn.
Donald L. Wyckoff, Pres.
May E. Walter, Secy.
R. Leigh Glover, Treas.
A nonprofit educational and cultural organization serving a national membership from its headquarters in New York City. Founded in 1943 to stimulate interest in and appreciation of the work of American craftspeople, the Council aims its programs at gaining general recognition of both the concept of craftsmanship and the contribution of the individual as indispensable to an improved environment. The Council is supported solely by membership dues and contributions. Mem. is open to all; dues from $18 annually.
Activities: National program which aids individual craftspeople with particular problems, urges governmental support for crafts, advises on the development of community and national program, works with crafts education programs in schools and colleges, and circulates exhibitions suitable for such institutions. Maintains Museum of Contemporary Crafts, Paul J. Smith, Dir, the only museum in the U.S. devoted solely to crafts and thematic exhibitions exploring the relationship between crafts and other areas of arts and design. Changing exhibitions; one-man shows. Publishes Craft Horizons, Rose Slivka, Editor, award-winning bimonthly magazine devoted to all aspects of craftsmanship. Maintains a Research and Education Department, Lois Moran, Dir, which includes the largest library of contemporary craft books in the U.S; operates a slide/film service called Your Portable Museum; and maintains portfolio files on craftspeople with both pictorial and biographical information useful to researchers, gallery owners. The Council operates an active regional program with representatives, elected periodically, to initiate Council-sponsored activities and to cooperate with other organizations' events throughout the country.
Following is a list of Regional Trustees:
Northeast Region:
Mary Nyburg, Box 24, Garrison, MD 21005
North Central Region:
James Dugdale, 1223 Clara Ave, Joliet, IL 60435
Northwest Region:
Ms. Lin Lipetz, 2207 Broadway E, Seattle, WA 98102

Southeast Region:
   Herb Cohen, Studios 2, Inc, Rte 1, Box 316,
   Blowing Rock, NC 28605
South Central Region:
   Bill Alexander, Art Dept, Colorado State University,
   Ft. Collins, CO 80521
Southwest Region:
   Ms. Dextra Frankel, 1970 S. Coast Hwy, Laguna Beach, CA 92651

THE AMERICAN FEDERATION OF ARTS
   41 E. 65th St, New York, NY 10021. Tel: (212) 988-7700
Mrs. Jacob M. Kaplan, Pres, Board of Trustees
Thomas M. Messer, V.Pres.
Mrs. Brooke Blake, V.Pres.
Francis E. Brennan, Secy.
David A. Prager, Treas.
Wilder Green, Dir.
Jane S. Tai, Asst. Dir.
Konrad Kuchel, Dir. of Exhibitions
Susie D'Alton, Exhibition Asst.
James Stephens, Exhibition Asst.
Steven Aronson, Film Coordinator
Michael Shroyer, Graphic Designer
Melissa Meighan, Registrar
Sara C. Fair, Dir. Mem. and Pub. Information
Stanley W. Berger, Controller
Estab. 1909 as a national, nonprofit, educational institution. Orga-
nizes circulating art exhibitions and film programs for museums, art
centers, universities, colleges, schools and libraries. National dues:
individuals $25 - $500, chapter (museums and universities) $75 and
up, corporations $250 and up.
   Exhibitions: The Heritage of American Art, Paintings from The
Collection of The Metropolitan Museum of Art; Beads, North Amer-
ican Indian Beadwork from The Museum of the American Indian, New
York; American Indian Collection from The Denver Art Museum;
American Master Drawings and Watercolors, Works on Paper from
Colonial Times to the Present; The Drawings of Morris Graves;
Master Drawings of American Architects; Contemporary Intaglios:
The Etching Process; The Graphic World of Giacometti; Contrasts:
Two Directions in 20th Century American Photographs; Ars Medica
from The Philadelphia Museum of Art; El Dorado: The Gold of An-
cient Columbia from El Museo de la Republica, Bogota; Primitive
Art, Masterworks, the Museum of Primitive Art, New York; Art
from Zaire, 100 Masterworks from the National Collection; The Art
of Tibet; Tsutsumu: The Art of the Japanese Package; The Arts of
Knowledge of Black Africa; Five Centuries of Tapestry, a Selection
from the Collection of The Fine Arts Museums of San Francisco;
The Last Empire: Victorian Photographs of India; The Dyer's Art:
Ikat, Batik and Palangi; American Abstract Artists, 1936-1976.
   Film Programs: Films on Art; The Arts Council of Great
Britain (32 films with catalog); New American Filmmakers, Selec-
tions from the Whitney Museum of American Art Film Program (240
films with catalog); The History of American Avant-Garde Cinema
(35 films, catalog and guest lecturers); Street and City Corridor,
Urban Proposals by Ulrich Franzen and Paul Rudolph.
   Activities: Art tours; lectures; museum exchange program.
   Publications: AFA Program Catalog; exhibition catalogs; Amer-
ican Art Directory; Who's Who in American Art; Sources of Films on
Art (jointly published with The Canadian Centre for Films on Art).

AMERICAN INSTITUTE OF ARCHITECTS
   1735 New York Ave. N.W, Washington, D.C. 20006.
   Tel: (202) 785-7300
William Marshall, Jr, Pres.
Hilliard T. Smith Jr, Secy.
William L. Slayton, Exec. V.Pres.
Free, Mon. - Fri. 8:30 AM - 5 PM. Estab. 1857 to organize and unite
the architects of the United States and to promote the aesthetic, sci-
entific and practical efficiency of the profession; supported by mem-
bership. Mem. 26,000.
   Library: 19,000 volumes; loans to members only; open to public
for reference.
   Publications: AIA Journal, monthly; memo.

AMERICAN INSTITUTE OF GRAPHIC ARTS
   1059 Third Ave, New York, NY 10021. Tel: (212) 752-0813
Karl Fink, Pres.
Flora Finn Gross, Exec. Dir.
For further information see p. 144.

THE AMERICAN NATIONAL RED CROSS
   National Headquarters, Washington, D.C. 20006.
Frank Stanton, Chairman; George M. Elsey, President
Estab. 1881. A voluntary organization of the American people dedicated to the relief and prevention of human suffering. The local
units of the American Red Cross are called chapters, of which there
are nearly 3150 serving the United States and its possessions. The
work of the organization is carried on for the most part by volunteers
and is financed mostly by funds raised through voluntary contributions. Red Cross services are given irrespective of race, creed, or
nationality. Membership is 30, 660, 438.
   Activities: Principal activities are nation-wide disaster relief and
preparedness services; assistance programs for members of the
armed forces, veterans and their families; various health and safety
services; youth service programs; a blood program that supplies
about 40 percent of the blood needs of the nation and conducts research; training of volunteers for Red Cross and community work;
government-requested help in carrying out the terms of international
agreements for the protection of war victims; and certain international services, including emergency disaster relief and goodwill
programs.
   Activities in art and related fields are arts and crafts instruction
programs for the hospitalized and the homebound and a Red Cross
intercultural school art program for youth.
   In the instruction programs carried on in hospitals, community
institutions, and the home, trained volunteers teach painting, drawing,
sculpture, ceramics, wood carving, weaving, jewelry-making, and
leather work. In the intercultural school art program, Red Cross
youth, under the leadership of their school art teachers, create original paintings and drawings expressing the experience and impressions of life in their communities and send their works to other
schools and community groups both in their own cities and in other
parts of the country.

AMERICAN NUMISMATIC ASSOCIATION
   818 N. Cascade, Colorado Springs, Colo. 80903.
Edward C. Rochette, Exec. Dir.
   Estab. 1891, chartered by the Congress of 1912, to encourage and
promote the science of numismatics—coins and medals—in the
United States and foreign countries; maintains a museum and library;
represents coin collecting interests. Semi-ann. meeting; mem. over
33,000; dues $12. Local activities conducted by 1000 branch socie-
ties.
   Coin collection maintained at the American Numismatic Associa-
tion's museum in the headquarters building in Colorado Springs.
   Library: 5000 volumes; lent free to members on request.
   Publications: The Numismatist, monthly, N. Neil Harris,
Editor.

AMERICAN SOCIETY FOR AESTHETICS
   Cleveland Museum of Art, University Circle, Cleveland, OH
   44106.
Herbert M. Schueller, Pres.
   94 McLean, Highland Park, MI 48203
James R. Johnson, Secy-Treas.
   School of Fine Arts, University of Connecticut, Storrs, Conn.
   06268. Tel: (203) 485-3016
   Estab. 1942, for the advancement of philosophical and scientific
study of the arts and related fields. Mem. open to the qualified persons in the fields of Society interest. Ann. meeting, regional meetings. Publishes Journal of Aesthetics and Art Criticism, quarterly,
John J. Fisher, Edicor, Temple University, Philadelphia, PA 19122.

AMERICAN SOCIETY OF BOOKPLATE COLLECTORS AND
   DESIGNERS
   Audrey Spencer Arellanes, Dir. & Editor, 429 N. Daisy Ave,
   Pasadena, Calif. 91107. Tel: (213) 681-6451
   Estab. 1922. Mem. limited to 250; dues $10 and higher; in-
cludes publications.
   Collections: Bookplates and books on the subject, gift from the
Society to Division of Fine Arts of the Library of Congress.
   Publications: Year Book; quarterly newsletter, Bookplates in
the News.

✠AMERICAN SOCIETY OF INTERIOR DESIGNERS
   730 Fifth Ave, New York, NY 10019. Tel: (212) 586-7111
John Hammon, Exec. Dir.
Estab. 1975, a consolidation of the American Institute of Interior
Designers and National Society of Interior Designers. Object: to
advance standards of interior design, to uphold in practice a code of
ethics and professional practices of mutual benefit in professional,
public, and trade relations, and to promote educational programs to
improve the art of interior design.
   Membership: 8000; active membership dues $150.
   Activities: Carried on through national committees; local activities conducted through 44 chapters. Annual competition for designers
of fabrics, furniture, floor coverings, wall coverings and lighting
produced and offered for sale during the year. Annual design competition for students in schools and colleges in the United States and
Canada offering courses in interior design; cash prize awards and
honorable mentions.
   The Society and its Educational Foundation issue grants and
scholarships to students and recent graduates, and maintain a national library of interior design books and publications.

ARCHAEOLOGICAL INSTITUTE OF AMERICA
260 W. Broadway, New York, NY 10013. Tel: (212) 925-7333
Frederick R. Matson, Pres.
Elizabeth A. Whitehead, Gen. Secy.
Estab. 1879, inc. 1906. Ann. meeting Dec; mem. over 6000; dues
$12 and higher. Managed by a council composed of its officers and
representatives of its schools, the president of each society and one
councilor for each fifth members.
Activities: Lectures provided each academic year for affiliated
societies; distributes career pamphlet; slide archives; 3-day annual
meeting for illustrated papers; tours. Oliva James Fellowship;
Harriet Pomerance Fellowship.
Publications: American Journal of Archaeology, scientific quarterly; Archaeology, popular quarterly; monographs.

Allied Institutions:
American School of Classical Studies in Athens
41 E. 72nd St, New York, NY 10021.
American Academy in Rome
Harold C. Martin, Pres.
41 E. 65th St, New York, NY 10021.
American Research Center in Egypt
Morroe Berger, Pres.
20 Nassau St, Princeton, NJ 08540.
American Schools of Oriental Research (Jerusalem, Baghdad,
Amman, Carthage)
Frank Moore Cross, Pres.
Room 102, 6 Divinity Ave, Cambridge, MA 02138.
School of American Research
Douglas W. Schwartz, Dir.
P.O. Box 2188, Santa Fe, NM 87501.
American Research Institute in Turkey
Hans G. Güterbock, Pres.
Oriental Institute, University of Chicago, Chicago, IL 60637.
American Institute of Iranian Studies
T. Cuyler Young, Jr, Pres.
West Asian Dept, Royal Ontario Museum, 100 Queens Park,
Toronto M5S 2C6, Can.
American Institute of Nautical Archaeology
George F. Bass, Pres.
P.O. Box 261, Philadelphia, PA 19105

ARCHIVES OF AMERICAN ART
41 E. 65th St, New York, NY 10021
For further information see p. 145.

ART DEALERS ASSOCIATION OF AMERICA, INC.
575 Madison Ave, New York, NY 10022. Tel: (212) 644-7150
Clyde M. Newhouse, Pres.
Ralph F. Colin, Admin. V.Pres. & Counsel
Leo Castelli, V.Pres.
Lucien Goldschmidt, V.Pres.
Gilbert S. Edelson, Secy. & Treas.
Estab. 1962 to promote the interests of the individuals, firms, as-
sociations, corporations and other organizations engaged in the busi-
ness of dealing in works of the fine arts, to improve the stature and
status of the fine arts business and to enhance the confidence and
good will of the public in the fine arts dealers. Meetings about four
times a year; mem. 97; annual dues $250. Election of Officers and
Board in May, effective the following October 1.

ARTISTS EQUITY ASSOCIATION, INC.
National Headquarters, 2813 Albemarle St. N.W, Washington,
DC 20008. Tel: (202) 244-0209
John Blair Mitchell, Pres.
Molly S. Brylawski, Exec. Dir.
Estab. 1947 to promote and protect the economic welfare of
professional artists. Mem. 2000; dues variable according to cate-
gory of membership and chapter. Chapters: Philadelphia, Maryland,
Washington, DC, Florida, St. Louis, Chicago, State of Washington,
Northern California, Southern California (Los Angeles and San Diego
Branches), Colorado, Albuquerque, Oregon, West Texas, Houston,
Santa Fe, Minnesota; also at-large members in every state of the
United States, including Hawaii and Alaska.
The Association is affiliated with Artists Equity Fund, Inc, for
the conduct of welfare and educational activities in the interest of
professional artists and American art. Contributions to the support
of this activity are deductible for income tax purposes.
The Association is actively engaged in promoting interests of
the artist through legislative means, on the national and local level,
and publishes a Newsletter at regular intervals to keep its membership and interested persons informed on all relevant matters, and
action kits on the following subjects: 1%; Ethical Guidelines for
Juried Exhibitions; Estate and Income Tazes; Marketing Art
through Galleries; Documentation of Art Works; Health Hazards for
Artists; Business Practices. AEA offers, as one of its member
benefits, a group health and life insurance plan.

ASSOCIATED COUNCILS OF THE ARTS
1564 Broadway, New York, NY 10036. Tel: (212) 586-3731
Louis Harris, Chmn. of Board
Michael Newton, Pres.
Marilyn Lazarevich, Admin. Dir.
Sandra Dilley, Ed, Publications
Nancy Bush, Dir. of Information & Advocates Coordinator
John Hightower, Chmn, Advocates for the Arts
Estab. 1960. Ann. meeting spring; mem. 900, including state and
community arts councils, libraries, universities, arts organizations
and volunteers. Advocates for the Arts estab. 1974 to provide op-
portunity for individuals to work together on behalf of the arts in
legal, economic and public issues; dues $60 - $500 according to
budget; individuals $30, student $20, business $200, libraries $35.
Activities: Seminars; research.
Library: Research materials on arts councils and arts administration maintained for members.
Publications: Trade publications; ACA Reports; quarterly Arts
Advocate; monthly Word from Washington.

ASSOCIATION OF ART MUSEUM DIRECTORS
P.O. Box 620, Lenox Hill Station, New York, NY 10021.
Evan H. Turner, Pres.
Dir, Philadelphia Museum of Art, Benjamin Franklin Parkway
at 26th St, Philadelphia, PA 19101.
Ian M. White, 1st V.Pres.
Dir, Fine Arts Museums of San Francisco, Lincoln Park, San
Francisco, CA 94121.
Rollin van N. Hadley, 2nd V.Pres.
Dir, Isabella Stewart Gardner Museum, 2 Palace Rd,
Boston, MA 02115
Paul C. Mills, Secy.
Dir, Santa Barbara Museum of Art, 1130 State St,
Santa Barbara, CA 93104.
Thomas W. Leavitt, Treas.
Dir, Herbert F. Johnson Museum of Art, Cornell University,
Ithaca, NY 14850.
Estab. 1916; meets twice a year for discussion of the work of art
museum executives. Mem. 112 active; 13 associate; 23 honorary.

ASSOCIATION OF COLLEGIATE SCHOOLS OF ARCHITECTURE, INC.
1735 New York Ave. N.W, Washington, DC 20006.
Tel: (202) 785-2324
Prof. Donlyn Lyndon, Pres.
David Clarke, Exec. Dir.
Estab. 1912 for the advancement of architectural education.
Full member schools 98, dues $500; affiliates 55, dues $75;
corresponding category has been dropped; individual members 260,
dues $20. Publishes Journal of Architectural Education, quarterly
during school year, subscription $9, Arthur Hacker, Editor;
ACSA Newsletter published 5 times during school year.

✠THE ASSOCIATION OF JUNIOR LEAGUES, INC.
825 Third Ave, New York, NY 10022. Tel: (212) 355-4380
Mary D. Poole, Pres.
Frances Verstandeg, Secy.
Edwin H. Marks, Jr, Exec. Dir.
The Association was founded in 1921 by the 30 Leagues then in existence to unite the member Leagues and to promote their individual
purposes by offering them leadership and assistance. The purpose of
each Junior League is to promote voluntarism, to develop the potential of its members for voluntary participation in community affairs,
to demonstrate the effectiveness of trained volunteers. Ann. Conference; mem. 228 Junior Leagues with 113,000 members.
Activities: The Junior Leagues are responsible for initiating the
arts council movement and subsequently have been involved in the
establishment of approximately 40 arts councils. They have acted as
catalysts in starting a number of arts, history and science centers
and arts festivals. They established the first museum docent programs in North America using volunteers. They are involved in
historic preservation. A recent thrust is programs relating to
building the arts into general education. Administrative, volunteer
and financial resources are invested by Leagues in these programs.
Publications: The AJL Review, 4 issues a year.

ASSOCIATION OF MEDICAL ILLUSTRATORS
6050 Northwest Hwy, Chicago, Ill, 60631. Tel: (312) 763 7350
Marvin Lurie, Exec. Dir.
Estab. 1945, inc. 1946 to encourage the advancement of medical illustration and allied fields of visual education; to promote understanding
and cooperation with the medical and related professions. Ann. meeting Oct; mem. 292 active, 62 associates, 5 honorary, 7 sustaining;
dues, active $35, assoc. $25, sustaining $100. Exhibition of mem-
bers' work at ann. meeting.
Publications: Newsletter, 6 times a year; Medical Illustration
(brochure); Journal of BioCommunications, 3 times a year.

CATHOLIC ART ASSOCIATION*
 c/o Mrs. William G. Finin, Exec. Secy, Box 113, Rensselaer-
ville, NY 12147. Tel: (518) 686-4211
Estab. 1937. Ann. national conventions in Aug; mem. 1198.
 Publications: Good Work (formerly the Catholic Art Quarterly);
Making and Thinking by Walter Shewring; Current Concepts of Art
by Sister M. Jeanne; Living Stones of Architecture by Graham Carey;
A Priest Speaks on Chalice Design by Rev. E. M. Catich.

COLLEGE ART ASSOCIATION OF AMERICA
 16 E. 52nd St, New York, NY 10022.
Albert Elsen, Pres.
George Sadek, V.Pres.
Marilyn Stokstad, Secy.
Gilbert S. Edelson, Hon. Counsel
Richard S. Ravenscroft, Hon. Treas.
Rose R. Weil, Exec. Secy.
Estab. 1912, for furtherance and promotion of the study and inter-
pretation of art. Ann. meeting; mem. about 7400; dues, institu-
tional $50, individual $17.50 - $40, depending on income.
 Activities: Maintains placement bureau and a service for buying
art books at a liberal discount for members.
 Publications: Art Bulletin, research quarterly, Howard Hibbard,
Editor. The Art Journal, Diane Kelder, Editor. A series of mono-
graphs on art and archaeology, Isabel Hyman, Editor.
 Awards: The Arthur Kingsley Porter Prize of $400 awarded
annually for a distinguished art historical article published in the
Art Bulletin by a scholar under 35 years of age of any nationality.
The Charles Rufus Morey Award for the most distinguished work
of art historical scholarship published each year. The Frank Jewett
Mather, Jr. Award for the best art criticism written by a North
American citizen. The Distinguished Teaching of Art Award of $500.
The Distinguished Teaching of Art History Award.

COUNCIL OF AMERICAN ARTIST SOCIETIES
 112 E. 19th St, New York, NY 10003. Tel: (212) 475-6650
Frank C. Wright, Pres.
Donald DeLue, 1st V.Pres.
John S. Dole, V.Pres, Treas. & Gen. Counsel
Katherine Thayer Hobson, Asst. Treas.
Florence Whitehill, Recording Secy.
Estab. Dec. 1962. The Council is a national organization, a tax-free,
non-profit, incorporated educational council; to educate, motivate
and protect art and artists; to further traditional art at the highest
esthetic level; policies and management controlled by artists. Ann.
meeting May; mem. 100; societies; endowed; no dues.
 Activities: Awards and citations for excellence in art; medals and
awards; circulates exhibitions; publishes monographs.

GENERAL FEDERATION OF WOMEN'S CLUBS
 1734 N St. N.W, Washington, DC 20036. Tel: (202) 347-3168
Mrs. John T. Crippen, Exec. Secy.
The purpose of the General Federation of Women's Clubs shall be to
unite the women's clubs and like organizations throughout the world
for the purpose of mutual benefit, and for the promotion of their common interest in educational, industrial, philanthropic, literary, artistic and scientific culture as interpreted and implemented by established policy.
 Founded in 1890, the General Federation of Women's Clubs is
an international organization with mem. in 36 countries and the
United States. This mem. figure includes 665,000 members who pay
per capita dues, in 13,500 clubs in the United States.
 State Federation and local clubs activities include: providing art
scholarships; sponsoring state and local contests for high school
seniors; art classes; presenting works of American artists as awards
to schools or clubs for outstanding services to art or to hospitals and
public buildings; conducting state art surveys; exhibiting the work of
state and local artists; observing American Art Week.
 Many of the above activities are financed through the Pennies
For Art Fund, established 1930, to which each member is asked to
donate just pennies. Proceeds are used within the State where collected.
 Official publication General Federation Clubwoman, monthly except June, July and August.

INDUSTRIAL DESIGNERS SOCIETY OF AMERICA
 1750 Old Meadow Rd, McLean, Va. 22101. Tel: (703) 893-5575
James F. Fulton, Pres.
Thomas Hal Stewart, Exec. Dir.
Estab. and inc. in the State of New York in 1965; created from the
merger of the American Society of Industrial Designers, the Industrial Designers Institute, and the Industrial Design Education Association. First professionally organized group dating back to 1938.
Ten chapters in five major areas of the country. Objectives include maintenance of high standards of design and professional

integrity, encouragement of sound design education, cooperation
with industry and government. Ann. meeting Fall; mem. 1100; full
mem. dues $125 annually.
 Activities: While IDSA does not sponsor lectures or classes at
present, members are available by special request to talk to appropriate groups on various subjects associated with industrial design.

INTERNATIONAL COUNCIL OF MUSEUMS COMMITTEE OF THE
 AMERICAN ASSOCIATION OF MUSEUMS
 2233 Wisconsin Ave. N.W, Washington, DC 20007.
 Tel: (202) 338-5300
Joseph Veach Noble, Pres.
Paul N. Perrot, V.Pres.
Susan M. Yecies, Prog. Coordinator
Open Mon. - Fri. 9 AM - 5 PM. Estab. 1946; the AAM represents
international museum interests within the United States through the
AAM/ICOM office which disseminates information on international
conferences, publications, travel and study grants, museum jobs,
training programs and museum collections. The AAM/ICOM office
also maintains an international network of museum professionals by
country and discipline and sponsors foreign museum professionals'
visits to United States museums. Financed by membership. Ann.
meeting June at the AAM's ann. meeting; mem. 500; dues individual
$15 associate and active, $50 supporting, $80 contributing; institu-
tional $100 - $400 associate, $800 supporting
 Publications: AAM/ICOM Newsletter, quarterly; ICOM News,
quarterly (from Paris).

INTERNATIONAL COUNCIL OF THE MUSEUM OF MODERN ART,
 NEW YORK
 11 W. 53rd St, New York, NY 10019. Tel: (212) 956-7090
August Heckscher, Chmn. of the Board
Mrs. Alfred R. Stern, Pres.
Mrs. Bagley Wright, V.Pres.
Mrs. Bertram Smith, Secy.
John Parkinson III, Treas.
 Founded in 1953, and inc. under the laws of the State of New York
in 1956, the Council in 1957 assumed sponsorship of The Museum of
Modern Art's program of international circulating exhibitions. A
nonprofit membership organization of approx. one-hundred seventy-
five art patrons and community leaders from the United States
and abroad, the Council is actively interested in contemporary art
and in furthering international understanding, believing that exchange
in the visual arts can provide an especially effective means for creating good will among peoples of different countries. Ann. dues,
$1500 U.S. members, $1250 foreign members; ann. meeting usually
Nov. (See also listings for Museum of Modern Art and Museum of
Modern Art, Department of Circulating Exhibitions).

INTERNATIONAL FOUNDATION FOR ART RESEARCH, INC.
 654 Madison Ave, New York, NY 10021. Tel: (212) 751-1520
Franklin Feldman, Pres.
Simon Sheib, Secy.
Elizabeth B. Burns, Exec. Secy.
Bonnie Burnham, Project Dir, Central Archive for Stolen Art
Office Hours: Mon. - Fri. 9 AM - 5 PM. Estab. 1968 to provide a
framework for impartial consideration by experts on questions concerning attribution and authentication of major works of art. Expanded 1975 to include a Central Archive for Stolen Art, for the collection and cataloguing of information on art theft. Financed by donations.
 Activities: The Foundation's primary function is the examination
of art objects by leading scholars and experts to provide impartial
opinions in the light of present day knowledge. The Foundation accepts paintings, sculpture, prints, pottery for study. An initial deposit of $300 covers stylistic examination and physical tests (in-
cluding x-ray, infrared, ultraviolet and chemical examinations; in
some cases, pigment identification by ionic spectrography, examination by autoradiography). A written report of the experts' conclu-
sions is issued to the owner in the name of the Foundation. Under
the Foundation's Museum Program, these services are offered to
smaller museums to aid in the resolution of questions dealing with
the proper attribution of works of art in their collections. Funds
are available to museums for the service through the aid of the NEA
and NYSC.
 The Central Archive for Stolen Art is a subsidiary research program of the Foundation, funded by special grant. This program was
undertaken in order to determine the feasibility of establishing
within the Foundation an international center where records of art
thefts might be collected and documented, for use by individuals,
institutions, government agencies, and other organizations involved
in the fine arts. This program is in the first phase of its development, which consists of a broad study of art theft, and the development of a system for cataloguing stolen art.
 Publications: Brochure and Bulletin available.

INTER-SOCIETY COLOR COUNCIL
   c/o Fred W. Billmeyer, Jr, Secy, Department of Chemistry,
   Rensselaer Polytechnic Institute, Troy, N.Y. 12181.
   Tel: (518) 270-6458
Charles W. Jerome, Pres.
S. Leonard Davidson, Treas.
Estab. 1931 to stimulate and coordinate the work being done by various societies, organizations and associations, leading to the standardization, description and specification of color, and to promote the practical application of these results to the color problems arising in science, art and industry. Ann. meeting in the spring; mem. 29 member-societies, and 500 individual members; dues: member-societies $75; individual members $15. Publishes Newsletter six times a year.

   Member Societies
American Artists' Professional League
American Association of Textile Chemists and Colorists
American Ceramic Society, Inc.
American Chemical Society
American College of Prosthodontists
American Institute of Architects
American Psychological Association
American Society for Testing and Materials
American Society of Interior Designers
American Society of Photogrammetry
The Color Association of the United States, Inc.
Color Marketing Group
Dry Color Manufacturers' Association
Federation of Societies for Coatings Technology
Graphic Arts Technical Foundation, Inc.
Gravure Technical Association
Illuminating Engineering Society
Industrial Designers' Society of America
Institute of Food Technologists
Manufacturers Council for Color and Appearance, Inc.
National Association of Printing Ink Makers, Inc.
National Paint and Coatings Association, Inc.
Optical Society of America
Society of Motion Picture and Television Engineers
Society of Photographic Scientists and Engineers
Society of Plastics Engineers, Inc.
Technical Association for the Graphic Arts
Technical Association of the Pulp and Paper Industry

KAPPA PI INTERNATIONAL HONORARY ART FRATERNITY
   Box 7843, Midfield, Birmingham, AL 35228. Tel: (205) 428-4540
   International Officers
Miss Garnet R. Leader, International Pres.
   Box 7843, Midfield, Birmingham, AL 35228
Dr. Ralph M. Hudson, 1st International V.Pres.
   University of Alabama in Huntsville, Box 1247
   Huntsville, AL 35607.
Dr. Donna Stoddard, 2nd International V Pres.
   Florida Southern College, Lakeland, FL 33802.
Elmer J. Porter, International Secy.
   3115 Margaret Ave, Terre Haute, IN 47802.
Myrtle Kerr, International Treas.
   Box 66553, Baton Rouge, LA 70806
Ed Wilwers, International Parliamentarian
   Russellville, AR 72801.
Charles Jones, Scholarship Chmn.
   Stephen F. Austin State University,
   Nacogdoches, TX 75961
Estab. 1911. The International honorary art fraternity for men and women in colleges, universities, and art schools. Biann. meeting in spring; mem. 40,000; dues, students in chapters $3, graduates $3, charter $25, initiates $10.
   Organizes traveling exhibitions of members' work; published annually The Sketch Book and Fall Bulletin; conducts contests of members' work in various media with appropriate recognition. Chapters hold local exhibitions, lectures, discussions.
   Awards scholarships annually to members. The Sketch Book arranges frequent competitions, with prizes.

   Chapter Roll
Alpha—University of Kentucky, Lexington, Ky. 40503
Theta—Birmingham Southern College, Birmingham, Ala. 35204
Iota—Iowa Wesleyan College, Mount Pleasant, Iowa 52641
Kappa—Lindenwood College, St. Charles, Mo. 63031
Lambda—Oklahoma City University, Oklahoma City, Okla. 73106
Mu—New Mexico Western College, Silver City, N.Mex. 88061
Nu—Fort Hays State College, Hays, Kans. 67601
Xi—University of Montevallo, Montevallo, Ala. 35115
Omicron—Western Montana College, Dillon, Mont. 59725
Pi—University of Georgia, Athens, Ga. 30601
Rho—Mississippi University for Women, Columbus, Miss. 39701

Sigma—Huntingdon College, Montgomery, Ala. 36106
Phi—Central State University, Edmond, Okla. 73034
Chi—Eastern Illinois University, Charleston, Ill. 61920
Psi—Southern Illinois University, Carbondale, Ill. 62901
Omega—Indiana State University, Terre Haute, Ind. 47809
Alpha Alpha—Samford University, Birmingham, Ala. 35209
Alpha Beta—Central Washington College, Ellensburg, Wash. 98926
Alpha Delta—University of Arkansas, Fayetteville, Ark. 72701
Alpha Epsilon—Mary Hardin—Baylor College, Belton, Tex. 76513
Alpha Eta—Florida Southern College, Lakeland, Fla. 33802
Alpha Theta—Winthrop College, Rock Hill, S.C. 29730
Alpha Iota—Depauw University, Greencastle, Ind. 46135
Alpha Kappa—Baylor University, Waco, Tex. 76706
Alpha Lambda—Sam Houston State University, Huntsville, Tex. 77340
Alpha Mu—University of Minnesota, Duluth, Minn. 55812
Alpha Xi—Kansas Wesleyan University, Salina, Kans. 67401
Alpha Omicron—Georgetown College, Georgetown, Ky. 40324
Alpha Pi—Southwest Texas State University, San Marcos, Tex. 78666
Alpha Rho—Brenau College, Gainesville, Ga. 30501
Alpha Sigma—Our Lady of the Lake College, San Antonio, Tex. 78207
Alpha Tau—John B. Stetson University, DeLand, Fla. 32720
Alpha Upsilon—Winona State College, Winona, Minn. 55987
Alpha Chi—Black Hills Teachers College, Spearfish, S.Dak. 57783
Alpha Psi—University of South Carolina, Columbia, S.C. 29208
Alpha Omega—Wichita State University, Wichita, Kans. 67208
Alpha Alpha Alpha—Oregon College of Education, Monmouth, Ore. 97361
Alpha Alpha Beta—Oklahoma Baptist University, Shawnee, Okla. 74801
Alpha Alpha Delta—Western State College, Gunnison, Colo. 81230
Alpha Alpha Epsilon—Southwestern College, Winfield, Kans. 61756
Alpha Alpha Zeta—Carthage College, Kenosha, Wis. 53140
Alpha Alpha Eta—University of Southern California, Los Angeles, Calif. 90007
Alpha Alpha Theta—University of Tampa, Tampa, Fla. 33606
Alpha Alpha Iota—University of Miami, Miami, Fla. 33124
Alpha Alpha Kappa—Arkansas State University, Jonesboro, Ark. 72467
Alpha Alpha Lambda—Southwestern State College, Weatherford, Okla. 73096
Alpha Alpha Mu—Eastern Washington College, Cheney, Wash. 99004
Alpha Alpha Nu—Texas Western College, El Paso, Tex. 79902
Alpha Alpha Xi—Phillips University, Enid, Okla. 73701
Alpha Alpha Omicron—Eastern New Mexico University, Portales, N.Mex. 88130
Alpha Alpha Pi—Oregon State University, Corvallis, Ore. 97331
Alpha Alpha Rho—University of Southern Mississippi, Hattiesburg, Miss. 39401
Alpha Alpha Sigma—New Mexico Highlands University, Las Vegas, N.Mex. 87701
Alpha Alpha Tau—West Liberty State College, West Liberty, W.Va. 26074
Alpha Alpha Upsilon—St. Cloud State College, St. Cloud, Minn. 56301
Alpha Alpha Phi—University of North Carolina, Chapel Hill, N.C. 27514
Alpha Alpha Chi—Murray State University, Murray Ky. 42071
Alpha Alpha Psi—Eastern Kentucky University, Richmond, Ky. 40475
Beta Alpha—Baker University, Baldwin City, Kans. 66006
Beta Beta—Kearney State College, Kearney, Nebr. 68847
Beta Gamma—Southeast Missouri State University, Cape Girardeau, Mo. 63701
Beta Delta—University of Alabama, University, Ala. 35486
Beta Epsilon—North Texas State University, Denton, Tex. 76201
Beta Zeta—Heidelberg College, Tiffin, Ohio 44883
Beta Eta—Marshall University, Huntington, W.Va. 25701
Beta Theta—Wayne State University, Wayne, Nebr. 68787
Beta Iota—Stephen F. Austin State University, Nacogdoches, Tex. 75961
Beta Kappa—Queen's College of the City University of New York, Flushing, N.Y. 11358
Beta Lambda—Hofstra University, Hempstead, N.Y. 11550
Beta Mu—Frostburg State College, Frostburg, Md. 21532
Beta Nu—Hunter College of the City University of New York, New York, N.Y. 10021
Beta Xi—University of Evansville, Evansville, Ind. 47704
Beta Omicron—Lewis and Clark College, Portland, Ore. 97212
Beta Pi—West Texas State University, Canyon, Tex. 79016
Beta Rho—State College of Iowa, Cedar Falls, Iowa 50613
Beta Sigma—Drew University, Madison, N.Y. 07940
Beta Tau—Lamar University, Beaumont, Tex. 77710
Beta Upsilon—Harris Teachers College, St. Louis, Mo. 63103
Beta Phi—Texas Wesleyan College, Fort Worth, Tex. 76105
Beta Chi—Hardin-Simmons University, Abilene, Tex. 79601
Beta Psi—Concord College, Athens, W.Va. 24712
Beta Omega—Seattle Pacific College, Seattle, Wash. 98119

Gamma Alpha—Northwest Missouri State College, Maryville, Mo. 64468

Gamma Beta—Fairmont State College, Fairmont, W.Va. 26554

Gamma Gamma—Union College, Barbourville, Ky. 40906

Gamma Delta—Wisconsin State University, Eau Claire, Wis. 54701

Gamma Epsilon—University of Houston, Houston, Tex. 77004

Gamma Zeta—Hastings College, Hastings, Neb. 68901

Gamma Eta—Nebraska State Teachers College, Chadron, Nebr. 69337

Gamma Theta—Montclair State College, Upper Montclair, N.J. 07043

Gamma Iota—Eastern Oregon College, LaGrande, Ore. 97850

Gamma Kappa—Madison College, Harrisonburg, Va. 22801

Gamma Lambda—Abilene Christian College, Abilene, Tex. 79601

Gamma Mu—Northwestern State University, Natchitoches, La. 71457

Gamma Nu—University of Southwestern Louisiana, Lafayette, La. 70501

Gamma Xi—Louisiana College, Pineville, La. 71360

Gamma Omicron—Centenary College of Louisiana, Shreveport, La. 71104

Gamma Pi—Western Kentucky University, Bowling Green, Ky. 42101

Gamma Rho—Northwestern State College, Alva, Okla. 73717

Gamma Sigma—Adelphi University, Garden City, N.Y. 11530

Gamma Tau—California State College at Los Angeles, Los Angeles, Calif. 90032

Gamma Upsilon—University of Alaska, Fairbanks, Alaska 99506

Gamma Phi—National Photographic, Box 7843, Midfield, Birmingham, Ala. 35228

Gamma Chi—Alaska Methodist University, Anchorage, Alaska 99500

Gamma Psi—San Diego State University, San Diego, Calif. 92115

Gamma Omega—West Virginia Wesleyan College, Buckhannon, W.Va. 26201

Delta Alpha—Northeast Louisiana State University, Monroe, La. 71201

Delta Beta—Mississippi College, Clinton, Miss. 39056

Delta Gamma—Mankato State College, Mankato, Minn. 56001

Delta Delta—Western Illinois University, Macomb, Ill. 61455

Delta Epsilon—University of Bridgeport, Bridgeport, Conn. 06602

Delta Zeta—New York State College, New Paltz, N.Y. 12561

Delta Eta—Northern Montana College, Havre, Mont. 59501

Delta Iota—Morehead State College, Morehead, Ky. 40351

Delta Kappa—University of the Philippines, Quezon City, Philippines

Delta Lambda—Delta State University, Cleveland, Miss. 38732

Delta Mu—Florence State University, Florence, Ala. 35630

Delta Nu—Belhaven College, Jackson, Miss. 39202

Delta Xi—Arkansas Polytechnic College, Russellville, Ark. 72801

Delta Omicron—C.W. Post College of Long Island University, Brookeville, N.Y. 11548

Delta Pi—Asheville-Billmore College, Asheville, N.C. 28801

Delta Rho—Ottawa University, Ottawa, Kans. 66067

Delta Sigma—Keuka College, Keuka Park, N.Y. 14478

Delta Tau—Alabama State University, Montgomery, Ala. 36101

Delta Upsilon—Troy State University, Troy, Ala. 36081

Delta Phi—College of Mount St. Vincent, Bronx, N.Y. 10471

Delta Chi—California State College, Fullerton, Calif. 93734

Delta Psi—Waynesburg College, Waynesburg, Pa. 15370

Delta Omega—Louisiana Polytechnic Institute, Rushton, La. 71270

Epsilon Alpha—Baldwin-Wallace College, Berea, Ohio 44012

Epsilon Gamma—Middle Tennessee State University, Murfreesboro, Tenn. 37130

Epsilon Delta—Minot State College, Minot, N.Dak. 58701

Epsilon Zeta—Dickinson State College, Dickinson, N.Dak. 58601

Epsilon Eta—University of Central Arkansas, Conway, Ark. 72032

Epsilon Theta—McMurry College, Abilene, Tex. 79605

Epsilon Iota—Harding College, Searcy, Ark. 72143

Epsilon Kappa—Montreat-Anderson College, Montreat, N.C. 28757

Epsilon Lambda—University of Wyoming, Laramie, Wyo. 82070

Epsilon Mu—Boise College, Boise, Idaho 83701

Epsilon Xi—John F. Kennedy College, Wahoo, Nebr. 68066

Epsilon Omicron—Herbert H. Lehman College of the City University of New York, Bronx, NY 10468

Epsilon Pi—Carson Newman College, Jefferson City, Tenn. 37760

Epsilon Rho—Friends University, Wichita, Kans. 67213

Epsilon Sigma—Ohio Northern University, Ada, Ohio 45810

Epsilon Tau—University of Alabama in Huntsville, Huntsville, Ala. 35807

Epsilon Upsilon—St. Mary's College, St. Mary's City, Md. 20686

Epsilon Phi—Mississippi State University, Mississippi State, Miss. 39762

Epsilon Chi—Bethany College, Bethany, WVa. 26032

Epsilon Omega—Instituto Allende, San Miguel de Allende GTO, Mexico

MID-AMERICA COLLEGE ART ASSOCIATION

c/o George Ehrlich, Pres, University of Missouri-Kansas City, Kansas City, MO 64110. Tel: (816) 276-1501

Dan Howard, V.Pres.

University of Nebraska-Lincoln, Lincoln NE 68508.

Geraldine Fowle, Treas.

University of Missouri-Kansas City, Kansas City, MO 64110

Estab. 1938 to promote better teaching of art and art history in colleges and universities. Ann. meeting Oct; ann. elections; mem. 200 college and university art departments in 24 states and 4 Canadian provinces. Average attendance 700.

NATIONAL ARCHITECTURAL ACCREDITING BOARD*

1735 New York Ave, Washington, DC 20006

Helen S. Steele, Exec. Secy.

Estab. 1940 by joint action of the American Institute of Architects, the Association of Collegiate Schools of Architecture and the National Council of Architectural Registration Boards. Publishes List of Accredited Schools of Architecture annually. Address requests for this list to: Executive Secretary.

NATIONAL ART EDUCATION ASSOCIATION

A National Affiliate of the NEA

1916 Association Dr, Reston, VA 22091. Tel: (703) 620-3855

John J. Mahlmann, Exec. Dir.

Charles M. Dorn, Pres. 1975-77

Head, Dept. Creative Arts, Purdue University, Lafayette, IN 46207.

Dr. Elliot W. Eisner

Prof. Art and Educ, Stanford University, Stanford, CA 94305

The National Art Education Association is a national organization devoted to the advancement of the professional interests and competence of teachers of art at all educational levels. It was founded in 1947 through the affiliation of four regional groups, Eastern, Western, Pacific, and Southeastern Arts Associations. Mem. fee, active $35, institutional comprehensive $100.

The program of the Association is financed through the mem. dues, sale of publications, and occasional grants for specific purposes. As a Department of the National Education Association, the NAEA maintains a permanent staff in the NEA Headquarters which carries out the policies and program as determined by the NAEA Board of Directors.

The purposes of the Association are to promote the study of the problems of teaching art; to encourage research and experimentation; to facilitate the professional and personal cooperation of its members; to hold public discussions and programs; to publish desirable articles, reports, and surveys; to integrate the efforts of others with similar purposes. Approx. 10,000 art teachers, administrators, supervisors, and students are members of the NAEA.

National Conferences are held annually. The NAEA Conference for 1974 was held in Chicago, April 7-12. The NAEA Conference for 1975 was held in Miami, April 6-11

Publications: The official Journal, Art Education, eight issues, subscription price, $15. Studies in Art Education, a journal of issues and research, issued three times a year, subscription price, $15. Art Teacher, a magazine for elementary and secondary art education, issued three times a year, subscription price, $7.50. Special publications include: Art for the Preprimary Child; Art Education: Elementary; Art Education: Middle/Junior High School; Art Education: Senior High School; Art in American Higher Institutions.

THE NATIONAL ASSOCIATION FOR HUMANITIES EDUCATION

P.O. Box 628, Kirksville, MO 63501.

Tel: (816) 665-5121, Exten. 3311

Robert C. Lamm, Pres.

Leon Karel, Exec. Secy.

Division Presidents:

Clara Wood, Division I

Arthur Mansure, Division II

Charles Harrington, Division III

Charles Bart, Division IV

Robert Larson, Division V

Leonard Berman, Division VI

Estab. 1967 to promote teaching of humanities, aesthetic education, and arts in the schools; supported by membership. Biennial Convention, even numbered years; mem. 600; dues $12.

Publications: Humanities Journal, 3-4 yearly; newsletter.

Income: $7000.

Attendance: 500 at convention

NATIONAL ASSOCIATION OF SCHOOLS OF ART

11250 Roger Bacon Dr, 5, Reston, VA 22090.

Tel: (703) 437-0700

Paul B. Arnold, Pres.

Chmn, Dept. Art, Oberlin College, Oberlin, OH 44074

Samuel Hope, Exec. Secy.

Formerly the National Conference of Schools of Design, holding its first conference in 1944. Changed name 1948, at which time its Constitution and By-Laws were adopted. Changed its name again in 1960 from National Association of Schools of Design to National Association of Schools of Art.

The organization is estab. to develop a closer relationship among schools and departments of art for the purpose of examining and improving their educational practice and professional standards in design and art.

Membership is open to schools and departments of art organized on a non-profit basis, estab. for the purpose of educating designers and artists in the visual arts and giving evidence of permanence and stability; possessing an approved organization, administration, faculty, and facilities; and maintaining standards agreed upon by the Association.

NATIONAL CARTOONISTS SOCIETY

9 Ebony Court, Brooklyn, NY 11229. Tel: (212) 743-6510
Bill Gallo, Pres.
Bill Kresse, Secy.
Marge Duffy Devine, Scribe
Estab. March 1946 to advance the ideals and standards of the profession of cartooning; to assist needy, or incapacitated cartoonists; to stimulate interest in the art of cartooning by cooperating with established schools; to encourage talented students; to assist with our talents, governmental and charitable institutes; supported by membership. Meetings monthly except June, July and Aug; annual Reuben Awards Dinner Apr. each yr; mem. 450; dues local $75, other $50.

Collections: National Cartoonists Society Collection; Milt Gross Collection.

Exhibitions: Manhattan Savings Bank, New York City, Graham Gallery, Museum of Cartoon Art.

Activities: Educational Department to supply material and information to students; traveling exhibitions organized and circulated; original cartoons lent to schools, libraries, galleries, etc; tape recordings; individual cartoonists to lecture, chalktalks can be arranged; occasional Cartoon Auctions; proceeds from traveling exhibits and auctions support Milt Gross Fund assisting needy cartoonists, widows and children.

Publications: Newsletter; The Cartoonist, annually.

NATIONAL COUNCIL OF ARCHITECTURAL REGISTRATION BOARDS*

1735 New York Ave. N.W, Suite 700, Washington, DC 20006
Tel: (202) 659-3996
Hayden P. Mims, Exec. Dir.
Estab. 1920 as a clearing house for architects registering from state to state. All now have laws regulating the practice of architecture. Ann. meeting June; San Francisco 1976; mem. 50 state registration boards, Puerto Rico, Canal Zone, Virgin Islands, and Guam. Publishes semi-annual newsletter, annual report.

NATIONAL ENDOWMENT FOR THE ARTS

Washington, D.C. 20506. Tel: (202) 634-6369
Miss Nancy Hanks, Chmn. of the Endowment and of the National Council on the Arts, the Endowment's advisory body.

The National Endowment for the Arts is an independent agency of the federal government created by Congress in 1965. The major goals of the Arts Endowment are to make the arts more widely available to millions of Americans; to preserve our rich cultural heritage for present and future generations; to strengthen cultural organizations including state and regional arts agencies representing the highest quality in the fields of architecture and environmental arts, dance, education, expansion arts, folk arts, crafts, literature, museums, music, public media (film, television, and radio), theatre, and the visual arts. Matching assistance is also available to official state arts agencies in form of bloc grants for their own arts programs. Grants to organizations with few exceptions, must be matched dollar for dollar while grants to individuals carry no matching provision.

Applications are reviewed by panels of experts in the field and referred to the National Council on the Arts, a body of 26 distinguished citizens appointed by the President. Upon the recommendations of these bodies final action is taken by the Chairman.

For Fiscal Year 1975 (July 1, 1974 - June 30, 1975) the total appropriation for the Arts Endowment was $74,750,000.

The Endowment's Museum Program awards fellowships for museum professionals to take sabbaticals; provides matching grants under the museum purchase plan for museums to purchase works by living American artists; provides aid to special temporary exhibitions and innovative permanent installations; assists in the publication of handbooks and catalogs; assists museums in support of conservation activities, training programs, renovation (climate control and security), and visiting specialists programs. For more information please write Museum Program, National Endowment for the Arts, Washington, DC 20506.

The Endowment's Visual Arts Program awards individual fellowships to visual artists, craftsmen, art and crafts critics and photographers of exceptional talent; awards matching grants to art schools, universities, museums, community centers, etc. for short-term residencies of artists, craftsmen, art critics and photographers

of national reputation; assists in the placing of works of art in public places, including inner city murals; provides assistance for professional workshops, photography and crafts exhibitions, craftsmen apprenticeship programs, and special artist's and craftsmen's projects that serve the field. For more information please write the Visual Arts Program, National Endowment for the Arts, Washington, DC 20506

Publications: The following are available from the Superintendent of Documents, U.S. Government Printing Office, Washington, DC 20402: New Dimensions for the Arts: 1971-1972, Stock No. 3600-0012. The following are available from Program Information Office, National Endowment for the Arts, Washington, DC 20506 free of charge: Guide to Programs; Artists in Schools.

NATIONAL INSTITUTE FOR ARCHITECTURAL EDUCATION

20 W. 40th St, New York, NY 10018. Tel: (212) 684-1948
Hugh N. Romney, Chmn. Board of Trustees
Byron Bell, V.Chmn.
Herman C. Litwack, Secy.
Sidney L. Katz, Treas.
Howard H. Juster, Dir. of Educ.
Lilian Marus, Exec. Secy.
Open Mon. - Fri. 9 AM - 5 PM. Inc. 1894 as Society of Beaux-Arts Architects, which was dissolved Dec, 1941; Beaux-Arts Institute of Design estab. 1916, name changed 1956 to above. Ann. meeting 1st week in Dec; mem. approx. 250; dues $20 per year.

Exhibitions: Prize-winning drawings of competitions held during year.

The Institute is Trustee for the Lloyd Warren Fellowship (Paris Prize in Architecture) for study and travel abroad; Hirons Alumni Scholarship to winner not enrolled in school; William Van Alen Architect Memorial Award (international competition) annual scholarship for further study or research project of some architectural nature; and other trust funds for prize awards for study and travel abroad and in the United States educational activities.

Publications: Yearbook, annually in Oct.

NATURAL SCIENCE FOR YOUTH FOUNDATION

763 Silvermine Rd, New Canaan, Conn. 06840.
John Ripley Forbes, Pres.
John F. Gardner, Exec. Dir.
Successor to the National Foundation for Junior Museums. A national organization engaged in conservation and educational work. Sponsor for Natural Science Centers, Trailside Museums, and Junior Nature Museums.

SOCIETY OF ANIMAL ARTISTS

151 Carroll St, City Island, Bronx, NY 10464.
Tel: (212) 885-2181
Paul Branson, Pres.
Patricia Allen Bott, Secy.
Beverly Bender, Treas
Albert Earl Gilbert, 1st V.Pres.
Estab. 1960 to make people more aware of the artists who explore the mystery, grandeur and grace of the animal kingdom and by so doing help ecology and conservation; financed by membership. Meetings about 4 times a year; mem. 127; dues $20.

Exhibitions: Art Gallery Manufacturers Hanover Trust Co; Abercrombie and Fitch Art Gallery; Grand Central Art Galleries; Southern Vermont Art Center.

Activities: To help students of animal art find the right teachers and books; extension department research in material on animal art; material available to artists conservation societies; no fees; traveling exhibitions organized and circulated; individual paintings and original objects of art lent; lectures with photos of wilderness and animals.

Library: Books illustrated and written by members but only for reference.

Publications: Newsletter, 8 annually.

SOCIETY OF ARCHITECTURAL HISTORIANS

1700 Walnut St, Room 716, Philadelphia, Pa. 19103.
Tel: (215) 735-0224, 735-0246
Spiro K. Kostof, Pres.
Elisabeth MacDougall, Secy
Rosann S. Berry, Exec. Secy.
Free daily 9 AM - 5 PM. Estab. to provide an international forum for those interested in architecture and its related arts, to encourage scholarly research in the field, and to promote the preservation of significant architectural monuments throughout the world; supported by membership. Mem. approx. 4000; dues individual and institutional $25.

Activities: Annual architectural tour in the United States and annual tour abroad.

Publications: Journal, quarterly; Newsletter, 5-6 annually.

SOUTHEASTERN COLLEGE ART CONFERENCE, INC.
    c/o Anne W. Thomas, Exec. Secy-Treas, P.O. Box 1022,
    Chapel Hill, NC 27514
John T. Carey, Pres.
    Chmn, Dept. Art, University of West Florida,
    Pensacola FL 32504
Jim Conlon, V.Pres.
    Dept. Art, University of South Alabama,
    Mobile, AL 36688
Gunther Stamm, Co-Ed. of Review/Newsletter
    Dept. Art, Florida State University,
    Tallahassee, FL 32306
Charles R. Mack, Co-Ed. of Review/Newsletter
    Dept. Art, University of South Carolina,
    Columbia, SC 29208
Meets annually at member institutions; dues institutional $15 - $25,
individual $10, student $3; mem. institutional 62, individual 324.

SOUTHERN ASSOCIATION OF SCULPTORS, INC.
    Art Dept, Appalachian State University, Boone, NC 28607.
    Tel: (704) 262-2220
Sherry Waterworth, Pres.
Ron Bennett, 1st V.Pres.
Mary Brownell, Treas.
    Regional V.Pres:
Don Boyd
Walter Jackson
Jerry Noe
Kenneth Weedman
Howard Woody
    Estab. 1965, inc. 1967, to promote the exchange of ideas and in-
formation among its members, assist institutions, museums and the
public in developing an understanding of sculpture through exhibi-
tions, demonstrations and publications. Ann. meeting fall; mem. 210;
dues $10. Participating mem. restricted to Ala, Ark, D.C, Fla,
Ga, Ky, La, Md, Miss, N.C, S.C, Tenn, Va, W.Va. Assoc. mem. open
to any U.S. sculptor.
    Exhibitions: Annual juried sculpture exhibition is national open
exhibits; area invitational exhibitions; Southern Sculpture, 1970;
Southern Small Sculpture, 1971; Regional Sculpture Exhibition, 1972;
National Sculpture, 1973, 74 & 75. $1900 in prizes.
    Activities: Traveling exhibitions organized and circulated; 500
loan slide library of southern sculpture.
    Publications: Southern Association of Sculptors Quarterly; Job
Information Center Bulletin, 9 times per year; periodic technical
publications; Illustrated Sculptors Directory, every 2 years.

STAINED GLASS ASSOCIATION OF AMERICA
    c/o Kenneth Urschel, Gen. Secy, 701 Elmhurst, Valparaiso,
    IN 46383.
Naomi M. Mundy, Exec. Secy.
    (1125 Wilmington Ave, St. Louis, MO 63111)
Estab. 1903, for appreciation of the ancient craft of stained glass,
and encouragement of fine craftsmanship. Ann. convention June;
full mem. is open to individuals, partnerships, or corporations engaged in the manufacture of stained or leaded glass. Associate
mem. open to those engaged in or interested in the craft but not
as proprietors.
    Publications: Stained Glass, quarterly, Dr. Norman L. Temme,
Editor; Story of Stained Glass, booklet.

✤UNITED STATES COMMITTEE OF THE INTERNATIONAL
    ASSOCIATION OF ART, INC.*
    41 E. 65th St, New York, NY 10021. Tel: (212) 988-7700 or
    (212) 707-7003
Dorothy Paris, Exec. Officer
    88 Seventh Ave. S, New York, NY 10014
The United States Committee of the International Association of Art
(an affiliate of UNESCO) comprises professional artists working in
the United States and belonging essentially to the fields of painting,
sculpture, and the graphic arts. The artists are represented in the
U.S. Committee by delegates from 13 national art societies (approx.
5000 total mem); two delegates from each society attend four board
meetings per year.
    Inc. March 1955 to promote greater appreciation of contemporary
Fine Arts, regardless of genre, to uphold the status of the artists and
to defend their rights, primarily on the national level, then on the
international level, evaluating by comparison and appraisal. The
purpose is also to stimulate international cultural relations and exchanges of art and artists free from any aesthetic or other bias. To
this end there are triennial Congresses—of which there have been
seven: Venice, Italy, 1954 (19 member nations); Dubrovnik, Yugo-

slavia, 1957 (34 member nations); Vienna, Austria, 1960 (52 member
nations); New York, 1963 (53 member nations); Tokyo, Japan, 1966
(56 member nations); Amsterdam, Holland, 1969; Varna, Bulgaria,
1973 (65 member nations).
    The International Organization is one of the largest in the
UNESCO cultural family and is a sister organization of the International Union of Architects. The Headquarters are in Paris at 6
Rue Franklin, Paris XVI, Dunbar Marshall, Secretary General.
    The bulletin of IAA now has a new title, Art (the journal of the
professional artists). It is usually produced at the end of autumn
and is supplied free to national committees with the aid of a subvention from UNESCO.
    National committees issue museum cards to artists who belong to
their member societies. These cards give them free access to museums in all parts of the world.

WESTERN ASSOCIATION OF ART MUSEUMS
    Mills College, Box 9989, Oakland, CA 94613.
    Tel: (415) 568-2400
Richard V. West, Pres.
    Dir, E. B. Crocker Art Gallery, 216 O St,
    Sacramento, CA 95814
Louise C. Tester, 1st V.Pres.
    Exec. Dir, Arizona Commission of the Arts & Humanities,
    6330 N. Seventh St, Phoenix, AZ 85014
E. F. Sanguinetti, 2nd V.Pres.
    Dir, Utah Museum of Fine Arts, University of Utah, 104 AAC
    Salt Lake City, UT 84112
Allen Dodworth, Secy.
    Dir, The Boise Gallery of Art, Julia Davis Park, Box 1505
    Boise, ID 83701
Lewis W. Story, Treas.
    Assoc. Dir, Denver Art Museum, 100 W. 14th Ave,
    Denver, CO 80204
Mary French, Exec. Dir.
Linda Evans, Coordinator, Special Educ. Expansion Dept.
Richard K. Marshall, Coordinator, Circulating Exhibition Dept.
Susan Melim, Asst. Coordinator, Circulating Exhibition Dept.
Mary Stofflet, Newsletter Ed.

    Regional Representatives:
Robert L. Shalkop, Alaska
    Dir, Anchorage Historical and Fine Arts Museum, 121 W.
    Seventh Ave, Anchorage, AK 99501. Tel: (907) 279-1553
Ronald D. Hickman, Arizona (Chmn, Regional Representatives)
    Dir, Phoenix Art Museum, 1625 N. Central Ave,
    Phoenix, AZ 85004   Tel: (602) 258-6164
Elizabeth Ross, Northern California
    Dir, Mills College Art Gallery
    Box 9973, Oakland, CA 94613   Tel: (415) 568-2773
Henry Gardiner, Southern California
    Dir, Fine Arts Gallery of San Diego, Balboa Park
    Box 2107, San Diego, CA 92112   Tel: (714) 232-7931
Willard Holmes, Western Canada
    Cur, Vancouver Art Gallery
    1145 W. Georgia St, Vancouver, BC. Tel: (604) 684-2488
Darrell Bohlsen, Colorado
    Dir, Sangre de Cristo Art and Conference Center
    210 N. Santa Fe, Pueblo, CO 81008. Tel: (303) 543-0130
Jim Hunt, Kansas
    Dir, Mulvane Art Center, Washburn University
    1700 College, Topeka, KS 66621. Tel: (913) 235-5341
Sister Joeann Daley, Montana
    Pres, Montana Gallery Director's Association, 709 E. Third,
    Anaconda, MT 59711. Tel: (406) 563-3068
George F. Kuebler, Oklahoma
    Dir, Oklahoma Art Center, 3113 Pershing Blvd,
    Oklahoma City, OK 73107. Tel: (405) 946-4477
Rachel Griffin, Oregon
    Cur, Portland Art Museum,
    S.W. Park & Madison, Portland, OR 97223. Tel: (503) 226-2811
Peter L. Myer, Utah
    Dir, B. F. Larson Gallery, Brigham Young University
    F-303 HFAC, Provo, UT 84602. Tel: (801) 374-1211
Marcia Jartun, Washington
    University of Puget Sound
    Tacoma, WA 98416
James T. Forrest, Wyoming
    Dir, University of Wyoming art Museum, Fine Arts Bldg,
    N. 19th St, Box 3138, Laramie, WY 82070. Tel: (307) 766-2374
Estab. 1921 to assemble and circulate exhibitions among both mem-
bers and nonmembers. Services include a group fine arts insurance
program, quarterly newsletter and annual conference.

United States Museums, Libraries and Associations

ALABAMA

BIRMINGHAM

BIRMINGHAM MUSEUM OF ART
  2000 Eighth Ave N, 35203. Tel: (205) 254-2565
William M. Spencer, Chmn. of Board
Mrs. William M. Rogers, Secy, Museum Board
John David Farmer, Dir.
Edward F. Weeks, Cur.
Carolyn T. Grimsley, Coordinator, Museum Art Educ. Council
Free 10 AM - 5 PM; Thurs. until 9 PM; Sun. 2 - 6 PM. Museum
opened Apr. 8, 1951; new building, 1959, enlarged 1965; further
additions 1966-67; new wing 1973. Board estab. 1950; mem. 1500;
dues $3 and higher.
  Collections: Lamprecht Collection of German cast iron art;
Kress Collection of European art, especially Italian art; 18th - 20th
century American painting and watercolors; Rives Collection of
ancient Palestinian art and archaeology; collections of Egyptian,
Oriental South Asian, African and American Indian art; British,
French, Dutch painting; German sculpture; Middle American and
Peruvian Pre-Columbian art (300); 400 prints, etchings, engravings
and woodcuts; British and American silver (250); New Guinea primi-
tive art (40); English and Continental ceramics (350); Art of the Old
West, including Remington bronzes (12); Wedgwood Collection (1500).
  Exhibitions: About 40 per year in all fields of art.
  Income and Purchases: Income, $350,000; annual purchases,
$20,000.
  Activities: Guided tours; members activities (with Bulletin);
lectures; concerts; studio classes for adults and children, art-
mobile for city schools and extension work with all schools in city
and counties, coordinated by The Museum Art Education Council.
  Library: Approx. 1500 volumes for reference only.
  Attendance: 100,000 annually.

BIRMINGHAM PUBLIC LIBRARY*
  2020 Seventh Ave, North, 35203. Tel: (205) 252-2538
Richardena Ramsay, Dir.
Free Mon. - Fri. 9 AM - 9 PM; Sat. 9 AM - 6 PM; Sun. 3 - 6 PM.
Estab. 1909; gallery opened 1927; Art Department opened 1946.
  Collections: Small permanent collection of prints and paintings;
Mexican pottery (small).
  Library: †16,000 books on fine arts, architecture, decorative
arts and landscape gardening; †1420 bound art magazines; †40,000
pictures mounted and unmounted, which are for circulation.
  Purchases: Annual purchases $13,000.

KAPPA PI INTERNATIONAL HONORARY ART FRATERNITY
  Box 7843, Midfield, 35228. Tel: (205) 428-4540
Miss Garnet R. Leader, International Pres.
Dr. Ralph M. Hudson, 1st International V.Pres.
Dr. Donna Stoddard, 2nd International V.Pres.
Elmer J. Porter, International Secy.
Myrtle Kerr, International Treas.
For further information see p. 7.

HUNTSVILLE

HUNTSVILLE ART LEAGUE AND MUSEUM ASSOCIATION, INC.
  206 B Bob Wallace, 35801. Tel: (205) 534-2511
Bill Nailen, Pres.
Gail Hansen, V.Pres.
Helen Vaughn, Secy.
Cora Gamblin, Treas.
Carolyn Wright, Gallery Exhibits Chmn.
Phyllis Eubanks, Gallery Exhibits Chmn.
Jeannie McLeish, Educational Chmn.
Louise Smith, Educational Chmn.
Richard C. Pope, Acting Dir.

Open Mon. - Fri. 10 AM - 2 PM. Estab. 1957. The League is a
nonprofit organization dedicated to promoting and stimulating the
appreciation of the visual arts. Ann. meeting Aug; mem. approx.
600; dues $7.50 adult, and higher for additional members of family;
$2 student.
  Exhibitions: 2 Annual Clothesline Shows at the Heart of Huntsville Mall; continuous artists exhibitions throughout Huntsville.
  Activities: Classes for adults and children; competitions;
film series.
  Publications: Monthly newsletter on activities plus exhibition
opportunities in the Southeast.
  Attendance: 10,000.

✤HUNTSVILLE MUSEUM OF ART
  Von Braun Civic Center, 700 Monroe St. S.W, 35801
  Tel: (205) 534-4566
Thomas A. Bowles, III, Dir.
Nancy W. Holliman, Business Officer
Carolyn H. Wood, Cur-Registrar
Giovanna M. Doyle, Cur, Museum Prog.
Daniel G. Halcomb, Preparator
Julia J. Marsh, Grantswriter
Katherine A. Gales, Museum Sales Gallery Mgr.
Denise Accardi, Secy-Photographer
Open Tues. - Sat. 10 AM - 5 PM; Sun. 1 - 5 PM; Thurs. 1 - 9 PM;
cl. Mon. The Huntsville Museum of Art occupied its permanent
quarters in the Von Braun Civic Center in Mar, 1975. Prior to that,
temporary offices and a small gallery were located on the University
of Alabama, Huntsville campus. The purpose of the museum is to
exhibit the visual arts and to establish educational and cultural programs that will improve the quality of life in Huntsville and its
environs. Income in derived from City of Huntsville special appropriation, $200,000 for fiscal year, 1975-76. No purchases for col-
lection are from city funds. Additional financial support is given by
the Women's Guild and the Museum Membership. Grants have been
made to the museum for programs and exhibits. Mem. 564; dues.
$5 - $500.
  Collections: Paintings and sculpture from the 19th - 20th centuries.
  Exhibitions: Four shows changing monthly. (1975) Ricardo de
Villodas; Gilbert Gaul Retrospective; broad-scoped Indian exhibition; walking tour and street fair in Mooresville. Special shows
planned for spring 1976 include a juried exhibition, an historical
exhibit on Huntsville and a show devoted to the chair.
  Activities: Docent training and education program; traveling
exhibits organized; concerts; films; lectures; workshops; volunteer
program; art enrichment program in public schools in conjunction
with Women's Guild. Museum sales gallery.
  Library: Art reference encyclopedia; general art information
books; some specialty books and slides.
  Publications: Ricardo de Villodas, Thomas A. Bowles, III;
Gilbert Gaul, James Reeves; Mooresville: Walking Tour.
  Attendance (Mar. 14 - Nov, 1975) Over 80,000.

✤UNIVERSITY OF ALABAMA IN HUNTSVILLE SGA FILM SERIES*
  P.O. Box 1247, 35807.

MODILE

ART PATRONS LEAGUE OF MOBILE, INC.
  Box 8055, 36608. Tel: (205) 344-2148
Mrs. Wythe Whiting, III, Pres.
Mrs. M. A. Norden, Secy. & Recording Secy.
Mrs. Wright Patton, Corresp. Secy.
Mrs. Carl Moore, Treas.
Mrs. Charles B. Bauer, American Crafts Gallery & Patio Gallery
Estab. May 1, 1964 to promote the education and appreciation of the

visual and graphic arts primarily in the Mobile area; financed by membership and fund raising projects. Ann. meeting May; mem. 350; dues $7.50 active, $10 assoc.

Exhibitions: Mobile Collects, 1972-1973, Objects d'Art from private collections; Environmental Design, 1973-1974, Interior Designers; Zelda, 1974-1975, works of Zelda Sayre Fitzgerald; Christmas Tree Potpourri, Dec. 1975; Hooray for Hollywood, spring 1976.

Activities: Lectures for members and guests; 5 visiting lecturers per year; scholarships.

Library: Clipping service, art clippings from magazines, journals, etc.

Publications: Newsletter (quarterly); Art Patrons League Calendar (annually).

Income and Purchases: Income $20,000; purchases $11,000.

Attendance: Outdoor Arts & Crafts Fair 50,000; exhibits 8000.

FINE ARTS COMMITTEE*
University of South Alabama
University Center, University Dr. S, 36688. Tel: (205) 460-6452
Annette McGowan, Chmn.
Judy Winter, V.Chmn.
Dr. Malcolm R. Howell, Dean of Students
Robert S. Holberg, Prog. Dir, University Center
Richard L. Nelson, Jr, University Center Dir.
Free 9 AM - 9 PM. Estab. July, 1971, to offer nationally famous contemporary works, exhibits of local artists, and traveling museums exhibits to further enrich the educational experience of the campus family while broadening community horizons; supported by appropriation and special student activity fees. Gallery with 60 linear feet of wall space upstairs, 50 feet downstairs specially luminated, and floor space for 3-D works. Meeting 2 - 5 times per academic quarter; mem. 10.

Collections: The Dove of Peace (print), Irving Amen; Spectrascopie Parrallex (sculpture), Barbara Soafford; New Politics '72 (silkscreen), Domingo Soto-Mendez; Reflections (drawing, pencil-ink), Anne Willet; a few student and professional works.

Exhibitions: Reproductions of Van Gogh; Original prints of Irving Amen; Original French Posters of 1890's; Ancient Buddhist Paintings of Japan; House of the Sun Exhibit; various local artists; regular student and faculty exhibits.

Activities: Lectures open to the public, 1 - 5 visiting lecturers per year; 1 - 5 gallery talks; concerts; dramatic programs; competitions. Library.

Publications: Kaleidoscope Brochure, arts; South Alabama Digest, review; Cinema Brochure, quarterly; Campus Calendar, monthly.

University Center Program Budget: $50,000.

⊕THE FINE ARTS MUSEUM OF THE SOUTH AT MOBILE
Langan Park, 36608. Tel: (205) 342-4642
Wayne F. Palmer, Chmn. of the Board
Mary O'Neill Victor, Dir. Gallery
Harold M Wittman, Asst. Dir.
Kathryn W. Lewis, Secy. & Records
Free Tues. - Sat. 10 AM - 5 PM; Sun. 12 AM - 5 PM. Estab. in 1964 to foster the appreciation of art and provide art education programs for the community; City appropriation. Board of directors meets monthly; mem. 600; dues life $1000, patron $100, supporting $50, family $25, individual $15.

Collections: 19th and 20th century American and European paintings, sculpture, prints and decorative arts; Wellington collection of wood engravings.

Exhibitions: American Watercolors 1850-1972; The Ancient Art of Orthodoxy; Sports in Art - Where the Action Is; American Porcelain Tradition; Art of the Old West; El Dorado: Gold of Ancient Colombia; The Preservation of a Heritage: A Half Century of Native American Art; Treasures of Jewish Art: Ceremonial and Symbolic.

Activities: Traveling exhibitions; original objects of art lent; lectures for public and members, visiting lecturers; art festivals, workshops, juried shows; concerts; competitions.

Library: 300 volumes for reference; 2000 slides for reference.

Publications: Calendar monthly.

Annual Income: Municipal and member support.

Attendance: Average 80,000 annually.

MOBILE ART ASSOCIATION, INC.
c/o Vasco Geer, Jr, Pres, 39 Alverson Rd, 36608.
Tel: (205) 344-7073
Mrs. George Ide, Secy.
Louis S Conover, Treas.
Estab. 1943 to promote and support a cultural program among artists, sculptors, and craftsmen in the field of fine arts; financed by mem. Ann. meeting May; mem. 436; dues $5.

Collections: Annual fall juried show collection.

Exhibitions: Fall jury show; Dauphin Island show; Old Mobile Show; Spring non-juried show.

Activities: Continuous art instruction to adults and children; competitions; co-sponsor of Mobile's Annual Outdoor Art and Crafts Fair to benefit Fine Arts Museum of the South at Mobile.

Publications: Mobile Art Association, Inc. Yearbook.

MONTGOMERY

ALABAMA ART LEAGUE
Montgomery Museum of Fine Arts, 440 S. McDonough St, 36104.
Tel: (205) 263-2519
Philip Coley, Pres.
Janice Ross, Secy.
Estab. 1929 to build a museum in the capitol city of Montgomery and help the artists of Alabama in every way possible; financed by endowment, city and state appropriation and membership. Ann. meeting first Sat. in Nov; mem. 300; dues $10.

Exhibitions by members at Montgomery Museum of Fine Arts, Birmingham Museum of Art, Mobile Art Gallery, George Washington Carver Museum, Tuskegee Institute, Goodwater Public Library, Convention Hall, Gadsden, The Governor's Mansion and WSFA-TV, Montgomery, Alabama.

Activities: Lending collection consisting of all media; lectures open to the public; 1 visiting lecturer per year; competitions; scholarships.

Publications: Newsletter; Alabama Art League Quarterly.

ALABAMA STATE DEPARTMENT OF ARCHIVES AND HISTORY
624 Washington Ave, 36130. Tel: (205) 832-6510
Milo B. Howard, Jr, Dir.
Free Mon. - Fri. 8 - 4:30 PM; Sat, Sun. and state holidays 8 - 11:30 AM, 12:30 - 4:30 PM, cl. on nat. holidays. Estab. 1901, exhibits depict the culture of Alabama and the Southeast and the territory embraced therein from the earliest times; state appropriation. Agency of the state government with no mem.

Collections: Portraits of prominent Alabamians, paintings depicting Alabama life, engraving and etchings of Alabama scenes.

Library: Reference photograph collection.

Publications: Alabama Historical Quarterly.

Income and Purchases: Income $190,000.

Attendance: 100,000 annual average.

⊕MONTGOMERY MUSEUM OF FINE ARTS
440 S. McDonough St, 36104. Tel: (205) 263-2519
Mrs. Robert S. Weil, President
Henry Flood Robert, Jr, Dir.
Theodore W. James, Asst. Dir.
Diane J. Gingold, Cur.
Sally Kingsbury, Cur. of Educ.
Denise M. Simoncini, Registrar
Audrey S. Gryder, Admin. Asst.
Free Tues, Wed, Fri. & Sat. 10 AM - 5 PM; Thurs. 10 AM - 10 PM; Sun. 2 PM - 5 PM; cl Mon. Estab. 1930 to promote fine arts; city museum with 5 changing exhibition galleries plus permanent collection galleries. Ann. meeting Apr; mem. 1300; dues $10 minimum with ascending categories.

Collections: Approx. 450 paintings, 350 works on paper including †19th and 20th century American paintings, American portrait collection (Freer and Goldthwaite Collections), †drawings and prints by contemporary American artists, †Old Master Print collection, †American and European sculpture.

Exhibitions: Dixie Annual, 11; Alabama Art League Annual, 20; First Family Christmas Card Competition, 4; 30 changing exhibitions per year. Special exhibitions: Photographs by Ralston Crawford; Edward Hopper: Selections from the Hopper Bequest; Thomas Coleman: Printmaker; Zelda Sayre Fitzgerald Retrospective; Realism and Surrealism in American Art; Marathon Art: Lotz, Eyfells and Gaudnek; James Foster Pinkston; Ride On! Exhibition of Antique Bicycles; Paolo Soleri: Arcology and the Future of Man.

Activities: 10 visiting lecturers per year covering predominately the permanent collections and special exhibitions; concert series; film series; staff lectures on art and art history; programs for children including puppet shows, improvisational tours, children's film series, slide-kit loans; intra-museum loans of permanent collections; art shop which maintains a permanent selection of replicas of major works and selected books on the history of art; annual art tour to a major city; local house and garden tour.

Library: Art reference library, approx. 500 volumes dealing with major artists and collections, in addition to a publication exchange program on an equal basis.

Publications: Exhibition catalogs; 4-5 publications per year.

Income: $200,000 per year including memberships. Annual purchases of $15,000 per year with special purchases every 3-5 years of approx. $75,000.

Attendance: 100,000 per year.

SELMA

STURDIVANT MUSEUM ASSOCIATION, INC.
713 Mabry St, P.O. Box 1205, 36701. Tel: (205) 872-5626
O. A. Marrow, Pres.
Dr. J. L. Stothart, V.Pres.
Judge B. M. Miller Childers, V.Pres.
Joe Traylor, V.Pres.
Mrs. Charles Hohenberg, V.Pres.
Sam A. Sommers, V.Pres.
Dr. Doy McCall, V.Pres.
Mrs. Edgar Stewart, Recording Secy.
Mrs. C. W. Wynn, Corresp. Secy.
Webster Manderson, Treas.
Open Tues. - Sat. 9 AM - 4 PM; admis adults $1.50, special youth
rates, under 12 free. Estab. 1957 by court order under Will of
Robert D. Sturdivant, to provide a museum, with emphasis on the
historical South, in the city of Selma. For this purpose Mr. and
Mrs. Sturdivant, wealthy plantation owners, left collections of books,
Indian artifacts, etc; endowed; city and county appropriation; in
addition, funds are raised each year by special events. Ann. meeting second Thurs. in Apr; mem. 270; dues $10, $25, $100, $1000.
Collections: †Period furniture of the fifties and earlier, to develop Sturdivant Hall as a historic house, built and owned by a
Southern cotton planter of wealth. Collections are increased by gifts
of manuscripts, textiles, objects of art, etc.
Exhibitions: Displays in exhibition cases include valuable and
antique dolls; bottles collected through the years by Mr. Sturdivant;
land grants, old libraries; genealogical material, expanding Mrs.
Studivant's collection, etc.
Activities: Book shop; historical publications for sale relating to
the community, such as cemetery records ($7.50-$10), local history;
information given to visitors daily.
Library: Several hundred volumes; the library is catalogued but
inactive with no librarian; large number of early magazines; DeBow's
Review, etc.
Publications: House leaflet.
Attendance: Approx. 5000 annually.

TUSCALOOSA

ARTS & HUMANITIES COUNCIL OF TUSCALOOSA COUNTY, INC.
P.O. Box 1117, 35401. Tel: (205) 553-3671
Mrs. J. D. Leapard, Pres.
John Boles, Secy.
Tom Boozer, Exec. Dir.
Free weekdays 8 AM - 5 PM. Estab. June 26, 1970 for the develop-
ment, promotion and coordination of educational, cultural and
artistic activities of the city and county of Tuscaloosa; financed by
endowment, city and state appropriation and membership. Quarterly
meetings with ann. meeting in June; mem. 410 individuals and 30
organizations; dues $5 individual, $25 organization.
Activities: Concerts, dramatic programs, competitions.
Publications: Lively Arts Calendar (quarterly).

TUSCUMBIA

TENNESSEE VALLEY ART CENTER
511 N. Water St, P.O. Box 474, 35674. Tel: (205) 383-0533
Mrs. Donald R. Brown, Pres.
Volunteer staff; part-time coordinator.
Open Tues. - Sun. 1 - 5 PM; admis. adults 50¢, children 25¢. Inc.
1964, organized for the building and operation of an art museum, the
creation of a higher level of culture in art, advancement of education
in all the arts in Northwest Alabama; mem. donations. New art
center bldg. opened Mar. 1973 with large main gallery and two
smaller for mo. exhibits of art work, workshops and group meetings.
Ann. meeting fourth Mon. in Mar; mem. 350; dues, patron $100,
sustaining $25, regular $5, student $3.
Exhibitions: Exhibition South, annual juried show with $1800 in
awards, in October, includes work from artists in all southeastern
states. Monthly exhibits represent all the arts: paintings, prints,
sculpture, fine handcrafts, photography from all over the country,
as well as members' work.
Activities: Small shows of members' paintings lent to schools,
libraries in area; 9 gallery talks per year; concerts, dramatic programs; classes for adults and children.

TUSKEGEE INSTITUTE

GEORGE WASHINGTON CARVER MUSEUM
Tuskegee Institute, 36088. Tel: (205) 727-8479
Mrs. Elaine F. Thomas, Dir. & Cur.
Mrs. Stefania Jarkowski, Art Gallery Dir.
Free Mon. - Sat. 10 AM - 4 PM; Sun. 1 - 4 PM. Estab. 1938 to house
Dr. Carver's extensive collections of native plants, minerals, birds,
his products from the peanut, sweet potato, and clay; the permanent

exhibit of vegetables that he had started in 1904, and his more than
100 paintings; financed by the college. Gallery maintains a permanent collection of traditional and contemporary paintings and
sculpture; traveling and monthly exhibitions.
Collections: Achievements of Dr. George Washington Carver in
science and art; African art; historical dioramas; artifacts of
Tuskegee Institute; paintings and sculpture.
Exhibitions: Stanislaw Noakowski, drawings; Contemporary
European posters; California National Water Color Society; 30
paintings by leading national artists; Art in Photography, Tuskegee
Institute; Washington Square Prizewinners; annual Student Art Show;
The Japanese Printmakers; Know Your Land and its Beauty (posters);
Ludwig Van Beethoven, 200 Anniversary Exhibit; Walery Kasprzyk,
watercolors; Kay Cassill; The Landscapes; Watercolors by Albert
Rinebold; Textile design by Dolores Ashley-Harris; Contemporary
Serigraphs; Moon Concept by Sara Winston, Carmine De Vivi; Christ-
mas Art Show; Contemporary Graphic Artists, Images and Reflec-
tions; The Black Experience in Print; Hilda Karniol; Bea Begman;
Bohdan Osyczka; Old Bergen Art Group; Claudia Steel; National
Society of Painters in Casein; Polish Posters; William H. Johnson;
Southern Vermont Art Center Group; Creative Past; Art of Africa;
Ethel Rabin, 20 caseins; Backgrounds of Modern Paintings; Artists
of Alaska; Jean Olds; Syed Yunus; Cecile Johnson; Cracow Water-
color Association; Women Painters of the West; Markand Thakar;
Faces of East Africa, L. Ayers; National Association of Women
Artists; Buffalo Kaplinski, Impressions of Southwest; Faces, Friends,
Forms, Fabrics of India, Elaine F. Thomas; Albert Rinebold; Alabama Art League.
Activities: Art classes; extension department serves the entire
United States; material available to museums and educational institutions; traveling exhibitions organized and circulated; individual paintings and original objects of art lent; photograph collection; lectures
open to the public; 5 visiting lecturers per year; 10 gallery talks;
daily tours; concerts; dramatic program; competitions. Book Shop.
Publications: Museum brochures, art gallery exhibition catalogues, historical dioramas.
Attendance: Approx. 13,000 annually.

UNIVERSITY (TUSCALOOSA)

ART GALLERY OF UNIVERSITY OF ALABAMA
35486. Tel: (205) 348-5967
Angelo Granata, Dir.
Free weekdays 8 AM - 5 PM; weekends 2 - 5 PM. Estab. 1946.
Collections: Small collections of †modern prints, drawings, paintings and photography; African and Mexican sculpture; Chinese ceramics; work by faculty and students.
Exhibitions: Approx. 15 temporary exhibitions a year, including
annual exhibitions by art faculty and students; traveling exhibitions
from collection available.

ALASKA

ANCHORAGE

ALASKA ARTISTS' GUILD, LTD.
Box 1888, 99510.
Teri Jo Hedman, Pres. Tel: (907) 272-6800
Barbara Mathews, V.Pres. Tel: (907) 344-4738
Norma McGee, 2nd V.Pres.
Marjorie Leavens, Recording Secy.
Sandy Mjolsnes, Corresp. Secy.
Ed Barrington, Treas.
Marie Shaughnessy, Funding Chmn.
Estab. 1958 to develop nondirective art, inc. 1959, to join in
selected activities of the arts, to improve quality and standard of
works, to establish communications between artist and public through
frequent exhibitions. Member of Arts Affiliates; nonprofit organiza-
tion; funding received in part from National Endowment for the Arts
for workshops. Monthly meetings, officers and board elected Jan;
mem. approx. 50; dues $10.
Exhibitions: Sponsors jointly with Anchorage Historical and Fine
Arts Museum annual statewide juried show; the Alaska Music
Festival Show; the annual juried Fine Arts Museum Show; the annual
South Central Alaska Artists' Guild Show.
Activities: Workshops conducted throughout state for adults and
children; lectures and film open to public; arts fair in conjunction
with Anchorage Community College. Guest instructors for workshops
open to the public.
Publications: Monthly newsletter.

✠ANCHORAGE HISTORICAL AND FINE ARTS MUSEUM
121 W. Seventh Ave, 99501. Tel: (907) 279-1553
R. L. Shalkop, Dir.
Juan Alvarez, Cur. Exhibits
John W. Carnahan, Cur. Collections

Patricia Wolf, Cur. Educ.
Diane Brenner, Archivist
Free, Tues. - Sat. 9 AM - 5 PM; Sun. 1 - 5 PM; cl. Mon. Estab.
1967 to collect and preserve materials relating to the art and history of Alaska, to exhibit them, as well as materials from other times and places and to interpret both through a variety of approaches; financed by city. Ann. meeting Oct; mem. 600; dues from $10 up.

Collections: †Prehistoric Alaskan artifacts; †Historic Alaskan native material (Eskimo, Aleut, Athapaskan, Tlingit-Haida); †Historic Alaskan Russian and American material; †Historic and contemporary Alaskan fine arts and crafts.

Exhibitions: Native Arts Festival; Earth, Fire and Fibre; National Invitational Biennial Print Exhibition; Russian Orthodox Art in Alaska, 1973; The Far North, 1973; Sydney Laurence, An Alaskan Impressionist, 1975; group, one-man and circulating exhibitions.

Activities: Educational department, training docent, guiding school and other groups, special classes for children; no fees; traveling exhibitions organized and circulated; lending collection, 200 photographs, 300 lantern slides, 4 motion pictures, 200 original prints, paintings and native artifacts; 1000 items lent in an average year; lectures open to the public; 12 visiting lecturers per year; 269 gallery talks and tours per year; concerts; dramatic programs; competitions. Book shop.

Library: 1000 volumes for reference; photograph collection of 5000 prints for reference; manuscripts, maps and current periodicals.

Publications: Exhibition catalogues; monthly newsletter; occasional papers.

Income and Purchases: Income approx. $300,000; purchases approx. $25,000.

Attendance: 90,000 annual average.

FAIRBANKS

ALASKA ASSOCIATION FOR THE ARTS
P.O. Box 2786, 99707. Tel: (907) 456-6485
Donna Matschke, Pres.
Walter Ensign, 1st V.Pres.
Carol Thomson, 2nd V.Pres.
Mary K. Barsdate, Secy.
Molly Heath, Treas.
Mildred Wenger, Historian
Irene Carr-Bayless, Exec. Dir.
Office hours: Mon. - Fri. 9 AM - 5 PM; gallery hours: weekdays 10 AM - 5 PM, weekends and holidays 2 - 4 PM. Estab. Nov, 1965 to expand the opportunities for citizens to enjoy and participate in cultural programs; to assist and promote the programs of existing arts organizations and to encourage formation of new ones in community; to encourage educational programs designed to strengthen and improve the arts; to facilitate touring of professional performers and exhibits; to act as coordinator between local arts groups and the national and state council on the arts; management of Civic Center Building at Alaskaland, through city, state and national grants. Ann. meeting in Apr; mem. 93, comprised of individuals, businesses and art groups.

Activities: Sponsorship of grand opera productions, chamber music and dance recitals; pops concerts with University-Fairbanks Symphony Orchestra; art exhibits and auctions; art balls, drama productions, film programs for adults and children, arts and crafts demonstrations and workshops, educational TV programs, student scholarships, Artist-in-the-Schools and Artist-in-Residence programs; provide administrative service on grants for other arts organizations.

Publications: Cultural Calendar, bimonthly, Sept. - May.

Annual Income: $24,000.

Attendance: 8000-10,000.

ELMER E. RASMUSON LIBRARY
University of Alaska, 99701. Tel: (907) 479-7224
H. Theodore Ryberg, Dir. of Libraries
Sharon West, Head Cataloging
David A Hales, Head Reader Services
Paul McCarthy, Head Archives
William Smith, Head Acquisitions
Patrick Ercolin, Head Media Services
Free Mon. - Thurs. 7:30 AM - 10 PM; Fri. 7:30 AM - 6 PM; Sat.
1 - 6 PM; Sun. 2 - 10 PM; when school not in session, Mon. - Fri.
8 AM - 5 PM. Estab. 1922 to support research and curriculum of the university; financed by state appropriations.

Collections: Paintings by Alaskan Artists, Eustace Ziegler, Ted Lambert, C. (Rusty) Heurlin, Raymond Eastwood, Nina Crumrine, Olaus Murie, Eudora Preston, and others; lithographs of Fred Machetanz; photographs of early Alaskan bush pilots; 400,000 volume library for lending via interlibrary loan; 40,000 print reference photograph collection on Alaska and the Polar Regions.

EXTENSION CENTER IN ARTS AND CRAFTS*
Division of Statewide Services
University of Alaska, P.O. Box 95204, 99701. Tel: (907) 479-7725
Dr. Charles W. Lafferty, Dean Div. of Statewide Services
Ronald W. Senungetuk, Staff Member
Estab. 1966 to provide learning center to Alaskan Eskimo and Indian artists and craftsmen for continuation of traditional arts and development of contemporary arts and crafts; financed by city & state appropriations.

UNIVERSITY OF ALASKA MUSEUM
99701. Tel: (907) 479-7505
L. Rowinski, Dir.
D. Larsen, Cur. of Ethnography
E. J. Dixon, Cur. of Archeology
Summer, daily 9 AM - 5 PM; winter, daily 1 - 5 PM; no admis.
Estab. 1929 to preserve, exhibit University of Alaska collections and make them available and useful for teaching and research; financed by state appropriations.

Collections: Alaskan Art; Ethnography; Archeology; Alaskan History; Natural History.

Activities: Book shop.

Publications: University of Alaska Museum Newsletter, irregular.

Attendance: 65,000 annual average.

JUNEAU

✣ALASKA STATE MUSEUM
Dept. of Education, Pouch FM, 99801. Tel: (907) 586-1224, 1221, 1262
Richard Engen, Div. Dir, Libraries & Museums
Alan Munro, Chief Cur. Museums
Dan Monroe, Educ. & Media Specialist
Ed Way, Cur. Exhibits
Martha Stevens, Cur. Multi-Media Educ. Prog.
Paul Dispier, Cur. Temporary Exhibits
Free winter Mon. - Fri. 8 AM - 4:30 PM; Sat. & Sun. 1 - 4:30 PM;
summer Mon. - Fri. 8 AM - 4:30 PM, 7 - 10 PM; Sat. & Sun.
1 - 4:30 PM, 7 - 10 PM; office open year round Mon. - Fri. 8 AM -
4:30 PM. Estab. 1900, opened to the public in 1920 to collect and maintain ethnological and archaeological material pertaining to Alaska, and for the collection of published and archival material on Alaska. Branch museums now in process of development, Arctic-Eskimo Museum, Barrow.

Collections: Ethnological and archaeological collections of Aleut, †Alaskan Eskimo, Coast Indian and Athapascan Indian items. †Historical collections of articles used by the Russians and the pioneers, †and present day items which have played a part in the contemporary history of Alaska, including art, sculpture, natural history and minerals. The present collection consists of approximately 12,000 items of history, ethnography, art, natural history, geology and archaeology, about half of which was collected prior to 1925. Ethnographic items represent a span of 10,000 years; some eskimo art forms predate the time of Christ.

Activities: Traveling exhibitions, lectures, films, multi-media learning kits; museology workshops; seminars.

Library: Research library and photo files; all other library, source material, maps and archival holdings were transferred to the Alaska Historical Library, State Capitol, Juneau in 1969.

Purchases: Approx. $25,000 annually.

Income: Approx. $300,000 annually, plus special grants for ethnographic and archeological studies and other museum related projects.

Attendance (The State Museum System): Approx. 100,000 annually; multi-media educational kits reach over 100 Alaskan villages and towns each year.

NOME

THE NOME ARTS COUNCIL
Box 233, 99762.
John J. Shaffer, Pres.
Delores Orman, Secy.
Barbara Shaffer, Treas.
Estab. to promote the arts for the benefit of the area community; endowed. Carrie McClain Memorial Library cooperates as a Museum.

Activities: Sponsor concerts, dramatic programs, classes and summer art excursions for children.

Income & Purchases: Income $1000 or less; purchases vary.

SITKA

SOUTHEAST ALASKA REGIONAL ARTS COUNCIL, INC.
P.O. Box 678, 99835. Tel: (907) 747-8581
Jan Craddick, Exec. Dir.
Elinora Brandner, Secy. & Coordinator

Linda Larsen, Pres.
Twyla Coughlin, V.Pres.
Judy Auger, Secy.
Corrinne Kenway, Treas.
Open 9 AM - 4:30 PM. Estab. in 1973 as a coordinating agency for arts organizations and community arts councils in Southeast Alaska; financed by grants from the Alaska State Council on the Arts, National Endowment for the Arts, American Revolution Bicentennial Commission, local school districts and municipalities, memberships and local contributions. Ann. meeting first weekend in Oct; mem: arts councils from 13 communities, serves additional communities in Southeast; dues $10 per delegate.

Activities: Two week camp for junior and senior high school students offering enrichment programs in dance, drama, music and visual arts; seven-community theatre design project; concert tours; workshops; classes.

Publications: Who Has An Idea (book of stories, articles and poems by children).

Total Budget: $200,000.

ARIZONA

DOUGLAS

DOUGLAS ART ASSOCIATION
Little Gallery
Box 256, 300 11th St, 85607. Tel: (602) 364-2633
Clarice Christensen, Pres.
Fran Wooldridge, First V.Pres.
Ray Levra, Second V.Pres.
Lucille Wilbourne, Treas.
Kitty Deiss, Secy. of Exec. Gallery Comt.
Free, daily 1:30 - 4 PM. Estab 1967 as a civic organization to bring to the people of this area art exhibitions of the highest quality and to encourage and nurture local talent; financed by mem. dues and donations. Gallery is an historic old building maintained for the association by the city of Douglas. Ann meeting June; mem. 135; dues $5.

Collections: †Two Flags Festival Collection for the cities of Douglas and Agua Prieta, Mexico.

Exhibitions: Exhibits alternate between membership shows, one man shows of area artists, and organizational shows such as the Tucson Southwest Watercolor Association; Two Flags Festival International Exhibits; also student and craft shows.

Activities: Special workshops, children's classes, college scholarships; lectures open to the public; 3 or 4 visiting lecturers per year; monthly association meetings and programs.

Publications: Newsletter, monthly.

FLAGSTAFF

MUSEUM OF NORTHERN ARIZONA
Northern Arizona Society of Science and Art, Inc.
Box 1389, Ft. Valley Rd, 86001. Tel: (602) 774-5211
Edward B. Danson, Pres.
David D. Chase, Treas.
Dorothy Pollock, Secy.
Hermann K. Bleibtreu, Dir.
Jane Metzger, Chmn. Art Comt.
Free 9 AM - 5 PM; Sun. 1:30 - 5 PM. Estab. 1928, inc. 1933, to tell the story of Northern Arizona, to increase knowledge and appreciation of science and art; building completed 1936. Ann. meeting Jan; mem. 1375; dues $10 and higher.

Collections: Contemporary †Hopi, †Navajo, Havasupai, and †other Indian arts and crafts, as well as †prehistoric objects; also †geology and †natural history; scientific collections.

Exhibitions: Annual exhibitions include Junior Art Show for Northern Arizona Indian Schools, April; Hopi Craftsmen, July; Navajo Craftsmen, July.

Library: Concentration on geology, biology, anthropology, meteorology, history, art of the Southwest. Books, 20,000; separates, 17,000; negatives, 70,000; slides, 11,000; maps, 4200.

Publications: Plateau (quarterly); bulletins, technical series, miscellaneous booklets, as published.

Income and Purchases: Income $880,962; annual purchases $3000.
Attendance: (1974) 101,569.

NORTHERN ARIZONA UNIVERSITY ART GALLERY
86001. Tel: (602) 523-3471
Joel S. Eide, Dir.
Open Tues. & Wed. 8:30 AM - 12 PM & 1 - 3 PM; Thurs. & Fri. 10 AM - 12 PM & 1 - 3 PM; Sun. 1 - 3 PM; also evenings Tues. & Thurs. 6:30 - 8:30 PM; cl. Mon. & Sat. Estab. 1962; frequent displays of the highest quality in all fields of art. Ann. meeting May; mem. 150 (Art Gallery Asn); dues $5.

Collections: Master prints of the 20th century and American Painting of the Southwest.

Exhibitions: Major traveling exhibitions since 1970: Lew Davis-40 year Retrospective 1970; Harmsen's Southwest Americana, 1972; Five Contemporary Printmakers, 1974; Varieties of Visual Reality, 1975; Ansel Adam's Photography, 1975; Noel Betts - Cities of the World, 1975; David Park's Paintings, 1975; Bill Owen's Photography, 1975; René Gelpi's Photography, 1975; NCAA Show, 1975; Dick Arentz Photography, 1976; Frank Jones' Paintings, 1976; Bruce McCombs' Print Show, 1976.

Activities: Extension service for Northern Arizona; traveling exhibitions; painting and objects of art loaned; lectures with 5 visiting lecturers per year; competitions.

Income: $5000.
Purchases: $400.
Attendance: 20,000.

JEROME

VERDE VALLEY ARTISTS INCORPORATED
Main St, P.O. Box 1017, 86331. Tel: (602) 634-5466
Diane Geoghegan, Pres.
Don Walsh, V.Pres. & Recording Secy.
Mary Johnson, Corresp. Secy.
Nelle Moffett, Dir. & Treas.
Free daily 10 AM - 5 PM. Estab. 1954 for the promotion of a united effort in the Verde Valley, and in other central Arizona communities of like interests, toward the advancement of the arts, art education, art appreciation, art exhibits, and for the maintenance of a permanent gallery and art center; financed by membership. Fine arts gallery for local amateur and professional artists. Gift shop. Ann. meeting June; mem. 100; dues $3 active, $5 exhibiting.

Collections: Small permanent collection containing 8 pieces.

Exhibitions: Jerome Theme Show 1975 (1st Annual); 3rd Annual El Valle Purchase Award Show; Yavapai College Fine Arts Faculty Show.

Activities: Lectures open to public; 12 visiting lecturers per year; concerts; classes for adults; competitions. Book shop.

Library: 30 volumes for reference only.

Publications: The Verde Artist Bulletin, monthly.

PHOENIX

ARIZONA ARTISTS GUILD
25 E. Coronado Rd, 85004.
Joan MacGillivray, Pres.
Sandra Thompson, 1st V.Pres. (Mem.)
Rae Evans, 2nd V.Pres. (Exhibitions)
Lydia Dillon, Recording Secy.
Katalin Ehling, Corresp. Secy.
Shirley Barefield Nelson, Treas.
Organized 1928. 5 meetings per year; officers elected annually; mem. 250 artists and associates; membership by jury of members; dues $10 annually.

Activities: Annual juried exhibitions, 2 - 5 per season, total awards 1970-1974, $6100; sponsors sketch groups, workshops, open to public; members available for demonstrations, programs.

ARIZONA WATERCOLOR ASSOCIATION
8122 N. Eighth Ave, 85021. Tel: (602) 943-6466
Frances Cole, Board Member
Lily Ham, Board Member
William Schimmel, Board Member
Adrian L. Hansen, Board Member
Val Muggeridge, Pres
Pat Dewitt, 1st V.Pres.
Sue Pohlman, 2nd V.Pres.
Pearl Ellis, 3rd V.Pres
Dick Phillips, Recording Secy.
Grace Grace, Corresp. Secy.
Jewel Bales, Treas.
Estab. 1960 to further activity and interest in watercolor and to reaffirm permance and importance of watercolor as a medium in its own right. Maintain exhibits of the highest professional quality; maintained by mem. Meeting dates, Oct, Dec, Feb, May; mem. 44; dues $8.

Exhibitions; Annual Winter Exhibit at Scottsdale Civic Center; others at Heard Museum, Phoenix Art Museum, Grady Gammage, Sedona, Prescott, Flagstaff, Yuma Art Center, Globe, Coolidge and Litchfield.

Activities: Traveling exhibitions organized and circulated.

Publications: Newsletter, mem. only.

✠HEARD MUSEUM
22 E. Monte Vista Rd, 85004. Tel: (602) 252-8848
Dr. Patrick T. Houlihan, Dir.
Free Mon. - Sat. 10 AM - 5 PM; Sun. 1 - 5 PM. Estab. 1929 by Mr. and Mrs. Dwight B. Heard. Ann. meeting Nov; endowed.

Collections: †Prehistoric and historic crafts of all primitive peoples, especially Southwestern Indian cultures.

Activities: Cooperates with City and County schools; lectures, exhibitions, craft demonstrations.

Library: 15,000 volumes.

✠PHOENIX ART MUSEUM
    1625 N. Central Ave, 85004. Tel: (602) 257-1222
Edward Jacobson, Pres.
Donald J. Kauffman, Secy.
Mary Dell Pritzlaff, V.Pres.
Sam Mardian, Jr, V.Pres.
Robert Applewhite, Treas.
Ronald D. Hickman, Dir.
Robert H. Frankel, Asst. Dir.
Sherwood D. Spivey, Jr, Bus. Mgr.
Shirley Haskin, Art Librn.
Daily 10 AM - 5 PM Wed. until 9 PM, Sun. 1 - 5 PM; cl. Mon. Estab. 1925; museum constructed 1959. Ann. meeting April; mem. 3200; dues $15 minimum membership.

Collections: Medieval, Renaissance; Baroque, 19th Century, Contemporary paintings, sculptures and graphics. Oriental arts collection; Mexican art and Western art. Thorne Miniature rooms.

Activities: Changing exhibitions in all areas of art including photography and graphics; art classes in art history, painting, sculpture and crafts. Lecture-movie series, concerts, symposia and research library facilities. Free tours by Docents; Junior Museum; Museum Shop.

Publications: Annual report; monthly calendar; exhibition catalogues; Catalogue of permanent collection.

Reference Library: 2500 volumes.
Income: $360,000.
Attendance: 150,000.

PUEBLO GRANDE MUSEUM
    4619 E. Washington St, 85034. Tel: (602) 275-3452
Donald H. Hiser, Archaeologist
Chad T. Phinney, Museum Asst.
Daily 9 AM - 5 PM; Sun. 1 - 5 PM; cl. Sat. and major holidays. Estab. 1929; a municipal archaeological Museum and research Laboratory for the interpretation of local history; City budget.

Collections: †Hohokam culture; †Arizona Indian Arts and Crafts.

Activities: Special training for students of anthropology; all-city public school program; lectures; classes for adults and children.

Library: 1850 volumes and a collection of photographs for reference only.

Attendance: 58,612.

SCOTTSDALE

SCOTTSDALE ARTISTS' LEAGUE
    P.O. Box 1071, 85252. Tel: (602) 271-9052
Jean Collet, Pres.
Anna Balentine, Secy.
Ann Schreiner, Corresp. Secy.
Floyd Armstrong, Treas.
Estab. Aug. 1961 to encourage the practice of art and to support and encourage the study and application of art as an avocation, to promote ethical principals and practice, to advance the interest and appreciation of art in all its forms and to increase the usefulness of art to the public at large; financed by membership. Maintains Upstairs Gallery in Camelview Plaza Mall. Monthly meetings 1st Tues; mem. 342; dues $10.

Exhibitions: Yearly juried exhibit for members only; yearly juried exhibit for Arizona artists (open show).

Activities: Lectures for members only; scholarships.

Publications: Art Beat (monthly bulletin to members).

TEMPE

ARIZONA STATE UNIVERSITY ART COLLECTIONS
    Matthews Center, 85281. Tel: (602) 965-2874
Rudy Turk, Dir.
Ken A. Smith-Brunet, Cur.
Mary Jane Williams, Registrar
Open Mon. - Fri. 10 AM - 5 PM; Sun. 1 PM - 5 PM; cl. Sat. Estab. 1950 with donations of American art by Oliver B. James. Intended to provide students with an opportunity to study and enjoy original works of art, the Collections are also an important cultural asset of the metropolitan Phoenix area and the State of Arizona.

Collections: †Collection of American Art with the following Divisions: I—Painting, beginning with portraits by colonial limners and including works from most periods and schools of American painting; II—Sculpture, consisting of works by contemporary and late 19th-century American sculptors; III—Graphics; IV—Ceramics, 19th and 20th century; V—Folk Art. †Collection of Historical and Contemporary Mexican Art. †Collections of European Art: Painting,

Sculpture, Graphics (notably, Orme and Barbara Lewis, Read Mullan, Lewis and Lenore Ruskin Collections).

Activities: Lectures, gallery talks, 30 temporary exhibitions annually, docent organization. Ethnic Arts Gift Shop.

Library: Books and catalogs.

Publications: Catalog and supplements, brochures, posters.

Attendance: Approx. 46,000 annually.

HOWE ARCHITECTURE LIBRARY
    Arizona State University, 85281. Tel: (602) 965-6400
Jane C. Henning, Architecture Librn.
Lois I. Schneberger, Soleri Archivist
Stanley G. Jones, Library Asst.
Free Mon. - Thurs. 8 AM - 10 PM; Fri. 8 AM - 5 PM; Sun. 5 - 10 PM. Estab. 1959 to serve as a regional resource center on the subject of architecture and to support the programs of Arizona State University; financed by state appropriation.

Collections: Paolo Soleri Archives. Library has 13,000 volumes for both lending and reference.

TUCSON

ARIZONA DESIGNER-CRAFTSMEN*
    c/o Patricia Reinking, Pres, 335 Spring Valley Dr, 85704.
    Tel: (602) 297-4233
Joe Harris, V.Pres.
Jacob Brookins, Treas.
Estab. 1959 to bring together the professional craftsmen of Arizona; to help maintain standards of excellence in crafts; to assist the craftsman in marketing his work; and to promote interest in crafts in Arizona; maintained by mem. Three chapters in Arizona, Northern-Flagstaff, Central-Phoenix, Southern-Tucson; local chapters meet mo; ann. meeting and conference held each May; approx. 140 juried mem, 160 gen. mem; dues juried $10, gen. $5.

Exhibitions: Annual Tucson Craft Market, Tucson Community Center; Annual Scottsdale Arts Festival; Ariz. Textile Competition, Ariz State Univ; Artist Craftsmen of intermountain West, ADC and Flagstaff Summer Festival Assoc, Flagstaff.

Activities: Lectures open to public, 2 visiting lecturers per year. Library.

Publications: ADC Newsletter 4 times a year.

✠CENTER FOR CREATIVE PHOTOGRAPHY
Univerisity of Arizona
    845 N. Park Ave, 85721. Tel: (602) 884-3094
Harold Jones, Dir.
Marguerite McGillivray, Admin. Asst.
Free Mon. - Fri. 8 AM - 5 PM. Estab. Sept. 16, 1975 as resource for the study of the history and nature of photography in the 20th century; financed by endowment, city and state appropriations. Changing exhibitions of photographs from Center collection and collections of other national institutions.

Collections: The complete archives of Ansel Adams, Wynn Bullock, Harry Callahan, Aaron Siskind and Frederick Sommer; a significant collection of the works of other major 20th century photographers.

Activities: Elementary, high school and senior citizens programs; traveling exhibitions; photograph collection; lectures open to public; 10 visiting lecturers per year; 10 gallery talks; gallery tours.

Library: Over 1000 volumes; photograph collection.

Publications: Bimonthly bulletin.

✠TUCSON MUSEUM OF ART, INC.
    235 W. Alameda, 85701. Tel: (602) 624-2333
Mrs. Ted F. Bloom, Pres.
Dr. Raymond H. Thompson, 1st V.Pres.
Richard T. Coolidge, 2nd V.Pres.
Joseph G. Gootter, Treas.
Mrs. Roger E. Armstrong, Recording Secy.
Marcia Grand, Corresp. Secy.
Paul M. Piazza, Dir.
Gerrit C. Cone, Asst. Dir.
Thomas W. Wiper, Dir. Educ.
Free Tues. - Sat. 10 AM - 5 PM; Sun. 1 - 5 PM. A nonprofit Arizona corporation founded in 1936 to promote public art education; faculty gallery for one-man shows by faculty members. Ann. meeting May; mem. 1500; dues student $7.50; individual $15; family $20; supporting $35; donor $50; sponsor $100; patron $250; benefactor $500; angel $1000; corporate $100-$1000.

Collections: Pre-Columbian; Spanish Colonial; Western Art; modern and contemporary fine arts and crafts.

Exhibitions: Arizona Crafts (juried, biannual, Arizona craftsmen); Arizona's Outlook (juried, biannual alternating with Arizona Crafts, Arizona artists); approx. 9 other exhibits annually, mostly organized by Tucson Museum of Art; some exhibition catalogs.

Activities: Annual arts and crafts fair; art rental and craft sales gallery; lectures, art appreciation and special subjects; speakers bureau; docent-guided tours; exhibitions prepared for circulation; music and dance programs; tours of Kino missions of southern Arizona and northern Mexico.

Library
119 N. Main, 85705. Tel: (602) 623-4881.
Dorcus Worsley, Art Librn.
General art reference with emphasis on pre-Columbian and other primitive arts of the world; approx. 16,000 slides, 3500 books, 5000 periodicals, pamphlets, miscellaneous publications.

La Casa Cordova
171 N. Meyer, 85701.
Mexican heritage museum and gift shop; restored home built in 1850's and 60's.

✠UNIVERSITY OF ARIZONA MUSEUM OF ART
Olive & Speedway, 85721. Tel: (602) 884-2173
William E. Steadman, Dir.
Free weekdays 10 AM - 5 PM; Sun. 2 - 5 PM. Estab. 1955; state and city appropriations.
Collections: The Samuel H. Kress Collection of 26 Renaissance works and 26 paintings from the retablo of the Cathedral of Ciudad Rodrigo; the Gallagher Memorial Collection of 171 international contemporary paintings and sculptures; the C. Leonard Pfeiffer Collection of American Painting; miscellaneous gifts of paintings, prints and furniture; the Samuel Latta Kingan Collection of 19th Century American Painting.
Exhibitions: First Retrospective in America of Paintings, Watercolors, Lithographs and Drawings by Cornelis Theodorus Marie (Kees) Van Dongen, 1971; The West and Walter Bimson (paintings and sculpture of western subjects), 1971; Childe Hassam Retrospective, 1972; Robert Vickrey Retrospective of Egg Temperas, Watercolors and Drawings, 1973; Isabel Bishop Retrospective of Paintings, Drawings, Etchings and Aquatints, 1974; Henri Manguin Retrospective of Paintings, Watercolors, Drawings, 1974; The Naked Eye (photographs by Edward Weston), 1975; Exhibition of Ansel Adams Photographs, 1975.
Activities: Educational department with Outreach Program to schools; docent program with tours of museum; traveling exhibitions; original objects of art lent; photograph collection; 400 gallery tours annually; book shop.
Library: 500 volumes.
Publications: Fully illustrated catalog for each special exhibition.
Attendance: 75,000.

YUMA
YUMA ART CENTER
P.O. Box 1471, 85364. Tel: (602) 782-9261
Laurel Meinig, Dir.
Open Tues. - Sun. 10 AM - 5 PM; cl. Mon. and national holidays.
Collections: Majority of work by contemporary Arizona artists.
Exhibitions: Program of changing exhibitions throughout the year. Major annual exhibition: Southwestern Invitational; Annual Arts Festival; Father Garces Celebration of the Arts includes art, music and performance.
Activities: Theatre Guild produces annual season of live theatre; in-house tour program and artist-in-residence program; cooperative lecture series with Arizona Western College; Rental-Sales Gallery.
Income: $50,000.

ARKANSAS

CLARKSVILLE

COLLEGE OF THE OZARKS ART DEPARTMENT LIBRARY
610 Johnson St, 72830.
Lyle Ward, Head, Art Dept.
Carolyn Green, Librn.
Free. Estab. 1834 as a four-year liberal arts college; den; endowed.
Collections: Original print collection; graduate students' painting collection.
Exhibitions: (Prints) Rebecca Witsell One-Woman Show, Arkansas Arts Center; Northern Illinois University traveling exhibition, DeKalb.
Activities: Elementary and Secondary Education programs meeting for state certification requirements; individual paintings lent to schools; 100 color reproductions and 3 16mm films; 100 items lent to 3 borrowers; lectures open to public; 9 visiting lecturers per year; concerts, dramatic programs; scholarships; book shop.
Library: 73,000 volumes.
Budget: $1000; purchases $100-$200.
Attendance: 570 total student enrollment.

CROSSETT

CROSSETT ART LEAGUE
125 Main, 71635. Tel: (501) 364-3606
Sunny Fisher, Pres.
Olivia Bingham, Secy.
Estab. to promote and encourage art skills and art appreciation; financed by membership and federal matching funds; mem. 41; dues $5.
Exhibitions held at El Dorado Art Center, Arkansas, Junior League Arts and Crafts Fair and Ashley County Fair.
Activities: Sponsor trips to cultural centers for sixth graders; adult and childrens' classes.
Publications: Monthly newsletter.

EL DORADO

SOUTH ARKANSAS ART LEAGUE
110 E. Fifth St, 71730. Tel: (501) 862-5474
Carl W. Egerer, Pres.
Ann S. Plair, Secy.
Free 9 AM - 5 PM. Estab. 1955 for the promotion, enrichment and improvement of the visual arts by means of exhibits, lectures and instruction, and through scholarships to be offered whenever possible; financed by city and state appropriation and membership. Gallery maintained to show ten guest artists annually; two months dedicated to local artists; works by local artists hanging in corridor year-round. Ann. meeting 4th Tues. in May; mem. 170; dues $5.
Collections: All paintings and collections are under jurisdiction of South Arkansas Arts Center.
Exhibitions: Various art shows in this and surrounding states.
Activities: Lectures open to public; 8 gallery talks per year; classes for adults and children; competitions; scholarships.
Library: 135 volumes for lending and reference.
Publications: Artifacts, quarterly.

SOUTH ARKANSAS ARTS CENTER
110 E. Fifth St, 71730.
Jerome Orr, Pres.
James L. Wilson, Dir.
Maurice Mims, Secy.
Free, 10 AM - 5:30 PM. Estab. 1964 to furnish arts to the South Arkansas Area; financed by endowments and contributions; two art galleries; art library.
Activities: Lectures open to the public; concerts; dramatic Programs; ballet company; classes for adults and children; competitions; scholarships.
Publications: Artifacts, quarterly.

FAYETTEVILLE

✠UNIVERSITY OF ARKANSAS ARTS CENTER GALLERY*
Arts Center, Garland Ave, 72701. Tel: (501) 443-4511 Exten. 561
Bruce Houston, Dir.
Free 8 AM - 10 PM; Sun. 2 - 5 PM. Estab. 1950. Used as educational gallery in fields of painting, drawing, sculpture, architecture, prints and the theatre arts.
Fine Arts Library: Library connected to Gallery contains approx. 14,000 books and periodicals on art, architecture, theatre and music (See Schools).

FORT SMITH

FORT SMITH ART CENTER
423 N. Sixth St, 72901. Tel: (501) 782-6371
Polly Crews, Dir.
Marcia Edwards, Pres.
Free daily 10 AM - 4 PM except Mon; Sun. 2 - 4 PM. Estab. 1957 to provide art museum, art association and art education; endowed. Sales Gallery. Mem. 292; ann. dues $15.
Collections: †American painting, graphic, drawings.
Activities: Adults art classes; films; lectures; traveling exhibitions; competitions. Library.
Publications: Bulletin monthly.
Annual Income: $25,000.
Attendance: 5000.

HELENA

PHILLIPS COUNTY MUSEUM
Helena Public Library, 623 Pecan St, 72342. Tel: (501) 332-3537
Mrs. J. F. Wahl, Pres.
Free 10 AM - 5 PM. Estab. 1929, as an annex to Library, estab. 1888; financed by Library.
Collections: American Indian material; portraits and manuscripts; two 16th century Italian paintings; china and glass; Civil War, Spanish-American War, World Wars I and II; Thomas A. Edison Display of Inventions.
Activities: Traveling exhibitions of paintings and prints by local and state artists; club meetings; cooperates with schools.
Attendance: 8000 annually.

HOT SPRINGS

SOUTHERN ARTISTS ASSOCIATION
Fine Arts Center, 815 Whittington Ave, 71901.
Tel: (501) 623-0836
John Baran, Pres.
Mrs. Charles Katz, Secy.
Mrs. J. B. Newcomb, Dir.
Lucile Chick, Staff Secy.
Free Wed. - Sat. 10 AM - 4 PM; Sun. 1:30 - 5 PM; cl. Mon. and
Tues. Estab. 1951 as Hot Springs Art Group. Provides the com-
munity with a yearly calendar of art exhibitions; provides gallery
space for members; educational program in art for community and
serves as state-wide art association. Meeting quarterly. Mem. 165;
dues $15 and higher.
Exhibitions: Annual Art Festival; Semiannual Outdoor Exhibitions;
one-man shows; traveling exhibitions from many sources.
Activities: Lectures; classes for adults and children; monthly
art films and open house; Wed. Workshop; one scholarship for youth
art student per year.
Attendance: 4700 visitors.

LITTLE ROCK

✿ARKANSAS ARTS CENTER
MacArthur Park, 72203. Tel: (501) 372-4000
James T. Dyke, Chmn of Board of Trustees
B. Finley Vinson, Pres.
A. F. Minor, Jr, Secy.
Townsend Wolfe, Exec. Dir.
Leon A. Kaplan, Asst. to Dir.
Norma Kirk, Exec. Secy.
Rebecca Rogers Witsell, Dir. of Educ.
Margaret Wickard, Registrar
Karren Miller, Dir. Pub. Information
Cater Cranford, Dir. Dance
June Freeman, Dir. State Services
Rand Hopkins, Dir. Children's Theatre
Evelyn McCoy, Dir. Library
Galleries free Mon.- Sat. 10 AM - 5 PM; Sun. 12 - 5 PM. Estab.
1937 as Museum of Fine Arts; formally dedicated as Arkansas Arts
Center May 18, 1963 to further the development, the understanding
and the appreciation of the visual and performing arts; mem. 3000;
dues $15.
Permanent Collection: Ceramics; glass; aluminum, bronze,
copper, pewter and silver; porcelain; drawings and wash drawings;
enamels; furniture; horology; jewelry; lamps; manuscripts; jade and
paper; paintings; photographs; prints; sculpture; textiles.
Exhibitions: 46 exhibitions; annual competitive exhibitions: Delta
Art Exhibition (for artists living or born in Arkansas, Mississippi,
Louisiana, Missouri and Tennessee), Young Arkansas Artists (for
the state's school children), Toys Designed by Artists, and the
Prints, Drawings and Crafts Exhibition.
Activities: State Services Program provides exhibitions, performing arts productions, AV materials to communities throughout state;
theatre programs; classes for students (age 3 to 70) in visual and
performing arts. (See Schools). Original objects of art and individual
paintings lent to schools and traveling exhibitions organized and
circulated (257 objects) to schools, churches and civic groups in the
State of Arkansas through Extension Department; 120 color reproductions, 10,000 lantern slides, 47 motion pictures and 85 film
strips; 332 items lent in average year to 5 active borrowers; photograph collection with 47 prints for lending; junior museum; 3 visiting lecturers per year open to public; 8 gallery talks; 301 tours; 15
demonstrations relating to current exhibitions; concerts, dramatic
programs, competitions; scholarships; book shop. Traveling seminar
programs twice a year to various countries of the world; neighborhood arts program in visual and performing arts to children in eco-
nomically disadvantaged neighborhoods.
Library: 5000 volumes for lending, with basic exceptions; photograph collection; John Reid jazz collection; collection of original
cartoons by George Fisher; books, magazines, films, filmstrips,
slides in all areas of the arts available to members on a noncircu-
lation basis.
Publications: Monthly bulletin for members; Arkansas Arts
Center Catalogue (annually).
Income: $781,386.
Attendance: 461,525.

ARKANSAS HISTORY COMMISSION
Old State House (West Wing), 300 W. Markham St, 72201.
Tel: (501) 371-2141
Dr. John L. Ferguson, Dir.
Free Mon. - Fri. 8 AM - 4:30 PM.
Museum includes gallery of †paintings of noted Arkansans. Li-
brary of †rare Arkansiana. Also included are the Harry B. Solmson
Collection of Confederate and Southern State Currency and the A.
Howard Stebbins Collection of Arkansas Obsolete Currency.

ARKANSAS TERRITORIAL RESTORATION
Territorial Square, 72201. Tel: (501) 374-5544
William B. Worthen, Jr, Dir.
Open daily 9 AM - 5 PM; Sun. 1 - 5 PM. admis. to museum houses,
adults $1, children (6 and under) 25¢, senior citizens (65 and over)
25¢; admis. free to reception center.
Restoration completed 1941; owned by the State, operated by the
Arkansas Territorial Restoration Commission. A group of 13 buildings dating from the 1820's-1840's, with permanent collection of
†furnishings of the period, †porcelain hands, †watercolors, some of
which are obtained through an annual Arts Festival purchase award,
and prints dating from the early 19th century, including early copies
and one original Audubon bird print of Arkansas birds.
Activities: New reception center opened 1973, with space for history and pre-tour lectures, slide shows, traveling and temporary
exhibitions of objects, photographs and art of historical and regional
interest; lending box program.
Library: Small collection of art, furniture, garden and history
books.
Attendance: Past two years, approx. 70,000.

PINE BLUFF

BRUSH AND PALLETTE GUILD*
71601.
Jackie Fish, Pres.
Mary Ann Stafford, Secy.
Estab. 1942 for the study and practice of painting, the promotion of
local exhibits and the arousing of community interests in an appreciation of painting; financed by membership. Help maintain the
sales and rental gallery of southeast Arkansas arts and science
center. Meetings second Thurs. of each month.
Exhibitions: Annual exhibit at southeast Arkansas rodeo and
livestock show.
Activities: Lectures open to the public; approx. 4 gallery talks;
competitions.

SOUTHEAST ARKANSAS ARTS AND SCIENCE CENTER
Civic Center, 71601. Tel: (501) 536-3375
Philip A. Klopfenstein, Dir.
Brad Ford, Dir. Theatre
James Loney, Cur. of Educ.
Chmn. of the Board changes yearly.
Free Mon. - Sat. 10 AM - 5 PM; cl. Sun. and holidays. Opened in
1968 in Civic Center Complex; governing authority, city of Pine
Bluff. Mem. 750; annual family dues $10, art school enrollment
100 students per quarter.
Collections: Contemporary art assembled by gifts and pur-
chases; prints of American college professors.
Activities: Art gallery exhibitions; annual art festival; annual
statewide competition; docent tours, theatre workshops, theatre
productions, concert series, music concerts; art sales gallery; regional advisory activities for cultural programs in 11 counties; film
series for adults and children; original art print sales, publications.
Annual Budget: $150,000.
Attendance: 55,000.

SPRINGDALE

ARTS CENTER OF THE OZARKS
Council of Ozark Artists and Craftsmen, Inc.
Arts Bldg, 216 W. Grove Ave, P.O. Box 725, 72764.
Tel: (501) 751-5441
Mrs. Fred McCuistion, Pres.
Geneva Powers, Dir. Arts Center
Mrs. Nick S. Matthews, V.Pres. Arts Div. & Exhibit Chmn.
Mrs. Luther S. Cammack, Workshop Chmn.
Rolf W. Brandt, Special Exhibit Chmn.
Free Mon- Fri. 1 - 5 PM. Estab. 1948, merged with the Springdale
Arts Center, to become Arts Center of the Ozarks, 1973, to preserve
the traditional handcrafts, to promote all qualified contemporary arts
and crafts, to help find markets for artists and craftsmen; financed
by city and state appropriations and memberships. Ann. meeting 3rd
Mon. in Aug; mem. 70; dues $10.
Exhibitions: Springdale Invitational Arts and Crafts Fair (an-
nually in June); Prairie Grove Clothesline Fair (annually on Labor
Day weekend).
Activities: Instruction in the arts, music, dance and drama, run
concurrently with other activities; evening classes in painting;
schedules workshops in handcrafts; rehearsals for the music and
dramatic productions.
Publications: Arts Center Events, monthly; bimonthly newsletter.

STATE UNIVERSITY

ARKANSAS STATE UNIVERSITY ART GALLERY, JONESBORO
Fine Arts Center, Jonesboro (Mailing Address: Box 846, State
University), 72467. Tel: (501) 972-3050
Evan Lindquist, Dir.

Free Mon. - Fri. 9 AM - 5 PM; cl. Sat. and Sun. Estab. 1967 adjunct to teaching program in Division of Art, Arkansas State University, affording opportunity for observation and study of original works of art; providing a showcase for contemporary working artists; appropriation.

Collections: Primarily works, †painting, sculpture, prints, drawing, by contemporary American artists; a few 19th and 20th century European artists represented in print collection.

Exhibitions: W. C. Estler Collection, 1972; Burke, Wittsell, Drasites, 1972; Ken Ryden, 1972; 3 Craftsmen, 1972, 1973; Oriental Rugs, 1972; Robert Andrew Parker, 1972; Memphis Academy of Arts Faculty, 1972; University of Missouri Faculty, 1973; Mary Sims, 1973; Walter Nichols, 1973; Al Allen, 1973; Frank Young Sculpture, 1974; American Craftsmen, 1974; Fabrics of Arizona Designer-Craftsmen, 1975; Wisconsin Watercolor, 1975; Original Watergate Cartoons, 1975.

Activities: 2-3 visiting lecturers per year; competitions.

Publications: Individual catalogs for each exhibit.

Attendance: 15,000 annual average.

STUTTGART

GRAND PRAIRIE ARTS COUNCIL, INC.*
P.O. Box 65, 72160. Tel: (501) 922-5231
Mrs. James R. Oliver, Jr, Pres.
Mrs. E.A. McCracken, Secy.
Estab. 1956, inc. 1964, to encourage cultural development in the Grand Prairie area; to sponsor the Grand Prairie Festival of Arts held annually in September at Stuttgart; and to work toward the establishment of an arts center for junior and senior citizens; maintained by contributions. Ann. meeting Jan. each year for election of officers; mem. 13, representing 4 civic organizations.

Collections: Very small permanent collection started by donations.

Activities: Schools divisions in festival.

Publications: Festival invitations in July; programs in Sept, yearly.

Annual Income: $3000-$4000.

Attendance: Approx. 9000 at Grand Prairie Festival of Arts.

CALIFORNIA

BAKERSFIELD

KERN COUNTY MUSEUM
3801 Chester Ave, 93301. Tel: (805) 861-2132
Richard C. Bailey, Dir.
Patti Binns, Secy.
Free Mon. - Fri. 8 AM - 5 PM; Sat. and Sun. 12 AM - 7 PM DST. Admission to Pioneer Village, adults 50 cents, adult groups 35 cents, juniors 35 cents and children 25 cents. Estab. 1945.

Collections: Minerals and ores, transportation, guns, California primitive paintings, Pioneer Village covering 12 acres; this includes more than 30 buildings, narrow guage railroad and station, log cabin, jail, church, a residence of 1884, blacksmith shop, first courthouse, country store, ranch residence with water tower, early drugstore, barber shop and other constructions.

Activities: Prepares data for circulation and program tours and visits by school and civic groups.

Library: 800 volumes for reference only; photograph collection of 500 prints for reference.

Publications: Guide to the Museum.

Attendance: 150,000 annually.

BERKELEY

BERKELEY PUBLIC LIBRARY
Art and Music Section
94704. Tel: (415) 644-6785
Bruce A. Munly, Head, Art & Music Section
Open Mon. - Thurs. 9 AM - 9 PM; Fri. & Sat. 9 AM - 6 PM; Sun. 1 - 5 PM. Estab. 1960; financed by city and state appropriations.

Collections: Art, Architecture, Crafts, Photography, Music, Dance, Costume.

Activities: 371 framed color reproductions, 9000 lantern slides, 75,000 books, 12,000 slides, 1400 framed reproductions, 7200 phonorecords and 196 cassettes in lending and circulating collection.

JUDAH L. MAGNES MEMORIAL MUSEUM
2911 Russell St, 94705. Tel: (415) 849-2710.
Dr. Daniel K. Oxman, Pres.
Dr. William Mandel, Secy.
Seymour Fromer, Dir.
Ruth Eis, Cur.
Ruth Rafael, Archivist
Vivian Kleinman, Librn.
Margaret Heilbronn, Office Mgr.
Free Sun. - Fri. 10 AM - 4 PM. Estab. 1962 for collection, preservation and exhibition of documents, artifacts, and art relating to the history of the Jewish people. Research, publication, and courses. Archives of the history of the Jews in the Western States; financed by mem. Changing exhibits gallery for bi-monthly exhibits of paintings, sculpture and photography. Mem. 700; dues $10-$1000.

Collections: Magnes Archives; Western Jewish Americana; world Jewish history; Holocaust collection recording the Nazi era; ceremonial art of the Jewish family; graphic and fine art; liturgical and Yiddish theater music; documents and artifacts of the Jews of India.

Exhibitions: (1974) Drawings by Al Hirschfeld; Jewelry by Israeli Craftsmen, Rachel and Eli Gera; A Tradition Revived, Contemporary Ketubot by David Moss; Jacob Pins, Israel's Master Woodcutter; Lithographs by Anatoli Kaplan; Sculptures by Elbert Weinberg. (1975) We Are the Wall Itself, Serigraphs by Albert Garvey; Creative Frontier; Magic and Superstition in the Jewish Tradition; Ruth Eis Paintings 1955-1975.

Activities: Lectures open to public, 5 visiting lecturers per year; 100 gallery talks; 100 tours; concerts; classes for adults. Gift shop.

Library: Reference library, 11,000 volumes; reference photograph collection, 2000 prints.

Publications: Art books, bibliographies and history, approx. 2 per year.

Income and Purchases: Income $50,000; purchases $5000.

Attendance: 12,000 annual average.

R. H. LOWIE MUSEUM OF ANTHROPOLOGY
University of California, Berkeley
103 Kroeber Hall, 94720. Tel: (415) 642-3681
Prof. William Bascom, Dir.
Frank A. Norick, Principal Anthropologist & Asst. Dir.
Albert B. Elsasser, Assoc. Research Anthropologist
Lawrence E. Dawson, Sr. Anthropologist
Dave D. Herod, Sr. Curatorial Anthropologist.
Open Mon. - Fri. 10 AM - 4 PM, Sat. & Sun. 12 - 4 PM; admis. 25¢ adults, 10¢ children. Estab. 1901 as a research museum for the training and educating of undergraduate and graduate students; a resource for scholarly research; Lowie Museum seeks to collect, preserve, educate and conduct research; financed by city and state appropriations.

Collections: Museum houses approximately 3.5 million objects of anthropological interest, both archaeological and ethnological. Excellent ethnological collections from Africa, Oceania, North America (Plains, Arctic and Sub-Arctic). Excellent archaeological collections from Egypt, Peru, California and Africa.

Anthropology exhibitions: Traditions in Transition; Games of Skill, Chance and Strategy; Indians of Panama; Artisans of India; Ishi, The Last Survivor of a California Indian Tribe; Sons of Vishvakarma—Artisans of India.

Activities: Lectures open to public; gallery talks and tours; adult classes; book shop.

Library: 2000 volumes for reference and research; photograph collection; 20,000 prints for reference.

Publications: Annual Report; Exhibition Guides.

Income & Purchases: Income over $250,000; purchases several thousand dollars.

Attendance: 65,000.

UNIVERSITY ART MUSEUM, BERKELEY
University of California, 94720. Tel: (415) 642-1207
James Elliott, Dir.
David Leonetti, Asst. Dir.
Bonnie Baskin, Cur. of Educ.
Joy Feinberg, Cur. of Collections & Exhibitions
Tom Luddy, Cur. of Film
Maria Eckstein, Special Events Coordinator
Carlos Gutierrez-Solana, Installation Coordinator
Mya Pelletier, Registrar
Free Tues. - Sun. 11 AM - 5 PM. Estab 1965; new museum building opened November 1970, designed by Mario Ciampi, Richard Jorasch, and Ronald E. Wagner of San Francisco; 95,000 square feet, ten galleries and sculpture garden; the Museum functions as a public museum and a teaching institution stressing involvement by students and faculty of the Univ. of California.

Collections: Hans Hofmann's gift of 45 of his paintings is housed in the Hans and Maria Hofmann Gallery; the permanent collection includes 20th century European painting, a major collection of 20th century American painting and sculpture (with a good representation of Hofmann School artists), a small group of Renaissance and Baroque paintings and sculpture, and a small but excellent group of Chinese paintings.

Exhibitions: The Museum originates four or five major exhibitions each year which are shows in Berkeley and then circulated nationally. Smaller exhibitions are originated for study purposes and are not circulated. In addition, selections from the permanent collection are exhibited, as well as selections from the collection of the Lowie Museum of Anthropology.

Activities: Gallery tours, art festivals, and workshops led by university students; weekly lectures, concerts, dance and music performances, and daily film showings. The Museum supports and houses the Pacific Film Archive, with the most extensive film exhibitions program on the west coast and film deposits of 3000 titles, including many Japanese features.

Publications: For most exhibitions originated by the Museum, informative and scholarly exhibition catalogues are published.

Library: The University Library at Berkeley and its various departmental branches house the largest collection of art books on the west coast. The Museum maintains a collection of exhibition catalogues and related materials for reference use.

Income and Purchases: Operating budget 1975-76: approx. $1,300,000, purchases $50,000.

Attendance: 381,000 (1973), 430,000 (1974).

CATHEDRAL CITY

MUSEUM OF ANTIQUITIES AND ART
Hotel Arner, Glenn Grove & Plumley Place, 92234
Samuel DeWalt Arner, Founder & Cur.
Free Nov 15 - May 1st, 3 - 5 PM & 7 - 9 PM. Estab. 1960 for educational purposes; financed by founder, Samuel DeWalt Arner. Permanent gallery of Western historical figures, mostly oil portraits by Arner over 50 year period.

Collections: Mostly Pre-Columbian artifacts, although some artifacts from Israel, Turkey, Lebanon, Egypt, Italy, India, Japan and China; ancient coins; ancient arms; fossils; gemstones; mineral specimens.

Activities: Lectures to visitors and large groups from schools and colleges.

Library: 3000 - 4000 volumes for reference on archaeology, anthropology, science, biography, politics, geography, metaphysics, geology, art and history.

CHERRY VALLEY

RIVERSIDE COUNTY ART AND CULTURE CENTER
Edward-Dean Museum of Decorative Arts
9401 Oak Glen Rd, 92223. Tel: (714) 845-2626
Mary Jo O'Neill, Museum Dir.
Barbara Jameson, Museum Asst.
Free daily 1 - 5 PM, except Mon. and legal holidays. Operated as a private museum from 1958 - 1964, then to County in 1964; Museum of Decorative Arts estab. as a permanent collection with some flexibility for showing loan collections; financed by county funding. North Gallery offers 11 changing exhibitions per year of art and decorative art.

Collections: European and Oriental Decorative Arts of the 17th and 18th centuries; permanent collections of furniture, paintings, porcelains, bronzes, Oriental rugs, paperweights, Chinese costumes, American pressed glass, art reference books and some rare books.

Exhibitions: Watercolors; American Indian; Fibre Forms; Photography; American Watercolor Society Traveling Show; Poster Nippon; Los Angeles Print Society; Sculpture; Watercolor West; Egyptian Folk Tapestries; Arthur Beaumont, US Naval Painter; Children's Art Exhibit; Wildlife Photography; Ceramics.

Activities: Lectures mainly for docents; average of 3 visiting lecturers and gallery talks per year; 126 tours; adult classes.

Library: 800 volumes for reference; periodical library.

Attendance: 21,000.

CHICO

TAYLOR HALL ART GALLERY
California State University, Chico
Art Dept, First St. & Normal Ave, 95929. Tel: (916) 895-5331
Catherine Sullivan, Gallery Technician
Richard Hornaday, Dept. Chmn.
Free, Mon. - Fri. 8 AM - 5 PM. Estab. as educational in relation to the art students and for the community in general; financed by state appropriations and assoc. students of University.

Collections: Permanent collection includes art department purchases and masters exhibits; Behrick Collection—Oriental ceramics; study collection of original prints available to teachers, student teachers and staff.

Exhibitions: One a month featuring one-man exhibitions of faculty sabbatical leave work and visiting artists of national prominence. Also exhibitions of student work, juried, and exhibitions organized by students. Also one to two major exhibitions of historical importance.

Activities: Individual paintings and original objects of art lent, 10 items lent in average year to 5 borrowers; lectures open to the public; 3 visiting lecturers per year; 2 gallery talks and tours per year.

Income: $2000.

Attendance: 5000 annual average.

CHULA VISTA

SOUTHWESTERN COMMUNITY COLLEGE ART GALLERY
900 Otay Lakes Rd, 92010. Tel: (714) 420-1080, Exten. 283
Geraldine Turley, Dir.
Free Mon. - Fri. 10 AM - 2 PM; Mon. - Thurs. 6 - 9 PM. Estab. 1961 to show contemporary artists' work who are of merit to the community and the school, as a service and an educational service; financed by city and state appropriations. Gallery is approx. 3000 sq. ft.

Collections: Permanent collection of mostly contemporary work, valued at approx. $45,000.

Exhibitions: (1974) Judy Dater; Les Krems; Neil White; Erik Gromborg; (1975) Don Hughs; Sterling King; Baldessari/Faculty Show.

Activities: Individual paintings and original objects of art lent; 22 color reproductions, 10 photographs and 70 original art works in lending collection; 100 items lent in average year; Junior Museum; lectures open to public; 3 visiting lecturers per year; 3 gallery talks; classes for adults; competitions. (See Schools)

Publications: Show announcements, on the average of every 3 weeks.

Attendance: 10,000.

CLAREMONT

GALLERIES OF THE CLAREMONT COLLEGES
(Lang Art Gallery, Scripps College and Montgomery Art Gallery, Pomona College)
Montgomery Art Center, 91711. Tel: (714) 626-8511, ext. 2241
David W. Steadman, Dir.
Anne LeVeque, Asst. Dir.
Free, daily 1 - 5 PM; cl. school holidays.

Collections: Young Collection of American Painting; †Graphics; Oriental art; Kress Collection of Italian Painting.

Activities: Traveling exhibitions organized and circulated; lectures open to public; 5 visiting lecturers per year; ceramics annual and print annual.

Income and Purchases: Income $20,000; purchases vary.

Attendance: 25,000 annual average.

CYPRESS

CYPRESS COLLEGE FINE ARTS GALLERY*
9200 Valley View St, 90630
Robert Hardy, Gallery Dir.
Free, Mon. - Fri. 11 AM - 3 PM; Tues. & Thurs. 7 - 9 PM during exhibitions. Estab. 1969 to bring visually enriching experiences to the school and community; financed by school budget.

Collections: Student works; purchase awards.

Exhibitions: Faculty Art Shows; Architectural Crafts Invitational; Collegiate Ceramics, American Ceramic Society; Annual Juried Student Show; Community College Ceramics; Annual High School Invitational; Craft Design Invitational; Aridian Techniques and Design; Seven from Washington: Printmaking Today; Roten Gallery of Baltimore, Maryland; plus many others.

DAVIS

MEMORIAL UNION ART GALLERY
University of California, Fourth Floor Memorial Union, 95616.
Tel: (916) 752-2885
Nancy L. Dickinson, Dir.
Marla Katz, Co-Dir.
Free weekdays 8 AM - 5 PM. Estab. 1966, the Memorial Union Art Gallery is sponsored by the Memorial Union.

Collections: †Modern prints and drawings, †contemporary sculpture, paintings, prints, weaving and photographs.

Activities: Traveling exhibitions circulated; lectures, concerts, poetry readings, competitions, gallery lectures.

Attendance: 10,000 annually.

DOMINGUEZ HILLS

ART GALLERY OF CALIFORNIA STATE COLLEGE, DOMINGUEZ HILLS
1000 E. Victoria, 90747. Tel: (213) 532-4300
Free Mon. - Fri. 12 - 2 PM. Estab. 1973 to exhibit faculty, student, and outside art exhibitions; financed by state appropriations.

DOWNEY

DOWNEY MUSEUM OF ART
10419 Rives Ave, 90241. Tel: (213) 861-0419
Robert Emirhanian, Pres.
Mrs. Beverly E. Inman, Exec. Dir.
Free 1 - 5 PM; cl. Mon. Estab. Oct. 1956 for education and civic development. Ann. meeting Apr; mem. 250; dues $10 and higher.

Collections: California Contemporary Artists.

Exhibitions: 6-8 changing exhibitions; portions of permanent collection shown once annually; Introductions program co-sponsored by Los Angeles County presents new talent in one-person exhibits all year long; Round Robin Art Competition held monthly among Southern California Art Association entrants, winners introduced.

Activities: Classes, lectures, docent service; extension service to Los Angeles environs; lends paintings and objects of art to schools; sponsors competitions; art rental gallery; artist materials cooperative.

Income: $50,000.

Attendance: 15,000-18,000.

EUREKA

HUMBOLDT ARTS COUNCIL
P.O. Box 221, 95501
Ardene Janssen, Pres.
Kathleen Timm, Secy.
Estab. Sept, 1966, to encourage, promote and correlate all forms of activity in the arts and to make such activity a vital influence in the life of the community; financed by membership. Ann. meeting 2nd Mon. in Oct; mem. 250; dues $10.

Collections: Art Bank, consists of the yearly award winner from the juried Redwood Art Association Spring Show, other purchases and donated works of art.

Activities: Traveling exhibitions organized and circulated; individual paintings and original objects of art lent; 16 items lent in average year to city and county schools; photograph collection; concerts, dramatic programs, competitions, scholarships.

Annual Income: $10,000.

FRESNO

✠FRESNO ARTS CENTER
3033 E. Yale Ave, 93703. Tel: (209) 485-4810
R. Andrew Maass, Exec. Dir.
Dorys L. Beck, Asst. to Dir.
Free Tues. - Sun. 10 AM - 4:30 PM, Tues, Wed. & Thurs. evenings 7:30 - 9:30 PM. Mem. 900; dues $5 students, $15 individual, $20 family and higher. Ann. meeting Mar.

Collections: Contemporary, Mexican including pre-Columbian and Oriental.

Exhibitions: San Joaquin Annual, Crafts Biennial, local and internationally known artists.

Activities: Docent tours and lectures, flims, art fair, classes for children and adults; gift shop and rental gallery featuring primarily local artists; recitals, city and county schools exhibitions.

Attendance: 40,000 annually.

FULLERTON

MUCKENTHALER CULTURAL CENTER
1201 W. Malvern, 92633. Tel: (714) 879-6860
William J. Gravesmill, Exec. Dir.
Dale Raoul, Prog. Supvr.
Ronald Salgado, Gallery Supvr.
Janis M. Gates, Exec. Secy.
Free Tues. - Sun. 12 - 5 PM. Estab. 1965 as a community center for the arts, operated for the City of Fullerton by the Cultural Groups Foundation of Northern Orange County. Maintains gallery.

Activities: Children's School of the Arts and adult classes; performing arts productions in cooperation with California State University, Fullerton.

Attendance: (1974-75) 75,000.

GARDEN GROVE

MILLS HOUSE ART GALLERY
12732 Main St, 92640. Tel: (714) 638-6707
Rachel Casey, Pres. of Mills House Volunteers
Barbara Burby, Secy. of Mills House Volunteers
Richard Conrad, Dir.
Sondra Evans, Cultural Arts Coordinator
Free Thurs. - Mon. Noon - 4 PM, cl. Tues. & Wed. Estab. July 1964 to promote the visual arts in the city of Garden Grove, serving student, local and regional artists; financed by city appropriation. Mem. 50; dues $10.

Exhibitions: (1974) Home Savings and Loan Contemporary Collection; Garden Grove Art Guild; 58 F Plaza Gallery; Mixed Media Photography Show. (1975) J. Alden Weir Prints; 8 Women Watercolorists; Garden Grove School District Show; Claes Oldenburg; 8 Los Angeles Photographers; Westways Cover Art; 2-man photography show.

Activities: Lectures open to public; 3 gallery talks and various gallery tours per year.

Attendance: 6000.

ORANGE COUNTY PUBLIC LIBRARY
Garden Grove Regional Branch, 11200 Stanford Ave, 92640.
Tel: (714) 530-0711
Harry M. Rowe, Jr, County Librn.
H. W. Kirkwood, Dir. Admin. Services
Margaret H. Ray, Dir. Pub. Services
Nadine Leffler, Dir. Special Services
Irmgard Bassen, Regional Librn.
Ann Ague, Regional Librn.
Katherine Spencer, Regional Branch Librn.
Carin Tong, Dir. Reference Center
Richard B. Dimmitt, Special Projects & AV Librn.
Free Mon. - Thurs, 10 AM - 9 PM; Fri. - Sat. 10 AM - 5 PM; cl. Sun. Estab. 1921 for public library services; financed by county and state appropriations; maintains gallery.

Collections: Reference books and periodicals collections; 400 color reproductions; 700 motion pictures; 14 original graphics; photograph collection.

Activities: Material available to the general public, no fees; traveling exhibitions organized and circulated; individual paintings and original objects of art lent (20,700 items in an average year to 600 active borrowers); lectures open to the public; classes for children.

Publications: Spurgeon Story; Ole Hanson's San Clemente; Quartet.

GLENDALE

BRAND LIBRARY AND ART CENTER
1601 W. Mountain St, 91201. Tel: (213) 956-2051
Jane Hagan, Librn.
Burdette Peterson, Exhibit Coordinator
Free Tues. & Thurs. 12 - 9 PM; Wed, Fri. & Sat. 12 - 6 PM; Sun. 1 - 5 PM; cl. Mon. Estab. 1956 as art and music departments of the Glendale Public Library; financed by city and state appropriations. A large and a small gallery with a contemporary art program and crafts.

Collections: †Works on history, theory, criticism and techniques, specialized encyclopedias, dictionaries, indexes and other guides to art and music literature; special collection of piano rolls, 78-rpm records, Dieterle picture collection, early photography journals.

Exhibitions: (1974-75) Los Hermanos; Ten Together-a Variety of Visual Expression; Martin Mondrus and Boris Kutchukov; Shirlee Prescott and Levrett Bradley; The New World and Beyond; Women Painters - West; Brand IV Ceramic Conjunction; Mary Moeller; Aida Fiscus; Frank Arcuri, Jean Wong; Nathaniel Bustion, Jr; Glendale Art Association Scholarship Competition; Stanley C. Wilson; Stephen Zaima; William S. Fenwick; 6 Painters/Watercolor Explored.

Activities: Lending collection, 2286 color reproductions, 4000 Kodachromes, 197 piano rolls, 360 cassettes; 127,169 items lent in an average year; lectures open to the public; 75 tours; concerts; competitions.

Library: 28,000 books on fine arts and music, 18,000 records, 300 cassettes, 4000 color slides on art.

Attendance: 72,000.

FOREST LAWN MUSEUM
1712 Glendale Ave, 91209. Tel: (213) 254-3131
Jane Llewellyn, Dir.
Wendy E. Clarke, Asst. Dir.
Free daily 10 AM - 6 PM. Estab. 1951 to continue the 'builder's creed' that Forest Lawn should be a memorial park, a place of service not only for the dead, but also for the living; a community museum, offering education and culture through association with the architecture and the art of world masters; endowed. There are 4 galleries in the museum and several smaller galleries in various buildings throughout the 4 parks.

Collections: American Western Bronzes; reproductions of Michelangelo's greatest sculptures; ancient Biblical and historical coins; stained glass window of the Last Supper; Crucifixion Painting by Paderewski (195 ft. x 45 ft); The Resurrection Painting-Robert Clark; reproductions and originals of famous sculptures, paintings, documents throughout 4 parks.

Exhibitions: Celebration of Michelangelo's Birthday; Exhibition of the Works of Jesse C. Beesley.

Activities: Reproductions of the crown jewels of England and documents for the Smithsonian Institution Bicentennial Collection lent; scholarships; memento shop which contains art works and books pertaining to Forest Lawn and artists whose works are displayed.

Library: 3000 volumes for employees' use.

Attendance: 200,000 annually.

HUNTINGTON BEACH

✠GOLDEN WEST COLLEGE ART GALLERY*
15744 Golden West St, 92647.
Cynthia Cardine, Dir.

IRVINE

UNIVERSITY OF CALIFORNIA, IRVINE ART GALLERY
92717.
Melinda Wortz, Dir.
Linda Rosengarten, Admin. Asst.
Free Oct - June, Tues. - Sat, 12 - 5 PM. Estab. 1965, for changing exhibitions devoted to contemporary art; financed by city and state appropriation and by interested private collectors.

Exhibitions: Roy Lichtenstein; Marcel Duchamp Symposium; Milton Avery; John McLaughlin; American Realist Painting of WWII; Bruce Nauman; Eric Orr; Sam Gilliam; UCI Master of Fine Arts Graduates; Private Spaces (Berlant, Cornell, Furman, Graham, Reiss, Westerman).

Activities: Monthly lectures on each exhibit.
Publications: Exhibition catalogs.

LAGUNA BEACH

✠LAGUNA BEACH MUSEUM OF ART
307 Cliff Dr, 92651. Tel: (714) 494-6531
Jim Moniz, Pres.
Mrs. Nick B. Willisma, 1st V.Pres.
Harry J. Lawrence, 2nd V.Pres.
Leon Jones, Treas.
Edward Behme, Secy.
Tom K. Enman, Dir.
Mary Jacob, Secy. to Dir.
Free six days a wk. 11:30 AM - 4:30 PM. Estab. 1918 as Laguna Beach Art Association. Gallery build in 1929; financed by endowment, membership and private donation; receives ann. grant from Festival of Arts of Laguna Beach and City of Laguna Beach. 4 galleries, museum store. Ann. meeting Sept; 900 mem; dues $18.

Collections: Early California painters from 1900 - 1940 and 1960 - 1970; photographs by Paul Outerbridge 1920 - 1936; Dr. Roland Fisher Collection of Mildred Bryant Brooks etchings; Ben Kutcher book collection.

Activities: Quarterly lecture series held by Paul Ballard.
Publications: Monthly newsletter.
Attendance: 35,000 annual average.

LA JOLLA

LA JOLLA MUSEUM OF CONTEMPORARY ART
700 Prospect St, 92037. Tel: (714) 454-0183
Sebastian Adler, Dir.
Arthur Fricker, Business Adminr.
Katheryn Jansen, Secy. to Dir.
Stephen Brezzo, Cur.
Richard Armstrong, Asst. Cur.
Patricia Quinby, Registrar
Gail Richardson, Librn.
Free Tues. - Fri. 10 AM - 5 PM; Sat. & Sun. 12:30 - 5 PM; Wed. 7 - 10 PM; cl. Mon, New Years, Thanksgiving and Christmas. Founded 1941 for exhibition and understanding of the visual arts. Nonprofit organization, tax exempt. 500-seat auditorium, classrooms, exhibition space; 6 acre sculpture garden under development. Mem. 1300; dues active $15, contributing $25, donor $50, patron $100, sustaining $250, benefactor $1000.

Collections: †Contemporary art including paintings, sculpture, drawings, prints; African art collection.

Exhibitions: Permanent, temporary and traveling exhibitions.
Activities: Films; lectures; gallery talks; guided tours, tours to other cities; concerts; Art to Schools lectures; formally organized education programs to children and adults; scholarships for children; docent program; intermuseum loans. Museum shop. Rental and sales gallery.

Library: 4000 volume library of books, periodicals, clippings, catalogs, slides.
Publications: Newsletter; exhibition catalogs.

LIBRARY ASSOCIATION OF LA JOLLA
The Athenaeum Music and Arts Library
1008 Wall St, 92037. Tel: (714) 454-5872.
Wilbert Hitchner, Pres.
Josephine Greer, Secy.
Lynn Neumann, Library Adminr.
Jody Evans, Cataloguer
Free Tues. - Sat. 10 AM - 5:30 PM. Estab. 1899 as a free and public institution, exclusively educational and cultural and not for profit; includes the operation of a fine arts library, financed by endowment and mem. Gallery. Ann. meeting third Tues. of July; mem. 600; dues $15.

Collections: †2600 art books; †600 music books; †3000 sheet music and scores; included is the Breitkopf and Hartel publication of Bach Werke, in 47 volumes, edited by the Bach Gesellschaft; 3000 records; 500 cassettes; 41 periodicals; 400 drama.

Activities: Lectures open to public; 3 visiting lecturers per year; concerts.
Library: 9000 volumes plus periodicals; picture file.
Income and Purchases: Income $24,000; purchases $4900.

MANDEVILLE ART GALLERY
University of California, San Diego
B-027, 92093. Tel: (714) 452-2860
Dr. Moira Roth, Dir.
Patricia H. Baxter, Cur.
Geraldine McAllister, Asst. Cur.
Free Sun. - Fri. 12 - 5 PM. Estab. 1967 to provide exhibitions of interest to the visual arts majors, university personnel and the community at large including an emphasis on contemporary art; financed by student registration fees and state appropriations.

Exhibitions: Southern California Indian Rock Art; Representational Painting; Japanese Prints; Fluxus, The Impure Image; Barbara Smith; Miriam Schapiro (The Shrine, The Computer and The Dollhouse); 18th Century English Graphics.

Attendance: 12,000 annual average.

LONG BEACH

CALIFORNIA STATE UNIVERSITY AT LONG BEACH ART GALLERIES*
6101 E. Seventh St, 90840. Tel: (213) 498-4367
A. James Bravor, Dean, School of Fine Arts
M. Thomas Ferreira, Chmn, Art Dept.
Free Mon. - Fri. 11 AM - 3 PM; Sun. & holidays 1 - 4 PM; cl. university & public holidays, Sat, June-Aug. Estab. 1949, affiliated with California State Universities and Colleges; financed by state appropriation.

Collections: Collections of the California State University and Colleges; collection attendant to the International Sculpture Symposium, 1966; contemporary American drawings.

Exhibitions: 10 exhibitions per year with purchase prizes on juried shows including annual drawing show, plus exhibits of painting, prints, graphic arts, sculpture and crafts; intermuseum loan exhibitions; temporary and traveling exhibitions.

Activities: Training programs for professional museum work workers; lectures; gallery talks; guided tours; films. Restaurant.
Library: Reading room and library.
Attendance: Approx. 20,000 annually.

✠CALIFORNIA STATE UNIVERSITY AT LONG BEACH LIBRARY
6101 E. Seventh St, 90840. Tel: (213) 498-4047
Charles J. Boorkman, Dir.
Lloyd Kramer, Assoc. Dir.
Henry J. DuBois, Fine Arts Librn.
Free Mon. - Thurs. 8 AM - 9 PM, Fri. 8 AM - 5 PM, Sat. 9:30 AM - 5:30 PM, cl. Sun. Estab. 1949 to support and augment the curriculum offered by the university's art department and to provide enrichment and recreational materials for all the campus community; financed by city and state appropriations. Graphics gallery exhibits prints and rare books owned by the library or loaned by other institutions.

Collections: Fine arts book collection of 21,996 volumes, 20,000 circulating, 2000 reference; 670 original prints; 3600 reproductions; 45,000 slides; photograph collection of 25 prints for reference, circulating to faculty; slide collection and art reproduction collections for circulation, fully cataloged.

Budget: Books $10,000, slides $1000, prints $300.

LONG BEACH MUSEUM OF ART
2300 E. Ocean Blvd, 90803. Tel: (213) 439-2119
Mr. Jan Ernst Adlmann, Dir.
J. Dennis Worley, Admin. Mgr.
David A. Ross, Deputy Dir, TV/Film
Free Wed. - Sun. Noon - 5 PM; cl. New Year's, Thanksgiving and Christmas. Opened in 1951 as a Municipal Art Center under the City Library Department; in 1957 the Long Beach City Council changed the Center to the Long Beach Museum of Art, a department of municipal government. New $8 million I. M. Pei facility, Arts Forum, underway, with 80,000 sq. ft, including Omitheatre and exterior Sculpture Garden/Forest, full video production and editing division, completion 1978.

Collections: †Paintings, †sculpture, †prints, †drawings, crafts and photography; 850 items with emphasis on West Coast and California contemporary; small collection of African artifacts; sculpture garden.

Exhibitions: Continuous exhibition of permanent collection; Arts of Southern California Exhibition (one every three years), a traveling exhibition of contemporary art, invitational, and organized by the museum under a grant from Los Angeles County; one-man and group exhibitions in diversified media; extensive video division.

Activities: Receptions, arts festivals, lecture series, docent tours, gallery talks, community extension work, children's and adult art classes, art rental and sales service, films and chamber music concerts. Book store with ceramics, jewelry, books, magazines, and original folk art objects for sale.

Library: Staff reference; restricted lending in books, publications and slides; Over 1500 books.

Publications: Quarterly bulletin, catalogues, announcements.

Attendance: Approx. 60,000.

LONG BEACH PUBLIC LIBRARY
Ocean & Pacific, 90802. Tel: (213) 597-3341
Mrs. Frances Henselman, City Librn.
Natalee Collier, Head Fine Arts Dept.
Free Mon. - Thurs. 10 AM - 9 PM; Fri. - Sat. 10 AM - 5:30 PM; Sun. 1:30 - 5 PM. Estab. 1909 to serve interests of general public; financed by city and state appropriations.

Activities: Individual paintings lent to schools; lending collection, 300 framed color reproductions, 800 motion pictures, 70 film strips; 3043 items lent in an average year.

Library: 26,000 volume library; 85,000 mounted pictures.

Income and Purchases: Income $9000; purchases $9000.

LOS ANGELES

AMERICAN ART SOCIETY
810 S. Lucerne Blvd, 90005. Tel: (213) 935-9728
Dr. H. M. Kurtzworth, Art Dir.
E. Franck Lee, Asst. Dir.
Payne Thebaut, Educ. Dir.
James De Marchi, Research Dir.
Founded 1935 as a nonprofit educational organization, to foster and develop the discovery and use of talent in the fine, decorative and industrial arts. Dedicated to the use of art as a national asset.

✛ARCHITECTURE AND FINE ARTS LIBRARY
University of Southern California
University Park, 90007. Tel: (213) 746-6783
Alson Clark, Librn.
Free Mon. - Thurs. 8:30 AM - 9 PM; Fri. 8:30 AM - 5 PM; Sat. Noon - 5 PM; Sun. 1 - 5 PM. Estab. 1925 to provide undergraduate and graduate level students and the teaching and research faculty materials in the areas of architecture and fine arts needed to achieve their objectives; branch library in the central library system supported by the University.

Collections: In the areas of fine arts and architecture (29,823 volumes): Monographs, periodicals, slides, pamphlets, art prints, as well as encyclopedias, dictionaries, indexes, bibliographies, guides, catalogs, some text books, maps, manuscripts and rare books. Also a 92,592 piece slide collection.

Annual Purchases: $33,413.

Attendance: 29,500.

CALIFORNIA MUSEUM OF SCIENCE AND INDUSTRY
700 State Dr, Exposition Park, 90037. Tel: (213) 749-0101
J. Howard Edgerton, Chmn of Board, Calif. Museum Foundation
William H. McAdam, Pres.
Maurice J. Dahlem, V.Pres.
Mrs. Howard Ahmanson, V.Pres.
Cyril Magnin, V.Pres.
Donald P. Loker, Secy.
Ernest J. Loebbecke, Treas.
G. E. Kinsey, Chmn. Exec. Comt.
William J. McCann, Museum Dir. & Exec. Secy. of Foundation
Free daily 10 AM - 5 PM. Dynamically tells the story of science, industry and commerce to the mass public by tempting each visitor to take part in a sensory learning experience and education adventure; appropriation and private foundation support. The museum has 9 halls housing 20 permanent exhibits and more than 60 temporary exhibits among which are Sister Cities Youth Art Exhib and Sister Cities in Focus that appear throughout the year. Currently underway is a permanent Space Museum, Nuclear Science Hall, the world's first Hall of Finance and a $6 million atomic energy complex. Financially supported by State of California and California Museum Foundation.

Permanent Exhibitions: Transparent hatcher-brooder where visitors can watch 150 chicks hatch daily and Embryo Exhibit telling story of development of egg; Communications Exhibit; Mathematica Exhibit; Automotive Exhibit; Electricity Hall; Air Traffic Control Exhibit; Energy Exhibit; Science of Aviation, a model of the Apollo Soyuz Text Project; Hall of Health; Dental Hall Exhibit with the world's largest mouth; Hall of Fame Exhibit.

Temporary Exhibitions: Annual Union Artist Exhibit, paintings and sculpture by all unions in AFL-CIO; Bonsai; Design West '76, annual showcase of the best in student design from jewelry to furniture to wallpaper; Hungarian Bicentennial Art Exhibit, paintings, ceramics, needlework, sculpture, wood carvings by Hungarian-

Americans; Key Art Awards, annual showing of posters, logos, word-styles promoting movies or TV shows; Ride the Big Red Cars, nostalgic display of the Pacific Electric Railway complete with an old car; National Hobby Show, creative hobby exhib; Of Medicine and Art, sculpture, paintings and medical memorabilia; Sharing Our Birthday with America, photographic essay of the total scope of Los Angeles Trade Tech facilities; Prospects of Scotland, an exhibition about the country, culture, traditions and quality of life of the Scottish people; Edge of Eternity, space and deep sea illustrations by artist Russell Arasmith of the LA Times; Eagle Eye and Apple Pie, graphics by 20 artists; Photography West, annual exhibit of color and black/white photographs sponsored by Professional Photographers West; L.A. Beautiful Posters, anti-litter posters by junior and senior high school students; Bill of Rights, poster art and 3-D interpretations by senior high students; Sons and Daughters, clay sculptures of children; Women Artists of the American West, an exhibition of paintings portraying the American West; Playtime '76 annual holiday surprise for children—playground equipment for them to play on; Sister Cities in Focus; Focus '76, outstanding high school and college photography; Festival of Holiday Ideas, to familiarize the public with the skills to create arts and crafts projects related to the holidays.

Activities: Formal science-art education programs are conducted regularly for school groups and the general public by a staff of 25 certified teachers and educators; educational programs include summer science workshop, exploring science on Saturdays, junior mathematics seminar, scientific lecture-demonstrations, teacher institutes, science film series; school tour programs; special health lectures and symposium, space symposium, and the Committee for Advance Science Training; competitions, scholarships. 500 seat auditorium to aid activities, community projects and Museum exhibition programs.

Publications: Notices of temporary exhibits, maps, pamphlets, etc.

Attendance: 3,000,000.

LOS ANGELES ART ASSOCIATION AND GALLERIES
825 N. La Cienega Blvd, 90069. Tel: (213) 652-8272
Stephen Longstreet, Pres.
Helen Wurdemann, Dir.
Free Tues. - Fri. Noon - 5 PM; Sat. Noon - 4 PM; Sun. 2 - 4 PM; Mon. 7:30 - 10 PM. Estab. 1925, reorganized 1933; patron supported. Ann. meeting 2nd Tues. in Apr; mem. 900; dues $25 and higher. Regional contemporary gallery showing established artists and new talent.

Exhibitions: Monthly exhibitions of painting, sculpture, graphics by Southern California artists.

Activities: Exhibition receptions, lectures and round table discussions; center for assistance for shows and information to visitors and surrounding communities.

Publications: In progress, a directory and the archive records of Southern California artists.

Attendance: 550 per wk.

LOS ANGELES COUNTY MUSEUM OF ART
5905 Wilshire Blvd, 90036. Tel: (213) 937-4250
Franklin D. Murphy, Chmn.
Richard Sherwood, Pres.
Anna Bing Arnold, V.Pres.
Mrs. F. David Frost, V.Pres.
R. Stanton Avery, V.Pres.
Mrs. Norman F. Sprague, Jr, Secy.
Dr. Charles Z. Wilson, Jr, Treas.
Kenneth Donahue, Dir.
Rexford Stead, Deputy Dir. Fine Arts
Mort Golden, Deputy Dir. Admin.
Jeanne D'Andrea, Cur. of Exhibitions
Ebria Feinblatt, Cur. of Prints & Drawings
Peter Fusco, Assoc. Cur. of Renaissance & Baroque Art
William E. Jones, Cur. of Decorative Arts
Mary Kahlenberg, Cur. of Textiles & Costumes
George Kuwayama, Cur. of Oriental Art
Pratapaditya Pal, Cur. of Indian Art
Maurice Tuchman, Cur. of Modern Art
Eleanor Hartman, Librn.
Patricia Nauert, Reg.
Permanent collection free (charge of $1 for adults and 50¢ for children in the Special Exhibitions Gallery); Tues. - Fri. 10 AM - 5 PM; Sat. & Sun. 10 AM - 6 PM. Estab. as Division of History, Science and Art in 1910; estab. separately in 1961; owned and maintained by the County of Los Angeles, policy by private Board of Trustees. Membership in excess of 30,000; dues $25 and higher.

Collections: Egyptian, Classical, Medieval, Renaissance, Baroque, American, Modern and Oriental. Distinguished specialties: Indian, Nepalese and Tibetan; Islamic Art; Peruvian textiles.

Special departmental collections: Textiles and costumes; prints and drawings, decorative arts.

Exhibitions: 4 major and 17 smaller exhibitions annually, with total attendance of 500,000.

Activities: Lectures on permanent collections, special lectures on changing exhibitions; films; chamber music concerts; recorded tours on permanent collection and special exhibitions; Art Rental Gallery for members; Textile and Costumes Research Center; members' travel program; book shop.

Library: 50,000 volumes.

Income and Purchases: Income $5,000,000; annual purchases $1,700,000.

Publications: Biennial Report; Members' Calendar (monthly); Bulletin; monographs; exhibition catalogs.

Attendance: 1,500,000 annual average.

LOS ANGELES INSTITUTE OF CONTEMPORARY ART
2040 Avenue of the Stars, 90067. Tel: (213) 553-2556
Joann Phillips, Pres.
Monroe Price, Secy.
Robert Lewis Smith, Dir.
Marcia Traylor, Gallery Coordinator
Free Tues. - Sat. 11:30 AM - 7:30 PM. Estab. Apr. 24, 1974 as a source of exposure and validation to artists working in the Southern California area through changing exhibitions using rotating curators; financed by endowment, city and state appropriation, membership. Gallery located in the ABC Entertainment Center, Century City, Calif. Ann. meeting June; mem. 1600; dues $15.

Exhibitions: 9 Senior Southern California Painters; Current Concerns, Parts I and II; Collage and Assemblage in Southern California; Object/Subject; Clay Works in Progress; 3 L.A. Sculptors; Collectors Choice.

Activities: Lectures open to public; gallery talks; concerts, dramatic programs; book shop.

Artists Registry consisting of approximately 8 slides per artist, with the work of over 450 artists. Open submission. Free of charge, open to the public.

Publications: Journal (bimonthly); LAICA Newsletter (monthly).

Income: $65,000.

Attendance: 50,000 annually.

LOS ANGELES PUBLIC LIBRARY
630 W. Fifth St, 90071. Tel: (213) 626-7461
Katherine Grant, Art & Music Librn.
Free Mon. - Thurs, 10 AM - 9 PM; Fri. & Sat. 10 AM - 5:30 PM; cl. Sun. & holidays. Estab. 1872. The Art and Music Dept. has for reference and circulation use 156,000 volumes on the fine arts and music (including music scores and recreation materials). Reference prints include 670 original etchings, woodcuts, lithographs and drawings; 54 Twin Prints and 270 Japanese prints, which include a complete set of Hiroshige's Tokaido Series.

Purchases: $56,300 plus $6000 special funds.

Income and Funds: Annual library budget $15,300,000; library book funds $2,176,642.

MALONE ART GALLERY
Loyola Marymount University
7101 W. 80th St, 90045. Tel: (213) 642-3050
Howard Myers, Dir.
Free Mon. - Fri. 10 AM - 4 PM. Estab. 1971 to hold exhibitions; financed by University.

Activities: Courses in display and exhibition design; traveling exhibitions organized and circulated; lectures open to public; 4 gallery talks and 4 tours per year; concerts, dramatic programs, classes for adults and children, competitions, scholarships.

Publications: Exhibition catalogs, irregularly.

Annual Income: $6500.

Attendance: 4800.

MOUNT ST. MARY'S COLLEGE ART GALLERY
Art Dept, 12001 Chalon Rd, 90049. Tel: (213) 272-8791
Jim Murray, Gallery Dir.
Free Wed. - Sun. 1 - 4 PM. Estab. to present works of art of various disciplines for the enrichment of students and community; financed by College.

Collections: Collection of and by Jose Drudis-Blada.

Exhibitions (1974): Selections from the Robert Rowen Collection; (1975) Three group shows of top Los Angeles Artists; John White, Sandtraps; (1976) Five Realists, Douke, Henderson, Murray, Pettibone, Wilf.

Activities: Lectures open to public, 2-3 visiting lecturers per year; scholarships.

Publications: Exhibition catalogs, 2-3 per year.

✣MUNICIPAL ARTS DEPARTMENT
Room 1500, City Hall, 90012. Tel: (213) 485-2433
Kenneth Ross, Gen. Mgr, Municipal Arts Dept.
Lawrence E. Deutsch, Pres, Municipal Arts Commission
Carl Dentzel, Pres, Cultural Heritage Board
John J. Pike, Pres. Municipal Art Patrons
Ileana Welch, Exec. Secy, Cultural Heritage Board
Josine Ianco-Starrels, Art Coordinator
Forrest Scott, Architect, A.I.A.
George Milan, Music Coordinator
Claire Isaacs Deussen, Dir, Jr. Arts Center
Estab. 1903; charter granted 1911; charter responsibilities include approval of design of municipal buildings, projections over public property and works of art acquired by the City; five commissioners. Bi-monthly meetings.
Municipal Art Gallery, Barnsdall Park, 4804 Hollywood Blvd, open Noon - 5 PM daily, cl. Mon. Hours vary for special exhibitions.
Junior Arts Center, 4814 Hollywood Blvd.

Collections: Small permanent collection includes portraits of former mayors.

Exhibitions: Annual All City Outdoor Art Festival, $10,000 purchase awards; major exhibitions co-sponsored with Municipal Art Patrons; Cubism: U.S.A, Maxfield Parrish; West Coast Now; Colonial Art of Mexico; Contemporary Japanese Drawings; Sonja Henie, Niels Onstad Collection from Norway; Soviet Union: Arts and Crafts in Ancient Times and Today.

Activities: Special exhibitions, lectures, demonstrations co-sponsored with art, civic, and business groups throughout the city; Bureau of Music youth and adult choruses and concerts, community sings, youth voice scholarships; declaration and preservation of historic-cultural buildings and sites by the Cultural Heritage Board; Junior Arts Center classes and workshops, special events, art exhibitions, and film programs for youth.

Publications: Newsletter, quarterly; Annual Report.

Attendance: Art Events 200,000; Music Events 177,085; Junior Arts Center 2500 Students.

NATIONAL WATERCOLOR SOCIETY (formerly California National Watercolor Society)
c/o Ruth Rossman, Pres, 401 Cascada Way, 90049.
Morten E. Solberg, 1st V.Pres.
Frank Nestler, Treas.
Sylvia Gavurin, Recording Secy.
Ruth Erlich, Corresp. Secy.
Barbara Day, Historian
Estab. 1921 to sponsor art exhibits for the cultural and educational benefit of the public. Ann. meeting Jan; mem. 400; dues $20 annually, but must be juried into membership.

Collections: Purchase award-winning paintings from 1954 to present.

Exhibitions: All-membership show, approximately $500 awards each year; annual exhibition, approximately $7000 each year.

Activities: At least 5 traveling shows each year; docent talks at annual exhibition; slide/cassette program of members' works.

Attendance: No actual record, but would total in the thousands.

NORTON SIMON INC. FOUNDATION
3440 Wilshire Blvd, 90010. Tel: (212) 380-2021
Norton Simon, Pres. & Dir.
Julia Mayer, Secy.
Darryl Isley, Cur.
Linda Traister, Registrar
Estab. 1954 to purchase and loan works of art; collection and exhibition of European painting and sculpture from Renaissance to the mid 20th century and Indian and Southeast Asian art.

Collections: †European painting and sculpture; †Indian and Southeast Asian art.

Activities: Traveling exhibitions; individual paintings lent to schools and others.

RUSKIN ART CLUB*
800 S. Plymouth Blvd, 90005. Tel: (213) 937-9641
Mrs. Bion A Provost, Pres.
Miss Alice Sturdy, V. Pres.
Estab. 1888, inc. 1905. Owns club building; ann. meeting April; mem. 60; dues $20. Weekly art study program. First two public art exhibitions in Los Angeles held by Ruskin Art Club were in 1890 and 1891.

SKIRBALL MUSEUM
Hebrew Union College
3077 University Mall, 90007. Tel: (213) 749-3424
Nancy Berman, Cur.
Alice Greenwald, Curatorial Asst.
Karen Seger, Admin. Asst.
Open Tues. - Fri. 11 AM - 4 PM; Sun. 10 AM - 5 PM. The Museum's collection was estab. in 1913 as part of the library of Hebrew Union College in Cincinnati, Ohio. In 1972, the collection was moved to the

California branch of Hebrew Union College and renamed the Skirball Museum. The collections consist of Jewish ceremonial art, paintings, drawings, sculptures by Jewish artists or on Jewish subject matters, and a large collection of Palestinian archaeology as well as prehistoric artifacts from Dr. Nelsen Glueck's revolutionary Negev site surveys.

Activities: Docent tours, lecture series, concert and drama; children's workshops, resource for scholarship in Jewish art.

Publications: Catalogs.

SOUTHWEST MUSEUM
Highland Park, 90042. Tel: (213) 221-2163
Carl S. Dentzel, Dir.
Bruce Bryan, Cur. & Ed. of Publications
Ruth M. Christensen, Lib.
Rose L. Ingraham, Casa de Adobe Hostess
Free 1 - 5 PM; cl. Mon. & certain holidays. Estab. 1907 to maintain a free public museum of history, science and art, as manifested in the native cultures of America and especially of the Southwest. Ann. meeting Feb; mem. approx. 1000; dues $10 and higher; students $7.50 Owns museum building, also Casa de Adobe, replica of a Spanish-California ranch house.

Collections: An extensive collection of Aboriginal American Art of Pre-Columbian and Post-Columbian periods; Caballeria collection of oil paintings from California missions; paintings of Western scenes and Indian subjects. Also collections of native American arts, crafts, textiles, ceramics and lithic arts.

Activities: Daily docent service for school children, mornings only. Christmas and Easter traditional California festivities at Casa de Adobe.

Library: An extensive collection exceeding 100,000 items for reference.

Publications: The Masterkey, quarterly; Southwest Museum Papers; Leaflets; Hodge Anniversary Publication Fund series. List on request.

Attendance: Approx. 85,000.

THORNE HALL*
Occidental College, 1600 Campus Rd, 90041. Tel: (213) 255-5151 Exten. 410
Constance M. Perkins, Prof. Art
Free Sept. 15 - June 15, Mon. - Fri. 9 - 3 PM. Estab. 1938, to provide material of contemporary interest and instructional value to the college community. Gallery is the foyer to the major auditorium.

Exhibitions: One man shows of: Jim Murray, Salvador Bru, Salvatore Pecoraro, Tom Holder, Philip Lewis, Jules Engel, Kathy Cross; group shows for: Robin Henderson and Donald Petersen, Ernest Rosenthal and Teruo Shida, Gene Gill, Fred Csentry, Mansaku Minashima and William Bradshaw; collections of contemporary Japanese Prints, Contemporary Prints, Black Art: The Black Experience; also student annual and senior comprehensive exhibitions.

Activities: Traveling exhibitions organized and circulated; Lectures open to the public; four gallery talks per year.

Income and Purchases: Income $1300.

Attendance: 7000.

UNIVERSITY OF CALIFORNIA, LOS ANGELES
405 Hilgard Ave, 90024.

Grunwald Center for the Graphic Arts. Tel: (213) 825-3783
Dr. E. Maurice Bloch, Dir. and Cur.
Thomas W. Travis, Asst. to Cur.
Phyllis Peet, Curatorial Asst.
Open Mon. - Fri. 9 AM - 12 PM, 1 - 5 PM.
Collections: †Permanent collection of prints and drawings, 15th century to the present. Major holdings include: German Expressionism, French Impressionism, Japanese woodblock, Tamarind Lithography Workshop impressions (complete), Ornament, Renoir, Picasso, Matisse and Rouault.

Activities: Research and study center; seminars, lectures and exhibitions (catalogues available).

Library: Reference materials on the graphic arts in addition to extensive holdings on the graphic arts in the UCLA Art Library.

Museum of Cultural History (formerly Museum and Laboratories of Ethnic Arts and Technology). Tel: (213) 825-4259
Christopher B. Donnan, Dir.
Marija Gimbutas, Cur. Old World Archaeology
Jay D. Frierman, Cur. N.E. Archaeology and Ethnography
George R. Ellis, Asst. to Dir, Adminr, Acting Cur, African and Oceanic Holdings
Raul A. Lopez, Head, Comt. Programs
Patricia Altman, Acting Cur. Folk Art
Beverly Freiburger, Admin. Asst.
Open 11 AM - 5 PM; Sat. & Sun. 1 - 5 PM. Estab. 1963. Ancient and Primitive Art, Archaeology, and Ethnography Museum: archaeology (R); art (R); textiles (R).

Activities: Guided tours, lectures, gallery talks; formally organized education programs for children and college students; temporary exhibitions of collections; community program: Satellite Museum exhibits, Peripatetic Museum program for children, practical museum training.

Library: 2000 volume library of books and periodicals relating to the collection.

Publications: Exhibition catalogues; occasional papers, slide sets.

The Frederick S. Wight Art Galleries.* Tel: (213) 825-1461
Gerald Nordland, Dir.
Jack Carter, Assoc. Dir.
Marian Eber, Administrative Asst.
Open 11 AM - 5 PM; Sat. and Sun. 1 - 5 PM; cl. during August. Estab. 1952. The Galleries serve both the University and the general public; their program is integrated with the curricula of the Art Department, and includes numerous exhibitions organized by the Galleries and scheduled to travel to other institutions.

Collections: Franklin D. Murphy Sculpture Garden, 45 sculptures from the 19th-20th centuries including Arp, Calder, Lachaise, Lipchitz, Moore, Noguchi and Smith; the Willitts J. Hole Collection of approximately 50 paintings of the Italian, Spanish, Dutch, Flemish and English schools, from the 15th to 19th centuries; 20th century painting, sculpture and photographic collections.

Exhibitions: Fifteen exhibitions annually, painting and sculpture, prints and drawings, architecture and design; operates in close conjunction with the (UCLA) Museum of Cultural History, and the Grunwald Center for the Graphic Arts, providing exhibitions space periodically.

Activities: Special lectures, either by the visiting lecturers or faculty members, average three per quarter.

Library: The Art Library is an integral part of the University Library; it houses 45,000 books; the Library also contains the Elmer Belt Library of Vinciana and a copy of Princeton's Index of Christian Art. A separate Slide Library contains 158,000 slides.

Attendance: (1967-68) 142,000; (1969-70) 148,000; (1971-72) 150,000.

⌘UNIVERSITY OF SOUTHERN CALIFORNIA GALLERIES
University Park, 90007. Tel: (213) 746-2799
Donald J. Brewer, Dir.
Free Mon. - Fri. 12 - 5 PM; cl. Sat. & Sun. (except for major exhibitions) & Aug. 1 - Sept. 15. Estab. 1939 by Mrs. Walter Harrison Fisher, who presented the Gallery and her collection of 72 paintings to the University; 48 additional paintings were given in 1964 by Dr. Armand Hammer. There has been a steady acquisition of 19th and 20th century European and American paintings, sculpture and graphics through the years. In 1973 the new School of Architecture and Fine Arts opened, containing a new foyer gallery primarily for student exhibitions. USC Council of Fine Arts supports gallery activities; mem. open to all; dues $100 annually.

Collections: The Galleries house the permanent collections of paintings of 17th century Dutch, Flemish and Italian, 18th Century British, 19th Century French and American landscape and portraiture schools. The galleries are an educational department of the University and have access to its libraries and slides.

Exhibitions: Changing exhibitions presented 10 months of the year.

Activities: Lecture series, films, gallery talks number approximately 25 annually.

Publications: In conjunction with exhibitions, the galleries publish an average of 3 catalogs annually.

Attendance: 18,000.

UNIVERSITY-STUDENT UNION ART GALLERY
California State University, Los Angeles
5151 State University Dr, 90039. Tel: (213) 224-2189
Frank Brown, Arts & Crafts Coordinator
Free Mon. - Thurs. 11 AM - 7 PM; Fri. 11 AM - 1 PM. Estab. Apr, 1975 as a fine arts gallery; financed by city and state appropriation.
Exhibitions: (1975-76): Regional American Art Series.

Activities: Traveling exhibitions organized and circulated; original objects of art and individual paintings lent; 20 items lent in average year; lectures open to public; 20 visiting lecturers per year; concerts; dramatic programs; classes for adults and children. Book shop.

Publications: Catalogs; artists books, 4 - 5 per year.

MALIBU

J. PAUL GETTY MUSEUM
17985 Pacific Coast Highway, 90265. Tel: (213) 459-2306 Admin; 454-6541 Reservations
Stephen Garrett, Deputy Dir.
Free 10 AM - 5 PM Mon. - Fri. (Apr. - Sept), Tues. - Sat. (Oct. - Mar.). Supported by Foundation.

Collections: Greek and Roman antiquities, Baroque and Renaissance paintings and 18th century French decorative arts housed in a reconstruction of an ancient Roman villa set in gardens overlooking the sea. Reservations suggested one week in advance for guaranteed parking and admission.
Library: 18,000 volumes.
Attendance: Since opening Jan. 1974 over half million visitors.

MENDOCINO

MENDOCINO ART CENTER, INC.*
P.O. Box 36, 540 Little Lake St, 95460. Tel: (707) 937-5818.
Mr. William Wallace, Pres.
Jennie Zacha, Secy.
William Zacha, Exec. Dir.
Dirk Myers, Admin. Asst.
Mary Buckaloo, Registrar and Secy.
Open 9 AM - 5 PM daily; e programs 7 days a wk. Estab. 1959, to provide a rounded cultural existence in an isolated community; financed by mem. Gallery is maintained and every mem. is permitted to submit three works. Ann. meeting last Thurs. in Aug. and one other date approx. 6 months later; mem. 830; dues $7.
Collections: We have attempted to buy a major work by each member of the faculty.
Exhibitions: Continuing exhibitions, new hanging opening with reception every two months.
Activities: Year round series of workshops every day of the week, and a resident program for high school seniors or graduates; 50 individual paintings and original objects of art lent in average year to 6 active borrowers; concerts, dramatic programs, classes for adults and children. Book Shop, books relating only to Mendocino area.
Library: 750 volumes for lending or reference.
Income and Purchases: Income $120,000; purchases $69,000.
Attendance: 1500 annual average.

MONTEREY

CASA AMESTI
516 Polk Street
Carole T. Scanlon, Coordinator, Interpretive Programs
Open Sat. & Sun. 2 - 4 PM; also by arrangement; admis. 50¢ & free to National Trust mem. A property of the National Trust for Historic Preservation, administered locally by Property Council.
Casa Amesti is an 1833 adobe structure reflecting phases of the history and culture of the part of California owned by Mexico, after the period of Spanish missions and before development of American influences from the Eastern seaboard. It is a prototype of what is now known as Monterey style architecture. The adobe was purchased in 1917 by Mr. and Mrs. Frances Adler Elkins. Mrs. Elkins, a popular interior decorator, added a sun porch, and worked with her architect brother David Adler, in designing the formal gardens. The furnishings, largely European, collected by Mrs. Elkins are displayed in a typical 1930's interior. Mrs. Elkins bequeathed the adobe to the National Trust in 1953. The property is a National Trust historic house which, although not operated as an historic house museum nor community preservation center, represents a unique adaptive use of the property involving three preservation groups. The Old Capital Club, a private organization, leases, occupies and maintains the property for social and educational purposes.
Activities: Volunteers from the Monterey History and Art Association provide interpretive services for visitors on weekends; visitation program initiated early 1975; special participation in Adobe tours in April and the Monterey Birthday Party in June.

MONTEREY PENINSULA MUSEUM OF ART
559 Pacific St, 93940. Tel: (408) 372-5477
June Elder Braucht, Dir.
Officers elected each January.
Free Tues. - Fri. 10 AM - 4 PM, Sat. & Sun. 1 PM - 4 PM; cl. Mon. and holidays. Estab. 1960, inc. 1963. Maintained by mem. Two changing exhibitions monthly plus permanent collections of museum and city. Ann. meeting Jan; mem. approx. 1000; dues, sliding scale from $7.50 individual active to $250 life.
Collections: Painting, sculpture, graphics, photography, folk art; City of Monterey collection of paintings by early American, California artists; international folk art collection.
Exhibitions: Two temporary collection galleries which change exhibitions each month; work from other areas in the fine arts, folk arts and crafts; early local art and contemporary local art; annual competitive, retrospective and invitational photographic shows.
Activities: Workshops for adults and children; lectures, films, bus tours; annual Festival of the Trees in December; annual competition; $1200 in annual prizes. Gallery Shop.

Library: 300 volumes for reference; color slides of master works.
Publications: Courier (monthly newsletter); World Events in Pueblo Times.
Annual Income: $45,000.
Attendance: 20,500 annual average.

MONTEREY PUBLIC LIBRARY
625 Pacific St, 93940. Tel: (408) 372-7391
Dorothy Steven, City Librarian
Free Mon. - Fri. 9 AM - 9 PM; Sat. 9 AM - 6 PM; Sun. 1 - 5 PM. Estab. 1849 as a library for the city of Monterey; financed by city and state appropriation.
Collections: Volumes on Raiquel, Elkins, Adler architecture collection (17th - 19th century English, Italian and French). Total of 114,000 volumes for lending and reference; photograph collection for reference only.

NEWPORT BEACH

✠NEWPORT HARBOR ART MUSEUM
2211 W. Balboa Blvd, 92663. Tel: (714) 675-3866
David Steinmetz, Pres.
Ben C. Deane, V.Pres.
George Jeffries, V.Pres.
Mrs. Richard S. Jonas, V.Pres.
Leon Lyon, V.Pres.
Mrs. C. Thomas Wilck, Secy.
Owen Metzler, Treas.
Betty Turnbull, Cur.
Phyllis J. Lutjeans, Curatorial Assoc.
Jean Smock, Mem. Secy.
Sue Henger, Registrar.
Admis. by contribution Tues. - Sun. Noon - 4 PM, Fri. evening 6 - 9 PM. Estab. 1962, the organization and presentation of the art of our own time as well as other cultures with related activities; maintained by mem. Ann. meeting second Tues. in June; mem. 1200; ann. dues $6, $15, $18, $25, $50, various fine arts patrons categories.
Collections: Small nucleus of permanent collection which includes Joseph Albers, Robert Irwin, Gene Davis, Ludwig Sander, Kenzo Okada, Julian Stanczak, Paul Wonner. Purchases made this year with matching NEA funds were paintings by John McLaughlin, John Paul Jones, Martha Alf, Lita Albuquerque, Masami Teroaka; additional funds were raised to purchase Gary Beydler drawing and a suite of 20 encaustic paintings by Jean St. Pierre.
Exhibitions: (Major) Paintings: Reginald Marsh a Retrospective Survey; Danny Lyon: Ten Years of Photographs; Walter Darby Bannard from West Coast Collections; Mary Cassatt: 15 Paintings; 10 Major Works by Mark Rothko; Emerson Woelffer, A Survey Exhibition, 1947-1974; Llyn Foulkes, 50 Paintings, Collages and Prints from Southern California Collections; A Survey Exhibition, 1959-1974; Artist as Collector, Art of Africa, Oceania, Amerindian art and the Santeros of New Mexico from the collections of John and Monica Haley, Erle and Clyta Loran, Lee Mullican and Luchita Hurtado, Emerson and Dina Woelffer; The Los Angeles Fine Arts Squad (Terry Schoonhoven) paints a Mural for the Newport Harbor Art Museum.
Activities: Organization of lecture series for members; bus trips to various museums and private collections; travel program; traveling exhibitions organized and circulated; active docent program as well as active membership comt; Museum Council of Women Volunteers; active men's committee; presentation of films, dance.
Library: 1000 volumes for reference.
Publications: Exhibition catalogs accompany most exhibitions 4 to 5 times a year.
Annual Income: $86,000.
Annual Attendance: 18,000

NORTHRIDGE

FINE ARTS GALLERY
California State University, Northridge
Nordhoff St, 91324. Tel: (213) 885-2192
Dr. Ralph Heidsiek, Dean College of Fine Arts
Dr. Dolores Yonker, Acting Chmn. Dept. Art History
Dr. Jean-Luc Bordeaux, Dir.
Louise Lewis, Asst. Dir.
Phil Morrison, Installations Dir.
JoAnn Case, Gallery Asst.
Free Sun. 1 - 4 PM, Tues. - Fri. 10 AM - 4 PM. Estab. 1971 to serve the needs of the four art departments and to provide a source of cultural enrichment for the community at large; financed by city and state appropriations. Mem. Arts Council for CSUN, 300; dues $25 annually.
Collections: Original prints, paintings, contemporary American art.

Exhibitions: Baroque Paintings and Greek and Roman Portraits from the J. Paul Getty Museum; Charles Garabedian; Art of India; Mark Tobey; faculty and student shows.

Activities: Docent program with approximately 350 tours annually; graduate museology program (art history department) coordinated with other public museums in the Greater Los Angeles area; visiting lecturers; catalog sales shop.

Publications: Catalogs of exhibitions.

Budget: $6000.

Attendance: 30,000 annual average.

OAKLAND

MEYER LIBRARY*
California College of Arts and Crafts
5212 Broadway, 94618. Tel: (415) 653-8118
Harry X. Ford, Pres. of College
Robert L. Harper, Head Librn.
Stephen L. Sorensen, Asst. Librn.
Ann E. Hardham, Acquisitions Librn.
Free weekdays 8 AM - 5 PM. Estab. to support the curriculum of the college.

Collections: †Fine arts, †graphic design, †crafts, †art education, †humanities; 23,029 volumes for lending and reference; clipping file.

MILLS COLLEGE ART GALLERY
94613. Tel: (415) 632-2700
Terry Pink Alexander, Acting Dir.
Free Wed. - Sun. 12 - 4 PM. Estab. 1925.

Collections: Regional collection of California paintings, drawings and prints; †extensive collection of European and American prints and drawings; Guatemalan textiles; photographs and slides.

Exhibitions: Contemporary painting, sculpture and ceramics and exhibitions from permanent collection and loan collections.

Purchases: $1500 annually.

Attendance: Approx. 5000.

✤THE OAKLAND MUSEUM
Art Department
1000 Oak St, 94607. Tel: (415) 273-3005
John E. Peetz, Dir. Oakland Museum
George W. Neubert, Cur. Art
Harvey L. Jones, Deputy Cur. Art
Therese Heyman, Sr. Cur. Prints & Photographs
Hazel Bray, Assoc. Cur.
Terry St. John, Assoc. Cur.
Marjorie Arkelian, Historian
Barbara Savinar, Registrar
Gary Lopez, Preparator
Ellen Lee, Secy. to Cur.
Frances Balcomb, Curatorial Asst.
Barbara Bowman, Asst. Museum Researcher
Bradford Claybourn, Preparator's Asst.
William Hollis, Curatorial Asst.
Elizabeth Jones, Office Aide
Charles Lokey, Curatorial Asst.
Jeffrey Long, Curatorial Asst.
Odette Mayers, Actg. Librn.
David Schuld, Preparator's Asst.
Brian Suen, Curatorial Asst.
Free Tues. - Thurs. & Sat. 10 AM - 5 PM; Fri. 10 AM - 10 PM; Sun. 10 AM - 6 PM; cl. Mon. The new Oakland Museum which opened to the public Sept. 20, 1969, is comprised of three departments, Natural Sciences (formerly the Snow Museum of Natural History, founded 1922), History (formerly the Oakland Public Museum, founded 1910), and the Art Department (formerly the Oakland Art Museum, founded 1916).

Internationally recognized as a brilliant contribution to urban museum design, The Oakland Museum occupies a four-square-block, tree-studded site on the south shore of Lake Merritt. Designed by Kevin Roche, John Dinkeloo and Associates, the Museum is a three-tiered complex of exhibition galleries, with surrounding gardens, pools, courts and lawns, constructed so that the roof of each level becomes a garden and a terrace for the one above.

The Oakland Museum Association is a separately incorporated auxiliary for all three departments with over 5000 members. From its membership, the OMA provides assistance and support for museum educational and cultural programs, through its Women's Board, Docent Council, and its Art, History, and Natural Sciences Guilds, which coordinate volunteer activities in the museum's three Departments. Among the Association's services are the Museum Store, Art Rental Sales/Service, and Gallery.

Collections: Paintings, sculpture, prints, illustrations, photographs, and craftwork created either by California artists or artists dealing with California subjects, in a range that includes sketches

and paintings by early artist-explorers, Gold Rush genre pictures, massive Victorian landscapes, examples of the California Decorative Style, as well as Impressionist, Post-Impressionist, Abstract Expressionist, and other contemporary works.

In addition to a large hall with 20 small exhibition bays for the permanent collections, the Art Department offers a gallery for one-man or group shows by contemporary California artists, and the Oakes Art Observatory and Gallery, containing the study collections, a multimedia presentation, and the photography and print collections. A wide variety of temporary monthly exhibitions are also held in the Museum's Great Hall.

Library: 5000 reference books and catalogs on American art, with emphasis on California and the West; Archives of California Art, special collection of archival materials on 15,000 artists, craftsmen and photographers of California.

OAKLAND PUBLIC LIBRARY
Fine Arts Section
Room 218, Main Library, 125 14th St, 94612. Tel: (415) 273-3309
William H. Brett, Dir. Library Services
Richard Colvig, Supervising Librn.
Open Mon. 12:30 - 9 PM, Tues. & Thurs. 9 AM - 9 PM, Fri. & Sat. 9 AM - 5:30 PM, cl. Sun. & holidays. Cooperation with the Oakland Museum and local groups. Free film programs are presented regularly.

†Circulating and reference books on architecture, costumes, dance, fine and applied arts, music, theatre and sports. †Musical scores, choral music, records and tape cassettes are available. †16mm films.

†For circulation and reference a picture collection established 1910; contains over 300,000 clipped and mounted pictures, posters, charts, post cards and stereographs; †100 framed and unframed reproductions of famous paintings.

Reference collections include biographical file of California artists; original prints; Kate Cole Collection of 225 oil paintings of California wildflowers.

Purchases: Approx. $24,000 annually.

WESTERN ASSOCIATION OF ART MUSEUMS
Mills College, Box 9989, 94613. Tel: (415) 568-2400
Richard V. West, Pres.
Louise C. Tester, 1st V.Pres.
E. F. Sanguinetti, 2nd V.Pres.
Allen Dodworth, Secy.
Lewis W. Story, Treas.
For further information see p. 10.

OJAI

THE COMMUNITY ART CENTER OF THE OJAI VALLEY, INC.
113 S. Montgomery St, P.O. Box 331, 93023. Tel: (805) 646-2769
Florence von Breyman, Pres.
Virginia Lumb, Secy.
Kent Madsen, DDS, Chmn. of Board
Nancy Genevieve McIsaac, Exec. Dir.
Open Mon. - Sat. 9 AM - 5 PM; special events weekend nights and Sun. Estab. 1936, nonprofit self-supporting foundation dedicated to the furtherance of the arts; financed by membership, donors, class and special event fees. Gallery has monthly exhibits of local and California artists. Ann. meeting 1st Mon. in Jan; mem. 350; dues $7.50 individual, $15 family.

Activities: Lectures open to the public; concerts, dramatic programs, classes in the theatre, dance, children, ceramic and music branches of the Art Center.

Library: Approx. 150 reference volumes.

Publications: Newsletter, bimonthly.

Income and Purchases: Income $15,000; purchases $15,000.

PACIFIC GROVE

PACIFIC GROVE ART CENTER
568 Lighthouse Ave, 93950. Tel: (408) 375-2208
Gerry Lukenas, Pres.
Martha Larson, Secy.
Michael Brown, Dir.
Free Tues. - Sat. 1 - 5 PM. Estab. 1068 to promote the arts on the Monterey Peninsula, their total diversities; financed by endowment, appropriation and membership. Gallery 1, major exhibition gallery for traveling, regional and local exhibits. Ann. meeting first of July; mem. 200; ann. dues $6-$100.

Activities: Adult class in fine art and music; extensive Junior Arts Program year around. Traveling exhibitions organized and circulated; individual paintings lent to schools; photograph collection, over 100 prints for sales. Junior Museum, art classes, over 200. Lectures open to public, 5 visiting lecturers per year; over 100 gallery talks or tours for schools and service organization; concerts, dramatic programs, classes for adults and children; competitions.

Publications: Mategot, six weeks bulletin.
Annual Income: $36,000.
Attendance: Open just one year, over 10,000.

PALM SPRINGS

✤PALM SPRINGS DESERT MUSEUM
101 Museum Dr, P.O. Box 2288, 92262
Walter Annenberg, Pres.
Dr. Roy F. Hudson, Secy.
Frederick W. Sleight, Exec. Dir.
Free to members, students, teachers and children; admis to general public $1, with Tues. free. Open Sept. - May, Tues. - Sat. 10 AM - 5 PM, Sun. 2 - 5 PM; cl. Mon. Estab. and inc. 1938. Ann. meeting Mar; mem. 1700; dues from $15 annually to $5000 life membership.
Collections: Modern American painting, prints and sculpture, specializing in California artists; interpretation of natural sciences of the desert; Southwestern Indian crafts.
Exhibitions: Approx. 30 per year.
Activities: A Museum of Art, Natural Sciences and the Performing Arts. Maintains photograph collection of 2500 prints for reference use; lectures, films, gallery talks and tours, concerts and other musical events, dance, classes for adults and children; docent training and Living Desert Reserve.
Publications: Calendar of Events (monthly); special exhibition catalogs; Parade (seasonal newsletter).
Library: Reference Library 2500 volumes.

PASADENA

PASADENA MUSEUM
Colorado & Orange Grove Blvds, 91105. Tel: (213) 449-6840
George Peters, Dir.
Sara Campbell, Cur.
Andrea Clark, Registrar
Open Thurs. - Sun. 12 - 6 PM, cl. Mon. - Wed. Estab. in 1924, the Museum was originally inc. as the Pasadena Art Institute; in 1954 the Museum received the Galka E. Scheyer Collection of over 400 works of 20th century western European art. Since this acquisition the main thrust of the Museum has been the collection and exhibition of 20th century art which includes painting, sculpture, graphics and photography. Mem. 1000; dues $500 life mem, $100 donor mem, $25 mem.
Collections: 20th century art and its origins—630 paintings, 70 sculptures, 3700 prints, 500 photographs, 120 drawings. The entire collection is constantly being enlarged, primarily through gifts from friends of the Museum. Portions of the permanent collection are always on view. In addition, extensive loans from the Norton Simon Foundation collections are permanently on view. These include works by Italian, Spanish, Dutch, Flemish and French Old Masters, as well as important sculpture from India and Southeast Asia.
Activities: Bookstore offers books on all fields of art, children's books, ceramics, frames, crafts, posters, cards and other related items.
Library: Approx. 500 books, periodicals, museum catalogs, gallery catalogs and numerous indexes related to all schools of art; use in restricted to museum personnel.
Annual Income: (fiscal year 1974-75) $599,000.
Attendance: (past 2 fiscal years) 100,000.

PASADENA PUBLIC LIBRARY
285 E. Walnut St, 91101. Tel: (213) 577-4049
Robert Conover, Library Dir.
Josephine Pletscher, Head, Fine Arts Div.
Free Mon. - Thurs. 9 AM - 9 PM; Fri. & Sat. 9 AM - 6 PM; cl. Sun.
Art Department estab. 1927, Alice Coleman Batchelder Music Library estab. 1955.
Collections: For reference and circulation 21,022 books on the Fine Arts and music scores; 12,796 records; 130,335 clipped and mounted pictures; 219 16mm sound films; 133 periodical subscriptions; beginning cassette tape collection; pamphlet file; scrapbooks on local architecture, artists and musicians; photocopy facilities.
Activities: Cooperates with local museums, schools, clubs, art, music and civic groups.
Income: $24,000 plus endowments and gifts, for materials only.

PLEASANT HILL

DIABLO VALLEY COLLEGE MUSEUM
Golf Club Rd, 94523. Tel: (415) 685-1230
Dr. William Niland, Pres.
Erda Labuhn, Cur.
Free 9:30 AM - 4:30 PM weekdays except Thurs, Sat. 1:30 - 5 PM.
Estab. 1960 as principally a science museum, but having a regular

schedule of small art shows in one section; financed by city and state appropriation.
Collections: Small print collections.
Activities: Docent tours.
Library: 125 volumes for reference; photograph collection; prints for reference.
Attendance: 13,804.

RANCHO PALOS VERDES

PALOS VERDES ART CENTER AND MUSEUM
Palos Verdes Community Arts Association
5504 W. Crestridge Rd, 90274. Tel: (213) 541-2479
Morton Rible, Pres.
Curt Wagner, V.Pres.
Mrs. G. R. Bynum, Secy.
William Balbirnie, Jr, Treas.
Inc. 1931, ann. meeting; mem. 1900; dues $15 and higher. Palos Verdes Art Center and Museum built May 1974.
Collections: Small permanent collection of prints and drawings.
Exhibitions: 8 shows a year; annual juried show.
Activities: 4 semesters of classes in all the visual arts; Music Conservatory offering seminar instruction on all musical instruments, family orchestra, bus trips to significant exhibits and shows in other areas, lectures, concerts, annual two-day art festival, Art for Fun(d)'s Sake; rental and sales gallery; museum gallery.
Publications: Chronicle (monthly).

REDLANDS

PEPPERS ART CENTER
University of Redlands
1200 W. Colton Ave, 92373. Tel: (714) 793-2121
Vernon E. Dornbach, Jr, Chmn, Art Dept.
Gallery free Tues. - Fri. 1 - 5 PM; Sat. & Sun. 2 - 5 PM. Estab. 1909, University, Liberal Arts College; endowed.
Collections: A small permenent collection including Ethnic Art, many graphics, some famous artists, mainly for teaching purposes.
Exhibitions: Exhibitions of various kinds during fall, winter, spring.
Activities: Art classes; lending slides, books, permanent collection to schools; library.

REDLANDS ART ASSOCIATION*
12 E. Vine St, 92373.
Beryl Larkin, Pres.
Marjorie Herms, Secy.
Ann Blesener, Gallery Mgr.
Free daily 10 AM - 2 PM; cl. Sun. Estab. 1964 to promote interest in the visual arts, to provide a gallery for artists; financed by memberships. Sales gallery for members' work. Meeting 4th Wed. each month; mem. 265; dues $6.
Exhibitions: Lyon Gallery exhibitions are presented at least 6 time yearly; many media mini juried shows at Vine St. Gallery for past 4 years.
Activities: Classes in painting, photography, ceramics, for children through teens; lectures open to the public; 4 visiting lecturers per year; 3 tours yearly; competitions; scholarships.
Publications: Redlands Art Association monthly bulletin.

RICHMOND

RICHMOND ART CENTER
Civic Center, 25th & Barrett Ave, 94804. Tel: (415) 234-0007 or 232-1212 Exten. 370
Ernie Kim, Dir.
James T. Soult, Cur.
A. Martin Cooke, Class Supvr.
Free Mon. - Fri. 10 AM - 4:30 PM; Thurs. evening 4:30 PM - 9:30 PM; Sun. 12 AM - 4:30 PM; cl. Sat. and holidays. Preliminary steps for formation, 1936-1944, formed 1944 to establish in the community a center for the arts. Ann. meeting May; mem. 1500; dues $5 and up.
Collections: Permanent collection, approx. 75 items, contemporary paintings, drawings, prints, sculpture.
Exhibitions: Group, one-man, Bay Area artists, 1 juried designer-craftsman per year; prizes vary.
Activities: Approximately 40 classes for adults, teens and children in painting, drawing, ceramics, weaving, jewelry, lapidary, batik, ballet, youth leadership training; gallery tours by Service League Docents; outreach program of art activities within surrounding community.
Library: Small library for staff and membership.
Publications: Brochures, catalogues, posters, announcements.
Income: $165,000.
Attendance: 35,000 (average for past two calendar years).

RIVERSIDE

✠RIVERSIDE ART CENTER AND MUSEUM
3425 Seventh, 92501. Tel: (714) 684-7111
Mary Jane Spiel, Pres.
Ruth Place, V.Pres.
Alan T. Garrett, Dir.
Daniel H. Smith, Exec. Secy.
Katie Miller, Sales & Rental Coordinator
Virginia Massingale, School Coordinator
Free Tues. - Sat. 10 AM - 5 PM; Sun. 1 - 5 PM; cl. Mon. Estab.
1931 to enlighten and refine the thinking of a particular people in a
particular location through the visual arts and crafts; financed by
membership. Exhibition gallery and sales and rental gallery main-
tained. Ann. meeting Apr; mem. 1000; dues student and senior citi-
zen $1.50, general $20, family $30, supporting $40, patron $75 and
up.
Collections: 50 pieces dating from late 1800's to present, a mix-
ture of media; fairly recent collection, additions made through Purchase Prize Competition and personal contributions.
Exhibitions: (1975-76) Buy Art for Christmas; Annual Members'
Show; Permanent Collection; Annual Purchase Prize Competition;
Watercolor West; Annual High School Press Enterprise Show; Art
Fun in the Sun; Neon Light Show.
Activities: Art classes, beginning to advanced studio instruction;
art program presented in public school system; staffs and funds
50% of free art class for disadvantaged children; lectures open to
public, 6 visiting lecturers per year; 100 tours; competitions;
scholarships.
Library: 400 volumes for lending and reference.
Publications: Artifacts, monthly, Sept. - July.
Total Revenue: $132,875; total expenditures $125,509.

UNIVERSITY OF CALIFORNIA ART GALLERY
Division of Fine Arts, 92502. Tel: (714) 787-4244
Kirk A. deGooyer, Dir.
William T. Bradshaw, Chmn, Art (Studio) Dept.
Barbara B. Maxwell, Cur. Slide/Print Collection, Art History Dept.
Victoria Fern, Special Projects Officer
Dr. Thomas O. Pelzel, Chmn, Art History Dept.
Free Mon. - Fri. 11 AM - 3 PM; Sun. 2 - 4 PM during school ses-
sions. Estab. 1963, the Art Gallery is integrated with the Art De-
partment curriculum.
Exhibitions: Two exhibits are scheduled each quarter (fall,
winter and spring) except summer. Exhibitions are organized by
the UCR Art History & Art (Studio) Department or obtained from
The American Federation of Arts and other exhibit rental
sources.
Publications: The Impressionists and the Salon, 1974; Joseph
Beuys, 1975; Fong Chung-Ray, 1976.
Attendance: 25,000.
The Museum of Photography
Barbara Parent, Sr. Preparator
Collections: The Bingham Collection, 3rd largest in United States.

ROSS

MARIN SOCIETY OF ARTISTS, INC.*
P.O. Box 203, 94957. Tel: (415) 454-9561
Doris Morrison, Pres.
Lynn Falch, Corresp. Secy.
Gallery free daily 1 - 4 PM. Estab. 1926 to foster cooperation
among artists and to further public interest in art. Semi-ann. meet-
ings May and Sept; mem. 712; dues $10.
Exhibitions: Ten exhibitions annually; annual exhibition in July or
Sept. with $3000 awards given.
Activities: Operates Rental Gallery all year; lectures, art appre-
ciation series, art seminars, technique demonstrations for artists.
Attendance: 50,000.

SACRAMENTO

CALIFORNIA STATE FAIR & EXPOSITION ART SHOW*
Box 15649, 95813
Thomas E. Blair, Mgr.
Miss Audrey Corcoran, Secy.
Edward J. Lynam, Exhibit Supv.
Free 10 AM - 10 PM Aug. 21 - Sept. 9 (an ann. event). Estab. 1854
to exhibit work of artists of the State of California.
Collections: Purchase awards have enlarged the permanent col-
lection which includes oils, watercolors, prints, ceramics and enam-
eling, textiles, photographs, color slides.
Activities: Art in Action demonstrations; Purchase Prize awards
available for loan; exhibitions circulated; individual paintings, ob-
jects of art and photographs for loan; dramatic programs.
Publications: Art catalog annually; Premium Book.
Budget and Awards: Budget $20,000; awards $5000.
Attendance: 450,000.

✠E. B. CROCKER ART GALLERY
216 O St, 95814. Tel: (916) 446-4677
Bert Geisreiter, Pres.
Richard Vincent West, Dir.
Roger Clisby, Chief Cur.
Free Tues, 2 - 10 PM; Wed. - Sun. 10 AM - 5 PM; cl. Mon. The
Gallery is the Art Museum of the City of Sacramento. Estab. in 1873
by Judge E. B. Crocker to house his collection of paintings, draw-
ings, prints and sculpture; the Gallery was presented to the city in
1885. Governed jointly by the City and the California Museum Asso-
ciation; dues $15-$250.
Collections: †16th-20th century paintings, †master drawings and
†sculpture; †19th century California painting; †Korean ceramics,
†Chinese and Japanese arts; †American glass and Victorian decora-
tive arts, costume and accessories.
Exhibitions: Crocker-Kingsley Annual, juried, open to Northern
California artists each spring; California Crafts, biennial, open to
California craftspeople.
Special Exhibitions: Master Drawings from Sacramento;
Sacramento Sampler I and II; Robert Bechtle Retrospective; The
Black Image; The Pre-Rembrandtists; The Collecting Muse.
Activities: Lectures, tours, films and musical concerts; The
Crocker Art Gallery Association sponsors an annual contemporary
exhibition, docent training program and other membership activity.
Library: Research library of books, exhibition catalogs, sales
catalogs, monographs and other art reference sources for staff and
membership by permission.
Attendance: 125,000.

SALINAS

HARTNELL COLLEGE GALLERY
156 Homestead Ave, 93901. Tel: (408) 758-8211
Judi Russell, Dir.
Free Mon. - Fri. 8 AM - 5 PM; Mon. - Thurs. 7 - 10 PM. Estab.
1938 as educational and cultural exposure for community; financed
by city and state appropriation.
Collections: †Watercolors, prints and sculpture; †5 Rouault
wood engravings; †6 original World War II posters.
Activities: Lectures open to public; dramatic programs, classes
for adults.

SAN BERNARDINO

COLLEGE ART GALLERY
California State College, San Bernardino
5500 State College Parkway, 92407. Tel: (714) 887-7459
Don Woodford, Dir. Gallery
Roger Lintault, Chmn. Art Dept.
Free Mon. - Fri. 9 AM - Noon & 1 - 3 PM; Wed. & Thurs. 6:30 - 9
PM; Sat. Noon - 4 PM; Sun. 1 - 5 PM. Estab. Dec. 6, 1972, to pro-
vide high quality exhibits of art for both the general and campus
communities. The work generally exhibited is contemporary; financed
by city and state appropriation.
Collections: Small collection of prints.
Exhibitions: Contemporary painting and sculpture from Los Ange-
les Galleries; Nicholas Krushenick, working drawings; Three Crafts-
men in Glass (Littleton, Marcus, Warehall); Jack Glenn Selects;
California Printmakers Invitational; Twelve Chicano Artistas; Women
and Wood (Nevelson, Marisol, etc); Renaissance Drawings; A Native
Genius: American Quilts; Robert Heinecken: photographic work;
Paper Works (Tom Wudl, Jay McCafferty, etc); Robert Rauschen-
berg: Hoarfrost Editions.
Activities: Lectures open to public; 1 - 3 visiting lecturers per
year; 1 - 4 gallery talks; tours; scholarships. (See Schools)
Attendance: 5300.

SAN BERNARDINO ART ASSOCIATION
1640 E. Highland (P.O. Box 2272), 92406. Tel: (714) 882-2054.
Vivian Kassel, Pres.
Catherine Dashbach, Secy.
Doris Jacka, 1st V.Pres.
Marie Hall, 2nd V.Pres. & Gallery Chmn.
Russell Brown, Treas.
Free Mon. - Sat. 12 - 4 PM. The Gallery Shop was formed for the
purpose of showing art to the residents of San Bernardino by artists
who reside in San Bernardino; a non-profit organization supported
by mem. Monthly meeting; mem. 160.
Activities: Art in the Schools Program; individual paintings lent
to schools and others; lectures open to public; 9 visiting lecturers,
5 gallery talks and tours per year; scholarships.
Publications: Newsletter, monthly.

SAN DIEGO

CALIFORNIA STATE UNIVERSITY, SAN DIEGO ART GALLERY
5402 College Ave, 92182
Dr. Winifred H. Higgins, Chairwoman, Dept of Art
Moira Roth, Dir.
Open 9 AM - 4 PM daily; no admis. Estab. to provide exhibitions of importance for the student-faculty and public of the San Diego environment; for study and appreciation of art and enrichment of the university; financed by city and state appropriations.
Collections: Contemporary Print Collection; Oriental Sculpture and Prints, on campus; Graduate Student Sculpture and Painting Crafts Collection.
Exhibitions: National Printmaking Annual; National Small Sculpture and Drawing; National Crafts Exhibition; Graduate & Undergraduate Students Exhibitions.
Activities: Original objects of art lent to university only; lectures open to the public.
Attendance: 35,000 annual average.

✠FINE ARTS GALLERY OF SAN DIEGO
Balboa Park, P.O. Box 2107, 92112. Tel: (714) 232-7931
Henry G. Gardiner, Dir.
Donald Crawford, Asst. Dir.
Martin E. Petersen, Cur. of Painting
Ellen Storjohann, Business Adminr.
Mary Chapman, Secy. to the Dir.
Dennis Komac, Cur. of Exhibitions
Barbara Pope, Curatorial Secy.
Harvey Miller, Activities Coordinator
Margaret A. Hughes, Mem. Secy.
Nancy Andrews, Librn.
Susan Naiman, Mgr, Book Store
Denise Draper, Mgr. Art Sales & Rental
Operated by the Fine Arts Society of San Diego. Free weekdays 10 AM - 5 PM; Sun. 12:30 - 5 PM; cl. Mon, Thanksgiving, Dec. 25 and Jan. 1. Estab. 1925, opened 1926; building owned by the City. Ann. meeting May; mem. 3800; dues $15 and higher; city and county appropriation.
Collections: Important Renaissance, Baroque and 18th Century European paintings of the Italian, Flemish, Spanish, Dutch, French and English schools. 19th and 20th century sculpture and paintings: American, Italian, English and French. Extensive print collection: American, European and Oriental. Oriental arts: sculpture, paintings, ceramics, and decorative arts. Decorative arts: American furniture and glass, Georgian silver.
Exhibitions: Special changing exhibitions of local and national interest; survey and one-man exhibitions; area shows include purchase awards.
Activities: Afternoon and evening programs, lectures and activities in cooperation with local art groups, gallery tours for school classes, classes for adults and young students. Art sales and rental gallery.
Library: Standard and specialized reference books, 10,000 volumes, plus extensive artist files, exhibition and priced catalogs, magazines and clippings; 12,291 slides. For members, serious art students and scholars; non-lending.
Attendance: 353,961.

FOUNDERS' GALLERY
University of San Diego
Alcala Park, 92110. Tel: (714) 291-6480
Prof. Therese T. Whitcomb, Dir.
Open weekdays 10 AM - 4 PM. Estab. Apr, 1971 to enrich the goals of the art department and university by providing excellent in-house exhibitions of all eras, forms and media, and to share them with the community; financed by department budget. Gallery is an architecturally outstanding facility with foyer, display area and patio, parking in central campus.
Collections: South Asian Textiles and Costumes of 19th and 20th centuries; Tibetian and Indian Looms, Ghandi etc, Spinning Wheels; †19th and 20th century American Folk Sculpture; 17th, 18th and 19th century French tapestries and furniture.
Exhibitions: Rico LeBrun; Georges Rouault; Francois Gilot; 19th Century Beaux Arts Drawings; California Adobes in Photos; Women Art of South Asia; Photo-Sculpture of Lou Brown; Di Guilio; Myrna Nobile Environmental; John Dirks Sculpture; 6 on Paper from Kentucky. 7 shows each year.
Activities: Original objects of art lent; 5000 lantern slides; lectures open to public; 10 tours per year; competitions; scholarships. (See Schools)
Annual Income: $500.
Attendance: 1500.

SAN DIEGO PUBLIC LIBRARY
Art and Music Section, 820 E St, 92101. Tel: (714) 236-5810
Charlotte Speik, Supervising Librn.
William Vere Wolf, Sr. Librn.

Gale Griffin, Picture Specialist
Marjorie Kooperman, Librn.
Open Mon. - Fri. 10 AM - 9 PM; Sat. 9:30 AM - 5:30 PM. Art and Music Section estab. 1954, to provide information and reference services in the fine arts with expanding collections of books, both reference and circulating, music scores, recordings, picture clipping file; City or State appropriation. Corridor Gallery, mo. exhibitions of art work by local artists and art groups are featured.
Collections: Special collections include the former library of a local architect, William Templeton Johnson, the former library of the late Donal Hord, sculptor; emphasis is on Spanish Mediterranean, Italian and French Renaissance architecture and oriental art, sculpture and ceramics, books on the theatre including biographies of famous actors and actresses, as well as histories of the American, London and European stages is another special collection, the gift of Elwyn B. Gould, local theatre devotee.
Exhibitions: Clairemont Art Guild; San Diego Watercolor Society; Designers' Workshop with one-man shows by local artists.
Activities: Color-slide shows and lectures to go with exhibits; lending collection, approx. 75,000 books both reference and circulating, approx. 15,000 recordings, approx. 427,000 pictures and postcards.
Purchases: Approx. $20,000 annually.

TIMKEN ART GALLERY
The Putnam Foundation
Balboa Park, 92101. Tel: (714) 239-5548
Walter Ames, Pres.
Allen J. Sutherland, V.Pres.
E. S. Larsen, Secy. & Treas.
Nancy A. Petersen, Adminr. of Timken Art Gallery
Free 10 AM - 4:30 PM; cl. Mon. & Sun. AM and entire month of Sept. Gallery opened Oct. 1965, Foundation was estab. 1951. A gallery was specially constructed to hold a collection of Old Master works and Russian Icons. Endowed by the late Misses Anne and Amy Putnam of San Diego. The name of the gallery is in recognition of a benefactor, The Timken Foundation of Canton, Ohio.
Collections: Flemish, Dutch, Italian, French, Spanish and American artists, including work by Rembrandt, Rubens, El Greco, Murillo, Bosch, Goya, Cotan, Ribera, Brueghel, Petrus Christus, Hals, Corot, Boucher, Fragonard, David, Veronese, Crivelli, Savoldo, Titian, Giotto, Guardi, Bellotto, Metsu, Van Ruisdael, Clouet, Lorrain, Cezanne, Bierstadt, Eastman Johnson, Inness, Benjamin West, Thomas Birch and countless others.
Activities: A docent is available two days per week for guided tours.
Publications: Catalog was published in 1969.
Attendance: 70,000 to 80,000 annually.

SAN FRANCISCO

ART COMMISSION—CITY AND COUNTY OF SAN FRANCISCO
165 Grove St, 94102. Tel: (415) 558-3465
Harold L. Zellerbach, Pres. of Commission
Martin Snipper, Dir. of Cultural Affairs
Joan Ellison, Asst. Dir.
Elio Benvenuto, Dir. of Visual Arts Progs.
Stephen Goldstine, Dir. Neighborhood Art Prog.
Howard Lazar, Coordinator, Street Artist Prog.
Estab. 1932; consists of 7 professional and 3 lay members appointed by the Mayor with advice of art societies, and 5 ex-officio members; monthly meetings.
Passes on all buildings and works of art placed on property of City or County; supervises and controls all appropriations made by the Board of Supervisors for music and the advancement of art and music; may volunteer advice to private owners who submit plans for suggestions; maintains a Civic Chorale and Neighborhood Arts program; adminsters ordinance providing 2% of cost of public construction for art ($400,000 in 1973); also, a municipal collection of art for embellishing public offices; purchases are made from the annual Art Festival; maintains art gallery and presents various concerts; licenses street artists; responsible for cataloging and maintaining all public works of art.
Purchases: Over $5000 annually.

ASIAN ART MUSEUM
Center of Asian Art & Culture, Golden Gate Park, 94118. Tel: (415) 387-5675
Mrs. Philip McCoy, Pres.
Marjorie D. Schwarz, Secy.
Betty F. Walters, Exec. Secy.
Estab. 1958 for illustrated lectures on specialized subjects by visiting scholars, American and foreign, small study groups on specific aspects of Asian art, support of the research library in the center, exhibitions arranged or co-sponsored by the society; financed by mem. Ann. meeting Apr. or May; mem. 1065; dues $15 active, $5 student.

Activities: Lectures open to the public; 6-8 gallery talks per year; classes for adults.

Publications: Society for Asian Art Newsletter, 3 per year.

CALIFORNIA HISTORICAL SOCIETY

2090 Jackson St, San Francisco, 94109
Tel: (415) 567-1848
1120 Old Mill Rd, San Marino, 91108
Tel: (213) 449-5450
Fred Farr, Pres.
J. S. Holliday, Secy. & Exec. Dir.
V. B. Gerhart, Asst. Dir.
Gary Kurutz, Dir. Library
Marilyn Ziebarth, Dir. Publications
Joan Kerr, Comptroller
Catherine Hoover, Cur. Exhibits
Monica Broucek, Community Services & Mem.
Jean Bruce Poole, Asst. to Dir. Southern California

Headquarters open Wed, Sat. & Sun. 1 - 5 PM; Library open Tues. - Sat. 10 AM - 4 PM; first Sat. each month free; free to Society members; gen. admis. $1, seniors, students and children 50¢. Estab. 1871 as a statewide, nonprofit educational institution with the purpose of stimulating and sustaining informed interest on the part of the general public in the history of California, and to collect, preserve, and disseminate information relating to the history of California and the Far West; financed by endowment and membership. Gallery has changing exhibitions of paintings, lithographs, drawings and fine arts from permanent collections, and works of others by California artists and photographers. Mem. 6500; dues vary.

Collections: Paintings, watercolors, drawings, lithographs, pen and ink sketches, sculpture, historic artifacts, photographs, costumes and ephemera relating to California and the Far West.

Exhibitions: Percy Gray Retrospective; The Redwood Empire; The Barns of California; The American Farm; New World Utopias; R. D. Ginther, Workingman Artist of the 1930's; Land for Sale; Adobes in the Sun; Ghosts of the Gold Rush; The Gold Rush Country; Lake Tahoe Album; Executive Order 9066; Workingmen's Party of San Francisco.

Activities: Nationwide exhibitions, primary area is statewide California; material available to museums, colleges and universities, fees vary $125-$450; material lent includes exhibitions of paintings, photographs (within themes); traveling exhibitions organized and circulated; original objects of art lent occasionally, but usually to museums only; numerous photographs and 15 motion pictures in lending collection; photographic collection of 160,000 prints, copies available for print price; lectures open to the public; 10-20 visiting lecturers per year; weekly gallery talks and tours; statewide programs and tours; classes for adults; docent program.

Library: 40,000 volumes noncirculating, reference and research only; manuscripts, diaries, journals, oral history, posters, scrapbooks, theater collection and ephemera.

Publications: CHS Quarterly; Historical Courier, 7 times yearly.

Attendance: 8000.

⚓THE FINE ARTS MUSEUMS OF SAN FRANCISCO

M. H. de Young Memorial Museum
Golden Gate Park, 94118. Tel: (415) 558-2887
California Palace of the Legion of Honor
Lincoln Park, 94121. Tel: (415) 558-2881
Ransom M. Cook, Pres.
Ian McKibbin White, Dir.
Dr. Thomas Carr Howe, Dir. Emeritus
Thomas K. Seligman, V.Dir, Educ.
Ronald Egherman, V.Dir, Admin. & Personnel
Marie S. Jensen, Exec. Secy. Board of Trustees
Ann Knoll, Development Officer
Thomas H. Garver, Cur. in charge Exhibitions
Susan Levitin, Asst. Cur. Exhibitions
D. Graeme Keith, Cur. in charge, Decorative Arts
Robert F. Johnson, Cur. in charge, Prints & Drawings
Fenton Kastner, Cur. Prints & Drawings
(Achenbach Foundation for Graphic Arts)
Elsa Cameron, Cur. in charge, Art School
William H. Elsner, Assoc. Cur.
Richard Fong, Asst. Cur. Educ.
Bruce Merley, Asst. Cur. Educ.
Charles Mills, Asst. Cur. Educ.
Anna Bennett, Assoc. Cur, Decorative Arts
Jane Nelson, Librn. & Cur, Dept. of Ancient Art
Frederic P. Snowden, Registrar (de Young Museum)
DeRenne Coerr, Registrar (Legion of Honor)
Charles Long, Pub. Relations
Roy Perkinson, Conservator, Paper
Teri Oikawa-Picante, Conservator, Painting
Gene Munsch, Conservator, Furniture

Open daily 10 AM - 5 PM; admis. adult 75¢, youth 25¢, senior citizens and children under 12 free; mem. free; first of month free. de Young Museum estab. 1895, Legion of Honor estab. 1924, merged 1972 as a department of the city and county of San Francisco. Museum Society mem. approx. 18,000; dues $20 and up.

Collections: de Young Museum—12th - 20th century European and American paintings, sculpture and decorative arts, including tapestries, silver, furniture, porcelain, glass and period rooms; arts of ancient Egypt, Greece and Rome; traditional arts of Africa, Oceania and the Americas. Legion of Honor—14th - 20th century French paintings, sculpture and decorative arts, including tapestries, furniture, porcelain, silver and period rooms; Rodin sculpture collection; Achenbach Foundation for Graphic Arts (Department of Prints and Drawings) holds approx. 100,000 works from Europe, America and Asia, 15th century to the present.

Activities: The de Young Museum Art School (studio classes), temporary exhibitions, lectures, films, concerts, Trip-Out Truck (community outreach); Docent Council (volunteer guided tours). Art book shops. Cafe.

Library at de Young Museum has 20,000 volumes on art research.

Archives of American Art West Coast Office (branch of Smithsonian Institution) microfilm library located in de Young Museum.

Publications: Members' monthly calendar; exhibition catalogs.

Income: Approx. $2 million annually (municipal).

Attendance: Approx. 1,500,000.

GALERÍA DE LA RAZA

2851 24th St, 94110. Tel: (415) 826-8009
Rene Yanez, Co-Dir.
Ralph Maradiaga, Co-Dir.
Elisa Borrego, Cur. & Researcher
Francisco Garcia, Documentation of Exhibits & Slides
Free Wed. - Sun. Noon - 5 PM. Estab. Nov. 1969 as a community gallery and museum to exhibit works by Mexican-American and Latin-American artists, contemporary as well as cultural folk art; plans are being made for a community design and art center; endowed. Meet once a month; mem. 150; dues $12.

Collections: Leopoldo Mendez Prints from Mexico; Huichol Yarn Paintings from Peter Young Collection; Folk Art from Mexico; Textiles from the Americas.

Exhibitions: 36 in last 3 years, 3-4 weeks duration per exhibit.

Activities: 750 Kodachromes, original objects of art and paintings lent and traveling exhibitions organized and circulated to community organizations, schools and universities at no charge; 25 items lent in average year to 35 borrowers. Lectures open to public; 24 visiting lecturers, gallery talks and tours per year; classes for adults and children; art book store.

Library: Resource material and photographs being acquired.

Publications: Galeria de la Raza Children's Coloring Book; Galeria Newsletter Bulletin (monthly); Calendar (yearly); original screen prints edition of 100.

Attendance: 35,000.

LONE MOUNTAIN COLLEGE ART DEPARTMENT

2800 Turk Blvd, 94118. Tel: (415) 752-7000, Exten. 240 & 241
Robert Brawley, Chmn.
Patricia Shih, Admin. Asst.
Free Mon. Tues, Thurs, Fri. & Sat. Noon - 4 PM; cl. Wed. & Sun. College estab. as San Francisco College for Women 1930, renamed Lone Mountain College, 1970. 25 ft. x 47 ft. gallery with 12 ft. ceilings, track lighting and hardwood floor.

Exhibitions: Bay Area Artists Series (3 exhibitions); Young Artist Exhibition Series (5 exhibitions); Tibetan Art Exhibition; Art of Retarded People; graduate, undergraduate and faculty exhibitions.

Activities: Concerts, dramatic programs, classes for adults.

Library: 175,000 volumes for lending and reference.

Publications: Lone Mountain College Gazette; undergraduate and graduate bulletins.

Attendance: 25 per day.

SAN FRANCISCO ART INSTITUTE

800 Chestnut St, 94133. Tel: (415) 771-7020
Mrs. Richard Swig, Chmn. Board of Trustees
David Robinson, 1st V.Chmn.
Maryanna G. Shaw, 2nd V.Chmn.
Robert C. Kirkwood, Secy.
D. E. Mundell, Treas.
Arnold Herstand, Pres.
Roy Ascott, Dir. College
Monroe Bush, Dir. Development
Tom Young, Dir. Admin.
Helene Fried, Assoc Dir. Pub. Affairs & Publications
Philip Linhares, Dir. Exhibitions
Elisabeth Cunkle, Librn.
Free Mon. - Sat. 10 AM - 4 PM. Estab. 1871, inc. 1889 to foster the appreciation and creation of the fine arts and maintain a school and museum for that purpose. Ann. meeting June; mem. 1300; dues $15-$100 and patron members.

Collections: Emanuel Walter Collection, San Francisco Art Institute Collection, Sloss Bequest. The San Francisco Art Institute Collection is on extended loan to the San Francisco Museum of Art; the Sloss Bequest is on extended loan to the California Historical Society.

Exhibitions: Emanuel Walter Gallery for exhibitions of contemporary art, open to the public, admission free; Atholl McBean Gallery for exhibitions of recent works by SFAI faculty on a two and three-man basis; Diego Rivera Gallery for exhibition of works by SFAI students; SFAI Photo Gallery for exhibitions of photographs by participating photographers invited by SFAI Photo Department.

SFAI Touring Exhibitions Program features group exhibitions of paintings, drawings, prints and photographs by prominent San Francisco Bay Area artists. These exhibitions are available for showing by college, university and private galleries for a minimal rental fee.

Library: The Anne Bremer Memorial Library of 21,000 volumes in art and the humanities, 6500 slides and 2000 reproductions.

Annual Gallery Attendance: Approx. 60,000.

SAN FRANCISCO MUSEUM OF ART
   McAllister St. at Van Ness Ave, 94102. Tel: (415) 863-8800
Eugene E. Trefethen, Jr, Pres.
Mrs. Walter A. Haas, Jr, V.Pres.
A. Hunter Land, II, Secy.
Alan L. Stein, Treas.
Henry T. Hopkins, Dir.
Michael McCone, Dep. Dir.
S. C. St. John, Controller
John Humphrey, Cur.
Mary Suzanne Foley, Cur.
Robert Whyte, Supvr. Educ. Dept.
Bonnie Hughes, Mem. Secy.
Eugenie Candau, Librn.
Phillip Goddard, Bookshop Mgr.
Julius Wasserstein, Gallery Supt.
Susan King, Registrar
Open Tues. - Fri. 10 AM - 10 PM; Sat. & Sun. 10 AM - 5 PM, cl. Mon; permanent collection is free; $1 charge for temporary exhibitions. Founded 1916, inc. 1921; operates as a museum of 20th century art; a cultural and educational center for the layman, with emphasis on arts of today. Ann. meeting of trustees May; dues $18 yearly and higher; mem. 5000. Museum occupies third and fourth floors, northern building of War Memorial, opened 1935.

Collections: †Museum collections of contemporary art; †Sarah and Michael Stein Collection; Latin American contemporary paintings, sculpture, drawings; Albert M. Bender collection of contemporary American and European paintings, drawings, prints, works by San Francisco artists; Harriet Levy collection of contemporary French paintings; William L. Gerstle collection contemporary paintings, drawings and prints.

Exhibitions: Roy DeForest; Louise Nevelson; Ansel Adams; Richard Diebenkorn; Peter Voulkos; Fred Martin; Ruth Asawa; Sol Lewitt; Jean Arp; Hassel Smith; Women of Photography; Clyfford Still.

Activities: Lectures, Film programs, concerts, poetry readings; book store.

Library: Reference library with emphasis on contemporary art and on periodicals. Slide library.

Income and Purchases: Annual income including funds, maintenance, approx. $800,000; purchases approx. $45,000 for 1973.

Attendance: 250,000.

SAN FRANCISCO PUBLIC LIBRARY
Art and Music Department
   Civic Center, 94102. Tel: (415) 558-3687
Mary Ashe, Librn. in Charge
Free Mon. - Fri. 9 AM - 9 PM; Sat. 9 AM - 6 PM; Sun. 1 - 6 PM. Estab. 1878; financed by city and state appropriations.

Collections: †Books and periodicals on all aspects of the visual and plastic arts as part of a department which also covers music, theatre, the performing arts and recreation; exhibition catalogs; clipping and ephemera files documenting local artists, organizations and activities; picture file: clippings and plates, chiefly from 19th and early 20th century books and periodicals, illustrating all subjects to the limits of the period.

SAN JOSE

✠ROSICRUCIAN EGYPTIAN MUSEUM AND ART GALLERY
   Rosicrucian Park, 95191. Tel: (408) 287-9171
Ralph M. Lewis, Dir.
Burnam Schaa, Cur.
Free Tues. - Fri. 9 AM - 5 PM; Sat, Sun. & Mon. 12 - 5 PM. Estab. 1929; operated by the Rosicrucian Order (AMORC), a non-sectarian philosophic fraternity, as an educational project and for preservation of Egyptian and Mesopotamian antiquities; endowed.

Collections: †Egyptian, Sumerian, Assyrian and Babylonian antiquities; a lending collection of photographs; †films in sound and color of expeditions made by the Rosicrucian Camera Expedition in

India, Tibet, Siam, Pakistan and Egypt. These films are loaned to the public without charge.
   Purchases: $10,000 annually.
   Attendance: 430,000 annually.

SAN JOSE MUSEUM OF ART
San Jose Museum of Art Association
   110 S. Market St, 95113. Tel: (408) 294-2787
Albert G. Dixon, Jr, Dir.
Elizabeth Gaidos, Cur.
Judith A. Bolin, Office Mgr.
Free Tues. - Sat. 10 AM - 4:30 PM; Sun. 12 - 4 PM. Estab. 1968 to provide the citizens of San Jose and the South Bay region with a changing exhibition schedule featuring local, regional, national and traveling shows; a permanent collection is also maintained; financed by city and state appropriations and membership. Ann. meeting June; mem. 750; dues, student and senior citizen $5, single $10, family $25, sustaining $25-$500.

Collections: Paintings, principally California and chiefly contemporary.

Exhibitions: 55-60 per year.

Activities: Two year docent fee paying student art survey program conducted in conjunction withCalifornia State University at San Jose; traveling exhibitions organized and circulated; original objects of art lent; reproductions given through outreach program; 80-100 oil paintings, prints and sculpture in lending collection, open to members; rental and sales gallery; lectures open to the public; 12 visiting lecturers and gallery talks per year; daily tours; classes for adults and children; competitions; traveling instructional museum - Lets Look at Art. Book shop.

Library: 200 volume reference library.

Publications: Monthly newsletter and exhibition catalogs.

Attendance: 35,000 annual average.

SAN JOSE STATE UNIVERSITY ART GALLERY
   Ninth and San Carlos, 95192. Tel: (408) 277-2716
Jessica Jacobs, Dir.
Free Mon. - Fri. 11 AM - 4 PM. Estab. 1960 as part of the university art department; financed by city and state appropriation.

Exhibitions: Primarily contemporary exhibitions.

Activities: Lectures; 4 - 5 gallery talks; 4 - 5 tours.

UNION GALLERY
San Jose State University
   Student Union, 95192. Tel: (408) 277-3222
Stephen Moore, Dir.
Dorothy Torres, Gallery Asst.
Free, Mon. - Fri. 10:30 AM - 4 PM. Estab. 1969 as an educational and community service; financed by city and state appropriations.

Collections: Small collection of contemporary work.

Exhibitions: Varied in nature from contemporary to traditional and cultural.

Activities: Community activities with blind and mental patients; lectures open to the public; varied number of visiting lecturers per year; gallery talks upon request.

Attendance: 40,000 annual average.

SAN MARCOS

PHIL H. PUTNAM MEMORIAL LIBRARY*
   Palomar College, 92069. Tel: (714) 744-1150
Esther W. Nesbin, Dean Instruction-Library Services
Mrs. Bonnie L. Smith, Reference Librn.
Free Mon. - Thurs. 7:30 AM - 9:45 PM; Fri. 7:30 AM - 4 PM; Sat. 9 AM - 2 PM. Estab. 1946 as a library service to college and community; financed by state and county tax.

Collections: Art collection including books, periodicals, pamphlets, recordings, tapes, photographs and slides; approx. 12,500 volumes in art and music.

Income and Purchases: Income $344,592; purchases $30,000 books and period, $3000 books in art and music.

Attendance: 78,047 annual circulation.

SAN MARINO

✠HUNTINGTON LIBRARY, ART GALLERY AND BOTANICAL GARDENS
   1151 Oxford Rd, 91108. Tel: (213) 681-6601 & 792-6141
James Thorpe, Dir.
Robert R. Wark, Cur. of Art Collections
Daniel H. Woodward, Librn.
Myron Kimnach, Cur. of Botanical Gardens
Suzanne W. Hull, Dir. of Admin. & Pub. Services.
Free daily except Mon, 1 - 4:30 PM, cl. Oct. & holidays; visiting groups may make reservations by mail or telephone, individual reservations are not necessary. Estab. 1919 by the late Henry E. Huntington as a free research library, art gallery, museum and botanical garden; exhibitions opened to the public in 1928. The Bo-

tanical Gardens include Japanese Garden, Zen Garden, Bonsai Court, 1500 varieties of camellias, 12 acre Desert Plant Garden, Cycad Collection, Palm Collection, Shakespeare Garden, Australian Garden, Subtropical Garden and Rose Garden.

Collections: Chiefly portraits of the British school of the 18th century and landscapes of the period exhibited in the Huntington house among the other objects of art, English and French furniture, French tapestries, Italian and French bronzes, English miniatures and Chelsea porcelain; extensive collections of British drawings and silver. The Arabella D. Huntington Memorial Art Collection in the west wing of the library building contains Italian and Flemish paintings of the 15th and 16th century, French sculpture, tapestries, furniture and porcelain of the 18th century.

Exhibitions: Art, manuscripts and rare books from the Huntington Collections.

Activities: Short informal dance, drama or musical programs presented outdoors; mini-talks; 3 week communications class for mentally gifted minors; regular tours of gardens and library's main exhibition hall; bookstore.

Library: Over 500,000 volumes, of which more than half are rare source material; 5,000,000 manuscripts; collections center on English and American history and literature. Library is available to qualified scholars and other persons engaged in research or creative work.

Publications: The Huntington Library Quarterly; books in the fields of English and American literature and history, art and horticulture; exhibition catalogs; guides.

Income and Purchases: Income $2,500,000; annual purchases approx. $325.000.

Attendance: 500,000 annually.

Friends of the Huntington Library

An independent organization of about 2000 Friends interested in promoting the activities and supplementing the collections of the Huntington Library, Art Gallery and Botanical Gardens; dues $25-$1000.

Society of Fellows

A support organization of individuals contributing $1000 per year; $10,000 for life membership. Corporate sponsors: $2500 per year.

SANTA ANA

✠BOWER'S MUSEUM*
2002 N. Main St, 92706. Tel: (714) 834-4024
Reilly P. Rhodes, Dir.
Charles N. Irwin, Cur. Anthropology & History
Larry L. Bruns, Cur. Art
Peter C. Bartlett, Cur. Natural Science
Margaret A. Key, Registrar
Paul Maull, Exhibit Specialist
Free Tues. - Sat. 9 AM - 5 PM; Sun. 1 - 5 PM; Wed. & Thurs. 7 - 10 PM; cl. Mon. Estab. 1934 to provide an active general museum for the community. The Charles W. Bowers Memorial Museum housed an authentic California mission-style home amid expansive fountain-studded grounds, originally devoted to the display of antique furniture, guns, Indian relics and historical items of early California families. A new wing has been added with an exhibition program of contemporary art. Financed by city appropriation supplemented by Foundation Board. Monthly meetings; mem. 400; dues student $5, individual $10, family $20, supporting $30, sponsor $50, patron $100, benefactor $500, life $1000; corporate $10 and $100.

Collections: 19th century American textiles, decorative arts and patterned glass; 19th and 20th century American Indian baskets; 19th and 20th century transportation; 19th and early 20th century North and South American costumes; late 19th century Oriental costumes; early California history; Orange County citraculture; Indian artifacts; Asian, African, contemporary American art; Pre-Columbian ceramics; conchology; oology; mammology; marine biology; mineralogy; paleontology; some 16th and 17th century items on loan.

Exhibitions: Temporary exhibits program supplemented by permanent exhibits, one added each year by purchase. Some of the exhibits housed in the new wing are Contemporary Reflections, works of 22 emerging New York painters; New Guinea Objects; Pre-Columbian Art of Mexico.

Activities: Lectures, gallery talks, concerts, scholarships; children's programs. Museum Shop.

Library: Reference library of 500 volumes, 500 photographs and study files.

Income: $141,270.

Attendance: 61,500.

SANTA BARBARA

✠THE ART GALLERIES
University of California, Santa Barbara, 93106.
Tel: (805) 961-2951
David Gebhard, Dir.

Phyllis Plous, Cur. of Exhibitions
Sonja Olsen, Admin. Asst. & Registrar
Steven Slaney, Designer of Exhibitions
Free Tues. - Sat. 10 AM - 4 PM; Sun. & holidays 1 - 5 PM; cl. Mon. Estab. 1962, an extension of programs in Art History and Studio, undergraduate and graduate level; state appropriation. Art Affiliates, UCSB, mem. 171; ann. dues $17.

Collections: Renaissance and Baroque medals and plaquettes, Morgenroth collection; Renaissance and Baroque paintings, Sedgwick collection; †Ala Story Graphic Arts Collection; †American architectural drawings, late 19th and 20th centuries.

Exhibitions: (1972) Sculpture of the 1920s and 1930s; Constructivist Tendencies; (1973) Roman Art in West Coast Collections; European and American Sculpture of the 40s; (1974) Indian Art of the Northern Plains; Drawings by 17th Century Italian Masters from the Collection of Janos Scholz; A Medieval Miscellany—Romanesque and Early Gothic Metalwork.

Activities: Traveling exhibitions organized and circulated; original objects of art lent; photograph collection, 4000 prints for references; archives of Southern California architecture; lectures open to public, 6 lecturers per year; 6 gallery talks or tours.

Publications: Catalogs, average 3 per year.

Attendance: Average 32,000 annually.

FAULKNER MEMORIAL ART WING
Santa Barbara Public Library, 40 E. Anapamu St, 93102.
Tel: (805) 962-7653
Robert A. Hart, Library Dir.
Open Mon. - Thurs. 10 AM - 9 PM; Fri. - Sat. 10 AM - 5:30 PM; Sun. 1 - 5 PM. Estab. 1930 and administered by the Library Trustees as a municipal art reading room and gallery.

Collections: Wing houses Public Library book collection in the fine arts as well as the †phonograph record collection, art reproductions and picture file.

Exhibitions: Regular exhibits of local contemporary paintings and sculpture through arrangements with the Santa Barbara Art Association.

Activities: Irregularly scheduled meetings, lectures and programs.

✠SANTA BARBARA MUSEUM OF ART
1130 State St, 93101. Tel: (805) 963-4364
Mrs. Edward R. Valentine, Pres.
Robert K. Straus, 1st V.Pres.
John Rex, 2nd V.Pres.
Mrs. William Joyce, Jr, 3rd V.Pres.
Mrs. Earnest Watson, Secy.
Reginald M. Faletti, Treas.
Paul C. Mills, Dir.
Mrs. Maxwell P. Ruston, Pub. Relations, Publications & Programs
Terrell Hillebrand, Registrar
Dean Dawson, Bldg. Supt.
Free Tues. - Sat. 11 AM - 5 PM; Sun. 12 AM - 5 PM; cl. Mon. Estab. 1938, bldg. opened 1941. Ann. meeting Jan. 1974; mem. 1845, dues $15 and higher.

Collections: American and European paintings, sculpture, drawings, prints; Oriental sculpture, paintings and ceramics; classical Greek and Roman art; African sculpture; Pre-Columbian art; Oriental musical instruments; Doll collection.

Exhibitions: Average about 30 per year; Guatemalan Folk art, California's Representation, New Realism, Cross-Cultural Iconography, Sculpture of George Kolbe, Photography in the Twentieth Century, Southern California Black Artists, African Art, Paul Jenkins.

Activities: Art classes and workshops for children and adults; lectures, weekly film series, special film programs, gallery tours, rental gallery, museum shop, annual treasure sale.

Library: A small general research library for staff and members.

Attendance: 135,000 annually.

✠UNIVERSITY OF CALIFORNIA, SANTA BARBARA ARTS LIBRARY
93106. Tel: (805) 961-2850
William R. Treese, Head
Susan Wyngaard, Asst. Art Librn.
Free Mon. - Thurs. 9 AM - 11 PM, Fri. & Sat. 9 AM - 6 PM, Sun. 2 - 11 PM. Estab. 1969 as the university art library to support academic programs; financed by city and state appropriation.

Collections: †Major collection of exhibition catalogs cataloged by computer based program; †research collection to support undergraduate and graduate instruction in the history of Greek, Roman and Etruscan art, Medieval art, Renaissance and Baroque art, 18th, 19th and 20th century art, Oriental, primitive and exotic arts and architecture.

Activities: Full program of instruction in studio art.

Library: 70,000 volumes for lending and reference; also over 18,500 art exhibition catalogs accessible via a computer based indexing system.

Attendance: 205,130 annual average.

SANTA CLARA

de SAISSET ART GALLERY AND MUSEUM
University of Santa Clara, 95053. Tel: (408) 984-4528
William Donnelly, S.J, Acad. V.Pres.
Lydia Modi Vitale, Dir.
Robert Bettencourt, Fiscal Consultant
George Bolling, Video Cur.
Paul Hoffman, Photography Cur.
Hope Hanafin, Special Events Coordinator
Susan Middleton, Preparator
Adrian Gallardo, Preparator
Gayle Feller, Secy.
Free Tues. - Fri. 10 AM - 5 PM, Thurs, 7 - 9 PM, Sat. & Sun. 1 - 5 PM, cl. Mon. and all national holidays, July - Sept. Estab. 1955, a major cultural resource in Northern California. In recent years, the Art Gallery and Museum has dramatically broadened its scope, exhibiting some of the world's leading avant-garde artists while not losing sight of the traditional. Maintained through membership in Gallery Associates and endowment; dues, ann. $15, sustaining $25, sponsor $100, benefactor $250, patron $500.
Collections: Videotapes, paintings, sculpture, graphics, china, silver, ivory, 17th and 18th century tapestries, California mission history, antiques, furniture.
Activities: Humanities forum, lectures, film festivals, volunteer program; permanent, temporary and traveling exhibitions; gallery shop; adult and children's art workshops.
Library: 250 volumes, California Mission period manuscripts and books; art reference books and periodicals for use upon special request of the director, video facilities and archives.
Income: $85,000; purchases $1500.
Publications: Magazine, Membership Quarterly; catalogs.
Attendance: Approx. 175,000.

✠TRITON MUSEUM OF ART
1505 Warburton Ave, 95050. Tel: (408) 248-4585
George Delucchi, Pres.
Dr. Hampton Gillespie, V.Pres.
Donna Scott Thomas, Dir.
Free Tues. - Fri. 12:30 - 4:30 PM; Sat. 10 AM - 5 PM; Sun. 1 - 5 PM; cl. Mon. Estab. 1965 to present a collection of creative art of the Western Hemisphere. Mem: 250; dues $5 and up.
Collections: 19th century Italian; late 19th century marble sculpture; Clare collection, English, 19th century; Early American; turn-of-the-century in-depth collections of Theodore Wores, Thomas A. McGlynn, Charles H. Harmon, A.D.M. Cooper, large collection of works by contemporary California artists and others; large collection of 19th century English and American majolica.
Exhibitions: 4 separate pavilions, each devoted to a different show. These change periodically, running from 1 to 4 months each; catalogs accompany most major exhibitions. In main building, works from permanent collection are constantly on exhibit in a rotating sequence.
Special Exhibitions (organized by the museum): Miniatures of the Mughals and Rajputs from Private Collection, Jan. 1972; Arts of the American Indians, Apr. 1972 (illustrated catalog); Antique and Contemporary Quilts, Mar. 1973; Max Pollak: In Retrospect, May 1973 (illustrated catalog); The Arts of Japan, June 1974; The Art of Writing, Sept. 1975; and monthly exhibits of outstanding contemporary and local artists.
Other Special Exhibitions (organized outside museum): Nation to Nation in the Visual Arts (contemporary Austrian art), original by Fresno Arts Center with California Arts Commission, July 1972; Great Drawings of the Renaissance, original by The American Federation of Arts, Aug. 1972; Prints and Drawings of Artists by Artists original by The American Federation of Arts, Aug. 1973; Charles Burchfield: Master Doodler, Nov. 1974.
Activities: Lectures by Director and guest speakers; demonstrations, guided tours; women's auxiliary and Docent Council; art rental program; annual art fair and sale; theater perfromances; small selection of art books, Unicef cards and postcards for sale; art classes for children and adults.
Library: c. 100 volumes including art encyclopedias; monographs on American artists; some periodicals; also approx. 75 exhibition catalogs.
Budget: Approx. $25,000 annually.
Attendance: 20,000 annually.

SANTA CRUZ

SANTA CRUZ ART LEAGUE, INC.
526 Broadway, 95060. Tel: (408) 426-5787
Elizabeth Morris, Pres.
Clem Schnabel, Secy.
June Baker, Cur.
Gallery open daily 1 - 5 PM. Founded 1919, inc. 1949. New Building, the Margaret Rogers Gallery, erected by members and art lovers. Ann. meeting 2nd Wed. in May, mo. meeting 2nd Wed; mem. approx. 200; dues lay $5, assoc $7, active $10.
Collections: Permanent home of wax figures of Last Supper (owned by Community of Santa Cruz).
Exhibitions: Annual state-wide exhibitions, selected by jury, open to artists painting in California; continuous exhibitions of members' work.
Activities: A month of summer sales of paintings; lectures; demonstrations; art classes; 12 gallery talks per year; scholarships.
Publications: Monthly bulletin to members.

SANTA CRUZ PUBLIC LIBRARY
Art and Music Department
224 Church St, 95060. Tel: (408) 423-6210, Exten. 37
Charles K. Atkins, Library Dir.
Alma Westberg, Head, Art & Music Dept.
Free Mon. - Fri. 9 AM - 9 PM; Sat. 9 AM - 6 PM. Estab. 1881 as a department of the Santa Cruz Public Library; financed by city and state appropriation. Gallery contains both contemporary and traditional art of various media; local artists, in cooperation with Santa Cruz City Museum.
Collections: General collection of books of art and music: reference, techniques, study.
Exhibitions: Paintings of Cor de Gavere, Dutch-American local artist; contemporary Santa Cruz artists in a variety of media and form; Frederick Billing, local 19th century artist of the West; Santa Cruz Camera Club; University of California, Santa Cruz, Bachelor of Fine Arts Candidates; Santa Cruz Weavers Guild; Santa Cruz Graphic Arts, Past and Present.
Activities: Special extension department serving Santa Cruz County, material available to residents of 2 months, free of charge; individual paintings lent to schools; 220 color reproductions and 175 motion pictures in lending collections, 10,000 items lent in average year. 220 prints for lending and reference, approx. 300 study prints. Lectures open to public, 2 visiting lecturers per year; 35 tours.
Annual Purchases: $10,000.

SANTA MONICA

SANTA MONICA COLLEGE ART GALLERY
Art Department, 1815 Pearl St, 90405. Tel: (213) 392-4911
William M. Hill, Dir.
Free daily 11 AM - 3 PM, cl. academic holidays. Estab. 1973 to provide a study gallery for direct contact with contemporary and historic works of art; financed by city and state appropriation.
Collections: †Permanent collection of Southern California prints and drawings.
Exhibitions: 8 per year.
Activities: Gallery talks by director; original objects of art lent; lectures open to public; 20 gallery talks and 40 tours per year.
Publications: Lists for major exhibitions.
Income and Purchases: Income approx. $10,000; purchases $1000 or more.
Attendance: 25,000.

SARATOGA

VILLA MONTALVO CENTER FOR THE ARTS*
Montalvo Association
P.O. Box 158, 95070. Tel: (408) 867-3421
R.Adm. Ralph M. Metcalf, U.S.N. Ret, Pres.
George Szudy, 1st V.Pres.
Mrs. R M. Davis, 2nd V.Pres.
George Barati, Exec. Dir.
Free daily 1 - 4 PM except Mon. and holidays. Estab. 1953; administered by Montalvo Association; Villa Montalvo is part of a cultural center for the development of art, literature, music and architecture by artists and promising students; facilities for artists in residence. The former home of the late U.S. Senator and Mayor of San Francisco, James Duval Phelan, was bequeathed as a Cultural Center, and is conducted as a non-profit enterprise by the Board of Trustees of the Montalvo Association. Ann. meeting Nov; mem. 800; dues $15 and higher.
Collections: Paintings; sculpture; decorative arts; graphics; manuscripts.
Activities: Lectures; gallery talks; guided tours; classes for adults and children; films; art festivals; concerts; dramatic programs. Carriage House Theatre; amphitheater.
Exhibitions: Monthly exhibitions of jewelry, ceramics, photography, paintings, drawings, crafts, graphic arts by California and other artists, and by students and faculty of Montalvo; traveling exhibitions.
Library: 500 volumes for reference.
Attendance: Over 50,000.

STANFORD

STANFORD UNIVERISTY MUSEUM OF ART
94305. Tel: (415) 497-4177 (tours: 497-3469)
Lorenz Eitner, Dir.
Nancy M. Doctor, Museum Secy.

Free weekdays 10 AM - 4:45 PM; Sat. & Sun. 1 - 4:45 PM. Opened 1891; mem. Committee for Art at Stanford; 1100 dues paying members; dues $15 and higher.
Collection: †Ancient Art (including parts of the Cesnola Collection of Cypriote Antiquities), †Oriental Art, †Renaissance to †Modern Painting, Graphics and Sculpture, Primitive Art; Cantor collection of Rodin bronzes.
Exhibitions: Six major and several lesser exhibitions during the year.
Activities: The Museum is actively involved in the program of research and teaching of the University; in addition, it offers docent service to school children and other interested members of the community; concerts, film showings and lectures are regularly offered; book shop.
Publications: Annual bulletin and some exhibition catalogs.
Attendance: (1974-75) 80,000.
Thomas Welton Stanford Art Gallery
94305. Tel: (415) 497-2842
Lorenz Eitner, Dir.
Free 10 AM - 4:45 PM; Sun. 1 - 4:45 PM; cl. Mon. Building completed 1917; houses changing exhibitions. Closed between exhibitions.

STOCKTON

PIONEER MUSEUM AND HAGGIN GALLERIES
Victory Park, 1201 N. Pershing Ave, 95203. Tel: (209) 462-4116 or (209) 462-1566
Michael N. Canlis, Pres.
Keith E. Dennison, Dir.
Free, Tues. - Sun. 1:30 - 5 PM; cl. Mon, Christmas, Thanksgiving and New Years. Estab. 1931. Mem. 800; dues $15 minimum; Ann. meeting Jan; building owned by San Joaquin Pioneer and Historical Society houses both art and history galleries.
Collections: The art collection is comprised mainly of †19th century French, American and European paintings; †graphics; and decorative arts. The extensive history collection contains items on Stockton, San Joaquin County and California history arranged in interpretive display settings.
Activities: Tours for children and adult groups conducted by appointment throughout the week; tour for the general public Saturdays; concerts; lectures; free Sunday films; identification service for art and history objects each month; periodically-changing art or history exhibitions; docent program.
Library: Approx. 7000 volumes mainly devoted to Californiana; extensive collection of original maps, records, diaries, documents and photographs concerned with city and county history. Open by appointment only.
Publications: Historical Diaries; Bi-monthly Calendar
Income: c. $120,000 annually.
Attendance: 65,000 annually.

UNIVERSITY CENTER GALLERY LOUNGE
University Center, University of the Pacific, 95211.
Tel: (209) 946-2171
Gary Kleemann, Dir.
Estab. 1975. Small collection of contemporary American prints; approx. one exhibition per month.

TURLOCK

✣CALIFORNIA STATE COLLEGE, STANISLAUS
800 Monte Vista Ave, 95380

Library. Tel: (209) 633-2232
R. Dean Galloway, Dir.
Bob Santos, Bibliographer
J. Carlyle Parker, Asst. Dir. & Head Pub. Services
Free daily 8 AM - 10 PM; Sat. 8 AM - 5 PM; Sun. 1 - 10 PM. Estab. 1957 to support curriculum of liberal arts, undergraduate and limited number of graduate programs; financed by state appropriation.
Collections: †Contemporary art; †general art history; †California art. 150,000 volumes and 5800 art books for lending.
Budget: $4000 for art books.

Art Gallery, Dept. of Art. Tel: (209) 633-2431
Martin Camarata, Chmn. Dept. Art
Free Mon. - Fri. Noon - 4 PM. Estab. 1965 for the purpose of community and cultural instruction; financed by state appropriation.
Exhibitions: Morton Grossman, watercolors; Ron Todd, photographs; Molly Schiff; Chet Kanowski, Computer Drawings; San Francisco Graphic Gallery, prints; Bocour Color Collection, Robert A. Nelson and Jean Schiff, drawings; Hansen Gallery Exhibition; Sandel and Alf.

VALENCIA

CALIFORNIA INSTITUTE OF THE ARTS LIBRARY
24700 McBean Parkway, 91355. Tel: (805) 255-1050
Donn B. Tatum, Chmn. of the Board
Luther Marr, Secy.

Robert J. Fitzpatrick, Pres.
Royal Clark, Exec. V.Pres.
Mel Powell, Provost
Elizabeth Armstrong, Head Librn.
Fred Gardner, Head, Pub. Services
James Elrod, Head, Technical Services
Vaughan Kaprow, Slide Librn.
Margie Hanft, Film Librn.
Joan Anderson, Music Cataloger
Open Mon. - Thurs. 9 AM - 10 PM, Fri. 9 AM - 5 PM, Sat. & Sun. 11 AM - 5 PM. Estab. 1961, first classes 1970, designed to be a community of practicing artists working in schools of art, design, film, music and theatre and dance. Emphasis is completely on contemporary works and thought, and the library serving all the separate schools reflects this emphasis; endowed.
Collections: 74,742 volumes on art, design, film, music, theatre, dance; 28,653 slides.
Exhibitions: Student work only, about 20 annually.
Activities: Material available to students, faculty and staff; all others in-house use only; no fees; material lent, books, slides, exhibition catalogs, bound scores, films to faculty and teaching assistants, scores; lending collection, 20,000 Kodachromes, 294 motion pictures; concerts; dramatic programs; scholarships. Book shop.
Publications: The Bridge, Cal Arts Bulletin.
Income and Purchases: $4,166,000.

WALNUT

MOUNT SAN ANTONIO COLLEGE ART GALLERY
1100 N. Grand Ave, 91789. Tel: (714) 598-2811
Michael Andrew Preble, Dir.
Myrtle Gebbie, Secy.
Open Tues. - Thurs. 10 AM - 2 PM, Sun. 1 - 4 PM, Tues. & Wed. 6 - 9 PM. Estab. c. 1950 as an art gallery for art and cultural exhibitions of interest and use by the college and resident communities; financed by city and state appropriation.
Collections: 20 works held by Gallery as the result of biennial exhibition awards; college has various small donated collections of art and artifacts.
Exhibitions: Ynez Johnston Retrospective; Arts of New Guinea from the Kennedy Collection; Michael Mollett Exhibition of Conceptual Art; Intaglio Prints by Eva and Paul Kolosvary.
Activities: 20 photographs and original objects of art lent; paintings lent to schools; traveling exhibitions organized and circulated; 10 items lent in average year to 5 borrowers; lectures open to public.
Publications: Occasional catalogs.
Attendance: 7000.

WALNUT CREEK

CIVIC ARTS THEATRE/EXHIBITION CENTRE
1641 Locust St, 94596. Tel: (415) 935-3300
Gary F. Schaub, Dir. of Civic Arts
Douglas Rankin, Performing Arts Supvr.
Jeanne Howard, Cur. Exhibitions
Lisa Bennett, Instructional Supvr.
Gallery free Tues. - Sat. 12 - 5 PM, Fri. 5 - 9 PM, Sat. 7 - 9 PM. Estab. 1963 by City of Walnut Creek Civic Arts Dept, comprised of an art gallery, theater and instructional center with the purpose of arts education for community involvement. Maintained by city and membership. Mem. 450; ann. dues $10-$100.
Activities: Classes for children and adults in painting, crafts, dance, ceramics, drama, art history, etc, with college credit; changing art exhibitions. Gallery education program which includes tour guide program, in-school program, artist-in-residence program; theater reperatory season; concerts, light opera, musicals.
Publications: Quarterly newspaper.

YOSEMITE NATIONAL PARK

YOSEMITE MUSEUM COLLECTIONS
National Park Service, U.S. Department of the Interior
Box 577, 95389. Tel: (209) 372-4461, ext. 61
Jack Gyer, Cur.
Stephen Medley, Librn.
Free, open on prior request. Estab. 1926 to interpret the natural sciences and human history of the Yosemite area; financed by federal appropriation. Yosemite Natural History Association members total 1000; dues $5 and up.
Collections: Photographic (with a special collection of early photographs of the area; Fine Arts; Indian cultural artifacts; pioneer Caucasian artifacts.
Activities: Original objects of art and paintings lent on special exhibit only; photograph collection; 20,000 prints for reference only; junior museum; lectures open to public; several visiting lecturers per year; book shop.

Library: 7000 volumes for reference.
Publications: Publication list available from Yosemite Natural History Association, Box 545, Yosemite National Park, CA 95389.

COLORADO

BOULDER

UNIVERSITY OF COLORADO FINE ARTS GALLERY
Fine Arts Building 104, 80302. Tel: (303) 492-6504
George Woodman, Chmn.
Jean-Edith Weiffenbach, Cur. & Exhibitions Dir.
Free Mon. - Fri. 8 - 12 AM & 1 - 5 PM. Estab. 1937. Monthly exhibitions; summer creative arts program; art and architecture library.
Attendance: Approx. 6500 (See Schools).
Henderson Museum
80302. Tel: (303) 492-6892
George Woodman, Chmn.
Jean-Edith Weiffenbach, Cur. & Exhibitions Dir.
Free Mon. - Fri. 8:30 AM - 5 PM, Sat. 9 AM - 4 PM, Sun. 10 AM - 4 PM. Continuous exhibitions; summer creative arts program.

CENTRAL CITY

GILPIN COUNTY ARTS ASSOCIATION
Opposite Opera House, Eureka St, 80427. Tel: (303) 582-5952
Kay Russell, Corresp. Secy.
Free daily 11 AM - 6 PM. Estab. and inc. 1948 to exhibit paintings, crafts and sculpture of Colorado artists; juried, $650 prizes awarded. Ann. meeting 1st Sun. in Sept; mem. 250; dues $1 and up.
Collections: Small permanent collection of works by Colorado artists.
Activities: Supports public school art program; artists' sales $25,000.
Income and Purchases: $28,000.
Attendance: 50,000.

COLORADO SPRINGS

AMERICAN NUMISMATIC ASSOCIATION
818 N. Cascade, 80903
Edward C. Rochette, Exec. Dir.
For further information see p. 4.

✤THE COLORADO SPRINGS FINE ARTS CENTER
(incorporating the Taylor Museum)
30 W. Dale St, 80903. Tel: (303) 634-5581
Brig. Gen. R. C. Crawford, Jr, Pres.
Mrs. John H. Lewis, Secy.
Dr. James H. Stauss, Treas.
Arne R. Hansen, Dir.
Mrs. Kendra Bowers, Interim Cur. Taylor Museum
Robert Morris, Interim Cur. Fine Arts Center
Betty Trotter, Mem. Secy.
Free 10 AM - 5 PM; Sun. 1:30 - 5 PM. Estab. 1919 as Broadmoor Art Academy, name changed 1936 with new building and program. Ann meeting Nov; mem. 3000; dues $15 and higher. Building opened 1936, gift of Mrs. Alice Bemis Taylor, with additions 1972; houses theater, lecture rooms, recital rooms, library, art school and galleries.
Collections: Drawings, prints, paintings, sculpture and design from pre-historic Indian to contemporary; survey collection of world art with emphasis upon the Southwest.
Exhibitions: 50 exhibitions annually in addition to permanent collection.
Activities: Regular membership programs and programs for the public; theater and music room facilities used by other groups for lectures, plays and performing arts; studio and art history instruction for children and adults; maintains book shop and museum shop.
Library: Approx. 10,000 items used by members, students and public.
Publications: Regular monthly calendar of events and special exhibition catalogs.
Attendance: Approx. 200,000.

DENVER

COLORADO WOMEN'S COLLEGE
Montview at Quebec, 80220. Tel: (303) 394-6012
Maynard Whitney, Assoc. Prof.
Financed by endowment and student tuition. Maintains gallery.
Exhibitions: 3 - 5 exhibitions per year, plus faculty show and student shows.
Activities: Lectures open to public; concerts; dramatic programs; classes for adults; scholarships; library. Book shop. (See Schools)

✤THE DENVER ART MUSEUM
100 W. 14th Ave. Parkway, 80204. Tel: (303) 297-2793
Frederick R. Mayer, Pres.
James L. Rumsey, V.Pres. & Treas.
Philip F. Anschutz, V.Pres.
Robert S. Gast, Jr, Secy.
Thomas N. Maytham, Dir.
Lewis W. Story, Assoc. Dir.
Robert Stroessner, Cur. New World Arts
Ronald Otsuka, Cur. Oriental Arts
Mrs. Cameron Wolfe, Cur. European Art
Mrs. Imelda DeGraw, Cur. of Textiles
Carolyn Stark, Cur. of Educ.
Georgianna Contiguglia, Honorary Cur. of American Art
Mrs. John Bunker, Research Assoc, Oriental
Mary Lanius, Research Assoc, Oriental
Marlene Chambers, Publ. Dir.
Linda Anderson, Pub. Relations
Anabel Nyman, Admin. Secy.
Cathey F. McClain, Development Dir.
Mary Pachello, Bursar
L. Anthony Wright, Jr, Registrar
Jeremy Hillhouse, Installation Designer
Free Sun. 1- 5 PM; Tues. - Sat. 9 AM - 5 PM; Wed. evenings 6 - 9 PM; cl. Mon. & national holidays. Estab. 1893 as Artists' Club of Denver, reorganized as Denver Art Association 1923 under present name. Ann. city appropriation for maintenance; collections owned by the Denver Art Museum Association. Ann. meeting Mar; dues $10 and up. New Art Museum Building designed by James Sudler Assoc. of Denver in collaboration with Gio Ponti of Milan, open May 1971; constructed on site of old galleries at south end of Civic Center.
Collections: Permanent and loan collection of Mediterranean, European, Oriental, American, Pre-Columbian, Spanish Colonial, American Indian, Oceanic, African Negro, Costumes and Textiles, Modern International Decorative Arts, Period Rooms. American, 1271 objects; American Indian 10,890; Ancient Mediterranean 200; African 501; European 1663; Pre-Columbian 682; Oceanic 546; Spanish Colonial 233; Oriental 1385; Textile 3077; Dolls and Doll Houses 1078.
Exhibitions: The museum presents an annual juried exhibition of works in all media. In the past, the exhibition has been open only to artists living in the state of Colorado. Top prize is a one-artist exhibition at the museum within a year of the show; award is based on juror recommendations and subsequent visits to studios of recommended artists by museum personnel.
Activities: Seminars; average 3 Cooke-Daniels Lecturers a year, 93,000 tours, Speakers Bureau talks in schools; Community Speakers lectures for organizations; artists' demonstrations; volunteer training program; special programs for members' children; Summer Workshop and scholarships; University of Denver Apprentice Program open to graduate students working for masters degree in art; Junior and Senior High School Seminars; movies, AV presentations; book shop.
Publications: Monthly members' newsletter and an annual report.
Budget and Purchases: 1972 $92,000 received and spent for accessions.
Income: City and County appropriation for 1975 $898,600; membership contributions 1974 $127,880; accessions averaged $62,660 (by purchase only, not including gifts).
Attendance: 550,000 annual average.

DENVER ARTISTS GUILD
c/o Dorothy Trent, 355 Ingalls St, Lakewood, 80226.
Emily F. Spillman, Pres.
Beulah Beardsley, Secy.
Estab. 1928 to promote the highest professional standards in original works of art by artists in the community, and appreciation of the fine arts. Ann. meeting 4th Wed. in Apr; mem. 90; dues $10.
Activities: Exhibitions, critiques, classes, lectures, etc.

DENVER PUBLIC LIBRARY
1357 Broadway, 80203. Tel: (303) 573-5152
Henry G. Shearouse, Jr, Librn.
Kurtz Myers, Head, Arts & Recreation Dept.
Free Mon. - Thurs. 10 AM - 9 PM; Fri. & Sat. 10 AM - 5:30 PM. Estab. 1889; art and music dept. organized 1926.
Collections: Reference and circulating collections of 65,391 books on the fine arts, costume, architecture, decorative arts, crafts, landscape gardening, music, theatre, sports and recreation. Houses the library of the State Board of Architects and the Friends of Folk Music Collection. 172,788 pamphlets, clippings and mounted pictures, 1366 framed prints, 960 16mm films and 13,032 phonograph records.
Activities: Frequent exhibitions from the book and picture collections; cooperates closely with the Denver Art Museum, schools, colleges and clubs throughout the region.

GOLDEN

FOOTHILLS ART CENTER
809 15th St, 80401. Tel: (303) 279-3922.
Alan Petersen, Pres.
Sybil Buerger, Secy.
Marian Metsopoulos, Dir.
Free, Mon. - Sat. 9 AM - 4 PM; Sun. 1 - 4 PM. Estab. 1968 to provide a cultural center for artists and the community (the Foothills
region including Metropolitan Denver), where all the arts may be
presented for the betterment of all of those involved; financed by membership. Ann. meeting; mem. 550; dues, individual $10, families $15.
Collections: 3 paintings in permanent collection have been
donated.
Exhibitions: Rocky Mountain National Watermedia Exhibition,
1974, 75 and in planning stage for 76; monthly exhibits in all media
in 8 galleries; open competitions in various media throughout the
year.
Activities: Original objects of art lent; lectures open to public; 4
visiting lecturers, 2 gallery talks and 30 tours per year; classes for
adults and children; competitions.
Library: Art library includes 489 volumes for lending and
reference.
Publications: Foothills Flyer, monthly.
Attendance: 10,000.

GRAND JUNCTION

WESTERN COLORADO CENTER FOR THE ARTS, INC.
1803 N. Seventh St, 81501. Tel: (303) 243-7337
Clara Mastrovich, Pres.
Ruth Moss, Secy.
Jean Todd, Exec. Secy.
Free Tues. - Sat. 10 AM - 5 PM; Sun. 2 - 5 PM. Estab. 1953 to
support the arts in western Colorado; financed by membership.
Gallery is a multipurpose room with a small stage. Ann. meeting
Feb; mem. 780; dues individual $5, family $10, patron $100,
benefactor $1000.
Collections: Small permanent collection of western art by Harold
Bryant, who was originally a member of this organization and later
became a well known western artist.
Exhibitions: 8-West Biennial, 1970, 72 & 74; Objects '71, '73 &
'75, National Craft Shows; Artist of the Month Series.
Activities: Concerts; dramatic programs; classes for adults and
children; competitions; traveling exhibits.
Library: 150 volumes for reference.
Publications: Monthly newsletter for members.
Income: $21,000.
Attendance: 8000 annual average.

GREELEY

JOHN MARIANI ART GALLERY
University of Northern Colorado
Department of Fine Arts, 80639. Tel: (303) 351-2143
Fredric L. Myers, Dir.
Free Mon. - Fri. 9 AM - 4 PM; Sun. 1 - 4 PM. Estab. Sept, 1973, to
bring in art exhibitions not usually seen in the area for benefit of
the University and the surrounding community; financed by endowment and city and state appropriation.
Publications: Quarterly schedule of exhibitions.
Attendance: 5000.

PUEBLO

CREATIVE AND PERFORMING ARTS CENTER
University of Southern Colorado
Belmont Campus, 2200 Bonfort Ave, 81001. Tel: (303) 549-2552
Jim Duncan, Dir.
Ed Sajbel, Art Dept.
Robert Hench, Gallery Dir.
Hours open vary. Estab. 1933 as an educational institution with
gallery. Music, dance and art center within the university;
financed by city and state appropriation.
Collections: Prints and drawings, mostly recent American;
student and faculty work, 2 and 3 dimensional.
Activities: Special educational department; original objects of
art and paintings lent; traveling exhibitions organized and circulated; lectures open to public; 3 - 10 gallery talks and 10 tours per
year; concerts; dramatic programs; adult classes; competitions;
book shop; library.
Publications: Creative Arts Quarterly for students and faculty,
issued 3-4 times per year.

CONNECTICUT

BRIDGEPORT

BRIDGEPORT ART LEAGUE*
528 Clinton Ave, 06605. Tel: (203) 335-6250
Mrs. Alexander Mazur, Pres.
Mrs. Matthew Bobowick, 1st V.Pres.
Mrs. Paul Lengyel, Art Chmn.
Free 10:30 AM - 5 PM; cl. Sun. Organized 1895, inc. 1916. Ann.
meeting May; mem. 150, 85 patrons, 25 voting and honorary mem;
dues $7.50 and higher.
Exhibitions: Special monthly shows by local artists; annual exhibition in April with jury and awards, open to non-members; Members Exhibition in May, of work completed in classes during the
year.
Activities: Lectures; classes in arts and crafts.
Library: Limited to reference works.
Attendance: 200 per year.

✠HOUSATONIC MUSEUM OF ART
Housatonic Community College
Art Department, 06608. Tel: (203) 366-8201
Vincent Darnowski, College Pres.
Burt Chernow, Dir. College Art Collection & Museum
Free Mon. - Fri. 9 AM - 6 PM. College Art Collection estab.
1967, the Housatonic Museum of Art estab. 1970; this collection of
original works of art is being developed by the Housatonic Community College as an expression of its serious commitment to cultural
enrichment through the living art of our times. The college considers it essential for students, faculty, administrators and campus
visitors to directly experience works of art as an everyday part of
the college's environment. The collection now just 8 years old, is
probably the largest and best collection of original contemporary
works of art by important artists at any American Junior College.
Collections: Primarily 19th and 20th century American and European drawing, painting, sculpture and graphics—Picasso, Matisse,
Rivers, Lindner, Derain, Warhol, DeChirico, Marisol, Lichtenstein,
Avery, Rauchenberg, Baskin, Wesselmann, Gottlieb, Darcangelo,
Katz, Cassat, Vasarely, Shahn, Daumier, Pavia and others.
Exhibitions: Rotating exhibitions from the permanent collection,
new acquisitions and changing shows by important contemporary
artists.
Activities: Lectures open to public; maintains slide and photograph collection for reference.
Library: College library, over 4000 volumes.
Publications: Catalogs.
Annual Income: Approx. $1000.

MUSEUM OF ART, SCIENCE AND INDUSTRY
4450 Park Ave, 06604. Tel: (203) 372-3521
Mrs. B. Franklyn Bulkley, Pres.
Bradley Brewer, Dir.
Leslie Birkmaier, Asst. Dir.
Galleries open Tues. - Sun. 2 - 5 PM; cl. Mon. and holidays. Estab.
1958 to provide exhibits and educational programs in the arts and
sciences for a regional audience. New building opened to the public
Jan. 1962. Financed by membership, endowment and city appropriations. Ann. meeting June; dues $10 - $500.
Exhibitions: Brandywine Heritage '74, featuring works by Andrew, N.C. and James Wyeth and Howard Pyle; Salvador Dali's Art-
in-Jewels.
Activities: Youth programs in science, programs in art, lectures,
classes for adults and children, exhibitions, planetarium shows;
demonstrations.
Attendance: Approx. 164,000.

BRISTOL

AMERICAN CLOCK AND WATCH MUSEUM, INC.
100 Maple St, 06010. Tel: (203) 583-6070
William S. Bristow, Pres.
Chris H. Bailey, Dir & Cur.
Open Tues. 1 - 5 PM Apr. - Oct. Estab. Oct, 1952; admis.
adults $1, children 8-16 50¢. Museum opened Apr. 1954, to preserve
items and history of the American Clockmakers. Ann. meeting Apr.
or May; mem. 325; dues $5.
Collections: †Clocks; †tools and library material.
Activitives: Lectures.
Library: 800 volumes; 500-600 prints.
Attendance: 5700.

DANBURY

DANBURY SCOTT-FANTON MUSEUM AND HISTORICAL SOCIETY
43 Main St, 06810. Tel: (203) 743-5200
Truman A. Warner, Pres.
Dorothy T. Schling, Dir.

Historic House Free; Wed. - Sun. 2 - 5 PM; cl. holidays. Estab. June 24, 1921 (merged with Museum and Arts Center by Legislative Act 1947). Operates the 1785 John and Mary Rider House as a museum of early Americana and 1790 Dodd House Hat Shop with exhibits related to hatting. Huntington Hall opened to the public Sept. 5, 1963 as an exhibit building for various displays changed periodically. Ives Homestead, located at Rogers Park in Danbury to be restored and opened to the public as a Memorial to American composer, Charles E. Ives. Supported by membership and endowment. Ann. meeting Nov; mem. 350; dues $5-$250.

Activities: Special exhibits, lectures, concerts, dramatic programs.

Library: Reference library of historic material only; photograph collection.

Publications: Monthly newsletter.

Attendance: 5000.

WOOSTER COMMUNITY ART CENTER*

Ridgebury Rd, 06810. Tel: (203) 743-6311
Roger O. Prince, Dir.
John D. Verdery, Headmaster, Wooster School
Open daily 10 AM - 5 PM. Estab. Apr. 1965 as a Community Art Center for exhibitions and art classes.

Exhibitions: Will Barnet, Ed Giobbi, B. Roll, Robert Andrew Parker, Mike Nevelson, Fred Baur, George Chaplin, Bryan Kay, Sperry Andrews, Thomas Stearns, Nancy Tholen and Roger Prince.

Activities: Community adult and high school classes and classes for Wooster School students in painting, drawing, sculpture, graphics, printmaking; lectures.

Library: Small library for lending and reference; collection of 2200 slides and 170 photographs.

Attendance: 3000.

ESSEX

ESSEX ART ASSOCIATION, INC.*

North Main St, 06426. Tel: (203) 767-8996
Mary Lohman, Pres.
Polly Murray, Secy.
E. Gould Chalker, Treas.
Marie Moore, Cur.
Open summer season only (mid-June through Labor Day) 1 - 5 PM; admis. 50¢. Estab. 1946 to maintain a non-profit organization for the encouragement of the arts and to provide and maintain suitable headquarters for the showing of art; maintained by mem. Small, well-equipped one floor gallery. Ann. meeting Sept; 160 assoc. mem. $10; 60 artist mem. $7.50.

Exhibitions: 3 regular annual exhibits each year plus 1 or 2 special exhibits each year. Usually one high school or grammar school exhibit each year.

Annual Income: $1300 average.

Attendance: Approx. 2500.

FARMINGTON

FARMINGTON MUSEUM
(Stanley-Whitman House)

37 High St, 06032. Tel: (203) 677-9222
Mrs. A.D. Barney, Pres.
Mrs. Mark Riemer, Cur.
Open Apr. 1 - Nov. 30 10 AM - 12 AM and 2 - 5 PM, cl. Mon; Dec. 1 - Mar. 31 Fri. and Sat. 10 AM - 12 AM and 2 - 5 PM; Sun. all yr. 2 - 5 PM. Estab. 1935 to preserve the 17th cent. house, furnished in the style of its period and used to display historical collections. The house and land on which it is located have been deeded in trust to the Farmington Village Green and Library Association, a specially chartered non-profit association. Ann. meeting Sept. The Stanley-Whitman House was designated a registered National Historic Landmark in October, 1960.

Attendance: Ann. average, 2900.

HILL-STEAD MUSEUM

06032. Tel: (203) 677-9064
Mrs. Erdman Harris, Pres.
H. P. Ziegler, Secy.-Treas.
Mr. and Mrs. Jarold D. Talbot, Cur.
Open Wed, Thurs, Sat. & Sun. 2 - 5 PM; groups other times by appointment; cl. Thanksgiving and Christmas; admis. $1 adults, 50¢ children. Estab. 1946 to preserve the atmosphere and complete furnishings of a turn-of-the-century country mansion. Ann. meeting twice a year.

Collections: English, French and American furniture, mainly 18th century; Chinese porcelains; Japanese prints; English and French clocks; a collection of paintings by Degas, Manet, Whistler, Monet, Cassatt; prints by Durer, Whistler, Meryon, Peronesi, Oriental rugs and Georgian Silver.

Activities: Guided tours of museum.

Library: 10,000 volumes on art, literature, politics, spiritualism and others, not available to general public.

Publications: Hill-Stead Museum, Hill-Stead Yesterdays.

Attendance: 9000 annually.

GREENWICH

THE ART BARN

143 Lower Cross Rd, 06830. Tel: (203) 661-9048
Blanche Hart, Pres.
Pheobe Biscow, Secy.
Rebecca Bernstein, Exec. Dir.
Mildred Birnbaum, Gallery Dir.
David Jensen, Treas.
Free Mon. - Fri. 9:30 AM - 3 PM, (also some weekends). Estab. Mar. 1962 to provide a stimulating atmosphere which encourages self-expression and growth without competitive pressures and by bringing sculptors, painters, printmakers and handcrafters from all parts of the country to exhibit at the Art Barn; nonprofit organization, financed by membership and from workshops, gallery and shop sales. Gallery located in a converted dairy barn. Ann. meeting June; mem. 350; dues individual $15, family $25.

Exhibitions: 10 per year.

Activities: Classes for adults and children; workshops; demonstrations; scholarships.

Library: 500 volumes loaned to members.

Attendance: 2500.

BRUCE MUSEUM

Bruce Park, 06830. Tel: (203) 869-0376
Raymond M. Owen, Jr, Dir.
Paul Griswold Howes, Dir. Emeritus
Gordon Schmidt, Cur. of the Art Dept.
Lee St. Germain, Secy. and Asst. to the Dir.
Free 10 AM - 5 PM; Sun. 2 - 5 PM; cl. Sat. Estab. 1908 by Robert M. Bruce as a natural history, historical and art museum; supported by the Town of Greenwich, Connecticut.

Collections: Paintings, sculpture, Oriental porcelains, art objects. Extensive collections: Zoo, †53 Dioramas pertaining to Natural History, and History of the Region, the American Indian.

Activities: Special exhibitions, lectures, films; cooperates with schools; loan collections.

Library: 1000 volumes.

Income: $115,000.

Attendance: 40,000.

THE GREENWICH ART SOCIETY AND ART CENTER

31 Lewis St, 06830. Tel: (203) 869-2610
Mrs. John Dixon, Publicity
Mrs. Walter I. Bradbury, Treas.
Mrs. George Huyer, Dir. Art Center
Estab. 1912, a nonprofit organization to further art education and to awaken and stimulate broader interest in arts and crafts in the town of Greenwich by means of classes, lectures, demonstrations, exhibitions and art scholarships; maintained by mem. The studio at the Art Center is used for classes and meetings. Ann. meeting Mar; mem. 500; dues $15 regular, $20 family, $3 junion (18 and under), $5 student (19 to 24 years).

Exhibitions: Annual Sidewalk Show, open to all artists in area; Juried Annual Fall Show held at Greenwich Public Library Gallery; additional exhibitions at Historical Society, Bruce Museum, Garden Club and Union Trust Banks.

Activities: Day and evening classes for adults, special classes for children, lectures, critiques and demonstrations; individual paintings lent to schools, lectures open to public; scholarships.

Publications: Bulletin of program for the year and class schedule.

Income and Purchases: (1975) Income $30,000; expenses $29,100.

Attendance: Students 200, visitors to exhibitions vary with each show.

HARTFORD

AUSTIN ARTS CENTER

Trinity College, 06106. Tel: (202) 527-3151
Michael Mahoney, Chmn. Dept. Fine Arts
John Woolley, Admin.
Open afternoons during term. Estab. 1957, creative and performing arts center with exhibition facilities in a liberal arts college; endowment. Gallery, exhibition facility mainly for student and faculty works and student generated projects; also outside shows.

Collections: Edwin M. Blake collection and archive.

Exhibitions: Sage Goodwin Paintings; John Taylor Retrospective; Joseph Shulman Collection; Works by Lutze; Hartford Collects; Edwin M. Blake Memorial Collection; George Chaplin Paintings; Mitch Pappas Retrospective; John Matt Sculpture; Robert Cale Prints; John Ferguson Sculpture; Selections from the Serge Lifar Collection of Diaghitev Drawings; plus selections from the George F. McMurray Collection annually.

Activities: Lectures open to the public, 9 visiting lecturers per year.

THE CONNECTICUT HISTORICAL SOCIETY

1 Elizabeth St, 06105. Tel: (203) 236-5621
George H. Gilman, Jr, Pres.
Frances A. Hoxie, Recording Secy. & Asst. to Dir.
Thompson R. Harlow, Dir.
Philip H. Dunbar, Cur. & Asst. Dir.
Elizabeth Abbe-Harlow, Librn.

Free 9:30 AM - 5:30 PM; cl. Sun. and holidays. Estab. 1825 for the preservation of material indigenous to Connecticut. Ann. meeting May; mem. 2100; dues $10 and higher.

Collections: Furniture, silver, pottery, pewter, paintings, prints, tavern signs, costumes, swords, war relics, guns, glass, china and memorabilia.

Exhibitions: Annual exhibition held Nov. - Jan. of little known early Connecticut artists.

Activities: Gallery talks monthly and upon request; lecture series Oct. - May; original objects of art loaned.

Library: 60,000 volumes for reference; 1500 Kodachromes; 10,000 prints and photos.

Income and Purchases: Annual income $187,000; purchases $17,000 for books, manuscripts and museum articles.

Publications: Quarterly Bulletin; Annual Report; 2-3 books a year.

Attendance: 18,000.

CONNECTICUT STATE LIBRARY MUSEUM

231 Capitol Ave, 06115. Tel: (203) 566-3056
David O. White, Museum Dir.

Free Mon. - Fri. 9 AM - 5 PM, Sat. 9 AM - 1 PM, cl. holidays and Sat. of weekend holidays. Estab. 1910 to house exhibits of Connecticut history and interest; financed by city and state appropriation.

Collections: Firearms, numismatics, horology, portraits, prints, contemporary bird prints, Shakespeare prints, panoramic maps.

Exhibitions: Permanent exhibit of portraits of Connecticut governors, chief justices and historical persons.

Activities: Original objects of art lent.

Library: Volumes and prints for reference; photograph collection.

Attendance: 36,000.

HARTFORD PUBLIC LIBRARY

Art and Music Department
500 Main St, 06103. Tel: (203) 525-9121
Vernon Martin, Dept. Head

A free public library estab. 1774, financed by city and state appropriation. There are 200 motion pictures and 300,000 pictures in a lending collection; concerts given.

MARK TWAIN MEMORIAL

351 Farmington Ave, 06105. Tel: (203) 247-0998
Edward Lane-Reticker, Pres.
William G. DeLana, 1st V.Pres.
Mrs. Thomas J. Groark, Jr, Secy.
Raymond A. Meany, Jr, Treas.
Dexter B. Peck, Acting Dir.
Wilson H. Faude, Cur.

Open June 1 - Aug, 10 AM - 4:30 PM; Sept. 1 - May, Tues. - Sat. 9:30 AM - 4 PM; Sun. 1 - 4 PM; cl. Mon, Jan. 1, Easter, Labor Day, Thanksgiving and Dec. 25. Guided tours $1.50 adults, 75¢ 16 and under, special group tour rates with advance arrangements. Estab. 1929 to restore and maintain Mark Twain's Hartford home, to collect research materials needed for the project and to keep before the public the life and work of Mark Twain. Ann. meeting May; mem. approx. 1000; dues $10 and higher. Maintains Historic House Museum with period interiors, museum room of memorabilia. National Shrine status, U.S. Dept. of Interior. Occasional exhibitions.

Collections: Mark Twain memorabilia, photographs, manuscripts; period and original furnishings; Tiffany collection; Candace Wheeler collection; Lockwood deForest collection.

Activities: Group tours; Frog Jump; Museum shop; Open House; Victorian Christmas.

Library: Reference library; photograph collection.

Attendance: Approx. 70,000.

Nook Farm Research Library
Some 13,000 volumes, 4500 pamphlets and 6500 manuscripts incorporating the Mark Twain Memorial Collection.

THE STOWE-DAY FOUNDATION

77 Forest St, 06105. Tel: (203) 522-9258
Jeremiah H. Bartholomew, Jr, Pres.
Thomas L. Archibald, Secy.
Joseph S. Van Why, Dir.
Diana Royce, Librn.
Ellice Schofield, Cur.
Mary Morrissey, Adminr, Nook Farm Visitors' Center
Harriet B. Stowe House open daily June thru Aug, 10 AM - 4:30 PM;
Sept. thru May, Tues. - Sat. 9:30 AM - 4 PM, Sun. 1 - 4; admis. adults $1.50, 16 & under, 75¢ & special group rates. Estab. 1941. Maintain the fully restored Harriet Beecher Stowe House and the Stowe-Day Memorial Library; operate programs on 19th century Americana thru publications, workshops, symposia; financed through endowment. Friends of the Harriet B. Stowe House and Research Library, organized 1975; mem. 75; dues single $10, couple $15, special $25.

Collections: 19th century wallpapers, carpeting and architectural drawings.

Exhibitions: †A Selection of 19th Century American Chairs; Architecture and the Decorative Arts in the Victorian Era; †The Curtain is Upon William Gillette; Harriet Beecher Stowe, Author and Artist; †Portraits of a 19th Century Family, with illustrated catalogue.

Activities: School tour program; ann 2 day workshop for teachers; photograph collection of 800 prints for reference and reproduction; lectures open to public; 5 visiting lecturers in 1975.

Library: 15,000 volumes, 85,000 manuscripts mostly non-circulating except c. 300; 2000 pamphlets.

Publications: Exhibition catalogues; Nook Farm, On Common Ground, reprint of Catharine Beecher and Harriet Beecher Stowe's, American Woman's Home.

Purchases: Approx. $15,000.

Attendance: 24,000.

✣WADSWORTH ATHENEUM

600 Main St, 06103. Tel: (203) 278-2670
Thomas R. Cox, Jr, Pres.
James B. Lyon, V.Pres.
Talcott Stanley, V.Pres.
John P. Britton, Treas.
Jared I. Edwards, Secy.
James Elliott, Dir.
Ms. Lynn Traiger, Asst. to the Dir.
Peter O. Marlow, Chief Cur. & Cur. Painting & Sculpture
Susan E. Gans, Educ. Dir.
Lavon H. Bair, Bus. Mgr.
Charles A. Edwards, Dir. Development & Pub. Affairs
Mrs. Jean C. Burnett, Pub. Relations Dir.
J. Herbert Callister, Cur. Textiles & Costumes
Phillip M. Johnston, Assoc. Cur, Dept. Decorative Arts
Mark Rosenthal, Asst. Cur. Paintings
Roland C. Cunningham, Conservator
David M. Parrish, Registrar
Elizabeth Hoke, Librn.
Margareta Lawler, Atheneum Shop Mgr.
A. Harrison Cromer, Pub. Prog. Dir.
Elizabeth Prager, Art Classes Coordinator
Mrs. Marion Lebel, Financial Secy.
William Clifford, Supt.

Free Tues. - Sat. 11 AM - 4 PM; Sun. 1 - 5 PM; cl. Mon, New Year's Day, July 4, Thanksgiving and Christmas. Estab. 1842 by Daniel Wadsworth as Atheneum Gallery of Fine Arts; now occupies entire city block square on Main St, downtown Hartford. Ann. meeting Mar; mem. 3200; dues $15 and higher. Privately supported. There are more than 60 galleries in 5 interconnected buildings, plus lecture room, classrooms, 299 seat theatre, Matrix Gallery of contemporary art and Lions Gallery of the Senses. Renovation and expansion of facilities completed in Feb. 1969 includes James Lippincott Goodwin Building, along with sculpture court, restaurant, additional classrooms, offices and a lecture room.

Collections: Collections illustrate the arts of Europe, Asia, Africa and the Americas. J. P. Morgan Collection of antique bronzes, Italian Majolica, English and American silver and French and Meissen Porcelain, the latter among the finest in existence. Wallace Nutting Collection of Furniture from the Pilgrim Century, gift of J. P. Morgan. †European and American painting from 1400 to the present, including fine examples of Baroque painting and arts of the Middle Ages and The Renaissance; European Tapestries; Armor; Pre-Columbian art; Lifar Collection of Ballet Designs; European and American prints and drawings; †American decorative arts; Continental decorative arts; Oriental art; †Modern art; American and European costumes; Colt guns.

Exhibitions: Varied major exhibitions of ancient-modern art.

Activities: Lectures and gallery talks by staff on art and related subjects (including docent talks and lectures), free gallery tours, art classes for children and adults, 6 outside lectures, 4 dance concerts, free Sunday concerts from Oct. to June, 6-10 film series per year, Children's Holiday Festival, members' exhibition previews and various special events. (See Schools.)

Library: Art reference library of over 15,000 books, plus pamphlets and catalogs; 35,000 slides.

Atheneum Shop: Cards, reproductions, photographs, books, gifts.

Publications: Monthly newsletter to members.

Attendance: 250,000 annual.

KENT

KENT ART ASSOCIATION, INC. GALLERY
Box 202 Route 7, 06757. Tel: (203) 927-4289
Arthur Hooton, Pres.
Frank Soltesz, 1st V.Pres.
George-Ann Gowan, 2nd V.Pres.
Elizabeth Miller, Recording Secy.
Frances Townley, Corresp. Secy.
Jayne McGarvey, Treas.
Open 2 - 5 PM during exhibitions only. Estab. 1923, inc. 1935. Ann. meeting Oct; mem. artists 50, assoc. 300; dues assoc. $5, sustaining $15, patron $25, life $100.
Exhibitions: Kent Art Association Exhibit, Aug. Spring exhibition May, Fall exhibition Oct, Associated Members Show, June.
Activities: Maintains gallery for changing exhibitions; lectures, demonstrations; portrait, still life and landscape; prize awards.
Attendance: 2500.

LITCHFIELD

LITCHFIELD HISTORICAL SOCIETY
On-the-Green, 06759. Tel: (203) 567-5862
John Mayher, Pres.
Philip Samponaro, Treas.
Lockett Ford Ballard, Jr, Dir.
Barbara Todd, Special Asst. to Dir.
Richard R. Quay, Secy.
Summer: Tues. - Sat. 11 AM - 5 PM; Winter: Tues. - Sat. 2 - 4 PM. Estab. 1856, inc. 1897 to encourage study and research, particularly relating to local history, biography, antiquities. Ann. meeting Sept; mem. 600; choice of memberships.
Collections: Paintings by Ralph Earl, the Jennys', George Catlin, and others; miniatures by Anson Dickinson; pewter, china, textiles, costumes; local products; laces, embroideries.
Ingraham Library: Local histories, biographies, Litchfield newspapers from 1786, maps, books by Litchfield authors, genealogy. Approx. 10,000 volumes, 40,000 manuscripts.
Activities: Changing exhibits, lectures, study classes. First Law School in America. Judge Tapping Reeve Home, built 1772; his Law Schoolhouse built 1784. Open May 15 - Oct 15 Tues. - Sat. 11 AM - 5 PM. Admis. adults $1.50, children 50¢, group reservations 50¢ each.
Collections: Period furnishings.
Attendance: c. 8000.

MERIDEN

ARTS AND CRAFTS ASSOCIATION OF MERIDEN, INC.*
P.O. Box 348, 06450.
Joseph Kuczynski, Pres.
Rose Cignatta, 1st V.Pres.
Stuart Grandy, 2nd V.Pres.
Arthur McCarthy, Treas.
Grace Ryan, Recording Secy.
Edna Pison, Mem. Secy. & Asst. Treas.
Marjorie McCarthy, Corresp. Secy.
Stuart Grandy, Prog. Secy.
Founded 1907, inc. 1950 to further interest in art in Meriden and surrounding areas; promote fellowship and exchange of ideas among active artists; encourage appreciation of art by educational programs; encourage beginners in the arts and crafts. Ann. meeting June; mem. 500; dues $5 and higher.
Collections: Small permanent collection of paintings and sculpture; additions being made; a permanent display place is expected within two years.
Exhibitions: Annual exhibition of painting, prints, crafts and sculpture, held in June with selection and awards by jury; special exhibitions; new exhibition opportunities appearing regularly.
Activities: Monthly meetings (except summer months) with speakers; annual contribution of art books to Curtis Memorial Library.

MIDDLETOWN

DAVISON ART CENTER
Wesleyan University
High St, 06457. Tel: (203) 347-9411
Dr. Richard S. Field, Cur.
Open Mon. - Sat. 10 AM - 4 PM; Sun. 2 - 5 PM; cl. weekends during summer.
Collection of Prints and Drawings: The majority of the collection has been presented to Wesleyan University by George W. and Harriet B. Davison, who began their donations in 1938 and continued to add to the collection until 1953 when George W. Davison died.

Since 1952 the collection, with its comprehensive and steadily growing reference library on the graphic arts, has been housed in the historic Alsop House (1838-1840), acquired by the University in 1949 and transformed into the Davison Art Center.
The print collection, comprising several thousand items, covers the entire field of print-making from the 15th century to the present day and contains many items of outstanding rarity and importance (Master E.S, Nielli, Mantegna, Pollaiuolo, and others). The European masters such as Dürer, Cranach, Rembrandt, Canaletto, Piranesi, Goya, Meryon and others are very well represented. The Millet collection, one of the finest and most complete collections of this master, deserves special mention. English and American printmakers of the second half of the 19th and the 20th century are comprehensively represented. A collection of about 600 Japanese prints supplements the collection of Western prints.
Since 1955 acquisition funds have made it possible to build up the collection in the field of contemporary art and to complete many areas in the field of old masters. The collection now comprises about 14,000 items.
Print exhibitions are frequently arranged in the gallery which was added to the Alsop House in 1952. Exhibitions 1973: Everything you always wanted to know about prints...; The Prints of Richard Hamilton; Offset Lithography; 1974: Alex Katz, Prints; The Fable of the Sick Lion, a 15th Century Blockbook; Sam Green; 1975: Images of Death; Prints and Drawings by Gabriel de Saint-Aubin; Prints and Drawings by Lee Bontecou; Recent American Etching; Oskar Kokoschka: Prints 1906-1923.

Friends of the Davison Art Center
Estab. 1961, a membership group formed for the purpose of supporting and augmenting the activities of the Davison Art Center. Through its membership contributions the acquisition fund of the collection has increased.

MYSTIC

MYSTIC ART ASSOCIATION, INC.
P.O. Box 259, 06355. Tel: (203) 536-7601 (during season)
Joanna M. Case, Secy.
Open June - mid-Sept. daily except Wed, 11 AM - 5:30 PM; admis. by donation. Estab. 1924, inc. 1926 to maintain an art museum to exhibit and sell works of art, promote cultural education, historical interest, local and charitable activities and to develop art association property for the beautification of the community. Operated by Board of Directors elected from both artist and general mem. Owns large gallery building on the Mystic River. Gen. mem. meeting early June; ann. meeting to elect artists to mem. Sept; dues $7 and higher.
Exhibitions: Annual regional juried show with money prizes; membership, invitational and others in main gallery; groups of one and two-man shows; works of historical interest running simultaneously in small gallery.
Activities: Musicals, motion pictures, lectures, receptions; post cards.

MYSTIC SEAPORT, INC.
Greenmanville Ave, 06355. Tel: (203) 536-2631
Francis Day Rogers, Chmn. of the Board
William C. Ridgway, Jr, Pres.
Oliver Denison, III, Secy.
Waldo C. M. Johnston, Dir.
Donald R. Judge, Librn.
J. Revell Carr, Cur.
Daily 9 AM - 5 PM; cl. New Year's & Christmas; admis. adults $4.25, children $1.75; winter rates adults $3.75, children $1.50; servicemen free; Library cl. Sun. Estab. and inc. 1929 to preserve America's maritime history with emphasis on exhibits on Southern New England in the mid-nineteenth century; financed by endowment, membership and gate admis. The R. J. Schaefer Gallery opened 1975. Ann. meeting July or Aug; mem. 13,250; dues individual $15, family $25 and higher.
Collections: Prints, paintings, models and figureheads; yachting trophies and memorabilia; early lamps; whaleship Charles W. Morgan; square-rigged training ship Joseph Conrad; Gloucester fishing schooner L. A. Dunton; other vessels and small craft. Museum buildings include Fire House, Spar Shed, Rope Walk, Shipsmith Shop, Counting House, Sail and Rigging Loft; Schoolhouse, Meeting House, Chapel, General Store, Apothecary Shop, Woodcarver's Shop; the Samuel Buckingham and Thomas Greenman Houses; Clock Shop; Weavers' Shop. Childrens' Museum; Planetarium; Art Gallery.
Exhibitions: Permanent collections are on display at all times. Schaefer Gallery opened with a showing of the work of James E. Buttersworth; showing work of John Faunce Leavitt currently.
Activities: Activated shops (Apr.-Oct), school group visits, lectures; mariner training programs; Munson Institute of American Maritime Studies, accredited graduate course; original objects of art lent to 26 borrowers; classes for adults and children; book shop.

Library: 30,000 imprints, 300,000 mss, periodicals, prints, ships' plans, microfilm, charts; open to the public for serious research.

Income: Approx. $2,400,000 and specific gifts.

Publications: Quarterly Log; monthly newsletter Windrose, reports to members; publications relating to maritime history at Mystic Seaport Museum Stores, Inc. Announcements for publications sent to members prior to publication date.

Attendance: 1975 estimate, 540,000.

NEW BRITAIN

MUSEUM OF CENTRAL CONNECTICUT STATE COLLEGE*
06050. Tel: (203) 225-7481
Isabel S. Fairchild, Dir.
Founded 1965; financed by state appropriation.

Collections: Paintings; sculpture; graphics; decorative arts; archaeology; folklore; anthropology; industry; textiles; architectural drawings and models.

Library: Books and other materials related to the history of art and art education available for reference.

NEW BRITAIN MUSEUM OF AMERICAN ART
56 Lexington St, 06052. Tel: (203) 229-0257
Charles B. Ferguson, Dir.
Mrs. Lois L. Blomstrann, Asst. Dir.
Free 1 - 5 PM; cl. Mon. Friends of the Museum; enrl. 550; dues $5.

Collections: †Permanent collection of 18th, 19th century and contemporary paintings, sculpture and watercolors.

Exhibitions: Special loan and one-man shows yearly from Oct. through June; permanent collection July through Sept.

Activities: Lectures on art, demonstrations and gallery talks, Oct. - June; bus trips.

Library
8 High St.
Henry Pelton, Secy.
Mrs. Virginia Dowell, Librn.

NEW CANAAN

SILVERMINE GUILD OF ARTISTS
06840. Tel: (203) 966-5617
George F. Lowman, Pres.
Miriam Broudy, V.Pres.
Spencer R. Stuart, V.Pres.
Bonnie Ford Woit, Secy.
Dorothy Robinson, Gallery Dir.
Free daily 12:30 - 5 PM. Inc. 1922 as a community undertaking for artists and laymen. It is one of the largest year-round, non-profit community art centers offering exhibits and instructions in the arts. (See Schools). 450 artist members, 325 supporting members.

Collections: Permanent collection of graphics by American artists, established in 1954; enlarged by purchase at each Biennial National Print Exhibition.

Exhibitions: Exhibitions change every 3 weeks; annual New England Exhibition of Painting and Sculpture with awards of $5000 in prizes; one-man, Members' and Invitational exhibits; Biennial National Print Exhibition.

Activities: Art Symposiums, summer series of chamber music concerts; rental and purchase plan; gallery talks and tours.

Library: Books on the arts and allied subjects - approx. 2000 items.

NEW HAVEN

THE MUNSON GALLERY, INC.
33 Whitney Ave, 06511. Tel: (203) 865-2121
Larom B. Munson, Pres.
Free, Tues. - Sat. 9 AM - 5:30 PM. Estab. 1860 for regular exhibitions, paintings, sculpture, graphics, framing and restoration.

Exhibitions: Elliot Orr; Mac Squires; Eugene Conlon; Frank Stella; Norman Ives; Josef Albers; Neal Cotton.

NEW HAVEN COLONY HISTORICAL SOCIETY
114 Whitney Ave, 06510. Tel: (203) 562-4183
Charles C. Kingsley, Pres.
Reverdy Whitlock, Secy.
Joseph Johnson Smith, Dir.
Robert Egleston, Cur.
Open Tues. - Fri. 10 AM - 5 PM; Sat, Sun. & major holidays 2 - 5 PM; cl. Mon. Estab. 1862 for the preservation, exhibition and research of local scholarly materials, memorabilia and arts. Ann. meeting Nov; mem. 1000; dues $15.

Collections: †Connecticut pewter, †New Haven silver, local furniture, paintings, drawings and graphics, toys, and items of local historic interest. Morris House (c. 1685-1780).

Exhibitions: One major show and many smaller ones annually. Major shows include Max Dellfant's Paintings - New Haven Artist 1865-1944; New England Arms Exhibit - 17th and 18th century arms, 1975; Tablewares of New Haven, 1640-1840, permanent decorative arts gallery; New Haven Industry Exhibit, 1975.

Activities: Exhibitions, morning and evening lecture series, active school program; gift shop.

Library: 14,000 volume research library specializing in genealogy and local history.

Publications: Quarterly Journal, Newsletter.
Attendance: Approx. 15,000.

NEW HAVEN FREE PUBLIC LIBRARY
133 Elm St, 06510. Tel: (203) 562-0151, Ext. 408
Meredith Bloss, Librn
Helen B. Worobec, Art Librn.
Open Mon. & Wed. 9 AM - 5:30 PM, Tues. & Thurs. 9 AM - 8 PM, Fri. & Sat. 9 AM - 5 PM; cl. Sun. Estab. 1886, art dept. 1921. Library includes books on †art, †music, †photography, †architecture and †gardening, †sports, †recreation, †theatre, †8mm films.

Activities: Circulating collection of mounted and unmounted pictures; continuous exhibitions, including work by local artists; cooperates with public schools; exhibits art work of children.

Purchases: Annual purchases $5300.

Art & Music Department

This department contains a large collection of art books, portfolios of plates, music books including both scores and music theory, phonograph records, and mounted pictures on a great variety of subjects. This picture collection is designed especially for schools, study clubs, religious education groups, and commercial artists. Exhibitions of the work of local artists are held in this room throughout the year.

Library is a member of the Film Cooperative of Connecticut, Inc.(which loans 16mm films).

NEW HAVEN PAINT & CLAY CLUB, INC.
The John Slade Ely House
51 Trumbull St, 06510. Tel: (203) 624-8055
Jordan Abeshouse, Pres.
Shirley Price, Secy.
Estab. 1900, inc. 1928. Annual meeting May; active mem. 230, assoc. & sustaining 60; active dues $10, assoc. $5, sustaining $20; life mem. $200 once. Mem. open to artists working in any media whose work has been accepted two times in the Annual juried show.

Exhibitions: Annual exhibition in spring open to all artists, working in any medium; selection and award of prizes by jury. Purchase fund: work added to club's Permanent Collection. In the fall there is an exhibition for members only.

Income & Purchases: Income in excess of $1000; annual purchases to $1000.

Permanent collection is on display in the Upstairs Galleries of the John Slade Ely House at all times when the House is open. Gallery hours, Tues. - Fri. 1 - 4 PM; Sat. & Sun. 2 - 5 PM; cl. Mon.

YALE CENTER FOR BRITISH ART AND BRITISH STUDIES
Box 2120 Yale Station, 06520. Tel: (203) 432-4594
Robert E. Kuehn, Asst. Dir.
Free. Estab. 1968. The Center is under development and construction; it will open to the public in 1977.

A part of Yale University, the Center is intended to house the collections of British art from the 16th through 19th century including paintings, drawings, prints, and rare books assembled by Mr. Paul Mellon; also to house research library and academic facilities for study of British art and culture.

Collections: 1500 British paintings, 30,000 rare illustrated books, 5000 drawings and watercolors.

Activities: The Center will sponsor a program in British studies; docent service will be available to the community; lectures; concerts; sales desk.

Library: Photographic collection of 40,000 works of British art for reference.

YALE MEDICAL LIBRARY
Yale University
333 Cedar St, 06510. Tel: (203) 436-4784
Stanley D. Truelson, Jr, Librn.
Ferenc A. Gyorgyey, Historical Librn.
Free Mon. - Fri. 8:30 AM - 12 PM; Sat. 8:30 AM - 10 PM; Sun. & holidays 11 AM - 12 PM. Estab. 1814, now the library of the Yale-New Haven Medical Center. Financed by endowment, tuition, gifts and grants. Ann. meeting of Associates, fall; mem. 332; dues $10, $25, $100, life mem. $1000.

Collections: Clements C. Fry Collection of Medical Prints and Drawings; Peter Parker Collection of Lam-Qua Paintings; Edward Clark Streeter Collection of Weights and Measures and Early Pharmacy Room; 430,000 volumes for lending and reference; photograph collection of 1200 prints for reference.

Exhibitions: Approximately 40 prints or drawings displayed in entrance corridor.

Publications: Annual Report, Users' Guide.

YALE UNIVERSITY ART GALLERY
1111 Chapel St, 06510. (Mailing Add: Box 2006, Yale Station, 06520.) Tel: (203) 436-0574.
Alan Shestack, Dir.
Mary Ann Nelson, Secy. to Dir.
Estelle M. Miehle, Admin. Asst.
Janet S. Dickson, Cur. Educ.
Mrs. Fernande E. Ross, Registrar & Cur. Intra-Univ. Loan Collection
Andrew F. Petryn, Consultant, Restoration
Charles F. Montgomery, Cur. Garvan & Related Collections of American Art
Theodore E. Stebbins, Jr, Cur. American Painting, Assoc Cur. Garvan Collection
Patricia E. Kane, Assoc Cur. Garvan & Related Collections of American Art
Edmund P. Pillsbury, Cur. of European Art; Asst. Dir.
James D. Burke, Cur. Drawings & Prints
George J. Lee, Cur. Oriental Art
Mary B. G. Neill, Asst. Cur. Oriental Art
Susan Burke, Assoc. Cur. for Ancient Art and the Dura Europos Collection
Sumner McK. Crosby, Cur. Medieval Art
George A. Kubler, Cur. Pre-Columbian & Primitive Art
Charles Seymour, Jr, Cur. Renaissance Art
Caroline Rollins, Information & Mem. Secy. (Art Gallery Assoc)

Free Tues. - Sat. 10 AM - 5 PM; Sun. 2 - 5 PM; cl. Mon, New Year's Day, July 4, Labor Day, Thanksgiving and Christmas. Estab. 1832 by Col. John Trumbull, aide-de-camp of Gen. Washington and his nephew-in-law, Benjamin Silliman. Present Gallery is an extension to the third art museum built and maintained by the University. The Trumbull Gallery (demolished in 1901) in which the patriot-artist's paintings of the Revolution were housed, was the earliest art gallery connected with a university in America. Street Hall (now used by the History of Art Department and the Slide & Photograph Collection) was the gift of Augustus R. Street, and the collections, including the early Italian paintings brought together by James Jackson Jarves, were installed there in 1868. The third building (about two-fifths of the proposed whole) opened in 1928; the additional wing was completed in Nov. 1953.

Collections: Objects illustrative of the ancient civilizations of the Orient, of Greece and Rome (Stoddard Collection of Greek and Roman vases) and antiquities from the University's excavations in Dura-Europos; the Near and Far East (Moore Collection); Europe, includes Jarves, Griggs and Rabinowitz Collection of Medieval and Renaissance paintings; America, includes Trumbull Revolutionary paintings, Garvan Collection of silver, furniture and paintings, recently reinstalled in an innovative setting, Morgan Collection of miniatures and the Edwin Austin Abbey Collection; modern paintings (Société Anonyme collection); prints and drawings, includes Achelis, Greene, Oppenheim, Tuttle, Steefel and other collections; Linton Collection of African Sculpture; Olsen Collection of Pre-Columbian Art.

Activities: During the academic year a public event held every Sunday at 3 PM: musical performances, dance, film, and scholarly lectures; guided tours, gallery talks, slide lectures to schools and clubs on appointment.

Library: Contains basic collection of 38,000 standard reference works, major monographs and periodicals. About 50,000 additional works available in Yale's Sterling Memorial Library and related material in the Beinecke Rare book and Manuscript Library. Photograph collection includes over 120,000 items available to the public for reference, although the slide collection of 161,000 items is for university use only.

Attendance: (1974-75) 93,631.
Yale University Art Gallery Associates
Mrs. Ralph Halsey, Chmn, Exec. Comt.
Caroline Rollins, Secy. to Mem.
Mem. c. 1350; dues $20 and higher. Informal organization of members (mem. open to any alumnus or friend of Yale) who receive the Bulletin, published irregularly, catalogs of exhibitions, special publications, monthly lecture and exhibition notices, invitations to openings and the opportunity to take two lecture series offered only to members. Associate contributions help to make possible publications, exhibitions and occasional acquisitions of works of art.

NEW LONDON

✠LYMAN ALLYN MUSEUM
100 Mohegan Ave, 06320. Tel: (203) 443-2545
Dr. Oakes Ames, Administrator
Dr. Edgar deN. Mayhew, Dir.
Roger Dennis, Conservator
Mrs. Edward Gipstein, Docent
Mrs. Willard O. Shepard, Secy.
Mrs. Arvin Karterud, Registrar
Open Tues. - Sat. 1 - 5 PM; Sun. 2 - 5 PM; cl. Mon. Dedicated 1932, inc. 1948, gift of Harriet Upson Allyn; contains 12 galleries, 3 classrooms, library and conservation laboratory. Mem. 1500; dues $10 and higher.

Collections: †American furniture, paintings and drawings, †Old Master drawings, †primitive art, †Oriental art, †Costumes, Palmer bequest of English and American furniture, †dolls and large doll houses. The Deshon-Allyn House (1829), a fine mansion of the Federal Period, has been restored and is open to the public during the hours the museum is open.

Exhibitions: (1967 to date) William Benton Collection of American Paintings; Henderson Collection; Selections from the Collection of Nathan Cummings; Dimitri Varley, Pottery: New London Whaling; Language of the Print, Karshan Collection; Paul Magriel Bronzes: 250 Years of American Art from Three Connection Museums (in connection with the Mattatuck Museum, Waterbury, Conn, and the New Britain Museum of American Art, New Britain, Conn), New London Silver, 1700-1835; Albert Hydeman Collection of Western and Oriental Paintings; Yngve Soderberg and Kenneth Bates, Retrospective; one-man show, Roger Dennis, Gund Collection of Western Art; New London County Furniture, 1640-1840; Retrospective Show, Tom Ingle; Jayne Kantor - Women Look at Women; Josef Presser; one-man show, Nelson C. White; local one-man shows; work of the children's and adults classes at the Museum.

Activities: Art classes for adults and children, gallery talks, tours for school children, art history lecture series, European and local tours; gift shop.

Library: Art reference library of 10,000 volumes.
Income and Purchases: Income $100,000; purchases $10,000.
Attendance: 40,000.

NIANTIC

EAST LYME ARTS COUNCIL*
Box 200, 06357.
Marvin Schutt, Pres.
Alice Gerber, Secy.
Jean Kondratenko, Chmn. Art Group
Nelson Smith, Chmn. Drama Group
Jayne Coale, Chmn. Youth Theater Workshop
Estab. 1963 to further all branches of the arts in the Southeastern Connecticut Community; financed by membership. Ann. meeting Jan; mem. 175.

Exhibitions: Ann. art show every July 4 weekend.
Activities: Drama workshops for youth and art classes; concerts; dramatic programs; classes for children.

NORWICH

SLATER MEMORIAL MUSEUM
The Norwich Free Academy
Converse Art Bldg, 06360. Tel: (203) 887-2505 Exten. 18
Joseph P. Gualtieri, Dir.
Free 9 AM - 4 PM, Sat. & Sun. 2 - 5 PM, Sept. - May; Tues. - Sun. June - Aug. 1 - 4 PM, cl. Mon; cl. holidays year round. Slater Building opened 1888 and houses Museum. Converse Building opened 1909 and houses exhibition galleries and art school.

Collections: Permanent collections of Far Eastern art of the 17th and 18th centuries including wood carvings, textiles, stencils, ceramics, metalwork and prints; Japanese ivory carvings; American furniture of the 17th, 18th and 19th centuries plus ceramics, pewter, and marine collection of the same era; furniture of the renaissance and post-renaissance; original classical and contemporary drawings and prints, American paintings of the 19th and 20th centuries; textiles from Coptic to contemporary; 17th and 18th century laces and jewelry; Persian tiles; Egyptian bronzes and potteries; Greek potteries.

Exhibitions: Special exhibitions changed monthly.
Activities: Gallery talks for school classes; Friends of the Museum sponsored monthly programs; topics of varied interest in the field of art.

Income: Financed by funds of the Norwich Free Academy.
Attendance: 30,600 annual average.

OLD LYME

LYME ART ASSOCIATION
P.O. Box 222, Lyme St, 06371.
Elisabeth Gordon Chandler, Pres.

Alex Poplaski, V.Pres.
H. Gil-Roberts, Treas.
Jessie Hull Mayer, Secy.
Doris Jorgensen, Asst. Secy.
Open daily 10 AM - 5 PM; Sun. 1 - 5 PM; Admis. 50¢. Estab. 1902.
Meetings June & Sept; mem. 455; dues $7.50 and higher; owns gallery building.
Exhibitions: Annual exhibitions of watercolors, graphics and small sculpture; annual oils and sculpture, both open to all artists working in or near Lyme; jury selection. Annual autumn exhibition, oils and sculpture, for members only; exhibition of children's work initiated in spring 1976.
Activities: Demonstrations of painting and sculpture held during exhibitions in season; gallery talks, art lectures and classes are in the planning stage.
Library: Maintains library of art reference books at Gallery on Lyme Street.
Purchases and Income: Purchases average from $8000 to $12,000 annually; income is minimal.
Attendance: 3500-4500 annually.

RIDGEFIELD

THE ALDRICH MUSEUM OF CONTEMPORARY ART
258 Main St, 06877. Tel: (203) 438-4519
Larry Aldrich, Founder & Pres.
Carlus & Ruth Dyer, Directors
Jacqueline Moss, Cur. Educ.
Open Sat. & Sun. 2 - 5 PM; admis. $1 adults, 50¢ children and students. Special tours for groups by appointment Wed. - Fri. Sculpture Garden, with over 25 major works, open to the public year round. Public institution estab. 1964 by Larry Aldrich for the exhibition of contemporary painting and sculpture to encourage appreciation and promotion of contemporary art. Friends of the Aldrich Museum, dues $100.
Exhibitions: Two exhibitions presented each year. From mid-Apr. to Labor Day, Contemporary Reflections presents the work of new artists who are not represented by galleries; mid-Sept. to mid-Dec. presents the works of established artists. Illustrated catalogs available.
Activities: Lectures and guided tours each Saturday. Art history seminars on contemporary art held 3 times annually on Friday mornings. Each seminar lasts 6 weeks and a fee is charged.
Attendance: Approx. 6000.

See Soho Center for Visual Artists, New York, NY.

STAMFORD

COUTURIER GALERIE
1814 Newfield Ave, 06903. Tel: (203) 322-2405
Marion B. Couturier, Dir.
Darrel J. Couturier, Coordinator & Assoc. Dir, International Operations
Open daily 11 AM - 4 PM; cl. Tues; no admis. Estab. 1961 as an art gallery and to promote community art education programs.
Exhibitions: 15th Anniversary Celebration—14th show for Josh Paskin and Evelyn Favus, impressionistic paintings; sculpture by Jaime Antunez, Stanley Marcus and Shay Rieger. International Christmas exhibition: works by artists from all over the world, including jewelry, pottery, paintings, original graphics, sculpture and weavings.
Activities: Material available to museums, schools and industry; fees for industry; traveling exhibitions organized and circulated; individual paintings and original objects of art lent.

THE FERGUSON LIBRARY
96 Broad St, 06901. Tel: (203) 325-4354
Marie V. Hurley, Dir.
Phyllis Massar, Art & Music Librn.
Open Mon. - Fri. 9 AM - 9 PM; Sat. 9 AM - 5:30 PM. Estab. 1880 as a public library dedicated to serving the information needs of the community; financed by city appropriation.
Collections: 11,000 books, both reference and circulation, on †art, †film, †photography, †theater, and †music (including librettos and scores). Also 7500 classical, popular and spoken †records and †cassette tapes; 2000 †color slides; †800 16mm films; picture file of 2700 circulating pictures as well as a comprehensive reference collection of photography of Old Stamford.
Exhibitions from the Stamford Collection as well as outside sources.
Annual Purchases: $10,000 art and music books, $7000 records, $16,000 films.

STAMFORD MUSEUM AND NATURE CENTER
High Ridge and Scofieldtown Roads, 06903. Tel: (203) 322-1646
F. D. Rich, Jr, Pres.
Gerald E. Rasmussen, Dir.
Free Mon. - Sat. 9 AM - 5 PM; Sun. & holidays 1 - 5 PM; Nov. -

Mar, Mon. 1 - 5 PM; cl. Thanksgiving, Christmas, New Year's Day; parking fee. Estab. 1936, Art Department 1955. Ann. meeting June; mem. 4000; dues $10 and higher; art class enrl. 1100.
Collections: Painting, sculpture, American crafts, American Indian, natural history.
Exhibitions: Art, sculpture, sculpture garden, children's farm, zoo, outdoor theater, observatory, planetarium.
Activities: Lectures to school groups, classes in painting, drawing, sculpture, ceramics, modern dance; also similar classes in natural history. Museum store, books, prints, crafts.
Publications: Monthly newsletter, pamphlets.
Income: $360,000.
Attendance: 250,000.

STONY CREEK

WILLOUGHBY WALLACE MEMORIAL LIBRARY ASSOCIATES
146 Thimble Islands Rd, 06405. Tel: (203) 488-8702
Elizabeth Brainerd, Pres.
Adeline Mix, Secy.
Margaret A. Thoms, Art Dir.
Free Mon. - Fri. 2 - 5 PM & 7 - 9 PM; Sat. 10 AM - 5 PM. Estab. 1960; financed by membership. Gallery is a nice, large, auditorium-type room. Annual meeting Aug; mem. 134; dues $5 - $100.
Exhibitions: Monthly exhibitions; one-man shows, group shows, sculpture shows, craft shows, etc.
Activities: Over 500 prints in photograph collection for reference; lectures open to public; 4 visiting lecturers per year; concerts; classes for children.
Publications: Notices of exhibitions.

STORRS

✠THE WILLIAM BENTON MUSEUM OF ART
The University of Connecticut, Building U-140, 06268.
Tel: (203) 486-4520
Paul F. Rovetti, Dir.
Stephanie Terenzio, Asst. Dir.
George Mazeika, Registrar
Free Mon. - Sat. 10 AM - 4:30 PM; Sun. 1 - 5 PM; cl. between exhibitions and major holidays. Estab. 1966. Friends of the Museum of Art; approx. 800 mem; student contributions $4, double $12.
Collections: Include the †Louise Crombie Beach Memorial Collection estab. in 1924 consisting primarily of American paintings, The Landauer Collection of Käthe Kollwitz Prints and Drawings, German prints.
Exhibitions: Approx. 7-9 varied, 2 major organized by Museum each academic year, some essentially teaching instruments for University and Art Department especially.
Activities: Concerts, lectures.
Publications: At least one major exhibition catalogue annually; bulletin.
Attendance: Approx. 25,000 per year.

TORRINGTON

TURNER MUSEUM
Torrington Library
12 Day Coeton Place, 06790. Tel: (203) 489-6684
Esther D. Carey, Librn.
Open Sat. 9:30 - 12 AM, 1:30 - 5 PM. Estab. 1900. The Museum, maintained by the Library, contains the Elisha Turner collection of old china, pictures; also a collection of early American pressed and blown glass given by Ella S. Coe of Litchfield; dolphin candlesticks; dolls; Staffordshire china.

WALLINGFORD

WALLINGFORD ART LEAGUE*
Box 163, 06492.
Inc. 1952 to foster arts and crafts in Wallingford and New Haven County. Ann. meeting Apr; mem. approx. 75.
Monthly meetings Sept. through June, 2nd Thurs. 8 PM. Lectures; annual outdoor exhibit last Sat. in Sept. for Conn. artists only.

WASHINGTON DEPOT

THE WASHINGTON ART ASSOCIATION
06794. Tel: (203) 868-2878
Philip F. Mygatt, Pres.
Mrs. F. Alexander Close, Exec. V.Pres.
Mrs. J. Owen Eames, Exec. Secy.
Mrs. W. C. Wetherill, Treas.
Dr. Philip Kappel, Chmn. Emeritus
Free Sun. - Fri. 2 - 5 PM; Sat. 10 - 12 AM & 2 - 5 PM; cl. Wed. Estab. 1952 to promote the understanding and appreciation of art, to encourage and facilitate the study and practice of the arts by individuals, to hold art exhibitions continually, to cooperate with schools, civic and youth organizations; supported by membership and contri-

butions and fund raising events. Gallery is housed in an old brick building; three rooms are contained within the gallery for exhibitions only. A fourth room on the second floor holds separate exhibitions. Ann. meeting Aug. 15-31; dues individual $8, family $12, patron $30, life $100.

Exhibitions: Approx. 30 exhibitions per year, some open, some by invitation, also one-man shows.

Activities: Adult and children workshops and classes in arts and crafts; films, bus tours and car trips; lectures open to public; visiting lecturers, gallery talks and tours.

Library: 250 volumes for lending and reference.

Publications: Washington Art Association Bulletin, 3 times a year; announcements for all shows and publicity material.

Attendance: 6900.

WATERBURY

MATTATUCK HISTORICAL SOCIETY
Mattatuck Museum
   119 W. Main St, 06702. Tel: (203) 754-5500
Mrs. Charles E. Spencer, III, Pres.
Rosemarie A. DiChiara, Exec. Secy.
Mrs. William W. Brown, Secy.
Olga M. Hughes, Dir.
Mary D. Michael, Dir. of Educ.
Free Tues. - Sat. 12 - 5 PM; Sun. 2 - 5 PM; cl. Mon; cl. Sun. during July & Aug. Estab. 1877, to collect and preserve documents and articles relating to Waterbury and the region known as Mattatuck. Ann. meeting Oct; mem. 1000; dues $10 and higher. Owns building containing offices, galleries and auditorium.

Collections: Objects of historic interest, including furniture, needlework and pottery; Indian artifacts of New England origin; paintings by Connecticut artists, historic to contemporary.

Activities: Lectures on art and history; Junior Museum conducts classes in local and national history for classes in Waterbury Public Schools.

Publications: Pictorical History of Waterbury 1674-1974; occasional publications and pamphlets on local history.

Attendance: 25,000.

SILAS BRONSON LIBRARY
   267 Grand St, 06702. Tel: (203) 755-2218
Stanford Warshasky, Dir.
Patricia Veneziano, Head, Art, Music & Theatre Dept.
Free Mon, Wed. & Thurs. 9 AM - 9 PM; Tues, Fri. & Sat. 9 AM-5:30 PM. Estab. 1869 to provide a free public library for the community; financed by endowment and city appropriation. A spotlighted gallery wall is used for art exhibits, also a locked glass exhibition case.

Exhibitions: By local artists in various media.

Activities: Lending collection, 265 motion pictures, 16 film strips in sets of 4, collection of 25,000 pictures, 135 framed art prints; 27,000 items lent in an average year; 26,000 active borrowers; lectures open to the public; concerts.

Library: 173,000 volumes for lending and reference; picture collection of 25,000 in children's dept.

WEST HARTFORD

ANNE BUNCE CHENEY LIBRARY
Hartford Art School
   University of Hartford, 200 Bloomfield Ave, 06117.
   Tel: (203) 243-4397
Jean J. Miller, Art Librn.
Open 8:30 AM - 7 PM and Sat. mornings; funds are allocated from University Library System budget.

Collections: 8800 volumes for lending and reference; 9100 mounted reproductions including photographs; 1780 pamphlets including exhibition catalogs.

CONNECTICUT ACADEMY OF FINE ARTS
   Box 204, 06101
Kenneth Davies, Pres.
Charles Ferguson, V.Pres.
Lilijean H. Metcalf, Secy-Treas.
Estab. 1910, inc. 1927. Ann. meeting May; mem. approx. 250; dues $10.

Exhibitions: Annual juried exhibition May at Wadsworth Atheneum; prizes, entry fee, open to all artists; members exhibition at New Britain Museum of American Art, March.

Income and Purchases: Income $4000; purchases $4000 annually.

Attendance: 7500 at annual exhibitions.

WESTON

THE SOCIETY OF MEDALISTS
   c/o Mary Louise Cram, Secy. & Treas, 34 W. Branch Rd,
   06880. Tel: (203) 226-5692
Donald A. Eifert, Pres.

Art Advisory Board:
Elvira Clain-Stefanelli
Frank Eliscu
Christopher Parks
Eric Sloane
Albert Wein
Estab. 1930 to stimulate interest in medallic sculpture. The Society of Medalists has granted two commissions annually since 1930 to American sculptors to execute bas-relief medallic sculpture. The finished high-relief fine art medals struck by the Society are then distributed to dues paying members of the nonprofit organization. Since its founding in 1930 by the late art patron, George Dupont Pratt (1869-1935), more than 90 American artists have been recipients of such commissions which are currently worth $2000 each. Free illustrated brochures, membership information and artists' submission inquiries will be accommodated by writing to the Society at the above address.

The Society has up to 2500 Bronze Members and 500 Silver Members. Its medals are exhibited annually at the American Numismatic Association Convention. Each August a News Bulletin is published featuring general information regarding collecting of medals.

Complete collections of Society medals are on permanent exhibit at the following locations: World Heritage Museum, University of Illinois, 484 Lincoln Hall, Urbana, IL 61801 and R. W. Norton Gallery, 4747 Creswell Ave, Shreveport, LA 71106.

WILTON

THE CRAFT CENTER MUSEUM*
   80 Danbury Rd, 06897. Tel: (203) 762-8363
Kenneth Lynch, Pres.
Otto Gust, Secy.
Carroll Cavanaugh, Dir.
Harvey Muston, Dir.
Joseph Henry, Cur.
Free Mar. - Dec. Mon. - Fri. 10 AM - 4 PM; cl. Jan. - Feb, national holidays. Estab. 1956 to exhibit and explain seventeenth to nineteenth century handwork, blacksmithing, casting, woodwork. Ann. meeting April; mem. 12.

Collections: Armor; tools and finished products in areas of metal spinning, furnishing; copper; lead; wood; leather; lighting; brass casting; silversmithing.

Activities: Maintains gallery for exhibitions; 3000 volume library and photograph collection for reference only.

DELAWARE

NEWARK

UNIVERSITY OF DELAWARE *
Student Center Art Gallery
   19711. Tel: (302) 738-2630
Jack S. Sturgell, Dir.
Open daily 12 AM - 5 PM; hours curtailed during vacations. Estab. 1926 to enlarge the student's acquaintance with art in its various aspects. The public is also invited to all exhibitions.

Exhibitions: Changed monthly; include traveling exhibitions from prominent museums and organizations as well as from the University collections. Annual exhibition of University students' work; yearly juried show of regional artists.

Attendance: Approx. 10,000.

University Art Collections
   19711. Tel: Archivist's Office, (302) 738-2750; Art History
   Collection, (302) 738-2418
John Clayton, University Archivist & Dir. Permanent Art Collection
Patricia Kent, Coordinator Cultural Programs
Sudie K. Lochridge, Cur. Slide & Photograph Library & Art History
   Teaching Collection
Morris Library open daily 8:30 AM - 10 PM; Clayton Continuing Education Center open Mon. - Fri. 8:30 AM - 5 PM; no admis. Estab. to consolidate the gifts of art to the University and to provide exhibitions of art objects from these collections to increase visual awareness on the University of Delaware campus; supported by State appropriation. Several exhibition areas around campus: Morris Library, Clayton Hall, Smith Hall mini-exhibition cases.

Collections: Permanent Collection of some 500 art objects including painting, sculpture and prints; Art History Teaching Collection of 600 art objects including painting, sculpture (primarily American, African and pre-Columbian), and prints.

Exhibitions: A University Grows, 1743-1934 (Morris Library); American Prints, Drawings, and Sculpture (Morris Library); Some French and German Prints of the 19th and 20th Centuries (Clayton Hall); two student shows, three professional artists' shows.

Publications: Continuing Education Center Fall and Spring Bulletins.

Attendance: 4000 average at exhibitions.

REHOBOTH BEACH

REHOBOTH ART LEAGUE, INC.
Henlopen Acres, P.O. Box 84, 19971. Tel: (302) 227-8408
Mrs. Howard W. Megee, Pres.
Sandford Leach, Exec. V.Pres.
Ruth Chambers Stewart, Exec. Secy.
Mrs. H. Duval Pearce, Asst. Exec. Secy.
Open 7 hours May - Sept. 31. Estab. 1938 to bring together inter-
ested people to inspire, encourage and sustain the art spirit in the
Rehoboth Beach community and all of Sussex County, Delaware.
Its classes are open to people of all ages. Ann. meeting last Mon.
in Aug; mem. approx. 1200, student enrollment 200; dues $10 and
higher.
Collections: Permanent collection of watercolors, oils, prints,
sculpture and pottery from gifts.
Exhibitions: Annual members' exhibitions in fine arts and in
crafts, student exhibitions in summer and at Thanksgiving; two and
three-man special and members shows; individual artist exhibitions,
exhibition schedule lasts from May to Oct. 1 plus Thanksgiving
show; annual awards $1000.
Activities: Lectures, concerts, Artists Costume Ball, Cottage
Tour of Art (artists' one-man shows in distinctive homes and cot-
tages plus 3 sculptors); outdoor show, flea market, film festivals;
classes in painting, drawing, sculpture, ceramics and weaving.
Publications: Spring brochure of exhibitions, events and classes;
newsletters.
Attendance: 10,000 annually.

WILMINGTON

COUNCIL OF DELAWARE ARTISTS
c/o Elinor H. Gray, Pres, 803 N. duPont Rd, Westover Hills,
19807. Tel: (302) 654-0249
Anne Genge, V.Pres.
Pauline McLean, Secy.
Estab. 1955 to educate the membership and the public about significant aspects of the creative arts including discussions, lectures
and exhibitions pertaining to the visual arts and to provide continuous exposure of members' work through exhibitions; to establish an
atmosphere of fellowship and cooperation among professional artist
members; financed by membership. Ann. meeting May; mem. 60;
dues $10.
Exhibitions: Wilmington Savings Fund Gallery; Wilmington Drama
League; University of Delaware; Luther Towers Gallery.
Activities: Traveling exhibitions organized and circulated; individual paintings lent to schools, public offices, retirement homes and
banks; items lent by invitation; slides of members' work at exhibitions; lectures open to the public; 9 visiting lecturers per year;
scholarships.
Publications: Newsletter, as indicated.

✣DELAWARE ART MUSEUM
Wilmington Society of the Fine Arts
2301 Kentmere Parkway, 19806. Tel: (302) 655-6288
Mrs. Alfred E. Bissell, Pres.
Charles L. Wyrick, Jr, Dir.
Rowland P. Elzea, Cur. of Collections
Mrs. Marion F. T. Johnson, Educ. Dir.
Mrs. Eugene R. Nixon, Librn.
Open daily 10 AM - 5 PM, Sun. 1 - 5 PM. Estab. 1911, inc. 1912 to
further the interest of art in Delaware. Ann. meeting last Tues. in
Oct; mem. approx. 1900; dues $15 and higher.
Collections: Bancroft Collection of English Pre-Raphaelite
paintings; Rosetti manuscripts; Howard Pyle paintings, drawings,
memorabilia and library; John Sloan paintings, drawings, etchings,
library and manuscripts; 19th and 20th century American paintings,
graphics and sculpture: Delaware artists; Pyle pupils; Charles Lee
Reese Collection of etchings; General Art Library.
Exhibitions: Annual Delaware Juried Exhibitions; The Calder
Family; American Painting 1857-69; The Independents of 1910; Andrew Wyeth; Edwin Dickinson; Life and Times of John Sloan; Jerome
Myers Centennial; The Golden Age of American Illustration: 1880-
1914; Howard Pyle, Diversity in Depth; Avant Garde Painting and
Sculpture in America: 1910-1925.
Activities: Lectures, film series, concerts, gallery talks, docent
service, classes for children and adults, circulating exhibitions,
travel program; Downtown Gallery.
Publications: Pre-Raphaelite, Howard Pyle, The Independents of
1910 catalogs; the Life and Times of John Sloan; monthly calendars
of events, annual reports, special catalogs for major exhibitions.
Annual budget: $400,000.
Attendance: Approx. 60,000.

HAGLEY MUSEUM
Barley Mill Rd. & Brandywine Creek, 19807. Tel: (302) 658-2401
Dr. Walter J. Heacock, Dir.
Joseph P. Monigle, Deputy Dir.

Open Tues. - Sat. 9:30 AM - 4:30 PM; Sun. 1 - 5 PM; cl. Mon; general admis. free; Jitney fare 25¢ children under 12, 50¢ adults.
Estab. 1957 to interpret the industrial history of the Brandywine as
it relates to the nation; endowed.
Collections: Manuscripts, including Du Pont Company records
from 1802 to 1966.
Activities: Maintains Fellowship program and cooperates with
schools.
Library: Museum Library consolidated in 1961 with Longwood
Library (Pa). The resultant Eleutherian Mills Historical Library is
co-equal with the Museum under the Foundation organization.
120,000 volumes, 5.5 million manuscript items and 225,000 photographs.
Attendance: Museum (1974) 140,000.

HISTORICAL SOCIETY OF DELAWARE*
Museum: Old Town Hall, 6th & Market Sts, 19806.
Library: 505 Market St, 19801. Tel: 655-7161
Walter J. Heacock, Pres.
William Poole, 1st V.Pres.
Dale Fields, Exec. Dir.
Roland H. Woodward, Museum Cur.
Mrs. Gladys M. Coghlan, Dir. of Libraries
George Gibson, Managing Editor
Free Tues. - Fri. 10 AM - 4 PM; cl. Mon, Sat, Sun, Holidays and
during Aug. Estab. 1864 to record and preserve Delaware History.
Ann. meeting Apr; mem. 1200; dues $10 and higher.
Collections: †Delaware pictures, †silver and †furniture;
manuscripts; costumes.
Activities: Educational programs, lectures, guided tours,
special programs as arranged.
Library: Over 45,000 volumes of Delaware and American history.
Income: Approx. $100,000.
Publications: Magazine Delaware History (biannual).
Attendance: 15,000.

WINTERTHUR

THE HENRY FRANCIS DU PONT WINTERTHUR MUSEUM
(Five miles northwest of Wilmington), 19735. Tel: (302) 656-8591
Lammot du Pont Copeland, Pres.
Charles van Ravenswaay, Dir.
John A. H. Sweeney, Sr, Coordinator of Research
Wesley A. Adams, Deputy Dir, Finance & Admin.
Charles F. Hummel, Cur.
Scott T. Swank, Head, Educ. Div.
Frank H. Sommer, III, Head, Libraries Div.
Nancy Goyne Evans, Registrar
Ian M. G. Quimby, Editor, Publications Office
Dorothy W. Greer, Head, Public Relations Office
Horace L. Hotchkiss, Jr, Cur, Corbit-Sharp House, Wilson-Warner
House
Main museum open by appointment only for guided tours, Tues. -
Sat. 9:30 AM - 4 PM, except national holidays and during spring
Garden Tour; fourteen rooms in the south wing open without ap-
pointment Tues. - Sat, 10 AM - 4 PM; sixteen rooms in main
museum open without appointment mid-April-May as
announced. Estab. 1930, opened as a museum, 1951, south wing
opened 1960, original house built 1839; enlarged by donor, the late
Henry Francis du Pont; privately supported. 195 display areas of
American decorative arts, 1640-1840, incl. over 100 period rooms.
Collections: Furniture, metalwork, ceramics, glass, textiles,
paintings, prints, and sculpture; also fabrics, lighting fixtures, pottery, porcelain, and carpets from England, Europe, and the Orient;
notable collection of Oriental export porcelains made for the American market.
Reference Library: American art history, technology and regional source material; extensive collections of books, manuscripts,
microfilm, photographs and slides; facilities for scholarly research available by application; over 45,000 volumes.
Activities: Tours of main museum for adults by appointment,
halfday tours $6; special subject tours and college and school tours
by arrangement; admis. charge varies seasonally for tours of 14
rooms in south wing; Winterthur Gardens open spring through
autumn as announced; lectures; seminars. Winterthur Program in
Early American Culture and Winterthur Program in the Conservation of Artistic and Historic Objects in cooperation with the University of Delaware, graduate course for M.A. and M.S. candidates.
Museum bookstore opened 1963; Copeland Lecture Hall opened 1966;
photographic facilities, conservation laboratories.
Publications: Publications and articles by staff, including annual
Winterthur Portfolio first issued 1963, and Annual Report, first is-
sued for 1962.
Income: Approx. $5,000,000.
Attendance: (1974) Approx. 90,000.
Historic Odessa: Corbit-Sharp House (1774), Wilson-Warner House
(1769).

Open to the public Tues. - Sat. 10 AM - 5 PM, Sun. 2 - 5 PM, except national holidays. John Janvier Stable (1791) and Brick Hotel (1822) also maintained by Winterthur Museum. Odessa, 23 miles south of Wilmington, a community of restored eighteenth and nineteenth century houses, many of which are fine examples of early Delaware Valley architecture. Single admission to Corbit-Sharp or Wilson-Warner House, $1.25, children under 16 50¢; combined admis. $2, children under 16, 75¢.

DISTRICT OF COLUMBIA

WASHINGTON

AMERICAN ASSOCIATION OF MUSEUMS
2333 Wisconsin Ave. N.W, 20007. Tel: (202) 338-5300
Joseph Veach Noble, Pres.
Richard McLanathan, Dir.
Roberta H. Faul, Ed.
For further information see p. 3.

AMERICAN ASSOCIATION OF UNIVERSITY WOMEN
2401 Virginia Ave. N.W, Washington, DC 20037.
Tel: (202) 785-7700
Helen B. Wolfe, Gen. Dir.
For further information see p. 3.

THE AMERICAN NATIONAL RED CROSS
National Headquarters, 20006.
Frank Stanton, Chmn.
George M. Elsey, Pres.
For further information see p. 4.

AMERICAN UNIVERSITY
Watkins Gallery
Massachusetts & Nebraska Aves, N.W, 20016.
Tel: (202) 686-2114 (art dept.)
Robert D'Arista, Dir. & Chmn, Art Dept.
Free Mon. & Tues. 10 AM - Noon & 1 - 7 PM; Wed. - Fri. 10 AM - Noon & 1 - 5 PM; Sat. 2 - 5 PM; cl. Sun. Estab. 1944 to exhibit original works of contemporary art and to serve students of the American University and the public.
Collections: Watkins Collection of 145 contemporary works of art; Crosby Collection of drawings and prints.
Exhibitions: (1975-76) Drawings and painting by Robert Gates; Work by Lothar Brabanski; Paintings by Grace Hartigan; Paintings by Gerry Wartofsky; Student Exhibitions; Kreeger Nominee Exhibit.
Activities: Lectures, films.
Library: Reference library of 1500 volumes; art library of 4000 volumes.
Publications: Tradition and Experiment in Modern Sculpture, by Charles Seymour, Jr.
Attendance: 5000.

ANDERSON HOUSE MUSEUM
Society of the Cincinnati
2118 Massachusetts Ave, N.W, 20008.
John D. Kilbourne, Dir.
Open Tues. - Sun. 2 - 4 PM; special hours on request by groups for guided tours; cl. Thanksgiving and Christmas. The Society of the Cincinnati was founded in May 1783; the Museum was opened to the public in 1938. Anderson House Museum is a National Museum for the custody and preservation of historical documents, relics and archives, especially those pertaining to the American Revolution. Because of its superb building (1905, Little and Browne, Boston, architects), original furnishings and collections of Western and Oriental art, Anderson House Museum is also a Historic House Museum.
Collections: Relics of the war of the American Revolution, swords and firearms; †documents of the Society of the Cincinnati, †autograph letters of officers who fought in the War of the American Revolution, and other historic documents; figurines of the French Regiments who fought at Yorktown, Va, 1781, and others; collection of paintings, 16 and 17 century Flemish tapestries, sculpture, period furniture; Oriental works of art, Japanese screens, bronzes, ceramics, jade, and others.
Exhibitions: Rotating exhibitions; the permanent collection.
Activities: Guided tours, gallery talks and lectures.
Library: 3000 volumes on American Revolution, Am. history and fine arts.
Publications: Annual Report of the Director: Sword and Firearm Collection of the Society of the Cincinnati...; The Society of the Cincinnati and its Museum; Swords voted to Officers of the Revolution...; Oriental Art at Anderson House; A Few Questions and Answers regarding the Society of the Cincinnati.
Attendance: 5600 annual average.

ARTISTS EQUITY ASSOCIATION, INC.
National Headquarters, 2813 Albemarle St. NW, 20008.
Tel: (202) 244-0209
John Blair Mitchell, Pres.
Molly S. Brylawski, Exec. Dir.
For further information see p. 5.

ARTS CLUB OF WASHINGTON
James Monroe House
2017 Eye St. N.W, 20006. Tel: (202) 331-7282
Dr. Henry Lea Mason, Pres.
C. Dudley Brown, V.Pres.
Albert L. Yarashus, Treas.
Mary Cates, Recording Secy.
Jeanne Rose, Corresp. Secy.
Exhibitions open daily 11 AM - 5 PM except holidays. Founded 1916. Ann. meeting Apr; mem. approx. 250. The James Monroe House (1803-1805) was built by Timothy Caldwell of Philadelphia. It is registered with the National Register of Historic Places, the Historical Survey 1937 and 1968, and the National Trust for Historic Preservation. Among noted occupants of the house was James Monroe, fifth President of the United States, who resided in the house while he was Secretary of War and State. During the first six months of his Presidency (1817-1825) the house served as the Executive Mansion, since the White House had been burned in the War of 1812 and had not yet been restored.
Activities: Programs of monthly lectures; periodic exhibitions; social and educational activities; the Anna Bartsch-Dunne scholarships and the Conrad Morton art scholarship are granted annually to the local universities who decide upon student recipients; the Lester Hereward Cooke sketch group meets at the Club semimonthly, continuing the activity initiated by the late Dr. Cooke, who was curator of painting at the National Gallery of Art.

ASSOCIATION OF COLLEGIATE SCHOOLS OF ARCHITECTURE, INC.
1735 New York Ave. NW, 20006. Tel: (202) 785-2324
Prof. Donlyn Lyndon, Pres.
David Clarke, Exec. Dir.
For further information see p. 5.

THE CATHOLIC UNIVERSITY OF AMERICA HUMANITIES LIBRARY
114 Mullen Library, 20064. Tel: (202) 635-5075
Dorothy M. King, Head
B. Gutekunst, Asst.
Open Mon. - Thurs. 9 AM - 10 PM; Fri. 9 AM - 6 PM; Sat. 9 AM - 5 PM; Sun. 1 - 10 PM.
Collections: The collection supports the academic program of the CUA art department.
Library: 6700 volumes for lending; 200 prints for lending.

COMMISSION OF FINE ARTS*
708 Jackson Place, N.W, 20006. Tel: (202) 343-5324
J. Carter Brown, Chmn.
Charles H. Atherton, Secy. & Admin. Officer
Open to the public daily 8 AM - 4:30 PM. Estab. by Act of Congress, 1910, to advise the President, Members of Congress, and various governmental agencies on matters pertaining to the appearance of Washington, D.C. Monthly meetings.
The Commission of Fine Arts is composed of seven members, three architects, one landscape architect, one painter, one sculptor, and one layman, who are appointed by the President for four-year terms. Report issued periodically.
Plans for all new projects in the District of Columbia under the direction of the Federal and District of Columbia Governments which in any important way affect the appearance of the city, and all questions involving matters of art with which the Federal Government is concerned, must be submitted to the Commission for comment and advice before contracts are made. Also gives advice on suitability of designs of private buildings in certain parts of the city adjacent to the United States Capitol, the White House, the headquarters of the various departments and agencies of the District and Federal Governments, the Central Mall, Rock Creek Park, and Georgetown.

CORCORAN GALLERY OF ART
17th St. & New York Ave. N.W, 20006. Tel: (202) 638-3211
David Lloyd Kreeger, Pres.
Roy Slade, Dir.
Jane Livingston, Chief Cur.
Dorothy Phillips, Cur. Collections
Susan Grady, Registrar
Robert Scott Wiles, Restorer
Connie Broadstone, Development Officer.
Free Tues. & Wed, $1.50 Thurs. - Sun, children under 12 and prearranged groups free. Open Tues. - Sun. 11 AM - 5 PM; cl. Mon, New Year's Day, Independence Day, Thanksgiving Day and Christmas Day. Estab. 1859 and inc. 1869, primarily for the encouragement of

American art. Mem. approx. 3000; dues student $15, single partici- pating mem. $25, family $35, Friends of the Corcoran $100, sponsor- ing $250, contributing $500 and up.

Collections: The William Wilson Corcoran collection consisting chiefly of †American paintings; James Parmelee collection of Amer- ican paintings and sculpture; Mary E. Maxwell collection of †Ameri- can prints from the 18th century to the present. The American col- lections of †paintings, watercolors, drawings and sculpture from the 18th century through the 20th century is being constantly increased by purchases, gifts and bequests. Edward C. and Mary Walker col- lection of 19th century paintings; bronzes by Antoine Louis Barye. The W. A. Clark collection includes paintings and drawings by Dutch, Flemish, English and American artists; Gothic and Beauvais tapes- tries; an important triptych by Andrea di Vanni; an 18th century French salon; furniture, laces, rugs, mostly of the Herat style; ma- jolica; Greek antiquities; a 13th century stained glass window; sculpture.

Exhibitions: One-man exhibitions of contemporary American artists; biennial exhibition of contemporary American painting; a program of exhibitions of Washington area artists, both one-man and group exhibits, and a program of historical exhibitions of Amer- ican art.

Activities: Free docent service; lectures, films, concerts, gal- lery shop; children's programs. Corcoran School of Art.

Library: Contains about 4500 volumes.

Publications: Calendar of Events (monthly), exhibition catalogues, color reproductions, handbooks of the collections.

Attendance: Approx. 200,000.

DAR MUSEUM (NATIONAL SOCIETY DAUGHTERS OF THE AMERI- CAN REVOLUTION)
1776 D St. N.W, 20006. Tel: (206) 628-4980
Mrs. Earl James Helmbreck, Cur. Gen.
Free Mon. - Fri. 9:30 AM - 4 PM. Estab. 1890 with a committee for the collection and preservation of historic and family-owned items prior to 1830. Ann. meeting Apr; mem. over 194,000.

Collections: †Furniture, †paintings, †silver, †pewter, †ceramics, ††textiles, †children's toys, and 28 Period Rooms furnished in styles of the 17th, 18th and 19th centuries.

Exhibits are held in the main museum gallery. Special exhibits arranged and changed periodically, usually every 3-6 months.

Activities: Tours for school groups throughout the year upon application; seminar held annually for volunteer docents who number just below 100; slides are available for lectures at cost of $2.50 (script included).

Library: General decorative arts and history library; color slides available for Building, Museum Collection and Period Rooms; 1500 research books.

Attendance: 12,000 annually.

DECATUR HOUSE
748 Jackson Pl. NW, 20006. Tel: (202) 638-1204
Shirley Markley, Adminr. & Property Council & Staff of National Trust Interpretors
Free during Bicentennial Year, Mon. - Fri. 10 AM - 2 PM; Sat. & Sun. 1 - 4 PM.

Decatur House is a property of National Trust for Historic Preservation. The house is a National Historic Landmark. It is preserved as a historic house museum but operated as a community preservation center.

Decatur House, a Federal period town house, was completed in 1819. Designed by Benjamin Henry Latrobe. Its first owner, Com- modore Stephen Decatur, was killed shortly in 1820. The house was later occupied by a series of important tenants. Among them: Henry Clay, Martin Van Buren, Judah P. Benjamin, and the French and Russian legations. Acquired by General Edward F. Beale, after the Civil War, it was the center of social and diplomatic life in the cap- ital until the death of its last owner, Mrs. Truton Beale. Mrs. Beale, a preservationist, restored the house in the 1940's and be- queathed it to the National Trust in 1958.

The first floor has a fine collection of Federal furniture and memorabilia representing the Decatur period, while on the second floor the Victorian, late 19th and 20th century furnishings signify the over 90 years that Beale lived in the house.

Property serves as headquarters of the National Trust and as a focal point for advancement of historic preservation. It develops new relationships among cultural, community preservation groups and National Trust members in its area. Responds to community preservation needs by acting as a link between community and appropriate headquarters offices of National Trust.

Activities: Provides interpretive programs which are related to Decatur House's own case study in historic preservation; programs include spring and fall lecture series, school program, walking tours, special Christmas programs; Members Day during National Historic Preservation Week in early May; programs coordinated, and often in conjunction, with Wilson House.

✠DUMBARTON OAKS RESEARCH LIBRARY AND COLLECTIONS
Harvard University
1703 32nd St, N.W, 20007. Tel: (202) 232-3101
William R. Tyler, Dir.
Collections and Gardens open Tues. - Sun. 2 - 5 PM; cl. Mon, holi- days and July through Labor Day. Conveyed in 1940 to Harvard University by Mr. and Mrs. Robert Woods Bliss as a research cen- ter in the Byzantine and Mediaeval Humanities and subsequently en- larged by them through gifts and bequests.

Collections: †Byzantine devoted to Early Christian and Byzantine mosaics, textiles, bronzes, sculpture, ivories, metalwork, jewelry, glyptics, and other decorative arts of the period; †Pre-Columbian devoted to sculpture, textiles, pottery, gold ornaments, and other objects from Middle and South America, dating from 800 B.C. to the early 16th century; also a small group of European and American paintings, sculpture, and decorative arts; †Garden Library, a collec- tion of rare books, prints, drawings, etc. on the history of landscape architecture, botanicals, and gardening.

Activities: Lectures and conferences on Byzantine subjects, Pre- Columbian, and landscape architecture and gardening.

Resources for Byzantine research include a library of 86,000 volumes (including periodicals), a photographic copy of the Prince- ton Index of Christian Art, the Dumbarton Oaks Census of Early Christian and Byzantine Objects in American Collections, and a col- lection of over 50,000 photographs. The Pre-Columbian Library con- sists of 4400 volumes. The Garden Library is a collection of 2400 rare books, prints and drawings and 10,000 other volumes.

Publications: Handbooks and catalogs of the Byzantine and Pre- Columbian Collections.

Attendance: Approx. 100,000 annually.

FOLGER SHAKESPEARE LIBRARY
E. Capitol St, from Second to Third, S.E, 20003.
Tel: (202) 546-4800
Hon. Willard W. Writz, Chmn, Library Comt.
John W. Ward, Pres. of Amherst College, Amherst, Mass, ex-officio member of the Comt.
O. B. Hardison, Jr, Dir.
Philip A. Knachel, Assoc. Dir.
James P. Elder, Dir. of Development
John F. Andrews, Dir. of Research Activities
Betty Ann Kane, Head, Pub. Prog.
Louis W. Scheeder, Producer, Folger Theatre Group
Lilly S. Lievsay, Chief Cataloger
Elizabeth S. Niemyer, Acquisitions Librn.
Exhibitions open to the public Mon. - Sat. 10 AM - 4:30 PM; Sun. from Memorial Day to Labor Day; reading room open to accredited scholars weekdays 8:45 AM - 4:45 PM, Sat. 8:45 AM - 4:30 PM. Estab. 1932 under administration of the Trustees of Amherst College, Amherst, Mass. Friends of the Folger Library; 400 mem. by invitation; dues $50; ann. meeting spring; Collectors Club.

Collections: World's largest collection of Shakespeariana, in- cludes books, oil paintings, watercolors, prints, busts and many art and museum objects. There is one of the best collections in the Western hemisphere for the study of the history of English civiliza- tion before 1700. Extensive collections of †English books of the 16th and 17th centuries, English manuscripts, †Renaissance books for both England and the Continent; large collection of †theatrical mate- rial (250,000 volumes).

Exhibitions: Traveling exhibits; exhibitions of books and manu- scripts in main gallery, exhibitions of contemporary arts and crafts in the Anne Hathaway Gallery.

Activities: Lectures, theatre performances, poetry readings, film series; specially scheduled tours for school groups are avail- able through docent program; Folger Institute of Renaissance and 18th century studies offers graduate and postgraduate seminars; sales shop; fellowships.

Attendance: Exhibition gallery attendance approx. 60,000; Reader attendance 1000.

FREER GALLERY OF ART
12th & Jefferson Dr. S.W, 20560. Tel: (202) 381-5344
Dr. Harold P. Stern, Dir.
Dr. Thomas Lawton, Asst. Dir.
W. T. Chase, Head Conservator, Technical Lab.
Dr. Esin Atil, Assoc. Cur, Near Eastern Art
Mrs. Hin-cheung Lovell, Asst. Cur. Chinese Art
Free daily 10 AM - 5:30 PM; cl. Christmas. Estab. 1900 under the Smithsonian Institution to exhibit its outstanding masterpieces of oriental art; devote staff work to research and publication in the his- tory of civilizations represented by objects in the collections.

Collections: †Art of the Near and Far East—paintings, sculpture, objects in stone, wood, jade, glass, porcelain, bronze, gold, silver, lacquer, metalwork; manuscripts (early Christian). Arts of the West are represented by a collection of works by James McNeill Whistler and some of his contemporaries. There are over 12,000 objects in the collections.

Activities: Five lectures annually on Near and Far Eastern Art; tours are by appointment only; a scholarship in conjunction with the American Oriental Society and a fellowship in conjunction with the University of Michigan are offered.

Library: 40,000 volumes relating to cultural and historical background of the collection.

Attendance: 230,000 average.

GENERAL FEDERATION OF WOMEN'S CLUBS
1734 N St. N.W, 20036. Tel: (202) 347-3168
Mrs. John T. Crippen, Exec. Secy.
For further information see p. 6.

GENERAL SERVICES ADMINISTRATION
Public Buildings Service-Fine Arts Program
18th & F Sts, N.W, 20405. Tel: (202) 963-5131
Donald W. Thalacker, Dir. Fine Arts Prog.

The Fine Arts Program office directs the work of artists commissioned to design and execute sculpture, murals, tapestries and other art work incorporated as part of the design of new Federal Buildings, except Post Offices and Veteran's Administration buildings. The scope of work is determined by the size and character of the building with allowances up to .5% of the estimated construction cost.

Artists are commissioned by direct selection by agency upon recommendation by a panel of distinguished art professionals appointed by the National Endowment for the Arts and the architect for the building.

Estimated annual budget: $1,000,000.

HIRSHHORN MUSEUM AND SCULPTURE GARDEN
Eighth & Independence Ave, S.W, 20560. Tel: (202) 381-6512
Abram Lerner, Dir.
Stephen Weil, Deputy Dir.
Joseph Sefekar, Adminr.
Charles Millard, Chief Cur.
Anna Brooke, Librn.
Edward P. Lawson, Chief, Educ. Dept.
Douglas Robinson, Registrar
Joseph Shannon, Acting Chief, Dept. of Exhibits & Design
Laurence Hoffman, Chief Conservator
Keith Cumberland, Building Manager
Estab. 1966 under the aegis of the Smithsonian Institution; building designed by Gordon Bunshaft of the architectural firm of Skidmore, Owings & Merrill. Opened in Oct. 1974.

Collections: Approximately 6000 paintings and sculptures donated to the nation by Joseph H. Hirshhorn, emphasizing the development of modern art from the latter half of the 19th century to the present. The major emphasis of the painting collection is on American art beginning with a strong group of Thomas Eakins' and going on to such important figures as Sargent, Eastman Johnson, Chase, Hartley, Gorky, De Kooning, Rothko, Noland, Rivers and Frank Stella. European painting is represented by works from the last 3 decades by such artists as Balthus, Bacon, Miro, Ernst, Agam and Vasarely. The sculpture collection is international in scope and is representative of major currents in the medium over the past 100 years. It includes in-depth representation by such sculptors as Daumier, Carpeaux, Barye, Rodin, Degas in the 19th century as well as more recent work by Brancusi, Calder, Giacometti, Arp, Moore, Manzu and David Smith.

Exhibitions: In addition to the permanent collection, a large gallery on the lower level of the Museum is used for special loan exhibitions.

Activities: The Museum maintains a lending program and responds to research and photographic requests from scholars, publishers and institutions. The Education Department of the Museum includes a docent program with guided tours given for school groups and organizations, and an extensive auditorium program including films, concerts and lectures.

Library: Research library containing approx. 8000 books, periodicals and catalogs available to scholars.

HOWARD UNIVERSITY GALLERY OF ART
College of Fine Arts
Sixth & Fairmont Sts, N.W, 20001. Tel: (202) 636-7047
Dr. James E. Cheek, Pres.
Dr. Vada E. Butcher, Dean, College of Fine Arts
Dr. Jeff R. Donaldson, Dir.
Dr. Albert J. Carter, Cur.
Free Mon. - Fri. 9 AM - 5 PM; Sat. 12 - 4 PM; cl. Sun. Estab. 1930 to stimulate the study and appreciation of the fine arts in the University and community.

Collections: Kress Study Collection of Renaissance Paintings and Sculpture; Alain Locke Collection of African Art; Irving R. Gumbel Collection of Prints; †Agnes Delano Collection of Contemporary American Watercolors and Prints; †University collection of painting, sculpture and graphic arts by African Americans.

Activities: Changing exhibitions monthly; bi-monthly gallery lectures and community programs.

Library: Art Seminar Library, a reference library for graduate and undergraduate work of 2100 volumes, 18,000 photographs and 12,000 lantern slides.

Attendance: Approx. 24,000.

Publications: Native American Arts (serial), exhibition catalogues, informational brochures; catalog of the African and African-American collections.

INDIAN ARTS AND CRAFTS BOARD
United States Department of the Interior
Room 4004, 20240. Tel: (202) 343-2773
Lloyd H. New, Chmn.
Royal B. Hassrick, Commissioner
Howard Rock, Commissioner
William H. Crowe, Commissioner
Gerald J. Gray, Commissioner
Robert G. Hart, General Mgr.
Myles Libhart, Dir. of Museums, Exhibitions, and Publications
Estab. 1935; serves Indians, Eskimos and the general public as an informational, promotional and advisory clearing-house for all matters pertaining to the development of authentic Indian and Eskimo arts and crafts. Through its varied activities the Board promotes the artistic and cultural achievements of contemporary Indian and Eskimo artists and craftsmen to create demand and interest in the production of authentic products, and endeavors to provide the stimulation necessary to broaden markets and production resulting in direct economic benefit to Indian and Eskimo peoples. Under its Museum Program, the Board administers and operates the Museum of the Plains Indian, Browning, Mont.(q.v.); the Sioux Indian Museum, Rapid City, South Dakota (q.v.); and the Southern Plains Indian Museum, Anadarko, Oklahoma (q.v.).

Collections: Contemporary Indian and Eskimo arts of the United States, including †decorative arts, †folk arts, †painting, †sculpture, †graphics.

Exhibitions: Traveling exhibitions include (1971) Photographs and Poems by Sioux Children, organized by the Board's Sioux Indian Museum, Rapid City, S.Dak, regional tour under auspices of the S.Dak. Arts Council and the Tipi Shop, Inc; (1972) Contemporary Southern Plains Indian Painting, organized by the Board's Southern Plains Indian Museum, Anadarko, Okla, state tour under auspices of the Okla. Arts and Humanities Council and the Okla. Indian Arts and Crafts Cooperative; (1972) Contemporary Indian Artists—Mont, Wyo, Idaho, organized by the Board's Museum of the Plains Indian, Browning, Mont, regional tour by the Museum; (1974) Painted Tipis by Contemporary Plains Indian Artists, organized by the Board's Southern Plains Indian Museum, Anadarko, Okla, toured by the Museum; (1974) Coyote Tales of the Montana Salish, with illustrations by Frederick Roullier, organized by the Board's Museum of the Plains Indian, regional tour by the Museum; (1973-June 1975) 57 one-person exhibitions organized and presented at the Board's 3 regional Museums and through arrangements by Board's Southeastern Regional Office at Museums and galleries in N.C, Fla, Miss. and La.

Publications: Source Directories of Indian and Eskimo owned and operated businesses marketing Native American arts and crafts; Bibliography of Native American arts and crafts of the United States.

Attendance: Average total attendance at national and international exhibitions organized by the Board: 1,500,000.

INTERNATIONAL COUNCIL OF MUSEUMS COMMITTEE OF THE AMERICAN ASSOCIATION OF MUSEUMS
2233 Wisconsin Ave. NW, 20007. Tel: (202) 338-5300
Joseph Veach Noble, Pres.
Paul N. Perrot, V.Pres.
Susan M. Yecies, Prog. Coordinator
For further information see p. 6.

INTERNATIONAL EXHIBITIONS FOUNDATION
1729 H St. N.W, Suite 310, 20006. Tel: (202) 298-7010
Mrs. John A. Pope, Pres.
Robert D. Papkin, Secy.
Inc. as a nonprofit, tax-exempt organization in 1965, to organize and circulate throughout the United States and Canada, a number of special loan exhibitions in the fields of paintings, drawings, prints, photographs, sculpture and the decorative arts.

The first exhibition was Chinese Art from the Collection of H.M. the King of Sweden, which started its six-museum tour at the National Gallery of Art, September, 1966; British Watercolors, 1750-1850, from the Victoria and Albert Museum, London, followed in November, 1966, opening in Houston, Texas; Festival Designs by Inigo Jones from the Devonshire collection in Chatsworth, England, started on March 18, 1967, at the National Gallery of Art prior to a nationwide tour.

Additional major exhibitions: Masters of Modern Italian Art; Painting in France, 1900-1967; William Sidney Mount; Views of Florence and Tuscany by Giuseppe Zocchi; German Expressionist

Watercolors; Old Master Drawings from Chatsworth; African Sculpture; La Belle Epoque; Tiepolo Drawings; Chinese Gold, Silver and Porcelain: The Kempe Collection; Edward Lear in Greece; Tamarind: A Renaissance of Lithography; La Scala: 400 years of stage design; Diaghilev and Russian Stage Designers; Walter Gropius: buildings, plans, projects 1906-1969; Old Master Drawings from Christ Church, Oxford; Dutch Genre Drawings; Namban Art; Dogon Art; Venetian Drawings from American Collections; Contemporary Spanish Painters; Marc Chagall: Works on Paper.

JOHN F. KENNEDY CENTER FOR THE PERFORMING ARTS
20566. Tel: (202) 872-0466
Roger L. Stevens, Chmn. of the Board of Trustees
Harry C. McPherson, Jr, V.Chmn. of the Board
Sen. Charles H. Percy, V.Chmn. of the Board
Henry Strong, V.Chmn. of the Board
Ralph E. Becker, Gen. Counsel
Charlotte Woolard, Acting Secy.
W. Jarvis Moody, Treas.
Martin Feinstein, Exec. Dir. Performing Arts
The Center opened on September 8, 1971. Facilities include the 2200-seat Opera House, 2750-seat Concert Hall, 1130-seat Eisenhower Theater and 224-seat film theater (film theater operated by the American Film Institute)
Established September 1958 by Act of Congress as the National Cultural Center. A bureau of the Smithsonian Institution, but administered by a separate Board of Trustees, the Center is the sole official memorial in Washington to President Kennedy.

KLUTZNICK EXHIBIT HALL-ART GALLERY*
1640 Rhode Island Ave, N.W, 20036. Tel: (202) 293-5284
Dr. Abram Kanof, Chmn.
Robert Skostech, Cur.
Free Mon. - Fri. 1:30 - 5 PM; Sun. 10 AM - 5 PM; cl. Sat, national & Jewish holidays. Estab. 1957 for exhibits of Jewish faith artists; financed by membership. Two gallery rooms.
Collections: American Jewish History and art; Jewish ceremonial objects; archives of B'nai B'rith.
Exhibitions: Approx. 9 one-man shows annually.
Activities: Traveling exhibitions organized and circulated; collections of graphics lent to other institutions; guided tours. Book Shop.
Library: 8000 volume Judaica library; photograph collection; manuscripts; reading room.
Publications: Brochures for art exhibits; occasional historical pamphlet; Portfolio, Lincoln and the Jews; Portfolio, Ceremonies of Jews.

✠LIBRARY OF CONGRESS
Prints and Photographs Division
First St, between E. Capitol St. & Independence Ave, 20540.
Tel: Reference (202) 426-6394; Offices 426-5836; Motion Pictures 426-5840
Daniel J. Boorstin, Librn. of Congress
Alan Fern, Chief, Prints & Photographs Division
Jerry L. Kearns, Head, Reference Section
John Kuiper, Head, Motion Picture Section
Jerald Maddox, Head, Curatorial Section
Exhibition Halls open 8:30 AM - 9:30 PM; Sat. 8:30 AM - 9:30 PM; Sun. 11 AM - 9:30 PM.
Reading Room of the Division Mon. - Fri. 8:30 AM - 5 PM (except legal holidays).
Founded in 1897, The Prints and Photographs Division contains about 177,000 prints and drawings (50% American), approximately 70,000 posters, an estimated 8 million photographic items and over 200,000 reels of motion pictures.
Collections: Original prints of all schools and periods, increased annually by the Gardiner Greene Hubbard and J. & E. R. Pennell endowments. †Pennell Collection of Whistleriana; †early American lithographs; Japanese prints; †original drawings by American illustrators; †pictorial Archives of Early American Architecture including the Historic American Buildings Survey; Archive of Hispanic Culture; †Civil War drawings, prints, photographs and negatives; †outstanding among the collection of photographs and photographic negatives are the Farm Security Administration Collection, Red Cross Collection, Arnold Genthe, F. B. Johnston, Toni Frissell, Look Magazine. †The Motion Picture Section contains over 3000 motion pictures made between 1894 and 1912 and a large collection of German, Japanese, and Italian documentaries and feature films made prior to 1945. The bulk of the collection consists of selections among films registered for copyright since 1942. A cooperative acquisition and preservation program between the Library and the American Film Institute attempts to collect American films printed on perishable nitrate stock and to preserve them through transfer on safety film.
Exhibitions: Biennial National Exhibition of Prints made within the preceding two years, of which a catalog is published and which is available on loan (the 24th Exhibition held in 1975, in collaboration

with National Collection of Fine Arts, Smithsonian). Exhibitions from the collection are held at intervals.
Publications: Guide to the Special Collections of Prints and Photographs in the Library of Congress (1955-out of print). American Prints in the Library of Congress, published for Library of Congress by The Johns Hopkins Press, Baltimore (1970); Viewpoints (1975), for sale by Superintendent of Documents, U.S. Govt. Printing Office.

MINIATURE PAINTERS, SCULPTORS AND GRAVERS SOCIETY OF WASHINGTON, D.C.
c/o Edith Trifiletti, Secy, 1711 Massachusetts Ave. N.W. 20036.
Evelyn A. Gladstone, Pres.
June T. Harriman, V.Pres.
Ralph Smith, Treas.
Dorothy Van H. Harrison, Historian
Eleanor Cox, Recorder
Organized 1931 to encourage art in Miniature. Mem. 59; dues $5. Holds annual exhibition which is an open International Show. No purchase awards; 6 prize awards at annual fall show.

✠MUSEUM OF AFRICAN ART
318 A St. N.E, 20002. Tel: (202) 547-7424
Warren M. Robbins, Dir.
Nancy Cromwell, Pub. Information Officer
Open Mon. - Fri. 11 AM - 5 PM; Sat. & Sun. Noon - 5 PM. Estab. 1963, opened 1964.
Collections: African sculpture, textiles, crafts and musical instruments (5000 items); 19th and 20th century Afro-American paintings and sculpture; photographic archives of 150,000 items including slides, films and prints.
Exhibitions: Traditional African art (changing exhibits); The Influence of African Sculpture on Modern Art; Animals in African Art; The Photography of Eliot Elisofon - African art and environment.
Activities: Public tours Wed. and Sat. 3:30 PM; lecture-discussion tours by appointment; extension programs (exhibits and lectures). Book shop with titles on African and Afro-American history, culture and art; African art reproductions; Boutique Africa, featuring quality crafts, jewelry and clothing imported from Africa.
Publications: Multimedia slide kit, The Creative Heritage of Africa; catalogues: The Language of African Art, African Art in Washington Collections, African Art: the de Havenon Collection; Tribute to Africa, the Sculpture and Photography of Eliot Elisofon; Miniature African Sculpture: the Weaving Pulley Collection of Harold Rome.
Attendance: 85,000.

MUSEUM OF THE UNITED STATES DEPARTMENT OF THE INTERIOR
C St. between 18th & 19th Sts. N.W, 20240. Tel: (202) 343-5016
Secy. of the Interior, ex-officio
Herbert Hallman, Exhibit Specialist
Free Mon. - Fri. 8 AM - 4 PM. Organized 1938 to visualize and explain to the public through works of art and other media the history, aims, and activities of the Department. The Museum occupies 10 galleries in a wing on the first floor of the Interior Department Building.
Collections: Oil paintings of early American explorers by William Henry Jackson; oil paintings of Western conservation scenes by Wilfrid Swancourt Bronson; Wildlife paintings by Walter Weber; Antarctic painting by Leland Curtis; murals; miniature dioramas; sculpture groups; watercolor and black and white illustrations; Indian arts and crafts; Colburn collection of Indian basketry; Gibson collection of Indian materials. †General collection of Indian, Eskimo and South Sea Islands and Virgin Islands arts and crafts, documents, maps, charts, etc.
Publications: Illustrated Museum brochure.
Attendance: Approx. 100,000.

NATIONAL AIR AND SPACE MUSEUM
7th & Independence Ave. SW, 20560. Tel: (202) 381-4156
Free, scheduled to open to the public, July 4, 1976, 10 AM - 9 PM during the summer; 10 AM - 5 PM during the winter. The Museum was established in 1946, with art acquisitions having been much more recent, to memorialize the national development of aviation and space flight with about 5000 square feet of gallery devoted to the theme, Flight and the Arts; financed through the Smithsonian Institution
Collections: Collection has been formed by donations only.
Exhibitions: Works from the collection have been exhibited continuously until June, 1975 at the Smithsonian Institution in Washington, D.C. and in various parts of the world under the auspices of the U.S.I.A; new exhibition will start July 4, 1976.
Activities: Special educational activities; lectures open to the public; Museum shop includes books.
Library: Extensive files of aerospace related photographs for reference.
Attendance: 6,000,000 expected.

NATIONAL ARCHITECTURAL ACCREDITING BOARD*
   1735 New York Ave, 20006.
Helen S. Steele, Exec. Secy.
For further information see p. 8.

✣NATIONAL COLLECTION OF FINE ARTS
   Eighth & G Sts, N.W, 20560. Tel: (202) 381-5180
Joshua C. Taylor, Dir.
Harry Lowe, Asst. Dir.
Harry Jordan, Asst. Dir. for Admin.
W. Robert Johnston, Registrar
Walter Hopps, Cur, 20th Century Painting & Sculpture
William H. Truettner, Cur. 18th & 19th Century Painting &
   Sculpture
Janet A. Flint, Cur. Prints & Drawings
Peter Bermingham, Cur. Educ.
Lloyd E. Herman, Dir, Renwick Gallery
Lois M. Fink, Research Cur.
Adelyn D. Breeskin, Consultant, 20th Century Painting & Sculpture
Abigail Booth, Coordinator, Bicentennial Inventory of American
   Paintings
David Keeler, Chief, Office of Exhibition & Design
Lois A Bingham, Chief, Office of Exhibitions Abroad
Thomas Carter, Conservator
Stefano Scafetta, Conservator
Katherine Eirk, Conservator
Carroll Clark, Ed, Office of Publ.
William B. Walker, Librn, National Collection of Fine Arts &
   National Portrait Gallery
Margery Byers, Chief, Office of Pub. Affairs
Michael Fischer, Photographer, Office of Registrar
Free daily 10 AM - 5:30 PM; cl. Christmas. Estab. 1846 as part of
the Smithsonian Institution and designated the National Gallery of Art
in 1906. Title changed to National Collection of Fine Arts in 1937.
The museum is now primarily concerned with the study and presenta-
tion of American art from its beginnings to the present.
   Collections: The collection of paintings, sculpture, prints, and
drawings numbers over 17,000. It represents a wide range of
American work, with particular strength in the late nineteenth and
early twentieth century. Major collections include those of Harriet
Lane Johnston (1906), William T. Evans (1907), John Gellatly (1929),
and more recently, the S. C. Johnson and Son collection of paintings
from the 1960s. There is a sizeable collection of portrait miniatures. All works not on display are available for examination by
scholars.
   Exhibitions: A representative selection of works from the collection are on permanent display in the galleries, providing a comprehensive view of the varied aspects of American art. Most temporary
exhibitions, some twenty-five a year, are originated by the staff,
many as part of the program to investigate less well-known aspects
of American art. They include both studies of individual artists,
such as W. H. Johnson, Ilya Bolotowsky and Lilly Martin Spencer,
and thematic studies such as Art of the Pacific Northwest, Pennsylvania Academy Moderns, and Academy: The Academic Tradition in
American Art. Major exhibitions are accompanied by authoritative
publications, small exhibitions by checklists. Exhibitions on design
and crafts are shown in the Renwick Gallery (q.v). A gallery, Explore, presents material of special interest to children, as well as
adults, and the gallery, Discover, serves the Department of Education for related exhibitions. A small area is devoted to a representation of other than American works. The museum also circulates exhibitions abroad on a regular basis.
   Activities: The Department of Education carries on an active program with the schools and the general public, offering imaginative
participatory tours for children, a Discover Graphics program which
includes a print workshop, and varied presentations of exhibitions,
lectures, symposia, and concerts. A research program in American
art is maintained for visiting scholars, and training is carried on
through internship in general museum practice and conservation.
The Bicentennial Inventory of American Paintings Executed Before
1914 is compiling a computer list of largely uncatalogued works from
throughout the country.
   National Collection of Fine Arts and National Portrait Gallery
Library: Contains 26,000 volumes, a photograph collection, a slide
library, clipping files, and original documents. The Archives of
American Art, a separate Smithsonian bureau, is located in the
library.
   Attendance: 322,000 average.
Renwick Gallery
   17th St. & Pennsylvania Ave. N.W, 20560. Tel: (202) 381-5811
Lloyd E. Herman, Dir.
Free daily 10 AM - 5:30 PM; cl. Christmas.
   James Renwick, Jr.'s 1859 building, designed as the first
Corcoran Gallery of Art, was reopened as a museum in Jan. 1972.
As the Renwick Gallery of the National Collection of Fine Arts, Smith-
sonian Institution, the building houses changing American crafts and
design exhibitions; films, lectures, and public programs to augment

the exhibitions; selected exhibitions from other countries. Restored
to its French Second Empire elegance after 67 years as the United
States Court of Claims, the building has two public rooms with period
furnishings, the Grand Salon and the Octagon Room, as well as eight
exhibition areas.
   Exhibitions: Since its opening, the Renwick Gallery has presented
36 special exhibitions including The Arts and Crafts Movement in
America 1876-1916, Form and Fire: Natzler Ceramics 1939-1972,
Shaker, The Goldsmith (organized in conjunction with the Minnesota
Museum of Art), Figure and Fantasy and Craft Multiples, an exhibition of 133 useful objects produced in multiples of at least ten, selected by national competition. In galleries devoted to exhibitions of
other nations, 200 Years of Royal Copenhagen Porcelain received
special attention. Major exhibitions are accompanied by publications,
smaller exhibitions by checklists.
   Activities: To augment the schedule of changing exhibitions, the
Renwick Gallery presents film programs and lectures emphasizing
the creative work of American designers and craftsmen as well as
complementing the exhibitions from other countries. Other special
educational activities have included tours of the building and of special exhibitions, a tour for children called 'The Design Experience,'
a series of craft demonstrations in conjunction with the Craft Multiples exhibition, and concerts of both traditional and contemporary
music.
   Attendance: (1974) 170,000.

NATIONAL COUNCIL OF ARCHITECTURAL REGISTRATION
   BOARDS*
   1735 New York Ave. N.W, Suite 700, 20006. Tel: (202) 659-3996
Hayden P. Mims, Exec. Dir.
For further information see p. 9.

NATIONAL ENDOWMENT FOR THE ARTS
   20506. Tel: (202) 634-6369
Miss Nancy Hanks, Chmn. of the Endowment of the National
   Council on the Arts, the Endowment's advisory body.
For further information see p. 9.

✣NATIONAL GALLERY OF ART*
   Constitution Ave. at Sixth St. N.W, 20565. Tel: (202) 737-4215
      Board of Trustees
The Chief Justice of the United States, Chmn.
The Secretary of State
The Secretary of the Treasury
The Secretary of the Smithsonian Institution
Paul Mellon
John Hay Whitney
Franklin D. Murphy
Lessing J. Rosenwald
Stoddard M. Stevens
      Officers and Staff
Paul Mellon, Pres.
John Hay Whitney, V.Pres.
J. Carter Brown, Dir.
David W. Scott, Consultant, Bldg. Program
Robert C. Engle, Construction Mgr.
Richard Bales, Asst to Dir, Music
W. Howard Adams, Asst. to Dir, National Programs
Katherine Warwick, Asst. to Dir, Pub. Information
Robert L. Pell, Asst. to Dir, Special Events
Elizabeth J. Foy, Administrative Asst.
Robert Amory, Jr, Secy. & Gen. Counsel
Mabel A. Barry, Gen. Attorney
Charles P. Parkhurst, Asst. Dir.
William P. Campbell, Cur. American Painting & Index of American
   Design
C. Douglas Lewis, Jr, Cur. Sculpture
Konrad Oberhuber, Research Cur.
J. M. Edelstein, Chief Librn.
Margaret I. Bouton, Chief Educ. & Pub. Programs
Alessandro Contini-Bonacossi, Cur. Photographic Archives
Theodore S. Amussen, Editor
Jack C. Spinx, Chief Exhibitions
Victor Covey, Chief Conservator
Peter Davidock, Jr, Registrar
Henry B. Beville, Chief Photographic Laboratory
David E. Rust, Cur. French Painting since 1700
Gaillard F. Ravenel, Cur.
H. Diane Russell, Cur.
Lloyd D. Hayes, Treas.
Joseph G. English, Adminr.
George W. Riggs, Asst. Adminr.
John Hand, Cur. Northern European Painting to 1700
Andrew Robinson, Jr, Cur. Graphic Arts
Sheldon Grossman, Cur. Later Italian Painting
Ross Watson, Cur. British Painting
E. A. Carmean Cur. 20th Century Art
David Brown, Cur. Italian Renaissance Painting

Anna M. Voris, Cur. Early Italian Painting
Robert L. Feller, Cur. Analytical Laboratory
Elsie V. H. Ferber, Cur. Art Information
Charles I. Suplee, Bldg. Supt.
Jacob Brickman, Captain of the Guard
Jeremiah J. Barrett, Personnel Officer
Max A. Leason, Chief Publ.
Donald Hand, Asst. Horticulturist
Free weekdays, 10 AM - 5 PM; Sun. 12 AM - 9 PM. Apr. 1 through
Labor Day, weekdays 10 AM - 9 PM, Sun. 12 AM - 9 PM; cl. Christ-
mas and New Year's Day. Estab. 1937; Gallery opened 1941; Fed-
eral appropriation and private endowment. Paintings, sculpture and
graphic arts, from the 12th to 20th centuries, belonging to the Nation,
to represent the best in the artistic heritage of America and Europe.

Collections: Contains the Andrew W. Mellon collection of 126
paintings and 26 pieces of sculpture, which included such masterpieces as Raphael's The Alba Madonna, the Niccolini-Cowper
Madonna, and St. George and the Dragon; van Eyck's Annunciation;
Botticelli's Adoration of the Magi; and nine Rembrandts. Twenty-one
of these paintings came from the Hermitage. Also in the original
gift were the Vaughan Portrait of George Washington, by Gilbert
Stuart, and The Washington Family, by Edward Savage. The National
Gallery's collection continues to be built by private donation, rather
than through government funds, which serve solely to operate and
maintain the Gallery, and other donations quickly followed Mr.
Mellon's. The Samuel H. Kress Collection, given to the nation over a
period of years, includes the great tondo of The Adoration of the Magi
by Fra Angelico and Fra Filippo Lippi, the Laocoön by El Greco, and
fine examples by Giorgione, Titian, Grünewald, Dürer, Memling,
Bosch, Francois Clouet, Poussin, Watteau, Chardin, Boucher, Fragonard, David, and Ingres. Also included were a number of masterpieces of Italian and French sculpture. The Widener Collection consists of fourteen Rembrandts, eight van Dycks, two Vermeers, major
works of Italian, Spanish, English, and French painting, and Italian
and French sculpture and decorative arts. The Chester Dale Collection included masterpieces by Manet, Cézanne, Renoir, Toulouse-
Lautrec, Monet, Modigliani, Pissarro, Degas, van Gogh, Gauguin,
Matisse, Picasso, Braque, and the American painter, George Bellows.
Several major works of art by some of the most important artists of
the last hundred years, such as Picasso, Cézanne, Gauguin, and the
American painter Walt Kuhn, were given to the Gallery in 1972 by the
W. Averell Harriman Foundation in memory of Marie N. Harriman.
Paintings to round out the collection have been bought with funds pro-
vided by the late Ailsa Mellon Bruce, daughter of Andrew W. Mellon.
Most important among them is the portrait of Ginevra de'Benci, the
only generally acknowledged painting by Leonardo da Vinci outside
Europe. Among others are Rubens' Daniel in the Lions' Den, Claude
Lorrain's Judgment of Paris, Saint George and the Dragon attributed
to van der Weyden, and a number of American paintings, including
Thomas Cole's second set of The Voyage of Life. Among recent
acquisitions is Picasso's Femme Nue, key work of the artist's analytical cubist period. The National Gallery's rapidly expanding
graphic arts holdings, in great part given by Lessing J. Rosenwald,
numbers about 30,000 items and dates from the 12th century to the
present. Mr. Rosenwald's gift, one of the world's great collections of
prints and drawings, forms the nucleus of the Gallery's holdings in
this field. The Index of American Design contains over 17,000 watercolor renderings and 22,000 photographs of American crafts and folk
arts.

Exhibitions (Selected exhibitions Jan. 1970 through Dec. 1973):
Masterpieces of African Sculpture; William Blake's Graphic Art from
the Rosenwald Collection; The Reality of Appearance, Trompe l'Oeil
Tradition in American Painting; 19th and 20th-Century Paintings from
the Collection of the Smith College Museum of Art; Selections from
the Nathan Cummings Collection; Mary Cassatt 1844-1925; British
Painting and Sculpture 1960 - 1970; Käthe Kollwitz; Prints and Drawings; Ingres in Rome; William Hogarth; Paintings from the Collection
of Mr. and Mrs. Paul Mellon; Dürer in America: His Graphic Work;
The Art of Wilhelm Lehmbruck; Old Master Drawings from Christ
Church, Oxford; Frederick Law Olmsted/USA; a Survey of the Mezzotint Technique; The Far North: 2000 Years of American Eskimo and
American Indian Art; Impressionist and Post-Impressionist Paintings
from the U.S.S.R; Etchings by Rembrandt; Prints of the Italian Renaissance; American Impressionist Painting; Drawings from the
Janos Scholz Collection; American Art at Mid-Century I; Drawings
by François Boucher.

Activities: Sunday lectures by distinguished guest speakers and
members of the Gallery staff are given throughout the year. The
A. W. Mellon Lectures in the Fine Arts are delivered as a series
each spring by an outstanding scholar (1973: J. Barzun; 1974: H. W.
Janson). General tours and lectures are given in the Gallery by
members of the Education department throughout the week. Special
tours are arranged for groups of visitors. An electronic guide service on exhibits in 30 rooms broadcasts brief lectures. This service,
called LecTour, as well as the Acoustiguide, which includes a "Director's Tour" and guides to special exhibitions, are available for a
small rental fee at the Mall entrance to the Gallery. Civilization,

Pioneers of Modern Painting, The American Vision, and other films
relating to the collections are given frequently free of charge in the
Gallery's auditorium. Concerts are held in the East Garden Court
each Sunday evening between September and June at 7 PM, also
without charge. The Office of Extension Services lends groups of
color slides with lecture texts and prints of motion pictures. The
borrower pays only the return postage. Color reproductions, slides,
slide strips, film strips, catalogues, and other publications may be
purchased from the Publications Office. Photographs of objects in
the Gallery's collection are available from the Photographic Service.

Library: 67,500 volumes on the history of fine arts and related
fields; photographic archives.

Attendance: Average daily attendance, fiscal 1972, 4710.
The National Gallery of Art offers four fellowship programs:

Samuel H. Kress Fellowship is based on recommendations by the
National Gallery Fellowship Committee under the chairmanship of
the Kress Professor-in-Residence. The duration of this fellowship
is one year's residence at the National Gallery. The purpose of the
Kress Fellowship is "to make the resources of the National Gallery
available to outstanding scholars and thereby expand the Gallery's
scholarly activities." This fellowship is made possible by a grant
from the Trustees of the Samuel H. Kress Foundation.

David E. Finley Fellowship is also based on recommendations
by the National Gallery Fellowship Committee under the chairmanship of the Kress Professor-in-Residence. The duration of this
fellowship is two and half years, the first two for study in Europe and
the last six months in residence at the National Gallery. The purpose
of the Finley Fellowship is "to encourage and train qualified candidates for professional careers in museum work." This fellowship,
which includes a travel stipend, is made possible by a grant from the
Andrew W. Mellon Foundation.

Chester Dale Fellowship is also based on recommendations by
the National Gallery Fellowship Committee under the chairmanship
of the Kress Professor-in-Residence. The duration of this fellowship is one year's residence at the National Gallery. It is made
possible under the will of Chester Dale.

Robert H. and Clarice Smith Fellowship, based on recommendations by the National Gallery Fellowship Committee, is also under
the chairmanship of the Kress Professor-in-Residence. The duration
of this fellowship is one year and may be taken either at the National
Gallery or abroad. The purpose of the Smith Fellowship is the study
of Dutch or Flemish art history. This fellowship is made possible by
a grant from Robert H. and Clarice Smith.

NATIONAL MUSEUM OF HISTORY AND TECHNOLOGY*
Constitution Ave. between 12th & 14th Sts, N.W, 20560.
Tel: (202) 381-5785
Brooke Hindle, Dir.
Vladimir Clain-Stefanelli, Chmn, Dept. Applied Arts
Eugene Ostroff, Cur. & Supv, Div. Photography
Dr. Elizabeth M. Harris, Assoc Cur, Div. Graphic Arts
Free daily 10 AM - 5 PM; extended spring and summer hours de-
termined yearly; cl. Christmas. Estab. 1846 as part of the Smith-
sonian Institution; the separate building for this museum opened in
1964; financed by federal appropriation.

Collections: †50,000 specimens of woodcuts, etchings, lithographs
and other prints including photo-mechanical work, and technical
equipment.

Exhibitions: Permanent, temporary and traveling exhibitions.

Activities: Docent program; lectures; gallery talks; guided
tours; concerts; TV and radio programs. Restaurant.

Library: 150,000 volumes of books and periodicals on American
history, technology, science, culture, military for interlibrary
loan and reference; manuscripts.

Publications: Catalogs; guidebooks; scholarly publications;
pamphlets; monographs.

Dept. of Cultural History: Harry T. Peters, America on Stone,
lithography collection of 1700 lithographs.

Section of Photography: †Photography collection starting with da-
guerre-o-types and other early methods and culminating in contemporary pictorial work. Frequent special exhibitions.

Section of Graphic Arts: Processes of the graphic arts including
hand methods and photo-mechanical operations shown through technical and historical exhibits. Frequent special exhibits.

Attendance: 7,000,000 average.

✠NATIONAL PORTRAIT GALLERY
F & Eighth Sts. N.W, 20007. Tel. (202) 381-5380
Marvin Sakik, Dir.
Douglas E. Evelyn, Asst. Dir.
Robert G. Stewart, Cur.
J. Michael Carrigan, Chief of Exhibits Design
Beverly Cox, Coordinator of Exhibits
Dennis O'Toole, Cur. of Educ.
Suzanne Jenkins, Registrar
Mona Dearborn, Keeper of the Catalogue of American Portraits
Felrath Hines, Conservator

Carol Cutler, Public Affairs Officer
Marc Pachter, Historian
William Walker, Librn.
Free daily 10 AM - 5:30 PM; cl. Christmas. Estab. 1962 under
the Smithsonian Institution as a museum of history and biography,
told through portraiture and statuary depicting the men and women
who have made significant contributions to the history, development, and culture of the people of the United States; financed by
government appropriation. The National Portrait Gallery
Commission meets two times a year.
Collections: Over 800 items; portraiture from 17th century
to the present; paintings, statuary, miniatures, reliefs, prints,
sculpture; on permanent exhibition is the Presidential Corridor,
an assemblage of portraits from George Washington onward.
All collections are constantly being enlarged. It is hoped that the
Gallery's charter will be rewritten to permit the purchase of
photographs.
Exhibitions: (1973-76) The Black Presence in the Era of the
American Revolution, 1770-1800; American Self-Portraits; In
the Minds and Hearts of the People: Prologue to the American
Revolution, 1760-1774; The Dye is Now Cast: The Road to
American Independence, 1774-1776; Portraits from the Americans:
The Democratic Experience.
Activities: Guided tours of permanent collections and tempo-
rary exhibitions; special presentations to school groups in the
field and in museum; traveling exhibitions organized and circulated; original objects of art lent, color reproductions, 1000
photographs, lantern slides, Kodachromes; lectures open to the
public; 1 tour per day for 6 weeks; fellowships. Restaurant; Book
Shop.
Library: 26,000 volumes on American art, biography and
history for reference; subscriptions to 850 publications.
Publications: Major historical books to accompany exhibitions;
teaching guides in booklet form prepared by the Gallery's Education Department primarily for secondary schools in the area
and throughout the country.
Attendance: 375,000.

NATIONAL TRUST FOR HISTORIC PRESERVATION
740-748 Jackson Pl, N.W, 20006. Tel: (202) 638-5200
Carlisle H. Humelsine, Chmn.
James Biddle, Pres.
Lawson B. Knott, Jr, Exec. V.Pres.
William G. Arey, Asst. Exec. V.Pres.
Terry B. Morton, V.Pres. & Ed, The Preservation Press
Russell V. Keune, V.Pres, Office of Preservation Services
James C. Massey, V.Pres, Office of Properties
William W. Morrison, V.Pres, Office of Public Affairs
Belle Grove, Middletown, Va; Casa Amesti and Cooper-Molera
Adobe, Monterey, Calif; Chesterwood, Stockbridge, Mass; Cliveden,
Philadelphia; Decatur House, Washington, D.C; Lyndhurst, Tarry-
town, N.Y; Oatlands, Leesburg, Va; Shadows-on-the-Teche, New
Iberia, La; Woodlawn Plantation and The Pope-Leighey House,
Mount Vernon, Va; The Woodrow Wilson House, Washington, D.C.
Chartered by Congress Oct. 26, 1949, as a non-profit, educational
organization to encourage public participation in historic preserva-
tion, and to own and administer for public benefit sites, buildings and
objects significant in American history and culture. Ann. conference
Oct; mem. individual 86,342, libraries, organizations, foundations,
2467, corporations 93; dues from $5.
Collections: At Trust properties.
Activities: Educational program; clearing house of information
on preservation; professional consultations; lecture series; administration of historic properties.
Publications: Historic Preservation, published quarterly;
Preservation News, monthly newspaper; technical leaflet series;
technical and advisory fact sheets; booklets of Trust-owned properties.

THE OCTAGON*
American Institute of Architects Foundation
1799 New York Ave, N.W, 20006. Tel: (202) 638-3105
Francis D. Lethbridge, Pres. of the AIA Foundation
David N. Yerkes, Chmn. of the Octagon Comt.
Jeanne F. Butler, Adminr. of the Octagon & Cur. of the AIA Gallery
Elinor E. Stearns, Asst. to the Adminr.
Free Tues. - Sat. 10 AM - 4 PM; Sun. 1 - 4 PM; cl. Mon. The
Octagon House was purchased by the American Institute of Archi-
tects in 1902 and in 1943 The American Institute of Architects
Foundation was incorporated. The significance of the Octagon is
twofold. Architecturally, it is an excellent example of Federal
period architecture designed by noted architect, Doctor William
Thornton, also architect of the Capitol. Built in 1800, the Octagon
served as a winter residence for the wealthy Virginia planter,
Colonel John Tayloe. Historically, the Octagon played an important
part in the War of 1812. After the burning of the White House by
the British in 1814, President James Madison and his wife Dolley

resided in the Octagon. The Treaty of Ghent, ending the War of
1812, was ratified in the second floor oval study of the Octagon.
Collections: The Octagon is furnished with pieces of the period
of Colonel Tayloe's residence, 1800-1828, though few are original
furnishings. These pieces represent fine examples of the Chippendale, Sheraton, and Hepplewhite styles of early nineteenth century.
The rooms are arranged and decorated as they are believed to
have been when the Tayloes occupied the Octagon.
Exhibitions: Generally photographic, change approximately every
six weeks and relate to architecture and its allied arts. Exhibits
have ranged from Contemporary Architecture of Brazil, 240 Years
of Courthouse Architecture in America, the Architecture of Bernard
Ralph Maybeck, among others, to planned exhibits such as Japanese
House and Temple Gardens, Mississippi Folk Architecture, and
Montana Ghost Towns, to name only a few.
Publications: Descriptive brochure.
Annual Income: Approx. $60,000 from endowment and AIA con-
tribution.
Attendance: Average past two years, approx. 25,000.

ORGANIZATION OF AMERICAN STATES - GENERAL
SECRETARIAT
17th St, Constitution Ave. & C St, N.W, 20006
Alejandro Orfila, Secy. General
Jorge L. Zelaya, Asst. Secy. General
Free 9 AM - 4:30 PM. Estab. 1890 to foster mutual understanding
and cooperation among the American Republics. Pan American
Union Building erected 1910, contains permanent exhibits, sculp-
tured Aztec fountain and busts of national heroes.
Activities: The Visual Arts Unit organizes monthly Latin
American art exhibits in the building and circulates art exhibits in
the United States and abroad, keeps photographic files on Latin
American art and produces documentary films on art subjects. The
Music and Folklore Unit promotes exchange of musicians and orga-
nizes concerts and triennial Inter-American music festivals.
Publications: Americas (monthly); Inter-American Review of
Bibliography, a quarterly with contributions in English, Spanish,
Portuguese and French.

✤THE PHILLIPS COLLECTION
1600 21st St, N.W, 20009. Tel: (202) 387-2151
Laughlin Phillips, Dir.
James M. McLaughlin, Assoc. Cur.
John Gernand, Registrar & Archivist
Willem de Looper, Asst. Cur.
Charles Crowder, in Charge of Music
Free weekdays 10 AM - 5 PM; Sun. 2 - 7 PM; cl. Mon. Estab. and
inc. 1918 as a gallery of modern art and its sources.
Collections: Permanent collection of paintings, primarily 19th and
20th century American and European, with frequent loan exhibitions.
Activities: Docent service; free lectures and concerts; color re-
productions, slides, catalogs and other publications may be purchased
at Publications Desk; weekly Sat. tour at 3 PM.
Attendance: 78,000 annually.

PRINT COUNCIL OF AMERICA
National Gallery of Art, 20565
Andrew Robison, Pres.
Grace M. Mayer, Treas.
Estab. 1956. A nonprofit organization fostering the appreciation
of fine prints, new and old. Ann. meeting Apr. or May. Occasional
publications on old and modern prints.

PUBLIC LIBRARY OF THE DISTRICT OF COLUMBIA*
Martin Luther King Memorial Library, 901 G. St. N.W, 20001.
Tel: (202) 727-1111
Milton S. Byam, Dir.
Lois Kent Stiles, Chief, Art Division
Free Sat. 9 AM - 5:30 PM; Sun. 1 - 5 PM; Mon. - Fri. 9 AM - 9 PM;
Estab. 1896. Art Division, in Central Library, contains †reference
and circulating books and periodicals on architecture, painting,
sculpture, photography, graphic and applied arts. †An extensive pamphlet file includes all art subjects, with special emphasis on individ-
ual American artists and on more than 400 artists active in the area
of the District of Columbia. †A circulating picture collection numbers over 65,118 mounted reproductions and †290 framed prints.
†Films and filmstrips on art are in the Film Division of the library.
Collections are used by individuals, clubs, colleges and universities;
public, private and parochial schools, and miscellaneous organizations. Special exhibitions held occasionally.
Income: $9081.

✤SMITHSONIAN INSTITUTION
1000 Jefferson Dr, SW, 20560. Tel: (202) 628- 4422
The Chief Justice of the United States, Chancellor of the Board of
Regents, which consists of the Vice President, three Members
of the Senate, three Members of the House of Representatives
and six Citizen Members.

S. Dillon Ripley, Secy.
Robert A. Brooks, Under Secy.
David Challinor, Asst. Secy. for Science
Charles Blitzer, Asst. Secy. for History & Art
Julian Euell, Asst. Secy. for Public Service
Paul N. Perrot, Asst. Secy. for
    Museum Programs
Free daily 10 AM - 5:30 PM; extended spring and summer hours
determined yearly; cl. Christmas; Bicentennial hours (1976), Apr.
through Labor Day open until 9 PM. Estab. 1846. James Smithson
bequeathed his fortune to the United States to found, at Washington,
under the name of the Smithsonian Institution, an establishment for
the increase and diffusion of knowledge among men. To carry out
Smithson's mandate, the Institution performs fundamental research;
publishes the results of studies, explorations, and investigations;
preserves for study and reference about 65 million items of scientific, cultural, and historical interest; maintains exhibits representative of the arts, American history, aeronautics and space exploration, technology, and natural history; participates in the international
exchange of learned publications; and engages in programs of education and national and international cooperative research and training.
Board of Regents meets three times yearly, January, May and September.
    The individual bureaus concerned with art under the Smithsonian
Institution (each reported separately) are as follows:

National Gallery of Art
    Constitution Ave. at Sixth St, N.W, 20565.
    (Administered under separate Board of Trustees)

Freer Gallery of Art
    12th & Jefferson Dr, S.W, 20560.

National Air and Space Museum
    7th & Independence Ave, S.W, 20560.

National Collection of Fine Arts (including the Renwick Gallery)
    Eighth & G St, N.W, 20560.

National Portrait Gallery
    Eighth & F St, N.W, 20560.

National Museum of History and Technology
    Constitution Ave. between 12th & 14th St, N.W, 20560.

John F. Kennedy Center for the Performing Arts
    20566.
    (Administered under separate Board of Trustees)
Archives of American Art
    41 E. 65th St, New York, N.Y. 10021.

Cooper-Hewitt Museum of Decorative Arts and Design
    9 E. 90th St, New York, N.Y. 10028.

Joseph H. Hirshhorn Museum and Sculpture Garden
    900 Jefferson Drive, S.W. 20560.

    Attendance: More than 20,000,000 (not limited to art bureaus).

SOCIETY OF FEDERAL ARTISTS AND DESIGNERS*
    c/o Charles R. Gailes, 715 E. Capital, 20003.
William Caldwell, Pres.
Estab. 1951 as a professional society of government employees involved in the planning, production and procurement of federal
visual communications; financed by membership. Meetings monthly,
Sept. - May; mem. 400; dues $10 and $15.
    Exhibitions: Annual Awards Show.
    Activities: Lectures for members only; 5-8 visiting lecturers
per year; 1-2 tours.
    Publications: Newsletter and Catalogue of annual exhibit, 10
issues yearly.

SOCIETY OF WASHINGTON PRINTMAKERS*
    c/o Prentiss Taylor, Pres, J 718 Arlington Towers, Arlington,
Va. 22209. Tel: (703) 522-3286
Isabella Walker, V.Pres.
Keiko Moore, Treas.
Lila Asher, Recording Secy.
Aline Feldman, Corresp. Secy.
Estab. 1934 as Society of Washington Etchers; name changed 1953.
Ann. meeting in Fall; mem. 60; dues $4. Presents National Print
Exhibitions, open to all printmakers and Members' Exhibitions,
alternating on a biennial basis. Purchase prizes presented to Li-
brary of Congress and Smithsonian Graphic Arts collections.

TEXTILE MUSEUM
    2320 S St, N.W, 20008. Tel: (202) 667-0441
John Ramsey Pugh, Pres. Board of Trustees
Arthur D. Jenkins, V.Pres.
Ward W. Dworshak, Treas.
Ralph S. Yohe, Secy.
Andrew Oliver, Jr, Dir.

Louise W. Mackie, Cur. Old World
Ann P. Rowe, Asst. Cur. New World
Patricia Fiske, Asst. Cur. Old World
Irene Emery, Cur. Emeritus, Technical Studies
Clarissa K. Palmai, Conservator
Katherine Freshley, Librn.
Petronel Lukens, Editor
Lilo Markrich, Museum Shop Dir.
May H. Beattie, Research Assoc. Islamic Rugs
Charles Grant Ellis, Research Assoc. Oriental Rugs
Mattiebelle Gittinger, Research Assoc. Southeast Asian Textiles
Mary Elizabeth King, Research Assoc. New World Textiles.
Free Tues. - Sat. 10 AM - 5 PM; cl. legal holidays. Founded by
George Hewitt Myers, inc. 1925 as a nonprofit, educational institu-
tion. The Museum is devoted to the preservation, exhibition and
study of ancient and modern handwoven rugs and textiles, New and
Old World, but generally excluding material from Western Europe
and other regions affected by the Industrial Revolution. Mem. approx. 1200; dues individual $20, family $30, contributing $50, sup-
porting $100, sustaining $500, sponsor $1000, patron (life asso-
ciate), $5000, benefactor (life associate) $10,000.
    Collections: 800 rugs and 9000 textiles from all areas of the
world where significant weaving was practiced except as stated
above. Old World: rich holdings of rugs from Asia Minor, the
Caucasus, Egypt, Islamic Spain, Persia, India and China. Strong
holdings of Coptic and Islamic archaeological textiles from Egypt,
also archaeological textiles from Syria, Iraq, Spain, India and more
recent textiles from Iran, Turkey, Greece, North Africa, India,
Indonesia, Japan and China. New World: one of the best collections
in the world of Peruvian archaeological textiles; also smaller collection of ethnographic textiles from Peru, Guatemala, Mexico and the
Southwest United States. Minor holdings of ethnographic textiles
from the Northwest coast and from Panama.
    Exhibitions: Changing exhibitions of rugs and textiles from the
collection as well as art from other institutions.
    Activities: Illustrated lectures; gallery tours; weekly rug appre-
ciation sessions; annual symposium, Irene Emery Round Table, on
various aspects of textiles. Rug convention held annually. Craft
classes in needlework and textile techniques. Museum shop.
    Conservation: The laboratory serves not only the Museum but
is available to other institutions that require specialty work on textiles.
    Library: Arthur D. Jenkins Library containing approx. 7000
volumes covering the collection and related areas with a cross-
indexed card catalog. Designed to be a library of record within the
field, it serves the research of the staff as well as visiting students
and scholars. Open to the public.
    Publications: Journal, annually; Museum Associates' Newsletter,
quarterly. Catalogs of exhibition and books relating to the Museum's
collection and activities, issued several times a year.

TRINITY COLLEGE LIBRARY
    Michigan Ave. & Franklin, N.E, 20017. Tel: (202) 269-2255
Sister Dorothy Beach, Librn.
Open Mon. - Thurs. 9 AM - 11 PM; Fri. 9 AM - 5 PM; Sat. 10 AM -
5 PM; Sun. 1 PM - 11 PM. Library estab. 1900.
    Volumes: (1975) 138,875.
    Budget 1975-76: Materials budget: $32,900; total budget: $107,467.

TRUXTUN-DECATUR NAVAL MUSEUM*
    1610 H St, N.W, 20006. Tel: (202) 783-2573
Vice Admiral W. S. DeLany, USN (Ret.), Pres.
Free daily 10:30 AM - 4 PM; cl. national holidays. Opened in
1950, the Museum is located in the carriage house adjoining the
historic home of Stephen Decatur, who distinguished himself in
the Tripolitan War. It is also named for Commodore Thomas
Truxtun, another naval figure of that period. Sponsored by the
Naval Historical Foundation, the exhibits cover the Merchant
Marine, U.S. Marine Corps, and Coast Guard in addition to the
U.S. Navy. Displays are changed periodically. The current
exhibit depicts 'Achievements of the Peace-time Navy in
Diplomacy and Science'. Much of the Foundation's extensive
collection of naval items is kept at the Library of Congress.

WOODROW WILSON HOUSE
    2340 S St, N.W, 20008. Tel: (202) 387-4062
Shirley Markley, Adminr & Property Council & Staff of National
    Trust Interpretors
Carole T. Scanlon, Coordinator, Interpretive Programs
Open daily 10 AM - 4 PM; cl. Christmas; admis adults $1.25, senior
citizens 60¢, also group rates.
    Woodrow Wilson House is a property of the National Trust for
Historic Preservation. The house is a National Historic Landmark.
    Wilson House was the house of Woodrow Wilson after he retired
at the end of his second term (1921), as 28th President of the United
States. A Georgian-Revival town-house, it was designed by Waddy
B. Wood, a prominent Washington architect of the day. The former

President received distinguished visitors there such as Lloyd George and Clemenceau. Wilson died there in his bedroom three years later on February 3, 1924. His widow Mrs. Edith Bolling Wilson continued to live in the house for almost 40 years after. At her death in 1961, she bequeathed the property to the American people under the guardianship of the National Trust for Historic Preservation.

The property serves as a focal point for advancing historic preservation. It develops new relationships among cultural, community preservation groups and National Trust members in its areas and responds to appropriate regional or headquarters offices of National Trust.

Activities: Provided is a series of interpretive programs related to Wilson House's own case study in historic preservation; included are walking tours which cover the Kalorama section of D.C; school programs; special Christmas program; rotating exhibits on preservation or on themes relating to Mr. Wilson's life; Members Day, during National Historic Preservation Week, in early May; Preservation Shop is located in Mrs. Wilson's trunk room.

Attendance: 14,000.

FLORIDA

BOCA RATON

ART GALLERY
Florida Atlantic University Art Department
   33431. Tel: (305) 395-5100, Exten. 2673
C. V. Dorst, Chmn. Dept. Art
Mary C. Dorst, Gallery Coordinator
Free Mon. - Thurs. 8 AM - 11 PM; Fri. 8 AM - 5 PM; Sat. 9 AM - 5 PM; Sun. Noon - Midnight. Gallery estab. 1970 to provide exhibit space for faculty and students and to provide an opportunity to bring to the area exhibits which would expand the cultural experience of the viewers; gallery located in University Library; financed by city and state appropriation and student activities fees.

Collections: The Art Department maintains a permanent collection of student work.

Exhibitions have included: Exhibits by faculty and former students; annual juried student show; work from area junior colleges; Exxon Foundation Exhibition; Alaskan Salon of Art; Pueblo Pottery; Invitational Weaving Exhibit; Mileo Photo Competition; America as I See It; Florida Craftsmen Traveling Exhibit; The Other Side of the Generation Gap; Rose Freid Abstract Collection; OAS sponsored Contemporary Printmakers of America; Constructions in Flexible Materials.

Activities: Slide collection in Art Department; lectures open to public; workshops sponsored by Student Art Society; scholarships.

Publications: Monthly notices.
Annual Budget: $2500.
Attendance: Over 6000.

BRADENTON

ART LEAGUE OF MANATEE COUNTY*
   Art Center, 209 Ninth St, West, 33505. Tel: (813) 746-2862
Mrs. Roger Murray, Dir.
Free Sept. - May, daily 9 AM - 4:30 PM, Sat. 9 - 12 AM; Sun. 2 - 4 PM; June 9 - 12 AM; cl. July & Aug. Estab. 1936. Ann. meeting April; mem. approx. 475; dues $15 and higher.

Exhibitions: Work by members, one-man shows and circulating exhibitions changing at three week intervals from Oct. through May. Members work June and Sept.

Activities: Art School instruction in painting, drawing, sculpture, copper enameling, clay techniques and variety of handcrafts; creative development for children; special art programs.

Library: Small but fine collection of art books of 750 volumes.
Attendance: Approx. 25,000.

CLEARWATER

✤FLORIDA GULF COAST ART CENTER, INC.
   222 Ponce de Leon Blvd. at Manatee Rd, Belleair, 33516.
   Tel: (813) 584-8634
Ellen C. Kaiser, Dir.
Free Tues. - Sat. 10 AM - 4 PM, Sun. 3 - 5 PM, Sept. - May; cl. Mon. Estab. to further the appreciation, practice and understanding of art in the community; provides school, exhibitions and various cultural activities. Mem. 1800 (open to all); dues $15 and higher.

Collections: Permanent collection; contemporary American paintings, including paintings from the Collection of Georgine Shillard-Smith.

Exhibitions: Traveling exhibitions, one-man shows, yearly members and Students Exhibition; exhibitions change every 3 weeks.

Activities: Lectures, films, musical programs, and demonstrations. School provides classes in painting, ceramics, sculpture,

literary interpretation, enameling, and jewelry design. Scholarship classes for all Junior and Senior High School Students.

Library: Art Library of 2000 volumes for member and student use.

Attendance: 10,000 - 15,000 annually.

CORAL GABLES

✤THE LOWE ART MUSEUM
University of Miami
   1301 Miller Dr, 33146. Tel: (305) 284-3535
John J. Baratte, Dir.
Paul E. Thompson, Asst. Dir.
Free Mon. - Fri. 12 - 5 PM; Sat. 10 AM - 5 PM; Sun. 2 - 5 PM. Estab. 1952 to bring outstanding exhibitions and collections to the community and to the University. Collections, exhibitions, library and other support material emphasize American art. Mem. 3500; dues $15 and higher.

Collections: Samuel H. Kress Collection of Old Masters; †Virgil Barker Collection of American Art; Alfred I. Barton Collection of Indian Art; †Oriental collection; †European art; Ancient art, print collection, pre-Columbian collection, sculpture collection.

Exhibitions: Exhibitions are specially assembled by the museum staff from the permanent collections and loans, approximately 20 exhibitions a year.

Activities: Lectures, gallery tours on request; demonstrations; film programs; studio activities for children and adults.

Library: 5000 volumes on art.
Attendance: 200,000 annually.

DAYTONA BEACH

MUSEUM OF ARTS AND SCIENCES
   1040 Museum Blvd, 32014. Tel: (904) 255-0285
David Sigerson, Pres.
Mrs. Tom Moore, Secy.
John H. Surovek, Dir.
Sharon Whempner, Exec. Secy.
Robert Hillenbrand, Planetarium Cur.
Steven Hartman, Science Cur.
Free Mon. - Sat. 9 AM - 5 PM; Sun. 1 - 5 PM; Wed. 7 - 9 PM; $1 to non-mem. to Planetarium. Estab. 1955; financed by mem. Gallery. Ann. meeting 3rd Thurs. in Nov; mem. 1130; dues single $10, family $15, contributing $25, sponsor $100, sustaining $500, life $1000.

Collections: 18th, 19th and 20th century collection of Cuban art donated by General and Mrs. Fulgencio Batista, former president of Cuba; permanent science collection including marine items, rocks and minerals, anthropological items.

Exhibitions: 108th American Watercolor Society; Sculpture on Canvas; Audubon on Paper; Printing Sampler; Volusia Through WW II; Norman Rockwell Sampler; Pre-Columbian; Volusia School Creates II.

Activities: Lending service, individual paintings and original objects of art; public lectures plus 3 visiting lecturers per year; classes for adults and children and competitions; art classes; science-planetarium related classes; nature trial studies. Book shop; Halifax Art Festival sponsored by the Ladies Guild.

Library: 25,000 items, science and art oriented.
Publications: News Letter, monthly.
Attendance: 74,000.

DELAND

STETSON UNIVERSITY ART GALLERY
   Sampson Hall, 32720. Tel: (904) 734-4121, Exten. 248
Fred Messersmith, Chmn. Art Dept.
Free, Mon. - Fri. 9 AM - 4:30 PM. Estab. 1964 and is maintained as an educational adjunct for our art department.

Exhibitions: American Watercolor Society; Northern Illinois Print Show; Boris Margo; Stetson Art Faculty; Charles White.

Activities: Lectures open to the public; competitions.
Purchases: Under $1000.
Attendance: 5000 annual average.

FORT LAUDERDALE

✤FORT LAUDERDALE MUSEUM OF THE ARTS
   426 E. Las Olas Blvd, 33301. Tel: (305) 463-5184
Elliott B. Barnett, Pres.
George S. Bolge, Dir.
Free Tues. - Sat. 10 AM - 4:30 PM; Sun. 12 - 5 PM; cl. Mon. 50¢ admis. charge from Dec. - Mar. Estab. 1958 to bring art to the community and provide cultural facilities and programs. Noncirculating library, reading room, exhibit space, classrooms. Ann. meeting Apr; mem. 1000; dues $20.

Collections: American and European graphics; paintings and sculpture from late 19th century to present; American Indian ceramics, stone and basketry; West African Tribal Sculpture; Pre-Columbian ceramics and stone artifacts.

Exhibitions: Changing monthly exhibitions, Annual Hortt Memorial Competition.

Activities: 2 major art oriented lecture series per year; guided tours; films; gallery talks; art festivals; docent program; intermuseum loan; classes for adults and children; 10 gallery tours per season; slide lecture in school program by request. Museum shop sales desk.

Library: Art reference 1000 volumes, 3000 Carnegie slides.

Publications: Quarterly bulletin; Calendar of Events, monthly; annual report in Sept.

Income and Purchases: Operating budget $118,300; purchases $20,000.

Attendance: 1200 per month past fiscal year.

GAINESVILLE

✠UNIVERSITY OF FLORIDA
University Gallery
   32611. Tel: (904) 392-0201
Roy C. Craven, Jr, Dir.
Marjorie Z. Burdick, Secy.
Free Mon. - Fri. 9 AM - 5 PM; Sun. 1 - 5 PM; cl. Sat. and holidays. Estab. Mar. 1, 1965, an arts exhibition gallery, open 11 months of the year, showing monthly exhibitions with various contemporary and historical content. The Gallery Guild meets annually in Oct; mem. 300; dues from $5 student to $1000 patron.

Collections: European, American, African and Oriental art, collections chiefly enlarged by gifts.

Exhibitions: (since opening date) Artists of the Florida Tropics; Miniatures and Small Sculptures from India, African Art, Yasuo Kuniyoshi, The Maya, Brazilian Architecture.

Attendance: 40,000.

Architecture and Fine Arts Library
   201A Architecture & Fine Arts Bldg, 32611. Tel: (904) 392-0222
Anna L. Weaver, Librn.
Open Mon. - Fri. 8 AM - 5 PM, 7 - 9 PM; Sat. 8 AM - Noon; Sun. 6 - 10 PM. Estab. 1940 to serve the faculty and students of the University of Florida, especially those in the College of Architecture and College of Fine Arts; financed by state appropriation.

Collections: 39,000 volumes.

Publications: New Book List, monthly.

JACKSONVILLE

✠CUMMER GALLERY OF ART
DeEtte Holden Cummer Museum Foundation
   829 Riverside Ave, 32204. Tel: (904) 356-6857
Suzanne S. Burns, Acting Dir.
Free Tues. - Fri. 10 AM - 4 PM; Sat. 12 - 5 PM; Sun. 2 - 5 PM; cl. Mon. Opened Nov. 1961. General art museum, collecting and exhibiting fine arts of all periods, all cultures.

Collections: †European, American painting, sculpture, graphic arts, decorative arts; Oriental collection of jade, ivory, Netsuke, Inro and porcelains. Collection of early Meissen porcelain is largest in United States.

Exhibitions: 6 - 8 special exhibitions annually.

Activities: Lectures, concerts, gallery tours.

Library: Art reference library of 4000 volumes; 10,000 color slides.

Attendance: 45,000.

✠JACKSONVILLE ART MUSEUM
   4160 Boulevard Center Dr, 32207. Tel: (904) 398-8336
Lyman T. Fletcher, Pres. & Chmn. of the Board
Peter H. Bos, Exec. V.Pres.
Marco L. Brown, Treas.
Bruce H. Dempsey, Dir.
Free Tues, Wed. & Fri. 10 AM - 4 PM; Thurs. 10 AM - 10 PM; cl. Mon, month of Aug. & legal holidays. Inc. 1948 as art center for the greater Jacksonville area.

Collections: Outstanding Oriental porcelains; 20th century paintings, prints and outdoor sculpture; Pre-Columbian and African works.

Exhibitions: 9 major exhibitions annually, featuring painting, sculpture, graphics, photography and crafts, nationally circulated; regional competitions; 10 exhibitions annually in gallery dedicated to showing local art groups.

Activities: Lectures, concerts, seminars, workshops, film series; expanding art education program, 12 week class sessions professionally instructed; daily tours; varied art-related events; museum shop.

Library: AV center; lending collections of over 6000 volumes, slides, reproductions.

Publications: Bimonthly newsletter; monthly calendar; brochures, catalogs.

JACKSONVILLE PUBLIC LIBRARY
Art and Music Department
   122 N. Ocean St, 32201
Jeff Driggers, Dept. Librn.
Free Mon. - Fri. 9 AM - 9 PM; Sat. 9 AM - 6 PM. Estab. 1905 to serve the public by giving them free access to books, films, phonograph recordings, pamphlets, periodicals, maps, plus informational services and free programming; financed by city appropriation. Open area on the mezzanine of the building serves as a display area for local artists.

Collections: Framed art reproductions; 550,512 volumes in library; photograph collection of 3000 prints.

Activities: Lending collection of 1000 color reproductions, 3000 photographs, 5100 lantern slides, 1690 motion pictures, 8060 phonograph recordings, 550,512 books; 73,227 items lent in average year, not including books; classes for adults; weekly film programs including presentation of 40 feature films per year.

Publications: Annual report.

KEY WEST

KEY WEST ART AND HISTORICAL SOCIETY
Martello Gallery and Museum
   S. Roosevelt Blvd, 33040. Tel: (305) 296-3913
Col. J. Paul Scurlock, Pres.
Edward G. Hefter, Corresp. Secy.
Maj. Louise V. White, Cur.
Mrs. John R. Bowman, Receptionist
Mario Borras, Custodian-Caretaker
Open 9:30 AM - 5 PM; admis. adults $1, youths (7-16 yr) 25¢. Estab. 1947 to sponsor an art gallery and local history museum; maintained by membership and admissions. Eight galleries in north wing of pre-Civil War fort. Ann. meeting May; mem. 550; dues active $7.50, contributing $25, student $2, patron $100, life $200.

Collections: Small collection of paintings and wood carvings presented to the historical society by the artists.

Exhibitions: Art exhibitions changed every 27 days except from June through Oct. when there is an annual summer show. A children's former playhouse with dolls, books, etc. A few books sold in entrance hall.

Library: Around 100 volumes for reference, mostly city tax books. Photographs on display in local history museum areas, such as turtling, fishing, sponging, etc.

Publications: Martello, yearly, local history articles and photographs sent to members only.

Attendance: Approx. 15,000 annually.

LAKELAND

POLK PUBLIC MUSEUM
   800 E. Palmetto, 33801. Tel: (813) 688-7744.
Janet Tucker, Pres.
Rev. Joseph Huntley, Secy.
Peter W. Ladue, Asst. Dir.
Kathleen Ewing Ladue, Asst. Dir.
Free Tues. - Fri. 10 AM - 5 PM; Sat. 10 AM - 1 PM; Sun. 1 - 4 PM. Founded in 1966 to bring changing exhibits of art, history and science to community and to provide cultural enrichment to the area; financed by membership. Five galleries. Mem. 398; dues $5 and up.

Collections: Barnun Collection (outstanding regional artists); Ellis Verink Photographs; 14th - 19th Century Stoneware and Pottery; Mineral and Fossil Collections; various individual pieces of notable art and furniture.

Exhibitions: The Eskimo as Artist; Indonesia: Jewel of the East Indies; The Nature of Things; Essay of a Young Photographer; Macrame, Creative Design in Knotting; Fossils Found by Children; The Curators Collection; Woodcuts by Winslow Homer; China: Her Opulent Past; William Bailey: Paintings and Drawings; Polk Collects; Makonde Sculpture; Art Nouveau.

Activities: Workshops, classes for adults and children, school tours, concerts, dramatic programs; photograph collection; 100 prints; lectures open to public; 6 visiting lecturers per year; 120 gallery tours. Suitcase Museum Program in which materials are made available to teachers on a short loan, free of charge.

Library: Over 300 volumes for reference.

Operating Budget: $40,000 - $50,000.

Attendance: 10,000 annual average.

MAITLAND

MAITLAND ART CENTER - RESEARCH STUDIO
231 W. Packwood Ave, 32751. Tel: (305) 645-2181
Mr. Rae Bennett, Pres.
Mrs. R. Field, Secy.
Charles L. Baker, Dir.
Roger F. Dumas, Cur. of Exhibits
Kären Neustadt, Cur. of Educ.
Free Tues. - Sat. 10 AM - 4 PM; Sun. 1 - 5 PM. Estab. 1939 to promote exploration and education in the visual arts and contemporary crafts; financed by city and state appropriation and membership. Maintains gallery. Ann. meeting May 1; mem. 780; dues $10.
Collections: 367 Graphics-Paintings of André Smith; architectural work including 9 acre compound and memorial chapel designed by Smith; 430 volumes of notes, books and records of André Smith.
Activities: Art training classes; lectures open to public; 4 visiting lecturers per year; 32 gallery talks and 160 tours; concerts, classes for adults and children, competitions; scholarships. Book shop.
Library: 430 volumes for reference.
Publications: Imagination, bimonthly.
Income and Purchases each over $50,000.
Attendance: 7500.

MIAMI

✖METROPOLITAN MUSEUM AND ART CENTER
7867 N. Kendall Dr, 33156. Tel: (305) 271-8450
Joseph R. Harrison, Jr, Pres.
J. Deering Danielson, Chmn. of the Board
Dr. Arnold L. Lehman, Dir.
Tom V. Schmitt, Asst. Dir.
Juanita May, School Dir.
Free Mon. - Thurs. 10 AM - 9:30 PM; Sat. & Sun. 1 - 6 PM; cl. Fri. Estab. 1962 to provide a complete museum and art school program; financed by endowment and membership. Includes permanent collection gallery, changing exhibitions galleries, historic costume gallery, Latin American gallery. Ann. meeting in May; mem. 5100; dues $15 to $5000.
Collections: 20th century Martinez-Canas collection of Latin American painting; Far Eastern art; African art; Historic costumes; pre-Columbian and American Indian; Antique toys; European and American painting and decorative arts.
Exhibitions: Beverly Pepper Monumental Sculpture; Philip Pearlstein: Nudes and Other Scenes; The American Woman: Images of 200 Years; American Painting 1920-1939; Judaica from American Collections; From Bustle to Hustle: 2 Centuries of Historic Fashion; Danish Designs of the 70's; Zuloaga: Paintings; Roy Lichtenstein: Drawings and Paintings.
Activities: Special education departments and children's museum presently being organized; extension department serves North Miami Branch of the Metropolitan Museum and Art Center; traveling exhibitions; individual paintings lent to schools and others; 100 items lent in an average year; lectures open to public; 10 visiting lecturers, 12 gallery talks and 100 tours per year; classes for adults and children; scholarships. Book shop.
Library: 2500 volumes for reference; also slide collection.
Publications: Newsletter, published 6 times per year; also various catalogues.
Attendance: 140,000.

MIAMI ART LEAGUE, INC.*
228 N.E. 82nd St, 33156. Tel: (305) 759-4003
Mrs. Elizabeth Spinks, Pres.
Mrs. Laura Tamme, Treas.
Mrs. Gladys Legge, Recording Secy.
Estab. 1928, inc. 1944. A non-profit organization to promote and develop art in Greater Miami. Mem. approx. 150; dues $5 and higher. Members participate in local and international shows annually. Monthly program meetings; workshops.

MIAMI-DADE JUNIOR COLLEGE ART GALLERY*
South Campus, 11011 S.W. 104th St, 33156. Tel: (305) 274-1281
Robert Sindelir, Dir.
Margaret Pelton, Art Dept. Chmn.
Estab. 1970 as teaching laboratory and public service; supported by college funds.
Collections: Permanent collections; prints; sculpture; paintings.
Exhibitions: Permanent collection and rentals; shows of visiting artist—Christo, Leslie Krimes, Wayne Thiebaud, Robert Arneson, Ray Parker.

✖MIAMI PUBLIC LIBRARY*
1 Biscayne Blvd, 33132
Carol Stone, Serials Librn.
Margarita Cano, Art Division

✖VIZCAYA
3251 S. Miami Ave, 33129. Tel: (305) 854-3531
R. K. Preston, Business Mgr.
Louise Drake, Cur. of Educ.
Susan W. Reiling, Cur. of Decorative Arts
Doris Littlefield, Curatorial Asst.
Kitty Harwood, Hon. Archivist
Open 9:30 AM - 5:30 PM every day except Christmas; admis. adults $2.50 to Palace and Gardens, $1 to Gardens; children and student groups 50¢. The Museum is operated by the Metropolitan Dade County Park & Recreation Department under the direct control of a four-man policy committee whose members are Edward P. Goodnow; Richard E. Danielson, Jr, Miami Corp; A. H. Peavy, Jr, Dir. Dade County Park & Recreation Dept; Supt. Museum Division, Dade County Park and Recreation Dept.
Vizcaya is an American realization of an Italian Renaissance Palace. It was inspired by several great European Houses but is not itself a copy. Architects F. Burrall Hoffman and Paul Chalfin built Vizcaya as a residence for the late James Deering of the International Harvester Family. Its extensive formal gardens, designed by Diego Suarez, are graced with fountains, statuary, baroque stairways and ornamental walls. The property was established in 1952 as a Museum of the Decorative Arts, and is being purchased by Dade County. The Heirs of James Deering have donated his art collections. The museum is assisted by two volunteer organizations. Guides are recruited and trained in an annual preparation course. An average of 150 people participate in this volunteer program. Another group called The Vizcayans is dedicated to providing for the care, maintenance, support, continuance, and success of Vizcaya as an art museum.
Collections: European interiors of the 16th to early 19th centuries; original paneling, wall coverings, ceilings, doors and appointments from palaces in Italy, France, Spain and England. The art objects include a Roman marble altar and sarcophagi, Renaissance tapestries, marbles and bronzes, outstanding examples of 18th century furniture. A notable collection of antique European and Oriental carpets is displayed on Vizcaya's floors.
Activities: Guided tours for school classes and other groups, concerts, special exhibits, membership lectures, loans to museums, Artist's Day; fashion shows and other programs including live television, network shows and radio. Museum Shop, Snack Bar.
Library: Art Reference Library pertaining to periods and objects represented in the museum.
Attendance: Average over 241,000 annually.

MIAMI BEACH

BASS MUSEUM OF ART
2100 Collins Ave, 33139. Tel: (305) 673-7530
P. C. Eckart, Chief Librn.
Free Tues. - Sat. 10 AM - 5 PM. Estab. 1963; art masterpieces for public viewing; financed by endowment and city appropriation.
Collections: Old Master paintings, medieval statues, tapestries; sculpture; vestments; decorative objects.
Exhibitions: Permanent collection only.
Library: The museum is under the administration of the public library and is next door, so the library's art collection is available to all museum visitors.
Annual Income: $41,400.
Attendance: 23,000.

OCALA

CENTRAL FLORIDA COMMUNITY COLLEGE
Box 1388, 3001 S.W. College Rd, 32670. Tel: (904) 237-2111
Henry Goodlett, Pres.
O. Joseph Fleming, II, Dir. Div. Fine Arts
Free Mon. - Fri. 8 AM - 9:30 PM. Estab. 1967 as a service to the community; financed by state appropriations. Gallery is the lobby to the auditorium, shows change generally monthly, with one show for the summer.
Collections: One small permanent collection of contemporary artists of varied media.
Activities: College level art instruction; concerts; dramatic programs; classes for adults; scholarships.
Library: 40,000 volume library.
Publications: Windfall.
Attendance: 5000 annual average.

ORLANDO

LOCH HAVEN ART CENTER, INC.
2416 N. Mills Ave, 32803. Tel: (305) 896-4231 & 896-4232
Mrs. John Duda, Jr, Pres.
David M. Reese, Dir.
Marena R. Grant, Asst. Dir.
Susan B. McKenzie, Exec. Secy.

Glenn Allred, Registrar
Mary Ann MacLean, Mem. Secy.
Free Tues. - Sat. 10 AM - 5 PM; Sun. 2 - 5 PM; cl. Mon. Estab. 1926; financed by membership, city, fund raising projects and donations.
> Collections: Pre-Columbian Art, prints and American paintings.
> Activities: Lectures, gallery tours, films, classes for adults and children.
> Exhibitions: Loan and circulating.
> Library: Reference library of 725 volumes.
> Publications: Bulletin (monthly).
> Attendance: 50,000 - 70,000.

PALM BEACH

THE HENRY MORRISON FLAGLER MUSEUM

Whitehall Way, 33480. Tel: (305) 655-2833
Mrs. Flagler Matthews, Pres.
William J. Moss, Secy.
Charles B. Simmons, Exec. Dir.
Cathryn J. McElroy, Cur.
Open daily 10 AM - 5 PM; cl. Mon; admis. adults $1.50, children 50¢, half price for groups of over 20. Estab. 1959 for preservation and interpretation of the Whitehall mansion, the 1901 residence built for Standard Oil founder and pioneer developer of Florida's east coast, Henry Morrison Flagler; financed by endowment and membership. Gallery, permanent collections in period room settings, traveling and special exhibits in West Room addition. Accredited by National Register of Historic Places. Ann. meeting first Fri. in Feb; mem. 602; dues $25.
> Collections: Furnishings, paintings, sculpture (mainly 19th century), porcelains, glass, silver, textiles, fans, laces, family memorabilia and archives of Flagler's Florida enterprises and local history, costumes.
> Library: 1000 volume reference library.
> Attendance: 62,000 annual average.

✠SOCIETY OF THE FOUR ARTS

Four Arts Plaza, 33480. Tel: (305) 655-7226
Walter S. Gubelmann, Pres.
Raymond J. Kunkel, Secy.
John Gordon, Dir.
Gabrielle Summerville, Asst. Dir.
Helen J. McKinney, Librn.
Free, galleries open Dec. to mid-Apr. Mon. - Sat. 10 AM - 5 PM; Sun. 2 - 5 PM; library open all year Mon. - Fri. 10 AM - 5 PM. Inc. 1936 to encourage an appreciation of art, music, drama and literature. Ann. meeting Mar; mem. 1500; dues $85 and higher.
> Exhibitions: (1972-73) Still Life and Flowers, from the collection of the Whitney Museum of American Art; Collecting Prints and Sculpture-In All Media, from the Lydia and Harry Winston Collection (Dr. and Mrs. Barnett Malbin); American Folk Art, collection of the late Edith Gregor Halpert; (1973-74) Drawings and Prints, lent by Art Institute of Chicago; Master Drawings and Watercolors, from the Yale University Art Gallery; Contemporary American Sculpture, assembled by the Howard and Jean Lipman Foundation and the Whitney Museum of American Art; (1974-75) Antique English Silver, the Folger Coffee Collection of coffee pots and accessories; Ferdinand Howald Collection, paintings from the Columbus Gallery of Fine Arts; Views of Florida by American Masters. Annual exhibition of contemporary American painting in Dec.
> Activities: Lectures open to public; 12 visiting lecturers per year; 2 gallery talks and 3 tours; concerts.
> Library: General lending library of 28,000 volumes.
> Publications: Calendar (Jan, Feb. & Mar.); annual schedule of events.
> Attendance: 64,000 (galleries and library).
Four Art Gardens
Open all year Mon. - Fri. 10 AM - 5 PM. Demonstration gardens in which over 150 varieties of exotic plants from many parts of the world may be found.

PENSACOLA

HISTORIC PENSACOLA PRESERVATION BOARD OF TRUSTEES

207 E. Zaragoza St, 32501. Tel: (904) 432-6051
William Guy Davis, Chmn.
Mrs. William Randolph, III, Secy.
James W. Moody, Jr, Dir.
George Demmy, Archaeology & Restoration Dir.
John C. Azab, Admin. Asst.
Russell E. Belous, Chief Cur.
Linda V. Ellsworth, Research & Publication Dir.
Free 9 AM - 4:30 PM. Estab. 1967 for preservation of historic architecture; research and publication of Gulf Coast history; history and transportation museums; city, county and state appropriation.

> Collections: Fishing Schooner (Buccaneer); early locomotive and cars; sawmill; transportation items; maps of Gulf Coast; archaeological collections; weapons; documents primarily of 18th and 19th centuries; local artists.
> Exhibitions (1975-1976): History of West Florida; Small Houses of Galveston; The Bicycle; frequent special exhibits.
> Activities: Photograph collection, prints for reference; grants for special research; school groups; museum store.
> Library: 500 volumes for reference.
> Publications: Proceedings: Gulf Coast Conference, annually; Campeche Days, Walking Tour of Historic Pensacola.
> Income: Approx. $250,000 annually.
> Attendance: Approx. 75,000 annually.

MUSEUM OF THE AMERICAS

105 W. Gonzalez St, 32501. Tel: (904) 438-6387
Earle W. Newton, Dir.
H. W. Olcott, Secy.
Estab. 1972. Collections are available by appointment at the temporary Anglo-American Center in Pensacola, but Anglo-American materials will be removed to a new Center in Vermont and Hispanic materials will be removed to St. Augustine in 1976. A new museum building will be erected in St. Augustine on land recently obtained adjacent to the educational centre. The San Miguel Center is primarily for educational work through the College of the Americas. The Museum of the Americas is projected as a new kind of museum with a strong educational mission; endowed. Ann. meeting May; dues $10.
> Collections: Pre-Columbian artifacts; Latin American and Spanish Folk Art; Anglo-American painting, especially Hogarth and his period; Colonial American.
> Activities: Educational department (College of the Americas) is a structural framework to permit joint use of museum and other community, national and international resource institutions for college level study in American life and culture; extension department; original objects of art lent on request to other museums.
> Library: 3000 volume reference library; English and American art and architecture; American history and life; Spanish and Latin American art and architecture.

PENSACOLA ART CENTER

407 S. Jefferson St, 32501. Tel: (904) 432-6247
Brigitte Huybregts, Dir.
Sue Stokes, Secy.
Dr. John Venettozzi, Pres.
Taris Savell, V.Pres.
Robert McDonnell, Treas.
Caroline Fletcher Eyster, Recording Secy.
Alma Dyson, Corresp. Secy.
Free Tues. - Sat. 10 AM - 5 PM; Sun. 2 - 5 PM. Pensacola Art Association founded 1953; Pensacola Art Center opened 1954; comprehensive selection of exhibits in all forms of the visual arts, annual juried show, educational exhibits. Ann. meeting Oct; mem. 550; dues $7.50 and up.
> Collections: Contemporary art.
> Exhibitions: Several annual shows, Great Gulf Coast Festival (juried visual arts) in cooperation with Pensacola Arts Council (all forms of visual arts, crafts, etc). Educational Exhibition especially designed for school age children; awards.
> Activities: Gallery tours, films, demonstrations, lectures, art classes in all media for children and adults. Gift Shop (art books, jewelry, crafts).
> Harry Thornton Library founded 1964; 350 volumes limited to fine arts and related fields.
> Income: $40,000.
> Attendance: 60,000 annually.

THE UNIVERSITY OF WEST FLORIDA ART GALLERY

32504. Tel: (904) 476-9500, Exten. 440
John T. Carey, Chmn. Art Dept.
Free 8 AM - 5 PM. Estab. 1969 as a teaching gallery to extend art education in the university and in the community; financed by state appropriation and student fees.
> Collections: Small permanent collection.
> Exhibitions: Shows of a national and regional level. Student, faculty and American Black History Week exhibits are also featured.

T. T. WENTWORTH, JR. MUSEUM

8382 Palafox Highway, P.O. Box 806, 32594. Tel: (904) 438-3638
T. T. Wentworth, Jr, Pres.
T. W. Wentworth, Secy.
Free Sat. & Sun. 2 - 6 PM. Estab. 1957, to conserve historical items and make them available to the public; art sections to encourage art and exhibit local art work; library; mem. and founder's contributions. Ann. meeting last Sat. of Aug.

Collections: Works local and some nationally famous artists; collection is constantly being enlarged by gifts.

Exhibitions: Special yearly art exhibit of some distinguished local artist.

ST. AUGUSTINE

FLORIDA ARTIST GROUP, INC.
6 South St, 32084. Tel: (904) 824-3187
Jean Wagner Troemel, Pres.
Dorothy Stewart, 1st V.Pres.
Inc. 1949, this organization has as its membership professional artists who have gained a degree of distinction through participation in national or state-wide exhibitions. All members come in as assoc. members and must be chosen by juror for annual exhibition 2 times within a 5 year period to qualify for full membership. The division of the state into 5 areas with area chairmen enables local showings to be held year around. Ann. meeting latter part of Apr; full mem. limited to 125, assoc. mem. unlimited; dues $10 and higher.

Exhibitions: One out-of-state juror of distinction selects the paintings for annual. Jurors of the past exhibitions include: Robert Parsons, Bartlett Hayes, Jr, Lamar Dodd, Homer Saint-Gaudens, Wilbur D. Peat, Thomas M. Beggs, Robert B. Hale, Fred Conway, Thomas Tibbs, Donald Mattison, John Taylor, Andree Ruellan, Gibson A. Danes, Carl Holty, James Byrnes, Albert Christ-Janer, Boris Margo, H. Lester Cooke (1973), William A. Fagaly (1974), Donelson F. Hoopes (1975) and Cleve K. Scarbrough (1976). Annual symposium and exhibition held in different part of state each year (1972 St. Augustine, 1973 Boca Raton held in conjunction with Florida League of Arts annual meeting, 1974 St. Petersburg, 1975 Norton Gallery, Museum of the Palm Beaches, West Palm Beach and 1976 Jacksonville Art Museum).

Publications: Illustrated catalog of members' work published 1975.

ST. AUGUSTINE ART ASSOCIATION GALLERY*
22 Marine St, 32084. Tel: (904) 824-2310
James E. Long, Pres.
William E. Twamley, 1st V.Pres.
Dr. Joseph Veber, 2nd V.Pres.
Harold M. Steele, Secy-Treas.
Miss Dorothy O. Smith, Corresp. Secy.
Gallery open Oct. - May, daily 1 - 5 PM; Sun. 2 - 5 PM; cl. Mon. Estab. 1924, inc. 1934, as a non-profit organization to further art appreciation and stimulate sales of members' work. Ann. meeting Mar; mem. 300; dues $6 and higher.

Collections: Permanent collection donated by area artists, consisting of 10 oils, 7 water colors, 3 graphics.

Exhibitions: Monthly exhibitions October through May with cash awards: New Talent Shows in November and April for those who have never before exhibited or won awards.

Activities: Lectures; sketch and portrait classes; 3 or more demonstrations per season; weekly open house discussions; sponsors art classes; is promoting Alice Lawton Library of Art in the public library building. Planned events throughout season.

Attendance: 600 per monthly exhibit; 5000 per year.

ST. AUGUSTINE HISTORICAL SOCIETY
271 Charlotte St, 32084. Tel: (904) 829-5514
Jacqueline Bearden, Office Mgr.
Open Mon. - Fri. 9 AM - Noon, 1 - 5 PM. Estab. 1883 to preserve and present historical material of St. Augustine and its environs. Officers elected yearly. Ann. meeting Jan; mem. 500; dues $5 and higher.

Collections: The Society owns three historic houses. One of these, the Oldest House (open daily 9 AM - 5:30 PM), is used as a historic house museum; another, The Tovar House is used for museum exhibits. The main museum is housed in a modern structure on the same grounds. Collections consist of furnishings appropriate to the periods of St. Augustine history (1565 to date); archaeological material recovered from this area, both aboriginal and colonial.

Activities: Quarterly meetings with lecturers.

Library: Specialized library of Florida history and related subjects, approx. 7000 items.

Publications: El Escribano, quarterly.

Attendance: 105,000 annually.

ST. PETERSBURG

✤MUSEUM OF FINE ARTS
255 Beach Dr. N, 33701. Tel: (813) 896-2667
Mrs. Acheson Stuart, Pres. Emerita
Wilbert R. Canning, Pres.
Lee Malone, Dir.
Alan Du Bois, Asst. Dir.

Open Tues. - Sat. 10 AM - 5 PM; Sun. 1 - 5 PM; cl. Mon, Christmas Day, New Year's Day. Estab. May 1961 to increase and diffuse knowledge and appreciation of art and art history. Ann. meeting Apr; mem. 2400; dues $5 and higher.

Collections: Far Eastern sculpture, especially Indian; 19th Century American and European paintings, graphics arts, decorative arts and sculpture; Contemporary American photographs; Jacobean and Early Georgian period rooms with furnishings; full schedule of loan exhibitions augments the permanent collections.

Activities: Illustrated lectures, 10-12 lecturers per year; special programs for children, junior and senior high school levels; art advisory clinic, docent service, sales desk.

Library: 4000 volumes, 4500 picture file, 8000 slides for reference only.

Publications: Pharos (quarterly) and catalogs.

Income and Purchases: Income $230,000; purchases $20,000.

Attendance: 40,000.

SARASOTA

✤JOHN AND MABLE RINGLING MUSEUM OF ART
Box 1838, 33578. Tel: (813) 355-5101
Richard S. Carroll, Dir.
Gerald Gartenberg, Adminr.
Robert B. Tonkin, Chief Cur.
Leslie Judd Ahlander, Cur. of Contemporary Art
Elizabeth S. Telford, Registrar
Val L. Schmidt, Librn.
John H. Hurdle, Cur, Ringling Museum of the Circus
M. James Czarniecki, III, Dir. of Educ. & State Services
James Bleyer, Dir. of Information
George D. Porter, Comptroller
Open Mon. - Fri. 9 AM - 10 PM; Sat. 9 AM - 5 PM; Sun. 1 - 5 PM; admis. $3, children under 12 free, Sat. free. Bequeathed to the State of Florida by John Ringling and operated by the state since 1946; built in Italian villa style around sculpture garden on 38 landscaped acres; original 18th century theater from Asolo, near Venice, in adjacent building; Ringling Residence and Ringling Museum of the Circus on grounds. Mem. Council dues $15 individual, $25 family.

Collections: †European painting, †sculpture, †drawings and †prints from the 16th, 17th and 18th centuries; noted for its Baroque pictures, especially those of Peter Paul Rubens; archaeology of Cyprus, medals and 18th century decorative arts; †developing collection of 19th and 20th century painting, sculpture and prints.

Activities: Monthly loan exhibitions, lecture series; state-wide chapter and affiliate programs of exhibitions and lectures; traveling exhibitions circulated to schools and colleges; art-related classes conducted in schools throughout the state and in institutions for the exceptional, delinquent and elderly; art carnival; crafts festival; volunteer training program; general and specialized tours of all facilities for school and other groups; classic and foreign film series; winter opera season; 6 month theatrical season of classical and modern performances by Asolo State Theater Company.

Library: Reference library of 7000 volumes, noted for Baroque; 20,000 museum and gallery catalogs; 20,000 auction sales catalogs.

Publications: Ringling Museums Newsletter, quarterly; SWAP News, monthly, for chapter and affiliate organizations.

Attendance: 750,000 annually.

SARASOTA ART ASSOCIATION
Civic Center, 707 N. Tamiami Trail, 33577. Tel: (813) 958-3175
Lloyd Gladfelter, Pres.
Beatrice DeBois, 1st V.Pres.
Paul Colmorgan, Treas.
Virginia Klemmer, Secy.
Free Oct. 1 - May 31 weekdays 10 AM - 5 PM; Sat. & Sun. 1 - 4 PM; (cl. occasionally on Sat). Estab. 1926, inc. 1940. Ann. meeting spring; mem. over 1000; dues $5-$15.

Exhibitions: 10 to 12 exhibitions for members only during an 8 month period, majority of which are juried and have cash awards.

Activities: Special events; lectures and demonstrations by local and nationally prominent artists; annual juried Sarasota County Public Schools Show; sidewalk benefits and auctions open to public.

Publication: Yearbook published each season in Sept. or Oct.

Attendance: Average 17,000 for 8 month period, last two seasons.

STUART

MARTIN COUNTY HISTORICAL SOCIETY
888 N.E. MacArthur Blvd, 33494. Tel: (305) 287-4256
Janet L. Hutchinson, Dir.

Gilbert's Bar House of Refuge Museum
Open daily 1 - 5 PM; cl. Christmas; admis. 25¢ over 12; school and other educational groups admitted free by appointment, weekday mornings. Estab. 1956 as a museum of maritime artifacts and local history. Hartman Aquarium; green turtle research.

Elliott Museum
Open daily 1 - 5 PM; admls. adults $1, children 0-14, 50¢, school and other educational groups admitted free by appointment, weekday mornings. Estab. 1960; donated by Harmon P. Elliott.
Collections: Florida history; Willoughby collection; Forrest shell collection; Killheffer Oriental collection; 12 Americana shops; antique cars; Elliott patents.
Exhibitions: Contemporary art.
Activities: Lectures; cultural events; Halpatiokee Chapter, Daughters of the American Revolution. General store.
Library: For reference only.
Publications: History of Martin County.

TALLAHASSEE

FLORIDA LEAGUE OF THE ARTS*
P.O. Box 6005, 32301. Tel: (904) 599-2720
Richard G. Fallon, Pres.
Mrs. Bette Logan, Secy.
Claire Cressman, Exec. Secy.
Open Mon. - Fri. 9 AM - 5 PM. Estab. 1963 to advance the arts in the State of Florida; financed by membership. Archives at state museum in Gainesville. Ann. meeting Spring; mem. 600.
Activities: Development of community art councils.
Publications: Newsletter quarterly.
Income and Purchases: Income $2000; purchases $1500.

FLORIDA STATE UNIVERSITY ART GALLERY
Fine Arts Building, 32306. Tel: (904) 644-6836/644-6474
J. L. Draper, Chmn, Dept. of Art
Free Mon. - Fri. 10 AM - 4 PM; weekends 1 - 4 PM; cl. school holidays. Estab. 1950; state supported. Art museum, lecture room and lounge.
Collections: Graphics, sculpture, paintings.
Exhibitions: Temporary exhibitions of collections, traveling exhibitions.
Activities: Lectures, gallery talks; formally organized education programs for graduate students.
Attendance: 60,000.

TAMPA

FLORIDA CENTER FOR THE ARTS
University of South Florida
4202 E. Fowler Ave, 33620. Tel: (813) 974-2271
John W. Coker, Acting Dir.
Jerry L. Bassett, Exhibitions Coordinator
Lloyd Bray, Jr, Events Coordinator
Dale AJ Rose, Programming Coordinator
Roy J. Trapp, Asst. Exhibitions Coordinator
Norma M. Prado, Staff Asst.
Fine Arts Gallery open Mon. - Sat. 10 AM - 1 PM, 2 - 5 PM, Sun. 1 - 5 PM; Teaching and Theatre Galleries open Mon. - Fri. 8 AM - 5 PM. Estab. as an arts management unit of the College of Fine Arts to develop and promote quality, professional visual and performing arts programs; to bring to the university community and public in general, an awareness of the best in all the arts, with accent on the contemporary scene.
Collections: Establishing a permanent collection with major emphasis on contemporary graphics, painting, sculpture and photography; minor emphasis on Pre-Columbian art, ceramics, folk and ethnic art.
Exhibitions: Conducts Art Bank package loan-exhibition program within Florida; presents and administers over 30 exhibitions and 250 performing arts events each year, involving students, faculty and visiting professional artists.
Activities: The Center manages the University Theatre, sponsors the University Artist Series, Film Art Series and Summer Chamber Music Series.
Attendance: 200,000.

LATIN QUARTER ART GALLERY
Ybor City Chamber of Commerce, 1509 Eighth Ave, 33605.
Tel: (813) 248-3712
Arthur M. Dosal, Pres.
Oscar Aguayo, Exec. Dir.
Free Mon. - Fri. 9 AM - 5 PM; cl. weekends. Estab. Jan. 1968 to give artists facilities to display their works and the general public opportunity to see original works by contemporary artists; financed by sales and Ybor City Chamber of Commerce funds. Mem. 339; dues $10 and higher.
Publications: Monthly memo to artists.
Income: $3500.

TAMPA BAY ART CENTER
320 N. Boulevard, 33606. Tel: (813) 253-5346, 5347
Jack Sahlman, Chmn, Board of Governors
James M. Bell, Dir.
Open Tues. - Fri. 10 AM - 5 PM; Sat. & Sun. 1 - 5 PM; cl. Mon. Estab. 1923. Dues individual and family $20, patron $100, business associate $250, benefactor $500, founder $1000.
Exhibitions: Gund Collection of Western Art; University of Tampa Faculty Exhibition; Avant Garde in Theatre & Art; Florida Bicentennial Architecture; Guilder Christmas Boutique; University of Tampa Student Exhibition; Austrian Tapestries; Charles Burchfield, Master Doodler; Paul Jenkins.
Activities: 3 artists in residence; free art classes for underprivileged children and adults, including senior citizens; scholarships; school tours guided by docents; sales rental gallery.
Guilder Gift Shop.
Library: Small art reference library with future plans for expansion.
Income: Over $90,000 annually.

TEQUESTA

LIGHTHOUSE GALLERY, INC.
100 Waterway Rd, 33458. Tel: (305) 746-3101
Marvin Potts, Pres.
Augusta Wells, Secy.
Elizabeth Long, Admin. Dir.
Evelyne Bates, Receptionist & Secy.
Free Tues. - Sat. 10 AM - 4 PM; Sun. 2 - 5 PM. Estab. 1964 to create public interest in all forms of the fine arts; financed by endowment and membership. Ann. meeting Apr; mem. 500; dues $25 minimum.
Exhibitions: Perhaps best known of the many featured artists, Moses family, including Grandma Moses; Henry Strater; A. E. Bachus; James Hutchison; Millard Wells.
Activities: Art classes; lectures open to public; classes for adults and children, competitions. (See Schools)
Library: Small library of art books and art magazines.
Publications: Monthly calendar of events.

WEST PALM BEACH

✴ART MUSEUM OF THE PALM BEACHES, INC.
Norton Gallery & School of Art
1451 S. Olive Ave, 33401. Tel: (305) 832-5194
James Y. Arnold, Jr, Pres.
Richard A. Madigan, Secy. & Dir.
R. Brant Snyder, Treas.
Christina Orr, Cur.
Alice Sturrock, Asst. to Dir.
Flanders Holland, School Mgr.
Kaye Fish, Registrar
Theresa E. Hickman, Mem. Secy.
C. Phelps Merrell, Supt.
Free Tues. - Fri. 10 AM - 5 PM; Sat. & Sun. 1 - 5 PM; cl. Mon. Estab. 1919, inc. 1940; Gallery dedicated 1941 for the education and enjoyment of the public; substantial additions were made in 1946, 1949, 1952 and 1966; building and major collections given by Mr. and Mrs. Ralph H. Norton. Ann. meeting Apr; mem. 1000; dues $35 and higher.
Collections: †The Norton Collection of paintings and sculpture includes European and American oils and watercolors; 20th century sculpture. The Chinese Collection includes Buddhist Sculpture, ritual bronzes, archaic jades, tomb statuettes, porcelains and pottery.
Exhibitions: Annual members' exhibition; students' work in April; regular schedule of special exhibitions.
Activities: Lectures, exhibitions, concerts, tours for children and civic organizations; maintains art school. (See Schools)
Library: Reference and lending library of over 2000 volumes.
Attendance: 80,000.

WINTER PARK

MORSE GALLERY OF ART
Rollins College, 32789. Tel: (305) 646 2526
Executive Offices: 151 E. Welbourne, 32789. Tel: (305) 645-5311
Hugh F. McKean, Dir.
Jeannette G. McKean, Assoc. Dir.
Valerie Morris, Secy.
Free Tues. - Sun. 1 - 5 PM. Estab. as a cultural and educational center for Rollins College and the community at large; financed by city and state appropriation. 3 galleries featuring work of Louis C. Tiffany and contemporaries, 19th and 20th century American artists. Office, serving porch, kitchen, garden patio. Advisory Group of 65 mem. meets monthly.

Collections: American art of the 19th and 20th centuries; French art glass of art nouveau period; stained glass of Louis Tiffany, LaFarge and Frederick Lamb.

Exhibitions: Arts and Crafts Movement in America, Princeton and Chicago; Norton Gallery, West Palm Beach; Ringling Museum, Sarasota.

GEORGIA

ATHENS

ATHENS ART ASSOCIATION
Unitarian Universalist Fellowship Church, 834 Prince Ave, 30601.
Mrs. Edward Lee Roberson, Pres. (new officers elected annually)
Open until 8 PM. Estab. 1919 to amplify art opportunities in Athens and develop appreciation in art interests and talents. Monthly meetings Sept. - June; mem. 95; dues $5 annually.

Exhibitions: Athens Regional Library; monthly exhibitions in about 10 different locations of members' art works; sponsor unusually good art works by local people.

Activities: Meetings once a month; program each month; special interest classes. two sidewalk sales per year.

Income and Purchases: One art purchase and donation to City Library of art books.

✤GEORGIA MUSEUM OF ART
The University of Georgia
Jackson St, Main Campus, 30602. Tel: (404) 542-3254
William D. Paul, Jr, Dir.
Ethel Moore, Cur.
Michael Kampen, Preparator
Janice Stanland, Registrar
Bernice Bowers, Secy. to Dir.
Vicky Brown, Secy. to Dir.
Judy Pace, Secy. to Cur.
Mary Virginia Bean, Secy. to Registrar
Free Mon. - Fri. 8 AM - 5 PM, Sat. 9 - 12 AM; Sun. 2 - 5 PM. Eva Underhill Holbrook Memorial Collection of 100 paintings covering 100 years of American Art was donated in 1945 by Mr. Alfred H. Holbrook, who founded the Georgia Museum of Art. Since then, the collection has been increased to 1000 paintings, over 2500 prints, 600 drawings and special collection of African primitive crafts, South Seas crafts, American Indian Art objects and Japanese prints and crafts.

Collections: Eva Underhill Holbrook Memorial Collection of American Art, Holbrook Collection, European paintings, prints and drawings, Kress Study Collection, Museum Patrons Collections, University of Georgia Collection, Pre-Columbian and American decorative arts. Represents nearly all schools of American art and includes oils, watercolors, prints, sculptures and miscellaneous works of art. All are open to additions.

Exhibitions: About 20 special exhibitions in addition to the permanent collection.

Activities: Temporary exhibitions and permanent collection utilized by classes throughout the University. Loans of paintings made to other museums; print collection circulates throughout the state; selection from the permanent collection circulated throughout the United States. Special exhibitions organized by the museum and shared with other institutions. Docent program for children and adults.

Library: Small museum library being consistently increased. Reference and general art books maintained by the University of Georgia Library.

Publications: A University Collects: Georgia Museum of Art; Highlights from the Collections, Georgia Museum of Art; The Kress Study Collection; American Paintings: The 1940's; American Paintings: The 1950's; American Paintings: The 1960's; Samuel Adler; The Paul A. Clifford Collection; Ronald Arnholm; Raphael Soyer; Joseph Hirsch; Lila Katzen; Philip Pearlstein; Alice Neel; quarterly bulletin.

Friends of the Museum; Georgia Museum Patrons, Inc: Advisory Board is composed of 10 members, and the Director, who is Chairman of the Advisory Board, to foster and promote the purchases of works of art for the Museum. An annual budget from the University is devoted to the expenses of the Museum.

ATLANTA

✤ARCHITECTURE LIBRARY
College of Architecture, Georgia Institute of Technology, 30332.
Maryellen LoPresti, Architecture Librn.
Mary Jane Warren, Library Asst. & Slide Cur.
Barbara Waters, Library Asst.

Open fall, winter and spring term Mon. - Thurs. 8 AM - 9:30 PM; Fri. 8 AM - 5 PM; Sat. 9 AM - Noon; Sun. 2 - 9:30 PM. Financed by state appropriation.

Library has a working collection of 10,000 book volumes, 13,000 pamphlets and 32,000 slides.

ATLANTA COLLEGE OF ART LIBRARY
1280 Peachtree St, N.E, 30309. Tel: (404) 892-3600, Exten. 210
Anne K. Wakefield, Head Librn.
Sarah Daniels, Visual Librn.
Open according to the season. Estab. 1931 to support the art history and studio work of the students of the college and develop a library devoted exclusively to the visual arts for the area; endowed.

Collections: Visual arts book and exhibit catalog collection of 13,000 titles with a speciality in contemporary art; lent to members with a deposit; 20,000 slide collection; microfiche collection.

Purchases: $21,500.

ATLANTA PUBLIC LIBRARY
Fine Arts Department
126 Carnegie Way, 30303. Tel: (404) 688-4636
Carlton C. Rochell, Dir.
Julie M. Compton, Head, Fine Arts Dept.
Open weekdays 9 AM - 9 PM; Sat. 9 AM - 6 PM; Sun. 2 - 6 PM.
Fine Arts Department estab. 1950, to provide materials in the fine arts by way of reference and circulating books, prints, recordings and cassettes; financed by city and state appropriation. Some exhibit space maintained.

Collections: 1400 framed prints for circulation; recordings and cassettes; books on art, theater, music, drama, etc.

Activities: 1100 motion pictures in lending collection; lectures open to public; classes for adults.

✤THE HIGH MUSEUM OF ART
1280 Peachtree St. N.E, 30309. Tel: (404) 892-3600
Robert Strickland, Chmn, Atlanta Arts Alliance
Frank M. Malone, V.Chmn. for the Museum
Gudmund Vigtel, Dir.
Free Mon. - Sat. 10 AM - 5 PM; Sun. 12 - 5 PM. Formerly known as the Atlanta Art Association, a founding member of the Atlanta Arts Alliance, estab. in 1965, which includes, in addition to the Museum, the Atlanta College of Art, the Atlanta Symphony Orchestra, the Alliance Theatre and the Atlanta Children's Theatre, for the benefit and enjoyment of the entire Southeastern community. Current membership of c. 8000, dues $10 and higher. Located in the Atlanta Memorial Arts Center.

Collections: American paintings, sculpture, graphics; European paintings, sculpture, graphics; African objects; some Oriental, Pre-Columbian, European and American decorative arts; Kress Collection of paintings and sculpture from the 14th-18th centuries; Uhry Collection of prints after 1850; Haverty Collection.

Exhibitions: About 12 special exhibitions per year.

Activities: Lectures, gallery tours, concerts, films, demonstrations; about 20 visiting lecturers per year; regularly scheduled gallery talks; full-time Department of Education with daily programs. Art Shop, rental service.

Publications: The Samuel H. Kress Collection (1958); Masterpieces in The High Museum of Art (1965); exhibition catalogs, including The Beckoning Land, The Düsseldorf Academy and the Americans, African Tribal Art from the Richman Collection in The High Museum of Art, Beyond India, Folk Art in America: A Living Tradition, Bauhaus Color; monthly calendars and museum reports published regularly.

Library: A growing library to serve all member organizations.
Operating Budget: $565,000 (1975-76).
Total Acquisitions: Approx. $450,000.
Attendance: 296,600 annual average.

AUGUSTA

GERTRUDE HERBERT INSTITUTE OF ART*
506 Telfair St, 30901. Tel: (404) 722-5495
Clemens de Baillou, Dir.
Open Tues. - Fri. 10 AM - Noon & 2 - 5 PM; Sat. 3 - 5 PM; groups by special arrangement, cl. Sun, Mon, Christmas and New Year's. Estab. 1937. Ann. meeting; mem. 250.

Collections: European Renaissance and modern paintings, sculpture, graphics.

Exhibitions: Monthly exhibitions, circulating exhibitions; one-man and group exhibitions.

Activities: Films, lectures, art classes.

Library: Small art library.

Income: $10,000.

COLUMBUS

COLUMBUS MUSEUM OF ARTS & CRAFTS, INC.
1251 Wynnton Rd, 31906. Tel: (404) 323-3617
Jack A. Bell, Chmn. of the Board
C. Clay Aldridge, Secy. of the Board & Mus. Dir.
Edward Swift Shorter, Dir. Emeritus
Free Tues. - Sat. 10 AM - 5 PM; Sun. 2 - 5 PM; cl. Mon, Thanksgiving, Christmas, New Year's. Estab. 1953 to build a permanent collection, to encourage work by Georgia and Southern artists and to establish loan shows and traveling exhibitions in all fields of art. Ann. meeting Jan; mem. dues $10 and higher.
Collections: †Early Masters; †American art; †Georgia artists; †sculpture and prints; †Indian section with extensive collection of ethnological and archaeological material relating to local Indians; a growing permanent collection includes portraits, landscapes and other paintings by English, Flemish, Dutch, Italian, early and contemporary American painters and others; †Oriental ivory collection; †antique American and foreign gun collection; African sculpture; †Persian rugs; †extensive American and foreign doll collection; needlework gallery, fans, costumes and jewelry.
Exhibitions: Morton Youth Wing with permanent and changing exhibits.
Activities: Gallery talks and tours, lectures, traveling exhibitions, art workshops for children and adults, active Museum Guild.
Library: All phases of art, Indian history.
Publications: Monthly Newsletter.
Income and Purchases: Income $125,800; purchases $15,000.
Attendance: 56,000.

DALTON

CREATIVE ARTS GUILD
Old Firehouse on Pentz St, P.O. Box 375, 30720.
Tel: (404) 278-0168
Bernice Spigel, Dir.
Free daily 10 AM - 5 PM. Estab. 1963 to recognize, stimulate and popularize creativity in the arts; maintained by membership. Total mem. 500; dues individual $10, family $15.
Exhibitions: Changing monthly shows of original art work, crafts, sculpture, photography, graphics.
Activities: Classes in art, drama, pottery, ballet, weaving, guitar, for children and adults. Sponsors Dalton Civic Pops Orchestra, Creative Arts Guild Writer's Group and summer youth theatre; traveling art exhibitions to city and county schools, annual Firehouse Arts Festival, Annual Student Arts Festival and Mid-Winter Crafts Festival.
Publications: Monthly bulletin.

DECATUR

DALTON GALLERIES
✠Agnes Scott College Art Department
Dana Fine Arts Bldg, 30030. Tel: (404) 373-2571
Dr. Marvin Banks Perry, Pres, College
Dr. Julia Gary, Dean Faculty
Dr. Marie Huper Pepe, Chmn. Dept.
Open Mon. - Fri. 9 AM - 9 PM; Sat. 9 AM - 5 PM; Sun. 2 - 5 PM. Estab. 1889 as a liberal arts college for women; financed by endowment.
Collections: Dalton collection on 19th and 20th century painting; Steffan Thomas collection of sculpture and painting.
Activities: Scholarships.

SAVANNAH

KIAH MUSEUM
505 W. 36th St, 31401. Tel: (912) 236-8544
Virginia J. Kiah, Dir. & Cur.
Nancy Walker, Asst. Cur.
Free Tues. & Thurs. 11 AM - 5 PM. Estab. Nov. 28, 1959; Kiah Museum is pioneer in offering a different approach to teaching. Educational center for many; not only art, but other subjects as well are taught through museum. Seeing, listening and touching are exciting experiences for many. Children and adults send and bring exhibit material from the United States and 17 foreign countries. Called Museum for the Masses; financed by Dr. Calvin Kiah.
Collections: Marie Dressler Collection; †18th, 19th and 20th century furniture; Howard J. Morrison, Jr. Osteological Exhibit; Civil War period collection; Indian artifacts; †fine arts exhibit of art work of student and adult artists from 18 countries; Harmon Foundation Collection of African wood carvings; †hobby collection; †folk art.
Activities: Traveling exhibitions organized and circulated; individual paintings and original objects of art lent; 500 prints in photograph collection; tours; concerts.
Attendance: 4000.

TELFAIR ACADEMY OF ARTS AND SCIENCES, INC.
Telfair Square, 121 Barnard St, P.O. Box 10081, 31402.
Tel: (912) 232-1177
A. G. Labrot, Pres.
Allan McNab, Dir.
Open Mon. - Sat. 10 AM - 4:30 PM; Sun. 2 - 5 PM; admis. $1; students 50¢; children under 12 25¢; free on Sun; guided tours.
Estab. June 1874, inc. 1920. Ann. meeting May; mem. 1260; dues $15 and higher.
Collection: †19th and 20th century paintings and decorative arts.
Exhibitions: Local and loan shows.
Activities: Lectures, gallery talks and tours, exhibitions, concerts and movies.
Attendance: 12,000.
Owens-Thomas House
124 Abercorn St, 31401. Tel: (912) 233-9743
Mrs. J. Allen Tison, Cur.
Admis. $1.50, special rates for groups of ten or more, free to members.
Estab. 1954 to exhibit the way of life in the early 19th century; administered by Telfair Academy of Arts and Sciences, Inc; collection of 18th and early 19th Century American and English furnishings; lectures; tours.

VALDOSTA

VALDOSTA STATE COLLEGE
North Patterson St, 31601. Tel: (912) 247-3319 & 3330
Irene Dodd, Head
Free Mon. - Fri. 9 AM - Noon, 1 - 5 PM. Estab. to expose both art and general education students to a variety of visual expressions; financed by state appropriations. Gallery is open rectangular room with approx. 122 running feet of exhibition space.
Exhibitions: Approx. 10-12; exhibition calendar changes each month.
Activities: Lectures at times, according to exhibition and funds; tours to museums in New York, Washington, Boston, etc.
Library on campus.
Attendance: 8000.

HAWAII

HONOLULU

THE ADVERTISER CONTEMPORARY ARTS CENTER OF HAWAII
605 Kapiolani Blvd, 96813. Tel: (808) 537-2977, Exten. 211
Laila Roster, Dir.
Free 8 AM - 5 PM. Estab. 1960 to provide a showcase for artists of Hawaii to show their work; nonprofit organization.
Collections: Permanent collection is the largest collection in Hawaii of works by Hawaii artists.
Exhibitions: One-man or group show each month. Purchases from shows are added to permanent collection. The State Foundation on Culture and Arts makes regular purchases for the State of Hawaii from monthly exhibitions.
Activities: Individual paintings and original objects of art lent; few items lent in an average year; gallery; slide library available for lending, includes slides of complete exhibitions as well as permanent collection.

ASSOCIATION OF HONOLULU ARTISTS
P.O. Box 10202, 96816.
Charles Graydon, Pres.
Harriett Holland, Secy.
Sharrel Terrell, 1st V.Pres. & Ed.
Teddi Scholz, 2nd V.Pres.
Suni Park, Corresp. Secy.
Jim Holland, Treas.
Ronald Kent, Mem. Chmn.
Estab. 1926 to promote cooperation and congeniality among Hawaii artists and those interested in art; to stimulate growth and ability among members by presenting programs designed to stimulate and educate; to contribute to the cultural life of Honolulu and the State of Hawaii. Mem. 210; monthly meetings; dues $10.
Exhibitions: Monthly exhibitions for members.
Activities: Lectures; demonstrations.
Publications: The Paint Rag, monthly.

THE FOUNDRY
899 Waimanu St, 96813. Tel: (808) 533-2609
Alan M. Leitner, Pres. & Dir.
Alice S. Leitner, Secy. Admin.
Christine Evans, Mgr.
William Evans, Chmn. of Artists-in-Residence
Free to public Mon. - Sat. 10 AM - 5 PM. Estab. 1969 as an art center with central exhibition gallery open to public in rustic envi-

ronment of old Hawaii. Workshops and artist studios surrounding gallery allow public to view artists at work in a creative environment. Art Center cultivates a community education of the arts, provides an interchange of knowledge; partially financed by city and state appropriation, partially self-supporting.

Exhibitions: Monthly exhibits open to public with shows of graduate art thesis; art organizations; one-man shows; educational shows.

Activities: Artists in residence; traveling exhibitions organized and circulated; junior museum; lectures open to public; 3 visiting lecturers per year, 3 gallery talks and 20 tours; concerts, classes for adults and children, competitions. (See Schools). Book Shop. Library.

Publications: Monthly exhibit bulletins.

Income: $50,000.

HAWAII STATE LIBRARY
Fine Arts - Audiovisual Section
478 S. King St, 96813. Tel: (808) 548-2340 Fine Arts, (808) 548-5913 Audiovisual.
Marion N. Vaught, Head Fine Arts-AV Section
Mary Lu Kipilii, Head AV Unit
Grace Hess, Librn. Fine Arts
Free Mon. - Thurs. 9 AM - 8 PM; Tues, Wed, Fri. & Sat. 9 AM - 5 PM. Estab. 1930 as central reference and circulating collection for both city and county of Honolulu and for the state of Hawaii; state appropriation.

Collections: Approx. 10,000 books on all of the fine arts including handcrafts, photography & costume; many major art journals, about 68,000 pictures covering a wide range of subjects including reproductions of famous paintings; some films and filmstrips on art and related subjects.

Exhibitions: Various local artists on a bi-weekly schedule exhibited in the courtyard area.

Activities: Traveling exhibitions organized and circulated; lending collection, 34,000 color reproductions, 300 photographs, 80 art motion pictures, 5 art film strips, approx. 10,500 art books; approx. 7500 art items lent yearly.

HAWAII WATERCOLOR AND SERIGRAPH SOCIETY
c/o Bonnie Ozaki, 927 17th Ave, 96816.
Bonnie Ozaki, Pres.
Marion Spinn, Secy.
Financed by membership. Mem. 75; dues $10.
Exhibitions: Amfac Plaza, Honolulu.
Activities: Lectures and workshop open to public.
Publications: Monthly bulletin.

✤HONOLULU ACADEMY OF ARTS
900 S. Beretania St, 96814. Tel: (808) 538-3693
Samuel A. Cooke, Pres.
M. L. Randolph, V.Pres.
James W. Foster, Dir. & V.Pres.
Selden Washington, Asst. Dir.
Litheia W. Hall, Secy. to Dir.
Ben Hyams, Spec. Asst. to Dir.
Sanna Deutsch, Registrar
Joseph Feher, Sr. Cur & Cur. of Graphic Arts & Studio Prog.
Howard A. Link, Cur, Asian Art & Keeper of Ukiyo-e Center
Marshall P. Wu, Asst. Cur, Asian Art
Gertrude Rosenthal, Consultant for Western Art
James H. Furstenberg, Cur, Prog. Development
Ruth Tamura, Cur, Extension Services
Violet A. Scott, Cur, Art Center
Roger Dell, Cur, Gallery Education Prog.
Sheila M. Kariel, Keeper, Alice Cooke Spalding House
Broné Jameikis, Keeper, AV Center
Barbara F. Hoogs, Keeper, Lending Collection
Anne T. Seaman, Librn.
Barbara W. Prock, Mem. Secy.
Alan Orman, Accountant
Marjorie Nickerson, Mgr, Academy Shop
Open Tues. - Sat. 10 AM - 4:30 PM; Sun. 2 - 5 PM; cl. Mon. and major holidays; admis. free to main building, modest fee for Spalding House, members free. Opened 1927, the only art museum of a broad general nature in the Pacific; established to provide Hawaii's people of many races with works of art representing their composite cultural heritage from both East and West. Main building is a Registered National Historic Place. Mem. 4500; dues $8 and higher.

Collections: Chinese painting, sculpture, ceramics, bronze, lacquerware, furniture; Japanese painting including screens, sculpture, prints, ceramics and folk arts; Korean ceramics; Islamic ceramics, ancient Mediterranean and medieval Christian art; European and American painting, prints, sculpture and decorative arts,

including the Kress Collection of Italian Renaissance painting; Western and Oriental textiles; traditional arts of Africa, Oceania and the Americas.

Exhibitions: More than 35 temporary exhibitions annually presenting a wide diversity of cultural, historic and contemporary forms of expression, utilizing loan and museum resources.

Activities: Guided tours, lectures, films, gallery talks, arts festivals, creative art classes for children and special exhibition program in the education department working with 50,000 children annually. Studio Program and Graphic Arts Center offer full and part-time professional courses in drawing, printing and printmaking. Resident Artist program invites master printmakers of international reputation to conduct printmaking workshops. (See Schools). Lending collection of paintings, prints, textiles, reproductions, photographs, slides and miscellaneous objects (about 21,000) available to schools and other educational organizations; AV library, extension program to neighbor islands; research in Asian art. Book and Gift Shop.

Library: About 23,000 books on history of art, especially Chinese and Japanese art; certain Oriental publications available for inter-museum loan for scholarly purposes.

Publications: Catalogs of special exhibitions, various art books and pamphlets of general or scholarly interest; Honolulu Academy of Arts Journal, biennial.

Income: $1,000,000; purchases $360,000.

Attendance: 124,000 annual average.

Alice Cooke Spalding House of the Honolulu Academy of Arts
2411 Makiki Heights Dr, 96822. Tel: (808) 537-9088
Spalding House opened in 1970, the Academy's extension for Asian decorative arts. House and gardens open Tues. - Sun. 1 - 4:30 PM; cl. Mon. and major holidays; admis. adults $1, senior citizens 50¢, students 25¢, Academy members, children under 12 and student groups with instructor free. Tues. admis. free to all. The gardens combine Oriental and Western horticulture and landscape art.

Exhibitions: Rotating exhibitions feature paintings, screens, calligraphy, stone rubbings, lacquerware, furniture, ceramics, costumes and folk-arts. An important part of Spalding House is the Ukiyo-e Center for the exhibition and study of Japanese woodblock prints. Monthly exhibitions are selected from the James A. Michener Collection of 5000 works by masters from the 17th century to modern times.

Activities: Guided tours of the exhibitions and gardens, lectures, demonstrations and dance and music programs. Book and gift shop.

POST MUSEUM*
Schofield Barracks
U.S. Army Support Command Hawaii, APO San Francisco 96557.
John A. Thacker, Dir.
Free Wed. - Sun. 10 AM - 4 PM. Estab. 1958 to preserve the military historical background in Hawaii; financed by military appropriations.

Collections: Military weapons of the past, present, flags, banners, manuals; military art; photograph collection.

Activities: Serves the islands of the state of Hawaii; material available to all persons both military and civilian; no loans.

Attendance: 40,000 annual average.

TENNENT ART FOUNDATION GALLERY*
203 Prospect St, 96813. Tel: (808) 531-1987
Hon-Chew Hee, Dir.
Open Tues. - Sat. 10 AM - Noon; Sun. 2 - 4 PM; cl. Mon; admis. adults $1, students 50¢, children under 12 25¢. Estab. 1954, dedicated to aesthetic portrayal of Hawaiian people and to house works of Madge Tennent; financed by trust. Gallery on slopes of Punchbowl below National Cemetery of Pacific. Mem. approx. 100; dues $3.

Activities: Individual paintings lent to schools, mobile unit; guided tours; lectures; gallery talks; training program for professional museum workers.

Library: 300 volume reference library.

Publications: Prospectus (monthly newsletter).

Attendance: 800 annual average.

KAILUA

WINDWARD ARTISTS GUILD
c/o Shirley Hasenyager, Box 851, 96734.
Estab. 1961 to promote art and art appreciation in Hawaii. Ann. meeting Nov; mem. approx. 130; dues $10.

Exhibitions: Easter Art Festival annually; many small exhibits at public libraries.

Activities: Lectures; gallery talks and tours; classes for adults and children; scholarships.

LANAINA

LAHAINA ARTS SOCIETY
649 Wharf St, 96761. Tel: (808) 661-0111
Daniel Vezzani, Pres.
Robert Kelsey, Secy.
Janet Allan, Mgr.
Free daily 10 AM - 4 PM. Estab. 1964 as a nonprofit organization interested in perpetuating native culture, art and beauty by providing stimulating art instruction, lectures and art exhibits; financed by membership and annual fundraising event, Beaux Arts Ball. Gallery located in old Lahaina Courthouse, Main Gallery is on ground floor, Old Jail Gallery is in the basement. Ann. meeting Sept; mem. 310; dues single $10, family $15.
Exhibitions: Exhibits change each month. One or two-man shows are in Old Jail Gallery, group, special or theme exhibits in Main Gallery. Honolulu Academy of Arts annual traveling exhibit held each year.
Activities: Classes are held as teachers become available; lectures open to public; 4 visiting lecturers per year; 36 gallery talks for schoolchildren; classes for adults and children, competitions; scholarships.
Library: 100 volumes for reference.
Publications: Monthly newsletter.
Income: $12,000.
Attendance: 25,000.

LIHUE

KAUAI MUSEUM
P.O. Box 248, 96766. Tel: (808) 245-6931
Juliet Rice Wichman, Pres.
Kathryn Hulme, Secy.
Robert A. Gahran, Dir.
Catherine Stauder, Researcher
Hazel Ward Gahran, Mgr Museum Shop
Open Mon. - Sat. 9:30 AM - 4:30 PM; cl. Sun; admis. adult $1, children thru age 15 free, accompanied by an adult. Estab. 1960 to provide the history of this island through the permanent exhibit, The Story of Kauai and through art exhibits, and ethnic cultural exhibits in the Wilcox building to give the community an opportunity to learn more of ethnic backgrounds; financed by mem. Ann. meeting Nov. each yr; mem. 500; dues $5, $10, $25, $50 & $100.
Collections: Hawaiiana collection with particular emphasis on items connected with the Island of Kauai.
Exhibitions: The first Americans: the first American Indian Exhibit in Hawaii; Annual Artists of Hawaii Exhibit; Pacific Northwest Indian Exhibit; Watercolors by Wai Hang Lai; Watercolors by Hubert Buel; Hawaiian Quilts; Watercolors and Prints of Emily Ehlinger; Oils by John Young; Filipino Cultural Heritage Exhibit Featuring the Badillo Collection; Attempted Russian Expansion on Kauai, 1815-1817; annual elementary and senior division school art exhibits each Mar. & Apr.
Library: Reference library of 2500 volumes; reference print, photograph collection; library is a research center specializing in material dealing with Kauai History.
Publications: Hawaiian Quilting on Kauai.
Attendance: 18,000 annual average.

KAUAI REGIONAL LIBRARY
4344 Hardy St, 96766.
Donna Marie Garcia, Regional Librn.
Free Mon, Wed. & Fri. 9 AM - 5 PM; Tues. & Thurs. 9 AM - 8 PM. Estab. 1922 to serve the public of Kauai through a network of a regional library, three community libraries, community/school library, reading room in community center and a bookmobile service. These libraries provide exhibit space for a variety of art works and individual art shows as well as participate in joint art exhibits with the local schools, community college and museum. Part of the Hawaii State Library System. Gallery provides display and exhibit area for one-man and group art shows.
Collections: Curator for Art in State Buildings Collection for the island of Kauai that is funded through the statewide program by the State Foundation on Culture and the Arts. This collection is a revolving collection available for all state buildings.
Exhibitions: Series of small one-man exhibits.
Activities: Lectures open to public; 4-8 visiting lecturers per year.
Library: 114,000 (includes all volumes in all public libraries); mounted picture collection.
Income: $400,000.

WAILUKU

MAUI HISTORICAL SOCIETY
Hale Hoikeike
P.O. Box 1018, 96793. Tel: (808) 244-3326
Dorothy Pyle, Pres.

Patricia Leffingwell, Secy.
Virginia Wirtz, Museum Dir.
Open daily 10 AM - 3:30 PM; cl. Sun; admis. adults $1.50, students and children 50¢. Estab. 1957 to preserve and promote interest in the history of Hawaii, particularly as it pertains to Maui County; supported by membership. Historic House Museum, former residence of Edward Bailey; his studio is now a gallery of his oil paintings and etchings. Ann. meeting 3rd Thurs. in March; mem. 410; dues annual $2, contributing $10, sustaining $25, life $100.
Collections: †Bailey Painting Collection; Neolithic Hawaiian Artifacts; early missionary furniture; rotating ethnic exhibits.
Activities: Lectures open to public, 5 visiting lecturers per year. Book Shop.
Library: Books, clipping file and photograph collection for reference only (collection currently being enlarged).
Publications: Annual Report; quarterly bulletins to members.
Income: Approx. $14,000.
Attendance: 4500.

IDAHO

BOISE

BOISE ART ASSOCIATION
Box 1505, 83701.
Boise Gallery of Art
Julia Davis Park. Tel: (208) 343-2923 or 343-2132
Allen Dodworth, Dir.
Beth Sellars, Asst. Dir.
Bee Clark, Admin. Asst.
Fae Roberts, Receptionist
Bill Campton, Preparator
Sally Casler, Sales Shop Mgr.
Open Tues. - Sun. 10 AM - 5 PM; cl. Mon. Association founded 1931, inc. 1961; gallery opened 1936.
Collections: American, European and Oriental collections of painting, sculpture and the minor arts; also a collection of works by Idaho artists.
Exhibitions: 20-24 exhibitions annually of painting, sculpture, photography, graphics, architecture, crafts, etc; annual exhibition for Idaho artists.
Activities: Arts Festival; classes in art and art appreciation, docent tours; public lectures, chamber concerts and films. Beaux Arts Société (fundraising auxiliary). Gallery Shop.
Library: 4000 items.
Publications: Bulletin, Annual Report, occasional catalogs of exhibitions.
Income: Approx. $90,000 annually.
Attendance: 80,000 annually.

MOSCOW

UNIVERSITY OF IDAHO MUSEUM
83843. Tel: (208) 885-6480
G. Ellis Burcaw, Dir.
Open Mon. - Fri. 9 AM - 4 PM when University is in session. Estab. 1963 to serve the University in all fields.
Collections: History, art and anthropology; most important exhibitions and collections in the field of ethnology, especially Africa and the Near East.
Exhibitions: 4-6 temporary exhibitions per year. Permanent exhibits in several campus buildings.
Activities: Classes in museology for college credit.
Publications: Occasional publications in museology and anthropology.
Income: $27,000.
Attendance: 4000 annually.

OROFINO

CLEARWATER ART ASSOCIATION, INC.
P.O. Box 1482, 83544
Betty Swineheart, Pres.
Leah Lumper, Secy.
Sam Swayne, V.Pres.
Marty Johnson, Treas.
Estab. 1958 to introduce and present an art program to the public in this small community; nonprofit, financed by membership. 25-30 mem. meet quarterly; dues $2 per year.
Activities: Extension, workshops and lessons serving Orofino City, available to anyone; classes for adults and children; scholarships. Support children's art contests and 4-H art projects.

POCATELLO

JOHN B. DAVIS ART GALLERY*
Fine Arts Center, Idaho State University, 83201.
Tel: (208) 236-3532
Ron Hinson, Dir.
Dennis R. Snyder, Chmn, Dept of Art.
Free Mon. - Fri. 12 - 4:30 PM; Tues, Wed. & Thurs. 11 AM - 4:30 PM; Sat. 2 - 4 PM. Estab. 1965 to serve as an art gallery and museum as part of the educational role of Idaho State University and to serve the residents of southeast Idaho in the same capacity; financed by endowment and city & state appropriations.
    Collections: Contemporary prints.
    Exhibitions: California Black Craftsmen; Joseph Albers; Action-Reaction; Western Faculty Invitational; Faculty Show; Bannock-Shoshone Indian Art; Eskimo Graphics; Jane Gehring Textiles and Archie Bray Foundation Glass; Cuna Indian Textiles; Oliveira and Adams Prints, Early 19th century Lithographs; Ceramics Show.
    Activities: Traveling exhibitions organized and circulated.
    Publications: Bulletin.
    Attendance: 3000 annual average.

TWIN FALLS

COLLEGE OF SOUTHERN IDAHO
Box 1238, 83301. Tel: (208) 733-9554
La Var Steel, Chmn Art Dept.
Kent Jeppesen, Gallery Dir.
Open 8 AM - 5 PM daily except Sun; no admis. Estab. 1967 as a college gallery for student and public; financed by community college and local support. Fine arts building and auditorium.
    Collections: Permanent collection.
    Exhibitions: Alexander Napote; various Waam Shows; Arthur Okamura; others.
    Activities: College art classes and workshops; lectures open to the public; concerts; dramatic programs; classes for adults and children; scholarships.
    Library: 100,000 volumes.
    Purchases: $1000 per year.
    Attendance: 15,000 annual average.

ILLINOIS

BLOOMINGTON

BLOOMINGTON NORMAL ART ASSOCIATION*
Russell Art Gallery
Withers Public Library, 202 E. Washington St, 61701.
Tel: (309) 824-7515
Mrs. Royal J. Bartrum, Pres.
Mrs. Ed Ringer, Corresp. Secy.
Open weekdays 10 AM - 9 PM; Sun. 2 - 5 PM except summer months. Estab. 1922. Ann. Meeting 1st Sun. in May, 3:00 PM; mem. approx. 625; dues $2 and higher.
    Activities: Monthly exhibitions; Junior Art Exhibits; Annual Competition for amateur painters and craftsmen of McLean County, Illinois; Alliance of the Arts—special programs in the arts fields. 1972-1973 season: 8 lecture exhibitions, gallery shows; 3 Alliance of Arts lectures and tea; bus trip to Chicago; trip to Rome and Florence, Italy; Amateur Show with 175 items submitted, prizes given.
    Attendance: 100-125.

ILLINOIS WESLEYAN UNIVERSITY SCHOOL OF ART
Alice Millar Center for the Fine Arts, 210 E. University St, 61701. Tel: (309) 556-3077
John Mulvaney, Dir.
Ruth Wentz, Secy.
Open Tues. - Sun. 1 - 4 & 7 - 9 PM. Estab. 1945; financed by endowment and membership. Merwin Gallery.
    Collections: Permanent collection of 190 pieces, including paintings and prints.
    Exhibitions: School of Art Faculty Exhibition; Monnett Experimental Aircraft Show; San Francisco Bay Area Printmakers; The Design Necessity: A Smithsonian Institution Exhibition; Second Annual Illinois High School Art Exhibition; Bloomington-Normal Art Association Amateur Exhibition; Chicago Area Show (Fine Arts Festival); Albion College Student Exchange Exhibition; Bachelor of Fine Arts Degree Exhibitions; School of Art Student Exhibition.
    Activities: Traveling exhibitions organized and circulated; original objects of art lent, on campus only; 190 items lent in an average year; lectures open to public; 5 visiting lecturers per year; many tours; concerts; dramatic programs; competitions; library.
    Publications: Exhibition posters and gallery schedule, monthly.

CARBONDALE

UNIVERSITY MUSEUM AND ART GALLERIES
Southern Illinois University at Carbondale
    62901. Tel: (618) 453-3493 or 453-5388
Dr. Basil C. Hedrick, Dir.
Evert A. Johnson, Assoc. Dir. for Art & Exhibits
Open Mon. - Fri. 10 AM - 4 PM. Art component of larger multi-discipline museum. Art section estab. in 1961 through the university. Galleries are located in the Home Economics and Faner buildings on campus.
    Collections: Contemporary painting, †drawing, †graphics, sculpture and crafts; also an extensive Melanesian collection.
    Exhibitions: Numerous exhibits covering a wide range of fine arts and crafts. Small environments, national drawing and synthetic color exhibits by invitation.
    Library on campus.
    Publications: Color slide catalog sets; yearly printed catalogs.
    Attendance: 50,000.

CHAMPAIGN

UNIVERSITY OF ILLINOIS
Krannert Art Museum
    College of Fine & Applied Arts, 500 Peabody Dr, 61820.
    Tel: (217) 333-1860
Mrs. Muriel B. Christison, Operating Dir.
Free 9 AM - 5 PM; Sun. 2 - 5 PM. Estab. 1874, with the John Milton Gregory collection of casts of classical sculpture.
    Collections: Spencer Ewing collection of Oriental art; L. E. Meyers collection of Early American furniture and art objects; Lorado Taft collection of sculpture; Merle J. and Emily N. Trees collections of paintings; W.P.A. paintings, sculptures, and prints; Olsen collection of Pre-Columbian art; Moore collection of classical and 18th & 19th century European and American decorative arts; †Oriental Arts collection, Class of 1908; †contemporary drawings and prints; contemporary American paintings and sculpture; †Mr. and Mrs. Hermon C. Krannert art collection of Old Masters.
    Exhibitions: Annual faculty exhibition, American Craftsmen exhibitions, architectural and home furnishing shows, Biennial Exhibition of Contemporary American painting & sculpture; occasional one-man shows; purchase awards.
    Activities: Public lectures under the Lorado Taft Lectureship Fund, gallery talks, demonstrations during Festival exhibitions, children's programs, graduate art museum training courses.
    Library: 30,000 volumes, 29,000 photographs, 29,000 slides.
    Income: Approx. $100,000 (exclusive of maintenance and purchase endowment).
World Heritage Museum
    College of Liberal Arts & Sciences, Lincoln Hall.
Georgette Merideth, Dir.
Free weekdays and Sun. 2:30 - 5 PM; Sat. during school term 9:30 - 12 AM.
    Collections: Originals and reproductions of Greek, Roman, Egyptian, Mesopotamian, African, Oriental and European art objects, including sculpture, pottery, glass, implements, coins, seals, clay tablets, inscriptions and manuscripts.

CHARLESTON

✠PAUL SARGENT GALLERY*
Eastern Illinois University
    Lincoln & 7th Sts, 61920. Tel: (217) 581-3410
R. Buffington, Dir.
Free Mon. - Fri. 8 AM - Noon & 1 - 4 PM; cl. School holidays.
Estab. 1948 as exhibition gallery; state and university supported.
    Activities: Temporary and traveling exhibitions.
    Publications: Exhibition catalogs.

CHICAGO

Direter Museum Alan Shestack 10/77

ART INSTITUTE OF CHICAGO
    Michigan Ave. at Adams St, 60603. Tel: (312) 443-3600
James W. Alsdorf, Chmn, Board of Trustees
E. Laurence Chalmers, Jr, Pres.
John Maxon, V.Pres. for Collections & Exhibitions
Donald J. Irving, V.Pres. for Acad. Affairs
Robert E. Mars, V.Pres. Admin. Affairs
Louise Lutz, Secy.
J. Patrice Marandel, Cur. Earlier Painting & Sculpture & Classical Art
A. James Speyer, Cur. 20th Century Painting & Sculpture
Harold Joachim, Cur. Prints & Drawings
David Chandler, Conservator, Prints & Drawings
Douglas Kenyon, Consultant in Conservation, Prints & Drawings
David Travis, Asst. Cur. Photography
Miles Barth, Preparator, Photography

Jack V. Sewell, Cur. Oriental Art
John W. Keefe, Cur. European Decorative Arts
Milo M. Naeve, Cur. American Arts
Christa Mayer-Thurman, Cur. Textiles
Elfrieda Bolyard, Preparator, Textiles
Evan M. Maurer, Cur. Primitive Art
Ingeburg Fiedler, Technician, Conservation
Wallace D. Bradway, Museum Registrar
Barbara Wriston, Dir. Museum Educ.
Jean L. Finch, Dir. of Libraries
Helen M. Lethert, Dir. of Museum Publicity
Margaret Blasage, Dir. Museum Publications
Edith B. Gaines, Dir. Annual Prog.
Howard Kraywinkel, Dir. Museum Photography
Roger Gilmore, Dean, School of the Art Institute
Open Mon, Tues, Wed, Fri. & Sat. 10 AM - 5 PM; Sun. & holidays
Noon - 5 PM; Thurs. 10 AM - 8:30 PM; cl. Christmas Day. Free
Thurs. Estab. and inc. 1879. Mem. (July 1975) 54,600; dues
single member $15, family $25.

Collections: Paintings, sculpture, arts of the Far East, prints,
drawings, photographs, decorative arts, primitive art. The painting
collection reviews the great periods of Western art, with an especially
fine sequence of French Impressionists and Post-Impressionists. The
print collection illustrates the history of printmaking from the 15th to
20th centuries with important examples of all periods. It is particularly rich in French works of the 19th century (Meryon, Redon, Millet,
Gauguin and Toulouse-Lautrec). In drawings there has been emphasis
on 18th and 19th century France. Outstanding in the collection of
earlier drawings is the group given by Mrs. Tiffany Blake and the
group given by Mrs. Joseph Regenstein. The photography collection,
begun in 1949, is also kept in the Department of Prints and Drawings.
The Glore Print Study Room is open to the public Tuesday through
Saturday. The Oriental Department displays the arts of China from
the pre-Han through the early Ch'ing dynasties; sculpture, painting,
jade, lacquer, textiles, ceramics, and the Lucy Maud Buckingham collection of Chinese bronzes. The Russell Tyson Collection, particularly
strong in Chinese and Korean ceramics, with notable examples of
Chinese furniture, is now a part of the permanent collection. Japanese
sculpture and painting of the great periods are represented, and woodblock printing is extensively surveyed in the Clarence Buckingham
collection of Japanese prints, the Gookin and Ryerson collections of
illustrated books, and the Arenberg gift of modern Japanese prints. A
special assemblage of Turkish and Greek Island embroideries is the
gift of Burton Y. Berry; other donors have made possible the creation
of a new gallery devoted to Indian sculpture and miniatures. The
Decorative Arts department collects American and European objects,
with notable groups of English pottery, including the Frank W Gun-
saulus collection of Wedgwood, the Amelia Blanxius collection of English pottery and porcelain, and English and American furniture and
silver. The Buckingham Medieval collection and Thorne Miniature
Rooms are on permanent view. Textiles are displayed in the Agnes
Allerton Textile Galleries, which include a Study Room. The collection of Primitive Art consists of African, Oceanic, and ancient
American objects.

Exhibitions: (1974-75) Paintings by Monet; Max Ernst: Inside the
Sight; 75th Exhibition by Artists of Chicago and Vicinity; Alberto
Giacometti, The Milton D. Ratner Family Collection; Persian and
Indian Miniatures from the Collection of Ann and Everett McNear:
A Promised Gift; American Institute of Architects Awards, 74;
African Art, The World of the Dogon.

Activities: Museum education programs for adults including
lectures, films and discussions; Junior Museum exhibitions, pro-
grams, games and library; Art Rental and Sales Gallery (work by
Chicago-area artists); Museum Store, Kenneth Sawyer Goodman
Memorial Theatre; School of Drama; School of the Art Institute.
(See Schools)

Libraries: Ryerson and Burnham Libraries; reference collections
in art and architecture, 95,584 volumes, 58,848 pamphlets, 166,692
slides (including school contribution) and 21,000 photographs.

Publications: Bulletin, Museum Studies, catalogs, Annual Report.
Income and Purchases: Income (1974-75) $9,201,426; purchases
(1974-75) $695,474.
Attendance: (July 1974 - July 1975) 1,026,948.

Woman's Board
    Art Institute
Mrs. Silas S. Cathcart, Pres. Estab. 1952. Ann. meeting May, mem.
86 (including ex-officio), ann. contribution. Supplement the Board of
Trustees in advancing the growth of the Institute and extending its
activities and usefullness as a cultural and educational institution.

The Auxiliary Board
    Art Institute
Michael J. Goodkin, Pres. Estab. 1973, ann. meeting June; mem. 54;
dues $25. Promotes interest in programs and activities of the Art
Institute among younger men and women.

Antiquarian Society
    Art Institute
Mrs. Edward Byron Smith, Pres. Estab. 1877. Ann. meeting Nov;
mem. 475, by invitation. Tours, trips, lectures and seminars for
members; gifts and decorative arts to the Institute.

Print and Drawing Club
    Art Institute
Frank B. Hubachek, Pres. Estab. and inc. 1922; mem. 150; dues
$25. Study of prints and drawings and their purchase for the Insti-
tute.

Society for Contemporary Art
    Art Institute
Mrs. Malcolm S. Kamin, Pres. Estab. and inc. 1940. Ann. meeting
May; mem. 181; dues $50 and higher. Lectures, seminars and an-
nual exhibition at the Institute. Assists the Institute in acquisition of
contemporary works.

The Orientals
    Art Institute
Jack Sewell, Secy-Treas. Estab. 1925. Mem. 72; dues $10 and
higher. Promotes interest in the Institute's collection of Oriental
Art.

⚓ARTS CLUB OF CHICAGO
    109 E. Ontario St, 60611. Tel: (312) 887-3997
Mrs. Alfred P. Shaw, Pres.
Franklin D. Trueblood, Secy.
Mrs. John Wentworth, 1st V.Pres.
Everett McNear, Chmn. Exhibition Comt.
Richard Christiansen, Chmn, Literary Comt.
Mrs. Maurice Cottle, Chmn, Music Comt.
Patricia M. Scheidt, Admin. Asst.
Free 10 AM - 5:30 PM. Estab. 1916 to maintain club rooms for
members and provide galleries for changing exhibitions open to the
public free of charge. Ann. meeting Nov; mem. 1120; dues lay mem.
$200, professionals $60, nonresident $25.
    Collections: Occasional purchases from bequests.
    Exhibitions: (1974-1975) Joan Mitchell, Recent Paintings; Univer-
sity of Notre Dame Collection; The Horse as Motif, 13th Century B.C. -
20th Century A.D; James Prestini, Sculpture; Kyle Morris, Paintings;
Jack Tworkov, Paintings; Kurt Krantz, Paintings and Drawings.
    Activities; Traveling exhibitions organized, lectures, concerts,
dramatic programs.
    Library: Reference library of 1600 volumes.

ASSOCIATION OF MEDICAL ILLUSTRATORS
    6650 Northwest Hwy, 60631. Tel: (312) 763-7350
Marvin Lurie, Exec. Dir.
For further information see p. 5.

THE BERGMAN GALLERY*
The College, University of Chicago
    5811 S. Ellis, 60637.
Louis Natenshow, Dir.
Joel Snyder, Dir. of Photographic Exhibitions
Mrs. Lisa Urbinato, Asst. to the Dir. & Registrar
Free, Tues. - Fri. 10:30 AM - 5 PM; Sat. 12 AM - 5 PM; during academic year only, cl. during summer. Estab. 1968 as an exhibition
gallery founded entirely by the college of the University of Chicago,
which provides changing shows of artistic and educational interest to
the University Community in all aspects of the visual arts; endowment.
    Exhibitions: Art Deco, Trends in Design; Lelde Kalmite, Paint-
ings; Larry Luckom, Paintings; Posters of WWI; Banners; Contemporary Paintings and Drawings from the Bill Bass Collection; Book
Hands and Decorated Manuscript Leaves 1200-1500; The Visionary
Art of Paul Laffoley; Midway Studio Faculty Show; Photography
Shows; Danny Lyon; Bob Hopkens, Sequences; Mirsky, Friends and
Neighbors.
    Activities: Have adjacent studio facilities used for visual studies
of photography; some courses through the University of Chicago extension are given in conjunction with the Bergman Gallery; material
available to the public; fees vary; traveling exhibitions organized and
circulated; original objects of art lent only in traveling exhibitions;
lectures open to the public; various gallery talks.
    Publications: Catalogues.
    Attendance: 5000 annual average.

CHICAGO HISTORICAL SOCIETY
    Clark St. at North Ave, 60614. Tel: (312) 642-4600
Harold K. Skramstad, Jr, Dir.
Joseph B. Zywicki, Chief Cur, Museum
Robert L. Brubaker, Librn.
Sarajane Wells, Chief, Education Prog.
Museum open Mon. - Sat. 9:30 AM - 4:30 PM, Sun. & holidays
12:30 - 5:30 PM; Library open Tues. - Sat. 9 AM - 5 PM; admis.
adults $1, children (6-17) 50¢, senior citizens 25¢, Mon. free.

Estab. 1856 to maintain a museum and library of American history with special emphasis on the Chicago region. Ann. meeting Oct; mem. 4100; dues $15 and higher.

Collections: Lincoln collection; Costume collection; Pioneer Life; Civil War; Chicago Decorative Arts.

Exhibitions: Permanent and changing exhibitions.

Activities: Gallery tours, auditorium programs and object demonstrations for school groups; pioneer craft demonstrations; "Please Touch" sessions for preschool through grade three; concerts, lectures and films for adults throughout the year.

Library: 142,000 volumes of books, pamphlets, periodicals, newspapers; 8200 reels of microfilm; over 4 million manuscripts, photographs, prints, broadsides, maps and other printed materials. Materials must be used within library.

Publications: Chicago History (members quarterly); occasional books and catalogs.

Attendance: Over 200,000 annually.

CHICAGO PUBLIC LIBRARY

Art Section, Fine Arts Division
    78 E. Washington St, 60602. Tel: (312) 269-2858
David L. Reich, Chief Librn.
Marjorie R. Adkins, Chief, Fine Arts Division
Nancy E. Harvey, Asst to Chief
Flora Footle, Head, Art Section
Ann Caplin, Asst. to Head
Yvonne Brown, Order Asst.
Rae Rondo Weeks, Catalog Asst.
Barbara Mello, Interagency Loan & Periodicals Asst.
Free Mon. - Thurs. 9 AM - 9 PM, Fri. 9 AM - 6 PM, Sat. 9 AM - 5 PM. Estab. 1897; financed by city and state appropriation. Gallery is under the auspices of the Cultural Center of the Chicago Public Library; no exhibits are held in the art section.

Collections: General books, periodicals, indexes and pamphlets in the subject areas of fine and applied art, dance, film and theater arts, costume, architecture, photography and decorative arts. Other divisions and sections of the library hold music, crafts, audiovisual and other related art materials. Special collections include a picture collection of over one million items of secondary source material covering all subject areas, also exhibition catalogs, beginning 1973, primarily English language catalogs; Folk Dance collection, 26 loose leaf volumes.

Activities: General participation in interlibrary loan through the regular channels, each application individually considered; 33,011 books in lending collection. Audiovisual material is handled by the audiovisual section of the library. Materials are restricted to use by Chicago area residents. Lectures open to public, conducted by the Cultural Center; concerts, dramatic programs.

Library: 33,011 volumes for lending and reference.

CHICAGO PUBLIC SCHOOL ART SOCIETY

    Art Institute of Chicago, Michigan Ave. at Adams St, 60603.
    Tel: (312) 922-5472
Mrs. Richard G. Forward, Pres.
Mrs. R. Jackson Coleman, V.Pres.
Mrs. Henry L. Schroeder, V.Pres.
Mrs. G. Barr McCutcheon, V.Pres.
Mrs. Lester Plotkin, Treas.
Mrs. Earl Bolton, Secy.
Office open Mon. - Fri. 9 AM - 5 PM. Estab. 1894; affiliated with Art Institute of Chicago 1942 to enrich public school children through involvement with art. Board meetings during school year. Mem. 700; dues $5 to $200.

Activities: Provides structured professional art appreciation program called Art Form in public schools; awards scholarships for School of the Art Institute to gifted elementary and secondary public school students for Saturday classes in Young Artists Studios; places reproductions in public schools as gifts or at substantial discount.

FIELD MUSEUM OF NATURAL HISTORY

    Roosevelt Rd. & Lake Shore Dr, 60605. Tel: (312) 922-9410
Blaine J. Yarrington, Pres.
E. Leland Webber, Dir.
Dr. Phillip H. Lewis, Acting Chmn, Dept. of Anthropology & Cur. of
    Primitive Art
Dr. Lorin I. Nevling, Chmn, Dept. Botany
Dr. Edward J. Olsen, Acting Chmn, Dept. Geology
Dr. Rupert L. Wenzel, Chmn. Dept. Zoology
Open 9 AM - 4 PM (winter); 9 AM - 6 PM (summer); 9 AM - 5 PM (spring and fall); 9 AM - 9 PM Fri; admis. $1 for adults, $2.50 for families (parents with children), 35¢ for ages 6-17, students with ID and senior citizens; free Fri. Estab. 1894 for the accumulation and dissemination of knowledge, preservation and exhibition of specimens of anthropology (including primitive art), botany, geology and zoology. Financed by membership, endowment and city appropriation, primarily endowment. Mem. approx. 22,000; dues $15 - $100,000. Maintains 22 anthropological exhibition halls including a Hall of Primitive Art.

Collections: Anthropological collections totaling over one third million specimens, including c. †100,000 art objects from North and South America, Oceania, Africa, Asia and prehistoric Europe.

Activities: Film and lecture series in fall and spring; free guided programs for organized groups; weekend Discovery program, participatory activities in exhibit halls; self-guided journeys.

Library: Reference library of 180,000 volumes on anthropology, botany, geology, zoology; photograph collection of thousands of prints.

Publication: Field Museum of Natural History Bulletin, monthly.

Attendance: Approx. 1,200,000.

THE MAURICE SPERTUS MUSEUM OF JUDAICA

    618 S. Michigan Ave, 60605. Tel: (312) 922-9012
Arthur M. Feldman, Dir.
Judith Benjamin, Asst. to Dir.
Grace Cohen Grossman, Cur. of Collections
Mary Dannerth, Registrar
Darcie Fohrman, Exhibitions Specialist
Open Mon. - Thurs. 10 AM - 5 PM; Fri. & Sun. 10 AM - 3 PM; admis. for special exhibitions $1, 50¢ students, senior citizens free. Estab. Dec, 1967, the Museum of Judaica is affiliated with the Spertus College of Judaica; financed by endowment and membership. One main, permanent exhibition gallery with 2 changing exhibition galleries. Mem. 148; dues $15 single, $25 family.

Collections: Ceremonial objects, paintings, sculpture, graphics, coins and medals, archaeological artifacts, a group of Yemenite manuscripts.

Exhibitions: Moshe Safdie; Leonard Baskin; David Moss; Israeli Art in Chicago Collections; Life in the Time of Solomon; Magic and Superstition in the Jewish Tradition; The Jews of Sandor; Jerusalem City of Mankind; Synagogue Architecture in America; Jewish Artists of the 20th Century, a survey.

Activities: Traveling exhibitions organized and circulated; original objects of art lent; 5 items lent in average year; slide collection of 5000 for reference; approx. 250 tours per year on request.

Library: 1000 volumes for reference; Jewish history archives.

Publications: Calendar of Events, annually.

Annual Income: $100,000.

Attendance: 20,000.

MUSEUM OF CONTEMPORARY ART

    237 E. Ontario St, 60611. Tel: (312) 943-7755
Edwin A. Bergman, Pres.
Donald Ludgin, Secy.
Stephen Prokopoff, Dir.
Alene Valkanas, Dir. Pub. Relations
Lynn Jorgenson, Bus. Mgr.
Beverly Kravitt, Mem. Dir.
Eleanor Childs, Secy. to Dir.
Helen Ratzer, Educ. Dir.
Ira Licht, Cur.
John Obuck, Preparator
Katherine McHale, Registrar
Open Mon. - Sat. 10 AM - 5 PM; Thurs. until 8 PM; Sun. 12 AM - 5 PM; admis. adults $1, children and students 50¢, members free. Estab. Oct. 1967; the Museum functions as a privately sponsored, nonprofit institution with a public commitment to encourage an interest in the arts of our time; endowed and financed by membership. Mem. are invited to preview reception of each exhibit; mem. 4500; dues $10, $20, $50, $100 and up.

Exhibitions: One or two exhibits during a 7 week period, closed for installation one week, then mount one or two different exhibits for another 7 week period.

Activities: Tours; community work; special lecture series, 10 visiting lecturers per year; concerts; dramatic programs. Museum gift shop.

Library: 400 volumes for reference; photograph collection and slides for reference.

Publications: Bimonthly calendar; catalogs of exhibits originating at museum.

Income and Purchases: Income $400,000; purchases $450,000.

Attendance: 125,000.

PALETTE AND CHISEL ACADEMY OF FINE ARTS

    1012 N. Dearborn St, 60610. Tel: (312) 337-9889
Cyril Mills, Pres.
Elsie T. Lowe, Secy.
Galleries free 2 - 5 PM; Tues. & Thurs. 7 - 9 PM. Estab. and inc. 1895; owns building containing galleries, classrooms, studios, library. Ann. meeting Jan; mem. over 100 established artists (national and international); dues $84.

Collections: Collection of oil paintings by members.

Exhibitions: Annual juried exhibition of members' work in oils, gold medal award; annual juried exhibition of members' work in watercolors, silver medal award; annual juried exhibition of members' work, mixed media, Diamond Medal Award and Harriet Bitterly cash award; regular exhibits of members' work; special and one-man shows.

Activities: Lectures; educational events.

UNIVERSITY OF CHICAGO
Art Library
  Goodspeed Hall 401, 5845 S. Ellis, 60637.
  Tel: (312) 753-3439
Scott O. Stapleton, Asst-in-charge of Art Library
Open Mon. - Thurs. 8:30 AM - 9 PM; Fri. & Sat. 9 AM - 5 PM; Sun. 1 - 5 PM; hours vary in summer quarter.
  Contains 53,000 volumes on history of art excepting Classical, Near Eastern, and city planning; pamphlet file (5000 pieces); auction sales catalogs (6000 pieces). Also, Union Catalog of Art Books in Chicago, listing the art titles in the following libraries: Chicago Public, Art Institute of Chicago Libraries, University of Illinois Chicago Circle Campus, Field Museum, Newberry, Northwestern University Library (Evanston) and the various divisions of the University of Chicago Libraries. Books on classical art, art of the Near East, and city planning, are housed in the Regenstein Library.

Art Slide Collection
  Tel: (312) 753-3896
Olivera Mihailovic, Cur.
Free 8:30 AM - 4 PM; cl. Sat. & Sun. Estab. 1938. (The slide collection will be moving this coming year into new quarters in the new Art Dept. Bldg.
  Reference collection of 75,000 black and white, 50,000 colored slides. Annual additions: 6000 slides; not available for loan.

Max Epstein Archive
  Tel: (312) 753-2887
Ruth R. Philbrick, Cur.
Free Mon. - Fri. 9 AM - 5 PM; cl. Sat. & Sun. Estab. 1938.
  Reference collection of 400,000 mounted photographs of works of art, also original material in history of prints. Annual additions, 8000 catalogued and mounted photographs.

Lorado Taft Midway Studios
  6016 Ingleside Ave, 60637. Tel: (312) 752-7708
Harold Haydon, Dir.
Free Mon. - Fri. 9 AM - 5 PM; Sat. 12 AM - 5 PM; cl. Sun.
  Studios of Lorado Taft and Associates, a Registered National Historic Landmark; exhibit of maquettes and portraits by Lorado Taft; tours arranged. Now University of Chicago, Department of Art, with exhibitions of student work in painting, sculpture, graphics and ceramics held in the Court Gallery.

The Renaissance Society
  Goodspeed Hall 108, 5845 S. Ellis, 60637.
  Tel: (312) 753-2886
Edward A. Maser, Pres.
Mrs. Jean Goldman, Exhibition Dir.
Free Mon. - Fri. 10 AM - 5 PM; Sat. 1 - 5 PM during exhibitions. Estab. 1915. Ann. meeting May; mem. approx. 500; annual dues $7 and higher. Student Membership (Univ. Chicago) $5.
  Changing exhibitions (about 6 per academic year); Annual Art for Young Collectors Sales Exhibition Nov.-Dec; lectures, gallery talks; catalogues. Only organization to regularly bring exhibitions to the University of Chicago campus. (See Schools).

CLINTON

FINE ARTS CENTER OF CLINTON
  119 W. Macon St, 61727. Tel: (217) 935-5055
Mrs. John Warner, III, Pres.
John Warner, III, Secy-Treas.
Robin McNeil, Dir.
Open Mon. - Fri. 10 AM - Noon, 1 - 5 PM. Estab. 1960, it was the deep conviction of John Smoot DuQuoin, in whose memory the Center was founded, that almost everyone is born with a latent talent and developing that talent, if possible, could be most rewarding; maintained by tuition fees, a nonprofit organization supported by Mr. and Mrs. J. Warner, III. Monthly exhibitions of original art work and photography in the gallery.
  Collections: Collection of contemporary art, Aaron Bohrod, Emil Gruppe, Tom Polston et al.
  Exhibitions: Old Bergen Art Guild (watercolors); American Federation of Arts exhibition; George Eastman House, photography by Dennis Stock; IBM exhibition, Watercolors by Americans; Graphics from Ferdinand Roten galleries and also The Lake Side Gallery, Smithsonian Institution, et al.

Activities: Classes in creative writing, dramatics, oil painting, music theory, drawing, dance, acrobatics, organ, voice, piano, guitar, weaving, jewelry, children's art; concerts, competitions.
Publications: Bulletin of Center activities annually.
Attendance: 550 students, 1000 visitors.

DECATUR

✠KIRKLAND GALLERY
  Millikin University, 62522. Tel: (217) 423-3661
Marvin L. Klaven, Dir.
Free, open during normal university schedule Mon. - Thurs. 12 AM - 8 PM; Fri, Sat, Sun. 12 AM - 5 PM. Part of Kirkland Fine Arts Center, opens Sept. 1970, property of Millikin Univ.
  Collections: Painting, drawings, sculpture, prints.
  Exhibitions: Monthly traveling exhibitions.

ELGIN

LAURA DAVIDSON SEARS FINE ARTS GALLERY
The Elgin Academy
  350 Park St, 60120
Robert Haggemann, Headmaster
D. Scott Irving, Fine Arts Chmn.
Robert Steinmiller, Drama Chmn.
Open to public during drama presentations. Academy founded 1839, chartered 1856 for the purpose of educational art and theater. One room gallery is dedicated primarily to 20th century local artists.
  Collections: Gilbert Stuart's George Washington; sculpture; furniture; Victorian silverplated items; decorative articles.
  Activities: Classes in ceramics, architectural design, painting, drawing and sculpture; photograph collection; 500-1000 prints; dramatic programs. Library.

ELSAH

SCHOOL OF NATIONS MUSEUM
  Principia College, 62028. Tel: (618) 466-2131 Exten. 334
Mary Elizabeth Wheeler, Cur.
Free Mon. - Fri. 8:30 AM - Noon, 1:30 - 4:30 PM.
  Collections: Excellent American Indian collection including baskets, blankets, pottery, leather, quill work, bead work, and silver. Asian Art Collection includes textiles, ceramics, arts and crafts from Japan, China, and Southeast Asia. European collections include glass, patch and snuff boxes, wood, metals, textiles. Dolls represent customs and costumes of the countries and regions of the world.
  Exhibitions: Changing exhibits on campus locations; permanent exhibits in School of Nations lower floor.
  Activities: A Youth Museum serves the Lower, Middle and Upper Schools of The Principia. Special museum programs offered throughout the year on the college campus. Museology courses offered on campus.

GALESBURG

GALESBURG CIVIC ART CENTER, INC.
  114 E. Main St, Box 258, 61401. Tel: (309) 342-7415
Judy Boynton, Pres.
Richard Strader, 1st V.Pres.
Mary Ann Contro, 2nd V.Pres.
Donald Bailey, Treas.
Steven Klindt, Gallery Dir.
Free Tues. - Fri. 11:30 AM - 4:30 PM; Sat. 10:30 AM - 3:30 PM. Estab. 1923; gallery and classroom opened 1965. Individual and family mem. 300, business mem. 75; dues $5 and up; business may sponsor exhibits for contribution of $500 (four week exhibit).
  Collections: Permanent collection of varied media, some gifts, most purchase.
  Exhibitions: Monthly exhibits except for annual Arts and Crafts Sale Nov. and Dec; one members' exhibit with cash prizes, annual Art Market (Indoor Art Fair), Galex juried competition prizes total $1500.
  Activities: Lectures, gallery talks, art exhibits, art demonstrations, art classes for adults and children, tours; offer Gallery for one meeting of various organizations in area (encourage art program for meeting).
  Income: $18,000 - $20,000 annually.
  Attendance: 5000 annually.

JACKSONVILLE

DAVID STRAWN ART GALLERY*
Art Association of Jacksonville
  331 W. College Ave, 62650. Tel: (217) 245-5075
Anthony M. Zaleski, Dir.
Free Sept. - May Tues. - Sun. 3 - 5 PM; also Fri. 7 - 9 PM; cl. Mon, Christmas & holidays. Estab. 1873, chartered by the State 1875; owns building; endowed 1915. Ann. meeting June; mem. 276; dues $3 and higher.

Collections: Valuable collection of pre-Columbian pottery.
Activities: Lectures, gallery talks, classes for children and
adults, traveling exhibitions.

KANKAKEE

KANKAKEE COUNTY HISTORICAL MUSEUM
Small Memorial Park, Eighth & Water St, 60901.
Tel: (815) 932-5279
Charles Stinson, Pres.
Mrs. David Ferris, Secy.
Joe Tolson, Treas.
Don DesLauriers, Cur.
Free Sat. & Sun 2 - 5 PM and by appointment. Estab. 1906, reorga-
nized 1947, to collect historical material relating to Kankakee
County and to display the collections for the public. Ann. meeting
Nov; mem. 400; dues $2 individual, $25 life.
Collections: Historical artifacts relating to the community;
15 George Grey Barnard studio plaster casts.
Exhibitions: Annual Christmas show; special exhibits all year.
Library: Small reference library; oral history library; photo-
graph collection.
Attendance: 2500.

LAKE FOREST

LAKE FOREST LIBRARY
360 E. Deerpath, 60045. Tel: (312) 234-0636
Louise Wells Kasian, Librn.
Sydney S. Mellinger, Asst. Librn.
Free Mon. - Fri. 9 AM - 9 PM; Sat. 9 AM - 5 PM; cl. Sun. Estab.
1898 to make accessible to the residents of the city, books and other
resources and services for education, information and recreation;
financed by city and state appropriation.
Collections: General art collection with particular strength in the
fields of painting and folk art.
Library: 72,000 volumes.
Annual purchases: $25,000.

MACOMB

WESTERN ILLINOIS UNIVERSITY ART GALLERY
61455. Tel: (309) 298-1355
Marie Czach, Dir, Museum-Gallery
Open Mon. - Fri. 8 AM - 5 PM and by arrangement. Estab. adjunct
to Art Department as community service for the University and its
constituency; state appropriation.
Collections: American Indian; contemporary painting; sculpture;
†crafts; †graphics; †Old Master Prints.
Exhibitions: Over 30 exhibitions per year including Annual National Print and Drawing Show; traveling exhibitions; one and two-
man shows of contemporary artists; faculty and student exchange
exhibitions.
Activities: Arts Development Office, serving West Central Illinois schools, banks, churches; traveling exhibitions organized and
circulated; original objects of art lent; lectures open to public,
4-6 visiting lecturers per year; scholarships and tuition waivers.
Attendance: Over 10,000.

MONMOUTH

BOONE ORIENTAL LIBRARY AND FINE ARTS COLLECTION*
Monmouth College, 61462.
A substantial private collection has been made available to the college by its owners, Commander and Mrs. G.E. Boone. The collection
is designed for study and display and is located near the Monmouth
campus. It consists of several thousand volumes and about 1000 art
objects.
Activities: Regularly scheduled classroom lecture courses;
guest artists; films; gallery critiques; special exhibitions.

MT. VERNON

MITCHELL MUSEUM
Richview Rd, Box 923, 62864. Tel: (618) 242-1236
Dr. Herbert Fink, Pres.
Ruby Miller, Secy.
Kenneth R. Miller, Exec. V.Pres.
Free Tues. - Sun. 1 - 5 PM; cl. Mon. Estab. Nov 4, 1973 to present
exhibitions of paintings, sculpture, graphic arts, architecture and
design representing contemporary art trends; to provide continued
learning and expanded education; financed by endowment and membership. Main Gallery, Hall Gallery and Lecture Gallery. Ann.
meeting Nov; mem. 550; dues $25 per person.

Collections: Paintings by late 19th and early 20th century American artists; some drawings and small sculptures; silver; small
stone, wood and ivory carvings; vases; Jade; cut glass; small
bronzes.
Exhibitions: 41 major exhibits since Nov. 1973, plus the
permanent collection.
Activities: Lectures open to public; 6 out-of-town tours;
concerts, classes for adults and children, competitions. Book shop.
Library: 400 volumes; photograph collection of 30 prints.
Publications: Newsletter (quarterly); Calendar of Events
(quarterly).
Attendance: 15,000.

NORMAL

✤CENTER FOR THE VISUAL ARTS GALLERY
Illinois State University, 61761. Tel: (309) 436-5487
Thomas R. Toperzer, Dir.
Gene A. Budig, Pres. of Univ
Charles W. Bolen, Dean, College of Fine Arts
Dr. Fred V. Mills, Chmn. Art Dept.
Open Tues. 9 AM - 10 PM; Wed. - Fri. 9 AM - 4:30 PM; Sat. 1 - 4:30
PM; Sun. 1 - 5 PM; cl. Mon. Estab. 1973; financed by state appro-
priations.
Collections: †Painting; †drawing; †prints; †photography; †sculp-
ture; †glass; †clay; †silver; †metals; †weaving; †fabrics.
Exhibitions: Biennial Crafts Invitational; Illinois Artists
Biennial; Faculty Biennial; rotating contemporary exhibitions.
Activities: Art for special education; serves Central Illinois
area; traveling exhibitions organized and circulated; lectures open
to the public; concerts; dramatic programs; classes for adults and
children; competitions; scholarships.

✤THE UNIVERSITY MUSEUMS
Illinois State University, 61761. Tel: (309) 829-6331
Roslyn A. Walker-Oni, Adminr.
Arlene A. Boggs, Secy. & Registrar
John A. Carlon, Cur, Funk Gem & Mineral Museum
Patricia A. Carlon, Assoc. Cur, Funk Gem & Mineral Museum
David L. Kuntz, Exhibits Technician
Dr. Barry E. Moore, Cur, International Collection of Child Art
Jean I. Shepherd, Curatorial Asst.
Virginia M. Wright, Curatorial Asst.
William V. White, Cur, Graphic Reproduction Collection
Dr. F. Louis Hoover, Dir. Emeritus, Special Consultant
Ewing Museum of Nations, Tues, Thurs. & Sun. 2 - 5 PM; The Univ.
Historical Museum, weekdays 10 AM - 5 PM, Sun. 2 - 5 PM; Funk
Gem & Mineral Museum, daily 2 - 5 PM, except Sat, cl. when classes
not in session; Stevenson Memorial Room, weekdays 2 - 5 PM, cl.
when classes not in session; Hudelson Museum of Agriculture,
Tues, Thurs. & Sun. 2 - 5 PM; Eyestone One Room School, Tues,
Thurs. & Sun. 2 - 5 PM, cl. when classes are not in session. Estab.
1945 to collect, preserve and interpret museum objects and act as a
service to the university community and the general public; city or
state appropriation. Numerous galleries and exhibit spaces which
are used for temporary and permanent exhibits.
Collections: †African Art, †Pre-Columbian Art of Middle America; †South Pacific Art; †Gem and Mineral; †International Dolls;
†North American Tribal Arts; natural history; agricultural, early
education, international collection of child art; Adlai Stevenson
Memorial Room; numerous historical collections.
Activities: Traveling exhibitions organized and circulated;
original objects of art lent; lectures open to the public.
Attendance: 15,000 annual average.

PEORIA

BRADLEY UNIVERSITY GALLERY
School of Art, 61625. Tel: (309) 676-7611, Exten. 285, 258, 385
Verne Funk, Dir.
Open Mon. - Fri. 1 - 4 PM; Sat. & Sun. 1 - 5 PM.
Collections: 100 prints from artists throughout the country.
Exhibitions: Biannual National Print Show; gallery has profes-
sional shows from artists and galleries in the U.S. with shows
changing every month; $2650 in purchases from 1975 show.
Purchases: Annual purchases $300.

✤LAKEVIEW CENTER FOR THE ARTS AND SCIENCES
1125 W. Lake Ave, 61614.
Dr. Ralph Claassen, Chmn, Board of Trustees
Mrs. Gerald Schwab, V.Chmn.
Judy Geary, Admin. Asst. & Interim Dir.
Free Tues. - Sat. 9 AM - 5 PM; Sun. 1 - 6 PM; Wed. 7 - 9 PM; cl.
Mon. Estab. 1964; new building opened 1965; organized to provide
enjoyment and education by reflecting the historical, cultural and
industrial life of the Central Illinois Area. Library facilities.
Dues $22 and higher.

Collections: Archaeological, art and general science.

Exhibitions: Monthly exhibitions dealing with the Arts and Sciences.

Activities: Demonstrations, art classes, planetarium, lectures, concerts.

Publications: Bimonthly bulletin.

Income: $220,000 annually.

Attendance: 300,000 for past 2 fiscal years.

PEORIA ART GUILD*
    1831 N. Knoxville Ave, 61603. Tel: (309) 685-7522
Mrs. Myron Hunzeker, Pres.
Mrs. Thomas Hunter, Secy.
Mrs. John Hansen, Sales Rental
Mrs. Lloyd Hedges, School
Mrs. Charles Roth, Mem.
Mrs. Russell Buster, Artist Chmn.
Stan Adams, Exhibit Chmn.
Free, Tues. - Sat. 10 AM - 4 PM, Sun. 1 - 4 PM; cl. Mon. Estab. 1900, Art Institute of Peoria; 1952, Art Center; 1965, Peoria Art Guild to carry on appropriate activities for the development of the arts, to form, preserve, and exhibit collections of art; financed by mem. Exhibit gallery with a new show every month, also an art sales rental gallery. Ann. meeting May 31; mem. 360; dues $5.

Collections: Guild collection of paintings, graphics, and sculpture is being enlarged by purchase awards from some of our exhibitions and from gifts.

Exhibitions: One-man shows and area exhibitions; Art Has No Sex Show; Craft Show; Black Art Show; membership exhibitions.

Activities: Education department, pre-school and grade school, drawing and painting, ceramics; young people, painting, drawing, printmaking, ceramics, sculpture; adults, painting, silkscreen, ceramics; extension department serves the inner city students; token fee; materials lent, brushes, paint, paper and clay; lending service, original paintings and graphics; 1800 items lent in average year; 200 active borrowers; 600 paintings and graphics for rent and exhibit in the sales rental gallery; lectures open to the public; 3 visiting lectures per year; 8 gallery talks; 15 tours; classes for adults and children; competitions; scholarships.

Publications: The Peoria Art Guild, bi-monthly.

Income and Purchases: Income $7700; purchases $500.

Attendance: 4800 annual average.

QUINCY

✤QUINCY ART CLUB*
Quincy Art Center
    1515 Jersey St, 62301. Tel: (217) 223-5900
William C. Landwehr, Dir.
Mrs. John T. Inghram, Exec. Pres.
Mrs. Paul T. Lambertus, Secy-Treas.
Free Tues. - Sun. 2 - 5 PM; cl. Mon, all legal holidays and during the summer months. Founded 1923, inc, 1951, to foster public awareness and understanding of the visual arts. Ann. meeting last Sun. in June; mem. approx. 400; dues Individual $6, family $10, annual patron $25, life member $250.

Collections: †Painting, sculpture, graphics and crafts by contemporary American and European artists.

Exhibitions: Quincy's Annual Art Show held in Nov. of each year and open to artists living within a 200 mile radius of Quincy; $1200 to $1500 in cash and purchase awards annually.

Activities: Guided tours, lectures, films, gallery talks, concerts; formally organized education program for children and adults; inter-museum loan; permanent, temporary and traveling exhibitions; scholarship program for art classes to underprivileged children.

Library: 350 volumes, periodicals and art books.

Publications: Quarterly calendar; catalogues of temporary exhibitions.

Income & Purchases: Vary from year to year.

Attendance: Approx. 6000.

QUINCY COLLEGE ART GALLERY
    1831 College Ave, 62301. Tel: (217) 222-8020
Robert Lee Mejer, Gallery Dir.
Free 8 AM - 10 PM. Estab. 1968 as a cultural enrichment and artistic exposure for the community; financed by the Quincy College Art Dept and College Art Program. Exhibitions held in the library foyer and the foundation room.

Collections: 19th Century Oriental and European Prints; 20th Century American Prints and Drawings; permanent collection of student and faculty works.

Exhibitions: Prints U.S.A; Contemporary American Drawings; Kathe Kollwitz; Norman Laliberte; New England Group; Blue Rider, New Objectivity, Bauhaus and Abstract Prints; African Sculpture; Byron Burford; Marc Chagall; Twenty-One Paint in Polymer; American Pop Posters; Syed J. Iqbal Geoffrey; Art Protis; Thomas Brown, O.F.M; Illinois Painters II; Contemporary Serigraphs; Contemporary Serigraphs; Contemporary American Drawings V: Norfolk Biennial; Don Crouch; Contemporary European and American Collage; The Quincy College Art Department Faculty; Student Show 73; Wunderlich and the School of Fantastic Realism; Rico Lebrun; Arnold Newman; Middle Western Landscape; Artemisia; Western Illinois University Faculty/Student Prints; Paolo Soleri-Arcology; Watercolor U.S.A; Multiple Media-Erie Art Center; Harvey Breverman; Dr. Grant Lund; Collographs; Martin Garhart; Mark Rogovin, Eskimo Art; Crossan Curry; Larry Rivers, Peter Paone, Louise Nevelson, Claes Oldenburg and Marisol.

Activities: Material available to anyone, no fees; traveling exhibitions organized and circulated; individual paintings and objects of art lent; 20,000 Kodachromes in lending collection; photograph collection; lectures open to public; 2-3 visiting lecturers per year; classes for adults; scholarships. Book shop.

Library: 6800 volumes.

Publications: Annual gallery calendars, brochures 3-5 times yearly.

Attendance: 5000 annual average.

QUINCY SOCIETY OF FINE ARTS
    1624 Maine St, 62301. Tel: (217) 222-3432
George M. Irwin, Pres.
Mrs. William Raufer, Secy.
Open Mon. - Fri. 9 - 12, Tues. 5 - 1. A community arts council estab. 1948 to coordinate and stimulate the visual and performing arts in Quincy and Adams County; a community arts service organization financed by endowment, membership and contribution. Mem. consists of 12 arts organizations.

Activities: Special free workshops in visual and performing arts developed for adults and students throughout the year.

Publications: Quarterly cultural calendars; occasional pamphlets and catalogs.

ROCKFORD

✤ROCKFORD ART ASSOCIATION
Burpee Museum of Art
    737 N. Main St, 61103. Tel: (815) 965-3131
Mrs. Thomas Killoren, Pres.
Mrs. Bay Kaufman, V.Pres.
Mrs. John Nagus, Secy.
Hazen Tuck, Treas.
Birney Grantz, Asst. Treas.
Joseph H. Ferguson, Dir. & Cur.
Mrs. Roger L. Harlan, Secy.
Open Tues. - Sat. 9 AM - 5 PM; Sun. 1 - 4 PM; cl. Mon. and holidays. Founded in 1914, the Rockford Art Association, Burpee Museum of Art has endeavored to promote and cultivate an active interest in all fields of fine and applied art, past and present, in Rockford and surrounding areas. Mem. 700; dues $15 regular, $20 family, $25 patron and $175 life.

Collections: The Association's growing permanent collection is directed toward contemporary American works of national and international importance in graphics, painting and sculpture. The collections in the American painting and printmaking fields are constantly being enlarged through major bequests and additions.

Exhibitions: Annual Exhibitions, Young Artists Show; Annual Juried Photographic Exhibit; Annual Rockford & Vicinity Jury Show; Greenwich Village Fair; Permanent Collection, plus numerous one-man shows and group exhibitions and traveling exhibitions. The Junior Gallery for Children is sponsored by the Women's Board of the Rockford Art Association.

Activities: Annual Greenwich Village Fair; Art Rental and Sales Gallery; studio classes for children and adults; demonstrations, art history seminars, gallery tours, films and special openings. The Show Me a Picture Program organized and implemented by the Association in conjunction with the Rockford Public School System.

Library: Katharine Pearman Memorial Art Library, an extensive collection of books and periodicals dealing with all aspects of the visual arts.

Publications: Burpee Art Museum / Rockford Art Association newsletter; exhibit announcements and brochures.

SPRINGFIELD

ILLINOIS STATE LIBRARY*
    62756. Tel: (217) 525-6683
Alphonse F. Trezza, Dir.
Mrs. Garnetta Cook, Head Audiovisual Section
Open weekdays 8 AM - 4:30 PM; cl. Sat. and Sun. Estab. 1839, Art Service 1916.

Collections: 54,800 †vertical file prints covering painting, sculpture, architecture; theatre, maps, and other items; 500 ††framed art prints; collection of original lithographs, etchings, and block prints; extensive collection of †art books and †magazines in general library.

Reference services are available to patrons of Illinois public libraries on inter-library loan requested through library systems.

Exhibitions: Framed art prints continuously displayed within the Library.

Purchases: $3000 yearly.

Annual Circulation: 500 (essentially a non-circulating collection).

✤ILLINOIS STATE MUSEUM OF NATURAL HISTORY AND ART

Spring & Edwards St, 62706. Tel: (217) 782-7386

Milton D. Thompson, Dir.

Robert J. Evans, Cur. of Art

Betty Carroll Madden, Cur. of Decorative Art and Illinois Art History

Free weekdays 8:30 AM - 5 PM; Sun. 1:30 - 5 PM. Estab. 1877 as a museum of natural history, art gallery added 1927; present museum building erected 1963.

Collections: Paintings, sculpture and graphics by American artists, especially those of †Illinois; midwestern prehistoric Indian artifacts; †Illinois folk and decorative art, including decoys, pottery and textiles; Benjamin Hunter collection of furniture, 150 coverlets and 55 antique clocks; Condell collections of American Indian (basketry, weaving, pottery and jewelry); Condell collection of Oriental art (textiles, bronzes, porcelains, inro and netsuke); Bartels hand-carved Victorian furniture; Carson Pirie Scott & Company miniature dioramas by Eugene Kupjack, featuring rooms and streets of historic Illinois; foreign and American glass, pottery and porcelain; antique dolls; contemporary crafts; foreign and American firearms and hand weapons. Anthropological collections include primitive art from North America, Oceania and Africa.

Exhibitions: Approximately 6 major exhibitions yearly featuring paintings, sculpture, graphics and crafts; Illinois Invitational, annual summer exhibit of contemporary Illinois artists; selections from museum collections exhibited periodically along with permanent displays.

Activities: Guest lectures, seminars, lecture service, guided tours and gallery talks, audio-museum tour; Educational Loan Service for Illinois, films and slides; service to 200,000 monthly; organize traveling exhibits (within Illinois).

Library: Technical, nonlending library of over 50,000 volumes.

Publications: Living Museum (bimonthly) in print and Braille; Arts, Crafts, and Architecture in Illinois; Condell Collection of Oriental Art; Clocks from the Hunter Collection; Carsons Illinois Rooms; G.P.A. Healy (catalog of Museum collection); exhibit catalogs; list of publications available on request.

Income and Purchases: Annual income for entire State Museum system, $1,200,000; annual art purchases, approx. $7000.

Attendance: 320,000 annually.

✤SPRINGFIELD ART ASSOCIATION

700 N. Fourth St, 62702. Tel: (217) 523-2631

Mrs. George Gillespie, Pres.

Mrs. William Telford, V.Pres.

Mrs. Donald Ferry, 2nd V.Pres.

Mrs. George Stickney, Jr, Recording Secy.

Mrs. David Spencer, Corresp. Secy.

Mrs. James Burton, Treas.

William Bealmer, Dir.

Open daily 2 - 5 PM; cl. Mon. Estab. 1900, inc. 1913 to promote the advancement of art in the city of Springfield; to provide to the community an opportunity to study and engage in creative art and to maintain and improve the property known as Edwards Place, donated to the Art Association by Mrs. Alice Edwards Ferguson.

Mem. approx. 1500; dues $10 and higher.

Collections: Permanent collection of 19th century and contemporary paintings, watercolors and prints; Thomas Condell loan collection of antiques; Oriental art; African collection; fabrics.

Exhibitions: Monthly exhibit by nationally known artists, exhibits on painting, prints, crafts and sculpture.

Activities: Lectures, films, gallery talks, instate mini-art tours, foreign art tours, workshops; sales and rental gallery; public school art program; classes for adults and children.

Library: Professional art library of 400 titles.

Publications: Yearly calendar; newsletters; exhibition brochures; membership brochure.

Income: Approx. $100,000 annually.

Attendance: Approx. 2200 per month.

WINNETKA

NORTH SHORE ART LEAGUE

Winnetka Community House, 620 Lincoln, 60093.

Tel: (312) 446-2870

Abby Block, Pres.

Marianne Hartnett, 1st V.Pres.

Peggy King, 2nd V.Pres.

John M. Butler, Jr, Treas.

Paula Fisher, Recording Secy.

Mildred Feinberg, Corresp. Secy.

Open Mon. - Sat. 9 AM - 6 PM. Estab. 1924, inc. 1954 to promote interest in creative art through education, exhibition opportunities, scholarship and art programs. Ann. meeting May; mem. 800 plus; dues $15.

Exhibitions: New Horizons in Painting and Sculpture Shows, juried for entry, nonmember; Old Orchard Art Festival, juried for entry, nonmember. Print and drawing show is shown first at studio, then moves to another location - such as the University of Illinois Circle Campus. Also held is an annual Members Show, a Student Show, Faculty Show and the annual members' fair, juried in all media, location may change from year to year. Annual Midwest Crafts Festival, juried, open to members and nonmembers, at the Old Orchard Shopping Center in Skokie.

Activities: Growth and expansion will be coordinating a number of fund raising events, including exhibits-sales-plus-auctions and other events. Classes for students 6 days a week, 4 evenings; scholarships; monthly evening programs feature lecture, demonstration, film, lively discussion on a variety of art-related topics.

Publication: A ten-issue Art League News during the year.

Income: (1974) Approx. $31,000.

Attendance: Approx. 400 students attend classes per week.

INDIANA

ANDERSON

ANDERSON FINE ARTS CENTER

226 W. Eighth St, 46016. Tel: (317) 649-1248

G. Eugene Yates, Pres.

W. Russell Merritt, Secy.

Dwight B. Stark, Dir.

Sharon L. Hart, Corresp. Secy.

Free Tues. - Sat. 10 AM - 5 PM; Tues. also 7 - 9 PM; Sun. 2 - 5 PM. Estab. July, 1966 for encouragement of the arts by exhibits, working with many cultural groups, being a facility for all the arts, existing for the enjoyment of the entire community; also functions as an arts council; maintained by membership. Three exhibition galleries totalling 1705 sq. ft; in addition, there is a reception area, gift shop, art rental gallery and school area. Ann. meeting first Fri. of May; mem. 1000; dues $2, $10, $15, $25, $50 & $100.

Collections: Group of pictures given to the Center by the Anderson Civic Art Association, recently merged into the Fine Arts Center, representative of Hoosier art of the past twenty years. Also, contemporary American art and European masters.

Exhibitions: In keeping with the Community Arts concept, about half of the yearly exhibits are devoted to artists and art organization within the Anderson community and the remainder from outside the area as rented traveling exhibits or selected one-man shows. The major exhibit each year is the Anderson Winter Show which is a competitive exhibit of watercolors and graphic prints. It is open to all artists in the five states of Indiana, Kentucky, Ohio, Michigan, and Illinois. Purchase prizes and cash awards in amounts of at least $1000 are given. Call for entries normally occurs in December each year.

Activities: Individual paintings lent to schools, original objects of art, 400 Kodachromes in lending collection, motion pictures; lectures open to public; approx. 100 tours during the year; concerts, dramatic programs, classes for adults and children, competition; scholarships.

Library: 200 volumes for reference.

Publications: Calendar of the Anderson Fine Arts Center, quarterly.

Income and Purchases: Income $42,000; purchases vary in amounts up to $2000.

Attendance: 26,000.

BLOOMINGTON

INDIANA UNIVERSITY ART MUSEUM

47401. Tel: (812) 337-5445

Thomas T. Solley, Dir. Art Museum

Free Tues. - Sat. 9 AM - 5 PM; cl. Sun. & Mon. New building completed 1962, includes Art Museum, Art Library, History of Art classrooms, studios, workshops.

Collections: †7,000 Objects of Ancient Art (including jewelry & coins); †2,000 primitive (African, Oceanic, Pre-Columbian), †3,000 Oriental; †1,500 prints and drawings; 500 Near Eastern and 300 other paintings, sculpture and decorative arts; †20th century painting and sculpture; †primitive and ancient art; †print collection.

Exhibitions: (1973-75) Henry Smith's Art; Bernard Greenwald Graphics; Fine Arts Festival; Burton Y. Berry Jewelry Show; Friends of Art Mini Sale; Photographs of Troyes Ruins; 18th-20th Century Drawings from Bloomington Collections; Paintings from Midwestern Collections; First National College Student Print Invitational; The Navajo Blanket; African Dolls; Japanese Master Drawings; New

Faculty Show (Vincent Falsetta); Indiana Printmakers; Master of Fine Arts Show; Henry Manguin Exhibition; Faculty Exhibition.
Attendance: Approx. 5800 visitors per month.
Friends of Art
Members 150. First year of organization, 1965-66.

EVANSVILLE

✠EVANSVILLE MUSEUM OF ARTS AND SCIENCE
411 S.E. Riverside Dr, 47713. Tel: (812) 425-2406
Donald B. Korb, Pres, Board of Directors
Siegfried R. Weng, Dir. Emeritus
John W. Streetman, III, Dir.
Kathleen Kelly, Asst. Dir.
Charlotte Stone, Registrar
Free 10 AM - 5 PM; Sun. 12 - 5 PM; cl. Mon. Estab. and inc. Oct. 25, 1926 to maintain and perpetuate a museum for the people of the City of Evansville and Vanderburgh County in which shall be kept art galleries and museum facilities of history and natural and applied sciences; the Museum to be used to foster the cultural development of the community. Ann. meeting, May; mem. 825; dues $8 and higher.
Collections: Collections include 20th century †American and 16th to 19th century European paintings, graphics and sculpture; Oriental art; †American Indian prehistoric and historic artifacts; medical and dental; arms and armor; †Natural History dioramas and specimens; Planetarium; †Lincolniana; Gothic Room; Pioneer Room; Victorian Rooms; 1910 kitchen and 1890 country store; Transportation including steam locomotive, cars and railroad station.
Exhibitions: Annual regional Mid-States Art Exhibition with awards, Nov; regional Mid-States Craft Exhibition with awards, Feb; High School Art Sch and Industrial Art by school children. Year's programs include traveling exhibitions, invitational artists shows, changing exhibits selected from the Museum collections, others. Total of purchase awards for last 2 years $7850; merit awards $1300.
Activities: Educational programs encompassing preschool through adult classes, docent tours; lectures, films; Civic Theatre; monthly philately, astronomy, camera, numismatic, artists guild programs offered to Evansville and Tri-State area. Planetarium programs. Museum shop, art rental and sales.
Henry B. Walker, Jr, Memorial Art Library: 3000 books on art, science and history. Archives.
Publications: Monthly bulletin.
Income and Purchases: Annual income from Civil City, County and Evansville School Corporation, donations, membership and sales.
Attendance: 112,100 (average last 2 calendar years).

FORT WAYNE

✠FORT WAYNE ART INSTITUTE
Museum of Art
1202 W. Wayne St, 46804. Tel: (219) 422-6467
John Krushenick, Dir.
Free Tues. - Sun. 1 - 5 PM, Sat. 10 AM - 5 PM; cl. Mon. Estab. and inc. 1921. Ann. meeting Apr; mem. 800; dues $15 and higher.
Collections: Permanent collection of †paintings, †prints, †sculpture and minor arts; Thieme Collection of Paintings; Hamilton Collection of Paintings and Sculpture; Fairbanks Collection of Paintings and Prints; Weatherhead Collection of Contemporary Paintings and Prints; William Moser Collection of African Art.
Exhibitions: Changing exhibitions; annual regional artists exhibition.
Activities: Lecture program; art lending service; docent program in cooperation with Fort Wayne and vicinity; school tours for all grades. Museum Shop.

School of Fine Arts Library
Tel: (219) 743-9796
Marilyn L. Murphy, Librn.
Estab. 1960. 5165 volumes, 5000 photographs and 16,000 slides for lending.
Attendance: 25,000.

FORT WAYNE FINE ARTS FOUNDATION
324 Penn Ave, 46805. Tel: (219) 484-9661
Darrell W. Huntley, Pres.
Jean Greenlee, Secy.
John V. McKenna, Exec. Dir.
Mary Brant, Mgr, Community Arts Center
Estab. 1955, dedicated to the development and support of the community artist in every arts discipline; city and county allocation, Annual United Arts Fund Drive. Exhibits in Ft. Wayne Arts Museum and Community Arts Center. Institutional membership organization.
Collections: Permanent Collection at Art Museum.
Activities: Develop programs between colleges, universities and community schools; Fort Wayne School of Fine Arts works with

Indiana-Purdue University on community arts council adult programs; concerts; dramatic programs; classes for adults and children; competitions; scholarships.
Publications: Fine Arts Calendar and Newsletter, quarterly.

PUBLIC LIBRARY OF FORT WAYNE AND ALLEN COUNTY
900 Webster St, 46802. Tel: (219) 742-7241
Charles E. Slater, Pres.
Mrs. Mark Knoblauch, Secy.
Mrs. Richard Belschner, Financial Secy.
Fred J. Reynolds, Head Librn.
Robert H. Vegeler, Asst. Head Librn.
Helen Colchin, Head, Fine Arts Dept.
Free Mon. - Fri. 9 AM - 9 PM, Sat. 9 - 6 PM. Estab. 1968, to provide a reference collection of the highest quality and completeness for the community and its colleges, and a place where local artists and musicians could exhibit their works and perform, and to provide a circulating collection of art prints, slides, and musical scores sufficient to meet the demand; city or state appropriation. Gallery on second floor features exhibitions of local artists, or groups, including painting, sculpture, graphics and photography.
Collections: Maintain framed art print and color slide collections.
Exhibitions: New exhibitions are mounted every six or eight weeks.
Activities: Lending service, framed prints and mounted pictures, 2658 color reproductions and prints, 80 photographs, 8 week loan period, 22,056 Kodachromes, approx. 293,000 mounted pictures; 14,000 framed prints, 14,000 color slides and 25,000 mounted pictures lent in average year; lectures open to the public; gallery talks by library art consult.
Library: Music and art reference library of 9480 volumes.
Publications: Pamphlets of local interest.
Income and Purchases: $10,000 budget.

INDIANAPOLIS

THE CLOWES FUND COLLECTION
Clowes Pavilion, Indianapolis Museum of Art, 1200 W. 38th St, 46208. Tel: (317) 923-1331
Allen W. Clowes, Cur.
Ian Fraser, Research Cur.
Free Tues. - Sun. 11 AM - 5 PM; cl. Mon. Estab. 1958; endowed; formed to display paintings of the Old Masters from the collection of the late Dr. G. H. A. Clowes. Board meeting Feb.
Collections: Italian Renaissance: Duccio, Fra Angelico, Bellini, Luini, Tintoretto, and others. Spanish: El Greco, Goya and others. Northern Renaissance: 17th and 18th Century Dutch, Hals, Rembrandt, and others. French: Clouet, Corneille de Lyon. English: Reynolds, Constable and others. Flemish: Breughel, Bosch, and others.
Exhibitions: Loan Exhibitions 1962, Lenten Exhibition loaned by The Clowes Fund Collection to the University of Notre Dame, South Bend, Indiana; Italian and Spanish Paintings from The Clowes Fund Collection to Indiana University Art Center, Bloomington, Indiana; Northern European Painting from The Clowes Fund Collection same location.
Attendance: 62,000 annual average.

HERRON SCHOOL OF ART
Indiana University-Purdue University at Indianapolis
1701 N. Pennsylvania St, 46202. Tel: (317) 923-3651

Herron Gallery
Kevin Byrne, Chairperson, Faculty Council Exhibition Comt.
Free Mon. - Fri. Noon - 5 PM. Estab. 1970 by Herron School of Art as an enrichment tool for the student body, and as a means of bringing the work of students and faculty to the public eye; financed as part of the school budget.
Exhibitions: Student and faculty shows; various traveling exhibits.

Library
Arthur Weber, Dean
Maudine B. Williams, Head Librn.
David V. Lewis, Asst. Librn.
School estab. 1891; library re-estab. in 1970, necessitated by the separation of the Museum from the School; the former Library was moved with the Museum. The Herron School of Art Library is a visual resource center for the support of the curriculum of the Herron School of Art; financed by state appropriation.
Collections: Collection strengths are in art history, and the studio areas of painting, printmaking, sculpture and illustration. The areas of American art history and American Indian art have received special impetus through soft money funding. Collection also includes 116 periodical subscriptions, and 22,000 slides. (See Schools)

HOOSIER SALON PATRONS ASSOCIATION, INC.
  951 N. Delaware, 46202. Tel: (317) 632-1736
Mrs. Gordon Hughes, Pres.
Mrs. Robert E. Gates, Secy.
Mrs. Ardath Burkhart, 1st V.Pres.
Corbin Patrick, Treas.
Kristin E. Blum, Exec. Dir.
Main gallery open Tues. - Fri. 9:30 AM - 4:30 PM; Sat. 11 AM -
4 PM; cl. Sun. & Mon. Estab. 1925 to promote work of Indiana art-
ists. Ann. meeting June; dues artist $5, member $10 and up.
  Exhibitions: Annual Hoosier Salon in Jan, then on tour; over
$5500 in prize money. Student Show, juried exhibit for undergradu-
ate Indiana University students in Apr; over $200 in prize money.
  Publications: Annual Salon Catelog; History of the Hoosier Salon.

INDIANA STATE MUSEUM
  202 N. Alabama St, 46204. Tel: (317) 633-4948
Carl H. Armstrong, Dir. Museums & Memorials
Jan Finney, Cur. Educ.
David McLary, Cur. Exhibits
Mary Jane Meeker, Cur. Research
Diane Alpert, Registrar
Free daily 9 AM - 5 PM, Sun. 2 - 5 PM. Estab. 1869 for preserva-
tion and interpretation of the natural and cultural history of the
State of Indiana; art collection limited to Indiana artists; financed
by state appropriation and membership. Indiana State Museum
Society Ann. meeting Apr; mem. 1300; dues $5 and higher.
  Collections: Early Indiana artists and leading contemporary
artists.
  Exhibitions: Permanent collection and annual invitational show-
ings of contemporary artists and wildlife artists; 4 art exhibits per
year.
  Activities: Tours, art programs. Gift and book shops.
  Library: 1000 volume general reference library.
  Publications: History-on-the-Move, bimonthly.
  Attendance: 75,000.

INDIANAPOLIS-MARION COUNTY PUBLIC LIBRARY
Arts Division
  40 E. St. Clair St, 46204. Tel: (317) 635-5662
Raymond E. Gnat, Dir.
Miss Helen Barron, Head Arts Division
Open Mon. - Fri. 9 AM - 9 PM; Sat. 9 AM - 5 PM; Sun. 1 - 5 PM.
Estab. 1873.
  Collections: Special collections include the †Julia Conner Thompson Memorial collection of more than 1000 volumes on domestic
architecture, interior decoration, furniture and landscape gardening
as well as the Carnegie Art Teaching Equipment set of 2100
mounted pictures.
  Activities: Circulates books, pictures, pamphlets, clippings and
provides opportunity for reference research for students and the
general public on all fine art subjects.

✠INDIANAPOLIS MUSEUM OF ART
  1200 W. 38th St, 46208. Tel: (317) 923-1331
Harrison Eiteljorg, Chmn. Board of Trustees
John R. Benbow, Pres. Board of Trustees
Robert A. Yassin, Dir.
Peggy A. Loar, Head, Educ. Prog & Asst to Dir for Special
  Projects
Peggy S. Gilfoy, Cur. Primitive Art & Textiles; in charge of Lilly
  Pavilion of Decorative Arts
Paul A. J. Spheeris, Cur. Oriental Art
Ellen Lee, Assoc. Cur. Western Art
Catherine Beth Lippert, Assoc. Cur. Decorative Arts
Martin J. Radecki, Conservator
Lorraine Price, Dir. Pub. Relations
Marian J. Gifford, Dir. Development & Membership
Bezie I. Droege, Head, Special Services
Krannert Pavilion free Tues. - Sun. 11 AM - 5 PM; cl. Mon. Lilly
Pavilion of Decorative Arts open Tues. - Sun. 1 - 4 PM; cl. Mon;
(admis. mem. and children under 12 free; nonmem. voluntary contri-
bution requested, scheduled school groups free). Estab. and inc.
1883, new facilities opened Oct. 1970, 150 acres including island and
lake. Mem. 12,000; dues $15 and higher. Branch galleries:
Indianapolis Museum of Art at Columbus; Downtown Gallery of IMA,
American Fletcher National Bank, 101 Monument Circle, Indianapolis.
  Collections: Pre-Columbian through contemporary art, all media
represented; of particular importance are 19th century American
and British paintings, collection of works by J. M. W. Turner, Oriental collection, 17th century Dutch and Flemish paintings, decorative arts of 18th century Germany, England, France and Italy.
  Exhibitions: (1975) George Deem; Rinaldo Paluzzi; English
Picturesque; Shreve Jade Collection; De Kooning; George Tooker
Retrospective; Cecelia Beaux; Lovis Corinth; IMA High School Artists; Twinrocker Handmade Paper; Alberto Giacometti; Three Centuries of Lace; Land and Sea; Architecture by Alexander Girard;

Charles Rennie Mackintosh; European Prints; Jade as Sculpture;
65th Indiana Artists; Objects & Crafts 1975; French Caricatures;
Harrison Eiteljorg Collection of Western Art; Robert Smithson; Alex
Katz Prints; Birdstones of North American Indian; Greentown Glass;
Recent Acquisitions Contemporary Prints; Indianapolis Collects:
European Furniture and Decorative Arts; Sculpture by Jacquard;
Currier & Ives; Robert Indiana Prints; Printed European Textiles;
European Drawings in the Collection; Raphael's Bible; Chinese Tex-
tiles & Costumes; Accessions: 1975; Illustrations from Dickens.
  Activities: State-wide traveling exhibition program; lectures;
concerts; films; art instruction for children and adults; gallery
tours; home study courses; circulating art exhibits to schools; extension lectures in schools; guided tours to other museums; seminars and workshops; musical presentations in outdoor theatron.
  Library: Art reference library of 18,000 books, 84 vertical file
drawers and extensive file of domestic and foreign museum publications.
  Slide Library, Education Department, Tues. - Sat. 1 - 5 PM;
30,000 art history color slides.
  Attendance: 575,000.

LAFAYETTE

✠LAFAYETTE ART CENTER
Lafayette Art Association
  101 S. Ninth St, 47901. Tel: (317) 742-4470
Suzanne Stafford, Dir.
Open daily 1 - 5 PM; cl. Mon, holidays & Aug. Association estab.
1909, inc. 1927, new Art Center estab. 1960. The new $100,000 Art
Center was paid for by the Association from bequests and accumulated interest through the years. The purpose of the Art Center is
to encourage and stimulate art and to present exhibitions of works of
local, regional and national artists and groups as well as representative works of American and foreign artists. Ann. meeting Oct; mem.
1050; dues begin at $5.
  Collections: 19th and 20th century paintings, drawings and prints;
contemporary works added to the collection each year.
  Exhibitions: New exhibitions installed monthly; juried exhibition
of regional artists and county artists with cash awards, held in
alternate years.
  Activities: Illustrated lectures on the gallery collection and
monthly exhibits are offered to schools, fraternal organizations and
business groups; adult and childrens classes in all art media,
scholarships available; lecture series and workshops. The shop:
work by local artists and craftsmen, museum replicas and imports,
art sales and rental gallery, open daily except Mon. 1 - 4 PM. Fall
Arts Fair. The Art League (volunteer organization).

MUNCIE

ARCHITECTURE LIBRARY
College of Architecture & Planning, Ball State University
  47306. Tel: (317) 285-4760
Marjorie H. Joyner, Librn.
Barbara Ayres, Clerical Asst.
Free Mon. 8 AM - 8 PM; Tues. - Thurs. 8 AM - 9 PM; Fri. 8 AM -
5 PM; Sat. & Sun. 1 - 5 PM. Estab. 1966 to provide materials in
fields of architecture, landscape architecture and planning; financed
by state appropriations.
  Collections: 15,000 bound volumes of books and periodicals;
collection of 29,000 slides; 300 active borrowers.
  Purchases: Approx. $10,000.

✠BALL STATE UNIVERSITY ART GALLERY
  2000 University Ave, 47306. Tel: (317) 285-5242
William E. Story, Dir.
Dolores Terhune, Asst. to Dir.
Open Mon. - Fri. 9 AM - 4:30 PM, 7 - 9 PM (except in summer
when it is closed at night); Sat. & Sun. 1:30 - 4:30 PM; cl. legal
holidays. Estab. 1936.
  Collections: Italian Renaissance art and furniture; 19th and
20th century American paintings, prints, and drawings; Kraft-Ball
Collection of Roman glass; graphics.
  Exhibitions: Traveling exhibitions from national associations;
invitational and special collection shows; national annual competition, juried, Drawing and Small Sculpture Show, with $2500 to $3000
in prizes.
  Activities: Guided tours, lectures, films, gallery talks, concerts, dance recitals, art festivals; formally organized education
programs for children, adults, and undergraduate and graduate
college students; inter-museum loan.
  Attendance: 45,000 annually.

MUNCIE ART ASSOCIATION, INC.*
  600 Court, 610 South Tillotson, 47303. Tel: (317) 747-0628
A. Ben Bennett, Pres.
Mrs. John Lantzius, V.Pres.

Mrs. Robert Kracht, Secy.
William P. Givens, Treas.
Open Tues. - Sat. 11 AM - 4 PM. Estab. 1906 to further interest in art. Cooperates with Ball State University Art Gallery. Board meets monthly; mem. 200; dues $3 and higher.
Collection: Primarily †Indiana artists' works; works may be borrowed by members.
Activities: Sponsors art sales, exhibitions, lectures; local exhibit in the spring; classes for children and evening classes for adults and talented high school students; active loan collection; scholarships; $2000 in prizes and awards.

NASHVILLE

BROWN COUNTY ART GALLERY ASSOCIATION*
#1 Artist Dr, 47448. Tel: (317) 988-4609
Marie J. Thompson, Pres.
Mr. C. R. Peckham, Exec. Secy.
Open every day Feb. 14 - Dec. 15, 10 AM - 5 PM; admis. non-mem. 25¢. Estab. 1926; included in the gallery is the Glen Cooper Henshaw Memorial Room, consisting of 75 permanent memorial works and approximately 100 Henshaw works which are available for purchase. Ann. meeting Oct; mem. 48 active artists, dues $25 annually; 800 supporting $5, $25, and $100.
Collections: Works of past and present members as well as other Indiana artists, contributed by friends of the gallery.
Exhibitions: Spring Show (Feb. 15), Summer Show (June 10), Fall Show (Sept. 10); a special assoc. mem. exhibition annually in Aug.
Activities: Church lectures, community organization meetings.
Youth Activities: Conducted tours for Girl Scouts, Boy Scouts, and special summer and winter camp groups, primarily in Brown County; special exhibitions, high school art works, and special one-man exhibits (approximately three weeks allotted to each of the active artists).
Attendance: 35,000 annually.

NOTRE DAME

ARCHITECTURE LIBRARY
University of Notre Dame
46556. Tel: (219) 283-6654
Geri Decker, Dir.
Open 8 AM - 10 PM. Estab. 1898 as a university branch; financed by endowment and students. Gallery maintained in lobby.
Exhibitions: Student theses; traveling shows.
Activities: Lectures open to public; scholarships.
Library: 15,000 volumes; photograph collection; 25,000 slides.
Annual Purchases: $8000.

ART GALLERY, UNIVERSITY OF NOTRE DAME
O'Shaughnessy Hall, 46556. Tel: (219) 284-6261, 7361
Dr. Dean A. Porter, Dir.
Rev. Richard J. Conyers, C.S.C, Cur.
Fred L. Geissel, Preparator
Free daily 10 AM - 5 PM; Sat. & Sun. 1 - 5 PM; cl. Christmas, New Year's Day, Good Fri. & July 4. Gallery estab. 1917; new building 1952, with five exhibition galleries, vaults, office and workshop; to present a standard of quality and to serve a didactic function within the University and community.
Collections: Permanent collection of over 4000 items including ancient to modern †painting, †sculpture, †prints, †drawings, †ceramics, tapestries and photographs. Of special interest is the F. J. Fisher Collection which consists mainly of 16th century Italian and 18th century French and English painting; the Kress Study Collection of painting and sculpture from the Trecento to 18th century Italian, Spanish and Dutch; the G. David Thompson gift of contemporary painting; †Dr. Tom Dooley Memorial Collection of Primitive Art.
Exhibitions: Exhibitions selected from the permanent collection are augmented by loan exhibitions from private collections and museums.
Activities: Lectures, tours, art seminars, concerts and poetry readings.
Library: A small library for reference.
Attendance: 45,000 annually.

MOREAU-HAMMES GALLERY
Art Department, Saint Mary's College, 46556.
Tel: (219) 284-4074
Dr. Edward Henry, Hon. Pres.
Mrs. Phil Zeitler, Pres.
Mrs. Sig Welber, Secy.
Dr. Joy Holmes, Chmn.
Jean Battles, Art History
Sister Cecelia Ann, Painting

Sarita Levin, Design
Jim Raymo, Photography
Kathleen B. McDonnell, Gallery Coordinator
Daily 1 - 9 PM; cl. Mon. Estab. 1956, for education and community-related exhibits; mem. and coll. support. Gallery presently occupies five rooms; all exhibits rotate; developing a children's gallery. Mem. approx. 50; dues patrons $25, mem. $10, students $5, children $2.
Collections: Cotter collection; Dunbarton collection of prints; Norman LaLiberte: various media.
Exhibitions: Ball State University collection of Drawings & Prints; The Master Gardener, E. Jerome Johnson: Sculpture; Sydney Chafits: Prints; Susan Chiang: Painting; Shalom Moskowitz: Painting; Alice Nichols: Painting; Alta Hertzler: Textiles.
Activities: Lectures open to the public; 3 visiting lecturers per year; 2 tours; concerts; dramatic programs; classes for adults.
Library: 5275 volume lending and reference library; 900 prints for reference.
Publications: Occasional catalogues.
Attendance: 2700-5400 annually.

OSCEOLA

NORTHERN INDIANA ARTISTS, INC.
The Artists Guild
P.O. Box 223, 46561.
Judy Ladd, Pres.
Ruth Davis, Chmn. of Board
Karen Pennino, Secy.
Betty Eming, Mem.
Joan Meyer, Treas.
Cecil Reader, Prog.
Estab. 1942, inc. 1946, for the purpose of promoting contemporary art. Mem. 130 active, 40 associates, 20 patrons; dues $7.
Exhibitions: 8 exhibitions a year; one out-door Art Mart.
Activities: Monthly demonstrations of techniques for members; visiting lecturers.
Publications: News Letter.

RICHMOND

ART ASSOCIATION OF RICHMOND, INDIANA
McGuire Memorial Hall, Whitewater Blvd, 47374.
Tel: (317) 966-0256
Hugh N. Ronald, Pres.
Mrs. W. Ralph Whisenhunt, Dir.
Dr. Denney French, Secy.
Free Sept. - June 8:30 AM - 4 PM; Sun. 2 - 5 PM; cl. Sat. and school holidays. Estab. 1897, inc. 1939, to provide the people of Richmond and surrounding areas with the opportunity for understanding and appreciating the rich cultural heritage of art in its many forms. McGuire Memorial Hall opened 1941, contains galleries, auditorium, art and music rooms. Ann. meeting third Mon. of Sept; mem. 600; dues adult $3, student $1, family $15, contributing any amount, benefactor $100.
Collections: †Paintings, †sculpture, †pottery, †prints, †textiles.
Exhibitions: Four annual exhibitions, ten special shows yearly. $750 in awards.
Activities: Lectures, tours, sponsors exhibitions of arts and crafts of foreign countries as well as American art, lending services.
Library: Library of 600 volumes; 30,000 catalogued reproductions.
Purchases: $500.
Attendance: 40,000.

LEEDS GALLERY
Earlham College Art Department
National Road W, 47374. Tel: (317) 962-6561
Franklin Wallin, Pres, College
Bernard Derr, Chmn, Art Dept.
Leeds Gallery open at all times 8 AM - 12 PM; no admis. fee. College estab. 1847 as a liberal arts college; privately financed, denominational; Leeds Gallery estab. 1970.
Collections: Well-represented regional artists: Marcus Mote, Bundy (John Ellwood), George Baker; prints by internationally known artists of 19th - 20th centuries.
Exhibitions: By individual artists, mostly regional; some traveling shows.
Activities: Traveling exhibitions organized and circulated; individual paintings and original objects of art lent; 1 or 2 items lent in average year; lectures open to public, 5-6 visiting lecturers per year; concerts, dramatic programs. Book store.
Library: 220,000 volumes including 4500 art books for lending and reference; 800 prints in photograph collection for reference.
Gallery Budget: Income $2500; Purchases $500-$800.

SOUTH BEND

✠SOUTH BEND ART ASSOCIATION, INC.
South Bend Art Center
   121 N. Lafayette Blvd, 46601. Tel: (219) 233-8201
Jack McGann, Pres.
Joan Beesley, Treas.
Andrew Nickle, Secy.
Vincenzo Mangione, Dir.
Open daily 9 AM - 5 PM; Sun. 2 - 5 PM; cl. Mon. Estab. 1947 with
the purpose of increasing awareness in the arts by presenting exhi-
bitions and lectures and offering classes in art instruction. Ann.
meeting 1st Sun. in Sept; mem. 900; dues $10 and higher.
   Collections: †Contemporary American art, †contemporary
ceramics.
   Exhibitions: Biennial Michiana Regional (Indiana & Michigan) and
Biennial Michiana Local (50 mile radius) with cash awards totaling
$2000; exhibitions by local artists and traveling shows.
   Activities: Lectures by specialists. Gallery talks and talks by
staff to community groups; foreign films; TV shows by staff; classes
for adults; Sat. classes for children; $400 worth of classes are
awarded to underprivileged children who either show promise in art,
or who would benefit by extra-curricular classes. Some are given on
a quarterly basis, names of children are given per the South Bend
Community School Corporation.
   Library: Small reference library, slide collection, reproductions
for study.
   Income: $95,000.
   Attendance: Approx. 20,000.

TERRE HAUTE

✠SHELDON SWOPE ART GALLERY
   25 S. Seventh St, 47807. Tel: (812) 238-1676
Mrs. Anton Hulman, Jr, Pres.
Mrs. John R. Haslem, Treas.
Ewing H. Miller, Secy.
James D. Bowne, Dir.
Mrs. Catherine Tackett, Cur.
Free daily 12 AM - 5 PM; Sun. 2 - 5 PM; cl. Mon, cl. Aug. Estab.
1942; endowed by bequest of Sheldon Swope.
   Collections: Paintings and sculpture, chiefly by contemporary
American artists; Oriental art.
   Exhibitions: Changed monthly; special Wabash Valley Annual in
March.
   Activities: Gallery talks for clubs, schools and other groups;
special tours for students of Indiana State University, Saint-Mary-
of-the Woods College, Rose-Hulman Institute and others.

UPLAND

CHRONICLE-TRIBUNE ART GALLERY
   Taylor University Art Department, 46989. Tel: (317) 998-2071
   Exten. 322
Ray E. Bullock, Art Gallery Supv.
Free Mon. - Sat. 9 - 12 AM, 1 - 4 & 7 - 9 PM; cl. Sun. Estab.
1972 as a permanent art collection, traveling art exhibitions, and
student art exhibitions; original gift of Gannet Foundation, supported
by the university.
   Collections: Includes all areas of visual art.
   Exhibitions: Rudy Pozzatti, prints; Thomas Thiery, watercolors;
Leland Boren Indian collection; numerous university and student
exhibitions.
   Activities: Dramatic programs; classes for adults; children's
classes.

VALPARAISO

SLOAN GALLERIES OF AMERICAN PAINTINGS
Valparaiso University
   Henry F. Moellering Memorial Library, 46383.
   Tel: (219) 462-5111
Dr. Warren Rubel, Chmn, Sloan Comt.
Richard Brauer, Cur.
Free during school year Mon. - Fri. 8 AM - 10 PM; Sat. 9 AM - 5
PM; Sun. 1 - 10 PM; special hours in the Summer and during school
holidays. Founded 1953; endowed. An extensive collection of works
by American artists and an endowment for their maintenance and ex-
pansion were given to the University by Percy H. Sloan as a memorial to his parents, Junius R. and Sara Spencer Sloan. In October,
1959, the initial exhibition of a monthly schedule of shows was installed in the galleries' first permanent home in the new Henry F.
Moellering Memorial Library.
   Collections: The Sloan Collection is composed of over 400 paintings by American artists in a range of time of little more than a
century. A cross section of styles represented reflect such European
influences as Romanticism, Impressionism, Realism, and Cubism,
while typical American works range from genre paintings to contemporary forms of Expressionism. The main body of the collection
comprises works by Junius R. Sloan and a number of his contemporaries of the Hudson River School. Recent purchases have extended
the collection in its representation of samples from the major movements of the last three decades. A schedule of acquisitions is
planned so that in the near future at least one work of every American painter of historical importance of the last fifty years will be included in the collection. A considerable section of the collection is
devoted to the Chicago-Indiana Dunes area. The permanent collection is distributed on loan to buildings throughout the university.
   Income and Purchases: Income $6000; purchases $3000.

IOWA

AMES

THE OCTAGON
Ames Society for the Arts
   232½ Main, 50010. Tel: (515) 232-5331
Richard Snyder, Pres. of the Board
Hazel Lipa, Secy.
Martha Benson, Dir.
Free Mon. - Fri. 1 - 5 PM; Sat. 10 AM - 5 PM; Sun. 2 - 5 PM; also
Mon. 5 - 9 PM. Estab. Jan. 1966, community art center providing
quality art experiences for people of all ages; financed by appropriation and membership. Ann. meeting Oct; mem. 600; dues
student $6, single $10, family $15, patron $25, benefactor $100.
   Exhibitions: Monthly exhibitions in two galleries of the work of
artists from throughout the region, the country and the world.
   Activities: Classes for adults and children in all media; circulating exhibits; rental material available, 5 sets of lantern slides;
lectures open to public, 5 visiting lecturers per year; 5 gallery
talks; 150 tours; concerts, dramatic programs, competitions. Book
Shop, Fibers to Fabric Shop, weaving, spinning and all textile supplies.
   Income: $80,000.
   Attendance: 20,000.

ANAMOSA

PAINT 'N' PALETTE CLUB
   R.R. 3, 52205. Tel: (319) 462-2601
Mrs. Jerry White, Pres.
Mrs. John Christophersen, Secy.
Dr. Gerald F. Brown, Exec. Dir.(elected)
Mildred B. Brown, Exec. Dir.(charter member)
Free Sun. afternoons from June 1 through middle of October; at any
other time for groups or individuals by appointment. Estab. 1955 for
the enjoyment and education of artists and interested public in the
area. The Antioch school (on the grounds of the gallery) was attended
by Grant Wood for 4 years as a boy. This building is maintained as a
historical museum, also open to the public; maintained by membership and donations. The gallery was constructed with funds donated
by Dr. Gerald F. Brown of the area; it is in the form of a Log Cabin,
therefore, Log Cabin Art Gallery. Ann. meetings 2nd and 4th Wed.
of each month regularly; other times by notice; mem. 37; dues $10.
   Collections: Two Grant Wood original litho's, three Mae Amelia
Rumple oils.
   Exhibitions: Three annual exhibitions in July of each year, Iowa
State Arts Council regional in 1970.
   Activities: Traveling exhibitions organized and circulated locally
in the area; individual paintings lent to schools; original objects of
art lent; lectures open to public; 5 or 6 visiting lecturers per year;
approx. 35 to 40 gallery talks or tours per year; classes for adults;
competitions. Book Shop.
   Publications: Annual brochure at time of the annual exhibit.
   Annual Income: $370 dues plus donations.
   Attendance: (1974) Approx. 4000.

CEDAR RAPIDS

✠CEDAR RAPIDS ART CENTER
   324 Third St, S.E, 52401. Tel: (319) 366-7503
Sutherland C. Ellwood, Pres.
Frank A. Davey, Treas.
Stan H. Widerspan, Dir.
Fred E. Easker, Jr, Asst. Dir.
Free Memorial Day - Labor Day, Tues. - Fri. 10 AM - 5 PM; Thurs.
5 - 8:30 PM; Sat. 10 AM - 1 PM; cl. Sun. & Mon. Labor Day -
Memorial Day, Tues. - Sat. 10 AM - 5 PM; Thurs. 5 - 8:30 PM;
Sun. 2 - 5 PM; cl. Mon. and all legal holidays. Inaugural opening
Dec. 3, 1966; permanent Grant Wood Gallery opened fall 1973. Ann.
meeting last Mon. in Jan; mem. 1800; dues student $5, individual
$10, family $15, contributing $25, supporting $50, sustaining $100,
patron $500, benefactor $1000.

Small permanent collections; 17-20 exhibitions a year; active education program including studio classes, films, lectures, Art Center Shop, Sales and Rental Gallery; Art Library, circulating exhibitions, Children's Gallery.
Publications: Newsletter.
Attendance: 35,000-40,000.

COE COLLEGE ART GALLERIES
1221 1st Ave. N.E, 52402. Tel: (319) 398-1637
Robert Kocher, Chmn. Art Dept.
Mrs. Robert Donaldson, Gallery Dir.
Free, Mon. - Fri. 8 - 10 PM; Sat. 10 - 12 AM; Sun 2 - 4 PM. Estab. 1942 for traveling exhibitions; financed by part of instructional college budget. Two galleries, both 60 x 18, 125 running feet exhibit space.
Collections: Coe Collection: Approx. 200 works by various persons; Marvin Cone Collection of 26 oils; Marvin Cone Alumni Collection; Conger Metcalf Collection; Forest M. Hinkhouse collection of contemporary art.
Exhibitions: 8-12 per year, mostly one-man shows of regional nature or rental print exhibitions.
Activities: Traveling exhibitions organized and circulated; individual paintings lent to schools; 1-3 items lent in an average year; 2 active borrowers; lectures open to the public; 1-2 visiting lecturers per year; 3 tours.
Library: 125,000 volumes.
Publications: College catalog.
Annual budget: $5500.
Attendance: 10,000 annual average.

CHEROKEE

SANFORD MUSEUM AND PLANETARIUM
117 E. Willow St, 51012. Tel: (712) 225-3922
Karl de Rochefort-Reynolds, Dir.
Patricia Williams, Asst. Dir.
Free 9 AM - Noon, 1 - 5 PM; Sun. 2 - 5 PM; cl. Sat. PM. Museum opened Apr. 1951; Endowed. Established by the late Mr. and Mrs. W.A. Sanford of Cherokee, as a memorial to their son, for the preservation and display of educational and historical objects. Ann. meeting Apr; mem. (Sanford Museum Asn.) 200; dues $5 and higher.
Collections: †Archaeological, †Natural History, †Historical.
Exhibitions: Traveling art, crafts and ethnological public school art.
Activities: Films, adult education courses, planetarium demonstrations for groups by appointment, lectures, art classes.
Library: Approx. 2000 volumes, mainly scientific, for reference only.
Publications: Northwest Iowa Archeaological Society Newsletter.
Income: $16,000.
Attendance: 20,000.

CLINTON

CLINTON ART ASSOCIATION GALLERY
P.O. Box 132, 708 25th Ave. N, 52732. Tel: (319) 242-9635, 242-8055
Hortense Blake, Dir.
Free Sat. & Sun. 1 - 5 PM, except holidays. Association estab. in 1947, Gallery, May 1968, to bring art to the community; no other Clinton organization has the furthering of interest in art as its sole aim; supported by membership. Gallery. Ann. meeting May; mem. approx. 300; dues single $5, family $10, patron $25, sustaining $40 or more.
Collections: Eighteen pieces, enlarging as possible; some donations.
Exhibitions: 265 since 1970; 10 Art Fairs (2 each year).
Activities: Lectures open to public, 3 visiting lecturers per year; 10 gallery talks; 10 tours; conserts, classes for adults and children.
Publications: Newsletter every two months.
Income: Approx. $3500.
Attendance: Approx. 3000.

DAVENPORT

✳DAVENPORT MUNICIPAL ART GALLERY
1737 W. 12th St, 52804. Tel· (319) 326-7804
Walter E. Neiswanger, Pres, Board of Trustees
Dudley Priester, 1st V.Pres.
Dorothy Edelen, Secy.
L. G. Hoffman, Dir.
Alex Edward Vance, Dir. Educ.
Della A. Dillon, Admin. Secy.
Jacqueline Ross, Bookkeeper-Clerk
Mimzi Litscher, Curatorial Registrar
Roberta Geheren, Mem. Secy.
Gladys Hitchings, Librn.

Free Tues. - Sat. 10 AM. - 4:30 PM; Sun. 1 - 4:30 PM; cl. Mon. & legal holidays. Estab. 1925 by City of Davenport.
Collections: Notable examples of European and Spanish-Colonial paintings; 19th and early 20th century American painting; Haitian art; European, Eastern and American collection of prints; paintings, drawings, and prints, Grant Wood Gallery.
Activities: Monthly changing exhibitions including Annual Mid-Mississippi Valley Competition; lectures, films, demonstrations, concerts; Art Force Gallery for Children; creative studio classes for adults and children with courses in painting, drawing, stoneware pottery, graphics and others; Rental-Sales Gallery; Gallery Shop, two annual out-of-doors Beaux Arts Fairs.
Library: Expanding Art Reference Library of 8000 volumes, slide index and reproductions of art.
Publications: Quarterly Preview; catalogues; collection research.
Income and Purchases: Operating income (1974) $328,153; purchases $5000-$10,000.
Attendance: 95,000.

Friends of Art
Davenport Municipal Art Gallery
Msgr. S. G. Menke, Pres.
Mary Allard, Treas.

Gallery Guild
Davenport Municipal Art Gallery
Mrs. William Swanson, Pres.
Mrs. George Friedl, V.Pres.
Ann Swanson, Treas.

PUTNAM MUSEUM
1717 W. 12th St, 52804. Tel: (319) 324-1933
Joseph L. Cartwright, Dir.
Janice Hall, Cur. Natural History
Jacqueline Denison, Cur. Exhibits
Betty Keen, Cur. Prints & Documents
Carol Hunt, Registrar
Peter Petersen, Cur. of Educ.
Open to the public Mon. - Sat. 9 AM - 5 PM; Sun. 1 - 5 PM. Estab. 1867 as Academy of Science. Ann. meeting May; mem. approx. 2500; dues individual $10, joint $15.
Collections: Art, History and Science Museum: natural history; ethnology; archaeology; botany; paleontology; anthropology; art prints, watercolors, drawings, and primitive art.
Activities: Lectures; films; gallery talks; formally organized education programs for children and adults; permanent and temporary exhibitions; manuscript collections; traveling exhibitions.
Income: Approx. $200,000.
Library: 50,000 volumes, science, art and history.
Attendance: 100,000.

DECORAH

VESTERHEIM
Norwegian-American Museum
517 W. Water St, 52101. Tel: (319) 382-5105
Dr. E. J. Nordby, Pres.
Phyllis Leseth, Secy.
Marion John Nelson, Dir.
Darrell D. Henning, Cur.
Betty Seegmiller, Admin. Asst.
Open May - Oct. 9 AM - 5 PM; Nov. - Apr. Sat. & Sun. 9 AM - 5 PM; weekdays by appointment; admis. adults $1.50, children 15 and under 75¢, children 6 and under free. Estab. 1877, inc. 1964 to engage in all activities necessary for the collection, preservation and exhibition of all artifacts which will throw light on the life of people in the United States of Norwegian birth and descent both in their home environment in Norway and in their settlements in America; endowed, maintained by membership, admis. and sales. Art objects and paintings distributed throughout the museum as they relate to the general display. Ann. meeting Oct; mem. 2500; dues $5, $10, $25 or $100, $500, $1000 once.
Collections: Nine historic buildings; decorative and applied arts and crafts; domestic articles; mementos, pictures, etc, all as apply to the Norwegians in America. Collections are being enlarged primarily by donations, but where possible by purchase.
Exhibitions: National Rose Painting Exhibition; Hooked Rug Display; Needlework Display (Hallmark Gallery, New York); Gausta Paintings, Minneapolis, 1967; Famous Barr, St. Louis; Indianapolis Children's Museum; Waterloo Dairy Congress; State Fair, Iowa, 1969.
Activities: Specialized classes in rose painting; weaving, embroidery (Hardanger, klostersom, etc); traveling exhibitions organized and circulated; original objects of art lent; photograph collection; lectures open to public; gallery talks or tours on appointment, mostly for school children and tour groups; competitions. Book and gift shop.

Library: 250 volumes for reference.

Publications: Newsletter, quarterly; Pioneer Cook Book; Time-Honored Norwegian Recipes; Norrøna Sketchbook; Rosemaling in Norway Today; Rosemaling in America Today.

Income and Purchases: Income $70,000; purchases for acquisitions $1500.

Attendance: 24,000.

DES MOINES

✠DES MOINES ART CENTER
Greenwood Park, 50312. Tel: (515) 277-4405
James T. Demetrion, Dir.
Peggy Patrick, Asst. Dir.
William F. Loebel, Dir. of Educ.
Julie Cramer, Asst. in Educ.
Clyde Johnson, Development Coordinator
Margaret Buckley, Librn.
Euphemia Conner, Registrar
Grace Owens, Secy. to Dir.
Helen Greer, Mem. Secy.
Ruth Green, Secy. to Educ. Dept.
Sara Mercer, Asst. Treas.
Elsa Godfrey, Mgr. Gallery Shop
Edmundson Art Foundation, Inc.
Mrs. Myron N. Blank, Pres.
James Cooney, V.Pres.
Robert Lubetkin, Treas.
John Pappajohn, Secy.
Free Sun & holidays Noon - 5 PM; other days 11 AM - 5 PM; cl. Mon. The will of J. D. Edmundson, Des Moines financier, provided for the erection of an art museum to serve as the Edmundson Art Foundation, which operates the Art Center. The Center was designed by Eliel Saarinen and was formally opened in June, 1948. In Oct. of 1968, the Art Center's gallery space was virtually doubled with the addition of a wing designed by I. M. Pei. Mem: 3500; dues $15 and higher.

Collections: †J. D. Edmundson Collection of American art including Bellows, Burchfield, Hartley, Hopper, Kuniyoshi, Lachaise, Lipchitz, Raymond Parker, Prendergast, Ben Shahn and Shinn; †Nathan Emory Coffin Collection includes works by Jean Arp, Barlach, Mary Cassatt, Corot, Courbet, Daumier, Diebenkorn, Goya, Paul Klee, Johns, Lichtenstein, S. Macdonald-Wright, Maillol, Marin, Monet, Henry Moore, Isamu Noguchi, Noland, Oldenburg, Pissarro, Rauschenberg, Rodin, Rothko and Sloan; †Rosenfield Collection includes works by Armitage, Dove, Grosz, Lipton, Matta and Nicholson. Gifts to the collection include works by Baziotes, Bourdelle, Brancusi, Gauguin, Graves, Gris, Kokoschka, Levine, Matisse, Picasso, Rouault, Gilbert Stuart, and other contemporary Americans. Prints and drawings numbering around 1000; small collection of Asiatic Art, African Primitive and Pre-Columbian Art.

Exhibitions: Iowa Artists Annual.

Activities: Lectures; films; demonstrations; concerts; Junior Art Museum; nonprofessional art school for adults with courses in painting, drawing, ceramics, weaving, design, jewelry, graphics and others; children's art classes for preschool through high school. Rental and Sales Gallery.

Library: Expanding art library of 6400 volumes including rare art reference books.

Publ: Bimonthly bulletins; catalogs of exhibits.

Income and Purchases: Income (operating) $500,000.

Attendance: 125,000, annual gallery attendance.

DUBUQUE

DUBUQUE ART ASSOCIATION*
596 W. 11th, 52001. Tel: (319) 588-9751
Mrs. Edward Schuster, Pres.
Art gallery at the Barn open daily 2 - 5 PM; week nights 7 - 9 PM. Estab. 1910, inc. 1956. Ann. meeting May; mem. 400; dues $5 and higher.

Collections: Paintings, drawings, prints, sculptures.

Activities: Monthly programs; lectures, gallery talks, films, slides; classes for all ages; bus tours, Beaux Arts Ball, Dubuqueland Area Annual Competition Show; Graphics U.S.A. (National Print Show 1970); 1973 Five Flags Sculpture Competition, $1000 prize for best entry.

FAIRFIELD

FAIRFIELD PUBLIC LIBRARY AND MUSEUM
Fairfield Art Association, Court & Washington, 52556.
Tel: (515) 472-3236
Mrs. Gary L. Cameron, Pres.
James Rabis, Librn.
Ben Taylor, Museum Dir.

Library open 11 AM - 8:30 PM; museum 11 AM - 6 PM; art gallery 6 - 8:30 PM. Library and museum financed by endowment and city appropriation; Art Association financed by endowment and membership.

Collections: Ornithology, minerals, Indian artifacts, pioneer implements, †paintings, †graphics.

Activities: Art Association offers classes for adults and children; lectures open to public; competitions; gallery.

FORT DODGE

BLANDEN ART GALLERY
920 Third Ave. S, 50501. Tel: (515) 573-2316
Robert A. Loomis, Pres, Board of Trustees
Craig E. Carlson, V.Pres, Board of Trustees
Robert J. Halm, Secy, Board of Trustees
Stephen L. Rhodes, Dir.
Free Tues. - Fri. 1 - 4:30 PM; Sat. 9 AM - Noon, 1 - 4 PM; Sun. 1:30 - 5 PM; cl. Mon. and holidays. Dedicated 1932, the Gallery was a gift to the city from Charles G. Blanden as a memorial to his wife; municipal art museum partially supported by city funds.

Collections: Paintings, sculpture and prints by contemporary American and European artists; †small collection of Japanese prints and screens; †paintings by minor American impressionists.

Exhibitions: Monthly loaned exhibitions augment continuous exhibitions of selections from the permanent collection.

Activities: Adult and children's art classes, films and lectures in cooperation with Iowa Central Community College and the Blanden Gallery Federation of Arts.

Library: Art reference library for use by the public on the premises.

Publications: Blanden Art Gallery Newsletter, monthly; catalogs for special exhibitions; annual report.

IOWA CITY

✠THE UNIVERSITY OF IOWA MUSEUM OF ART
Riverside Dr, 52240. Tel: (319) 353-3266
Jan Muhlert, Dir.
Richard Wickstrom, Assoc. Cur. of Prints & Photography
Free Mon. - Sat. 10 AM - 5 PM; Sun. 1 - 5 PM. Estab. 1969. Mem. approx. 500; dues $5 and higher.

Collections: Owen and Leone Elliott collection of early 20th century paintings, old master prints, English silver and Chinese jade; University collection of paintings, prints and sculpture; primitive pre-Columbian and African art; Lithographs from Tamarind Workshop; other loan collections of European and American paintings and prints.

Exhibitions: Approx. 20 exhibitions a year drawn from the permanent collection and loan exhibitions.

Activities: Print and Drawing Study Club; guided tours, lectures and gallery talks by artists, critics, historians and collectors.

Publications: Catalogs of exhibitions.

Attendance: 40,000.

KEOKUK

KEOKUK ART CENTER*
Box 871, 52632.
Mrs. Richard Gammon, Pres.
Mrs. Richard Lofton, Secy.
Richard Stebbings, V.Pres.
Delbert Chapman, Treas.
Bruce Busey, Prog. Dir.
Free Mon. - Sat. 9 AM - 5 PM. Estab. 1954 to promote art in tri-state area, supported by membership. Keokuk Public Library, 210 N 5th St. gives use of gallery. Ann. meeting 1st Mon. in May; dues individual $5, family $8.

Collections: Starting permanent collection, approx. 10 paintings and sculpture.

Exhibitions: One per month, runs for 3 weeks, all media.

Activities: Individual paintings lent to schools; original objects of art lent; 10 items lent in an average year to 3 active borrowers; lectures open to public; 2 gallery talks; classes for adults and children; competitions.

Publications: Newsletter, quarterly.

Income: $1500.

Attendance: 2000.

MARSHALLTOWN

CENTRAL IOWA ART ASSOCIATION, INC.
Fisher Community Center, 50158. Tel: (515) 753-9013
Mrs. Stanley Doerr, Pres.
Mrs. LeRoy Ackerson, Secy.
Open 1 - 4 PM. Inc. 1959. Ann. meeting May; mem. approx. 600; dues $7.50, students $5.

Collections: Fisher collection includes Utrillo, Cassatt, Sisley, Vuillard, Monet, Degas, Signac, Le Dourge, Vlaminck, Montioolli; sculpture—Christian Petersen, Romenilli, Bourdelle and ceramic study collection including Gilhooly, Arneson, Nagle, Kottler, Babu, Geraedts, Boxem, Leach, and traditional Japanese wares.

Activities: Monthly exhibits; reference library; classes for adults and children; classes in ceramics, sculpture; jewelry, painting. Exhibits begin the first Sun. of the month and are open weekdays thereafter. Approx. 6 gallery talks a year.

Library: Art reference library.

Attendance: Approx. 30,000.

MASON CITY

✤CHARLES H. MacNIDER MUSEUM
303 Second St. S.E, 50401. Tel: (515) 423-9563
Frank R. Jeffrey, Pres.
Robert Zimmer, Treas.
Pauline Hedgecock, Secy.
Richard E. Leet, Dir.
Miss Glyde J. Wheeler, Dir. of Educ.
Mrs. John Hoblit, Secy.
Free Tues. & Thurs. 10 AM - 9 PM; Wed, Fri. & Sat. 10 AM - 5 PM; Sun. 2 - 5 PM; cl. Mon. and holidays. Opening date, Jan. 9, 1966; estab. to provide North Central Iowans and Southern Minnesotans with a complete arts program. Mem. approx. 600 individuals and families.

Collections: Permanent collection being developed with an emphasis on †American and Iowa art, containing prints, paintings and pottery. Artists represented include Oliveira, Dove, Davies, Levine, Francis, Healey, Prior, Lasansky, Burchfield, Graves, Burford, Metcalf, Wood, Maurer, Benton, Baziotes.

Exhibitions: Monthly art exhibitions of regional, national and international scope are featured; Annual Iowa Crafts Competition ($800 in awards); Annual Area Competitive Show ($350 in awards); Aaron Bohrod; Alfred Maurer (collection Univ. of Nebr); Kaethe Kollwitz; American Paintings from the Winston Collection; African Textiles and Jewelry; Light Sculpture; A Sense of Place; Biennial Staff Show.

Activities: The Museum program features art classes, lectures, films, concerts, summer arts festival and guided tours. Classes are conducted year-round.

Library: Reference library information.

Publications: Regular newsletter.

Income and Purchases: Income $63,000; amount of purchases varies.

Attendance: Average 28,000.

MASON CITY PUBLIC LIBRARY
225 Second St. S.E, 50401. Tel: (515) 423-7552
Lowell R. Wilbur, Library Dir.
Reath Snyder, Art Librn.
Free 9 AM - 9 PM. Estab. 1883. Special art room of 3400 circulating books. Exhibit hall with monthly exhibitions. Purchases of paintings small and limited to regional artists. Circulating collection of 420 originals and reproductions; small permanent collection; 120,424 volumes in library.

Activities: Occasional lectures.

Income: Library, $166,919; art dept. varies.

MT. VERNON

ARMSTRONG GALLERY
Cornell College
52314. Tel: (319) 895-8811
Doug Hanson, Dir. Gallery & Chmn. Dept. of Art
Free Mon. - Fri. 7:30 AM - 4:30 PM. Estab. to display artists' work; financed by Cornell College.

Collections: Thomas Nast Drawings and Prints; Sonnenschein Collection of 57 15th-17th Century European Drawings.

Exhibitions: 6 exhibits each year, plus 10-20 student thesis shows each year.

Activities: Lectures open to public, 1 visiting lecturer each year.

ORANGE CITY

NORTHWESTERN COLLEGE ART GALLERY
Ramaker Library
51041.
John Kaericher, Dir. Gallery & Chmn. Art Dept.
Free Mon. - Fri. 9 AM - 4 PM (except college vacations). Estab. 1968 to provide original visual art exhibitions and programs for the campus and surrounding towns; financed by endowment.

Exhibitions: Stuart Edie Paintings; Pratt Graphic Shows; Roten Gallery Shows; Japanese Woodcuts; Area Artists; Faculty and Student Shows; many contemporary artists' shows.

Activities: Traveling exhibitions organized and circulated; individual paintings and original objects of art lent.

SIOUX CITY

SIOUX CITY ART CENTER
Art Center Association of Sioux City
513 Nebraska St, 51101. Tel: (712) 279-6272
Peggy Parris, Dir.
Free Tues. - Sat. 10 AM - 5 PM; Sun. 2 - 5 PM; cl. Mon. holidays, Aug. Sponsoring group estab. 1914 as Sioux City Fine Arts Society, reorganized 1938 as Art Center Association. Ann. meeting Dec; mem. 450; dues $15 to $250 annually.

Collections: Municipal Gallery has small contemporary collection of †regional and national work (400 pieces).

Exhibitions: Circulating alternating exhibitions, local shows, one regional competition, painting and prints, drawings and sculpture.

Activities: Exhibitions of the best of contemporary and traditional arts, gallery tours, art forum programs, chamber music and concerts, films, children's and adult art courses, junior activity programs. Rental Gallery, Gift Shop.

Library: Collection of current magazines, dealing with all phases of art; art books and folios, slides, for reference only.

Income and Purchases: Income, $65,000; annual purchases $1600.

Publications: Monthly bulletin, exhibition catalogs.

Attendance: 25,000.

WATERLOO

WATERLOO ART ASSOCIATION
420 W. 11th St, 50702. Tel: (319) 232-1984
James L. Smith, Pres.
Ilene Cook, Secy.
Edna Reeck, V.Pres. & Gallery Chmn.
Arlo Johnson, Treas.
Free Wed. 10 AM - 4:30 PM; Sat. & Sun. 2 - 4:30 PM. Estab. 1960 to encourage area artists and provide for the exhibition of their work; maintained by membership. Rented building providing three gallery rooms, workshop room, art supply sales room and storage rooms. Ann. meeting last Tues. in Jan; mem. 100; dues $10.

Exhibitions: The work of a professional guest artist of this area each month.

Activities: Operate a sales and rental gallery for the benefit of members; individual paintings lent to schools by special arrangement; lectures generally open to public, two visiting lecturers per year; classes for adults; competitions.

Attendance: 1200.

WATERLOO MUNICIPAL GALLERIES
225 Cedar St, 50704. Tel: (319) 291-4491
Clarence Alling, Gallery Dir.
Free Mon. - Fri. 9 AM - 5 PM; Sat. 9 - 12 AM; Sun. 2 - 5 PM. Estab. 1957 to provide an art forum for the Waterloo area; appropriation. Ann. meeting 2nd Thurs. of Jan; mem. 500; dues $3 single and up.

Collections: Small new collection of contemporary American painting, prints, and sculpture.

Exhibitions: Monthly exhibitions of regional painting, sculpture, prints and fine crafts.

Activities: General art classes for children and adults in the Waterloo area; Junior Museum, attendance 16,000; lectures open to public; approx. 10 gallery talks or tours per month; dramatic programs; competitions.

Attendance: 35,000.

WEST BRANCH

HERBERT HOOVER PRESIDENTIAL LIBRARY
52358. Tel: (319) 643-5301
Thomas T. Thalken, Dir.
Open year-round, Mon. - Sat. 9 AM - 5 PM; Sun, May - Labor Day 10 AM - 6 PM, Sept. - May 2 - 5 PM; admis. adults 50¢, children under 16 and school groups free.

Estab. 1962, governed by National Archives and Records Service; books, memorabilia, personal papers and other material reflecting Hoover's life. Forty-five additional manuscript collections are included within the Library's holdings. National Historic Site surrounding the Library is administered by the National Park Service and includes the birthplace, gravesite, Quaker meeting house, blacksmith shop and park.

KANSAS

ABILENE

DWIGHT D. EISENHOWER PRESIDENTIAL LIBRARY
67410. Tel: (913) 263-4751
Dr. John E. Wickman, Dir.
William K. Jones, Museum Cur.

Open daily 9 AM - 5 PM; cl. Thanksgiving, Christmas Day, New Year's Day; admis. adults and children over 16, 50¢, children accompanied by parents admitted free. Library estab. May 1, 1962, Museum April 6, 1954; Federal Government appropriation.

Collections: Research Library and Museum contains papers of Dwight D. Eisenhower and his associates, together with items of historical interest connected with the Eisenhower Family. Mementos and gifts of General Dwight D. Eisenhower both before, during, and after his term as President of the United States.

Library: Reference library of 23,000 volumes and reference collection of 75,000 prints.

Attendance: Center, 400,000 .

HARPER

HARPER ART ASSOCIATION, INC.
  67058.
Dorothy Scarlett, Pres.
Ruth Staugh, Secy.
In process of relocating gallery in Santa Fe Art Depot which will curtail shows and services a bit because of space. Financed by membership. Ann. meeting 2nd Sat. in Apr; mem. 26; dues $5.

Collections: Permanent collection of past and present members' works; art instructors' works.

Exhibitions: Rural Urban District Shows, Kansas State University.

Activities: Classes for adults and children, competitions.
Library.

HAYS

FORT HAYS KANSAS STATE COLLEGE ART GALLERY
  67601. Tel: (913) 628-4287
John Thorns, Jr, Chmn. Art Dept.
Zoran Stevanov, Chmn. Exhibition
Free Mon. - Fri. 8 AM - 5 PM. Estab. 1953 to exhibit creative work on a college campus; financed by city and state appropriations.

Collections: †Contemporary Prints; Regionalist (1930's) Print Collection; †Graduate thesis work.

Exhibitions: B. Cook, Paintings, Prints and Drawings; J. Bass, Sculpture; Kansas First National Small Painting, Drawing and Print Exhibition; C. J. Eastman, Paintings; Faculty Exhibition, FHKSC Art Department; B. Alexander and K. Hendry, Ceramics.

Activities: Traveling exhibitions organized and circulated; individual paintings and original objects of art lent; 50 color reproductions, 75 photographs, 30,000 lecture slides, 100 motion pictures, 35 film strips in lending collection; 25 shows lent in an average year to 10-12 active borrowers; photograph collection of 200 prints for lending and reference; lectures open to the public; 2 visiting lecturers per year.

Attendance: 10,000 annual average.

HUTCHINSON

HUTCHINSON ART ASSOCIATION
  c/o Mrs. Laura Barr, Secy.-Treas, 321 E. First St, 67501.
  Tel: (316) 662-6242
Shirley Schmidt, Pres.
Jane Dronberger, V.Pres.
Marvel Senti, Exhibit Chmn.
Estab. 1949 to bring exhibitions to the city of Hutchinson and maintain a permanent collection of 50 watercolors, prints, oils circulated in the public schools. Ann. meeting; mem. 125; dues $5 and higher. Exhibitions are held in the Hutchinson Public Library, and include an all-member show as well as annual Art Fair. Prize awards $3500.

KANSAS STATE FEDERATION OF ART
  c/o Winston A. Schmidt, Dir, 510 E. 14th St, 67501.
Estab. 1932 to sponsor exhibitions of various types at low cost. Ann. meeting spring; mem. 35 organizations, dues $15; 100 individuals, $2 and $5. At present inactive.

INDEPENDENCE

INDEPENDENCE MUSEUM*
Ladies Library and Art Association
  123 N. Eighth, 67301. Tel: (316) 331-3515
Mrs. Harold Bullock, Pres.
Mrs. James Gilmore, Secy. & Chmn. Board of Dirs.
Mrs. Edgar Beahm, Chmn. Board of Trustees
Open Sun, Wed, Sat. 1 - 5 PM; open other times by appointment; admis. 50¢ Estab. 1882 to foster the arts and help make them available to all. Gallery contains many original works plus artifacts. Meeting once a month Oct.-May; mem. 150; dues $6.

Exhibitions: Monthly exhibitions; Institute of Lopedics Exhibit; Annual Arts & Crafts Show.

Activities: Present one-man shows; have had 20 annual art exhibits, open to all within a 200 mile radius; facilities available to the public; work closely with the schools; annual exhibit from both the high school and college classes.

LAWRENCE

✠UNIVERSITY OF KANSAS MUSEUM OF ART
  66044. Tel: (913) 864-4710
Charles Eldredge, Dir.
David Curry, Asst. to Dir.
Bill Hennessey, Cur. Collections
James L. Enyeart, Cur. Photography
Dolores Brooking, Cur. Museum Educ.
Free Tues. - Fri. 9 AM - 4:45 PM; Sat. & Sun. 1:30 - 4:45 PM; cl. major holidays. Museum estab. 1928 to provide the community with the opportunity to enjoy original works of art and to supplement with original material the studies of the various departments of art and art history offered at the University. The Museum aims to illustrate, both by means of its permanent collection and by loans from other institutions, the various forms and aspects of the visual arts. The Museum collections are available to the general public for study at any time. Advance notice must be given by those desirous of viewing some portion of the collection not on display. Mem. c. 500 renewable annually; dues students $5, regular mem. $10-$49, patrons $50-$99, benefactors $100 or more.

Collections: European and American painting and sculpture from medieval to modern times; European and Oriental decorative arts; medals and placquettes from the Renaissance to the present; Samuel H. Kress Study Collection of Medieval and Renaissance Painting; W. B. Thayer Memorial Collection (includes Oriental and European art); Gene Swenson Collection of American modern art.

Exhibitions: (1970-73) Gene Swenson: Retrospective for a Critic; The Arcadian Landscape: 19th century American Painters in Italy; 150 Years of American Quilts; Invisible in America: Photos by Marion Palfi; American Drawings & Watercolors; John Steuart Curry. (1973-75) The Stouse Collection: The Arts of Costa Rica; Spanish Baroque Drawings in North American Collections; Stitches in Time: Samplers in the Museum's Collection; Glimpses of Fugitive Pleasures: Japanese Prints from the Museum Collection; The Art of the Indian Basket in North America.

Activities: Frequently the opening receptions of the various changing exhibitions are highlighted with introductory lectures concerning the exhibition. Tours of the Museum of Art, accompanied by short lectures, are available if arrangements are made in advance.

Library: Reference library related to collections only.

Publications: The Register of the Museum of Art, twice annually, exhibition catalogs, the Handbook of the Museum of Art, 1962.

Attendance: 100,000 annually.

LINDSBORG

THE BIRGER SANDZEN MEMORIAL GALLERY
Bethany College Campus
  401 N. First St, 67456. Tel: (913) 227-2220
Dr. C. P. Greenough, III, Co-Dir.
Carl William Peterson, Co-Dir.
Open daily 1 - 5 PM; cl. Mon. and major holidays; admis. charged. Estab. 1957 for the purpose of permanently exhibiting Dr. Birger Sandzen's graphics and paintings, in addition to exhibiting work of other artists.

Permanent Exhibitions: Oil paintings, watercolors, graphics, ceramics and sculpture; 17th century Japanese bronzes.

Monthly Exhibitions: Prints and oils by nationally known artists on display each month, with an average of 25 changes annually. A special exhibition, estab. in 1899 is held during Easter Week; this exhibition is the oldest annual art exhibition in Kansas.

Gallery Courtyard: The Little Triton fountain, the only major work of the Swedish sculptor Carl Milles to be found in Kansas.

Activities: Gallery talks, lectures.

Library: 180 art books.

Publications: Graphic Work of Birger Sandzen.

Attendance: 7000-9000.

THE McPHERSON COUNTY MUSEUM AND OLD MILL COMPLEX
  Mill St, 67456. Tel: (913) 227-3595
T. S. Anderson, Cur.
Pauline Glendening, Secy.
Open weekdays 9:30 AM - 5 PM (May-Oct); 1 - 5 PM (Nov-Apr); Sun. 1 - 5 PM; cl. Mon. and major holidays; admis. charged.

The McPherson County Museum, located by the Smoky Hill River, contains not only the Bethany College Museum collection, but items of the early history of the Midwest and the Scandinavian heritage of the Lindsborg area. Adjacent is the old Runbeck Mill, the only existing water-driven flour mill still standing in the county today.

The complex across the street contains an early little red school-house, the Thomas Pavilion which housed the Swedish Government Exhibit at the 1904 St. Louis World's Fair Exhibition, the first class-room building used on the Bethany College campus in 1881, and Sweadal (the first U.S. Post Office in McPherson County in 1869 and first county courthouse of 1870).

THE MINGENBACK ART CENTER*
Bethany College Campus, 67456.
Daniel Mason, Dept. Head
Art classroom building, Department of Art, Bethany College, completed in 1970.
College Collection consists of numerous oil paintings, water-colors, prints, etchings, wood engravings, lithographs, ceramics, and sculpture. Material is used as general education reference, not for public display.

TOPEKA

ARTS COUNCIL OF TOPEKA, INC.
216 W. Seventh St, 66603. Tel: (913) 357-71119
Gabriel Morales, Pres.
Stewart Entz, Pres-Elect
Susan Ellis, Exec. Dir.
Open Mon. - Fri. 9 AM - 4 PM. Estab. 1959, reorganized late 60's, to enrich the quality of life for all Topekans by seeing that they are exposed to arts-related opportunities and experiences; financed by appropriations from Kansas Arts Commission and membership. 63 mem. organizations; 179 individual mem.
Activities: Arts information and central ticket center; speakers' bureau; identification of local artists; special services to arts organizations. Lectures hosted; gallery trips organized; sponsoring program on art therapy; coordinated art exhibit for West Lake Bi-centennial Committee. The Arts Council also sponsored a Street Arts Happening, bus tours to points of artistic interest and coordinated a special ticket program for those individuals who normally do not have the opportunity to attend arts events. All programs free to public.
Publications: Monthly newsletter; calendar of arts activities.

GALLERY OF FINE ARTS
Topeka Public Library
1515 W. Tenth St, 66604. Tel: (913) 233-2040
James C. Marvin, Head Librn.
Gladys Davis, Secy.
Tom Muth, Asst. Librn.
Robert H. Daw, Head, Fine Arts Dept.
Larry D. Peters, Gallery Dir.
Free Mon. - Fri. 9 AM - 9 PM; Sat. 9 AM - 6 PM; Sun. in winter 2 AM - 6 PM; cl. Sun. in summer. Estab. 1871 to provide the community with exposure to changing exhibitions including the gal-lery's permanent collections; financed by city and state appropria-tion. New 30 x 40 ft gallery with carpeted walls and track lighting. Approved alarm systems for fire and theft; various cases and pedestals. Separate collections room and office with alarms.
Collections: †Kansas Artist Collection; Art Glass; Prints; Miscellaneous Chinese Textiles; Early 1900's Pottery.
Exhibitions: Art of the West; Kansas Artist Craftsman Traveling Exhibition. Emphasis is being put on exhibitions which are built rather than renting.
Activities: Original objects of art lent on specific occassions to other institutions; Over 1200 color reproductions, 300 motion pictures, over 3000 Kodachromes and 100 art objects and reproduc-tions in lending collection; lectures open to public; concerts.
Library has 30,000 volumes.

MULVANE ART CENTER
Washburn University, 66621. Tel: (913) 235-5341
R. J. Hunt, Dir. & Head, Art Dept.
Free 9 AM - 4 PM; Sun 2 - 5 PM; cl. Sat. & Holidays. Estab. 1924; building, gift of Margaret Mulvane, provides 3 galleries, studios and classrooms for Department of Art. Mem. approx. 750; dues $7.50 and higher.
Collections: International paintings, sculpture, prints, and crafts.
Exhibitions: Continuous program of exhibitions; students' exhibi-tion, May.
Activities: Frequent gallery programs; films open to the commu-nity without charge; popular art lectures in Topeka by staff and visit-ing artists; classes for adults and children.
Library: 3,000 volumes on art.
Publications: Exhibition brochures.
Income and Purchases: Income approx. $60,000; purchases approx. $2000.
Attendance: Approx. 20,000 annually. (See Schools).

TOPEKA ART GUILD*
P.O. Box 701, 66601. Tel: (913) 272-9660
Charles L. Marshall, Pres.
Harry B. Nelson, Cur.
Free weekdays 9 AM - 5 PM; Sun. 3 - 5 PM. Estab. 1916, inc. 1936. Ann. meeting May; mem. approx. 250; dues $2 and higher.
Collections: About 17,000 prints and photographs which are circulated to schools and organizations in the State.
Activities: Exhibitions changing every two or three weeks through the school year; lectures; demonstrations.

WICHITA

✣EDWIN A. ULRICH MUSEUM OF ART
Wichita State University
67208. Tel: (316) 689-3664
Dr. Martin H. Bush, V.Pres. Univ. & Dir. Museum
Gary Hood, Asst. Cur.
James W. Johnson, Curatorial Asst.
Sheryl Wolfe, Registrar
Free Wed. 9:30 AM - 8 PM; Thurs. & Fri. 9:30 AM - 5 PM; Sat, Sun. and holidays 1 - 5 PM. Estab. Dec. 1974; the Museum not only serves a student body of 15,000 by presenting over 46 important ex-hibitions each year, it also shares freely its cultural and educational facilities and programs with the greater Wichita area and the State of Kansas; financed by endowment. Gallery, 6000 square feet of ex-hibition space with movable walls.
Collections: The Museum's collection of over 3500 examples of American art is one of the largest west of the Mississippi. The painting collection is particularly strong in 20th century American art with beautiful examples by Max Weber, George L. K. Morris, Ernest Trova, Arnold Blanch, Robert Goodnough, Frank Stella, Thomas Cole and hundreds of others. There are 1250 prints in the print section; approximately 210 Pre-Columbian and American Indian items; numerous major sculptures by individuals such as Alexander Calder, Louise Nevelson, Lynn Chadwick, Ernest Trova, Gerhardt Marcks, August Rodin, Alexander Archipenko, George Rickey, Chaim Gross, George Kolbe and others. In addition to a small collection of African art, the Museum has 150 paintings by ma-rine artist, Frederick J. Waugh.
Exhibitions: (1975) Frederick J. Waugh 1861-1940; Yousuf Karsh; James Abbott McNeill Whistler, 1834-1903; Rembrandt Harmensz Van Rijn, 1606-1669; Robert Goodnough; Selections from the Permanent Collection; Isabel Bishop Retrospective; Käthe Koll-witz, 1867-1945; Honoré Daumier, 1808-1899; Dorothea Lange, 1895-1965; George Grosz, 1893-1959; Wayne Thiebaud; Will Barnet; Childe Hassam, 1859-1935; American Pop Art; Walker Evans; Lyonel Feininger, 1871-1956; Clayton Staples; Photo-Realism; Lawrence Calcagno; Lewis Hine, 1874-1940; Ernest Trova; Our Only World; Abraham Walkowitz Retrospective, 1880-1965; First Biennial Wichita State University Faculty Exhibition; Alfred Eisenstaedt; Hair; Charles Grafly, 1862-1929; Henri Manguin; Executive Order 9066; African Textiles and Jewelry; Photographs of Kertesz, Rodchenko, and Moholy-Nagy; Richard Pousette-Dart; Harry Sternberg; Eugène Atget; Richard Anuszkiewicz; Cork Marcheschi; Civil War Drawings; Milton Glaser; Antwerp's Golden Age; 18th and 19th Century Por-traits; Leonardo da Vinci; Models based on the Madrid Manuscripts.
Activities: Over 500 Wichita State University students study all aspects of art, design and art history. (See Schools) Continuing education material available to everyone; photograph collection; lec-tures open to public, 10 visiting lecturers and 10 gallery talks per year; concerts, classes for adults; scholarships. Book shop.
Publications: Goodnough; Harry Sternberg: A Catalogue Raisonné; numerous exhibition brochures.
Attendance: 80,000.

KANSAS WATERCOLOR SOCIETY*
1545 Willow Lane, 67208.
Kean Tilford, Pres.
Jean Shelito, Secy.
Estab. 1968 to promote watercolor in Kansas by annual competition, traveling shows, workshops, scholarships, and others; financed by mem. and entry fees. Ann. meeting Fall; mem. 66; initiation dues.
Exhibitions: Competition each fall.
Activities: Two traveling shows in Kansas; materials lent, watercolor; traveling exhibitions organized and circulated; lectures open to the public; workshop.
Income: Non profit organization.

WICHITA ART ASSOCIATION, INC.
9112 E. Central, 67206. Tel: (316) 686-6687
Olive Ann Beech, Chmn. of Board
Gladys Wiedemann, Pres.
John R. Rouse, Dir. & Cur.
Oliver Witterman, Secy.
John T. Sheffield, Treas.
Galleries open 1 - 5 PM; cl. Mon. Estab. 1920, inc. Apr. 1932. Ann. meeting May; mem. 1000; dues $25 and up.

Collections: Prints and drawings, paintings, sculpture, decorative arts and crafts.

Exhibitions: National Graphic Arts and Decorative Art-Ceramics exhibitions alternate biennially, with $2500 prizes given for Decorative Arts; traveling exhibitions change each month; one-man shows; special programs.

Activities: Lectures, gallery talks, concerts, workshops, films, demonstrations. Sales gallery. Wichita Children's Theatre is a subsidiary of the Association; Garden Club, Antique Collectors Club and Monday Morning Group are also subsidiaries.

Library: Over 2500 art reference volumes.

Publications: Monthly newsletter.

Attendance: 25,000.

✤WICHITA ART MUSEUM
619 Stackman Dr, 67203. Tel: (316) 264-0324
Howard E. Wooden, Dir.
Mrs. Kenneth Brasted, Chairperson of the Board
Mrs. Leonard Metzker, Treas.
Jon Roe, Secy.
Open 10 AM - 5 PM; Sat. & Sun. 1 - 5 PM; cl. Mon. Original building completed in 1935, enlarged by the addition of three new wings in 1963. The Museum is owned and operated by the city assisted by a board of 10 members.

Collections: Roland P. Murdock Collection of American Art; L. S. & Ida L. Naftzger Collection of European Prints, Florence N. Evans European and Oriental Porcelain and Faience Collection; Kansas Artists Collection; Lucy T. Powell Ivory Collection; Edmund L. and Faye Davison Collection; M. C. Naftzger Collection of Charles M. Russell.

Exhibitions: Major exhibitions yearly. Biennial state-wide exhibition of paintings, sculpture and prints; Kansas Artists Biennial, awards total $6450; traveling exhibitions.

Activities: Lectures on art history and appreciation; visiting lectures; docent service for school children and interested groups; films and concerts.

Library: Over 2000 volumes with an emphasis on American art.

Income and Purchases: Income $190,000 City of Wichita; purchases by the Wichita Art Museum Members Foundation, Inc.

Attendance: 60,000.

WICHITA PUBLIC LIBRARY
223 S. Main, 67202. Tel: (316) 265-5281
Ford A. Rockwell, Head Librn.
Gary D. Hime, Asst. Librn.
Virginia Dillon, Circulation Dept. Head
Viola Tidemann, Reference Dept. Head
Bonnie Rupe, Acquisitions Dept. Head
Wilma Brooks, Art & Music Dept. Head
Barbara Fischer, Children's Room Dept. Head
William Hoffman, Business & Technical Dept. Head
Sondra Koontz, State-Wide Film Service
Betty Spriggs, Talking Books for the Blind
Free Mon. - Thurs. 8:30 AM - 9 PM; Fri. & Sat. 8:30 AM - 5:30 PM; Sun. 1 - 5 PM. Estab. 1876 and grown to be an informational center and large free public library to improve the community with educational, cultural and recreational benefits through books, recordings, films, art works and other materials. No dues. Total registered borrowers: 127,299.

Collections: Driscoll Piracy Collection; John F. Kennedy Collection; Harry Mueller Philately Book Collection; Kansas Book Collection.

Annual Exhibitions: Kansas Scholastic Art Awards Show; Wichita Area Girl Scout Exhibit; Annual Best News Photographs Exhibit; Wichita Women Artists; Senior High School Students Spring Exhibit; plus numerous other exhibits throughout the year.

Activities: 8 branch libraries; Mail-A-Book to county residents; free service to everyone; lending collection of 1100 framed pictures, 1450 16mm films, 9200 recordings and 925 liturgical music; large genealogy collection; noon-time programs of speakers through fall and winter; puppet shows put on by Children's Department; 1,100,000 volumes loaned in average year; 4500 microfilms; dozens of tours each year.

Income: $1,400,000 (from local taxes).

Attendance: Several thousand daily.

KENTUCKY

ANCHORAGE

ART CENTER ASSOCIATION*
1622 Stary Ave, 40223. Tel: (502) 583-6300
Junius Prince III, Pres.
Mrs. Edwin Middleton, V.Pres.
J. Stuart Mitchell, Treas.

Mrs. Robert A. Dean, Jr, Secy.
Jerome A. Donson, Dir. of School
Bruce H. Yenawine, Registrar
Juanita Duncan, Office Mgr. School
Open Mon. - Fri. 9 AM - 5 PM; Sat. 9 - 12 AM; Sun. 2 - 5 PM; July and Aug. Mon. - Fri. 9 AM - 4 PM. Estab. 1942 by merger of Louisville Art Center, founded 1929, and the Louisville Art Association, founded 1909, to promote art and art education in Louisville. Ann. meeting June; mem. 750; dues $10 and up.

Collections: Permanent collection of international art.

Exhibitions: 11 contemporary art exhibits in the School Gallery; children's shows; Christmas sale.

Activities: Gallery talks, members' lectures series, movies, demonstrations and an annual auction.

Library: Art books, etc, 5000 volumes.

Publications: Announcements, catalogs, school newspapers.

BEREA

BEREA COLLEGE*
Art Dept, 40403. Tel: (606) 986-8946
Lester Pross, Chmn.
Open Mon. - Fri. 8 AM - 6 PM; Sat. 8 - 12 AM. Estab. 1935.

Collections: Small collection of †paintings, †prints, †sculpture, †weaving, †ceramics and †minor arts; Kress study collection of Renaissance paintings.

Exhibitions: Biennial Drawing Exhibition.

Activities: Lends objects of art, conducts classes on college level; lectures open to the public.

Library: About 3000 volumes for reference only; 1500 color reproductions for loan and reference; 8000 photographs; 25,000 slides.

Purchases: (1970-73) $750.

KENTUCKY GUILD OF ARTISTS AND CRAFTSMEN
Box 291, 40403. Tel: (606) 986-3192
Garry Barker, Exec. Dir.
Officers & Trustees change each year.
Estab. Jan. 1961 to develop the arts and crafts of Kentucky, to assist artists and craftsmen in bettering their skills, and to help in the marketing of their products. Ann. meeting Nov; mem. approx. 500; dues individual $7.50, Centers $15.

Exhibitions: The Kentucky Artist/Craftsmen exhibit on tour through 1976 in Kentucky.

Activities: Workshops, fairs, competitions; annual fair (10th in 1976) in Oct.

Publications: Kentucky Guild Newsletter, monthly; Guild Record.
Guild Gallery
811 Euclid Ave, Lexington
Open daily 10 AM - 5 PM; cl. Sun. Sale of members' work; approx. $75,000 per yr.

Office Gallery
213 Chestnut St.
Rotating monthly exhibits.

BOWLING GREEN

KENTUCKY MUSEUM AND LIBRARY
Western Kentucky University, 42101. Tel: (502) 745-2592
Riley Handy, Ky. Librn.
A. Bruce MacLeish, Cur.
Anne R. Johnston, Cataloguer
Open Mon. - Sat. 9 AM - 4:30 PM; Museum also open Sun. 11 AM - 3 PM; cl. during school vacation period. Building dedicated 1939.

Collections: Kentucky historical material, †natural history, Indian and pioneer relics, †handicrafts, costumes, portraits and furniture; Snell Collection of Prints, Miniatures, Furniture and Oil Paintings from Southern Europe.

Library: Approx. 25,000 volumes and manuscripts on Kentuckiana.

Attendance: Average 20,000-25,000 annually.

✤WESTERN KENTUCKY UNIVERSITY ART GALLERY
Ivan Wilson Center for Fine Arts, 42101. Tel: (502) 745-3944
John Warren Oakes, Gallery Dir.
Free Mon. - Fri. 8 AM - 4 PM. Building constructed 1973 to house educational and cultural exhibits relating to university and community needs; financed by state appropriation.

Collections: Print and painting collections both being enlarged annually.

Exhibitions: Average 1 per month.

Activities: Traveling exhibitions organized and circulated; lectures, workshops.

FRANKFORT

KENTUCKY HISTORICAL SOCIETY
Old State House, 40601. Tel: (502) 564-3018
William R. Buster, Dir.
Dr. Hambleton Tapp, State Historian & Editor.
Estab. 1836, inc. 1838, to collect, maintain and preserve authentic records, information, facts and relics connected with the history of the Commonwealth and the genealogy of her peoples; to promote a wider appreciation of the American heritage, with particular emphasis on the advancement and dissemination of knowledge of the history of Kentucky. Ann. meeting 1st Fri. after 1st Mon. in Nov; mem. 10,400; dues $5 annually, $50 life.
Activities: Guided tours at all museums; library encourages researchers and historians.
Publications: The Register, quarterly; Kentucky Ancestors, quarterly; The Bulletin, bimonthly newsletter; Kentucky Heritage, 3-4 issues per year.
Income: $471,400 state appropriation; $83,000 agency funds.

Old Capitol Restoration
Broadway at St. Clair Mall
Free Tues. - Sat. 9 AM-4 PM; Sun. 1 - 5 PM; cl. Mon. except by special arrangement. Restored legislative halls, period rooms, Kentucky Art Galleries.

Kentucky History Museum
Broadway at St. Clair Mall, Old Capitol Annex
Free Mon. - Sat. 9 AM - 4 PM; Sun. 1 - 5 PM. Displays arranged chronologically to depict Kentucky history; includes Indian artifacts, interior of log cabin, clothing, political history, Hall of Governors.

Historical and Genealogical Library
Broadway at St. Clair Mall, 3rd Floor Old Capitol Annex
Free Mon. - Sat. 8 AM - 4:30 PM; Sun. 9 AM - 4:30 PM. Over 50,000 volumes, manuscripts, microfilm about Kentucky history and genealogy.

Kentucky Military History Museum
Old State Arsenal, E. Main St.
Free Mon. - Sat. 9 AM - 4 PM; Sun. 1 - 5 PM. Traces Kentucky's rich military heritage and the development of today's modern weapons.
Attendance: Approx. 2000 per month.

LEXINGTON

MOXLAN GALLERY
Mitchell Fine Arts Center
Transylvania College, 40508. Tel: (606) 255-6861
John R. Bryden, Prof.
Financed by endowment, the Moxlan Gallery holds approximately 6 exhibitions a year during sessions when students are on campus.

UNIVERSITY OF KENTUCKY ART GALLERY
105 Fine Arts Bldg, Rose St, 40502. Tel: (606) 258-2808
Nancy Coleman Wolsk, Dir.
Stephen Johnson, Asst. Dir.
Free 9 AM - 5 PM; Sat. & Sun. 1 - 5 PM. Building erected in 1949 which houses Art Gallery.
Collections: Historical and contemporary prints and drawings; 19th and 20th century paintings.
Exhibitions: Temporary exhibitions including an annual exhibition of contemporary graphics.
Activities: Lectures and tours on major exhibitions.
Library: Art library of 3000 volumes, 500 prints and 15,000 slides.
Publications: Annual graphics catalogues; periodic additional catalogs for temporary exhibitions.
Attendance: 18,000 annually.

LOUISVILLE

ALLEN R. HITE ART INSTITUTE
University of Louisville, Belknap Campus, 40208.
Tel: (502) 636-4233
Dr. Jay M. Kloner, Dir.
Dorothy Jared, Secy.
Gail R. Gilbert, Head, Art Library
Estab. 1946 through bequest of Allen R. Hite for instruction in art. Coordinates all University art activities. Permanent and periodic exhibitions of small collection of 100 paintings, †600 prints, 75 drawings. 5 or 6 exhibitions annually, one-man and group, old master and modern. Lectures endowed annually. Publishes exhibition catalogs.
Margaret M. Bridwell Art Library
Gail Gilbert, Librn.
Free Mon. - Thurs. 8 AM - 10 PM; Fri. 8 AM - 5 PM; Sat. 9 AM - 5 PM; Sun. 2 - 6 PM. Estab. 1936. Contains 29,000 volumes.

Slide Collection
Ann S. Coates, Slide Cur.
Anne F. Oppenheimer, Asst Slide Cur.
Contains 100,000 slides.
Photographic Archives
James C. Anderson, Dir.
Contains 600,000 negatives and prints, including Standard Oil of New Jersey Collection and Roy Stryker Collection.

FILSON CLUB
118 W. Breckinridge St, 40203. Tel: (502) 582-3727
J. Alexander Stewart, Pres.
James R. Bentley, Secy.
Richard L. Hagy, Asst. to Pres.
Lois Price, Dir. of Museum Planning
Martin F. Schmidt, Librn.
Free weekdays 9 AM - 5 PM; Sat. 9 AM - Noon Oct. - June. Estab. 1884 to collect, preserve and publish historical material, especially pertaining to Kentucky. Monthly meeting Oct. - June; mem. 2200; dues $15, $300 life.
Collections: †Books and manuscripts, family heirlooms, large collection of portraits of Kentuckians.
Library: 38,000 volumes for reference and research; photograph collection.
Publications: Filson Club History Quarterly; Series 1 and Series 2 Publications (38 volumes).

✠J. B. SPEED ART MUSEUM
2035 S. Third St, 40208. Tel: (502) 637-1925
William H. Abell, Pres.
Mrs. Berry V. Stoll, V.Pres.
Addison Franklin Page, Dir. & Cur.
John S. Speed, Secy-Treas.
Bertha Brackin, Asst. Secy-Treas.
Mrs. Mary Carver, Registrar
Free 10 AM - 4 PM; Sun. 2 - 6 PM; cl. Mon. & holidays. Estab. 1925 for the diffusion of knowledge and appreciation of art for public benefit by Mrs. Hattie Bishop Speed as a memorial to her husband, James Breckinridge Speed; building opened 1927; in 1947 name changed from J. B. Speed Memorial Museum; Satterwhite Wing opened Oct. 1954 with five new galleries and added service facilities. Hattie Bishop Speed Music Room addition opened April 1973 with six new galleries and sculpture garden. Owned and conducted by Board of Governors; endowed. Mem. about 2000; dues $15 and higher.
Collections: †European and American paintings, sculpture, prints, decorative and useful arts; Kentucky Portrait Gallery; Kentucky art; †Preston Pope Satterwhite collection of European decorative arts, including Elizabethan Hall, tapestries, sculpture and furniture of Gothic, Renaissance and Baroque periods; Robert Bacon Conway collection of miniatures; 18th century porcelains; Frederick Weygold collection of North American Indian objects, †historic and †modern art.
Exhibitions: Average about 10 special exhibitions per twelve-month season in four galleries; regular exhibits in twenty galleries; monthly exhibitions emphasizing regional, national and international art, modern and historic, for the general public.
Activities: Lectures, concerts, gallery talks with approx. 10 visiting lecturers; films.
Library: Art reference library open to the public Tues. through Fri.
Publications: Quarterly bulletin, calendar and exhibition catalogues, Handbook of Art Accessions, 1947 to 1960, publ. 1960; Museum Handbook, publ. 1973.
Attendance: Approx. 65,000.

MOREHEAD

✠CLAYPOOL-YOUNG ART GALLERY
Morehead State University
40351. Tel: (606) 783-3232
Dr. Bill R. Booth, Head Dept. Art
Brenda Whitt, Secy.
Free Mon. - Fri. 7 AM - 11 PM; Sat. - Sun. 1 - 4 PM. Estab. 1922 to provide undergraduate and graduate programs in studio and art education; the department maintains an exhibition gallery for traveling exhibitions, faculty, and student work; financed by appropriation. The Claypool-Young Art Gallery is tri-level with 2344 square feet of exhibition space.
Collections: Establishing a permanent collection which to date consists principally of prints by major contemporary figures; several works added each year through purchase or bequest. Additions to lending collection include, The Maria Rilke Suite of lithographs by Ben Shahn, consisting of 23 pieces, The Laus Pictorum Suite by Leonard Baskin, consisting of 14 pieces, and 3 lithographs by Thomas Hart Benton (Jesse James, Frankie and Johnny, and Huck Finn).

Exhibitions: (Principal Exhibition) Figures and Faces; 19th and 20th Century European Master Drawings; Sculpture In Bronze Casts from Florence, Italy by Prof. John Kehoe; The Mortimer Brandt Collection of Medieval Manuscript Illuminations, a religious art exhibition which included a large collection of Santos, wall hangings and liturgical objects; a large number of one-man exhibitions along with invitational shows and group exhibits.

Activities: Student and faculty exhibitions to schools and libraries; traveling exhibitions organized and circulated; individual paintings lent to schools; 200 items in lending collection, prints, photographs available upon request; lectures open to public; 5 visiting lecturers per year, 10 gallery talks, 30 tours; concerts; competitions.

Library: 5000 volumes.

Budget: $4000.

PADUCAH

PADUCAH ART GUILD, INC.
Second & Broadway, 42001. Tel: (502) 442-2453
Jas. C. Pullen, Pres.
Juanita Gilliam, Secy.
Free daily Noon - 4 PM; Sun. 1 - 5 PM. Estab. and inc. 1957 to bring monthly exhibitions of original art works to the community with a final goal of establishing an art museum for the city; new gallery opened in present location in Mar. 1963. Monthly meetings; mem. 150; dues $5 and higher.

Exhibitions: Annual Members' Exhibition, judged by professional jurors from various art centers such as Memphis Academy of Art, Art Institute of Chicago, Southern Illinois University and regional colleges with art faculties; exhibitions of the works of local and regional artists; traveling exhibitions.

Activities: Lectures, workshop sessions and demonstrations; conducts sketch classes.

Attendance: Approx. 8500 per yr.

LOUISIANA

ALEXANDRIA

CENTRAL LOUISIANA ART ASSOCIATION, INC.
P.O. Box 5791, 71301.
Mrs. Cedric Lowrey, Pres.
Mrs. Ward T. Jones, 1st V.Pres.
Mrs. William J. Defee, III, 2nd V.Pres.
Mr. & Mrs. Windsor P. Thomas, Jr, Secy-Treas.
Mrs. Leonard Fuhrer, Dir.
Estab. 1937 to foster art appreciation and to encourage development of artists; inc. 1969. Ann. meeting Apr; 400 mem. available in patron, sustaining, contributing, participating, family, student and general.

Activities: Art exhibits from American Federation of Arts, Smithsonian Institute, Artists Collections and Art Galleries; lectures and films, member show annually and Young People's shows, docent program, and art workshops.

Income and Purchases: Approx. $5500 annually.

Attendance: 15,000 annually.

BATON ROUGE

ANGLO-AMERICAN ART MUSEUM
Memorial Tower, Louisiana State University, 70803.
Tel: 388-4003
Robert B. Smythe, D.D.S, Pres.
Mrs. Richard A. Mornhinveg, Secy.
Oscar G. Richard, Dir.
H. Parrott Bacot, Cur.
Anelia G. Miller, Secy.
Free, weekdays 9 AM - 4 PM; Sat. 9 AM - 12 AM & 1 PM - 4 PM; Sun. 1 PM - 4 PM. Estab. 1959, opened to public 1962, estab. by an anonymous donor to serve as a constant reminder of the major cultural heritage the United States received from the British peoples; city or state appropriation and mem. Two temporary galleries house loan exhibitions and local art work. Ann. meeting twice yearly; mem. 303.

Collections: English and American period rooms, paintings and decorative art.

Exhibitions: Seven loan exhibitions and numerous sampler exhibitions from the museum's collection.

Activities: Lectures for members only; 2 visiting lecturers per year.

Library: 400 volume reference library.

Publications: Guide to the Anglo-American Art Museum, Anglo-American Art Museum Catalogue, paintings, prints, drawings approx. every 2 years; temporary exhibition catalogues.

Income and Purchases: Income $27,484; purchases $27,484.

Attendance: 25,000 annual average.

LOUISIANA STATE ART, HISTORICAL AND CULTURAL PRESERVATION AGENCY ART GALLERIES
Old State Capitol, corner North Blvd. & St. Phillip St, 70801.
Tel: (504) 389-5086 & 5087
Jay R. Broussard, Dir.
Charles Ford, Exhibits Dir.
Galleries free daily 10 AM - 4:30 PM; Sat. & Sun. 1 - 5 PM; cl. state holidays. Estab. 1938 by state legislature to promote contemporary art throughout the state; total funds come from state legislature.

Exhibitions: Sponsors annual competitions open to all Louisiana artists without fee, juried, prizes; photography in May; paintings, sculpture, ceramics and graphics in Oct; conducts annual exhibitions for students in Mar; holds international watercolor exhibition in Nov; exhibitions in galleries changed every 2-4 weeks.

Activities: Furnishes lectures, slide talks and assistance to clubs anywhere in the state.

Publications: Annual Report; announcements and catalogs of exhibitions.

Income and Purchases: Income $25,000 (state funds only); purchases approx. $500 annually.

Attendance: Approx. 70,000 annually.

✠LOUISIANA STATE UNIVERSITY
Department of Fine Arts, 70803. Tel: (504) 388-5402
Don Bruce, Acting Head Dept.
Free 8 AM - 5 PM.
Estab. 1934. Special exhibitions planned by faculty committee. Lectures and gallery talks; invitational exhibitions of contemporary works.

Circulates exhibitions of students' art, consisting of 30 to 40 works by Louisiana State University students. Department collection of contemporary graphic works (prints and drawings). (See Schools)

Attendance: 10,000 annually.

✠LOUISIANA STATE UNIVERSITY UNION ART GALLERY
P.O. Box BU, 70803. Tel: (504) 388-5117
Judith R. Stahl, Art Dir.
Art Gallery free daily 9 AM - 9 PM. Estab. 1964, designed for exhibitions for university and community interests; traveling exhibitions as well as local exhibits are held annually; supported by appropriations and membership. Gallery is centrally located on the main floor of the LSU Union, with 1725 square footage.

Exhibitions: (1970-71) Lavern Krause Show; Bill Iles Show; Contemporary Belgian Prints; Small Paintings from Museum Collections and others. (1971-72) Painterly Realism; Jack Wilkinson Exhibit; Simmone Stern Gallery Show; Master Printmakers from Cooper-Hewitt Museum; Marcia Marcus Show. (1972-73) American Pop Posters; Faith Ringgold; Sidney Garrett Show; Paris Poster Review and others. (1973-74) Walter Anderson Exhibit; Louisiana Chapter of the American Crafts Council Invitational Exhibit; Landfall Press Prints; (1974-75) John Desmond; Tamarind Renaissance of Lithography; Clark Print Exhibit; French Sculpture Photo Exhibit; Jack Wilkinson Retrospective; Southern Sculpture Association Show; Jewelry Exhibit; plus the permanent collection, faculty and student shows annually.

Activities: Lectures open to public, 2 visiting lecturers per year; photograph collection; free art films.

Publications: Brochures for local exhibitions, quarterly.

Attendance: 55,000.

Arts and Crafts Shop
Louisiana State University Union, 70803.
Judith R. Stahl, Arts & Crafts Shop Mgr.
Open Mon. - Fri. 1 - 9 PM; LSU students and Union members participants. Estab. 1964, designed to assist and instruct students and Union members in basic pottery making, jewelry making, photography, silkscreening, woodworking, batik, stained glass, drawing.

Attendance: 4500.

LAFAYETTE

ART CENTER FOR SOUTHWESTERN LOUISIANA
P.O. Drawer 4290, University of Southwestern Louisiana Station, 70501. Tel: (318) 232-1169
Mrs. John Love, Dir.
Free Mon. - Fri. 10 AM - 4:30 PM; Sun. 2 - 5 PM. Estab. 1968 to house permanent collection, special monthly exhibits and seminars; financed by endowment and membership. Mem. 2500; dues $10 - $500.

Collections: Louisiana 19th century paintings; 19th and 20th century French work; 18th and 19th century English art, including Corot, Kneller, Reynolds, Ibbetson, Healy, Sully, Renoir, Monticelli, Rinck; contemporary Louisiana artists.

Exhibitions: Designfair; Art for Youth; George Rodrique; H. Alvin Sharpe; French Paintings (1800-1970); Steamboat in Art; Oriental Art; Oriental Rugs; 18th Century Louisiana French Furnishings.

Activities: Junior museum, Nov. attendance 7000; lectures open to public, 12 visiting lecturers per year; 100 or more gallery talks and tours; classes for adults and children, competitions.

Publications: 6 newsletters per year; 18th Century Louisiana French Furnishings; Oriental Rugs (Antique); Permanent Collection of the Art Center for Southwestern Louisiana.

Attendance: 20,000 annual average.

STUDENT UNION ART GALLERY

University of Southwestern Louisiana

P.O. Box 2611, 70501. Tel: (318) 233-3850, Exten. 779

Glen Menard, Dir, Student Union

Clay Edwards, Dir. Programming

Charles Cook, Prog. Advisor

Michael Flaherty, Craftshop Dir. & Art Gallery Mgr.

Open on variable schedule; no admis. Estab. 1970 to expose the area and the campus to new and innovative ideas through the arts; financed by city and state appropriation. Reference library. Gallery has approx. 1500 sq. ft. floor area and 153 ft. running wall space.

Exhibitions: Lee J. Sonnier; Dutch Kepler; Allan Jones; Annual Faculty Shows; Annual Student Juried Shows; Tom Secrest; Herman Mhire; Charles Richardson; plus others.

Activities: Junior Museum; lectures open to public; 3 visiting lecturers per year; 15 - 25 gallery talks; classes for adults; competitions; arts and crafts workshops. Book shop.

Publications: Gallery schedule, every semester.

Annual Income: Approx. $200.

Attendance: 12,000 visitors.

MONROE

MASUR MUSEUM OF ART

Twin City Art Foundation

1400 S. Grand St, 71201.

Fred Westrom, Chmn.

Jean Taylor, Secy.

U. Schmidt, Dir.

Carolyn McGough, Secy.

Free Tues. - Thurs. 10 AM - 6 PM; Fri. 1 - 4 PM; Sat. & Sun. 2 - 5 PM. Estab. 1963 to encourage art in all media, to enrich the cultural climate of this area; financed by appropriations and membership. Gallery has 500 running ft. hanging space. Mem. 250; dues $10, $25, $100.

Collections: †Permanent Collection, contemporary art all media, approx. 100 works.

Exhibitions: Picasso Ceramics; Rolland Golden; 7th, 8th, & 9th annual competitive exhibitions; Robert Addison; Don Cincone; Peter Poskas; Werner Mayer Günther; Monroe Collectors; Walter Davis Collection; Henry Guerriero.

Activities: Presentation of programs to the public; lectures open to the public; 4 visiting lecturers per year; 20 tours; classes for adults and children; competitions.

Library: 30 volumes.

Publications: Brochures of shows, monthly.

Income and Purchases: Income $46,000; purchases $3000.

Attendance: 5000 annual average.

NEW IBERIA

SHADOWS-ON-THE-TECHE

117 E. Main St, (P.O. Box 254), 70560. Tel: (318) 369-6446

Inez V. Hebert, Adminr. & Property Council & Staff of National Trust Interpreters

Carole T. Scanlon, Coordinator, Interpretive Programs

Open daily 9 AM - 4:30 PM; cl. Christmas; admis adults $1.50, senior citizens, 50¢; group rates available.

The Shadows is a property of the National Trust for Historic Preservation. Preserved as a historic house museum; operated as a community preservation center, it is a National Historic Landmark.

A townhouse on the Bayou Teche, it faces the main street of modern New Iberia, but is surrounded by three acres of landscaped gardens shaded by live oaks. Built in 1831, the Shadows represents a Louisiana adaptation of classical revival architecture. Fashionable balls and masquerades as well as everyday activities are reflected in the possessions of five generations of the Weeks family on display in the house. The property fell into ruin after the Civil War but was restored during the 1920's by Weeks Hall, great grandson of the builder. Mr. Hall revived the spark of antebellum hospitality at the Shadows, entertaining such celebrities as W. C. Fields, Mae West, and H. L. Menken. Mr. Hall bequeathed the Shadows to the National Trust in 1958.

The house contains furnishings typical of those owned by a planter's family between 1830 and 1865. Collection includes two fine paintings by Louisiana itinerant artist Adrian Persac (1857-72) as well as paintings by the donor, Weeks Hall.

Property serves as a focal point for advancement of historic preservation. It develops new relationships among cultural, community preservation groups and National Trust members in its area. Responds to community preservation needs by acting as a link between community and appropriate regional or headquarters offices of National Trust.

Activities: Interpretive programs which are related to the Shadows particular historic preservation program; community produced programs include Sugar Cane Festival and sidewalk art show; Members Day during National Historic Preservation Week, in early May.

Attendance: 24,250.

NEW ORLEANS

THE HISTORIC NEW ORLEANS COLLECTION

Kemper and Leila Williams Foundation

533 Royal St, 70130. Tel: (504) 523-7146

Benjamin W. Yancey, Chmn. of Board

Stanton M. Frazar, Dir.

Open Tues. - Sat. 10 AM - 5 PM; admis. adults $1, children 50¢. Building constructed in 1792 by Jean Francois Merieult; recently renovated by Koch and Wilson to accommodate the 11 galleries which house a collection of paintings, prints, documents, books and artifacts relating to the history of Louisiana from the time of its settlement, gathered over a number of years by the late L. Kemper Williams and his wife; the foundation was established with private funds to keep it intact.

Collections: Material on the Battle of New Orleans, containing many originals and every known print; includes oil paintings, watercolors, lithographs, engravings, pencil drawings and illustrated diaries. A series of 1814 drawings of forts on the lower Mississippi by Barthelemy Lafon; a series of orginal drawings by James Gallier, Sr, architect of Gallier Hall, and his son, James, Jr; included in the series is an original drawing of the exterior and interior of the third Christ Church at Canal and Dauphine. In the collection's archives is a group of 106 military letters written during the War of 1812, city directories dating back to 1805, a set of privateer papers of Jean Lafitte and Dominique You, and an extremely rare book published in 1770 by Captain Philip Pittman.

Exhibitions: The collection will be exhibited on a rotating basis in 11 galleries; the first deals with important periods of Louisiana history, ranging from Colonial Louisiana to The World's Industrial and Cotton Centennial Exposition in 1884-1885. Three galleries are devoted to Andrew Jackson and the Battle of New Orleans, one to The Mississippi River, one to Cartography and the Fourth Estate, and others to the face of the city, its environs and its commerce and industry.

LAMPE GALLERY OF FINE ART

3920 Old Gentilly Rd, 70126. Tel: (504) 949-6387

Mr. & Mrs. Frederick Lampe, Owners

Gallery free Mon, Tues, Thurs. & Fri. 10 AM - 5:30 PM; Wed. 1 - 5:30 PM; Sat. 10 AM - 3 PM. Estab. 1965 to teach art and art appreciation. Gallery maintained to teach all forms of sculpture, Old Master techniques, and to show student work as well as European art.

Collections: American Primitives; Clementine Hunter Oils.

Exhibitions: Semi-annual art shows of student and professional artists.

Activities: Classes for adults and children.

LOUISIANA STATE MUSEUM

Office: 751 Chartres St, 70116. Tel: (504) 581-4321

F. Clancy Dupepe, Chmn. Board of Dir.

Robert R. Macdonald, Dir.

Housed in 8 buildings—The Cabildo, The Old Arsenal, Jackson House, Creole House, The Presbytere, Lower Pontalba Building, Madame John's Legacy and Old United States Mint. Office in The Presbytere (see above). Estab. 1906 as a state institution for the exhibition of historical materials relating to the development and current life of Louisiana. The Cabildo, built in 1795-1799, was formally opened as a museum in 1911. Friends of The Cabildo, c. 6000 mem; dues $6 and higher. Open daily 9 AM - 5 PM except Mon. Admis. adults 50¢, children 25¢, children under 12 free.

Collections: Arts, crafts, portraits, clothing, Mardi-Gras and military costumes, weapons, jewelry, furniture, minor and industrial arts, especially as made or used in Louisiana.

Exhibitions: Permanent—The history of Louisiana is portrayed in exhibitions in The Cabildo. The Cabildo was the seat of the Spanish Colonial civil government and the scene of transfer ceremonies of the Louisiana Purchase. The Cabildo Complex includes the Old State Arsenal, a Greek Revival building by R. Dakin, Creole House (1842) and the Jackson House (1842).

In the restored Presbytere are exhibited a selection of original 18th and 19th century maps, drawings, documents and paintings portraying Louisiana history and a part of the extensive collection of important works of art, especially portraits of early French and Spanish families and persons prominent in 19th century Louisiana military, political and business affairs. The history of costume and decorative arts used in Louisiana is displayed along with smaller groups of military and Mardi-Gras costumes. Playthings of the Past (dolls and toys) and Louisiana's original Elephant Folio of Audubon's Birds of America subscribed to by the Legislature in 1835, are of special interest.

The Pontalba House (1850), a restored historic apartment or town house of the 1851-1870 period in New Orleans, is located in the Lower Pontalba Building.

Madame John's Legacy (1788) has just been completed and opened to the public as a historic house museum.

Educational Activities: Six lectures or programs yearly co-sponsored by the Friends of The Cabildo. Guided tours for school and other groups provided by trained Junior League docent program.

Archives: 40,000 documents of the official French and Spanish Colonial Archives, 1717-1803; other manuscripts, business documents, family papers, etc, relating to Louisiana. Photographic archives on New Orleans and Louisiana; also maps and prints.

Library: 32,000 volumes and periodicals on Louisiana history and general reference.

Attendance: Approx. 300,000.

✠NEW ORLEANS MUSEUM OF ART
Isaac Delgado Museum, Stern Auditorium, Wisner Education Wing
City Park, Lelong Ave, 70179. Tel: (504) 488-2631
Robert A. Peyroux, Pres.
James J. Coleman, Jr, 1st V.Pres.
Frederic B. Ingram, 2nd V.Pres.
Mrs. P. Roussel Norman, Secy.
Richard A. Peneguy, Treas.
E. John Bullard, Dir.
Joan Caldwell, Asst. to Dir.
William A. Fagaly, Cur. Collections
Pamela P. Bardo, Cur.
Charles Mo, Registrar
Annabelle Hebert, Sr. Cur. Educ.
David C. Swoyer, Cur. Educ.
Alice Yelen, Cur. Educ.
Barbara H. Neiswender, Adminr.
Jacqueline Sullivan, Accountant
William L. Hyde, Librn.
Open Tues. - Sat. 10 AM - 5 PM; Sun. 1 - 6 PM; cl. Mon. & holidays; admis. adults (18-65) $1, children (12-18) 50¢. Estab. 1911; building given to city by Isaac Delgado, maintained by municipal funds. Three new wings, including Stern Auditorium and Wisner Education Wing, added in 1971, tripling size of original building. Ann. meeting in Nov; mem. 2500; dues $15 and higher.

Collections: †Old Master paintings of various schools; The Samuel H. Kress collection of masterpieces of the Italian Renaissance; Special concentration: †pre-Columbian masterworks from Mexico, Central and South America and †Latin colonial and contemporary painting and sculpture; Stern-Davis Collection of Peruvian Colonial Painting; †19th and 20th century American Art; †19th and 20th century Louisiana painting; The Chapman H. Hyams Collection of Barbizon and late 19th century Salon paintings and sculpture; †special collection of the work of Edgar Degas; †20th century European art, with concentration on surrealism; †Chinese and Japanese art; Morgan Whitney Collection of jades, mostly Ming; †African art; †photography and graphics; The Melvin P. Billups Glass Collection (over 10,000 objects from antique to 19th century); †Latter-Schlesinger Collection of European Portrait Miniatures.

Exhibitions. (1973) Walker Evans Retrospective; Andy Warhol - Mao Tse Tung; James Rosequist, Horse Blinders; Graphic Art of German Expressionism; 1973 Artists Biennial ($3350 in purchase awards); Graphics '72 Japan; Multiple Interaction; Wayne Thiebaud Graphics; African Art of the Dogon; Don Potts, My First Car. (1974) Kurt Kranz: Bauhaus and Today; Arshile Gorky Drawings; Clarence John Laughlin: The Personal Eye; Fritz Bultman Drawings; Art and Landscape of Italy: Too Late to be Saved?; Contemporary American Indian Artists; The Camera; 1973 Artists Biennial Winners: Beasely, Childers, Colville, Gordy, Kohlmeyer, Pramuk, Templer, Umlauf; Diane Arbus Photographs; Richard Clague Retrospective. (1975) Photographs by Robert Doisneau and August Sander; Jacob Lawrence Retrospective; A Panorama of American Painting: The John J. McDonough Collection; The Cotton Office, New Orleans and Twenty Bronze Sculptures by Edgar Degas; 1975 Artists Biennial; Folk Art in America: A Living Tradition; John McCrady Retrospective; German and Austrian Expressionism.

Activities: Formally organized education programs for children; lectures; film series, concerts, dance recitals; docent program; adult and children's art classes. Museum shop.

Library: Art reference library of approx. 5000 volumes for staff and members.

Publications: Monthly Calendar of Events; annual report; catalogs of permanent collection and special exhibitions.

Income: Municipal appropriation and private donations provide funds for operating expenses, exhibitions and education programs and acquisitions. Budget 1975, excluding acquisitions funds, $670,000; approx. $50,000-$70,000 available annually for acquisitions.

Attendance: (1975) Approx. 200,000.

NEW ORLEANS PUBLIC LIBRARY
Art and Music Division
219 Loyola Ave, 70140. Tel: (504) 586-4938
M. Eugene Wright, Head Library
Marilyn Wilkins, Head Div.
Joe Clark, Library Assoc. II
Pat Green, Library Assoc.
Free Mon. - Fri. 9 AM - 9 PM; Sat. 9 AM - 5 PM. Estab. 1958; financed by city and state appropriations.

Collections: Westfeldt Art Collection of 712 framed prints; picture file of 46,342 mounted pictures; collection of reference and circulating books in the Fine Arts, Sports and Recreation Division; 20,000 phonograph records; 8mm motion pictures; 200 audio cassettes.

Exhibitions: Graphics, paintings and watercolor exhibits by local artists; community group non-art exhibits; library originated exhibits; library sponsored contests by schools; graphics, sculpture, crafts and photography.

Activities: 16,000 items lent in an average year; lectures open to public; concerts, classes for adults and children, competitions.

Publications: Book lists; handout sheets; Irons in the Fire.

Income and Purchases: Total library budget $2,045,958; total materials budget $160,000.

TULANE UNIVERSITY
Newcomb Art Department Exhibition Gallery
60 Newcomb Pl, 70118. Tel: (504) 865-4631
Dr. Jessie Poesch, Chmn. Art Dept.
Mr. Pat Trivigno, Assoc. Chmn.
Free 9 AM - 4:30 PM.
Exhibitions: Exhibitions are planned as an integral part of the Art Department program. (See Schools)

Architecture Library
Division of Howard Tilton Library
About 2500 volumes; 3000 slides, prints and photographs. The library also contains an extensive file of pictorial material, including architectural photographs relating to New Orleans. A small working reference library of architectural material is maintained in Stanley Thomas Hall, in the quarters of the School of Architecture.

UNIVERSITY OF NEW ORLEANS FINE ARTS GALLERY
Lake Front Dr, 70122. Tel: (504) 288-3161 Exten. 493
W. Thomas Young, Chmn.
Molly Matthews, Secy.
Doyle Gertjejansen, Gallery Dir.
David Foley, Asst.
Free Mon. - Fri. 8 AM - 4:30 PM. Estab. August, 1974 to expose the students and community to historic and contemporary visual arts; financed by state appropriation. Gallery consists of 1800 square feet, 112 lineal feet of wall space, 20 feet ceiling heights, natural and artificial lighting.

Exhibitions: (1974) 13 New Orleans Sculptors; U.N.O. Fine Arts Faculty; U.N.O. Fine Arts Seniors; (1975) Lucille Reed-Weavings & Gwen Norsworthy-Light Paintings; Art of Africa and Oceania; Thomas Arndt, Photography; F.A. Student; N.O. Pyramid Artists Group; U.N.O. FA Faculty; Leon Hushcha-Drawing/Painting; Walmsley & Short, Printmakers; Bill Ludwig, Sculpture; FA Dept. Seniors; (1976) Reese, Prints, & Lewis, Batik; American Indian Art; Southeastern Sculptors; FA Students.

SHREVEPORT

LOUISIANA STATE EXHIBIT MUSEUM
3015 Greenwood Rd, 71109. Tel: (318) 635-2323
Heber E. Long, Dir.
Free 9 AM - 5 PM; Sun. 1 - 5 PM. Estab. 1939; state financed; features dioramas, displays, and murals showing state's history, resources, and natural beauty.

Exhibitions: About 15 a year by local and regional art groups and artists; also ceramic and china painting shows.

Attendance: 600,000 annually.

THE R. W. NORTON ART GALLERY
4747 Creswell Ave, 71106. Tel: (318) 865-4201.
Mrs. Richard W. Norton, Jr, Pres.
Jerry M. Bloomer, Secy.
Free Tues. - Sun. 1 - 5 PM; cl. Mon. Easter, Thanksgiving, Christmas, New Years, and July 4. Estab. 1946, opened 1966; endowed;

founded to present aspects of the development of American and European culture through exhibition and interpretation of fine works of art and literature, both from the Gallery's own collections and from those of other institutions and persons. Ann. meeting April.

Collections: Large collections of paintings and sculpture by Frederic Remington and Charles M. Russell; paintings and sculpture relating to early American history; portraits of famous Confederate leaders; American miniatures and early American silver; European paintings and sculpture; 16th century Flemish tapestries; Wedgwood collection.

Exhibitions: Annual Holiday In Dixie exhibit (April); annual Christmas exhibit incl. antique doll collection; Antique Gun Collection (1969, 1971, 1973); One-man exhibitions of paintings by regional artists; special exhibits of porcelain, glass, silver, and others.

Activities: Guided tours weekday mornings by appointment; slide lectures.

Library: Reference & research (non-circulating), open Wed. & Sat. 1 - 5 PM; 5000 volumes (incl. periodicals) covering the fine arts, history, literature, and bibliography; James M. Owens Memorial Collection of Early Americana (700 volumes on Colonial history, particularly Virginia); rare books and atlases; Elephant folio edition of Audubon's Birds of America; complete set of John Gould ornithological works.

Publications: Catalogs, brochures and leaflets on all special exhibitions (47 through 1975).

Attendance: (1973-74) 58,278.

✤SHREVEPORT ART GUILD*
P.O. Box 346, 71162.

MAINE

BATH

BATH MARINE MUSEUM
04530. Tel: (207) 443-6311
George F. Miller, Pres.
Ralph L. Snow, Dir.
Harold E. Brown, Emeritus Cur.
Marion S. Lilly, Registrar
Open 10 AM - 5 PM Memorial Day - mid-Oct; admis. charged. Estab. May 1964; displays artistic-historical presentation of maritime history of the Bath area of Maine. Ann. meeting Oct; mem. 1150; dues $7 and higher.

Collections: 200 paintings, prints, drawings and lithographs of ships, people and places relating to the area; 300 models and half-models of vessels built in the area; numerous photographs and other artifacts.

Activities: Junior touch-me room; lectures; guided tours for groups. Gift shop.

Library: 3600 maritime history volumes for reference.

Publications: Newsletter, quarterly.

Attendance: (1972) 35,000.

BRISTOL

PEMAQUID GROUP OF ARTISTS
04539. Tel: (207) 677-2633
Gene Klebe, Pres.
Ernest Thompson, V.Pres.
Florence Thompson, Secy.
Cynthia Brackett, Treas.
Frances Curtis, Gallery Hostess
Gallery open weekdays 10 AM - 5 PM. Organized 1929. Ann. meeting day after Labor Day; mem. 35; dues $1, entry fee $5.

Exhibitions: Summer exhibitions by local artists and those sojourning in the vicinity, July 1 - Labor Day.

Attendance: Approx. 8000.

BRUNSWICK

BOWDOIN COLLEGE MUSEUM OF ART
Walker Art Bldg, 04011. Tel: (207) 725-8731, Exten. 275
Dr. R. Peter Mooz, Dir.
Lynn Yanok, Exec. Secy.
Betty S. Smith, Asst. to Dir. & Cur, Peary-Macmillan Arctic Museum
Russell J. Moore, Cur.
Free weekdays 10 AM - 4 PM; Sun. 2 - 5 PM; July & Aug. 10 AM - 5 PM; Sun. 2 - 5 PM; cl. major national holidays. Erected 1894; original collection estab. 1811. Mem. 850, contributions $10 and higher.

Collections: American portraits of Colonial and Federal periods, including Smibert, Feke, Badger, Blackburn, Copley, West, Stuart; †American paintings, 19th and 20th centuries; †European paintings, 14th-19th centuries; †European sculpture, 16th-19th centuries;

†European and American master drawings, 16th-20th centuries; Assyrian reliefs from Palace of Assurnasirpal II; Greek & Roman sculpture, vases, bronzes, coins; English & American silver; Chinese ceramics & jades.

Exhibitions: Major exhibitions originated by the Museum 1962-70: Art of Leonard Baskin; Portrayal of the Negro in American Painting 1710-1963; The Salton Collection of Renaissance and Baroque Medals and Plaquettes; As Maine Goes, The Maine Coast and Its Despoilment; Winslow Homer at Prout's Neck; Language of the Print, The Karshan Collection; Hands to Work and Hearts to God, The Shaker Tradition in Maine; Rockwell Kent, The Early Years; The Winslows: Pilgrims, Patrons and Portraits; The Art of American Furniture; The Molinari Collection of Renaissance and Baroque Medals and Plaquettes; James Bowdoin: Patriot and Man of the Enlightenment.

Activities: Lectures, gallery talks, films.

Publications: Catalogs of major exhibitions; occasional papers.

Attendance: 40,000 annually.

DEER ISLE

HAYSTACK MOUNTAIN SCHOOL OF CRAFTS
04627. Tel: (207) 348-2816
Jack Lenor Larsen, Chmn. of Board
Charles R. Gailis, Pres.
Ethel Clifford, Secy.
Francis S. Merritt, Dir.
Roger W. Harding, Treas.
Free Sat. & Sun, June - Sept. Estab. 1950, for research and instruction in crafts and related extension services of exhibitions, consultation and conferences; financed by tuition income plus annual donations. Gallery maintained for continuous summer exhibition of important American and other national craftsmen.

Collections: †American Ceramics, †American Glass, †American Jewelry.

Exhibitions: 5 American Jewelers-Ebendorf, Fisch, Kreigman, Seppa, Skoogfors; Woodblock Prints by Toshi Yoshida; Glass by Dale Chihuly, Sam Herman, Michael Boylen; Graphics by Michael Rothenstein; Ceramics by Bill Sax, Gerry Williams, Byron Temple, William Wyman, Robert Winokur; Wood by Bob Stockdale; Contemporary Nigerian Graphics, Textiles, Ceramics, Metal; Prints by Bruce Onobrakpeya, Robert Broner, Jon Hall; Photographs by Nicholas Callaway; Senegalese Paintings by Alioune Cissoko; Sculpture by Clark FitzGerald; Glass by Dale Chihuly and Jamie Carpenter; Quilts by Beth Gutcheon; Ceramics by Erik Gronborg, Victor Spinsky, Starr Sutherland, Richard Schneider, Mutsuo Yanagihara.

Activities: Educational department, 12-week summer session in ceramics, graphics, glass, jewelry, weaving and photography; national extension department; crafts and slide material to schools, galleries and museums; traveling exhibitions organized and circulated; original objects of art lent; lending collection, 1000 Kodachromes, 50 items lent in average year; approx. 6 borrowers per year; lectures; 25 gallery talks; scholarships.

Library: 500 volume reference library; examples of American crafts since 1950 and numerous important craftsmen represented in Kodachrome collection.

Publications: Annual brochure.

Income: $100,000.

Attendance: 300 annual attendance, 2000 visitors.

ELLSWORTH

COLONEL BLACK MANSION
04605. Tel: (207) 667-8671
Col. Haskell Cleaves, Pres.
Mrs. Morton C. Whitcomb, Secy.
Open June 1 - Oct. 15 daily Mon. - Sat. 10 AM - 5 PM; cl. Sun; admis. $1. Historical mansion with guided tours; operated by the Hancock County Trustees of Public Reservations. Ann. meeting 2nd Tues. in Aug; mem. 225; no dues.

Collections: Authentic period furniture, china, glass and decorative objects in their fine original setting.

Attendance: 5500.

KENNEBUNK

THE BRICK STORE MUSEUM*
117 Main St, 04043. Tel: (207) 985-4802
Alan S. Nelson, Pres.
Mrs. Donald D. Kimball, Cur.
Free 10 AM - 4:30 PM; cl. Sun, Mon. & holidays. Estab. 1936, inc. 1940, to collect and preserve local historic records and objects and to further art interest in Maine. Housed in Old Brick Store, built in 1825. Additional buildings given to Museum in 1957 and 1959 and 1961 (The Barry Workshop, 4 Dane St, with classes year round) for more space for exhibitions, storage and carriages. Ann. meeting 4th Tues. in June; mem. 440; dues $5 and higher.

Collections: †Costumes, †historic documents, †ship models, †maritime material, †Early Americana, †paintings and prints.

Exhibitions: Annual members' exhibition of paintings and prints in August, total prizes $350; changing exhibits from April to October.

Activities: Lectures, demonstrations, local history talks for school children and adults, classes at Workshop for children and adults.

Library: Good reference library of 3500 volumes on local history, antiques, maritime, art and genealogy.

Publications: Booklets on Historic Monuments of Kennebunk, Old Family Portraits of Kennebunk, Old Houses of Kennebunk and Kennebunkport, Reprint of Bryant List of Sailing Vessels Built in District of Kennebunk, 25th Anniversary Pamphlet, Ancient History of Kennebunk To 1785 (1970).

Attendance: 7500.

LEWISTON

TREAT GALLERY
Bates College, 04240. Tel: (207) 783-6535
Synnove Haughom, Cur.
Free Mon. - Fri. 1 - 5, 7 - 8 PM; Sun. 2 - 5 PM; cl. major holidays. Estab. 1955 in honor of Mr. and Mrs. George W. Treat to acquaint the student body and the community with the works of recognized artists.

Collections: Marsden Hartley drawings (99) and paintings (2); Sylvan Lehman Joseph Collection of Prints including one Rembrandt and 19 Cassatts; 4 Thompson Family portraits (ancestors of George W. Treat); 17th and 18th century English, Dutch, French and Italian landscapes and portraits; 19th and 20th century American and European paintings and prints; 1 Zorach sculpture; Freeman Hinckley (former Bates College trustee) Collection of Chinese objects.

Exhibitions: Changed monthly.
Activities: Lectures.
Attendance: Approx. 6800.

MACHIAS

UNIVERSITY OF MAINE AT MACHIAS ART GALLERY*
04654. Tel: (207) 2553313
Chenoweth Hall, Chmn. Cultural Affairs
Free 8 AM - 8 PM. Estab. 1968; financed by city and state appropriation.

Collections: John and Norma Marin Collection.

Exhibitions: D'Amico Collection; Francis Merrill-Haystack School; Picasso prints; National Gallery Collection; plus many one-man shows.

Activities: Extension department serves Washington County; material available to residents and summer visitors; material lent, books, records, prints, slides; traveling exhibitions organized and circulated to Calais Technical Institute; individual paintings and original objects of art lent; lending collection, 100 color reproductions, 2000 lantern slides, 6000 Kodachromes, 30 film strips; lectures; 12 visiting lecturers per year; Classes for adults.

Library: 1640 volume lending and reference library; 156 prints for lending and reference.

Attendance: 1200 annual average.

OGUNQUIT

✠MUSEUM OF ART OF OGUNQUIT
Shore Rd, 03907. Tel: (207) 646-8827
Nicholas Sewall Strater, Pres.
Frances Mawn, Clerk & Registrar
George D. Varney, Treas.
DeWitt Hardy, Assoc. Dir.
Peter R. Mawn, Cur.
Free daily 10:30 AM - 5 PM; Sun. 1:30 - 5 PM. Estab. and inc. 1951 as a non-profit organization; opened 1953 to show sculpture and painting by North American artists during July and Aug; endowed. Ann. meeting Aug; mem. 18, of whom 8 are trustees; Friends 150, dues individual $15, couple $25.

Collections: American †sculpture, †painting, †drawing, chiefly 1920-.

Exhibitions: Americans of Our Times, sculpture, painting and drawing from permanent collection, shown jointly with loans. Special past exhibitions: Winslow Homer, Wyeth, Luks, Carl Walters, Karolik Collection, Morris Graves, Hartley, Kuhn, Kuniyoshi, Tobey, Cassatt, Flannagan, Curtis, Demuth, Burchfield, Alexander Brook, Henry Strater, William Muir, Rudolph Dirks, William von Schlegell, Jack Levine, DeWitt Hardy, Reginald Marsh, Harmon Neill, Peggy Bacon, John Heliker, Edward Hopper and John Laurent.

Publications: Annual illustrated catalogs; life catalog of Carl Walters.

Attendance: Average 20,000 each summer.

OGUNQUIT ART ASSOCIATION
The Barn Gallery
Shore Rd. & Bourne's Lane, 03907. Tel: (207) 646-5370
Michael Palmer, Pres.
Evelyne Harper, V.Pres.
Eugene Sullivan, Secy.
Ted Jaslow, Treas.
Vivian Berman, Dir.
John Laurent, Dir.
Betty Bryden-Wills, Dir.
Open mid-June - mid-Sept. Mon. - Sat. 10 AM - 5 PM & 8 - 10 PM; Sun. 2 - 5 PM. Estab. 1929; composed of professional artists chosen by jury; must be residents in Ogunquit of state of Maine. Ann. meeting held twice during summer months; mem. approx. 50; dues $15.

Exhibitions: Three, July, Aug, and Sept, held at the Barn Gallery. The Barn Gallery Associates is a charitable, educational institution; their building includes 2 main galleries plus a Collector's Gallery featuring unframed works, the J. Scott Smart outdoor Sculpture Court and the Judson Dunaway Room (new 1966) which permanently houses the Hamilton Easter Field Art Foundation Collection.

Activities: Sponsored by the Barn Gallery Associates include illustrated lectures, art and avant garde films and demonstrations; workshops; concerts; about 20 to 25 programs during season; Art Auction of Ogunquit Art Association members' work in August.

Attendance: 15,000.

ORONO

UNIVERSITY OF MAINE ART GALLERY
Carnegie Hall, 04473. Tel: (207) 581-7165
Howard Neville, Univ. Pres.
Vincent A. Hartgen, Cur.
Free weekdays 9 AM - 5 PM; Sun. when announced. Estab. 1946 to add to the cultural life of the University of Maine student, to be a service to Maine artists, and to generally promote interest in good and important art, both historic and modern. Patrons of the Fine Arts - mem. 125; dues $25, $50, $100.

Collections: By purchase and gifts, the †University Collection has grown to a stature which makes it a nucleus in the state for outstanding contemporary art, in all media. It includes 1600 paintings and graphic art and historic and European items. There are six galleries on the campus.

Exhibitions: A full schedule of exhibitions of all media by outstanding American and European Artists; conducts an Art Program of Exhibitions in annual Art Festivals and year-round exhibitions; maintains Artists of Maine Gallery to show examples of Maine art at all times.

Activities: Evening seminars and classes for adults; maintains slide collection, 2500 photographs, 15,000 kodachromes, 22,000 prints. Lecture open to the public; gallery talks and tours on demand.

Purchases: Approx. $3000.
Attendance: 13,000.

POLAND SPRING

SHAKER MUSEUM*
Sabbathday Lake, 04274. Tel: (207) 926-4865
Theodore E. Johnson, Dir.
Helen M. Haley, Asst. to Dir.
Kenneth N. Hatcher, Registrar
David W. Serette, Cur. Graphic Arts & Photography
Sr. R. Mildred Barker, Cur. Manuscripts
Sr. Frances A. Carr, Archivist
Open May 30 - Sept 30, Mon. - Sat. 10 AM - 4:30 PM; admis. adults, $1.50, children 6-12 75¢, under 6 free with adult. Founded 1931; inc. 1971, to preserve for educational and cultural purposes Shaker artifacts, publications, manuscripts, and works of art, to provide facilities for educational and cultural activities in connection with the preservation of the Shaker tradition, to provide a place of study and research for students of history and religion. Ann. meeting 2nd Wed. in Jan.

Collections: Shaker †textiles, †metal and wooden ware, †furniture, †community industries, †paintings and drawings by Shaker artists, †manuscripts.

Activities: Guided tours, library, inter-museum loan exhibitions, lectures, gallery talks; educational program in collaboration with the University of Maine at Portland-Gorham. Book Shop.

Library: Shaker imprints, works on Shakerism, photographs, manuscripts and ephemera; over 13,800 items.

Publications: The Shaker Quarterly.

PORTLAND

✠PORTLAND MUSEUM OF ART*
Portland Society of Art
111 High St, 04101. Tel: (207) 774-4058
John Holverson, Dir.

Free 10 AM - 5 PM; Sun. 2 - 5 PM; cl. Mon. and holidays. Portland Society of Art estab. and inc. 1882, L. D. M. Sweat Memorial building (dedicated 1911), adjoining McLellan-Sweat Mansion (registered National Historic Landmark). Society owns buildings and collections; maintains Museum and Portland School Art. Ann. meeting May; mem. 800; dues $10 and higher.

Collections: †Permanent collection of American painting, sculpture, decorative and graphic arts; James A. Healy collection of American and European paintings; collection of Franklin Simmons sculpture; †Frank H. Swan collection of Portland Glass, †Charles Freeman Edgecomb collection of Glass, †Francis O. Libby collection of Japanese Sword Guards.

Exhibitions: A Century of Portland Painters, 1820-1920; Alan Gussow—Painter of Places; Contemporary Scottish Paintings; 100 Drawings from the Skowhegan School; 1970 Faculty Show, School of Fine and Applied Art; 5 Minnesota Photographers; Aaron Draper Shattuck—Forgotten Connecticut Painter; Lights (light sculpture); O'Neal Ingram Paintings; 1971 Student Show, School of Fine and Applied Art; Robert Indiana Number Series; Tribal Art of West Africa; Early Maine Weathervanes; 1971 Faculty Show, School of Fine and Applied Art; 5 Photographers; Whitman Sampler Exhibition; 1972 Faculty Show, School of Fine and Applied Art; Come and See: A Museum Collects; Portland: Heritage and Future of a City; 1972 Faculty Show, School of Fine and Applied Art; Paul Laffoley, 12 Paintings; John Eide Photographs; 1973 Student Show, Portland School of Art; traveling exhibitions from The American Federation of Arts and the Smithsonian Institution.

Activities: Lectures, gallery talks, chamber music concerts, workshops and excursions.

Publications: Monthly Bulletin, periodic catalogues.

Income: $80,000.

Attendance: 45,000.

McLellan-Sweat House

Free 10 AM - 5 PM; Sun. 2 - 5 PM; cl. Mon. and holidays; admis. adults $1, children 50¢; members of Society, servicemen, educational tours excepted. A Federal mansion erected by John Kimball, Sr, in 1800 for Hugh McLellan. Willed to the Portland Society of Art by Margaret Mussey Sweat in 1908. Furnished in the Federal period.

VICTORIA SOCIETY OF MAINE WOMEN
Victoria Mansion
    109 Danforth St, 04101. Tel: (207) 772-4841
Mrs. Richard C. Coyne, Pres.
Mancy E. Braun, Recording Secy.
Mrs. James Dewolfe, Corresp. Secy.
Mrs. Hadley S. Ward, Treas.
Mrs. Elias C. Thomas, Jr, Restoration
Open Tues. - Sat. 10 AM - 4 PM Mid-June to Labor Day; cl. Mon. and holidays; admis adults $1, children 50¢. Estab. 1943 to foster and promote the arts and education; to preserve, further restore and maintain Victoria Mansion (built 1859) as an historic landmark and as the best standing example of early Victorian art, architecture and decoration. Ann. meeting June; mem. 450; dues $5.

Collections: Features of Victoria Mansion include carved panellings of rare woods; paintings on walls and ceilings; Royal Family portrait woven in silk; oil painting of Queen Victoria's favorite residence, Osborne House, presented by King George VI; rare books, bronzes and marble mantels and other historic items.

Attendance: 2500.

ROCKLAND

WILLIAM A. FARNSWORTH LIBRARY AND ART MUSEUM
    Elm St, 04841. Tel: (207) 596-6457
Boston Safe Deposit & Trust Company, Trustee
Wendell S. Hadlock, Dir.
Mrs. Beatrice B. Grant, Admin. Asst.
Free Tues. - Sat. 10 AM - 5 PM; Sun. 1 - 5 PM; cl. Mon, except June through Sept. Estab. 1948 by the bequest of the late Lucy C. Farnsworth to present a cultural program in fine and applied arts to the residents of Rockland and adjacent areas. In addition to the main exhibition galleries and the library, the museum is equipped with a large studio, auditorium with projection booth and stage, lecture hall and workshop. Board meeting Jan.

Collections: †American and European paintings, drawings and prints of the 18th, 19th and 20th century; special emphasis on the work of contemporary artists who interpret the Maine scene.

Activities: Exhibitions, concerts, lectures, classes.

Library: 2000 volumes for reference.

Attendance: 75,000.

ROCKPORT

MAINE COAST ARTISTS
    Russell Ave, 04856. Tel: (207) 236-2875
Mrs. Brampton Parker, Pres, Board of Trustees
Laurie V. Buffinton, Dir.

Mrs. Stephen Kent Biggs, Asst. Dir.
Free July - Aug. Mon. - Sat. 10 AM - 6 PM; Sun. 1 - 6 PM. A non-profit art center, estab. in 1968, dedicated to exhibiting a broad representation of work by accomplished Maine artists; maintained by sponsorship and all work is for sale. Gallery is a former firehouse. Ann. meeting of the Incorporators, Sept; sponsors 125, who contribute $15-$500.

Exhibitions: Two exhibitions, July and August; painting, sculpture, graphics.

Attendance: 5000 persons per season.

SEARSPORT

PENOBSCOT MARINE MUSEUM
    04974. Tel: (207) 548-6634
Richard V. Palmer, Dir.
Open Memorial Day weekend - Oct. 15, Mon. - Sat. 9 AM - 5 PM; Sun. 1 - 5 PM; admis. adults $2, children 50¢. Estab. 1936, opened 1937. Mem. 300; dues $10 and higher.

Collections: Paintings and prints; American and Oriental Furnishings; shipbuilding tools and builders half-models; navigational instruments and charts; ship models and nautical memorabilia. Four homes of former shipmasters are included in the nine building complex.

Library: 3000 Volumes.

Attendance: 9000.

SPRINGVALE

HILDRETH GALLERY
Anderson Learning Center
    Nasson College, 04083. Tel: (207) 324-5340
George Burk, Cur.
Robert J. Berkley, Dir. Anderson Learning Center
Free, Mon. - Fri. 9 AM - 5 PM; Sat. & Sun. 2 - 5 PM. Estab. 1969; the gallery is an exhibition and lecture area which establishes new facilities for the study of humanities at Nasson and, with the adjoining outdoor court, provides a unique location for the display of the college's permanent art study collection; the appealing location and design of these areas should easily promote the success of those art exhibition and guest lecture programs offered by the college to the community; endowment.

Collections: 20th century paintings, sculpture and graphic works.

Exhibitions: Seven exhibitions of prominent artists per year; historical exhibitions and student shows.

Activities: Individual paintings lent to schools; originial objects of art lent, exhibits only; photograph collection of 700 prints, on request; lectures open to the public; 6 visiting lecturers per year; 6 gallery talks, on request.

Library: 115,000 volumes.

Publications: Poster for each exhibit.

Purchases vary.

Attendance: 6000 annual average.

WATERVILLE

✠COLBY MUSEUM OF ART
    04901. Tel: (207) 873-1131, Exten. 221
Hugh J. Gourley, III, Dir.
Open Mon. - Sat. 10 AM - Noon & 1 - 4:30 PM; cl. major holidays. Estab. in 1959 to serve as an adjunct to the Colby College Art Program and to be a museum center for Central Maine. Friends of Art at Colby, mem. 625; dues $10 and higher.

Collections: The American Heritage Collection (about 85 American Folk Art objects) presented to Colby College by Mr. and Mrs. Ellerton Jette; The Helen Warren and Willard Howe Cummings Collection of American Art; The Pulsifer Collection of Winslow Homer (13 paintings and drawings); the John Marin Collection of 25 works by Marin; other examples of American Art of the 18th, 19th and 20th centuries; Pre-Columbian Mexico; Far Eastern ceramics; Etruscan art and certain European artists also represented.

Library: 1500 volumes for reference only.

Publications: Quarterly newsletter.

THOMAS COLLEGE
    W. River Rd, 04354. Tel: (207) 873-0771
John L. Thomas, Pres.
Dr. Donald F. Brown, Dir.
Free Mon. - Fri. 8 AM - 5 PM. Estab. 1968 for presentation of instructional shows for student audience.

Exhibitions: 1 or 2 exhibitions a month during school year of Maine artists only. Included are Lois Dodd, Bernard Langlais, David Ellis, John Beuregard, Harry Stump.

Library for reference only; over 1000 in slide collection.

Attendance: 1500.

WISCASSET

LINCOLN COUNTY CULTURAL AND HISTORICAL ASSOCIATION
Wiscasset, 04578.
John Heyl, Pres.
Dr. Robert L. Bradley, Cur.
Gerry M. Bradley, Admin. Asst.
See hours and admission for individual buildings below. Inc. 1954 to
preserve buildings of historic interest. Presents 200 years of
Maine's crafts and skills including the work of craftsmen who spend
part of the year in Maine. Presents the works of contemporary pro-
fessional artists, working in Maine, by means of two juried summer
exhibitions. Displays a rare collection of fire engines. Ann. meet-
ing July; mem. approx. 1000; dues $5 and higher. The Association
maintains 3 museums and one art gallery. (See below).
 Collections: Prison equipment and ephanera; hand tools; textiles;
furniture, household articles.
 Exhibitions: Maine Art Gallery, one show each month; Lincoln
County Museum, permanent exhibit on the history of punishment,
changing exhibits on 200 years of Maine crafts and skills.
 Activities: School programs and tours; slide shows; reference
library (local history and penology); lectures; concerts.
 Publications: Association newsletter and occasional monographs.
Income: Approx. $10,000.
 Attendance: Lincoln County Museum approx. 8000; Maine Art
Gallery approx. 4500 (summer only).

Lincoln County Museum
 Open June 1 - Sept. 15, daily 10 AM - 5 PM, Sun. 12:30 - 5 PM;
Winter, Sat. 10 AM - 5 PM, Sun. 12:30 - 5 PM, weekdays by appoint-
ment.

Lincoln County Fire Museum
 Open June 1 - Labor Day, 10 AM - 5 PM.

Maine Art Gallery (Wiscasset)
 Open July 2 to Sept. 4.

Pownalborough Court House (1761, Dresden)
 Open June 26 to Sept. 4.

YORK

OLD GAOL MUSEUM
 York St, 03909. Tel: (207) 363-3872
Mrs. Sewall Winton, Dir.
Mrs. Henry Cadwalader, Chmn.
Mrs. Owen Jones, Corresp. Secy.
Open June 15 - Sept. 30 weekdays 9:30 AM - 5 PM; Sun. 1:30 - 5 PM;
admis. adults $1, children 25¢. Estab. 1900, inc. 1972 to preserve
local history as seen in historic buildings (Old Gaol 1720; Emerson-
Wilcox House 1740), records and decorative arts; endowed. Ann.
meeting Aug.
 Collections: 17th, 18th and 19th century furniture, needlework,
china, lighting equipment.
 Activities: Conducts museum tours for school classes, special
exhibits. Museum shop, reproductions of 18th century porcelain,
pewter, silver, brass and crewelwork.
 Library: 3300 volumes and 600 photographic prints and manuscripts for reference only; decorative arts, local history and
genealogies subject matter. Open Oct. 1 - June 15 Mon. - Fri,
10 AM - Noon, 1 - 4 PM.
 Income: Annual income for Old Gaol and Wilcox House, approx.
$30,000.

SOCIETY FOR THE PRESERVATION OF HISTORIC LANDMARKS*
 Lindsay Rd, 03909.
Owen R. Jones, Pres.
Richmond Hooper, Treas.
Society estab. 1941 to operate the Elizabeth Perkins House, 1730, the
Old School House, Jefferds Tavern and John Hancock Warehouse (see
below). Ann. meeting Aug; mem. 50; dues $2.

Elizabeth Perkins House
 Open June 22 - Sept. 7, weekdays 9:30 AM - 5 PM; Sun. 1:30 - 5
PM; admis. adults 50¢, children free. A Colonial house as lived in
by a Victorian family; built 1730; contains 18th and 19th century fur-
niture, china, and prints.
 Attendance: 2300 per season.

Old School House
 Open May 30 - Sept. 15, weekdays 9:30 AM - 5 PM; Sun. 1:30 -
5 PM. Original school built in 1745; figures of the schoolmaster and
children are in period costumes.
 Attendance: 11,500 per season.

Jefferds Tavern
 Open May 30 through Labor Day, daily 9:30 AM - 5 PM; Sun.
1:30 - 5 PM; admis. adults 50¢, children free. An ancient hostelry
built before the Revolution by Capt. Samuel Jefferds.

John Hancock Warehouse
 Free open June 22 - Sept. 7, weekdays 9:30 AM - 5 PM; Sun.
1:30 - 5 PM. Owned by the signer of the Declaration of Independence
at the time of his death; listed in the National Register of Historic
Places; exhibits of old tools and antique ship models.
 Attendance: 4500 per season.

MARYLAND

ANNAPOLIS

UNITED STATES NAVAL ACADEMY MUSEUM
 21402. Tel: (301) 267-2108
Dr. William W. Jeffries, Dir.
James W. Cheevers, Sr. Cur.
Capt. A. G. Ellis, Cur. Prints
Robert F. Sumrall, Cur. Ship Models
David E. Christie, Visual Information Specialist
Free Tues. - Sat. 9 AM - 5 PM; Sun. 11 AM - 5 PM; cl. Mon, New
Year's, Thanksgiving and Christmas. Estab. 1845 to collect, preserve and utilize tangible evidence of American naval history with
emphasis on naval officers and their contributions in the development
and events of the Navy, nation and mankind; financed by endowment
and federal government. Museum proper contains two galleries
totaling about 9000 sq. ft. Art and historic objects are also exhibited
in other buildings on campus.
 Collections: Paintings, drawings, prints, sculpture, medals, ship
models, flags, uniforms, weapons, silver, manuscripts and personal
memorabilia. All collections are being enlarged, but mainly by donations.
 Exhibitions: (1972-75) Ships of Bone; Selections from the Permanent Art Collection; The Legacy of Two Admirals: John A. Dahlgren
(inventor) and Henry Walke (artist); American Colonial Wars at Sea.
 Activities: Traveling exhibitions organized and circulated; original objects of art lent; 960 items lent in average year; material
available to faculty, students and visiting scholars of Academy ($2
fee for photographs); lectures for Academy only; 50 tours per year.
 Library: 3000 volumes for reference; 3000 prints in photograph
collection for lending and reference.
 Attendance: Approx. 1,000,000.

BALTIMORE

ART COMMISSION OF BALTIMORE CITY*
 City Hall, 21202.
William Donald Schaefer, Chmn.
Estab. 1895 to pass upon designs for all public structures. Composed
of the Mayor and 7 representatives of independent art organizations
of the City and the Park Board.

✠THE BALTIMORE MUSEUM OF ART
 Art Museum Dr, 21218. Tel: (301) 396-7100
J. Paul Bright, Jr, Pres.
E. Kirkbride Miller, Jr, V.Pres.
Mrs. Robert H. Levi, Secy.
Charles S. Garland, Jr, Treas.
Tom L. Freundenheim, Dir.
Ronald J. Goff, Asst. Dir. for Admin.
William Voss Elder, III, Chmn, Curatorial Div. & Cur.
 Decorative Arts
Victor I. Carlson, Cur. Prints & Drawings
Brenda Richardson, Cur. Painting & Sculpture
Glenn L. Long, Chmn, Div. Educ. & Cur-in-Charge of African,
 Oceanic & Pre-Columbian Collections
J. Benjamin Katzner, Dir. Capital Campaign
Martha L. Parkhurst, Dir. Mem. & Development
Alice C. Steinbach, Dir. Pub. Information
Brenda Edelson, Dir. Prog.
Ann Boyce Harper, Managing Ed.
Sona K. Johnston, Assoc. Cur. Painting & Sculpture
Jay McK. Fisher, Asst. Cur. Prints & Drawings
Mary Beale Munford, Asst. Cur. Decorative Arts
Dena S. Katzenberg, Consultant Cur. Textiles
Diana C. Schramm, Registrar
Margaret M. Powell, Installationist
Robert A. Zimmerman, Designer
Free Tues. - Sat. 11 AM - 5 PM; Thurs. evenings (except summer)
7 - 10 PM; Sunday 1 - 5 PM; cl. Mon. Estab. and inc. 1914; Museum
opened 1923 in Garrett House, Mt. Vernon Place; present building
completed 1928; Jacobs Wing 1938; Saidie A. May Art Center 1950;
William Woodward Wing 1956; Cone Wing 1957, renovated 1974;
American Wing doubled 1970. Municipally and privately funded.
Mem. 5500; dues $15 and higher.
 Collections: Cone collection 19th and 20th century French paintings, sculpture and drawings with special emphasis on Matisse;
collection of textiles, laces, jewelry, etc; Saidie A. May collection of

modern European paintings and sculpture; Gallagher Memorial collection of 20th century American painting; Mary Frick Jacobs collection of European Old Masters, Aubusson tapestries and objects d'art; Jacob Epstein collection of Old Masters, Rodin and Barye bronzes; Daingerfield collection of 18th century English and American paintings; Antioch mosaics; classical objects; Wurtzburger collections of art from Africa, the Americas and the Pacific, 20th century sculpture; 50,000 prints and drawings from 15th century through modern; a group of American primitive paintings given by Edgar William and Bernice Chrysler Garbisch; Renaissance Room; Oriental Gallery; Maryland Wing with period rooms, paintings and Americana; Woodward collection of English sporting art; White collection of Maryland silver and American decorative arts; Mabel Garrison Siemonn collection of 20th century French art; Nelson and Juanita Greif Gutman collection of art since 1850; Thomas E. Benesch Memorial Collection of contemporary drawings; Lucas collection of French 19th century paintings and prints on indefinite loan from the Maryland Institute College of Art.

Exhibitions: Changing exhibitions covering many different phases of art since 1500. Maryland Biennial Exhibition open to artists born or residing in Maryland; selections are made by an out-of-town jury; awards approx. $5000 yearly. Approx. 50 temporary exhibitions per year. Man in Sport Photography, 1968; From El Greco to Pollock, Early and Late Works, 1969; The Partial Figure in Modern Sculpture, 1970; Washington Twenty Years, 1970; Baltimore Painted Furniture, 1972; Moshe Safdie: For Everyone A Garden, 1973; Walter Darby Bannard, 1973; Blue Traditions: Indigo Dyed Textiles and Related Cobalt Glazed Ceramics from the 17th through the 19th Century, 1973-74; Max Klinger: Selections from his Graphic Work, 1974-75; Andy Warhol: Paintings, 1962-1975, 1975; Anywhere So Long As There Be Freedom: Charles Carroll of Carrollton, His Family and His Maryland, 1975.

Activities: Study courses; creative art classes for adults and children; gallery talks; illustrated lectures; films, concerts, children's theatre.

Library: Research library of about 18,000 volumes, pamphlets, catalogs and magazines. Lending collection of about 6000 slides and 2000 facsimiles and reproductions.

Publications: Monthly calendar of events; exhibition catalogs; permanent collection catalogs.

Income and Purchases: Income $1,600,000; purchases approx. $65,000 yearly.

Attendance: 250,000 annually.

COMMUNITY COLLEGE OF BALTIMORE ART GALLERY

2901 Liberty Heights Ave, 21215. Tel: (301) 462-5800, Exten. 250
Bennard B. Perlman, Dir.
Free Sun. 1 - 5 PM; Mon. - Fri. 10 AM - 4 PM; cl. Sat. Estab. 1965 to bring to the Baltimore and college communities exhibitions of note by regional and national professional fine artists; financed by city and state appropriations.

Collections: Permanent collection consists chiefly of graphics (from the 16th century to the present), together with paintings by some notable American (Milton Avery, Louis Eilshemius) and regional artists.

Exhibitions: WPA: Art of the Depression Years; Teachers as Artists; Maryland Crafts Council; The Artist's Studio; Contemporary Maryland Artists; plus an annual art faculty, art student and one-person faculty show.

Activities: Lectures open to the public.

✤THE DECKER GALLERY

The Maryland Institute College of Art
1300 Mt. Royal Ave, 21239. Tel: (301) 669-9200
William J. Finn, Pres.
Joseph S. Czestochowski, Dir.
Free Mon. - Fri. 10 AM - 4 PM & 6 - 10 PM; Sat. 10 AM - 4 PM; Sun. 1 - 4 PM. Exhibiting since 1826; financed by endowment and student tuition.

Collections: Maryland Institute - George A. Lucas Collection donated in 1909 comprising over 400 paintings and drawings by Corot, Daumier, Greuze, Manet, Pissarro, Delacroix, Millet and Whistler, bronzes by Antoine Barye and a collection of 17,000 graphics.

Exhibitions: Alphonse Mucha; Selections from The Lucas Collection.

Activities: Traveling exhibitions organized and circulated; original objects of art lent; lectures open to public; gallery talks; tours; concerts, dramatic programs. Book shop.

Library: 32,000 volumes for lending and reference.

Publications: Two major publications per year, several small catalogs, handouts of the works in the Lucas Collection.

Attendance: 10,000.

ENOCH PRATT FREE LIBRARY OF BALTIMORE CITY

Fine Arts Department
400 Cathedral St, 21201. Tel: (301) 396-5490
Ernest Siegel, Dir. of Enoch Pratt Free Library
Miss Howard Hubbard, Chief Pub. Relations Div.

James Dickson, Head Fine Arts Dept.
Free Mon. - Thurs. 9 AM - 9 PM; Fri. - Sat. 9 AM - 5 PM; Sun. 1 - 5 PM. Estab. 1882; main building opened 1933; includes books and periodicals on art subjects.
Purchases: $25,000 (includes art and music).
George Peabody Branch
17 E. Mt. Vernon Place, 21201. Tel: (301) 396-5540
Gail Juris, Head
Free Mon. - Sat 9 AM - 5 PM; cl. Sun.

Activities: Lends picture collection of 157 framed prints and 405,000 unframed pictures. There are 13 exterior display windows and additional exhibits in interior display cases, corridors and special departments. Lectures and film showings. Booklets issued periodically.

THE JOHNS HOPKINS UNIVERSITY

Archaeological Collection
Gilman Hall, Homewood, Charles & 34th Sts, 21218.
Free Mon. - Fri. 11 AM - 3 PM. Archaeological Collection consists of changing exhibitions of Egyptian, Greek and Roman material. Estab. 1876 as part of the University's Archaeological Dept. (See Schools)

The Milton S. Eisenhower Library Galleries
Quadrangle Level
Alan R. Taylor, Assoc. Librn.
Free Mon. - Fri. 9 AM - 5 PM. Changing exhibitions of paintings, sculpture and photography by Baltimore artists.

Evergreen House
4545 N. Charles St, 21210.
Open to the public Mon. - Fri. 2 - 5 PM. The former house of John W. Garrett which he bequeathed to the University; collections of fine arts, rare book library, changing exhibitions. It also contains a collection of paintings left by Mrs. Garrett to the Evergreen House Foundation.

Welch Medical Library
Johns Hopkins Medical School, 1900 E. Monument St, 21205
Portraits of medical men, medical artifacts, rare book library, changing exhibitions.

MARYLAND HISTORICAL SOCIETY

201 W. Monument St, 21201. Tel: (301) 685-3750
John L. McShane, Pres.
S. Vannort Chapman, Rec. Secy.
P. William Filby, Director
Mrs. Romaine Somerville, Gallery Curator
A. Hester Rich, Librarian
Gallery free Tues. - Sat. 11 AM - 4 PM; Sun. 1 - 5 PM, library ($1 day for non-mem) Wed. - Sat. 9 AM - 4:30 PM. Inc. 1844 to collect, preserve and disseminate information on the history of Maryland and the United States. Ann. meeting Feb; mem. about 4600; dues $12.

Collections: Of historical interest the collection includes portraits and landscapes in oil; miniatures, furniture, silver, glass, ceramics, textiles and arms.

Exhibitions: Original manuscript of The Star-Spangled Banner in the handwriting of Francis Scott Key; Bonaparte Room; Confederate and Union collections; Washington prints; Chesapeake Bay maritime museum of models, paintings and prints; costumes, Colonial kitchen; Darnall Young People's Museum of Maryland History.

Activities: Guided tours for school classes; monthly lectures; illustrated afternoon talks on American arts and crafts; lectures by staff on local and national history given before clubs, patriotic societies and schools.

Library: Includes collections of American history in maps, prints, 2 million manuscripts and 70,000 bound volumes.

Publications: Maryland Historical Magazine, quarterly; News and Notes of the Maryland Historical Society, 6 issues ann; Archives of Maryland; various books, pamphlets and exhibition catalogs.

Attendance: 43,000.

MUNICIPAL ART SOCIETY OF BALTIMORE CITY

c/o Beverley C. Compton, Jr. Pres, 135 E. Baltimore St, 21202. Tel: (301) 727-1700
Alan P. Hoblitzell, Treas.
Estab. 1899, the Society contributes primarily to the painting of murals in public buildings and the adornment of public places with statuary. Conducts series of lectures on art by outstanding critics. Offers an annual traveling scholarship at the Rinehart School of Sculpture conducted at the Maryland Institute. Annual income about $5000. Mem. 150; dues $15.

PEALE MUSEUM
(Municipal Museum of Baltimore)
225 Holliday St, 21202. Tel: (301) 396-3523
George D. Hubbard, Pres.
Wilbur H. Hunter, Dir.
Thomas E. Eader, Asst. Dir.
Paul A. Amelia, Archivist
Free Tues. - Fri. 10:30 AM - 4:30 PM; Sat. & Sun. 1 - 5 PM; cl. national holidays. Built 1814 by Rembrandt Peale as Peale's Baltimore Museum and Gallery of Fine Arts; City Hall, 1830-1875; restored as Museum of the Life and History of Baltimore in 1929.
Collections: Extensive collection of prints, paintings and photographs of Baltimore; Hambleton Collection of Baltimore Views; portraits painted by Peale for the City.
Activities: Program includes annual contemporary art and photo shows, historic art and architecture, modern civic problems; lectures; traveling exhibitions and tours; Historical Information Center in the Washington Monument.
Publications: Bulletins and Historical Series published irregularly; Historical Guide to Baltimore.
Income and Purchases: Income $60,000; purchases $1000.
Attendance: 25,000 annual average.
Carroll Mansion
800 E. Lombard St, 21202. Tel: (301) 396-4980
Built 1812. furnished in early 19th century style. Last home of Charles Carroll of Carrollton, signer of Declaration of Independence.

✠**WALTERS ART GALLERY**
600 North Charles St, 21201. Tel: (301) 547-9000
Francis D. Murnaghan, Jr, Pres, Board of Trustees
Richard H. Randall, Jr, Dir.
William R. Johnston, Asst. Dir.
Edward P. McCracken, Admin. Officer
Jeanny Vorys Canby, Cur. of Egyptian and Ancient Near Eastern Art
Dorothy Kent Hill, Cur. of Greek and Roman Art
Edgar Peters Bowron, Cur. of Renaissance and Baroque Art
Lilian M. C. Randall, Cur. of Rare Books & Manuscripts
Elisabeth C. G. Packard, Dir, Dept. of Conservation
Theodore L. Low, Dir, Dept. of Educ.
Emily C. Schilpp, Librn.
Leopoldine Arz, Registrar
Ursula Eland McCracken, Editor of Publications
Mary Ann Daily, Pub. Relations
Irene Butterbaugh, Book Shop Manager
Open Mon. 1 - 5 PM; Tues. - Sat. 11 AM - 5 PM (closes at 4 PM during July and August); Sun. & Holidays 2 - 5 PM; cl. New Years Day, Fourth of July, Thanksgiving Day, Christmas Eve and Day. Estab. 1931 by will of Henry Walters, who gave the city his gallery, adjoining residence, the contents of both and an endowment fund for maintenance; inc. in 1933; gallery reopened in 1934; new 100,000 square feet addition opened in Nov. 1974. Mem. 1900; dues students $5, individual $10, family $15.
Collections: The collections cover the entire history of art from Egyptian times to the beginning of the 20th century, including important groups of †Roman sculpture, †Etruscan, †Byzantine and †Medieval art, †Sevres porcelains, †Near Eastern art and †2000 European paintings; †illuminated manuscripts; †Oriental art; †jewelry; †arms and armor.
Exhibitions: (1973) Merchants and Mandarins: The Mutual Influence of China and Europe; Ancient Masterpieces in Bronze; Jean Leon Gerome; Indian Art. (1974) William and Henry Walters: Collectors and Philanthropists; Armenian Manuscripts.
Activities: Lectures, gallery tours, concerts, extensive children's programs integrated with school work; 556 events. Book shop.
Library: Approx. 65,000 volumes of reference works on history of art and on decorative objects.
Publications: Exhibition and collection catalogs.
Income: (1974) $859,745.90.
Attendance: 87,000 annual average.

COLLEGE PARK

✠**UNIVERSITY OF MARYLAND ART GALLERY**
J. Millard Tawes Fine Arts Center, 20742. Tel: (301) 454-2717
Eleanor Green, Dir.
William Hommel, Assoc. Dir.
George Levitine, Chmn. Dept. of Art
Free Mon. - Sat. 9 AM - 5 PM; Sun. 1 - 5 PM. Estab. 1966 to present exhibitions related to the programs of the Department of Art of the University and to serve the Museum Training Program of the Department; State appropriation. Gallery is part of the Department of Art.
Collections: Small collection of 20th-century paintings, sculpture, and prints, mostly works executed on the WPA Federal Art Project and the Dept. of the Treasury, Section of Painting and Sculpture.

Exhibitions: Jasper F. Cropsey, a retrospective view of America's painter of Autumn; Hommage a Baudelaire; Retrospective for a Critic, Duncan Phillips; Drawings of Arshile Gorky; Martin Johnson Heade; Thomas Couture, Paintings and Drawings in American Collections; American Pupils of Thomas Couture; Biennial exhibition of the Studio Faculty; Annual Graduate Thesis Exhibition; Chinese Art from the Ferris Luboshez Collection; The Apocalypse; The Private Collection of Martha Jackson; 20th Century Masterpieces from the Musee de Grenoble; Tony Smith, Painting and Sculpture; Art of the Mende; Richard Klank, Painting and Drawing; Rockne Krebs; (photo) (photo) $2 \ldots$ (photo)^n: Sequenced Photographs; Search for Innocence: Primitive and Primitivistic Art of the 19th Century; The Late Landscapes of William Morris Hunt.
Activities: Lectures open to public, 8 visiting lecturers per year; scholarships.
Publications: Catalogs for all exhibitions.
Attendance: 20,000.

EASTON

EASTON ACADEMY OF THE ARTS
Box 605, 21601. Tel: (301) 822-0455
W. Thomas Fountain, Pres.
Mrs. Kurt L. Lederer, Prog. Dir.
J. Robert Seyffert, Cur.
Free weekdays 10 AM - 4 PM, weekends 2 - 4 PM during shows. Estab. 1958 to encourage pursuit and promotion of arts and creative arts, (architecture, crafts, drama, graphics, literature, music, painting, sculpture); maintained by membership. Ann. meeting third Wed. in May, monthly meeting of council (10 months); mem. 800; dues junior $5, individual $10, husband & wife $15, sustaining $30.
Collections: †Permanent Collection.
Exhibitions: Annual members show, juried, primary school, high school, college student (1969-1970); one-man shows, invited shows.
Activities: Extension work, three-county area, art appreciation, Maryland public schools; lectures open to public, three visiting lecturers per year; concerts, classes for adults and children, competitions; bus trips to museums and performing arts centers.
Library: 100 volumes for lending and reference.
Attendance: 5000.

FRIENDSVILLE

MUSEUM WITHOUT WALLS, RCEDA INC.
P.O. Box 45, Morris Ave, 21531. Tel: (301) 746-5712
Richard Kibbey, Museum Dir.
William F. Robinson, Exec. Dir, RCEDA Inc.
Frank DuVal, Cur. Exhibitions
Lynda Waggoner, Assoc. Cur.
Randall Overdorff, Technical Dir.
B. David Gaither, Asst. Cur.
Richard Johnson, Business Mgr.
Deborah C. L. Smith, Admin. Supvr.
Free 8:30 AM - 4 PM. Estab. Sept, 1971 to circulate 30 to 40 traveling exhibitions primarily through school systems in New York State, Pennsylvania, Maryland, Florida and a few other states. Each exhibition is accompanied by an artist-in-residence-lecturer; financed by endowment, city and state appropriation and earned income. Small gallery for temporary exhibitions for local patrons.
Collections: Contemporary monumental stone sculpture and small bronzes, wood sculpture, etc; †20th Century paintings; †etchings, engravings, lithographs, silkscreens, woodcuts, Renaissance to contemporary; †photographs.
Exhibitions: Bremoils of Edward Bafford; To See Ourselves; Record of the Moment: I/Jacob Riis; Record of the Moment: II/Lewis Hine; Ukiyo-e and the Japanese Print; Four Photographers; The Graven Image; Hiers to Wisdom; Plain 'n Fancy, needlework; Turn of the Century Photographers; The Jolly Corner Suite by Peter Milton; plus others.
Activities: Development of workshops, lectures, festivals for community center, libraries and colleges; traveling exhibitions organized and circulated; individual paintings and original objects of art lent; 5000 lantern slides and 400 photographs in lending collection; 2000 items lent in average year; lectures usually open to public; 6 - 8 visiting lecturers per year; 5 full-time lecturers; 4000 gallery talks; concerts; dramatic programs; classes for adults and children; scholarships.
Library: 2000 volumes for reference only; 400 prints in photograph collection for lending and reference.
Publications: Bimonthly newsletter
Income and Purchases: Income $1,500,000; purchases to $30,000.
Attendance: 500,000.

HAGERSTOWN

✠WASHINGTON COUNTY MUSEUM OF FINE ARTS
   City Park, 21740. Tel: (301) 739-5727
Richard G. Wantz, Pres.
H. Paul Kotun, Dir.
Robert E. Preszler, Cur.
Free 10 AM - 5 PM; Sun. 1 - 6 PM; cl. Mon, Christmas and
New Year's Day. Estab. and inc. 1929; building opened 1931;
new wings opened 1949. Board of Trustees meet quarterly; mem.
500; dues $10 and higher.
   Collections: The initial collection, gift of Anne Brugh Singer, includes 19th and 20th century French, Dutch, and †American paintings,
sculpture, ceramics, and prints; Eichberg collection of Italian †Re-
naissance objects, furniture and tapestries; Glover collection of
paintings; Tack collection of Chinese paintings; a collection of Tibetan banners; Friedberg collection of Chinese jades; collection of
early Italian, Dutch and Flemish masters; display of regional historical relics.
   Exhibitions: Annual Cumberland Valley Artists (prizes $1500)
Annual Photographic Salon; Public School Art annually; permanent
collection installations; special monthly exhibitions.
   Activities: Lectures on the history of art and related subjects by
visiting speakers and staff personnel; concerts, gallery tours, film
programs; regular Saturday morning Youth Program; Museum art
classes for adults and children. Sales desk.
   Library: 2500 volumes on art and history; collection of films,
filmstrips, tapes and slides.
   Income and Purchases: Income $95,000.
   Publications: Monthly announcements, special catalogs, annual
report.
   Attendance: 55,000.
William H. Singer Memorial Gallery
   Opened 1949; permanent collection.

ROCKVILLE

CITY OF ROCKVILLE MUNICIPAL ART GALLERY
   Civic Center Mansion, 603 Edmonston Dr, 20851.
   Tel: (301) 424-3184
Bernard R. Loiselle, Dir.
Jane Loiselle, Civic Center Supvr.
Free Mon. - Fri. 1 - 5 PM; Sun. 2 - 5 PM. Estab. 1959; financed by
city appropriation.
   Collections: Small permanent collection.
   Exhibitions: Gallery exhibits of 12 shows per year. One of these
is a youth show.
   Activities: Classes for adults.
   Attendance: 7500 annual average.

SILVER SPRING

MARYLAND SCHOOL OF ART
   640 University Blvd. E, 20901. Tel: (301) 439-7200
Terrence James Coffman, Pres.
Judy Lewis, Secy.
Kenneth Allen, Chmn.
Marjory Gross, V.Pres.
Oscar Chilimsky, Chmn. Foundation Prog.
Ellen Vincent, Admis. Counselor
Free 9:30 AM - 4:30 PM. Estab. 1973 for the purpose of education.
Exhibitions by faculty and area artists.
   Activities: Visual communications; traveling exhibitions orga-
nized and circulated; lectures open to public, 3 visiting lecturers
per year; classes for adults, competitions; scholarships.
   Library: 300 volumes; 5000 prints in photograph collection.
   Publications: Point (every 3 months); school catalogs.

TOWSON

✠GOUCHER COLLEGE
   21204.
Dr. Eric Van Schaack, Chmn, Dept. of Visual Arts
H. Brown, Dir. Exhibitions
Free, open when college is in session 9 AM - 5 PM. Estab. 1885 to
serve the educational needs of Goucher College and the local com-
munity; financed by endowment.
   Collections: †20th century painting, sculpture and graphic art;
†Oriental textiles; Oriental and Pre-Columbian art.
   Exhibitions: Works of art from the Goucher College Collection.
   Activities: Photograph collection of 26,000; classes for adults.
   Library: 188,700 volumes for lending or reference to authorized
students; photograph collection.

✠TOWSON STATE COLLEGE ART GALLERY*
   21204
Christopher Bartlett, Dir.

MASSACHUSETTS

AMHERST

JONES LIBRARY
   01002. Tel: (413) 256-0246
Anne M. Turner, Dir.
Free Mon. & Fri. 9 AM - 5:30 PM; Tues, Wed, Thurs. 9 AM - 9:30
PM; Sat. 10 AM - 5:30 PM.
Inc. 1919; opened 1921. In addition to library of 94,000 volumes,
includes art gallery. Owns paintings by Ruth Payne Burgess and
paintings presented by the family of William A. Burnett. Picture
lending reproductions. Special exhibitions and lectures during the
year.

✠MEAD ART BUILDING OF AMHERST COLLEGE
   01002. Tel: (413) 542-2335
Frank Trapp, Dir.
Lewis A. Shepard, Cur.
Anne Mannarino, Registrar
Free during academic year Mon. - Fri. 9 AM - 5 PM; Sat. & Sun.
Noon - 5 PM; summer 10 AM - Noon & 1 - 4 PM; cl. Aug. Building
erected 1949.
   Collections: Main collection devoted to †American art, English
art and Ancient art; other Western European and Oriental collec-
tions; †material on art history now being increased.
   Exhibitions: Exhibitions change frequently for both college
curriculum needs and for specialized loan exhibitions; War a la
Mode;American Painters of the Arctic; American Folk Art.
   Library: Art library of 9000 volumes.
   Publications: Catalogs published for major exhibitions.
   Attendance: 35,000.

UNIVERSITY OF MASSACHUSETTS ART COLLECTION*
   Art Dept, Bartlett Hall, 01002. Tel: (413) 545-2574
Randolph Bromery, Chancellor
George Wardlaw, Chmn. Art Dept.
Walter Kamys, Dir. Univ. Collection
Estab. 1963 to form best possible collection of contemporary Ameri-
can drawings.
   Collection: Contemporary American drawings, paintings and
sculpture. The collection in dispersed around the campus until
completion of Fine Arts Center and Gallery in 1974.

   University Art Gallery
William Forwood, Dir.
Open weekdays 10 AM - 4 PM; Sat. & Sun. 2 - 5 PM. Gallery conducts regular series of exhibitions for the University. Publication
of catalogue with most shows.

   Art Slide Library
Dorothy Perkins, Cur.
Open Mon. - Fri. 8 AM - 4 PM. 65,000 slides, 24,500 titles.

ANDOVER

✠ADDISON GALLERY OF AMERICAN ART*
   Phillips Academy, 01810. Tel: (617) 475-3403
Christopher C. Cook, Dir.
Susan J. Clarke, Cur. Painting & Sculpture
John M. Snyder, Cur. Photography
Antoinette Thiras, Secy, Registrar
Free 10 AM - 5 PM; Sun. 2:30 - 5 PM. Phillips Academy founded
1778; Addison Gallery of American Art estab. 1930, in memory of
Mrs. Keturah Addison Cobb, in order to enrich permanently the lives
of the students of Phillips Academy, by helping to cultivate and foster
in them a love for the beautiful. The gift also included a number of
important †American paintings, †prints and †sculpture. Mem. c. 300;
dues voluntary.
   Collections: Permanent collection is limited to American art.
   Exhibitions: Originated by the Addison Gallery, Feelies, the
nature of things perceived through touch, 1967; Alumni Treasures,
1968; Noise, An examination of the aural environment, 1968; Effigy
and Ritual, effigies of four different cultures, 1968; Seven Decades
(1900-1969), painting and sculpture by alumni of Phillips Academy,
1969; The Works, a comprehensive survey of the Addison Gallery
Collection, 1969; The Black Photographer, 1971; Larry Stark, 1971;
Beverly Hallam, 1971; Art Therapy at Danvers, 1971; John Laurent,
1972.
   Activities: Real Art Data, formed to produce special exhibitions
and publish new kinds of art information.
   Library: 1500 volumes
   Publications: Exhibition catalogues.
   Attendance: 25,000.

ATTLEBORO

ATTLEBORO MUSEUM, INC.
Capron Park, 02703. Tel: (617) 222-2644
Pasquale Masiello, Pres.
Vera Cross, Dir.
Charles Calverly, Secy.
William Bott, Treas.
Free Tues. - Fri. 12:30 - 4 PM; Sat. & Sun. 2 - 5 PM; cl. Mon. New building opened Oct. 1951. Ann. meeting May; mem. 400; dues $6 individual, $10 family.
Collections: Historic and art collections.
Exhibitions: Art and craft exhibits changed monthly in 3 galleries; competitive juried painting exhibit with $600 in prizes.
Activities: Each exhibit opens with a lecture or demonstration by visiting speaker; scholarships.
Attendance: 7200.

BEVERLY

BEVERLY HISTORICAL SOCIETY
117 Cabot St, 01915. Tel: (617) 922-1186
Robert Lovett, Pres.
Ray Standley, Secy-Treas.
Mrs. Walter D. Pratt, Financial Secy.
Roger Hanners, Chmn, Balch House
Esther Herrick, Chmn, Hale House
Mrs. Dan Coffey, Historian-Librn.
Open throughout the year, Wed, Thurs, Fri, 10 AM - 4 PM; July & Aug. daily 10 AM - 4 PM; Balch House open June through Sept, daily 10 AM - 4 PM, cl. Sun, other times by appointment; Hale House open June 15 - Sept. 15, daily 10:30 AM - 4 PM, cl. Sun. & Mon, other times by appointment; admis. adults $1, children 25¢. Estab. and inc. 1891, to investigate, record and perpetuate local history. Occupies house built by John Cabot in 1781. The Balch House, built in 1636 by John Balch, contains old furniture. The Hale House was built by the first minister, John Hale, in 1694. Ann. meeting Oct; mem. about 380; dues $5.
Collections: An extensive collection of objects pertaining to the sea, instruments, ship models, shells, tapa cloths, ship portraits, etc; portraits by Gilbert Stuart of early merchants and seamen; large collection of glass, porcelain, pewter, embroideries, colonial and Revolutionary documents.

BOSTON

ART COMMISSION OF THE CITY OF BOSTON*
Faneuil Hall, 02201.
Nelson Aldrich, Chmn.
David McKibbin, Clerk & Secy.
Estab. 1890. Five members appointed by the Mayor, one each year for 5 year term. No work of art can become the property of the City without approval of the Art Commission.

⌘BOSTON ARCHITECTURAL CENTER
320 Newbury St, 02115. Tel: (617) 536-3170
Urs Gauchat, Pres.
Herbert H Glassman, V.Pres.
H. P. Goeters, Secy.
Frederick Norris, Treas.
Arcangelo Cascieri, Dean
Peter Blake, Chmn.
Elsie M. Hurst, Dir. of Admin.
Estab. 1889 for professional and educational architectural purposes. Ann. meeting 3rd Tues. in June; mem. 500; dues assoc. mem. $20, regular mem. $25. Gallery facilities.
Exhibitions: Continual program of exhibitions, special and student.
Activities: Conducts evening architectural courses; lectures with visiting lecturers annually; offers scholarships and competitions.
Library: 12,000 volumes.
Publications: Architecture and the Computer; Forces Shaping the Role of the Architect; The City as a System; Systems; The New John Hancock Building: An Example of Public and Private Decision Making; Transportation; International Systems Building Round Table Conference.
Income: Approx. $400,000.

BOSTON ATHENAEUM
10½ Beacon St, 02108. Tel: (617) 227-0270
Rodney Armstrong, Dir. & Librn.
David M. K. McKibbin, Art Dept.
Free Mon. - Fri. 9 AM - 5:30 PM; cl. Sat. June 1 - Oct. 1. Estab. 1807; financed by membership and endowment. Ann. meeting Feb; mem. 1049 shares.
Collections: †Topographical prints and photographs of New England.

Exhibitions: Exhibitions of books and prints from permanent collection of the library; monthly exhibitions of contemporary arts
Library: 435,000 volumes, mainly history, literature and fine arts.

BOSTON PUBLIC LIBRARY
Copley Square, 02117. Tel: (617) 536-5400
Philip J. McNiff, Dir. & Librn.
Central Library building contains mural decorations by Pierre Puvis de Chavannes, Edwin A. Abbey, John Elliott, and John Singer Sargent; bronze doors by Daniel Chester French; sculptures by Frederick MacMonnies, Louis St. Gaudens, Bela Pratt, Francis Derwent Wood; illustrations by Howard Pyle; paintings by Duplessis and Copley; and bust of John Deferrari by Joseph A. Coletti.
Fine Arts
G. Florence Connolly, Cur. of the Fine Arts
Free 9 AM - 9 PM; Sat. 9 AM - 6 PM; Sun. 2 - 6 PM in winter, cl. in summer.
Collections include 73,000 books and over 410,000 pictures.
Albert H. Wiggin Gallery (Prints)
Sinclair H. Hitchings, Keeper of Prints
Free 9 AM - 9 PM; Sat. - 6 PM; Sun. 2 - 6 PM in winter, cl. in summer. Study Room Mon. - Fri. 9 AM - 5 PM; cl. Sat. and Sun.
Collection contains 49,500 prints, photographs, drawings and watercolors; 1554 books; 23 oil paintings; 258 foredge paintings; porcelain figurines of 13 Cries of London. Eight to nine exhibitions each year.

⌘BOSTON UNIVERSITY*
George Sherman Union
775 Commonwealth Ave, 02215.
Maura Burns, Prog. Dir.

BOSTON WATERCOLOR SOCIETY
c/o Charles A. Mahoney, Pres, 30 Ipswich St, 02215.
Glen G. MacNutt, V.Pres.
Fletcher P. Adams, Secy-Treas.
Estab. 1885. Ann. meeting Jan; mem. by majority vote of members based on excellence of candidates' work; mem. approx. 100; dues $10 annually. Selected traveling exhibitions available on request by Accredited Museums.

GIBSON SOCIETY, INC.
137 Beacon St, 02116. Tel: (617) 267-6338
Stephen T. Hibbard, Pres.
Charles F. Woodard, Jr, Treas.
Mr. & Mrs. David Sweeney, Custodians.
Open daily 2 - 5 PM; cl. Mon. & holidays; admis. $1. Estab. 1957. A Victorian House Museum open to the public.
Attendance: Approx. 1000 annually.

GUILD OF BOSTON ARTISTS
162 Newbury St, 02116. Tel: (617) 536-7660
Robert Douglas Hunter, Pres.
Charles A. Mahoney, V.Pres.
Ruth Wynn, Secy.
Phyllis Church Maloney, Cur.
Free Tues. - Sat. 10:30 AM - 5:30 PM; cl. Sun. & July & Aug. Estab. and inc. 1914. Ann. meeting Apr; mem. 65-80 active, under 100 assoc. A cooperative organization. The Guild owns its bldg; one gallery with continuous exhibitions in which each member is entitled to show one work. The second gallery devoted to one-man shows, each member by turn at regular intervals. Three yearly general exhibitions by entire active membership.
Attendance: 100-200 daily.

⌘INSTITUTE OF CONTEMPORARY ART
955 Boylston St, 02115. Tel: (617) 266-5151
David H. Thorne, Pres.
Gabriella Jeppson, Dir.
Open Tues. - Wed. 10 AM - 5 PM; Thurs. - Sat. 10 AM - 9 PM; Sun. 12 - 5 PM; admis. $1. Estab. 1936 to bring contemporary art to Boston; financed by city and state appropriation, membership and private contributions; gallery recently opened in a 19th century rennovated police station. Ann. meeting Nov; mem. approx. 1500; dues $20 and higher.
Exhibitions: Major shows of local, national and international significance, organized by the I.C.A. staff and guest curators.
Activities: As a laboratory of contemporary art, the Institute presents not only traditional art forms, but also music, dance, video, film and lectures. Urban education program and active public art program, administrating such projects. Book Shop.
Publications: Exhibition catalogs; reports; newsletters.
Income and Purchases: Income $300,000; purchases $300,000.
Attendance: 5000 annually.

ISABELLA STEWART GARDNER MUSEUM
280 Tho Fonway, 02115
Office: 2 Palace Rd, 02115. Tel: (617) 566-1401
G. Peabody Gardner, Pres.
Malcolm D. Perkins, V.Pres. & Secy.
John Lowell Gardner, Treas.
Rollin van N. Hadley, Dir.
Linda V. Hewitt, Asst. Dir.
Free (except for $1 charge on Sun) Sept. - June Tues. 1 - 9:30 PM;
Wed. - Sun. 1 - 5:30 PM; cl. Mon, national holidays. July & Aug.
Tues. - Sun. 1 - 5:30 PM; cl. Mon. & July 4. Free music programs
Tues. at 8 PM; Thurs. & Sun. at 4 PM; no music in July & Aug. Inc.
1900 to exhibit the works of art collected by Mrs. John Lowell
Gardner.
Collections: 14th to 20th century European and American paint-
ings, notably paintings of the Italian Renaissance; Classical, Roman-
esque, Gothic and Renaissance sculpture; 15th to 18th century tapes-
tries and other textiles; Oriental objects; furniture, metalwork, and
ceramics; building in the style of the Italian 15th century.
Attendance: 196,000.

MacIVOR REDDIE GALLERY
The Art Institute of Boston
700 Beacon St, 02215. Tel: (617) 262-1223
William H. Willis, Jr, Dir.
Free Mon. - Fri. 9 AM - 5 PM; Mon, Wed, Thurs. 5 - 8 PM. Estab.
1967 to provide exhibitions at the Art Institute of Boston; supported
by budget from the Institute; 2500 square feet of gallery.
Exhibitions: (1970-1973) Seven faculty shows, nine student shows;
outside exhibitions included six photographers, thirteen painters,
five illustrators, four sculptors and eight graphic designers.
Activities: Lectures open to the public, six visiting lecturers
per year; eight gallery talks; classes (See Schools).
Attendance: Approx. 2000 annually.

✠MUSEUM OF FINE ARTS*
465 Huntington Ave, 02115. Tel: (617) 267-9300
George C. Seybolt, Pres.
William A. Coolidge, V.Pres.
John Coolidge, V.Pres.
Mrs. Frank L. Christian, V.Pres.
John L. Gardner, V.Pres. & Treas.
James Peabody, Secy.
Merrill C. Rueppel, Dir.
Arthur D. Larson, Asst. Treas.
James Griswold, Development
Diggory Venn, Speical Projects Mgr.
Linda Thomas, Registrar
Trinita Petersen, Secy. to Dir.
Jan Fontein, Cur. Asiatic Art
Yashiro Iguchi, Conservator Asiatic Art
Johnathan Fairbanks, Cur. American Decorative Arts
Robert C. Moeller, Cur. European Decorative Arts
Kenworth Moffett, Cur. Contemporary Art
Larry Salmon, Cur. Textiles
Eleanor A. Sayre, Cur. Prints & Drawings
William Kelly Simpson, Cur. Egyptian Art
Cornelius C. Vermeule, Cur. Classical Art
Barbara Lambert, Keeper Musical Instruments
Clifford S. Ackley, Asst. Cur. Prints & Drawings
Mary B. Comstock, Assoc. Cur. Classical Art
John McKeon, Asst. Cur. Classical Art
Suzanne Chapman, Assoc. Cur. Egyptian Art
William J. Young, Head Research Laboratory
Francis W. Dolloff, Conservator Prints & Drawings
Roy Perkinson, Asst. Conservator Prints & Drawings
Richard Finlayson, Conservator Paintings
Philip Vance, Assoc. Conservator Paintings
William Lillys, Dean Educ.
William Bagnall, Dean Museum School
Carl F. Zahn, Graphics Designer
Margaret Jupe, Ed. Dept. Publ.
Clementine Brown, Mgr. Pub. Relations
William Wilson, Mgr. Purchasing
John E. Morrison, Supt.
Open daily 10 AM - 6 PM; Tues. & Thurs. evenings until 9 PM; cl.
New Year's Day, July 4, Thanksgiving and Christmas; admis. adults
$1; free Sun. 10 AM - 1 PM; children under 16 free; 65 and over free
Mon. 10 AM - 12 PM. Estab. and inc. 1870; Present building opened
1909. Mem. about 13,000; dues $20 and higher.
Collections: Outstanding Chinese, Japanese and Indian art;
exceptional † Egyptian, †Greek and †Roman art; †master paintings
of Europe and America; †superb print collection from fifteenth century to present; also †sculpture, †decorative and minor arts including
period rooms, porcelains, †silver, †tapestries, †textiles, †costumes
and †musical instruments.

Exhibitions: Specially organized exhibitions are continually on
view in addition to exhibitions of the permanent collections.
Activities: Department of Public Education offers lectures, seminars and films for adults and school groups; lectures, exhibitions
and slides for schools; special activities for young people in creative
and visual arts such as Children's Room and High School Scholarship
Class; art classes for adults and children; television programs in
cooperation with WGBH-TV; study and performance of Early Music.
Library: Contains about 180,000 books and pamphlets and clip-
pings; slide library of 70,000 slides.
Income and Purchases: Income c. $3,500,000; purchases
$1,000,000.
Publications: Bulletin (quarterly), Calendar of Events (monthly).
Attendance: Average 650,000.

MUSEUM OF THE NATIONAL CENTER OF AFRO-AMERICAN
ARTISTS*
122 Elm Hill Ave, 02121. Tel: (617) 442-8820
Edmund B. Gaither, Dir-Cur.
Rachelle Puryear, Asst. Cur.
Dr. Elma Lewis, Dir.
Free Tues. - Sat. 12 AM - 9 PM; Sun. 2 - 5 PM. Estab. Jan. 1, 1970
to collect, exhibit and promote Black American and West Indian art,
financed as part of the NCAAA. Gallery with area of approx. 250 sq.
ft.
Collections: East and West African sculptures, drawings and paintings, photographs, by black American artists including Henry Tanner
and Charles White; 4500 original slides of black Americans' work.
Exhibitions: Twenty exhibitions since museum was established in
1970.
Activities: Projected extension work, New England area, schools,
civic groups, churches, etc, variable fees; traveling exhibitions organized and circulated; individual paintings lent to schools; lectures open to public; 4-8 gallery talks or tours per show; concerts,
dramatic programs, classes for adults and children; scholarships.
Library: Photograph collection for reference, approx. 200 prints.
Publications: Catalogues.
Annual Income: $65,000.
Attendance: Average 10,000 annually.

ST. BOTOLPH CLUB*
199 Commonwealth Ave, 02116. Tel: (617) 536-7570
William H. Forbes, Pres.
Charles B. Blanchard, Secy.
Free 2 - 5 PM during exhibitions. Estab. 1880. Ann. meeting Apr;
mem. men interested in art and literature.
Club owns house. Permanent collection of members' work.
Exhibitions; lectures; concerts.

SOCIETY FOR THE PRESERVATION OF NEW ENGLAND
ANTIQUITIES
Otis House, 141 Cambridge St, 02114. Tel: (617) 227-3956
Mrs. Gemmell Jainschigg, Pres.
Abbott L. Cummings, Exec. Dir.
Ellen F. Dewald, Admin. of Membership & Pub. Affairs
Morgan W. Phillips, Architectural Conservator
Richard C. Nylander, Cur. Collections
Roy A. Petre, Interpreter of Properties & Collections
Richard P. Thompson, Asst. to the Exec. Dir.
Daniel M. Lohnes, Librn.
Frederick E. Eayrs, Jr, Dir. of Properties and Collections
Lynne M. Spencer, Properties Adminr.
Christina H. Nelson, Registrar
Stanley M. Smith, Dir. of Development
David M. Hart, Dir. of Consulting Services
Frederic C. Detwiller, Architectural Historian
Maximilian L. Ferro, Architect
William B. Hart, Dir. of Field Service
Kathryn Welch, Preservation Planner
Open 10 AM - 4 PM; cl. Sat, Sun. & holidays; admis. $1 to non-
members. Estab. and inc. 1910. Ann. meeting May; mem. 3650; dues
$10 and higher.
The Otis House serves as both headquarters and museum for the
Society. Tours of the newly restored period rooms are given at 10,
11, 1, 2 & 3, Mon. - Fri. In addition, the library contains study col-
lections of New England architecture in the form of 5000 fragments,
3000 measured drawings, 200,000 photographs and 200 pattern books.
Other collections include textiles and wallpaper. Owns over 00 his
toric houses throughout New England, which are open to the public.
Publications: Old-Time New England, biannual bulletin.

BROCKTON

BROCKTON ART CENTER
Fuller Memorial
Oak St. on Upper Porter's Pond, 02401. Tel: (617) 588-6000
Marilyn Friedman Hoffman, Dir

Roger Dunn, Cur.
Philip O'Brien, Pub. Affairs
Carol Heepke, Ed. Coordinator
Open Tues. - Sun 1 - 5 PM, Thurs. until 10 PM; cl. Mon, national holidays and Thurs. evenings during July & Aug. Admis. adults $1, children under 16 and members free. Estab. 1969. Total mem. 1600; dues students $5, single $12, family $20, sustaining $50, sponsor $100, patron $200, benefactor $300.
Collections: Art museum with collection of 19th century American and contemporary painting; photographs.
Exhibitions: Temporary exhibitions of 19th century American and contemporary art; annual historical exhibition on loan from Museum of Fine Arts, Boston during the school year.
Activities: Guided tours; lectures; films; formally organized education programs for children and adults; fall, spring and summer art classes; books, color reproductions, jewelry, note cards, glass, china, children's items for sale. Art Rental Service. Auditorium.
Library: 600 volume art reference library, for use by members, museum staff and students.
Publications: Newsletter and calendar of events, bimonthly; exhibition catalogs.
Attendance: 15,000 annual average.

THE BROCKTON PUBLIC LIBRARY SYSTEM
Municipal Gallery, 304 Main St, 02401. Tel: (617) 587-2516
Ernest J. Webby, Jr, Libr. Dir.
Free Mon. - Fri 9 AM - 9 PM; Sat. 9 AM - 6 PM; cl. Sun. Special room for monthly art exhibitions.
Collections: W. C. Bryant collection of 19th and 20th century American paintings, chiefly by New England artists; loan collection of 20th century painters from the Woman's Club of Brockton; gifts of 20th century paintings which include 4 paintings by Hendricks Hallett and an oil painting by Mme. Elisabeth Weber-Fulop; mounted photographs of Renaissance art and watercolors by F. Mortimer Lamb; 5000 books on fine and applied art.
Exhibitions: Monthly exhibitions by local and nationally known artists.
Attendance: 20,000.

BROOKLINE

PUBLIC LIBRARY OF BOOKLINE
361 Washington St, 02146. Tel: (617) 734-0100
Theresa A. Carroll, Town Librn.
Leona A. Gifford, Asst. Town Librn.
Free Sept. - June, Mon. - Fri. 9 AM - 9 PM, Sat. 9 AM - 6 PM, Sun. 2 - 6 PM; July & Aug, Mon, Wed. & Fri. 9 AM - 9 PM, Tues. & Thurs. 9 AM - 6 PM. Estab. 1857; the library provides information, books, records, pictures, etc, for the use of the community. Special programs including films, lectures, demonstrations, concerts, and discussions are sponsored for both children and adults; supported by appropriation. Exhibition hall-auditorium facility; separate Art & Music Room.
Collections: †Over 300,000 books; †6000 records; †700 periodical and newspaper subscriptions; †600 catalogued maps; †several thousand pamphlets; 20,000 mounted †photographs, †prints, and †pictures. †Special reference collection of pictures and photographs of Brookline.
Exhibitions: Brookline Library Society of Artists (estab. 1950) membership and juried annual exhibits; rotating exhibits by individual members.
Activities: Library sponsors Brookline Library Society of Artists ($15 mem. fee) which conducts exhibitions, weekly workshop, various monthly programs open to public; publishes monthly newsletter for members; c. 500,000 items lent in an average year.
Publications: Booklists (varying topics), c. 25 each year.
Purchases: Books and materials, $178,000.

CAMBRIDGE

BUSCH-REISINGER MUSEUM
Harvard University
Kirkland St. & Divinity Ave, 02138. Tel: (617) 495-2338
Charles W. Haxyhausen, Asst. Cur.
Elaine A. Slater, Staff Asst.
Free Mon. - Sat. 9 AM - 4:45 PM; cl. Sun. & holidays; also cl. Sat. July 1 through Labor Day.
Collections: Works of art of the Middle Ages, Renaissance and Modern Times; extensive collection of Expressionist and Bauhaus works; Bauhaus and Lyonel Feininger Archives; reproductions of works of Germanic art of the Middle Ages and Renaissance; special exhibitions as announced.

CAMBRIDGE ART ASSOCIATION*
23 Garden St, 02138. Tel: (617) 876-0246
Jane Marsh Beveridge, Pres.
Robert Warshawer, 1st V.Pres.

Frances Henderson, 2nd V.Pres.
Priscilla Montgomery, 3rd V.Pres.
Linda Hirschmann, Recording Secy.
Ruth Glass, Corresp. Secy.
Rowland Stebbins, Treas.
Edward Cooper, Exec. Dir.
Regina Lee, Sales & Rental Dir.
Free Tues. - Sat. 10:30 AM - 5 PM; Wed. until 9 PM; Sun. 2 - 6 PM; cl. Sun. in July, cl. in Aug. Estab. 1944 to exhibit, rent and sell members' work and to encourage an interest in fine arts and crafts in the community. Ann. meeting June; mem. 700; dues artists $20, friends $15, students $5.
Exhibitions: Members' juried exhibitions in Main Gallery every two weeks, some invited shows and a foreign exhibition each year. Invited shows in Rental Gallery and Craft Gallery. Prizes award approximately $1000 annually.
Activities: Rental services of art works; spring auction; lectures and demonstrations. Print Box; classes for adults; exhibit and sale of books by members.
Publications: Monthly Bulletin

CARPENTER CENTER FOR THE VISUAL ARTS
Harvard University
19 Prescott St, 02138. Tel: (617) 495-3251
Eduard F. Sekler, Dir.
Estab. 1963 as an undergraduate department of Harvard University, offering a B.A. in visual and environmental studies; financed by endowment.
Exhibitions: (1973-74) The Social Question: a Photographic Record 1895-1910; Experimental Color Photography; An Exhibition of Art Work by Students of Josef Albers; Graphic Design-a Kinetic Presentation of Contemporary Trends; The Other Twenties; Recent Photographic Work of William Eggleston; Patchworks: An Exhibition of Contemporary American Quilts by Radka Donnell, Susan Hoffman and Molly Upton; plus others.
Activities: Traveling exhibitions organized and circulated; regular film showings; individual paintings lent to other Harvard departments or houses; no actual lending collection but will lend certain films in our collection; photograph collection for reference; lectures open to public, 8 visiting lecturers per year.
Library: Small reference library for staff use only.
Publications: 1-2 exhibition catalogs per year; 1 work of art (multiple) per year for distribution to members of the Carpenter Center for the Visual Arts Association.

HAYDEN GALLERY
Massachusetts Institute of Technology, Room 14W-111, 02139. Tel: (617) 253-4400
Jerome B. Wiesner, Pres.
Wayne Andersen, Chmn. Comt. Visual Arts
Marjory Supovitz, Projects Coordinator
Steven Ringle, Gallery Mgr.
William A. Baker, Cur. Hart Nautical Museum
Free Mon. - Sat. 10 AM - 4 PM; cl. Sun. and holidays. Estab. 1950.
Collections: The MIT Art Collection includes a fine collection of 20th century painting, sculpture, drawings, and graphics, the Catherine N. Stratton Collection of Graphics, and a collection of archival quality photographs. The Allen Forbes Collection of Whaling Prints and the Arthur H. Clark Collection of Marine Prints housed in the Hart Nautical Museum.
Exhibitions: Eight exhibitions per year.
Activities: Gallery talks, openings with the artists present, special events related to the specific exhibitions, films.
Attendance: 36,000 per year.

ROTCH LIBRARY OF ARCHITECTURE AND PLANNING
Massachusetts Institute of Technology, 77 Massachusetts Ave, 02138. Tel: (617) 253-7052.
Margaret DePopolo, Librn.
Florence Doksansky, Acquisitions Librn.
Micheline Jedrey, Processing Librn.
Ann Longfellow, Reference Librn.
Lenis Williams, Slide Librn.
Open Mon. - Thurs. 9 AM - 11 PM; Fri. 9 AM - 8 PM; Sat. 10 AM - 6 PM; Sun. 1 - 11 PM; special hours when school not in session. Estab. 1868, to serve the students and faculty of the School of Architecture and Planning and other members of the M.I.T. community.
Collections: †Books, journals, pamphlets, slides, photographs, microfiche; major subject areas are architectural design and history of architecture; history of art (19th and 20th century painting and sculpture); urban studies; regional, economic and social planning.
Library: 91,000 volume reference library; 30,750 pamphlets (cataloged); photograph collection, 41,000 prints, 117,000 slides; borrowing privileges restricted to members of M.I.T. community and purchasers of library cards.
Publications: Selected Rotch Library Acquisitions, irregular.

SEMITIC MUSEUM
Harvard University
    6 Divinity Ave, 02138. Tel: (617) 495-4631 & 5756
Prof. Frank Moore Cross, Jr, Dir.
Dr. C. E. S. Gavin, Cur. Ancient Near Eastern Art & Archeology
Prof. William C. Moran, Cur. Cuneiform Collections
Collections cl. to the general public. Admittance by appointment
with the curators and to Friends of the Museum. Founded 1889 to
promote sound knowledge of Semitic languages and history by pro-
viding home for Harvard departments, library, research collections,
public education programs and overseas explorations.
    Research collections of archaeological materials from the Near
East, chiefly from Palestine-Syria, Mesopotamia and Egypt. Manuscript collections currently stored in Houghton Library.
    Publications: Regular publications include Harvard Semitic
Series and Harvard Semitic Monographs.

WILLIAM HAYES FOGG ART MUSEUM
Harvard University
    Quincy St. & Broadway, 02138. Tel: (617) 495-2378
Seymour Slive, Dir.
Suzannah Doeringer, Asst. Dir.
Marcy Coburn, Asst. to Dir.
David Mitten, Cur. Ancient Art
Arthur Beale, Chief Conservator
Marjorie B. Cohn, Assoc Conservator
Louise Bluhm, Asst. Conservator
Agnes Mongan, Cur. Drawings
Eunice Williams, Asst. Cur. Drawings
Stuart C. Welch, Hon. Cur. Indian & Islamic Art
Jeanne Wasserman, Hon. Cur. 19th & 20th Century Sculpture
Wolfgang Freitag, Fine Arts Librn.
John Rosenfield, Cur. Oriental Art
Louise Cort, Asst. Cur. Oriental Art
C. Adrian Rubel, Assoc. in Oriental Art
Henri Zerner, Cur. Prints
Colles Baxter, Asst. Cur. Prints
Davis Pratt, Assoc. Cur. Photographs
Margaret C. Scott, Cur. Univ. Loans
Louise T. Ambler, Cur. Univ. Portrait Collection
Phoebe Peebles, Archivist
Mary Mills Thierry, Secy, Friends of the Fogg
Janet Cox, Dir of Publications & Pub. Relations
Louisa Sprague, Sales Secy.
Jane Watts, Registrar
Michael Nedzweski, Photographer
Maryline Altreri, Ed. Asst.
Laurence Doherty, Supt.
Free weekdays 9 AM - 5 PM, Sun. 2 - 5 PM; cl. holidays and Sat. &
Sun. from July 1 - Labor Day. Original building opened 1895; present
building 1927; the Museum serves as a laboratory for the Dept. of
Fine Arts which trains art historians and museum professionals.
The Center for Conservation and Technical Studies operates a
training program for conservators and technical specialists.
    Collections: Egyptian antiquities; sculpture from Persepolis;
Greek and Roman sculpture and vases; ancient coins; Chinese sculpture, bronzes, jades, crystals, paintings and prints; Cambodian
sculpture; Japanese art; Romanesque and Gothic sculpture; European
and American sculpture; Early Italian, Spanish, Flemish painting;
European painting of the 17th - 20th centuries; American painting;
English and American watercolors; English painting of the 18th and
19th centuries; drawings, including an extensive collection of 19th
century French drawings; prints; contemporary art; photographs;
English and American silver; Wedgwood.
    Activities: Special exhibitions, lectures, gallery talks.
    Library: The Library is one of the largest and most specialized
in the world, having a collection of some 150,000 volumes, 665,164
photographs and 195,000 slides. There are several special photographic archives.
    Publications: Annual Report; Newsletter.

CONCORD

CONCORD ANTIQUARIAN SOCIETY MUSEUM
    Lexington Rd. & Cambridge Turnpike, 01742.
    Tel: (617) 369-9609
John H. Demer, Dir.
Open Mar. 13 - Nov. 1, 10 AM - 4:30 PM; Sun. 2 - 4:30 PM; admis.
adults $1.50, children 14 and under 75¢. Estab. 1886 to preserve,
collect and exhibit antiques from Concord families. Ann. meeting
Mar; mem. approx. 650; dues $15 and higher.
    Collections: Furnishings from Concord families arranged chrono-
logically in a series of 15 Period Rooms. Emerson Study; Thoreau
Room; Revolutionay relics; set of Cincinnati china which belonged
to Benjamin Lincoln. Collection includes Paul Revere lantern.
    Activities: Guided tours for visitors and school children; lectures;
special exhibitions; docent tours of museum.

    Publications: Ruth Wheeler's Concord; Climate for Freedom; The
Flavour of Concord, cookbook published in conjunction with the Concord Garden Club.
    Attendance: Approx. 23,000 annually.

CONCORD ART ASSOCIATION
    15 Lexington Rd, 01742. Tel: (617) 369-2578
Alice Moulton, Pres.
Frances Mellen, Secy. & Cur.
Open Tues. - Sat. 11 AM - 4:30 PM, Sun. 2 - 4:30 PM; cl. Mon;
admis. 50¢ for adult nonmembers. Estab. 1916 for the encouragement, promotion, advancement of art and art exhibitions, to establish and maintain in the town of Concord an art museum, to acquire
and dispose of works of art; financed by endowment and membership.
Ann. meeting Oct; mem. 402; dues $10-$15.
    Collections: Miniatures, bronzes, early American art prints,
engravings, lithographs and some American glass.
    Exhibitions: Annual summer exhibit for tourists; America art of
the revolutionary war period and early 19th cent; changing exhibits
rest of year; painting, sculpture, contemporary crafts; member exhibitions.
    Activities: Lectures open to the public; 6 visiting lecturers per
year; competitions.
    Attendance: 10,000 annual average.

DEDHAM

DEDHAM HISTORICAL SOCIETY
    612 High St, 02026. Tel: (617) 326-1385
Courtenay P. Worthington, Pres.
Mrs. Muriel N. Peters, Librn.
Open to public daily 2 - 5 PM; cl. Sun, cl. Sat. during July and Aug.
Estab. 1859, inc. 1862, to preserve local material of historical importance; to provide data for historical research and to maintain a
library of genealogies and histories. Ann. meeting first Tues. in
Mar; mem. 394; dues, individual $5, family $8, life $150.
    Museum: Contains relics pertaining to Dedham history or Ded-
ham families: some 17th century furniture; china, silver, pewter,
oil paintings, clothes, household implements, Indian relics, guns and
swords, etc.
    Exhibitions: (1968) Dedham Pottery.
    Library: About 7000 volumes of Histories and Vital Records of
Dedham and other New England towns; Genealogical material; manuscripts.
    Publications: Dedham Pottery (book); A Brief Guide to Dedham
Village (pamphlet).
    Attendance: 2500.

FALL RIVER

GREATER FALL RIVER ART ASSOCIATION
    80 Belmont St, 02720. Tel: (617) 673-7212
Michael Hurley, Pres.
Mrs. Sumner Waring, V.Pres.
Mrs. William Mullen, V.Pres.
Mrs. Roger Buffington, V.Pres.
Mrs. Andrew Weelock, Clerk
Mrs. George Aronis, Corresp. Secy.
Miss Anna Fuller, Treas.
Mrs. Edward A. Doyle, Dir.
Open Sept. - June daily 1 - 4 PM. Estab. 1955 for the cultural en-
richment of the community; supported by membership. Seven rooms
of our building, a large Victorian house, are used for art exhibitions.
Ann. meeting -3rd Mon. in June; mem. 310; dues $6, $10 and $25.
    Collections: †Graphics; †ceramics, slides of paintings of the
Fall River School.
    Exhibitions: Three or four one-man shows annually, Members
Show; National Competitive Exhibition, Classes Exhibition; Fall
River Collects Art, semi-annually; (1970) Fall River School of
Painting 1853-1932; Annual Traditional Open Show-New England
Artists.
    Activities: Extension work, Greater Fall River organizations;
approx. 50 individual paintings and original objects of art lent to in-
stitutions, 53 lantern slides; lectures open to public, 8 visiting lec-
turers per year; classes for adults and children; competitions;
scholarships. Gift shop of original graphics, ceramics, etc.
    Publications: Bulletin monthly.
    Income and Purchases: Income $800 after expenses; purchases
$100.
    Attendance: 10,000.

FITCHBURG

FITCHBURG ART MUSEUM
    25 Merriam Pkwy, 01420. Tel: (617) 345-4207
Jay M. Rome, Pres.
Mrs. Abbott T. Fenn, Secy.

Myrtle F. Parcher, Treas.
Peter Timms, Dir.
Open daily except Mon. 9 AM - 5 PM; Wed. also 6 - 9 PM; Sun. 2 - 5
PM; cl. July 1 until Labor Day. Estab. and inc. 1925 with the Eleanor
A. Norcross Bequest; owns fire-proof building. Ann. meeting Dec;
mem. c 1000; annual dues $5 to $500.
Collections: †Paintings, †drawings, †prints, †18th century French
provincial furniture, †china, textiles, †ceramics, †sculpture, †Ameri-
can and English silver.
Exhibitions: Annual regional exhibition open to artists within 25
miles; prize awards; frequent current exhibitions of traditional and
contemporary fine arts and crafts and loans of great art of past.
Activities: Exhibition previews, Endowed lectures and demonstrations, docent service; 15 weekly classes Oct. to June for adults and
children, 215 students registered.
Publications: Catalogs and events notices.
Attendance: 7000.

GARDNER

MOUNT WACHUSETT COMMUNITY COLLEGE GALLERY
Art Department, 01440. Tel: (617) 632-6600
Jean C. Tandy, Asst. Prof. & Art Dept. Coordinator
Wm. Gruters, Gallery Dir.
Gene Cauthen, Chmn. for Exhibitions Throughout College
Free Mon. - Fri. 8 AM - 9:30 PM. Estab. 1971, two year art cur-
riculum concurrently developing a private college collection of
prints, paintings, sculpture and a gallery; financed by city and
state appropriation. Exhibit between 12-14 exhibitions per school
year in temporary quarters.
Collections: Approx. 25 works, including a Gottlieb and Leonard
Baskin, annually add 3-4 works.
Exhibitions: Local and Boston artists' works; student competition
with prizes in categories of painting, sculpture, drawing and ceramics.
Activities: Educational department, evening and summer studio
courses in all areas; collection of 10 sculpture reproductions, 24
color reproductions, 11 motion pictures, 24-30 film strips and 6000
art slides; lectures open to the public, 4 visiting lecturers per year,
6-10 tours; concerts, dramatic programs, classes for adults and
children, competitions; visual arts film series; visual arts institute.
Book shop.
Library: 2753 volumes on art for lending and reference use.
Over 6000 art slides for reference; portrait collection, Gale International Portrait Gallery for lending and reference.
Income and Purchases: Income, student funds for purchases,
$1500-$2000.

GLOUCESTER

CAPE ANN HISTORICAL ASSOCIATION
27 Pleasant St, 01930 Tel: (617) 283-0455
Caroline E. Benham, Asst. Cur.
Open Tues. - Sat. 11 AM - 4 PM; cl Sun. & Mon; admis. Inc. 1876
for the preservation of ancient houses, one built c. 1650, one in
1750 and one in 1803. Ann. meeting May; mem. 425; dues $5 and
higher.
Collections: Paintings and drawings by Fitz-Hugh Lane, antique
furniture, porcelain, glass, silver, jewelry, ship models, mementos
of the Revolutionary period.
Activities: Lectures, exhibitions, occasional classes.
Library: 500 volumes for reference only.
Attendance: 5000.

HAMMOND CASTLE
80 Hesperus Ave, 01930. Tel: (617) 283-2080 & 2081
Virgil Fox, Artist in Residence
Daily guided tours, Labor Day - May, Tues. - Fri. 10 AM - 3 PM;
Sat. & Sun. 11 AM - 4 PM; May 1 - Labor Day, guided tours week-
days 11 AM - 5 PM; open museum weekends; cl. Mon, Thanksgiving
Day, Christmas and New Years; admis. adults $2, children under
12 $1; group rates (min. 25 people) adults $1.50, children under 12
75¢. Estab. 1931, former home of famous inventor, John Hays
Hammond, Jr; building in spirit of the Middle Ages.
Collections: Gothic and Renaissance sculpture, stained glass,
furniture and other objects in appropriate arrangement. †Princess
Zalessky Collection on loan and some donated.
Activities: 8600 pipe organ with concerts by national and inter-
nationally famous organists. Castle Gift Shop and Coffee Shop.
Publications: Hammond Castle Guide Book; Cook Book; Gallery
Catalog.
Attendance: 72,500 annual average.

NORTH SHORE ARTS ASSOCIATION, INC.
Rear, 197 E. Main St, 01930.
Ronald Brake, Pres.
James Hooley, V.Pres.

Roger Curtis, Treas.
Free 10 AM - 5:30 PM; Sun. 2:30 - 5:30 PM, July, Aug. & Sept.
Estab. and inc. 1922. Owns gallery. Ann meeting Aug; mem. approx.
300; dues assoc. $5, patrons $10, artists $15.
Exhibitions: Summer exhibition of members' work; jury, prizes.
Activities: Lectures; demonstrations; art classes in painting and
drawing from life; Artists at Work day in gallery in July and August
with artists demonstrating all media; Silent Auction.
Attendance: 3000-4000 annually.

GREAT BARRINGTON

SIMON'S ROCK EARLY COLLEGE
Alford Rd, 01230. Tel: (413) 528-0771
Dr. Baird Whitlock, Pres.
Stephen H. Stackpole, Chmn, Board of Trustees
Dr. Perry Whitmore, Dean, Academic Affairs
Catherine B. Miller, Dean, Students
Eunice Agar, Chmn, Dept. Art
Free daily. Estab. 1964 as a liberal arts college with AA and BA
degree programs, interdisciplinary majors, open to students who
have completed tenth grade of secondary school; financed by endow-
ment. Gallery maintained for monthly exhibits during school year.
Exhibitions: 10 one-man shows per year, plus student exhibits
and occasional rental shows.
Activities: Students teach art classes in local schools; student
exhibit is circulated to high schools in New England; 5500 lantern
slides in lending collection; lectures open to public; 4 - 6 gallery
talks per year; 6 tours; concerts, dramatic programs; scholarships.
Book shop. (See Schools)
Library: 30,000 volumes for lending and reference.

GROTON

GROTON HISTORICAL SOCIETY
Boutwell House, Main St, 01450.
Gladys P. Farwell, Pres.
Leroy E. Johnson, Jr, 1st V.Pres.
Isabel C. Beal, Secy. & Cur.
Henry C. Hallowell, Treas.
Open during summer Sat. 3 - 5 PM. Estab. 1894. Ann meeting
Oct; mem. 150; dues $3.
Collection of articles relating to Groton. Four meetings with
programs yearly; library specializing on history of Groton and sur-
rounding towns.

HADLEY

HADLEY FARM MUSEUM ASSOCIATION
147 Russell St, 01035.
Earle P. Parsons, Pres.
Mildred Howell, Secy.
Robert Saunders, Cur.
Open May 1st - Oct. 12th, 10 AM - 4:30 PM; Sun. 1:30 - 4:30 PM; cl.
Mon. Museum estab. 1930, Association 1963, to give a practical
picture of the lives of those who settled and lived in Hadley and its
environs; financed by endowment. Ann. meeting Mar; mem. 60.
Collections: Farm tools and household implements.
Attendance: 5040.

HARVARD

FRUITLANDS MUSEUMS
Prospect Hill, 01451.
Bailey Aldrich, Pres.
William Henry Harrison, Dir.
Open May 30 to Sept. 30, Tues. - Sun. 1 - 5 PM; cl. Mon. except
when a holiday. Estab. 1914, inc. 1930, by Clara Endicott Sears.
Fruitlands was the scene of Bronson Alcott's experiment in community life. House contains †furniture, household articles, pictures,
books and valuable manuscript collection of Alcott family and Transcendental group.
Old Shaker House contains †relics, handicrafts and displays
illustrating life of the Shakers
American Indian museum contains ethnological exhibits;
weapons; specimens of Indian lore, art, culture and dioramas
illustrating historical events of the Indians of the region; sculpture by Philip Sears.
Picture Gallery contains †portraits by itinerant artists and
landscapes by Hudson River School.
Library contains †manuscripts and publications relative to
museum collections; Transcendental Movement, Shakers, American
Indian North of Mexico, American art history, c. 10,000 volumes.
Attendance: Approx. 18,000.

HAVERHILL

HAVERHILL PUBLIC LIBRARY
99 Main St, 01830. Tel: (617) 373-1586
Virginia Bilmazes Bernard, Librn.
Janice Christensen, Arts Librn.
Free 9 AM - 9 PM; Sat. 9 AM - 5:30 PM. Estab. 1873; exhibition gallery.
Collections: 19th and 20th century prints, including Picasso, Kollwitz, Renoir, Whistler, Toulouse-Lautrec, Sloan, Degas, Cassatt, Daumier, Legros, Matisse, Chagall, Dufy, and others; mid-19th century photographs, work by Frith, Beato and Robertson, Naya, Bourne, O'Sullivan, Gardner, and others; illuminated manuscripts; small group of paintings, including William S. Haseltine, Joseph A. Ames, Thomas Hill, Harrison Plummer, Winfield Scott Thomas, Henry Bacon, Sidney M. Chase. †Non-circulating arts book collection of 8000 volumes on the fine and applied arts.
Exhibitions: Monthly exhibition program of regional artists and traveling shows.
Activities: Periodic film, videotape, and slide presentations; instruction in photography, film-making, and videotape production.
Income and Purchases: Approx. $1500 annually for art books, $1200 of which is from a special fund for non-circulating art books.

HOLYOKE

CITY OF HOLYOKE MUSEUM—WISTERIAHURST
238 Cabot St, 01040. Tel: (413) 536-6771
Mary Griffin, Chmn, Holyoke Historical Commission
Mrs. William S. Quirk, Museum Dir.
Open Tues. - Sat. 1 - 5 PM; Sun. 2 - 5 PM; cl. holidays & July. Sponsored by the City of Holyoke under the jurisdiction of the Holyoke Historical Commission. Dues junior $3, active $5, regular $10, family $25, contributing $50, cooperating $100, sustaining $500, benefactor $1000.
Collections: †Paintings; †antique furniture; historical dioramas; period rooms; †glass and china; science and natural history; †Oriental art.
Activities: Special art shows; Sunday afternoon concerts; painting classes for children; sponsors films and lectures; special exhibits and festivals of ethnic culture featured periodically; special programs and illustrated lectures planned for visiting school classes. Youth Museum in Carriage House. (See Children's and Junior Museums)
Income: $86,000.

LINCOLN

DE CORDOVA AND DANA MUSEUM AND PARK
Sandy Pond Rd, 01773. Tel: (617) 259-8355
Janet Daniels, Pres.
Frederick Walkey, Exec. Dir.
Miriam Jagger, Asst. Dir.
Ann Russell, Development Dir.
Merrie Blocker, School Dir.
Open Tues. - Sat. 10 AM - 5 PM; Sun. 1:30 - 5 PM; admis adults $1.50, under 21 50¢. An arts center inc. 1950. Mem. 3200; dues $30 and higher.
Collections: 20th century †sculpture, †painting, †drawings and †prints.
Exhibitions: Year-round program of special exhibitions, with emphasis on contemporary New England art.
Activities: Art classes for adults, teenagers and children; lectures; films; concerts.
Library: 1500 art books and publications.
Income and Purchases: Income $600,000; purchases $5000.
Attendance: 50,000 annually.

LOWELL

LOWELL ART ASSOCIATION*
243 Worthen St, 01852. Tel: (617) 452-7641
John A. Goodwin, Pres.
Open 2 - 4:30 PM. Estab. 1878 to maintain birthplace of James A. M. Whistler, promote interesting art in area, exhibit works in public gallery; supported by membership. Ann. meeting May; mem. 200; dues life $100, couple $8, individual $5, student $2.
Activities: Plan art classes for adults and children, monthly lectures, exhibits; 6 visiting lecturers per year; gallery talks or tours by appointment; concerts, competitions.
Library: 300 volumes for reference.

MALDEN

MALDEN PUBLIC LIBRARY
36 Salem St, 02148. Tel: (617) 324-0218
Dina G. Malgeri, Librn.
Dr. Roland Wilder, Chmn Art Comt.

Free Mon. - Thurs. 9 AM - 9 PM; Fri. & Sat. 9 AM - 6 PM; cl. Sun. & holidays; cl. Sat. during summer. Estab. 1879, inc. 1885. Ann. meetings Jan.
Collections: Art Gallery (3 rooms) contains over †100 paintings by American and European artists; sculpture; etchings and lithographs. Purchases made from Elisha S. and Mary D. Converse Art funds.
Exhibitions: Exhibitions by Malden and other artists from time to time.
Activities: Lectures.
Library: More than †6000 mounted prints; 185,699 books of all types; †16,400 art books; †phonograph records; †microfilms, motion picture films and filmstrips.
Income: $353,439 plus $30,000 for works of art.
Publications: Annual report; Art Catalog (in preparation).

MARBLEHEAD

MARBLEHEAD ARTS ASSOCIATION, INC.
King Hooper Mansion
8 Hooper St, 01945. Tel: (617) 631-2608
Arthur W. Hughes, III, Pres.
Capt. R. Tate Simpson, Secy.
Miss Garnet Conniers, Exec. Secy.
Open year-round 2 - 5 PM; cl. Mon; admis. 50¢. Estab. 1922, inc. 1927. Ann meeting June; mem. approx. 400; dues $10 and higher. Owns and occupies the historic King Hooper Mansion (1728) which contains fine paneling, ballroom, gallery, and garden by Shurclif.
Exhibitions: Continuous exhibitions of members' work and invited guest exhibitors.
Activities: Sponsors Friends of Contemporary Prints, yearly exhibitions; lectures; concerts and other programs; classes during winter months for children and adults. Youth art classes.
Attendance: 2500.

MARBLEHEAD HISTORICAL SOCIETY
161 Washington St, 01945. Tel: (617) 631-1069
Hammond Bowden, Pres.
Mrs. Frederic L. Woods, Jr, Recording Secy.
Open May 15 - Oct. 12 9:30 AM - 4 PM; cl. Sun. Estab. 1898, inc. 1902, to preserve the historic Col. Jeremiah Lee mansion which was built in 1768. Ann. meeting Aug; mem. 650; dues $3 and higher.
Collections: †Furniture, silver, glass, books, pictures, portraits, log books, ledgers, wills, deeds, Revolutionary and Town records. Noted for finely carved staircases and columns, original handpainted wallpapers; one of the finest examples of Colonial architecture in America.
Activities: Tours, winter lectures by members.
Attendance: 2500 (6 mo).

MARION

MARION ART CENTER
Main St, 02739. Tel: (617) 748-1266
Sarah R. Brown, Pres.
Rita Cain, Secy.
Nina Campbell, Exec. Secy.
Alice Phinney, Asst. Secy.
Open Tues. - Sun. 1 - 5 PM. Estab. 1957 to provide theater and visual arts exhibitions for the community and to provide studio classes for adults and children; financed by membership. Gallery is 70 ft. of wall space, 280 sq. ft. floor space; indirect lighting; entrance off Main St. Ann. meeting 2nd Tues. in July; mem. 300; dues $7.50 single, $12.50 family.
Exhibitions: (1975) Willoughby Elliot, Prints; Roseann Radosavich, Prints & Drawings; George Mellor, Sculpture; Brooks Kelly, Paintings and Collage; Sarah Brown and Marcia Ingraham, Paintings and Sculpture; Anne Powers, Paintings; A. D. Tinkham, Paintings; Andrew Hepburn and Albert Bigelow, Marine Paintings; scholarship competition and show; members show, all media; sidewalk show and sale; Christmas craft show.
Activities: Rental of paintings and prints, available to anyone for a fee of $10 - $20 per 2 month period; original objects of art lent; approx. 100 items lent in average year; lectures open to public; 5 visiting lecturers per year; concerts, dramatic programs, classes for adults and children, competitions; scholarships.
Publications: Monthly invitations to opening; annual membership folder.
Attendance: 1200.

NANTUCKET

KENNETH TAYLOR GALLERIES OF ARTISTS ASSOCIATION OF NANTUCKET*
Straight Wharf, 02554. Tel: (617) 228-0722
Schuyler Bradt, Pres.
Free Mon. - Sat. 10 - 12 AM, 2 - 5 PM; cl. Sun. Estab. 1944, inc. 1969. The Artists Association of Nantucket operates upstairs and

downstairs galleries in a one hundred year old whaling era warehouse owned by the Nantucket Foundation; also operates the adjacent Little Gallery; organized to promote, assist, encourage and develop interests of artists and to aid in development of Nantucket as center for artists, to present shows and programs of interest to the community. Ann. meeting c. Aug. 15; mem. approx. 155 artists, 110 associates, 175 patrons; dues for artists $10.

Collections: Permanent collection of †paintings, prints, chromos, photographs, enlarged by gift program; on exhibition occasionally through season; also on loan to schools during winter.

Exhibitions: Member exhibitions change every two weeks; one-man and two-man shows in Little Gallery change every week; Paintings, prints, photographs, sculpture, crafts; awards, both honorary and cash, to artists; paintings or sculpture ($930 in 1969) awarded to patrons on Patron Night.

Activities: Lectures, demonstrations, concerts, films for members and their guests; annual benefit auction.

Library: Collection of art books has been donated to the Nantucket Atheneum by the Association for use of residents and visitors to the island; this collection is enlarged each year.

Income: Approx. $12,000.

Attendance: 15,000 (late June to mid-Sept.).

NEEDHAM

BOSTON PRINTMAKERS
c/o Mrs. S. M. Rantz, Secy-Treas, 299 High Rock St, 02192.
Tel: (617) 444-2692
Vivian Berman, Pres.

Estab. 1947. Exec. Board meetings as needed; ann. meeting June; mem. 125; dues $10. Sponsors Annual National Print Exhibition open to all printmakers; awards approx. $1500. Gallery talks; traveling exhibition for 1 year following each exhibition.

Attendance: 15,000-20,000.

NEW BEDFORD

FREE PUBLIC LIBRARY
Box C902, 02741. Tel: (617) 999-6291 or 9-6292
Laurence H. Solomon, Dir
Thelma Paine, Reference Dept.
Free Mon. - Thurs. 9 AM - 9 PM; Fri. & Sat. 9 AM - 5 PM; cl. Sun. & holidays. Estab. 1853.

Collections: Permanent art collection; collection of pictures for circulation to schools, adults and juveniles. Permanent collection especially strong in works by New Bedford artists, Bierstadt, Bradford, C.H. & R. Swain Gifford, Wall, Millet, Eldred and Clifford Ashley. On display also are a group of framed plates from the original Audobon Elephant Folio of the Birds of America. The Melville Whaling Room (Opened in April, 1962) in addition to its large collection of whaling documents (over 90,000 items) displays a collection of paintings and prints dealing with the whaling industry. A bronze statue commemorating the whaling industry stands in front of the Library. This monument, done in 1913, was created by Bela Pratt.

OLD DARTMOUTH HISTORICAL SOCIETY AND WHALING MUSEUM
18 Johnny Cake Hill, 02740. Tel: (617) 997-0046
Eliot S. Knowles, Pres.
Edward D. Hicks, Secy.
Richard C. Kugler, Dir.
Open winter daily 9 AM - 4 PM, Sun. 1 - 4 PM; summer daily 9 AM - 5 PM; Sun. 1 - 5 PM. Estab. 1903 to maintain a whaling and marine museum and a museum of local history. Ann. meeting May; mem. 1450.

Collections: Half-scale model of whaleship, whaling pictures, implements, models, scrimshaw, furniture, dolls, etc.

Special Exhibitions: (1970) William Bradford (1823-1892); (1972) Albert Bierstadt; (1973) Clifford W. Ashley (1881-1947); (1974) R. Swain Gifford (1840-1905); (1975) New Bedford and Old Dartmouth: Portrait of a Region's Past.

Activities: Visiting lectures on art and historical subjects (6 per year); loans to other museums; gallery tours for school groups. Book Shop.

Library: Reference library of 6000 volumes; photograph collection of 5000 prints for reference and sale.

Publications: The Bulletin (quarterly), other publications occasionally; catalogs of the above exhibitions.

Income and Purchases: Annual income, $130,000; purchases, about $15,000.

Attendance: 80,000.

✠SWAIN SCHOOL OF DESIGN
William W. Crapo Gallery
19 Hawthorn St, 02740. Tel: (617) 999-4436
Dr. Jean S. Lozinski, Pres.

Free Mon. - Fri. 10 AM - 4 PM; cl. Sat. & Sun. Estab. 1881.
Exhibitions: Monthly exhibitions.
Activities: Lectures, gallery talks.
Library: 9500 volumes on fine arts and design.
Attendance: 200 (See Schools).

NORTH ANDOVER

MERRIMACK VALLEY TEXTILE MUSEUM
800 Massachusetts Ave, 01845. Tel: (617) 686-0191
Dr. Walter Muir Whitehill, Pres.
Dr. James B. Peabody, Secy.
Thomas W. Leavitt, Dir.
Peter M. Molloy, Cur.
Betty D. Goddard, Asst. Cur. Books & Periodicals
Helena Wright, Asst. Cur. Prints & Manuscripts
Katherine R. Koob, Asst. Cur. Textiles
Robert A. Hauser, Conservator
Betsy W. Bahr, Asst. Cur. Educ.
Open Mon. - Fri. 9 AM - 5 PM; Sat. & Sun. 1 - 5 PM; free (except Sun. for demonstrations & guided tours). Estab. 1960 to preserve the artifacts, documents and pictorial descriptions of the American textile industry; financed by endowment. Two exhibit galleries maintained.

Collections: Collection of hand implements, tools and machines for manufacture of textiles; textile collection; books and periodicals; manuscripts; prints and photographs.

Activities: School group visits to galleries; special events; museum teachers and materials to classrooms; traveling exhibitions organized and circulated; 200 Kodachromes and handcraft artifacts lent; lectures open to public occasionally; 100-200 gallery talks and tours; scholarships. Book Shop.

Library: 33,500 volumes for interlibrary loans only; 20,000 prints in photograph collection for reference only; also includes textile study collection, including sample pattern books; print collection; manuscript collection.

Publications: Occasional Reports of the Museum.

Attendance: 6000.

NORTHAMPTON

FORBES LIBRARY
20 West St, 01060. Tel: (413) 584-8550
James F. Hazel, Librn.
Hollee Haswell, Art & Music Librn.
Free Mon. - Sat. 9 AM - 9 PM; Sun. 2 - 6 PM; holidays 2 - 6 PM, except cl. all day Memorial Day, July 4, Thanksgiving and Christmas. Estab. 1894 as a general public library serving Northampton.

Collections: 302,155 volumes; 7214 micro holdings. Completed renovations make possible purchase and programming of audiovisual materials including graphics.

Special Collections: Official White House portraits of President and Mrs. Calvin Coolidge; the Holland House collection of English miniatures; works of regional artists displayed on the walls of the art gallery. Connecticut Valley History; Early American Children's Literature; Genealogical Records; Japan and Japanese Books, including original Japanese color prints; Library of Charles E. Forbes; Walter E. Corbin Collection of photographic prints and slides.

Activities: Monthly exhibitions of local artists' and photographers' works in the gallery. Bookmobile.

Income and Purchases: (fiscal 1975) Income $251,786; purchases, books $31,109, periodicals $7692, micro holdings $394, audiovisual materials $6485.

✠SMITH COLLEGE MUSEUM OF ART*
Fine Arts Center, 01060. Tel: (413) 584-2700 Exten. 236, 740
Charles Chetham, Dir.
Elizabeth Mongan, Cur. of Prints
Mary Varriano, Registrar
Patricia Welch, Secy.
Wilda Craig, Museum Mem. Secy.
Free Tues. - Sat. 11 AM - 4:30 PM; Sun. 2 - 4:30 PM; cl. Mon. & academic holidays; summer by appointment. The Smith College Museum of Art has completed construction of a new museum building as part of the fine arts complex.

Collections: 725 paintings, including works by Rembrandt, Ingres, Gauguin, Juan Gris, Seurat, Picasso, Monet, De Kooning and others; over 700 prints; 39 drawings; Orientalia; Mexican sculpture; especially strong in 19th century European paintings.

Exhibitions: Selections from the 18th Century Collection; Toulouse-Lautrec Lithographs; Faculty Exhibition; Prints and Drawings of the 19th and Early 20th Century from the Collection of Selma Erving, A Gift to the Museum.

Attendance: Approx. 20,000 annually.

NORTON

WHEATON COLLEGE
Watson Gallery
    Watson Hall, 02766. Tel: (617) 285-7722
Ann H. Murray, Dir.
Ronald J. Onorato, Cur.
Open Mon. - Sun. 1 - 5 PM; other hours by appointment.
    Collections: Over 120 19th and 20th century paintings, mostly
American; over 250 16th - 19th century old master prints and
drawings.
    Exhibitions: Temporary exhibitions changed each month,
sponsoring works by artists on campus.
    Activities: Gallery talks; Shippee Memorial lecture (annual).
    Publications: Catalogs about 4 times per year.

✠Fine Arts Library
    Watson Hall
Gertrude Martin, Librn.
    13,500 books and folios; 67 periodicals (current); 12,000 photo-
graphs and reproductions; 40,000 slides; 2700 scores; 1900 records.
The Shippee Memorial Collection of 250 framed reproductions and
50 original prints are for rental to students.

PITTSFIELD

BERKSHIRE ART ASSOCIATION
    P.O. Box 385, 01201. Tel: (413) 684-3090
Mrs. Glenn Jorn, Pres.
Mrs. Richard Lynch, Secy.
Estab. 1950 to encourage art in the New England and New York
State regions; financed by membership. Ann. meeting Nov; mem.
artists 540, nonartists 500; dues $10.
    Exhibitions: Semi-annual exhibitions are hung in the Berkshire
Museum.
    Activities: Individual paintings and original objects of art lent;
competitions; scholarships.
    Publications: Exhibition brochures and catalogs, twice a year.

BERKSHIRE MUSEUM
    39 South St, 01201. Tel: (413) 442-6373
Paul K. Fodder, Pres.
Stephen B. Hibbard, V.Pres-Treas
Mrs. Lawrence K. Miller, Secy.
Stuart C. Henry, Dir.
Bartlett Hendricks, Cur, Science Dept.
Samuel A. Spratlin, Financial Secy.
Thomas G. Smith, Head, Junior Dept.
Free 10 AM - 5 PM; Sun. 2 - 5 PM; cl. Mon.(except in July & Aug).
Estab. 1903, reorganized 1932. Ann. meeting Jan; mem. 1331; dues
$7.50 and higher. Building, gift of Zenas Crane, contains nine †art
galleries, eight †science galleries, auditorium, children's room,
art classrooms and library, which includes Carnegie reference art
set.
    Collections: Original sculpture, paintings and objects from
Egyptian times to modern. Interiors from Aston Magna. Old
Master's Gallery with works by Van Dyck, Reynolds, Raeburn,
Patinir and others. Early American and large Hudson River group.
Gallery with Spalding Collection of Chinese Art. Science Dept. con-
tains birds and animals in realistic settings, Biology and mineral
Rooms, Animals of the World in Miniature with dioramas by Louis
Paul Jonas, and Hall of Man, which includes Peary Arctic Sledge.
Berkshire Historical Room contains original One Hoss Shay and
William Stanley's first transformer.
    Activities: Many classes on art and other subjects; lectures,
plays and field trips. Nature Hour; Junior department. Little Cin-
ema, an air-conditioned professional theatre, shows finest foreign
and American films and runs periodically.
    Attendance: Approx. 100,000 annually.

PITTSFIELD ART LEAGUE
    Berkshire Museum, 01201.
Ora W. Burke, Pres.
Dorothy Huntley, Advisor
Patricia Trahanas, V.Pres.
Suzanne Brown, Treas.
Olive Murphy, Secy.
Open weekdays 10 AM - 5 PM; Sun. 2 - 5 PM; cl. Mon. Estab. 1923.
Ann. meeting May; mem. 100; dues $6.
    Exhibitions: Annual exhibition in Nov. at the Berkshire Museum.
    Attendance: Average attendance of League 100.

SHAKER COMMUNITY, INC.
    (Albany Road, Hancock)
    Mail: Box 898, Pittsfield, 01203. Tel: (413) 433-0188
Mrs. Lawrence K. Miller, Pres.
John H. Ott, Dir. & Cur.

Open June 1 - Oct. 31, 9:30 AM - 5 PM. Estab. 1960 for the restoration of Hancock Shaker Village, and for displays of Shaker life.
    Collections: †Shaker drawings; †furniture in 22 buildings.
    Library: By appointment.
    Attendance: Approx. 50,000.

PLYMOUTH

PLYMOUTH ANTIQUARIAN SOCIETY
    c/o Curator, 27 North St, 02360. Tel: (617) 746-0012
Mrs. Lee W. Gregory, Pres.
Margaret G. Clark, Cur.
Open June through Labor Day daily, 10 AM - 5 PM; Antiquarian
House, admis. adults $1, children 25¢; Spooner House, admis. adults
$1, children 25¢; Harlow Old Fort House, admis. adults $1, children
25¢. Estab. 1920 to preserve and exhibit houses and objects of
antiquarian interest. Ann. meeting Nov; mem. 500; dues, annual $3,
life $25.
    Collections: Furniture, household items, implements, dolls.
Antiquarian House now has a special storage and study area that
houses the several hundred garments and accessories worn by
Plymouth men, women and children from the mid-18th century
through the 1920's and 1930's. These are available for study, by
appointment, in the storage and study area by students engaged in
research on costumes. The collection is called the Rose T.
Briggs Costume Collection.
    Exhibitions: Items from the Society's collections. Annual exhi-
bitions.
    Activities: Guided tours, children's classes, household crafts;
visitor participation.
    Attendance: Approx. 30,000 annually.

PROVINCETOWN

PROVINCETOWN ART ASSOCIATION
    460 Commercial St, 02657. Tel: (617) 487-1750
Ciriaco G. Cozzi, Pres.
Sheila Miles, Dir.
Open daily June through Aug. 11 AM - 5 PM & 8 - 10 PM; Sun.
2 - 5 PM. Admis. 50¢, mem. free. Estab. 1914, inc. 1921, to promote and cultivate the practice and appreciation of all branches of
the fine arts; to assemble a permanent collection; provide forums,
concerts and similar activities for the public; operating within its
charter as a non-profit organization. Ann. meeting Aug; mem. 800,
dues $10 and higher.
    Owns three exhibition galleries, Hawthorne Memorial Gallery,
Art Library, and a permanent collection of paintings. Exhibition
galleries show 175-200 paintings, sculpture and prints in each show.
Special Charles W. Hawthorne Exhibitions. Winter program, children's classes, sketch classes.
    Attendance: For all activities—8 to 10,000.

ROCKPORT

ROCKPORT ART ASSOCIATION
    The Old Tavern, 12 Main St, 01966. Tel: (617) 546-6604
Martin Ahearn, Pres.
S. Ohrvel Carlson, V.Pres.
John W. Pettibone, Cur.
John Wentworth, Art Chmn.
Open summer Mon. - Sat. 9:30 AM - 5 PM; Sun. 1 - 5 PM; winter
Mon. - Sat. 9:30 AM - 4:30 PM; Sun. 1 - 5 PM. Founded 1921, inc.
1928, to advance the art of the community and to benefit the public
through exhibitions of paintings, prints and sculpture of artist members. Ann. meeting Aug; mem. 1100 (artists, 250, lay mem. 850);
dues $7.50 and higher.
    Exhibitions: 3 major exhibitions each summer; in winter, monthly
membership shows, one-man shows every two weeks, special exhibitions. Local crafts in year-round display.
    Activities: Sat. morning classes for young people; adult sketch
groups, life and portrait painting; lectures, concerts, demonstrations,
panels. Lends small exhibitions, on request, to galleries, theatres,
and others. Offers scholarship annually (for one year) to apply on
tuition for worthy student graduating from Rockport High School, de-
siring further art training.
    Publications: Exhibition catalogs; bimonthly newsletter to mem-
bers, Book of Rockport Artists (publ. 1940, 1946, 1956, 1964, 1970),
Calendar of Exhibitions and Activities; The Rockport Sketchbook.
    Attendance: 50,000 annually.

SALEM

ESSEX INSTITUTE
    132 Essex St, 01970. Tel: (617) 744-3390
Bryant F. Tolles, Jr, Dir
Katherine W. Richardson, Asst. to Dir.

Mrs. Gilbert R. Payson, Cur.
Mrs. Charles A. Potter, Librn.
Open Tues. - Fri. 9 AM - 4:30 PM; Sun. 2 - 5 PM. Estab. and inc. 1848. Ann. meeting May; mem. 1000; dues $15 and higher. The Essex Institute is an Essex County collection of furniture and furnishings, dolls, portraits, books and manuscripts of the 17th-19th centuries.
Publications: Historical Collections (quarterly); Newsletter (quarterly); occasional books.
Attendance: 100,000.
Period Houses owned and operated by the Institute are listed below.
Crowninshield-Bentley House, 120 Essex St.
Open June 1 through Oct. 15 (except July 4); guided tours Tues. - Sat. 10 AM - 4 PM; Sun. 2 - 4:30 PM; admis. $1. Built in 1727, this $2\frac{1}{2}$ story frame house contains many fine period pieces.
Pingree House, 128 Essex St.
Open all year Tues. - Sat. 10 AM - 4 PM; June through Oct. 15 Sun. 2 - 4:30 PM; admis. $1. Built in 1804 by Samuel McIntire and furnished in that period.
Peirce-Nichols House, 80 Federal St.
Open all year Tues. - Sat. 2 - 4:30 PM; admis. $1. Built by Samuel McIntire in 1782; some original furnishings and a counting house.
John Ward House, on grounds of Essex Institute.
Open June 1 through Oct. 15, Tues. - Sat. 10 AM - 4 PM; Sun. 2 - 4:30 PM; admis. $1. Dates from 1684 and is furnished in the manner of the time. In the lean-to are an apothecary's shop (1825), a Salem cent shop (1840) and a weaving room.
Lye-Tapley Shoe Shop (1830) and Vaughan Doll House, on grounds of Essex Institute.
Free June 1 through Oct. 15, Tues. - Sat. 10 AM - 4 PM; Sun. 2 - 4:30 PM.
Assembly House, 138 Federal St.
Open all year Tues. - Sat. 2 - 4:30 PM; admis. $1. Built in 1782 and remodeled by Samuel McIntire in 1796.

400,000 volume library of books and manuscripts relating to civil history of Essex County; museum offers slide show, tours of museum and houses; exhibits, 4-6 lectures per year; publications and gift shop; educational seminars; scholarships arranged by outside university programs.

PEABODY MUSEUM OF SALEM
East India Marine Hall, 161 Essex St, 01970. Tel: (617) 745-1876
Augustus P. Loring, Pres.
Walter M. Whitehill, Secy. & Historian
Ernest S. Dodge, Dir.
Philip C. F. Smith, Cur. Maritime History
Peter Fetchko, Cur. Ethnology
Sarah P. Ingalls, Cur. Natural History
Barbara B. Edkins, Librn.
Open year round 9 AM - 5 PM; Sun. & holidays 1 - 5 PM; admis. adults $1, children 6-16 50¢. Estab. 1799 to collect marine, ethnological worldwide, and natural history specimens of Essex County; endowed. Ann. meeting Sept; mem. 1400; dues fellows $100, friends $20 annually.
Collections: 35,000 maritime; 75,000 ethnological and †10,000 natural history items.
Exhibitions: About six special exhibitions a year.
Activities: Exhibitions, lectures, classes, guided tours for school classes.
Income and Purchases: Annual income $150,000; annual purchases $12,000.
Library: 100,000 volumes specializing in the three departments; 500,000 photographs.
Publications: Books, bulletins, catalogues.
Attendance: 140,000.

SANDWICH

HERITAGE PLANTATION OF SANDWICH
Grove St, Box 566, 02563. Tel: (617) 888-3300
Nelson O. Price, Dir.
H. R. Bradley, Cur. Arts & Crafts
Open daily 10 AM - 5 PM, May 1 - Oct. 15; admis. adults $2.50, children 6 and over 75¢; group rates available by reservation. Estab. 1969 to preserve and display specific examples of arts and crafts which show excellence of workmanship and ingenuity in their conception and creation in an American museum; financed by membership and private foundation. Galleries for permanent collections and a gallery for special exhibitions. Ann. meeting June; mem. 1250; dues $10 single, $15 family, $35 sustaining, $250 life.
Collections: †19th century paintings; †shop and cigar store figures; †carousel animals; †weathervanes; †decoys; †scrimshaw; †mechanical banks; †bronze sculpture; †pewter; †glass; †tole ware; †tools; †antique automobiles and firearms and related items in separate museums.

Exhibitions: The Herbert Waide Hemphill, Jr. Collection of American Folk Art, 1974; The Art of Frank Vining Smith (1879-1967), Marine Artist, 1975; Unsung Patriots of the American Revolution, 1976.
Activities: Education department serves elementary and high schools, program with Cape Cod Community College; prints for reference in photograph collection; lectures as part of college art course; concerts; classes for adults and children.
Library: Approx. 1000 volumes for reference, but loan to students taking art course.
Publications: View from the Cupola, quarterly; exhibition catalogs.
Attendance: 87,000 annual average.

SHARON

KENDALL WHALING MUSEUM
02067. Tel: (617) 784-5642
K. R. Martin, Dir.
Mrs. A. Waldman, Bookkeeper
Open Mon. - Fri. 10 AM - 4 PM; admis. adults 50¢, children 25¢.
Collections: Manuscripts, paintings, scrimshaw, objects relating to the whaling industry.
Research library: 3500 volumes; photograph collection of 5000 prints; 300 charts; 800 engravings.
Publications: Kendall Whaling Museum Paintings Book; Kendall Whaling Museum Prints Book.

SOUTH HADLEY

MOUNT HOLYOKE COLLEGE ART MUSEUM
01075. Tel: (413) 538-2245
Jean Harris, Chmn. Dept. Art
Janet B. Murrow, Dir. Museum
Wendy M. Watson, Cur.
Free Mon. - Fri. 11 AM - 5:30 PM; Sat. 1 - 5 PM; Sun. 2:30 - 4:30 PM. Building erected 1971 to house the equipment and collections of the Dept. of Art of Mount Holyoke College. It contains lecture rooms, painting and sculpture studios, art library; art museum with 5 galleries houses the permanent collection.
Collections: European and American paintings, sculpture, prints and drawings; Egyptian, Greek, Roman, Pre-Columbian and East Asian art; also a collection of Italian Trecento paintings. Recent purchases include works by Glackens, Prendergast, Robinson, Guercino, Nicholson, Bellows, Wen Cheng-Ming, Lu Chi, Wu Wei, Hua Yen; Nottingham alabaster. Recent gifts include paintings by Harnett, Isabel Bishop, Kay Sage, Davies, Tanguy, Grosz and Henri; also drawings by Kandinsky, Jordaens and Soyer; sculpture by Zorach and Stankiewicz; Roman frescoes and Medieval sculpture.
Exhibitions: Temporary monthly exhibitions sponsored by the Mount Holyoke Friends of Art are held in the museum, as well as the display of the permanent collection.
Library: 14,260 volumes on art and archaeology; slide collection of 20,000 black and white and 30,000 color slides; several thousand photographs.
✢Mount Holyoke College Friends of Art
Estab. 1931 to provide art exhibitions for the College and the community. Mem 300; dues $10. Sponsors monthly exhibitions in the art museum as well as films, gallery talks, lectures and trips to view other collections.
Exhibitions: (1974-1975) Recent Paintings by Susan Mangam; American Posters of the 90's; Edward Curtis' Photographs of Indians of the Southwest; Dorothy Cogswell Retrospective; Gregorian Collection of Antique Oriental Rugs; Northeastern Regional Photography Exhibition; Art as a Muscular Principle (10 San Francisco Artists 1950-1965); Modern Chinese Painting and Calligraphy by Tong Yang-Tze and Ho Hwai-Shouh; Annual Student Show. (1975-76) Harold Weston, A Retrospective of Paintings; Recent Work, Barry Seace; From Pedestal to Pavement: The Image of Woman in American Art, 1875-1975; Pre-Columbian Art; Second Biennial National Prints and Drawings Exhibition; Annual Student Show.

SOUTH SUDBURY

LONGFELLOW'S WAYSIDE INN
Boston Post Rd, Rte. 20, 01776. Tel: (617) 443-8846
Lawrence Coolidge, Chmn, Trustees
Open 9 AM - 9 PM.
This old hostelry made famous by Longfellow, was first built by David Howe in the 18th century and was known as "Howe's Tavern." Some years later, a new sign went up, reading Red Horse Tavern. After publication of Tales of a Wayside Inn, it acquired its present name. The inn remained in the Howe family for years, being handed down from father to son. It was visited by Coolidge, Edison, and many others. It was damaged by fire in December, 1955, and was restored by a grant from the Ford Foundation.

The inn is open daily all year. There is a 50 cent admission charge. No charge for admission to dining room and overnight guests. Guided tours by arrangement. It is administered by a special group of Trustees.

Attendance: 250,000 annually.

SPRINGFIELD

BABSON LIBRARY ART GALLERY
Springfield College
263 Alden St, 01109. Tel: (413) 787-2332
William Blizard, Chmn, Art Dept.
Free daily 8 AM - 11 PM. Estab. 1975 to bring a wide range of quality exhibits in all areas of the visual arts to the Springfield College campus; financed by Cultural Affairs Committee.

Collections: †Paintings, sculpture, drawings and prints in permanent collection.

Exhibitions: 21 exhibits over last 3 years, including one-man shows and national juried exhibition, Works on Paper.

Activities: Original objects of art lent; paintings, drawings and prints in lending collection; 100 items lent in average year; lectures open to public; 6 visiting lecturers per year; 3 gallery talks; concerts; dramatic programs; classes for adults; competitions; scholarships. Book shop. (See Schools)

Library: Over 110,000 volumes for lending and reference.

Income and Purchases: Income $12,000; purchases $1000.

Attendance: Over 10,000.

CONNECTICUT VALLEY HISTORICAL MUSEUM
194 State St, 01103. Tel: (413) 732-3080
Juliette Tomlinson, Dir.
Cecelia F. Callazzo, Secy.
Free 1 - 5 PM; Sun. 2 - 5 PM; cl. Mon. Estab. 1871.

Collections: China, glass, pewter, period rooms relating to Springfield and the Connecticut Valley.

Exhibitions: Special exhibitions including Pewter of the Connecticut Valley; American Silver; Scalamandre Textiles; James S. Ellsworth, American Miniature Painter; Painting and Prints from Connecticut Valley Collectors.

Library: Contains material relating to early Springfield, including the Account Books of John Pynchon, 1651-1713; photograph collection for lending and reference.

Income: $20,000 annually.

✤GEORGE WALTER VINCENT SMITH ART MUSEUM
222 State St, 01103. Tel: (413) 733-4214
Donald Reichert, Dir.
Emil Schnorr, Cur.
Jean Frank, Exec. Secy.
Free 1 - 5 PM; Sun. 2 - 5 PM; cl. Mon. except by appointment; cl. major holidays. Estab. 1895 as a unit of the Springfield Library and Museums Association, to house collections given by the late Mr. and Mrs. George Walter Vincent Smith. Sixteen galleries, loan exhibition gallery, Children's Workshop, Classroom, Library.

Collections: 16th, 17th and 18th century jades; 17th, 18th century porcelains, cloisonné enamels (Ming); Chinese robes and bronzes; 17th and 18th century Japanese lacquers, ivories, arms, armor; pottery, metals; India and the Near East metals, stuffs, arms and armor; Oriental rugs; 19th century American paintings; European glass, manuscripts, furniture, armor, paintings, textiles.

Exhibitions: Annuals: Work of faculty and student classes, Springfield Art League, Regional; exhibits of nationally known craftsmen in glass, ceramics, metal; one-man shows of accredited artists of the Connecticut Valley, as well as one-man shows of artists of historic significance, i.e. 19th century painters; recipient of State grants money for exhibits of local importance.

Activities: Lectures, demonstrations, documentary and foreign films, docent service, adult classes, gallery talks, radio and television. Children's Workshop and art classes, clubs, summer program.

Library: Reference library of 2700 volumes on decorative arts.

Publications: Bulletin, bimonthly Oct. - June; exhibition catalogs.

Attendance: Approx. 75,000.

Friends of the Quadrangle

Membership jointly shared by Smith Art Museum, Springfield Museum of Fine Arts, Science Museum and the Connecticut Valley Historical Museum.

MUSEUM OF FINE ARTS
49 Chestnut St, 01103. Tel: (413) 733-5857
Ramona Corriveau, Pres, Board of Trustees
Geraldine Lockwood, Exec. Secy.
Pauline M. Reynolds, Registrar
Laila Kain, Educ. Coordinator
Marion Freeman, Mem. Secy.
Lee Sheridan, Dir. Pub. Relations

Free Tues. - Sat. 1 - 5 PM; Sun. 2 - 5 PM; cl. Mon. & holidays. Estab. 1933 as a unit of the Springfield Library and Museums Association through the bequests of Mr. and Mrs. James Philip Gray. Building contains 18 galleries, library theater, offices.

Collections: Pre-historic Chinese to 19th Century; Persian Miniatures from 10th - 20th Century; Japanese Woodblock Prints, Paintings and Sculpture; Gothic to Renaissance: 17th, 18th, 19th and 20th Century Italian, Dutch, French and British; Primitive to Contemporary American Paintings, Sculpture and Graphics; Print Collection from Old Masters to Present.

Exhibitions: Special exhibitions, historic to contemporary, are continually on view in addition to permanent collection.

Activities: Education Department offers lectures, films, tours, concerts, audiovisual programs, docent study program; in-classroom public schools program coordinated with student tours.

Library: Reference library of 5000 volumes; slides; library of permanent collection and other art masterpieces.

SPRINGFIELD ART LEAGUE
220 State St, 01103.
Estab. 1918, to stimulate art expression and appreciation in Springfield. Ann. meeting Apr; dues $7.

Exhibitions: Special nonjuried show in Nov, open to all artists, to promote sale of work; Annual jury exhibition in Apr. with cash awards.

Activities: Lectures; demonstrations; exhibits each year at the Smith Museum of Art.

SPRINGFIELD CITY LIBRARY
220 State St, 01103. Tel: (413) 739-3871
Ramona L. Corriveau, Pres.
Francis P. Keough, Dir.
Karen A. Dorval, Head, Fine Arts Dept.
Fine Arts Dept. free Mon. - Fri. 9 AM - 9 PM; Sat. 9 AM - 5 PM; cl. holidays. Estab. 1857, Fine Arts Department opened 1905. In addition to the City Library system, the Springfield Library and Museums Association owns and administers, as separate units, the George Walter Vincent Smith Museum, the Springfield Museum of Fine Arts, the Science Museum, and the Connecticut Valley Historical Museum.

Exhibitions: Monthly exhibitions from the Library's collections and of work by local artists. Loan exhibitions.

Library: Art Dept. of Library has 17,500 volumes; 60 periodicals; †25,000 pictures including American wood engravings and blockprints, photographs, color reproductions and a circulating collection of framed prints.

Income and Purchases: $8000.

STOCKBRIDGE

CHESTERWOOD
Box 248, 01262. Tel: (413) 298-3579
Paul H. Ivory, Adminr.
Susan Frisch, Curatorial Asst.
Arthur Dutil, Buildings & Grounds Supt.
Kathleen Oppermann, Admin. Asst.
Carole T. Scanlon, Coordinator, Interpretive Programs
Open Memorial Day weekend through Oct. 31, 10 AM - 5 PM; candlelight tours Wed. evenings during July & Aug. 8 - 10 PM; open May on appointment basis; cl. end of Oct. till May; admis. adults $1.75, senior citizens 80¢, children 75¢, group rates by arrangement; free to National Trust members.

Chesterwood is a property of the National Trust for Historic Preservation. Preserved as a historic house, operated as a community preservation center. Chesterwood was the summer home and studio of sculptor Daniel Chester French (1850-1931). Here he worked for 6 months of the year over a period of 30 years. Henry Bacon designed the 30-foot stucco and frame cubical studio (1897), as well as the Colonial Revival mansion (1900). Margaret French Cresson donated the house to the National Trust in 1969. The collective includes sculpture, bronzes, plaster casts and paintings by Daniel Chester French, Mrs. French and their contemporaries as well as manuscripts, 2000 photographs and a 5000 volume reference library.

Property serves as focal point for advancement of historic preservation. It develops new relationships among cultural, community, community's present needs by action as a resource look between community, preservation groups, and Trust members in its area. Responds to community preservation needs by acting as a link between community and appropriate regional or headquarters offices of National Trust.

Provides interpretive programs which are related to Chesterwood's particular case study in historic preservation. Programs include pre-visit school material and tour program, National Trust

summer intern program, college field experience program; special exhibits, participation in Daniel Chester French Retrospective - 1976-1977. Members Day during part of National Preservation Week early part of May. Preservation Shop.
Attendance: (1975) 15,000.

STOCKBRIDGE MISSION HOUSE ASSOCIATION
Box 422, 01262. Tel: (413) 298-3383
Andrew R. Mack, Chmn.
John Rogers, Secy.
Carol Patten, Cur.
Open Tues. - Sat. 10 AM - 5 PM; Sun. 11 AM - 4 PM.
Built 1739, restored by Mabel Choate, 1928, as a memorial to her parents, Mr. and Mrs. Joseph H. Choate. Originally the home of John Sergeant, first missionary to the Stockbridge Indians, it is now an Early American Museum containing household objects, portraits and decorations of the period, and Indian relics. Ann. meeting June. Annual average attendance, 3000.

STURBRIDGE

OLD STURBRIDGE VILLAGE
Sturbridge, 01566. Tel: (617) 347-3362
Edward L. Clifford, Chmn. Board of Trustees
Alexander J. Wall, Pres.
Larry Morrison, Dir. Pub. Information
Open daily 9:30 AM - 5:30 PM except Christmas and New Year's; admis. $4 to all 40 buildings and exhibits; special school, children's and group rates. Estab. 1936 to perpetuate and interpret the New England social, economic and cultural heritage. Ann. meeting Sept; mem. 11,000; dues $7.50 and up.
Collections: Buildings, furnishings, †pottery, †glass, †iron, †tin, †textiles, †tools, †firearms, †folk arts, †clocks, †New England rural paintings, and others.
Activities: Annual antiques forum and other special programs; school visitation program.
Library: 21,000 volumes; 120 running feet of manuscript.
Publications: The New England Galaxy, The Rural Visitor (quarterlies); Guidebook; pamphlet series; annual report.
Attendance: 670,000.

TYRINGHAM

TYRINGHAM INSTITUTE (JEAN BROWN ARCHIVE)
Shaker Seed House, 01264. Tel: (413) 243-3216
Mrs. Leonard Brown, Dir.
Free, open by appointment. Estab. 1970 as an aide to scholars doing research within the context of the collections; primarily a study collection, privately financed.
Collections: †Dada; †Surrealism; †Concrete Poetry; †Happenings; †Fluxus; †Conceptual art; †Intermedia, which includes music, dance, performance and video. The paintings in the collection are on permanent loan to Princeton University Museum.
Activities: Original objects of art lent to schools; photographs made on specific request, depending on use.
Library: Thousands of volumes and hundreds of prints for reference.
Attendance: 25 researchers from United States, South America and Europe.

WALTHAM

ROSE ART MUSEUM
Brandeis University, 02154. Tel: (617) 647-2402
Carl I. Belz, Dir.
Marjorie Groggins, Registrar
Kathe Tuttman, Secy.
Walter Soule, Bldg. Supvr.
Free every day except Mon. 1 - 5 PM; cl. major national holidays. Estab. and opened June 1961; a repository of a general collection of art objects.
Collections: Mr. and Mrs. Edward Rose Collection of †18th and †19th century English and French china; †19th and 20th century painting and sculpture; Helen S. Slosberg Collection of †Oceanic Art and Ethnographic Objects.
Exhibitions: Paintings, sculpture, prints, drawings and photography exhibitions organized during the academic year. Portions of the permanent collection exhibited several times during the year.
Activities: Openings and occasional gallery talks.
Attendance: 25,000 annually.

WELLESLEY

WELLESLEY COLLEGE MUSEUM
Jewett Arts Center, 02181. Tel: (617) 235-0320, ext. 314
Ann Gabhart, Dir.
Free 8:30 AM - 5:00 PM, Sun. 2 - 5 PM during college year; cl. in

summer. Estab. 1875; A small teaching museum serving Wellesley and nearby communities.
Collections: †Major works of sculpture, Classical through Modern, also African. †Paintings, 14th through 20th centuries. Watercolors, prints and drawings, 15th through 20th centuries.
Exhibitions: Teaching, traveling and loan shows.
Library: 15,200 books; 37,000 slides; 50,000 photographs and color reproductions.

WELLESLEY SOCIETY OF ARTISTS*
c/o Mary Nugent, Secy, 31 Ledyard Rd, 02181.
Harry Senger, Pres.
Rosalie Wentworth, V.Pres.
Helen Sherman, Dir.
Harold Lindergreen, Dir.
Joe Havens, Dir.
Free 9 AM - 5 PM.
Estab. 1932, to bring together painters, sculptors and workers in the graphic arts, living in Wellesley and its environs, and to encourage talented students. Ann. meeting Fall; mem. active 61, associate 80; dues $3 and $5. Annual exhibition at Wellesley Free Library. Five meetings-demonstrations by well-known artists; 2 sketch trips; 4 portrait sketch classes and 2 exhibitions of artists' work during the season.

WENHAM

WENHAM HISTORICAL ASSOCIATION AND MUSEUM, INC.
132 Main St, 01984. Tel: (617) 468-2377
Mrs. Dean Cogswell, Pres.
Mrs. George V. Upton, III
Irene Dodge, Dir.
Open Mon. - Fri. 1 - 4 PM; Sun. 2 - 5 PM; cl. Sat, holidays and month of Feb; admis. adults $1, children 6-14 25¢, mem. free. Estab. 1917, inc. 1952, to exhibit collections of literary, scientific, religious and historic interest and to provide educational and cultural service and facilities for better understanding of different races and religions. Ann. meeting Apr; mem. 675; dues $5 and higher.
Collections: †4000 dolls and figurines; costumes and accessories 1800-1960; quilts; fans; needlework and embroideries, mostly 19th century; two shoe shops with tools and lasts; agricultural tools; kitchen utensils.
Exhibitions: Changing exhibits of art and historical material. Permanent ice industry exhibit.
Activities: Craft classes; series of lectures on antiques and the decorative arts; guided lectures and tours for school and youth groups.
Library: 1000 volumes for reference. Headquarters for Massachusetts Society for Promoting Agriculture (1792).
Publications: Books on local records and history; Annual Report.
Annual Income: $23,000.
Attendance: 6000-7000.

Historic House c. 1661.

WESTFIELD

JASPER RAND ART MUSEUM
Westfield Athenaeum, Public Library, 01085. Tel: (413) 568-7833
Mrs. Edmund S. Piszczek, Pres.
Franklin P. Taplin, Dir.
Mrs. John E. Reed, Secy.
Free 9 AM - 9 PM; cl. Wed. & Sat. at 6 PM. Estab. 1927. Supported by special and City funds. Continuous local and traveling exhibitions. Art classes for children; ceramics classes for adults and children. Monthly film programs. Ann. meeting 4th Mon. in Oct.

WILLIAMSTOWN

STERLING AND FRANCINE CLARK ART INSTITUTE
South St, 01267. Tel: (413) 458-8109
George Heard Hamilton, Dir.
John H. Brooks, Assoc. Dir.
Charles C. Cunningham, Chief Cur.
David B. Cass, Asst. Cur.
Rafael Fernandez, Cur. of Prints & Drawings
Martha Asher, Registrar
Michael Rinehart, Librn.
Dustin Wees, Photograph and Slide Librn.
G. Louis McManus, Supt.
Free daily 10 AM - 5 PM; cl. Mon. Museum building opened May, 1955 for the exhibition of Fine Arts.
Collections: Paintings 14th, 15th and 16th century Italian and Netherlands; 17th, 18th and 19th century American and European,

particularly French 19th century. Extensive collection of old English silver. Photographs of all paintings and slides of most paintings for sale.

Exhibitions: The permanent collection and changing exhibitions.
Activities: Guided tours, lectures, films.
Attendance: 100,000.

✣WILLIAMS COLLEGE MUSEUM OF ART
Main St, 01267. Tel: (413) 597-2429
S. Lane Faison, Jr, Dir.
Eugene J. Johnson, Cur.
Free 10 - 12 AM, 2 - 4 PM; Sun. 2 - 5 PM. Estab. 1926. Original building, designed by Thomas Tefft and given in 1846 by Amos Lawrence. Nine exhibition galleries and lecture rooms. During college year, frequently changing temporary exhibitions. Permanent collection developing to provide a broad representation of world art in original examples especially in fields not already covered by collections of the Clark Art Institute (q.v.)

Collections: †European and American paintings, drawings and prints; Roman glass; †Ancient Art; Assyrian sculpture; †European and American sculpture; textiles; ceramics; †Medieval art; Mayan pottery; early American furniture; †Spanish art; African art.

Library: Art library of 15,000 volumes; 50,000 slides; 500 color reproductions.

Income: Approx. $13,000.
Attendance: Approx. 12,000.

WORCESTER

AMERICAN ANTIQUARIAN SOCIETY
185 Salisbury St, 01609. Tel: (617) 755-5221
Marcus A. McCorison, Dir. & Librn.
Georgia B. Bumgardner, Cur. Graphic Arts
Free 9 AM - 5 PM; cl. Sat, Sun. & holidays. Inc. 1812; mem. hon. 275.

Collections: Early American portraits; Staffordshire pottery, †bookplates, †prints, †lithographs, †cartoons, †engravings, colonial furniture.

Library: 750,000 titles, contains books, newspapers and manuscripts dating before 1877; early American books on art; 20th century books and periodicals relating to the history and culture of the United States before 1877.

Publications: Proceedings, (semi-annually); monographs.
Income and Purchases: Income $200,000; purchases $50,000.

CRAFT CENTER
25 Sagamore Rd, 01605. Tel: (617) 753-8183
Dr. Robert Bennett, Pres.
Mrs. Alfred M. Whiting, Jr, Secy.
Angelo Randazzo, Dir.
Free Mon. - Sat. 9 AM - 5 PM; Sun. 2 - 5 PM Sept. - Aug. Nonprofit educational institution to foster an interest in crafts and to assist individuals by education in the crafts. Ann. meeting Oct; mem. 900; dues $10 and higher.

Activities: Maintains gallery; exhibits; lectures; colored slides; tours; gallery talks; classes for adults and children; summer school; reference and lending library; demonstrations; annual invitational Craft Fair 3rd week in May. Craft Shop.

Attendance: 12,000.

JOHN WOODMAN HIGGINS ARMORY, INC.
100 Barber Ave, 01606. Tel: (617) 853-6015
Mrs. M. L. Wilding-White, Pres.
George H. Gage, Dir.
Albert J. Gagne, Cur.
Open Tues. - Fri. 9 AM - 4 PM; Sat. 10 AM - 3 PM; Sun. 1 - 5 PM; cl. national holidays; admis. Estab. and inc. in 1928 at Worcester, Massachusetts. Ann. meeting with Incorporators; no dues.

Collections: Art of the Stone Age, Bronze Age, and Iron Age; ancient Greek and Roman armor; over 100 suits of medieval and Renaissance armor for combat, joust and parades; many helmets and other elements of armor; weapons of all types; artistic objects of the iron smith's craft; paintings; tapestries; stained glass; wood carvings; armorial banners and furniture.

Activities: An audio-visual educational program emphasizes the relationship of the collection to art and history. Approx. 40,000 visitors are received annually including school classes, scout groups and adult organizations from the New England States, New York and New Jersey.

Library: The John Woodman Higgins Memorial Library contains books, monographs, clippings and prints on armor and related subjects. Students may use research facilities on request.

✣WORCESTER ART MUSEUM
55 Salisbury St. at Tuckerman St, 01608. Tel: (617) 799-4406
Milton P. Higgins, Pres.
Richard Stuart Teitz, Dir.
John W. Curtis, Treas.
Laurence Maloy, Clerk, Adminr. & Asst. Treas.
John C. Ewer, Development Officer
Dagmar E. Reutlinger, Cur. of the Collections
Stephen B. Jareckie, Registrar & Assoc Cur, Photography
Merle S. Harbach, Cur. of Educ.
Penny Mattern, Librn.
Jean Connor, Head, Pub. Relations
Sante Graziani, Dean, School of Worcester Art Museum
Richard Lindgren, Supt.
Free 10 AM - 5 PM; Sun. 2 - 6 PM; cl. Mon, July 4, Thanksgiving, Christmas & New Year's Day. Estab. and inc. 1896 for the promotion of art and art education. Building enlarged 1921, 1933, 1940 and 1970. Ann. meeting Oct; mem. 6100; contributions $12 and higher.

Collections: Mesopotamian, †Egyptian, †Greek and Roman sculpture; †Greek vases; mosaic pavements from Antioch; †Persian and Indian sculpture and miniatures; Chinese bronzes, ceramics, paintings and sculpture; †Japanese prints and bronzes; †Pre-Columbian pottery, sculpture, gold; Romanesque chapter house; †European sculpture of the Middle Ages and Renaissance; †European and American paintings; Italian, French and English furniture and ceramics; Flemish, French and Norwegian tapestries; early American furniture and silver; †European and American prints and drawings.

Special Exhibitions: (1973) Homer-Hassam-Hopper; The American Portrait: from the Death of Stuart to the Rise of Sargent; Photographs of Diane Arbus; An American Impressionist: Theodore Robinson; The Popper Collection of Oriental Art. (1974) Three Realists: Close, Estes, Raffael; American Pieced Quilts; European Paintings from the Collection of the Worcester Art Museum; Irish Directions; Paintings by Husain. (1975) Ansel Adams; The Graphic Work of Kandinsky; Bicentennial I: The Colonial Epoch in America; Ross Moffett; Three Israeli Artists, Gross, Kupferman, Neustein; American Art Since 1945. (1976) Naives and Visionaries; Bicentennial II: The Early Republic.

Activities: Lectures; courses; gallery talks; docent service; study groups; graduate seminars on special exhibitions; public film programs; films for members; concerts, jazz and classical; children's and adult art classes; conducts art school. Sales and rental gallery; gift shop.

Library: Reference library of 25,374 volumes; lending collection of 29,569 slides.

Publications: Worcester Art Museum Bulletin, 3 issues a year; quarterly calendar of events; Annual Report.

Attendance: 150,596.

MICHIGAN

ALBION

✣ALBION COLLEGE, DEPARTMENT OF VISUAL ARTS
49224. Tel: (517) 629-5511
Vernon L. Bobbitt, Chmn. Art Dept.
Free Mon. - Fri. 9 AM - 5 PM; Sat. 9 - 12 AM; Sun. 2 - 5 PM; Mon - Thurs. 7 - 9 PM when college is in session. Estab. 1835 to offer art education at college level, general art exhibition program for campus community and public; endowed. New $1,000,000 building having five large gallery areas.

Collections: Prints, 15th-20th centuries decorative arts, painting, drawing, folk art, etc.

Exhibitions: Continuous changing exhibitions.

Library: Large number of volumes for reference; photograph collection.

Attendance: Approx. 5000 per year.

ALPENA

✣JESSE BESSER MUSEUM
491 Johnson St, 49707. Tel: (517) 356-2202
Dennis R. Bodem, Museum Dir.
Eugene A. Jenneman, Planetarium Coordinator
Robert E. Haltiner, Cur.
Harry Zolnierek, Exhibits Preparator
Open Mon. - Fri. 9 AM - 5 PM; Sun. 1 - 5 PM; Tues. & Thurs. 7 - 9 PM; Museum free, Planetarium 25¢. Founded 1965, a museum of history, science, and art serving the northern Michigan area.

Collections: 19th and 20th century graphics, paintings, and sculpture; period furnishings and decorative arts; North American archaeological materials; agricultural and lumbering tools; historical shop interiors; historical buildings; manuscript collection.

Activities: Planetarium programs (Sun. 2 & 4 PM; in summer, Thurs. 7:30 PM); guided tours; lectures; art festivals; study clubs; formally organized education programs for children and adults; inter-museum loans; permanent, temporary and traveling exhibitions; school loan service; TV programs.

ANN ARBOR

KELSEY MUSEUM OF ANCIENT AND MEDIAEVAL ARCHAEOLOGY
434 S. State St, 48104. Tel: (313) 764-9304
John G. Pedley, Dir. Res. Cur.
Louise A. Shier, Cur.
Elaine K. Gazda, Asst. Cur.
John H. Humphrey, Asst. Cur.
Free, currently undergoing major renovation, call for opening date to public. Still open for research and business transactions. Collections begun in 1893, estab. as a museum in 1928; archaeological expedition currently in Carthage, Tunis, Tunisia. Research, instruction, and exhibits; publications available for sale.
    Objects of the Graeco-Roman period from excavations conducted by the University of Michigan in Egypt and Iraq; antiquities chiefly from Egypt, Greece, Italy, North Africa and Palestine. Guided tours by appointment only. Research library.

✣THE UNIVERSITY OF MICHIGAN MUSEUM OF ART
Alumni Memorial Hall, 48104. Tel: (313) 764-0395
Bret Waller, Dir.
John Holmes, Asst. Dir.
Nesta Spink, Cur. of Collections
Marjorie H. Swain, Asst. to Dir.
Lilli Milder, Exec. Secy, Friends of the Museum
Jacquelynn Slee, Registrar
Jo Lau, Admin. Secy.
Free Mon. - Sat. 9 AM - 5 PM; Sun. 2 - 5 PM. Estab. 1946, as a university art museum and museum for the Ann Arbor community; financed by city and state appropriation. Mem. 1500; dues individual $15, family $25.
    Collections: Arts of the Western world from the 6th century A.D. to the present; Far Eastern, Near Eastern, African and Oceanic, including †painting, †sculpture, †decorative art, †graphic arts, †contemporary art, ceramics and manuscripts.
    Exhibitions: (1972) Art and the Excited Spirit; The Gosman Collection; (1974) The Poet Painters: Buson and His Followers; Ann Arbor Architecture: A Sesquicentennial Selection; European Drawings from the Sonnenschein Collection.
    Activities: Docent training program; original objects of art lent; photograph collection; lectures open to public; classes for children; scholarships.
    Publications: The University of Michigan Museum of Art Bulletin (annually).
    Attendance: 55,000.

BATTLE CREEK

BATTLE CREEK CIVIC ART CENTER
265 Emmett St, 49017. Tel: (616) 963-7385
William Kitchen, Pres.
Darwin R. Davis, Dir.
Free daily 9:30 - 4:30 PM; Sun. 1 - 4 PM; cl. Mon. & legal holidays. Estab. 1947 to offer classes for children and adults, to plan monthly exhibitions of professional work. Ann. meeting May or June; mem. 500; dues $10 and higher.
    Collections: Small permanent collection of prints and paintings.
    Exhibitions: Exhibitions of photography, crafts, paintings, prints and drawings; student exhibits; group and one-man shows; Battle Creek 100, sponsored by Battle Creek Gas Co, $1000 purchase awards.
    Activities: Educational and informative movies, lectures and demonstrations; illustrated talks on art appreciation for elementary schools in the area through trained volunteers; classes in painting, photography, pottery, sculpture, etc; maintains gift and rental gallery for the public.
    Library: Slide library, art books.
    Budget: (1975-76) $64,000.

BATTLE CREEK COMMUNITY UNITED ARTS COUNCIL
450 North Ave, 49016. Tel: (616) 965-3931
Mrs. M. Burton Easter, Pres.
John Nequist, Secy.
Marguerite Yarger, Coordinator
Estab. 1964 to provide more participation and appreciation for the arts; conduct annual patron fund drive to subsidize arts; mem.
    Publications: Newsletter, bi-monthly.

BIRMINGHAM

BIRMINGHAM-BLOOMFIELD ART ASSOCIATION
1516 S. Cranbrook Rd, 48009. Tel: (313) 644-0866
Jennie Jones, Pres.
Doris Roeder, Secy.
Kenneth R. Gross, Exec. Dir.
Mrs. Joe Higuchi, Exec. Secy.
Gallery hours Mon. - Sat. 9:30 AM - 4:30 PM; Sun. 2 - 5 PM. Estab. 1956 to provide a community-wide, integrated studio-gallery art center. Program of outstanding art exhibits, lectures, movies, classroom instruction and events designed to foster appreciation of art in its many forms; supported by membership. Ann. Meeting June; mem. approx. 700; dues individual $20, family $35, contributing $50, supporting $100, life $500.
    Exhibitions: Eight or nine local and national exhibitions per year.
    Activities: Lectures and workshops open to the public; 9 gallery tours per year; classes for adults and children; scholarships; competitions.
    Publications: Calendar, monthly; exhibition notices and catalogs, approx. nine per year.
    Attendance: Approx. 2400 students annually.

BIRMINGHAM GALLERY INC.
1025 Haynes St, 48011. Tel: (313) 642-7455
John W. McKinney, Pres.
Douglas Webster, V.Pres.
Free Tues. - Sat. 10 AM - 6 PM. Estab. 1968 for exhibition of contemporary sculpture, painting, graphics and crafts.
    Exhibitions: One-man shows; Cranbrook Academy of Art Printmakers.
    Activities: Rental collection of original prints; lectures to private groups; gallery.
    Library: 1450 volume library.
    Publications: Catalogues and announcements, eight times a year.

BLOOMFIELD HILLS

✣CRANBROOK ACADEMY OF ART MUSEUM
500 Lone Pine Rd, 48103. Tel: (313) 645-3300
John D. Peterson, Dir. of Museum
Mary Riordan, Cur. of Collection
Beth Peterson, Coordinator Community Activities
Open Tues. - Sun. 1 - 5 PM; cl. Mon. and holidays; admis. Estab. 1924 as part of Cranbrook Academy of Art; Museum Community Activities Center estab. 1959.
    Collections: Sculpture by Carl Milles, ceramics by Maija Grotell, decorative arts by Eliel Saarinen; contemporary paintings, nineteenth century prints, study collection of textiles and porcelains by Adelaide Robineau.
    Exhibitions: Contemporary painting, sculpture, architecture, design and crafts. Annual Student Exhibition, June through Aug.
    Activities: Lectures; museum tours; film programs; art classes for adults and children. (See Schools)
    Attendance: 60,000.

DEARBORN

GREENFIELD VILLAGE AND HENRY FORD MUSEUM
48121. Tel: (313) 271-1620, for information 271-1976
William Clay Ford, Chmn.
Dr. Donald A. Shelley, Pres.
Frank Caddy, V.Pres.-Admin.
Robert G. Wheeler, V.Pres.-Research & Interpretation
Robert Dawson, Dir. Pub. Relations
Ronald Kanack, Dir. Special Events
Kenneth Wilson, Dir. of Collections & Preservation
Open weekdays 9 AM - 5 PM; holidays, weekends and July - Aug. 9 AM - 6 PM. Separate admission charges to the Village and Museum, adults $2.75, children 6 - 12 $1.25. Estab. 1929 as a general museum of American culture and history for educational purposes. Publicly supported through admissions and the Friends of Greenfield Village and Henry Ford Museum.
    Collections: Includes decorative arts, folk art, transportation, power, communications, agriculture and home arts. Greenfield Village has over 100 historic buildings including homes of famous Americans and public and industrial buildings. Most buildings are furnished or equipped, and many were moved from their original sites to Dearborn.
    Exhibitions: (1975-76) Old Time Summer Festival; Industrial Heritage U.S.A.; The Circus; Colonial Military Muster; Old Car Festival; Autumn Harvest Weekend; Christmas in Greenfield Village (annual); Henry Ford Museum Christmas Exhibit; Famous Americans Exhibit; Warp and Weft; Sports Cars in Review (annual); Special

Bicentennial Exhibit, The Struggle and the Glory; Law Day U.S.A.; County Fair of Yesteryear; Muzzle Loaders Festival; A History of Political Parties in the U.S.; Let Freedom Ring; American Folk Art.

Activities: Group tours for elementary and secondary school children; bicentennial group tours; lesson tours with advance classroom materials for teachers, and a day in a one-room school house; adult conference center for crafts and enrichment courses with enrollment in excess of 1000 per term; crafts classes afternoon schedule and weekends for children; concerts, dramatic programs.

Library: 30,000 volumes, plus rare book collections, manuscript and photograph collections. Henry Ford Archives contain some 14 million documents.

Publications: The Herald (Museum quarterly issued to mem.); publications on exhibits and individual collections, issued as published.

Attendance: Approx. 1.75 million annually.

DETROIT

CENTER FOR CREATIVE STUDIES-COLLEGE OF ART AND DESIGN
245 E. Kirby St, 48202. Tel: (313) 872-3118
Walter B. Ford, II, Pres.
Wendell W. Anderson, Jr, V.Pres.
Mrs. George E. F. Brewer, V.Pres.
Charles Wright, III, Secy.
Pierre Heftler, Treas.
Walter Midener, Dir. Art School
Open 9 AM - 4 PM & 6:30 - 9:30 PM. Estab. 1906, inc. 1915; School estab. 1926, to provide a thorough education in any field of art. Ann. meeting in Fall; mem. 210; dues $15 and higher. Ann. student exhibition in May. Maintains Art School. (See Schools)

Publications: Art and A City by Joy H. Colby. A history of the Society published 1956.

Library: Approx. 8200 books, 17,000 slides.

Income: $1,250,000.

DETROIT ARTISTS MARKET
1452 Randolph St, 48226. Tel: (313) 962-0337
Douglas K. Semivan, Art Dir.
Anne H. Silven, Chmn, Board of Dir.
Margaret Conzelman, Mgr.
Open daily 10 AM - 5 PM; cl. Aug. Estab. 1932. A non-profit organization that exhibits and sells the work of Detroit area artists and craftsmen. Dues $5, $10 and $25.

Exhibitions: Include one-man shows as well as group and theme shows, changing every four weeks. All work is juried.

Activities: Visiting jurors and lecturers; gallery talks; gallery tours; museum tours; opening receptions.

Publications: Newsletter biannually.

Attendance: 20,000.

✣THE DETROIT INSTITUTE OF ARTS
5200 Woodward Ave, 48202. Tel: (313) 833-7900
Lee Hills, Pres. City of Detroit Arts Commission
Ralph T. McElvenny, V.Pres. City of Detroit Arts Commission
Frederick J. Cumings, Dir.
William A. Bostick, Adminr. & Secy.
Francis W. Robinson, Cur. Emeritus Medieval Art
Larry J. Curry, Cur. American Art
William H. Peck, Cur. Ancient Art
Dewey F. Mosby, Cur. European Art
Ellen Sharp, Cur. Graphic Arts
John H. Neff, Cur. Modern Art
Audley M. Grossman, Jr, Cur. Theatre Arts
Michael Miners, Coordinator Detroit Youtheatre
Richard Mühlberger, Chmn. Educ.
Robert R. Rodgers, Dir. Pub. Relations
Margaret M. DeGrace, Press Relations Officer
Susan F. Rossen, Coordinator of Publ.
Charles H. Elam, Registrar
F. Warren Peters, Librn.
Lawarnce W. Jackson, Bldg. Supt.
Joseph Klima, Jr, Photographer
James L. Greaves, Chief Conservator
Voluntary admis. Wed. - Sun. 9:30 AM - 5:30 PM; cl Mon, Tues, and holidays. Estab. and Inc. 1885 as Detroit Museum of Art; chartered as municipal department 1919 and name changed; original organization continued as Founders Society Detroit Institute of Arts; present building opened 1927; South Wing addition completed 1966; North Wing addition opened 1971.

Collections: Representative examples of the arts from prehistory to the present time, including Egypt, Mesopotamia, Greece and Rome, the Orient, Europe, Africa, the South Seas, and the Americas. Comprehensive collection of textiles and of American decorative arts.

Special Collections: Paul McPharlin Puppetry, Theatre and Graphic Arts Collections; Grace Whitney Hoff Collection of Fine Bindings; Robert H. Tannahill Bequest of Impressionist and Post-Impressionist paintings, traditional African objects, French silver; Elizabeth Parke Firestone Collection of 18th century French silver; William Randolph Hearst Collection of arms and armor and Flemish tapestries. Central court decorated with Diego Rivera frescoes (1932-33). Incorporated in American Wing galleries is Whitby Hall, furnished with important collection of furniture.

Exhibitions: Michigan Artists and Michigan Artist-Craftsmen (alternate years); Master Paintings from the U.S.S.R.; French Painting 1774-1830; Cobra and Contrasts; Twilight of the Medici; Akhenaten and Nefertiti; French Impressionists and Post-Impressionists from the U.S.S.R.; African Art of the Dogon; African Terracottas South of the Sahara.

Activities: Art workshops; gallery talks and tours; films; cooperative programs with metropolitan area schools, university groups and special interest groups. Two museum shops.

Special Activities: Detroit Youtheatre; Puppetry; Detroit Film Theatre; many lectures and lecture series; Brunch with Bach; Concert Series; midwest area office of Archives of American Art.

Library: Research library of art, archaeology, architecture and allied subjects; auction sales catalogs; photograph and clipping files; 50,000 books; 40,000 slides.

Publications: Bulletin; Calendar of Events; handbooks and catalogs of various collections, and catalogs of special exhibitions.

Income and Purchases: Average income City and Founders Society $3,287,417; acquisitions through gifts and purchases 860 (1972), $1,788,000; 365 (1973), $2,522,000; 300 (1974), $1,258,000.

Attendance: 846,110 annual average.

(See Archives of American Art under National Organizations)
Detroit Institute of Arts Founders Society
5200 Woodward Ave, 48202. Tel: (313) 833-7950
Stanford C. Stoddard, Chmn. of Board
Norman B. Weston, Pres.
Mrs. Gaylord W. Gillis, Jr, V.Pres.
Mrs. Alan E. Schwartz, Secy.
Alfred M. Pelham, Treas.
Frederick J. Cummings, Exec. Dir.
Frank A. Morgan, Mgr.
Estab. and Inc. 1885; public membership philanthropic society contributing to the growth of the Detroit Institute of Arts. Ann. meeting Feb; mem. 12,000; dues individual $25, family $40, patron $150, corporate mem. $250, corporate contributor $1,000, corporate sponsor $5,000, corporate patron $10,000. Underwrites Educ. Dept. activities, publications, special exhibitions, and most purchases of works of art. Sponsors rental collection of original work by Michigan artists and reproductions, museum shops and other special activities.

DETROIT PUBLIC LIBRARY
5201 Woodward Ave, 48202. Tel: (313) 833-1467
Clara S. Jones, Dir.
Shirley Solvick, Chief Fine Arts Dept.
Free Mon. - Sat. 9:30 AM - 5:30 PM; Wed. until 9 PM; Sun. 1 - 5 PM Oct. - May.

Fine Arts Dept. estab. 1921. Over †50,000 books and bound periodicals; †500,000 pictures for reference and circulation; †1000 color reproductions; †clippings on subjects related to the department.

Purchases: $25,000.

✣WAYNE STATE UNIVERSITY*
McGregor Memorial, Community Arts Gallery
450 W. Kirby at Cass, 48202. Tel: (313) 577-2400
Richard J. Bilaitis, Gallery Coordinator
Free Mon. - Fri. 9 AM - 9 PM; Sat. & Sun. 1 PM - 5 PM. Estab. 1956 as a facility for university and community oriented exhibitions and programs.

Collections: Small collection of American as well as European painting, sculpture and graphics.

Exhibitions: Monthly exhibitions are shown with no permanent installation. Graphics from the collection of Dr. and Mrs. Ernst Scheyer; Distinguished Alumni Exhibition; Fine Arts Section, Michigan Academy of Science, Arts and Letters; Retrospective Exhibition of Sculpture by George Zambrzcki 1924-1969; Painting and Drawing by Professor of Art, Mary Jane Bigler; Annual Exhibitions of Art by WSU Students.

Activities: Exhibitions, concerts, lectures for adults, students and the community; monthly exhibitions.

EAST LANSING

MICHIGAN STATE UNIVERSITY
Kresge Art Center
48824. Tel: (517) 355-7612; Gallery (517) 355-7631
Roger Funk, Chmn. Dept. of Art

Joseph Ishikawa, Dir. of the Gallery
Free daily 9 AM - 5 PM; Tues. 7 - 9 PM; Sat. & Sun. 1 - 4 PM.
Collections: Permanent collection of paintings, †prints and
†sculpture.
Exhibitions: Rental shows; staff and student shows making up a
yearly calendar of about 10 exhibitions supplementing the permanent
collection.
Activities: Lectures, classes, art films; conducts summer art
school. (See Schools)
Publications: Yearly exhibition calendar; regular bulletin;
occasional announcements of art lectures and films; catalogs.

FLINT

✠FLINT INSTITUTE OF ARTS
DeWaters Art Center, 1120 E. Kearsley St, 48503.
Tel: (313) 234-1695
Dr. G. Stuart Hodge, Dir.
Thomas A. Kayser, Asst. Dir.
Dorothy Booth, Registrar
Gerna Rubenstein, Head, Educ.
Evelyn N. Lee, Mem./Pub. Relations
Barbara Lippincott, Museum Shop Mgr.
Open Mon. - Sat. 10 AM - 5 PM; Sun. 1 - 5 PM; Tues. 7 - 9 PM.
Inc. 1930. Ann. meeting June; mem. 2500; dues $10 and higher.
Collections: Renaissance Decorative Arts (tapestries, furniture,
ceramics, sculpture, etc.); Chinese paintings, bronzes, jades, ivo-
ries; 18th & 19th Century European Glass; 19th & 20th Century
painting and sculpture; Paperweights.
Exhibitions: Greater Flint Area Show; All Michigan Biennial;
special monthly exhibitions organized by the Flint Institute of Arts;
Annual Flint Art Fair.
Activities: Lectures, gallery talks, chamber music, concerts,
film series; art survey lectures; non-credit classes for adults and
children include painting, sculpture, ceramics, weaving, and others;
docent service; Friends of Modern Art; Founders Society; Art Rental.
Museum shop.
Library: Reference library.
Publications: Scholarly catalogues of all major exhibitions (Art of
the Great Lakes Indians, Art of Black Africa, Art of the Armorer, 1st
& 2nd Flint Invitationals).
Income and Purchases: Income, $300,000; purchases $100,000.
Attendance: 100,000.

FLINT PUBLIC LIBRARY
1026 E. Kearsley, 48502. Tel: (313) 232-7111
Ransom L. Richardson, Dir.
Forrest Alter, Head, Art, Music & Drama Dept.
Free Mon. - Thurs. 9 AM - 9 PM; Fri. & Sat. 9 AM - 6 PM. Art,
Music & Drama Dept. estab. 1958; a division of Flint Board of Educ.
Continuous program of exhibition of department's materials and
materials borrowed. 31,000 books and 2171 bound periodicals in
art, music and drama for lending and reference; 70 vertical file
drawers of pictures; 10 vertical file drawers of mounted reproductions for study and lending; many clippings on fine arts; many
exhibition catalogs.

GRAND RAPIDS

✠CALVIN COLLEGE CENTER ART GALLERY
Art Department
49506. Tel: (616) 949-4000, Exten. 2826
Edgar G. Boeve, Chmn. Art Dept.
Chris Stoffel Overvoorde, Dir. Exhibitions
Free Mon. - Fri. 9 AM - 9 PM, Sat. 10 AM - 4 PM. Gallery estab.
1974, college estab. 1876, for purpose of education.
Exhibitions: Gabor Peterdi Prints; International Photo Competi-
tion; Sculptural Invitational; Nigerian Art; Felix Bracquemond;
William Kurelek; M.S.U. Faculty; plus several student, faculty and
alumni exhibitions.
Activities: Lectures open to public; 2 or 3 visiting lecturers per
year.
Attendance: 13,000 per academic year.

✠GRAND RAPIDS ART MUSEUM
230 East Fulton, 49502. Tel: (616) 459-4676
Fred A. Myers, Dir.
Free 10 AM - 5 PM; Sun. 2 - 5 PM. Estab. 1910, inc. 1913; owns
building. Ann. meeting May; mem, contributors.
Collections: Permanent collections include early and contemporary American; German Expressionists; early and contemporary
French; Italian Renaissance; early and contemporary English art.
Activities: Lectures; gallery tours; Saturday Creative Art
classes for 1-12 grades; University of Michigan Art Extension
classes for adults; special art lectures and films; school talks for
grades 3-12.

Library: Art reference library of 1300 volumes.
Income & Purchases: Imcome $175,000; purchases and gifts
$10,000.
Attendance: 65,000.

GRAND RAPIDS PUBLIC LIBRARY
60 Library Plaza, N.E, 49502. Tel: (616) 456-4400
Alberta Massingill, Dir.
Free Mon. - Thurs. 8:30 AM - 9 PM; Fri. & Sat. 8:30 AM - 5:30
PM; Sun. 2 - 5 PM, except July & Aug. Estab. 1871. Over 15,000
books on art, including furniture and landscape architecture.
Income and Purchases: Income $1,302,702; annual purchases
of books $110,000.
Books Circulated: 899,100.

HARTLAND

HARTLAND ART COUNCIL
P.O. Box 127, 48029. Tel: (313) 632-5200
William P. Nelson, Pres.
Bruce Sdunek, V.Pres.
Helen J. Nelson, Secy.
Sandra Scherba, Treas.
Estab. 1967 to promote arts in Hartland community; financed by
membership. Gallery space in local library and Hartland High School
Media Center. Mem. 50; dues $3 - $100.
Collections: Approximately 50 works - paintings, sculptures and
photos. Collection enlarged each year through purchased awards
from Hartland Art Show, funds donated by community and Hartland
Foundation.
Exhibitions: Annual Art Show.
Activities: Extension Department material available to Michigan
art councils and schools for a $25 fee; traveling exhibitions orga-
nized and circulated; 200 Kodachromes and commentaries on winning works of art in Hartland art shows in Lending collection; photograph collection of 20 prints; lectures open to public; concerts,
dramatic programs, competitions; scholarships.
Income and Purchases: Income $3000 - $4000; purchases $1500 -
$2000.
Attendance at Annual Art Show: 2000.

JACKSON

ELLA SHARP MUSEUM*
3225 Fourth St, 49203. Tel: (517) 787-2320
James D. Marler, Dir.
Lynn Loftis, Cur. Historical Educ.
Cynthia Gaetzi, Cur. Art Educ.
Open Tues. - Fri. 10 AM - 5 PM; Sat. and Sun. 1:30 - 5 PM; admis.
to Sharp Home, Hillside, 25¢. Estab. 1965 to serve the people of
Jackson and to provide a place for cultural education in the com-
munity; supported by endowment and membership. A temporary
gallery where a variety of exhibits are held; large and small gallery. Ann. meeting May; mem. 1000; dues, $1, $5, $10, $25, $50
and $100.
Collections: Clothing and accessories from 1840-1940; furniture from several periods during Victorian period; china; porcelain; coverlets and quilts; †oil paintings; †prints.
Exhibitions: Egypt; Influence of the Flower; Contemporary
Graphics; Furniture.
Activities: Traveling exhibitions organized and circulated; objects of art lent to schools, kits of museum artifacts; photograph
collection for lending and reference; lectures open to the public,
seven visiting lecturers per year; four gallery talks, three tours;
concerts, dramatic programs; classes for adults and children;
competitions, scholarships. Book Shop.
Library: 250 volumes for lending and reference; 2000 photographs.
Publications: Newsletter, quarterly; annual report; research
material as requested.
Income and Purchases: Income $78,000; purchases $2000.
Attendance: 10,000 annual average.

KALAMAZOO

GENEVIEVE AND DONALD GILMORE ART CENTER
Kalamazoo Institute of Arts
314 S. Park St, 49006. Tel: (616) 349-7775
Harry Greaver, Dir. of Art Center.
Mrs. Logan Weaver, Business Mgr.
Kirk Newman, Assoc. Dir. for Educ.
Free winter hours, Tues. - Fri. 11 AM - 4:30 PM; Sat. 9 AM - 4 PM;
Sun. 1:30 - 4:30 PM; cl. Mon. Summer hours (July 4 - Labor Day),
Tues. - Sat. 10 AM - 4 PM. Cl. all major holidays and last two weeks
of Aug. Inc. 1924 to further interest in the arts, especially the visual
arts; new building 1961. Ann, meeting June; mem. 4200; dues $10 and
higher.

Collections: †20th Century American Art, †sculpture, †art on paper - drawings, watercolors, graphics and photographs

Exhibitions: Temporary exhibit program covers all aspects of visual arts; Kalamazoo Area Show; Art Fair first Sat. in June.

Activities: Traveling exhibits to area schools; general art lectures by staff; 5 visiting lecturers per year; gallery tours; film program; June workshops; non-credit studio classes in art for adults and children; teaching staff of 20, mostly part-time. (See Schools.)

Library: 4500 volumes; 7000 slides; 60 current art periodicals.

Income and Purchases: Income $350,000.

Attendance: 75,000.

LANSING

MICHIGAN STATE LIBRARY
735 E. Michigan Ave, 48933. Tel: (517) 373-1580
Francis X. Scannell, State Librn.
Open Mon. - Fri. 8 AM - 5:30 PM; Sat. 9 AM - 1 PM Oct. - May; cl. Sun.

Art Department estab. 1900. Over 4000 large, unframed pictures covering architecture, sculpture, graphic arts and painting, for exhibition by schools, clubs, churches, etc. Also 1343 posters, 120,000 smaller pictures. Good collection of art books and bound magazines.

Purchases: Annual purchases, $5000.

MIDLAND

✤MIDLAND ART COUNCIL
The Midland Center for the Arts
1801 W. St. Andrews Dr, 48640.
Carol B. Coppage, Coordinator
Exhibitions open to public daily including weekends, 1 - 5 PM; Thurs. 7 - 9 PM. Estab. 1956 to foster the understanding and enjoyment of art through exhibitions of recognized works of art; through films and demonstrations, classes in appreciation, history and techniques; and to maintain a fully-equipped workshop for practicing artists. Ann. meeting Mar; mem. 425; dues $6 and higher; for use of workshop $60 individual per year.

Activities: As above, plus slide-lectures, gallery talks; art auctions, flea markets, holiday sales, other special sales; classes open to public in ceramics, painting, weaving, photography, metalsmithing and children's art.

Exhibitions: (1975) Bill Adair's paintings of wildlife; Dr. James Kane's collection of antique duck decoys; Midland Camera Club Photography; Delta College Faculty Exhibition; Mary Beard's paintings; Bracquemond Etchings; Holiday Invitational Sale; Indian Jewelry Sale; Dow Corning Christmas Card Display; Mid-Michigan Exhibition; Rose Traines and Virginia Seitz, paintings and sculptures; Public School Art Show; Bicentennial Exhibition: Mary Cassatt and Edgar Degas Exhibition with Battle Creek paintings, drawings and sculptures; Capitol City Traveling Exhibition; Studio Art Exhibition; Eras and Epochs, Bicentennial Exhibition with Historical Society; Annual Outdoor Art Fair.

Publications: Newsletter for mem. (monthly).

Attendance: Over 12,000 at all exhibitions.

MONROE

MONROE CITY-COUNTY FINE ARTS COUNCIL
1555 S. Raisinville Rd, 48161. Tel: (313) 242-7300
Robert P. Merkel, Pres.
Bernice Iott, V.Pres.
Hugh Baker, Secy.
Elsie Little, Treas.
Estab. 1967 to promote greater understanding and appreciation of the arts for citizens of Monroe County, Michigan; financed by city and state appropriations and membership. Mem. 40; dues $2.

Activities: Art exhibits; Literature Club; music compositions commissioned; historical architecture awards; art and dance scholarships, music grants.

Publications: Music in Monroe County (in progress).

MOUNT CLEMENS

THE ART CENTER
One Grand Ave, 48043. Tel. (313) 469-8666
Roy E. Calcagno, Pres.
Marjorie U. DeFrancis, Exec. Secy.
Gallery hours Tues. - Sun. 1 - 4 PM; cl. Mon. Estab. May 10, 1970, to promote interest in fine arts, to introduce art of good quality for display and to encourage and guide people to self expression in the arts; supported by mem. Corporation was organized, money raised to renovate former Carnegie Library building owned by City; City also donated funds, has agreed to pay utilities. Detroit Institute of Art has helped by loans of fine exhibits and training of volunteers. Ann. meeting June; mem. 200; dues student $5, individual $10, family $15, etc.

Exhibitions since May 1970: Mother and Child, Cross-Currents U S A, Museum Director's Choice, Call It Calif, Michigan Annual.

Activities: Lectures open to public; tours; classes for adults and children; ethnic night festivities; scholarships. Rental and Sales Gallery. Gift Shop of hand crafts.

MUSKEGON

✤HACKLEY ART MUSEUM
296 W. Webster Ave, 49440. Tel: (616) 722-6954
Shirley Howarth, Dir.
Ann Archambault, Asst. to Dir.
Margaret Bobian, Receptionist
Dr. Robert Boelkins, Chmn. of Board of Trustees
Free daily 9 AM - 5 PM; Sun. 2 - 5 PM; cl. national holidays. Estab. 1911; Trustees are Board of Education; building contains 7 galleries, sculpture court, auditorium and studio.

Collections: American and European paintings representing 450 years; sculpture, drawings, prints, manuscripts, early printed pages, Persian miniatures, decorative arts and the L. C. Walker Collection of Old Master etchings, drypoints, engravings, etc; Japanese prints.

Exhibitions: Annual Regional Exhibition, traveling exhibitions and other changing exhibitions each month.

Activities: Picture Rental Service; lectures; slide programs; films; art classes for children and adults; Friends of Art weekly meetings.

Income and Purchases: Income $80,000; purchases and gifts $100,000.

Attendance: 50,000.

Friends of Art
Inc. 1921 to cooperate with Hackley Art Museum; study class on Wed. from Oct. to April. Ann. meeting April; mem. 200.

OLIVET

ARMSTRONG MUSEUM OF ART AND ARCHAEOLOGY
Olivet College, 49076. Tel: (616) 749-7000
William Whitney, Dir.
Estab. 1960 to collect artifacts and display for educational purposes.

Collections: †Modern American Prints; Mesopotamian Artifacts; Thailand Artifacts; Philippine Artifacts; two Barlach, two Klee and other items.

Exhibitions: 6 invitational shows; 6 one-man shows; 5 student shows; 2 traveling shows.

Library: (Olivet College) 70,000 volumes for reference and lending; 350 prints for reference only.

Purchases: Approx. $1000.

Attendance; 1200 per yr.

PONTIAC

PONTIAC CREATIVE ARTS CENTER, INC.
47 Williams St, 48053. Tel: (313) 333-7849
Frederick Poole, Pres.
Yolanda Flores, Secy.
Ian R. Lyons, Exec. Dir.
Free Mon. - Fri. 10 AM - 4 PM. Estab. 1968, to educate and uplift minority and culturally deprived people through the exposure of art; financed by endowment, city and state appropriation and mem. Gallery. Ann. meeting March; mem. 400; dues $5, $10, $100, $500.

Activities: Educational department; lectures open to the public; 4 visiting lecturers and gallery talks per year; dramatic programs; classes for adults and children; competitions; many exhibitions; scholarships.

Publications: Educational schedules.

Income: $84,000.

PORT HURON

MUSEUM OF ARTS AND HISTORY*
1115 Sixth St, 48060. Tel: (313) 982-0891
Mrs. Walter K. Brooks, Pres.
Dale Northrup, Art Chmn.
Free Wed. - Sun. 1 - 4:30 PM. Estab. 1968 to preserve area historical and marine artifacts and to provide a cultural center for the community; maintained by appropriation and mem. Two galleries feature loaned exhibitions, changed each month. Meetings third Tues. in Oct, third Tues. in Feb; mem. 513 not incl. family; dues $5, $10, $25, $100.

Collections: Extensive rock collection, birds, lepidoptera; 19th century American furniture, farm implements; 19th century American paintings; Civil War and Thomas Edison artifacts; local newspapers from 1868.

Exhibitions: John Sloan etchings; area juried art show; Mother and Child in paintings; Vinnorma Shaw McKenzie retrospective;

prints from J.L. Hudson art galleries; Michigan on Canvas by Robert Thom; Cross Currents, U.S.A; Bronzes from D.I.A; Museum Director's Choice from D.I.A. and others.

Activities: Photograph collection, 150 prints for reference; lectures open to public, 6 visiting lecturers per year; classes for adults and children; competitions.

Publications: Newsletter, quarterly.
Annual Income: $13,000.
Attendance: Approx. 14,000.

ROCHESTER

MEADOW BROOK ART GALLERY
Oakland University, 48063. Tel: (313) 377-3005
Kiichi Usui, Cur.
Free Tues. - Fri. 1 - 5 PM; Sat. - Sun. 2 - 6:30 PM; evening hours in conjunction with the Meadow Brook Theater performances, 7:30 - 8:30 PM. Estab. 1962 to provide a series of changing exhibitions and to develop a collection of art as a cultural force for the students and the university community. In 1972 the name was changed from the University Art Gallery, and joined the Office of Cultural Affairs with the Meadow Brook Music Festival and Theater to enhance Oakland University's cultural contributions to serve a greater community. Mem. Meadow Brook Gallery Assoc. dues $20, student $1.

Collections: Approx. 300 pieces of art of Africa, Oceania and pre-Columbia Americas, donated by former Governor of Michigan, G. Mennen Williams, Mr. and Mrs. Ernst Anspach of New York and other individuals; also contemporary European and American paintings and graphics.

Exhibitions: Changing exhibitions with emphasis on contemporary art, oriental art and art of Preliterate Peoples (Africa, Oceana, pre-Columbia). Recent exhibitions include: A Point of View (contemporary art from the collection of Richard Brown Baker), Personal Preference (paintings and sculptures from Mr. and Mrs. S. Brooks Barron), Art of the Decade, 1960-1970, American Realism Post-Pop, Chinese Fan Painting of Ming and Ching, and Japanese Ink Painting of the Edo Period; Minoru Yamasaki: A Retrospective.

Activities: Lectures, film and slide presentations, music; dance performances in relation to art exhibitions sponsored in collaboration with other academic departments and the Office of Cultural Affairs of the University.

Library: University Library.
Publications: Exhibition catalogs.
Income and Purchases: Yearly budget approx. $15,000.
Attendance: 25,000.

SAGINAW

SAGINAW ART MUSEUM
1126 N. Michigan Ave, 48602. Tel: (517) 754-2491, 2492
James K. Chase, Dir.
Henry S. Smith, Pres. of Board
Free Tues. - Sat. 10 AM - 5 PM; Sun. 1 - 5 PM; cl. Mon. Estab. 1947. Ann. meeting May; mem. 800; dues $15 and higher.

Collections: †Oils and †watercolors, †prints; Rogers Groups.
Exhibitions: Special exhibitions during year; annual area exhibition; children's exhibitions.

Activities: Art lending service; lectures; art school, workshops, children's educational program; puppet festival. Gift Shop.

Library: †Art reference library, new publications.
Publications: Monthly Bulletin.
Income: $150,000.
Attendance: 50,000.

TRAVERSE CITY

MARK OSTERLIN LIBRARY
Northwestern Michigan College, 49684. Tel: (616) 946-5650
Bernard C. Rink, Librn.
Free daily 8 AM - 5 PM; summers 9:30 AM - 4:30 PM. Estab. 1960; financed by city and state appropriation. One area in lobby as gallery.

Collections: †Eskimo Art from Canadian Arctic; rest of collection spans the continuum from prints to egg tempera on Masonite.

Exhibitions: Annual Eskimo Print and Sculpture Show in August.
Library: 2000 volume library; 1000 volumes of special Italian Renaissance art history.
Income and Purchases: Income $3500; purchases $1000.

MINNESOTA

DULUTH

THE TWEED MUSEUM OF ART
University of Minnesota, Duluth, 55812.
William G. Boyce, Dir.
Robin Poynor, Cur.

Larry Gruenwald, Technician
Free daily 8 AM - 4:30 PM; Sat. & Sun. 2 - 5 PM. Estab. 1950, new gallery occupied 1958, to serve both the University and community as a center for exhibition of works of art and related activities; Alice Tweed Tuohy wing completed in 1965 to house the permanent collection. Subscriber's fees $5 to $10.

Collections: George P. Tweed Memorial Art Collection of approx. 500 paintings with emphasis on Barbizon School. Jonathan Sax Collection of Contemporary Prints.

Exhibitions: Approx. 15 major exhibitions a year with additional supplementary exhibitions. Major retrospective exhibition given to a guest artist once a year. Other exhibitions: Third Biennial Lake Superior International Craft Exhibition, Swedish Design Today, Duluth: A Painterly Essay, Paintings by Francis Chapin, Drawings U S A, American Watercolor Society

Activities: Gallery talks and tours; members previews; exhibition and sale of student art; gallery practice courses for University students; biweekly art program for children in cooperation with public schools and the Friends of Tweed Museum. Alice Tweed Tuohy purchase awards for student art. Groups from schools, civic organizations, convention delegates and others, visited the gallery during the last year.

MANKATO

✤LINCOLN ART GALLERY*
207 Lincoln Hall, Box 42, Mankato State College, 56001.
Tel: (507) 389-6413
Donald R. Byrum, Dir. & Cur. of Art Collections
Harlan H. Bloomer, Designer of Publications
Open weekdays 8 AM - 5 PM; Tues. evenings 7 - 9 PM; no admis. Estab. 1960 to promote the visual arts throughout the college and town community and southern Minnesota; financed by city and state appropriations.

Collections: American bookplates; †prints; †contemporary prints, drawings, paintings, sculpture, photographs, and crafts; †extensive collection of student art works in all media.

Exhibitions: Graphics by modern masters; six Belgian photographers; artists of the western frontier; recent British prints; California national watercolors; Peter Milton etchings; drawings by Leonard Baskin; war-game: Jacques Callot and Stefano Della Bella; AFA: Museum purchase fund collection; MMA: Drawings USA; Josef Albers prints.

Activities: In cooperation with Mankato State College conducts art courses by demand relating to exhibiting, collecting and art history; extension department serves southern Minnesota and art centers in north central America and on demand; material available to any art center, school or organization; fees, to $75 monthly plus shipping; traveling exhibitions organized and circulated; individual paintings and original objects of art lent; photograph collection of 200 prints for lending and reference; junior school with art department of college; lectures open to the public; 2 visiting lecturers per year; gallery talks and tours on demand.

Publications: Annual report from the director.
Income and Purchases: Income $7500; purchases $3000.

MINNEAPOLIS

AMERICAN SWEDISH INSTITUTE
2600 Park Ave, 55407. Tel: (612) 871-4907
Leonard F. Ramberg, Pres.
Dr. Wesley M. Westerberg, Dir.
Open Tues. - Sat. 1 - 4 PM; Sun. 1 - 5 PM; cl. Mon; nominal admis. fee. Estab. and inc. 1929. Building donated by Swan J. Turnblad and contains in a home setting a fine collection of Swedish artifacts plus many items of general cultural interest pertaining to Scandinavia. The Grand Hall, paneled in African mahogany, is considered the finest installation on this continent. Throughout the gallery there are eleven porcelain tile fireplaces: nine of Swedish and two of German design. Dues: regular (single) $10, regular (husband and wife) $15, sustaining (husband, wife and all children under age 21, living at home) $25, supporting $50, patron $100, life $1000, student (boy or girl, attending school, below the age of 21) $5, non-resident (single, or husband and wife outside a fifty mile radius of Twin Cities) $10.

Collections: Paintings, sculpture, tapestries, ceramics, china, glass, pioneer items and textiles.

Activities: Special exhibitions, lectures, concerts, films, classes in Swedish and Swedish folk dancing; summer language camp. Gift shop. Book store.

Publications: Happenings (monthly newsletter).
Attendance: Approx. 50,000.

COFFMAN UNION GALLERY
University of Minnesota, 55455. Tel: (612) 373-7604
Roselyn Rezac, Coordinator
Elaine Ward, Chairperson

Marlene Vernon, Advisor
Free 10 AM - 5 PM. Estab. Jan. 1976 for use to campus and local
artists. Financed by student fees.
Activities: Films, lectures, demonstrations.

METROPOLITAN CULTURAL ARTS CENTER
1530 Russell Ave, N, 55411. Tel: (612) 522-4111
Robert H. Samples, Board Chmn.
Patricia Samples, Exec Dir.
Open 9 AM - 10 PM. Estab. 1967 to offer training in the arts to
people who could not afford it otherwise and to bring people of dif-
ferent cultural backgrounds together to experience the arts; main-
tained by membership and contributions for social and civic groups.
Ann. meeting 3rd Mon. in Sept; mem. 106; dues $10.
Activities: Training in theatre, dance, music, writing, art;
classes for adults and children; dramatic programs.
Publications: MCAC newsletter, monthly.
Annual Income: $50,000.
Attendance: 400.
Shoestring Playhouse
2639 Thomas Ave. N, 55411.
Northeast Workshop
670 N.E. Broadway, 55413.

✠MINNEAPOLIS INSTITUTE OF ARTS*
Minneapolis Society of Fine Arts
201 E. 24th St, 55404. Tel: (612) 339-7661
Samuel Sachs II, Dir.
Orrel E. Thompson, Assoc. Dir. & Dir. of Educ.
Arnold Jolles, Conservator
Merribell Parsons, Cur. Decorative Arts.
John Ittmann, Cur. Prints & Drawings
JoAnn Reedquist, Coordinator Exhibitions
Carroll T. Hartwell, Cur. Photography
Harold Peterson, Librn.
Free Tues. 10 AM - 10 PM; Wed. - Sat. 10 AM - 5 PM; Sun. &
holidays 1 - 5 PM; cl. Mon. Founded in 1883. The Minneapolis So-
ciety of Fine Arts was established to maintain museums, galleries
and libraries, including The Minneapolis Institute of Arts, to acquire
books and manuscripts, and objects of fine and industrial arts, and to
provide lectures, instruction and entertainment in furtherance of the
general purposes of the Society. Ann. meeting Oct; mem. 5291; dues
individual $15, family $25, differing rates for students, educators
and non-residents.
Collections: The Institute's excellent and comprehensive collections present distinguished examples of world art. Among major
holdings are the celebrated Pillsbury collection of Chinese bronzes;
the collection of Chinese jewelry, jades, textiles and ceramics; the
Pre-Columbian collections; †the collections of British silver and
American decorative arts; †the print collection; †and the distinguished collections of European decorative arts, including a celebrated collection of tapestries and European and American paintings
and sculpture; masterpieces of Fra Angelico, Nardo di Cione, Titian,
El Greco, Poussin, Rubens, Rembrandt, Guercino, Chardin, Prud'hon,
Goya, as well as superb examples of European and American paintings
of the 19th and 20th centuries.
Exhibitions: 1970-73 exhibitions included Richard Avedon; Painting in Italy in the 18th Century: Rococo to Romanticism; Art Deco;
Dutch Masterpieces from the 18th Century: Painting and Drawing
1700-1800; The J. Paul Getty Collection; American Indian Art: Form
and Tradition, Fakes and Forgeries and Other Deceptions.
Activities: Tours and lectures; concerts; films, classes; seminars
and workshops for adults and children; the Museum Shop; Artmobile
and Inner City Mobile Gallery; Arts Opportunity Program.
Library: Reference library of 20,000 volumes with large photographic and reproduction holdings.
Publications: Annual Bulletin; monthly Calendar; catalogues; picture books, postcards; note cards; gallery guides.
Attendance: 450,000 annually.

The Friends of the Institute
Mrs. Charles V. Krogness, Pres.
Estab. in 1922 to broaden the influence of the Institute throughout the community. Ann. meeting May; mem. 1500 women members
of The Minneapolis Society of Fine Arts. Sponsors the Volunteer
Docent Program, the Museum Shop, the Visitors' Center, special
lectures, publications, improvement projects and other supportive
programs.

MINNEAPOLIS PUBLIC LIBRARY
300 Nicollet Mall, 55401. Library Tel: (612) 372-6500
Joseph Kimbrough, Dir.
Mary L. Dyar, Assoc. Dir.
Muriel A. Wogsland, Admin. Clerk

Marlea R. Warren, Head, Art/Music/Films Dept.
Free Mon. - Thurs. 9 AM - 9 PM; Fri. & Sat. 9 AM - 5:30 PM.
Library estab. 1889. Art Department contains about †32,000
books, exhibition catalogs and bound periodicals on fine arts; over
1,000,000 small mounted pictures and clippings for circulation.
Income and Purchases: Income of entire library is over
$5,200,000; current art purchase budget, books $16,160; periodicals
$2700, continuations $2575.

MINNESOTA ARTISTS ASSOCIATION
c/o Al Olson, Pres, 1012 Marquette Ave, 55403.
Tel: (612) 335-4781
Tom Hessel, V.Pres.
Yvonne Duda, Secy.
Mary Shoquist, Treas.
Chartered 1937, to make the citizens of Minnesota more aware of
the role art plays in their lives and to promote the welfare of
Minnesota Artists. Ann. election May; monthly meetings Sept. -
May; mem. 180; dues assoc. $10, active $10.
Exhibitions: Exhibitions of members work in rotating shows;
annual juried shows for members.
Archives: Archives, biographical file, photographic file of
members' works; volume of Bulletins on file at Minneapolis Public
Library.
Publications: Monthly newsletters (Sept. - May); current mem-
bership rosters.

MINNESOTA STATE ART SOCIETY*
Kilbride Art Gallery, 3208 Hennepin Ave, 55408.
Tel: (612) 825-3434
Robert Kilbride, Pres.
Estab. 1903 to promote and encourage the fine arts in Minnesota.
11 Board members appointed for four year terms by the Governor of
the State.

UNIVERSITY GALLERY
University of Minnesota
Northrop Memorial Auditorium, 55455. Tel: (612) 373-3424, 3425
Barbara J. Shissler, Dir. (on leave)
Lyndel King, Acting Dir.
Charles P. Helsell, Cur.
Susan Brown, Cur.
Linda M. Djerf, Registrar
Free Mon. - Fri. 11 AM - 4 PM; Sun. 2 - 5 PM; cl. Sat. and holidays.
Estab. 1933. The program of the University Gallery is planned to
provide for the all-University function of meeting the broad ob-
jectives of an all-University art museum, and for the in-service
function of meeting the specific teaching and research needs of the
Art History Department of the University of Minnesota.
Collections: The permanent collection of the University Gallery
is largely devoted to †paintings, †drawings and †prints by American
artists working in the first half of the twentieth century, and contains
notable works by Avery, Dove, Feininger, MacDonald-Wright, Marin
and O'Keeffe. A sculpture collection of major works by contemporary artists includes sculpture by Baizerman, Bertoia, Richier,
David Smith and others. A developing print collection includes
works by artists of all schools and periods. Collections on extended loan from Ione and Hudson Walker and Mrs. B. J. O. Nordfeldt include major holdings in Hartley, Maurer and Nordfeldt.
Exhibitions: The University Gallery stresses a program of frequently changing major loan exhibitions, held concurrently with
smaller exhibitions organized for specific teaching purposes, or of
the permanent collections. Exhibitions organized by the University
Gallery during 1974-75 included: Works by John Rood: A Memorial
Exhibition, the Art and Mind of Victorian England; Printings from
the Forbes Magazine Collection; Richard Serrin: Portrait of the
Artist as an Old Master; Inhabitants of the Enchanted Isle: French
Pleasure Gardens in the Age of Grandeur; Studio Arts Faculty
Exhibition.
Activities: Two lending programs are provided for University of
Minnesota students, faculty and staff: Office Loan Collection of
framed paintings and prints for staff offices; Student Rental Collec-
tion of framed prints for student homes.
Attendance: Approx. 50,000.

UNIVERSITY OF MINNESOTA ART LIBRARY
12 Walter Library, 55455. Tel: (612) 373-2875
Herbert Scherer, Librn.
Roxanne Markoff, Library Asst.
Open Mon. - Thurs. 8 AM - 9 PM; Fri. 8 AM - 5 PM; Sat. & Sun.
1 - 5 PM; Summer hours 8 AM - 4:30 PM weekdays. Estab. 1950
to serve the art research needs of the students and faculty of the
University; the public is served through statewide interlibrary lending and the public is welcome to use materials in the Art Library; fi-

nanced by city and state appropriation and membership. Friends of the Art Library meet fall, winter and spring; mem. 125; dues $10 regular, $25 and up, patron.

Collections: Collection covers the fine arts: painting, sculpture, architecture and photography. Particular strengths are: Scandinavian Art, Baroque Art and American Art. Special feature is the art exhibition catalog collection of over 4000 items, fully cataloged and accessible to patrons.

Library: Lending and reference collection of 49,703 volumes.

Annual Purchases: Books and periodicals $25,676.

✤WALKER ART CENTER
Vineland Place, 55403. Tel: (612) 377-7500
Thomas M. Crosby, Jr, Pres.
Roger L. Hale, V.Pres.
Mrs. James K. Wittenberg, V.Pres.
Martin Friedman, Dir, Secy. Board of Dir.
Donald C. Borrman, Adminr, Treas. Board of Dir.
Dean Swanson, Chief Cur.
Philip Larson, Cur.
Mildred Friedman, Coordinator, Design; Editor, Design Quarterly
Carolyn DeCato, Registrar
James E. Johnson, Graphic Designer
Suzanne Weil, Coordinator, Performing Arts
Melinda Ward, Coordinator, Film
Mary Hooper, Coordinator, Public Information
Eric Sutherland, Photographer
Miriam Swenson, Office Mgr.
Joan Benson, Admin. Secy.
Geraldine Owens, Library Asst.
Kathy Mack, Mgr, Center Book Shop
Museum open summer: Tues. - Sat. 10 AM - 8 PM (after 5 PM special exhibition galleries only); Sun. noon - 6 PM; winter: Tues. & Thurs. 10 AM - 8 PM; Wed. - Sat. 10 AM - 5 PM; Sun. noon - 6 PM; cl. Mon, national holidays. Office hours Mon. - Fri. 9 AM - 5 PM. Walker Art Center estab. 1879 by T. B. Walker, reorganized 1939 as Walker Art Center, inc. 1946; building erected 1927; new museum building opened May 15, 1971. Emphasis on contemporary art in temporary exhibitions and permanent collection. Supported by T. B. Walker Foundation and membership. Ann. meeting May; mem. 4000; dues $20, educational and senior citizen $12.50, sponsor $100, donor $500, patron $1000.

Collections: Oriental jade collection; 19th century American paintings by Frederic E. Church, Thomas Cole, Asher B. Durand, James Hamilton, Albert P. Ryder, Worthington Whittredge; 20th century paintings, sculptures and graphics including works by Josef Albers, Carl Andre, Alexander Archipenko, George Ault, William Baziotes, Larry Bell, Rudolf Belling, Charles Biederman, Lee Bontecou, Alexander Calder, Anthony Caro, Chryssa, Ralston Crawford, Stuart Davis, Raymond Duchamp-Villon, Dan Flavin, Lyonel Feininger, William Glackens, Adolph Gottlieb, Robert Grosvenor, Marsden Hartley, Hans Hofmann, Robert Indiana, Robert Irwin, Donald Judd, Craig Kaufmann, Ellsworth Kelly, Nicolas Kruschenick, Jacques Lipchitz, Morris Louis, Giacomo Manzu, Franz Marc, Conrad Marca-Relli, Marino Marini, Alfred H. Maurer, Joan Miro, Henry Moore, Robert Morris, Robert Murray, Louise Nevelson, Isamu Noguchi, Kenneth Noland, Georgia O'Keeffe, Claes Oldenburg, Jules Olitski, Robert Rauschenberg, Theodore Roszak, Lucas Samaras, George Segal, Ben Shahn, Charles Sheeler, John Sloan, David Smith, Richard Smith, Tony Smith, Frank Stella, Nicolas de Stael, Niles Spencer, Clifford Still, George Sugarman, Mark di Suvero, Ernest Trova, Andy Warhol.

Exhibitions: (July 1973 to present) Sottsass/Superstudio: Mindscapes**; Printmakers: Midwest Invitational**; Photographers: Midwest Invitational**; c. 7500; Novelson: Wood Sculptures**, Diane Arbus; New Learning Spaces and Places**; Willem de Kooning: Drawings/Sculptures**; Ellsworth Kelly: Paintings/Sculptures/ Drawings; Invitation 1974**; James Nutt; Alberto Giacometti: A Retrospective; Eight Artists: Prints from Gemini G.E.L**; Projected Images**; Naives and Visionaries**; Robert Israel/Design for Opera**; Selections from the Martha Jackson Collection**; Oldenburg: Six Themes**; Akagawa/Byrne/Kahn/Leicester**; Americans in Florence: Europeans in Florence; Gaston Lachaise: Sculpture and Drawings; Axelrod, Bjorklund, Herdegen, Sorman**; Greene and Greene; Anthony Caro; and other group and one-man exhibitions of paintings, sculpture, prints, drawings, design and photography. (Exhibitions marked ** originated by Walker Art Center)

Publications: Exhibition catalogs; Design Quarterly; Calendar of Events (11 issues a year); brochures, announcements and checklists.

Library: Reference collection of 2000 volumes, 30,000 catalogs, 12 vertical files, 80 periodical subscriptions, slides and small collection of primary materials including tapes and correspondence. Program emphasis is contemporary art, design and architecture.

Attendance: (1974) 454,632.

O'ROURKE ART GALLERY MUSEUM AND ROURKE GALLERY
523 S. Fourth St, 56560. Tel: (218) 233-7137
James O'Rourke, Pres. & Dir.
Aldrich C. Bloomquist, V.Pres.
Dr. John D. Wahl, Secy.
Free Wed. - Sun. Noon - 5 PM; cl. Mon. & Tues. Estab. 1960 to foster and promote a knowledge and love of art in our community and to provide a repository for the artistic heritage of this area, to operate and maintain an art gallery and museum, to promote the extension and improvement of education in the arts, to provide facilities for the exhibition and conservation of the art in this area, both of the past and the present; financed by membership Ann. meeting June 18; mem. 510; dues $10 - $1000.

Collections: †North American Indian Art; †West African Art; †Pre-Columbian Mexican Art; Oriental Art; Persian Manuscripts and Pottery; †19th and 20th Century Graphic Art; †20th Century Painting and Sculpture; 19th Century Decorative Art.

Exhibitions: West African Sculpture; Eskimo Art; Perian 800 BC to 1900 AD; North American Indian Art (pre 1900); Western Mexico Sculpture; Jean Dubuffet Prints; Marc Chagall Lithographs; Leonard Baskin Sculpture and Graphic Art; Robert A. Nelson Paintings and Sculpture; and 26 others mostly of regional artists.

Activities: Extension Department serves Western Minnesota and North Dakota; material available to colleges, schools, art centers and galleries; fees; material lent, paintings, sculpture, prints, drawing, photographs, Indian, African and Persian art; traveling exhibitions organized and circulated; individual paintings and original objects of art lent; lending collection, 250 photographs for lending and reference, 3800 original art; 1000 items lent in average year; 12 active borrowers; lectures open to the public; 4 visiting lecturers and gallery talks per year; 30 tours; concerts; classes for adults and children; museum intern program. Book shop.

Library: Reference collection of 5000 volumes, 1200 print photograph collection and 3800 pieces in slide collection.

Publications: Slaytons Pictorial, monthly.

Income and Purchases: Income $60,000; purchases $8000.

Attendance: 15,200.

OWATONNA ART CENTER
P.O. Box 134, 55060. Tel: (507) 451-9990
Mary E. Leach, Pres.
Beatrice Spencer, Secy.
Open daily except Mon, 2 - 5 PM; gallery open 3 wks, cl. 2; admis. varies with shows. Inc. July, 1974; gallery opened May 3, 1975; to preserve works of local professional artists; to provide display of various collections, exhibits and competitive shows; to provide classes in the arts and to promote performing arts; financed by membership and donations. Ann. meeting 1st Tues. in Oct; mem. 340; dues individual $5, student $3, family $10, patron $50.

Collections: Collection of works by local professional artists; world costume collection.

Exhibitions: (1975-76) Steele County Show; Assimilation Japan; Americana - Quilts and Paintings Prior to 1914; Phil Barrager Serigraphs; Lynette Schmidt, one-woman show; Marianne Young World Costume Collection.

Activities: World costume collection organized and circulated; concerts; classes for adults and children; competitions.

Library: 60 volume reference library for members only; periodicals for reference.

Publications: Newsletter, monthly or bimonthly, depending on time of year.

Income and Purchases: Income $17,301; purchases $13,396.

Attendance: Approx. 5000.

ROCHESTER ART CENTER*
320 E. Center St, Mayo Park, 55901. Tel: (507) 282-8629
Thomas R. Toperzer, Dir.
Free daily 10 AM - 4 PM; Sun. 1 - 5 PM; cl. Mon. and all special holidays. Inc. 1946 as a non-profit organization. Ann. meeting Nov; mem. 800; dues $7.50 and higher.

Exhibitions: Annual Area Art Show with awards totaling $275 annually.

Activities: Lectures, classes, programs, tours; six visiting lecturers per year; six or eight gallery talks; lending services; scholarships and fellowships; annual high school student awards.

Library: 500 volumes for art reference.

Budget: $75,000 (two buildings).

Attendance: 30,000 annually.

ST CLOUD

ST. CLOUD STATE UNIVERSITY
Atwood Center, 56301. Tel: (612) 255-2202
Patricia A. Krueger, Prog. Dir.
Free daily 8 AM - 11 PM. Atwood Center estab. 1966; exhibit and feature art program for college campus, gallery lounge in college union; extracurricular in nature with student committees selecting schedule; supported by student activity fee.
Collection: Only a few permanent pieces as part of general decorum.
Activities: Lectures open to the public; concerts; dramatic programs; competitions; films; art and craft sales and demonstrations; exhibitions arranged by students. In music listening lounge there is a collection of records for use by students on premises, private listening headsets.

ST. PAUL

HAMLINE UNIVERSITY GALLERIES
Dept of Art, 55104.
Dr. Frederick D. Leach, Gallery Dir. & Chmn, Dept. of Art
Free 9 AM - 4:30 PM; cl. Sat. & Sun. Estab. 1943 to display outstanding works of art in all media for instruction of and appreciation by the public and students; financed by the University.
Collections: Paintings, prints, drawings and sculpture.
Exhibitions: Continuous exhibitions; annual purchase award exhibits in painting and in graphic arts. (See Schools)
Library: Rental library of original modern works and reproductions. Extensive color slide library of paintings, architecture, sculpture, minor arts and graphics.

JAMES JEROME HILL REFERENCE LIBRARY
Fourth St. at Market, 55102. Tel: (612) 227-9531
Dr. Virgil F. Massman, Exec. Dir.
Mon. - Thurs. 9 AM - 9 PM; Fri. & Sat. 9 AM - 5:30 PM during school year; Summer 9 AM - 5:30 PM. Estab. 1921. 5000 volumes in art collection, 215,000 volumes in entire library.
Collections: Highlights are Original Seth Eastman watercolors, Albers, Josef, Interaction of Color, Audubon, John James, The Birds of America. Fairy Tales of the Brothers Grimm; Illustrations by Arthur Rackham, 1st edition, signed and numbered copy. Bodmer, Karl, 81 hand colored plates. Other major areas are architecture, Oriental art, North American Indian art, and the Masters with special emphasis on Rembrandt.
Exhibitions: Eastman Exhibit, 1972; CLIC Exhibits '72 and '74; Donovan Photography Show, 1973.

MINNESOTA HISTORICAL SOCIETY
Cedar & Central Ave, 55101. Tel: (612) 296-2747
Ronald Hubbs, Pres.
Russell W. Fridley, Dir.
Robert C. Wheeler, Assoc. Dir.
John J. Wood, Deputy Dir.
Donn Coddington, Field-Archaeology-Historic Sites Dir.
John Yust, Museum Cur.
Lucile Kane, Archivist
James D. Thueson, Librn.
Lila Johnson Goff, Head, AV Library
June D. Holmquist, Asst. Dir. for Publications
Kenneth A. Carley, Editor, Minnesota History
Judy Posely, Editor, Roots
Museum open Mon. - Fri. 8:30 AM - 5 PM; other depts. Mon. - Fri. 8:30 AM - 5 PM; Sat. Museum & Library 10 AM - 4:30 PM; Sun. Museum only 2 - 5 PM. Estab. 1849 to collect and preserve material relating to the history of Minnesota and to cultivate a knowledge of the development of the State; present building erected 1917. Ann. meeting Oct; mem. 6000; dues $10 and higher.
Collections: Over 50,000 paintings, photographs and prints; furniture; glass; a fine collection of Indian and pioneer objects.
Exhibitions: Exhibitions relate to history and development of Minnesota; changed regularly.
Activities: Historic tours; lectures; museum exhibits; guided building tours for school and adult groups. Maintains Mille Lacs Indian Museum; Fort Snelling; Charles A Lindbergh Home; General William G. LeDuc Home; Lower Sioux Agency; Alexander Ramsey House; Oliver H. Kelley Homestead; Connors' Fur Post; Grand Mound; Fort Ridgely; Jeffers Petroglyphs; State Capitol.
Library: Reference library of more than 300,000 volumes of Americana devoted principally to the Northwest, with special collections on genealogy, Civil War, Scandinavian elements in the U.S. The Society's collection of newspapers contains more than 25,000 bound volumes of Minnesota newspapers, beginning with the first paper published in the State. An extensive state project for the microfilming of the collection is under way. The Manuscript collection consists of over five million manuscripts on Minnesota and the Northwest.

Publications: Minnesota History, four times a year; Roots, three times a year for school classes of Minnesota history; educational bulletins; Newsletter, six times a year.
Income and Purchases: Annual income $3,500,000; purchases $100,000.
Attendance: 500,000 annually.

✠**MINNESOTA MUSEUM OF ART**

Permanent Collection Gallery
305 St. Peter St, 55102
Community Gallery
30 E. Tenth St, 55101. Tel: (612) 227-7613

Malcolm E. Lein, Pres. & Exec. Dir.
Laurene Tibbetts, Asst. to Exec. Dir.
Dr. Robert J. Poor, V.Pres, Plans & Programs; Cur. Asian Art
Ann Walton, Dir, Museum Div; Cur. Painting, Sculpture, Prints & Decorative Arts
Miriam B. Lein, Cur. Drawings & African Art
Patricia J. Heikenen, Dir, Prog, Publ & Pub. Relations
Betty S. Runyon, Dir, Visitor Services & Asst. Dir. Pub. Relations
Lola Plaisted, Dir, Development
Otto Theuer, Designer; Dir, Community Service Prog.
Mary Theuer, Dir. Operations & Registrar Temporary Exhibitions
Sandra Lipshultz, Registrar, Permanent Collection
Sam Scott Douglas, Exhibitions Dir.
Jan Swearer, Dir, Museum Educ.
Heidi Heffelfinger, Coordinator, Museum Educ.
Lucy McAllister, Dir, Arts Awareness
Leanne Klein, Librn.
Joseph Gianetti, Consultant, Photography Apprenticeship Prog.
Permanent Collection Gallery open day after Labor Day through Memorial Day, Tues. - Sat. 11 AM - 5 PM; day after Memorial Day to July 31, Tues. - Fri. 11 AM - 5 PM; cl. Aug; admis. 50¢ adults, 25¢ children. Community Gallery open Mon. - Wed. 9 AM - 5 PM; Thurs. - Sat. 9 AM - 9:30 PM; Sun. 1 - 9:30 PM; no admis charge. St. Paul Art Center incorporated as St. Paul Gallery and School of Art in 1927; until 1963, located in private mansion on Summit Ave, St. Paul; moved to new Arts and Science Center, 30 E. Tenth St. in 1964; name changed to Minnesota Museum of Art in 1969; Permanent Collection Gallery established in distinguished Art Deco building in 1972. Museum purpose is to act as trustee in preserving important works of art for the benefit of present and future generations, and to use its resources and collection actively as an educational force to enrich the community. Member agency of the St. Paul-Ramsey Arts and Science Council. Ann. meeting Sept; dues family $25, professional, student and nonresident $15.
Collections: †20th century drawings, sculpture, paintings and prints; contemporary †American, †African, and Northwest Coast Indian crafts; †Asian sculpture, †ceramics, †paintings, †prints, screens, drawings, textiles, and furniture; American and European lace.
Exhibitions: (1974) Legacy from the East**; John G. Flannagan - Sculpture/Drawings 1924-1938** sponsored jointly with Weyhe Gallery, New York; Encounter with Artists 12, Evelyn Raymond and Marjorie Kreilick**; Encounter with Artists 13, Minnesota Craftsmen**; Encounter with Artists 14, Private College Art Faculty Exhibition**; Encounter with Artists 15, Mary Barrett and Walter Nottingham**; Lace, Fans and Photographs**; Best 100**; Gunduz Golonu, Turkish Printmaker**; Encounter with Artists 16, Smith Park Craftsmen**; The Goldsmith** sponsored jointly with the Renwick Gallery of the National Collection of Fine Arts, Washington, D.C. with the cooperation of the Society of North American Goldsmiths; Greenland: Arctic Denmark sponsored jointly with the Science Museum of Minnesota; (1975) Jade as Sculpture; African Heritage**; Talent VI, Minnesota State College System**; Best 100**; Highlights from the Atlanta University Collection of Afro-American Art; Drawings USA, 75**; Contemporary Japanese Prints**; Leroy Neiman, Retrospective Exhibition**. (Exhibitions marked ** originated by Minnesota Museum of Art).
Activities: Education Department operates a Youth School in the Community Gallery; tours for St. Paul elementary school children, junior and high school students. Other tours for school children and interested groups offered on request in both locations. Special art films and lectures offered; also rare films of earlier vintage; National biennial competition Drawings USA tours museums throughout the United States; also traveling exhibitions of prints, crafts, textiles and metalwork. Members' study tours.
Library: Reference collection of approx. 1500 volumes, with special emphasis on drawings, prints, contemporary American crafts; African, Northwest Coast Indian and Oceanic art; textiles, needlework, photography, posters.
Publications: Exhibition catalogs, brochures, announcements, checklists, newsletter.
Income and Purchases: Projected budget 1976-77 $627,000; Acquisition Purchases range from $40,000 - $110,000 annually.
Attendance: 375,000.

ST. PAUL COUNCIL OF ARTS AND SCIENCES
30 E. Tenth St, 55101. Tel: (612) 227-8241
Marlow Burt, Exec. Dir.
Open Tues. & Wed. 9 AM - 5 PM; Thurs. - Sat. 9 AM - 9:30 PM; Sun.
1 - 9:30 PM; cl. Mon. Estab. 1958, opened in 1964.
Activities: Conducts annual united arts and science fund drive;
cooperative promotion and other activities for the five member
agencies including the Minnesota Museum of Art, Community Programs in the Arts and Sciences, Science Museum, Schubert Club, St.
Paul Chamber Orchestra and KSJN Radio Station. Administers the
St. Paul Arts and Science Center which houses the galleries, the
member agencies and the Crawford Livingston Theatre.
Attendance for the building: (1967-69) 350,000.

ST. PAUL PUBLIC LIBRARY
Fourth & Washington Sts, 55102. Tel: (612) 224-3383
J. Archer Eggen, Dir. of Libraries
Delores A. Sundbye, Supvr, Arts & AV Services
Open Mon. - Thurs. 9 AM - 9 PM; Fri. & Sat. 9 AM - 5:30 PM.
Collections: 16,000 books and 90 periodicals on art; file of 23,000
mounted pictures; 10,000 slides; 1500 large reproductions in color,
of which 800 are framed for loan to the public; 150 sculpture reproductions, also for free loan. Title and artist index of illustrations
in art books; complete collection of the first edition of Arundel
prints. There is a notable collection of books on †costume, †jade,
and †furniture. Gallery with changing exhibitions where various organizations hold meetings.
Purchases: Annual purchases $10,000 for books, pictures, and
sculpture.

SCHOOL OF THE ASSOCIATED ARTS GALLERIES
344 Summit Ave, 55102. Tel: (612) 224-3416
Virginia Rahja, Pres.
Ronald Swenson, Dean
Dean DuVander, Chmn. Interior Design
John Lenertz, Chmn. Commercial Arts
Free, Mon. - Fri. 9 AM - 4 PM. Estab. 1924, changing exhibitions
relate to the art college; financed by endowment.
Collections: Emphasis on Modern Art.
Exhibitions: Shows change every 3 weeks.
Activities: Lectures open to the public; scholarships. Book
shop. (See Schools)
Library: 7000 volume library; books and prints for reference;
photograph collection of 15,000 slides for reference.
Publications: 4 or 5 per year.

MISSISSIPPI

CLEVELAND

✠ **FIELDING L. WRIGHT ART CENTER**
Delta State College
Box 1955, 38732. Tel: (601) 843-2151
Malcolm Norwood, Head Dept. Art
Terry Simmons, Exhibitions Chmn.
Dr. Don Sontag, Art Educ. Chmn.
Open Mon. - Fri. 8 AM - 5 PM except school holidays; Sun. 3 - 5 PM
on opening of shows; no admis. Estab. 1968 primarily as an educa-
tional gallery for the benefit of students, but serves the entire area
for changing shows of art since it is the only facility of this nature
in the Mississippi Delta Region; financed by state appropriations.
Collections: Marie Hull Art Collection; Whittington Memorial
Collection; Delta State College Permanent Collection; Smith-Patter-
son Memorial Collection.
Exhibitions: Burton Callicott; Theora Hamblett, Paintings; Alvin
Sella Paintings and Constructions; Hal Carney, Paintings; Bill Dunlap; Mississippi Folk Architecture Traveling Show of rendered
drawings and photographs from the Smithsonian Institution; Mississippi Art Colony Show; (1975-76) Marie Hull Retrospective; William De Leftwich Dodge and Sarah Dodge Kimbrough; Maltby Sykes,
Printmaker; Northwest Louisiana University Faculty; plus others.
Activities: Educational department for training artists and
teachers of art; extension department serves Mississippi Delta region; material available to students in extension courses; fees,
$20 per semester hour credit; traveling exhibitions organized and
circulated; individual paintings and original objects of art lent; lending collection, 350 color reproductions, 6 motion pictures, 35 film
strips, approx. 6000 color slides, not loaned outside art department;
lectures open to the public; 10 visiting lecturers per year; 5 gallery
talks; 25-50 tours; classes for adults; competitions; scholarships.
Publications: Announcements of exhibitions, monthly during Fall,
Winter and Spring.
Purchases: Vary per appropriations.
Attendance: Approx. 2500-3000.

COLUMBUS

MISSISSIPPI UNIVERSITY FOR WOMEN
Art Gallery and Museum
Fine Arts Bldg, 39701.
Charles E. Ambrose, Dir. of Gallery, Cur. of Museum & Permanent
Collection
Free Mon. - Fri. 8 AM - 5 PM. Estab. 1948.
Collections: 350 pieces in the collection of †paintings, drawings,
prints; †permanent collection of Mississippi artists; †American art.
Exhibitions: Frequent special and circulating exhibitions. Selec-
tions from Permanent Collection periodically; international exhibition.
Activities: Visiting artists program; illustrated lectures; art
films in connection with Department of Art and student art organi-
zations; visiting foreign artists workshops; childrens art classes.

JACKSON

✠ **MISSISSIPPI ART ASSOCIATION**
P.O. Box 824, 39205. Tel: (601) 354-3538
Mrs. Wirt Yerger, Jr, Pres.
Mrs. Davenport Mosby, Jr, V.Pres.
Charles Burnham, Treas.
D. Michael Ogden, Dir.
Ray Parish, Educ. Dir.
Dan Matusiewicz, Dir of Mem. & Pub. Relations
Ruth Carr, Secy.
Gallery open Tues. - Sat. 9 AM - 5 PM; cl. Mon. Organized 1911,
inc. 1926, new charter received 1953, for purpose of education, ex-
hibition and acquisition. Ann. meeting May; mem. 2100, dues $5 and
higher.
Collections: Paintings and prints, sculpture, tapestry, pottery;
collections added to annually include Mississippi Collection, First
National Bank and Mississippi Art Association Collection. All collections become the property of the Association for the permanent
collections.
Exhibitions: Mississippi Competitive Exhibition; Collegiate Exhibition; annual membership exhibition in Dec; outstanding monthly
exhibitions year-round; national exhibitions presently exhibited by
M.A.A. at the State Historical Museum until the completion of the
Arts Center-Planetarium.
Activities: Travel-lecture program; traveling exhibition program; sales gallery; lectures and workshops; gallery exhibitions;
slide lending library; art classes for children and adults; sponsoring
of visual arts exhibitions at Mississippi Arts Festival; Civic Arts
Center Planetarium Development; art education and docent program;
speakers bureau; art activities for young people; billboard art;
state-wide program assistance.
Publications: Newsletter, monthly; exhibition calendars.

MISSISSIPPI DEPARTMENT OF ARCHIVES AND HISTORY
Archives & History Bldg, Box 571, 39205. Tel: (601) 354-6218
Old Capitol Museum, Box 571, 39205. Tel: (601) 354-6222
William F. Winter, Pres. Board of Trustees
Elbert R. Hilliard, Dir.
Byrle Kynerd, Dir, Old Capitol Museum
Charlotte Capers, Dir. Information & Educ.
Patti Black, Dir. Archives & Library
Open, Dept of Archives and History, Mon. 8 AM - 9 PM; Tues. -
Sat. 8 AM - 5 PM; cl. Sun. Old Capitol Museum, Free Mon. - Sat.
8 AM - 5 PM; Sun. 12:30 - 4:30 PM; cl. Mon.
Estab. 1902 for the care and custody of official archives; to col-
lect material relating to the history of the State from the earliest
times and to impart knowledge of the history and resources of the
State. Maintains the State Historical Museum housed in the Old
Capitol. Includes a portrait gallery of distinguished Mississippians.
Exhibitions: Special exhibitions monthly; folk songs and folk
crafts programs.
Activities: Guided tours on appointment; lectures, films.
Attendance: Archives and History 6394; Old Capitol Museum
83,587.

MUNICIPAL ART GALLERY*
839 N. State St, 39201. Tel: (601) 352-0128
Mike Ogden, Dir.
Free Tues, Wed, Fri, Sat. 9 AM - 5 PM; Thurs. 12 - 5 PM; Sun. 2 -
5 PM; cl. Mon.
Old residence owned by City. Permanent collection and monthly
exhibitions of Mississippi Art Association. Serves as meeting place
for women's clubs and visitors to gallery.

LAUREL

✠ **LAUREN ROGERS LIBRARY AND MUSEUM OF ART**
Fifth Ave. at Seventh St, 39440. Tel: (601) 428-4875
(Mail: P.O. Box 1108)
Robert C. Hynson, Chmn.
Nell Davis, Librn. & Acting Dir.

Stewart J. Gilchrist, Pres.
Kalford C. Ralcliff, Secy. & Treas.
Free 10 - 12 AM and 2 - 5 PM; Sun. 2 - 5 PM; cl. Mon. Estab. and
inc. 1922 for the advancement of learning and of the arts. Ann.
meeting June; supported by Eastman Memorial Foundation; owns
building.
Collections: Includes 102 †paintings, among which is a Millet,
Corot, Constable, Crome, Homer, Sargent, Sloan, Turner, Whistler;
140 Japanese color prints; American and European furniture; 600
baskets; 60 pieces of Georgian silver.
Exhibitions: Monthly exhibitions; co-operates with local organizations.
Activities: Art classes for adults and children; some type of
entertainment is given on the Sunday afternoon openings of exhibits;
chamber music, choral groups, soloists, Little Theatre, lectures.
Guided tours of students and other groups are given upon request.
Library: 15,750 volumes make up collections of genealogy, art
books and special collections of Mississippiana.
Income: $30,500.
Attendance: 8000.

MERIDIAN

✠MERIDIAN MUSEUM OF ART
Box 5773, 25th Ave. at Seventh St, 39301. Tel: (601) 693-1501
Dr. William Thornton, Pres.
Betsy Weems, Secy.
William Myers Watkins, III, Exec. Dir.
Rosanne Knight, Admin. Asst.
Free Tues. - Sun. 1 - 5 PM. Estab. 1969 to give cultural enrich-
ment and educational benefits to the people of East Mississippi, West
Alabama, The South, and the United States; supported by appropria-
tion and membership. Three galleries. Ann. meeting 2nd week in
Dec; mem. 600; dues $10-$1000 and over.
Collections: Lithographs, paintings, oil and acrylic; ink drawings;
photographs.
Exhibitions: Approx. 150 since 1970.
Activities: Docent program; school tours; lectures for members
only (some open to public), 2 visiting lecturers per year; 12 gallery
talks; classes for adults and children; competitions.
Library: 200 volumes for reference.
Publications: Gallery Review, quarterly newsletter.
Attendance: 20,000.

MISSISSIPPI ART COLONY*
c/o Alex M. Loeb, Dir, 2741 38 St, 39301. Tel: (601) 482-2827
Jean R. Loeb, Secy-Treas.
Mrs. Scott Tennyson, V.Pres.
Estab. 1945 to hold workshops at least twice yearly, for painting in-
struction and occasionally other areas; to select show with prizes
awarded, which travels state of Mississippi between workshops.
Financed by mem. Ann. meeting Oct. and May, sometimes April;
mem. 40; dues $3.
Exhibitions: Seven exhibitions since 1970; juried show of 20-25
paintings has toured state, being exhibited in 5-6 localities, museums,
libraries and galleries.
Activities: Traveling exhibitions organized and circulated.
Publications: Mississippi Art Colony Bulletin Newsletter.
Attendance: 70 at workshops annually.

OXFORD

MARY BUIE MUSEUM*
510 University Ave, 38655. Tel: (601) 234-3151
Mrs. G. L. Eatman, Dir.
Open Tues, Wed. & Sat. 10 - 12 AM & 1:30 - 4:30 PM; Thurs. & Fri.
1:30 - 4:30 PM; Sun. 2 - 5 PM; cl. Mon, and last two weeks in Aug.
Estab. 1939, by gift from Mrs. Mary Skipwith Buie and her sister
Kate A. Skipwith, to the city of Oxford, to preserve the Skipwith and
Buie historical relics and to further interest in fine arts.
Collections: Paintings by Mary Skipwith Buie; historical documents; relics of the Revolutionary and Civil War periods; glass;
china; fine old costumes; silver; jewelry, and two St. Memin engravings. Over 250 antique dolls, earliest about 1650 to 1916 Schoenhut;
over 300 fans, early 19th century from all over the world.
Exhibitions: Museum of Modern Art, Smithsonian Institution, International Exhibitions, Local and Regional Artists, Cybis and
Ispanky Porcelain Figurines, Oriental Carpets; local artist competition shows; nursery and kindergarten yearly show; National Association of Women Artists; National Watercolor Exhibition (sponsored by
Junior League, Jackson, Miss); and numerous one-man exhibitions.
Activities: Classes in painting, oil and water color; china painting; also classes in painting sponsored by the Museum in neighboring towns; home of the Skipwith Genealogy Society; school groups,
club meetings, teas and receptions.
Attendance: 7000-10,000 yearly.

TUPELO

LEE COUNTY LIBRARY
219 Madison St, 38801. Tel: (601) 844-2377
Mrs. Gilmer Garmon, Chmn.
Betty R. Kemp, Dir.
Miss Manie Berry, Reference Librn.
Ann Wallace, Business Reference Librn.
Mrs. Marion Cagle, Children's Librn.
Open Mon. - Thurs. 9 AM - 8 PM; Fri. - Sat. 9 AM - 5 PM. Estab.
1941 to provide books and other sources of information to serve the
intellectual, recreation, cultural needs of its users. A sustained
cultural effort is the provision of bimonthly exhibits of art objects
and the visual arts exhibit in the Mezzanine Gallery; financed by
city or state appropriation. The Mezzanine Gallery and the Helen
Foster Room are used as exhibit space for exhibits by University art
students, local professional artists and occasionally art exhibits
from national museums.
Collections: The Tupelo Gum Tree Festival purchase prizes are
placed in the Lee County Library each year; these have included
paintings and pottery.
Activities: 118 color reproductions in lending collection.

UNIVERSITY

UNIVERSITY GALLERIES
Fine Arts Center
University of Mississippi, 38677. Tel: (601) 232-7193
Gale Hammond, Secy.
Robert L. Tettleton, Dir. Galleries & Chmn. Dept. Art
Free daily 8 AM - Noon & 1 - 4:30 PM. Estab. 1954 as a teaching
gallery; financed by city and state appropriation.
Collections: Former faculty and student work; some work
bought from traveling exhibitions over the years; collections consists of more than 200 pieces.
Exhibitions: 10 exhibitions per year.
Activities: Extension courses in art history and methods and
materials of the artist available to anyone for $15 per semester
hour; traveling exhibitions organized and circulated; individual
paintings lent to schools; original objects of art lent; 20,000 lantern
slides and 50 color reproductions in lending collection; 150 items
lent in average year; lectures open to the public, 2 visiting lecturers
per year, 2 gallery talks and 5 tours; scholarships.
Library: Main library of the University has 7000 volumes.
Publications: One gallery schedule per year.
Income and Purchases: Income $1500, purchases $500.
Attendance: 2000.

VICKSBURG

VICKSBURG ART ASSOCIATION
1204 Main St, 39180
James S. Reasoner, Pres.
Elizabeth Pajerski, 1st V.Pres.
Estab. 1962 to promote the production and appreciation of fine art
through instruction, exhibitions, traveling shows, and lectures for
all age groups. The care and preservation of an historically significant building as an art gallery, which is housed in the Old Vicksburg Constitutional Firehouse, c. 1870; financed by membership.
Monthly meetings; mem. 267; dues $6 - $25.
Exhibitions: 4 membership exhibitions annually; 2 - 4 exhibitions presented annually of well-known regional artists and state-
sponsored exhibitions.
Activities: Lectures open to public, 8 - 12 visiting lecturers per
year; 2 - 4 gallery talks; classes for adults and children; competitions.
Annual Income: $4000.
Attendance: 800.

MISSOURI

CAPE GIRARDEAU

KENT LIBRARY
Southeast Missouri State University
63701. Tel: (314) 334-8211
Duane Ed. Henricks, Reference/Documents Librn.
Open daily. Utilize main level areas for exhibitions.
Collections: 240,000 volumes in library; fine arts collection of
5000 volumes. On permanent display is the extensive Thomas Beckwith collection of MoundBuilders Indian pottery from the Missis-
sipian cultural period (900-1500 A.D). The Jake K. Wells Mural,
800 sq. ft. in size, covers the West wall of the library foyer. One of
the largest murals in the state, it depicts the nature and development
of Southeast Missouri. The 800 volume Charles L. Harrison
Library, housed in the Rare Book Room, is especially strong in

volumes containing illustrations by the Cruikshanks, Gustave Dore, Arthur Rackham and John James Audubon. Atlas Coelestis by Andree Celarii is also in the collection.

Exhibitions: Art student work and traveling exhibitions; faculty shows; exhibits from other college and university art departments.

COLUMBIA

DANIEL BOONE REGIONAL LIBRARY
100 W. Broadway, 65201. Tel: (314) 443-3161
Gene Martin, Dir.
Free Mon. - Fri. 9 AM - 9 PM; Sat. 9 AM - 6 PM; Sun. 1 - 5 PM. Estab. 1959.

Exhibitions: Touring exhibits through the Missouri State Council on the Arts; exhibits by local artists through the year (no prizes).

Activities: Individual paintings and original objects of art lent; 238 color reproductions, 200 Kodachromes, 883 filmstrips and 103 sculpture reproductions in lending collection; mem. of Missouri libraries film coop.

FINE ARTS GALLERY
University of Missouri-Columbia
A126 Fine Arts Center, 65201. Tel: (314) 882-3555
Lawrence Rugolo, Chmn.
Free Mon. - Fri. 9 AM - 3 PM; Sun. 2:30 - 4:30 PM. Estab. 1960 to augment the art student's education and provide the community with important exhibitions of art; financed by state appropriation. Gallery is set between the drama department and the art department, the 40 x 80 foot, well-lit gallery is central to the fine arts complex and has approximately 200 feet of wall space with a 12 foot ceiling.

Exhibitions: Some 8-10 exhibitions are held each year, ranging from shows rented from the AFA and other major museums to shows of local students and faculty work.

Activities: Material available to schools and galleries; no fees; traveling exhibitions organized and circulated; original objects of art lent; occasional gallery talks.

Attendance: 16,000 annual average.

THE LEWIS JAMES AND NELLIE STRATTON DAVIS ART GALLERY
Stephens College, 65201. Tel: (314) 442-2211 Exten. 302
Gardiner McCauley, Dir. Davis Gallery & Head Art Dept.
Free Sept. 10 - May 10, Mon. - Fri. 8 AM - 5 PM. Estab. 1964 to provide exhibitions of art for the general interest of the local community and for the education of the student body in general; endowed. Gallery.

Collections: Modern paintings; †modern graphics; primitive sculpture.

Exhibitions: 33 exhibitions since 1970 - 1975-76 schedule includes Hiroshige Prints; Melanesian Sculpture; Harry Lum; Contemporary San Francisco Artists; Russell Green; Imogene Cunningham; Quilts from Nebraska Collections; Student Graduates.

Activities: Lectures open to public, 6 visiting lecturers per year; 6 gallery talks.

Income and Purchases: Operating budget $3000; purchases $250.

Attendance: 7000.

MUSEUM OF ART AND ARCHAEOLOGY
University of Missouri-Columbia
Ellis Library 4D11, 65201. Tel: (314) 882-8363
Saul S. Weinberg, Dir.
Gladys D. Weinberg, Asst. Dir.
Ruth E. Witt, Admin. Asst. & Registrar
Ryntha J. Gibbs, Secy.
Jane C. Biers, Cur. Ancient Art
Richard G. Baumann, Cur. Renaissance & Modern Art
Sarla D. Nagar, Assoc. Cur. S. Asian Art
Free daily 2 - 5 PM. Estab. 1957 to furnish a collection of universal art as an adjunct to the teaching program of the department of art history and archaeology of the university, secondly to afford a museum for Columbia and Central Missouri; financed by state appropriations. Series of galleries with exhibitions of ancient, Mediaeval and modern art of all varieties.

Collections: Primitive art of Oceania, Africa, Central and South America; Far Eastern Art; Southeast and Central Asian Art; Ancient Near Eastern Art; †Greek and Roman art; †Early Christian and Byzantine Art; †Prehistoric and Pre-Renaissance art of Europe; †European art-Renaissance to 1800; †European and American art, 1800 to present.

Exhibitions: Ancient Mediterranean and Near Eastern Art; Recent Acquisitions of Modern and Contemporary Art; Turn of the Century Poster Art; Art of Gandhara; Masks and Images - African and Oceanic Art; Echoes from the East - China and Japan; Tel Anafa in Upper Galilee, Israel; Thomas Hart Benton Memorial Exhibition; Paul Revere Silver Casters - First Bicentennial Exhibition; Contemporary American Paintings and Prints; Recent Acquisitions.

Activities: Original objects of art lent; tours.

Library: 2000 volumes for lending and reference; 6000 prints in photograph collection for lending and reference.

Publications: MUSE-Annual of the Museum of Art and Archaeology, University of Missouri-Columbia, annually.

Income and Purchases: Income $100,000-$110,000; purchases $25,000-$30,000.

STANLEY HALL GALLERY
University of Missouri-Columbia
Department of Housing and Interior Design, 65201.
Tel: (314) 882-7224
Gary L. Hennigh, Dir.
Robert Kabak, Assoc.
Free Mon. - Fri. 8 AM - 5 PM; cl. holidays. Estab. 1960 to provide aesthetic and learning experiences for students and the public dealing with interior design and related arts; financed by city and state appropriation.

Collections: Historic textiles.

Exhibitions: Crafts, painting, computer graphics, interior design, textile design, furniture design, weaving.

Activities: Classroom learning experiences; original objects of art lent, less than 5 items lent in average year; lectures open to public; 3 - 4 gallery talks per year.

INDEPENDENCE

THE HARRY S TRUMAN LIBRARY AND MUSEUM
64050. Tel: (816) 252-1144
Dr. Benedict K. Zobrist, Dir.
Milton F. Perry, Museum Cur.
Open daily 9 AM - 5 PM; admis. adults 50¢. Estab. July 6, 1957 to preserve and make available for study and exhibition the papers, objects and other materials relating to President Harry S Truman and his contemporaries. Gravesite of President Truman in the courtyard. Administered by the National Archives and Records Service of the Federal Government.

Collections: Portraits of President Truman; Art Collection of President Truman; original cartoons; mural by Thomas Hart Benton, Independence and the Opening of the West; historical collections relating to the history of the U.S. Presidency.

Activities: Educational tours; approximately 200 gallery talks or tours a year; maintains sales desk.

Library: 40,000 volumes for reference; 65,000 prints from the photograph collection for research only. The Library houses an estimated ten million papers. Inquiries as to the availability of research materials should be addressed to the Director. (Note: The admission fee pertains only to the Museum. Offices and research areas are not open to the public.)

Exhibitions: 1963-1965: Combat Drawings and Paintings of the 35th Division by Olin Dows, 1963; John F. Kennedy and The Truman Library, 1964; President Truman, 1945 (1965); Truman and Churchill, 1966; 1945: Year of Decision, 1970; The Whistle Stop Campaign, 1973-1976.

Attendance: 250,000.

JACKSON COUNTY HISTORICAL SOCIETY
217 N. Main St, 64050. Tel: (816) 252-1892
Susannah Gentry, Pres.
Mrs. H. H. Haukenberry, Secy.
Mrs. Kenneth L. Graham, Coordinator

1859 Jail Museum and Marshal's House
217 N. Main St, 64050.
Mrs. Kenneth L. Graham, Dir.
Open June, July & Aug, Mon. - Sat. 9 AM - 5 PM; Sun. 1 - 5 PM; Sept. - May, Tues. - Sat. 10 AM - 4 PM; Sun. 1 - 5 PM; admis. 50¢, 12 and under free. Estab. 1959. Elementary school tours emphasizing local and regional history; sales desk.

1858 John Wornall House
61st Terrace & Wornall Rd, Kansas City, 64113.
Tel: (816) 444-1858
Laurie Ekstrom, Cur.
Open Tues. - Sat. 10 AM - 4:30 PM; Sun. 1 - 4:30 PM; admis. adults $1, students 75¢, children 25¢. Estab. 1972. Wide selection of craft classes and workshops for various age groups.

Research Library and Archives
Independence Square Courthouse
Nancy Ehrlich, Dir.
Free Mon. - Thurs. 11 AM - 3 PM. Estab. 1960. Photograph collection for reference.

Financed by membership. Ann. meeting last Sun. in Jan; mem. 2500; dues $5 - $100.

Collections: Furnishings and interior decor at both Museums: circa 1850-1875; original portraits and other material to 1830's;

displays featuring pioneer life in the period of the westward expansion; selected memorabilia of Harry S Truman, 33rd President of the United States.

Exhibitions: Mid-19th century Christmas displays and fine early handmade quilts at both museums; 19th century toys (on loan) and 200 years of Presidential election campaign materials (on loan) at 1859 Jail Museum.

Activities: Lectures open to public; 3 visiting lecturers per year; classes for adults and children.

Library: Volumes limited, primarily archival material, for reference only.

Publications: Jackson County Historical Society Journal, quarterly.

Attendance: 1859 Jail Museum: 25,000; Wornall House: 15,000.

JOPLIN

DOROTHEA B. HOOVER JOPLIN HISTORICAL SOCIETY MUSEUM*
110 Joplin St, 64801.
Helen Chickering, Corresponding Secy.
Open Tues. - Sat. 11 AM - 4 PM; Sun. 1 - 4 PM; cl. Mon. Estab. 1973.

Collections: Nineteenth century furniture, pictures and accessories with local connections; primitive tools and implements; photographs of early Joplin; glass cases of documents, china, glass, ladies accessories, memorabilia; old costumes, quilts, coverlids, dolls, toys, valentines and books; paintings by well known artists, Robert Higgs and Duke Wellington; large miniature circus; large collection of circus books and magazines, circus posters, photographs and oil paintings.

✠SPIVA ART CENTER, INC.
Newman & Duquesne Roads, Missouri Southern Fine Arts Bldg, 64801. Tel: (417) 623-0183
Mrs. William Rainey, Pres.
Mrs. John Duffy, V.Pres.
Mrs. John Cragin, Secy.
Mrs. Elroy Thomas, Treas.
Priscilla Eberle, Exec. Secy.
Darral A. Dishman, Dir.
Free Tues. - Fri. 10 AM - 4 PM; Sat. 9 AM - Noon; Sun. 2 - 5 PM; cl. Mon. & national holidays. Estab. June, 1959, inc. 1969, as a nonprofit educational, social and cultural community center with the purpose of collecting, preserving and exhibiting works of art for encouragement and advancement of art education. Ann. meeting Mar; mem. 650; dues $5 and higher.

Collections: 19th century paintings; New Guinea sculpture; Mary Gregory glass; American Indian prints; early American glass.

Exhibitions: Changing monthly exhibitions including one-man and group; May competitive exhibition; purchases and prizes $1500.

Activities: Classes in various phases of the visual arts for adults and children; lectures; scholarships, competitions; Film Classic Series; Gallery tours; 2 week summer painting workshops.

Library: Maintains reference library of art books.

Publications: Calendar; newsletter.

Attendance: 15,000 annual average.

KANSAS CITY

AVILA COLLEGE
Fine Arts Department
11901 Wornall Rd, 64145. Tel: (816) 942-8400, Exten. 259
Sister Olive Louise Dallavis, Pres.
G. Richard Scott, Academic Dean
Dr. W. Louis, Chmn.
Margaret Reinhart, Coordinator
Free 9 AM - 4:30 PM. College estab. 1945 to give students a preparation for life and making a living through Liberal Arts studies and work in major or professional areas, in a Catholic atmosphere; Dean's scholarships available; a contributed service of the religious Sisters. Art Department gallery is 14 ft. x 30 ft; track lighting; sculpture stands, etc.

Collections: Artifacts, paintings and sculpture are placed throughout the buildings on the campus. 4000 Kodachrome slides.

Exhibitions: Painting; Sculpture; Ceramics; Textiles.

Annual Income: $300.

Attendance: 100 each month.

KANSAS CITY ART INSTITUTE
4415 Warwick Blvd, 64111. Tel: (816) 561-4852
John W. Lottes, Pres.
Jerome L. Grove, Dean of the College
Michael J. Greene, V.Pres. Institutional Advancement
Ronald Cattelino, Dir. Finance & Facilities
Susan Hubbard, Dir. Development
Mary Woods, Dir. Alumni

Catherine Burgoin, Dir. Communications
Sharon Stites, Dir. of Admis.
Open Mon. - Fri. 8:30 AM - 5 PM; Sat. 8:30 - 12 AM. Estab. 1885, inc. 1887; professional education for the visual arts; four-year college course leading to B.F.A. degree in five fields. Fifteen-acre landscaped campus with 14 buildings, classrooms and studio space for every student, auditorium, library, administrative offices, dining hall, student lounge, exhibition gallery and housing for men and women. Mem. 1000; dues $25 and higher.

Activities: Gallery program; lectures, concerts, films, demonstrations; visiting artists; scholarships; classes for adults; Saturday precollege program; summer semester; Mid-America Regional Film Center; Student Mobility to nine other colleges of art. Complete supply store.

Library: 24,000 volumes, reproductions and collection of original drawings and paintings.

Media Center: Collection of 29,500 slides, tape collection, audiovisual services to all departments and staff, including equipment for audiovisual presentations.

Attendance: Full-time enrl. 600; total enrl. including summer school and extension courses 1350.

Charlotte Crosby Kemper Gallery
4415 Warwick, 64111.
George E. Powell, Jr, Chmn, Board Governors
Mrs. Robert G. Evans, V.Chmn. of Board & Chmn. Mem. Comt.
Gallery open daily. Estab. Sept. 1963 to provide exhibitions of interest to the college and regional community.

Exhibitions: (1975-76) John Kreigshauser and William Philyaw (designer craftsman); Roger Shimomura, Oriental Masterpieces and Masterprints; Richard Matthews, ten year retrospective; Summer High School Studio Work, Painting, Drawing, Ceramics, Photography; Michael Walling; The Frank Collection-American Indian-New Mexican Spanish Colonial Art; Master Fiber Works; Central American Ceramics; Invitational Photography Exhibit; Robert Venturi, Architectural Presentation; Invitational Crafts, Wendell Castle, wood, Sherrie Smith, fiber, Robert Winokur, clay; Lester Goldman; Robert Natkin, Retrospective; K.C.A.I. Graduating Senior Exhibition.

KANSAS CITY (MO.) PUBLIC LIBRARY
311 E. 12th St, 64106.
Harold R. Jenkins, Librn.
Robert M. Ross, Head Art & Music Dept.
Open Mon. - Wed. 8:30 AM - 9 PM; Thurs. - Sat. 8:30 AM - 5 PM; cl. Sun. Estab. 1873.

Lending collection of 12,500 color reproductions; 1300 16mm films; art books collection of 30,000 volumes.

Income and Purchases: Income $2,084,376; purchases $10,000.

MUNICIPAL ART COMMISSION
City Hall, 415 E. 11th St, 64106. Tel: (816) 274-1866
Mayor Charles B. Wheeler, Jr, Chmn.
Lynn Bauer, V.Chmn.
Mary Louise Dudding, Exec. Dir.
K. E. Coombs, AIA, Secy.
Created by 1925 Charter. Three ex-officio members and 6 appointed by Mayor. Approves all works of art that are to become property of the city whether by purchase or gift. Approves design of buildings, bridges and other structures to be erected upon city property. Approves issuance of permits for construction of marquees projecting over streets or boulevards. City Council may dispense with approval by the Art Commission.

✠WILLIAM ROCKHILL NELSON GALLERY OF ART
Atkins Museum of Fine Arts
4525 Oak St, 64111. Tel: (816) 561-4000
Milton McGreevy, Trustee
M. D. Blackwell, Trustee
Herman R. Sutherland, Trustee
Laurence Sickman, Dir.
Ross E. Taggart, Senior Cur.
Ralph T. Coe, Asst. Dir. & Cur, Paintings & Sculpture
George L. McKenna, Assoc. Cur, Prints & Registrar
Jeanne A. Harris, Assoc. Cur, Oriental Art
Marc Wilson, Cur. Chinese Art
Larry Eikleberry, Dir. Educ.
Kathleen Taggart, Exec. Secy, Society of Fellows
Ellen Goheen, Assoc. Cur. Paintings & Sculpture
Michael Hagler, Asst. Cur, Exhibitions
Anne Tompkins, Librn.
June Finnell, Secy. to Dir.
Janet Patterson Waller, Secy. to Cur.
Karen Dean Bunting, Asst Cur, Sales & Rental
Glenna Youngstrom, Exec. Secy, Friends of Art
Forrest Bailey, Conservator
Bobby J. Hornaday, Supt. of Galleries
Phillip Brimble, Publicity

Sherwood Songer, Supt.
Jeanne Baldwin, Asst. in Educ.
Mary Evans, Asst. in Educ.
Dr. Chu-tsing Li, Research Cur. in Far Eastern Art
Dr. Marilyn Stokstad, Research Cur. in Western Art
Effie M. Harnden, Secy. to Dir. of Educ.
Open Tues. - Sat. 10 AM - 5 PM; Sun. 2 - 6 PM; cl. Mon; free Sat. &
Sun; other times admis adults 50¢, children 6-12 years of age 25¢.
Estab. 1926 by William Rockhill Nelson Trust; collection started 1930
with income from a fund of about $12,000,000. Building dedicated in
1933, contains 60 galleries, auditorium, library, classrooms.

Collections: †European paintings, prints, drawings, and sculpture; †Egyptian and Classic art; †Chinese, †Japanese, †Persian and
†East Indian arts; †decorative arts including Spanish, Italian, English, French, East Indian and Chinese period rooms; †American
painting and decorative arts, including 5 Early American rooms; the
F. P. Burnap Collection of English Pottery; †Starr Collection of
European and American Portrait Miniatures; †primitive arts; †Pre-
Columbian and American Indian art; Children's Museum devoted to
exhibitions designed for children.

Exhibitions: Special exhibitions 1973 through 1975 included: Ed-
ward Hopper: Selections from the Hopper Bequest; The Navajo
Blanket; Ancient Chinese Bronzes from the Pillsbury Collection;
Chinese Gold, Silver and Porcelain: The Kempe Collection; The
Fresh Air School; Graphics by Six Swiss Sculptors; Photographs by
Peter Fink; Mid-America Invitational: Howard Jones and Arthur
Osver; Max Ernst: Inside the Sight; Greek, Etruscan and Roman
Jewelry from the Carl Kempe Collection; African Art of the Dogon;
40th Anniversary Exhibition; Mid-America V; 19th Century American
Painting; Thirty Miles of Art; Whistler Prints; Later Persian and
Indian Art from the Permanent Collection; Mystics and Mandalas;
Old Master Prints from the Permanent Collection; Antwerp's
Golden Age; Wood Sculptures by Louise Nevelson; Thomas Hart
Benton: An Artist's Selection, 1908-1974; The Graphic Work of
Kandinsky; Treasures from the Musée Guimet; Works of Art by
Jacob Lawrence; Friends of Wen Cheng-ming: A View from the
Crawford Collection; Tom Wesselmann: The Early Years; Archaeo-
logical Finds of the People's Republic of China; Felix Bracquemond
and the Etching Process; Three Centuries of French Satire,
1614-1914; Bingham's Missouri; Campbell Museum Collection.

Activities: Staff lectures; visiting lecturers (varying subjects,
often related to special exhibitions), approx. 12 per year; daily
tours; concerts; film programs; dance programs.

Junior Education: Supervised tours of approx. 114,000 children
annually; art and marionette classes for children.

Library: Art history library of approx. 30,000 volumes; junior
library devoted to books and rental reproductions for children, approx. 2094 volumes.

Publications: Calendar of Events, monthly; occasional Bulletin.
Attendance: 330,000.

Friends of Art of Kansas City
4525 Oak St, 64111. Tel: (816) 561-4000
Stuart Hutchison, Pres.
Gary Gradinger, Selections Chmn.
Glenna Youngstrom, Exec. Secy.
Byron Cohen, Chmn. of the Guild.
Estab. and inc. 1934 to encourage contemporary art. Ann. meeting
Nov; mem 6693 (including Guild members); dues $20 and higher
(Guild membership limited to those under 30 years of age; estab.
1960, mem 1400); dues $15.

The Friends of Art provides guest lecturers, study programs,
operated Sales and Rental Gallery, coffee lounge, docent service.
The organization also acquires contemporary art for the Nelson-
Atkins Gallery, and has presented over 190 paintings, drawings,
watercolors and sculptures to the collection.

KIRKSVILLE

THE NATIONAL ASSOCIATION FOR HUMANITIES EDUCATION
P.O. Box 628, 63501. Tel: (816) 665-5121, Exten. 3311
Robert C. Lamm, Pres.
Leon Karel, Exec. Secy.
For further information see p. 8.

MARYVILLE

NORTHWEST MISSOURI STATE UNIVERSITY
64468. Tel: (816) 582-2145
James Broderick, Gallery Dir. and Chmn. Dept. of Art
Open Mon. - Fri. 1 - 4 PM; special hours Sat. and Sun.
Collections: American paintings and prints; American and Euro-
pean furniture and decorative arts.
Exhibitions: Special exhibitions of national and regional scope.
Activities: Visiting Artist Series with exhibitions and lectures by
outstanding artists in all fields; three to five per year.

MEXICO

MEXICO-AUDRAIN COUNTY LIBRARY
305 W. Jackson, 65265. Tel: (314) 518-4939
Mrs. Ernest Gantt, Pres.
Rebecca Gibbs, Secy.
Eldon R. Burgess, Dir.
Mary Jane Geary, Reference Librn.
Karen Stephens, Reference Librn.
Doris Alexander, Acquisitions Librn.
Violet Lierheimer, Acquisitions Librn.
Erselle Moore, Children's Librn.
Nancy Archer, Bookmobile Librn.
Laura Waage, Bookmobile Librn.
Free, Winter hours, Mon. - Thurs. 9 AM - 9 PM; Fri. - Sat. 9 AM -
5:30 PM; Sun. 1 - 4 PM. Estab. 1912 to provide library services to
the residents of Audrain County, Missouri; financed by city and
county appropriations. Exhibit room with different exhibits each
month; local school children have a continuously changing exhibit in
the childrens department. Ann. meeting monthly for board of trustees.

Collections: †Books, films, filmstrips, art slides, records, art
prints, art objects; small statuary and object d'art; permanent display of about one dozen original painting done either by locally connected artists or of local scenes; permanent collection of David
Douglas Duncan prints.

Exhibitions: Local Federated Women's Club sponsored a different exhibit each month during the fall, winter and spring, these included local artists, both adult and young people and recognized
artists of the area; The Missouri Council of the Arts also provides
traveling exhibits that we display.

Activities: Bookmobile serves the county with 52 stops per month,
also have 3 branch libraries at Vandalia, Laddonia and Farber, Missouri; material available to all residents of the county; fees, none
to county residents, $3 per year to non-residents; individual paintings
and original objects of art lent; lending collection, 100 art print color
reproductions, 1200 Kodachromes, 48 motion pictures, 1869 film
strips, over 92,519 books, 2946 records, 86 periodicals, 10 newspapers; 285,816 items lent in an average year, 20,000 active borrowers; classes for children, story hour 45 minutes each Tuesday.
Income: $147,535.45.

POINT LOOKOUT

RALPH FOSTER MUSEUM
School of the Ozarks College
65726. Tel: (417) 334-6411, Exten. 407
Dr. M. Graham Clark, Pres.
Col. Charles J. Hackett, Secy.
Marvin E. Tong, Jr, Dir.
Ron Miller, Asst Dir.
John Paul Butler, Cur. Monies
Herbert L. Thomason, Museum Construction Supvr.
Brian Middleton, Cur Arts & Armor
Steve Finkemeier, Registrar
Anita & Juanita Wilson, Curators of Art
Janie Shafer, Secy. to Dir.
Free Mon. - Sat. 8 AM - 5 PM; Sun. 1 - 5 PM. Estab. 1959 as a
nonprofit educational, scientific, historical, cultural institution to
portray the Ozarks region; financed by endowment and membership.
Ann. meeting May; mem. 200; dues $5 - $1000.
Collections: †Art of the Ozarks; †Firearms and armour;
†monies; †historical items of the Ozarks; †Art of the West and by
the American Indian; Big Game exhibits; Indians of the Ozarks;
Ozarks Hall of Fame.
Exhibitions: Continuing exhibits; local art shows and traveling
exhibits.
Activities: Lectures open to public, 4 visiting lecturers per
year; 300 gallery talks; 345 tours. Book shop.
Library: 500 volumes for reference; 10,000 prints in photograph
collection.
Publications: Ralph Foster Museum Newsletter, quarterly.
Income and Purchases: Income $80,000; purchases $5000.
Attendance: 17,500.

ST. CHARLES

HARRY D. HENDREN GALLERY
The Lindenwood Colleges
Department of Art, 63301. Tel: (314) 723-7152, Exten. 241 or
946-6912, Exten. 241.
W. Dean Eckert, Chmn.
Nancy Follis, Secy.
Free daily 9 AM - 10 PM; Sat. 9 AM - 4 PM; Sun. Noon - 4 PM.
Estab. 1969 as a college exhibition gallery; financed by endowment.
Gallery is approx. 3600 sq. ft. with skylight and one wall of side
light.

Collections: More than 40 contemporary American and European prints in various media including works by Paul Jenkins, William Hayter, Picasso, Villon, and others.

Activities: Traveling exhibitions organized and circulated through the Missouri State Council on the Arts; original objects of art lent; photograph collection; lectures open to public; 5 - 6 visiting lecturers per year; 5 - 6 gallery talks; 3 - 4 tours; classes for adults; scholarships; Book shop. Library.

Attendance: 3000 - 4000 for exhibitions.

ST. JOSEPH

ALBRECHT ART MUSEUM
Albrecht Gallery Corporation
2818 Frederick Blvd, 64506. Tel: (816) 233-7003
Dorothy Wenz, Pres.
Dr. H. C. Willumsen, 1st V.Pres.
Mrs. Richard Optican, Secy.
Jack Killackey, Treas.
Mrs. Bartlett Boder, Historian
James M. Ray, Dir.
Open Tues. - Fri. 10 AM - 4 PM; Sat. and Sun. 1 - 5 PM; cl. Mon, Thanksgiving, Christmas and New Year's; admis. adults 25¢, children 10¢. Opened May, 1966, after an extensive campaign by members of the Corporation raised a fund of over $115,000 to maintain an art gallery in the Albrecht house. The gallery receives additional support from the city of St. Joseph and from the members. The gift of the Albrecht Mansion to the league was made by Mr. and Mrs. W. Conger Beasley of St. Joseph. Mrs. Beasley was the only daughter of Mr. and Mrs. William Albrecht, who built the Georgian Mansion in the center of four and a half acres of landscaped gardens in the late thirties. Ann. meeting 2nd Wed. of April; dues $10 and higher.

Collections: 19th and 20th century American paintings, drawings, prints and sculpture; 19th and 20th century European prints.

Exhibitions: (1973) Drawing-America 1973; Measuregraph Corporation Collection; Paintings by Fritz Scholder; Paintings by Contemporary American Indians; Art in A Time/Space Dimension; Daisy Cook-Painter from Missouri; Missouri Craft Council Exhibition; Kansas City Art Institute Faculty Exhibit; Bob Byerly-Realist; Lithuanian Bookplates; Charles Burchfield, Master Doodler; Bernard Buffet Prints; Western Art from Local Collections; Paintings by Dhimitri Zonia; Architecture of St. Joseph Photographic Exhibit; Missouri Botanical Gardens Exhibit; (1974-75) Engraving America 1974; A Sense of Place; Paintings by Jo Sickbert; Architecture of St. Joseph Photographic Exhibit; Missouri Crafts Council Exhibit; Drawing America 1975; The Stained Glass Windows of St. Joseph Photographic Exhibit; Tamarind: A Renaissance of Lithography; Eight State Print Exhibition; Paintings by Archie Musick; Paintings and Drawings by Werner Wildner.

Activities: Gallery talks, formally organized educational programs for children and adults; guided tours, lectures, films, concerts; library reading room; luncheons. Art Shop sells Museum jewelry, reproductions of prints and sculpture, pottery, postcards, Christmas cards, note cards, gifts; sponsors an Annual Art Fair and special one-day sales.

Publications: Monthly newsletter to members; The Architecture of Saint Joseph (catalog); Drawing America 1973; Engraving America 1974.

Income and Purchases: (1974) Income $45,000; purchases $10,000.
Attendance: (1974) 15,000.

ALLIED ARTS COUNCIL OF ST. JOSEPH, MISSOURI
510 Francis St, 64501. Tel: (816) 233-0231
Robert G. Powell, Pres.
Mrs. Philip Thompson, Secy.
Mrs. Edward Y. Barlow, Exec. Dir.
Free, Sept. - May daily Mon. - Fri. 9 AM - 3 PM. Estab. 1963 to co-ordinate arts efforts in our city; financed from mem. Ann. meeting June; mem. 13 organizations; dues vary.
Publications: Bi-monthly calendar of events.

ST. JOSEPH MUSEUM
11th & Charles Sts, 64501. Tel: (816) 232-8471
Richard A. Nolf, Dir.
Don L. Reynolds, Asst. Dir.
June M. Swift, Secy.
Free May through mid-Sept, Mon. - Sat. 9 AM - 5 PM; Sun. 2 - 5 PM. Mid-Sept. through Apr, Tues. - Sat. 1 - 5 PM; Sun. and holidays 2 - 5 PM. Estab. 1927 to increase and diffuse knowledge and appreciation of history, art and the sciences. Ann. meeting Jan; mem. 300; dues $5.
Collections: One of the finest †American Indian collections in the U.S.; Natural History and History of the area.
Activities: Guided tours; lectures; films; study clubs; hobby workshops; formally organized education programs for children and adults; permanent and temporary exhibitions; manuscript collections; traveling exhibitions.

Library: 5000 volumes for reference only.
Publications: Museum Graphic, irregular.
Income and Purchases: Income $80,000; purchases $3500 annually.
Attendance: 70,000.

Pony Express Stables Museum
914 Penn St, 64503. Tel: (816) 279-5059
Richard A. Nolf, Dir.
Don L. Reynolds, Asst. Dir.
June M. Swift, Secy.
Free May through mid-Sept. Mon. - Sat. 9 AM - 5 PM; Sun. 2 - 5 PM; cl. mid-Sept. through Apr; groups by appointment. Estab. 1950 to diffuse knowledge and appreciation of the Pony Express and its relation to the expansion of the West; under administration of St. Joseph Museum.
Collections: Western history, archaeology with emphasis on the Pony Express.
Activities: Guided tours, lectures, films, permanent and temporary exhibitions, traveling exhibitions.
Library: 300 volumes for reference only.
Attendance: 35,000.

ST. LOUIS

ARTISTS GUILD OF ST. LOUIS*
277 E. Lockwood Ave, Webster Groves, 63119.
Paul A. McHugh, Exec. Mgr.
Open daily 11 AM - 3 PM; Sun. 1 - 5 PM; cl. Tues. Founded 1886, inc. 1906, as a non-profit organization; owns large building containing 3 galleries, and recreational facilities; owns large collection of purchase-prize art for exhibition locally and out-of-town. Mem. 382; dues $35 and higher.

Exhibitions: Sept. - May, continuously in 3 galleries; 3 week open-competitive juried exhibits with cash prizes; a money-raising prestige Special Event show is usually an annual event; 3 plays are also given on stage. Competitive exhibitions are usually Crafts and Sculpture; Watercolors and Pastel; Young Artists (18 yrs. to 25 yrs); Prints and Drawings; Portraits; Painting; Artists Guild Art Section. When possible, there is a two-man or small group exhibition, in small gallery.

Activities: Opening art show receptions, weekly weaving classes, lectures, dinners, plays.

Publications: A roster of members and exhibition schedule is printed annually.

Income and Prizes: Income $18,000; prizes $4000 average, annually.

ARTS AND EDUCATION COUNCIL OF GREATER ST. LOUIS
607 N. Grand St, 63103. Tel: (314) 531-6450
Homer E. Sayad, Chmn.
H. E. Wuertenbaecher, Jr, Pres.
H. O. Johnston, Secy.
Anthony Turney, Exec. Dir.
Estab. March, 1963. The purpose of the organization consists of coordinating, promoting and assisting in the development of cultural and educational activities in the Greater St. Louis area through the cooperative efforts of citizens acting in council; to offer generally, planning, coordinating, promotional and fund-raising service to eligible organizations and groups, thereby creating a valuable community-wide association. Mem. 111 agencies.
Publications; Calendar of Cultural Events monthly.

MISSOURI HISTORICAL SOCIETY
Jefferson Memorial Bldg, 63112. Tel: (314) 726-2622
John L. Gillis, Pres.
John H. Lindenbusch, Exec. Dir.
Mrs. Ernst A. Stadler, Manuscript Librn.
Nancy Smith, Librn.
John F. Lesser, Museum Cur.
Mrs. Carey W. Judah, Cur. Costume Collection
Gail Guidry, Cur. Pictures
Frances Starr, Supvr. Educ. Dept.
Free daily 9:30 AM - 4:45 PM; Library cl. Sun. & Mon. Estab. 1866 to collect and preserve objects and information relating to the history of Missouri and the Louisiana Purchase Territory. Ann. meeting Sept; mem. 4000; dues from $15.
Collections: †Historical and genealogical library, †newspapers, †manuscripts, †paintings, †prints, †photographs, †costumes, †early Midwestern arts and crafts, †other museum objects.
Activities: Lectures and tours for members; children's programs.
Libraries: Research library. Pictorial Dept, 75,000 photographs, prints, and other material.
Publications: Bulletin, quarterly.
Attendance: 400,000.

✠THE ST. LOUIS ART MUSEUM
  Forest Park, 63110. Tel: (314) 721-0067
George S. Rosborough, Jr, Pres.
James Nowell Wood, Dir.
Alan Brimble, Secy. & Controller
Clements L. Robertson, Conservator
Richard S. Cleveland, Design Coordinator
Christy B. Shreffler, Pub. Information Officer
Rick Gaugert, Program Coordinator
Martha O'Neil, Exec. Secy, Friends of the St. Louis Art Museum
Ann Abid, Librn.
Thelma R. Stockho, Acting Cur. Educ.
William E. Trampier, Bldg. Supt.
Mrs. Herbert M. Patton, Jr, Registrar
Scott Vogel, Mgr. Museum Shop
John Bloecher, Supt. Security
Thomas T. Hoopes, Cur. Emeritus
Richard S. Cleveland, Assoc. Cur. Oriental Art
Jack Cowart, Assoc. Cur. 19th & 20th Century Art
Nancy Ward Neilson, Assoc. Cur. Prints & Drawings
Lee A. Parsons, Assoc. Cur. Pre-Columbian & Primitive Art
Lynn E. Springer, Assoc. Cur. Decorative Arts
Free 10 AM - 5 PM; Tues. 2:30 - 9:30 PM; cl. Mon, Christmas &
New Year's Day. Special exhibitions, admis. voluntary amount.
Estab. 1909 as City Art Museum succeeding the St. Louis Museum of
Fine Arts, estab. 1879 by Washington University; supported by City
and County of St. Louis property tax. Ann. meeting May; mem. 6500;
dues $18.50 and higher.
  Collections: Spanning 5000 years, the Museum's collections are
representative of the best visual arts of Europe, Africa, Asia and
Oceania, as well as the Americas. Particularly fine are the collections of 15th and 16th century Northern European painting; 17th century Dutch painting; 18th - 20th century American painting; 19th and
20th century French painting; 20th century European sculpture;
American and European decorative arts; Chinese bronzes and porcelains; Oriental rugs; African sculpture; pre-Columbian art; arts
of the South Seas. Due to limitations of space, only a portion of the
total collections can be viewed at any one time. Therefore, the
Museum reserves a number of galleries for rotation exhibitions to
ensure that the public may view as many of the best works as possible. The Museum is currently undergoing extensive renovation
which will greatly improve gallery space.
  Special Exhibitions: (1974-75) Mughal and Deccani Paintings
from the Collection of Edwin Binney, III; Second St. Louis Area Art-
ists Exhibition: Sculpture by Marie Taylor and Paintings by Wallace
Herndon Smith; The Architecture of St. Louis; Aspects of Irish Art;
Mid-America 5; The Rediscovered Work of William J. Hinchey;
Jacob Lawrence in Retrospect; Georgia O'Keeffe in St. Louis; The
Black Presence in Art; Artists from the Royal Botanical Gardens,
Kew; On View: American Watercolors and Drawings, Recent Acquisi-
tions, the Barbizon School; The Steinberg Gifts; Third St. Louis Area
Artists Exhibition: Muriel Nezhnie Helfman and Heikki Seppa; The
Eads Bridge; Tribute to Mark Tobey; Wallace Duck Prints; Costumes
from the Collection of Steven Edison; New Japanese Photography;
Three New England Watercolor Painters; Chris Wilmarth: Nine
Clearings for a Standing Man; Charles Meryon - Prints and Draw-
ings; Venetian Drawings from American Collections; Robert
Rauschenberg "Pages" and "Fuses;" A Retrospective of Arthur G.
Dove; 20th Century Sculpture from the Permanent Collection; Ritual
Arts of the South Seas; Bingham's Missouri.
  Activities: Special exhibitions of national importance; film se-
ries; seminars; children's programs; courses of study for adults
and children; gallery talks and guided tours. The Teachers Re-
source Center makes available to area teachers slides, information
sheets on works of art in the collection and other classroom aids.
Restaurant. Museum Shop.
  Library: First-rate reference library containing 20,000 volumes;
pamphlet files; slides; photographs and rare books.
  Publications: Bimonthly Bulletin; biennial Museum Monographs;
Museum Newsletter for area schools; special exhibition catalogs.
  Attendance: 500,000.

✠ST. LOUIS PUBLIC LIBRARY
  1301 Olive St, 63103. Tel: (314) 241-2288
Paxton R. Price, Librn.
Martha Hilligoss, Chief Art Dept.
Open Mon, Wed, Thurs. & Fri. 9 AM - 9 PM; Tues. & Sat. 9 AM -
5 PM; cl. Sun. Art Dept. estab. 1912. About 44,000 volumes on fine
and applied arts; Steedman Architectural Library of 1290 volumes;
15,000 color slides on art history; framed and unframed reproductions and sculpture replicas loaned free.
  Income and Purchases: Annual income of Library $4,953,289;
purchases (Art Dept) $13,620.

WASHINGTON UNIVERSITY GALLERY OF ART
  Steinberg Hall, 63130. Tel: (314) 863-0100 Exten. 4128
Graham W. J. Beal, Dir.

Hours: Mon. - Fri. 9 AM - 5 PM; Sat. 10 AM - 4 PM; Sun. 1 - 5 PM.
Collection estab. 1879, building 1960.
  Collections: Paintings, drawings and prints 16th through 20th cen-
tury; 19th and 20th century sculpture; Greek vases and Artifacts;
Greek and Roman coin collection.
  Exhibitions: About four circulating exhibitions a school year plus
annual faculty and student exhibitions.
  Activities: Educational work from the Department of Art and
Archaeology in History of World Art; original objects of art lent.
  Library: (serving School of Architecture, School of Fine Arts,
Dept. of Art and Archaeology and public) 50,000 volumes, books,
periodicals, pamphlets, and other publications.

SEDALIA

SEDALIA ART ASSOCIATION, INC.
  P.O. Box 643, 65301.
W. J. Eschbacher, Pres.
Mrs. Lonnie Schott, Secy.
Estab. 1971 for promotion and enjoyment of visual arts; financed by
mem. Mem. 60; dues $10.
  Exhibitions: Annual art show.
  Activities: Lectures open to the public; 4 to 6 visiting lecturers
per year; classes for adults and children; competitions.
  Library: 30 volume library.
  Publications: Monthly bulletin.
  Attendance: 30 annual average.

SPRINGFIELD

SOUTHWEST MISSOURI MUSEUM ASSOCIATES
  1111 Brookside Dr, 65807. Tel: (417) 866-2716
Officers change each year.
  Estab. 1928 as Springfield Art Museum, which it created and
gave to the City of Springfield in 1947. Ann. meeting May; mem.
1380, dues $7 nonresident $4.50. Has 75 art study groups of about
20 members each, meeting monthly. Publishes Bulletin monthly;
annual report in May.

✠SPRINGFIELD ART MUSEUM*
  1111 E. Brookside Dr, 65807. Tel: (417) 866-2716
Kenneth M. Shuck, Dir.
Dudley C. Murphy, Educational Cur.
Greg G. Thielen, Librn.
Free 9 AM - 5 PM; Sun. 1 - 5 PM; Tues, Wed. and Thurs. 6:30 -
9:30 PM. Estab. and inc. 1928; museum became municipal in 1947;
founding group reincorporated as Southwest Missouri Museum As-
sociates. Mem. 1234; dues $5.
  Collections: Permanent collection of †American art, †graphic art,
†ceramics and †Americana.
  Exhibitions: Sponsors annual exhibition Nov, open to all artists of
Missouri, Oklahoma, Arkansas, Iowa, Kansas, Nebraska, Louisiana,
Mississippi, Alabama and Tennessee. Purchase and prize awards
$2000; 1963-1973, sponsors national competition Watercolor U.S.A,
May. Purchase and prize awards $10,000; 1968-1973. Monthly cir-
culating exhibitions and temporary historical gallery.
  Activities: Associates conduct 62 study groups in Springfield and
9 in surrounding towns.
  Library: Art reference library of 300 volumes and 5000 clippings,
both available for lending.
  Income: $120,000.
  Publications: Bulletin for members; exhibition catalogues; weekly
news release.
  Attendance: 100,000.

UNIVERSITY GALLERY
Southwest Missouri State University
  901 S. National, 65802. Tel: (417) 531-1561, Exten. 204
Dennis H. Rexroad, Gallery Dir.
Dianne Strickland, Asst. Dir.
Rodney S. Frew, Chmn. Gallery Installations
Anna Dawson, Secy.
Free Mon. - Sat. 8 AM - 10:30 PM; Sun. 2 - 10:30 PM. Estab. 1963
to present exhibitions of interest and educational value to the uni-
versity community and general public; financed by state appropria-
tion.
  Collections: All exhibitions are temporary, however a collection
of contemporary and historical prints is being enlarged yearly.
  Exhibitions: 10 shows per year. African sculpture from private
collections; prints by pop, op and super-realists; Goya prints; Wayne
Thiebaud paintings, drawings and prints; 19th century Japanese
woodcuts; Les Krims photographs; Arline Fisch body jewelry,
Arthur Sandoval tapestries; German graphic arts.
  Activities: Photograph collection for reference and instruction;
lectures open to public; visiting lecturers; gallery talks and tours.
  Annual income: $2600.

MONTANA

ANACONDA

COPPER VILLAGE MUSEUM AND ARTS CENTER OF DEER LODGE COUNTY
Eighth & Main, P.O. Box 29, 59711. Tel: (406) 563-3604
Jack Boley, Pres.
Marian Geil, Secy.
Mary Jane Brimhall, Dir.
Betty Dotson, Admin. Asst.
Free Sun, Tues, Thurs, Fri. & Sat. 1 - 5 PM; Wed. 7 - 9 PM; June - Aug. Tues. - Fri. 9 AM - 5 PM (cl. noon); Wed. 7 - 9 PM; Sat. & Sun. 1 - 5 PM. Estab. Sept. 1971 to provide for the cultural enrichment for the community; financed by city and state appropriation and membership. Maintains gallery of 48 ft. x 36 ft burlap panelled walls; track lighting; black ceiling; no windows; portable panels; cubes with plexiglas covers. General membership meeting annually; board meets monthly; mem. 150.
Collections: Local historical items only.
Exhibitions: (1975-76) Art and Artifacts of South America; Albrecht Durer - The Apocalypse; Native Funk & Flash; Currier and Ives; Sr. Joeann Daley, European Sketchbook; Toys, Handmade and Antique; Brian Persha, pottery; Brenda Herndon, batiks; Kevin Red Star, paintings; Coyote Tales of the Montana Salish; Lela Autio, fabric sculpture, Dennis Smith, raku; Judy Nansel, paintings; Whistler, prints; Local Artists Show; Hogarth, original prints; Daumier, original prints; Shirley Bentley Cleary; Copper Fest; Orlin Helgoe, paintings; Classical Narratives in Master Drawings.
Activities: Classes and workshops and demonstrations as well as films and lectures to fit with exhibits; lectures open to public, 4 visiting lecturers per year; 4 gallery talks; concerts, dramatic programs, classes for adults and children, competitions; Sales gallery.
Library: 15 volumes of great masters and of an art historical nature for reference; photograph collection.
Publications: Monthly exhibit brochures.
Attendance: Approx. 12,000.

BILLINGS

BILLINGS ART ASSOCIATION*
2523 Beartooth Dr, 59102.
Archie Elliot, Pres.
Terry Palm, V.Pres.
Connie Landis, Secy.-Treas.
Estab. in 1948 as a branch of the Montana Institute of the Arts to preserve the heritage of the State as found in its history and folklore and to stimulate creative work in the several arts. The Institute sponsors an annual Festival of the Arts, a film competition and publishes a magazine, Montana Arts, six times yearly. The Association holds monthly meetings in the interest groups of fine arts, crafts, weaving and writing and three meetings per year of the combined membership. Exhibitions and demonstrations are also sponsored. MIA has approx. 1000 members, BAA approx. 125.

✤YELLOWSTONE COUNTY FINE ARTS CENTER
401 N. 27th St, 59101. Tel: (406) 259-1869
Richard C. King, Pres, Yellowstone Art Center Foundation
Robert E. Fehlberg, Chmn, Yellowstone County Fine Arts Center Commission
Donna M. Forbes, Dir, Yellowstone Art Center
Free daily Tues. - Sun. Noon - 5 PM; Thurs. & Fri. evenings 7 - 9 PM; cl. Mon. Estab. Oct. 1964; the Yellowstone Art Center is devoted to exhibitions in the visual arts, music, dance and lectures. Ann. meeting June; mem. approx. 800; dues $10 individual, $15 family and other higher. Operation and maintenance by Yellowstone County.
Collections: Permanent collections being formed in paintings and ceramics.
Exhibitions: Local, regional and traveling exhibitions from the U.S. and abroad. New Western Room Gallery.
Activities: Children's classes in art and ceramics; adult classes in drawing, ceramics, photography and painting; lectures; gallery talks and tours; concerts; dramatic programs and films; library.
Publications: Bulletins monthly; Newsletter monthly.
Attendance: 30,000 annual average.

BOZEMAN

KETTERER ART CENTER
35 North Grand, 59715. Tel: (406) 586-5021
Raymond W. Campeau, Dir.
Rand Honadel, Cur.
Free Sept. - May, Tues. - Sun. 1 - 5:30 PM; June - Aug, Tues. - Sun. 10 AM - 5:30 PM. Estab. 1968 to enrich the cultural environment of the community of Bozeman; a regional gallery exhibiting work of living artists; 12 shows a year.

Activities: Traveling exhibitions organized and circulated; individual paintings lent to schools; 50 items in an average year; lectures open to public, 5 visiting lecturers per year; 12 gallery talks; 25 tours; classes for adults and children in jewelry, ceramics, graphics, painting; competitions.
Income: $30,000.
Attendance: 10,000.

MONTANA STATE UNIVERSITY*
Museum of the Rockies
59715. Tel: (406) 994-2251
Leslie C. Drew, Dir.
This community-university museum, located on the campus in its specifically designed buildings, supplements classroom instruction from the elementary levels through the graduate level with specific attention to the out-of-school visitor. Collections include 545 original paintings, prints, drawings and sculptures. The exhibition programs utilizing collections are interpreting the physical and social heritages of the Northern Rockies Region.

Exit Gallery
Student Union Building, 59715. Tel: (406) 994-4501
Exhibitions are co-sponsored by MSU Art Club and the Associated Students of Montana State University. Traveling and local exhibitions, principally contemporary. Adjunct programs: lectures, workshops for faculty, students, and public, sponsored by the School of Art.

BROWNING

MUSEUM OF THE PLAINS INDIAN AND CRAFTS CENTER
Box 400, 59417. Tel: (406) 338-2230
Myles Libhart, Dir. of Museums, Exhibitions & Publications
Rosemary Ellison, Supvr. Indian Arts & Crafts Board Museum Prog.
Free June 1 - Sept. 15 Mon. - Sun. 8 AM - 8 PM; Sept. 16 - 30 Mon. - Sun. 8 AM - 5 PM; Oct. 1 - May 31 Mon. - Fri. 9 AM - 5 PM; cl. Sat, Sun. & nat. holidays during Oct. 1 - May 31. Estab. 1941, administered and operated by the Indian Arts and Crafts Board, US. Department of the Interior.
Collections: Historic and contemporary arts of the Plains Indian, including †decorative arts, †folk arts, †paintings, †sculpture, †graphics.
Exhibitions: Permanent exhibitions of historic and contemporary arts of the Plains Indian; presents at Museum continuing series of one-person exhibitions of work by contemporary Indian and Eskimo artists and craftsmen of the U.S; traveling exhibitions include (1972) Contemporary Indian Artists—Montana/Wyoming/Idaho, with regional tour scheduled by the Museum; Coyote Tales of the Montana Salish.
Activities: Gallery tours for schools and other groups, loans of slide lecture kits to schools.
Sales Shop: Operated by the Northern Plains Indian Crafts Association; offers a wide variety of authentic contemporary craft products and fine arts by Indian artists and craftsmen of the Plains and other areas.
Publications: One-person exhibition brochure series; Contemporary Indian Artists— Montana/Wyoming/Idaho; Coyote Tales of the Montana Salish.
Attendance: Average 85,000.

DILLON

WESTERN MONTANA COLLEGE ART GALLERY
710 S. Atlantic, 59725. Tel: (406) 683-7232
Jim Corr, Dir.
Free weekdays 8 AM - 5 PM. Estab. Oct. 1, 1969 to provide a viewing opportunity for Southwestern Montana; financed by endowment.
Activities: Teacher training program; traveling exhibitions organized and circulated; individual paintings and original objects of art lent; 60 paintings and drawings in lending collection.
Attendance: 6000.

GLASGOW

FORT PECK FINE ARTS COUNCIL
59230. Tel: (406) 228-4341
Paul Ressmeyer, Pres.
Kathy Makich, Secy.
Carl Dix, Treas.
Inc. 1970 to promote fine arts, theatre and other entertainment for eastern Montana. Summer theatre with gallery type showing in lobby, changed weekly.
Income and Purchases: $24,000.
Attendance: 14,000.

GREAT FALLS

✤C. M. RUSSELL MUSEUM AND ORIGINAL STUDIO
   1201 Fourth Ave. N, 59401. Tel: (406) 452-7369
Ray W. Steele, Dir.
Open summer, Mon. - Sat. 10 AM - 5 PM; Sun. - 1 - 5 PM; winter,
Tues. - Sat. 10 AM - 5 PM; Sun. 1 - 5 PM. Estab. 1953. Ann. mem.
student $2, individual and family $15, assoc. $35, supporting $50,
sustaining $100, sponsor $500.
   Collections: Works by Charles M. Russell and other Western
works, historical and contemporary.
   Exhibitions: Traveling exhibitions in contemporary arts; more
than a dozen exhibitions are offered yearly along with related pro-
grams within the arts.
   Activities: Gift shop, books, reproductions, jewelry; children's
theatre, creative dramatics; film program; Arts/Science Fair.
Creative workshops, annual C. M. Russell Auction.
   Library: Western Americana, 500 items.
   Operating Budget: $125,000.
   Attendance: (1974) 50,000.

HELENA

ARCHIE BRAY FOUNDATION
   2915 Country Club Ave, 59601. Tel: (406) 442-2521
Peter Meloy, Chmn. Board of Dir.
Branson Stevenson, Secy.
David Cornell, Dir.
Judy Cornell, Asst. Dir.
Free Mon. - Sat. 9 AM - 5 PM; cl. Sun. Inc. 1952 to make a fine
place to work available for all who are seriously and sincerely interested in any of the branches of the ceramic arts; financed by the sale
of the pottery and clay materials. Revolving monthly shows of contem-
porary ceramics and glass; also permanent collection of ceramics.
   Collections: †Permanent collection of 107 pieces of ceramics,
continually being expanded.
   Exhibitions: Approx. 25 one-man ceramics shows.
   Activities: Slides of the permanent collection for rent; classes for
adults; resident crafts program, for those wishing to study 1 to 2 years
to see if they could do it for a living.
   Library: Approx. 160 volumes for lending and reference.
   Income and Purchases: Income $40,000; purchases approx. $1000.
   Attendance: Estimated 3500.

MONTANA HISTORICAL SOCIETY
   225 N. Roberts St, 59601. Tel: (406) 449-2694
Ken Korte, Dir.
Vivian A. Paladin, Publ.
Harriett Meloy, Librn.
Open Mon. - Fri. 8 AM - 5 PM; Sat. and Sun. 12 AM - 5 PM.
Summer hours, daily 8 AM - 8 PM, June 1 - Labor Day. Estab.
1865; State appropriation. Mem. 10,000; dues $10 includes maga-
zine.
   Collections: Large collection of the works of Charles M. Russell;
Poindexter Collection of Modern Art.
   Exhibitions: Some special shows each year; formal museum
featuring frontiers of Montana; Territory Junction, street scene '80s;
new wing opened summer of 1970 with antique car display; rotating
exhibits; annual Western Art Show.
   Library: Specializes in history of Montana and the West. 100,000
volumes, including books, newspapers of the Territory and State,
manuscripts, personal papers, state archives, business record and
30,000 photographs.
   Publications: Montana, Magazine of Western History, quarterly
magazine; Montana Post, membership bulletin, quarterly. Society
publishes and sells many art reprints of works of Charles M. Russell, orginal Russell bronzes; good western books.
   Income and Purchases: Income $400,000; purchases vary.
   Attendance: (1974) 122,218.

KALISPELL

✤HOCKADAY CENTER FOR THE ARTS
Flathead Valley Art Association
   Second Ave. E. & Third St. (Box 83), 59901. Tel: (406) 755-5268
Karen J. Lauder, Dir.
Marsha Davis, Secy.
Free Mon. - Sat. 12 AM - 5 PM. Estab. 1967 to encourage interest
and particpation in all art forms through a program of traveling
exhibits, classes, films and recitals; supported by city or state
appropriation and membership. The center is housed in the old Carnegie Library Building which has three galleries on the main floor
and one downstairs. Ann. meeting 3rd Mon. in Nov; mem. approx.
250; dues individual $5.
   Collections: The main collection includes eight portrait studies
by Hugh Hockaday, the center's late namesake, as well as several
other of his works.

   Exhibitions: Changed monthly; include a wide variety of art forms
from Japanese posters to fabric sculpture by Dana Boussard. An-
nual juried art competition with $450 in awards.
   Activities: Lectures open to the public, several visiting lecturers
per year; concerts, drama programs; classes for adults and children;
pottery lab with full-time resident potter; darkroom facilities.
   Library: 100 volumes for lending and reference.
   Publications: Monthly bulletin to members.
   Income: $24,000.
   Attendance: Approx. 9000 per year.

MISSOULA

GALLERY OF VISUAL ARTS*
   Turner Hall, University of Montana, 59801.
   Tel: (406) 243-5416
Dean Douglas, Dir.
Grove Hull, Cur.
Michelle B. Wurth, Cur. Asst.
Free, Mon. - Fri, Summer & Academic year, 10 AM - 5 PM, Sat. &
Sun, Academic year, 2 - 5 PM. Estab. 1970 to provide exhibit space
for students and faculty of the Art Dept. at the University of Montana
and for periodical showings of the University's permanent art col-
lection; to sponsor outside exhibitions in an effort to acquaint the
community and the university with significant comtemporary artists
nationwide; to provide guest lecturers to the community; financed
by city and state appropriation. Gallery, 60 x 40 ft. exhibit space;
spot and flood lighting; moveable panels; 14 ft. ceilings.
   Collections: Dana Collection; Poindexter Collection.
   Exhibitions: Armajani Exhibition; Art of the North American
Plains Indians; Bruce Barton Exhibition; Ceramics Exhibition; Con-
temporary Indian Art Exhibit; Drawing Exhibition; Durer, Al-
brecht; Faculty Exhibition (every Fall); Fakeye, Lamidi; Helgoe,
Orlin; Indian Art Show; Invisible/Visible; Kuo, Alex; Pratt Graphics
Center; Rocky Mountain Print Show; Student Thesis Shows (every
Spring); Xerox - 1st Annual Xerox Open; Zucker; Multiples & Change-
Student Show; Phil Navasya-Paintings; John Smart-Photographs; Ivan
Karp Slide Show; George Longfish Paintings; Art Auction & Exhibit
(every Dec); Chamberlain, Zucker, Cosgrove.
   Activities: Original objects of art lent; lending collection, 100
Kodachromes; lectures, open to the public; 5 visiting lecturers per
year; competitions; scholarships.
   Income: $3000.
   Attendance: 10,261 annual average.

SIDNEY

J. K. RALSTON MUSEUM AND ART CENTER
   221 Fifth St. S.W./basement, P.O. Box 50, 59270.
   Tel: (406) 482-3500
Charles Evanson, Pres.
Mrs. Jean Gladowski, Secy.
Linda K. Mann, Museum Dir.
Free 1 - 5 & 7 - 8:30 PM summer; 1 - 5 PM winter; cl. Mon. & Sat.
Estab. 1972 to preserve our area's historical value and bring it to
the public's attention and to bring a cultural awareness of the arts
to young and old alike; financed by city and county appropriations.
Ann. meeting Mar; mem. approx. 300; dues $5 per member.
   Exhibitions: J. K. Ralston; Bob Southland; MIA Festival; Roscoe
White Eagle; Bill Stockton; David Dreisbach; Coyote Tales; Isabelle
Johnson Collection; Norwegian Prints; Costumes and Native Dress
from Guatemala; Bohdan Osycika; Markand Thakar; Leonard Scheu;
Julie Bush; W.P.A. Prints; Tipi Design Exhibit; Norwegian Crafts
and Rosemaling; Daumier Prints; Classical Narratives of Old
Masters; Helcoe Exhibit; Steven McLeod; Juried art show; local
artists-children; young adults and adults.
   Activities: Classes in various art media for all ages; panels
available for local and traveling exhibits; photograph collection for
reference; dramatic programs; classes for adults and children.
Sales shop.
   Historical Reference Library contains reference material, old
photographs, catalogs, magazines, newspapers, microfilm, school
annuals; early Montana published works with emphasis on Montana
and Mon-Dak area.
   Attendance: 2300 annual average.

NEBRASKA

BROWNVILLE

BROWNVILLE HISTORICAL SOCIETY, INC.
   68321. Tel: (402) 825-6001
The Museum, Carson House and Wheel Museum open 2 - 5 daily,
June, July & Aug; Sun. May through Oct; cl. Mon; admis. adults 50¢,
children under 16, 25¢. Estab. 1956 to preserve the heritage and
culture of early Nebraskans. Supported by festivals and members.
Mem. over 450; dues $7.

Activities: Festivals held three times a year; Antique Flea Market; Muzzle Loaders; National Old Fiddlers Contest; tour of restored homes.

Publications: Quarterly bulletin.

Attendance: 3000 to 30,000 per festival.

Carriage House Art Gallery
Brownville Fine Arts Association, 68321.
Open Wed. - Fri. 1 - 5 PM; weekends 10 AM - 6 PM; cl. Mon. & Tues. Founded 1970 to promote the cultural activities of early and present Nebraska and to establish a place for new artists to work. Supported by mem. and festivals. Mem. 400; dues $7.

Activities: Fine Arts Day; Folk Life Festival; seminars, concerts, summer music workshops for teenagers, dance and symphony.

Attendance: 300 to 10,000.

MUIR HOUSE*
Corner Atlantic and 2nd St, 68321. Tel: (402) 825-4671
Mrs. Harold Dihel Le Mar, Owner & Mgr.
Cecelia Kudron, Asst.
Open 10 AM - 6 PM on Festival Days; Sun. and special tours by appointment; admis. 75¢, 35¢ for youth 10-16, younger free accompanied by adult. Built 1868-1870, restored 1961, solely to show what living was during the pre-1900 years; educational; furnished historically correct.

Collections: All collections are permanent; many art books, and history-school childrens books; Bibles of early years, music, and stereoscape views as early as they were made.

Exhibitions: Dolls and furniture.

Activities: Material loaned to historic societies of approved nature, up to 25 photographs; kodachromes taken and shown but not loaned; approx. 15 gallery tours in summer only (Tours by appointment, 556-6010).

Attendance: 800.

CHADRON

CHADRON STATE COLLEGE ART GALLERY
Division of Fine Arts, 69337. Tel: (308) 432-4451, Exten. 317
Free Mon. - Fri. 9 AM - 4 PM; other times by request. Estab. 1970 to have a showplace for student and faculty work as well as visiting artists and traveling shows; financed by city and state appropriation.

Collections: Works of former students and faculty. No attempt to purchase works from specific artist or period.

Exhibitions: Sence of Place; Nebraska Centennial Quilt Show.

Activities: Individual paintings lent to schools; 50 color reproductions in lending collection; lectures open to public; 1 or 2 gallery talks per year; concerts, dramatic programs, classes for adults; scholarships. (See Schools)

Attendance: 2000.

CHAPPELL

CHAPPELL MEMORIAL LIBRARY AND ART GALLERY
69129. Tel: (308) 874-2626
Doris McFee, Librn.
Gallery open Mon. & Wed. 2 - 5 PM, 7 - 9 PM; Sat. 2 - 6 PM. Estab. 1935, by gift of Mrs. Charles Henry Chappell to the City.

Collections: Paintings; etchings and other prints; Indian paintings; Japanese and Chinese prints and paintings. The collection is a permanent one and was the personal collection of Mrs. Charles Henry Chappell.

GERING

SCOTTS BLUFF NATIONAL MONUMENT
Department of the Interior, National Park Service, Box 427, 69341. Tel: (308) 436-4340
Donald R. Harper, Supt.
Lary D. Barney, Supv. Park Ranger
Linda Hahn, Admin. Officer
Free, Day after Labor Day through May 29, 8 AM - 4:30 PM, May 30 through Labor Day 8 AM - 8:30 PM. Estab. 1919 for commemoration of the Oregon Trail; supported by Federal Government. Gallery has three exhibit rooms, Oregon Trail Room, Landmark Room, and William H. Jackson Memorial Wing.

Collections: †Permanent collection of original watercolor paintings.

Library: 100 volume reference library.

HASTINGS

HASTINGS MUSEUM
1330 N. Burlington, 68901. Tel: (402) 463-7126
O. J. McDougal, Jr, Pres.
Charles Osborne, Secy.

Burton R. Nelson, Dir.
Geraldine S. Shuman, Admin. Asst.
Michael J. Reiners, Exhibits Specialist
Chanda A. Miller, Accessions Registrar
Milburn Erickson, Cur. of Astronomy
Open Sun. & Holidays, 1 - 5 PM, Sept. - May 8 AM - 5 PM, June - Aug. 8 AM - 8 PM; admis. adults 75¢, children 25¢. Estab. 1926 for a program of service and exhibits to augment and stimulate the total educative program of schools and the general public; financed by city appropriation. Mem. 950, dues $1.

Collections: George W. Cole Smith & Wesson Collection; Richards Coin Collection; Richard Conroy Big Game Trophies; bird and mammal habitat groups; gems & precious stones; J. M. McDonald Planetarium; American Indian exhibits and artifacts; over 700 firearms; early farm equipment; antique automobiles; glassware, furniture.

Activities: Educational department gives talks and tours to school groups, several educational pamphlets; photograph collection for lending and reference. Book shop.

Library: 1000 volume reference library, at museum only.

Publications: Yester News, monthly except July, Aug. & Sept.

Income and Purchases: Income $83,000; purchases $25,000.

Attendance: 42,875.

LINCOLN

ELDER ART GALLERY
Nebraska Wesleyan University
50th & St. Paul Sts, 68504. Tel: (402) 466-2371
William J. Evans, Dir.
Free Tues. - Fri. 10 AM - 5 PM; Sat. 10 AM - 4 PM; Sun. 3 - 5 PM; cl. Mon. Estab. 1966 for the display of student work, one-man shows, group shows and exhibition of permanent collection; university budget. 4 meetings per year; mem. 30; no dues.

Collections: †Permanent Collection of Prints, Paintings and Sculpture (purchases made with university funds and grants from private foundations); Campus Collection (works donated by university alumni).

Activities: Lectures open to public; 2 gallery talks and 4 tours per year; concerts.

Income and Purchases: Income $7500; purchases $5000.

Attendance: 8000 annual average.

LINCOLN COMMUNITY ARTS COUNCIL
Room 508 Lincoln Center Bldg, 68508. Tel: (402) 477-5930
Larry Lusk, Pres.
Mary Alice Snider, Secy.
Patsy Davidson, Coordinator
Open 8:45 AM - 4:45 PM. Estab. 1967 to promote and encourage the community-at-large and all its arts organizations to grow, develop, use all the resources available, avoid over-lapping of energy, money, talent, and to enrich the entire community; clearing house for arts activities scheduling; financed by endowment, city and state appropriation and membership. Monthly meetings; 50 groups representing 100 members; dues prorated.

Publications: Newsletter; arts calendar (6 per year).

✠NEBRASKA ART ASSOCIATION
Sheldon Memorial Art Gallery
University of Nebraska, 68508.
Mrs. Carl H. Rohman, Pres.
Mrs. John H. Ames, 1st V.Pres.
Mrs. James A. Rawley, Secy.
Mrs. Dwight Cherry, Treas.
Open Tues. 10 AM - 10 PM; Wed. - Sat. 10 AM - 5 PM; Sun. 2 - 5 PM; cl. Mon. Estab. 1888 as Haydon Art Club, inc. 1900 with present name. Ann. meeting June; mem. 1025.

Collections: †Nebraska Art Association collection of American paintings, sculpture, prints, drawings, and ceramics; †Nelle Cochrane Woods collection of American paintings, purchased through endowment; †Thomas C. Woods collection of American paintings purchased through endowment.

Activities: Annual exhibitions of contemporary art in conjunction with University of Nebraska Art Galleries, with lectures and purchases.

Purchases: Approx. $15,000 annually available for restricted purchases.

NEBRASKA STATE HISTORICAL SOCIETY
1500 R St, 68508. Tel: (402) 432-2793
Nellie Snyder Yost, Pres.
Marvin F. Kivett, Society Dir.
Ann Reinert, Librn.
James Potter, Archivist
Free 8 AM - 5 PM; Sun. 1:30 - 5 PM; cl. some major holidays. Estab. 1867 to preserve and disseminate information regarding the history of Nebraska and the West. Ann. meeting spring and fall; mem. 5200; dues $3

Collections: Chiefly of the Plains Indians and Nebraska Pioneers; Archaeological Collection; some regional paintings.
Library: Reference library of 60,000 volumes; photograph collection of 60,000 prints.
Publications: Nebraska History, quarterly; Historical News Letter, monthly; publications in anthropology, and history, and educational leaflets, irregularly.
Income: $1,000,000 yearly.
Attendance: 100,000.
Branch Museums (open during summer months): Fort Robinson Museum, near Crawford; George W. Norris Home, McCook; Thomas P. Kennard Home, Lincoln; Neligh Mills, Neligh; Chimney Rock, Bayard; John G. Neihardt Center, Bancroft; Three Mobile Museums.

UNIVERSITY OF NEBRASKA ART GALLERIES

Sheldon Memorial Art Gallery, 68508. Tel: (402) 472-2461, 2463
Norman A. Geske, Dir.
John Nelson, Asst. to Dir.
Mrs. A. Douglas Anderson, Dir, Educational Services
Dan Ladely, Dir. Sheldon Film Theater
Helen Duven, Secy.
Ruth York, Secy.
Mrs. Robert Spence, Mgr, Art Shop
Free Tues. 10 AM - 10 PM; Wed. - Sat. 10 AM - 5 PM; Sun. 2 - 5 PM; cl. Mon, Thanksgiving, Christmas, New Year's, July 4th, Labor Day; other holidays open 2 - 5 PM.
Collections: †Frank M. Hall Collection of contemporary paintings, sculpture, prints, drawings, photographs, ceramics, purchased through endowment; †Nebraska Art Association Collection of American paintings, sculpture, prints, drawings, ceramics; †Howard S. Wilson Memorial Collection of American paintings and drawings; Bertha Schaefer Bequest.
Exhibitions: Prints by Michael Nushawg; Paintings by Clayton Pond; Rope sculptures by Bill Lockhart; Quilts from Nebraska Collections; Serigraphs by Barry Lewis; Folgers Silver Collection; Joe Miller Paintings; Photographs by Michael Simon; Prints by Winslow Homer; Photographs by Robert Grier; Paintings and Drawings by Ralph Albert Blakelock; Paintings by Walter B. Wilson; John Stewart Prints; Three Lithographers: Bruce Lowney, John Himmelfarb, Don Eddy; Photographs by Carl Sesto; Posters ca. 1900; Photographs by Richard Faller; Photographs by Ellen Landweber; Illustrated Books; Weavings by Mary Kester.
Activities: Gallery talks, concerts, films and Lincoln Friends of Chamber Music. Art shop, sale and rental of original works in all media.
Purchases: $30,000 annually.
Attendance: 115,300.

McCOOK

HIGH PLAINS MUSEUM*
423 Norris Ave, 69001. Tel: (308) 345-3661
Ray Search, Pres.
Open daily 1:30 - 4:30 PM; no admis. Estab. 1966 to preserve the items pertaining to the local history and to interpret them to the public; financed by membership. Ann. meeting Jan; mem. approx. 50; dues $2.
Collections: Donated paintings; paintings made on the barracks walls of prisoners of war camp near McCook.
Activities: Lectures open to the public; 2 gallery talks; 60 tours. Book shop.
Library: Approx. 500 volumes for reference; photograph collection of several hundred.
Income and Purchases: Income approx. $1200; purchases approx. $400.
Attendance: 2000 annual average.

OMAHA

✠THE ART GALLERIES
University of Nebraska-Omaha

The New Gallery
Annex 22, 133 S. Elmwood Rd, 68101. Tel: (402) 554-2486
Laurence J. Bradshaw, Gallery Dir.
Ann Mactier, Secy
Jerome Birdman, Dean School of Fine Arts
Free weekdays 9 AM - 7:30 PM. Estab. 1975 to heighten cultural and aesthetic awareness of the metropolitan and midlands area; financed by state appropriation.
Exhibitions: (1975-76) Omaha Collector's Show; Abraham Kamberg Collection of Bauhaus Prints; U.N.O. Art Faculty Show; 23rd National Exhibition of Prints; Tricia Smith One-Woman Show; Riverfront, Noguchi and Carl Jonas; Evelyn Garfinkel One-Woman Show; Artists Residents of Chicago; Laliberte Banners Show; Senior Thesis Show.

The Administration Gallery
Admin. Bldg, Room 371, 68101. Tel: (402) 554-2420
Free weekdays 9 AM - 4 PM. Estab. 1967 to heighten cultural and aesthetic awareness of the metropolitan and midlands area; financed by state appropriation.
Exhibitions: (1975-76) Nutmeg Suite; New Generation Drawings; U.N.O. Art Collection; U.N.O. Student Art Competition; Ferdinand Roten Galleries Sale; U.N.O. Senior Thesis Show; U.N.O. Design Students' Show; Henry Serenco One-Man Show; World Print Competition '73; Student Juried Show; Student Art Competition.
Activities at both locations: Photograph collection in the planning stage; lectures open to public, 2 visiting lecturers per year, 2 gallery talks, 4 tours; competitions; scholarships.
Publications: 1974 Geometric Abstractions (catalog); 1975 The Omaha Collectors Show (catalog).
Annual Purchases: $5000.
Attendance: 14,000.

CREIGHTON UNIVERSITY FINE ARTS GALLERY

2500 California St, 68178. Tel: (402) 536-2509
Bidez Embry Moore, Dir.
Frances Kraft, Chmn. Fine & Performing Arts Dept.
New gallery facility opened 1973. Gallery handles 10 exhibits per academic year; space provided for student thesis exhibits.
Collections: Graphics, paintings, drawings, sculpture, ceramics, photography and pottery.
Exhibitions: Don Doll; Robert Nelson; Jerry Uelsman.
Activities: Lectures open to the public, 1 visiting lecturer per year.

✠JOSLYN ART MUSEUM

2200 Dodge St, 68102. Tel: (402) 342-3996
Stanley J. How, Chmn. Board Trustees
Laurance R. Hoagland, Pres. & Managing Dir.
Michael B. Yanney, V.Pres.
Francis T. B. Martin, Secy.
Edgar M. Morsman, Jr, Treas.
Burdette R. Fredrickson, Business Adminr.
Ruth H. Cloudman, Chief Cur.
Mildred Goosman, Cur. Western Collections
Harrison C. Taylor, Cur. Exhibitions
Berneal Anderson, Registrar
Evelyn A. Sedlacek, Librn.
Joanne Evans, Publicity & Programming
James Mangimeli, Gen. Supt.
Open weekdays 10 AM - 5 PM; Sun. 1 - 5 PM; cl. Mon, holidays; admis. 50¢, children under 12 free with adult; free Sat. AM.
Joslyn Art Museum was inc. May 3, 1928, under the laws of the State of Nebraska, opened Nov. 29, 1931, a gift of Mrs. Sarah H. Joslyn in memory of her husband, George A. Joslyn, Omaha businessman. Purpose of the Museum is to care for and expand the collections, offer exhibitions, promote education in and cultivation of the fine arts. Total mem. is 5000, with annual dues of $15 for family, $10 individual, $5 student, $25 friend, $50 associate, $100 sustainer, $250 sponsor, $500 donor, $1000 patron, $2500 benefactor. The Museum is governed by the Board of Trustees. The Trustees are the voting members with the ann. meeting third Tues. in Dec.
The Museum, a marble building covering a two-block area, contains ten large galleries with small exhibit areas surrounding a large central court and 1200-seat Witherspoon Concert Hall on the main floor. The concert hall is used for programs by major community music and cultural organizations. The ground floor includes exhibit areas, Library, studios, Lecture Hall, Museum Shop, Rental and Sales Gallery, and the offices.
Collections: The Joslyn permanent collections are arranged chronologically. More than half the exhibit area on the main floor is devoted to period collections, starting with the Classical through the Renaissance, to European art of the Seventeenth, Eighteenth, Nineteenth Centuries, to the Impressionists, and Contemporary American Arts. The exhibits combine painting, sculpture, the decorative and graphic arts. New Acquisitions are being added in all areas. Artists in the permanent collections include: DiCredi, Titian, Veronese, El Greco, Ribera, Rembrandt, Goya, Reynolds, Raeburn, Corot, Stuart, Renoir, Monet, Henri, Grant Wood, Benton, Pollock, and others.
In the Court balcony are works by Karl Bodmer, Alfred Jacob Miller, and George Catlin. The Bodmer Collection, owned by the Northern Natural Gas Company, Omaha, is housed at Joslyn and includes 400 watercolor sketches.
The collections on the ground floor are devoted to the Great Plains Region, outlining development of art and design in the Middle West from earliest times to today, with emphasis on the Nineteenth Century. Native arts of the North American Indians are included in this Early West section.
Exhibitions: The Midwest Biennial Exhibition, a juried show open to artists in a 16-state area around Nebraska, is held in even-numbered years, includes paintings, sculpture and graphics; addi-

tions to the Museum's permanent collection are purchased from the exhibition. Temporary exhibitions include traveling shows of national significance, Joslyn-organized shows, one-man and group shows in all media, student art.

Joslyn-organized shows include: Midwest Biennial Exhibition; Mary Cassatt Among the Impressionists; Looking West 1970; The Thirties Decade: American Artists and Their European Contemporaries; A Sense of Place: The Artist and the American Land; A Rich Inheritance: Oriental Rugs of the 19th and Early 20th Centuries; The Growing Spectrum of American Art.

Activities: Creative and art appreciation classes for children (pre-school through high school) and adults, plus special workshops; exhibition gallery talks and lectures; monthly film programs; tours of the collections and special exhibitions; special tour program of the permanent collections and special exhibitions maintained for public school children; Joslyn Chamber Music Series.

Library: Art reference library of 10,000 volumes; periodicals; pamphlet and clipping files; special files on Nebraska art and artists; circulating material of mounted pictures and folios; plus a library of 15,000 slides.

Publications: Monthly calendar September through June; special exhibition catalogues; Annual Review; Guide to the Museum; brochures.

Attendance: (1970-72 average) 160,000.

RED CLOUD

WILLA CATHER PIONEER MEMORIAL AND EDUCATIONAL FOUNDATION
    68970. Tel: (402) 746-2653
Miriam Mountford, Pres.
Marcella Van Meter, Secy.
JoAnna Lathrop, Dir.
Open May 1 - Oct. 1 10:30 AM - 5 PM Mon. - Fri; weekends 1 - 5 PM; remainder of year by appointment; admis. adults 50¢, students and children 25¢, student groups free. Estab. 1955 to foster an interest in the work of Willa Cather, identify and restore places made famous in her writings, to encourage scholarship in the humanities, to bond, insure and house art, literature and historical items relating to the life and work of Willa Cather; financed by endowment and membership. Maintains book shop. Ann. spring conference May 1; mem 1500; dues $10 individual.

Collections: All collections concern Willa Cather's life or art; rare books, foreign books (translations of Cather), general collection, periodicals, pamphlets, clippings, photographs, microfilm.

Exhibitions: Lucia Woods Photographs of Catherland.

Library: 500 volumes and 800 prints in photograph collection for lending and reference (to individual students).

Publications: Willa Cather Pioneer Memorial and Educational Foundation Newsletter, quarterly.

Annual Income: Approx. $35,000.

Attendance: 8200.

SEWARD

KOENIG ART GALLERY
    Concordia College, 800 N. Columbia Ave, 68434.
    Tel: (402) 643-3651
Richard Wiegmann, Dir.
Open weekdays 8 AM - 5 PM, Sun. 2 - 5 PM. Estab. 1959 as part of the total program of Concordia College, its purpose is primarily educational, providing the campus community and the people of our region an opportunity to experience a wide variety of original works of visual art and craft; financed by tuition and support by the governing church body of the institution.

Collections: †Contemporary prints—American and Foreign; †Ceramics and glass.

Exhibitions: Temporary exhibitions on a monthly basis.

Activities: Extension department serves city of Seward; material available to Concordia staff and students and Seward residents; Minimal fees; individual paintings and original objects of art lent; lending collection, 400 color reproductions; 200 items lent in an average year, 75 active borrowers.

NEVADA

ELKO

NORTHEASTERN NEVADA MUSEUM
    1515 Idaho St. (Mailing, P.O. Box 503), 89801.
    Tel: (702) 738-3418
Morris F. Gallagher, D.D.S, Pres.
Howard Hickson, Dir.
Tammy Robison, Registrar
Free Mon. - Sat. 9 AM - 5 PM; Sun. 1 - 5 PM. Museum opened Apr. 5, 1968; historical, Indian and natural history of Northeastern Nevada; exhibits, research files, library; maintained by appropriation, memorials, contributions and donations. One gallery 30 by 50 ft. usually 25-50 paintings, omni equipment. 3 meetings per year, no specific dates; mem. 1160; dues $5 - $1000.

Collections: Regional art (donated); 20 paintings to date.

Exhibitions: 20 one-man exhibits, local, state, Idaho and Utah artists.

Activities: Historical and Indian lectures; extension work for northeast Nevada schools, service groups; slide shows, taped with equipment; original objects of art lent; 1500 photographs and 2000 Kodachromes in lending collection; lectures open to public, 5 visiting lecturers per year; concerts, classes for adults and children, competitions. Book shop.

Library: 1250 volumes and 1400 prints in photograph collection for reference.

Publications: Quarterly; Newsletter, quarterly.

Income: Estimated $60,000.

Attendance: 47,532.

LAS VEGAS

LAS VEGAS ART MUSEUM
Las Vegas Art League
    3333 W. Washington, 89107. Tel: (702) 648-1868
Jerry Motto, Pres.
Mary Shaw, Secy.
Cookie Best, Gallery Dir.
Free, winter Noon - 4 PM daily; summer 1 - 5 PM daily. Estab. 1950 to offer fine arts to the citizens of Las Vegas, to offer artists a place to show, work and study, to offer good education in fine arts to adults and children of the community; financed by membership. Ann. meeting May; mem. 400; dues $10.

Collections: Present day artists, majority of which have been winners in annual national competition.

Exhibitions: New exhibit each month, some are one-man shows, others are traveling shows; sponsor 2 competitions a year, a local Clark County and a national.

Activities: Educational department offers a full curriculum for adults and children; lectures open to the public; 3- 4 visiting lecturers per year; gallery talks; 15 - 20 tours; classes for adults and children; competitions; scholarships.

Library: 75 volume lending library.

Publications: Monthly bulletin.

Income and Purchases: Income $24,000; purchases $1000-$5000.

Attendance: 8000.

UNIVERSITY OF NEVADA, LAS VEGAS, ART GALLERY*
    4505 Maryland Parkway, 89109. Tel: (702) 736-6111 Exten. 237
Michael McCollum, Chmn. Art Dept.
Open 8 - 12 AM, 1 - 5 PM. Gallery measures 55 by 30 ft; monthly exhibitions by faculty and traveling shows; suggested by appropriation and membership. Mem. 50; dues $10.

Collections: 125 prints, †23 paintings, †sculpture, †3 ceramics and 30 Oriental pieces.

Exhibitions: Contemporary Spanish Art, Mary Sharp; Rocky Mountain Show; Cliff Segerblom; Invitational Drawing Exhibit; Luminists Competition & Invitational; Misch Kohn, Prints; Marie Mason; Roland Peterson; Rita Deanin Abbey; Dick Volpe & Mary Sharp; Frank Steiner; Erik Gronborg, Sculpture; Mary Cady Johnson; Rocky Mountain Oil Paintings; Comic Art Exhibition; Graduating Seniors Exhibition; Michael McCollum, Ceramics; Jack Garver; Young Americans, 69; Peter L. Myer; Annual Student Show, Spring Student Sale.

Activities: Traveling exhibitions organized and circulated; 15,000 Kodachromes in lending collection; lectures open to public, 2 visiting lecturers per year; 15 gallery talks or tours; concerts, dramatic programs, classes for adults and children; competitions; scholarship. Book shop.

Library: 200,000 volumes for lending and reference.

Publications: Announcements only.

Income and Purchases: Income $2000; purchases $500-$1000.

Attendance: 5000.

OVERTON

MOAPA VALLEY ART GUILD*
    Box 75, 89040. Tel: (702) 397-2531
Max E. Bunnell, Dir.
Estab. 1960 to awaken area to art, sponsor annual spring exhibit, featuring art from Kindergarten through to professional; good attendance. Supported by state appropriation, mem, work projects. Sept. through May, meetings Wed. 8 - 10 PM for instruction; mem. 35; dues $5.

Collections: Paintings by Paul Lauritz, Farrel Collett, R.V. Bullough, Peter Myer, A.E. Johnson, Leslie B. DeMille, Theo Glen, Max Bunnell, Glen D. Anderson, Floyd E. Brienholt, Harrison T. Groutage.

Exhibitions: Three, Annual Spring Show.

Activities: Junior Art Guild, weekly meetings, annual trip to museums and galleries in Calif; individual paintings lent to schools; lectures open to public, 2 visiting lecturers per year; classes for adults and children 12 and over.

Income and Purchases: Income $1000; purchases $150.

NEW HAMPSHIRE

CONCORD

✠THE ART CENTER IN HARGATE
St. Paul's School
    03301. Tel: (603) 225-3341, Exten. 58
Thomas R. Barrett, Head, Art Dept.
Juanita White, Secy.
Open Tues. - Sat. 10 AM - 4:30 PM; during school year. June, Mon. - Fri. 1 - 4 PM. Estab. 1967 to house the Art Department of St. Paul's School, provide a cultural center for the school community as well as the central area of New Hampshire; endowed. Secure gallery consisting of subdivided room approx. 60 by 40 ft. Friends of the Arts at St. Paul's School, 150 mem; dues $10-$50.

Collections: Painting, sculpture, drawings, graphics, chiefly gifts to the school; collection represents varied periods and nationalities.

Exhibitions: (1973-74) The Monotype (SITES); Indian Paintings (Welch); Art Department Faculty; Mark Tobey Graphics (IEF); Milton Avery Prints (IEF); Benjamin Rowland Watercolors (FOGG); (1974-75) Makonde Sculpture (SITES); Robert Rogers Photos; Audubon Animals; Direct Vision; John Flannagan: Sculpture and Works on Paper (IEF); (1975-76) American Posters (Currier and National Endowment); Young Artists from Bali (Black); Civil War Drawings (IEF); New Architecture in New England (IEF); Mallorca (Miro Prints) (IEF); plus annual student shows.

Activities: Original object of art lent; lectures for mem. only, 4 visiting lecturers per year; approx. 6 gallery talks or tours; classes for students.

Library: 150 volumes, facsimile reproductions of Old Master drawings (500 drawings represented, 14th-19th century) for use of students enrolled at St. Paul's School.

Attendance: 6500.

LEAGUE OF NEW HAMPSHIRE CRAFTSMEN
    205 N. Main St, 03301. Tel: (603) 224-3375
Merle D. Walker, Dir.
Open weekdays 9 AM - 5 PM. Estab. 1931, inc. 1932, to develop the educational and economic values in arts and crafts. Gallery, featuring traveling and members' craft exhibits, located at League headquarters, open weekdays 10 AM - 4 PM. Ann. meeting Oct; mem. 5000; dues $3.50 and higher.

Collections: Approx. 50 objects from early 30's to today.

Exhibitions: Members work at Annual Craftsmens Fair, juried with cash awards and purchase prizes to permanent collection.

Activities: Seminar for Advanced Craftsmen held early each year in 5 major crafts. Organized more than 24 member groups which do craft work under league direction; operates about ten marketing centers, and annual Craftsman's Fair in summer; members' work selected for exhibition by jury. Lectures; study courses throughout New Hampshire. Cooperates with the State Board of Education in conducting craft classes.

Library: Small library of books and magazines for members.

Publications: League Letter, 6 times a year; other bulletins.

NEW HAMPSHIRE HISTORICAL SOCIETY
    30 Park St, 03301. Tel: (603) 225-3381
Richard F. Upton, Pres.
John F. Page, Secy. & Dir.
Mary Lyn Ray, Asst. to Dir.
Richard C. Frantz, Asst. Cur.
Robinson Murray, III, Assoc. Librn.
Open Mon, Tues, Thurs. & Fri. 9 AM - 4:30 PM; Wed. 9 AM - 8 PM; cl. Sat. & Sun. Estab. 1823 to preserve materials of New Hampshire history; financed by endowment and membership. Gallery maintained. Ann. meeting 1st Sat. in May; mem. 2000; dues $10 and up.

Collections: †New Hampshire decorative arts; †domestic artifacts; †historical memorabilia.

Exhibitions: Decorative Arts of New Hampshire, 1973; True Gospel Simplicity: Shaker Furniture - New Hampshire, 1974; Walter Ingalls, Sahbornton Artist, 1975.

Activities: Lectures open to the public and occasionally for members only, 10 visiting lecturers per year; concerts, classes for adults and children. Book shop.

Library: Volumes and prints for reference only.

Publications: Historical New Hampshire, quarterly.

CORNISH

SAINT-GAUDENS NATIONAL HISTORIC SITE
    c/o National Park Service, U.S. Dept. of Interior, P.O. Box, Windsor, VT, 05089.
John Dryfhout, Cur.
Open May 25 - Oct 31, daily 8:30 AM - 5 PM; admis. 50¢, under 16 years of age free. Estab. 1919 as Saint-Gaudens Memorial, to preserve the home, studio, gardens and collections of sculpture of Augustus Saint-Gaudens (1848-1907), who lived and worked here. Transferred as of Oct. 15, 1965, to the Federal Government; financed by the National Park Service.

Collections: More than †100 examples of Saint-Gaudens' work are exhibited in the permanent collection in the studio and sculpture court; American sculpture.

Exhibitions: Gallery for exhibitions of contemporary and historic painting and sculpture, May - October.

Activities: Original objects of art lent; conducted tours on request; summer concerts in studio. Book Shop.

Library: 600 volumes; photograph collection of 1500 prints.

Income and Purchases: Income $125,000; purchases $15,000.

Attendence: 10,000.

EXETER

THE LAMONT GALLERY
Phillips Exeter Academy
    03833. Tel: (603) 772-4311, Exten. 324
Stephen G. Kurtz, Prin.
John Wharton, Dir.
Bridget Paddock, Asst. Dir.
Free daily Tues. - Sat. 9 AM - 5 PM; Sun. 2 - 5 PM; cl. Mon. Estab. 1953 to provide an Art Center and studios for art instruction. Dedicated to the memory of Thomas William Lamont, II, lost in action in 1945.

Collections: 19th century English prints; 19th century American prints; portraits; †contemporary prints and paintings.

Exhibitions: 15 exhibitions per year; annual student exhibition with awards.

Activities: Classes for Academy students; lectures; concerts; dramatic programs, films—all open to the public.

HANOVER

DARTMOUTH COLLEGE GALLERIES AND COLLECTIONS
    Hopkins Center, Carpenter Hall, Wilson Hall, 03755.
    Tel: (603) 646-2808
Jan van der Marck, Dir.
Free daily 11 AM - 4 PM & 7 - 10 PM; Sun, holidays and intersessions, 2 - 5 PM. Situated in the Hopkins Center for the Visual and Performing Arts (1962) along with extensive facilities for theatre, music, studio, film, workshops.

Collections: Assyrian reliefs; early Christian mosaics; Greek and Roman icons; Chinese paintings, sculpture, ceramics, bronzes; 17th to 20th century European, 19th to 20th Century American paintings, sculpture, drawings, graphics; frescoes by Jose Clemente Orozco (Baker Memorial Library); early Massachusetts silver.

Exhibitions: Approx. 30 at Hopkins Center, 10 at Carpenter Hall, 6 at Wilson Hall annually, in addition to selections from the permanent collection at all three places.

Art Library (Carpenter Hall): Approx. 40,000 volumes.

Publications: Catalogs for Artist-in-Residence, special features, selections from the permanent collection.

Attendance: Approx. 100,000 annually.

KEENE

LOUISE E. THORNE MEMORIAL ART GALLERY
    Keene State College, 03431. Tel: (603) 352-1909
Dr. Leo Redfern, Pres. of the College
Jocelyn Brodie, Dir.
Mrs. M. Plaut, Chmn. Friends of the Thorne Art Gallery
Free Mon. - Sat. 1 - 4:30 PM; Sun. 3 - 5 PM. Estab. 1965 to present a continuous schedule of quality art exhibits for the college and regional communities. Friends mem. 500; dues $3.

Collection: Small collection of works by noted regional artists.

Activities: Exhibitions, lectures, gallery talks.

Attendance: 10,000.

MANCHESTER

✠CURRIER GALLERY OF ART
    192 Orange St, 03104. Tel: (603) 669-6144
Raymond H. Daniels, Pres.
Ernest A. Sweet, Jr, Treas.

Gene E. Tobias, Admin. Asst.
Mrs. Lawrence Shirley, Clerk
~~David S. Brooke~~, Dir. *Robert McIntyre Doty* 12/77
Melvin E. Watts, Cur.
Robert Eshoo, Supvr, The Currier Art Center
Free 10 AM - 4 PM; Sun. 2 - 5 PM; cl. Mon. & holidays. Estab. and inc. 1915, by will of Mrs. Hannah M. Currier, which included endowment. Building opened 1929, contains six galleries, auditorium, library. Ann. meeting Mar; mem. 800; dues $10 and higher; student rates $5.
Collections: †European Masters 13th to 20th century; †American paintings and sculpture 18th century to present; †fine American decorative art 17th to early 19th century including furniture, textiles, glass and silver.
Exhibitions: Special exhibitions of paintings, sculpture, decorative and industrial art.
Activities: A regular fall program of lectures; eight concerts yearly; film program; docent service; extension service to schools. The Currier Art Center offers an annual program in creative work to children 6 to 18 years of age. Bookshop carries postcard reproductions of collections, and publications.
Publications: Bulletin; exhibition catalogues.
Attendance: 35,000.

MANCHESTER CITY LIBRARY
405 Pine St, 03104. Tel: (603) 625-6485
John J. Hallahan, City Library Dir.
Ann Frank, Fine Arts Librn.
Free Mon. - Thurs. 9 AM - 9 PM; Fri. 9 AM - 6 PM; Sat. 9 AM - 5 PM; cl. Sun.
Lending collection of over 8500 books on art; mounted pictures; †16mm films (105). Collection of Canadian Travel films available for loan to groups. 20 art magazines, 95 filmstrips. †Cooperative film collection available for loan; monthly film program to public; interlibrary loan; teletype.

MANCHESTER HISTORIC ASSOCIATION
129 Amherst St, 03104. Tel: (603) 622-7531
John R. Reilly, Jr, Pres.
Virginia Gerken Plisko, Dir.
Elizabeth B. Lessard, Librn.
Free Tues. - Fri. building open 9 AM - 4 PM; Sat. 10 AM - 4 PM; cl. Sun. & Mon, nat. & state holidays and Tues. following Mon. holidays. Inc. 1896 to collect, preserve, and make known Manchester's historical heritage. Ann. meeting Apr; mem. 145; dues $10 and higher.
Collections: Permanent collection of †furniture, †glass, †pewter, †maps, †prints, †paintings, †ceramics, †costumes, †textiles, and †artifacts of all types, household, business, home and shop industries and agriculture relating to the early and later history of Manchester. The †Indian artifact collection of over 10,000 pieces found at Manchester sites and the collection of fire apparatus and equipment are especially noteworthy.
Exhibitions: Permanent and changing exhibitions reflecting all aspects of Manchester history.
Activities: Spring and fall program series.
Library: Research library containing †maps, †prints, †photographs, †printed and †manuscript material available for use by the public, includes many early textile mill records and swatch sample books. Over 35,000 pieces.
Publications: Bi-monthly newsletter (The Bulletin); annual report; occasional catalogues; special bulletins each on an individual subject.
Income: $22,000 annually.
Attendance: 7651.

NEW HAMPSHIRE ART ASSOCIATION, INC.
Box 1075, 03105.
Gallery, 24 W. Bridge St, 03105. Tel: (603) 622-0527
Grace Casey, Exec. Dir.
Jafar Shoja, Pres.
Elaine Biganess Livingstone, 1st V.Pres.
Calvin Libby, 2nd V.Pres.
Lucie Duhaime, Treas.
Alice Coync, Corresp. Secy.
Virginia Hurt, Recording Secy.
Sales and central gallery open year-round, Tues. - Fri. 10 AM - 4 PM. Summer gallery in Strawberry Banke Historic Preservation Area, Portsmouth, N.H. Estab. 1940, inc. 1962, as a non-profit organization. Ann. meeting June; mem. 300; dues $20.
Exhibitions: Annuals at Currier Gallery of Art; Spring, which travels to museums and galleries in N.H, Mass, Maine; Summer, combined with New Hampshire League of Arts and Crafts at Mount Sunapee State Park, Sunapee, N.H. Various one-man and group shows at gallery.

NASHUA

THE ARTS AND SCIENCE CENTER
14 Court St, 03060. Tel: (603) 883-1506
Gerald Q. Nash, Pres.
J. Herman Pouliot, Chmn. Exec. Comt.
Ronald D. Deane, Exec. Dir.
Barbara Saltmarsh, Coordinator, Children's Museum
Free Mon. - Fri. 10 AM - 5 PM; Thurs. 6 - 9 PM; Sat. 10 AM - 5 PM; Sun. 1:30 - 5 PM. Inc. 1961 to provide educational programs, exhibitions, lectures, film programs, musical performances and productions by theater arts groups. New facility opened Nov, 1973, includes two large exhibition galleries, Rental and Sales Department, Museum Shop, Theater with capacity of 250 for performances and productions, six classrooms, Coffee Shop, large meeting room, storage and office space. The Children's Museum, the only one of its kind in New Hampshire, is designed to allow children to experience more through participation instead of observation. Special tours and programs for school and children's groups. There is a nominal admission fee. Monthly meeting of the Board of Trustees first Tues. each month, ann. meeting Board and members, May; mem. 954; dues $5, $10, $15, $25, $50, $100, $250, $500, $1000.
Activities: Classes for preschool, primary, secondary, and adults in arts, crafts, languages; lectures; films; scholarships.
Publications: Newsletters; releases; invitations to openings.
Attendance: 30,250.

PETERBOROUGH

THE SHARON ARTS CENTER, INC.
R.F.D. 2, Box 361, 03458. Tel: (603) 924-3582
George Kendall, Pres.
Carl M. Jackson, Dir.
Free daily 10 AM - 5 PM; Sun. 1 - 5 PM. Estab. 1945 to promote appreciation of the arts and crafts in the Monadnock Area. Member of the League of New Hampshire Craftsmen. Financed by membership and endowment. Ann. meeting Sept; dues $7. Conduct art and craft classes. Exhibition gallery and Shop open May - Dec. 24.

PORTSMOUTH

MOFFATT-LADD HOUSE*
154 Market St, 03801. Tel: (603) 436-8221
Mrs. Robert P. Booth, Chmn. Advisory Comt.
Open to visitors from May 15 - Oct. 15, 10 AM - 5 PM; Sun. 2 - 5 PM. Estab. 1913. Eighteenth century mansion, garden, and counting-house. Home of William Whipple, signer of the Declaration of Independence. Furnished in the period and maintained as an historical museum by the National Society of Colonial Dames in the State of New Hampshire.
Activities: Tours for school children.
Attendance: Approx. 2000.

PORTSMOUTH HISTORICAL SOCIETY*
43 Middle St, 03801.
Arnold J. Grover, Pres.
Marion Call, Secy.
Open 10 AM - 5 PM; cl. Sun; admis. 50¢. Estab. 1919. Headquarters in the John Paul Jones House, built in 1758 by Gregory Purcell, a merchant sea-captain. Purchased and restored in 1920 by the Portsmouth Historical Society. Ann. meeting Sept; mem. approx. 200; dues $2.
Collections: China, glass, silver, books, documents, furniture, portraits and costumes pertaining to the early history of Portsmouth.

NEW JERSEY

CALDWELL

CALDWELL COLLEGE ART GALLERY
07006. Tel: (201) 228-4424
Sister M. Gerardine, Dir.
Free weekdays 8:30 AM - 5 PM; weekends by appointment. Estab. 1970 to provide students and area community with exposure to professional contemporary talent, to afford opportunities for qualified artists to have one-man shows.
Exhibitions: Matteo Jannicello; Markand Thakar; Edward Sokol; Robert Cariola; Esther Fuhrman; Margery Ryerson; Howard Conant; R. T. Kahn; Eileen Shreiber; Robert Phillips; Tela Banks; Jane Bearman; Ugo Giannini; Sister Mary Compassion; Marlene Lenker; Anne Steele Marsh; Simon Cohen; Frances McQuillan; William Gorman; Ina Golub; Annie Lenney; Ralph Stein; Carmen Cicero; James Kearns; Robert Henri; Sherman Edwards.

Activities: Educational department in connection with the college art department; lending collection of 25 lantern slides, 10,000 Koda-chromes, 5 motion pictures, 6 film strips and 4 cartridges; 2000 items lent in average year; lectures open to public; 3 visiting lecturers per year; scholarships.

NEW JERSEY WATERCOLOR SOCIETY
c/o Nat Lewis, 51 Overlook Rd, 07006.
Don Voorhees, Pres.
Edwin Havas, V.Pres.
John Bermingham, Secy.
Nessa Grainger, Corresp. Secy.
J. Luigina, Treas.
Mem. 110; dues $8.
Exhibitions: Annual Members' Shows; Annual Open Juried Exhibitions-alternating between Morris Museum of Arts and Science, Morristown, N.J. and the Monmouth Museum, Lincroft, N.J.
Activities: Traveling exhibitions organized and circulated.
Publications: Newsletter, 4 times yearly.

CAMDEN

CAMPBELL MUSEUM
Campbell Pl, 08101. Tel: (609) 964-4000 Exten. 2688
Ralph Collier, Pres.
R. G. Calder, Jr, Secy.
Ellen Berger, Museum Asst.
Free, Mon. - Fri. 9:30 AM - 5 PM. Estab. 1966 to assemble and exhibit to the public a collection of tureens, bowls, and utensils made for food service dating from 500 B.C. to the present; financed by fund from Campbell Soup Co.
Exhibitions: At Abby Aldrich Rockefeller Museum, Williamsburg, De Young Museum, San Francisco, Mint Museum of Art, Charlotte, Art Institute of Chicago, Brooks Memorial Art Gallery, Memphis, Joslyn Art Museum, Omaha, Smithsonian Institution Museum of History and Technology, Washington, D.C, High Museum of Art, Atlanta, Delaware Antiques Show, Baltimore Museum of Art, Milwaukee Art Center, Boston Museum of Fine Arts, Toledo Museum of Art and the Royal Ontario Museum.
Activities: Lending collection, traveling exhibitions organized and circulated; 70 items lent per exhibition; unlimited photograph collection; slide presentation or film; gallery.
Library: 25 volume reference library.
Publications: The Campbell Museum Collection Catalogue, every three years.
Attendance: 24,000.

CLINTON

CLINTON HISTORICAL MUSEUM
56 Main St, 08809. Tel: (201) 735-4101
Bruce D. Herrigel, Pres.
Elizabeth Nelson, Secy.
Gloria Lazor, Dir.
Claire Young, Cur. of Exhibits
Open weekdays 1 - 5 PM, weekends Noon - 6 PM; admis. adults $1.50, children under 12 50¢, senior citizens $1, members and preschoolers free. Estab. 1960 for preservation and display of historical artifacts; financed by membership and donations. Ann. meeting 2nd Mon. in Apr; mem. 120; dues $5 - $1000.
Collections: 18th and 19th century artifacts of American domestic, agricultural and industrial life.
Activities: Concerts; Craft Fair.
Income: $35,000.
Attendance: 12,000 - 13,000.

HUNTERDON ART CENTER
Old Stone Mill, Center St, 08809. Tel: (201) 735-8415
Helen Axel, Pres.
John C. Marsh, V.Pres.
Richard Dieterly, Secy.
Free Tues. - Sun. 1 - 5 PM; cl. Mon. Estab. 1952, opened 1953, a nonprofit organization to provide opportunity for adults and children to participate in the enjoyment of the arts and crafts in all forms. Ann. meeting Mar; mem. approx. 1000; dues student $5, single $10, family $15, sustaining $25, patron $100.
Exhibitions: Annual exhibitions include National Print Exhibition; Annual Exhibit; Members' Exhibition; Holiday Exhibition (Professional); Antiques Show; Craft Exhibition; Invitational group shows.
Activities: Classes for adults and children; lectures; concerts; dramatic programs; films.
Publications: Newsletter, monthly.
Purchases: Prints (purchase prizes) $100 or more.
Attendance: 10,000 average.

EAST ORANGE

ART CENTRE OF THE ORANGES, INC.
Art Centre Galleries, 16 Washington St, 07017.
Tel: (201) 674-8445
George Schwacha, Pres.
Ethel I. Brehm, Admin. Asst.
Open Sept. - May, Mon, Wed, Thurs, Fri, 1 - 4 PM; Regional Show Mon. - Sun. 1 - 4 PM. Inc. 1924. Ann. meeting May; mem. 300; dues $10; monthly meetings Sept. - May of Board of Dir.
Exhibitions: Members' exhibition fall and spring; classes exhibition in Dec; Regional Show Mar. (N.J, Pa, N.Y, Conn. artists), prize awards, 2-year total $4000; Invitational Show (all art organizations of N.J.) Feb.
Activities: Painting demonstrations, oil, watercolor, acrylics; lectures; classes fall and winter, oil portrait, pastel portrait; watercolor; landscape (outdoor, fall and spring); still life; life drawing and painting.

ELIZABETH

THE FREE PUBLIC LIBRARY OF ELIZABETH, N.J.
11 S. Broad St, 07202. Tel: (201) 354-6060
Hazel Hulbert Elks, Library Dir.
Roman Sawycky, Head Art & Music Dept. & Supv. Librn.
Doris Fichtelberg, Principal Art & Music Librn.
Daisy Tamayo, Sr. Art Librn.
Free daily 9 AM - 9 PM; Sat 9 AM - 5 PM; cl. Sun. Estab. 1913, the art department functions within the area library system, it offers free service to patrons of Elizabeth and also to patrons of neighboring towns, Roselle Park, Kenilworth, Union and Cranford; financed by city and state appropriations. Special exhibit area for displaying paintings and miscellaneous objects d'art.
Collections: †15,000 books on fine arts; †200,000 mounted pictures, illustrations and photographs on miscellaneous subjects for lending; †800 large art reproductions, some framed, all for lending; reference collection of Japanese prints by various artists.
Exhibitions: Works by local artists and photographers; Black History; history of Elizabeth or other historical objects such as a stone from the Wall of China, original leaves from rare Bible editions; original embroidery and Easter Eggs from Ukraine; Cuban Art.
Activities: Furnish information on history and current trends in art education; extension Department serves Elizabeth and towns of Union, Kenilworth, Roselle Park, Cranford; material available to patrons of these municipalities; no fees; individual prints lent to schools; 250 motion pictures, 400 filmstrips and projection equipment in lending collection; 37,000 items lent in average year; lectures open to the public; 15 visiting lecturers per year; concerts; dramatic programs.
Purchases: $5000.

HOPEWELL

HOPEWELL MUSEUM
28 E. Broad St, 08525.
Dr. Donald M. Bergen, Pres.
Marie Chartier, Secy.
E. Forrest Lowe, Treas.
Alice B. Lewis, Cur.
Beverly Weidl, Asst. Cur.
Open Mon, Wed. & Sat. 2 - 5 PM; donation suggested. Estab. 1922 as a museum of local history from early 1700 through 1900, to show what this community was like for almost 300 years. Financed by endowment, membership and donations.
Collections: A colonial parlor; a Victorian parlor; Colonial furniture and furnishings; antique china, glass, silver and pewter; early kitchen utensils and spinning wheels; early deeds, documents, charters and pictures; antique guns, powder horns and swords; costumes from colonial days to the present; genealogical material, books and manuscripts; Indian handicrafts and relics; early farm implements; early needlework; natural history exhibits.
Activities: Clothing occasionally loaned to local institutions; photograph collection of 60 prints.
Library of local history books for reference use within quarters.
Publications: Hopewell valley Heritage; Pioneers of Old Hopewell; maps.
Attendance: 2000.

JERSEY CITY

HUDSON COUNTY COURT HOUSE
Board of Chosen Freeholders
595 Newark Ave, 07306. Tel: (201) 792-3737
Hon. Anne H. O'Malley, Dir.
Hon. Edward F. Clark, Jr. County Supv.

Mural Paintings: Howard Pyle, The Coming of the Dutch, The Coming of the English, In Old Dutch Days and decorations in Superior Court Room; Frank D. Millet, The Purchase of Pavonia and A Skirmish With the Indians; Charles Yardley Turner, Washington Watching the Assault on Fort Washington from Fort Lee and The First Trip of the Clermont in the upper gallery of the Rotunda. Dome decorations by Edwin Howland Blashfield installed 1911.

JERSEY CITY FREE PUBLIC LIBRARY—FINE ARTS LIBRARY*
678 Newark Ave, 07306. Tel: (201) 435-6262 Exten. 66
Alfred Trattner, Librn. in Charge
Open Mon. & Thurs. 1 - 9 PM; Tues, Wed. & Fri, 12 AM - 6 PM; Sat. 10 AM - 5 PM, cl. Sat. during summer.
Library: 9,000 volumes art and music; 4000 records, languages, documentary, music; 16mm. films, New Jersey Library Film Circuit; 200 films in private collection of the library; film showings Mon. 7 PM, Wed. 1 PM; 150 8mm. films; 900 35mm. filmstrips; 200 framed reproductions; a small collection of art slides. All materials loaned to the public.

JERSEY CITY MUSEUM ASSOCIATION
Jersey City Free Public Library Bldg.
472 Jersey Ave, 07302. Tel: (201) 435-6262
J. Owen Grundy, Pres.
Arthur Hansen, Treas.
M. Theresa Bender, Recording Secy.
Adelaide Dear, Corresp Secy.
Estab. 1932; inc. educational membership association whose purpose is the establishment in Jersey City of a museum building for art, science, history, and technology.
Exhibitions: Juried and one-man shows, New Jersey Painters & Sculptors Society Annual, and Hudson Artists.
Activities: Sponsors and administers the museum program of the Jersey City Free Public Library; public lectures at meetings and gallery functions listed elsewhere.

JERSEY CITY MUSEUM GALLERIES
Jersey City Free Public Library Bldg, 472 Jersey Ave, 07302. Tel: (201) 435-6262, Exten. 68
Ben Emmet Grimm, Dir, Jersey City Pub. Library
J. Owen Grundy, Pres, Jersey City Museum Asn.
Cindy Sanford, Cur.
Collections of both Public Library and Jersey City Museum Association are undergoing cleaning, restoration and cataloging. Museum temporarily closed. Visiting art exhibitions to continue.
Art exhibitions of selections from permanent collections of paintings, sculpture and graphic art; one-man and small group shows; Annual Exhibitions of The Painters & Sculptors Society of New Jersey in April and The Hudson Artists, Inc. in November. Gallery lectures and demonstrations.

PAINTERS AND SCULPTORS SOCIETY OF NEW JERSEY, INC.
c/o May Heiloms, Hon. Life Pres, 340 W. 28th St, New York, NY 10001.
Estab. 1941. Meetings Mar. and Nov; mem. 115; dues $15. New members by invitation only, through election by membership committee. 1976 annual exhibitions held at National Arts Club Gallery, New York City; jury, prizes. Exhibition open to all artists nationally and internationally. Nonmembers subject to jury of selection. Exhibitions usually one-third members and two-thirds nonmembers.
Attendance: In last two years 10,437.

ST. PETER'S COLLEGE ART GALLERY
O'Toole Library, Glenwood Ave, 07306.
Tel: (201) 333-4400, Exten. 360 & 433-2527, Exten. 223
Oscar Magnan, Dir.
Edward Brohel, Dir. Special Programs
Mary Ann Henninger, Exec. Secy.
Free Mon, Tues, Fri. & Sat. 11 AM - 4 PM; Wed. & Thurs. 11 AM - 9 PM. Estab. Sept. 1971 to show general views of art trends, especially contemporary.
Collections: Collection is placed in different buildings on the campus; †Greek and Roman pieces; †Italian masters of the 17th Century; †contemporary art works.
Exhibitions: Hudson River School of Painting; The Constructive Line: From Naum Gabo to Tony Smith; Three New Jersey Artists; History of the Poster; The Greco-Roman World as Seen in Their Crafts.
Activities: Traveling exhibitions organized and circulated; individual paintings and original objects of art lent; lectures open to public; 12 visiting lecturers per year; 10 gallery talks; 20 tours; concerts; dramatic programs. Book shop.

LAVALLETTE

FEDERATED ART ASSOCIATIONS OF NEW JERSEY, INC.
31 Pershing Blvd, 08735. Tel: (201) 793-0803
Barbara L. Jost, Pres.
Rose Reilly, Secy.
Jane Whipple Green, Exec. Secy.
Mary Keim Tietze, Judge and Jury Chmn.
Lucy Worley, Parliamentarian
Estab. 1969 to provide communication and exchange of ideas among art associations; financed by membership. Ann seminar: 4 sections meet separately, Oct, Nov, Feb. and Mar; 35 clubs, approx. 2000 mem; dues $10 per year, per club.
Activities: Lectures open to the public and other interested art clubs at section meetings; supply information to member groups on running state shows, selection of judges, program suggestions.
Publications: Newsletter, 4 times a year, Directory of Art Organizations in New Jersey, annually in Sept.

LINCROFT

✠THE MONMOUTH MUSEUM
761 Newman Springs Rd, 07701. Tel: (201) 747-2266
Charles B. Harding, Chmn.
William B. Leonard, Pres.
Milton J. Bloch, Dir.
Open Tues. - Sat. 11 AM - 5 PM; Fri. 7 - 9 PM; Sun. 1 - 5 PM; cl. June, July and Aug. Estab. 1963 to advance interest in art, science and nature in this area; new building opened Sept, 1974. Mem. 900; dues student $3, individual $7.50, family $15, contributing $25, associate $50, supporting $100, patron $500, life (charter mem) $1000.
Exhibitions: Modern French Paintings, Wild Flowers, Collectors' Choice, Paper Is...; Flags of Freedom; Treasures of Tibet; Inside Outer Space; Canadian Contrasts; Three Centuries of Art in New Jersey; As Eye See It (optical illusion); Hoofprints (history of the horse); New Jersey Arts & Crafts; The Colonial Expression.
Activities: Variety of lectures, films, workshops, etc, in conjunction with each new exhibit; total approximately 35-40 annually.
Library: Small library related to past exhibits, perhaps 300 volumes.
Income & Purchases: Operating budget approx. $65,000.
Attendance: Approx. 30,000 annually.

LONG BRANCH

THE LONG BRANCH HISTORICAL MUSEUM
1260 Ocean Ave, 07740. Tel: (201) 229-0600, 222-9879
Edgar N. Dinkelspiel, Pres.
Mrs. Elsie B. Netter, Secy.
Open by appointment; no admis. Estab. 1953 for Post Civil War displays, also two art shows annually on the grounds, one in July over the Fourth, the second in Mid Aug. Biennial meeting; mem. 16; dues $1.
Exhibitions: Art shows for the past 14 years.
Activities: Educational department; lecture tours open to the public.
Attendance: 15,000 annual average.

MADISON

COLLEGE ART GALLERY
Drew University
07940. Tel: (201) 377-3000, Exten. 320
Robert Ackerman, Dean
Peter Chapin, Chmn, Art Dept.
Free weekdays 1 - 4 PM; Sat. 9 AM - Noon and by appointment. Estab. 1968 to provide 8 or 9 exhibitions each school year to augment program of courses and to serve the community. Notices are sent to a mailing list of about 700 people, outside the campus. Often a discussion session takes place with the artist(s) in the Gallery during the shows. Maintains a slide library for art history courses. Financed by university instructional budget, general budget and donations. Friends of the College Gallery consisting of 60 Friends and student members.
Collection: Study collection of serigraphs, lithographs and intaglio prints; pottery; large sculpture by Robert Mallary.
Exhibitions: One-person shows, Margo Hoff, Stephen Pace, Jerome Witkin, William Umbreit, Linae Frei, John Opper and others; Wolf Kahn and Emily Mason; Berger Collection of Prints; The Printmaking Council of New Jersey Benefit Show; Aspects of Drawing; Student Show and others. Some shows on loan from major New York galleries.

MILLBURN

PAPER MILL PLAYHOUSE*
Brookside Dr, 07041. Tel: (201) 379-3636
Frank Carrington, Dir.

Gene Carrington, Cur.
Gallery open during all performances, Sept. through July.
    Estab. 1929, inc. 1930; building purchased 1934; Gallery, above
lobby, opened 1936. Collection of paintings and prints. Changing
exhibitions throughout season include work by local groups and individual artists of standing.

MONTCLAIR

✠THE MONTCLAIR ART MUSEUM
    South Mountain & Bloomfield Ave, 07042. Tel: (201) 746-5555
S. Barksdale Penick, Jr, Pres.
Mrs. George C. Bluestone, V.Pres.
Edward N. Lippincott, Jr, Secy.
Howard D. Brundage, Treas.
Kathryn E. Gamble, Dir.
Ann S. Rogerson, Cur.
Elsie W. Dillon, Supvr. Educ.
Lillian Bristol, Pub. Relations
Edith A. Rights, Librn.
Adelaid R. Birnie, Bursar
Patricia P. Barnes, Art School Registrar
Joan P. Lorenson, Curatorial Registrar
Mary DiMaio, Secy. to Dir.
Free Tues. - Sat. 10 AM - 5 PM; Sun. 2 - 5:30 PM; cl. Mon. and July
& Aug. Estab. and inc. 1911; building opened 1914, wing 1931, general
remodeling 1957. Ann. meeting Oct; mem. 1087; dues $20 and higher.
    Collections: †American painting and sculpture; prints, laces,
costumes and accessories; Chinese snuff bottle collection; Rand collection of American Indian art; furniture; Graeco-Roman pottery and
glass; Oriental objects; tapestries and needlepoint; Whitney silver
collection.
    Exhibitions: Approx. 30 exhibitions each season; invitational ex-
hibitions for New Jersey artists.
    Activities: Lectures, gallery talks, concerts, classes for adults
and children. (See Schools)
    Library: Reference collection of over 8000 books, catalogs and
periodicals; 13,000 slides; lending collection of reproductions.
    Publications: Bulletin, bimonthly, 5 issues; exhibition catalogs.
    Attendance: 39,000.

MONTCLAIR STATE COLLEGE
    07043. Tel: (201) 893-5103
David W. D. Dickson, Pres.
Donald M. Mintz, Dean Sch. Fine & Performing Arts
Harry Rosenzweig, Dir. Cultural Programming
Free Mon. - Fri. 9 AM - 5 PM; Sat. & Sun. selected hours. Estab.
1908 as an institution of higher education; designated one of two
regional centers of influence in the arts for New Jersey; financed by
state appropriations, private and corporate contributions. Mem.
approx. 1000 students, over 100 artist/faculty.
    Exhibitions: Gallery One - Patricia Johanson; Peter Agostini;
Richard Mayhew; Angela Jansen; Andrew Stasik; Marilyn Levine,
Richard T. Notkin, Kenneth Price; Will Barnet; Collections in New
Jersey; Carmen Cicero; New Jersey Print Makers - Peter Chapin,
Minna Citron, David Finkbeiner, Jacob Landau, Stefan Martin, Reginald Neal; Adrian Piper; Lida Hilton and William McCreath.
    Activities: Professional training in the arts (See Schools); Weekly
Art Forum of visiting professional artists, critics and curators;
Events in the Arts (series of evenings of poetry, dance, music,
films); resident string quartet; professional summer stock theater;
award winning educational theater series; over 100 musical performances per year on and off campus; student recitals, exhibitions and theatrical productions; strong liaison with community
and other arts and educational institutions.
    Library: 245,085 bound volumes; 10,850 microfilm reels.
    Attendance: Approx. 85,000 annually.

NEW BRUNSWICK

UNIVERSITY ART GALLERY
Rutgers University, 08903. Tel: (201) 932-7237
Dr. Edward J. Bloustein, Pres. of Univ.
Phillip Dennis Cate, Cur. Fine Arts Collection
Janie Chester, Cur. Educ.
Free daily 10 AM - 4:30 PM; Sun. 1:30 - 4:30 PM. Estab. 1966.
The University Art Gallery houses the Fine Arts Collection of Rut-
gers University and presents outside loan exhibitions throughout
the school year.
    Collections: 15th and 17th century Italian, 17th century Dutch,
18th, 19th and 20th century American, 18th and 19th century English
paintings; †19th and 20th century French and American prints.
    Activities: 20 gallery talks per year; organizes a series of loan
exhibition throughout the school year with concentration on 19th cen-

tury European Prints; tours by appointment; concerts; Friends of the
Rutgers University Art Gallery (dues single $10, family $15, patron
$25, endowment $100).
    Publications: 4 exhibition catalogs annually; Friends Newsletter.
    Attendance: 40,000.

NEWARK

THE NEW JERSEY HISTORICAL SOCIETY
    230 Broadway, 07104. Tel: (201) 483-3939
Milford A. Vieser, Pres.
Reeve Schley, Jr, Chmn. of Board of Trustees
Robert M. Lunny, Dir.
Miss Joan C. Hull, Asst. Dir.
Arthur V. Irwin, Jr, Asst. Dir.
Robert C. Morris, Librn.
Howard W. Wiseman, Cur.
Mrs. Clifford Crawbuck, Business Mgr.
Free 9:30 AM - 5 PM; cl. Sun, Mon. & Tues. Estab. and inc. 1845 as
a museum and library of New Jersey history. Ann. meeting Apr;
mem. 4000; dues $15 and higher.
    Collections: †New Jersey portraits, landscapes and genre; †draw-
ings and prints; †transportation; †period rooms; furniture and decorative arts; †New Jersey History Gallery.
    Activities: Special events include historical lectures and openings
of exhibitions; annual meetings of the Society and Women's Branch;
annual New Jersey Historical Conference since 1951; traveling exhibitions; annual dinner; class groups and gallery talks; student
activities.
    Library: Historical and genealogical library of 50,000 volumes
and 100,000 manuscripts and documents, newspapers, maps, etc.
    Publications: New Jersey History, historical quarterly since
1845; New Jersey Messenger, newsletter 4 times a year; Collections of the Society: works of New Jersey history and allied subjects; The Cockpit and The Crossroads.
    Attendance: Approx. 10,000.

✠NEWARK MUSEUM ASSOCIATION
    49 Washington St, 07101. Tel: (201) 733-6600
Robert M. Krementz, Pres.
Samuel C. Miller, Dir.
Dorothy McNally, Asst. to Dir.
Wilmot T. Bartle, Admin. Asst.
Audrey F. Koenig, Registrar
Edward Chandless, Exhibits Dir.
Sally O'C. Townsend, Dir. of Educ.
Gary Swangin, Planetarium & Observatory
Sheryl Bouler, Jr. Museum
Ruth Hessler, Lending Dept.
Jean West, Arts Workshop
Irving H. Black, Science Dept.
Susan Auth, Classical
Dorothy B. Bartle, Coins & Fire Museum
Fearn Thurlow, Painting & Sculpture
Valrae Reynolds, Oriental Collections
Phillip H. Curtis, Decorative Arts
Anne Spencer, Ethnology
Marjorie H. Fredricks, Prog. & Publ.
Free 12 AM - 5 PM; Sun. & holidays, 1 - 5 PM; cl. Thanksgiving, Dec.
25, Jan. 1 & July 4. Estab. and inc. 1909, to exhibit articles of art,
science, history and technology, and for the study of the arts and
sciences. Building gift of Louis Bamberger, opened 1926; held in
trust by the Museum Association for the City which gave the site.
Adjoining building purchased by Museum 1937. Supported by city,
state and county. Ann. meeting Jan; mem. 3000; dues $10 and higher.
    Collections: †American painting and sculpture of all periods with
primitives well represented. †Tibetan, †Chinese, †Japanese, †Indian,
†Islamic art. †Mediterranean antiquities, including Eugene Schaefer
Collection of ancient glass. †Decorative arts; †African, †South Pacific, †American Indian and †Pre-Columbian material; †crosses and
crucifixes; †coins; †science collections; Planetarium and Observatory.
    Exhibitions: Exhibitions continuing indefinitely: Newark's Oldest
Schoolhouse (1784); 1800 House; Tibet; Africa; American Indians;
Decorative Arts; Oriental Masterpieces; Physical Sciences; Earth
Sciences; Animal Kingdom; Mechanical Models; Newark Fire Museum. Approximately 40 changing exhibitions during the year including paintings and sculpture from the Museum's collection.
    Activities: Tours and lectures for adult groups by appointment;
gallery talks, demonstrations, films, concerts, free during the year.
Planetarium performances: adults 50¢, children 25¢. Docent service
for schools and groups (80,000 in 1974). Lending service of three-
dimensional objects to schools (20,000 objects). Arts workshop in
ceramics, weaving, painting, sculpture, graphics. Two sales desks.
Junior Museum (see separate listing under Junior Museums).

Library: 30,000 books and pamphlets; 20,000 photographs of Museum collections and activities; 1000 Tibet Photos; 3000 slides.
Publications: News Notes monthly; The Newark Museum Quarterly; catalogs and bulletins on most major exhibitions.
Attendance: 190,000.

NEWARK PUBLIC LIBRARY
Art and Music Department
 5 Washington St, 07101. Tel: (201) 733-7840
J. Bernard Schein, Dir. of Library
William J. Dane, Supv. Art & Music Librn.
Joan Burns, Prin. Art Librn.
Open Mon, Wed, Thurs. 9 AM - 9 PM; Tues. & Fri. 9 AM - 6 PM;
Sat. 9 AM - 5 PM; cl. Sun. & legal holidays. Estab. 1910.
 Collections: †50,000 books on the fine and applied arts; †1650 portfolios of design; †1,000,000 illustrations and reproductions of paintings for reference and lending. Also a valuable collection of †10,000 original prints for exhibit and study, including 2000 Japanese prints and printed books by various artists. Also a collection of †3100 rare and finely printed books, manuscript leaves, etc. to illustrate the history of writing and of the printed word. †14,000 slides on paintings, architecture, decorative arts and sculpture. †1000 illustrated books from the 19th and 20th centuries and †2000 posters on travel, World Wars I and II, motion pictures, music and from galleries and museums.
 Exhibitions: Exhibits of new accessions, graphic media of various kinds, works of local artists and topical exhibits; circulating exhibits for the New Jersey State Council on the Arts.
 Activities: Film programs and concerts.
 Purchases: $15,000 annually.

NUTLEY

MINIATURE ART SOCIETY OF NEW JERSEY
 200 Chestnut St, 07110. Tel: (201) 661-2280
John Barnwell, Pres.
Pat Longley, V.Pres. Publicity
Marilyn Brill, V.Pres. Programs
Vivian Noyes Fikus, Secy.
V. Egan, Treas.
Adele Landfear, Recording Secy.
Financed by membership. Meeting 1st Wed. each month; mem. 100; dues $10.
 Exhibitions: Annual National Show; 4-5 traveling shows a year.
 Activities: Traveling exhibitions organized and circulated; competitions.
 Publications: Newsletter, 4-5 times a year.

PARAMUS

BERGEN COMMUNITY MUSEUM
 Ridgewood Ave. at Farview, 07652.
Spencer B. Newman, Pres.
Joan M. Schuster, Dir.
Open Wed. - Sat. 1 - 5 PM; Sun. 2 - 6 PM; suggested minimum donation 50¢ adults, 25¢ children. Inc. May 21, 1956, to provide a creative and recreative museum center for arts and sciences in Bergen County, N.J, showing this area's nature and importance as a threshold of American history, industry and culture. Ann. meeting Apr. or May; 32 member Board; mem. dues $5 and higher, students $2.
 Collections: Graphics, painting, photography and sculpture by New Jersey and international artists. Cultural objects of local prehistoric people, Lenni-Lenape, Dutch, English and later settlers. Nature and science materials, fossil to contemporary, including Mastodon find with other Ice-Age animals.
 Exhibitions: Salute to Women; Latin American Show Through New Jersey; The Hermitage Clothing and Textile Committee; Architect B. Spencer Newman and 19th National Print Exhibition (1975), including 10 county artists among 111 in show; Paul Ortlip, Dorothea Vann, James Gordon Irving, Bergen County Artists Guild, Art Center Affiliates, Jerome Gordon, Ethelyn Woodlock, Julius Kramer, Grant Reynard, Bom's Cumpelik; William Anerbach-Levy, Charles Shedden, Ralph Didriksen, Anita Friend, Ruth Cowell; New Jersey Designer-Craftsmen, George Fish, Shirley Yudkin, Marion Lane, Paul Burns, Charles Vukovich, Jack Osborn, Joel Krauser, Kay Seiler, A.A.P.L, Arnoldo Miccoli; Modern Artists Guild, Solomon Rothman, Lillian Marzell, Paul Sisko, Grace Bogerto; Curator's Choice, Yvette Davison.
 Activities: Seminars, field trips, extension exhibitions in schools; libraries and shopping centers; films, demonstrations; museum workshops; series of classes; photography workshops.
 Attendance: 12,000 annually.

PITTSTOWN

ASSOCIATED ARTISTS OF NEW JERSEY
 R.D. 1, 08867. Tel: (201) 735-5831
Alexander Farnham, Pres.
Carolyn Keskulla, V.Pres.
Anne S. Marsh, Corresp. Secy.
Jane Oliver, Recording Secy.
Ruth Kreiger, Treas.
 Estab. 1941. Ann. meeting May; mem. 50 professional artists; new members voted in by Board of Directors; dues $7. Two annual exhibitions held in New Jersey.

PLAINFIELD

PLAINFIELD PUBLIC LIBRARY
 Eighth St. at Park Ave, 07060. Tel: (201) 757-1111
L. A. Moore, Dir.
Free 9 AM - 9 PM; Sat. 9 AM - 5 PM; cl. Sun. & holidays.
 Estab. 1881. Includes †Lincoln Fine Arts Collection. 175,000 volumes in Library collection, and color slides, film collection, video-tapes. Exhibits held by Plainfield Art Association and other groups. Art and Photograph Exhibitions; Chamber Music Concerts; Drama Readings; Film Programs.
 Income: $575,000.

PRINCETON

✠PRINCETON UNIVERSITY
The Art Museum
 08540. Tel: (609) 452-3787
Peter C. Bunnell, Dir.
Allen Rosenbaum, Asst. Dir.
Frances Follin Jones, Cur. Collections
Free Tues. - Sat. 10 AM - 4 PM; Sun. 2 - 4 PM; cl. Mon. and major holidays. Estab. 1882 to make original works of art available to students in Dept. of Art and Archaeology. (See Schools). New building dedicated 1966. Friends of the Art Museum; mem. 1200. Docent tours available.
 Collections: 25,000 prints, drawings and photographs of various schools; 600 Chinese paintings; Chinese ritual bronzes; 600 American and European paintings; 1000 examples of pottery and porcelain, ancient and modern; numerous examples of sculpture, including the Putman Collection of contemporary monumental sculpture and the various minor arts.
 Exhibitions: 12 to 15 temporary exhibitions annually which supplement the installation of the permanent collection.
 Publications: Publishes the Record of the Art Museum (semi-annually); numerous catalogs.
 Attendance: 86,000.

Index of Christian Art
 McCormick Hall
Rosalie B. Green, Dir.
Free Mon. - Fri. 9 AM - 5 PM; cl. Aug. & holidays.
 Estab. 1917. Over 500,000 cards and 100,000 photographs and photostats. Some inquires answered by mail; fee for compilations and prints.

SOUTH ORANGE

ARCHAEOLOGICAL SOCIETY OF NEW JERSEY
 Room 106 Humanities Bldg, Seton Hall University, 07079.
 Tel: (201) 762-6680
Herbert C. Kraft, Pres.
John H. Gustafson, Secy.
Estab. 1931. Four meetings per year; mem. 650; dues $5 active.
 Promotes and encourages the study of archaeology; investigates archaeological sites and preserves artifacts; circulates small exhibits on local archaeology; encourages and assists in research of archaeological sites. Society maintains a circulating library of books on anthropology and ethnology available to membership. The Society is a member of the Eastern States Archaeological Federation.

SETON HALL UNIVERSITY ART CENTER
 South Orange Ave, 07079. Tel: (201) 762-9000
Louis de Foix-Crenascol, Dir.
Barbara W. Kaufman, Cur. Exhibitions
Lou H. Mitchell, Cur. Collections
Petra t.D. Chu, Cur. Slides & Educational Media
Free daily 9 AM - 10 PM. Estab. 1963 as Student Center Art Gallery, renamed Art Center 1973. For the permanent collection of contemporary American art, the Troast Memorial Gallery was established in 1974.

Major Exhibitions: (1973-75) Chinese Brush Painting: David Kwo, I Chao Chu, Ming Wang, Lai Chin-Cheng; Graphics: Louis Lozowick; Painting: Anthony Triano, Carter; Watercolor: Edwin Havas.
Activities: Free public lectures, gallery talks.
Library: 7000 slides of painting.
Attendance: Approx. 35,000 annually.

SUMMIT

SUMMIT ART CENTER, INC.
68 Elm St, 07901. Tel: (201) 273-9121
Mrs. Alex Aidekman, Pres.
Robert Reid, Dir.
Exhibits open daily 2 - 4 PM. Estab. 1933. Ann. meeting Apr; mem. 2000; dues $15.
Exhibitions: New exhibitions every 3-4 weeks; Annual Statewide Juried Show; one and two-man shows.
Activities: Art classes for adults and children; lectures; musical events.

TRENTON

FREE PUBLIC LIBRARY OF TRENTON, N.J.
Art and Music Department
120 Academy St, 08608. Tel: (609) 392-7188
Veronica F. Cary, Library Dir.
B. Adele Knepley, Head, Art & Music Dept.
Open Mon. - Fri. 9 AM - 9 PM; Sat. 9 AM - 5 PM; cl. Sunday & legal holidays; no admis. to city residents. Library estab. 1750; Art and Music Dept. estab. 1966.
Collections: 53,000 pictures, 4600 record discs, over 100 motion pictures; New Jersey State Music Educators collection of choral and orchestral music (choral music: 228 titles, 42,000 pieces; orchestral music: 168 titles, 16,200 pieces); vocal and orchestral scores and libretto for operas; books on and about art and music.

MERCER COUNTY COMMUNITY COLLEGE LIBRARY
1200 Old Trenton Rd, 08690. Tel: (609) 586-4800
Frank G. Butorac, Chmn, Library Services Dept.
Free 9 AM - 5 PM. Estab. 1891 to provide library services for the college. Triangle Gallery primarily for exhibiting student work; portion of the library main floor is devoted to permanent display cabinets, in addition display panels are used in the library for faculty exhibits, community exhibits and travelling exhibits, on a rotating basis.
Collections: Cybis Collection; Bronislaw Cybis; Ceramics Collection; Kelsey Collection; Painting by Wolf Kahn; Mexican Art and Handicrafts.
Exhibitions: Faculty Art Exhibition; Kahlil Gibran, Exhibit of Original Drawings; Cybis Collection; Bronislaw Cybis; Mexican Art & Handicrafts; Student Paintings; Photography by Students; 10 exhibitions of student work: paintings, printmaking, drawings, graphic design; Children's Art Exhibit; Mercer County Artists '73.
Activities: Extension department; lending collection, 627 motion pictures; lectures open to the public; 4 gallery talks; classes for adults and children. Book Shop.
Library of 48,000 volumes; photograph collection of 200 prints.
Publications: College catalog, every 2 yrs.

✳NEW JERSEY STATE MUSEUM
Cultural Center
205 W. State St, 08625. Tel: (609) 292-6300 for dir. or (609) 292-6464 for 24-hour recorded program information.
Leah P. Sloshberg, Dir.
Karen G. Cummins, Asst. to Dir.
John S. Moore, Admin. Asst.
Zoltan F. Buki, Cur. Bureau Arts
Lorraine E. Williams, Cur. Bureau Archaeology/Ethnology
Suzanne Corlette, Cur. Bureau Cultural History
Raymond J. Stein, Cur. Bureau Science
Wallace X. Conway, Cur. Bureau Exhibits
Raymond J. Howe, Cur. Bureau Educ.
Richard D. Perry, Planetarium
Allen C. Hilborn, Press & Publications
Free Mon. - Fri. 9 AM - 5 PM; weekends 1 - 5 PM; cl. Jan. 1, July 4, Dec. 25, Thanksgiving. Estab. 1890; since 1945 a division of N.J. Department of Education; moved October 1965 into new State Cultural Center with four-floor museum building, adjoining 150-seat planetarium and adjacent 416-seat auditorium building which also includes exhibition galleries; under construction are large galleries for major natural sciences and cultural history exhibits; operates book and gift shop.
Collections: †Paintings, drawings, prints and sculpture with special emphasis on New Jersey and other American works; †all areas of decorative arts with special emphasis on New Jersey ceramics, glass, furniture; †18th and 19th century craft and tech-

nological artifacts; †natural history, geology, paleontology with New Jersey emphasis; †archaeology and ethnology with emphasis on New Jersey and the New World; Sisler Memorial Collection of North American Mammals.
Exhibitions: Bimonthly changing exhibitions in fine and decorative arts; contemporary New Jersey Artists series featuring works by two selected painters, photographers or craftsmen in six-week showings; also temporary exhibitions relating to science and history.
Activities: For school children lecture-demonstrations cover natural history, New Jersey Indians, astronomy, government (including State House tours), fine and decorative arts. For teachers there are workshops, classes in astronomy and classroom use of Museum services and facilities. Public activities and services include planetarium programs, lectures, films, performing arts, concerts, identification of specimens and objects and information verification in natural sciences and astronomy. Special consultation is available on costs and mechanics of planetarium operation. Film loan service and circulating exhibitions are provided for schools, libraries, community centers and nonprofit groups.
Publications: (All on irregular basis) bulletin series of reference handbooks devoted to New Jersey natural history, the sciences and the arts; report series devoted to in-depth New Jersey research and surveys; investigation series based on research and field work in the natural sciences and the humanities; exhibition catalogues; calendars.
Library: Appropriate research material is maintained by each bureau and section—art, archaeology, ornithology, paleontology, etc.
Purchases: In excess of $100,000.
Attendance: Half-million plus.

NEW MEXICO

ALBUQUERQUE

ALBUQUERQUE ARTS COUNCIL*
5900 Domingo Rd. N.E, 87108. Tel: (505) 265-3271
Crawford MacCallum, Pres.
Alma McGovern, Secy.
Jane Mabry, V.Pres.
Ed Meadows, Treas.
Debbi Vick, Secy.
Open Mon. - Fri. 10:30 - 12:30 AM. Estab. 1970 to unify the arts of Albuquerque. Meeting 2nd Wed. of every mo; mem. 200; dues $3 yr. - $10 mo.
Activities: Lectures open to the public.
Publications: Cultural Calendar, monthly.

ALBUQUERQUE PUBLIC LIBRARY*
Fine & Performing Arts Department, 423 Central N.E, 87101.
Tel: (505) 766-7722
Alan B. Clark, Dir.
Hester Miller, Head Fine & Performing Arts Dept.
Open Mon. - Thurs. 9 AM - 9 PM; Fri. - Sat. 9 AM - 5:30 PM.
Estab. 1967 to provide study, research, and recreational materials in the arts for the people of the city, county, and state; financed by city and state appropriations.
Collections: †9000 volumes on non-performing arts; †39,500 circulating pictures; †37 framed circulating original graphics; †88 framed circulating reproductions; †1863 slides.
Activities: Individual paintings, reproductions and original graphics lent to schools; lending collection, 88 framed color reproductions, 1863 lantern slides, 37 framed original graphics, 39,241 pictures; (art & general subject); 6673 items lent in an average year.
Income and Purchases: Income $5000, purchases $5000.

THE CLASSICAL SCHOOL GALLERY
614 Indian School Rd. N.W, 87102. Tel: (505) 843-7749
Dr. C. M. Flumiani, Pres.
Open daily 10 - 12 AM, 3 - 5 PM. Estab. 1969 to foster the classical approach to the arts and art education; endowed; new 2500 sq. ft. building. Mem: 15; dues $200.
Collections: Italian masters.
Activities: Art instruction for adults; lectures open to public; scholarships. Book shop.
Library: 2000 volumes.
Publications: Art & Life, quarterly.

MUSEUM OF ALBUQUERQUE
P.O. Box 1293, 87103. Tel: (505) 766-7878
Richard A. Bice, Chmn. Board of Trustees
Suzanne de Borhegyi, Dir.
Open Tues. - Fri. 10 AM - 5 PM; Sat. & Sun. 1 - 5 PM; admis. Tues. - Sat. adults 25¢, children 10¢. Estab. Sept 1967 as a regional history museum devoted to the collection and preservation of local cultural history, ranging from 20,000 BC to the present.

The Museum sponsors and maintains a temporary exhibition schedule showing the art, history and science aspects of our environs and that of the world; maintained by city appropriation.
Mem. 569; dues $5, $10, $25, $50; $100 Business and Professional.

Collections: General, decorative arts, costumes, photography.

Exhibitions: Una Casa de Nuevo Mexico; Edward Curtis Photogravures; The Museum as a Custodian; Weapons as Western Tools; Ranching in New Mexico; Watercolor Southwest One; Women in New Mexico; Five Critical Elections; Ten Centuries of Mexican Jewelry; Textile Biennial; Fred Harvey Fine Arts Collection; Albuquerque Foundry & Machine Works; New Mexico Santero Art; Our Lady of Guadalupe; Pan American Costumes; Fifteen of Mexico's Artists; Metro Youth Art; Introductions 1974; 300 Years of French Posters.

Activities: Volunteer docent program for school tours, 1974-216 tours for 5591 children, 1973-291 tours for 8677 children. Book shop.

Library: Approx. 1000 volumes.

Publications: Las Noticias (Newsletter, 10 per year); Exhibition catalogs as needed.

Annual Income: $141,782.

Attendance: 31,600 annual average.

NEW MEXICO ART LEAGUE OLD TOWN GALLERY
400 Romero St. N.W, 87104. Tel: (505) 243-0398
Paul Sanchez, Pres.
Pat O'Connell, V.Pres.
Doris Brooks, Treas.
Pat Durgin, Secy.
Jean Rosenburg, Dir.
Sales gallery open 10 AM - 5 PM. Founded 1930 at Univ. New Mexico as an art patronage organization with purpose of collecting fine art and social and cultural activities for the citizens; present gallery opened in 1966 under Peter Walker, Pres. Ann. meeting 1st Mon. in Oct; mem. over 500.

Collections: Paintings and sculpture at Old Town Gallery and Albuquerque National Bank Gallery, Wyoming Blvd. Branch.

Activities: Show for members, changing every month; one-man or group shows changing every month; monthly meetings with demonstrations open to the public; gallery available for outside groups. National small painting show in Feb, $2000 in prizes each year; statewide mall show each Oct. or Nov, $2000 in prizes each year. Church Street Festival in June.

Publications: Monthly newsletter.

Income: Average $50,000 per year.

Attendance: Average 100 per day; 250-550 at receptions.

⚵UNIVERSITY OF NEW MEXICO
University Art Museum
Fine Arts Center, 87131. Tel: (505) 277-4001
VanDeren Coke, Dir.
Thomas Barrow, Assoc. Dir.
Open Tues. - Fri. 10 AM - 5 PM; Sun. Noon - 5 PM; cl. Mon. & Sat; admis. adults 50¢, children 25¢, faculty, staff and students free. Estab. 1963. Friends of Art, ann. meeting 3rd Wed. in May; mem. 300.

Collections: †Contemporary American painting, prints and sculpture with emphasis on artists who have worked in New Mexico; †Old Master prints; †19th and 20th century lithographs and creative photographs; Santos and Spanish-Colonial silver (Field Collection).

Selected Exhibitions 1970-1973: Marin In New Mexico; Colonial Art of Mexico; Sources for Tomorrow: Drawings of Gaston Lachaise; The Graphic Work of Jasper Johns; Robert Rauschenberg in Black and White; Annual Faculty and Student Exhibitions; Ilya Bolotowsky: Paintings and Columns; Paul Harris Sculpture; Eliot Porter Retrospective; National Craft Invitational; Light and Substance; New Acquisitions Under NEA and Friends of Art Grants.

Publications: Bulletin annually; numerous exhibition catalogs.

Attendance: 35,000 annually.

Fine Arts Library (Branch of the Zimmerman Library)
87131. Tel: (505) 277-2901
Free Mon. - Thurs. 8 AM - 10 PM; Fri. 8 AM- 5 PM; Sat. 8 - 12 AM; Sun. 2 - 5 PM.

Estab. 1963 to meet the needs of the students and faculty within the subjects covered. Special emphasis on pre-Columbian and Spanish colonial art and architecture, American Indian art, 19th and 20th century art and architecture, including urban planning, history of the graphic arts, including photography. Supplemented by collections of general University Library which is especially strong in anthropology. 40,000 volumes, 100,000 slides, 13,500 photographs and reproductions, 4000 exhibition catalogs.

Jonson Gallery
1909 Las Lomas Rd. N.E, 87106. Tel: (505) 243-4667
Raymond Jonson, Dir.
Arthur H. Johnson, Cur.
Free 12 AM - 6 PM; cl. Mon. Estab. 1950 for preservation of works by Raymond Jonson and other artists; exhibitions by contemporary

artists with emphasis on New Mexico artists; living and working areas for Raymond Jonson. Gallery.

Collections: Jonson Retrospective Collection, 569 pieces; Jonson Collection, works by other artists, 430 pieces; Jonson Theatre Collection, 83 pieces.

Exhibitions (paintings unless otherwise noted): (1971) Jerry Romotsky; William Vaughan Howard; J. Frederick Laval (photo/serigraphs); William Patterson; Ray Kiihne; Julia La Fon; 22nd Annual Summer Exhibition, Raymond Jonson; Mariellen Blackburn; Ed Garman; Howard B. Schleeter; Permanent Collection. (1972) Maera; Joseph A. Chavez (sculpture); Jack Garver; University of New Mexico Art Education Faculty; Catherine Fisher; 23rd Annual Summer Exhibition, Raymond Jonson; Quinn Mizer; John Skolle; Ralph Lewis; Ed Garman and Raymond Jonson, two-man show. (1973) Donald Hugh Harrelson; Mickey McConnell; Peggy Hight-Robb; Twelve Photographers; Catherine Fisher; Burton Quincy Phillips; 24th Annual Summer Exhibition, Raymond Jonson.

Library: 1000 volumes for reference.

Publications: Announcements of forthcoming exhibitions; occasional catalogs of exhibitions.

Attendance: 2000-3000.

GALLUP

MUSEUM OF INDIAN ARTS AND CRAFTS
Chamber of Commerce Building, 103 W. 66 Ave, 87301.
Tel: (505) 863-6849
Octavia Fellin, Chmn. Comt.
Free, weekdays, 9 - 12 AM; 1 - 5 PM. Estab. 1947 to display various arts and crafts capabilities of the Hopi, Zuni, and Navajo Indian tribes, for visitiors and local residents; financed by Chamber of Commerce budget.

Activities: Lectures open to the public; slide program during summer.

Attendance: 3000 annual average.

LOS ALAMOS

LOS ALAMOS ARTS COUNCIL
P.O. Box 284, 87544.
Jane Bennorth, Pres.
Judy Gursky, Secy.
Estab. 1967 for coordination of cultural activities in Los Alamos and environs; financed by city and state appropriation and membership. Gallery for a permanent collection and exhibits. †Permanent collection just beginning. Meetings Sept. & Mar; mem. 200; dues $5, $8 and $20; 17 mem. organizations.

Activities: Sponsor various types of cultural activities, including an annual four day arts festival in the summer, two Northern New Mexico Crafts Fairs, monthly cultural programs, monthly Morning Musicale, master classes in music, sack lunch musicales, student musicales, photography; plus serving as an advisory board to the county on matters concerning cultural activities and the maintenance of Fuller Lodge.

Publications: Los Alamos Arts Council Newsletter, monthly.

Income and Purchases: Under $2000.

Attendance: 100 (small events), 7500 (Arts Festival), 4000 (Crafts Fair).

ROSWELL

ROSWELL MUSEUM AND ART CENTER
11th and Main Sts, 88201. Tel: (505) 622-4700
Donald B. Anderson, Pres.
Robert V. Ely, V.Pres.
Martha Gillespie, Secy.
Ralph McIntyre, Treas.
Wendell Ott, Dir.
William D. Ebie, Asst. Dir.
Mrs. Doyle M. Denney, Exec. Secy.
Margaret Detwiler, Mem. Secy.
Free Mon. - Sat. 9 AM - 5 PM; Sun. & holidays 1 - 5 PM. Estab. 1937; founded as a Museum of Art, History and Archaeology. Mem. 500; dues $5 and higher.

Collections: †20th century American paintings and sculpture; †European and American prints; †Southwestern painting; †collection of paintings and prints of Peter Hurd and Henriette Wyeth; †Witter Bynner collection of Chinese paintings and jade; ethnological and archaeological collection of southwestern Indian art; historical material of southeastern New Mexico; aquarium and natural history exhibits; Robert H. Goddard Rocket Wing.

Exhibitions: Peter Hurd paintings and eight traveling painting and sculpture exhibitions a year; permanent collection; Witter Bynner Chinese paintings and jade; Pre-Columbian sculpture; Southwestern Indian Art.

Activities: Planetarium programs; chamber music concerts; lectures; Extension courses from Eastern New Mexico University; Great Books Discussion Groups; Archaeological and Historical Societies; studio classes for adults and children; tours and gallery talks; astronomy club and science clubs (HS age).

Library: Specializing in southwestern art and archaeology, with reproductions, photographs, books and magazines available for loan.

Publications: Quarterly Bulletin; Exhibition catalogs; Publications in Arts and Science.

Income and Purchases: Income, $50,000; purchases, $7000.

Attendance: 65,000.

SANTA FE

INSTITUTE OF AMERICAN INDIAN ARTS MUSEUM
Cerrillos Rd, 87501. Tel: (505) 988-6281
Charles Dailey, Dir.
Manuelita Lovato, Cur. Functions
Free, Mon. - Fri. 9 AM - 5 PM; cl. on weekends. Estab. 1962 to instruct in all aspects of arts and crafts to Americas' native American peoples from all of United States; museum serves as a support to curriculum and as a repository for the only major collection of contemporary Indian arts and crafts, provides opportunity for study of museology as applies to Indian visitors centers as well as study of the unique collection; traveling shows important for reservation areas; financed by federal government. Gallery approx. 4000 sq. feet of exhibition area; revolving shows constantly featuring primarily student work and material from permanent collection.

Collections: Only major collection of contemporary Indian arts and crafts in America. Not only is the traditional material collected, but also the most avant garde and experimental directions in Indian Art. Vital and comprehensive collection in fields of paintings, graphics, textiles, ceramics, sculpture, jewelry, photographs, printed textiles, costumes, ethnological materials such as drums and paraphanelia for general living.

Exhibitions: Earth Color; Quiet Emphasis; yearly student sales exhibit held in June - September each year; 10 Year Retrospective; photograph traveling show.

Activities: Assisting any Indian reservation in setting up their own visitor centers or museum in America; material available to Indian reservations, museums, cultural centers and universities, with fees, transportation and insurance provided; traveling exhibitions organized and circulated; individual paintings and original objects of art lent; eight shows of about thirty items lent in average year; lectures open to the public; competitions; scholarships.

Library: 30,000 volume library, specializing in Indian related materials; arts books.

Income: $40,000.

Attendance: 15,000 annual average.

MUSEUM OF NAVAJO CEREMONIAL ART, INC.
704 Camino Lejo, 87501. Tel: (505) 983-8321
(Mailing address: Box 5153)
Steven H. Tremper, Dir.
Constance Darkey, Librn.
Lynda M. Nonno, Acting Cur.
Mel Lawrence, Pub. Relations
Lorraine Cervone, Admin. Asst.
Free Tues. - Sat. 10 AM - 5 PM; Sun. 2 - 5 PM; cl. Mon. Estab. 1937 to perpetuate for the general public, for research students, and for the Indians themselves, this great example of an indigenous people's culture. Ann. meeting Feb; mem. 425; dues $25 and higher. Founded by the late Miss Mary Cabot Wheelwright, the museum is built in a symbolic form of a ceremonial hogan, to function as an integral background of the exhibitions of sandpaintings and other Navajo materials.

Collections: †In addition to the collection of sandpainting reproductions (casein, watercolor and wool tapestry reproductions) there are complete sets of ritual objects; †slides, †tapes, †photographs; and other comparative objects.

Exhibitions: †Sandpainting reproductions of various Navajo ceremonials; also †ritual material, masks, baskets, medicine pouches, †jewelry, †textiles, etc. Live exhibits by Navajo artists and photographers of Navajo subjects, and displays of current specimens such as Navajo weaving, pottery, etc, are interspersed with permanent collections, as occasions arise.

Activities: Guided tours, lectures, films, music, lectures to colleges and cults. Pertinent lectures are presented from time to time, covering all aspects of anthropology and related subjects, particularly those dealing with the Navajo. Museum shop.

Library: Specialized collection of books and manuscripts for research.

Publications: Bulletins, books on Navajo culture.

Attendance: Approx. 17,000-20,000.

MUSEUM OF NEW MEXICO
P.O. Box 2087, 87501. Tel: (505) 827-2834
George Ewing, Dir.
Michael Weber, Assoc. Dir. & Dir. History Div.
Donald O. Strel, Dir. Fine Arts Div.
Yvonne Lange, Dir. International Folk Art Museum
Stewart Peckham, Dir, Laboratory of Anthropology
Susan J. Dewitt, Pub. Information Officer
Free Museum buildings open Mon. - Sat. 9 AM - 5 PM; Sun. & holidays 2 - 5 PM. Estab. 1909. Museum of New Mexico Foundation supports acquisitions, programs and fund raising; 650 members; dues $12.50

The Museum of New Mexico, a state institution, operates in four major fields of interest, Fine Arts, International Folk Art, History and Anthropology (archaeology and ethnology), which are housed in four separate buildings. In addition to the Museum buildings in Santa Fe, the Museum of New Mexico also maintains the following State Monuments located in various parts of the state: Kuaua (Coronado) Pueblo Ruins, Jemez Mission and Pueblo Ruins, Abo and Quarai Mission Ruins, Fort Sumner and Fort Selden.

Collections: Over 65,000 items in collections.

Exhibitions: The Museum of New Mexico offers a variety of in-the-field services to the state-wide public. In the area of traveling exhibitions, a major completely packaged exhibit and several circulating exhibits are scheduled yearly. One of the exhibits, the Museum on Wheels, which travels to schools, contains a fixed display of curriculum-oriented material with educational electronic equipment.

Activities: Educational kits with hands-on materials are sent to schools throughout the state; extensive docent program serving 15,000 school children during school year.

Libraries: The Museum houses four separate research libraries on Folk Art, Fine Arts, History and Anthropology; 24,000 volumes.

Publications: Bimonthly Newsletter; quarterly El Palacio; exhibition catalogs, annual reports, monographs, pamphlets, books, magazines and guides.

Income: State appropriation $1,200,000 annually.

Attendance: 500,000 plus 100,000 at monuments annually.

Fine Arts Building (Built 1917)
107 W. Palace Ave.
Collections: National and International with emphasis on artists of the Southwest.
Exhibitions: (1975) New Mexico Fine Arts Biennial Competition-Exhibition; permanent collection: Laura Gilpin; Louis Ribak; Women of Photography; Field Painting; Indian Paintings.

Museum of International Folk Art (Built 1953)
P.O. Box 2087, Camino Lejo, 87501. Tel: (505) 827-2544
Dr. Yvonne Lange, Dir.
Paul Winkler, Asst to Dir.
Carol Steiro, Cur. Collections
Nora Fisher, Cur. Textiles
Christine Mather, Cur. Spanish Colonial Collections
Judy Chiba, Cur.
Charlene Cerny, Cur.
Alan Vedder, Conservator
Judith Gleye, Librn.
Free Mon. - Sat. 9 AM - 5 PM; Sun. 1 - 5 PM. Estab. 1950 to collect, exhibit and research objects related to folk culture and to encourage the art of the craftsman. Financed by endowment and city and state appropriation. Mem. only through Museum of New Mexico Foundation.
Collections: International folk art, with emphasis on Spanish Colonial and Hispanic-related culture; costumes and textiles.
Exhibitions: What is Folk Art?; African Fabrics; Navajo Pictorials; Mexico: Fantasy and Imagination; New Mexico Crafts Biennial; Southwest Crafts Biennial; Traveling Limners; Village Embroidery Workshops; plus numerous smaller exhibitions.
Activities: Lends complete exhibits to libraries, community centers, schools, universities and private organizations which have exhibition space (22 educational aid exhibits; 9 circulating exhibits; 1 mobile turck unit); lectures open to the public; 4 visiting lecturers per year; 84 gallery tours; concerts; dramatic programs; classes for adults and children; competitions. Book Shop.
Library: 4000 volumes for reference and copying; 5000 slides and 80,000 prints for reference and copying; tape and manuscript collection of folk dramas of New Mexico.
Attendance: 67,892.

Palace of the Governors (Built 1610)
Palace Ave.
Exhibitions: Southwestern History, Spanish-Colonial and Territorial Periods; The Palace Press, a working exhibit of frontier printing.

Hall of the Southwestern Indian—Contemporary Indian Civilizations of the Southwest.

Laboratory of Anthropology (Built 1936)
Old Santa Fe Trail (Camino Lejo)
Research laboratory in archaeology and ethnology.
Collections: Materials from various Indian cultures of the South-west—pottery, textiles, jewelry, etc.
Exhibitions: Ceremonial paraphernalia; Indian silverwork.

SCHOOL OF AMERICAN RESEARCH
P.O. Box 2188, 87501. Tel: (505) 983-4629
Daniel Kelly, Jr, Pres.
Philip Shultz, V.Pres.
Jason Kellahin, Secy.
David Davenport, Treas.
Dr. Douglas W. Schwartz, Dir.
Inc. 1917 as a center for advanced studies in anthropology. Collections are exhibited under loan agreements at the Museum of New Mexico. The School conducts advanced seminars in anthropology, supports scholars working in Southwestern anthropology, publishes anthropological books, conducts basic research in archaeology. Membership program includes lecture series and field trips. The school is a privately funded institute, supported by foundation grants, private donations and endowment. Ann. meeting Nov. or Dec.
Collections: Archaeological; fine arts.
Library: Small library, with emphasis on anthropology.
Publications: Advanced Seminar Series; Southwestern Indian Arts Series; Arroyo Hondo monographs.

SOCORRO

SOCORRO ART LEAGUE
1212 North Dr. N.W, 87801. Tel: (505) 835-0651
Wyveta LeRoy, Pres.
Sylvia Gormley, V.Pres.
Joan Zahm, Secy.
Dr. W. D. Crozier, Corresp. Secy. & Treas.
Estab. 1960 for the sponsorship of art classes and study groups, presentation of art exhibitions, furnishing art books to the public library and sponsorship of art lectures and demonstrations; financed by mem. Meetings monthly except in summer; mem. 26; dues $5.
Exhibitions: Approx. 12.
Activities: Lectures open to the public; 4 visiting lecturers per year; classes for adults; exhibitions in local banks and library; workshops.
Attendance: 240 annual average.

TAOS

HARWOOD FOUNDATION OF THE UNIVERSITY OF NEW MEXICO
Box 766, 87571. Tel: (505) 758-3063
Dorothy Brandenburg, Pres. of Board
Stephen R. Brogden, Dir.
Dixie M. Gillette, Acting Dir.
Dr. Rupert A. Trujillo, Dir, Division of Continuing Educ, Univ. of New Mexico
Free 10 AM - 5 PM; cl. Sun. and holidays. Buildings and contents given to the University of New Mexico by Elizabeth Case Harwood, 1936, to be maintained as an art, educational and cultural center; maintained by the University with all activities open to the public.
Collections: Old New Mexico Santos; Indian Artifacts; †permanent collection of works by Taos artists; primitive New Mexico wood sculpture and tin ware; Persian miniatures.
Library: Only public library in Taos County, approx. 20,000 volumes. Special collections of Southwest literature and art library; D. H. Lawrence first editions.

KIT CARSON MEMORIAL FOUNDATION, INC.
P.O. Box B, 87571.
Jacob M. Bernal, Pres.
Jack K. Boyer, Secy. & Exec. Dir.
Open summer 7:30 AM - 7:30 PM; winter 8 AM - 5 PM; spring and autumn 8 AM - 6 PM. Admis. adults (16 yr. and older) 50¢; youths (12-15 yr.) 25¢, children (6-11 yr.) 15¢, children under 6 yr. free with parents; family rate, $1.50; special tour rates. Ann. meeting 1st Wed. of March; mem 230; dues contributing $10, participating $15, share $25, sustaining $50, subscribing $100, supporting $250, benefactor $500, sponsor $750, patron $1000.
Estab. August, 1949, to maintain and operate the home of Kit Carson and to perpetuate his name and deeds. The Kit Carson Home is now classified as a Registered National Historic Landmark by the National Park Service. Articles of incorporation were amended in 1960 to include acquisition of other historic, archaeological, and cultural sites.
In 1962 the home of Ernest L. Blumenschein, co-founder of the Taos Art Colony, was given to the Kit Carson Memorial Foundation by Miss Helen G. Blumenschein. In May, 1966, the Blumenschein home was designated as a Registered National Historic Landmark by National Park Service. This historic house will be opened to the public in the future.

In 1967, Mrs. Rebecca S. James, Taos artist, gave the Foundation the Ferdinand Maxwell House and Property on Governor Bent St, Taos, in memory of her late husband, William James. The 6 room house, an excellent example of the New Mexican Territorial Period, will be opened to the public in the future.
In 1972, acquired the Hacienda de Don Antonio Severino Martinez, prominent Taos merchant and official during the Spanish Colonial Period. The Hacienda will be restored to that period and opened to the public. The National Park Service designated the Martinez Hacienda as a Registered National Historic Landmark in May, 1973.
Collections: A small collection of paintings for sale; collections currently being expanded are those within the Kit Carson Home itself and the Historical and Archaeological Collections. An excellent collection of Western Americana is in the Museum Shop. Pieces of art done by the members of the original Taos Society of Artists and other Taos Artists (1890-1930 period) are being collected for future exhibition in the Art Museum to be established in part of the Blumenschein Home. Furniture and furnishings belonging to the Blumenschein family are also being collected. Furniture and furnishings of the New Mexican Territorial Period are being collected for the development of the Ferdinand Maxwell House.
Activities: Conducted tours for groups by arrangement; Director is available for lectures on historical and archaeological subjects. As a non-profit organization for educational purposes, the Museum has expanded to include historical and archaeological exhibits of the Taos ares.
Library: A growing library for reference of 25,000 volumes and more than 5000 photographs and negatives; Map section contains 285 maps. Library is also a depository for the Taos County Historical Society.
Income and Purchases: Income, $33,796. Purchases, $20,840.
Attendance: Approx. 53,000 annually.

TAOS ART ASSOCIATION, INC.
P.O. Box 198, 87571. Tel: (505) 758-2052
Emil Bisttram, Pres.
Johanna Jones, Secy.
Sue McCleery, Exec. Dir.
Thom Andriola, Dir, Stables Gallery
Free daily 10 AM - 5 PM. Estab. Apr, 1952 as an art association composed of artists and businessmen to encourage the understanding of the arts, both plastic and performing; financed by membership. Ann. meeting Apr; mem. 450.
Exhibitions: The Modern Artist in Taos 40's and 50's; Annual Awards Show for Taos County, over $500 in prizes.
Activities: Children's program in painting and theater; traveling exhibitions organized and circulated; lectures open to public; concerts; dramatic programs; classes for adults and children; competitions.
Publications: Monthly calendar of events to membership and with map to hotels.
Attendance: 15,000.

NEW YORK

ALBANY

⚜ALBANY INSTITUTE OF HISTORY AND ART
125 Washington Ave, 12210. Tel: (518) 463-4478
Herbert A. Jones, Pres.
Norman S. Rice, Dir.
Kenneth H. MacFarland, Librn.
Free 10 AM - 4:45 PM; Sun. 2 - 6 PM; cl. Mon. Estab. 1791, inc. 1793 as the Society for the Promotion of Agriculture, Arts, & Manufactures; 1829 as Albany Institute; 1900 as Albany Institute and Historical and Art Society. Present name adopted 1926. Ann. meeting mid-May; mem. about 2000; dues $15 and higher.
Collections: Art and historical material, chiefly related to artists and craftsmen of the region. †Silver; †pewter; †furniture; †glass; †ceramics; †18th and 19th century painting and sculpture by artists of the Hudson River area; Export Ware; Chelsea, Bow china; English 18th century furnishings and paintings; †contemporary paintings and sculpture.
Exhibitions: American decorative arts centered around Albany; some area history; Annual Regional Exhibition by Artists of the Upper Hudson; Biennial, Contemporary American Printmakers; changing exhibition program in contemporary design and fine arts.
Activities: Lectures, varied from theatre, art and antiques to travelogues and dance; adult painting classes and education projects in cooperation with area schools and colleges; children's classes in drawing, painting; lectures for children on Albany history and ancient arts of the world, on appointment through public schools.

Library: Reference library on fine arts, contemporary arts, Albany history. Manuscripts related to Albany families. 6500 books, 150,000 manuscripts.

Income and Purchases: Income $350,000; purchases $25,000.

Attendance: 80,000.

THE ART GALLERY OF THE COLLEGE OF SAINT ROSE
432 Western Ave, 12203. Tel: (518) 471-5111
Sister Marion Charlene Honors, Dir.
Free Sun. - Fri. 2 - 5 PM; cl. Sat. Estab. 1969 to provide a facility that presents fine art both to the college community and to the public and provide a place for college art students to display their works; financed by college funds.

Collections: Very small permanent collection consisting of paintings, prints, and a few pieces of sculpture.

Exhibitions: (1975-76) Martin Benjamin and Allen Yarinsky: Photography; Satish Joshi: Paintings; 1976 Olympic Posters from Kennedy Galleries: Graphics by 15 American Artists; Robert Kaupelis: Paintings and Drawings; plus senior, faculty and student shows.

Attendance: Few hundred for each show.

NEW YORK STATE HISTORY COLLECTIONS
State Education Bldg, 12234. Tel: (518) 474-5353
Louis L. Tucker, State Historian
John S. Still, Chief Cur.
John S. Watson, Prin. Cur.
Permanent exhibits being planned for new State Museum, to open in July 1976—Cultural Education Center, Empire State Plaza, 12238.

†Collections: Edward Lamson Henry sketchbooks, paintings, photographs and other memorabilia; Shaker materials; New York furniture, silver, pewter, glass; country store collection; lighting devices, tools, toys; farm equipment, transportation; firearms, swords; uniforms, costumes, textiles; prints and paintings; professional equipment (photographic, medical, etc); heavy industrial. Some available for viewing by prior arrangement.

NEW YORK STATE LIBRARY
State Education Bldg, 12234. Tel: (518) 474-5958
John A. Humphry, Asst. Commissioner for Libraries
Peter J. Paulson, Dir.
Mildred Ledden, Gen. Reference
Peter Christoph, Manuscripts & History
Darrell Welch, Rare Books
Free Mon. - Fri. 8:30 AM - 6 PM. Estab. 1818.
Collections: Over 35,000 titles in a collection of 4,800,000 items, especially strong in architecture, painting, sculpture, and music (texts). A picture collection of over 50,000 on New York State is maintained in the Manuscripts and History section. Most materials available on interlibrary loan.

Exhibitions: Exhibit program involves mainly printed and manuscript materials.

Income and Purchases: Book budget $670,000.

NEW YORK STATE MUSEUM AND SCIENCE SERVICE
State Education Building, 12224. Tel: (518) 474-5841
Noel C. Fritzinger, Asst. Commissioner
G. Carroll Lindsay, Dir. Museum Services
Daily 9 AM - 4:30 PM except Thanksgiving, Christmas, and New Year's Day. Estab. 1870 as part of the University of the State of New York; natural history and history museum stressing New York State.

Collections: †Geology, †paleontology, †biology, †history, †anthropology of New York State, Lithgow Murals in Iroquois Indian groups, Bird Art in Science and The World of Gems, the science of gemology.

Exhibitions: Major bicentennial exhibit and new series of regional exhibits scheduled for opening July 1, 1976 in the Cultural Education Center.

Activities: Temporary exhibits; classes for school students by appointment.

Attendance: 300,000.

THE PRINT CLUB OF ALBANY*
125 Washington Ave, 12210. Tel: (518) 463-4478
Alice Pauline Schafer, Pres.
Mrs. John F. Bowen, Secy.
Estab. 1934. Mem. limited to 150; dues $10 and higher. Sponsors the †print collection of the Albany Institute; biennial open print show; annual exhibit of members' work, monthly meetings and exhibits at the Institute. Issues a contemporary artist's print annually.

SCHUYLER MANSION
Clinton & Catherine Sts, 12202. Tel: (518) 463-2577
Robin Michel, Historic Site Mgr.
Free 9 AM - 5 PM, Wed. - Sun.
A 1762 Georgian Mansion built by General Philip Schuyler that has in its permanent collection, †Queen Anne, Chippendale and Hepplewhite furnishings. Special tours arranged by appointment.

STATE UNIVERSITY OF NEW YORK
State Education Department
State Education Bldg, 12234. Tel: (518) 474-2121
Ewald B. Nyquist, Pres. of Univ. & Commissioner of Educ.
Gordon M. Ambach, Exec. Deputy Commissioner of Educ.
Thomas D. Sheldon, Deputy Commissioner for Elementary, Secondary and Continuing Educ.
William L. Bitner, III, Assoc. Commissioner for Instructional Services
Vivienne Anderson, Asst. Commissioner for General Educ. & Curricular Services
Vincent J. Popolizio, Chief, Bureau of Art Educ.
Ernest Andrew Mills, Assoc. in Art Educ.
James V. Gilliland, Assoc. in Art Educ.
Robert L. Reals, Assoc. in Art Educ.
The State Education Department through its various supervisors, determines the policy and directs the courses and the supervision and inspection of work in art in the elementary, secondary schools, including the junior and senior high schools. The Department also passes upon applications for licenses to teach art in the public schools, and upon college programs for teachers of the subjects.

THE UNIVERSITY ART GALLERY
State University of New York at Albany
1400 Washington Ave, 12203. Tel: (518) 457-3375
Donald Mochon, Dir.
Nancy Liddle, Asst. Dir.
Francoise Yohalem, Asst. Dir.
John Wisniewski, Preparator
Free, Mon. - Fri. 9 AM - 5 PM; Sat. & Sun. 1 - 5 PM. Estab. 1967; financed by state appropriations.

Collections: Study collection of contemporary prints and drawings.

Exhibitions: Changing exhibitions of contemporary art in all media; Constructivist Tendencies; New York State Craftsmen; 13 Women Artists; Civilization of Lluhros; Childrens Theater Designs, Sets, Costumes, etc; Roman Vishniac; 8 Women Potters; Paintings by Leonard Rossoman; The Representational Spirit; Six Corner Neons; Masterpieces of Australian Bark Painting; Artists of the Mohawk-Hudson Region.

Activities: Lectures open to the public; 2-3 visiting lecturers per year; 6 gallery talks; tours by advance arrangement; concerts.

Publications: Exhibition catalogs, 6-8 per year.

Attendance: 50,000 annual average.

AMSTERDAM

WALTER ELWOOD MUSEUM AND ART GALLERY
300 Guy Park Ave, 12010. Tel: (518) 843-3180, Exten. 287
Joseph Todak, Coordinator
Free weekdays Sept. 1 - June 31, 8:30 AM - 4 PM; July 1 - Aug. 31, 8:30 AM - 3 PM; cl. legal holidays. Founded 1940 by the late Walter Elwood; sponsored by the Board of Education.

Collections: Early American, Victorian, Natural History, Local History (bicentennial), Space Travel, Thomas Edison Science. Period rooms.

Activities: Guided tours, special topic tours; multi-media kits on request.

Attendance: 10,000.

ANNANDALE-ON-HUDSON

WILLIAM COOPER PROCTER ART CENTER
Bard College, 12504. Tel: (914) 758-8494
Matt Phillips, Dir.
Sandra Phillips, Secy. & Cur.
Free, 10 AM - 5 PM, daily. Estab. 1964 as an educational center. The art center has a gallery, slide library and uses the college library for its teaching.

Collections: Assorted contemporary paintings and sculptures.

Exhibitions: Monotypes of Maurice Prendergast; major photography shows including Edward Steicher, Paul Caponigro; A Siskind retrospective forthcoming.

Activities: Photograph collection of 2000 prints; children's art classes; lectures open to the public; 4-8 gallery talks; scholarships.

Publications: Catalogs, major one every 2 years.

AUBURN

CAYUGA MUSEUM OF HISTORY AND ART
203 Genesee St, 13021. Tel: (315) 253-8051
Richard Hamilton, Pres.
Sue Near, V Pres.
Yvonne Rubenfeld, Secy.
Prof. Walter K. Long, Dir.

Free 1 - 5 PM; Sat. 9 AM - Noon & 1 - 5 PM; cl. Mon. Estab. 1936. Ann. meeting Jan; mem. 850; dues $5 and higher. Division of art, history, industry, children's work, music and drama. Meeting place for many organizations. Art classes use Greenhouse as art studio. Branch Museums: Memorial Log Cabin (1791), replica of birthplace of Millard Fillmore, 13th President of United States, Owasco Stockaded Indian Village at Emerson Park; Sherwood Library and Museum at Sherwood.

Collections: Beardsley collection of Filipino material; Herter collection of 14th - 18th century textiles, Stanton collection; Cayuga Indian artifacts; Victorian Room; Gov. Throop Room; American painting.

Exhibitions: Annual Art Exhibit; special exhibitions; one-man shows.

Activities: Lectures; children's classes; groups of objects lent to small museums and schools in the region; 10 gallery talks on art and 10 on history each year; annual presentation of cornplanter medal. Gift shop.

History Library: 10,000 volumes.

Income and Purchases: Income $30,000; purchases $1500.

Attendance: 44,000.

BAYSIDE

QUEENSBOROUGH COMMUNITY COLLEGE LIBRARY

56th Ave. & Springfield Blvd, 11364. Tel: (212) 631-6340
Prof. Charles Pappalardo, Chief Librn.
Free Mon. - Thurs. 9 AM - 10 PM; Fri. 9 AM - 5 PM; Sat. 9 AM - 2 PM. Estab. 1961 to serve the students and faculty of the college; appropriation.

Collections: Book and periodical collection which includes material on painting, sculpture and architecture; reproductions of famous paintings on walls throughout the library and reproductions of artifacts and sculpture; print collection; extremely valuable vertical file collection.

Exhibitions: Exhibit cases are changed about every two months; Examples of exhibits, Black Art, Mosaics, Pop art, Posters, Women in Art, etc.

Publications: Queensborough Community College Library Newsletter, monthly.

Income and Purchases: Budget $80,000; purchases $80,000.

BINGHAMTON

✠ROBERSON CENTER FOR THE ARTS AND SCIENCES

30 Front St, 13905. Tel: (607) 772-0660
Edward A. Harmes, Jr, Pres.
Keith Martin, Dir.
Laura B. Martin, Asst. Dir.
Richard Barons, Cur. History
Richard DeLuca, Planetarium Cur.
Roslyn Tunis, Cur. Art
Arket Lewis, Controller
Philip Carey, Educational Services
Joan Kunsch, Dir, Ballet School
General Museum and Educational and Cultural Housing, and Administering Binghamton Museum of Fine Arts and Historical Collections.
Integrated Societies:
Astronomical Society of Broome County
   Joseph Campfield, Chmn.
Civic Theater of Binghamton
   Marc Ferro, Pres.
Roberson Fine Arts Society
   Anne Cotton, Pres.
Roberson Folk Dancers
   Jeannine Wright, Chmn.
Roberson Garden Center
   Mrs. Robert Cart, Chmn.
Broome County Historical Society
   David Mapes, Pres.
Performing Arts Society
Roberson Photographic Center
   Marilyn Ross, Pres.
Broome County World Affairs Council
   Dr. Arthur Smith, Chmn.
Free Mon. - Fri. 10 AM - 5 PM; Sat. & Sun. Noon - 5 PM. Estab. and inc. 1934, opened 1954 to create and maintain an educational center to promote the advancement and understanding of literature, art, science, history, government, music and kindred subjects. Mem. 3657; dues student $7.50; associate $15 and higher.

Collections: Historical, fine arts and natural history.

Exhibitions: (1974-75) William Bingham-America; A Good Investment; Collector's Choice; Christmas Forest 1974 and 1975; Oh, Yesterday; Ricardo's Miniature Circus; The Iconography of Binghamton; Civilization of Llhuros; Swedish Design Today; Light and Lens; Still Life Today; Fine Arts Members' Show; 1975 Susquehanna Regional; plus others.

Activities: Gallery talks, illustrated lectures, deomonstrations, films, dance, concerts and plays, musicals, children's programs; guided tours for school children and groups; classes for adults and children; studio, craft, dance and art workshops, exhibitions, members' sales gallery, museum shop; planetarium programs, astronomy courses, celestial observation.

Attendance: (1973-74) 251,200.

Two Rivers Gallery
   22 Front St, 13905. Tel: (607) 723-6921
Judith M. Carey, Mgr.
Open Wed. - Sun. 10 AM - 5 PM.

Kopernik Observatory
   Underwood Rd, Vestal, 13850. Tel: (607) 772-0660
Open spring, summer and fall.

UNIVERSITY ART GALLERY

State University of New York at Binghamton
13901. Tel: (607) 798-2634
Michael Milkovich, Dir.
Katherine R. Gleason, Secy.
Walter Luckert, Gallery Technician
Free: Mon. - Sat. 11 AM - 5 PM; Wed. 7 - 10 PM; Sun. 1 - 5 PM.
The Gallery opened in 1967.

Collections: †Teaching collection from Egyptian to Contemporary Art.

Exhibitions: A balanced exhibition program with catalogues between the contemporary arts and historical arts; (1971) recent Works by the Art Studio Faculty and Staff; Master Craftsmen Invitational; (1972) Traditional Art of West Africa; (1973) 8 Contemporary American Artists; Recent Works; (1974-75) Strictly Academic; Marshall Galsier; Frans Wildenhain; Binghamton Collects; Angelo Ippolito Retrospective; Islam and the Medieval West.

Activities: Lectures, musical programs and tours for the special exhibitions are organized regularly.

Library: The Gallery Library is supplemented with the University Library and very adequate for research.

Publications: Yearly publication of the University Art Gallery Bulletin, of which Number One appeared in the form of a concise catalog of Collections. Following issues deal with objects.

Income and Purchases: Irregular, depending on state appropriations and gifts.

BLUE MOUNTAIN LAKE

ADIRONDACK LAKES CENTER FOR THE ARTS

12812. Tel: (518) 352-7715
L. Robert Webb, Pres.
Edith Mitchell, Treas.
Abbie Verner, Secy.
James E. Hutt, Dir.
Open year round. Estab. 1967, the center offers an extensive art and craft instruction program. During July and August the Center's activities include classical, traditional and contemporary music programs; a film program, and coffeehouse performances. The Shop, featuring one of a kind crafts, is open year-round 10 AM - 4 PM daily, except Sun. The center is maintained by memberships and contributions and assistance from The New York State Council on the Arts; mem. dues, adults $3, students $1, family $8.

Library: 300 books plus magazines for reference.

Publications: Bimonthly newsletter.

ADIRONDACK MUSEUM OF THE ADIRONDACK HISTORICAL ASSOCIATION

12812. Tel: (518) 352-7311
H. K. Hochschild, Pres.
Craig A. Gilborn, Dir.
Open June 15 - Oct. 15, daily incl. Sun. 10 AM - 5 PM; admis. adults $3, children under 15 years $1; special group rates. Estab. 1955 to show the relationship of man to the Adirondacks. Ann. meeting Aug.

Collections: Paintings and prints; outdoor life and economy; special collection of Adirondack boats; transportation; logging; research library, photographs and memorabilia.

Special exhibitions: One each year; has included printings by Winslow Homer, A. F. Tait, photographs by Eliot Porter.

Library: 5000 volumes for research; photograph collection of approx. 33,000 prints.

Attendance: Average 90,000 per season.

BRIARCLIFF MANOR

BRIARCLIFF COLLEGE ART GALLERY

10510. Tel: (914) 941-6400 Exten. 740
Dr. Harold C. Simmons, Dir.
Free weekdays 10 AM - 5 PM; weekends 2 - 5 PM. Estab. 1964 to exhibit works of art by professional artists residing or working in Westchester County, New York and faculty and student works of the college; financed by the college.

Collections: Small permanent collection.
Activities: Lectures open to the public; one - two gallery talks per year.
Attendance: 500 annual average, plus college community.

BRONX

BRONX MUSEUM OF THE ARTS*
851 Grand Concourse, 10451. Tel: (212) 681-6000
Sol Shaviro, Pres.
Ernestine Hill, Secy.
Elizabeth Beirne, Dir.
Kathleen Cunningham, Admin. Asst.
Madeline Dejesa, Exhibition Coordinator
Free, 10 AM - 4:30 PM. Estab. 1971 as a conduit for other museums of the city to bring their works to the community and for local artists to have their works viewed, we reach out to the community making art available, free and easily accessible to the Bronx community; financed by city and state appropriations and membership. Community Gallery for local artists. No ann. meeting; mem. 75; dues initial fee of $15.
Exhibitions: Paintings from the Met; A Child's World; Games!!! Juegos!!!; International Posters; Hillman Paintings and Sculpture; Bronx Week Business Exposition; Containers!; Vanishing Africa; Puerto Rican Art and Heritage; B.C.A. Photography Annual; Art by People who work in The Bronx County Building; Arts and Crafts by Retarded Children; Bronx Museum Annual; Contemporary Crafts Bazaar; Oversize Drawings and Multiples; Alice in Wonderland; Flora and Fauna of the Bronx.
Activities: Multi-media art workshops for school children and the community; concerts; classes for adults and children.
Income: (1972-73) $75,000-$100,000.
Attendance: (1971-1972) 120,000; (1972-1973) 336,200.

SOCIETY OF ANIMAL ARTISTS
151 Carroll St, City Island, 10464. Tel: (212) 885-2181
Paul Branson, Pres.
Patricia Allen Bott, Secy.
Beverly Bender, Treas.
Albert Earl Gilbert, 1st V.Pres.
For more information see p. 9.

VAN CORTLANDT MUSEUM*
Van Cortlandt Park, 246th St. & Broadway, 10471.
Tel: (212) 546-3323
Mrs. Norbert Hansen, Chmn.
Open 10 AM - 4:30 PM; Sun. 2 - 4:30 PM; cl. Mon; admis. adult 50¢, children under 12, no charge; Fri. & Sat. free to all. Estab. 1898.
Collections include furniture and objects relating to the Colonial period of American history; also Delftware, pottery and glass.
Activities: Classes for school children each day; slide programs for all visitors.
Attendance: 30,000.

BRONXVILLE

BRONXVILLE PUBLIC LIBRARY
201 Pondfield Rd, 10708. Tel: (914) 337-7680
Mrs. G. R. Connor, Dir.
Free, Winter, Mon, Wed, Fri. 9:30 AM - 5:30 PM, Tues, Thurs. 9:30 AM - 9 PM; Sat. 9:30 AM - 5 PM; Summer, Mon, Wed, Thurs, Fri. 9:30 AM - 5 PM; Tues. 9:30 AM - 9 PM; Sat. 9:30 AM - 1 PM. Financed by city and state appropriations.
Collections: Many American painters represented such as Winslow Homer, Frederick Waugh, Childe Hassam, Bruce Crane and William Henry Howe; 25 Original Currier and Ives prints and a collection of Japanese art prints.
Exhibitions: Original paintings and prints on walls throughout. An exhibit room, also, is for use by current artists, and changed monthly.

SARAH LAWRENCE COLLEGE LIBRARY
Glen Washington Rd, 10708. Tel: (914) 337-0700
Rose Anne Burstein, Librn.
Carol Shaner, Maintains Exhibits
Free 9 AM - 5 PM. Estab. Jan, 1974 to provide library facilities for students and members of the community; includes timely exhibits; financed by endowment. Gallery space used by faculty and other organizations from nearby areas. 131,446 volumes; slide collection.
Exhibitions: Visual arts, including photography; pottery, The Japan Society; old books and manuscripts, many illustrated; sculpture; early American artifacts; Japanese ceramics; contemporary ceramics.
Activities: Lectures open to public; 5 visiting lecturers per year.

BROOKLYN

BROOKLYN INSTITUTE OF ARTS AND SCIENCES
200 Eastern Pkwy, 11238. Tel: (212) 783-6500
Edward S. Reid, Chmn. of Board
Seth S. Faison, V.Chmn.
Robert A. Levinson, V.Pres.
John J. McAtee, Jr, Secy.
James Q. Riordan, Treas.
Thomas A. Donnelly, V.Chmn. Admin.
Estab. 1823, re-inc. 1890; organized into three departments, The Brooklyn Museum, Brooklyn Children's Museum, Brooklyn Botanic Garden. Ann. meeting Jan; mem. approx. 8,000. For information on exhibitions, educational activities, library and publications in the field of art see listings for The Brooklyn Museum and Brooklyn Children's Museum.
Income and Purchases: Income $6,000,000; purchases $3,000,000
Attendance: 2,500,000 annually.

✠THE BROOKLYN MUSEUM*
Eastern Pkwy. & Washington Ave, 11238. Tel: (212) 638-5000
Robert E. Blum, Hon. Chmn.
Robert A. Levinson, Chmn, Governing Board
Michael Kan, Acting Dir. & Cur. African, Oceanic & New World Art
Carlin Gasteyer, Asst. Dir. Admin.
Robert J. Hayden, Asst. Dir. Operations
J. Stewart Johnson, V.Dir. for Collections & Cur, Decorative Arts
Julia Hotton, Asst. Dir. Interpretation
Hagop Kervorkian, Chief Cur.
Bernard V. Bothmer, Cur, Egyptian & Classical Art
Richard Fazzini, Asst. Cur, Ancient Art
Patricia Davidson, Research Assoc, Ancient Art
Eleanor F. Wedge, Wilbour Librn.
Jo Miller, Cur, Prints & Drawings
Elizabeth Anne Coleman, Cur, Costumes & Textiles
Dianne H. Pilgrim, Asst. Cur. in Charge, Decorative Arts
Dorothy Tricarico, Fashion-Textile Coordinator, Design Laboratory
Sarah C. Faunce, Cur, Paintings & Sculpture
Linda Ferber, Asst. Cur, Paintings & Sculpture
Robert Moes, Cur, Oriental Art
Hanna T. Rose, Cur, Educ. Div.
Lynn Kohl, Asst. Cur, Educ. Div. & Chmn, Junior Mem.
David LeVita, Musicologist
Charles K. Wilkinson, Cur, Middle Eastern Art & Archaeology
Margaret B. Zorach, Librn, Art Reference Library
Susanne P. Sack, Conservator
Sheldon Keck, Consultant Conservator
George Mangini, Mgr, Gallery Shop
Barbara LaSalle, Registrar
Jolyon Hofsted, Dir, Art School
Bruce North, Asst. Dir, Art School
Sylvia Hochfield, Editor
Bernard Wolff, Graphic Designer
Scott Hyde, Photographer
Free Wed. - Sat. 10 AM - 5 PM; Sun. 11 AM - 5 PM; holidays 1 - 5 PM; cl. Mon, Tues, Christmas; admis. charge to some special exhibitions. Estab. 1889; building dedicated 1897. Mem. approx. 3000; dues annual $15, family $20, sustaining $25, fellow $50, contributing $100, patron $250, donor $500, life $1000.
Collections: 1st floor: Prehistoric and †Primitive Art including American Indian Art, Pre-Colombian Central and South American, Peruvian textiles, Costa Rican pottery and basketry, models of Maya temples; collection from Malaysia, Polynesia, Melanesia and Africa; Education Dept; Special Exhibitions Galleries; Gallery Shop; Restaurant. 2nd floor: †Japanese, Indian, †Middle Eastern, Persian and Chinese collections; Prints and Drawings Dept; Special Exhibition Gallery; Design Laboratory; Art Reference Library; Art School. 3rd floor: †Nine galleries of Egyptian Art; Kevorkian Gallery of Ancient Middle Eastern Art; one gallery of Greek and Roman Art and synagogue mosaics; one gallery of Coptic Art; Auditorium; Lecture Hall. 4th floor: 28 period rooms dating from 1675 to 1970 including whole houses; period furniture; American pewter; ceramics; Silver Gallery; Emily Winthrop Miles Wedgwood Collection; Costume Theater. 5th floor: †American painting from Colonial to modern times; Sculpture Court of European and American work; 19th and 20th century European painting; Renaissance and Medieval painting; Paintings Study Gallery, American and European watercolors. Outdoor Sculpture Garden comprised of architectural ornament from buildings no longer standing in New York.
Exhibitions: Exhibitions in 1975 included Of Men Only; The Mark of Ancient Man; European and American Male Finery from 1750 to 1975; National Print Biennial. Each year the Community Gallery has 12 exhibitions of works by local Brooklyn artists; the Brooklyn Museum Art School presents exhibitions of works by students and by the faculty; the Gallery Shop presents 6 exhibit sales during the year including Engravings from the Louvre, Woodcraft, Textiles and American Folk Craft.

Activities: Education Division has art courses for children, teachers and adults; docent service; studio workshops; lectures; films; concerts; folk and national dance programs. Lending services include slides in black and white and in color; 16mm films; mounted pictures. Lecture series and gallery talks for Museum members; Art Study Tours around the world; art school for adults, amateur and professionals. (See Schools)

Library: Art reference library of 60,000 volumes; Wilbour Egyptological library of 14,000 volumes.

Attendance: (1969-70) 864,238.

BROOKLYN PUBLIC LIBRARY
Grand Army Plaza, 11238. Tel: (212) 636-3111
Kenneth F. Duchac, Dir.
William R. Johnson, Chief Art & Music Div.
Kenneth Axthelm, Chief AV Div.
Free Mon. - Thurs. 9 AM - 8 PM; Fri. & Sat. 10 AM - 6 PM; Sun. 1 - 5 PM (fall-spring, tentative). Estab. 1892; financed by city and state appropriation.

In Art and Music Division Collection: Materials on fine and applied arts, music; book collection of 116,350 volumes for reference and circulation; circulating picture files of over 60,000 items, 470 framed prints for lending or reference, works on architecture, special costume collection. In Audiovisual Division Collection: Nearly 2000 motion pictures, over 15,000 phonograph records, 225 tape cassettes, filmstrips.

Exhibitions: Art works, photographs, crafts, historical and cultural displays, etc.

Activities: Films, classes for children, other programs; exhibitions in lobby and on 2nd floor. Brooklyn Art Books for Children Citations, annual awards given jointly for children's books outstanding as works of literature and of art.

Publications: Brooklyn Public Library Bulletin, bimonthly.

NATIONAL CARTOONISTS SOCIETY
9 Ebony Court, 11229. Tel: (212) 743-6510
Bill Gallo, Pres.
Bill Kresse, Secy.
Marge Duffy Devine, Scribe
For further information see p. 9.

THE NEW MUSE COMMUNITY MUSEUM OF BROOKLYN
1530 Bedford Ave, 11216. Tel: (212) 774-2900, 2901.
Eduardo J. Standard, Chmn. Board of Dirs.
Robert O. Lovell, Secy. Board of Dirs.
Andrew J. Gill, Exec. Dir.
Maria Parks, Admin. Asst.
Charlene Van Derzee, Asst. Dir.
Sophie Johnson, Coordinator of Cultural Arts
Reginald Workman, Coordinator of Music
Martha McPhatter, Secy.
Open Tues. - Fri. 2 - 10 PM; Sat. & Sun. 1 - 5 PM; admis. free (donations and contributions accepted). Estab. Jan, 1973 to establish an African-American educational and cultural institution of high calibre in the Crown Heights and Bedford-Stuyvesant sections of Brooklyn; financed by city and state appropriation and membership. Gallery contains cultural and historic exhibitions; fine arts exhibitions, 3 - 6 week durations, permanent and semi-permanent. Ann. meeting Jan. 31st; mem. 150; dues $5 - $100.

Collections: Small nucleus of Haitian, African and Afro-American artifacts.

Exhibitions: Black Artists of Brooklyn; Crafts-75; The Black Man and the Sea; Jazz in the First Person; Where We at Black Women Artists.

Activities: Workshops in the visual and performing arts; cultural resource material available to schools and community groups for a minimal charge; traveling exhibitions organized and circulated; 150 prints in photograph collection; lectures open to public; 5 visiting lecturers per year; 15 gallery talks; 250 tours; concerts; classes for adults and children; competitions. Book shop containing workshop related material primarily.

Annual income: $180,000.

Attendance: 650,000.

PRATT INSTITUTE LIBRARY
Art & Architecture Department
11205. Tel: (212) 636-3685
Richardson Pratt, Pres.
Louis D. Sass, Librn.
Sydney Starr Keaveney
Ann Marie Bergholtz
Estab. 1887 for the students, faculty, staff and alumni of Pratt Institute; private school, financed by tuition and endowment. School maintains several galleries.

Collections: Approx. 22,000 art and architectural volumes; collections of pictures and reproductions from magazines and books; 60,000 piece slide collection.

Publications: Periodicals in the Library (computerized listing).

SCHOOL ART LEAGUE OF NEW YORK CITY
131 Livingston St, 11201. Tel: (212) 875-5381
Charles M. Robertson, Pres.
Eleanor Greenan, 1st V.Pres.
Sybil C. Simon, 2nd V.Pres.
Reynolds Girdler, Jr, Treas.
Arnold Roston, Secy.
Dorothy G. Evans, Dir.
Estab. 1909 to foster art education in the public schools of the City of New York, the League is co-sponsored by a Board of Trustees and the Board of Education of the City of New York. Its purpose is to enrich and enlarge the arts programs available to our young people in our city's schools. Interdisciplinary arts activities are offered as a supplement to existing arts programs through the use of New York City's cultural resources. Support is provided for innovative programs within the schools, and scholarships and grants are given to encourage gifted students. Mem. approx. 3000; dues $5 and higher. Public school pupils may join for $1 a school term. Ann. Junior mem. approx. 22,000. Annual awards, an average of 50 scholarships to professional art schools and colleges to graduates of the academic and vocational high schools; approx. 500 medals each year to graduates of elementary, academic, and vocational high schools

Activities: Special awards to needy students doing graduate art work, through contributions from foundations, commercial firms and philanthropic institutions. Visits to galleries, artists studios, private film showings, and museum openings; Arts Career Exposition's attendance 50,000; Awards Ceremony at the Metropolitan Museum of Art, attendance 7000; workshops, seminars, classes, inservice training for teachers.

BUFFALO

✠ALBRIGHT-KNOX ART GALLERY
The Buffalo Fine Arts Academy
1285 Elmwood Ave, 14222. Tel: (716) 882-8700
Seymour H. Knox, Pres.
Samuel D. Magavern, V.Pres.
Albert R. Gurney, Secy.
Northrup R. Knox, Treas.
Robert T. Buck, Jr, Dir.
James N. Wood, Assoc. Dir.
Charlotte Buel Johnson, Cur. Educ.
Open Tues. - Sat. 10 AM - 5 PM; Sun. Noon - 5 PM; cl. Thanksgiving, Christmas and New Year's Day. The Buffalo Fine Arts Academy founded 1862; gallery opened 1905; new wing added 1962; Academy owns building and collections. Annual grants from City and County go toward operating expenses; purchases made through special funds; Gallery managed by Academy Board of Directors. Ann. meeting Oct; mem. c. 3600; dues $20 and higher.

Collections: †1200 paintings and drawings; †400 sculpture and constructions; †1750 prints ranging from 3000 B.C. to the present with special emphasis on American and European contemporary art.

Exhibitions: Art Today: Kinetic and Optic; Plus X Minus; Today's Half Century; Painters of the Section d'Or; Nassos Daphnis: Works Since 1951; Joseph Cornell: Collages and Boxes; Some Cornered Installations in Fluorescent Light from Dan Flavin; Modular Painting; Rockne Krebs: Day and Night Passage; Ellsworth Kelly: The Chatham Series; Sam Francis Retrospective Exhibition; Paintings by Auguste Herbin: The Plastic Alphabet: The Buffalo Society of Artists; Western New York Artists (juried); Patteran Artists; Duayne Hatchett: Recent Paintings and Sculpture; Robert Motherwell; A la pintura and Four Related Paintings; Nancy Graves: Drawings 1971-73; Stephen Antonakos: Recent Drawings and Sculpture; Sheila Isham: Paintings 1968-73; Max Bill: Paintings, Sculpture, Graphics 1928-74; Era of Exploration: Photographs of the Western Landscape, 1850-1880.

Activities: Lectures, concerts, films, plays, gallery talks, art appreciation study groups; creative art classes for children; tours for adults and children. Total number of tours: 1176; total number serviced by Education Dept, 122,745 (both figures 1971-72).

Library: Art reference library for members of approx. 12,000 volumes.

Operating Income: (1973-74) $756,544.

Attendance: (1973-74) 277,051.

BUFFALO AND ERIE COUNTY PUBLIC LIBRARY
Lafayette Square, 14203. Tel: (716) 850-7525
Paul M. Rooney, Dir. Library
Winifred M. Wynne, Deputy Dir, Reference Service
Free Mon. - Thurs. 9:30 AM - 9 PM; Fri. & Sat. 9:30 AM - 5:30 PM; Sun. 2 - 6 PM; June - Sept. cl. Sat. & Sun. Buffalo and Erie County Library estab. 1954 through merger of the Buffalo Public, Grosvenor and Erie County Public Libraries.

Collections: 30,000 volumes on art and architecture (includes 6000 on costumes); rare book room with emphasis on fine printing.

Purchases: Approx. $10,000 for art books annually.

CHARLES BURCHFIELD CENTER
   1300 Elmwood Ave, 14222. Tel: (716) 862-6011
Dr. E. K. Fretwell, Jr, Chmn.
Dr. Carlton E. Bauer, Co-Chmn.
Walter Hoetzer, Asst. Cur. Collections
Edna M. Lindemann, Dir.
Barbara Lewczyk, Archivist & Registrar
Open Mon. - Fri. Noon - 5 PM; Thurs. Noon - 9 PM; Sat. & Sun. 1 -
5 PM. Estab. 1965 to exhibit paintings, drawings, related works,
by Charles Burchfield, Western New York and America's outstanding
watercolorist, and to make his journals and records available for
study; to develop as a center for the exhibition, study and encourage-
ment of significant art expression in the Western New York area; fi-
nanced by endowment, city and state appropriation and membership.
Ann. meeting about Jan. 15; mem. 500.
   Collections: Burchfield paintings, watercolors, drawings and
wallpapers; works of living American artists; Western New York
Artists (historical).
   Exhibitions: Wallpapers by Charles Burchfield; Matha Visser't
Hooft; Works by Living American Artists; Patteran Artists; Buffalo
Society of Artists; George William Eggers Collection; Second Western
New York Purchase Award Collegiate Drawing Exhibition; Charles
Burchfield: Facets of the Artist's Expression; Young Collectors: An
Exhibition of Their Favorite Works; Six Corporate Collectors;
Prochownik: Drawings for You the People; Our Best in 1975; Buffalo
Youth in Art; The Language of Wood.
   Activities: Work with schools and colleges in the area; material
available to galleries with appropriate security; nominal fees; travel-
ing exhibitions organized and circulated; original objects of art lent;
lending collection of motion pictures; photograph collection; lectures
open to public, and other programs for adults, youths and children.
Sales desk.
   Library: Items including slides, photographs, books, exhibition
catalogs and vertical file material on Burchfield and Western New
York artists; Charles Burchfield and George William Eggers
archives.
   Publications: Catalogs of exhibitions, 6-8 yearly.
   Income: $100,000 supplementing gifts.
   Attendance: 20,000.

GALLERY 219*
State University of New York at Buffalo
   University Union Activities Board-Arts Committee, Room 261,
   Norton Hall, 3435 Main St, 14214. Tel: (716) 831-5112, 831-5113
Walter Behnke, Pres.
Sharon Till, Arts Committee Dir.
Mrs. Pulvino, Secy. & Receptionist
Free, Sun. 1 - 5 PM; Tues. & Fri. 12 AM - 4 PM, 8 - 10 PM; Mon,
Wed, Thurs. 11 AM - 5 PM; cl. Sat. Estab. to expose the campus to
a wide variety of art, ranging from contemporary painting and sculp-
ture, prints, photographic design, crafts, and media related arts;
financed by student fees. Small gallery located in student union
bldg.
   Collections: No permanent collection; we take exhibits on loan
from other galleries or agencies and also work from individual artists and students.
   Exhibitions: Recent Canadian Painting and Sculpture: A Selection.
   Activities: Lectures open to public; occasional educational workshops; competitions.
   Publications: Publicity done on a monthly basis.

CANAJOHARIE

CANAJOHARIE LIBRARY AND ART GALLERY
   Church St, 13317.
Mrs. William Crangle, Pres.
Edward Lipowicz, Cur.
Mrs. James Dern, Secy.
Mrs. Richard Raine, Librn.
Free winter Mon. - Fri. 10 AM - 5:15 PM, also Fri. 7 - 9 PM, Sat.
10 AM - 2 PM; summer Mon. - Fri. 9 AM - 4 PM, also Fri. 7 - 9
PM, Sat. 9 AM - 1 PM. Estab. 1927 as a memorial to Sen. James
Arkell. Ann. meeting Apr; supported by State and village grants and
endowments.
   Collections: †Paintings by American artists.
   Exhibitions: From permanent collection, changed each month.
   Library: 20,817 volumes; yearbooks, periodicals, magazines.
   Attendance: Average 3000-5000.

CANTON

ST. LAWRENCE UNIVERSITY ART GALLERY
   Griffiths Art Center, 13617. Tel: (315) 379-5192
Sarah E. Boehme, Cur.
Free daily 9 AM - 5 PM. Estab. 1967 to establish a permanent collection of art as an educational resource and to sponsor exhibitions
of artistic interest for the university and community; financed by
endowment.

   Collections: †Graphics from 15th - 20th centuries; †Contempo-
rary painting and sculpture; †Photography; †Oriental art; African
art.
   Exhibitions: Annual Acquisitions, Prints from the St. Lawrence
University collection, Eskimo art, Fritz Janschka: A tribute to
Joyce's Ulysses; Susan Hauptman, A.I.R. Cooperative Gallery,
other traveling exhibitions, faculty and student exhibitions.
   Activities: Traveling exhibitions organized and circulated;
original objects of art lent to museums, galleries and schools free
of charge; photograph collection; lectures open to public.

CENTERPORT

VANDERBILT MUSEUM COMMISSION OF SUFFOLK COUNTY
   Box F, Little Neck Rd, 11721. Tel: (516) 261-5656
Charles H. Stoll, Chmn.
Benjamin T. Greshin, Secy.
Raymond H. McKay, Treas.
Walter Fasbender, Exec. Dir.
Open May 1st - Oct. 31, Tues. - Sat. 10 AM - 4 PM; Sun. & holidays
12 AM - 5 PM; cl. Mon; admis. adults 75¢, children 25¢. Estab.
1949. The Museum is the former home of the late Mr. William K.
Vanderbilt, who left a $10,000,000 trust fund together with the mansion
and museum for the enjoyment of the public. In 1949 the gift was
presented to the County of Suffolk and is administered by The Suffolk
County Vanderbilt Museum Commission. The New York State Department of Education's Board of Regents issued a charter to the
Board of Trustees at the same time. The Museum was opened to the
public for the first time in July, 1950. The original country home
was transformed through landscaping and painstaking care for au-
thenticity and drama in architecture into a 24-room mansion of Span-
ish-Moroccan design. In addition, a 2-story structure in the same
architectural theme was built to house the Hall of Fishes and Shell
Collection.
   Collections: Marine and wild life from all over the world.
   Income: $270,000.
   Attendance: 272,000 annually.
Vanderbilt Planetarium was completed in Jan, 1971. Tel: (516)
   757-7500.
The complexity of the shows at the Vanderbilt Planetarium is made
possible by nearly a half-million dollars worth of technical apparatus, including a main sky projector, capable of portraying over
11,300 stars - more stars than any other such device in the world.
In Addition, hundreds of auxiliary projectors and an elaborate sound
system are used to produce the countless special visual effects and
dramatic sequences which are the hallmark of the new planetarium.
The entire experience takes place above and around the viewer on
a giant domed projection screen measuring 60 feet in diameter.

CHAPPAQUA

ART RESEARCH SERVICE
   P.O. Box 95, 855 Hardscrabble Rd, 10514. Tel: (914) 238-4039
Dr. H. G. Hesslein, Pres.
Open by appointment only. Estab. 1962; research on the history of
art done for museums, collectors, art dealers.

CHAUTAUQUA

CHAUTAUQUA GALLERY OF ART
Chautauqua Art Association
   Summer: Wythe Ave, Chautauqua, N.Y.
      14722. Tel: (716) 357-2771
   Winter: 1192 Parkside Dr, Alliance, Ohio
      44601. Tel: (216) 821-0468
Dr. Helen B. Cleveland, Dir.
Marilyn Glendening, Secy.
Mrs. Robert Bargar, Secy.
George Weaver, 1st V.Pres.
Petrina Neher, Gallery Asst.
Douglas Miller, Gallery Asst.
Conrad Brunner, Gallery Asst.
Free Mon. - Sat. 1 - 7:30 PM; Sun. 12:30 - 2:30, 4 - 7:30 PM.
Estab. 1949 to promote quality art, culture and appreciation of the
arts; financed by membership. Six annual meeting dates; mem.
1200; dues $4.
   Exhibitions: Approx. 68.
   Activities: Art appreciation; individual paintings lent to schools;
75-100 items lent in an average year; 150-200 active borrowers;
junior museum, 1000 annual average attendance; lectures; 24 visiting lecturers per year; 30 gallery talks; 15 tours; concerts; dramatic programs; classes for adults and children; competitions;
scholarships; art magazines in library. Book shop.
   Publications: Art Gallery Magazine; publications in art magazine; national jury show program activities schedule.
   Attendance: 12,000 annual average.

CLINTON

EDWARD W. ROOT ART CENTER
Hamilton College, 13323. Tel: (315) 859-7331
Ms. Lettie Tourville, Supv.
Free Mon. - Fri. 8:30 AM - 10:30 PM; Sat. 9 - 12 AM & 2 - 6 PM;
Sun. 2 - 10:30 PM. Estab. 1958 to make available to Hamilton
College students and to the entire community fine examples of art,
music and literature. Financed by Hamilton College appropriations
and private donations.
Exhibitions: 7 exhibitions throughout the academic year arranged
by the Joint Exhibitions Committee of Hamilton and Kirkland Colleges.
Activities: Maintains library of music records and recorded
literature; library of books on art and related subjects; lectures,
gallery talks and tours; concerts.
Attendance: Approx. 15,000 per year.

KIRKLAND ART CENTER
On-The-Park, 13323. Tel: (315) 853-8871
Bernardine T. Lohden, Dir.
William English, Pres.
Open Tues. - Fri. 10 AM - Noon, 1 - 5 PM; Sun 15 - Aug. 14; Tues. -
Fri. 1 - 5 PM; cl. Aug. 15 - 31. Estab. June 1960; certificate of
incorporation filed with the Supreme Court of the State of New York;
to provide instruction to all age groups mainly in the visual arts and
to provide programs and exhibitions to augment the classes. Ann.
meeting 2nd Mon. in June; mem. 1200; dues student (kindergarten
through 12th grade) $2, college $2.50, single $5, couple $8, family
$15, sustaining $12, sponsor $25, patron $50.
Collections: Limited collection of about eight pieces.
Exhibitions: Annual Membership Show, Nov; Annual Juried Exhibition, Apr; Annual Photography Exhibition, Jan.
Activities: Art classes for children Kindergarten through 12th;
theater classes for children 4th-6th grade; adult classes in sculpture, ceramics, printmaking, life drawing, watercolor, oil and
acrylic painting, crafts, and workshops; children's cinema program; Lunch Hour Book Review, Meet the Artist Series, musical
and dance programs, demonstrations, lectures of general interest.
Art Shop.
Library: Approx. 200 art books and magazines.
Income & Purchases: Annual budget of approx. $50,000.
Attendance: 15,000.

COOPERSTOWN

THE BRUSH AND PALETTE CLUB
P.O. Box 446, 13326.
Nancy Larbig, Pres.
Mrs. Persis H. Van Cleef, Secy.
Linda Cole, V.Pres.
Virginia Hawxhurst, Treas.
Estab. June 14, 1966 to encourage groups for sketching and painting,
exhibiting among artists in the group, visits to exhibitions and lec-
tures, assisting in sale of members' works, and to hold an annual
exhibition; financed by membership. Meetings Oct. and May; mem.
110; dues $3.
Exhibitions: Fire House Gallery, each year June - Sept; Fine
Arts Exhibition, each Oct; Outdoor Show, each Labor Day weekend.
Activities: Classes for adults.
Attendance: Approx. 4600 for all three exhibitions.

COOPERSTOWN ART ASSOCIATION
13326. Tel: (607) 547-9777
Thomas Natoli, Pres.
Henry S. Fenimore Cooper, M.D, Treas.
Margaret S. Bellows, Secy.
Open daily 10 AM - 5 PM; Sun. 1 - 5 PM. Estab. 1928, inc. 1957, to
stimulate art interest in central New York state. Ann. meeting
Sept; mem. 800; dues $5 and up.
Collections: Permanent collection of reproductions of Old Masters
and Moderns plus continuing purchases of original paintings and
sculptures from the annual shows.
Exhibitions: Annual National Exhibition in Aug; prizes, $3000;
annual shows, purchases $16,000 value accumulated.
Activities: Winter classes in painting and crafts.
Purchases: $500 annually.
Attendance: 4500.

**THE HISTORICAL SOCIETY OF EARLY AMERICAN DECORATION,
INC.**
Fenimore House, 13326. Tel: (607) LH7-2533
Mrs. Edwin Rowell, Pres.
Mrs. John C. Miller, Corresp. Secy.
Mrs. E. A. Nibelink, Secy.
Mrs. Spencer G. Avery, Cur.
Exhibition Hall in Farmer's Museum of the New York State Histori-
cal Association open summer 9 AM - 5 PM; winter, Tues. - Sat.

9 AM - 5 PM; cl. Sun. AM & Mon; admis. fee; special educational
group rate. Estab. 1946. To perpetuate Early American Decoration as an art, promote research in that field, record and preserve
examples of the decorative arts, with emphasis on Americana;
maintain exhibits and publish works on the subject of Early American Decoration and the history thereof; to elevate the standards of
its reproduction and utilization. Ann. meeting May; mem. 800;
dues. $15.
Collections: †Stenciled and painted tin of all kinds; †decorated
chairs, painted chests, etc.
Activities: Lectures; two exhibitions each year other than in the
permanent gallery at the Farmer's Museum; awards to members for
outstanding craftsmanship at each exhibition.
Library: 150 volumes for reference; lantern slides; photograph
collection; recordings of original antiques by Esther Stevens Brazer
and Walter H. Wright, for members' use.
Publications: The Decorator, twice a year; The Ornamented
Chair, The Decorator Digest, The Ornamented Tray, An Illustrated
Glossary of Decorated Antiques; also, reprinted from Antiques
Magazine, 27 Articles by Esther Stevens Brazer.
Attendance: Average 136,000.

NEW YORK STATE HISTORICAL ASSOCIATION
Fenimore House-Central Quarters, 13326. Tel: (607) 547-2533
Minor Wine Thomas, Jr, Dir & Chief Cur.
Milo V. Stewart, Assoc. Dir. & Chief Educ.
Salvatore G. Cilella, Jr, Registrar
Open May, June, Sept, Oct. 9 AM - 5 PM; July, Aug 9 AM - 9 PM;
winter 9 AM - 5 PM; cl. Mon; admis. adults $2, children 75¢, special
educational group rate. Estab. 1899. House built 1932. Ann. meeting July; mem. adults 2800, junior 9000; dues $12.
Collections: †American Folk Art; J. H. I. Browere Life Masks;
†portraits, landscapes, genre paintings of New York State; memorabilia of James Fenimore Cooper.
Exhibitions: Special bicentennial exhibit.
Activities: Seminars on American Culture annually in history,
arts, folklore course, crafts; history workshops; conferences; very
active junior program; Cooperstown Graduate Programs in conjunc-
tion with State Univ. College at Oneonta offering masters degree in
History Museum Training and American Folk Culture and Conserva-
tion of Historic and Artistic Works.
Library: Basically New York State history and folklore in all its
phases.
Publications: New York History, quarterly; The Yorker, junior
magazine.
Attendance: 58,000.
Farmers' Museum
Tel: (607) 547-2533
George P. Campbell, Cur.
Lawrence Nelson, Assoc. Cur.
Virginia D. Parslow, Asst. Cur.
Open summer 9 AM - 5 PM; winter Tues. - Sat. 9 AM - 5 PM; cl.
Sun. AM & Mon; admis. adults $2.50, children 75¢, special educa-
tional group rate. Estab. 1943. Operated by New York State Histor-
ical Association.
Folk Museum of rural life in upstate New York, 1785-1860. Main
building with collections and craft demonstrations; recreated New
York State village with 13 buildings brought in from nearby area; ex-
amples of folk and popular art in the Lippitt Farmhouse, the Bump
Tavern.
Publications: New York Folklore Quarterly.
Attendance: 129,000.
Carriage and Harness Museum
Elk St, 13326. Tel: (607) 547-2533
Open daily 9 - 12 AM & 1 - 5 PM; admis. adults $1, children 50¢.
Estab. 1966; building erected 1901; operated by the New York
Historical Association.
Collections: Houses over thirty horse-drawn sporting vehicles
with the harness and accoutrements, displayed to tell the story of
sport driving in the early 20th century.

CORNING

CORNING GLASS CENTER
14830. Tel: (607) 962-0102
John P. Fox, Jr, Dir.

The Corning Museum of Glass
14830. Tel: (607) 937-5371
Thomas S. Buechner, Dir.
Dwight Lanmon, V.Dir. Collections
John H. Marin, V.Dir. Admin.
Jane S. Spillman, Assoc. Cur.
Sidney Goldstein, Assoc. Cur.
David Donaldson, Asst. Cur.
Robert H. Brill, Research Scientist.
Adrian Baer, Operations Mgr.

Free July & Aug. daily 8:30 AM - 5 PM; Sept. - June, daily 9:30 AM - 5 PM; cl Mon. Nov. - May. Parking fee in summer months. Estab. 1951 to present to the public the entire story of glass, its history, art, science and actual manufacture. Contains The Corning Museum of Glass, Hall of Science and Industry, Steuben Factory, Community Center, Cafeteria and Shops, special exhibit hall, lecture and conference rooms. Ann. meeting Nov.

Collections: A most comprehensive collection of glass (over 14,500 objects) dating from 1500 B.C. to the present, print collection (400 prints) dealing with glass.

Exhibitions: Glass Vessels in Dutch Painting of the 17th Century; The Story of American Glass; American Historical Flasks; Ancient Glass from the Collection of Mr. Ray Winfield Smith; American Pressed Glass of the Lacy Period, 1825-1850; Asian Artists in Crystal; Venite Adoremus; Three Great Centuries of Venetian Glass; Glass 1959; Toledo Glass National I, II and III; Edris Eckhardt, Artist in Glass, a Retrospective Exhibition; Dominick Labino, A Retrospective Exhibit, 1964-1969; Four British Schools, Design in Glass: Maurice Marinot, Great Glassmaker; American Glass Now.

Activities: Lectures, films, concerts, theatre programs; seminars; circulating exhibitions; domestic and overseas tours.

Library: 15,000 volumes for reference; manuscripts, incunabula, rare books; color slides and photograph collection for reference and lending; microforms; periodicals.

Publications: Catalogues of exhibitions; annual Journal of Glass Studies; monographs, reprints, booklets, postcards, prints, slides; microfiche.

Attendance: 700,000; community use 200,000.

CORTLAND

CORTLAND FREE LIBRARY ART GALLERY
32 Church St, 13045. Tel: (607) 753-1042
Warren S. Eddy, Library Dir.
Free 9:30 AM - 9 PM; Wed. & Sat. 9:30 AM - 5:30 PM.
Art Gallery opened 1938. Monthly exhibitions. Approx. 1200 art books, general in subject coverage.

DOUGLASTON

NATIONAL ART LEAGUE
44-21 Douglaston Parkway, 11360. Tel: (212) 229-9495
Leo Breslau, Pres.
Estab. 1932, inc. 1950, as Art League of Long Island, Inc. Mem. over 200.

Exhibitions: Two annual major shows (one National); Gallery exhibitions.

Activities: Lectures; demonstrations; art classes for adults and children, in all media.

Publications: Bulletins; catalogues; brochures.

EAST HAMPTON

✠GUILD HALL OF EAST HAMPTON
158 Main St, 11937. Tel: (516) 324-0806.
Walter J. Fried, Chmn. Board of Trustees
Mrs. Enez Whipple, Dir.
Free 10 AM - 5 PM; Sun. 2 - 5 PM; open evenings during performances in John Drew Theatre, Guild Hall. Estab. and inc. 1931 to foster music, drama and the arts. Ann. meeting Apr; mem. 1800; dues $17.50 and higher.

Collections: †Permanent collection of paintings and sculpture with emphasis on artists of the region.

Exhibitions: About 20 a year including annual artist members' exhibition in May; invitational exhibition of artists of the region; outdoor sculpture show; special loan and theme exhibitions; †permanent art collection; special educational exhibitions; Outdoor Clothesline Exhibition in July.

Activities: Classes in arts and crafts, lectures, concerts, foreign and art films, summer theatre (professional). Museum shop.

Publication: Monthly Newsletter to members.

Attendance: Over 80,000 annually.

ELMIRA

✠ARNOT ART MUSEUM
235 Lake St, 14901. Tel: (607) 734-8651
Howard H. Kimball, Jr, Pres.
Kenneth H. Lindquist, Dir.
Mrs. Josef Stein, Secy.
Boyd McDowell, II, Treas.
Alan Lee Voorhees, Cur. of Educ.
Free Tues. - Fri. 10 AM - 5 PM; Sat. & Sun. 2 - 5 PM; cl. Mon.
Estab. 1911, inc. 1913. The Arnot Art Museum is a museum pledged to serve the people of the community with a regular schedule of changing exhibits from the permanent collection and travelling shows

as well as providing other free cultural activities not ordinarily available in the area. Ann. meeting May; owns building; endowed; mem. 650; dues $3 and higher.

Collections: Flemish, Dutch, French, English, German, Italian, Spanish, and †American paintings; †Contemporary prints; European and †American sculpture.

Exhibitions: Changed monthly; assembled from the permanent collection, rented from traveling exhibition services, or borrowed from private collectors or institutions. Regional exhibition for artists living in 60 mile radius of Elmira held annually, prizes $650; regional (60 mile radius of Elmira) craft exhibition annually, prizes.

Activities: Lectures related to current exhibits; three to five visiting lecturers per year; art classes for children; ten gallery talks per year on current exhibits; free film programs; also free concerts. Art Rental Service.

Library: Art library with approximately 300 books, 11 periodicals; slide collection.

Income and Purchases: Endowment approx. $36,000, other approx. $20,000; acquisition endowment, $22,000.

Attendance: Approx. 16,000 annually.

ELMIRA ART CLUB*
Arnot Art Gallery, 235 Lake St, 14901.
Mrs. Howard Pierce, Pres.
Earl Canfield, V.Pres.
Open daily 2 - 5 PM. Estab. 1935 to foster art in the community.
Meetings second Wed. of each month; mem. 55; dues $6.

Exhibitions: Monthly exhibitions in club room.

Activities: Criticisms, painting exhibitions, films, lectures, demonstrations, outings.

Attendance: About 30-50 each month.

WATSON ART GALLERY
Elmira College
14901. Tel: (607) 734-3911, Exten. 273
William Lee, Dir.
Free Mon. - Fri. Noon - 3 PM.
Activities: Exhibitions; concerts.

FLUSHING

QUEENS COLLEGE ART COLLECTION
Queens College, 11367. Tel: (212) 520-7243
Prof. Robert Muller, Chief Librn.
Prof. Neal W. Richmond, Art Librn.
Free Mon. - Fri. 9 AM - 9 PM; Sat. 10 AM - 2 PM. Estab. 1957 for study collection for Queens College students; appropriation; administered by Paul Klapper Library of Queens College of City Univ. of New York and attached to Art Library. Small exhibition gallery, loan shows and selections from permanent collection in changing exhibitions.

Collections: Approx. 800 objects covering most fields of art history and media, all acquired by gift.

Exhibitions: The Group Theatre, 1933-1941, photographs by Alfredo Valente; Animal Art of the Ancient Near East. One-man shows—drawings by William Bailey, Marvin Bileck, Margit Beck; prints by Ronald Markman, Michael Mazur, Mel Leipzig; changing photography exhibitions.

Activities: Original objects of art, 8000 lantern slides in lending collection.

Library: 20,000 volumes for lending and reference.

Publications: Queens College Art Collection (1960) and Supplement (1961); Man in the Ancient World (1958); The World as a Symbol: an Exhibition of Medieval Art (1959); Costume and Scenic Designs from the R. Eric Gustafson Collection (1970); Animal Art from the Ancient Near East (1968); West African Vision: Weapons, Jewelry, Costume (1971); The Group Theatre, 1933-1941.

✠THE QUEENS MUSEUM
(Queens County Art and Cultural Center)
New York City Bldg, Flushing Meadow-Corona Park, 11368.
Tel: (212) 592-2405
Janet Langsam, Chmn. Board of Trustees
Saunder Schaevitz, Pres.
Sid Feinberg, Secy.
Catherine Monroe, Interim Asst. to Deputy Dir.
Open Tues. - Sat. 10 AM - 5 PM; Sun. 1 - 5 PM; suggested contribution, adults 50¢, children 25¢. Estab. 1972 to promote and exhibit art in the Borough of Queens as an educative institution; financed by city and state and private funds. Nonmembership corporation.

Patrons: Benefactor, sponsor, sustaining, supporting, contributing, family, individual, artist/craftsman, student/senior citizen.

Collections: Small collection of 20th century painting, sculpture and graphics.

Exhibitions: Gallery has changing exhibitions of art.
Activities. Guided tours, lectures; films; gallery talks; concerts; children and adult art classes; sales desk/gift shop; craft gallery.
Publications: Catalogs of exhibitions.
Income: (1974-75) $145,000
Attendance: 66,000.

FREDONIA

MICHAEL C. ROCKEFELLER ARTS CENTER GALLERY
State University College, 14063. Tel: (716) 673-3537
Cheryl R. Towers, Dir.
Free Mon, Wed. & Fri. 1 - 5 PM; Tues. & Thurs. 10 AM - 5 PM
(schedule subject to change). Estab. 1963 and relocated in 1969 to new quarters designed by I. M. Pei and Partners.
Collections: Primarily 20th Century American Art and Architectural archival material.
Exhibitions: Approx. 10 per year. 1975-76 Highlights: SLUJ Internationale 1975: An Exhibition of Junk/Correspondence Art; CAPS Painters; Ceramics Invitational; Small Sculpture Exhibition; 19th Century American Paintings from Area Collections; Chautauqua County Folk Art; National Print Competition; Architecture in Chautauqua County; student and faculty exhibits.
Activities: Lectures; tours; demonstrations; films; cooperative efforts with Lakeshore Association for the Arts.
Publications: Exhibition catalogs.
Purchases: $20,000.
Attendance: 30,000.

GENESEO

STATE UNIVERSITY OF NEW YORK, GENESEO, FINE ARTS GALLERY
Fine Arts Building, 14454. Tel: (716) 245-5401
Bertha V. B. Lederer, Coordinator, Fine Arts Activities
Dora J. Scorsone, Secy.
Estab. 1967; general purpose gallery serving college and community; shows are mostly originated here; state appropriation.
Collections: Small collection including paintings, ceramics, prints, furniture, sculpture.
Exhibitions: Horses and Hounds of the Geneseo Exhibition, 1973; Early Arts in the Genesee Valley Exhibition, 1974; Early Architecture in the Genesee Valley, drawings by Carl F. Schmidt, photographs by Roger B. Smith, 1975.
Activities: Individual paintings and original objects of art lent; photograph collection of 300 prints for reference; lectures open to public, 3-4 visiting lecturers per year; catalogs from previous shows are sold in college administration building or by writing gallery directly; concerts.
Library: 400-600 volumes for reference.
Publications: The Hudson River School, Horses and Hounds of the Genesee, Early Arts in the Genesee Valley, Early Architecture in the Genesee Valley. $5 per catalog.
Attendance: 4000.

GLENS FALLS

THE HYDE COLLECTION
161 Warren St, 12801. Tel: (518) 792-1761
The Hyde Collection Trust, Owners
A. Morton Raych, Acting Dir.
James Kettlewell, Cur.
Open Tues, Wed, Fri, Sat. & Sun. 2 - 5 PM; free, and by appointment for groups. Estab. 1952. Volunteer Council of about 100 members as guards, guides, office help and public relations committees.
Collections: Sculpture, tapestries, furniture; paintings by El Greco, Rembrandt, Rubens, Botticelli, Tintoretto, Renoir, Picasso, Homer, and others; drawings by da Vinci, Degas, Tiepolo, Matisse, Claude, and others.
Exhibitions: Artists of Lake George 1776-1976, summer 1976; 10 additional temporary exhibitions through the year.
Activities: Lectures, concerts, classes for adults.
Library: Reference and lending library of 300 volumes, color reproductions, 800 Kodachromes.
Publications: Rembrandt's Christ; The Art of Henry Ossawa Tanner; The Sculpture of John Rogers; David Smith of Bolton Landing; Rockwell Kent (1882-1971); American Quilts - European and American Samplers; Elihu Vedder; Annual Report.
Attendance: 15,000 annually.

GOSHEN

HALL OF FAME OF THE TROTTER
240 Main St, 10924. Tel: (914) 294-6330
E. Roland Harriman, Pres.
Delvin G. Miller, Secy.
Philip A. Pines, Dir.

Mrs. Jean Musgrave, Registrar
Mrs. J. C. Dill, Educ. Officer
Open daily, 10 AM - 5 PM; Sun. & holidays 1:30 - 5 PM; no admis. Estab. 1949 to collect and preserve the memorabilia associated with the American trotting horse and the sport of harness racing; honors people and horses of the sport; endowment, mem. and sport supported. Gallery, two galleries, the smaller schedules 6-8 different shows annually, the larger given to longer exhibits, also used for lectures, concerts, movies. Mem. approx. 1000; dues $15, $30 and $100.
Collections: Lithographs (mainly Currier & Ives); oils and other media; †sculpture; Sulkies of famous trotters and pacers; horse shoes, equipment; library continually being expanded with new volumes.
Exhibitions: A wide variety ranging from exhibits on weathervanes to champion horses, each designed to tell the story of the art and history of harness racing.
Activities: Visits to classrooms; guided tours; lectures; films for classes in the museum; tours of horse farms; material available to race tracks, associations and schools; no fees; material lent includes free standing exhibit units and individual panels; photograph collection; lectures by appointment only; concerts. Gift shop.
Library: 9000 volumes.
Publications: Bimonthly newsletter.
Income: $86,000.
Attendance: 35,000.

GREENVALE

C. W. POST CENTER ART GALLERY
Long Island University
11548. Tel: (516) 299-2788
Joan Vita Miller, Dir.
Free Mon. - Fri. 10 AM - 5 PM; Tues. til 9 PM; Sat. & Sun. 1 - 5 PM. Estab. Oct, 1973 to present the highest caliber of art to student body and to the surrounding community; financed by private university funds.
Collections: 19th and 20th century American art.
Exhibitions: Louise Nevelson; Gertrude Stein and Her Friends (works by Gris, Matisse, Renoir, Braque, Picasso, Picabia and Tchelitchew); Long Island Art Collectors Exhibition (works by Monet, Matisse, Giacometti, Warhol, Pearlstein and Vasarely); Wreck (paintings and sculpture using the automobile in art - Chamberlain, Seley, Salt and Balsey).
Activities: 30 photographs (30 x 40) in lending collection; individual paintings and original objects of art lent; traveling exhibitions organized and circulated; material available to all galleries, schools and libraries in Long Island and New York for fees of $250 - $400 per month; lectures open to public; 3 visiting lecturers per year; 5 gallery talks; concerts.
Publications: Catalogs, every 2 months.
Attendance: 146,000.

HAMILTON

THE PICKER ART GALLERY
Colgate University
Charles A. Dana Creative Arts Center, 13346. Tel: (315) 824-4132
Prof. Edward A. Bryant, Dir.
Faith H. Deyoe, Registrar & Secy.
Free Mon. - Fri. 9 AM - 5 PM; Sat. 9 AM - 5 PM; Sun. 1 - 5 PM.
Estab. 1966 for its value in a liberal arts education; an affiliate of Colgate University.
Collections: Luis deHoyos collection of Pre-Columbian art; Thomas Nast cartoon collection; Herbert A. Mayer collection; †Oriental art; paintings, sculpture, prints.
Exhibitions: (1974-75) The World of James Van Der Zee; Movie Palace Modern, a collection of drawings influenced by the Art Deco style; Against the Wall: Protest Posters from the American Revolution to Viet Nam; Selected Prints from the Herbert F. Johnson Museum of Art, Cornell University; Puerto Rican Prints; Our Only World, Photographs from the U.S. Environmental Protection Agency; The American Painter as Printmaker; Terry Gips, Photographs and Silkscreens; Watercolors by Geraldine Greig; Susan Eder, Drawings and Sculpture; Autobiography: Painting/Photography; Independent Filmmaking: 1943-1975; T. T. Kwo Collection of Chinese Painting and Calligraphy; The March Eleven, Perspective of 7 Painters and 4 Sculptors; Roger A. Birn, Photographs; David R. MacDonald, Stoneware Sculpture; Edward A. Curtis Photographs: The Hopi; Modern Chinese Woodblock Prints: 1936-1947; plus annual faculty, exhibitions, student art shows and exhibitions from the permanent collection.
Activities: Lectures open to public; 5 visiting lecturers per year; 5 gallery talks.
Publications: Exhibition catalogs, 8 times a year.
Attendance: 7000.

HASTINGS ON HUDSON

HUDSON VALLEY ART ASSOCIATION
   243 S. Broadway, 10706. Tel: (914) 478-1097
Rayma M. Spaulding, Pres.
Perry Alley, Treas.
Joan Rudman, Secy.
Estab. 1928, inc. 1933, to perpetuate the artistic traditions of American artists such as made famous the Hudson River School of Painting through exhibitions of painting and sculpture with public support. Membership by invitation; ann. meeting May; mem. 300; dues $10, special exhibits extra.
   Exhibitions: Annual exhibition each May, open to all artists of the U.S. who work in realistic tradition, to compete for money awards and gold medals of honor, juried; other exhibits from time to time.
   Activities: Free demonstrations, lectures, and exhibitions.

HEMPSTEAD

EMILY LOWE GALLERY
Hofstra University
   11550. Tel: (516) 560-3275
Robert R. Littman, Gallery Dir.
Emma Knutsen, Secy.
Helen Carr, Pub. Relations
Open Mon. - Fri. 10 AM - 5 PM, Wed. & Thurs. 6 - 9 PM; Sat. & Sun. 1 - 5 PM for special exhibitions. Estab. 1963 as a university art gallery serving Hofstra University students and the nearby Nassau County community, as well as frequent visitors from out of town. Theme exhibitions, traveling shows; financed by University budget.
   Collections: †Small and varied collection ranging from primitive, Asian, contemporary art to 20th century photographs.
   Exhibitions: (1972-73): Decoy: The Print and the Painting of Jasper Johns; Victorian Art; Landscape and Discovery: A Photographic Survey; Fibre Work; Say It With Flowers; (1973-74) The Book Stripped Bare: 20th Century Illustrated Books; The Male Nude; Diaghliev/Cunningham; Wish You Were Here: History of the Picture Postcard; (1974-75) Art Pompier: Anti-Impressionism; Bradley Walker Tomlin; The Silent Majority from Francois Boucher to Walter Keane—Over Two Hundred Years of Very Very Popular Art; (1975-76) Fashion Photography: Six Decades.
   Activities: Traveling exhibitions organized and circulated; lectures open to public; 1 - 3 visiting lecturers per year; ongoing gallery talks; concerts; competitions.
   Publications: Scholarly catalogs are published for all exhibitions.

HUNTINGTON

✠HECKSCHER MUSEUM
   Heckscher Park, Prime Ave, 11743.
   Tel: (516) 421-1000, Exten. 244 or (516) 271-4440
Miner D. Crary, Jr, Chmn. Board of Trustees
Eva Ingersoll Gatling, Dir.
Roth Solomon, Asst. Dir.
Elisabeth Kaplan Boas, Mem. & Prog. Coordinator
William H. Titus, Registrar
Free 10 AM - 5 PM; Sat, Sun. & Holidays, 1 - 6 PM; cl. Mon. Estab. by gift of Mr. and Mrs. August Heckscher to the people of Huntington, 1920; inc. 1957 for the maintenance, preservation and operation of the Museum building together with the preservation, exhibition and display of all objects and works of art located therein. Ann. meeting June; mem. 375; dues $10 and higher.
   Collections: Paintings, sculpture, drawings and prints by 16th - 20th century European and American artists.
   Exhibitions: Art Deco and Its Origins; Fairfield Porter; Windows and Doors; Mistaken Identity; Stanley Twardowicz, Retrospective; Ibram Lassaw, Retrospective; Artists of Suffolk County is an annual invited exhibition: 1974, Photographers; 1973, Craftsmen; 1972, Graphics; 1971, New Directions. Huntington Township Art League sponsors annual Long Island Artists Exhibition.
   Activities: Gallery lectures; guided tours to school classes, special groups by appointment; summer art workshops for children; adult lectures series; reference file on artists of Suffolk County.
   Publications: Exhibition catalogs; quarterly newsletter.
   Income: $169,000.
   Attendance: (1974 average) 45,350.

HYDE PARK

FRANKLIN D. ROOSEVELT LIBRARY AND MUSEUM
   Albany Post Rd, 12538. Tel: (914) 229-8114
William R. Emerson, Dir.
Dr. James L. Whitehead, Cur. of Museum
Open daily 9 AM - 5 PM; cl. Christmas Day; admis. adults, 50¢, children free up to 16 years of age. First opened to public, 1941.

   Collections: Papers of President and Mrs. Roosevelt and of various members of his administrations. Museum objects illustrative of their lives, careers, and special interests, including personal things; gifts from heads of state, friends, and admirers; and items collected by President Roosevelt—paintings and prints, ship models, documents and relics on the history of the U.S. Navy, as well as other marine items and prints and paintings of the Hudson Valley.
   Exhibitions: Two temporary changing exhibitions per year on subjects related to the Roosevelt era.
   Library: 50,000 books, periodicals, pamphlets, etc, devoted to life, career, and special interests of Franklin D. Roosevelt and Anna Eleanor Roosevelt.
   Attendance: 200,000.

ITHACA

✠HERBERT F. JOHNSON MUSEUM OF ART
Cornell University
   14853. Tel: (607) 256-6464
Thomas W. Leavitt, Dir.
Jason D. Wong, Asst. Dir.
Martie W. Young, Cur. Asian Art
Elizabeth Evans, Asst. Cur.
Nancy S. Press, Coordinator of Educ. & Cur. of Crafts
Carol Murray, Registrar
Donald Feint, Supt.
Genya M. Yarkoni, Admin. Supvr.
Open Tues. - Sat. 10 AM - 5 PM; Wed. 10 AM - 9 PM; Sun. 11 AM - 5 PM; cl. Mon. Estab. 1973, replacing Andrew Dickson White Museum, originally founded in 1953 as Cornell University's Art Museum.
   Collections: European and American paintings, drawing and sculpture; graphic art; George and Mary Rockwell Galleries of Asian Art (permanent installation); Medieval and Primitive (permanent installation).
   Exhibitions: Directions in Afro-American Art; Gaston Lachaise; Clarence Schmidt; Four Centuries of Scenic Invention; Alan Sonfist: An Autobiography; Ed Thompson Paintings; The Bicentennial Series by Benny Andrews; Irish Directions of the 70's.
   Activities: Daily tours upon request; Art Insights: Making Senses classes for children and adults.
   Publications: Directions in Afro-American Art; Gaston Lachaise.
   Annual Income: $400,000; purchases $50,000.
   Attendance: 125,000.

JAMAICA

QUEENS BOROUGH PUBLIC LIBRARY*
   89-11 Merrick Blvd, 11432. Tel: (212) 739-1900
John Solomita, Acting Dir.
Dorothea Wu, Head, Art & Music Div.
Free Mon. - Fri. 10 AM - 9 PM; Sat. 10 AM - 5:30 PM; Sun. 1 - 5 PM, except June to Sept.
   Estab. 1896; Art & Music Division estab. 1933. 40,000 volumes on art and music for home loan; †14,000 volumes exclusive of bound periodicals for reference; includes a picture collection of over 1,500,000 items, classified by subject, mounted for circulation.
   Budget: Annual budget $15,000.

QUEENS BOROUGH SOCIETY OF ALLIED ARTS AND CRAFTS, INC.*
   90-22 155th St, 11432. Tel: (212) 219-2223
Frank Angrisani, Pres.
Russell Bruce, V.Pres.
Jessie Hershenhart, Treas.
Aaron Hershenhart, Financial Secy.
Free Mon. 11 AM - 1 PM; Tues. 7:30 - 9:30 PM; Sat. 2 - 4 PM. Inc. 1922. Ann. meeting Sept; mem. 70; dues $15 annually.
   Activities: Classes in painting; Outdoor Show; publishes Newsletters and catalogues of exhibitions.
   Income: $700.

JAMESTOWN

JAMES PRENDERGAST LIBRARY ASSOCIATION
   509 Cherry St, 14701. Tel: (716) 484-7135
Murray L. Bob, Dir.
Gallery free Mon. - Fri. 9 AM - 9 PM; Sat. 9 AM - 6 PM; Sun. 1 - 4 PM, Oct. to May.
   Gallery estab. 1891 as part of Library. Permanent collection includes 19th century American, French, German and Italian paintings. †Approx. 5000 volumes in art section available for loan. †Records, films, art prints, art slides, sculpture reproductions for loan.
   Exhibitors: Traveling exhibitions, local organizations and individuals.
   Income: $292,000.

KATONAH

THE KATONAH GALLERY
28 Bedford Rd, 10536. Tel: (914) 232-4988
Mrs. Volney Righter, Pres.
Beverly Shapiro, Secy.
Anne Baren, Dir.
Joan Pace, Asst. Dir.
Beth McCorkle, Secy. & Bookkeeper
Free Tues. - Thurs. & Sun. 2 - 5 PM; Fri. & Sat. 10 AM - 5 PM.
Estab. 1954 to bring creative art at its finest, to the community of
Northern Westchester, to encourage local artists and to add enrich-
ment of the arts to the school children in the surrounding towns;
does not maintain a permanent collection but borrows from private
collectors and museums; financed by endowment, city and state
appropriation and membership. Ann. meeting fall; mem. 800; dues
$10 and up.
Exhibitions: Realism Now; American Quilts: 1850-1970; Ceramics
of China and Southeast Asia; Bill Barrett and Elaine Krause; Calder;
Art of the Maya; Oceania; New Painting Stressing Surface; Wood,
Paper, Cloth, Glass, Feathers, String and Clay; Ming-Ch'i; Clay
Figures Reflecting Life in Ancient China; Modern Sculpture, The
Beginnings of Modernism, 1900-1934.
Activities: Visiting artists; docent in-school slide lectures on
painting, architecture and sculpture; teachers and student workshops;
educational exhibitions; creative outlets course in local women's
prison; workshops in local home for disadvantaged children.
Traveling exhibitions organized and circulated; individual paintings
and original objects of art lent; 20 photographs, 200 Kodachromes
and 5 film strips in lending collection; 500 items lent in average
year; lectures open to public; 6 visiting lecturers per year; 4 gallery
talks; 15 tours; concerts, classes for adults and children, competitions; scholarships.
Library: 300 catalogs for reference work.
Publications: Ming-Ch'i: Clay Figures Reflecting Life in Ancient
China; American Painting: 1900-1975.
Attendance: 50,000.

KINGSTON

SENATE HOUSE AND SENATE HOUSE MUSEUM
312 Fair St, 12401. Tel: (914) 338-2786
Kenneth Hasbrouck, Pres. of the Board
James P. Gold, Site Mgr.
Free Wed. - Sat. 9 AM - 5 PM; Sun. 1 - 5 PM; cl. Mon. & Tues.
First meeting place of the New York State Senate in 1777. Senate
House acquired by New York State in 1887, Senate House Museum
constructed 1927-28. Under The New York State Division of
Historic Preservation, Albany.
Collections: Furnishings of the Revolutionary Period; †J. Vander-
lyn Collection; †New York State Governors' Papers; local records.
Library is primarily Ulster County 18th - 19th century related,
research only.
Attendance: 13,000.

LONG BEACH

LONG BEACH PUBLIC LIBRARY*
111 West Park Ave, 11561. Tel: (516) 432-7201
Dr. John Pisacano, Pres.
Mrs. Ruth Selnick, Secy.
Samuel L. Simon, Dir.
Daniel M. Groden, Asst. Dir.
Mrs. Moira Ryan, Secy to Dir.
Mrs. Carol Donner
Free, Mon, Wed, Thurs. 9 AM - 9 PM, Tues. & Fri. 9 AM - 6 PM;
Sat. 9 AM - 5 PM; Sun. Sept. - June, 1 - 5 PM. Estab. 1928 to cir-
culate books and other materials which are recreational, educa-
tional and informational; exhibit cultural works of artists in all
media; financed by city and state appropriations. Gallery main-
tained in cooperation with the Long Beach Art Association to exhibit
works of local and county artists.
Collections: †93,674 books, †5855 phonograph records; †3900
cassettes; †132 films, †photographs; †12,079 pamphlets.
Exhibitions: Painting; Needlework; Sculpture; Photographs; Arts
and Crafts; approx. 98 exhibits from January 1970 thru June 1972.
Activities: Extension department serves City School District,
City of Long Beach; material available to homebound, no fees; material lent, books, magazine, pamphlets, records, films, cassettes,
photographs and pictures; traveling exhibitions organized and circulated; lending collection, 289 photographs, 132 motion pictures,
21 film strips; 222,919 items lent in average year; 18,205 active
borrowers; lectures open to the public; 50 visiting lecturers per
year; 23 gallery talks; concerts; dramatic programs; classes for
adults and children; competitions.
Publications: The Long Beach Calendar Newsletter, monthly.
Budget: $367,347.
Attendance: 150,000 annual average.

MONROE

MUSEUM VILLAGE OF SMITH'S CLOVE
10950. Tel: (914) 782-8247
George C. Paffenbarger, Jr, Pres.
James Steinmetz, Asst. Treas.
Christopher E. Belson, Dir.
Virginia Gunter, Cur.
Open May 15 - Nov 15, 10 AM - 5 PM; admis. adults $2.50, children
8-17 $1.25, under 8, free; group rates available; school and youth
groups by advance reservation only.
Smith's Clove is an outdoor museum of the crafts and technology
of 19th century America. Its purpose is to collect, preserve and
interpret to the public artifacts related to rural life in northeastern
United States in the 1800's. Opened to the public in 1950, Museum
Village of Smith's Clove was created from the personal collections of
Roscoe W. Smith, who began collecting Americana in 1915. In 1961
Mr. Smith surrendered his entire ownership interest and, by authority of the Board of Regents of the State of New York, the Museum became a not-for-profit educational corporation, with membership
open to any member of the general public interested in joining. Approx. 200 Friends of Museum Village; membership drive is underway; dues $5 students, $10 adults, $25 family; four supporting
membership categories ranging from $50 - $500.
The Museum usually has on exhibit approximately 30 buildings,
such as a one-room schoolhouse, general store, apothecary, dress
emporium, blacksmith's shop, etc. Several special exhibits and
other events, annually.
Activities: Winter Education Program for area students in
4th and 7th grades; craft demonstrations.
Publications: Friend of Truth, occasional newsletter.
Attendance: Approx. 90,000.

MOUNT VERNON

MOUNT VERNON PUBLIC LIBRARY
28 S. First Ave, 10550. Tel: (914) 668-1840
Emanuel Dondy, Library Dir.
Free Mon. - Fri. 9 AM - 9 PM; Sat. 9 AM - 6 PM; Sun. 1 - 5 PM;
cl. Sat. & Sun. during July and Aug. Doric Hall, murals by Edward
Gay, N.A; Exhibition Room, frescoes by Louise Brann Soverns.
Exhibitions: Semi-annual shows by Mount Vernon Art Association.
Others, changing monthly, cover a wide range of subjects: one-man
shows of painting and sculpture; woodcarving; metalwork; silver;
porcelains; costume dolls; fans; stamps, etc. Norman Wells Print
Alcove, estab. 1941.
Library: More than 4000 books on art, specifically architecture,
ceramics, costumes, decoration, design, painting, photography and
prints. Lending collection of pictures on many subjects for practical
purposes, as well as framed prints and sculptures.

MOUNTAINVILLE

STORM KING ART CENTER
10953. Tel: (914) 534-3115
H. Peter Stern, Pres.
Dorothy Mayhall, Dir.
David Collens, Asst. to Dir.
Eleanor Andersen, Registrar
Ted Newhook, Horticulturist
Open Apr. - Oct. Tues. - Sun. 1 - 5:30 PM; cl. Mon. Estab. 1959.
Collections: 200 acre sculpture garden with over 125 large scale
outdoor contemporary sculptures including 13 works by David Smith;
works by Hepworth, Moore, Caro, Snelson, Lewitt, Stankiewicz,
Rickey, Ferber, Calder, Grosvenor, Von Schlegell, Bill, Myers,
Ginnever, and others.
Exhibitions: Permanent sculpture collection, plus over 100 loan
sculptures in special Sculpture in the Fields exhibitions; changing
exhibitions in the galleries of prints, paintings and sculpture.
Activities: Lecture series on contemporary painting and
sculpture; lectures by artists; gallery and garden tours.
Library: 1000 volumes, art from 1850; exhibition catalog file of
one-man shows since 1960; all art periodicals since 1965.
Attendance: 25,000 annually.

NEW PALTZ

THE COLLEGE ART GALLERY
State University College, 12561. Tel: (914) 257-2439
William A. Bartsch, Dir.
Daniel Scully, Asst. to Dir.
During academic year open Mon. - Fri. 10 AM - Noon & 1 - 4 PM; cl.
academic holidays; summer semester, Mon. - Fri. 10 AM - 4 PM.
The exhibitions program is intended primarily as support for the
courses in studio art and art history offered by the Art Division.
Functioning in this way, the Gallery displays material in traditional
media ranging from the antique to contemporary.

Collections: Painting, principally 20th century American; †prints, primitive, African and New Guinea; Pre-Columbian; Oriental prints and some sculpture.

Exhibitions: (1970) George Wexler, One-Man Show; Anonima Group; Third Intercollegiate Exhibition, Plastics; Critic's Choice; Faculty Exhibition; (1971) American Painters as Printmakers; Arts of Antiquity, Greece, Etruria, Rome; Molas from San Blas; Ken Green, Ceramics; Craftsmen from Norway; Master Printmakers from the Cooper-Hewitt Collection; Kammerer, Sculpture; (1972) CERAMICS 1972; Arts of China; C. C. Wang; (1973) Dale Stein, Drawings.

NEW ROCHELLE

NEW ROCHELLE ART ASSOCIATION
New Rochelle Public Library, 662 Main St, 10805
Len Gorelick, Pres.
Estab. 1912. Monthly meeting; mem. 200; dues $10. Exhibitions; lectures.

NEW ROCHELLE PUBLIC LIBRARY
662 Main St, 10805. Tel: (914) 632-7878
Eugene L. Mittelgluck, Dir.
Mrs. Willie R. Carrington, Fine Arts Librn.
Art Gallery and Library free Mon. - Thurs. 9 AM - 9 PM; Fri. 9 AM - 6 PM; Sat. 9 AM - 6 PM; cl. Sun. & holidays, also on Sat. during July & Aug.
Estab. 1893. Art Gallery for showing work of members of New Rochelle Art Association; changing exhibitions October through May; case displays, illustrated lectures and demonstrations at Association meetings; framed prints and art slides for lending.
Fine Arts library of over 7800 books. Clipping and picture file of 500,000 prints for circulation, mounted and unmounted. Headquarters for audiovisual service for Westchester Library System, serving 38 libraries.

NEW YORK CITY

ALLIED ARTISTS OF AMERICA, INC.
1083 Fifth Ave, 10028
Dale Meyers, Pres.
William Gorman, V.Pres.
Moses Worthman, Treas.
Reta Soloway, Corresp. Secy.
Estab. 1914, inc. 1922, as a self-supporting exhibition cooperative, with juries elected each year by the membership, to promote work by American artists. Ann. meeting Mar; active mem. 450, assoc 225; dues $15 and $12 respectively.
Exhibitions: Annual exhibition in the fall at National Academy of Design; numerous awards, medals; prizes total approx. $4500 each year.
Activities: Conducts demonstrations during the period of Annual Exhibition. Awards scholarship through the National Academy of Design.

✠AMERICAN ACADEMY IN ROME*
41 E. 65th St, 10021. Tel: (212) 683-2725
Henry T. Rowell, Pres.
Walker O. Cain, Secy.
William H. Johnstone, Treas.
Henry A. Millon, Dir.
Frank E. Brown, Head, Classical School
Martha Peitzke Wilson, Exec. Secy.
Estab. 1884; inc. by Congress 1905; consolidated with School of Classical Studies 1913; Dept. of Musical Composition estab. 1921; Ann. meeting Oct; Board in Jan.
Fellowships in architecture, landscape architecture, environmental design, classical studies, post-classical humanistic studies, history of art, musical composition, painting and sculpture, are open to citizens of the United States for two years beginning October first with the option of accepting a single year. In total, approx. 15 fellowships are awarded each year. Though there is no age limit, the Academy aims to give the awards to young persons of outstanding promise, when such candidates apply. Stipend and travel allowances $4600; free residence, studio or study, library and other facilities at the Academy. Applications must be received at the New York office before January first of each year.
Address in Rome, Via Angelo Masina 5, 00153.

AMERICAN ACADEMY OF ARTS AND LETTERS
633 W. 155th St, 10032. Tel: (212) 286-1480
Richard Wilbur, Pres.
Malcolm Cowley, Chancellor
John Hersey, Secy.
Gilmore D. Clarke, Treas.
Margaret M. Mills, Exec. Dir.
Free admis. during exhibitions 1 - 4 PM; cl. Mon, holidays, and summer. Estab. 1904 by the National Institute of Arts and Letters.

Ann. meeting Dec, special meeting May; mem. limited to 50, chosen from mem. of the National Institute of Arts and Letters for further distinction. Owns two buildings containing offices, art galleries, museum, art reference library and auditorium.
Collections: Permanent collection of sculpture, paintings, and drawings by members; large collection of works by Childe Hassam and Eugene Speicher.
Activities: Together with the National Institute of Arts and Letters holds six or more exhibitions a year, an annual ceremonial, and conducts a program of Art Awards. Award of Merit medals for sculpture and painting are given in rotation every fifth year. Awards may not be applied for.
Publications: The Academy publishes jointly with the National Institute of Arts and Letters annual Proceedings and exhibition catalogues.
Purchases: Annual purchases of paintings by living American artists, approx. $50,000 from the Childe Hassam Fund, given to museums and art galleries across U.S.

AMERICAN ARTISTS PROFESSIONAL LEAGUE, INC.
112 E. 19th St, 10003. Tel: (212) 475-6650
Frank C. Wright, Pres.
Mary Keim Tietze, Secy.
For further information see p. 3.

AMERICAN COUNCIL FOR THE ARTS IN EDUCATION
115 E. 92nd St, 10028.
Eldon Winkler, Pres.
Robert Glidden, V.Pres.
Gerry J. Martin, Secy-Treas.
For further information see p. 3.

AMERICAN CRAFTS COUNCIL
44 W. 53rd St, 10019. Tel: (212) 977-8989
Mrs. Vanderbilt Webb, Chmn. of Board
John L. Baringer, V.Chmn.
Donald L. Wyckoff, Pres.
May E. Walter, Secy.
R. Leigh Glover, Treas.
For further information see p. 3.

AMERICAN FINE ARTS SOCIETY
215 W. 57th St, 10019. Tel: (212) 247-4510
Stewart Klonis, Pres.
Arthur J. Foster, Secy.
Inc. 1889; estab. to provide facilities for art activities as owner of the American Fine Arts Society Building. Ann. meeting Jan. Gives lectures by prominent persons in the art world.

AMERICAN INSTITUTE OF GRAPHIC ARTS
1059 Third Ave, 10021. Tel: (212) 752-0813
Karl Fink, Pres.
Flora Finn Gross, Exec. Dir.
Anne E. Kantor, Assoc. Dir.
Open weekdays 9:30 AM - 5 PM. Estab. 1914. A national nonprofit educational organization devoted to raising standards in all branches of the graphic arts. Mem. 1850; annual dues $36 and $60; company mem. $275, $400, $550, $1100; professional mem. $93; student $17. Institute chapters and affiliates include professional groups in Washington, D.C, Detroit, Mich, Philadelphia, Pa, Los Angeles and San Francisco, Calif. and Houston, Tex.
Exhibitions: Covers Show and Inside Show in alternating years; Learning Materials Show and Children's Book Show in alternating years; Packaging Show and Illustration Show in alternating years; Communication Graphics Show; Fifty Books of the Year. Rotating monthly exhibits of University Press books, private press books, and Guild of Book Workers exhibition.
Activities: Clinics on aspects of book production and seminars on design and production problems; plant tours. The Guild of Bookworkers (fine bindings) is an affiliated organization. Medal for distinguished contributions to the Graphic Arts awarded 1975 to Bradbury Thompson.
Publications: AIGA Journal, published three times yearly.
Attendance: Gallery shows and traveling shows viewed by over 1,000,000 annually.

AMERICAN INTERNATIONAL SCULPTORS SYMPOSIUMS, INC.
799 Greenwich St, 10014. Tel: (212) 242-3374
Verna Gillis, Pres. & Treas.
David Gillis, Secy.
Bradford Graves, V.Pres.
Joshua Cohn
Open 9 AM - 5 PM; no admis. Estab. 1971 to promote art in public places and to educate the general public in the process of making art; to aid sculptors in building works that would not be possible in their own studios; financed by endowment and city or state appropriation. Ann. meeting four times a year; open mem; no dues.

Exhibitions: Permanent exhibitions at Vermont Interstate Highway rest areas of sculptures completed during symposium in summer of 1971; Graduate Center Mall, City University of New York, 73.

Activities: Film rentals and slide-lectures in Universities on public art; photograph collection of several hundred prints; lectures open to the public; 12 visiting lecturers per year.

Poetry in Public Places, a special project of A.I.S.S, in Dec, 1974 began placing one poem per month in 1000 New York City buses. The project was awarded a Certificate of Merit by the Municipal Art Society of New York in 1975 for humanizing public transport. For 1976, the project expands to include 2020 buses per month throughout the state of New York, presenting an overview of 200 years of American verse as a Bicentennial project. It is expected that the project will expand nationwide in 1977. The 11 inches x 28 inches poem cards are available for purchase for individuals or institutions at the rate of $5 per card, or $50 for the set of 12.

Income: $35,000.

THE AMERICAN MUSEUM OF NATURAL HISTORY
Central Park West at 79th St, 10024. Tel: (212) 873-1300
Robert G. Goelet, Pres.
Dr. Thomas D. Nicholson, Dir.
Weekdays 10 AM - 4:45 PM; Sun. & holidays 11 AM - 5 PM; cl. Thanksgiving and Christmas; admis. by contribution (suggested, adults $1, children 50¢). Estab. and inc. 1869. A museum for the study and exhibition of all aspects of natural history; includes ceremonial objects, artifacts, clothing, weapons and architecture of primitive peoples and earlier civilizations. Mem. 325,000.

Exhibitions: The Museum's renowned habitat dioramas of mammals, birds, forest and ocean life, Examples are the Hall of Small Mammals of North America, the Hall of Primates, the Hall of Man in Africa, the Hall of Indians of the Plains, the Hall of Early Dinosaurs, the John Lindsley Hall of Earth History, the Hall of Mexico and Central America, the Hall of Peoples of the Pacific.

Activities: Adult evening lecture series; field trip program; People Center; archeological tour of Mezo-America; courses for science teachers, the Natural Science Center for Young People; gallery talks, slide lectures and films.

Library: More than 275,000 books and periodicals on every aspect of natural history from anthropology to zoology as well as maps and books on travel and exploration. The Library has an exceptional collection of rare books on natural history; many of them are first-editions monographs and folios of great value.

Attendance: (Fiscal 1973-74) 2,000,000 (including The American Museum-Hayden Planetarium).

New York State Theodore Roosevelt Memorial
Equestrian statue of Theodore Roosevelt by the late James Earle Fraser at entrance. Mural painting by William Andrew Mackay in hall.

The American Museum-Hayden Planetarium
81st St. near Central Park West (entrance also through Museum) Admis. adults $1.75, children through age 17 and students with ID $1, senior citizens (with identification) $1.25.

The history and lore of celestial bodies in motion across the sky narrated and shown on 75-ft. dome by means of the Zeiss Projector. Performances, two to seven times daily, utilize controlled lighting, music, special sound effects and narration, for such themes as Trip to the Moon, From Galileo to Palomar, Exploring the Milky Way, Messengers from Space, Color in the Sky and the Christmas show, The Star of Bethlehem. The world's first blacklight murals illustrating various celestial phenomena, and other astronomical paintings and graphics; laser light concert weekday evenings.

AMERICAN NUMISMATIC SOCIETY
Broadway at 156th St, 10032. Tel: (212) 286-3030
Samuel R. Milbank, Pres.
Leslie A. Elam, Dir.
Margaret Thompson, Chief Cur.
Free 9 AM - 4:30 PM; Sun. 1 - 4 PM; cl. Mon. and holidays. Estab. 1858. Ann. meeting Jan; mem. 1745; fel. $25, assoc. $15. Owns museum and library building.

Collections: †American and foreign coins and medals, †ancient coins, †decorations and war medals.

Activities: Special exhibitions; occasional lectures; circulates exhibits; graduate seminar; fellowships and grants.

AMERICAN SOCIETY OF CONTEMPORARY ARTISTS
c/o Mark Freeman, Pres, 307 E. 37th St, 10016
Howard Kuh, 1st V.Pres.
Theresa Lindner, Coresp. Secy.
Constance Scharff, Recording Secy.
Seymour Nydorf, Treas.
Estab. and inc. 1917. Ann. meeting Apr; mem. 130, associate mem. 75; dues $15.

Exhibitions: Annual exhibitions, alternating at National Arts Club, National Academy Galleries, Lever Brothers and Union Carbide Corp, all New York. National traveling watercolor and print shows. Awards for outstanding service to distinguished citizens in or contributing to artists and the art world; prizes; demonstrations; awards $3000.

✠AMERICAN SOCIETY OF INTERIOR DESIGNERS
730 Fifth Ave, 10019. Tel: (212) 586-7111
John Hammon, Exec. Dir.
For further information see p. 4.

AMERICAN VETERANS SOCIETY OF ARTISTS, INC.*
c/o J. Lamberg, Secy, 6345 Saunders St, Rego Park, 11374. Tel: (212) 459-1265
Founded 1937, inc. 1942; mem. 150. Veterans of military service who are professional artists. Promotes interest in art; sponsors exhibitions of members' work; seeks to maintain comradeship with those who serve or have served in the armed forces of the United States.

Exhibitions: Annual Exhibitions and Summer Festival Exhibition with awards in oils, watercolors, sculpture and graphics. Occasional film lectures showing various techniques.

AMERICAN WATERCOLOR SOCIETY, INC.
1083 Fifth Ave, 10028.
Mario Cooper, Pres.
Mina Kocherthaler, Recording Secy.
Estab. 1866, inc. 1903; N.Y. Watercolor Club amalgamated with society in 1941. Ann. meeting Apr; mem. by jury based on excellence of work; mem. 543; dues $15.

Exhibitions: International exhibitions: Japan, 1957; Great Britain, 1959; Exchange, Great Britain, 1962; Mexico, 1970; Canada, 1972; Australia, 1975. Special exhibition in 1966/67 at the Metropolitan Museum commemorating Centennial of A.W.S; Annual Exhibition in Apr. at National Academy of Design; $12,000 in awards. Two traveling shows selected annually from exhibition.

Publications: History of American Watercolor Society by Ralph Fabri published in 1968; newsletter, summer and winter.

Attendance: Average 4000.

ARCHAEOLOGICAL INSTITUTE OF AMERICA
260 W. Broadway, 10013. Tel: (212) 925-7333
Frederick R. Matson, Pres.
Elizabeth A. Whitehead, Gen. Secy.
For further information see p. 5.

ARCHITECTURAL LEAGUE OF NEW YORK
41 E. 65th St, 10021. Tel: (212) 628-4500
Robert A. M. Stern, Pres.
Marita O'Hare, Admin. Dir.
Walter Rooney, Treas.
Liz Show, Secy.
Open weekdays 10 AM - 5 PM; admis. seminars $2.50, mem. free. Ann. meeting Apr; mem. 650; dues $40 (under 35 yr), $75 (over 35 yr), $15 student

Exhibitions: Street Works, Your Worst Work, The Architecture of Speed, The Bruce Goff Show. Annual Exhibition of Architectural Renderings (juried).

Activities: Lectures, slide lectures, walking tours.

ARCHIVES OF AMERICAN ART
Smithsonian Institution
Administrative Headquarters, 41 E. 65th St, New York, N.Y. 10021. Tel: (212) 628-1251
Archives Center, Eighth & G Sts. N.W, Washington, D.C. 20560. Tel: (202) 381-6174
New York Area Office, 41 E. 65th St, New York, N.Y. 10021. Tel: (212) 628-1251
Mid West Area Office, 5200 Woodward Ave, Detroit, Mich. 48202. Tel: (313) 833-2199
North East Area Office, 87 Mt. Vernon St, Boston, Mass. 02108. Tel: (617) 523-2460
West Coast Area Office, M. H. De Young Memorial Museum, Golden Gate Park, San Francisco, Calif. 94121. Tel: (415) 668-1880
Mrs. Otto L. Spaeth, Chmn. Board of Trustees
Irving F. Burton, Pres.
Mrs. Alfred Negley, V.Pres.
Mrs. E. Bliss Parkinson, V.Pres.
Joel S. Ehrenkranz, Treas.
Henry de Forest Baldwin, Secy.
William E. Woolfenden, Dir.
Garnett McCoy, Archivist
Arthur Breton, Cur. of Manuscripts
Paul Cummings, Oral Historian
Dennis Barrie, Mid West Area Dir.

Robert Brown, North East Area Dir.
Jerry Bywaters, Tex Area Dir.
Paul Karlstrom, West Coast Area Dir.
Open 10 AM - 5 PM Mon. through Fri. Founded in 1954 and joined
the Smithsonian Institution in 1970. A national research institute
whose purpose is to collect basic documentary source materials on
American painters, sculptors, and craftsmen. It aims to simplify the
problems of the working scholar by having such material readily
available on microfilm.

Collections: Research collection of documentary material on
American art, either in original manuscript or printed form or microfilm (5000 rolls, containing five million items). Covers American
painters, sculptors, printmakers; art collectors; dealers; critics and
historians; museums, societies and institutions.

Current field projects: Oral History Program; Regional
Collecting Programs.

Publications: Archives of American Art Journal (quarterly).

ART COMMISSION OF THE CITY OF NEW YORK
    City Hall, 10007. Tel: (212) 566-5525
Muriel Silberstein, Pres.
Donald J. Gormley, Exec. Secy.
Irene Andrejko, Supervising Stenographer
Whitney North Seymour, Jr, Secy.
    Estab. 1898. The Art Commission, with offices in City Hall, is
composed of eleven members serving without compensation and consisting of the Mayor, the Presidents of the Metropolitan Museum of
Art, the New York Public Library, the Brooklyn Institute of Arts and
Sciences, or an appointed trustee of each institution, one painter,
one sculptor, one architect, one landscape architect, three laymen,
all residents. They meet once a month and pass upon the designs
for all works of art and public structures to go into, over, or on City
property. Also supervises the restoration of portraits and frames
in City-owned buildings, inspects installation of works of art and
construction of City-owned buildings in accordance with Charter
provisions; inspects park monuments in collaboration with the Department of Parks and advises accordingly.

ART DEALERS ASSOCIATION OF AMERICA, INC.
    575 Madison Ave, 10022. Tel: (212) 644-7150
Clyde M. Newhouse, Pres.
Ralph F. Colin, Admin. V.Pres. & Counsel
For further information see p. 5.

ART DIRECTORS CLUB, INC.*
    488 Madison Ave, 10022. Tel: (212) 838-8140
Herbert Lubalin, Pres.
Jo Yanow, Exec. Secy. & Communications Dir.
Exhibition gallery open Mon. - Fri. 9 AM - 5 PM. Estab. 1920.
Ann. meeting May; mem. 610.
    Sponsors Annual Show on Advertising and Design - Worldwide;
publishes Annual; honors greats in the field in Annual Hall of Fame;
conducts Encounters with Students and Faculty and gives scholarships to recognized art schools and art students in city high schools
and colleges; circulates commercials and slides as part of Traveling
Graphics Library; numerous special educational and professional
programs on premises for members throughout year. Sponsors
Annual New York City Communications Week Conference - International visitors on all themes. Hosts visits to New York communications working environments. Annual Show travels abroad
under United States Information Agency.

ART INFORMATION CENTER, INC.
    189 Lexington Ave, 10016. Tel: (212) 725-0335
Directors:
Betty Chamberlain, Managing Dir.
May Asher, Asst. Dir.
Stanley William Hayter
Jacob Lawrence
Andrew C. Ritchie
Open Mon. - Fri. 2 - 5:30 PM by appointment.
    Organized 1959, inc. 1963; free tax-deductible clearing house of
contemporary fine arts. Maintains †files of living artists with their
gallery affiliations (c. 40,000 artists); files of galleries, their rosters
of artists and catalogs of current and recent shows (c. 450 in New
York, 300 in other U.S. cities, 50 in foreign cities); †files of slides
of work by unaffiliated artists (c. 750 artists and 8-12 slides each)
for use by dealers looking for new talent. The Center helps to chan-
nel the many artists in New York, and those coming to New York,
seeking New York outlets for their work. It aids new galleries to
start, helps artists to find out where they can learn special disciplines and skills and where to exhibit in summer. Furnishes information on many aspects of contemporary art to museums, art
schools, collectors and the public. All documentation kept constantly up to date.

✠ART STUDENTS LEAGUE OF NEW YORK
    215 W. 57th St, 10019. Tel: (212) 257-4510
Lisa M. Specht, Pres.
Barbara R. Swanson, Recording Secy.
Stewart Klonis, Exec. Dir.
Estab. 1875 to maintain art school and membership activities. Ann.
meeting Dec; mem. 5000 plus; dues $5 except for life members.
    Exhibitions: Various exhibitions in League Gallery by members,
students and instructors.
    Activities: Lectures; sponsors approx. 130 scholarships annually,
plus Traveling Scholarships; additions are made to the collections by
purchases of outstanding examples of students' work annually, and of
instructors and other prominent members of League. Maintains
school. (See Schools)
    Library: Reference library for students and members only.
    Publications: Art Students League News, monthly.
    Attendance: 2250.

ARTIST-CRAFTSMEN OF NEW YORK, INC.*
    130 E. 28th St, 10016. Tel: (212) 679-8154
R. Leigh Glover, Pres.
Joan Zimet, 1st V.Pres.
Donald O. Mauros, 2nd V.Pres.
Muriel Barnes, Treas.
Nell Znamierowski, Recording Secy.
Mary Walker Phillips, Corresp. Secy.
Estab. 1958 as successor to New York Society of Craftsmen and New
York Society of Ceramic Arts. Ann. meeting Mar; mem. approx.
300. Affiliated with American Craftsmen's Council.
    Annual exhibition in New York City; periodic exhibitions at
National Design Center and other New York City locations. Purpose
to promote interest in quality craftsmanship. Admittance as an
artist-craftsman member to the Society is by submission of work
to membership jury. Emphasis is laid upon professional standards
of craftsmanship and the quality of work. Persons having demonstrated great interest in the crafts but who are not craftsmen may
become associate or contributing members on election by the Board
of Governors. A Newsletter is published 4-6 times a year, and there
are about 6 membership meetings a year. Exhibitions and demonstrations are arranged for the purpose of broadening public interest
in and knowledge of crafts and developing standards of taste in design and workmanship.

ARTISTS EQUITY ASSOCIATION OF NEW YORK, INC.
    1780 Broadway, 10019. Tel: (212) 586-0554
Alton S. Tobey, Pres.
Domenico Facci, V.Pres.
Bernard Simon, Treas.
Bea Begman, Recording Secy.
Bernard Kassoy, Corresp. Secy.
Open 10 AM - 4 PM. Estab. 1947 to advance, foster and promote the
fine arts and economic and professional interests of those who work
in the fine arts; to protect and secure the economic and professional
rights of such artists. A nonpolitical, esthetically nonpartisan organization representing the artist in the New York area. Mem. meetings Feb, Apr, Oct. & Dec; mem. 750; dues $20.
    Activities: Committees of Government and Art, Welfare, Griev-
ance, Special Events; Artists' Housing; Forums; Research Projects.
Operates Artists Welfare Fund, Inc, primarily to help artists in need
of temporary financial assistance, publishes brochures on economic
problems.
    Publications: AEA Newsletter.

ARTISTS' FELLOWSHIP, INC.
    1083 Fifth Ave, 10028.
Furman J. Finck, Pres.
Gerard A. Knipscher, V.Pres.
Martin Hannon, Recording Secy.
J. B. Adams, Corresp. Secy.
Elliot Liskin, Treas.
Russell Rypsam, Historian
    Estab. 1859, reorganized 1889 as Artists' Aid Society, inc. 1925
as Artists' Fellowship, Inc. Its purpose is to aid artists in need of
hospitalization. Ann. meeting Dec; mem. 173. Controls an endowed
bed in Presbyterian Hospital. Awards the Gari Melchers medal for
distinguished service to the arts and the Clinedinst medal for out-
standing achievement in the arts and crafts.

THE ARTISTS GUILD INC
    Mezzanine Floor, 25 W. 36th St, 10018
Dean Powell, Pres.
Joan De Katch, Corresp. Secy.
    Estab. 1920. Members benefit by several services the Guild pro-
vides for their protection and guidance. Advice and exchange of ideas
with experienced people in the field. Interesting meetings, guest
speakers, presenting newest techniques and products in our business.
Ann. exhibitions. Charter mem. of Joint Ethics Committee. Mem.

open to free-lance or employed artists; mem. 200-300; dues $25 active, $20 assoc, $15 nonres. mem, $15 students; ann. meeting May; monthly meetings Sept. through May.

ARTISTS TECHNICAL RESEARCH INSTITUTE, INC.
207 W. 106th St, 10025. Tel: (212) 749-7819
Stuyvesant Van Veen, Pres.
Ralph Mayer, Dir.
Bena F. Mayer, Admin. Asst.
Estab. 1959 for the publication of results of scientific laboratory investigations of the materials of creative painting and sculpture, appropriations and grants from NEA and private donations.
Activities: Publication of Audio-Visual Materials.
Publications: Quarterly Journal.

✤ASIA HOUSE GALLERY
The Asia Society
112 E. 64th St, 10021. Tel: (212) 751-4210
George W. Ball, Chmn. Board of Trustees
Phillips Talbot, Pres.
Lionel Landry, Exec. V.Pres.
Allen Wardwell, Gallery Dir.
Virginia Field, Assoc. Gallery Dir.
Open weekdays during exhibitions 10 AM - 5 PM; Sat. 11 AM - 5 PM; Sun. 1 - 5 PM. The Asia Society is a non-profit organization, inc. 1957 to further greater understanding and mutual appreciation between the United States and the peoples of Asia; Asia House Gallery was inaugurated 1960 to acquaint Americans with the historic art of Asia. Annual meeting of Corporation in May; mem. (May, 1973) 1980; dues $15 and higher.
Collections: No permanent collection, loans obtained from the U.S. and foreign collections for special exhibitions.
Exhibitions: (1973) Ceramic Art of Japan: 100 Masterpieces from Japanese Collections; A Flower from Every Meadow: Indian Paintings from American Collections; Shah 'Abbas and the Arts of Isfahan; (1974) The Colors of Ink: Chinese Paintings and Related Ceramics from The Cleveland Museum of Art; Rajasthani Temple Hangings of the Krishna Cult; The Poet-Painters: Buson and His Followers; (1975) Asian Art: Selections from the Collection of Mr. and Mrs. John D. Rockefeller 3rd, Part II; Rarities of the Musee Guimet; Photographs from the Himalayas: Abode of the Snows; Nepal: Where the Gods are Young.
Activities: One or more lectures for members given by guest specialists in connection with each exhibition and recorded lectures by the gallery director available to visitors. Film, dance, musical and additional lecture programs presented by other Asia Society Departments. Color slides of loans to the exhibitions made available through commercial distributors.
Publications: Fully illustrated, book-length catalogs published for each exhibition; Archives of Asian Art published annually.
Attendance: 43,400.

ASSOCIATED COUNCILS OF THE ARTS
1564 Broadway, 10036. Tel: (212) 586-3731
Louis Harris, Chmn. of Board
Michael Newton, Pres.
Marilyn Lazarevich, Admin. Dir.
Sandra Dilley, Ed, Publications
Nancy Bush, Dir. of Information & Advocates Coordinator
John Hightower, Chmn, Advocates for the Arts
For further information see p. 5.

ASSOCIATES OF THE ART COMMISSION, INC.
City Hall, 10007.
Bethuel M. Webster, Pres.
Allyn Cox, Secy.
Estab. 1913, inc. 1942. Composed of former members of the Art Commission; acts in an advisory capacity to the Commission. Ann. meeting Jan; mem. approx. 45; dues $20.

ASSOCIATION OF ART MUSEUM DIRECTORS
P.O. Box 620, Lenox Hill Station, 10021.
Evan H. Turner, Pres.
Ian M. White, 1st V.Pres.
Rollin van N. Hadley, 2nd V.Pres.
Paul C. Mills, Secy.
Thomas W. Leavitt, Treas.
For further information see p. 5.

✤THE ASSOCIATION OF JUNIOR LEAGUES, INC.
825 Third Ave, 10022. Tel: (212) 355-4380
Mary D. Poole, Pres.
Frances Verstandeg, Secy.
Edwin H. Marks, Jr, Exec. Dir.
For further information see p. 5.

AUDUBON ARTISTS, INC.
1083 Fifth Ave, 10028. Tel: (212) EN9-4880
Domenico Facci, Pres.
Mark Freeman, Sr. V.Pres.
E. Raymond Kinstler, V.Pres. for Oil
Serge Hollerbach, V.Pres. for Aquarelle
Jacques Hnizdovsky, V.Pres. for Graphic
Gaetano Cecere, V.Pres. for Sculpture
Jan Gary, Recording Secy.
Therese Censor, Corresp. Secy.
Alice Gross, Treas.
Open 1 - 5 PM. Estab. 1942. Open to artists of every school, technique, subject matter, in all accredited media. Ann. meeting Apr. or May; mem. approx. 400; dues $15. Annual Exhibition held at the National Academy of Design. Demonstrations during exhibition. Over $4000 in awards and medals.

CARAVAN OF EAST AND WEST INC.
Caravan House Galleries
132 E. 65th St, 10021. (212) 744-4793
Elsie Clarke, Pres.
John Lally, Secy. & Gallery Dir.
Duncan Sterling, Treas.
Mrs. John Lally, V.Pres. & Asst. Gallery Dir.
Free Tues. - Sat. 11 AM - 6 PM. Estab. Mar, 1929 as a nonprofit organization to help artists display their work to the general public, to increase communication between peoples of the world, and to give lectures and talks on important topics; financed by endowment and membership. Two galleries located on same premises for one-man exhibits. Ann. meeting 1st Mon. in Apr; mem. 465; dues family $15, single $10.
Exhibitions: Two artists are exhibited for a 17-day period Jan. to June and Oct. to Dec. 31.
Activities: Foreign language classes; lectures open to public; 14 visiting lecturers per year; 14 gallery talks; 10 tours; concerts; classes for adults.
Publications: Pen Friend Guide, worldwide circulation, issued twice a year.
Annual Income: $40,000.
Attendance: 9000.

CATHARINE LORILLARD WOLFE ART CLUB, INC.
802 Broadway, 10003
Mae Berlind Bach, Pres.
Helen DeCozen, 1st V.Pres.
Lucille Hampton, Treas
Sara Boal, Recording Secy.
Jacquie-Louise Gray, Corresp. Secy.
Estab. 1896, inc. 1963, to further fine, representational American art. A club of professional women painters and sculptors. Mem. accepted on an international basis subject to jury. Monthly meetings; mem. over 200; dues $10.
Exhibition: 2 annuals; 1 open, 1 members; several other members shows. Approx. 45 awards each year, cash, medals and materials.
Activities: Lectures, programs, scholarship, annual Metropolitan Museum benefit for travel grant and research in U.S.A.

CENTER FOR INTER-AMERICAN RELATIONS ART GALLERY
680 Park Ave, 10021. Tel: (212) 249-8950
James Wolfe, Dir. Visual Art Prog.
Nita M. Renfrew, Gallery Adminr.
Sharon L. Schultz, Gallery Asst.
Open daily Noon - 6 PM. Gallery opened Sept, 1967 as a major program element of the Center for Inter-American Relations to enlarge knowledge and appreciation in the United States of the art and cultural heritage of other areas in the Western Hemisphere; maintained by contributions and memberships. Three galleries, 5 - 6 loan exhibitions a year of Latin American and Canadian art. Mem. over 600; dues $25 - $200.
Collections: Limited collection of contemporary Latin American paintings, drawings and prints; 19th century Mexican, Colonial and Pre-Columbian objects on permanent loan; 17th and 18th century French, English, Italian and Spanish furniture and decorative arts as house furnishings.
Exhibitions: (1973-75) About 30 works by Michael Snow; Rogelio Polesello; Santiago Cardenas/Carlos Rojas, 10 Argentine Artists for the United Nations; Peruvian Paintings on Textile, 800 B.C. to 1700 A.D; Frank Bowling; Latin American Prints from Museum of Modern Art; El Dorado, The Gold of Ancient Colombia; Margin of Life, Cornell Capa; Hectoe Poleo; 6 Cuban Painters Working in New York; Omar Rayo Intaglios 1960-1975 from the Rayo Museum; Juan Downey; Tapestries by Luis Montiel; Pre-Columbian Ceramics from Ecuador; Leonora Carrington Retrospective.
Activities: Traveling exhibitions organized, individual works lent; photograph collection, artist files. Book shop for catalog sales.

Publications: Exhibition catalogs.
Income: $106,000 as allocated from the Center's overall budget.
Attendance: 25,000.

CHINA HOUSE GALLERY
125 E. 65th St, 10021. Tel: (212) 744-8181
John M. Crawford, Jr, Chmn. Art Comt.
F. Richard Hsu, Dir.
Amy McEwen Wolf, Asst. Dir.
Free Mon. - Fri. 10 AM - 5 PM; Sat. 11 AM - 5 PM; Sun. 2 - 5 PM, during exhibitions only. Estab. 1966 for exhibitions of classical Chinese art; financed by endowment and sponsors. Gallery has two loan exhibitions of classical Chinese art per year; painting, sculpture, decorative arts. Gallery Sponsors 25; dues $500.
Exhibitions: Chinese Silk Tapestry-K'o-ssu; Early Chinese Gold and Silver; Dragons in Chinese Art; Wintry Forests, Old Trees-Some Landscape Themes in Chinese Painting; Ceramics in the Liao Dynasty; China Trade Porcelain; Tantric Buddhist Art; Friends of Wen Cheng-Ming-A view from the Crawford Collection; Ancient Chinese Jades, from the Buffalo Museum of Science (Awarded NEA grant); Art of the Six Dynasties.
Activities: Films and lectures available to school and adult education groups on exhibitions and Chinese culture and art in general; 6 visiting lecturers per year; 50 gallery talks; concerts; classes for adults.
Publications: Catalogues are published on each exhibition presented, two annually.
Income: $35,000.
Attendance: 12,000 annual average.

COLLEGE ART ASSOCIATION OF AMERICA
16 E. 52nd St, 10022.
Albert Elsen, Pres.
George Sadek, V.Pres.
Marilyn Stokstad, Secy.
Gilbert S. Edelson, Hon. Counsel
Richard S. Ravenscroft, Hon. Treas.
Rose R. Weil, Exec. Secy.
For further information see p. 6.

COLUMBIA UNIVERSITY
Avery Architectural Library
117th St. West of Amsterdam Ave, 10027. Tel: (212) 280-3501
Adolf K. Placzek, Librn.
Open Mon. - Thurs. 9 AM - 10 PM; Fri. 9 AM - 5 PM; Sat. 1 - 5 PM, Sun. 2 - 6 PM during school year. Estab. 1890, present building 1912; School of Architecture occupies upper floors. (See Schools)
Collections: Contains over 110,000 books on architecture and the allied arts, including nearly all architectural incunabula and the rare books of the profession from the 15th century to the present. Supplemented by the †Fine Arts Library, †Ware Library of the School of Architecture, †Teachers College and the †General Library of the University, there are over 300,000 volumes on the various fields of the fine arts. Avery Library receives over 300 current architectural and planning periodicals. Collection of 10,000 original architectural drawings, mainly American.

Fine Arts Library
Morningside Heights, 10027. Tel: (212) 280-3982
Mary M. Schmidt, Fine Arts Librn.
Estab. 1922 to provide bibliographical support to the teaching of Art History at Columbia University; endowed.
Collections: 55,000 volumes of monographs and journals on painting, sculpture, drawing and prints.
Publications: Guide to Art Research Collections in the New York City Area, 1972.

COOPER-HEWITT MUSEUM OF DECORATIVE ARTS AND DESIGN
9 E. 90th St, 10028. Tel: (212) 860-2011
2 E. 91st St. & Fifth Ave, 10028.
Lisa S. Taylor, Dir.
Christian Rohlfing, Adminr.
John Dobkin, Prog. Mgr.
Elaine Evans Dee, Cur. Drawings & Prints
Milton Sonday, Cur. Textiles
Alice Baldwin Beer, Consultant, Dept. Textiles
J. Stewart Johnson, Cur. Decorative Arts
Robert Kaufmann, Librn.
Estab. 1896, opened 1897 as The Cooper Union Museum For The Arts of Decoration; joined the Smithsonian Institution in 1968, and name changed then; offers a major assemblage of decorative arts materials, and serves as a design research laboratory for professionals and students; closed to general public for renovation at present; will re-open early 1976, currently collections are available for study by prior arrangement.
Collections: Textiles, from 1500 B.C. to the present; furniture, woodwork, metalwork, ceramics, lace, embroidery, costume acces-

sories, and other decorative arts; collection of over 5000 wallpapers; drawings and prints, including Decloux collection of about 500 original drawings for ornament and decoration by 16th, 17th and 18th century French masters; important collection of French, Italian, German and American theater and stage designs; Piancastelli collection of 12,000 original drawings for ornament and decoration; drawings by Arnold W. Brunner, William M. Chase, Frederic E. Church, Kenyon Cox, Childe Hassam, Winslow Homer, Daniel Huntington, Thomas Moran, Walter Shirlaw, and F. Hopkinson Smith; George Cameron Stone bequest of Japanese sword mountings. The total collections include over 100,000 objects.
Exhibitions: Immovable Objects, subtitled, An Outdoor Exhibition About City Design on View Throughout Lower Manhattan from Battery Park to Brooklyn Bridge.
Activities: During the present period of renovation of the property many objects from the collections are on loan to other museums for the duration or for loan exhibitions. When the Museum re-opens, a full complement of extension services will be provided for students, professionals and the general public, including lectures, films, exhibitions, workshops, a book and sales shop.
Library: Reference Library contains 25,000 volumes and pamphlets on fine and applied arts, including 1100 rare books of designs for architecture, ornament and decoration; an encyclopedic picture archive of 1,500,000 classified illustrations in the fields of fine and applied arts, and specialized archival collections of Color, Symbols, Pattern, Technology, Fashion and Materians and Advertising Design.

COUNCIL OF AMERICAN ARTIST SOCIETIES
112 E. 19th St, 10003. Tel: (212) 475-6650
Frank C. Wright, Pres.
Donald DeLue, 1st V.Pres.
John S. Dole, V.Pres, Treas. & Gen. Counsel
Katherine Thayer Hobson, Asst. Treas.
Florence Whitehill, Recording Secy.
For further information see p. 6.

✠THE DECORATORS CLUB, INC.*
41 East 65 St, 10021.
Jane Cunningham, Pres.

FASHION INSTITUTE OF TECHNOLOGY LIBRARY*
227 W. 27th St, 10001. Tel: (212) 239-7695, 96
Eunice Walker, Acting Librn.
Marjorie Miller, Art Reference Librn.
Sweetman R. Smith, Reference Librn.
Open Mon. - Thurs. 8:30 AM - 9:30 PM; Fri. 8:30 AM - 5 PM; Sat. 10 AM - 4 PM. Estab. 1952 as a technical community college library designed to serve students and faculty of the institution, open to other institutions, the fashion industry and the general public for reference only; financed by city and state appropriations.
Collections: 38,776 general college book and periodical collection, with strengths in fine and applied arts, interior design, costume, fashion, textile design and technology, management and merchandising; picture file; clipping files on textile arts; original fashion sketches.

FEDERAL HALL NATIONAL MEMORIAL*
National Park Service, Department of the Interior
Corner of Wall & Nassau Sts, 10005. Tel: (212) 264-4367
Vernon D. Dame, Superintendent
Free Mon. - Fri. and all holidays 9 AM - 4:30 PM; weekends in summer. Site of the old Federal Hall, first capitol of the United States, where Washington took his oath of office as President and where the Bill of Rights was adopted. Book and memento shop.
Exhibits on: †George Washington, †Bill of Rights, and John Peter Zenger.
Educational Activities: Tours are provided for all school groups upon request in advance.
Library: Contains c. 1000 books, the majority dealing with the Colonial and Federal Periods; a few books are on the National Parks and Conservation.
Attendance: 100,000.

FEDERATION OF MODERN PAINTERS AND SCULPTORS, INC.
340 W. 72nd St, 10023. Tel: (212) 362-4608
Ahmet Gursoy, Pres.
Barbara Krashes, V.Pres.
Elisabeth Model, Corresp. Secy.
Estab. 1940; professional painters and sculptors united to promote the cultural interests of artists working in the United States, to facilitate the showing of their work, and to improve their professional and economic welfare. Mem. approx. 70; dues $8.
Exhibitions: Exhibitions in New York City, nationally, traveling shows.
Activities: Art Forums, film showings, symposia, lectures; sponsors of Museum Gift Plan, whereby major museums throughout

the country are able to acquire members' work for their permanent collections. Permanent collections comprised exclusively of members' work are installed in many museums of art in the United States. Recipient 1975 of grant from the New York State Council on the Arts. Gallery Association of New York is sponsoring one year traveling show within New York State for this group, catalog to be published in 1976.

Publications: Occasional exhibition catalogs.

FINE ARTS FEDERATION OF NEW YORK
44 W. Ninth St, Room 20, 10011. Tel: (212) 477-2124
Margot Gayle, Pres.
Minor Bishop, Secy.
Bradford Greene, Treas.

Estab. 1895, inc. 1897, to secure united action by the art societies of New York in all matters affecting their common interests, and to foster and protect the artistic interests of the community. Ann. meeting April; membership consists of six delegates from each of the 20 constituent organizations making up the Federation, making an approximate membership represented of some 7000; dues for each representative $7, making $42 for each society.

Members of the Art Commission of the City of New York are appointed by the Mayor from nominations provided to him by the Federation.

FREDERICK THOMPSON FOUNDATION, INC.
441 E. 20th St, 10010. Tel: (212) 533-6631
Mrs. Humbert Cofrances, Pres.
Mrs. Frederick Thompson, Exec. Dir.

Open Sat. and by appointment. Estab. 1956, inc. 1962, to provide a Center where there may be study, discussion and the production of creative arts. A program of activities planned to create a sense of appreciation of art and particularly the art of painting. Ann. meeting Oct; board meets quarterly.

Collections: Over 300 paintings by Frederick Thompson, all excellent examples of Trompe L'Oeil technique.

Exhibitions: Lincoln Center Museum of the Performing Arts, New York.

Activities: Loan collection of color plates from American and European museums on Giotto, Raphael, Hals, Vermeer, Rembrandt, Chardin, Copley, Homer, Cezanne, Eakins and van Gogh; slide and film shows; essays by Frederick Thompson on the above Masters available upon request. Programs with color slides and tapes free to New York City residents for presentations. Instructional outlines also available.

Attendance: Over 5000.

FRENCH INSTITUTE - ALLIANCE FRANCAISE
22 E. 60th St, 10022. Tel: (212) 644-1820
Robert G. Goelet, Pres.
Vincent Milligan, Sr. Dir.
Jean Vallier, Exec. Dir.

Free Mon. - Thurs. 10 AM - 8 PM; Fri. 10 AM - 6 PM. Estab. 1911. Ann. meeting Oct; mem. 2300; dues $20 ($15 for teachers and students).

Building opened 1926, contains auditorium, circulating French library, collection of ceramics. Annual purchases for library only, $5000. Library contains 35,000 volumes on French literature and art. Weekly French lectures during the winter. Year-round classes in French.

✤FRICK ART REFERENCE LIBRARY
10 E. 71st St, 10021. Tel: (212) 288-8700
Helen Clay Frick, Dir.
Mildred Steinbach, Librn.

Admittance by appointment (telephone or letter) Mon. - Fri. 10 AM - 4 PM, Sept. - May, Sat. 10 AM - Noon; cl. Sun, holidays and Aug.

Estab. 1920; new building dedicated 1935. A reference library of over †450,000 photographs, over †165,000 catalogs and †books on the history of European and American painting, drawing, sculpture, illuminated manuscripts available to graduate students and others interested.

Attendance: 8000 annually.

✤FRICK COLLECTION
1 E. 70th St, 10021. Tel: (212) 288-0700
Henry Clay Frick, II, Pres.
Martha F. Symington, Secy.
Everett Fahy, Dir.
Edgar Munhall, Cur.
Bernice Davidson, Research Cur.
David M. Collins, Business Adminr.
Dean Walker, Lectr. & Curatorial Asst.
Susan Caroselli, Lectr. & Curatorial Asst.
Martha Hackley, Manager, Sales and Information
William Fleming, Supt.

Free 10 AM - 6 PM; Sun. and holidays 1 - 6 PM; cl. Mon; cl. Jan. 1, July 4, Thanksgiving and Dec. 24th and 25th; special summer hours June, July & Aug, Wed. - Sat. 10 AM - 6 PM; Sun. 1 - 6 PM; cl. all day Mon. & Tues. Children under ten not admitted; those under sixteen must be accompanied by adults. Opened 1935; bequeathed and endowed by Henry C. Frick; controlled by a Board of Trustees.

Collections: 14th to 19th century paintings, with fine examples of Western European masters and suites of Boucher and Fragonard decorations; 16th to 19th century drawings and prints; 15th to 18th century sculpture, of which Renaissance bronzes are most numerous; 16th century Limoges enamels; 17th to 18th century Chinese and French porcelains; Renaissance and French 18th century furniture.

Activities: Lectures, concerts.

Publications: The Frick Collection, An Illustrated Catalog, Vols. I - II; Paintings (1968), Vols. III - IV; Sculpture (1970), Vol. VII; Oriental and French Porcelains (1974); other volumes in preparation; Masterpieces of the Frick Collection (1970); Handbook of Paintings (1971).

Attendance: Average (1971-72) 225,000.

GRAND CENTRAL ART GALLERIES*
Painters and Sculptors Gallery Association
40 Vanderbilt Ave, 10017. Tel: (212) 867-3344
Peter Grimm, Pres.
Cleo F. Craig, V.Pres.
Stanley C. Allyn, V.Pres.
Jack S. Parker, Secy. & Treas.
J. Porter Brinton, Jr, Asst. Secy. & Treas.
Erwin S. Barrie, Dir. & Mgr.

Free 9:30 AM - 5:30 PM; cl. Sun; cl. Sat. in summer. Estab. 1923, a non-profit organization operated solely in the interest of living American artists. The officers serve without pay. All works of art are for sale. 100 lay members of these galleries pay annual dues of $400 for which they receive works of art contributed by artist members.

Exhibitions: Continuous exhibitions, changed bi-weekly. Annual Founders Exhibition in Oct.

GROLIER CLUB
47 E. 60th St, 10022. Tel: (212) 838-6690
H. W. Liebert, Pres.
F. S. Streeter, Secy.
Robert Nikirk, Librn.

Four exhibitions yearly, free weekdays 10 AM - 5 PM; Sat. 10 AM - 3 PM; Library cl. Sat. & Sun. Founded 1884, devoted to book collecting and all the arts of the book. Owns building; permanent reference library, 60,000 volumes, 5000 prints. Library principally bibliographical and typographical, large collection bookseller and auction catalogues from 17th century. Mem. 625.

Publications: About one per year, often a major work.
Purchases: Approx. $15,000.

GUILD OF BOOK WORKERS
1059 Third Ave, 10021. Tel: (212) 752-0813
Mary C. Schlosser, Pres.

Estab. 1906 to stimulate and develop interest in the several handbook crafts. Affiliated with the American Institute of Graphic Arts. Mem. 250; dues $60 in metropolitan area; $36 elsewhere.

Exhibitions: Handbook binding, case-making, restoration, calligraphy and illumination, and hand-decorated papers on request.

Activities: Several meetings yearly, lectures, workshops or tours, intermittent exhibitions.

Library: Approx. 500 items relevant to the handbook crafts; available on a mail order basis to members only.

Publications: Journal of the Guild of Book Workers, three times annually as a service to members; available to institutional libraries on a subscription basis.

Attendance: Average at meetings 35.

THE HISPANIC SOCIETY OF AMERICA
Broadway, between 155th & 156th Sts, 10032. Tel: (212) 926-2234
A. Hyatt Mayor, Pres.
Theodore S. Beardsley, Jr, Dir.
Vivian A. Hibbs, Cur. Archaeology
Ruth M. Anderson, Cur. Costume
Jean R. Longland, Cur. Library
Florence L. May, Cur. Textiles
Priscilla E. Muller, Cur. Museum
Martha M. de Narváez, Cur. Manuscripts-Rare Books

Museum free Tues. - Sat. 10 AM - 4:30 PM; Sun. 1 - 4 PM; Library Tues. - Fri. 1 - 4:30 PM; Sat. 10 AM - 4:30 PM; buildings cl. Mon. and Jan. 1, Feb. 12, Easter Sunday, May 30, July 4, Thanksgiving Day, Dec. 24, 25, 31; Reading Room also cl. during the month of Aug, from Dec. 24 to Jan. 1 inclusive, Feb. 22, Good Friday and Oct. 12. Founded 1904 by Archer Milton Huntington in order to estab. a public museum and library to present culture of Hispanic peoples.

Mem. elective, limited to 100, corresponding mem. to 300. Recorded tours in English and Spanish.

Collections: Permanent exhibition of paintings, sculpture and decorative arts representative of Hispanic culture from pre-historic times to the present.

Activities: An orientation program consisting of 62 color slides of the collections with a recorded commentary in either Spanish or English is available for educational institutions. The Information Desk sells publications of the Society, slides, post cards, note cards and reproductions of objects in the collection.

Library: †Reference library of manuscripts, some 15,000 early imprints, and more than 90,000 books printed after 1700, relating to the art, history, and literature of Spain and Portugal. †Reference file of photographs and prints.

Publications: Works by members of the Staff and of the Society on Spanish Art, History, Literature, Bibliography, with special emphasis on the collections of the Society.

Attendance: Average approx. 36,000 annually for the past two years.

INTERNATIONAL CENTER OF MEDIEVAL ART, INC.
The Cloisters, Fort Tryon Park, 10040. Tel: (212) 923-3700
Carl D. Sheppard, Pres.
Whitney S. Stoddard, V.Pres.
Barbara Dirlam, Secy.
Sumner McK. Crosby, Jr, Treas.
Estab. 1963 as The International Center of Romanesque Art, Inc. The International Center of Medieval Art was founded to promote greater knowledge of the arts of the Middle Ages, and to contribute to and make available the results of new research. Nonprofit organization supported by members and benefactors. Ann. meeting Jan. (in conjunction with College Art Association of America); mem. 600; dues student $7.50, active (individual, institutional) $15, contributing $100, lifetime $500, benefactor $1000.

Activities: Organize and sponsor public lectures, exhibitions and symposia; financial support given to excavations of important medieval sites at Spoleto, Caen, and the Abbey of Psalmodi; sponsors sessions at the annual Conferences of The Medieval Institute of Western Michigan University, Kalamazoo.

Publications: Gesta, 2 issues per year.

INTERNATIONAL FOUNDATION FOR ART RESEARCH, INC.
654 Madison Ave, 10021. Tel: (212) 751-1520
Franklin Feldman, Pres.
Simon Sheib, Secy.
Elizabeth B. Burns, Exec. Secy.
For further information see p. 6.

JAPAN HOUSE GALLERY
Japan Society, Inc.
333 E. 47th St, 10017. Tel: (212) 832-1155
Isaac Shapiro, Pres, Japan Society
David MacEachron, Exec. Dir. Society
Rand Castile, Gallery Dir.
Maryell Semal, Asst. Gallery Dir.
Open at exhibition times Mon. - Fri. 10 AM - 5 PM; Sat. 11 AM - 5 PM; Sun. 1 - 5 PM; contributions accepted from nonmembers. Estab. 1907 as a bicultural society to promote understanding and friendship between the United States and Japan; financed by memberships. Gallery has major loan exhibitions of Japanese art. Ann. meeting Fall; mem. 2000; dues vary.

Collections: No permanent collection; small study collection.

Exhibitions: Rimpa; Rosanjin; Contemporary Posters; The Greenfield Collection (lacquer); Namban; Ledoux Heritage: Ukiyo and Prints; The Courtly Tradition in Japanese Art and Literature; Ikeda and Ida: Two new Japanese Printmakers; Tsutsumu: The Art of the Japanese Package: The Fleeting World: Ukiyo-E Prints from the Edith Ehrman Collection.

Activities: Lectures open to the public; visiting lecturers; approx. 100 gallery talks and tours per year; concerts; dramatic programs; classes for adults and children; library; photograph collection.

Library: 4500 volume library on Japanese art and history available on premises or for loan to society members.

Publications: Monthly newsletter; exhibition catalogs.

Attendance: 50,000.

THE JEWISH MUSEUM
1109 Fifth Ave. (92nd St), 10028. Tel: (212) 860-1888
Joy G. Ungerleider, Dir.
Susan Goodman, Cur.
Cissy Grossman, Asst. Cur. for Judaica
Henry Korn, Adminr.
Open Sun. 11 AM - 6 PM; Mon. - Thurs. Noon - 5 PM; cl. Fri. & Sat. and major Jewish holidays; admis. adults $1.50, children (6-16) and students with ID card 50¢; senior citizens pay-what-you-wish. Group admis. rates. Estab. 1947, under the auspices of The Jewish Theological Seminary of America. Mem. dues $10 and up.

Exhibitions: Permanent exhibitions include the largest collection of Jewish ceremonial objects in the United States, archaeology from the Holy Land, Samuel Friedenberg Collection of coins and medals. Changing contemporary exhibitions include painting, sculpture and photography. Recent exhibitions have included Moshe Safdie: For Everyone a Garden; Berggassee 19: The Office and Antiquities of Dr. Sigmund Freud and Jewish Experience in the Art of the 20th Century.

Activities: Guided tours, lectures, films, concerts, children's programs, courses, walking tours of the Lower East Side. Gift shop.

JOHN SIMON GUGGENHEIM MEMORIAL FOUNDATION
90 Park Ave, 10016. Tel: (212) 687-4470
Gordon N. Ray, Pres.
James F. Mathias, V.Pres.
Estab. and inc. 1925. The Foundation awards Fellowships to assist persons engaged in research in any area of knowledge or creation in the fine arts. The Fellowships are available to advanced scholars and artists who have already demonstrated unusual capacity in their given fields. Applications are due by October 1 and awards are announced in March.

Fellowships in the fine arts were awarded in 1975 to artists: Guy Irving Anderson, Jeffery Francis Beardsall, Lynda Benglis, Billy Al Bengston, Natvar Bhavsar, Stanley Boxer, Fritz Bultman, Bruce Conner, Mel Edwards, Jackie Ferrara, Peter L. Gourfain, Aristodimos Kaldis, Michael Lekakis, Norman Lewis, Clement Meadmore, David Rabinowitch, Michelle Stuart and Marvin Torffield; to scholars and writers: Wayne E. Begley, Bruce Cole, Sidney Geist, Ellen H. Johnson, Steven Lattimore, Kathleen Weil-Garris Posner and Margit Rowell.

LINCOLN CENTER FOR THE PERFORMING ARTS, INC.
Amsterdam, Plaza, and Main Galleries
1865 Broadway, 10023. Tel: (212) 765-5100
Amyas Ames, Chmn. of the Board
John W. Mazzola, Managing Dir.
Open daily 10 AM - Midnight; admis. varies. First building opened 1962, Center completed 1969 to present the performing arts to the broadest cross-section of the community; financed by endowment, city, state and federal appropriations and membership; mem. guilds or associations that support the Center or a constituent; dues $15-$1000.

Collections: Amsterdam, Plaza, and Main Galleries collections consist of original designs for stage settings and costumes, drawings and models of theatres, graphics for posters and lithographs, photographs. There are other works of are at the Lincoln Center, located at the New York State Theater, Avery Fisher Hall, Lincoln Center Plaza North, Metropolitan Opera House, Vivian Beaumont Theater, The Juilliard School and Alice Tully Hall.

Exhibitions: Exhibits of the collections change frequently.

Activities: Photograph collection for lending and reference; lectures for subscribers; 5000 tours; concerts; dramatic programs; scholarships.

Library: General Library of circulating and information collections; Children's Library; Research Library.

Publications: Calendar of Events; newsletters or magazines.

Income and Purchases: Income $71,000,000; purchases $76,000,000.

Attendance: 2,600,000 paid audiences; 90,000 tours; one million attend free performances in the parks and on the Plaza.

LOTOS CLUB*
5 E 66th St, 10021. Tel: (212) 737-7100
Open 10 - 12 AM & 2 - 5 PM during exhibitions. Estab. 1870 as a social club for men, to which many artists belong. Occasional exhibitions annually. Publishes Lotos Leaf monthly.

LOUIS COMFORT TIFFANY FOUNDATION*
1083 Fifth Ave, 10028. Tel: (212) 831-5015
Lewis Iselin, Pres.
Paul Smith, V.Pres.
Henry Allen Moe, Secy.
Sergei Kolochov, Treas.
The Tiffany Foundation, estab. in 1918 was reorganized with the permission of the Courts in 1947. The estate at Oyster Bay together with its art collection was sold and the funds thereby derived added to the capital assets.

The Tiffany Foundation operates by making annual grants of cash up to two thousand dollars, each, to advanced students of painting, sculpture and the graphic arts. The Foundation also offers grants in the creative crafts. The grants are awarded by jury from recommendations of selected artists, craftsmen and art educators.

LOVIS CORINTH MEMORIAL FOUNDATION, INC.
55 Liberty St, 10005. Tel: (212) 964-4424
M. Weinstein, Treas.
Thomas Corinth, Secy.

Open by appointment. Estab. 1969-70 as a tax-exempt, nonprofit, educational Membership Corporation to exhibit works by Lovis Corinth and Charlotte Berend in American museums, to dispense educational information about German art as represented by Lovis Corinth, and to provide access to educational material relating to the lives and works of said artists, to researchers; supported by mem. Ann. meeting Oct. 1st; contributing mem. $1000 initiation fee.

Lovis Corinth Prints and Drawings exhibition held at U.S. National Museum of Smithsonian Institution, Washington, D.C, in Apr, 1970; Lovis Corinth traveling exhibition held through Smithsonian Institution at M. H. de Young Museum, San Francisco, Stanford University, Stanford, Calif, and other museums during 1971, 1972 and 1973. Charlotte Berend paintings traveling exhibition held through V.Arsdale at American museums 1972-74. Lovis Corinth Memorial Exhibition held at Indianapolis Museum of Art, 1975.

✠THE METROPOLITAN MUSEUM OF ART
Main Building, Fifth Ave. at 82nd St, 10028. Tel: General Information (212) 736-2211, Museum Offices (212) 879-5500.
The Cloisters, Fort Tryon Park, 10040. Tel: (212) 923-3700
Douglas Dillon, Pres. Board of Trustees
Thomas Hoving, Dir.
Ashton Hawkins, Secy. & Counsel
Arthur Rosenblatt, V.Dir. Architecture & Planning
Philippe de Montebello, V.Dir. Curatorial & Educational Affairs
Daniel K. Herrick, V.Dir. Finance
Ann R. Leven, Treas.
Richard Dougherty, V.Dir. Pub. Affairs
Richard R. Morsches, V.Dir. Operations
Karl Katz, Chmn. for Special Projects
John T. Conger, Mgr. Personnel
John K. Howat, Cur. American Paintings & Sculpture
Berry B. Tracy, Cur. in Charge, American Wing
Morrison H. Heckscher, Cur. American Wing
Vaughn E. Crawford, Cur. in Charge, Ancient Near Eastern Art
Prudence Oliver Harper, Cur. Ancient Near Eastern Art
Helmut Nickel, Cur. Arms & Armor
Jacob Bean, Cur. Drawings
Christine Lilyquist, Cur. Egyptian Art
Henry G. Fischer, Lila Acheson Wallace Cur. in Egyptology
Elizabeth E. Gardner, Cur. European Paintings
Wen Fong, Special Consultant for Far Eastern Affairs
Martin Lerner, Research Fellow Far Eastern Art
Dietrich von Bothmer, Chmn. Greek & Roman Art
Anne M. McCann Taggart, Consultant on Archaeology, Greek & Roman Art
Richard Ettinghausen, Consultative Chmn. Islamic Art
George Szabo, Cur. Robert Lehman Collection
Carmen Gomez-Moreno, Cur. Medieval Art
Laurence Libin, Assoc. Cur. in Charge, Musical Instruments
Douglas Newton, Chmn. Primitive Art
Julie Jones, Cur. Primitive Art
Janet S. Byrne, Cur. Prints & Photographs
Colta Feller Ives, Assoc. Cur. Acting in Charge, Prints & Photographs
Henry Geldzahler, Cur. 20th Century Art
Olga Raggio, Chmn. Western European Arts
Yvonne Hackenbroch, Cur. Western European Arts
James Parker, Cur. Western European Arts
John Brealey, Conservator, Paintings
Merritt Safford, Conservator, Prints & Drawings
Catherine Chance, Assoc. Museum Educ. Community Prog.
David Kusin, Assoc. Museum Educ. High School Prog.
Elizabeth Flinn, Assoc. Museum Educ. in Charge, Junior Museum
Elizabeth R. Usher, Chief Librn, Library
Margaret P. Nolan, Chief Librn, Photograph & Slide Library
Melanie Yaggy Snedcof, Assoc. Museum Educ, Acting in Charge Pub. Educ.
John Buchanan, Registrar
Marica Vilcek, Assoc. Cur. Central Catalog
Hilde Limondjian, Prog. Mgr. Concerts & Lectures
Jerry Mirelli, Mgr. Data Processing
Inge Heckel, Mgr. Development & Promotion
Jack Frizzelle, Mgr. Pub. Information
Bradford D. Kelleher, Publisher
Katharine Stoddert Gilbert, Ed. Bulletin
Leon Wilson, Ed-in-Chief
Stuart Silver, Admin. Design
Charles F. Webberly, Mgr. Office Service
William F. Pons, Mgr. Photograph Studio
Theodore Ward, Mgr. Purchasing
Allen Gore, Assoc. Mgr. in Charge of Security
Joseph P. McMahon, Mgr. Buildings
Main Building open Tues. 10 AM - 8:45 PM; Wed. - Sat. 10 AM - 4 4:45 PM; Sun. 11 AM - 4:45 PM; cl. Mon; pay-what-you-wish admis. policy. Estab. and inc. 1870. Ann. meeting of Corporation Oct; mem. 33,000; dues $25 and higher.

Collections: Covering about 5000 years and representing the arts of Egypt, including the Temple of Dendur, The Ancient Near East, Greece and Rome, Islamic, The Far East, Europe and The United States and the rest of the Americas, including paintings, sculpture, prints, drawings, glass, ceramics, metalwork, furniture, architecture and period rooms, textiles, costumes, arms and armor, musical instruments, etc. Notable collections given or bequeathed include: Benjamin Altman collection of European paintings and decorative arts; Jules S. Bache collection of European paintings and decorative arts; George Blumenthal Collection of Medieval and Renaissance painting and decorative arts; Crosby Brown collection of musical instruments; Michael Friedsam collection of European paintings; Edward S. and Mary Stillman Harkness collection of European paintings, Egyptian art, textiles; H. O. Havemeyer Collection of European paintings; Kress-Hillingdon collection of 18th century French furniture and decorative arts; J. Pierpont Morgan collection of Medieval and Renaissance decorative arts; Catherine D. Wentworth collection of European silver and goldsmiths' work; R. Thornton Wilson collection of European ceramics; Nathan Cummings collection of Pre-Columbian art; John D. Rockefeller, Jr. collection of Chinese porcelains; Stephen C. Clark collection of paintings and drawings; Julia A. Berwind collection of European paintings and decorative arts; Robert Lehman collection of European paintings, drawings and decorative arts; Michael C. Rockefeller collection of primitive art; The Lesley and Emma Sheafer Collection of paintings, furniture and decorative arts; The Harry G. C. Packard Collection of Asian Art.

Exhibitions: (1973) 19th Century American Landscape Paintings; The Painterly Photograph; Masterpieces of Indian Art in the Metropolitan Museum; Dutch Couples: Pair Portraits by Rembrandt and his Contemporaries; Precious Cargoes from the East; Paul Strand Photographs 1915-1968; George Bellows Lithographs; Victorians in Togas: Paintings by Sir Lawrence Alma-Tadema; The World of Balenciaga; Gold; American Paintings and Drawings from the Collection of Mr. and Mrs. Raymond Horowitz; Drawings and Prints by the Carracci; Photographs by Imogene Cunningham; The Art Heritage of Puerto Rico; Helen Frankenthaler Painted Book Covers; An Architect and His Client: Frank Lloyd Wright and Francis W. Little; Nudes in Landscapes; Early Renaissance Sculpture from Northern Italy; Sculpture by Augustus St. Gaudens from the Metropolitan's Collection; In Prayse of the Needle: English Domestic Embroidery 1650-1750; Quoth the Raven: Homage to Edgar Allan Poe; Philip Guston Drawings 1938-1972; Man Ray: Photographs and Rayographs; Giovanni di Paolo Paintings; Abraham Bloemaert: Prints and Drawings; Photographs by Francis Frith and Other Travelers to Egypt and Palestine; The Arts of Ancient China; Understanding Silver; Works by Mary Cassatt from the Metropolitan's Collection; Masterworks from the Museum of the American Indian; Van Gogh as Critic and Self Critic; Sung and Yuan Paintings; Hidden Treasures of Japanese Art: A Selection of Prints, Netsuke and Inro from the Metropolitan Museum; Landscape/Cityscape; The Art of Imperial Turkey and its European Echoes; The Apocalypse; Permanent Installation of the Salon from the Hotel de Cabris; The 10s, 20s, 30s: Inventive Clothes: 1909-1939; Jewelry, Goldsmith's Work and Horology; Masterpieces of Tapestry from the 14th to 16th Century. (1974) From David to Picasso: French Drawings from the Collection of the Metropolitan Museum; Saints and their Legends; 20th Century Accessions, 1967-1974; Photographs by Ansel Adams; Venetian Paintings in The Metropolitan Museum of Art; Twelve Great Quilts from the American Wing; The David and Bathsheba Tapestries; New York City Public Sculpture by 19th Century American Artists; Currier and Ives Lithographs; Indian Miniatures from the Jeffrey Paley Collection; The Art of Oceania; The Belles Heures of Jean, Duke of Berry; A Portfolio of Prints in Honor of Meyer Schapiro; Italian Renaissance Drawings from the Musee du Louvre, Paris; The Grand Gallery; Romantic and Glamorous Hollywood Design; Five Paintings by Maxwell Hendler; The Impressionist Epoch. (1975) The Great Wave: The Influence of Japanese Woodcuts on French Prints; Momoyama: Japanese Art around 1600; The Bronzes of India and Southeast Asia; The Royal Academy Revisited; Paintings by Francis Bacon; The Secular Spirit; Life and Art at the End of the Middle Ages; The Passover Story; From the Lands of the Scythians; Ancient Treasures from the Museums of the U.S.S.R, 3000 B.C. to 100 B.C; Era of Exploration; Opening of the Robert Lehman Collection; French Painting 1774-1830: The Age of Revolution; George Washington: Icon for America; Images of the New World; To Touch and See.

New Installations: Andre Mertens Galleries of Musical Instruments; The Costume Institute; European Paintings Galleries; Far Eastern Galleries; Islamic Art Galleries; Robert Lehman Collection.

Activities: Free lectures on subjects related to the fine arts for adults and children; subscription series of concerts and lectures in the Auditorium for members and public; courses for academic credit in cooperation with Columbia and New York Universities; Auditorium programs for children and high school students. Children's activities available Saturday and Sunday. Gallery tours: Tuesdays - Fridays for school classes, group gallery tours by appointment, gallery tours in Spanish Thursdays and Saturdays.

Library: Collection of 200,000 volumes, 12,000 periodical subscriptions; reference collection of 277,000 black and white photographs and 6100 color prints; lending collection of 166,500 black and white slides and 150,000 color slides. Lending collection open to the public; a rental fee is charged. Sales of photographs of objects in the Museum's collections. In addition to staff and members of the Museum, the Reference Library is also open to students at graduate schools, research workers, and scholars.

Publications: Bulletin, 4 issues a year; Newsletter-Calendar of Events, 6 issues; handbooks and guides of various departments; catalogs of special exhibitions; Scholarly Journal.

Attendance: Calendar years (1973) 2,573,953; (1974) 3,008,540 (These figures include Main Building and The Cloisters).

The Costume Institute
  Stella Blum, Cur. A center for costume research and study.

The Cloisters
  Fort Tryon Park, 10040. Tel: (212) 923-3700
J. L. Schrader, Cur. in Charge
Jane Hayward, Cur.
Open Tues. - Sat. 10 AM - 4:45 PM; Sun. 1 - 4:45 PM; pay-what-you-wish admis. policy. A branch of the Museum opened in 1938, devoted to European medieval art. Among the architectural elements incorporated in the building are four cloisters reconstructed with original stonework from French monasteries, a Romanesque chapel from France, a complete chapter house of the 12th century, a 13th century sculptured portal, and a 12th century Spanish apse.

In this setting are exhibited sculpture, paintings, stained glass, metalwork and furniture of the Middle Ages. Outstanding are the set of 14th century tapestries, the Nine Heroes, and the famous tapestries representing The Hunt of the Unicorn. The Chalice of Antioch, earliest known Christian chalice and two famous Books of Hours from the library of the Duke of Berry are on view in the Treasury. Paintings include the 15th century Altarpiece of the Annunciation with Saint Joseph and donors by Robert Campin, known as the Master of Flemalle. An important addition to the collections was the 14th century, carved ivory Cross from Bury St. Edmunds, England.

The site of The Cloisters, the building, and in large part the collections, are the gifts of John D. Rockefeller, Jr.

MUNICIPAL ART SOCIETY OF NEW YORK*
  41 E. 65th St, 10021. Tel: (212) 628-4553
Brendan Gill, Pres.
Gordon Hyatt, Secy.
Kent Barwick, Exec. Dir.
Estab. 1892, inc. 1898. The Society is the one organization in New York through which the layman, professional and the business firm can work together to encourage high standards for public art, architecture, planning, landscaping and preservation in the five boroughs. Ann. meeting May; mem. about 1200; dues $15 and higher.

MUSEUM OF AMERICAN FOLK ART
  49 W. 53rd St, 10019. Tel: (212) 581-2475
Barbara Johnson, Pres.
Adele Earnest, V.Pres.
Kenneth Page, Secy.
Ralph Esmerian, Treas.
Bruce Johnson, Dir.
Open Tues. - Sun. 10:30 AM - 5:30 PM; cl. Mon; admis. 50¢, under 12 free. Estab. 1961. The Museum is a New York showcase for changing exhibitions presenting various aspects of the American folk artist and his work. Mem. dues, annual $15, family $25, contributing or organizational $100, life $1000.
  Collection: Permanent collection.
  Exhibitions: Five special exhibitions each year.
  Library: For reference only; photograph collection.

MUSEUM OF CONTEMPORARY CRAFTS OF THE AMERICAN
  CRAFTS COUNCIL
  29 W. 53rd St, 10019. Tel: (212) 977-8467, 8468
Mrs. Vanderbilt Webb, Chmn. of the Board
Donald L. Wyckoff, Pres, American Crafts Council
Paul J. Smith, Dir. of Museum
Open Tues. - Sat. 11 AM - 6 PM; Sun. and holidays 1 - 6 PM; admis. 75¢, children (under 12) 25¢; members free; student groups by special appointment, no charge. Estab. 1956.
  Collections: Beginning stages of permanent collection of †20th century American crafts all media.
  Exhibitions: Handcrafts and design, including decorative arts, folkcrafts, technological works; textiles, metal, ceramics, wood, and visitor participation exhibitions.

Research and Education Department
  44 W. 53rd St, 10019.
Lois Moran, Dir.

Maintained by American Crafts Council, including 2000 volume library, biographical/pictorial portfolios for use on the premises; also extensive rental/sales service.
  Attendance: Approx. 90,000.

✣THE MUSEUM OF MODERN ART
  11 W. 53rd St, 10019. Tel: (212) 956-6100
William S. Paley, Chmn. of Board
Gardner Cowles, V.Chmn.
David Rockefeller, V.Chmn.
Mrs. John D. Rockefeller III, Pres.
J. Frederick Byers III, V.Pres.
Mrs. Bliss Parkinson, V.Pres.
Neal J. Farrell, Treas.
Richard E. Oldenburg, Dir. Museum
Richard Koch, Dir. Admin.
William Rubin, Dir. Painting & Sculpture Collection
William S. Lieberman, Dir. Drawings
Riva Castleman, Dir. Prints & Illustrated Books
Arthur Drexler, Dir. Dept. Architecture & Design
John Szarkowski, Dir. Dept. Photography
Edward (Ted) S. Perry, Dir. Dept. Film
Richard Palmer, Coordinator of Exhibitions
Waldo Rasmussen, Dir. International Prog.
William Burback, Special Asst. for Educ.
Carl Morse, Dir. Dept. Publ.
Inga Forslund, Librn.
John Limpert, Dir. Mem. & Development
Elizabeth Shaw, Dir. Pub. Information
Open Mon, Tues, Fri, Sat. & Sun. 11 AM - 6 PM; Thurs. 11 AM - 9 PM; cl. Wed. & Christmas; admis. adults $2, students $1.25, children and senior citizens 75¢; Tues. pay-what-you-wish. Estab. 1929 to help people enjoy, understand, and use the visual arts of our time. Collections and changing exhibitions (drawn from all over the world) include painting and sculpture, architecture, films, prints and illustrated books, photography, drawings, design and other practical applications of today's art. Nonprofit, educational organization supported primarily by admission fees, membership dues, sales of publications and other services and contributions. Mem. 28,000; dues $25 and up (student $15).

Collections: 3000 works of paintings and sculptures; 2600 drawings; 10,000 prints; 800 illustrated books; 3000 posters and graphics; 14,000 photographs; 400 architectural drawings; 60 architectural models; 2500 design objects; 4500 films; 3,000,000 film stills.

Exhibitions: Among exhibitions shown in New York, 1974-1975 were: Miro in the Collection of The Museum of Modern Art; Published in Germany 1923; Unfamiliar Places: A Message from Bill Dane; Giorgio Morandi: Prints; Painters for the Theatre: An Invitation to the Theatre Arts Collection; Portraits; Marcel Duchamp; Projects: Barry Flanagan; Kertesz, Rodchenko, Moholy-Nagy: Photographs from the Collection; Architectural Models from the Collection; Felix Vallotton: Woodcuts of the 1890's; Works on Paper; Recent Acquisitions I: Painting and Sculpture; Projects: Giulio Paolini; Adolph Gottlieb: 1903-1974; Louis Kahn: 1901-1974; New Japanese Photography; Recent Acquisitions II: Painting and Sculpture; The Painting of Gerald Murphy; Projects: Rafael Ferrer; Jacob Israel Avedon: Photographed by Richard Avedon; Printed, Folded, Cut and Torn; Painting and Sculpture; Projects: Sonia Landy Sheridan and Keith Smith; Seurat to Matisse; Drawing in France; Photographs from the Harvard Social Ethics Collection; Recent Drawings Acquisitions; Projects: Marlene Scott V; Projects: Video I; Gods, Heroes and Shepherds; German Drawings: The Expressionists; Arakawa: Recent Prints; Public Landscapes: An Exhibition of Photographs; Projects: Michael Hurson; Projects: Helen Levitt in Color; Works from Change, Inc; Contemporary Soviet Artists; Eight Contemporary Artists; Projects: Translations by Jess; Projects: Video II; Chasubles designed by Henri Matisse; Ludwig Mies van der Rohe: 5 Projects; Furniture by Charles Rennie Mackintosh; Reinstallation of the Collection; American Prints: 1913-1963; Posters in the Penthouse; Lee Friedlander; Projects: John Walker; Edward Weston; Projects: Video III; Furniture from the Design Collection; Projects: Loren Madsen; Joseph Koudelka: Photographs; Lucas Samaras; Points of View; Architectural Studies and Projects; In the Twenties; Projects: Ger van Elk; Walker Evans: 1903-1975; Five Recent Acquisitions; Anthony Caro; Projects: Video IV; From the D. W. Griffith Collection; Irving Penn Recent Works; Prints by Sculptors; Barbara Hepworth Memorial; Milton Glaeser; Tinguely: La Vittoria; Jacques Villon: 1875-1975; Projects: Video V; Modern Masters: Manet to Matisse; Picture Puzzles; Drawings: Recent Acquisitions; 76 Jefferson; Projects: Walter Pichler; Printsequence; The Architecture of the Ecole des Beaux-Arts; Projects: Video VI; New Design Acquisitions; Eugene Buechel, S.J: Rosebud and Pine Ridge Photographs, 1922-42. Selections from the collection are always on view on the 2nd and 3rd floors, on the ground floor, and in the Museum's Sculpture Garden.

Films: Films presented in conjunction with Marcel Duchamp exhibition; Henry Hathaway; Warner Bros; Panavision Day; James

Broughton; Argos Films; New Acquisitions; Special Thursday evening, Murray Lerner: Two films concerning popular music festivals; Soviet Silent Cinema, Part 1: 1916-1925; New Directors/New Films; Raoul Walsh; New Mexican Cinema; Special Acquisition; Metro-Goldwyn-Mayer: 1924-1974; Happy 80th Birthday, Jean Renoir; Yakuza Films; Zagreb '74 in New York; French Critics Week; New Swiss Films; The Wedding March; D. W. Griffith Centennial Part 1: The Biograph Films, 1908-1913; Films on Edward Weston; The Films of Francesco Rosi; Perspectives on French Cinema; D. W. Griffith Centennial Part 2: The Feature Films, 1914-1931; Emile de Antonio; Re-View; John Ford in the Collection, 1917-1937; Happy Birthday, John Randolph Bray; A Day with Voskovec - Werich; John and Faith Hubley; Recent Films from West Germany; Soviet Silent Cinema, Part 2: 1926-1927; Films from the German Democratic Republic. Continuing film programs include: Films from the Archive; Requests from the Archive; History of Film; What's Happening? (films exploring current social and political issues); Shorts and Documentaries; Cineprobe (experimental films by independent filmmakers); Films for Young People.

Activities: Film showings, international in scope, illustrating the historic and esthetic development of the motion picture; lectures; symposia; summer concerts; art lending service; national circulating exhibitions; circulating film programs.

Library: 30,000 titles in 16 languages on the modern visual arts. Reference collection of 100,000 photographs. Bookstores for publications, reproductions, postcards, note and seasonal cards, posters, slides, appointment calendars, gift items.

Publications: 78 books in print on exhibitions, artists, monographs and catalogs.

Attendance: Approx. 1,000,000.

Affiliated Organizations: International Council of The Museum of Modern Art; Junior Council of The Museum of Modern Art.

MUSEUM OF THE AMERICAN INDIAN
Heye Foundation
Broadway at 155th St, 10032. Tel: (212) 283-2420
Dr. Frederick J. Dockstader, Dir.
Free 1 - 5 PM; cl. Mon. & holidays and the month of Aug. Estab. 1916; building opened 1922. Mem. 1000; $15 to $1000.

Collections: World's largest collection of art and culture of the Indians of North, Central, and South America, West Indies, and the Eskimo. Outstanding collections of Pre-Columbian art and historical materials. Extensive collection of photographs and Kodachrome slides pertaining to Indian art. All collections being added to regularly from special purchase funds.

Exhibitions: Temporary and permanent exhibitions of all phases of Indian life; regular special and annual shows; research facilities available to qualified scholars. Special exhibits feature American Indian art.

Activities: Bookshop with wide selection of original art works.
Library: 40,000 volumes.
Publications: Active publication program on regular basis.
Attendance: 75,000.

MUSEUM OF THE CITY OF NEW YORK
1220 Fifth Ave. between 103rd to 104th Sts, 10029.
Tel: (212) 534-1672
Louis Auchincloss, Pres.
Mrs. Randolph B. Marston, Secy.
Joseph Veach Noble, Dir.
Richard Haberlen, Asst. Dir.
Jacqueline Adams, Pub. Relations
Albert K. Baragwanath, Senior Cur, Librn. & Cur. Portraits & Prints, Military, Marine & Fire
Margaret Stearns, Cur Decorative Arts
Jo Anne Olian, Cur. Costumes
Theodore H. Fetter, Cur. Theatre & Music
John Noble, Cur. of Toys
Billie Nielsen, Dean of Educ. Dept.
Anne Goodman, Sales Desk
Charlotte LaRue, Photo Library
Free Tues. - Sat. 10 AM - 5 PM; Sun. & holidays 1 - 5 PM; on holiday Mondays, open 1 - 5 PM; cl. Mon. & Christmas. Estab. and inc. 1923 as a nonprofit corporation, to illustrate the culture and history of the City of New York. Present building opened 1932. Ann. meeting Jan; mem. approx. 1750; dues student $10, individual $15, family $25, contributing $50, supporting $100, sustaining $500, patron $1000, life $5000.

Collections: Many thousand items of outstanding costumes, period 1880-1930 most heavily represented; furniture including research collection on Duncan Phyfe and John Henry Belter; silver, by New York City silversmiths; decorative arts; fire fighting equipment; manuscripts and maps; marine memorabilia, ship models; portraits and miniatures; prints, photographs, reproductions; half a million views of New York City—the Harry T. Peters Collection of Currier & Ives, the Percy C. Byron photographs, 1885-1930, the Jacob A. Riis photographs, 1877-1910; Garvan Collection of Street Cries by

N. Calyo; J. Clarence Davies Collection, all media and periods; theatrical and musical memorabilia, the most extensive and comprehensive collection of New York City material in existence, including largest collection of the works of Robert Edmond Jones; theatre library 4000 volumes together with the Dazian Library; toys and doll houses, including Stettheimer doll house; dioramas; military memorabilia. All collections relate to the City of New York.

Exhibitions: (Permanent) The Dutch Galleries, an exciting presentation relating and communicating the social, political, and economic aspects of the settlement of New Amsterdam; other permanent exhibitions include period alcoves and costumes, prints and photographs, portraits, furniture by New York cabinet-makers, silver, toys, shop models, theatrical memorabilia, maps, fire engines, and dioramas that vividly recreate important events relating to New York City from the time Verrazzano sailed into the harbor until the present day. CITYRAMA, a new type of multi-media, audiovisual exhibition utilizing authentic three-dimensional objects to trace the history of New York from 1524 to the present. The museum has an active special exhibition program, the purpose of which is to highlight parts of the museum's vast collection not on permanent exhibition and artifacts that are timely in subject matter.

Activities: Cooperative program with N.Y. Public Schools, lecture, demonstration (Please Touch), gallery tour for school classes by appointment; Sat. puppet shows and Please Touch demonstrations for adults and children; Sun. concerts; walking tours, pointing out historical and architectural landmarks in selected neighborhoods of New York, for adults, and children, every other Sun. from April through Oct. (request Walking Tour brochure); Sales desk, including mail order.

Library: Reference library open by appointment; 10,000 volumes; 25,000 manuscripts.

Publications: Annual Report; bi-monthly Calendar of Events.
Attendance: (1971) 435,500; (1972) 439,400.

NATIONAL ACADEMY OF DESIGN
1083 Fifth Ave, 10028. Tel: (212) 369-4880
Umberto Romano, Secy.
Alice G. Melrose, Dir.
Open during exhibitions 1 - 5 PM. Estab. 1825, inc. 1828. Ann. meeting Mar; mem. 194 Academicians, 157 associates; no dues. Owns building, opened 1942. Library.

Collections: Permanent collection includes portrait of and a work by every Academician from S. F. B. Morse, the first President, to the present day.

Exhibitions: Annual exhibitions, jury; awards, open to nonmembers. Other societies hold their exhibitions in the Academy's building.

Other organizations having headquarters in the building are: American Water Color Society; Artists Fellowship; Society of American Graphic Artists; Audubon Artists; the L. C. Tiffany Foundation. Maintains National Academy School of Fine Arts at 5 E. 89th St. (See Schools)

THE NATIONAL ARTS CLUB GALLERY*
15 Gramercy Park South, 10003 & 119 E. 19th St, 10003.
Tel: (212) 475-3424
Walter Borten, Pres.
Gallery free 12 AM - 7 PM incl. Sun; cl. Mon. Estab. and inc. 1898, to promote the mutual acquaintance of art lovers and art workers; to assist talented artists; encourage discussions relating to the arts and to maintain in the City of New York a building having facilities to promote the enjoyment of the arts including studio rooms and a gallery for exhibitions, concerts and other presentations of the arts. Ann. meeting May; mem. approx. 600; owns clubhouse containing galleries, restaurant and adjoining studio building.

Collections: Paintings and sculpture by life members.
Exhibitions: Annual exhibition of painting and sculpture by members in Jan; watercolor, oil, sculpture exhibitions (members and non-members) with prizes and awards. Special exhibitions.

Library: Maintains a comprehensive library on art and kindred subjects.

Activities; Lectures, music programs and dramatic presentation; art classes. Cooperates with other art organizations in allowing them use of the facilities for meetings and art presentations.

NATIONAL ASSOCIATION OF WOMEN ARTISTS, INC.
156 Fifth Ave, 10010. Tel: (212) 675-1616
Esther K. Gayner, Pres.
Beverly Boxer, Exec. Secy.
Estab. 1889 as the Women's Art Club of New York; known as National Association of Women Painters and Sculptors from 1914 to 1941, when present name was adopted. Ann. meeting May; general meeting Nov; mem. about 700 in 44 states; dues exhibitors $20, assoc. $25.

Exhibitions: Annual members' exhibition in Spring with awards; annual traveling exhibitions of oils, watercolors, graphics; Annual foreign exchange exhibition.

Activities: Demonstrations and lectures at annual exhibition.

Publication: Annual Exhibition Catalog.

NATIONAL INSTITUTE FOR ARCHITECTURAL EDUCATION
20 W. 40th St, 10018. Tel: (212) 684-1948
Hugh N. Romney, Chmn. Board of Trustees
Byron Bell, V.Chmn.
Herman C. Litwack, Secy.
Sidney L. Katz, Treas.
Howard H. Juster, Dir. of Educ.
Lilian Marus, Exec. Secy.
For further information see p. 9.

NATIONAL INSTITUTE OF ARTS AND LETTERS
633 W. 155th St, 10032. Tel: (212) 286-1480
Harrison E. Salisbury, Pres.
William Meredith, Secy.
Ross Lee Finney, Treas.
Margaret M. Mills, Exec. Dir.
Lydia Kaim, Admin. Asst.
Open 1 - 4 PM during exhibitions. Estab. 1898 by the American Social Science Association; inc. 1913 by Act of Congress for the furtherance of literature and the fine arts in the United States. Ann. meeting Jan; no dues; mem. limited to 250 persons, chosen for notable achievement in art, music and literature.

Occupies headquarters in the building of the American Academy of Arts and Letters with which it cooperates in holding six or more exhibitions a year, an annual ceremonial, and conducts a program of Art Awards. The Institute also awards The Gold Medal for Graphic Art, Painting, Sculpture and Architecture, rotating each every fifth year; the Marjorie Peabody Waite Award for art, given every 3rd year; the Arnold W. Brunner Award for Architecture and the Richard and Hinda Rosenthal Award for Painting, given annually. Awards may not be applied for.

The Institute publishes jointly with the American Academy of Arts and Letters annual Proceedings and exhibition catalogs. The Library of the Institute and the Academy also includes books by and about members of the Department of Art.

✠NATIONAL SOCIETY OF INTERIOR DESIGNERS
See American Society of Interior Designers, p. 4.

✠NATIONAL SOCIETY OF MURAL PAINTERS, INC.*
41 E. 65th St, 10021.   Tel: (212) 988-7700
Buell Mullen, Pres.
Dean Fausett, 1st V.Pres.
Alton Tobey, 2nd V.Pres.
John Manship, Secy.
Anthoney Toney, Treas.
Estab. and inc. 1895 to encourage and advance the standards of Mural Painting in America; to formulate a code for decorative competitions and by-laws to regulate professional practice. Ann. meeting Apr; mem. 150; dues $15, non-res. $10.

Activities: Annual Bulletin of photographs of contemporary work of members; biographies and articles pertinent to the mural painting profession. Exhibitions held in collaboration with allied professions. Ernest Piexotto Prize awarded to young artists for work in relation to architecture. The Society is a constituent member of the Fine Arts Federation of New York, of the American Federation of Arts and of the United States Committee of the International Association of Art (an affiliate of UNESCO).

NATIONAL SOCIETY OF PAINTERS IN CASEIN AND ACRYLIC, INC.
1083 Fifth Ave, 10028
Mark Freeman, Pres.
Mina Kocherthaler & Howard Mandel, Co-V.Pres.
Lily Shuff, Corresp. Secy.
Constance Scharff, Recording Secy.
Ralph Fabri, Founding Pres.
Elias Newman, Hon. Pres.
Estab. 1952 to afford artists an opportunity to exhibit paintings in casein and acrylic, regardless of style, technique, etc. Accepted as an educational organization by the New York Department of State, Albany; nonprofit organization since Feb, 1960. Legacies, devises, transfers or gifts to or for the Society are deductible for Federal estate and gift purposes under the provisions of Sections 2055, 2106 and 2522 of the Code. Ann. meeting Apr. or May; mem. 90; dues $15.

Exhibitions: 8th Annual, National Arts Club, 1962; 9th Annual, Riverside Museum, 1963; 10th Anniversary Show, National Arts Club, 1964. All annuals thru 1972 held at National Arts Club with medals and over $1000 in cash awarded in each. In recent exhibitions approx. 115 artists from 22 states participated. The 23rd annual exhibition will be held in the galleries of the National Academy of Design, Dec, 1976.

Activities: Lectures; gallery talks and painting demonstrations during exhibitions; individual paintings lent to schools, traveling exhibitions arranged.

NATIONAL SCULPTURE SOCIETY
75 Rockefeller Plaza, 10019. Tel: (212) 582-5564
Robert A Weinman, Pres.
Claire Stein, Exec. Dir.
Open to public Mon. - Fri. 9 AM - 5 PM. Estab. 1893, inc. 1896 to foster the development and appreciation of sculpture in the United States. Ann. meeting 2nd Tues. in Jan; mem. approx. 350; mem. categories, fellow, member (both sculptors), allied professionals (chiefly architects), patrons; dues patrons $50, fellows $20, mem. and nonres. fellows $15, nonres mem. $10.

Exhibitions: Annual exhibition of sculpture in the round and relief, open to all sculptors in the United States. Prizes include gold, silver and bronze medals, $500 Hexter prize, $300 Richard prize for portraits, $200 Dietsch prize, $150 Lindsey Morris prize for relief, Mrs. Louis Bennet prize for relief ($50), other additional ones from time to time. Traveling exhibitions of photographic enlargements of sculpture circulated free of charge; sponsors other exhibitions.

Awards: In addition to the exhibition awards listed above, $500 and $250 youth awards, scholarships to National Academy of Design in New York, Pennsylvania Academy of Fine Art. The Medal of Honor awarded to individuals for notable achievement in and for encouragement to American sculpture. The Herbert Adams Memorial Medal to those who make notable contributions in the promotion of art. The Henry Hering Memorial Medal awarded when the occasion warrants for outstanding collaboration between architect, owner and sculptor.

Activities: The Society maintains a photographic file of members' work in the office and one at the Frick Art Reference Library, and answers technical and historical questions relevant to American sculpture. Maintains an advisory committee to assist any person or group planning public or private sculpture; advises on establishing rules for competitions, copyright information is shared, carries on an educational program through endowments and gifts. Assists in research and collects archival materials about American sculptors.

Publications: National Sculpture Review, quarterly magazine; Enduring Memory; past exhibition catalogs.

✠NEW SCHOOL FOR SOCIAL RESEARCH*
66 W. 12th St, 10011.
John R. Everett, Pres.
Allen Austill, Dean
Julian Levi, Chmn, Art Workshops
Paul Mocsanyi, Dir, Art Center
Exhibits of New School Art Center, located at 65 Fifth Avenue, free (please call OR5-2700 for hours). A university for adults estab. 1919, to advance education of both the scholar and the layman, with work centering in the social sciences and the humanities. Includes large non-credit program; Graduate Faculty of Political and Social Science, Center for New York City Affairs and undergraduate New School College. In 1970, the Parsons School of Design affiliated with The New School. Occupies six buildings, dedicated 1931, 1956, 1959, 1969, and 1972. Mural decorations by Thomas Hart Benton, Jose Clemente Orozco, Camilo Egas, Michel Cadoret and Gonzalo Fonseca.

Collections: †Sculpture including works by Lipchitz, Hadzi, Noguchi, Penalba, Baskin, Zogbaum, Konzal, Lipton, King, Gross, Trajan and others. Paintings by Rattner, Carlo Dolci, Cleve Gray, Youngoman.

Publications: Monthly Bulletin; Social Research quarterly.

Attendance: 17,000.

NEW YORK CHAMBER OF COMMERCE*
65 Liberty St, 10005. Tel: (212) 732-1123
Thomas N. Stainbach, Exec. V.Pres.
Miss A. Randolfi, Librn.
Free 9:30 - 11:30 AM & 2 - 4:30 PM by applying at office. Estab. 1768. Ann. meeting May; mem. 1800.

Collections: Portraits of business leaders of the United States from the late 18th century to the present.

Library: Approx. 10,000 volumes.

Publications: Irregular.

NEW YORK HISTORICAL SOCIETY
170 Central Park West (77th St.), 10024. Tel: (212) 873-3400
Robert G. Goelet, Pres.
Robert S. Beekman, M.D, Secy.
James J. Heslin, Dir.
Richard J. Koke, Cur. Museum
Kathleen Luhrs, Ed.
Mary Black, Cur. Paintings, Sculpture & Decorative Arts

Joyce M. Crawford, Supvr. Educ. & Pub. Relations
Robert Muntmer, Supt. Building
Free 1 - 5 PM; Sat. 10 AM - 5 PM; Sun. 1 - 5 PM; cl. Mon. Estab.
1804, inc. 1809, to collect and preserve whatever may relate to the
history of the United States in general and New York in particular,
and to carry on educational work in the field of American history.
Present building erected 1908; wings opened 1939. Maintains art
gallery, museum and library. Mem. about 1500; dues $20 and
higher.

Collections: †Over 3000 American portraits in oil, miniatures
and sculpture; 19th century American landscapes; Old Master paintings of the Italian, early Flemish and Dutch, French, English, German and Spanish schools. The Society's paintings derive largely
from the New York Gallery of Fine Arts (1858); Thomas J. Bryan
collection of Old Masters (1867); Louis Durr collection of European
and American paintings (1822); and Peter Marie collection of miniatures of prominent women of New York (1905). Perhaps the greatest
jewel of the Society's art gallery is the unique collection of 433 original watercolor drawings by John James Audubon for his elephant
folio Birds of America.

Exhibitions: †From the Society's permanent collections of Early
American glass, china, pottery, pewter, silver, dolls, and toys;
household utensils, lighting devices; John Rogers' sculpture; costume
figurines; the J. Insley Blair collection of historic kerchiefs; the
Prentis collection of New England colonial furniture in three period
rooms; The New York Fire Department; and a gallery of New York
coaches of the late 19th century. All collections except Old Masters
currently enlarged by gift and purchase.

Activities: Lectures; demonstrations; films for school children
and adults; concerts.

Library: 600,000 bound volumes; 200,000 pamphlets and 10,000
volumes of newspapers; large collections of manuscripts, prints,
drawings, photographs, maps, broadsides and caricatures.

Income and Expenditures: Income $808,000, expenditures
(budget) $1,142,850; purchases $100,000.

Publications: Quarterly and occasional volumes.

Attendance: 375,000.

NEW YORK PUBLIC LIBRARY
Astor, Lenox and Tilden Foundations
Fifth Ave. & 42nd St, 10018. Tel: (212) 790-6262
Richard C. Couper, Pres.
John M. Cory, Dir.
Estab. 1895. Book collection over 8,500,000 (Central Research Li-
brary, over 5,000,000; Branch Libraries, over 3,500,000).
†Prints Division, Room 308
Elizabeth Roth, Cur.
Free, for information about hours call 661-7220. Estab. 1899; admis.
by application to Research Libraries; Administrative Office estab.
1899.

Total number of prints and drawings about 162,000. Represents
all periods and media, 15th - 20th centuries. Special emphasis on the
American print. Study of print appreciation, print history and pro-
cesses are featured. Extensive exhibitions always on view.
†Spencer Collection, Room 324
Joseph T. Rankin, Cur.
Free, for information about hours call 661-7220; admis. by applica-
tion to Research Libraries; Administrative Office estab. 1917.

A choice collection (8000 volumes) of illuminated medieval and
Renaissance manuscripts and illustrated books from the 15th to 20th
centuries, representative of the history of book and manuscript
illustration.
†Art Division, Room 313
Donald Anderle, Chief
Free, for information about hours call 661-7220.

Over 100,000 books covering the fine and applied arts. Large col-
lection of ephemeral biographical and illustrative material, filed
under artists and subjects. Large color reproductions.
†Schomburg Center for Research in Black Culture, 103 W. 135th
St, 10030
Jean Blackwell Hutson, Cur.
Free Mon. - Wed. 10 AM - 8 PM; Thurs. - Sat. 10 AM - 6 PM; cl.
Sun. & holidays.

The largest collection (55,000 volumes; 250,000 archives) in the
country of books on black culture and art. Permanent collection of
African art.
†Picture Collection, Room 73
Lenore Cowan, Cur.
Free Mon, Wed. & Fri. 10 AM - 5:45 PM; Tues. & Thurs. Noon -
7:45 PM; cl. Sat, Sun. & holidays. Estab. 1915.

Approximately 2,250,000 classified pictures encyclopedic in sub-
ject scope may be borrowed by those who live, work or study in New
York State except for exhibition of classroom use.
†Donnell Library Center Art Library, 20 W. 53rd St, 10019.
Rebecca Siekevitz, Librn.
Free Mon. - Thurs. 9:30 AM - 8:30 PM; Fri. & Sat. 9:30 AM - 5:30
PM; cl. Sun. & holidays.

Over 13,000 circulating books and 2800 reference volumes
covering the fine and applied arts. Vertical files of catalogs and
clippings on contemporary artists and art movements. Over 00
periodicals for reference use.
†General Library and Museum of the Performing Arts, 111 Amsterdam Ave, 10023. Tel: (212) 799-2200
Dr. Robert Henderson, Chief
Free Mon. & Thurs. 10 AM - 9 PM; Tues, Wed. & Fri. 10 AM - 6 PM;
Sat. Noon - 6 PM; cl. Sun. & holidays.

Reference collections in dance, music and theatre, plus a circulating library of books, scores, and recordings in the performing
arts. There are four galleries, in addition to museum areas, which
hold exhibitions relating to the performing arts. A variety of free
performing arts programs, seminars, etc. offered in auditorium
seating 200.

NEW YORK SOCIETY LIBRARY
53 E. 79th St, 10021. Tel: (212) 288-6900
Sylvia C. Hilton, Librn.
Free for reference 9 AM - 5 PM; cl. Sun. and holidays; summer cl.
Sat. Estab. 1754, inc. 1772; free reference service; circulation of
books limited to subscribers and shareholders. Ann. meeting last
Tues. in Apr; mem. 2128; dues $27 a year; $18 for six months.

The †John C. Green collection contains illustrated reference
books on painting, costume, decoration and ornament. Library has
180,000 volumes. Art; Americana and New York historical sources;
biography and travel; belles lettres, etc.

Publications: Informal history of the library since 1907; New
Books, bulletins bi-monthly; Annual Report.

Income and Purchases: Income $262,780; purchases (books,
binding, and periodicals) $29,542.

NEW YORK SOCIETY OF ARCHITECTS
101 Park Ave, 10017. Tel: (212) 683-2244
M. Milton Glass, Pres.
Robert A. Brisson, Secy.
Margot A. Henkel, Exec. Dir.
Open 11 AM - 4 PM. Inc. 1906. Ann. meeting Dec, lecture meetings
monthly; mem. approx. 500; res. mem. dues $40.

Activities: Conducted through 25 committees; awards medals to
outstanding architectural students.

Library: New York City Building Codes 1910 to present.

Publications: Bulletin, monthly; Architects, annually; New York
City Building Code Manual, annually; New York City Electrical Code,
annually; New York City Fire Prevention Code, annually.

NEW YORK UNIVERSITY
Washington Square, 10003
(For educational activities see Schools)
Founded in 1831, New York University has the largest graduate
and professional enrollment of any private university in the nation.
The university offers more than 2500 courses leading to more than
20 different degrees. Its 13 schools, colleges and divisions are located at five major centers in Manhattan. New York University also
administers Town Hall, the celebrated midtown cultural center.

✠New York University Art Collection
1 Washington Square Village, 10012. Tel: (212) 598-3479
Ruth Bowman, Cur.
Joy Gordon, Asst. Cur. Educ.
Howard Conant, Chmn. Art Collection Comt.
Estab. 1958, the Collection is installed throughout the University as
an environmental collection, in lounge areas of the student centers
and dormitories, in seminar rooms, and in faculty and administrative offices. Maintained by gifts and University appropriation.

Collections: Approx. 2000 paintings, sculptures, drawings, prints
and photographs, primarily 20th century, acquired almost entirely
through donations from artists, alumni and friends of the University,
approved by the Art Collection Committee.

Exhibitions: Special exhibitions coordinated for classes and
seminars within the University; loan shows to other universities and
museums.

Activities: Gallery talks by the curator; panel discussions; lectures.

✠Grey Art Gallery and Study Center
100 Washington Square E, 10003.
Tel: (212) 598-3479
Joy L. Gordon, Cur. & Acting Dir.
Jane Sharrard, Admin. Secy.
Liz Papageorgiou, Registrar
Howard Conant, Head, Art Collection Comt.
Free Mon. - Thurs. 11 AM - 6 PM; Sat. Noon - 4 PM. Collection
estab. 1958; Grey Art Gallery and Study Center estab. 1974; the gift
of Abby Weed Grey of St. Paul, the Grey Art Gallery and Study
Center opened in Apr, 1975, the first such facility at a major uni-
versity in the city. It will bring under one roof New York Univer-
sity's extensive but scattered collection of 20th century art objects

and some 500 contemporary Asian and Middle Eastern works presented by Mrs. Grey. Gallery has changing exhibitions relating to interdisciplinary courses throughout the University, and open to the public. Exhibitions supported with slide shows, talks, films, etc.

Collections: Over 2500 works, primarily 20th century American and European, with new collection of over 500 contemporary Asian and Middle Eastern paintings, drawings and sculpture.

Exhibitions: Contemporary Asian and Middle Eastern Art; Lion Rugs from Fars (Southern Iran); Report from SoHo (artists work from the SoHo District NY); Irish Directions (contemporary art from Ireland); American Realism: 1920-1960 - from the Sara Roby Foundation Collection.

Activities: Individual paintings lent to other museums and galleries for formal exhibitions; original objects of art lent; lectures open to public.

NICHOLAS ROERICH MUSEUM
319 W. 107th St, 10025. Tel: (202) 864-7752
Katherine Campbell Stibbe, Pres.
Elina Yussupoff, Secy.
Sina Fosdick, Exec. V.Pres.
Joseph Weed
Robert Leser
Dorothy Blalock
Dr. D. Fogel
Svetoslav Roerich
Elisabeth Fogel
Edgar Lansbury
Ingeborg Fritschi
Free, daily 2 - 5 PM; cl. Sat. & holidays. Estab. 1958 to show a permanent collection of paintings of Nicholas Roerich, internationally known artist, to promote his ideals as a great thinker, writer, humanitarian, scientist, explorer, to promote his Pact and The Banner of Peace; financed by membership. Gallery in which works of contemporary artists are shown. Mem. dues, assoc. $10, contributing $25, sustaining $50.

Collections: †Nicholas Roerich Collection.
Exhibitions: Paintings, watercolors and graphics.
Activities: Literature and pamphlets freely distributed to countries, scholars, students, artists and cultural institutions; lectures open to the public; several visiting lecturers per year; many gallery talks and tours; concerts.
Library: Pamphlets and publications being catalogued for reference; photograph collection for reference; colored reproductions; postcards.
Publications: Literature, books, pamphlets pertaining to Nicholas Roerich.
Attendance: Approx. 5000.

THE ONCE GALLERY, INC.
Automation House
49 E. 68th St, 10021. Tel: (212) 628-1010
Alfred S. Goldfield, Pres.
Clare Fisher, Dir.
Free 10 AM - 5 PM; cl. Sun. & major holidays. A nonprofit, nonmembership service organization inc. May, 1974, opened Nov, 1974, to provide first one-person exhibits for artists who have not shown in New York City at no cost to artists. Exhibitors chosen by panel of professional curators. Funded by corporations, foundations, private donors, etc. Governed by Board of Directors and Advisory Board of prominent persons in the arts.
Exhibitions: Charles O'Connor; Jim Alinder; Dale Chisman; George Richmond.
Activities: Planned panel discussions; lectures; symposiums.
Publications: Catalog of each exhibit.
Attendance: 3500 (annual estimate).

THE PEN AND BRUSH, INC.
16 E. Tenth St, 10003. Tel: (212) 475-3669
Harriet M. Hagerty, Pres.
Amanda Van Der Voort, 1st V.Pres.
Rosemary Harris, Recording Secy.
Margaret Sussman, Corresp. Secy.
Margaret W. Martin, Exec. Secy.
Janice Lourie, Treas.
Open 1 - 5 PM except holidays during exhibitions. Estab. 1893, inc. 1912; clubhouse purchased 1923, contains rooms, dining room and exhibition galleries. Ann. meeting Feb; mem. about 250 professional women writers, artists, sculptors, and craftsmen.
Exhibitions: Ten annual exhibitions of members' work; occasional one-man shows.
Activities: Lectures and workshops.
Library: 1500 volumes; fiction, non fiction by members, plus reference and current best sellers.

✤PIERPONT MORGAN LIBRARY
29 E. 36th St, 10016. Tel: (212) 685-0008
Henry S. Morgan, Pres.
Haliburton Fales, Secy.
Charles Ryskamp, Dir.
Francis S. Mason, Jr, Asst. Dir.
Priscilla C. Barker, Asst. to Dir.
Hugh J. Hubbard, Admin. Asst.
Miss Elizabeth Dodd, Registrar & Secy.
Dr. Curt F. Buhler, Research Fel. for Texts Emeritus
Dr. Paul Needham, Cur. Printed Books & Bindings
Dr. John H. Plummer, Cur. Mediaeval & Renaissance Manuscripts; Research Fel.
William Voelkle, Assoc. Cur. Mediaeval & Renaissance Manuscripts;
Miss Felice Stampfle, Cur. Drawings & Prints
Mrs. Cara Dufour Denison, Assoc. Cur. Drawings & Prints
Dr. Edith Porada, Hon. Cur. Seals & Tablets
Herbert Cahoon, Cur. Autograph Manuscripts & Later Printed Books; Dir. Library Services.
Reginald Allen, Cur. of Gilbert & Sullivan Collection
Gerald Gottlieb, Cur. Ball Collection of Children's Books
Evelyn Semler, Reference Librn. & Asst. Cur. Heineman Collection
Robert Riggs Kerr, Supvr. Catalog
Anne Gallagher, Reference Assoc.
Alexander Jensen Yow, Conservator
Mrs. Patricia Reyes, Asst. Conservator
Miss Deborah Evetts, Bookbinder
Charles Passela, Supv. Photography
Mrs. Marie Blankenship, Sales Desk Mgr.
Free Tues. - Sat. 10:30 AM - 5 PM; Sun. 1 - 5 PM; July, open Tues. - Fri. 10:30 AM - 5 PM; cl. Aug. Reading Room open Mon. - Fri, incl. Aug. Estab. and inc. 1924; endowed and collection placed in custody of a Board of Trustees by the late J. P. Morgan.
Collections: †Illuminated manuscripts, †autograph manuscripts, letters and documents; †printed books from c. 1450; †bookbindings; †original drawings from 14th to 19th centuries; †Rembrandt etchings; †modern calligraphy; mezzotints; art objects.
Library: Reference library; cards for use of Reading Room issued to accredited scholars. Occasional lectures. Special exhibitions.

PRINT COUNCIL OF AMERICA
National Gallery of Art, Washington, DC, 20565
For information see p. 50.

PRINTMAKING WORKSHOP
114 W. 17th St, 10011. Tel: (212) 989-6125
Robert Blackburn, Dir.
Madeleine-Claude Jobrack, Mgr.
Anthony Kirk, Workshop Foreman
Open weekdays 8 AM - 11 PM; weekends 9 AM - 5 PM. Estab. 1949 as a workshop space for artists to print etchings and lithographs; night classes and edition printing; financed by endowment, city and state appropriation and membership. Gallery maintained with 2000 contemporary prints for sale and exhibition rental. Mem. 800; dues vary.
Exhibitions: Wilkes Barre, Pa; The American Federation of the Arts Traveling Show; Queensboro College; many galleries and universities.
Activities: Classes in graphic arts; material available to local areas with mobile print programs; traveling exhibitions organized and circulated; original objects of art lent; lectures open to public; classes for adults, scholarships.

SALMAGUNDI CLUB
47 Fifth Ave, 10003. Tel: (212) 255-7740
Martin Hannon, Pres.
Ruth R. Reininghaus, Corresp. Secy.
Gallery free during exhibitions 1 - 6 PM. Estab. 1871, inc. 1880. Ann. meeting Apr; mem. 600; dues res. artists $212, res. layman, $288; nonres. artist $162, nonres layman $174, junior $120. Scholarship, graduated in scale.
Building purchased 1917. Clubhouse, with living quarters (for men), restaurant, gallery and library of over 6000 volumes with notable books on art. Collection of paintings by members. The Salmagundi Club also acts as the organizing and screening agency between the U.S. Navy and all qualified American artists. Under its Naval Art Cooperation and Liaison (NACAL) Committee, artists are chosen and sent on short painting trips around the world to interpret the daily life and traditions of the U.S. Navy.
Activities: Seven exhibitions each year by artist members with cash awards; regular schedule of art demonstrations, lectures, art classes, etc.

Publications: 1972 Centennial Roster (includes all past and present members from 1871 to date); Salmagundi Membership Roster (every two years); Salmagundian (monthly except for summer months).

SCALAMANDRE MUSEUM OF TEXTILES*

201 E. 58th St, 10022. Tel: (212) 361-8500
Franco Scalamandre, Founder & Pres.
Serena Hartian, Dir.
Free 9 AM - 5 PM; cl. Sat. & Sun, also national holidays. Estab. 1947 to encourage interest in Textile design for decoration.

Collections: 2000 old documentary pieces of textile; reproductions of old textiles; contemporary textiles showing modern motifs in textured weaves of today.

Activities: Traveling Exhibits in the various periods of decorative art for circulation throughout the United States to museums only; 15 Small Students Exhibits for art schools, colleges (must be requested by faculty member). Permanent display of textiles used in †Historic Restorations; lectures given on History of Textile Design, including the Classification of Textiles, both Period and Modern.

SCHOOL OF VISUAL ARTS LIBRARY

214 E. 21st St, 10010. Tel: (212) 679-7350, Exten. 67, 68
Zuki Landau, Chief Librn.
Vanessa Lynn, Asst. Librn.
Susan Kramer, Slide Librn.
Open Mon. - Thurs. 9 AM - 7:30 PM; Fri. 9 AM - 5 PM for students and faculty only. Estab. 1961 to serve needs of School of Visual Arts students and faculty; financed by tuition.

Collections: †Art history, fine and graphic arts, commercial art, films, photography and humanities; 20,000 Kodachromes in lending collection; 10,000 volumes for lending and reference; 10 large drawers in picture collection; approx. 700 pamphlets.

Publications: Accessions lists, monthly.

SCULPTORS GUILD, INC.

75 Rockefeller Plaza, 10019. Tel: (212) 484-6382
Herbert Kallem, Pres.
Cleo Hartwig, Exec. Dir.
Sidney Simon, V.Pres.
Elizabeth Klavun, Exec. Secy.
Chaim Gross, Treas.
A nonprofit organization estab. in 1937 to maintain a high standard in presenting works expressing all aspects of the constantly evolving and varying sculptural scene. The Sculptors Guild does not try to mold public taste; it tries to present a wide variety of excellent contemporary sculpture. Ann. meeting May; mem. 100; dues $20.

Exhibitions: Annual exhibition (Oct. - Nov) held at Lever House, Park Avenue, New York City. Over the years the Guild has also presented a series of large outdoor exhibitions in central locations in New York City.

Activities: Assembles traveling exhibitions of sculpture; initiates educational programs connected with sculpture; maintains office for public, with files on members' works.

Publications: Fully illustrated catalogs of exhibitions.

Friends of the Sculptors Guild
A sponsoring group interested in the programs and projects of the Sculptors Guild.

SCULPTURE CENTER

167 E. 69th St, 10021. Tel: (212) 737-9870
Janak K. Khendry, Dir.
Marjorie Fields, Pres.
Frank R. Donahue, Treas.
Barbara Lekberg, Secy.
Gallery free to the public, 11 AM - 5 PM; Tues. through Sat.
Estab. 1929 as Clay Club of New York, to gurther the interest of student and professional sculptors. Inc. in 1944 as Sculpture Center (a non profit organization) for the cultivation of the art of sculpture and to provide facilities for work. Moved into new building 1950 at which time the present name was adopted. Approx. 55 professional sculptors represented in the gallery.

Activities: Maintains school and studies for beginners, advanced and professional sculptors. (See Schools) Gallery presents one-man, group and feature sculpture exhibitions. Monthly lectures on art by famous sculptors, museum directors, art historians; traveling sculpture exhibitions; visits to sculptors studios in New York area. (Lectures are free to the public.)

Library: Approx. 200 books.
Publications: Over 50,000 catalogues printed every year.
Attendance: 35,000.

SOCIETY OF AMERICAN GRAPHIC ARTISTS, INC.

1083 Fifth Ave, 10028. Tel: (212) 289-1507
Martin Barooshian, Pres.

Estab. 1915, as Brooklyn Society of Etchers; inc. 1932 under name of Society of American Etchers; became the Society of American Etchers, Gravers, Lithographers and Woodcutters in 1947; present name adopted in 1951. Meetings in Spring and Fall. Mem. about 230 artists, dues $10, assoc. about 250 who receive a print each year, executed for this purpose only, dues $25.

Purpose of the Society is to promote the association of individuals interested in the arts, especially in graphic arts, as defined by the intaglio, relief and planographic media and to advance the interests of the graphic arts by exhibitions and other means, without financial profit. Most important professional printmaker organization in U.S.A.

Collections: Permanent collection of 250 prints consisting of the Diploma Prints of the members.

Exhibitions: National exhibition with jury and between 10 and 20 prizes of $3000-$5000. Overseas traveling shows for U.S. Information Agency.

Activities: Forums on printmaking; demonstration of printmaking in all media.

Publications: Newsletter.

SOCIETY OF ILLUSTRATORS

128 E. 63rd St, 10021. Tel: (212) 838-2560
Alvin J. Pimsler, Pres.
Gerald McConnell, 1st V.Pres.
Dean Ellis, Treas.
Marylin Hafner, Secy.
Roland Descombes, House Chmn.
Prof. M. Carr Ferguson, Counselor
Terry Brown, Asst. to Dir.
Gallery open to the public weekdays 10 AM - 5 PM. Estab. 1901; owns building opened 1939, with meeting rooms and gallery. Monthly meetings.

Activities: Exhibitions, lectures; annual National Exhibition of Illustration; educational material.

SOCIETY OF MEDALISTS

For information see p. 44.

SOHO CENTER FOR VISUAL ARTISTS

110-114 Prince St, 10012. Tel: (212) 226-1993, 1995
Larry Aldrich, Founder & Pres.
Carlus Dyer, Dir.
Bernard Karpel, Library Consultant
Open Tues. - Fri. 1 - 5 PM; Sat. 11 AM - 5 PM; cl. summer months. Estab. 1974, a nonprofit activity sponsored by The Aldrich Museum of Contemporary Art. (See Ridgefield, Connecticut)

Exhibition Center: Established for the purpose of showing the work of new artists chosen through an annual survey by The Aldrich Museum. No commission is taken on sales of work and no fees charged to artists selected for presentation. Changing monthly exhibitions. Free admis.

Reference Library: Books, pamphlets and periodicals specially selected for the working artist. Free to all artists who register. Registration approx. 2000.

Attendance: Approx. 50,000.

✠SOLOMON R. GUGGENHEIM MUSEUM

1071 Fifth Ave, 10028. Tel: (212) 860-1300; 860-1313 for hours and exhibition information.
Peter Lawson-Johnston, Pres, The Solomon R. Guggenheim Foundation
Thomas M. Messer, Dir.
Henry Berg, Deputy Dir.
Susan L. Halper, Exec. Asst.
Linda Konheim, Prog. Adminr.
Agnes R. Connolly, Auditor
Louise Averill Svendsen, Cur.
Diane Waldman, Cur. of Exhibitions
Margit Rowell, Cur. of Special Exhibitions
Angelica Rudenstine, Research Cur.
Linda Shearer, Asst. Cur.
Carol Fuerstein, Ed.
Karen Lee, Curatorial Coordinator
Mary Joan Hall, Librn.
Ward Jackson, Archivist
Orrin Riley, Conservator
Lucy Belloli, Asst. Conservator
David Roger Anthony, Registrar
Saul Fuerstein, Preparator
Robert E. Mates, Photographer
Dana Cranmer, Technical Mgr.
Miriam Poser, Pub. Affairs Officer
Miriam Emden, Mem. Representative
Carolyn Porcelli, Coordinator
Darrie Hammer, Information
Peter Loggin, Building Supt.

Open Tues. 11 AM - 8 PM; Wed. - Sun. & holidays 11 AM - 5 PM; cl. Mon. except holidays; cl. Christmas; admis. $1; students with validated ID and visitors over 62, 50¢; groups of school children accompanied by teacher, 25¢; children under 7 free; Tues. evenings 5 - 8 PM free. The Solomon R. Guggenheim Foundation, estab. in 1937 by Solomon R. Guggenheim and founded for the promotion and encouragement of art and education in art. Its main purpose is to foster an appreciation of art by acquainting museum visitors with significant painting and sculpture of our time.

Collections: The Guggenheim Museum Collection reflects the creative accomplishments in modern art from the time of the Impressionists to the constantly changing experimental art of today. The collection of nearly three thousand works, augmented by the Justin K. Thannhauser Collection of 75 Impressionists and Post-Impressionist masterpieces, includes the largest group of paintings by Vasily Kandinsky to be seen in any of the world's museums; the largest number of sculptures by Constantin Brancusi in any New York museum; numerous important paintings by Chagall, Delaunay, Klee, Leger, Marc, Picasso and others. The development of modern art, from European Impressionism to contemporary American painting, is represented in the permanent collection. A partial list of these masters includes: Bacon, Bonnard, Braque, Cezanne, Dubuffet, Malevitch, Miro, Modigliani, Mondrian, Moore, Rousseau, and Seurat among the Europeans, and such Americans as Davis, de Kooning, Gottlieb, Guston, Lichtenstein, Louis, Noguchi, Pollock, Stuart and Warhol. Painting, drawing and print collections are being enlarged by gifts and purchases. The Museum also acquires the work of artists of younger reputation working in this country and abroad, including Christensen, Korman, Mangold, Nauman, G. Ritcher, Serra.

Exhibitions: The exhibition program at the Guggenheim Museum averages 8-12 shows per year. Among exhibitions since 1965 are: Nicholas de Stael; Edvard Munch; Egon Schiele; Paul Klee; Masterpieces of Peru; Neo Impressionism; Peggy Guggenheim Collection; Joseph Cornell; Roy Lichtenstein; David Smith; Alexander Calder; Carl Andre; Fangor; Contemporary Japanese Art; Francis Picabia; Joaquin Torres-Garcia; Pol Bury; John Chamberlain; Robert Mangold; Mondrian Centennial; Robert Ryman; Joan Miro; Magnetic Fields; Eva Hesse; A Memorial Exhibition; Ferdinand Hodler Retrospective; Jean Dubuffet: A Retrospective; Kasmir Malevich; Futurism: A Modern Focus; Alberto Giacometti: A Retrospective; Illya Bolotowsky; Jesus Rafael Soto: A Retrospective; Max Ernst: A Retrospective; Brice Marden; Jiri Kolar; Frantisek Kupka 1871-1957: A Retrospective; Aristide Maillol: 1861-1944; as well as smaller group and one-man shows and periodic selections from the Museum's permanent collection. The Guggenheim International Exhibition, held approximately every three to four years, is intended to be a comprehensive survey of contemporary art gathered from all parts of the world. Young Talent Exhibition, sponsored by a private foundation, is also held every three or four years.

The Museum maintains a membership program known as The Society of Associates. Dues are $250. Corporate memberships are also available at $1000 and up. These contributions help make possible the acquisition of important works by living artists for the permanent collection; the presentation of internationally significant exhibitions; special performing arts events; half-rate admission price for students and senior citizens; free Tuesday evenings; guided tours of the Museum. Privileges of membership include: invitations to private openings, complimentary catalogs published by the Museum, free admission to the Museum, bookstore discounts, use of the Museum reference library, special tours and events for members only and courtesies extended by selected major museums abroad.

Activities: The Museum offers a program of special events. Films are shown and lectures are given by museum staff members and visiting authorities in the museum auditorium. Performing arts events, including music and dance concerts, and theatrical productions, are occasionally scheduled in the auditorium or in the main gallery. Guided tours of temporary exhibitions and the Thannhauser Collection are given by museum-trained docents. Poetry readings, sponsored by The Academy of American Poets, are given on selected evenings during the year. Information and tickets for the readings may be obtained from The Academy of American Poets, 1078 Madison Avenue, New York, NY 10028.

Library: Research library oriented around the collection of 19th and 20th century paintings and sculpture. Approx. 10,000 volumes; 20,000 catalogs; extensive files of reference material. Open by appointment only.

Publications: Exhibitions are accompanied by illustrated and fully-documented catalogs. Art books, original lithographs, prints, posters, slides, postcards, notecards and greeting cards are available. A handbook of the Museum's permanent collection is also available.
Attendance: 350,000 - 400,000 annually.

TRAPHAGEN SCHOOL OF FASHION
Museum Collection
257 Park Ave. S, 10010. Tel: (212) 673-0300
Florita Raup, Cur.
Open to the general public by appointment.
The Collection was assembled for the purpose of providing artistic inspiration for students of design, and includes over a thousand national and period costumes and costume accessories (lace, fans, jewelry, buttons, etc.); dolls, including figurines, puppets, manikins and minikins; antique chests; armoirs; cassones; brasses from all over the world; textiles and textile prints; American Indian pottery, baskets, blankets; Meissen, Chinese and Japanese porcelains; miscellaneous objects of beauty.
Library
Evelyn Snyder, Librarian
The Library is primarily for the use of the students but is open to the public by appointment for special research for publication purposes if credit is given.
The Library consists of over 16,000 volumes and approx. 75,000 pamphlets, photographs, and other unmounted material. Special collections include the Denks Collection of Old German works on painters and sculptors; the William Robinson Leigh Collection of works on the American Indian; Mrs. Henry E. Coe Collection of Folk Songs of all Nations (with appropriate costumes); Wilbur Macey Stone Collection of the work of Famous Illustrators; Old and Rare Fashion Magazines (over 1000 volumes and 50 titles).
Important subjects, in addition to Costume and Fashion are Architecture, Art Anatomy and Art History, Dolls, Lettering and Typography, Interior Decoration, Military Uniforms, Textiles, Theatre, Travel and Nature.

✣UNITED STATES COMMITTEE OF THE INTERNATIONAL
ASSOCIATION OF ART, INC.*
41 E. 65th St, 10021. Tel: (212) 988-7700 or (212) 787-7063
Dorothy Paris, Exec. Officer
88 Seventh Ave. S, New York, NY 10014
For further information see p. 10.

THE UNIVERSITY CLUB LIBRARY*
1 W. 54th St, 10019.
Fred McKechnie, Dir.
R. Smith, Gen. Asst.
T. Pascal, Sr. Aid
A. Jackson, Sr. Aid
Members only 9:30 AM - 5 PM weekdays. Estab. 1865 for the promotion of the arts and culture in post university men; financed by endowment and membership. Art is hung in all areas of the building. Ann. meeting Mar. 17; mem. 4250; dues $600.
Collections: Art and architecture; fine binding; 135,000 volume library and photograph collection for reference only.
Exhibitions: New York Historical; The Hispanic; New York Public; American Association University Presses; New York Zoological.
Activities: Material available to members only; lectures for members only; approx. 4 gallery talks; tours; concerts; dramatic programs.
Publications: Library & Club Bulletin, Nov. - May.
Attendance: 7000 annual average.

WASHINGTON HEADQUARTERS ASSOCIATION
Morris-Jumel Mansion
Roger Morris Park, W. 160th St. & Edgecomb Ave, 10032.
Tel: (212) WA3-8008
Mrs. J. Frank Wood, Pres, Washington Headquarters Association
Natalie Bunting, Adminr, Morris-Jumel Mansion
Open Tues. - Sun. 10 AM - 4 PM. Historic house museum, built by Roger Morris, 1765, Washington's headquarters from mid-Aug. to mid-Oct, 1976; bought and restored by Stephen Jumel, 1810, acquired by New York City, 1903, opened as a museum, 1907 under auspices of Washington Headquarters Association (inc. 1904) and the City of New York. Appointment necessary for groups of 10 or more and for guided group tours. Mem. 400; dues individual $10, student $5, sponsor $15, family $25, sustaining $50, nonprofit organizations $50, patron $100, life $500, corporate $1000.
Collection: Mid-18th and 19th century pieces (Georgian, Federal, Empire); colonial flower and herb garden.
Activities: Performing arts series; illustrated lectures on history, art, architecture, antiques, colonial herbs and flowers, fashion, food, cookery, religion, and education. Celebrations of Washington's Birthday, Battle of Harlem Heights, Annual Meeting and Garden Party, Flag Day.
Attendance: 8000 - 10,000.

✣WHITNEY MUSEUM OF AMERICAN ART
945 Madison Ave, 10021. Tel: (212) 794-0600
Flora Whitney Miller, Hon. Chmn. Board of Trustees
Howard Lipman, Pres.
Flora Miller Irving, V.Pres.

Arthur G. Altschul, Treas.
Thomas N. Armstrong III, Dir
Palmer B. Wald, Adminr.
Nancy McGary, Registrar
Marcia Tucker, Cur.
Barbara Haskell, Cur.
Patricia Hills, Adjunct Cur, 18th & 19th Century Art
John G. Hanhardt, Assoc. Cur. Film
Libby W. Seaberg, Librn.
David Hupert, Head, Educ. Dept.
Donald LaBadie, Pub. Relations
Doris Wilk Palca, Head Publications & Sales
Walter Poleshuch, Development Officer
Open daily 11 AM - 6 PM; Sun. & holidays Noon - 6 PM; Tues.
evening to 10 PM; cl. Christmas; admis. $1, $1.50 weekends and
holidays, free Tues. evenings, children under 12, free accompanied
by an adult; annual unlimited admis. pass $15; annual student's pass
$5. Estab. 1930, inc. 1931, by Gertrude Vanderbilt Whitney for the
advancement of contemporary American art; Museum opened 1931;
moved to 54th St. in 1954; new building opened in 1966; financed by
endowment.
   Collections: 1727 paintings and drawings, 472 sculptures, 430
drawings, 1250 prints, 30 photographs; the Hopper Bequest of approx.
300 oils, 300 watercolors, 1275 drawings and 57 prints. Work in the
collection is mainly by 20th century American artists; acquisitions
chiefly work by living artists.
   Exhibitions: (Dec. 1973-Dec. 1975) Lee Krasner: Large Paintings;
Larry Zox; George Ault: Nocturnes; Michael Lekakis; Richard
Haas; Anne Truitt; Marvin Torfield; William Allan; The Flowering of
American Folk Art 1776-1876; Alice Neel; Frank O'Hara, A Poet
Among Painters; John McLaughlin; Ree Morton; Joan Mitchell;
American Pop Art; Johan Sellenraad; Jacob Lawrence; The 20th
Century: 35 American Artists; Jack Whitten; Jim Nutt; Alex Katz;
The Painter's America: Rural and Urban Life, 1810-1910; Jim Roche;
Al Held; Joan Moment; Richard Pousette-Dart; Photography in Amer-
ica; Tony Robbin; George Tooker; Permanent Collection; 1975 Bi-
ennial Exhibition of Contemporary American Art; Betye Saar; Roy
De Forest; Isabel Bishop; Jon Schueler; The Whitney Studio Club
and American Art 1900-1932; Seascape and the American Imagina-
tion; Minnie Evans; American Abstract Art; Sheldon Peck; Richard
Tuttle; The Sculpture and Drawings of Elie Nadelman; Dennis Ash-
baugh; Mark di Suvero; Doug Wheeler; Arthur Dove; Portrait of
Young America; Brenda Miller.
   Library: Comprehensive collection on American artists for re-
search only.
   Publications: Exhibition catalogs and the following books:
Calder's Circus; Auto Polaroids; The Flowering of American Folk
Art 1776-1876; American Pop Art; Photography in America; Seascape and the American Imagination. Sales desk in main lobby.
   Attendance: 320,000.
Friends of the Whitney Museum of American Art
   The Friends of the Whitney Museum of American Art is the Museum's only individual membership body of which there are approximately 700 members. Since their founding in 1956, the Friends have
contributed a large number of important works of art to the permanent collection as well as supporting other parts of the Museum's
program. The annual dues in the Friends are $250 for an individual
or couple. A Junior Membership at $100 is available to persons up
to age 30; in the case of couples, the older person's age determines
eligibility. Junior members have the same rights and privileges as
other members. There is also a specialized membership category,
the Historic Art Associates, which supports the museum's work in
the field of 18th and 19th century historic art. They receive regular
Friend's benefits.

The Downtown Branch
   55 Water St, 10041. Tel: (212) 483-0011
Staffed by students in the Whitney's Independent Study Program.
Free 11 AM - 3 PM, weekdays only. Opened Sept, 1973 to service
the lower Manhattan area. Changing exhibitions.

WOMEN'S SLIDE REGISTRY
   Artists Space, 155 Wooster St, 10012
   Slide Registry Comt.
Mary Miss
Michelle Stuart
Sandy Gellis
Paula Tavins
Jean Feinberg
   The Women's Slide Registry was formed in 1970 by the Ad Hoc
Women Artists' Committee to make available a collection of slides
by women artists. Open for viewing to everyone, no charge, but is
aimed at specialists in the visual arts. There are 3 registries,
all artists are represented by 1 slide in each registry. A folder
containing additional slides, a biography and related materials is
also available for viewing at Artists Space. The registry, which is
nonprofit is used solely as a source of information and used by directors seeking artists for shows.

Activities: 2 duplicate traveling registries which are rented to
colleges, lecturers, etc, for a fee of $25 plus postage.

NORTH SALEM

HAMMOND MUSEUM
Museum of the Humanities
   Deveau Rd, 10560. Tel: (914) 669-5033
Natalie Hays Hammond, Dir.
Mrs. Elizabeth H. Taylor, Assoc. Dir.
Open May - Dec, Wed. - Sun. 11 AM - 5 PM; admis. adults, $1 each
to Museum, Gardens; children, 75¢ each to Museum, Gardens. Inc.
in 1957 as a non-profit, educational institution; absolute charter
from New York State Board of Regents, 1962; financed by membership and contributions. Mem. is open to all who are in sympathy with
its aims and purposes; mem. dues, donations, and contributions to
Hammond Museum are tax deductible; mem. over 1600.
   A Museum of the Humanities, presenting changing exhibitions of
international scope and varied historic periods and topics, supplemented by programs of related special events such as dramatic presentations, concerts, lectures, and documentary films. The Oriental
Stroll Gardens, comprising fifteen individual gardens on 3½ acres,
include a lake, a reflecting pool, a dry landscape, a waterfall, and a
Zen Garden. Museum Shop; luncheon by reservation in Terrace
Restaurant, May - Oct.
   Attendance: Approx. 20,000 annually.

NORTHPORT

NORTHPORT PUBLIC LIBRARY
   151 Laurel Ave, 11768. Tel: (516) 261-6930
Victoria Wallace, Dir.
Frances Ingram, Asst. Dir.
Free, Mon. - Fri. 9 AM - 9 PM; Sat. 9 AM - 5 PM; Sun, Oct. - Apr.
1 - 5 PM. Estab. 1914; financed by local tax levy. Mem. 22,150.
   Collections: Rex Brasher, Birds and Trees of North America;
Jack Kerouac, Manuscript of the Town and the City.
   Exhibitions: Monthly exhibits of local artists and photographers.
   Activities: Dramatic programs.
   Library: 6350 volumes of art books, approx. 125 in reference,
rest for lending; 60 titles in periodicals on art and photography, total
book collection 151,000 volumes.
   Income and Purchases: Income $688,101; annual purchases
$100,000 book budget.

OGDENSBURG

FREDERIC REMINGTON MUSEUM
   303 Washington St, 13669. Tel: (315) 393-2425
Mildred B. Dillenbeck, Acting Dir.
John G. Ward, Chmn. Board of Trustees
Open all year Mon. - Sat. 10 AM - 5 PM; June - Sept. Sun. 1 - 5 PM;
cl. holidays; admis. adults $1, students 50¢, youth under 12 free
accompanied by an adult.
   Frederic Remington Art Museum is housed in an interesting mansion built in 1809. This is the most complete single collection of the
bronzes, oil paintings and other art works and mementos of Frederic
Remington (1861-1909), who was born in Canton, New York and lived
in Ogdensburg. He is famed for his depictions of the days of exploration and warfare with the Indians on the American Frontier. Recreated studio. Other exhibits include collections of furniture, glass,
china, silver and cameos. Additional exhibit areas now available with
the opening of the new Addie Priest Newell Galleries.
   Attendance: 14,000.

OLD CHATHAM

THE SHAKER MUSEUM
   12136. Tel: (518) 794-9105, 9100
John S. Williams, Sr, Chmn. of the Board
Warden McL. Williams, Pres.
Keith G. Flint, Secy.
John S. Williams, Jr, Treas.
Robert F. W. Meader, Dir.
Mrs. Malcolm Wheeler, Asst. Secy. & Asst. Treas.
Open May 1 - Oct. 31 daily 10 AM - 5:30 PM; cl. Nov. 1 - Apr. 30;
admis. adults $2, youths 15-21 $1, sr. citizen $1, children 6-15 50¢,
under 6 free. Estab. 1950 to perpetuate the life, culture and arts of
the Shaker Church, and to relate their achievements to the modern
world; financed by endowment. Ann. meeting, June.
   Collections: Costumes, †furniture, †tools, craft shops, medi-
cines, †books and manuscripts.
   Exhibitions: Spiral photograph exhibit 1973.
   Activities: Approx. 30 school and adult group tours.
   Library: Reference library of 1200 volumes; mss. 2409; photograph collection c. 2000.

Publications: Shaker Seed Industry; The Shaker Museum; The Shaker Adventure; numerous pamphlets.
Income and Purchases: Income $74,500; purchases $2000.
Attendance: 17,450.

OLD WESTBURY

NEW YORK INSTITUTE OF TECHNOLOGY
Wheatley Rd, 11568. Tel: (516) 686-7543
Dr. F. T. Lassiter, Chmn, Fine Arts Dept.
Open Mon. - Fri. 9 AM - 5 PM. Estab. 1964; gallery maintained for many exhibits held during the year.
Exhibitions: Annual faculty shows and student shows; Young Artists; Contemporary Artists Invitational; The Art of Collecting; Winslow Homer Prints; Art Happening, involving Dorothy and Herbert Vogel.
Activities: Custom silk-screen printmaking for artists, galleries, publishers, etc. Also serves as an atelier.

ONEONTA

COLLEGE UNION*
State University College, 13820. Tel: (607) 431-2550
Robert McLaughlin
Estab. 1972 to offer students, staff and visitors an opportunity to view current as well as past artistic styles and works; financed by city and state appropriation.
Exhibitions: The Chuck Winters Exhibition; two-woman show; IBM's Inventions of Leonardo Da Vinci; several student shows; additional photography shows, a black exhibition; women's exhibition.
Activities: Lectures open to the public; 8 visiting lecturers per year; gallery.
Attendance: 20,000 annual average.

POTSDAM

POTSDAM PUBLIC MUSEUM
Village of Potsdam Civic Center, 13676. Tel: (315) 265-6910
Mrs. A. D. Palmer, Pres.
Mrs. F. A. Ramsdell, Secy.
Dee Little, Dir. & Cur.
Klara Lovass-Nagy, Asst. Cur. & Exhibits Designer
Kay Wyant, Educational Asst.
Radka Zuman, Curatorial Asst.
Patricia Irwin, Educational Asst.
Dorothy Routh, Staff Asst.
Free Tues. - Sat. 2 - 5 PM. Estab. 1940 as a museum of decorative arts and history serving St. Lawrence County to expand the cultural horizons of area residents through permanent collections and exhibits temporary exhibits and a variety of programs; financed by city and state appropriations.
Collections: Burnap Collection of English Pottery; pressed glass and art glass of the 19th and early 20th century; costumes of the 19th and 20th centuries; Mandarin Chinese hangings, china and costume; history and development of the local area with displays, craft demonstrations, special exhibits, and much research materials.
Exhibitions: Annual Outdoor Art Show; Potsdam at the Turn of the Century; Art Nouveau; Old Fashioned Christmas; Potsdam Sandstone.
Activities: Photograph collection of 200 antique prints; lectures open to the public; craft workshops for adults and children. Book shop.
Library: 300 volume reference library.
Publications: Monthly newsletter.
Attendance: 6000.

✣STATE UNIVERSITY COLLEGE AT POTSDAM ART GALLERY
Brainerd Hall, Pierrepont Ave, 13676. Tel: (315) 268-5041
Dr. Roger W. Lipsey, Art Dept. Chmn.
Benedict Goldsmith, Gallery Dir.
Carol Belshaw, Secy.
Free weekdays 1 - 5 PM & 7 - 9 PM; Sat. & Sun. 1 - 5 PM. Estab. 1967 to serve college and community as a teaching gallery; financed by state appropriation. Gallery associated with Art Department.
Collections: Roland Gibson Collection, contemporary Japanese, Italian and American art - painting, sculpture and prints; †contemporary print collection; †contemporary drawing collection; †contemporary painting collection; †contemporary sculpture collection.
Exhibitions: National Print Exhibition; National Drawing Exhibition; New Realism Revisited; African Sculpture, Anspach Collection; Potsdam Plastics; William T. Gambling, Retrospective; Abstraction: Living and Well; New Surrealism.
Activities: Traveling exhibitions organized and circulated; Original objects of art lent; beginning photograph collection; lectures open to the public; 6 visiting lecturers per year; gallery talks; tours; concerts; William King, Artist in Residence.

College Library: 10,666 art volumes; college collection distributed throughout campus.
Operating Budget: $15,000.
Attendance: 18,000 (estimate).

POUGHKEEPSIE

✣VASSAR COLLEGE ART GALLERY
Taylor Hall, 12601. Tel: (914) 452-7000, Exten. 2645
Peter Morrin, Dir.
Innis Shoemaker, Cur.
Christine Havelock, Cur. Classical Collection
Free 9 AM - 4:30 PM; Sun. 2 - 5 PM, during academic year. Dedicated 1915; seven exhibition galleries; library; three lecture halls, seminar and study rooms.
Collections: Charles M. Pratt gift of Far Eastern ceramics and jades and Italian paintings; Matthew Vassar collection of American paintings of Hudson River School and 19th century English architectural watercolors; Mary Thaw Thompson collection of 17th century French engravings including works of Nanteuil, Morin; Dexter M. Ferry collection of paintings and etchings; Felix M. Warburg collection of Mediaeval sculpture and of graphics including 54 by Durer and 68 by Rembrandt; Olga Hasbrouck collection of Chinese ceramics; †European paintings, sculptures and drawings ranging from the Renaissance to the 20th century, including Bacchiacca, Valentin de Boullogne, Cézanne, Salvator Rosa, Claesz, Robert, Corot, Courbet, Delacroix, Tiepolo, Van Gogh, Munch, Klee, Bourdelle, Laurent, Kolbe, Gabo, Calder, Moore; †20th century American and European paintings including Bacon, Nicholson, Rothko, de Kooning, Hartley, Weber, Ryder; graphics ranging from Rembrandt to Rouault, Picasso, Matisse and Braque. The Classical Collection, which was established 1938, includes Greek vases; Egyptian, Etruscan and Mycenaean objects ranging from a mummy to tiny bronzes; Roman glass; marble portraits; jewelry; other archaeological finds.
Exhibitions: Monthly exhibitions.
Library: Van Ingel Art Library of 25,000 volumes, 40,000 slides, 30,000 photographs.

PURCHASE

✣ROY R. NEUBERGER MUSEUM
State University of New York, College at Purchase, 10577.
Tel: (914) 253-5087
Jeffrey Hoffeld, Dir.
Simon Zalkind, Asst. Cur.
John Cassidy, Museum Mgr.
Friends of the Neuberger Museum
Leonard Yaseen, Chmn.
Margot Linton, Pres.
Free Tues. - Sat. 11 AM - 5 PM; Sun. 1 - 5 PM. Estab. 1971, opened May, 1974, to serve college and community.
Collections: Roy R. Neuberger Collection of 19th and 20th century American art. Other gifts and long term loans include: Rickey Collection of constructivist art, Hans Richter Collection of American and European artists, including Richter's own art. Eliot P. Hirshberg Collection of African art. Cleve Gray's Threnody, a sequence of 14 paintings.
Exhibitions: George Grosz Theatrical Drawings; Harry Holtzman photographs: Village Gods of South India; Cletus Johnson: Theaters; Cleve Gray: Studies for Threnody; Ben Cunningham: Corner Paintings; Ruth Vollmer: Sculpture and Drawings; Jacques Villon Retrospective; William Scharf: Continuum.
Activities: Guided tours; film showings; lectures and symposia; Yaseen lecture series.
Liberal arts college library of 112,000 volumes with special strength in the performing and visual arts; includes collection of 20,000 art slides; photograph collection.

ROCHESTER

INTERNATIONAL MUSEUM OF PHOTOGRAPHY
George Eastman House
900 East Ave, 14607. Tel: (716) 271-3361
Robert J. Doherty, Dir.
James Card, Dir, Dept. Film
Andrew Eskind, Asst. to Dir.
Open 10 AM - 5 PM; cl. Mon; admis. adults $1, students 50¢, children 25¢, Wed. free. Estab. and inc. 1947 to foster interest and to show progress in the art and science of photography. Eastman House, built in Georgian Colonial style, is a distinguished piece of architecture which became a Registered National Historic Landmark in 1969. Mem. dues assoc. $10 per year. Associates receive a book and a quarterly publication.
Collections: †Photographs; †apparatus; †books; †films; George Eastman Collection of Old Master Paintings.

Exhibitions: Permanent chronological survey of history of photography; permanent exhibition of history and technology of cameras and photographic processes.

Activities: Special exhibits; traveling exhibitions; symposia; print service; book and slide service; film series (except Aug). Book shop. Intern program.

Library: 10,000 volumes for reference.

Publications: 2 catalogs per year; Image, quarterly.

Attendance: Approx. 150,000.

✤MEMORIAL ART GALLERY

The University of Rochester

490 University Ave, 14607. Tel: (716) 275-3081

William J. Maxion, Pres. Board of Managers

Mrs. Frederick W. Post, Secy. Board of Managers

John A. Mahey, Dir.

Langdon F. Clay, Asst. Dir. for Educ.

Robert Henning, Jr, Asst. Dir. for Curatorial Services

Bernice Meyer, Adminr.

Margaret Bond, Head, Pub. Relations

Margaret Bennett, Head, Mem.

Robert A. Young, Supt.

Open Sun. 1 - 5 PM; Tues. 10 AM - 9 PM; Wed. - Sat. 10 AM - 5 PM; admis. adults $1, students and senior citizens 50¢, children 25¢. Estab. and inc. 1913 by gift of Mrs. James S. Watson to the University of Rochester as a public art center and university dept. Considerably enlarged in 1926 by joint gift of Mr. and Mrs. Watson. Renovated and expanded in 1968 with addition of new wing doubling former size. In addition to exhibition galleries it contains 300-seat auditorium, art library, lecture and class rooms, and adjacent Creative Workshop with painting, printmaking, weaving, and metal studios. Mem. 8800; dues $20 and higher; 225 corporate supporters.

Collections: Coverage of all major periods and cultural areas from Assyria and predynastic Egypt to the present. †Collection of paintings includes works by Orcagna, El Greco, Catena, Strozzi, Feti, Magnasco, Tintoretto, Rembrandt, Hals, Steen, de Vos, Rubens, Constable, Ingres, Cezanne, Monet, Degas, Cassatt, Braque, Delacroix, Courbet, Renoir, Matisse, Picasso, and 19th and 20th century American masters. †Sculpture represents Assyrian, Egyptian, Classical, Chinese, Persian, Pre-Columbian, African, Romanesque, Gothic, and Renaissance periods. Contemporary sculptors include Rodin, Maillol, Marini, Manzu, Bourdelle, Barlach, Marcks, Lipchitz, Moore and Noguchi. †Decorative arts comprise collections of ceramics, tapestries, textiles, silver, Chinese and Luristan bronzes, ivories, manuscripts, furniture and American folk art.

Exhibitions: Changing exhibitions ranging through historic and contemporary periods of painting, sculpture, decorative arts, and prints. Annual regional Rochester-Finger Lakes Exhibition open to all artists and craftsmen of nineteen counties in West-Central New York, judged by an out-of-town jury. Unjuried annual Clothesline Art Show and Sale with purchases averaging over $125,000.

Activities: Weekly study courses, public lectures, gallery talks, concerts, films, and demonstrations; seventy creative art classes weekly for children and adults, workshops for recreation and playground leaders, in-service courses for teachers, modeling classes for handicapped children and blind adults, summer school for children and adults; Lending and Sales Gallery of original paintings, prints, and sculptures; Gallery Shop; loan prints for University students; active school service program with gallery talks, classroom loans, traveling exhibits, visiting artists; neighborhood services program including free Allofus Art Workshop with enrollment of 500 adults and children.

Library: Circulating and reference library of 10,000 books and bound periodicals and 5000 slides supplementing the University library.

Publications: Gallery Notes, 9 times yearly; exhibition catalogs.

Income: Annual income for operation $930,000, of which $370,000 is in membership dues.

Attendance: 150,000.

PRINT CLUB OF ROCHESTER*

Memorial Art Gallery, 490 University Ave, 14607.

Tel: (716) 275-3081

Estab. 1930. Ann. meeting Oct; mem. 80; dues $10. Exhibitions at Rochester Public Library and Memorial Art Gallery. Eight meetings a year with annual presentation of print in Oct.

ROCHESTER HISTORICAL SOCIETY

485 East Ave, 14607. Tel: (716) 271-2705

Sydney Weinberg, Pres.

Helen Brooks, Secy.

Mrs. James S. Watson, Dir. Woodside (the Society's Museum)

Free daily 10 AM - 4 PM; cl. Sat, Sun. & holidays. Inc. 1861 to collect, preserve and display historic material including books and manuscripts relating to Rochester and the Genesee Valley District. Ann. meeting May; mem. 350, dues $5 and higher.

Activities: Lectures; maintains gallery and photograph collection.

Library for reference only.

RUSH RHEES LIBRARY

Fine Arts Library

University of Rochester, 14627. Tel: (716) 275-4476

Stephanie Frontz, Librn.

Archie M. Miller, Chmn. Dept. Art

Fine Arts Library contains 32,000 volumes, 169 periodicals, 56,600 slides, 14,000 mounted photographs.

SANBORN

NIAGARA COUNTY COMMUNITY COLLEGE GALLERY

3111 Saunders Settlement Rd, 14132. Tel: (716) 731-3271, Exten. 342

Dorothy H. Westhafer, Gallery Dir.

Open Mon. - Fri. Noon - 4 PM; Wed. & Thurs. 7 - 9 PM; Sun. 2 - 4 PM. Estab. Jan, 1973 to present high quality exhibitions of a diverse nature to broaden student and community interests and understanding; financed by county and state appropriations, student fees and Fine Arts Division funds.

Collections: †Alumni and student work; ceramics, glass from School for American Craftsmen; 20th century prints.

Exhibitions: Rochester Institute of Technology's School for American Craftsmen; Rochester Folk Art Guild; William King, sculpture; Gallery Association of New York circulating shows; Pratt Graphics Exhibit; Smithsonian Exhibits; Design Works-Bedford Stuyvesant; Line '75; 10 Designing Women, America at Work/at Play 1880-1920; Design for Living (from Youngstown Design Center); plus alumni, faculty and student shows.

Activities: 32 color reproductions, 9000 Kodachromes, 36 motion pictures, 10 filmstrips and 960 sound slides in Library Learning Center lending collection; 6 visiting lecturers per year; concerts, dramatic programs, classes for adults and children.

Income and Purchases: Income $2500; purchases $0 - $250.

Attendance: 3000 - 4000.

SARATOGA SPRINGS

NATIONAL MUSEUM OF RACING, INC.

Union Ave, 12866. Tel: (518) 584-0400

John W. Hanes, Chmn.

Charles E. Mather, II, Pres.

Paul R. Rouillard, Secy.-Treas.

Elaine E. Mann, Dir.

Elizabeth Clute, Asst.

Free all year round 10 AM - 5 PM; Sat. Noon - 5 PM (except Feb); Sun. Noon - 5 PM (June 15 - Sept 15); August racing season, daily 9:30 AM - 7 PM; children under 12 must be accompanied by parents. Estab. 1950 to establish a museum for the collection, preservation and exhibition of books, documents and other printed or written material, statuary, paintings and memorabilia associated with the origin, history and development of horse racing and the breeding of thoroughbred horses; privately supported. Seven galleries on first floor of building housing paintings, racing trophies and statuary, auditorium on second floor featuring steeplechase exhibit and films during the race meet.

Collections: Equine art-paintings, racing trophies, racing colors, photographs, films, prints, other racing memorabilia.

Exhibitions: Collection of equine art by Vaughn Flannery; Woodward Collection of sporting art from Baltimore Museum; from private collectors-Paintings by Sir Alfred J. Munnings.

Activities: Individual paintings lent to schools; traveling exhibit of colored photos titled Thoroughbred World, Its Color & Action now on permanent loan to Calder Race Course, Miami, Fla; 20 items lent in an average year; lectures given during racing season. Book shop.

Attendance: 69,000 annual average.

SKIDMORE COLLEGE ART GALLERY*

Hathorn Studio, 12866. Tel: (518) 584-5000

Earl B. Pardon, Chmn. Art Dept.

Free Mon. - Fri. 9 AM - 10 PM; Sat. 9 AM - 5:30 PM; Sun. 2 - 10 PM; cl. during college vacations. Estab. 1928 as part of the Dept. of Art.

Collections: Small permanent collection of †prints, †drawings, †paintings, †sculpture, †textiles and †ceramics, †photographs, †reproductions and †slides.

Exhibitions: Temporary exhibitions changed every three weeks.

Activities: Lectures, concerts, circulating exhibitions.

Library: Art Library adjoins the Gallery. Contains 7000 books and folios; 37 periodicals; 13,000 photographs and plates of illustrative material; 525 original prints; 6443 black and white slides, and 7017 colored slides. The Main Library has additional art books, folios and bound periodicals.

Budget and Purchases: Budget $18,000; purchases $5000.

Attendance: 6000 year.

YADDO
Saratoga Springs, 12866.
Newman E. Wait, Jr, Pres.
Curtis Harnack, Exec. Dir.
Estab. 1926. The country estate of the Late Mr. & Mrs. Spencer Trask at Saratoga Springs, N.Y; open all year; provides room, board, and studio space for limited number of artists in writing, visual arts, and music composition. Open to all who have achieved some measure of professional accomplishment. Applications must be received by Feb. 15; work must be shown to an Admis. Comt. Invitations are issued by Apr. 15, for periods up to two months. No cash grants.

SCHENECTADY

THE SCHENECTADY MUSEUM
Nott Terrace Heights, 12308. Tel: (518) 372-3386
Prof. Joseph Finkelstein, Pres.
Joseph Flora, V.Pres.
Mrs. Robert L. Fullman, Secy.
Joseph A. Matocha, Treas.
Mark Winetrout, Acting Dir. & Cur. Art Collection & Exhibits
Marjorie B. Foote, Cur. Costumes
Sarah R. Mason, Assoc. Cur. Educ.
William Kinsella, Planetarium Dir. & Cur. Science
Virginia Strull, Dir. Development
Open Tues. - Fri. 10 AM - 4:30 PM; Sat. & Sun. Noon - 5 PM. Founded 1934, chartered by the New York State Regents in 1937 to increase and diffuse knowledge in appreciation of art, history, industry, and science by providing collections, exhibits, lectures, and other programs. Ann. meeting Oct; mem. 2200; dues $5, $12.50, $15, $25, $50, $100, $250, and $500 and up.
Collections: 19th and 20th century costumes and textiles; x-ray tubes, electrical equipment and instruments; mollusks; minerals; fossils, North American Indian, African, birds, decorative arts; 19th and 20th century art.
Exhibitions: Artists of the Mohawk-Hudson Region; Regional Crafts Show, purchases and awards $600; temporary exhibits of costumes and textiles, art, natural science, ethnology, and technology.
Activities: Art and craft classes; planetarium programs for school pupils and public; guided tours for school pupils; bus tours to other museums, historic sites, and cultural events; European and Central American tours; loan materials and exhibits for area schools, colleges, and libraries; amateur radio station; lecture and movie series; annual indoor plant show, Haunted House; Festival of Nations; Crafts Fair; Rock Festival; Sales and Rental Gallery; Gift shop.
Library: 5000 reference and technical volumes.
Publications: Monthly calendar and annual report.
Income: $190,000.
Attendance: 68,000.

SKANEATELES

SKANEATELES LIBRARY ASSOCIATION
49 E. Genesee St, 13152. Tel: (315) 685-5135
Frederick G. Martin, Pres.
Mrs. J. W. Thorne, Secy.
Mrs. Samuel Townsend, Librn.
Mrs. Edward D. Ramage, Asst. Librn.
Free 10 AM - 5:30 PM; cl. Sun. Estab. 1877.
Collections: Paintings by American artists and etchings by American and foreign artists. 200 paintings by John D. Barrow in separate wing.
Exhibitions: Occasional special exhibitions.
Library: 25,000 volumes.

SOUTHAMPTON

THE PARRISH ART MUSEUM
25 Jobs Lane, 11968. Tel: (516) 283-2118
Mrs. Arthur Boyer Schoen, Pres.
Franklin O. Canfield, 1st V.Pres.
Winslow M. Lovejoy, Jr, Secy.
Dudley F. Cates, Treas.
Free Tues. - Sat. 10 AM - 5 PM; Sun. 2 - 5 PM; cl. Mon, cl. to change exhibitions several times a year. Estab. 1897 to collect and exhibit art objects, establish art workshops and instruction; to hold or sponsor special exhibitions of educational and cultural interest and value. Mem. 1100; dues $10 and higher.
Collections: Samuel L. Parrish Collection, owned by Southampton Village, of North Italian Renaissance paintings; museum collection of over 900 paintings by American artists dating from latter part of the 18th century to the present including 43 by William Merritt Chase.

Exhibitions: Changing exhibitions, approx. 25 a year.
Activities: Traveling exhibitions circulated; concerts, films; art workshops for children.
Library: 2000 volumes of art reference.

STATEN ISLAND

JACQUES MARCHAIS CENTER OF TIBETAN ARTS, INC.
338 Lighthouse Ave, 10306. Tel: (212) 987-3874
Ruth Sprute, Dir.
Sigred Sidrow, Librn.
Rosemary Tung, Cur.
Open Apr. 1 - Nov. 30, Sat. & Sun. 2 - 5 PM; June, July & Aug, open Tues. & Thurs. 2 - 5 PM; admis. 50¢. Estab. 1946 for maintenance of library and museum in Buddhist philosophy, art and religion, with particular emphasis on Tibetan Buddhism; financed by endowment, earned income and some government grants.
Collections: Jacques Marchais permanent collection of Tibetan Art.
Activities: Special lectures and tours are available by appointment; photograph collection is being catalogued for reference; lectures open to the public; 6 visiting lecturers per year; limited numbers of reproductions and woodblock prints available.
Library: 1100 volumes for reference only.
Attendance: 4000.

STATEN ISLAND INSTITUTE OF ARTS AND SCIENCES*
75 Stuyvesant Place, St. George, 10301. Tel: (212) 727-1135
Terence H. Benbow, Pres.
George O. Pratt, Jr, Dir.
Mathilde P. Weingartner, Cur. of Science
Barry Leo Delaney, Cur. of Art
Gail K. Schneider, Editor & Librn.
Freda Mulcahy Esterly, Museum Lecturer
Elsie Verkuil, Asst. to the Dir.
Free Tues. - Sat. 10 AM - 5 PM; Sun. and holidays, 2 - 5 PM; cl. Mon, Thanksgiving, Christmas, New Year's, Fourth of July, Labor Day. Estab. 1881, inc. 1906. Mem. approx. 900; dues $10 and higher.
Collections: In addition to the art collections, the Institute maintains in its Museum collections in †geology, †ornithology, entomology, botany, zoology and †American Indian archaeology, all with emphasis on Staten Island. The collection of cicadidae is outstanding. Permanent exhibits include habitat groups and an Indian burial, excavated on Staten Island, recreated as a diorama.
Exhibitions: Annual Spring Members Show; group and collection shows.
Activities: Lectures on art and science; annual series of lectures and films on natural history; fall and spring terms of adult classes; complete program of lectures in art and in natural history for school children with annual registration of 30,000; four Weissglass awards totaling $400 presented each year.
Library: Reference collection of 30,000 publications in science, art history, history, and genealogy; a choice collection of Staten Island newspapers from 1834-1934 on microfilm (reader in Library); letters, documents, journals, files of clippings, and old photographs relating to the history of Staten Island and the metropolitan region; the George W. Curtis Collection of books, manuscripts, and memorabilia.
Publications: The New Bulletin (indexed), monthly except for the summer; Proceedings, 3 times a year; catalogs; Annual Reports.
Attendance: 105,000 annually.
Department of Art
Collections: †American paintings of the 19th and 20th centuries; †prints; small sculptures; Oriental, Greek, Roman and Primitive art objects.
Exhibitions: Exhibitions in decorative arts; design exhibitions in various media; major loan shows of paintings and prints; special exhibitions of graphic arts and of photography.

STONY BROOK

THE MUSEUMS AT STONY BROOK
11790. Tel: (516) 751-0066
Mrs. Ward Melville, Pres, Board of Trustees
Susan Stitt, Dir.
Nicholas Langhart, Adminr.
The Carriage Museum, Art Museum, period buildings, and Museums' store are open 10 AM - 5 PM Wed. - Sun. & most Mon. holidays. The Carriage Museum and period buildings are open from mid-Apr. through Thanksgiving weekend; the Art Museum and Museums' store are open year round. All Museums closed Thanksgiving Day, Christmas and New Year's Day. Admis. to all Museums, Apr. - Nov, adults $2, senior citizens and students $1.50, children (ages 6-12) 75¢; Nov. - Apr, adults 75¢, senior citizens and students 50¢, children (ages 6-12) 25¢. Museums members free. The Craft

Center is open 10 AM - 5 PM daily, year round, except during exhibit changes; admis. free.

The Museums at Stony Brook, formerly called the Suffolk Museum at Stony Brook, Long Island, was founded in 1935 and received its charter as a nonprofit educational institution in 1942. This charter states that The Museums' purpose is to collect and preserve objects of historic and artistic interest and to offer popular instruction and opportunities for aesthetic enjoyment. Mem. 1100; dues $10 and higher.

Collections: †Paintings by William Sidney Mount, his artist brothers, Shepard and Henry, and other 19th century artists; Long Island birds; †carriage collection; costume and textile collections.

Activities: Exhibitions; lectures; school tours; Colonial workshop for school groups; bus trips. At the Craft Center, an extensive program is offered of craft classes and workshops.

Library: Contains 1000 books on the history of carriages and transportation; trade catalogs (19th century); craft publications.

Income: (73-74 fiscal year) $170,000.

Attendance: (1974) 25,000.

SYRACUSE

ERNEST STEVENSON BIRD LIBRARY

Waverly Ave, 13210. Tel: (315) 423-2440
Donald C. Seibert, Dept. Head
Barbara A. Opar, Architecture Librn.
Ramona Roters, Slide Librn.
Jeannette T. Sullivan, Art Librn.
Open weekdays 8 AM - 11 PM; Sat. 10 AM - 5 PM; Sun. Noon - 10 PM. Estab. to serve faculty and students teaching and studying in the fine arts field. Located in Syracuse University Library.

Library: 38,000 volumes; 5000 exhibition catalogs, 110 slides, 26,000 pictures in picture file.

Purchases: $36,000 for books and periodicals.

✤EVERSON MUSEUM OF ART

401 Harrison St, 13202. Tel: (315) 474-6064
Ronald A. Kuchta, Dir.
Sandra Trop-Blumberg, Asst. Dir. Exhibitions
Barbara Beckos, Cur. Educ.
Letty Murray, Mem. Chmn.
Rob Harper, Registrar
Richard Simmons, Assoc. Cur. Video Arts
Peg Weiss, Cur. Collections
Free Tues. - Fri. Noon - 5 PM; Sat. 10 AM - 5 PM; Sun. Noon - 5 PM; PM; cl. Mon. & major holidays. Estab. and inc. 1896. Ann. meeting May; mem. 2700; dues individual $15 and higher, corporate $100 and higher.

Collections: Contemporary American painting and sculpture; traditional American painting; Cloud Wampler Collection of Oriental Art; 17th, 18th and 19th century English porcelain; contemporary American ceramics; African Collection.

Major Exhibitions: American Art in Upstate New York; Ceramic National; Children's National Book Awards; Roy Simmons, Jr. Collages; Meredith McClouth, photos; Judd Rosebush, Computer Animations; Ant Farm; Contemporary Irish Directions; Lila Katzen; On My Own Time, industrial exhibit; Dieter Froese; John Willenbecher; Romare Beardon; Andy Mann; Lawrence Condon; Donald Lipsky, photos; David Hayes; Mony Scholastic; Charles James; Yeffe Kimbal; Brass Rubbings; Stanley Boxer; Ruth Reed Cummings, primitive; Marcia Marcus; Electronic Movers; Tibetan Art, Regional; Bill Viola, video; Masters in Contemporary Ceramics; Polish Constructivists; James Burgess; George Rhodes; American Heroes in Ceramics; Art/Tapes; Leo Manso; Art Deco; 200 years of Royal Copenhagen Porcelain; 3 women painters, May Stevens, Alice Neal, Sylvia Sleigh; Zuniga; Navajo Blankets; Permanent Collection.

Activities: Annual lecture series; guest lecturers related to exhibitions; adult studio courses in drawing, printmaking and introduction to art media; children's art classes Sat. mornings and weekdays during summer; docents for all exhibitions; sales gallery featuring work of local professional artists and craftsmen, contemporary posters and graphic works; luncheon restaurant open to public.

Library: General noncirculating art reference library of 4000 volumes, including a slide collection, traveling education exhibitions to schools and a video tape library.

Income and Purchases: Annual operating income $579,350; annual purchases $30,000.

Attendance: 300,000.

JOE AND EMILY LOWE ART GALLERY

Syracuse University
Sims Hall, 13210. Tel: (315) 432-2380
August L. Freundlich, Dean, Col. of Visual & Performing Arts
Stanton L. Catlin, Dir. Exhibitions
Free Tues. - Sat. Noon - 5 PM; Sun. 1 - 5 PM. Estab. 1870 as both an educational and cultural resource for the students and faculty of Syracuse University, and the people of the community; private university.

University Art Collections: American art of the 20th century (Burchfield, Curry, Marsh, Sloan, etc); Collections of American printmakers (Margo, Schrag, Florsheim, Castellon, Peterdi), and master prints (Rembrandt, Whistler, etc); sculpture of James Earle Frazier, Ivan Mestrovic, and Doris Caesar; limited editions porcelain sculptures by Edward Marshall Boehm.

Exhibitions: (1974-76) A Sense of Scale, contemporary large scale paintings by artists of central New York State; 500 Years of Printmaking and Varieties of Realism, both from University Collections; Sculpture, Drawings and Watercolors by Sir Jacob Epstein, Retrospective.

Activities: Traveling exhibitions organized and circulated.

Attendance: 20,000.

TARRYTOWN

LYNDHURST

635 S. Broadway, 10591. Tel: (202) 638-5200
William C. Taggert, Adminr. & Property Council & staff of National Trust Interpretors
Carole T. Scanlon, Coordinator, Interpretive Programs
Open May 1 - Oct. 31. 10 AM - 5 PM. & legal holidays; Nov. 1 - Apr. 30, 10 AM - 4 PM; cl. Christmas & New Year's; admis. adults $2.25; senior citizens $1.25; group rates by arrangement; free to National Trust members.

A property of the National Trust for Historic Preservation, preserved as a historic house museum operated as a community preservation center. It is a National Historic Landmark.

Lyndhurst is a Gothic Revival castle designed in 1838 for General William Paulding by Alexander Jackson Davis, one of America's most influential 19th century architects. Commissioned by second owner, George Merritt, to enlarge the house, Davis in 1865 continued the Gothic Revival style in the additions. It was purchased in 1880 by Jay Gould and willed to his daughter, Helen. Later acquired by another daughter, Anna, Duchess of Talleyrand-Perigord, Lyndhurst was left to the National Trust in 1964.

The property is located on spacious grounds along the Hudson River. Visitors are free to explore the magnificent park which is being restored to an 1873 site plan. Other highlights include a carriage house stocked with period vehicles, stables and the remains of what was once one of the world's private greenhouses.

Highly important collection of Gothic furniture designed by architect A. J. Davis in the 1830's and again in the 1870's. Other fine 19th century furnishings and paintings. Windows attributed to L. C. Tiffany.

The preservation of Lyndhurst is a composite of the contributions of the three families who lived in it. Property serves as a focal point for advancement of historic preservation. Through it are developed new relationships among cultural, community, preservation groups and National Trust members in its area. Responds to community preservation needs by acting as a link between community and appropriate regional or headquarters offices of National Trust.

Provides interpretive programs which are related to Lyndhurst's particular case study in historic preservation. The National Trust Restoration Workshop, located in a portion of the stable complex, carries out restoration craft services for National Trust properties. Many special programs are produced at Lyndhurst in cooperation with community groups such as outdoor summer concerts, antique and auto shows and Christmas programs. A set of 10 in. x 8 in. measured drawings of Lyndhurst taken by Historic American Buildings Survey is available from Preservation Shop.

Attendance: (1975) 51,000.

SLEEPY HOLLOW RESTORATIONS, INC.

Box 245, 10591. Tel: (914) 631-8200
Dana S. Creel, Pres.
John W. Harbour, Jr, Exec. Dir.
Saverio Procario, Deputy Dir. Admin.
Open 10 AM - 5 PM; cl. Thanksgiving Day, Christmas and New Year's; admis. to Sunnyside, Philipsburg Manor and Van Cortlandt Manor, adults $2.25 each property, juniors 6-14 $1.50 each property. Three-visit tickets valid one year adults $5.75, juniors $3.75. Groups of 20 or more must make reservations in advance.

Chartered 1951 as a nonprofit educational foundation. Owns and operates historic properties which are Sunnyside in Tarrytown, the home of author Washington Irving; Philipsburg Manor in North Tarrytown, a Dutch-American gristmill-farm site of the early 1700s; Van Cortlandt Manor in Croton-on-Hudson, a manorial estate of the Revolutionary War period.

Collections: 17th, 18th and 19th century decorative arts; memorabilia of Washington Irving and of the Van Cortlandt Family.

Activities: Guided tours; lectures; demonstrations of 17th and 18th century arts and crafts; organized education programs; exhibition of collections.

Library: Specialized reference library with particular emphasis on 17th, 18th and 19th century living in the Hudson River Valley.

Publications: The Van Cortlandts of Croton: York State Patriots; The Loyalist Americans; America's Wooden Age; Life of George Washington; Life Along the Hudson; The Mill at Philipsburg Manor; Rip Van Windle and The Legend of Sleepy Hollow; Washington Irving's Sunnyside; Philipsburg Manor: A Guidebook; The Knickerbocker Tradition; The Worlds of Washington Irving; Six Presidents from the Empire State; Aspects of Early New York Society and Politics; Washington Irving: A Tribute; The Family Collections at Van Cortlandt Manor; plus prints and documents including Declaration of Independence, Howe Map and A Portfolio of Sleepy Hollow Prints.

Films: Lords of the Manor: The Story of Philipsburg, The Mill at Philipsburg Manor.

Attendance: 200,000.

TROY

✠THE NEW GALLERY*
Russell Sage College
Schacht Fine Arts Center, 12180. Tel: (518) 270-2263
Ruth Healey, Gallery Dir.
Free, Mon. - Fri. 9 AM - 3:30 PM. Estab. 1972 for monthly exhibitions of paintings, sculpture and crafts; financed by the college.

Collections: †Paintings; †Graphics; †Sculpture; †New Guinea artifacts.

Exhibitions: Paintings from New York Galleries including Martha Jackson Gallery, Betty Parsons Gallery, O. K. Harris Gallery; Exhibition of New Guinea sculpture from the permanent collection; student work; one man shows.

Activities: 2 semesters in museum theory and practice for students, taught at the Rensselaer County Historical Society; photograph collection; lectures for students only.

Attendance: 800 for 9 months.

RENSSELAER COUNTY HISTORICAL SOCIETY
59 Second St, 12180.
Dorothy Donnelly Long, Pres.
Mrs. Frederick R. Walsh, Dir.
Mrs. Arthur F. Brod, Jr, Cur-Registrar
Open Tues. - Sat. 10 AM - 4 PM; cl. major holidays. Inc. 1927 to promote historical research, preservation of historic records; to gather and preserve American fine arts, painting and decorative arts; endowed and supported by members. Ann. meeting second Mon. in Sept; mem. 500; dues $2-1000.

Collections: Hart-Cluett Mansion (National Register of Historic Places); 11 period rooms of 19th century furniture, portraits, silver, ceramics, costumes, quilts and coverlets.

Exhibitions: Changing exhibitions of art and history; traveling architecture exhibit.

Activities: 8 members' meetings, special tours, Christmas Greens Show.

Library: Approximately 800 volumes related to local history; large photographic collection.

Publications: Monthly newsletter.

Income and Purchases: $40,000; purchases vary from $400 per year to $1000.

Attendance: 10,000.

THE RENSSELAER NEWMAN FOUNDATION CHAPEL AND CULTURAL CENTER
2008 19th St, 12180. Tel: (518) 274-7793
John I. Millett, Pres.
Rev. Thomas Phelan, Secy.
Charles H. Saile, Dir.
Shirley Broderick, Secy.
Free 8 AM - 11 PM. Estab. 1968 to provide religion and culture for members of Rensselaer Polytechnic Institute and Troy area, a broadly ecumenical service; supported by contributions. Gallery.

Collections: Medieval sculpture; contemporary paintings, sculpture and needlework; liturgical vestments and artifacts.

Exhibitions: Laliberté banners; Picasso traveling exhibition; New York State Council on the Arts; Smithsonian Institution traveling exhibition; local one-man shows.

Activities: Lectures open to public, 10 visiting lecturers per year; concerts; dramatic programs; classes for adults and children.

Publications: Sun and Balance, 3 times a year.

Income: $110,000.

Attendance: 100,000.

UTICA

✠MUNSON-WILLIAMS-PROCTOR INSTITUTE
310 Genesee St, 13502. Tel: (315) 797-0000
William C. Murray, Pres.
William P. White, Treas.
Edward H. Dwight, Dir. Museum of Art

Joseph S. Trovato, Asst. to Dir. Museum of Art
John R. Manning, Dir. School of Art.
Timothy L. Trent, Mgr. Communications
Free weekdays and Sat. 10 AM - 5 PM; Sun. 1 - 5 PM; cl. holidays. Estab. 1919, provisional charter granted by The Board of Regents of the University of the State of New York, changed to absolute charter in 1941, and amended in 1948 additional power to provide instruction in higher education at the college level in the fine arts; became active in 1935. Museum of Art with auditorium, and Fountain Elms, the restoration of a mid-19th century house, opened in 1960. Meetinghouse, restored residence on Institute grounds for group meetings. Museum mem. fee $7.50 (those living within a 20-mile radius of Utica); nonres. mem. fee $3 (those living outside the 20-mile radius); student mem. fee $1.50.

Collections: †18th, 19th and 20th century American paintings, sculpture, and decorative arts; Greek, Persian and pre-Columbian art; †arts of central New York; †contemporary European paintings and sculpture; †drawings and prints; †Archives of Central New York Architecture.

Exhibitions: Periodically changing exhibitions; Artists of Central New York Annual; Annual Utica Arts Festival.

Activities: Lectures, concerts; film series; guided tours for school children and groups; lending library of pictures and sculpture; sales and rental gallery (regional artists work); Lending and Listening Library of Records; Art Shop; Great Artists Series (6 concerts annually).

Library: 12,000 volumes on the arts; 20,000 slides; 50 current periodicals

Publications: Monthly Bulletin; annual year book; monthly calendars; exhibition catalogs. (See Schools)

Attendance: 85,000.

WATERTOWN

ROSWELL P. FLOWER MEMORIAL LIBRARY
229 Washington St, 13601. Tel: (315) 788-2352
Antony F. Cozzie, Library Dir.
Bonnie L. Ross, Reference Librn.
Free Mon. - Fri. 8:30 AM - 8:30 PM; Sat. 9 AM - 5 PM. Estab. 1903.

Collections: Paintings by American artists, sculpture, local antique furniture, murals.

Exhibitions: Promotes art exhibitions of local artists. Exhibitions are held in the library and number approx. 12 yearly.

WEST POINT

✠WEST POINT MUSEUM
United States Military Academy, 10996. Tel: (914) 938-2203
Richard E. Kuehne, Dir. Museum
Robert W. Fisch, Cur. Arms & Armor
Ray W. Moniz, Cur. Design
Michael J. McAfee, Cur. History
Michael E. Moss, Cur. Art
Walter J. Nock, Museum Specialist
Free 10:30 AM - 4:15 PM. Estab. 1854, supplementing the academic, cultural and military instruction of cadets; collections open to the public.

Collections: Sully portrait collection; Rindisbacher watercolors; †military paintings and prints; †military artifacts including weapons, flags, uniforms, medals, etc; paintings and prints of West Point.

Library: Small reference library of military subjects; photograph collection of 2500 items for lending or reference.

Income and Purchases: Income, c. $100,000; purchases, c. $5000.

Attendance: Approx. 370,000 annually.

WESTFIELD

✠PATTERSON LIBRARY
40 S. Portage St, 14787. Tel: (716) 326-2154
Cecily Moot Johnson, Pres
Rosanne Benson, Secy.
James M. Wheeler, Librn. & Dir.
Joseph Koshute, Art Dir.
Free Mon. - Sat. 9:30 AM - 5 PM; Mon, Wed, Thurs. evenings 7 - 9 PM. Estab. 1896 to provide opportunity for education and recreation through the use of literature, music, films, paintings, and other art forms; financed by endowment, local and state appropriations. Gallery has 2 rooms, one of 1115 sq. ft., octagon shaped, 11 ft. ceilings, 2nd room of 1400 sq. ft, semicircular, 15 ft. ceilings, 8 ft. high display walls burlap over plywood x 70 ft. length. Ann. meeting 2nd Sat. in July.

Collections: †30,000 books; 300 species of seashells; 100 specimens mounted of birds; 50 WWI posters; photograph collection of local history, 5000 prints for reference; †160 periodicals.

Exhibitions: Traveling exhibits; other painting, sculpture, and photography from western New York, Ohio and Pennsylvania artists.

Activities. Material available to anyone; fees for rental loan from local artists painting in members' gallery; framed reproductions, sculpture replicas and original paintings by local artists in lending collection ($500 value limit); also lent are 60 color reproductions, 5000 slides, 50 motion pictures on art subjects through county library system; 500 items lent in average year; WWI poster collection for tour; lectures open to the public; 6 visiting lecturers per year; 3 gallery talks; 6 tours; classes for adults and children; recitals; 40-seat film theater.

Income and Purchases: Income $60,000; purchases $30,000.
Attendance: 15,000.

YONKERS

THE HUDSON RIVER MUSEUM
511 Warburton Ave, 10701. Tel: (914) 963-4550
Donald M. Halley, Jr, Dir.
Mary Jean Madigan, Cur. History
Sutherland McColley, Cur. Art
Robert Conaway, Planetarium Dir.
Open Tues. - Sat. 10 AM - 5 PM; Sun. 1 - 5 PM; Wed. 7 - 10 PM; cl. Mon; open holidays (except New Year's Day, Thanksgiving, Christmas Eve, Christmas Day, New Year's Eve) from 1 - 5 PM; admis. by contribution. Estab. 1924 as Yonkers Museum of Science and Art, present name adopted 1940, inc. 1948; privately supported, maintained by city. New award-winning poured concrete addition opened 1969. New building houses Andrus Space Transit Planetarium, Troster Geophysical Hall. Major temporary exhibitions in art, history and technology.

Collections: 19th century decorative arts, paintings from the Hudson River School and restored period rooms are housed in the Museum's historic Trevor Mansion, Glenview.

Activities: Year around programs of concerts, lectures, films and gallery talks. Young People's Art Festival provides programs of drama, dance, poetry, music and films on weekends. Classes in arts and crafts for both children and adults. Winter and summer sessions.

Attendance: Approx. 200,000.

PHILIPSE MANOR HALL STATE HISTORIC SITE
29 Warburton Ave, 10701. Tel: (914) 965-4027
Edward v.K. Cunningham, Jr, Chmn, Taconic State Park & Recreation Commission
Peter F. Rain, Regional Adminr.
Nichol J. Forsht, Regional Historic Preservation Supvr.

Built 1682-1745; given to the state in 1908; opened 1912; currently open Wed. - Sun. Noon - 5 PM; to be open June 1, 1976, Wed. - Sun. 9 AM - 5 PM; guided tours on the hour and half hour. Presently undergoing restoration to be completed July 1976, under the administration of the New York State Office of Parks and Recreation, Taconic Region. The primary collection is the Cochran Collection of Art; the site is noted for the 18th century Rococo plaster ceiling.

YONKERS ART ASSOCIATION
Hudson River Museum, 10701.
Janice C. Tate, Coordinator
Estab. and inc. 1915. Mem. approx. 300; dues $15. Ann. exhibition, at Hudson River Museum, open to all artists; jury, award. Lectures, studio visits, workshops.

NORTH CAROLINA

ASHEVILLE

✠ASHEVILLE ART MUSEUM
Civic Center, 28801. Tel: (704) 253-3227
F. Thomas Gilmartin, Dir.
Estelle Marder, Registrar
Ronald Meisner, Field Services Coordinator
Deanna Napoli, Exhibitions Cur.
Free Tues. - Fri. 10 AM - 5 PM; Sat. & Sun. 1 - 5 PM; cl. Mon. & nat. holidays. Estab. 1948, to provide educational services to the western North Carolina community. First permanent home opened Feb, 1970. The Museum currently has an active purchase program to acquire additional contemporary works by southeastern contemporary artists.

Collections: Contemporary and indigenous arts and crafts of the Southeast includes active collecting of southern Appalachian works.

Activities: Mobile Museum Program; tours; lectures; workshops; films; circulating exhibitions and annual invitational exhibitions; reference library. Sales shop.

Publications: Bimonthly newsletter; periodic events calendars.
Attendance: Approx. 40,000 annually.

PACK MEMORIAL PUBLIC LIBRARY
Pack Square, 28801. Tel: (704) 252-8701
Kenneth Brown, Librn
John Bridges, Community Activities Dir.
Free Mon. - Fri. 9 AM - 9 PM; Sat. 9 AM - 6 PM; cl. Sun. Estab. 1879. Exhibition Room shows monthly topical displays of general interest and literary exhibitions assembled from the library's holdings.

Circulating collection of 16mm sound films and LP records; circulating and reference collection of general books on art. Monthly presentations of outstanding films Oct. through Apr. sponsored by Friends of the Library. Weekly films during summer. Series of popular art lectures in fall. Some recitals on Sunday afternoons jointly sponsored by library and Friends of the Library.

Attendance: (Main library program), 7000.

SOUTHERN HIGHLAND HANDICRAFT GUILD
P.O. Box 9145, 15 Reddick Rd, 28805. Tel: (704) 298-7928
Guild Shops:
Allanstand, 16 College St, Asheville, N.C. 28801. Tel: (704) 253-2051
Guild Crafts, 930 Tunnel Rd, Asheville, N.C. 28805.
Tel: (704) 298-7903
Guild Gallery, 501 State St, Bristol, Va. 24201. Tel: (703) 669-0821
Parkway Craft Center (summer only), Blowing Rock, N.C.
Tel: (704) 295-7938
Robert W. Gray, Dir.
James Gentry, Educ. Dir.
Alan W. Ashe, Comptroller
Carol R. Smith, Secy.
Estab. 1930, inc. 1945 to promote cooperation among agencies and individuals in conserving and developing Southern Mountain handicrafts. Ann. meeting spring; mem. 475 individual craftsmen; 75 centers, 225 friends, 44 assocs, 36 life, 19 honorary mem; dues $6 and higher. Two Craftsmen's Fairs annually—second Monday in July, Asheville, N.C; third Tuesday in October, Gatlinburg, Tenn.
Attendance at Fairs: July 25,000; October 38,000.

BELHAVEN

FANNIE MEBANE RALPH LIBRARY AND GALLERY*
27810. Tel: (919) 943-3051
Mrs. J.W. Lloyd, Pres.
Miss Loyce Brinson, Secy.
Mrs. W.E. Bateman, Jr, Art Dir.
Free Mon, Wed. & Fri. 2 - 5 PM. Estab. 1914, permanent building 1952, to serve the public and to furnish material for research and to enrich the cultural life of the community with exhibitions of art. Quarterly meetings; dues.

Collections: †Old Master prints; Metropolitan miniatures; James Walker serigraphs; Ethel Parrot Hughes tempera; Effie Raye Bateman portraits, woodcuts, seascapes and abstracts. These are lent for exhibitions on request.

Activities: Special lecture tours for local school groups; paintings and art objects lent to schools; exhibitions of noncompetitive shows (philanthropic project of Effie Raye Bateman in conjunction with Library Association); library for reference and lending.

CHAPEL HILL

✠WILLIAM HAYES ACKLAND MEMORIAL ART CENTER
University of North Carolina, 27514. Tel: (919) 933-3039
Joseph Curtis Sloane, Dir.
Robert Schlageter, Assoc. Dir.
Wanda Calhoon, Registrar
John Minor Wisdom, Cur.
Free Tues. - Sat. 10 AM - 5 PM; Sun. 2 - 5 PM; cl. Mon. Dedicated in 1958, The Ackland Art Center serves as a center for the visual arts and houses the Department of Art. It has galleries for temporary and permanent exhibitions, a library, and the Joseph Palmer Knapp rooms of antique furniture and decorative arts.

Collections: †Paintings, †prints, †drawings, †sculpture, †minor arts.

Exhibitions: Six to ten exhibitions a year.
Activities: Regular Art Department lectures.
Library: Research library of 123,000 volumes in addition to study collections of slides, photographs and colored reproductions.
Attendance: 40,000.

CHARLOTTE

✠THE MINT MUSEUM OF ART
501 Hempstead Place, 28207. Tel: (704) 334-9723
Cleve K. Scarbrough, Dir.
William C. Landwehr, Cur. Exhibitions
M. Mellanay Delhom, Cur, The Delhom Gallery & Institute for Study & Research in Ceramics
Drue Ann Sheesley, Cur. Educ.

Elizabeth Crouch, Asst. Dir. for Admin.
Robert Pierce, Head, Performing Arts Dept.
Stuart Schwartz, Cur, Hezekiah Alexander House
Free Tues. - Fri. 10 AM - 5 PM; Sat. & Sun. 2 - 5 PM; cl. national
and city holidays. Erected 1837 as 1st branch of the U.S. Mint;
moved and opened as a museum in 1936; inc. 1933. Ann. meeting
Jan; mem. 3000; dues $10 and up.
Collections: 3500 works of art; 2000 of these comprise the Delhom collection of ceramics; the remainder Renaissance, 18th century, 19th and 20th century American, Pre-Columbian; gold coin
collection, artifacts and documents; Hezekiah Alexander House,
c. 1774, historic restoration.
Exhibitions: Annual juried shows; painting and sculpture,
crafts (at least 3 purchases annually from each), one-man shows,
traveling exhibitions.
Activities: Lectures, concerts, films, docent training, guided
tours, Drama Guild productions, puppet shows, art classes, outdoor
festival, sales and rental gallery, museum shop.
Library: Art reference library of 2100 volumes.
Income and Purchases: Income $441,000; purchases $10,000.
Attendance: 135,000.

CULLOWHEE

ASSOCIATED ARTISTS OF NORTH CAROLINA, INC.
c/o Perry I. Kelly, Pres, P.O. Box 755, Cullowhee, 28723.
Tel: (704) 293-7210
Dr. Perry Kelly, Pres.
Tim Gilmartin, V.Pres.
Estab. 1959, a volunteer organization working toward the advancement of the fine arts in North Carolina through education and exhibits in cooperation with the various museums, galleries and other
art institutions in the state. A major project is effort to obtain more
art instruction in the public schools. Ann. meeting Oct; mem. 400.
Exhibitions: Circulates traveling exhibition composed of selec-
tions from the Spring Members' Show.
Publications: Exhibition catalogs.

DAVIDSON

CUNNINGHAM ARTS CENTER
Davidson College, 28036. Tel: (704) 892-8021
Douglas Houchens, Chmn. Art Dept.
Herb Jackson, Dir. Davidson National Print & Drawing Competition
Larry Ligo, Art Historian
The Cunningham Arts Center is the campus home for music,
drama and the fine arts. Exhibits change monthly in the Stowe Gal-
leries and often the artist attends the opening and speaks about his
work. The Davidson National Print and Drawing Competition is the
largest in the country and brings the finest graphics to the campus
each spring. Purchase awards amount to $3250. Recent acquisitions
include work by Isabel Bishop, Alexander Calder, Robert Goodnough,
Jack Levine, Peter Milton, Raphael Soyer, Carol Summers and Mark
Tobey. There are also prints and drawings by Corinth, Corot, Goya,
Hogarth, Lautrec, Miro, etc.
The new E. H. Little Library was completed in the summer 1974.
A structure of 100,000 sq. ft, it has a capacity of 500,000 volumes.
Special collections include a unique collection of materials on Peter
Stuart Ney, a designer of the college seal and reputed to be Napo-
leon's Marshal Ney; a collection of works of Bruce Rogers, book de-
signer; works by and about Woodrow Wilson, a former student. In
the near future, a portion of the Horton Collection, including jade,
porcelain, silver and furniture will be on permanent display in the
library.

DURHAM

✠DUKE UNIVERSITY MUSEUM OF ART
6877 College Station, 27708. Tel: (919) 684-5135
William K. Stars, Dir.
Nancy L. Passman, Asst. to Dir.
Paul A. Clifford, Asst. Cur.
Free Mon. - Fri. 9 AM - 5 PM; Sat. & Sun. 2 - 5 PM. Estab. 1969
as a research and study museum for the University and as a cultural center for the Durham and University communities; financed
by private and University funds, gifts, endowment. Seven galleries
exhibiting permanent and loan collections. Friends, mem. 138;
dues $5 - $1000.
Collections: Ernest Brummer Collection of Medieval and
Renaissance sculpture and decorative arts; Paul A. Clifford Collection of Pre-Columbian Art; Dr. and Mrs. John Gibbons Collection
of Bronzes of the Renaissance and later periods; Dr. and Mrs.
James H. Semans Collection; Col. and Mrs. Van R. White Oriental
Art Collection; Duke University Classical Collection; Kenneth W.
Clark Coin Collection; Duke University Graphic Collection; †Collec-
tion of Contemporary North Carolina Art.

Exhibitions: Woodcuts of Winslow Homer; Italian Paintings from
the Mary and Harry L. Dalton Collection; Prints of Josef Albers;
Sculpture of Raimondo Puccinelli; Traditional African Art; plus
others.
Activities: Docent program; individual paintings and original ob-
jects of art lent; lectures open to public; 5 visiting lecturers per
year; 20 gallery talks; 156 tours; classes for adults and children.
Publications: Exhibition catalogs; brochures; postcards.
Total budget: $33,448 (not including endowment funding).
Attendance: 15,000.

DUKE UNIVERSITY UNION GRAPHIC ARTS COMMITTEE
Box KM, Duke Station, 27706. Tel: (919) 684-2911
Tina I. Finkel, Pres.
Free 8:30 AM to Noon. Estab. to bring to the university community
exhibits of every type of graphic arts, to bring artists to campus
for workshops; financed by endowment. Galleries, large room in
Union and wall and shelf space in Booklovers Room in East Campus
Library. Monthly meetings; mem. approx. 15.
Exhibitions: Professional and local artists, approx. twice
monthly.
Activities: Lectures open to the public; 1 visiting lecturer per
year; classes for adults; competitions.
Income: 10% commission on exhibited works sold.

NORTH CAROLINA CENTRAL UNIVERSITY MUSEUM OF ART
27707. Tel: (919) 683-6211
Nancy C. Gillespie, Dir.
Free Mon. - Fri. 1 - 4 PM; Sun. 2 - 5 PM, when exhibits are up or
anytime by cooperation of director. Estab. 1971 to serve as a repository for the work of Afro-Americans and other minority groups; to
serve as a vehicle of education for majors through exhibits and the
future establishing of films, photos, museum training courses; financed by university. The gallery is physically a part of the art department; a new facility is planned for the biennium.
Collections: Small permanent collection of some 44 pieces, most
of which are paintings by well known black artists; a few pieces from
Africa, a student collection, currently negotiating for more work
from Africa and will expand collection as funding permits.
Exhibitions: Pan Africa 1971 (opening exhibit in collaboration
with Pan Africa Track Meet held in Durham); Toussaint L'Ouverature
series by Jacob Lawrence; Figures on the Beach III by Robert Reid;
Black Experience in Prints (Pratt Graphics); Ah Haiti, Glimpses of
Voodoo (Museum of National Center of Afro-American Artists);
Phillip Lindsay Mason, Paintings and Prints, 1973; Photographs by
George Walker III; Paintings by David Driskell; Paintings by Ernie
Barnes.
Activities: Individual paintings and original objects of art lent;
lending collection, 127 color reproductions; lectures open to the
public.
Income and Purchases: Income $2500-$3000; purchases con-
tingent upon funding.
Attendance: 200-300 per show.

GREENSBORO

✠WEATHERSPOON ART GALLERY
University of North Carolina at Greensboro, McIver Building,
27412.
James E. Tucker, Cur. Weatherspoon Art Gallery
Gilbert F. Carpenter, Dir.
Free Tues. - Fri. 10 AM - 5 PM; Sat. & Sun. 2 - 6 PM; Cl. Mon,
major academic holidays and between terms. Estab. 1942. Mem.
in the Weatherspoon Gallery Assoc. is open to everyone. Ann.
meeting Apr; mem. 450; dues $5 and higher.
Collections: Modern and contemporary †paintings, †sculpture,
†prints, †drawings.
Exhibitions: Annual Art on Paper Show; Annual exhibition of students' work; Selections from the Permanent Collection; American
and European Prints; Artists of North Carolina; Contemporary American Painting, Sculpture and Design.
Activities: Visiting lecturers from Dept. of Art; gallery talks by
faculty members and visitors, announced to students and members of
Gallery Association; scholarships and fellowships available in Dept.
of Art; traveling exhibitions; docent training program.
Purchases: Approx. $50,000 annually.

GREENVILLE

GREENVILLE ART CENTER
802 S. Evans St, 27834. Tel: (919) 758-1946
Edith G. Bradley Walker, Dir.
Open Sept. - June Mon. - Sat. 9 AM - 5 PM. Estab. 1939, inc.
1960 to foster public interest in art and to form a permanent collection. Sponsored by East Carolina Art Society. Ann. meeting
Feb; mem. 600; dues $10 and higher.

Collections: Photograph collection for reference and lending; †sculpture, crafts, †graphics, †contemporary paintings.

Exhibitions: Changing exhibitions from national traveling exhibition sources; exhibitions of local artists' work.

Activities: Lectures, demonstrations; art classes for adults and children; musicals, poetry readings.

Library: 200 art (graphic) books; 150 magazines.

Publications: Newsletter, monthly.

Income: $12,000 for operation, plus Foundation income for acquisition of art.

Attendance: 19,000.

KATE LEWIS GALLERY*
School of Art, East Carolina University, Box 2704, 27834.
Tel: (919) 758-6665
Dr. Wellington B. Gray, Dean
M. Tran Gordley, Mem. Acquisition Comt.
Robert Edmiston, Mem. Acquisition Comt.
Wesley V. Crawley, Mem. Acquisition Comt.
Free Mon. - Fri. 8 AM - 5 PM when the University is in session. Estab. 1959 as a teaching gallery for the University and for the display of senior exhibitions and master's theses; financed by state appropriation. Gallery is a subsidiary operation of the School of Art on the campus and is under the control of the faculty of the School of Art and its Dean.

Collections: Small collection in American art, being enlarged; a good portion of the collection is in the area of prints with some painting and a few pieces of sculpture.

Exhibitions: Exhibitions mounted by the staff of the school, traveling exhibitions from other colleges and organizations, faculty and student shows, a total of nine shows per year. During the summer permanent collection is exhibited.

Activities: Art classes for public school age children during regular school year.

Library: 900 volume technical library; approx. 32,000 2x2 color slides.

HICKORY

HICKORY MUSEUM OF ART
Third St. & First Ave. N.W, 28601. Tel: (704) 327-8576
Hugh M. Boyer, Pres.
George Blackwelder, Jr, V.Pres.
Virginia Neagle, Secy.
Mildred M. Coe, Dir. & Treas.
Free Mon. - Fri. 10 AM - 5 PM; Sun. 3 - 5 PM. Estab. 1944; new building dedicated 1960; serves principally the upper Piedmont region of the State. Ann. mem. drive Apr; mem. 497. Hickory Museum Guild formed in 1970 with approx. 100 mem.

Collections: Permanent collection of †American paintings as well as some Dutch, German, Italian and English examples; rare Chinese porcelains.

Exhibitions: Six nationally known artists shown annually; other regional and local exhibits supplement the year's program.

Activities: Art classes, lectures, docent tours, annual school art contests and local art exhibitions.

Library: Modest collection of technical books on the arts; miscellaneous papers and brochures; small collection of books on artists and the history of art.

Income and Purchases: Approx. $18,000 income; purchases $2000.

Attendance: 12,000.

NEW BERN

TRYON PALACE RESTORATION COMPLEX
613 Pollock St, 28560. Tel: (919) 638-5109
Donald R. Taylor, Dir.
Mrs. John A. Kellenberger, Chmn.
Dabney M. Coddington, Cur. Educ.
Julia B. Claypool, Educ. Specialist
Mrs. Robert A. Ipock, Registrar
James A. Thomas, Maintenance
W. H. Rea, Horticulturist
Open Tues. - Sat. 9:30 AM - 4 PM; Sun. 1:30 - 4 PM; cl. Mon. (unless national holiday); admis. adults $2, children through high school age $1; other tours available and combination ticket adults $4, children $1.50. Estab. 1959; historic house museums (Tryon Palace, Stevenson House, John Wright Stanly House) with fine portraits, paintings, mid-18th century, Federal and Empire antiques, furnishings, silver, porcelain, objet d'art; financed by state appropriation and admis. fees, Tyron Palace Commissions' private funds. Semi-annual meeting Apr. & Oct. for Tryon Palace Commission members.

Art collections: Paintings by Richard Wilson, Thomas Gainsborough, Claude Lorrain, School of Claude Lorrain, School of Sir

Joshua Reynolds, School of Sir Godfrey Kneller, E. Van Stuven, Matthew William Peters, Charles Phillips, Richard Paton, David Martin, Jan Olbercchts, Alan Ramsay, Nathaniel Dance, etc; graphics.

Activities: Information, publicity, audio-visual orientation program; annual symposium on the 18th century decorative arts; visiting lecturers; lending program with 36 slides with narrative; Mirror of the Past, 28-minute color and sound film; continuous tours by costumed hostesses. Museum Shops.

Library: 3000 volumes for reference and display available for use with special permission; photograph collection for reference.

Publications: Seven books, many leaflets.

Attendance: 40,400 annual average.

RALEIGH

HARRYE LYONS DESIGN LIBRARY
209 Brooks Hall, North Carolina State University, 27607.
Tel: (919) 737-2207
Helen Zschau, Librn.
Gloria Close, Libr. Asst.
Lynn Crisp, Libr. Asst.
Jane Myatt, Libr. Asst.
Free Mon. - Thurs. 8:30 AM - 9:30 PM; Fri. 8:30 AM - 5 PM; Sat. 9 AM - 1 PM; Sun. 1 - 5 PM. Estab. 1946; to serve the reading, study, and reference needs of the faculty and students of the school of design; financed by city and state appropriations.

Collections: Books and periodicals on urban design, product design, landscape design, †art and architecture. Slides on art, architecture, landscape design, †urban design; 15,953 volumes of lending and reference books; 33,772 slide collection; 370 print collection; 914 maps and plans; 215 bibliographies compiled by the design library.

Purchases: $15,000.

Attendance: 30,200 annual average.

NORTH CAROLINA ART SOCIETY
107 E. Morgan St, 27601.
Mrs. Isaac V. Manly, Pres.
Mrs. Charles M. Reeves, Jr, V.Pres.
Charles Lee Smith, Jr, Secy-Treas.
Mrs. Christopher R. Webster, Exec. Secy.
Estab. 1927 to formulate programs to promote public appreciation of visual art, to encourage talent, to disseminate information on art through publications, to encourage private acquisition of works of art and to support the State Art Museum's programs by membership. Ann. meeting Dec; mem. 3000; dues $5 (student) and higher.

The Art Society's collection has been given to the North Carolina Museum of Art and all purchases are given either to that or other art centers in the State.

Exhibitions: Annual North Carolina Artists' Exhibition held at North Carolina Museum of Art, financed, including medal awards and purchases, by the Art Society.

Income: $25,000; art purchases (Phifer Fund) - $3000 N.C. Artists' Exhibition; $50,000 (Phifer Fund) annually for work of art for State Art Museum.

✦NORTH CAROLINA MUSEUM OF ART
107 E. Morgan St, 27611. Tel: (919) 829-7568
Moussa M. Domit, Dir.
Justus Bier, Dir. Emeritus
Charles J. Robertson, Assoc. Dir.
Michael W. Brantley, Head, Educ. Services
Benjamin F. Williams, Head, Collections Care & Preparation
Gay M. Hertzman, Head, Collections Research & Publ.
Dorothy B. Rennie, Head, Prog. Research & Coordination
Peggy Jo D. Kirby, Registrar
Cheryl S. Warren, Librn.
Free Tues. - Sat. 10 AM - 5 PM; Sun. 2 - 6 PM; cl. Mon, New Year's Day, Christmas, Thanksgiving & state holidays. Estab. 1947, open to public 1956.

Collections: European and American painting, sculpture, decorative arts; ancient art; Pre-Columbian, African, Oceanic and North American Indian art; Kress Collection; Phifer Collection; Mary Duke Biddle Gallery for the Blind.

Exhibitions: Approx. 10 per year; annual North Carolina artists competitions; traveling exhibition program.

Activities: Lectures, concerts, guided tours, seminars-workshops, statewide extension program. Bookshop.

Library: A reference library of approx. 10,500 volumes, 2000 color slides, 4000 black and white photographs and 700 color transparencies.

Publications: Bulletin, quarterly; Calendar, 10-11 per year; exhibition and permanent collection catalogs, brochures.

Income: State legislative appropriation $900,000 including purchase fund.

Attendance: Approx. 84,000.

ROCKY MOUNT

ROCKY MOUNT ARTS AND CRAFTS CENTER
Old Nashville Rd, P.O. Box 4031, 27801.
Tel: (919) 977-2111 Exten. 257
Julia Jordan, Dir.
William A. Rawls, Dir. Theatre
Free Mon. - Fri. 9 AM - 1 PM and 2 - 5 PM; Sun. 3 - 5 PM; cl.
Sat. except for classes. Estab. 1957 to promote the development
of the creative arts in the community through education, partici-
pation, and appreciation of music, dance, painting, drama, etc,
and to provide facilities and guidance for developing talents and en-
riching lives through artistic expression and appreciation. Financed
by membership and sponsored by the City Recreation Dept. Mem.
approx. 600; dues $5 and higher.
Exhibitions: Permanent collection and traveling shows change
each month. Outdoor Art Exhibition in the Spring, part of the Arts
Festival.
Activities: Conducts art classes; maintains small lending library;
lectures, concerts, year-round theatre program, classes for adults
and children.
Attendance: Approx. 25,000.

WILMINGTON

ST. JOHN'S ART GALLERY, INC.*
114 Orange St, 28401. Tel: (919) 763-0281
John R. Oxenfeld, Pres.
Mrs. Frederick Willetts, Jr, Secy.
Margaret T. Hall, Dir.
Hester Donnelly, Art Teacher
Ruth Johnson, Secy.
Birta Anderson, Student Aid
Open Mon. - Sat. 10 AM - 5 PM; Sun. 2 - 5 PM; cl. Sat. & Sun. in
June, July and Aug. Estab. 1962; art center for Southeastern North
Carolina; restore and preserve historic building, St. John's Masonic
Lodge, No. I; to estab. an art collection, provide special exhibitions
and art classes, lectures and music programs; supported by mem.
Exhibitions are rented or borrowed and changed each month. A sales
Gallery for artists in the area also. Ann. meeting 2nd Tues. in June;
mem. 1250; dues $7.50 individual, $15 family.
Collections: Paintings by Elizabeth Chant, glass scent bottles,
Jugtown pottery, †contemporary American painting.
Exhibitions: 12 to 14 exhibits each year; one-man shows of area
artists, travelling exhibits from other museums, exhibits from local
collectors.
Activities: Classes in drawing and painting for children and
adults; lectures and musicals for the membership, 4-5 visiting lec-
turers per year; gallery talks or tours average 30-60 a year.
Library: 200 volumes for lending.
Publications: St. John's Bulletin, monthly from Oct. through June.
Annual Income: $12,000-$14,000.
Attendance: 14,500-17,000.

WINSTON-SALEM

THE ARTS COUNCIL, INC.
610 Coliseum Dr, 27106. Tel: (919) 722-2585
Elizabeth M. Booke, Pres.
Milton Rhodes, Exec. Dir.
Allan H. Cowen, Assoc. Dir.
Open weekdays 9 AM - 5 PM. Estab. 1949, The Arts Council is a
housing, coordinating, promoting, and fund raising organization for
39 member groups, including Associated Artists, Arts and Crafts
Association, the Winston-Salem Symphony Association, The Little
Theatre, South Eastern Center for Contemporary Art, Childrens'
Theatre.
Housing facilities include a theatre, rehearsal rooms, art and
craft studios and an exhibition gallery. Financed by endowment,
city and state appropriation and fund drives. Ann. meeting May;
mem. 15,000; member groups are autonomous of Arts Council, but
management counsel, promotion and funds are provided for various
arts programs.

ASSOCIATED ARTISTS OF WINSTON-SALEM
Arts Council Gallery
610 Coliseum Dr, 27106. Tel: (919) 723-9075
Elsie Dinsmore Popkin, Pres.
Kay Geroy, Secy.
Dorothy Hitchcock, Gallery Exhibit Chmn.
William C. Carter, Treas.
Christie Taylor, Mgr.
Free 9 AM - 5 PM. Estab. 1955 to conduct and promote creative and
educational activities in fine art through exhibitions, programs, and
demonstrations; financed by membership and Arts Council. Public
gallery in Arts Council Building open whenever the building is open.
Meetings are 2nd Tues. of each month, elections in Apr; mem. 314;
dues $7 associate, $10 exhibiting.

Exhibitions: Rotating exhibits by exhibiting artist members, plus
juried shows, 1 print and drawing show each October; Painting and
sculpture juried show each March; juried photography show; David
Lund; Walter Barker and Peter Agostini.
Activities: Individual paintings and original objects of art lent;
lectures open to public; 10 - 12 visiting lecturers per year; 1 - 2
gallery talks; competitions.
Publications: Monthly newsletter.
Annual Income: $6000.
Attendance: 2200.

MUSEUM OF EARLY SOUTHERN DECORATIVE ARTS
924 S. Main St.(mailing Drawer F, Salem Station), 27108.
Tel: (919) 722-6148
Arthur Spaugh, Jr, Pres. of Old Salem, Inc.(owner)
Frank L. Horton, Dir.
Carolyn Weekley, Cur.
Open Mon. - Sat. 11 AM - 6 PM; Sun. 1:30 - 4:30 PM; cl. Christmas;
admis. adults $2, students $1. Opened to the public Jan, 1965 to re-
search, collect, preserve and exhibit the early (1600-1820) decora-
tive arts of Maryland, Virginia, the Carolinas, Georgia, Kentucky and
Tennessee; endowed. 15 period rooms and 4 galleries exhibiting
early southern decorative arts. Mem. 300; dues $15 individual.
Collections: †Furniture, †period rooms, †metalwork, †ceramics,
†textiles, †prints, †paintings by early southern artists or of southern
subjects.
Exhibitions: 2-3 special exhibitions yearly.
Activities: Slide programs loaned to classes, clubs, individuals,
nominal rental, approx. 50 per year; several thousand Kodachromes
in lending collection; lectures open to public; daily gallery talks or
tours; classes for adults.
Library: Approx. 1800 volumes for lending to staff, reference to
others; cataloged slide and photograph library of southern decorative arts in museum collections and private collections; data files on
Southern artisans.
Publications: Journal of Early Southern Decorative Arts (twice
yearly).
Attendance: (1974) 17,862.

NORTH CAROLINA MUSEUMS COUNCIL
Old Salem, Inc, Drawer F Salem Station, 27108.
Tel: (919) 723-3688
William J. Moore, Pres.
John D. Ellington, Secy-Treas.
Cleve K. Scarbrough, V.Pres.
Belinda B. Riggsbee, Newsletter Ed.
Estab. 1964 to stimulate public interest, support and understanding
of museums, to provide a medium for cooperation and communica-
tion among museums and museum personnel; financed by member-
ship. Ann. meeting spring; mem. 200; dues $5 individual.
Activities: Lectures for members only; 2 visiting lecturers per
year.
Publications: North Carolina Museums Council Newsletter,
spring and fall.

✠REYNOLDA HOUSE, INC.
Reynolda Rd, P.O. Box 11765, 27106. Tel: (919) 725-5325
Barbara B. Lassiter, Pres.
Nicholas B. Bragg, Exec. Dir.
Open daily 9:30 AM - 4:30 PM; Sun. 1:30 - 4:30 PM; cl. Mon,
Christmas Day and month of Jan; admis. $2 adults, 75¢ children
or students. Estab. 1964 for the advancement of education and
the arts; endowed. Gallery.
Collections: American paintings, American and imported antique
furnishings, complete collection of American birds by Dorothy
Doughty; costume collection dating from 1905 to 1940's.
Activities: Lectures open to public, 4 or 5 visiting lecturers per
year; chamber music concerts; humanities classes, 15 hours college
credit.
Library: 2000 volumes on American art and artists for reference.
Attendance: 40,000.

SOUTHEASTERN CENTER FOR CONTEMPORARY ART
500 S. Main St, 27101. Tel: (919) 725-9104
T. Hilliard Staton, Pres.
Ted Potter, Dir.
Mrs. Noel L. Dunn, Asst. to Dir.
Mrs. Peter T. Wilson, Jr, Business Mgr.
Free Mon. - Sat. 10 AM - 4:30 PM; Sun. 2 - 4:30 PM. Estab. and
inc. 1956, the Center is a nonprofit organization serving the South-
east. Its purpose is to bring the work of the finest artists of the
Southeast to the viewing and buying public. Ann. meeting May; mem.
700; dues $10.
Exhibitions: The Center holds Semi-Annual Southeastern Juried
Competitions judged by a prominent figure in the art world. The
remaining 10 exhibits are invitational one and two-man and group
shows, making a total of 12 shows a year. The Center has no per-

manent collections. A number of Center works are available for rent, and rental payments may be applied to the purchase price, $15,000 in cash awards have been given over a three-year period.

Activities: The Center primarily has an educational function and offers lectures and art demonstrations to the public. Center docents attend a preopening lecture on each new show. Numerous school groups tour the Center, and Center Art Kit docents give lectures and show slides in the public school system.

Income: Average annual budget $100,000.

Attendance: For past two calendar years, 50,000.

NORTH DAKOTA

DEVILS LAKE

LAKE REGION ART ASSOCIATION
P.O. Box 11, 58301.
Dikka Ballentine, Co-Chairwoman
Ann Schroeder, Co-Chairwoman
Mrs. L. E. Campbell, Secy.
Estab. 1957 to further art appreciation and provide exhibits from throughout the State of North Dakota; encourage art and art appreciation to young and old alike; financed by endowment and mem. State Art Gallery, open Memorial Day - Labor Day; admis. free. Meeting dates, monthly, Sept. - May; mem. 60; dues $2.

Exhibitions: Annual Spring Art Show.

Activities: Lectures open to the public; scholarships.

GRAND FORKS

UNIVERSITY ART GALLERY
University of North Dakota
Box 8136 University Station, 58201. Tel: (701) 777-4195
Laurel J. Reuter, Dir.
Leigh Herndon, Asst. to Dir.
Free. Estab. 1970 to house temporary exhibitions of contemporary American art with related educational events; financed by city and state appropriation.

Activities: The University has a separate College of Fine Arts (See Schools). Traveling exhibitions organized and circulated; lectures open to the public; 4-5 gallery talks.

Publications: Exhibition catalogs.

Attendance: 50,000 annually.

MINOT

LINHA ART GALLERY
Minot Art Association
Box 325, 58701. Tel: (701) 838-4445
Trish Hoeuen, Pres.
Judy Smith, Secy.
Galen R. Willert, Gallery Dir.
Mary Ann Brosnahan, Permanent Collection Comt.
William Lange, Treas.
Ardie Huss, V.Pres.
Open daily 1 - 5 PM; cl. Mon; admis. adults 50¢, children 10¢.
Estab. 1970 to promote means and opportunities for the education of the public with respect to the study and culture of the fine arts and the enjoyment and wholesome utilization thereof; sponsoring a fine arts gallery; financed by endowment and membership. Ann. meeting 1st Tues. in Apr; mem. over 200; dues $5 - $500.

Collections: †Regional, national and international prints and paintings.

Exhibitions: Different exhibition every three weeks; Annual All North Dakota Art Competition.

Activities: Lectures open to the public; 2-3 visiting lecturers per year; 34 tours; classes for adults and children; competitions. Gift shop.

Publications: Newsletters and class brochures; Calendars of Forthcoming Exhibitions and Events, 4-6 issues per year.

Attendance: 6000 annual average.

Downtown Linha Art Gallery
Balcony Floor, Ellisons Dept. Store
Estab. Feb. 1, 1975. Exhibitions changing monthly.

Collections: Prints, paintings, macrame, pottery and sculpture in a permanent collection that has been exhibited locally and in other towns in the northwestern part of state.

VALLEY CITY

✤2ND CROSSING GALLERY
Room 210 McFarland Hall, Valley City State College, Box 1319, 58072. Tel: (701) 845-2690
Floyd Martin, Co-Dir.
Mrs. Riley Rogers, Co-Dir.
Open Mon. - Fri. 1 - 4 PM; Mon. & Wed. 7 - 9 PM; Sun. 2 - 4 PM.

Estab. Oct, 1973 to provide local, state, national and international shows for the people of this area; competitions; financed by endowment and membership. Small but very professional gallery 29 x 40 ft, with track lighting and movable standards. Mem. approx. 130; dues $15 resident.

Collections: †Collection of 16 pieces purchased over a 3 year period.

Exhibitions: 11 separate exhibitions per year (closed Aug).

Budget: $8000; purchases, $465 (last fiscal year).

Attendance: Over 6000.

OHIO

AKRON

✤AKRON ART INSTITUTE
69 E. Market St, 44308. Tel: (216) 376-9185
Louis S. Myers, Pres.
Mrs. Henry Saalfield, Secy.
Richard Herberich, Treas.
Robert M. Doty, Dir. *to Currie gallery*
David Verbeck, Adminr.
D. Lawrence Smith, Dir. Educ. Programming
Denis Conley, Gallery Asst.
Marjorie Harvey, Registrar/Librarian
Free daily Noon - 5 PM. Estab. 1921, inc. 1928, reorganized 1944; remodelled Carnegie Library building owned by Institute, provides downtown location with 9 galleries, six studios, lecture hall, offices and work rooms. Ann. meeting May; mem. 2018, incl. individuals, clubs and industrials; dues $20 and higher.

Collections: 20th century American—a growing collection containing Warhol, Judd, Segal, Davis and others; Dutch and Flemish 16th and 17th century; Italian 15th, 16th and 17th century; German 16th century; French 18th and 19th centuries; educational collection providing kits of objects and slides for loan to teachers; contemporary in emphasis.

Exhibitions: 15 to 20 exhibitions.

Activities: Over 90 special events scheduled for the public annually result in increased attendance; 30 exhibitions, 10 of which feature local artists; 25 adult classes and 12 student classes; 7284 students toured by docents and 50 special tours; 8 concerts, 9 gallery lectures, 5 workshops; 13 free Sat. workshops for children; 8 member openings. Museum shop.

Library: 4000 volumes covering fine arts, architecture and design; 59 art, design, architecture and sculpture periodicals. Classified and indexed exhibition catalog; 6100 slides, mounted reproductions and biographical and clipping file for reference.

Income and Purchases: Income $250,000; purchases average $30,000 annually.

Attendance: 50,000.

BIERCE LIBRARY
University of Akron
44325. Tel: (216) 375-7495
H. Paul Schrank, Jr, Librn.
Open Mon. - Fri. 7:30 AM - Midnight; Sat. 9 AM - 5 PM; Sun. 2 PM - Midnight. Estab. 1870.

Library contains 436,000 volumes, approx. 9000 covering art.

ASHLAND

ASHLAND COLLEGE
Art Department
College Ave, 44805. Tel: (419) 289-4005
Leon F. Schenker, Chmn.
Carl M. Allen, Dir. of Exhibitions
Free Tues. - Sun. 1 - 4 PM; Tues. 7 - 10 PM. Estab. 1969-70. Gallery maintained for continuous exhibitions, with accent on contemporary works, some historical, occidental and Oriental.

Exhibitions: German Expressionist 20th Century Prints; European Drawing From the Baroque Period; George Biddle Retrospective; David Dreisbach, Print Retrospective; Sidney Chafetz, Portraits and Satires; Contemporary Painting Invitational; Iranian Ceramics; Noel Martin, Designer; Ed Mieczkowski, Paper Paintings; Ed Mayer, Sculpture with Options; Modern Korean Paintings; John Pearson, Large Works, etc.

Activities: Original objects of art lent to Akron Art Institute and Cleveland Museum of Art; lectures open to public; 2 - 3 gallery talks; tours; concerts, dramatic programs, classes for children; scholarships. (See Schools)

Income and Purchases: Income base amount $2500, plus occassional assists; purchases $500 - $20,000.

ATHENS

✠ANTHONY G. TRISOLINI GALLERY
Ohio University
    48 E. Union St, 45701. Tel: (614) 594-5664
Dr. Henry H. Lin, Dir.
Doreen H. Pallini, Asst. Dir.
Free Mon. - Fri. 10 AM - 4 PM; Sun. 1 - 4 PM. Estab. Apr, 1974
to serve as a center for the permanent collection of Ohio University and to enrich the cultural sphere of the University and Athens
communities by presenting exhibitions from varied sources; financed by the University. 120 gallery volunteers meet monthly;
dues $4.
    Collections: Major collections and those presently being en-
larged by purchase are works by contemporary printmakers.
    Exhibitions: (1974) Marison Exhibition; Carol Townsend;
Richard Maury Williams Collection; Juan Genoves Suite Silencio,
Silencio; Leuty McGuffy Manahan Paintings; Jacques Lipchitz Drawings; (1975) Tom Wesselman Drawings; Italian Renaissance Paintings;
Donald Whitlach; Jim Dine Prints; De Steiguer Portraits; Margaret
Krecker Awards; Donald and June Roberts Collection.
    Activities: Work is lent to on-campus buildings and other gal-
leries; lectures open to public; 3 gallery talks; competitions.
    Publications: Catalogs for most shows.
    Annual Purchases: $5000.
    Attendance: 3000.

✠OHIO UNIVERSITY FINE ARTS LIBRARY
    45701. Tel: (614) 594-5065
Anne Braxton, Art Librn.
Timothy Daum, Asst. Art Librn.
Free Mon. - Fri. 8 AM - Midnight; Sat. & Sun. 1 PM to Midnight; financed by state appropriations.
    Collections: Research collection in history of photography; small
collection of original photographs for study purposes.
    Library: 30,000 volume lending library; photograph collection
of 7500 prints for lending; 3500 exhibition catalogs.

BEREA

✠ART GALLERY
Baldwin-Wallace College
    95 E. Bagley Rd, 44017. Tel: (216) 826-2152
Harold D. Cole, Head Dept. Art
Helen A. Leon, Dir. Art Gallery
Terry Speer, Conservator
Free Sun. - Fri. 2 - 5 PM. Art Gallery is considered to be a part
of the art program of the department of art, its purpose is that of
a teaching museum for the students of the college and the general
public; financed through budgetary support of the college.
    Collections: Approx. †200 paintings and sculptures by mid-west
artists of the 20th century; †approx. 1900 drawings and prints from
16th-20th century, with a concentration in 19th-20th century
examples.
    Exhibitions: Approx. 50 exhibitions since 1972, including Recent
Works by M. C. Gellman; Prints by Milton Avery; Sculpture by Gwen
Lin Goo; Retrospective Work of David Driesbach; Stoneware by
Harriet and Tom Spleth; work from the permanent collection.
    Activities: Individual paintings lent to schools; 20 items lent in
an average year; photograph collection begun in 1972, 10 prints;
lectures open to the public; 4 gallery talks; 10 tours; competitions.
    Publications: Exhibition catalogs are published for important
exhibitions, 1-2 per year.
    Attendance: 2500.

CANTON

✠THE CANTON ART INSTITUTE
    1001 Market Ave. N, 44702. Tel: (216) 453-7666
E. Lang D'Atri, Pres.
Mrs. Kenneth Adams, V.Pres.
Paul Basner, Treas.
John P. Van Abel, Secy.
Jesse G. Wright, Jr, Dir.
Joseph R. Hertzi, Asst. to Dir.
Shirley A. Hawk, Admin. Asst.
Free Sept. - July 15, Tues. - Sat. 10 AM - 5 PM; Tues, Wed. &
Thurs. 7 - 9 PM; Sun. 2 - 5 PM. Summer, July 15, - Aug 16, Tues. -
Sat. Noon - 5 PM; Sun. 2 - 5 PM. Estab. 1935, inc. 1941. Ann.
meeting in Apr; mem. 1680; dues $10 and higher.
    Collections: American, Italian, and Spanish paintings; eighteenth
and nineteenth century English and American portraiture; twentieth
century regional art; graphics; art library; sculpture; decorative
arts; costumes; art objects.
    Exhibitions: Approximately 40 to 50 traveling or collected
exhibitions of painting, sculpture, commercial and industrial arts
annually.

    Activities: Guided tours; lectures; films; gallery talks; arts
festivals; formally organized education programs for children and
adults.
    Library: Art library of 4000 volumes.
    Attendance: 75,000.

CINCINNATI

CINCINNATI ART CLUB
    1021 Parkside Place, 45205. Tel: (513) 762-9484
Gene P. Hinckley, Pres.
Robert B. Schoellkopf, Secy.
Joseph O. Emmett, Treas.
Estab. 1890, inc. 1923. New Gallery completed. Ann. meeting May;
mem. approx. 250; dues active $45, assoc. $35. Small collection of
paintings by American artists.
    Exhibitions: Exhibition of members' work changed monthly.
Open to the public each Sunday afternoon Sept. to May. Annual Club
Shows Sept, Jan, and Christmas Art Bazaar. Sales $6000-$7000
annually.
    Activities: Lectures and demonstrations by important artists
each month (Sept. to May); a Forum open to the public each month.
Maintains small library of books on art.
    Gallery Attendance: Averages 3500.

✠CINCINNATI ART MUSEUM
    Eden Park, 45202. Tel: (513) 721-5204
John J. Emery, Chmn.
John W. Warrington, Pres.
Millard F. Rogers, Jr, Dir.
Betty Zimmerman, Asst. Dir.
Denny T. Carter, Assoc. Cur. Painting
Kristin L. Spangenberg, Cur. Prints, Drawings·
Dr. Carol M. Macht, Cur. Decorative Arts, Sr. Cur.
Daniel S. Walker, Assoc. Cur. Ancient & Near Eastern Art
Mary L. Meyer, Cur. Costumes & Textiles
Roslynne Wilson, Cur. Educ.
Carolyn R. Shine, Registrar & Asst Gen. Cur.
Patricia Rutledge, Librn.
Clay W. Pardo, Adminr.
Open 10 AM - 5 PM; Sun. & holidays 1 - 5 PM; cl. Thanksgiving &
Christmas; admis. adults $1, children 12-18 50¢; free on Sat; free
to mem. all times. Estab. 1880, inc. 1881. Ann. meeting Mar; mem.
2300; dues $25 - $100.
    Collections: Paintings from 14th to 20th century European; 13th
to 17th century Chinese; 18th to 20th century American. Includes
collections of Mary M. Emery, John J. Emery, Mary Hanna, Mary
E. Johnston, Emilie Heine and Eva Belle and Harry S. Leyman;
Sculpture includes Nabataean antiquities from Khirbet Tannur;
Egyptian, Greek, Medieval, Renaissance, Near and Far Eastern
and Modern, as well as the collection of Millard F. and Edna F.
Shelt; (15th to 20th century) European and (17th to 20th century)
American prints and drawings including the collections of Herbert
Greer French, Allyn C. Poole, Ross W. Sloniker and Albert P.
Strietmann (color lithographs); miniature paintings from India and
Persia; art objects from North and South America and Africa;
Chinese bronzes, textiles and pottery; near Eastern textiles, pottery, bronzes and gold; French, English and American rooms of
the 17th to 19th centuries; European and American ceramics,
silver, glass, lace, tapestries and costumes; W. T. H. Howe
collection of early American glass; William Howard Doane collection of musical instruments; U.S. Playing Card Co. collection
of Playing Cards and the Arthur Joseph collection of Meissen
porcelain on permanent loan.
    Exhibitions: (1970-1975) Paintings of the 1950's from the Gug-
genheim Museum; prints by Rolf Nesch; Guggenheim collection
painters and printmakers; Worthington Whittredge: A Retrospective Exhibition of an American Artist; Children's art from the
Museum classes; American paintings from Newport; Objects: U.S.A;
Annual Exhibition by Art Academy of Cincinnati students; Figures/
Environments; books and prints by William Blake; sculpture from
Cincinnati private collections; Cincinnati Biennial Awards Exhibi-
tion; Albrecht Durer in his 500th year; The American City: Yester-
day, Today and Tomorrow; drawings by Carl Friedrich Lessing;
recent prints by Julian Stanczak; Robert Duncanson Centennial Exhi-
bition; Annual Exhibition of Children's Art from Museum classes;
Annual Art Academy of Cincinnati Students Show; E. Paul Wilhelm
Memorial Exhibition; Decorative Arts in Review; The Passionate
Years: Eastman Johnson Retrospective Exhibition; Mark Tobey: A
Decade of Printmaking; Honore Daumier and Thomas Nast: Political Commentary Through Prints; The Mary E. Johnston Collection
of late 19th and 20th century European and American paintings; The
1972 Cincinnati Invitational Exhibition; Winter Celebrations and
Pageants in Prints; San Francisco Bay area comtemporary printmakers; Edward Lear in Greece; The Mathews: Masterpieces of
the California Decorative Style; Homage to Maurits C. Escher;
Dine/Kitaj; Annual Art Academy of Cincinnati Students Show;

Tarot Cards; Masterpieces from Pennsylvania Academy of Fine Arts; Louise Nevelson as Printmaker; Campbell Museum Collection; Eastern European Printmakers; George L. K. Morris, Abstract Art of 1930's.

Activities: Subscription lecture series offered to members and their guests, with fall series relating to Decorative Arts and spring series on Cincinnati area architecture. Regular season of art classes for members and their children age 4 - 18, meeting Sept. - Dec, Feb. - Apr; summer classes from mid-June through July. Tour and lecture programs for adults and children by appointment. Special members' programs for openings of major exhibitions. Monthly gallery lectures for members sponsored by Women's Committee. Volunteer-managed and staffed Museum Shop which sells books, publications, two and three-dimensional reproductions, all relating to Museum's permanent collections and temporary exhibitions. Cafeteria open to public Mon. - Fri. 12:30 - 3:30 PM; Sat. 11:30 AM - 2 PM.

Library: 33,000 books, 250,000 pamphlets and clippings, 17,000 mounted reproductions, color slides of collections, to cover the history of arts and artists. Open to public for reference, with lending privileges limited to members.

Publications: Exhibition catalogs for major shows originated by the Museum; issues of the Museum Bulletin (approx. twice a year); seasonal program booklets; information brochures; Children's Guides to the Collections; invitations and special announcements.

Attendance: 322,000.

CINCINNATI INSTITUTE OF FINE ARTS
2649 Erie Ave, 45208. Tel: (513) 871-3325
Morley P. Thompson, Pres.
James M. E. Mixter, Secy.
Paul George Sittenfeld, Exec. Dir.
Estab. and inc. 1927 to provide for the continuance and growth of education and culture in the various fields of fine arts in the metropolitan community of Cincinnati. Ann. meeting Oct. Management of endowments and coordination of financial policies of Cincinnati Symphony Orchestra, Cincinnati Art Museum, Cincinnati Opera, Taft Museum (q.v.). Manages the Fine Arts Fund of Cincinnati, conducting an annual campaign for public support in behalf of the four participating institutions named above.

THE CONTEMPORARY ARTS CENTER
115 E. Fifth St, 45202. Tel: (513) 721-0390
Nancy McIntosh, Chmn.
Jack Boulton, Dir.
Open Tues. - Sat. 10 AM - 5 PM; Sun. Noon - 5 PM; cl. Mon. & holidays. The Contemporary Arts Center is an independent organization. It is the successor to the Cincinnati Modern Art Society, which was estab. and inc. in 1939. Ann. meeting July; mem. approx. 900; dues $25 and higher.
Exhibitions: Approx. eight exhibitions a year devoted exclusively to the art of the 20th century in all media.
Activities: Plans special tours for members in other cities and countries; lectures; film series; gallery talks; concerts; docent training program; originates traveling exhibitions.

✠DESIGN, ARCHITECTURE & ART LIBRARY, UNIVERSITY OF CINCINNATI
45221. Tel: (513) 475-3238
Suzanne Yoder, Acting Librn.
Estab. to serve the teaching and research needs of the College of Design, Architecture & Art; financed by appropriations.
Collections: †Approx. 28,000 volumes of books and periodicals.
Income and Purchases. Income approx. $45,000; purchases approx. $20,000.

EMERY GALLERY
Edgecliff College
2220 Victory Parkway, 45206. Tel: (513) 961-3770
Sister Margaret Molitor, Pres.
Dorothy M. Kiel, Dir.
Free 1 - 5 PM daily. Estab. 1967 to present to students and the public at large outstanding artists of local, national and international fame; privately financed.
Exhibitions: Joan Graff, fine art prints; Peach Mountain Fibers, wall hangings by Cincinnati Weaver's Guild; American Crafts Exhibition; Art Students of Edgecliff College.
Activities: Individual paintings lent to schools; lectures open to public; classes for adults and children; scholarships. Book shop.

✠TAFT MUSEUM
316 Pike St, 45202. Tel: (513) 241-0343
Frank T. Hamilton, Pres.
John W. Warrington, Chmn.
Katherine Hanna, Dir.
Jan Weigel, Designer

Free 10 AM - 5 PM; Sun. & holidays, 2 - 5 PM; cl. Thanksgiving and Christmas. In 1927 Mr. and Mrs. Charles P. Taft gave to the Cincinnati Institute of Fine Arts their art collection, the House and all endowment fund for maintenance. Active control was taken by the Institute in 1931; Museum opened in 1932. The historic House, built in 1820, is one of the finest examples of Federal architecture in this country. Its interior is decorated in the period. An architectural green, formal garden was opened in 1949.
Collections: 150 paintings including work by Rembrandt, Hals, Turner, Goya, Corot, Gainsborough, Raeburn and other Masters; 200 notable Chinese porcelains; 120 French Renaissance enamels; Renaissance jewelry and 18th century watches from many countries; furnishings of the House include antique toiles and satins and a large collection of Duncan Phyfe furniture.
Exhibitions: (1973-75) 100 Years of Toys: 1820-1920; You Name It, Part Two; Soft and Light; Dutch Couples: Rembrandt and His Contemporaries; About Pottery and Porcelain... Plus; American Painting and Sculpture Today; Kinetic Light Sculpture by Claudio Marzollo; Ming to Ch'ing; Ming Seventeenth Century Ink and Color Paintings.
Activities: Free lectures and tours for children and adults; special lectures by visiting lecturers; free Sunday Chamber Music concerts and recitals; approx. 500 gallery tours, 10 lectures by staff; 70 In-School classroom demonstrations (four year pilot project in 8 schools grades 2 - 5); a total of 800 educational events annually.
Library: 1000 books and portfolios relating to Taft Art Collection, noncirculating.
Publications: Catalog of the Taft Collection; Booklet on History of the Historic House and Art Collection; special exhibition catalogs.
Attendance: Average 50,000.

UNIVERSITY OF CINCINNATI FINE ARTS COLLECTION
403 Tangeman, 45221. Tel: (513) 475-3462
Gilbert Young, Co-dir./Conservator
Elizabeth B. Sittenfeld, Co-dir./Cur.
Free Mon. - Fri. 8 AM - 5 PM. Estab. 1967 to preserve and maintain the University's art collection through University funding; to maintain Tangeman University Center Art Gallery, open to public seven days a week, 12 AM - 5 PM.
Collections: Persian miniatures; Japanese woodblock prints; Indian basketry; some 250 paintings by European artists executed in the 1950's, donated by Mr. and Mrs. Julius Fleischmann. Over 2000 paintings hung in offices across the campus; the collection is strongest in early Cincinnati art.
Exhibitions: The usual painting exhibitions by area artists, highlighted by a variety of exhibitions: Appalachian quilts, German Expressionist woodcuts, Japanese woodblock prints, Candy Wrappers from the 1930's, The Cincinnati Union Terminal Building (a fine example of Art Deco), Art from the Cincinnati public schools, Black Art Exhibit, a mini exhibit of graphics by Josef Albers.
Activities: Small traveling exhibitions organized and circulated; individual paintings and original objects of art lent, 10 items lent in an average year; lectures open to public, 2 visiting lectures per year; numerous gallery talks.
Attendance: 10,000.

CLEVELAND

AMERICAN SOCIETY FOR AESTHETICS
Cleveland Museum of Art, University Circle, 44106
Herbert M. Schueller, Pres.
James R. Johnson, Secy-Treas.
For further information see p. 4.

CLEVELAND ART ASSOCIATION
Cleveland Institute of Art, 11141 East Boulevard, 44106.
Mrs. Robert Little, Pres.
Joseph McCullough, Secy.
(c/o Cleveland Institute of Art)
Estab. and inc. 1916, re-incorporated 1950 as a non-profit organization. Ann. meeting Nov; mem. about 200; dues $5.
Activities: †Collection of pictures by local artists may be borrowed by members; endowment fund for scholarships in Cleveland Institute of Art; donated funds to the Institute for student prizes, awards and special projects aimed in general at the promotion of local artists' work. Donates work by Cleveland artists to the Cleveland Museum.
Income and Purchases: Income $6000; purchases $5200.

✠CLEVELAND INSTITUTE OF ART
11141 East Blvd, 44106. Tel: (216) 421-4322
Joseph McCullough, Pres.
Ann Roulet, Dean of Students
John Swift, Dir. Admis. & Financial Aid
Gallery free 9 AM - 4 PM; Tues. & Wed. 7 - 9 PM; Sun. 2 - 5 PM for special receptions as well as outside shows. Estab. 1882 to provide professional education in the visual arts. Ann. meeting Nov.

Collections: Small collection of student work.
Exhibitions: Special exhibition program throughout the year.
Activities: Visiting artists and lectures each year.
Library: 27,230 volumes for lending and reference; approx. 200 prints; vertical file of 90,000 items; 29,500 slides; 1217 micro-forms; 454 audio cassettes; 162 current periodical subscriptions.
Publications: School Catalog. (See Schools)

✠CLEVELAND MUSEUM OF ART
11150 East Boulevard, 44106. Tel: (216) 421-7340
Lewis C. Williams, Pres.
Sherman E. Lee, Dir. & Chief Cur. Oriental Art
A. Beverly Barksdale, Gen. Mgr.
Ursula Korneitchouk, Admin. Asst. to Dir.
Edward B. Henning, Cur. Modern Art
William S. Talbot, Assoc. Cur. Paintings
Ann T. Lurie, Assoc. Cur. Paintings
Louise S. Richards, Cur. Prints & Drawings
Dorothy G. Shephard, Cur. of Textiles
Wai-Kam Ho, Cur. Chinese Art
Stanislaw Czuma, Cur. Indian Art
William E. Ward, Asst. in East Indian Art, Museum Designer
Arielle P. Kozloff, Asst. Cur. in Charge Ancient Art
John D. Cooney, Research Cur. for Egyptian Art
William D. Wixom, Cur. Decorative Arts (Medieval & Renaissance)
Henry Hawley, Cur. Decorative Arts (Post-Renaissance)
Gabriel P. Weisberg, Cur. Educ.
Karel Paukert, Cur. Musical Arts
Daphne Cross Roloff, Head Librn.
Judith Frost, Assoc. Librn.
Merald E. Wrolsted, Ed. Museum Publ.
Frances Stamper, Mgr. Pub. Relations & Mem.
Delbert R. Gutridge, Registrar
Albert J. Grossman, Operations Admin.
George R. Schoeffel, Personnel Mgr.
John Yencho, Plant Operations Mgr.
Free Tues, Thurs, Fri. 10 AM - 6 PM; Wed. 10 AM - 10 PM; Sat. 9 AM - 5 PM; Sun. 1 - 6 PM; cl. Mon. & nat. holidays. Estab. and inc. 1913. Building opened 1916, New Wing, 1958, New Education Wing, 1970. Ann. meeting Nov; mem. approx. 9700; dues $15 and higher.
Collections: European and American paintings of all periods and styles, especially strong in works of seventeenth and nineteenth centuries; European and American Decorative arts of all periods, notably medieval and eighteenth century; Oriental art, including important collections of Chinese and Japanese painting and ceramics, and Indian sculpture; drawings and prints; Classical and Egyptian art; Near Eastern Art; textiles. Included are the †Holden, †J.H. Wade, †John L. Severance, Elisabeth Severance Prentiss, Grace Rainey Rogers, †Mr. and Mrs. William H. Marlatt, and †Leonard C. Hanna, Jr, Collections.
Exhibitions: Annual exhibition, May Show—work by artists and craftsmen of the Western Reserve, awards by jury. Annual exhibition, Year in Review, all acquisitions made during the year, in Fall or early Winter. Special exhibitions included Paths of Abstract Art; Japanese Decorative Style; Style, Truth and the Portrait; Neo-classicism—Style and Motif; 50 Years of Modern Art; Medieval Treasures from France; Chinese Art Under the Mongols; Cara-vaggio and His Followers (each with a Museum-published book-catalog).
Activities: Lectures, concerts, study courses; gallery talks; classes; films; special exhibits for children; extension exhibitions in schools and other groups.
Library: Over 83,000 volumes; over 152,000 slides.
Publications: Bulletin 10 times a year; News & Calendar 6 times a year; book-catalogs of special exhibitions; monographs and Evolution in the Arts: And Other Theories of Culture History; Chinese Art Under the Mongols: The Yuan Dynasty (1279-1368); The Many Ways of Seeing; Fabergé and His Contemporaries; African Tribal Images; Lyonel Feininger: A Definitive Catalogue of His Graphic Works.
Income and Purchases: Income $6,582,300; purchases $2,839,600.
Attendance: Average 500,000.

CLEVELAND PUBLIC LIBRARY
325 Superior Ave, 44114. Tel: (216) 241-1020
Dr. Ervin J. Gaines, Dir.
Stephen G. Matyi, Head, Fine Arts Dept.
Arnold G. McClain, Head, Audio Visual Dept.
Estab. 1869. Books in Main Library, thirty-six branches, hospital libraries, institution libraries, extension services libraries, schools and recreational centers, plus traveling book service. Total collection 3,318,514 volumes.
Fine Arts Department has over †200,000 volumes; †850,000 pictures, chiefly clippings and smaller reproductions, some in color;

12,000 phonodiscs. The book collection is strong in architecture, design, costume, peasant art, art history, paintings and painters reproductions of illuminated manuscripts; history, theory, and literature of music, musical scores.
In the Audio Visual Department are †4000 slides and †3160 educational films, 500 filmstrips.
The John G. White collection of †Folklore, Orientalia and Chess included primitive art, Oriental architecture and sculpture, and Oriental illuminated manuscripts. Total 122,000 volumes.
The Main and Branch libraries offer lectures, films, concerts and exhibitions.

COOPER GALLERY
Cooper School of Art
2341 Carnegie Ave. S.E, 44115. Tel: (216) 241-1486
Joseph C. Hruby, Dir.
Donald H. Wright, Pres.
Howard Hammerlund, Secy.
Free 8 AM - 4:30 PM; Mon, Tues. & Thurs. 6 - 10 PM; Sat. 9 AM - 2 PM. Estab. 1936 as a private art school with emphasis in communicating visual arts and photography; financed by tuition and fees.
Exhibitions: Local and regional professional artists showing in one-man or small group exhibits; 8 exhibits plus faculty and student shows.
Activities: High school and adult avocational art programs; extension material available to high school art instructors; traveling exhibitions organized and circulated; individual paintings and original objects of art lent; 5000 lantern slides in lending collection; lectures for students only, 30 visiting lecturers per year; 12 gallery talks; 50 tours; classes for adults and children; competitions; scholarships. Book Shop.
Library: 3000 volumes for lending and reference; 15,000 slides.

DEZIGN HOUSE III
Park Centre 9F, 1701 E 12 St, 44114. Tel: (216) 621-7777
Ramon J. Elias, Dir.
Margery M. Elias, Assoc.
Free, open only by previous appointment. Estab. 1962 to maintain an art and design center where only honest art and design by honest artists may be seen.
Collections: †Textile Designs; Painting, North East Ohio; Sculpture.
Exhibitions: 10 major exhibitions.
Activities: Traveling exhibitions organized and circulated; individual paintings and original objects of art lent; lectures open to the public; gallery.
Library: 3000 volumes.
Attendance: 24,000 annual average.

THE PRINT CLUB OF CLEVELAND
The Cleveland Museum of Art, 11150 East Blvd, 44106.
Tel: (216) 421-7340
Moselle T. Meals, Pres.
Shirlee Dalton, Secy.
Estab. and inc. 1919. Ann. meeting Jan; mem. 250 (limited to residents of the Western Reserve); dues $50 and higher.
†Purchases prints for collection of The Cleveland Museum of Art; lectures and programs throughout the year. Issues a print by an outstanding artist periodically for members.

SALVADOR DALI MUSEUM
24050 Commerce Park Rd, 44122. Tel: (216) 464-0372
A. Reynolds Morse, Pres.
Eleanor R. Morse, Secy.
Laura Fazio, Dir.
Joan Kropf, Asst. Dir.
Open Tues. - Sat. 10 AM - Noon & 1 - 4 PM; appointments suggested. Estab. 1971 to show works by Salvador Dali exclusively; privately supported. Gallery has several hundred works by Dali housed on second floor of the IMS Building.
Exhibitions: Dali retrospective including, Cancelled Graphic Plates, Important Statements and Manifestos by Dali, The Horses and The Hippies Suites; Space Graffeti; permanent addition hologram.
Activities: 50 framed color reproductions available; photograph collection; lectures open to the public. Book shop (all publications by, on, or about Mr. Dali).
Publications: Exhibition catalogs as needed.
Income and Purchases: $25,000.
Attendance: 18,760 annual average.

THE WESTERN RESERVE HISTORICAL SOCIETY
10825 East Boulevard, 44106. Tel: (216) 721-5722
Meredith B. Colket, Jr, Dir.
Kermit J. Pike, Chief Librn.
Kenneth B. Gooding, Dir. Auto-Aviation Museum
Jairus B. Barnes, Cur. Museum

Open Tues. - Sat. 10 AM - 5 PM; Sun. 2 - 5 PM; cl. Mon; admis. adults $1, student 50¢. Estab. 1867. Collects, preserves, displays, and makes available for research, materials relating to the history of Cleveland and the Western Reserve (northeastern Ohio). Buildings consist of a 1918 mansion (Library), 1910 mansion (Museum), a Florentine style central addition (galleries and exhibits), and a special museum housing an auto-aviation collection. Mem. 2800; dues $15 and up.

Museum Collections: Portraits of early Clevelanders, costume and accessories including fans, glass, ceramics, Indian exhibit, period rooms, spinning and weaving demonstrations, dioramas, Napoleon room, and changing exhibits.

Library: 200,000 books, 25,000 volumes of newspapers; 1050 collections of manuscripts and archives. Areas of interest include local history and genealogy, Civil War, slavery and abolitionism, Shakers, American Revolution, and New England history.

Activities: Weekly programs and tours; lectures and tours for school classes and other visiting groups; occasional special lectures.

Publications: Historical Society News monthly, and averages one additional book per year.

Attendance: Average 90,000.

WOMEN'S CITY CLUB OF CLEVELAND*
Women's Federal Bldg, 320 Superior Ave. N.E, 44114.
Tel: (216) 696-3760
Norma S. Huey, Exec. Dir.
Mrs. George N. Seltzer, Pres.
Mrs. Harold Fallon, Gallery Chmn.
Gallery open Mon. - Fri. 9 AM - 5 PM. Estab. and inc. 1916. Mem. approx. 1000; resident club dues $75.

Exhibitions: Continuous exhibitions with paintings and handicrafts in the Club Gallery.

Activities: Lectures on art and music. Club sponsors the Cleveland Arts Prize Awards each spring with awards in the fields of visual art, architecture, music, literature.

COLUMBUS

AMERICAN CERAMIC SOCIETY, INC.—DESIGN DIVISION
65 Ceramic Dr, 43214. Tel: (614) 268-8645
Frank P. Reid, Exec. Dir.
For further information see p. 3.

✣ THE COLUMBUS GALLERY OF FINE ARTS
480 E. Broad St, 43215. Tel: (614) 221-6801
Mrs. Richard M. Ross, Pres.
Mahonri Sharp Young, Dir.
Edmund K. Kuehn, Cur. of Collections
Katherine W. Paris, Registrar & Cur. Decorative Arts
Donna H. Turner, Cur. Educ.
Herbert W. Moore, Business Mgr.
Wilda Terrible, Mem. Secy.
Free daily Noon - 5 PM; cl. major holidays. Estab. 1878. Ann. meeting May; mem. 4000; dues $25 and higher.

Collections: †Ferdinand Howald Collection—American (especially strong in Demuth, Dickinson, Hartley, Marin, Prendergast and Sheeler) and modern French; †Frederick W. Schumacher Collection—Renaissance, Baroque, 19th and 20th century American and European paintings; †Lillie Gill Derby Collection—Old Masters (especially English and Dutch portraiture); †leading collection of paintings by George Bellows.

Exhibitions: (Special) British Art: 1890-1928, Irish Art. (Annual) Central Ohio Camera Club Council, Columbus Art League, Beaux Arts Designer/Craftsmen.

Activities: Collector's Gallery, visiting lecturers, 16 gallery talks a year, daily tours for children; tours for adults on request; children's museum programs, workshops, regular exhibitions by and for children; docent training; workshops.

Library: 8000 volumes.
Attendance: 150,000.

FINE ARTS LIBRARY
Ohio State University
1813 N. High St, 43210. Tel: (614) 422-6184
Prof. Hugh C. Atkinson, Dir, University Libraries
Jacqueline Sisson, Head, Fine Arts Library
Open Mon. - Thurs. 8 AM - 10 PM; Fri. 8 AM - 5 PM; Sat. 10 AM - 4 PM; Sun. 2 - 10 PM. Between quarters: 8 AM - 5 PM; cl. Sat. & Sun. Estab. to support teaching programs and faculty research of the university in the fields of art and archaeology; financed by city and state appropriation.

Collections: Collection supports research for advanced degrees in all phases of the visual arts except photography. In conjunction with agreement between members of Art Research Libraries of Ohio, retrospective purchases concentrate on Medieval and Renaissance periods. Strong collection of Serbo-Croatian publications on Byzantine art, Russian and Polish publications. Microfiche and microfilm collection includes the Turner Bequest of drawings and numerous runs of Indic journals. Depository of Art Research Libraries of Ohio Author Union Card Catalog collections complemented by other campus libraries with strong holdings on architecture, archaeology and photography. 54,165 volumes for lending and reference; 1200 photographs in the Decimal Index of the Art of the Low Countries for reference only.

Activities: Lectures on library research; lends library materials through interlibrary loan to students and faculty of other institutions, no fee.

Publications: ARLO Union List of Serials.

Library Materials: $30,616 including serials (does not include salaries and wages).

Attendance: 128,000.

THE SCHUMACHER GALLERY
Capital University
2199 E. Main St, 43209. Tel: (614) 236-6203
Dr. Thomas Langevin, Pres.
Prof. Richard G. Bauer, Dir.
Free Mon. - Fri. 1 - 5 PM; Sun. 2 - 4 PM; evenings by appointment. Estab. 1966 to provide the students with the best available in the visual arts; to serve the community via the permanent collection, monthly travelling shows, and community programming; endowed. The gallery consists of 16,000 sq. feet, including a community reception room, lecture hall seating 60, lecture space seating 250, fabrication room, vault, offices, and six display galleries.

Collections: 16th-17th century Flemish paintings, †prints; 19th century paintings; †Oceanic collection of Tribal Arts and artifacts; †20th century American painting, sculpture, graphics; Ohio painters.

Exhibitions: Nine visiting shows (individual and group) per year, plus selected works from permanent collection. Individual shows include exhibits by Clarence Carter, William Zorach, George Bellows, Pietro Montana, Italy, sculpture by Nevelson. Group shows include works loaned from American Watercolor Society, shows from Kennedy and Downtown Galleries, New York City; Black art Show from Africa. Annual group exhibits: Central Ohio Watercolor Society, Bexley Area Art Guild, Ohio Liturgical Art Guild, Senior Student Show.

Activities: Youth Art Institutes during the summer (ages 12-18); community art classes and lecture programs during school year; loans on special request, prints and paintings; lectures open to the public; 2-4 visiting lecturers per year; 3-6 gallery talks; concerts; classes for adults and children; competitions; framed reproductions available on loan to campus community.

Art Library of 2000 volumes.
Attendance: 4000-5000 per year.

COSHOCTON

JOHNSON-HUMRICKHOUSE MEMORIAL MUSEUM
Sycamore & 3rd Sts, 43812. Tel: (614) 622-3155
Mrs. S.S. Shaw, Dir.
Free Tues. - Sat. 1 - 4:30 PM; Sun. and holidays 2 - 5 PM; cl. Mon. except Memorial Day, July 4, Labor Day. Estab. 1931; gift of two pioneer residents; occupies a school building erected in 1853; managed by Library Board.

Collections: American Indian baskets and bead work; Eskimo artifacts; material from Coshocton County Mound Builders; Chinese and Japanese porcelains, prints, embroideries; European prints, porcelains, glass and laces; Aztec, Toltec and Mayan pottery heads. In 1947 acquired Miller-Preston bequest of furnishings and implements used by Coshocton County pioneer families.

Exhibitions: Out-of-town exhibitions; permanent collection exhibitions changed periodically.

Activities: Program, in close cooperation with City, parochial and county schools, includes gallery talks, lectures.

Library: Technical books for research supplied by City Library on permanent loan.

CUYAHOGA FALLS

RICHARD GALLERY AND ALMOND TEA GALLERY
Divisions of Studios of Jack Richard, 2250 Front St, 44221.
Jack Richard, Dir.
Fran Nancarrow, Agent
Open weekdays 9 AM - 5:30 PM; Sat. 9:30 AM - 12:30 PM; no admis. Estab. Almond Tea Gallery 1964, Richard Gallery 1960, for exhibition of local, regional and national works of art; financed privately.

Collections: Brackman; Grell; Gleitsmann; Terry Richard; Ball; Cornwell; Loomis; and others.

Exhibitions: Maria von Trapp; Mitsuka Sakata; Susan Shoemaker; Brackman; Grumbacher Palette Collection; Akron Society of Artists; Dalton Collection of Japanese Art; Fletcher Collection of Indian Art; African Art; Pottery; Antique glassware; Longnecker Collection.

Activities: Traveling exhibitions organized and circulated; individual paintings and original objects of art lent; lending collection of

300 paintings and prints; 300 items lent in average year; 10 active borrowers; photograph collection of 5000 prints; lectures open to the public; 3 visiting lecturers per year; 20 gallery talks; 20-25 tours; competitions; scholarships. Book shop. Frame shop. Art supplies.

Library: 1000 volumes for reference and some lending; 50,000 reference clipping file.

Attendance: Several hundred.

DAYTON

✠DAYTON ART INSTITUTE
Forest & Riverview Ave, 45405. (Box 941, 45401).
Tel: (513) 223-5277
Harry S. Price, Jr, Pres.
Robert L. Bates, V.Pres.
Mrs. Vincent Bolling, Jr, Secy.
Robert A. Stein, Treas.
Mrs. Edward C. Schmidt, Pres. Assoc. Board
Bruce H. Evans, Dir.
Andrew J. Hieftje, Business Mgr.
Helen L. Pinkney, Librn.
Marie D. Ferguson, Dir. Development
Phyllis Heiden, Mem. Secy.
Kathryn F. Pinkney, Musical Programs
Sharon Berlo, Secy. to Dir.
Gerald L. Boehner, Supt.
Michael A. Quick, Cur. of Collections
Mark A. Clark, Cur. of Decorative Arts & Registrar
Helen L. Pinkney, Cur. of Textiles
Kathy K. Foley, Asst. Cur.
John Daley, Fellow in Rome
Honoré S. David, Cur. Community Services
Amelia E. Banister, Curatorial Asst.
Craig A. Subler, Coordinator Studio Classes
Free Tues. - Fri. & Sun. Noon - 5 PM; Sat. 9 AM - 5 PM; cl. Mon. & holidays. Inc. 1919, building erected 1930, art school building erected 1965. Ann. meeting Apr; mem. 1600; dues $20 and higher.

Collections: †Western paintings and sculpture, †Near and Far Eastern arts, †Mediterranean arts, †Pre-Columbian arts, †decorative arts, †prints, †textiles, †contemporary arts.

Exhibitions: Annual All-Ohio Selection. Among recent exhibitions: Jean Leon Gerome; Paintings by Edward Edmondson; Paul Storr Silver in American Collections.

Activities: Art classes for adults and children; public school lecture tour program; rental and sales gallery; art advisory clinics; conferences on urban design; special exhibition previews; lectures; movie programs. Auditorium and Lecture Hall use extended to other cultural organizations for modest fees.

Library: Art reference library of 20,000 books, plus magazines, periodicals, reproductions and slides.

Publications: Members Bulletins, Calendars and Annual Reports; Catalogs.

Income and Purchases: Income $650,000; purchases (1975) $54,000.

Attendance: 145,000-165,000.

WRIGHT STATE UNIVERSITY ART GALLERY
45431. Tel: (513) 873-2896
William H. Spurlock, II, Dir.
Kathleen Letson, Gallery Asst.
Free Mon. - Fri. 10 AM - 4 PM; Sun. Noon - 4 PM; cl. Sat. Estab. Oct, 1974 to continuously exhibit temporary exhibitions of the work of the nations leading contemporary artists, artists of national and international reputation, regional artists, and lesser known contemporary artists; to provide an educational forum for the exploration of the most contemporary ideas in the visual arts; financed by city and state appropriation.

Collections: Small but growing permanent collection of contemporary paintings and prints.

Exhibitions: (1974-75) Robert Irwin, Sculpture; Stephen Antonakos, Neon Sculpture; Paul Zelevansky, Environments; Dennis Adams, Paintings; (1975-76) Craig Lucas, Paintings; David Cort, Nam June Paik, Doug Davis and Et Al, Projection and Video Art; Patrick Ireland, Rope Sculpture; Arnold Belkin, Paintings; Hans Haacke, Carl Andre, Robert Mangold, Lucio Pozzi and Stephen Rosenthal; Lucas Samaras, Photos; Richard Nonas, Sculpture; Douglas Sanderson, Paintings; also numerous regional artists.

Activities: Material available on rental to greater University community; original objects of art lent; 10 photographs in lending collection; 200 items lent in an average year; 10 prints in photograph collection for lending and reference; lectures open to public; 12 visiting lecturers per year; 16 gallery talks. Book shop.

Publications: Exhibition catalogs.

Attendance: 12,000.

DELAWARE

OHIO WESLEYAN UNIVERSITY
Department of Fine Arts
Humphreys Art Hall, 43015. Tel: (614) 369-4431, Exten. 650
Justin Kronewetter, Head & Dir. of Exhibitions
Free 9 AM - 4 PM daily; Sat. 9 AM - Noon. Gallery estab. 1915.

Collections: Paintings, sculpture, prints, photographs, drawings, ceramics, tribal artifacts.

Exhibitions: Monthly exhibitions in Lynn Mayhew Gallery; exhibition of professional and student work. Annual exhibition of contemporary photography.

Activities: Public lectures; visiting artists; workshops; art programs.

Library: 2200 books, 40,000 slides.

FINDLAY

EGNER FINE ARTS CENTER
Findlay College
1000 N. Main St, 45840. Tel: (419) 422-8313
Douglas Salveson, Asst. Prof. Art
Free Mon. - Fri. 7 AM - 5 PM. Estab. as a college art department, plus gallery; financed by endowment.

Collections: †Primarily contemporary prints.

Exhibitions: 18 exhibitions of contemporary art and crafts and one retrospective exhibition during last three years.

Activities: Concerts, dramatic programs, classes for adults and children, competitions; scholarships. Book shop. Library.

GRANVILLE

✠THE DENISON UNIVERSITY ART GALLERY
Burke Hall, 43023. Tel: (614) 587-0810, Exten. 255
Steven W. Rosen, Dir. & Chief Cur. of Collections
Jane Terry Bailey, Cur. of Burmese Art
Ann Munro Kessler, Registrar
Free Mon. - Fri. 10 AM - 5 PM. Estab. 1946; endowed.

Collections: †European and American drawings, paintings, prints and crafts; †Burmese sculpture, manuscripts, paintings and crafts; Chinese ceramics, rubbings, sculpture, crafts; American Indian Pottery and Central American arts and crafts.

Exhibitions: G. B. Piranesi: Views of Rome; John Sloan: Graphics; Chinese Dynastic Art; Burmese Crafts; Ralph Komives: Recent Sculpture; Michael Jung: Paintings & Photograms; Jeanne Otis: Ceramics; Graphics 1904-1905 Piscasso; J. L. Forain: The War Sketches; Tom's Mola Show; student exhibitions annually, new exhibitions annually.

Activities: School tours, community services; photograph collection for lending and reference; lectures open to the public; reference library.

Publications: Catalogues, bi-monthly.

KENT

ARCHITECTURE/URBAN STUDIES LIBRARY
Kent State University Libraries
Kent State University, 44240. Tel: (216) 672-2854
Edward J. Hall, Jr, Librn.
Judy Meyer, Supvr.
Free 8 AM - 5 PM. Estab. 1967; financed by state appropriations.

Activities: Lending collection of 6400 Kodachromes.

Library: 6435 books, 885 bibliographies, 106 microfilm, 1575 bound periodicals, 52 vertical files, 275 periodical titles.

Publications: Urban Scene-newsletter, quarterly.

Attendance: 11,450.

MANSFIELD

✠THE MANSFIELD ART CENTER*
Mansfield Fine Arts Guild, Inc.
700 Marion Ave, 44903. Tel: (419) 756-1700
Walter Stevens, Pres.
Mrs. Chandler Stevens, Secy.
H. Daniel Butts, III, Dir.
Mrs. Henry Van Horn, Exec. Secy.
Free Tues. - Sun. 12 AM - 5 PM. Estab. 1945, inc. 1956, to maintain an art center in which exhibitions, lectures, gallery talks, special programs, symposia and series of classes for children and adults are provided for the North Central Ohio area; maintained by membership, commission on sales and classes. Gallery 5000 sq. ft. with flexible lighting, movable walls, props, etc. to facilitate monthly exhibition changes. Meeting dates April & Oct; mem. 1050; dues $3 student, $15 family, $10 adult, $25 supporting, $50 sustaining, $100 patron, $500 benefactor.

Exhibitions: Changing exhibitions of member artists work, traveling shows & locally organized one-man, group and theme exhibitions changing monthly throughout the year. Exhibitions since the opening of The Mansfield Art Center April 3, 1971—Saalfield-Sundell Collection; 26th Annual May Show; 8 Artists From Kent; 1st Childrens Classes Show; Trio Show: George Olson, Prints, Harley Francis, Paintings, David Miller, Drawings; Ohio Craft Invitational Show; 5th Annual Fall Members Show; 2nd Annual Holiday Fair; Alan and Richard Chiara; Cleveland Institute of Art Faculty; Women: James Alley, Photo Paintings, David Hostetler, Sculpture and Roger Williams, Sculpture and Drawings; Richard Treaster; 27th Annual May Show: Carl Allen, Relief, David Appleman, Paintings, Edward Mayer, Sculpture and Michael Walusis, Paintings; Ohio Craft Invitational Show 2; 6th Fall Members Show; 3rd Holiday Fair; Behold These Stones: Rubbings by Ward Patterson; Brenda Fuchs, Ilona and Reed Thomason, Paintings and Drawings; Richard Anuszkiewicz and Julian Stanczak; Contemporary Indian Paintings from the Philbrook Art Center; 28th Annual May Show; 3-D Work from Ohio University; A Summery Summary of Member Artists Work; 3rd Children's Classes Show; Ohio Craft Invitational Show 3; 7th Annual Fall Members Show and the 4th Holiday Fair.

Activities: Original objects of art lent through a rental gallery with minimal fees, 100 borrowers, 150-200 items per year; lectures open to public, an average of 6 visiting lecturers per year; film series; over 100 gallery talks mainly for school groups; classes for adults and children; competitions; scholarships.

Library: 750 volumes; the library is basically a collection of monographs and studies of styles and periods for teacher and student reference.

Publications: Bimonthly newsletter and annual report.

Annual Income: $45,000.

Attendance: 15,000.

MARIETTA

CAMPUS MARTIUS MUSEUM AND OHIO RIVER MUSEUM*

Saint Clair near Front St, 45750. Tel: (614) 373-3717

Mrs. Catherine B. Remley, Cur.

Mrs. Juanita Etter, Asst.

Open daily 9 AM - 5 PM; Sun. & Holidays 1 - 5 PM; cl. Christmas, Thanksgiving and New Years Day; admis. $1 adults, children under 13 free with an adult, 50¢ otherwise. Estab. 1920 commemorating the first settlement of the Northwest Territory and the history of the Ohio River; financed by endowment, city and state appropriation and mem.

Collections: Paintings by Sala Bosworth, Charles Sullivan and Lily Martin Spencer; photographs by S. Durward Hoag and Capt. Frederick Way, Jr; portraits by Chandler, Edward Savage, Duncanson, Mather Brown, Slack; river scenes by William Reed, Capt. Jesse Hughes, Thomas Anshutz.

Activities: Lectures for schools and interested groups; photograph collection, over 1000 prints for reference; lectures open to the public. Book Shop.

Library: 2000 volume reference library.

Attendance: 60,000 annual average.

GROVER M. HERMANN FINE ARTS CENTER

Marietta College Art Department

45750. Tel: (614) 374-5173

William Gerhold, Chmn.

Free Mon. - Fri. 8 AM - 11 PM; Sat. 8 AM - 5 PM; Sun. 1 - 11 PM. Gallery maintained.

Collections: Permanent collection of contemporary American painters, sculptors and craftspeople; significant collection of African and Pre-Columbian art.

Exhibitions: (Annual) Mainstreams, Marietta College International Competition; Marietta College Crafts National.

Activities: Traveling exhibitions organized and circulated; lectures open to public; competitions. Book shop. Library.

Publications: Marietta College Crafts Directory, semi-annually.

Attendance: 20,000.

MASSILLON

MASSILLON MUSEUM

212 Lincoln Way E, 44646. Tel: (216) 833-4061

Mrs. Marion Wilson, Chmn. Museum Comt.

Mary M. Merwin, Dir.

Free Tues. - Sat. 10 AM - 5 PM; Sun. 2 - 5 PM; cl. Mon. Estab. 1933; operated by City School District Library. Ann. meeting Jan; mem. 1000; dues $5 and higher.

Collections: Pease archaeological and ethnological objects; †paintings by William T. Mathews; †Abel Fletcher photographic material; †folk art; †19th century furniture, china and glass; †contemporary American paintings and sculpture; †historical collection pertaining to Massillon and to Stark County and Ohio; †scientific material.

Exhibitions: Ohio Artists and Craftsmen Show in July and Aug; Regional Painting Show in Mar; total prizes and purchases, $3000. Annual Sidewalk Show, first full weekend in June. Exhibitions are changed monthly.

Activities: School tours; adult group tours; lectures on art and history; demonstrations in crafts; film and music series for adults and students, classes in painting, ceramics, enameling, jewelry and photography for students and adults. Rental Gallery of original art work.

Annual purchases: Approx. $2000-$3000.

Attendance: 25,600.

MIDDLETOWN

THE MIDDLETOWN FINE ARTS CENTER*

116 S. Main St, 45042. Tel: (513) 424-2416

Mrs. Frank R. Myers, Pres.

Mrs. Edward A. Scanlon, Secy.

Edward Burroughs, Dir.

Open Mon. - Fri. 9:30 AM - 3 PM; Sat. 9 - 12 AM; Mon. & Thurs. evenings 7:30 - 9:30 PM. Estab. 1957 to provide facilities, program, and instruction, for the development of interests and skills in the visual arts, for students of all ages, from Middletown and its surrounding communities; endowment through funds donated to Arts in Middletown (our funding agency). Ann. meeting March.

Exhibitions: Annual Student Show; annual Area Art Show; sponsored the showing of the Mead Corporation's Collection; joint sponsorship of many varied shows with the Miami University, Middletown.

Activities: Classes in painting, ceramics, enameling on copper, calligraphy, design, silk screen and others from time to time; lectures open to public, 3-4 visiting lecturers per year; gallery talks or tours occasionally, 3-4 per year; competitions.

Library: 472 volumes for lending and reference.

Attendance: Average 400 paid registrations for classes.

NORTH CANTON

THE LITTLE ART GALLERY

North Canton Public Library, 185 North Main St, 44720.
Tel: (216) 499-4712

Mrs. R. T. Warburton, Pres.

Mrs. Ed Hill, Secy.

Mrs. John L. Zumkehr, Dir.

Free during regular library hours Mon. - Fri. 10 AM - 9 PM; Sat. 10 AM - 5 PM. Estab. 1936 to encourage and promote appreciation and education of fine art, graphic arts, commercial art and other related subjects; recognizes and encourages local artists by promoting exhibitions of their work; financed by city and state appropriation.

Collections: †Original works by contemporary artists.

Exhibitions: Monthly shows featuring the works of many northeastern Ohio artists, some of them nationally known; competitive May show each year with cash awards totaling $270; art from the classrooms of the North Canton Public Schools (April); shows featuring our collection of famous reproductions of religious subjects as well as secular.

Activities: 110 color reproductions in lending collection; 446 circulations in 1974; lectures open to the public; 2 gallery talks and tours per year; classes for adults and children; competitions.

Income and Purchases: Budget $1200; purchases average $500.

Attendance: 5053.

OBERLIN

✠DUDLEY PETER ALLEN MEMORIAL ART MUSEUM

Oberlin College, 44074. Tel: (216) 775-8665

Richard E. Spear, Dir.

Chloe H. Young, Cur.

Katherine J. Watson, Cur. of Before 1800 Art

Ellen H. Johnson, Hon. Cur. Modern Art

Closed for renovation and expansion until latter 1976. Building erected 1917 in memory of Dr. Dudley Peter Allen by his wife; wing added 1937 by Mrs. Dudley P. Allen Prentiss. Collections begun 1896. Society of Oberlin Friends of Art, mem. dues $4 student, $7.50 and higher.

Collections: Examples of †sculpture, †painting, †graphics and †decorative arts from the early Egyptian period to the present day.

Exhibitions: Frequent traveling exhibitions and specially assembled exhibitions.

Activities: Lectures; seminars; gallery tours. Part of Oberlin College teaching plant and serving college curriculum including 81 art courses, historical and practical.

Library: Approx. †27,000 volumes, †150,000 lantern slides; †20,000 photographs and †color plates. †Rental library of originals and reproductions. (See Schools)

Publications: Bulletin of the Allen Memorial Art Museum, twice yearly.

Attendance: 24,000.

INTERMUSEUM CONSERVATION ASSOCIATION
Intermuseum Laboratory, Allen Art Bldg, 44074.
Tel: (216) 775-7331
James Woods, Pres.
Richard Spear, Secy.
Marigene H. Butler, Dir.
Free daily 9 AM - Noon & 1 - 5 PM. Estab. 1952 for examination and treatment of works of art; financed by mem. Mem. 18 member museums.
Library: Technical books and publications on restoration of works of art.
Publications: ICA Newsletter, semi-annually.

OXFORD

MIAMI UNIVERSITY ART CENTER
Rowan Hall, 45056. Tel: (513) 529-2232
Sterling Cook, Coordinator, Museum Art Collection
Bonnie Masson, Asst. in Charge of Folk Art
Free daily 1 - 5 PM, when exhibitions are up. Estab. 1972 to care for and exhibit University art collections, to arrange for a variety of exhibitions from other sources, and for the educational and cultural enrichment for the University and community; financed by endowment and state appropriation. Gallery is approx. 180 ft of wall space.
Collections: †Paintings; †prints; †sculpture; decorative arts; †folk art, largely Middle European, Middle Eastern, Mexican, Central and South American.
Exhibitions: 19 exhibitions during last 3 years.
Activities: Items from folk art collections lent to University and local public schools; 2500 Kodachromes and 5 motion pictures in lending collection; 500 items lent in average year; 1500 prints in photograph collection; lectures open to public; 4 visiting lecturers per year; 25 gallery talks and 25 tours.
Library: 200 volumes for reference only.
Publications: Brochures and/or small catalogs for exhibits, approx. 6-8 per year.
Annual Purchases: $2000 - $70,000.
Attendance: 8000.

SPRINGFIELD

CLARK COUNTY HISTORICAL SOCIETY
Memorial Hall, 45504. Tel: (513) 324-0657
R. Carlton Bauer, Pres.
Linda Davis, Secy.
George H. Berkhofer, Exec. Dir & Cur. of Society's Museum
Open Mon. - Thurs. 9 AM - Noon & 1 - 4 PM; Sat. 9 AM - Noon; 2nd & 4th Sun. 2 - 4 PM; cl. Fri. Estab. 1897 for collection and preservation of Clark County history and historical artifacts; financed by appropriation. One ann. meeting in Nov; Board of Trustees, once monthly; mem. over 400; dues $5 individual, $7.50 family.
Collections: Books, paintings and items of everyday life; approx. 60 oil paintings, mostly mid-late 19th century, of prominent Springfielders plus some European landscapes, a few early 19th century.
Exhibitions: Annually at Clark County Fair in August.
Activities: Meetings and lectures once a month open to public. Books for sale.
Library: Several thousand volumes and a photograph collection for lending and reference; large collection of early newspapers back to 1830's.
Publications: Monthly newsletter.
Annual Income: $7500; purchases $7500.

SPRINGFIELD ART CENTER
107 Cliff Park Rd, 45501. Tel: (513) 325-4673
Orsino H. Bosca, Pres.
George McCleary, Secy.
Patricia D'Arcy Catron, Dir.
Free Tues. - Fri. 9 AM - 5 PM; Sat. 9 AM - 3 PM; Sun. 2 - 4 PM. Estab. 1967 as school for education in fine arts for children and adults and twelve exhibitions per year; classes in 4 semesters per year; ages 6 years through adults of any age; financed by membership. Three galleries plus hanging corridors. Ann. meeting June; mem. 1000; dues $15, $25, $35.
Collections: †Small permanent collection.
Exhibitions: 12 exhibitions per year of area artists.
Activities: Classes in the fine arts, drawing, painting, sculpture, printmaking, jewelry making, pottery; children's work organized and circulated; lectures open to the public; 6 visiting lecturers per year; 15 gallery talks; 100 tours; classes for adults and children; scholarships.
Library: 1000 volume reference library; lending to membership only.

Publications: Monthly newsletter.
Income and Purchases: Income $60,000; purchases variable.
Attendance: 35,000 annual average.

TOLEDO

TOLEDO ARTISTS' CLUB*
1456 W. Sylvania, 43612. Tel: (419) 478-5222
Cordella Treece, Pres.
Ernest Spring, 1st V.Pres.
George Stahl, 2nd V.Pres.
Lowell Skilliter, Treas.
Helen Packard, Recording Secy.
Open Mon. - Fri. 1 - 5 PM; Sat. 10 AM - 2 PM; other times by appointment. Estab. 1943, inc. 1944, to provide an opportunity for members to study and exhibit; provides studios and galleries, meeting place for artists, craftsmen and laymen; clubhouse also maintained for educational purposes. Ann. meeting May; mem. 800 (state, national, and international); dues $12.
Activities: 34 exhibits in and and around greater Toledo in which members exhibit monthly, and sponsors 6-8 yearly outdoor type shows; juried shows annually and two juried shows for high school age. Many gallery talks; hosts outside groups; provides art lessons in the school it maintains; underprivileged and handicapped children scholarships available. More than $25,000 sold at outdoor shows in 1972; more than 300 exhibiting artists.
For the past five years the club has had a booth at the International Festival and in 1970, 1971, and 1972 won an award; club has had a booth at the Annual Toledo Hobby Show sponsored by the City, won an award in 1969; has at least two national personalities to lecture and demonstrate each year. Co-sponsors The Toledo Festival of the Arts, Crosby Park, held last Sat. and Sun. of June.
Publications: Year Book annually; The Sketch Pad monthly.
Income: (1972) Over $30,000.

TOLEDO FEDERATION OF ART SOCIETIES
c/o The Toledo Museum of Art, Monroe St. at Scottwood Ave, 43601. Tel: (419) 255-8000
Helmut P. Beckmann, Pres.
Dale Keiser, V.Pres.
Marti Werner, Recording Secy.
Theda Wagenknecht, Corresp. Secy.
Dorothy Price, Treas.
Estab. 1917 to promote mutual understanding and cooperation between the artists and the public; to further art education and to exhibit and promote sales of work by Toledo artists. Mem. 15 societies; dues $10. Each organization sends two delegates to monthly meetings of the Federation Council. The Federation consists of: Artklan; Art Instructors in the Public Schools of Toledo; Art Interests, Inc; Athena Art Society; Bedford Artists Club; Craft Club of Toledo; Palette Club; Port Clinton Artists' Club; Spectrum; Tile Club of Toledo; Toledo Artists' Club; The Toledo Museum of Art; The Toledo Museum School of Design; Toledo Potters' Guild; Toledo Area Women's Art League; Delegates at Large.
Collections: †Permanent collection of work of area artists; collection of more than 100 items includes paintings and crafts. Federation selects additional entries annually through purchase awards.
Exhibitions: Annual exhibition of work by artists of Toledo and region, selected by nationally known jury, chosen by Federation, shown during May at The Toledo Museum of Art; Annual Toledo Area Exhibition now covers 15 Ohio and 2 Michigan counties.

✠THE TOLEDO MUSEUM OF ART
Monroe St. at Scottwood Ave, 43609. (Mail: Box 1013, 43697). Tel: (419) 255-8000
Marvin S. Kobacker, Pres.
Otto Wittmann, Dir.
Roger Mandle, Assoc. Dir.
Charles F. Gunther, Asst. Dir. Educ.
Samuel F. Hunter, Admin. Asst.
Leonard C. Urbanski, Comptroller
Patricia Whitesides, Registrar
William Hutton, Chief Cur.
Robert F. Phillips, Cur. Contemporary Art
Kurt T. Luckner, Cur. Ancient Art
William J. Chiego, Assoc. Cur, European Paintings
Roger M. Berkowitz, Asst. Cur, Decorative Arts
Joyce Young, Supvr. Music
Anne O. Reese, Librn.
George F. Hartman, Jr, Superintendent
Free 9 AM - 5 PM; Sun. & Mon. 1 - 5 PM; cl. major legal holidays. Estab. and inc. 1901; building erected 1912; additions 1926 and 1933. Ann. meeting Dec; mem. 6000; dues $15 and higher.
Collections: †Edward Drummond Libbey and Arthur J. Secor collection paintings; †Maurice A. Scott galleries of American paintings; †George W. Stevens collection of books and manuscripts; †sculpture; †prints; †ancient and modern glass; †stained glass; †ceramics; †Ori-

ental, †Egyptian, †Assyrian and †classical antiquities; †medieval art; †contemporary art in Glass Gallery.

Exhibitions: (1973-75) The Campbell Museum Collection; The Fresh Air School; The Toledo Modern Art Group Exhibition; The Kempe Collection-Chinese Gold, Silver, Porcelain; Black Artists of Toledo; Men Who Make Our World-Photographs by Karsh; Edward Hopper-American Realist; African Art of the Dogon; Art of the Comic Strip; Masterpieces of Irish Art; The Great Wall of China; Charles Meryon Prints and Drawings; Graphics '74: Spain; 70 Years of Steuben Glass; Contemporary American Painting; Dominick Labino-A Decade of Glass; El Dorado: Ancient Colombian Gold; Dr. Seuss Illustrations; The Age of Louis XV: French Painting, 1710-1774. Annual exhibitions of the work of Toledo area artists.

Activities: Lectures; concerts; classes; talks for public school groups; conducts Museum School of Design. (See Schools)

Library: 30,000 volumes for reference; 40,000 slides.

Publications: Quarterly Museum News; monthly Calendar Guide to the Collections; Art in Glass.

Attendance: Average 463,000.

VERMILION

GREAT LAKES HISTORICAL SOCIETY
480 Main St, 44089. Tel: (216) 967-3467
Alexander C. Meakin, Pres.
Arthur N. O'Hara, Bus. Mgr.
Open daily in summer 11 AM - 6 PM; winter weekends 11 AM - 5 PM; spring and fall daily 11 AM - 5 PM, cl. Mon. Inc. 1944, nonprofit organization, to promote interest in discovering and preserving material on the Great Lakes and surrounding areas. Museum. Mem. 2100 incl. 288 libraries, univ. and coll; dues range $10-$500.

Collections: Unparalleled collection of ship models, marine relics, paintings and photographs dealing with the history of the Great Lakes; also a collection of marine engines and navigational instruments. The Inter-Lake Yachting Asn. Room houses eighty years of yachting history on the Great Lakes.

Exhibitions: One-man exhibits of models, photographs and drawings.

Activities: Model boat show conducted each June for scratch built ship models with award for best of lake type. Conducted tours available on appointment with special rates for groups; Museum Store has items identified with the Great Lakes including books. Two general membership meetings with outstanding speakers dealing in Great Lakes history.

Publications: Inland Seas (quarterly journal).

Attendance: 23,500.

WILLOUGHBY

FINE ARTS ASSOCIATION
AKA The School of Fine Arts
38660 Mentor Ave, 44094. Tel: (216) 951-7500
Brian Sherwin, Pres.
Mrs. Ronald Chapnick, Secy.
James J. Savage, Exec. Dir.
Doris Foster, Visual Arts Coordinator
Free weekdays 9 AM - 9 PM; Sat. & performance times 9 AM - 5 PM. Estab. Aug. 27, 1957 to bring arts education to all people regardless of their ability to pay, race or social standing; financed by membership and donations. Gallery maintained. Ann. meeting Apr; mem. 1152; dues $15 and up.

Exhibitions: Monthly exhibitions, theme, one-man and group; annual juried exhibit for area artists.

Activities: Art classes; in-school programs; lectures open to public; 10 - 15 visiting lecturers per year; three-county area served by Extension Department; material available to schools and organizations; gallery talks; tours; concerts, dramatic programs, classes for adults and children, competitions; scholarships. (See Schools)

Library: 5000 volumes for reference only.

Attendance: 20,000.

WOOSTER

COLLEGE OF WOOSTER ART CENTER
College Art Museum, 44691. Tel: (216) 264-1234, Exten. 388
Dr. Arnold Lewis, Dir.
Phyllis Clark, Asst. to Museum Dir.
Free weekdays 8:30 AM - Noon & 1 - 5 PM; Sun. 2 - 5 PM; cl. summers. Founded 1944 to provide an opportunity for students, faculty and the local community to view original works of art.

Collections: Paintings, prints, sculpture, tapestries, Chinese bronzes, and porcelains.

Exhibitions: Monthly exhibitions from the collection and traveling exhibitions; Invitational Functional Ceramics Exhibition with sale and workshop in Apr.

Activities: Lectures, concerts and art programs.

Library: Collection of framed prints and reproductions for lending. Also a library of slides, filmstrips. (See Schools)

YELLOW SPRINGS

✠NOYES GALLERY
Antioch College Art Department
45387. Tel: (513) 767-7331, Exten. 464
James Jordan, Chmn. Dept.
Barbara Kohn, Exhibitions Coordinator
Free daily 1 - 4 PM. Estab. 1971 to present a variety of art to the college and area community and to offer a place for student and professional artists to show work.

Collections: Small collection of original prints.

Exhibitions: James Van Der Zee, Photos; Will Peterson, Prints; Michael Jones, Ceramics; Antioch Art Faculty; Don Kelly, Sculpture and Prints; student exhibits; area invitational benefit sale; Jerry Skuba, Prints and Sculpture; Robert Whitmore, Painter; James Pierce Turf Maze Exhibit; Jon Hudson and James Kline, Sculpture and Prints; GLCA Sponsor Japanese Caligraphy; Anthony McCall, Filmmaker.

Activities: Student prints traveling exhibitions organized and circulated; 1 show lent per year; lectures open to the public; 4 visiting lecturers per year; 4 gallery talks.

Attendance: 500.

YOUNGSTOWN

✠THE BUTLER INSTITUTE OF AMERICAN ART
524 Wick Ave, 44502. Tel: (216) 743-1711
Dr. Joseph G. Butler, Dir. & Pres.
Clyde Singer, Assoc. Dir.
Dr. Eric C. Hulmer, Cur.
Joseph G. Butler, IV, Treas.
Alice Goldcamp, Educ. Dir.
Free daily 10 AM - 4:30 PM; Sun. 1 - 5 PM; cl. Mon. Estab. and inc. 1919; endowed. Building erected 1919, additions 1931, 1951, 1968; has 16 galleries. First museum building to be devoted entirely to American art. Friends of American Art mem. 700.

Collections: American paintings dating from 1750 to 1975; †Oils, †watercolors, †drawings by American artists; †sculpture and ceramics; prints; †paintings and drawings of American Indians; †32 paintings of Clipper Ships, From Sail to Steam; seven scale ship models.

Exhibitions: Annual Midyear Show; Ohio Ceramic Annual. Other exhibitions include Polish Arts Club Show; Area Artists Annual; Youngstown State University Annual; numerous traveling exhibitions.

Activities: Lectures, demonstrations, tours, concerts and classes. (See Schools)

Library: Several hundred volumes, biographical and general, on American art; large color reproductions.

Publications: Catalog of Permanent Collection with numerous reproductions issued Sept. 1951; Supplements issued 1954, 1959, 1960, 1966 and 1969.

Attendance: Average 80,000.

ZANESVILLE

ZANESVILLE ART CENTER
Maple at Adair Aves, 43701. Tel: (614) 452-0741
James Stubbins, Chmn. Board of Trustees
Dr. Charles Dietz, Dir. & Instr.
Mrs. Joseph Howell, Registrar & Librn.
Open daily 9:30 AM - 5 PM; Sun. 2 - 5 PM; July daily 1 - 5 PM; Sun. 2 - 5 PM; cl. Fri, holidays & Aug. Estab. 1936 to maintain a cultural center for teaching fine arts, crafts, and to present and maintain permanent collections and traveling exhibitions of art, historical objects and industrial design; endowed. Ann. meeting June.

Collections: †European paintings; †American paintings; †sculpture; †drawings and prints; †Oriental art objects; †ceramics; †Early American glass; English paneled room c. 1700; material ranges through ancient to contemporary.

Exhibitions: (1974-75) Recent Accessions to the Permanent Collection; The Everett S. Greer Glass Collection; The Meissen Urn and Lattice Border Milk White Glass Collection, bequest of Dr. Harry C. Powelson; The Russell P. Herrold Glass Collection; Paintings and Prints of Mexico and the American West by David Campbell; Ceramics by Gene Friley; Weavings by Nancy Crow; Jewelry by Fred and Dianne Rundell; Paintings by James Laughman; Photographs by Don Decherd; Ceramics by Jean Anderson; Paintings by Paul Jenkins. Multiplemedia Exhibition from the Erie Art Center; Photographs by Charles Cauliflower; American Woven Coverlets; Paintings by Paul Samuelson; exhibition and Sale of Original Works of Art from Ferdinand Roten Galleries; Plexiglass and Paper Constructions by Nancy Miller; Cloth Collages by Penney Denning;

Paintings and Woodcuts by Gert Smith; Paintings by Sue Wall; 20th Annual AAUW Children's School Art Exhibition; Muskingum County Council of Garden Clubs Flower Show; 34th Annual May Arts and Crafts Exhibition; Salon des Refusés Exhibition; Zane's Trace Commemoration Celebration Exhibition from the Permanent Collection.

Activities: Lectures, gallery tours; classes for adults and children in art, crafts and languages; entertainments and recitals; gallery tours for school children; consultation and advisory service.

Library: Art Reference Library of 4200 volumes, files of pamphlets and reproductions; 4000 photographs; 6000 slides.

Publications: Monthly bulletins.

Income: Approx. $6000.

Attendance: Average daily attendance 65.

Friends of Art:

Estab. 1944; 418 members; contributions $5 and up. Funds for acquiring accessions to the permanent collection and promotion of Art Center program.

Beaux Arts Club

Estab. 1954; 44 members; dues $2. Young Women's Auxiliary to the Art Center; art related projects for benefit of Art Center.

OKLAHOMA

ANADARKO

SOUTHERN PLAINS INDIAN MUSEUM AND CRAFTS CENTER
   Box 749, 73005. Tel: (405) 247-6221
Myles Libhart, Dir. of Museums, Exhibitions, & Publications
Rosemary Ellison, Cur.
Free June 1 - Sept. 30, Mon. - Sat. 9 AM - 5 PM; Sun. 1 PM- 5 PM; Oct. 1 - May 31, Tues. - Sat. 9 AM - 5 PM; Sun. 1 - 5 PM; cl. Mon. New Year's Day, Thanksgiving and Christmas. Estab. 1948; administered and operated by the Indian Arts and Crafts Board, U.S. Department of the Interior, U.S. Government.

Collections: Historic and contemporary arts of the Southern Plains Indian, including †costumes, †decorative arts, †folk arts, †paintings, †sculpture, †graphics.

Exhibitions: Permanent exhibitions of historic and contemporary arts of the Kiowa, Comanche, Cheyenne, Arapaho, Wichita, Caddo, Fort Sill Apache, Kiowa-Apache and Delaware; presents at Museum continuing series of one-person special exhibitions of work by contemporary Native American artists and craftsmen of the U.S; traveling exhibitions include (1972) Contemporary Southern Plains Indian Painting, organized by the Museum with state tour under auspices of the Oklahoma Arts and Humanities Council and the Oklahoma Indian Arts and Crafts Cooperative, (1970) Contemporary Indian and Eskimo Basketry of the United States, scheduled by the Museum.

Activities: Gallery tours for schools and other groups, loans of slide lecture kits to schools.

Publications: One-person exhibition brochure series; Contemporary Southern Plains Indian Painting, published by Oklahoma Indian Arts and Crafts Cooperative; Painted Tipis by Contemporary Plains Indian Artists.

Sales Shop: Operated by the Oklahoma Indian Arts and Crafts Cooperative, offers a wide variety of contemporary craft products and fine arts by Indian artists and craftsmen of Oklahoma and other areas.

Attendance: Average 80,000.

ARDMORE

THE CHARLES B. GODDARD CENTER FOR THE VISUAL AND PERFORMING ARTS
   First Ave. & D St. S.W, 73401. Tel: (405) 226-0909
Mrs. Leon Daube, Pres.
Richard Colvert, Secy.
Laurence London, Managing Dir.
Jerome Westheimer, Treas.
Joyce Harris, Office Secy.
Free Mon. - Sat. 9:30 AM - 4 PM. Estab. Mar. 1970 to bring fine art programs in the related fields of music, art and films to local community at minimum cost; supported by membership. Gallery to bring traveling exhibitions to Ardmore. Monthly advisory board meeting; mem. 450; dues $12-$1000.

Collections: Portraits, paintings, drawings.

Exhibitions: Santa Fe Museum Exhibit; Paintings by Luis Oncins; American Watercolor Association; Ardmore Annual Art Show; Masters Photographic Exhibit; High School Art Exhibit; McAlister Prison Show; East Central State Exhibit; Cowboy Hall of Fame Exhibit; New Mexico Santero Religious Exhibit; Prize Indian Paintings; Library of Congress 25th National Exhibition of Prints & An American Sampler; Texas Watercolor Association, Oklahoma Designer Craftsmen; Taos Art Association; Stephen Parrish: Nineteenth Cen-

tury Picturesque; Old Bergen Art Guild; National Society of Painters in Casein and Acrylics; F. Roten Galleries Exhibit; Valton Tyler Exhibit.

Activities: Classes for strings for children and adults, classes for dancing, guitar, art and Spanish; concerts available for membership, dramatic programs by the Little Theatre Group. Book shop.

Annual Income: $35,000.

Attendance: 30,000.

BARTLESVILLE

WOOLAROC MUSEUM
   Route 3, 74003. Tel: (918) 336-6747
R. R. Lansdown, Dir.
Lucinda Simmons, Cur. Art
Free 10 AM - 5 PM. Estab. 1929 to house art and history of the Southwest. Reference library.

Collections: †Oil paintings, †archaeological Indian material, †Indian arts and crafts, †bronzes, †Southwest Pioneer materials; 55,000 items now displayed.

Attendance: 243,450.

CLAREMORE

WILL ROGERS MEMORIAL*
   P.O. Box 157, 74017. Tel: (918) 341-0719
Robert W. Love, Mgr.
Patricia A. Lowe
Free, 8 AM - 5 PM daily incl. holidays and weekends. Estab. 1938 to perpetuate the name and deeds of the great American, Will Rogers; financed by state appropriations.

Collections: Personal items belonging to Will Rogers; dioramas; original oils of Will Rogers by Count Tamburini, Leon Gordon, Leyendecker; mural by Ray Piercey; library collections include photographs, original manuscripts, movies, magazines and other items; original oils and cartoons in storage including Borein etchings.

Activities: Photograph collection of 2500 prints; 75 for lending or reference.

Library: 500 volumes; 22 minute film short on Will Rogers available to schools and non-profit organizations; small but complete research library on Will Rogers which is available by appointment only to students.

Attendance: 500,000 annually.

GOODWELL

NO MAN'S LAND HISTORICAL SOCIETY—NO MAN'S LAND HISTORICAL MUSEUM
   Panhandle State University, 73939. Tel: (405) 349-2670
Lona Neff Graham, Pres.
Joan Overton Kachel, Secy.
Dr. Harold S. Kachel, Cur.
Free Tues. - Fri. 9 AM - 5 PM; Sat. & Sun. 1 - 5 PM; cl. Mon. Estab. 1934 to preserve and perpetuate the history of the Panhandle of Oklahoma; financed by appropriation and membership. Ann. meeting in Apr; dues $5 individual, $10 organizational, $100 life.

Collections: The museum divisions are: archives, anthropology, art gallery, biology, geology, pioneer history and library. Notable collections: William E. Baker Archaeological Collection; Billye Sewell Barbed Wire Collection; Earl Gilson Pitcher and Book Collections; Phillips Brothers Biological Collection; historical materials of the region, rocks, minerals.

Exhibitions: 9 one-man art shows each year, usually local artists.

Library: 1000 volumes; 200 prints in photographic collection.

Attendance: 6000.

LAWTON

MUSEUM OF THE GREAT PLAINS
   Elmer Thomas Park, 73501. (Mail: P.O. Box 68).
   Tel: (405) 353-5675 .
Dr. David Miller, Pres.
Steve Wilson, Dir.
Towana Spivey, Cur. Anthropology
Cynthia Seamans, Cur. Collections
Dianne Redfield, Cur. Exhibits
Free Mon. - Fri. 8 AM - 5 PM; Sat. 10 AM - 5 PM; Sun. 1:30 - 5 PM. Estab. 1960 to portray the broad sweep of human history in the Great Plains of North America; financed by membership and endowment. Ann. meeting Oct; mem. 800; dues $7.50.

Collections: †Plains Indian, †historical items, †fine arts of all media, †pioneer vehicles.

Activities: Tours; monthly films concerning various aspects of the Trans-Mississippi West; lectures and gallery talks upon request. Gift shop.

Library: 14,000 volumes; 175,000 piece archival materials; 5000 photos.

Publications: Great Plains Journal, twice yearly.

MUSKOGEE

THE FIVE CIVILIZED TRIBES MUSEUM

Agency Hill, Honor Heights Dr, 74401. Tel: (918) 683-1701
John T. Griffin, Jr, Pres.
Charlene Adair, Secy.
Mrs. Spencer Denton, Dir.
Maxeene Bridwell, Field Representative
Open Mon. - Sat. 10 AM - 5 PM; Sun. 1 - 5 PM; admis. 50¢ adults, 25¢ students, special group rates. Estab. 1966 to exhibit artifacts, relics, history, and traditional Indian art of the Cherokee, Chickasaw, Choctaw, Creek, and Seminole Indian Tribes; financed by membership. Gallery shows only paintings of these Five Tribal Indians done in traditional Indian Art. Biannual meetings Apr. & Oct; mem. 1100; dues $5-$300.

Collections: Permanent collection is of Traditional Indian Art by known artists.

Exhibitions: Competitive Art Show and Students Competitive Art Show held annually; plus numerous one-man shows.

Activities: To show slides about the Museum and Indian History to schools and other organizations; guided tours upon request; reference photograph collection.

Library: 3500 volume research and reference library.

Publications: The Five Civilized Tribes Museum Newsletter, 4 times yearly.

Attendance: 29,800 average.

NORMAN

MUSEUM OF ART

University of Oklahoma
Fred Jones, Jr, Memorial Art Center, 410 W. Boyd St, 73069.
Tel: (405) 325-3272
Sam Olkinetzky, Dir.
Edwin J. Deighton, Asst. Dir.
Free Tues. - Fri. 10 AM - 4 PM; Sat. 10 AM - 1 PM; Sun. 1 - 4 PM; cl. Mon. and holidays. Estab. 1936 to preserve art collections and present circulating exhibitions. Ann. meeting Sept; mem. 65; dues $10-$100.

Collections: †Contemporary American paintings; †contemporary American and European graphics; †Oriental painting, sculpture and minor arts; American Indian paintings; Flemish and Dutch paintings.

Exhibitions: Circulating, originating, and permanent. 30 purchases and prize awards, $3000, 1970-1973.

Activities: Weekly color slide series; 24 gallery talks; art classes; occasional lectures series; art lending service; traveling exhibit program; docent program. Book shop.

University Art Library: 8000 volumes.

Publications: Occasional exhibition catalogs, brochures, posters.

Income and Purchases: Income $10,000; purchases $2000.

Attendance: 125,000.

STOVALL MUSEUM OF SCIENCE AND HISTORY

University of Oklahoma, 73069. Tel: (405) 325-4711
J. K. Greer, Dir.
Candace Greene, Asst. to Dir.
M. Farwell, Dir. Educ.
D. Ross, Dir. Exhibitions
Free weekdays 9 AM - 5 PM; Sat, Sun. & holidays 1 - 5 PM; Museum was originally founded as a geology and natural history museum by the Territorial Legislature in 1899. In 1943 the Board of Regents of the University consolidated the collections into a general museum and in 1948 the collections were moved into the present quarters. Mem. dues $15 family, $7.50 student.

Collections: More than two million cataloged specimens are departmentalized under the following departments: Archaeology, Ethnology, Classical Art and Archaeology, History, Geology, Botany, Zoology and Art (historical and primitive paintings).

Exhibits: Permanent exhibits include among others, wildlife dioramas, paleontology and archaeology exhibits; Roman statuary, frieze and tile mosaics.

Activities: Lectures, workshops, films; open house programs; field trips; sales desk.

Publications: Yearly calendar of museum activities, scientific publications by faculty members, Stovall Museum Publications, published at irregular intervals; monthly newsletter. Current books include: Oklahoma Archaeology, An Annotated Bibliography (No. 1); Reptiles of Oklahoma (No. 2); Wilderness Bonanza, The Tri-State District of Missouri, Kansas and Oklahoma (No. 3).

Attendance: 50,000.

OKLAHOMA CITY

NATIONAL COWBOY HALL OF FAME AND WESTERN HERITAGE CENTER

1700 N.E. 63rd St, 73111. Tel: (405) 478-2250
J. B. Saunders, Chmn. Board of Dir.
Joe Watt, Pres. Board of Dir.
Dean Krakel, Managing Dir.
Bryan Rayburn, Deputy Dir.
Richard Muno, Art Dir.
Juan Menchaca, Cur.
Esther Long, Educ. Dir.
Bill Wilson, Pub. Relations Dir.
Open daily 9:30 AM - 5:30 PM; cl. Thanksgiving, Christmas and New Years Day; admis. $2 adults, $1 children, under 6 free, group rates available. Estab. 1965 as a memorial shrine to great Westerners; financed by membership. Ann. meeting Apr; mem. 5000; dues $25 - $200.

Major Collections: Charles Russell Collection; Charles Schreyvogel Memorial Studio; Nicolai Fechin Collection; James and Laura Fraser Studio Collection; Albert K. Mitchell Russell-Remington Collection; Thomas Moran; Albert Bierstadt.

Exhibitions: Royal Western Watercolor Show; National Academy of Western Art Exhibition.

Activities: Docent guided tours, special programs; seminars; traveling art exhibits organized and circulated; Book Shop.

Library: 6000 volume reference library.

Publications: Persimmon Hill Magazine, quarterly.

✤OKLAHOMA ART CENTER

Plaza Circle-Fair Park, Pershing Blvd, 73107.
Tel: (405) 946-4477
Robert E. Lee, Pres.
William Hulsey, V.Pres.
Jerome M. Westheimer, V.Pres.
Charles Buchwald, Treas.
James E. Work, Attorney
George F. Kuebler, Dir.
Mary Catherine Connery, Asst. to Dir.
Free Tues. - Sat. 10 AM - 5 PM; Sun. 1 - 5 PM. Estab. 1936, inc. 1946 to encourage regional art activity and to present an educational program for adults and children. Dues $15 and higher.

Collections: †Contemporary prints, drawings, watercolors; †historical survey of prints and drawings; †American masters paintings; †American contemporary paintings and sculpture (including Washington Gallery of Modern Art complete collection and Eight State purchase awards).

Exhibitions: Annual Eight State Exhibition of Painting and Sculpture; National Exhibition of Prints and Drawings; Oklahoma Designer-Craftsmen Exhibition; Young Talent in Oklahoma (juried high school show with awards of seven $150 one-year college scholarships).

Activities: A program of changing national loan exhibitions; gallery tours; art films; circulating OAC collection exhibitions; lectures by guest speakers; gallery talks; family art events; Book Store; Sales & Rental Gallery.

Library: Approx. 1500 volumes, magazines and files back to 1936.

Attendance: 50,000.

OKLAHOMA HISTORICAL SOCIETY

Division of Museums
Historical Building, 73105. Tel: (405) 521-2491
George H. Shirk, Pres. Board of Trustees
Jack Wettengel, Exec. Dir. & Ex-Officio Secy.
Bruce E. Joseph, Educ.
LaJeanne McIntyre, Finance
C. E. Metcalf, Historic Sites
Martha Blaine, Indian Archives
Alene Simpson, Library
Mary Moran, Newspaper Archives
Dr. Kenny Franks, Publications
R. W. Jones, Museums
Joe L. Todd, Cur. of Collections
Roy T. Pope, Exhibit Technician
John R. Hill, Exhibit Technician
Mark L. Cantrell, Evening Attendant
Ann Covalt, Admin. Asst.
Inez Orr, Registrar
Esther Phillips, File Clerk
Free Mon. - Fri. 8 AM - 9 PM; Sat. 8 AM - 6 PM; Sun. 1:30 - 4:30 PM. Estab. 1893 to provide an overview of the history of the state of Oklahoma, presented in graphic and three-dimensional forms, through the use of artifacts with which the history was made, to tell the story in chronological order, pointing out the highlights of history; financed by state appropriations and membership. Gallery has a feature of the month program to place focus on prominent Oklahoma artists whose works deal with historical interests. Annual meeting April; mem. 2000; dues $5.

Collections: Historical nature-agricultural, anthropological, archaeological, art, costumes, ethnological, folk, history, Indian, oil industry, medical, mineralogical, military, numismatic, transportation; specialized collections at historic sites and museums over the state.

Exhibitions: Chronologically progressive display areas of the main museum (depicting pre-history, Plains Indian history, the Five Civilized Tribes' occupancy of Indian territory, the land openings of the late nineteen and early twentieth centuries, statehood, and progress since statehood) are permanent; feature of the month program.

Activities: Guided tours for school groups and other groups; junior historian clubs; special presentations and study programs for children and adults; other interpretative programs; lectures open to the public; approx. 40 visiting lecturers per year; approx. 500 gallery talks; approx. 2200 tours. Book shop.

Library: Reference library of approx. 40,000 volumes; photograph collection for reference.

Publications: Mistletoe Leaves, monthly newsletter; The Chronicles of Oklahoma, scholastic quarterly; and various brochures and reprints.

Income and Purchases: Income $1.2 million; society depends on donations for additions to its collections.

Attendance: 50,000 annual average.

OKLAHOMA MUSEUM OF ART
7316 Nichols Rd, 73120. Tel: (405) 840-2759
Dr. Robert Sukman, Pres.
J. Howard Christy, Secy.
James K. Reeve, Dir.
Mrs. William Greenwood, Business Secy.
Carol Chatham, Secy. to Dir.
Open Tues. - Sat. 10 AM - 5 PM; Sun. 1 - 5 PM; cl. Mon. & national holidays; nonmember admis. adults $1, children under 12 50¢, members free. Estab. 1958, reorganized 1975, the Museum is committed to those ideals which hold that great traditional values of art not only provide the soundest basis for continuing artistic expression but offer a stability against which merits of contemporary art can be weighed. Museum sponsors exhibitions and offers studio and lecture art classes which explore realism in art idioms; financed by membership. Six galleries used for permanent collection and monthly changing temporary loan shows. Ann. meeting 3rd Sun. in Jan; mem. 1200 adults, 1077 students; dues $15, $25, $100, $500.

Collections: Small painting collection of 19th and 20th century works; slightly larger collection of 20th century prints and drawings. Both areas now being added to through purchases and donations. Museum is expanding collections to include works in all art media, furniture, minor arts, sculpture, etc.

Exhibitions: For the most part one-man and group shows of regional artists displayed on monthly basis; annual competitive juried shows include Statewide High School Drawing show, Members' Juried Annual, Annual Artists Salon; a major old master show in 1975, Oklahoma Collects (Tintoretto to Wyeth).

Activities: Starting Jan, 1976, 13 adult studios in painting, sculpture, drawing; 2 young people's studios, 3 art history lecture classes; workshops. Lectures open to public; 6 visiting lecturers per year; 16 gallery talks; 25 tours; competitions; scholarships. Book shop.

Library: 100 volume reference library; small slide library being formed.

Publications: Monthly calendar; exhibition catalogs.

Attendance: 3735.

OKLAHOMA SCIENCE AND ARTS FOUNDATION, INC.
3000 Pershing Blvd, Fair Park, 73107. Tel: (405) 946-5566
Richard Harrison, Pres.
Mrs. Ronald Rosser, Secy.
Mrs. James H. Ross, Dir.
Ronald P. Olowin, Planetarium Dir.
Robert Sciamada, Assoc. Planetarium Dir.
Larry Blain, Sci-Technol. Cur.
Mrs. Erich P. Frank, Art Dir.
Mrs. Ralph McCracken, Admin. Asst.
Open Mon. - Sat. 10 AM - 5 PM; Sun. 1 - 5 PM; Planetarium charge only, $1.25 adults, 75¢ children under 12. Estab. 1958 to create and expanded interest in and understanding of the pictorial and graphic arts and developments in the field of various sciences and technologies; to supplement educational facilities offered in the public schools in the fields of arts and sciences. Meetings as called by Pres. Mem. (JAM with Oaklahoma Art Center) 2000; dues $25 for JAM, $15 for OSAF only. Contributions made through city-wide Allied Arts Foundation campaign.

Collections: Foucault Pendulum, space, Ships Bridge and Periscope; scientific exhibits such as laser beam, minerals, energy bicycle, calculator, etc. Art and science traveling exhibits every 6-10 weeks. Gallery houses Gerrer collection of ancient artifacts and Kirkpatrick ivory collections.

Activities: Art classes for children and adults; preschool program; films; science lectures; summer junior science classes; adult science classes. Theatre presentations for groups on science, ancient civilizations and art; bibliomania book sale. Planetarium programs for preschool to adult with repertoire of ten shows, public shows on weekends; tours available on request; reference library. Book shop included in sales desk.

Publications: Monthly newsletter.

Attendance: 250,000 annually.

PONCA CITY

PONCA CITY ART ASSOCIATION
Box 1394, 819 E. Central, 74601. Tel: (405) 765-9746
Bob Westmoreland, Pres.
Arzella Walz, Secy.
Free Wed. - Sun. 1 - 5 PM. Estab. 1947 to encourage creative arts, to furnish place and sponsor art classes, sponsor art exhibits and workshops; financed by membership and flea market. Ann. meeting first Tues. in Apr; mem. 600; dues $5 family.

Collections: Permanent fine arts collection, additions by purchases and donations.

Exhibitions: 8 per year.

Activities: Education committee has spring and fall classes, lectures, workshops in all media, competitions, scholarships, annual fine arts festival, prizes and purchase awards.

Publications: Association Bulletin, quarterly.

Income: $10,000.

PONCA CITY CULTURAL CENTER AND INDIAN MUSEUM
1000 E. Grand, 74601.
Delia F. Castor, Museum Cur.
Leon Nelson, City Mgr-in-Charge
Free daily 10 AM - 5 PM; Sun. and holidays 1 - 5 PM; cl. Tues, Christmas and New Year's. Indian Museum estab. 1939, Cultural Center at present location May 26, 1968, for the social and cultural use of the citizens; maintained by appropriation. The Art Association changes exhibitions on main floor, Garden Center rooms show paintings, and Museum exhibits paintings of Indian Artists in addition to permanent collection.

Collections: Three E. W. Lenders paintings, Indian paintings, Kiowa paintings collected by O. B. Jacobson, University of Oklahoma; one original Mopope, one Blue Eagle, one Woody Crumbo, in addition to the limited edition prints of 6 Ship Shee; a life sized self-portrait of D. Buongiorno, 1905, N.Y. A mural sized painting Mr. Marland had painted by Randel Davey. One painting in the English Landscape manner. Antiques in D.A.R. Room 101 Ranch Collection, picture and artifacts concerning the 101 Ranch activities, people and buildings; Ray Falconer Collection of old glass negatives and photographs.

Exhibitions: Many local painters have exhibits. One traveling exhibit of Oklahoma Art sponsored by the Oklahoma Arts and Humanities. Indian exhibitions.

Activities: Craft program. The museum is concerned with the revival of the Indian yarn work, fingerweaving. We are teaching Indians and others how to do it to revive and hopefully popularize a beautiful craft. It is time consuming and takes yarn. Photograph Collection; gathering Indian stories; lending library of copied material on Indian tribes, etc; 100 gallery talks or tours; 100 gardening books in Garden Center; 100 Indian and history in museum.

Attendance: 25,000.

SHAWNEE

THE GERRER COLLECTION
Art Gallery and Museum of St. Gregory's Abbey
74801. Tel: (405) 273-9878
Rt. Rev. Robert G. Dodson, Pres.
Rev. Joachim J. Spexarth, Secy.
Free daily 2 - 4 PM; cl. Sat. Estab. 1915 as a cultural and educational contribution to the local community as well as to the students of St. Gregory's College; endowed.

Collections: American School; French School; English School; Italian School; Spanish School; German School; Low Countries School; some 700 works of art, paintings, sculpture, engravings and etchings; American Indian (paintings). Over 6000 museum artifacts: Babylonian, Persian, Syrian, Cyprian, Grecian, Roman, African, Oriental (Chinese, Japanese and Indian), American Indian (Alaskan, North American, Central American and South American), and others.

Exhibitions: Local exhibition of most works of art and artifacts.

Activities: Branch display in Oklahoma City; program for schools of Oklahoma in art and art history; original objects of art lent; lectures open to public; classes for adults and children.

Library: Extensive holdings all housed in St. Gregory's College Library and available to public and students.

Publications: Catalog only at present.

Attendance: 100,000 annual average.

STILLWATER

GARDINER ART GALLERY
Oklahoma State University, Department of Art, 74074.
Tel: (405) 372-6211, Exten. 332, 7222
B. J. Smith, Dir.
Open Mon. - Fri. 8 AM - 5 PM; Sat. 9 AM - Noon; Sun. 2 - 5 PM.
Estab. as Gardiner Art Gallery Sept. 1970, formerly Whitehurst Art
Gallery; Gallery run by Department of Art.
Exhibitions: Shows changed every 3 weeks.
Attendance: 1000.

TAHLEQUAH

CHEROKEE NATIONAL HISTORICAL SOCIETY, INC.
P.O. Box 515, TSA-LA-GI, 74464. Tel: (918) 456-6007
W. W. Keeler, Pres.
J. I. Monroe, Secy.
M. A. Hagerstrand, Exec. V. Pres. & Acting Dir.
Open Tues. - Sat. 10 AM - 5 PM; admis. adults 25¢, children 10¢.
Organization estab. 1963, museum, 1974, to preserve the history and
traditions of the Cherokee Tribe of Indians; to serve as an agency
for the education of tribal members and the general public in the
history and heritage of the Cherokees; to conduct research into
matters relating to history and heritage; financed by membership.
Cherokee National Archives and Library; collection of Indian
art in the Cherokee National Museum. Over 1000 mem; dues $5,
$50, life $100, endowment $500 or more.
Collections: Principal Chief (of the Cherokees) W. W. Keeler collection of personal papers and memorabilia; Trail of Tears collection of Indian art and sculpture; †Permanent archives collection on
Cherokee history and culture; smaller miscellaneous collections
pertaining to Cherokee history and culture.
Exhibitions: Indian Images (Smithsonian Institution); Trail of
Tears Indian Art Show; Cherokees in the News (A Century of News
about the Cherokees - 100 original newspapers from 1768-1875).
Activities: Slides and special programs available on request;
1 motion picture, over 2000 Kodachromes and 1000 photographs in
lending collection, 30 sets lent in an average year; lectures open to
public; village schedules tours; art shows; scholarships.
Library; Over 1500 volumes for reference; 1000 prints in
photograph collection for lending and reference.
Annual Purchases: Over $2000 (archives only).
Attendance: 100,000.

TULSA

ELOISE J. SCHELLSTEDE GALLERY OF FINE ARTS*
4956 S. Peoria, Camelot Inn, 74105. Tel: (918) 582-4134
Eloise J. Schellstede, Pres.
Richard Lee Schellstede, Dir.
Wilma D. Morgan, Area Promotions
Open Mon. - Fri. 9 AM - 5 PM. Estab. November 1969 for the promotion of living artists and their works; endowed. Gallery, paintings
and sculpture on display from area artists and other guest artists.
Activities: Sponsored approx. 20 shows in area; lectures; winter
classes for adults in painting and sculpture; twenty gallery talks or
tours.
Library: 180 volumes for reference; Slide Library of great artists from Museums; also from living artists (living artists works
available for sale or commissions).

GREEN COUNTRY ART ASSOCIATION
Green Country Art Center, 1825 E. 15th St, 74104
Tel: (918) 932-4259
Eloise J. Schellstede, Pres.
Pierce St. John, V.Pres.
Richard L. Schellstede, Secy-Treas. & Coordinator
Open Mon. - Fri. 10 AM - 5 PM. Estab. Apr. 1968; an area organi-
zation to promote the artist and his work and to present the artist's
work to the public; supported by membership. There are now 3
annual shows set up plus each artist may display a limited number of
paintings or sculpture. Mem. 300 from Okla, Ark, Mo, Kans. & Tex.
by application.
Exhibitions: Dogwood Art Festival, Eastern Oklahoma, to be announced in Jan; Green Country Air Fair, Camelot Inn; Bicentennial
Green Country Special 1976; all of these are annual shows and 1976
will be the eighth year; Special at the Independent Petroleum Exposition in Tulsa, 76; special shows and exhibits are announced to the
membership, in addition to the annual shows.
Activities: Scholarship awarded at the Green Country Art Fair
to a member artist for advance study; scholarship awarded to an
area college for their Art Dept. (See Schools)
Publications: Green Country Art News, monthly.
Attendance: Average 20,000, Art Fair; average 5000, other shows
in outlying areas.

GREEN COUNTRY ART FOUNDATION, INC.
Green Country Art Center, 1825 E. 15th St, 74104.
Tel. (918) 932-4259
Eloise J. Schellstede, Founder & Pres.
Pierce St. John, V.Pres.
Richard L. Schellstede, Secy-Treas. & Exec. Dir.
Open Mon. - Fri. 10 AM - 5 PM; Sun. 1 - 5 PM. Estab. 1973 as a
foundation to promote works of area living artists through the Green
Country Art Association and other similar art associations and orga-
nizations; to promote and encourage the artists to use area subjects of
Oklahoma and the Five State Area, thus showing the world the beauti-
ful heart of the United States; to establish a permanent facility in
Tulsa for the exhibition of artistic works of living artists, and be a
center of art oriented activities, and center for Green Country Art
Association and Green Country Art Foundation, Inc.
Activities: To develop and maintain a cooperative relationship
with local and national museums and other cultural organizations;
to provide financial assistance in the form of scholarships, grants,
or loans to deserving member artists for further formal training;
to provide financial assistance to colleges, universities and recognized schools of art, to further develop artistic talents; to obtain
necessary funds from public or private resources to adequately
meet the goals and objectives of the foundation. Assistance is given
to the Green Country Art Association for their scheduled shows and
activities.

✠PHILBROOK ART CENTER
2727 S. Rockford Rd, 74114. Tel: (918) 742-2459
Alexander Stoia, Dir. & Pres.
Marcia Manhart, Educ. Dir.
Raymond Watkins, Gallery Supvr.
Open 10 AM - 5 PM; Sun. 1 - 5 PM; admis. $1.50, children under 15
free, students with ID 75¢. Estab. in 1939 as an art center for exhibiting art of all historical periods including the present; encourages
regional art activity and art education. Ann. meeting Apr; mem. dues
$18 and higher. Governing body, Southwestern Art Association.
Collections: European, Early American and contemporary American Oils, watercolors and prints; American Indian paintings;
sculpture; period furniture; Indian pottery, baskets, six period
rooms; Samuel H. Kress Collection of Italian Renaissance paintings
and sculpture; Laura A. Clubb Collection of paintings; Clark Field
collection of American Indian baskets and pottery; Roberta Campbell Lawson collection of Indian costumes and artifacts; American
Indian murals and paintings; Gussman Collection of African Sculpture.
Exhibitions: Regular changing exhibition program of exhibits
(Oct-May); permanent collection shown June-Sept. Oklahoma Artists Annual with awards; American Indian Annual open to artists of
Indian descent; Oklahoma Designer-Craftsmen Exhibition, annual
Collectors Choice exhibit.
Activities: Monthly morning gallery talks and evening gallery
talks on current exhibitions or special topical series given by di-
rector. Education program includes fall and spring 12-week adult
and childrens art classes (adults, weekdays, children, Sat. morn-
ings); Junior Studio, mornings, June and July. Ruskin Rental and
Sales Gallery, paintings for rent.
Library: 1800 volumes, also the Roberta Campbell Lawson library of source material on Indians.
Attendance: 100,000.

THOMAS GILCREASE INSTITUTE OF AMERICAN HISTORY AND ART
2500 W. Newton St, 74127 (Mail: R.R. 6).
Tel: (918) 581-5311
Cecille Bales, Chmn. of the Board
W. R. Best, Dir.
D. M. McPike, Cur. Anthropology
Carolyn Tannehill Bradshaw, Cur. Art
G. P. Edwards, Cur. History
Museum free Mon. - Sat. 9 AM - 5 PM; Sun. and holidays 1 - 5 PM;
cl. Christmas. Library free for research, cl. weekends and holidays. Estab. by the late Thomas Gilcrease as a private institution;
acquired by the City of Tulsa 1954; governed by a Board of Directors
and City Park Board; building addition completed Oct. 1963. Mem.
1600; dues $15 and up.
Collections: American art from Colonial period to present, with
emphasis on art of historical significance. Much of the work shown
is of documentary nature, with considerable emphasis on the American Indian and the opening of the West. Art collections include 4000
paintings by 400 American artists; artifact collections include 10,000
objects from Mid-Americas, and North America, and include both
prehistoric and historic materials from most of the Indian cultures of
these areas.
Exhibitions: A special or rotating exhibit during fall-winter-
spring seasons; special exhibitions periodically; public school art
exhibit.

Activities: Film program and lectures on art and history; gallery tours; lectures to school groups outside the museum.

Library: Contains 65,000 books and documents, many rare books and manuscripts of the American discovery period, as well as materials concerning the Five Civilized Tribes.

Publications: The American Scene (quarterly) devoted to articles on American History and art with illustrations from Gilcrease Art Collections; The Curator (bimonthly) contains articles pertaining to Gilcrease collections and various programs; The Gazette (bimonthly) contains news and articles concerning activities; published on alternate months.

Book Shop: Books, magazines, pamphlets, covering such subjects as the American Indian, art and history, and western artists in the collection; slides and reproductions from Gilcrease collections; artifacts and jewelry handcrafted by Indian artists.

Attendance: 80,000 annually.

OREGON

ASHLAND

STEVENSON UNION ART GALLERY*
Stevenson Union, Southern Oregon College
  97520. Tel: (503) 482-6461
Mrs. Marythea Grebner, Dir. of Stevenson Union
Edith L. Morrill, Asst. Dir. Activities
Free Mon. - Thurs. 9 AM - 9 PM; Fri. 9 AM - 5 PM. Estab. 1966 to provide members of the Southern Oregon College community and the greater Ashland area an opportunity to experience a well rounded selection of art and crafts; financed by student fees.

Collections: †Small permanent collection of prints, paintings by local artists and a sculpture by Bruce West.

Exhibitions: Phil Tyler: Photography; 2nd Annual Rogue Valley Women; Betty La Duke; Paintings from India; Monica Setziol: Weavings; Sculpture by Lavelle Foos and painting by Walter Peterson; Southern Oregon College Faculty Exhibit 11/33; Pop Prints of the 60's.

Activities: Special lectures; artist workshops; short programs for educational TV; exhibiting artists lecture to art classes when possible; lectures open to the public; 3 visiting lecturers per year; 8 gallery talks yearly.

Income and Purchases: Income $2500; purchases $100-150.
Attendance: 4000 annual average.

BANDON

RIVER'S END ARTS AND CRAFTS GALLERY*
  P.O. Box 1166, 97411.
E. Michelman, Pres.
Mae Fellows, Secy.-Treas.
Irene Ranta, Gallery Decorator
Freda Lowe, Mem. Coordinator
Open Summer 10 AM - 4 PM; no admis. Estab. in this area as an outlet for the talent demonstrated; financed by membership. Meeting first Tues. of every month; dues $12 per yr.

Activities: Material is available to anyone; individual paintings and original objects of art lent; lending collection, color reproductions and photographs; 12 items lent in an average year; 12 active borrowers; classes for adults.

COOS BAY

COOS ART MUSEUM
  515 Market Ave, 97420. Tel: (503) 267-3901
Robert Abel, Chmn. Board
Frederick Kruse, V.Chmn.
Peggy Champagne, Secy.
Nina Grunwaldt, Treas.
Maggie Karl, Dir.
Helen Thom, Rental Sales Gallery
Mary Lee Flanagan, Gift Shop
Jo-Ann Andrews, Educ. Chmn.
Mabel Garner, Cataloger
Gan Martin, Cur.
Museum Galleries open daily & Sun. 1 - 4 PM; cl. Mon. Estab. 1950, inc. 1960, a non-profit group formed for the purpose of encouraging interest in the fine arts; incorporated for the purpose of estab. a permanent headquarters for the Coos Artists League and to raise a building fund for a fine arts museum and art school; acquired the original Carnegie Library Building for this purpose, and the formal opening of the museum was held September 17, 1966. Ann. meeting Jan; mem. totals 550 active and assoc; dues $10 and $15 annually, organizational dues $10, sustaining, donor, patron, $25 and higher; sixty honorary members composed of exhibiting fine artists.

Collections: Permanent collection of contemporary American Art including sculpture, paintings, prints and drawings; recently received a matching fund grant from the National Endowment of the Arts to improve permanent collection.

Exhibitions: Monthly exhibitions in painting, sculpture, photography and weaving by professional artists. Special exhibitions, Junior Art Show with all the grade, junior and high school students participating (held in May). Juried craft exhibition held in July; juried painting and sculpture exhibition in Nov; juried photography exhibition in Mar. Prize money up to $1500 for each exhibition. Purchases for the permanent collection are made from the various exhibitions.

Activities: Summer and winter workshops; a school for art with classes in weaving, paintings, sculpture, jewelry making, calligraphy, woodcarving, drawing, silver smithing, stitchery, and many others held on a regular term basis. Classes for children of all ages all year long. Museum tours arranged for school art departments and school students from all over Southwestern Oregon.

Publications: Bulletin (Monthly); brochures on current exhibits and the annual report.

Attendance: Approx. 20,000.

COQUILLE

COQUILLE VALLEY ART ASSOCIATION
P.O. Box 224, 97423. Tel: (503) 396-3294
Myrtle McCollum, Chmn. Board of Dir.
Open Tues. - Sun. 1 - 4 PM. Estab. 1950 to furnish instructors in manual arts to all interested and to promote art appreciation. Ann. meeting Apr; mem. 125; dues $12 per year.

Collection: Permanent collection donated and/or purchased from teachers and members.

Exhibitions: From throughout state of Oregon.

Activities: Summer workshops by visiting artists; regular classes in painting and drawing convene in Sept. through May.

CORVALLIS

HORNER MUSEUM
Oregon State University
  Gill Coliseum, 97331
Thyrza J. Anderson, Cur.
Wallace Weltzin, Asst. Cur.
Free Tues. - Fri. 10 AM - 5 PM; Sat. 10 AM - 2 PM; Sun. 2 - 5 PM. Estab. 1880 to reveal the holdings in an informative way, to enhance shows, to engage students and faculty in participation, to seek the support and cooperation of the community; financed by city and state appropriation and membership. Gallery maintained. Mem. 70; dues $10.

Collections: Stuffed animals and birds, butterflies, carriages, quilts, minerals, tools, dishes and glassware, clocks, Oriental rugs and dishes, vases, Indian and Eskimo artifacts, dolls, guns, clothing and jewelry.

Exhibitions: Textiles - Historic and Contemporary; Lights - Old, Modern and Student Designed; Africa and the World; Portraits, Past and Present; Historic Oregon Architecture; Chairs; Objects for Preparing Food; Summertime - 1900; Eskimo Artifacts and Art; Doll Houses; The Farm; The 30's; The Culture and Crafts of the Indians of Oregon.

Activities: Photograph collection; lectures open to public, 7 visiting lecturers per year; concerts; dramatic programs; classes for adults and children.

Income and Purchases: Income $35,000; purchases $250.
Attendance: 30,000.

⌘MEMORIAL UNION ART GALLERY
  Oregon State University, 97331. Tel: (503) 754-2416
George F. Stevens, Secy. & Dir.
Free daily 8 AM - 10 PM. Estab. 1928. Ann. meeting May; mem. 15,000.

Collections: The William Henry Price Memorial Collection of Oil Paintings.

Exhibitions: American Prints Today; Contemporary Prints from Holland; Way of Chinese Landscape Painting; Art Faculty Exhibits; Exchange Exhibits; Japanese Prints; Contemporary Painting and Sculpture.

Activities: Educational program integrated with the exhibit schedule; Extension Dept. serves the State; material available to responsible galleries for fees ranging to $85; traveling exhibitions; paintings lent to schools; lectures.

Library: For reference and lending; collection of color reproductions.

Publications: Calendar and exhibition pamphlets.
Income: Annual income, $70,000; purchases variable.
Attendance: 50,000.

DELAKE

LINCOLN COUNTY ART CENTER
P.O. Box 622, 97367. Tel: (503) 994-5839
Fae Reddick, Pres.
Fern Johnson, Secy.
Maude Walling Wanker, Dir.
Dorothy Wilson, Treas.
Gallery free 2 - 5 PM daily; cl. Mon. Estab. 1942 as a non-profit
art educational institution. Ann. meeting Jan; mem. approx. 300.
 Exhibitions: Local, national and international.
 Activities: Lectures by art instructors from various colleges;
classes in painting, drawing, design, weaving, ceramics, metal-
craft, etching, and sculpture.
 Library: 500 volumes for reference and lending.
 Income: Approx. $5000.
 Publication: Artcentergram, monthly.
 Attendance: Approx. 1000.

EUGENE

THE ERB MEMORIAL STUDENT UNION ART GALLERY
University of Oregon
 13th Ave. & University St, 97403. Tel: (503) 686-4373
Shelia Wheeler, Activities Dir.
Adell McMillan, Asst. Dir. for Programs.
Frank Geltner, EMU Cultural Forum Representative for the Arts
Free Sun. Noon - 11 PM; Mon. - Thurs. 7:30 AM - 11 PM; Fri. &
Sat. 7:30 - Noon. Estab. 1950 to provide exhibitions for enjoyment
and appreciation of art for campus and its guests. Mem. of Art
Gallery Committee is composed of a Chairman and 15 students.
Special exhibitions within the Student Union and throughout the
campus.
 Collections: †Pacific Northwest Art. Purchases made annually
following Pacific Northwest Art Annual invitational exhibition. Began
in 1961 with a show of oils by Northwest Artists.
 Purchases: Annual purchases $100-$2000

MAUDE KERNS ART CENTER
1910 E. 15th Ave, 97403. Tel: (503) 345-1126
Thomas C Moreland, Pres.
Mrs. John Alltucker, Secy.
John F. Connor, Dir.
Jane Raffeld, Admin. Asst.
Free Sat. - Thurs. 1 - 5 PM. Estab. 1943 to foster ethical standards
in arts and crafts, community art education through classes and gal-
lery exhibitions; financed by membership. Monthly shows in Gallery
of paintings, prints and crafts, exhibiting mostly local work. Ann.
meeting Apr; mem. 1350; dues $10 adult, $15 family.
 Exhibitions: Paintings, drawings, ceramics, terrariums, stained
glass, textiles, prints, fashions, photographs, jewelry.
 Activities: Traveling exhibitions organized and circulated; 30
tours; classes for adults and children; competitions; scholarships.
 Publications: Bimonthly newsletter.
Income and Purchases: Income $80,000; purchases $78,000.
 Attendance: 3000 annual average.

SCHOOL OF ARCHITECTURE AND ALLIED ARTS LIBRARY,
UNIVERSITY OF OREGON
 Lawrence Hall, 97403. Tel: (503) 686-3637
Betty H. Shafer, Librn.
J. Gail Burkart, Slide Librn.
Open Mon. - Thurs. 8 AM- 10 PM, Fri. 8 AM - 5 PM, Sat. 1 - 5 PM,
Sun. 2 - 10 PM; cl. weekends during summer. Estab. 1919 to pro-
vide resources for the courses, degree programs and research of
the departments in the School of Architecture and Allied Arts and
for its Institute for Community Art Studies and the Center for En-
vironmental Research; financed by endowment and state appropriation.
 Activities: Photograph collection contains 22,000 mounted photographs, primarily teaching resources and not loaned.
 Library: Approx. 20,000 volume library; collection of 125,000
slides for School of Architecture and Allied Arts.

✠UNIVERSITY OF OREGON MUSEUM OF ART
97403. Tel: (503) 686-3027
Richard C. Paulin, Dir.
Michael Whitenack, Supvr. Statewide Services
Tommy Griffin, Acting Chief Preparator
Mrs. William Zentner, Registrar
Norine Arens, Admin. Asst.
Richard Nigh, Museum Clerk
Lucille Johnston, Secy. Statewide Services
Open Tues. - Sun. Noon - 5 PM, all galleries including Rental
Sales and Museum Shop. Estab. 1933 by popular subscription as a
memorial to Prince Lucien Campbell (University President 1902-
1925) to provide an art museum at the University for use by students,
faculty, and general public, to promote an active and continued interest in the visual arts, both past and present.
 Collections. The Murray Warner Collection of Oriental Art includes over 3200 accessioned objects, representing principally the
cultures of China and Japan. However, the collection also includes
works from Cambodia, Korea, Mongolia, Russia, and American and
British works which show oriental influence. Many major acquisitions, both by gift and purchase, have been added in the oriental area,
more than doubling the initial Warner collection and including such
new areas as Ghandaran and Indian sculpture, Chinese funerary
jade, Persian miniatures, and Syrian glass. However, in the past
few years, this museum has been actively and successfully collecting in the Contemporary American, European and Great Pacific
Basin areas, with particular emphasis on artists and craftsmen
from the Northwest. This collection alone now includes over 900
works and a new permanent gallery is devoted exclusively to this
area. Two new and outstanding collections are the over 500 works,
both archival and major, executed by the internationally renowned
painter, Morris Graves, and over 137 photographic architectural
documentational pieces of buildings throughout this nation designed
by the famed Northwest architect, Pietro Belluschi.
 Exhibitions: Exhibitions are local, national, and international in
scope and are museum organized or traveling; each year the exhibitions committee of this museum strives to create varied and diverse
programs of exhibitions in order to reach as many people as possible.
 Activities: The Friends of the Museum maintains an active state-
wide membership which helps to support the exhibitions, acquisitions, Statewide Services circulating exhibitions program, docent
training and the Rental-Sales gallery, and many other activities,
both aesthetic and social in nature. Friends of the Museum founded
in 1958; annual meeting in spring; membership 500; dues $3 (stu-
dent), $15 (regular), and higher.
 Publications: Exhibition catalogues periodically.
 Income: $105,071.
 Attendance: 6000 per month; 6000 more per year in scheduled
tours.

KLAMATH FALLS

KLAMATH ART ASSOCIATION
P.O. Box 955, 97601
Warren Kerr, Pres.
James Leard, V.Pres.
Don Ross, Treas.
Nina Pence, Chmn. Exhibits
Beth Grigg, Secy.
Gallery, 120 River St, free Mon. - Sat. 1 - 4 PM, Sun. 2 - 5 PM &
special occasions. Association estab. 1948 to provide art training
for local residents; Gallery estab. 1960 to provide display and
teaching space for the Association's activities. Ann. meeting
Sept; mem. over 200; dues $7 and higher.
 Collections: Paintings, ceramics, weaving; owned by members.
 Exhibitions: 12 annually, one membership show, one juried
show and remainder varies.
 Activities: Annual arts festival, Mid-Sept. Classes in painting,
drawing, ceramics, weaving. Children's summer art classes.
Visiting lectures; workshops.
 Annual Income: $7000 (membership, gallery sales, tuition).
 Attendance: Approx. 5000.

KLAMATH COUNTY MUSEUM
1451 Main St, 97601. Tel: (503) 882-2501, Exten. 208
Harry J. Drew, Dir. & Cur.
Museum Advisory Board:
Douglas Ernst, Chmn.
Norma Smith, Secy.
Free Tues. - Sun; cl. Mon. Estab. 1953 to preserve and exhibit his-
torical and cultural materials related to Klamath Country; County &
State appropriations.
 Collections: Etchings by Rembrandt; primitive art objects; glass-
ware; paintings by local artists.
 Activities: Traveling school exhibits, guided tours, lectures.
 Library: Small reference library of c. 5000 volumes; photograph
collection of 10,000 prints and negatives for reference; out-of-print
material on local history.
 Attendance: 30,000.

MEDFORD

ROGUE VALLEY ART ASSOCIATION
P.O. Box 763 (gallery 40 S. Bartlett), 97501. Tel: (502) 772-8118
Ben Trowbridge, Pres.
Phil Patterson, V.Pres.
Dunbar Carpenter, Treas.
Jan Sawyer, Secy.
Gigi Dobbs, Gallery Coordinator

Free Mon. - Sat. 9 AM - 4 PM. Estab. 1960 to provide the surrounding area with changing exhibits in what is going on in the world of art; supported by membership. Maintains the Rogue Gallery. Ann. meeting April; mem. 330; family $10, single $7.50, patron $25, student $2.

Exhibitions: New exhibit each month.

Activities: Summer art education for children 7-18, scholarships offered; adult education classes throughout year have included calligraphy, drawing and workshops in stained glass and printmaking; tours and artist lectures. Auxiliary Board initiated in 1971.

Publications: Newsletter, approx. 4 annually.

Income: (1974) $17,500.

Attendance: Average 8000 annually.

MONMOUTH

GALLERY 107

Oregon College of Education
   97361. Tel: (503) 838-1220
Peter G. Stone, Comt. Chmn.
   Comt. Mem:
John Casey
Leo J. Kirk
Donald Hoskisson
Free Mon. - Fri. 8 AM - 5 PM during scheduled exhibits. Estab. to bring work of contemporary and traditional artists and craftsman to the community and the college for study and familiarity; financed by state appropriation and student funds.

Collections: Contemporary Northwest Ceramics.

Exhibitions: Spray Works; Fountain Figure Show; Buena Vista Clay Works Show; American Student Show (Kiln Dried); Fiber Sculpture by Mike Walsh; Cooper Super Show; Higher Education Invitational Exhibition; Oregon High School Invitational.

Activities: Educational department conducts tours for public schools, encounters in the gallery; material available to Oregon schools; pay mailing fees; traveling exhibitions organized and circulated; original objects of art lent; 500 lantern slides concerning Oregon artists and methods; 50 items lent in average year; 30 active borrowers; photograph collection of 8000 slides; lectures open to the public; 3-5 visiting lecturers per year; 6-8 gallery talks and tours; library.

Income and Purchases: Income $2200; purchases $300.

Attendance: 3000.

PORTLAND

BASSIST INSTITUTE

923 Southwest Taylor St, 97205. Tel: (503) 228-6528
Donald H. Bassist, Pres.
Ernest Buhlinger, Secy.
Free, 9 AM - 5 PM. Estab. 1964 to provide practical instruction in retail merchandising, interior design, display, fashion design, advertising and promotion, fashion history and textiles.

Collections: Definitive collection of fashion and costume history books, also notable collection in furniture and interior decoration fields.

Activities: Lending collection of 150 motion pictures; lectures open to the public; scholarships. Book shop.

Library: Approx. 7000 volume library; clip file of current materials in our fields.

Attendance: 150 per week.

CONTEMPORARY CRAFTS ASSOCIATION

3934 S.W. Corbett Ave, 97201. Tel: (503) 223-2654
William J. Hawkins, III, Pres.
Melody Teppola, V.Pres.
C. Herald Campbell, Treas.
Jan de Vries, Dir.
Free Mon. - Fri. 11 AM - 5 PM; Sat. 11 AM - 4 PM; Sun. 1 - 4 PM. Estab. and inc. 1937; maintained by volunteers to promote high standards of design and workmanship among creative artists in the Northwest. Mem. 900; dues $10 and higher.

Collections: Collection of contemporary crafts in all mediums, currently being enlarged.

Activities: Maintains exhibition galleries for invitational shows, one-man and group; sales gallery for sculpture, pottery, weaving, jewelry, etc, by Northwest Artist-Craftsmen. Group tours for schools and others interested; scholarship for resident potter. Craftsmen-in-the-Schools program.

HOFFMAN GALLERY

School of the Arts and Crafts Society of Portland
   616 N.W. 18th Ave, 97209. Tel: (503) 228-4741
Callum Mac Coll, Gallery Dir.
Free Mon. - Thurs. 9 AM - 10 PM; Fri. & Sat. 9 AM - 4 PM; cl. Sun. The Julia E. Hoffman Gallery, estab. 1956, is a small well designed area occupying part of the building's first floor. It presents thoughtfully planned and well installed exhibitions of work both by contemporary artists and craftsmen and by traditional, folk and primitive cultures. It aspires to exemplify the highest standards of design and workmanship, to set goals and provide stimulation of ideas for students, to elevate the capacity for judgment and appreciation in all viewers. It adheres to no bias toward the avant garde or the traditional, but seeks instead to call attention to quality, in whatever mode it comes. Gallery talks by trained guides are available to groups upon request.

The Arts and Crafts Society as Resource Center. Grants from the National Endowment for the Arts and the Oregon Arts Commission and the Metropolitan Arts Commission provide opportunities for artists and craftsmen who share common aesthetic and technical interests to come together in a situation in which they derive stimulation from one another's presence and ideas. Outside lecturers are brought in. A slide bank is being built up for use by artists, craftsmen and teachers in the area. It is a center from where things happen in the art community, like the Oregon Designer Craftsmen's Guild and the Northwest Mural Beautification Project. Mem. 1000, each paying $7 or more annually. Ann meeting May.

Library: 600 volumes for reference; slides, periodicals.

Publications: Quarterly catalog; monthly gallery announcements; newsletters; descriptive brochure.

Income and Expenditures: $133,000 income; $133,000 expenditures.

Attendance: Approx. 1200.

LIBRARY ASSOCIATION OF PORTLAND, OREGON

Multnomah County Library
   801 S.W. Tenth Ave, 97205. Tel: (503) 223-7201
James H. Burghardt, Librn.
Barbara J. Kern, Head Art & Music Dept.
Free Mon. - Thurs. 9 AM - 9 PM; Fri. & Sat. 9 AM - 5:30 PM; cl. Sun. & holidays. Estab. 1864; dept. of Public Library. Ann. meeting 3rd Tues. in Sept.

Collections: c. †14,000 titles on art; c. †2,000,000 circulating unmounted pictures; †707 large color reproductions for circulation; †11,553 colored slides for circulation.

Purchases: $18,000 annually.

METROPOLITAN ARTS COMMISSION

522 S.W. Fifth Ave, 97204. Tel: (503) 248-4569
Henry Stanley, Chmn.
Robert Jones, V.Chmn.
Emily Carpenter, Exec. Dir.
Liz Thorsten, Staff Secy.
Office open 8 AM - 5 PM. Estab. Feb. 1973 to promote and encourage programs to further the development and public awareness of and interest in the visual and performing arts; financed by city and county appropriation.

Publication: Newsletter, quarterly.

OREGON HISTORICAL SOCIETY

1230 S.W. Park Ave, 97205. Tel: (503) 222-1741
Thomas Vaughan, Dir.
Millard McClung, Assoc Dir.
Robert Stark, Museum Adminr.
Louis Flannery, Chief Librn.
Priscilla Knuth, Managing Ed.
Free Mon. - Sat. 10 AM - 4:45 PM. General formation 1873, inc. 1898, to collect, preserve, exhibit and publish materials pertaining to the Oregon Country. Ann. meeting 2nd Fri. in Nov; mem. 5500; dues $10.

Museum Collections: Approx. 50,000 museum objects, approx. 20,000 square feet of exhibit space.

Activities: Lectures, field trips, films, exhibits; educational programs for all ages; maintain historic 1856 Bybee-Howell House, Sauvie Island.

Library: Reference library of more than 50,000 volumes; photograph collection of over 1,000,000 prints; 10 million pieces of manuscript material; over 10,000 maps, over 9000 reels microfilm.

Publications: Oregon Historical Quarterly; books; maps, pamphlets; newsletter.

Income: $650,000 annually.

Attendance: 125,000.

✠PORTLAND ART MUSEUM

Portland Art Association
   1219 S.W. Park, 97205. Tel: (503) 226-2811
Donald Jenkins, Dir.
Kathryn Gates, Registrar
Betty Engel, Conservator
Mary Brown, Bookkeeper
Mary Ann Mees, Librn.
Robert Peirce, Ed. & Research Asst.
Pauline Illo Eyerly, Educ. & Publicity
Elizabeth Donally and Jan Liss, Membership
Diana Turner, Asst. Cur.

Evelyn Lamon, Exec. Asst. to Dir.
Pat Howe, Preparator
Warren Wolf, Dean, Museum Art School
Marjorie Eastman, Registrar, Museum Art School
Open Noon - 5 PM; Fri. Noon - 10 PM; cl. Mon. Estab. and inc.
1892. Ann. meeting Nov; mem. 5700; dues $15 and higher.
Collections: Rasmussen Collection of Northwest Coast Indian Art,
†European painting and sculpture from the Renaissance to the 20th
century, including Samuel H. Kress Collection of Renaissance Art;
French painting from the 17th - 20th century; German Expressionist
painting; †American art from the 18th - 20th centuries; †Chinese
sculptures, bronzes, furniture, ceramics and painting; Japanese
screens; Mary Andrews Ladd collection of Japanese prints; Lewis
Collection of classical antiquities, mainly Greek vases from Attica
and Italy; †Gebauer Collection of Cameroon art; †Pre-Columbian
art; †Alice B. Nunn Collection of English silver, concentrating on
Huguenot silver of the 18th century; †Persian and Indian miniatures;
†Drawings and prints of all periods; Hirsch Collection of Oriental
rugs; Lawther Collection of Ethiopian crosses; Gayer-Anderson Col-
lection of Egyptian scarabs; †painting and sculpture by Northwestern
artists.
Exhibitions: (1974) Hilda Morris; Artists Under 35; Calligraphy;
Testimony to a Process; Objects for Preparing Food; Warren Wolf;
Charles Heaney; Museum Art School Thesis; The Navajo Blanket
Exhibition; Bryon Gardner; Fritz Scholder and Leonard Baskin;
Darcelle XV; Sculpture for Public Places; Erte: Original Designs;
Anne Breivik; Art of the Pacific Northwest; Rembrandt Etchings from
Sloane Collection; Solange and Hank Kowert; John Young; Kertesz,
Rodchenko, Moholy-Nagy; Truman Phillips; World War I Posters
from the Portland Art Museum; Oriental Gallery Opening; Charlot
Lithographs; Christmas Toy Show; Textiles from Portland Art Mu-
seum Collection; (1975) Rolf Nesch; Masterworks in Wood: The 20th
Century; Image and Word: The Art of Illustration; Four Wood Build-
ings: A Walking Tour; Masterworks in Wood: The Christian Tradition; Sally Haley, Paintings; Selection from the Collections of Dr.
Francis J. Newton; Wooden Musical Instruments; (1976) Masterworks
in Wood: Woodcuts and Wood Engravings; Artists of Oregon: Paper-
works II; New Japanese Photography; Peking Illuminations - An Environment by Milton Wilson; Dimitri Hadzi and Hugh Townley: Two
Sculptors; Photographs by Ernest Bloch; Photographs by Michael
Mathers: American Portraits; European Paintings from the Collection of the Portland Art Museum; Wood Pieces from the Collection of
the Portland Art Museum; C. S. Price: 25 Years Later.
Activities: Professional Art School, adult instruction, children's
classes (See Schools); competitive entrance scholarships; five honor
scholarships. Rental-Sales Gallery; lectures; slide-tape programs
accompanying special exhibitions; guided tours for children and
adults; previews and teas for members; various benefits given by
auxiliary groups for the Board of Trustees.
Library: Reference library of about 6000 books; 35,000 slides.
Income: $950,000.
Publications: Museum Calendar; Annual Report; occasional exhibition catalogs; a series of Notes on the Collections by invited
scholars.
Attendance: 88,000 per year; average student registration, 540.

PORTLAND CENTER FOR THE VISUAL ARTS
117 N.W. Fifth, 97209. Tel: (503) 222-7107
Michele Russo, Pres.
Mel Katz, Secy.
Mary L. Beebe, Exec. Dir.
Free Tues. - Sun. Noon - 6 PM, Fri. Noon - 9 PM. Estab. 1972 to
provide educational opportunities to the public in general, and to
artists and art students in particular, in the various visual arts, to
bring quality exhibits of contemporary art by living artists from all
regions of the United States to this community; financed by member-
ship, federal and state grants. Gallery has 5000 sq. ft. of unob-
structed space. Ann. meeting fall; mem. over 700; dues $6-$240.
Exhibitions: (1974-75) Jack Tworkov; T. R. Uthco; Don Judd;
Nicholas Krushenick; Robert Scull: American Pop Collector (film);
Alice Neel; John Baldessari; Milton Glaser; Peter Teneau; Jim
Nutt; outdoor exhibition of painted cars; Oregon Arts Commission
exhibition for high school artists-in-residence; Chuck Close.
Activities: Educational department enables special studies
students to earn credit; lectures open to the public; 12 visiting lec-
turers per year; 16 gallery talks; concerts; dramatic programs;
small library; Oregon artists slide archives.
Attendance: 25,000, 9 mo. season.

REED COLLEGE ART ASSOCIATES
Faculty Office Building Gallery
3203 S.E. Woodstock Blvd, 97202. Tel: (503) 771-1112
Prof. Charles S. Rhyne, Chmn. Dept. Art & Dir. Art Gallery
Mrs. Paul Feldenheimer, Pres. Art Assocs.
Joan White, Dir. Campus Events
Free Sat. & Sun. Noon - 5 PM, or by appointment. Estab. 1962 to
bring to Reed and the Portland community, shows of significant

art from New York and other art centers. Many shows relate to
advanced art courses at Reed or to important exhibitions at the
Portland Art Museum of P.C.V.A.
Collections: 20th century paintings, drawings, prints and sculp-
ture; pre-20th century prints.
Exhibitions: (1973-74) Paintings and Drawings by William Wiley;
Wall Painting by David McKenzie; Sculpture by Lewis Rakosky;
Black as Color, Paintings and Sculpture by Ilya Bolotowsky; Paint-
ings by Bill Ivey, Prints by Stella and Serra; (1974-75) Paintings by
Elaine Pelosini; Works on Paper by Jack Tworkov; Drawings by
Barry Kahn; Drawings by Joan Snyder; Collages and Prints by
Nicholas Krushenick; Wall Sculptures by Robert Maki; Paintings and
Drawings by Bill Hoppe; Lithographs by Jean Dubuffet; (1975-76)
American Realism; Paintings by Gene Davis, Paintings by David
Reed; Photographs by Irving Penn; Paintings by Ron Kleeman; Paint-
ings by Scott Sonniksen; Christo's Oceanfront.
Activities: Public events connected with exhibitions each year
include gallery talks by artists, visiting lecturers, films and slide
presentations.
Library: Reference and study library of 10,000 books and 100
periodicals on art; 50,000 slide collections. (See Schools)

WHITE GALLERY
Portland State University Art Exhibition Committee
2nd Floor of Smith Memorial Center, S.W. Broadway at Harrison
St, P.O. Box 751, 97207. Tel: (503) 229-4463
Catherine Kumlin, Chairperson
Terry Tambara, Gallery Asst.
Robert Kasal, Art Dept. Adviser
Free weekdays 7 AM - 10 PM; Sat. 9 AM - 5 PM. Estab. 1965 as a
student operated, noncommercial gallery which provides a variety
of exhibitions and programs throughout the year for the educational
enrichment and enjoyment of the university and community; financed
by city and state appropriations and student incidental fees.
Collections: Small permanent collection of about 200 works,
mostly by Northwest area artists, and installed throughout the university; two acquisitions a year.
Exhibitions: Continual program of exhibits changing every month.
Activities: Lectures open to the public; 3-4 visiting lecturers per
year; 8-10 gallery talks.
Income and Purchases: Budget $4000; purchases $500.

SALEM

SALEM ART ASSOCIATION
Bush House, Bush Barn Art Center
600 Mission St, 97301. Tel: (503) 363-4714, 581-2228
Tom Hallman, Pres.
Helen Ward, V.Pres.
Mrs. William Lindburg, Exec. Dir.
Maxine E. Cooper, Exec. Secy.
Bush Barn open year around, Tues. - Fri. 9:30 AM - 5 PM; Sat. & Sun.
1 - 5 PM; admis. free. Bush House open Sept. through May, Tues. -
Sun. 2 - 5 PM; June, July, Aug, Tues. - Sat. 12 AM - 5 PM; Sun. 2 -
5 PM; admis. adults 75¢, students 25¢, children (under 12), 10¢;
Wed. free during winter only. Inc. 1938, Museum opened 1953;
Bush Barn Art Center opened 1965 to preserve the best of the past
and encourage the arts of the present. Ann. meeting May; mem.
1000; dues $10 and higher.
Exhibitions: Changed monthly.
Attendance: 25,000 annually.

SPRINGFIELD

EMERALD EMPIRE ARTS ASSOCIATION*
P.O. Box 104, 97477.
Mrs. Frank Light, Pres.
Michele Thorp, Secy.
Nellie Mae Ayres
Ethel Lyngholm
Bob Forehand
Willis Washburn
Estab. 1957 to advance art in our community and to build up funds
for a workshop and gallery; financed by membership. Meeting third
Tues. of each month; mem. 150-170; dues $5 per yr.
Activities: 10 week classes each year plus 2-3 workshops; area
served is Willamette Valley; material available to anyone; traveling
exhibitions organized and circulated; individual paintings and original
objects of art lent; 18 active borrowers; lectures open to the public;
8 gallery talks and 10 tours annually; classes for adults and children;
competitions; exhibitions twice a year at local shopping center.
Book shop.
Library: 150 volume library.
Publications: Monthly Art League Bulletin.

THE DALLES

THE DALLES ART ASSOCIATION - THE DALLES ART CENTER
Fourth & Washington, 97058. Tel: (503) 296-4759
Jeanne Hillis, Pres.
Muriel Harrison, Secy.
Ray Hotka, V.Pres.
Carl Kramer, Exhibit Chmn.
Free Thurs, Fri. & Sat. 1 - 4 PM. Estab. 1959 for presentation of
community arts activities; financed by membership. Gallery main-
tained. Ann. meeting 1st Mon. in June; mem. 60; dues $10.
Exhibitions: State services exhibits, member and guest exhibits.
Activities: Traveling exhibitions organized and circulated; indi-
vidual paintings lent to schools; lectures open to public, 4 visiting
lecturers per year; 4 gallery talks; classes for adults and children;
competitions. Junior Art Club with 15 members.
Publications: Monthly bulletin.
Attendance: 3000.

PENNSYLVANIA

ALLENTOWN

✤ALLENTOWN ART MUSEUM
Fifth at Court Sts, 18105. Tel: (215) 432-4333
Bernard Berman, Pres.
Richard N. Gregg, Dir.
Olive F. Ponstingl, Asst. to Dir.
Peter F. Blume, Cur.
Miriam C. Miley, Cur. Educ.
David S. Miller, Supt.
Free Tues. - Sat. 10 AM - 5 PM; Sun. 1 - 5 PM; cl. Mon. & holidays.
Estab. Dec. 1959 to encourage the understanding and enjoyment of
the arts and the best examples of the human heritage in the Lehigh
Valley. New building addition of 30,000 sq. ft. opened Nov. 1975 with
expanded gallery space and programs. Ann. meeting Apr; mem.
2500; dues $12.50 and higher.
Collections: Samuel H. Kress Memorial Collection of Italian and
Northern European Schools; †Society of the Arts Collection of Original Prints; †J. I. and A. Rodale Collection of American Etchings.
Exhibitions: 10 temporary exhibitions each year principally from
Museum sources coast to coast and overseas. Important exhibitions
subject of illustrated catalogs. Area Artists' Annual Exhibition,
juried.
Activities: Regular gallery talks for school classes; gallery
tours for groups by appointment; extension service to schools; members lectures, visiting lecturers and scholars; concerts, dramatic
readings, art and classic films. Junior Museum Adventure Club
(visiting lecturers, programs for children aged 8-13). Lending
services, slides and reproductions. Bookshop.
Library: Research and reference library of 6000 volumes.
Publications: Monthly Calendar of Events and catalogs of major
exhibitions.
Income: $300,000.
Attendance: 80,000.

BETHLEHEM

LEHIGH ART GALLERIES
Lehigh University, 18015. Tel: (215) 691-7000, Exten. 525
Ricardo Viera, Dir.
Open daily 9 AM - 5 PM; Sat. 9 AM - Noon; Sun. 2 - 5 PM. Estab.
1927 under Dept. of Fine Arts. Collection enlarged through gifts
and donations from alumni and friends.
Collections: The Permanent Collection is a reservoir of visual
resources maintained to further the cultural, educational policies of
the University. Other collections include Contemporary American
Art, oils, watercolors, etc; Old and Contemporary Prints; Grace
Collection of Paintings (Goya, Raeburn, Romney, Reynolds, Inness,
Gainsborough, Hobbema, Corot, Daubigny, etc); Dreyfus Collection of
French paintings (Bonnard, Fantin-Latour, Sisley, Vuillard, Courbet,
Redon, Picasso and others); Wilson Collection containing oils, The
Eight (Henri, Davies, Sloan, Lawson, Bellows, Beal, Hartlet, etc);
Watercolors (Burchfield, Gaertner, Marin, Blampied, etc); Prints
(Arms, Whistler, Marsh, Kent, Warhol, Oldenburg, Feininger, Johns,
Rembrandt, Motherwell, Marin, etc); Prasse Collection of Prints
(Blampied, Munkata, Delacroix, Matisse, and French, Dutch, German,
Italian); Isaacs Collection of prints and paintings (early American
prints of local area); Baker Collection of Chinese porcelains (Ming
and Ch'ing).
Exhibitions: 16 exhibitions annually; monthly exhibitions (Alumni
Memorial and DuBois Galleries); one-man shows; group shows;
international shows; student exhibitions; Alumni Exhibition; annual

contemporary print exhibition; annual contemporary American
painting exhibition.
Activities: Lectures; independent studies; volunteers; programs
for students; tours; gallery talks; demonstrations; loans; prints and
ceramic sales.
Library: 15,000 art magazines, catalogs, slides and books; Reproduction Rental Service, 500 units.
Publications: Catalogs issued monthly; fall and spring exhibition
schedule.
Income and Purchases: Income $7500; purchases $1000-$4000.

BOALSBURG

COLUMBUS CHAPEL, BOAL MANSION AND MUSEUM
16827. Tel: (814) 466-6210
Mathilde Boal Lee, Pres.
Christopher Lee, Dir.
Mrs. John C. Major, Cur.
Open June 1 to Labor Day 10 AM - 5 PM; May, Sept, Oct. 2 - 5 PM;
admis. adults $1.25, students 50¢, children 25¢, group rate (groups
over 10) $1 for adults. Estab. 1952; education in art, religious
artifacts, and American and Spanish history, also, French history;
supported by tourist fees and donations.
Collections: Paintings in the Columbus Chapel and the Boal
Mansion, Spanish, Italian, Flemish, American, and French. Paint-
ings of the Columbus Family Chapel, paintings of the Boal Family
collections of paintings.
Activities: Guided tours.
Publications: Columbus and Related Family Papers, 1451 to
1902: An Inventory of the Boal Collection.
Attendance: 1000 adults, 800 young, 250 group.

BUCK HILL FALLS

BUCK HILL ART ASSOCIATION
18323.
Winthrop Neilson, Pres.
Free 9 AM - 9 PM. Estab. 1933. Ann. meeting Aug; mem. 110; dues
$5.
Small permanent collection of paintings. Annual Midsummer
Purchase Prize Exhibition. Classes, exhibitions, lectures, programs,
mostly in summer season.

CHADDS FORD

BRANDYWINE RIVER MUSEUM
The Tri-County Conservancy of the Brandywine, Inc.
Box 141, 19317. Tel: (215) 388-7601, 459-1900
George A. Weymouth, Chmn.
Henry A. Thouron, Pres.
James H. Duff, Museum Dir.
Anne E. Mayer, Cur. Collections
Joan H. Gorman, Asst. Cur.
Nancy H. Carter, Registrar
Andrew L. Johnson, Exec. Dir. Tri-County Conservancy
Open 9:30 AM - 4:30 PM; admis. $1.50 adults; children, students and
senior citizens 75¢. Estab. 1971, devoted to the documentation,
exhibition and interpretation of Brandywine Valley art, with
particular attention to the expanse of the Brandywine Tradition en-
gendered by Howard Pyle, the relationship of regional art to the
natural environment; financed by membership. Mem. 2282; dues
vary.
Collections: Brandywine regional artists and illustrators of the
19th century and Howard Pyle and his many students through N. C.
Wyeth, Peter Hurd, John McCoy, Andrew and James Wyeth.
Exhibitions: The Brandywine Heritage; N. C. Wyeth; Maxfield
Parrish; The Paintings of Clifford W. Ashley; other exhibitions
change regularly.
Activities: Photograph collection for reference; library; lec-
tures; concerts; special educational programs; tours. Book shop.
Publications: The Brandywine Heritage; Three Sculptors of Amer-
ican Realism; Whalers, Wharves, and Waterways (the paintings of
Clifford W. Ashley); regular exhibition catalogs; quarterly members'
newsletter.
Attendance: 200,000 annual average.

CHESTER

DESHONG MEMORIAL ART GALLERIES*
11th St. & Edgmont Ave, 19013.
J. Edward Clyde, Sr. Trustee
Free daily 3 - 8 PM; Sat. 9 - 12 AM. Estab. 1913; endowment.
Collections: 18th and 19th century Oriental art objects; 19th
century European landscape and genré pictures.

COLUMBIA

NATIONAL ASSOCIATION OF WATCH AND CLOCK COLLECTORS
  MUSEUM AND LIBRARY*
  514 Poplar St, 17512 (P.O. Box 33). Tel: (717) 684-8261
Earl T. Strickler, Cur.
Open Weekdays 8 AM - 5 PM; Sat, Sun. & holidays by appointment.
  Collections: Clocks, watches, horological tools and artifacts,
horological books and memorabilia.

DOYLESTOWN

MERCER MUSEUM
The Bucks County Historical Society
  Pine & Ashland Sts, 18901. Tel: (215) 345-0210
Wm. F. Heefner, Pres.
Gary D. Schuman, Exec. Dir.
M. M. Lawrence, Adminr.
Lynne F. Poirier, Chief Cur.
Terry McNealy, Library Dir.
Open Mar. through Dec, Tues. - Sat. 10 AM - 5 PM; Sun. 1 - 5 PM;
admis. adults $1.50, children under 18, 75¢; special group rates by
appointment. Library, same except 10 AM - 1 PM Sat. Estab. 1880,
inc. 1885. Ann. meeting Nov; also spring meeting; mem. 2000; dues
$10 and up.
  Collections: 35,000 items housed in an especially designed and
constructed building; these items, termed The Tools of the Nation
Maker, comprise all the goods and gear used for living, as well
as the crafts and trades from the first settlers until the emergence
of the machine age. Also extensive American Folk Art collection.
  Activities: 8000 school groups, given demonstration lecture;
special membership programs. Museum Shop lecture series;
annual folk festival; tours.
  Library: 44,000 books, large manuscript collection.
  Publications: Journal, semi-annually; Headlines, monthly news-
letter; frequent other special publications.
  Income: $150,000.
  Attendance: Approx. 40,000.

DUNCANSVILLE

LEE ATKYNS STUDIO-GALLERY
  Box 171, R. D. 2, 16635. Tel: (814) 695-0186
Lee Atkyns, Dir.
Open by appointment. Estab. 1950 as an exhibition gallery.
  Collections: Liberated Lines, Series of paintings plus derivative
works showing conception of the style over a period of 25 years.
  Exhibitions: Paintings Expressing Music, 1970; Paintings For
Intellectuals, 1971; Liberated Lines Paintings, 1972.
  Activities: Lectures open to public; guided tours.

ERIE

ERIE ART CENTER
  338 W. Sixth St, 16507. Tel: (814) 459-5477
John Patton, Pres.
Virginia Grean, Secy.
John L. Vanco, Exec. Dir.
Free Fri, Sat, Sun. 1 - 5 PM; Tues. - Thurs. 1 - 9 PM. Estab. 1898,
inc. 1900, for exhibition and encouragement of the visual arts; supported by membership. Four exhibition rooms with approx. 230
lineal feet of wall space. Ann. meeting May; mem. 725; dues $10
individual, $15 family, $2 student, $25 and $50 Corporate Assoc.
and Patron.
  Collections: Oils, graphics, sculpture by American artists.
  Exhibitions: Over 30 exhibitions, including group shows, annual
competitive shows (1973 was 50th annual) and one-man shows of
works by Richard Anuszkiewicz, Dennis Oppenheim, Corita Kent,
Carl Hirsch, Sig Rennels, Anthony Ko and others. Assembles and
circulates nationally the following traveling exhibitions: Graphic
Work of the Vienna Secession; Multiplemedia (an exhibition of new
world photographs, prints and multiple sculpture by artists from
all over the U.S.); The Roycroft Shops 1894-1915: A Propelling
Force of the American Arts and Crafts Movement.
  Activities: Organization of exhibitions outside own facilities,
as well as other art-oriented projects, commissions, print publications, etc. Material available to nonprofit and charitable organizations at no charge, businesses and corporations for nominal fees.
Individual paintings lent to schools, original objects of art lent, 850
Kodachromes in lending collection; one film has been produced by
the Art Center. Lectures open to public, 4-5 visiting lecturers per
year; 25-35 gallery talks or tours; concerts, classes for adults and
children; competitions; scholarships. In-house Frame Shop.
  Library: Small reference library.
  Publications: Monthly Bulletin, various exhibition catalogs.
  Income and Purchases: Income (1974-75) $60,000; purchases
$2000.
  Attendance: 15,000.

ERIE PUBLIC LIBRARY*
  3 S. Perry Square, 16507. Tel: (814) 456-7057
Dr. Joseph P. Scottino, Pres.
Mrs. Carole Wunner, Secy.
Kenneth G. Sivulich, Dir.
Open, Winter Mon. - Fri. 9:30 AM - 9 PM, Sat. 9 AM - 5:30 PM, cl.
Sun; Summer Mon. & Fri. 9:30 AM - 9 PM, Tues, Wed. & Thurs.
9:30 AM - 6 PM, Sat. 9 AM - 5:30 PM, cl. Sun; no admis. Estab.
1899 to provide public library services to the community; financed
by city and state appropriations. Gallery contains original paintings, drawings, prints and reproductions of paintings and sculpture.
  Exhibitions: Nationwide Currier & Ives Exhibition; local exhibits.
  Activities: Material available to all adult patrons, no fees;
material lent includes original paintings, prints, drawings, painting
and sculpture reproductions; lending collection, 700 color reproductions; 6000 items lent in an average year; photograph collection.
  Income and Purchases: Income $4000; purchases $4000.

GREENSBURG

WESTMORELAND COUNTY MUSEUM OF ART
  221 N. Main St, 15601. Tel: (412) 837-1500
Louis E. Sensenich, Pres.
John Barclay, Jr, Treas.
Paul A. Chew, Dir. & Secy.
Regina L. Narad, Secy. to Dir.
Free Tues. 1 - 9 PM; Wed. - Sat. 10 Am - 5 PM; Sun. 2 - 6 PM; cl.
Mon. & holidays. Inc. 1949; opened to the public May, 1959, to ex-
tend community, educational, and cultural services; endowed. Ann.
meeting 4 times a year; mem. 825; dues $5 and higher.
  Collections: American Painting, sculpture, prints and drawings,
furniture and decorative arts; Pennsylvania folk art; European
prints, drawings, and decorative arts; four American mid-Victo-
rian period rooms; two eighteenth century English period rooms.
The emphasis of the Museum's permanent collection is chiefly
American from the Colonial period to the present.
  Exhibitions: (1973-75) Richard Devlin; Frank Dolphin; Permuta-
tions: Earth, Sea, Sky by Lawrence Calcagno, lent by the Smith-
sonian Institution Traveling Exhibition Service; 10th Invitational
Regional Art Exhibition; James Nichols; Oriental Rugs from Collec-
tions in Western Pennsylvania; The Figure in Recent American
Painting; Tom Brunger; Alfred B. Charley; John Silk Deckard; Art
and the Kitchen; 11th Invitational Regional Art Exhibition; Bill
Davis, Prints and Drawings; The John J. McDonough Collection-
A Panorama of American Painting.
  Activities: Lectures; art educational courses for adults; gallery
talks and tours; art classes for adults and children; concerts; films;
dramatic programs; annual print sale.
  Library: 4500 volumes primarily in the field of American art;
50 periodicals; 9500 2 x 2 colored slides.
  Attendance: 73,000.

HARRISBURG

PENNSYLVANIA DEPARTMENT OF EDUCATION
Division of Arts and Humanities
  Box 911, 17126. Tel: (717) 787-8714
Russell P. Getz, Chief
Arts in Education Program:
Aledra Braddell, Assoc, Ways & Meaning Place
Christine Myers Crist, Special Prog. Asst.
Arthur Gatty, Dir, Pa. Governor's School for the Arts
Bernice J. Gottschalk, Prog. Adviser
Lola Kearns, Dir, Pilot Arts Curriculum Prog.
Joe McCarthy, Prog. Adviser
Clyde M. McGeary, Sr. Prog. Adviser
Mike Opalko, Learning Environments Specialist
Robert Revicki, Prog. Adviser
Bill Thompson, Dir, Ways and Meaning Place
  The Arts in Education Program provides leadership and con-
sultative and evaluative services to all Pennsylvania schools in arts
program development. Infusion of arts processes into differentiated
curriculums for all students is a particular thrust. The program offers model programs at several sites, ongoing staff development
programs, assistance in designing aesthetic learning environments
and consultation in identifying and employing regional and community
resources for arts education. A monthly newsletter, Arts-File,
provides over 4000 teachers with current information on innovative
arts programs as well as opportunities for professional growth presented in workshops, conferences, performances and exhibits sponsored by institutions, professional arts associations and school
districts.

PENNSYLVANIA HISTORICAL AND MUSEUM COMMISSION
  William Penn Memorial Museum & Archives Bldg, 17120.
  Tel: (717) 787-3362
William J. Wewer, Exec. Dir.

Michael J. Ripton, Dir. Bureau of Museums
Harry E. Whipkey, Dir. Bureau of Archives & History
State Museum, State Archives, Historical Commission and Historical
Properties combined into one agency in 1945.
Activities: Guided tours in William Penn Memorial Museum,
Pennsylvania Farm Museum of Landis Valley, and at most historical
properties. Special exhibitions at William Penn Memorial Museum.
Craft and Harvest Days at Farm Museum.
Income: $5,000,000 for entire Commission.
William Penn Memorial Museum (formerly State Museum), Harris-
burg
J. Duncan Campbell, Dir.
Museum open Mon. - Sat. 9 AM - 5 PM; Sun. 1 - 5 PM. Offices
Mon. - Fri. 8:30 AM - 5 PM.
Collections: Fine Art Gallery, Period Rooms, Craft Shops;
Decorative Arts, Folk Art; Halls of Archaeology, Natural History,
Technology and Industry and Military History; Planetarium.
Other Museum of the Commission: Pennsylvania Farm Museum
of Landis Valley, Lancaster, q.v.; Fort Pitt Museum, Pittsburgh;
Somerset Historical Center, Somerset; Pennsylvania Lumber Mu-
seum, Galeton; Pennsylvania Military Museum, Boalsburg; being de-
veloped—Railroad Museum of Pennsylvania, Strasburg; Anthracite
Museum Complex (Eckley Village, Ashland, Scranton).
Historic Sites and Properties of the Commission: Pennsbury
Manor, Morrisville; Pottsgrove Mansion, Pottstown; Cornwall
Furnace, Cornwall; Conrad Weiser Memorial Park, Womelsdorf;
Daniel Boone Homestead, Birdsboro; Ephrata Cloister, Ephrata;
Old Economy, Ambridge; Drake Well Park, Titusville; Flagship
Niagara, Erie; Fort Augusta, Sunbury; Hope Lodge, Whitemarsh;
Admiral Peary Park, Cresson; Robert Fulton Homestead, Lancaster
Co.; Old Stone House, Butler Co., Graeme Park, Horsham; Johnston
Tavern, Leesburg; McCoy House, Lewistown; Bradford House, Wash-
ington; Brown's Mill School, Marion; Bushy Run Battlefield, Jean-
nette; Fort LeBoeuf, Waterford; Hughes House, Jefferson; Morton
Homestead, Prospect Park; Peace Church, Camp Hill; Priestley
House, Northumberland; Gov. Printz Park, Essington; Searights
Toll House, Uniontown; Tuscarora Academy, Academia; Warrior
Run Church, McEwensville.

HAVERFORD

MAIN LINE CENTER OF THE ARTS
Old Buck Rd. off Lancaster Ave, 19041.
Eleanor Daitzman, Dir.
Open Mon. - Fri. 10 AM - 4 PM; Sat. 10 AM - Noon. Estab. and inc.
1937 to encourage creative endeavor. Mem. approx. 550; dues $8
and higher.
Activities: Day and evening classes for adults and children in
painting, sculpture, music and crafts; workshops; lectures; demon-
strations and monthly exhibitions, $600 prizes 1970-72. (See Schools)
Income: Approx. $25,000.

INDIANA

✠KIPP GALLERY
Indiana University of Pennsylvania, 15720. Tel: (412) 357-2530
Ned O. Wert, Exhibition Chmn.
Free daily 9 AM - 4 PM; Sat. & Sun. by appointment. Estab. 1970 as
a complete gallery exhibition program; financed by endowment and
student coop funding.
Exhibitions: Bruce Davidson Photographs; Contemporary Reflec-
tions 71-75; Women in Art; Harry Holland, Painter; Student Show;
Faculty Show Annual; James Myford, Sculptor, New Work, New
York; The American Federation of the Arts Print Show.
Activities: Lectures open to public, 4 visiting lecturers per
year.
Publications: Flyers for each show.
Annual budget: $6000.

JENKINTOWN

ALVERTHORPE GALLERY*
511 Meetinghouse Rd, 19046. Tel: (215) 884-0466
Lessing J. Rosenwald, In Charge Collection of Prints and Rare Books
Ruth Fine Lehrer, Cur.
Open Mon. - Fri. by appointment; no admis. Estab. 1939 for the
study of prints and rare books.
Collections: Small collection of drawings; prints and rare books
15th-20th centuries; Blake Collection.
Exhibitions: Works included in various loan exhibitions.
Activities: Works lent on limited basis to institutions meeting
established qualifications; photograph service for purchase.
Library: 3000 volume reference library.

KUTZTOWN

SHARADIN ART GALLERY
Kutztown State College, 19530. Tel: (215) 683-3511, Exten. 342
Eldon Katter, Gallery Coordinator
Free Mon. - Fri. 10 AM - 4 PM; Sat. 10 AM - Noon, 2 - 5 PM; Sun.
2 - 5 PM. Estab. 1956 to make the best of the contemporary arts
available to the town and gown communities; financed by city and
state appropriations.
Collections: Approx. 400 works in prints, drawings and paintings.
Exhibitions: Art Protis; Dan Young Ceramics; Prints and Draw-
ings of Artists by Artists; Small Paintings for Museum Collections;
Contemporary New Zealand Painting; Recent British Prints: 15
Artists; Color in Series; 104th Annual Watercolor Exhibition; Con-
temporary Law and Justice and the Original Print; Ed and Mary Lou
Higgins: Jewelry and Weaving; 4th Annual Miniature Print Exhibition;
Japanese and Burundi Children's Art; Michael Mazur: Airbrush
Drawings; Printmaker William Weege and Sculptor David Elaharty;
Leonard Baskin's Divine Comedy; 4 Porcelain Ceramists: Winokur,
Winokur, Stewart, and Bloom; Bruce Davidson, Photographer; Fabric
Sculptress Louise Todd; Realist Revival; Advertising Amalgam;
Sewn, Stitched, and Stuffed: Fiber Sculpture; Art Marks: Drawings by
Blum, Gigliotti, and Stewart; Photographers Jerry Uelsmann and
Leslie Krims; New Directions in Printmaking; Hairy, Knotty, Slinky
Things: Sculpture by Neda Al Hilali; The Textured Surface: 8 Paint-
ers from the Phoenix Gallery; Two Weavers: Warren Seelig and
Lewis Knauss; No-Man's Land: Sculpture by Carolee Thea; Art/Pa-
per.
Activities: Lectures open to the public; 2 gallery talks per year.
Publications: Brochure listing a gallery season's collection of
shows.
Purchases: $5000.

LANCASTER

COMMUNITY GALLERY OF LANCASTER COUNTY
15 W. Grant St, 17603.
Helen Woolworth, Pres. Gallery Council
Genevieve D. Libhart, Dir.
Free Oct. 1 - May 30 daily Noon - 4 PM; Sun. 1 - 5 PM. Estab. 1965
and inc. 1975. Supported by individual and business sponsors in addition to Lancaster County funds. Annual meeting held each Apr; mem.
500; dues $5 general, $50 patron, $100 sustaining.
Exhibitions: 10 exhibits a year - Benton Spruance, Leavitt Collection, Robert Indiana, Chaim Gross, Luigi Rist, George Gach,
Eric Sloane, Hattie Brunner, Charles Parks, Grace Pugh, and exhibits from local artists and collections.
Activities: Guided gallery tours to sixth grade city and county
school children; lectures also open to public.
Publications: Brochures for each exhibit, semi-annual newsletter.
Attendance: 10,000.

LANCASTER COUNTY ART ASSOCIATION*
Art Center, 22 E. Vine St, 17602. Tel: (717) 392-9258
John G. Gates, Pres.
Estab. 1936, inc. 1950. Ann. meeting 2nd Tues. in May; mem. 320;
dues $10.
Collections: Currently being enlarged by purchases.
Exhibitions: Monthly exhibitions; Spring and Fall Member &
Student Shows; three 3-man shows, and others.
Activities: Demonstrations, lectures, classes, programs, tours;
six visiting lecturers per year; two gallery talks; free classes for
Retired Citizens Association; sponsors Lancaster County Day tour of
fine homes and gardens annually as a project to raise funds for com-
munity projects. Sponsors traveling exhibitions.
Library: Technical only. Association supplies funds to the Public
Library for purchase of art books and publications.

PENNSYLVANIA FARM MUSEUM OF LANDIS VALLEY
2451 Kissel Hill Rd, 17601. Tel: (717) 569-0401
Carroll J. Hopf, Dir.
John B. Brooks, Cur. Crafts & Educ.
Vernon S. Gunnion, Preparator
Open Mon. - Sat. 8:30 AM - 4:30 PM; Sun. 1 - 5 PM; admis. adults
$1, children under 12 free, group rate 65¢. Estab. 1925; owned and
operated by the Pennsylvania Historical and Museum Commission,
Bureau of Museums, Michael J. Ripton, Acting Dir.
More than 250,000 items depicting rural life in the late 18th and
19th centuries. A museum of agriculture, domestic arts and crafts,
tools, furnishings, wagons, carriages, Pennsylvania German folk art.
Furnished 18th century log cabin, federal period brick house, late
Victorian farmhouse and crossroads hotel, print shop, tinsmith
shop, blacksmith shop, school house, fire house, country store.
Attendance: 130,000.

LEWISBURG

BUCKNELL UNIVERSITY
Ellen Clarke Bertrand Library
   17837. Tel: (717) 524-3056
George M. Jenks, Univ. Librn.
Open Mon. - Fri. 8:30 AM - 11 PM; Sat. 9 AM - 5 PM; Sun. 1 - 11
PM. Estab. 1952.
   Library contains 8500 art books; Kress Study Collection of
Renaissance art, 21 items; Sordoni Collection of Oriental art,
several hundred items; other works of art.

MERION

BUTEN MUSEUM OF WEDGWOOD
   246 N. Bowman Ave, 19066. Tel: (215) 664-9069
Nettie M. Buten, Pres. & Cur.
Cecily Darwin Littleton, Secy.
David Buten, Dir.
Free Oct. ‡ May, Tues, Wed. & Thurs. 2 - 5 PM; Sat. 10 AM - 1 PM.
Estab. 1957 to promote the culture that is Wedgwood; maintained by
membership. Five display galleries of the comprehensive Wedgwood
story. Mem. 1750; dues $15 plus three other classes.
   Collections: †Wedgwood.
   Activities: Lectures for members only, 8 visiting lecturers per
year; gallery talks and tours for the public. Books and Wedgwood
Sales desk.
   Library: 750 volumes, 2000 photographs and slides for lending
and reference; colored 2 by 2 slides on sales desk.
   Publications: Annual book on Wedgwood.
   Attendance: 9000.

NEW BRIGHTON

MERRICK ART GALLERY
   Fifth Ave. & 11th St, 15066. Tel: (412) 846-1130
Robert S. Merrick, Trustee
Toby C. Weiss, Dir.
Patricia K. Bellan, Dir. Educ.
Free, fall and winter hours, Tues. - Sat. 10 AM - 5 PM; Sun. 1 - 5
PM; cl. Mon; summer hours vary. Estab. 1880 by Edward Dempster
Merrick; gallery devoted to 19th century American and European
painting for the free enjoyment of the people of New Brighton and for
the cultural enlightenment of other young artists; financed by endow-
ment. Ann. meeting usually Jan. or Feb; mem. 287; dues $10, $15,
$25.
   Collections: 19th Century European Paintings; 19th Century
American Hudson River School Paintings.
   Exhibitions: Gallery has sponsored exhibitions by local Beaver
County and Allegheny County artists.
   Activities: Merrick Family Memorabilia collection for reference
only; lectures open to public; visiting lecturers; gallery talks and
tours; dramatic programs; classes for adults and children; con-
certs; competitions.
   Publications: Quarterly newsletter for Merrick Art Gallery Asso-
ciates.
   Attendance: Over 10,000.

NEW CASTLE

HOYT INSTITUTE OF FINE ARTS*
   124 E. Leasure Ave, 16105. Tel: (412) 658-9418
John L. Wilson, Pres. Board of Trustees
William Craig McBurney, Exec. Dir.
Free Tues. - Sat. 9 AM - 4 PM. Estab. 1968 to encourage the de-
velopment of the arts within the community; endowed; supported by
membership. Mem. 440 including honorary; dues $5, $10, and $25.
   Collections: Local artists.
   Activities: Lectures open to public; concerts; dramatic programs;
classes for adults and children; competions; scholarships.
   Publications: Newsletter to members, semi-annually.
   Attendance: 27,000.

NEW WILMINGTON

✤**WESTMINSTER COLLEGE ART GALLERY**
   16142. Tel: (412) 946-8761
Robert Godfrey, Dir.
Free Mon. - Sat. 10 AM - 7 PM; Sun. 2 - 7 PM. Estab. 1854 to
organize and present 9 exhibitions per season, to organize traveling
exhibitions, publich art catalogs of national interest; visiting artists
program; financed by endowment.
   Collections: †20th century prints and drawings; 19th and 20th
century paintings.
   Exhibitions: In Praise of Space-The Landscape in American Art;
19th Century Landscape Drawings and 20th Century Painting, Drawing, Watercolor; The Figure in Recent American Painting; The Pieced

Quilt; Drawings Shows of 20th Century Figurative Artists including
William Bailey, Marvin Bileck, Larry Day, Emily Nelligan and
George Hildrew; Painting Shows include Alfred Leslie, Alex Katz,
Philip Pearlstein, Neil Welliver, Paul Georges, Bonnie Sklarski,
Barbara White and Andy Marcus.
   Activities: Traveling exhibitions organized and circulated; lec-
tures open to public; 4 visiting lecturers per year; gallery talks.
   Publications: Westminster College Art Gallery, annually; occa-
sional catalogs.
   Annual Income: Over $2000.
   Attendance: 15,000.

NEWTOWN

HICKS ART CENTER
Bucks County Community College
   Fine Arts Department, 18940. Tel: (215) 968-5861
Bruce Katsiff, Chairperson
Gallery free Mon. - Fri. 8 AM - 4 PM. Estab. 1970 to bring outside
artists to the community; financed by city and state appropriation.
   Exhibitions: Art Faculty Exhibition; Three Young Men; Chelten-
ham Printmakers; Ben Cunningham; Focus on Women; Alumni Show;
American Folk Art; Crafts Show.
   Activities: Traveling exhibitions organized and circulated.

PHILADELPHIA

AMERICAN COLOR PRINT SOCIETY*
   2022 Walnut St, 19103. Tel: (215) 248-4114
Richard Hood, Pres.
Bernard A. Kohn, Treas.
Ethel V. Ashton, Secy.
Mildred Dillon, V.Pres.
Stella Drabkin, V.Pres.
Estab. 1939 to exhibit and sell color prints. Ann. meeting Oct; mem.
approx. 100; dues $5 and higher.
   Exhibitions: (Annuals) National juried exhibition held at Print
Club, Philadelphia, in March. There are 6 annual prizes, 3 of which
are Purchase Prizes with the prints becoming a part of the American
Color Print Society's Collection housed in the Philadelphia Museum
of Art. Printmaking demonstrations at the Print Club in March.
   Activities: Society has published a presentation print each year,
until 1960, in an edition of 50 which have been given to the Associate
Members.
   Purchases: Annual purchases approx. $100.

AMERICAN SWEDISH HISTORICAL FOUNDATION
American Swedish Historical Museum
   1900 Pattison Ave, 19145. Tel: (215) 389-1776
Michael S. Shapiro, Dir.
Charles L. Seeburger, Cur. Collections
Open Tues. - Fri. 10 AM - 5 PM; Sat. & Sun. 12 AM - 5 PM; cl.
national holidays; non-mem. admis. 50¢. Estab. 1926. Ann. meeting
June; mem. 1200; dues $10 and higher.
   Collections: †History and culture of Americans of Swedish de-
scent; special collections include Jenny Lind, John Ericsson, Fredrika
Bremer.
   Exhibitions: Temporary exhibitions of paintings, arts and crafts
by Swedish and Swedish-American artists.
   Activities: Group tours by appointment; Lucia Fest - Valsborgs-
mässoafton; lectures; slide/film strip shows.
   Library: General reference library; special libraries, Rambo
Research of genealogical and colonial material, Jenny Lind, Fredrika
Bremer. Total volumes, 10,000.
   Publications: Yearbook, annually.
   Attendance: 3000.

CLIVEDEN
   6401 Germantown Ave, 19144. Tel: (215) 848-1777
Raymond V. Shepherd, Jr, Adminr. & Property Council & staff of
   National Trust Interpretors
Carole T. Scanlon, Coordinator, Interpretive Programs
Open year round 10 AM - 4 PM; cl. Christmas Day; admis. adults
$1.25, senior citizens 60¢, group tours by arrangement, free to
National Trust members.
   Cliveden is a property of the National Trust for Historic Preservation. Preserved as an historic museum operated as a community
preservation center, it is a National Historic Landmark. Cliveden
was build in 1763-67 as the country house of Benjamin Chew, a distinguished Philadelphia lawyer and political leader. Surrounded by
six acres of centuries-old trees, it has continued to be used through
seven generations.
   Chew family furnishings include extremely important Philadelphia
pieces made by such prominent cabinetmakers as Thomas Affleck,
Jonathan Goste Lowe, and Daniel Wood. There is also some Penn
family furniture, as well as paintings by Smibert, Wollaston, Pine

and Henry. Chew papers include over 100,000 manuscript pages plus 3000 volumes and the law library of Chief Justice Benjamin Chew.

Property serves as a focal point for advancement of historic preservation. It develops new relationships among cultural, community, and preservation groups, and Trust members in its area. Responds to community preservation needs by acting as a link between community and appropriate regional or headquarters offices of National Trust. Adaptive use, is a preservation project of 1976-77. Interpretive programs are provided which relate to Cliveden's particular care study in historic preservation. Special Christmas program, Members Day during National Historic Preservation Week early May. Set of 16 in. x 8 in. measured drawings, taken by Historic American Building Survey, available from Cliveden's Preservation Shop.

DREXEL UNIVERSITY ART GALLERY AND MUSEUM COLLECTION*
    Chestnut & 32nd Sts, 19104. Tel: (215) 895-2424
Geraldine Peterson Staub, Cur.
Free 9 AM - 5 PM; Sat. 9 AM - 1 PM; cl. Sun. Estab. 1891; Picture Gallery 1902.
    Collections: Museum collection includes examples of decorative arts of India, China, Japan and Europe; hand printed India cottons, European textiles; Sevres and other ceramics. Randell Hall Gallery contains the John D. Lankenau and the Anthony J. Drexel collections of German and French paintings of the 19th century. (See Schools)

FAIRMOUNT PARK ART ASSOCIATION*
    25th & Benjamin Franklin Parkway, 19103. Tel: (215) 763-1468
C. Clark Zantzinger, Jr, Pres.
Eileen H. Wilson, Exec. Secy.
    Estab. 1871, inc. 1872, charter amended 1906, to embellish Fairmount Park and City Parks with sculptures, fountains and other suitable decoration, to promote interest in civic improvements and city planning. Ann. meeting April; mem. dues $15 and higher; annual report.

FELLOWSHIP OF THE PENNSYLVANIA ACADEMY OF THE FINE ARTS
    The Peale House, 1811 Chestnut St, 19103. Tel: (215) 299-5082
Dorothy Pere, Pres.
Lucy Glick, Secy.
L. A. D. Montgomery, Treas.
Estab. 1897 to provide opportunities for creative incentive and sharing in responsibilities for the development of facilities and activities in the field of art for its members, and to maintain relations with the students of The Pennsylvania Academy of the Fine Arts. Meetings Sept, Oct, Feb. & May; mem. approx. 700; dues $6, nonresident $3.
    Collections: Loan collection of 600 paintings and sculptures.
    Exhibitions: Annual exhibition of oils, sculpture, watercolors and graphics partly invitational and partly juried, with awards. Annual prizes awarded at exhibitions $1050.
    Activities: Lectures, films, classes.
    Income: Approx. $3000.

THE FRANKLIN INSTITUTE SCIENCE MUSEUM AND PLANETARIUM
    Benjamin Franklin Pkwy. at 20th St, 19103. Tel: (215) 448-1000
Dr. Bowen C. Dees, Pres.
Joel N. Bloom, V.Pres. & Dir. Science Museum
H. George Hamilton, Dir. Fels Planetarium
D. E. Gates, Dir. Museum Operations
Emerson Hilker, Dir. Library
William G Brown, Mgr, Special Projects
Open daily 10 AM - 5 PM; extended hours during summer 1976 are anticipated. Estab. 1824 by a group of concerned Philadelphia citizens whose purpose was to provide a place where scientists and craftsmen could meet to study and solve technological problems. New building opened in 1934. Mem. approx. 10,000; dues individual $15, family $25, educator family $12.50, supporting $100, sustaining $250, sponsor $500, patron $1000, benefactor $5000, student $5.
    Exhibitions: Museum contains exhibits and demonstrations relating to physical science and technology; approximately 12 new temporary exhibits a year, including special exhibitions, which address contemporary socio-technological issues. Planetarium shows change several times a year.
    Activities: Conducts laboratories for scientific and technical research and development; lectures; annual medal awards for distinguished achievements in science and technology. Educational activities include: adult and student Saturday and Summer Workshops; daily lectures, tours and demonstrations for school children; seminars for gifted high school students.
    Library: 300,000 volumes, 4000 periodicals in nearly every language in the world, and the largest patent file outside the U. S. Patent Office in Washington, D. C.
    Publications: Journal of the Franklin Institute, monthly; Franklin Institute News, 4 times a year.
    Attendance: Approx. 700,000 annually.

FREE LIBRARY OF PHILADELPHIA
Art Department
    Logan Square, Room 208, 19103. Library Tel: (215) MU6-5403; Art Dept. Tel: (215) 686-5403.
Keith Doms, Dir. of Library
Miriam L. Lesley, Head, Art Dept.
Open Mon. - Thurs. 9 AM - 9 PM; Fri. 9 AM - 6 PM; Sat. 9 AM - 5 PM; Sept. - June Sun. 1 - 5 PM. Library estab. 1891, Art Dept. 1896.
    Reference and circulating collection of approx. 131,000 cataloged volumes on costumes, architecture, fine and useful arts; †pamphlet file of uncataloged exhibition catalogs, artists' bibliographies, unbound pamphlets, clippings (7700); 193 current periodicals in art, architecture, costume, decoration; 597 older periodical titles; Index of artists especially American (10,700 names); Index of exhibition catalogs of the Pennsylvania Academy of the Fine Arts, by artist (10,000 names). Special collections—18th and 19th century architectural pattern books; Philadelphia chapter, American Institute of Architects, original measured drawings of colonial Philadelphia buildings (368); John Frederick Lewis collection of books on fine prints and print making (2645).

Print and Picture Department
    Room 211. Tel: (215) 686-5405
Robert F. Looney, Head.
Open 9 AM - 5 PM; cl. Sun; also cl. Sat. June - Sept. Estab. 1954 by combining the Print Department and the Picture Collection.
    Special print collections (non-circulating): †John Frederick Lewis Collection of portrait Prints (211,000); Hampton L. Carson Collection of Napoleonic Prints (3400); Americana (1200); †Philadelphiana (8000); †graphic arts (2000); †greeting and tradesmen's cards (27,000). Circulating Picture Collection of pictures in all media, universal in subject coverage (500,000). Print exhibitions, Library-owned and traveling. Original drawings—Rosenthal Collection, American (847); Bendiner Collection, International (102). Samuel Castner Collection of Philadelphia—scrapbooks, 46 volumes; prints, drawings, photos, clippings.

Rare Book Department
    3rd Floor. Tel: (215) 686-5416.
Howell J. Heaney, Rare Book Librn.
Open Mon. - Sat. 9 AM - 5 PM. Estab. 1949.
    Cuneiform tablets and seals, 2800 Babylonian and Sumerian (John Frederick Lewis Collection); †Mediaeval and Renaissance manuscripts, 250 volumes, 2000 individual leaves—mostly with miniatures (Lewis Collection); †Oriental manuscripts, 155 volumes (Lewis Collection); Oriental Miniatures, 1250, mostly Mughul, Rajput and Persian (Lewis Collection); †Angling Prints, 1000 from 17th to 20th century (Evan Randolph Collection); †Prints of Philadelphia, 400 from 1800 to 1950 (Randolph Collection); †Howard Pyle and His School, books and original drawings (Thornton Oakley Collection); †Legal Prints, 8000 (Hampton L. Carson Collection); †Pennsylvania German Fraktur, 1000 (Borneman and Yoder Collections); †Horn Books, 150 (Elisabeth Ball Collection); †original drawings, paintings, prints, and other illustrative material relating to the works of Dickens, Goldsmith and Thackeray; early American prints and engravings. †Arthur Rackham (Grace Clark Haskell Collection); †Kate Greenaway; †Beatrix Potter. Early American children's books (15,000) including Rosenbach Collection (1682 - 1836); American Sunday-School Union historical collections; 300 caricatures, prints and drawings (Alfred Bendiner Collection).

HISTORICAL SOCIETY OF PENNSYLVANIA
    1300 Locust St, 19107. Tel: (215) 732-6200
James E. Mooney, Dir.
Open daily Apr. through Nov. 30, 1976 9 AM - 9 PM. Regular hours Mon. 1 - 9 PM; Tues. - Fri. 9 AM - 5 PM; cl. Sat, Sun. & Aug; $1 per day for nonmember use of library. Estab. 1824. Ann. meeting Mar; mem. approx. 2700; dues $15.
    Collections: Unmatched collection of papers, prints, paintings, furniture, household and personal effects, and other memorabilia from pre-Revolution through 1800; more than 800 paintings and miniatures by early American artists, Stuart, Sully, Copley, Peale, Wright, Birch, Inman, Neagle and others. More than 14 million manuscripts.

HOUSTON HALL
    University of Pennsylvania, 19174.
Anthony S. Codding, Dir.
Estab. 1896 for the enhancement of social living, providing opportunities for self-expression, and experiences which are educational and relaxing. Includes an art gallery.
    Activities: Art Exhibits, a film series, lectures, Cultural Theatre Series.

INDEPENDENCE NATIONAL HISTORICAL PARK
    311 Walnut St, 19106. Tel: (215) 597-7132
Hobart G. Cawood, Supt.

Douglass C. Warnock, Asst. Supt.
John C. Milley, Supervisory Cur.
Free 9 AM - 5 PM. Estab. as part of the National Park System, Jan. 1, 1951, and administered by the National Park Service of the United States Department of the Interior. Includes Independence Hall, Congress Hall, and Old City Hall, First and Second Bank of U.S, Philadelphia (Merchants) Exchange, Bishop White and Dolley Todd Houses, Graff House, City Tavern, Deshler-Morris House and Kosciuscko House.
Collections: Colonial and early American portraits, including the Peale and Sharples Collections; American and English Decorative Arts; †relics of Colonial, Revolutionary and post-Revolutionary periods which are the famed Liberty Bell, Syng inkstand, and Rising Sun chair.
Attendance: 3,500,000.

INSTITUTE OF CONTEMPORARY ART
University of Pennsylvania, 34th and Walnut Sts, 19174.
Tel: (215) 243-7108
Suzanne Delehanty, Dir.
Michael A. Quigley, Asst. Dir.
Carla B. Hultman, Curatorial Asst.
Free Mon. - Fri. 10 AM - 5 PM; Sat. & Sun. Noon - 5 PM; Tues. 10 AM - 7:30 PM. Estab. 1963 to provide a continuing forum for the active presentation of advanced developments in the visual arts; financed by membership and the University of Pennsylvania.
Mem. 800; dues $15, $50, $125, $500 and up.
Exhibitions: The Highway; Will Insley, Two Generations of Color Painting, Against Order: Chance and Art, Allan D'Arcangelo, Rafael Ferrer, William T. Wiley, Grids, The Topography of Nature, Nancy Graves, Inside Philadelphia, Agnes Martin, Made in Philadelphia, Robert Morris, Six Visions, Cy Twombly, Video Art and others.
Activities: Lecutres open to the public; 3-4 visiting lecturers per year; 3-4 gallery talks; concerts; 4 children's programs, events and concerts.
Publications: Exhibition catalogs; Calendar of Events; member's Newsletters.
Attendance: 80,000.

JOHN GRAVER JOHNSON COLLECTION*
Parkway and 25th St, 19101. Tel: (215) 763-2490
Joseph J. Rishel, Cur.
Irene Konefal, Secy.
Open daily 9 AM - 5 PM; admis. $1. Upon his death in 1917, prominent Philadelphia lawyer, John Graver Johnson left his extensive collection intact to the people of Philadelphia, since 1933 the collection has been housed in the Philadelphia Museum of Art; administration and trusteeship of the collection is maintained separately from the other collections in the museum.
Collections: Early and later Italian Renaissance paintings; northern European schools of Flanders, Holland and Germany in the 15th, 16th and 17th century; French 19th century paintings.
Activities: Special lectures and related activities; occasional lending of collection to significant exhibitions.
Library: Johnson Collection Library has approx. 4500 volumes for reference; rare sales catalogues.
Publications: Several catalogues for various parts of the collection including Catalogue of Italian Paintings and Catalogue of Flemish and Dutch Paintings.
Attendance: (1971) 573,575; (1972) 589,887.

LA SALLE COLLEGE GALLERY FOR THE STUDY COLLECTION OF ART
20th St. & Olney Ave, 19141. Tel: (215) VI8-8300, Exten. 365
Thomas M. Ridington, Cur. & Dir.
Free Mon. - Thurs. 2 hrs. per day. Collection begun 1965 as support for art history program, as a service to community and as a bridge to larger collections in center city; financed by college. Re-opened in new and larger quarters Nov. 1975. Gallery of seven large spaces, four set up to suggest 16th, 17th, 18th and 19th centuries and to contain paintings of those centuries.
Collections: †16th century and later religious works; †17th, 18th and 19th century portraiture (English, French, American); †landscapes; †large collection of graphic works, mostly 20th century.
Exhibitions: Regular collection; work of local artists, about 3-5 per year.
Publications: Exhibition catalogs, occasionally.
Annual purchases: In excess of $10,000.

MOORE COLLEGE OF ART
20th & Race Sts, 19103. Tel: (215) LO8-4515
Mellicent Allen, Acting Pres.
Gregory Peters, V.Pres. Finance
James G. Perrin, Dir. of Development

Hilda Schoenwetter, Dean
Delores Lewis, Registrar;
Patti Stapleford, Admis. Dir.
Tom Meehan, Admin. Asst.
Dianne Vanderlip, Gallery Dir.
Eloise Held, Dir. Pub. Relations
Open Mon. - Fri. 9 AM - 4:30 PM; gallery free. Estab. 1831 as a professional and fine arts college for women; financed by endowment and tuition. Gallery with exhibitions from entire U.S.
Exhibitions: (1972-73) H. C. Westerman, Artists Books, Paintings, an exhibition of six New York artists; (1973-74) C. 7500, an exhibition organized by Lucy R. Lippard, Oyvind Fahlstrom, Clay Things, East Coast Invitational; (1974-75) Wm. Copley, Hopi Kachina Dolls, North, East, West & South & Middle Drawing Show, Edwardian Album.
Activities: Traveling exhibitions organized and circulated; lectures open to public, 10 visiting lecturers per year; 10 gallery talks; classes for adults and children; scholarships. Book shop.
Library: 29,000 volumes for lending and reference; 49,000 prints in collection; 149 file drawers; slides.
Publications: MCA Alumnae Journal; MCA Bulletin, quarterly.
Attendance: 600 students.

✤MUSEUM OF THE PHILADELPHIA CIVIC CENTER
34th St. & Civic Center Blvd, 19104.
William G. Chadwick, Chmn. of the Board
John Pierron, Exec. Dir.
Ronald L. Barber, Asst. to Dir. of Museum
Frank Bartell, Cur. Educ.
Robert Nobel, Cur.
Marian Aguilera, Cur.
Albina DeMeio, Registrar
Henry Spector, Promotion & Publicity Specialist
Zenon L. Feszczak, Dir. Design
Open Tues. - Sat. 9 AM - 5 PM; Sun. 1 - 5 PM; cl. Mon. Estab. 1894 to present the museum's permanent collection of international primitive and folk arts and of a frequently changing series of exhibits of contemporary crafts, architecture and industrial design from all parts of the world, with a regular program of lectures, social and cultural events.
Collections: Oriental and African crafts and musical instruments; Philippines, South Pacific, Siberian and Latin American crafts.
Exhibitions: (Permanent) Other Sounds of Music; Oriental Crafts; African Crafts; Latin American Crafts. Temporary exhibitions of local and international arts and crafts. During Bicentennial year, Design For Fun, exhibits on leisure time activities of America over past two centuries, also electronic fun-devices of the future; admis. $1.50 adults, 75¢ children.
Activities: Lessons by Curator of Education and public school teachers to school children and civic and educational groups; lends objects of art; lectures; gallery talks and tours; concerts; classes for children.

✤PENNSYLVANIA ACADEMY OF THE FINE ARTS
Broad & Cherry Sts, 19102. Tel: (215) 299-5060
Peale House: 1811 Chestnut St, 19103.
Peale Club: 1819 Chestnut St, 19103.
John Gribbel II, Pres.
Richard J. Boyle, Dir.
Robert Stubbs, Adminr. & Secy.
Henry Hotz, Jr, Dean of School
Frank H. Goodyear, Jr, Cur.
Joseph S. MacLaughlin III, Development Asst.
Free 10 AM - 5 PM; cl. Mon, New Year's, Thanksgiving and Christmas. Museum and School of Fine Arts estab. 1805 by C. W. Peale, Thos. Sully, Benj. West, et al, to encourage cultivation of art in the United States. Mem. 3800; dues $25 and higher.
Collections: The collections excel in 18th and 19th century American paintings (1617), sculpture (302), drawings and prints (2700). Alston, C. W. Peale, Stuart, Sully, West are each represented in numerous important works. A European Collection, including 65,000 prints and drawings, is accessible to qualified persons.
Exhibitions: Recent exhibits include Hopper, Sloan, Bierstadt, Anshutz, Susan Macdowell Eakins, 15th & 16th century woodcuts, Wm. Trost Richards, Thos. Doughty, Pittman, Pearlstein, etc. One exhibition during the Bicentennial year will display the whole range of American art from the Academy's historic collections with a comprehensive catalog.
Activities: Concerts; gallery talks by staff and visiting scholars; fine arts school winter (day and evening) and summer. (See Schools) Museum Shop, art safaris to Europe and Asia and in the U.S.
Library: Art reference library of approx. 4000 items available to students and members.
Attendance: 90,000.

THE PHILADELPHIA ART ALLIANCE

251 S. 18th St, 19103. Tel: (215) KI5-4302
Raymond S. Green, Chmn. of the Board
George A. D'Angelo, Pres.
Raphael Sabatini, V.Pres. in Charge of Art
James Kirk Merrick, Secy. & Exec. Dir.
Arthur Klein, Treas.
Free Mon. - Fri. 10:30 AM - 5 PM; Sat. & Sun. 1 - 5 PM. A unique,
educational and cultural organization founded in 1915, catering to all
the arts: music, drama, painting, sculpture, prints, design, literary
arts, illustration, architecture. Ann. meeting Mar; mem. approx.
2400 individuals and organizations; dues from $50. Galleries open
free to members, guests and the public; restaurant for members and
their guests.

Activities: Exhibitions, paintings, sculpture and crafts; dance
and music programs; lectures and demonstrations and films.

Publications: The Art Alliance Bulletin, published 9 times a
year, Oct. - May; Philadelphia Art Alliance Press publishes 3 or 4
art-related volumes annually.

Attendance: Approx. 100,000.

PHILADELPHIA ART COMMISSION

Room 1329, City Hall Annex, 19107. Tel: (215) 686-4470
John T. Dorrance, Jr, Pres.
Beverly T. Volk, Exec. Secy. & Dir.

Former Art Jury created by Act of Legislature 1907, re-enacted
1919. City Charter, adopted by the Electors April 17, 1951, abolished
the Art Jury and created the Art Commission. Consists of eight
members appointed by the Mayor and the Commissioner of Public
Property, ex officio. Department of the City government which
passes upon the design and location of all buildings and other structures or fixtures to be erected by the City, or for which the City or
any other authority furnishes a site; any structure or fixture to be
erected by any person upon or to extend over any highway or other
public place within the City; any work of art acquired by the City or
the removal, relocation, alteration to any existing work of art. Also
passes upon the design and location of all private structures or fixtures within 200 feet of the Benjamin Franklin Parkway and in areas
abutting the Independence Hall and Independence Mall.

✠ PHILADELPHIA COLLEGE OF ART

Broad & Pine Sts, 19102. Tel: (215) KI6-0545
Thomas F. Schutte, Pres.
Richard H. Reinhardt, Dean of Faculty
Janet Kardon, Dir. Exhibitions
Gallery open Mon. - Fri. 9 AM - 5 PM; no admis. College estab.
1876 to prepare artists and designers for careers in business, industry, education and the fine arts; financed by endowment and city
appropriation. Gallery's varied exhibition program serves to
stimulate its own community as well as the general public in its
center city location. The work of younger but innovative, recognized
artists is features. Book shop.

Exhibitions: Tibetan Tankas, Black Mountain College - Summer of
'52, Labyrinths, Lewis Baltz Photographs, Sketchbooks by Artists
and Projects for PCA

Library: Approx. 38,000 volumes for lending or reference, half
of which are devoted to the arts, with strong emphasis on books of
the cinema; 100,000 pictures on a variety of subjects. Policy of the
library is to assist the art community in general and cooperate
actively with other libraries of all types. Open Mon. - Fri 8:15 AM -
10 PM; Sat. 10 AM - 2 PM; summer Mon. - Fri. 9 AM - 4 PM.

Publications: Alumni Magazine, twice yearly; a general newspaper, twice monthly.

✠ PHILADELPHIA MUSEUM OF ART

Parkway at 26th St, 19130. Tel: (215) 763-8100
George M. Cheston, Pres.
William P. Wood, Treas. & V.Pres.
George B. Clothier, Solicitor
George Howard, Acting Secy.
Evan Hopkins Turner, Dir.
John Sharpe, Controller
Carl A. Colozzi, Asst Dir. for Services
Arnold Jolles, Asst. Dir. for Art
Lawrence Snyder, Asst. Dir. for Personnel
Philip Thompson, Asst. Dir. for Development
Anne d'Harnoncourt, Cur. 20th Century Art
David T. Dubon, Cur. Decorative Arts: Medieval & Renaissance
Henry P. McIlhenny, Advisor Decorative Arts
Darrel Sewell, Cur. American Art
Joseph Rishel, Cur. Paintings before 1900
Kathryn Hiesinger, Cur. European Decorative Arts after 1700
Jean Gordon Lee, Cur. Far Eastern Art
Stella Kramrisch, Cur. Emeritus, Indian Art
Kneeland McNulty, Cur. Prints, Drawings & Photographs
Carl Zigrosser, Cur. Emeritus, Prints & Drawings
Elsie Siratz McGarvey, Cur. Costume & Textiles

Michael Hoffman, Advisor, Alfred Stieglitz Center
Theodor Siegl, Conservator
David Katzive, Chief, Div. Educ.
William Miller, Asst. Chief, Div. Educ.
Mary Anne Justice, Cur. Slide Dept.
Barbara Chandler, Registrar
Barbara Sevy, Librn.
Sandra Horrocks, Pub. Relations Mgr.
Robert Lipsey, Museum Supt.
Shelley Hodupp, Mgr. Museum Shop
George Marcus, Publications Ed.
Leslie Moneta, Park Houses
Penny Bach, Head, Dept. Urban Outreach
Caroline Thiermann Gladstone, Volunteer Guides
Jane Copeland, Mem. Supvr.
Beatrice Lertzman, Admin, Services Officer
Alfred J. Wyatt, Photographer
Open daily 9 AM - 5 PM with possible extended hours during Bicen-
tennial period; admis. adults $1.50, children 75¢; cl. legal holidays.
Estab. and inc. 1876. Formerly known as Pennsylvania Museum of
Art, present name adopted 1938. Ann. meeting Oct; mem. 16,000;
dues $15 individual, $25 family. Buildings owned by City, opened
1928; wings 1931 and 1940; Fashion Galleries 1949, 1951 and 1953;
Gallatin and Arensberg collections 1954; Far Eastern Wing 1957;
Decorative Arts Galleries 1958; Charles Patterson Van Pelt Auditorium 1959; Nepalese-Tibetan Gallery 1960; New Galleries of Italian
and French Renaissance Art 1960; Museum contains 250 Galleries.

Collections: Cover the general history of European, American
and Eastern Art since the beginning of the Christian era. Ensembles
include Chinese palace hall; Chinese temple; Chinese scholar's
study; Japanese temple; Japanese tea house; Indian temple; Sasanian
units from Iran; Romanesque cloister and facade; Gothic chapel;
French Renaissance choir screen; and many period rooms, European
and American. Sculpture, especially medieval Renaissance, French
18th century and work from India. Comprehensive collection of Old
Masters (†Wilstach, †Elkins, McFadden and John G. Johnson collections) and 19th and 20th century art (Gallatin, Arensberg, Tyson,
White and Stern collections). World famous collection of the paintings of Thomas Eakins. The American Art Galleries, newly installed
and opening Dec. 1976 will contain architectual elements, Philadelphia furniture and silver, Tucker porcelain, Stiegel glass, Geesey
Collection of Pennsylvania Dutch Folk Art; Barberini-Kress Foundation Tapestry Series, The History of Constantine the Great; The
Nepalese-Tibetan Gallery collection; Italian and French Renaissance
art collection includes architectural elements, furniture, bronzes and
decorative arts from Edmund Foulc and other collections. In Eastern
art, imported Persian, Chinese (Crozier collection), Nepalese and
Tibetan art. In prints some 100,000 items (including 60,000 on
deposit from the Pennsylvania Academy of Fine Arts).

Exhibitions: (1973) Gauguin Monographs; Frank Furness Architecture; (1974) Marcel Duchamp, The Invisible Artist; Clarence
Laughlin Photographs; A Decade of Gifts; Stanzione Arms and
Armour from the Kienbusch Collection; (1975) The Greenfield Collection; American Silver; The Nude in Philadelphia.

Activities: (Division of Education) The Charles Patterson Van
Pelt Auditorium seats 400 for lectures, concerts and film showings,
classes for children; continuous art field program for school children; Mini-Museum Mobile with traveling exhibitions for children;
gallery tours and talks; art history survey and specialized lecture
series; series of circulating exhibitions and films; adult workshop
classes; art films; lecture series; slide lectures; concerts; Art
Sales and Rental Gallery; tours by Volunteer Guides daily, available
in 9 languages.

Library: Contains more than 85,000 volumes dealing with the
field of art; large slide and film library.

Income: Income in city funds plus approx. $2,092,850 private
funds for the year of 1974-75.

Attendance: 622,400 annual average.

John G. Johnson Collection
Joseph Rishel, Cur.
Open daily 9 AM - 5 PM; cl. holidays.

Collection left to the city in 1917 by the late John G. Johnson.
Formerly housed in the Johnson house, the collection is now installed
in 20 especially finished galleries at the Philadelphia Museum.
There are 1286 paintings illustrating the history of art from the 14th
to the 19th centuries, including notable examples from Italian, Flemish, Dutch, German, Spanish, French and English Schools. Of the
total number of pictures in the collection, about one-half are constantly on display, the remaining ones being available to students on
request.

Rodin Museum, Parkway at 22nd St.
Open daily 9 AM - 5 PM; contributions suggested.

Collection of sculpture, drawings and watercolors by Auguste
Rodin, bequeathed by Jules E. Mastbaum. Largest Rodin Collection
outside Paris. The Rodin Museum has been re-installed with trea-

sures from the Philadelphia Museum of Art through Jan. 1976, reopening with the Rodin sculptures and drawings Mar, 1976.

Mount Pleasant, Fairmount Park
Open daily 10 AM - 5 PM; admis. 25¢ adults, 10¢ children.
Built 1761, restored 1926. One of the finest and richest houses of the Colonies; mid-Georgian style carvings and Chippendale style furnishings.

Cedar Grove, Lansdowne Dr, Fairmount Park
Open daily 10 AM - 5 PM; admis. 25¢ adults, 10¢ children.
Built in Frankford about 1721, moved 1927. Ancestral home of Morris family; contains original furniture of William and Mary, Chippendale, and Hepplewhite periods; Colonial kitchen.

The Women's Committee
Mrs. Robert Dripps, Pres.
Estab. 1877, inc. 1915; takes active interest in the Museum. Mem. 40 active, 10 sustaining, and 2 honorary. Sponsors Art Sales and Rental; Park Houses, Volunteer Guides.

PHILADELPHIA SKETCH CLUB*
235 S. Camac St, 19107. Tel: (215) 545-9298
Free during exhibitions 2 - 5 PM. Estab. 1860, inc. 1889 for artistic practice and social intercourse. Owns buildings with gallery and art library; collection of members' work. Ann. meeting Jan; mem. approx. 200; dues $50 per yr. Art classes, as announced, Sept.-June.
Exhibitions: Annual exhibition of watercolors in Oct; prints, Mar; small oils, May. Many other exhibitions.

PHILADELPHIA WATER COLOR CLUB*
c/o Mili D. Weiss, Secy, Randall Rd, Wyncote, 19095.
Charles Taylor, Pres.
Estab. 1900. Ann. meeting Apr; mem. 370; dues $7.50 and $10.
Permanent collection housed at the Philadelphia Museum of Art; endowment fund for purchases and awards. Emergency fund estab. 1946 to aid by purchase members in need.
Exhibitions: Biennial exhibitions Nov. at Pennsylvania Academy of the Fine Arts; members' exhibition annually, June through summer, at Philadelphia Art Alliance; Civic Center Museum, 1970.
Water Color Club Medal awarded yearly for outstanding work in furthering water color painting in general; other medals awarded annually are the Dana, Dawson, Eyre and Pennell. Two cash awards annually: Philadelphia Water Color Club Prize of $400 and Thornton Oakley prize of $50.

THE PHILIP H. & A. S. W. ROSENBACH FOUNDATION MUSEUM
2010 DeLancey Pl, 19103. Tel: (215) 732-1600
Clive E. Driver, Dir.
Open for guided tours daily 2 - 5 PM except Mon; group tours from 10 AM - 5 PM by appointment; Library open Mon. - Fri. to scholars 10 AM - 6 PM by appointment; cl. Aug. & nat. holidays; cl. weekends June & July; admis. adults $1.50, students 50¢, groups of 8 or more $1 per person; exhibit only 50¢. Estab. 1948 as a nonprofit corporation.
Collections: 18th century English antiques and silver, paintings, prints and drawings, porcelain, rugs and objets d'art; rare books and manuscripts, consisting of British and American literature, Americana, and book illustration; 100,000 manuscripts; 25,000 books; Marianne Moore Archive.
Exhibitions: Changing exhibitions of aspects of the collections.

PLASTIC CLUB*
247 Comac St, S, 19107. Tel: (215) 545-9324
Sarah F. Crumb, Secy.
Free during exhibitions Mon. - Fri. 1 - 4 PM. Organized 1897, inc. 1903, a woman's club to promote a wider knowledge of art. Ann. meeting May; mem. approx. 200; dues $10 and higher. Owns clubhouse with gallery; paintings by members.
Exhibitions: Annual exhibition of water-colors by members in Jan; oils and sculpture in Mar; Gold and Silver Medals awarded, as well as cash prizes at Annual Oil and Water Color Shows; work of sketch classes in May; summer work in Oct. Rotary exhibitions through northern cities, Nov. to June. Lectures; sketch classes for members and guests.

PRINT CLUB
1614 Latimer St, 19103. Tel: (215) 735-6090
Donald McPhail, Pres.
Anne F. Wetzel, Secy.
Margo Devereux, Dir.
Free 10 AM - 5:30 PM; Sat. Noon - 4 PM. Estab. 1914, inc. 1921. Ann. meeting Jan; mem. 1400; dues $12.50 and higher. Owns clubhouse with galleries.
Collections: Collection of prints and bookplates. Print Club †permanent collection housed at Philadelphia Museum of Art.

Exhibitions: Annual competitive exhibition of original prints, prizes awarded; changing monthly exhibitions of contemporary graphics. Annual purchase awards $1000.
Activities: Lectures; demonstrations; etching press. Book shop.

SAMUEL S. FLEISHER ART MEMORIAL
719 Catharine St, 19147. Tel: (215) WA2-3456
Mrs. Stuart F. Louchheim, Chmn.
George B. Clothier, Treas.
David H. Katzive, Coordinator
Thora E. Jacobson, Adminr.
Louis P. Hirshman, Dir. Instruction
Free Mon. - Fri. 10 AM - 4 PM, during exhibitions; Mon. - Thurs. 7 - 9:30 PM; Sat. 1 - 3 PM. Estab. 1898 as a free art school and sanctuary (Museum of Religious Art), an Italian Romanesque Revival building; financed by endowment; administered by the Philadelphia Museum of Art. Gallery used primarily for school-related exhibitions, also for special shows of contemporary artists.
Collections: Medieval and Renaissance religious painting and sculpture; 18th - 19th century Portuguese liturgical objects; 17th - 20th century Russian icons; 20th century paintings and prints; some sculpture.
Exhibitions: (1972-74) Painting and Photography, Something in Common; A Child's Garden of Art; James Rosenquist Slush Thrust; Open Studio Work in Progress; L. A. Flash/Phila. Flash; In Her Own Image; plus annual student, faculty, adult and childrens' exhibitions.
Activities: Traveling exhibitions organized and circulated; original objects of art lent, 2 items lent in average year; lectures open to public; 26 gallery talks; concerts, classes for adults and children. (See Schools)
Annual Income: Approx. $160,000.

SCHOOL ART LEAGUE
Philadelphia Public Schools
Administration Bldg, 21st St. & Parkway, 19103.
Tel: (215) 299-7727
Jack Bookbinder, Dir. Div. Art Educ.
Leon Cohen, Supv.
Estab. 1922 to provide advanced art instruction in various media for Philadelphia school children. Mem. approx. 1600.
Activities: Sat. morning classes in 12 centers throughout the city; instruction by professional artists and art teachers in the fields of painting, sculpture, graphics, commercial design, photography and crafts; trips to art galleries and museums.
Exhibition of students' work held annually at the Museum of the Philadelphia Civic Center. Instructions and materials without charge.

SOCIETY OF ARCHITECTURAL HISTORIANS
Room 716, 1700 Walnut St, 19103.
Tel: (215) 735-0224, 0246
Spiro K. Kostof, Pres.
Elisabeth MacDougall, Secy.
Rosann S. Berry, Exec. Secy.
For further information see p. 9.

TYLER SCHOOL OF ART LIBRARY
Temple University, Beech & Penrose Ave, 19126.
Tel: (215) CA4-7575, Exten. 245
Ivy Bayard, Librn.
Open 8:30 AM - 9 PM & Sat. & Sun. 1 - 4 PM during academic sessions; 8:30 AM - 4 PM when school is not in session.
Collections: Books and periodicals on all aspects of art and art history, emphasizing studio and 20th century art; 13,500 volumes for lending and reference; book collection includes exhibit and auction catalogs.
Budget: $13,650 for books and periodicals.

THE UNIVERSITY MUSEUM
University of Pennsylvania
33rd and Spruce St, 19174. Tel: (215) 386-7400
Howard C. Petersen, Chmn. of the Board
Froelich G. Rainey, Dir.
James B. Pritchard, Assoc. Dir.
David J. Crownover, Exec. Secy.
William P. Coe, Cur. American Section
Margaret Plass, Hon. Cur. African Art
James B. Pritchard, Cur. Biblical Archaeology
David O'Connor, Assoc. Cur. Egyptian Section
Derk Bodde, Assoc. in Chinese Studies, Far Eastern Section
Rodney S. Young, Cur. Mediterranean Section
G. Roger Edwards, Assoc. Cur. Mediterranean Section
Robert H. Dyson, Jr, Cur. Near Eastern Section
Ake W. Sjöberg, Cur. of Babylonian Tablet Collection
William H. Davenport, Cur. Oceania Section

Ward H. Goodenough, Cur. Oceanic Ethnology
Loren C. Eiseley, Cur. Early Man
Wilton M. Krogman, Cur. Physical Anthropology
Jeffrey L. Kenyon, Dir. Educ. Dept.
Jean Adelman, Librn.
Free 10 AM - 5 PM; Sun. 1 - 5 PM; cl. Mon. Estab. 1887 for the
study of man. Mem. 2300; dues $15 and higher.
    Collections: Archaeological collection from Babylonia, Egypt,
Palestine, the Mediterranean and the Americas. Art of China, India,
Persia, Ethnology of American Indian, Oceania and Africa, including
outstanding collection of Negro art. Museum's collections have been
built through its more than 200 expeditions. Loan collections to museums and schools of specimens, photographs, lantern slides, and
other visual aids. Casts, postcards of Museum objects, publications
and film strips are available.
    Activities: Films, music, rotating special exhibits for public;
special activities for children and members.
    Publications: Expedition, the Magazine of Archaeology/Anthro-
pology, 4 times a year; Museum Monographs (reports on excavations, collections, linguistic investigations), irregularly; Museum
Applied Science Center Newsletter.
    Attendance: 350,000 yearly.

VIOLET OAKLEY MEMORIAL FOUNDATION, INC.
    627 St. George's Rd, 19119. Tel: (215) CH7-0633
Edith Emerson, Pres. & Cur.
Open by appointment; guest cards $1.50. Estab. 1962, inc, 1972, to
encourage the activities to which Violet Oakley's career was dedicated; financed by membership. The building is in Pennsylvania
Register on Historic Sites. Large studio maintained, with Violet
Oakley works. Ann. meeting May; mem. 250.
    Collections: Memorial paintings, drawings by Violet Oakley;
plus furniture and objects d'art. Records, archives, press books
and art library.
    Exhibitions: June exhibition by artist members.
    Activities: A few original objects of art lent to well-known art
museums; lectures for members and guests; concerts, dramatic
programs.

WILLET STAINED GLASS STUDIOS
    10 E. Moreland Ave, 19118. Tel: (215) 247-5721
Henry Lee Willet, Chmn.
E. Crosby Willet, Pres.
Marguerite Gaudin, V.Pres.
Augusta W. Willet, V.Pres.
William R. Eagan, Secy-Treas.
Helene Weis, Librn.
Aaron R. Knopman, Sales Representative
Free 8 AM - 4:30 PM weekdays by appointment. Estab. 1890 as the
largest stained glass studio in the United States.
    Activities: Apprentice school; library open for student re-
search; classes for hobbyists; traveling exhibitions organized and
circulated; individual paintings and original objects of art lent;
lending collection, photographs, Kodachromes and motion pictures;
lectures; 3 tours per wk.
    Library: Approx. 1000 volumes; photograph collection of
approx. 11,650 prints; original sketches.

THE WOODMERE ART GALLERY
    9201 Germantown Ave, 19118. Tel: (215) 247-0476
Carl Helmetag, Jr, Chmn of the Board
Dr. John H. Wolf, Pres.
Wallace S. Martindale, Jr, Treas.
Mrs. Michael Puchek, Secy.
Edith Emerson, Cur.
Harry A. Harris, Dir. & Chmn. Exhibitions
Free daily 10 AM - 5 PM; Sun. 2 - 5 PM; cl. holidays. Estab. 1940;
founded by Charles Knox Smith, in trust for benefit of the public.
Original collection and building increased. A large addition in 1965
provides additional gallery and studio space. Ann. meeting April;
mem. 1500; dues $8 and higher.
    Collections: Smith Collection of European and American paint-
ings; Oriental rugs, furniture, porcelains; European porcelains and
furniture; European and American sculpture; contemporary American
†paintings, †sculpture, and †graphics.
    Exhibitions: 8 current exhibitions annually; prizes awarded in
Members', Annual Juried and Special Exhibitions.
    Activities: Classes for adults and children; Philadelphia Guild
of Handweavers' classes; concerts, lectures, gallery tours.
    Attendance: 14,000.

PITTSBURGH

ART INSTITUTE OF PITTSBURGH GALLERY
    536 Penn Ave, 15222. Tel: (412) 471-5651
John A. Johns, Pres.

Open to public free of charge. Institute estab. 1921 as an art school
and proprietary trade school. Scholarships available. Library.
(See Schools)
    Exhibitions: Local art group shows; student and faculty members;
local artists; technical art exhibits; Andy Warhol; Franklin Mc-
Mahon; Day-Glo Contest Winners; Coca-Cola Exhibit; Ray Simboli;
Graphic Communications Through the Ages.
    Publications: Catalog, brochures, School Newspaper.

ARTS AND CRAFTS CENTER OF PITTSBURGH
    Mellon Park, Fifth & Shady Aves, 15232. Tel: (412) 361-0873
Donal Pierucci, Pres.
Audrey Bethel, Exec. Dir.
Open Tues. - Sat. 10 AM - 5 PM; Sun. 2 - 5 PM. Estab. 1944, inc.
1947. Headquarters for nonprofit organizations in the creative arts.
15 resident and 2 affiliated member groups (1600 individuals). Ann.
meeting Jan; administered by board of resident group and community
representatives; resident members pay per capita dues according
to own memberships; affiliated members, group dues.
    Exhibitions: Galleries maintained for monthly contemporary ex-
hibitions, group and one-man shows. Special exhibitions: Artist of
the Year, retrospective show honoring a Pittsburgh artist chosen
by Board; Invitational one-man or group show.
    Activities: Non-credit arts and crafts classes conducted for
adults and children; Mart operated for outlet for members' work;
rental facilities provided for outside groups for art programs; professional workshops offered to artists throughout state (3 per year).
    Publications: Center brochure, class brochure 4 times a year.
    Income and Sales: Approx. gross income $225,000; gross sales
$75,000.
    Attendance: 85,000.

ASSOCIATED ARTISTS OF PITTSBURGH
Arts and Crafts Center
    Fifth and Shady Aves, 15232. Tel: (412) 361-4235
Marjorie Firsching Shipe, Pres.
Robert Bowden, V.Pres.
Teresa Rozewski, Secy.
David Andreaco, III, Treas.
Open 10 AM - 5 PM. Estab. 1910, inc. 1930. Ann. meeting May;
mem. 500; dues $20.
    Annual exhibit of work by members in Mar.-Apr; jury, prizes.

CARNEGIE LIBRARY OF PITTSBURGH*
    Art Division, Music and Art Department, 4400 Forbes Ave,
    15213. Tel: (412) 622-3107
Mrs. Ida Reed, Librn in Charge
Free, Mon. - Sat. 9 AM - 9 PM, Sun. 2 - 5 PM; cl. Sat. eve. & Sun,
Memorial Day-Labor Day. Estab. 1930 to provide reference and circulating materials and information on all aspects of art; financed by
city and state appropriations.
    Collections: Reference and circulating collection of 40,000
volumes in all areas of art; special collections of architecture and
costume books; lending photograph collection of 300,000 prints; lending collection of 80,000 slides.

THE FRICK ART MUSEUM
    7227 Reynolds St, 15208. Tel: (212) 371-7766
Virginia E. Lewis, Dir.
Mrs. John F. Connors, Exec. Secy.
Mrs. C. W. Cox, Registrar
T. L. Dennis, Supt. of Maintenance
Rocco E. Giorgianni, Head of Security
Free, Wed. - Fri. 10 AM - 4 PM; Sat. 10 AM - 5 PM; Sun. 1 - 5 PM;
cl. Aug. Estab. 1970 as an art museum for public enjoyment and edu-
cation; endowment.
    Collections: †Italian, Flemish, French paintings from the early
Renaissance through the 18th century; French 18th Century Period
Room; Italian and Flemish bronzes of the 15th, 16th and 17th cen-
turies; 16th to 18th century Italian furniture; 18th century French
furniture; Chinese 18th century porcelains; 18th century English and
Irish silver; 18th century Russian silver; Sculpture, Houdon, Clodion;
Tapestries, French mille fleurs and Flemish 16th century.
    Activities: Lectures open to the public; 3-5 visiting lecturers per
year; 24 gallery talks; 50 tours; concerts; small working library.
    Publications: Five Lectures by Dr. W. R. Hovey; The Arts in
Changing Societies: Reflections Inspired by Works of Art in the
Frick Art Museum, Pittsburgh; Check List; Madame Jean Antoine
Houdon (reprinted from The Art Bulletin); The Treasures of the
Frick Art Museum.
    Attendance: 15,350 annual average.

IVY GALLERIES
Ivy School of Professional Art
    University Ave, 15214. Tel: (412) 323-8800
M. B. Kirshenbaum, Pres. & Dir.
Dr. Seymour Blinderman, Provost

Victor Willem, Asst. Dir.
Free daily 9 AM - 5 PM & 7 - 9:30 PM. Estab. Jan. 1960 as a professional art school with 8 quarter programs in fine arts and commercial arts. Several galleries throughout school for periodic shows.
Exhibitions: 6-8 general shows a year, graphics, paintings, prints and sculpture.
Activities: Lectures open to public, 2-3 visiting lecturers per year; classes for children; scholarships; book shop.
Library; Over 1000 volumes for reference only.
Publications: The Ivy Leaf, published every other month.

✠MUSEUM OF ART, CARNEGIE INSTITUTE
4400 Forbes Ave, 15213. Tel: (412) 622-3200
James M. Walton, Pres.
Richard M. Scaife, Chmn. Museum of Art Comt.
Leon Anthony Arkus, Dir.
William D. Judson, Cur Film Section
Anthony N. Landreau, Cur. Educ. Section
David T. Owsley, Cur. Section of Antiquities, Oriental & Decorative Arts
Herdis Bull Teilman, Cur. Painting & Sculpture
Walter Read Hovey, Advisor for Asiatic Art
Emily J. Roberts, Exec. Secy.
Charles W. Cathey, Registrar
Open Tues. - Sat. 10 AM - 5 PM; Sun. 1 - 6 PM; cl. Mon. Free Sat; contribution requested other days. Estab. 1896, inc. 1926; financed by endowment, Carnegie Institute membership, grants from foundations and trusts and corporate gifts. Scaife Gallery for permanent collection opened fall 1974; Heinz Galleries for special exhibitions opened fall 1975; new decorative arts galleries opened spring 1975. Mem. approx. 9000; dues $1000 sponsoring, $500 contributing, $100 sustaining, $50 participating, $25 family, $15 individual, $5 student, $100-$10,000 corporate.
Collections: American and European Paintings and Sculpture; Drawings, Prints and Watercolors; Antiquities, Oriental and Decorative Arts; Ailsa Mellon Bruce Collection; Photographs and Films.
Founder-Patrons Day Exhibitions: (1970-75) Pittsburgh International Exhibition of Contemporary Art; Ailsa Mellon Bruce Collection of European Furniture, Porcelain and Silver; Fresh Air School: Sam Francis, Joan Mitchell, Walasse Ting; Art in Residence: Art Privately Owned in the Pittsburgh Area; Celebration; Pittsburgh Corporations Collect.
Annual Exhibitions: Associated Artists of Pittsburgh; series of one-man exhibitions by local artists; Neapolitan Creche; Three Rivers Arts Festival.
Other Exhibitions: Forerunners of American Abstraction; Jean Dewasne; Mr. and Mrs. Henry Pearlman Collection; many print and photographic exhibitions.
Activities: Two free gallery talks daily; member receptions and previews; Film Section (Directors' Film Series, History of Film Series, Independent Film Maker Series); adult and childrens' classes; travel-lecture series (18 films); gift shop; domestic and international tours; free "Man and Ideas" lecture series.
Publications: Carnegie Magazine, 10 times annually; catalogs of permanent collection and of special exhibitions.
Building Attendance: Approx. 500,000 annually.
Three Rivers Arts Festival
Tel: (412) 687-7014
Alexander H. Jackson, Chmn.
Mrs. W. Peirce Widdoes, Exec. Dir.
Mrs. Ralph R. Atlas, Exec. Secy.
Festival supported by City, County, State Arts Council, Foundations and interested corporations and individuals.
Estab. 1960, 10-day festival (May-June) including visual and performing arts—painting, sculpture, crafts, photography and music, dance, drama, film, all free to the public and held on the grounds of Gateway Center, downtown Pittsburgh; also demonstrators, children's activities, magician, special shows.

PITTSBURGH PLAN FOR ART
1251 N. Negley Ave, 15206. Tel: (412) 362-1234
Sylvester Damianos, Pres.
James Winokur, V.Pres.
Eva Ada Weill, Secy.
Rebecca Borman, Exec. Dir.
Joyce Walsh, Secy.
Free Tues. - Sat. 10 AM - 4 PM; Sun. 2 - 5 PM. Estab. 1955 as a nonprofit educational facility for the borrowing, browsing and purchasing of Pittsburgh artists' work; financed by membership and fees from rentals and sales commissions. Four modern gallery rooms and office; large sculpture court and a sculpture garden; Victorian architecture. Mem. 450.
Exhibitions: 30 exhibitions by artist members.
Activities: Traveling exhibitions organized and circulated; individual and original objects of art lent; lending collection, 700 paint-

ings, drawings and prints, 100 sculptures; 1200 items lent in average year; lectures; 2 gallery talks and tours; classes for adults; films; scholarships. Book shop.
Income and Purchases: $110,000.
Attendance: 10,000 annual average.

✠UNIVERSITY OF PITTSBURGH
Henry Clay Frick Fine Arts Building, 15260.

✠Henry Clay Frick Fine Arts Library. Tel: (412) 624-4124
Elizabeth Crampton Booth, Librn.
Open Mon. - Thurs. 9 AM - 10 PM; Fri. - Sat. 9 AM - 5 PM; Sun. 2 - 5 PM. Estab. 1927. 47,500 volumes incl. 299 periodical subscriptions; Western and Oriental art history, archaeology, architecture, sculpture, painting, manuscripts, fine painting.

University Art Gallery. Tel: (412) 624-4116
Carl Nordenfalk, Dir.
Open to public Tues. - Sat. 1 - 5 PM; Sun. 2 - 5 PM.
Exhibitions: The Art Gallery sponsors a year-round program of art exhibitions, incl. traveling shows each year originating at other institutions and several shows each year organized and first displayed in Pittsburgh.
Educational Activities: Program of community events, incl. lectures, is held each year.

See Art School Section for Department of Fine Arts and Department of Studio Arts.

READING

BERKS ART ALLIANCE
Wyomissing Institute of Art Bldg, Trent & Belmont St, 19610.
Regina D. Gouger, Pres.
Merri Woolley, V.Pres.
Estab. 1941 to maintain active art center in Reading and Berks County. Mem. 150; dues $10; meetings 2nd Tues. of odd months.
Exhibitions: Three annual membership shows, plus solo or two-person shows of a two week period each, all open to public, free of charge.
Activities: Life drawing workshops, Thurs. 9:30 AM - 12:30 PM and Thurs. 7 - 9 PM; open painting session Thurs. afternoon; sponsors one day painting class with visiting artist once a year; sponsors annual trip to American Watercolor Society show in New York.

✠READING PUBLIC MUSEUM AND ART GALLERY
500 Museum Rd, 19611. Tel: (215) 373-1525
J. Daniel Selig, Dir. & Acting Cur. Fine Arts
Richard C. Koch, Cur. Botanical Science
Free 9 AM - 5 PM; Sat. 9 AM - 12 M; Sun. 2 - 5 PM; summer mid-June through Labor Day 9 AM - 4 PM; Sun. 2 - 5 PM; cl. Sat. Estab. 1904, art gallery 1913, inc. 1921; maintained by Reading School District, but accessions come from public contributions and private donations. Mem. Friends 600; annual dues, single $10; family $15.
Collections: Over 1200 paintings by American and foreign artists, mainly 16th - 20th century; sculpture; graphics and watercolors; decorative arts: Egyptian, Greek, Roman, European, African, North American, Indian, Pre-Columbian, Chinese, Japanese, Pennsylvania-German; armour; ethnology: Oceanic, the Americas, Australian, Latvian; natural history: lepidoptera, North American birds and mammals, Pennsylvanian paleontology, minerals.
Exhibitions: Regional exhibition open to artists living within 35 miles; jury selection. Special exhibitions.
Activities: Formally organized educational program for children with 6 regularly scheduled city classes each day in geography, history and natural science; gallery tours for non-Reading students; concerts, lectures and special programs for adults.
Library: Reference library of 15,000 volumes.
Income and Purchases: Income $10,700; expenditures $5,000 annually.
Attendance: Approx. 90,000.

SCRANTON

EVERHART MUSEUM
Nay Aug Park, 18510. Tel: (717) 346-7186
Judge Otto P. Robinson, Chmn. Trustees
Carl E. Ellis, Cur. Art & Assoc. Dir.
William E. Speare, Cur. Natural History & Assoc. Dir.
Free 10 AM - 5 PM; Sun. 2 - 5 PM; cl. Mon. & holidays. Estab. and inc. 1908; gift to the City from Dr. Isaiah F. Everhart; supported by endowment and City appropriations; building re-built 1928-29. Ann. meeting June; mem. 1200; dues $7.50 and higher.
Collections: †American folk art; Oriental art; African, Oceanic; †American Indian material; European and American painting, prints and sculpture; †natural history and science, birds, animals, reptiles and fishes of Pennsylvania; Dorflinger Glass (1852-1921).

Exhibitions: Monthly exhibitions in both art and natural history departments.

Activities: Monthly membership lecture series (art and science); weekly classes in art and science for children and adults; guided tours; outside lectures. Annual member Ball; Artist-in-residence programs.

Library: Approx. 8500 volumes for reference, art and history.

Income and Purchases: Income $67,150; purchases $2000.

Attendance: 200,000 annually.

SWARTHMORE

FRIENDS HISTORICAL LIBRARY
Swarthmore College, 19081. Tel: (215) 328-2625; 544-7900, Exten. 436 (Peace Collection)
Dr. J. William Frost, Dir.
Jane A. Rittenhouse, Assoc. Dir.
Bernice Nichols, Cur. Peace Collection
Free weekdays 8:30 AM - 4:30 PM; Sat. 9 AM - Noon; cl. Aug, Sat. during college vacations and certain other holidays. Estab. 1871 to preserve and make available to the public material by and about Quakers and their concerns; supported by endowment and by Swarthmore College.

Collections: Quaker paintings; Quakers as subject in art; Meeting House picture collection; portraits; group pictures, residences; Swarthmore College pictures; other Quaker schools; silhouettes and sketches of individual Friends are conveniently arranged for consultation. Also a large collection of manuscripts, autographs, and records of Quaker and peace organizations. Books, pamphlets and periodicals, approx. 35,000 altogether, contain many rare items from the 17th century, Quaker and anti-Quaker. The Peace Collection consists primarily of archival material: records of peace organizations in U.S. and 59 foreign countries, and papers of peace leaders, including Jane Addams, Emily Greene Balch, Elihu Burritt, A. J. Muste, Wilhelm Sollmann, and others. Includes 1400 peace posters and war posters; 1300 periodical titles.

The Whittier Collection includes virtually every edition and every variant printing as well as nearly every periodical contribution of the Quaker poet John Greenleaf Whittier. On the walls of the Library are paintings including two Edward Hicks originals.

Attendance: More than 2500 annually.

UNIVERSITY PARK

✠THE PENNSYLVANIA STATE UNIVERSITY, UNIVERSITY PARK
Museum of Art
16802. Tel: (814) 865-7672
William Hull, Dir.
William D. Davis, Asst. Dir.
Olga Preisner, Registrar
Free daily Noon - 5 PM; cl. Mon. Estab. 1972 to make variety of visual experiences through a program of changing exhibitions; financed by state appropriations and private gifts. Museum store.

Collections: Mainly American paintings, drawings, prints with some emphasis on Pennsylvania artists. Limited materials in Oriental, African and Near Eastern areas. The Kehl and Nena Markley Collection of Ancient Peruvian Ceramics.

Attendance: 60,082.

Arts Library
E405 Pattee Library, 16802
Dr. Stuart Forth, Dean Libraries
Jean Smith, Arts Librn.
Carole Franklin, Music Librn.
Free weekdays 8 AM - Noon, Sat. 8 AM - 5 PM, Sun. 1 PM to Midnight. Several areas utilized within the university library where changing exhibits of local artists' work is shown.

Collections: Lending and reference library of 31,050 volumes, not including music materials; collection of 500 original prints for study purposes and display.

WAYNE

WAYNE ART CENTER
413 Maplewood Ave, 19087. Tel: (215) 688-3553
Virginia Bradley Clark, Pres.
Open Mon. - Fri. 10 AM - 4 PM. Estab. 1929, inc. 1932 to promote art knowledge and induce the use of free time creatively. Ann. meeting May; mem. 300; dues $10 - $100.

Exhibitions: Local, regional and specialized shows at the art center as well as exhibits in the community at corporations and Radnor Township building; 20 per year.

Activities: Classes for adults Mon. through Fri, day and evening; classes for children Sat. AM.

WILKES-BARRE

SORDONI ART GALLERY
150 S. River St, 18703. Tel: (717) 824-4651
Phil Richards, Dir.
Cara Berryman, Gallery Coordinator
Free weekdays & Sun. 1 - 5 PM; Sat. 10 AM - 5 PM; Estab. 1973 to encourage art appreciation in the Wilkes-Barre community; financed by endowment. Gallery located on campus at Wilkes College; 30 x 40 ft. with elaborate alarm system.

Collections: 19th century academic European paintings and sculpture.

Activities: Lectures open to public; 12 tours.

YORK

THE HISTORICAL SOCIETY OF YORK COUNTY
250 E. Market St, 17403. Tel: (717) 848-1587
Harry L. Rinker, Exec. Dir.
James Gergat, Cur.
Norwood Miller, Cur. Educ.
Robert Nawrocki, Librn.
Henry S. McFall, Pres.
G. William Schaumann, 1st V.Pres.
Byron H. LeCates, Secy.
Marvin Sedam, Treas.
Open Mon. - Sat. 10 AM - 4 PM; Sun. 1 - 5 PM; admis. charged (gallery at museum is free). Estab. 1895 to record, preserve, collect and interpret the history of York County and Pennsylvania, including music and art of the past and present. Ann. meeting Apr; mem. 3500; dues $12 and higher.

Collections: Works by Lewis Miller and other local artists; Titus Geesy Toy Collection; †Fraktur and other Pennsylvania folk art; James Shettel Collection of theater and circus material.

Restoration Properties: General Gates House (1751), Golden Plough Tavern (1741) and Log House (1812), 157 W. Market; Bonham House (1870), 152 E. Market.

Exhibitions at Museum, 250 E. Market: Five gallery shows per year featuring living artists; two major shows on some aspect of regional and national decorative or folk arts; three to four secondary shows featuring subject areas (e.g, textiles, fractur, etc) from the collection.

Activities: Guided tours; education program; lecturers; concerts; classes for adults and children; summer internship program. Gift shops.

Library: Reference library of 15,000 volumes; photograph collection of 10,000 prints; large collection of genealogical manuscripts and records.

Publications: Monthly Newsletter; Lewis Miller Sketches and Chronicles; Regional Aspects of American Folk Pottery; The Kentucky Rifle.

Income: $160,000.

Attendance: Approx. 30,000.

MARTIN MEMORIAL LIBRARY
159 E. Market St, 17401. Tel: (717) 843-3978
Marycatharine Weaver, Dir.
Free Mon. - Fri. 9 AM - 9 PM; Sat. 9 AM - 5 PM. Estab. 1935.

Exhibitions: Frequent exhibitions of paintings, arts and crafts, manuscripts and books.

Activities: Lectures; concerts; programs for adults and children.

Library: †125,999 volumes; †12,481 mounted pictures; †16,874 pamphlets; †7900 recordings; 192 16mm films.

Publications: Bulletin, monthly; occasional bibliographies of special collections; Annual Reports; Martin Memorial Library Historical Series; Martin Memorial Library.

Income and Purchases: Income $285,000; annual purchases $55,000.

RHODE ISLAND

KINGSTON

THE SOUTH COUNTY ART ASSOCIATION, HELME HOUSE
1319 Kingstown Rd, 02881. Tel: (401) 783-2195
Dr. George L. Young, Pres.
Dr. Conrad Hill, Recording Secy.
Matthew L. Vollucci, Treas.
Open to the public Tues. - Sun. 2 - 5 PM during exhibitions which are usally of 2 weeks duration 10 or 12 times per year. Estab. Aug. 1929, inc. 1937; took title to property (present home, Helme House) April 1945; To promote an interest in art and to encourage artists in Washington County, Rhode Island, and to support in every way the aesthetic interests of the community. Ann. meeting Oct; mem. approx. 300; dues, artist $7.50, lay member $10, sustaining $15, student $3.

No large permanent collection. Paintings by early members, not usually on display.

Exhibitions: Open Show in April, juried with prizes totaling $275; Members Show in August; Regional Open Earthworks Show, juried with prizes totaling $250.

Activities: Exhibitions, demonstrations, lectures; classes offered through the year in oil, watercolor, ceramics and sculpture with an approximate enrollment of 100 to 130 in both Workshop and Helme House.

NEWPORT

ART ASSOCIATION OF NEWPORT
Howard Gardiner Cushing Memorial Gallery
76 Bellevue Ave, 02840. Tel: (401) 847-0179
Bruce Howe, Pres.
Mrs. W. R. Michael, V.Pres.
Mrs. Paul C. Rogers, Exec. Secy.
Ralph O. Udall, Treas.
Mrs. James Silvia, Dir.
Free 10 AM - 5 PM; Sun. 2 - 5 PM. Estab. 1912, inc. 1915 for the promotion of art, literature, music and science. Ann. meeting June; mem. 700; dues $5 and higher. Owns building.

Exhibitions: Annual exhibition, oils and small sculptures, watercolors, drawings, pastels, prints; open to American artists with jury selection. Continuous special exhibitions.

Activities: Lectures; maintains art school; choral society; picture rental library; print loans to schools; scholarships. (See Schools).

Income & Purchases: Income $55,000.

NEWPORT HISTORICAL SOCIETY
82 Touro St, 02840. Tel: (401) 846-0813
William A. Sherman, Pres.
Theodore E. Waterbury, Exec. Dir.
Free Tues. - Fri. 9:30 AM - 4:30 PM; Sat. 9:30 AM - 12 AM; cl. Sun. & Mon. Estab. and inc. 1853 to preserve articles and manuscripts relating to Newport history. Ann. meeting May; mem. 500; dues $10 and higher. Owns Seventh Day Baptist meeting house built in 1729 and the Wanton-Lyman-Hazard House of 1675.

Exhibitions: Marine Museum and extensive exhibits of silver, china, glass, furniture, Newport scenes and portraits.

Library: 8000 books and 1700 manuscript volumes of log books, custom house papers, mercantile records; also 60,000 loose manuscripts of the 17th and 18th centuries.

Publications: Newport History, quarterly.

Attendance: 8000.

REDWOOD LIBRARY AND ATHENAEUM
Bellevue Ave, 02840. Tel: (401) 847-0292
Dr. Donald B. Fletcher, Pres.
Donald T. Gibbs, Librn.
Free 10 AM - 6 PM; cl. Sun. & holidays. Inc. 1747. Ann. meeting Aug; dues, shareholders $15, subscribers $25.

Collections: 130,000 books, pictures, statues; portraits by Stuart (6), Sully, Feke, Healy, Rembrandt Peale, Charles Wilson Peale, and other early American painters; many paintings by Charles B. King.

Exhibitions: Bi-monthly exhibits of prints, bindings and rare books.

Income and Purchases: Income $103,000; purchases $14,000 (books).

PAWTUCKET

SLATER MILL HISTORIC SITE
Roosevelt Ave, P.O. Box 727, 02860. Tel: (401) 725-8638
Dr. Patrick M. Malone, Dir.
Gary Kulik, Cur.
Open June 1 - Sept. 5 Tues. - Sat. 10 AM - 5 PM; Sun. 1 - 5 PM; Sept. 6 - May 31 Mon. - Fri. group reservations only; Sat. and Sun. 1 - 5 PM; admis. adults $1.50, children (6-14 yr.) 75¢. Estab. 1955 for historic and educational purposes. The Museum of Early American Crafts and Industry is owned and administered by the Old Slater Mill Association. Ann. meeting June; mem. 650; dues $10 and higher.

The site now consists of three buildings. The museum shows early textile machines, reproductions of early cotton mill equipment, paintings, prints, and photographs.

Attendance: Approx 30,000.

The Slater Mill
The cotton mill built in 1793 by Samuel Slater, was restored in 1925. On the first floor there is an exhibit of early cotton machines illustrating each step in the process of turning a blae of cotton into finished cloth. Many machines, dating from 1775 to 1920, are demonstrated for visitors. On the second floor, there is an exhibit developed through a grant from the National Endowment for the Humanities illustrating the home manufacture of cloth from 1790-1840, which displays the collection of hand looms, spinning wheels, and early 19th century implements for the processing of flax and wool. Gift Shop.

The Wilkinson Mill
Built in 1810, this stone building contains a recreation of a working machine shop of the mid-nineteenth century period, on the very site of one of the earliest machine shops in New England, with the old shafts and belts powering a variety of machine-tools dating from 1825 to 1875.

The Sylvanus Brown House
Built in 1758 and recently moved to this site, restored and furnished in strict accordance with an inventory made in 1824, this house is a rare example of life at home in an urban-industrial community of the early 19th century.

PROVIDENCE

DAVID WINTON BELL GALLERY
Brown University, List Art Building, 64 College St, 02912.
Tel: (401) 863-2421
Kermit Champa, Chmn.
Nancy Versaci, Cur.
Open exhibitions only, Mon. - Fri. 11 AM - 4 PM; Sat, Sun. & holidays 2 - 5 PM; no admis. Estab. 1971 to present exhibitions of interest to students and other members of the community; endowment.

Collections: Approx. 1000 prints and works by several major contemporary artists.

Exhibitions: (1973-74) Images and Words; American Paintings in the Rhode Island Historical Society Collection; Quilt Raising; The Brown Art Department Collects; (1974-75) Henry Moore, Prints from the Collection of Giles A. Abroux; Drawings for Krazy Kat Cartoons; Hans Hoffman-Works on Paper; Brown Faculty Exhibition; Rubenism; Goldberger Exhibition - James Carpenter, Italo Scanga, Duff Schweninger, Willoughby Sharp, Miles Varner; French Drawings and Watercolors from the Collection of the Museum of Art, R.I.S.D.; various student exhibitions.

Activities: Lectures open to public; 5 visiting lecturers per year.

✠MUSEUM OF ART
Rhode Island School of Design
224 Benefit St, 02903. Tel: (401) 331-3507
Bayard Ewing, Chmn. Board of Trustees
Dr. Lee Hall, Pres.
Houghton P. Metcalf, Jr, Chmn. Museum Council
Dr. Stephen E. Ostrow, Dir.
Diana L. Johnson, Acting Chief Cur./Assoc. Cur. Prints & Drawings
Elizabeth T. Casey, Cur. Aldrich Collection & Cur. Oriental Art
Eleanor A. Fayerweather, Cur. Costume Center
Dr. Patricia Mandel, Visiting Cur. American Painting
R. Ross Holloway, Consultant Cur. Antiquities
Cora Lee Gibbs, Cur. Educ.
Susan S. Lukesh, Assoc, Cur. Antiquities
Carol C. Sanderson, Asst. Cur. American Painting
Sheila K. Smith, Prog./Publ.
Sofia W. Vervena, Head, Exten. Service & Mgr. Museum Shop
Elmina M. Malloy, Registrar
Catharine S. Lantz, Mem. Secy.
Open Sun. and holidays, 2 - 5 PM; Tues. - Sat. 11 AM - 5 PM; cl. Mon, Jan. 1, July 4, Thanksgiving, Christmas and Aug; admis. adults 19 and over $1, children 5-18 25¢, no charge to members or children fours years and under; groups of ten and over will be charged half price; free Sat. Rhode Island School of Design estab. and inc. 1877 to collect and exhibit art for general education of the public; present buildings opened in 1897, 1906 and 1926. Biannual meeting of governing board in Nov. and May; Museum mem. 3180; dues family $25, single $15, students and faculty $10.

Collections: Ancient, Oriental and ethnographic art; 15th through 18th century European art; †19th and early 20th century French art from Romanticism through Post-Cubism; American painting; English watercolors; †contemporary graphic arts; Lucy Truman Aldrich Collection of European Porcelains and Oriental Textiles; Abby Aldrich Rockefeller Collection of Japanese Bird and Flower Prints; †Nancy Sayles Day Collection of Modern Latin American Art; †The Albert Pilavin Collection of 20th Century American Art, the Pendleton House Collection (18th century American furniture and decorative arts). A Costume Center and a Prints and Drawings Cabinet are open to the public by appointment.

Exhibitions: Due to the installation of an atmospheric control system begun in the Fall of 1974, the Museum will not be scheduling any further special exhibitions until the work is completed in the Spring of 1976. While selections from all areas of the nucleus collection should be available during this period, a call in advance to the Museum is suggested.

Activities: Lending exhibition of slide units and objects from the Museum Resources Program; slide lectures, gallery talks, concerts, poetry readings, adult and childrens courses; tours. Museum Shop.

Library: 52,072 volumes.

Publications: Museum Notes (Selection Series), published each April; Calendar of Events (5); brochures, catalogs.

Attendance: 85,000.

PROVIDENCE ART CLUB

11 Thomas St, 02903. Tel: (401) 331-1114
Walter G. Ensign, Pres.
John W. Steere, Secy.
Marilyn L. Poland, Club Secy.
Marjory Dalenius, Gallery Secy.
Gallery free Mon. - Fri. 10 AM - 4 PM; Sun. 3 - 5 PM. Estab. 1870 and inc. 1880 for art culture. Financed by membership. Gallery is two rooms of an historic building built in 1790. Ann. meeting first Wed. in June; mem. 837; dues artist $80, non-artist $130. Owns clubhouse.

Collections: Permanent collection of paintings.

Exhibitions: Annual exhibition of members' work, changed every two weeks, Oct. - June; 3 open shows each season.

Activities: Lectures for members only; 20 visiting lecturers per year; dramatic programs; classes for adults; competitions; scholarships.

Attendance: 4320.

PROVIDENCE ATHENAEUM

251 Benefit St, 02903. Tel: (401) 421-6970
Edward O. Handy, Jr, Pres.
Peter Hewitt, Secy.
Free 8:30 AM - 5:30 PM; cl. Sun. & holidays.

The Providence Library, estab. 1753, and the Providence Athenaeum, estab. 1831, were united and chartered 1836; building opened 1838. Ann. meeting Sept. Collection of portraits and miniatures including The Hours by Malbone. Publishes Bulletin 2 to 3 times a year. Book collection, 150,000 volumes.

PROVIDENCE PUBLIC LIBRARY

150 Empire St, 02903. Tel: (401) 521-7722
F. Charles Taylor, Librn.
Susan Waddington, Head, Art & Music Dept.
Free Mon. - Tues. 8:30 AM - 9 PM; Wed. - Thurs. 8:30 AM - 6 PM; Fri. - Sat. 8:30 AM - 5 PM; cl. Sun. Estab. 1878. Art Department has about 35,000 books on art, 160,000 loose pictures, over 200 posters, and reproductions for loan. Continuous exhibitions, changed bimonthly. Library material and loan exhibitions.

Collections: †Architecture, †jewelry, photographs of Rhode Island Mill Village architecture; collection of circulating reproductions and posters.

Income and Purchases: Income $1,400,000; purchases for art $4250.

PROVIDENCE WATER COLOR CLUB

6 Thomas St, 02903.
Barbara Green, Pres.
Leslie Swuift, V.Pres.
A. E. S. Peterson, Secy.
Robert Pomfret, Treas.
Rose D. Roman, Asst. Treas.
Open Tues. - Fri. 12:30 - 3:30 PM; Sun. 3 - 5 PM; during exhibitions 1 - 3 PM. Estab. 1898. Ann. meeting Mar; mem. 230; dues $15.

Collections: Small collection of paintings and drawings by early members; prints and paintings by contemporary members.

Exhibitions: Annual exhibition of members' works; Annual Christmas exhibition; Annual Print Show; Annual Open Juried National Show; six or more one-man exhibitions per year.

Activities: Lectures; slide lectures; demonstrations.

THE RHODE ISLAND HISTORICAL SOCIETY

52 Power St, 02906. Tel: (401) 331-8575
Duncan Hunter Mauran, Pres.
Bradford Swan, Secy.
Albert T. Klyberg, Dir.
Nancy Peace, Librn.
Richard K. Showman, Ed, Nathanael Greene Papers
Admis. adults $1.50, students 50¢. Estab. 1822 to preserve, collect and interpret Rhode Island historical materials, including books, manuscripts, graphics, films, furniture and decorative arts; financed by endowment, city and state appropriation and membership. Ann. meeting Jan; mem. 2500; dues $15 and higher.

Exhibitions: American Paintings in the Rhode Island Historical Society.

Activities: Childrens tours; 10,000 prints for reference and copying; lectures open to the public, 4-6 visiting lecturers per year;

4-6 gallery talks; tours; concerts; film programs; classes for adults and children. Book Shop.

Publications: Rhode Island History, quarterly; The John Brown House Loan Exhibition of Rhode Island furniture; American Paintings in the Rhode Ialand Historical Society (catalog); Nathanael Greene Papers; occasional monographs; bimonthly newsletter.

Purchases: Largely through donations.
John Brown House (1786)
52 Power St, 02906.
Open Tues. - Fri. 11 AM - 4 PM; weekends 2 - 4 PM. Estab. 1942, carefully restored and furnished with fine examples of Rhode Island heritage. Guided tours for groups or individuals are available.

Collections: †Pieces by Rhode Island cabinetmakers, some original to the house; †portraits; †china, †glass, †pewter, and †other decorative objects; Rhode Island furniture, silver, porcelain, paintings, textiles; Carrington Collection of Chinese export objects; McCrellis Collection of antique dolls; Greene Collection of childrens' tea sets and dishes.

Attendance: 5000.
The Historical Society Library
121 Hope St, 02906.
Open Tues. - Sat. 9 AM - 5 PM; June, July and Aug. Mon. - Fri. 9 AM - 5 PM; admis $1 per day, $5 for four months. Estab. as a research library housing an outstanding historical and genealogical collection.

Collection: †1000 manuscripts, dating from 17th century; †Rhode Island imprints, 1727-1800; †Rhode Island Broadsides; †Providence Postmaster Provisional Stamps; †Rhode Island post office covers; †genealogical sources; all state newspapers; maps; films, TV news films and movies; graphics; architectural drawings; 20,000 photographs and 200,000 volumes for reference.

Attendance: 9000.
Aldrich House and Gardens
110 Benevolent St, 02906.
Garden open May - Sept. Fri. 1 - 4 PM. Aldrich House was acquired in 1974 and is being developed as a museum of Rhode Island history. Will open to the public in late 1976.

SAUNDERSTOWN

GILBERT STUART MEMORIAL, INC.

Gilbert Stuart Rd, 02874. Tel: (401) 294-3001
Mrs. C. Gordon MacLeod, Pres.
Mrs. Wallace Campbell, 1st V.Pres
Edward F. Hindle, Recording Secy.
Mrs. Henry L. P. Beckwith, Corresp. Secy.
Alice D. Greene, Treas.
A. E. Cummings, Cur.
Open summer daily 11 AM - 5 PM; winter 11 AM - 4 PM; cl. Fri; admis. adults $1, children 25¢.

A national historic landmark, estab. 1930, inc. 1940 to restore and preserve Gilbert Stuart's birthplace, built 1751; intact is an 18th century Snuff Mill and Grist Mill. Ann. meeting 3rd Sat. in July; mem. approx. 250; dues $2 to $5. Small collection of photographs of Gilbert Stuart paintings, period furniture. Guided tours of the house.

Attendance: 13,000.

WARWICK

RHODE ISLAND JUNIOR COLLEGE ART DEPARTMENT GALLERY

Knight Campus, 400 East Ave, 02886. Tel: (401) 825-1000
Rita C. Lepper, Chmn.
Open Mon. - Fri. 8 AM - 4 PM. Estab. 1960 to exhibit local artists.

Exhibitions: Exhibitions are changed monthly.

Activities: Original objects of art lent; 300 color reproductions, 200 photographs, 10,000 Kodachromes, 15 motion pictures, 20 film strips and 200 clippings/small prints in lending collection; lectures open to the public. Book Shop. Library. (See Schools)

Providence Branch
235A Promenade St, Providence, 02908. Tel: (401) 331-5500
Blackstone Valley Campus
Louisquisset Pike, Lincoln, 02865.

WARWICK ARTS FOUNDATION

P.O. Box 726, Pilgrim Station, 02920. Tel: (401) 942-2399
Doris Halloway Arlen, Pres.
Bernadette Messa, Admin. Asst.
Estab. 1963 as a non-profit organization which promotes and fosters programs related to music, art, theatre and dance within the city of Warwick, Rhode Island; financed by city and state appropriations and memberships. Ann. meeting April.

Exhibitions: Festival of the Arts, 1973; F. Roten Galleries Exhibition, 1975.

Activities: 1 Lecture; 7 programs.

Publications: Art calendar, quarterly.

Income and Purchases: Income $3500; purchases approx. $4500.

Attendance: 10,000.

WESTERLY

WESTERLY ARTS COUNCIL
Box 131, 02891.
Jillian Barber, Pres.
Mrs. H. L. DeVore, Secy.
Frederick Eckel, Jr, V.Pres.
Mrs. Victor Orsinger, Treas.
Jane Perry, Corresponding Secy.
Estab. 1968 to sponsor, promote, encourage and coordinate artistic and cultural activities in the area; financed by some state appropriations and membership. Ann. meeting first Wed. of June; mem. 120; dues $5.
    Activities: Sponsor exhibits; provide arts and crafts lessons; workshops to school children, adults and the elderly; lectures open to the public; concerts; dramatic programs.
    Income: Dues, grants plus performance revenues.

WESTERLY PUBLIC LIBRARY
Broad St, 02891. Tel: (401) 596-2877
Ardis S. Moorhead, Dir.
Free 9 AM - 9 PM; Sat. 9 AM - 5:30 PM. Estab. 1894.
    Collections: Permanent collection of paintings, chiefly 19th century American; lustreware collection; mineral collection; Civil War Relics; library art collection contains approx. †10,000 items including Charles H. Davis Memorial Collection of books; †1200 classified museum objects; John Francis Brines Collection of small bronzes.
    Exhibitions: Exhibits changed monthly in Art Gallery.

SOUTH CAROLINA

CHARLESTON

THE CHARLESTON MUSEUM
121 Rutledge Ave, 29401. Tel: (803) 722-2996
Arthur M. Wilcox, Pres.
Robert L. Clement, Jr, Secy.
Donald G. Herold, Dir.
Albert E. Sanders, Cur. of Natural History
J. Kenneth Jones, Cur. of Decorative Arts
Mrs. Edward Webb, Cur. Historic Houses
Allen Liss, Cur, Anthropology
Daniel Johnson, Cur. Educ.
James Carter, Registrar
Nancy Hackney, Librn.
Open Mon. - Sat. 9 AM - 5 PM; Sun. 1 - 5 PM; admis. adults $1, children 50¢. Estab. 1773 as an educational institution, collects, preserves and uses artifacts of natural history, history, anthropology, and decorative arts; oldest museum in Western Hemisphere; financed by endowment, city and state appropriations and memberships. Exhibit halls, permanent and temporary, period rooms and 2 historic houses. Ann. meeting Feb; mem. 1000; dues $12.50 single, $18 family.
    Collections: †Furniture; †Silver; china; glass; †textiles; †prints.
    Exhibitions: Lion Rugs from Fars; Archaeological Excavations at the Heyward-Washington House.
    Activities: Material available to schools; no fees; traveling exhibitions organized and circulated; lending collection, photographs, ethnology and natural history objects; 250 items lent in an average year; lectures open to the public; 12 visiting lecturers per year; 700 tours; classes for adults and children. Book shop.
    Library: 30,000 volume reference library; photograph collection; mainly reference.
    Publications: Members Newsletter.
    Income: $190,000
    Attendance: 225,000.
Heyward-Washington House
    87 Church St, 29401.
Open daily 10 AM - 5 PM. Home of Thomas Heyward, Jr, signer of the Declaration of Independence, temporary residence of George Washington while visiting in 1791. Contains a superb collection of Charleston made furniture. A National Landmark.

Joseph Manigault House
    350 Meeting St, 29401.
Adam style planter mansion designed by architect, Gabriel Manigault, and built in 1803. A National Landmark.

Hunley Museum
    Church and Broad Sts, 29401.
Free daily 10 AM - 5 PM. Building dates to 1798, houses display of Charleston Civil War naval history.

⚓GIBBES ART GALLERY
Carolina Art Association
    135 Meeting St, 29401. Tel: (803) 722-0133
O. Johnson Small, Pres.
Col. D. D. Nicholson, 1st V.Pres.

Mrs. C. E. Graham Reeves, Secy.
C. Stuart Dawsin, Jr, Treas.
William C. Coleman, Dir.
Mrs. Leo J. Manske, Cur. of Collections
Mrs. Elio Leby, Supt. Gallery School
Open Tues. - Sat. 10 AM - 5 PM; Sun. 2 - 5 PM; small admis. for non-members. Estab. 1857, inc. 1858. Gallery built from the James S. Gibbes bequest; opened 1905. It is managed by the Carolina Art Association which is assisted with funds from city and county of Charleston. Ann. meeting Oct; mem. 2300; dues $15 and higher.
    Collections: Paintings, sculpture, graphics, and miniature portraits; American art; strongest in 18th and 19th century American Art.
    Exhibitions: Monthly exhibitions of national, international and regional art.
    Activities: Films, lectures, concerts; art classes for adults and children; gallery tours and outside presentations for schools and other groups.
    Library: 2295 volumes on fine arts
    Income and Purchases: Income $150,000; purchase approx. $5000.
    Attendance: 50,000

CLEMSON

⚓RUDOLPH E. LEE GALLERY
College of Architecture, Clemson University, 29631.
    Tel: (803) 656-3081
Harlan E. McClure, Dean
Tom Dimond, Coordinator of Educational Media & Exhibits
Free Mon. - Fri. 9 AM - 4:30 PM; Sun. 2 - 5 PM. Estab. 1956 to provide cultural and educational resources; to collect, preserve, interpret and display items of historical, educational and cultural significance; supported by appropriation.
    Collections: Contemporary American paintings and graphics; †Clemson Architectural Foundation Collection.
    Exhibitions: (1973-75) Foundry Art; James Mills, Paintings; Charles Warren Callister, Architecture; Semester review of student work; Mt. Angel Library, Photographs; John Kehoe, Sculpture; Student Exhibit; 4 Craftsmen from East Carolina; Mercer College faculty; Bruce Miletto, Paintings; Poems and Fibers, Weaving; 1974 Architectural Thesis Projects; Robert Church Memorial Traveling Exhibit, Architecture; Pueblo Pottery of New Mexico; Clemson Art Faculty; Bernard Freemesser, Photographs; Springs Mills Traveling Art Show 1974; Student Exhibit; Dismantling of a landmark, Architecture; South Carolina Arts Commission Invitational Exhibit; Graphic work of the Vienna Secession; F. Clark Stewart, Drawings ASLA Awards Traveling Exhibit; Herb Jackson, Paintings. Prints; Suzanne Davis, Recent Tapestries; Phil and Sharon Whitley, Sculpture; Dan Brown, M.F.A. Thesis Exhibit; Thesis Projects and Student work from College of Architecture, Clemson Architectural Foundation Permanent Collection; Louise Nevelson, Prints; Harris and Ros Barron, Paintings, Sculpture.
    Activities: Extension work in the Southeast; Material available to museums, universities, etc, fees where necessary; traveling exhibits organized and circulated; individual paintings and objects of art; approx. 400 items lent per year, 8-10 borrowers; photograph and slide collection for reference; lectures open to public, 12-15 visiting lecturers per year; 20-25 gallery talks and tours.
    Library: 10,000 volumes for reference; 38,000 slides; 200 periodical titles; art and architecture rare book room.
    Publications: Annual Exhibition Bulletin; Monthly Posters on Exhibits; exhibit catalogs.
    Attendance: 20,000.

COLUMBIA

⚓COLUMBIA ART ASSOCIATION
Senate & Bull Sts, 29201. Tel: (803) 799-2810
Dr. J. R. Craft, Dir.
Ambrose G. Hampton, Jr, Pres.
Mrs. Richard C. Slocum, Secy.
    Estab. 1916. Ann. meeting last Thurs. in Jan; mem. 1800; dues $15 and higher. Operating agent for the Columbia Museum of Art. Lectures; exhibitions; concerts; films; art reference library.

⚓COLUMBIA MUSEUM OF ART
Senate & Bull Sts, 29201. Tel: (803) 799-2810
Ambrose G. Hampton, Jr, M.D, Pres.
Edwin H. Cooper, Museum Commission Chmn.
Mrs. Richard C. Slocum, Secy.
John Richard Craft, Dir.
John S. Davis, Asst. Dir.
Sarah A. Cahill, Exec. Secy.
David Van Hook, Cur.
F. Edward Barnwell, Registrar

Ruth Sutton, Business Mgr.
Cassandra Baker, Educational Coordinator
Christopher H. Craft, Science Head
William Lazarus, Planetarium Dir.
J. Bardin, Art School Supv.
Free. Tues. - Sat. 10 AM - 5 PM; Sun. 2 - 6 PM; cl. Mon. Estab.
and opened 1950 to extend art understanding, to assist in the conservation of a valuable cultural heritage, and to recognize and assist
contemporary art expression. Ann. meeting Jan; mem. 2000; dues
single $15, family $25 and higher. Science Museum opened Jan. 1960
to correlate youth activities in the natural history and physical sciences.
    Collections: Samuel H. Kress Collection of Italian Renaissance
paintings; Chinese calligraphy; Seibels Collection; Barringer Collection; †contemporary art; Hammond Collection, Spanish Colonial Collection; Neuhoff Collection of English Furniture; Erin Kohn Doll
Collection; †European and American paintings and interior arts.
    Exhibitions: (1975-76) Folk Art in America: A Living Tradition;
Retrospective Survey of Paintings by William de Leftwich Dodge;
Sculpture by Jane Armstrong; Graphics/Spain '74; Survey of Painting
by Frederick Frieske; Silver Anniversary Exhibits; An American
Impressionist: Paintings by Gertrude Fiske; Rosenthal Porcelain
Placques; Recent Paintings by Barkley L. Hendricks; Seth Eastman's
Mississippi; American Watercolor Society; Americana Collection of
C. Thomas May; America's First Architect: Robert Mills; British
Silver; African Art; Notable Women of South Carolina; Photography
by Constantine Manos and others.
    Activities: Art and science lectures; demonstrations; decorative
art seminars; concerts; dramas; touring exhibitions to statewide
colleges; film study groups; and correlated educational activities.
    Library: Reference library of 3500 art books and current art
periodicals; slide collection and film strip library.
    Publications: Monthly News; Annual Report; exhibit catalogs.
    Income: Operations budget $335,000.
    Attendance: 150,000.

GUILD OF SOUTH CAROLINA ARTISTS
    1112 Bull St, 29201.
Dr. Diane Chalmers Johnson, Pres.
Edwin Ritts, Jr, Pres. Elect
Bette Lee Coburn, V.Pres.
Steven A. Jordan, Secy./Treas.
Sally Cahill, Admin. Asst.
Estab. 1951 for the purpose of promoting the visual arts in South
Carolina; programs, workshops, newsletter, annual juried exhibit
supported by membership. Ann. meeting approx. Nov. 1; mem. 400;
dues assoc $5, active $10, patron $25, commercial patron $50.
    Exhibitions: Annual exhibition, juried, by members; rotates from
Columbia Museum of Art, Greenville County Museum of Art, Florence
Museum of Art, and Gibbes Art Gallery in Charleston; host gallery
receives purchase award ($1000 annual purchase award).
    Activities: Workshops, programs; photograph collection of award
winner and work from annual exhibition; lectures open to the public,
one or two visiting lecturers per year; competitions.
    Publications: Brochure; annual membership directory.
    Income: (1974) $8,906.

SOUTH CAROLINA ARTS COMMISSION
    829 Richland St, 29201. Tel: (803) 758-3442
Rick George, Exec. Dir.
Open Mon. - Fri. 8:30 AM - 5 PM. Estab. 1967 as a state agency
designed to promote and develop the arts in South Carolina. Financed
by state and federal appropriations and private funds. The agency
has three programming divisions: arts-in-education, contemporary
arts, and professional arts development.
    Art Truck: A mobile arts studio equipped for classes and
experimentation in painting, drawing, printmaking, filmmaking,
photography, and video arts. The truck conducts 26 two-week
residencies throughout the state each year.
    Crafts Truck: Similar in operation to the Art Truck, the crafts
unit is equipped for classes and workshops in folk arts and crafts
native to South Carolina: pottery, basketweaving, jewelrymaking,
glassblowing, etc.
    State Art Collection: A collection of paintings, drawings, crafts,
and graphics by native and resident South Carolina artists. With
over 100 art works, the collection tours the state as a traveling
exhibit.
    Artists-in-the-Schools: Sends visual and performing artists into
South Carolina schools to work side by side with students and teachers.
This very popular program involves poets, actors, filmmakers and
visual artists.
    Publications: Quarterly arts magazine about the arts in South
Carolina and the activities of the South Carolina Arts Commission.
    Grants: The Commission awards approx. $165,000 each year in
grants to local arts organizations and individual artists.

FLORENCE

FLORENCE MUSEUM
    Spruce at Graham St, 29501. Tel: (803) 662-3351
Richard S. Wallace, Pres.
William A. Burns, Dir.
Lynn Robertson Myers, Cur.
Free Tues. - Sat. 10 AM - 5 PM; Sun. 2 - 5 PM; cl. major holidays.
Estab. 1924, inc. 1936, to collect, preserve, and exhibit cultural and
natural history; maintained by appropriation and membership.
Twelve galleries for permanent collection and separate curatorial
facility. Ann. meeting Spring; mem. 500; dues $5.
    Collections: World Art—African, internationally important ex-
amples of 19th century sculpture (20), weapons (15); Ancient, small
collection of outstanding Egyptian, Babylonian and Greco-Roman
sculpture (15) plus numerous classical artifacts (200); American
Indian, Pueblo ceramics (70) and jewelry (30), Central American
textiles (50), others (100); Oceanic (20); Oriental, Chinese ceramics (T'ang-Ch'ing 100), costumes (75), Japanese (20), Korean (5),
other (20); 20th century paintings (40), other (50); American furniture (20), paintings (40), other (200); †European, tapestries (2),
ceramics (20), furniture (5), painting and sculpture (30). Local history (200) and natural history (30), primarily works of visual significance.
    Exhibitions: Rotate collection; recent acquisitions; loan. Limited
to collecting, preserving, exhibiting, and a publications program.
    Publications: Bimonthly newsletter, occasional papers.
    Income: $46,000.
    Attendance: (1973-74) 19,000.

GREENVILLE

BOB JONES UNIVERSITY MUSEUM AND ART GALLERY
    29614. Tel: (803) 242-5100
Dr. Bob Jones, Chmn. of the Board
Joan Davis, Dir.
Kathy Pflug, Restorer/Conservator
Free Sept. through May, Tues. - Sat. 1 - 5 PM; Sun. 1:30 - 5 PM;
June through Aug. and Christmas vacation, Tues. - Sun. 2 - 4 PM;
cl. Mon, July 4, Christmas Eve, Christmas Day, New Year's Eve,
New Year's Day. The Bowen Collection of Biblical Antiquities was
presented to the University by Mr. and Mrs. Frank Bowen in 1942.
The permanent sacred art collection was begun by Dr. Bob Jones,
Chancellor of Bob Jones University, and was opened to the public
with the completion of the University Museum and Art Gallery building
in 1951. Termed one of the most remarkable collections of famous
religious paintings in the world, the gallery was opened for the
purpose of showing how universal is the Word of God in its appeal
to human hearts in every generation.
    Collections: Bowen Collection of Biblical Antiquities and Illustra-
tive Material, including artifacts from Palestine, Syria, Lebanon,
Egypt, and Jordan; Bob Jones University Collection of Sacred Art,
including only religious art by the Old Masters from the 13th through
the 19th centuries, and numbering works by such artists as Botticelli,
Tintoretto, Veronese, del Piombo, Rubens, Van Dyck, Rembrandt,
Titian, Cranach the Elder, G. David, Reni, Gentileschi, Domenichino,
Ribera, Murillo, Zurbaran; furniture and sculpture.
    In 1963 Bob Jones University acquired, for its War Memorial
Chapel, a series of important paintings on Revealed Religion by
Benjamin West. These were originally executed for King George
III, to be placed in his new Chapel at Windsor Castle. Because of the
illness of the King, plans for the construction of the Chapel were
abandoned and the completed paintings were returned to the painter.
The posthumous sale of West's works, in 1829, included a number of
the pictures on Revealed Religion. Joseph Neeld, M.P, was the successful bidder, and the pictures hung in his home until 1962. At that
time, they were offered for sale by Christie's of London. Six were
acquired for the Bob Jones University with funds provided for that
purpose by an anonymous friend of the University.
    Activities: Gallery talks; illustrated talks to schools and other
groups; special lectures; special exhibits for children. (See Schools).
    Publications: Catalogues; illustrated booklets.
    Attendance: 29,291.

GREENVILLE COUNTY MUSEUM OF ART
    420 College St, 29601. Tel: (803) 271-7570
Russell A. Graham, Chmn.
Jack A. Morris, Jr, Exec. Dir.
Edwin Ritts, Jr, Chief Cur.
Caryl C. Palmer, Admin. Asst.
Martha Gray, Business Mgr.
Sylvia L. Marchant, Assoc. Dir. Educ.
Georgia Prease, Educ. Asst.
Sharon Whitley, Assoc. Dir. Museum School of Art
Ken Howie, Assoc. Dir. Electragraphics
Free Mon. - Sat. 10 AM - 4 PM; Sun. 1 PM - 5 PM. Art Association
estab. 1945, Museum estab. previous building in 1958 and new 56,000

square foot facility in March 1974, to provide by means of exhibitions, lectures, classes, etc., a broad program in the visual arts which will be both educational and stimulating. Ann. meeting June; mem. 1200; dues $10 and higher.

Collections: North American with special emphasis on contemporary painters, sculptors and printmakers.

Exhibitions: Organized special exhibitions of private, corporate and foundation collections. Other exhibitions include state and local competitions, one-man shows, and traveling exhibitions from Smithsonian Institution, Museum of Modern Art and The American Federation of Arts.

Activities: Operates Museum School of Art (See Schools); Education Department; Sales Department; Southeastern Regional Conservation Laboratory; complete color television production studios known as Electragraphics Department; maintains a cooperative relationship with county art reference library, next door; presents lectures; classes for adults and children.

Purchases: $10,000.
Attendance: 108,000.

GREENWOOD

THE MUSEUM
Phoenix St, P.O. Box 3131, 29646. Tel: (803) 229-4700
I. G. Wooten, Pres.
Dr. R. J. Lund, Secy.
J. W. Durst, Cur.
Free daily 9 AM - 5 PM; Sun. 2 - 5 PM; cl. Sat. Estab. 1967; through the eyes of a general museum, an effort to bring a new cultural element to the area; closest other museum about 75 miles; financed by membership. Quarterly meetings; mem. 400.

Library started.
Attendance: 10,000.

MURRELLS INLET

BROOKGREEN GARDENS
Murrells Inlet, 29576. Tel: Pawleys Island (803) 237-4657
C. Paul Jennewein, Pres.
A. Hyatt Mayor, 1st V.Pres.
Joseph V. Noble, 2nd V.Pres.
Michael Rapuano, Treas.
Eric S. Malm, Secy.
Gurdon L. Tarbox, Jr, Dir.
Open daily 9:30 AM - 4:45 PM; ground cleared at 5:30 PM; cl. Christmas Day. Estab. and inc. 1931 to exhibit and preserve flora and fauna of the Southeast, and to collect and present a museum of American Sculpture, chiefly shown out-of-doors; 380 pieces presently exhibited.

Library: Books and periodicals relating to subjects for which Brookgreen Gardens was established.

Publications: Catalogs, folders, photographs and postcards of the collections.

Attendance: 175,000.

SPARTANBURG

THE ARTS COUNCIL OF SPARTANBURG COUNTY, INC.
385 South Spring St, 29301. Tel: (803) 583-2776
Mrs. Charles N. Gignilliat, Pres.
Georgia Allen, Exec. Dir.
Open Mon. - Fri. 9 AM - 5 PM; Sat. - Sun; 2 - 4 PM. Estab. Nov. 1968 to coordinate all cultural activities in the Spartanburg area. The Arts Council acts as a chamber of commerce for its 29 affiliates, and is completely supported by donations. Two large galleries downstairs, with additional gallery space upstairs. Sponsor changing exhibits from Sept. - June. The member organizations are open for membership at varied yearly dues. Ann. meeting Mar; mem. 6000.

Collections: Small collection of work by Southeastern artists of note, all donated by the artists to the Council.

Exhibitions: Shows have included Charles Parks, Ireland Regnier, Thomas Engles, etc. Group shows by the Artists' Guild of Spartanburg, and students and teachers from the Art Association classes.

Activities: Art classes for adults and children (any class will be offered for 10 or more interested students); classes in puppetry, make-up, creative dramatics, mime, and dance for pre-school through adults; ticket sales for the Spartanburg Concert Series, Little Theatre, Youth Theatre, Ballet Guild, etc.

Publications: Bimonthly cultural arts calendar listing events in the Spartanburg area.

Yearly Budget: $60,000.
Attendance: Over 25,000.

THE GALLERY
385 S. Spring St, 29301. Tel: (803) 582-7616
Mrs. Jacky Dietrich, Chmn.
Sharon McCullough, Treas.

Mary Schweder, Cur.
Open Sept. - July, Mon. - Fri. 10 AM - 5 PM. Estab. 1969 to promote work of artists through showing and offering for sale their art work, to bring to the public the best work that is being produced nationally. A non-profit organization staffed daily by volunteers, financed by the Spartanburg County Foundation and by the Spartanburg County Art Association, for which The Gallery is the major project.

Exhibitions: Since opening the work of such distinguished artists as Jean McWhorter of Columbia, Darell Koons of Greenville, Betty Jane Branlett of Spartanburg, Dr. Leo Twiggs of Orangeburg, Arthur Rose of Orangeburg, Bette Lee Coburn of Greenville, Sallie Middleton of Asheville, and Elizabeth O'Neill Verner of Charleston has been shown. In addition, other noted North Carolina & Georgia artists have presented successful exhibitions at the Gallery. There are 9 one-man shows every year.

Activities: Tours and gallery talks by appointment; Sponsors annual purchase award exhibit for Spartanburg Bank & Trust Company, a purchase award for First Citizens Bank & Trust; Assists other local banks and organizations with purchases and sponsors occasional cash award design competitions for local firms.

Publications: Newsletters twice a year, others when needed.
Attendance: An average since opening of over 3000 annually.

SUMTER

SUMTER GALLERY OF ART
219 W. Liberty St, 29150. Tel: (803) 755-0543
J. Eugene Matthews, Chmn. Board Dir.
Margaret U. Britt, Gallery Dir.
Free, Tues. - Sun. 3 - 6 PM. Estab. 1970 to bring to this area exhibits of works of recognized artists, to provide an outlet for local artists for the showing and sale of their work, and to serve as a facility where visual art may become a part of the life and education of the people, particularly the children, of this community. Financed by membership plus support from Artists Guild and the South Carolina Arts Commission. Gallery is primarily an exhibiting gallery, each exhibit running for three weeks; our season is from September - May. Ann. meeting March; mem. 230; dues individual $5, family $7.50, patron $25, life $100.

Exhibitions: Individual and group exhibits of paintings, sculpture collages, photography and crafts by well-known artists, primarily from South Carolina and neighboring states; Annual Young People's Exhibit, presenting work of young artists of the local schools.

Activities: Classes for adults and children; competitions.
Publications: Monthly newsletter.
Income: Approx. $4000.
Attendance: 4200 annual average.

SOUTH DAKOTA

BROOKINGS

✤SOUTH DAKOTA MEMORIAL ART CENTER
South Dakota State University, Medary Ave. at Harvey Dunn St, 57006
Robert Carey, Pres.
Mrs. C. L. Ferguson, V.Pres.
C. F. Cecil, Secy-Treas.
Joseph M. Stuart, Dir.
Rex Gulbranson, Asst Dir.
Cora Sivers, Cur.
Geraldine Bushard, Secy.
Free Mon. - Fri. 8 AM - 5 PM, 7 - 10 PM; Sat. 10 AM - 5 PM; Sun. 1 - 5 PM. Estab. 1969 as a center for the arts in South Dakota; state and privately supported. Mem. 200; dues $1 - $1000.

Collections: 60 Harvey Dunn Paintings; 1750 Marghab Linens; 240 pieces in general collection, mainly state and regional art.

Exhibitions: Gaston Lachaise; Howard Pyle; Art of South Dakota; South Dakota Biennial; Northwestern Biennial.

Activities: Films, gallery talks, circulated exhibits, lectures, workshops, art classes; music, dance and dramatic presentations.

Library: 500 volumes for reference; periodicals; slides; Archives of South Dakota Art.

Publications: Quarterly News; exhibition catalogs.
Income and Purchases: Income $60,000; acquisitions $3000.
Attendance: 125,000.

DEADWOOD

DEADWOOD GULCH ART GALLERY
665½ Historic Main St, 57732. Tel: (605) 578-3636
J. D. Sulentic, Pres.
Margaret Sulentic, Secy.

Open 9 AM - 5 PM April - Dec; no admis. Estab. 1967 to display and sell works of art; the gallery is operated in conjunction with a Chinese Museum Tunnel Tour, for which a charge of 25¢ per person is made.

Book shop.

RAPID CITY

DAKOTA ART GALLERY (formerly Civic Art Gallery)
Dakota Artists Guild
Dahl Fine Arts Center, 713 Seventh St, 57701.
Tel: (605) 342-2144
Thomas J. Winn, Dir.
Free Mon. - Sat. 10 AM - 5 PM. Estab. 1965 as Civic Art Gallery by Dakota Artists Guild; financed by membership and public contributions. Approx. 200 mem; dues $10.
Exhibitions: Continuing local exhibits and exhibits of national artists by invitation. All exhibits changed monthly.
Activities: Public lectures, monthly meetings open to public, gallery tours, classes of instruction, scholarships, community art projects.
Publications: Brochure; monthly newsletter
Income: Approx. $38,000 - $40,000.
Attendance: Approx. 5000 - 6000.

SIOUX INDIAN MUSEUM AND CRAFTS CENTER
Box 1504, 57701. Tel: (605) 348-0557
Myles Libhart, Dir. of Museums, Exhibitions & Publ.
Rena McGhan, Cur.
Rosemary Ellison, Supvr, Indian Arts & Crafts Board Museum Prog.
Free June 1 - Sept. 30, Mon. - Sat. 8 AM - 5 PM; Sun. 1 - 5 PM; Sept. 1 - May 31, Tues. - Sat. 10 AM - 5 PM; Sun. 1 - 5 PM; cl. Mon. during Sept. 1 - May 31, New Year's Day, Thanksgiving, Christmas. Estab. 1939; administered and operated by the Indian Arts and Crafts Board, U.S. Dept. of the Interior, U.S. Government.
Collections: Historic and contemporary arts of the Sioux, including †costumes, †decorative arts, †folk arts, †paintings, †sculpture, †graphics.
Exhibitions: Permanent exhibitions of historic and contemporary arts of the Sioux, or Dakota, of the Northern Plains; presents at Museum continuing series of one-person exhibitions of work by contemporary Indian and Eskimo artists and craftsmen of U.S, traveling exhibitions include (1971) Photographs and Poems by Sioux Children, organized by the Museum with state tour under auspices of South Dakota Arts Council and Tipi Shop, Inc; Contemporary Sioux Painting; Contemporary Sioux Quillwork; Contemporary Sioux Quilts.
Activities: Gallery tours for schools and other groups, loans of slide lecture kits to schools.
Sales Shop: Operated by Tipi Shop, Inc, offers a wide variety of authentic contemporary craft products and fine arts by Indian artists and craftsmen of North and South Dakota, Nebraska, Minnesota, Iowa, and other areas.
Publications: One-person exhibition brochure series; Contemporary Sioux Painting, and Photographs and Poems by Sioux Children, published by Tipi Shop, Inc.
Attendance: Average 100,000.

SIOUX FALLS

✠CIVIC FINE ARTS ASSOCIATION
235 W. Tenth St, 57102. Tel: (605) 336-1167
Mrs. H. W. Farrell, Pres.
Mrs. Frank Wallner, Secy.
Raymond Shermoe, Dir.
Free Tues. - Sat. 11:30 AM - 5 PM; Sun. 2 - 5 PM. Estab. Apr, 1961 as a contemporary museum and arts center; financed by membership. Gallery maintained. Ann. meeting June; mem. 12,000; dues $10.
Collections: The Center has acquired 45 original works of art, drawings, prints, paintings, sculpture, by such well-known artists as Amland, Baskin, Buchanan, Bucher, Eide, Fern, Frasconi, Howe, Kudlacek, Martin, Munce, Rembrandt and H. Moore; collection of posters.
Exhibitions: The twelve exhibits offered each year are free to the public; 45,000 visitors view the exhibits of contemporary, historical examples of the visual arts, painting, prints, sculpture and crafts. Recent exhibitions include David Stone Martin; National Small Painters Exhibition; Sioux Quill Work.
Activities; Traveling exhibitions organized and circulated; original objects of art lent; lectures open to public; 7 visiting lecturers per year; 25 gallery talks; 120 tours; classes for adults and children; competitions; workshops; scholarships. Book shop. Library.
Publications: Monthly newsletter
Income and Purchases: Income $32,000; purchases $500.
Attendance: 100,000 (2 years).

SPEARFISH

BLACK HILLS ART CENTER*
Little Gallery, 57783.
Mrs. Harry Henderson, Dir.
Open daily during school hours. Estab. 1936 to encourage art expression and greater appreciation in the Black Hills area. Mem. approx. 500; dues $5 and higher. Work of the Art Center is promoted jointly by Black Hills State College and by the local Chapter of Kappa Pi, National Honorary Art Fraternity, and by Spearfish Paint and Palette Club.
Exhibitions: Local exhibits are quarterly; traveling exhibitions occasionally; annual exhibition for May 15 to June 15; Black Hills Art Exhibit in Student Union.
Activities: Classes for adults, and programs held each semester; summer workshop; traveling exhibitions; summer Art Colony in August, annually.
Library: Approx. 200 art books; Carnegie gift library contains 1000 prints and 150 art books. Films, books and reproductions are being added annually.
Attendance: Approx. 1500.

VERMILLION

COYOTE STUDENT CENTER
University of South Dakota, 57069. Tel: (605) 677-5334
Gerry Gebhart, Arts Chmn.
Mark Stephens, Prog. Dir.
Open Mon. - Thurs. 7 AM - 11 PM; Fri. & Sat. 7 AM - 9 PM. Estab. 1965 to provide students and the university community the opportunity to view and review various types of art and art forms; appropriation from student fees. Gallery maintained.
Activities: Lectures open to public, 1 - 2 visiting lecturers per year; gallery talks or tours; concerts, dramatic programs; limited collection; touring exhibitions.

W. H. OVER MUSEUM
University of South Dakota, 57069. Tel: (605) 677-5228
June Sampson, Dir.
H. Russell Howard, Exhibits Designer
Dr. Oscar Howe, Artist-in-Residence
Free Mon. - Fri. 8 AM - 4:30 PM; Sat. 10 AM - 4:30 PM; Sun. 2 - 4:30 PM.
Collections: Anthropology, art, natural history, history with major emphasis on the North American plains cultures; Oscar Howe studio and gallery; Arne B. Larson musical instrument collection; David Clark Memorial Collection of Plains Indian Ethnology.
Activities: Traveling and loan exhibits; museum techniques training, publication, tours; library; special children's classes; research in Plains Indian culture, lectures, etc.
Attendance: 8500.

YANKTON

DURAND ART COLLECTION OF YANKTON COLLEGE
James Lloyd Library, 57078.
Prof. Jerome E. Gallagher, Cur.
Estab. 1909. †The collection of about 10,000 photographs and color reproductions, chiefly serves the Art Department. A few original paintings, sculpture and prints. Exhibitions frequently changed, are open to students, faculty and townspeople. Occasional lectures for schools and clubs and loan exhibits circulated. College library with comprehensive section on art history.

TENNESSEE

CHATTANOOGA

HOUSTON ANTIQUE MUSEUM
201 High St, 37403. Tel: (615) 267-7176
Mary E. Baker, Dir.
Open Tues. - Sat. 10 AM - 4:30 PM; Sun. 2 - 4:30 PM; cl. Mon. and holidays. Estab. 1961, inc. 1949, collection willed to Chattanooga by the late Mrs. Houston. Ann. meeting Apr. 27; mem. 500; dues person $5, couple $7.50, family $10, life $100.
Collections: Rare collection of glass, porcelains, 15,000 pitchers, Early American furniture; 600 patterns of pressed glass, all types art glass, etc.
Activities: 6 lectures per year; lending library for members; slide program for elementary schools.
Library: Books on antiques.
Publications: The Fabulous Houston.
Income and Purchases: Income fluctuates, no purchases.
Attendance: 10,000.

⊁HUNTER MUSEUM OF ART
Bluff View, 37403   Tel: (615) 267-0968
Scott L. Probasco, Jr, Chmn. of Board
Budd H. Bishop, Dir.
Jean P. Stansell, Business Adminr.
Meredith Davis, Cur. of Educ.
Open Tues. - Sat. 11 AM - 4:30 PM; Sun. 1 - 4:30 PM; cl. Mon;
admis. adults $1.50; children 50¢; Tues. free to all. Estab. 1924;
Museum opened 1952. Ann. meeting May; mem. 1200; dues $15 and
higher. Museum Store for sales and rental.
   Collections: American painting and sculpture, 18th to 20th
centuries; American decorative arts.
   Exhibitions: Approx. 30 changing exhibitions annually, including
eleven-state competition with $2200 in prizes; local Art Festival
and Exhibitions; traveling exhibits in painting, sculpture, photography, architecture, and decorative arts; one-man exhibits by
regional artists.
   Activities: Day and evening classes for adults and high school
students; afternoon and Sat. classes for children; elementary school
education program, lectures; gallery talks, arts festival; film series.
   Library: 600 volume reference library.
   Income and Purchases: Income $250,000; purchases limited.
   Attendance: 100,000, annual estimate.

CLARKSVILLE

MARGARET FORT TRAHERN GALLERY*
   Art Department, Austin Peay State University, 37040.
   Tel: (615) 648-7236
Charles T. Young, Pres.
Lewis B. Burton, Cur.
Free, workdays 9 AM - 3 PM. Estab. 1962 as a university-commu-
nity service to exhibit a variety of visual media from regional professionals and university art majors; financed by university appropriations.
   Collections: Regional artists, primarily watercolors, graphics
and sculpture.
   Exhibitions: Average 8-10 per year.
   Activities: Education and extension department; occasional
faculty travel show; collection, 100 color reproductions, 300 lantern
slides, 17,000 Kodachromes, 8 motion pictures, 19 film strips, items
used at gallery, no loan system; lectures open to the public; 20 visiting lecturers per year; 12 gallery talks; dramatic programs; classes
for adults and children; competitions; scholarships.
   Publications: Announcements of shows and artist biographies,
monthly.
   Purchases: $3000 annual average.
   Attendance: 52 daily average.

GREENEVILLE

GREENEVILLE ARTS GUILD, INC.*
   P.O. Box, 37743.
Mrs. Patt Hurst, First National Bank
   (First National Bank, 37743)
Mrs. Nayland Clark, Secy.
Kyle Boyd, V.Pres.
Mrs. Jesse Musick, 2nd V.Pres.
Christopher Saville, Treas.
Estab. 1968 to sponsor free art service programs for all ages in the
community, its schools and its hospitals (medical and 1500 bed state
hospital and school for the mentally retarded); maintained by mem-
bership. Mem. 300 family and business; dues $10 up.
   Collections: Recently commissioned collection of 34 photographs
by John E. Schrader, Professor of Photography at East Tennessee
State Univ, now being circulated by the Tennessee Arts Commission
as part of its Touring Arts Program.
   Exhibitions: (1972-1973) 25th Anniversary Faculty Show, Univ. of
Tennessee Department of Art; Photography of John Schrader; antique
furniture and accessories (assembled from local sources); Guild
Painters (local students); Area Public School Works (exhibited with
reception).
   Activities: Exhibitions tours by city and county children, slide-
lectures on art history in schools; gifts of art books and reproductions to schools and public library; film program at hospital for
retarded; 34 photographic prints for lending; lectures open to public,
two visiting lectures per year; 4 gallery talks or tours; concerts;
classes for adults and children; Sinking Creek Film Celebration
financially supported; fall gallery dinners preceeding local little
theatre productions; Art Cart; workshop in creative stitchery.
   Publications: Greeneville Arts Guild Newsletter, three yearly.
   Income and Purchases: Income approx. $4000.
   Attendance: 15,000.

JACKSON

JACKSON ART ASSOCIATION*
   38301.
W. J. Tenison, Jr, Pres.
Mrs. Sara O'Neal, Secy.
Gary Jantzen, Treas.
Mrs. Cheri Henderson, V.Pres. Programs
Mrs. Mary Robinson, V.Pres. Publicity
Mrs. Norma Dennison, V.Pres Mem.
Kenneth Grissom, Co-V.Pres Exhibits
Grove Robinson, Co-V.Pres. Exhibits
Estab. 1959 to promote a better understanding and appreciation of
the visual arts among the citizens of Jackson and the surrounding
area; financed by mem. Ann. meeting second Tues. each month;
mem. 70; dues $5.
   Exhibitions: Annual Arts and Crafts Show and Sale.
   Activities: Lectures open to the public; 8-10 gallery talks; schol-
arships.
   Publications: President's News Letter, Monthly.
   Income and Purchases: Approx. 1000.

UNION UNIVERSITY ART GUILD
   Highway 45 Bypass, 38301. Tel: (901) 668-1818
Diane Styers, Pres.
Joy Morris, Secy.
Free 8 - 10 AM. Estab. Sept, 1973 to further art as a beneficial and
needed factor of life; financed by membership; gallery maintained.
Mem. 43; dues $2.
   Collections: Eli Prouty Collections; individual student collections.
   Activities: Lectures for members only; 1 tour per year; concerts,
dramatic programs, competitions.
   Annual Income: $150.

JOHNSON CITY

EAST TENNESSEE STATE UNIVERSITY
⊁Carroll Reece Museum
   37601. Tel: (615) 929-4392 and 929-4283
Harvey A. Dean, Dir.
Helen Roseberry, Registrar.
Audaleen H. McNutt, Museum Secy.
Free Mon. - Fri. 12:45 - 4:45 PM; Sat. - Sun. 1 - 5 PM. Estab. 1964
to enhance the cultural and educational advantages of the University
and the people of Upper East Tennessee. Friends of the Reece Museum annual memberships; purpose of the group is to acquire paintings to be part of the Permanent Collection.
   Collections: 3 permanent exhibitions, Tennessee Frontier Room,
a reconstructed scene of Frontier Life in the latter part of the 18th
century and early 19th century; Reece Room, an exhibition of memorabilia of former U.S. Congressman from Tennessee, B. Carroll
Reece; Music from the Past, a collection of early musical instruments.
   Exhibitions: Three galleries of traveling exhibitions, some rented
and some organized by Museum staff.
   Activities: Musical concerts, film series, educational programs;
meetings, receptions and other activities are carried on during the
year.
   Library: Located on campus as part of the University, approximately 2500 volumes of art literature.
   Purchases: 19th and 20th century art; Appalachian crafts, historical materials of East Tennessee.
   Attendance: 28,000 annually.

Elizabeth Slocum Gallery
   Art Department, 37601. Tel: (615) 929-4292, 929-4247
Dr. D. P. Culp, Pres. of Univ.
Daniel K. Teis, Chmn. Art Dept.
George Moldovan, Dir. Exhibitions
Lloyd Sheets, Cur.
Free daily 8 AM - 5 PM; Sat. 9 - 12 AM. Estab. to augment all the
programs and areas of instruction within the Department of Art and
to foster interest in various modes of artistic expression in the
campus at large.
   Collections: A small teaching collection of prints, paintings, ce-
ramics and weaving. (University collections are located at Reece
Museum. See above).
   Exhibitions: Original and traveling exhibits.
   Activities: Full art education program; courses for credit are
taught at East Tennessee State University branches at Kingsport,
Greenville and Bristol, Tenn; classes for adults and children; schol-
arships and fellowships; frequent lectures, seminars and workshops.
   Attendance: 15,000.

KINGSPORT

KINGSPORT FINE ARTS CENTER
Church Circle, 37660. Tel: (615) 246-9351
James Cochrane, Pres.
Marian Stras, Secy.
Katherine Thomas, Dir.
Debbie Watkins, Secy.
Free weekdays 9 AM - 5 PM; Sat. Noon - 4 PM. Estab. 1968 to promote and present all the arts to all the people in area; this includes performing arts, visual arts, and classes; financed by membership. Ann. meeting May; mem. 548; dues $10, $20, $30, $50, $100, $250.
   Exhibitions: Winslow Homer, Wood Engraver; Man in Sport; 10 Watercolors by Andrew Wyeth; Faces From American Theatre— Original Etchings and Engravings of Al Hirshfeld.
   Activities: Several gallery talks; 5-10 tours; concerts; dramatic programs; classes for adults and children; competitions. Craft Shop.
   Publications: Newsletter, bimonthly.
   Income: $20,000.
   Attendance: 10,000.

KNOXVILLE

✤DULIN GALLERY OF ART
3100 Kingston Pike, 37919. Tel: (615) 525-3100
Earnest B. Rodgers, Pres.
W. R. McNabb, Dir.
Open Tues. - Sun. 1 - 5 PM; admis. 50¢. Estab. 1962. The Gallery is dedicated to the presentation and interpretation of the finest works of art available. The gallery is located in the historic house designed in 1915 for H. L. Dulin by John Russell Pope. Mem. 1200; dues $15 and up.
   Collections: Approx. 200 works, predominately contemporary; graphics; Thorne miniature rooms.
   Exhibitions: Temporary exhibits changing monthly; annual Dulin National Print and Drawing Competition; permanent collections.
   Activities: Lectures; tours conducted for groups when requested in advance.
   Library: Reference library of 200 volumes.
   Publications: Occasional exhibition catalogs; Guide to Dulin House; Thorne Rooms Booklet.
   Purchases: $2400.
   Attendance: 12,000.

FRANK H. McCLUNG MUSEUM
University of Tennessee
1327 Circle Park Dr, 37916. Tel: (615) 974-2144
Alfred K. Guthe, Dir.
Joseph W. Hopkins, Exhibits Coordinator
Elaine A. Evans, Cur. of Collections
Free Mon. - Fri. 9 AM - 5 PM. Estab. 1961 to collect, maintain and interpret paintings, works of art, items of natural history and historical objects. Emphasis is placed on the Tennessee area. A major purpose is to provide research materials for students and faculty of the university; financed by city and state appropriation.
   Collections: Lewis-Kneberg Collection (Tennessee Archaeology); Frederick T. Bonham Collection (18th - 20th century furniture, art objects); Grace Moore Collection (memorabilia of her career 1920's - 40's).
   Exhibitions: Birds: Identification and Documentation; Woman: 2nd World Exhibition of Photography; Southern Highland Handicraft Guild; Baskets of the Western Indians; The Dead Sea Scrolls; The Capture of Solar Heat; Faculty Art Shows, Thesis Exhibitions; Christmas Art Sales; Normal Illinois Faculty Exhibition; American Institute of Graphic Art; National Sculpture; Surrealist Prints from Durer to Dali.
   Activities: Materials available to recognized organizations in the Southeast at no charge; original objects of art lent. approx. 100 prints in photograph collection; lectures open to public; gallery talks; 80 tours; competitions.
   Attendance: 32,500.
Eleanor Dean Audigier Art Collection
Hoskins Library, 1401 Cumberland Ave, 37916.
Tel: (615) 974-2122
Free 15 hours a week. Estab. 1934; financed by state appropriations.
   Collections: The Audigier Collection contains over 800 art objects: 19th century copies of Italian Renaissance paintings, sculpture, furniture and silver; 19th century cameos; Chinese, French and German porcelain; personal jewelry, ivory miniatures; Turkish and Arabic trays; Ancient Egyptian scarabs, shawbtis; Greco-Roman jars and lamps.
   Attendance: 5000.

✤UNIVERSITY OF TENNESSEE ART EXHIBITIONS*
306 University Center, 37916.
Kevin Majut, Dir.

MARYVILLE

MARYVILLE COLLEGE FINE ARTS CENTER GALLERY
37801. Tel: (615) 982-6950
Harry H. Harter, Chmn, Dept. Fine Arts
William H. Swenson, Sr. Art Prof.
Open daily except Sun.
   Ten to twelve traveling exhibitions during college year; art movies four times a year; gallery programs in connection with circulating exhibitions. Paintings of local and visiting artists exhibited twice a year. †Print Collection.

MEMPHIS

✤BROOKS MEMORIAL ART GALLERY
Overton Park, 38112. Tel: (901) 726-5266, 4762
Dr. John J. Whitlock, Dir.
Gail Chumley, Secy. to Dir.
Joseph S. Czestochowski, Cur. of Collections
Diana DuWitt, Cur. Educ.
Judy Taylor, Coordinator Pub. Information
Maurine F. Newell, Registrar
Letitia B. Proctor, Librn.
Henry C. Harris, Chief of Security & Maintenance
Free Tues. - Sat. and holidays 10 AM - 5 PM; Sun. 2 - 5 PM; cl. Mon, New Year's, Thanksgiving, Christmas and Good Friday. Estab. 1914 by gift from Mrs. Samuel H. Brooks; maintained by the City of Memphis to promote interest and development in cultural arts and activities of the citizens; original building opened 1916; first addition 1955; second addition 1973. Brooks Memorial Art Gallery Foundation, Inc. Ann. meeting 2nd Wed. in June; dues educational $10, family and individual $25, patron $100, life $1000 and up, corporate $500, $1000, $5000 and $25,000.
   Collections: Kress Collection of 28 Italian paintings and 2 sculptures, 13th through 18th centuries; 16 Dutch and Flemish paintings, 16th through 18th centuries; 21 English paintings, 17th through 19th centuries; 7 French paintings, 16th through 19th centuries; 29 American paintings and sculptures, 18th through 20th centuries; †International Collection of 30 paintings and sculptures, 19th and 20th centuries; Dr. Louis Levy Collection of 1000 American prints; 27 piece Eastern and Near-Eastern Decorative Arts Collection (Han, T'ang and Ching Dynasty Chinese, 19th century Japanese and 15th and 16th Dynasty and New Empire Egyptian; 150 piece Mid-South Collection of 20th century paintings and sculptures; Porcelain, Glass and Textile Collection.
   Exhibitions: Biennial Mississippi River Craft Show, fall, 1977, prizes $2000; Biennial Mid-South Exhibition, Mar.-Apr., 1977, prizes $2350; Annual Junior Mid-South (children and young adults) held in Apr; three changing exhibitions monthly.
   Activities: Artworks, an educational experience center; school tours, seminars, fine arts lectures, film series, gallery lectures; reproduction lending service to schools; Sales Shop and Book Store; special programs for members, museum studies program with Memphis State University and Southwestern College and museum internships in cooperation with colleges and universities throughout the U.S; 194-seat auditorium.
   Library: 11,500 volume reference library on books on art, history, artists, and art works, decorative arts.
   Publications: The Samuel H. Kress Collection; Sixty Paintings; Selections from the American Collection; A Question of Regionalism; bimonthly newsletter.
   Income and Purchases: 1975-76 operating budget $287,331; acquisitions endowment $350,000.
   Attendance: 115,675.

✤G. PILLOW LEWIS MEMORIAL LIBRARY
Memphis Academy of Arts
Overton Park, 38112. Tel: (901) 726-4085
Patricia C. Hayley, Librn.
Sandra Wade, Asst. Librn.
No admis; financed by city and county appropriations.
   Collections: Collection of 14,000 volumes, lends to students, faculty and trustees; 22,000 slides for use by faculty and students only; 104 periodicals; 28 drawer vertical file; small collection of original prints and reproductions.
   Income: Approx. $8500.

MEMPHIS PINK PALACE MUSEUM
232 Tilton Rd. & Central Ave, Chickasaw Gardens, 38111.
Tel: (901) 458-8587
Robert P. Sullivan, Dir.
Maxine Spencer, Secy.
   In the midst of a $5.3 million expansion program which will not be completed until Jan. 1, 1977.

MURFREESBORO

MIDDLE TENNESSEE STATE UNIVERSITY PHOTOGRAPHIC GALLERY
Box 305, 37132. Tel: (615) 898-2787
Harold L. Baldwin, Cur.
Free Mon. - Thurs. 8 AM - 10 PM; Fri. 8 AM - 6 PM; Sat. 8 AM - 5 PM; Sun. 2 - 10 PM. Estab. Sept, 1969, for the purpose of exhibiting photographs only, to include professionals as well as students; financed by endowment.
Collections: 268 photographs from all over the world and most artist photographers.
Exhibitions: (1974-75) Charles W. Sanders; Harry Callahan; Fred Pleasure; Oliver A. Schuchard; Roger Camp; Roger Williams; Edward Weston; (1975-76) Henry Holmes Smith; Therold Lindquist; George Hardin; Mirle Freel; Diana Hulick; Dominick Fucci; Peter Menzel; Don Rutledge; plus annual student exhibitions.
Activities: Extension Department serves anyone in Middle Tennessee area free of charge; traveling exhibitions organized and circulated; photograph collection for lending and reference; gallery talks; competitions; scholarships.
Publications: Photographic Annual.
Income and Purchases: Income $3000; purchases approx. $1500.
Attendance: Several thousand, including students.

NASHVILLE

COHEN MEMORIAL MUSEUM OF ART
George Peabody College for Teachers
Box 513, 37203. Tel: (615) 372-8178
Dr. Walter Rutkowski, Dir.
Lucius B. DuBose, Cur.
Patricia S. Irwin, Secy.
Free Mon. - Fri. 1 AM - Noon & 1 - 4:30 PM. Galleries are used to exhibit student works, faculty works, and visiting artist's works; on occasion, permanent collection is exhibited; college funded.
Collections: Kress Study Collection; Algernon Sydney Sullivan Collection of 19th Century Paintings and other items collected through the years. (These items are stored and brought out occasionally).
Exhibitions: 6 visiting artists, Middle Tennessee High School Art Exhibit, Peabody Senior Exhibition, 4 graduate exhibitions, Peabody Centennial Exhibition.
Activities: Lectures and exhibits open to the public; slide library for student and faculty use only.
Attendance: 3000.

FISK UNIVERSITY MUSEUM AND GALLERY
18th & Jackson Sts, 37203. Tel: (615) 329-9111, Exten. 255
David Driskell, Dir. Museum
Robert Hall, Cur. Educ. & Collections
Pearl Cresswell, Registrar
Christine Johnson, Secy.
Free daily 9 AM - 5 PM. Estab. 1949 to acquaint the Fisk and Nashville communities with traditional and contemporary art forms and to offer extension and resource material to other institutions and individuals; financed by university.
Collections: General collection includes works by Hans Moller, Milton Avery, photos by Carl Van Vechten; Afro-American Collection: sculpture, prints, paintings by contemporary Black Americans; African Art Collection: contemporary and traditional art from West Africa; Alfred Stieglitz Collection of Modern Art: 101 works, primarily painting, drawings and prints.
Exhibitions: Amstad II: A Survey of Afro-American Art; African Art Exhibit, Bakuba; Paintings by William T. Williams; Elizabeth Cattlett, Sculptor; Paintings by Nelson Stevens and James Phillips.
Activities: 150 Afro-American paintins and prints in lending collection; 75 items lent in average year; original objects of art lent; traveling exhibitions organized and circulated; Extension Department serves individuals and other institutions in continental Unites States. Photograph collection for reference; lectures open to public, 5 visiting lecturers per year; tours. Book shop. Reference library.
Publications: Exhibition catalogs, 6 times a month and twice a year; Fisk Art Report.
Attendance: Approx. 5000.

✤**TENNESSEE BOTANICAL GARDENS AND FINE ART CENTER**
Cheekwood Division, Cheek Rd, 37205. Tel. (615) 352-5310
Julia C. Haworth, Exec. Secy.
Duncan P. Callicott, Garden Dir.
Richard C. Page, Asst. Garden Dir.
Randall E. Lantz, Horticulturist
John Henry Nozynski, Dir. Fine Arts Center
Linda Thompson, Cur. Educ.
Alan Seneker, Exhibit Designer
Mrs. Victor White, Gift Shop Mgr.
Mamie Smiley, Tea Room Mgr.

Mrs. Seawell Brandeau, Pres, Friends of Cheekwood
Ann Alexander, Docent Chmn.
Mrs. Alford O. Sinclair, Mansion Guide Chmn.
Open Tues. - Sat. 10 AM - 5 PM; Sun. 1 - 5 PM; cl. Mon. and major holidays; admis. fee; members and children under 12 and pre-arranged school groups no charge; special group rates. Founded 1957; Art Center and Botanical Gardens housed in 1928-32. Mem. dues: student $2, nonres. $10, res. $15, participating $25, contributing and corporate $100, sustaining $250, life $3000.
Collections: Chinese snuff bottles and porcelain; Japanese woodblock prints; 17th - 19th century European glass, sculpture; 17th - 20th century American and European art, graphics and sculpture.
Exhibitions: Permanent, temporary and traveling exhibitions.
Activities: Guided tours; lectures; films; gallery talks; formally organized education programs for children and adults; docent and mansion guide programs.
Library: 5000 volume library of botany and fine arts available for interlibrary loan and for use on premises.
Publications: Cheekwood Mirror, monthly newsletter; exhibition catalogs.

TENNESSEE STATE MUSEUM*
War Memorial Building, 37219. Tel: (615) 741-2692
Jean Du Val Kane, Dir.
Peg Schneider, Cur.
Paul Schrag, Preparator
Carl Spitzer, Artist
Carol Kaplan, Registrar
Free weekdays 9 AM - 4 PM; cl. Sat, Sun. and national holidays. Estab. 1937 to preserve and exhibit historical objects and scientific exhibitions, Indian artifacts, portraits and general museum exhibits. The Museum is under the direction of the Tennessee Arts Commission and is financed from that budget.
Collections: Portraits of Governors of Tennessee, prominent statesmen, Presidents from Tennessee; Civil War portraits and paintings. Other items include pioneer relics; Indian beadwork, baskets, bows, arrows, ceremonial pieces, skeletons from mound builders and cave burial places; Tennessee wildlife exhibits; Smoky Mountain Crafts; dolls from foreign countries; the Weems-Slayden collection of historical trophies including pistols, swords, carvings, medals; Oscar Baynard egg collection; war relics from all wars beginning with the Revolutionary War; relics from the Battleship Tennessee.
Attendance: 150,000.

WATKINS INSTITUTE
Sixth Ave. at Church St, 37219. Tel: (615) 242-1851
C. H. Sargent, Dir.
Anton Weiss, Art Dir.
Dorris Stone, Exec. Secy.
Free 8 AM - 9:30 PM. Estab. 1885 as an adult education center for art, home economics, business education, adult evening high school, and courses of a general nature; rent from business property is source of income.
Collections: All-State artist collection (oldest collection of Tennessee art in the state); this is a purchase-award collection, oil, pastel, watercolor, graphics, and sculpture; several other collections of lesser value.
Exhibitions: Six or eight per year.
Activities: Traveling exhibitions organized and circulated; individual paintings lent to schools; original objects of art lent; lectures open to public, 6 or 8 visiting lecturers per year; classes for adults and children; competitions.
Library: 20,000 volumes.
Publications: Quarterly catalogue listing courses; art brochure.
Attendance: 5000 students.

OAK RIDGE

✤**OAK RIDGE COMMUNITY ART CENTER**
P.O. Box 105, 37830. Tel: (615) 482-1182
Tanyia Creasey, Pres.
Sue Lindemer, Secy.
Jewell Stallions, Receptionist & Secy.
Paul Swenson, Exhibits Chmn.
Open weekdays 10 AM - 2 PM; Sat. & Sun. 2 - 5 PM; no gallery fee. Estab. and inc. 1952 to provide pleasure and education for its members and the community in the field of art; maintained by membership. Gallery maintained. Two membership meetings per year, announced a month in advance; mem. 763; dues family $15, individual $10, student and children $5, retired persons half-price.
Exhibitions: Monthly exhibits including both local and traveling shows.
Activities: Classes in oils, watercolors, drawing, ceramics, sculpture, jewelry making, children's art, weaving, batik, folk guitar, poetry; extension dept. serving Anderson, Knox and Roane County;

basic art supplies donated for classes in underprivileged areas, approx. 300 participants; local one-man shows displayed in various community buildings; Sidewalk Show; Children's Art Show; various other special events. Rental of 375 original-paintings, reproductions and sculpture. Gift Shop offering local crafts. Film Series including vintage and modern classic films.

Library just instituted.

Publications: Oak Ridge Community Art Center Newsletter, monthly.

Income and Purchases: Income $12,500; expenditures $12,000.

Attendance: 10,000.

SEWANEE

THE UNIVERSITY OF THE SOUTH GALLERY OF FINE ARTS.
Guerry Hall, 37375.
Dr. Edward Carlos, Dir.
Open Daily 2 - 5 PM except holidays and non-university sessions.
Art Gallery estab. 1938; Monthly exhibitions during school year (2 - 4 per month, changing shows); two lectures per year; tours regularly by request). Museum chambers estab. 1972 featuring period rooms, collection of paintings, prints, furniture and artifacts, sculpture, photography.

Attendance: 5000-6000.

TULLAHOMA

THE TULLAHOMA FINE ARTS CENTER, INC.
401 S. Jackson, 37388. Tel: (615) 455-4560
Mrs. Lonnie E. Ray, Pres.
Mrs. Richard Hawkins, Secy.
Mrs. Charles Mullins, Exhibit Chmn.
Free Wed. 2 - 4 PM; Sun. 2 - 5 PM. Estab. 1968 to encourage art appreciation; a place where painting and sculpture are exhibited, painting and sculpture classes taught and slide lectures presented; financed by membership. Mem. 200; dues student $5, regular $10, patron $25 or more.

Exhibitions: Local artists and artists from surrounding towns in middle Tennessee.

Activities: Paintings of local artists are placed in bank; lectures open to public; concerts, classes for adults and children.

Library: 15 volumes for reference.

Publications: Tullahoma Fine Arts Center Newsletter, bimonthly.

Income and Purchases: Income $5500; purchases c. $2800.

TEXAS

ABILENE

RYAN FINE ARTS GALLERY
McMurry College Art Department
Sayles Blvd. & S. 14th St, 79605. Tel: (915) 692-4130, Exten. 280
Dr. Thomas Kim, Pres, College
Sherwood Suter, Chmn. Art Dept.
Open during regular school hours, no admis. fee. Estab. 1923; financed through endowment.

Activities: Student exhibitions; lectures open to public, 2 visiting lecturers per year; 20 tours; concerts, classes for adults; scholarships.

Attendance: 2500.

AMARILLO

✠AMARILLO ART CENTER
Box 447, 79178. Tel: (806) 372-8356
Betty Bivins Childers, Pres.
James Fisher, Dir.
Thomas Livesay, Cur. of Art
Patrick McCracken, Cur. of Educ.
Teresa Scott, Admin. Asst.
Free Tues. - Fri. 10 AM - 5 PM; Sat. and Sun. 1 - 5 PM; Wed. E. 7 - 10 PM. Estab. 1967 as a small city art museum with broad educational and cultural program. Gallery is approx. 8000 square feet, two to four concurrent exhibitions changing monthly. Ann. meeting Sept; mem. 700; dues $25 and higher.

Exhibitions: Approximately eighty exhibitions during last three years, including all phases and types of art.

Activities: Extensive lending collection; lectures, AV prog, some art classes available to schools and interested groups, no fee; lectures open to public, 2 visiting lecturers, 3 gallery talks, 200-300 tours per year; classes for adults and children; competitions; scholarships primarily to disabled or deprived children and young adults; book shop.

Library: 500 volumes, reference only.

Publications: Bimonthly newsletter; numerous exhibition catalogs.

Income and Purchases: Income $3000-4000; purchases $1000 currently.

Attendance: 55,000.

✠AMARILLO ART CENTER ASSOCIATION
Amarillo College Campus, Van Buren St, P.O. Box 447, 79105

AUSTIN

✠LAGUNA GLORIA ART MUSEUM
P.O. Box 5568, 78763. Tel: (512) 452-9447
Jerry C. Porter, Exec. Dir.
Cathryn Dorsey, Asst. to Dir.
Open Tues. - Fri. 9 AM - 5 PM; Sat. 10 AM - 5 PM; Sun. 1 - 5 PM; cl. Mon. Estab. 1961; operated as an art museum by a board of trustees; financed by private and municipal funds. Ann. meeting Nov; mem. 800; dues $20 and higher.

Exhibitions: Varied exhibitions from national and regional sources; Annual Arts and Crafts Fiesta for artists in May.

Activities: Conducts art school all year; members' previews; lectures, docent and others.

Library: Small library of Art books and colored slides which may be used here or checked out by art instructors.

Attendance: Average attendance has increased to approx. 60,000 annually.

✠ST. EDWARD'S UNIVERSITY
Fine Arts Exhibit Program
78704. Tel: (512) 444-2624, Exten. 316
Dr. Henry Altmiller, Academic Dean
Brother Hilarion Brezik, Dir. Fine Arts Exhibit Prog.
Free weekdays 8 AM - 6 PM; Sun. 1 - 5 PM. Estab. 1961 to present for the university population and general public a monthly schedule of exhibits in the visual arts as a means of orientation toward established and current trends in art styles in terms of their historical-cultural significance and aesthetic value, through teaching exhibitions, art films, public and private collections from distributing and compiling agencies, museums, galleries, artists.

Exhibitions: Southwest Sweet Funk; The Flying Circus—Sculpture and Graphics by Fred and Barbara Whitehead; Contemporary Prints of Japan; Two Printmakers in Paris—Etchings by Jean Lodge and Angelica Caporaso; A Jerusalem Journal—a personal documentary by an Emmy Award-Winning CBS cameraman; Paintings and Drawings by Jerry Lefevre; Drawings for Dante's Divine Comegy by Leonard Baskin; Visionary Projects by Reginald Malcolmson; annual faculty and art student exhibitions.

Activities: Tours; lectures; one visiting lecturer per year; classes; literature.

Library: Maintains library of over 2000 volumes for lending and reference.

Income and Purchases: Income $4000-$6000; purchases $300-$400.

Attendance: 9000 - 10,000.

TEXAS FINE ARTS ASSOCIATION
State Headquarters, Laguna Gloria Art Museum, P.O. Box 5023, 78763. Tel: (512) 453-5312
J. Louis Murfee, Jr, Pres.
Mrs. Jphn D. Haltom, Exec. Dir.
Open 10 AM - 5 PM. Estab. 1911. Ann. meeting May; mem. 4200 (25 chapters).

This association annually sponsors three exhibitions: The Annual (open), The State Citation (membership), and The State High School Scholarship. Also sponsors ten traveling exhibitions shown in museums, colleges, libraries and smaller communities in Texas and Mexico.

Elisabet Ney Museum
304 E. 44th St, 78751.
Museum is former home, studio and grounds of Elisabet Ney, whose sculpture is preserved here; also exhibition galleries where works of Texas artists are shown.

THE UNIVERSITY OF TEXAS AT AUSTIN ART LIBRARY
23rd at San Jacinto, 78712. Tel: (512) 471-1636
Joyce Hess, Art Librn.
Free Mon. - Thurs. 8 AM - 10 PM; Fri. 8 AM - 5 PM; Sat. 10 AM - 4 PM; Sun. 2 - 6 PM. Estab. to support the curriculum of the art department and to provide materials for research for advanced students and faculty; financed by city and state appropriations.

Collections: Library collection includes materials on art history, painting, sculpture, drawing, crafts, graphic arts, photography, monographs and biographies of artists, art education; 30,000 volumes for lending and reference; 5000 lending and reference photograph collection; vertical file of exhibition notices and brochures.

BANDERA

FRONTIER TIMES MUSEUM*
P.O. Box 212, 78003.
Sandra Doane Turk, Pres.
Mrs. E. B. Batto, Cur & Mgr.
Open daily 10 - 12 AM, 1 - 4:30 PM; cl. Mon; admis. 25¢ ten yrs. and
over, children must be accompanied by an adult. Estab. 1933 to pre-
serve records, photographs, and artifacts of the American West with
emphasis on those of the local Texas hill country area; endowed.
Ann. meetings 3 times a yr; mem. 17; no dues.
    Collections: F. B. Doane collection of western paintings; Louisa
Gordon collection of antiques, including bells from around the world;
J. Marvin Hunter collection of photos, artifacts, memorabilia of
American West and the Texas hill country, and many rare items.
    Exhibitions: Occasional one-man shows by Texas artists whose
work coincides with the theme of the museum.
    Activities: Photograph collection. Book shop.
    Income: $10,000.
    Attendance: 6500 annual average.

BEAUMONT

BEAUMONT ART MUSEUM
    1111 Ninth St, 77702. Tel: (713) 832-3432
Betty W. Hirsch, Dir.
Charles Hill, Pres.
Patrick Boyt, 1st V.Pres.
Lynn Milam, Secy.
Tom Page, Treas.
Open Tues. - Fri. 10 AM - 5 PM; Sat. & Sun. 2 - 5 PM; cl. Mon. and
holidays. Estab. and inc. 1950. Ann. meeting May; mem. 1200;
dues $20, $35, $50, $100, $500.
    Collections: Paintings, sculpture, graphics, 20th century Ameri-
can art; 19th century decorative arts; Eskimo and Thai prehistoric
artifacts.
    Exhibitions: Biennial Invitational Exhibition of Texas Painters
and Sculptors, Apr, even-numbered years, $2000 in purchase prizes;
Southeast Texas Photography Competition, Apr, odd-numbered
years. Program of changing exhibitions: painting, sculpture,
graphics, decorative arts, archaeology.
    Activities: 6 lectures, 2 concerts and 7 film programs per year
for members; gallery talks for public; archaeology studies and arts
awareness programs for junior members; tours for all fifth grade
classes; monthly slide lectures for eighth grade American history
classes; special slide lectures for grades 1 - 5; monthly seminars
for high school classes. Sales gallery, book shop.
    Library: Art library of 500 books.
    Publications: Beaumont Art Museum News, monthly membership
newsletter; exhibition catalogs.
    Attendance: 35,000.

THE BEAUMONT ARTS COUNCIL
    c/o Mrs. Burton Doiron, Co-Chmn, 3360 Beard St, 77703.
Tel: (713) 892-0336.
Estab. 1969 to foster total esthetic involvement in the community and
improved communications among cultural organizations. Meetings
one spring, one fall.
    Activities: Sponsored forum for city election candidates to discuss
their attitudes toward cultural environment.

BUCHANAN DAM

THE BUCHANAN ARTS AND CRAFTS INC.*
    Highway 29, 78609. Tel: (512) 793-2858
Jaynet Buze, Chmn. of Board
Babbie Baxter, Pres.
Mae Brown, Secy.
Margaret Crenshaw, Exec. Secy.
Alma Howerts, Treas.
Free Mon. - Fri. 10 AM - 5 PM; Sun. 1 - 5 PM; cl. Wed, Jan. 1 - Apr.
1. Estab. 1963 to increase the interest in our community by meet-
ings, exhibits, classes and lectures; supported by membership. Own
building with approx. 1800 ft. of floor space. Ann. meeting 2nd Tues.
in Jan; mem. 90, assoc. 10; dues $15, assoc. $5.
    Exhibitions: Monthly exhibits in Burnet First State Bank, Burnet,
Texas; Blue Bonnet Trail Exhibit and Aqua Festival Exhibit, both
annuals, open to the general public; The Highland Lakes Arts & Crafts
Trails Exhibit, Oct; Starving Artist in June.
    Activities: Lectures open to public, approx. 4 visiting lecturers
per year; gallery talks or tours when qualified speakers are available; members meet at the building each Tues. to paint; three teachers for persons wishing art instruction and various instructors who
teach a requested craft.
    Attendance: Weekday average 8; Sundays 20-25 or more; atten-
dance at exhibitions much higher.

CANYON

PANHANDLE-PLAINS HISTORICAL SOCIETY
Panhandle Plains Historical Museum
    2401 Fourth Ave, 79015. Tel: (806) 655-2567
Joseph Pool, Pres.
James S. Kone, 1st V.Pres.
Dr. James A. Hanson, Exec. Secy, Treas. & Dir. of Museum
Jack Downing, Asst. Dir.
Olive Vandruff Bugbee, Cur. of Art
B. R. Harrison, Cur. of Anthropology
Carol Cline, Exhibits Designer
Claire Kuehn, Archivist & Librn.
Jackie Wilson, Secy.
Mrs. Sidney Shaller, Registrar
Free weekdays 9 AM - 5 PM; Sun. 2 - 6 PM. Estab. 1921 to preserve
history of the region, including all phases of history, fine arts and
natural sciences. Ann. meeting May; mem. 1000; dues $5 and higher.
    Collections: Over 1300 paintings by early and contemporary
American painters.
    Exhibitions: Exhibitions normally changed monthly.
    Library: Reference library of 8000 volumes; photograph collec-
tion of 2000 prints.
    Publications: Panhandle-Plains Historical Review, annually.
    Attendance: 125,000.

CORPUS CHRISTI

ART MUSEUM OF SOUTH TEXAS*
✠Corpus Christi Art Foundation
    1902 North Shoreline, P.O. Box 1010, 78403. Tel: (512) 884-3844
Edwin Singer, Pres.
Norma Urban, Secy.
Mrs. Thomas Gallander, Dir.
Mrs. Marilyn Smith, Exec. Secy.
Mrs. Archie Walker, Adminr. Asst.
Mrs. Michelle W. Locke, Lecturer-Librn.
Miss Katina Simmons, Cur. Educ.
Tom Bower, Cur. Exhibitions
Free Tues. - Sat. 10 AM - 5 PM; Sun. 1 - 5 PM. Estab. 1960 to col-
lect and preserve objects of artistic importance and to present a pro-
gram of education which enlarges and enriches the public knowledge
and understanding of the arts; supported by appropriation and mem-
bership. First floor Gallery, 1500 sq. ft; Art Rental Gallery, 600 sq.
ft; Great Gallery, 4300 sq. ft; Upper Gallery, 1890 sq. ft. Mem. 2200;
dues $15 and higher.
    Exhibitions: (1970) Paintings and Sculpture by Richard Scherpe-
reel; Abstract Expressionism; Romantic Art at the Time of Beethoven; American Paintings: 19th and 20th Century; Corpus Christi
Art Foundation Annual Exhibition; William Sinday Mount, Rural
America; Sculpture by Ron Sullivan; Christmas Tree Forest. (1971)
Selections from James A. Michener; Tri-Group Show; Opportunity
for Feat in Place; South Texas Collections; Corpus Christi Art
Foundation Annual Exhibition; Psychedelic Posters; American Folk
Art; Maxine McClendon Show; Christ Mass Prints Show. (1972) 19th
Century French Lithography; Eve Sonneman: Photographer; Selec-
tions by New and Old Collections; Corpus Christi Art Foundation
Annual Exhibition; Works in a Series: Johns, Stella, Warhol; Christmas Tree Forrest; Michael Tracy. (1973) Print Sale; William
Wilhelmi; George Catlin; Velox Ward; Corpus Christi Art Foundation Annual Exhibition; Colla/Shiloja.
    Activities: Lectures open to the public, 2-3 visiting lecturers per
year; classes for adults and children, eleven exhibitions a year,
films, guided tours; competitions. Book Shop.
    Library: 900 volumes for reference; Slide Library of 3000 slides.
    Income and Purchases: Income $299,005; purchases $267,529.
    Attendance: 106,562.

DEL MAR COLLEGE DEPARTMENT OF ART GALLERY
    Baldwin at Ayers, 78404. Tel: (512) 882-6231
Free Mon. - Fri. 8 AM - 9:30 PM. Estab. 1932 to teach art and to
provide exhibition showcase for college and community; financed by
city and state appropriation. Gallery consists of over 200 running
feet space, plus other smaller areas.
    Collections: †Del Mar permanent collection consisting of pur-
chases from Annual National Drawing and Small Sculpture Show;
plus donations.
    Exhibitions: Regular schedule of local and traveling shows, Sept.
through May; Annual National Drawing and Small Sculpture Show in
May.
    Activities: Junior museum; lectures open to public; 2 - 3 visiting
lecturers per year; 6 - 8 gallery talks; concerts, classes for adults,
competitions; scholarships.
    Budgeted funds and donations: $1500 - $2000.
    Attendance: 10,000 - 15,000.

DALLAS

✠DALLAS MUSEUM OF FINE ARTS
Fair Park, 75226. Tel: (214) 421-4187
Mrs. Eugene McDermott, Chmn. of the Board
John D. Murchison, Pres.
Harry S. Parker, Dir.
Eugene W. Mitchell, Asst. Dir. Admin.
John Lunsford, Cur.
Robert M. Murdock, Cur. Contemporary Art
Barney Delabano, Cur. Exhibitions
Carol Robbins, Curatorial Asst.
Mrs. John Houseman, Registrar
Fred Mitcham, Librn.
Mrs. J. O'C. Rodgers, Dir. Development & Mem.
Free Tues. - Sat. 10 AM - 5 PM; Sun. 1 - 5 PM; cl. Mon. and Christmas. Estab. 1903; building completed 1936; new addition 1965; merged with Dallas Museum for Contemporary Arts 1963. Ann. meeting May; mem. 4000; dues $25 and higher.
Collections: †19th and 20th century European and American painting and sculpture including Arp, Bellows, Bernard, Brooks, Calder, Cassatt, Chase, Dine, Dubuffet, Gauguin, Gorky, Gottlieb, Harnett, Hepworth, Hicks, Hopper, Kandinsky, Kline, Lindner, Louis, Maillol, Monet, Moore, Morris, Motherwell, Murphy, Nevelson, Nicholson, Pissarro, Pollock, Prendergast, Redon, Rodin, Rothko, Smith, Stuart, Tobey, Vasarely, Wyeth, Zox; †pre-Columbian including Mesoamerica and South America; †antiquities including Egyptian, Etruscan, Greek, Roman, and Near Eastern; Stillman collection of Congo sculpture; Schindler Collection of African Sculpture; †Far Eastern painting, ceramics, and sculpture; European painting of the 17th and 18th centuries; Old Master and contemporary prints and drawings.
Exhibitions: About ten exhibitions a year, half assembled by Museum staff. Major exhibitions of last two years include Burgoyne Diller, Kempe Collection, James Brooks, Robert Graham, African Art from Dallas Collections, Interchange, Geometric Abstraction 1926-1942, Exposition Architecture, 19th Exhibition of Southwestern Prints and Drawings, Options for Tomorrow's City, The Hand and The Spirit: Religious Art in America 1700-1900, Sam Francis Paintings 1947-1972, Amsterdam/Paris/Düsseldorf, Velox Ward, Old Master Prints, Max Ernst, North Texas Painting and Sculpture, Southwestern Photography, The Sculpture of Thailand. Periodic regional exhibitions.
Activities: Education Department offers school tours, general tours of collection and special exhibitions, lectures by both visiting scholars and staff, gallery talks, film series; sunday concerts. Museum Shop. Gallery Buffet (October - May).
Library: Reference library of approx. 11,000 volumes.
Income: City of Dallas $317,000 annually and private support $356,500 annually.
Publications: Catalogs issues on major exhibitions; monthly newsletter.
Attendance: 225,000.

DALLAS PRINT AND DRAWING SOCIETY
Dallas Public Library, Commerce St, 75201. Tel: (214) 748-9071
Thomas Campbell, Pres.
Estab. 1935; reorganized 1958. Meetings six times a year; mem. 85; dues $10.
Activities: Co-sponsors with the Museum the Southwest Print and Drawing Exhibition; lectures; demonstrations in printmaking and drawing; print workshop for members.
Purchases: $250-$500.

DALLAS PUBLIC LIBRARY
Fine Arts Division
1954 Commerce St, 75201. Tel: (214) 748-9071
Mrs. Lillian M. Bradshaw, Library Dir.
George Henderson, Fine Arts Librn.
William Haddaway, Art Librn.
Free Mon. - Fri. 9 AM - 9 PM; Sat. 9 AM - 6 PM.
Library estab. 1901, Fine Arts estab. as separate division in 1954, to furnish the citizens of Dallas materials and information concerning the arts; appropriation. Exhibits in the division on various subjects.
Collections: Books, both reference and circulating, concerning the †arts; picture files; collection of †original prints co-sponsored by the Dallas Print and Drawing Society; circulating collection of †framed reproductions; film library; photograph collection.
Exhibitions: Various exhibits on art, crafts, books, personalities relating to the arts, etc.
Publications: Occasional exhibit catalogs.
Income and Purchases: Income $48,000; purchases $35,000 for books, periodicals and prints; $13,000 for recordings.

✠POLLOCK GALLERIES*
Owen Arts Center
Southern Methodist University, 75222. Tel: (214) 692-2489
William A. Robinson, Dir.
Free Mon. - Sat. 9 AM - 5 PM; Sun. 1 - 5 PM. Estab. 1965 to present monthly exhibitions of art in all media of interest to the University and to the community; special funds annually. Four large galleries.
Collections: Small collection of contemporary American and European art.
Exhibitions: Gyorgy, Kepes, Latin American Painters, Japan Art Festival, Contemporary Italian Painters, The American Poster, Contemporary Watercolors, American Folk Art, Many Approaches to Drawing, Jasper Johns Graphics, etc.
Activities: Traveling exhibitions organized and circulated; original objects of art lent; lectures open to public, 4 visiting lecturers per year; 40 gallery talks or tours; concerts; sale of exhibit catalogues.
Publications: Exhibition catalogues.
Attendance: (1968) Estimated 72,000; (1969) estimated 108,000.

DENTON

ART DEPARTMENT GALLERY*
North Texas State University
76203. Tel: (817) 788-2071
Ken Havis, Gallery Dir.
Free, Mon. - Fri. 9 AM - 4 PM. Estab. 1960 for teaching; financed by city & state appropriations.
Collections: †Fashion Collection; †Print Collection; †Voertman Collection (permanent student collection).
Exhibitions: Invitational; Art of Collecting, Edward Marcus, Stanley Marcus, John Murchison, and Ed Weiner; Student Exhibition; Architecture without Architects; Faculty Exhibition; Voertmen Exhibition; Collecting, Edward Mattil; Hiram Williams; Twenties and Thirties—Fashion and Art.
Activities: Teaching art; slides for teaching; lectures open to public; 8 visiting lecturers per year; library; scholarships.

TEXAS WOMAN'S UNIVERSITY ART GALLERIES
76204. Tel: (817) 382-8923
Dr. Donald E. Smith, Chmn. Art Dept.
Oleta Ash, Secy.
Free 8 AM - 5 PM daily.
Collections: Kwakiutl Indian masks, Tlingit masks, African sculpture, †Prints, †small collection of modern paintings, Eskimo Ivories.
Activities: Circulates exhibitions; lectures, concerts, classes for adults and children; scholarships; maintains lending and reference library; 8000 slides, 40 filmstrips, 600 color reproductions.

EL PASO

DEPARTMENT OF ART GALLERIES
The University of Texas at El Paso
79968. Tel: (915) 747-5181
Clarke H. Garnsey, Chmn.
Department Studios and Galleries open Mon. - Fri. 8 AM - 5 PM; no admis. fee. University estab. 1916, Department of Art estab. 1940; financed by city and state appropriation. Art Alumni Group in process of becoming established; 365 mem. thus far.
Collections: Small collection of prints from old and modern masters, and growing collection of student works.
Exhibitions: Best of Show Exhibitions out of the Texas Fine Arts Association; Annual Student Shows and Faculty Exhibitions.
Activities: Extension work is offered through the regular University Extension Service to anyone over high school age, variable fees. Lectures open to public; 2 - 4 gallery talks per year; 2 - 4 tours; general university scholarships available; classes for adults.
Publications: Exhibition catalogs.

✠EL PASO MUSEUM OF ART
1211 Montana Ave, 79902. Tel: (915) 543-3800
Leonard P. Sipiora, Dir.
William Rakocy, Cur. Collections
Patricia Davenport, Cur. Educ.
Free Tues. - Sat. 10 AM -5 PM; Sun. 1 - 5 PM; cl. Mon. and national holidays. Estab. 1960. Ann. meeting Jan; mem. 1000; dues $15.
Collections: Kress collection of 14th-17th century European paintings; 18th, 19th, and 20th century American art, contemporary graphics, Pre-Columbian Mexican Colonial art; Heritage collection of decorative arts.
Exhibitions: 16-20 exhibitions yearly; Treasure of the Month.
Activities: Creative Art for children and adults, Art Appreciation for children and adults: monthly lectures, foreign films, concerts.
Library: 400 art volumes.
Attendance. 75,000.

FORT WORTH

AMON CARTER MUSEUM OF WESTERN ART
   3501 Camp Bowie Blvd, 76101. (Mail: P.O. Box 2365).
   Tel: (817) 738-1933
Mrs. J. Lee Johnson III, Pres.
Mitchell A. Wilder, Dir.
Dr. John A. Diffily, Dir. Educ.
Dr. Ron C. Tyler, Cur. History
Peter H. Hassrick, Cur. Collections
Marjorie Morey, Cur. Photographic Collections
Nancy G. Wynne, Librn.
Frances M. Gupton, Registrar
Free daily 10 AM - 5 PM; Sun. & holidays 1 - 5:30 PM; cl. Mon.
Opened to the public Jan. 22, 1961, incorporated as a non-profit
educational institution Oct. 13, 1961.
   Collections: A notable collection of paintings and sculptures,
especially Remington and Russell.
   Acquisitions: †In general field of American Art, especially as-
pects of American culture which find their identification as Western.
   Exhibitions: Special exhibitions and publications concerned with
the study and documentation of the American West.
   Library: 13,500 volumes, principally related to the field of interests in which the Museum exhibitions and publications program
operates. Microfilm archives of 19th century newspapers; photographic archives.
   Attendance: 110,835.

⚜THE FORT WORTH ART MUSEUM
   1309 Montgomery St, 76107. Tel: (817) 738-9215
Sid R. Bass, Pres.
Mrs. Warren McKeever, Secy.
Richard Koshalek, Dir.
Jay Belloli, Cur.
Anne Livet, Performing Arts Dir.
Free Tues. - Sat. 10 AM - 5 PM; Sun. 1 - 5 PM. Estab. 1901 as a
museum of 20th century art; financed by city and state appropria-
tion and membership. 5 large galleries for exhibition on the main
floor. Ann. meeting Jan. 28, 1976; mem. 1500; dues $25.
   Collections: †20th century paintings, sculpture, drawings and
prints.
   Exhibitions: (1974-76) 20th Century Art, Ft. Worth/Dallas Pri-
vate Collections; Roy de Forest Retrospective; Stephen Antonakos:
Outdoor Neon; Brice Marden: Drawings 1963-1973; Arman - Selected
Works: 1958-1974; 4 From Austin; Tarrant County
Annual Exhibition; Exchange/DFW/SFO; Larry Bell: Recent Work;
Dan Flavin: Installations in Fluorescent Light; The Great American
Rodeo.
   Activities: Orientation gallery for 4th grade students; original
objects of art lent only to museums; 30 items lent in average year;
some lectures open to public, some for members only; concerts;
dramatic programs; competitions. Book shop. Reference library.
   Publications: Calendar, monthly.

FORT WORTH PUBLIC LIBRARY ARTS DEPARTMENT
   Ninth & Throckmorton, 76102.
   Tel: (817) 335-4781, Exten. 34
Miss Lirl Treuter, Dept. Head
Thomas K. Threatt, Asst.
Free Mon. - Fri. 9 AM - 9 PM; Sat. 9 AM - 6 PM; cl. Sun. Estab.
1902; supported by appropriation. Not a commercial gallery, but exhibit areas for framed and matted reproductions of paintings which
are displayed and available for circulation to the public; also frequent small exhibits of original works and crafts.
   Collections: †Books; sheet music, †music scores, tune cards,
phonorecords; †framed and matted reproductions of paintings;
special files of clipped pictures, articles, pamphlets and programs;
other special collections of original cartoon art, Hal Coffman collection; bookplates, Nancy Taylor collection, and historic picture
and photograph collection autographed by various celebrities.
   Activities: Traveling exhibitions organized and circulated; 280
circulating reproductions; 150 photographs and 115 albums; also
photograph collection for reference; classes for adults; competitions.
   Publications: Bibliographies and occasional catalogs.

KIMBELL ART MUSEUM
   P.O. Box 9440, Will Rogers Rd. W, 76107. Tel: (817) 332-8451
A. L. Scott, Pres.
Dr. Richard F. Brown, Dir.
David M. Robb, Jr, Cur.
Dr. Max W. Sullivan, Head, Administrative Services
Liz Johnson, Secy.
Ilse Rothrock, Librn.
Free daily 10 AM - 5 PM; Sun. 1 - 5 PM; cl. Mon. and Jan. 1, July
4, Thanksgiving and Christmas. Estab. 1964, opened to public 1972,
for the collection, preservation, research publication and public
exhibition of art of all periods; endowed.

   Collections: Continuing acquisitions program.
   Exhibitions: Special exhibitions.
   Activities: Lecture, film, music and docent programs; research
library; conservation center.
   Publications: Collection catalog and other occasional publications.
   Attendance: 190,000.

GALVESTON

THE ROSENBERG LIBRARY
   2310 Sealy, 77550. Tel: (713) 763-8854
Robert K. Hutchings, Pres.
Edward J. Fox, Secy.
John D. Hyatt, Librn.
Frieda Sheel, Public Services Dir.
Larry J. Wygant, Cur. Special Collections
Margaret Culbertson, Rare Books Librn.
Free, Mon. - Thurs 9 AM - 9 PM, Fri. - Sat. 9 AM - 6 PM. Estab.
1900 to provide library services to the people of Galveston, together
with lectures, concerts, exhibitions; financed by endowment and city
and state appropriation. Library includes the Harris Art Gallery,
The James M. Lykes Maritime Gallery, The Hutchings Gallery to-
gether with miscellaneous art and historical exhibit galleries and
halls. Mem. 523; dues $5 - $100.
   Collections: 19th century American and European paintings and
sculptures; Lalique crystal; 19th century Japanese art; †Texas art;
†contemporary American graphics; †historical artifacts relating to
Texas, 15th century to present; incanabula through fine contemporary printing.
   Exhibitions: Average approx. 18 exhibitions per year; History of
Shipping in the Gulf of Mexico; Three Centuries of Spanish Art;
Lalique; Ten Notable Texans; The Emil Bunjes 75th Birthday Exhibition; numerous one-man shows.
   Activities: Extension department serves Galveston County;
material available to individuals and organizations; film, framed
pictures and film strips; traveling exhibitions organized and circulated; original objects of art lent; lending collection, 18,444 color
reproductions, 810 motion pictures, 310 film strips, 487 framed pictures, 17 sculptures; 1961 items lent in average year; photograph
reference collection; lectures; gallery talks; concerts; dramatic
programs; classes for adults and children; 438,395 volume lending
and reference library.
   Publications: The Rosenberg Library Bulletin, irregular, semi-
annual.
   Income and Purchases: Income $358,000; purchases $61,000.

HOUSTON

THE ART LEAGUE OF HOUSTON
   1953 Montrose Blvd, 77006. Tel: (713) 523-9530
Warren W. Curlee, Pres.
Mrs. W. D. Moody, Secy.
Charlene Harris, Coordinating Dir.
Open Mon. - Fri. 10 AM - 4 PM; Sun. 1 - 5 PM. Estab. 1948, inc.
1953, a nonprofit organization for the furtherance of the arts and
artists in the Houston area; supported by membership. Gallery for
periodic exhibition (juried competitions) of members' works and
specified invitational exhibits. Ann. meeting 3rd Thurs. in May;
mem. 650; dues $15 active, $25 patron.
   Exhibitions: Monthly exhibits of members' works or invitational
exhibits.
   Activities: Lectures open to public, 8 visiting lecturers per year;
classes for adults; competitions.
   Publications: Year Book, annually; Newsletter, monthly.
   Attendance: 3000.

CONTEMPORARY ARTS MUSEUM
   5216 Montrose, 77006. Tel: (713) 526-3129
Mrs. Sanford McCormick, Pres.
Mrs. Alvin Lubetkin, Chmn. Board
Ford Hubbard, Jr, Exec. V.Pres.
Mrs. A. Knox Tyson, Secy. & Parliamentarian
James Harithas, Dir.
Mrs. D. L. Prince, Asst. Dir.
Paul Schimmel, Cur.
Joanie Whitebird, Cur.
Vidal Briscno, Cur.
Ann Bunn, Cur. Educ.
Open Tues. - Sat. 10 AM - 5 PM; Sun. Noon - 6 PM; cl. Mon. Estab.
1948 to promote a better understanding of contemporary art; no
permanent collection. Ann. meeting May; mem. 2000; dues $10
students, others $25 and higher.
   The 15,000 square foot building was designed by Detroit archi-
tect Gunnar Birkerts, for an approximate total cost of $550,000. The
parallelogram shaped structure consists of two floors. The upper
level houses an 8000 square foot gallery with a ceiling height of 20

feet. The lower level houses shipping and receiving, bookshop, research library, multipurpose room, staff offices and storage.

Exhibitions: Exhibitions covering contemporary art in all media: painting, sculpture, drawing, video, dance, theater, poetry, music, etc. with an emphasis on Texas artists.

Activities: Wide ranging educational program including the prototypical Art After School, a program of art classes in selected elementary schools; docent program; special events; book store.

Annual Budget: $250,000.

Attendance: 300,000.

HOUSTON PUBLIC LIBRARY
Fine Arts and Recreation Department
500 McKinney Ave, 77002. Tel: (713) 224-5441
John Harvath, Jr, Head, Fine Arts & Recreation
Open Mon. - Fri. 9 AM - 9 PM; Sat. 9 AM - 6 PM. Library departmentalized in 1959; supported by city appropriation.

Collections: In general, all DDC 700's; building in areas of antiques and collectibles, film and motion pictures, 19th - 20th century art, and ethnic art, particularly African and Afro-American; 42,000 volumes, about 90% of which are for lending; 17,500 mounted pictures of art works for lending; 2000 photographs of celebrities in all fields for lending; 700 circulating color framed reproductions; 21 circulating sculpture replicas; 5000 Kodachromes for lending; 6000 photograph records; 600 cassettes, including music and audio texts; 2000 auction and exhibition catalogs; 300 noncirculating departmental periodicals; 8500 pieces of sheet music, including popular and classical; foundation collections of microfiche and microfilm format materials.

Exhibitions: Monthly exhibitions of the work of local artists which vary each month to represent the diverse subjects located in Fine Arts and Recreation.

Bibliographies available: African and African-American Arts, North American Indian Arts, Screen Plays, Silver, A Bibliography. (Annotated bibliographies based on departmental holdings).

✠INSTITUTE FOR THE ARTS
429 Sewall Hall, Rice University, P.O. Box 1892, 77001.
Rice Museum
University at Stockton Sts, Rice University, 77001.
Tel: (713) 528-0630
Mrs. John de Menil, Dir.
Harris Rosenstein, Adminr.
Jesse Lopez, Mgr.
Sandra Curtis, Registrar
Susan J. Barnes, Research Assoc.
Rice Museum free Tues. - Sat. 10 AM - 5 PM; Sun. Noon - 6 PM. Estab. to organize and present art exhibitions.

Exhibitions: (1974) Gray is the Color; African Art as Philosophy; Cartier-Bresson; Hommage to Picasso; (1975) Antwerp's Golden Age; Mardin, Novros, Rothko; Form and Freedom.

Activities: Art-to-Schools Program; group of docent volunteers deliver slide lectures on art in local elementary, junior and senior high schools; lectures, slides and equipment provided by Institute for the Arts. Paintings, sculpture, prints, posters loaned to local colleges and universities, selected public service organizations; lectures open to the public; concerts.

Library: 26,000 volumes for lending
Publications: Exhibition catalogs.
Attendance: 38,000.

✠THE MUSEUM OF FINE ARTS, HOUSTON
1001 Bissonnet St, 77005. Tel: (713) 526-1361
Harris Masterson, Pres.
Isaac Arnold, Jr, V.Pres.
Mrs. Robert N. Murray, V.Pres.
Mrs. Theodore N. Law, Secy.
E. L. Wehner, Treas.
William C. Agee, Dir.
David B. Warren, Assoc Dir. & Sr. Cur. Bayou Bend Collection
Kent Sobotik, Chief Cur.
Linda D. Henderson, Assoc. Cur. Modern Art
Thomas P. Lee, Jr, Assoc. Cur.
Alvia Wardlaw Short, Assoc. Cur. Educ.
Patrice Jones Day, Mem. & Fund Drive Coordinator
Anne Feltus, Publicist
Jack Key Flanagan, Conservator
Sarah Mendell Keagy, Activities Coordinator
Edward B. Mayo, Registrar
Linda Nelson, Librn.
Clare Spangler, Exec. Asst. to Directors
Robert Spangler, Preparator
Albert D. Sterkx, Business Mgr. & Controller
Marjorie S. Thompson, Docent Coordinator
Zelma Wells, Bookkeeper
Clem Barron, Admin. Dean, Museum School of Art
Kenneth R. Jewesson, Dir, Museum School of Art

Barry Greenlaw, Cur, Bayou Bend Collection
Katherine S. Howe, Assoc. Cur, Bayou Bend Collection
Free Tues. - Sat. 9:30 AM - 5 PM; 9:30 AM - 9 PM first Wed. each month Oct. - May; Sun. Noon - 6 PM; cl. Mon, July 4, Labor Day, Thanksgiving, Christmas. Estab. 1900 as Houston Art League, dedicated to the promotion and perpetuation of art; inc. 1924 as The Museum of Fine Arts, Houston. Owns building; major additions, Cullinan Hall designed by Mies van der Rohe, completed 1958, and Brown Pavilion designed by Mies van der Rohe, completed Jan, 1974; owns branch institution, Bayou Bend, former home of Miss Ima Hogg, which houses Museum's collection of American decorative arts, formally dedicated 1966. Mem. 3800; dues student $5, contributing $25, sustaining $50, patron $100, donor $500, benefactor $1000.

Collections: Permanent Collection, paintings, sculpture and artifacts; Annette Finnigan Collection, sculpture and decorative arts, including ancient Egyptian, Greek and Roman ceramics, jewelry, glass and coins; Edith A. and Percy S. Straus Collection of Italian and Northern European painting and sculpture, mostly from the 15th century; Samuel H. Kress Collection of Italian and Spanish 16th and 17th century paintings; Hogg Brother Collection of works by Frederic Remington; collection of Southwest American Indian art and artifacts and collection of German Expressionist watercolors, drawings and prints, and European and American graphics, gifts of Miss Ima Hogg; A. T. McDannald Collection, moundbuilder artifacts and Mississippian antiquities; Fabacher-Griffith Collection of pre-Columbian art, gift of Mrs. Harry C. Hanszen; native arts from Africa, Australia and South Pacific Islands; contemporary American, contemporary European and European Old Master paintings and sculpture, including purchases from Agnes Cullen Arnold Endowment Fund and Laurence H. Favrot Bequest Fund; Bayou Bend Collection of American Decorative Arts; 17th - 20th century European and American paintings and sculpture, gift of Mr. and Mrs. Raymond H. Goodrich and Esther Florence Whinery Goodrich Foundation; primitive and contemporary sculpture; gifts of Houston Endowment, Inc. and D. and J. de Menil.

Exhibitions: (Jan. - Aug. 1975) The Collection of John A. and Audrey Jones Beck: Impressionist and Post-Impressionist Paintings; Diane Arbus; Willem de Kooning Drawings and Sculptures; Dorothy Hood Drawings; Texas Public Buildings of the 19th Century; 18th and Early 19th Century Design Books; Vienna 1920: Children's Woodcuts from the Cizek School; Primitive Art Masterworks; Oriental Art from Houston Collections; Edward Weston Photographs; Gifts from the Masterson Collection of European Decorative Art; Modern Painting 1900 to the Present; American Chairs from The Bayou Bend Collection; Selections from the Romansky Collection; Memorial Tribute to Miss Ima Hogg.

Activities: Lectures on art history and techniques of artistic expression; concerts; film classics; travel and art films; gallery tours; gallery talks; recitals; dramatic programs; travel tours within the U.S. and to foreign countries.

Library: Specialized art and research library of 12,100 volumes.

Publications: Bulletin, quarterly; Calendar, monthly; exhibition catalogs for Museum-organized exhibitions.

Attendance: (1974) 301,898.

SARAH CAMPBELL BLAFFER GALLERY
University of Houston
114 Fine Art Bldg, 4800 Calhoun, 77004. Tel: (713) 749-1320
William A. Robinson, Dir.
Toni Beauchamp, Asst. to Dir. & Registrar
Michael J. Metyko, Gallery Mgr.
Free. Estab. Mar, 1973 as an educational art facility for University of Houston campuses (40,000 students) and Houston community; financed by city and state appropriation.

Collections: †14th - 20th century European and contemporary American paintings and drawings, under the auspices of the Blaffer Foundations; †Charles and Katherine Fleetwood pre-Columbian Collection; other miscellaneous collections.

Exhibitions: (1974-75) Larson/Walsh Sculpture; Manns/Utterback; Earl Staley; Smithsonian Royal French Jewels; Gaston Lachaise; Creative Collaboration (AIA); 1975 Houston Area Exhibition (juried); student exhibit; (1975-76) The Onderdonks; Three Centuries of the American Nude (Bicentennial); Faculty Exhibit; Picasso, Braque and Leger; Edvard Munch (originating); Houston Designer Craftsmen. Inaugural show of Blaffer Collections. Permanent collections are selectively displayed each year.

Activities: Traveling exhibitions organized and circulated; original objects of art and individual paintings lent; lectures open to public; competitions.

Annual Income: $64,000; purchasing done through Foundations.

Attendance: 19,465.

INGRAM

HILL COUNTRY ARTS FOUNDATION*
Box 176, 78025. Tel: (512) 367-5710
John R. Banister, Pres.

Eleanore Collier, Secy.
Gene Ball, Dir.
Free, 8 AM - 10:30 PM, summer; Mon. - Fri. 0 AM - 4 PM in other seasons. Estab. to provide a place for creative activities in the area of the visual arts and performing arts; to provide classes in arts, crafts, drama and music; financed by membership. Very small Gallery. Ann. meeting 2nd Sat. in Aug; mem. 625; dues $10, $25, $100 and up.
  Exhibitions: Many one-man and group shows.
  Activities: Art workshops, drama courses; lectures open to public; various visiting lecturers per year; concerts; dramatic programs; classes for adults and children; competitions; scholarships.
  Publications: Spotlight, 6 per year.
  Income and Purchases: $55,000.
  Attendance: 15,000-20,000.

LUBBOCK

✠MUSEUM OF TEXAS TECH UNIVERSITY
  P.O. Box 4499, 79409. Tel: (806) 742-5151
Charles M. McLaughlin, Acting Dir.
Free Tues. - Sat. 10 AM - 5 PM; Sun. 1 - 5 PM. Estab. 1929 for teaching, research, and public service; financed by state appropriations and West Texas Museum Association.
  Collections: Permanent collections are essentially in the fields of art, history, anthropology, biological science, and geoscience; art fields are primarily contemporary American in all media and Western American; study collections relating to arid land cultures the world over are being started; permanent exhibitions in art, history and natural sciences.
  Exhibitions: Monthly changing exhibitions in temporary galleries.
  Activities: Traveling exhibitions organized and circulated; original objects of art lent; lectures open to the public; over 2 visiting lecturers per year; over 2 tours. Book Shop.
  Publications: Museum Quarterly, Museum Journal, occasional papers and special publications.

MC ALLEN

✠McALLEN INTERNATIONAL MUSEUM*
  P.O. Box 3486, 78501.
Rudolph V. Pharis, Dir.

MIDLAND

MUSEUM OF THE SOUTHWEST*
  1705 W. Missouri, 79701. Tel: (915) 683-2882
Leon G. Byerley, Jr, Pres.
Mrs. William Jowell, Secy.
Ronald D. Deane, Dir.
Mrs. Theron D. Vaughan, Office Mgr.
Free, Mon. - Sat. 10 AM - 5 PM, Sun. 2 - 5 PM. Estab. 1965 to promote and exhibit art, history and science, specifically from the Southwest and carry out an educational program for the public, relating to the objects displayed; financed by mem. Mem. 455; dues $1-$10,000.
  Collections: †Small collection of paintings, prints and pottery; historical and scientific items of the Southwest.
  Exhibitions: 65 exhibitions from January 70 - July 73; South Africa Costume, Fantasia, Annual Southwestern Area Art Shows, The Western Scene, Water, Quilts, American Masters, Robert Marshall-one man show, Pueblo Pottery, Greenland Arctic, Denmark, Why Midland, The Cow and the Cowboy, The Wyeth Family.
  Activities: Docenting program which tours three or four exhibits per year; traveling exhibitions organized and circulated; individual paintings and original objects of art lent; lending and reference photograph collection; lectures open to the public; visiting lecturers; 123 tours; concerts; classes for adults and children; competitions. Book shop.
  Library: Reference library of approx. 200 volumes.
  Publications: Museletter, monthly.
  Attendance: 26,000 annual average.

ODESSA

PRESIDENTIAL MUSEUM
  622 N. Lee, 79761. Tel: (915) 332-7123
John Ben Shepperd, Chmn.
Alzada Malone, Cur.
Free 9 - 12 AM & 1 - 5 PM. Estab. 1965 to heighten appreciation of and respect for the responsibilities of the Office of the President, to dramatize in non-partisan manner the background, accomplishments, trials, and human side of all the Presidents of the United States, of Texas; supported by membership. Portraits of all presidents, wives and vice-presidents on one canvas in oil; gallery of vice-presidents, Also-Rans, and Pets of Presidents, as well as wood mosaics of all Presidents. Ann. meeting Feb; mem. 500; dues $25 and $100.

Collections: Portrait Galleries of Presidents, †also-rans, †pets of Presidents, †Acetate brush drawings of Vice Presidents, wood mosaics of all Presidents, †1st lady dolls in inaugural gowns, Presidents of Texas, †White House china, churches of Presidents, †mothers and fathers of Presidents, †personal items of Presidents, †Memorial Library, †signatures, †birthplace replicas of the Presidents, †hand-carved caricatures of the Presidents.
  Exhibitions: Pate Collection of Abraham Lincoln First Ladies of the White House; Honoring the Memory of the Presidents (everything in U.S. named for a President); Presidential Postcard Exposition; British Ties with Early Presidents; Homes of the Presidents; †Campaigns and Conventions; †Presidential Cartoons; †Signatures, first in a three-year series in connection with Bicentennial Celebration: Presidents on Wheels; special commemorative exhibits.
  Activities: Special programs for schools, teachers, and service groups, including tours and visual instruction; lectures open to public.
  Library: 3000 volumes for reference; photograph collection; books only relating to the Presidency; tape recordings.
  Publications: Presidential Museum Newsletter, monthly.
  Income and Purchases: Income $20,000; purchases $18,500.
  Attendance: 40,000.

ORANGE

STARK MUSEUM OF ART
  P.O. Drawer 909, 77630. Tel: (713) 883-3513
Nelda C. Stark, Chmn. Foundation
David C. Hunt, Museum Cur.
Anna Jean Caffey, Museum Registrar
Owned and operated by the Nelda C. and H. J. Lutcher Stark Foundation, a Texas nonprofit corporation, Stark Museum of Art was established to preserve and display the Stark collection of art, promote interest in subjects relative to same through future exhibits, publications and educational programs; financed by endowment.
A museum building under construction and is schedules for completion in 1976.
  Collections: Primarily American and American-Western paintings and sculpture, both 19th and 20th centuries well represented; also large collection of American and English ceramics, porcelain and crystal.
  Collector's library of several hundred rare volumes on subjects of art, ethnology and natural history; a future reference or research collection.

SAN ANGELO

HOUSTON HARTE UNIVERSITY CENTER
Angelo State University
  Box 11027, 76901. Tel: (915) 942-2062
Wes Davis, Dir, University Center.
Larry Howard, Prog. Consultant
Ms. Arcie Cervantes, Chairperson, Art Comt.
Free Mon. - Fri. 9 AM - 4 PM; Wed. 7 - 9:30 PM. Estab. 1970 to provide entertainment and informal education for the students, faculty and staff; financed by city and state appropriation. Gallery maintained.
  Collections: In Our Image, collection of 32 wax drawings done by Guy Rowe as basis for illustrating the book, In Our Image, written by Houston Harte.
  Exhibitions: Historical artifacts, weaving, photography, sculpture, pottery, modern drawings, etc. IBM Da Vinci; Robert Fainter; In Our Image; Leeber-Piccolo; Hallmark Greeting Cards; Joan Bankston; children's, students and faculty exhibitions.
  Activities: Lectures open to public; 2 visiting lecturers per year; 5 gallery talks; 1 tour; concerts; dramatic programs; competitions.
  Annual Income: $3000.
  Attendance: 250.

THE SAN ANGELO ART CLUB
Kendall Art Gallery
  119 W. First St. (Box 3362), 76901.
Roxye Bynum, Pres.
Rosa Gray, Secy.
George Maxwell, Exhibit Chmn.
Gallery open year round, Sun, Wed. & Sat. 2 - 5 PM. Art Club estab. 1928, Kendall Art Gallery estab. 1949, to promote the fine arts in the City of San Angelo; Memorial Endowment Fund estab. 1972 by friends of the gallery. Ann. meeting Aug; mem. approx. 100; dues $12, includes newsletter.
  Permanent Collection: Paintings by Xavier Gonzales, Gladys Rockmore Davis, Bryon Browne, Frederick Waugh, Iver Rose and many others.
  Activities: Classes in oil painting and other media; monthly exhibits from area artists; cooperative program with city under study. Special workshops arranged, approx. 2 per year.

Publications: Splashes, gallery newsletter.
Income and Purchases: $8000 for upkeep and prizes.
Attendance: Approx. 4800 aggregate.

SAN ANTONIO

THE COPPINI ACADEMY OF FINE ARTS
    115 Melrose Place, 78212. Tel: (512) 824-8502
Dr. Warren Hester, Pres.
Ed Willmann, 1st V.Pres.
Joyce Ward, Treas.
Margaret Jones, Corresponding Secy.
Virginia Fitzgerald, Recording Secy.
Susanne Gottuk, Parliamentarian
Ruth Duncan, Historian
Dan Burt, Pres. Ex-officio
Erwin O. Wesp, Exhibition Chmn.
Free Sat, Sun. or by appointment 2 - 5 PM. Estab. 1945 to foster a
better acquaintance and understanding between artists and patrons;
to encourage worthy accomplishment in the field of art and to
serve as a means of public exhibition for active members works
and other works of art; financed by membership. Upstairs gallery
donated by founder Dr. Pompeo Coppini to the academy for exhibition of works. Annual meeting third Sun. in Jan; mem. 191; dues
$10 active, $2 assoc, $10 sustaining: $100 life.
    Collections: Oil paintings by Rolla Taylor; sculpture by
Waldine Tauch and Pompeo Coppini.
    Exhibitions: Panhandle Plains Museum; Central Texas Museum;
Coppini Garden and Gallery Show; Coppini Show; exhibitions year
round, different artists and exhibits in Victoria, Houston, Clifton and
Georgetown, Texas.
    Activities: Gives educational programs and art demonstrations
and sponsors workshops; photograph collection for exhibition and
reference; lectures open to the public; approx. 5 tours; competitions;
scholarships.
    Publications: Coppini News Bulletin, monthly.

✠MARION KOOGLER McNAY ART INSTITUTE
    6000 N. New Braunfels St, 78209. Tel: (512) 824-5368
Mrs. Edgar Tobin, Pres.
John Palmer Leeper, Dir.
Free Tues. - Sat. 9 AM - 5 PM; Sun. 2 - 5 PM; cl. Mon. Inc. 1950
for the encouragement and development of modern art; endowed.
Ann. meeting May; mem. 400; dues $50.
    Collections: Large collection of French 19th century painting,
particularly Impressionist and Post-Impressionists including
Gauguin, Cezanne, Matisse, Picasso, etc; †American watercolors
of distinction, from Winslow Homer to present; New Mexican arts
and crafts; the Dr. and Mrs. Frederic Oppenheimer collection of
Gothic and mediaeval art; distinguished print collection; the Sylvan
and Mary Lang Collection of 19th and 20th century French and American art.
    Activities: Lectures; concerts; films; gallery talks; monthly ex-
hibitions, both traveling and from the permanent collection; guided
tours for children (15,000 in 1972).
    Library: 7000 volumes, general reference for art, and specialized
Southwestern section, specialized Oriental section, especially Japanese prints reference material.
    Publications: Exhibition catalogues; permanent collection cata-
logs; postcards of the collection.
    Income and Purchases: Income $200,000; purchases $30,000.
    Attendance: (1971) 100,000; (1972) 100,000.

SAN ANTONIO ART LEAGUE
    310 W. Ashby, 78209. Tel: (512) 732-6048
Mrs. E. H. CuBose, Pres.
Mrs. Joseph Satel, Secy.
Mrs. Jack Casey, Exec. Dir.
Charles Long, Museum Consultant
Free Tues. - Fri. 10 AM - 4 PM; weekends 1 - 4 PM; cl. Mon.
Estab. 1912 as a public art gallery for San Antonio, and for the pro-
motion of a knowledge and interest in art by means of exhibitions; fi-
nanced by membership and fund raising projects. Meetings are 1st
Tues. of month, Oct. - May; mem. 1000; dues $10 - $100.
    Collections: Permanent collection of around 350 items consisting
of paintings, sculpture, crafts.
    Exhibitions: Annual exhibitions are: San Antonio Artist of the
Year, one-man show; Annual San Antonio Art League Artists exhibition, juried show for San Antonio and the surrounding area with approx $4000 in prizes. Traveling exhibitions, Martha Jackson Collec-
tion presented 1974; permanent collection on exhibit during summer.
Collection of approx. 100 prints.
    Activities: Individual paintings lent to schools upon request;
original objects of art lent; 50 items lent in an average year; lectures open to public; 3 gallery talks per year; 2 tours; competitions.

Library: 350 volumes for reference.
    Publications: Monthly calendar of events; exhibition catalogs, 3
per year.
    Income and Purchases: Income approx. $28,000; purchases $1500.

✠SAN ANTONIO MUSEUM ASSOCIATION
Witte Memorial Museum
    3801 Broadway, 78209. Tel: (512) 826-0647
Jack R. McGregor, Dir.
P. J. Bauman, Business Mgr.
Open Mon. - Fri. 9 AM - 5 PM; Sat. & Sun. 10 AM - 6 PM; admis. by
voluntary contribution, suggested adults 50¢, children under 12, 25¢.
    Natural History Museum: The Lone Star Hall of Wildlife and
Ecology; geology, the E. M. Barron mineral and gem collection;
paleontology; anthropology; pre-Columbian anthropology and archaeology.
    History Museum: Items relating to Early Texas history; period
rooms, fiesta costumes, American Indian.
    Historic Houses: Of the period 1800-1840. Twohig House, Ruiz
House, Navarro House, Hill Country Log Cabin, East Texas Log
Cabin.
    Art Museum: Early American art; early Texas painters; con-
temporary regional art; sculpture, drawings, prints, glass, china,
procelain, deocrative arts; U.S. and international circulating exhibitions.
    Actitivies: Guided tours, lectures, films, gallery talks, library,
educational programs for children and adults. Gift Shop.

San Antonio Museum of Transportation
    HemisFair Plaza, 78205. Tel: (512) 226-1201
Open daily 10 AM - 6 PM; admis. by voluntary contribution, suggested adults 50¢, children under 12 25¢.
    Permanent Exhibition: Transportation Hall where the history of
transportation is traced. Classic and antique automobiles, a stage-
coach, street cars, horsedrawn carriages, World War I Jenny air-
plane, miniature train.
    Activities: Guided tours, lectures, films, educational programs.
Gift shop.

SOUTHWEST CRAFT CENTER
    300 Augusta St, 78205. Tel: (512) 224-1848
    Gallery, 420 Paseo de La Villita, 78205. Tel: (512) 222-0926
Mrs. William Larsen, Exec. Dir.
Mrs. Donald Saunders, Chmn. of Board
Mrs. Thomas Berg, Pres.
Chartered 1963, shop estab. 1968, to keep crafts alive by giving
craftsmen an outlet for their work, to educate the public in crafts
by putting good crafts before them and also maintaining a school
where these media can be taught; supported by endowment and membership. Sat. morning Discovery Class, free to San Antonio school
district children. Gallery open daily 10 AM - 5 PM selling juried
crafts of over 110 craftsmen; also one-man and group shows throughout the year. School open 9:30 AM - 10 PM. Ann. meeting May;
1500 students, 35 craftsmen on faculty; dues $10 and up.
    Exhibitions: Approx. 12 one-man and group craft shows; pottery,
weaving, batik, jewelry, ceramic sculpture at gallery. School:
Student-faculty show in Apr. and Dec.
    Activities: Crafts workshop programs with visiting artists;
classes open to public in ceramics, design, jewelry, furniture,
guitar, sculpture, metal, quilting, spinning and dyeing, stained
glass, weaving, woodcarving, photography, printmaking; meetings,
special events for members.
    Library: Reference library of craft books, slides and films.
    Publications: Yearbook; schedule of classes; opening invitations.
    Attendance: 100,000 at openings and events.

SHERMAN

IDA GREEN GALLERY
Austin College
    75090. Tel: (214) 892-9101 Exten. 218
C. R. Neidhardt, Dir.
Open weekdays 9 AM - 5 PM; no admis. Estab. 1972 to serve campus
and community; endowment.
    Collections: Minor collection of approx. fifty prints.
    Exhibitions: Monthly, September through May; one or two during
summer.
    Activities: Lectures open to the public; 2-4 visiting lecturers per
year; 6-10 tours.
    Attendance: 5000 annual average.

TYLER

✠TYLER MUSEUM OF ART
    1300 S. Mahon, 75701. Tel: (214) 595-1001
Ralph Davis, Pres.
Mrs. Ralph Spence, Secy.

Ronald R. Gleason, Dir.
Martha Surls, Cur. Educ.
Carolyn Goldwater, Admin. Asst.
Herbert Allen, Preparator
Free Tues. - Sat. 9 AM - 5 PM; Sun. 1 - 5 PM; cl. Mon. and holi-
days. Financed by membership. Gallery maintained. Mem. 750;
dues. $15 - $2500.
    Exhibitions: George T. Green; Jack Mims; Jim Roche; Robert
Wade; Vernon Fisher; James Surls; Juergen Strunck; Jim Love: In
Pursuit of the Bear.
    Activities: Organized tours; workshops for children and teachers;
Day at the Museum program for local and area fourth grades; travel-
ing exhibitions organized and circulated; lectures open to public,
4 visiting lecturers per year; 4 gallery talks; 150 tours; classes for
children. Sales shop.
    Library: 500 volume reference library.
    Publications: Bulletins; exhibition catalogs.
    Annual Income: $111,343.
    Attendance: 10,000.

WACO

BASE ARMSTRONG BROWNING LIBRARY
    Baylor University, 700 Speight, 76703. Tel: (817) 755-3566
Dr. Jack W. Herring, Dir.
Betty Coley, Librn
Rita Humphrey, Admin. Asst.
Free daily 9 AM - Noon & 2 - 4 PM; Sat. 9 AM - Noon. Estab. 1918
to provide a setting for the personal possessions of the Brownings
and to have as complete as is possible a collection for the use of
Browning scholars; financed by endowment.
    Collections: Meynell; Hagedorn; Shields; Kress; gallery collec-
tion of portraits given by the Kress Foundation; portraits of Robert
Browning by his son, Pen Browning; portraits of Elizabeth Barrett
Browning; portraits of donors; photograph collection of 1200 prints;
8000 volume reference library.
    Activities: To provide complete information to students and
scholars on the Brownings; material available to all for use within
the building only; no fees; lectures open to the public; 3-4 visiting
lecturers per year; dramatic programs; classes for adults; scholarships.
    Publications: Studies in Browning and His Circle, Armstrong
Browning Library Newsletter, two issues yearly; Baylor Browning
Interests Series, published irregularly.
    Income: $75,000.
    Attendance: 15,000.

BAYLOR ART MUSEUM
    Baylor University, 76703. Tel: (817) 772-1867
J.B. Smith, Dir.
Free daily 8 AM - 5 PM; Sat. 8 - 12 AM. Estab. 1967 to take care of
works given to the University and to make special collections for
teaching purposes; financed from university appropriations. The Department of Art maintains a gallery.
    Collections: Small collection of New Guinea sculpture, African
sculpture, and regional paintings. Large collection of original prints.
    Exhibitions: Regional show through Art Department.

✡WACO CREATIVE ARTS CENTER*
    414 Franklin, 76710
Mrs. M. Hardesty, Adminr.

UTAH

BRIGHAM CITY

BRIGHAM CITY MUSEUM-GALLERY
    24 North 3rd West, 84302. Tel: (801) 723-6769
Delone B. Glover, Chmn. of the Board
Phyllis K. Owen, Dir. & Secy.
    Assts:
Ellen Siggard
Ruth Pierce
Fern Burt
Free Mon. - Sat. 11 AM - 7 PM; cl. holidays. Estab. 1970 to
stimulate all ages in their interest and appreciation for art; financed
by city and state appropriations. Museum-Gallery board of local
citizens meets monthly.
    Collections: Paintings; art objects, historical books; photographs;
Indian Pottery; artifacts; book collection - Western History; 10
commissioned oils depicting early modes of western transportation.
    Exhibitions: Competitive Art Festival, two new divisions in
this annual event include, Our Town, paintings of familiar structures
in city and Bicentennial theme. Paintings will be purchased from
both catagories. A number of permanent exhibits are displayed in
fields of history and natural science; monthly art shows by local,

state and national artists, including an annual School Art on Parade
by local students; in addition to 25 art shows, a collector's corner
is featured; Annual Quilt Exhibition and Quilting Bee
    Activities: A Community Art Week with a theme, Portraits of
Liberty, was made possible through a grant from Utah Fine Arts
and the National Endowment for the Arts. The community was
involved with exhibits, concerts, stage productions, contests, and
fire hydrants were painted to represent Revolutionary patriots.
40 tours per year. Book Shop.
    Publications: Monthly announcements and invitations.
    Income and Purchases: Income $9130; purchases vary.
    Attendance: (1973) 10,500; (1974) 11,300.

CEDAR CITY

BRAITHWAITE FINE ARTS GALLERY
    Southern Utah State College, 84720. Tel: (801) 586-4411
Thomas A. Leek, Cur. of Art
Glen Dale Anderson, Asst. to Cur.
Free Mon. - Sat. 9 AM - 6 PM. Estab. for cultural edification,
through the visual arts, of the Southern Utah State College student
body, staff, faculty and the tri-state geographic area which includes
Southern Utah, Southern Nevada, and Northern Arizona; financed by
city and state appropriations.
    Collections: †General permanent collection of two and three-
dimensional art; emphasis on expansion is currently being made on
graphic art.
    Activities: Traveling exhibitions organized and circulated;
invididual paintings and original objects of art lent; 100 color reproductions, 5000 Kodachromes; lectures open to the public; 2 visiting
lecturers per year; 2 gallery talks; concerts; classes for adults;
scholarships. (See Schools)
    Purchases: $5000.

FILLMORE

TERRITORIAL STATEHOUSE
    50 W. Capitol Ave, 84631. Tel: (801) 743-5316
C. Max Martin, Ranger-in-charge
Free June 1 - Sept. 1 8 AM - 9 PM; all other months 9 AM - 5 PM.
Estab. 1930, dedicated by Gov. George H. Dern as a museum for
pioneer relics; restored by the State and local Daughters of Utah
Pioneers. Funds to maintain the Museum are appropriated by the
State; run by State Parks, Division of Parks and Recreation.
    Collections: Over fifty paintings formerly in the Legislative
Hall; seven good pieces of sculptor, some silk screen prints,
charcoal and pencil sketches, lithographs, and Pioneer Portraits in
beautiful antique frames that in themselves are a work of art. Over
200 prints in photograph collection, used for reference.
    Activities: Local art classes and schools make several tours each
year; art classes come for sketching; motion pictures taken by
schools and other organizations, sometimes shown here as courtesy;
lectures open to public, two visiting lecturers per year; several informal gallery talks and tours.

KAYSVILLE

KAYSVILLE COMMUNITY ART LEAGUE
(LeConte Stewart Art Gallery)
    611 Crestwood Rd, 84037. Tel: (801) 376-4438
Gerald Purdy, Pres.
Mrs. Eldean Holliday, Secy.
    Bd. of Dirs:
Mrs. N. V. Sanders
Mrs. Lawrence Welling
Henry Heath
Stephen Whitesides
Robert Bitner
Free Tues. - Fri. 3 - 5 PM; Sun. & Mon. 7 - 9 PM. Estab. 1971
to administer affairs of LeConte Stewart Gallery of Art in Kays-
ville and provide source of funds for its maintenance; financed by
membership. Small gallery near community center remodelled
from historical building. Annual meeting upon call of pres; mem.
655; dues $2.
    Collections: Paintings, lithography and other work of LeConte
Stewart.
    Exhibitions: Utah, 1972 Capitol Building Exhibit; running retro-
spective of LeConte Stewart paintings.
    Activities: Lectures open to the public; 3 gallery talks per year.
    Attendance: 1000 annual average.

OGDEN

ECCLES COMMUNITY ART CENTER
    2580 Jefferson Ave, 84401. Tel: (801) 392-6935
Ronald D. Hales, Pres.
Mrs. Horace Gillespie, Secy.

Mrs. Robert G. Gale, Dir.
Kenneth Davidson, Exhibit Chmn.
Free Mon. - Sat. 9 AM - 5 PM; Sun. 2 - 5 PM; cl. holidays. Estab.
1958 to increase and broaden the opportunities for area citizens to
enjoy and to participate in cultural activities, to render service to all
participating groups in the Center; financed by appropriation and
membership. Gallery, approx. 15 exhibits are held yearly. Ann.
meeting 3rd Mon. of May; mem. 400; dues $5 up to $1000; organizations $20.
   Exhibitions: Local and national exhibits, changing each month.
   Activities: Classes for adults and children; competitions.

PROVO

BRIGHAM YOUNG UNIVERSITY
Harris Fine Arts Center, B. F. Larsen Gallery
   84602. Tel: (801) 374-1211 Exten. 2881
Peter L. Myer, Dir.
Free Mon. - Fri. 8 AM - 10 PM. Estab. 1963 to bring to the University students and faculty a wide range of new experiences in the
visual arts.
   Collections: International collection of prints; Utah artists; 19th
and 20th century American paintings; drawings, sculpture; †Western
art.
   Exhibitions: Monthly exhibitions of one-man shows by invitation;
student and faculty work; circulating exhibits and works from the
permanent collection.
   Activities: Lectures, dramatic programs, concerts.
   Attendance: 150,000.

THE SONS AND DAUGHTERS OF UTAH PIONEERS OF PROVO
   500 N. 500 West St, 84601. Tel: (801) 375-1822
J. Rulon Morgan, Pres.
Lela De. St. Jeor, Secy.
Josephine Bird, Chmn. Museum
Free June - Sept. Mon. - Fri. 9 AM - 5 PM; other times by appoint-
ment. Estab. 1933 to display pioneer relics, artifacts and art;
financed by city and state appropriation. Gallery. Ann. meeting
Mar; mem. 20; dues $1.
   Collections: Relics, artifacts, pioneer cabins, art.
   Activities: Lectures open to the public; 4 gallery talks; concerts.
Book Shop.
   Library: 200 volumes for lending and reference; 200 prints
for lending and reference.
   Income and Purchases: (1975) Income $5000; purchases $5000.
   Attendance: 15,000.

SALT LAKE CITY

COUNCIL HALL
Utah Travel Council
   Capitol Hill, 84114. Tel: (801) 533-5681
Michael D. Gallivan, Dir.
Milt Jolley, Asst. Dir.
Billie Van Pelt, Exec. Secy.
Maury Christensen, Information Dir.
Anne Brillinger, Publicity Dir.
Free Memorial Day - Labor Day 8:30 AM - 6 PM; rest of year 8:30
AM - 5 PM.
   Constructed in 1864-1866, served for almost 30 years as the seat
of government of Salt Lake City and the meeting place of the terri-
torial legislature. Reconstructed on Capitol Hill and formally pre-
sented to the State of Utah in July of 1963, now an official state infor-
mation center and home of Utah Travel Council. Contains small
museum of pioneer and historic significance with paintings and furniture.
   Activities: Traveling exhibitions organized and circulated; photograph library of 2000 photographs, 5000 transparencies, 63 prints
(motion pictures) for lending to organizations, and general public.
   Publications: In-house newsletter; travel newsletter, quarterly.

INFORMATION CENTER AND MUSEUM
Church of Jesus Christ of Latter-day Saints
   Temple Square, 84101. Tel: (801) 531-2675
Keith E. Garner, Dir.
Free winter 8 AM - 6 PM, summer 6:30 AM - 9 PM. Museum estab.
1869, Information Center 1904 to disseminate information and display
historical memorabilia to the visiting public; church financed.
   Collections: Historical and religious paintings and museum
objects.
   Exhibitions: Continuous exhibitions.

✣SALT LAKE ART CENTER
   54 Finch Lane, Reservoir Park, 84102. Tel: (801) 328-2762
Max Smith, Pres.
Thomas Frank, 1st V.Pres.
Boyd Mullins, 2nd V.Pres.

Mrs. Harmon Eyre, Treas.
Mrs. Douglas A. Muir, Secy.
Wayne F. Gledhill, Dir.
Free year-round Tues. - Sun. 1 PM - 5 PM; cl. Mon. and holidays.
Estab. 1931 to foster and develop generally all fine arts and to
educate the public to an appreciation of art. Ann. meeting Sept;
mem. 700; dues from $15.
   Collections: †Primarily 20th century art of the Intermountain
region.
   Exhibitions: Monthly exhibitions of art from Sept. through May,
including Biennial of Intermountain Painting and Sculpture, Inter-
mountain Crafts, Children's World of Art series, and 20th Century
Design series. Notable exhibitions organized by the Center include
100 Years of Utah Painting, Contemporary Bolivian Painting, Com-
puter-Generated Drawings, Program for the Blind, Stimuli, and
Earth Show. Summer exhibitions of selections from the Permanent
Collection.
   Activities: Art Center School and Workshop; Rental-Sales Gal-
lery; docent-guided tours; lectures and panel critiques; films;
annual Arts Festival; annual Beaux Arts Ball; biennal Art Auction;
Archives of Intermountain Art. Gift Shop.
   Publications: Monthly Bulletin; catalogs of key exhibitions;
Annual Report to Members.
   Income: $85,000.
   Attendance: 10,000.

✣UTAH MUSEUM OF FINE ARTS
   104 Art & Architecture Center, University of Utah, 84112.
   Tel: (801) 322-7332
E. F. Sanguinetti, Dir.
Thomas Southam, Asst. Cur.
Jack Hicks, Gallery Supt.
Josephine Theodore, Secy.
Ann Friedman, Registrar
Free weekdays 10 AM - 4 PM; Sat. - Sun. 2 - 5 PM. Estab. 1951,
a museum of fine arts under the administration of the College of
Fine Arts. The Museum's holdings include a wide variety of objects
with an emphasis on 19th century American and French landscape
paintings.
   Collections: There are collections of French 18th century fur-
nishings and tapestries, English 17th and 18th century furniture and
pictures, contemporary graphic works, Egyptian antiquities, and objects from Buddhist cultures. Italian Renaissance paintings and
furniture. Winifred Kimball Hudnut Collection; Marion Sharp Robinson Collection; Bartlett Wicks Collection; Natacha Rambova Egyptian
Collection; Ann McQuarrie Hatch Collection; Franken Japanese Print
Collection; Trower and Michael Collections of English, American
and Peruvian silver.
   Exhibitions: Continuous series of temporary exhibitions organized
by staff; occasional traveling exhibitions; annual faculty exhibition.
Arthur B. Davies Retrospective; A. H. Wyant Retrospective, Robert
Beauchamp, Frank Roth, Wayne Thiebaud, John Marin Drawings,
Adja Yunkers, Homage to Seurat, Alex Katz Retrospective, The
Etching Renaissance in France: 1850-1880, Gene Davis, Prehistoric
Petroglyphs and Pictographs in Utah, Mel Ramos Retrospective, Art
of the Navajo Weaver; (1975-76) Social Concern and the Worker:
French Prints 1830-1910; Abraham Walkowitz Retrospective; Edward
Hopper Exhibition; Works by Joseph Hirsch; David Chihuly: Glass
Cylinders; Point Source: Star Maps, a recent project by Charles
Ross; American Painting 1850; Graphic Styles of the American Eight;
Indian Basket Designs of the Greater Southwest; Utah Painting and
Sculpture 76; Patterns and Sources of Navajo Weaving: the W. D.
Harmsen Collection.
   Activities: Lectures; 7 illustrated lectures on American Folk
Art; scheduled tours for school children; concerts; film series.
   Library: 500 volumes for reference.
   Publications; John Marin Drawings; Drawings by New York
Artists; 20th Century American Drawings - Jacobson Collection;
Social Concern and the Worker: French Prints 1830-1910; Abraham
Walkowitz Retrospective.
   Attendance: 65,000.

UTAH STATE DIVISION OF FINE ARTS
   609 E. South Temple St, 84102.
   Tel: (801) 533-5895, 5896, 5303, 6050
Franz Johansen, Chmn.
Ruth R. Draper, Exec. Dir.
Estab. 1899 as the Utah Art Institute by Utah State Legislature to
promote the fine arts in Utah. Presently a division within the Department of Development Services, State of Utah. Financed by state
and federal appropriations.
   Collections: State-owned collection of paintings, watercolors
and sculpture housed in state-owned buildings. Strong emphasis
on WPA period.
   Exhibitions: Statewide Painting and Sculpture Competition and
Exhibition annually; special exhibits at Carriage House Gallery,
609 E. South Temple.

Activities: Division sponsors traveling exhibitions, regional art shows and statewide competitions in painting and sculpture, literature, drama, and music in cooperation with arts organizations throughout the state. The Division helps to support over 60 arts organizations statewide.

State Appropriation: (1975-76) $324,800.

SPRINGVILLE

SPRINGVILLE MUSEUM OF ART
126 E. 400 S, 84663. Tel: (801) 489-7305
L. Ross Johnson, Dir.
Free Tues. - Fri. 10 AM - 5 PM; Sat. & Sun. 2 - 5 PM; cl. Mon. During Feb, High Schools of Utah Art Exhibit and April, National Show, open every day 10 AM - 9 PM. Collection began 1903; art association inc. 1925; originally started to help young people know the pleasure and encouragement of good art values and study. In addition to big shows, many one-man shows held which help them to know and appreciate good art. City-wide drive each spring, in which federated, civic, sports clubs, churches, schools, etc, participate, quite well accepted and supported.

Collections: Permanent collection consists of 259 †paintings and sculpture; a gift, the Steed Collection, consists of 141 additional paintings.

Exhibitions: Annual National April Art Exhibit; usually two one-man shows each month, one held over, a new one beginning; High Schools of Utah Art Exhibit, February.

Activities: Art classes (usually in the Fall); club meetings, art interested groups; plays in Little Theatre Room; docent classes, receptions, banquets, etc. for which we rent the building. Many state-based and out-of-state schools bring students, mostly art and humanities classes, to tour gallery.

Library: Approx. 200 volumes on art and art history; 500 slides of art work.

Publications: Monograph: Cyrus E. Dallin; catalog of permanent collection.

Attendance: Approx. 10,000.

VERNAL

LITTLE GALLERY OF ARTS
155 E. Main St, 84078.
LeOra Jacobe, Pres.
Free 1 - 9 PM. Estab. 1952; financed by city and state appropriation and membership. Meetings in January, April, July and October; mem. 60; dues regular $5, exhibiting $10.

Exhibitions: Dinosaur Land Art Festival each summer; Crafts and Arts Show each October; Uintah Potters Guild Show; one-man shows.

Activities: Competitions and special events.

Publications: Arty Facts, quarterly.

VERMONT

BENNINGTON

BENNINGTON MUSEUM, INC.
W. Main St, 05201. Tel: (802) 442-2180
Peter W. Cook, Chief Cur.
Stanley R. Pike, Jr, Adminr.
Eugene R. Kosche, Cur. of Military & Mechanical Arts
Charles G. Bennett, Librn.
Open Mar. 1 - Nov. 30, 9 AM - 4:30 PM; summer, 9 AM - 6 PM; cl. Dec, Jan. & Feb. Inc. 1876, opened building 1928; local historical museum with gallery. Grandma Moses Schoolhouse Museum. Ann. meeting Spring; mem. 650; dues $10 and higher.

Collections: Largest collection of Bennington Pottery on public display, rare collections of American Blown and Pressed Glass, a gallery of Grandma Moses paintings, collections of furniture, rare documents, historical costumes and uniforms, firearms and swords, toys and dolls, Early American household items, contemporary Vermont and other European paintings and sculptures, and the famous Bennington Flag.

Activities: Lectures; gallery tours for organized classes of school children; gallery of changing exhibitions. Gift shop.

Library: Genealogical reference file for Bennington and surrounding area; full time librarian.

Income: Approx. $150,000.

Attendance: 80,000.

BURLINGTON

UNIVERSITY OF VERMONT
Robert Hull Fleming Museum
05401. Tel: (802) 656-2090
Richard H. Janson, Dir.

Nina Parris, Cur.
Free Mon. - Fri. 9 AM - 5 PM; Sun. 1 - 5 PM; cl. Sat. and most holidays. Estab. by Act of Legislature 1826 as College (Society) of Natural History; reorganized 1931. Mem. 300; dues $4 and higher.

Collections: †American and †European painting, sculpture, drawings, and prints; †American design and costumes; Oriental and †Primitive art (African, Oceanic, Pre-Columbian, Read collection of American Plains Indian art); Egyptian and †Classical antiquities; Assyrian sculpture.

Changing Exhibitions of mostly 20th century art.

Activities: Visiting lecturers; gallery talks; film series; school tours.

Library: 1200 volumes.

Publications: 2 or 3 exhibition catalogues per year.

Purchases: $15,000 annually.

Attendance: 20,000 per year.

FAIRLEE

WALKER MUSEUM
Route 5, 05045. Tel: (802) 333-9572
Herbert Brooks Walker, Pres.
Brooks & Noel Walker, Dirs.
Free July - Sept. daily 10 AM - 5 PM; donations accepted. Estab. 1960; temporarily closed for reparations.

Collections: †Japanese Room; Iranian Bazaar; †Chinese porcelains; †Americana, kitchen aids, toys, furniture; †Canadian displays; †Amerindian; †18th and 19th century American paintings; †minerals; †Polynesia; †costumes.

Exhibitions: Open air exhibits.

Activities: Materials and items lent to libraries and schools, ethnographic, illustrative, economic surveys, etc; Wagon loans by appointment.

Library: 1000 volumes for reference; photographic collection of 1000 items and 500 Kodachromes.

Attendance: Approx. 1000.

MANCHESTER

SOUTHERN VERMONT ART CENTER
05254. Tel: (802) 362-1405
Dr. Ilsley S. Zecher, Pres.
James L. Montague, Dir.
Mrs. Arthur Pierce, Dir. Public Relations
Open June - mid-Oct daily except Mon, 10 AM - 5 PM. Estab. 1929 to promote education in the arts and to hold exhibitions of art in its various forms. Ann. meeting Sept; mem. 1100; dues, artist $10, layman $15 and higher.

Collections: †Permanent collection of contemporary American sculptors and painters and loan collection; permanent collection additions by gift.

Exhibitions: Annual exhibition for members; Fall Show; one-man and special exhibitions.

Activities: Summer classes in painting, drawing, graphic arts, photography, creative writing, sculpture.

Library: 500 volumes of arts and history.

Publications: Annual catalog.

Sales: $35,000 yearly.

Income: $100,000 from all sources.

Attendance: 15,000 during the season.

MIDDLEBURY

✠JOHNSON GALLERY
Middlebury College
05753. Tel: (802) 388-2762
David A. Bumbeck, Dir.
Free daily 1 - 5 PM; Sat. 9 AM - Midnight. Estab. 1968 primarily as a teaching collection but also sponsor exhibitions of selected artists; fianaced by Middlebury College.

Collections: †Paintings, †Prints, †Drawings, †Sculpture.

Publications: Annual Report.

SHELDON ART MUSEUM
Park St, 05753. Tel: (802) 388-2117
Harold M. Curtiss, Pres.
Mrs. Nina R. Mudge, Cur.
Open June 1 - Oct. 15, Mon. - Sat. 10 AM - 5 PM; winter hours by appointment. Admis. Adults $1, children 50¢. Estab. 1882 for the preservation of portraits, furniture and artifacts of Middlebury. Seventeen rooms arranged as a 19th century Vermont home. Mem. approx. 400; dues $3 and higher. New library and research center.

Attendance: Average 2500.

MONTPELIER

VERMONT ARTS AND CRAFTS SERVICE
   136 State St, 05602. Tel: (802) 828-3128
D'Ann Calhoun Fago, Dir.
Lois E. Jackson, Asst. Dir.
   Arts and Crafts Council:
Irma Hegard, Acting Chmn.
Angela Hinchey
Arthur Ericson, Dir, Vocational-Technical Educ.
Open 8 AM - 4:30 PM. Estab. 1941 by Act of State Assembly,
carrying on a state-wide program for young people and adults to
improve design and workmanship, encourage participation in the
applied arts and stimulate interest through bulletins, talks and exhibitions; offers Marketing and Design Consulting Service, emphasis
on development of functional cottage crafts with high standards of
workmanship and greater use of natural resources abundant within
the state (i.e, wool, wood, etc); Workshop/Demonstration Program
coordinates a program that takes practicing craftsmen into the
schools on a regular basis. Revolving fund makes loans to craftsmen for purchases of materials.
   Library: Small but comprehensive craft library.
   Publications: Bi-monthly Newsletter.

T. W. WOOD ART GALLERY
   Kellog-Hubbard Library Bldg, Main St, 05602.
Ronald Slayton, Cur.
Edmund Dunstan, Pres.
Mrs. H. R. Seivright, Secy.
Ralph Geer, Treas.
Free Tues. - Sat. Noon - 4 PM; cl. Sun. & Mon. Estab. 1895, inc.
1896 to house paintings by Thomas Waterman Wood; later
acquired works by American artists of 1920's and 30's. Ann.
meeting Dec; solicit town every year for patrons; dues single $3,
family $5, patron $25, contributor $100.
   Exhibitions: Eight special or one-man shows are held.
   Publications: Monograph on T. W. Wood, $3.
   Attendance: 4000.

RUTLAND

CHAFFEE ART GALLERY
Rutland Area Art Association, Inc.
   16 S. Main St, 05701. Tel: (802) 775-0356
Edith Smith, Pres.
Free daily 11 AM - 5 PM; Sun. 1 - 4 PM. Estab. 1961, inc. 1962
and sponsored by the Rutland Area Art Association, to promote and
maintain an educational and cultural center in Rutland for the
area artists, photographers, craftsmen and others in the art field;
appropriation from the City of Rutland. Ann. meeting Oct; dues
exhibiting artists $10, inactive artists and laymen $5 and higher.
   Exhibitions: Annual Members Exhibit, juried; Autumn Members
Exhibit, juried; one-man and invitational exhibits. Art-in-the-Park
outdoor festival mid-August; Foliage Festival, mid-October.
Displays of photography, flower arrangements, hobby collections,
special shows.
   Activities: Special events in performing arts, art lectures,
musicals, craft and art demonstrations, slide shows; art classes
in summer for children, teens and adults.
   Publications: Calendar of Events annually.
   Attendance: 6000 registered guests annually.

ST. JOHNSBURY

**ST. JOHNSBURY ATHENAEUM PUBLIC LIBRARY AND ART
   GALLERY**
   30 Main St, 05819. Tel: (802) 748-8291
Arnold Munkittrick, Pres, Board of Trustees
Catherine E. Dyer, Secy, Board of Trustees
Jean F. March, Librn.
Free 10 AM - 5 PM; also Mon. & Fri. 5 - 8 PM; Sat. 10 AM - 2 PM.
Estab. 1873, inc. 1882. Ann. meeting Jan.
   Art Gallery contains about 100 paintings, chiefly American
and European 19th century and copies of Old Masters; several
Hudson River School. Art Library contains some rare and many
standard works.
   Attendance: 2500.

SHELBURNE

SHELBURNE MUSEUM
   05482. Tel: (802) 985-3344
J. Watson Webb, Jr, Pres.

Kenneth E. Wheeling, Acting Dir.
Joseph J. Quinn, Asst. Dir.
Open May 15 - Oct. 15, daily 9 AM - 5 PM; admis. adults $4; stu-
dents $2. Estab. Nov. 18, 1947. Ann. meeting June.

Outdoor Museum
   Over 35 buildings and houses on 45 acres. Five furnished period
houses, early as 1733. Lighthouse; Shaker Horsestand Shed; Country Store and Apothecary Shop; Meeting House; Horseshoe Barn;
Stage Coach Inn; Slate Jail; Hunting Lodge and Art Gallery; Blacksmith and Wheelwright Shop; School House; 10-Wheel Locomotive;
Railroad Cars and Station; Sidewheeler S.S. Ticonderoga; Circus
Parade Building.
   Collections: (All active) Carriages, coaches, wagons, sleighs,
craftsmen's hand tools, fire fighting equipment, toys, model railroad,
pewter, china, glass, paintings, prints, dolls, doll houses, clocks,
decoys, weaving, quilts, coverlets, samplers, rugs, razors, sculptured folk art, farm equipment and tools, brass and bronze foundry
patterns, live bee exhibit, one-inch model circus parade and 40 car-
ousel figures.

Webb Gallery
   American 18th and 19th century primitives and academic painting, 65 known artists represented.

Electra Havemeyer Webb Memorial Building
   Collection of European Art, furniture and furnishings of the late
Mr. and Mrs. J. Watson Webb, co-founders.
   Library: Reference library and photograph collection.
   Attendance: Approx. 150,000.
   Note: The Shelburne Museum and the University of Vermont offer
jointly a study program in American Art and Design at the museum
in the summer months.

SPRINGFIELD

SPRINGFIELD ART AND HISTORICAL SOCIETY
   9 Elm Hill, 05156. Tel: (802) 885-2415
Dr. Jeremy Brown, Pres.
Mrs. Fred R. Herrick, Secy. & Receptionist
Free Mon. - Fri. 12 AM - 4:30 PM; appointment only Sat, Sun, and
holidays.
Since the Miller Art Center was first organized in 1955, there has
been a gradual but consistent expansion of the types of activities and
exhibits sponsored by this Organization. While the emphasis on Art
has been continuous, there has been a redirection of purpose to include hand crafts, ballet classes, and historical exhibits. Because
of the demonstrated interest in and support for the historical activities, and to reflect the multiple purposes of the Center, the name of
the Organization has been changed to the Springfield Art and Historical Society.
   Collections: Primitive portraits by Horace Bundy, Aaron D.
Fletcher, Ashel Powers; dolls and doll carriages, toys and banks;
Richard Lee pewter; Bennington Ware.
   Exhibitions: Paintings changing monthly; historical material
associated with the early days of Springfield.
   Activities: Classes in painting, drawing, early American
decorating; lectures; reproductions of Horace Brown's painting,
Long View, are for sale. Small Sales Gallery of Paintings. Give
Art for Christmas Sale in December.
   Library: Small reference library.
   Attendance: Approx. 2800.

WAITSFIELD

BUNDY ART GALLERY
   P.O. Box 19, 05673. Tel: (802) 496-3713
Harlow Carpenter, Dir.
Elizabeth Joslin, Adminr.
Free July 1 - Aug 31 weekdays 10 AM - 5 PM; Sun. 1 - 5 PM; cl.
Tues. and July 4. Estab. 1962, inc. 1963 to make contemporary art
and an art library accessible to the public and to enhance the cul-
tural life of surrounding communities.
   Collections: †Contemporary painting and sculpture.
   Activities: Concerts.
   Library: Small library of reference and lending.
   Attendance: Approx. 2000.

WINDSOR

SAINT-GAUDENS NATIONAL HISTORIC SITE
   United States Department of the Interior, National Park
   Service, Saint Gaudens Rd, P. O. Box, Windsor, VT 05089.
John H. Dryfhout, Cur.
For information see Cornish, New Hampshire.

VIRGINIA

ALEXANDRIA

THE ATHENAEUM
Northern Virginia Fine Arts Association
    201 Prince St, 22314. Tel: (703) 548-0035
Mrs. Robert Bruce Rogers, Jr, Pres.
Capt. Donald E. Willman, 1st V.Pres.
Stanley L, Krejci, 2nd V.Pres.
Benjamin R. Achenbach, Secy.
R. Sherrard Elliot, Jr, Treas.
Mrs. James S. Lacy, Jr, Coordinator
Open Sept. - May Tues. - Sat. 10 AM - 4 PM; Sun. 1 - 4 PM; cl.
Mon; also open summer 1976. Estab. 1964 to promote education,
appreciation, participation and pursuit of excellence in all forms of
arts and crafts; to enrich the cultural life of the metropolitan area
and Northern Virginia. Mem. approx. 600; dues single $20, double
$25 and higher.
    Exhibitions: (1975-76) Art in Stitches, 1975; Horace Day's 30
Years Ago: A Soldier/Artist in World War II; Seven Trees of
Christmas; Michael Loyer One Man Show (Winner 1975 Juried Show);
American Primitives; The Athenaem Show: 7th Annual Juried;
Alexandria Heritage: Antique Silver, Furniture and Porcelain;
Alexandria Seaport City (last two are Bicentennial Shows).
    Activities: Lectures, including Clement Conger, Fred Cain,
safaries to Virginia Museum and other cultural attractions, Civili-
zation series.
    Publications: Monthly Newsletter.
    Attendance: 15,000.

BLACKSBURG

THE BLACKSBURG REGIONAL ART ASSOCIATION
    c/o Bernard J. Sabaroff, Pres, 2501 Capistrano St, 24060.
Bernard J. Sabaroff, Pres.
Pat Furey, Secy.
Estab. 1950, a chapter of the Virginia Museum of Fine Arts
dedicated to the encouragement and the enjoyment of the arts.
Meetings several times per year; dues single $5, family $7.50.
    Collections: †Collection of paintings (12) by contemporary
artists who have exhibited in Blacksburg.
    Exhibitions: Nine in last three years.
    Activities: Traveling exhibitions organized and circulated from
Virginia Museum of Fine Arts; lectures open to the public, 3-5
visiting lecturers per year; concerts; dramatic programs;
competitions.

VIRGINIA POLYTECHNIC INSTITUTE AND STATE UNIVERSITY
College of Architecture Library
    24060. Tel: (703) 951-6182
Charles Burchard, Dean
Robert E. Stephenson, Architecture Librn.
Free Mon. - Thurs. 8 AM - 11 PM; Fri. - Sat. 8 AM - 5 PM; Sun.
2 - 11 PM. Estab. 1928 to provide library service to the College of
Architecture and the other divisions of the University; financed by
state appropriation and membership.
    Collections: 25,600 volumes for lending and reference on
architecture, art, building construction, urban affairs and planning;
planning file of 2000 pieces.
    Income and Purchases: Income $38,930; purchases $38,930.

VIRGINIA POLYTECHNIC INSTITUTE AND STATE UNIVERSITY
Department of Art, Owens Hall
    24061. Tel: (703) 951-5547
Dean Carter, Head Dept. & Prof.
Gallery hours indefinite for new location, probably Mon. - Fri. 8 AM -
5 PM, plus some evenings; no admis. fee. Estab. 1969 to provide
situation for students to display work, as well as work of faculty,
other artists in area and nation, and traveling exhibitions. To supplement art curriculum as well as to provide stimulating visual presentations for academic community and public; financed by city and
state appropriation. Gallery maintained.
    Exhibitions: Egyptian Folk Tapestries and Sculpture; African
Textiles; Southeastern Graphics Council Traveling Exhibition; Woodcuts by Bernard Solomon; shows of various faculty members, several
yearly exhibitions of student works; yearly calendar allows approximately 14 exhibition time slots.
    Activities: Faculty traveling exhibition organized and circulated;
original objects of art lent to other colleges and departments at
University; lectures open to public; classes for adults; scholarships.
(See Schools)
    Publications: Gallery announcements; department newsletter.
✠Squires Art Gallery*
    Squires Student Center, 24061. Tel: (703) 951-5535
Thomas C. Lile, Dir. of Squires
Thomas F. Butterfield, Dir. Arts

Free Mon. - Sat. 8 AM - Noon; Sun. 9 AM - Noon. Estab. Sept,
1969, to provide interesting and informative exhibits on the local and
national level for the students, faculty and the college community;
financed by student activity fee and building operation. Weekly meetings of students and advisor to plan shows and events.
    Activities: Lectures open to public, approx. 3 visiting lecturers
per year; competitions.
    Income and Purchases: Income $3000-$5000 per year; purchases
$300 per year.
    Attendance: For one year of operation, 50,000 visitors.

CHARLES CITY

WESTOVER
    Charles City County, 23030.
Mrs. B. C. Fisher, Owner
Mrs. B. C. Pearce, Mgr.
Grounds and Garden open daily 9 AM - 6 PM; admis. $1. (House not
open).
    Built about 1730 by William Byrd II, Founder of Richmond, the
house is considered an outstanding example of Georgian architecture
in America, with steeply sloping roof, tall chimneys in pairs at both
ends, the elaborate Westover doorway; three story central structure
with two end wings. The path from the Caretakers House near the
gate to the house is lined with tulip poplars over 100 years old; former kitchen is a separate small brick building, believed to be older
than the residence. East of the house is the foundation of an old ice-
house, a dry well with passageways leading under the house to the
river; The Westover gates of delicate ironwork incorporate initials,
WEB; lead eagles on the gateposts, supporting fence columns topped
with stone finials cut to resemble pineapples, bee-hives, and other
symbolic designs. Long-established boxwood garden with tomb of
William Byrd II. Members of his family, and Capt. William Perry,
who died Aug. 6, 1637, are located in old church cemetary one-fourth
mile west of house.

CHARLOTTESVILLE

FISKE KIMBALL FINE ARTS LIBRARY
    University of Virginia, 22903. Tel: (804) 924-7024
Mary C. Dunnigan, Librn.
Theresa McDaniel, Slide Librn.
Free Mon. - Fri. 8 AM - 5 PM; Sat. & Sun. during school terms
8 - 11 AM. Architecture and Art Libraries combines in 1970, as
a research facility for School of Architecture, Art and Drama
Departments; financed by city and state appropriation.
    Library: $41,000 collection, approx. 50 percent non-circulating;
4000 prints for lending; slides (architecture) 50,000.
    Income: $20,000 - $40,000 (book and slide purchases).

THOMAS JEFFERSON MEMORIAL FOUNDATION
Monticello
    P.O. Box 316, 22902. Tel: (804) 295-2657
Walter M. Whitehill, Pres.
James A. Bear, Jr, Cur.-Dir.
Open Mar. 1 - Nov. 1, 8 AM - 5 PM; Nov. 1 - Feb. 28, 9 AM - 4:30
PM; admis. adults $2, children 6-11 years and school groups, 50¢.
    Monticello is owned and maintained by the Thomas Jefferson
Memorial Foundation, a non-profit organization founded in 1923.
The home of Thomas Jefferson, designed by him and built 1769-
1809 contains many original furnishings.

UNIVERSITY OF VIRGINIA ART MUSEUM
    Thomas H. Bayly Memorial Bldg, Rugby Rd, 22903.
    Tel: (804) 924-3592
Frederick Hartt, Dir.
David B. Lawall, Cur.
Open Tues. - Sun. 1 - 5 PM; cl. major holidays. Mem. 260; dues
student $5, other $15-250.
    Collections: 19th and 20th centure American; 17th and 18th
century European; Asian.
    Attendance: 10,347.

FARMVILLE

BEDFORD GALLERY
Longwood College Art Department
    23901. Tel: (804) 392-9359
Barbara L. Bishop, Chmn. Dept. of Art
Free Mon. - Fri. 9 AM - Noon & 1 - 5 PM; Sat. & Sun. 2 - 6 PM;
cl. holidays. Estab. Sept. 1970 to present works by professional
artists for benefit of college and local community; financed by
city and state appropriation.
    Collections: Contemporary work by Virginia artists; works by
Thomas Sully, 19th century American artist; Art Department
Collection, 20th century prints, paintings, crafts.

Exhibitions: (1974-75) Drawings, Prints, and Sculpture by Ida Trusch and Katharine Gilbert; Recent Work, Paintings and Prints by Janice Lemen; The Miles C. Horton, Jr, Collection; Longwood College Student Exhibit; African Collection from Permanent collection of Hampton Institute; Watercolors by Lee Montgomery; (1975-76) Summer 75, Barbara Ames, Etta Edwards, Gwendolyn Hain, and Lyn Yeatts; American Prints from collection of Roanoke Fine Arts Center; Craft Collectables, Enamels by Virginia Bedford, Furniture by Tom Wessells, Knotted Wall Hangings and Small Items by Gertrude Shook, Pottery by June Kapos, Jim Lane, and Julia Phillips, Sculpture to Wear by Peter Wreden; Prints, Drawings, Photographs by Barbara L. Bishop; Jewelry and Weaving by Ron and Barbara Wyancko; Works by Bernard Martin.

Activities: Individual objects of art and paintings lent; lectures open to the public, 6 visiting lecturers per year; 2 gallery talks; tours by request.

Publications: Fine Arts Calendar, invitations to individual exhibits.

Purchases: Average up to $1000.

Attendance: 5000.

HAMPTON

HAMPTON INSTITUTE COLLEGE MUSEUM

23668. Tel: (804) 727-5308
Mrs. Julia Roberts Vodicka, Dir.
Free Mon. - Fri. 8 - 5 PM. Estab. 1911.

Collections: †African, Oceanic, †Pre-Columbian American Indian; †contemporary graphics, drawings and paintings.

Activities: Lectures, gallery talks.

Library: Art reference; 500 volumes.

Budget: $34,000.

Attendance: 8500.

HARRISONBURG

DUKE FINE ARTS GALLERY

Madison College Art Department
Main at Grace Sts, 22801. Tel: (703) 433-6216
J. David Diller, Head, Art Department
Free Mon. - Fri. 8 AM - Noon & 1 - 4:30 PM; and by special appointment. Estab 1968 for temporary exhibition, for both teaching purposes and public enjoyment; financed by city and state appropriation.

Collections: Very small permanent collection includes Staples Collection of Indonesian Art; most other works 20th century art.

Exhibitions: (1973-74) The Disasters of War; Contemporary American Art; Virginia Fraktur; Faculty Art Show; Image of an Age; Leonardo Da Vinci Inventions; Senior Art Show; Designs for Theater; 20th Century American Sculpture; Graduate Art Students Exhibits; (1975-76) Robert Sowers, Stained Glass; Clifford Earl, Sculpture; Primitive Arts and Crafts from the Shenandoah Valley and Other Early American Objects; William Marriot, through the Privacy of the Mail; Samuel Reese, Prints Produced in Prison; Art Department Faculty; Experiments with Gallery Space, Students at Madison College; The American Coverlet, From the Collection of the Smithsonian Institution, Douglas Withers, Needlepoint; Communication Graphics 1974-1975, From the American Institute of Graphic Arts; Charles Renick, Sculpture Work of the Mentally Ill, from the New York Area; Allen Carter and Michael Platt, Drawing, Painting, Sculpture; Video Works, Students at Hartwick College, Oneonta, New York; Street Scene 1776' A Fine Arts Festival Honoring Founders' Day and Our Nation's Birthday; Harvey Breverman, Prints and Bronze Reliefs; Madison College Student Work.

Activities: Loans limited to faculty and a few students at Madison College, 300 color reproductions, 100 lantern slides, 25,000 Kodachromes, 20 motion pictures, 100 film strips in lending collection; photograph collection; lectures open to the public, 4 visiting lecturers per year; one gallery talk; classes for adults; scholarships.

LEESBURG

OATLANDS

Rte. 2, Box 352, 22075. Tel: (703) 777-3174
Miriam G. Rabb, Adminr. & Property Council & staff of National Trust Interpretors
Carole T. Scanlon, Coordinator, Interpretive Programs
Open Apr. 1 - Oct. 31, Mon. - Sat. 10 AM - 5 PM; Sun. & legal holidays 1 - 5 PM; cl. end of Oct. - Mar. 31; admis. adults $1.50, senior citizens 75¢, group rates by arrangements; free to National Trust members.

Oatlands is a Classical Revival Mansion constructed by George Carter, son of Robert (Councillor) Carter (circa 1800-06). Oatlands is a property of National Trust for Historic Preservation operated as an historic house museum and a community preservation center. It was partially remodelled in 1827 when the front portico with hand carved Corinthian capitals added. Confederate troops were billeted here during the Civil War. The home remained in possession of the Carters until 1897.

In 1903, Mr. and Mrs. Corcoran Eustis of Washington, D.C, bought Oatlands. Their daughters gave the property to the National Trust for Historic Preservation.

Oatlands is essentially a Carter House with the Eustis collection of furniture. Greek-Revival ornament adorns the interior. Terraced boxwood, magnolias, a bowling green and a gazebo grace the elaborate formal gardens.

Property serves as a focal point for advancing historic preservation and develops new relationships among cultural, community preservation groups and National Trust members in its area. Responds to community preservation needs by acting as a link between community and appropriate regional or headquarters offices of National Trust.

Located in the heart of Northern Virginia hunt country, the property is protected by 261 preservation easements which help insure the estate's continuing role as a center for equestrian sports and events which are produced by various groups in Loudon County. Interpretive Programs provide focus on Oatlands particular case study in historic preservation. 'Christmas at Oatlands' and Members Day during National Historic Preservation Week in early May. The Carriage House conference room may be reserved for meetings. Preservation Shop.

Attendance: (1975) 21,200.

LEXINGTON

WASHINGTON AND LEE UNIVERSITY

DuPont Gallery
24450. Tel: (703) 463-9111, Exten. 351
Dr. Gérard Maurice Doyon, Dir.
Prof. I-Hsiung Ju, Exhibitions
Open Sept. - May 9 AM - 4:30 PM; no admis. Estab. 1942, mostly as a teaching gallery consisting of monthly shows of contemporary work of living artists and student shows; endowment.

Exhibitions: Mostly student shows.

Activities: Museum apprenticeship with the Virginia Museum, Richmond, and the North Carolina Museum, Raleigh; lectures open to the public; 1 - 5 gallery talks; scholarships.

Library: Over 3000 art volumes in university library.

Art Budget: $12,000 plus salaries.

Attendance: Students 200-300 per day, others 5 - 10 per day.
University Collection
24450. Tel: (703) 463-9111, Exten. 350 or 351
Prof. Marion M. Junkin, Cur.

Collection in storage until the university obtains a museum; financed by endowment.

Collections: Major collection of 18th and 19th century American paintings; minor collection of 17th - 19th century European paintings; a major collection of Chinese export porcelain, one of the best and largest in United States.

Activities: Traveling exhibitions organized and circulated; individual paintings lent to schools; original objects of art lent; Chinese export porcelain and American paintings in lending collection; photograph collection.

LORTON

GUNSTON.HALL PLANTATION

22079. Tel: (703) 550-9220
Mrs. Frederick Frelinghuysen, First Regent
Capt. Walter W. Price, Jr, Dir.
Louise L. Stockdale, Mgr.
Bennie Brown, Jr, Librn.
Margaret C. Roudabush, Exec. Secy.
Open 9:30 AM - 5 PM; admis. adults $2, students 6-16 50¢. Estab. to acquaint the public with George Mason, Colonial patriot and his 18th century house and gardens; owned and operated by Commonwealth of Virginia.

Activities: School programs, films, slides on architecture, archaeology, furnishings and decorative arts, and gardens, as well as history; extension department serves Northern Virginia; material available to schools; no fees; traveling exhibitions organized and circulated; lending collection, 5 slide presentations, 5 motion pictures, 7 film strips; photograph collection; lectures for members only; 8 visiting lecturers per year; concerts.
Museum Shop.

Library: Reference library extensive rare book collection, archives.

Attendance: 42,000.

LYNCHBURG

LYNCHBURG FINE ARTS CENTER, INC.
1815 Thomson Dr, 24501. Tel: (804) 846-8451
Ralph E. Burnette, Pres.
Orion A. Templeton, Secy.
Jane McKee Mundy, Adminr.
Mrs. Donald Hudson, Secy. & Bookkeeper
David Gilbert, Guest Orchestral Conductor
Rudy Hazucha, Asst. Conductor
George B. Clarke, Asst. Conductor
Stephen Endres, Art Dir.
Phillip Sommer, Theatre & Technical Dir.
Vallerie Sommer, Asst. Theatre & Technical Dir, Children's
Theatre Dir.
Open Mon. - Fri. 9 AM - 5 PM; other hours depending upon programs; no admis. to building, $3 for theatre production and concerts, $3.50 for musical play. Estab. 1958 to promote interest in and appreciation and talent for art, music, dramatic literature and other fine arts; supported by membership. Ann. meeting 2nd Tues. after 1st Sun. in June; mem. 1800 (goal 2200); dues single $25, double $45, student $15.
Exhibitions: Ten each year, plus twice-annual visit by Virginia Museum Artmobile.
Activities: Art sales gallery; lectures and programs open to public; concerts, dramatic programs; theatre classes for children, art classes for children and adults, dance classes for children and adults.
Publications: FACets, monthly newspaper (except August).

RANDOLPH-MACON WOMAN'S COLLEGE
2500 Rivermont Ave, 24504. Tel: (804) 846-7392
William Quillian, Pres. of Coll.
Elliott R. Twery, Chmn. Art Dept.
Kent Ahrens, Cur.
Open 9 AM - 9 PM. Estab. a collection of American painting for general and specific educational use; endowment. Art gallery was built in 1952 in cooperation with the National Gallery of Art, it houses part of the permanent collection and is used for special exhibitions; open by appointment.
Collections: Extensive collection of American painting.
Activities: Objects lent; photography collection; lectures; concerts; dramatic programs; library.

MC LEAN

INDUSTRIAL DESIGNERS SOCIETY OF AMERICA
1750 Old Meadow Rd, 22101. Tel: (703) 893-5575
James F. Fulton, Pres.
Thomas Hal Stewart, Exec. Dir.
For further information see p. 6.

MIDDLETOWN

BELLE GROVE
Box 57, 22645. Tel: (703) 869-2028
George Smith, Adminr.
Wynn Lee, Asst. Adminr, Property Council & staff of volunteers
Carole T. Scanlon, Coordinator, Interpretive Programs
Open Apr. 1 - Oct. 31 Mon. - Sat. 10 AM - 4 PM; Sun. & legal holidays 1 - 5 PM; cl. Oct. 31 - Mar. 31; admis. adults $1, senior citizens 50¢, group rates by arrangement; free to National Trust members.
A property of the National Trust for Historic Preservation. Preserved as an historic house, operated seasonally as a center for community programs.
Belle Grove was built in 1794 for Major Isaac Hite, Jr, a Revolutionary War officer. During the Civil War Battle of Cedar Creek, the house served as the headquarters of General Phillip Sheridan. The late Francis Welles Hunnewell bequeathed Belle Grove to the National Trust. Built of dressed native limestone, the classical one-story structure has two porticos and interior architecture with fine paneling, cornices, and refinements suggested by Thomas Jefferson.
Belle Grove is an historical farm in the heart of the Shenandoah Valley. The rooms of the farmhouse are often filled with the activities of spinning and weaving, oral history workshops, or open hearth cooking workshops, as it fulfills a role as a center for the interpretation of rural folk life.
Seasonal programs include summer archaeological program for students, Farm Craft Days co-produced with surrounding community groups as well as a railsplitting contest. Members Day during National Historic Preservation Week is in early May. A set of 10 x 8 inch measured drawings of Belle Grove, taken by Historic American Buildings Survey, are available from the Preservation Shop.

MOUNT VERNON

MOUNT VERNON
22121. Tel: (703) 780-2000
Mrs. Thomas Turner Cooke, Regent
Mt. Vernon Ladies' Association
Charles C. Wall, Resident Dir.
Open to the public every day in the year from 9 AM; ent. gate closes Mar. 1 - Oct. 1 at 5 PM; Oct. 1 - Mar. 1 at 4 PM; admis. $1.
The home of George Washington, purchased 1858 from his great-grand-nephew by the Mt. Vernon Ladies' Association of the Union, which maintains it. Ann. meeting Oct.
The Mansion is fully furnished with original and period furniture, silver, portraits and prints. Large collection of relics. Library theme, George Washington. Personal papers; biographical; life of the period and locale. The estate includes spinning house, coach house, various quarters, restored flower and kitchen gardens. Also the tomb of George and Martha Washington.
Attendance: Approx. 1,250,000.

POPE-LEIGHEY HOUSE
22121. Tel: (703) 780-3118
George Smith, Adminr.
Susan Smith, Asst. Adminr, Property Council & staff of National Trust Interpretors
Carole T. Scanlon, Coordinator, Interpretive Programs
Open early Apr. - end of Nov, Sat. & Sun. 9:30 AM - 4:30 PM; cl. end of Nov. - end of Mar; admis. adults $1.25, senior citizens 60¢; combination ticket with Woodlawn mansion, adults $2, senior citizens $1, group tours by special arrangement with Administrator; appointments available for study groups and architects.
Pope-Leighey is a house museum of the National Trust for Historic Preservation, located on the grounds of Woodlawn.
This residence was designed in 1940 by Frank Lloyd Wright for his client, the Loren Pope Family. Built of cypress, brick, and glass, the Usonian structure contains such features as a flat roof, radiant heat, indirect lighting and build-in furniture all designed by Frank Lloyd Wright, and all considered unusual for their time.
Threatened by proposed construction of an interstate highway in 1964, Mrs. Majorie Folsom Leighey, second owner, presented the property to the National Trust for Historic Preservation. It was then moved to the Woodlawn grounds.
Publications: Brochure and paperback history of house.
Attendance: (1975) 7500.

WOODLAWN
22121. Tel: (703) 780-3118
George Smith, Adminr.
Susan Smith, Asst. Adminr, Property Council and staff of National Trust Interpretors
Carole T. Scanlon, Coordinator, Interpretive Programs
Open daily 9:30 AM - 4:30 PM, including legal holidays; cl. Christmas; admis. adults $1.25, senior citizens 60¢, group rates by arrangement. Combination ticket (in season) with Pope-Leighey House (on grounds) adults $1.25, senior citizens 60¢, group rates for both houses.
The land, a grist mill, and the site for the mansion were presented by General George Washington to Eleanor and Lawrence Lewis. After the Lewis period, the property was purchased by a Quaker business firm. Many Quakers settled on the original 2000 acres and the lands were divided into small farming lots. One family, the John Mason family of New Hampshire, bought the Woodlawn mansion and some adjacent acreage. They built Grand View, and permitted the families of the surrounding farms to use Woodlawn Mansion as a school and meeting place for the social, religious and civic groups in and around Woodlawn. The Mason period covers 1851 until 1892. Later owners of Woodlawn included Broadway playwright and producer Paul Kester (1900-1905) who initiated some preservation efforts within Woodlawn mansion, which were continued by the next owner, Mrs. Frances Sharp. By 1924, Woodlawn was purchased by U.S. Senator Oscar W. Underwood. The property remained in the Underwood family until 1948. When it was offered for sale it was purchased by the Woodlawn Public Foundation. In 1951 the foundation's trustees decided that the visiting public would be better served if Woodlawn was administered by the National Trust.
The mansion furnishings are largely from the Federal and early Empire periods, and include Lewis family memorabilia and gifts from the Robert Woods Bliss and Colonel Garbish collection.
Property serves as a focal point for advancement of historic preservation in Northern Virginia. Through it are developed new relationships among cultural, community, preservation groups and National Trust members in its area. Responds to community preservation needs by acting as a link between community and appropriate regional or headquarters offices of National Trust. Operates as a small conference center for preservation-education programs produced by

the National Trust such as the annual Woodlawn Conference for Historic Site Administration; participates in the National Trust Summer Intern Program.

Interpretive programs emphasize Woodlawn's particular case history in historic preservation. Needlework exhibit each March with accompanying needle point classes. Carols by candlelight in December.

Attendance: (1975) 53,000.

NEWPORT NEWS

THE MARINERS MUSEUM
Museum Dr, 23606. Tel: (804) 595-0368
Dr. William J. Hargis, Jr, Pres.
William D. Wilkinson, Dir.
John O. Sands, Cur. Prints & Paintings
John L. Lochhead, Librn.
Open Mon. - Sat. 9 AM - 5 PM; Sun. 12 AM - 5 PM; cl. Dec. 25; admis. adults $1, children 6-16 50¢, under 6 free. Estab. 1930 by Archer M. Huntington. The most extensive marine collection in this country which has enchanted millions. The thousands of artifacts exhibited in nine galleries include hundreds of famous prints and paintings, models of famous ships from sail to steam and navigation equipment including full-size operating lighthouse lens. Huge cannons, anchors, bells on the grounds with picnicking in 880-acre park and fishing on 167-acre lake.

Collections: †Paintings and prints, numbering about 12,000, of sailing ships, steamships, harbors, naval ships and battles, whaling, fishing and yachting; over 80 figureheads; †800 ship models; †navigational instruments; †whaling and fishing equipment; †sailors' handiwork and tools; †lighthouse and lifesaving equipment; †full-sized small craft; ships' equipment; †ceramics, †silver and glassware designed in nautical motifs.

Exhibitions: Selections from the above collections are displayed in 9 exhibition halls. Permanent exhibitions include Chesapeake Bay, Marine Painting and Decorative Arts, History of Seapower, and the August F. Crabtree Exhibition of Miniature Ships. In a courtyard is a display of small boats. There are outdoor displays of anchors and cannon. There is also statuary by Anna Hyatt Huntington. Special exhibitions on maritime subjects are held periodically.

Activities: Rotating exhibitions of the museum's material annually; Junior League guides; other tours are arranged.

Library: More than 46,000 books and pamphlets, a large group of periodicals; 3000 ship papers; 6000 maps and charts; and more than 100,000 photographs are available for reference.

Attendance: 150,000.

PENINSULA ARTS ASSOCIATION
10207 Warwick Blvd, P.O. Box 1546, 23601.
Tel: (703) 596-8175
Ralph Tudor, Pres.
Henry L. Gordner, 1st V.Pres.
Judge Nelson Durden, 2nd V.Pres.
Thelma Akers, Dir.
Free Tues. - Sun. Noon - 5 PM. Estab. 1962. Ann. meeting May; mem. 579; dues $10 and higher.

Exhibitions: Rotating gallery of crafts from all parts of state; monthly one- and two-man exhibits; Annual Members Show; Statewide Juried Show with nationally recognized juror (with Virginia Museum of Fine Arts); Artists and Craftsmen in residence; Annual Craft Festival with art exhibit and craftsmen demonstrating; Annual Christmas Craft Show; Artmobile Exhibits from Virginia Museum of Fine Arts of which we are a chapter.

Activities: Children's art and craft classes; classes for adults.
Publications: Monthly newsletter.
Attendance: 4000.

NORFOLK

CHRYSLER MUSEUM AT NORFOLK
Mowbray Arch and Olney Rd, 23510. Tel: (804) 622-1211
Walter P. Chrysler, Jr, Pres. & Dir.
Dennis R. Anderson, Cur. of Western Art & Senior Cur.
L. Lindsey Jones, Cur. of Decorative Arts
Shirley H. Ganse, Cur. of Eastern Art
Paul E. Doros, Cur. of Glass
Michael B. Goodwin, Cur. of Photography
Thomas W. Styron, Registrar
Ann Dearsley-Vernon, Cur. of Educ.
Morris L. Jones, Dir. of Special Projects
Donald E. Harris, Pub. Relations
Frederick H. Wahlig, Adminr.
Free daily 10 AM - 5 PM; Sun. 11 AM - 5 PM; cl. Christmas, New Year's. Founded 1926. Mem. 2700; dues individual $10, family $20, sustaining $50, friend $100, business $100.

Collections: Arts from Egypt, Greece, Rome, Near East, Middle East, Far East, Africa, Orient, pre-Columbian America; Italian, French, Dutch, Flemish, English, German, American paintings and sculptures of all periods; ancient to modern glass from Asia, Africa, Europe, Sandwich, Tiffany, Galle, New England glass; American, English, French, Italian, German furniture, decorative arts; textiles; costumes, jewelry; silver; china; artifacts.

Activities: Docent program; lectures; gallery talks; guided tours; films; drama; concerts; dance recitals; ballet; puppet shows; formally organized education programs for adults, children and for undergraduate college students; inter-museum loans, permanent and temporary exhibitions.

Publications: Newsletter and Calendar monthly; exhibition catalogs.

Attendance: 128,300.

Adam Thoroughgood House (c. 1656)
Thoroughgood Lane and Parrish Rd, Thoroughgood Estates, Virginia Beach, Va. 23455. Tel: (804) 622-1211. 16th century.

Moses Myers House (1791)
323 E. Freemason, Norfolk, Va. 23510. Tel: (804) 622-1211. 18th century.

Willoughby-Baylor House (1794)
Freemason and Cumberland Sts, Norfolk, Va. 23510. Tel: (804) 622-1211. 18th century.

Open Apr. - Nov. Sun. Noon - 5 PM; Mon. - Sat. 10 AM - 5 PM; Dec. - Mar. Noon - 5 PM; cl. Christmas, New Year's; admis. 50¢, students and children 25¢.

THE HERMITAGE FOUNDATION
7637 North Shore Rd, Lochhaven, 23505. Tel: (804) 423-2052
Philip R. Morrison, Dir.
Open 7 days a week, 10 AM - 5 PM; cl. Christmas; admis. $1, children 25¢. Estab. 1937 to maintain and operate museum. Ann. meeting Oct; mem. 350; dues $17.50.

Collections: Paintings; furniture; Oriental and Near-Eastern arts including bronzes, ceramics, textiles and rugs; European decorative arts.

Activities: Art classes; 10 lectures per year; gallery tours.
Library: Approx. 600 volumes, general art.
Income: $60,000-$70,000.
Attendance: Over 20,000 annually.

IRENE LEACHE MEMORIAL ASSOCIATION
c/o Mrs. Charles R. Dalton, Pres, 556 Mowbray Arch, 23507.
Mrs. Charles R. Dalton, Pres.
Mrs. Frank Nash Bilisoly, Secy.
Estab. 1905. Ann. meeting May; mem. 25. Maintains a Memorial Room in the Chrysler Museum at Norfolk, containing early Renaissance paintings and sculpture.

Activities: Biennial Art Exhibition; Spring Literary Festival; 5 lectures a year.

MacARTHUR MEMORIAL
City Hall Ave. and Bank St, 23510.
Tel: (804) 441-2256 Office & Library; 441-2382 Reception Desk
R. H. Alexander, Dir.
Janice Dudley, Secy. to Dir.
Open weekdays 10 AM - 5 PM; Sun. 11 AM - 5 PM.
In 1962 the Old Court House building, built originally in 1847, was remodeled and re-built with a rotunda and exhibition rooms to house the extensive memorabilia given to the City of Norfolk by General of the Army, Douglas MacArthur. The Memorial was opened Jan. 26, 1964, General MacArthur's 84th birthday. The late General's remains are entombed in the Memorial. Operated by City of Norfolk.

Library: MacArthur Archives; General MacArthur's personal library of 4000 volumes; collection of periodicals, newspapers, speeches.

Budget: (1976) $168,843.
Attendance: 120,000.

RESTON

NATIONAL ASSOCIATION OF SCHOOLS OF ART
11250 Roger Bacon Dr, 5, 22090. Tel: (703) 437-0700
Paul B. Arnold, Pres.
Samuel Hope, Exec. Secy.
For further information see p. 8.

RICHMOND

AGECROFT ASSOCIATION
Agecroft Hall
Sulgrave Rd, 23221. Tel: (703) 353-4241
John C. Williams, Pres.-Dir.
Open Tues. - Fri. 10 AM - 4 PM; Sat. & Sun. 2 - 5 PM; admis. adults $1, students 50¢. Open to the public July 1969; house of

the 15th century transported from England in 1926-28 showing collection of furniture; endowed.

Collections: †Tudor furniture; photograph collection, audio-visual slide commentary; portraits in oils.

ASSOCIATION FOR THE PRESERVATION OF VIRGINIA* ANTIQUITIES
2705 Park Ave, 23220. Tel: (804) 359-0239
Elbert Cox, Pres.
Robert A. Murdock, Exec. Dir.
Conover Hunt, Cur. Collections
Estab. 1889 to acquire and preserve historic buildings, grounds, and monuments in Virginia. Ann. meeting May; mem. 6000; dues student $1, adult $5, couple $8, contributing $25, sustaining $50, life $300, institutional $10.

Twenty-six Branches administering forty properties in Virginia. Among the properties: Jamestown Island; Walter Reed Birthplace, Gloucester; Rolfe-Warren House, Surry County; John Marshall House, Richmond, Scotchtown, Hanover County; Mary Washington House and Rising Sun Tavern, Fredericksburg; Prestwould, Clarksville; Smithfield Plantation, Blacksburg; Farmers Bank, Petersburg; Cape Henry Lighthouse, Virginia Beach. Hours and admissions vary according to location.

Permanent collections of decorative arts; quarterly newsletter, Discovery; occasional publications; library at headquarters housing approximately 1700 volumes on art and history available for use on premises.

THE FEDERATED ARTS COUNCIL OF RICHMOND, INC.
The Carillon, 1300 Blanton Ave, 23221. Tel: (804) 353-8182
Norruth D. Graham, Jr, Pres.
Mrs. C. Coleman McGehee, Secy.
Thomas P. Bryan, Chmn. of the Board
Mrs. R. Spencer Hines, V.Pres.
Mrs. J. Clarke Chase, Exec. Secy.
Open Mon. - Fri. 9 AM - 1 PM. Estab. 1949 to increase the artistic expression and experiences of Richmond's citizens of all ages; to serve as a unified voice for all the arts; to protect the position of the arts as a vital and necessary part of life; to foster the growth of the arts; to consider the needs of the community in the arts and to seek ways and means of providing adequate and coordinated programs and projects to meet these needs; financed by city and state appropriations and membership. Ann. meeting May.

Collections: 130 volume library.
Activities: Concerts and dramatic programs; Arts Center Development.
Publications: Calendar of Events, 150,000 copies are circulated with telephone books; quarterly newsletter.
Income and Purchases: Income $15,000; purchases $6520.
Attendance: (1974) 74,300.

HAND WORK SHOP, INC.
316 North 24th St, 23223. Tel: (804) 649-0674
Katherine Tevepaugh, Pres.
T. Jackson Abernathy, Secy.
Ruth T. Summers, Exec. Dir.
Carol Ellyson, Coordinator Educ.
Mrs. Grayson Crawford, Bookkeeper
Free Mon. - Sat. 10 AM - 4:30 PM. Estab. 1963 to promote interest in the hand crafts and arts, teaching these skills to children and adults; to provide an outlet where craftsmen can sell their work; endowment. Two room gallery where solo and duo shows of crafts are shown Sept-June. Annual meeting 4 times yearly; 20 board mem; no dues.
Collections: †Pottery and weaving.
Activities: Classes for adults and children; workshops.
Income and Purchases: Income $50,000; purchases $10,000.
Attendance: 10,000 annual average.

SCHOOL OF ARTS LIBRARY
Virginia Commonwealth University
325 N. Harrison St, 23284
Alice B. Deal, Dir.
Joan L. Muller, Asst.
Nancy S. Brantley, Asst.
Free Mon. - Fri. 9 AM - 5 PM. Estab. 1926 to support the teaching program of eleven departments of the School of the Arts; financed by state appropriation.
Collections: A slide collection of approx. 110,000 2 x 2 inch colored transparencies of art works (architecture, painting, sculpture, applied arts). A collection of 12,500 exhibit catalogs, worldwide in scope, from galleries and museums.
Activities: 200,000 items lent in average year; 110,000 Kodachromes, 19 motion pictures, 13 film strips and 10 video tapes in lending collection.

VALENTINE MUSEUM
1015 E. Clay St, 23219. Tel: (804) 649-0711
Henry T. Wickham, Pres.
Mrs. John H. Cronly, Chmn.
Jean Du Val Kane, Dir.
Meredith Beal, Cur. House
Elizabeth T. Childs, Cur. Collections
Mrs. Luther C. Wells, Cur. Costumes
Linda B. Berlekamp, Cur. Textile Resource & Resource Center
Mrs. Stuart B. Gibson, Cur. Research Library
Open Tues. - Sat. 10 AM - 4:45 PM; Sun. 1:30 - 5 PM; cl. Mon; admis. adults $1, students 59¢, family group not to exceed $2.50, adults in groups of 12 or more, 50¢ per person, military free. Estab. 1892. Mem. 2000; dues (July 1-June 30) $10 and higher; Junior Center mem. 5-18 (May-May) $3.

A general museum dealing in all aspects of man's environment, interpreting the life and history of the area through its diversified collections. Four-building complex includes Wickham-Valentine House (1812) maintained as a typical 19th century Richmond residence and teaching building; Indian collection; pipe collection; costume collection, Textile Resource and Research Center; Research Library; Junior Center (junior museum and activities center); special rotating exhibits interpreting area history including biennial art show; 19th century Sculpture Studio.

Exhibitions: Richmond in Paintings and Drawings.
Activities: Lectures; tours; Junior Center activities; classes for adults and children; scholarships.
Publications: Valentine Profile (bimonthly for Museum members); occasional catalogs; Silhouette (quarterly for Textile Resource and Research Center Members).
Income and Purchases: $224,000.
Attendance: 10,000.

VIRGINIA HISTORICAL SOCIETY
Battle Abbey
428 North Blvd, 23221. Tel: (804) 358-4901
Joseph C. Robert, Pres.
John Melville Jennings, Secy. & Dir.
Howson W. Cole, Librn.
William M. E. Rachal, Ed. of Publ.
Mrs. Kenneth W. Southall, Cur. of Special Collections
Galleries open Mon. - Fri. 9 AM - 5 PM; Sat. & Sun. 2 - 5 PM; library open Mon. - Fri. 9 AM - 5 PM; admis. $1. Estab. 1831 for collecting, preserving, and making available to students and scholars research materials relating to the history of Virginia; endowed; maintained by membership. Gallery with historical portraiture and paintings. Mem. 3300; dues vary according to class.
Collections: †Manuscripts; †printed books; †newspapers; †maps; †engravings and photographs; †portraits and other paintings.
Activities: Lectures for members only. Book Shop.
Library: Printed books, approx. 250,000 for reference only; m manuscripts, approx. 3,500,000; photograph collection of 125,000 prints for reference; maps; newspapers; broadsides; sheet music.
Publications: Virginia Magazine of History and Biography, quarterly; and Occasional Bulletin, semi-annually; Documents Series, full-length books.
Attendance: (1974) approx. 20,000.

✠VIRGINIA MUSEUM OF FINE ARTS
Boulevard & Grove, 23221. Tel: (804) 770-6344
Dr. William H. Higgins, Jr, Pres.
James M. Brown, Dir.
Fred Haseltine, Asst. to Dir. & Head Pub. Information Dept.
George Cruger, Head, Publications Dept.
William Ryan, Head, Design Dept.
Helen Dohn, Secy. of the Museum
Collections Division
Pinkney Near, Head
Elizabeth Culler, Registrar & Asst. Cur.
Betty Stacy, Librn.
Programs Division
William Gaines, Head & Programs Dir.
Fred Brandt, Asst. Head
Phyllis Houser, Asst. Head
Charlotte Major, Supv. Educ. Services
Catherine Grinnan, Supv. Art Services
Judy King, Supv. State Services
Robert Albertla, Chapter Coordinator
Lisa Hummel, Loans Registrar
David Pittman, Artmobile Coordinator
Julia Williams, Supv. Loan-Own Art Services
Theatre Division
Keith Fowler, Producing Dir.
Loraine Slade, Mgr.
Administrative Division
Donald A. Nicholas, Adminr.
A. W. Stalnaker, Asst. Adminr.

Kenneth Beam, Controller
Louise Wilcox, Mem.
Open Tues. - Sat. 11:00 AM - 5 PM; Sun. 1 - 5 PM; cl. Mon; admis.
50¢, free Sat. & Sun. Estab. 1934; building opened 1936; Theatre
opened 1955; South Wing added 1970. Ann. meeting May; mem.
13,700; dues $25 and higher.
    Collections: Representative examples of the arts from early
Egypt to the present time, including paintings, sculpture, furniture
and objets d'art. Comprehensive collections of early Greek vases
(8th century to 4th century B.C); archaic Chinese bronzes; archaic
Chinese jades. Special Collections: The John Barton Payne collection of paintings, prints and Portuguese furniture; T. Catesby Jones
collection 20th century European paintings and drawings; Lillian
Thomas Pratt collection of Czarist Jewels by Peter Carl Faberge;
†Arthur and Margaret Glasgow collection of Flemish and Italian
Renaissance paintings, sculpture and decorative arts; Mrs. Arthur
Kelly Evans collection of pottery and porcelain; Lady Nancy Astor
collection of English china; †Adolph D. and Wilkins C. Williams
collection of paintings, tapestries, china and silver; Branch collection
of Italian Renaissance paintings, sculpture and furniture. Nasli and
Alice Heeramaneck collection of art of India, Nepal, Kashmir and
Tibet; Ailsa Mellon Bruce Collection of 18th century furniture and
decorative arts; Meissen Porcelain Collection of Dr. and Mrs.
Arthur Mourot.
    Exhibitions: (Biennials) Virginia Artists; Virginia Designers;
Virginia Interior Designers; Virginia Architects/Planners; Virginia
Photographers; Virginia Craftsmen. American Painting quadrennial;
25 special exhibitions annually.
    Activities - Gallery Activities: Lectures in relation to current
loan exhibitions; morning and evening classes for children and adults
in painting, drawing, graphics, ceramics, weaving and dramatics;
awards 10-15 fellowships annually to Virginia artists; 3 Artmobiles
travel to large and small communities throughout the State with exhibitions; one additional Artmobile travels exclusively to college campuses; circulates more than 100 traveling exhibitions throughout the
State; Statewide activities include 30 confederated organizations.
Theatre Activities: Seven drama productions each year; professional
dance events; music concerts; and ten films yearly; Repertory
Equity Theatre Company; lectures, workshops and demonstrations.
    Library: 30,000 volumes on art techniques and history of art.
The Library is growing rapidly.
    Publications: 9 Bulletins annually; catalogs for special exhibi-
tions and collections; Arts in Virginia 3 times annually; brochures,
programs and invitations.
    Participating in the Museum's programs are The Fellows of the
Virginia Museum, who meet yearly to counsel the Museum on its
future plans; The Women's Council, which sponsors and originates
special programs; the Collectors' Circle, a group of Virginia art
lovers who meet four times a year to discuss various aspects of
collecting; the Corporate Patrons, State and local business firms
who lend financial support to Museum programs; and Virginia
Museum Youth Guild.
    Attendance: 265,000-270,000 average at headquarters build-
ing; 1,250,000 average entire state-wide system.

ROANOKE

ROANOKE FINE ARTS CENTER
    301 23rd St, S.W, 24014. Tel: (703) 342-8945
Hugh Fletcher, Jr, Pres.
David R. Goode, 1st V.Pres.
Mrs. Ronald B. Harris, 2nd V.Pres.
Mrs. James B. Feltner, Secy.
Dr. Robert Murray, Treas.
Walter M. Hathaway, Dir.
Shirley N. Coffey, Secy.
Ann Masters, Program Coordinator
Dori B. Blay, Center Hostess
Pat Kinder, Business Manager
Cary Jones, Downtown Gallery Hostess
Hawthorne Bigler, Registrar
Roanoke Fine Arts Center open to public Tues. - Fri. 10 AM - 5 PM;
Sun. 1 - 5 PM. Gallery in Public Library open Tues. - Sat. 12 AM -
5 PM. Estab. 1951 to encourage and develop interest in the arts, to
provide ways and means for the purchase of works of art, to add to
the cultural enrichment of the Roanoke Valley. Mem. 1300; dues
$12.50 and higher.
    Collections: Virginia artists; American prints and drawings;
Mediterranean antiquities; Decorative Arts Gallery.
    Exhibitions: Town Square—Sidewalk Art Show, June, $4000
prizes; Area Photo Show, April. Roanoke Fine Arts Center—two
monthly exhibits. Downtown Library Gallery—Area Artist Show,
Oct; juried and loan exhibitions.
    Activities: Borrow or Buy Gallery; Art Mart; members events,
classes.

Library: Small reference library.
Publications: Monthly Calendar of Events.
Income and Purchases: Income approx. $65,000 annually; purchases
$1500.
    Attendance: 20,000.

STRASBURG

STRASBURG MUSEUM
    King St, 22657. Tel: (703) 465-3428
Virginia H. Cadden, Pres.
Ellen H. Hatmaker, Secy.
Volunteer Staff
Open May - Oct. 10 AM - 4 PM; admis. family $1.25, adults 50¢,
children 25¢. Estab. 1970 as a repository of artifacts from a
rural Shenandoah Valley community; a center of ceramic study
and production based on the historical significance of pottery to
this community; financed by membership. Ann. meeting Jan;
mem. 300; dues $2.50.
    Exhibitions: (1974) Oil paintings and watercolors from local
artists.
    Activities: Classes for adults and children.
    Income: $3000.
    Attendance: 4000.

VIRGINIA BEACH

VIRGINIA BEACH ARTS CENTER
    1916 Arctic Ave, 23451. Tel: (804) 428-9294, 425-5987
Carol Doyle, Coordinator
Jo Dyckman, Secy.
Open to public Mon. - Fri. 10 AM - 5 PM. Estab. 1951, inc. 1953,
to promote the Arts in the Tidewater Area, particularly in the City
fo Virginia Beach; a chapter of the Virginia Museum of Fine Arts.
Mem. 1000; dues $8 and higher.
    Exhibitions: Exhibitions monthly; Annual Summer Boardwalk
Art Show: $5000 prizes, $180,000 sales.
    Activities: Lectures, tours; classes; films.
    Publications: Newsletter.

WILLIAMSBURG

✠ABBY ALDRICH ROCKEFELLER FOLK ART COLLECTION
    23185. Tel: (804) 229-1000 Exten. 2424
Beatrix T. Rumford, Dir.
Donald Walters, Assoc. Cur.
Barbara Luck, Registrar
Free daily summer 10 AM - 9 PM; Sun. Noon - 9 PM; winter daily
Noon - 8 PM. Estab. 1939.
    The Abby Aldrich Rockefeller Folk Art Collection is one of the
country's leading collections of American folk art of the 18th and
19th centuries.
    Collections: Over 2000 paintings, sculptures, and decorative
useful wares which are shown in a building especially designed for
this purpose and which borders the colonial area.
    Exhibitions: (1974) Collectors' Choice: Paintings of James
Sanford Ellsworth, Collectors' Choice: Paintings from the Collection
of Mr. and Mrs. Peter H. Tillou, European Traditions Reflected
in American Folk Art, Printed Sources of American Folk Art,
Virginia Fraktur; (1975) Paintings of Queena Stovall, Three New
England Watercolor Painters, Folk Pottery of the Shenandoah
Valley, Sheldon Peck: 19th Century Folk Portrait Painter, American
Historical Decorated Stoneware; plus yearly Christmas shows
developed around varying themes.
    Activities: Special tours for school and study groups, traveling
exhibitions, lecturers, and a series of film sequences on folk art
subjects.
    Library: Approx. 1500 volumes, including a collection of 19th
century drawing book sources, chiefly concerning American art and
artists.
    Publications: Annual catalogue of special exhibit; revised and
updated catalogue of the collection to be published in 1977.
    Attendance: Approx. 123,000 annually.

THE COLONIAL WILLIAMSBURG FOUNDATION
    P.O. Drawer C, 23185. Tel: (804) 229-1000
Carlisle H. Humelsine, Pres.
Donald J. Gonzales, V.Pres. & Dir. Pub. Relations
Hugh De Samper, Dir, Press Bureau
Graham S. Hood, Dir. & Cur. of Collections
Exhibition buildings and craft shops open 9 AM - 5 PM. Folk Art
Collection free daily 12 AM - 6 PM.
    The colonial area of this 18th century capital of Virginia, en-
compassing 173 acres with nearly 500 homes, shops, taverns,
public buildings, and dependencies, has been carefully restored to

its original appearance. Included are 90 acres of gardens and greens. The work was initiated by the Late John D. Rockefeller, Jr, in 1926.

There are more than 30 exhibition homes, public buildings and craft shops where guides and craftsmen in colonial costume show visitors the arts and decorations as well as the way of life of pre-Revolutionary Virginia. In addition, there are historic Bruton Parish Church, the Abby Aldrich Rockefeller Folk Art Collection and the Courthouse of 1770. The exhibition properties include 211 furnished gallery rooms.

The principal Exhibitions are:

†The Capitol—one of colonial America's most important buildings—scene of Patrick Henry's oration against the Stamp Act.

†The Gaol—where debtors, criminals and Blackbeard's pirates were imprisoned.

†Raleigh Tavern—one of the most famous taverns of colonial times, where Virginia patriots plotted Revolutionary action, and social center of the capital.

†Brush-Everard House—small well-appointed home, typical of a comfortable but not wealthy colonial.

†Governor's Palace and Gardens—residence of royal governors. Outstanding English and American 18th century furnishings and extensive formal colonial gardens.

†Wythe House—home of George Wythe, signer of Declaration of Independence and teacher of Jefferson and John Marshall.

†Public Magazine—arsenal of the Virginia colony, now exhibiting colonial arms.

†Peyton Randolph House—original residence of the first president of the Continental Congress.

†Wetherburn's Tavern—among the most famous of 18th-century Virginia's hostelries, over 200 years old.

†James Geddy House—original dwelling and workshop of a well-known colonial silversmith and businessman.

†Wren Building of the College of William and Mary—the oldest academic building in British America, with six rooms open to the public and the remainder still in use for college classes and faculty offices.

†Craft Shops—the trades and crafts of 200 years ago are carried on in 20 authentically furnished Craft Shops where artisans use the tools and methods of the 18th century.

Collections: Colonial Williamsburg, presents a cross-section of colonial Virginia life in the furnishings of the public buildings, taverns, shops and homes. The collections of American and English furnishings, with frequent additions, include representative pieces, rare English pieces in the Palace, 18th century American paintings, English pottery and porcelains, English silver, exceptionally fine textiles and rugs.

Information Center: Outside the Historic Area this modern center houses graphic exhibits of the restoration and colonial life. Continuous showings of a full-color, Vista Vision film, Williamsburg: The Story of a Patriot.

Activities: Williamsburg Forum Series, annual events including Antiques Forum; Garden Symposium; regular performance of 18th-century dramas, organ recitals and concert music; slide lectures. Limited grant-in-aid program for researchers.

Publications: Books and brochures on Williamsburg and colonial life; gallery book of the Folk Art Collection; documentary motion pictures; audiovisual material.

Attendance: Approx. 1,000,000.

✣DEPARTMENT OF FINE ARTS
College of William and Mary
  23185. Tel: (804) 229-3000, exten. 385 or 650.
Dr. R. K. Newman, Chmn. Dept.
Louise Kale, Interim Registrar
Free Mon. - Fri. 10 AM - 4 PM and by appointment. Art Collection and exhibition of works began in 18th century for purposes of teaching, research and pleasure; financed by endowment, city and state appropriation and donation. Small exhibition room used for rotating exhibits.

Collections: 18th-19th century American portrait collection; The Jean Outland Chrysler Collection of Modern Paintings; The Alice Aberdein Collection of Oriental Arts and Crafts.

Exhibitions: Loan shows; items from College Art Collection; faculty and student exhibitions.

Activities: Original objects of art lent occasionally; lending collection, lantern slides; photograph collection of 300 prints for reference; lectures open to the public; 3 visiting lecturers.

WASHINGTON

BELLEVUE

PACIFIC NORTHWEST ARTS AND CRAFTS ASSOCIATION*
  376 Bellevue Square, 98004. Tel: (206) 454-0234
Ralph Garhart, Pres.
Mrs. George D. Salisbury, Secy.
Roger Peterson, Treas.
Estab. 1947. Principle purpose to exhibit the work of artists and craftsmen of the Pacific Northwest. All work is for sale. Monthly Board meeting; mem. approx. 40. Special exhibitions; annual Outdoor Fair in July. Annual awards approx $8500 all media.

Collections: Pacific Northwest Arts and Crafts Permanent Collection presently housed at the Bellevue Public Library.

BELLINGHAM

WHATCOM MUSEUM OF HISTORY AND ART
  121 Prospect St, 98225. Tel: (206) 676-6981
Mrs. Richard Fleeson, Chmn. Museum Bd.
Susan H. L. Barrow, Dir.
George E. Thomas, Cur.
Emil Mierson, Admin. Coordinator
Open Tues. - Sun. 12 AM - 5 PM; cl. Mon. Estab. 1942 to collect, preserve, and interpret regional historical objects and art; maintained through joint appropriation from City of Bellingham and Whatcom County. Museum is housed in a restored building constructed in 1892 as a city hall. Ann. meeting last Thurs. in Jan; mem. 750; dues $15.

Collections: Aboriginal with emphasis on Northwest Coast; pioneer and settlers objects; art with emphasis on contemporary. Permanent display of aboriginal artifacts; regional period rooms; logging dioramas and tools; mounted birds of the area.

Special Exhibitions: Arts of a Vanished Era (catalog), northwest Indian material; Green Gold Harvest (catalog), logging history; The Fourth Corner (book), early settlement of the area; Whatcom Seascapes (catalog), waterfront history; regular exhibits of regional artists; changing historical exhibits.

Activities: Classes for college credit in Museology, and ceramics; classes in art history, crafts, children's art; guided tours for school classes; lectures; school loan exhibits. Museum Shop.

Publications: The Fourth Corner, Eighteen Men and a Horse, The Harris Journal, Booming and Panicking on Puget Sound, Skqee Mus, Arts of a Vanished Era, Green Gold Harvest, Whatcom Seascapes, A Report: Master Carvers of the Lummi, Guide to Bird Finding in Washington.

Income and Purchases: Income $117,000; purchases $10,000.

Attendance: (1974-75) Over 100,000.

CLARKSTON

VALLEY ART CENTER INC.
  842 Sixth St, 99403. Tel: (509) 758-8331
Pat Rosenberger, Pres. & Exec. Dir.
Erma Holcroft, Secy.
Open weekdays 9 AM - 4 PM; Sun. 2 - 5 PM; admis. by donation. Estab. July, 1968 to foster the education and enjoyment of the visual arts in the area, through lecture, exhibits and classes in art; financed by membership. Exhibiting space for 200 paintings; exhibits change each four weeks. Ann. meeting last Wed. in Jan; mem. 156; dues $6, $10, $25.

Exhibitions: Alfred Dunn Watercolor; Bronze Artist Pamella Harr; other Northwest artists.

Activities: Conduct year around art classes, an affiliate of Walla Walla Community College for credit courses, specialized art classes; traveling exhibitions organized and circulated; paintings by local artists lent to public places and libraries; lectures open to public; 4 gallery talks per year; 4 - 6 tours; classes for adults and children; competitions.

Publications: Quarterly Newsletter to patrons.

Attendance: 7800.

ELLENSBURG

FINE ARTS GALLERY
Central Washington State College
  98926. Tel: (509) 963-2665
James M. Sahlstrand, Dir.
Free, Mon. - Fri. 8 AM - 5 PM. Estab. 1970 to present as many and as varied exhibits as possible of both local and national origin; as a space for the presentation of student work; to be of service to both the college and the community; financed by city and state appropriations.

Exhibitions: New Photographics (National Competitive Exhibit); Invitational and Competitive Print and Jewelry Exhibits; other invitational shows throughout the year.
Activities: Lectures open to the public; competitions; films.
Publications: Catalogs for all national and invitational exhibits.

MARYHILL

MARYHILL MUSEUM OF FINE ARTS
98620. Tel: (509) 773-4792
Robert Campbell, Dir.
Open Mar. 15 - Nov. 15 daily 9 AM - 5 PM; admis. adults $1, students 50¢, children 8 and under free. Estab. 1922 and endowed by Samuel Hill to provide a general Museum for the Mid-Columbia area of the Northwest. Ann. meeting May. Building contains 22 galleries. National Historic Site.
Collections: Rodin sculpture and drawing; 19th century American and French sculpture; royal furniture designed by Marie, Queen of Roumania, and memorabilia; European and American paintings; American Indian baskets; Columbia River Basin prehistoric arts; antique and modern chessmen; World War II costumed French Fashion mannequins, a gift of La Chambres de la Coutiere Parisienne; portraits of Columbia River Gorge wildflowers by Sally Haley.
Library: Small library for staff use only.
Income: $80,000.
Attendance: Over 80,000.

OLYMPIA

✤STATE CAPITOL HISTORICAL ASSOCIATION
State Capitol Museum
211 W. 21st Ave, 98504. Tel: (206) 753-2580
Gerry Alexander, Pres.
Mrs. Judson McKinley, Secy.
Kenneth R. Hopkins, Dir.
Delbert J. McBride, Cur.
Free Tues. - Fri. 10 AM - 4 PM; Sat. 12 AM - 4 PM; Sun. 1 - 4 PM. Estab. 1941; primarily a historical museum, but operates a fine arts program, including changing exhibits of non-local origin, traveling exhibits and various class activities; financed by appropriation and membership. Museum contains one gallery devoted to changing art exhibitions. Ann. meeting in summer; mem. 350; dues $6 regular.
Collections: Collection of Northwest paintings and sculpture; collection of Indian arts.
Exhibitions: Annual Governor's Invitational Exhibition.
Activities: Develop and present school programs for museum visitation, training docents, extension service to schools, etc; extension service to Southwest Washington for schools and public; traveling exhibitions organized and circulated; original objects of art lent; concerts; classes for adults and children. Gift Shop.
Attendance: 50,000-60,000.

PULLMAN

WASHINGTON STATE UNIVERSITY MUSEUM OF ART
99163. Tel: (509) 335-1910, 1603
Harvey L. West, Dir.
Bruce Guenther, Cur.
June Harbour, Exec. Secy.
Free Mon. - Fri. 10 AM - 4 PM & 7 - 10 PM; Sat. & Sun. 1 - 5 PM. Estab. Sept, 1974 to house the university's collection of 19th and 20th century American art and provide through a varied exhibition schedule access for the college community to the broadest possible range of human creative endeavor; financed by city and state appropriation.
Collections: Late 19th century to present day American art with particular strength in the areas of the Ash Can School and Northwest regional art scene.
Exhibitions: Faculty Exhibition, Greco-Roman Artifacts/Goya/ Daumier/NW Indian Tools, Wright Collection/Symposium, Hofmeister, Dickinson/Mason, Permanent Collection, The Chair, The Northwest Painter, Larsen Textile, NW Sculpture, Print Exhibit/ Symposium, Laisner, Student Reviews.
Activities: Washington State Art Services Program makes material available to city and county arts organizations, private art associations and to individuals for set fee, plus transportation; traveling exhibitions organized and circulated; original objects of art lent; 100 items lent in average year; lectures open to public, 7 visiting lecturers per year; 8 gallery talks; 3 tours; concerts. Book shop.
Publications: Two exhibition catalogs; monthly posters and mailers.
Attendance: 38,000.

RICHLAND

ARTS COUNCIL OF THE MID-COLUMBIA REGION
P.O. Box 735, 99352. Tel: (509) 943-0524
Helen B. Maurer, Pres.
Marjorie Peterson, Secy.
Steven R. Markstrom, Arts Coordinator
Free Mon. - Fri. 9 AM - 5 PM. Estab. April 2, 1968, to encourage, promote and coordinate the arts; financed by membership. Board meetings 3rd Thurs. of each month; mem. 140; dues $5, $10, $25.
Exhibitions: Promotes several invitational and juried shows each year.
Activities: Artist-in-residence program covering 2 counties; concerts; dramatic programs; classes for adults and children; competitions; scholarships; library.
Publications: Monthly Calendar/Newsletter.
Income: $10,000.

SEATTLE

ALLIED ARTS OF SEATTLE, INC.*
107 S. Main St, 98104. Tel: (206) 624-0432
Paul E. S. Schell, Pres.
William E. Talley, 1st V.Pres.
Mrs. Jonathan Whetzel, 2nd V.Pres.
Mrs. D. F. Ellsworth, Secy.
Nancy Erickson, Treas.
Alice Rooney, Exec. Dir.
Free, 9 AM - 5 PM. Estab. 1954 to promote and support the arts and artists of the Northwest and to help create the kind of city that will attract the kind of people who support the arts; financed by membership. Ann. meeting Jan; mem. 750; dues $2.50-$25 depending on category.
Exhibitions: Occasionally co-sponsor an exhibition in a Seattle gallery or museum.
Activities: Co-sponsorship with Seattle Public Schools of visits by school children to artists studios; scholarships.
Publications: Allied Arts Newsletter, eleven times per year; quarterly calendar of cultural events; directory of arts organizations in Puget Sound area, biannual.
Income: $21,000.

CHARLES AND EMMA FRYE ART MUSEUM
P.O. Box 3005, 704 Terry Ave, 98114. Tel: (206) 622-9250
Mrs. Walser C. Greathouse, Pres.
Free weekdays 10 AM - 5 PM; Sun. Noon - 6 PM. Estab. 1952; endowed. Ann. meeting Oct.
Collections: Charles and Emma Frye collection of 230 paintings, 19th and 20th century European and American, primarily Munich and Barbizon Schools; †accessions in American art of 19th and 20th centuries.
Exhibitions: Puget Sound Area Show by artists of the Puget Sound area ($500 in prizes); American Watercolor Society Traveling Exhibition and other traveling exhibitions and one-man shows.
Activities: Gallery tours, complimentary printed gallery guides to permanent collection.
Publications: Frye Vues monthly.
Library: Art library for research and reference, staff only.
Attendance: Approx. 52,000.

FRIENDS OF THE CRAFTS
311½ Occidental Ave. South, 98104. Tel: (206) 623-5191
Ruth Penington, Pres.
Anne Todd, Secy.
Catherine Munter, Dir.
Sue Everett, Mgr.
Free Tues. - Sat. 12 AM - 5 PM. Estab. 1965 to help establish crafts as an art form, to keep the craftsman and the public in touch with the best of ethnic and contemporary work available and to help establish criteria of excellence in the craft field; financed by mem. and grants. Gallery about 3000 sq. ft. in old brick bldg. on third floor. Natural brick and woodwork provide warm setting for craft objects. Ann. meeting Jan; mem. 720; dues $12 for active mem.
Collections: †Craft object collection.
Activities: Lending collection, 800 Kodachromes; lectures frequently for public, dialogues for members only; 3 visiting lecturers per year; 10 gallery talks; many tours. Book shop.
Library: 100 volumes, in process of expanding circulars and bound books.
Publications: Monthly membership bulletin.
Attendance: 23,000 annual average.

KING COUNTY ARTS COMMISSION
400 King County Court House, 98104. Tel: (206) 344-4040
Ray Meuse, Pres.
Ina Beay, Treas.
Yankee Johnson, Exec. Secy.

Barbara McDonald, Program Coordinator
Office open 8:30 AM - 4:30 PM. Estab. 1966 to further public awareness of and interest in the visual and performing arts; financed by county appropriation. Publishes The Arts, jointly with Seattle Arts Commission.

MODERN ART PAVILION
Seattle Art Museum
Seattle Center, 2nd N. & Thomas St, 98109. Tel: (206) 447-4795
John H. Hauberg, Pres. of Board
Richard E. Fuller, Pres. & Dir. Emeritus
Willis Woods, Dir.
Charles Cowles, Cur.
Sarah Clark, Asst. Cur.
Tore Hoven, Mgr.
Open Tues. - Sun. 11 AM - 6 PM; Thurs. 11 AM - 8 PM; cl. Mon, New Year's Day, Thanksgiving, Christmas. A Branch of the Seattle Art Museum in the former British Pavilion at Seattle World's Fair, remodeled through a gift from Poncho (Asn.) and a bequest from the late Richard Dwight Merrill into a year around exhibition facility, officially opened June 4, 1965. Permanent collection and temporary exhibits of 20th century art.
Exhibitions: (1974-75) 59th Annual Exhibition of Northwest Artists; Skagit Valley Artists; Max Beckmann Graphics; Alexander Calder; Museum Permanent Collection; Art of Pacific Northwest (organized by Smithsonian Institution); Mark Tobey (organized by Smithsonian Institution); 60th Annual Exhibition of Northwest Artists; William Ivey Retrospective; 20th Century Museum Collection; M.F.A. University of Washington Thesis Show; Helen Frankenthaler: Paintings 1969-1974; Jean Arp; Claes Oldenburg: Six Themes; Northwest Artists Today: Part II—61st Annual Exhibition; Roy Lichtenstein: Recent Works; Willem DeKooning, Recent Works; The Artist and the City, C.E.T.A; Recent Work of Jack Tworkov; Photographs by Ansel Adams; Lucas Samaras, Photo-Transformations.
Activities: Docent service; Rental-Sales Gallery; Book Shop.
Attendance: Approx. 108,000 annually.

MUSIC AND ART FOUNDATION*
710 E. Roy St, 98102. Tel: (206) 324-2660
Mrs. Walter Ricker, Pres.
Estab. 1923 to stimulate and encourage young people to develop their talents in Creative Arts, Literature and Music. Ann. meeting May; mem. 2000; dues $2 and higher.
Activities: Contributes to purchase funds of local groups; maintains Free Creative Art School for Children; sponsors of concerts, dramatic programs. Since 1954 has operated the Cornish School of Allied Arts in Seattle which was founded in 1914 by Miss Nellie Cornish.
Articles of Incorporation specifically state that assistance limited to legal residents of the state of Washington.

*SEATTLE ART MUSEUM
Volunteer Park, 98112. Tel: (206) 447-4710
John H. Hauberg, Pres. of Board
Richard E. Fuller, Pres. & Dir. Emeritus
Willis F. Woods, Dir.
Henry Trubner, Cur. Dept. of Asian Art
Charles Cowles, Modern Art Cur.
Mrs. Coe V. Malone, Exec. Secy.
Jeri McDonald, Dir. Public Relations
Marilyn Miller Davis, Business Mgr.
Pauline DeHaart Adams, Registrar
Elizabeth de Fato, Librn.
Mrs. William J. Lahr, Dir. of Educ.
Jo H. Nilsson, Photography & Slide Librn.
Mrs. Frank H. Molitor, Book Shops
Paul Macapia, Photographer
H. Neil Meitzler, Designer
William J. Lahr, Shipping Supv.
Volunteer Park open weekdays 10 AM - 5 PM; Thurs. 7 - 10 PM; Sun. & holidays Noon - 5 PM; cl. New Year's, Memorial Day, Thanksgiving & Christmas. Estab. 1906, inc. 1917; building opened 1933, gift to the city from Mrs. Eugene Fuller and Richard Eugene Fuller, for the recreation, education and inspiration of its citizens. Ann. meeting Oct; mem. c. 4200; dues $10 and higher.
Collections: Eugene Fuller memorial collection with special emphasis on Japan, China, India, also Egypt, Ancient Greece and Rome, European, Near Eastern, Primitive and contemporary Northwest art; major holdings in Northwest art, including Tobey, Callahan, Graves, as well as contemporary art, expecially American, i.e. Gorky, Pollock, Warhol and Lichtenstein; Thomas D. Stimson memorial collection with special emphasis on Far Eastern art; selected highlights on Asian Collection on permanent display with special emphasis on Japanese art (screens, paintings, sculptures and lacquers); also extensive Chinese and Indian collections; Norman Davis collection with emphasis on Classical art; Manson

F. Backus collection of prints; LeRoy M. Backus collection of drawings and paintings; Samuel H. Kress collection of 14th-18th century European paintings, Nash and Alice Heermaneck collection of Primitive art; Henry and Martha Isaacson collection of 18th century European porcelain; Eugene Fuller memorial collection of Chinese jades from archaic throuth 18th century; indefinite loan of 18th century Drawing Room furnished by the National Society of Colonial Dames of America in the State of Washington.
Exhibitions: (1973-75) Jack Youngerman; Venetian Splendor: Canaletto and Guardi; The Sculpture of Thailand; Leo Kenney Retrospective; Surprise Exhibitions: Casals in Rehearsal; The Campbell Museum Collection; European and American Porcelain and Silver Soup Objects; The Poet-Painters: Buson and His Followers; Museum Treasures: Four Decades of Collecting; Man and Society I: Far-out Beginnings; Early Epochs of Chinese and Japanese Art; the Art of India: The Engagement Calendar; Art for the Holiday Season; Hidden Treasures: Masterworks on Paper; Asian influence on motifs and shapes - European porcelains; Ancient Art; Man and Society II: Making the Unseen Visible; Morris Graves; New Acquisitions and on Approval; Art of the Western World; The Oriental Point of View; Hans Popper Collection of Oriental Art; 1973-1974 Acquisitions; Worcester Porcelain from Collections of Seattle Ceramic Society Members and Museum Collections; Egyptian Sculpture; Photographs by Ray Meuse; Jacob Lawrence Retrospective; Man and Technology; Reality and Deception; Primitive Art/Masterworks; Behind the Great Wall of China; Smith Family Collects; Photographs by David Watanabe; 20th Century Sculpture; Works on Paper from the Virginia Wright Fund; El Dorado: The Gold of Ancient Colombia; Man and Technology; Tobey and Graves Paintings.
Activities; Lectures by visiting lecturers average about 12 a year; docent service; film programs; chamber music concerts; TV and radio programs; double lecture course under the Museum Guild; monthly programs for Senior Citizens (except July, Aug, Sept.); adult art history classes; around 300 Treasure Box visits yearly to King County Public Schools' 5th-6th grade classrooms and special groups; about 700 docent tours a year. Book Shops net c. $44,000 per year.
Library: Reference library of nearly 9000 volumes; slide collection of c. 44,000.
Publications: Bimonthly exhibits and activities calendar; annual report; Greek Coins and Cities, 1967; Tobey's 80, a Birthday Retrospective, 1969; Chinese Snuff Bottles, 1969; Chinese Jades, 1971; American Art: Third Quarter Century, 1973; Asiatic Art in the Seattle Art Museum, 1973; Four Decades of Collecting, 1973; Skagit Valley Artists, 1974.
Income and Purchases: (1975) Operating income, c. $492,000; annual purchases vary.
Attendance: 225,939.

SEATTLE PUBLIC LIBRARY
1000 Fourth Ave, 98104. Tel: (206) 624-3800
Ronald A. Dubberly, Librn.
Open Mon. - Thurs. 9 AM - 9 PM; Fri. & Sat. 9 AM - 6 PM; cl. Sun.
Art Department opened 1907. Includes †68,146 books, †8469 of which are bound periodicals; approx. †24,283 mounted color reproductions, †26,771 photographs of Northwest architecture and views, †657,821 pictures, †1536 large color reproductions, †902 original prints, drawings, paintings and sculpture.
Income: (1975) $27,670 (for books and pictures).

SEATTLE WEAVER'S GUILD
c/o Museum of History & Industry, 2161 E. Hamlin St, 98112.
Carlene Striker, Pres.
(15540 168th Ave. N.E, Woodinville, WA 98072)
Anita Peckham, Recording Secy.
Eleanor Helliwell, Corresponding Secy.
Estab. 1937 to further interest in hand weaving. Monthly meetings except Dec, June, July and Aug; mem. 242; dues $10.
Exhibitions: Northwest Craftsmen's Exhibition at the Henry Gallery; Northwest Association of Handweavers biannual conference, Best of Show 1975.
Activities: 4 regular monthly meetings are study sessions and 4 are program meetings, open to members and guests only; workshops throughout the year.
Library: Lending library for members only.

THOMAS BURKE MEMORIAL WASHINGTON STATE MUSEUM
University of Washington, 98195.
George I. Quimby, Dir.
Dr. James Nason, Cur. Ethnology
Dr. Sievert Rohwer, Cur. Zoology
Bill Holm, Cur. Northwest Coast Indian Art
Dr. V. Standish Mallory, Cur. Invertebrate Paleontology
Dr. John M. Rensberger, Cur. Vertebrate Paleontology

Free, Tues. - Sat. 10 AM - 4:30 PM; Sun. 1 - 4:30 PM. Estab. 1889 for research and exhibitions.
  Collections: Anthropology and Natural History of the Northwest and the Pacific; specializing in primitive art of these regions.
  Activities: Circulates study collections; conducts museum classes.

THE UNITED ARTS COUNCIL OF PUGET SOUND
  305 Harrison St, Seattle Center, 98109. Tel: (206) 447-4726
Robert E. Gustavson, Exec. Dir.
Open 9 AM - 5 PM. Estab. 1968 to raise corporate money for the sustaining budgets of arts organizations; to provide opportunities for communication, cooperation, and increased administrative efficiency among its arts mem; financed by corporate contributions. Ann. meeting first Wed. in Nov.
  Publications: Quarterly corporate membership report.
  Income: $300,000.

✠UNIVERSITY OF WASHINGTON
  Henry Art Gallery, 98195. Tel: (206) 543-2280
Richard Grove, Dir.
Free Mon. - Fri. 10 AM - 5 PM; Thurs. 7 - 9 PM; Sat. & Sun. 1 - 5 PM. Estab. 1927 by gift of Horace C. Henry.
  Collections: 19th century American and European paintings; †contemporary paintings, sculpture, prints, drawings and ceramics; †contemporary Japanese pottery.
  Exhibitions: Changing exhibitions including all media and wide historical range.
  Activities: Concerts; lectures; musical programs; poetry readings; Archives of Northwest Art.
  Publications: In addition to exhibition catalogs, the gallery publishes an Index of Art in the Northwest, distributed by the University of Washington Press (currently comprising 9 volumes, with 11 volumes to be completed in the future).
  Attendance: 62,000.

UNIVERSITY OF WASHINGTON ART LIBRARY
  101 Art Building, 98115. Tel: (206) 543-0648
Marietta M. Ward, Librn.
Free Mon. - Fri. 8 AM - 5 PM; Tues. - Thurs. 7 - 10 PM; Sun. 1 - 4 PM; hours vary during summer. Estab. 1950 primarily to provide resources for the courses, degree programs and research of the School of Art; also serves as the Art Library for the University community as a whole; financed by state appropriation.
  Approx. 19,500 volumes primarily for lending, some reference; photograph collection of approx. 9000 prints for reference. Areas of emphases include art history, art education, painting, graphic design, sculpture, interior design, ceramic art, industrial design, printmaking and metal design.

WOMEN PAINTERS OF WASHINGTON*
  c/o Mrs. Don Haldeman, Pres, 29-10th Ave. S, Kirkland, 98033.
Mrs. George McLeod, V.Pres.
Mrs. Milton Munter, 2nd V.Pres.
Mrs. Norman Pletz, Treas.
Mrs. A.G. Stahl, Secy.
  Estab. 1930. Mem. 100; dues $6. Two annual exhibitions held, a Christmas Show and annual exhibition at Frederick & Nelson's Little Gallery. Occasional special exhibitions. Monthly meetings held at Seattle Art Museum from Sept. through May. Programs include lectures, and demonstrations by University professors or prominent artists in painting, sculpture and crafts.

SPOKANE

✠CHENEY COWLES MEMORIAL MUSEUM
Eastern Washington State Historical Society
  2316 W. First Ave, 99204. Tel: (509) 456-3931
Albert H. Culverwell, Dir.
Lee J. Sahlin, Pres.
Mrs. Ronald Broom, Secy.
Open Tues. - Sat. 10 AM - 5 PM; Sun. 2 - 5 PM; cl. Mon. Estab. 1916; Museum of history and art; maintained by State appropriation, some city and county money and memberships. Fine arts gallery with regular monthly art exhibitions of Pacific Northwest Artists. Ann. meeting usually in May; mem. 1100; dues $5 per person.
  Collections: Regional history including collection of Indian arts and handicrafts; birds and mammals; historic house of 1898 by architect Kirtland K. Cutter, interior restored and decorated in period; fine arts gallery.
  Exhibitions: Approx. 105 since 1967.
  Activities: Traveling exhibitions organized and circulated; approx. 500 Kodachromes in lending collection; lectures open to public; concerts. Museum Shop.

Library: 3682 volumes for reference; photograph collection, approx. 15,000 prints and negatives; newspaper clipping file; manuscripts; library use only, copies available on request.
  Publications: Museum Notes to all members, 10 issues per year.
  Attendance: 82,800.

SPOKANE PUBLIC LIBRARY
  W. 906 Main St, 99201. Tel: (509) 838-3361
Betty W. Bender, City Librn.
Janet Miller, Fine Arts Librn.
Free, Mon. - Fri. 9 AM - 9 PM; Sat. 9 AM - 6 PM. Estab. 1962; financed by city and state appropriations.
  Exhibitions: One each month.
  Activities: Individual paintings and original objects of art lent; lending collection, †600 color reproductions, †400 photographs, lantern slides, †2500 Kodachromes, †200 motion pictures, †60 film strips, 100 cassett cartridges; 1,164,676 items lent in average year; 87,631 active borrowers; lectures open to the public; concerts; dramatic programs; classes for children; gallery.

TACOMA

KITTREDGE ART GALLERY*
  1500 N. Warner St, 98416. Tel: (206) 759-3521 Exten. 326
Marcia Jartun, Gallery Dir.
Free, Mon. - Fri. 9 AM - 4 PM; Sun. 1 - 4 PM. Estab. for showing of student and professional works; university operated.
  Collections: Abby Williams Hill, who painted Northwest scenes from the 1880's to the 1930's.
  Publications: Monthly show bulletins.
  Attendance: 1000 annual average.

✠TACOMA ART MUSEUM
  12th and Pacific, 98402. Tel: (206) 272-4258
George Davis, Pres.
Mrs. R. Gene Grant, V.Pres.
Donald V. Rhodes, Treas.
Mrs. Reed Hunt, Secy.
Jon W. Kowalek, Dir.
Open daily, 10 AM - 4 PM; Sun. Noon - 5 PM. Estab. 1891 as the Tacoma Art League; inc. in 1963, and name changed to Tacoma Art Museum in 1964; Ann. meeting between May 27 and June 27; mem. 1200; dues individual $15, couples $25 and up; all funds come from individual and corporate memberships.
  Collections: American and European paintings of the 19th and 20th centuries; sculpture, prints, drawings, decorative objects,
  Exhibitions: Circulating exhibitions; national and international sources; also organizes major exhibitions nationally.
  Activities: Distinguished art lecturers, active Women's Committee, programs on art, docent lecturers, children and adult art classes, seminars for collectors, member's previews, art rental program.
  Library: Art Reference Library contains many important art reference books and magazines.
  Income and Purchases: Over $150,000.
  Attendance: Approx. 200,000.
Sara Little Center of Design Research
  A recreation and restoration of the private studio, library and reference collection of Sara Little.

TACOMA PUBLIC LIBRARY
Handforth Gallery
  1102 S. Tacoma Ave, 98402. Tel: (206) 572-2000
Kevin Hegarty, Dir, Tacoma Public Library
Sadie Uglow, Head, Library Fine Arts Dept. & Dir. Handforth Gallery
Free Mon. - Thurs. 9 AM - 9 PM; Fri. & Sat. 9 AM - 6 PM. Estab. 1952 to extend library service by providing the public with a program of local and traveling art shows; to provide local artists with exhibit space; appropriation. The Handforth Gallery adjoins and extends the services of the Fine Arts Department of the Library.
  Collections: Thomas S. Handforth collection of etchings, lithographs, drawings and paintings; †paintings and prints by local artists.
  Exhibitions: Monthly change of exhibits.
  Library: 1000 volumes on art, architecture and crafts; 38,000 picture collection.

WASHINGTON STATE HISTORICAL SOCIETY
  315 N. Stadium Way, 98403. Tel: (206) 593-2830
Bruce LeRoy, Dir.
Open Tues. - Sat. 9 AM - 4:30 PM; Sun. 2 - 5 PM; cl. Mon. & holidays. Estab. 1891. Ann. meeting May; mem. 964; dues $7 and higher. Owns three buildings; Art Gallery under direction of Society.
  Collections: Pre-historic relics; †Indian and Eskimo artifacts, baskets, clothing, utensils; Oriental items; †Washington-Northwest pioneer relics.

Exhibitions: Changed monthly.
Activities: Special school tours.
Library: Specializes in Northwest history with 10,000 volumes, maps, 750,000 manuscripts and 200,000 pictures; general history of Washington.
Publications: News Notes and sponsors Pacific Northwest Quarterly with the State University. Books and pamphlets on Pacific-Northwest history.
Attendance: 225,000 annually.

YAKIMA

ALLIED ARTS COUNCIL OF THE YAKIMA VALLEY, INC.
5000 W. Lincoln Ave, 98908. Tel: (509) 966-0930
Nick Mason, Pres.
Frances Marble, Secy.
Bootsy Semon, Exec. Dir.
Free, Mon. - Fri. 9 AM - 5 PM, Sept. - May, 9 - 12 AM, June - Aug. Estab. 1962 to coordinate and promote the arts, financed by mem. The Warehouse Gallery, a display gallery and sales gallery, exhibits by invitation. Member groups 36, individual mem. 1000; dues $5-150.
Exhibitions: Governors' Invitational, local and area artists.
Activities: Art classes throughout the year; Attic Rental and Sales Gallery.
Publications: Artscope, monthly calendar of events.
Income: $12,000-15,000.

WEST VIRGINIA

ATHENS

ALEXANDER ARTS CENTER*
Concord College
24712
M. R. Coiner, Dir.

CHARLESTON

THE CHARLESTON ART GALLERY OF SUNRISE
755 Myrtle Rd, 25314. Tel: (304) 344-8035
Gene A. Schott, Exec. Dir. Sunrise
Mary Black, Cur. Fine Arts
Mrs. Dormal E. Cometti, Asst. Cur. Fine Arts
Free Tues. - Sat. 10 AM - 5 PM; Sun. 2 - 5 PM; cl. Mon. Estab. 1960 (consolidated with Sunrise Foundation, Inc, Apr, 1974) to present exhibitions of outstanding stature which will provide a stimulus for the public and for state artists and lead to growth and development in both appreciation and execution of art works; Sunrise maintained by memberships and donations. Patron $500 or more, special gift contributor $50-499, family $15, adult (single) $10, student or children $1. Ann. meeting Apr; mem. 2500 (1975).
Collections: Contemporary paintings and graphics and a small collection of sculpture and ceramics.
Exhibitions: (1974) Wood sculpture by A. K. Morton, West Virginia; Modern Masters Tapestries; paintings by Lee Savage, New York; Phenomenon of Peter Max; watercolors by Mary Virginia Roberts, California; Sesame Street; paintings by William H. Johnson; Allied Artists of West Virginia 43rd Annual; Gund Collection of Western Art; 11th Annual Rental Gallery Exhibition; Persistant Crafts of Poland; photographs by Amelia Bent Burnett; watercolors by Edna Way, Ohio; Memorial Exhibition of paintings by Ruby Chamness, West Virginia; Kanawha Valley Collectors Exhibition, featuring portraits; 12th Annual Gallery Exhibition of Graphics and Drawings; paintings and sculpture by Cubert Smith, West Virginia; drawings by Children of Eek, Alaska; Folk Paintings from Dalarna; Trees of the Nations; (1975) photography by Charleston Press Photographers; duo-photography by Stiles and Manthorpe; miniature paintings, Paul Klein, West Virginia; Heritage: American Historic Buildings; Allied Artists of West Virginia 44th Annual; Antwerp's Golden Age; 4th Appalachian Corridors Biennial; photography by Will Endres, Jr, West Virginia; 12th Annual Rental Gallery Exhibition; Gallery Instructors and Students; Permanent Collection, featuring new accessions; Alaskan Artists with Eskimo Artifacts; Monumental Brass Rubbings by Laurence Lawson, Ohio; 13th Annual Gallery Exhibition of Graphics and Drawings; Soft Prints by Leila Daw, Missouri; Trees of the Nations. Annual exhibitions include selections from the permanent collection at least twice a year; many one-man shows by area artists; Renal Gallery Exhibit; Allied Artist of West Virginia Exhibition; Competitive Gallery Graphics and Drawings Exhibition; exhibits by area university and college faculty and students; Trees of the Nations. Biennial Exhibitions include Appalachian Corridors and Kanawha Valley Collectors. Traveling Exhibitions include Mountain Artisans; West Virginia Artists; Selections from Permanent Collection. Purchase and Prize awards (1974) Gallery Graphics and Drawings Exhibition, $1600; Allied Artists of West Virginia Annual Exhibition, $3700; (1975) Allied

Artists of West Virginia Annual Exhibition, $3000; Gallery Graphics and Drawings Exhibition $1000; Appalachian Corridors Biennial, $8625.
Activities: Art in School and Portfolio Loan Program; rental and sales gallery for art works, color reproductions, motion pictures and slides in lending collection; lectures open to the public; concerts; non-credit studio classes for adults and children; special lectures for organizations and schools; tours; competition for art lessons scholarships for students, grade school through high school; art instructors, 20, mostly part-time; art books in Gallery Shop.
Library: 1400 volumes for reference.
Publications: Teacher's Guides, Class Schedule and Volunteer Activities, yearly; Calendar of Events, 3 times a year; Newsletter, quarterly; brochures of exhibitions approximately 8 times a year.
Attendance: Approx ann average: 50,000.

HUNTINGTON

HUNTINGTON GALLERIES
Park Hills, 25701. Tel: (304) 529-2701
Mrs. Robert K. Emerson, Dir.
Eason Eige, Dir. of Educ.
William Sargent, Cur.
Barbara Krumholtz, Prog. Coordinator
Constance Ford, Admin. Secy.
Jean Cummings, Bookkeeper
Ruth Boyd, Mem. Secy. & Receptionist
Bernice Dorsey, Librn.
Jay Adkins, Supt.
Open Tues. - Sat. 10 AM - 4 PM; Sun. 1 - 5 PM; voluntary admis. Founders Herbert Fitzpatrick and Rufus M. Switzer provided a woodland tract of 50 acres for the erection of an art museum, arboretum and bird sanctuary. The museum was opened in Nov. 1952. A grant by the Henry L. and Grace Doherty Foundation provided for a building addition doubling the size of the museum complex which opened in 1970; the addition was designed by Walter Gropius for the Architects Collaborative. Mem. 2300; dues $5-25 depending on status.
Collections: Daywood collection of American art including Henri, Sloan, Prendergast, Luks, Glackens, Shinn, Lawson, Hassam, Homer, Hopper, Wyeth; Bagby collection includes Stuart, Bierstadt and Reynolds. Fitzpatrick gifts include Georgian silver collection, European paintings and oriental rugs; Herman P. Dean collection of arms; prints and drawings numbering 800; small collection of Oriental and Pre-Cortesian art; recent acquisitions include Calder, Lipton, Rhodes, Bertoia and Albrizio.
Activities: Changing exhibitions and annual Exhibition 280; chamber orchestra, films, lectures, demonstrations; gallery talks and tours; Junior Art Museum; studio art classes for adults and children in painting, drawing, ceramics, weaving, graphics, photography, etc. Galleries Gift Shop.
Library: Expanding art reference library with audio visual slide index center; Open 1 - 4 PM; Tues. - Sat.
Income and Purchases: Operating income $240,000; purchases by gift.
Annual Gallery Attendance: 60,000.

PARKERSBURG

PARKERSBURG ART CENTER*
P.O. Box 131, 26101. Tel: (304) 485-4748
Ann Randolph, Dir.
Free 2 - 5 PM; cl. Mon. Estab. 1955; education through exhibits, classes, lectures; maintained by membership. Gallery. Ann. meeting 3rd Tues. of June; mem. 350 (families); student $1, single $5, family $15, patron $25 and business $50.
Exhibitions: Art From the Netherlands, The duPont Show, Annual Juried Show, Richard Proctor Art in Textiles, Adult Amateur, Art Work of Bess Widmeyer, New Life for Landmarks, Children's Exhibit, Hippiedon, Heaven or Hell, Circus Exhibit, William Gerhold, Christmas Show, Culture of the Middle East; Framing, Right and Wrong; How to Look at a Painting.
Activities: Individual paintings lent to schools, original objects of art lent; 110 color reproductions in lending collection; lectures open to public; 145 gallery talks or tours; classes for adults and children; competitions; scholarships.
Publications: Monthly and yearly publications.
Annual Income: $10,000-$12,000.
Attendance: 10,000.

ROMNEY

HAMPSHIRE COUNTY PUBLIC LIBRARY
Main St, 26757. Tel: (304) 822-3185
Carol Winland, Pres.
Mary Pugh, Secy.
Brenda Riffle, Librn.

Free, Mon. - Fri. 10 AM - 5 PM; Sat. 10 AM - 3 PM. Display cases, changed every month.

Collections: 18,000 volume library.

Exhibitions: Various local artists' collection; private collections of rocks, antiques, displays of items of other countries; weaving; children's art.

Activities: Concerts; dramatic programs; classes for adults and children.

Income and Purchases: $14,534.

Attendance: 16,470.

WHEELING

OGLEBAY INSTITUTE MANSION MUSEUM
Oglebay Park, 26003. Tel: (304) 242-4200
(Museum (304) 242-7272)
S. H. Coulling, Exec. Dir.
John A Artmberger, Museum Dir.
Museum open 9:30 AM - 5 PM; Sun. & holidays 1:30 - 5 PM; cl Thanksgiving, Dec. 24, 25 and 30 & Jan. 1; admis. $1.50, children 12 and under free. Estab and inc. 1930 to promote educational, cultural, and recreational activities in Wheeling Tri-State area. Building and grounds property of City. Mem. approx. 1000; dues $10 and higher.

Collections: Contains period rooms; and a collection of †early glass made in the Wheeling area; †early china, †pewter and guns.

Exhibitions: Current exhibits of art and other allied subjects change monthly in an exhibition wing adjoining the main house.

Activities: Day-long Antiques Seminars twice a year; antique classes (furniture, glass and china); six gallery talks.

Library: Highly specialized library on the early history of the area. Many source books, prints, documents and maps.

Attendance: Approx. 30,000.

Oglebay Institute Mansion Museum Committee
Mrs. R. C. Miller, Chmn.
Mr. R. C. Haylett, Jr, V.Chmn.
Mrs. R. E. DiBartolomeo, Secy.

WISCONSIN

BELOIT

THEODORE LYMAN WRIGHT ART CENTER
Beloit College, 53511. Tel: (608) 365-3391
Jeanne A. Dalzell, Dir.
Free weekdays 9 AM - 5 PM, 7 - 9 PM; Sat. 11 AM - 5 PM; Sun. 2 - 5 PM. Estab. 1892; building dedicated 1930 and contains galleries, lecture rooms and studios.

Collections: Especially strong in Oriental and contemporary collections; Pitkin Collection of Oriental Art; Gurley Collection of Korean Pottery, Japanese sword guards, Chinese snuff bottles and jades; Morse Collection of paintings and other art objects; †Neese Fund Collection of Contemporary Art; Fisher Memorial of Greek casts; furniture and sculpture of various periods; prints by Rembrandt, Durer, Whistler and others; †Ross Collection of Graphics, Photographs and Slides. Total collection of over 6000 items.

Exhibitions: Monthly exhibitions; Annual Beloit and Vicinity in May with $2500 in prizes for 1975; Annual Student Exhibition in April; Annual Faculty Exhibition.

Activities: Lecture series; demonstrations; art classes (See Schools); films, gallery talks.

Publications: Special Catalogs and Brochures of Exhibitions.
Art League of Beloit
Mem. 100; dues $5 and higher. Monthly meeting Oct. to May.

EAU CLAIRE

DEPARTMENT OF ART
University of Wisconsin-Eau Claire
100 Waler St, 54701. Tel: (715) 836-3278
Charles Campbell, Acting Dir, Dept. Art
Anders C. Shafer, Dir, Foster Art Gallery
Gallery open Mon. - Fri. 11 AM - 5 PM; Sun. 1 - 4 PM. Financed by city and state appropriation.

Collections: Permanent collection, includes works by Knaths, Stamos, Dine, Falstrom and many others.

Exhibitions: (1975-76) Permanent Collection; A Year of the Woman Exhibition; Ceramist, Metalsmith, Weaver; Peter Bilan and Wayne Kimball; John Lawler and William Pearson; John Thomas; Julius Schmidt; Kind Gallery Artists; plus B.F.A. exhibits and shows, annual faculty shows and annual student art show and festival.

Activities: Teaching children with special problems; lectures open to public; 1 - 6 visiting lecturers per year; 5 - 10 gallery talks; tours.

Attendance: Approx. 10,000.

GREEN BAY

NEVILLE PUBLIC MUSEUM
129 S. Jefferson St, 54301. Tel: (414) 432-7791
Mrs. Glorian Johnson, Pres.
James L. Quinn, Dir.
Donn P. Quigley, Chief Cur.
Jeanne Schuldes, Assoc. Cur.
James Kreiter, Cur. Art
Ruth Little, Cur. Educ.
Bonita Cagle, Museum Registrar
Free Mon. - Sat. 9 AM - 5 PM; Sun. 2 - 5 PM. Estab. 1915 as Green Bay Public Museum; name changed 1926. Inc. Ann. meeting in spring; mem. approx. 350; dues individual $5, family $10.

Collections: Contemporary and historical †paintings, †drawings, †prints and sculpture; Neville family portraits; David Belasco collection of Victoriana; antique furniture; †china, †glass, †silver, †fans, laces, costumes and accessories; musical instruments. Other permanent collections and exhibits deal with history, geology, biology, archaeology, ethnology, etc.

Exhibitions: Local art clubs exhibit annually; Northeastern Wisconsin Art Show annually with cash awards, plus rotating art exhibits changed monthly.

Activities: Guided tours; lecturers; films, gallery talks; sponsor Friends of Art Club, Geology Club and Astronomical Society; formally organized education program; inter-museum loan; permanent, temporary, and traveling exhibitions; school loan service.

Library: Books and magazines concerning all phases of the museum interests. Library use available to the public, but loans of books rarely made.

Publications: Annual Report.

Income: Museum budget appropriated by City and County.

Attendance: Approx. 100,000.

✤UNIVERSITY OF WISCONSIN-GREEN BAY*
120 Circle Dr, 54302.
W. F. Prevetti, Cur. Art

KENOSHA

KENOSHA PUBLIC MUSEUM
Civic Center, 53140. Tel: (414) 652-4512
Kenneth Dearolf, Dir. & Secy.
Harry J. Martin, Cur. of Preparation
Paula Touhey, Cur. of Educ.
Free 9 - 12 AM & 1 - 5 PM; Sat. 9 - 12 AM; Sun. 1 - 5 PM. Estab. 1936 as a cultural center. Friends of the Museum, ann. meeting June; mem. 100; dues $5-$500.

Collections: †American Indian and Oriental artifacts; wildlife; Lorado Taft dioramas; †paintings and crafts; †Wisconsin pottery, carved ivory, New Guinea Carvings, African Art, Eskimo Artifacts.

Activities: 12 illustrated travel lectures; art classes for adults and children; lapidary, ceramics, painting, and watercolor classes; monthly art exhibits; annual Kenosha Art Show with prizes; school loan service of 1770 items. Sales desk.

Library: 1163 volumes on science and art.

Income & Purchases: Income $90,000; purchases $5000.

Attendance: (1971) 82,000.

MADISON

✤ELVEHJEM ART CENTER
University of Wisconsin-Madison
800 University Ave, 53706. Tel: (608) 263-2240, 263-2246
Eric S. McCready, Dir.
Carlton E. Overland, Cur. Graphics
John S. Hopkins, Registrar & Asst. to Dir.
William Bunce, Librn. Kohler Art Library
Free Mon. - Sat. 9 AM - 4:45 PM; Sun. 12 - 7:45 PM; cl. major holidays. Estab. Sept. 12, 1970; University art museum providing galleries for permanent collection, exhibition space for temporary shows, and classrooms and office facilities for Art History Department. State appropriation, endowment, private funds. Friends of EAC, mem. 1100.

Collections: General art collection from ancient to modern periods, approx. 2000 objects, with special importance in fields of Russian Icons, Italian and Dutch paintings, ancient Greek vases, prints and drawings, and Indian and Southeast Asian art. (All of these areas are being enlarged by purchase).

Exhibitions: Indian Miniature Painting, 1971; Canadian Landscape Painting, 1973; Italian Rennaissance Festival Designs, 1973; Rare Porcelain: European and Oriental Export, 1974; American Hand-woven Coverlets of the 19th Century, 1975.

Activities: Lectures open to public, visiting lecturers each year; docent program, gallery talks or tours. Museum Shop.

Library: Approx. 70,000 volumes for lending and reference, limited to University of Wisconsin staff and students.

Publications: Bulletin/Annual Report, each autumn; exhibition catalogues, several per year.

Attendance: 75,000 annually.

MADISON ART CENTER, INC

720 E. Gorham St, 53703. Tel: (608) 257-0158
Robert Chambless Hendon, Dir.
Mollie Buckley, Publicity & Membership
Leonard T. Heinen, Pres. Board of Dir.
Free daily 9 AM - 5 PM; Tues. - Thurs. 9 AM - 9 PM; Sun. 1 - 5 PM; cl. Mon, holidays & Aug. Asn estab. 1901, present building 1964, inc. 1970. 7 galleries: Sales & Rental Gallery, Gallery Shop, special photo gallery, Rudolph E. Langer Print Study Room; studio class rooms, auditorium-theatre, dark room, film editing; print shop; large park like grounds on lake. Ann meeting May; mem. 1500; dues $10 up.

Collections: †Large print & drawing collection (Japanese, European, Mexican, American); †paintings, †sculpture, 16th and 17th century tapestries; current emphasis on contemporary Americans.

Exhibitions: Over 40 shows annually; 8-10 major shows usually organized by the staff of the center; occasional loan or rented exhibitions; smaller shows include one-man shows, print exhibitions, photographic exhibitions, group shows and theme exhibitions. The center has organized and circulated its own exhibitions. Annuals include Salon of School Art and Madison Art Guild Annual, usually in Apr. and May.

Activities: Extensive film showing program weekly with guest filmmakers; special lectures and demonstrations (approx. 8-10 annually); bus tours to special exhibitions, programs, etc, outside of Madison; Print Club; Docent Program; Loan program to public schools (4 exhibitions now circulating). Sidewalk Art Fair (one of the midwests largest); gallery talks for all major shows; Annual Arts Ball. Over 600 students participate in classes during the spring-summer and fall semesters. Photography, filmmaking that includes animation and sound sync is offered; ceramics, sculpture, drawing, life drawing, painting, multi-media and pre-school workshops, parent-child workshops, printmaking that includes relief, intaglio and serigraphy and paper-making workshops.

Library: Small selection of books, catalogs and slides in addition to Print Study Room which functions as a working library for the study and research of graphics.

Publications: Posters and announcements usually accompany each exhibition; catalogs are published for approx. 6-10 shows each year.

Income and Purchases: Budget in excess of $100,000; purchases $10,000.

Attendance: 90,000 in 11 months.

STATE HISTORICAL SOCIETY OF WISCONSIN

816 State St, 53706. Tel: (608) 262-3266
James Morton Smith, Dir.
Richard A. Erney, Assoc. Dir.
William H. Applegate, Asst. Dir.
Thurman O. Fox, Dir. Museum
Raymond S. Sivesind, Dir. Historic Sites and Markers
Charles Shetler, Librn.
Paul H. Hass, Dir. Editorial Division
Barbara J. Kaiser, Dir. Field Services
William F. Thompson, Dir. Research
F. Gerald Ham, State Archivist
Free weekdays, Mon. - Fri. 8 AM - 10 PM; Sat. 8 AM - 4 PM; Sun. 12 - 4 PM; cl holidays. Estab. 1846, museum added 1854; organized to promote a wider appreciation of the American heritage, with particular emphasis on the collection, advancement, and dissemination of knowledge of the history of Wisconsin and of the Middle West. State supported. Ann. meeting June; mem. 7000; dues $7.50 and higher.

Collections: Costumes, furniture, dolls, china, glass, coins, stamps, guns, machinery, craft and agricultural tools and models, and other items of social, political and economic history of Wisconsin and the Midwest. Historymobile and other traveling exhibitions. Iconographic collection, paintings and prints of over 355,000 photos and slides. State archives of over 26,000 cu. ft. Americana library including public documents collection, over 388,000 volumes, 400,000 pamphlets; newspaper collection of more than 35,000 volumes and 95,494 reels of microfilm. Manuscripts collection of 25,175 cu. ft; Mass Communications History Center; Center for Theatre Research;

McCormick Collection of Agricultural History. All collections being enlarged. Materials lent in state and to out-of-state museums and libraries.

Historic Sites: Villa Louis, Prairie du Chien; Old Wade House and Carriage Museum; Greenbush; Stonefield Farm and Craft Museum, Cassville; Circus World Museum, Baraboo; Madeline Island Historical Museum, La Pointe; Pendarvis Historical Site, Mineral Point.

Exhibitions: Frequent special exhibitions; 4 annual gallery changes; TV and radio programs; films, participation exhibits.

Activities: Elementary school program; Founders Day (Jan); regional meetings of local historians.

Attendance: (Incl. mobile unit and historic sites) 487,000 annually.

UNIVERSITY OF WISCONSIN-MADISON
Wisconsin Union

Memorial Union, 800 Langdon St, 53706. Tel: (608) 262-2263
Union South, 227 N. Randall Ave, 53706. Tel: (608) 263-2543
Ted Crabb, Dir. & Secy.
Jan Marshall Fox, Art Coordinator
Free 10 AM - 8 PM. Organization estab. 1907 to provide a cultural program for the members of the university community. Ann. meeting May; mem. 46,500 faculty, alumni and townspeople, plus 38,000 students; dues $30. Owns two fireproof buildings with 3 galleries.

Collections: Oil and watercolor paintings, prints, and sculptures, mostly by contemporary American artists.

Exhibitions: Student Art Exhibit in spring, with jury awards of $1000. Student Craft Show in spring with jury awards of $900. Year round traveling exhibitions shown.

Activities: Informal classes in arts and crafts. Periodic gallery talks and films; 4 sidewalk art sales. Loan collection available on rental to students and members. (See Schools)

Purchases: $1500 annually.

Attendance: 192,300.

MANITOWOC

THE RAHR PUBLIC MUSEUM AND CIVIC CENTER

610 N. Eighth St, 54220. Tel: (414) 684-4181
Joseph S. Hutchison, Dir.
Richard Quick, Exec. Secy. & Registrar
Free daily 9 AM - 5 PM; Sat. & Sun. 2 - 5 PM; cl. legal holidays. Estab. 1950 to promote art in the county and to serve as an historical museum. New addition open Nov, 1975. Board meets monthly. The Rahr Public Museum Association mem. 300; ann. meeting Mar.

Collections: Oils, watercolors, graphics and drawings by American, European and Japanese artists. Collection being added to by purchases. New permanent addition, the Schwartz Collection of Chinese Ivory Carvings.

Exhibitions: Monthly changing exhibitions of regional-national arts; Manitowoc County Annual Art Shows; Elementary and Secondary Grades Art Shows of Manitowoc Public School; traveling exhibitions.

Activities: Guided tours through art exhibits for students of elementary and secondary schools and colleges.

Library: Basic reference library of literature, art and art history magazines; collection of catalogs of art exhibits in the U.S; file of black and white and color reproductions of U.S.A. and World Art.

Attendance: 34,000.

MENOMONIE

✠UNIVERSITY OF WISCONSIN-STOUT
Gallery 209

Applied Arts Bldg, 13th Ave. & 4th St, 54751. Tel: (715) 232-1428
Orazio Fumagalli, Cur.
Free Mon. - Fri. 9 AM - 5 PM; Sat. 1 - 5 PM. Estab. 1966; the gallery is conceived of as a community facility as well as university. Exhibitions are, on the average of once a month, changed for added interest. State appropriation.

Activities: Art appreciation course for high school and elementary school groups; tours for visiting community groups; Sat. Art and Drama classes for young people.

Attendance: Approx. 13,000.

MILWAUKEE

ALVERNO COLLEGE

3401 S. 39th St, 53215. Tel: (414) 671-5400
George Brownlee, Gallery Dir.
Free Mon. - Fri. 9 AM - 5 PM; Sun. 2 - 5 PM; cl. non-school days. Estab. for the aesthetic enrichment of community and the aesthetic education of students. Gallery maintained.

CARDINAL STRITCH COLLEGE
Studio San Damiano

6801 N. Yates Rd, 53217. Tel: (414) 352-5400
Sister Mary Thomasita, Head Dept.

Free, daily 9 AM - 5 PM. Estab. 1947 to encourage creative art in each individual; financed by endowment, city and state appropriations and tuition.

Collections: Folk crafts; paintings.

Exhibitions: Professor's works; senior graduating exhibitions; well known area artists; acquisitions from distant lands; children's art; approximately five exhibitions of student's work.

Activities: Traveling exhibitions organized and circulated; individual paintings and original objects of art lent; few items lent in average year; approx. 20 visiting lecturers and tours per year; concerts; dramatic programs; classes for adults and children; competitions; scholarships. Book shop.

Library: Art collection of 200 volumes; photograph collection.

Publications: CSC News, monthly.

Attendance: 1972-600, 1973-750.

MARQUETTE UNIVERSITY GALLERY*
University Committee on the Fine Arts
53233. Tel: (414) 224-7263
Prof. John Pick, Chmn.
Free daily 8 AM - 10 PM. Estab. 1953 to exhibit the growing University collection of art, to sponsor an annual major art show and to exhibit traveling art exhibitions.

Collections: †Renaissance religious art; Durer collection. Collections enlarged mostly by gifts; average past three years $50,000.

Exhibitions: Colonial Religious Art of Ecuador; Dali's Art-in-Jewels; Grandma Moses Retrospective; Ex Voto Paintings.

Activities: Maintains a library, photograph collection; lectures; concerts; dramatic programs.

Attendance: 32,000.

MILWAUKEE AREA TECHNICAL COLLEGE
Kronquist Craft Gallery
1015 N. 6th St, 53203. Tel: (414) 278-6600
John Strachota, Dir. Gallery
Open daily; no admis. Estab. 1961 to stimulate appreciation for fine metalwork; financed by gifts.

Collections: Permanent collection of sterling hollowware, flatware, jewelry, and bronze castings by Emil F. Kronquist.

Exhibitions: Continuous graphic and applied art student and faculty showings.

Attendance: 2000 annual average.

✠MILWAUKEE ART CENTER*
750 N. Lincoln Memorial Dr, 53202. Tel: (414) 271-9508
R. V. Krikorian, Pres.
Richard G. Jacobus, V.Pres.
Thomas W. Godfrey, V.Pres.
R. D. Hevey, Treas.
Mrs. Ernest J. Philipp, Secy.
Tracy Atkinson, Dir. Milwaukee Art Center & Cur. Layton Collection
Dr. Joseph J. Reis, Dir. Div. Interpretation
J. Eugene Felsch, Dir. Div. Presentation
Hugh E. Morgan, Dir. Div. Administration
Elliott L. Judd, Development Asst.
Mrs. Ann H. Kohl, Cur. Villa Terrace
Mrs. Barbara Coffman, Cur. Collector's Gallery
Barbara Brown, Cur. Adult Educ.
Thomas H. Beckman, Registrar
Mrs. Marguerite Atkinson, Exec. Asst.
Catherine Lamb, Mgr. Gallery Shop
Free daily 10 AM - 5 PM; Sun. 1 - 5 PM; Thurs. 10 AM - 10 PM. Inc. 1888, to collect, exhibit, interpret, preserve its collection and to engage in research. Located in War Memorial Center, designed by Eero Saarinen, completed in 1957. The Center has recently opened a three-level 150,000 square foot addition on the shore of Lake Michigan, to house the collection of Mrs. Harry Lynde Bradley. Ann. meeting May; mem. 3200; dues family $20, individual $17.50.

Collections: The Layton collection of late 19th and early 20th century American and European paintings; the Bradley collection of 800 paintings and sculptures; permanent collection of sculpture, paintings, drawings, prints. Permanent Light Gallery. Villa Terrace, branch museum for decorative arts.

Exhibitions: (Biennials) Wisconsin Painters and Sculptors; Wisconsin Designer-Craftsmen. Special Exhibitions: Wisconsin Collects, 1964; Pop Art and the American Tradition, 1965; The Inner Circle, 1966; Botero, 1967; Light/Motion/Space Show, 1967; Directions I, Options, 1968; Von Schleinitz Collection, 1968; Bradley Collection, 1968; Art of the Congo, 1968; Art Treasures of Turkey, 1967; Directions II, Aspects of a New Realism, 1969; A Plastic Presence, 1969; Contemporary Acquisitions, 1970; Seymour Lipton, 1969; Portraits from Milwaukee Collections, 1971; Six Painters, 1972; The Urban River, 1973; The Art of Haiti, 1973.

Activities: Tours, lectures, films, concerts, matinees; Junior Education classes in art, creative theatre. Children's Art Lending

Library; Collectors' Corner; Garden Club. Friends of Art activities include Bal du Lac, Lakefront Festival of Arts, luncheon program meetings, tours, Antiques Show. Gallery Shop, Children's Exhibition Gallery, Circulating Exhibitions for Adults and Young People.

MILWAUKEE PUBLIC LIBRARY
Art and Music Department
814 W. Wisconsin Ave, 53233. Tel: (414) 278-3000
Henry E. Bates, Jr, City Librn.
Kirk L. Pressing, Supvr, Central Library Services
Nancy W. Boone, Coordinator Fine Arts
Free Mon. - Fri. 8:30 AM - 9 PM; Sat. 8:30 AM - 5:30 PM; Sun. 1 - 5 PM. Estab. 1897.

Collections: Approx. 100,000 volumes on art including costume in the Milwaukee Public Library system; 38,000 bound periodicals; 15,000 posters; 60,000 mounted pictures; framed and unframed reproductions; cassettes; newspaper clippings on local artists and art activities. Subjects include fine and applied arts, history of art, architecture, city planning, landscape architecture, numismatics, philately, crafts, decorative and household arts, costume, photography, auction and exhibition catalogs.

Exhibitions: Art exhibits included in general exhibit program at Central Library.

Publications: Milwaukee Reader, weekly, includes articles and bibliographies on art subjects as well as notices of current exhibitions and events in Milwaukee. Occasional bibliographies are published as pamphlets.

Income and Purchases: $10,000 from budgeted funds and additional income from endowments spent annually on Central Library collection.

Charles Allis Art Library
1630 E. Royall Place, 53202. Tel: (414) 278-3010
Margaret Fish Rahill, Librn-in-charge
Free Tues. - Sun. 1 - 5 PM; Wed. 7 - 9:30 PM.

The Charles Allis Art Collection is an extension of the Art and Music Department of the Milwaukee Public Library. The Allis home and art collection were presented to the city in 1945, including a $200,000 endowment fund to help maintain the building and collection. The collection contains the personal library of Mr. Allis; Chinese, Japanese, Persian and Korean pottery and porcelain; Chinese jade; ancient glass; French silver and Limoges enamel; Japanese netsuke; Barye bronzes; 16th and 17th century Italian bronzes; Oriental rugs; paintings by French, American, Dutch, German, Italian and Norwegian artists; etchings and engravings by Durer, Rembrandt, Whistler, Meryon, Haden and Zorn; French furniture and art objects of the 14th, 15th and 16th centuries.

Temporary exhibitions include paintings, prints, sculpture and crafts of local artists and traveling exhibitions. Activities include meetings of cultural groups, concerts, tours of the collection, and film programs.

Attendance: Allis Art Library 21,000 annually.

MILWAUKEE PUBLIC MUSEUM
800 W. Wells St, 53233. Tel: (414) 278-2700
Dr. Kenneth Starr, Dir.
Wallace N. MacBriar, Asst. Dir.
Shirley Marine, Pub. Affairs (incl. TV-Radio)
Dr. Nancy Oestreich Lurie, Cur. American Indians
Dr. Rudolph Dornemann, Cur. History
Lon Mericle, Underwater Archaeology (Research Assoc.)
Dr. Arthur Niehoff, Ethnology-Asia (Hon. Cur.)
Bernard Brown, Primitive Art (Hon. Cur.)
Dr. Allan Corre, Biblical Archaeology (Research Assoc.)
Mrs. Aaron Tilton, Hon. Cur. Ceramics
Dr. Richard G. Peske, Archaeology-North America, Great Lakes Area (Research Assoc.)
Dr. Martyn Dibben, Botany
Dr. Robert West, Cur. Geology
John Luedtke, Oriental History & Decorative Arts
Arthur Frank, Classical History (Hon. Cur)
Frederick Benkovic, U.S. History & Military History (Hon. Cur)
Homer Lynn, U.S. History (Hon. Cur)
Dr. Allan Young, Cur. Invertebrate Zoology
Dr. Gerard R. Noonan, Asst. Cur. Invertebrate Zoology
James Neidhoefer, Lepidoptera (Research Assoc)
Dr. Max Nickerson, Cur. Vertebrate Zoology
Dr. Merlin Tuttle, Cur. Mammals
Dr. Richard E. Spieler, Cur. Ichthyology
Leo Johnson, Photography
Edward Green, Graphic Arts & Exhibit Design
Edith Quade, Educ.
Vernon Hagen, Acting Head AV Library
Judith Turner, Librn.
James Burnham, Conservationist
Open daily 9 AM - 5 PM, except major holidays; free for Milwaukee County residents; admis. charge for non-County residents; adults $1,

children 25¢. Estab. 1882 fourth largest natural history museum in the United States; now building completed in 1963; total space, 350,000 sq. ft; exhibit space, 150,000 sq. ft. A natural history and history museum operated by the city of Milwaukee.

Collections: Bading Spanish Colonial art collection; Nunnemacher collection of guns; Northwest Coast Indian masks; I. A. Dinerstein Art Collection; Western African Art; Dietz Typewriter Collection; Pre-Columbian Collection.

Exhibits, 1st floor: A Trip Through Time and Space; 2nd floor: Wonders of Life and The World and Its Peoples; 3rd floor: The World and Its Peoples.

Wonders of Life, scientific classification of plant and animal life, Man and Culture, biological principles, interrelationships of life forms with one another and with their environment; North America, a geographic and ecological tour of the North American continent; Tapestry Hall shows furnishings from 16th century Habsburg Europe, 17th century German States, and 18th century France, including: three tapestries from Brussels, Spanish Netherlands, depicting the Roman legend of Vertumnus and Pomona; German and French suits of armor and a Milanese halfsuit of armor; a Danish bridal chest c. 1700; Dutch chairs upholstered in pieces of tapestry and a German tooled leather chair, gilded and enameled and decorated with a Prussian eagle; an 18th century clock believed to have been owned by Maria Theresa, Empress of Austria and Queen of Hungary.

Middle-South American and Oceanic Cultures, a geographic and ecological tour of Indonesia, Melanesia, Micornesia, Polynesia, South and Central America and the Caribbean; the Ecuadorian Room houses the museum's famous Bading Collection of Spanish Colonial art and furniture; exhibit includes a Middle American rain forest, a Mexican market street and a Guatemalan highlands' market; Pre-Columbia America; Circumpolar, Asian areas, the oceans of the world, African continent (veldt, rain forest) with some of the largest dioramas in any museum; area includes Western African Art collection.

Youth Center has a Period House furnished in Colonial American style, a Living World Corner with (small animals, snakes, and fish), Homes of the World. Audiovisual Center houses the museum's film collection; films can be borrowed by registered Milwaukee groups, organizations and home borrowers, special out-of-town film service is also available. Shop International, sale items from around-the-world and a publications section.

On the exterior of the museum there are the Haida Totem Pole, a cedar totem pole obtained in 1922 from the Haida Indians of Canada, carved about 1860 on Queen Charlotte Island, British Columbia, a 12-foot high bronze figure of Indian and four swans in flight, symbolizing Great Lakes area, designed and sculptured by Marshall Fredericks of Detroit, Michigan, the Fladoes Memorial Fountain, Boy and the Sea Gull, a green bronze statue and lake trout symbolizing the Great Lakes, designed by Joseph McDonnell of Michigan and donated in memory of Martin Fladoes, the Conrad Memorial Fountain, designed by Edward Green, museum artist, donated in memory Ernst Conrad; Milwaukee's last street Tower clock, donated by Thomas Bliffert; Wild Garden of native and naturalized plants in south lawn.

Activities: School visits, workshops, lecture and film programs, guided tours; special events including ethnic programs; puppet shows. Loans exhibit cases to schools. Reference library. Youth Museum.

Publications: Bibliography of Museums and Museum Work, 1900-1960; The Museum Visitor: Selected Essays and Surveys of Visitor Reaction to Exhibits in the Milwaukee Public Museum; Outdoor Museums; The Gull Lake Site: A Prehistoric Bison Drive Site in Southwestern Saskatchewan; Pre-Columbian America: The Art and Archaeology of South, Central and Middle America; Menomini Lexicon; Battle Flags of the Confederate Army of Tennessee; Art of the Congo: Function and Form in Masks and Figures; Native Money of Palau; The Mexican Kickapoo Indians; The Effigy Mound Culture of Wisconsin; Factory Workers in India; East Indians in the West Indies; Cameroons Village: An Ethnography of the Bafut; The Clam River Focus; Spider Divination in the Cameroons; Bilbao, Guatemala: An Archaeological Study of the Pacific Coast Cotzumalhuapa Region, Vols. I and II; Portfolio of Sioux Indian Drawings; Masks of the Northwest Coast; Iroquois False-Face Masks; Mambilla—Art and Material Culture; Air Guns; The Nye-Terry-Greene Breech-Loader Complex; Ivory Sculpture Through the Ages; Historic Wisconsin Buildings: A Survey of Pioneer Architecture, 1835-1870; Air Gun Batteries; The Scheiffel and Kunitomo Air Guns; Milwaukee Landmarks: An American Architectural Heritage, 1850-1950; A Checklist and Key to the Amphibians and Reptiles of Belize, Central America; The Hellbenders: North American Giant Salamanders; Systematics and Natural History of the American Milk Snake, Lampropeltis triangulum; Resource Partitioning Among the Snakes of the University of Kansas Natural History Reservation; Additions to the Herpetofauna of Belize; Control of the Circadian Rhythm of Locomotion in the Tough-skinned Newt, Taricha granulosa; The Reptiles of the Upper Amazon Basin, Iquitos Region, Peru Island Lizards and Amphisbaenians; State Regulations for Collecting Reptiles and Amphibians; A Bibliography of Wisconsin Vegetation; The Hawthorns of Wisconsin; Contributions to the Taxonomy of Crataegus; Silurian Trilobites of Southeastern Wisconsin: A Guide for Fossil Collectors;

A Half Century of Change in Bird Populations of the Lower Chippewa River, Wisconsin; Birds of Wisconsin; Occasional Papers in Natural History; Popular Science Handbook Series; Lore Leaves (reprints from Lore, the quarterly publication of the Friends of the Museum); plus bulletins and yearbooks.

Attendance: 800,000.

TOWER GALLERY
Mount Mary College
  2900 Menomonee River Parkway, 53222. Tel: (414) 258-4810
Sister M. Regina Collins, Chairperson
Free, weekdays 8 AM - 4:30 PM; Sat. & Sun. 1 - 4 PM. Estab. 1940 to provide both students and local community with exposure to art experiences and to provide artists, both estab. professionals and aspirants with a showplace for their work; financed by private funds.

Collections: Antique furniture, 16th century and Victorian period; contemporary print collection; Watercolor-Wisconsin artists.

Exhibitions: Six exhibitions a year.

UNIVERSITY OF WISCONSIN-MILWAUKEE, FINE ARTS GALLERIES
School of Fine Arts, 53201. Tel: (414) 963-4946
Fred R. Parker, Dir.
Free daily 10:30 AM - 4 PM; Sat. 10 AM - 3 PM; cl. Sun. Estab. 1967 to function as university 'museum/galleries' in conjunction with the art department and/or other colleges on campus; also serves outside urban community; financed by city and state appropriation.

Collections: †Large graphic collection, primarily current art.

Exhibitions: Local artists, national artists, international artists; crafts and design shows; photography; MFA graduates; varied museum calibre exhibitions.

Activities: Small photograph collection; lectures open to public; 2 - 3 visiting lecturers per year; 4 - 5 gallery talks; competitions.

WISCONSIN PAINTERS AND SCULPTORS, INC.
c/o Tom Uttech, Pres, 2582 N. Cramer, 53211.
Quido Brink, V.Pres.
Claudia Gorecki, Secy.
Muriel Mennen, Treas.
Estab. 1900 to promote the welfare of Wisconsin painters and sculptors and to promote and develop Wisconsin art. Ann. meeting Nov; mem. approx. 150; dues $8 and higher. Bi-annual exhibition in April at Milwaukee Art Center. Active program of exhibitions and lectures in cooperation with the Art Center and allied groups in the State.

Income and Purchases: Income approx. $800.

NEENAH

BERGSTROM ART CENTER AND MUSEUM
  165 N. Park Ave, 54956. Tel: (414) 722-2912
Anthony V. Garton, Dir.
Geraldine J. Jasper, Asst. Dir. & Cur. Paperweights
Free Wed, Thurs, Sat, Sun. 1 - 5 PM throughout the year, except holidays other than Easter; also Tues. 1 - 5 PM during June, July & Aug. Estab. 1959 to operate and maintain in the City of Neenah, an institution devoted to providing cultural and educational benefits for the public.

Collections: Evangeline Bergstrom collection of glass paperweights; Ernst Mahler collection of Ceramic glass; permanent collection of paintings and drawings.

Exhibitions: Rotating exhibitions in Mahler Gallery; performing arts events, including film series, chamber recitals; workshops; outdoor arts festival.

Activities: Classes for children and adults; lectures, sales and rental gallery, and book and postcard sales desk sponsored by Friends of the Bergstrom Art Center organization. Museum maintains art reference library and paperweight research center, the latter open by appointment with the Curator; gallery talks also offered to groups by appointment.

Attendance: (1974) 15,000.

OSHKOSH

OSHKOSH PUBLIC MUSEUM
  1331 Algoma Blvd, 54901. Tel: (414) 424-0452
Roy Martin, Board Pres.
John H. Kuony, Dir. & Cur. of Art
Robert J. Hruska, Asst. Dir. & Cur. of Anthropology
Free Tues. - Sat. 9 AM - 5 PM; Sun. 1 - 5 PM; cl. Mon. Estab. in 1924 to collect and exhibit historical, Indian and natural history material relating to the area and fine and decorative arts. City owned mansion near University of Wisconsin-Oshkosh campus.

Collections: Moderate permanent collection of work by †American artists and 18th century English portraits. Notable exhibitions of †pressed glass; †Indian artifacts.

Activities: Monthly changing exhibits; lectures; conducts art school. Art classes for children and adults and courses jointly with University in museum techniques; Annual Art Fair in July with awards of about $1600 each year. Sales Shop.

Library: 5000 volumes for reference plus periodicals in the arts, sciences and history; large collection of manuscripts and photographs.

Income: Approx. $135,000

Attendance: Approx. 85,000 per year.

THE PAINE ART CENTER AND ARBORETUM

1410 Algoma Blvd, 54901. Tel: (414) 235-4530

Ralph A. Bufano, Dir.

John D. Green, Arboretum Mgr.

Free Sun, Tues, Thurs. & Sat. 2 - 5 PM; from Memorial Day to Labor Day open daily 2 - 5 PM; cl. Mon. & holidays. Estab. 1948 to stimulate interest in the fine and decorative arts and English architecture and furnishings; financed by endowment. Formally affiliated with the University of Wisconsin-Oshkosh undergraduate program. English gardens.

Collections: Antique Persian carpets; French, English and American 18th and 19th century paintings and sculpture; English period furniture; silver; collection of Chinese porcelains, jades and bronzes; Russian and Greek icons; American and European prints; American glass.

Activities: Organizes special loan exhibitions. Inness, Daubigny, Remington, Adolf Schreyer, J. M. W. Turner, etc; films and lectures, group tours available upon advance request.

Library: Art reference and periodical library; 1000 reference books; subscriptions of 10 periodicals related to art, museums and horticulture.

Publications: Catalogs of exhibits (Barbizon, Schreyer, Turner, L. Lhermitte, etc); Helen Farnsworth Mears; Lion Rugs from Fars.

Attendance: 85,000.

RACINE

CHARLES A. WUSTUM MUSEUM OF FINE ARTS

2519 Northwestern Ave, 53404. Tel: (414) 632-2747

Joseph Cranley, Chmn.

Joyce VandeBunt, Secy.

George Richard, Dir.

Free Mon. - Thurs. 11 AM - 9 PM; Fri. - Sun. 11 AM - 5 PM. Estab. 1939, Museum opened 1941; financed through an endowment given to the city by Mrs. Jennie E. Wustum and by the city of Racine. Educational program financed by the Racine Art Association.

Collections: Incompletely cataloged; include several hundred WPA Project works, plus a number of contemporary watercolors by Wisconsin artists.

Exhibitions: Changed monthly, with emphasis on art of the area. Annual jury exhibition, Watercolor Wisconsin, which then tours state.

Activities: Classes for adults and children; film program and art lectures; sales, rental gallery; work on premises by young and established artists who need use of specialized facilities; meetings of art-related clubs; flower gardens on 12 acre estate.

Annual Combined Budget: Over $120,000.

Attendance: 40,000.

RACINE ART ASSOCIATION

2519 Northwestern Ave, 53404. Tel: (414) 636-9177

Officers change annually

George M. Richard, Dir.

Open Mon. - Thurs. 11 AM - 9 PM; Fri. - Sun. 11 AM - 5 PM. Estab. 1939. Ann. meeting May; mem. approx. 300; dues $10 and higher. Sponsors exhibits, lectures, films, classes for children and adults and other activities at the Wustum Museum of Fine Arts.

Attendance: Approx. 45,000.

RIPON

RIPON COLLEGE ART GALLERY

Harwood Union Bldg, 54971. Tel: (414) 748-8110

E. M. Breithaupt, Dir.

Free Mon. - Fri. 9 AM - 4 PM. Estab. 1965 to provide student body with changing exhibits.

Exhibitions: Paintings, sculpture, print, multi-media.

Activities: Individual paintings lent to schools; 20,000 lantern slides.

Attendance: 4000.

RIVER FALLS

UNIVERSITY OF WISCONSIN-RIVER FALLS

Gallery 101

54022. Tel: (715) 425-3236

David George Burzynski, Cur/Dir.

Free daily 9 AM - 5 PM & 7 - 9 PM. Estab. Sept, 1973 to exhibit

artists of regional and national prominence and who have displayed professional achievement in the arts; financed by state appropriation.

Collections: The collection is divided into two areas, regional artists and national-international artists.

Exhibitions: (1975) Jerry Rudquist - paintings and drawings; Invitational Ceramics Exhibit; Sculpture Exhibit; Contemporary Religious Art; (1976) Drawing USA - Retrospective.

Activities: Lectures open to public; 3 visiting lecturers per year; 12 gallery talks; 30 tours.

Attendance: 80,000.

SHEBOYGAN

✠JOHN MICHAEL KOHLER ARTS CENTER*

608 New York Ave, 53081. Tel: (414) 458-6144

Miss Ruth Kohler, Dir.

Dr. Edward Schott, Pres.

Mrs. Elizabeth Jacobson, V.Pres.

Miss Bernice Scott, Secy.

Richard Pauls, Treas.

Free Tues. - Sun. 1 - 5 PM; Mon. 7 - 9 PM, cl. national holidays. Estab. 1967 to provide aesthetic and educational opportunities in the creative visual and performing arts; maintained by membership. Five exhibition galleries, theater, four studio-class rooms, library, sales gallery. Ann. meeting Feb; mem. 650; dues student $7.50, active $15, contributing $25-$50, sustaining $50-$100, supporting $100-$250, sponsor $250-$500; Patron $500.

Collections: Kuehne collection of 6000 Prehistoric Wisconsin Indian artifacts; contemporary prints including Warhol, Hunt, Piene, Wunderlich, and others.

Major Exhibitions: 1970—Games; Wisconsin Photographers; The Human Image; Miniatures; Outdoor Sculpture; Graphics '70: Germany, The Expressionist Revolt; Paul Wunderlich and Peter Dean; Posters by German and Austrian Expressionists; John Wilde, Drawings and paintings; Joyous Shapes, paintings by Richard Lazzaro; Pop Graphics. 1971—Feathered Splendor, use of feathers in costume decoration and ceremony from 900-1971 A.D; Art by the Second Sex: Clay Sculpture and Paintings by James Leedy; The Midtown Environment: Interim and Ultimate Solutions; Israeli Art '71; Goldsmith '70; Iris x 7, paintings by Lowell Nesbitt; 5 Star; Nineteenth Century Comtoise Clocks, Glass 2000 B.C. - 1971 A.D; Porcelains by Jack Earl, Fabrics by Sister Mary Remy Revor. 1972—Haitian Paintings, Serigraphs and Mental Sculpture; Landscape, paintings of contemporary America; 18th and 19th Century European Porcelains; Graphics '72: Japan; Graphics '72: Wisconsin; Salt-Glaze Ceramics by Nancy Dudchenko; American Folk Art Textiles, Three Centuries; Cartoon and Comic Strip Art; 1, 2, 3 ...Wham, calligraphic images in contemporary art; Man and Spirit in New Guinea Art; The Scroobious Pip and Other Delights: Paintings and Drawings by Nancy Ekholm Burkert; Wisconsin Painters: Recent Trends; Corita Kent Retrospective; Printmaking: A History of Techniques; 52nd Annual Wisconsin Designer/Craftsmen Exhibition; Plastic Earth: A National Ceramics Invitational; Leather: 1000 Years.

Activities: Pre-school; classes for adults and children in all phases of the visual arts as well as dance, theatre and music; lectures; demonstrations; summer theatre; children's theatre; film series; concerts; tours. Sales Gallery.

Library: Art books and periodicals.

Publications: Newsletters, quarterly; exhibition catalogs; annual report.

Income and Purchases: Income $50,000; purchases $89,000.

Attendance: 100,000.

WAUSAU

MARATHON COUNTY HISTORICAL SOCIETY AND MUSEUM

403 McIndoe St, 54401. Tel: (715) 848-6143

Wm. F. McCormick, Pres.

Edward T. Schoenberger, Exec. Dir.

Free daily 9 AM - 5 PM; Sun. 2 - 5 PM; cl. Sat. & holidays. Estab. 1952. Ann. meeting 2nd Tues. of Sept. mem. 1800; dues $1 and higher.

Collections: Largest collection in mid-west of 1880 glass baskets, 160 items in collection.

Exhibitions: Changing monthly exhibitions; Annual Festival of Arts; Annual Wisconsin Designer Craftsmen Exhibit; movie program each Sunday. Exhibits in the museum on lumbering, Indians, prehistoric life, geology, music, clothes, toys, early occupations, farming, and many others. $3,000 in awards, 1970-1973.

Activities: Extension service to all schools in the county, public and private; objects lent to schools; maintains photograph collection of 3500 items; lectures; concerts; classes for children; competitions. The Society has been the first winner of the Reuben Gold Thwaites award as the most outstanding Historical Society in Wisconsin.

Library: Mainly reference; 3000 volumes and 5000 photographic prints.
Income: $35,000.
Attendance: 60,000.

WEST BEND

⚹THE WEST BEND GALLERY OF FINE ARTS
300 S. Sixth Ave, 53095.
Miss Joan Pick, Pres.
E. G. Kocher, Exec. Dir.
F. J. Derer, Exec. Secy.
Free daily 1:30 - 4:30 PM except Mon. & Tues. Estab. 1961 to encourage the varied art interests of the community; supported by endowment and membership. A large colonial style building with seven gallery exhibit rooms. Ann. meeting Feb; mem. 300; dues $5.
Collections: Largest Carl Von Marr Collection in separate Von Marr Wing including 40 paintings and 30 drawings.
Exhibitions: Monthly exhibitions; one annual show with approx. $1000 in awards.
Activities: Original objects of art lent; painting and pottery classes for adults; children's summer art classes; competitions; monthly travelogues.
Library: 280 art books plus current art magazines.
Purchases: Approx. $1200.
Attendance: 3000 ann. average.

WYOMING

BIG HORN

BRADFORD BRINTON MEMORIAL RANCH MUSEUM
Box 23, 82833. Tel: (307) 672-3173
James T. Forrest, Dir.
Ed Smyth, Asst. to Dir.
Free May 15 - Labor Day, daily 9 AM - 5 PM. Estab. 1960, a memorial to Western American art and history; financed by endowment.
Collections: American art of 19th century and early part of 20th century; permanent collection of 600 paintings, sculpture and graphics; mostly by American artists but some English.
Exhibitions: Hans Kleiber Retrospective; Bill Gollings Retrospective; Exhibit of the works of Richard Evans; The Sporting Scene, The works of Edward Borein; The Art of Etching; The Plains Indians; permanent collection.
Activities: 300 Lantern slides; photograph collection, 1000 prints for reference; lectures open to public, visiting lecturer; daily gallery talks or tours.
Library: 4000 volumes on art and art history for reference by appointment.
Publications: Monographs on artists in collection; approx. one a year.
Annual Income: $50,000.
Attendance: 13,000 summer season.

CASPER

CENTRAL WYOMING MUSEUM OF ART
Foundation for the Visual Arts
104 Rancho Rd, 82601. Tel: (307) 235-5247
John Albanese, Pres.
Mrs. Malvin Cole, Secy.
Mrs. Russell Pitts, Dir.
Free daily 1 - 5 PM; also by special request; cl. Mon. Estab. and inc. 1967 to show good traveling shows to the public and school children; financed by membership and Art Council grant. Public art gallery. Mem. dues $5 and higher.
Collections: Starting new collection.
Exhibitions: National Gallery of Art; Smithsonian; American Federation of Crafts; plus other traveling shows.
Activities: Lectures open to the public; dramatic programs; competitions; small library.
Publications: Monthly newsletter.
Income and Purchases: $25,000.
Attendance: 30,000.

CHEYENNE

CHEYENNE ARTISTS GUILD, INC.*
1010 E. Sixteenth St, 82001.
June Kauffman, Pres.
Billie Griske, Secy.
Steve Rodriquez, V.Pres.
Dorothy Feldman, Treas.
John Richards, Exhibit Chmn.
Penny Yost, Prog. Chmn.

Jack Brown, Bldg. Chmn.
Cherrie Read, Hospitality Chmn.
Sherry McCann, Calling Chmn.
Rosella Nimmo, Mem. Chmn.
Carol Deknek, Newsletter
Gloria Stevens, Publicity Chmn.
Peggy Alberts, Educ. Chmn.
Free, Tues. - Fri. 12 AM - 4:30 PM; Sat. 10:30 AM - 4:30 PM; Sun. 2 - 4:30 PM. Estab. 1949 to be an educational non-profit organization and to further the efforts and studies of its members, to sponsor exhibits, and to promote interest in art; financed by endowment and memberships. Meetings dates: Board meeting, first Monday every month; general meeting, second Monday every month; mem. approx. 168; dues $10.
Collections: Guild members and other artists.
Exhibitions: Approx. 12 exhibitions yearly.
Activities: Educational department; lectures open to the public; approx. 11 gallery talks; 11 tours; classes for adults and children; scholarships. Art supply shop and gift store.
Publications: Monthly newsletter.
Income and Purchases: Income $31,348; purchases $16,591.

WYOMING COUNCIL ON THE ARTS
State of Wyoming Offices, 82002. Tel: (307) 777-7742
Robert F. Barlow, Pres.
Margaret Peck, Secy.
Michael F. Haug, Exec. Dir.
Joan Westphall, Admin. Secy.
Free Mon. - Fri. 8 AM - Noon & 1 - 5 PM. Estab. 1967, The Wyoming Council on the Arts is an agency of the State of Wyoming, created in 1967 to encourage and assist cultural and artistic programs throughout the state. The Council consists of ten Governor-appointed members from over the state, meeting approximately five times during the year; financed by endowment and city and state appropriation. Gallery consists of the five rooms of offices; 12-14 pieces can be hung, depending on size.
Exhibitions: Mainly by state artists (amateur, semi-professional and professional), hung for a period of two to three months; high school student art work.
Activities: Artists in Schools program places visual artists, poets, and filmmakers in schools in the state for periods ranging from a few days to three months; traveling exhibitions organized and circulated; individual paintings lent to schools.
Library: 200 volumes for reference, extra copies may be lent.
Publications: Bimonthly Calendar of Events; Arts in Wyoming, quarterly newsletter; Annual Report.

WYOMING STATE ARCHIVES AND HISTORICAL DEPARTMENT
State Office Building, 82002. Tel: (307) 777-7518
William H. Williams, Dir.
Laura Hayes, Cur.
Wyoming State Museum, Wyoming State Art Gallery, Free weekdays 9 AM - 5 PM; Sun. 9 AM - 5 PM; Sat, Memorial Day to Labor Day, 9 AM - 5 PM.
Fort Bridger Subject Museum, April 1 to Sept. 15, daily 8 AM - 7 PM; Sun. & Mon. 12 AM - 7 PM. Sept. 15 - Dec. 15, Sat. 8 AM - 4 PM and Sun. 12 AM - 4 PM only.
Fort Fetterman Subject Museum, daily 8:30 - 12 AM & 1 - 5 PM; Sun. 12 AM - 6 PM.
Estab. 1895; collects, conserves, exhibits of material related to the ethnology, archeology and history of Wyoming and the surrounding region of the West.
Library: Reference library of 5000 volumes; photo section, 60,000 prints.
Attendance: 60,000 annually.

WYOMING STATE ART GALLERY
State Office Bldg, 82002. Tel: (307) 777-7519
William H. Williams, Dir.
Mrs. Laura M. Hayes, Cur.
Free, Mon. - Fri. 8:30 AM - 5 PM; Sat. 9 AM - 5 PM. Estab. 1969; financed by state appropriation.
Exhibitions: State western artists.
Library: Reference library of 300 volumes.
Attendance: 60,000 annual average.

CODY

BUFFALO BILL MEMORIAL ASSOCIATION
P.O. Box 1020, 82414. Tel: (307) 587-2268
Mrs. Henry H. R. Coe, Chmn.
Melvin C. McGee, Secy.
Don Hedgpeth, Dir.
Joyce Mayer, Exec. Secy.
Leo A. Platteter, Cur, Plains Indian Museum
Richard I. Frost, Cur, Buffalo Bill Museum

Open daily May - Sept. 8 AM - 5 PM; June - Aug. 7 AM - 10 PM.
Estab 1917 to preserve and exhibit art, artifacts and memorabilia
of the Old West; operator of Buffalo Bill Museum, Plains Indian
Museum, Whitney Gallery of Western Art, and Winchester
Firearms Museum; financed by admis. and private funds.
  Collections: Original paintings and sculpture by foremost
artists of the Old West; historical memorabilia of Col. William F.
"Buffalo Bill" Cody; hundreds of items of the Plains Indians.
Book Shop.
  Library: Reference library for the serious student.
  Attendance: Over 200,000.

CODY COUNTRY ART LEAGUE
  836 Sheridan Ave, 82414. Tel: (307) 587-3597
Mrs. George W. Tresler, Pres.
Richard B. Frazier, V.Pres.
Mrs. Jesse Frost, Secy.
Mrs. Gordon Way, Dir.
Mrs. L. A. Johnson, Exhibiting Chmn.
Mrs. S. J. Duggleby, Publicity Chmn.
Mrs. James Gilbert, Educ. & Prog. Chmn.
Mrs. William Mack, Representative of Past Pres.
Free Noon - 8 PM. Estab. June 1964 for promotion of artistic
endeavor among local and area artists; exhibits, displays, and
sales; education, and art classes; financed by endowment, mem-
bership, grants from Wyoming Council on the Arts; yearly auction;
sponsors. Ann. meeting 2nd week in Dec; mem. 115; dues $10.
  Collections: One work each by Nicholas Eggenhoffer and
Robert Myers.
  Exhibitions: Western States Art Exhibit ($500 purchase award
and over $1000 in other prizes); one-man shows.
  Activities: Lectures open to the public; 2-3 visiting lecturers
per year; workshops; films; dramatic programs; classes for
adults and children; competitions.
  Income and Purchases: Income $18,365; purchases $18,064.
  Attendance: 15,000.

WHITNEY GALLERY OF WESTERN ART*
  P.O. Box 1020, 82414. Tel: (307) 587-2777
Harold McCracken, Dir.
Joyce Mayer, Exec. Secy.
Ernest J. Goppert, Pres.
Melvin C. McGee, Secy.
Open May 1 - June 1, 8 AM - 5 PM; June 1 - Sept. 1, 7 AM - 10
PM; Sept. 1 - Oct. 1, 8 AM - 5 PM. Estab. 1959 for exhibition
and preservation of documentary Western art; self-supporting.
One annual meeting and periodic local board meeting.
  Collections: Catlin, Russell, Remington, Sharp, Bierstadt, Mil-
ler, and all documentary artists of the Old West.
  Exhibitions: In addition to our permanent collection we have a
yearly feature exhibition of the work of prominent contemporary
Western artists.
  Library: 2000 volumes, photograph collection, for reference.
  Income and Purchases: Income (1969) $132,000; purchases vary.
  Attendance: (1969) 200,000.

LARAMIE

✠UNIVERSITY OF WYOMING ART MUSEUM
  Box 3138, University Station, 82070. Tel: (307) 766-2374
James Taylor Forrest, Dir.
Jerry Berger, Cur.
William Little, Asst. Cur.
Open Sun. - Fri. 2 - 5 PM. Estab. 1968 as Art Museum.
  Collections: †American and †European painting, prints and
sculpture.
  Exhibitions: Circulate state-wide series of exhibits; faculty,
student shows; loan, permanent collection.
  Activities: Visiting lecturers, films demonstrations.
  Library: 600 volumes on works of art.
  Income and Purchases: $8000-10,000 per year.
  Attendance: 25,000.

ROCK SPRING

SWEETWATER COMMUNITY FINE ARTS CENTER
  400 Center, 82901.
Al Kenney, Dir.
Estab. 1965, opened 1966 with federal funding, to create a way
for children and adults to witness and participate in the performing
arts. Federal funding ended 1970; financed by city appropriation,
Sweetwater County Library, and School District No. 1.
  Collections: Over 200 paintings owned by Rock Springs High
School, which is acclaimed to be the best owned by American
High Schools.
  Exhibitions: (1975-76) Robert I. Russin; Casper Symposium;
Thomas Connell Lander; Rock Springs Artist Show; Casper Jr.

College Faculty Exhibit; Terrence Hick, wildlife artist; Dick
Hutt, Cheyenne watercolor artist; Green River Local Artist Show;
William E. Wright, versatile Sheridan artist; Rock Springs Art
Guild National Exhibit and Competition; Alexander Scourby,
Whitney America; Western Wyoming College Regional Photography
Workshop and Exhibit; four exhibits from Shared Touring Exhibits
Program.
  Activities; Traveling exhibits; lectures; demonstrations;
musical and dramatic performances.

TORRINGTON

SOUTHEASTERN WYOMING ART ASSOCIATION*
  Box 212, 82240.
Linda Dodge, Pres.
Maxine Fisher, Treas.
Ruth Kelly, Secy.
Art Shack open weekdays 1:30 - 4:30 PM or by appointment; no
admis. fee. Estab. to give artists a group to belong to, to exchange
ideas, to hold classes; The Art Shack is an outlet for members
works, to acquaint the community with our artists; financed by
endowment and mem. Small sales gallery through which members
sell their paintings and crafts. Mem. 45; dues $5.
  Activities: We work through the Eastern Wyoming Community
College and serve the entire community and county; fees for classes;
original objects of art lent from members private collections; lectures open to the public; dramatic programs; classes for adults and
children; competitions; donate books to the county library, also feature an artist of the month at the county library.
  Publications: Monthly newsletter.
  Income: Commissions and dues.

AMERICAN SAMOA

PAGO PAGO

JEAN P. HAYDON MUSEUM
  P.O. Box 1540, 96799. Tel: 633-4347
Palauni Tuiasosopo, Chmn. Board of Trustees
Fa'ailoilo Lauvao, Cur.
Diana P. Saulo, Asst. Cur.
Open Weekdays 10 AM - 4 PM; Sat. 10 - 12 AM; no admis. Estab.
1971 for preservation of Samoan culture, history and custom; fi-
nanced by city or state appropriations and grants from the National
Endowment for the Arts.
  Collections: Samoan village life; U.S. Navy history; natural
sciences; Polynesian artifacts.
  Library: Reference library; photograph collection for reference;
16mm films and slides.

PUERTO RICO

PONCE

MUSEO DE ARTE DE PONCE
(Ponce Art Museum)
  Avenida de las Americas, Apartado 1492, 00731.
  Tel: 842-6215, 9394
Dr. Rene Taylor, Dir.
Open daily 10 AM - 4 PM; cl. Mon; admis. adults $1, children
under 12 25¢. Dedicated and opened 1965. Administered and
supported by the Luis Ferre Foundation. The donor of this new
museum, Luis A. Ferre, a native of Ponce, wished to establish a
museum for the people of Puerto Rico and the many visitors from
numerous countries. The two-story contemporary museum was
designed by Edward Durell Stone.
  Collections: Paintings, ceramics and sculpture, including the
works of Valazquez, Gainsborough, Rubens, Reynolds and Van Dyke.
Noteworthy are its Pre-Raphaelite and Italian Baroque Paintings.
The museum also has 150 paintings by Puerto Rican artists.
  Activities: Lectures, concerts; art library; exhibitions are
held monthly.

SAN JUAN

✠INSTITUTO DE CULTURA PUERTORRIQUENA
(Institute of Puerto Rican Culture)
  Apartado 4184, 00905. Tel: (809) 724-0700
Luis M. Rodriguez-Morales, Exec. Dir.
Created in 1955 for the conservation of the national heritage of the
people and the education of the young; to discover the history and
culture of their proud heritage.
  Collections: Archaeological, historical and artistic collections
have been accumulated to represent a treasure of incalculable worth.
  Activities: 15 museums established to date with 5 in preparation;
mobile and regional museums.

LA CASA DEL LIBRO
(The House of Books)
    Calle del Cristo 255, 00901; or Box S2265, 00903.
    Tel: (809) 723-0354
David Jackson McWilliams, Dir.

Sponsoring organization: Amigos de Calle del Cristo 255, Inc.
    Rafael Fabregas, Pres.
    Max Goldman, V.Pres.
    Miguel A. Ferrer, Treas.

Free Mon. - Fri. 11 AM - 5 PM; Sat. 2 - 5 PM. Estab. 1955 as a museum-library devoted to the history and arts of the book and related graphic arts; financed by state appropriation and membership in the sponsoring organization. Mem. approx. 350; dues $10 and higher.

Collections: Bibliography of graphic arts; early printing, especially 15th and 16th century Spanish; modern fine printing; calligraphy; binding; book illustration; papermaking; approx. 5000 items in library.

Exhibitions: Gallery has displays on the first floor relating to printing and other arts of the book, such as: Spanish Incunables; Printing of Music in Books; The Boundaries of the World; Concrete Poetry; Editions of the ''Quixote''; ''Por los Caminos del Dia''; Original Art Work for ''The Emperor's New Clothes''; The Illustrated Book in Puerto Rico; Book Plates; ''Objetivos'' de Julio Plaza; Fifteen Years of Posters at La Casa del Libro.

Activities: Visits from school groups, students of library science and workers in graphic arts; material available; no fees; traveling exhibitions organized and circulated to schools and colleges in Puerto Rico; original objects of printing arts lent; material must by used on the premises; occasional lectures open to the public; gallery talks vary per year; some classes for adults. Book Shop.
    Income: $26,000.
    Attendance: 14,000.

United States Children's and Junior Museums

CALIFORNIA

LOS ANGELES

JUNIOR ARTS CENTER
 4814 Hollywood Blvd, 90027. Tel: (213) 666-1093
Mrs. Gavin Miller, Chmn. Board of Trustees
Claire Isaacs Deussen, Dir.
Thomas Mathews, Admin. Asst.
Ron Layborteaux, Art Cur.
Richard Ellis, Educ. Coordinator
Free Mon. - Sat. 9 AM - 5 PM. Estab. May, 1967 to stimulate and assist in the development of art skills and creativity. A Division of Municipal Arts Department, City of Los Angeles; financed by city appropriation and membership. The Gallery offers exhibitions of interest to children and young people and those who work with the young. Ann. meeting of the Friends of the Junior Arts Center first wk. of May; mem. 350; dues $5, $10, $25, $50, $100, $500, $1000.
 Collections: Permanent collection of two-dimensional works on paper and of Super 8mm film by former students.
 Exhibitions: (1970-75) Cola (Coherent Light Art); Faculty Exhibition; Bread; Folk Art of India; Is There Anything in Particular? (student organized); Toys and Things Japanese, Designs by Shigeo Fukuda; Picasso Prints; K-12 East (from E. Los Angeles City Schools); African Masks and Artifacts; Tibetan Mandalas; Students Prints; Proof! (student drawing and photography); Flash (media exhibit); Rotunda of City Hall, Children's Art; Artist as Teacher as Artist; Tube City; Mechicano at the Junior Arts Center; Word Show (Experience with words, possibilities with language); Wallnuts (mural exhibition); Toy Show (Exhibit and participation utilizing wheel, box and suspension techniques); 3 to 1 (Art exhibit designed by California based artists); Festivals and Celebrations (International Children's exhibit); What About Art? (Student Art Exhibit); What a Relief! (Bas-relief-sand casting); In-House Floaters (13 JAC photographers).
 Activities: Classes for young people ages 5-17, 100 hours weekly for 40 weeks in painting (all media), drawing, etching, general printmaking, photography, filmmaking, photo silkscreen, three-dimensional photography, ceramics, environmental education, dollmaking, writing, pantomime and improvisation, playwriting, music appreciation, creative dance, cooking, bookmaking, and film animation; two-thirds of this program offered after school, evenings and weekends and one-third in the morning hours to classes transported by the local schools. Workshops for teachers and other adults who work with children; concerts; lectures; films and improvisational groups scheduled for students and the public; special activities in schools, parks, and other appropriate sites throughout the city.
 Library: 700 volumes for reference; 5000 slides for reference; 10,000 slides-documentation.
 Publications: Quarterly schedule of art classes; exhibition notices.
 Income: $247,000 city; $12,000 Friends of the Junior Arts Center.
 Attendance: 50,000 including workshops, special events and Gallery programs.

OAKLAND

JUNIOR CENTER OF ART AND SCIENCE
 3612 Webster St, 94609. Tel: (415) 655-3226
Jane McCaffery, Dir.
Open Tues. - Fri. 10 AM - 5 PM; Sat. 10 - 12 AM. Estab. May 1949, to provide classes in music, drama, art, dance, science; for the children of the East Bay. Mem. dues family $10, contributing $25, sustaining $50, sponsor $100, business $25 - $500. Sponsored by the Art League of the East Bay and East Bay Children's Theatre. Junior Center Guild.
 Activities: Exhibitions; art and craft classes; music and movies.

PALO ALTO

PALO ALTO JUNIOR MUSEUM AND ZOO
 250 Hamilton Ave, 94301. Tel: (415) 329-2111
 Location: 1451 Middlefield Road
Mearl Carson, Supvr.
Gale Bruce, Instr. Arts & Crafts
Open Tues. - Fri. 10 AM - 5 PM; Sat. 9 AM - 5 PM; Sun. 1 - 4 PM. of the recreation department of the City in 1943; completely renovated and transferred to Nature and Science in 1969.
 Collections: Art and artifacts; natural science specimens; zoo animals of an indigenous nature; all collections continuously increased by donations.
 Activities: Conducts crafts and nature classes both at Museum and extension classes at community centers; guided tours; exhibits; and, sciencemobile for transporting special exhibits to schools.
 Library: Books and magazines on arts, crafts, natural science, ethnology, etc, 1000 items.
 Publications: Monthly notes; Prehistoric Palo Alto (brochure).
 Income: Budget $60,000.
 Attendance: 100,000.

SAN FRANCISCO

JOSEPHINE D. RANDALL JUNIOR MUSEUM
 199 Museum Way, 94114. Tel: (415) 863-1399
Dr. A. Kirk Conragan, Dir.
Thomas A. Mandas, Natural Science Cur.
John R. Dillon, Natural Science Cur.
Marie Anido, Cur. Arts & Crafts
Free Tues. - Sat. 10 AM - 5 PM; Sun. Noon - 5 PM; cl. Mon. Estab. 1945, part of the San Francisco Recreation and Park Department.
 Activities: Classes in natural science, natural history, Indian of California, seismology, marine biology, physical science, botany horticulture, chemistry, geology, rocks and minerals, ceramics, weaving, leaded glass, painting, art history, jewelry, and stitchery. Special field trips to neighboring biotic communities, nature by horseback, and week-end and one week camp-outs.
 Library: Books of art and natural history; map files; geological publications and seismological information.
 Attendance: 120,000 annual average, not including 6800 school children.

SAN MATEO

COYOTE POINT MUSEUM
 Coyote Point, 94401. Tel: (415) 573-2595
Maryann Danielson, Dir.
Carol J. Kemnitz, Cur.
Free Mon. - Sat. 9 AM - 5 PM; Sun. 1 - 5 PM. Inc. 1953, opened 1954. Mem. dues $10 and higher.
 Collections: Natural history, science.
 Exhibitions: Permanent dioramas depicting wildlife habitats of the county; temporary displays telling nature stories coinciding with the seasons; terraria of local reptiles and amphibians; a sanctuary where many native birds and mammals are on display.
 Activities: Conducted tours; special classes; supervised field trips; animal loan program; maintains a science reference library and bookstore; Counselling Service and Teacher Workshops.
 Library: Natural history, environment.
 Attendance: 80,000.

SAN RAFAEL

LOUISE A. BOYD MARIN MUSEUM OF SCIENCE
 76 Albert Park Lane, 94901. Tel: (415) 454-6961
Bruce Blake, Exec. Dir.
William Wallace Sterling, Pres.

Open Tues. - Sat. 10 AM - 5 PM; cl. Sun, Mon, Thanksgiving, Christmas, New Year's. Estab. July 3, 1953, to provide wildlife refuge and nature education center. Ann. meeting Jan; mem. 1100; dues family $12.50, other catagories.

Collections: Marin County wildlife and ecology exhibits; small collection of live native animals.

Activities: Wildlife refuge providing emergency and long-term medical care to any native animals; visitor center open Free to the public; nature and ecology education activities for children, families and adults; classes and field trips offered year round for nominal fees; extensive school program; Docent Council; speakers bureau; camping and backpack trips; nature-related craft classes, nature classes for children 3 yrs. old and up; changing exhibitions; Museum Store.

Library: Nature and ecology and wildlife, 500 volumes; available to members and local teachers, others by arrangement; no loan except to county residents.

Publication: Quarterly class announcements.

Finances: 80% private support, from donations, fees, memberships ships; 20% county support; annual budget (1975-1976); expense $85,000; income $85,000.

Attendance: 70,000.

CONNECTICUT

MANCHESTER

LUTZ JUNIOR MUSEUM
126 Cedar St, 06040. Tel: (203) 643-0949
Pamela Saloom, Dir.
Nina S. Dvornek, Pres.
Free Tues. - Sun. 2 - 5 PM; cl. Mon, holidays and month of Aug. Founded 1954, opened 1958; non-profit children's museum. Ann. meeting May; adult and family mem. 370; junior mem. 700; dues junior $2, single adult $5, family $10, contributing $25.

Collections: Participatory exhibits in history, science, ethnology and fine arts.

Activities: Classes in fine arts and science, cultural programs and field trips; store.

School Services Department: 500 loan exhibits, tours, resource people.

Attendance: 23,500.

MYSTIC

THE CHILDREN'S MUSEUM
Mystic Seaport, Inc.
06355. Tel: (203) 536-2631
Waldo C. M. Johnston, Dir. Mystic Seaport, Inc.
Open daily summer 9 AM - 5 PM; grounds close at 6 PM; admis. adults $4.25, children $1.75; winter 10 AM - 4 PM; grounds close at 5 PM; admis. adults $3.75, children $1.50, adult & child tickets good for two consecutive days admis. to museum in winter; cl. Christmas & New Year's; special two day admis. adults $6, children $2.25; group rates on request. Estab. as a view into the life of children who went to sea in the late 19th century. A representation of a ships cabin depicts the living quarters of a captain's family, complete with furnishings typical of a large sailing vessel. Yard with a boat and mast for climbing.

Collections: Reproduction of toys, dolls clothing and games that 15th century children played with at sea.

Exhibitions: Children Who Went to Sea.

NEW BRITAIN

NEW BRITAIN YOUTH MUSEUM
30 High St, 06051. Tel: (203) 225-3020
Alan J. Krauss, Dir.
Free Mon. - Fri. 1 - 5 PM; Sat. 10 AM - 5 PM; cl. Sat, June, July and Aug. Founded 1956; sponsored by the City and New Britain Institute.

Collections: Ethnic, natural history, American Indian, Americana.

Activities: Exhibits, loan service, lectures, participation and demonstration, clubs on arts and crafts of man and nature, from primitive and pioneer to highly civilized cultures.

NEW LONDON

THAMES SCIENCE CENTER*
Gallows Lane, 06320. Tel: (203) 442-0391
Kathie Haeni, Chief Naturalist
Free Mon. - Sat. 9 AM - 5 PM; July 1 - Sept. 1 8 AM - 4 PM; Sun. 1 - 5 PM. Sponsored by the Board of Directors and the Public of New London County. Mem, dues $4 to $50.

Collections: All collections are active.

Exhibits: Emphasizing biological and earth sciences; cultural history.

Activities: Exhibits in the Center; clubs and classes for people of all ages; field trips, special programs, lectures and films, programs for schools; monthly publication to members.

Income: $56,000.

WEST HARTFORD

ENVIRONMENTAL CENTERS INC.

Children's Museum of Hartford
950 Trout Brook Dr, West Hartford, 06119. Tel: (203) 236-2961
Maxine Valitsky, Admin. Dir.
Rosemary Campominosi, Registrar
Carol Bower, Aquarium Dir.
John Roberts, Planetarium Dir.
Gail Collins, Special Programming
Open Mon. - Fri. 2:30 - 5 PM; Sat. 10 AM - 5 PM; Sun. 1 - 5 PM; mornings reserved for school groups; no charge except for Planetarium Shows and Aquarium, adults $1.50, children 75¢, group rates for 10 or more. Founded 1927, non-profit corporation. Dues for ECI mem. junior (thru age 17) $5, individual $15, family $20, sustaining $100, patron $250.

Collections: Colonial America, American Indian, The Orient, biology, geology, natural history, earth sciences, wild animals, snakes and birds, 62 foot model of Sperm Whale.

Activities: Tours, lectures, films, formally organized classes for school groups, teacher workshops, permanent and temporary exhibitions, loan service department for educational institutions, store.

Roaring Brook Nature Center
176 Gracey Rd, Canton, 06019. Tel: (203) 693-0263
Jay Kaplan, Naturalist-Dir.
Gail Johnson, Naturalist
Open Tues. - Sat. 10 AM - 5 PM; Sun. 1 - 5 PM.

Collections: Mounted birds, animals, habitat materials, fossils, rocks, live animals and reptiles.

Activities: Lectures, workshops, formally organized education programs for schools, teacher workshops, out-reach program in schools, permanent and temporary exhibitions, walks on five nature trails, store.

Attendance: Approx. 200,000.

WESTPORT

MID-FAIRFIELD COUNTY YOUTH MUSEUM*
10 Woodside Lane, 06880. Tel: (203) 227-7253
John F. Gardner, Dir.
Free Mon. - Sat. 9 AM - 5 PM; Sun. 2 - 5 PM; cl. national holidays. Founded 1958, opened 1961. Maintains 53 acre wildlife sanctuary: self guided trails. Mem. 2500; dues junior $5, friend $50, subscribing $250, sustaining $500.

Collections: Natural Science—fossils, birds, marine life, minerals, etc.

Activities: School tours; lectures, gallery talks; films; workshops; training programs for professional museum workers; intermuseum and school loans; traveling exhibitions organized and circulated; mobile vans.

Library: 2500 volumes on natural science for reference.

Publications: Monthly magazine, Connecticut Naturalist; bulletins; quarterly Research Journal.

Attendance: 80,000.

FLORIDA

JACKSONVILLE

THE JACKSONVILLE CHILDREN'S MUSEUM, INC.
1025 Gulf Life Dr, 32207. Tel: (904) 396-7061
Dr. G. Dekle Taylor, Pres.
Mrs. Edward Baker, 1st V.Pres.
Mrs. Leonard Moseby, 2nd V.Pres.
Mrs. Robert Myers, Secy.
Doris Whitmore, Dir.
Open Tues. - Sat. 9 AM - 5 PM; Sun. 2 - 5 PM; cl. Mon. & Sept; summer hrs. vary. Estab. and inc. 1941. Mem. total enrollment 500; dues junior $7.50, individual $15, family $25, subscriber $50, patron $100, sponsor $250, honorary $500.

Collections and Exhibitions: Natural Science department with shells, rocks, minerals, fossils, birds, live Florida wildlife; Planetarium, astronomy; ethnology of Africa, Alaska, Japan, India, Seminole Indians, Southwest Indians; Antique dolls, ancient Egypt, anthropology, natural history, paleontology, environmental displays.

Activities: Spring, summer and fall classes in arts and crafts, painting, ceramics, stitchery, science, astronomy, pre-school program (plus school year kindergarten for 5 yr. olds). Guided tours and lectures given by Women's Guild and volunteers. Museum Gift Shop; various holiday and seasonal activities such as Indian Summer Harvest Festival in Nov; Haunted House and Halloween Party, Cracker Crafts, Spring Festival, Christmas Festival and Party.

Library: 500 volume library of encyclopedias; nature books, science publications, Life Nature Library series; books on Antique Dolls, Indians, astronomy, rocks, birds, lands and peoples, history, art techniques, etc; plus many monthly publications.

Publications: Annual bulletin to teachers; monthly bulletin to schools and members; monthly bulletin to astronomy club and Weather Watchers bulletin.

Attendance: Approx. 200,000.

MIAMI

MUSEUM OF SCIENCE
3280 S. Miami Ave, 33129. Tel: (305) 854-4242
Don J. Starkey, Exec. Dir.
Jack Horkheimer, Planetarium Dir.
Diane Sceltzman, Coordinator of Educ. Prog.
Free Mon. - Sat. 9 AM - 5 PM; Sun. Noon - 10 PM; Fri. & Sat. 7:30 - 10 PM; Space Transit Planetarium Shows daily 1, 2:30, 4 & 8 PM, Fri. & Sat. 10 PM, Spanish narration Sat. 5:30 PM, Sun. 5:30 & 9:30 PM, admis. charged to planetarium shows. Inc. 1949. Ann. meeting May; mem. 2200; dues $10 and higher.

Collections: Art objects; ethnology, †ornithology; geology; physical sciences, †oceanic fish, Florida tree snails; Florida ecology-mammals.

Activities: Exhibits, lectures, films, observatory, planetarium.

Library: General science oriented, 3000 volumes.

Publications: Museum, monthly.

Budget: (1975) 615,000.

Attendance: 450,000.

TALLAHASSEE

TALLAHASSEE JUNIOR MUSEUM*
3945 Museum Dr, 32303. Tel: (904) 576-1636
Bruce Culpeper, Pres.
Sam W. Kates, Dir.
Ann Matthews, Cur.
Tiffany West, Coordinator of Educ.
Open Tues. - Sat. 9 AM - 5 PM; Sun. 2 - 5 PM; cl. Mon, one wk. at Christmas, holidays; admis. adults 50¢, children under 16 10¢, members no charge. Estab. 1957, museum for the family with changing exhibits in the arts, social sciences, and the natural sciences; financed by mem, county and city school board appropriation. Dues $5-100. A pioneer Florida restoration of the 1880's consisting of eleven log building.

Collections: Pre-historic Florida Indian pottery; a complete 1880 Florida farm-furnishings and tools.

Activities: Crafts, nature; educational department; traveling exhibitions; lending service to schools; lectures open to the public; gallery talks; concerts.

Income: $105,000.

Attendance: 75,000.

GEORGIA

MACON

MUSEUM OF ARTS AND SCIENCES, INC.
4182 Forsyth Rd, 31204. Tel: (912) 477-3232
Douglas R. Noble, Dir.
Open Mon. - Fri. 9 AM - 5 PM; Sat. 11 AM - 5 PM; Sun. 2 - 5 PM; cl. national holidays; admis.

Collections: Contemporary art; historical, natural science artifacts.

Exhibitions: Georgia reptiles, amphibians and fish in Nature Center Building; limestone cave; nature trails; traveling art and science exhibits in Main Exhibit Hall.

Activities: Classes for children and adults; art exhibits; lectures; movies; special events.

Planetarium
William M. Stallings III, Dir.
Groups by appointment Mon. - Fri; public shows Fri. 8 PM; cl. national holidays; admis. for public shows adults $1, children 50¢.

SAVANNAH

SAVANNAH SCIENCE MUSEUM, INC.
4405 Paulsen St, 31405. Tel: (912) 355-6705
Elizabeth Labrot, Pres.
Ann Trosdal, Secy.
Charles E. Milmine, Dir.
Gerald C. Williamson, Cur.
Jean T. Milmine, Educ. Dir.
Free Weekdays 10 AM - 5 PM; Sun. 2 - 5 PM. Estab. 1954 to foster interest in science, history and industry in the community. Supported by membership. Ann. meeting April; mem. 700; dues $15 and higher.

Activities: Work with school systems in Chatham County; 50 items lent per year to 30 active borrowers; lectures open to the public, 4 or 5 visiting lecturers per year; Teacher's and Youth Group Resource Center. Book Shop.

Library: 700 volumes for lending and reference.

Publications: Newsletter, monthly.

Attendance: 40,000.

ILLINOIS

CHICAGO

THE JUNIOR MUSEUM OF THE ART INSTITUTE OF CHICAGO
Michigan Ave. at Adams St, 60603.
Tel: (312) 236-7080 Exten. 253
Lois Raasch, Asst. Dir. Museum Educ, Junior Museum
Open Mon, Tues, Wed, Fri. and Sat. 10 AM - 4:30 PM; Thurs. 10 AM - 8 PM; Sun. Noon - 4:30 PM. Estab. by the Woman's Board of the Art Institute with the co-sponsorship of the Junior League of Chicago, inc. 1964.

The rooms, galleries, studio and auditorium were designed to offer unique educational opportunities for children aged nine and over, whether they visit the Institute in groups, alone, or with their families. Among the facilities of the Junior Museum—The Sol and Celia Hammerman Gallery "America and the Artist," works of art from The Art Institute's vast collection in an illustrative exhibition for young people; The Rainbow Gallery—colors projected on a white wall and a rainbow-like spectrum demonstrate the physical properties of light and color; Picnic Room—exhibitions of children's art; The Little Library in memory of Joan Farwell open to children 6 years through high school for browsing and reference work; Junior Museum Store and other points of interest and instruction.

Activities: Lectures provided by the Department of Museum Education to schools and youth organizations. Gallery Games, I Spy and Round Up.

Publications: Gallery Games; Heritage Hikes; Round-up Games.

Attendance: 180,000 annually.

INDIANA

INDIANAPOLIS

CHILDREN'S MUSEUM OF INDIANAPOLIS*
3010 N. Meridian St, 46208. Tel: (317) 925-9263
Mildred S. Compton, Dir.
Weimer K. Hicks, Jr, Cur. Collections
Free Tues. - Sat. 9 AM - 5 PM; Sun. 2 - 5 PM; cl. Mon. Estab. 1925, inc. 1946. Sponsored by individual membership, private endowment and public grant; ann. meeting 3rd Wed. in Feb; mem. $10 and higher.

Collections: American history; social culture of other lands; Indian; transportation; toys; prehistory.

Activities: School group tours; Lending Exhibit Service to schools, libraries, hospitals and churches, covering every subject in the permanent collection; after school activities including hobby, nature and craft groups; classes; conducted tours and demonstrations; field trips; films; pioneer fair; international fair; theater.

Library: 3000 general volumes, reference only.

Attendance: 200,000.

KENTUCKY

LOUISVILLE

✠JUNIOR ART GALLERY, INC.
Louisville Free Public Library, 4th & York Sts, 40203.
Tel: (502) 583-7062
Roberta L. Williams, Exec. Dir.
Free Mon. - Sat. 9 AM - 5 PM; cl. Sun; cl. Sat. & Sun. during June & July; cl. Aug. Inc. 1950 under auspices of the Junior League,

thereafter jointly sponsored by the Junior League, The Louisville Fund, and the Louisville Free Public Library; presently sponsored by the Louisville Fund and the Louisville Free Public Library.

Collections: †Small collection begun in 1955 by purchases from exhibitions.

Exhibitions: Five exhibitions a year of work by adult artists designed for and interpreted to children attempting to increase their awareness of aesthetic experiences. With a few exceptions these exhibitions are assembled by the Gallery. Sample topics are: Beautiful Things, Seven Ways with Wood, Fiber Form.

Activities: Gallery tours; workshops; special appreciation activities; loan exhibitions; slide sets; annual street painting contest; special films.

Income: Budget $48,200.

Attendance: 30,000 annually.

LOUISIANA

BATON ROUGE

LOUISIANA ARTS AND SCIENCE CENTER
502 North Boulevard and 100 South River Rd, 70801.
Tel: (504) 344-9463
Mrs. Allan R. Brent, Dir.
Mary E. Bailey, Asst.
Kathleen Loe, Cur.
Jeff C. Gregory, Cur.
Harold Arbour, Planetarium Supvr.
Jane Menville, Planetarium Supvr.
Museum free Tues. - Sat. 10 AM - 5 PM; Sun. 1 - 5 PM; cl. Mon; Planetarium admis. children 25¢, adults 50¢. Estab. 1906 to widen the world of wonderment for children and serve as an extension to an enrichment of formal classroom education; financed by Parish School Board and City-Parish appropriations. Mem. 800; dues youth $2, adult $5, family $7.50, sponsor $50, life $200.

Collections: Ivan Mestrovic sculpture, bronze; Francois Brochet sculpture, wood polychrome; original graphics; photography collections include Irving Olson, Lynn Lennon, and Richard Balzer; Eskimo soapstone carvings, prints, artifacts; contemporary art; American Indian art and artifacts; Egyptology; Tibetan Religious Art Collection; Man and the Mississippi River and The Story of Plastics, audiovisual presentations of special interest.

Activities: Traveling exhibitions organized and circulated; liaison with schools and colleges; special school loan service; lectures; tours; starlight concerts, movies. Gift Shop, Soupçon, Sculpture Garden, Restored Governor's Mansion.

Publications: Happenings, Heavenly Facts, quarterly; Planetarium Study Guide and subject study guides for teachers.

Income: $160,000.

Attendance: 100,000.

MASSACHUSETTS

BOSTON

THE CHILDREN'S MUSEUM
Jamaicaway, 02130. Tel: (617) 522-4800
Michael Spock, Dir.
Phyllis D. O'Connell, Assoc. Dir. & Dir. Resource Center
Elaine Heumann Guriau, Dir. Visitor Center
Jim Zien, Dir. Community Services
Open schooldays 2 - 5 PM; weekends and school holidays and vacations 10 AM - 5 PM; free Fri. 6 - 9 PM; closed New Year's, July 4th, Thanksgiving, Christmas, Sept; admis. adults $2, children $1, groups from Metropolitan Parks District no charge. Founded 1913. Mem. individual child $4, individual adult $8, double $12, family $16; City of Boston residents, individual child $2, individual adult $4, double $6, family $8.

Collections: Natural history and ethnological. Resource Center for teachers including 400 kit reference collection of three dimensional teaching materials in science, math, social studies, humanities and language arts; 700 circulating exhibits and curriculum units in the natural and social sciences. Publications, educational materials and toys sold in gift shop.

Activities: Temporary and permanent exhibits; scheduled group visits and programs; informal Discovery programs, demonstrations and films; circulating exhibits and kits; teacher workshops; undergraduate and graduate internships; curriculum development; exhibit and learning research; consulting services.

Library: 2500 volume library of books and periodicals on museology, education, child development, the natural and social sciences.

Attendance: 200,000.

HOLYOKE

CITY OF HOLYOKE YOUTH MUSEUM—WISTARIAHURST
238 Cabot St, 01040. Tel: (413) 536-6771
Mrs. William S. Quirk, Dir.
Open Mon. - Sat. 1 - 5 PM; Sun. 2 - 5 PM. Opened May 3, 1964 in Carriage House on Wistariahurst estate. Sponsored by the City of Holyoke, under jurisdiction of Holyoke Historical Commission.

Exhibitions: In 20th Century Science Area-Whaling, An Early New England Industry; Scrimshaw, An Early Folkart; Equipment Used Today in Exploring the Ocean; Satellite Communications by Telstar (One third scale model of Telstar); Interplanetary Space Display; Dinosaurs and Conservation; Natural History Room opened June 1966. North American Indian Hall opened May 1973 on the second floor; twelve exhibits encompassing Northeast, Southeast, Plains, Southwest, Northwest Coast and California Indian tribes; also, mineralogy and geology exhibits. Guided tours incl. film and slides on Indians.

Activities: Nature study classes for children; loan exhibits, paintings and objects of art. Sun. afternoon concerts; Sat. afternoon film program; lectures on Arts and Crafts; art classes for children; traveling exhibits, and Museum in a Box for local schools.

Attendance: 18,000 annually.

MICHIGAN

DETROIT

CHILDREN'S MUSEUM, DETROIT PUBLIC SCHOOLS
67 E. Kirby St, 48202. Tel: (313) 873-2670
Beatrice Parsons, Dir.
Free Mon. - Fri. 1 - 4 PM; Sat. 9 AM - 4 PM Oct. - May; school classes and other groups by appointment. Estab. 1917. Sponsored by Detroit Board of Education.

Collections: Folk crafts, ethnology, geology, natural history, history, primitive crafts; dolls and toys, musical instruments.

Activities: Demonstrations; lending department; school classes; lectures; Saturday programs; Planetarium.

Reference Library: Art, ethnology, science and technical books; 2000 volumes.

Attendance: 60,000.

MINNESOTA

DULUTH

A. M. CHISHOLM MUSEUM
St. Louis County Heritage and Arts Center
506 W. Michigan St, 55802. Tel: (218) 722-8563
B. Cusick, Cur.
Open Mon. - Sat. 9 AM - 5 PM. Sponsored by Board of Education and Citizen's Board of Directors.

Collections: Cultures of the world; American history; American Indian history; natural history; geology.

Activities: Class groups; art classes and hobby class for youth.

MISSOURI

KANSAS CITY

✠JUNIOR GALLERY AND CREATIVE ARTS CENTER
Nelson Gallery-Atkins Museum
4525 Oak St, 64111. Tel: (816) 561-4000
Larry Eikleberry, Dir. Educ. & Creative Arts Center
Open Tues. - Sat. 10 AM - 5 PM; Sun. 2 - 6 PM. Estab. 1960 to create a greater awareness of the world around us through art. Museum mem. $100.

Activities: Creative art classes, holiday, art-and-nature, mixed-media, watercolor, marionettes; adult sculpture, drawing, painting, Oriental brushwork, and design classes. Tours are scheduled through this department for the collection in the Nelson Gallery. Special workshops for group leaders working with children; also for groups such as Girl Scouts; annual open house for participating families; Jr. League production for children; training courses for high school museum tour aides.

Library: For children and guides; 2537 books, 105 reproductions.

Income and Expenses: Income (1974) $42,581 fees and gifts; expenses (1974) 72,919 (deficit paid through trust fund).

Attendance Jr. Gallery: (1973) 204,860; (1974) 155,747.

NEW HAMPSHIRE

NASHUA

CHILDREN'S MUSEUM
The Arts and Science Center
 14 Court St, 03060. Tel: (603) 883-1506
Gerald Q. Nash, Pres.
Barbara Saltmarsh, Dir.
Cindi Goldberg, Asst.
Scott Wilson, Asst.
Open Tues. - Fri. 9:30 - 11:30 AM & 1:30 - 4:30 PM; Sat. 10 - 12
AM & 2 - 4:30 PM; Sun. 2 - 4 PM; cl. Mon; admis. 25¢. Estab.
Nov. 23, 1975, a participatory learning facility designed especially
for children; consists of 7 specific exhibit areas related to the
arts, history and science; financed by membership.
 Activities: Lectures open to the public, visiting lecturers;
concerts; dramatic programs; varied courses for adults and
children.
 Publications: Monthly newsletter; education flyer quarterly.

NEW JERSEY

MORRISTOWN

MORRIS MUSEUM OF ARTS AND SCIENCES*
 Normandy Heights & Columbia Rds, 07960 (mail: P.O. Box 125,
 Convent, 07961). Tel: (201) 538-0454
Chester H. Newkirk, Dir.
Robert J. Koenig, Asst. Dir.
Mary Chandor, Art Cur.
Free Mon. - Sat. 10 AM - 5 PM; Sun. 2 - 5 PM. Summer, July and
August, Tues. - Sat. 10 AM - 4 PM; cl. major holidays. Inc. 1943.
Ann. meeting 3rd Wed. in Jan; mem. 1300; dues $10 and higher.
 Collections: American historic and foreign; rocks and minerals;
New Jersey wildlife; North American Indians; dolls and toys.
 Exhibitions: Art, history, natural and physical sciences.
 Activities: Lectures, audio-visual, music, dance and drama pro-
grams, art and nature workshops; gallery talks and guided tours.
 Library: 1000 volumes of art and science; reading room.
 Attendance: 135,000 annually.

NEWARK

✣JUNIOR MUSEUM
 Newark Museum, 49 Washington St, 07101. Tel: (201) 733-6604
Sheryl B. Bouler, Supvr.
Open 12 AM - 5 PM. Estab. 1926. Ann. meeting May 15; mem.
10,123; dues 10¢.
 Collections: Art, science, industry.
 Exhibitions: Mini-zoo: live fish, turtles, snakes, alligators, birds,
iguanas, other small animals; changing exhibits; annual exhibition of
children's work.
 Services: Advice given to young hobbyists and collectors in the
fields of rocks and minerals, seeds and leaves, coins and fossils.
 Activities: After-school Sat. and summer workshops in art, sci-
ence, anthropology for ages 6-18; daily workshops available to Jr.
Museum members; pre-school workshops in art Tues, Wed. and
Thurs. mornings. Special holiday programs; awards.
 Attendance: 12,125 workshops and special programs.

NORTH BRUNSWICK

JOHNSTON HISTORICAL MUSEUM
Boy Scouts of America
 Routes 1 & 130, 08902. Tel: (201) 249-6000
William Harrison Fetridge, Chmn.
H. Avery Chenoweth, Dir.
Ilmar Pleer, Mgr.
Free Tues. - Sat. 9 AM - 4:30 PM; Sun. 1 - 4:30 PM; cl. Mon.
Estab. June 4, 1960, to preserve history of the Boy Scouts of
America.
 Collections: Scout memorabilia, Rockwell paintings.
 Attendance: 50,000.

NEW YORK

NEW YORK

JUNIOR MUSEUM
 Metropolitan Museum of Art, Fifth Ave. at 82nd St, 10028.
 Tel: (212) 879-5500
Elizabeth Flinn, Assoc. Museum Educator
Open Tues. - Sat. 10 AM - 4:45 PM; Sun. and holidays 11 AM - 4:45
PM; cl. Mon. incl. Mon. holidays. A department of The Metro-
politan Museum of Art, Junior Museum estab. 1941; new Junior
Museum opened 1957, with greatly expanded exhibition area, art
reference library for children, an auditorium seating 279, modern
snack bar and sales desk.
 Exhibitions: (Major) Archaeology-Exploring the Past, 1966-
1968, and the Artist's Workshop—Tools and Techniques, 1968-.
Changing exhibitions of children's work. (minor)
 Collections: Junior Museum draws upon the collections of the
Metropolitan Museum of Art.
 Activities: Exhibitions; school program; library; publications;
auditorium programs; studio hours; treasure hunts, etc.
 Attendance: 300,000 (estimated).

STATEN ISLAND

JUNIOR MUSEUM OF THE STATEN ISLAND MUSEUM*
 75 Stuyvesant Place, 10301. Tel: (212) 727-1135
Mrs. Freda Mulcahy Esterly, Museum Lectr.
Sponsored by the Staten Island Institute of Arts and Sciences.
 Collections: Art and artifacts of the Museum available to the
Junior Museum.
 Weekday lectures for school children on art and science; Sat.
AM programs of an educational nature.

UTICA

MOHAWK VALLEY MUSEUM
 620 Memorial Pkwy, 13501. Tel: (315) 724-2075
Dr. James Meyer, Pres. of Board
Dr. Eino Kivisalu, Dir.
Open Tues. - Sat. 10 AM - 5 PM; Sun. 12 AM - 5 PM. Estab. Oct.
1963, inc. April 1966, to foster knowledge and interest among the
children of the community in the natural sciences and history with
particular attention to areas of local cultural and historic interest.
School tours and classroom demonstrations by appointment. Com-
munity Board, open mem; dues $5 annually, patron $15, contri-
buting $25, supporting $100.
 Exhibitions: Science, natural history, history. (Permanent)
Iroquois Exhibit, How they built barns, Dioramas of Early Utica.
Also temporary exhibits.
 Attendance: 21,000.

NORTH CAROLINA

CHARLOTTE

CHARLOTTE NATURE MUSEUM
 1658 Sterling Rd, 28209.
Russell I. Peithman, Dir.
Navar Elliot, Cur. Exhibits
John Karn, Cur. Educ.
James Seebach, Cur. Planetarium
Free Mon. - Sat. 9 AM - 5 PM; Sun. 2 - 5 PM. Inc. 1947 to develop
an appreciation of man and nature. Ann. meeting May; mem. 1000;
dues $10-500.
 Collections: †Primitive Art—Oceania, South America, Alaskan
Eskimo, Africa; †Pre-Columbian—Mayan, Peruvian, North Ameri-
can.
 Activities: Art workshops in nature sketching and museum
methods; lectures on African kingdoms, ancient civilizations.
 Library: Nature and Anthropology.
 Income and Purchases: Income $228,000; purchases $4000.
 Attendance: (1974-75) 405,000.

GREENSBORO

NATURAL SCIENCE CENTER*
 4301 Lawndale Dr, 27408. Tel: (919) 288-3769
Edward J. von der Lippe, Exec. Dir.
Nancy L. Blount, Cur. Educ.
Janis M. Thompson, Cur. Collections
Free Mon. - Sat. 9 AM - 5 PM; Sun. 2 - 5 PM; cl. New Year's,
Easter, Thanksgiving, Christmas. Estab. 1957, sponsored by
Greensboro Parks and Recreation Department. Mem. dues indivi-
dual $5, contributing $10, family $15, sponsor $25, business $50
or more, donor $100, patron $500 or more.
 Collections: Natural sciences; Indian artifacts.
 Activities: Docent program or council; training program for
professional museum workers; temporary and traveling exhibitions
organized and circulated; lectures; gallery talks; guided tours;
study clubs; school loan service; mobile vans; classes; junior
museum.
 Library: Library of natural sciences and books about birds
available for use by members of the museum; museum reproductions.
 Publications: Annual brochure; newsletters.

ROCKY MOUNT

ROCKY MOUNT CHILDREN'S MUSEUM
Sunset Park, 27801. Tel: (919) 442-5181
Mrs. Mae W. Bell, Dir.
Free Mon. - Fri. 10 - 12 AM, 2 - 5 PM; Sat. & Sun. 2 - 5 PM. Estab. 1952. Sponsored by the City of Rocky Mount.
Collections: Indian, fossil, art, Colonial and other general museum collections, †coastal and regional habitats.
Activities: Arts, crafts, natural history, science, photography, astronomy workshops. Planetarium.
Library: Reference library of approx. 600 volumes, mostly science.
Attendance: 95,000 annually.

OHIO

BAY VILLAGE

LAKE ERIE JUNIOR NATURE AND SCIENCE CENTER
Huntington Park Reservation, 28728 Wolf Rd, 44140.
Tel: (216) 871-2900
Elberta W. Fleming, Dir.
Open May - Oct. daily 1 - 5 PM except Wed, weekends only during Aug; Nov. - Apr. daily 1 - 5 PM; cl. Sun; Planetarium open Sat. - Sun. 3 PM. Estab. 1945; sponsored by Board of Trustees.
Collections: Live animals, natural history, creative crafts, sciences.
Activities; Animal lending library; classes in natural and physical sciences, conservation, arts, scientific fields, nature and creative crafts. Planetarium; Gift Shop.
Library: Approx. 3000 volumes on related subjects.
Income and Purchases: Annual income $50,000; purchases $5000.
Attendance: Approx. 95,000 annually.

OREGON

PORTLAND

PORTLAND CHILDREN'S MUSEUM
3037 S.W. Second Ave, 97201. Tel: (503) 227-1505
R. G. Bridgeford, Dir.
Dianne Kornberg, Art School Cur.
Free June 1 - Sept. 30 Mon. - Fri. 10 AM - 5:30 PM; Oct. 1 - May 30 Mon. - Fri. 10 AM - 6 PM; Sat. 10 AM - 3 PM. Estab. 1949; sponsored by Portland Bureau of Parks and Recreation.
Collections: Natural history, art gallery, toys, dollhouses, miniatures.
Activities: Art classes in painting, photography, filmmaking, jewelry, graphics, pottery, calligraphy, weaving for children 4-18; lectures and tours on selected art and natural history subjects.
Attendance: Museum & lectures 65,000.

SOUTH CAROLINA

COLUMBIA

✠COLUMBIA SCIENCE MUSEUM
1519 Senate St, 29201. Tel: (803) 799-2812
Christopher H. Craft, Supv.
William Lazarus, Palnetarium Dir.
Tom Fleming, Asst. Planetarium Dir.
Mary Galloway, Secy.
Steve Holm, Science Asst.
Free Tues. - Sat. 10 AM - 5 PM; Sun. 2 - 6 PM; cl. Mon. Estab. 1959, a division of the Columbia Museum of Art. Sponsored by the Columbia Art Association to serve the science interests of youth and adults.
Collections: Dr. Robert Gibbes Collection of Shells; Kendall Collection of Pan American Pots; Edmund R. Cuthbert Collection of Fossils; Burt B. Reid Collection of Mounted African Mammals; Mrs. Toshiko McCall Collection of Caribbean Sealife; mounted mammals, birds and reptiles; mineral collection; bird skins and nests; and others.
Exhibitions: Live reptilian exhibits; panoramas; South Carolina nature garden; Planetarium; South Carolina Underwater Archeology; Prehistoric Dinosaur Exhibit; and others.
Activities: Youth clubs; photo club; bird club; astronomy club; gem and mineral society; Planetarium demonstrations; field trips; education; library; films; lectures; South Carolina Archeological Society.
Attendance: 154,860.

ROCK HILL

THE MUSEUM OF YORK COUNTY
Route 4, Box 211, 29730. Tel: (803) 366-4116
Charles W. Hall, Exec. Dir.
Chris Houmes, Asst. Dir.
Ray Liguori, Itinerate Programer
John Schneider, Taxidermist
Kathie Moore, Head Tour Guide
Sue Mitchell, Secy.
Free Mon. - Fri. 9 AM - 4:30 PM; Sat. 1 - 5 PM; Sun. 2 - 5 PM. Estab. 1949 primarily as a natural and physical science museum; contains world's largest collection of mounted hoofed African animals; financed by county appropriation. Art Gallery maintained by the Artist League of the Museum.
Activities: Workshops, lectures open to public, dramatic programs, classes for adults and children.
Library: Reference library.
Attendance: 80,000-125,000.

TEXAS

FORT WORTH

FORT WORTH MUSEUM OF SCIENCE AND HISTORY
1501 Montgomery St, 76107. Tel: (817) 732-1631
Helmuth J. Naumer, Exec. Dir.
Max Ary, Planetarium Dir.
Aubyn Kendall, Collections Cur.
Donald R. Otto, Dir. of Museum School
Dennis Bartz, Dir. of Interpretation
William J. Voss, Science Cur.
Michael Sievers, History Cur.
James Pollard, Building Supt.
Free Mon. - Sat. 9 AM - 5 PM; Sun. 2 - 5 PM. Estab. May 21, 1941, to maintain a place where anthropological, historical, ethnological, and scientific collections may be housed and exhibited; to increase and diffuse a knowledge and appreciation of history, art and science; to preserve objects of historic, artistic and scientific interests; to offer popular instruction and opportunities for esthetic enjoyment.
Collections: Art, historical, archaeological, ethnological, natural science, geological.
Exhibitions: Instructive exhibits in anthropology, astronomy, biology, geology, paleontology, art, medical science, and history, particularly that of Texas.
Educational Activities: School Services program for area schools designed to supplement regular classroom work by use of artifacts to touch. (1973-1974 attendance 161,579)
Museum School: An average of 60 classes per session in five annual sessions offered for ages six through adult, in art, history, and science.
Special Features: Noble Planetarium.
Library: 5600 volumes, science, history and art primarily, for reference by the staff and junior volunteers working on special research projects.
Attendance: (1973-74) 927,963.

WEST VIRGINIA

CHARLESTON

✠SUNRISE FOUNDATION, INC.
Children's Museum Department and Planetarium, 746 Myrtle Rd, 25314. Tel: (304) 344-8053
Douglas E. Bradley, Cur.
Free Tues. - Sat. 10 AM - 5 PM; Sun. 2 - 5 PM; cl. Mon. Inc. 1949, reorganized 1974. Ann. meeting Apr; mem. 2300; dues $15.
Collections: Anthropological specimens; rocks; minerals; fossils; shells; antique dolls and toys.
Exhibitions: Three long-term exhibit halls, one short-term, various revolving cases.
Activities: Exhibits; planetarium; classes; bird, stamp, doll and astronomical clubs; workshops; suitcase loans; puppetry programs; invitational performing arts. Museum Shop.
Library: General research, 2000 volumes for staff and members only.
Income and Purchases: Income as part of Sunrise Foundation, Inc; purchases made from budgeted or designated funds for collection development.
Attendance: 100,000.

Canadian Art Organizations

CANADIAN ARTISTS' REPRESENTATION (CAR)
  Box 3154, Station A, Edmonton, Alberta T5J 2G7.
  Tel: (403) 423-3126
Sylvain Voyer, National Representative
Giuseppe Albi, Exec. Secy.
Estab. Sept. 1967 as an association of professional artists, national
in membership, with provincial and city chapters; deal with artists'
rights in government dealings, payment of artists' fees by public
galleries, and in general any matters that deal with the welfare
of artists in society; financed by membership and Canada Council
Grant. Local members meet on local schedule, National Provin-
cial Representatives meet twice a year; mem. 1500 nationally;
dues $5-10. Small collection of art periodicals.
  Publications: National CAR News, Ontario (CAROT), and
Maritimes (CARGO), quarterly.

CANADIAN CONFERENCE OF THE ARTS
  3 Church St, Suite 47, Toronto, Ontario M5E 1M2.
  Tel: (416) 364-6351
Richard Courtney, Pres.
Russell Disney, Treas.
Julian Porter, Secy.
John Hobday, National Dir.
  Estab. 1945 to influence public opinion and government action at
all levels to create a climate more favourable to the arts. Inde-
pendent non-profit, non-governmental association of arts organiza-
tions, artists, and supporters of art across Canada. Ann. meeting
during Apr; mem. (1975) organizations 300, individuals 500.
  Publications: Direction Canada Report, April 1973; Comminique,
semi-annual; monthly bulletin; The Arts and the Media, 1975;
The Arts and the Municipalities, 1975; The Arts and Education,
1975.

CANADIAN CRAFTS COUNCIL
  16-46 Elgin St, Ottawa, Ont. K1P 5K6. Tel: (613) 235-8200
Leslie C. Manning, Pres.
Douglas Mantegna, Secy.
Peter Weinrich, Exec. Dir.
Open Mon. - Fri. 8 AM - 5 PM. Estab. 1974 to encourage the highest
quality Canadian crafts in all media and improve the living standards
of craftsmen in the country through education and information; financed by membership. Ann. meeting summer; mem. 4500; dues individual $25, group $50 per head.
  Collections: Massey Foundation collection of contemporary Canadian crafts.
  Exhibitions: Festival Canada Exhibition, 1974; Bicentennial Ex-
hibition-Washington, 1975.

CANADIAN GUILD OF POTTERS
  100 Avenue Rd, Toronto, Ont. M5R 2H3. Tel: (416) 923-1803
Peter Coviello, Pres.
Marlene Smith, Secy.
Mrs. Marion Maynard, Mgr.
Open Mon. - Sat. 10 AM - 6 PM; Thurs. 10 AM - 9 PM. Estab.
1933, inc. 1962, to promote the best in pottery. Ann. meeting
May; mem. approx. 1000; dues $15.
  Activities: Sponsors exhibitions of Canadian pottery in Canada
and overseas; conducts yearly workshop with visiting instructor;
presents are shows at the center.
  Publications: Tactile, six times a year.

CANADIAN MUSEUMS ASSOCIATION
  c/o R. R. Inglis, Exec. Dir, 500-56 Sparks St, Ottawa, Ont.
  J9H 5A9.
Mary Sparling, Pres.
Estab. 1947. Ann. meeting May; dues institutions $15-300,
individuals $15.

Activities: Provides resource support for training programs.
  Publications: Quarterly journal, Gazette; monthly newsletter,
Museogramme.

CANADIAN SOCIETY FOR EDUCATION THROUGH ART
  Faculty of Educ, Univ. of Regina, Regina, Sask. S4S 0A2.
John M. Emerson, Pres.
Dr. Les Groome, Secy. Gen.
Estab. 1954 to promote art education in Canada; financed by mem-
bership. Ann. meeting Oct; mem. approx. 1000; dues affiliate $2,
professional $20.
  Activities: Scholarships; workshops: research; annual conference.
  Publications: Newsletter, quarterly; Journal; Research Bulletin.
  Attendance: 300 annual average.

CANADIAN SOCIETY OF GRAPHIC ART*
  100 Simpson Ave, Toronto, Ont. M8Z 1E3.
Avrom Yanosky, Pres.
Joy Bain, Secy.
Inc. 1933. Ann. meeting Oct; mem. approx. 75. Holds annual
exhibition; traveling exhibitions. Merged late 1975 with Society
of Canadian Painter-Etchers and Engravers; new name to be
announced.

CANADIAN SOCIETY OF PAINTERS IN WATER COLOUR
  c/o Julius Griffith, Secy, 102 Hillsdale Ave, W, Toronto,
  Ont. M5P 1G3.
John Bennett, Pres.
Estab. 1925, inc. 1936. Ann. meeting May; mem. 92; dues $20.
  Exhibitions: Annual exhibition opening in a different Canadian
city each November, with a second showing in Jan. or Feb. in another large center.
  Activities: Organizes traveling exhibitions in Canada and other
countries through National Gallery, and Art Gallery of Ontario Extension Services; holds a seminar about every two years on water
colour and related media; awards annual Canadian Society of Painters in Water Colour prize.

COMMUNITY PLANNING ASSOCIATION OF CANADA
  425 Gloucester St, Ottawa Ont. K1R 5E9. Tel: (613) 238-7834
John D'Eath, Pres.
Jacques Ledoux, Dir. Nat. Affairs
Estab. 1946 as citizens' organization to promote public understanding of and participation in the process of planning the growth of urban
areas. Open to all interested persons. Ann. meeting Sept. - Oct;
mem. 6000; dues $10 and higher. Attendance annual National Plan-
ning Conference, 500.
  Activities: Distributes literature on planning; conducts national
and local conferences; nine divisions conduct programs at local
level.
  Publications: Community Planning Review, monthly; occasional
case studies.
  Library: Reference library.

MARITIME ART ASSOCIATION*
  767 Churchill Row, Fredericton, New Brunswick.
I. C. Easton, Pres.
  (Halifax)
Mrs. M. German-van Eck, Corresp. Secy.
  (Box 87 Site 17 RR 5, Armdale, Halifax, NS)
G. Gillard, Treas.
  (40 West Lane, Moncton, NB)
Estab. 1934 to co-ordinate work of art societies in New Brunswick,
Newfoundland, Nova Scotia and Prince Edward Island. Ann. meeting
May. Mem. 27 societies paying corporate dues of $5 and higher.
Organizes traveling exhibitions of Maritime Artists. Lecture tours;
loan collection of lantern slides.

Member Organizations
Clare Arts Council, College Ste-Anne, Church-Point, NS; Dartmouth Heritage Museum, Dartmouth, NS; Fredericton Society of Artists, Fredericton, NB; Moncton Art Society Inc, Moncton, NB; St Andrews Music, Art and Drama Club, St. Andrews, NB; Town of Amherst, Amherst, NS; Western Counties Regional Library, Yarmouth, NS; Woodstock Art Club, Woodstock, NB; and individual members.

PROFESSIONAL ART DEALERS ASSOCIATION OF CANADA
65 Queen St. W, Suite 1800, Toronto, Ont.
John K. Robertson, Pres.
Barbara Ensor, Secy.
Sam Markle, V.Pres.
Avrom Isaacs, Treas.
David Tuck, Dir.
Delores Booth, Dir.
Ian Muncaster, Dir.
Thomas Beckett, Dir.
Leon Lippel, Dir.
Estab. 1966 to further art in Canada; financed by membership. Ann. meeting; mem. 41; dues $200 per annum.

ROYAL ARCHITECTURAL INSTITUTE OF CANADA
Exec. offices: 151 Slater St, Ottawa, Ont. K1P 5H3.
Tel: (613) 232-7165
Fred T. Hollingsworth, Pres.
Charles Cullum, 1st V.Pres.
Michael Byrne, V.Pres. Finance
Alexander Leman, V.Pres. Administration
Bernard Wood, Immediate Past Pres.
Marcel J. B. Tardif, Exec. V.Pres.
Robert A. Christie, Exec. Secy./Treas.
Open 9 AM - 5 PM; summer 9 AM - 4 PM. Estab. 1907, inc. 1908, granted permission by King Edward VII to use the prefix Royal in 1909 and inc. under the present name in 1912. The purpose of the Institute is to establish and maintain a bond between the societies recognized by the Institute as Component Associations and to promote the welfare of the Architectural Profession in Canada. There are nine Provincial Associations (q.v.) Mem. 2851, limited to those who hold mem. in a Provincial Association (Order of Architects of Quebec, mem. 1099, not a Component Association of the R.A.I.C. as of March 31, 1974). Annual Assembly once a year in various centres of Canada (Annual Assembly 1976 in Ottawa, May 16-20).
Library: Volumes on architecture, building, construction, etc.
Activities; Allied Arts Medal every year for outstanding achievement in the Arts allied to Architecture such as mural painting, sculpture, decoration, stained glass, industrial design, etc; medals each year to outstanding student in the final year of each of the accredited Canadian schools of architecture.
Publications: Architecture Canada Directory, annually.

ROYAL CANADIAN ACADEMY OF ARTS/ACADEMIE ROYALE DES ARTS DU CANADA
40 University Ave, Toronto, Ont. M5J 1T1. Tel: (416) 361-0659
John C. Parkin, Pres.
Ray V. Cattell, Exec. V.Pres.
Ian R. Maclennan, Hon. Treas.
Ann J. Nelles, Exec. Dir.
Estab. 1880 by the Marquis of Lorne and H.R.H. Princess Louise; inc. 1882 by Royal Charter, to encourage the arts of painting, sculpture, architecture, design, photography and filmmaking. Receives grant from Canadian Government. Members elected as Academicians. Ann. meeting Nov; mem 375; dues $35.
Activities: National exhibitions every two or three years; Award, Royal Canadian Academy Medal for distinguished contribution to the visual arts in Canada.

SCULPTOR'S SOCIETY OF CANADA
c/o Visual Arts of Ontario, 8 York St, Toronto, Ont. M5J 1R2.
Tel: (416) 366-1607
Irene Blogg, Pres.
Richard Green, Secy.
Louis Temporale, Treas.
May Marx, Past Pres.
Estab. 1928 for the furtherance of sculpture and sculptors. Ann. meeting June; mem. 100; dues $25.
Exhibitions: First Traveling Show, 1970-1971; Second Traveling Show, 1971-1972; Toronto-Dominion Show, 1972-1973; Hamilton Place, 1974; Second Traveling Show, 1975.
Activities: Traveling exhibitions organized and circulated to Canadian and U.S. Art Galleries, sculpture, drawings and prints; individual sculptures lent to schools; 35 lantern slides for lending;

lectures open to public; one or two gallery talks per year; photograph collection for lending and reference.
Publications: Bimonthly newsletter.
Attendance: 30.

SOCIETY OF CANADIAN PAINTER-ETCHERS AND ENGRAVERS
600 Markham St, Toronto 4, Ont.
M. Kathleen Cardiff, Pres.
Anne Smith Hook, Treas.
(32 Mountview Ave, Toronto, M6P 2L3)
June Bird, Secy.
Estab. 1916, inc. 1935. Ann. meeting Mar; mem. 100; dues $12.
Activities: Annual exhibition in Mar. Organizes traveling exhibitions; maintains three print cabinets in Royal Ontario Museum, Toronto; Public Library and Museum, London, Ont; and University of Toronto. Administers G.A.Reid Silver Memorial Award for best print in annual exhibition; Nicholas Hornyansky Memorial Award; Edits print of the year, selected by vote, to subscribers. Maximum edition 75 prints. Maintains Archives & Prints of 3-4 purchase awards, annually.
Seminars in Printmaking held in 1966 in conjunction with the Society of Graphic Arts, with Gabor Peterdi, of Yale University, as lecturer; and in 1967, with Andrew Stasik of the Pratt Institute as lecturer. A third such seminar was held in 1969 under the guidance of John Ihle.
Merged late 1975 with Canadian Society of Graphic Art; new name to be announced.

ALBERTA

ALBERTA ART FOUNDATION
11th Floor, CN Tower, 10004 104th Ave, Edmonton.
W. B. McMullen, Pres. Tel: (403) 429-5211
W. H. Kaasa, Secy. Tel: (403) 427-2553
W. Tin Ng, Coordinator. Tel: (403) 427-2031
Estab. Sept. 29, 1972 to collect and to exhibit art works pertinent to the Province of Alberta; financed by city and state appropriation.
Collections: †Alberta Art Foundation collection.
Exhibitions: Premier Exhibition in Calgary and Edmonton, 1973; Atlanta, Georgia Exhibition, 1975; Premier International Exhibition in London, Brussels and Paris, 1975-76.
Activities: Extension Department serves provincial, national and international public galleries, museums and educational institutes; traveling exhibitions organized and circulated; individual paintings and and original objects of art lent; 300 items lent in average year; 90 prints in photograph collection for lending.
Publications: Quarterly newsletters; Annual Report.
Income and Purchases: Income $50,000; purchases: less than $50,000.

ALBERTA ASSOCIATION OF ARCHITECTS
217 Revillon Building, 10201 104th St, Edmonton, T5J 1B2.
M. E. Evamy, Pres.
J. B. Jamieson, Hon. Secy.
Mrs. H. L. Bond, Exec. Secy.
Open 8:30 AM - 4:30 PM. Estab. 1906. Ann. meeting; Council meets once a month; mem. 280; dues $170.

ALBERTA SOCIETY OF ARTISTS
Room S545, Alberta College of Art, Calgary, T2M 0L4.
Barbara Roe Hicklin, Pres.
Dr. Archie F. Key, Dir. Information & Research Centre
Estab. 1931 as an association of professional artists designed to foster and promote the development of visual and plastic fine arts primarily within the province. Ann. meeting May; mem. approx. 100; dues $15.
Activities: Annual and group shows in cities and communities of Alberta; reciprocal exchanges with societies elsewhere.
Publications: Highlights-Newsletter, bimonthly.

CALGARY

ALBERTA COLLEGE OF ART
Southern Alberta Institute of Technology, 1301 16th Ave. N.W, T2M 0L4. Tel: (403) 289-6641
Kenneth Sturdy, Head of College
Hazel Churchill, Secy.
Cheryl Patterson, Admin. Asst.
Ron Moppett, Sr. Cur.
Adelle Kimick, Library Supvr.
Gallery free Mon. - Fri. 4 - 8:30 PM; Tues. - Fri. Noon - 1 PM; Sat. & Sun. 2 - 5 PM. Gallery estab. 1958 as an academic-didactic function plus general fine art exhibition service to the public; city and province appropriation provide financing. Two galleries with full security and controls. No membership.

Collections: Permanent collection of paintings, graphics, student honors work, gifts plus antiques.

Exhibitions: Local, Provincial, National Gallery of Canada; Western Association of Art Museums (U.S.A); Embassy Offerings (Ottawa); North American commercial and public gallery offerings.

Library: 4000 volume branch library; students have access to the Learning Resources Center, Southern Alberta Institute of Technology (7000 art volumes); 44 periodical subscriptions; 13,000 slides; 3000 art reproductions; 500 exhibition catalogs.

CALGARY ARTISTS SOCIETY
c/o Zaidee Finch, Secy, 3728 35th Ave. S.W, T3E 1A5.
Tel: (403) 249-1385
Pat Gordon, Pres.
Ted Ranshaw, Treas.
Estab. 1965 to foster and improve standard of art of members and community; financed by membership and government grant. Monthly meeting 1st Thurs; mem. 40; dues $15.

Exhibitions: Allied Arts Building; Public Library; Kensington Art Gallery, Calgary.

Activities: original objects of art lent; 75 items lent in average year; photograph collection available to certain members only; lectures for members only, 3 visiting lecturers per year; 4 gallery talks; classes for adults and children, competitions.

Annual Income: $1000.

GLENBOW-ALBERTA INSTITUTE
Art Department
Ninth Ave. & First St. E. Tel: (403) 245-4741
Lorne E. Render, Dir. of Exhibitions
Andrew Oko, Asst. Cur.
Charles S. Tomsik, Installation Supvr.
Glenbow-Alberta Institute was chartered in 1966 by special act of the Legislature of the Province of Alberta to govern the Glenbow Foundation. The Foundation was estab. in 1955 by Eric L. Harvie to collect and document material related to western Canada.

Collections: Major collection of paintings and prints related to the art and history of western Canada.

Exhibitions at Glenbow Centre, open daily: Permanent display of Western Canadian art and periodic temporary displays. Representative historical displays of material from the Institute's collections, with particular emphasis on Western Canadian life.

THE UNIVERSITY OF CALGARY ART GALLERY
First Floor Library Block, 2920 24th Ave. N.W, T2L 1B4.
Tel: (403) 284-5987
J. Brooks Joyner, Cur.
Open Mon. - Fri. 11 AM - 5 PM; Sat. & Sun. 1 - 5 PM; Tues. & Thurs. 6 - 9 PM. Estab. to provide exhibitions for the university community and for the Calgary metropolitan area, and to conserve and maintain the permanent art collection of the university; financed by city and state appropriation. Gallery consists of 3500 sq. ft, with preparation area and storage area of approx. 1500 sq. ft.

Collections: Over 425 works, including paintings, drawings, prints and ceramics, mostly by artists of Western Canada.

Activities: Lectures open to public; 8 - 10 gallery talks per year; 20 - 30 tours; classes for adults.

Annual Purchases: $10,000.

EDMONTON

ARTS AND CRAFTS DIVISION[*]
Department of Culture, Youth and Recreation
Government of the Province of Alberta
11650-142 St. Tel: (403) 452-6960
Leslie F. Graff, Supv. Arts and Crafts Div.
Robert W. Whyte, Asst. Supv. Leadership Training
Sheelagh Dunlap, Asst. Supv. Exposure Programs.
Pierre Guy
Phyllis Ponech
Free, Mon. - Fri. 8:15 AM - 4:30 PM. Estab. to provide assistance to the Province of Alberta in the development of the visual arts and crafts; financed by city and state appropriations. A small, informal gallery approx. 400 sq. ft. created for the purpose of training community personnel in the handling of exhibitions.

Exhibitions: Local sculpture and paintings.

Activities: Leadership training for instructors who work with adults and/or children; serves entire province; material available to residents of Alberta; course fees only; traveling exhibitions organized and circulated; individual paintings and original objects of art lent; lending collection, 2-3 photograph exhibitions; 150 Kodachrome slide exhibitions; photograph collection for reference; lectures open to the public; competitions; scholarships.

Library: 500 volume reference library.

Publications: Various technical journals, articles of history, and others, 10-15 per year.

Attendance: 150,000-200,000.

EDMONTON ART CLUB
11306 123rd St, T5M 0E9. Tel: (403) 454-5498
A. D. Herbert, Pres.
J. H. Horton, Secy.
Mrs. G. Stuart, V.Pres.
Mrs. B. Farrell, Treas.
Estab. 1925 for the propagation of interest in art; financed by membership. Monthly meetings, 2nd Thurs; mem. 42; dues $6.

Exhibitions: 2 annual exhibitions, spring and fall.

Activities: 20 - 30 paintings and drawings lent in average year; lectures for members only, 8 visiting lecturers per year; 3 gallery tours.

Library: 100 volumes.

Publications: Monthly newsletter.

THE EDMONTON ART GALLERY
2 Sir Winston Churchill Square, T5J 2C1. Tel: (403) 429-6781
Terry Fenton, Dir.
Andrew Sidlo, Business Mgr.
Karen Wilkin, Sr. Cur.
Open daily 10 AM - 5 PM; Wed. & Thurs. 10 AM - 10 PM; Sun. & holidays 1 - 5 PM. Inc. 1923. Ann. meeting Mar; mem. 1500; dues $15 and higher. Receives municipal appropriation, provincial and federal grants, and Canada Council grant.

Collections: †Canadian paintings, sculpture and graphic arts.

Exhibitions: Over 40 exhibitions annually.

Activities: Art classes for adults and children, lectures, guided tours and talks; art rental service; junior gallery; gallery shop.

Library: 1000 periodicals and books on art and education.

Publications: Exhibition catalogs.

Attendance: 200,000.

EDMONTON WEAVERS' GUILD
13816 110th Ave, T5M 2M9. Tel: (403) 455-5602
Margaret Berg, Pres.
Monica Hughes, Secy.
Estab. to foster arts of weaving, spinning and dyeing in Edmonton district and to encourage beginners and aim for high standard of workmanship; financed by membership. Meetings 3rd Wed. of Sept, Nov, Jan, Mar. and May; mem. 130; dues $3.

Activities: 5 members' workshops meeting every 2 weeks; occasional workshops given by craftspeople from other regions or countries, usually 3-day; public lecture with slides often given along with workshops.

Library: 187 volumes for lending; periodicals dealing with weaving, spinning, dyeing; yarn sample cards.

Publications: Newsletter, two per month.

Annual Income: Approx. $500.

MARIAN CENTRE HANDICRAFT
10528 98th St, T5H 2N4. Tel: (403) 424-3544
Linda Lambeth, Dir.
Open daily except Sun. 10 AM - 5 PM. Estab. Feb, 1973 to promote arts and crafts within the city, especially for the poor; to provide a cultural meeting place for all levels of society - Friendship Centre; financed by donations.

Activities: Craft classes available on a city-wide basis.

PROVINCIAL ARCHIVES OF ALBERTA
Department of Culture
12845 102nd Ave, T5N 0M6. Tel: (403) 452-2150
A. D. Ridge, Provincial Archivist
E. A. Ference, Chief, Archives Services
Open Mon. - Fri. 9 AM - 4:30 PM. Estab. 1967.

Collections: Provincial archives, historical photographs, maps, tapes, private manuscripts; oral history.

Activities: Exhibitions; publications.

Library: 8000 volumes, open for public reference.

Budget: (1975-76) $267,110.

Attendance: 3000 in 2 years.

PROVINCIAL MUSEUM OF ALBERTA
Alberta Culture, Government of Alberta
12845 102nd Ave, T5N 0M6. Tel: (403) 452-2150
B. A. McCorquodale, Dir.
Dr. D. Richeson, Head Cur, Human History Section
D. A. E. Spalding, Head Cur, Natural History Section
J. Villa-Arce, Extension Supvr.
Open winter, Mon. - Sat. 9 AM - 5 PM; Sun. 11 AM - 9 PM; summer, 9 AM - 9 PM daily. Estab. 1967.

Collections: Birds, mammals, fish, reptiles, minerals, fossils, history, Indians, archaeology.

Activities: School programs; guided tours; bookshop; publications.

Budget: (1975-76) $1,255,000.

Attendance: 450,000.

UNIVERSITY ART GALLERY AND MUSEUM
Ring House 1, University of Alberta, T6G 2E2. Tel: 432-5818
R. A. Davey, Cur.
Helen Collinson, Curatorial Asst.
Free weekdays 11 AM - 4 PM. Estab. 1964 to house the university
permanent collection and to display and initiate traveling exhibi-
tions; financed by university appropriation.
Collections: †Paintings, †sculpture, †graphics, †constructions;
artifacts from Geology, Anthropology, Dentistry, Medicine, and
Classics Departments.
Exhibitions: (1973-74) B.F.A. Students - sculpture and prints;
media show; J. B. Taylor sketches and Joe Fafard; M.V.A. student
show; Velma Foster Prints and pieces from the University Collections; Jim Dow photos; Edmonton weavers; Molas of the Cuna
Indians and drawings of Jeff Funnell; Department of Art and Design
Staff Show; Robert Downing sculptures and Dorothea Dean quilts;
Robert Motherwell; Don Maybe - Wendy Toogood and Hnizdovsky;
Opening Doors - Visual Communications Design students; (1974-75)
William Townsend and Artifacts for a Future Atlantis; Department
of Art and Design Staff Show and Student Exhibition; Barbara Caruso
prints; Art and Design: Painting Division, Visual Communications
Design, and Prints and Sculpture; M.V.A. Presentation; Inuit Art and
paintings by M.V.A. students.
Library: Approx. 400 volumes, mainly on contemporary Canadian
art.
Publications: M.V.A. Catalog, graduate students in the Master of
Visual Arts program at University of Alberta.

LETHBRIDGE

THE ALLIED ARTS COUNCIL OF LETHBRIDGE
The Bowman Arts Centre
811 Fifth Ave. S, T1J 0V2. Tel: (403) 327-2813
C. R. Baunton, Pres.
Carol Watkinson, Visual Arts Officer
L. H. Watkinson, Treas.
Karen Kay, Secy.
Joan Waterfield, Performing Arts Officer
Open weekdays 10 AM - 11 PM; no admis. Estab. 1958 to encourage
and foster cultural activities in Lethbridge to cooperate with persons,
groups and organizations engaged in the promotion of cultural activities; and to provide facilities for such cultural activities; financed by
city and state appropriations and membership. Small gallery mainly
for the use of our member organizations but also used to promote the
work of Alberta and Western Canadian Artists. Ann. meeting Feb;
37 member organizations; dues $10.
Exhibitions: Locals exhibitions include painters, potters, fabric
makers and childrens' art, provincial government traveling exhibits;
one-man shows included sculpture and silversmithing, photography,
prints.
Activities: Performing and visual arts program; photograph collection for reference and classes; lectures open to public; gallery
talks; concerts; dramatic programs; classes for adults and children;
scholarships.
Publications: Calendar of the Arts, weekly.
Income: $20,000.

UNIVERSITY OF LETHBRIDGE ART GALLERY*
Lethbridge-West
Dr. W. E. Beckel, Pres.
B. J. McCarroll, Gallery Dir.
Free, Mon. - Fri. 8:30 AM - 4:30 PM; Sun. 1 - 4 PM. Estab. 1968
for public service and the teaching mechanism; financed by city
and state appropriations.
Collections: Some professional prints and drawings; student
work.
Exhibitions: Local and regional shows in addition to those travel-
ing exhibitions by the National Gallery, The Winnepeg Gallery and
The Western Association of Art Museums, approx. ten shows per
year.
Activities: Individual paintings and original objects of art lent;
lending collection, 10,000 Kodachromes, 20-25 motion pictures; 10-
15 active borrowers; lectures open to the public; 4-5 gallery talks;
10-12 tours; library.
Income and Purchases: Income $2000; purchases $800.
Attendance: 1000 annual average.

MEDICINE HAT

ALLIED ARTS COUNCIL
8, 503A Third Ave. S.E, T1A 2M2.
G. P. J. Parish, Pres.
Kay Cooney, Secy.
Estab. approx. 10 years ago to encourage and promote activities of a
cultural nature in our community; financed by membership. Organization has not been active for the past two years. Many of the functions formerly carried out by the Council have been undertaken by the
local community college. A meeting is planned soon to decide
whether or not to continue or to dissolve organization and transfer
remaining funds to other community groups interested in the visual
arts.

SPIRIT RIVER

PEACE REGION ARTS SOCIETY
P.O. Box 297, T0H 3G0. Tel: (403) 864-3035
E. C. Stacey, Chmn.
Mrs. M. Moulds, Exec. Secy.
D. Gibson, Mem. Officer
Mrs. F. Calk, Finance Officer
Miss K. Hoskin, Recording Secy.
Estab. Nov. 2, 1974; a unified body of people concerned about the
betterment of the arts atmosphere in the Peace Region of Alberta.
Society is a source of contact with and information about the artists
and performers in the area; exposure through selling and per-
forming exhibitions; financed by membership and provincial and
government grants. Board meetings are open to guests, ann.
meeting Apr; mem. 320; dues $2.
Exhibitions: Peace Region Arts Festival, held in Fairview College, 1975.
Publications: Bimonthly Newsletter.
Attendance at Festival and Annual Meeting: Approx. 3150.

BRITISH COLUMBIA

THE CRAFTSMEN'S ASSOCIATION OF BRITISH COLUMBIA
801, 207 W. Hastings St, Vancouver, V6B 1H7.
Tel: (604) 681-9613
Walter Dexter, Pres.
Stan Tait, Secy.
Open Mon. - Fri. 10 AM - 3 PM. Estab. 1972 as a nonprofit organization working in the interests of craftsmen in the Province of British Columbia and for communication in the crafts; financed by membership and provincial government grant. Upstairs Gallery recently
established for the exhibiting and/or selling of work of British Columbia craftsmen. Ann. meeting Mar; mem. 400; dues $8.50.
Exhibitions: Craft Annual, juried exhibition of original hand-
crafted work.
Activities: Compiling of a Commissions Registry of British Columbia craftsmen to be used by architects, shopkeepers, and the
individual buyer. Workshop program instigated and organized on
demand.
Library: Composed of periodicals and books relating to many
crafts.
Publications: Craft Contacts, monthly.

BURNABY

BURNABY ART GALLERY
6344 Gilpin St, V5G 2J3. Tel: (604) 291-9441
Norman Howard, Pres.
Douglas Staughton, 1st V.Pres.
Patrick Brown, Treas.
J. Walker, Acting Adminr.
Arthur Kilgour, Chief Museums Asst.
Open Mon. - Sat. 10 AM - 5 PM; Sun. 1 - 5 PM; Wed. 7 - 9 PM; ad-
mis. 25¢, free on Wed. Estab. 1967; financed by federal, provincial
and municipal appropriations and membership. 1 - 3 meetings per
year; mem. 385; dues $10 single, $5 student, $15 family, $25 group,
$100 business, $250 life.
Collections: Primarily original prints.
Exhibitions: Program of Fine Arts Exhibitions, changing monthly,
approx. 25 individual exhibitions per year, plus related events and
activities.
Activities: Workshops in film, poetry, dance and music taken to
schools or offered in the gallery; extension department tours serve
communities through the province, some major shows tour nationally; material available to galleries, art centers and schools;
individual paintings and original objects of art lent through rental
service to members; lectures open to public; competitions.
Library: Primarily monthly publications for members' use.
Publications: Exhibition catalogs.
Income and Purchases: Income approx. $200,000; purchases
$1000 - $5000.
Attendance: 30,000.

THE SIMON FRASER GALLERY
Centre for Communications and the Arts
Academic Quadrangle 3004, Simon Fraser University, V5A 1S6.
Tel: (604) 291-4266
James Warren Felter, Cur. & Dir. Exhibitions

Open Mon. 1:30 - 4 PM & 5 - 8 PM; Tues. - Fri. 10 AM - 1 PM &
2 - 4 PM; cl. Sat. & Sun. Estab. 1971; financed by public university
appropriations.
Collections: The Simon Fraser Collection, including contemporary
and Eskimo art; international graphics.
Exhibitions: The Art of the Eskimo; Comics as an Art Form;
British Columbia: Photographers; N. E. Thing Co. Ltd; Banners;
Recycled-The New Folk Art; Goya-The Disasters of War; Contempo-
rary Hungarian Photographers; British Columbia Crafts Exhibition;
John K. Esler Graphics; The Private Patron: British Columbia;
Tibetan Woodblock Prints; China Fan Paintings; Folk Art of Ecuador
and Jungle Crafts of South America; The Workshop Collection:
GRAFF; Convocation 73; L.I.P: Vancouver Art; The Lumia Recital
Hall; Manitoba Etchings; Joel Smith-Postal Paintings; Infinite
Images: Domingo Alvarez; Paintings by Guayasamin: White Bird
Flying; M. C. Escher-Beyond Reality; Emily Carr's Contemporaries;
The Graphic Art of Sylvia Tait; Dana Atchley-Fragments 1963-
1973; Artists' Stamps and Stamp Images; 50 X 50 Netherlands
Graphics; The Art of Ching-Ku Chang; La Guilde Graphique; Vehicle
Art Inc; Pacific Rim Consciousness; British Columbia Rugs; The
First Year; Hand Coloured Prints; Brooker and Fitzgerald: Their
Drawings; Through the First Decade; Chinese Brush Techniques;
India: A Photographic Essay; International Women's Year.
Activities: Extension program; traveling exhibitions organized
and circulated; individual paintings and original objects of art lent;
500 items lent in average year.
Library: Slide library, artists file, and art gallery file for
reference.
Publications: Occasional exhibition catalogs.
Attendance: 27,000.

WESTERN CANADA ART ASSOCIATION INC.
c/o Centre for Communications and the Arts, Simon Fraser
University, V5A 1S6. Tel: (604) 291-4266
James Warren Felter, Chmn.
Betty Anne Yuill, Secy-Treas.
Estab. 1970 to promote high standards of excellence and uniform
methods in the care and presentation of works of art; to assist developing visual art centres in Western Canada; to encourage cooperation among members, and between members and other art
gallery and museum associations; financed by membership. Mem.
47 organizations; dues individual subscribing $5, associate $10,
active $20.
Activities: Training committee, organization and presentation of
gallery training workshops.
Library: Lending and reference library for members only.
Publications: WCAA Newsletter, 6 - 8 per year.

CHILLIWACK
COMMUNITY ARTS COUNCIL OF CHILLIWACK
Box 53, V2P 6H7. Tel: (604) 792-2069
Murray Mackie, Pres.
Susan Hohby, Secy.& Coordinator
Ed Classen, Financial Advisor
Clint Hames, V.Pres.
Open 9 AM - 4 PM. Arts Council estab. 1960, Arts Centre estab.
1972, to encourage all forms of art in the community; financed by
endowment and membership. Ann. meeting June; mem. 200; dues
$3 single, $5 organizational.
Collections: 26 Salish weavings.
Exhibitions: Local artists' exhibitions, including oils, water-
color, prints, pottery, wood carving, weavings and other fabric arts.
Activities: Concerts, dramatic programs, classes for adults and
children; scholarships.
Publications: Arts Council Newsletter, 8 per year.

COQUITLAM
PLACE DES ARTS
166 King Edward St, V3K 4T2. Tel: (604) 526-2891
Leonore Peyton, Dir.
Free Mon. - Thurs. 9 AM - 10 PM; Fri. & Sat. 9 AM - 4 PM. Estab.
Sept. 1, 1972, as a cultural, community crafts, and resource center,
an art school and gallery; financed by municipal and fine arts
council program funds.
Exhibitions: Bi-weekly shows of artists and craftsmen throughout
the year.
Activities: Special Education Department serving retarded young
adults, school children, senior citizens and womens' groups; satellite
courses within the school of the district on request; lectures open to
public; 12 - 15 gallery talks per year; concerts, dramatic programs,
classes for adults and children; scholarships; small library of 20
volumes.
Publications: Newsletter and program, every two months.
Attendance: Approx. 3000.

DAWSON CREEK
SOUTH PEACE ART SOCIETY*
Dawson Creek Art Gallery
Alaska Ave. & 13th St, P.O. Box 875.
M. Wanka, Pres.
D. Hillhouse, Secy.
E. McPhail, Treas.
S. Ravelli, V.Pres.
Open 9 - 12 AM, 1 - 5 PM; admis. 35¢. Estab. 1962 as a promotional
of local talent and community appreciation of art; financed by city and
provincial appropriations and membership. Museum and art gallery
combined function with Tourist Bureau. Ann. meeting third Tues. of
Mar; dues $3.
Activities: Original objects of art lent; color reproductions and
lantern slides in lending collection; lectures open to the public; 3 gal-
lery talks; 8 tours; classes for adults and children; exhibitions.
Income: $2500 - $3000.

KELOWNA
KELOWNA CENTENNIAL MUSEUM
470 Queensway Ave, V1Y 6S7. Tel: (604) 763-2451
T. Hamilton, Pres.
Sadie Conrad, Secy.
Ursula Surtees, Chief Cur.
Leslie Hopton, Museum Educator
Free summer, June - Sept. 10 AM - 5 PM & 7 - 9 PM; winter 2 - 5
PM. Estab. 1935 as a community museum, a national exhibit center
where traveling exhibits are received and circulated; financed by
city and state appropriation and membership. Gallery maintained
for local art exhibits and small traveling exhibits. Ann. meeting
Mar.
Collections: †Local collection, including all phases from natural
history to water travel; special collections of †lamps and lighting,
†lace, †Oriental toys.
Exhibitions: National and provincial exhibitions on festive beads,
lighting, multi-culture items, archeological items, stern wheeler
travel and conservation; many private exhibitions, including silver,
pottery, weapons and coins.
Activities: Traveling exhibitions organized and circulated; individual items lent to schools; 2000 lantern slides in lending collection; lectures open to public; classes for adults and children.
Library and photograph collection.
Publications: 2 volumes of interior Salish Indians 'Lak-La-Hai
Ee' on food and dwellings; 1 pictorial book of Kelowna.

PRINCE GEORGE
GORDON GALLERIES
Prince George Art Centre
1362 Seventh Ave, V2L 3P1. Tel: (604) 563-6447
Colina Wilson, Pres.
Frances Evans, Secy.
Mrs. J. Parker, Treas.
Jane Shaak, Dir. Exhibitions
Free 10 AM - 5 PM. Estab. 1970 to display work of local artists and
craftsmen and display traveling exhibits of Canadian art; financed by
membership. Ann. meeting May; mem. 200; dues $5.
Exhibitions: 2001 Central, traveling exhibition.
Activities: 25 tours; classes for children.
Publications: Gordon Galleries News Bulletin, 12 yearly.
Income: $5200.
Attendance: 12,000.

PRINCE RUPERT
MUSEUM OF NORTHERN BRITISH COLUMBIA
P.O. Box 669, McBride St. & First Ave. E, V8J 3S1.
Tel: (604) 624-5637 or 624-5638
Dr. R. G. Large, Pres.
Jocelyn Bolton, Secy-Treas.
Ms. M. J. Patterson, Cur.
Linda Schuster, Temporary Mgr.
Free summer 9 AM - 9 AM - 9 PM; winter 9 AM, except Sun. Estab.
1924. Owned by the city of Prince Rupert. New building opened
Aug, 1958, houses Museum-Tourist Bureau. Ann. meeting May;
dues $1.
Collections: Totem Poles; North Coast Indian collections, in-
cluding robes, masks, fishing gear, utensils, baskets, tools, shells
and marine life; stern wheelers; coins; Eskimo art from Dorset Bay
and Baffin Island; many other objects.
Attendance: Approx. 40,000 - 45,000.

PRINCE RUPERT ART CLUB

c/o Ms. Johan C. Woodland, Corresp. Secy, 658 Seventh Ave. E,
V8J 2J6. Tel: (604) 624-9045
Anna Thornton, Pres.
Isobel Moore, Treas.
Estab. 1949. Ann. meeting June; mem. 50; affiliated Picture Loan
Society, 200; dues $3 per year, which includes membership in the
Prince Rupert Community Arts Council.
Activities: Exhibit local and outside art in hotel lobbies, air
terminals, restaurants, etc; organize art classes during winter; arrange workshops throughout the year in a wide variety of arts and
crafts, some of them taught by professionals; finance opening nights
for exhibits given by Prince Rupert artists; encourage participation
in the arts by sponsoring a social evening each week in the Art Room,
at which each person attending may work on whatever project he
chooses, in whatever medium he chooses. Informal help is available
when necessary from other members of the Art Club. Frame, display, rent and sell through the Picture Loan Society paintings and
prints of young artists in Canada and the U.S, watercolors, silk
screen collage, woodcuts, etc.

RICHMOND

RICHMOND ARTS CENTRE

767 Minoru Gate, V6Y 1R8. Tel: (604) 278-1755
William Anderson, Dir.
Free daily 2 - 5 PM; Mon. - Fri. 7 - 9 PM. Estab. 1967; financed by
city appropriation.
Collections: Oil paintings, ink and wash and pencil and ink
sketches of local or related importance.
Exhibitions: Change every three weeks.
Activities: 200 prints in photograph collection for reference;
junior museum; dramatic programs; classes for adults and children;
gallery.
Library: 60 volume reference library; approx. 400 hours taped
interviews on local history, summarized and indexed.
Publications: Newsletter, bimonthly.
Attendance: 36,000.

VANCOUVER

ARTISTS GALLERY

555 Hamilton St, V6B 2R1. Tel: (604) 687-1345
Frances Fitzgibbon, Dir.
Leo LaBelle, Assoc. Dir.
Free Mon. - Fri. 9 AM - 5 PM. Estab. Jan, 1971 to administer employment programs for hiring artists, to purchase local and contemporary art, frame it and show it, to operate free loan art library
to public buildings; currently in process of becoming a nonprofit
organization; financed by city and state appropriation. Gallery has
2000 sq. ft. space.
Exhibitions: Continual 3-week exhibits of local contemporary
artists, both group and single exhibitions.
Activities: Framed original works of art available on free loan
to all public agencies, hospitals, schools in greater Vancouver and
outlying municipalities; traveling exhibitions organized and circulated; 3000 art works in lending collection, 2500 items lent in average
year; 250 prints in photograph collection for lending; competitions;
scholarships.
Income and Purchases: Income approx. $100,000; purchases
$80,000.

CENTENNIAL MUSEUM

1100 Chestnut St, V6J 3J9. Tel: (604) 736-4431
Dr. G. M. Shrum, Exec. Dir.
Open daily 10 AM - 5:30 PM.
Collections: Natural history, history, archaeology and anthropology chiefly of the Pacific Northwest Coast.
Exhibitions: Archaeology and ethnology of British Columbia;
pioneer, Victorian history of British Columbia; natural history of
the North-West (not yet completed).
Activities: Vancouver Museums Association; films and lecture
series; gift shop. Junior Museum, archaeology, history, ethnology
programs for schools, guided school tours.
Library: Staff reference but available by appointment to students,
researchers, etc; 6000 items chiefly on Pacific Northwest Coast.
Attendance: 230,000.

COMMUNITY ARTS COUNCIL OF VANCOUVER

315 W. Cordova St, V6B 1E5. Tel: (604) 683-4358
Mrs. R. Michael LePage, Pres.
F. R. Carey, V.Pres, Civic Arts
Ralph J. Flitton, V.Pres, Performing Arts
Mrs. J. B. Jarvis, V.Pres, General Arts
Hope Gaynor, V.Pres, Admin. & Hon. Secy.
N. H. Bunning, Hon. Treas.

Office open Mon. - Fri. 8:30 AM - 4:30 PM; gallery open Mon. - Fri.
10 AM - 4 PM. Estab. 1946, a society dedicated to the support of
arts; wide range of interest in the arts; promotes standards in all art
fields including civic arts. Ann. meeting Sept; mem. 1000; dues
individual $5, group $10.
Exhibitions: Office serves as small gallery to show works of
emerging artists who have not exhibited before; approx. 12 shows
per year.
Publications: Membership Newsletter, 9 times per year.

FINE ARTS GALLERY

University of British Columbia, V6T 1W5. Tel: (604) 228-2759
David Cottington, Cur.
Erika Gerson, Asst. Cur.
Free Tues. - Sat. 10:30 AM - 5 PM; cl. Sun, Mon. and holidays.
Estab. 1955; financed by endowment and university appropriation.
Exhibitions: Continuing exhibitions of fine art.
Activities: Occasional lectures relative to exhibitions; other lec-
tures open to the public; gallery talks and tours; concerts, happenings
and performances.
Library: 2000 exhibition catalogs.
Publications: Exhibition catalogs, approx. 3 per year.
Attendance: 70,000.

MUSEUM OF ANTHROPOLOGY

University of British Columbia
V6T 1W5.
Dr. Michael M. Ames, Dir.
Ria T. Rowe, Admin. Asst.
Madeline Bronsdon, Cur. Ethnology
Audrey Hawthorn, Cur. Ethnology
Dr. Margery Halpin, Cur. Ethnology
Dr. Elvi Whittaker, Cur. Ethnology
Dr. R. G. Matson, Cur. Archaeology
As of June 1, 1976, open Tues. summer and winter Noon - 9 PM;
Wed. - Sun. winter, Noon - 5 PM, summer, Noon - 7 PM; cl. Mon;
admis. adults $1, children 50¢. Museum specializes in cultures of
the Northwest Coast Indians, also other non-Western cultures. The
Museum has pioneered a unique concept of visual storage galleries
in which its ethnographic collections are on public view. Computerized catalog data.
Collections: Northwest Coast Indian cultures, non-Western cultures, including North and South America.
Activities: School programs and adult education programs;
lectures open to public; gallery talks and tours; concerts; dramatic
programs; classes for adults and children; competitions.
Library: 1200 volumes for teaching and reference only; photographs of items in collection available to other museums and institutions.

✤THE VANCOUVER ART GALLERY*

1145 W. Georgia St, V6E 3H2. Tel: (604) 682-5621
Gary R. Bell, Pres.
Luke Rombout, Dir.
Doris Shadbolt, Sr. Cur. & Assoc. Dir.
Peter Hendrie, Financial Admin.
Marguerite Pinney, Special Events Coordinator
Millie McKibbon, Educ. Officer
Willard Holmes, Asst. Cur.
Jean Martin, Librn.
Free Mon. - Sat. 10 AM - 5 PM; Wed. & Fri. 10 AM - 10 PM; Sun.
2 - 5 PM; Estab. 1931; site provided by City, which makes annual
grant; building enlarged to present size in 1951. Ann. meeting Mar;
mem. 1830.
Collections: 17th to 20th century European painting; Canadian
painting, sculpture, graphics; Emily Carr Collection; contemporary
American painting and graphics.
Exhibitions: (1970) Ronald Bladen & Robert Murray; Intermedia;
Pasadena Art Museum Collection; Gathie Falk, Horizontal Line,
Glenn Lewis; Jack Chambers Retrospective. (1971) Emily Carr
Centennial; Sculpture of the Inuit; Claude Breeze. (1972) West Coast
Lokas; Survey of Canadian Art Now; Structural Cinema; Maxwell
Bates. (1973) Don Potts, My First Car; Collection of Ian Davidson.
Activities: Free noon hour programmes of music, poetry and
drama on Wed, Thurs. and Fri. Evening lectures and events, daily
school tours, films, picture loan for members, Satellite programme
and other activities in Vancouver and around the province.
Library: Books, periodicals, slides, catalogues, and reproduc-
tions, for reference.
Income: Annual income $560,270.

VICTORIA

✤ART GALLERY OF GREATER VICTORIA*

1040 Moss St, V8V 4P1. Tel: (604) 384-3123
Richard Simmins, Dir.
Will Hoare, Asst. Dir.

C. D. Graham, Cur.
Open 11 AM - 5 PM Tues. - Sat; also 7:30 - 9:30 PM Thurs; 2 - 5 PM
Sun; cl. Mon. Estab. 1945. Ann. meeting Oct; mem. 2100; dues
$7.50 and higher.

Collections: Contemporary †Canadian, †American and European;
European painting and decorative arts from 16th to 19th century;
†Primitive arts; †Japanese art from Kamakura to contemporary;
†Chinese art; Tibetan art; †Indian art; †Persian art.

Exhibitions: Contemporary Canadian and international oriental;
annual Vancouver Island Jury Exhibition ($300 in prizes) approx. 35
shows per annum changing every two or three weeks.

Activities: Classes for children; lectures; films; recitals; drama;
art rental.

Library: 3000 volumes on art and art history.

Income and Purchases: Income $110,000; purchases $12,000.

Attendance: 46,000.

MALTWOOD ART MUSEUM
4509 W. Saanich Rd. Tel: (112) 479-4468
Martin Segger, Cur.
Free June through Aug, Tues. - Fri. 10 AM - 4 PM. Estab. 1964 to
collect, preserve, and exhibit furniture, glass, china; objects d'art
of, and relating to, the Arts and Crafts movement; assist university
museum training program; endowed.

Collections: Chinese pottery, Han, Wei, Tang, Sung, Ming; medieval Persian pottery, object d'art; Oriental rugs, 16th - 19th century;
17th & 18th century English furniture; sculptures by Catherine Maltwood F.R.S.A; paintings and prints, 17th century to 1940; †arts and
crafts furniture, †silverware, †glassware, †pottery, †pewter and
†19th and early 20th century stained glass.

Exhibitions: Oriental bronzes and pottery from National Museum,
Ottawa; (1968) Selections from permanent collection; (1969) Arts and
Crafts collection; (1970) Stained glass, 17th century English furniture,
Medieval English Brass Rubbings.

Activities: Traveling exhibitions organized and circulated; original objects of art, photographs and color slides in lending collection,
approx. 250 items per yr. Photograph collection, 500 prints for
lending and reference; lectures open to public, eight visiting lecturers per yr; 30 gallery talks or tours; dramatic programs. Book
shop.

Library: 700 volumes for lending and reference through Mac-
Phearson Library, University of Victoria.

Publications: Books: King Carters Church; Brass Rubbings; The
Railway Hotels and the Development of Chateau Style in Canada;
Arts of the Forgotten Pioneers.

PROVINCIAL ARCHIVES OF BRITISH COLUMBIA*
Parliament Buildings. Tel: (604) 327-3621
J. W. Mossop, Cur. & Display Dir.
Free, Mon. - Fri. 8:30 AM - 5 PM. Estab. 1910, our painting collec-
tion is a section within visual records division, collection includes
paintings as historical records; financed by provincial appropriations.
Medium sized gallery incorporated in Archives Building.

Collections: Paintings of historic interest by content as visual
records; representative collections of works by British Columbia
artists or those who have painted within the province.

WEST VANCOUVER

WEST VANCOUVER VISUAL ARTS SOCIETY
Box 91514, V7V 3P2
Norma Sorensen, Pres. Tel: (604) 922-1450
Myrtle Mayall, Secy.
Mrs. F. Lightheart, V.Pres.
Mrs. W. D. M. Patterson, Treas.
Estab. 1968, inc. as a nonprofit society 1970, to provide a greater
opportunity for people in the community to participate in the enjoyment of the visual arts; special emphasis has been directed toward
exhibitions of high quality; financed by provincial and municipal
government grants, membership and private foundations. Part-time
gallery maintained until the heritage building which housed it was
moved; efforts are being made to have this building restored as an
arts center, to be part of a beautiful waterfront historic square.
Ann. meeting Sept; mem. 35; dues $2.

Exhibitions: Latest work of Jack Shadbolt; Under Thirty; British
Print Show; Design 74; Woman, a two-part exhibition done in con-
junction with Burnaby Art Gallery, in which works by Toulouse
Lautrec and Gustave Klimt were displayed.

MANITOBA

MANITOBA ASSOCIATION OF ARCHITECTS
710-177 Lombard Ave, Winnipeg R3B 0W9. Tel: (204) 942-7767
L. Plotkin, Pres.
M. Brownie, Exec. Secy.

Estab. 1906, inc. 1910. Provincial Architectural Registration Board
and professional governing body. Ann. meeting Jan; mem. 220; dues
$110.

The Manitoba Association of Architects has established a joint
lectureship fund with the School of Architecture at the University of
Manitoba, and has established a practice of bringing three or more
outstanding lecturers to Winnipeg each year for university and public
lectures. The Association has established a yearly donation of $300
in prizes awarded to students pursuing the course at the School of
Architecture, University of Manitoba.

MANITOBA SOCIETY OF ARTISTS*
c/o Betty Dimock, 249 Elm St, Winnipeg R3M 3N6.
Robert Bruce, Pres.
Estab. 1925. Ann. meeting Feb; mem. approx. 50; dues $2 and
higher. Annual exhibition Mar. - Apr.

BRANDON

BRANDON ALLIED ARTS CENTRE*
Brandon Allied Arts Council
1036 Louise Ave. Tel: (204) 727-1036
Joyce I. Murray, Art Dir.

WINNIPEG

MANISPHERE GROUP OF ARTISTS
c/o Ellen B. Cringan, 82 Cordova St, R3N 0Z8.
Tel: (204) 489-4417
Hans Osted, Pres.
Ethel Percy, Secy.
Mo Renaud, Gen. Mgr.
George Prost, Pres, Board of Dir.
Estab. 1970 to further the work of the artist at the local and commu-
nity levels; financed by membership. Ann. meeting Oct. 1st; mem.
60; dues $8.

Collections: Organization purchases one of the works from the
annual juried show.

Exhibitions: Juried shows of one American segment and one
Canadian segment; four exhibitions of members works yearly.

Activities: Educational department activities, teaching in rural
areas, regular classes plus workshops in oils, printmaking, watercolors, pottery, acrylics and pastels; traveling exhibitions organized
and circulated; individual paintings and original objects of art lent;
lectures open to the public; 2 gallery talks yearly; 1 tour; competitions; scholarships.

✤UNIVERSITY OF MANITOBA GALLERY III
School of Art, R3T 2N2. Tel: (204) 474-9586
William Kirby, Art Gallery Comt.
Free Mon. - Fri. 9 AM - 9 PM. Estab. 1946, Gallery III estab. 1965
to provide exhibitions for students and faculty on the university
campus; exhibitions also open to the public.

Collections: †Contemporary Canadian and American Painting,
sculpture and prints.

Exhibitions: Exhibitions from Museum of Modern Art, American
Federation of Arts, Smithsonian Institution, National Gallery of
Canada, and others; annual exhibitions by the students of the School
of Art.

Activities: Lectures, gallery talks, discussion groups, workshops.

Attendance: 20,000.

Faculty of Architecture Exhibition Centre Architecture Building
Donald Ellis, Dir. of Exhibitions
Free Mon. - Fri. 9 AM - 10:30 PM; Sat. 9 AM - 5 PM. Estab. 1959
with the opening of the new Faculty of Architecture Building to provide architectural and related exhibitions for students and faculty
on the University Campus and, particularly for Architecture students;
exhibitions also open to the public.

Exhibitions: Exhibitions from National Gallery of Canada, Smithsonian Institution, American Federation of Arts, Museum of Modern
Art and from other private and public sources; annual exhibitions by
the students in the Faculty of Architecture.

Activities: Lectures; gallery talks; symposia.

Art Libraries at School of Art, Faculty of Architecture and the
University Library.

Attendance: 15,000.

THE WINNIPEG ART GALLERY
300 Memorial Blvd, R3C 1V1. Tel: (204) 786-6641
Roger L. Selby, Dir.
Michael J. Scholl, Pub. Information Officer
Free Tues. - Sat. 11 AM - 5 PM; Sun. Noon - 5 PM. Estab. 1912,
inc. 1963, to present a diversified, quality level program of art in
all media, representing various cultures, past and present. Educa-

tional function to the surrounding community and act as major art resource for the Canadian prairies. Ann. meeting spring; mem. 2500; dues $5 and up.

Collections: Painting, sculpture, graphics and other media. Particular emphasis is given to Canadian art. Inuit (Eskimo) art collection of over 4000 pieces.

Exhibitions: Traveling and original exhibitions.

Activities: Lectures, children's and adult classes, special events programs, film series, concerts, tours, extension work, numerous Women's Committee projects, Film Series, Art Rental and Sales Gallery and restaurant.

Library: 13,500 books, catalogs and periodicals, plus 5000 35mm slides.

Publications: Monthly Calendar of Events; exhibition catalogs.

Annual Budget: $1.2 million; annual purchases $100,000.

Attendance: 257,000.

THE WINNIPEG SKETCH CLUB
434 Assiniboine Ave, R3C 0Y1. Tel: (204) 943-4772
Hugh McVarish, Pres.
Douglas A. Newey, Treas.
Lily Hobbs, Secy.
(14-149 Langside St, R3C 1Z5)

Open to the public by appointment. Formed 1914 as Winnipeg Art Students Sketch Club; name changed in 1920 to present name; to provide a meeting place for members to advance their studies by means of sketch meetings, and for encouragement of work done independently; an organization of art lovers to meet and profit by mutual help and example through the study of the living model and the practice of sketching from nature. Ann. meeting Jan; mem. approx. 75; dues $10.

Exhibitions: Annual exhibition at the Winnipeg Art Gallery, usually in Nov. or Dec; also Sketch Club openhouse and various local activities.

Activities: Weekly sketching sessions each Tues. and Thur. with model, Sept. to early May; outdoor sketching each Tues. May - Sept. Takes part in various other art activities, particularly during 1970, which was Manitoba's Centennial year; occasionally takes part in activities in other parts of the Province of Manitoba.

Library: Contains numerous art books and the Club Archives.

NEW BRUNSWICK

ARCHITECTS ASSOCIATION OF NEW BRUNSWICK*
13 Germain St, Saint John. Tel: (506) 652-8340
Freda M. Large, Exec. Secy, Box 910, Rothesay E0G 2W0
Inc. 1933. Ann. meeting Jan; mem. 41; dues $100 and higher.

FREDERICTON

BEAVERBROOK ART GALLERY
703 Queen St, P.O. Box 605. Tel: (506) 455-6551
Lady Beaverbrook & Sir Max Aitken, Custodians
Ian G. Lumsden, Cur.
Paul A. Hachey, Asst. Cur.
Open winter, Sept. 15 - May 31, Sun. & Mon. Noon - 5 PM; Tues. - Sat. 10 AM - 5 PM; summer, June 1 - Sept. 14, Tues. - Sat. 10 AM - 9 PM; Sun. & Mon. 2 - 9 PM. Estab. Sept. 1959; operates on endowment fund and Beaverbrook Canadian Foundation. 800 Friends of the Beaverbrook Art Gallery; dues $5 minimum.

Collections: †British paintings, †Canadian paintings, English porcelain, †sculpture.

Exhibitions: Diverse program of traveling and gallery-sponsored exhibitions; provincial extension program.

Activities: Art education program consisting of tours, lectures and films. Sales desk.

Attendance: Approx. 60,000.

NEW BRUNSWICK CRAFT SCHOOL
Hut 3, Woodstock Rd. Tel: (506) 453-2305
Hazel T. Gorman, Dir.
Lucy Fellows, Jewelry
Jeannine Dugas & Adele Ilves, Weaving
Judy Young, Design & Textiles
Peter Wolcott, Pottery
Mary Clover, Designer
Lise Bourque, Supvr. Training
Open Mon. - Fri. 8:30 AM - 5 PM. Estab. 1946 to encourage and promote a creative craft program in the Province of New Brunswick; financed by Province of New Brunswick Government. Gallery is 30 x 24 ft. for the display of crafts.

Collections: An exhibition of New Brunswick crafts to be added to each year.

Activities: 2-year craft program to train producing craftsmen in the areas of jewelry, pottery, weaving, fabrics, woodworking and design; recreational evening classes offered also. Summer recreational one-day programs at Fundy National Park, Alma.

Library: 650 volumes for lending and reference; growing collection of audiovisual equipment and slides.

Publications: Dimensions, quarterly; Craftsmen of New Brunswick, School of Crafts Brochure; Directory of New Brunswick Craftsmen and Craft Shops; Craft Horizons; Rock and Gem; Design.

Attendance: 36 students, 2-year program; 4000, recreational summer program.

SAINT JOHN

THE NEW BRUNSWICK MUSEUM
277 Douglas Ave, E2K 1E5. Tel: (506) 693-1196
David Ross, Dir.
M. Robertson, Archivist
D. Christie, Cur. Natural Science
G. Finley, Cur. History
R. Percival, Cur. Art
L. N. Atcheson, Bus. Mgr.
Open summers 10 AM - 9 PM. Open winters 2 - 5 PM; admis. adults 50¢, children 25¢. Gesner Museum estab. 1842, Natural History Society Museum estab. 1862, New Brunswick Museum estab. and inc. 1930. Ann. meeting June; mem. dues $5 and higher.

Collections: †Canadian paintings (many by New Brunswick artists), †drawings, †prints, †handicrafts; †European and Oriental arts; primitive art. Natural History Dept. includes paintings by Audubon. Canadian History Dept. includes Indian and New Brunswick crafts; †portraits and †historical pictures by West, Trumbull, Copley, and Romney.

Activities: Special exhibitions; lectures; courses and conducted tours for schools; films. Conducts extension work throughout New Brunswick. Loan collections of slides, paintings, publications.

Library: All departments have fine reference libraries, and that of the Art Dept. is one of the best in the Maritime Provinces.

Publications: Museum Memo, quarterly; Annual Report.

Income and Purchases: Income approx. $800,000; annual purchases approx. $20,000.

Attendance: 70,000.

MONCTON

GALERIE D'ART
Universite de Moncton. Tel: (506) 858-4081
Raoul Dionne, Pres.
Edward E. Leger, Dir.
Free Mon. - Fri. 1:30 - 4:30 PM; Sat. & Sun. 2 - 4 PM; Mon. & Wed. 7 - 9 PM. Estab. 1965 for art exhibitions; financed by university appropriation.

Collections: †Canadian Prints, Drawings and Paintings.

Library: 4000 volume lending and reference library.

Income and Purchases: Income $8000; purchases $1000.

Attendance: 3000.

ST. ANDREWS

SUNBURY SHORES ART AND NATURE CENTRE, INC.
139 Water St, P.O. Box 100.
Mrs. Ernest Frederick Eidlitz, Founder
James Oppe, Pres.
Mrs. Donald McLeese, Secy.
Mrs. Ralph Brinkhurst, Exec. Secy.
Thomas Moffatt, Dir.
Estab. 1964 as a nonprofit charitable, educational organization, to promote, establish and maintain at St. Andrews and elsewhere in the province of New Brunswick, opportunities for study and practice of the arts and crafts, and for natural history study and conservation education. Ann. meeting July; mem. approx. 400; dues $5 or more.

Activities: Workshops on syper realism and wildlife art; regular art exhibitions, children's art courses, weaving, spinning, dyeing, jewelry, batik, raku pottery, nature workshops and field trips for all ages, beach walks, photography and rocketry; outdoor education workshops for New Brunswick school teachers twice yearly in French and English.

NEWFOUNDLAND

ST. JOHN'S

ART GALLERY, MEMORIAL UNIVERSITY OF NEWFOUNDLAND
Prince Phillip Dr. Tel: (709) 753-6716
Edythe Goodridge, Acting Cur.

E. Cadigan, Cur. of Installations
E. Jane, Art Gallery Asst.
B. Murphy, Art Gallery Asst.
P. Miskell, Sr. Clerk
R. Green, Secy.
Open daily 10 AM - 10 PM. Estab. 1961; financed by Memorial University. Three galleries.
   Collections: †Memorial University of Newfoundland Permanent Collection of approx. 800 works; Rental Collection of 250 works.
   Exhibitions: Approx. 90 exhibitions per year.
   Activities: Traveling exhibitions organized and circulated; individual paintings and original objects of art lent; lending collection of 2000 lantern slides; lectures open to public, 12 - 15 lectures per year.
   Income and Purchases: Income $180,000; purchases $10,000.
   Attendance: 180,000.

NEWFOUNDLAND MUSEUM
   Duckworth St. Tel: (709) 726-5987
Martin L. Bowe, Dir. Historic Resources
F. Vallis, Chief Historic Sites
Donagh O'Dea, Extension Officer
Andrew Wilson, Cur. Maritime History.
Free daily 9 AM - 5 PM. Estab. 1952 as three museums (Newfoundland Museum; Naval and Military Museum; Maritime Museum) devoted to portraying a general history of Newfoundland; provincial financing.
   Collections: Native People; †Furniture; †Nautical.
   Activities: Conducts historic lectures in schools; traveling exhibitions organized and circulated; individual paintings and original objects of art lent; photograph collection of 10,000 for reference; tours during summer months.
   Publications: Technical papers.
   Attendance: 57,022.

NOVA SCOTIA

NOVA SCOTIA ASSOCIATION OF ARCHITECTS
   Suite 630, 5991 Spring Garden Rd, Halifax B3H 1Y6
Officers change annually; address correspondence to Exec. Secy.
Estab. 1932. Ann. meeting Feb; mem. 116.

DARTMOUTH

DARTMOUTH HERITAGE MUSEUM
   Wyse Road.
G S. Gosley, Dir.
Mrs. R. Gargan, Secy.
Mrs. E. Richter, Asst. Art.
Open Summer (July & Aug), 9 AM - 9 PM; Winter, 1 - 5 PM; admis. adults 35¢, family mem. $1 per yr. Estab. Feb. 1968; Story of the City of Dartmouth; City appropriation. Art Gallery. Ann. meeting June; mem. 50; dues $2.
   Collections: †Nova Scotia glass; dolls; †Artifacts (local history); aircraft models; †works of art.
   Activities: Tours of school classes; classes for adults and children.
   Attendance: 44,000.

HALIFAX

ANNA LEONOWENS GALLERY
Nova Scotia College of Art and Design
   153 Granville St. Tel: (902) 422-7381, Exten. 184
Garry Neill Kennedy, Pres.
James Davies, Dean
Robert MacKeeman, Dir.
Open daily. Estab. for educational purpose; financed by city and state appropriations and tuition. One small and one large gallery.
   Exhibitions: 30 - 40 exhibitions per year.
   Activities: Extension department has courses throughout the province.
   Library: 7000 volume lending and reference library; 320 periodicals; 20,000 slides.
   Publications: Ten books, one periodical.

EYE LEVEL GALLERY
   Marble Building, 1672 Barrington St. Tel: (902) 425-6412
Roger Savage, Pres.
Hattie Prentice, Secy.
Susan Beaver, Coordinator.
Free Mon. - Sat. Noon - 5 PM. Estab. 1973 as an artist cooperative gallery to provide exhibition opportunities for contemporary regional artists; financed by endowment and membership. Gallery consists of

three rooms, located on 2nd floor. Meetings, last Thurs. of each month; mem. 57; dues $5.
   Exhibitions: Peggy's Cove Syndrome; Ron Suebrook, Grassroots; Recent Works; David Haigh; First Annual Little Print and Drawing Show; Censorship; Eye Opener; Fernandes; plus others.
   Activities: Traveling exhibitions organized and circulated; original objects of art lent; lectures open to public; 4- 5 gallery talks per year; 7 tours; demonstrations; dramatic programs; classes for adults; competitions. Slide collection of Nova Scotia artists.
   Publications: Eye Level Newsletter, monthly.

MOUNT SAINT VINCENT UNIVERSITY ART GALLERY
   Seton Academic Centre, B3M 2I6. Tel: (902) 443-4450
Mary Sparling, Dir.
Free Mon. - Fri. 9 AM - 5 PM; Tues. 9 AM - 9 PM; Sat, Sun. and holidays Noon - 5 PM. Estab. 1971 to offer continuously changing exhibitions of local, regional, national and international origin, featuring a balance between fine arts and crafts; financed by Mount Saint Vincent University.
   Collections: The art gallery is custodian of a collection of pictures, ceramics and pottery of the late Alice Egan Hagen of Mahone Bay, noted Nova Scotia potter and ceramist, which is on permanent display in Rosaria Hall. It also has a growing permanent collection of works of Canadian contemporary artists.
   Exhibitions: Pacific Coast Consciousness; Jude; Art, Craft, Baking, Hobby and Talent Show; Duguay Woodcuts; Veneer; Jane Austen Photographs; A Sense of Meaning; Calendar 1976, exhibit of linoleum-cut prints by Linda Jurcisek; Images of Women in Sacred Art; Tapestries from Poland; Inuit Women in Transition; From Craft into Art; African Masks; Homage to Sarain Stump; Hines on Hines; plus the permanent collection.
   Activities: Traveling exhibitions organized and circulated; individual paintings and original objects of art lent; lectures open to public, 10 visiting lecturers per year; 5 gallery talks; 35 tours; films; workshops; concerts; classes for adults and children; competitions.
   Publications: Schedule of Events, every second month.
   Attendance: 17,000.

NOVA SCOTIA MUSEUM OF FINE ART*
   P.O. Box 2262.
C. A. E. Fowler, Pres.
Mrs. T. Housser, Secy.
Mrs. H. P. Connor, V.Pres.
Bernard Riordon, Cur.
Free summers Mon. - Sat. 10 AM - 7:30 PM, Sun. 12 AM - 7:30 PM; winters Mon. - Sat. 10 AM - 5 PM, Sun. 12 AM - 5 PM. Estab. 1908, to erect a museum for the preservation and exhibition of works of art, to make, maintain and exhibit collections of such works, and afford instruction in the fine arts; supported by membership and Provincial Government Grant. Centennial Art Gallery estab. 1967 situated in the Powder Magazine of the Halifax Citadel. Mem. 360; dues individual $5, family $10, student $1.
   Collections: 190 works of art.
   Exhibitions: (1971) Honari Daumier, lithographs; Peter Dobush, W. C. Draro, graphics; Artists in Action; Brent Homans, oil paintings; Potters S. Weaver, N.S.C. of A.R.D; Canadian Student Printmakers; Contemporary Artists in Nova Scotia; Robert Percival, paintings, drawings, The Art of W. J. Phillips, woodcuts and wood engravings; Violet Woens, drawings; Raimonde Demopoulis, weaving, rugs to baskets, pillows to clothing; Don Wright, monoprints, watercolours. (1972) Watercolour Paintings of Saskatchewan; Adrian Hebert, Thirty Years of His Work (1923-53); Halifax Portraits, covering 200 years; Gary Morton, acrylic, inks, oils; Artists in Action; Artists in Action Work; Gerald Trottier, paintings and drawings; Permanent Collection selections; Selections from Permanent Collection of Nova Scotia Museum of Fine Art; Christopher Pratt, serigraphs; Artario '72; Focus: Photographic Essays Exhibition; Nadezda Pliskova. (1973) Sharon Carver and Richard Fauteux; Concepts of Shape and Color; Alan Wylie; Nova Scotia Artists; McAlpine Collection.
   Activities: Traveling exhibitions organized and circulated; lectures open to the public, two visiting lecturers per year; 20 gallery talks, 100 tours; classes for adults and children; Art Sales and Rental Service.
   Publications: Bulletin, twice a year.
   Attendance: 50,000 annually.

PUBLIC ARCHIVES OF NOVA SCOTIA
   Coburg Road, B3H 1Z9. Tel: 423-7040
Dr. C. Bruce Fergusson, Provincial Archivist
Open Mon. - Fri. 8:30 AM - 10 PM; Sat. 9 AM - 6 PM; Sun. 1 - 10 PM. Estab. 1931; financed by appropriation. Gallery.
   Collections: Mainly portraits and historical paintings.
   Library: 36,000 volumes for reference; 8000 photographs for reference.

Publications: Numerous special publications; Nova Scotia Series; bulletins; archives; all for sale in Book Shop.
Attendance: 8500.

ONTARIO

ASSOCIATION OF CANADIAN INDUSTRIAL DESIGNERS (ONTARIO)*
Suite 208, 159 Bay St, Toronto M5J 1J7. Tel: (705) 366-4981
Mace Mair, Secy.
Estab. 1948, to promote and foster a high standard of design in industrial products as a service to the public, the manufacturing industries, and the national culture and economy. Ann. meeting Nov; mem. 120; dues $75.

ONTARIO ASSOCIATION OF ARCHITECTS*
50 Park Rd, Toronto M4W 2N5. Tel: (416) 929-0623
Brian Parks, Exec. Dir.
Estab. 1890. Mem. 1,400.
Activities: Sponsors exhibition of new building materials and techniques. Awards annual cash prizes through School of Architecture, University of Toronto, and Ryerson Institute of Technology, Ontario College of Art, University of Waterloo, and Carleton University.

ONTARIO CRAFTS COUNCIL
346 Dundas St. W, Toronto M5T 1G5 (offices, gallery and craft resource centre). Tel: (416) 921-4272
140 Cumberland St, Toronto (commercial outlet)
Paul Bennett, Exec. Dir.
Ontario Crafts Council recently formed by the merger of the Canadian Guild of Crafts (Ontario) and another multicraft organization within the province; Council consists of 25 affiliated groups and cooperating institutions. Ann. meeting spring; dues not yet established.
Collections: Permanent collection of contemporary crafts.
Exhibitions: Varied exhibition program, including biennial show, traveling exhibitions, regional shows, the Craft Gallery with exhibitions of a month's duration.
Activities: Awards and bursary program; 10% of profits from the Council store go directly to a bursary program; bursaries are given to professional craftsmen who wish to study beyond Ontario.
Craft Resource Centre has a library, portfolios of practicing craftsmen, a slide library, research material on the Canadian craft movement.
Publications: Crafts, bimonthly.

ONTARIO SOCIETY OF ARTISTS*
559 Jarvis St, 3rd Floor, Toronto
Gerald Sevier, Pres.
Nomi Cameron, Secy.
(643 Yonge St, Toronto 285)
Estab. 1872 for the encouragement of original art in Ontario. Ann. meeting Mar.
Activities: Holds annual exhibition in spring, open to all Canadian artists; jury; makes awards. Annual small picture exhibition. Organizes traveling exhibitions in Ontario. Exhibitions circulated.

VISUAL ARTS ONTARIO
8 York St, 7th Floor, Toronto M5J 1R2. Tel: (416) 366-1607
Kenneth B. McKay, Pres.
Kemp Kieffer, Secy.
William J. S. Boyle, Exec. Dir.
Janni de Savoye, Exec. Asst.
Gail Habs, Communications Officer
Louise Chenier, Ed.
Open 9 AM - 5 PM. Estab. 1973 to coordinate activities of professional art societies in Ontario, to initiate programs to further awareness of visual arts in Ontario, an association of artists; financed by city and provincial appropriation. Ann. meeting June; 8 organizations, 2700 members.
Exhibitions: Over 25 exhibitions throughout Canada.
Activities: Traveling exhibitions organized and circulated; competitions; grants to professional visual artists.
Publications: Artviews, bimonthly bulletin; Visual Arts Handbook, every 2 years.

AMHERSTBURG

THE GIBSON GALLERY*
Fort Malden Guild of Arts and Crafts
140 Richmond St. Tel: 736-5110
Wm. G. Wight, Pres.
Mrs. W. T. Ashby, Secy.
Florence Gatfield, Treas.

Open Sun. 2 - 5 PM; donation. Estab. 1968 to encourage and develop the cultural life of the community; financed by city and state appropriations and membership. Gallery a converted railway station and caboose. Ann. meeting Sept; mem. 450; dues $2.
Exhibitions: Area artists; one, two or three-man shows; two traveling exhibitions; Art Gallery of Windsor Selected Paintings.
Activities: Lectures open to the public; 3 gallery talks and tours; concerts; dramatic programs; classes for adults and children; competitions.
Publications: Bi-monthly newsletter.
Income: Approx. $3500.
Attendance: 1200 annual average.

BRAMPTON

PEEL MUSEUM AND ART GALLERY
7 Wellington St. E, L6W 1Y1. Tel: (416) 451-9051
Grant Clarkson, Pres.
R. E. Jones, Secy.
Mrs. R. H. Bull, V.Pres. & Museum Comt. Pres.
John Jacobs, Treas.
Lenore Kummell, Art Gallery Comt. Pres.
Lydia A. Ross, Dir.
Open daily 1:30 - 4:30 PM; admis. adults 35¢, students and children 15¢, mem. free. Estab. 1968; financed by appropriations and membership. Ann. meeting May 15; mem. over 200; dues $2.
Collections: †Pioneer Artifacts-19th Century Ontario; †Indian Artifacts-Iroquois.
Exhibitions: Changing art shows promoting local artists.
Activities: Free school tours through both museum and art gallery; archives; lectures open to the public; 3 visiting lecturers per year; classes for adults and children; pioneer craft classes.
Library: Reference library of 200 volumes.
Income and Purchases: Income approx. $7000; purchases art gallery $1000, museum $1000.
Attendance: 5000 annual average.

BRANTFORD

GLENHYRST ARTS COUNCIL OF BRANTFORD INC.
20 Ava Rd, N3T 5G9. Tel: (519) 756-5932
John S. Canning, Pres.
William S. Bragg, Exec. Dir.
Free Tues. - Fri. 2 - 8 PM; Sat. & Sun. 2 - 6 PM; cl. Mon. Estab. 1957; Arts Centre supported by membership and fund-raising events. 11 room house left to the city by the late E. L. Cockshutt, maintained by the city.
Collections: †Small permanent collection.
Exhibitions: Held on regular basis.
Activities: Lectures open to public, visiting lecturers; classes for adults and children; competitions.
Library: Very small reference library.
Publications: Monthly newsletter.
Attendance: 20,000.

CHATHAM

THAMES ARTS CENTRE
75 William St. N, N7M 4L4. Tel: (519) 354-8338
Lloyd Groombridge, Chmn. Board of Trustees
Barry E. Morrison, Dir.
David K. McNeil, Tech. Dir.
Joan Crummer, Educ. Supvr.
Office open Mon. - Fri. 9 AM - 5 PM; public viewing hours Tues. - Sun. 1 - 5 PM; cl. Mon; no admis. fee. Estab. Dec. 4, 1963, inc, to encourage, educate and develop the arts and the awareness of the arts in the community by providing top quality artists to perform, teach and exhibit; to preserve cultural heritage; financed by endowment, city and state appropriation and membership. Ann. meeting 3rd Mon. in Oct; mem. 500; dues $5 individual, $10 family.
Exhibitions: Historical Quilt Exhibition; Group of Seven and Their Contemporaries; Antique Oriental Rug Exhibition; Chatham-Kent Heritage Exhibition; local artists, one-man and group exhibitions, local juried exhibitions and photography shows.
Activities: Docent program; lectures; tours; classes for adults and children; films; concerts; dramatic programs; competitions.
Library: Small selection, for reference only.
Publications: Bimonthly bulletin.
Attendance: 6000.

DOWNSVIEW

ART GALLERY OF YORK UNIVERSITY
Ross Bldg. N. 145, 4700 Keele St, M3J 1P3. Tel: (416) 667-3427.
Michael Greenwood, Cur.
Open Mon. - Fri. 10 AM - 4:30 PM; Sun. 2 - 5 PM. Estab. 1970 to provide for a large university community and for the general public

a program of changing art exhibitions covering a wide spectrum of historical periods and cultures; financed by federal and provincial appropriations.

Collections: Permanent and enlarging collection of modern Canadian painting, sculptures, graphics, tapestries, and electric works for the enhancement of the building and openair sites.

Exhibitions: Members of Faculty of Fine Arts Exhibition; Robert Downing: Sculpture and Drawings; Eskimo Prints; Light and movement: International artists; African carving and objects from Toronto collections; Eskimo Carvings; Ted Godwin: Paintings and Prints; El Greco: St. Francis Meditating on Death; Richard Hamilton: Graphic Work; Claude Breeze: 10 Years; Viktor Vasarely: Paintings & Graphics; Douglas Morton: Retrospective; Michael Semak: Italy; Tim Whiten: Sculpture & Drawings; Marcel Duchamp: Readymades & Graphics; Signals Electric; David Gilhooly: Gifts from the Frog World: Hidden Treasure from Central Africa; Ron Kostyniuk: Relief Structures; Cozic and Delavalle; The N. E. Thing Co, Ltd; (1974-75) Japanese Scroll Exhibition; Henry Moore Drawings and Sculpture Exhibition; Charles Band Memorial Exhibition of Canadian Painting and Sculpture; 18th Century Stage, Britain; Anne James; German Expressionist Graphic Exhibition; William Vazan; Electric Currents; Dialogues - African Sculpture from Toronto Collections; National Gallery Print Exhibition; Fernand Leduc, Tapestries and Screen Prints; Inuit Women in Transition; Toronto Collectors: Dr. Henry Levison; Roger Hilton Works on Paper.

Activities: Original objects of art lent; photograph collection; library.

Publications: Catalogs of most exhibitions.

HAMILTON

ART GALLERY OF HAMILTON*
Main W. at Forsythe St, L8S 4K9. Tel: (416) 527-6610 & 6619
Glen E. Cumming, Dur.
Keith Courtney, Cur.
Free daily 10 AM - 5 PM; also Thurs. 8 - 10 PM; Sun. 2 - 5 PM; cl. Mon. Estab. 1914. Date varies for ann. meeting.
Collections: †Canadian painting including Blair Bruce Memorial; †British, †French and †American works.
Activities: Special exhibitions; classes for adults and children; conducted tours for school children.

DUNDURN CASTLE
Dundurn Park, York Blvd, L8R 3H1. Tel: (416) 522-5313
Brig. Gen. Willis Moogk, Dir.
Open mid-June to Labour Day daily 10 AM - 5 PM; evening appointments for groups of 25 or more; Labour Day to mid-June, booked tours mornings and evenings, open to public 1 - 4 PM, except school holidays 10 AM - 4 PM; cl. Christmas and New Year's Day; children must be accompanied by adults. Owned and operated by the City of Hamilton.
Dundurn, the home of Sir Allan Napier MacNab; Hamilton's Centennial Project has been the restoration of this historic house. Built in 1832-35 it was tenured by MacNab until his death in 1862. The terminal date of the furnishings in 1855. Approximately 37 rooms are shown and a 3-room on site museum; demonstrations of cooking, baking, butter and candle making using 19th century methods. Seminars.
Attendance: 90,000.

JORDAN

JORDAN HISTORICAL MUSEUM OF THE TWENTY
Vintage House. Tel: (416) 562-5242
Barbara Coffman, Secy.
H. L. Crowfoot, Dir.
Free May - Oct. daily Noon - 6 PM. Estab. 1953 to preserve the material and folklore of the area, known as The Twenty. Ann. meeting Dec; mem. 820.
Collections: Archives, textiles, agricultural implements, giant cider press, fracturs, furniture.
Activities: Special displays as requested by the community; Pioneer Day first Sat. after Canadian Thanksgiving holiday.
Budget and Income: $14,500.
Attendance: 17,000.

KINGSTON

AGNES ETHERINGTON ART CENTRE
Queen's University, K7L 3N6. Tel: (613) 547-6170
Michael Bell, Dir.
Frances K. Smith, Cur.
William Muysson, Assoc. Cur.
Open Mon. - Fri. 9 AM - 5 PM; Sat. & Sun. 1 - 5 PM; Tues. & Thurs. 7 - 9 PM. Estab. 1957, exten. 1962 and 1975. Gallery Association of 900 mem; annual fee family $10, individual $6, student $2, patron $25.

Collections: Zacks' collection, Canadian paintings, drawings, sculpture, European prints and drawings; paintings; British domestic silver. Catalog of collection, with 207 illustrations, published 1968.
Exhibitions: International, national and regional exhibitions, with catalogs.
Activities: Gallery tours, film programs, public lectures, loan and circulating exhibitions, recitals, studio workshop classes for adults and students.
Library: Canadian reference material; art history reference library under Department of Art History available on Campus.
Attendance: Average 70,000 annually.

KITCHENER

THE KITCHENER-WATERLOO ART GALLERY
43 Benton St, N2G 3H1. Tel: (519) 745-6671
L. H. Marsland, Pres.
Robert Ihrig, Gallery Dir.
Mrs. R. Hodgson, Gallery Secy.
Fergus Tomlin, Cur, Extension Dept.
Brad Blain, Asst, Extension Dept.
Free Tues. - Sat. 10 AM - 5 PM; Sun. 1 - 5 PM; Tues. - Fri. 7 - 9 PM. Estab. 1956 to promote the visual arts in the community; financed by city and state appropriation and membership. Ann. meeting June; mem. 550; dues $3, $8, $12.
Collections: Small collection based on Canadian works with the main emphasis on contemporary work.
Exhibitions: Monthly exhibitions with occasional gallery created exhibits.
Activities: Extension department serves Waterloo region, material available to anyone, no fees; traveling exhibitions organized and circulated; individual paintings and original objects of art lent; lending collection, 50 color reproductions, 500 Kodachromes, books; 100 active borrowers; lectures; concerts; classes for adults and children; competitions; scholarships.
Library: 400 volume library.
Publications: Annual report, monthly bulletins.
Income and Purchases: Income: $50,000; purchases $3000.
Attendance: 15,000 annual average.

KITCHENER-WATERLOO SOCIETY OF ARTISTS*
c/o Mrs. K. E. Chestney, 11 Southwick Place, Waterloo
Rev. Frank Rose, Pres.
Estab. 1931 to stimulate and encourage the development and appreciation of art in the community and to arrange and hold exhibitions annually. Ann. meeting May; mem. approx. 42; dues $3 and higher. Sponsors a scholarship for the Doon School of Fine Arts.

KLEINBURG

THE McMICHAEL CANADIAN COLLECTION
L0J 1C0. Tel: (416) 893-1121
Dr. Robert McMichael, Dir.
J. Allyn Taylor, Chmn. Board Trustees
R. E. Dowsett, V.Chmn. Board Trustees
Diane McQueen, Corresp. Secy.
Open Tues. - Sun. Noon - 5:30 PM. Mornings reserved for school tours by appointment; free admis. and parking. Estab. 1965 to give a better understanding of Canadian art to people of all ages.
Collections: Permanently hanging collection of Canadian Group of Seven works and their contemporaries (Emily Carr, Tom Thomson, David Milne, etc), as well as Canadian Eskimo and Indian art; continually being enlarged through gifts and purchases. The McMichael Canadian Collection is wholly owned by the Province of Ontario.
Library: Mainly archival material.
Publications: The McMichael Canadian Collection book available in The Gallery Shop.
Attendance: 184,690.

LONDON

LONDON ART GALLERY ASSOCIATION
c/o London Public Library and Art Museum, 305 Queens Ave, 14.
George Bowie, Pres.
Nancy Postian, Secy.
Janet Delaney, Exec. Dir.
Open Mon. - Fri. 9 - 12 AM. Inc. 1964, estab. 1969, generally to assist and promote the activities of the Art Gallery in the community. Ann. meeting May; mem. 1018; dues student $2, single $7, family $10, sponsor $15, patron $40, benefactor $90, founder $490, charter donor $990.
Activities: Sponsors lectures and special events, raises funds for acquisitions, promotes educational activities, provides art tours, to build a separate art gallery for London.
Income and Purchases: Income first year approx. $16,000; $4000 donated to Art Gallery's purchase fund.

LONDON PUBLIC LIBRARY AND ART MUSEUM
305 Queens Ave, N6B 1X2. Tel: (519) 432-7166
E. S. Beacock, Dr. & Secy-Treas.
Mrs. Paddy O'Brien, Cur. Art Museum
Miss J. Kelly, Asst. Cur. Registration
Donald DeGrow, Asst. Cur. Educ. & Extension
Anne Garwood Roney, Asst. Cur. Installations
Kate McCabe, Docent Supvr.
Daniela Presetnik, Extension Officer
Valerie Greenfield, Communications Officer
Free Mon. - Fri. 9 AM - 9 PM; Sat. 9 AM - 5 PM; Sun. & public &
civic holidays, gallery only 2 - 5 PM. Present building opened in
1940, additions 1951, 1967; receives municipal appropriation.
London Art Gallery Association and Women's Committee member-
ships total approx. 1000; dues (LAGA) $2-$10.
 Collections: Canadian †painting, †sculpture and †graphics; some
British paintings.
 Exhibitions: Average of 35 per year; two branch galleries, 12
each per year; One annual open juried exhibition, Annual Western
Ontario Exhibition; purchase awards approx. $3000 annually.
 Activities: Children's classes, docent training, lectures, films,
demonstrations, special events; Gallery Shop; two picture rental
services; tours, lecture series, high school art classes; extension
services.
 Library: Special reference, approx. 200 †books.
 Income and Purchases: Income, Library and art gallery, approx.
$2,160,000; purchases approx. $8000.
 Attendance: (1970-72) average 80,000 per year.

McINTOSH MEMORIAL ART GALLERY
University of Western Ontario, N6A 3V1. Tel: (519) 679-3181 or
6027
Maurice Stubbs, Univ. Art Cur.
Alexandre Haldare, Asst. Cur.
Free daily Noon - 5 PM; Wed. 7 - 10 PM. Estab. 1942 to encourage
the support of the arts in the community and on campus. Friends of
the McIntosh Gallery, 60; dues student $5, individual or family $15,
supporting $50, patron $100, life $500.
 Collections: Works in various media dating from the early 19th
century to the present; emphasis is on 20th century Canadian
graphics and painting.
 Exhibitions: Approximately 12 per year, no annual or award
shows.
 Activities: Lectures and/or films and/or demonstrations to supplement each exhibit; gallery talks.
 Library: Small collection of reference books for staff and
museology students.
 Publications: Catalog/checklist per exhibit; news bulletins for
major events, plus listing of events every two months.
 Purchases: Approx. $3500 allotted by McIntosh Committee per
annum.
 Attendance: Approx. 17,000.

NIAGARA FALLS

OAK HALL (Human History Museum)
c/o The Niagara Parks Commission, Box 150, L2E 6T2.
Tel: (416) 356-2241
Open daily mid-June - Labor Day 11 AM - 7 PM; admis. adults (over
12 years) 50¢, children (12 and under) free. Estab. 1959, the re-
stored home of late Sir Harry Oakes; financed by Niagara Parks
Commission, a self-sustaining provincial agency.
 Collections: Early Niagara prints and oils on display in gallery.
 Publications: Historical Niagara Frontier Revisited, annual pro-
motional brochure.

OAKVILLE

OAKVILLE PUBLIC LIBRARY AND CENTENNIAL GALLERY
120 Navy St, L6J 2Z4. Tel: (416) 845-3405
R. B. Moses, Chief Librn.
Esther Demeny, Gallery Cur.
Free Mon. - Fri. 10 AM - 9 PM; Sat. 10 AM - 5 PM; Sun. 2 - 5 PM.
Estab. 1967 for a greater awareness of the diversified role of the
gallery in the total visual arts scene; financed by city and provincial
appropriations. Fine Arts Gallery has 2000 sq. ft. area, with 150
running feet of wallspace and 20 x 18 sculpture court.
 Collections: †Original paintings, drawings, prints and sculpture;
†native Canadian arts; also 41 pieces of sculpture replicas.
 Exhibitions: 67 exhibitions since 1970, including 3-4 major ones
yearly.
 Activities: Extension department serves Oakville and area; material available to general public; fees are 1% of works value; material lent, original art works and sculpture replicas; traveling exhibitions organized and circulated; individual paintings and original
objects of art lent; lending collection, 63 originals, 41 replicas;

photograph collection of 34 prints; lectures open to the public; visit-
ing lecturers and tours varies; constant gallery talks.
 Publications: Happenings, monthly; 2 - 3 exhibition catalogs
yearly.
 Income: $40,000 - $50,000 plus residence within library complex.
 Attendance: 25,035.

TARAS H. SHEVCHENKO MUSEUM AND MEMORIAL PARK
FOUNDATION
1363 Dundas St. W. Tel: (416) 827-2651
Toronto Office: 42 Roncesvalles Ave, Toronto M6R 2K3.
 Tel: (416) 535-1063
Peter Prokop, Pres. & Cur.
Stanley Dobrowolsky, Secy.
Open Sun, July & Aug. Noon - 5 PM; others by appointment; admis.
by voluntary donation. Estab. 1952, a 16.5 acre park, complete with
monument and museum opened to the public as a symbol of the unity
and brother of Ukrainian Canadians with Canadians of all national
origins; financed by donations.
 Collections: Reproductions and copies in oil and watercolor of
Taras H. Shevchenko's own paintings and sketches and also paintings
done by other artists and authors representing some aspects of T. H.
Shevchenko's life. Display and handicrafts - ceramics from
Ukraine, handicrafts made by Ukrainian Canadians and exhibits of
Ukrainian pioneer life in Western Canada.

OSHAWA

THE ROBERT McLAUGHLIN GALLERY*
Civic Centre. Tel: (416) 576-3000
E. F. Bastedo, Pres.
Joan Murray, Dir.
Peggy Dancey, Exec. Secy.
John Pool, Treas.
E. Samuel, V.Pres.
Kate McCabe, Educ. & Exten. Officer
Chesley Taylor, Gallery Asst.
Free Mon. - Fri. 12 AM - 5 PM & 7 - 9 PM; Sat. 12 AM - 5 PM;
Sun. 2 - 5 PM. Estab. May 1967; The Robert McLaughlin Gallery
offers a programme of exhibitions and lectures to Oshawa and Dis-
trict, to offer the highest quality of professional exhibitions, lec-
tures, films, etc; City appropriation and membership. Ann. meet-
ing March of each year, monthly meetings end of each month; mem.
approx. 500; dues family $15, student $2.50, adult $10, benefactor
$100.
 Collections: More than 300 works: Alexandra Luke collection
(one of †Painters Eleven), Fenwick Lansdowne Bird Charts, Douglas
M. Duncan collection; also many other individual donations.
 Exhibitions: The Gallery changes exhibitions every three weeks.
Some exhibitions come from the Art Gallery of Ontario, National
Gallery of Canada; also many arranged and organized by the Robert
McLaughlin Gallery.
 Activities: Special Education Department starting Sept. 1970;
Extension Department serving Oshawa and District since Jan. 1970,
paintings, prints, sculpture, etc, available to schools, clubs, City
buildings, etc. for very minimal fee on a trial basis. Lectures open
to public; concerts, classes for adults and children. Book shop.
 Publications: Seasonal bulletin and monthly bulletin.
 Attendance: Average 60,000 per year.

OTTAWA

LAURIER HOUSE
335 Laurier Ave. E. Tel: (613) 992-8142
Valerie Proctor, Cur.
Free Tues. - Sat. 10 AM - 5 PM; Sun. 2 - 5 PM; July & Aug, Tues. -
Sat. 10 AM - 9 PM, Sun. 2 - 9 PM; cl. Mon. Estab. 1951; historical
site, the former home of two Canadian Prime Ministers, Sir Wilfrid
Laurier and Mr. Mackenzie King; contains the study of a third Prime
Minister, Lester B. Pearson.

✠THE NATIONAL GALLERY OF CANADA
Elgin St, K1A 0M8. Tel: (613) 992-4636
Jean Sutherland Boggs, Dir.
G. V. Shepherd, Asst. Dir. & Cur. European Art
R. H. Hubbard, Chief Cur.
J-R Ostiguy, Research Cur. Canadian Art
P. Theberge, Curatorial Adminr. & Cur. Contemporary Canadian Art
D. Reid, Cur. Post-Confederation Canadian Art
C. C. Hill, Asst. Cur. Post-Confederation Canadian Art
J. Trudel, Cur. Early Canadian Art
J. R. Porter, Asst. Cur. Early Canadian Art
Miss R. L. Tovell, Asst. Cur. Canadian Prints & Drawings
J. W. Borcoman, Cur. Photography
A. McNairn, Asst. Research Cur.
Miss L. D'Argencourt, Asst. Research Cur.
M. Laskin, Jr, Research Cur. European Art

B. Smith, Cur. Contemporary Art
Mrs. M. C. Taylor, Cur. Drawings
D. Druick, Cur. Prints
M. Ruggles, Head, Restoration & Conservation Laboratory
Dorothea Coates, Registrar
Mrs. M. N. Balke, Librn.
Helen Clark, Photograph Librn.
R. Graburn, Head, National Prog.
Miss J. Smiter, Head, Pub. Relations & Information Services
M. Pantazzi, Chief Educ. Services
L. D. Allatt, Bldg. Coordinator
Nancy Clark, Ottawa Exhibitions
P. Smith, Head Publications
Mrs. A. Armstrong, Chief, Reproduction & Rights
Free 10 AM - 6 PM; Tues. & Thurs. 10 AM - 10 PM; Sun. & holidays 2 - 6 PM; cl. Christmas Day; cl. Mon. Oct. - Apr. Founded 1880 under the patronage of the Governor-General, the Marquess of Lorne, and his wife the Princess Louise; first inc. 1913 and charged with the development and care of the National Collections and the promotion of art in Canada. Since Apr. 1, 1968 the Gallery has been a part of the National Museums of Canada reporting to a Board of Trustees established for the Corporation. The Gallery is housed (since 1960) in the Lorne Building, with 8 floors devoted to exhibition space, auditorium, workshops, offices, laboratories and cafeteria.

Collections: Canadian painting, sculpture and decorative arts from 17th to 20th century; European painting and sculpture from 14th to 20th century; contemporary American art; prints and drawings of principal schools; photography; diploma works of the Royal Canadian Academy of the Arts. Among the principal acquisitions 1970-1972 were European painting, sculpture including Klimt (Hope I), Mondrian (Composition 1936-42) Bartolomeo Veneto (Portrait of a Young Woman), Il Morazzone (The Raising of Lazarus), Benson (Portrait of a Man), de Hondecoeter (Landscape with a Musical Gathering), Carpeau (Bacchante), Dalou (Seated Woman Reading) and a group of medieval works. Poussin (Martyrdom of St. Erasmus); Puget (Bust of a King); Patel (Landscape with Rest of the Flight to Egypt); Poelanburgh (Clorinda Savug Alinda & Safronia from the Stake); Bernini (Bust Urban VIII); American painting and sculpture including Noland (Untitled), Serra (Davidson Gate), Gorky (Charred Beloved II), Marden (3 Deliverate Greys for Jasper Johns), Graves (Variability and Repetition of Variable Forms). Prints and drawings by Lewis Sutherland, Bartlett, Oldenburg, Picasso, Rouault, Rauschengerg, Lichtenstein, Warnol, Joh, Gainsborough, Cezanne, Bandinelli, Hamilton, Hayter. Canadian works by Patterson, Snow, Wieland, Pilot, Borduas, Fitzgerald, Milne, Tousignant, Walker, Breeze, Peel, Levine, Vaillancourt, Urquhart, Zelenak, Lafrance, and Sasseville.

Exhibitions: Principal exhibitions 1970-75 include The Group of Seven; Two Painters of Quebec, Antoine Plamondon, 1802-1895, Theophile Hamel, 1817-1870; Tiepolo Drawings from Stuttfart and Würzburg; Gift from the Douglas M. Duncan Collection and the Milne-Duncan Bequest: True Patriot Love; Erich Heckel; Progress in Conservation; Paul Kane; Art and the Courts; Fontainebleau, Art in France, 1528-1610; Boucherville/Montreal/Toronto/London 1973; Robert Harris 1849-1919; People's Art: Naive Art in Canada; Ozias Leduc: Silver in New France; Canadian Paintings in the Thirties; The Calvary at Oka; High Victorian Design; Donald Judd.

Exhibitions sent abroad: Canada 4 + 3 to Paris; Canadian Watercolours of the 19th Century to Paris and London; Eight Artists from Canada to Tel-Aviv; participation in Venice Biennale and the Biennale de Paris; The Canadian Landscape in Painting in Peking and Shanghai.

Loan exhibitions are sent annually to all parts of Canada, and individual loans of thousands of works of art are sent to other museums and institutions for exhibitions and for extended loan.

Activities: Lectures, films, gallery talks and guided tours at the Gallery and lecture tours throughout Canada; broadcasts and telecasts; loan collection of films on art; slides for sale; conservation; sales desk for publications, reproductions and postcards.

Library: Reference library of 44,000 volumes; pamphlet files; files on Canadian art and artists; photograph reference library.

Publications: Annual reviews; Bulletin, semi-annual; exhibition catalogs; Canadian Artists Monographs; National Programme Journals.

Attendance: 450,000.

NATIONAL MUSEUM OF MAN
Victoria Memorial Bldg.
Dr. W. E. Taylor, Jr. Dir.
Mary Ahearn, Pub. Relations
Estab. 1974. Exhibits illustrating the archaeology, ethnology and history of Canada. The Canadian Centre for Folk Culture Studies has material on Canadian and Ethnic Oral Literature, Rites of Passage, Cyclic and Calendar Feasts of the Year, Material Culture, Folk Arts and Popular Language. The Canadian War Museum contains military artifacts, trophies and pictures of wars in which Canada has participated.

NATIONAL MUSEUM OF NATURAL SCIENCES*
Metcalfe and McLeod St, Victoria Memorial Building, K1A 0M8.
Dr. Louis Lemieux, Dir.
This Museum deals with the sciences of botany, mineralogy, palaeontology and zoology. The main exhibit halls of Birds, Botany, Mammals, Life Through The Ages, (Dinosaurs and other fossils) The Earth, and two Halls of Animal Life are presented in the Victoria Memorial Museum Building. Large research collections are held in various buildings in Ottawa and are available to qualified persons for research projects. The National Herbarium Collection contains over 357,000 sheets of vascular plants and some 126,000 sheets of mosses and liverworts, 38,000 lichens, and 14,000 algae. The National Zoological Collections contain more than 2,500,000 specimens of molluscs, 635,000 crustaceans, 662,000 other invertebrates, 214,000 fishes, 70,000 reptiles and amphibians, 62,500 birds, and 41,000 mammals. The National Collection of Display Minerals includes an estimated 66,000 mineral specimens; The Palaeontological Collections include 8,000 fossil specimens. The Canadian Oceanographic Identification Centre was organized in 1967 and now has some 500 reference species. The Zooarchaeology Research Unit, established in 1972, is designed to assist in the identification and interpretation of animal remains found in archaeological investigations.

The Interpretation and Extension Division, also established in 1972, is engaged in a new program of travelling exhibits, museumobiles and loans of exhibit materials to other museums. That Division also provides a general information service to the public in matters pertaining to the natural sciences.

NATIONAL MUSEUM OF SCIENCE AND TECHNOLOGY
1867 St. Laurent Blvd. at Russell Rd, K1A 0M8.
Tel: (613) 998-9520 (for Museum Guide), 998-9520 or 4566 (for General Information)
Dr. D. M. Baird, Dir.
R. W. Bradford, Cur. Aviation & Space
T. A. Brown, Cur. Agricultural Technology
R. J. Corby, Cur. Industrial Technology
E. A. DeCoste, Cur. Communications Technology
J. J. Dost, Cur. General Technology
Tours mid-Sept. - mid-May 9 AM - 9 PM, cl. Mon, guides available for general or topic-oriented visit; mid-May - mid-Sept. open daily 9 AM - 9 PM.

Participation and test of skills is part of the learning experience at this museum which exhibits Canada's role in Science and Technology with locomotives and trains, vintage automobiles, carriages and sleighs, aircraft, agricultural implements, a physics hall, communications, marine transport, timepieces, meteorology and astronomy.

The National Aeronautical Collection, housed mainly at Rockcliffe Airport, has more than 90 historic aircraft demonstrating the history of aviation with especial interest on the importance of the flying machine in the development and exploration of Canada and the protection of our lifestyle during two world wars, dating back to the Silver Dart—the first powered heavier-than-air flight in Canada.

Library: 10,000 volume library with especial strength on a retrospective collection of Canadian aviation.

Attendance: Approx. 3/4 million visitors a year.

NATIONAL MUSEUMS OF CANADA
Century Building, 360 Lisgar St, K1A 0M8. Tel: (613) 995-9832
Bernard Ostry, Secy-Gen.
Miss J. Boggs, Dir. National Gallery of Canada
Dr. W. E. Taylor, Jr, Dir. National Museum of Man
L. F. Murray, Cur. Canadian War Museum
Dr. Louis Lemieux, Dir. National Museum of Natural Sciences
Dr. D. M. Baird, Dir. National Museum of Science & Technology
The Museums are open daily, winter 9 AM - 5 PM; summer 9 AM - 9 PM. The Museums originated in the Geological Survey of Canada (founded 1843); the name National Museum of Canada was applied in 1927; changed to National Museums of Canada by House of Commons legislation in 1968. The individual museums under the National Museums of Canada (each reported separately) are as follows:

National Gallery of Canada
Elgin and Slater Sts. Tel: (613) 992-4636

National Museum of Man
Victoria Memorial Building. Tel: (613) 992-3497
Canadian War Museum
330 Sussex Dr. Tel: (613) 992-2774

National Museum of Natural Sciences
Victoria Memorial Building. Tel: (613) 996-3102

National Museum of Science and Technology
St. Laurent Blvd. and Smyth Rd. Tel: (613) 998-4566
National Aeronautical Collection
Rockcliffe Air Force Base. Tel: (613) 993-2010

The purposes of the corporation are to demonstrate the products of nature and the works of man, with special but not exclusive reference to Canada, so as to promote interest therein throughout Canada and to disseminate knowledge thereof. (The Corporation was created by an Act of Parliament in 1968.)

Activities: Lectures for adults and children; conducted tours for schools; talks and lectures; each museum maintains a sales desk that sells prints, books, bulletins, recordings, model animals, artifacts, postcards, slides, etc; traveling exhibitions.

Library: The library contains 80,000 volumes, with periodicals, books, microforms, and manuscripts about related fields to all the disciplines of the Museums. Miss A. E. Dawe, Librarian.

Purchases (1974-75) $2,385,124.

Attendance: Exceeds $2\frac{1}{2}$ million annually for all museums.

PUBLIC ARCHIVES OF CANADA
395 Wellington St, K1A 0N3. Tel: (613) 992-3047
Dr. W. I. Smith, Dominion Archivist
Free 8:30 AM - 4:45 PM. Estab. 1872; collection of pictures began in 1906; supported by appropriation from the Government of Canada.

Collections: Manuscripts, maps, books, paintings, drawings, prints, photographs, slides, films, machine readable archives.

Exhibitions: Documents, prints, pictures, and maps.

Publications: Catalogue of Pictures; Image of Canada; Braves and Buffalo: Plains Indian in 1837; The W. H. Coverdale Collection of Canadiana; A. J. Miller's West—The Plains Indian - 1837; Quebec and its Environs; Western Odyssey 1881—With the Marquis of Lorne; Alfred Jacob Miller.

ST. CATHARINES

✤THE ST. CATHARINES AND DISTRICT ARTS COUNCIL
109 St. Paul Crescent, L2S 1M7. Tel: (416) 684-2925
Dr. D. Steele, Pres.
Arnel Pattemore, Secy.
A. Peter Harris, Dir.
Mrs. Joanne Rolfe, Secy. to the Dir.
Open Tues. - Sun. 1 - 5 PM. Estab. 1956; Art Centre activities, to stimulate greater public interest in all phases of cultural activity, provide increased opportunity for public enjoyment of drama, music, painting and the allied arts, and to support encourage and endeavour to effect the establishment of a civic centre to provide auditorium facilities, space for suitable display and housing of fine art, and headquarters for all affiliated organizations interested in arts and letters; financed by city and provincial grants. 4 galleries display monthly exhibitions of all types as well as concerts and recitals, etc. Ann. meeting Sept; mem. 900; dues single $7, family $10, sustaining $40, patron $500, life $300, Founder $1000.

Collections: Collections of contemporary Canadian art.

Activities: Traveling exhibitions organized and circulated; individual paintings lent to schools; original objects of art lent; 1000 lantern slides in lending collection; lectures open to public, 6 visiting lecturers per year; weekly gallery talks or tours; concerts, drama programs, classes for adults and children; competitions. Book shop.

Library: 100 volumes for reference only; Art Rental Gallery, manned by Women's Committee of St. Catherines and District Arts Council; rent only to individual members and member organizations.

Publications: Bulletin and advance invitations, monthly.

Income and Purchases: Income $42,000; purchases $3000.

Attendance: 35,000.

SARNIA

SARNIA PUBLIC LIBRARY AND ART GALLERY
N7T 2M6. Tel: (519) 337-3291
R. T. Bradley, Dir.
Free Mon. - Fri. 9 AM - 9 PM; Sat. 9 AM - 5:30 PM; Sun. Oct. - May 2 - 5 PM. A collection of Canadian paintings instituted in 1919 and administered by the Women's Conservation Art Association of Sarnia. The collection was turned over to the Sarnia Library Board in 1956 and additions are being made from time to time.

Collections: Canadian paintings; a collection of old photographs of Sarnia and Lambton County are stored in the gallery.

Exhibitions: Twelve to fifteen shows a year, either traveling from other galleries or initiated by the Sarnia Art Gallery.

Activities: Children's art classes in July and August.

Gallery Attendance: 33,320.

SIMCOE

EVA BROOK DONLY MUSEUM
109 Norfolk St. S. Tel: (519) 426-1583
William Yeager, Cur.
Kenneth S. McArthur, Managing Dir.
Open Wed. - Sun. 1:30 - 5 PM; other times by appointment; admis. 50¢ adult, 25¢ student, children under 12 free, $3 per year mem, children free if with adult, tours $5 per 35, 10¢ each additional person. Estab. 1946 to display and aid research in the history of Norfolk County; financed by endowment, city and provincial appropriations and membership. Mem. dues $3 individual, $5 family.

Collections: Large collection of important early documents and newspapers; library of local history and much genealogical data; 370 paintings of historic Norfolk by W. E. Cantelon; display of artifacts of the 19th century Norfolk County; various other artifacts and displays related to history including an emphasis on native fauna.

Exhibitions: Concerned mainly with focusing new light on some aspects of the permanent collection.

Library: Reference library; photograph collection for reference and display.

Attendance: 2800.

STRATFORD

THE GALLERY/STRATFORD
54 Romeo St. N, N5A 4S9. Tel: (519) 271-5271
Robert F. Swain, Dir.
A. J. Lawson, Pres, Stratford Art Association
Open May - Oct. Mon. - Sat. 10 AM - 8 PM, Sun. Noon - 6 PM, admis. 50¢; Nov. - Apr. Tues, Wed. & Thurs. 1 - 10 PM, Fri. 1 - 5 PM, Sat. 10 AM - 5 PM, Sun. 1 - 5 PM, cl. Mon, no admis. Estab. 1967; a nonprofit permanent establishment open to the public and administered in the public interest, for the purpose of studying, interpreting, assembling and exhibiting to the public. Ann. meeting Sept; monthly meetings; mem. 600.

Collections: Growing collection of prints and drawings, paintings, sculpture, theater designs.

Exhibitions: Average change once a month, large international exhibition June, July and August.

Activities: Art classes for adults, children and teens; school tours; art in the schools programme; docent training; art appreciation classes; travelling exhibitions organized; picture rentals; lectures and films open to public; gallery tours on demand; concerts; dramatic programmes; competitions; scholarships.

Library: Small but growing reference library.

Publications: Monthly Calendar of Events; exhibition catalogs.

Income: $130,000.

Attendance: (1973) 54,600.

SUDBURY

LAURENTIAN UNIVERSITY MUSEUM AND ARTS CENTRE
Department of Cultural Affairs, P3E 2C6.
Tel: (705) 675-1151, Exten. 497 and 498
Dr. E. J. Monahan, Pres.
Eric Woodward, Dir.
Free Tues. - Sun. from Noon. Estab. 1967 for students and community; owned and financed by the university, and supported by the Boards of Education and the Ontario Arts Council.

Collections: Canadian Heritage Foundation permanent collection; plus own purchases and donations.

Exhibitions: Ivan Wheale; Art of the Canadian Eskimo; Drawings by Michelangelo; Italian master drawings; Enore Szasz; Group of Seven; Emily Carr; Brazilian Artists; Patchwork Quilts; New Zealand Prints.

Activities: Lectures open to the public; concerts.

Publications: Communiques, monthly.

THUNDER BAY

LAKEHEAD VISUAL ARTS*
c/o Robert Boorman, Pres,
301 S. Vickers St. Tel: (807) 622-4090
Robert Boorman, Pres.
Mrs. Lorraine Campbell, Secy.
Summer Gallery open 2 - 10 PM; admis. Estab. 1952 for the promotion of the visual arts; city and state appropriations and membership. Summer Gallery open June-Sept. Meeting 1st Mon. of the month; mem. 89; dues $7.50 per person, $10 family.

Collections: Silver Collection.

Exhibitions: Spring Show every year in May.

Activities: Lectures open to the public; 6 visiting lecturers and gallery talks per year; classes for adults; competitions; scholarships.

Publications: Newsletter, bi-monthly.

Income and Purchases: Income $1500, purchases $1000.

Attendance: 6000 annual average.

TORONTO

✤ART GALLERY OF ONTARIO
Grange Park, M5T 1G4. Tel: (416) 361-0414
Marvin B. Gelber, Pres.
William J. Withrow, Dir.
Michael E. George, Secy-Treas.

Richard J. Wattenmaker, Chief Cur.
Roald Nasgaard, Cur. Contemporary Art
Jeremy Adamson, Cur. Canadian Historical Art
Margaret S. Machell, Custodian of The Grange
William C. Forsey, Dir. Educ. & Extension
Open weekdays 10 AM - 5 PM; Sun. & holidays Noon - 5 PM; Wed. & Thurs. during the season 10 AM - 10 PM. Admis. voluntary. Estab. 1900 in Grange House (1817), bequeathed by Mrs. Goldwin Smith; art gallery building adjoins. The Grange, a Georgian manor house restored and furnished in the style of the 1830s; open to the public the same hours as the gallery. Ann. meeting June; mem. 14,000; dues $15 and higher.

Collections: Representative collection from 14th century to the present day; 5,000 paintings, sculptures, watercolours, prints, drawings, miniatures, pastels and tapestries, †Canadian, †European, †American; Henry Moore Sculpture Centre, the Zacks Wing, Alan Garrow collection of 19th century illustrated English Books (200).

Exhibitions: Scultura Italiana; From Delacroix to Degas; Group of Seven; International Paintings of the '50s and '60s; Realisms '70; Hector Guimard; Jack Chambers; Hamel/Plamondon; Archipenko; Modern Tapestries; Francis Picabia; Frank Stella; Edouard Vuillard 1868-1940; The Art of Tom Thomson; Recent Vanguard Acquisitions; Art in Revolution; The True North; Flower Pieces by Robert Holmes; Contemporary Canada; The Work of Frei Otto; de Chirico by de Chirico; French Master Drawings of the 17th and 18th Centuries in North American Collections; Canadian Heritage; Ontario Society of Artists: 100 Years; French Printmakers of the 19th Century; Toronto Painting: 1953-1965; Appel's Appels; The Art of the Comic Strip; The Art of Jean Hugo; Puvis de Chavannes and the Modern Tradition; Exposure: Canadian Contemporary Photographers. Summer, changing selection from collection.

Activities: Circulating 50 exhibitions to 90 centres, including Artists with Their Work, through Province of Ontario; conducted tours; Sunday concerts; art classes for adults and children; films; panel discussions; special lectures; art demonstrations. Loan collection of 32,000 slides; 200 slides for sale; study collection of prints; Gallery Shop—books, catalogs and reproductions; Art Rental Service; assistance in museum training program.

Art Reference Library: 18,500 volumes.

Income and Purchases: Income $3,432,000; purchases $100,000.

Attendance: 425,000.

ART METROPOLE
Art Metropole Building, 241 Yonge St, M5B 1N8.
Tel: (416) 368-7787
Jorge Saia, Pres.
Michael Tims, Secy.
Robert Handforth, Dir.
Peggy Gale, Video Mgr.
Free Mon. - Sat. Noon - 6 PM. Estab. Oct, 1974, a nonprofit agency formed to promote, collect, document, archive, and distribute work by artists in nontraditional media; distribute books, recordings, film and videotapes by artists; maintain a library of artists books and videotapes; financed by federal grants and sales income.

Collections: †Videotapes by artists; publications by artists, specifically †conceptual, †fluxus, †correspondence artists.

Activities: Lend and rent videotapes by artists to institutions and individuals for a rental fee; 60 videotapes and 9 16mm motion pictures in lending collection; lectures open to public, 6 visiting lecturers per year. Book shop.

Library: Reference library, largely still uncatalogued; photograph collection for reference.

Publications: Art Metropole Catalog (lists items for sale and rent only), quarterly.

ARTS AND LETTERS CLUB *
14 Elm St, 2.
Robert Christie, Pres.
John Galilee, Secy.
Estab. 1908. Ann. meeting May; mem. 500; dues $75 and higher. Clubhouse has art library of several hundred volumes, dining room; frequent exhibitions.

GALLERY SEVENTY SIX
The Ontario College of Art
76 McCaul St, M5T 1W1. Tel: (416) 366-4977, Exten. 62
Dr. Paul D. Fleck, Pres. College
Brian Kipping, Cur.
Free Mon. - Fri. 10 AM - 5 PM; Sat. & Sun. Noon - 5 PM. Art College estab. 1876, gallery estab. c. 1970 for faculty and student exhibitions and to exhibit outside work to benefit the college; financed by the Ontario College of Art.

Collections: Small print collection.

Exhibitions: Approximately 30 exhibitions a year. Experimental Art Faculty Show; Shitbandit Exhibition; Paintings by Peter Hill; Memory Drawings - Brian Kipping; Geigy Psychotherapeutic Art

Exhibition (from mental institutions across Ontario); Lily Maley Memorial Exhibition; Napolean Brousseau; Billy Barkhouse-Skeletal Figures.

Activities: Traveling exhibitions organized and circulated; individual paintings and original objects of art lent; concerts; dramatic programs; competitions. Slide library of past exhibitions.

Publications: Invitations; small scale catalogs.

Attendance: 10,000 - 15,000.

HART HOUSE
University of Toronto, M5S 1A1
Jean Georges Lengelle, Warden
J. Schwartz, Program Advisor
Open to the public daily; Sun. 2 - 5 PM.
Estab. 1911; presented 1919 to University of Toronto as a men's union; The Deed of Gift was changed and women are now able to be members of Hart House. Since its opening, has been acquiring a collection of Canadian painting, with the co-operation of a student committee. Works of the Group of Seven and others displayed in principal rooms. Gallery for regular exhibitions. Reference library; photograph collection. Collection of paintings now numbers over 200 canvases. Art classes conducted; one lecture given on each exhibition, if possible, by the artist himself.

LYCEUM CLUB AND WOMEN'S ART ASSOCIATION OF CANADA*
23 Prince Arthur Ave, 5. Tel: (416) 922-2060
Mrs. R. T. Bogle, Pres.
Mrs. J. L. Callis, Recording Secy.
Open 9:30 AM - 4:30 PM; Sat. 10 AM - 1 PM. Estab. 1885. Ann. meeting Apr; mem. approx. 250.
Activities: Special exhibitions; drawing, painting; study groups. Awards founder's memorial scholarship to art students annually. Scholarships given to Ontario College of Art, Royal Conservatory of Music, National Ballet.

Library: Approx. 500 volumes including extensive Canadiana.

Branches in Ontario in Hamilton, Owen Sound, St. Thomas, Peterborough and Oshawa.

METROPOLITAN TORONTO CENTRAL LIBRARY
214 College St, M5T 1R3. Tel: (416) 924-9511
John T. Parkhill, Dir.
Free daily 9 AM - 9 PM; Sat. 9 AM - 5 PM; Sun. Mid-Oct. - Mid-May 1:30 - 5 PM. Estab. 1883.

John Ross Robertson Historical Collection
4400 Early Canadian prints, drawings and paintings.

Toronto and Early Canada Picture Collection
Estab. 1960. †25,000 prints, photographs, drawings and paintings.

Fine Art Section
Estab. 1960. †40,000 books, periodicals, pamphlets on fine and decorative arts, photography, costume, printing. †Circulating picture collection of 500,000 items; †private press books of 1000 items; †19th and 20th century posters, 600 items.

⚜ROYAL ONTARIO MUSEUM
100 Queen's Park, M5S 2C6. Tel: (416) 928-3691
G. D. Wotherspoon, Chmn. Board
Dr. James E. Cruise, Dir.
J. H. Harvey, Asst. Controller Operations
H. Hickl-Szabo, Cur. European Dept.
E. S. Rogers, Cur. Ethnology Dept.
A. D. Tushingham, Chief Archaeologist
Hsio-Yen Shih, Cur. Far Eastern Dept.
N. Millet, Cur. Egyptian Dept.
Neda Leipen, Cur. Greek & Roman Dept.
D. B. Webster, Cur. Canadiana Dept.
Dorothy K. Burnham, Cur. Textiles Dept.
T. C. Young, Jr, Cur. West Asian Dept.
Dorothea Hecken, Registrar
B. Leech, Assoc. Cur-in-Charge, Conservation Dept.
J. Anthony, Chief, Display Gen.
Dr. Walter M. Tovell, Head. Educ. & Extension Services
Judith Morgan, Head Librn.
Denis K. Brown, Pub. Relations Mgr.
L. Warren, Chief Photographer
Jane Court, Information Asst.
Open Mon. - Sat. 10 AM - 5 PM; Sun. 1 - 9 PM. (Canadiana Building 1 - 5 PM); admis. 50¢ adults; Sigmund Samuel Canadiana Building, 14 Queen's Park Crescent W, 5, free. Estab. 1912 as the Provincial Museum. Mem. 4500; dues $25 - $5000.

Collections: The outstanding features are the world-famous Chinese collections and the Lord Lee of Fareham collection of medieval and Renaissance objets d'art; also extensive collections of American Indian and world ethnological material; pre-historic Greek and Roman art and archaeology; European Medieval, Renaissance and post-Renaissance art; Egyptian and Western Asian art and archaeology; Harry Wearne collection of printed and painted textiles; early Ontario weaving; Japanese and Indian art; French-Canadian collection; Sigmund Samuel Canadiana collection; paintings; books; maps, house in a separate building at 14 Queen's Park Crescent, West.

Activities: Special exhibitions; research facilities; archaeological and ethnological field work in Canada and overseas; courses for Ontario schools and universities; adult courses; lectures and film showings; maintains reference library and Far East library.

Publications: Rotunda, quarterly.

Attendance: (1974) 1,116,822.

TORONTO SPINNERS AND WEAVERS*
c/o Mrs. E. Forrest, 280 Bessborough Dr.
Estab. 1939. Ann. meeting May. Participates in exhibitions of Canadian Guild of Crafts.

WATERLOO

ART GALLERY, UNIVERSITY OF WATERLOO
N2L 3G1. Tel: (519) 885-1211 Exten. 2493
Marlene Bryan, Admin.
Free Mon. - Fri. 9 AM - 4 PM; also open Sun. 2 - 5 PM. during fall and winter terms. Estab. 1961 to provide a series of monthly traveling exhibitions, related programmes such as seminars, lectures, films, concerts and a permanent collection; financed by university administrative funds.

Collections: Permanent collection mostly contemporary Canadian art plus international works of art donated by twenty embassies.

Exhibitions: 61 exhibitions since 1970.

Activities: Lectures open to the public; concerts.

Publications: Brochure is published for each exhibition, approx. 10-12 yearly.

Attendance: 50,000 annual average.

WINDSOR

THE ART GALLERY OF WINDSOR
445 Riverside Dr. W, N9A 6T8. Tel: (519) 258-7111
R. A. Goodwin, Pres.
Kenneth Saltmarche, Dir.
E. D. Fraser, Jr, Cur.
Megan Bice, Educ. Cur.
Kenneth Ferguson, Business Mgr.
Free Tues, Thurs, Fri. & Sat. 10 AM - 6 PM; Wed. 10 AM - 10 PM; Sun. 1 - 5 PM; cl. Mon. and statutory holidays. Gallery estab. 1943, inc. 1944. Ann. meeting Mar; mem. 2500; dues $10 and up.

Collections: Over 1200 paintings, graphics, sculpture, Eskimo prints and carvings emphasizing the arts of Canada from the 18th century to the present.

Exhibitions: Annual exhibition of the work of artists of the Southwestern Ontario region; Art for All, annual collector's exhibition and sale brings together works of the 19th and 20th century from across Canada.

Activities: Visual and performing arts are presented in lectures, demonstrations, concerts held Friday mornings, Wednesday evenings and Sunday afternoons weekly from September through May. Special program held in cooperating with local Boards of Education involves tours conducted by volunteer docents for over 7000 children annually; Art in The Park, a two-day outdoor festival of the arts held at Willistead Park is sponsored by the Gallery Guild and features work of 200 artists and craftsmen, free musical presentations, demonstrations, etc. The Gallery Guild also operates a picture rental and sales gallery open to the public 30 hours weekly.

The Uncommon Market, operated by the Women's Committee, features Canadian and other fine crafts, books, prints and other publications, Eskimo carvings. Open during all gallery open hours.

Attendance: (1974-75) 120,000.

WOODSTOCK

WOODSTOCK PUBLIC LIBRARY AND ART GALLERY
445 Hunter St, N4S 4G7. Tel: (519) 539-6761
Alexandra Prytulak, Chmn. of Library Board
Lillie Telfer, Cur. of Art Gallery
Free Mon, Wed, Thurs. & Fri. Noon - 8 PM; Tues. Noon - 9 PM; Sat. 10 AM - 6 PM. Estab. 1966 to bring art to the people; financed by city and provincial appropriations. Two galleries, picture loan collection. Mem. 300.

Collections: Small Canadian collection.

Exhibitions: Change every three weeks.

Activities: Tours of exhibitions; lectures open to the public; concerts; films; classes for adults and children; competitions.

Library: Record lending library; audiovisual department.

Gallery Attendance: 23,000.

PRINCE EDWARD ISLAND

CHARLOTTETOWN

CONFEDERATION CENTRE ART GALLERY AND MUSEUM
P.O. Box 848, C1A 7L9. Tel: (902) 892-2464
Dr. S. A. MacDonald, Pres.
Dr. L. I. Duffy, Secy.
Dr. Moncrieff Williamson, Dir.
Janet MacGregor, Personal Asst. & Secy.
Mark Holton, Cur.
Judy MacDonald, Registrar
Open daily 10 AM - 5 PM; Sun. 2 - 5 PM; cl. Mon; July-Aug. daily 10 AM - 9 PM; admis. 25¢, mem, students and children free. Estab. 1964 as a national collection devoted to Canadian art and fine crafts; financed by federal, provincial, city and the private sector. Four major display areas, classrooms and workshops. Mem. 400; dues $5 individual, $10 family.

Collections: Robert Harris paintings and drawings; †Canadian art early and contemporary; †Canadian fine crafts.

Exhibitions: Average thirty exhibitions a year from our own and circulating collections; special exhibitions each July and August to coincide with our summer festival.

Activities: Educational department conducts art classes for ages 5-18, also creative drama and contemporary dance; student teachers art courses in conjunction with the University of Prince Edward Island; extension department serves province; material available to schools, service clubs and groups; fees by arrangement; materials lent, paintings, audio visual films, film strips and slides; traveling exhibitions organized and circulated; individual paintings and original objects of art lent; lending collection, 7000 Kodachromes, 12 motion pictures and 50 film strips; number of items lent varies with the number of active borrowers; junior museum; lectures open to the public; various visiting lecturers per year; tours by request; concerts; dramatic programs; classes for children; scholarships.

Library: 1547 volumes for reference; reference and loan photograph collection of 200 prints.

Publications: Exhibition catalogues when required.

Attendance: 100,000 annual average.

QUEBEC

ASSOCIATION DES GRAVEURS DU QUÉBEC*
(Association of Engravers of Quebec)
3684 St-Laurent, Montreal. Tel: (514) 844-7609
Gerard Tremblay, Pres.
Marc Beaulé, Secy.
Estab. 1970 to promote etching and engraving and diffuse it; financed by provincial subvention. Ann. meeting November 30; mem. 100; dues $10.

Exhibitions: Salon des Metiers D'Art, 1971 & 1972; Museum of Fine Arts, 1972.

Activities: Traveling exhibitions organized and circulated; photograph collection for lending and reference; competitions.

Publications: Catalogue.

Income: Approx. $3000.

CHATEAU DE RAMEZAY*
Antiquarian and Numismatic Society of Montreal
290 Notre-Dame St. E, Montreal, 127. Tel: (514) 861-3708
John D. King, Cur.
Estab. 1895 in residence (1705) of Claude de Ramezay, governor of Montreal.

Collections: Early Canadian portraits; woodcarving; handicrafts; furniture; numismatic collection.

Income: Approx. $25,000.

Attendance: Approx. 40,000.

GUILDE CANADIANNE DES METIERS D'ART, QUEBEC
(Canadian Guild of Crafts, Quebec)
2025 Peel St, Montreal H3A 1T6. Tel: (514) 849-6091
Ann. meeting Apr; dues $15 and higher.

Exhibitions: Works by professional craftsmen and artists from Canada; group and one-man shows.

Collections: Permanent collection of Eskimo and Indian arts and crafts.

Library: Reference library.

Activities: Instruction in weaving, on-loom and off-loom, macrame, decoupage, design for wall hangings and silversmithing.

LA SOCIETE DES DECORATEURS-ENSEMBLIERS DU QUEBEC
(Interior Decorators' Society of Quebec)
Studio G, 451 St-Sulpice St, Montreal. Tel: (514) 878-1113
Anselme Lapointe, Pres.
Ginette Levesque, V.Pres.
Rene Studler, 2nd V.Pres.

Marie Jose Ratelle, Secy.
Real Chevalier, Treas.
Open 9 AM - 5 PM. Estab. 1935 as a non-profit professional
association; financed by membership. Ann. meeting Jan; mem.
285; dues $125.
  Exhibitions: Travelling Exhibit in the Province of Quebec.
  Activities: Education Committee to improve the level of teaching
in interior design; lectures for members only.
  Publications: News Bulletin, 10 per year.
  Income: $30,000.

ORDER OF ARCHITECTS OF QUEBEC
  1825 Dorchester Blvd. W, Montreal H3H 1R4.
  Tel: (514) 937-6168
Paul-Andre Tetreault, Pres.
Antoine Ghattas, Secy.
Open to the public 9 AM - 5 PM. Estab. 1890. Ann. meeting May;
mem. 1303; dues $275.
  Library: Reference library of documentary and architectural
books.
  Publications: Register.

SOCIETE DES ARTISTES PROFESSIONNELS DU QUEBEC*
(Society of Professional Artists of Quebec)
  7575 Milan Brass, Montreal. Tel: (514) 656-1070
Reynald Piché, Pres.
Julien Patenaude, Secy.
Serge Lemoyne, Treas.
Mrs. Maurice Demers, V.Pres.
Andre Fournelle, V.Pres.
Claude Gosselin, Coordinator
Free, 9:30 AM - 5:30 PM. Estab. 1966 in defense of the artists in
visual arts; promotion of members; consultants in the establishment
of new policies in arts; financed by city and state appropriations
and membership. Experimental gallery. Ann. meeting 1st Jan;
mem. 200; dues $15.
  Activities: Documentation Center, possibility of lectures and
films in the gallery; photograph collection of 2000 slides for lending
and reference; lectures open to the public; concerts; dramatic
programs.

ARVIDA

LE COMITE DES ARTS D'ARVIDA
  C. P. 53, G7S 4K6.
Mrs. E. L. Lavoie, Pres.
Mrs. Claire Freve, Secy.
Free weekdays 9 AM - 5 PM & 7 - 10 PM; weekends 2 - 5 PM &
7 - 10 PM. Estab. 1942 to provide exhibitions in the entry of the
City Hall, Arvida; financed by membership. Ann. meeting Sept;
mem. 200; dues $1.
  Exhibitions: Albert Rousseau, Vladimir Horik, Andree Boileau,
Jerome Legare, Lucienne Langevin, J. P. Lapointe, Jean Laforge,
JeanPaul Landry, Vladimir Smirnoff, Leopold Tremble, B. J.
Zubrzycki, plus others.

DORVAL

DORVAL CULTURAL CENTRE
  1401 Lakeshore Dr, H9S 2E5. Tel: (514) 636-4043
Louise B. Rivet, Cultural Agent
Danyelle Brodeur, Animator
Offices open 9 AM - 9 PM; Gallery open 2 - 9 PM. Estab. 1967
to promote culture and art; financed by city and province appro-
priation.
  Exhibitions: Eskimo Art, Paintings (Local and International
Artists), Tapestries, Alluchromies, Prints, Photography, Local
Handicrafts, Sculptures, Collages, Fleche, Poetry.
  Activities: Concerts (indoor and outdoor), theatre play, courses
for adults and children, film presentation and discussion, classical
ballet and jazz ballet show.

JOLIETTE

LE MUSEE D'ART DE JOLIETTE
  455 Blvd. Base-de-Joc, J6E 5P3.
Father Wilfrid Corbeil, Pres.
J. A. Desormiers, Secy./Treas. of the City of Joliette
Hon. Justice Jacques Dugas, V.Pres.
Serge Joyal, Member of Parliament for Maisonneuve-Rosemont
Free to public. Estab. 1961 for educational purposes; made public
1973; financed by city and state appropriations and membership.
Mem. 25.
  Collections: Sculptures from the Middle-Ages to the Renaissance;
paintings from 16th, 17th, 18th and 19th centuries; modern collection
of Canadian paintings.

MONTREAL

✣BIBLIOTHEQUE*
  L'Universite du Quebec, 1180 Rue de Bleury, 111.

GALERIE D'ART KEBEC
  College de Saint-Laurent, 625, Blvd Sainte-Croix, H4L 3X7.
  Tel: (514) 747-6521 Exten. 314
Gerard Lavalle, Dir. & Cur.
Free Sept. - May, Mon. - Fri. 10 AM - 4 PM. Estab. 1962 as
Free, Sept. - May, Mon. - Fri. 10 AM - 4 PM. Estab. 1962 as
educational; French Canadian art; ancient and modern permanent
collections and periodical exhibitions; state appropriations.
  Collections: †Painting; †tools; traditional arts of French
Canada from 17th-19th century; †furniture; †sculpture; †wood
carving; †silver; †textiles; †ceramics; †metal work; †artifacts;
Indian artifacts, †costumes, †ceramics, †tools.
  Activities: Lectures; guided tours; gallery talks; photograph
collection of 2000 prints for reference.
  Publications: Images Taillées du Québec (album).

McGILL UNIVERSITY MUSEUMS
Peter Redpath Museum
  On the Campus. Tel: (514) 392-5994
Prof. John B. Lewis, Dir.
Prof. Robert L. Carroll, Cur. Vertebrate Paleontology
Prof. Henry M. Reiswig, Invertebrate Zoology
Vincent Conde, Cur. Invertebrate Zoology, Malacology
Louise S. Stevenson, Cur. Geology
Prof. Delphine MacLellan, Hon. Cur. Marine Sciences Collection
Prof. Bruce G. Trigger, Hon. Cur. Anthropology
Cl. to the general public. Estab. 1882. The collections (Geology,
Mineralogy, Vertebrate Paleontology, Vertebrate and Invertebrate
Zoology, and Anthropology) art primarily designed to serve the
faculty and students of the University.

McCord Museum
  690 Sherbrooke St. W, H3A 1E9. Tel: (514) 392-4778
Harriet C. Campbell, Interim Dir.
Nancy J. Dunbar, Cur. of Collections
Cynthia B. Eberts, Cur. of Costume
Stanley G. Triggs, Cur. of Photography
Clifford Williamson, Designer
Open Fri, Sat. & Sun. 11 AM - 6 PM; research by appointment.
Estab. 1919, affiliated with McGill University and the Montreal
Museum of Fine Arts. Canadian history and prehistory.

✣THE MONTREAL MUSEUM OF FINE ARTS
  3400 Ave. du Musee, H3G 1K3.
  Tel: (514) 285-1600
Dr. Sean B. Murphy, Pres.
David Giles Carter, Dir.
Léo Rosshandler, Deputy Dir.
John M. Wynn, CA, Deputy Dir. for Bus. Admin.
Ruth Jackson, Registrar & Cur. Decorative Arts
Dr. Myra Nan Rosenfeld, Research Cur.
Edith Archambault, Assoc. Cur. Educ.
Luis de Moura Sobral, Assoc. Cur. Research, Prints and Drawings
Simon Laflamme, Assoc. Cur. Educ.
Germain Lefebvre, Assoc. Cur. Canadian Art
Louise Vernier, Assoc. Cur. Educational Programming
Janet Brooke, Asst. Cur. Western Sculpture
Claudette Hould, Asst. Cur. 19th Century Painting
A. L. Maranzi, Conservator
Richard Halliday, Dean, School of Art & Design, Art Centre
Miss Juanita Toupin, Librn.
The Museum is now closed for expansion until May 1976. Estab.
1860 for exhibition of paintings; museum estab. 1916. Ann. meeting
Sept; mem. 6000; dues $15 and higher.
  Collections: †Paintings, including French 19th century, Spanish,
Dutch, British, Canadian and other schools; †European decorative
arts; †textiles; Harry A. Norton collection of ancient glass; †Chinese,
Near Eastern, Peruvian and primitive art.
  Exhibitions: Special exhibitions.
  Activities: Classes for adults and children; guided tours; lec-
tures; gallery talks; film programmes. Maintains School of Art and
Design (see Canadian Schools).
  Library: Reference only; 22,700 volumes fine and applied arts;
13,000 exhibition catalogues; 19,000 art sales catalogues.
  Publications: M, a quarterly review; Handbook to the Collection
(1960); Catalogue of Paintings (1960); Guide (1976).
  Attendance: 275,000.

✣MUSEE D'ART CONTEMPORAIN
  Cité du Havre, 103. Tel: (514) 873-2878/79
Branch of the Ministry of Cultural Affairs of Quebec
Fernande Saint-Martin, Dir.

Alain Parent, Dir. of Exhibitions
Hector Thisdale, Admin. Officer
Free daily 10 AM - 6 PM; cl. Mon. Estab. 1964; Exhibitions of visual arts, conferences, films, happenings; collection of works of art since 1940; appropriation.
Collections: Permanent collection of Quebec, Canadian and foreign artists.
Exhibitions: Monthly exhibitions of Quebec, Canadian and foreign contemporary visual arts; approximately 25 exhibitions yearly.
Activities: Guided tours, conferences, art films to students and general public; Extension Department serving anyone, free of charge; materials for loan, paintings, sculptures, 3000 slides, 5000 photographs, 10 films, etc; approx. 200 items loaned to ten borrowers per year. Lectures open to public, 6 visiting lecturers per year; 200 gallery talks or tours; competitions; scholarships. Book shop.
Library: 3000 volumes for reference; photographs, periodicals, art catalogues, slides, films, etc.
Publications: Art catalogues on the occasion of exhibitions.
Attendance: 150,000.

MUSEE DE L'EGLISE NOTRE-DAME
430, St. Sulpice St, H2Y 2V5. Tel: (514) 842-2925
Father Fernand Lecavalier, Pastor
Open Mon. - Sat. 9:30 AM - 4 PM; Sun. 1 - 4 PM; admis. adults 50¢, children 25¢. Estab. 1937 as a historic and religious museum; financed by the Church of Notre-Dame.
Collections: Silverware, medals, paintings, Old Greek and Roman coins, religious ornaments, furniture, statues, volumes; manuscripts and documents pertaining to the history of Canada.
Activities: Original objects of art lent for exhibitions.
Income: (1974) $11,350.
Attendance: 25,000 annual average.

PAVILION OF HUMOUR
Man and His World, H3C 1A0.
Tel: (514) 872-6079
Robert La Palme, Cur.
Andre Carpentier, Deputy Cur.
Paula Kirouac, Asst.
Josee Vanier, Secy.
Open June 21 - Labor Day 10 AM - 8:30 PM. Estab. 1968 to show graphic humour from 60 countries, plus humorous sculptures borrowed from anywhere; financed by endowment and city and state appropriations. The Pavilion of Humour is part of Man and his World.
Collections: Strip-cartoons; Drawings from Pulitzer Prize winners; Drawings from Reuben Award winners; Drawings on International Salon of Cartoons winners; Collection of American Editorial Cartoon from 1867 to now; Collection of Panel Cartoon from eighteen sixties to now.
Activities: Material available to universities and museums; traveling exhibitions organized and circulated; original objects of art lent; competitions, the International Salon of Cartoons has a Grand-Prix of $5000, first prize of $1000, plus $2000 in lesser prizes awarded by a 5 member jury invited from all over the world, to 12 winners; books and money are also distributed to winners in a junior cartoon exhibition.
Library: 2744 volumes for reference.
Publications: Catalogues for Cartoonist of the Year exhibition and International Salon of Cartoons.
Income: $250,000.
Attendance: 300,000 annual average.

SIR GEORGE WILLIAMS UNIVERSITY COLLECTION OF ART
1435 Maisonneuve Blvd, 107.
Edwy F. Cooke, Dir.
Donald F. P. Andrus, Cur.
Patrick Landsley, Registrar
Free 11 AM - 9 PM. Estab. 1966 to exhibit Canadian works of art both of historical and contemporary interest. In general only Canadian artists are exhibited in order to acquaint the University students and the general public with the most significant movements in the development of Canadian art; financed through the University budget.
Collections: †Painting, †graphics, †sculpture, †mixed media, decorative arts.
Exhibitions: As the Gallery is composed of three exhibition halls, exhibitions are changed every two to three weeks. Exhibitions include two large students shows, staff shows, retrospectives and thematic exhibitions.
Activities: Paintings, graphics, and sculpture loaned to Central and Eastern Canada, university and public galleries for shipping and insurance fees; lectures open to public, 2-3 visiting lecturers per year; Gallery used for talks by staff members; concerts, dramatic programs.

Publications: Catalogue of the Collection, every 2 years; exhibition catalogues for the Carl Schaefer Exhibition, Fritz Brandtner Exhibition, Anne Savage Exhibition.
Attendance: 110,000.

PERCE

LE CENTRE D'ART DE PERCE
G0C 2L0.
Suzanne Guite, Pres.
Michelle Tommi, Secy.
Thomas Tommi, Dir.
Josee Tommi, Dir.
Frederic Tommi, Dir.
Free July - Aug. 10 AM - 10 PM. Estab. 1955 to promote art in all its forms; financed by endowment. Gallery of contemporary arts and crafts.
Collections: Permanent collections of Alberto Tommi's late paintings.
Exhibitions: Alberto Tommi; Suzanne Guite; Francoise Bujold; Jeannie Guillaume; Hugh Barret.
Activities: Photograph collection; concerts, dramatic programs; classes for children.
Publications: Le Centre D'Art de Perce, annually.
Income: $10,000.
Attendance: 15,000.

QUEBEC

MUSEE DU QUEBEC
Parc des Champs de Bataille, G1S 1C8.
Tel: (418) 643-2150
Andre Juneau, Dir.
Claude Thibault, Conservator of Ancient Art
Ginette Masse, Conservator of Contemporary Art
Therese La Tour, Conservator & Ethnographer
Francois Lafortune, Chief Librn.
Guy Paradis, Dir. of Educ. Services.
Free 9 AM - 5 PM; Sun. & holidays 1 - 5 PM. Estab. 1933 under Government of Province of Quebec. Branch Museums, Hôtel Chevalier, 5 Champlain St, Quebec; Old French Canadian Homestead.
Collections: †Painting, †sculpture, †furniture by Quebec artists and carvers from the 17th century to the present. (Note: the Archives of the Province which occupy the ground floor of the Museum possess a collection of mss. and historical objects.)
Activities: Special exhibitions; circulating exhibitions; lectures.
Library: Reference library; photograph collection of 6000 prints; 7000 books; 23,000 slides; 655 microcards; 183 microfilms; 73 records.
Purchases: $75,000.
Attendance: 544,000.

MUSEE DU SEMINAIRE DE QUEBEC
6, rue de l'Université.
Jean M. Thivierge, Cur.
Open Mon. - Fri. 10 AM - 4 PM; July & Aug, Sat. 1 - 4 PM; admis. 25¢. Estab. 1874.
Collections: Canadian, Italian, French, Flemish, Spanish and British paintings; coins, stamps, old silver, etc.

RIMOUSKI

LE MUSEE REGIONAL DE RIMOUSKI
35 W. Saint-Germain, G5L 4B4. Tel: (418) 724-2272
Open June - Aug. 10 AM - 9 PM; Sept. - May 9 AM - Noon, 1 - 6 PM & 7 - 9 PM. Estab. 1972, a museum of fine arts housed in a restored and concerted 1823 stone church. In the 3-story building, one story is reserved for a small permanent collection. The other two stories are reserved for travelling exhibitions, film showings and recitals. National Exhibition Center since 1973. Library developing regional art documentation. Ann. meeting Fall; dues regular $5, groups or societies $50, life $100.
Collections: Canadian art, paintings, sculpture and silversmithing; 3 European paintings, including 2 by Ribera.
Attendance: 60,000.

SHAWINIGAN

CENTRE CULTUREL DE SHAWINIGAN
2100 Dessaules, G9N 6V3. Tel: (819) 539-4822 and 5333
Open Mon. - Fri. 9 AM - Noon & 1:30 - 5 PM; Mon. & Wed. 7 - 9 PM; show days 1:30 - 9 PM; no admis. fee. Estab. Oct. 15, 1967, to promote the visual and performing arts; financed by city and state appropriation. Art gallery for touring exhibitions, permanent collection and for sales.
Collections: Paintings; sculpture.

Exhibitions: 60 in 3 years; multi-national exhibitions including paintings, sculpture, handicrafts and photography.

Activities. Painting, drawing, copper enameling, dance, theatre and music workshops available to students for $35; original objects of art lent; photographs and slides in lending collection; 100 items lent in average year; concerts, dramatic programs, classes for adults and children; competitions.

Income and Purchases: Income $2000; purchases $2000.

Attendance: 30,000.

SHERBROOKE

CENTRE CULTUREL DE L'UNIVERSITE DE SHERBROOKE
(University of Sherbrooke Cultural Center)
    Cite Universitaire, J7K 2R7. Tel: (819) 565-5445
Andre Lachance, Admin. Dir.
Robert Beaudoin, Asst. Admin. Dir.
Andre Vigeant, Art Dir.
Jean Rene Tetreault, Publicist
Art Gallery free Mon. - Thurs. 12:30 - 4:30 PM & 7 - 9:30 PM; Sun. 1 - 5 PM; cl. Fri. & Sat. Estab. 1964; the Cultural Centre takes care of the cultural life on the campus and in the city of Sherbrooke; exhibitions, theater, music, lectures, movies, etc. More than 150 ft. of walls; all equipped; used only for professional artists. Mem. 2300; dues $15.

Collections: †Engravings, paintings, sculptures of Canadian artists; a few engravings from international artists.

Exhibitions: 12 per year in Art Gallery, 40 in different halls, principally Canadian artists.

Activities: Gallery talks, tours; concerts, dramatic programs, many classes for adults and children.

Attendance: (1974-75) 505,000.

TROIS RIVIERES

CENTRE CULTUREL DE TROIS RIVIERES
(Cultural Center of Trois Rivieres)
    Place de l'Hotel de Ville
Jacqueline Pothier, Hostess
Francois Lahaye, Dir. Production
Open 9 AM - Noon, 1:30 - 5 PM & 7 - 10 PM. Estab. 1967; financed by city and state appropriations. Gallery maintained. Monthly meetings.

Activities: Educational department; expositions.

VAUDREUIL

MUSEE HISTORIQUE DE VAUDREUIL
(Vaudreuil Historical Museum)
    431 Blvd. Roche, J7V 5V5. Tel: (514) 455-2092
Lucien Theriault, Pres.
Pierre Emond, Secy.
Fernande Letourneau, V.Pres.
David Aird, Dir.
Andree Boileau, Mgr.
Open Tues. - Sat. 9 AM - Noon & 1 - 5 PM; Sun. Noon - 5 PM; admis. adults 75¢, children 25¢. Estab. 1953; financed by endowment. Ann. meeting May 26; mem. 100; dues $5.

Collections: Paintings, portraits and sculpture; historic documents; antique implements for weaving, woodworking and farming; antique pottery, utensils, clothing, furniture and toys; antique butter and candy-making utensils; Edison Gramophone, c. 1915.

Exhibitions: 10 local artists' exhibitions; Les instruments d'eclairage; Les moules et le moulage domestique.

Activities: Original objects of art lent; 100 items lent in average year; concerts; classes for children. Book shop.

Library: Volumes for reference only; 80% of photograph collection for reference; collection of 600 cylinders.

Publications: Vaudreuil Soulanges, Western Gateway of Quebec; Musee de Vaudreuil Catalog (Selectif).

Attendance: 10,000.

SASKATCHEWAN

SASKATCHEWAN ART ASSOCIATION*
    c/o Mrs. Jackie Clark, Pres, Box 2013, Nipawin.
    Tel: (306) 862-4401
Wayne Morgan, Secy.
Estab. June, 1969; an association of B. and C. Gallery Directors set up to circulate information on the availability of exhibitions; back-up programs and educational programs on an adult level; financed by provincial appropriation. Meetings annually or when deemed necessary; mem. approx. 20 galleries and exhibiting centers; no dues.

Activities: Beginning to promote educational programs on a limited scale but main function is to acquaint exhibiting centers with the sources of such programs.

Publications: Saskatchewan Art Association Bulletin, as necessary, 5 or 6 times per year.

SASKATCHEWAN ASSOCIATION OF ARCHITECTS
    2426 Hanover Ave, Saskatoon S7J 1E8
A. E. Smith, Pres.
    (3039 Quinn Dr, Regina S4P 2W3)
T. Okeren, Secy-Treas.
    (306 Avenue Bldg, Saskatoon S7K 1M1)
Estab. 1911. Ann. meeting Feb; mem. 75; dues $175. Memorial scholarship given to architecture student at University of Manitoba, Winnipeg (1 hr. $200). Book prize given to architectural technology student at Saskatchewan Technical Institute, Moose Jaw ($25).

LLOYDMINSTER

LLOYDMINSTER BARR COLONY MUSEUM COMMITTEE
    c/o City Hall, 5011 49 Ave, S9V 0T8. Tel: (403) 825-5655, 825-3726
Richard Larsen, Chmn.
Blaire L. Bowsfield, Secy.
Mrs. D. Barradell, Cur.
Open 9 AM - 9 PM; admis. adult 50¢; student 25¢, children 10¢. Estab. 1965 to promote an interest in the history of our city; financed by donations. Imhoff paintings and Fuch's Wildlife and Antique Museum. Ann. meeting at the call of the chairman; mem. 5; dues donation.

Collections: Photograph collection.

Activities: Lectures for visiting schools.

Attendance: 1972, 3224; 1971, 2676.

PRINCE ALBERT

JOHN M. CUELENAERE LIBRARY
Grace Campbell Gallery
    125 12th St. E. Tel: (306) 763-8496
Free weekdays 10 AM - 8:30 PM; Sat. 9 AM - 5 PM. Estab. 1974 as a public library which has an art gallery of approx. 100 linear ft; financed by city and state appropriation.

Exhibitions: Local shows; shows loaned by Norman Mackenzie Art Gallery and Mendel Art Gallery; few out-of-province shows.

Activities: Lectures open to public, 2 visiting lecturers per year; 2 gallery talks; 10 tours; concerts.

Publications: Cuelenaere Contact, bimonthly.

REGINA

NORMAN MACKENZIE ART GALLERY
    University of Regina, S4S 4A2. Tel: (306) 523-5801
Nancy E. Dillow, Dir.
P. McCann, Secy.
Free Mon. - Fri Noon - 5 PM; Wed. - Thurs. 7 - 10 PM; weekends 1 - 5 PM. Estab. 1934; new gallery built 1953.

Collections: †Canadian and Saskatchewan paintings; †Old Master drawings; †sculpture and art objects.

Activities: Special and traveling exhibitions; lectures; recitals; films.

Library: Prints and reproductions and authoritative literature on painting and art history.

Purchases: Approx. $9000.

Attendance: Approx. 30,000.

REGINA PUBLIC LIBRARY
    2311 12th Ave, S4P 0N3. Tel: (306) 523-7621
M. Anderson, Chmn. Regina Pub. Library Board
R. Yeo, Chief Librn.
Estab. 1909, new building 1962, new mezzanine 1972; municipally funded by the city of Regina.

Income and Purchases: Income $1,598,157; purchases $239,425.

Dunlop Art Gallery
W. P. Morgan, Dir. & Cur.
Free Mon. - Fri. 9:30 AM - 9 PM; Sat. 9:30 AM - 6 PM; Sun. 1:30 - 5 PM; cl. holidays. Art Gallery opened 1947, financed as a Department of the Public Library.

Collections: †Small permanent collection of paintings and drawings; †Art rental; Children's Art Loan (reproductions).

Exhibitions about 18 per year. These include local, provincial, national, international professional artists; loan exhibitions; amateur, children's and grassroots art. A broad exhibition policy.

Library: (part of the Regina Public Library's 250,000 volumes)
†10,000 art books; †films on Art; †artist biographies; †exhibition
catalogues; †picture file.
Activities: Include concerts, poetry reading, plays, films, etc.
Publications: Exhibition catalogs; annual report.
Attendance: 80,000.

Prairie History Room
Mrs. D. Hayden, Librn.
Free Mon. - Fri. 1 - 5:15 PM; Tues. & Fri. 6 - 9 PM; Sat. 9:30 AM -
5:15 PM. Opened 1973, financed as a Department of the Public Library.
Collections: †1,600 volumes Canadiana, also †maps, †photographs,
†clippings, †tapes and †pamphlets on Regina area.
Activities: Room is used for research, tours and lectures; seeks
and compiles information on Regina area with frequent displays of
material.

SASKATCHEWAN ARTS BOARD
200 Lakeshore Dr, S4S 0A4. Tel: (306) 584-1122
Paul Rezansoff, Chmn.
Vern Bell, Exec. Dir.
Lea Collins, Visual Arts Officer
Jean Freeman, Literary & Theatre Officer
James Ellemers, Arts Extension Officer & Dir. Saskatchewan
    School of the Arts
Office open 8:30 AM - 5 PM; summer hours 8:30 AM - 4:30 PM.
Estab. 1948 as an autonomous agency for promotion and development
of the arts in Saskatchewan; financed by annual provincial govern-
ment grant. The Board is composed of 7 - 15 appointed, unpaid
board members, whose major concern at the present time is the
support and development of professionals and professional standards
within the province.
Collections: †Permanent collection containing over 600 works by
Saskatchewan artists and artisans only, dating from 1950 to present;
purchased mainly from current exhibitions around the province.
Part of the permanent collection hangs in the Saskatchewan Centre
of the Arts, Regina.
Exhibitions: Assistance is given in the organizing and circulating
of traveling exhibitions; works from the Permanent collection were
circulated in such exhibitions as: Sioux Handcrafted Rugs, 1970;
Saskatchewan Art and Artists, 1971; Prairie Ceramics, 1973-75;
From Realism to Abstraction, 1973-75; Colour Now, 1975-76; Monuments Reduced, 1975-76. Items from the Permanent Collection were
in a number of special exhibitions including Swift Current '74, items
are on permanent loan in the Estevan City Hall, the Moose Jaw Art
Centre, and the Yorkton Regional High School.
Activities: Programs include individual and group assistance
grants, workshop assistance, aid for exhibitions, community assistance for the performing arts, script reading service, play-script
duplication subsidy, community artists program, and consultative
services. Operates Saskatchewan School of the Arts at Echo Valley
Centre, summer classes for young people and fall and spring
classes for adults are offered in a wide variety of crafts, visual and
performing arts.
Publications: Annual Report; Services and Programs Brochure;
Brochures for Saskatchewan School of the Arts Classes.

SASKATOON

MEMORIAL LIBRARY AND ART GALLERY
Nutana Collegiate Institute
    411 11th St, E, S7N 0E9.
Philip Listoe,
Free, Mon. - Fri. 8 AM - 4 PM. Estab. 1925, paintings by Canadian
artists were dedicated to students who lost their lives in World War
I, the library commemorates students from the same collegiate who
lost their lives in World War II. Main hallway of the collegiate as
well as the main office and library houses the collection of about 50
paintings.
Collections: Lending and reference library of 10,000 volumes;
audio visual aids; art books.
Exhibitions: Mendel Art Gallery.
Publications: Brochures.
Attendance: 2000 annual average.

THE SASKATOON GALLERY AND CONSERVATORY CORPORATION
Mendel Art Gallery and Civic Conservatory
    950 Spadina Crescent E, Box 569, S7K 3L6. Tel: (306) 652-8355
John E. Climer, Dir.
Open daily 10 AM - 10 PM. Estab. 1944 (Saskatoon Art Centre) by
Saskatoon Art Association, Saskatoon Camera Club and Archaeological Society as a step towards a community centre. Facility built and
opened Oct, 1964, with grants from Fred S. Mendel, industrialists, the
Provincial Government and Civic Government; inc. Jan, 1966 to es-
tablish and maintain in the city of Saskatoon, public art galleries,
schools, museums, exhibitions, workshops for the preservation, collection, development, creation of works of art and to carry on activities conducive to the above, with special emphasis on the visual arts.
Two and one-half story extension built 1975 with capital grants from
The National Museums of Canada and city of Saskatoon. Ann. meeting Jan. or Feb.
Collections: Canadian painting, sculpture, graphics, watercolors;
Eskimo sculpture, graphics; European paintings, sculpture, drawings,
etc; all collections being increased. The permanent collection is installed in the Mendel Salon at the Mendel Art Gallery.
Exhibitions: Annual traveling exhibitions organized by the Gallery.
Activities: Classes for all age groups; adult lecture series; film
series; Picture Sales and Rental Gallery; tours for school groups,
conventions, etc; extension services to all schools within the city
of Saskatoon; exhibition services provided for recognized community
groups throughout Canada.
Library: 3919 volumes with emphasis on art; slide collection of
4323.
Income: $350,000.
Attendance: 300,000.

UNIVERSITY OF SASKATCHEWAN, SASKATOON
The Art Department Gallery
    S7N 0W0. Tel: (306) 343-4528
Otto Rogers, Head, Dept. Art
Robert Christie, Gallery Supvr.
Free weekdays, hours vary from term to term. Estab. approx. 1960
(formerly Marquis Gallery) for the education of both students and
local public, showing both art exhibitions as well as more didactic
shows; financed by endowment.
Collections: Regional and national works of art; international
works of art, primarily prints. Collection is added to yearly.
Exhibitions: Approximately 60 exhibitions over last three years,
of which approximately 30 were organized by the gallery. The
other exhibitions were arranged for via other galleries and gallery
circuits.
Activities: Original objects of art lent; lectures to students.
Publications: Exhibition catalogs or brochures.

WESTERN DEVELOPMENT MUSEUM
2610 Lorne Ave. S, S7K 3S5. Tel: (306) 652-8900
Gordon A. Wilson, Exec. Dir.
Robert W. Unruh, Accountant
Open 9 AM to dusk all year; branches at North Battleford and Yorkton open May to Oct; admis. adults $1, under 16 years 50¢, preschool,
free, family rate $3; school groups free. Estab. 1947 to acquire, pre-
serve, restore, display, and activate pioneer machinery, furnishings,
and the way of life of the prairie pioneer.
Museums housed at Yorkton, featuring an ethnic display; North
Battleford, featuring an outdoor Pioneer Village; and at Saskatoon,
a new multi-million dollar museum complex featuring an indoor
pioneer street of the period 1905-1910 and featuring the agricultural
and transportation history of the Canadian prairies. This collection
features the most outstanding and largest agricultural and transportation history exhibit in Canada and one of the largest on the North
American continent. New branch of Western Development Museum at
Moose Jaw opening mid-1976, featuring transportation and aviation
exhibits.
Activities: Annual pioneer show at Saskatoon, Saskachimo, held
each July featuring the actual demonstration of early farm machinery, methods of transportation and household articles. Attendance at the show, 150,000 paid admissions. A small reference library is maintained at the Museum.
Attendance: 210,000.

Major Museums Abroad

ARGENTINA

BUENOS AIRES

CENTRO DE ARTE Y COMUNICACION (CAYC)
(Center of Art and Communication)
    Elpidio Gonzalez 4070. Tel: 566-8046 and 7774
Jorge Glusberg, Dir.
Amelia Montes, Mgr.
Edward Ring, Cur.
Diana Larronde, Exec. Secy.
Ruben Fraga, Theatre Coordinator
Ing. Oscar Sevlever, Video Coordinator
Arch. Luis Lentini & Arch. Diego Forero, Architecture
    Coordinators
Luis Chemes, Films Coordinator
Open 11 AM - 9 PM; cl. Sun; free except for special events. Estab.
Aug, 1969 to introduce in Argentina, on a pedagogycal level, the most
important events of experimental and avant-garde art from interna-
tional art centers and also present the Latin American art made by
young artists at those centers; create a Latin American circuit from
the artistical activities; financed by membership. Gallery consists
of three floors, each 8 m x 20 m; documentation center consists of
two floors, each 9 m. x 30 m.
    Exhibitions: Joseph Kosuth; Christo; Donald Burgy; Barry
Flanagan; John Baldesarri; Joe Tilson; Experimental Polish Photography; H. Kielholz and C. Rothacher (Switzerland); 121 Checoslovak
Engravings; Otto Piene (Germany); Sol Le Witt (U.S.A); Hungarian
Festival 1974; Graphics with Computers (Germany); Yayanagi and
Kimura, engravings (Japan); Dick Higgins (U.S.A); Visual Poetry
organized by Jasia Reichardt.
    Activities: Seminaries of art, sociology of art, communication,
epistemology, research in architecture, theatre, etc; traveling
exhibitions organized and circulated; 90 motion pictures and 210
videotapes in lending collection; photograph collection of 4000 prints;
lectures open to public paying admission and for members; 30 gallery talks per year; concerts, dramatic programs, classes for
adults; competitions. Book shop.
    Library: 4654 volume reference library.
    Publications: Bulletin describing activities and work of artists,
10 per year.

MUSEO NACIONAL DE ARTE DECORATIVO*
(National Museum of Decorative Art)
    Av. del Libertador 1902.
Dr. Federico Aldao, Dir.
Estab. 1902.
    Collections: Furniture; sculptures; tapestries; European and
South American works.
    Activities: Lectures and concerts.
    Publications: Exhibition catalogues, guide.

MUSEO NACIONAL DE BELLAS ARTES*
(National Museum of Fine Arts)
    Avda. Libertador Gen. San Martin 1473. Tel: 83-8814
Samuel F. Oliver, Dir.
Raquel Edelman, Library Dir.
Open Wed. - Mon. 3 - 7 PM. Founded 1885.
    Collections: European paintings (16th to 20th centuries);
sculpture; Argentine painting.
    Activities: Auditorium for audiovisual programs, films, con-
certs and lectures. Modern pavilion for special exhibitions.
    Art Library: More than 20,000 volumes.

ROSARIO

MUSEO MUNICIPAL DE BELLAS ARTES JUAN B. CASTAGNINO*
(Municipal Museum of Fine Arts)
    Avda. Pellegrini, 2202 Parque Independencia. Tel: 27310

Pedro Sinopoli, Dir.
Pedro Alberto Sinopoli, Exec. Secy.
Free Wed. - Sat. 4 - 7 PM; Sun. & holidays, 10 - 12 AM & 4 - 7 PM.
Estab. 1920; The present building was inaugurated 1937; appropriation.
    Collections: An important collection of European and American
paintings and sculpture from 16th century to contemporary.
    Exhibitions: Exhibition of Argentine Engravings, 1968; Interna-
tional Biennal of Comics, 1969; Exhibition of Kinetic Art, 1969; Exhibition of Art and Cibernetic, 1970; Argentine Paintings, 1969; Exhibitions of Argentine Engravings 1970, etc.
    Activities: Concerts, dramatic programs, competitions.
    Library: 15,000 volumes for reference.
    Publications: Catalogs of the exhibitions.
    Attendance: (1968) 103,444; (1969) 88,714.

AUSTRALIA

ADELAIDE

THE ART GALLERY OF SOUTH AUSTRALIA
    North Terrace, 5000. Tel: 223.8481
John Baily, Dir.
Ron Appleyard, Asst. Dir.
Mon. - Sat. 10 AM - 5 PM; Sun. 2 - 5 PM. Estab. 1881. Friends of
The Art Gallery of South Australia estab. 1969 to foster interest in
the activities of the Gallery; mem. 1125.
    Collections: Collections of paintings, drawings, sculpture, prints,
applied art, furniture, ceramics, coins, South Australian Historical
collection.
    Activities: Mobile exhibition with lecturers visiting country areas
annually. Education section provides lectures in Gallery and reproduction lending service. Film evenings, music concerts and lectures held in Gallery. Sale of reproductions and books at Sales Desk.
    Publications: Quarterly Bulletin of the National Gallery of South
Australia, 1939-1967; Quarterly Bulletin of The Art Gallery of
South Australia, 1968 to date.
    Income: $100,000 per annum for the purchase of works of art;
administrative costs, building maintenance and salaries met by the
State Government.
    Attendance: 155,000.

BRISBANE

QUEENSLAND ART GALLERY
    Fifth Floor (6th Floor Administration), M.I.M. Bldg, 160 Ann St,
    4000 (temporary premises). Tel: 292138
Raoul Mellish, Dir.
Robert Cunningham, Asst. Dir.
Open Mon. - Sat. 10 AM - 5 PM; Sun. 2 - 5 PM; cl. Christmas, Good
Friday & Anzac Day. Estab. 1895. Queensland Art Gallery Society.
    Collections: Predominantly Australian art, various media, with
some European.
    Exhibitions: Continuous exhibition program from the Gallery's
Collection as well as loan exhibitions from overseas. Annual Trustees' Prize $2500; biennial L. J. Harvey Memorial Prize for Drawing
$500.
    Activities: Educational programs for school, tertiary and adult
audiences; children's creative art class; monthly evening lectures
and occasional exhibition openings.
    Library: Small special library with emphasis on Australian art;
slides, tapes, film.

HOBART

TASMANIAN MUSEUM AND ART GALLERY
    5 Argyle St, G.P.O. Box 1164M, 7001
D. R. Gregg, Dir.

Carl Andrew, Cur. Art
Open Mon. - Fri. 10 AM - 5 PM; Sat. 11 AM - 4 PM; Sun. 2:30 - 5
PM. Estab. 1843.
 Collections: Tasmanian historical pictures, Australian contempo-
rary paintings and sculpture.

LAUNCESTON

QUEEN VICTORIA MUSEUM
 Wellington St, 7250. Tel: (003) 316777
David Gunn, Mayor
C. A. Allen, Town Clerk
W. F. Ellis, Dir.
J. A. McPhee, Gallery Officer
R. Hamilton, Registrar
Free Mon. - Fri. 10 AM - 5 PM; Sun. 2 - 4 PM. Estab. 1891 as the
headquarters of a professionally conducted complex of art galleries,
theatres, museums and educational services conducted mainly as a
city authority but extending over half the state; financed by city and
state appropriations. Gallery.
 Collections: Visual art collections, relating to Australia; colonial
period (1803-1900); †contemporary work.
 Exhibitions: Approx. 15 annually.
 Activities: Liaise with and service schools, plan and conduct
juvenile services; serves 13,000 square miles; material available
to local galleries and schools; no fees; traveling exhibitions organized and circulated; individual paintings and original objects of art
lent; 300 items lent in an average year; 30 active borrowers; lectures open to public; 10 visiting lecturers per year; 20 gallery talks;
200 tours; concerts; dramatic programs; competitions.
 Library: 8000 volumes for reference; photograph collection of
750 prints for reference; planetarium; trailside museums.
 Publications: Records of the Queen Victoria Museum, approx. 4
per year.
 Income and Purchases: Income $210,000; purchases $3000.
 Attendance: 90,000 annual average.

MELBOURNE

NATIONAL GALLERY OF VICTORIA*
 Victorian Arts Centre, 180 St. Kilda Rd, 3004. Tel: 62 7411
Gordon Thomson, Dir.
Kenneth Hood, Sr. Cur.
William McCall, Secy.
Open Tues. - Sat. 10 AM - 5 PM; Wed. 10 AM - 9 PM; Sun. 10 AM -
5 PM. Estab. 1859.
 Collections: Old Master and modern paintings, prints and draw-
ings, sculpture including Rembrandt, Tiepolo, van Dyck, Turner,
Veronese, Titian, Goya, Constable, Gainsborough, Sargent, Bonnard,
Frankenthaler, Monet, Rodin, Bernini and many others; William
Blake watercolours, Asian collection, antiquities, period furniture,
ceramics, bronzes, glass, silver.
 Activities: Education Section: 1000 students, primary to tertiary
level are handled per week. Bookshop: art books, postcards and re-
productions; National Gallery Society with approx. 7000 members and
full programme of lectures; daily lecture tours by voluntary guides.
 Library: 6000 volumes, 30 periodicals.
 Income and Purchases: $210,000 Aust. annually.
 Attendance: Approx. 15,000 per month.

PERTH

THE WESTERN AUSTRALIAN ART GALLERY
 Beaufort St, 6000. Tel: 28 7233.
Frank Norton, Dir.
Bertram Whittle, Deputy Dir.
Lou Klepac, Sr. Cur.
Open Mon. - Fri 10:30 AM - 5 PM; Sat. 9:30 AM - 5 PM; Sun. 2 PM -
5 PM; during special exhibitions Wed evening 7:30 - 10 PM. The Art
Gallery was established in 1895 as part of the Western Australian
Museum and became an autonomous body by Act of Parliament in
May, 1960.
 Collections: 584 oils, 238 watercolors, 1600 prints and drawings,
66 sculptures, Australian Aboriginal artifacts and primitive art,
antique and modern furniture, antique and modern silver and gold
ware, ceramics, glass and pottery.
 Exhibitions: Biennially, Perth Prize for Drawing International,
alternating with Western Australian Artists Exhibition.
 Activities: Guided tours of Gallery, educational and holiday
activities, touring exhibitions.
 Library: 1200 volumes.
 Income and Purchases: Annual income $389,077 (1974-75);
annual purchases $78,414 (1974-75).
 Attendance: (2 years) 224,235.

SYDNEY

ART GALLERY OF NEW SOUTH WALES
 Art Gallery Road, Domain, 2000. Tel: (02) 211.2100
Peter Laverty, Dir.
Gil Docking, Deputy Dir.
Daniel Thomas, Sr. Cur.
Renée Free, Cur. European & American Art
Nicholas Draffin, Cur. Prints & Drawings
Bernice Murphy, Sr. Educ. Officer
W. M. Boustead, Conservation
Open Mon. - Sat. 10 AM - 5 PM; Sun. 2 - 5 PM; cl. Christmas Day
and Good Friday. Estab. 1874; the state art museum, under the
Department of Culture, Sport and Recreation. In 1972 the Art Gal-
lery reopened after being closed for some time to allow remodelling
and extensions to the building to take place.
 Collections: Australian art, fully comprehensive, the most com-
plete in existence, except for 19th century decorative arts. Primi-
tive art, Australian aboriginal, including notable burial posts and
bark paintings; Melanesian. European painting and sculpture—
British includes Hogarth, R. E. Pine, Reynolds, Wilson, Turner,
Constable, Etty, Danby, John Gibson, Madox Brown, Burne-Jones,
Leighton, Poynter, Fildes, Sickert, Gore, Nash, Ben Nicholson,
Sutherland, Moore, Hepworth, Pasmore, Davie. Other European col-
lections less complete—Strozzi, Stomer, Van Bijlert, Van Bloemen,
Hubert Robert, Tiepolo, Corot, Boudin, Fantin-Latour, Pissarro,
Bonnard, Monet, Vlaminck, Hayden, Leger, Zadkine, Albers,
Vasarely, Morris Louis. Prints and drawings—a good systematic
collection including Mantegna, Durer, Callot, Rembrandt, Piranesi,
Canaletto, Goya, Turner, Constable, Meryon, Whistler, Munch,
Matisse, Picasso. Oriental art, a small collection—Chinese ceram-
ics, Chinese bronzes; Tibetan, Japanese and Chinese paintings;
Japanese ceramics; Japanese woodcuts; Thai sculpture; Persian
ceramics; good Persian and Indian miniatures. Decorative arts—
a famous collection of British pewter, 17th to 18th century; English
porcelain, 18th century and Victorian; contemporary tapestries,
Lurcat and Matisse. All collections except decorative arts are being
actively enlarged.
 Exhibitions: (1973-75) Recent Australian Art; Opening of New
Primitive Art Gallery; John Constable; 17th Century Pastoral Holland; Some Recent American Art; Exhibition of 'Blue Poles' Pollock;
Cartier Bressons France; Paul Klee; Two Masters of the Weimar
Bauhaus; Hirshfield-Mack and Lyonel Feinger; Ladies in Land-
scapes; Modern Masters: Manet to Matisse; Victorian Olympians;
Project shows (small scale) including Grace Crowly; Objects of
the Imagination and Poynter Drawings.
 Activities: Lectures and films in conjunction with Gallery Society
at least once a week; visits to private collections with talks by gal-
lery staff; volunteer guide floor tours; New South Wales traveling
art exhibition. Small Bookshop.
 Research Library for staff only.
 Publications: Art Gallery Annual; special exhibitions catalogs.
 Attendance: 300,000.

MUSEUM OF APPLIED ARTS AND SCIENCES
 659-695 Harris St, Broadway, 2007. Tel: 02-211 3911
Sir John Hurley, Pres.
J. L. Willis, Dir.
H. H. G. McKern, Deputy Dir.
Free, daily 10 AM - 5 PM; Sun. 2 - 5 PM; cl. Good Friday and
Christmas Day. Estab. 1880 to display and scholarship in the applied arts and sciences; financed by endowment and state appropriation.
 Collections: †Ceramics; glass; metalwork; ivory; textiles;
costume; musical instruments; numismatics; Asian arts; arms
and armour; horology; ship models; pure and applied sciences;
physics; chemical technology; biology; electronics; transport;
communication; engineering.
 Activities: Educational department conducts teaching sessions,
primarily for school classes; liaison with school teachers; provides a guide-lecturer service; use of photograph collection on approval from director. Book shop.
 Library: 10,000 volume reference library.
 Publications: Annual report.
 Attendance: 230,000 annual average.

AUSTRIA

GRAZ

NEUE GALERIE AM LANDESMUSEUM JOANNEUM
(New Gallery at Provincial Museum)
 Sackstrasse 16, 8010 Graz
Prof. Dr. Wilfried Skreiner, Dir.
Open 9 AM - 6 PM; admis. 5 Sh. Financed by province and state
appropriations.

Collections: Painting of the 19th and 20th century, especially Austrian, Biedermeier; Styrian painters of the 19th century, two pictures of Egon Schiele; drawings and watercolors (20,000) of Austrian and German artists; international graphic art of the 20th century.

Exhibitions: Approx. 50 Austrian, Italian and Yugoslavian painters exhibitions since 1970.

Activities: Extension department serves Styria, Italy and Yugoslavia; traveling exhibitions organized and circulated; individual paintings and original objects of art lent; lending collection of photographs; lectures open to public; 30 visiting lecturers and gallery talks yearly; concerts; competitions; scholarships.

Library: Reference collection of approx. 5000 volumes.

Income and Purchases: Income approx. $50,000; purchases approx. $10,000.

Attendance: Approx. 10,000.

LINZ

WOLFGANG-GURLITT-MUSEUM
Neue Galerie Der Stadt Linz
(New City Gallery)
Linz, Hauptplatz 8. Tel: 24 04
Peter Baum, Dir.
Open Mon. - Fri. 10 AM - 6 PM; Sat. 10 AM - 1 PM; cl. Sun. Estab. 1947.

Collections: †19th and 20th century paintings, drawings, sculpture and prints from Central Europe; 430 paintings and small sculptures; 4000 graphics and prints; International collection of reproductions and slides.

Exhibitions: Own collection year round; 10 changing exhibitions a year of one-man, group, retrospective, of famous artists of international 20th century art.

Activities: Permanent lectures with the adult education school; lending service, reproductions, for schools and private lectures.

Library: 6000 volumes.

Attendance: 25,000.

SALZBURG

SALTZBURGER MUSEUM CAROLINO AUGUSTEUM*
(Salzburg Museum)
Museumsplatz 1, Postfach 525, A-5010. Tel: 43 1 45, 41 1 37 (06222).
Dr. Freidrike Prodinger, Dir. Ethnology, History of Civilization, Arts and Crafts.
Dr. Albin Rohrmoser, Art History
Dr. Kurt Conrad, Ethnology
Dr. Josef Gassner & Hermine Holzbauer, Library & Archives
Ing. Fritz Moosleitner, Prehistory
Dr. Volker Kutschera, Theatrical Sciences & Pub. Relations
Annemarie Fiebich-Ripke, Restoration
Otto Rainer, Admin.
Open daily 9 AM - 5 PM; cl. Nov. 1. Estab. 1834.

Collections: Prehistoric and Roman archaeology; medieval art; baroque, 19th century, modern art; approx. 20,000 prints and drawings; weapons; coins; musical instruments; furniture; local history of civilization; historical chambers; All collections being enlarged by purchase and donations.

Attached museums:

Volkskunde-Museum
(Folklife Museum)
Monatsschlösschen near Castle of Hellbrunn, Salzburg
Open Apr. - Oct, daily 10 AM - 6 PM. Estab. 1924.

Collections: Folklife—furniture, costumes, faience, miniature farmhouses, perchten-masks, immigration.

Burgmuseum
(Castle of Hohensalzburg)
Open daily 9 AM - 5 PM; cl. Nov. 1st. Estab. 1959.

Collections: Local history of defense; arms and armor; guilds furniture; flags; wrought iron; history of law, etc.

Museum Pavilion
Mirabellgarten
Open daily 9 - 12 AM, 2 - 6 PM.

Exhibitions: Frequent special changing exhibitions at the Salzburg Museum and at the Museum Pavilion.

Activities: Symposia on important changing exhibitions; gallery talks, demonstrations (research) on historical musical instruments; concerts on old instruments; tours; lending services to other exhibitors; books edited by the museum for sale; production of silent and sound pictures on Austrian national customs, local theatre history and on the research work on toys.

Library: Approx. 70,000 volumes; technical literature; local archives. Open Mon. - Fri. 9 - 12 AM.

Publications: Jahresschrift, annually; Schriftenreihe, occasionally; catalogues on each major exhibition; postcards, slides, posters.

Income and Purchases: Annual Income 1,600,000 Austrian schillings; annual purchases regular budget 500,000 Austrian schillings; further possible purchases from extra budget 500,000 Austrian schillings.

Combined attendance for Salzburg Museum and all attached museums: (1971) 430,193; (1972) 440,666.

VIENNA

GEMÄLDEGALERIE DER AKADEMIE DER BILDENDEN KÜNSTE IN WIEN
(Art Gallery of the Academy of Fine Arts)
A1010 Schillerplatz 3, 1. Tel: (0222) 579616
Dr. Heribert Hutter, Dir.
Open Tues. 10 AM - 2 PM; Wed. 10 AM - 1 PM & 3 - 6 PM; Thurs. & Fri. 10 AM - 2 PM; Sat. 9 AM - 1 PM; Sun. 9 AM - 1 PM; cl. Mon. Estab. 1822.

Collections: Originate from the collections of Count Anton Lamberg-Sprinzenstein who, at his death in 1822, willed his collections to serve as teaching materials and examples for the students of the Academy of Art. Other collections followed: Prince Liechtenstein, W. v. Wurzbach, etc. collection is mainly paintings of the 12th - 18th centuries, Hieronymus Bosch, Hans Grien, 17th century Dutch (Rembrandt, Ruisdael, Goyen, Jan Both, and others); Flemish (Rubens, Jordaens, Van Dyck, etc); also Tiepolo, Magnasco, Francesco Guardi.

Exhibitions: Annual exhibit from the Reserve (Sonderausstellungen) during the study year.

Publications: Bildhefte der Akademie, annually.

Attendance: 14,000.

Kupferstichkabinett der Akademie der bildenden Künste
(Print and Drawing Collection of the Academy of Fine Arts)
Dr. Albert Massiczek, Dir.
Open Mon. - Fri. 10 - 12 AM, 2 - 4 PM after notification; time-to-time expositions Mon. - Sat. 9 - 12 AM. Estab. 1876.

Collections: Drawings and prints of the 15th to 20th centuries, especially Italian, Netherland, German. Gothic architectural drawings, Dürer, Rembrandt etc, Nazarenes, Daffinger (watercolors of flowers), Thomas Ender, Rudolf von Alt. More than 28,000 drawings and 60,000 prints.

Attendance: 1400.

GRAPHISCHE SAMMLUNG ALBERTINA
(Albertina Graphic Art Collection)
Augustinerstrasse 1
Dr. Walter Koschatzky, Dir.
Study Room open Mon. - Thurs. 1 - 4 PM; cl. during July & Aug.
Exhibition Mon, Tues, Thurs, Fri. 10 AM - 4 PM; Wed. 10 AM - 6 PM; Sat. & Sun. 10 AM - 1 PM. Estab. late 18th century.

Collections: Drawings, watercolors and prints of all schools 14th to 20th centuries. All collections active. This is one of the largest and best print collections in Europe, total holdings about 1,800,000 items.

Library: 45,000 volumes.

Attendance: 80,000.

KUNSTHISTORISCHES MUSEUM*
(Museum of Fine Arts)
1 Burgring 5.
Dr. Erwin M. Auer, Chief Dir.
Open daily 10 AM - 3 PM; Sun. 9 AM - 1 PM; Tues. & Fri. also 8 - 10 PM. Estab. 1891.

Collections: Egyptian and Oriental collections; antiques; ceramics; jewelry and tapestries; paintings; weapons; old music instruments; historical carriages and costumes; the collection of Schloss Ambras.

Exhibitions: Vienne à Versailles; Canaletto; Die Neue Galerie des Kunsthistorischen Museums.

Library: 70,000 volumes; photograph collection and 50,000 prints.

MUSEUM DES 20. JAHRHUNDERTS*
(Museum of the 20th Century)
1010 Vienna Schweizergarten. Tel: 0222/ 65 51 21, 65 06 42
Dr. Alfred Schmeller, Dir.
Wilhelm Gaube, Asst.
Open Mon, Thurs, Fri, Sat. 10 AM - 4 PM; Sun. 10 AM - 1 PM; Wed. 2 - 9 PM; cl. Thurs; admis. ÖS 5.-, special exhibitions ÖS.-10, students, children free. Estab. 1962 for the collecting and conservation of modern art; financed by city and state appropriations.

Collections: Works of the 20th century; special exhibitions.

Exhibitions: Bruno Gironcoli; Live-Haus Rucker Co; Osteuropäische Volkskunst; Comic Strips; Bohuslav Kokoschka; Der Mensch in Weltraum; Peter Pongratz; Adolf Loss für junge Leute; Anfänge des Informel in Öst; Aspekte und Probleme des ital. Design; Brauer;

Kornelius Kolig; Walter Pichler Objekte; Jaques Lipchitz; Arena 70; Arena 73; Revolutionsarchitektur; Graphiken und Objekte aus der Werkstatt GEMINI G. E. L; Ernst Haas-Photos aus Wien; Kulturpolitiker malen und zeichnen; Wiener Schule des Phantastischen Realismus; Rudolf Richly; Tomi Ungerer; Arena 73; Ad Reinhardt; Objekte der Gruppe Missing Ling.

Activities: Weekly seminar with instructions; extension department; traveling exhibitions organized and circulated; lectures open to public; concerts; dramatic programs; classes for adults.

Library: Photograph collection.

Publications: Catalogues.

ÖSTERREICHISCHE GALERIE
(Austrian Gallery)
Prinz Eugen-Str. 27, Oberes Belvedere, A 1030.
Tel: 72 64 21, 72 43 58
Dr. Hans Aurenhammer, Dir.
Dr. Hubert Adolph, Cur.
Dr. Elfriede Baum, Cur.
Dr. Gerbert Frodl, Cur.
Dr. Michael Krapf, Cur.
Open Tues. Noon - 4 PM; Wed, Thurs. & Sat. 10 AM - 4 PM; Fri. & Sun. 9 AM - 1 PM; admis. 5 Austrian shillings (ticket valid for all three collections). Estab. 1903 for the collection, exhibition and publication of Austrian art, (excepting drawings, watercolors, prints and arts and craft) from the Middle Ages until the present day; supported by State appropriation.

Collections are shown in the following subdivisions: †Austrian Gallery of 19th and 20th century, †Museum of Austrian Baroque Art, and Museum of Austrian Medieval Art.

Exhibitions: (1970-75) Mittelalterliche Wandmalerei in Österreich; Oskar Kokoschka; Tina Blau; Medieval Art in Carinthia; Anton Faistauer; Joseph Floch; Late Gothic Art in Tyrol; Thomas Schwanthaler; The Szolnok School of Painters.

Library: Reference library with approx. 4000 volumes; photograph collection, (not open to public).

Publications: Mitteilungen der Oesterreichischen Galerie, annually.

Attendance: 160,000.

BELGIUM

ANTWERP

INTERNATIONAL CULTURAL CENTRE
Meir 50, B-2000. Tel: (031) 31.91.81
Flor Bex, Dir.
Jean-Paul Coenen, Asst.
Jan Debbaut, Asst.
Free daily 10 AM - 5 PM. Estab. 1970 by the Ministry of Culture as a governmental documentation and exhibition centre on contemporary arts. Organizing 4 exhibitions per month on avant-garde art, photography and architecture; video shows and weekly film program.

Collections: Belgian and international artist-tapes, experimental films; contemporary art.

Activities: Video equipment available for video productions by artists.

Library: 2000 volumes (including catalogs) and 80 magazines on contemporary art for reference.

Publications: Exhibition catalogs in Dutch, French and English.

KONINKLIJK MUSEUM VOOR SCHONE KUNSTEN
(Royal Museum of Fine Arts)
Plaatsnijdersstraat 2.
Dr. G. Gepts, Cur-in-Chief
Dr. A. Monballieu & J. Buyck, First Assistants
L. Wuyts, Librn.
M. De Vos-De Jong, Educational Service
Open daily except Mon; admis. 5 Belgian francs. Free Sun. Wed. & Sat. afternoon. Estab. 1843.
Collections: More than 4000 Masterpieces; five centuries of Flemish painting; a Survey of Western painting.
Exhibitions: Special shows according to the year-program.
Activities: Visiting lecturers, gallery talks; Junior museum.
Library: 35,000 volumes
Publications: Jaarboek van het Koninklijk Museum voor Schone Kunsten Antwerpen, annually, 1954-60; catalogs.
Attendance: 60,000 annually.

MUSEUM MAYER VAN DEN BERGH
(Mayer van den Bergh Museum)
Lange Gasthuisstraat 19, 2000. Tel: 031 324237
Joz. De Coo, Dir.
Free 10 AM - 5 PM. Estab. 1904 for the conservation and exhibition of collections of Fritz Mayer van den Bergh (+ 1902); financed by endowment and appropriation.

Collections: Art and antiquities of the 14th, 15th, 16th and 17th centuries.

Publications: Catalogue of Paintings, Drawings and Manuscripts; Catalogue of Sculpture and Plaquettes; The Breviary M.v.d.B.

MUSEUM PLANTIN-MORETUS*
(Plantin-Moretus Museum)
Vrijdagmarkt 22. Tel: 33.06.88
Dr. L. Voet, Cur.
Mrs. L. Peeters-Demaeyer, Librn.
Free everyday 10 AM - 1 PM. Estab. 1876; 16th-17th century printing plant and patrician's house; City appropriation.

Collections: Old Belgian and foreign prints, 16th-18th century; manuscripts, designs, punches and matrices, moulds, wood blocks and copper plates.

Activities: Advanced Institute for printing art; photograph collection.

Library: Approx. 30,000 volumes.

MUSEUM SMIDT VAN GELDER*
(Smidt van Gelder Museum)
Belgiëlei 91, 2000. Tel: 03-39.06.52
Maria Snoeckx, Chief Asst.
Free, 10 AM - 5 PM, cl. on Mon. and also on even dates from Oct. 1 - May 1. Estab. 1949 as a private collection given to the City; financed by city appropriations.

Collections: Museum arranged as a 18th century aristocratic living house with French furniture and paintings (18th century) and Dutch paintings from the 17th & 19th centuries, tapestries and, most important 18th century Chinese and European porcelain.

Library: Reference library of 600 volumes; approx. 1000 prints for reference in photograph collection.

Attendance: 8,500 annual average.

OPENLUCHTMUSEUM VOOR BEELDHOUWKUNST (MIDDELHEIM)
(Open air Museum for Sculpture Middelheim)
Middelheimlaan 61, 2020. Tel: 031/ 27 15 34
L. Craeybeckx Burgomaster, City of Antwerp, Pres.
F. Baudouin, Cur. of the Art Historical Museums, City of Antwerp
Mrs. M.R. Bentein, Deputy Keeper, Museum Middelheim
Free every day from 10 AM until sunset except during biennial exhibitions. Estab. 1950; Contemporary sculpture from its origins (Rodin, Martini etc) up to the present day, as well for the collection as for the biennial exhibitions.

Collections: Contemporary sculpture mainly outdoors in the surroundings of a beautiful park; smaller sculpture in pavilions.

Exhibitions: 9th Biennial 1967, 10th Biennial 1969; Calder; Caille; Drawings by sculptors; Colored Objects; 1970 Collection Peeters, Bruges; Metalsculptures; Woodsculptures - 1971 Sofu Teshigahara; 11th Biennial - 1972 Graphics by Pierre Caille; Nino Cassani - 1973 12th Biennial; 1974 Belgian Sculpture; 1975 13th Biennial; Middelheim 25.

Activities: Gallery talks or tours at request only.

Library: 25,000 volumes for lending and reference; photograph, film and slide collection for reference.

Publications: Catalogs of collections and exhibitions.

RUBENIANUM
Belgiëlei 91, B 2000. Tel: 031/ 39 10 90
Frans Baudouin, Keeper of the Art Historical Museums of the City of Antwerp
Nora de Poorter, Asst. Keeper
Prof. R. A. d'Hulst, Univ. of Ghent
Open Mon. - Fri. 8:30 AM - 4:30 PM. Estab. 1950 as the art-historical department and documentation center of the City of Antwerp concerning Rubens and Flemish Art of the 16th and 17th centuries. Its first aim is the publication of the Corpus Rubenianum Ludwig Burchard; financed by city appropriation.

Collections: Library and documentation of the National Centrum voor de Plastische Kunsten van de 16de En de 17de Eeuw are incorporated.

Library: c. 27,000 volumes and c. 48,000 prints in photograph collection for reference only.

Publications: Corpus Rubenianum Ludwig Burchard (an illustrated Catalogue Raisonne of the work of P. P. Rubens in 26 parts, based on material of Dr. Ludwig Burchard).

STEDELIJK PRENTENKABINET*
(Municipal Gallery of Graphic Arts)
Vrijdagmarkt 23. Tel: 03/322455
Dr. L. Voet, Dir.
R. de Belser, Chief-Asst.
Free Mon. - Fri. 10 AM - 4 PM; Estab. 1936; research-work on Flemish graphic art; City appropriation. No permanent exhibition.

Collections: Old drawings—Rubens, Van Dyck, Jordaens, E. and A. Quellin, Schut, etc. Modern drawings—J. Ensor, Rik Wouters,

W. Vaes, Fl. Jespers, H. Leys, etc. Old engravings—Galle, Wiericx, Jegher, Goltzius, W. Hollar, Hogenbergh, etc. Modern engravings—Ensor, W. Vaes, Masereel, Cantre, J. Minne, etc.

Activities: Photograph collection of approx. 15,000 prints; Antwerp iconographic collection.

Library: Approx. 9000 volumes, mainly reference books; Photograph collection, 800 prints.

BRUGES

GROENINGEMUSEUM*
(City Gallery of Art)
Dyver, 12.
Dr. A. Janssens de Bisthoven, Dir.
Open daily, during summer (March-Sept. 30) 9:30 - 12 AM & 2 - 6 PM, also (July-Sept. 30) 8 - 10 PM; during winter (Oct.-Feb. 28) 10 - 12 AM & 2 - 5 PM; cl. New Year's Day; admis. 10 francs.

Collections: †An exceptionally rich collection of paintings, including some of the most famous masterpieces by Jan van Eyck, Hugo van der Goes, Jan Memling, Gerard David, Adriaen Isenbrant, Hieronymus Bosch and Pieter Pourbus.

Attendance: 65,000.

BRUSSELS

MUSEES ROYAUX D'ART ET D'HISTOIRE
(Royal Museums of Art and History)
10 Parc du Cinquantenaire, 1040. Tel: 7.33.96.10
René De Roo, Cur.
Open 9:30 AM - 12:30 PM & 1:30 - 5 PM; cl. Mon. Estab. 1835.

Collections: †Egyptian, Oriental and classical art; †Roman Belgium; †Medieval, Renaissance and modern art (furniture, tapestries, textiles, lace, glass, ceramics, silver, etc); † Far Eastern art; †American archaeology; †ethnography; †folklore.

Educational Activities: Lectures organized by Educational Service on subjects relating to the collections, principally ancient art and archaeology, Medieval & Renaissance manufacturing arts, folklore, ethnography; 50 visiting French & Dutch lecturers per year. Gallery talks (1450 per yr. for schools, 100 per yr. for adults, organized by the Educational Service; 25 per yr. organized by the Museum); 7 tours per yr. to exhibitions, cities, etc. organized by the Educational Service.

Library: 105,000 volumes
Attendance: Average 80,000.

MUSEES ROYAUX DES BEAUX-ARTS DE BELGIQUE
(Royal Museums of Fine Arts of Belgium)
rue du Musee 9. Tel: 02/513.96.30
Philippe Roberts-Jones, Dir.
Henri Pauwels, Cur. Ancient Art
Francine-Claire Legrand, Cur. Modern Art
Estab. 1830.

Collections: Medieval, Renaissance and modern paintings, drawings and sculpture.

Musée d'Art Ancien
rue de la Regence 3.
Collections: Paintings and drawings, 15th-19th century, and old and modern sculpture.

Musée d'Art Moderne
place Royale 1.
Collections: Paintings, drawings and sculpture of the 19th-20th century (temporary exhibitions only).

Musée Wiertz
rue Vautier 62.
Collections: Paintings of Antoine Wiertz.

LIEGE

MUSEES D'ARCHEOLOGIE ET D'ARTS DECORATIFS
(Liege Museums of Archeology and Decorative Arts)
13, Quai de Maastricht. Tel: 04/23.20.68
Joseph Philippe, Dir.
Jean Beguin, Asst. Cur.
Open 10 AM - 12:30 PM and 2 - 5 PM; Sun. & holidays 10 AM - 2 PM. Curtius Museum estab. 1909, Ansembourg Museum in 1905 and the Glass Museum in 1959; supported by city appropriation.

Collections (100,000 pieces): Musee Curtius, archeology; decorative arts from prehistory to 18th century; Musee du Verre, history and art of glass; Musee d'Ansembourg, 18th century decorative arts of Liege, housed in a mansion of the same period.

Activities: Guides are available for visitors; lectures; book shop.

Library: Approx. 10,000 volumes; photograph collection of approx. 5000 prints.

Publications: Bulletin de l'Association Internationale pour l'Histoire du Verre (annually); plus Annales of the Association.

VERVIERS

MUSEES COMMUNAUX BEAUX-ARTS ET ARCHEOLOGIE
(Community Museum of Fine Arts and Archaeology)
Beaux-Arts-rue Renier, 17 (Archéologie-rue des Raines, 42).
Tel: 087/331695
V. Bronowski, Cur.
Free Mon. - Thurs. & Sat. 9 AM - Noon & 2 - 5 PM; Sun. 10 AM - 1 PM & 3 - 6 PM. Estab. 1884; supported by appropriation.

Collections: Ancient and modern painting and sculpture; graphic arts; ceramics; furniture; Roman antiquities; regional archaeology; folk arts.

Exhibitions: Eight exhibitions of fine arts and archaeology a year.

Activities: Classes for children; lectures open to public.

Library: Approx. 5000 volumes, photograph collection for reference.

Publications: Guide books.

BOLIVIA

LA PAZ

MUSEO NACIONAL DE ARQUEOLOGIA*
(National Museum)
Calle Tihuanacu 93, Casilla oficial 64. Tel: 29624
Gregorio Cordero Miranda, Dir.
Olga Joffre Chávez, Asst. Dir.
Victor Vera, Secy.
Federico Diez de Medina, Cur. Archaeology
Estab. 1846, reinaugurated 1960.

Collections: Anthropology; ethnology; archaeology; zoology; numismatics; folklore; traditional native arts and crafts; colonial art; Lake Titicaca district exhibitions.

Activities: Study of Archaeology, cultural exchange with the exterior, services to tourists, college, & institutions.

Library: 3000 volumes.

Publications: Anales del Museo, Centenario del Museo 1940.

Attendance: 9350.

BRAZIL

OURO PRETO

MUSEU DA INCONFIDENCIA
(History of Democratic Ideals and Culture in Minas Gerais)
Praca Tiracentes, 139, 35.400. Tel: 332
Rui Mourao, Dir.
Open Noon - 5:30 PM. Estab. 1938.

Inaugurated 1944 to honor the first movement towards Brazil's independence, the Inconfidencia Mineira, which took place in Ouro Preto, then the capitol of Minas Gerais; to explain how this movement and its ideals first appeared; to show a general view of the cultural development of Minas Gerais to the public through the collections.

The Museum belongs to the Federal Government and is an organ of the Ministry for Education's Department for the Preservation of the National Historic and Artistic Property. It has no Board of Trustees and no membership. All expenditures are paid directly by the Federal Treasury.

Collections: Objects related to the 1789 revolutionaires of Minas Gerais (the Inconfidentes); †wood carvings; †furniture; painting; sacred arts; silver. Special collections: tombs containing the remains of the Inconfidentes who died exiled in different regions of Africa; original drawings, documents, and wood carvings by Antonio Francisco Lisboa, the Little Cripple, who is Brazil's most important artist and who was also a sculptor and architect.

Library: Specializes in Brazil's history and history of art, with emphasis on Minas Gerais problems; small representation of Portugese, Spanish, and Latin American arts and history. Contains more than 1600 works and periodic publications, totaling more than 2200 volumes.

Archives: Documents that belonged to Barao de Camargos, an ancient Senator who lived in Ouro Preto and documents from all the Ouro Preto's offices of notary public during the colonial period.

Attendance: 150,000.

RIO DE JANEIRO

MUSEU DE ARTE MODERNA DO RIO DE JANEIRO
(Museum of Modern Art)
Avenida Beira-Mar s/n°, Caixa Postal 44 - ZC 00
Tel: 222-6816
Heloisa Aleixo Lustosa, Exec. Dir.
Regina Pinto Zingoni, Assoc Exec. Dir.
Open daily Noon - 7 PM; Sun. 2 - 7 PM; cl. Mon. Estab. 1948.

Exhibitions: Monthly shows of painting, sculpture and engraving by Brazilian and foreign artists.

Activities: Theoretical and practical courses on painting; engraving workshop for pupils; film library; permanent collection.

Library: 7159 volumes.

Publications: Catalogs and bulletins.

MUSEU NACIONAL DE BELAS ARTES*
(National Museum of Fine Arts)
Av. Rio Branco 199.
Maria Elisa Carrazzoni, Dir.
Estab. 1938.

Collections: Brazilian and European paintings and sculpture; graphic arts; furniture; primitive art; numismatics; posters; photographs.

Exhibitions: Holds an annual exhibition of painting, sculpture, engraving, architecture, and fine arts.

Library: 8000 volumes.

Publications: Anuario, Boletim, catalogues, etc.

SAO PAULO

MUSEU DE ARTE
(Sao Paulo Art Museum)
Av. Paulista 1578
P.M. Bardi, Dir.
Open 2 - 6 PM. Founded 1947.

Collections: †Ancient and modern paintings and sculptures. Italian, 13th to 20th century; French, 16th to 20th century; Spanish and Portugese, 16th to 19th century; Flemish, Dutch, and German, 15th to 20th century; British, 18th to 20th century; American, 19th to 20th century; Brazilian, 17th to 20th century.

Activities: Conducts history of art school.

CHILE

SANTIAGO

MUSEO DE ARTE POPULAR AMERICANO*
(Art of the American Peoples Museum)
University of Chile, Faculty of Fine Arts,
Gerro Santa Lucia. Tel: 30138.
D. Oreste Plath, Dir.
Free, Tues. - Sat. 10 AM - 5:30 PM; Sun. 3 - 6 PM. Estab. for the study and exposure to popular American art. Three rooms with showcases and panels for exhibition.

Collections: Popular art of the American peoples; collection of araucarian silver.

Exhibitions: Pesebres, retablos e imagineria religiosa; Tejidos indigenas y populares de America; Artesania Popular Mexicana; Arte Popular Chileno; Arte Popular Rumano; Arte y Artesanias de China Popular.

Activities: Extension department activities are related to the faculty of fine arts; traveling exhibitions organized and circulated; lectures.

Library: Reference collection of 3500 volumes; photograph collection.

Publications: Exhibition catalogues, annually.

MUSEU NACIONAL DE BELLAS ARTES*
(National Museum of Fine Arts)
Parque Forestal, Casilla 3209.
Lily Garafulic, Dir.
Estab. 1880.

Collections: Paintings, engravings and etchings, 9668; 367 pieces of sculpture.

Exhibitions: Holds an annual exhibition of painting, sculpture, engraving, architecture and fine arts.

Library: 892 volumes.

REPUBLIC OF CHINA (TAIWAN)

TAIPEI

NATIONAL PALACE MUSEUM
Wai-shuang-hsi, Shih-lin. Tel: (02) 881-2021
Chiang Fu-tsung, Dir.
Ho Lien-kwei, Deputy Dir.
Li Lin-ts'an, Deputy Dir & Acting Cur. Dept. Antiquities
Wang Pu, Secy-Gen. & Head Conservation Dept.
Peter Chang, Head Library & Documents Dept.
Chiang Chao-shen, Cur. Dept. Painting & Calligraphy
Wang Chi-wu, Chief Publications Div.
Richard C. T. Wang, Chief Exhibition Div.
She Cheng, Registrar

Open daily 9 AM - 5 PM; admis. NT$15 adults, NT$4 children and students. Estab. Oct. 10, 1925, moved into the present building Nov. 12, 1965 to supervise the preservation, cataloguing and exhibition of the art objects in the collection, to encourage research on the art objects in the collection, to promote Chinese ancient cultural arts, and to cooperate with other national research institutions; funded by the central government.

Collections: Jades, bronzes, pottery, porcelain, oracle bones, enamelware, carved lacquer, painting, calligraphy, tapestry, embroidery, writing implements, miniature crafts, rare and old books, Ch'ing dynasty court and governmental documents. All collections are of Chinese origin.

Exhibitions: (1973) Paintings from Ta-feng-t'ang and Lan-ch'-en-ke; Calligraphic Rubbings; Ninety Years of Wu School Painting; Sung Album Leaf Painting; (1974) Paintings of Catholic Artists; Tapestry and Embroidery; (1975) Fan Paintings from the Orecuiys Box of Mist and Clouds Collection; Masterpieces of Sung Painting; Figure Painting; Paintings of Yun Shou-p'ing; Four Great Masters of the Yüan.

Activities: Educational activities arranged by the Exhibition Department include sponsoring lecture series on Chinese art in both English and Chinese, hosting special lectures by visiting scholars, encouraging student tours of the museum, handling junior museum and arranging traveling exhibitions throughout Taiwan. 14,576 4 x 5 in. color photos, 20,134 4 x 5 in. black and white photos, over 50,000 enlarged photos and 9648 color slides in collection; photograph collection of art objects in museum for reference and for sale; classes for adults. Book shop.

Library: Approx. 20,000 volumes and art objects not contained in Museum, for reference (this number does not include rare books or Ch'ing documents). Photograph collection of over 3000 prints for reference.

Publications: Newsletter, monthly; Bulletin, bimonthly (both in English; Quarterly (in both English and Chinese); numerous catalogs; reprints of rare books.

Attendance: Approx. 1,200,000.

COLOMBIA

BOGOTA

MUSEO DE ARTE COLONIAL
(Museum of Colonial Art)
Carrera 6 N19-77. Tel: 416017
F. Gil Tovar, Dir.
Open 10 AM - 7 PM. Estab. 1942. Formerly part of The National University; actually, Instituto Colombiano de Cultura. The building erected by The Jesuits in 1604. Has been closed for a year, being restored and reorganized 1975.

Collections: †Paintings, †sculpture, †furniture, †silver work of the Spanish Colonial period (16th, 17th, 18th centuries).

Activities: Concerts every Tuesday at 7 PM.

CYPRUS

NICOSIA

CYPRUS MUSEUM*
Museum Ave.
Kyriakos Nicolaou, Cur.
Mrs. Angeliki Pieridou, Asst. Cur.
Mrs Ino Nicolaou, Asst. Cur, Records
Open 8 AM - 1 PM & 2:30 - 4:45 PM; admis. 50 mils for residents; 100 mils non-residents. Estab. 1908 to illustrate the ancient cultures of Cyprus; State appropriation. There are 12 galleries with exhibits dating from Neolithic to Graeco-Roman times.

Collections: Pottery, sculpture, bronzes, jewelry, inscriptions and various minor works of art.

Exhibitions: A special exhibition has been opened with finds from current excavations.

Library: Reference library; photograph collection.

Publications: Guide to the Cyprus Museum, postcards.

CZECHOSLOVAKIA

BRATISLAVA

SLOVENSKA NARODNA GALERIA
(Slovak National Gallery)
Razusovo nabr. 2, 89013. Tel: 383 04, 321 66
Dr. Stefan Mruskovic, Dir.
Dr. Karol Vaculik, Chief, Dept. Slovak & European Art to 19th Century
Dr. Silvia Ileckova, Chief, Dept Contemporary Art

Dr. Eva Trojanova, Chief, Dept. Graphic Art
Dr. Katarina Schreiberova, Chief, Dept Nonprofessional Art
Founded 1948; the leading National Art Institution with collections
of Slovak and European painting, mostly Italian, Netherland, Flemish
and Dutch, c. 4500 items; sculpture, c. 1700 items; graphics and
drawings, c. 17,000 items; insitic art, 700 items; applied arts, 1400
items.

The main exhibition halls in Bratislava under reconstruction
since 1972; at present all the collections concentrated in the castle
of the central Slovakian city of Zvolen and in the castle of the local-
ity of Červený Kameň. Open 10 AM - 6 PM. The permanent installation of paintings and graphics by one of the leading artists of the
Slovak modern art, Ľudovít Fulla, in the city of Ružomberok.

Exhibitions: Apart from the permanent installations in own
premises, specialized exhibitions in Czechoslovakia and abroad.
Regular international exhibitions in Bratislava organized by the
Slovak National Gallery: Biennale of Illustrations Bratislava (BIB),
exhibitions of children's books illustrations, held since 1967;
Triennale of Insitic (Naive) Art, exhibitions held since 1966, in 1975
extended to include all forms of nonprofessional art. In connection
with both exhibitions prizes and awards by an International Jury. In
addition, both national and international symposiums and seminars on
selected topics.

Publications: Selected materials from each symposium (e.g, The
Problems of Contemporary Children's Books Illustrations, The
Gothic Art in Slovakia, On the Nonprofessional Art, On the Contemporary Slovak Art, etc. Bulletin Ars Populi appears irregularly 2 or
3 times a year, dedicated to the problems of nonprofessional art.

Library: c. 30,000 volumes.

BRNO

MORAVSKÁ GALERIE V BRNĚ
(Moravian Gallery at Brno)
Husova ulice 14, 66 226 Brno. Tel: 20 151 / 24 809
Jiří Hlušička, Art Historian & Dir.
Open daily 10 AM - 6 PM; cl. Mon; admis. 1,-,2,-,4,-Czech crowns.
Estab. 1817 as a regional gallery of fine arts; collects all-world art;
specialised in Moravian Art; financed by state appropriation.

Collections: †Fine art collection: painting, sculpture, graphic art
since 14th century to present; †Applied Art collection: glass, furniture, textiles, jewellery, ceramics, graphic design, photography;
Oriental art collection. Over 100,000 pieces in both collections.

Exhibitions: Biennale of Graphic design; Cut glass trienale;
Biennale of Czechoslovak contemporary photography; and other exhibitions from own collections or lent exhibitions from other Czech
and foreign institutions.

Activities: Extension department serves south Moravia; material
available to all small regional galleries or museums free of charge;
traveling exhibitions organized and circulated; original objects of
art lent for exhibitions only; visiting lecturers and gallery talks vary
per year; tours; concerts; classes for adults.

Library: Lending collection of approx. 60,000 volumes; public
art library.

Publications: Bulletin of Moravian Gallery, 3 per year; catalogs; Museology Papers, 4 per year.

LITOMERICE

GALERIE VYTVARNEHO UMENI*
(Gallery of Fine Arts)
412 47 Litoměřice, Michalská 7, Czechoslovakia 2338
Otakar Votoček, Dir.
Open Mon. - Fri. 10 - 12 AM; 2 - 5 PM; Sat. & Sun. 10 AM - 5 PM;
admis. adults 2.-Kčs, students Kčs 1.-- Estab. 1958 as a collection
of the North-Bohemian paintings and sculptures 13th-20th century;
financed by city and state appropriations.

Collections: Gothic art of the 14th-15th century; Renaissance
paintings and sculptures of the 15th-16th century; Barok art of the
17th-18th century; †Art of the 19th century and the collection of the
contemporary art.

Exhibitions: Approx. 10 mutual exhibitions yearly; Dutch paintings of the 17th century; North-Bohemian county in the works of
the painters a graphikers; Art Protis, tapestry; Russian Ikons;
Naive Art.

Activities: Extension department serves the North Bohemian
county; material available to the schools and clubs; fees; material
lent, pictures, sculptures, graphics and books; traveling exhibitions
organized and circulated; individual paintings and original objects of
art lent; lending collection, 41 color reproductions, 4000 lantern
slides, 15 exhibitions of graphics; 70 active borrowers; photograph
collection for lending; lectures open to the public; 8 visiting lecturers and gallery talks per year; 1-2 tours; concerts; classes for
children.

Library: Lending and reference library of 5000 volumes.

PRAGUE

NARODNI GALERIE V PRAZE*
(National Gallery)
Hradcanske nam. 15, 119 04 Praha 012. Tel: 352441-3, 536637
Prof. Dr. Jiri Kotalik, Pres.
Dr. Libuse Jandova, Deputy Dir. & Chief Graphic Art Collection
Doc. Dr. Jiri Masin, Chief Ancient Art Collection
Dr. Vaclav Prochazka, Chief Modern Art Collection
Dr. Lubor Hajek, Chief Oriental Art Collection
Open daily 10 AM - 6 PM; cl. Mon. Estab. 1796 as picture gallery
of the Society of Patriotic Friends of Arts; 1901 established Gallery
of Modern Art; 1945 both collections united in the National Gallery;
to collect and expertly safeguard the collections of Czech and world
paintings, sculptures and graphic art works; financed by state appropriations.

Collection: Ancient, Modern, Graphic and Oriental Art Collections.

Exhibitions: Basic exhibitions approx. 25 per year.

Activities: Provides methodical help to 25 regional galleries and
coordinates their professional activity; traveling exhibitions organized and circulated abroad, approx. 25 per year; photograph collection of 62,000 prints for lending; lectures open to public; 402 gallery
talks and 362 tours per year; concerts; classes for adults and children; competitions.

Library: 33,000 volumes for lending; 10,000 photographs in
archives; concentrates complete editions of Czech and foreign professional magazines; elaborates the collection of Czech and foreign
exhibition catalogues.

Publications: Bulletin of National Gallery; catalogues of permanent exhibitions, collections and short-time exhibitions.

Attendance: 1971-750,000; 1972-701,000.

STATNI ZIDOVSKE MUZEUM*
(State Jewish Museum)
Jáchymova 3, 110 01 Prague 1. Tel: 633-74
Erik Klíma, Dir.
Doc. Dr. V. Sadek, Chief of the Scientific Dept. & the Dept. of Col-
lections
Prom.hist. A. Franková, Chief of the Dept. of Expositions
Open 9 AM - 5 PM; cl. Sat; admis. adults 5 Kčs, students 3 Kčs.
Founded in 1950, to inform the public about the history of Jews in
Bohemia and Moravia; Jewish Cemetery of the 15th century and the
oldest synagogue in Gothic Style of the 13th century.

Collections: Silver liturgical objects; textiles from synagogues
of historic interest; library of ancient books with a collection of
Hebrew manuscripts; historical archival materials of Bohemian
and Moravian Jewish religious communities; children's drawings
and works of painters from Terezín (Theresienstadt).

Activities: Exhibitions, scientific research on the field of the
history of Jews in Bohemia and Moravia.

Library: 80,000 volumes.

Publications: Judaica Bohemiae, biannually.

Attendance: 700,000 visitors annually.

DENMARK

AALBORG

NORDJYLLANDS KUNSTMUSEUM
(The Art Museum of Northern Jutland)
Kong Christians Alle 50 DK 9000. Tel: 08-138088
J. A. Lorck, Governor
Lars Rostrup Bøyesen, Dir.
H. P. Jensen, Leader of Pub. Relations Dept.
Open Apr. - Oct. daily 10 AM - 5 PM; Nov. - Mar. daily 11 AM -
4 PM; cl. Mon; admis. 5 Kr. Estab. 1972; financed by endowment
and city and state appropriation.

Collections: Anna and Kresten Krestensen Collection; large collections of Danish and international paintings, sculptures and graphics
from 1900 and up to date; COBRA collection.

Exhibitions: Graphics from USSR, W. Hasior, Modern Art from
West Germany, Joan Miro, Art from Africa, World Press Photo,
Asger Jorn, Emil Nolde, Jean Dewasne, Reidar Aulie, Naiv Art from
Scandinavia, Pierre Alechinsky, New Art from Jugoslavia, Art from
Moderna Museet i Stockholm, Photos by Stuart Fox, Art from the
Swedish Kings Collection, 100 Silent Film Posters, Art Nouveau
from Hungaria, Heinz Mack, Modern Swedish Graphics, Stoneware
from Saxbo, Modern Art from U.S.A, West Germany, Italy, France,
Sweden, Great Britain and Denmark, Sculptures, Drawings and
Etchings by Henry Moore.

Activities: Educational department conducts guided tours in the
collections; conferences; traveling exhibitions organized and circulated; individual paintings and original objects of art lent; photograph collection; lectures open to the public; concerts; dramatic programs.

Library: Large archives of international art catalogs, cuttings from papers and other sort of documentation.
Publications: Catalogs and bulletin, 6-8 yearly.
Attendance: 100,000 annual average.

AARHUS

AARHUS KUNSTMUSEUM
(Aarhus Art Museum)
Vennelystparken, Dk 8000. Tel: 06 - 135255
Johan Richter, Pres.
Kristian Jakobsen, Dir.
Free Tues. - Fri. 10 AM - 4 PM; Sat. - Sun. 10 AM - 5 PM; cl. Mon. Estab. 1858. Endowed; appropriation.
Collections: Danish art, painting, sculpture, graphic arts, c.1750 to present time; European art, mostly graphic art, recent works; a few outstanding works 17th century and later.
Exhibitions: Several every year.
Activities: Junior museum; lectures open to public; concerts.
Library: Photograph collection.
Annual Purchases: Approx. $30,000.
Attendance: Approx. 70,000.

CHARLOTTENLUND

THE ORDRUPGAARD COLLECTION
Vilvordevej 110, 2920. Tel: 01 OR 11 83
Dr. Haavard Rostrup, Dir.
Open May - Sept. daily except Mon. 2 - 5 PM; Oct. - Apr: Sat. & Sun. 2 - 4 PM; admis. 2 Danish crowns.
Collections: Wilhelm Hansen Collection, paintings by Delacroix, Corot, Courbet, Manet, Degas, Renoir, Pissarro, Sisley, Gauguin, Cezanne and other French and Danish artists from the 19th century.

COPENHAGEN

DET DANSKE KUNSTINDUSTRIMUSEUM
(Museum of Decorative Art)
Bredgade 68, 1260. Tel: (0) 149452
Jørgen Trolle, Pres.
Erik Lassen, Dir.
Vibeke Woldbye & Jørgen Schou-Christensen, Keepers
Eva Steinaa & Kristen Olesen, Librns.
Free daily 1 - 4 PM & from Sept. 1st - May 31st Tues. 1 - 9 PM; cl. Mon. Library open weekdays 10 AM - 4 PM & from Sept. 1st - May 31st Tues. 10 AM - 9 PM; cl. Mon. Estab. 1894.
Collections: European decorative art from the middle ages till the present—Furniture, carpets and tapestries, porcelain and pottery, silverware, jewelry, textiles and bookbindings. Chinese and Japanese art and handicrafts.
Exhibitions: Approx. 20 exhibitions a year.
Activities: Lectures, 2-3 visiting lecturers per year.
Library: 50,000 volumes for lending; photograph collection.
Publications: Kunstindustrimuseets Virksomhed.

KØBENHAVNS BYMUSEUM
(Copenhagen City Museum)
Vesterbrogade 59, 1620. Tel: 01-210772
Steffen Linvald, Dir.
Jørgen Ahlefeldt-Laurvig, Archaeologist
John Erichsen, Cand. Mag. Inspector
Open summer, daily 10 AM - 4 PM; winter, 1 - 4 PM; cl. Mon; all year, Tues. 7 - 9 PM. Admis. adults 1 crown, children 0,5 crown, Wed. & Fri. free. Estab. 1901 to preserve history and topography of Copenhagen.
Collections: Søren Kierkegaard Collection
Exhibitions: Different exhibitions about Copenhagen history.
Activities: Lending service of archaeological material, original objects of art, approx. 200,000 photographs; 4500 items lent per year to c. 400 borrowers.
Library: Approx. 2000 volumes; photograph collection.
Publications: Historiske Meddelelser om København, Saertryk, annually.

NATIONALMUSEET
(The National Museum)
Prinsens Palae, Frederiksholms Kanal 12
Dr. P.V. Glob, Dir.
Estab. 1807.
Collections: Consists of 10 divisions: The Danish Prehistoric Collection, The Danish Historical Collection, The Danish Folk Museum, The Ethnographic Collection, The Collection of Classical Antiquities, The Royal Collection of Coins and Medals, The Open-air Museum at Sorgenfri, The Department of Natural Sciences, The Museum of the Danish Resistance Movement 1940-1945 and Public Relation Department.

NY CARLSBERG GLYPTOTHEK
(The Carlsberg Gallery)
Dantes Plads, 1556
M. Gjødesen, Dir.
H. Rostrup, Cur. French & Danish Art
F. Johansen, Cur. Greek & Roman Art
J. Christiansen, Cur. Greek & Roman Art
Open Summer daily 10 AM - 4 PM; Winter weekdays 12 AM - 3 PM; Sun. 10 AM - 4 PM; admis. 3 kroner; Wed. & Sun. free; cl. Mon. all year. Estab. 1897.
Collections: †Egyptian, †Greek, †Etruscan, and †Roman sculpture, etc; †Danish and †French paintings and sculptures from 19th century.
Library: Reference library of 35,000 volumes.
Attendance: 155,000.

STATENS MUSEUM FOR KUNST
(Royal Museum of Fine Arts)
1307 Sølvgade
Jørn Rubow, Dir.
Open daily 10 AM - 5 PM; Wed. 10 AM - 10 PM; cl. Mon. Reading-room, Dept. of Prints & Drawings, Tues. - Sat. 10 AM - 5 PM; Wed. 10 AM - 5 PM & 7 - 10 PM; cl. Sun. & Mon.
Department of Paintings and Sculpture: Chief collection of Danish works of art, 18th-20th century; Scandinavian artists 19th and 20th century; modern French Art. Old Master collection of the Italian, Flemish, Dutch, German, and French schools. Library of approx. 50,000 volumes.
Department of Prints and Drawings: Containing nearly 200,000 drawings and prints of Danish and foreign origin, as well as a library.
Publications: Kunstmuseets Arsskrift, annual.

THORVALDSENS MUSEUM
Porthusgade 2, 1213.
Alsing Andersen, Mayor
Dr. Dyveke Helsted, Dir.
Dr. Bjarne Jørnaes, Cur.
Dr. Torben Melander, Res. Asst.
Open May - Sept. 10 AM - 4 PM; Oct. - Apr. 10 AM - 3 PM; Sun, Wed, Fri. free; admis. other days 1 Kr. Estab. 1848; financed by the city of Copenhagen.
Collections: †Works by Bertel Thorvaldsen, his collections of paintings, drawings, antiquities.
Exhibitions: Fra Thorvaldsens Samlinger; C. A. Lorentzen; Møde Med Italien; Childrens Drawings; H. W. Bissen; Maegtige Schweiz; Romantisk tegnekunst fra Tyskland; Danish Museums 1648-1848; Fransk Nyklassicisme; Tegningen fra Leningrad.
Activities: Lectures open to the public; concerts. Book shop.
Library: Reference library and photograph collection.
Publications: Meddelelser Fra Thorvaldsens Museum, irregular.
Attendance: 70,700.

HUMLEBAEK

LOUISIANA MUSEUM OF MODERN ART
Gammel Strandvej ad, 3050. Tel: 03-190719
Knud W. Jensen, Pres.
Hugo Arne Buch, Cur.
Hans Erik Wallin, Ed.
Børge Hansen, Chief Accountant
Open 10 AM - 5 PM; admis. kr. 8. Estab. Aug. 14, 1958, to introduce international modern art to the Danish public; financed by endowment and city and state appropriation.
Collections: Arp, Giacometti, Naum Gabo, Calder, Henry Moore, Alechinsky, Carl Henning Pedersen, Sekine, Kawaguchi, Onosato.
Exhibitions: (1973) Naive Art; Extreme Realism; Alfred Jensen; Jean Tinguely Jorn; Public Design in Holland; Pol Bury; Dali; Eisenstein; Visible-Invisible; (1974) Chr. Boltanski; Tapies; Christo; Fellini; Dubuffet; Dewasne; Anon. Design; Tantra; Japanese Art - Old and New; (1975) Miro; Jan Groth; Villalba; Morris Louis; Monory; Moderna Museet visits L; Duane Hanson; Luginbühl; Ipousteguy; Edvard Munch; Navaho Blankets; CAYC.
Activities: Concerts.
Publications: Louisiana Revy, 3-4 times a year,
Attendance: 200,000.

EGYPT

ALEXANDRIA

GRECO-ROMAN MUSEUM*
Museum St.
Dr. Henry Riad, Dir.
H. Comber, Librn.
Estab. 1892.

Collections: Exhibits from the Coptic, Roman and Greek eras.
Library: 8000 volumes.

CAIRO

COPTIC MUSEUM*
 Masr Ateeka, Cairo
Dr. Shafik Farid, Dir.
Open 8 AM - 1 PM (summer); 9 AM - 4 PM (winter). Estab. 1910.
 Collections: Sculpture; architecture; ivory; pottery; glass;
manuscripts. textiles; icons; bone.
 Library: 7000 volumes.

EGYPTIAN NATIONAL MUSEUM
 Midan-el-Tahrir, Kasr El-Nil.
Dr. Gamal Moukhtar, Dir.
Dr. ABD el-Kader Selim, Chief Cur.
Dr. Dia'Abou-Ghazi, Librn.
Open (winter) 9 AM - 4 PM; (summer) 8:30 AM - 1:30 PM. Estab.
1900.
 Collections: From prehistoric times until 6th century A.D. Museum houses the Organization of Antiquities; the organization administers the archaeological museums and controls excavations.
 Exhibitions: Selection of items added to the Museum in the last
ten years; special shows.
 Library: 333,830 volumes.
 Publications: Annales du Service des Antiquities de l'Egypte,
annually, supplements, irregularly; Catalogue General du Musee,
irregularly; Fouilles a Saggarah; Catalogue de la Bibliotheque du
Musee Egyptien du Caire.

ETHIOPIA

ADDIS ABABA

THE MUSEUM, INSTITUTE OF ETHIOPIAN STUDIES
Addis Ababa University
 P.O. Box 1176
Dr. Girma Kidane, Cur.
Open weekdays 8:30 AM - 12:30 PM & 2:30 - 4:30 PM; Sat. & Sun.
8:30 AM - 12:30 PM; admis. 50¢, students free. Estab. 1963, primarily as an ethnological museum with substantial collection of
traditional Ethiopian paintings starting with 15th century; financed
by city and state appropriation, membership, Society of Friends of the
Institute of Ethiopian Studies. Monthly meetings; dues $50.
 Collections: 5585 pieces in ethnological collections; 383 pieces in
collection of paintings, the oldest c. 15th century; 1334 pieces in
collection of crosses, the oldest c. 11th - 12th centuries.
 Exhibitions: Stuttgart, Germany, 1973; Zürich, Swizterland,
Vienna, Austria and Stockholm, Sweden, 1973-74; Paris, France,
1975.
 Activities: Lectures for members only.
 Library: Reference library; over 7000 negatives in photograph
collection; 1200 color slides.
 Publications: Catalogs and albums, published irregularly.
 Income and Purchases: Income approx. $5000; purchases approx.
$10,000.

FINLAND

HELSINKI

SUOMEN KANSALLISMUSEO*
(The National Museum of Finland)
 00101 Helsinki 10, Box 913. Tel: 441181
Dr. Riitta Pylkkanen, Dir.
The National Board of Antiquities and Historical Monuments (previously the Archaeological Commission), of which the National Museum
is a branch, estab. 1884. A research institute and museum. In 1893
the Historical-Ethnographical Museum of the Helsinki University, the
collections of the Finnish Archeological Society and the Ethnographical Museum of the Finnish Undergraduates Corporation were united
under the name of the State Historical Museum, and later as the National Museum. In 1916 the first departments were opened to the
public. The library, including that of the Finnish Archeological
Society, contains approx. 73,000 volumes.
 The Museum comprises a Prehistoric Department with Finnish
and Comparative Collections, a Finnish Historical Department combined with a Collection of Coins and Medals, and an Ethnographical
Department with Finnish, Finno-Ugrian and Comparative Ethnographical Collections. The Open-Air Museum at Seurasaari (Fölisön) and
the museums at Suomenlinna (Sveaborg) are branches of the National
Museum.

TURKU

TURUN TAIDEMUSEO*
(Turku Art Association and Museum)
 Puolalanpuisto. Tel: 11 810
Leif B. Sourander, Pres.
Erik Bergh, Dir.
Lector Osmo Laine, V.Pres.
Carl-August Doepel, Treas.
Open weekdays 10 AM - 4 PM; Thurs. also 6 - 8 PM; Sun. 10 AM -
6 PM, cl. Mon. Sept. 11 - May 31; admis. adults 1 mk, students and
children 0.50 mk. Estab. Turku Art Association 1891, Turku Art
Museum 1904; supported by State and City. General meeting in Mar;
mem. 1324 (12.31.69); dues 7 mk, permanent mem. 140 mk.
 Collections: Outstanding collections of 19th and 20th century Finnish art, paintings, drawings, prints and sculpture. International
print collection, 19th and 20th century.
 Exhibitions: Total of 37, including Bauhaus 1919-25, Hommage à
Picasso, Erik Bryggman 1891-1955 memorial exhibition, Plakat Polski, James Ensor (prints), Aristide Maillol, Paul Delvaux (prints),
Markus Leppo, New York (photos), 40 Deutsche unter 40; furthermore annual exhibitions with invited guests, 1969 e.g. Giò Pomodoro
(Italy) and Ole Sporring (Denmark).
 Activities: Continuing program of changing exhibitions, 25 conducted gallery tours and gallery talks; lectures open to the public;
loan program of original objects of art. Turku Art School, the oldest
in Finland, estab. 1830.
 Library: Number of volumes for reference; photograph collection of c.500 prints for reference; poster collection.
 Income and Purchases: Income approx. $28,300; purchases approx. $4000-$5000.
 Attendance: (1968) 41,115; (1969) 45,280.

FRANCE

ANGERS

MUSEE DES BEAUX-ARTS
(Museum of Fine Arts)
 10 rue du Musee, 49000. Tel: (41) 88.64.65
Viviane Huchard, Conservator, Musees d'Angers
Catherine Lagrue, Asst. Conservator
Genevieve Thomas, Librn.
Genevieve Pellefigues, Librn.
Open Oct. 1 - May 31 10 AM - Noon & 2 - 3 PM; Apr. 1 - Sept. 30
daily 9 AM - Noon & 2 - 6 PM; admis. 1 F, .50 F for children and
senior citizens; financed by city appropriation.
 Collections: Galerie David d'Angers and sculpture of the 19th
century; objects of art and sculpture of the Middle Ages and
Renaissance; 19th century French and foreign primitive paintings;
contemporary tapestries.
 Exhibitions: (1974) Art Negre; Barbauet; (1975) Art de la
Vallee de la Loire; Examples de Miro; Tapisseries du Stage de
formation textile du Festival d'Aujou; Un quatier antique a Angers.
 Activities: Concerts. Book shop.
 Library: 1000 prints in photograph collection and 2000 volumes
for reference only.

LILLE

MUSÉE DES BEAUX-ARTS DE LILLE
(Museum of Fine Arts)
 Place de la République 59000, Lille
Open 10 AM - 12:30 PM, 2 - 5 PM; cl. Tues; admis. 2 F. Financed
by city and state appropriations.
 Collections: Paintings of 15th-20th century Western Europe;
sculptures; ceramics and objects of art.
 Exhibitions: (1973) Beckmann; L'ameublement et l'habillement de
la Renaissance a nos jours; Images d'une France (photographies d'A.
Martin) et "Esteve" (lithographies); (1974) Peintures prehistoriques
du Tassili; Exposition d'art indien; Exposition Peintres suedois; La
collection d'Alexandre Leleux; Cent ans de peinture francaise dans
les collections; (1975) Peinture anglaise contemporaine; Villi
Baumeister; Tapisseries brabanconnes d'aujourd'hui; Tapis et
gravures de l'Azerbaidjan; Peinture est allemande.
 Activities: School improvement; photograph collection.
 Library: Not open to the public.

LYON

MUSEE DES BEAUX ARTS, PALAIS ST. PIERRE*
(Museum of Fine Arts)
 20 place des Terreaux, 69001. Tel: 28-07-66
Mme. Madeleine Rocher-Jauneau, Cur.
Open daily 10 - 12 AM & 2 - 6 PM; admis. free. Estab. in the 17th
century in the Monastry of the Nuns of St. Pierre; museum of paint-

ing, sculpture and objets d'art. Association of the Friends of the Museum, 1100 mem; ann. dues 10 F.

Collections: Greek and Roman sculpture; Gothic and Renaissance art; ancient and modern painting; objets d'art; oriental art; painting of the Lyonnaise school since the 17th century; Egyptian, Greek and Roman antiquities; Islamic art; French art since the Middle Ages.

Exhibitions: (1968) U.S.A Groupe 68; Gaston Chaissac; Survage; Musée de Werkusen. (1969) Alexandre Archipenko; Emil Voldo; Nathalie Gontcharova. (1970) Les Psaumes de Benn; Tony Garnier; Jawlensky; Werner Scholz. (1971) Ludwig Kirchner; Theatre exceriture theatrale de la region Rhone-Alpes. (1972) Tapisseries anciennes; aut dessins du liusee Kroller-Muller; Baliks de Jerome Wallace. (1973) Art ancien du Mexique et du Peron; Ryas Jeulandais; Georges Filiberti; Le Nuagisme; Gravieres de l'ecole de Fontainebleau.

Activities: Lectures for high school and college students; photographs; book shop.

Publications: Bulletin des Musées et Monuments Lyonnais, quarterly.

PARIS

MUSEE COGNACQ-JAY
(Cognacq-Jay Museum)
   25 Boulevard des Capucines, 75002. Tel: 0735566
Mlle. Thérèse Burollet, Dir.
Open 10 AM - 6 PM, cl. Mon. & Tues. Estab. 1928; City appropriation.

Collections: 18th century works of art; paintings of Boucher, Fragonard, Tiepolo; Quentin de La Tour pastels; drawings by Fragonard, Watteau; furniture; porcelain; sculpture by Lemoyne, Clodion, Falconet, Houdon; art of silversmiths; miniatures.

MUSEE CONDE
   Chateau de Chantilly, 60500.
Andre Chamson, Pres.
Raymond Cazelles, Conservator
Open Mar. - Nov. 10:30 AM - 6 PM; admis. 5 F. Estab. 1897.
Collections: Paintings, sculpture, drawings, prints, manuscripts, books, medals and archives.
   Activities: Educational and extension departments.
   Publications: Le Musee Conde, semi-annually.

MUSEE D'ART MODERNE DE LA VILLE DE PARIS*
(Museum of Modern Art)
   11 Ave du President Wilson, 16e.
Jacques Lassaigne, Cur.
Open daily 9:45 AM - 5:15 PM; cl. Tues. Estab. 1750.
   Collections: Modern painting and sculpture.

MUSEE DE CLUNY
(Cluny Museum)
   6 Place Paul Painleve (V) 75005.
Francis Salet, Dir.
Open daily 10 AM - 12:45 PM & 2 - 5 PM; cl. Tues. Library.
   Collections: †Tapestries, enamels, sculptures and ivories of the Middle Ages.

MUSEE DES ARTS DECORATIFS
(Museum of Decorative Arts)
Bibliotheque des Arts Decoratifs
   107 rue de Rivoli, 75001. Tel: 260 32.14
Robert Bordaz, Pres.
Pierre Meilhac, Secy.
Francois Mathey, Chief Cur.
Olivier Lepine, Cur.
Yvonne Brunhammer, Cur.
Marie-Noële de Gary, Cur.
Nadine Gasc, Cur.
Odile Nouvel, Cur.
Open Wed. - Sat. 10 AM - Noon & 2 - 5 PM; Sun. 10 AM - 5 PM; admis. 5 F. Estab. 1863 to adapt beauty to industry; financed by city and state appropriation and membership. Gallery maintained for exhibition of decorative art, architecture and art. Ann. meeting end of June; mem. 3200; dues 50 F.

Collections: Home decor of the French Middle Ages; Oriental art; tapestry collection; Dubuffet bequest; department of design; †textiles; †paper paints.

Exhibitions: Des dolelotiers aux Passementiers; Equiveques, French Paintings of the 19th century; Les Bronzes Ilamiers; Molieres; Les tapisseues de le Corbusier; David Hockney; Le Surrelisme; plus others.

Activities: Lectures with guided tours; films; educational sessions in firms connected with decorative arts, painting, engraving and pottery; traveling exhibitions organized and circulated; original

objects of art lent; 10,000 black and white prints and 500 Ektachromes in photographic department for reference only.
   Library: 80,000 volumes; 1000 photographs.
   Publications: Exhibition catalogs.
   Attendance: 80,000.

MUSEE DU JEU DE PAUME
(Gallery of Impressionists)
   Place de la Concorde
Hélène Adhemar, Cur.
Open daily 9:45 AM - 5:15 PM; cl. Tues. Annex of The Louvre.
   Collections: 19th century Impressionist paintings.

MUSEE DU LOUVRE*
(The Louvre Museum)
   Palais du Louvre. Tel: 231-59-40
Pierre Quoniam, Dir.
Open daily 9:45 AM - 5:15 PM; cl. Tues. & holidays. Estab. 1793.
   Collections: The †collections are divided into six departments and offer a panorama of the arts of all periods: Greek and Roman antiquities; Oriental antiquities; Egyptian antiquities; sculpture of the Middle Ages, the Renaissance and modern times; paintings; Objets d'Art of the Middle Ages, Renaissance and modern times.
   Special Collections: Drawings; Islamic Art; Coptes Antiquities; the Edmond de Rothschild Collection.
   Library: †100,000 volumes.
   Attendance: Paying 1,500,000; free 1,500,000.

MUSEE DU PETIT PALAIS
(Municipal Museum)
   Av. W. Churchill. Tel: 265-99-21
Mlle. Adeline Cacan, Chief Cur.
Open daily 10 AM - 6 PM; cl. Mon. & Tues. Estab. 1902. Temporary exhibitions.
   Collections: Egyptian, Greek, Etruscan antiquities; Roman bronzes, ceramics, coins; objets d'art of the Middle Ages and the Renaissance; paintings and drawings of the 17th and 18th centuries; tapestries, furniture, porcelains of Sevres and Saxe, etc; Chinese collections; drawings and paintings of the 19th century.
   Library: 10,000 volumes; 7000 prints.

MUSEE NATIONAL DES MONUMENTS FRANCAIS
(National Museum of French Sculpture and Murals)
   Palais de Chaillot, 16.
Museum open Wed. - Mon. 9:45 AM - 12:30 PM & 2 - 5 PM; cl. Tues. Library open to students of the Louvre and archeologists, Mon. - Fri. 10 AM - Noon & 2 - 5 PM; cl. Sat. & Sun. Founded 1880.
   Collections of the Museum: Full scale casts of the principal French monuments and sculpture from the Middle Ages to the 19th century. Full scale reproductions of medieval murals.
   Collections of the Library: Archeology, history of art, photograph collection of c. 20,000 prints; collection of c. 2000 copies of medieval murals.

MUSEE NATIONAL DU CHATEAU DE FONTAINEBLEAU
(National Museum of Fontainebleau)
   77 Fontainebleau. Tel: 422.27.40
Jean-Pierre Samoyault, Cur.
Open 10 AM - Noon & 2 - 6 PM (Oct. 1 - Apr. 1 2 - 5 PM). Founded in the 12th century; financed by state appropriation.
   Collections: 16th to 19th century furniture and interiors.
   Activities: Photograph collection; book shop; library.

REIMS

MUSEES DE REIMS
   8 Rue Chanzy, 51100. Tel: (26) 47 28 44
F. Pomarede, Conservator
J. P. Bonnal, Asst. Conservator.
M. Guillemain, Asst.
Free 10 AM - Noon & 2 - 6 PM. Estab. 1795 as a museum of art, archeology and local history; financed by city appropriation.
   Collections: †10 designs by Cranach; †paintings on canvas of the 15th - 16th centuries; 16th century tapestries of de Saint Revii; 17th - 18th century paintings; †25 paintings by Corot; †French paintings of the 19th century; ceramics; art and archeological antiques.
   Exhibitions: (1973) Sculptures de Noll; Le Cirque; (1974) La Revolution de 1848 a Reives; La feorue au 19th century; (1975) Brascanat.
   Activities: Expositions, classes and service for scholars.
   Library: 2000 volumes and 1000 prints in photograph collection.

STRASBOURG

MUSEE DE L'OEUVRE NOTRE DAME*
(Cathedral Museum)
3, Place du Chateau. Tel: 32.59.00
Victor Beyer, Conservator
Hours and admis. same as Musée des Beaux-Arts. (see below).
Collections: Houses dating from 14th, 16th and 17th centuries, grouped around the House of Charity. Romanesque Rooms: Sculptures of the 11th and 12th centuries; stained glass windows from Strasbourg's former Romanesque Cathedral. Gothic Rooms: Originals of the finest 13th century sculptures from the Cathedral; Drawings of the cathedral's Houses of Charity of the 13th to 15th centuries; Meeting-room of the Lodge of Stone-masons and Stone-cutters (1580). 15th Century Rooms: Sculptures, stained glass, Alsatian paintings. Renaissance Rooms: Graphic Arts and Illustration of books produced at Strasbourg from 1500 to 1600; paintings, drawings and stained glass by Grien; archives; rooms devoted to Renaissance furniture and sculpture; Still-life room; development of gold and silverware in Strasbourg from 15th to 19th century. Excellent collection of glass.

MUSEE DES BEAUX-ARTS*
(Museum of Fine Arts)
2 Place du Chateau. Tel: 35.47.27
Victor Beyer, Dir.
Open: Summer (April-May) daily 10 - 12 AM, 2 - 5 PM; cl. Good Friday, Easter, & May 1. (June-Sept.) daily 10 - 12 AM, 2 - 6 PM; cl. July 14. Winter (Oct. 1-Mar. 31) 10 - 12 AM, 2 - 4 PM daily; cl. Tues, Nov. 1, Dec. 25, Jan. 1. Admis. 1 F; half fee for groups of ten, students, children, and the military.
Occupies two floors of the Rohan Castle, which also contains the Archaeological Museum, the Museum of Decorative Arts, the Print Department, and the Library.
Collections: Important collection of paintings of the chief European schools (14th to 19th century) from Giotto to modern times. Works by Filippino Lippi, Corregio, Veronese, Tintoretto, Tiepolo, Guardi, El Greco, Zurbaran, Goya, Memling, Lucas of Leyden, van Heemskerk, Rubens, Van Dyck, De Hoogh, Marmion, Valentin, Vouet, Tassel, Watteau, Boucher, Chardin, Fragonard, etc; also Corot, Rousseau, Pissaro, Sisley, Degas, Monet, Renoir and others. Gauguin, Signac, Vuillard, Dufy, Braque and others of the modern school.

TOULOUSE

MUSEE DES AUGUSTINS
(Museum of Augustins)
2 ter rue Alsace-Lorraine, 31000. Tel: (61) 21-68-00
Denis Milhau, Cur.
Alfred Deflandre, Secy.
Open daily except Tues. 10 AM - Noon & 2 - 6 PM; admis. 1 Franc. Financed by city and state appropriation. Maintains gallery.
Collections: Romanesque, gothic and modern sculpture of Languedoc; paintings of the 16th-20th centuries, French, Italian, Flanders, Spanish.
Activities: Visits and comments for schools; traveling exhibitions organized and circulated; lectures open to public; 200 visiting lecturers per year; classes for children.
Library: 4000 volumes and 1000 prints in photograph collection for reference only.

TOURS

MUSEE DES BEAUX-ARTS
(Museum of Fine Arts)
18 Llau Francais Sicard, 37000. Tel: 05-68-73
Mrs. M. N. Linot De Villechenon, Chief Conservator
Miss S. Guillot De Suduiraut, Asst. Conservator
Open Nov. - Feb. 9 AM - Noon & 2 - 5 PM; cl. Tues; Mar. - Oct. 9 AM - Noon & 2 - 6 PM; June - Sept. 9 - 11 PM; cl. Jan. 1, May 1, July 1, Nov. 1, Dec. 25; admis. 2 F 50. Created as a museum of the French Revolution, installed into the Palais of the Archbishop in 1910; financed by municipal appropriation.
Collections: Italian paintings of the 13th-16th centuries, primitives, Mantegna; French paintings and furniture of the 18th century, work of Largillieu, Laucret, Boucher, Lerroneau, Challot, Demoulin, Rembrandt, Rubens, Delacroix, Boulanger, Chasseriau, Monct, Dourdelle, Calder.
Exhibitions: (1973-75) Peintures francais du XVII's du musee du Louvre; E. Debat-Ponsan; Images d'une France; La soierie touraugelle et le costumes au XVIII's; La ceramique touraugelle au XIX's; Lithographics de Max Ernst; L'Art de la Vallee de la Loire du XV's a l'epoque classique; Raoul Michau; Gravures de Picasso.
Activities: Overhead photographs for viewing; 2 lectures per week open to the public; library for reference.

VERSAILLES

MUSEE NATIONAL DU CHATEAU DE VERSAILLES
(National Museum of the Chateau of Versailles)
78000. Tel: 950-58-32
Open 10 AM - 5 PM; admis. 5 F. Estab. summer 1837 for the conservation and display of the Royal Apartments and the collections they contain.
Collections: Furniture, paintings and objects of art contained in the Royal Apartments; paintings of the 16th - 19th centuries contained the History Museum of France.
Activities: Bureau of Cultural Affairs organizes visiting conferences for the purpose of educating scholars; original objects of art lent; lectures open to the public.
Library: For reference only.

GERMANY

BERLIN

STAATLICHE MUSEEN PREUSSISCHER KULTURBESITZ
(State Museums, Foundation for Prussian Cultural Treasures)
Stauffenbergstr. 41, 30. Tel: 030-2609-
Prof. Dr. Stephan Waetzoldt, Dir.
Founded 1830; Museum Dahlem built 1912 and 1970; Nationalgalerie built 1968. Museums in Dahlem open Tues. - Fri. 9 AM - 5 PM, Sat. - Sun. 9 AM - 5 PM; cl. Mon. Museums in Charlottenburg open Sat. - Thur. 9 AM - 5 PM; cl. Fri. Nationalgalerie open Mon. Noon - 8 PM, Tues. - Sun. 9 AM - 5 PM; cl. Fri. Antiquities Collection open Mon, Thurs. & Fri. 9 AM - 5 PM, Sat. - Sun. 10 AM - 5 PM, Wed. 2 - 9 PM; cl. Tues.

Collections in Dahlem (1 Berlin 33, Arnimallee 23/27)
Picture Gallery: †Paintings from 13th to 18th century, Old Dutch, Old German, Italian, Netherlands and French works, including Durer and 26 paints by Rembrandt.
Dept. of Sculpture: †Late antiquity to classicism, among others Riemenschneider, Donatello.
Dept. of Prints and Drawings: †300,000 drawings, prints and illustrated books of all epochs of European art; greatest collection of Durer drawings, Bruegel and Rembrandt.

Museum of Ethnology (1 Berlin 33, Lansstr. 8)
†300,000 items of different cultures. Dept. of Oceania, ships, houses, masks; Ancient America, ceramics, gold; South Asia, masks, string puppets; Africa, North America, East Asia (China, Tibet) and Europe; Junior Museum; Museum for the Blind.
Museum of Indian art: †Central Asiatic Frescoes of the early middle ages from Turfan and Indian Sculpture.
Museum of Far Eastern Art: Paintings, ceramics of China and Japan.
Museum of Islamic Art: †Glass, ceramics, tapestry, stucco, metal, ebony and book design from Near East, North Africa and Spain.
Museum of German Folklore: On exhibit from 1976.

Museums in Charlottenburg
Egyptian Antiquities: †All periods, bust of queen Nofretete and sculptures from Tel el Amarna.
Greek and Roman Antiquities: †Bronzes, vases, marble sculptures, gold jewelry up to the Byzantine period, Hildesheimer Silberfund (silvertrove).
Museum of Pre- and Protohistory: †Objects found by excavation and in settlements in Europe and Asia from Old Stone Age to the height of the Middle Ages.
Museum of Arts and Crafts: †Objects from the middle ages to the 20th century, Welfenschatz.
Plaster cast House: 7000 different forms.
In the Center of Berlin:
Art Library and Lipperheide Costume Library: †11,000 drawings of architecture and design, prints and rare books, 125,000 volumes of history of art and costume.
Nationalgalerie: †Paintings, sculptures and drawings 19th and 20th centuries, C.D. Friedrich, Mensel, French and German impressionists; modern exhibitions.
Attendance: Approx. 1,500,000 annually.

BONN

RHEINISCHES LANDESMUSEUM*
(Rhineland Museum)
Colmantstrasse 14-16, 53 Bonn. Tel: 02221/632158
Dr. Christoph B. Rüger, Dir.
Open daily 10 AM - 5 PM; Wed. 10 AM - 9 PM; cl. Mon. admis. 1 DM. Estab. 1820 for collecting, conservation, scientific examination and research, publication and exhibition to the public of the cultural remains and works of art of the Rhineland from prehistoric times to the present day; financed by city and state appropriations.

Collections: Archeological remains and monuments of the prehistoric, Roman, early Christian and early medieval periods of the
Rhineland; †Medieval and modern art, sculpture, painting, decorative art (furniture, pottery, glass, silver etc.) of the Rhineland; †Dutch
and Flemish paintings of the 16th and 17th centuries; †Contemporary
art of the Rhineland.

Exhibitions: (1970) Art of the Rhineland from Renaissance to Ex-
pressionism. (1971) Gerhard Wind; Georg Meistermann. (1972) The
Painter School of the Hague, Dutch painters 100 years ago; Hann
Trier. (1973) Fortunato Depero, an artist of futurism; Werner
Gilles; Joseph Fassbender; 300 years of Delft ceramics.

Activities: Special programs for children and the young, also
for old people; courses for teachers and students, excursions, lectures.

Library: Reference library of approx. 40,000 volumes; photograph
collection for reference.

Publications: Das Rheinische Landesmuseum Bonn, bulletin, 6th
ed; Bonner Jahrbücher, annual, scientific publication; exhibition catalogues.

Attendance: 132,000 annual average.

STÄDTISCHES KUNSTMUSEUM BONN*
(Art Museum of the City of Bonn)
Rathausgasse 7, 53. Tel: 77686.
Dr. Eberhard Marx, Dir.
Dr. Dierk Stemmler, Asst. Dir.
Free daily 10 AM - 5 PM, Thurs. 10 AM - 9 PM, cl. Mon. Supported
by the city administration.

Collections: Art of the 20th century, especially August Macke and
the Rhenish expressionists; German art since 1945; graphic arts.

Exhibitions of contemporary art.

Library: Reference library of approx. 4000 volumes.

Publications: Auswahlkatalog der Sammlung 1966; Katalog der
Neuerwerbungen 1962-76; 20. Jahrhundert, Bilder, Plastiken,
Aquarelle; numerous catalogs for exhibitions.

BREMEN

KUNSTVEREIN BREMEN*
(Bremen Art Association Gallery)
28 Bremen, Am Wall 207. Tel: 32.47.85
Konsul Hermann Helms, Pres.
Dr. Rudolf Blaum, Secy.
Dr. Günter Busch, Dir.
Dr. Jürgen Schultze, Cur.
Dr. Annemarie Winther, Asst. Cur.
Dr. Gerhard Gerkens, Asst. Cur.
Open Tues. 10 AM - 4 PM and 7 - 9 PM; Wed. & Thurs. 10 AM - 4
PM; Fri. 10 AM - 4 PM and 7 - 9 PM; Sat. & Sun. 10 AM - 2 PM; cl.
Mon; admis. to Gallery DM -.50; for special exhibitions, DM 1 to
DM 2. Estab. 1823. Gallery houses European art since the Middle
Ages. Ann. meeting; mem. 2730; dues DM 15 and higher.

Collections: European paintings, Middle Ages to modern, especially French and German art of the 19th century; drawings;
prints; 17th to 20th century plastic collections; coins and medals
up to the end of the 19th century.

Exhibitions: 63 exhibits including Emile Bernard, Ernst Barlach,
Max Slevogt and his time, from Delacroix to Maillol, Max Beckmann
and the German expressionists, Maurice Denis, Edvard Munch, Emil
Nolde, Ernst Ludwig Kirchner.

Activities: Traveling exhibitions; objets d'art lent; 4600 photographs; lectures open to the public (15-18 visiting lecturers per year);
approx. 50 gallery talks; adult classes; scholarships.

Library: Reference library of 40,000 volumes; 400 prints; photographs.

Publications: Schriften zu Kunstwerken der Kunsthalle Bremen;
exhibition catgolues; Meisterwerke der Kunsthalle Bremen; Katalog
der Lemalde des 19. und 20. Jahrhunderts in der Kunsthalle Bremen.

BRUNSWICK

HERZOG ANTON ULRICH - MUSEUM
(Duke Anton Ulrich Museum)
Museumstrasse 1; Medieval section: Burg Dankwarderode,
Burgplatz, D-33 Braunschweig. Tel: 0531/49589 - 49378
Dr. Rüdiger Klessman, Dir.
Dr. Bodo Hedergott, Chief Cur.
Dr. Christian von Heusinger, Cur.
Dr. Sabine Jacob, Asst.
Open Tues. - Sun. 11 AM - 4 PM; Wed. 11 AM - 8 PM; Medieval
Section open Tues. - Sun. 10 AM - 4 PM; cl. Mon. Estab. 1754; fi-
nanced by state appropriations.

Collections: Egyptian, Greek and Roman Antiquities; Medieval
Art; †European paintings of the 15th - 18th centuries; †prints and
drawings from the 15th century to the present time; illustrated
books; †European Renaissance and Baroque decorative art, including
bronzes, wood and ivory carvings, Italian majolica, French 16th cen-

tury enamels, porcelain, glass, clocks, furniture, laces, waxes, etc;
Chinese lacquers.

Exhibitions: Pferd und Reiter; Burgkmair und die graphische
Kunst der deutschen Renaissance; Kunst des Barock in Polen;
Deutsche Kunst des Barock.

Activities: Lectures; concerts.

Library: 30,000 volumes for reference.

Publications: Catalogs and guides.

Attendance: 57,150.

COLOGNE

MUSEEN DER STADT KOLN
(Cologne City Museums)
An der Rechtschule. Tel: 221-2372
Dr. Gerhard Bott, Gen. Dir.
Dr. Hubertus Froning

Wallraf-Richartz Museum
An der Rechtschule. Tel: 221-2370
Dr. Gerhard Bott, Dir.
Dr. Horst Keller, Dir. Modern Art
Dr. Kurt Löcker, Cur. Ancient Art
Dr. Evelyn Weiss & Dr. Rainer Budde, Cur. Modern Art
Dr. Hella Robels, Cur. Engravings
Dr. Dieter Route, Cur. Engraving after 1945
Dr. Rolf Wallrath, Records
Dr. Albert Schug, Dir, Library
Dr. Frank Otten, Library
Open daily 10 AM - 5 PM, Tues. and Fri. until 10 PM. Founded 1824.

Collections: †Paintings from 1300 A.D. to present; †sculpture
from 1800 A.D. to present; †engravings.

Exhibitions: 1967: Zoltan Kemeny, 1907-1965; Marc Chagall (in
the Art Gallery); new talent sponsored by the Wallraf-Richartz Museums since 1966; Graham Sutherland. 1968: Selected drawings and
watercolors; Ars multiplicatā, and Art of the world from private
collections (in the Art Gallery); Hahn collection; Icons—One hundred
masterpieces from the Icon Museum of Recklinghausen; Max Beckmann and the German expressionists. 1969: E.W. Nay memorial
exhibition; Art of the sixties—Ludwig collection. 1970: Herbert
Giradet collection; Autumn of the Middle Ages—late Gothic in Cologne and the lower Rhine (in the Art Gallery).

Junior Museum: Starting in 1965, the Cologne Museums organize
exhibitions for young people, generally at the Wallraf-Richartz
Museum.

Activities: Lectures, discussions, university seminars, gallery
talks and tours.

Library: 70,000 volumes.

Attendance: 283,393 (1968), 417,617 (1969).

Romisch-Germanisches Museum
Roncalliplatz. Tel: 221-2304
Dr. Hugo Borger, Dir.
Dr. Peter La Baume, Cur. Prehistory, Provincial Roman Archaeology
Dr. Jörgen Bracker, Cur. Classical Archaeology.
Dr. Günther Ristow, Cur, Early Christian Archaeology
Dr. Walter Meier-Arendt, Cur. Prehistory
Opening times: Schatzkammer in der Alten Wache (Treasures in the
Old Guardhouse), daily 10 AM - 5 PM, Thurs. until 10 PM; Dionysos-
Mosaik, daily 10 AM - 8 PM, Tues. and Fri. 7 - 10 PM; Prätorium,
daily 10 AM - 5 PM. Founded 1946.

Collections: †Pre- and early historic discoveries; †Roman excavations; †Roman glass and industrial arts; †gold ornaments of the
era of migrating tribes.

Exhibitions (shown in the Art Gallery): 1967, Romans on the
Rhine; 1968, Art of the world from private collections; 1969, Romans
in Romania.

Activities: Lectures, discussions, university seminars, gallery
talks and tours.

Library: 18,000 volumes.

Attendance: 258,156 (1968), 299,288 (1969).

Rautenstrauch-Joest Museum für Völkerkunde (Ethnography)
Ubierring 45. Tel: 311065/66
Dr. Axel von Gagern, Dir.
Dr. Ingeborg Bolz, Cur. American Indian Art
Dr. Waldemar Stöhr, Cur. Art of Indonesia and the South Seas
Dr. Klaus Volprecht, Cur. African Art
Open daily 10 AM - 5 PM; Thurs. - Sat. until 8 PM. Founded 1906.

Collections: †Culture and art of the non-European peoples.

Exhibitions (shown in the Art Gallery) (1971) Black Isles of the
South Seas; (1972) Childrens manual work; Toys of Foreign Peoples;
(1973) Asiatic Shadow Shows; Firuzkuhi - Nomads of the Blue
Mountains; (1974) Mimus and medicine - Ceylonese masks; (1975)
East Africa- figure and ornament.

Activities: Lectures, discussions, university seminars; films;
gallery talks and tours.

Library: 38,000 volumes.

Attendance: 82,000.

Kolnisches Stadtmuseum (Cologne City Museum)
Zeughaustrasse 1 - 3. Tel: 221-2352
Dr. Hugo Borger, Dir.
Dr. Werner Jüttner, Cur. Art History
Dr. Max-Leo Schwering, Cur. Cologne Folklore
Dr. Maria Schmidt, Cur. Folk Art
Dr. Liesel Franzheim, Cur. Graphics
Dr. Elisabeth Reiff, Cur. Photograph Collection
Open daily 10 AM - 5 PM, Thurs. until 10 PM. Founded 1888.
   Collections: †National history; †national development; †religious
and rural art and culture; †trade and industrial arts of Cologne;
†graphic arts of Cologne and the Rhineland; †photograph collection
of the Rhineland (145,000 prints).
   Exhibitions: 1967, Wasa 1628 und 1961—shipboard journal. 1968:
Art of the world from private collections (in the Art Gallery);
Sveagold and Viking ornaments. 1969: Justice in the Rhineland;
Counsel and silver in Cologne. 1970: Ships and Ports; Play in two
centuries.
   Activities: Lectures, discussions, university seminars, gallery
talks and tours.
   Library: 12,000 volumes.
   Attendance: 102,242 (1968), 107,119 (1969).

Kunstgewerbemuseum (Arts and Crafts Museum)
Eigelsteintorburg. Tel: 221-3860

Dr. Brigitte Klesse, Dir.
Dr. Carl-Wolfgang Schumann, Cur. Sculptures, Mobiles, Gold,
   Bronze and Pewter Crafts.
Dr. Gisela Reineking-von Bock, Cur. Ceramics, Glass, Textiles
Open daily 10 AM - 5 PM. Founded 1888.
   Collections: †Arts and crafts from early Middle Ages to modern.
   Exhibitions: 1967: Manfredo Borsi works 1957-1967; Romanian
crafts; Majolika; Polish crafts. 1968: Art of the world from private
collections (in the Art Gallery); pewter-bronze-iron; Folk art of
Germany, Austria and Switzerland (in the Art Gallery). 1969: Con-
temporary decorative arts of the Netherlands; Selection from the
standing collection of the Arts and Crafts Museum; Richard-Bampi-
Preis. 1970: Autumn of the Middle Ages—late Gothic in Cologne and
the lower Rhine (in the Art Gallery).
   Activities: Lectures, discussions, university seminars, gallery
talks and tours.
   Attendance: 8606 (1968), 9808 (1969).

Museum für Ostasiatische Kunst (East Asian Art)
Kattenbug 18 - 24. Tel: 221-3863
Dr. Roger Goepper, Dir.
Dr. Edith Dittrich, Cur.
Open daily 10 AM - 5 PM. Founded 1913.
   Collections: †Art of China, Japan and Korea.
   Exhibitions: 1967: Tomioka Tessai 1836-1924; Masterpieces of
East Asian art. 1968: Buddhist art of East Asia; Art of the world
from private collections (in the Art Gallery); Children's paintings
from East Asia. 1969: Japanese woodcarvings from the collection
of Theodor Scheiwe, Münster; Art of the Tokugawa Period; Municipal
and temple treasures from Japan (in the Art Gallery). 1970: Chinese
art.
   Activities: Lectures, discussions, university seminars, gallery
talks and tours.
   Library: 7000 volumes.
   Attendance: 13,387 (1968), 11,813 (1969).

Schnutgen Museum
Cacilienstrasse 29 (Cäciliendirche). Tel: 221-2310
Dr. Anton Legner, Dir.
Dr. Anton von Euw, Cur. Art of the Middle Ages.
Open daily 10 AM - 5 PM, Wed. 7 - 10 PM. Founded 1906.
   Collections: †Religious art, early Middle Ages to Baroque.
   Exhibitions: 1968, Art of the world from private collections; 1970,
Autumn of the Middle Ages—late Gothic in Cologne and the lower
Rhine (both in the Art Gallery).

Kunsthalle Köln (Cologne Art Gallery)
Josef-Haubrich-Hof 1. Tel: 221-2335
Dr. Helmut R. Leppien, Dir.
Open daily 10 AM - 8 PM, Mon. and Fri. until 10 PM. Founded 1967
for showing special exhibitions.
   Exhibitions: 1967: Romans on the Rhine; Marc Chagall. 1968:
Ars multiplicata; Art of the world from private collections; Italian
art of the 20th century; Wilhelm Busch; Folk art of Germany,
Austria and Switzerland. 1969: Romans in Romania; Indians of
North America—treasures from the Museum of American Indians;
National and temple treasures of Japan. 1970: Now—art in Germany
today; Autumn of the Middle Ages—late Gothic in Cologne and the
lower Rhine.
   Activities: Lectures, discussions, university seminars, gallery
talks and tours.
   Attendance: 153,403 (1968), 163,637 (1969).

DUSSELDORF
KUNSTSAMMLUNG NORDRHEIN-WESTFALEN*
(Nordrhein-Westfalen Art Collection)
Jacobistrasse 2, Schloss Jägerhof, 4 Dusseldorf 1.
Tel: 0211/357525
Prof. Dr. Werner Schmalenbach, Dir.
Dr. Joachim Büchner, Cur.
Open Tues. - Sun. 10 AM - 5 PM; Wed. 10 AM - 8 PM; cl. Mon;
admis. DM 1. Estab. 1961 as a 20th century art collection; financed
by city and state appropriations.
   Collections: Permanent collection includes main pieces of inter-
national 20th century painting, starting from Fauvism, Expressionism
and Cubism, it represents the main streams of contemporary art
until today.
   Exhibitions: Annual didactical exhibitions, Paul Klee (1971);
Cubism (1972); Surrealism (1973).
   Activities: Programs for children and grownups; material available to museums and editors; different fees only for materials of
reproduction; traveling exhibitions organized and circulated; original
objects of art lent; lending collection, 300 photographs, 95 lantern
slides, 140 Kodachromes.
   Library: 30,000 volumes for reference.
   Publications: Bulletin Düsseldorfer Museen (in connection with
other museums in Düsseldorf), 4 times a year.

STÄDTISCHE KUNSTHALLE
(City Art Gallery)
Grabbeplatz 4, 4 (Postfach 1120). Tel: 0211/365783
Jürgen Harten, Dir.
Renata Sharp, Exec. Secy.
Dr. Katharina Schmidt, Delegate Dir.
John Matheson, Asst.
Dr. Jaroslav Borovicka, Asst.
Open 10 AM - 8 PM; cl. Mon; admis. 2,- DM, students 0,50 DM.
Estab. 1967, financed by city and state appropriations.
   Exhibitions: (1975) Konrad Klapheck; Richard Gessner; Enrico
Baj; Karl Arnold, Hoppla, wir leben; Pop-Jeans, Levi's denim art;
Granz Gertsch, Gemälde; Franz Hanfstaengl, Portraits; 18. Juni
bis 13. Juli; Norbert Kricke; Ernst Oberhoff, Gemälde; John
Latham, Zeit und Schicksal; Richard Paul Lohse; Jan J. Schoon-
hoven; Sehen um zu hören, Objekte und Konzerte zu visueller Musik;
W. Knoebel, Bilder und Zeichnungen; Jonas Hafner, Lacrimae;
Wilhelm Rudolph, Gemälde; Peruanische Erdzeichen; Chronik der
Kunsthalle, Plakate, Editionen, Kataloge 1967-1975.
   Activities: Concerts, dramatic programs.
   Publications: Exhibition catalogs.

FRANKFURT
STAEDELSCHES KUNSTINSTITUT
(Staedel Art Institute)
Schaumainkai 63. Tel: 617092
Estab. 1817. Open Tues. - Sun. 10 AM - 5 PM; Wed. 10 AM - 8 PM;
cl. Mon. City Art Gallery integrated to the Städel Institute. Founded
1907.
   Collections: European painting of all periods; department of
prints and drawings (c. 65,000 prints and c. 25,000 drawings) from
15th century to the present; collection of paintings of the 19th and
20th centuries.
   Exhibitions: Special exhibitions of old and modern art.
   Library: 34,000 volumes.
   Attendance: 65,000.

MUSEUM FÜR KUNSTANDWERK*
6 Frankfurt a.M, Schaumainkai 15. Tel: 0611/212-4037
Dr. Peter Wilhelm Meister, Dir.
Dr. Annaliese Ohm, Cur.
Free, daily 1 - 5 PM; Wed. 1 - 8 PM; cl. Mon. Estab. 1877 for
decorative arts from the Middle Ages till 20th century and Asiatic
art; financed by city appropriations.
   Collections: Ceramics, furniture, glass, bronzes, silverwork,
pewter, iron work, textiles and manuscripts.
   Exhibitions: Liu Kuo-sung, the Way of a Modern Chinese Painter;
Persian Rugs; Form and Colour, Chinese Bronzes and Early Ceram-
ics, Collection; H. W. Siegel, Hong Kong; Japanese Roofs; British
Potters; Art from Japan.
   Activities: Photograph collection of 2000 prints for reference.
   Library: 5000 volumes for reference.
   Purchases $20,000.
   Attendance: 1971, 19,620; 1972, 22,396.

HAMBURG
HAMBURGER KUNSTHALLE
(Hamburg Art Hall)
Glockengiesserwall. Tel: 248251
Dr. Werner Hofmann, Dir.

Open daily except Mon. 10 AM - 5 PM; Wed. 10 AM - 7 PM; admis. DM 1. Estab. 1869.

Collections: Recent schools of Western Art for paintings and sculptures. Masterworks of painting from 14th century to present, including Master Bertram, Master Francke, Cranach, Rembrandt, Ticpolo, Runge, Menzel, Manet, Liebermann, Kokoschka, Kandinsky, Picasso, Claude Lorrain, Boucher, Friedrich, Munch, Nolde, Arp, Beckmann, Klee, Leger, Jones Hockney. Sculpture of 19th and 20th centuries, including masterpieces by Schadow, Hildebrand, Rodin, Maillol, Kolbe, Barlach, Lehmbruck, Marini, Moore, Giacometti, Rickey, Calder, Arp, Uhlmann, Segal, Nachi, Man Ray, Luginbühl, Gräsel. Medals from 15th - 20th centuries; ancient coins; 60,000 prints and 15,000 drawings from 14th - 20th centuries.

Exhibitions: (1970) Max Ernst - Inside the Sight (Coll. de Menil); Examination of a Taste (G. C. Schwabe Bequest 1886); (1971) Revolutionary Architecture (Ledoux, Boullee, Lequeu); one-man shows of 1971-72: Cesar (Baldaccini), Walter Dexel, Walter Pichler, Shusaku Arakawa; (1973) Nana - Myth and Reality (about a painting by Manet); Art in Germany 1898-1973; Kunst um 1800 (Art of about 1800), cyclus of exhibitions 1974-1977: Ossian and Art of 1800; Caspar David Friedrich; Johann Heinrich Fuessli; William Blake; Johan Tobias Sergel; William Turner and the Landscape of his Time; Philipp Otto Runge.

Activities: Ten lectures per winter (each repeated the day after).
Library: 70,000 volumes.
Publications: Catalogs of permanent collection and exhibitions.
Series (irregular): Zur Sache. Special issues.
Attendance: (1974) 340,000.

HANNOVER

KESTNER-MUSEUM*
3000 Hannover, Trammplatz 3. Tel: 0511/168-2120
Dr. Peter Munro, Dir.
Dr. Christel Mosel, Cur.
Dr. Margildis Schlüter, Asst Cur.
Free Tues, Wed, Fri. 10 AM - 4 PM; Sat. 10 AM - 6 PM; Sun. 10 AM - 1 PM; cl. Mon. Estab. 1889, financed by city appropriations.

Collections: Egyptian, Greek and Roman antiquities; gems, coins, medals, European arts and crafts (medieval to modern); graphic arts.

Exhibitions: (1970) Klingende Kostbarkeiten, Tischglocken aus 5 Jahrhunderten, Slg. Anselm Lange, Hannover; Otto-Gleichmann, Handzeichnungen und frühe Aquarelle; Französische Jugendstil-Plakate für Zeitschriften und Ausstellungen; Heinz Trökes, Graphik; HAP Grieshaber Graphic aus eigenen Beständen des Kestner-Museums. (1971) Deutsche Buchkunst 1900-1970; Dürer Graphik, Einzelblätter; Delfter Fayence, Begegnung mit den Niederlanden; Paul Wunderlich: Dürer Paraphrasen. (1972) Kunsthandwerk im Umbruch, Jugendstil und zwanziger Jahre; Max Ernst, Jenseits der Malerei; Hansen-Bahia: Holzschnitte aus 25 Jahren. (1973) Englische Keramik, British Potters; Schmuck und Gerät, gestern und heute; Deutsche keramische Kunst der Gegenwart Sammlung Wolf.

Activities: Photograph collection of approx. 10,000 prints; lectures open to public; concerts.
Library: 17,000 occasionally for lending or reference.
Publications: Catalogues of exhibitions, irregular.

KARLSRUHE

STAATLICHE KUNSTHALLE KARLSRUHE
(State Art Gallery)
Staatliche Kunsthalle, Hans Thoma Str. 2-6, D 75 Karlsruhe.
Tel: (721) 135-3355
Prof. Dr. Horst Vey, Dir.
Dr. Werner Zimmerman, Deputy Dir.
Dr. Johann Eckart von Borries, Dir. Engraving
Dr. Anneliese Reuter-Rautenberg, Dir. Dept. Educ.
Dr. Juergen Rohmeder, Dir Publications
Free daily 10 AM - 5 PM; cl. Mon. Estab. 1803 for collecting and exhibiting; financed by state appropriations. Mem. 72.

Collections: 15th-20th century German painting and graphics; 17th-20th century French paintings and graphics; 16th-17th century Dutch and Flemish paintings and graphics.

Exhibitions: 40 exhibitions from 1970-1972.

Activities: Education department has courses in art administration, special school exhibits in art instruction for adults and children; material available to institutions, schools, instructors and others; no fees; traveling exhibitions organized and circulated; 3000 color reproductions, 2000 photographs and 25,000 lantern slides in lending collection; lectures for public and members; 10 visiting lecturers per year; 79 gallery talks; competitions.
Library: Reference collection of approx. 62,000 volumes; photograph collection.
Publications: Yearbook.

MUNICH

BAYERISCHE STAATSGEMALDESAMMIUNGEN
(Bavarian State Galleries of Art)
2 Meiserstrasse 10. Tel: 55911
Prof. Dr. E. Steingraber, Gen. Dir.
Curators:
Leo Cremer, Restoration
Dr. Wolf-Dieter Dube, 20th Century Art
Dr. Christoph Heilmann, 19th Century Art
Dr. Eberhard Rukman, 19th Century Art
Dr. Carla Schuls-Hoffmann, 20th Century Art
Dr. Peter Eikemeier, Netherlandish Paintings
Dr. Gisela Goldberg, Old German Paintings
Dr. Rudiger an der Heiden, German Baroque Paintings
Dr. J. G. Prinz von Hohenzollern, French Paintings
Dr. Ulla Krempel, Flemish Paintings
Dr. Rolf Kultzen, Italian Paintings
Richard Lohe, Restoration
Dr. Liselotte Camp, Pub. Relations
This organization administers art galleries of the Bavarian State, in Munich, as well as other Bavarian State galleries located in Augsburg, Aschaffenburg, Passau, Regensburg and Bamberg. Those located in Munich include:

Alte Pinakothek
(Old Picture Gallery)
Barerstrasse 27. Tel: 286105
Open 9 AM - 4:30 PM; Tues. & Thurs. 7 - 9 PM; cl. Mon. Estab. 1836; founded upon the collections of the Bavarian Princes.
Collections: Old Masters.
Library: Approx. 28,000 volumes.

Neue Pinakothek and Staatsgalerie Moderne-Kunst
(New Picture Gallery and State Gallery of Modern Art)
Prinzregentenstrasse 1. Tel: 292716
Open daily 9 AM - 4:30 PM; Thurs. 7 - 9 PM; cl. Mon.
Collections: 19th and 20th century art.

Schackgalerie
Prinzregentenstrasse 9.
Open daily 9 AM - 4:30 PM; cl. Tues.
Collections: Late Romantic German art.

Doerner-Institute
2 Meiserstrasse 10. Tel: 55911
Dr. Hubert Falkner von Sonnenburg, Dir.
Bruno Heimburg, Restoration
Dr. Frank Preusser, Chemo-Physiker
Dr. Johann Koller, Chemo-Physiker
Doerner Institute is a laboratory for conservation and scientific research, part of the Bavarian State Galleries of Art.

BAYERISCHES NATIONALMUSEUM
(Bavarian National Museum)
Prinzregentenstrasse 3, 8 München 22. Tel: 089/22 25 91
Dr. L. Kriss-Rettenbeck, Gen. Dir.
Dr. J. Bauer, Folk Art
Dr. G. Himmelheber, Furniture
Dr. H. Huesmann, Theater
Dr. K. Maurice, Clocks
Dr. E. Noelle, Theater
Dr. R. Rückert, Ceramics
Dr. A. Schädler, Sculpture
Dr. A. Voelker, Textiles
Dr. P. Volk, Sculpture
Dr. R. Wackernagel, Conservation
Open Apr. - Sept. Tues. - Fri 9:30 AM - 4:30 PM; Oct. - May 9 AM - 4 PM, Sat. & Sun. 10 AM - 4 PM. Estab. 1855. Branch museums: Theatermuseum, 8 München 22, Galeriestr. 4a. Tel: 22 24 49; Meissener Porzellan-Sammlung, Stiftung Ernst Schneider, Schloss Lustheim bei Schleissheim. Freundeskreis der Bayerischen Nationalmuseums.

Collections: European art from 900-1850; paintings, sculpture, decorative arts; bronze, ceramics, clocks, furniture, glass, ivory, metal work, stained glass, tapestries; folk art; cribs.
Activities: 50 visiting lecturers per year. Book shop.
Art Library: 45,000 volumes.
Publications: Münchner Jahrbuch der bildenden Kunst, annually; Bildfuehrer; Forschungshefte.

STAATLICHE GRAPHISCHE SAMMLUNG MÜNCHEN
(National Graphic Collection)
Meiserstrasse 10, D 8 München 2, Bavaria. Tel: 55 91 341
Dr. Herbert Pee, Dir.
Dr. Annegrit Schmitt, Nat. Cur.
Dr. Dieter Kuhrmann, Chief Cur.
Dr. Gisela Scheffler, Cur.

Free Mon. - Fri 9 AM - 1 PM & 2 - 4:30 PM. Estab. 19th century as a royal order; financed by city and state appropriations.

Collections: †European drawings and graphic arts of the 15th till the 20th century.

Exhibitions: (1970) Rembrandt das druckgraphische werk; Frühzeit des Holzschnitts; Munch, Zeichnungen; (1971) Albrecht Dürer, Druckgraphik; Emil Nolde, George Grosz, J. Gonzalez; Schweizer Zeichnungen im 20. Jahrhunderts; (1972) Hundert Meister werke; (1973) Baselitz; König-Ludwig-Album; Max Klinger, Druckgraphik; (1974) Niederländische Zeichnungen des 16. Jahrhunderts; Karl Hubbuck, Frühe Zeichnungen und Druckgraphik; Alt-deutsche Zeichnungen aus der Universitätsbibliothek Erlangen; Neuerwerbungen der Jahre 1971-1974; Paul Eliasberg; (1975) Niederländische Zeichnungen des 17. Jahrhunderts; Französische Farbstiche des 18. Jahrhunderts aus dem Kupferstichkabinett der Veste Coburg; Michael Mathias Prechtl; Ernst Wilhelm Nay.

Library: 20,000 volumes for reference; photograph collection for sale; collection of portraits and etchings.

Publications: Netherlands drawings of the 15th - 18th century, catalog of National Graphic Collection; catalogs of expositions, irregular.

STADTISCHE GALERIE IM LENBACHHAUS
(Lenbach House City Gallery)
Luisenstrasse 33, München 2, 8000. Tel: 0811/52 14 31
Dr. Armin Zweite, Dir.
Dr. Erika Hanfstaengl, Cur.
Dr. Rosel Gollek, Cur.
Open daily 9 AM - 4:30 PM; cl. Mon; admis. adults 1.50 DM; students .50 DM. Estab. 1925 to collect objects of art produced in Munich and Bavaria, mainly paintings and sculptures; financed by city and state appropriations.

Collections: †Paintings of the 19th century (Munich school); Franz von Lenbach, his paintings and his private collection of art objects; †The Blue Rider and Jawlensky and Klee; Art Nouveau; Neue Sachlichkeit; †Contemporary art, prints and drawings (19th and 20th century).

Exhibitions: Arakawa, Segal, Fruhtrunk, Bilder, Objekte, Filme, Konzepte (Collection Herbig); Gerhard Richter, Nikolaus Lang, Anton Hiller, Die Maler der Brücke und der deutsche Expressionismus (College Buchheim); Cy Twombly, paintings and drawings.

Activities: Collaboration with schools, guided tours, courses in paintings; lectures open to the public; 10 visiting lecturers per year; concerts.

Library: 3000 volumes; photograph collection.

Income and Purchases: Income $80,000; purchases $30,000.

Attendance: 100,000.

NUREMBERG

GERMANISCHES NATIONALMUSEUM*
(Germanic National Museum)
Kornmarkt I. Tel: 20.39.71
Dr. Arno Schönberger, Chief Dir.
Open (Oct. 1-Mar. 31) Tues. - Sat. 10 AM - 4 PM; Sun. 10 AM - 1 PM; (Apr. 1-Sept. 30) Mon. - Sat. 10 AM - 5 PM; Sun. 10 AM - 4 PM; admis. DM 0.50. Estab. 1852. Mem. 8000; dues DM 10.

Collections: Paintings; graphics; sculpture; weapons; instruments; coins; musical instruments; archives; textiles; furniture; toys; ancient historical objects, etc.

Activities: Lectures; gallery talks and tours; concerts.

Library: 300,000 volumes; photograph collection with 50,000 negatives.

Attendance: 190,000.

GHANA

ACCRA

GHANA NATIONAL MUSEUM*
Barnes Rd, P.O. Box 3343. Tel: 22 2-1633
Dr. Oku-Ampofo, Chmn. of the Board
R. B. Nunoo, Dir.
Free Tues. - Sun. 8 AM - 6 PM. Estab. 1957 to display archaeological, ethnographic, historic and artistic materials from Ghana and neighboring countries; financed by government subvention. One section of the museum is devoted to works by modern Ghanaian artists and sculptors working mostly with traditional themes.

Collections: Ghanaian and African archaeology, history, ethnography, modern art and sculpture.

Exhibitions: If this is the time; Winneba 1972; The Life and Work of Sri Aurobindo; Ike Muse-gouaches; The Work of Leo Frobenias.

Activities: Lecturing to schools both at the school and at the museum; showing films to schools; guiding schools around the museum; photograph collection of about 1000 prints for reference; lectures open to the public; 6 visiting lecturers per year.

Library: Approx. 1100 volumes for reference and lending to museum staff.

Publications: Museum Handbook, occasional papers, irregular.

Attendance: 69,000 annual average.

GREAT BRITAIN

BATH

AMERICAN MUSEUM IN BRITAIN
Claverton Manor, BA2 7BD
E. L. Richards, Chmn. Board of Trustees
Ian McCallum, Dir.
Sheila Little, Director's Secy.
Michael Candler, Deputy Dir. & Dir. Educ.
Kay Bond, Assoc. Cur.
Open Mar. through Oct. daily except Mon. 2 - 5 PM. Estab. July 1961. A Museum of the American Decorative Arts estab. as a tribute to Anglo-American Friendship.

Activities: Lectures, tours and films.

Publications: America in Britain (private circulation 3 times a year).

Attendance: Approx. 95,000 annually.

BIRMINGHAM

BARBER INSTITUTE OF FINE ARTS*
University of Birmingham
B15 2TS. Tel: (021) 472-0962
H. A. D. Miles, Dir.
R. E. W. James
R. B. Lockett
Open Mon. - Fri. 10 AM - 5 PM; Sat. 10 AM - 1 PM. Estab. 1932 for the enjoyment of fine art and music within the university; endowment. Four main galleries.

Collections: Chiefly paintings from 14th century to early 20th century.

Activities: Lectures; concerts; private library and photograph collection.

BRIGHTON

ROYAL PAVILION, ART GALLERY AND MUSEUMS
BN1 1UE. Tel: Brighton 63005-7
J. H. Morley, Dir.
J. M. A. Dinkel, Deputy Dir. & Keeper of the Royal Pavilion & Principal Keeper of Art
E. R. Bradley, Principal Keeper, Conservation & Design
R. E. Budd, Prin. Asst. (Adminr, Sales & Security)
D. M. B. Cordingly, Principal Keeper, Antiquities & Interpretation
C. A. B. Steel, Prin. Keeper Natural Sciences
Dr. D. Simpson, Exhibitions Officer
Dr. G. H. A. Bankes, Keeper of Ethnography
Miss C. E. A. Dudley, Keeper of Archaeology
Miss J. Rutherford, Keeper of Applied Art
Miss W. Patchin, School Loans Officer
P. R. M. Conner, Keeper of Art
Miss M. J. Waller, Keeper of Preston Manor & Rottingdean Grange
M. Jones, Sr. Designer

The Royal Pavilion
Open daily Oct. - June 10 AM - 5 PM; July - Sept. 10 AM - 8 PM; cl. Christmas Day, Boxing Day & three days at end of June; admis. charges under review. Original furniture and decorations.

Exhibitions: Annual Regency Exhibition (July - Sept, inclusive). Guided tours.

Attendance: 333,500.

Museum and Art Gallery
Church St.
Estab. 1851; local authority, Brighton district, from Apr. 1, 1974. Free admis.

Collections: Old Master paintings, Sussex Archaeology and folklife, ethnography and natural history. There is also the famous Willett collection of pottery and porcelain, the Spencer collection of musical instruments and a gallery devoted to an important collection of 20th century fine and applied art of the Art Nouveau and Art Deco periods.

Regular temporary exhibitions.

The Grange, Rottingdean
Open summer Mon. - Fri. 10 AM- 7 PM; Sun. 2- 6 PM; winter Mon. - Fri. 10 AM - 6 PM; Sat. 10 AM - 5 PM; Sun. 2 - 5 PM; cl. Christmas Day, Boxing Day and Good Friday. Toy collection, temporary exhibitions, etc.

Preston Manor
Open daily 10 AM - 5 PM; Sun. 2 - 5 PM; cl. Christmas Day,
Boxing Day and Good Friday; charges are under review. Georgian
manor house, original furniture and decorations.

Booth Natural History Museum
    Dyke Rd.
Open Mon. - Sat. 10 AM - 5 PM; Sun. 2 - 5 PM; free admis.

    Annual expenditure of all sections: £491,400.
    Income: £212,000 from sales, admissions, rents, etc; the balance
of expenditure from Local Authority.

BRISTOL

CITY ART GALLERY*
    Queen's Rd, BS8 1RL. Tel: Bristol (0272) 299771
A. D. P. Wilson, Dir.
F. W. Greenacre, Cur. of Fine Art
Miss E. C. Witt, Cur. of Applied Art
P. Hardie, Cur. of Oriental Art
Open Mon. - Sat. 10 AM - 5:30 PM. Estab. 1905; City appropriation.
    Collections: †Paintings, drawings, sculpture, British, Continental,
13th-20th century; †English pottery, porcelain, silver, glass, furniture,
etc; †Bristol porcelain and glass etc; †Schiller collection of Oriental
ceramics, glass and metalwork.
    Exhibitions: Circulating exhibitions from Arts Council etc. The
Bristol School of Artists, Francis Dantz and Painting in Bristol, 1810-
1840; Bristol Hardpaste Porcelain Exhibition; Exhibition of Oriental
Carpets from R. G. Hübel Collection; Retrospective Exhibition of work
of Peter Blake; Victorian Narrative Paintings from the Store; Exhibition of the work of Reuben Chappell; Paintings and Drawings by W. J.
Miller.
    Activities: Concerts; lectures, etc.
    Library: Over 600 volumes for references.
    Publications: Abstracts, once every quarter.
    Annual Purchases: $25,000 Basic.

Red Lodge
    Park Row, Bristol.
Early 17th century mansion, panelled interiors, period furnishings.

Georgian House
    Great George St, Bristol.
Late 18th century Town House, period furnishings.

CAMBRIDGE

FITZWILLIAM MUSEUM
    Trumpington St, CB2 1RB. Tel: 0223.69501-3
M. A. Jaffe, Dir.
J. G. Pollard, Deputy Dir. Coins & Medals
R. V. Nicholls, Antiquities
M. Cormack, Paintings & Drawings
J. M. Huskinson, Admin.
R. A. Crighton, Applied Arts
P. Woudhuysen, Librn.
E. C. Chamberlain, Prints
D. D. Robinson, Paintings & Drawings
T. R. Volk, Coins & Medals
Miss J. Bourriau, Egyptology
Free Tues. - Sat. 10 AM - 5 PM; Sun. 2:15 - 5 PM; cl. Mon. with ex-
ception of Easter Monday and Spring & Summer Bank Holidays,
23-26 December, New Year's Day and Good Friday. Estab. 1816;
financed by endowment and University of Cambridge.
    Collections: Antiquities; Coin Room; Applied Arts, including
European ceramics, Oriental works of Art, Textiles, arms and
armour, furniture and sculpture; Print Room; paintings and drawings;
Library includes manuscripts, collections of autographs and music.
All collections are being enlarged by purchase, gift and bequest.
    Exhibitions: Approx. 8 exhibitions a year in the Exhibition Gal-
lery; 8 exhibitions a year in the Drawings and Prints Departments.
    Activities: Lectures for the Friends of the Fitzwilliam (oldest
in U.K.); loans are authorized as agreed by Syndicate of the Museum;
concerts. Book shop.
    Library: 60,000 volumes, 7500 photographic prints for reference.
    Publications: Catalogs and handbook, as needed. Colour cards,
slides, replicas.
    Income and Purchases: Income for purchases approx. £20,000,
purchases vary.
    Attendance: 130,000.

LINCOLN

USHER GALLERY
    Lindum Rd, LN2 1NN. Tel: 0522-27980
A. J. H. Gunstone, Dir.
R. H. Wood, Keeper of Art

Free weekdays 10 AM - 5:30 PM; Sun. 2:30 - 5 PM. Estab. 1927;
financed by appropriations.
    Collections: Peter De Wint Collection; Topographical Collection:
paintings and drawings of Lincoln 18th-20th centuries; James Ward
Usher Collection; Exley Loan Collection; Tennyson Room.
    Exhibitions: Lincolnshire and South Humberside Artist's Spring
Exhibition; Paintings by Richard Whittern Australian Artists Exhibition; Paintings by Ian Fraser; Art Nouveau Pewter; International
Ceramics; William Tom Warrener 1861-1934; Paintings and Reliefs
by Endre Hevezi; Paintings by Stuart Walton; Art in Lincolnshire;
Four Printmakers; The English Landscape; Paintings by Shirley
Teed; Paintings and Ceramics by Neil Macdonell, Stuart Walsh and
Pauline Philp; Contemporary Weavings; Paintings by Susan Anderson; John Smith, Potter.
    Activities: Material available to inhabitants of Lincolnshire; fees
per picture annually £2.00, old age pensioners £1; paintings, drawings
and prints lent from permanent collection; original objects of art lent;
lending collection of 200 paintings, drawings and prints; 134 items
lent in an average year; school prints loan scheme; lectures open to
public; occasional visiting lecturers; gallery talks and tours as requested. Book shop.
    Publications: Catalog of Peter deWint Collection; Catalog of the
Usher Collection of Watches.
    Attendance: Approx. 57,900 annually.

LIVERPOOL

WALKER ART GALLERY
    William Brown St, L3 8EL. Tel: (051) 207-1371
Timothy Stevens, Dir.
Edward Morris, Keeper of Foreign Art
Mary Bennett, Keeper of British Art
Free, 10 AM - 5 PM, Sun. 2 - 5 PM. Estab. 1873 as a permanent
collection of paintings, drawings, prints, watercolours, and sculp-
ture; financed by appropriations.
    Collections: European paintings, drawings, prints, †watercolours,
sculpture, post 1200 century A.D.
    Exhibitions: Taste of Yesterday; New Italian Art, 71 & 72; G. H.
Wedgwood; Joseph Gott; M. G. Lightfoot; Edvard Munch; J. H. Hay;
Magic and Strong Medicine; John Moores Liverpool Exhibitions.
    Activities: Lectures and guide tours for children and teachers;
material available to schools and hospitals; nominal fees; material
lent includes paintings and prints; 350 items lent in an average year;
140 active borrowers; lectures open to the public; 3 visiting lecturers per year; 30 gallery talks. Book shop.
    Library: Reference library of 10,000 volumes.
    Publications: Annual reports; Bulletin of Walker Art Gallery.
    Attendance: 277,863.

LONDON

ART INFORMATION REGISTRY LTD.
    125/129 Shaftesbury Ave, WC1.
Norma Binnie, Company Secy.
    Directors:
John Hubbard
Malcolm Hughes
Bryan Kneale
Richard Leachman
Bridget Riley
Peter Sedgley
Peter Townsend
W. A. West
Free, 9:30 AM - 6 PM. Estab. 1969 as a catalyst organization im-
partially providing two way information between artists and their
public; it maintains a visual library of current and experimental
work, open to professional artists; financed by endowment and
membership. Mem. 1000; dues £2.00.
    Exhibitions: Will mount and promote exhibitions using material
of artists on the registry when requested to do so.
    Activities: Lending collection of 12,000 Kodachromes; items lent
and active borrowers vary per year; lectures open to public.
    Library: For reference only.
    Publications: AIR Mail, annually; AIR Newsletter, monthly;
Artists Mailing List.

THE BRITISH LIBRARY, REFERENCE DIVISION
(formerly The British Museum Library)
    Great Russell St, WC1B 3DG. Tel: 01-636 1544
Viscount Eccles, Chmn, British Library Board
Dr. H. T. Hookway, Chief Exec.
D. T. Richnell, Dir. Gen, Reference Div.
Free; Galleries open Mon. - Sat. 10 AM - 5 PM; Sun. 2:30 - 6 PM;
Reading Room open Mon, Fri. & Sat. 9 AM - 5 PM; Tues, Wed. &
Thurs. 9 AM - 9 PM. Until July 1973, was the British Museum
which was estab. 1795; organization's purpose is to make its 10

million books and manuscripts available to readers in the reading rooms, to give photographic and other services and to run exhibitions; financed by city and state appropriation. Maintains four galleries of printed books and manuscripts.

Collections: Approx. 8 million printed books, 75,000 Western and 30,000 Oriental manuscripts, 100,000 charters and rolls, 18,000 detached seals and casts of seals, 3000 Greek and Latin papyri, and a fine collection of Egyptian papyi. Admission for research to the Public Reading Rooms at Great Russell Street is by ticket.

Exhibitions: Chinese & Japanese Maps; English Restoration Bookbindings; Petrarch; Modern Literary Manuscripts; The Written Word on Papyrus; Milton Tercentenary; Churchill the Writer; Charles Lamb; Thomas Manor; American War of Independence (1975) Boccaccio; Jane Austen.

Activities: Photograph collection; lectures open to public; 2 tours daily. Book shop.

Science Reference Library: Principal public reference library in the United Kingdom for contemporary literature of physical sciences, technology, engineering and the life sciences. No admission ticket is required.

Publications: The British Library Journal, six monthly.
Annual Income: $24,000,000.
Attendance: 600,000.

THE BRITISH MUSEUM
   Great Russell St, WC1B 3DG. Tel: 01-636-1555
Sir John Pope-Hennessy, Dir.
Miss M. Webb, Deputy Dir.
J. A. G Gere, Keeper of Prints & Drawings
G. K. Jenkins, Keeper of Coins & Medals
T. G. H. James, Keeper of Egyptian Antiquities
E. Sollberger, Keeper of Western Asiatic Antiquities
D. E. L. Haynes, Keeper of Greek & Roman Antiquities
I. H. Longworth, Keeper of Prehistoric & Romano-British
   Antiquities
N. M. Stratford, Keeper of Medieval & Later Antiquities
R. L. S. Bruce-Mitford, Keeper of Sutton Hoo (Research & Publication)
D. E. Barrett, Keeper of Oriental Antiquities
M. D. McLeod, Keeper of Ethnography (Museum of Mankind)
M. Tite, Keeper of the Research Laboratory
H. Barker, Keeper of Conservation
S. P. Cooper, Head of Pub. Services
Mrs. M. R. Bruce-Mitford, Pub. Relations Officer
Open weekdays 10 AM - 5 PM, Sun. 2:30 - 6 PM; cl. Good Fri, Christmas Eve, Christmas Day, Boxing Day and New Year's Day. Estab. 1753.

Collections: †Collections and exhibitions of prehistoric, ancient, medieval, Oriental and other arts; drawings, prints, coins, ceramics. The ethnographical collections are at the Museum of Mankind, 6 Burlington Gardens, W1X 2EX.

Activities: Two public lectures, six days per wk. throughout the year; film shows; programs available on request.

Publications: Numerous publications on the collections, including British Museum Quarterly.
Attendance: 2,210,000.

GUILDHALL ART GALLERY
   King St, Cheapside, EC2P 2EJ. Tel: 01-606-3030
Godfrey Thompson, Dir.
Nora E. Wilson, Adminr.
Open Mon. - Fri. 9:30 AM - 5 PM. Estab. 1886 to provide gallery facilities for art organizations connected with City of London and to exhibit from the permanent collection; financed by city and state appropriation.

Collections: Ceremonial works connected with corporation of City of London; Victorian paintings; works depicting London life and topography; works by Matthew Smith.

Exhibitions: (Annual Exhibits) Lord Mayor's Art Award; City of London Art Exhibition; Royal Drawing Society; Royal Photographic Society; Royal Society of Marine Artists; Sir John Cass College Exhibition; exhibitions from permanent collections.

Activities: 1000 prints in photograph collection; maintain a kiosk for selling publications, slides and reproductions.
Attendance: Approx. 20,000.

NATIONAL GALLERY
   Trafalgar Square, WC2N 5DN. Tel: 839-3321
Michael Levey, Dir.
Open Mon. - Sat. 10 AM - 6 PM; Sun. 2 - 6 PM; June-Sept, until 9 PM Tues. & Thurs. Cl. Christmas Eve, Christmas Day, Boxing Day, Jan. 1st and Good Friday. Estab. 1824.

Collections: A representative collection of Italian, Dutch, Flemish, Spanish and German schools. French painting up to 1900. A selection of British paintings from Hogarth to Turner.

Educational Activities: Public lectures free of charge given at varying times. Other lectures can also be given free of charge to schools and special parties of not more than 30 persons.

Publications: The functions of the Publications Department include photography and publication of coloured prints and transparencies, photographs, postcards, books and catalogs.
Income: Annual grant £990,000.
Attendance: 1,622,725.

THE QUEEN'S GALLERY
Buckingham Palace
   Lord Chamberlain's Office, St. James's Palace, S.W.1
   (Entrance on Buckingham Palace Road)
J. L. Titman, Registrar
Open Tues. - Sat. and bank holidays 11 AM - 5 PM; Sun. 2 - 5 PM; cl. Mon. except bank holidays; admis. adults 30p, 10p children, students on production of valid student's card and old age pensioners. The Queen's Gallery at Buckingham Palace is a small art gallery where items in the Royal Collection are put on view to the general public.

Exhibitions: Landscapes from the Royal Collection, these will be complemented by a group of drawings from the Royal Library.

SOUTH LONDON ART GALLERY
   Peckham Rd, SE5 8UH. Tel: (01) 703-6120
K. A. Doughty, Cur.
P. W. Taylor, Deputy Cur.
Kenneth Sharpe, Keeper
Open during exhibitions weekdays 10 AM - 6 PM; Sun. 3 - 6 PM; no admis. Estab. 1891 for changing exhibitions; financed by municipal appropriations.

Collections: †Collection of Victorian Paintings and Drawings; †Small collection of Contemporary British Art; †Collection of 20th Century Original Prints; †Comprehensive Collection of Topographical Paintings and Drawings of Local Subjects.

Exhibitions: South London Artists; Paintings from the Southwark Collection; Paintings, Sculptures, Photographs: Alfred Janes, Peter Johns, Livia Rolandini, Jørgen Sedgwick; Books at your service; Lord Carron Prize Award and Richard Briginshaw Prize Award; South East London Art Group; IV Painters; Aspect '74; Jane Ford, Jane Lloyd, Laetitia Yhap: Paintings; Paintings and Sculpture: Dante Elsner, Shelley Fausset, Jeff Hoare; Paintings 1914-1924; Dorothy King Retrospective; One plus Four; Clarissa Cooks, Vera Lane, Jim Russell, Martin Ware: Painting, Etching and Jewellery; Adrian Daintrey, Jean Young: Paintings and Drawings; Women and Work: A document on the division of labour in industry; Christine Roberts: Environmental Art - Peckham Rye Station; 25 years of Embroidery 1950 to 1975.

Activities: Concerts; classes for adults and children; competitions.
Attendance: (1971-73) 32,000.

THE TATE GALLERY
   Millbank, SW1P 4RG. Tel: 01-8281212
Sir Norman Reid, Dir.
Open weekdays 10 AM - 6 PM; Sun. 2 - 6 PM; cl. Good Friday, Christmas Eve, Christmas Day, Boxing Day and New Year's Day. Estab. 1897 by Sir Henry Tate.

Collections: British painting from the 16th century to today; modern foreign painting from Impressionism onwards, and modern sculpture. Especially fine examples of the works of Hogarth, Blake, Turner and the Pre-Raphaelites.

Exhibitions: Special exhibitions held regularly throughout the year.

Activities: Public lectures free of charge are given on Tues. at 1 PM; on Thurs. at 1 PM & 3 PM Sat. & Sun. at 3 PM.

Publications: The functions of the Publications Department include photography and publication of coloured prints and transparencies, Photographs, postcards, books and catalogues.
Attendance: Approx. 900,000.

VICTORIA AND ALBERT MUSEUM
   Cromwell Rd, S.W. 7. Tel: 589.6371
Open weekdays incl Sat. & Bank Holidays 10 AM - 6 PM; Sun. 2:30 - 6 PM; cl. Good Friday, Christmas Day, Christmas Eve, Boxing Day, New Year's Day. Estab. 1852.

Collections: †Collections of fine and applied arts of all countries, periods and styles, including Oriental art. European collections are mostly post-Classical. Included in the collections: architectural details, arms and armour, the art of the book; bronzes, calligraphy, carpets, ceramics, clocks, costumes, cutlery, drawings, embroideries, enamels, engravings, fabrics, furniture, glass, gold and silversmiths' work, ironwork, ivories, jewelry, lace, lithographs, manuscripts, metalwork, miniatures, musical instruments, oil paintings, posters, pottery and porcelain, prints, sculpture, stained glass, tapestries, theatre art, vestments, watches, water-colours, woodwork.

Educational Activities: Numerous lectures monthly; temporary exhibition programme.
Library: 400,000 volumes.
Attendance: 1,500,000.

THE WALLACE COLLECTION
Manchester Square W1M 6BN. Tel: 01-935 0687/8
C. D. F. P. Brocklehurst, Chmn. of Trustees
T. W. I. Hodgkinson, Dir.
R. A. Cecil, Asst. to Dir.
A. V. B. Norman, Asst. to Dir.
Free weekdays 10 AM - 5 PM; Sun. 2 - 5 PM. Estab. 1900, to display the collection of works of art formed by the 3rd and 4th Marquess of Hertford and Sir Richard Wallace; bequeathed to the nation by Lady Wallace in 1897.
Collections: Paintings by Old Masters of the British, French, Flemish, Dutch, Spanish and Italian Schools; outstanding representation of the arts of France in the 18th century, including furniture, sculpture, Sevres porcelain, miniatures and goldsmithswork; Mediaeval and Renaissance works of art and ceramics. European and Oriental arms and armour.
Attendance: (1974) 108, 215.

WELLINGTON MUSEUM
(Apsley House)
149 Piccadilly, W1V 9FA. Tel: 01-499-5676
H. V. T. Percival, Officer-in-charge.
Free Mon. - Sat. 10 AM - 6 PM; Sun. 2:30 - 6 PM. Estab. 1952 to house the First Duke of Wellington's Collection in his London home; financed by state.
Collections: Paintings, silver plate, porcelain, furniture, sculpture, medals, swords, orders, uniforms, snuff boxes and personal relics of the Duke of Wellington.
Exhibitions: Duke of Wellington in Caricature.
Activities: Lectures open to the public; occasional tours; photograph collection and library are for staff use only. Book shop.
Publications: V & A, annually.
Attendance: 65,000 - 70,000.

THE WORSHIPFUL COMPANY OF GOLDSMITHS
Goldsmiths Hall, Foster Lane, EC2. Tel: 01-606-8971
Graham Hughes, Art Dir.
Mr. Forbes, Deputy Warden of Assay Office
Miss Hare, Librn.
Miss Wallis, Cur.
Peter Jenkins, Clerk
Free 10 AM - 5 PM by strict appointment only and usually for people associated with the craft. Estab. 1175, royal charter in 1327, as a guild for craftsmen of gold and silver and as a centre of London hallmarking; self-supporting.
Collections: †Antique plate; †modern silver, jewelry and medals.
Exhibitions: Extensive exhibitions of the 4 collections both in U.K. and abroad.
Activities: Placing graduate apprentices; motion pictures, lantern slides and photographs in lending collection; photograph collection; lectures open to public, once each month; concerts; competitions; scholarships.
Library: Approx. 3000 volumes and a photograph collection for reference; lantern slides available for brief periods for teachers.
Publications: The Review, annually.

MANCHESTER

UNIVERSITY OF MANCHESTER
Whitworth Art Gallery
Whitworth Park, M15 6ER. Tel: 061-273-1880
Prof. C. R. Dodwell, Dir.
Francis W. Hawcroft, Keeper
Joan Allgrove, Keeper of Textiles
C. J. Allan, Asst. Keeper
Robert Hopper, Asst. Keeper
Michael Regan, Exhibitions Officer
Robin Vousden, Pub. Relations Officer
Jean M. Thomas, Secy.
Free Mon. - Sat. 10 AM - 5 PM; Thurs. 10 AM - 9 PM; cl. Christmas & Good Friday. Founded by Royal Charter 1889.
Collections: Permanent collections of †English watercolors and drawings; †Old Master paintings, drawings and prints; †historic and modern textiles; †contemporary works of art; Japanese color prints; †modern and historic wallpapers.
Exhibitions: Biennial exhibition of Northern Young Contemporaries with six prizes of £100 each; usually five exhibitions each year, with both historic and contemporary themes.
Activities: Maintains library and photograph collection; lectures; gallery talks and tours; objects of art lent to loan exhibitions.
Attendance: 42,275.

OXFORD

ASHMOLEAN MUSEUM
Tel: 57522
David Piper, Dir.
Founded 1683.
Collections: Art and archaeological collections of the Univ. of Oxford; British, European, Mediterranean, Egyptian and Near Eastern archaeology; Italian, Dutch, Flemish, French and English oil paintings; Old Master and modern drawings, watercolours and prints; miniatures; European ceramics; sculpture and bronzes; English silver; objects of applied art; Hope collection of engraved portraits; coins and medals of all countries and periods; Chinese and Japanese porcelain, paintings and lacquer; Chinese bronzes, Tibetan art; Indian sculpture and painting; Islamic pottery and metalwork.
The Museum building also houses the Cast Gallery and the Ashmolean Library which specialises in Archaeology, Western and Eastern Art, Ancient History, Classical Philology and Numismatics; the Griffith Institute Library for Near Eastern Archaeology and Egyptology; and the Grenfell and Hunt Papyrological Library.

PLYMOUTH

CITY MUSEUM AND ART GALLERY
Drake Circus
Alexander A. Cumming, Dir.
James Barber, Deputy
Robin M. Thomas, Keeper of Art
Jeremy Pearson, Asst. Keeper of Art
James Manning, Technical Officer
Free weekdays 10 AM - 6 PM; Fri. 10 AM - 8 PM; Sun. 3 - 5 PM. Estab. 1897; this institution houses all the art treasures belonging to the City of Plymouth; we also hold monthly exhibitions and operate a School Service; supported by local taxes.
Exhibitions: Henry Moore; Young Contemporaries; Sculpture and Painting 69; Barbara Hepworth 70; Sir Joshua Reynolds Exhibition 1973.
Activities: Educational Department for school loans and visits; certain material available to local schools; traveling exhibitions organized and circulated; individual paintings lent to schools; original objects of art lent; color reproductions in lending collections; 5000 items lent in an average year to approx. 130 borrowers.
Income and Purchases: Income $210,000; purchases $17,500.
Attendance: 172,000.

SHEFFIELD

SHEFFIELD CITY ART GALLERIES
Surrey St, S1, 1XZ.
H. F. Constantine, Dir. City Art Galleries
Michael Diamond, Deputy Dir.
Julian Spalding, Keeper Mappin Art Gallery
Sheffield Corporation-Sheffield City Art Galleries maintains two galleries:

Graves Art Gallery
Surrey St, 1. Tel: 0742 734780-82
Free weekdays 10 AM - 8 PM; Sun. 2 - 5 PM. Estab. 1934.

Mappin Art Gallery
Weston Park, 10. Tel: 0742 26281
Free weekdays 10 AM - 5 PM (June - Aug. 8 PM); Sun. 2 - 5 PM. Estab. 1887.
Collections: †British Art, 17th-20th centuries (2000 works); †Italian Art, 15th-18th centuries (40 works); †Dutch and Flemish Art, 16th-17th centuries (100 works); †French Art, 19th-20th centuries (90 works); Chinese Ivories, 14th-19th centuries (200 works); †Indian Paintings and Sculpture (40 works); †Islamic, Greek and Roman Art (150 works); †European Watercolours, 17th-20th centuries (1500 works).
Exhibitions: Annual Open Art; Annual Children's Art; Annual College of Education; Annual School of Art; approx. 40 special exhibitions and events per annum.
Activities: Schools lending service; home loans service; classes for children and adults; concerts; competitions; six visiting lectures per year; coach tours to major cities and abroad.
Publications: Provisional Catalogue of Foreign Schools Paintings, 1966; Early English Watercolours (booklet), 1965; The Grice Collection of Chinese Ivories; Exhibition catalogues, slides, postcards.
Annual Purchase Grant: £18,500.
Annual Attendance: 357,000.

YORK

YORK CITY ART GALLERY
Exhibition Square, York, England
John Ingamells, Cur.
Michael Clarke, Art Asst.
Free, weekdays 10 AM - 5 PM; Sun. 2:30 - 5 PM. Estab. 1879; appropriations.

Collections: European Painting 1350 onwards; English Old Masters; prints and drawings of local topography, 17th-19th century; 20th century stoneware.

Exhibitions: Francis Place 1647-1728; The Beautifullest Church; A Candidate for Praise.

Activities: Lectures open to the public; approx. 6 visiting lecturers per year; approx. 12 gallery talks and 30 tours yearly; concerts; dramatic programs.

Library: 7000 volume reference library.

Publications: Preview, 3 times a year.

Attendance: 50,000 annual average.

SCOTLAND

DUNDEE

DUNDEE CITY ART GALLERY AND MUSEUM
Albert Square, DD1 1DA. Tel: 0382-25492
J. D. Boyd, Dir.
Wm. R. Hardie, Deputy Dir.
J. J. Perkins, Keeper Exten. Serv.
A. B. Ritchie, Keeper Natural History
C. A. Zealand, Keeper Antiquities
Free Mon. - Sat. 10 AM - 5:30 PM. Estab. 1873; financed by city and state appropriations.

Collections: Permanent collection of Scottish paintings (largely 19th century); Dutch, Flemish and Italian 17th century paintings; modern local paintings and sculpture collection (1500 items at present, including paintings, drawings and sculpture).

Exhibitions: Three Scottish Colourists (Cadell, Hunter and Peploe); Sir W. Q. Orchardson; Donald Bain; Hills of Dreams, Wm. McLance.

Activities: School loan service; traveling school exhibitions; in-service courses for teachers; museum lecture service; reproductions of collection approximately 300 for lending and sale; classes for adults and children.

Publications: Art Catalogue; Dundee Museum Guide; 100 Years of Dundee City Museums; publications in fields of natural history, folklore, geology, archaeology, history and art.

Purchases: £17,000.

Attendance: Over 260,000.

EDINBURGH

NATIONAL GALLERIES OF SCOTLAND
17 Ainslie Pl, EH3 6AU. Tel: 031-556-8921
Jack Kane, Chmn. Board of Trustees
Miss R. J. Johnston, Secy.
Hugh Scrutton, Dir.

National Gallery of Scotland
The Mound, EH2 2EL. Tel: 031-556-8921
Colin Thompson, Keeper Paintings
Keith Andrews, Keeper Prints & Drawings
Open weekdays 10 AM - 5 PM; Sun. 2 - 5 PM. Estab. 1859 as Scottish National Collection of European and British paintings and sculpture from the 15th century to 1900; financed by state appropriation. Library for curatorial use only.

Collections: Includes comprehensive collection of Scottish paintings; long term loans include the Trinity Altarpiece by Hugo van der Goes on loan from H.M. The Queen and 30 pictures from Bridgewater House on loan from the Duke of Sutherland. All collections gradually being enlarged.

Exhibitions: Pictures for Scotland—The National Gallery of Scotland and Its Collection: a study of the changing attitude to painting since the 1820's. Photograph collection.

Publications: Bulletin, 3-4 times per year.

Purchases: Grant-in-aid, £168,000, plus some trust funds.

Attendance: 164,000.

Department of Prints and Drawings
Open Mon. - Fri. 10 AM - 12:30 PM & 2 - 3:30 PM. Contains a large collection of old master drawings (15th to 19th centuries) with special emphasis on Italian and Scottish artists. There is also a fine group of English watercolors, including 38 by Turner from the Vaughan Bequest. Prints comprise large series by Durer, Rembrandt and Goya.

Scottish National Gallery of Modern Art
Royal Botanic Garden, EH3 5LR. Tel: 031-332-3754
Douglas Hall, Keeper
Open 10 AM - 6 PM, or dusk if earlier. Estab. 1960 as department of National Galleries of Scotland, in temporary accommodation as the Scottish National Collection of 20th century art; financed by state appropriation. Small working library.

Collections: 20th century paintings, drawings and sculpture of all schools; recent contemporary Scottish art; graphic art. All collections currently being enlarged by purchase.

Exhibitions: (1970) The Art of the Letter; Henry Gotlib; Barbara Hepworth; Seven Painters in Dundee; Recent Acquisitions of the Scottish Arts Council; (1971) Magritte, sculptures; William Scott, drawings; Gerald Laing; Julio Gonzalez; (1972) Aleksander Zyw; Ian Hamilton Finlay; Henri Gaudier-Brzeska; Toys by Artists; (1973) Edvard Munch, graphic art; William Johnstone; Bridget Riley; Earth Images.

Publications: Bulletin, 3-4 times per year.

Purchases: Grant-in-aid, £177,000, plus some trust funds.

Attendance: 87,000.

Scottish National Portrait Gallery
1 Queen St, EH2 1JD. Tel: 031-556 8921
R. E. Hutchison, Keeper
Open weekdays 10 AM - 5 PM; Sun. 2 - 5 PM. Estab. 1889 to collect and exhibit portraits of the principal figures in Scottish history; financed by state appropriation. Library for curatorial use.

Collections: Portraits in various media; large collection of D. O. Hill calotypes; photographic record of Scottish portraiture.

Exhibitions: A View of the Portrait, Portraits by Alexander Moffat 1968-1973; A Face for Any Occasion; Painting in Scotland 1570-1650; some 400 items from a collection of over 2000 items are regularly exhibited.

Activities: Original objects of art lent to approved exhibitions; a collection of 14,000 engravings and 20,000 photographs for reference; occasional lectures. Book shop.

Publications: Bulletin, 3-4 times per year.

Purchases: Grant-in-aid £25,000, plus some trust funds.

Attendance: 59,904.

THE ROYAL SCOTTISH MUSEUM*
Chambers St, EH1 1JF. Tel: 031-225 7534
Dr. Norman Tebble, Dir.
Department of Art and Archaeology:
C. Aldred, Keeper
R. Oddy, Asst. Keeper
Miss J. M. Scarce, Asst. Keeper
Miss D. Idiens, Asst. Keeper
M. C. Baker, Asst. Keeper
Department of Natural History:
Dr. A. S. Clarke, Keeper
E. C. Pelham-Clinton, Asst. Keeper
I. H. J. Lyster, Asst. Keeper
Dr. G. Smaldon, Asst. Keeper
D. Heppell, Sr. Scientific Officer
A. Rodger Waterston, Keeper Emeritus
Department of Geology:
Dr. Charles D. Waterston, Keeper
Dr. H. G. Macpherson, Asst. Keeper
Dr. A. Livingstone, Asst. Keeper
Dr. S. M. Andrews, Sr. Scientific Officer
Department of Technology:
Dr. A. G. Thomson, Keeper
J. D. Storer, Asst. Keeper
A. D. C. Simpson, Asst. Keeper
Dr. R. G. W. Anderson, Asst. Keeper
Exhibitions and Design Section:
H. O. A. F. Fernandez, Exhibitions Officer
M. J. Moore, Asst. Keeper
Education and Public Relations Section:
Miss M. S. Thomson, Education & Public Relations Officer
Administrative Office:
A. Falconer
Free weekdays incl. Sat. 10 AM - 5 PM; Sun 2 - 5 PM; cl. Dec 25, Jan 1st & 2nd. Estab. 1854; a national museum administered by the Scottish Education Department. The Friends of the Royal Scottish Museum, a society, is connected with the Museum.

Collections: The decorative arts of the world and the natural and applied sciences.

Exhibitions: Special temporary exhibitions are held from time to time.

Activities: Public lectures and film programmes are held in the Museum's Lecture Theatre, Gallery Talks in the halls and galleries. The Museum has a bookstall and a public tea-room.

The Museum Library: Contains works relevant to the Museum's fields.

Average annual attendance: 550,000.

GLASGOW

GLASGOW MUSEUMS AND ART GALLERIES
Kelvingrove, G3 8AG. Tel: 041 334 1134
T. A. Walden, Dir.
George Buchanan, Deputy Dir.
Jack Scott, Keeper of Archaeology
William Wells, Keeper of Burrell Collection
Charles Palmar, Keeper of Natural History

Anthony Browning, Keeper of Technology
Alasdair Auld, Keeper of Fine Art
Brian Blench, Keeper of Decorative Art
Free weekdays 10 AM - 5 PM; Sun. 2 - 5 PM. Estab. 1856 as a scientific institution responsible for the recording of local history, archaeological excavations and biological and geological field work throughout the West of Scotland, always willing to deal with enquiries from the public; concerned with the quality of life, the organization offers, in addition to permanent collections, a continuous program of special loan exhibitions; financed by city appropriation.

Collections: Pictures (regarded as the finest municipal art collection in Great Britain); arms and armour; ship models; archaeology and ethnography collections. All are being enlarged by purchase or gift.

Exhibitions: 15 per year, 25% organized by Glasgow museums.

Activities: Intra-mural teaching; classes are brought from schools and other establishments to the museums; film program; Saturday art club; courses for teachers; visits to schools; 5000 prints in photograph collection; lectures open to public; 28 visiting lecturers per year; gallery talks; tours; concerts; classes for adults and children; competitions. Book shop.

Library: 12,500 volumes for reference.

Publications: Scottish Art Review, biannually; Calendar of Events, quarterly; Programs of exhibitions, monthly; What's Happening, quarterly.

Income and Purchases: Income $65,000; purchases $90,000 (with central government grant-in-aid).

Attendance: 934,000.

WALES

CARDIFF

NATIONAL MUSEUM OF WALES
    Cathays Park, CF1 3NP. Tel: 26241
Dr. A. B. Oldfield-Davies, Pres.
Col. H. Morrey Salmon, Treas.
Dr. G. O. Jones, Dir.
D. W. Dykes, Secy.
Dr. D. A. Bassett, Geology
J. A. Bateman, Zoology
R. L. Charles, Art
S. G. Harrison, Botany
Dr. H. N. Savory, Archaeology
D. M. Rees, Industry
Free weekdays 10 AM - 5 PM (Oct.-Mar); 10 AM - 6 PM (Apr.-Sept); Sun. 2:30 - 5 PM; bank holidays and Tues. following 10 AM - 6 PM; cl. Christmas Eve, Christmas Day, Boxing Day, New Year's Day and Good Friday. Estab. by Royal Charter 1907; financed by city and state appropriations. Ann. meeting Oct.

Collections: Geology, botany and zoology exhibits show the geologic forces which give the country its present shape, the plants which appear there, and the animals which have lived and now live upon it. Archaeology and Art show the work of Man: the earliest traces of his occupation of Wales, his mastery over materials with the passage of time and his works of art up to the present. The art collections include portraits of eminent Welshmen, pictures of the Welsh scene, and works of Welsh artists, including many by Richard Wilson; and, among the objets d'art Swansea and Nantgarw china and Pontypool and Usk japan ware. There are also many things which are not Welsh, in particular a remarkable collection of French 19th century paintings.

Attendance: 295,100.

ST. FAGANS

WELSH FOLK MUSEUM*
    near Cardiff. Tel: Cardiff 561357
T. M. Owen, Cur.
J. G. Jenkins, Keeper Material Culture
Vincent H. Phillips, Keeper Oral Traditions & Dialects
Open April - Sept, weekdays 10 AM - 7 PM; Sun. 2:30 - 7 PM. Oct. - Mar, weekdays 10 AM - 5 PM; Sun. 2:30 - 5 PM. Open all Bank Holidays incl. Good Friday, Easter Monday, Whit-Monday; cl. Christmas Day and Boxing Day; admis. adults 10p, children 5p. Estab. 1947.

In the village of St. Fagans, four miles west of Cardiff, is the Welsh Folk Museum. It comprises an open air museum, including the Elizabethan mansion of St. Fagans Castle, the rooms of which are furnished in period style, its gardens and grounds, and an adjoining area of eighty acres of woodland. Buildings from all parts of Wales are re-erected where, craftsmen may be seen practicing their crafts, and a selection of the diverse material which is the study of folk-life is exhibited in a new museum block. With these collections and activities the Welsh Folk Museum illustrates the old way of life in Wales.

Attendance: 170,000.

GREECE

ATHENS

BENAKI MUSEUM*
    1 Odos Koumbari. Tel: 611-617
Anthony E. Benaki, Founder
M. Lambros Eftaxias, Chmn.
Open Jan. 1 - Feb. 28, 9:30 AM - 2 PM; Mar. 1 - Dec. 31, 9:30 AM - 1:30 PM & 4:30 - 7:30 PM; admis. 10 drachmae. Estab. Apr. 1930; endowed by the Founder; grant from the State.

Collections: Ancient Greek art, chiefly jewelry; Byzantine and Post-Byzantine art, Icons and minor crafts; modern Greek popular art, national dresses and embroideries; Greek historical relics; Greek historical archives. Collections of Christian and Moslem art of Egypt. Chinese Art (porcelain); textiles and embroideries from Near and Far East.

Library: 16,000 volumes for reference only; 6000 prints in photograph collection; book shop for the editions of the museum only.

Publications: Catalogues and Guides.

NATIONAL PINACOTHEK AND ALEXANDER SOUTZOS MUSEUM
    50, Vas. Constantinou Ave, 516. Tel: 711-010
Dr. Dimitrios Papastamos, Gen. Dir.
Mrs. E. Karagianni, Restorer
Open winter 9 AM - 6 PM; Apr. - Oct. 9 AM - 1 PM & 4 - 8 PM; cl. Tues; admis. Drachmae 30. Estab. 1900 as a picture gallery for Greek and European painting; financed by endowment and city and state appropriation. Gallery maintained for periodic exhibitions of contemporary art.

Collections: 14th - 20th century European painting, including El Greco, Caravaggio, Jordaens, Poussin, Tiepolo, Mondrian and Picasso; engravings including Dürer, Rembrandt, Goya; impressionist, post-impressionist and contemporary drawings; †17th - 20th century Greek paintings, †sculptures and †engravings; furniture.

Exhibitions: Watercolors and drawings by E. Ziller; Drawings by George Grosz; Drawings by Edward Lear; Exhibition of Contemporary Rumanian painting, Greek and French impressionism, contemporary Italian sculpture; Greek-Illyrian treasures from Yugoslavia; Retrospective exhibitions of N. H. Ghikas, Giallinas, Sikeliotis, Vassiliou.

Activities: Lectures and tours for students; traveling exhibitions organized and circulated; individual paintings and original objects of art lent; photograph collection of about 4000 prints for reference; lectures open to public; concerts. Book shop.

Library: 2500 volumes for reference.

Publications: Exhibition catalogs, 3 per year.

HONG KONG

HONG KONG MUSEUM OF ART
    City Hall, Edinburgh Place. Tel: 5-224127
John Warner, Cur.
L. C. S. Tam, Asst. Cur.
Irene Kho, Asst. Cur.
Free Sun. & pub. holidays 1 - 6 PM; weekdays 10 AM - 6 PM; cl Thursday. Estab. 1962 to provide, through the museum's collections, displays and specialized staff, an education centre for all residents of Hong Kong; financed by the Hong Kong taxpayers.

Collections: Local art, Chinese art, decorative art and crafts.

Exhibitions: Permanent display of Chinese art plus regular special exhibitions such as Contemporary Hong Kong Art 1975, Contemporary Prints by Chinese artists, Exhibition of Chinese Blue and White Porcelain, Chinese Puppets and Crafts of the Middle Kingdom.

Activities: Guided tours for schools; competitions on museum's exhibits; children's art competitions.

Publications: Exhibition catalogs and books; reproductions and postcards. Free monthly newsletter.

Income and Purchases: Income HK$50,000; purchases HK$300,000.

Attendance: 300,000.

HUNGARY

BUDAPEST

MAGYAR NEMZETI GALERIA
(Hungarian National Gallery)
    Budavari Palota B,C,D epület, 1250 Budapest Postafiok 31.
    Tel: 161-280
Dr. G. E. Pogany, Dir. Gen.
Dr. Istvan Solymar, Deputy Dir. Gen.
Dr. Eva Bodnar, Chief of the Painting Dept.
Olga Heil, Chief, Graphic Dept.
Erzsebet Csap, Chief, Sculpture Dept.
Dr. Zsuzsa Nagy, Chief, Medallion Dept.
Dr. Eva Visy-Strobl, Chief, Library
Ilona Gerevich, Chief, Old Hungarian Art Collection

Open every day except Mon. 10 AM - 6 PM; admis. 3 forints, free Sat. Estab. 1957 to display and preserve Hungarian art works of the 12th century of till the present time; financed by government appropriation. The Hungarian National Gallery is being moved to its new building, the former Royal Palast, and its collection having been completed by the old Hungarian art, the gallery will offer a complete survey of Hungarian art in its entirety.

Collections: Hungarian Romanesque, Gothic, Baroque panel paintings and carvings; 19th and 20th century Hungarian paintings, sculptures, graphic art works, medallions; all currently being enlarged either by purchase or by endowment.

Exhibitions: 150 in the Gallery and in several country museums.

Activities: Traveling exhibitions organized and circulated; original objects of art lent; photographs available if needed for reproduction; 25,000 prints; lectures open to public; 500 gallery talks or tours; concerts, classes for children, competitions.

Library: 25,000 volumes for reference.

Publications: Catalogs of exhibitions; Bulletin de la Galerie Nationale Hongroise; Annales de la Galerie Nationale Hongroise.

Income and Purchases: Income 1,000,000 forints; purchases 1,000,000 forints.

Attendance: 600,000.

MUSEE HONGROIS DES BEAUX-ARTS*
(Museum of Fine Arts)
Dozsa György ut 41, 1396. Tel: 429-759
Dr. Klara Garas, Dir-Gen.
Dr. A. Czobor, Head Prints & Drawings
Dr. E. Eszlary, Head Old Sculpture
Dr. D. Pataky, Head Modern Art
Dr. T. Szentleleky, Deputy Dir.
Dr. J. Gy. Szilagyi, Head Greek & Roman Antiquities
Dr. M. H. Takacs, Head Old Pictures
Dr. V. Wessetzky, Head Egyptian Antiquities
Open weekdays 10 AM - 6 PM; Sun. 10 AM - 6 PM; cl. Mon; admis. 3 florins per person, free for schools and students. Estab. 1906 to collect works of art within the spheres of classic archaeology and European art history, 13th-20th century; financed by city and state appropriations. Annual meetings 4 times yearly; mem. 500.

Collections: †Old pictures, 13th-18th century; †prints and drawings, 14th-20th century; †modern paintings and sculpture, 19th-20th century; †Egyptian, Greek and Roman antiquities.

Exhibitions: Raphael; Italian Landscapes; The Esterhazy Collection; Prints and Drawings from the Esterhazy Collection; Dürer; Old Hungarian Art; Decline of the Middle Ages; French Graphic Art; Masterpieces from Paris Museums; Cranach and his Age; European Landscapes, 16th-17th century; British Portraits; Russian Icons.

Activities: Educational department, guided tours for schools and groups and educational programme for adults; free university; traveling exhibitions organized and circulated; original objects of art lent; lectures open to public; gallery talks; classes for adults and children.

Library: 50,000 volumes, 1200 periodicals and photograph collection for lending and reference.

Publications: Bulletin, semi-annually; catalogues.

Attendance: 500,000 annual average.

ICELAND

REYKJAVIK

THE EINAR JONSSON MUSEUM
Reykjavik
Open winter, Sun. & Wed. 1:30 - 4 PM; summer (May - Aug), daily except Mon, 1:30 - 4 PM. Financed by state appropriation.

Collections: The museum contains almost all originals of Einar Johsson's (sculptor) works and some paintings of his.

THJODMINJASAFN
(National Museum of Iceland)
Sudurgata. Tel: (91) 16779, (91) 13264
Thor Magnusson, Dir, Fil.kand.
Gisli Gestsson, Cur.
Elsa E. Gudjonsson, Cur. of Textiles
Halldor J. Jonsson, Cur.
Arni Bjornsson, Cur.
Thorkoll Grimooon, Cur.
Free Sept. 1 - May 31, Sun, Tues, Thurs, Sat. 1:30 - 4 PM; June - Aug, daily 1:30 - 4 PM. Estab. 1863; archaeology, ethnology, folklore; State appropriation.

Collections: Archeological and ethnological artefacts, portraits, numismatics.

Exhibitions: Greenland the Past, 1968; Icelandic Folk Costumes, 1969; Twelve Artists of Former Times, 1970.

Library: Unknown number of volumes; photograph collection for lending and reference.

Publications: Árbok (year-book), published by the Archaeological Society.

Income and Purchases: Income approx. $4000; purchases vary.

Attendance: Approx. 40,000.

INDIA

BARODA

MUSEUM AND PICTURE GALLERY*
Sayaji Park, 5. Tel: 4605
Dir. Vacant
Shri P. G. Gupte, Keeper Science Sections
Shri M. N. Gandhi, Keeper Art & Archaeology Sections
Shri S. K. Bhowmik, Asst. Dir.
Open weekdays 9:30 AM - 5 PM; Thurs. 10 AM - 5 PM. Museum estab. 1894, Picture Gallery estab. 1920.

Collections: Indian art, archaeology and natural history; Eastern and Far Eastern civilization and art, ethnology; Greek, Roman and European art, a very representative collection of European paintings.

Exhibitions: Four exhibitions are arranged every year.

Activities: Film shows and lecture series are a regular feature of the Museum; 5 distinguished visiting lecturers are invited every year.

Library: 15,000 books and periodicals.

Publications: Bulletin annually.

Attendance: Over 600,000 annually.

CALCUTTA

THE INDIAN MUSEUM
27 Jawaharlal Nehru Road, 13. Tel: 239855
Shri A.K. Bhattacharyya, Dir.
Open winter, 10 AM - 4:30 PM; summer, 10 AM - 5 PM. Estab. in 1814 through the efforts and collections of the Asiatic Society of Bengal which had been founded in 1784. Being under a Board of Trustees and subsidized by the Union Government of India, the Board meets 4 times a year; annual general meeting 3rd week of March.

Collections: Art—textiles, miniature paintings, ivory, metalware, ceramics, woodcarvings, bronzes, papier mache, jade, crystal, gold and silver ornaments. Archaeology—copper and stone implements of prehistoric and proto-historic origin; stone sculptures; terracotta objects; bronze figures; steatite objects; stucco figures; coins, etc. Anthropology—tribal and regional objects including sets of cultural objects represented by garments, headdress, ornaments, weapons, utensils, etc. Zoology—type specimens of fauna in India including some specimens from abroad, skeleton and skeletal remains of extinct animals, fish and all types of mammals, invertebrates and vertebrates, including a large collection of reptiles, birds, and insects. Geology—large collection of fossils; mammals; reptiles and trees; meteors, meteorites, stones, minerals. Industrial (Botany)—collections of plants, productive and decorative; specimens of cereals, floral plants, fruits and fruit-plants, fibrous plants, economic plants and a large collection of ethnobotanic specimens. All the above sections are being added to by purchase, gifts and permanent loan.

Exhibitions: Indian Monuments; combined exhibitions from the six different sections above; Museums in Education; Modern Indian Paintings.

Activities: Lectures, discussion seminars, University classes in archaeology, art, the sciences and museology; special programmes of Students' Day held on every Saturday with documentary films and special guided tours of the Museum.

Library: 4000 volumes, 1500 periodicals, books, journals, pamphlets, reports, memoirs.

Income and Purchases: Grant-in-aid from Union Govt, approx. Rs. 1,000,000; annual purchases approx. Rs. 80,000.

Attendance: (1967-68, 1968-69) Approx. 4,000,000.

NEW DELHI

LALIT KALA AKADEMI
Rabindra Bhavan, 110001. Tel: 387241
Karl J. Khandalavala, Chmn.
Estab. Aug, 1954, as the national academy of art, founded for the promotion of visual arts; financed by state appropriation. Gallery only for holding exhibitions of the Akademi, other organizations or artists.

Collections: 507 paintings, graphics and sculptures. The Akademi buys new works of art every year.

Exhibitions: 25 Years of Indian Art, 1972-73; National Exhibition of Art, 1973; Retrospective Exhibition of Bendre, 1974; Third Triennale-India, 1975.

Library: 4002 volumes for reference only; photograph collection and a collection of 3306 color transparencies for reference.

Publications: Lalit Kala Newsletter; Lalit Kala (journal on ancient art); Lalit Kala Contemporary (half-yearly on modern art); art books and multicolor reproductions, prints, etc.

NATIONAL GALLERY OF MODERN ART
Jaipur House, Dr. Zakir Husain Rd, 110003.
Tel: 382835, 384560, 384640
Dr. L. P. Sihare, Dir.
Sukanta Basu, Restorer
Dr. Anis Farooqi, Deputy Keeper, Educ.
K. S. Mathur, Deputy Keeper, Art Collection
Y. C. Gajwe, Deputy Keeper, Publication
S. K. Sahni, Sr. Guide Lecturer
Chintamani Vyas, Sr. Technical Asst.
Shri R. N. Batham, Guide Lecturer
B. K. Pant, Technical Asst.
P. K. Ray, Photographer.
Free weekdays 10 AM - 5 PM; cl. Mon. Inaugurated Mar. 29, 1954 to develop a representative collection of Indian and international modern art, essentially painting, sculpture and graphic covering a span of more than a hundred years and make them on view to the public at large. The Museum has a very intensive special exhibition, educational and publication programme. The National gallery of Modern Art is financed by the Government of India, Union Ministry of Education and Social Welfare, under whom it is functioning as a subordinate office.

Collections: Indian contemporary paintings, sculptures and graphics. These are displayed in a chronological order as far as possible so as to give a bird's eye view of the evolution of modern Indian art since 1857. The collection of art objects is made through purchase and gifts. There is an art purchase committee comprising of Indian experts and on their recommendations, art objects are acquired for the permanent collection of the Gallery.

Activities: Two guide lecturers who conduct lectures in the Gallery at 11 AM & 3 PM daily for the visitors. Groups of students, Indian and foreign tourists and other V.I.P's are provided conducted tours of our galleries on prior appointment. Short term art appreciation seminars for students and teachers are being organized; traveling exhibitions organized and circulated; art objects lent only under special circumstances; 3000 Kodachrome slides in lending collection. Mobile Exhibition Bus.

Library: Approx. 4900 volumes and 300 prints for reference.
Publications: Post cards; color reproductions; monographs; Hand Book of Paintings and Graphics; Hand Book of Sculptures; Handbook of Bengal School; exhibition catalogs.

NATIONAL MUSEUM OF INDIA*
Janpath
C. Sivaramamurti, Dir.
Open 10 AM - 5 PM; cl. Mon. Estab. 1949.
Collections: Large in scope. All collections active. Prehistory; Indus Valley culture; †sculptures (stone and terra cottas) from 3rd century B.C. to 18th century; Bronzes; †miniatures and drawings, c. 14,000; mural paintings; †sanskrit, Persian, Arabic, Indian language manuscripts, c. 10,000; †coins, c. 40,000; †arms; †decorative arts; †ethnology; Central Asian antiquities and murals; Museum Conservation Laboratory.

Exhibitions: 4 to 5 per year.
Educational Activities: Guided tours; lectures; cultural programs; educational movies related to archaeology, monuments, art; approx. 10-20 outside lecturers.
Library: Archaeology, art, Indology; approx. 15,000 volumes, 100 periodicals.
Income and Purchases: Annual budget approx. Rs 2,200,000; Annual purchases approx. Rs 600,000-Rs 1,200,000.
Attendance: Over 200,000 annually.

IRELAND

MUNICIPAL GALLERY OF MODERN ART
Charlemont House
Parnell Square 1. Tel: (01) 741903
Ethna Waldron, Cur.
Open Tues. - Sat. 10 AM - 6 PM; Sun. 11 AM - 2 PM; cl. Mon. Estab. 1908; in present premises since 1933.
Collections: Lane collection; †works by contemporary painters; frequent temporary exhibitions.
Activities: Gallery lectures, film shows, talks for children, guided tours. Book shop.
Attendance (1974) 61,481.

NATIONAL GALLERY OF IRELAND
Merrion Square West, 2. Tel: 67571, 61699
James White, Dir.
Michael Wynne, Asst. Dir.
Eibhlin McCarthy, Registrar
Ann Stewart, Librn.
Andrew O'Connor, Restorer

Maighread McParland, Restorer
Frances Ruane, Educ. Officer
Free weekdays incl Sat. 10 AM - 6 PM; Thurs. 10 AM - 9 PM; Sun. 2 - 5 PM. Estab. 1864; contains 42 rooms of †paintings of all European schools and an †American Room; special rooms of †drawings and †watercolors. Changing exhibitions.
Activities: Lecture theatre, Tourifon sound guide, demonstrations for children. Sales Desk: Photographs of all works, catalogues, reproductions, postcards, slides and souvenirs. Restaurant open during Gallery hours.
Art Reference Library: Open to the public on weekdays 10 AM - 5:15 PM; approx. 10,000 volumes.
Attendance: Average 1000 per day.

NATIONAL MUSEUM OF IRELAND
Kildare St. Tel: 765521
A. T. Lucas, Dir.
Open Tues. - Sat. 10 AM - 5 PM; Sun. 2 - 5 PM; cl. Mon. Estab. 1877.
Comprises †Irish Antiquities Division, †Art and Industrial Division, †Natural History Division, Folklife Division.
Library: c. 10,000 books.
Publications: Occasional guides to collections and specialist catalogs of particular collections.
Attendance: 173,000.

ISRAEL

MUSEUM OF ANCIENT ART
4 Bialik St, P.O. Box 4811.
Dr. J. Elgavish, Dir.
Municipal Museum. Estab. 1948.
Collections: †Greek and Roman sculpture and terracottas; †Canaanite and Biblical terracottas; findings from excavations at Shikmona (ancient Haifa); coptic textiles and portrait painting from Egypt; †provincial Roman coins.
Educational Activities: Teen-agers' circles in Israeli archaeology; children's courses on Ancient art; lectures to school classes.
Publications: Album Shikmona, The City Museum of Ancient Art, Haifa; The excavations of Shikmona, A Seleucian Garrison Camp from Hasmonean Times.

MUSEUM OF MODERN ART
Haifa Municipality. 4 Bialik St. Tel: 04-640775
G. Tadmor, Dir-Cur.
J. Shen-Dar, Cur.
N. Vodnizky, Pub. Relations
Open Mon. - Thurs. 10 AM - 1 PM & 4 - 7 PM; Fri. 10 AM - 1 PM; Sat. 10 AM - 2 PM; cl. Sun. Estab. 1951.
Collections: †Israel paintings, sculpture, drawings and prints; †Modern French, English, American and German paintings; 19th and 20th century prints; †archives of reproductions; †posters. Permanent installation, special collection - M. Shemi Hall, paintings by the late artist.
Exhibitions: Special biannual shows, Young Israeli Artists' Show, in honor of the late Dr. Schiff, with prize awards.
Activities: Weekdays, student lectures, films, lectures, gallery talks; Sat, lectures for tourists in English. Lending services of reproductions and slides for schools.
Library: 8000 items with emphasis on modern art.
Annual Income and Purchases: $13,000.
Attendance: 10,500 annually.

ISRAEL MUSEUM
91000. Tel: (02) 36231
Daniel Gelmond, Dir.
Miriam Tadmor, Cur. Samuel Bronfman Biblical & Archaeological Museum
Martin Weyl, Cur. Bezalel National Art Museum
Magen Broshi, Cur, Gottesman Centre for Biblical MSS, at the Shrine of the Book
Ayala Gordon, Cur. Youth Wing.
Open 10 AM - 5 PM daily except Fri. & Sat. afternoons; Tues. 10 AM - 10 PM. Estab. 1965, the Israel Museum includes the Samuel Bronfman Biblical and Archaeological Museum, the Bezalel National Art Museum, the Billy Rose Art Garden and the Shrine of the Book, which houses the Dead Sea Scrolls. Ann. meeting Spring; local mem. 4000 families; dues IL 50, International Organization of Patrons 343; dues $1000.
Exhibitions: (1970-75) 120 different exhibitions covering archaeology, sculpture, painting, graphics and ethnology.

Activities: 2500 children attending weekly classes in Youth Wing; guided tours for children; didactic exhibitions; weekly art history lectures; weekly Film Club. monthly Chamber Concerts.
Library: 60,000 volumes on archaeology and art.
Publications: Catalogs; Israel Museum News; posters.
Attendance: 500,000.

TEL-AVIV

MUSEION HA'ARETZ
(Ha'aretz Museum)
Museum Center, Ramat Aviv, P.O. Box 17068, 61170.
Tel: 415244-248
Mayor of Tel Aviv, Chmn. of Board of Trustees
Dr. K. A. Moosberg, Chmn. of Exec. Comt.
Y. L. Prag, Dir. of Museum Ha'aretz
Mrs. S. Dagan, Secy. of Museum Ha'aretz
A. Kindler, Dir, Kadman Numismatic Museum
D. Davidovitch, Dir, Museum of Ethnography & Folklore
Dr. J. Kaplan, Dir, Museum of Antiquities of Tel Aviv-Yafo
Miss G. Lehrer, Cur, Glass Museum
Mrs. U. Zevulun, Cur. Ceramics Museum
Mrs. A. Kaplan, Cur. Tel Aviv History Museum
Dr. B. Rothenberg, Cur. Nechushtan Pavilion
Prof. Dr. S. Avitsur, Adam Ve Amalo Museum
M. Megiddon, Cur, Tel Qasile Excavations
Dr. E. Landau, Educ. & Pub. Relations
E. Heinemann, Librn, Central Library
Open 9 AM - 4 PM; Fri. 9 AM - 1 PM; Sat. 10 AM - 2 PM; admis.
fees on weekdays, Sat. & holidays free. Museum founded in 1952, opened to public in 1959; originally founded as a pavilion-style museum of the east Mediterranean, aiming to familiarize the public, and especially the youth, with the rich cultural heritage of this cradle region of humanity; financed by city appropriation.
Collections: †Ancient glass; †ceramics; †coins; Prehistoric finds; †Jewish ritual and secular art objects; †Jewish costumes; †scientific and technical apparatus; historical documents, etc, of Tel Aviv-Yafo; traditional work tools and methods.
Exhibitions: Approx. two temporary exhibitions are mounted each year in the individual museums of the Ha'aretz Museum framework.
Activities: Art and Science Centre (creativity working groups); original objects of art lent; photographs of objects in the collections are made available on request; collections of films and film-strips are available in Science Museum, Museum for the History of Tel Aviv, Museum of Ethnography and Folklore. Photograph collection for reference; lectures for members only, approx. 6-8 visiting lecturers per year. Printed guides, postcards, etc. are sold from counter in each museum.
Library: Approx. 6000 volumes for reference.
Publications: Yearbook of the Museum Ha'aretz (Hebrew and English editions), annually.
Attendance: Approx. 325,000.

THE TEL AVIV MUSEUM*
Helena Rubinstein Pavilion, 6 Tarsat St. Tel: 247196
New Building, 27 Shderot Shaul Hameleh, Tel: 257361
Dr. Haim Gamzu, Dir. & Chief Cur.
Miss Mira Friedman, Cur.
Open 10 AM - 1 PM & 4 - 7 PM. Helena Rubinstein Pavilion estab. 1959; New Building estab. 1971.
Collections: Old Masters—fine examples of the English, Italian, French, Dutch Schools of the 16th to 18th century. French School: 19th Century—Delacroix, the Barbizon School, Corot (oils and drawings), major works by Impressionists including Renoir, Degas, Pissarro, Monet, Whistler and Post Impressionists (Signac, etc); 20th Century: Fauves and their generation; Van Dongen, Vlaminck, Marquet, Marie Laurencin, Suzanne Valadon, Utrillo; Cubism: Juan Gris, Leger, Jacques Villon, Picasso; Dada Surrealism—about 50 significant works by Arp, Taeuber-Arp, Janco, Herold, Lam, Matta, Ernst, Picabia, de Chirico, Tanguy, Masson, Charles Seliger, etc; Jewish Parisian School: a large number of Chagall, Kisling, Pascin, Modigliani, Lipchitz, Soutine and others. National Schools: 19th and 20th century—Russian: among others, a collection of 28 works by Archipenko. Belgian: 17 major works by Ensor and works by others. German Expressionists: oils, drawings by Schmidt-Rottluff, Nolde, Pechstein, Heckel, Kokoschka. American: paintings from the Ash-Can School to Baziotes, Jackson Pollock, Noland and Morris Louis. English: Pre-Raphaelites, significant series of 18th and 19th century watercolours. Italian: Morandi, Boccioni, Prampolini, Marino Marini, Rotella, and others. South American: Portinari, Rivera, Tamayo, Siqueiros, Morado, Lazar Segal, and others. Polish: Lebenstein. A comprehensive collection of Jewish and Israeli painters of the 19th and 20th century. Good examples of sculpture, 19th and 20th century by Rodin, Degas, Epstein, Barlach, Lehmbruck, Lipchitz, Henry Moore.

Exhibitions: (1967) Rodin, Léger; (1969) Vienna School of Fantastic Realism; (1971) Art and Science; (1972) Picasso; (1973) Tou Louse-Lautrel, Agam. The Museum organizes about 20 exhibitions annually on one-man, group exhibitions, Israeli and Foreign. The Graphic Department (12,000 items) includes Rembrandt, Goya, Daumier and a large survey of modern and contemporary graphics.
Activities: Chamber music concerts, lectures, films, classes for children and adults, traveling art exhibitions, youth centers, etc.
Library: The Helena Rubinstein Art Library at the New Building, 27 Shderot Shaul Hameleh, has a collection of c. 18.000 volumes (books and periodicals) covering most fields of art.

ITALY

FLORENCE

GALLERIA D'ARTE MODERNA DI PALAZZO PITTI*
(Gallery of Modern Art)
Piazza Pitti. Tel: 055/287096
Dr. Sandra Pinto, Dir.
Gualberto Carrai, Secy.
Open daily 10 AM - 4 PM; Sun. 9 AM - 1 PM; cl. Tues; admis. L 1.50. Estab. 1924 as a show of the permanent collections of Italian art of the 19th and early 20th century existing in Florence; financed by state and city appropriations.
Collections: Italian, mainly Tuscan art of the 19th and 20th century.
Exhibitions: Cecioni; Lo Opere; Arte Americane; Nuovi Termini; Sfortuna della Cianemia; Lascito A. Magnelli.
Activities: Photograph collection; lectures; library.
Publications: Catalogues of exhibitions.

GALLERIA DEGLI UFFIZI*
(Uffizi Gallery)
Piazzale Uffizi
Dr. Luciano Berti, Dir.
Estab. 16th century.
The finest collection of Florentine Renaissance painting in the world. In addition to other very important collections in the Uffizi Gallery, one of the best in Italy for antique statues, tapestries, miniatures, not to mention the famous drawing collection, there is a unique and complete collection of artists' self-portraits, ranging from the sixteenth century to the twentieth century; this was begun in the seventeenth century by Cardinale Leopoldo de'Medici, and continued by his successors.

GALLERIA PALATINA, PALAZZO PITTI, MUSEI
(Palatine Gallery)
Piazza Pitti, 1, 50125. Tel: 260695-270323
Dr. Marco Chiarini, Dir.
Dr. Sandra Pinto, Museu degli Argenti
Dr. Christina Piacenti, Galleria de'Arte Moderna
Open Mon. - Sat. 8:30 AM - 2 PM; Sun. & holidays 9 AM - 1 PM; cl. Tues; admis. 200 Lire, 100 holidays, Sun. free. Supported by Gov. appropriation. Gallery.
Collections: Galleria Palatina: Paintings from 15th to 18th centuries Raffaello, Tiziano, Andrea del Sarto. Museo degli Argenti: Silver, enamels, ivories, tapestries, amber, jewels, etc. Appartamenti Monumentali: Tapestries, furniture, pictures, etc. Galleria di Arte Moderna: Modern Neoclassic paintings and sculpture.
Exhibitions: Galleria Palatina: Landscapes, Cherubs & Views of 17th Century Rome (since 1967); Restored paintings from Gallery of Florence (since 1969); Paintings on Stone (since 1970). Appartamenti Monumentali: Artists to the Grand Ducal Court (since 1969); Caravaggio and His Paintings from the Gallery of Florence (since 1970); Florentine and English Exhibition of Art and Culture from the 16th to 20th Centuries.
Activities: Approx. 12 gallery talks and tours each year. Book shop.

GENOA

GALLERIA DI PALAZZO BIANCO
(White Palace Gallery)
via Garibaldi 11
Dr.Arch. Vincenzo Oddi, Dir.
Open Tues. - Sat. 9:30 - 11:45 AM & 2:30 - 5:45 PM; Sun. 9:30 - 11:45 AM; cl. Mon, legal and religious holidays. Estab. 1892.
Collections: Paintings by Genoese and Flemish masters and other schools, sculpture and tapestries; treasures include Paganini's violin and the letters of Columbus, preserved in Palazzo Tursi.

LUCCA

MUSEO NAZIONALE DI VILLA GUINIGI*
(National Museum of Villa Guinigi)
via della Quarquonia. Tel: 0583/46033
Dr. Licia Bertolini Campetti, Dir.
Free summer, 9:30 AM - 1 PM, 3 - 6 PM; winter, 9:30 AM - 2 PM;
cl. Mon. Estab. July 20, 1968; documentation of art and crafts in
Lucca throughout the centuries (from prehistory to approx. 1850);
appropriation.
   Collections: Prehistoric and archaeological materials; sculpture and architecture decoration, 11th to 19th century; Old Master
paintings, 12th to 18th century; wooden inlays and sculpture; ancient
clothes 15th to 19th century.
   Photograph Collection: Approx. 1000 prints.

PINACOTECA NAZIONALE*
(National Picture Gallery)
Palazzo ducale, piazza Napoleone, 55100. Tel: 0583/55315
Dr. Licia Bertolini Campetti, Dir.
Open 8 AM - 2 PM; Sun. 9 AM - 1 PM; cl. Mon; admis. 1 L. Estab.
1875 for exhibition of Lucchese works of art; financed by appropria-
tions.
   Collections: Paintings from churches and palaces of the city and
territory, also from the Medici family; photograph collection.
   Attendance: (1971) 2396; (1972) 2651.

MANTOVA

GALLERIA E MUSEO DEL PALAZZO DUCALE
(Gallery and Museum of the Palazzo Ducale)
Piazza Sordello, 46100. Tel: 0376/20283
Dr. Ilaria Toesca Bertelli, Dir.
Open Tues. - Sat. 9 AM - 2 PM; Sun. 9 AM - 1 PM; admis. L.150.
Estab. as a monument to the Gonsaga family who lived here for
centuries; contains capital works of art, including Mantegna
frescoes, Castello and Pisanello murals.
   Collections: Classical antiquities; Renaissance and later
paintings; classical sculpture; prehistorical relics from Mantuan
territory; Egyptian antiquities; Medieval sculpture; Renaissance
and Baroque sculpture; 13th-19th century paintings; numismatic
collection.
   Exhibitions: 1974: Tesori D'Arte Nella Terra Dei Gonzaga.
   Library: Approx. 2000 volumes for reference, not open to
public; photograph collection of 17,000 prints for reference.
   Attendance: 69,040 annual average.

MILAN

MUSEO D'ARTE ANTICA
(Museum of Ancient Art)
Castello Sforzesco
Dr. Mercedes Garberi, Dir.
Open 9:30 AM - 12:30 PM & 2:30 - 5:30 PM; cl. Mon. Estab. 1879.
   Collections: Sculpture from Middle Ages to 16th century; paint-
ings including works by Mantegna, Lippi, Bellini, Lotto, Tintoretto,
Tiepolo, Guardi, Foppa and others; ancient and contemporary
drawings.
   Library: 41,000 volumes.

Civiche Raccolte de Arte Applicata
(Collections of Minor Arts)
Castello Sforzesco
Dr. Clelia Alberici, Dir.
Open 9:30 AM - 12:30 PM & 2:30 - 5:30 PM; cl. Mon.
   Collections: Minor arts—furniture, ceramics, tapestries, etc.
Musical instruments.

Stamp Collection Bertarelli
Castello Sforzesco
Dr. Clelia Alberici, Dir.
Open 9 - 12 AM & 3 - 6 PM; cl. Sat. & Sun.

Raccolte Archeologiche e Numismatiche
Castello Sforzesco & Corse Magenta 15
Dr. Ermanno Arslan, Dir.
Open 9:30 AM - 12:30 PM & 2:30 - 5:30 PM.
   Collections: Castello Sforzesco - Prehistoric and later; ancient
Egyptian, antique and modern coins; Corso Magenta - Greek,
Etruscan and Roman collections.
   Exhibitions: (Castello Sforzesco) Gli Etruschi; nuove ricerche e
scoperte, 1973; Arte preistorica della Valcamonica, 1974; Archeolo-
gia della nuova Cina, 1974. (Corso Magenta) La medaglia polacca
contemporanea, 1973; I medaglioni romani, 1974; Le monete di
Traiano, 1974; Il tesoretto di Vigevano, 1975.
   Activities: Student guidance; lectures for adults; shop for publi-
cations and postcards.
   Library: 4423 volumes specializing in antique coins.

Publications: Notizie dal Chiostro del Monastero Maggiore, twice
yearly; coin collection catalog; exhibition catalogs.

Museo di Milano
(Museum of Milan)
Vedi Sant'Andrea 6.
Dr. Ermanno Arslan, Dir.
Open 9:30 AM - 12:30 PM & 2:30 - 5:30 PM; cl. Mon.
   Collections: Paintings of Milan subjects of the 19th century.

MUSEO POLDI PEZZOLI
(Poldi Pezzoli Museum)
Via Manzoni, 12, 20121. Tel: (02) 794889
Dr. Alessandra Mottola Molfino, Dir.
Open daily 9:30 AM - 12:30 PM & 2:30 - 5:30 PM; holidays 9:30 AM -
12:30 PM & 2:30 - 5:30 PM; Thurs. also 9 - 11 PM; cl. Mon, New
Year's, Easter, May 1st, Aug. 15, Nov 1, Christmas. Admis. 500
lire. Assembly of members of Associazione Amici del Poldi
Pezzoli; mem. 600.
   Collections: Paintings, Italian and foreign from 14th to 18th
centuries; archaeology, carpets, fabrics, antique weapons and ar-
mour; pottery, glasses, glass windows, gold, jewels, furniture,
bronzes, Islamic objects, clocks and watches.
   Exhibitions: (1970) Milan 1870-1970: A Century of Art; (1971)
Japanese Masks and Costumes; (1973) Belgian XX Century Jewels;
(1974) Treasures of Mosan Art X-XIII centuries; Engravings of
Ensor and Munch; Grafics of Ennio Morlotti; (1975) Landscape woodcuts by Hokusai and Hiroshige; 1301/Bonifacio VIII.
   Activities: Photograph collection, 2047 prints for reference; lectures open to public, approx. 130 visiting lecturers per year; classes
for adults; scholarships; educational section for children; restoration of ancient arms and armours.
   Library: Approx. 3000 volumes for reference.
   Publications: Catalogs of exhibitions indicated above and of the
museum collections; brief guide to the museum.

PINACOTECA AMBROSIANA*
(Ambrosian Picture Gallery)
Piazza Pio XI, 2, 20123. Tel: 800146
Dr. Angelo Paredi, Dir.
Open daily 9:30 AM - 5 PM; admis. Lire 200; children and students,
till 15 years, free. Estab. 1609; endowed. Gallery.
   Collections: Apulian, Venetian and Neapolitan paintings and
sculpture from the 11th century to the 19th century.

PINACOTECA DI BRERA*
(Brera Picture Gallery)
Via Brera 28.
Prof. Franco Russoli, Dir.
Open Summer: 9:30 AM - 1 PM, 2 - 6:30 PM; Winter: 9:30 AM - 4
PM; Fri. also 9 - 11 PM; cl. Mon. The proceeds derived from ad-
mission fees go to the State Treasury for the support of the Museums
of the State.
   Collections: Paintings and drawings of the 14th to 19th centuries.
   Educational Activities: The Pinacoteca, in collaboration with
the Friends of Brera and Museums of Milan, sponsors special
courses which are open to the public. In these courses the more
important works in the Pinacoteca collection are explained in eight
lessons.
   Attendance: Approx. 100,000.

NAPLES

MUSEO E GALLERIE NAZIONALI DI CAPODIMONTE*
(Mt. Capodi National Museum & Gallery)
Palazzo di Capodimonte. Tel: 910801
Prof. Raffaello Causa, Dir.
Open weekdays 9:30 AM - 4 PM; holidays 9:30 AM - 1 PM; cl. Mon.
   Collections: †Italian and foreign paintings from 13th to 19th cen-
turies; small bronzes and medals from the Renaissance; tapestries
from 16th to 18th centuries; ivory and objects of minor art; Italian
Majolica; Italian and foreign porcelains; Murano glass; Armour
from 15th to 19th centuries; furniture, 18th and 19th centuries; draw-
ing and print collections of 15th-19th century.
   Library: 10,000 volumes and pamphlets and magazines specializing in the History of Art.
   Attendance: 75,000 annually.

MUSEO NAZIONALE*
(National Museum)
Prof. Alfonso de Franciscis, Dir.
Estab. 18th century.
   Collections: Works of art from Farnese, Borgia, and Noia Col-
lections, and works recovered from excavations in Southern Italy,
particularly in Pompeii and Herculaneum. A foremost collection
of ancient bronzes, wall paintings and mosaics.

PADOVA

MUSEO CIVICO DI PADOVA
(Municipal Museum)
Piazza del Santo, 10. Tel: 049-23106; 049-23713
Dr. Alessandro Prosdocimi
Open 9:30 AM - 1:30 PM. Financed by city appropriations.
  Collections: Lapidary Collection; Archaeological Museum; Gallery of Pictures; Bottacin Museum (Numismatic); other collections.
  Library: 350,000 volumes; photograph collection.
  Publications: Bollettino del Museo Civico di Padova, semi-annual.

PERUGIA

GALLERIA NAZIONALE DELL'UMBRIA
(Umbrian National Gallery)
Palazzo Dei Priori, Corso Vannucci, 06100
Dr. Francesco Santi, Dir.
Open 9 AM - 2 PM; admis. 150 lire. Estab. 1863; documentation of the arts (painting, sculpture, jewels) in Umbria from the 13th century to the 18th century; financed by state appropriation.
  Collections: School of painting (Italian) in Umbria from the 13th to the 18th century; 13th, 14th, 15th century sculpture; Medieval ivory; jewels (Umbria-Siena) 13th and 14th centuries; furniture of the Renaissance.
  Exhibitions: Annual shows (lasting a week at the museum) on the restoration of art works in cooperation with two churches and museums in the region of Umbria.
  Library: 3995 volumes; photograph collection, 25,000 negatives (inactive), 25,000 positives (active), all for specialized study only.
  Publications: F. Santi, Itinerary of the Gallerie Nazionale dell' Umbria (brief guide); catalog of Romanesque and Gothic works.
  Annual Income: (1974) 2,625,900 Lire.
  Attendance (1974): 41,296 (free and paid).

PISA

MUSEO NAZIONALE E MUSEO CIVICO DI SAN MATTEO*
(St. Matteo National Museum)
Piazza S. Matteo in Soarta, 56100. Tel: 050/23750
Dr. Licia Bertolini Campetti, Dir.
Dr. Antonino Caleca, ispettore
Open summer, 9:30 AM - 4 PM; winter, 9:30 AM - 2 PM; cl. Mon; admis. Lit. 100.-. Estab. 1846; documentation of art in Pisa throughout the centuries; appropriation.
  Collections: Old Master paintings, 11th-18th centuries; marble and wooden sculpture 10th-18th century; mediaeval illuminated manuscripts; renaissance tapestries; Roman and Italian coins, etc.
  Exhibitions: Mostra del restauro, 1967, 1971, 1972.
  Activities: Photograph collection, approx. 1000 prints; concerts.

ROME

CAPITOLINE MUSEUM AND PALAZZO DEI CONSERVATORI*
(Museum of Sculpture)
Tel: 682862
C. Pietrangeli, Chief Officer
Open daily 9 AM - 2 PM; Tues. - Thurs. also 5 - 8 PM; Sat. also 9 - 11:30 PM; cl. Mon.
  Collections: †3500 ancient sculptures, †paintings, pottery, †bronzes, ††tapestry and other works of art.
  Attendance: (1968) 209,509; (1970) 231,373.

GALLERIA DORIA PAMPHILJ
(Dorian Gallery)
Piazza del Collegio Romano 1/A, 00186.
Dr. Eduard A. Safarik, Dir.
  Collections: Paintings by Correggio, Titian, del Piombo, Lorrain, Filippo Lippi, Velazquez, Carracci, Caravaggio.

GALLERIA NAZIONALE D'ARTE ANTICA IN PALAZZO CORSINI
(National Gallery in Corsini Palace)
10 via della Lungara. Tel: 65-23-23
Dr. Nolfo di Carpegna, Dir.
  Collections: Paintings by Ribera, Rubens, Van Dyck, Caravaggio, Saraceni, Borgianni, Honthorst, Terbrugghen, Maratta, Dolci, Murillo, Pietro da Cortona, Lanfrances and others.

Galleria Nazionale d'Arte Antica in Palazzo Barberini
(National Gallery in Barberini Palace)
33 via delle Quattro Fontane. Tel: 45-51-84
Dr. Nolfo di Carpegna, Dir.
  Collections: Paintings by Simone Martini, Beato Angelico, Piero di Cosimo, Filippo Lippi, Giulio, Romano, Perugino, Raffaello, Lotto, Tintoretto, El Greco and others.

MUSEO GALLERIA BORGHESE*
(Borghese Gallery)
Piazzale Scipione Borghese, 00197. Tel: 858577-861174-860756
Dr. Luciana Ferrara Grassi, Dir.
Open 9 AM - 2 PM; festive 9 AM - 1 PM; cl. Mon.
  Collections: Sculptures (G. Bernini, Canova); paintings by Lorenzo di Credi, Andrea del Sarto, Dosso Dossi, Domenichino, Raffaello, Veronese, Antonello da Messina, Tiziano, Caravaggio.

SASSARI

MUSEO NAZIONALE G. A. SANNA - SASSARI
(G. A. Sanna National Museum)
Via Roma 64, 07100. Tel. 079/ 272203
Prof. Ercole Contu, Supt-Dir. of Museum
Open 9 AM - 2 PM; admis. 100 lire; Settimana dei Musei exhibition free. Estab. 1930; enlargement and reorganization in line with didactic standards and modern esthetics; financed by state appropriation.
  Collections: Archeological collections, picture gallery, collection of Sardiniam ethnography.
  Exhibitions: Museum weeks.
  Activities: Visiting students; lectures open to the public with special permission; 30 visiting lecturers per year.
  Library: 2000 volumes; photograph collection.

TORINO

MUSEO CIVICO*
(Municipal Museum)
Via Magenta, 31 Tel: 011-541822
Dott. Aldo Passoni, Asst. Dir.
Dott. Anna Serena Fava, Cur. Numismatics
Dott. Silvana Pettenati, Cur. Antique Art Collection
Open 9 AM - 8 PM; cl. Mon; admis. £100; free on holidays. Financed by city and state appropriations.
  Collections: Antique and modern art from 4th-20th century.
  Exhibitions: Many exhibitions from 1970 to the present.
  Activities: Traveling exhibitions organized and circulated; original objects of art lent; 50 items lent in average year; photograph collection of 27,200 prints; lectures open to the public.
  Library: 32,894 volumes.
  Publications: Catalogues for temporary shows and for each section of the museum.

TRIESTE

CIVICO MUSEO REVOLTELLA-GALLERIA D'ARTE MODERNA*
(Revoltella Civic Museum-Gallery of Modern Art)
Via Diaz 27, 34123. Tel: 040-35429
Dr. Giulio Montenero, Cur.
Free daily 9 AM - 1 PM; holidays 10 AM - 1 PM; cl. Mon. Estab. 1872 to maintain the buildings inherited by the foundation in their proper original decor; increasing the number of pictures, sculptors, and graphic arts from 800 to 900. The temporary exhibits come prepared in the communal hall of art at the Constanzi Palace in Trieste.
  Collections: About 1200 paintings and sculptures and 4000 graphic arts are represented; All the artists from the regione of Friuli-Venezia Giulia; many artists are Italian, some artists European, especially central Europe.
  Activities: Educational Dept; traveling exhibitions organized and circulated.
  Library: 4000 volumes, photograph collection, 5000 prints.

VATICAN CITY

MUSEI E GALLERIE PONTIFICIE
(Vatican Museums and Galleries)
Vatican City
Deoclecio Redig de Campos, Dir. Gen.
  Pope Julius II in 1503 had the statue of the Apollo del Belvedere brought to the Vatican. That was the beginning of the Vatican collections.
  Hours for all museums, 9 AM - 2 PM; July through Sept. 9 AM - 5 PM.

Greek and Roman Sculpture:
  Georg Daltrop, Cur.
Museo Pio-Clementino, founded by Clemens XIV and Pius VI in 1784; Museo Chiaramonti and Braccio Nuovo, founded by Pius VII in 1810 and 1822; Museo Gregoriano Profano, formerly Lateranense, founded by Gregory XVI in 1844.

Etruscan Art:
  Francesco Roncalli, Cur.
Museo Gregoriano Etrusco, founded by Gregory XVI in 1837.

Egyptian Art:
Gianfranco Nolli, Cur.
Museo Gregoriano Egizio, founded by Gregory XVI in 1839.

Early Christian Art:
Museo Pio Cristiano, formerly Lateranense, founded by Pius IX in 1854.

Mediaeval and Modern Art:
Fabrizio Mancinelli, Cur.
Chapel of Nicholas V, painted by Beato Angelico 1448-1450; Sistine Chapel, built by Sixtus IV 1475-1483, and frescoed by several masters of the 15th century and by Michelangelo 1508-1512 and 1535-1541; Borgia Apartment with frescoes by Pinturicchio 1492-1495, and others; Loggia and Stanze painted by Raphael 1508-1520; Pinacoteca Vaticana, founded by Pius XI in 1932.

Ethnographical Collection:
Giuseppe Penkowski, Cur.
Museo Missionario Etnologico, formerly Lateranense, founded by Pius XI in 1926-1927.

Collection of Modern Religious Art:
Prof. Dandolo Bellini, Hon. Cur.
Inaugurated by Paul VI in 1973.

JAPAN

KURASHIKI

OHARA MUSEUM OF ART*
1-1-15 Chuo. Tel: 0864-22-0005
Shin-ichiro Foujita, Cur.
Open Apr. - Oct. 9 AM - 5 PM; Nov. - Mar. 9 AM - 4 PM; admis. 100yen, student 50yen. Estab. 1930 to exhibit, collect and keep for fine arts.
Collections: Modern European and American paintings and sculpture; Modern Japanese Oil Paintings and Sculpture; Ancient Egyptian and Persian Arts; Asiatic Arts and another Modern Japanese Potterys.
Exhibitions: Permanent exhibition.
Activities: Lectures open to the public; gallery talks; library. Book shop.

KYOTO

KYOTO KOKURITSU HAKUBUTSUKAN*
(Kyoto National Museum)
Higashiyama Shichi-cho, Higashiyama-ku
Takaaki Matsushita, Dir.
Haruki Kaoeyama, Chief Cur.
Estab. 1899 as Imperial Kyoto Museum and in 1952 became the National Museum.
Collections: Fine and industrial arts; historical materials of Asia.

KYOTO KOKURITSU KINDAI BIJUTSUKAN
(The National Museum of Modern Art, Kyoto)
Enshoji-cho, Okazaki, Sakyo-ku
Michiaki Kawakita, Dir.
Tadao Ogura, Chief Cur.
Kenji Suzuki, Cur.
Takeo Uchiyama, Cur.
Yashuhiro Shimada, Cur.
Ruiko Kato, Asst. Cur.
Open 10 AM; admis. 80 yen adults & students (senior high school, university and college). Estab. Mar, 1963 for the exhibition, research and preservation of modern art at home and abroad; financed by city and state appropriation. 23 mem. meet twice a year.
Collections: Kawakatsu Collection (potteries made by Kanjiro Kawai and donated by Kenichi Kawakatsu, 418 pieces).
Exhibitions: (1972) Japanese Artists in Europe; James Ensor; (1973) Japanese Artists in the Americas; Bird's Eye View of Contemporary Handicraft; (1974) Handicraft in Okinawa; Andrew Wyeth; 8 - 10 exhibitions per year.
Activities: Lecture of the exhibitions which are held in the museum for a fee of 600 yen a year; traveling exhibitions organized and circulated; original objects of art lent; lectures for members only; 30 visiting lecturers per year, 10 gallery talks, 2 tours.
Library: 1000 domestic books, 500 foreign books; photograph collection.
Publications: MIRU, monthly bulletin; Handicraft in Okinawa; catalog of exhibitions;
Attendance: 206,778.

NARA

NARA KOKURITSU HAKUBUTSUKAN*
(Nara National Museum)
Noborioji-cho 50, Nara Park.
Dr. O. Kurata, Dir.
H. Naito, V.Dir.
H. Nishimura, Chief Cur.
Open 9 AM - 4:30 PM; cl. Mon; admis. adults 80 yen, children 30 yen. Estab. April 1902; reorganized Aug. 1952 and attached to the Committee of the Protection of the Cultural Properties. Originally established to display relics of the large Buddhist temples of the area.
Collections: Classification of Buddhist arts: iconographies in sculptures, pictures, and ritual tools; styles of Buddhist statues, 6th to 14th century; Forms of Temple: formal development of the temples and detailed techniques of architecture; other statues, relics, scrolls. Tea House, originally installed in the garden of the Imperial Monastery and later moved to the garden of the Museum.
Exhibitions: Special annual exhibitions—Shosoin Treasure, last of Oct. to early Nov. (2 wk); Buddhist Art on some special theme, Apr. - May.

TOKYO

BRIDGESTONE MUSEUM OF ART*
1-1, Kyobashi, Chuoku. Tel: (563)0241
Shojiro Ishibashi, Pres.
Yasuo Kamon, Exec. Dir.
Takatsugu Rokujo, Chief Cur.
Open 10 AM - 5:30 PM; cl. Mon; admis. Yen 100. Estab. 1952; permanent display of Ishibashi Collection; endowed. 5 exhibit rooms, 1 lobby.
Collections: Foreign paintings, mainly Impressionism and after; Japanese Western Style paintings; late 19th century to present age; foreign sculptures, from ancient times to present age; foreign original prints, from 17th century to present age; foreign glass wares, bronze wares and pottery, from ancient times to early modern times.
Exhibitions: Shigeru Aoki; Retrospective Exhibition.
Activities: Educational Department; lectures open to public, 44 visiting lecturers per year.
Library: 2200 volumes for reference; photograph collection.
Publications: Catalogue in Japanese, Catalogue in English, Catalogue in French; Illustrated Catalogue (in Japanese and English), large size, small size; Annual Report.
Income and Purchases: Income ¥99,830,000; purchases ¥99,630,000.
Attendance: 99,054.

KOKURITSU SEIYO BIJUTSUKAN
(The National Museum of Western Art)
Ueno Park, Taito-ku, 110. Tel: 03-828-5131
Dr. Chisaburo F. Yamada, Dir.
Kazuo Anazawa, Chief Cur.
Hideya Saski, Cur.
Open 9:30 AM - 5 PM; cl. Mon; admis. ¥ 80. Estab. 1959 to display French paintings and sculptures of the Matsukata Collection (Expressionists and Rodin) and to build up a collection of European art for display in order to show to Japanese public the tradition of European art and its historical development, and at the same time to give Japanese the opportunity to appreciate the aesthetic achievement of Europeans in visual arts; financed by state appropriations. Gallery designed by Le Corbusier, display approximately 100 paintings and 50 sculptures.
Collections: Matsukata Collection which was built up by Kojiro Matsukata in the early 1920's consists of 300 paintings and 63 sculptures, collection consists of impressionists paintings including 12 by Monet and 3 by Renoir; 55 Rodin sculptures including The Gate of Hell, Les Bourgeois de Calais and Le Pensur; †paintings by old masters.
Exhibitions: English Landscape Paintings of the 18th and 19th Centuries; German Expressionism; From Cezanne through Picasso; 100 Drawings from the Collection of the Museum of Modern Art, New York; Roman Baroque Paintings; Goya; Dürer and German Renaissance; Cezanne; Hodler; English Portraits.
Activities: Traveling exhibitions organized and circulated; lectures open to the public.
Library: Reference only.
Publications: Bulletin Annuel du Musee National d'Art Occidental; catalogues of our collection and catalogues of special exhibitions being held twice annually.
Purchases: $200,000-$350,000.
Attendance: 680,000 annual average.

NIPPON MINGEI-KAN*
(Japanese Folk-craft Art Museum)
    861 Komaba-machi, Meguro-ku
S. Hamada, Cur.
    Collections: 20,000 objects of folk-craft arts from all parts of
the world.

TOKYO KOKURITSU HAKUBUTSUKAN*
(Tokyo National Museum)
    Ueno Park, Daito-ku
Seisuke Inada, Dir.
Open 9 AM - 4 PM; cl. Mon. Founded 1871.
    Collections: Japanese and Far Eastern paintings; calligraphy;
sculpture; metalwork; ceramic arts; textiles; lacquer ware; archae-
ological items.
    Publications: Museum, monthly.

TOKYO KOKURITSU KINDAI BIJUTSUKAN*
(The National Museum of Modern Art, Tokyo)
    3 Kitanomaru Koen, Chiyoda-ku, 102. Tel: 03-214-2561, 2565
Jô Okada, Dir.
Masayoshi Homma, Deputy Dir.
Shûichi Okada, Admin. Chief
Tamon Miki, Chief Cur.
Yukinobu Toba, Chief, Nat. Film Center
Museum open 10 AM - 5 PM; cl. Mon, year-end and New Year
holidays. Film Center in Kyobashi open 1 - 7:30 PM; cl. Sun, Nat.
holidays, year-end and New Year holidays. Estab. 1952. New mu-
seum building completed in 1969; old museum building at Kyobashi,
Chuo-ku, now used by the National Film Center. Monthly meeting;
mem. approx. 1,000; ann. fee Y1,000.
    Collections: Japanese paintings 528, oil paintings 604, prints
898, sculpture 179, crafts 23, drawings 100, watercolours 54,
caligraphies 18. Motion picture films—feature play films 735,
documentary films and news reels, etc, 3,340.
    Exhibitions: (1970) The Retrospective Exhibition of Kenkichi
Tomimoto; Ben Shahn; Preview show in Japan of the 5th Japan Art
Festival; Aug. 1970, Aspects of New Japanese Art; Contemporary
British Art; Contemporary Indian Painting; The 7th International
Biennial Exhibition of Prints in Tokyo; 50 years Bauhaus. (1971)
Around 1930 in Modern Japanese Art; René Magritte; Preview show
in Japan of the 6th Japan Art Festival; New Acquisitions; Post-
humous Exhibition of Yamaguchi Kaoru; Contemporary German Art,
Zeitgenössische Deutsche Kunst; Contemporary Ceramic Art, Can-
ada, United States, Mexico and Japan; Development of Postwar
Japanese Art—Figurative Art. (1972) Contemporary Swedish Art;
Masters of Modern Italian Art; New Acquisitions 1972; Today's
Focus—on Modern Japanese Art; The 8th International Biennial Ex-
hibition of Prints in Tokyo; Japanese Artists in Europe; The Retro-
spective Exhibition of Denchu Hirakushi. (1973) Contemporary
Yugoslav Art; Development of Postwar Japanese Art—Abstract and
Non-Figurative; Modern Japanese Art and Paris; Giacomo Manzù;
Japanese Artists in America.
    Activities: Art lectures twice a year, a series of 5 lectures at a
time; 10 visiting lecturers per year; lending services for the purpose
of enlightenment in art and by the requests of the local museums.
Film showing at the National Film Center twice a day at 3 & 6:15 PM.
Reference Materials of different types regarding motion pictures exhibited at the National Film Center. Book Shop.
    Library: Books in Japanese, 2,918; books in foreign languages,
745; all books are concerned with art.
    Publications: Bulletin of the National Museum of Modern Art,
Tokyo Gendai no Me (Today's Focus), monthly annual report; exhibition catalogue for each exhibition; comments on each film program.
    Income and Purchases: (1972) Income ¥20,898,105; expenses paid
¥232,627,467; purchases ¥25,000,000.
    Attendance: Museum 159,800; National Film Center 68,937.

TOKYO-TO BIJUTSUKAN*
(Tokyo Metropolitan Art Museum)
    Ueno-Park, Taito-ku, 110. Tel: 03-823-6921
Takeshi Niijima, Dir.
Akira Asahi, Cur. in Chief
Free Tues. - Sun. 9 AM - 4:30 PM; cl. Mon. & Dec. 29 - Jan. 3.
Estab. 1926; new building opened Sept. 1, 1975, contains gallery,
auditorium, library and studios and provides rental galleries.
    Collections: †Contemporary paintings, sculptures and crafts.
    Exhibitions: The museum originates three or four major exhibi-
tions each year. 160 art groups exhibitions a year at the rental
galleries.
    Activities: Visiting lecturers; films; painting class.
    Library: Approx. 7000 volumes, mainly on Japanese art; 70
periodicals. Open to the public.
    Publications: News of Museum, monthly; catalog of special exhi-
bition.
    Attendance: 1,320,000.

WAKAYAMA
KOYASAN REIHOKAN
    Koyasan, Ito-gun
Chikyo Yamamoko, Dir.
Open 8 AM - 5 PM or 9 AM - 4 PM; admis. 200 yen. Estab. 1921 to
keep the treasures handed down in Koyasan, one of the centers of
Japanese Buddhism.
    Collections: More than 25,000 pieces of painting, sculptures,
calligraphy, manuscripts, etc.

KOREA

SEOUL

THE NATIONAL MUSEUM OF KOREA
    Kyongbok Palace, 1 Sejongro, Chongro-ku. Tel: 72-9295
Sunu Choi, Dir.
Byongsam Han, Chief Cur.
Yangmo Chong, Chief Cur.
Nanyoung Lee, Cur. in Charge of Registrar
Ingu Kang, Cur. in Charge of Archaeology.
Open 9 AM - 6 PM; admis. 100 won for adults; 50 won for children.
Estab. 1915; financed by governmental appropriations. Branch Mu-
seums: Kyongju Museum, Puyo Museum and Kongju Museum.
    Collections: Pottery, ceramics, bronze wares, Buddhist sculp-
ture, painting and calligraphy. (historical and artistic materials)
    Special Exhibitions: Prehistoric Bronze of Korea; Yi Ceramics
of Dr. Byungrae Park's Collection; Treasures of Silla Dynasty; Folk
Arts of Korea.
    Activities: Lectures open to the public; concerts. Book shop.
    Library: 10,000 volumes for reference.
    Publications: Misul Jaryo, a magazine on fine arts, biannually;
Museum News, monthly.
    Income: $52,000.
    Attendance: 347,000 (1974).

LEBANON

BEIRUT

ARCHAEOLOGICAL MUSEUM
    American University of Beirut
Evette Bridi, Secy.
Leila Badre, Cur.
Free Mon. - Fri. 10 AM - Noon & 2 - 4 PM. Estab. 1868 as part of
University cultural and educational endeavour; financed by Univer-
sity. Gallery consists of two large galleries, in which there are 51
show cases.
    Collections: A selection of flint implements, pottery, bronzes,
figurines and coins from the Palaeolithic Age to the 18th century
A.D; glass, sculptures, jewelry.
    Activities: Daily exhibitions; Educational Department teaches
archaeology; photograph collection of 10,000 prints for reference.
Book shop. Library.
    Income and Purchases: Income $1000; purchases $1000.
    Attendance: 3000.

MUSEE NATIONAL*
(National Museum of Lebanon)
    rue de Damas. Tel: 293068
Emir Maurice Chehab, Dir. Gen. of Antiquities
Open winter 9 - 12 AM & 2 - 5 PM; summer 9 - 12 AM & 3 - 6 PM.
    Collections: Objects and statues of the prehistoric period; col-
lections of jewelry and statues of the Phoenician period; sarcophagus
of Ahiram (13th Century B.C), depicting the prototype of the whole
modern alphabet; anthropological sarcophagi of the Greco-Persian
period; collections of jewelry in gold of the Roman, Byzantine and
Arabic periods; sacrophagi and reliefs, mosaics and goblets of the
Greco-Roman period; collections of monies in gold, in sliver, and in
bronze, of the Phoenician, Helenistic, Roman, Byzantine and Arabic
periods; ceramics and wainscotting of the Arabic period.
    Publications: Bulletin du Musee de Beyrouth, annually; Etudes et
Documents d'Archeologie (Publications des fouilles entreprises au
Liban); texts and historical documents.

MALTA

VALLETTA

NATIONAL MUSEUM*
    Kingsway, 25293.
Francis X. Mallia, Dir.
Marius J. Zerafa, Fine Arts Dept.
Tangred Gouder, Archeological Dept.

Open winter 8:30 AM - 1:30 PM, 2 - 4:30 PM; summer 8:30 AM - 1:30 PM; admis. 10¢. Estab. 1905; financed by government.

Collections: Prehistoric archeological remains; 17th and 18th century works of art; collection of works by Martha Prati; †contemporary art.

Exhibitions: Council of Europe Exhibition; regular exhibitions of contemporary art.

Activities: Lectures; tours; scholarships.

Library: Approx. 2000 volumes.

Publications: Museum annual report.

Attendance: 500,000 annual average.

MEXICO

GAUDALAJARA

MUSEO DEL ESTADO*
(National Museum)
Founded 1700 as a seminary.

Collections: Early Mexican objects; folk art and costumes; archaeological discoveries.

MEXICO CITY

MUSEO DE ARTE MODERNO
(Museum of Modern Art)
Bosque de Chapultepec, 5. Tel: 553-63-13
Fernando Gamboa, Dir.
Juan Acha, Coordinator
Mariana Frenk-Westheim, Coordinator
Maria Elena C. de Christensen, Coordinator
Jorge Guadarrama, Cur.
Alfredo Ramirez Herrara, Adminr.
Eva Ramirez Pena, Secy.
Open Tues. - Sun. 11 AM - 7 PM. Estab. 1964; financed by state appropriation.

Collections: Jose Maria Velasco, academic bridge to 20th century Mexican Painting, 51 works; first six decades of 20th century Mexican painting, 124 works; contemporary art (1950-1973), Mexican and foreign, 70 works; international works, a donation which is on temporary exhibition in the Museo de Arte Moderno.

Exhibitions: (Jan. - Dec, 1975) Helen Escobedo, Objetos y Espacious Artisticos; Nadine Prado y Raul Herrara, Dos nuevos valores de la pintura Mexicana; Ricardo Martinez; Oswaldo Guayasamin, La Edad de la Ira; Bryan Nissen, pinturas-Arte y Critica Social; Arnold Belkin, Muertes Historicas; Roberto Matta, Arte Comprometido; Robert Motherwell, Restrospectiva del Gran Pintor Norteamericano; Fernando Ramos Prida, pinturas; Julio Le Parc, Arte cinetico y optico; La Mujer Creadora y Tema del Arte; Adja Yunkers, obras recientes; Manuel Rodriguez Lozano, pinturas, Arte Contemporaneo de Polonia; Feliciano Bejar, Objetos opticos; Edmundo Aquino, pinturas; Retrospectiva y Prospectiva Diseno Mexicano; Waldemar Sjolander, Myra Landau, pinturas; Cordelia Urueta, pinturas; Pierre Soulages, pintura y grabado; Pintura Primitiva y Moderna Haitiana; Arte contemporaneo de Yugoslavia; Color como Lenguaje.

Activities: Guided tours; lectures and round table discussions; films. Book shop.

Publications: One catalog published in conjunction with each exhibition; Artes Visuales, tri-annual magazine.

Attendance: Approx. 50,000 per month.

MUSEO NACIONAL DE ANTROPOLOGIA*
(National Museum of Anthropology)
Paseo de Reforma y Calzada de la Milla 5. Tel: 40/4-10; 553-62-66
Ignacio Bernal, Dir.
Open Tues. - Fri. 9 AM - 7 PM; Sat, Sun. & holidays 9 AM - 6 PM; cl Mon.

Collections: Anthropological, ethnological, archaeological. Some 600,000 exhibits.

Library: 300,000 volumes.

MUSEO NACIONAL DE ARTES E INDUSTRIAS POPULARES
(National Museum of Industrial Arts)
Av. Juarez 44, Mexico 1, D.F. Tel: 5-10-34-04 & 5-21-66-79
Dr. Daniel F. Rubin de la Borbolla, Dir.
Open daily 10 AM - 7-8 PM. Estab. May 1951 for exhibit and sale of traditional Mexican crafts. The Museum supports 3 regional museums of crafts: Museo Regional de la Ceramica, Tlaquepaque, Jal; Museo Regional de Arte Popular de la Huatapera, Uruapan, Mich; Museo de la Laca, Chiapa de Corzo, Chis.

Collections: Major †permanent collections of Mexican popular arts and crafts with emphasis on native pottery, textiles and lacquer.

Exhibitions: Exhibit of Mexican Pottery.

Activities: Operates workshops for the training of craftsmen; scholarships to craftsmen; operates provincial museums of arts and crafts; contests.

Library: Arts and crafts with emphasis on Mexico and Latin America.

Publications: Books and booklets on crafts; Ceramica Popular Mexicana.

Annual Purchases: 160 dolares.

MUSEO NACIONAL DE HISTORIA*
(National Historical Museum)
Castillo de Chapultepec
Antonio Arriaga Ochoa, Dir.
Estab. 1822; moved to Chapultepec Castle 1941, opened 1944.

Collections: History of Mexico since the Spanish Conquest; Mexican and European porcelain, ceramics, mosaics, jewelry, textiles; 19th century paintings; statues, religious art and cultural history.

MUSEUM OF SAN CARLOS
Puente de Alvarado 50, 1. Tel: 35-48-48 (for guided tours)
Open Tues. - Sun. 10 AM - 5 PM; cl. Mon, Jan. 1, Feb. 5, Mar. 21, Good Friday, May 1, Sept. 1 and 16, Nov. 20 and Dec. 25; admis. weekdays, 2 pesos; Sun. free, children under 5 years of age, student art teachers and groups from official schools are free.

Collections: The last room in the museum displays a choice collection of drawings by artists of the caliber of Da Vinci, 'Tintoretto', Raphael, Rubens, 'of Velvet', Jose de Ribera 'el Espanoleto', Goya, as well as other important artists.

Activities: Guided tours conducted in Spanish, English, or French; lectures, conferences, films, concerts and other cultural activities. Publications shop. Cafeteria.

Library: The Museum has an Art Library, which exchanges publications with similar institutions all over the world.

PUEBLA

MUSEO DE ARTE JOSE LUIS BELLO Y GONZALEZ
(Museum of Art)
3 Poniente 302. Tel: 41-94-75.
Alicia Torres De Araujo, Dir.
Maria Teresa Aguilar Galicia, Secy.
Open 10 AM - 5 PM; admis. $2. Estab. 1944 to diffuse art; financed by by state appropriations and admis. fee.

Activities: Lending collection, 8 color reproductions, 50 photographs, 1 motion picture and several film strips; 5000 catalogues and 2000 post cards; lectures open to public; 400 gallery talks; 6 tours; concerts; dramatic programs; classes for adults and children.

Library: 876 volumes for lending.

NETHERLANDS

ALKMAAR

STEDELIJK MUSEUM ALKMAAR
(Alkmaar Municipal Museum)
Doelenstraat 3. Tel: 073-10737
K. J. Kriek, Dir.
Open Mon. - Thurs. 10 AM - Noon & 2 - 5 PM; Fri. 10 AM - 5 PM; Sun. 2 - 5 PM; cl. Sat; admis. f.0.50, children under 16 f.0.25, groups of 15 persons f.0.25. Estab. 1873; history of Alkmaar; art, exhibitions in winter; financed by appropriation.

Collections: Concerning history and art of Alkmaar and environments; also modern; collection of antique children's toys.

Exhibitions: Mostly work from artists of the province; further Japanese Art, Rumenian Art, Thibetan Art, Pre-Columbian Art, Postage Stamps, Book-printing, history of the Alkmaar Chemist's shops.

Activities: Individual paintings lent to schools.

Library: A small hand-library; 100 photographic prints.

Annual Purchases: $5000.

AMSTERDAM

REMBRANDTHOUSE MUSEUM
Jodenbreestraat 4-6. Tel: 020-249486
Open weekdays 10 AM - 5 PM; Sun. 1 - 5 PM; admis. ƒ 1,50 children, ƒ 0,50 groups, ƒ 1,00 per person. Estab. 1911; financed by endowment and membership. Mem. 1000; dues ƒ 10,00 minimal.

Collections: 250 Rembrandt etchings, 6 drawings and paintings by his masters and pupils; library.

Attendance: (1971) 127,825; (1972) 130,272.

RIJKSMUSEUM
(State Museum)
Stadhouderskade 42. Tel: 73.21.21
Dr. S. H. Levie, Gen. Dir.

J. W. Lugard, Gen. Secy.
Dr. J. W. Niemeijer, Printroom
Dr. P. J. van Thiel, Dir. Dept. Paintings
Dr. A. L. den Blaauwen, Dir. Dept Sculpture & Applied Art
Dr. W. H. Vroom, Head, Dept. National History
Dr. K. W. Lim, Head Dept. Asiatic Art
A. J. M. van der Vaart, Dir. Sales Dept.
Open weekdays 10 AM - 5 PM; Sun. 1 - 5 PM; admis. f 2.00, Sat. &
Sun. f. 1.00. The Rijksmuseum was estab. as a National Gallery of
Art in 1808. The actual building was completed in 1883 and contains
250 rooms open to the public.
    Collections: Dept. of Painting contains the most complete and
famous collections of Dutch paintings ranging from the 15th to the
19th century, including Rembrandt's Night Watch; works by Frans
Hals and Vermeer; a small group of the Italian, Spanish, French and
Flemish Schools. Other collections include sculpture, furniture,
decorative arts, an outstanding museum of Asiatic art; a print room
with remarkable collection of prints and drawings from all parts of
the world. The Historical Dept. contains many excellent paintings,
models, relics showing the past of the Netherlands up to the 19th
century.
    Library: An extensive art reference library of 50,000 titles.
    Attendance: 1,290,375 average.

RIJKSMUSEUM VINCENT VAN GOGH*
    Paulus Potterstraat 7. Tel: 020-764881
Dr. E. R. Meijer, Dir.
Dr. H. van Crimpen
Mrs. L. Couvée-Jampoller
Mrs. L. Van Leeuwen
Open 10 AM - 5 PM; Sun. 1 - 5 PM; admis. f 2. Estab. 1973;
financed by city and state appropriations.
    Collections: †The Vincent van Gogh Collection (paintings, draw-
ings and letters); The Theo van Gogh Collection (contemporary artists of the second half of the 19th century, documents)
    Activities: Lectures open to public; concerts; dramatic programs;
classes for adults and children; competitions. Book shop.
    Library: Approx. 5000 volumes; photograph collection; letters
of Vincent van Gogh, Theo van Gogh and other contemporaries; other
documentation.
    Publications: Catalogues of the collection; bulletin Vincent, quar-
terly.
    Attendance: Since opening date approx. 115,000.

STEDELIJK MUSEUM—AMSTERDAM*
(Municipal Museum)
    Paulus Potterstraat 13. Tel: 020-73.21.66
E. L. L. de Wilde, Dir.
A. J. Petersen, Chief Cur. Painting & Sculpture
J. van Loenen Martinet, Cur. Printroom
W. Bertheux, Cur. Applied Art & Design
J. M. Joosten, Research Cur.
E. Ebbinge, Cur. Communication Dept.
W. H. Brabänder, Intendant
Open Mon. - Fri. 9:30 AM - 5:30 PM & 7 - 10:30 PM; Sat. 9:30 AM -
5 PM; Sun. 1 - 5 PM. Estab. 1895, new wing 1954.
    Collections: International paintings and sculptures dating from
1850 to the present day, especially to be seen from June - Sept.
Highlights are Cézanne, Monet, Van Gogh, European expressionism,
Chagall; the extensive collection of paintings by Malevich, Mondriaan,
Matisse, Dubuffet, Cobra-groep, European and American tendencies
after 1960 (Pop Art, Zero, Nouveau Réalisme, Colorfield Painting,
Conceptual Art); Dutch art 1850 until now. Printroom—drawings,
graphic art, especially Werkman, Cobra, recent tendencies; applied
art and design—especially ceramics, glass, textiles, furniture
(Rietveld), posters, typography, photography, bibliophil editions.
    Exhibitions: From Sept. - May c. 30 exhibitions (group exhibi-
tions and one-man shows) are organized, dedicated to art tendencies
since 1960.
    Activities: Guided tours for Amsterdam school children (from 10
to 13), about 11,000 participants every year; concerts of contemporary
music (Oct. - Apr. Sun. afternoons); music on mechanical organ, films
and other activities usually in the evening (Mon. - Fri) Information
Desk; Reproduction Department—posters, reproductions, postcards,
books, catalogues for sale; subscriptions and season-tickets;
Restaurant with terrace.
    Library: Open Mon. - Sat. 9:30 AM - 5 PM; Modern art 1850 up
to the present; 11,000 books, 55,000 catalogues, 110 magazines.
    Income and Purchases: Income, subsidy of the Municipality of
Amsterdam Hfl. 6,571,000 which includes the sum of Hfl. 900,000
for purchases.
    Attendance: (1971) 430,000; (1972) 447,000.

DELFT
STEDELIJK MUSEUM "HET PRINSENHOF"
("Het Prinsenhof" State Museum)
    St. Agathaplein 1. Tel: 015/133111, Exten. 335/339
Dr. R. A. Leeuw, Dir.
Dr. P. Biesboer, Cur.
Open daily 10 AM - 5 PM; Sun. & festive days 1 - 5 PM. Begun
as the Museum "Historische Zaal" in 1883, became City Museum
and archives, 1906; estab. 1947 as a museum for fine arts of Delft
and Holland and for the history of William the Silent and the 80-year
war; financed by city and state appropriation. Gallery, De Volle
Maan, for contemporary art, mainly Delft artists.
    Collections: Dutch art of the 15th, 16th, 17th and 18th centuries;
Delftica; Delft silver; †Delft ware; Delft tapestries; collection
of paintings of Orange-Nassau family, especially William the
Silent and the 80-year war.
    Exhibitions: Buitenplaatsen bedreigd (Dutch historical manors
and their collections); Gerard Houckgeest; Meta-realisten; D.P.G.
Humbert de Superville; Collectie Rust.
    Activities: Original objects of art lent; concert.
    Library: 3800 volumes for reference; photograph collection for
reference.

EINDHOVEN

MUNICIPAL VAN ABBEMUSEUM
(Eindhoven Municipal Museum)
    Bilderdijklaan 10, Postbox 235. Tel: 040-68811
Alderman for Cultural Affairs, Pres.
R. H. Fuchs, Dir.
J. Bremer, Cur.
J. Ober, Educ. Officer
Open Mon. - Sat. 10 AM - 5 PM; Sun. & holidays 1 - 5 PM; admis.
Dfl. 1. Estab. 1936; museum of the art of the 20th century; city
property.
    Collections: Collection ranges from Cubism to the latest trends
in art; specialties, neoconstructivism, Zero, Postpainterly Abstrac-
tion, Lissitzky-collection (85 works) graphics, prints, concept art,
etc.
    Exhibitions: Moholy-Nagy, Fontana, Robert Morris, Beuys, Van
Doesburg, Tatlin, Judd, Compas IV West Coast, Gemini-prints,
Bouwen 20-40 (Dutch architecture 1920-1940), Di Suvero, Warhol,
Sol LeWitt, Daniel Buren, Lawrence Weiner, etc.
    Activities: Museum course for primary and high schools; lec-
tures open to public; 60 museum talks or tours; concerts, different
programs.
    Library: Approx. 18,500 catalogs, 4000 books, 8500 magazines,
500 photographic prints for reference, films, video, slides.
    Publications: Exhibition catalogs; publication of the collection.
    Yearly Purchases: Dfl. 190,000.
    Attendance: 100,000.

GRONINGEN

GRONINGER MUSEUM VOOR STAD EN LANDE
(Groningen Museum)
    Praediniussingel 59. Tel: 050-17292
Drs. A. Westers, Dir.
P. I. M. Vries, Adjunct-Dir. & Cur. Paintings & Drawings
P. ter Hofstede, Scientific Asst.
Miss J. M. Cochius, Cur. Oriental Ceramics
J. H. Leopold, Scientific Asst. Silver
Dra. E. A. J. Boiten, Cur. Mediaeval & Later History
Drs. J. W. Boersma, Cur. Archaeology
Open 10 AM . 5 PM; cl. Mon; admis. fl.0.50. Estab. 1894; State ap-
propriation.
    Collections: Oriental ceramics, European ceramics, silver, local
archeology, local history; paintings and drawings from the 16th to the
20th century, mainly Dutch (including Hofstede de Groot collection,
17th century; and Veendorp collection second half 19th century).
    Exhibitions: Principally modern art.
    Activities: Original objects of art lent; 1500 prints for reference;
concerts.
    Library: 1000 volumes for reference.
    Publications: Annual report.
    Attendance: 36,500.

HAARLEM

FRANS HALSMUSEUM*
    Groot Heiligland 62. Tel: 023/31.41.40
D. H. Couvee, Dir.
Open daily 10 AM - 5 PM; Sundays from 1 PM. Founded in 1862 in
the old Townhall; in the present building since 1913.
    Collections: Group portraits by Frans Hals; Works by Haarlem's
leading portrait, genre, landscape and still-life painters (from 1500

to present day); Ancient main building and inner court of beautiful architecture by Lieven de Key (1608); 17th and 18th century interiors, period room, sculpture, and industrial art; collection of oldest specimens of printing (Costeriana); silver; Old Apothecary Shop; Doll's House.

Activities: Guided tours on request.
Library: 6000 volumes.
Attendance: (1969) 95,000.

Vishal and Vleeshal De Hallen (annex Frans Halsmuseum, Modern Department): Temporary exhibitions. Attendance: 36,500.

TEYLERS MUSEUM
Spaarne 16. Tel: 023-320197
Directors:
L.H. Graaf Schimmelpenninck
H.E. Stenfert Kroese
L. van Nouhuys
G. Beets
C.W.D. Vrijland, Secy.
Dr. J. Kistemaker, Cur. Physics
Dr. C.O. van Regteren Altena, Cur. Paleontology
J.H. van Borssum Buisman, Resident Cur.
J.G. de Bruijn, Librn.
Dr. H. Enno van Gelder, Numismatics
Open Mar. 1 - Oct. 1, 10 AM - 5 PM; Oct. 1 - Mar. 1, 10 AM - 4 PM; admis. Dfl. 1.- Estab. 1778 to present art, science, public welfare; endowed. Gallery containing drawings, paintings, physical instruments, fossils, minerals, coins and medals, library natural sciences.
Collections: Paintings 19th-20th century; drawings Italian, Dutch, French 15th-20th century.
Exhibitions: Temporary exhibitions of drawings.
Activities: Photographs; lectures; concerts.
Library: 120,000 volumes for reference.
Publications: Editions of Teylers 1e en 2e Genootschap; catalog, Drawings from the Teyler Museum.

THE HAGUE

HAAGS GEMEENTEMUSEUM
(Municipal Museum of The Hague)
Stadhouderslaan 41, P.O. Box 72, 2076. Tel: 070-51.41.81
Dr. L. J. F. Wijsenbeek, Dir.
Dr. Beatrice Jansen, Deputy Dir. & Head, Dept. Ancient Art
P. A. Frequin, Adminr.
Dr. J. L. Locher, Head, Dept. Modern Art
Dr. C. C. J. von Gleich, Head, Music Dept.
Dr. W. M. van der Mast, Head, Dept. History of The Hague
Dr. C. H. A. Broos, Head, Dept. Prints
Dr. H. Overduin, Head Educ. Dept.
Free weekdays 10 AM - 5 PM; Sun. & holidays 1 - 5 PM; Wed. 8 - 10 PM; special fees for temporary exhibitions; special reduced fees for groups. Estab. 1883. The present museum was built by the well-known architect Dr. H. P. Berlage in 1935; extension for temporary exhibitions since 1962. Society of Friends of the Municipal Museum of The Hague; subscription fee f. 15 annually; approx. 1700 members.
Collections: Ancient Decorative Arts collection includes Delft pottery, Italian and Spanish majolica, Chinese pottery and porcelain, Islamic pottery; Hague silver 17th-19th century; Hague porcelain 1776-1784; Egyptian, Roman, Islamic, Venetian and Dutch glass; objects in bronze and Dutch pewter; Dutch Period Rooms 1680-1780; art of the Ancient World: Greek pottery, terracotta's, Coptic textiles; ancient Indonesian art, Dutch colonial furniture. Modern Art Collection includes paintings, sculpture and decorative arts of the 19th and 20th century. Dutch artists, notably: Jongkind, Weissenbruch, van Gogh; largest collection of works (257) by Piet Mondrian, van Doesburg and other members of the Stijl group; recent trends: Karel Appel, Constant, Westerik and Visser. Foreign artists, notably: Bonington, Monet, Redon; expressionists: Kirchner, Kokoschka; Picasso, Lissitzky; sculptures by Arp, Moore, Lipchitz; Bacon, Vasarely, Kitaj. Printroom: large collection of prints and drawings of Dutch and foreign masters of the 19th and 20th century, notably: Redon, Bresdin; Toulouse Lautrec, German expressionists; Mondrian, Werkman; Escher, Heyboer and living Dutch artists. Music Department: unique survey of musical instruments from four centuries and five continents. Amongst the about 2600 instruments (of which one half is on permanent exhibition) are famous Italian and Flemish harpsichords (Celestini, Rückers), Dutch stringed instruments (Jacobs, Rombouts), German and French wind instruments (Grenser, Gautrot). From Indonesia a complete gamelan-orchestra. Frequent museum-concerts. Guided tours (cassette recorders). Research Music Library (c. 75,000 items).
Activities: Winter Program (Sept-May); lectures, concerts; film programs; courses for adults and children in basic principles of modern art; history of art; applied arts; gallery talks; explicatory slide-shows relating to exhibitions; museum lessons for schools

(10,000 children); visual quizzes for children during holidays; children's workshop (only children of visitors); guided bus tours viewing i.e, important monuments in The Hague, art nouveau architecture in The Hague and Brussels; exchange market held regularly for collectors of art reproductions.
Publications: General and specific publications related to each department. Modern Art: catalog of paintings (1962) and sculptures (1972); Mondrian (1974). Ancient Decorative Arts: catalogs of Dutch glass (1962) and Hague silver (1962); guides to the collections of European and Islamic Decorative Arts; many picture books concerning the various collections (also in English). Music Department: catalog of wind instruments, volume I (1970); selection of old European instruments; catalogs of the music library I and II (1969, 1973).
Attendance: 218,100.

HET NEDERLANDS KOSTUUMMUSEUM
(Museum of Costume)
Lange Vijverberg 14, P.O. Box 72, 2076.
Dr. L.J.F. Wijsenbeek, Dir.
Miss M.C. de Jong, Head
Open weekdays 10 AM - 5 PM; Sun. & holidays 1 - 5 PM; Wed. evening 8 - 10 PM; admis. f. 0.25. The collection was founded by the well-known actor Cruys Voorbergh and acquired by the municipality in 1951; since 1957 open to the public.
Collections: This museum contains a fine collection of European fashion from the second half of the 18th century up to the present time and is housed in a mansion, dating back to 1757, in the centre of the town. The costumes and accessories are partly displayed in Period Rooms and partly in show cases.
Library: The Library offers the student and those interested, the possibility of studying any subject in relation to the collection (on request).
Publications: Catalogs; picture books.
Attendance: 16,200.
Museum Bredius
Prinsegracht 6, P.O. Box 72, 2076. Tel: 070-63.16.03
Dr. L. J. F. Wijsenbeek, Dir.
Open weekdays 10 AM - 5 PM; Sun. & holidays 1 - 5 PM; Wed. 8 - 10 PM; admis. f. 0.25. This museum is the former private house with the collections of the well-known Dutch art historian, Dr. A. Bredius.
Collections: Decorative arts and Dutch paintings of the 17th century.

KONINKLIJK KABINET VAN SCHILDERIJEN (MAURITSHUIS)*
(Royal Picture Gallery)
Korte Vijverberg 8
H. R. Hoetink, Dir.
Open weekdays 10 AM - 5 PM; Fri. 8 - 10 PM; Sun. 11 AM - 5 PM. Building erected 1633; museum estab. 1816.
Collections: Dutch and Flemish Schools of the 17th century.

MUSEUM BREDIUS*
Prinsegracht 6, 2076.
Dr. L.J.F. Wijsenbeek, Dir.
Open weekdays 10 AM - 5 PM; Sun. & holidays 1 - 5 PM; Wed. 8 - 10 PM; admis. f. 0.25. The well-known art-historian, Dr. A. Bredius, donated his collection and private 17th century house, since 1923 in loan to the municipality of The Hague, in 1946.
Collections: Paintings by Rembrandt, Steen, Seghers, Terborch, Ruisdael and others; drawings by Breughel, van Goyen, Rembrandt (8), Ruisdael (5) and others; furniture, silver, glass, porcelain.
Attendance: (1970) 2249; (1971) 2167; (1972) 2519.

HERTOGENBOSCH

NOORDBRABANTS MUSEUM
Bethaniëstraat 1. Tel: 073 130713
Dr. M. M. A. van Boven, Dir.
Open Mon. - Fri. 10 AM - 5 PM; Sat. & Sun. 1 - 5 PM; admis. f 1, - f 0,50. Financed by city and state appropriation.
Collections: Archaeological collection; paintings and drawings from the 16th - 20th centuries; gold and silver.
Exhibitions: Giorgio de Chirico; Brabantse monumenten croeger en nu; Zingende Kathedraal; Felix Timmermans.
Activities: Traveling exhibitions organized and circulated; photograph collection; lectures open to public; 12 visiting lecturers per year; concerts.

HOORN

WESTFRIES MUSEUM
(Westfrisian Museum)
Rode Steen 1, 1900. Tel: 02290-5783
W. A. Braasem, Dir.
Mrs. T. Y. v. d. Walle, Archaeology Dept.
H. W. Saaltink, Sr. Research Asst.
Mrs. W. N. Mallekote, Admin.

Open, April - Oct. daily 10 AM - 5 PM; Sun. 12 AM - 5 PM; Oct. - April, daily 10 - 12 AM, 2 - 5 PM; Sun. in Oct. & Mar. 2 - 5 PM; admis. ƒ.1, children ƒ.0,50; families consisting of more than 3 persons ƒ.2,50. Estab. 1880; financed with appropriations.

Collections: 17th and 18th interiors with fine fittings; †16th-19th century paintings; †china; †glass; †silverware; †objects of trade; †navigation; and †business; costumes; †objects of folk art; collections from the Westfrisian area and the town culture of the old trading-town Hoorn; 20th century naive painting.

Exhibitions: Several expositions each year.

Activities: Original objects of art lent; 20 items lent in an average year; photograph collection for reference; concerts.

Library: 200 volume reference library.

Publications: Annual report.

Income and Purchases: Income f.350,000-; purchases f.20,000-.

Attendance: 40,000.

LEYDEN

STEDELIJK MUSEUM DE LAKENHAL
(Leyden Municipal Museum)
Oude Singel 28-32. Tel: 071-144044 / 144045
M. L. Wurfbain, Dir.
Miss I. W. L. Moerman, Cur, History Dept.
J. P. Sizoo, Cur, Modern Art
A. R. Andre de la Porte, Asst.
Miss A. L. H. Redele, Asst.
Open daily 10 AM - 5 PM; Sun. 1 - 5 PM; admis. Fl .75 - Fl 1.50. Founded 1869, opened to the public 1-5-1874, to house the municipal collection of works of art and other artifacts; financed by city appropriation. Museum with objects of artistic and/or historical value and interest.

Collections: †Painting, †sculpture, †applied arts of the Leyden region from the beginning until the present day; historical collection.

Exhibitions: 30 exhibitions, including Treasures from the Leyden University Library, In Rembrandt's Circle, Vanity of Vanities, Dutch Vanitas representations from the 17th century.

Activities: Art classes and introduction courses for children; Extension Department serving mainly Leyden and surroundings; material available to all who apply, for insurance fees. Individual paintings lent to schools, original objects of art lent; photographs solely for sale; approx. 4000 lantern slides in lending collection; Kodachromes made on request. Lectures open to public, visiting lecturers vary per year; approx. 250 gallery talks or tours per annum; concerts.

Library: Approx. 4800 volumes, 2000 photographic prints for reference.

Publications: Approx. 10 catalogues annually.

Income and Purchases: Income $300,000; purchases $15,000.

Attendance: Approx. 45,000.

OTTERLO

RIJKSMUSEUM KROLLER-MULLER
(Kroller-Muller State Museum)
National Park, Otterlo. Tel: 08382-241
Drs. R. W. D. Oxenaar, Dir.
Drs. E. Joosten, Asst. Dir.
Dr. P. H. Hefting, Cur.
Open daily 10 AM - 5 PM; Sun. 1 - 5 PM. Estab. 1938.

Collections: 276 works by Vincent van Gogh and a selection of 19th and 20th century works of art including Seurat, Redon, Braque, Picasso, Gris, Mondrian; a small number of works by old masters including Baldung Grien, Cranach, Tintoretto; sculptures by Rodin, Maillol, Lehmbruck, Moore, Hepworth, Giacometti, Marini, Raedecker, etc; old and modern ceramics, drawings, and graphic art; †sculpture garden.

Library: Approx. 3000 volumes.

ROTTERDAM

MUSEUM BOYMANS-VAN BEUNINGEN
Mathenesserlaan 18, P.O. Box 2277, 3002. Tel: 36.05.00
J.C. Ebbinge Wubben, Dir.
Open weekdays 10 AM - 5 PM; Wed. 7:30 - 10 PM; Sun. 11 AM - 5 PM. Estab. 1847.

Collections: Paintings of the Netherlands from the brothers Van Eyck to Vincent Van Gogh, Italian and French paintings from the 15th to the 19th century and contemporary paintings. Old and modern drawings and graphic art; ceramics, glass, pewter, silver, lace, furniture. Works by Kandinsky, Franz Marc, Oscar Kokoschka, and others. Some of the outstanding works in the collection include Hubert and Jan Van Eyck's The Three Marys at the Open Sepulchre; Heronimus Bosch's The Prodigal Son; Pieter Breughel's The Tower of Babel; Rembrandt's Portrait of Rembrandt's Son Titus. There are also 21 paintings by Rubens.

Library: 90,000 volumes.

NEW ZEALAND

AUCKLAND

AUCKLAND CITY ART GALLERY
Private Bag, Wellesley St. Tel: 74650, Exten. 663
Councillor Dr. R. H. L. Ferguson, Pres.
Dorothy J. Wherry, Secy.
Ernest Smith, Dir.
Eric Young, Registrar & Cur. Paintings & Sculpture
John Maynard, Exhibitions Officer
Anne Kirker, Cur. Prints & Drawings
Eileen Maitland, Conservator
Tim Garrity, Librn.
Ross Ritchie, Designer
Don Soloman, Outreach Mgr.
Free Mon. - Thurs. 10 AM - 4:30 PM; Fri. 10 AM - 8:30 PM; Sat. & Sun. 1 - 5:30 PM. Estab. 1887 as a general purpose gallery of the fine arts with collections for exhibition and study and facilities for the organization and receipt of touring exhibitions. Provides art services to general public, schools and university and support to New Zealand artists; financed by endowment, city and state appropriation and membership. Seven exhibition areas with full facilities devoted to permanent and special exhibitions. Ann. meeting Aug. or Sept; mem. 650; dues $8, $12 family, $3 student.

Collections: General collection of European paintings and sculpture from 12th century on; American and Australian paintings; European and American prints and drawings; New Zealand art (except Maori). All collections being added to with special emphasis on contemporary international prints, British painting and New Zealand art of all media and dates.

Exhibitions: (1973) John Constable; (1974) 17th Century Pastoral Holland; Some Recent American Art; (1975) Van Gogh in Auckland; New Zealand Women Painters; plus many others.

Activities: Outreach Program serving particularly Polynesian communities in Auckland; concerts, dramatic programs. Book shop.

Library: 5500 volumes for reference; photograph collection and color slide collection for reference.

Publications: Auckland City Art Gallery Quarterly.

Income and Purchases: Income $400,000; purchases $35,000.

Attendance: 135,000.

DUNEDIN

DUNEDIN PUBLIC ART GALLERY
Logan Park. Tel: 78 770
E. C. S. Falconer, Pres.
T. Grant, Hon. Treas.
L. C. Lloyd, Dir.
Free weekdays 10 AM - 4:30 PM; weekends & holidays 2 - 5 PM. Estab. 1890 as an art gallery society; financed by endowment. Gallery built 1925; 12 exhibition galleries; modern storage block and conservation laboratory; national conservation training centre. Mem. 1175.

Collections: Major holdings are in New Zealand and Australian paintings and prints and European paintings; Smythe Collection of over 1000 18th and 19th century English watercolors and drawings; various private gift collections of paintings and engravings; English and continental glass and ceramics; antique English and colonial furniture; sculpture; Oriental rugs.

Exhibitions: Extensive program forming and touring exhibitions from New Zealand and overseas; regular rehanging of own holdings; annual average of 22 special exhibitions.

Activities: Schools art education program; children's and adults' classes in painting, sculpture and crafts; 4-year training program for students in conservation; lectures; tours; touring exhibition vehicle to country towns and schools.

Publications: Annual Report, Gallery Handbook quarterly News and Views; conservation and art education pamphlets.

Income and Purchases: From Dunedin City Council (administration and salaries grant), members' subscriptions, revenue from bequests and gift funds; income (1973074) NZ$25,000; New Zealand art purchases (1973-74) NZ$15,000.

Attendance: 30,000.

NAPIER

HAWKE'S BAY ART GALLERY & MUSEUM (INC)*
Herschel St.
H. William Youren, Pres.
John E. Broad, Secy.
James S. B. Munro, Dir.
Helena M. Hull, Asst. Dir.
Open Mon. - Fri. 12:30 - 4:30 PM; weekends 2:30 - 4:30 PM; admis. 20¢ non-members. Estab. 1932 as a regional historical museum featuring the arts of man both European and Polynesian; financed by en-

dowment, city and state appropriations and membership. Ann. meeting May; mem. 1200; dues $3.

Collections: Maclean Collection of Maori Artifacts; Simcox Collection of Moa-hunter Artifacts.

Exhibitions: Seven Invited Potters; Annual Exhibition of Painting; International Road Safety Posters; A Taste of Yesterday—Victoriana; Olumpic Posters; New Zealand Painting—a Survey 1900-1920; Watercolours by John Kinder; Print Exhibition; German Postage Stamps; Reproductions of Dutch Landscapes.

Activities: Educational department, social studies for primary and intermediate schools, pottery group, chamber music group, gallery music group, recorded music listening group, painting class, local historical affairs, collectors group; lectures open to public; 6 gallery talks per year; concerts; classes for adults.

Library: 4500 volume reference library; photograph collection of 4000 prints for reference; 370 plans.

Publications: Annual report; quarterly newsletter; Picture of a Province, Naming of Napier, British Regiments in Napier, Kiwis in Captivity, 100 years on the Taupo Road.

Income and Purchases: $24,000; purchases $700.

Attendance: 36,000 annual average.

WANGANUI

SARJEANT ART GALLERY*
Queen's Park.
H. D. Robertson, Hon. Cur.
Collections: European Old Masters, English watercolours and pre-Raphaelite paintings; representative New Zealand collection; Gilfilan Collection; Barraud Collection; drawings by Bernadino Poccetti.

WELLINGTON

NATIONAL ART GALLERY OF NEW ZEALAND
Buckle St. Tel: 859703
M. N. Day, Dir.
I. A. Hunter, Educ. Officer
G. Packwood, Cur.
Carol Quirk, Asst. Cur.
Free daily 10 AM - 4:45 PM. Estab. 1936 to house National Collection of art works, archival preservation, acquisition of good representative works of art to augment collection, educative centre in art for New Zealand; supported by gov. appropriation.

Collections: Sir John Ilott prints; Archdeacon Smythe Collection, Harold Wright Collection. †John Weeks Collection.

Exhibitions: (1973) Wellington through the Artist's Eye; Contemporary Australian Painting and Sculpture; Raymond McIntyre; (1974) Inigo Jones; William Blake Collotypes; 100 Master Prints from the Ilott Collection; Molly Morpeth Canaday Exhibition; Australian Aboriginal Arts; Swiss Engineering Photographs; French Photographs; Recent Acquisitions; Japanese Suiboku Painting; Six New Zealand Artists.

Activities: Direction of art education programs in schools and universities of New Zealand; traveling exhibitions organized and circulated; original objects of art lent, 500 objects lent in average year; photograph collection for lending and reference. Publications Desk.

Library: 2000 volumes for reference.

Publications: Catalogs in conjunction with exhibitions.

Income and Purchases: Income NZ$14,000; purchases NZ$35,000.

Attendance: 84,550.

NORWAY

BERGEN

VESTLANDSKE KUNSTINDUSTRIMUSEUM
(Western Norway Museum of Applied Art)
Nordal Brunsgate, 9, 5000. Tel: (47 5) 21 51 08
Frithjof Meidell Andersen, Hon. Consul, Pres.
Peter M. Anker, Museum Dir.
Mrs. Thale Riisöen, Cur.
Mrs. Lini Richter Salvesen, Librn.
Mrs. Turid Hagelsteen, Secy-Accountant
Open May 15th - Aug. 31st, weekdays 10 AM - 3 PM; Sun. Noon - 3 PM; off season every day except Mon. Noon - 3 PM; free admis. Estab. 1887 to encourage Norwegian industry and crafts as regards tastefulness and appropriate work, and to try to develop the taste of the general public in a similar way; financed by endowment, government appropriation and membership. Approx. 4 meetings a year in connection with lectures, opening of temporary exhibitions etc; mem. approx. 350; dues 1974, $2350.-

Collections: The General Munthe collection of Chinese art; the Singer collection of art and antiquities from the Norwegian home of Anna B. and William H. Singer. (Both are bequeathed collections be-

sides the Museum's collections). †Collections of old European arts and crafts, antique Bergen silver, contemporary Norwegian and foreign ceramics, glass, furniture, textiles, metalwork, Chinese arts. A total of about 20,000 objects.

Exhibitions: (1973) Jon Sandsmark - Embroideries; Martin Borgord and William H. Singer - paintings; Frida Hansen - The European in Norwegian weaving; Western Norway's crafts of today; British Jewellers 1973; Erik Nyholm ceramics; Mesopotamian embroidered tapestries; (1974) Sigurd Bentzon's Bequest - furniture, etc; Polish graphic designer Stanislaw Zamecznik; Tendencies in Norwegian crafts 1974; Alf Rongved - ceramics; Dagny and Finn Hald - decorative and sculptural ceramics; Fra Haus til Kongens København - Norwegian folk costumes as seen with an artist's eye 1750-1850; (1975) Old folk costumes in Fana; Molle-Cecilie Major - handwoven tapestries; Claudie Tardits - applique; Edvard Munch and Henrik Ibsen - scenery sketches etc; Olle Ohlsson - a Swedish goldsmith and designer; Status and poverty; Laying the table.

Activities: Receives classes from the primary school level upwards, also students from art colleges and from the University Department of Art History, for teaching and lectures given by the staff. Certain courses are also arranged in cooperation with various popular educational organizations. Photograph for internal use, about 15,000; 800 (8x8 cm) slides; 3800 (5x5 cm) Kodachromes; lectures open to public, a few for members only, 2-3 visiting lecturers per year; gallery talks and tours; concerts; scholarships.

Library: Approx. 15,000 volumes and 3800 booklets; lending services.

Publications: Vestlandske Kunstindustrimuseums Arbok (Yearbook every 3-5 years); exhibition catalogs.

Income and Purchases: Income (1974) $120,000.-; purchases (1974) $2460.-.

Attendance: 23,500.

LILLEHAMMER

LILLEHAMMER BYS MALERISAMLING
(Lillehammer Art Museum)
Kirkegaten 69. Tel: N 062 51944
Knut Ramberg, Pres. of Board & Editor
Ole Rønning Johannesen, Chief Exec.
Open weekdays 10 AM - 3 PM; Sun. Noon - 4 PM; Wed. also 6 - 8 PM; cl. Mon; admis. N.kr. 3,-. Estab. 1921, opened for the public 1927 as a permanent art gallery; financed by city and state appropriation.

Collections: Norwegian paintings, sculpture and graphic art from the 19th and 20th centuries.

Exhibitions: In addition to the permanent collection, the Art Museum arranges some 8 - 10 special exhibitions each year.

Activities: Public lectures; instruction for public schools; traveling exhibitions organized and circulated; 10 gallery talks; 20 tours; concerts.

Library: 2000 volumes and photograph collection for reference only.

Publications: Lillehammer Bys Malerisamling Arbok, every third year.

OSLO

KUNSTINDUSTRIMUSEET I OSEO*
(The Oslo Museum of Applied Art)
St. Olavs Gate 1. Tel: 02-203578
Per M. Hansson, Pres.
Lauritz Opstad, Dir.
Mrs. Inger Marie Kvall, Cur.
Mrs. Anse Bay Sjovold, Cur.
Free Jan. 15 - May 1 & Sept. 15 - Dec 1, daily 11 AM - 3 PM; Tues. & Thurs. 7 - 9 PM; cl. Mon. Estab. 1876 to further the aesthetic value of the products of artisans and promote the understanding for these values among the public; city and state appropriation. Gallery.

Collections: Furniture, silver, ceramics, glass, textiles, and others, old and modern.

Exhibitions: Approx. 10 every year.

Activities: Lectures open to the public; concerts; classes for adults; guided tours; photograph collection, prints for sale; traveling exhibitions in preparation. Book Shop.

Library: 28,000 volumes.

Publications: Yearbook, biannually.

Attendance: 33,000.

NASJONALGALLERIET
(National Gallery)
Universitetsgaten 13, 1. Tel: 20 04 04
Knut Berg, Dir.
Open Mon. - Fri. 10 AM - 4 PM, Sat. 10 AM - 3 PM, Sun. Noon - 3 PM, Wed. & Thurs. also 6 PM - 8 PM. Estab. 1837.

†Collections: Norwegian painting and sculpture; European paintings with examples of modern French, Danish and Swedish art; icons; prints and drawings; small collection of Greek and Roman sculpture.
Library: c. 20,000 volumes; collection of exhibition catalogs and slides.

NORSK FOLKEMUSEUM
(Norwegian Folk Museum)
Bygdöy, 2. Tel: 55.80.90
Halvard Björkvik, Dir.
Open summer 10 AM - 6 PM; winter, 10 AM - 4 PM; admis. 5 Kr. Estab. 1894.
Collections: †The Open Air Museum totals about 150 old buildings, all original. Among them are the Stave Church from Hallingdal; farmsteads from different districts of the country; single buildings of particular interest; The Old Town—18th century town houses. †Urban Collections—Norwegian town interiors from the Renaissance to the present; Henrik Ibsen's Study; The first Parliament Hall of Norway (1814); Post-renaissance costumes. †Other collections include peasant art and furniture; post-medieval church art; woven tapestries; tools and technics of old Norwegian farming; toys and dolls; modern and primitive musical instruments. Total number of items in collections, 130,000.
Library: 32,000 volumes.
Publications: Annual yearbook.
Income: $650,000.
Attendance: 300,000.

NORSK SJÖFARTSMUSEUM
(Norwegian Maritime Museum)
Bygödoynes, 2. Tel: 556395
Svein Molaug, Dir.
Bard Kolltveit, Cur.
Else Marie Thorstvedt, Librn.
Boat Hall open Apr. 15 - Sept. 30, 10 AM - 8 PM; Oct. 1 - Apr. 14, 10:30 AM - 4 PM; Tues. & Thurs. 10:30 AM - 9 PM; Library open Oct. - Apr. 8:30 AM - 4 PM; May - Sept. 8:30 AM - 3 PM; Sat. 8:30 AM - 2 PM; Tues. 8:30 AM - 9 PM. Estab. 1914 to collect and exhibit items illustrating Norwegian maritime civilization. Ann. meeting May; mem. 500.
Collections: Ship models, paintings, photographs of ships, tools, instruments and other items pertaining to maritime collections. The Polarship Gjöa. Special exhibitions of small crafts. Archives pertaining to maritime history.
Activities: Instruction of school classes; underwater excavations; semi-weekly meetings during the winter for divers; 40 slide programs; courses in rope-work, seamanship, etc. Training ship, Svanen (one-week expeditions during the summer). Souvenir Shop.
Library: 16,000 volumes; 200 current periodicals.
Attendance: 103,000.

UNIVERSITETETS OLDSAKSAMLING
(University Museum of National Antiquities)
Frederiks gate 2, 1. Tel: 330070
Dr. Sverre Marstrander, Dir.
Irmelin Martens, Head, Stone & Bronze Age Dept.
Wencke Slomann, Head, Early Iron Age Dept.
Charlotte Blindheim, Head, Viking Age Dept.
Martin Blindheim, Head, Medieval Age Dept.
Free summer 11 AM - 3 PM, winter Noon - 3 PM. Estab. 1828 for the exhibition of finds from the prehistoric periods, mediaeval church art and objects from mediaeval towns; the Viking ship finds with magnificent grave goods in the Viking Ship Museum at Bygdöy (branch museum); responsibility for archaeological finds and for the preservation of prehistoric monuments in the southeastern and southern part of Norway; educational and research institution (Scandinavian archaeology); financed by state appropriation. Universitetets Oldsaksamling is an institute of the University of Oslo.
Collections: Material from the Norwegian Stone, Bronze and Iron age; church art and profane objects from the Mediaeval Age.
Activities: Lecture in Scandinavian archaeology; special lectures open to public.
Library: 30,000 volumes; 30,000 prints in photograph collection.
Publications: Universitetets Oldsaksamlings Arbok (yearbook); Skrifter (proceedings); guides.
Annual Purchases: $100,000.

PAKISTAN

KARACHI

NATIONAL MUSEUM OF PAKISTAN*
Burns Garden.
Toswir Husain Hamidi, Supt.

Open 10 AM - 5 PM. Estab. 1950.
Collections: The exhibits include material from the earliest time in Pakistan to the late Moghul period, e.g. palaeolithic stone implements (500,000 to 200,000 years ago); fine specimens of pottery, chert implements and terra cotta objects from Kot Diji (3000 to 1800 B.C); relics of the world famous Indus Valley Civilization (2500 to 1800 B.C); specimens of Gandhara art both in stone and stucco (1st to 5th century A.D); glass, terra-cotta, stone, bronze, iron, bone, ivory, and silver objects along with gold jewelry from Taxila; a number of sculptures depicting incarnations of Hindu gods and goddesses belonging to the 8th and 12th centuries from East Pakistan; objects of Muslim arts and crafts in glass, metal, ceramics and garments.
The Museum also has different sections for †manuscripts, †paintings, †specimens of calligraphy, †Faramin and royal documents, †coins, and †ethnological collections.
Exhibitions: Books on Japan; Sikh Royal Treasures.
Educational Activities: Lectures on museology and archaeology; conducted tours for school, college, and university students.
Library: Books on museology, archaeology, and allied subjects.
Income and Purchases: Annual income £3520; annual purchases £50,000.
Attendance: Over 1,000,000 average per year.

LAHORE

LAHORE MUSEUM
Lahore
Dr. Saifur Rahman Dar, Dir.
F. M. Anjum Rahmani, Keeper of Islamic Collections
Shahbaz Khan, Keeper of Pre-Islamic Collections.
Tahira Azam Beg, Keeper of Coins & Medals
Nighat Ismat, Keeper of Miniature Paintings
Estab. 1864.
Collections: 16 galleries devoted to various subjects of archaeology, history, fine arts, crafts and ethnology. Largest Collections in the world of Gracco-Buddhist sculptures, Indo-Pakistan coins and miniature paintings of the Mughal, Rajput and Kangra Schools. Good collections of modern paintings, specimens of industrial arts and crafts, Arabic and Persian manuscripts, Buddhist, Hindu and Jaina sculptures, carpets, rugs, wood carvings and armoury.
Exhibitions: Every 2 months on paintings, books and manuscripts.
Activities: Periodical lectures on art, archaeology, museology and history by eminent local and foreign scholars. Research Conservation Laboratory; Modeling Workshop; Photographic Section.
Library: 14,000 volumes on art, history, archaeology and museology. Open summer, 9 AM - 5 PM; winter, 8 AM - 4 PM; cl. Fri.
Publications: Guide Book; Catalogs of manuscripts and rare books.
Income: From admission tickets: average Rs.1,00,000 annually.
Expenditures: Rs.3,02,740 for developments; Rs.4,48,000 for nondevelopments.
Attendance: 250,000.

PESHAWAR

PESHAWAR MUSEUM*
Grand Trunk Rd.
S.M. Jaffar, Cur.
Estab. 1907.
Collections: Mainly sculptures of the Gandhara School, containing images of the Buddha, Bodhisattvas, Buddhist deities, reliefs illustrating the life of the Buddha and Jataka stories; architectural pieces and minor antiquities.

TAXILA

ARCHAEOLOGICAL MUSEUM*
Rawalpindi, Taxila District.
M. A. Halim, Custodian
Open winter 9 AM - 4 PM; summer 9 - 12 AM, 3 - 6 PM. Estab. 1928; membership of the Museums Association of Pakistan.
Collections: Sculptures of Gandhara and Indo-Afghan School of Arts with other antiquities from Taxila Sites ranging from 7th century B.C. to 5th century A.D.
Exhibitions: Temporary exhibitions are held on special occasions.
Activities: Lectures on the archaeology of Pakistan with special reference to Taxila are arranged for the college and University students.
Library: 1500 volumes.
Attendance: 40,000 annually.

PERU

MUSEO DE ARTE*
(Museum of Art)
Paseo Colon 125.
Dr. Carlos Neuhaus, Presidente del Patronato de las Artes
Dr. Alberto Santibanez Salcedo, Dir.
Open Thurs. - Sun. 10 - 12 AM & 3 - 7 PM; admis. 30¢, students
free; Sun. morning free. Estab. 1960; permanent exhibits of Peruvian
art from the different historical periods; educational programs for
students; temporary exhibits; Gov. appropriation; Membership. 6
galleries. 25 patrons.
Collections: Pre-Inca and Inca collections, ceramic, textiles;
Colonial painting, metals, sculpture; Republic paintings; modern
paintings, sculpture.
Exhibitions: Permanent exhibitions; temporary exhibitions usually changed monthly.
Activities: Guidance of groups of students, teaching; public
cinema, fees; traveling exhibitions organized and circulated; color
reproductions, photographs, slides, kodachromes; lectures open to
public, 12 visiting lecturers per year; gallery talks and tours, two
in English, two in Spanish weekly; classes for children, competitions.
Book shop.
Library: 1000 volumes for reference.
Publications: Guides and catalogues.
Annual Income: $4600.
Attendance: Near 200,000.

MUSEO NACIONAL DE LA CULTURA PERUANA*
(National Museum of Peruvian Culture)
Avenida Alfonso Ugarte 650
Dr. Luis E. Valcarcel, Dir.
Estab. 1946.
Collections: Popular art; ethnography of Amazonic tribes; folk-
lore; ethnology; linguistics.

PHILIPPINES

MUSEUM OF ARTS AND SCIENCES
University of Santo Tomas, Manila
Calle Espana. Tel: 47-22-31 Local 269
Jesus M. Merino-Antolinez, Dir.
Maria Teresa Del Mar, Secy.
Free 9 AM - Noon & 2 - 5 PM. Collections began in 1682, estab.
formally as museum in 1848 to assist the students and professors of
the university in the study of science, art, ethnology and history; financed by university aid. Art gallery, due to extreme space limita-
tion, is more of an art repository of rich collections covering the
art in the Philippines.
Collections: Fauna of the Philippines: vertebrate, invertebrate,
†conchology, †corals, †insects; mineralogy and petrology; history;
†coins, †medals, †philately, †archaeology; †art: †paintings,
†sculpture, †applied art; ethnology: †Philippine, †Oriental.
Exhibitions: The Christianization of the Philippines, 70; The
History of the Coin, 72; collaboration with several repositions of
other institutions.
Activities: Assistance to students and their projects is available;
original objects of art lent; photograph collection.
Attendance: 24,000.

POLAND

MUZEUM NARODOWE W KRAKOWIE
(National Museum in Cracow)
ul. Manifestu Lipcowego 12. Tel: 281-40, 273-03
Tadeusz Chruscicki, Dir.
Dr. Zofia Alber, Far Eastern Art
Dr. Jerzy Banach, Polish Iconography
Dr. Irena Grabowska, Arms and Armour
Dr. Adam Homecki, Manuscripts
Janina Klosinska, Icons
Dr. Maria Kopff, Polish Painting & Sculpture of the 14th-18th
Centuries
Dr. Barbara Miodonska, Polish Illuminated Manuscripts
Dr. Janusz Ostrowski, Greek & Roman Art
Prof. Dr. Mieczyslaw Porebski, Polish Modern Art
Dr. Janusz Reyman, Polish Coins
Dr. Marek Rostworowski, European Painting of the 15th-17th
Centuries

Dr. Anna Rozycka Bryzek, Italian Painting
Dr. Stefan Skowronek, Ancient Coins
Dr. Franciszek Stolot, Deputy Dir, Polish Art of the 16th-18th
Centuries
Dr. Maria Taszycka, Textiles, Polish Costumes
Dr. Zdzislaw Zygulski, Jr, Arms & Armour, Near Eastern Minor
Arts
Estab 1879 for historic and artistic collections of Polish and foreign
art and objects of culture. Association of Museum Friends.
Collections: National Museum in Cracow consists of serveral
departments with various collections. The Director and Administra-
tion seat is in the Palace of E.Hutten Czapski. Czartoryski Library
and Archives, ul. Sw.Marka 17: 13,300 documents, illuminated
codices, incunabula, approx. 208,000 volumes on history, art and
culture. The Emeryk Hutten-Czapski Department, ul.Manifestu
Lipcowego 12: 120,000 graphics, 250,000 in numismatic collections,
45,000 old books. Department of Textiles, ul. Smolensk 9 Dzolayski
House, pl.Szczepanski 9: Departments of arms and armour, Far
Eastern Art, Icons.
Activities: 1-2 temporary exhibitions per month; guided tours;
lectures for schools; films on art; traveling exhibitions; concerts;
classes for children.
Reference library: Approx. 50,000 volumes.
Publications: Rozprawy i Sprawozdania Muzeum Narodowego w
Krakowie, annually; various catalogs, guides and monographs.
Attendance: Approx. 350,000.

Galeria Polskiego Malarstwa i Rzeźby od 14 do 18 wieku
(Gallery of Polish Painting and Sculpture of the 14th-18th Centuries)
pl. Szczepański 9, Kamienica
Szolayskich. Tel: 570-21
Open daily 10 AM - 4 PM; Mon. 12 AM - 6 PM, Sun. 10 AM - 4
PM; cl. Tues and days after holidays; admis. zl.4.
Collections: Very valuable and exquisite collection of Polish
painting and sculpture, mostly of Cracow school, from the 14th
through 18th century, among them the famous sculpture Madonna
of Kruzlowa (c. 1400).

Galeria Malarstwa Polskiego w.XIX
(Gallery of Polish Painting of the 19th Century)
Rynek Główny, Sukiennice. Tel: 571-46
Open daily 10 AM - 4 PM; Thurs. 12 AM - 6 PM; Sun. 10 AM - 4
PM; cl. Tues. and days after holidays; admis. zl.4.
Famous collection of Polish paintings, which formed a foundation
of the National Museum in Cracow; the Nero's Torches by Siemirad-
zki, the historical compositions by Matejko; The Prussian Homage,
among others.

Galeria Sztuki Polskiej w.XX
(Gallery of Polish Painting and Sculpture of the 20th Century)
al. Trzeciego Maja 1. Tel: 333-77
Open daily 10 AM - 4 PM; Wed. 12 AM - 6 PM; Suns. 10 AM - 4 PM;
cl. Mon. and days after holidays; admis. zl.4.
Very outstanding collection of Polish painting and sculpture from
the Modern Art Movement (Mloda Polska) until the present time with
a large representation of the artists of Cracow.

Zbiory Czartoryskich
(The Czartoryski Collection)
ul. Pijarska 15. Tel: 535-16
Open daily 10 AM - 4 PM; Thurs. 12 AM - 6 PM; Sun. 9 AM - 3 PM;
cl. Wed. and days after holidays; admis. zl.4.
Polish national relics, decorative and oriental art, arms and
armour, Egyptian, Greek and Roman art, painting gallery (Leonardo
da Vinci, Lady with an Ermine; Rembrandt Landscape).

Dom Jana Matejki
ul. Florianska 41. Tel: 575-62
Open daily 10 AM - 4 PM; Fri. 12 AM - 6 PM; Sun. 9 AM - 3 PM;
cl. Mon. and days after holidays; admis. zl 4
Biographic museum of Jan Matejko, the outstanding Polish
painter of the second half of the 19th century who with his great
historical compositions largely contributed to the national culture
and consciousness.

PANSTWOWE ZBIORY SZTUKI NA WAWELU
(The Wawel State Collections of Art)
Wawel 5
Dr Jerzy Szablowski, Pres.
Stefan Zajac, Mgr.
Stanislaw Ciećkiewicz, Mgr.
Open 9 AM - 5 PM; admis. zl.10. Estab. 1925; research works of
archeology, history of art and history connected with the monuments
situated on the Wawel Hill and in the Wawel Museum; Restoration of
the works of art; educational works; organization of permanent and
temporary exhibitions. Gov. appropriation.
Collections: King Sigismond August's 16th century collection of
Flemish tapestries, †western European painting, Italian Renaissance
furniture, †western-European and Oriental pottery, †Polish, western-

European and Oriental weapons, Oriental carpets and tents; Royal Treasury: crown jewels, historical relics, banners, gold objects.

Exhibitions: Thousand years of Polish-Hungarian relations (together with the National Museum of Budapest), Thousand years of art in Poland (two exhibitions in Paris and in London organized together with the National Museum of Cracow).

Activities: Special courses for staff members; lectures open to public; concerts, classes for adults and children, competitions.

Library: 7651 books, 1533 periodicals for reference; no permanent lending collection but any print supplied on request.

Publications: Studia do Dziejow Wawelu, Zrodla do Dziejow Wawelu, Biblioteka Wawelska, irregularly.

WARSAW

MUZEUM NARODOWE
(The National Museum)
    Al. Jerozolimskie 3, 00-495. Tel: 21 10 31
Dr. Stanislaw Lorentz, Dir.
Dr. Kazimierz Michalowski, V.Dir.
M. Plominska, Keeper of Educ. Dept.
Open Tues. 10 AM - 8 PM; Thurs. Noon - 6 PM; Sun. & holidays 10 AM - 5 PM; other days 10 AM - 4 PM; cl. Mon; admis. adults zl.7, children zl. 5, Thurs. free. Estab. 1862; financed by state appropriations. Branch museums: Palaces in Warzaw-Wilanow, Lazienki, Krolikarnia and outside Warsaw - Nieborow and the museum in Lowicz.

Collections: †Antiquities; Mediaeval Art; †Polish and European Art from the 15th century till today; Numismatics; Graphic Art; Drawings and Prints; †Decorative Art.

Exhibitions: 23 temporary exhibitions 1973-74, including Max Slevogt, 30 years of the Polish museums, Russian painting of the 19th Century, American West, Baroque Art in Germany, Italian Painting of the 18th Century and The World of Franklin and Jefferson.

Activities: Educational department service to the visitors at the national museums, action of the popularization of art, cycles of popular talks and discussions, art film shows; traveling exhibitions organized and circulated; original objects of art lent; 8000 slides in lending collection; photograph collection of 106,000 negatives; approx. 60 lectures yearly to public; concerts; classes for adults; competitions; Club of Young Friends of the Museum. Book shop.

Library: 90,000 volumes.

Publications: Rocznik Muzeum Narodowego w Warszawie (Annual of the National Museum in Warsaw); Bulletin du Musee National de Varsovie, quarterly; exhibition catalogs and others.

Attendance: 298,900.

MUZEUM NARODOWE WE WROCLAWIU*
(National Museum)
    Plac Powstańców Warszawy 5, 50-153 Wroclaw. Tel: 38839
Dr. Leszek Itman, Dir.
J. Gebczak
A. Chrzanowska
M. Hermansdorfer
D. Ostowska
I. Rylska
J. Skibinska
D. Stankiewicz
M. Starzewska
B. Steinborn
M. Jedrzejczak
W. Swiderska
A. Zawisza
A. Ziomecka
J. Piatek
W. Gluzinski
Free, Tues, Fri. 12 AM - 7 PM; Wed, Thurs. & Sat. 11 AM - 4 PM; Sun. 11 AM - 6 PM; cl. Mon. Estab. 1948 for collecting, conservation, scientific research, education and the organization of cultural activities; financed by appropriations.

Collections: †Collection of Silesian stone carvings 12th-16th centuries; †Collection of Mediaeval Art 14th-16th centuries; †Polish Painting 18th-20th Centuries; †Collection of Silesian art 16th-18th centuries; †Collection of decorative hunters arms 16th-18th centuries; †Collection of contemporary art, painting, sculpture, glass and ceramics.

Exhibitions: Mezzotint XVII-XIX; Contemporary art of Norway; Bohemian glass; Glass of T. Kiriazopoulos; Paintings of I. Moncada; Polish art of book 1900-1970; Gielniak's Graphic; E. Garztecka-Collection; Faience of Wloclawek.

Activities: Educational-extension department; shows; cinema programs; traveling exhibitions organized and circulated; individual paintings and original objects of art lent; lending collection, 7 sets of

color reproductions, 2 sets of photographs, 6 motion pictures, 100 film pictures relating to art, lent from film producers; 16 items lent in an average year; 20 active borrowers; lectures open to public; 12 visiting lecturers per year; 40 gallery talks; 1000 tours; concerts; dramatic programs; classes for adults and children; competitions; constantly adding catalogs and guides to collections, prepared by staff. Book shop.

Library: Reference library of 55,000 volumes; photograph collection.

Publications: Roczniki Sztuki Slaskiej and Roczniki Etnografii Slaskiej, annually; catalogues, guides and others.

Attendance: 70,000 annual average.

PORTUGAL

LISBON

MUSEU NACIONAL DE ARTE ANTIGA
(National Museum of Ancient Art)
    Largo 9 de Abril. Tel: 664151 & 672725
Maria Alice Beaumont, Dir. & Cur. Painting
Sergio de Andrade, Cur. Sculpture
Rafael Calado, Cur. Ceramics
Natalia Correia Guedes, Cur. Textiles
Maria Fernanda Passos Leite, Cur. Jewelry, Goldsmith Art
Maria Helena Mendes Pinto, Asst. Cur. Furniture
Jose Luis Porfirio, Cur, Pub. Relations & Cultural Activities
Madalena Cabral, Educational Service.
Open 10 AM - 1 PM & 2:30 - 5 PM; Thurs. & Sat. till 7 PM; cl. Mon. & public holidays; admis. 5$00; free Sat. & Sun. Estab. 1884. Friends of the National Museum of Ancient Art dues 50$00 minimum.

Collections: Portuguese art—paintings from the 15th to the 19th centuries; sculpture from the 13th to 18th centuries; ornamental art (goldsmith art, ceramics, furniture, textiles). Foreign art—painting and sculpture, goldsmith art, ceramic, church vestments. Persian carpets, Oriental art of Portuguese influence.

Exhibitions: About 6 temporary exhibitions per year.

Activities: Lectures in connection with the current exhibitions; guided tours for every school grade; accompanied visits. Workshop. Bookshop.

Library: Approx. 16,000 volumes and 2000 publications, mainly on history of art, both Portuguese and universal, conservation, museology, etc.

Publications: Catalogs of temporary exhibitions.

Income and Purchases: Annual endowment by the state for the purchase of specimens of interest to any of the collections, and of books.

Attendance: 40,000.
Museu da Madre de Deus
Free.

Special collection of colored glazed tiles, 14th - 20th centuries. Permanent installations of special collections: Patino Room—Late 18th century French designed boiseries, decoration, furniture, Savonnerie carpet; Gulbenkian donation; Capela das Albertas, 16th-17th centuries.

MUSEU NATIONAL DE ARTE CONTEMPORANEA*
(National Museum of Contemporary Art)
    Rua Serpa Pinto 6
Maria de Lourdes Barthold, Dir.
Founded 1911.
    Collections: Contemporary painting and sculpture.

PORTO

MUSEU NACIONAL DE SOARES DAS REIS
(National Museum of Soares das Reis)
    Rua de D.Manuel II. Tel: 27110
Maria Emilia Amaral Teixeira, Dir.
Dr. Quaresma, Cur.
Dr. Viana, Cur.
Open 10 AM - 5 PM; admis. 5$00. Financed by city and state appropriation.

Collections: Paintings, sculptures, goldchmidts, glass, jewelry.

Exhibitions: Hap Grieshaber, Educational Department; The Flowers; Emmerico Nunes; Alvaro de Bree; Jose Francisco de Paiva; The Lusiadas; Aurelia de Sousa Antonio Carneiro, Manessier, 20th Century in Oporto.

Activities: Atelier, visits, games; traveling exhibitions organized and circulated; individual paintings and original objects of art lent; 20 color reproductions, 1789 photographs and 830 lantern slides

in lending collection; lectures open to public; concerts; dramatic programs; classes for children; competitions. Book shop.
Library: 7890 volumes.
Publications: Museu, 2 per year.

RHODESIA

NATIONAL GALLERY OF RHODESIA*
20 Kings Crescent
Frank McEwen, Dir.
Open daily Tues. - Sun. 9 AM - 5 PM; cl. Mon. Estab. 1957.
Collections: Ancient and modern European paintings and sculpture; tapestries; African traditional and local contemporary sculpture and paintings; large loan collections exhibited.
Activities: Friends of the Gallery organization, lectures and films. African sculpture workshop functioning since 1961. Annual exhibition of Rhodesian artists.
Library: Art reference library of over 1600 books; newspaper and periodicals section.

ROMANIA

MUSEUM OF ART CLUJ-NAPOCA
Piata Libertatii 30. Tel: 26952
Dr. Virgil Vatasiano, Pres. Scientific Council
Alexandra Rus, Dir.
Open Mon. & Thurs. 11 AM - 7 PM. Estab. 1951; financed by state appropriation.
Collections: Romanian and European art including paintings, graphics and sculpture of the 15th - 20th centuries.
Exhibitions: Romanian Art, paintings of the 19th and 20th centuries; Ion Sima; Elena Popea; Iosif Bene; Sava Hentia; Alexandru Mohi.
Activities: Traveling exhibitions organized and circulated; individual paintings and original objects of art lent; junior museum; concerts, dramatic programs, classes for adults and children; scholarships. Book shop.
Library: 3000 volumes; photograph collection of 2000 prints; Romanian books of art and catalogs of art.
Publications: Exhibition catalogs, semi-annually.

REPUBLIC OF SOUTH AFRICA

MICHAELIS COLLECTION
Old Town House, Greenmarket Square
Mayor of Capetown, Chmn. Board of Trustees
John Cecil Haak, Cur.
Open 10 AM - 5:30 PM; admis. 10¢. Estab. 1917 to house collection of 16th and 17th century Dutch and Flemish masters donated to the nation by Sir Max Michaelis.
Collections: †Michaelis collection; †graphic art collection.
Activities: Lectures, concerts, dramatic programs, classes for children and adults.
Library: 500 volumes of reference works.
Publications: General catalogue; special catalogue; annual reports.
Income and Purchases: Annual income $30,000; annual purchases $3000.
Attendance: 30,000.

SOUTH AFRICAN NATIONAL GALLERY
Government Ave, P.O. Box 2420. Tel: 45-1628 Sangal
Hans Fransen, Acting Dir. & Dir. Dept. Prints & Drawings
Valerie Leigh, Dept. Painting & Sculpture
Lynn McClelland, Dept. Educ.
Josephine Minicki, Librn.
Open Mon. - Sat. 10 AM - 5:30 PM, Sun. 10 AM - 5 PM; cl. Christmas Day, Good Friday and New Year's Day. Estab. 1871, inc. 1895, present building 1931. Society of Friends of the Gallery, meetings arranged monthly; mem. 530; dues R5, family R7; subscribing bodies of a cultural nature R10, subscribing business corporations, not less than R50, life R75.
Collections: 370 South African, 500 foreign paintings; 600 South African and 420 foreign drawings and watercolors; 450 South African and 1280 foreign prints; 90 South African, 40 traditional African and 90 foreign pieces of sculpture. Very small collections of photography and applied art.
Exhibitions: (1973) Contemporary French Painting; DUO, exhibition for the blind (art and music); Contemporary British Art; Vasarely; German Graphic Art; Portraits from the Prints Room; Goya etchings; (1974) Henry Moore; Three Centuries of French Painting; Maurits Escher; Involvement, a Participatory Exhibition for the Sighted and the Blind; French Art of the Turn of the Century; Maurice van Essche Retrospective; Giacomo Balla; Antoine Bourdelle; South African Printmakers; (1975) Contemporary French Tapestries; Cecil Higgs Retrospective; African Motifs; Charles Peers; and many smaller exhibitions.
Activities: Evening art lectures; lunch-hour film shows; guided tours; modelling classes for the blind. Bookshop.
Library: 4800 books, 270 periodicals; pamphlets, catalogs; South African newspaper cuttings.
Annual Income: (1974-75) R220.417.
Attendance: 102,175.

DURBAN ART GALLERY
City Hall, Smith St. Tel: 27535, Exten. 351
P.A. Clancey, Dir.
E.S.J. Addleson, Cur.
Open daily 9:30 AM - 5 PM; Wed. 9:30 AM - 2 PM; Sun. 2:30 - 5 PM. Estab. 1892 to provide current, contemporary exhibitions of paintings and historical works, including painting, sculpture, and objets d'art, for the benefit of the public and the city's cultural programme, and to provide a free service of identification and classification of paintings and the detection of fakes. Gallery financed by donations, bequests, and municipal yearly funds. Mem. 350; dues R3.50 and higher. Durban Art Gallery Association inaugurated March 1965.
Collections: †Sculpture of English, French, German, Russian, Norwegian and South African Schools; also Rhodesian and Zambian; †paintings of the English, French, Dutch, Flemish, Spanish, and South African Schools; Chinese and Japanese ivories; bronze medals and plaques, French 19th century; †Chinese porcelain and Oriental objets d'art; European porcelain and objets d'art. Glass Lalique; laces, English, Irish, French, Italian. †Graphic art of South African, Spanish, German, Dutch, French and English Schools, also Italian and Australian schools. †South African contemporary pottery.
Exhibitions: (1973-75) Paintings and Graphics by Victor Vasarely; Modern Dutch Paintings; The Quiet Eye-photographs by Felicitas Vogler; Retrospective Exhibition of Paintings by the South African artist, Cecily Sash; Sculpture by Giacomo Balla; The Royal Crown Jewellers of Lesotho; The Sanlam Collection of South African Paintings; Etchings by Francisco Goya; The Art and Craft of Rorke's Drift; Graphics by Nawits Escher; Contemporary Graphics from American Universities; Naval Paintings by the South African Artist, Herbert Hastings McWilliams; Paintings by 3 19th century Artists in South Africa: Bowler, Angas and I'ons; Chinese Snuff Bottles; Art-South Africa-Today 1975; Sculpture by Antoine Bourdelle; Contemporary French Tapestries.
Activities: Lectures; guided tours; films; loan of reproductions from the Gallery collection; art classes for children on a Saturday morning.
Library: Current publications from overseas and South Africa, 6000 volumes.
Publications: Guide to the collection of the Durban Art Gallery, exhibition catalogs, monthly review of the art scene.
Income and Purchases: Annual income total for Natural History Museum, Art Gallery, Local History Museum and Old House (all one department) R187, 380; Annual purchase grant for the Art Gallery R10,000.
Attendance: 240,000.

MUNICIPAL ART GALLERY
Joubert Park. Tel: 725-3130
Miss P.M. Erasmus, Dir.

Free Tues. - Sun. 10 AM - 5 PM; Oct. 1 - Apr. 30, 8 - 10 PM Wed, Sun, public holidays except Christmas day & Good Friday. Estab. 1910; City appropriation.

Collections: Paintings, 17th century Dutch; 19th and 20th century French paintings and sculpture; British painting and sculpture; 20th century South African painting and sculpture; graphic collection from Rembrandt and Durer to present day; textiles, mainly lace of various European countries, 16th-19th century; ceramics, Han. to late Ming.

Exhibitions: Le Corbusier; Contemporary French Tapestries; Contemporary British painting; The Scientific Investigation of paintings; Ernst Barlach/Käthe Kollwitz joint exhibition; Bonnard exhibition; Retrospective and memorial exhibitions, South African artists; Various from Print Cabinet 18th and 19th century English watercolors and drawings.

Activities: Conducted tours on application; lectures during exhibitions; lectures open to public, 150 gallery talks or tours per year; concerts.

Library: 15,000 volumes including catalogs, photograph collection, for reference only.

Publications: Guide list to Collections and temporary exhibition catalogs.

Attendance: 72,000.

PIETERMARITZBURG

TATHAM ART GALLERY
City Hall, Pietermaritzburg, 3201 Natal. Tel: (0331) 27031, Exten. 127
L. A. Ferguson, Cur.
Open daily 10 AM - 5 PM; cl. Sun. & pub. holidays. Estab. 1906 as a municipal gallery for the benefit of the citizens of Pietermaritzburg.

Collections: Whitwell Collections—18th, 19th and 20th century English and French paintings and graphic art. Includes work by Sisley, Boudin, Daubigny, Harpignies, Corot, Cotman, Sickert, Steer, Stanley Spencer, Mark Gertler, and Spencer Gore objets d'art.
†General collection includes Ivon Hitchens, Manessier, Miro, Clave, Tapies, Vilacasas, Picasso, Braque, Bonnard, Chesgall, Roualt, Delain, Whistler, Gericault.

Activities: Film shows; lunch hour record recitals; lectures on graphic art, art appreciation, etc.

Annual Purchases: £6000.

Attendance: 6500.

PRETORIA

PRETORIA ART MUSEUM
Pretoria, Transvaal. Tel: 444271/2
Councillor L. A. Cloete, Chmn. Museum Board
A. J. Werth, Dir.
Open Tues. - Sat. 10 AM - 5 PM; Sun. 1 - 6 PM; Wed. 7:30 - 10 PM. Estab. May 20, 1964, to display mainly South African painting, graphics and sculpture as well as the art of countries outside South Africa which have influenced South African art. Friends of the Museum association estab; mem. approx. 900.

Collections: 17th century Dutch; †19th and 20th century South African; and †a miscellany of other arts including some applied arts.

Educational Activities: Public lectures, film shows, guided tours.

Library: Reference library of 750 volumes, 1000 photographs, 300 lantern slides.

Purchases: Annual purchases approx. R75,000.

Attendance: Approx. 266 per day.

SPAIN

BARCELONA

MUSEO DE ARTE CATALUNA*
(Museum of Ancient Art)
Palacio Nacional, Parque de Montjuich
Juan Ainaud de Lasarte, Dir.
Estab. 1934. Scholarships given.

Collections: †Romanesque and Catalan Gothic paintings and sculpture; Renaissance and Baroque paintings.

MUSEO DE ARTE MODERNO
(Museum of Modern Art)
Palacio de la Ciudadela
Juan Barbeta Antones, Dir.

Open 9:30 AM - 1:45 PM; cl. Mon. Estab. 1946. Scholarships given.
Collections: Modern art.
Exhibitions: Commemorative expositions.
Library: 49,600 volumes.
Publications: Exhibition catalogs.

MADRID

MUSEO DEL PRADO
(Museum of Paintings and Sculpture)
Calle de Felipe IV. Tel: 2.39.22.29, 4.68.09-50
Xavier de Salas y Bosch, Dir.
Open 10 AM - 5 or 6 PM according to the season of the year. Estab. 1819.

Collections: 14th - 19th century paintings. Sections of 19th and 20th century in the Cason of Buen Retiro. Ancient and Renaissance sculptures; drawings, jewels and medals.

Activities: Weekly public lectures.

Library: Over 10,000 titles.

MUSEO ROMANTICO*
(Museum of the Romantic Epoch)
San Mateo 13, 4. Tel: 257-18-17
Maria Elena Gomez-Moreno, Dir.
Raul Diez, Secy.
Manuel Llanes, Librn.
Manuel Perez Tormo, Restorer
Open 11 AM - 6 PM; Sun. 10 AM - 2 PM. Estab. 1924.

Collections: †Paintings, †furniture, †books and †decorations of the Spanish romantic period.

Educational Activities: Lectures and concerts.

Library: Books on history, literature, art of the Romantic period; collection of 5000 engravings, lithographs.

Attendance: 10,000.

TOLEDO

CASA Y MUSEO DEL GRECO*
(El Greco's House & Museum)
Calle de Samuel Levi. Tel: 2400
Maria Elena Gomez-Moreno, Dir.
Open 10 AM - 2 PM & 3 - 6 PM; Summer until 7 PM; admis. 15 pesetas.

Collections: Furniture, objects of the period; Paintings of El Greco, including the series of Christ and the Apostles; Other paintings of various periods (15th to 18th century).

Library: Works referring to Toledo and El Greco. Use by permission only.

Publications: Catálogo de las Picturas de la Casa y Museo del Greco, 1968.

The Casa y Museo del Greco is supported by the Fundaciones Vega-Inclán. Estab. 1910.

Attendance: 250,000.

VALENCIA

MUSEU DE BELLAS ARTES DE VALENCIA
(Valencia Fine Arts Museum)
C. San Pio V, 9. Tel: (96) 360-57-93
Felipe-Vincente Garin Llombart, Dir. & Conservator.
Open 10 AM - 2 PM; financed by city and state appropriation.

Collections: Paintings and sculpture of the 15th - 20th centuries; archeological section; photograph collection.

SWEDEN

GOTHENBURG

GÖTEBORGS KONSTMUSEUM
(Gothenburg Art Gallery)
Götaplatsen 412 56
Karl-Gustaf Hedén, Dir.
Open 11 AM - 4 PM; Sun. 12 AM - 4 PM. Estab. 1861. Present building 1923, new wing 1968.

Collections: †Scandinavian art; †old masters, especially Italian, Flemish and Dutch; †French art from impressionists.

Library: Art library of 7000 volumes.

Attendance: 150,000.

RÖHSSKA KONSTSLÖJDMUSEET
(The Roehss Museum of Arts and Crafts)
  Vasagatan 37-39, 41137.
Jan Brunius, Dir.
Open weekdays 11 AM - 4 PM; Sun. 12 AM - 4 PM; also Tues. 7 - 9
PM; cl. Mon.
  Collections: Swedish and foreign furniture, pottery, porcelain,
glass, silver, pewter, forged ironwork, textiles; series of interiors;
Oriental collection of bronzes, ceramics, glass and textiles from
China and Japan. Modern exhibition halls for temporary displays of
Modern Swedish.
  Library: 22,000 volumes.

MARIEFRED

SWEDISH STATE PORTRAIT GALLERY
  Gripsholm Castle
Ulf G. Johnsson, Keeper
Lars Sjoeberg, Asst. Keeper
Open May 15 - Aug. 31 daily 10 AM - 5 PM; opening hours reduced
during the winter months; admis. Swedish crowns 4:50. Administrated
by Nationalmuseum, Stockholm.
  Collections: Portraits, mainly Swedish, from 15th century to
modern time, approx. 3500 items.
  Activities: Authorized guides May - Aug. for schools and visiting
groups.

STOCKHOLM

KUNGL MYNTKABINETTET STATENS MUSEUM FÖR MYNT
  MEDALJ OCH PENNINGHISTORIA
(Royal Coin Cabinet Museum of Monetary History)
  Storgatan 41, Box 5405, S-114 84. Tel: 08/63 07 70
  (Museum entrance: Narvavägen 13-17)
Dr. Brita Malmer, Dir.
Open daily 11 AM - 4 PM. Estab. July 1, 1975, this museum was
separated from the Museum of National Antiquities.
  Collections: Coins, banknotes, other means of exchange,
medals.
  Exhibitions: 4 rooms of permanent exhibitions; temporary exhi-
bitions.
  Numismatic section of library owned by the Royal Swedish
Academy of Letters, History and Antiquities.
  Activities: Lectures to university students, schools and special
groups; guided tours.
  Attendance: 90,000.

NATIONALMUSEUM
  Box 16 176, S-10324. Tel: 08/24.42.00
Dr. Bengt Dahlbäck, Dir.
Open daily 11 AM - 5 PM; Tues. 11 AM - 9 PM. Estab. 1792.
  Collections: †Paintings, miniatures, icons, sculpture, prints and
drawings, arts and crafts. Administers the State collections of
paintings and sculptures in the royal castles and Gustaf III's
antikmuseum (The Collection of Antiquities of Gustaf III) in the
Royal Palace of Stockholm. Collections of 20th century paintings
and sculptures, housed in Moderna museet (The Museum of Modern
Art). Collections of ancient Far Eastern Art In Ostasiatiska museet
(Museum of Far Eastern Art).
  Library: 138,370 volumes.
  Attendance: 494,800 average.

NORDISKA MUSEET
(Swedish Museum)
  Djurgarden. Tel: 63.05.00
Dr. Sune Zachrisson, Dir.
Kersti Holmquist, Keeper of Buildings, Household & Furnishings
Dr. Elisabet Hidemark, Keeper of Textiles & Dress
Dr. Göran Rosander, Keeper of Cultural Field Research
Skans Torsten Nilsson, Head Educ. & Pub. Relations
Dr. Sten Lundwall, Librn.
Greger Oxhammar, Head Adminr.
Prof. Mats Rehnberg, Keeper of the Chair, Institute of Folk Life
  Research
Open Tues. - Fri. 10 AM - 4 PM; Sat. & Sun. Noon - 5 PM; cl. Mon.
Founded 1873 to further the knowledge of the culture and history of
the Swedish people through scientific research on one hand and popu-
lar teaching and instructing on the other.
  Collections: †Folk art, †handcrafts, †period furnishings, †cos-
tumes, etc.
  Exhibitions: Permanent exhibitions giving a survey representa-
tive of the field of action of the museum, with about eight temporary
exhibitions a year.

Activities: Guided visits and prize competitions for school children and a lively collaboration with educational organizations. Two
or three lecture series per year.
  Library: 100,000 volumes.
  Attendance: 200,000.

STATENS HISTORISKA MUSEUM
(Museum of National Antiquities)
  Storgatan 41, Box 5405, S-114 84 (Museum entrance, Narvavägen
  13-17). Tel: 08/63 07 70
Dr. Olov Isaksson, Dir.
Open daily 11 AM - 4 PM. Estab. 17th century; open to the public
since 1847.
  Collections: Stone, Bronze and Iron Age, including Viking Period;
gold treasures, medieval art, armour and textiles.
  Activities: Lectures to schools; public special temporary exhibi-
tions; guided tours.
  Library owned by The Royal Swedish Academy of Letters, History
and Antiquities, has collection of 145,000 volumes.
  Junior Museum and workshop opened 1963.
  Attendance: 90,000.

SWITZERLAND

BASEL

MUSEUM FUR VOELKERKUNDE UND SCHWEIZERISCHES MUSEUM
  FUR VOLKSKUNDE BASEL
(Museum of Ethnological Collections and Folklore)
  Augustinergasse 2. Tel: 061 258282
Dr. Gerhard Baer, Dir.
Open 10 AM - Noon, 2 - 5 PM; cl. Mon. Estab. 1893.
  Collections: Melanesia, Polynesia, Asia, East Indonesia, Africa,
America, Switzerland; collection of textiles.
  Exhibitions: Permanent and special exhibitions.
  Activities: Talks and conducted tours.
  Library: 25,000 volumes
  Attendance: 80,000.

OFFENTLICHE KUNSTSAMMLUNG - KUNSTMUSEUM BASEL
(Museum of Fine Arts)
  St. Albangraben 16, CH-4010. Tel: 061/22.08.28
Dr. Franz Meyer, Dir.
Verena Trueb, Secy.
Dr. Paul-Henry Boerlin, Cur. Paintings
Dr. Dieter Koepplin, Cur. Prints & Drawings
Open June - Sept, 10 AM - 5 PM; Oct. - May, 10 AM - Noon & 2 - 5
PM; cl. Mon. Estab. as private collection about 1550; founded as
public collection 1662; new building 1936.
  Collections: †15th and 16th century paintings, including Konrad
Witz, Grünewald, Holbein and others; †17th century Dutch paintings;
†19th and 20th century paintings from Corot to the present.
  Exhibitions: Regular exhibitions from the collections of prints
and drawings.
  Library: 60,000 art books.
  Attendance: 217,200.

BERNE

KUNSTMUSEUM BERN
(Museum of Fine Arts Berne)
  Hodlerstrasse 12, CH, 3011. Tel: (31) 22-09-66
Dr. Hugo Wagner, Dir.
Dr. Sandor Kuthy, Cur.
Open 10 AM - Noon & 2 - 5 PM, Tues. 8 - 10 PM; cl. Mon. AM.
Estab. 1879; enlarged 1936.
  Collections: †Italian Masters; †Niklaus Manuel; Deutsch and con-
temporary artists; †Swiss Baroque Masters; †Swiss 19th and 20th
century Masters; †French and other European Masters of the 19th
and 20th centuries. A great collection of †Paul Klee works of 2600
items; †Foundation Hermann and Margrit Rupf, important Cubist
collection.
  Library: 30,000 volumes.
  Publications: Berner Kunstmitteilungen, issued 8 times a year;
catalogs of collections and temporary exhibitions.
  Attendance: 42,500 average.

CHUR

BÜNDNER KUNSTMUSEUM CHUR
(Bündner Art Museum)
  Postplatz, 7000. Tel: 081 / 22.17.63
Hans Hartmann, Dir.
Trudy Caflisch, Secy.
Open daily except Mon. 10 AM - Noon & 2 - 5 PM; 1st & 3rd Fri. each
month open also 7:30 - 10 PM; admis. to permanent exhibit, SFr. 1-;

special show, 3.- to 4.-. Estab. 1900 for support of local art, Swiss art and modern art; financed by endowment, city and state appropriation and membership.

Collections: Angelika Kauffmann; Giovanni Segantini; Ferdinand Hodler; Giovanni, Augusto, Alberto Giacometti; E. L. Kirchner; Swiss painting; plastic art, 19th and 20th centuries.

Exhibitions: Alois Carigiet; Leonhard Meisser; 75 Jahre Bündner Kunstsammlung; five exhibitions a year.

Activities: Traveling exhibitions organized and circulated; photograph collection and library for internal use only; concerts; dramatic programs; competitions. Book shop.

Publications: Exhibition catalogs.

GENEVA

MUSEE D'ART ET D'HISTOIRE
(Museum of Art and History)
 rue Charles-Galland (Mailing Address: Case Postale 395, 1211 Geneve 3). Tel: 29.00.11
Claude Lapaire, Dir.
Open daily 10 AM - Noon & 2 - 6 PM except Mon. morning. Estab. 1910.

Collections: Fine arts, decorative arts, archaeology, numismatics.

Library: 60,000 volumes.

Publications: Genava, annually; Musees de Geneve, monthly.

PETIT PALAIS
Modern Art Museum
 2, Terrasse Saint-Victor, 1206. Tel: 46.14.33
Dr. Oscar Ghez, Pres-Founder
Open 10 AM - Noon & 2 - 6 PM; cl. Mon. AM. Admis. Frs. 5, students Frs. 3.50. Estab. Nov. 1968; motto, Art in the Service of Peace.

Collections: Impressionists and postimpressionists; nabis; neo-impressionists; fauves; painters of Montmartre; Painters of Montparnasse; French expressionists; naifs (primitives of the 20th century); School of Paris: cubists.

Permanent Exhibitions: Renoir, Guillaumin, Caillebotte, Vallotton, Serusier, Gauguin, Denis, Moret, Valtat, Derain, Vlaminck, Marquet, Van Dongen, Jean Puy, Camoin, Manguin, Permeke, Forain, Steinlen, Utrillo, Valadon, Gleizes, Lhote, Survage, Maria Blanchard, Hayden, Picasso, Kisling, Mane-Katz, Pascin, Chagall, Soutine, Foujita, Signac, Cross, Luce, Dubois-Pillet, Henri Martin, Charles Angrand, etc.

Publications: Catalogs for most exhibitions; 2 Vol. L'Aube du XX Siecle, From Renoir to Chagall; reproductions of the main master pieces visible at the Petit Palais.

Attendance: 50,000.

LA CHAUX DE FONDS

MUSE DES BEAUX-ARTS ET SOCIETE DES AMIS DES ARTS*
(Museum of Fine Arts)
 2300 La Chaux de Fonds, 33 rue des Musees
M. Andre Sandoz, Pres.
Paul Seylaz, Dir-Conservator
Open daily 10 AM - 12 PM, 2 - 5 PM; mem. free on Mon. except for special exhibits. Estab. 1864 for the enrichment of the permanent collection and the organization of exhibitions, information and essentially of modern art; financed by state and city appropriations and membership. Gallery. Ann. meeting biennially; mem. 500; dues 25 Fr.

Collections: Works of local artists; †works by Leopold Robert a Le Corbusier; Swiss works from the 19th-20th century; foreign and contemporary artists works.

Exhibitions: Biennial exhibition of regional artists; private Swiss collections of black Africa; private exhibitions of foreign artists; Perie, Zenderoudi, Palazuelo, Perilli, Iglesias and Perales.

Activities: Original objects of art lent occasionally to other Swiss and foreign museums.

Publications: Illustrated catalogues for each exhibition.

ST. GALLEN

HISTORISCHES MUSEUM IN ST. GALLEN
(Historical Museum)
 Museumstrasse 50, CH-9000. Tel: 071/24.78.32
Dr. Ricco Labhardt, Dir.
Open daily 2 - 5 PM; cl. Mon; admis. 2 Fr. (free Wed, Sat. afternoon, Sun).

Collections: Weapons; porcelain; pewter; glass and glass painting; period rooms; Burgundian standards of 1476.

Exhibitions: (1972) Porzellan und Fayeuce aus Zürich und Nyon; Schweizerische Kleinmeister des 18th and 19th Jahrhunderts; (1973) Masken aus dem Jarganserland.

Activities: Photograph collection; lectures open to the public.

Publications: Museumsbrief, 1-2 per year; Jahresbericht.

Attendance: 19,000.

SCHAFFHAUSEN

MUSEUM ZU ALLERHEILIGEN
(All Saints' Museum)
 Klosterplatz
Dr. Max Freivogel, Dir.
Open Apr. - Oct. 9:30 AM - Noon & 1:30 - 5 PM; Nov. - Mar. 10 AM - Noon & 1:30 - 4:30 PM; cl. Mon. Estab. 1928.

Collections: Prehistoric; Roman; 19th century art; industrial art.

WINTERTHUR

KUNSTMUSEUM WINTERTHUR
(Art Museum)
 Museumstrasse 52, CH-8400. Tel: 052/845162
Dr. Rudolf Koella, Cur.
Open 10 - 12 AM & 2 - 5 PM; cl. Mon. AM. Estab. 1866.

Collections: Swiss painting and sculpture since 1700; portraits by Anton Graff; French, Italian and German painting and sculpture of the 19th and 20th centuries.

Exhibitions: Annual show of local artists; Tri-annual show of artists from Canton of Zurich; 2 to 3 exhibitions a year of contemporary Swiss and International art; retrospective exhibits.

Educational Activities: 2 lectures a year, generally on contemporary art.

Library: 3200 volumes.

Attendance: 12,000.

ZURICH

KUNSTHAUS ZURICH
(Art Gallery)
 Heimplatz 1
Dr. F. Baumann, Dir.
Open Tues. - Sun. 10 AM - 5 PM; Mon. only 2 - 5 PM; Tues. - Fri. also 8 - 10 PM. Estab. 1910.

Collections: Mainly 19th and 20th century †European and †Swiss artists; J. Fussli Collection; F. Hodler Collection; A Giacometti Foundation; Ancient and Medieval sculptures and medieval paintings.

Library: 25,000 volumes.

Attendance: 200,000.

MUSEUM RIETBERG ZURICH
 Gablerstrasse 15, 8002. Tel: 25.45.28
Dr. Eberhard Fischer, Dir.
Dr. Helmut Brinker, Cur. East Asia Dept.
Open Tues. - Sun. 10 AM - 5 PM; Wed. also 8 - 10 PM; cl. Mon. Estab. 1952.

Collections: †Art of the Americas, †Asiatic art; †African and Oceanic Arts.

Library: 6000 volumes.

Attendance: 28,500.

Museum Rietberg Zurich am Hirschengraben 20
8001. Tel: 47 96 52
Open Tues. - Fri. 2 - 7 PM; Sat. & Sun. 2 - 5 PM; Thurs. also 8 - 10 PM; cl. Mon. Estab. 1974.

Special temporary exhibitions on non-European art.

SCHWEIZERISCHES LANDESMUSEUM
(Swiss National Museum)
 Museumstrasse 2, P. O. Box 2760, CH-8023. Tel: (051) 25.79.35
Dr. Hugo Schneider, Dir.
Dr. Jenny Schneider, V.Dir.
  Curators
Dr. Rudolf Degen
Dr. H.-U. Geiger
Dr. Alain-Charles Gruber
Dr. Rudolf Schnyder
Dr. Walter Trachsler
Dr. Lucas Wüthrich
Dr. René Wyss
Dr. Bruno Muhlethaler, Chemist-Physicist
Klaus Deuchler, Pub. Relations
Free Summer 10 AM - Noon & 2 - 5 PM; Mon. only 2 - 5 PM. Estab. 1898.

Collections: Medieval art, Carolingian frescoes and ivory tablets, 9th century; Romanesque ecclesiastical sculpture (painted wood-carvings) and textiles, architectural ceramics; Late Gothic paintings, shrine-altars, ecclesiastical sculptures, furniture, goldsmith's works, living rooms; 16th to 18th century-silverware (partly belonging to the old trade guilds of Zurich), reliquaries, chalices, monstrances; heraldry and genealogy; arms and armours; clocks, bells, costumes, stained glass, furniture; period rooms; prints and drawings; large section of prehistory. All collections being added to.

Activities: Conducted tours on Thurs. 6 PM, attendance 3000 per year.

Library: 80,000 volumes, 900 periodicals.

Publications: Annual report; Zeitschrift für schweizerische Archäologie und Kunstgeschichte, 4 per year.

Purchases: Annual purchases $100,000 (Museum and Branch Museum).

Attendance: 240,000.

Branch Museum: In the old guildhouse Zur Meisen, Münsterhof 20 (2nd floor). Choice porcelains from Swiss factories of the 18th and 19th centuries. Wildegg Castle, Canton of Argovie.

SYRIA

DAMASCUS

NATIONAL MUSEUM*
  Syrian University St, 4.
Abdul Hamid Darkal, Dir.
Estab. 1919.
  Collections: Ancient Oriental, Greek, Roman, Byzantine, Islamic and modern art.
  The Directorate-General of Antiquities is located here to preserve and conserve Syrian antiquities and to supervise the archaeological museums and the excavations.

TUNISIA

LE BARDO

MUSEE NATIONAL DU BARDO
(Bardo National Museum)
  Le Bardo. Tel: 261-002
Ennaifer Mongi, Dir.
Open 8 - 12 AM - 2:30 - 6 PM. Supported by Gov. appropriation.
  Collections: Greek and Roman antiquities; Islamic art.
  Activities: Guides for student and adult tours; traveling exhibitions; photograph collection.
  Library: The library has a photograph collection.
  Publications: Antiquités Africaines, also notés and articles; (the National Institute of Archaeology is the publisher).

TURKEY

ISTANBUL

ISTANBUL ARKEOLOJI MÜZELERI
(Archaeological Museum of Istanbul)
  Sultanahmet. Tel: 279069, 279070
Necati Dolunay, Dir.
Lüfti Tugrul, Asst. Dir.
  Curators
Nezih Firatli, Classical
Edibe Üzünoglu, Ancient Orient
Fatma Yildiz, Cuneiform Tablets
Veysel Donbaz, Cuneiform Tablets
Ibrahim Artuk, Islamic Coins
Nekriman Olcay, Non-Islamic Coins
Nejat Özatay, Workshop
Fehamet Camcioglu, Workshop
Open every day except Mon. 9 AM - 5 PM; July and Aug, every day until 7 PM. Estab. 1846; comprising Museum of Classical Antiquities, Museum of Oriental Antiquities, Museum of Mosaics.
  Collections: Prehistoric, Greek, Roman, Byzantine and Cypriote antiquities; coins and medals; Sumerian, Hittite, Assyrian and Egyptian antiquities in the Museum of Ancient Orient; Cuneiform Tablets.
  Exhibitions: Annual open air exhibitions of paintings, sculptures and ceramics.
  Activities: Bookshop selling the museum publications, postcards, slides, copies of museum objects.
  Library: 45,000 volumes; books on archaeology, art history, history.
  Publications: Annual of the Archaeological Museums of Istanbul.
  Attendance: 114,370.

MUSEUM OF TURKISH AND ISLAMIC ART
  Süleymaniye
Can Kerametli, Dir.
Open daily 10 AM - 5 PM; cl. Mon. Estab. 1914.
  Collections: Collection of the oldest Turkish carpets; old Korans; books with miniatures and illumination; metalwork and ceramics, sculpture in stone and stucco; fermans and monograms of the sultans, and other monuments of Islamic art.

TOPKAPI PALACE MUSEUM*
Kemal Çiğ, Dir.
Palace built by Mohammed II, and enlarged by other Ottaman Sultans.
  Collections: Turkish armour, cloth, embroidery, tiles, glass and porcelain, Chinese and Japanese porcelains, clocks, copper and silverware, paintings, miniatures, illuminated manuscripts, baldachin; library and archives; and other collections.

URUGUAY

MONTEVIDEO

MUSEO NACIONAL DE ARTES PLASTICAS*
(National Museum of Fine Arts)
  Tomás Giribaldi 2283 esq. Julio Herrera y Reissig, Parque Rodó
  Tel: 43 800
Angel Kalenberg, Dir.
Free winter 2 - 6 PM; summer 6 - 10 PM; cl. Mon. Estab. 1911; Gov. appropriation.
  Collections: Juan Manuel Blanes, Carlos Federico Sáez, Rafael Barradas, Pedro Figari, Joaquín Torres García, Alfredo de Simone, José Cúneo, Carlos González.
  Exhibitions: Permanent Collection; Paul Klee, drawings; Alexander Calder, sculpture, jewels, engravings; Surrealism, painting and sculpture; Paris and the contemporary art, painting; Rodin, sculpture and watercolors; Rafael Pérez Barradas, painting, drawing, etc.
  Activities: Extension Dept; material available to Museums, no charge; traveling exhibitions organized and circulated; original objects of art lent; lectures open to public, six visiting lecturers per year; gallery talks or tours weekly; concerts, competitions.
  Library: 4500 volumes for reference.
  Publications: Exhibition catalogues, four yearly.
  Attendance: Average 290,000.

VENEZUELA

CARACAS

MUSEO DE BELLAS ARTES*
(Museum of Fine Arts)
  Parque Sucre, Los Caobos, 105. Tel: 543792
Miquel G. Arroyo C, Dir.
Prisca Dale de Moleiro, Secy.
Carlos Duarte, Head, Conservation Dept.
Gerd Leufert, Cur. Prints & Drawings
Iris P. de Muller, Registrar
Isabel Morasso de Navas, Librn.
Alvaro Sotillo, Asst. to the Curators.
Open daily 9 - 12 AM & 3 - 5:30 PM; cl. Mon. Estab. 1938; enlarged 1953, 1957, 1963.
  Collections: Venezuelan Painting from the end of the 19th century to the present; contemporary sculpture; Pre-Colombian art; Egyptian art; Chinese porcelain; European porcelain; Latin American paintings and sculpture, incl. primitives; European painting, collection of prints and drawings.
  Exhibitions: Approx. 24 per year.
  Educational Activities: 12 lectures per year; 48 gallery talks per yr; art education for children three times per wk.
  Library: Approx. 2155 books on painting, sculpture, architecture, applied arts; catalogues and magazines.
  Purchases and Prize Awards: Approx. $50,000 per yr.
  Income: $125,019.
  Attendance: Approx. 200,000.

YUGOSLAVIA

LJUBLJANA

MODERNA GALERIJA*
(Modern Art Gallery)
  Tomšičeva 14, 61000. Tel: (061) 21-709
Zoran Kržišnik, Dir.

Open 10 AM - 6 PM; cl. Mon; admis. adults 3 Din; students 2 Din; groups 1 Din. Estab. 1947 to collect contemporary works of art in Slovenia; permanent collection of Slovene art; temporary exhibitions of Slovene, Yugoslav and foreign art; giving place for international exhibitions of graphic art in Ljubljana; financed by appropriations.

Collections: Permanent collections of Slovene painting, sculpture and graphic art, from 1900 until today.

Exhibitions: Retrospective exhibitions: Richard Jakopič, Frančišek Smrdu, Stane Kregar; 25 years of Slovene graphic art; French naives; IX. and X. International Exhibition of Graphic Art in Ljubljana.

Activities: Educational department; traveling exhibitions organized and circulated; photograph collection of 15,000 prints; lectures open to public; 12 visiting lecturers per year; 65 tours; concerts.

Library: Reference library of 14,000 volumes.

Attendance: 11,900 annual average.

NARODNA GALERIJA
(National Art Gallery)
Prezihova ulica 1. pp. 432, Yu-61001. Tel: 21-765; 21-249; 21-570
Dr. Anica Cevc, Chief Exec.
Dr. Ksenija Rozman, Asst.
Polonca Vrhunc, Asst.
Open Tues. - Sun. 10 AM - 6 PM; cl. Mon; admis. adults, N din 3.-, students, groups, etc, N din 2.- Estab. 1918; presentation of Slovenian art from Middle Ages to the beginning of 20th century; financed by government appropriation.

Collections: Collection of Slovenian pictures, sculptures, and graphic arts from the beginning of 13th century to the end of World War I; copies of frescoes in Slovenia from Middle Ages to 19th century; 1807 pictures, 2791 graphic arts, 684 sculptures.

Exhibitions: Old Serbian Art, 1970; Mihael Stroj, 1971; Gothic Sculptures of Slovenia, 1973; Venetian Masters of the 18th century, 1974; Czech Painting of the 19th and the beginning of the 20th century, 1975.

Activities: Lectures about Slovenian, Jugoslav, and West-European art; guidance through permanent or contemporary exhibitions in the National Art Gallery; traveling exhibitions organized and circulated; photograph collection of 13,027 negatives and 10,533 prints for reference; 3 gallery tours per year; concerts; dramatic programs; 2-6 visiting lecturers per year, 181-192 gallery talks.

Library: Books and exhibition catalogs of West-European art, especially Jugoslav and Slovenian Art; 9436 volumes for reference.

Publications: Exhibition catalogs.

Attendance: 40,290.

ZAGREB

GALERIJE GRADA ZAGREBA
(City Art Galleries)
Offices: Rokov perivoj 4, 41000. Tel: 041 424 490

Radoslav Putar, Dir.
Open 11 AM - 1 PM; 5 - 8 PM; admis. 3 dinars. Estab. 1961; financed by endowment.

Activities: Traveling exhibitions organized and circulated; original objects of art lent; 200 items lent in average year; photograph collection; library. Book shop.

Publications: Bit International, Spot (photography journal) and regular catalogs.

Attendance: 20,000.

Galerija suvremene umjetnosti
(Gallery of Contemporary Art)
Katarinin trg 2, 41000. Tel: 041-443-227
Bozo Bek, Chief Cur.
Marijan Susovski, Cur.
Davor Maticevic, Cur.
Estab. 1954. Collection of contemporary art, sculpture and paintings.

Galerija primitivne umjetnosti
(Gallery of Primitive Art)
Cirilo-metodska ulica 3, 41000. Tel: 041-443-294
Boris Kelemen, Chief Cur.
Estab. 1952. Collection of naive paintings and sculptures.

Atelje Mestrovic
(Studio Mestrovic)
Mletacka 8, 41000. Tel: 041-445-075
Vesna Barbic, Chief Cur.
Estab. 1959; financed by endowment. Private studio of Ivan Mestrovic and works (sculptures).

Zbirka Benko Horvat
(Collection Benko Horvat)
Rokov perivoj 4, 41000. Tel: 041-424-490
Dimitrije Basicevic, Chief Cur.
Estab. 1948; financed by endowment. Collections of prints, drawings and paintings of the 15th-19th centuries.

STROSSMYER'S GALLERY OF OLD MASTERS OF THE YUGOSLAV ACADEMY OF SCIENCES AND FINE ARTS
Zrinjski Trg 11, 41000.
Dr. Grga Novak, Pres.
Prof. Vinko Zlamalik, Dir.
Prof. Ljerka Gasparovic, Cur.
Open Tues. 5 - 7 PM; Wed. & Fri. 10 AM - Noon; Thurs. & Sun. 10 AM - 1 PM; admis. 5 and 10 dinar. Estab. 1884 for the preservation, exhibition and explanation of old Masters; financed by city and state appropriation.

Collections: Paintings and sculpture with emphasis on the Italian school from Renaissance to 18th century, 15th - 16th century Austrian painting, 16th century German art, 16th - 18th century Flemish and Dutch school and the French school from 18th - 20th centuries.

Activities: Photograph collection for reference only.

Library: 13,000 volumes.

ART SCHOOLS

ARRANGEMENT AND ABBREVIATIONS
KEY TO ART SCHOOLS

This section includes professional art schools; colleges and universities that offer technical courses in art and lecture courses in the history and appreciation of art; schools of architecture and of landscape architecture; and individual artists who conduct classes of professional standards.

The colleges and universities offer a major in Art unless otherwise noted. The returned questionnaires provided the information. The first year, in many art schools, is a Foundation Course where the student acquires basic skills and principles of creative design as preparation for choice of advanced study in a specific department.

Junior colleges and some art schools offer credit at the end of two year courses—Associate in Arts and Associate in Fine Arts—which are accepted by senior colleges and universities. Graduate courses lead to the Master Degree. College and university scholarships are usually awarded to students of outstanding scholarship who are in need of financial aid. The number of studio, lecture and laboratory courses include only those in the Art Department.

ARRANGEMENT OF DATA

Name of institution and address; zip code and telephone number where possible.
Name of Director (Dir), Chairman (Chmn) or head (Head) of school or department.
Number of full time (FT) and part time (PT) instructors.
Year when school or Art Department was established (Estab).
Control of institution, whether public (pub), private (pvt), or denominational (den).
Student body is co-educational unless noted as for men (M), women (W).
Classes are held during the day (D) unless otherwise noted, evening (E), Saturday (Sat), morning (AM), afternoon (PM).
Admission requires high school graduation or equivalent unless otherwise noted as, no entrance requirements (no ent. req), or examination (exam).

Number of years required for graduation.
Whether degrees are conferred (degree).
Scholarships (schol) and fellowships (fel) offered.
Number of studio courses (SC), lecture courses (LC), and graduate courses (GC).

Enrollment (enrl) is of students majoring in art and of others taking art courses unless otherwise noted.
Tuition (tui) is for the academic year of approximately nine months. Fees for children's Saturday classes are usually on a monthly basis.

Summer School: name of Head of Art Department or Director of Summer Session; courses; fee; date of opening; duration and enrollment.

ABBREVIATIONS AND SYMBOLS

Acad—Academic
Admis—Admission
AM—Morning
Approx—Approximate, Approximately
Assoc—Associate
Asst—Assistant
c—circa
C—Course
Cert—Certificate
Chmn—Chairman
Cl—Closed
Co-ed—Co-educational
Coll—College
Cr—Credit
D—Day
Den—Denominational Control
Dept—Department
Dipl—Diploma
Dir—Director
Div—Division
Dorm—Dormitory
E—Evening
Educ—Education

Enrl—Enrollment
Ent—Entrance
Ent. Req—Entrance Requirements
Estab—Established
Exam—Examination

Fel(s)—Fellowship(s)
FT—Full Time Instructor

GC—Graduate Course
Gen—General
Grad—Graduate

HS—High School
Hr—Hour
Incl—Including
Instr—Instructor
Jr—Junior

Lab.C—Laboratory Course
LC—Lecture Course
Lect—Lecture(s)
Lectr—Lecturer(s)

Maj—Major in Arts
Mo—Monthly
PM—Afternoon
Pres—President
Prin—Principal
Prog—Program
PT—Part Time Instructor
Pts—Points
Pub—Public
Pvt—Private
Reg—Registration
Req—Requirements
Res—Residence, Resident
SC—Studio Course
Schol—Scholarship
Sr—Senior
Tui—Tuition
TV—Television
Undergrad—Undergraduate
Univ—University
W—Women
Wk—Week
Yr—Year(s)

⌖Chapter of The American Federation of Arts

*No response to questionnaire
‡National Architectural Accrediting Board
    for architectural schools
American Society of Landscape Architects
    for courses in landscape architecture.

United States Art Schools

ALABAMA

ATHENS

ATHENS COLLEGE, Art Department, Beaty St, 35611.
   Tel: (205) 232-1802 Exten. 203
Dennis Johnson, Head; 1 FT instr. Estab. 1832; state upper div;
D & E; ent. req. HS dipl; 2 yrs; degrees, B.S, B.A; scholar; 26 SC,
6 LC. total coll enrl. D 951, E 590, maj. 15. Campus res. $1080.

Art Education	History of Art & Archaeology
Ceramics	Painting
Commercial Art	Photography
Costume Design & Construction	Sculpture
Drawing	Stage Design
Graphic Arts	Teacher Training
Handicrafts	Theatre Arts

   Summer School: Term of 15 wks. beginning June 4; 1973 enrl.
471.

AUBURN

AUBURN UNIVERSITY, School of Architecture and Fine Arts,
Department of Art, 36830. Tel: (205) 826-4373
E. K. McPheeters, Dean; C. Hiers, Head; 18 FT, 3 PT instr.
Estab 1928; pub; D; co-ed; ent. req. HS dipl, ACT/SAT; degrees,
4 yrs. req. for B.F.A, 2 yrs. for M.F.A; 48 SC, 9 LC, 19 GC; enrl.
300. Tui. incl. room and board $1660 per yr. res, $2185 non-res.

Design	Painting
Drawing	Printmaking
Illustration	Sculpture

Adult hobby courses, drawing, painting; tui. $25 per course.

BIRMINGHAM

BIRMINGHAM-SOUTHERN COLLEGE,* Art Department, 800 Eighth
Ave. W, 35204. Tel: (320) 328-5250
Dr. Virginia Pitts Rambert, Chmn; 4 FT instr. Estab. 1946; den;
D; ent req. HS dipl, ACT or SAT scores, C average; 4 yr; degrees,
A.B, B.S, B.F.A, B.M, B.M.E; financial aid awarded, some leadership scholarships available on variable basis; 22 SC, 8 LC, interim
term courses of 4 or 8 wk, 4 required of each student in 4 yr.
period; approx. enrl. 500, maj. 50. Tui. $1500 per yr, monthly full-
time $166, part-time $250 per unit; campus res. $950.

Art Education	History of Art & Archaeology
Drawing	Painting
Graphic Arts	Sculpture
Graphic Design	

Children's classes in Art as laboratory for training teachers; tui.
$5 for 4 wk; enrl. approx. 20.
   Summer School: Paul Bailey, Dean; tui. $125 per course for term
of 8 wk. beginning June 11 & Aug. 10; 1973 enrl. approx. 250.

Advanced Painting, Graphics,	Painting & Drawing
Sculpture	Problems in Composition
Art and Music	

✠SAMFORD UNIVERSITY, Art Department, 800 Lakeshore Dr,
35209. Tel: (205) 870-2840, 2849
Dr. Lowell C. Vann, Chmn; 3 FT, 1 PT instr. Estab. 1841; pvt; D;
ent. req. HS dipl, ent exam, ACT/SAT; 4 yr; degrees, B.A, B.S.Educ;
24 SC, 4 LC, 1 GC. Tui. $46 per semester hr. plus fees; campus
res. $450 per semester.

Advertising Design	Handicrafts
Art Education	History of Art & Archaeology
Ceramics	Painting
Commercial Art	Photography
Costume Design &	Sculpture
Construction	Stage Design

Drawing	Teacher Training
Graphic Arts	Theatre Arts
Graphic Design	

Adult hobby classes, ceramics, drawing, painting; enrl. 40.
   Summer School: Regular semester courses on rotating basis;
tui. $46 per hr. for term of 5 wk. beginning June 7.

UNIVERSITY OF ALABAMA IN BIRMINGHAM, Department of Art,
University Station, 35294. Tel: (205) 934-4941
Edith Frohock, Acting Chmn; 4 FT, 3 PT instr. Estab. 1972; pub;
D & E; ent. req. HS dipl, ent. exam; 4 yr; degree, BA; 27 SC, 9 LC;
enrl. D 429, E 282, maj. 50. Tui. $525 per yr.

Aesthetics	Graphic Design
Art Education	History of Art and Archaeology
Drawing	Painting
Graphic Arts	Sculpture

   Summer School: Tui. $175 for term of 8 wks. beginning June 15.

BREWTON

JEFFERSON DAVIS STATE JUNIOR COLLEGE,* Art Department,
Alco Dr, 36426. Tel: (205) 867-4832
John B. Spicer, Instr; Jerry Jones, Instr. Estab. 1965; pub; D & E;
co-ed; ent. req. HS dipl. or equivalency cert; 2 yr; degrees, A.A.,
A.S; 10 SC, 1 LC; enrl. D 700, E 332, maj. 25. Tui. $67.50 per quar-
ter, part-time $16.50 per cr. hr, non-res. $122.50 per quarter; no
campus res.

Introduction to Art	Crafts
Basic Design	Drawing
Beginning Painting	Fundamentals of Photography
Ceramics	

   Summer School: Jerry Jones, Instr; Ceramics, Drawing, Introduction to Art; tui. $67.50, non-res. $122.50 per quarter; enrl. 200.

HUNTSVILLE

UNIVERSITY OF ALABAMA IN HUNTSVILLE,* Department of Art,
P.O. Box 1247, University Dr, 35807. Tel: (205) 895-6114
Dr. Ralph M. Hudson, Chmn; 4FT, 2 PT instr. Estab. art maj. 1969;
pub; D & E; co-ed; ent. req. HS grad, ent. exam, mature students on
nonmatriculation basis; 4 yr; degree, B.A; 39 SC, 15 LC; enrl. D 150,
E 115, maj. 85, others 180. Tui. $525 per yr, non-res. $1050; campus res.

Advertising Design	Graphic Design
Aesthetics	History of Art & Archaeology
Art Education	Illustration
Commercial Art	Lettering
Drafting	Painting
Drawing	Sculpture
Graphic Arts	Teacher Training

Adult hobby classes, Commercial Design, Drawing, Painting, Sculpture; tui. approx. $45 per course; enrl. 40.
   Summer School: Dr. Ralph M. Hudson, Chmn; Art Education,
Drawing, Communication Graphics, Painting, Sculpture; $175 per
term of 11 wk, non-res. $350 per term, beginning 2nd wk. in June;
enrl. 180.

JACKSONVILLE

JACKSONVILLE STATE UNIVERSITY,* Art Department, 36265.
   Tel: (205) 435-9820 Exten. 293
Lee R. Manners, Head; 4 FT instr. Estab. 1883; pvt; D & E; ent.
req. HS dipl, ent. exam, ACT; 4 yr; degrees, B.A, B.S, with Art
Minor; 4 SC, 2 LC; enrl. D 275, E 25, minors 92. Tui. $445;
room $200-$300.

Advertising Design	Graphic Arts
Art Education	History of Art & Archaeology

Ceramics
Commercial Art
Drawing

Painting
Sculpture

LIVINGSTON

LIVINGSTON UNIVERSITY,* Division of Fine Arts, 35470.
Tel: (205) 652-5241
Dennis P. Kudlawiec, Chmn; 3 FT instr. Estab. 1835; state; co-ed;
degrees, B.A, B.S, B.Mus, M.Ed, M.Sc; schol; enrl. 1800. Tui.
$115 per quarter, room and board, $220 per quarter.

Art Appreciation
Art Education
Art for the Teacher
Ceramics
Crafts
Design
Freehand Drawing

Graphics
History of Art
Industrial Design
Painting
Mechanical Drawing
Metal Work
Woodworking

MARION

JUDSON COLLEGE,* Art Department, 36756.
Tel: (205) 683-2011
Sara Lucille Parker, Coordinator; 1 FT, 1 PT instr. Estab. 1838;
den; D (a few evening classes); W; ent. req. HS grad, adequate HS
grades and ACT scores; 3-4 yr; degree, B.A; schol, workshops,
loans, grants; 12 SC, 6 LC; enrl. total 450. Tui. $2330 per yr. for
3 yr. degree; campus res. Special projects courses according to
students' needs.

Crafts
Commercial Art
Design

Drawing
Painting
Watercolor

Adult hobby classes, studio drawing and painting; tui. $30; enrl. 5
Children's classes, studio drawing; tui. $30; enrl. 15.

MOBILE

SPRING HILL COLLEGE, Department of Fine Arts, 36608.
Tel: (205) 460-2371
Rev. Daniel A. Creagan, Chmn; 3 FT, 2 PT instr. Estab. 1960; den;
D & E; ent. req. HS grad, ent. exam; 4 yr; degree, A.B; 8 SC, 4 LC;
enrl. D 100, E 20, maj. 25. Tui. $1900 per yr, PT $65 per semester
hr; campus res. $790.

Aesthetics
Art Education
Drawing

Graphic Arts
History of Art & Archaeology
Painting

UNIVERSITY OF SOUTH ALABAMA, Department of Art, 307 University Blvd, 36688. Tel: (205) 460-6335
John H. Cleverdon, Chmn; 10 FT instr. Estab. 1964; pub; D & E;
ent. req. HS dipl, ACT, early admis. prog. for students with 3 yrs.
HS and superior ACT scores; 4 yr, 3 yr prog. for students with
HS dipl. and superior ACT scores; degrees, B.A, B.F.A. and B.A.
in Art History; 32 SC, 27 LC; enrl. D 452, E 48, maj. 120. Tui.
$597; campus res. $1152.

Advertising Design
Ceramics
Commercial Art
Drawing
History of Art

History of Architecture
Lettering
Painting
Printmaking
Sculpture

Summer School: John H. Cleverdon, Chmn; summer schedule
varies considerably due to projected student enrl. and available
faculty; tui. $199; campus res. $384; 1975 enrl. 155.

MONTEVALLO

UNIVERSITY OF MONTEVALLO, College of Fine Arts, Art Department, 35115. Tel: (205) 665-2521 Exten. 224
John Stewart, Dean; John Spicer, Chmn; 4 FT instr. Estab. 1896;
pub; D & E; co-ed; ent. req. ACT; 4 yr; degrees, B.A, B.S, B.F.A;
schol, work study; 35 SC, 10 LC, 7 GC; enrl. maj. 80, others 2800.
Tui. incl. room and board $1270 to $1540 per session, non-res.
$210 additional per session; campus res.

Advertising Design
Art Education
Art History
Ceramics
Crafts

Design
Painting
Photography
Printmaking
Sculpture

Summer School: John Spicer, Dir; six courses; room and board
$220 per session; two 5 wk. sessions beginning June 5 and July 5;
enrl. 1000.

MONTGOMERY

AUBURN UNIVERSITY AT MONTGOMERY, Art Department, 36109.
Tel: (205) 279-9110 Exten 292
Charles Shannon, Acting Head; 2 FT, 1 PT instr. Estab. 1972; pub;
D & E; ent. req. HS dipl; 4 yr; degree, B.A, major or minor in art;
14 SC, 3 LC; enrl. D 400, maj. 50. Tui. $175 per quarter; no campus
res.

Art Education
Design Fundamentals
Drawing

History of Art
Painting

Adult hobby classes, drawing and painting; tui. $35 per quarter.

HUNTINGDON ART INSTITUTE,* 1500 E. Fairview Ave, 36106.
Tel: (205) 263-1611 Exten. 55
Mae Belle Gay, Dir; 8 PT instr. Estab. 1973; non-credit continuous
education program; enrl. 119. Tui. $50 per course, per sem;
evening classes.

Architectural Drafting
Architectural Rendering
Creative Thinking
Graphics
Lectures

Open Studio
Painting
Photography
Sculpture

HUNTINGDON COLLEGE, Division of Visual Art and Art Institute,
1500 E. Fairview Ave, 36106. Tel: (205) 263-1611
Dr. Mae Belle Gay, Dir; 1 FT, 7 PT instr. Estab. 1854; den; D & E;
co-ed; ent. req. HS grad, ent. exam; 4 yr; degrees, B.A, B.S; 19 SC
enrl. 250; 8 LC enrl. 250; enrl. maj. 28. Tui. $575 per semester;
campus res. $1040.

Advanced Studio
American Art History
(seminar)
Art Appreciation
Art in Religion
Design
Drawing
Elementary School Art
Figure Drawing

Foundations of Art
History of Art
Independent Study, Theory &
Practice
Modern Art
Painting
Photography
Pottery

Adult classes, drawing, painting, photography, tui. $50; creative
thinking, tui. $30; also, children's classes.
Summer School: Classes vary, incl. workshops, seminar, studio.

TROY

*TROY STATE UNIVERSITY, Department of Art, 36081.
Tel: (205) 566-3000 Exten. 278
Dr. R. C. Paxson, Head; 7 FT instr. Estab. 1957; pub; ent. req. HS
grad, ent. exam; degrees, B.A, B.S. (Arts and Sciences), B.A, B.S,
M.S. (Art Education); maj granted in Aesthetics and Art History;
schol. and fel; 23 SC, enrl. 100; 11 LC, enrl. 175. Tui. $165 per
quarter, non-res. from Fla, Ga, Miss, or Tenn. $225, other non-res
$365; campus res.

Aesthetics
Art History
Commercial Art
Crafts
Design
Drawing
Graphic Arts
Jewelry
Summer School.

Lettering
Museology
Painting
Photography
Pottery
Sculpture
Teacher Training

TUSKEGEE INSTITUTE

TUSKEGEE INSTITUTE,* Division of Humanities, College of Arts
and Sciences, Arts and Crafts Department, 36088.
E. F. Thomas, Head; 3 FT instr. Estab. 1881; pvt; 4 yr; degree.

Applied Art
Art Appreciation
Basic Design
Color
Crafts

Interior Design
Teacher Training
Textile Design
Weaving

UNIVERSITY

UNIVERSITY OF ALABAMA, College of Arts and Sciences, Department of Art, 35486. Tel: (205) 348-5967
Angelo Granata, Chmn; 11 FT instr. Estab. 1919; pub; D; co-ed; 4
yr; degrees, B.A, B.F.A, M.A, M.F.A; 50 SC, 12 LC, 20 GC; enrl.
950, maj. undergrad. 225, grad. 20. Tui. $297.50 per semester,
non-res. $595 per semester.

Art Education (College of
Education)
Art History

Graphic Design
Painting
Photography

Ceramics/Glass   Printmaking
Drawing/Design   Sculpture
    Summer School: Angelo Granata, Dir; courses same as above;
tui. $180, non-res. $360; enrl. undergrad. 280, grad. 20.

ALASKA

ANCHORAGE

ALASKA METHODIST UNIVERSITY,* Department of Art, Wesley Dr,
99504. Tel: (907) 272-4401
Gerald Conaway, Head Dept; 2 FT instr. Estab. 1960; pub; pvt; den;
D & E; ent. req. HS dipl, ent. exam; degree, B.A. in Art; 7 SC, 1 GC;
enrl. D 50, E 15, maj. 6. Tui. $2150 per yr; campus res. $1500.

Art Education   Photography
Drawing   Sculpture
Graphic Arts   Theatre Arts
Painting

ANCHORAGE COMMUNITY COLLEGE, University of Alaska, Department of Art, 2533 Providence Ave, 99504. Tel: (907) 279-6622
Keith Appel, Facilitator; 4 FT, 5 PT instr. Pub; D & E; open enrl; 4
yr; degrees, A. A. in art, B.A. in art; schol; 22 SC, 3-5 LC; enrl.
approx. 800. Tui. $170 per semester; no campus res.

Art Education   Painting
Ceramics   Photography
Drawing   Sculpture
Graphic Arts   Stage Design
History of Art & Archaeology   Teacher Training
Jewelry   Theatre Arts
Metalcraft   Weaving
Adult hobby classes same as in regular program.
    Summer School: Courses offered, Ceramics, Drawing, Painting;
tui. $20 per credit for term of 13 wk. beginning May; 1974 enrl. 150.

FAIRBANKS

UNIVERSITY OF ALASKA, Department of Art, Fine Arts Complex,
99701. Tel: (907) 479-7530
Charles W. Davis, Acting Head; 4 FT, 1 PT instr. Estab. 1963; pub;
D & E; ent. req. HS dipl; 4 yr; degree, B.A; schol; 28 SC, 4 LC;
enrl. D 293, E 50, maj. 45. Tui. $160 per sem, non-res $300 per
sem, grad. $240 per sem, under 8 cr. $20 per cr. hr; campus res.
c. $1600 per yr.

Ceramics   Lettering
Drawing   Painting
Graphic Arts   Sculpture
History of Art & Archaeology   Textile Design
Jewelry
Adult hobby classes, crafts, drawing, painting, under the direction
of the community college; tui. $90 per 3 cr. hr; enrl. 30 per class.
Children's classes on Sat, ceramics, drawing & painting, sculpture,
under the direction of the community college; $45 per 8 wk; enrl. 40.
    Summer School: Dr. William Pennebaker, Dir; $63 per studio
course, plus lab fee $20, for term of 3 or 6 wk.

Drawing   Sculpture
Painting   Watercolor
Printmaking

ARIZONA

FLAGSTAFF

NORTHERN ARIZONA UNIVERSITY, Art Department, 86001.
    Tel: (602) 523-4612
Dr. James P. Anderson, Chmn; 16 FT, 1 PT instr. Estab. 1912; pub;
D & E; co-ed; 4 and 5 yr; degrees, B.F.A, M.A; 55 SC, 10 LC, 9 GC;
enrl. maj. 450, others 100, total univ. 10,000. Tui. $195 per sem,
$378 non-res; campus res. room $155 per sem, board $660.

Advertising Design   Jewelry
Ceramics   Lettering
Drawing   Painting
Graphic Arts   Sculpture
History   Teacher Training
Career and continuing educ. prog. both on and off campus; tui.
$10-$30 per credit hr; enrl. 200.
    Summer School: Dr. Virgil Gillenwater, Dir; 5 wk. from June 10.
Tui. $22 per sem. hr.

Art History   Jewelry
Ceramics   Painting
Drawing   Sculpture
Graphics   Teacher Training

MESA

MESA COMMUNITY COLLEGE, Department of Art, 1833 W.
    Southern Ave, 85202. Tel: (602) 833-1261 Exten. 270
Gene Corno, Chmn; 6 FT instr. Estab. 1963; pub; D & E; co-ed;
ent. req. HS grad, GED, or over 21; 2 yr; degree, A.A; schol; 18 SC,
3 LC, enrl. D 4662, maj. 285. Tui. free to local students, $1430 per
yr. non-res; no campus res.

Advertising Design   Jewelry
Basic Design   Life Drawing
Ceramics   Painting
Drawing   Sculpture
History of Art
    Summer School: Gene Corno, Dir; tui. $12 per sem hr, two terms
of 5 wk. beginning June 18.

Art History   Design
Ceramics   Drawing

PHOENIX

GRAND CANYON COLLEGE, Art Department, 3300 W. Camelback
    Rd, P.O. Box 11097, 85061. Tel: (602) 249-3300 Exten. 227
Dr. C. L. Russell, Chmn; 1 FT, 2 PT instr. Estab. 1948; pvt; D & E;
co-ed; ent. req. HS dipl, ent. exam; 4 yr; degrees, B.A, B.S; schol;
26 SC, 8 LC; enrl. D 250, E 75, maj. 45. Tui. $37.50 per sem. hr,
plus fees; campus res. $1109.

Advertising Design   History of Art & Archaeology
Aesthetics   Jewelry
Art Education   Lettering
Ceramics   Painting
Commercial Art   Sculpture
Drawing   Stage Design
Fashion Arts   Teacher Training
Graphic Arts   Theatre Arts
Handicrafts
Adult hobby classes, ceramic sculpture, fibers, figure drawing, metal
casting, Raku ceramics, silver and turquoise, water colors, weaving,
wheel throwing; tui. $37.50 per credit hr, plus fees.
    Summer School: Dr. C. L. Russell, Dir; courses, same as adult
hobby classes; tui. $37.50 per credit hr, plus fees, for two 5 wk.
terms, beginning June 4 and July 10.

KACHINA SCHOOL OF ART,* 3801 N. 30th St, 85016.
    Tel: (602) 955-5930
Jay Datus, Dir; 4 FT, E 2 FT instr. Estab. 1947; pvt; 36 mo; dipl,
cert; schol; 5 SC, 1 LC. Children's classes 4 Sat. AM.

Advertising Design   Industrial Design
Display   Interior Design
Drawing   Lettering
Fashion Illustration   Painting
Graphic Arts   Textile Design
Illustration
    Summer School: Jay Datus, Dir; 12 wk. beginning June 1.

PHOENIX COLLEGE, Department of Art & Photography, 1202 W.
    Thomas Rd, 85013. Tel: (602) 264-2492 Exten. 256
Doug Brooks, Chmn; 7 FT, 22 PT instr. Dept. estab. 1948; pub;
co-ed; ent. req. HS grad; 2 yr; degree, A.A; schol; enrl. maj. 125,
others 500, E 100. Tui. $45 res.

Art Appreciation   Life Drawing
Basic Design   Mexican Arts & Crafts
Ceramics   Oil Painting
Commercial Art   Photography (basic & color)
Crafts   Sculpture
Drawing & Composition   Watercolor Painting
Drawing & Perspective   Weaving
Interior Design

TEMPE

ARIZONA STATE UNIVERSITY, Department of Art, 85281.
    Tel: (602) 965-3469
Clyde W. Watson, Chmn; 51 FT, 33 PT instr. Estab. 1885; pub;
D & E; co-ed; degrees, B.A, B.S, B.F.A, M.A, M.F.A, Ed.D; grad.
assistantships and associateships, non-res. tui. schol. for some grad.
students; 95 SC, 48 LC, 86 GC; enrl. undergrad. maj. 1300, M.F.A.
maj. 05, M.A. maj. 100, art educ. maj.(Ed.D), 15, total univ. 31,000.
Tui. $200 per sem, non-res. $585 additional per sem; campus res.

Art Education   Interior Design
Art History   Painting
Ceramics   Photography
Crafts   Printmaking
Drawing   Sculpture
Graphic Design
    Summer School: Clyde W. Watson, Dir; $20 per sem. hr; two 5
wk. sessions c. May 31 to July 2, July 6 to Aug. 6.

THATCHER

EASTERN ARIZONA COLLEGE, Art Department, 85552.
Tel: (602) 428-1133 Exten. 63
Justin Fairbanks, Head; 2 FT, 6 PT instr. Estab. 1890; pub; D & E;
ent. req. HS dipl, GED, or 18 yrs. old; 2 yr; A.A. (Art or Art Educ);
tui. schol. for res; 17 SC, 3 LC; enrl. D 144, E 131, maj. 11, others
264. Tui. $153 per yr, $19 mo. FT, $3-5 mo. PT, $400 non-res;
campus res. $1140.

Art Appreciation	Jewelry
Art Education	Lapidary
Ceramics	Lettering
Design	Painting
Drawing	Photography
History of Art & Archaeology	Sculpture

TUCSON

✠TUCSON MUSEUM OF ART SCHOOL, 179 N. Main Ave, 85705.
Tel: (602) 622-1327
Thomas William Wiper, Dir. of Educ; 21 PT instr. Estab. 1924; pvt;
D & E; co-ed; no ent. req; schol; 42 SC, 2 LC; total enrl. D & E 1139.
Tui. varies per course; no campus res.

Assemblage	Modern Dance
Basket Weaving	Painting
Ceramics	Photography
Drawing	Sculpture
Fencing	Textile Design
Graphic Arts	Three Dimensional Design
Handicrafts	Weaving
History of Art & Archaeology	Woodwork
Jewelry	

Adult hobby classes; also, children's classes, art, crafts, ceramics,
sculpture, drawing & painting, theatre workshop, dance.
Summer School: Enrl. 300.

UNIVERSITY OF ARIZONA, College of Fine Arts, Department of
Art, 85721. Tel: (602) 884-1251
Robert W. McMillan, Head; 29 FT, 15 PT instr. Estab. 1885; pub;
4 yr; degrees, B.A. (Art History), B.F.A. (Art Educ. and Studio),
M.A. (1 yr. 30 units, Art History and Art Educ.), M.F.A. (2 yr. 60
units, Studio); schol; 26 SC, 34 LC, 37 GC; enrl. maj. 615, others
890, average per sem. Tui. non-res. $545 per sem. plus reg. fee
$275 per sem; campus res.

Art Education	Metalwork
Art History	Painting
Ceramics	Photography
Drawing	Printmaking
Graphic Design	Sculpture

ARKANSAS

ARKADELPHIA

OUACHITA BAPTIST UNIVERSITY, School of Arts and Sciences,
Department of Art, Box 785, 71923. Tel: (501) 246-4531 Exten 282
Phares Raybon, Chmn; 2 FT instr. Estab. 1886; den; D; co-ed; ent.
req. HS dipl; 4 yr; degrees, B.A. in Commercial Art, B.S.E. in Art
Educ; 11 SC, 2 LC; enrl. 93, maj. 35. Tui. $1210 per yr; campus res.
$990.

Advertising Design	History of Art & Archaeology
Art Education	Painting
Ceramics	Sculpture
Commercial Art	Teacher Training
Drawing	

Summer School: Phares Raybon, Dir; Art Education, Design;
tui. $32 per sem. hr. for term of 5 wk, beginning June 1; enrl. 35.

CLARKSVILLE

COLLEGE OF THE OZARKS, Department of Art, 72830.
Tel: (501) 754-3431
Lyle Ward, Chmn; 1 FT instr. Estab. 1836; den; D; co-ed; ent.
req. HS grad, ent. exam, ACT; 4 yr; degrees, B.A, B.S; schol;
7 SC, 2 LC; enrl. D 560, maj. 16. Tui. $810 per yr; campus res.
$350 room, $600 board.

Art Appreciation	History of Art
Art Education	Painting
Ceramics	Teacher Training
Drawing	

Summer Art Workshop: Art Education, Studio Painting; tui.
$30 per hr. for term of 3 wk; enrl. 15 minimum.

CONWAY

UNIVERSITY OF CENTRAL ARKANSAS, Art Department, 72032.
Tel: (501) 329-2931 Exten. 331
Dr. Jerry D. Poole, Head; 6 FT teachers. Estab. 1908; pub; co-ed;
ent. req. HS grad; 4 yr; degrees; 14 SC, 4 LC. Campus res.

Advanced Design	Crafts
Art Appreciation	Drawing & Painting
Art History	Printmaking
Ceramics	Sculpture
Color & Design	Teacher Training
Commercial Art	
Summer School.	

FAYETTEVILLE

✠UNIVERSITY OF ARKANSAS,* Art Department, 72701.
Tel: (501) 575-5202
Thomas D. Turpin, Chmn; 13 FT, 13 PT instr. Estab. 1872;
pub; 4 yr; degrees, B.A, B.S, M.F.A; schol, grad. assistantships;
51 SC, 20 LC, 40 GC; enrl. maj. 250, others 1800. Tui. $200 per
sem. or $20 per sem. hr, non-res. $465 per sem. or $46.50 per
sem. hr; res. fee $475 per sem.

Art Education	Drawing
Art History	Jewelry
Ceramics	Painting
Commercial Art	Printmaking
Design	Sculpture

Summer School: Thomas D. Turpin, Chmn; tui. $15 per sem.
hr, non-res. $35 per sem. hr.

HELENA

PHILLIPS COUNTY COMMUNITY COLLEGE,* Department of
English and Fine Arts, Box 785, 72342. Tel: (501) 338-6496
Exten. 61
Dr. Jean Knowlton, Chmn; 3 FT, 1 PT instr. Estab. 1966; pub;
D & E; ent. req. HS dipl, ent. exam, GED equivalency; 2 yrs;
degrees, A.A, A.A.S; schol; 8 SC, 1 LC; enrl. D 72, E 17. Tui.
$100 sem. county residents, $150 sem. state residents, $175 sem.
out-of-state; non-residential.

Ceramics	History of Art & Archaeology
Drafting	Painting
Drawing	

LITTLE ROCK

✠ARKANSAS ARTS CENTER, MacArthur Park, 72203.
Tel: (501) 372-4000
Townsend Wolfe, Exec. Dir; Becky Rogers Witsell, Dir. of Educ;
6 FT, 8 PT instr. Estab. 1960; pvt (funds to operate school come
from memberships and tuition and other fees; classes, however, are
offered to the public); D & E; co-ed; ent. req. age req. only by class
(accreditated courses offered in conjunction with Univ. Ark, Little
Rock); schol; 50 SC, 1 LC; total enrl. 2200. Tui. varies per course
for mem. and non-mem.

Art Education	Painting
Ballet	Photography
Creative Dramatics	Pottery
Drawing	Printmaking
Enameling	Puppetry
Film Making	Sculpture
Glassblowing	Theatre Crafts
Jewelry	Watercolors
Modern Dance	Yoga
Movement	

Summer School: Same courses as for fall and spring sem.

PHILANDER SMITH COLLEGE,* Art Department, 812 W. 13th St,
72203.
Eugenia V. Dunn, Chmn; 1 FT, 3 PT instr. Estab. 1952; pvt; 4 yrs;
degrees, B.A, in cooperation with the Arkansas Arts Center; schol;
4 LC, 12 SC; enrl. total 600, maj. 5, others 35. Tui. $475 for 36 wk.

Art Appreciation	Drawing
Arts & Crafts	Painting
Afro-American Art History	Printmaking
Art History	Sculpture
Basic Design	

Summer School: Dr. Crawford Mims, Dir.

UNIVERSITY OF ARKANSAS AT LITTLE ROCK,* Department of Art,
32nd & University Sts, 72204. Tel: (501) 565-7531 Exten. 323
Al Allen, Head; 6 FT, 4 PT instr. Estab. 1928; pub; D & E; ent. req.
HS grad; 4 yr; degree, B.A; schol; SC, LC; enrl. 5000. Tui. $200
per sem.

Art Education	Drawing
Art History	Painting

Commercial Art
Crafts
Design
Pottery
Printmaking
Sculpture

MAGNOLIA

SOUTHERN STATE COLLEGE, Department of Art, 71753. Tel: (501) 234-5120 Exten. 224
Willard Carpenter, Chmn; 3 FT instr. Estab. 1909; pub; D & E; co-ed; ent. req. HS grad; 4 yr; degrees, B.S.E, B.A; 16 SC, 3 LC; enrl. D c. 2300, maj. 45. Tui. $200 per sem; campus res. $488.
Advanced Art Studio II
Advertising Design
Art Education
Ceramics
Drawing
Handicrafts
History of Art & Archaeology
Painting
Printmaking
Sculpture
Teacher Training

Summer School: Dr. L. A. Logan, Vice Pres. for Academic Affairs; basic art courses; tui. $75 for term of 5 wk, beginning June 8.

PINE BLUFF

SOUTHEAST ARKANSAS ARTS AND SCIENCE CENTER, and Little Firehouse School, Civic Center, 71601. Tel: (501) 536-3375
Philip A. Klopfenstein, Dir. Estab. 1958; pub; no ent. req; no degree. Mo. exhibits.
Drawing
Graphic Arts
Handicrafts
Painting
Photography
Sculpture
Theatre Arts

Adult hobby classes; instr. from various local and area colleges.

RUSSELLVILLE

ARKANSAS POLYTECHNIC COLLEGE, Art Department, 72801. Tel: (501) 968-0244
Edward M. Wilwers, Head; 3 FT, 2 PT instr. Estab. 1909; pub; D & E; ent. req. HS grad, ent. exam; 4 yr; degrees, B.A, B.S; schol, fel; 5 LC, 22 SC; enrl. maj. 65, others 1750. Tui. $205 per sem, non-res. $265 per sem.
Advertising Design
Architecture
Ceramics
Display
Drafting
Drawing
General Design
Illustration
Industrial Design
Lettering
Painting
Printmaking
Teacher Training
Textile Design

Summer School: Edward M. Wilwers, Dir; $75 for each term of 5 wk.

SILOAM SPRINGS

JOHN BROWN UNIVERSITY, Division of Arts and Literature, Department of Art, 72761. Tel: (501) 524-3131
Ralph C. Kennedy, Div. Chmn; 1 FT instr. Estab. 1919; pvt; D; co-ed; ent. req. HS grad; 9 SC, 3 LC; no maj. Tui. $1300 per yr; campus res. $2400 per yr.
Commercial Art
Crafts for Teachers
Drafting
Drawing
History of Art & Archaeology
Painting
Teacher Training

STATE UNIVERSITY

ARKANSAS STATE UNIVERSITY, College of Fine Arts, Division of Art, Fine Arts Center, 72467. Tel: (501) 972-3050
Karl Richards, Chmn; 13 FT instr. Estab. 1909, Art Prog 1938; pub; D & E; co-ed; ent. req. HS dipl; 4 yr; degrees, B.F.A, B.S, B.S.E; schol; 29 SC, 9 LC; enrl. D 6000, maj. 195. Tui. per yr. $400, non-res. $700, res. $17 per cr. hr, non-res. $27 per cr. hr; campus res. $390 to $490.
Advertising Design
Art Education
Ceramics
Commercial Art
Drawing
Glassblowing
Graphic Arts
Graphic Design
History of Art & Archaeology
Illustration
Jewelry
Lettering
Painting
Sculpture
Teacher Training

Adult hobby classes, enrl. 40 in ceramics, 15 in jewelry, 40 in painting.

Summer School: Karl Richards, Chmn; tui. $90, non-res. $150 for term of 5 wk, two sessions beginning first wk. in June and early in July; 1975 enrl. 239.
Art Appreciation
Art Education
Drawing
Jewelry
Art History
Ceramics
Design
Painting
Sculpture

WALNUT RIDGE

SOUTHERN BAPTIST COLLEGE, Humanities Department, 72476. Tel (501) 886-6741 Exten 34
Gerry Gibbons, Chmn; 1 FT, 1 PT instr. Estab. 1941; den; D; co-ed; ent. req. HS dipl, ent. exam; 2 yr; degree, A.A; schol; 4 SC, 2 LC; enrl. 60. Tui. $32 per sem. hr; campus res. $940 per yr.
Art Education
Ceramics
Drawing
Graphic Design
History of Art & Archaeology
Painting

CALIFORNIA

APTOS

CABRILLO COLLEGE, Visual Arts Division, 6500 Soquel Dr, 95003. Tel: (408) 425-6464
Holt E. Murray, Chmn; 9 FT, 10 PT instr. Estab. 1959; pub; D & E; ent. req. HS dipl; 2 yr; degree, A.A; 46 SC, 7 LC; enrl. 24 each SC, 45 each LC. Summer School.
Ceramics
Drawing
Graphic Arts
Graphic Design
Handicrafts
History of Art & Archaeology
Jewelry
Painting
Photography
Sculpture
Textile Design

ARCATA

HUMBOLDT STATE UNIVERSITY,* Art Department, 95521. Tel: (707) 826-3625
J. Pauley, Chmn; 20 FT instr. Estab. 1913; pub; D & E; degrees, B.A, 4 yr. B.A. with credential, 5 yr; schol; 35 SC, 11 LC, 11 GC. Tui. $48; campus res.
Ceramics
Graphic Design
Design
Jewelry & Metalsmithing
Painting
Photography
Printmaking
Sculpture
Teacher Training

Children's classes, art 12; $5 fee; enrl. 10.

Summer School: Dr. John C. Hennessy, Dean, Continuing Education; tui. $96 for 6 wk. from June 22; enrl. 800.

BAKERSFIELD

BAKERSFIELD COLLEGE, Art Department, 1801 Panorama Dr, 93305. Tel: (805) 871-7120
Victor Bracke, Head; 10 FT, 2 PT instr. Estab. 1913; pub; D & E; ent. req. ent. exam, open door policy; 2 yr; degree, A.A; 16 SC, 4 LC; enrl. D 6000, maj. 150-200. No tui.
Architecture
Ceramics
Commercial Art
Drafting
Drawing
Glassblowing
Graphic Arts
History of Art & Archaeology
Illustration
Jewelry
Lettering
Painting
Photography
Sculpture
Stage Design
Theatre Arts

Adult hobby classes, ceramics, painting; enrl. 100-150.

Summer School: Dr. Richard Harkins, Dir; term of 6 wk. term beginning June; 1973 enrl. 150.
Ceramics
Design
Drawing
Figure Drawing
Photography

BELMONT

COLLEGE OF NOTRE DAME, Department of Art, 1400 Ralston Ave, 94002. Tel: (415) 593-1601
Robert David Ramsey, Chmn; 2 FT, 6 PT instr. Estab. 1951; den; D & E; co-ed; ent. req. HS grad, ent. exam; $3\frac{1}{2}$-4 yr; degrees, B.A, M.A.T; schol; 18 SC, 12 LC; enrl. D 200, E 70, maj. 50. Tui. $1850 per yr; campus res. $1300 per yr.
Aesthetics
Art Education
Ceramics
Costume Design
Drawing
Environmental Design
Etching
History of Art & Archaeology
Interior Design
Painting
Photography
Sculpture
Silk Screen
Weaving

Summer School: Sister Mary Emmanuel Donnelly, Dir; upper division courses as in regular program plus special art education workshops; tui. $32 per unit for 6 wk. term; §974 enrl. 1047.

BERKELEY

UNIVERSITY OF CALIFORNIA, BERKELEY, College of Letters and Science, Department of Art and History of Art, 94704. James Cahill, Co-Chmn, History of Art, 11 FT, 2 PT, 2 visiting instr; Robert Hartman, Co-Chmn, Art, 15 FT, 4-6 visiting instr. Estab. 1902; pub; D; ent. req. sames as undergrad. to Univ, B.A. B.A.(Art) for admis. to M.A.(Art) prog.

Drawing
Graphic Art
History of Art
Painting

Sculpture
Teacher Training with
    School of Education

CARMEL

CARMEL ART INSTITUTE, P.O. Box 9, 93921.
    Tel: (408) 624-9951
John Cunningham, Pres. & Dir; 3 FT instr. Estab. 1938, inc. 1955; pvt; D (Mon. through Fri); 4 yr. course for Fine Arts, objective painter; Certificate of Completion. Tui. $85 per mo; reg. limited to 30; approved for veterans.

Aesthetics
Anatomy
Design

Etching
Lithography
Painting

    Summer School: two 6 wk. sessions.

CHICO

CALIFORNIA STATE UNIVERSITY AT CHICO, School of Humanities and Fine Arts, Art Department, W. First & Normal Sts, 95926.
    Tel: (916) 345-5331
Richard Honraday, Head; 24 FT, 3 PT instr. Pub; D & E; ent. req. ent. exam; 4 yr; degrees, B.A, M.A; schol. to art maj; 24 SC, 11 LC, 12 GC; enrl. D 1500, E 500, maj. 450, grad. 80. Tui. $83 per sem.

Art Education
Ceramics
Drawing
Glass
History of Art

Painting
Printmaking
Sculpture
Teacher Training

    Summer School: Richard Hornaday, Head; tui. $27 per unit for term of 10 wk. beginning June 7.

Art Education
Ceramics
Design
Drawing

History of Art
Painting
Sculpture
Teacher Training

CLAREMONT

PITZER COLLEGE,* Department of Art, 91711.
    Tel: (714) 626-8511
C. H. Hertel, Prof. of Art; 3 FT, 1 PT instr. Estab. 1964; pvt; D; co-ed; ent. req. HS dipl, various criteria, apply Dir. of Admis; 4 yr; degree, B.A; schol; 8 SC, 6 LC; enrl. Sept-June maj. 19, grad. 10 (Claremont Grad. School). Tui. $2000; campus res. $1350.

Aesthetics
Ceramics
Drawing
Environments
Graphic Arts

History of Art & Archaeology
Painting
Photography
Sculpture
Weaving

As one of the Claremont Colleges, cross-registration in Ceramics, Environments, Film Arts, Graphic Arts and Weaving.

POMONA COLLEGE, Art Department, 91711.
    Tel: (714) 626-8511 Exten. 2241
Gerald M. Ackerman, Chmn; 6 FT instr. Estab. 1887; pvt; D; 4 yr; degree, B.A; schol. and fel; 18 SC, 21 LC; enrl. maj. 15, others 300. Tui. $1650 per sem; campus res.

Ceramics
Drawing
History of Art

Painting
Photography
Sculpture

SCRIPPS COLLEGE,* Art Department, 91711.
    Tel: (714) 624-2616
Paul G. Darrow, Prof of Art; 8 FT, 3 PT instr. Estab. 1926; pvt; W; 4 yr; degree, B.A; res. schol; normal enrl. 485.

COMPTON

COMPTON COMMUNITY COLLEGE, Art Department, 1111 E. Artesia Blvd, 90221. Tel: (213) 635-8081 Exten. 283
Dr. Bill Hart, Chmn Fine Arts; 1 FT, 5 PT instr. Estab. 1929;

pub; D & E; ent. req. HS dipl, 21 yrs. of age; 2 yr; degree, A.A; schol; 16 SC, 6 LC; enrl. D 3500, E 2000, maj. 18.

Advertising Design
Afro-American Art
Art Education
Design
Drafting
Drawing
General Crafts

History of Art and Archaeology
Lettering
Painting
Photography
Showcard Writing
Theatre Arts (separate dept.)

    Summer School: Floyd Hopper, Dir; courses offered, Art Appreciation, History.

CORONA DEL MAR

BRANDT PAINTING WORKSHOPS, 405 Goldenrod Ave, 92625.
    Tel: (714) 675-0093
Rex Brandt, Co-Dir; 4 PT instr. Estab. 1946; summer program only; pvt; D; ent. req; HS dipl. or age 21; 5 SC; enrl. 150. Tui. $65 per wk; no campus res.

Drawing
Painting

CORONADO

CORONADO SCHOOL OF FINE ARTS, 176 C Ave, P.O. Box 156, 92118.
Monty Lewis, Dir; D 2 FT, 6 PT, E 1 FT instr. Estab. 1944; pvt; 3-4 yr; dipl; SC, LC; enrl. D 50, E 25, children 15. Tui. $120 per 4 wk, PT $78 per 4 wk, children 4 Sat. AM $20. Approved for Veterans and Foreign Students.

Advertising Design
Art History
Commercial Art
Fine Arts
Graphic Arts

Illustration
Mural Decoration
Painting
Sculpture

    Summer School: Monty Lewis, Dir; 8 wk. session; tui. FT $120 per 4 wk; enrl. 75; Watercolor Seminar $76 per 4 wk, $120 per 8 wk.

COSTA MESA

ORANGE COAST COLLEGE, Fine Arts Department, 2701 Fairview, 92626. Tel: (714) 556-5514
Paul Cox, Chmn; 38 FT, 55 PT instr. Estab. 1946; pub; D & E; ent. req. ent. exam; 2 yr; degree, A.A; schol; 288 SC, 52 LC; enrl. D 1500, E 1400, maj. 2397. No tui; no campus res.

Advertising Design
Architecture
Art Education
Basic Crafts
Ceramics
Commercial Art
Display
Drafting
Drawing
Exhibition Design
Fashion Arts
Graphic Arts
Graphic Design
History of Art & Archaeology
Illustration

Industrial Design
Interior Design
Jewelry
Landscape Architecture
Lettering
Museum Staff Training
Occupational Therapy
Painting
Photography
Sculpture
Stage Design
Teacher Training
Textile Design
Theatre Arts
Weaving Fibers

Adult hobby classes, furniture refinishing.
    Summer School: Dr. Blakley, Dir; courses offered same as above.

CYPRESS

CYPRESS COLLEGE, Fine Arts Division, 9200 Valley View St, 90630. Tel: (714) 826-2220 Exten. 292
Lester Johnson, Chmn; 9 FT, 9 PT instr. Estab. 1967; pub; D & E; 2 yrs; degree, A.A; schol; 25 SC, 5 LC; enrl. D 2089, E 758. No tui; no campus res.

Advertising Design
Ceramics
Display
Drawing
Film Making
Graphic Arts
Handicrafts

History of Art & Archaeology
Leather
Macrame
Painting
Printmaking
Sculpture
Silkscreen

    Summer School

Ceramics
Crafts
Design & Color
Drawing

Introduction to Art
Museum Seminar
Painting

DAVIS

UNIVERSITY OF CALIFORNIA, College of Letters and Science,
Art Department, 95616. Tel: (916) 752-0105
Prof. Richard D. Cramer, Head; 17 FT instr. Estab. 1952; pub;
D; 4 yr; degrees, B.A, M.A, M.F.A; schol; 28 SC, 35 LC; enrl. maj.
130, others 1000. Tui. $244.50, non-res. $1045.50.

Architectural Design	Graphic Arts
Art History	Painting
Ceramics	Photography
Drawing	Sculpture
Film Making	

Laboratory for Research in the Fine Arts and Museology.
Tel: (916) 752-0106
R. D. Cramer, Acting Dir; Gerald Hoepfner, Staff.
Along with the basic study of conservation and museum techniques
and the training of museum workers, the Laboratory is building
archives which will list the contents and appropriate date of collections in California from major museums which share the cooperative effort with the Laboratory.

DOMINGEUZ HILLS

CALIFORNIA STATE COLLEGE, Department of Fine Arts,
Dominguez Hills, 90747. Tel: (213) 532-4300
Prof. Marshall Bialosky, Chmn; 9 FT, 3 PT instr. Estab. 1965;
pub; D & E; co-ed; ent. req. upper one-third of HS class; 4 yr;
degree, B.A; 35 SC, 25 LC; enrl. maj. 130. Tui. free; no campus
res.

Aesthetics	History of Art & Archaeology
Design	Painting
Drawing	Sculpture
Graphics	Teacher Training

EL CAJON

GROSSMONT COLLEGE, Art Department, 8800 Grossmont College
Dr, 92020. Tel: (714) 465-1700
Marj Hyde, Chmn; 11 FT instr. Estab. 1961; pub; D & E; no ent.
req; unit and curriculum req. for grad; degree, A.A; schol; 22 SC,
1 LC; total enrl. 1000. Tui. free; no campus res.

Ceramics	Painting
Composition	Photography
Drawing	Primitive Art
History of Art	Sculpture

Summer School: K. Nobilette, Dir; courses offered, Ceramics,
Drawing, Photography.

EL CAMINO COLLEGE

EL CAMINO COLLEGE, Division of Fine Arts, 16007 Crenshaw
Blvd, 90506.
Dr. Lewis E. Hiigel, Dean; 20 FT, 21 PT instr. Estab. 1947; pub;
D & E; ent. req. HS dipl; 2 yr; degree, A.A; schol; 37 SC, 4 LC;
enrl. maj. approx. 600, total 5200. Tui. free; no campus res.

Advertising Design	History of Art & Archaeology
Art Education	Industrial Design
Art In Modern Life	Jewelry
(Appreciation)	Lettering
Ceramics	Painting
Costume Design & Construction	Sculpture
Crafts	Stage Design
Display	Theatre Arts
Drawing	Three-Dimensional Design
Gallery	Two-Dimensional Design

Summer School: Extension of regular yr; courses offered,
beginning classes.

EUREKA

COLLEGE OF THE REDWOODS, Art Department, 95501.
Tel: (707) 443-8411
Reginald R. Mintey, Chmn; 5 FT, 8 PT instr. Estab. 1964; pub;
D & E; ent. req. HS grad; 2 yr; degree, A.A; schol; 15 SC, 3 LC
per quarter; enrl. 4000, art maj. 75. Campus res. $900 per yr.

Art Fundamentals	History of Art & Archaeology
Ceramics	Jewelry
Commercial Art	Lettering
Drafting	Painting
Drawing	Photography
Fabrics	Sculpture
Graphic Arts	

Summer School: Dale Collins, Dir; courses to be announced;
tui. free.

FRESNO

CALIFORNIA STATE UNIVERSITY, FRESNO, Art Department,
Shaw & Maple Aves, 93740. Tel: (205) 487-2516
Roger Bolomey, Chmn, 25 FT, 5 PT instr. Estab. 1911; pub; ent.
req. HS dipl. with 7 rec. units, or with 5 rec. units; pass ent. exam
in top 30 percentile, or 21 yr. of age; 4 yr; degree, A.B, 5 yr. teaching credential, M.A. program; schol; 36 SC, 8 LC. Summer School,
Extension.

Art History	Intaglio
Art Tours	Lithography
Ceramics	Museum Techniques
Crafts	Painting
Design	Photography
Drawing	Printmaking
Graduate Seminars and Exhi-	Sculpture
bitions	Teacher Training with Depart-
Independent Study	ment of Education

FULLERTON

CALIFORNIA STATE UNIVERSITY, FULLERTON, Department of
Art, 800 N. State College Blvd, 92634. Tel: (714) 870-3471
G. Ray Kerciu, Acting Chmn; 31 FT, 22 PT instr. Pub; D & E; ent.
req. ent. exam, SAT or ACT; 4 yr; degrees, B.A, M.A; 105 SC,
9 LC, 23 GC; total enrl. 22,000, maj. 838, grad. students 134.
Tui. $190 per yr; no campus res.

Advertising Design	Illustration
Art Education	Industrial Design
Ceramics	Jewelry
Commercial Art	Lettering
Display	Painting
Drawing	Photography
Graphic Arts	Sculpture
Graphic Design	Teacher Training
Handicrafts	Textile Design
History of Art & Archaeology	Weaving

Summer School: Courses varied; tui. $88 for 3 units for term of
6 wk.

FULLERTON COLLEGE, Fine Arts/Art Department, 321 E. Chapman
Ave, 92634. Tel: (714) 871-8000
Donald E. Widen, Chmn; 20 FT, 8 PT instr. Estab. 1913; pub; D & E;
ent. req. HS dipl, ent. exam; 2 yr; degree, A.A; schol. No campus res.

Advertising Design	History of Art & Archaeology
Aesthetics	Illustration
Architecture	Industrial Design
Art Education	Jewelry
Ceramics	Landscape Architecture
Commercial Art	Lettering
Costume Design & Construction	Painting
Drafting	Photography
Drawing	Sculpture
Fashion Arts	Stage Design
Graphic Arts	Teacher Training
Graphic Design	Textile Design
Handicrafts	Theatre Arts

GILROY

GAVILAN COLLEGE, Art Department, 5055 Santa Therese Blvd,
95020.
Kent Child, Chmn. Humanities Div; 2 FT, 6 PT instr. Estab. 1919;
pub; D & E; ent. req. HS dipl. or 18 yr. age; 2 yr; degree, A.A.(Art);
15 SC, 2 LC; enrl. D 150, E 75, maj. 30. Tui. free to res, non-res.
$27 per unit, foreign student $15 per unit; no campus res.

Ceramics	Painting
Drafting	Photography
Drawing	Sculpture
Graphic Arts	Teacher Training
History of Art & Archaeology	Theatre Arts
Jewelry	

Adult hobby classes, ceramics; tui. $6; enrl. 25.
Summer School: Courses offered, Ceramics, Drawing,
Painting.

GLENDALE

GLENDALE COLLEGE,* Department of Fine & Applied Art, 1500 N.
Verdugo Rd, 91208. Tel: (213) 240-1000
Milton Young, Chmn; 8 FT, 3 PT instr. Estab. 1927; pub; D & E; ent.
req. HS grad, ent. exam; 2 yr; degree, A.A; 20 SC, 12 LC; enrl. D
3500, E 3000, maj. 200. Tui. free; no campus res.

Advertising Design	History of Art
Architecture	Industrial Design
Ceramics	Jewelry
Commercial Art	Lettering

Costume Design & Construction
Drafting
Drawing
Graphic Arts
Graphic Design
    Painting
Photography
Sculpture
Stage Design

Summer School: Dr. Charles Wheelock, Dir; Art History; June 23 to July 30.

HAYWARD

CALIFORNIA STATE UNIVERSITY, HAYWARD, Art Department, 25800 Hillary St, 94542. Tel: (415) 881-3111
Lynn Couden, Chmn. Dept; 20 FT instr. Estab. 1960; pub; D & E; ent. req. HS dipl, ent. exam, ACT; 4 yr; degree, B.A; schol; 30 SC, 12 LC; enrl. 1100. Tui. varies per unit and type of program. Summer School.

Aesthetics	Leather
Architecture (lecture)	Lettering
Ceramics	Museum Staff Training
Drawing	Painting
Graphic Arts	Photography
Graphic Design	Printmaking
Handicrafts	Sculpture
History of Art & Archaeology	Wood
Jewelry	

CHABOT COLLEGE, Humanities Division, 25555 Hesperian Blvd, 94545. Tel: (415) 782-3000 Exten. 287
R. Glenn Leuning, Chmn; 240 FT, 400 PT instr. Estab. 1961; pub; D & E; ent. req. HS dipl; 2 yr; degree, A.A; schol; 27 L-SC, 5 LC; enrl. (Oct. 1969) D 6707, E 4462, maj. 293. Tui. free to res, non-res. $9.33 per quarter unit, 15 units of more, $420 per yr, fees $70 per quarter; no campus res.

Advertising Design	History of Art & Archaeology
Art Education	Illustration
Ceramics	Lettering
Commercial Art	Painting
Costume Design & Construction	Sculpture
Drafting	Stage Design
Drawing	Theatre Arts

Summer School: Dr. Shanon L. Christiansen, Dir; term of 6 wk. beginning July 6, 1970; 1969 enrl. 3410.

Art History	Introduction to Art
Drawing	Sculpture

HOLLYWOOD

HOLLYWOOD ART CENTER SCHOOL,* 2025 & 2027 N. Highland Ave, 90028. Tel: (213) 851-1103
Mona Lovins, Dir; 1 FT, 7 PT instr. Estab. 1912; pvt; D & E; ent. req. HS dipl, submission of art work; 3 yrs; cert; 6 SC; enrl. D 40, E 12. Tui. $1052 per yr, enrl. fee $50.

Advertising Design	Graphic Design
Ceramics	History of Art
Commercial Art	Illustration
Costume Design & Construction	Industrial Design
Display	Interior Design
Drafting	Lettering
Drawing	Painting
Fabric Design	Sculpture
Furniture	Textile Design
Graphic Arts	

HUNTINGTON BEACH

✠GOLDEN WEST COLLEGE, Fine and Applied Arts Division, 15744 Golden West St, 92647. Tel: (714) 892-7711 Exten. 553
John Wordes, Chmn. Estab. 1966; pub; D & E; ent. req. HS dipl. or 18 yr. of age; 2 yr; degree, A.A; 27 SC, 10 LC; enrl. D 8530, E 13,442.

Advertising Design	Jewelry
Animation	Lettering
Cartooning	Painting
Commercial Art	Photography
Display	Printmaking (Photo
Drawing	Silk-Screen & Etching)
Film Making	Sculpture
Graphic Design	Stage Design
History of Art	Textile Design
Illustration/Rendering	Theatre Arts

Summer School: Dr. Loren Moll, Dir.

IDYLLWILD

UNIVERSITY OF SOUTHERN CALIFORNIA, IDYLLWILD CAMPUS, Idyllwild School of Music and the Arts (ISOMATA), P.O. Box 38, 92349. Tel: (714) 659-2171
Dr. Philip N. James, Acting Exec. Dir; 7 instr, 7 asst. Estab. 1950; pvt; D; ent. req. HS dipl; no degrees; schol; 4 SC, 5 GC; enrl. summer 1975 434 student wk. Tui; campus res. Entirely a Summer School.

Ceramics	Indian Weaving
Handicrafts	Jewelry
Indian Basketweaving	Painting
Indian Pottery	Sculpture

Children's classes, pottery, painting, dance, drama, music; teen prog, painting & drawing, ceramics, music, dance, drama; enrl. 1477 student wk.

IRVINE

UNIVERSITY OF CALIFORNIA, IRVINE, School of Fine Arts, Studio Art Department, 92717. Tel: (714) 833-6648
Clayton Garrison, Dean; John Paul Jones, Acting Chmn; 8 FT, 4 PT. Estab. 1965; pub; D; ent. req. HS dipl; 4 yr; degrees, B.A.(Studio Art), M.F.A.(Art); schol; 24 SC, 2 LC, 4 GC. Tui. $228 per yr.

Ceramics	Painting
Costume Design & Construction	Sculpture
Drawing	Stage Design
History of Art & Archaeology	Theatre Arts
Motion Pictures	

KENTFIELD

COLLEGE OF MARIN, Department of Art, 94904.
Martin Stoelzel, Chmn; 12 FT, 21 PT instr. Estab. 1926; pub; D & E; ent. req. HS dipl. or ent. exam; 2 yr; A.A; schol; 43 SC, 8 LC; enrl. D 5000, E 2000. No tui, lab fees for art classes.

Advertising Design	History of Art and Archaeology
Architecture	Jewelry
Art Education	Painting
Ceramics	Photography
Costume Design & Construction	Sculpture
Drafting	Stage Design
Drawing	Textile Design
Graphic Arts	Theatre Arts

Adult hobby classes, jewelry, ceramics, painting, sculpture, photo, puppetry; tui. $6 plus lab fees of $5, $6 & $10.

Summer School: Cal Darrow, Dir.

LA JOLLA

UNIVERSITY OF CALIFORNIA, SAN DIEGO, Visual Arts Department, B-027, 92093.
Newton Harrison, Chmn; 16 FT, 3 PT instr. Estab. 1967; pub; D & E; ent req. HS dipl, univ. req; 4 yr; degrees, B.A.(Art), B.F.A.(Art), M.F.A. and (pending) B.A.(Art Hist); fel; enrl. maj. 150, grad. 35. Tui. $600, non-res, $2100; campus res. $1425 per yr.

Art Theory & Criticism	Painting
Drawing	Photography
History & Criticism of Film	Video
History of Art & Archaeology	

Summer School: Dr. Quelda Wilson, Dir; courses offered vary from year to year.

LA VERNE

LA VERNE COLLEGE, Division of Humanities, 1950 Third St, 91750. Tel: (714) 593-3511 Exten. 269
Joella Mahoney, Asst. Prof. of Art; 2 FT, 3 PT instr. Estab. 1899; pvt; D & E; ent. req. HS dipl; 4 yr; degree, B.A.(Art); schol; 12 SC, 4 LC; enrl. D 125, E 60, maj. 6. Tui. $2600 per yr; campus res. $1200.

Batik	Photography
Ceramics	Quilt & Patch Work
Drawing	Sculpture
History of Art & Archaeology	Stained Glass
Painting	Theatre Arts

LONG BEACH

CALIFORNIA STATE UNIVERSITY AT LONG BEACH, Art Department, 6101 E Seventh St, 90840. Tel: (213) 498-4376
Thomas Ferreira, Chmn; 50 FT, 25 PT instr. Estab. 1949; pub;

ent. req. HS grad, ent. exam; 4 yr; degrees, B.A, B.F.A, M.A,
M.F.A; 164 SC, 26 LC, 23 GC; enrl. 2000. Fees $180 per yr; campus
res $1050-1275 per yr.

Art Education	Illustration
Art History	Industrial Design
Ceramics	Interior Design
Display & Exhibition	Metalsmithing & Jewelry
Drawing	Painting
General Art	Printmaking
General Crafts	Sculpture
Graphic Design	Textile Design

    Summer School: Dr. Roderick Peck, Dir; $30 per unit for one
6 wk. session from June 22.

LOS ANGELES

ART IN ARCHITECTURE/JOSEPH YOUNG, 1434 S. Spaulding Ave,
    90019. Tel: (213) 933-1194
Dr. Joseph L. Young, FIAL, Dir; 3 FT, 1 PT instr. Estab. 1955;
pvt; D; co-ed; ent. req. HS dipl; schol; 2 yr; degree, M.A; 2 SC,
1 LC, 2 GC; enrl. D 15, maj. 3, grad. 3, others 9. Tui. $900,
monthly FT $100, monthly PT $50.

Drawing	Polyphonoptics
Graphic Design	Precast Concrete
History of Architecture	Sculpture
Mosaics	Stained Glass
Photography	

Program of workshop participation in actual commissions with
emphasis on creative apprenticeship of two years in all media.

EAST LOS ANGELES COLLEGE, Art Department, 5357 E. Brooklyn
    Ave, 90022. Tel: (213) 263-7261
William V. Newman, Chmn; 7 FT, 21 PT instr. Estab. 1949; pub;
D & E; ent. req. ent. exam; 2 yr; degree, A.A; 35 SC, 10 LC; enrl.
D 700, E 620, maj. 1320.

Advertising Design	Graphic Design
Aesthetics	History of Art & Archaeology
Ceramics	Illustration
Commercial Art	Jewelry
Costume Design & Construction	Lettering
Display	Painting
Drawing	Sculpture
Fashion Arts	Textile Design
Graphic Arts	Weaving

Children's classes, ceramics, drawing, painting, sculpture; enrl.
120.
    Summer School: Ethel Rose Orloff, Dir.

LOS ANGELES CITY COLLEGE,* Department of Art, 855 N.
    Vermont, 90029. Tel: (213) 663-9141
Dr. Russell D. Cangialosi, Chmn; 9 FT 2 PT instr. Estab. 1929; pub;
D & E; co-ed; ent. req. HS grad, over 18 yr. of age; 2 yr; degree, A.A;
26 SC, 6 LC. Tui. free, $6 reg, no campus res.

Advertising Design	Graphic Arts
Aesthetics	Graphic Design
Architecture	Handicrafts
Art Education	History of Art & Archaeology
Ceramics	Lettering
Commercial Art	Painting
Display	Sculpture
Drawing	

    Summer School: Dr. Russell D. Cangialosi, Chmn; restricted to
basic courses.

LOYOLA MARYMOUNT UNIVERSITY, Department of Art and Art
    History, 7750 Fordham Rd, 90045. Tel: (213) 670-1370 Exten. 380
Mary N. Parent, Chmn; 6 FT, 3 PT instr. Estab. 1948, merged with
Loyola Univ. 1973; pvt; D; ent. req. HS grad; 4 yr; degree, B.A;
schol; 28 SC, 21 LC; enrl. 350; maj. 80. Tui. undergrad. $1250 per
sem.(programs of 15-18 units); campus res, room $700, board
$720-$776 per acad. yr.

Aesthetics	Painting
African Art (every other year)	Photography
Art Education	Pre-Columbian Art (every other
Ceramics	year)
Drawing	Printmaking
History of Art & Archaeology	Sculpture
Jewelry & Metalsmithing	Teacher Training
Lettering	

Children's classes, painting and ceramics; tui. $20 per quarter; enrl.
30.

OCCIDENTAL COLLEGE, Art Department, 1600 Campus Rd, 90041.
    Tel: (213) 259-2749
Robert Hansen, Chmn; 5 FT, 3 PT instr. Estab. 1887; pvt; D; ent.
req. HS dipl, coll. transcript, SAT, recommendations; 4 yr; degree,

B.A; coll. schol. & grants according to need; 19 SC, 25 LC, 5 GC;
enrl. maj. 50, others 300, coll. 1800. Tui. $1007, res. $400-$555
per term (3 terms, plus summer session).

Art Education	Painting
Art History	Sculpture
Drawing	Theory & Criticism
Graphics	

    Summer School: Dr. Lewis Owen, Dean of Faculty; tui. $383 per
course ($1067 for 3 courses); enrl. art dept. 25, school 400.

Art Education	Ceramics (SC)
Art History	Glass Blowing (SC)

OTIS ART INSTITUTE of Los Angeles County, 2401 Wilshire Blvd,
    90057. Tel: (213) 387-5288
Gurdon Woods, Dir; Stewart Baron, Dean; 12 FT, 17 PT instr.
Estab. 1918; pub; D & E; 4 yr. starting at 3rd yr. coll. level;
degrees, B.F.A, M.F.A; schol; ent. req. 30 sem. hr. academic subjects and 20-30 sem. hr. of art, portfolio of art work; ent. req. grad.
level B.F.A. and portfolio; enrl. degree program 185. Tui. $500
per sem. Maj. and Minor chosen from the following depts:

Ceramics	Painting
Drawing	Printmaking
Inter-media	Sculpture

    Summer Session: 6 wk. undergrad. and grad. courses in all
depts. except academic; $56 or $135 per course D & E; 6 unit
maximum.

UNIVERSITY OF CALIFORNIA, LOS ANGELES, Department of Art,
    405 Hilgard Ave, 90024. Tel: (213) 825-1770
Raymond Brown, Acting Chmn; 53 instr. Estab. 1919; pub; 4 yr;
degrees, A.B, M.A, M.F.A, Ph.D; teaching assistantships; enrl.
maj. 700. General Catalog may be obtained from Office of Admis.
for information on admis. req, fees, schol.

Ceramics Design	New Forms & Concepts
Costume Design	Painting
Drawing	Photography
Glass Design	Prints
Graphic Design	Sculpture
History of Art	Textiles Design
Industrial Design	Video Design

UNIVERSITY OF SOUTHERN CALIFORNIA, Department of Fine
    Arts, 90007. Tel: (213) 746-2788
Charles D. Weber, Assoc. Dean; 16 FT, 6 PT instr. Fine Arts estab.
1887; pvt; D & E; 4 yr; degrees, A.B, B.F.A, A.M, M.F.A, Ph.D; enrl.
maj. in Fine Arts 187. Tui. $108 per unit.

Art Education	Three-Dimensional Arts
Art History	Two-Dimensional Arts

Junior art program, 2-dimensional & 3-dimensional art; tui. $30
per sem; enrl. 55.
    Summer School: Tui. $108 per unit; 7 wk. session from June
18-August 4.

WOODBURY COLLEGE,* Division of Professional Arts, 1027
    Wilshire Blvd, 90017. Tel: (213) 482-8491
Rosalie F. Utterbach, Chmn. Estab. 1884; pvt; D & E; Accredited
Western Assoc of Schools & Coll. as a 5 yr. specialized institution
of higher learning; degree, B.S. in Professional Arts; enrl. maj.
525, others 1600; accelerated study.

Art Education	Fashion Design
Commercial Art	Interior Design

MALIBU

PEPPERDINE UNIVERSITY,* Fine Arts Division, 24255 Pacific
    Coast Hwy, 90265.
L. E. McCommas, Chmn; 4 FT, 1 PT instr. Estab. 1937; pvt; D;
grad. 8 trimesters, with credential 10 trimesters; degrees, B.A,
M.A; schol; 5 LC, 23 workshop; enrl. maj. 35, others 135. Tui. 2
trimesters $2550, room and board $1250; campus res. semi-pro-
fessional.
Crafts
Fine Arts
Teacher Training (Professional, 5 yr)
    Summer School: Dr. Olaf Tegner, Dir; tui. $82 sem. unit.

MARYSVILLE

YUBA COLLEGE, Fine Arts Division, North Beale Rd, 95901.
    Tel: (916) 742-7351
Carol McGee, Chmn; 14 FT, PT (varies) instr. Estab. 1927; pub;
D & E; ent. req. HS grad. or 18 yr. of age; 2 yr; degree, A.A;
schol; 23 SC, 2 LC; enrl. total 1437, maj. 493. Tui. none for res,
non-res $420 per yr, foreign (Visa) $200 per yr; campus res. $1200
per yr.

Advertising Design	Lettering
Aesthetics	Painting

Art Education	Photography
Ceramics	Sculpture
Drafting	Stage Design
Drawing	Theatre Arts
Graphic Arts	

Summer School: Rex McDougal, Dean & Assoc. Dean Community Educ. Serv; term of 6 wk. beginning mid-June; 1969 enrl. 500.
Full curriculum, plus:

Home Decorative Arts	Navajo Silversmithing
Lapidary	Non-Loom Weaving

MENDOCINO

MENDOCINO ART CENTER, 540 Little Lake St, P.O. Box 36, 95460. Tel: (707) 937-5818
William Zacha, Dir. Estab. 1959; non-profit, tax-exempt pvt. corporation; D & E; ent. req. interest in art advancement; no degrees granted; enrl. summer session, average daily enrollment 100, can accomodate 11 res. students during the winter. Tui. for a single workshop is $35 per wk, $21 per weekend, res. program $3000, incl. room, board, art supplies and all tui. for a minimum of 60 workshops in as many media.

Aesthetics	Painting
Basketry	Patternmaking
Batik	Photography
Bookbinding	Rubbings
Ceramics	Sculpture
Drawing	Serigraphy
Dyeing	Sewing
Graphic Arts	Spinning
History of Art & Archaeology	Stage Design
Jewelry	Stained Glass
Kitemaking	Stitchery
Life Drawing	Textile Design
Macrame	Theatre Arts
Music	Weaving
Origami	

Adult hobby classes; tui. $35 for 15 hour workshop, $21 for 9 hour workshop, 9 hours weekend; enrl. average 8. Children's classes; tui. $15 for 15 hour workshop; enrl. class limited to 14.

Summer School: Ten week session, June 24 through August 30.

MODESTO

MODESTO JUNIOR COLLEGE, Art Department, College Ave, 95350. Tel: (209) 526-2000 Exten. 308
Paul J. Corrigan, Chmn; 8 FT, 16 PT instr. Estab. 1921; pub; D & E; ent. req. HS dipl or special status; 2 yr; degree, A.A; schol; 37 SC, 5 LC; enrl. total 1563. Tui. for non-res and foreign students only.

Advertising Design	Jewelry
Ceramics	Lapidary
Commercial Art	Lettering
Display	Metal Enameling
Drafting	Painting
Drawing	Photography
Graphic Arts	Sculpture
Graphic Design	Theatre Arts
History of Art & Archaeology	

Summer School: Dr. Julius Manrique, Dir; courses offered, Ceramics, Drawing, Watercolor; term of 6 wk. beginning June 14.

MONTEREY

MONTEREY PENINSULA COLLEGE, Division of Creative Arts, Art Department, 980 Fremont St, 93940.
Tel: (408) 649-1150 Exten. 229
J. L. Hysong, Chmn; 6 FT, 4 PT instr. Estab. 1947; pub; D & E; ent. req. HS dipl, ent. exam. for non-HS grad, 18 yr; 2 yr; degrees, A.A, A.S; schol; 13 SC, 17 LC; enrl. D 1343, E 623, maj. 160. Tui. free to res, non-res. $28 per unit; no campus res.

Aesthetics	Metal Arts
Ceramics	Painting
Design	Sketching
Drawing	Weaving
History of Art & Archaeology	

Summer School: Morgan Stock, Chmn. Div. of Creative Arts; tui. same as above for 6 wk. term beginning 2nd Mon. in June; 1969 enrl. 130. Two wk. drawing, design, ceramics and painting institutes (60 hr) offered in addition.

Art History	Drawing
Design	Painting

NORTHRIDGE

CALIFORNIA STATE UNIVERSITY, NORTHRIDGE,* Department of Art 2-Dimensional Media, 18111 Nordhoff St, 91324. Tel: (213) 885-2348
William Mitchell, Chmn; 19 FT, 3 PT instr. Estab. 1956; pub; D, E & Exten; ent. req. HS grad; 4-5 yr; degrees, B.A, M.A; enrl. maj. undergrad. 1000, grad. 65. Tui. res. $82 per sem. over 6 units, $62 under 6 units.

Drawing	Photography
Graphic Design	Printmaking
Painting	

Summer School: John J. Hannah, Acting Chmn; $27 per unit for 6 wk.

NORWALK

CERRITOS COMMUNITY COLLEGE, Art Department, 11110 Alondra Blvd, 90650.
Wilburt Fenner, Chmn; 9 FT, 20 PT instr. Estab. 1956; pub; D & E; ent. req. HS dipl. or 18 yr. of age; 2 yr; degree, A.A; schol; 36 SC, 6 LC. Tui. free for res, non-res. $29 per unit.

Aesthetics	History of Art & Archaeology
Architecture	Jewelry
Ceramics	Lettering
Commercial Art	Museum Staff Training
Display	Painting
Drawing	Photography
General Crafts	Sculpture
Graphic Arts	Theatre Arts
Graphic Design	

OAKLAND

CALIFORNIA COLLEGE OF ARTS AND CRAFTS, 5212 Broadway, 94618. Tel: (415) 653-8118
Harry X. Ford, Pres; 84 FT, 34 PT instr. Estab. 1907; pvt; ent. req. HS grad. with C average; 4 yr; degrees, B.F.A, M.F.A, M.A.Ed; enrl. 1090. Tui. per trimester $1195 entering, $1090 continuing. Teaching Credential Program, concurrently with Art Major for B.F.A. or as post-Baccalaureate program.

Ceramics	Metal Arts
Design	Painting
Drawing	Photo
Environmental Design	Printmaking
Film	Sculpture
General Crafts	TV
General Fine Arts	Textile Arts
Glass	Teacher Education
Graphic Design	

Sat. classes for children.

Summer School: Tui. $100 entering, $71 continuing per unit for each session from May 12 to June 12, June 16 to July 17 or July 21 to Aug. 21.

HOLY NAMES COLLEGE, Art Department, 3500 Mountain Blvd, 94619. Tel: (415) 436-0111
Robert G. Yaryan, Chmn; 2 FT, 7 PT instr. Estab. 1917; pvt; D & E; ent. req. HS dipl; 4 yr; degree, B.A; schol; 30 SC, 3 LC. Tui. $1700 per yr; campus res. $700.

Art Education	Lettering
Bookbinding	Painting
Calligraphy	Photography
Ceramics	Printmaking
Drawing	Textile Design
History of Art & Archaeology	Weaving
Jewelry	

LANEY COLLEGE,* Art Department, 900 Fallon St, 94607.
Carol Joy & Ted Odza, Chmn; 10 FT, 9 PT instr. Estab. 1962; pub; D & E; ent. req. HS dipl; 2 yr; degree, A.A; 52 SC, 8 LC; enrl. art dept. D 1600, E 600.

Advertising Design	Illustration
Architecture	Industrial Design
Cartooning	Interior Design
Ceramics	Jewelry
Commercial Art	Kinetic Art
Costume Design and Construction	Landscape Architecture
Display	Lettering
Drafting	Macrame
Drawing	Painting
Fashion Arts	Photography
Graphic Arts	Sculpture
Graphic Design	Stage Design
History of Art & Archaeology	Textile Design
	Theatre Arts

MILLS COLLEGE, Division of Fine Arts, Art Department, 94613.
Tel: (415) 632-2700
Robert A. Dhaemers, Head; 7 FT, 3 PT instr. Estab. 1852; pvt; D;
W (men in GC); 4 & 6 yrs; degrees, B.A, M.F.A; schl; enrl. under-
grad. 900, maj. in Art Technique 212, maj. in Art History, 125,
grad. 150, maj. in Art Technique 20. Tui. $2925, grad. $1270.

Art History (undergrad)	Fine Arts (grad)
Art Technique (undergrad)	Teacher Training (with Dept. Educ)

PALM DESERT

COLLEGE OF THE DESERT, Art Department, 43-500 Monterey Ave,
92260. Tel: (714) 346-8041
Hovak Najarian, Chmn; 3 FT, 4 PT instr. Estab. 1962; pub; D & E;
ent. req. HS dipl, ent. exam; 2 yr; degree, A.A; schl; 10 SC, 3 LC;
enrl. D 150, E 150, maj. 15. No tui. fee; no campus res.

Ceramics	Painting
Crafts	Photography
Drawing	Printmaking
History of Art	Sculpture
Introduction to Art	

PASADENA

ART CENTER COLLEGE OF DESIGN, 1700 Lida St, 91103.
Tel: (213) 577-1700
Don Kubly, Dir. & Pres; 40 FT, 84 PT instr. Estab. 1930; pvt;
D & E; 4 yr; degrees; 168 SC, 82 LC, 29 GC; enrl. D & E approx.
1030. Tui. $1100 (15 wk. trimester).

Advertising Design	Industrial Design
Advertising Illustration	Painting
Environmental Design	Photography & Film
Fashion Illustration	Product Design
Graphic Design & Packaging	Transportation Design
Illustration	

PASADENA CITY COLLEGE, Art Department, 1570 E. Colorado
Blvd, 91106.
Dr. Armen Sarafian, Pres; Richard F. Cassady, Chmn; D 22 FT,
E 20 PT instr. Estab. 1928; pub; 2 yr; degree, A.A; schl; 40 SC,
5 LC.

Advertising Design	Drawing & Painting
Apparel Arts	Graphics
Art History	Illustration
Ceramics	Interior Design
Cinematography	Photography
Crafts	Sculpture
Design	

Summer School: William G. Norris, Admin. Dean; 2 sessions of
6 wk. beginning 3rd wk. in June.

PORTERVILLE

PORTERVILLE COLLEGE, Division of Fine and Applied Arts, 900
S. Main St, 93257. Tel: (209) 781-3130
Mike Rost, Chmn; 5 FT, 2 PT art instr. Estab. 1927; pub; D & E;
ent. req. HS dipl, over 18 yr. age; 2 yr; degrees, A.A, A.S;
schl; 15 SC, 3 LC; enrl. D 190, E 105, maj. 10. Tui. free for
res. and approved foreign students, non-res. $547.50 per sem;
no campus res.

Ceramics	Painting
Drafting	Photography
Drawing	Sculpture
Graphic Arts	Stage Design
History of Art & Archaeology	Teacher Training
Jewelry	Theatre Arts
Leather	Weaving
Mosacis	

Summer School: Nero Pruitt, Dir; courses offered same as
above; tui. non-res. $37 per unit for term of 6 wk. beginning
June 7; enrl. 600.

REDDING

SHASTA COLLEGE,* Art Department, Old Oregon Trail, 96001.
Tel: (916) 241-3523
Donald C. Boyd, Chmn. Creative Arts; 7 FT, 5 PT instr. Estab.
1950; pub; D & E; ent. req. HS dipl; 2 yrs; degree, A.A; schl; 19
SC, 3 LC; enrl. D 3500, E 5000. Campus res. $840.

Ceramics	History of Art & Archaeology
Commercial Art	Jewelry
Drawing	Painting
Figure Drawing	Pen, Brush & Ink
Form, Design & Color	Photography
Freehand Drawing	Printmaking

General Crafts	Sculpture
Glass Blowing	Shades, Shadows & Perspective
Handicrafts	Watercolor

REDLANDS

UNIVERSITY OF REDLANDS,* Department of Art, 1200 W. Colton
Ave, 92373.
Vernon Dornbach, Jr, Chmn; 5 FT instr. Estab. 1909; pvt; D & E;
ent. req. HS grad, ent. exam; 4 yr; degrees, B.A, B.S, M.A, M.E,
M.A.T; schol. and fel; 18 SC, 12 LC; enrl. 1500. Tui. $1950; campus
res.

Art History	Jewelry
Ceramics	Painting
Drawing & Painting	Sculpture
Ethnic Art	Teacher Training
Graphic Arts	

Summer School: Dr. William Umbach, Dir; tui. $42.50 per unit,
three terms (two for 5 wk. and one for 3 wk), June 1-19, June 22-
July 24, and July 23-Aug. 28.

RIVERSIDE

LOMA LINDA UNIVERSITY, Art Department, 92505.
Tel: (714) 785-2170
R. A. Churches, Head; 3 FT, 3 PT instr. Estab. 1950; den; D & E;
ent. req. HS dipl, ent. exam; 4 yrs; degrees, B.A, B.S; schol; 19 SC,
6 LC, 1 GC; enrl. D 800, E 150, maj. 40, grad students 5. Tui.
$1800 per yr; campus res. $2919 with full tui, 16 units or more per
quarter.

Aesthetics	Occupational Therapy
Art Education	Painting
Ceramics	Photography
Drafting	Sculpture
Drawing	Stained Glass
History of Art & Archaeology	Teacher Training

Adult hobby classes, subjects on demand; tui. $30 per course.

RIVERSIDE CITY COLLEGE, Fine Arts Division, Department of
Art, 4800 Magnolia Ave, 92506. Tel: (714) 684-3240 Exten. 267
O. K. Harry, Head; 6 FT, 4 PT instr. Estab. 1917; pub; D & E;
ent. req. HS dipl. or over 18 yr. age; 2 yr; degree, A.A; 20 SC,
3 LC; enrl. D 910, E 175. Tui. free, non-res. $31 per unit, maximum
$465 per sem; no campus res.

Advertising Design	History of Art & Archaeology
Art Education	Illustration
Ceramics	Jewelry
Commercial Art	Lettering
Drawing	Painting
Graphic Arts	Sculpture
Graphic Design	Teacher Training

Summer School: James Duncan, Dir; term of 6 wk. beginning
June 21, 1976; enrl. 225.

Art for Elementary Teachers	Drawing
Art History	Painting
Ceramics	Sculpture

UNIVERSITY OF CALIFORNIA, RIVERSIDE, College of Humanities
and Social Sciences, Department of Art History, 92507.
Tel: (714) 787-4241
Thomas O. Pelzel, Chmn; 4 FT, 1 PT instr. Estab. 1962; pub; D;
ent. req. HS dipl, ent. exam; 4 yr; degrees, B.A, M.A; 17 LC, 5 GC;
enrl. D 135, maj. 20.

Division of Fine Arts, Program in Art (Studio).
Tel: (714) 787-4621
William Bradshaw, Chmn; 4 FT, 1 PT instr. Degree, B.A; 14 SC;
enrl. D 214, maj. 50.

Drawing	Painting
Graphic Arts	Photography

Summer School: Thomas Broadbent, Dir.

ROHNERT PARK

CALIFORNIA STATE COLLEGE, SONOMA, Art Department, 1801
E. Cotati Ave, 94928. Tel: (707) 664-2151
Susan Moulton, Chmn; 11 FT, 5 PT. Estab. 1961; pub; D; ent. req.
HS dipl; 4 yr; degrees, B.A.(Art Studio), B.A.(Art History); 50 SC,
25 LC; enrl. D approx. 1200, maj. 286, unclassified grad. in art
therapy 20. Tui. FT $86 per sem, PT $77 per sem, non-res.
$650 per sem.

Aesthetics	History of Architecture
Animation	History of Art & Archaeology
Art Education	Painting
Ceramics	Photography

Drawing	Sculpture
Graphic Arts	Theatre Arts
Graphic Design	

Summer School: Len Swensen, Dir; courses offered, Art Education, Crafts; tui. $30 per unit for term of 10 wk.

SACRAMENTO

AMERICAN RIVER COLLEGE, Department of Art, 4700 College Oak Dr, 95841.
James Kaneko, Chmn; 8 FT, 3 PT instr. Estab. 1957; pub; D & E; ent. req. HS grad. or 18 yr. old; 2 yr; degrees, A.A, 2 yr. terminal cert; schol; 17 SC, 4 LC; enrl. D 1309, E 262, maj. 371.

Advertising Design	Jewelry
Art Education Crafts for Teachers	Lettering/Calligraphy
	Painting
Ceramics	Photography & Film Making
Drafting	Printmaking
Drawing	Stained Glass
History of Art	Theatre Arts

Summer School: Owen Stewart, Dir; 6 wk. beginning June 22; enrl. 3.

Basic Design	Introduction to Art
Drawing	Painting

CALIFORNIA STATE UNIVERSITY, SACRAMENTO, Department of Art, 6000 Jay St, 95819. Tel: (916) 454-6166
R. L. Bohr, Chmn; 30 FT instr. Estab. 1950; pub; D; ent. req. HS grad, ent. exam; 4 yr; degrees, B.A, M.A; schol; 40 SC, 18 LC, 12 GC; enrl. maj. 606.

Art Education	Drawing
Art History	Jewelry
Ceramics	Painting
Cinematography	Printmaking
Crafts	Sculpture

Summer School: R. L. Bohr, Dir; 1 wk. pre-session, 6 wk; enrl. 225.

SACRAMENTO CITY COLLEGE, Division of Humanities and Fine Arts, 3835 Freeport Blvd, 95822. Tel: (916) 449-7551
M. W. Nunes, Chmn; 12 FT, 2 PT instr. Estab. 1916; pub; D & E; ent. req. HS dipl; 2 yr; degrees, A.A, A.S; schol; 16 SC, 9 LC. No tui; no campus res.

Advertising Design	History of Art & Archaeology
Art Education	Painting
Ceramics	Photography
Commercial Art	Sculpture
Drawing	Theatre Arts
Graphic Arts	

Summer School: Herbert Blossom, Dir; courses offered similar to regular session; no tui.

SALINAS

HARTNELL COLLEGE, Art and Photography Departments, 156 Homestead Ave, 93901. Tel: (408) 758-8211
Robert Lee, Chmn. Fine Arts; 3 FT, 3 PT instr. Estab. 1922; pub; D & E; ent. req. HS dipl; 2 yr; degree, A.A; 14 SC, 3 LC; enrl. D 350, E 160, maj. 30. Tui. free; no campus res.

Architecture	Jewelry
Ceramics	Metalsmithing
Commercial Art	Painting
Drafting	Photography
Drawing	Sculpture
Graphic Arts	Stage Design
History of Art & Archaeology	Theatre Arts

Summer School: Dr. Norman Berdan, Dir; tui. free; begins approx. June 15; enrl. 150.

Art Appreciation	Film Making
Ceramics	Photography
Drawing	

SAN BERNARDINO

CALIFORNIA STATE COLLEGE, SAN BERNARDINO, Art Department, 550 State College Pkwy, 92407. Tel: (714) 887-7459
Roger Lintault, Chmn; 6 FT, 8 PT instr. Estab. 1965; pub; D & E; ent. req. HS dipl, ent. exam; 4 yr; degree, B.A; schol; 31 SC, 14 LC, 5 GC; enrl. D 260, E 90, maj. 120. Tui. $192 per yr; campus res. $1150.

Art Education	Photography
Ceramics	Printmaking
Drawing	Sculpture
Glassblowing	Weaving

History of Art & Archaeology	Wood Crafts Design
Painting	

Summer School: Stephen A. Bowles, Dean; tui. $20 per unit.

Art Education	Ceramics
Art History	Woodworking

SAN BERNARDINO VALLEY COLLEGE, Art Department, 701 S. Mt. Vernon Ave, 92403. Tel: (714) 885-9231
David Lawrence, Head; 224 FT, 510 PT instr. Estab. 1926; pub; D & E; ent. req. HS dipl, 18 yr. of age; 2 yr; degrees, A.A, A.S; schol; enrl. D 750, E 400, maj. 230. Tui. free to res, non-res. $1020 per yr; no campus res.

Advertising Design	Drawing
Architecture	History of Art & Archaeology
Art Education	Landscape Architecture
Artistic Weaving	Lettering
Ceramics	Photography
Costume Design & Construction	Sculpture
Drafting	Theatre Arts

Summer School: Dr. Harold Chandler, Dir; no tui.

SAN DIEGO

CALIFORNIA STATE UNIVERSITY, SAN DIEGO, Department of Art, 5402 College Ave, 92182. Tel: (714) 286-6511
Winifred H. Higgins, Chmn; 32 FT, 20 PT instr. Estab. 1897; pub; D & E; ent. req. HS dipl, ent. exam, portfolio; 4 yr; degrees, B.A, M.A; schol; 110 SC, 33 LC, 32 GC; enrl. D 4000, maj. 1200, grad. 150. Tui. $161; campus res. $576 room incl. deposit, $560 board.

Advertising Design	Handicrafts
Aesthetics	History of Art & Archaeology
Art Education	Illustration
Ceramics	Industrial Design
Commercial Art	Jewelry
Costume Design & Construction	Lettering
Display	Museum Staff Training
Drawing	Painting
Environmental Design	Photography
Fashion Arts	Sculpture
Graphic Arts	Teacher Training
Graphic Design	Textile Design

Summer School: Winifred H. Higgins, Dir; tui. $27 per unit for term of six 3 wk. courses beginning June & Aug; 1973 enrl. 175.

MESA COLLEGE, Fine Arts Department, Mesa College Dr, 92111. Tel: (714) 279-2300 Exten. 239
Albert J. Lewis, Chmn; 10 FT, 2 PT instr. Estab. 1962; pub; D & E; ent. req. ent. exam; 2 yr; degree, A.A.(Fine Arts); 17 SC, 4 LC; total coll. enrl. D 8500, E 5000, maj. 150. Tui. free, student fees; no campus res.

Ceramics	Life Drawing
Drawing	Orientation
Fibers	Painting
General Crafts	Sculpture
History of Art	Three-Dimensional Design
Jewelry	Two-Dimensional Design
Lettering	

Summer School: Tui. free; 2 sessions of 6 wk. each; enrl. 92 D.

Ceramics	Design
Crafts	Drawing

UNITED STATES INTERNATIONAL UNIVERSITY, School of Performing and Visual Arts, 10455 Pomerado Rd, 92131. Tel: (714) 271-4300
Netter Worthington, Dir. Visual Arts & Dean Sch; 4 FT, 2 PT instr. Estab. 1966; pvt; D; ent. req. HS dipl, interview, portfolio, letters of recommendation; 4 yr; B.A.(Advertising, Costume, Set Design, Painting & Drawing or Teaching), B.F.A; schol; 27 SC, 4 LC; enrl. D 300. Tui. $850 per quarter, $60 per unit; campus res. $545 per quarter.

Advertising Design	Graphic Design
Art Education	History of Art & Archaeology
Ceramics	Illustration
Commercial Art	Painting
Costume Design & Construction	Sculpture
Drafting	Stage Design
Drawing	Teacher Training
Fashion Arts	Theatre Arts
Graphic Arts	

Summer School: Netter Worthington, Dir; courses offered, Drawing, Introduction to Visual Thinking, Painting; tui. $60 per unit for term of 8 wk. beginning June 14.

UNIVERSITY OF SAN DIEGO, Art Department, Alcala Park, 92110. Tel: (714) 291-6480
Therese Truitt Whitcomb, Chmn; 2 FT, 3 PT instr. Estab. 1952;

pvt; D & E; ent. req. HS dipl, SAT; 4 yr; degree, B.A; schol;
19 SC, 7 LC; enrl. univ. 2300, maj. 50. Tui. $65 per unit; campus
res. $1400.

Art in Elementary Education	History of Modern Art
Ceramics	History of Oriental Art
Design	Painting
Drawing	Photography
Enameling	Printmaking
Exhibition Design	Sculpture
History of American Art	Survey of Art History
History of Art Seminars	Weaving
History of Contemporary Art	

Summer School: Dr. Raymond Brandes, Dir; 4 courses offered;
tui. $65 per unit for terms of 3 wk, 6 wk, 3 wk. beginning June 1.

SAN FRANCISCO

ACADEMY OF ART COLLEGE, 625 Sutter St, 94102.
  Tel: (415) 673-4200
Richard A. Stephens, Pres; 20 FT, 10 PT instr. Estab. 1928; pvt;
D & E; ent. req. HS dipl, transcripts, portfolio (12 current pieces);
4 yr; degrees, cert, B.F.A, co-op B.F.A through Univ. of San
Francisco; schol; 50 SC, 50 LC; enrl. D 550, E 150, maj. 490. Tui.
$1500 per yr, $65 per single unit.

Advertising Design	History of Art
Ceramics	Illustration
Commercial Art	Jewelry
Drawing	Painting
Fashion Arts	Photography
Graphic Arts	Sculpture
Graphic Design	

Summer School: Richard A. Stephens, Dir; courses offered same
as above; tui. $375 for term of 6 wk. beginning June 14; enrl. 350.

ARTHUR W. PALMER ART SCHOOL, Studio 303, 545 Sutter St,
  94102. Tel: (415) 982-0152
Arthur W. Palmer, Head. Estab. 1945; pvt; D & E; ent. req. ent.
exam; non-credit; 4 SC. Tui. four 3 hr. lessons $30.
Drawing
Painting
Portrait Drawing & Painting
Adult hobby classes, portrait, figure, still life; tui. 4 lessons for
$30; continuous enrl.

BRANDON ART SCHOOL, 2441 Balboa St,
  94121.
Warren Brandon, Head; 3 FT, 3 PT instr. Estab. 1960; pvt; D & E;
no ent. req; no degrees; 4 SC. Tui. $50 per 8 wk. or 8 lesson
course. Summer School.

Art Education	History of Art & Archaeology
Drawing	Painting

LONE MOUNTAIN COLLEGE, Art Department, 2800 Turk Blvd,
  94118. Tel: (415) 752-7000 Exten. 240/241
Robert J. Brawley, Chmn; 3 FT, 9 PT instr. Estab. 1930 as San
Francisco Coll. for Women, became Lone Mountain Coll. 1970;
pvt; D & E; ent. req. HS dipl, ent. exam; 4 yr; degrees B.A, B.F.A,
M.A, M.F.A; schol; 32 SC, 14 LC, 25 GC; enrl. maj. 75, grad.
61. Tui. $2176; campus res. $1400.

Advertising Design	Lettering
Aesthetics	Museum Staff Training
Art Education	Occupational Therapy
Ceramics	Painting
Commercial Art	Photography
Costume Design & Construction	Sculpture
Drawing	Stage Design
Fashion Arts	Stained Glass
Graphic Arts	Teacher Training
Graphic Design	Textile Design
Handicrafts	Theatre Arts
History of Art	Weaving
Jewelry	

Summer School: Robert Brawley, Dir; Studio Art Program; tui.
$580 for term of 6 wks; enrl. 25.

RUDOLPH SCHAEFFER SCHOOL OF DESIGN, 2255 Mariposa St,
  94110. Tel: (415) 863-0715
Rudolph Schaeffer, Dir; 7 FT, 4 PT instr. Estab. 1926; pvt; D & E;
schol; 3 yr. for dipl. in Interior Design, Color Design; 4 LC, 7 SC;
enrl. 20 per class. Tui. $2000.

Art of Arrangement	Design
Asian and Western Art	Drawing & Drafting
Color	Humanities
Color-Design	Interior Design
Crafts	Presentational Design

Summer School: One 5 wk. session.

SAN FRANCISCO ART INSTITUTE (formerly California School of
  Fine Arts), 800 Chestnut St, 04133. Tel: (415) 771-7020
Arnold Herstand, Pres; Roy Ascott, Dean of the College; Alice
Erskine, Dean for Student Affairs. Dept. Chmn: Jack Fulton,
Photography; Bill Geis, Sculpture; Richard Graf, Printmaking;
David Hannah, Painting; Larry Jordan, Filmmaking; Raymond
Mondini, World Studies. Estab. 1871; pvt; 3 yr; degrees, B.F.A,
M.F.A; schol. and grants-in-aid; enrl. FT, 676, PT 269. Tui.
$1080 per sem.

Ceramics	Photography
Drawing	Printmaking
Filmmaking	Sculpture
Painting	World Studies

Summer School: Three 4 wk. sessions; tui. $300 per course.

SAN FRANCISCO COMMUNITY COLLEGE, Department of Art, 50
  Phelan Ave, 94112. Tel: (415) 587-7272 Exten. 158
Richard Moquin, Chmn; 17 FT, 22 PT instr. Estab. 1935; pub;
D & E; ent. req, ent. exam; 2 yrs; degree, A.A; 18-20 SC, 6 LC;
enrl. D 3500, E 350. No tui.

Advertising Design	History of Art & Archaeology
Aesthetics	Illustration
Architecture	Industrial Design
Art Education	Jewelry
Basic Design	Landscape Architecture
Ceramics	Lettering
Commercial Art	Metal Arts
Drafting	Painting
Drawing	Photography
Fashion Arts	Sculpture
Graphic Arts	Stage Design
Graphic Design	Theatre Arts
Handicrafts	

Summer School: Richard Moquin, Chmn; courses offered same as
regular yr.

SAN FRANCISCO STATE UNIVERSITY, School of Creative Arts,
  Department of Visual Arts, 1600 Holloway Ave, 94132.
  Tel: (415) 469-2176
Seymour Locks, Chmn; 29 FT, 8 PT instr. Estab. 1899; pub; 4 yr;
degrees, B.A, M.A; 70 Lab.C and SC, 10 LC; enrl. maj. 500, master
candidates 80. Tui. $95.50 per sem.

Art Education	Painting
Art History	Photography
Ceramics	Printmaking
Design	Sculpture
Metal Arts-Jewelry	Textiles

SAN JOSE

SAN JOSE CITY COLLEGE, Department of Art, 2100 Moorpark Ave,
  95128. Tel: (408) 298-2181 Exten. 214
Rotating chmn; 8 FT, 12 PT instr. Estab. 1923; pub; D & E; ent. req.
HS dipl, over 18 who are deemed to profit from education; 2 yr;
degree, A.A; 10 SC, 3 LC; enrl. D 6000, E 8000.

Art Education	History of Art & Archaeology
Ceramics	Jewelry
Commercial Art	Lettering
Crafts	Painting
Drawing	Printmaking
Figure Drawing	Sculpture

Adult hobby classes, beginning painting for seniors; no tui; enrl.
18-24.

SAN JOSE STATE UNIVERSITY, Art Department, 95192.
  Tel: (408) 277-2541
Kathleen Cohen, Chmn; 60 instr. Estab. 1921; pub; 4 yr; degrees,
B.A, M.A.(Art), M.F.A.(Art); 108 SC, 25 LC, 30 Lab.C, 34 GC; enrl.
maj. 1400, course enrl. 4737. Fee $72 per sem.

Graphic Design	Teacher Training (with
Interior Design	Department of Education)

SAN LUIS OBISPO

CALIFORNIA POLYTECHNIC STATE UNIVERSITY AT SAN LUIS
  OBISPO, School of Communicative Arts and Humanities, Art
  Department, 93407.
Dr. Thomas V. Johnston, Head; 10 FT, 2 PT instr. Pub; D & E;
ent req. HS dipl, ent. exam; degrees, B.S, B.A.(no art maj);
26 SC, 11 LC. Tui $67, PT $53-$61 per quarter, non-res. $1299

Advertising Design	Leather
Ceramics	Metals
Display	Painting
Drawing	Plastics
Glassblowing	Sculpture
Graphic Arts	Teacher Training

Graphic Design
History of Art & Archaeology
Jewelry

Textile Design
Wood

Adult hobby classes, sculpture, painting, fiber design, weaving; tui. $16.25 per unit; enrl. 24 per class.

Summer School: Fred Wolf, Dir. of program for entire university; variable courses; tui. $18 per unit for term of 4 wk. beginning June 18; 1973 art dept. enrl. 48.

SAN MARCOS

PALOMAR COLLEGE, Art Department, 92069.
Tel: (714) 744-1150
Rita A. White, Chmn; 10 FT, 5 PT instr. Estab. 1950; pub; D & E; ent. req. ent. exam; 2 yr; degree, A.A; 51 SC, 5 LC; enrl. D 11,000, E 5000, maj. 150. Tui. no fee; no campus res.

Aesthetics
Ceramics
Commercial Art
Drawing
General Crafts
Glass Blowing
Graphic Arts
Graphic Design
History of Art & Archaeology

Jewelry/Metalsmithing
Illustration
Lettering
Life Drawing
Museum Staff Training (Gallery
    Design)
Painting
Sculpture

Summer School: Howard Brubeck, Dir.

SANTA ANA

SANTA ANA COLLEGE, Art Department, 17th at Bristol, 92706.
Tel: (714) 835-3000 Exten. 285
James Utter, Chmn; 11 FT, 18 PT instr. Estab. 1915; pub; D & E; ent. req. HS dipl, 18 yr. of age; 2 yr; degrees, A.A.(Art, Commercial Art); 31 SC, 6 LC; enrl. D 970, E 542, maj. 600. Tui. free; no campus res.

Advertising Design
Ceramics
Commercial Art
Costume Design & Construction
Drafting
Drawing
Fashion Arts
Graphic Arts

History of Art & Archaeology
Illustration
Lettering
Painting
Photography
Sculpture
Stage Design
Theatre Arts

Summer School: Dean Brunell, Dir; courses offered, Art Appreciation, Basic Photography, Ceramics; tui. free for term of 8 wk.

SANTA BARBARA

UNIVERSITY OF CALIFORNIA, Department of Art, 93106.
Tel: (805) 961-2454
Bruce S. McCurdy, Chmn; 31 FT instr. Estab. 1916; ent. req. HS grad. or exam; 4 yr; degrees, B.A, M.A, M.F.A, Ph.D; schol; 24 SC, 56 LC, 28 GC; enrl. maj. 450, others 1745. Fees $219 per quarter, non-res. $719; campus res.

Ceramics
History of Art
Painting
Printmaking

Sculpture
Special Secondary & General
    Secondary Art Credential

Summer School: $165 for 6 wk.

SANTA CRUZ

UNIVERSITY OF CALIFORNIA AT SANTA CRUZ, Art Board of
    Studies, Performing Arts Building, 95060
Rotating chmn; 13 FT, 1 PT instr. Pub; D; ent. req. HS dipl; 4 yr; degree, B.A; 11 SC per quarter, 3 LC per quarter; enrl. D approx. 7000, maj. 80.

Aesthetics
Ceramics
Drawing
Graphic Arts
History of Art & Archaeology

Painting
Photography
Sculpture
Stage Design
Theatre Arts

Summer School: Carl Tjerandsen, Dir.

SANTA MARIA

ALLAN HANCOCK COLLEGE,* Fine Arts Department, 800 S. College
    Dr 93454. Tel: (805) 922-7711
George Muro, Head; 11 FT, 7 PT instr. Estab. 1920; pub; D & E; co-ed; ent. req. HS dipl, over 18 and educable; 2 yr; degree, A.A; 24 SC, 4 LC; enrl. D 800, E 220, maj. 115. Tui. $20; no campus res.

Advertising Design
Art Education
Ceramics
Costume Design & Construction

Jewelry
Lettering
Painting
Photography

Display
Drawing
Graphic Arts
History of Art & Archaeology

Serigraphy
Stage Design
Theatre Arts
Weaving

Adult hobby classes, painting and life drawing; tui. $3; enrl. 35.

Summer School: Tui. $2 per unit (maximum $10) for term of six wk. beginning June 18; enrl. 230.

Ceramics
Crafts
Drawing

Opera Workshop
Repertory Theatre
Watercolor

SANTA MONICA

RUSTIC CANYON ARTS & CRAFTS CENTER, Los Angeles City
    Department of Recreation and Parks, 601 Latimer Rd, 90402.
    Tel: (213) 454-9872
Carlyn Medaglia, Dir; 14 PT instr. Estab. 1963; pub; D & E; no degrees; classes for adults and children; 10 wk. sessions; 38 SC.

Ceramics
Copper Enameling
Drawing

Jewelry
Painting
Sculpture

SANTA ROSA

SANTA ROSA JUNIOR COLLEGE, Department of Art, 1501 Mendocino
    Ave, 95401. Tel: (707) 527-4298
Jim Rosen, Chmn; D 6 FT, 7 PT, E 27 instr. Estab. 1918; pub; D & E; ent. req. HS dipl; 2 yr; degree, A.A, no major in art; schol; D 33 SC, 6 LC, E 48 SC, 4 LC; enrl. D 918, E 1120. Tui. non-res. $29 per unit.

Advertising Design
Ceramics
Commercial Art
Costume Design & Construction
Display
Drafting
Drawing
Fashion Arts
Graphic Arts
Graphic Design
History of Art & Archaeology

Jewelry
Lettering
Museum Staff Training
Painting
Photography
Sculpture
Stage Design
Textile Design
Theatre Arts
Weaving

Summer School: Max Hein, Dir; term of 6 wk. beginning June 16, 1976.

Ceramics
Drawing
Introduction to Art
Jewelry

Painting
Photography
Printmaking
Watercolor

SARATOGA

VILLA MONTALVO,* Center for the Arts, P.O. Box 158, 95070.
    Tel: (408) 867-3421
Mrs. Jean Ryan, Chmn. Classes Comt; 8 FT instr. Estab. 1953; pvt; 8 SC, 1LC; enrl. 120. Tui. $25 for eight 3 hr. lessons. Children's classes $25 for 6 Sat. AM; enrl. 14.

Ceramics
Drawing
Painting

Summer School: Mrs. Joseph Ryan, Chmn; $25 for 8 wk. term beginning mid-June; enrl. 90.

WEST VALLEY COLLEGE, Art Department, 14000 Fruitvale Ave,
    95050. Tel: (408) 867-2200
David Ogle, Chmn; 11 FT, 37 PT instr. Estab. 1964; pub; D & E; ent. req. HS dipl. or 18 yr. of age; 2 yr; 8 degrees; 51 SC, 12 LC; enrl. D 1260, E 801. Reg. fee under $10; no campus res.

Aesthetics
Architecture
Ceramics
Commercial Art
Costume Design & Construction
Drafting
Drawing
Furniture Design
Graphic Arts
History of Art & Archaeology
Jewelry
Landscape Architecture

Lettering
Man & Materials
Museum Staff Training
Occupational Work Experience
Painting
Photography
Sculpture & Metal Casting
Stage Design
Stained Glass
Theatre Arts
Weaving

Adult hobby classes, many classes offered by Community Services Dept; tui. varies.

Summer School: David Ogle, Dir; tui. under $10 for term of 6 wk. beginning mid-June.

Ceramics
Drawing

Jewelry
Sculpture

STANFORD

STANFORD UNIVERSITY, Department of Art, Cummings Art
Building, 94305. Tel: (415) 497-3404
Lorenz Eitner, Chmn; 19 FT, 2 PT instr. Estab. 1891; pvt; 4 & 5
yr; degrees, B.A, M.A, PhD; schol; 15 SC, 30-250 LC, 5-15 GC;
enrl. univ. 12,000. Tui; campus res.

Art Education (with School of Education)	Lithography
	Photography
Art History	Sculpture
Design	Stage Design (in Department of
Drawing/Painting	Speech & Drama)

Summer School: Lorenz Eitner, Dir; tui. as announced for 8 wk.
from mid-June; enrl. art dept. 307.

STOCKTON

SAN JOAQUIN DELTA COLLEGE, Art Department, Kensington &
Alpine, 95204. Tel: (209) 466-2631 Exten. 307
Bruce Duke, Head; 7 FT instr. Estab. 1935; pub; D & E; ent. req.
HS grad; 2 yr; degree, A.A; schol; 12 SC, 2 LC; enrl. D 7000,
E 6000, maj. 100. Tui. free; no campus res.

Ceramics	Lettering
Drafting	Painting
Drawing	Photography
Graphic Arts	Sculpture
History of Art & Archaeology	Stage Design
Jewelry	Theatre Arts

Adult classes, ceramics, drawing, jewelry, painting; tui. $6 per
class; enrl. 25 per class.
Summer School: Dr. Joseph Laurin, Dir.

UNIVERSITY OF THE PACIFIC, Department of Art, 95204.
Tel: (209) 946-2242
Larry Walker, Chmn; 7 FT, 1 PT instr. Estab. 1851; pvt; ent. req.
HS grad. with 20 semester grades of recommending quality earned
in the 10th, 11th and 12th years in traditional subjects, twelve of
these grades must be in academic subjects; 4 yr. & grad. school
available (4-1-4 calendar prog); 15 (4 unit) full courses, 16 (2 unit)
SC, 5 LC, Independent Study; enrl. maj. 60-75, 800 per yr. Tui.
$3380 per yr, $145 per unit (6½ to 11½ units), $113 (½ to 6 units);
campus res. $1720.

Applied Arts	Drawing & Painting
Art Education	Fine Arts
Consumer Design	Museology & Art History
Crafts	Sculpture & Ceramics

Summer School: Two 5 wk. sessions.

SUISUN CITY

SOLANO COMMUNITY COLLEGE, Suisun Valley Rd, P.O. Box
246, 94585. Tel: (707) 643-2761
Dorothy Herger, Instr; 3 FT, 4 PT instr. Estab. 1945; pub; D & E;
ent. req. HS dipl; 2 yr; degree, A.A; 16 SC, 5 LC; enrl. D 215, E 60.
Tui. free; no campus res.

Ceramics	Lettering
Commercial Art	Painting
Drawing	Printmaking
Form & Composition	Sculpture
Fundamentals of Art	Stained Glass Window Making
History of Art	Survey of Modern Art
Jewelry Design	

Summer School: William Cochran, Dean Summer Session;
courses offered, Art Appreciation, Art Workshop.

THOUSAND OAKS

CALIFORNIA LUTHERAN COLLEGE, Art Department, Olson Rd,
91360. Tel: (805) 492-2411, 12, 13
B. M. A. Weber, Head; 3 FT, 2 PT instr. Estab. 1961; den; D & E;
ent. req. HS dipl, ent. exam; 4 yrs; degree, B.A; 18 SC, LC & SC, 5,
LC, 6; enrl. D & E 297, maj. 46, grad. students 9. Tui. $2400-
$3650 per yr, PT $70 cr; campus res. $1000.

Advertising Design	Lettering
Ceramics	Painting
Costume Design & Construction	Photography
Drawing	Sculpture
Fashion Arts	Stage Design
Graphic Arts	Teacher Training
History of Art & Archaeology	Textile Design
Illustration	Theatre Arts
Industrial Design	

Summer School: Dr. John Cooper, Dir; courses offered are
varied; tui. $70 cr. for two 4 wk. terms beginning June 18 & July
23; 1973 enrl. 52.

TURLOCK

CALIFORNIA STATE COLLEGE, STANISLAUS, Department of Art,
95380. Tel: (209) 633-2431 Exten. 431, 432
Martin Camarata, Chmn; 7 FT instr. Estab. 1957; pub; ent. req. HS
grad, ent. exam; 4 yr; degree, B.A.(Liberal Arts); 26 SC, 11 LC;
enrl. maj. 95, total 2000. Tui. $83.50.

Art History	Printmaking
Drawing	Sculpture
Painting	

Summer School: Richard Farnsworth, Assoc. Dean of Educational
Services; tui. $30 per sem. unit; enrl. 750.

Art Experience in Elementary School	Arts in Contemporary Society
	Ceramics
Art Experiences for Excep-	Graphic Design
tional Child	Two Dimensional Design

VALENCIA

CALIFORNIA INSTITUTE OF THE ARTS, School of Art, 24700
McBean Pkwy, 91355. Tel: (805) 255-1050
Robert Fitzpatrick, Pres; Stephan Von Huene, Acting Dean; 10 FT
instr. Estab. 1970; pvt; ent. req. portfolio, health cert; 2-4 yr;
degrees, B.F.A, M.F.A; schol; SC, Projects; Accrd. WCA; enrl.
D 130 first yr; 150 in 1973. Tui. $3450 for 32 wk; campus res.
Summer School.

Drawing	Post Studio
Graphics	Sculpture
Painting	Video
Photography	Visual Information

VENTURA

VENTURA COLLEGE, Fine Arts Division, 4667 Telegraph Rd,
93003. Tel: (805) 642-3211 Exten. 229
Harry D. Korn, Chmn; 13 FT, 15 PT instr. Estab. 1925; pub; D & E;
ent. req. HS dipl. or 18 yr. of age; degrees, A.A, A.S; schol; 50 SC,
15 LC; enrl. D 500, E 500, maj. 300. Tui. free to res; no campus
res.

Advertising	Graphic Design
Art Education	History of Art & Archaeology
Ceramics	Illustration
Commercial Art	Industrial Design
Costume Design & Construction	Jewelry
Display	Painting
Drafting	Photography
Drawing	Sculpture
Fashion Arts	Stage Design
General Crafts	Textile Design
Graphic Arts	Theatre Arts

Extensive non-credit evening prog.
Summer School: Eric Nicolet, Dir; many of the regular session
courses are offered.

WALNUT

MOUNT SAN ANTONIO COLLEGE, Art Department, 1100 N. Grand
Ave, 91789. Tel: (714) 598-2811 Exten. 259
Ronald B. Ownbey, Chmn; 14 FT, 3 PT instr. Estab. 1945; pub;
D & E; ent. req. over 18 yr. of age; 2 yr; degrees, A.A, A.S; 24 SC,
5 LC; enrl. D 2254, E 852, maj. 500. Tui. free to res, non-res.
$36 per unit, with maximum of $540 per sem; no campus res.

Advertising Design	Illustration
Ceramics	Lettering
Commercial Art	Metals & Enamels
Drafting	Painting
Drawing	Photography
Fibers	Sculpture
Graphic Arts	Theatre Arts
History of Art	

Summer School: Term of 6 wk. beginning June 21; enrl. art 150.

Ceramics	Life Drawing
Drawing	Printmaking
History of Art	

WEED

COLLEGE OF THE SISKIYOUS, Art Department, 800 College Ave,
96094. Tel: (916) 938-4463 Exten. 21
Barry R. Barnes, Art Area Chmn; 3 FT, 2 PT instr. Estab. 1959;
pub; D & E; ent. req. HS dipl; 2 yrs; degree, A.A; schol; 12 SC,
1 LC; enrl. D 1000, E 2600, maj. 40. Tui. none for res; campus
res. $1000.

Art Education	History of Art & Archaeology
Ceramics	Painting
Drafting	Photography

Graphic Arts
Graphic Design
Handicrafts

Sculpture
Theatre Arts
Weaving

WHITTIER

RIO HONDO COLLEGE, Fine Arts Department, 3600 Workman Mill
Rd, 90608. Tel: (213) 692-0921 Exten. 361
John R. Jacobs, Chmn; 12 FT, 13 PT instr. Estab. 1963; pub;
D & E; ent. req. HS dipl; 2 yr; degrees, A.A, A.S; schol.

Advertising Art	Jewelry
Ceramics	Lettering
Costume Design & Construction	Painting
Display	Photography
Drawing	Sculpture
Graphic Arts	Stage Design
History of Art & Archaeology	

Summer School: Dr. Josh Michaels, Dir; no tui. for term of 6
wk. beginning June 25; 1973 enrl. 3190.

American Art History	Fibres & Fabrics
Art Appreciation	History of Mexican Art
Art for Classroom Teacher	Introduction to Art
Art for Early Childhood	North American Indian Art
Art Therapy	Painting
Arts of Asia	Photography
Ceramics	Printmaking
Clothing Design	Scenic Design
Design	Sculpture
Design in Glass	Weaving
Drawing (freehand & life)	

WHITTIER COLLEGE, Department of Art, Stauffer Art Center,
90608. Tel: (213) 693-5032 Exten. 299
Robert W. Speier, Chmn; 2 FT, 2 PT instr. Estab. 1901; pvt; D &
E; ent. req. HS dipl, credit by exam, CLEP, CEEBA; 4 yr; degree, B.A;
schol. & fel; 12 SC, 12 LC; enrl. approx. 552-560 per sem. Tui.
$2650, FT $60 per unit, PT $95 per unit, audit $47.50 per unit,
grad. $95 per unit; campus res. $1334.

Art Education	History of Art & Archaeology
Ceramics	Painting
Drawing	Photography
Graphic Arts	Sculpture

Adult and children's classes for special students; tui. $4.

Summer School: Courses offered, California Landscape
Painting, Color, Elementary Art Education Workshops; tui. $60
per unit; $120 or $180 per session; July 7 - July 31, Aug 4 - Aug 29;
enrl. approx. 25.

WILMINGTON

LOS ANGELES HARBOR COLLEGE, Department of Art, 1111 Figue-
roa Place, 90744. Tel: (213) 835-0161
John Cassone, Chmn. Art Dept; 5 FT, 12 PT instr. Estab. 1949; pub;
D & E; ent. req. HS dipl; 2 yrs; degree, A.A; 30 SC, 3 LC, 1 GC;
enrl. D 6000, E 2000.

Advertising Design	Handicrafts
Architecture	History of Art & Archaeology
Ceramics	Illustration
Commercial Art	Jewelry
Costume Design & Construction	Lettering
Drawing	Painting
Fashion Arts	Photography
Graphic Arts	Sculpture

Summer School: John Cassone, Dir.

Beginning Design	Life Drawing
Beginning Drawing	Painting

COLORADO

BLACK HAWK

BLACKHAWK MOUNTAIN SCHOOL OF ART, 251 Main St, 80422.
Tel: (303) 582-5235
Michael S. Parfenoff, Dir; 6 FT instr. Estab. 1962; pvt; D & E; ent.
req. letter of recommendation, personal contract; 10 SC, 5 LC; enrl.
25. Summer School only; tui. $800, incl. room and board and bulk art
materials, for term of 6 wk. beginning June 25.

Aesthetics	Illustration
Ceramics	Painting
Drawing	Photography
Graphic Arts	Sculpture

BOULDER

UNIVERSITY OF COLORADO, Fine Arts Department, 80302.
Tel: (303) 492-6504
George Woodman, Chmn; 32 FT instr. Estab. 1920; pub; co-ed; 4 yr;
degrees, B.A, B.F.A, M.A.(Art Educ), M.A.(Art Hist), M.F.A;
ent. schol. and others to res; 36 SC, 60 LC, 55 GC; enrl. maj. 600,
grad. 100, others, 2578. Tui. $265.50 per sem; non-res. $1061.50;
campus res. $1490.

Art Education	Jewelry
Art History	Painting
Ceramics	Photography
Drawing	Sculpture
Graphics	

Summer Session.

COLORADO SPRINGS

COLORADO COLLEGE, Art Department, 80903.
Tel: (303) 473-2233 Exten. 418
James Trissel, Chmn; 6 FT instr. Estab. 1874; pvt; D; ent. req. HS
dipl. or equivalent and selection by admis. comt; 4 yr; degrees, B.A,
M.A.T; schol. to students with financial need only; 20 SC, 20 LC;
enrl. D 700, maj. 40. Tui. $3100; campus res. $1200.

Art Education	Painting
Drawing	Photography
Graphic Arts	Sculpture
History of Art	Theory

Summer School: Gilbert Johns, Dean; tui. $60 per cr. hr. for term
of 8 wks. beginning June 15.

Architecture	Painting
Drawing	Photography
Film	Sculpture

DENVER

COLORADO INSTITUTE OF ART, 16 W. 13th Ave, 80204.
Tel: (303) 825-4715
John Jellico, Pres; Billy G. Travis, Dir; 5 FT, 5 PT instr. Estab.
1952; pvt; D & E; co-ed; ent. req. HS dipl, ent. exam, portfolio of
current work; 24 mo; dipl; 15 SC; enrl. D 150, E 35. Tui. $1500
per yr; FT $125 per mo; no campus res.

Advertising Design	History of Art & Archaeology
Aesthetics	Illustration
Anatomy	Layout
Commercial Art	Lettering
Display	Outdoor Sketching, Production
Drawing	Painting
Fashion Arts	Perspective
Graphic Arts	Photography
Graphic Design	

COLORADO WOMEN'S COLLEGE, Art Department, Montview Blvd.
& Quebec, 80220. Tel: (303) 394-6012
Maynard Whitney, Coordinator of Fine Arts; 3 FT, 2 PT instr.
Estab. 1888; pvt; D; W; ent. req. HS grad. (with 15 units in English,
Foreign Languages, Social Science, Science and Math), SAT or ACT
ent. exam; 4 yr; degrees, B.A, B.S, B.F.A; schol; 6 SC, 9 LC; enrl.
total 700. Tui. and campus res. $2320.

Art Education	Fiber & Fabric
Art History	Painting
Ceramics	Printmaking
Design	Sculpture
Drawing	

Summer School and Evening Classes: Write to registrar for
schedule. Photography and Jewelry taught summers and
occasionally during year.

LORETTO HEIGHTS COLLEGE,* Art Department, 3301 S. Federal
Blvd, 80236. Tel: (303) 922-4011
Max Di Julio, Prog. Dir; 2 FT, 3 PT instr. Estab. 1880; pvt; D & E;
ent. req. HS dipl, ent. exam; 4 yrs; degrees, B.A, B.S, B.F.A; 8 SC,
4 LC. Tui. $2200 per yr; campus res. $1200.

Art Education	Jewelry
Ceramics	Lettering
Drawing	Painting
Graphic Arts	Sculpture
History of Art and Archaeology	Weaving

Summer School: William Joseph, Dir.

Ceramics	Printmaking
Glass	Weaving
Jewelry	

ROCKY MOUNTAIN SCHOOL OF ART, 1441 Ogden St, 80218.
Tel: (303) 832-1557
Philip J. Steele, Dir; 10 FT instr. Estab. 1963; pvt; D & E; ent. req.

portfolio of work; 2 yr; cert; schol; enrl. D 100, E 25. Tui. $1260 per yr; FT $110, PT varies; no campus res.

Advertising Design	Graphic Design
Commercial Art	History of Art & Archaeology
Drawing	Illustration
Fashion Arts	Lettering
Fine Art	Painting

Summer School: June 5 through Aug. 19.

UNIVERSITY OF DENVER, School of Art, University Park Campus, 80210. Tel: (303) 753-2846
Mel Strawn, Dir; John E. Billmyer, Acting Dir; 17 FT, 3 PT instr. Estab. 1929; pvt; D; ent. req. HS grad. in upper 40% of class; 4-5 yr; degrees, B.A, B.F.A, M.A, M.F.A; schol; enrl. 1000. Tui. $1050 per quarter.

Art Education	Pre-Professional Design
Ceramics	(Communications, Physical
Design	Structures, Environment &
Drawing	Habitat, Photography)
History of Art	Printmaking
Painting	Sculpture

FT. COLLINS

✠**COLORADO STATE UNIVERSITY,** Art Department, G100 Visual Arts Bldg, 80523. Tel: (303) 491-6774, 6775
Dr. Perry Ragouzis, Chmn; William F. Imel, Admin. Asst; 30 FT, 2 PT instr. Art Dept. estab. 1950; pub; 4 yr; degrees, B.F.A, B.A, M.F.A; 61 SC with enrl. 3600, 14 LC with enrl. 2200, enrl. maj. 547. Tui. res. $656.50, non-res. $2082.50; campus res. $1310.

Advertising Design	Printmaking
Ceramics	Sculpture
Drawing & Composition	Silversmithing
Graphic Design	Teacher Training
Illustration	Textile Design
Interior Design	Typography
Jewelry	Weaving
Painting	

Summer School: Dr. Perry Ragouzis, Chmn; one 5 wk. session, one 8 wk. session.

GRAND JUNCTION

MESA COLLEGE, Art Department, 81501. Tel: (303) 248-1323
Donald E. Meyers, Chmn; 3 FT, 1 PT instr. Estab. 1925; pub; D & E; ent. req. HS dipl or GED; 4 yr; degrees, A.A, B.A.(Visual & Performing Arts); schol; 12 SC, 4 LC; enrl. D maj. 100. Tui. $345 per yr, non-res. $1374, all students pay $10 application and evaluation fee.

Advanced Studio	Early Childhood Art
Art in the Home	Figure Drawing
Ceramics	History of Art
Civilization and the Arts	Jewelry
Color	Man Creates
Craft Survey	Painting
Critical Analysis	Printmaking
Drawing	Sculpture

Adult hobby classes, painting.
Summer School: Robert Youngquist, Dir; Ceramics, Drawing, Jewelry; tui. $45 for 4 wk; enrl. 40.

GREELEY

UNIVERSITY OF NORTHERN COLORADO, Department of Fine Arts, 80639. Tel: (303) 351-2143
Robert B. Turner, Chmn; 17 FT, 2 PT instr. Estab. 1889; pub; D; ent. req. HS grad; 4-5 yr; degrees, B.A, M.A; 37 SC, 3 LC, 18 GC, campus laboratory school; enrl. maj. 430, grad. 60, others 2000. Tui. $16 per cr. hr, non-res. $30 per cr. hr; campus res. Summer School.

Ceramics	Painting
Crafts	Printmaking
Design	Sculpture
Drawing	Teacher Education
Graphics	Textile Design
History of Art	Weaving

GUNNISON

WESTERN STATE COLLEGE OF COLORADO, Art Department, 81230. Tel: (303) 943-3083
August Grosland, Head; 7 FT instr. Estab. 1911; pub; D & E; ent. req. HS dipl, special exam; 4 yr; degree; 29 SC, 7 LC, 8 GC; enrl. art dept. 850, total coll. 3000.

Art Education	Jewelry
Calligraphy	Painting

Ceramics	Printmaking
Design	Sculpture
Drawing	Studio Art
Introduction to Art	Weaving

Summer School: Dr. Edwin H. Randall, Dir; tui. res. $102 plus fees, non-res. $405 plus fees per quarter; 2, 5, 8 and 10 wk. courses.

LA JUANTA

OTERO JUNIOR COLLEGE, Art Department, 81050. Tel: (303) 384-4446
Kenneth Brandon, Head; 1 FT instr. Estab. 1941; pub; D & E; ent. req. HS grad; 2 yr; degrees, A.A, A.A.S; schol; 12 SC, 3 LC; enrl. 776. Tui. $363 per quarter; campus res. $900 per yr.

Ceramics (E only)	Metal Sculpture
Creative Design	Oil Painting (D & E)
Drawing (D & E)	Watercolor
History of Art	

PUEBLO

SOUTHERN COLORADO STATE COLLEGE, * Art Department, Belmont Campus, 81001. Tel: (303) 549-2201
Edward R. Sajbel, Head; 9 FT, various PT instr. Estab. 1964; pub; D & E; open enrl, G.E.D. test, HS dipl; 2-4 yrs; degrees, B.A. in Fine Art, B.S. in Art Educ; schol; 43 SC, 15 LC. Tui. $450 per 3 quarters; non-res. $1389; room and board $975.

Advertising Design	Jewelry
Aesthetics	Lettering
Art Education	Metals-Enameling
Ceramics	Painting
Drafting	Photography
Drawing	Sculpture
Graphic Arts	Theatre Arts
Graphic Design	Weaving
History of Art & Archaeology	Woods
Illustration	

Adult hobby classes, ceramics, drawing, painting, photography, sculpture; tui. $19 per quarter hr.
Children's classes in conjunction with Sangre de Cristo Art Center; tui. varies.
Summer School: Edward R. Sajbel, Head Art Dept; 2 terms of 5 wk. each beginning June 15 & July 20; total school enrl. 1973 approx. 800.

Art Education	Drawing
Art History	Painting (oil, acrylics)
Ceramics	Watercolor

UNIVERSITY OF SOUTHERN COLORADO, BELMONT CAMPUS, Art Department, 2200 Bonforte Ave, 81005.
Jim Duncan, Dir. Creative and Performing Arts Center; 8 FT 2 PT instr. Estab. 1933; pub; D & E; ent. req. HS dipl, open door policy; 4 yr; degrees in Art, with emphasis in Art Education, Graphic Design and Commercial Art; schol; enrl. D 700, E 100, maj. 150. Tui. $561 per yr, non-res. $1600 per yr, $23 per quarter hr. cr.

Advertising Design	Illustration
Aesthetics	Jewelry
Art Education	Painting
Ceramics	Photography & Film
Commercial Art	Sculpture
Drafting	Teacher Training
Drawing	Theatre Arts
Graphic Arts	Weaving
Graphic Design	Woods
History of Art & Archaeology	

Summer School: Dr. Don Janes, Dir; tui. $175; two 5 wk. terms beginning June 11 and July 19; enrl. total 1000, art 200.

Art Education	Drawing
Art History	Painting
Ceramics	Watercolor

STERLING

NORTHEASTERN JUNIOR COLLEGE, * Art Department, 80751. Tel: (303) 522-6600 Exten. 671
Peter L. Youngers, Head; 2 FT instr. Estab. 1950; pub; D & E; ent. req. HS dipl, ent. exam; 2 yr; degree, A.A; schol; 16 SC, 2 LC; enrl. D 50, E 30, maj. 20. Tui; campus res.

Art Education	History of Art & Archaeology
Ceramics	Lettering
Drawing	Painting
Graphic Arts	Sculpture

Adult hobby classes, ceramics, painting; tui. $15; enrl. 10-20 per class.
Summer School: J. D. Gregory, Dir.

CONNECTICUT

BRIDGEPORT

✠HOUSATONIC COMMUNITY COLLEGE, Art Department, 06608.
Tel: (203) 366-8201 Exten. 346
Vincent Darnowski, Pres; Burt Chernow, Chmn; 4 FT, 8 PT instr.
Estab. 1970; pub; D & E; ent. req. HS grad; 2 yr; degree, A.A;
schol; SC, LC. Tui. FT $100.

Ceramics	Independent Projects
Color	Introduction to Studio Art
Contemporary American Art	Lettering
Design	Modern Art
Drawing I, II, III, IV	Painting
History & Appreciation of Art	Sculpture
I & II	Teaching Children Art
History & Appreciation of	Three-Dimensional Design
Cinema	Visual Organization

JUNIOR COLLEGE OF CONNECTICUT,* Art Department, University
of Bridgeport, 06602. Tel: (203) 384-0711 Exten. 348
Bruce Glaser, Chmn; 16 FT, 6 PT instr. Estab. 1927, in conjunction with the University of Bridgeport; pvt; D & E; ent. req. HS
dipl, HS equivalency exam; 2 yr; A.A; schol; 39 SC, 17 LC (with
Univ); tui. $2200.

Advertising Design	Industrial Design
Aesthetics	Jewelry
Art Education	Lettering
Ceramics	Painting
Commercial Art	Photography
Costume Design & Construction	Sculpture
Drafting	Stage Design
Drawing	Teacher Training
Graphic Arts	Textile Design
Graphic Design	Theatre Arts
History of Art & Archaeology	Weaving

Summer School: Prof. Bruce Glaser, Chmn. Art Dept; same
courses as during academic year.

UNIVERSITY OF BRIDGEPORT,* Art Department, 06602.
Tel: (203) 384-0711
Prof. Bruce Glaser, Chmn; 16 FT, 7 PT instr. Estab. 1927; pvt;
D & E; ent. req. HS grad with 16 units, SAT; 4 yr; degrees, B.A,
B.S, B.F.A, M.S; schol; enrl. maj. 350, others 8000. Tui. incl.
room and board $3400.

Art Education	Graphic Design
Art History	Painting
Ceramics	Printmaking
Fine Arts	Sculpture

Summer School: Prof. Bruce Glaser, Chmn; 10 wk. from June -
Aug.

HAMDEN

PAIER SCHOOL OF ART, INCORPORATED,* 6 Prospect Court,
06511. Tel: (203) 777-7319
Edward T. Paier, Pres; 18 FT, 17 PT instr. Estab. 1946; pvt; D & E;
co-ed; ent. req. HS grad, presentation of portfolio, transcript of records, recommendation; 3, 4, 5 yr; no credit; 10 SC, 6 LC, 1 GC; enrl.
D 385, E 150. Tui. $1450 per yr.

Advertising Design	Illustration
Commercial Art	Interior Design
Drawing	Lettering
Fashion Arts	Painting
Graphic Arts	Photography
Graphic Design	Technical Illustration
History of Art & Archaeology	

Summer School: E. T. Paier, Dir; tui. $300 for term of 6 wk.
beginning July 6, part-time and unit subjects available; enrl. 150.

HARTFORD

TRINITY COLLEGE, Department of Fine Arts, Summit St, 06106.
Tel: (203) 527-3151 Exten. 230
George Chaplin, Dir. Studio Arts Prog; Michael Mahoney, Chmn;
4 FT, 2 PT instr. Estab. 1823; pvt; D; ent. req. HS dipl, ent. exam,
portfolio; 4 yr; degree, B.A; schol; 16 SC, 15 LC; enrl. D 650, maj.
40. Tui. $3325 per yr, audit $100 per course; campus res. $1560.

Basic Design	History of Art
Color	Painting
Drawing	Sculpture
Graphic Design	

KENT

✠KENT SCHOOL,* Department of Art and Art History, Box 401,
06757.

MIDDLETOWN

WESLEYAN UNIVERSITY, Art Department, 06457.
Tel: (203) 347-9411 Exten. 257, 253
John Frazer, Chmn; 10 FT, 8 PT instr. Univ. estab. 1831, Art Dept.
estab. 1928; pvt; D; 4 yr; degree, B.A; 33 SC, 27 LC; enrl. maj. 76,
others 885. Tui. $3600; campus res.

Architecture Drawing &	History of Film
Design	History of Prints
Calligraphy	Painting
Ceramics	Photography
Color	Printmaking
Design	Silver Craft
Drawing	Typography
Film Production	Video Workshop
History of Art	

Summer School: James Steffensen, Dir.

NEW BRITAIN

CENTRAL CONNECTICUT STATE COLLEGE, Art Department,
1615 Stanley St, 06050. Tel: (203) 225-6351
Walter J. LaVoy, Chmn; 15 FT, 20 PT instr. Estab. 1846; pub; ent.
req. screening by faculty and student representatives, portfolio,
art ent. exam; 4 yr; degrees, B.A, B.S, M.A, M.S; schol; SC & LC
vary with sem; enrl. undergrad. 6173, grad. 400, E 4774. Tui.
$300 per sem, other fees (higher for non-res).

Art History	Graphics
Ceramic Sculpture	Jewelry
Ceramics	Mural Design
Crafts	Museum Planning
Design	Painting
Display Design	Puppetry
Drawing & Composition	Sculpture

Young people's Sat. arts workshop, 6 to 18 yr.
Summer School & Evening College: R. Tupper, Dir; same
courses; tui. $30 per cr. undergrad, $35 per cr. grad.

NEW CANAAN

SILVERMINE GUILD SCHOOL OF THE ARTS, 1037 Silvermine Rd,
06850. Tel: (203) 866-0411
Robert Franco, Dir; 27 PT instr. Estab. 1939; pvt; yr-round D & E,
Sat. AM; children from age 6 and adults; no ent. req; non-credit PT,
4 yr. cert. FT; schol; 25 SC; enrl. 450. Fall and spring, 15 wk.
sem, summer, 8 wk. session.

Advanced Painting Seminar	Life Drawing & Painting
Ballet	Mime
Basic Drawing & Painting	Modern Dance
Ceramics	Photography
Color	Portrait Painting
Design	Sculpture
Figure Sketch	Weaving
Graphics	

NEW HAVEN

ALBERT MAGNUS COLLEGE, Art Department, 700 Prospect St,
06511. Tel: (203) 777-6631
Sister Thoma Swanson, Chmn; 1 FT, 6 PT instr. Estab. 1925, Art
Dept. 1970; pvt; D & E; W, M admitted to classes; ent. req. HS dipl,
SAT, CEEB; 120 credits, 8 sem; degree, B.A; 26 SC, 9 LC; art enrl.
D 124, E 25, maj. 20. Tui. $2300 per yr, PT matriculating, $75 per
cr. hr, PT week-end coll, $50 per cr. hr; campus res. $1600.

Aesthetics	History of Art & Archaeology
Art Education	Painting
Art Therapy	Photography
Ceramics	Sculpture
Drawing	Stage Design
Graphic Arts	Theatre Arts
Handicrafts	

SOUTHERN CONNECTICUT STATE COLLEGE, Art Department,
501 Crescent St, 06515. Tel: (203) 397-2101
Manson Van B. Jennings, Pres; Marshall S. Kuhn, Chmn; 27 FT,
9 PT instr. Normal School estab. 1893, Teachers College estab.
1937; pub; D & E; ent. req. HS grad, SAT; 4 yr; degrees, B.S,
M.S.(Art Educ), B.A.(Art History), B.A.(Studio Art); enrl. undergrad.
maj. 400, grad. maj. 525. Tui. and fees res. $500 per yr, non-res.
$1400; campus res.

Art Education	Glassblowing
Art History	Metalworking & Jewelry
Batik	Painting
Ceramics	Photography

Design
Drawing

Printmaking
Sculpture

Summer School: George Cole, Dir; 6 wk. from June 25; tui. $32 undergrad. cr, $40 grad. cr; enrl. 1800.

YALE UNIVERSITY, School of Art, 180 York St, 06520.
Tel: (203) 436-4380
Andrew Murray Forge, Dean; William Bailey, Dir. of Studies in Painting; Alvin Eisenman, Dir. of Studies in Graphic Design; David Von Schlegell, Dir. of Studies in Sculpture; Jerry L. Thompson, Dir. Undergrad. Studies. Estab. 1869; pvt; co-ed; two 16 wk. terms; 2 yr. for M.F.A. degree for those with B.A. or B.F.A; enrl. 140 maximum. Tui. $3350.

Graphic Design
Filmmaking
Painting

Photography
Printmaking
Sculpture

Department of the History of Art (Yale College and Graduate School), Box 2009, 56 High St, 06520. Tel: (203) 436-8853
David J. Cast, Dir. Undergrad. Studies; George L. Hersey, Dir. Grad. Studies; Nancy A. Walchli, Admin. Asst; Anne C. Hanson, Chmn; 27 FT, 2 PT instr. Estab. 1940; pvt; D; co-ed; undergrad. maj. leading to B.A, grad. prog. ent. req. B.A. and foreign language, offering Ph.D. degree; training for small groups in all principal fields of History of Art, museum training; schol, fel, and assistantships; courses change each yr. Tui. $4050 grad. school.

School of Architecture, 180 York St, 06520.
Tel: (203) 436-0550
Herman D. J. Spiegel, Dean. Estab. 1869; pvt; co-ed; ent. req. Bachelor's degree, Grad. Record Exam; M.Arch.(3 yr), M.Environ. Design (2 yr); enrl. 150 maximum. Tui. two 16 wk. terms $3650.

NEW LONDON

CONNECTICUT COLLEGE,* Art Department, 06320.
Tel: (203) 442-5391 Exten. 496
David A. Smalley, Chmn; 8 FT, 3 PT instr. Estab. 1916; pvt; co-ed; ent. schol. and others; 4 yrs; degrees; 11 SC, 15 LC; enrl. maj. 100, others 475. Tui. res. $3750, non-res. $2630; campus res.

NORWICH

THE NORWICH ART SCHOOL, The Norwich Free Academy, 108 Crescent St, 06360. Tel: (203) 887-2505 Exten. 217
Mrs. Lawrence R. Browning, Dir. of Sch & Head Art Dept. of Norwich Free Academy; 9 FT, 4 PT instr. Estab. 1890; pvt; D & E; ent. req. HS dipl. or equivalency and portfolio; basic one yr. course. Tui. c. $1000, non-res. HS pupils $1264; no campus res.

Ceramics
Design & Screenprinting
Drawing & Composition
Fashion Arts
Figure Drawing
Graphic Arts
History of Art
Jewelry & Metalsmithing

Lettering
Painting
Photography
Poster & Layout
Sculpture
20th Century History of Art
Watercolor
Weaving

Adult classes, metalsmithing, pottery; tui. $25 per 15 wk. session. Children's classes, Sat. mornings, 3 through 8 grades, $32 per 30 wk. session. Special Fine Arts Prog. for Norwich Free Academy students beginning 10th grade.

STORRS

UNIVERSITY OF CONNECTICUT, School of Fine Arts, Art Department, 06268. Tel: (203) 486-3930
Gerard Doudera, Head; 24 FT, 10 PT instr. Estab. 1950; pub; 4 yr; degrees, B.F.A, B.A.(Art History); 42 SC, 21 LC; enrl. maj. 300, others, 3125. Tui. $350, non-res. $850; campus res. $1030-$1260 per yr.

Architecture
Ceramics
Design
Drawing
Graphic Design
History of Art

Oil Painting
Photography
Printmaking
Sculpture
Watercolor

Summer School: Stuart H. Manning, Dir; two 6 wk. terms; tui. $35 per cr, enrl. 100 per term.

Design
Drawing
History of Art

Painting
Sculpture

VOLUNTOWN

FOSTER CADDELL'S ART SCHOOL, RFD 1, Rte. 49, 06384.
Tel: (203) 376-9583
Foster Caddell, Head; 1 FT instr. Estab. 1955; pvt; D & E; ent. req. reasonable talent and desire to work; no degree; schol; enrl. D 85, E 50. Tui. $500 per day, per wk. for a yr.

Aesthetics
Art History
Drawing

Painting
Pastels

Summer School: Landscape Painting.

WEST HARTFORD

HARTFORD ART SCHOOL OF UNIVERSITY OF HARTFORD, 200 Bloomfield Ave, 06117. Tel: (203) 243-4393
Bernard Hanson, Dean; 17 FT, 19 PT instr. Estab. 1877; pvt; D & E; ent. req. HS dipl, ent. exam, portfolio review; 4 yr; degrees, B.F.A, B.F.A.(Art Educ), M.A.(Art Educ), M.F.A; schol; 72 SC, 5 LC, 50 GC; enrl. D 300, grad. 75, E 150. Tui. $2650; campus res. $1894.

Advertising Design
Art Education
Ceramics
Drawing
Filmmaking
Movement Exploration

Painting
Photography
Printmaking
Sculpture
Teacher Training
Video

Summer School: Bernard Hanson, Dean; $75 per cr. hr; enrl. 150.

Art Education
Ceramics
Crafts
Drawing
Filmmaking

Painting
Photography
Printmaking
Sculpture

SAINT JOSEPH COLLEGE,* Department of Fine Arts, 1678 Asylum Ave, 06117. Tel: (203) 232-4571
Vincenza A. Uccello, Head; 2 FT, 1 PT instr. Estab. 1932; pvt; D & E; W; ent. req. HS dipl, CEEB; 4 yr; degrees, B.A, B.S, M.A; schol; 5 SC, 7 LC; enrl. D 104. Tui. $1800; campus res. $1320.

Art Education
Batik
Drawing
Enameling
Fundamentals of Design

History of Art
Mosaic
Painting
Weaving

WEST HAVEN

UNIVERSITY OF NEW HAVEN, School of Arts and Sciences, Department of Fine Arts, 300 Orange Ave, 06516.
Tel: (203) 934-6321 Exten. 365, 258
Elizabeth Moffitt, Chmn; 3 FT, 12 PT instr. Estab. 1971; pvt; D & E; ent. req. HS dipl; 2-4 yr; degrees, A.S.(Commercial & Advertising Art), B.A.(Fine Arts, Interior Design, Fashion Design), B.S.(Biological Illustration); 27 SC, 5 LC; enrl. D 250, E 100, maj. 47. Tui. $2010 per yr, PT D $81.25 per cr, E $45 per cr; campus res. $2090.

Advertising Design
Basic Design
Ceramics
Commercial Art
Drawing
Fashion Arts
Graphic Arts
Graphic Design
History of Art & Archaeology
Illustration

Interaction of Color
Lettering
Painting
Photography
Sculpture
Textile Design
Three-Dimensional Art
Two-Dimensional Art
Weaving

Summer School: Richard Lipp, Dir.

Ceramics
History of Art
Photography

Sculpture
Studio Art

WESTPORT

FAMOUS SCHOOLS, 17 Riverside Ave, 06880.
Tel: (203) 227-8471
Fritz Henning, Dir. Estab. 1948; pvt; no ent. req; home-study courses:

Commercial & Fine Art
Photography
Writing

WILLIMANTIC

EASTERN CONNECTICUT STATE COLLEGE, Art Department, Windham St, 06226. Tel: (203) 456-2331 Exten. 258
Julian Akus, Chmn; 4 FT, 1 PT instr. Estab. 1881; pub; D & E; ent. req. HS dipl; 4 yr; degrees, B.A.(Fine Arts), B.S.(Art); schol; enrl. D 300, E 75, maj. 40. Tui. $450 per yr, plus $250 fee; campus res. $870.

Ceramics
Crafts

History of Art
Painting

Drawing	Sculpture
Graphic Arts	

Summer School: Kenneth H. Lundy, Dir; Art & Craft Workshop.

WOODSTOCK

ANNHURST COLLEGE, Art Department, R.R. 2, 06281.
Tel: (203) 928-7773 Exten. 65
Sister Claire Pelletier, Chmn; 3 FT, 1 PT instr. Estab. 1970; pvt;
D & E; ent. req. HS dipl, ent. exam, scholastic aptitude, recommendation from HS principal, 15 units of academic preparation from HS;
4 yrs; degree, A.B; schol; 17 SC, 3 LC; enrl. D 105, E 16, maj. 33,
minors 10. Tui; $1800 per yr; campus res. $1350.

Art Education	History of Art
Ceramics	Lettering
Design	Painting
Drawing	Photography
Graphic Arts	Sculpture

Adult classes, painting; tui. $70 per cr; enrl. 16.

Summer School: Sister Lucille Denomme, Dir; courses offered,
art education and others; tui. $70 per cr. hr. for term of 6 wk; 1973
enrl. 18.

DELAWARE

DOVER

DELAWARE STATE COLLEGE,* Art Education Department,
19901.
Miss Kathleen Berhalter, Chmn; 3 FT, 1 PT instr. Estab. 1960; pub;
D & E; ent. req. HS dipl, SAT; 4 yrs; degree, B.A. in Art Educ; schol;
13 SC, 9 LC; enrl. over 60 maj. and non-maj. Tui. non-res. $575 per
yr; campus res. $750.

Advertising Design	Illustration
Aesthetics	Jewelry
Art Education	Lettering
Ceramics	Painting
Commercial Art	Photography
Drawing	Sculpture
Graphic Arts	Stage Design
Handicrafts	Teacher Training
History of Art and Archaeology	Theatre Arts

NEWARK

UNIVERSITY OF DELAWARE,* College of Arts and Sciences, Department of Art, 19711. Tel: (302) 738-2244
Dept. Art: Daniel K. Teis, Chmn; 14 FT instr. Estab. 1914; pub; ent.
req. HS grad; degrees, M.A; schol.

Art Education	Jewelry & Metalwork
Crafts	Painting
Drawing	Printmaking
Graphic Design	Sculpture
Interior Design	Textile Design

REHOBOTH BEACH

REHOBOTH ART LEAGUE, INC, P.O. Box 84, 19971.
Tel: (302) 227-8408
Mrs. Ward H. Tanzer, Chmn. Educ. Dept; 6 PT instr. Estab. 1938;
pvt; D & E; classes open to all; 6 SC; enrl. D 95. Tui. for series
of lessons.

Ceramics	Sculpture
Drawing	Weaving

Children's classes, arts & crafts, drawing, painting.

DISTRICT OF COLUMBIA

WASHINGTON

AMERICAN UNIVERSITY, Department of Fine Arts, Massachusetts
& Nebraska Aves. N.W, 20016.
Helene M. Herzbrun, Chmn; 14 FT, 14 PT instr. Estab. 1925; den;
ent. req. ent. exam; 4 yr; degrees, B.A, M.F.A, M.A; schol; 27 SC,
12 LC, 29 GC; enrl. maj. 400, grad. 70. Tui. $360 per full course
plus res.

Art History	Painting
Design	Sculpture
Drawing	Teacher Training
Graphics	

Summer School: Ben L. Summerford, Chmn.

THE CATHOLIC UNIVERSITY OF AMERICA, Michigan Ave. N.E,
20064. Tel: (202) 529-6000
Pvt; D; 4-5 yr; degrees; schol.

School of Engineering and Architecture
Donald Marlow, Head; 30 FT, 10 PT instr. Estab. 1911; undergrad.
and grad.
‡Architecture

Graduate School of Arts and Sciences, Division of Art
Thomas P. Rooney, Head; 6 FT, 2 PT instr. Estab. 1937; degrees.

Ceramics	History of Art
Design	Metalsmithing
Drawing	Painting
Graphic Arts	Sculpture

Summer School: Thomas P. Rooney, Chmn; 6 wk.

CORCORAN SCHOOL OF ART, New York Ave. & 17th St. N.W, 20006.
Tel: (202) 628-9484
Roy Slade, Dean of Sch; Peter Thomas, Dean; Rona Slade, Chmn.
Found; Blaine Larson & William Christenberry, Co-Chmn. Fine Art;
Kaywal Ramkissoon, Chmn. Visual Communication; Bill Lombardo,
Chmn. Ceramics; A. Brockie Stevenson, Chmn. Drawing & Design;
Jack Perlmutter, Chmn. Printmaking; Andrew Hudson, Chmn.
Complementary Studies; Joe Cameron, Chmn. Photography; 15 FT,
32 PT instr. Estab. 1890; pvt; D & E; ent. req. HS dipl; Corcoran
dipl. granted for successful completion of 4 yr. coordinated and
structured study, dipl. prog. offered in Visual Communication and
Fine Art; enrl. D 500, E 350, Sat. 230, Summer 345. Reg. fee
$15, tui. $1000 per term FT; $220 per three cr. course. Young
people and adult Summer and Sat. classes; Corcoran School of
Art Abroad.

GEORGE WASHINGTON UNIVERSITY, Department of Art, 20052.
Tel: (202) 676-6085
William A. MacDonald, Chmn; 17 FT, 35 PT instr. Estab. 1893;
pvt; D & E; 4 yr; degrees, A.B, M.A, M.F.A, Ph.D; ent. schol; SC and
LC at Univ. and Corcoran School of Art; enrl. maj. 250, others 1800.
Tui. $96 per cr. Summer School.

Ceramics	Museum Studies
Design	Painting
Drawing	Photography
Graphics	Sculpture
History & Theory of Art	

GEORGETOWN UNIVERSITY, College of Arts and Sciences, Department of Fine Arts, 20007. Tel: (202) 625-4085
Clifford T. Chieffo, Chmn; 7 FT, 5 PT instr. Estab. 1958; den;
D & E; ent. req. 2 yr. in approved coll. plus portfolio approved by
head of dept; 4 yr; degree, A.B.(Fine Arts); 17 SC, 18 LC; enrl. open.
Tui. regular yr. of Georgetown Univ, Coll. of Arts and Sciences.

Drawing	History of Music
Graphics	History of Theatre
History of Art	Sculpture
History of Film	Studio Painting

Adult art classes vary each yr, see bulletin.
Summer School: Joe Pettit, Dean; tui. and courses same as
regular session, smaller choice.

HOWARD UNIVERSITY,* Department of Art, College of Fine Arts,
6th St. & Fairmount St. N.W, 20001. Tel: (202) 636-7047
Vada E. Butcher, Dean; Jeff R. Donaldson, Chmn. 16 FT instr.
Estab. 1921; pvt; D & E; 4 yr; degrees, B.F.A, M.A. History of Art,
Art Educ; M.F.A. (2 yr.), schol. fel; average enrl. per sem. 200,
others 450. Tui. $450 per sem; campus res.

Art Education	Painting
Art History	Photography
Ceramics	Printmaking
Design	Sculpture

IMMACULATA COLLEGE OF WASHINGTON, Division of Fine Arts,
4300 Nebraska Ave, 20016. Tel: (202) 966-0040
Yolanda R. Frederikse, Chmn; 3 FT, 1 PT instr. Estab. 1905; den;
D; W; ent. req. HS dipl (15 units in a secondary school approved by
state accreditation agency), students from other countries must take
English for Foreign Students Test; 2 yr; degree, A.A.(Art); Basic
Educ Opportunity Grant; 6 SC, 3 LC; enrl. D 25. Tui. $1400 per yr;
campus res. $1600.

Basic Design	Introduction to Art
Commercial Art	Painting & Composition
Drawing	Teacher Training
Handicrafts	Watercolor
History of Art	

Children's summer craft classes at Dunblane Elementary School.

TRINITY COLLEGE, Art Department, Michigan Ave. at Franklyn N.E, 20017.
Dr. Liliana Gramberg, Chmn; 2 FT, 4 PT instr. Estab. 1900; pvt; D & E; W; ent. req. HS dipl, ent. exam; 4 yr; degrees, B.A, B.S, M.A.T; schol; 8 SC, 2-3 LC; enrl. D 120, maj. 17, grad. 20.

Aesthetics	Lettering
Art Education	Painting
Drawing	Photography
Graphic Arts	Sculpture
Graphic Design	Teacher Training
History of Art & Archaeology	Textile Design
Jewelry	3-D

    Summer School: Dr. Jean Willke, Dir; various courses offered.

FLORIDA

BOCA RATON

COLLEGE OF BOCA RATON, Department of Art, Military Trail, 33431. Tel: (305) 395-4301.
E. J. Ranspach, Head; 1 FT, 3 PT instr. Estab. 1963; pub; D & E; open door ent; 2-4 yr; degrees, A.A, B.A; schol; 6 SC, 2 LC; enrl. D 50, E 20, maj. 6.

Advertising Design	Industrial Design
Commercial Art	Painting
Drawing	Photography
Fashion Arts	Sculpture
Graphic Arts	Stage Design
History of Art & Archaeology	Textile Design

FLORIDA ATLANTIC UNIVERSITY, Art Department, 33432. Tel: (305) 395-5100 Exten. 2673
Claire V. Dorst, Chmn; 7 FT, 1 PT instr. Estab. 1964; pub; D & E; ent. req. A.A; 2 yr; degrees, B.F.A, B.A; 37 SC, 14 LC, 1 GC; enrl. D 1600, maj. 150, grad. 8, special students 7. Tui. $16 per quarter cr; campus res. $570.

Aesthetics	Jewelry
Applied Art	Lettering
Art Education	Museum Staff Training
Ceramics	Painting
Commercial Art	Photography
Costume Design & Construction	Sculpture
Drawing	Stage Design
Graphic Arts	Teacher Training
Handicrafts	Theatre Arts
History of Art	Weaving
History of Architecture	

    Summer School: Claire V. Dorst, Dir.

BRADENTON

ART LEAGUE SCHOOL OF THE ART LEAGUE OF MANATEE COUNTY,* 209 9th St, W, 33505. Tel: (813) 746-2862
Betty Mac Coll, Exec. V. Pres; D 7 PT, E 3 PT instr. Estab. 1952; pvt; D & E; 17 SC. Sat. AM children's classes.

Ceramic Sculpture & Design	Portrait
Drawing	Pottery
Landscape	Sketching
Oil Landscape	Watercolor, experimental
Painting	

MANATEE JUNIOR COLLEGE, Department of Fine Arts, 26th St. W, 33507. Tel: (813) 755-1511
James R. McMahon, Chmn; 4 FT, 2 PT instr. Estab. 1958; pub; D & E; ent. req. HS grad; 2 yr; degree, A.A; schol; 12 SC, 4 LC; enrl. D 312, E 80, maj. 103, general educ. 150. Tui. plus fees non-res, $22 per sem. hr, fee varies for res; no campus res.

Architecture	Lettering
Art Education	Painting
Ceramics	Photography
Commercial Art	Sculpture
Drafting	Stage Design
Drawing	Theatre Arts
History of Art & Archaeology	

Adult classes, painting, drawing, sculpture; tui. $10 per sem.
    Summer School: Dr. Kermit Johnson, Dir.

Art History	Drawing
Ceramics	Painting

CLEARWATER

✤FLORIDA GULF COAST ART CENTER, 222 Ponce de Leon Blvd. at Manatee Rd, 33516. Tel: (813) 584-8634
Ellen C. Kaiser, Dir; 23-25 PT instr. Estab. 1949; pvt; D & E; no ent. req; no degrees; schol; 20 SC, 3 LC; enrl. 200. Tui. $50 a term per class, four terms a yr. for adults, no res. facilities.

Ceramics	Jewelry
Creative Writing	Painting
Crewel	Photography
Drafting	Sculpture
Drawing	Weaving
Handicrafts	Wood Carving
History of Art & Archaeology	

Opera Workshop; intern program for college seniors at an art center.
Children's classes, drawing, sculpture, painting, art sampler, ceramics; tui. $25 per class per term; enrl. 35-50 per term.

CORAL GABLES

UNIVERSITY OF MIAMI, Department of Art, P.O. Box 248106, 33124. Tel: (305) 284-2542
Gerald G. Winter, Chmn; 17 FT, 2 PT instr. Estab. 1930; pvt; D & E; ent. req. HS grad, coll. board grades; 4 yr; degrees, B.A, B.F.A, M.A.(Art History), M.F.A; schol; 83 SC, 14 LC; 30 GC; enrl. maj. 450, grad. 41, others 750. Tui. $2900; campus res. room $750.

Art History	Photography
Ceramics	Printmaking
Graphic Design	Sculpture
Painting	Weaving

Children's classes available at Loew Art Museum.
    Summer School: Dr. M. Robert Allen, Dir; two 6 wk. sessions, plus workshops; tui. $70 per cr.

DELAND

STETSON UNIVERSITY, Art Department, 32720. Tel: (904) 734-4121 Exten. 248
Fred Messersmith, Head; 3 FT instr. Estab. 1880; den; ent. req. coll. boards; 4 yr; degrees; schol; 5 SC, 5 LC, 5 Lab.C; normal enrl. 200. Tui. $2000 per yr.

Art Education	Drawing & Painting
Art History	Graphics
Commercial Art	Introduction to Art
Crafts	Photography
Design	Sculpture

FORT LAUDERDALE

ART INSTITUTE OF FT. LAUDERDALE,* 3000 E. Las Olas Blvd, 33316. Tel: (305) 525-4197
Mark K. Wheeler, Dir; 9 FT, 7 PT instr. Estab. 1968; pvt; D & E; ent. req. HS dipl; 2 yrs; dipl; schol; enrl. D 250, E 50. Tui. $450 per quarter; campus res. $1000.

Advertising Design	Illustration
Commercial Art	Lettering
Drawing	Painting
Fashion Arts	Photography
Graphic Design	

✤FORT LAUDERDALE MUSEUM OF THE ARTS, Art School, 426 E. Las Olas Blvd, 33301. Tel: (305) 463-5184
George S. Bolge, Dir; 3-4 PT instr. Estab. 1959; pvt; 2-3 hr. per wk, no cr; grad courses in Art Appreciation, Internship in Museum work; enrl. limited to 20 per class, 3 terms per yr. Tui. adults painting $70 per 10 wk. term, sculpture $100; children $35 per 10 wk. term. Summer classes, two children's.

Art Appreciation	Slab Pottery
Painting	Watercolor
Photography	Weaving
Sculpture	

FORT MYERS

EDISON COMMUNITY COLLEGE, Department of Art, College Pkwy, 33901.
1 FT, 1 PT instr. Estab. 1962; pub; D & E; ent. req. HS dipl; 2 yr; degrees, A.A, A.S; schol. Tui. free to res, plus matriculation fee $11, non-res. $15 per cr. hr, plus matriculation fee $11.

Art Education	Interior Design
Commercial Art	Jewelry
Dimensional Design	Lettering
Drawing	Painting
History of Art & Archaeology	Sculpture

Adult classes of Continuing Education, any non-cr. activity of interest to 20 or more adults for which a teacher is available; tui. $10.

GAINESVILLE

✣UNIVERSITY OF FLORIDA, College of Fine Arts, Department of
Art, 302C AFA, 32611. Tel: (904) 392-0211.
Joseph J. Sabatella, Dean; Eugene E. Grissom, Chmn; 23 FT instr.
Estab. 1925; pub; 4 yr; degrees; schol; GC; enrl. undergrad. 200,
grad. 20. Tui. $14-22 per hr, non-res. $37-59 per hr; campus res.

Art Education	History of Art
Crafts	Painting
Creative Photography	Printmaking
Graphic Design	Sculpture

INDIALANTIC

ELIOT McMURROUGH SCHOOL OF ART, 306 Fifth Ave, 32903.
Tel: (305) 723-8876
Eliot S. McMurrough, Faculty Dir; 1 FT, 4 PT instr. Estab. 1954;
pvt; D & E; ent. req. applicants must have genuine desire for study;
4 yr; dipl; schol; enrl. D 24, E 10, maj. 24. Tui. $1008 per yr,
FT $112 mo, PT varies mo, 1-3 classes per wk. $4.50 per class,
4-7 classes per wk. $4 per class, random $6 per class; no campus
res.

Anatomy	Design
Art Education	Drawing
Basic Forms	Painting
Color	Perspective
Commercial Art	Sculpture
Composition	Tools & Uses

JACKSONVILLE

FLORIDA JUNIOR COLLEGE AT JACKSONVILLE, SOUTH CAMPUS,
Art Department, Beach Blvd, 32216. Tel: (904) 646-2150
Jim Schupp, Chmn. Div. Fine Arts, Humanities, Speech, Drama,
Foreign Language; 6 FT instr. Estab. 1966; pub; D & E; ent. req. HS
dipl; 2 yr; degrees, A.A, A.S; schol; 14 SC, 6 LC; art enrl. D 150,
E 75. Tui. $10 per cr. hr. all terms; no campus res.

Batik	Handicrafts
Blockprinting	History of Art & Archaeology
Ceramics	Leathercraft
Drawing	Macrame
Glaze Techniques	Painting
Graphic Design	Weaving

Adult hobby classes, ceramics, painting, photography; tui. $2 per
course; enrl. 150 per term.
Summer School: Jim Schupp, Dir; tui. $50 for term of 6 wk.
beginning June 19; 1973 enrl. 75-80.

Art Appreciation	Drawing
Crafts	Painting

JACKSONVILLE UNIVERSITY, College of Fine Arts, Department
of Art, University Blvd. N, 32211. Tel: (904) 744-3950
S. Barre Barrett, Chmn; 4 FT, 8 PT instr. Estab. 1932; pvt; D & E;
ent. req. HS dipl, ent. exam; 4 yr; degrees, B.F.A.(Studio Art, Art
History), B.A.Ed; schol; 29 SC, 16 LC; enrl. D 403, maj. 80. Tui.
$1850 per yr; campus res. $1380.

LAKE CITY

LAKE CITY COMMUNITY COLLEGE,* Art Department, 32055.
Tel: (904) 752-1822 Exten. 274
1 FT, 2 PT instr. Estab. 1962; pub; D & E; ent. req. HS dipl;
2 yrs; degree, A.A; 9 SC, 2 LC; enrl. D 160, E 80, maj. 10. Tui.
$8.50 per wk.

Ceramics	Jewelry
Composition	Painting
Drawing	Sculpture
Handicrafts	Weaving

LAKE WORTH

PALM BEACH JUNIOR COLLEGE,* Department of Art, 4200 Congress Ave, 33460. Tel: (305) 965-8000 Exten. 257
Dr. James B. Miles, Chmn. Dept. 8 FT, 5 PT instr. Estab. 1935;
pub; D & E; ent. req. HS dipl. or over 25; 2 yrs; degrees, A.A, A.S;
20 SC, 5 LC; total coll. enrl. D 3400, E 3200, maj. 200. Tui. in-
state $260 per yr, PT $36 per sem. hr; out-of-state $330 per yr,
PT $83 per sem. hr.

Advertising Design	Handicrafts
Architectural Drawing	History of Art & Archaeology
Basic Design	Interior Design
Ceramics	Jewelry
Commercial Art	Lettering
Drawing	Painting
Enamelling	Photography
Graphic Arts	Sculpture
Graphic Design	Typography

Adult hobby classes, floral design, picture frame making, jewelry,
weaving; tui. $15-$25; enrl. 15-30.
Summer School: Dr. James B. Miles, Dir.

Art Appreciation	History of Art
Design	Photography
Drawing	

LAKELAND

FLORIDA SOUTHERN COLLEGE, Art Department, 33802.
Tel: (813) 683-5521 Exten. 431
Dr. Donna M. Stoddard, Coordinator of Art; 4 FT instr. Estab. 1885;
den; co-ed; D; ent. req. HS dipl. (13 academic units, 4 English, 3
math, 6 sciences-history, foreign language); 4 yr; degrees, A.B,
B.S; schol; 17 SC, 5 LC; enrl. FT 1389, PT 412; also directed and
independent study. Tui. and fees approx. $1480 per sem. incl. room
and board. Art courses preparatory for teaching and graduate study.
Summer Session: Dr. Donna M. Stoddard, Coordinator of Art
Dept.

Art for Teachers	Directed & Independent Study
Art History	Survey
Crafts	

MARIANNA

CHIPOLA JUNIOR COLLEGE, Art Department, 32446.
Tel: (904) 482-4935
Richard H. Vait, Chmn; 1 FT, 1 PT instr. Estab. 1954; pub; D & E;
ent. req. HS dipl; 2 yr; degree, A.A; schol; 14 SC, 2 LC; enrl. D 60.
Tui. $10 per sem. hr, non-res. $20; campus res. $1000.

Ceramics	Jewelry
Drafting	Painting
Drawing	Sculpture
History of Art & Archaeology	Stage Design
Industrial Design	Theatre Arts

MIAMI

ART INSTITUTE OF MIAMI, 7808 N.E. Second Ave, 33138.
Tel: (305) 754-5688
Elwin Porter, Dir; 2 FT, 4 PT instr. Estab. 1958; pvt; D; ent. req.
HS dipl. or equivalent; 2-4 yr; cert; schol; 10 SC, 2 LC. Tui. $800
per yr; no campus res.

Advertising Design	Illustration
Anatomy	Landscape Architecture
Art Education	Lettering
Basic Design & Composition	Painting
Commercial Art	Photography
Display	Sculpture
Drawing	Watercolor
History of Art & Archaeology	

Summer School: Elwin Porter, Dir; courses offered, same as
above; tui. $50-$200 for term of 9 wk. beginning June 25.

MIAMI-DADE COMMUNITY COLLEGE, South Campus, 11011 S.W.
104th St, 33156. Tel: (305) 274-1281
Margaret M. Pelton, Chmn; 14 FT, 4 PT instr. Estab. 1960; pub;
D & E; ent. req. HS dipl, 18 yr. old; 2 yr; degrees, A.A.(Fine Art,
Art Educ); schol; 21 SC, 7 LC; enrl. D 60,000, E 1000, maj. 350.
Tui. $125 per sem, non-res. $325, $5 reg. plus some studio fees;
no campus res.

Art Education	Graphic Arts
Ceramics	History of Art
Design	Jewelry
Drawing	Painting
Elementary Education	Photography
Fabric & Fibers	Sculpture

Adult classes in all art areas; tui. $15.

MIAMI SHORES

BARRY COLLEGE, Department of Art, 11300 N.E. Second Ave,
33161. Tel: (305) 758-3392
Joseph M. Ruffo, Chmn; 4 FT, 3 PT instr. Estab. 1940; pvt; D & E;
ent. req. HS dipl, portfolio for B.F.A; 4 yr; degrees, B.A, B.F.A,
B.A.(Educ), B.F.A.(Educ); schol; 8 SC, 2 LC; enrl. D 300, E 60, maj.
40. Tui. $1700 per yr; campus res. $1200.

Advertising Design	Illustration
Art Education	Jewelry
Ceramics	Painting
Commercial Art	Photography
Costume Design & Construction	Sculpture
Drawing	Stage Design
Fashion Arts	Teacher Training
Graphic Arts	Textile Design
Graphic Design	Theatre Arts
History of Art & Archaeology	

OCALA

CENTRAL FLORIDA COMMUNITY COLLEGE, Fine Arts Division,
P.O. Box 1388, 32670. Tel: (904) 237-2111 Exten. 84
O. Joseph Fleming, Dir; 2 FT instr. Estab. 1958; pub; D & E; ent.
req. HS dipl; 2 yr; degree, A.A; schol; 2 SC, 2 LC; enrl. 1500. Tui.
$10 per sem. hr, non-res. $20 per sem. hr; no campus res.

Art Appreciation	Ceramics
Art Fundamentals	Drawing
Basic Design	Printmaking

PENSACOLA

PENSACOLA JUNIOR COLLEGE, Visual Arts Department, 1000
College Blvd, 32504. Tel: (904) 476-5410 Exten. 268
Carl F. Duke, Head Dept. of Art; 11 FT 1 PT instr. Estab. 1948;
pub; D & E; ent. req. HS dipl; 2 yr; degrees, A.S, A.A; schol; enrl.
maj. approx. 100. Tui. $24 per cr. hr; no campus res. Summer
School.

Advertising Design	Lettering
Ceramics	Macrame
Drawing	Painting
Graphic Arts	Photography
History of Art & Archaeology	Sculpture
Illustration	Weaving
Jewelry	

UNIVERSITY OF WEST FLORIDA, Faculty of Art, 32504.
Tel: (904) 476-9500 Exten. 440
Dr. John T. Carey, Chmn; 7 FT, 2 PT instr. Estab. 1967; pub;
D & E; ent. req. equivalent of 2 yr. training at jr. coll. or 4 yr.
inst; 1 yr. in res. required; degree, B.A; schol; 25 SC, 20 LC;
enrl. D 4668, E 933, maj. 60. Tui. fees per cr. hr. per quarter;
$15 per quarter hr, non-res. $47 per quarter hr.

Art Education	Painting
Ceramics	Photography
Commercial Art	Sculpture
Drawing	Teacher Training
Graphic Arts	Textile Design
Jewelry	

Summer School: Dr. John T. Carey, Dir; courses offered, Art
Education, Art History, Studio; reg. fee $190, housing $160 for
term of 9 wk. beginning mid-June.

ST. PETERSBURG

ST. PETERSBURG JUNIOR COLLEGE,* Department of Humanities,
6605 Fifth Ave. N, 33733. Tel: (813) 546-0011
Dr. Edwin L. Stover, Chmn; 7 FT instr. Estab. 1927; pub; D & E;
ent. req. HS dipl; 2 yr; degrees, A.A, A.S; schol; 13 SC, 3 LC; total
enrl. fall term, 1969, D 7031, E 2478. Full-time students pay matriculation fee of $200 per acad. yr; additional tui. out-of-district $60,
out-of-state $240; no campus res.

Advertising Design	History of Art & Archaeology
Aesthetics	Painting
Ceramics	Photography
Design I & II	Sculpture
Drafting	Stage Design
Drawing	Survey in Crafts
Graphic Arts	Theatre Arts

Summer Session: Session III of year-round calendar; majority of
the above courses; tui. as above, in-district $10 per cr. hr, out-of-
district $13, out-of-state $22; total enrl. 4669 (both campuses).

Clearwater Campus, 2465 Drew St, 33515.
Karl Garrett, Chmn, Department of Humanities. Estab. 1965; same
information as above.

SARASOTA

HILTON LEECH ART STUDIO, 4433 Riverwood Ave, 33581.
Tel: (813) 924-5770
Mrs. Elden Rowland, Exec. Secy; 3 FT, 3 PT instr. Estab. 1946;
pvt; D; no ent. req; no degree; schol; 6 SC; enrl. 75, all PT enrl.
Various fees per instruction; no facilities.

Drawing	Photography
Painting	Watercolor

Adult hobby classes, painting-all media; tui. $10 a lesson; enrl. 75.
Summer School: Mrs. Hilton Leech, Virginia City, Mont;
courses offered, Drawing & Painting; 8 wk. beginning July 1st.

NEW COLLEGE OF THE UNIVERSITY OF SOUTH FLORIDA,
Humanities Division, Fine Arts Department, 5700 N. Tamiami
Trail, 33578. Tel: (813) 355-1151
Jack Cartlidge, Head; 4 FT instr. Estab. 1963; pvt; D; ent. req.

ent. exam, SAT; 3 yr; degree, B.A.(Fine Arts); 6 SC, 5 LC; enrl. D
150-200, maj. o. 15. Tui. $715 per yr. res; campus res. $2400.

Aesthetics	History of Art & Archaeology
Ceramics	Painting
Drawing	Sculpture
Graphic Arts	Stained Glass

RINGLING SCHOOL OF ART, 33580.
Tel: (813) 355-5259
Robert E. Perkins, Pres; George R. Kaiser, Jr, Dean of Admis;
18 FT instr. Estab. 1931; pvt; D; ent. req. HS grad; degrees, 3 yr.
cert, B.F.A; 51 SC, 2 LC; enrl. maj. 450. Tui. $960; campus res.
$110.
Advertising Design
Interior Design
Painting

TALLAHASSEE

FLORIDA A & M UNIVERSITY,* Art Department, Box 512, 32307.
Tel: (904) 222-8030 Exten. 246
Howard E. Lewis, Chmn Dept; 10 FT, 1 PT instr. Pub; D & E; ent.
req. HS dipl, score on Florida State-Wide Test or its equivalent; 4
yrs; degrees, B.Sc, B.A; 34 SC, 13 LC, 4 GC; enrl. D 3592, E 297,
maj. 135. Tui. $570 per yr; out-of-state $350 per quarter; campus
res. $942.

Advertising Design	History of Art & Archaeology
Aesthetics	Lettering
Art Education	Painting
Ceramics	Photography
Design	Sculpture
Drawing	Teacher Training
Graphic Arts	Textile Design

Adult hobby classes, ceramics workshop, tui. $48 per quarter; enrl.
30 per quarter.
Summer School: Howard E. Lewis, Dir; tui. $190 for term of 9
wk. beginning June 14.

Art Appreciation	Ceramics
Art Education	Humanities

FLORIDA STATE UNIVERSITY, School of Visual Arts,
32306.
J. L. Draper, Acting Dean. Pub; D & E; schol. Tui. $240, plus
$350 non-res. per quarter.

Department of Art. Tel: (904) 644-6474
Jerry L. Draper, Head; 25 FT instr. Estab. 1906; degrees, B.A,
B.F.A, M.A, M.F.A, Ph.D; schol. and fel; enrl. D 400, grad. 74.

Cinematography	Photography
Design	Printmaking
Fashion Illustration	Sculpture
History & Criticism of Art	Visual Communication
Painting	

Department of Art Education and Constructive Design, 123
Education Building. Tel: (904) 644-5473, 5474
Dr. Ivan E. Johnson, Head; 9 FT, 3 PT instr. Estab. 1928; ent. req.
ent. exam; 4 yr; degrees, B.S, B.A, M.A. and Ph.D.(Art Educ),
B.S, B.A. and M.S.(Constructive Design), B.F.A.(pending); schol;
62 SC, 12 LC, 20 GC; enrl. D 521, E 30, maj. 135, grad. 29.

Art Education	Museum Staff Training
Ceramics	Occupational Therapy
Industrial Design	Teacher Training
Jewelry	Textile Design

Summer School: Dr. Garth Blake, Dean.

TALLAHASSEE COMMUNITY COLLEGE, Art Department, 444
Appleyard Dr, 32303. Tel: (904) 576-5181
Ruth Deshaies, Prog. Chmn; 1 FT, 2 PT instr. Estab. 1966;
pub; D & E; ent. req. HS dipl; 2 yr; degrees, A.A, A.S; 2 SC,
1 LC; enrl. 2500. Tui. $120 per 15 wk. sem; no campus res.

Basic Design	Painting
Drawing	Photography
History of Art & Archaeology	

TAMPA

UNIVERSITY OF SOUTH FLORIDA, College of Fine Arts, Art
Department, 4202 Fowler Ave, 33620. Tel: (813) 974-2360
George Pappas, Chmn; D 20 FT instr. Estab. 1956; pub; ent. req. HS
grad, 14 units cert. by HS, ent. exam; minimum 180 quarter hr. for
B.A.(Art) and 72 quarter hr. for M.F.A. Tui. undergrad. res. $14
per hr., non-res, $37 per hr, grad. res. $20 per hr, non-res. $57 per
hr.

Art History	Graphics
Ceramics	Painting

Cinematography   Photography
Drawing   Sculpture
     Summer School: One of four equal yearly quarters.

UNIVERSITY OF TAMPA,* Department of Art, Plant Park, 33606.
     Tel: (813) 253-8861
Wallace F. Green, Chmn. Dept. Art; 5 FT instr. Estab. 1930; pvt;
D & E; 4 yr; degrees; 17 SC, 8 LC.

Art Education   History of Art
Ceramics   Painting
Design   Printmaking
Drawing   Sculpture

WEST PALM BEACH

✣NORTON SCHOOL OF ART, 1451 S. Olive Ave, 33401.
     Tel: (305) 832-5194
Richard A. Madigan, Dir; Flanders Holland, Mgr; 4 FT instr.
Sept-July, 5 FT instr. Nov-Apr, 3 E instr. Estab. 1941; pvt; no
ent. req; no degree; enrl. adults 250, children and teenagers 150.
Fee children's courses $10-16 per mo, adult courses various rates.

Art History   Painting
Ceramics   Sculpture
Drawing

WINTER PARK

ROLLINS COLLEGE,* Department of Art, Main Campus, 32789.
     Tel: (305) 646-2000
Hallie LuHallam, Chmn; 4 FT instr. Estab. 1885; pvt; D & E; 4 yr;
degree; schol; 11 SC, 10 LC; D & E enrl. 250.

Aesthetics   Drawing & Painting
Art History   Humanities Foundation
Art History Survey   Principles of Art
Design   Sculpture

GEORGIA

ATHENS

UNIVERSITY OF GEORGIA, Franklin College of Arts & Sciences,
     Division of Fine Arts, 30602. Tel: (404) 542-2121
Opened 1801, chartered 1875; 4 yr; degrees; schol. & fel. ($2725,
9 mo. masters level, $2925, 9 mo. doctorate level, grad. assistant-
ships available through grad. school of Univ. of Georgia and others).
Tui. $519; campus res.

     Department of Art
Edmund B. Feldman, Head; 54 FT, 1 PT instr. Estab. 1932; degrees;
75 SC, 29 LC, 69 GC; enrl. undergrad. maj. 800, grad. 100, others
1500.

Art Education   Interior Design
Art History   Jewelry & Metal Work
Art—Home Economics   Painting & Drawing
Ceramics   Photographic Design
Fabric Design   Printmaking
Graphic Design   Sculpture
     Summer School: Edmund B. Feldman, Dir; $169 for 11 wk.

ATLANTA

ATLANTA COLLEGE OF ART, 1280 Peachtree St. N.E, 30309.
     Tel: (404) 892-3600 Exten. 231
William J. Voos, Dean; Mrs. Guthrie Foster, Asst. Dean; Jean Dyer,
Dir. Admis; 17 FT, 12 PT instr. Estab. 1928; pvt; D; ent. req.
portfolio of 8 examples of art work (slides), HS grad, HS and coll.
transcripts, SAT, application form, $15 fee; 4 yr; degree, B.F.A;
28 SC, 14 LC; enrl. D 250, E 500. Tui. $1800.

Drawing   Sculpture
Painting   Video Imagery
Photography   Visual Communication
Printmaking
Adult Extension Program, Sat. Morning Workshop and Summer
Foundation Workshop for HS students.
     Summer School: Jean Dyer, Dir; tui. varies with course;
enrl. 300.

Drawing   Printmaking
Painting   Television
Photography

CLARK COLLEGE, Art Department, 240 Chestnut St. S.W, 30314.
     Tel: (404) 681-3080 Exten. 252
Dr. Emmanuel V. Asihene, Chmn; 3 FT. Estab. 1869; pvt; D; ent.

req. HS dipl, ent. exam; 4 yr; degree, B.A; SC, LC; enrl. D 45,
maj. 12, grad. 12. Tui. $2675.30 per yr; campus res. $994.

Advertising Design   Illustration
Commercial Art   Lettering
Graphic Arts   Photography
Graphic Design   Visual Communication

EMORY COLLEGE OF EMORY UNIVERSITY, Department of the
     History of Art, 30322. Tel: (404) 377-2411 Exten. 7511
John Howett, Chmn; 5 FT, 3 PT instr. Estab. 1965; den; D; ent.
req. HS grad; 4 yr; degrees, B.A, M.A, Ph.D; 3 SC, 30 LC, 3 GC;
enrl. 2600. Tui. $950 per quarter.

✣GEORGIA INSTITUTE OF TECHNOLOGY, College of Architecture,
     225 North Ave. N.W, 30332. Tel: (404) 894-4885, 4886
Vernon D. Crawford, Acting Dean; Paul M. Heffernan, Dir; 38 FT,
16 PT instr. Estab. 1908; pub; co-ed; ent. req. HS dipl, SAT; 4 yr;
degrees, B.S, B.S.(Building Construction), B.S.(Industrial Design),
M.Arch, M.City Planning; 54 SC, 118LC, 58 GC; enrl. 900. Tui.
(incl. fees) $560, non-res. $1680; campus res. One yr. Study Abroad
Program, Paris, France, for 4th yr. architectural students.

Architecture   Graduate City Planning
Building Construction   Industrial Design
Graduate Architecture

GEORGIA STATE UNIVERSITY,* 33 Gilmer St, S.E, 30303.
     Tel: (404) 577-2400 Exten. 332, 333
Prof. Joseph S. Perrin, Head; D 20 FT, 2 PT, E 18 FT, 2 PT instr.
Estab. 1914; pub; ent. req. HS grad, ent. exam, college board, interview; 4 yr; degrees, Bachelor of Visual Arts, A.B. in Art; schol;
80 SC enrl. 600, 17 LC enrl. 300; enrl. maj. 300, others 20. Tui.
$423 per yr, approx. $37 per mo, matriculation and other expenses
approx. $100; campus res.

Advertising Design   Illustration
Art History   Interior Design
Ceramics   Lettering
Drawing   Painting
Graphic Arts   Sculpture
Handicrafts-Weaving, Jewelry,   Teacher Training
     Metalwork   Textile Design
     Summer School: Joseph S. Perrin, Dir; Tui. $141 for term of 9
wk. beginning June 10; enrl. 450.

AUGUSTA

AUGUSTA COLLEGE, Department of Fine Arts, 2500 Walton Way,
     30904. Tel: (404) 828-3211
Dr. Eloy Fominaya, Chmn; 4 FT, 1 PT instr. Jr. Coll. estab. 1925,
Sr. Coll. 1962; pub; D & E; ent. req. HS grad, ent. exam; 4 yr;
degrees, B.A, B.S, B.Bus.Admin, M.Bus, M.Educ; schol; 11 SC, 3 LC;
total enrl. 4000. Tui. $345; no campus res.

Art Education   History of Art & Archaeology
Ceramics   Painting
Design   Sculpture
Drawing
Adult hobby classes, recreational painting; tui. $30; enrl. 10-20.

CARROLLTON

WEST GEORGIA COLLEGE, Art Department, 30017.
     Tel: (404) 834-1235
Derrill M. Maxwell, Chmn. Estab. 1975; pub; D; ent. req. HS dipl,
ent. exam; 4 yr; degrees, A.B.(Studio, Art Educ); schol; 24 SC,
10 LC, 1 GC; enrl. maj. 124. Tui. $444 per yr, PT $11 per quarter
hr; campus res. $960.

Aesthetics   Painting
Art Education   Photography
Ceramics   Sculpture
Graphic Arts   Teacher Training
Graphic Design   Textile Design
History of Art & Archaeology   Weaving
Adult hobby classes, ceramics, drawing, painting; tui. $15.
     Summer School.

Art Education   Graphics
Drawing   Painting

CLEVELAND

TRUETT-McCONNELL COLLEGE,
     30528.
Maurice Blaine Caldwell, Head; 1 FT instr. Estab. 1946; den; D & E;
ent. req. HS dipl; 2 yr; degrees, A.A, A.S; schol; 8 SC, 2 LC; enrl.
D 35, maj. 15. Tui. $2300 per yr.

Aesthetics   History of Art & Archaeology
Ceramics   Painting
Drawing   Stage Design
Graphic Design

COCHRAN

MIDDLE GEORGIA COLLEGE (Junior College Unit of the University of Georgia), Department of Art, 31014.
Tel: (912) 934-6221 Exten. 288
Robert R. Nason, Chmn; 2 FT instr. Pub; D & E; co-ed; ent. req. HS dipl, GED; 2 yr; degree, A.A; 6 SC; enrl. D 270, E 45. Tui. 3 quarters $330, payable one third in advance each quarter; campus res. $290 per quarter.

Art Education	Drawing
Ceramics	Lettering
Commercial Art	Painting

Summer School: Robert R. Nason, Dir; courses offered same as above; tui. $110 for term of 10 wk. beginning approx. June 15; 1976 enrl. 30.

COLUMBUS

COLUMBUS COLLEGE, Department of Art, Algonquin Dr, 31907.
Tel: (404) 568-2047
Dr. Josiah L. M. Baird, Head; 7 FT, 1 PT instr. Estab. 1949; pub; D & E; ent. req. HS dipl, ent. exam; 4 yr; degrees, B.S.(Art Educ), B.A.(Art), M.Ed.(Art Educ); schol; 29 SC, 7 LC, 14 GC; enrl. D 300, E 50, maj. 130, grad. 20. Tui. $132, plus $16.50, for 12 or more quarter hr, non-res, $348, plus $16.50; no campus res.

Art Education	Painting
Ceramics	Photography
Costume Design & Construction	Sculpture
Drawing	Stage Design
Graphic Arts	Teacher Training
History of Art & Archaeology	Textile Design
Illustration	Theatre Arts
Jewelry	Weaving
Macrame	

Adult hobby classes and children's classes, various subjects; enrl. each 60.
Summer School: Dr. Josiah L. M. Baird, Dir; courses offered, Art History, Studio; term of one quarter; enrl. 200.

DECATUR

✣AGNES SCOTT COLLEGE, Art Department, 30030.
Tel: (404) 373-2581
Dr. Marie Huper Pepe, Chmn; 3 FT instr. Reorganized in 1943 forming University Center in cooperation with Emory University, Georgia Institute of Technology, University of Georgia (Athens), Oglethorpe University, Columbia Theological Seminary and Atlanta Art Association; pvt; W; 4 yr; degree, B.A; schol; 10 SC, 12 LC.

Art Structure & Design	History of Art
Ceramics	Painting
Drawing	Sculpture

GAINESVILLE

BRENAU COLLEGE, Art Department, 30501.
Tel: (404) 532-4341 Exten. 254
Bill Singles, Head; 3 FT, 1 PT instr. Estab. 1878; pvt; D & E; W; ent. req. HS dipl; 4 yr; degrees, B.A, B.S; schol; 30 SC, 5 LC; enrl. D 450, E 100, maj. 25. Tui. $1440 per yr; campus res. $1260 per yr.

Advertising Design	History of Art & Archaeology
Aesthetics	Illustration
Art Education	Interior Design
Basic Design	Jewelry
Ceramics	Lettering
Commercial Art	Metalsmithing
Costume Design & Construction	Painting
Crafts	Photography
Drawing	Sculpture
Fabric Design	Stage Design
Fashion Arts	Textile Design
Graphic Design	Theatre Arts
Handicrafts	Weaving

Summer School: John Sites, Dean; tui. $25 per cr. hr. for term of 3 wk. beginning June; 1976 enrl. 250.

Art Education	Fabric Design
Ceramics	Graphic Design
Crafts	Painting/Drawing
Commercial Art	Photography

LA GRANGE

LAGRANGE COLLEGE, Art Department, 30240.
Tel: (404) 882-2911 Exten. 491
John Lawrence, Head; 2 FT instr. Estab. 1831; pvt; D & E; ent.

req. HS dipl, ent. exam; 4 yr; degree, B.A; schol; 11 SC, 2 LC; enrl. maj. 40. Tui. $1250, incl. room and board.

Art Education	Photography
Commercial Art (Textile)	Printmaking
History of Art	Sculpture
Painting	

MACON

MERCER UNIVERSITY,* Art Department, 1400 Coleman Ave, 31207.
Tel: (912) 743-1511 Exten. 235
Marshall Daugherty, Chmn; 4 FT instr. Estab. 1945; den; D; ent. req. HS grad; 4 yr; degree, B.A; 9 SC, 7 LC, 2 GC; enrl. maj. 15. Tui. $2000 per yr; campus res. room and board, $1000 per yr.

Art Education	Graphic Arts
Ceramics	History of Art
Drawing	Sculpture

Summer School: Dr. Paul Cable, Dir; courses offered, Drawing, Painting, Sculpture; tui. $436 for term of 9 wk. beginning June 16.

WESLEYAN COLLEGE, School of Fine Arts, 31201.
Tel: (912) 477-1110
Thomas A. Prochaska, Acting Chmn; 3 FT instr. Estab. 1836; pvt; W; ent. schol. & others; 4 yr; degree, B.F.A; 39 SC, 9 LC; enrl. approx. 600. Tui. res. $3395 per yr.

Art Education	Graphic Arts
Ceramics	Painting
Commercial Art	Sculpture

MT. BERRY

BERRY COLLEGE, Art Department, 30149.
Dr. Tommy Mew, Head; 3 FT, 1 PT instr. Estab. 1904; pvt; D & E; ent. req. HS dipl, ent. exam; 4 yr; degrees, B.A, B.S; schol; 23 SC, 6 LC; enrl. maj. 115. Tui. $1500 per yr; campus res. $2805. Summer School.

Advertising Design	Graphic Art
Aesthetics	History of Art & Archaeology
Art Education	Painting
Ceramics	Photography
Drafting	Sculpture
Drawing	Teacher Training

ROME

SHORTER COLLEGE, Art Department, Shorter Ave, 30161.
Tel: (404) 232-2463
Jane M. McCord, Head; 2 FT instr. Estab. 1873; den; D; ent. req. combination of tests; 4 yr; degree, A.B.(Art); schol; 9 SC, 4 LC; enrl. D 500, maj. 25. Tui. $1575 per yr; campus res. $1050.

Art Education	History of Art & Archaeology
Batki	Hooked Tapestry
Ceramics	Painting
Drawing	Photography
Enamel	Sculpture
Graphic Arts	Silk Screen
Graphic Design	Teacher Training
Handicrafts	Textile Design

Summer School: George Hayes, Art Dir; courses offered, Art Appreciation, Ceramics, Sculpture.

VALDOSTA

VALDOSTA STATE COLLEGE, Department of Art, Patterson St, 31601. Tel: (912) 247-3319, 3330
Irene Dodd, Head; 9 FT instr. Estab. 1911; pub; D; ent. req. SAT; 4 yr; degrees, A.B. and B.F.A.(Art Educ); 25 SC, 10 LC, 9 GC; enrl. 400, maj. 120, total 4278. Tui. 12 or more quarter hr, res. $139, non-res. $319; less than 12 quarter hr, res. $9.75 per hr, non-res. $23.73 per hr. Summer School.

Advertising Design	History of Art
Art Education	Illustration
Ceramics	Museum Tour
Commercial Art	Painting
Drawing	Sculpture
Graphic Arts	Teacher Training
Graphic Design	Weaving

Children's classes, crafts, drawing, sculpture, watercolor.

WALESKA

REINHARDT COLLEGE,* Department of Art, 30183.
Tel: (404) 479-2119
Curtis A. Chapman, Head; 1 FT, 3 PT instr. Estab. 1966; den;

D; ent. req. HS dipl, ent. exam; 2 yr; degrees, A.A, A.S; schol; 4 SC, 1 LC; enrl. D 270. Tui. $810; campus res. $1800.

Aesthetics
Art Appreciation
Drawing
Graphic Arts

Handicrafts
History of Art & Archaeology
Painting
Sculpture

Summer School: Dennis Harris, Dir; courses offered, Printmaking, Art Appreciation.

YOUNG HARRIS

YOUNG HARRIS COLLEGE, Department of Art, 30582.
Tel: (404) 379-2161
Ezra L. Sellers, Chmn; 2 FT instr. Estab. 1886; den; D; ent. req. HS dipl; 2 yr; degree, A.F.A; schol; 6 SC, 4 LC; enrl. D 540, maj. 48. Tui. $765 per yr; PT $407; campus res. $1245.

Design
Drawing

Painting
Sculpture

History of Art & Archaeology
Adult classes, painting; no tui; enrl. 18. Children's classes, 4 wk. in summer; no tui; enrl. 20.

HAWAII

HONOLULU

THE FOUNDRY ART CENTER, 899 Waimanu St, 96813.
Tel: (808) 533-2609
Alice S. Leitner, Dir; 5 FT, 10-20 PT instr. Estab. 1969; pvt; D & E; ent. req. prerequisites according to course; cert. of completion; 10 SC, 2 LC. Tui. $50 per course.

Aesthetics
Ceramics
Copper Enameling
Drawing
Graphic Arts
Handicrafts
Language of Art

Language of Drawing
Macrame
Painting
Sculpture
Textile Design
Weaving
Woodcarving

Children's classes, arts and crafts; tui. $25.
Summer School: Alice S. Leitner, Dir; tui. $50 for term of 8 wk.

✢HONOLULU ACADEMY OF ARTS, Studio Program, 900 Beretania St, 96814. Tel: (808) 538-3693
Joseph Feher, Cur; 3 FT, 1 PT instr. Estab. 1946; pvt; ent. req. 16 yr. of age with talent; 3 yr; schol. Tui. $220 half day, $440 full day per sem.

Drawing
Painting

Printmaking: Etching &
Lithography

Summer School: Joseph Feher, Dir; Drawing, Painting and Printmaking; tui. $75 for 6 wk, half days.

KAPIOLANI COMMUNITY COLLEGE, Pensacola Campus, 620 Pensacola St, 96814; tel: (808) 531-4654 Exten. 142. Diamond Head Campus, 4303 Diamond Head Rd, 96816; tel. (808) 735-3127
Gretchen Andersen, Instr; 1 FT, 3 PT instr. Coll. estab. as a community coll. in 1965; pub; D & E; ent. req. ent. exam; 1-2 yr; degrees, A.S, A.A; schol; 6 SC, 7 LC; enrl. D 3800, E approx. 500. Tui. $45, non-res. $455, res. $3.50 per sem. unit, non-res. $38 per sem. unit; no campus res.

Art Appreciation
Art History: Asian & Western
Ceramics & Macrame
Drawing & Painting
Introduction to Visual Arts

Jewelry
Light & Color
Perception
Textile Design

Adult classes, ceramics & macrame, drawing & painting, jewelry, textile design; tui. depends on amount of units; enrl. 25 per class.
Summer School: James Embrey, Dir; courses offered change each summer; tui. depends on amount of units taken; term of 6 wk; enrl. 700.

UNIVERSITY OF HAWAII, Department of Art, 2535 The Mall, 96822.
Tel: (808) 948-8251
Prithwish Neogy, Chmn; 30 FT instr. Estab. 1907; pub; 4 yr; degrees, B.A, B.F.A, M.A, M.F.A; 55 SC, 25 LC, 35 GC; enrl. 21,000. Tui. non-res. $562.50 per sem, $48 per cr. hr.

Ceramics & Glassblowing
Design
Drawing
History of Art
Painting

Photography
Printmaking
Sculpture
Textile Design
Weaving

Summer School: Robert K. Sakai, Dean; primarily undergrad. courses; tui. $30 per cr. hr.

KAHULUI

MAUI COMMUNITY COLLEGE, 310 Kaahumanu Ave, 96732.
Barbara D. Miller, Art Prog. Coordinator; 1 FT, 3 PT instr. Estab. 1967; pub; D & E; ent. req. ent. exam; 2 yr; degree, A.S; schol; 8 SC, 2 LC; enrl. D 300, E 100. Tui. non-res. $350 per sem.

Advertising Design
Architecture
Batik
Ceramics
Copper Enameling
Display
Drafting
Drawing
Graphic Arts

Graphic Design
History of Architecture
History of Art & Archaeology
Jewelry
Painting
Photography
Sculpture: Welding
Textile Design
Weaving

Adult hobby classes, batik, silk screen jewelry; tui. $10-$30; enrl. 60.
Summer School: Walter Onyl, Dir; courses offered, Introduction to the Visual Arts; tui. $35 for term of 6 wk. beginning June; enrl. 40.

LIHUE

KAUAI COMMUNITY COLLEGE,* Department of Art, RRI, Box 216, 96766. Tel: (808) 245-6741
2 FT, 1 Pt instr. Estab. 1965; pub; D & E; ent. req. HS dipl; 2 yrs; degrees, A.A, A.S; schol; 6 SC, 2 LC; enrl. D 965, E 468. Tui. FT $50; out of state students $700.

Ceramics
Drafting
Drawing
Graphic Arts

History of Art & Archaeology
Painting
Photography
Watercolor

Summer School: courses offered, Ceramics, photography, watercolor; tui. 1-3 sem. hrs. $5, 4-6 sem. hr. $10 for term of 6 wk. beginning June 12 and July 20.

IDAHO

BOISE

BOISE STATE UNIVERSITY, Art Department, 1910 College Blvd, 83725. Tel: (208) 385-1247
Louis A. Peck, Chmn; 21 FT, 11 PT instr. Estab. 1932; pub; D & E; ent. req. HS dipl; 4 yr; degrees, B.A, B.F.A, B.A. and B.F.A.(Educ), B.A. and B.F.A.(Advertising Design); schol; 51 SC, 8 LC, 4 GC; enrl. D 2539, maj. 441, grad. 14. Tui. $362 per yr, PT $20 per cr; campus res. $1500.

Advertising Design
Art Education
Ceramics
Commercial Art
Drawing
Graphic Arts
Graphic Design
History of Art & Archaeology
Illustration

Jewelry
Lettering
Metal
Painting
Photography
Sculpture
Teacher Training
Textile Design

Summer School: Dr. Louis A. Peck, Dir; tui. $20 per cr.

Art Education
Art History
Design

Drawing
Introduction to Art
Painting

NORTHWEST NAZARENE COLLEGE, Art Department, Holly at Dewey, 83651. Tel: (208) 467-8412
Dr. Mary Shaffer, Head; 3 FT instr. Den; D & E; ent. req. HS dipl; 4 yr; degrees, A.A, A.B; schol; 12 SC, 5 LC; enrl. D 200, E 40, maj. 24. Tui. $1590 for 3 terms; campus res. $995.

Advertising Design
Art Education
Ceramics
Commercial Art
Crafts for Teachers
Drafting
Drawing

Graphic Arts
History of Art & Archaeology
Illustration
Lettering
Painting
Sculpture
Teacher Training

Adult hobby classes, crafts; tui. $120 per course.
Summer School: Dr. Lilburn Wesche, Dir; course offered, Art Education.

LEWISTON

LEWIS-CLARK STATE COLLEGE, Art Department, 83501.
Tel: (208) 746-2341
Robert Almquist, Discipline Coordinator; 2 FT instr. Estab. 1893;

pub; D & E; ent. req. HS dipl; 4 yr; degrees, B.A.(Drawing, Painting, Sculpture); schol; 10 SC, 2 LC; enrl. D 120, E 15, maj. 5. Tui. 3285 per yr, non-res. $985, PT (up to 7 cr.) $12 per cr; campus res. $270.

Art Education	Painting
Composition	Sculpture
Drawing	Survey
History of Art & Archaeology	Teacher Training
Independent Study	Watercolor

MOSCOW

UNIVERSITY OF IDAHO, Department of Art and Architecture, 83843. Tel: (208) 882-2672
Paul L. Blanton, Head; 20 FT instr. Estab. 1923; pub; D & E (limited evening courses); 4-5 yr; degrees, B.F.A, B.A, B.Arch, B.L.Arch, B.F.A.(Interior Design), M.F.A, M.A, M.Arch; SC, LC, GC; schol. and teaching assistantships; enrl. 450. Tui. $200 per sem, non-res. $700. Limited extension courses in painting and jewelry.

Architecture	Landscape Architecture
Art Education (maj)	Painting
Design	Sculpture
Interior Design (maj)	

Work in crafts, jewelry, ceramics, photography, and others.
Summer School and Summer Traveling Workshop on Wheels in Idaho.

POCATELLO

IDAHO STATE UNIVERSITY, Department of Art, Box 8004, 83209. Tel: (208) 236-2361
Dennis Snyder, Chmn; 7 FT, 4 PT instr. Estab. 1901; pub; D & E; ent. req. HS grad. or GED, ACT; 4 yr; degrees, B.A, B.F.A, M.F.A; 32 SC, 6 LC, 22 GC; enrl. maj. 75, grad. 15, total 500. Reg. fee $205, non-res. tui. $425; campus res. $650. Continuing Education evening classes; Summer Session.

Art Education	Metals
Art History	Painting
Ceramics	Printmaking
Design	Sculpture
Drawing	Weaving

REXBURG

RICKS COLLEGE, Department of Art, 83440. Tel: (208) 356-2276
Arlo Coles, Coordinator; 6 FT instr. Estab. 1888; pvt; D; co-ed; ent. req. HS dipl, ent. exam; degrees, A.A.(2 yr), cert.(1 yr); schol; 18 SC, 1 LC; enrl. D. 4684, maj. approx. 50-75. Tui. $270 LDS per sem, $375 non-LDS; campus res. $470 per sem.

Art for Elementary Teachers	Graphic Design Studio
Art History	Illustration
Ceramics	Layout
Design	Lettering
Drawing	Oil Painting
Figure Drawing	Sculpture
General Art	Watercolor Painting

Summer School: Brent Kinghorn, Dir; tui. $250 for term of 10 wk. beginning June 10; 1973 enrl. 417.

TWIN FALLS

COLLEGE OF SOUTHERN IDAHO, Fine Arts Department, P.O. Box 1238, 83301. Tel: (208) 733-9554 Exten. 260
Lavar Steel, Chmn; 3 FT, 2 PT instr. Estab. 1965; pub; D & E; ent. req. HS grad, ent. exam, ACT; 2 yr; degree, A.A; schol; 18 SC, 2 LC, 285 GC; enrl. D 1800, E 200, maj. 30. Tui. $400.

Art Education	Painting
Ceramics	Photography
Commercial Art	Sculpture
Drafting	Stage Design
Drawing	Teacher Training
History of Art	Theatre Arts
Lettering	

Adult hobby classes, all subjects; tui. varies (about $15); enrl. 20 or 30 each class. Children's classes, general art; tui. $15 (10 wk); enrl. 20.
Summer School: Dr. P. J. Smith, Dir; tui. $5 per cr. hr. for term of 8 wk. beginning June 1; 1969 enrl. 200.

Art Education	Drawing
Art History	Painting
Ceramics	

ILLINOIS

BALLEVILLE

BELLEVILLE AREA COLLEGE, Department of Art, 2500 Carlyle Rd, 62221.
Wayne Shaw, Chmn; 3 FT, 15 PT instr. Estab. 1948; pub; D & E; ent. req. HS dipl, ent. exam; 2 yr; degrees, A.A.(Art & General Studies), A.S; schol; 36 SC, 9 LC; total enrl. D 3800, E 3500, art maj. 210. Tui. $400 per yr, $9 per sem. hr; no campus res.

Advertising Design	Painting
Art Education	Photography
Ceramics	Printmaking
Commercial Art	Sculpture
Drawing	Teacher Training
History of Art & Archaeology	Theatre Arts
Jewelry	

Adult hobby classes under dir. of Dr. Warren E. Nieburg, Dean of Community Services, ceramics, design, drawing, jewelry, painting, photography, sculpture; tui. $9 per hr; enrl. 175.
Summer School: Wayne Shaw, Dir; tui. $9 per sem. hr. beginning June 7; 1975 enrl. 175.

Art History	Jewelry
Ceramics	Photography
Drawing	

BLOOMINGTON

ILLINOIS WESLEYAN UNIVERSITY, School of Art, 61701. Tel: (309) 556-3077
John Mulvaney, Dir; 5 FT, 1 PT instr. Estab. 1932; den; D; 4 yr; degrees; 27 SC, 14 LC; schol; enrl. maj. 100, others 80. Tui. $2580 per yr. including campus res.

Art Education	Photography
Ceramics	Printmaking
History of Art	Sculpture
Painting	

CARBONDALE

SOUTHERN ILLINOIS UNIVERSITY,* Art Department, College of Communications and Fine Arts, 62901.
C. B. Hunt, Jr, Dean; Herbert L. Fink, Chmn. Art Dept; 18 faculty members. Estab. 1874; pub; D & E; 4 yr; degrees; schol; SC, LC; enrl. maj. 165.

Art Education	Printmaking
Art History	Sculpture
Metalcraft	Silversmithing
Painting	Weaving
Pottery	

Summer School: 8 wk. or 12 wk.

Department of Design, School of Fine Arts
Harold L. Cohen, Chmn; 10 faculty members. Estab. 1956; pub; 4 yr. for B.A, 2 additional yr. for M.S. degrees; students transferring from another Univ. cannot receive cr. for design courses but will be evaluated on the basis of his or her work; enrl. maj. 120.
Basic Design
Product-Shelter Design
Visual Design

CARLINVILLE

BLACKBURN COLLEGE, Department of Art, 62626. Tel: (217) 854-3231
James M. Clark, Chmn; 2 FT, 2 PT instr. Estab. 1949; pvt; D & E; ent. req. HS grad; 4 yr; degree, B.A; schol; 14 SC, 7 LC; enrl. maj. 40. Tui. $1800 per yr; campus res, $350 plus work plan (all res. students work 15 hr. per wk).

Art History	Printmaking
Ceramics	Teacher Training
Drawing & Painting	Theatre Arts
Painting	

CHARLESTON

✠EASTERN ILLINOIS UNIVERSITY, Department of Art, 61920. Tel: (217) 581-3410
John Linn, Head; 23 FT instr. Estab. 1899; pub; 4 yr; degrees, B.A.(Art Educ, Studio, Art History), M.A.(Art Educ, Studio); schol; 55 SC, 22 LC, 18 GC; enrl. maj. 264, others 1606. Tui. $250 (9-11 sem. hr), $300 (12-17 sem. hr).

Art Education	Jewelry & Metalsmithing
Ceramics	History of Art

Commercial
Crafts
Design
Drawing

Painting
Printmaking
Sculpture

CHICAGO

AMERICAN ACADEMY OF ART, 220 S. State St, 60604.
   Tel: (312) 939-3883
Clinton E. Frank, Pres; I. Shapiro, Dir; 15 FT, 7 PT instr. Estab.
1923; pvt; ent. req. HS grad; 2-3 yr; degree, A.A; enrl. 300 FT,
400 PT. Tui. $1550 FT, fall, spring and summer terms; E & Sat.
classes available. Commercial & Fine Art.

CHICAGO ACADEMY OF FINE ARTS,* 65 E. Southwater, 60601.
   Tel: (312) 782-1140
Richard Hamper, Dir; James Paulus, Dean; Paula Buchwald, Asst.
Dean; 41 faculty mem. Estab. 1902; pvt; D & E, Sat; ent. req. HS
grad. and portfolio; 2-3-4 yr. program with academic subjects taken
at Univ. of Chicago or Roosevelt Univ; cert, dipl, B.F.A; schol; 120
sem. hr. art, 30 sem. hr. acad; enrl. 600. Tui. $1250 per yr, $42.50
per sem. hr; no campus res. Sat. classes available.

Advertising Design	Illustration
Animation (film making)	Interior Design
Cartooning	Lettering & Typography
Commercial Art	Mechanical Drawing
Crafts	Mechanical Equipment (building
Drawing	systems)
Fashion Illustration	Photography
Furniture Design & Construc-	Problem Solving
tion	Visual Communications
History of Design	

Summer School: 6 wk. beginning June 22, minimum 4 sessions;
$50 reservation fee.

Advanced Design	Figure Drawing
Color	Figure Painting
Commercial Art	Interior Design
Design	Photography
Drawing & Painting	Printmaking
Fashion Illustration	

CITY COLLEGES OF CHICAGO,* Central Administration Offices,
   180 N. Michigan Ave, 60601. Tel: (312) 269-8000
Pub; D & E; co-ed; ent. req. HS dipl, completion of ACT; 2 yr; degrees, A.A, dipl, A.A.S, dipl. applied science. Tui. free to Chicago
res, gen. service fee part-time $10, full-time $20; out-of-city
$33.50 per sem. hr, out-of-state $50 per sem. hr, lab fees vary; no
campus res. Adult educ. courses; fee $1 reg. charge.

   Kennedy-King College, Art and Humanities Department,
   6800 S. Wentworth Ave, 60601. Tel: (312) 962-3200
Estab. 1935; enrl. 9010.

Art Education	Painting
Drafting	Photography
Drawing	Radio-TV
History of Art & Archaeology	Theater Arts
Industrial Design	

   Loop College, Art and Humanities Department, 64 E Lake
   St, 60601. Tel: (312) 269-8000
Estab. 1962; enrl. 10,600.

Art Education	Industrial Design
Drafting	Painting
Drawing	Theater Arts
History of Art & Archaeology	

   Malcolm X College, Art and Humanities Department, 1900
   W. Van Buren St, 60612. Tel: (312) 942-3000
Estab. 1911; enrl. 5000.

Art Education	Industrial Design
Ceramics	Painting
Drafting	Radio-TV
Drawing	Sculpture
History of Art	Theater Arts

   Mayfair College, Art and Humanities Department, 4626 N.
   Knox Ave, 60630. Tel: (312) 286-1323
Estab. 1956; enrl. 3800.

Art Education	Industrial Design
Ceramics	Painting
Drafting	Photography
Drawing	Theater Arts
History of Art & Archaeology	

   Olive-Harvey College, Art and Humanities Department, 10001
   S. Woodlawn Ave, 60628. Tel: (312) 568-3700
Estab. 1957; enrl. 4700

Art Education	Industrial Design

Drafting
Drawing
History of Art & Archaeology

Painting
Theater Arts

   Southwest College, Art and Architecture Department, 7500
   S. Pulaski Rd, 60652. Tel: (312) 735-3000
Estab. 1960; enrl. 4700.

Art Education	History of Art & Archaeology
Ceramics	Illustration
Drafting	Painting
Drawing	Photography
Graphic Arts	Sculpture
Graphic Design	Weaving

   Wright College, Art and Humanities Department, 3400 N.
   Austin Ave, 60634. Tel: (312) 777-7900
Bernard J. Brille, Chmn; 5 FT instr. Estab. 1934; pub; D & E; ent.
req. HS dipl; 2 yrs; degree, A.A; 15 SC, 5 LC; enrl. D 3000, E 2500.
Tui. No tui. for Chicago res; outside of Chicago, but in Illinois,
$34.50 per cr. hr.

Advertising Design	Graphic Design
Architecture	History of Art & Archaeology
Ceramics	Lettering
Commercial Art	Painting
Drafting	Sculpture
Drawing	Textile Design

Adult hobby classes, water color, oil painting, interior design; tui.
$3 for 8 sessions; enrl. 30 per class.
   Summer School, courses offered, painting, figure drawing; no tui.
for Chicago res, outside of Chicago but in Illinois, $34.50 cr. hr. for
term of 8 wk. beginning July 2; 1973 enrl. 25.

CONTEMPORARY ART WORKSHOP, 542 W. Grant Pl, 60614.
   Tel: (312) 525-9624
John Kearney, Dir; 2 FT, 5 PT instr. Estab. 1950; pvt; D & E;
no ent. req; schol; enrl. D 45, E 40; approx. 30 studios for artists.
Tui. $70 for 10 wk; no campus res.
Graphic Arts
Painting
Sculpture

DEPAUL UNIVERSITY, Department of Art, 2323 N. Seminary,
   60614. Tel: (312) 321-8194
William Conger, Chmn; 5 FT, 4 PT instr. Estab. 1898; pvt; D & E;
co-ed; ent. req. HS dipl, univ. evaluation; 4 yr; degree, B.A; 18 SC,
19 LC; enrl. D 600, maj. 50. Tui. $2130 per yr; see Univ. Bulletin.

Art Education	Painting
Design	Photography
Drawing	Printmaking
History of Art	Sculpture

HARRINGTON INSTITUTE OF INTERIOR DESIGN, 410 S. Michigan
   Ave, 60605. Tel: (312) 939-4975
Robert C. Marks, Dean; D 6 FT, 15 PT, E 4 FT, 8 PT instr. Estab.
1931; pvt.(affiliated with Roosevelt Univ); ent. req. HS grad; 3 yr.
for professional dipl, plus additional courses for B.A. or B.G.S;
enrl. 1974-75 D 134, E 142. Tui. D $900 per sem, E $400 per sem.
Interior Design (Complete Professional Training)

ILLINOIS INSTITUTE OF TECHNOLOGY,* Department of Architec-
   ture, 3300 S. Federal St, 60616. Tel: (312) 225-9600
George Edson Danforth, Dir; 9 FT instr. Estab. 1895 as Armour
Institute, consolidated with Lewis Institute of Arts and Sciences,
1940; pvt; 5 yr; degrees, B.Arch, M.S.Arch, M.S.City and Regional
Planning; normal enrl. 200.
‡Architecture

INSTITUTE OF DESIGN OF ILLINOIS INSTITUTE OF TECHNOLOGY,
   3360 S. State St, 60616. Tel: (312) 225-9600 Exten. 471
17 FT, 2 PT instr. Estab. 1937; pvt; D & E; ent. req. CEEB exam,
schol. standing; 4 yr; degrees, B.S.(Design), M.S.(Visual Education,
Visual Design, Product Design, Photography); schol; enrl. D 275,
E 115. Tui. $1150 per sem.
   Summer School: Jack Weiss, Dir; Grad. Art Educ. Prog.

INSTITUTE OF LETTERING AND DESIGN, 202 S. State St, 60604.
   Tel: (312) 341-1300
Sidney Borden, Dir; 1 FT, 4 PT instr. Estab. 1937; pvt; D; 3 yr;
dipl. Tui. $1250, each 4 wk. $150. Summer School.

Display	Lettering
Graphic Arts	Sign Painting

NORTH PARK COLLEGE, Fine Arts Division, 5125 N. Spaulding,
   60625. Tel: (312) 583-2700 Exten. 228
Monroe B. Olson, Chmn; 2 FT, 3 PT instr. Estab. 1957; den; D & E;

ent. req. HS dipl, ent. exam; 4 yr; degree, B.A; schol; 11 SC, 4 LC; enrl. D 80, E 20, maj. 19. Tui. $2385 per yr, $280 per course; campus res. $1290.

Advertising Design	Industrial Design
Art Education	Jewelry
Ceramics	Painting
Commercial Art	Photography
Drawing	Sculpture
Graphic Arts	Teacher Training
Graphic Design	Textile Design
History of Art & Archaeology	

Adult hobby classes, jewelry making, painting; tui. $35; enrl. 15-25.
Summer School: Paul J. Larson, Asst Dean; courses offered, Drawing, Painting, Studio; tui. $180 for term of 8 wk. beginning late June; enrl. 15-20 per course.

NORTHEASTERN ILLINOIS UNIVERSITY, Art Department, St. Louis at Bryn Mawr Ave, 60625. Tel: (312) 583-4050 Exten. 580, 581
Russell Roller, Chmn; 12 FT, 2 PT instr. Estab. 1869; pub; D & E; ent. req. HS dipl, GED test, upper half high school class or higher ACT score; 4 yr; degree, B.A; schol; 44 SC, 22 LC; total enrl. 10,200, art maj. 175, grad. 1583, others 798. Tui. $210 per term, PT $32 per sem. hr, non-res. $633 per term, PT $95 per sem. hr; no campus res.

Art Education	Lettering
Ceramics	Metal Enameling
Crafts	Painting
Drawing	Photography
Graphic Design	Printmaking
History of Art & Archaeology	Sculpture
Industrial Design	Teacher Training
Jewelry	

RAY-VOGUE SCHOOLS, 750 N. Michigan Ave, 60611.
Tel: (312) 787-5117
Wade Ray, Dir; 14 FT, 5 PT instr. Estab. 1916; pvt; D & E; ent. req. HS grad; 1-2 yr; enrl. 500. Tui. $1530 per yr.

Commercial Art	Interior Design
Dress Design	Photography
Fashion Illustration	Window Display
Fashion Merchandising	

Summer School: $420 for 10 wk. beginning in June; enrl. 200.

SCHOOLS OF THE ART INSTITUTE OF CHICAGO, Michigan Ave. at Adams St, 60603. Tel: (312) 443-3700
Donald J. Irving, Dir; 75 FT, 20 PT instr. Estab. 1866; pvt; ent. req. portfolio; 4 yr; degrees, B.F.A, M.F.A; 103 SC, 22 LC; enrl. 750 FT, 400 PT. Tui. $1650.

Ceramics	Printmaking
Environmental Design	Sculpture
Fashion Design	Teacher Education
Film Making	Textile Design
Glassworking	Video
History of Art	Visual Communications
Painting	Weaving
Photography	

Summer School: Donald J. Irving, Dir; tui. $390 for 4 full days for 8 wk; enrl. 500.

UNIVERSITY OF CHICAGO, Department of Art, History of Art, Cochrane-Woods Art Center, 5540 S. Greenwood Ave, 60637.
Tel: (312) 753-3880
Herbert L. Kessler, Chmn; 13 FT instr. Estab. 1882; pvt; D & E; ent. req. Coll. level exam; admis. at opening of any quarter; degrees, B.A, M.A, Ph.D; schol, fel; 31 LC, 22 GC; enrl. 130. Tui. approx. $3500; annual prizes for scholarship.

History and Theory of Art and Architecture

Baroque	Indian Art
Byzantine & Early Christian	Islamic Art
Chinese Art	Medieval Art
Classical Art & Archaeology	19th & 20th Century Art
European & American Art	Renaissance

Practice of Art, Midway Studios, 6016 Ingleside Ave, 60637.
Tel: (312) 752-7708
Thomas Mapp, Dir. Admis. at opening of any quarter; degrees, B.F.A, M.F.A; schol, fel; 26 SC; enrl. 15. Tui. as above.
Prizes for excellence in practice of art; Historic Studios of Lorado Taft and associates, includes workshops and the Court Gallery.

Ceramics	Graphics
Design	Photography
Drawing & Painting	Sculpture

UNIVERSITY OF ILLINOIS AT CHICAGO CIRCLE, College of Architecture and Art, P.O. Box 4348, 60680.
Tel: (312) 996-3000 Art Exten. 3337, Architecture Exten. 3335, History of Architecture & Art Exten. 3326
Alfred Maurice, Acting Dean; Richard Whitaker, Head Dept. of Architecture; Edward Colker, Head Dept. of Art; Donald Ehresmann, Chmn. Dept. of History of Architecture & Art; 68 FT, 27 PT instr. Estab. 1946; pub; D; ent. req. Architecture: English 3, algebra 2, plain geometry 1, trigonometry $\frac{1}{2}$, one foreign language 2, 5 additional units, 3.25 transfer average; Art & History of Architecture & Art: English 3, algebra 1, geometry 1, one foreign language 2, 5 additional units; 3.25 transfer average; Architecture 5 yr, Art & History of Architecture & Art, 4 yr; degrees, B.A, B.Arch; enrl. 1084. Tui. res. $212, non-res. $542.

Architecture—Construction	History of Architecture & Art
Architecture—Design	Industrial Design
Architecture—Humanities	Painting
Architecture—Technology	Photography—Film Design
Art Education	Printmaking
Communications Design	Sculpture
Comprehensive Design	
Comprehensive Plastic & Graphic Arts	

UNIVERSITY OF ILLINOIS AT THE MEDICAL CENTER, CHICAGO, Medical Art (Main Campus at Champaign-Urbana), 1853 W. Polk St, 60612. Tel: (312) 663-7337
A. Hooker Goodwin, Head; 5 FT instr. Estab. 1921; pub; ent. req. same as Coll. of Fine and Applied Arts, Urbana; 5 yr.(3 yr. Coll. of Fine and Applied Arts, Urbana, 2 yr. Medical Center Campus).

CHICAGO HEIGHTS

PRAIRIE STATE COLLEGE, Art Department, 197th & Halsted, 60411. Tel: (312) 756-3110
Dr. Albert Piarowski, Chmn; 3 FT, 14 PT instr. Estab. 1958; pub; D & E; ent. req. HS dipl, ACT; 2 yr; degree, A.A; 24 SC, 6 LC; enrl. dept. 300, maj. 200. Tui. $420 per yr.

Advertising Design	Life Drawing
Design	Materials Workshop
Drawing (Multi-Media)	Painting
History of Art	Photography
Illustration	Production Processes
Interior Design	Sculpture

Summer School: Dr. Albert Piarowski, Dir; tui. $14 per cr. hr. for term of 8 wk.

Art History Tour	Materials Workshop
Design	Painting
Drawing	Photography

DECATUR

MILLIKIN UNIVERSITY, Art Department, 1184 W. Main, 62522.
Tel: (217) 424-6227
Marvin L. Klaven, Chmn; 3 FT, 1 PT instr. Estab. 1904; pvt; D & E; ent. req. HS dipl, ACT; 4 yr; degrees, B.A, B.F.A; schol; 10 SC, 2 LC; enrl. D 100, E 20, maj. 45. Tui. $2700 per yr; campus res. $1250. Kirkland Gallery, monthly exhibits, lectures, discussions, Fine Arts Series, Honors Program.

Aesthetics	Jewelry
Art Education	Painting
Ceramics	Printmaking
Commercial Art	Sculpture
Drawing	Teacher Training
Graphic Arts	Theatre Arts
History of Art & Archaeology	Watercolor

Summer School: Dr. William Lewis, Dir; courses offered, Drawing, Painting, Printmaking; tui. $180 for term of 4 wk. beginning June; enrl. 25.

DE KALB

NORTHERN ILLINOIS UNIVERSITY, Department of Art, 60115.
Tel: (815) 753-1473
Robert L. Even, Chmn; 75 FT instr. Estab. 1921; pub; D & E; ent. req. HS class standing, ACT score; 4 yr; degrees, B.S.(Educ), B.A, B.F.A, M.A, M.S.(Educ), M.F.A; schol; 119 SC, 40 LC, 84 GC; enrl. maj. 1400, service courses in other depts. 12,000, total 23,000. Tui. $298.50, non-res. $629. Campus res. required for graduation. Summer School.

Art Education	Fine Arts
Art History	Foreign Study Programs
Crafts	Liberal Arts
Design	

Artists-in-res. and special workshop programs offered during summer.

EDWARDSVILLE

✤SOUTHERN ILLINOIS UNIVERSITY AT EDWARDSVILLE, School of
  Fine Arts, 62025.
    Tel: (618) 692-3071
David C. Huntley, Chmn; 20 FT instr. Estab. 1869; pub; D & E; ent.
req. ACT; 4 yr; degrees, B.A, B.S, M.S.(1 yr), M.F.A.(2 yr); schol;
27 SC, 12 LC, 20 GC; enrl. 13,500; campus res. fee.

ELMHURST

ELMHURST COLLEGE, Art Department, 190 Prospect, 60126.
    Tel: (312) 279-4100
Sandra Jorgensen, Chmn; 4 FT, 4 PT instr. Estab. 1947; pvt;
D & E; ent. req. HS dipl, ent. exam; 4 yr; degree, B.A; schol;
12 SC, 7 LC; enrl. D 259, E 90, maj. 32. Tui. $2630 per yr,
PT D $70 per hr, E $53 per hr; campus res. $1450.

Art Education	History of Art & Archaeology
Art Therapy	Painting
Ceramics	Photography
Drawing	Sculpture
Graphic Arts	

Weekend college offering experimental courses.

EVANSTON

NORTHWESTERN UNIVERSITY,* College of Arts and Sciences,
    Department of Art, 60201. Tel: (312) 492-7346
Wilbert A. Seidel, Chmn; 7 FT, 5 PT instr. Estab. 1924; pvt;
4 yr; degrees, A.B, M.A, M.F.A; schol. and fel; 15 SC, 8 LC,
5 GC; normal enrl. 300-500. Tui. $3180 per year.

Interior Architecture and	Practice of Art
Design	Teaching of Art

Department of Art History, 60201. Tel: (312) 492-7077
James D. Breckenridge, Chmn; 8 FT, 5 PT instr. Estab. 1972; pvt;
4 yr; degrees, A.B, M.A, Ph.D; schol. and fel; 22 LC, 12 GC; normal
enrl. 400-600. Tui. $3180 per year.
History of Art

FREEPORT

HIGHLAND COMMUNITY COLLEGE, R.F.D. 2, Pearl City Rd,
    61032. Tel: (815) 235-6121
Jody Schultz, Instr; 1 FT, 4 PT instr. Estab. 1962; pub; D & E;
ent. req. HS dipl, ent. exam; 2 yr; degrees, A.S, A.A, A.B.A, A.A.S;
schol; 6 SC, 1 LC. Tui. $10 per sem. hr. for in-district students;
enrl. 126.

Art History	Introduction to Art
Art Materials & Processes	Painting
Design	Pottery
Drawing	Printmaking

Continuing Education classes, basic drawing, oil, charcoal,
printmaking, sculpture, pottery, handweaving & related crafts,
rosemaling, macrame, needlepoint; tui. $10 per sem. hr; enrl.
278. Occasional summer workshops for High School and Elementary
School students.
    Summer School: One course offered each year.

GLEN ELLYN

COLLEGE OF DUPAGE, Lambert Rd, 60137.
    Tel: (312) 858-2800 Exten. 2057
Pamela B. Lowrie, Art Coordinator; 9 FT, 25 PT instr. Estab.
1966; pub; D & E; open ent. req; 2 yr; degrees, A.A (Art),
A.A.S.(Interior & Fashion Design); schol; 20 SC, 5 LC. Tui. $10
per cr. hr; no campus res. Summer School.

Aesthetics	Landscape Architecture
Architecture	Occupational Therapy
Ceramics	Painting
Costume Design & Construction	Photography
Drafting	Sculpture
Drawing	Stage Design
Fashion Arts	Textile Design
History of Art & Archaeology	Theatre Arts
Jewelry	

Adult hobby classes. Children's classes, ceramics.

GODFREY

LEWIS & CLARK COMMUNITY COLLEGE,* Art Department,
    Godfrey Rd, 62035. Tel: (618) 466-3411 Exten. 275
Dr. Paul Cooke, Chmn. Humanities Div; 2 FT, 3 PT instr. Estab.
1970, formerly Monticello College; pub; D & E; ent. req. HS dipl,
ent. exam, open door policy; 2 yrs; degree A.A; schol; 13 SC, 2 LC;
enrl. D 1800, E 600, maj. 40. Tui. $10 per sem. hr; commuting
coll.

Advertising Design	Handicrafts
Basic Design	History of Art
Ceramics	Painting
Drafting	Sculpture
Drawing	Weaving

Adult hobby classes, interior design, introduction to drawing &
painting, antiques; tui. $10 per sem. hr; enrl. 30.
    Summer School: Dr. Paul Cooke, Chmn. Humanities Div; pre-
summer 4 wk. session painting on-location, 4 hrs. daily; $30 for
3 sem. cr. hr; enrl. 15; summer courses, painting, advanced and
beginning; tui. $30 per 3 cr. hr. for term of 8 wk. beginning
June 18; total 1973 art enrl. 30.

GREENVILLE

GREENVILLE COLLEGE, Department of Art, 62246.
    Tel: (618) 664-1840 Exten. 295
Paul J. Wolber, Chmn; 3 FT, 1 PT instr. Estab. 1965; pvt; D; ent.
req. HS dipl, C average, ACT; 4 yr; degrees, B.A.(Art), B.S.(Art
Education); schol; 15 SC, 5 LC; enrl. D 250, maj. 40. Tui. $1930
per yr; campus res. $1300.

Advanced Studio	Handicrafts
Art Education	History of Art & Archaeology
Ceramics	Independent Study
Commercial Art	Painting
Drawing	Sculpture
Graphic Arts	Teacher Training

Summer School: Dr. David Dickerson, Dir; courses offered,
Art Education, Introduction to Fine Arts.

JACKSONVILLE

MACMURRAY COLLEGE,* Art Department, 62650.
    Tel: (217) 245-6151
Howard F. Sidman, Head; 2 FT instr. Estab. 1846; den; 4 yr; degrees; 29 SC, 6 LC.

Advertising Design	Industrial Design
Ceramics	Interior Design
Costume Design	Teacher Training
Drawing & Painting	Textile Design

JOLIET

COLLEGE OF ST. FRANCIS,* Art Department, 500 Wilcox, 60435.
    Tel: (815) 726-7311, Exten. 270
Robert G. Cosgrove, Chmn; 4 FT instr. Maj. estab. 1950; pvt;
D & E; ent. req. HS grad, ent. exam; 4 yr; degrees, B.S, B.A.(Art
or Art Educ); 19 SC, 6 LC; enrl. D 150, E 20, maj. 70. Tui. $1100;
campus res. $900.

Aesthetics	History of Art & Archaeology
Architecture	Jewelry
Art Education	Lettering
Ceramics	Painting
Drawing	Sculpture
Enameling	Teacher Training
Graphic Arts	Textile Design

Children's classes, art in variety of media; tui. $80, 16 wk. lessons,
2 hr. Sat AM; enrl. 20 (limit).
    Summer School: Art courses, Ceramics, Calligraphy; tui. $105
for term of 6 wk. beginning June 23; 1969 enrl. 35.

LAKE FOREST

BARAT COLLEGE,* Department of Art, 700 E. Westleigh Rd, 60045.
    Tel: (312) 234-3000 Exten. 328
Albert Pounian, Chmn; 4 FT, 4 PT instr. Estab. 1858; den; D;
W only; ent. req. HS dipl, ent. exam; 4 yrs; degree, B.A; schol;
32 SC, 16 LC; enrl. maj. 58. Tui. $1800 per yr; PT $65 per cr.
hr; campus res. $1400.

Architecture	History of Art & Archaeology
Ceramics	Illustration
Drawing	Painting
Graphic Arts	Photography
Graphic Design	Theatre Arts

Summer School: G. Donald Hollenhorst, Dir; courses offered,
ceramics, drawing, painting.

LAKE FOREST COLLEGE, Department of Art, Sheridan Rd, 60045.
    Tel: (312) 234-3100
Alex F. Mitchell, Chmn; 5 FT instr. Estab. 1857; pvt; D; ent. req.
HS dipl, ent. exam; 4 yrs; degree, B.A; schol; 7 SC, 21 LC; enrl. D
1100, maj. 65. Tui. $3050 per yr; campus res. $1280 including fees.

Aesthetics	History of Art & Archaeology
Architecture	Painting

Art Education
Drawing
Graphic Arts

Photography
Sculpture
Teacher Training

MACOMB

WESTERN ILLINOIS UNIVERSITY, Art Department, 61455.
  Tel: (309) 298-1549
Dr. Neil A. Chassman, Chmn. Estab. 1901; pub; D; ent. req. HS
dipl; 4 yr; exten. courses; enrl. maj. 400. Tui. $473.75 per term.
Art Education
Art History
Ceramics

Jewelry/Metals
Painting
Sculpture

HS Summer Art Camp; tui. $85; enrl. 50.
  Summer School: Dr. Neil A. Chassman, Chmn; 8 wk. term.

MOLINE

BLACK HAWK COLLEGE, Department of Art, 6600 34th Ave,
  61265. Tel: (309) 796-1311
Joseph F. Ramsauer, Chmn; 4 FT, 4 PT instr. Estab. 1946; pub;
D & E; ent. req. HS dipl; 2 yr; degree, A.A; 9 SC, 4 LC; enrl. D
780, E 100, maj. 85. Tui. $13.50 per sem. hr; no campus res.
Ceramics
Crafts Workshop
Drawing
History of Art & Archaeology
Jewelry

Lettering
Painting
Sculpture
Visual Design

  Summer School: Courses offered, Art Appreciation, Ceramics,
Visual Design; tui. $40.50 for term of 6 wk. beginning June 7;
1974 enrl. 45.

MONMOUTH

MONMOUTH COLLEGE, Department of Art, Art Center, N. Ninth
  St, 61462. Tel: (309) 457-2341
Harlow B. Blum, Head; 2 FT, 2 PT instr. Estab. 1930; pvt; D; ent.
req. 15 units incl. English, history, social science, foreign language,
mathematics & science, SAT or ACT tests; degree, B.A; schol,
grants; 16 SC, 4 LC; enrl. (1975-76) maj. 25, total coll. 700. Tui.
$945 per term; campus res. $400 per term.
Advanced Special Topics
Contemporary Art
Drawing
Filmmaking
Independent Study
Introduction to History of Art
  Sequence
Introductory Art Workshop

Painting
Photography
Printmaking
Sculpture
Secondary Art Methods
Seminar in Oriental Art
Senior Art Seminar
Studio A, B & C

  Summer School: Dr. Milton Bowman, Registrar; courses
offered, Beginning Drawing, Beginning Printmaking.

NORMAL

✠ILLINOIS STATE UNIVERSITY, Department of Art, 61761.
  Tel: (309) 438-5621
Dr. Fred V. Mills, Chmn; 50 FT instr. Estab. 1857; pub; D & E;
ent. req. HS grad; 4 yr; degrees, B.A, B.S, M.A, M.S, M.F.A, Ed.D;
47 SC, 26 LC, 31 GC; enrl. undergrad. maj. 575, grad. 80, total art
5300. Tui. and fees res. and grad. $305.50, non-res. $636.
Art Appreciation
Art History
Ceramics
Cinematography
Design
Drawing
Glass

Graphic Design
Jewelry
Painting
Photography
Printmaking
Sculpture
Textiles

Adult recreation classes, ceramics, jewelry; enrl. 150.
  Summer School: Dr. Fred Mills, Dir; tui. $151.75, non-res.
$266.25; enrl. 160
Art Activities in Elementary
  School
Art for the Exceptional Child
Crafts in Elementary School
Drawing
Metal
Painting

Participation in Elementary Art
  Photography
Printmaking
Sculpture
Teaching Art in the
  Elementary School
Teaching Art in High School

PEORIA

BRADLEY UNIVERSITY, School of Art, 61606.
  Tel: (309) 676-7611 Exten. 258, 385, 285
Verne Funk, Dir; 10 FT instr. Pvt; ent. req. HS grad; 4 yr; degrees,
A.B, B.S, B.F.A, M.A, M.F.A; schol; enrl. maj. 116, others 400. Tui.
$1050 per sem.
Art History
Art Metal

Jewelry
Painting

Ceramics
Drawing
Film
Graphic Design

Photography
Printmaking
Sculpture

QUINCY

QUINCY COLLEGE, Department of Art, 62301.
  Tel: (217) 222-8020
Rev. Thomas Brown, Chmn; 2 FT, 2 PT instr. Estab. coll. 1860,
art dept. 1953; ent. req. HS grad, ACT or SAT ent. exam; 4 yr;
degrees, A.A, B.A, B.S, B.F.A; 21 SC, 13 LC; enrl. maj. 45, total
enrl. D 1350, E 130. Tui. $900 per sem; campus res. $250-300 per
sem.
Aesthetics
Ancient & Mediaeval Art
Art Seminar
Ceramics
Commercial Art
Contemporary Art Seminar
Drawing
Film Making
Fundamentals (Two Dimen-
  sional & Three Dimensional)

Modern Art
Non-Western Art
Painting (Oil & Mixed Media)
Photography
Printmaking
Renaissance & Baroque Art
Sculpture
Special Problems
Watercolors

Seminar in Europe (summer); optional Junior Year Abroad.
  Summer School: Rev. Thomas Brown, Dir. in Art; $40 per sem.
hr. for 6 wk. beginning June 20.

RIVER GROVE

TRITON COLLEGE, School of University Transfer Studies, 2000
  Fifth Ave, 60171. Tel: (312) 456-0300 Exten. 467
Norm Wiegel, Chmn; 5 FT, 6 PT instr. Estab. 1965; pub; D & E;
ent. req. HS dipl, some adult students are admitted without HS
dipl. but with test scores indicating promise; 2 yr; degree, A.A;
17 SC, 3 LC; enrl. D 650, E 150, maj. 138, adults and non-cr.
courses. Tui. $11 per sem. hr, out-of-district $30.78; no campus
res.
Advertising Design
Art Education
Ceramics
Commercial Art
Drawing
Experimental Design
Graphic Arts
Graphic Design

History of Art & Archaeology
Illustration
Lettering
Painting
Printmaking
Recreational Arts & Crafts
Sculpture
Theatre Arts

Adult hobby classes and Continuing Education classes, drawing,
painting, ceramics, theatre arts, jewelry, crafts, sculpture,
candle making, stained glass, quilling, plastics; tui. $11 per hr;
enrl. 550.
  Summer School: Dr. G. L. Hinrichs, Dir; most of above courses
offered; tui. $11 per sem. hr. for term of 8 wk. beginning June.

ROCK ISLAND

AUGUSTANA COLLEGE, Art Department, 61201.
  Tel: (309) 794-7000
Alvin Ben Jasper, Chmn; 3 FT, 5 PT instr. Estab. 1860; den; D & E;
ent. req. HS grad. plus exam; 4 yr; degree; schol, fel; 8 SC, 9 LC,
3 Lab.C; enrl. 2000. Tui. $770.
Art History
Ceramics
Crafts
Design
Drawing
Elementary School Art Methods
Fabric
Introduction to Visual Arts
Sat. classes for children.

Jewelry
Life Drawing
Painting
Photography
Printmaking
Sculpture
Secondary School Art Methods

ROCKFORD

ROCK VALLEY COLLEGE, Department of Art, Division of Mathe-
  matics and Humanities, 3301 N. Mulford Rd, 61111.
  Tel: (815) 226-2600.
R. David Gustafson, Chmn. Div; 3 FT instr. Estab. 1965; pub;
D & E; ent. req. HS dipl. 2 yrs; degrees, A.A, A.S; 9 SC, 3 LC;
approx. enrl. D 250, E 80, maj. 60. Tui. $15 per cr. hr; no campus
res.
Aesthetics
Drafting
Drawing
Graphic Arts

Graphic Design
History of Art & Archaeology
Painting
Three dimensional design

Adult hobby classes, painting, drawing, ceramics, weaving; tui.
$16 - $19. Children's classes, crafts; tui. $15.

Summer School: courses offered, Drawing, Design, Painting, Special Projects; tui. $15 per cr. hr. for term of 8 wk. beginning June 13; 1973 enrl. 50.

ROCKFORD COLLEGE, Art Department, 61101.
Tel: (815) 965-5711
Tim Mather, Head; 4 FT, 4 PT instr. Estab. 1847; pvt; ent. req. HS grad. plus test; 4 yr; degrees, B.A, B.F.A; schol; 10 SC, 6 LC; enrl. maj. 75, others 260 D & E. Tui. incl. room and board and fees $3880.

Art History	Photography
Ceramics	Relief Printmaking
Drawing & Painting	Sculpture
Graphic Arts (Etching, Engraving, Serigraphy)	Teacher Training
	Textile Arts
Mechanical Drawing	Theatre Arts
Paper Making	Weaving

Summer School: $35 per cr. hr. for 6 or 8 wk. from June 15; enrl. 15 art students, others 200.

URBANA

UNIVERSITY OF ILLINOIS, College of Fine and Applied Arts, 110 Architecture Building, 61801. Tel: (217) 333-1661
Jack H. McKenzie, Dean; 260 FT, 150 PT instr. Estab. 1931; pub; D; co-ed; ent. req. HS grad, ent. exam; 4 yr; Bachelors, Masters, Doctors degrees; schol, fel, assistantships; enrl. undergrad. 2600, grad. 585. Tui. $496, non-res. $1486.
Adult hobby classes scheduled through University Extension. Children's Sat. classes, summer youth classes. Summer School.

Department of Art and Design, 143 Fine Arts Building, 61820.
Tel: (217) 333-0855
James R. Shipley, Head; 70 FT, 68 PT instr. Estab. 1876; pub; D; ent. req. ACT scores; degrees, B.F.A.(4 yr), M.A.(1 yr), M.F.A.(2 yr), Ph.D.(3 yr), D.Ed.(3 yr); 111 SC, 39 LC, 16 GC; enrl. undergrad. 639, grad. 118.

Art Education	Industrial Design
Ceramics/Metal	Medical Art
Drawing	Painting
Graphic Design	Photography
History of Art	Printmaking
Independent Studies	Sculpture

Adult hobby classes scheduled through University Extension. Children's Sat. AM classes. Visual Research Laboratory.
Summer School: Tui. $124, fees $66, for 6 hr. or 1½ units; enrl. undergrad. 198, grad. 62.

WHEATON

WHEATON COLLEGE, Department of Art, 60187.
Tel: (312) 682-5050
Alva Steffler, Dept. Chmn; 4 FT, 2 PT instr. Estab. 1861; pvt; D & E; ent. req. HS dipl; 4 yrs; degree, B.A; schol; 20 SC, 5 LC; total enrl. 2378, maj. 50. Tui. $2490 per yr; campus res. $1380.

Advertising Design	Graphic Design
Aesthetics	History of Art & Archaeology
Art Education	Painting
Ceramics	Photography
Drawing	Sculpture
Graphic Arts	Teacher Training

WINNETKA

NORTH SHORE ART LEAGUE, 620 Lincoln, 60093.
Tel: (312) 446-2870
Abby Block, Pres; 25 PT instr. Estab. 1924; pvt; D & E; no ent. req; no degrees; schol. to Chicago Art Inst. grad; 28 SC; enrl. D 280, E 75. Tui. 16 wks, 3 hr. a session, $60; no campus res.

Critique	Painting
Drawing	Photography
Graphic Arts	Pottery
Graphic Design	Sculpture
Handicrafts	Stitchery
Jewelry	Wood Cut

Children's classes, multi-media in the arts.

INDIANA

ANDERSON

ANDERSON COLLEGE, Art Department, E. Fifth & College, 46011.
Tel: (317) 644-0951 Exten. 458
Raymond A. Freer, Chmn; 2 FT, 4 PT instr. Estab. 1928; pvt; D & E; ent. req. HS dipl, ent. exam, recommendations; 4 yr; degrees,

A.A, B.A; schol; 16 SC, 6 LC; enrl. D 120, E 75, maj. 45. Tui. $2030 per yr; campus res. $920.

Art Education	Museum Staff Training
Ceramics	Occupational Therapy
Commercial Art	Painting
Drawing	Sculpture
Graphic Design	Stage Design
History of Art & Archaeology	Teacher Training
Jewelry	Textile Design

Adult hobby classes and children's classes; $85 per cr. hr.
Summer School: Prof. Robert Smith, Dir; tui. $68 per cr. hr for term beginning June 1.

BLOOMINGTON

INDIANA UNIVERSITY, Department of Fine Arts, 47401.
Tel: (812) 337-7766
W. Eugene Kleinbauer, Chmn; 35 FT, 58 PT instr. Estab. 1911; pub; D; ent. req. admis. to the Univ; 4 yr; degrees, A.B, B.F.A, B.S, M.A, M.F.A, M.A.T, Ph.D; schol; 55 SC, 100 LC, 110 GC; enrl. maj. undergrad. 430, grad. 135 (65 Art History, 70 Studio), others 5600. Tui. $361 per sem, non-res. $820; campus res.

Ceramics	Printmaking
Drawing	Printed Textiles
Graphic Design	Sculpture
History of Art	Woven Textiles
Jewelry & Silversmithing	Teacher Training (with Sch.
Painting	of Educ)
Photography	

Summer School: Tui. $31 per cr. hr, non-res. $69.

EVANSVILLE

INDIANA STATE UNIVERSITY, EVANSVILLE, Art Department, 8600 University Blvd, 47712. Tel: (812) 426-1251
Dr. Blevins, Head; 5 FT, 1 PT instr. Estab. 1969; pub; D & E; ent. req. HS dipl; 4 yr; degrees, B.S.(Art Educ), B.A.(Art); schol; 27 SC, 4 LC; enrl. D 150, E 30, maj. 90. Tui. $600 per yr; no campus res.

Aesthetics	History of Art & Archaeology
Art Education	Jewelry
Ceramics	Painting
Commercial Art	Photography
Drafting	Sculpture
Drawing	Stained Glass
Furniture Design	Teacher Training

Adult hobby classes, silkscreen; tui. $20; enrl. 25.

UNIVERSITY OF EVANSVILLE, Art Department, 1800 Lincoln Ave, 47714. Tel: (812) 479-2043
Leslie Miley, Jr, Chmn; 6 FT, 6 PT instr. Estab. 1854; pvt; D & E; ent. req. HS dipl, ent. exam; 4 yr; degrees, B.A, B.S.(Art Educ); B.S.(Art Therapy), B.F.A, M.A.(Art Educ); schol; 21 SC, 10 LC, 9 GC; enrl. D 740, E 421, undergrad. maj. 112, grad. 32. Tui. $22 per quarter hr.

Aesthetics	History of Art & Archaeology
Art Education	Jewelry
Ceramics	Lettering
Commercial Art	Museum Staff Training
Drawing	Painting
General Crafts	Sculpture
Graphic Arts	Teacher Training
Handicrafts	Weaving

Children's classes, studio art activities, understanding the arts; tui. $25 per 10 wk. session.
Summer School: Leslie Miley, Jr, Dir.

Art Education	Painting
Ceramics	Printmaking
Drawing	Textiles

FORT WAYNE

✦FORT WAYNE ART INSTITUTE, School of Fine Arts, 1026 W. Berry St, 46804. Tel: (219) 743-9796
Russell L. Oettel, Dir; D 8 FT, 2 PT, E 6 PT, Sat. young people's classes 5 PT instr. Estab. 1888; pvt; ent. req. HS dipl. and portfolio; 4 yr; degree, B.F.A, cert; schol; enrl. D 200, E 140, Sat. 120. Tui. per yr. D $1000, adult E $100, Sat. $32.50.

Ceramics	Painting & Drawing
Design	Photography
Graphic Design	Printmaking
History of Art	Sculpture
Illustration	Weaving
Metalsmithing	

ST. FRANCIS COLLEGE, Art Department, 2701 Spring St, 46808.
   Tel: (219) 432-3551 Exten. 236
Maurice A. Papier, Head; 2 FT, 5 PT instr. Estab. 1890; den;
D & E; ent. req. HS dipl, ent. exam, rank in upper half of grad.
class, others will be interviewed; 2-4 yr; degrees, A.A.(Commercial
Art), B.A, B.S, M.S; schol; 20 SC, 3 LC, 12 GC; enrl. maj. 50. Tui.
$525 per sem, PT undergrad. $42 per sem. hr, grad. $46 per sem.
hr; campus res. $600 per sem.

Art Education	Life Drawing
Ceramics	Painting
Drawing	Photography
Engraving	Sculpture
Etching	Silk Screen
Graphic Arts	Teacher Training
History of Art	Two Dimensional Composition
Jewelry	Weaving
Lettering	Woodcuts

Adult hobby classes, painting; tui. $20 for 12 wk; enrl. 25. Chil-
dren's classes, grades 1 - 6; elem. art; tui. $20; enrl. 40-50.
   Summer School: Maurice Papier, Dir; tui. undergrad. $35 sem.
hr, grad. $38 sem. hr. for term of 3 or 6 wk. beginning June; 1973
enrl. 100-120.

Ceramics	Painting
Graphics	Sculpture
Jewelry	Weaving

FRANKLIN

FRANKLIN COLLEGE, Art Department, 46131.
   Tel: (317) 736-8441
Luigi Crispino, Chmn; 1 FT, 1 PT instr. College estab. 1834; den;
D; ent. req. HS grad; 4 yr; degree, B A; 9 SC, 4 LC; enrl. 700. Tui.
incl. room and board $3670 per yr.

Art Education	Painting
Basic Design	Print Shop
Ceramics	Sculpture
Drawing	

GOSHEN

GOSHEN COLLEGE, Department of Art, 1700 S. Main St,
46525.
Abner Hershberger, Chmn; 2 FT, 4 PT instr. Estab. 1950; den;
D & E; ent. req. HS dipl; 4 yr; degrees, B.A, B.S.(Educ); schol;
20 SC, 6 LC; enrl. D 80, E 40, maj. 40. Tui. $1550 per yr; campus
res. $800.

Art Education	Painting
Art Therapy	Sculpture
Ceramics	Teacher Training
Drawing	Textile Design
Graphic Arts	Weaving
History of Art	

   Summer School: Abner Hershberger, Dir; tui. $165 for term of
$3\frac{1}{2}$ wk. beginning May 1.

Advanced Ceramics	Art Education
Advanced Painting	Design

GREENCASTLE

DE PAUW UNIVERSITY, Department of Art, 46135.
   Tel: (317) 653-9721 Exten. 455
Ray H. French, Head; 4 FT, 2 PT instr. Estab. 1837; pvt; den; 4 yr;
ent. schol. and others; degree; 18 SC, 8 LC, E GC; enrl. maj. 100,
others 300. Tui. $3150; campus res. Junior sem. apprenticeship
program in New York City.

Ceramics	Painting
Commercial Art	Sculpture
Crafts	Printmaking
History of Art	Teacher Training (with Dept.
Jewelry	of Educ.)

HANOVER

HANOVER COLLEGE, Art Department, 47243.
   Tel: (812) 866-2151
J. W. Shaffstall, Chmn; 2 FT, 2 PT instr. Coll. estab. 1827, art
dept. 1968; pvt; D; ent. req. HS dipl; 4 yr; degrees, B.A, B.S; schol;
10 SC, 4 LC; enrl. D 200, maj. 10, special students 4. Tui. $2075
per yr; campus res. $1090.

Aesthetics	Jewelry
Art Education	Painting
Ceramics	Photography
Drawing	Sculpture
Enameling	Stage Design
Graphic Arts	Teacher Training
History of Art & Archaeology	Theatre Arts

INDIANAPOLIS

HERRON SCHOOL OF ART, 1701 N. Pennsylvania St, 46202.
   Tel: (317) 923-3651
Arthur Weber, Dean; 28 FT, 9 PT instr. Estab. 1891; pub, school
of Indiana-Purdue University at Indianapolis; 4 yr; degrees, B.F.A,
B.A.E, M.A.E; schol. and honor awards; enrl. 300 degree seeking
students, 1200 others. Tui. $21 per cr. hr, non-res. $42 per cr. hr.

Art Education	Printmaking
Art History	Sculpture
Clay	Silk-Screening
Drawing	Typography
Fine Arts	Visual Communication
Painting	Woodworking
Photography	

   Saturday School: Don Moore, Dir; schol. for junior and senior
HS students; enrl. 200.
   Summer Pre-College Workshop (Examination of and Guidance in
Art Careers): Aaron Law, Dir; $50 for 12-day, 5 hr. sessions, two
sessions available; enrl. 25 each session.

Design	Printmaking
Drawing	Three-Dimensional Work

INDIANA CENTRAL UNIVERSITY, Fine Arts Department, 1400 E.
   Hanna Ave, University Heights, 46227. Tel: (317) 788-3368
Gerald G. Boyce, Chmn; 3 FT instr. Estab. 1902; den; D & E; ent.
req. upper half of HS grad. class; 4 yr; degrees, B.A, B.S, M.A;
schol; 8 SC, 6 LC, 8 Lab.C; enrl. maj. 35, others 175. Tui. $850
per yr; campus res.

Aesthetics	Prints
Clay	Sculpture
General Art	Teacher Training (with Dept.
History of Art	of Educ.)
Jewelry	Textile
Painting	Weaving
Pottery	

MARIAN COLLEGE,* Art Department, 3200 Cold Spring Rd, 46222.
   Tel: (317) 924-3291 Exten. 244
Sister Sarah Page, Chmn; 2 FT, 2 PT instr. Estab. 1937; pvt; dem;
D & E; co-ed; ent. req. 2 yr. same foreign language, algebra, geometry; 4 yr; degrees, B.S, B.A; 28 SC, 6 LC; enrl. D 721, E 114, total
835. Tui. $1450 per yr, student asn. & coll. fees $90 per yr; campus
res. room & board $900 per yr.

Advertising Design	Graphic Arts
Aesthetics	History of Art
Art Appreciation	Interior Design
Art Education	Lettering
Ceramics	Painting
Drawing	Sculpture
Fashion Arts	Teacher Training

LAFAYETTE

✤PURDUE UNIVERSITY, School of Humanities, Social Science, and
   Education, Department of Creative Arts, Art & Design Section
   47907. Tel: (317) 494-8702
Charles M. Dorn, Head; 33 FT instr. Estab. 1925; pub; 4 yr; degrees,
B.A, M.A; schol; 50 SC, 22 LC, 22 GC, some E classes; enrl. maj.
394, others 1746. Tui. non-res. $950; campus res. $1340.

Art History	Painting
Ceramics	Photography
Film & Video	Sculpture
Graphics	Teacher Education
Industrial Design	Visual Design
Interior Design	Weaving
Jewelry	

MUNCIE

✤BALL STATE UNIVERSITY, Art Department, 47306.
   Tel: (317) 285-5638
Dr. Ned H. Griner, Head; 27 FT instr. Estab. 1928; D & E; ent.
req. HS grad, portfolio required of students transferring credits
from other institutions; 4 yr; degrees, B.A, M.A, D.Educ; schol;
grad. assistantships and doctoral teaching fels; normal enrl. 18,000.
Tui. undergrad. res. $240 per quarter.

Art Education	Jewelry
Art Gallery	Lithography
Art History	Painting
Ceramics	Photography
Drawing	Sculpture
Graphic Design	Silk-Screen
Intaglio	Weaving

Interior Environmental Design
   Summer School: Two sessions; also visiting artists, art workshops, festivals and field trips.

NORTH MANCHESTER

MANCHESTER COLLEGE,* Art Department, College Ave, 46962.
Tel: (219) 982-2141 Exten. 276
Max I. Allen, Chmn. Dept; 3 FT, 1 PT instr. Estab. 1895; den;
D; ent. req. HS dipl; 4 yrs; degrees, A.B, B.S; schol; 16 SC, 3 LC;
enrl. D 152, maj. 10. Tui. $1950 per yr; campus res. $910.

Advertising Design	Painting
Art Education	Sculpture
Batik	Spinning
Ceramics	Stitchery
Commercial Art	Teacher Training
Graphic Arts	Textile Design
Handicrafts	Vegetable Dyeing
History of Art & Archaeology	Weaving
Lettering	

Summer School: Dr. Howard Book, Dean; courses offered vary; tui. $175 per course.

NOTRE DAME

ST. MARY'S COLLEGE, Department of Art, 46556.
Tel: (219) 284-4074
Dr. Joy A. Holm, Chmn; 8 FT, 1 PT instr. Estab. 1855; pvt; D & E;
W; ent. req. CEEB, standing, recommendations, others; 3½-5 yr;
degrees, B.A, B.F.A; schol, fel; 21 SC, 10 LC; enrl. maj. 117, others
418. Tui. $2250, fees $3590.

Art Education	Photo Silkscreen
Ceramics	Photography
Design	Printmaking
Drawing	Sculpture
Jewelry	Weaving
Painting	

Rome program, both studio and lecture, Art History, Design, Drawing.

UNIVERSITY OF NOTRE DAME, Department of Art, 46556.
Tel: (219) 283-7602
Rev. James Flanigan, Chmn; 9 FT, 2 PT instr. Estab. 1855; pvt;
D; co-ed; ent. req. upper third HS class, ent. exam; 4 yr; degrees,
A.B, B.F.A, M.A, M.F.A; fel; 38 SC, 8 LC, 20 GC; enrl. maj. 100.
Tui. $2616; campus res.

Advertising Design	Painting
Art History	Photography
Ceramic Sculpture	Pottery
Drawing	Printmaking
Fibre	Sculpture
Industrial Design	Welding Sculpture

Summer School: Rev. James Flanigan, Chmn; 15 courses in
Studio and Art History, chiefly for high school art teachers working
on advanced degrees; tui. $70 per cr. point; enrl. 50.

OAKLAND CITY

OAKLAND CITY COLLEGE, Division of Fine Arts, 47660.
Tel: (812) 749-4781 Exten. 53
Dr. Marie M. McCord, Chmn; 4 FT, 1 PT instr. Estab. 1961; den;
D & E; ent. req. HS dipl, SAT; 2 & 4 yr; degrees, A.A, B.A, B.S;
schol; 10 SC, 5 LC; enrl. maj. 35. Tui. $1665 per yr; campus res.
approx. $1200.

Advertising Design	Macrame
Art Education	Painting
Ceramics	Pottery
Drawing	Sculpture
History of Art & Archaeology	Teacher Training
Lettering	Weaving

Summer School: Dr. Marie M. McCord, Dir; courses offered,
Painting, Pottery and others; two 5 wk. terms; 14 art maj.

RICHMOND

EARLHAM COLLEGE, Art Department, 47374.
Tel: (317) 962-6561 Exten. 403
Prof. Bernard Derr, Head; 4 FT, 1 PT instr. Estab. 1847; pvt;
D; 4 yr; degree, B.A; schol; 6 SC, 3 LC; term enrl. D 125, maj.
6. Tui. incl. campus res. $4400.

Ceramics	Photography
Drawing	Sculpture
Graphic Arts	Teacher Training
History of Art	Theatre Arts
Jewelry	Weaving
Painting	

ST. MARY-OF-THE-WOODS

SAINT MARY-OF-THE-WOODS COLLEGE, Art Department, 47876.
Tel: (812) 533-2181
Sister Richard D. Ancona, Chmn; 3 FT, 5 PT instr. Estab. 1841; den;

W; 4 yr; schol; degrees; enrl. maj. 26, others 215.

Art Appreciation	History of Art
Basic Art	Metalcraft
Ceramics	Painting
Design	Philosophy of Art
Drawing	Sculpture
Graphic Arts	Teacher Training

Summer School: For Sisters of Providence only; enrl. 70; Sat.
classes for children.

ST MEINRAD

ST. MEINRAD COLLEGE, Department of Art, 47577.
Tel: (812) 357-6575
Donald Walpole, Head; 4 PT instr. Estab. 1854; pvt; D & E; ad-
mission and registration in the sch; 3 SC, 3 LC; enrl. D 36, E 30.

Advertising Design	Graphic Design
Aesthetics	History of Art & Archaeology
Ceramics	Painting
Drawing	Theatre Arts

Adult hobby classes, painting, ceramics; tui. $2 per session; enrl. 30.

SOUTH BEND

INDIANA UNIVERSITY AT SOUTH BEND, Fine Arts Department,
1825 Northside Blvd, 46615. Tel: (219) 237-4282
Harold R. Langland, Chmn; 4 FT, 3 PT instr. Estab. 1965; pub;
D; ent. req. HS dipl; 4 yr; degree, B.A.(Fine Arts); schol; 15 SC,
7 LC; enrl. D 1075, maj. 200. Tui. $21 per cr. hr; non-res. $42
per cr. hr; no campus res.

Drawing	History of Art & Archaeology
Graphic Arts	Painting
Handicrafts	Sculpture

Summer School: Harold R. Landland, Chmn. Dept; courses
offered, art history, drawing, painting; tui. $21 per cr. hr, non-res
$42.

TERRE HAUTE

INDIANA STATE UNIVERSITY, Department of Art, 47809.
Tel: (812) 232-6311 Exten. 2222
Whitney J. Engeran, Jr, Chmn; 22 FT instr. Estab. 1870; pub; D & E;
ent. req. HS grad; 4 yr; degrees, B.A, B.S, B.F.A, M.A, M.F.A, M.S;
60 SC, 10 LC, 50 GC. Tui. $24 per cr. hr, non-res. $47; campus res.
$471 per sem. dorm. fee.

Art History	Museology
Art Theory & Criticism	Painting
Ceramics	Photography
Commercial Design	Plastics
Furniture Design	Printmaking
Metal Sculpture (Foundry & Other)	Teacher Training (with Dept. of Educ.)
Metalry & Silversmithing	Wood Sculpture

Children's Sat. AM classes.
Summer School: Dr. Harriett Darrow, Dir; courses offered
same as above; two 5 wk terms; fees same as above.

UPLAND

TAYLOR UNIVERSITY, Department of Art, 46989.
Tel: (317) 998-2751 Exten. 306
Jack D. Patton, Head; 2 FT, 1 PT instr. Estab. 1846; pvt; D; ent. req
req. HS dipl; 4 yr; degrees, A.B, B.S; 8 SC, 3 LC; art enrl. 590,
maj. 55. Tui. $2190 per yr; campus res. $1235 per yr.

Advertising Design (visual) & Lettering	History of Art
Aesthetics	Jewelry
Art Education	Painting
Ceramics	Photography
Drawing	Sculpture
General Design	Teacher Training
Graphic Arts	Theatre Arts (in Speech Dept)

Summer School: Ron Keller, Dir; 1975 courses, Art for Teachers,
Introduction to Art Education, Survey of Fine Arts; term of 5 wk.
beginning June; total school enrl. 1440.

IOWA

AMES

IOWA STATE UNIVERSITY, College of Home Economics, Department of Applied Art, 50010. Tel: (515) 294-6724
Clair B. Watson, Head; 34 FT, 8 PT instr. Estab. 1923; pub; D;
ent. req. 4 yr; degrees, B.A, M.A; 55 SC, 10 LC, 7 GC; enrl. D 725.
Summer School.

Department of Architecture, College of Engineering
Maring Gehner, Head

Department of Landscape Architecture. Tel: (515) 294-5676
Thomas A. Barton, Head; 10 FT instr. Estab. 1929; pub; D; ent.
req. HS dipl, upper half of class; 4 yr; degrees, B.S.(Landscape
Arch), M.Landscape Arch; assistantships; 13 SC, 5 LC, 10 GC,
6 SLC; enrl. maj. 122, grad. 10, urban planning undergrad. 65,
grad. 8. Tui. $600; campus res. $870.
Landscape Architecture
Urban Planning

CEDAR FALLS

UNIVERSITY OF NORTHERN IOWA, Department of Art, 50613.
  Tel: (319) 273-2077
Kenneth Lash, Head; 20 FT, 1 PT instr. Estab. 1948; pub; D & E;
ent. req. HS grad, ACT and others; 4-5 yr; degrees, B.A, B.A.(Educ),
B.A.(Design), M.A, M.A.(Educ); 17 SC, 1 LC, 9 GSC, 12 GLC; school
enrl. 9000. Tui. $315 per sem, grad. $330, non-res. $600 per sem,
grad. $690; campus res.

Ceramics	Painting
Crafts	Photography
Design	Printmaking
Drawing	Sculpture
History of Art	Teaching of Art
Jewelry and Metalwork	

CEDAR RAPIDS

COE COLLEGE, Department of Art, 52402.
  Tel: (319) 364-1511 Exten. 302, 206
Robert L. Kocher, Chmn; 3 FT, 2 PT instr. Estab. 1851; pvt; D;
ent. req. SAT or ACT and/or portfolio; 4 yr; degree, A.B; schol;
15 SC, 8 LC; enrl. 1200. Tui. incl. campus res. $3765.

Art History	Painting
Ceramics	Photography
Drawing	Printmaking

Summer School: Robert Kocher, Head; each course 17 days in
length; tui. $175 per course; enrl. average 90.

American Art History	Drawing
Ceramics	Painting

KIRKWOOD COMMUNITY COLLEGE,* Department of Art, Kirkwood
  Blvd, 52401.
Ray Mullen, Head; 2 FT, 2 PT instr. Estab. 1967; pub; D & E; ent.
req. HS dipl; 2 yrs; degree, A.A.S; 8 SC, 2 LC; enrl. D 180, E 30.
Tui. $11 per sem. hr; off campus res.

Ceramics	History of Art & Archaeology
Drawing	Lettering
Graphic Arts	Painting
Graphic Design	Sculpture

Adult hobby classes, ceramics; tui. $10 per ten wk; enrl. 20.
  Summer School: Ray Mullen, Dir; tui. $11 per sem. hr.

Ceramics	Painting
Drawing	Prints

MOUNT MERCY COLLEGE, Art Department, 1330 Elmhurst Dr.
N.E, 52402. Tel: (319) 363-8213 Exten. 284
Charles Barth, Chmn; 3 FT, 1 PT instr. Estab. 1960; pvt; D & E;
ent. req. HS dipl; 4 yr; degree, B.A; 14 SC, 5 LC; enrl. 900, maj.
30. Tui. $1935, $175 per course; campus res. $990.

Art Education	Printmaking
Art Introduction	Sculpture
Basic Design	Senior Thesis & Exhibit
Drawing	Teacher Training
History of Art	Textile
Painting	

Summer School: Dr. Travis Houser, Dir; courses offered,
Art for Teachers, Drawing, Painting; tui. $175 for term of 5 wk.

CLINTON

MOUNT SAINT CLARE COLLEGE, Art Department, 400 North Bluff,
  52732. Tel: (319) 242-4023
Sister Mary Veronica Langner, Art Instr; 1 FT, 1 PT instr. Pvt; D;
co-ed; ent. req. HS dipl; 2 yr; schol; 9 SC, 1 LC; enrl. D 25. Tui.
$1000; campus res. $1030.

Art Appreciation	Drawing
Basic Design	Lettering
Ceramics	Painting

Summer Session: Sister Mary Veronica Langner, Dir; Art
Appreciation, Painting; tui. $70 per course.

CRESTON

SOUTHWESTERN COMMUNITY COLLEGE,* Art Department, 50801.
  Tel: (515) 782-7081
Paul Kerry McDowell, Head; 1 FT instr. Pub; D & E; ent. req.
HS dipl; 2 yrs; degree, A.S; 6 SC, 4 LC; enrl. D 400. Tui. $185 per
yr.

Aesthetics	History of Art & Archaeology
Art Education	Lettering
Ceramics	Painting
Drawing	Sculpture
Graphic Design	Teacher Training

Adult hobby classes: All subjects; tui. $8; enrl. 30.

DAVENPORT

MARYCREST COLLEGE, Art Department, 1607 W. 12th St, 52804.
  Tel: (319) 326-9512
Sister Clarice Eberdt, Chmn; 3 FT, 6 PT instr. Estab. 1939; den;
D & E; ent. req. HS dipl; 3-4 yr; degrees, B.A, M.A; schol; 35 SC,
15 LC, 13 GC; enrl. D 446, E 129, maj. 68, grad. 56. Tui. $2100
per yr, $20 activity fee; campus res. $1270.

Advertising Design	History of Art & Archaeology
Aesthetics	Illustration
Art Education	Jewelry
Ceramics	Lettering
Commercial Art	Museum Staff Training
Costume Design & Construction	Painting
Drafting	Photography
Drawing	Sculpture
Fashion Arts	Stage Design
Graphic Arts	Teacher Training
Graphic Design	Theatre Arts

Summer School: Dr. R. Schwieso, Dir; courses offered, Independent Study, Painting, Readings; tui. variable; 1975 enrl. 20.

SAINT AMBROSE COLLEGE, Art Department, 518 W. Locust St,
  52803. Tel: (319) 324-1681 Exten. 344, 242, 243
John Schmits, Chmn; 4 FT, 1 PT instr. Estab. 1892; den; D & E;
ent. req. HS dipl; 4 yr; degree, B.A; schol; 17 SC, 12 LC; enrl.
D 450, E 40, maj. 55. Tui. $67 per sem hr; campus res. room
$330 per sem, board $391 per sem.

Advertising Design	Graphic Design
Art Education	History of Art & Archaeology
Calligraphic Study	Illustration
Ceramics	Lettering
Commercial Art	Painting
Drafting	Photography
Drawing	Sculpture
Graphic Arts	Teacher Training

DECORAH

LUTHER COLLEGE,* Art Department, 52101.
  Tel: (319) 387-1110
Orville M. Running, Chmn; 4 FT, 3 PT instr. Estab. 1861; den;
D; ent. req. HS dipl. or ent. exam; 4 yrs; degree, B.A; schol; 13 SC,
5 LC; enrl. D 160. Tui. $2110 per yr; campus res. $950.

Aesthetics	Lettering
Art Education	Painting
Ceramics	Stage Design
Drawing	Teacher Training
Graphic Arts	Theatre Arts
History of Art & Archaeology	

Summer School: Dr. Warren G. Berg, Dir; courses offered,
drawing, painting.

DES MOINES

DRAKE UNIVERSITY, Art Department, 2501 University Ave, 50311
  Tel: (515) 271-2863
Prof. Condon Kuhl, Chmn; 19 FT instr. Estab. 1881; pvt; D & E;
ent. req. 2 pt. average in HS or previous coll; 4 yr; degrees, B.F.A,
M.F.A; schol, fel; 54 SC, 15 LC, 33 GC; enrl. maj. 350, grad. 15,
others 500. Tui; campus res.

Advertising Design	Painting
Art Education	Pottery
Art History	Printmaking
Crafts	Sculpture
Drawing	Silversmithing & Jewelry
Interior Design	

Summer School: Two 5 wk. sessions for 6 cr. hr. each.

DUBUQUE

CLARKE COLLEGE, Department of Art, 52001.
  Tel: (319) 583-9751
Sister Joan Lingen, Chmn; 4 FT, 2 PT instr. Estab. 1843; den.

(Catholic but all den. accepted); D & E; W (men in art dept); ent. req. HS grad, 16 units and Coll. Ent. Bd; 4 yr; degree, B.A. (Art); 15 SC, 4 LC; enrl. maj. 50, others 200.

Art History	Lettering
Ceramics	Printmaking
Drawing & Painting	Sculpture
Jewelry	Teacher Training

Adult Continuing Education Program; D & E.
　　Summer School: $50 per sem. hr. for three 3 wk. sessions; enrl. art 50; address all inquiries to Registrar, Summer Session.

FOREST CITY

WALDORF COLLEGE, Art Department, 50436.
John Nellermoe, Chmn; 1 FT, 1 PT instr. Estab. 1903; den; D; ent. req. HS dipl, ACT or SAT; 2 yr; degrees, A.A, A.C, A.A.S; schol; 4 SC; enrl. D 80, maj. 15. Tui. $845 per yr; campus res. $560.

Ceramics	History of Art
Drafting	Painting
Drawing	Woodcrafts

GRINNELL

GRINNELL COLLEGE, Department of Art, Division of Humanities, 50112. Tel: (515) 236-6181 Exten. 521
Richard Cervene, Chmn; 4 FT, 1 PT instr. Estab. 1930; pvt; ent. req. HS grad; 4 yr; degree, B.A; schol; 9 SC, 9 LC, independent study and extra-curricular workshops; enrl. c. 150 per sem. Tui. incl. room, board and fees $4620; campus res.
Art History Major
Studio Art Major

INDIANOLA

SIMPSON COLLEGE, Art Department, 50125.
　　Tel: (515) 916-6251
Jack W. Ragland, Head; 2 FT instr. Coll. estab. 1860, art dept. 1965; pvt; D; ent. req. HS dipl, ent. exam, portfolio desired; 4 yr; degree, B.A; schol; 16 SC, 8 LC; enrl. D 50, maj. 20. Tui. $2400 per yr; campus res. board $610, room $450.

Art Education	Painting
Ceramics	Photography (occasionally)
Drawing	Sculpture
Graphic Arts	Stage Design
History of Art & Archaeology	Theatre Arts

IOWA CITY

UNIVERSITY OF IOWA, School of Art and Art History, Division of Fine Arts, 52242. Tel: (319) 353-4551
Wallace J. Tomasini, Dir; 38 FT, 50 PT instr. Estab. 1911; pub; 4 yr; degrees, B.A, B.F.A, M.A, M.F.A, Ph.D; schol, fel; 65 SC, 18 LC, 55 GC; enrl. maj. undergrad. 435, grad. 240. Tui. undergrad. $341 per sem, grad. $390, non-res. undergrad. $775 per sem, grad. $825; campus res. Apply to Dir. of School for forms and financial aid applications.

Art Education	Photography
Ceramics	Printmaking
Drawing	Sculpture
Graphic Design	Textile Design
History of Art	Theatrical Production Design
Metalwork & Jewelry	Theory & Criticism
Multimedia	Three-Dimensional Design
Painting	

　　Summer School: Wallace J. Tomasini, Dir. of School of Art and Art History Program; tui. undergrad. $269, grad. $331, non-res. undergrad. $583, grad. $680; 8 wk. beginning June 1.

LE MARS

WESTMAR COLLEGE, Art Department, 51031.
　　Tel: (712) 546-7081 Exten. 231
Gary R. Bowling, Head; 1 FT instr, 1 PT artist-in-residence. Estab. 1890; pvt. (formerly affiliated with the United Methodist); D; ent. req. ACT, SAT or PSAT; 4 yr; degrees, B.A, B.M.Ed, B.A.S.(accepts credit for prior vocational technical training); enrl. 700, maj. 22.

Art Education	Drawing Techniques
Art History	Foundations of Art
Art Philosophy & Criticism	Graphic Communications
Business World of Art	Life Drawing
Ceramics	Oil Painting Techniques

Commercial Art Principles	Sculpture Techniques
Crafts	Synthetic Media & Color
Design	Watercolor

JANUS Continuing Education for retired persons.
　　Summer School: Mary Dise, Registrar.

MASON CITY

NORTH IOWA AREA COMMUNITY COLLEGE,* Department of Art, 500 College Dr, 50401. Tel: (515) 423-1264 Exten. 204
Kenneth C. Franks, Head; 1 FT instr. Estab. 1964; pub; D & E; ent. req. HS dipl; 2 yr; degree, A.A; schol; 4 SC, 2 LC; enrl. D 198, E 25, maj. 30. Tui. $350 in district or state, $525 out-of-state, plus $10 lab fee, $30 activity fee per yr; no res. facilities.

Art Education	History of Art & Archaeology
Basic Design	Painting

Adult hobby classes, subjects vary greatly, primarily painting and crafts; tui. approx. $3 per hr; enrl. 30.
　　Summer School: Dr. Frank Hoffman, Dir; Art Essentials; tui. $45 for term of 5 wk. beginning early June; 1969 enrl. 8.

MOUNT PLEASANT

IOWA WESLEYAN COLLEGE,* Art Department, 52641.
　　Tel: (319) 385-2211
Theodore Rasmussen, Head; 2 FT instr. Estab. 1842; den; 4 yr; degrees; schol; 10 SC, 4 LC; enrl. maj. 32.

Art Education	Painting
Art History	Sculpture
Ceramics	Secondary Art
Drawing	Special Problems
Graphic Arts	Twentieth Century Art History
Introduction to Art	

　　Summer School.

MOUNT VERNON

CORNELL COLLEGE, Art Department, Armstrong Hall, Fine Arts, 52314. Tel: (319) 895-8811 Exten. 128
Doug Hanson, Head; 3 FT, 1 PT instr. Estab. 1853; den; D; ent. req. HS grad; 4 yr; degrees, B.A, B.S.S, B.Phil; schol; 30 SC, 3 LC; normal enrl. 950. Tui. total cost per yr. $2600.

Art History	Jewelry
Batik	Metal & Fiber Design
Ceramics	Painting
Conceptual Art	Sculpture
Design	Weaving
Drawing	

ORANGE CITY

NORTHWESTERN COLLEGE, Art Department, Bushmer Art Center, 51041. Tel: (712) 737-4904
John Kaericher, Chmn; 2 FT instr. Den; D; ent. req. HS grad, ent. exam; 4 yr; degree, B.A; schol; 20 SC, 3 LC; enrl. D 150, maj. 35, others 120. Tui. incl. campus res. $2788 per yr.

Aesthetics	Layout Design (with Journalism
Art Education	Program)
Ceramics	Painting
Drawing	Photography
Gallery Program	Printmaking
History of Art	Sculpture
Honors Studies	Stage Design (with Theatre Dept)
Independent Studies	Teacher Training
Introduction to Studio	

　　Summer School: Harold Van der Laan, Acting Dir; tui. $45 per cr. hr.

OTTUMWA

OTTUMWA HEIGHTS COLLEGE, Division of Fine Arts, 52501.
John Bowitz, Chmn; 1 FT, 1-4 PT instr. Estab. 1913; pvt; D & E; ent. req. HS dipl; 2 yrs; degree, A.A; schol; 12 SC, 2 LC; enrl. D 80, E 30, maj. 18. Tui. $480.

Ceramic Sculpture	History of Art & Archaeology
Ceramics	Painting
Drawing	Sculpture
Handicrafts	

Adult hobby classes, drawing & crafts; tui. $18; enrl. 45.
Children's classes: ceramics; tui. $30; enrl. 25.
　　Summer School: John Bowitz, Dir; courses offered, Art Appreciation, Art Tools, Ceramics; tui. $100 for term of 5 wk. beginning June 5; 1973 enrl. 20.

PELLA

CENTRAL COLLEGE OF IOWA,* Art Department, 50219.
Tel: (515) 628-4151
John A. Vruwink, Chmn; 1 FT, 1 PT instr. Estab. 1937; den; 4 yr;
degree; schol; 9 SC, 8 LC; enrl. maj. 10, others 120. Tui. $750;
campus res.

Art Education, with Dept. of Educ.	Design
	Drawing & Painting
Art History & Appreciation	Graphic Arts
Ceramics	Sculpture

SIOUX CITY

BRIAR CLIFF COLLEGE, Department of Art, 3303 Rebecca St,
51104. Tel: (712) 279-5321 Exten. 452
William J. Welu, Chmn; 2 FT, 1 PT instr. Estab. 1930; pvt; D; co-
ed; ent. req. HS grad, ent. exam; 4 yr; degrees, B.A, B.S; schol; 9
SC, 4 LC; enrl. maj. 30. Tui. $1820; campus res. $1075.

Art I, II, III, IV	Drawing
Art Education	Independent Study
Art History	Reading Seminar
Design	

Summer School: William J. Welu, Dir; courses as above; tui.
$33 per cr. hr. for term of 10 wk. beginning June 15.

MORNINGSIDE COLLEGE,* Art Department, 1501 Morningside Ave,
51106. Tel: (712) 277-5212
John Gordon, Chmn; 2 FT instr. Pvt; D & E; co-ed; ent req. HS dipl;
4 yr; degrees, B.A, B.S.Art Educ; 17 SC, 4 LC; enrl. D 161, maj. 35.
Tui. $1320; campus res. $790.

Art Education	Photography
Ceramics	Sculpture
Drawing	Teacher Training
Painting	Textile Design

Summer School: Glen R. Rasmussen, Dir; Art History and Art
Education, (2nd term) Art History and Ceramics; tui. $30 per hr. for
two 5½ wk. terms, beginning June 8 and July 15.

KANSAS

ATCHISON

BENEDICTINE COLLEGE, Art Department,
66002.
Prof. Dennis McCarthy, Chmn; 2 FT instr. Estab. 1971; den; D; ent.
req. HS dipl, ent. exam; 4 yrs; degree, B.A; 23 SC, 6 LC; enrl. D
1000, maj. 29. Tui. $1400 per yr.

Aesthetics	Lettering
Art Education	Painting
Ceramics	Photography
Drawing	Sculpture
Graphic Arts	Stage Design
Graphic Design	Teacher Training
History of Art & Archaeology	Theatre Arts

BALDWIN

BAKER UNIVERSITY,* Department of Art, 66006.
Tel: (913) 594-3362 Exten. 538
Walter J. Bailey, Chairperson; 2 FT, 1 PT instr. Estab. 1858;
pvt; D; ent. req. HS dipl, provision made for entrance without HS
dipl. by interview and committee action; 4 yrs; degree, A.B. in
Art; schol; 11 SC, 3 LC; enrl. D 105, maj. 28. Tui. $1450, PT $175
per full course; campus res. $950.

Art Education	Painting
Ceramics	Sculpture
Drawing	Teacher Training
Graphic Arts	Textile Design
History of Art & Archaeology	

Seminar on the Creative Process.
Summer School: Don D. Donihue, Acting Dean.

COLBY

COLBY COMMUNITY COLLEGE, Art Department, 1255 South
Range, 67701. Tel: (913) 462-3984 Exten. 259
Kenneth Eugene Mitchell, Dept Representative. 2 FT, 2 PT instr.
Estab. 1965; pub; D & E; no ent req, HS dipl. before graduating;
2 yr; degree, A.A; schol; 20 SC, 5 LC; enrl. D 200 per sem, E 150,
maj. 22. Tui. $420 in state, $1800 out-of-state; $15 per cr hr;
campus res. $550 sem.

Art History I, II, III	Figure Drawing
Ceramics	Lettering
Color Structure	Painting

Commercial Art (Fashion Design)	Photography
	Overseas Art History Tours
Design	Three Dimensional Design
Drawing	

Summer School: Kenneth E. Mitchell, Dir; courses offered same
as fall and spring sem; tui. $15 per cr. hr. for term of 4 wk. be-
ginning May 16; 1973 enrl. 27.

EL DORADO

BUTLER COUNTY COMMUNITY JUNIOR COLLEGE,* Division
of Fine Arts, Haverhill & Towanda Rd, 67042.
Tel: (316) 321-5083 Exten. 51
Robert H. Chism, Chmn. Div. 2 FT, 1 PT instr. Estab. 1927; pub;
D & E; ent. req. HS dipl; 2 yrs; degree, A. A; schol; 8 SC, 2 LC;
enrl. D 1176, E 410. Tui. $5 per cr. hr; campus res. $800.

Ceramics	Painting
Drawing	Photography
History of Art	Textile Design

EMPORIA

THE COLLEGE OF EMPORIA,* Art Department, 66801.
Tel: (316) 342-3670 Exten. 89
Lloyd G. Roser, Head Dept; 1 FT, 1 PT instr. Estab. 1882; pvt;
D; ent. req. HS dipl; scholastic aptitude test; 4 yrs; degrees,
B.A, B.S, B.M.E, B.M; schol; 18 SC, 3 LC; enrl. D 450. Tui. $1480;
campus res. $1020.

Art Education	Introduction to Art
Ceramics	Painting
Color & Design	Sculpture
Drawing	Stage Design
Graphic Arts	Three-Dimensional Design
History of Art & Archaeology	

Summer School: Lloyd G. Roser, Dir; courses offered, printmaking, sculpture, and others; tui. $30 hr. term of 5 wk. beginning
June 3; 1973 enrl. 92.

EMPORIA KANSAS STATE COLLEGE, Art Department, 66801.
Tel: (316) 343-1200
Rex Hall, Chmn; 9 FT, 3 PT instr. Estab. 1865; pub; 4 yr; degrees,
B.S.E, B.F.A, M.A; schol; 47 SC, 15 LC. Summer School.

Art History	Metalry
Ceramics	Painting
Commercial Art	Printmaking
Drawing	Sculpture
Glassblowing	

HAYS

FORT HAYS KANSAS STATE COLLEGE, Department of Art, 67601.
Tel: (913) 628-4287
John C. Thorns, Jr, Chmn; 10 FT, 1 PT instr. Estab. 1902; pub;
ent. req. ACT scores; 4 yr; degrees; A.B.Art, B.F.A.Art; M.A.Art;
schol; 43 undergrad. SC, 20 grad. SC, 12 undergrad LC, 7 grad LC;
enrl. 900 Tui. (Fall) $237.25, non-res. $484.75.

Ceramics	Painting
Design	Sculpture
Drawing	Silversmithing
Graphics	

Summer School: 7 wk. beginning June 7; tui. $15.25 per hr, non-
res. $32.25; enrl. 300.

HUTCHINSON

HUTCHINSON COMMUNITY JUNIOR COLLEGE, 1300 N Plum,
67501. Tel: (316) 663-5781 Exten 113
Russell Dickenson, Chmn; 3 FT, 2 PT instr. Estab. 1928; pub; D &
E; ent. req. HS grad; 2 yr; degree, A.A; schol; 17 SC, 5 LC; enrl.
maj. 37, 2416 total. Tui. $356 per yr; campus res. $880.

Art Education	Jewelry
Ceramics	Painting
Design, 2D & 3D	Printmaking
Drawing	Sculpture
History of Art & Archaeology	

Summer School: James Stringer, Dean; Painting, Drawing; tui.
$10 per cr. hr. for term of 4 wk.

LAWRENCE

UNIVERSITY OF KANSAS, School of Fine Arts, 66044.
Tel: (913) 864-4401
Peter G. Thompson, Assoc. Dean. Pub; 4-5 yr; degrees, B.F.A,
B.A.E, B.S, M.F.A; schol. and fel. Tui. $268 per sem, non-res.
$663; campus res. Freshman Common Curriculum (required for
all new freshmen), Roger Shimomura, Advisor, enrl. 250.

Department of Design
Richard Branham, Chmn; 24 FT, 12 PT instr. Estab. 1921; 83 SC, 32 LC, 26 GC; enrl. maj. 250, grad. 40.

Advertising Art	Industrial Design (5 yr)
Ceramics	Interior Design (5 yr)
Design	Jewelry
Editorial Art	Silversmithing
Graphic Design	Textile Design in Weaving

Department of Painting and Sculpture
Michael Ott, Chmn; 18 FT, 5 PT instr. Estab. 1885; 50 SC, 25 GC; enrl. maj. 150.

Art History	Sculpture
Painting	Theatre Design
Printmaking	

Department of Occupational Therapy
Joan Wyrick, Chmn; 8 FT, 4 PT instr. Estab. 1965; 25 LC, 10 Lab.C, hospital field work; enrl. 200. Courses in occupational therapy.

Department of History of Art (College of Liberal Arts and Sciences), Spooner Hall, 66044. Tel: (913) 864-3616
Chu-Tsing Li, Chmn; 7 FT, 8 PT instr. Estab. 1951; pub; D; 4 yr; degrees, B.A, B.F.A, M.A, Ph.D; 23 LC, GC; enrl. maj. 75, grad. 30, others 900.

Chinese & Japanese Art	North American Art
History of Art	Western European Art

School of Education
Dr. Philip Rueschhoff, Chmn. Courses in art education.

Summer School: 8 wk. in all depts.

LINDSBORG

BETHANY COLLEGE, 67456.
Tel: (913) 227-3312 Exten. 44
Daniel Mason, Head; 4 FT instr. Estab. 1881; den; D; co-ed; ent req. HS grad; 4 yr; degree, B.A; schol; 16 SC, 4 LC. enrl. 750. Tui. $2700 per yr. incl. tui, fees and room and board.

Art Education	Painting
Art History	Photography & Filmmaking
Ceramics	Printmaking
Drawing	Sculpture

Summer School: One 6 wk. term. Write Dir. of Summer School for Bulletin.

MANHATTAN

KANSAS STATE UNIVERSITY, 66506.
Tel: (913) 532-5950
Pub; ent. req. HS grad; 4-5 yr; degrees; schol. Tui. $263, non-res. $658, grad. $57 plus $14 per cr. hr; campus res.

College of Architecture and Design
Bernd Foerster, Dean; 53 FT instr. Estab. 1904; degrees, B.Arch. (5 yr), B.Interior Arch.(5 yr), B.Landscape Arch.(5 yr), M.Arch, M.Landscape Arch, M.Regional and Community Planning; enrl. approx. 1150.

‡Architecture	‡Landscape Architecture
‡Interior Architecture	‡Regional & Community Planning

Summer School: Bernd Foerster, Dean; 8 wk. from June 4.

College of Arts and Sciences, Department of Art
Jerrold Maddox, Head; 22 FT instr. Estab. 1965, combined art from H.E.(1914) and art from Arch.(1904); 4-5 yr; degrees, B.S.(Art Educ), jointly with Coll. Educ.(4 yr), B.A.(4 yr), B.F.A.(4 yr), M.A.(Art); enrl. 200.

Art Education	Graphic Design
Ceramics	Metalsmithing & Jewelry
Crafts	Painting
Design	Prints
Drawing	Sculpture

Summer School: Jerrold Maddox, Head; 8 wk. from June 4.

College of Home Economics, Department of Clothing, Textiles and Interior Design
Theresa Perenich, Head. Estab. 1914; enrl. 420, Fashion Marketing maj. 221, Textile Science maj. 10, Fashion Design maj. 43, Interior Design maj. 146.
Summer School: Theresa Perenich, Head; 8 wk. from June 7.

McPHERSON

McPHERSON COLLEGE, Art Department, 67460.
Tel: (316) 241-0731 Exten 72
Mary Ann Robinson, Chmn; 2 FT instr. Estab. 1887; den; D; ent req. HS dipl, ent. exam; 4 yr; degree, B.A; schol; 12 SC, 2 LC; enrl. D 450, maj. 14. Tui. $1550 per yr; $50 per hr; campus res. $400.

Art Appreciation	History of Art

Art Education	Interior Design
Ceramics	Lettering
Craft Workshops	Painting
Drawing	Teacher Training

Summer School: Dr. Dayton Rothrock, Dir; tui. $50 per hr.

OTTAWA

OTTAWA UNIVERSITY, Department of Art, Tenth & Cedar Sts, 66067.
Pal T. Wright, Dir; 2 FT, 1 PT instr. Estab. 1865; pvt; D; ent. req. HS grad, SAT or ACT test; 4 yr; degree B.A; schol; 16 SC, 5 LC; enrl. D 35, maj 5. Tui. 76-77 yr. $2160, $270 per course; campus res. $1170.

Art Education	Graphic Design
Ceramics	History of Art & Archaeology
Drawing	Painting
Fashion Arts	Photography
Graphic Arts	Sculpture

PITTSBURG

KANSAS STATE COLLEGE OF PITTSBURG, Art Department, 1701 S. Broadway, 66762. Tel: (316) 231-7000 Exten. 353
Reed Schmickle, Chmn; 8 FT instr. Estab. 1921; pub; 4 yr; degrees, B.S.A.E, B.F.A, M.A, M.S; schol; undergrad. 33 SC, 8 LC; grad 18 SC, 13 LC; normal enrl. 140 maj, others 550. Fees $195, non-res. $442.75; campus res.

Art Education	Fine Arts
Art Therapy	

Summer School: Reed Schmickle, Dir; Grad. and undergrad. res. $12.65 per cr. hr, non-res. $29.65.

SALINA

KANSAS WESLEYAN UNIVERSITY,* Art Department, Santa Fe & Clafin St, 67401. Tel: (913) 827-5541
George F. Chlebak, Assoc. Prof. Art; 1 FT instr. Estab. 1886 den; 4 yr; degree, A.B; schol; 8 SC, 3 LC; enrl. maj. 15, others 500 for two sem. Tui. $1800 per yr; campus res.
Design
Drawing & Painting
History of Art
Summer School: $42.50 per cr. hr. for 8 wk. June & July; enrl. 125.

STERLING

✤STERLING COLLEGE, 67579.
Gordon Zahradnik, Chmn; 1 FT, 1 PT instr. Estab. 1876; den; D & E; ent. req. HS grad; 120 hrs; schol; 16 SC, 4 LC; enrl. D 70, maj 9. Tui. $1600 per sem.

Art Education	Macrame
Ceramics	Painting
Display	Paper Mache
Drawing	Sculpture
Enameling	Tooling
Handicrafts	Theatre Arts
Jewelry	

Adult Hobby Classes: Varied; tui. $20 per sem; enrl. 27.
Summer School: Dr. George Stone, Dir; tui. $40 per hr.

TOPEKA

WASHBURN UNIVERSITY OF TOPEKA, Department of Art, Mulvane Art Center, 17th and Jewell Sts, 66621.
R.J. Hunt, Head, 4 FT, 4 PT instr. Estab. 1000; pub; ent req. HS grad; 4 yr; degrees, A.B, B.F.A; 11 SC, 5 LC; enrl. maj. 60, others 280. Tui. $20 per sem. hr, non-res. $36; campus res.

Art History & Appreciation	Drawing
Ceramics	Metalcraft & Jewelry
Design	Painting

Childrens classes, tui. $18 for twelve 1½ hr sessions. Adult classes, tui. $22 for twelve 3 hr sessions.

WICHITA

FRIENDS UNIVERSITY, Art Department, 2100 University Ave, 67213. Tel: (316) 263-9131 Exten. 391
Dee M. Connett, Head; 2 FT, 2 PT instr. Estab. 1898; pvt; D & E; ent. req. HS dipl, recommendation and application through admissions bd; 4 - 5 when in work-study program; degrees, A.B, B.S; schol; 19 SC, 5 LC; enrl. D 332, maj. 30. Tui. $1650 per yr, $825 sem, part time $65 per hr; campus res. $553 sem.

Aesthetics	History of Art & Archaeology
Art Education	Illustration
Ceramics	Jewelry

Design	Metalsmithing/Blacksmith Forging
Drafting	Painting
Drawing	Photography
Enameling	Sculpture
Graphic Arts	Teacher Training
Graphic Design	Weaving
Handicrafts	

Summer School: Dee M. Connett, Dir; courses offered, Art Appreciation, Ceramics, Arts and Crafts for Elementary School, Metalsmithing; tui. $34 per hr, beginning June 5 to Aug. 24; 1973 enrl. 28.

SCHOOL OF THE WICHITA ART ASSOCIATION, 9112 E Central, 67206. Tel: (316) 686-6687
John R. Rouse, Dir; 20 instr. Estab. 1923; pvt; D & E; schol, enrl. 300. Tui $20 per sem hr. for 14 wk. sem.

Art History	Painting
Ceramics	Photography
Commercial Art	Pottery
Drawing	Printmaking
Enameling	Silversmithing
Fashion Design	Weaving

Summer School: 6 wk. June-July.

✠WICHITA STATE UNIVERSITY, Division of Art, College of Fine Arts, 67208. Tel: (316) 689-3555
Robert M. Kiskadden, Asst. Dean; 18 FT, 6 PT instr. Estab. 1907; pub; ent. req. HS dipl; 4-5 yr, degrees, B.F.A, B.A.E. in Educ. M.A. in Educ. and Graphic design, M.F.A, 60 hrs; schol. and fel; SC, LC; enrl. maj. 400. Tui. $282 per sem.

Art Education	Graphic Design
Art History	Painting
Ceramics	Printmaking
Drawing	Sculpture

KENTUCKY

ANCHORAGE

✠LOUISVILLE SCHOOL OF ART, 100 Park Rd, 40223.
Tel: (502) 245-8836
Bruce H. Yenawine, Dir; 6 FT, 5 PT instr. Estab. 1929; pvt; D & E; ent. req. HS dipl; 4 yr; degree, B.F.A. Tui. $625 full-time.

Ceramics	Painting
Commercial Art	Printmaking
Crafts/Design	Sculpture
Jewelry Design	Textiles Design
Metalsmithing	Weaving

BARBOURVILLE

UNION COLLEGE, Art Department, College St, 40906.
Tel: (606) 546-4151
Elizabeth Burke, Dept. Head; 1 FT, 1 PT instr. Den; D & E; ent. req. HS dipl; 4 yr; degrees, B.S, B.A, M.A.(Educ). Tui. $1630 per yr; campus res. $2474.

Art Appreciation	Painting
Art Education	Recreational Arts and Crafts
Art Fundamentals	Teacher Training
Drawing	Theatre Arts
History of Art	

BEREA

BEREA COLLEGE, Art Department, 40403.
Tel: (606) 986-8946
Lester Pross, Chmn; 6 FT, 3 PT instr. Estab. 1935; pvt; ent. req. HS grad; 4 yr; degree, B.A; all students on full tui. schol. and all participate in student labor program, other schol. and loan funds; 20 SC enrl. 275, 10 LC enrl. 73; enrl. maj. 40, others 1082. No tui; other expenses $150; campus res. $440.

Art History	Sculpture
Ceramics	Teacher Training
Drawing	Textile Design
Printmaking	

BOWLING GREEN

WESTERN KENTUCKY UNIVERSITY,* Art Department, 42101.
Tel: (502) 745-3940
Verne K. Shelton, Head; 14 FT, 1 PT instr. Pub; D; co-ed; ent. req. HS dipl; 4 yr; degrees, B.A, B.F.A; 7 SC, 2 LC; enrl. maj. 220. Tui. $125, non-res. $375, or $9 per hr. non-res. $30; campus res. $610, non-res. $860.

Aesthetics	History of Art & Archaeology
Art Education	Painting
Ceramics	Sculpture

Drawing	Teacher Training
Graphic Arts	Weaving

Summer School: Dr. John Scarborough, Dir; tui. $62.50, non-res. $187.50 for term of 8 wk. beginning June 16; 1969 enrl. 50.

Art Education	Drawing
Art History	Painting
Design	

CAMPBELLSVILLE

CAMPBELLSVILLE COLLEGE, Department of Fine Arts, 42718.
Tel: (502) 465-8158
Robert Stapp, Chmn; 2 FT, 4 PT instr. Estab. 1923; den; D & E; ent. req. HS dipl, ent. exam; 4 yr; degrees, B.A, B.S; schol; 9 SC, 30 LC; art enrl. D 28, E 9. Tui, room and fees $2340.

Aesthetics	History of Art & Archaeology
Art Education	Jewelry
Batik	Macrame
Candle Making	Painting
Ceramics	Sculpture
Commercial Art	Stage Design
Drafting	Stitchery
Drawing	Theatre Arts
Handicrafts	Tie-dyeing

Summer School: Tui. $300 for term of 8 wk. beginning June 10; 1975 art enrl. 42.

COVINGTON

NORTHERN KENTUCKY STATE COLLEGE, Art Department, 526 Johns Hill Road, Highland Heights, 41076.
Tel: (606) 781-2600 Exten. 139, 151, 152, 167
Dr. Bill Parsons, Chmn: 15 FT, 2 PT instr. Founded 1968; pub; D & E; ent. req. HS grad, ACT scores; 4 yr; degrees, B.F.A, B.A.(Art Educ), B.Mus, B.Mus.Educ; 31 SC, 10 LC. Tui. per sem. $210; part-time $18 per cr. hr; non-res. per sem; $475, part-time $40 per cr. hr. Summer as above.

Art Education	Photography
Ceramics	Printmaking
Drawing	Radio & TV
History of Art & Archaeology	Sculpture
Journalism	Speech
Music	Theatre Arts
Painting	

DANVILLE

CENTRE COLLEGE OF KENTUCKY, Art Department, 40422.
Tel: (606) 236-5211
Tom Gaines, Chmn; 4 FT instr. Estab. 1819; pvt; 4 yr; degree; SC, LC; enrl. D 750-800.

Ceramics	History of Art
Commercial Art	Printmaking
Design	Sculpture
Drawing & Painting	

Adult hobby classes, painting, drawing, ceramics.

FORT MITCHELL

THOMAS MORE COLLEGE, Department of Art, Box 85, Turkeyfoot Rd, 41017. Tel: (606) 341-5800
Bernard L. Schmidt, Chmn. Dept; 3 FT, 3 PT instr. Estab. 1921; den; D & E; ent. req. ACT, SAT; 4 yr; degrees, B.A, B.E.S; schol; 20 SC, 8 LC; enrl. D & E 1768, maj. 30, grad. students 4. Tui. $49.50 per cr. hr.

Art Education	Painting
Ceramics	Photography
Drawing	Sculpture
Graphic Arts	Teacher Training
History of Art	Visual Communication

Summer School: Father Ed Bauman, Dir; courses vary from summer to summer.

GEORGETOWN

GEORGETOWN COLLEGE, Fine Arts Division, Art Department, 40324. Tel: (502) 863-8351.
Charles James McCormick, Chmn: 2 Ft, 1 PT instr. Estab. 1829; den; D; ent. req. ACT score and HS transcript; 4 yr; degree, B.A; schol. and grants; 14 SC, 6 LC; enrl. 1150. Tui. $215, $900 non-res. 4-1-4 curriculum; Jan. interterm; Travel Classes.

Advanced Painting	Oil Painting
Art Appreciation	Photography
Art History	Public School Art
Art Survey	Secondary Art
Ceramics	Sculpture

Drawing   Three-Dimensional Design
Graphics   Two-Dimensional Design
     Summer School: Charles James McCormick, Chmn; courses offered, Art Humanities, Art Education, Studio Classes; three 3 wk. modules of one course each; $200 per course.

LEXINGTON

TRANSYLVANIA UNIVERSITY, Fine Arts Department, 300 N. Broadway, 40508. Tel: (606) 233-8179
Dr. Charles D. Haller, Chmn; 2 FT, 1 PT instr. Pvt; D; ent. req. HS grad, HS record, coll. boards, comt. approval; 4 yr; degree, A.B; schol; 20 SC, 10 LC; enrl. 750. Tui. $3320; campus res. $2190. tui. guaranteed.

Art Education   Painting
Ceramics   Sculpture
Drawing   Stage Design
Graphic Design   Teacher Training
History of Art & Archaeology   Theatre Arts

UNIVERSITY OF KENTUCKY, College of Arts & Sciences, Department of Art, 40506. Tel: (606) 258-9000 Exten. 2452, 2453
Prof. Joseph Fitzpatrick, Chmn; 20 FT, 1 PT. Estab. 1918; pub; 4 yr; degrees, B.A, M.A, M.F.A; schol. & grad. assistantships; 23 SC, 19 LC, 6 GC; enrl. maj. 200, others 800. Tui. res. $240, non-res. $605; campus res.

Art Education   Painting
Ceramics   Printmaking
Drawing   Sculpture
History of Art   Textiles
     Summer School: Prof. Joseph Fitzpatrick, Chmn; courses offered, Art Education, Drawing, History of Art, Painting; tui. res. $80, non-res. $200 for 8 wk. beginning June 5; enrl. 200.

LOUISVILLE

UNIVERSITY OF LOUISVILLE,* Allen R. Hite Art Institute, Belknap Campus, 40208. Tel: (502) 636-4233
Dr. Jay M. Kloner, Dir; Dorothy Jared, Secy; 12 FT instr. Estab. 1946 through bequest of Allen R. Hite for instruction in art; coordinates all Univ. art activities; pub; D; ent. req. admis. to coll; 4 yr; degrees, B.A, M.A; schol; 31 SC, 27 LC, 30 GC. enrl. undergrad. 120, grad. 30. Tui. res. $950, non-res. $1950.

Art Education   Painting
Ceramics   Photography
Design   Printmaking
History of Art   Sculpture
     Summer School: Tui. undergrad. res. $360, non-res. undergrad. $738; full-time for two 5 wk. sessions from June 8.

MIDWAY

✤MIDWAY COLLEGE, Art Department, Stephens St, 40347.
     Tel: (606) 846-4423 Exten. 27
Virginia Hutton, Chmn; 1 FT instr. Den; D; W; ent. req. HS dipl, ACT; 2 yr; schol; 7 SC, 3 LC; enrl. 55.

Art Education   Drawing
Basic Design   Historical Furniture
Ceramics   Lettering
Decorative Textiles   Painting

MOREHEAD

✤MOREHEAD STATE UNIVERSITY, Art Department, Claypool-Young Art Building, 40351. Tel: (606) 783-3232, 2193
Dr. Bill R. Booth, Head; 9 FT, 1 PT instr, 2 grad. teaching assts. Estab. 1922; pub; D & E; ent. req. ACT; 4 yr (128 sem. hr), 30 sem. hr. for M.A; schol, workshops, lab. assistantships and grad. assistantships; 40 undergrad. courses, 28 grad. courses, special workshops and seminars; enrl. 380. Tui. res. undergrad. $210 per sem, grad. $235 per sem, non-res. undergrad. $475 per sem, grad. $500 per sem.

Art Education   History of Art
Ceramics   Photography
Color & Design   Printmaking
Commercial Art   Sculpture
Crafts   Teacher Training (Art Education)
Drawing   Watercolor
General Art
     Summer School: Dr. Bill R. Booth, Dir.

MURRAY

MURRAY STATE UNIVERSITY, College of Creative Expression, Art Department, 42071. Tel: (502) 762-3784
Robert W. Head, Chmn; 18 FT instr. Estab. 1925; degrees, B.S, B.A,

B.F.A, M.A, M.A.Ed, M.A.(Studio), M.A.C.T; enrl. maj. 250. Tui. $481; campus res.

Art Appreciation   Graphic Design
Art History   Metalsmithing & Jewelry
Ceramics   Photography
Design I & II   Printmaking
Drawing & Painting   Sculpture
Design Materials   Textile Design & Weaving
     Summer School: Robert W. Head, Chmn; tui. $238 for term of 8 wk. beginning mid-June.
     Summer Arts Academy. Workshops for high school students, mid-July; studio activities.

OWENSBORO

BRESCIA COLLEGE, Art Department, 120 W. Seventh St, 42301.
     Tel: (502) 685-3131 Exten. 289
Fred Stephens, Chmn; 6 FT. Estab. 1950; den; D & E; ent. req. HS dipl, ent. exam, ACT, GED; 4 yr; degrees, A.A, B.A, B.S, B.M. (Music & Music Educ); schol; 22 SC, 10 LC; enrl. D 400, E 360, maj. 50. Tui. $37 per sem. hr, gen. fee $15 per sem, activity fee $16 per sem; campus res. room $300 per year, room and board $500 per sem.

Advertising Design   History of Art
Aesthetics   Lettering
Architecture   Painting
Art Education   Photography
Ceramics   Teacher Training
Drafting   Textile Design
Drawing   Three-Dimensional Design
Graphic Arts
Adult hobby classes, same as above; tui. $37 per cr. hr, audit $15 per sem. hr.
     Summer School: Courses offered, Ceramics, Drawing, Photography; tui. $37 per sem. hr. for term of 6 wk. beginning June; enrl. 50.

KENTUCKY WESLEYAN COLLEGE,* Department of Fine Arts, 3000 Frederica St, 42301.
Dr. Emil G. Ahnell, Chmn; 1 FT instr. Dept. estab. 1950; den; 4 yr; degree, B.A; schol; 11 SC, 4 LC; enrl. maj. 40. Tui. $30 per cr. hr; campus res.

Advertising Design   Drawing, Painting, & Design - 4 yr.
Art Appreciation   Graphic Arts
Art History   Illustration
Arts and Crafts   Jewelry
Ceramics and Sculpture   Teacher Training
Commercial Art   Watercolor
     Summer School: Art Survey and Art for the Elementary Schools; enrl. 60.

PIPPA PASSES

ALICE LLOYD COLLEGE, Art Department,
     41844.
Golden Glen Hale, Chmn; 1 FT, 1 PT instr. Estab. 1922; pvt; D & E; ent. req. HS dipl, ent. exam; 2 yr; degrees, A.A, C.A; schol; 6 SC, 1 LC; enrl. maj. 5. Tui. incl. campus res. $1650 per yr.

Drawing   Photography
Painting   Sculpture
Adult hobby classes, ceramics; tui. free; enrl. 40

RICHMOND

EASTERN KENTUCKY UNIVERSITY,* Art Department, 40475.
     Tel: (606) 622-2040
Daniel N. Shindelbower, Chmn; 14 FT, 2 PT instr. Estab. 1910, pub, D; co-ed; ent. req. HS grad; 4 yr; degrees, B.A, B.F.A, M.A. in Educ; 30 SC, 6 LC, 6 GC (5 of which may be repeated twice). Tui. res. undergrad. $217.25, grad. $242.25 per sem, non-res. undergrad. $482.25, grad. $507.25 per sem, plus fees; campus res. $156-166 per sem.

Drawing Media   Metal Casting
Figure Drawing   Painting Media
Figure Painting   Sculpture, Synthetic Media
Graphics II   Senior Exhibition
Greek & Roman Art   Twentieth Century Painting
     Summer School: Daniel N. Shindelbower, Dir; June 10 through Aug. 2; tui. res. undergrad. $90, grad. $96, non-res. undergrad $219, grad. $225; campus res. available.

WILLIAMSBURG

CUMBERLAND COLLEGE, Department of Art, Walnut St, College Sta. Box 523, 40769. Tel: (606) 549-0498
Russell A. Parker, Acting Head Dept; 4 FT instr. Estab. 1959; den; D & E; ent. req. HS dipl, special approval may be granted for

admission; 4 yr; degrees, B.S, B.A; schol; 26 SC, 12 LC; enrl. D 720, E 90, maj 38. Tui. $1086 per yr; campus roo. $760.

Aesthetics	History of Art & Archaeology
Art Education	Jewelry
Basketry	Lettering
Batik	Museum Staff Training
Ceramics	Painting
Drawing	Sculpture
Enameling	Teacher Training
Graphic Arts	Weaving
Handicrafts	

Summer School: R. A. Parker, Acting Head Dept; courses offered, Art Appreciation, Art History, Two and Three Dimensional Studio; tui. $218 per term for term of 5 wk. beginning June 5; 1976 enrl. 110.

WILMORE

ASBURY COLLEGE, Art Department, 40390.
Tel: (606) 858-3511 Exten. 245
Rudy Medlock, Head; 4 FT instr. Estab. 1890; D; pvt; 4 yr; degrees, A.B, B.A; 15 SC, 9 LC; sch. enrl. 1200. Tui. $40 per cr. hr, $500 per quarter; campus res. Summer School.

Art History-Survey	Painting
Arts and Crafts	Photography
Ceramics	Sculpture
Drawing	Teacher Training
Graphic Arts	Weaving
Lettering	

LOUISIANA

BATON ROUGE

LOUISIANA STATE UNIVERSITY, BATON ROUGE,* Fine Arts Department, 70803. Tel: (504) 388-2166
Mr. Jack Wilkinson, Head; 26 FT, 6 PT instr. Estab. 1934; pub; 4 yr; degrees, B.F.A, M.A; grad. assistantships; 55 SC, 32 LC, 18 GC; enrl. 2590. Fees $160 in-state, $410 out-of-state; campus res.

Art Education	Graphic Arts
Art History	Interior Design
Ceramics	Painting
Crafts	Sculpture
Design	Teacher Training with College of
Drawing	Education

HAMMOND

SOUTHEASTERN LOUISIANA UNIVERSITY, Department of Art, University Station, 70401.
Paul Lawrence, Head; 6 FT instr. Univ. estab. 1925, dept. art 1964; pub; D; ent. req. HS dipl; 4 yr; degrees, B.A.(Art Educ, Art); 27 SC, 5 LC, 1 GC; enrl. maj. 127, others 400. Tui. non-res. undergrad. $630 per yr, grad. $200; campus res. $664 per sem.

Art Education	History of Art & Archaeology
Design	Painting
Drawing	Sculpture

LAFAYETTE

UNIVERSITY OF SOUTHWESTERN LOUISIANA, School of Art and Architecture, 70501. Tel: (318) 233-3850 Exten. 521, 522
R. Warren Robison, Dir; 30 FT, 1 PT instr. Estab 1900; pub; 4-5 yr; degrees, B.F.A, B.Arch; enrl. univ. 13,000.

Advertising Design	Choreographic Design
Architecture	Fine Arts
Art Education	Interior Architecture
Ceramics	Photography

LAKE CHARLES

McNEESE STATE UNIVERSITY, Department of the Visual Arts, 4000 Ryan St, 70601.
Nowell A. Daste, Dept. Head; 5 FT instr. Estab. 1952; pub; D & E; ent. req. HS dipl; 4 yrs; degree, B.A; schol; 27 SC, 1 LC; enrl. D 250, maj. 110. Tui. FT $335; campus res. $500 per sem. with 5 day meal ticket.

Architecture	History of Art & Archaeology
Art Education	Macrame
Drafting	Painting
Drawing	Papier Mache
Dyeing	Photography
Graphic Arts	Sculpture
Graphic Design	Stitchery
Handicrafts	Teacher Training

Summer School: Courses offered, Architectural Graphics, Art Education, Art History Survey, tui. $74.50 for term of 8 wk. beginning June 3, 1975; enrl. 100.

METAIRIE

DAVID SCHOOL OF BASIC ART, INC, 5050 W. Esplanade, 70002.
Tel: (504) 888-3630
David W. Jenks, Pres; 4 FT instr. Estab. 1969; pvt; D & E; no particular ent. req; no degree; 6 SC; enrl. 125 students per wk. Tui. $48 per 8 lesson course.

Aesthetics	Painting
Drawing	

Children's classes, 8 wk. course Sat. and weekdays after school.

MONROE

NORTHEAST LOUISIANA UNIVERSITY, Department of Art, 71201.
Tel: (318) 342-3110
Dr. James B. Edwards, Head, Dept. of Art; 11 FT instr. Estab. 1931; pub; D & E; co-ed; ent. req. HS grad; 4 yr; degrees, B.F.A, M.Ed; schol; 43 SC, 5 LC, 8 GC; enrl. D 250, E 20, maj. 230. Tui. $220, part time $10 per cr. hr, activity fee $14 per sem; campus res. $664.

Advertising Design	Jewelry
Art Education	Lettering
Ceramics	Occupational Therapy
Commercial Art	Painting
Drawing	Photography
Graphic Arts	Teacher Training
History of Art & Archaeology	Weaving

Summer School: Tui. $45; two 6 wk. terms beginning June 1 and July 9.

NEW ORLEANS

DELGADO JUNIOR COLLEGE,* Department of Fine Arts, 615 City Park Ave, 70119. Tel: (504) 486-5403
Benjamin John Ploger, Chmn; 2 FT, 2 PT instr. Dept. estab. 1967; pub; D & E; ent. req. HS dipl, 18 yr. old; 2 yr; degrees, A.A, A.S; schol; 12-20 SC, 12-20 LC; enrl. D 150, E 65, maj. 60. Tui. $200 per yr; no campus res.

Art Appreciation	History of Art & Archaeology
Drawing	Painting

THE JOHN McCRADY ART SCHOOL OF NEW ORLEANS,* 910 Bourbon St, 70016. Tel: (504) 529-5628
Mary B. McCrady, Dir; 4 PT instr. Estab. 1942; pvt; D & E; co-ed; ent. req. HS dipl, ent. exam, examples or color slides of work; 3 yr; no degree; schol; 4 SC.

Advertising Design	History of Art & Archaeology
Commercial Art	Illustration
Drawing	Lettering
Fashion Arts	Painting
Graphic Design	Textile Design

Adult hobby classes, painting (various mediums and techniques); tui. $34 and $27; enrl. 30.
Children's classes, all subjects; tui. $15; enrl. 10.
Summer School: Mary B. McCrady, Dir; tui. $34 for monthly term June and July; 1969 enrl. 20.

LOYOLA UNIVERSITY, Department of Visual Arts, 6363 St. Charles Ave, 70118. Tel: (504) 866-5471 Exten. 240
Brother Gebhard Fröhlich, Chmn; 3 FT, 2 PT instr. Den; D & E; ent. req. HS dipl, ent. exam; 4 yr; degrees, B A.(Visual Arts); schol; 9 SC, 3 LC; enrl. D 150, E 45, maj. 28. Tui. $2000 per yr; campus res. $1400.

Ceramics	Sculpture
Drawing	Teacher Training
Painting	

Summer School: Brother Gebhard Fröhlich, Dir; courses offered, Drawing, Painting, Sculpture; tui. approx. $500 for term of 6 wk. beginning in June; enrl. 40.

NEW ORLEANS ART INSTITUTE, 2926 Canal St, 70119.
Tel: (504) 822-1453
Walter A. Labiche, Dir; 1 FT, 2 PT instr. Estab. 1970; pub; D & E; ent. req. acceptable visual interest, plus samples of work; 2.5 yrs; no degree; schol; enrl. D 25, E 24. Tui. FT $93.50, PT $47; no campus res.

Advertising Design	Graphic Arts
Art Education	Graphic Design
Calligraphy	Illustration
Commercial Art	Isometrics
Drafting	Lettering

Drawing	Painting
Fashion Arts	Technical Illustration

Adult hobby classes, oils, watercolors, acrylics, ink, anatomy; tui. $30 mo; enrl. 10.

SOUTHERN UNIVERSITY, NEW ORLEANS,* Department of Fine Arts and Art Education, 6400 Press Dr, 70126.
Tel: (504) 282-4401 Exten. 267, 268
Eddie Jack Jordan, Head Dept. 4 FT instr. Estab. 1960; pub; D & E; ent. req. HS dipl; 4 yrs; degree, B.A; schol; 27 SC, 9 LC; enrl. art maj. 39, other art courses, approx. 600. Tui. $105, non-res. $350 per sem; commuter coll.

Art Education	Handicrafts
Ceramics	History of Art & Archaeology
Commercial Art	Painting
Drawing	Sculpture
Graphic Arts	Teacher Training
Graphic Design	

TULANE UNIVERSITY, School of Architecture, 70018.
Tel: (504) 865-6472
William K. Turner, Dean; 18 FT, 3 PT instr. School estab. 1907; pvt; 5 yr; degrees, B.Arch, M.Arch; enrl. 310. Tui. $3000 per yr; campus res.
‡Architecture

Newcomb College, Art Department, 60 Newcomb Pl, 70118.
Tel: (504) 865-4631
Prof. Jessie Poesch, Chmn; 13 FT instr. Estab. 1885; pvt; D & E; ent. req. admis. to one of Coll. of Tulane Univ; 4 yr; degrees, B.A.(Art History, Studio Art), B.F.A.(Studio Art), M.A.(Art History), M.F.A.(Studio Art), M.A.T; 22 SC, 20 LC, 17 GC; enrl. D 828, E 96, maj. 46, grad. 117. Tui. $3000 per yr; campus res. $550.

Art Education	History of Art & Archaeology
Ceramics	Painting
Drawing	Photography
Graphic Arts	Sculpture

Summer School: Dean Robert C. Whittemore, Dir; tui. $220 per unit for term of 8 wk. beginning in June; enrl. 144.

Art Survey	Painting
Ceramics	Photography
Drawing	Sculpture
Modern Art	

UNIVERSITY OF NEW ORLEANS, Department of Fine Arts, 70122.
Tel: (504) 288-3161
Dr. Thomas Young, Chmn; 9 FT, 2 PT instr. Estab. 1970; pub; 4 yr; degree, B.A; 16 SC, 8 LC; enrl. maj. 150. Tui. $145 per sem; campus res.

Art Education	Graphic Arts
Art History	Painting
Design	Sculpture
Drawing	

XAVIER UNIVERSITY OF LOUISIANA,* Art Department, Palmetto & Pine Sts, 70125. Tel: (504) 486-7411 Exten. 284
Numa Joseph Rousséve, Chmn; 6 FT, 1 PT instr. Estab. Sept. 1934; den; D; ent. req. HS dipl, ent. exam, plus scores from CAB SAT; 4 yr; degrees, B.A. (Art maj), B.A.Art Educ; B.F.A; schol; 27 SC, 6 LC; enrl. univ. 1500, E 50. Tui. $1070; campus res. $804.

Advertising Design	Graphic Arts & Design
Aesthetics (Philosophy Dept.)	History of Art & Archaeology
Art Appreciation	Lettering
Art Education (Secondary)	Painting
Art Essentials	Photography
Art Seminar, 20th Century	Process of Development, Art
Ceramics	Therapy
Drawing	Sculpture
Fashion Arts	Teacher Training

Summer School: Sister M. Petra, S.B.S, Dir; Art Essentials, Art Appreciation.

PINEVILLE

LOUISIANA COLLEGE, Department of Art, 71360.
Tel: (318) 487-7262
John T. Suddith, Chmn; Charles Jeffress, Asst. Prof. Art. Den; ent. req. HS grad; 4 yr; degrees, B.A, B.S; LC, Lab.C; enrl. maj. 30; 49 hr. of art req. plus 78 hr acad. for degree.
Art Education
Studio Arts

RUSTON

LOUISIANA TECH UNIVERSITY, School of Art and Architecture, Box 6277, Tech Station, 71270. Tel: (318) 257-3909
Jack Beard, Dir; 19 FT, 6 PT instr. Estab. 1904; pub; D; ent. req.

HS dipl; 4 yr; degrees, B.A, B.F.A, M.A, M.F.A; 98 SC, 8 LC, 87 GC; normal enrl. maj. 652, others 538. Tui. $116.50 per quarter. Summer School. Year Round Program on Rome, Italy Campus.

Architecture	Interior Design
Commercial Art	Photography
Crafts	Teacher Training
Design	Textiles, Clothing &
Fine Arts	Related Art (in Home Econ)
General Art	

SHREVEPORT

CENTENARY COLLEGE OF LOUISIANA, Department of Art, Centenary Blvd, 71104. Tel: (318) 869-5011
Willard Cooper, Chmn; 2 FT, 2 PT instr. Estab. 1825; den; D & E; ent. req. HS dipl, ent. exam; 4 yr; degree, B.A; schol; 15 SC, 8 LC; enrl. D 350, E 30, maj. 15. Tui. $1500 per yr; campus res. $1000.

Aesthetics	Jewelry & Metalsmithing
Art Education	Materials & Techniques
Ceramics	Painting
Costume Design & Construction	Stage Design
Drafting	Teacher Training
Drawing	Theatre Arts
Graphic Arts	Weaving
History of Art & Archaeology	

Summer School: Willard Cooper, Dir.

Art for Teachers	Drawing
Art History	Painting

SOUTHWESTERN INSTITUTE OF ARTS,* 657 Jordan St, 71101.
Tel: (318) 221-9926
Arthur C. Morgan, Dir; 2 PT instr. Estab. 1934; pvt; D & E; schol; enrl. 40 part-time adults and children; all classes limited to 10 students each. Tui. $14 to 42 per mo.
Drawing
Painting
Sculpture

THIBODAUX

NICHOLLS STATE UNIVERSITY, Department of Art, Box 2025, 70301.
Dr Ronald T. Benson, Head; 5 FT instr. Estab. 1948; pub; D & E; ent. req. HS grad; 4-5 yr; degree, B.A; enrl. D 1000, E 60, maj. 100. Tui. $151; campus res. $375.

Aesthetics	Neon
Art Education	Painting
Ceramics	Photography
Drawing	Plastics
Film Making	Sculpture
Graphic Arts	Teacher Training
History of Art & Archaeology	

Summer School: Dr. O. E. Lovell, Dir; tui. $76.50 for term of 9 wk. beginning June 8, 1973; enrl. 2700 total.

Advanced Drawing	Ceramics
Art Appreciation	Independent Study in Drawing
Art Education	Individual Exhibits
Beginning Drawing	Intermediate Drawing

MAINE

BRUNSWICK

BOWDOIN COLLEGE,* Department of Art, 04011.
Tel: (207) 725-8731
Philip C. Beam, Chmn; 3 FT instr. Estab. 1893; pvt; co-ed; 4 yr; degree, B.A, schol; 6 SC, 14 LC; enrl. 1150. Tui. $2700 per yr.
Courses in all fields and periods of art history; courses via lectures, conferences and studio practice.

DEER ISLE

HAYSTACK MOUNTAIN SCHOOL OF CRAFTS, 04627.
Tel: (207) 348-2816, 6946
Francis S. Merritt, Dir; 20 FT instr. Estab. 1951; pvt; D & E; ent. req. HS grad; schol; 16 SC; enrl. 90; courses certified for coll. cr. Tui with room and board $125 per wk for 12 wk.

Ceramics	Photography
Glass	Weaving
Graphics	Wood
Jewelry	

Summer School: Francis S. Merritt, Dir; tui. $125 per wk.

GORHAM

UNIVERSITY OF MAINE, PORTLAND-GORHAM, Art Department, 04038. Tel: (207) 839-3351 Exten. 477
Juris Ubans, Chmn; 7 FT, 5 PT instr. Estab. 1956; pub; ent. req. HS dipl, art portfolio; 4 yr; degrees, B.A, B.S, B.F.A. Tui. $500, non-res. $1500; campus res. $1400.

Art Education	Photography
Art History	Printmaking
Ceramics	Sculpture
Design	Watercolor
Drawing	Weaving
Painting	

   Summer School: William G. Mortensen, Dir; tui. $25 per cr. hr.

KENNEBUNKPORT

ROGER DEERING SCHOOL OF OUTDOOR PAINTING, Ocean Ave. & Elm St, 04046   Tel: (207) 967-2273
Roger Deering, Dir; Winifred Deering, Registrar and Secy. Estab. 1940; pvt; D; outdoor painting classes June 28 - July 30, 1976; limited to 15 students in each course; folder on request; Marine and land-scape oil and watercolor painting, lectures, demonstrations during 5 wk. period.

LEWISTON

BATES COLLEGE, Liberal Arts College, Art Department, 04240. Tel: (207) 783-3941
Donald Lent, Chmn; 3 FT, 1 PT instr. Estab. 1864, dept 1964; pvt; D; 4 yr; degree, B.A; 9 SC, 13 LC; enrl. 1200 total. Tui. incl. room and board and fees $4650.

Ceramics	Painting
Drawing	Printmaking

ORONO

UNIVERSITY OF MAINE, College of Arts and Sciences, Department of Art, Carnegie Hall, 04473. Tel: (207) 581-7691
Michael H. Lewis, Chmn; 7 FT instr. Present program estab 1946; pub; 4 yr; degrees, B.A, B.S; 16 SC, enrl. 140, 10 LC; enrl. 800. Tui. same as Univ. tui; campus res.

Art Appreciation	Graphic Arts
Art History	Sculpture
Design	Teacher Training
Drawing & Painting	

Children's classes, art education; spring semester; enrl. approx. 40.
   Summer School: Michael H. Lewis, Dir; courses offered, Art Appreciation, Art Education, Studio Courses; tui. $25 per cr. hr. and fees.

PORTLAND

PORTLAND SCHOOL OF ART of the Portland Society of Art, 97 Spring St, 53 Danforth St and 61 Pleasant St, 04101. Tel: (207) 775-3052
William C. Collins, Dir; 12 FT, 6 PT instr. Estab. 1882; pvt; D & E; ent. req. HS grad. or equivalent, transcripts, letters of recommenda-tion, statement of purpose, portfolio; 4 yr; degrees, B.F.A. or dipl; enrl. D 160, E 50; Sat. classes. Tui. FT $1680 per yr.(Sept-June), E $65 per 10 wk. term (materials extra).

Ceramics	Photography
Fine Arts	Sculpture
Graphic Art	Silversmithing & Jewelry
Graphic Design (Commercial)	

   Summer School: William C. Collins, Dir; tui. $65 per cr; enrl. 50.

Ceramics	Photography
Design	Sculpture
Fine Arts	

SKOWHEGAN

SKOWHEGAN SCHOOL OF PAINTING AND SCULPTURE, Box 449, 04976. Tel: (207) 474-9345 (Winter Office: 329 E. 68th St, New York, N.Y. 10021. Tel: (212) 861-9270)
John Eastman, Jr, Exec. V.Pres; Roy Leaf, V.Pres; Joan C. Franzen, Dir; 5 FT, 8 PT instr. Estab. 1946; schol; lectures by visiting artists; enrl. 65. Tui. incl. room and board $1750; 9 wk. July and Aug.

Drawing	Painting
Fresco	Sculpture

SPRINGVALE

NASSON COLLEGE,* Art Department, 04083. Tel: (207) 324-5340
George Burk, Dir; 2 FT instr. Estab. 1935; pvt; D & E; co-ed; ent. req. coll. ent. exam, etc; 4 yr; degrees; SC, LC.

WATERVILLE

COLBY COLLEGE, Art Department, 04901. Tel: (207) 873-1131 Exten. 215
James M. Carpenter, Head; 4 FT instr. Estab 1944; pvt; ent. req. HS grad; 4 yr; degree, A.B; schol; 6 SC, 8 LC; enrl. maj. 50, total 500. Tui. $3000.

Drawing	Painting
History of Art	Sculpture

MARYLAND

BALTIMORE

COLLEGE OF NOTRE DAME OF MARYLAND, Art Department, 4701 N. Charles St, 21210. Tel: (301) 435-0100 Exten. 17
Prof. Ruth Nagle Watkins, Chmn; 3 FT, 2 PT instr. Estab. 1895; den; W; 4-1-4 Calendar; D & E; ent. req. HS grad, ent. exam; 4 yr; degree, A.B. schol. and tui grants; 9 SC, 9 LC; enrl. maj. D 41, E 25. Tui. $2100, room and board $1400.

Advanced Painting	History of Art
Ceramics	Introductory Painting
Communication Arts	Metal Sculpture & Welding
Crafts	Printmaking
Drawing & Design	Sculpture

   Summer School: Sister Mauro Manna, Dir; education, contempo-rary society course; tui. $180 per course; enrl. 200.

COMMUNITY COLLEGE OF BALTIMORE (formerly Baltimore Ju-nior College), Art Department, 2901 Liberty Heights Ave, 21215. Tel: (301) 462-5800
Bennard B. Perlman, Chmn; D 7 FT, E 10 PT instr. Estab. 1947; pub; ent. req. HS grad; 2 yr; degree, A.A; 27 SC, 3 LC; enrl, maj. 175, total D 4300, E 7000. Tui. $170.75 per sem. city res, $328.25 per sem. state res, $485.75 per sem. out-of-state.

Advertising Design	Fundamentals of Design
Anatomy & Life	Graphic Arts
Arts & Crafts	History of Art
Ceramics	Photography
Drafting (architectural &	Sculpture
mechanical)	Theatre Art
Drawing	Television

   Summer School: Joseph S. Culotta, Dean; $15 per cr. city res, $30 per cr. state res, $45 per cr. out-of-state res. for two 5 wk. sessions beginning June 14 & July 19; enrl. 3600.

COPPIN STATE COLLEGE, Art Department, 2500 W North Ave, 21216. Tel: (301) 383-5929/5925
Luke A. Shaw, Asst Prof; 3 FT, 3 PT instr. Estab. 1975; pub; D & E; ent. req. HS dipl. & ent. exam; 4 yr; degrees B.A, B.S, M.A; 7 SC, 7 LC; enrl. D 37, E 15, others 38. Tui. $200 per yr.

Advertising Design	Illustration
Art Education	Jewelry
Ceramics	Lettering
Commercial Art	Painting
Drawing	Photography
Graphic Arts	Sculpture
Graphic Arts	Sculpture
Graphic Design	Theatre Arts
History of Art & Archaeology	

   Summer School: Peggi Graves, Dir; tui. $20 per cr. for 8 wk. beginning June 21; enrl. 150.

Art Appreciation	Ceramics
Art Education	Sculpture

JOHNS HOPKINS UNIVERSITY, Charles & 34th Sts, 21218. Tel: (301) 366-3300 Exten. 381, 1234

Department of the History of Art
Egon Verheyen, Chmn; 7 FT, 2 PT instr. Estab. 1947; pvt; co-ed; D & E; 4 yr; degrees; schol; LC; enrl. 10-30 in advanced courses, c. 200 in introductory courses. Tui. $3500 per yr; campus res.
History of Art

   Johns Hopkins Medical School, Department of Art as Applied to Medicine, 725 N. Wolfe St, 21205. Tel: (301) 955-3213
Ranice W. Crosby, Dir; 3 FT, 5 PT instr. Estab. 1911; 2 yr. grad. course; degree, M.A; enrl. 8-10. Tui. $3500 per yr.
Medical & Biological Illustration

✠MARYLAND INSTITUTE, College of Art, 1300 W. Mt. Royal Ave,
21217. Tel: (301) 669-9200
William J. Finn, Pres, Theodore E. Klitzke, Dean; 49 FT, 46 PT
instr. Estab. 1826; pvt; D & E; ent. req. HS grad, exam; 4 yr; degrees, B.F.A, M.F.A, dipl, cert; schol; enrl. D 1107, E 554, Sat.
280. Tui. $2530 D, $106 per cr.

Art Teacher Education	Interior Design
Designer-Craftsman	Painting
Drawing	Photography
Graphic Design & Illustra-	Printmaking
tion	Sculpture

Summer School: Dean Tom Scott, Dir; tui. $50 per cr; enrl.
654.

Hoffberger School of Painting
Grace Hartigan, Artist-in-Residence; limited tuition, fel. awarded
annually for study at the graduate level.

Rinehart School of Sculpture
Norman Carlberg, Sculptor-in-Residence; limited tuition, free
fels. awarded annually for study at the graduate level.

Maryland Institute School of Painting
Seymour Shapiro, Artist-in-Residence; limited tuition, fels.
awarded annually for study at the graduate level.

✠MORGAN STATE UNIVERSITY, Department of Art, Hillen Rd at
Coldspring Lane, 21239. Tel: (301) 893-3020
Oliver Patrick Scott, Chmn; 9 FT, 4/5 PT instr. Estab. 1950; pub;
D & E; ent. req. HS dipl, ent. exam; 3½ to 5 yr. undergrad, 1½ to 2 yr.
grad; degrees A.B.(Art), B.S.(Art Educ), M.F.A.(Studio, Art Hist,
Museol); schol, $600 to $1500, awarded for one yr. annually; 28 SC,
12 LC, 17 GC; enrl. E 30, maj. 130, grad. 13, other 30. Tui. $1197
per yr; Md. res $737 per yr; campus res. $1440.

Aesthetics	Jewelry
Architecture	Lettering
Art Education	Museum Staff Training
Ceramics	Painting
Display (Environmental Design)	Photography
Drafting	Sculpture
Drawing	Stage Design
Graphic Arts	Teacher Design
Graphic Design	Theatre Arts (Interdisciplinary)
History of Art & Archaeology	

Children's classes: drawing, crafts, painting and printmaking; tui.
$15 per sem; enrl. 25 to 40.
Summer School: Visual Arts, Jewelry, Photography; tui. $25 cr.
& fees for term of 6 wk. beginning June.

SCHULER SCHOOL OF FINE ARTS, 5 E Lafayette Ave, 21202.
Tel: (301) 685-3568
Hans C. Schuler, Dir; 2 FT, 1 PT instr. Estab. 1959; pvt; D & E;
4 yr; 9 SC, 3 GC; enrl. D 50, E 30, grad. 2. Tui. $1000 per yr, part-
time students pay by schedule for sem.

Drawing	Painting
Graphic Arts	Sculpture

Children's summer classes: Age over 14 yr; tui. $165/$225.
Summer School: Hans C. Schuler, Dir; watercolor, oil paint-
ing, drawing and sculpture; tui. $165 for term of 6 wk. beginning
June 21, 1976, 6 hr. $225; enrl. 30.

TOWSON STATE COLLEGE, Department of Art, 21204.
Tel: (301) 823-7500 Exten 297
Tom Supensky, Assoc Prof; 24 FT, 8 PT instr. Estab. 1866; pub;
D & E; ent req. HS grad; 4 yr; degrees, B.S, B.A, M.Ed Art Educ.

Art Education	Jewelry
Art History	Painting
Ceramics	Sculpture
Drawing	Textile Design
Enameling	Weaving & Textiles
Graphic Arts	Wood & Metal

Summer School: Tom Supensky, Dir; two 5 wk. sessions; enrl.
450 per session.

BEL AIR

HARFORD COMMUNITY COLLEGE, Humanities Division, 401
Thomas Run Rd, 21014. Tel: (301) 838-1000 Exten. 293
Dr. Claire Eckels, Chmn. Div; 4 FT, 5 PT instr. Estab. 1957; pub;
D & E; ent. req. HS dipl; 2 yrs; degree, A.A; schol; 17 SC, 4 LC;
enrl. FT 1000, PT 1000. Tui. FT per sem. $180, PT per sem. hr.
$15; no campus res.

Architectural Drawing	History of Art & Archaeology
Ceramics	Interior Design
Design	Painting
Drawing	Photography
Graphic Arts	Sculpture

BOWIE

BOWIE STATE COLLEGE, Department of Art, Jericho Park Rd,
20715. Tel: (301) 262-3350 exten. 441/442
Amos White, IV, Chmn; 4 FT, 1 PT. Estab. 1968; pub; D & E; ent.
req. HS dipl; 4 yr; degrees B.A.(Fine Arts), B.S.(Art Educ); 24 SC,
7 LC, 5 GC; enrl. D 300, E 60, maj. 60, grad. 20. Tui. $620 per
yr, $1070 per yr. out-of-state res, $25 per cr. hr; campus res.
$1200.

Art Education	Painting
Ceramics	Photography
Drawing	Sculpture
Graphic Arts	Teacher Training
History of Art & Archaeology	

Summer School: Amos White, IV, Chmn; tui. $25 per cr. hr. for
term of 6 wk. beginning June 23.

Art for the Elementary School	Multi-Media Workshop
Art Fundamentals	Sculpture
Art Survey	Visual Design
History of Modern Art	

CATONSVILLE

CATONSVILLE COMMUNITY COLLEGE, Art Department, 800 S
Rolling Rd, 21228. Tel: (301) 747-3220
Dedree Drees, Div Asst; 10 FT, 4 PT instr. Estab. 1956; pvt; D
& E; ent. req. HS dipl; 2 yr; degree A.A; schol; 22 SC, 3 LC; enrl.
D 900, E 400, maj. 250. Tui. $300 per yr, $13 cr. hr; no campus
res.

Advertising Design	Lettering
Commercial Art	Painting
Display	Photography & History of Photog-
Display	raphy
Drafting	Production & Agency Skills
Graphic Design	Sculpture
History of Art & Archaeology	Stage Design
Illustration	Theatre Arts

Adult hobby classes, ceramics, silk screen and frame building; tui.
$15; enrl. 60 per yr.
Summer School: Jim Linksz, Dir; tui. $13 per cr. hr. beginning
June 24, 2 summer terms; enrl. 90.

Design	Photography
Drawing	Sculpture
Painting	Watercolor

COLLEGE PARK

UNIVERSITY OF MARYLAND, Art Department, J. Millard Tawes
Fine Arts Center, 20742. Tel: (301) 454-2717
Dr. George Levitine, Chmn; 35 FT, 3 PT instr. Estab. 1944; pub;
D; co-ed; ent. req. HS dipl, upper half of class; 4 yr; degrees, B.A,
M.A, M.F.A, Ph.D; 37 SC, 26 LC, 17 GC; enrl. 3500, maj. 700, grad.
100. Tui. $979, part-time $31 per cr. hr; campus res. $400.

Art Education	Museum Training
Drawing	Painting
Graphic Arts	Sculpture
History of Art & Archaeology	Studio Art

Summer School: John Lembach, Dir; courses same as above;
tui. $31 per cr. hr. for term of 6 wk; first session May 26 through
July 2, second session July 8 through Aug 13 (1976)

CUMBERLAND

ALLEGANY COMMUNITY COLLEGE, Art Department, Willow Brook
Rd, 21502. Tel: (301) 724-7700
Jerry L. Post, Head; 1 FT instr. Estab. 1966; pub; D & E; ent. req.
HS dipl; 2 yr; degree, A.A; schol; 6 SC, 1 LC; enrl. D 30, E 9. Tui.
$300 per yr; $45 per 3 cr. hr. courses; no campus res.

Ceramics	Survey of Art History
Drawing	Theatre Arts
Painting	Two & Three Dimensional Design

Summer School: Jerry L. Post, Dir; courses offered, Painting,
Two-Dimensional Design; tui. $15 per cr. hr. for term of 6 wk. be-
ginning July 1; 1975 enrl. 15.

FREDERICK

✠HOOD COLLEGE,* Fine Arts Department, 21701.
Tel: (301) 663-3131
A. Russo, Chmn; 3 FT instr. Estab. 1893; pvt; W; 4 yr; degrees;
10 SC, 7 LC. Tui. $1400; enrl. 750.

Art Appreciation	Painting
Design & Applied Arts	Sculpture
History of Art	

FROSTBURG

FROSTBURG STATE COLLEGE, Department of Art & Art Education, 21532. Tel: (301) 689-4351
George Kramer, Head Dept; 8 FT instr. Estab. 1898; pub; D; ent. req. HS dipl; 4 yr; B.S, B.A.(Art, Art Educ), M.Ed.(Art Educ); 25 SC, 5 LC; enrl. D 230, maj. 150; grad. students 13. Tui. $200 per yr; fees $446; campus res. $690 room, $624 meals.

Advertising Graphics	Painting
Art Education	Photography
Art History	Printmaking
Ceramics	Sculpture
Drawing	Teacher Training
Graphic Design	Textile Design
Jewelry	Two & Three Dimensional Design

Children's classes, Sat. sch. prog; tui. $5.
    Summer School: David Sanford, Dean Admissions; tui. $25 per cr. hr. for term of 4½ wk, beginning May.

ST MARY'S CITY

✠ST. MARY'S COLLEGE OF MARYLAND,* Department of Art, 20686. Tel: (301) 994-1600
Dr. Glenn Martin, Chmn; 5 FT, 1 PT instr. Estab. 1966; pub; D & E; ent. req. HS dipl, ent. exam; 4 yrs; degree, B.A; 17 SC, 17 LC; enrl. D 989, E 126, maj. 189, others 76. Tui. $300; campus res. $1025.

Art Education	Painting
Ceramics	Photography
Drawing	Sculpture
Glass Blowing	Silversmithing
Graphic Arts	Teacher Training
History of Art & Archaeology	Theatre Arts
Jewelry	Weaving

Adult hobby classes, watercolor; enrl. 10.
Children's classes: 3 sessions offered during the summer; tui. $30; enrl. 40.
    Summer School: Dr. Oak Winters, Dir; courses offered: creating with stained glass, pottery making, watercolor; tui. $25 for term of 7 wk. beginning June 25.

SALISBURY

SALISBURY STATE COLLEGE, Art Department, Camden & College Ave, 21801. Tel: (301) 546-3261
Kent Kimmel, Chmn; 5 FT, 3 PT instr. Estab. 1925; pub; D & E; ent. req. HS dipl, ent. exam, satisfactory SAT and/or coll. boards; 4 yr; degrees, B.A, B.S, M.Ed, M.A.(Hist); schol; 20 SC, 5 LC, 1 GC; enrl. D 317, E 167, concentrates 50. Tui. $200 Md. res, $650 out-of-state, 1 course - 1 sem. $25 hr. undergrad, 1 course - 1 sem. $38 hr. grad; campus res room $510, board $600.

Advertising Design	Handicrafts
Aesthetics	History of Art & Archaeology
Art Education	Painting
Ceramics	Photography
Drawing	Sculpture
Graphic Arts	Teacher Training
Graphic Design	

Adult hobby classes, woodcarving, Bas-Relief.
    Summer School: Dr. H. O. Schaffer, Dir; courses offered vary depending on need; tui. $25/$38 per hr. for term of 5 wk. beginning second wk. of June, 1976, enrl. 40.

SILVER SPRING

THE MARYLAND SCHOOL OF ART, 640 University Blvd. E, 20901.
Terrence Coffman, Dean; 4 FT, 15 PT instr. Estab. 1969; non-profit, tax-exempt; D & E; open admissions, students on probation for first quarter of instruction; 2 yr. cert, 3 yr. dipl; schol; 42 SC, 1 LC; enrl. D 250 per quarter, E 60 per quarter. Tui. $585 per quarter; no campus res.

Advertising Design	Occupational Therapy
Air Brush	Painting
Ceramics	Photography
Commercial Art	Relief Printmaking
Drawing	Sculpture
History of Art & Archaeology	Silkscreen Printmaking
Illustration	Watercolor
Lettering	

    Summer School: Terrence Coffman, Dir; tui. $65 per cr. hr. for term of 2 five-wk. sessions beginning June 25; 1973 enrl. 100.

Drawing	Painting
Junior Workshop	Sculpture
Life & Anatomy	Watercolor

TOWSON

✠GOUCHER COLLEGE, Department of Visual Arts, 21204.
    Tel: (301) 825-3300
Dr. Eric Van Schaack, Chmn; 5 FT, 2 PT instr. Estab. 1885; pvt; D; W; ent. req. SAT and three achievement tests of CEEB or ACT; 4 yr; degree, A.B; 27 SC, 17 LC; enrl. undergrad. 1029, maj. 40 (1974-75).

Art Conservation	History of Art (many specialized
Art of Motion Picture	courses)
Ceramics	Painting
Drawing	Printmaking
Historic Preservation	Sculpture

WESTMINSTER

WESTERN MARYLAND COLLEGE, Art Department, 21157.
    Tel: (301) 848-7000 Exten. 241
Wasyl Palijczuk, Head; 3 FT, 1 PT instr. Estab. 1867; independent; D & E; ent. req. HS dipl, ent. exam, scholastic aptitude test; 4 yr; degrees, B.A, B.S, M.Ed; 15½ SC, 12½ LC, 6 GC; enrl. D 1113, maj. 45, grad. art students, 3. Tui. $2150 per yr; campus res. $1050.

Aesthetics	Jewelry
Art Education	Lettering
Ceramics	Painting I & II
Design I & II	Photography
Drawing I & II	Printmaking
History of Art & Archaeology	Sculpture I & II
Illustration	Teacher Training
Introduction to Art	Watercolor

Children's classes, Sat. mornings conducted by college students; enrl. over 12.
    Summer School: Wasyl Palijczuk, Dir; two 5 wk. terms beginning June 18.

Ceramics	Sculpting
Painting	Weaving
Printmaking	

MASSACHUSETTS

AMHERST

✠AMHERST COLLEGE, Department of Fine Arts, Mead Art Building, 01002. Tel: (413) 542-2335
Carl N. Schmalz, Jr, Chmn; 6 FT, 2 PT instr. Estab. 1822; pvt; D; ent. req. HS dipl; 4 yr; degree, B.A; 15 SC, 15 LC. Tui. approx. $4525 per yr; campus res. approx. $4650.

Aesthetics	Photography
Graphic Design	Sculpture
History of Art & Archaeology	Serigraphy
Painting	

UNIVERSITY OF MASSACHUSETTS, College of Arts and Sciences.

    Department of Art, 01002. Tel: (413) 545-1902
Prof. George Wardlaw, Chmn; 41 FT instr. Art Dept. estab. 1958; pub; ent. req. HS grad, portfolio required, 15 units HS, ent. exam; 4 yr; degrees: B.A.(Studio, Art History), B.F.A.(Studio, Interior Design, Art Educ), M.A.(Art History), M.F.A.(Ceramics, Painting, Printmaking, Sculpture), M.S.(Interior Design), M.A.T; 40 SC, 19 LC, 20 GC; enrl. maj. undergrad. 600, grad. 65. Tui. $300 per sem, non-res. $600 per sem.

Art Education	Light Workshop
Ceramics	Painting
Computer Graphics	Photography
Design Graphics	Printmaking
Drawing	Sculpture
Glassblowing	Teacher Training
History of Art	Three-Dimensional Design
Interior Design	Two-Dimensional Design

    Department of Landscape Architecture and Regional Planning, College of Food and Natural Resources
Dr. Ross S. Whaley, Head; 18 FT, 6 PT instr. Estab. 1905; pub; D; ent. req; 4-6 yr; degrees, B.S, M.L.A, M.R.P; schol; 6 SC, 15 LC, 26 GC; enrl. maj. undergrad. 325, grad. 105. Tui. $300 per sem, non-res. $600 per sem; campus res.

Environmental Design	Park Administration
Landscape Architecture (grad.)	Regional Planning (grad.)

AUBURNDALE

LASELL JUNIOR COLLEGE, 1844 Commonwealth Ave, 02166.
Leonie S. Bennett, Head; 5 FT, 1 PT instr. Estab. 1851; pvt; D & E; W; ent. req. HS dipl, ent. exam in some depts, portfolio in art dept;

2 yr; degrees, A.A, A.S; schol. Tui. including room, board and fees $4585, non-res. including tui. and fees $2590.

Advertising Design	History of Art & Archaeology
Aesthetics	Jewelry
Art for Child Study	Painting
Ceramics	Photography
Design & Color	Three-Dimensional Design
Drawing	

BEVERLY

ENDICOTT COLLEGE, Department of Art, 376 Hale St, 01915.
Tel: (617) 927-0585
Prof. J. David Broudo, Head; 7 FT, 2 PT instr. Estab. 1939; pvt; D; W; ent. req. HS dipl. with 16 units of work, SAT, a record that indicates talent and promise of successful achievement in some field for which Endicott offers training; 2 yr; degrees, A.S, A.A; schol; 16 SC. Tui. $3900 (incl. board and room).

Architectural Design	Jewelry
Art Studio	Painting (Oil & Watercolor)
Ceramics	Pattern Drafting
Commercial Art	Photography
Costume Design & Construction	Sculpture
Crafts	Teacher Training
Drafting & Sketching	Textiles
Drawing & Composition	Three-Dimensional Design
Fashion Illustration	Two-Dimensional Design
Graphics	Weaving
History of Art	Window Display
Interior Design	

BOSTON

THE ART INSTITUTE OF BOSTON, 718 Beacon St, 02215.
Tel: (617) 262-1223
William H. Willis, Dir; D 31 FT, 20 PT, E 10 FT, 6 PT instr. Estab. 1912; pvt; D & E; ent. req. HS grad, portfolio and interview; 3-4 yr; dipl; B.S.(Applied Art), B.S.(Photography), B.F.A, through Univ. Coll, Northeastern Univ; schol; enrl. 450, E 140. Tui. $1400, fees $200.

Advertising Design	Lettering
Ceramics	Painting
Display	Photography
Drawing	Printmaking
Fashion Illustration	Sculpture
Graphic Design	Textile Design
Illustration	

Summer School: Tui. $240 for term of 8 wk. beginning July 8; enrl. 200.

BOSTON CENTER FOR ADULT EDUCATION, 5 Commonwealth Ave, 02116. Tel: (617) 267-4430
Laura Bernard, Asst. Dir; 25 PT instr. Estab. 1933; pvt; D & E; schol; 48 SC, 7 LC. Tui. average course fee $42.

Aesthetics	Lettering
Architecture	Macrame
Basketmaking	Needlework
Blacksmithing	Painting
Ceramics	Photography
Commercial Art	Quilting
Drafting	Rya Rugs
Drawing	Sculpture
Fashion Arts	Stained Glass
Graphic Arts	Theatre Arts
Graphic Design	Toys
History of Art & Archaeology	Weaving
Illustration	Whittling
Jewelry	Woodworking
Leather	

Children's classes, painting for parents and children; tui. $25.
Summer School: Same courses as above.

✤BOSTON UNIVERSITY, School for the Arts, School of Visual Arts, 855 Commonwealth Ave, 02215. Tel: (617) 353-3371
Edward F. Leary, Acting Dir; 25 FT, 8 PT instr. Estab. 1919; pvt; ent. req. HS dipl, SAT, portfolio; 4 yr; degrees, B.F.A, M.F.A; schol; enrl. 400. Tui. $3280; campus res.

Art Education	Painting
Drawing	Printmaking
Graphic Design	Sculpture

Summer School: Courses offered at Boston, Art Education, Drawing, Painting; tui. $70 per cr.

BUTERA SCHOOL OF ART, 111 Beacon St, 02116.
Tel: (617) 536-4623
Joseph Butera, Dir; 4 FT, 6 PT instr. Estab. 1932; pvt; D & E; ent. req. HS transcripts, 2 letters of recommendation and port-

folio; 2-4 yr; dipl; enrl. D 100, E 75. Tui. D $1300 per yr, E $400.
Sign Painting Division originally Wagner School of Sign and Commercial Art.

Commercial Art	Illustration
Fashion Illustration	Sign Painting

CHAMBERLAYNE JUNIOR COLLEGE, 128 Commonwealth Ave, 02116. Tel: (617) 536-4500
Herbert T. Anderson, Chmn; 7 FT, 5 PT instr. Estab. 1892; pvt; D & E; ent. req. HS dipl; 2 yr; A.A; schol; CSS req; 30 SC, 94 LC, 28 Lab.C; enrl. D 900, E 200. Tui. $1800; campus res. $1980.

Art Department

Architectural Drafting for the Interior Designer	History of Furniture Interior Design
Business Orientation for the Designer	Jewelry Leather Work
Ceramics	Materials for the Designer
Commercial Design	Technical Drawing
Freehand Drawing	Textile Weaving
History of Architecture	Visual Elements
History of Art	Watercolor & Rendering

Fashion Department

Apparel Design	Fashion Materials
Fashion & Style	Textile Design
Fashion Illustration	Textile Printing

EMMANUEL COLLEGE, Art Department, 400 The Fenway, 02115.
Tel: (617) 277-9340 Exten. 204
Sister Mary Francis, Pres; Michael Jacques, Chmn; 4 FT, 3 PT instr. Estab. 1923; pvt; D; W; ent. req, HS dipl, ent. exam, portfolio; 4-5 yr; degrees, A.B, B.F.A; schol; 26 SC, 9 LC, 6 GC; enrl. art dept. D 300, maj. approx. 80; grad. students 2. Tui. $1050 per yr; tui, room and board $2000.

Advertising Design	History of Art & Archaeology
Aesthetics	Illustration
Art Education	Life Drawing
Artistic Heritage of Boston	Painting
Batik	Philosophy of Art
Ceramics	Portrait Painting
Copper Enamel	Sculpture
Design & Composition	Teacher Training
Drawing	Technical Drawing
Graphic Arts	Watercolor
Handicrafts	Weaving

GARLAND JUNIOR COLLEGE,* Art Department, 409 Commonwealth Ave, 02215. Tel: (617) 266-7585
Robert McCue, Chmn, 6 FT, 6 PT instr. Estab. 1872; pvt; D; W; ent. req. HS dipl, portfolio, interview; 2 yr; degree, A.S; schol; 21 SC, 5 LC; enrl. D 120, maj. 50. Tui. $2100; campus res. $2050.

Ceramics	Metalsmithing
Fashion Design	Painting
Illustration and Advertising Design	Photography
Interior Design	Printmaking

MASSACHUSETTS COLLEGE OF ART, 364 Brookline Ave, 02215.
Tel: (617) 731-2340
Jack Nolan, Pres; 49 FT, 54 PT instr. Estab. 1873; pub, conducted under Mass. Div. of State Colleges-Board of Trustees; D & E; ent. req. CEEB, HS or coll. transcripts, art portfolio or slides; 4 yr; degrees, B.F.A, 2 yr; M.F.A, M.S.A.Educ; 361 SC, 161 LC, 16 GC; enrl. D 1053, grad. 41, E 530. Tui. res. $500 per yr, non-res. $1200 per yr, continuing educ. $25 per hr.

Art Education	Industrial Design
Art History	Interrelated Media
Architecture Design	Jewelry & Silversmithing
Ceramics	Painting
Fashion Design	Photography
Filmmaking	Printmaking
Glassblowing	Sculpture
Graphic Design	Weaving
Illustration	

Continuing Education courses, rotating selection of regular courses; tui. $25 per cr. hr; enrl. c. 530 per sem.
Summer School: Dr. Dorothy Simpson, Assoc. Dir; courses offered, Critical Studies, Art Education, Design, Fine Arts, Media & Performing Arts; tui. $25 per cr. hr; enrl. 516.

THE NEW ENGLAND SCHOOL OF ART AND DESIGN, 28 Newbury St, 02116. Tel: (617) 536-0383
J. W. S. Cox, Pres; 30 PT instr. Estab. 1923; pvt; D & E; ent. req. HS dipl, portfolio, interview; cr. transferable to Univ. Coll. of Northeastern Univ and other colls; enrl. 250. Tui. $1325.

Fashion Illustration	Graphic Design
Fine Arts	Interior Design

THE SCHOOL OF FASHION DESIGN, 136 Newbury St,
02116.
Richard F. Alartosky, Pres; approx. 10 FT, approx. 20 PT instr.
Estab. 1934; pvt; D & E; ent. req. HS dipl, interview, portfolio,
references and transcripts; 2 yr. cert, 3 yr. dipl; schol; approx.
30 SC, approx. 10 LC; enrl. D 80, E 125. Tui. $1400 day school,
$575 eve school; campus res. from $500-$1500 per yr.
Costume Design & Construction
Fashion Arts
  Summer School: Richard F. Alartosky, Dir; same courses
offered as regular yr; tui. $575 for term of 6 wk. beginning July &
Aug; 1973 enrl. 20.

✠SCHOOL OF THE MUSEUM OF FINE ARTS, 230 The Fenway,
02115. Tel: (617) 267-9300 Exten. 485
Joseph Hodgson, Acting Dean; D 31 FT, 14 PT, E 25 PT instr. Estab.
1876; pvt; D & E; ent. req. HS dipl, portfolio; 4 yr; dipl, degree, 5th yr; E
cert, B.F.A, B.S.Educ, M.F.A. in affiliation with Tufts Univ; schol.(sev-
eral travel schol. annually); 57 SC, 6 LC; enrl. D 470, E 550. Tui. and
fees D $1100 per sem, E $140 per course per sem; no campus res.
Ceramics   Photography & Film
Fibers   Plastics
Graphic Design   Printmaking
History of Art   Sculpture
Jewelry & Metalsmithing   Stained Glass
Multi-Media   Video/Performance
Painting

VESPER GEORGE SCHOOL OF ART,* 44 St, Botolph St, 02116.
  Tel: (617) 267-2045
Fletcher Adams, Dir; D 21 FT, E 5 FT instr. Estab. 1924; pvt; 3 yr;
ent. schol. Children and Sat. lessons.
Advertising Art   Fine Arts
Design   Illustration
Fashion Illustration   Interior Decoration

BROCKTON

BROCKTON ART CENTER, Art Workshops, Oak St, 02401.
  Tel: (616) 588-6000
Beverley Edwards, Workshop Coordinator; 18 PT instr. Estab.
1970; pvt; D & E; schol; 27 SC, 2 LC; enrl. approx. 200 each term,
3½ terms per yr. Tui. per 10 wk. term, children $33-$38, adults
$39-$50.
Aesthetics   Painting
Architecture   Photography
Ceramics   Sculpture
Drawing   Stitchery
Graphic Arts   Textile Design
Graphic Design   Theatre Arts
History of Art & Archaeology   Weaving
Jewelry
Children's classes, clay, clown troupe, creative drama, drawing,
film-animation, painting, printmaking, sculpture; tui. $33-$38 per
term; enrl. 40-50 per term.
  Summer School: Beverley Edwards, Dir; courses offered, approx.
same as other terms; tui. $33-$38 per term of 5 wk. beginning July-
1st wk. Aug; enrl. approx. 150.

CAMBRIDGE

HARVARD UNIVERSITY,* 02138
  Tel: (617) 495-1000

  Department of Fine Arts, Fogg Museum, 02138.
  Tel: (617) 495-2377
John Rosenfield, Chmn; 14 FT instr. Estab. 1874; pvt; Men (Radcliffe Coll. for W); 4 yr; degrees; schol. and fel; 26 LC incl. 12 GC;
enrol. undergrad. Harvard, 53, Radcliffe, 49, grad. Harvard (incl. W)
80. Tui. $3200 undergrad. & grad.
History of Art only.

  Carpenter Center for the Visual Arts, 19 Prescott St, 02138.
Eduard F. Sekler, Dir; Len Gittleman, Co-ordinator Light & Com-
munication; 14 FT, 10 PT instr. Estab. 1963; pvt; Men (Radcliffe
Coll. for W), 4 yr; degree, A.B; schol; enrl. Harvard 937, Radcliffe
307. Tui. $3200 undergrad.
Descriptive Drawing & Graphics   Perception & Expression
Design for Stage   Photography
Design Fundamentals   Photography as Sociological
Form from Technology   Description
Fundamentals of Environmental   Special Projects
  Design   Studies of the Environment
Light & Communication Work-   Style & Language of Film
  shops

  Graduate School of Design, Departments of Architecture, City
  & Regional Planning, Landscape Architecture, and Urban De-
  sign Program, Gund Hall, 02138.
Maurice Dorney Kilbridge, Dean; 90 FT and PT instr. Ent. req;
degrees, A.B, S.B, B.L.A, B.C.P. or B.Arch. or equivalent; schol.
and fel; enrl. 500.
Architecture   Landscape Architecture
City & Regional Planning   Urban Design

MASSACHUSETTS INSTITUTE OF TECHNOLOGY, School of Archi-
  tecture and Planning, Departments of Architecture and Urban
  Studies and Planning, 77 Massachusetts Ave, 02139.
  Tel: (617) 253-1000
William L. Porter, Dean; N. John Habraken, Head, Dept. of Archi-
tecture; Langley C. Keyes, Head, Dept of Urban Studies and Plan-
ning; 72 FT, 38 PT instr. Estab. 1865; pvt; 2, 4 & 6 yr; degrees,
S.B.(Art & Design), S.B.(Urban Studies), M.Arch, A.S.(Advanced
Studies), M.C.P, Ph.D.(City Planning), Ph.D.(Arch, Art & Environ-
mental Studies); SC, LC, GC; enrl. 504. Tui. $3700; campus res.

DOVER

CHARLES RIVER CREATIVE ARTS PROGRAM, 56 Centre St, 02054.
  Tel: (617) 785-0068
Priscilla B. Dewey, Dir, Multi-Arts School; 40 FT instr. Estab.
1970; pvt; D; ent. req. none; schol; enrl. D 175. Tui. $235 per mo;
campus res.
Ceramics   Mask Making
Colonial Crafts   Painting
Costume Design & Construction   Photography
Drawing   Puppetry
Graphic Arts   Sculpture
Graphic Design   Soapstone Carving
Illustration   Stage Design
Lettering   Theatre Arts
Macrame   Weaving
Children's classes, art, dance, drama, music, gymnastics; winter
children's theatre; tui. $235 for 4 wk; enrl. 175.
  Summer School: Priscilla B. Dewey, Dir; July and August.
Art   Drama
Dance   Music

FRAMINGHAM

FRAMINGHAM STATE COLLEGE, Art Department, 01701.
  Tel: (617) 872-3501 Exten. 333
Stephen Durkee, Head; 6 FT, 3 PT instr. Estab. 1839, Art Major,
1970; pub; D; ent. req. HS dipl, ent. exam, performance session, in-
terview; 4 yr; degree, B.A; schol; 20 SC, 16 LC; enrl. maj. 120.
Tui. $350 per yr. res; campus res. $400.
Architecture   Jewelry
Art Education   Museum Staff Training
Art Therapy   Painting
Batik   Photography
Drawing   Three-Dimensional Design
Graphic Arts   Teacher Training
History of Art & Archaeology   Weaving

FRANKLIN

DEAN JUNIOR COLLEGE, Visual and Performing Arts Dept, 99
  Main St, 02038. Tel: (617) 528-9100
Lawry Reid, Chmn; 6 FT, 1 PT instr. Estab. 1865; pvt; D & E;
ent. req. HS grad, Coll. Ent. Exam. Board Schol. Aptitude Tests;
2 yr; degrees, A.A, A.S; schol; 12 SC, 8 LC; enrl. D 80. Tui.
$2700, $40 sem. hr; campus res. $1500.
Art of Renaissance   Modern Art
Art Therapy   Painting
Creative Art   Photography
Drawing   Theatre Arts
Graphics   Three-Dimensional Design

GREAT BARRINGTON

SIMON'S ROCK EARLY COLLEGE, Studio Arts Department, Alford
  Rd, 01230. Tel: (413) 528-0771
Eunice Agar, Chmn; 2 FT, 2 PT instr. Estab. 1964; pvt; D; ent. req.
personal interview; 2-4 yr; degrees, A.A, B.A, interdisciplinary
arts major; schol; 7 yr. SC, 8 sem. SC, 1 yr. LC, 8 sem. LC. Tui.
incl. campus res. $4700 per yr.
Aesthetics   Painting
Ceramics   Photography
Drawing   Sculpture
Graphic Arts   Stage Design
History of Art & Archaeology   Theatre Arts

HOLYOKE

HOLYOKE ACADEMY OF FINE ARTS, 225 High St, 01040.
  Tel: (413) 534-0045
Stephen J. Treston, Dir; 2 FT, 3 PT instr. Estab. 1971; pvt; D & E;
ent. req. HS dipl preferred or the equivalent; 2 yr; cert; 10 SC, 4 LC;
10 GC; enrl. 115. Tui. 25 hr. per wk. $2008, 15 hr. per wk. $2510,
12 hr. per wk. $2635, 9 hr. per wk. $3062, 6 hr. per wk. $3765.

Advertising Design	Illustration
Aesthetics	Industrial Design
Cartooning	Interior Design
Commercial Art	Lettering
Drafting	Painting
Fashion Art	Technical Illustration
History of Art	

Adult hobby classes, basic drawing, foundation courses, painting;
tui. $2 per hr; enrl. 20.
Children's classes, tui. $2 per hr; enrl. 13.
  Summer School: Stephen J. Treston, Dir; courses offered same
as above.

HOLYOKE COMMUNITY COLLEGE, 303 Homestead Ave, 01040.
  Tel: (413) 538-7000 Exten. 270
Frank Cressotti, Head; 3 FT, 1 PT instr. Estab. 1946; pub; D & E;
ent. req. HS dipl, portfolio; 2 yr; degree, A.A; schol; 7 SC, 4 LC;
enrl. D 115, E 20, maj. 50. Tui. $300 per yr.

Art Education	History of Art & Archaeology
Drawing	Painting
Graphic Arts	Photography
Graphic Design	

  Summer School: William Murphy, Dir; courses offered depends
on demand; tui. $20 per cr. hr.

LONGMEADOW

BAY PATH JUNIOR COLLEGE,* Department of Art, 588 Longmeadow
  St, 01106. Tel: (413) 567-0621
Charles B. Hayward, Chmn; 2 FT, 10 PT instr. Estab. 1947; pvt;
D & E; W only; ent. req. HS dipl; 2 yrs; degree, A.F.A; schol;
18 SC, 2 LC; enrl. D 475, E 200, maj. 40. Tui. $2700 yr; campus
res. $1000.

Ceramics	History of Art & Archaeology
Drawing	Painting
Foundation Art	Photography
Graphic Arts	Sculpture

Adult hobby classes, 12 subjects; tui. $36; enrl. approx. 175.
  Summer School: Charles B. Hayward, Chmn; courses vary
annually; tui. $36 for term of 6 wk. beginning June; 1973 enrl. 50.

MEDFORD

✤TUFTS UNIVERSITY (In affiliation with the Boston Museum of
  Fine Arts School), Fine Arts Department, 11 Talbot Ave, 02155.
  Tel: (617) 628-5000 Exten. 281
Madeline H. Caviness, Chmn; 5 FT, 25 PT instr. Boston Museum
School estab. 1876, Tufts affiliation, 1940-1945; pvt; D & E; ent.
req. ent. exam; 4 yr; degrees, B.A, B.F.A, M.A, M.F.A; schol; 12
SC, 19 LC, 9 GC; enrl. Coll. Liberal Arts (M) 1560, Jackson Coll.
(W) 1527, total studio enrl. Tufts E 562, maj. 40-50, grad. 30
(M.F.A). Tui. $3600; campus res. $2000.

Ceramics	Occupational Therapy
Drawing	Painting
Graphic Arts	Photography
History of Art & Archaeology	Sculpture
Jewelry	

  Summer School: Robert L'Hommedieu Miller, Dir; tui. $190 for
term of 6 wk. beginning June 25; 1973 enrl. 65-70.

Design	Painting
Drawing	Photography

NEW BEDFORD

✤SWAIN SCHOOL OF DESIGN, 19 Hawthorn St, 02740.
  Tel: (617) 997-3158
Dr. Jean S. Lozinski, Dir; 10 FT, 1 PT instr. Estab. 1881; pvt; ent.
req. HS grad; 4 yr; degree, B.F.A; enrl. D 180, Sat. (children's
classes) 90. Tui. $1850, Sat. (children) $50. Approved for veterans
and foreign students.

Design	Painting
Drawing	Sculpture
Graphic Arts	

  Summer School: Painting workshop, tui. $75; enrl. 15. Chil-
dren's classes, tui. $50; enrl. 30.

NORTH DARTMOUTH

SOUTHEASTERN MASSACHUSETTS UNIVERSITY, College of Fine
  and Applied Arts, 02747. Tel: (617) 997-9321
Dietmar R. Winkler, Interim Dean; Peter London, Chmn, Dept. Art
Educ; Evan Firestone, Chmn, Dept. Art History; Margot Neugebauer,
Chmn, Dept. Design; T. Frank McCoy, Chmn, Dept. Fine Arts; 30 FT
instr. Estab. 1948; pub; ent. req. HS grad, CEEB and portfolio; 4 yr;
degrees, B.F.A.(Art Educ, Visual Design, Painting, Textile Design),
M.F.A.(Visual Design, 3 yr), M.A.E.(Art Educ); schol; enrl. 450.
Tui. undergrad. and grad. $300, non-res. $700. E and summer
classes.

Art Education	Jewelry & Metalworking
Calligraphy	Painting
Ceramics	Photography
Color & Design	Printmaking
Composition	Sculpture
Drawing	Structural Representation
Figure Drawing	Textile Design
Graphic Reproduction	Typography
History of Art	Visual Design
Illustration	

NORTHAMPTON

SMITH COLLEGE, Department of Art, 01060.
  Tel: (413) 584-2700
Elliot M. Offner, Chmn; 17 FT, 3 PT instr. Estab. 1875; pvt; D;
W; 4 yr; degrees; schol. and fel; 15 SC, 32 LC, 7 GC; enrl. art
history approx 75, studio art approx. 75, total 1021. Tui. $4980
including room and board; campus res.
History of Art
Studio Art

NORTON

✤WHEATON COLLEGE, Art Department, 02766.
  Tel: (617) 285-7722
Thomas J. McCormick, Chmn; 7 FT instr. Estab. 1834; pvt; W;
4 yr; degree, A.B; schol; 6 SC, 18 LC; enrl. 1143. Tui. $5450 incl.
room and board.

Basic Design	History of Art
Drawing & Painting	Sculpture
Graphic Arts	

PAXTON

ANNA MARIA COLLEGE, Department of Art, Sunset Lane, 01612.
  Tel: (617) 757-4586
David T. Green, Chmn; 3 FT instr. Estab. 1948; pvt; D & E; ent.
req. HS dipl, ent. exam; 4 yrs; schol; 15 SC, 12 LC; enrl. D 190,
E 144, maj. 56. Tui. $1700 per yr, $60 per cr. hr; campus res.
$1200.

Advertising Design	Modelling
Aesthetics	Occupational Therapy
Art Education	Painting
Ceramics	Photography
Drawing	Rug Design
Enameling	Sculpture
Handicrafts	Silk Screen
History of Art	Stitchery
Lettering	Teacher Training
Macrame	Weaving

  Summer School: Sr. Clarice Chauvin, Dir; tui. $60 cr. hr. for
term of 6 wk. beginning June 15; 1973 enrl. 20.

Crafts for the Retarded	Oil Painting
Lettering	Watercolor Techniques

PITTSFIELD

BERKSHIRE COMMUNITY COLLEGE, Fine Arts Department, West
  St, 01201.
Robert M. Boland, Chmn; 4 FT, 1 PT instr. College estab. 1960,
Fine Arts Dept. with maj. 1967; pub; D & E; ent. req. HS dipl, ent.
exam, interview and portfolio for art maj; 2 yr; degrees, A.A, A.S;
schol; 10 SC, 4 LC; enrl. D 975, E 512, maj. 100. Tui. $250; no
campus res.

Aesthetics	Graphic Design
Ceramics	History of Art & Archaeology
Commercial Art	Lettering
Costume Design & Construction	Painting
Drawing	Stage Design
Graphic Arts	Theatre Arts

Adult hobby classes in ceramics; tui. $77 per sem.
  Summer School: Dr. Geng Kamp, Dir; courses offered change
yearly; tui. $77 for term of 6 wk. beginning July; 1969 enrl. 672.

PROVINCETOWN

CAPE SUMMER SCHOOL OF ART, 02657.
  Tel: (617) 487-0703
Henry Hensche, Dir. Estab. 1930; pvt; schol. Tui. $40 per wk, $80 per mo. $150 per 2 mo. from July 1 to Aug. 30.
Composition
Drawing
Painting

MORRIS DAVIDSON SUMMER SCHOOL OF MODERN PAINTING,
  Miller Hill Rd, 02657.
Morris Davidson, Dir. Estab. 1944; pvt; D AM; ent. req. previous study; no dipl, no degrees; all instruction individual; schol. (2). Tui. $275 per mo.
Modern Painting (Spatial Organization)
Special orientation course for art teachers.

THE PROVINCETOWN WORKSHOP, A SCHOOL OF PAINTING AND
  DRAWING, 492 Commercial St, 02657. Tel: (617) 487-0973
Victor Candell and Leo Manso, Dirs; 2 FT instr. Estab. 1958; pvt; D & E, summers only; co-ed; ent. req. ent. exam; schol. recommendation by Dept. Heads or Prof. Tui. summer (9 wk.) $285, $175 per mo, $45 per wk; reg. fee $5.
Art Education   Graphic Arts
Drawing   Painting

SOUTH HADLEY

MOUNT HOLYOKE COLLEGE, Department of Art, 01075.
  Tel: (413) 538-2245
Jean C. Harris, Chmn; 10 FT, 1 PT instr. Estab. 1837; pvt; W; 4 yr; degrees; schol. and fels; 32 LC, 13 SC; enrl. maj. 75, others 1840. Tui. $3150; campus res. $1750.
Graphics   Painting & Drawing
History of Art & Archaeology   Sculpture

SPRINGFIELD

SPRINGFIELD COLLEGE, Department of Visual and Performing
  Arts, Dana Fine Arts Center, 263 Alden St, 01109.
  Tel: (413) 787-2332.
William Blizard, Chmn; 3 FT, 6 PT instr. Estab. 1885; pub; D & E; co-ed; ent. req. SAT art portfolio; 4 yr; degrees, B.S, B.A, B.H; schol; 40 SC, 10 LC; enrl. D 2200, E 200, maj. 40, grad. 400. Tui. $66 per cr. hr.
Aesthetics   History of Art & Archaeology
Art Education   Painting
Ceramics   Photography
Drawing   Sculpture
General Crafts (wood,   Stage Design
  cloth design)   Teacher Training
Graphic Arts   Textile Design
Adult classes, painting, ceramics, drawing, sculpture, photography and others; tui. $66 per cr. hr; enrl. 350. Children's classes, all media; tui. free; enrl. 100.
  Summer School: Dave Wuerthele, Dir; tui. $66 per cr. hr. for two five wk. terms beginning June 22 and July 27; 1969 enrl. 400.
Ceramics   Painting
Crafts   Photography
Drawing   Sculpture
Note: All art classes are 2 studio hr. cr.

STOCKBRIDGE

BEAUPRE, A Creative and Performing Arts Center,
  01262.
Mrs. Stanley North, Dir; 2 FT instr. Estab. 1944; pvt; D; W; ent. req. none. Tui. $1025 for term of 6 wk. beginning June 27. Summer school only and offers a Major in Art for girls, 9-15.
Ceramics   Painting
Drawing   Stitchery
Lettering   Tie Dyeing
Macrame   Weaving
Mobiles

TRURO

TRURO CENTER FOR THE ARTS AT CASTLE HILL, INC, Castle
  Rd, 02666. Tel: (617) 349-3714
Joyce Johnson, Dir; 40 instr. Estab. 1972; pvt; D & E summers only; no degrees or cert; schol; enrl. 400. Tui. $85 for two wk. workshops, $45 for one wk; no campus res.
Ceramics   Painting
Drawing   Sculpture

Graphic Arts   Silversmithing
Handicrafts   Weaving
Jewelry
Children's classes, 6 - 8 wk; tui. $50 - $150.

WALTHAM

BRANDEIS UNIVERSITY, Department of Fine Arts, 02154.
  Tel: (617) 647-2555
Robert W. Berger, Chmn; 11 FT instr. Estab. 1948; pvt; D; ent. req. high ranking HS grad, coll. board ent. exam; 4 yr; degree, B.A; schol; 10 SC, 28 LC; enrl. 2600. Tui. $3550; campus res.
Design   History of Art, (Specialized courses)
Drawing   Painting
Graphic Arts   Sculpture

WELLESLEY

WELLESLEY COLLEGE, Art Department, 02181.
  Tel: (617) 235-0320 Exten. 307
Peter J. Fergusson, Chmn; 13 FT, 5 PT instr. Estab. 1875; pvt; W; 4 yr; degree, B.A; schol. and fel; 15 SC, 29 LC, 10 Seminars; enrl. maj. 100, others 1450.

WESTFIELD

WESTFIELD STATE COLLEGE, Art Department, Western Ave,
  01085. Tel: (413) 568-3311 Exten. 256.
Arno Maris, Chmn; 8 FT instr. Pub; D; ent. req. ent. exam, interview; 4 yr; degree, B.A.(Fine Arts); 32 SC, 15 LC, 10 GC; enrl. 107. Tui. $600 per yr; campus res. $500 per yr.
Art Education   Industrial Design
Ceramics   Lettering
Drawing   Painting
Graphic Arts   Photography
Graphic Design   Sculpture
History of Art & Archaeology   Teacher Training
Illustration   Theatre Arts

WESTON

REGIS COLLEGE, Art Department, 235 Wellesley St, 02193.
  Tel: (012) 893-1820
Sister M. Louisella Walters, Chmn; 2 FT, 4 PT instr. Estab. 1944; pvt; D; W; ent. req. ent. exam; 4 yr; degree, A.B; schol; enrl. D 160, maj. 60. Tui. $2300 per yr; campus res. $1450.
Aesthetics   History of Art & Archaeology
Art Education   Jewelry
Batik   Painting
Ceramics   Sculpture
Drawing   Stained Glass
Enameling   Teacher Training
Graphic Arts   Weaving
  Summer School: Sister Anna Mary Kelly, Dir; courses offered, Printmaking, Painting.

WILLIAMSTOWN

WILLIAMS COLLEGE, Art Department, 01267.
  Tel: (413) 597-2377
Whitney S. Stoddard, Chmn; 10 FT, 6 PT instr. Estab. coll. 1793, dept. 1903; pvt; D; co-ed; ent. req. HS dipl. and tests; 4 yr. (M.A. 2 yr); degrees; 8 SC, 30 LC, 12 GC. Tui. $4200; campus res.
Architecture   Graphic Arts
Basic Design   History of Art

WORCESTER

CLARK UNIVERSITY, Department of Visual and Performing Arts,
  01610. Tel; (617) 793-7711
Donald Krueger, Chmn, Visual Arts. Estab. 1887; pvt; D & E; ent. req. HS dipl, ent. exam, portfolio for studio art maj; 4 yr; degrees, B.A. in cooperation with the school at the Worcester Art Museum, B.F.A. in E coll; schol; enrl. approx. D 100, E 12, maj. approx. 40. Tui. $3450 per yr; campus res. $2000.
Advertising Design   Illustration
Aesthetics   Museum Staff Training
Art Education   Painting
Ceramics   Photography
Commercial Art   Printmaking

Drawing
Graphic Design
History of Art

Sculpture
Teacher Training
Theatre Arts

Extensive opportunity for special projects in visual arts.
    Summer School: Various courses offered in Coll. of Professional and Continuing Education, some in cooperation with the Worcester Craft Center.

COLLEGE OF THE HOLY CROSS, Fine Arts Department, 01610. Tel: (617) 793-2011
John Reboli, Chmn; 9 FT instr. Estab. 1843; den; D; ent. req. HS dipl; 4 yr; degrees, 14; schol; 9 SC, 18 LC; enrl. 471. Tui. $3200 per yr, infirmary $50, student activity fee, $37; campus res. $1400.

Art Education
Ceramics
Drawing
Graphic Arts

History of Art & Archaeology
Painting
Sculpture

✤CRAFT CENTER, 25 Sagamore Rd, 01605.
    Tel: (617) 753-8183
Angelo Randazzo, Dir; 7 FT, 6 PT instr. Estab. 1951; pvt; D & E; ent. req. none; 10 SC; enrl. D 150, E 300. Tui. $45 per 10 wk. session of 3 hr. per wk.

Ceramics
Design
Enameling
Graphic Arts

Graphic Design
Jewelry
Photography
Woodworking

    Summer School: Angelo Randazzo, Dir; tui. $125 for term of 3 wk. beginning July 5-23; enrl. 12 students per class.

Ceramics
Enameling
Graphics

Jewelry
Photography
Woodworking

SCHOOL OF THE WORCESTER ART MUSEUM, 55 Salisbury St, 01608. Tel: (617) 799-4406
Sante Graziani, Dean; 10 FT, 2 PT instr. Estab. 1898; pvt; D; ent. req. HS transcript, portfolio; 3 yr. cert. program; schol. for all three yr; 19 SC, 3 LC; enrl. 135. Tui. $1350 per yr.

Advanced Painting
Art History since 1900
Basic Drawing & Painting
Color Research
Composition
Figure Sketch
Graphics
History of Art

Illustration
Introduction to Sculpture
Life Drawing & Painting
Perspective
Photography
Technics
Three Dimensional Design
Visual Design

MICHIGAN

ADRIAN

ADRIAN COLLEGE, Art Department, 49221.
    Tel: (517) 265-5161 Exten. 246
Michael Cassino, Chmn; 3 FT, 2 PT instr. Estab. 1961; den; D & E; 4 yr; degrees, B.A, B.A.(with teaching cert), B.F.A; schol and fel; 26 SC, 6 LC; internship; enrl. maj. 50, others 350. Tui. $2200 per year; campus res $1300.

Art Education
Art History
Ceramics
Design & Drawing

Figure Drawing
Painting
Printmaking
Sculpture

    Summer School: Dr. Jan Hoffer, Dir; tui. $60 per cr. hr. for 3 or 6 wk. term from May 23 - Aug. 15.

SIENA HEIGHTS COLLEGE, Art Department, Siena Heights Dr, 49221. Tel: (313) 263-0731.
Dr. S. Jeannine Klemm, Dir; 8 FT instr. Estab. 1919; pvt; D & E; ent. req. HS dipl, C+ average; 4 yr; degrees, B.A, B.F.A; 6 SC, 2 LC, 4 GC; enrl. maj. 139, others 201. Tui. $750, board $550, $50 per sem. hr; campus res.

Ceramics
Drafting
Drawing & Painting
Graphic Arts
Metal Arts

Photography
Printmaking
Sculpture
Textile Design

    Summer School: $50 per cr. hr. for 6 wk. beginning June 24.

ALBION

✤ALBION COLLEGE, Department of Visual Art, 49224.
    Tel: (517) 629-5511 Exten. 249
Vernon L. Bobbitt, Chmn; 5 FT instr. Estab. 1835; pvt; D; ent. req. HS grad. and ent. exam; 4 yr; degree, B.A; schol; 14 SC, 6 LC; enrl. maj. 50, others 450. Tui, room and board $3610; campus res.

Art & Liberal Education
Ceramics

Pre-Professional Art
Sculpture

ALLENDALE

GRAND VALLEY STATE COLLEGES, College of Arts and Sciences, Art Department, 49401. Tel: (616) 895-6611 Exten. 486
Prof Beverly Berger, Head; 8 FT, 3 PT instr. Estab. 1963; pub; D & E; ent. req. HS dipl; 4 yr; degrees, B.A, B.S; schol; 22 SC, 10 LC; enrl. D 500, E 100, maj. 140, special students 15. Tui. $630 per yr; campus res. $2239.

Aesthetics
Art Education
Ceramics
Drawing
Graphic Arts
History of Art

Jewelry
Painting
Photography
Sculpture
Teacher Training
Theatre Arts

    Summer School: Chmn. Art Department; tui. $210 for term of 10 wk; total 1975 enrl. 7200

Art Appreciation
Art Education
Drawing
Fiber
Independent Study

Jewelry
Painting
Photography
Printmaking

ALMA

ALMA COLLEGE, Art Department, 48801.
    Tel: (517) 463-2141 Exten. 323, 405
Kent Kirby, Head; 3 FT, 1 PT instr. Estab. 1886; den; D & E; ent. req. HS dipl, ent. exam; 4 yr; degrees, B.A, B.F.A; schol; 19 SC, 4 LC; enrl. D & E 200, maj. 50. Tui. $2504 per yr; campus res. $1246.

Art Education
Ceramics
Design Theory
Drawing
Environmental Design
Furniture Design
Graphic Design
History of Art & Archaeology
History of Film

Independent Studio Projects
Interior Design
Jewelry
Painting
Photography
Printmaking
Sculpture
Textile Design
Weaving

ANN ARBOR

UNIVERSITY OF MICHIGAN, School of Art, 2000 Bonisteel Blvd, 48105. Tel: (313) 764-0397
George V. Bayliss, Dean; 39 FT, 5 PT instr. Estab. 1905; pub; D; ent. req. HS dipl, SAT, portfolio; 4-6 yr; degrees, B.F.A, M.A, M.F.A; schol; 75 SC, 6 LC, 86 GC; enrl. maj. 406, grad. 37. Tui. $424 per sem, grad. $580, non-res. $1378, grad. $1504.

Advertising Design
Art Education
Ceramics
Drafting
Drawing
Graphic Arts
Graphic Design
Handicrafts
Illustration
Industrial Design

Interior Design
Jewelry
Lettering
Painting
Photography
Sculpture
Teacher Training
Textile Design
Weaving

    Summer School: George Bayliss, Dean; courses as above; tui. $212, grad. $333, non-res. $689, grad. $755.

    Department of History of Art* (College of Literature, Science and the Arts). Tel: (313) 764-5400
Clifton Olds, Head; 11 FT instr. Dept. estab. 1910; pub; degrees, B.A, M.A, Ph.D; schol. and fel; enrl. maj. 100, grad. 75.

History of Art
Museology

BATTLE CREEK

KELLOGG COMMUNITY COLLEGE,* Visual Arts Department, 49016.
Will Collopy, Chmn; 3 FT, 9 PT instr. Estab. 1962; pub; D & E; no ent. req; 2-4 yrs; degree, A.A; schol; enrl. D 2200, E 2000, maj. 50. Tui. $11 cr. hr. res.

Advertising Design
Architecture
Art Education
Ceramics
Commercial Art
Costume Design & Construction
Drafting
Drawing
Graphic Arts

Illustration
Industrial Design
Jewelry
Lettering
Painting
Photography
Sculpture
Stage Design
Teacher Training

Graphic Design   Theatre Arts
History of Art & Archaeology
Adult hobby classes in all areas; tui. $11 cr. hr.
     Summer School: Will Collopy, Dir; courses offered, basic art; tui.
$11 cr. hr.

BENTON HARBOR

LAKE MICHIGAN COLLEGE, Art Department, 2755 E. Napier Ave,
     49022. Tel: (616) 927-3571
2 FT, 2 PT instr. Estab. 1943; pub; D & E; ent. open door; 2 yr;
degree, A.F.A; 10 SC, 6 LC. Tui. $160 per sem. Summer School.

Art Appreciation   History of Art
Art Education   Jewelry
Basic Design   Painting
Ceramics   Sculpture
Crafts   Textiles
Drawing   Watercolor
Graphics

BERRIEN SPRINGS

ANDREWS UNIVERSITY, 49104.
     Tel: (616) 471-7771
Greg Constantine, Chmn; 4 FT instr. Estab. 1952; den; D & E; ent.
req. HS grad; 4 yr; degrees, B.S.(Art Educ), B.A, M.A.T; 18 SC,
5 LC; enrl. 130, maj. 35. Tui, room and board $1000 per quarter.

Advertising Design   Painting
Art Education   Photography
Ceramics   Printmaking
Design   Sculpture
Drawing   European Study
     Summer School: Dr. D. Ford, dir; tui. $53 per cr. hr. for 8 wk.
session beginning June 16.

BIRMINGHAM

BIRMINGHAM-BLOOMFIELD ART ASSOCIATION, 1516 S. Cranbrook
     Rd, 48009. Tel: (313) 644-0866
Kenneth R. Gross, Exec. Dir; over 40 PT instr. Estab. 1956; pub;
D & E; no ent. req; no degree; term of 10 wk. beginning Sept, Jan,
Apr. and July; schol; 85 SC, 3 LC; enrl. youth and adult 786. Tui.
from $3 for single workshop to maximum of $85 for class; no campus
res.

Aesthetics   History of Art & Archaeology
Applique   Jewelry
Ceramics   Lettering
Commercial Art   Metal
Drawing   Occupational Therapy
Fiber Preparation (Spinning,   Painting
     Dyeing)   Pottery
Fibers   Quilting
Glass   Sculpture
Graphic Arts   Teacher Training
Graphic Design   Textile Design
Youth classes, calligraphy, cliche verre, silk screen. Children's
classes, color & design, crafts, drawing & painting; tui. $30-$50.

BLOOMFIELD HILLS

✣CRANBROOK ACADEMY OF ART, 500 Lone Pine Rd, 48013.
     Tel: (313) 645-3300
Wallace Mitchell, Pres; John F. Mills, Registrar; 11 FT instr.
Estab. 1927; pvt; degrees, 2 yr. for B.F.A with 2 yr. at accredited
coll, 2 yr. for M.F.A and M.Arch; non-degree students admitted;
schol; undergrad. and grad. courses; enrl. 150. Tui. $1200 per sem.

Architecture   Painting
Ceramics   Photography
Design   Printmaking
Fiber   Sculpture
Metalsmithing

DEARBORN

HENRY FORD COMMUNITY COLLEGE, Art Department, 5101 Ever-
     green Rd, 40121. Tel: (313) 271-2750 Exten. 295
Robert J. Ferguson, Chmn; 6 FT, 15 PT instr. Estab. 1938; pub;
D & E; ent. req. HS dipl; 2 yr; degree, A.A; schol; 25 SC, 9 LC;
enrl. D 3500, E 7500, maj. 600. Tui. $10 per cr. hr, non-res. $15
per cr. hr, plus lab. fees; drive in campus.

Advertising Design   Jewelry
Art Education   Materials
Ceramics   Painting
Commercial Art   Photography
Drafting   Sculpture
Drawing   Teacher Training

Graphic Arts   Textile Design
History of Art & Archaeology   Weaving
     Summer School: Robert J. Ferguson, Dir; tui. $10 per cr. hr,
non-res. $15.

Advanced Drawing   Black & White Photography
Art Appreciation   Ceramics
Art History   Directed Study
Basic Drawing   Life Drawing
Basic Two-Dimensional Design

DETROIT

CENTER FOR CREATIVE STUDIES-COLLEGE OF ART AND
     DESIGN, 245 E. Kirby St, 48202. Tel: (313) 872-3118
Walter Midener, Dir; D 32 FT, D & E 44 PT instr. Estab. 1926; pvt;
4 yr; degree, B.F.A.(Painting, Sculpture, Advertising Design,
Graphics, Glass, Fabric Design, Metalcraft, Ceramics, Photography,
Industrial Design); 1 FT schol. through Scholastic Magazine, 3 FT
schols. to grads. of Detroit Public HS; 23 SC; enrl. D & E total 950
Tui. $1950 per yr, $975 per sem.

Advanced Drawing   Illustration Drawing
Advertising Design   Industrial Design
Advertising Illustration   Lettering
Art History   Life Drawing & Anatomy
Automotive Illustration   Mechanical Illustration
Basic Design   Metal & Jewelry
Basic Drawing & Perspective   Painting
Ceramics   Photography
Fabric Design   Sculpture
Glass   Watercolor
Graphics & Lithography
Children's Sat. AM classes; tui. $110.
     Summer Session: Walter Midener, Dir; tui. $485 for 8 wk; enrl.
288.

Basic Design   Metalcraft
Basic Drawing   Painting
Ceramics   Sculpture
Life Drawing   Watercolor

WAYNE STATE UNIVERSITY,* College of Liberal Arts, Department
     of Art and Art History, 450 W. Kirby St. 48202. Tel: (313) 577-
     2980
G. Alden Smith, Chmn; D 40 FT, 35 PT instr. Estab. 1868; pub;
D & E; 4-5 yr; univ. course in History of Art cooperates with Detroit Institute of Arts; degrees, B.A, B.F.A, M.A, M.F.A; schol &
fel; 80 SC, 40 LC, 88 GC; enrl. 3100. For registration fee and tui.
see catalog.

Costume Design & Construc-   Drawing, Painting & Graphics
     tion, in H.E.   History of Art
Crafts-ceramics, metal, weaving   Photography
Design-Advertising, Industrial,   Sculpture
     Interior
     Summer School: 4 quarters annually, same administration.

EAST LANSING

MICHIGAN STATE UNIVERSITY, College of Arts and Letters, De-
     partment of Art, 48824. Tel: (517) 355-7612
Roger Funk, Chmn; 38 FT, 2 PT instr. Estab. 1855; pub; 4 yr;
degrees, B.A, B.F.A, M.A, M.F.A; schol. and fel; SC, LC, GC; enrl.
maj. 600, others 2100; campus res.

Art Education   History of Art
Crafts   Industrial Design
Fine Arts   Photography
Graphic Design
Children's Saturday Art Program, fabrics & fibers, painting & draw-
ing, photography, printmaking, sculpture, three-dimensional media,
two-dimensional media; tui. $7 per term; no enrl. limit.
     Summer School: See Leland, Michigan

FLINT

CHARLES STEWART MOTT COMMUNITY COLLEGE,
     Fine Arts Division, 1401 E. Court St, 48503.
     Tel: (313) 235-7541 Exten. 243
Samuel E. Morello, Chmn; 8 FT, 12 PT, E 4 FT instr. Estab. 1923;
pub; D & E; ent. req. HS grad. or equivalent, GED test; 62 sem. hr.
for grad; degree, A.A; limited schol; 13 SC, 5 LC; enrl. maj. 200,
others 10,000. Tui. district res. $12 per cr. hr, state res. $22,
out-of-state res. $32; matriculation and other fees approx. $30.

Ceramics   Jewelry
Design   Metalsmithing
Drawing   Painting

History of Art   Sculpture
Independent Studies   Teacher Training
    Summer School: Courses offered, Art History, Teacher Training, limited studio courses; term of 8 wk. from June 12; tui. same as above; enrl. 3500.

GRAND RAPIDS

AQUINAS COLLEGE, Art Department, 1607 Robinson Rd. S.E, 49506.
    Tel: (616) 459-8281
4 FT, 1 PT instr. Estab. 1960; den; D & E; ent. req. HS grad; 4 yr; degrees, B.A, B.F.A; 33 SC, 10 LC; D 203; E 69; maj. 22. Tui. $2260; campus res. $1200.

Art Education	Painting
Art History	Printmaking
Design	Sculpture
Drawing	

CALVIN COLLEGE, Art Department, 1801 E. Beltline, 49506.
    Tel: (619) 949-4000
Prof. Edgar G. Boeve, Chmn; 6 FT, 4 PT instr. Estab. 1876; den; D & E; ent. req. HS dipl. or ent. exam; 4 yr; degrees, A.B, A.B. (Educ), B.F.A; schol; over 16 SC, 4 LC; enrl. D 1200, E 165, maj. 105, total coll. enrl. 3500. Tui. $1960 per yr; campus res. $1030.

Advertising Design	Graphic Arts
Aesthetics	Graphic Design
Architecture	History of Art & Archaeology
Art Education	Jewelry
Casting	Painting
Ceramics	Photography
Commercial Art	Sculpture
Costume Design & Construction	Stage Design
Drafting	Teacher Training
Drawing	Theatre Arts
Enameling	

    Summer School: Edgar G. Boeve, Dir.

Design	Principles of Art Education
Painting	Printmaking

GRAND RAPIDS JUNIOR COLLEGE, Art Department, 143 Bostwick N.E, 49502. Tel: (616) 456-4572
Glenn T. Raymond, Chmn; 4 FT, 4 PT instr. Estab. c. 1920; pub; D & E; ent req. HS dipl. or ent. exam; 2 yr; degree, A.A; schol; 17 SC, 2 LC; enrl. D 250, E 75, maj. 60. Tui. city res. $12 per cr. hr, state res. $20, out-of-state $30; no campus res.

Art Education	History of Art & Archaeology
Ceramics	Jewelry
Drafting	Painting
Drawing	Sculpture
Graphic Arts	Teacher Training

    Summer School: Courses offered, Art History & Appreciation, Teacher Training; tui. same as above for term of 8 wk. beginning June 10.

KENDALL SCHOOL OF DESIGN, 1110 College N.E, 49503.
    Tel: (616) 451-2886
17 FT, 4 PT instr. Estab. 1928; pvt; D; 3 yr; cert; schol. Tui. $1000 per yr.

Advertising Design	Illustration
Furniture Design	Interior Design

    Summer School: May through July.

HILLSDALE

HILLSDALE COLLEGE, Art Department, 49242.
    Tel: (517) 437-7341 Exten. 257
Rosamond Joy Stewart, Head; 2 FT, 1 PT instr. Estab. 1844; pvt; ent. req. HS grad. or exam; 4 yr; degrees; 12 SC, 5 LC; enrl. coll. 1000. Tui. and fees, board and room $3642 per yr.

Art Education	Jewelry
Ceramics	Painting
Design	Printmaking
Drawing	Sculpture
History of Art	

HOLLAND

ART SCHOOL OF THE CRAFTS GUILD, 0-380 S. 168th Ave, Rte. 7, 49423. Tel: (616) 335-3402
Alleene Lowery Fisher, Dir; 1 FT instr. Estab. Detroit 1927, Holland 1948; pvt; W; cert; enrl. limited to 20. Tui. including studio res. $300 per month yr. round.
Design
Drawing & Painting
Home study courses in Landscape, Oil Painting Fundamentals, Portraiture, Still Life; $300 each.

HOPE COLLEGE, Art Department, Rusk Building, 49423.
    Tel: (616) 392-5111 Exten. 2275
Delbert Michel, Chmn; 5 FT, 1 PT instr. Pvt; D; ent. req. HS grad, ent. exam, art maj. requires dept. approval; 4 yr; degree, B.A; 15 SC, 10 LC; enrl. D 350, maj. 50. Tui. $2370; campus res. $3550.

African Art	Modern Architecture
American Art	Modern Painting & Sculpture
Ancient Art	Non-Western Art
Art Education	Painting
Baroque & Rococo Art	Photography
Ceramics	Recent Art Seminar
Design	Renaissance Art
History of Art	Sculpture
Life Drawing	Teacher Training
Medieval Art	

    Summer School: Delbert Michel, Dir; tui. $45 per sem. hr. for terms of 6 and 8 wk. beginning June 22; 1969 enrl. 40.

Art Methods	Painting
Ceramics	Printmaking
Introduction to Art (Studio)	Sculpture
Life Drawing	

JACKSON

ELLA SHARP MUSEUM, 3225 Fourth St, 49203.
    Tel: (517) 787-2320
Elise Cole, Curator of Art Education for Young People; 3 FT, 20 PT instr. Estab. 1965; pvt; D & E; ent. req. museum mem; schol; 10 SC, 5 LC; enrl. adults and children approx. 200. Tui. varies with type of course being offered. Courses offered in conjunction with the Adult Enrichment Dept, Jackson Community College, Jackson.

Art Education	Painting
Ceramics	Photography
Drawing	Quilting
Fabric & Fiber Arts	Sculpture
Graphic Arts	Stitchery
Graphic Design	Textile Design
Indian Crafts	Theatre Arts
Macrame	Weaving
Museum Staff Training	

KALAMAZOO

KALAMAZOO COLLEGE,* Department of Art, Academy St, 49001.
Marcia J. Wood, Head; 3 FT instr. Pvt; D; 4 yr; degree, B.A; schol; 12 SC, 10 LC; total enrl. D 1384, maj. 20. Tui. $505 per quarter, miscellaneous fees $135 per quarter; campus res. $460 per quarter.

Aesthetics	History of Art & Archaeology
Art Education	Lettering
Ceramics	Painting
Costume Design & Construction	Sculpture
Dimensional Design	Teacher Training
Drawing	Theatre Arts
Graphic Arts	

KALAMAZOO INSTITUTE OF ARTS, 314 S. Park St, 49006.
    Tel: (616) 349-7775
Kirk Newman, Assoc, Dir. for Educ; 2 FT, 23 PT instr. Estab. 1924; pvt; D & E; co-ed; no ent. req; schol; 18 SC, 3 LC; enrl. D 650, E 650. Tui. $21 to $44 per class per sem; no campus res.

Ceramics	Jewelry
Drawing	Painting
Graphic Arts	Photography
History of Art & Archaeology	Sculpture

    Summer School: Kirk Newman, Assoc. Dir.

Ceramics	Printmaking
Painting	Sculpture
Photography	Weaving

⚜WESTERN MICHIGAN UNIVERSITY, Art Department, 49008.
    Tel: (616) 383-1858
Charles E. Meyer, Head; 29 FT, 8-10 PT instr. Estab. 1904; pub; D & E; ent. req. available at Admissions; 4 yr; degrees, B.S, B.A, B.F.A, M.A, M.F.A; 53 SC, 20 LC, 32 GC; enrl. maj. 500, grad. 50. Tui. $315, grad. $435, non-res. $795, grad. $1035; campus res. $690 per sem.
    Summer School: Same as above; enrl. c. 150 maj.

LANSING

LANSING COMMUNITY COLLEGE, Performing and Creative Arts Department, 419 N. Capitol Ave, 48914. Tel: (517) 373-7170
David Machtel, Head; 3 FT, 24 PT instr. Estab. 1967; pub; D & E;

ent. req. HS dipl; 2 yr; degrees, A.A. and cert; schol; 18 SC; total enrl. 1000. Tui. $7.50 per cr. hr; no campus res.

Advertising Design	Interior Design
Art Education	Jewelry
Ceramics	Leather Work
Commercial Art	Life Drawing
Decoupage	Macrame
Design	Painting
Drawing	Sculpture
Graphic Design	Serigraphy
History of Art	Weaving
Illustration	

LELAND

LEELANAU SUMMER ART SCHOOL,* 49654. (Sponsored by Michigan State University, Art Department)
Erling B. Brauner, Chmn. Estab. 1939. Tui. $21 per term hr; visitors $65 for 1-5 wk; enrl. 29.

LIVONIA

MADONNA COLLEGE, Art Department, 36600 Schoolcraft Rd, 48150. Tel: (313) 425-8000 Exten. 8
Sister M. Angeline, Chmn; 1 FT, 4 PT instr. Estab. 1949; pvt; D & E; ent. req. HS dipl; 1-4 yr; degrees, Cert. of Achievement, A.A, A.B; schol; 15 SC, 2 LC; enrl. coll. 1700. Tui. $950 per yr; campus res. $425-$525 semi-private room, $525-$575 board.

Art for the Aging	History of Art
Ceramics	Jewelry
Commercial Art	Lettering
Drawing	Painting
Graphic Arts	Sculpture
Graphic Design	Teacher Training

Adult hobby classes, beginning and advanced painting, mixed media painting, drawing, lapidary & jewelry, ceramics, card design; tui. $40 per sem. of 10 wk; enrl. 50 per sem.

SCHOOLCRAFT COLLEGE,* Department of Art, 18600 Haggerty Rd, 48151. Tel: (313) 591-6400
Robert Dufort, Dept. Chmn; 4 FT, 3 PT instr. Estab. 1961; pub; D & E; ent. req. sometimes ent. exam; 2 yrs; degree, A.A; schol; 13 SC, 3 LC.

Art Education	Jewelry
Ceramics	Painting
Graphic Arts	Photography
Handicrafts	Sculpture
History of Art & Archaeology	

MARQUETTE

NORTHERN MICHIGAN UNIVERSITY, Department of Art and Design, 49855. Tel: (906) 227-3703
Thomas Cappuccio, Head; 10 FT, 2 PT instr Estab. 1889; pub; D & E; ent. req. HS grad; 4-5 yr; degrees, B.S, B.A, B.F.A.(teaching cert), M.A; state schols; 64 SC, 8 LC, 24 GC; total enrl. 8200. Tui. $312 per sem, non-res. $690.

Art Education	Physical Aspects of Art
Cinematography	Physical Basis of Form
Drawing Illustration	Printmaking
Environmental Design	Psychological Aspects of Art
Furniture Design	Psychological Basis of Visual
Graphic Design	Communications
Industrial Design	Sculpture
Interior Design	Social Aspects of Art
Jewelry	Value and Form
Painting	Weaving
Photography	Wood Crafts

Summer School: Studio, Education courses.

MIDLAND

✤MIDLAND CENTER FOR THE ARTS, 1801 W. St. Andrews, 48640.
Carol Coppage, Dir. Exceptional facilities and faculty for community use; college credit to Northwood Institute (Midland) students; enrl. 100 per session; tui. $35-$45.

Ceramics	Photography
Metalsmithing	Weaving
Painting	

Children's classes, multi-media (grades 1-4), drawing (grades 5-9); tui. $20; enrl. 30 per session.

MOUNT PLEASANT

CENTRAL MICHIGAN UNIVERSITY, Art Department, 48859.
Tel: (517) 774-3025
Peter A. Jacobs, Chmn; 21 FT, 1 PT instr. Estab. 1892; pub; ent. req. HS grad; 4 yr; degrees, B.A, B F A, A.B, M.A; 50 SC, 9 LC; enrl. 14,500. Tui. undergrad. $18.50 per sem. hr, grad. $25 per sem. hr, non-res. undergrad. $45 per sem. hr, grad. $50 per sem. hr; campus res. $1300 per yr.

Ceramics	Photography
Commercial Art	Printmaking
Design	Sculpture
Drawing	Teacher Training
Metalsmithing	Weaving
Painting	

Summer School: Dir. L. Cochran, Dir; tui. res. variable, non-res. $228 for 6 wk. beginning June 19; enrl. 2500.

OLIVET

OLIVET COLLEGE, Department of Art, 49076.
Tel: (616) 749-7000
Donald Rowe, Chmn; 6 FT instr. Estab. 1844; pvt; ent. req. HS dipl. or exam; 4 yr; degrees, B.A, M.A; SC, LC; schol. Tui. $1200 per sem.

Advanced Independent Work	Metalwork
Baroque Art	19th Century Art
Basic Design	Non-Figurative Sculpture
Drawing	Painting
Figurative Sculpture	Primitive Art
Graphics	Renaissance Art
History of Visual Art	Research Paper
Medieval Art	20th Century Art

PONTIAC

THE PONTIAC CREATIVE ARTS CENTER, 47 Williams St, 48053.
Tel: (313) 333-7849
Ian R. Lyons, Exec. Dir; 15 PT instr. Estab. 1964; pub; D & E; schol; 22 SC. Tui. PT $80 mo.

Ceramics	Painting
Drawing	Photography
History of Art & Archaeology	Sculpture
Jewelry	Weaving

Adult hobby classes, ceramics, drawing, jewelry, painting, sculpture, weaving; tui. $45; enrl. 168. Children's classes, ceramics, painting, sculpture, violin; tui. $25; enrl. 27.

PORT HURON

ST. CLAIR COUNTY COMMUNITY COLLEGE, Fine Arts Department, 323 Erie St, 48060. Tel: (313) 984-3881
Patrick Bourke, Discipline Chmn; 4 FT, 1 PT instr. Estab. 1923; pub; D & E; ent. req. HS dipl, ent. exam; 2 yr; degrees, A.A, A.A.S; schol; 30 SC, 5 LC; enrl. D 60. Tui. $12.50 per cr. hr.

Advertising Design	History of Art & Archaeology
Art Education	Illustration
Ceramics	Lettering
Commercial Art	Painting
Display	Photography
Drawing	Sculpture
Graphic Arts	Theatre Arts
Graphic Design	

ROCHESTER

OAKLAND UNIVERSITY, Art and Art History Department, 48063.
Tel: (313) 377-3375
Carl F. Barnes, Jr, Chmn; 6 FT instr. Estab. 1957; pub; 4 yr; degree, B.A.(Art History); schol; 6 SC, 14 LC; enrl. maj. 75. Tui. $20.50 per cr, non-res. $58 per cr; campus res. $709 per sem.
Art History
Drawing
Painting

SAUGATUCK

OXBOW SUMMER SCHOOL OF ART,* 49453.
Tel: (616) 857-5811
Dick Dell, Board Pres; 5 FT instr. Estab. 1910; pvt; credit toward graduation recognized by schools which operate during regular school calendar; work schol. undergrad. and grad; students currently in school 9 wk. season, enrl. weekly. Tui. $40; campus res, send for catalogue.

Ceramics	Painting
Graphics	Photography
Metalwork	

UNIVERSITY CENTER

SAGINAW VALLEY STATE COLLEGE, Art Department,
48710.
Barron Hirsch, Chmn; 2 FT, 4 PT instr. Estab. 1970; pub; D & E;
ent. req. HS dipl; 4 yr; degree, B.A; schol; 40 SC; 12 LC; enrl. D
210, E 25, maj. 55. Tui. $17 per cr. hr; campus res. $1100-$1300
single occupancy, $25 deposit.

Advertising Design	Jewelry
Art Education	Painting
Ceramics	Photography
Drawing	Sculpture
Graphic Arts	Teacher Training
Graphic Design	Theatre Arts
History of Art	Weaving
Illustration	

Children's classes, painting, drawing, sculpture; tui $3 per unit;
enrl. 75.

WARREN

MACOMB COUNTY COMMUNITY COLLEGE, Art Area, 14500
Twelve Mile Rd, 48093. Tel: (313) 779-7138
D. L. Wing, Assoc. Dean of General Education; 5 FT, 5 PT instr.
Estab. 1962; pub; D & E; ent. req. HS dipl; 2 yr; degrees, A.A,
A.A.S; schol; 13 SC, 6 LC; enrl. D 800 E 400, maj. 125. Tui.
$13 per cr. hr, non-res. county $24, non-res. state $34.

Advertising Design	Handicrafts
Architecture	History of Art & Archaeology
Ceramics	Illustration
Commercial Art	Industrial Design
Costume Design & Construction	Jewelry
Display	Painting
Drafting	Photography
Drawing	Sculpture
Graphic Arts	Watercolor
Graphic Design	

Summer School: Courses offered, Basic Drawing, Ceramics.

YPSILANTI

EASTERN MICHIGAN UNIVERSITY, Art Department, 48197.
Tel: (313) 487-1268
Kingsley M. Calkins, Head; 35 FT instr. Estab. 1849; pub; D & E;
4 yr; degrees; 34 SC, 5 LC, 12 GC; enrl. undergrad. maj. 598; 93
courses offered. Tui. 12 hr. $246, non-res. 12 hr. $666; campus
res.

Fine Arts	Photography
Foundry Techniques	Public Works of Art
Multi-Media	Teacher Training

Summer School: Kingsley M. Calkins, Dir; tui. 1 cr. $33 to 6 cr.
hr. $123, non-res. 1 cr. $60 to 6 cr. hr. $240.

MINNESOTA

BEMIDJI

BEMIDJI STATE UNIVERSITY, Art Department, 56601.
Tel: (218) 755-3939
A. Keith Malmquist, Head; 8 FT, 1 PT instr. Estab. 1922; pub; D &
E; ent. req. HS dipl; 4 yr; degrees, A.S. & B.S. in Technical Illustration & Commercial Design, B.A.(Art), B.S.(Teaching of Art);
schol; 27 SC, 14 LC, 2 GC; enrl. dept. D 500, E 100, maj. 150, grad.
students 2, special minority groups 30. Tui. $7.25 per quarter hr.
res, $15.50 per quarter hr. non-res; campus res. $854.

Advertising Design	History of Art & Archaeology
Aesthetics	Industrial Design
Architecture	Jewelry
Art Education	Lettering
Ceramics	Painting
Drafting	Photography
Drawing	Sculpture
Fabric	Stage Design
General Crafts	Teacher Training
Graphic Arts	Textile Design
Handicrafts	Theatre Arts

Summer School: Keith Malmquist, Dir; tui. $7.25 per quarter hr.
$15.50 non-res. for term of 5 wk, beginning June 17 & July 23; 1973
enrl. 200.

Art Education	Design
Art History	Painting
Ceramics	Sculpture

COLLEGEVILLE

ST. JOHNS UNIVERSITY, Department of Art, 56321.
Tel: (612) 363-3192
Bela Petheo, Chmn; 4 FT instr. Estab. 1870-1880; pvt; D; ent.
rcq. HS dipl, ent. exam, portfolio; 4 yrs; degrees, B.A, B.S; schol;
18-19 SC, 10 LC; enrl. D 300-400, E 50, maj. 40. Tui. $1850 per yr,
$50 activity fee; campus res. approx. $1000.

Art Education	Museum Staff Training
Ceramics	Painting
Costume Design & Construction	Photography
Drawing	Sculpture
Graphic Arts	Stage Design
History of Art & Archaeology	Teacher Training
Jewelry	Theatre Arts
Lettering	

Adult hobby classes, ceramics, drawing, painting, prints; tui. $20 per
cr; enrl. 20-25.
Summer School: Sister Dennis Frandrup/Bela Petheo, Dir;
courses offered, Drawing, Painting, Printmaking; tui. $20 per cr.
for term of 4 wk. beginning July 1; 1973 enrl. 10-15.

DULUTH

COLLEGE OF ST. SCHOLASTICA,* Art Studio I and II, Kenwood
Ave, 55811. Tel: (218) 728-3631
Roberta Jensen, Art Dir; 1 FT instr. Estab. 1972; pvt; D; 3-4 SC
per quarter; enrl. 1000, free and open studio on liberal arts campus
for use of all students. Tui. $1700 per yr.

Ceramics	Painting
Drawing	Photography
Graphic Arts	Sculpture
Handicrafts	Weaving
Jewelry	

UNIVERSITY OF MINNESOTA, DULUTH, Art Department, 55812.
Tel: (218) 726-8225
James H. Brutger, Head; 11 FT, 10 PT instr. Pub; 4 yr; degrees,
B.F.A, B.S, M.A; schol. and fel; 53 SC, 28 LC, 33 GC; enrl. maj.
210, others 1250. Tui. $250, non-res. $625 plus incidental fee and
hospitalization.

Ceramics	Photography
Crafts	Printmaking
Design	Sculpture
Gallery Practice	Teacher Training
History of Art	Weaving & Fibers
Painting	

Summer School: Two terms of 5 wk; tui. $13.50 per cr. plus
incidental fee and hospitalization.

ELY

VERMILION COMMUNITY COLLEGE, Art Department, 55731.
Tel: (218) 365-3239
Daniel Wood, Art Instr; 1 FT instr. Estab. 1922; pub; D; co-ed; ent.
req. HS grad. 2 yr; degree, A.A; 17 SC, 5 LC; enrl. D 150, E 15,
maj. 5, others 160. Tui. $360; campus res. $850.

Aesthetics	Lettering
Ceramics	Painting
Drafting (mechanical)	Photography
Drawing	Sculpture
Graphic Arts	Special Design (2D, 3D)
History of Art & Archaeology	

Adult hobby classes, ceramics; tui. $10; enrl. 15.

GRAND MARAIS

GRAND MARAIS ART COLONY,* 55604.
Tel: (218) 387-1541
Birney Quick and Byron Bradley, Dirs; 3 FT instr. Estab. 1947; pvt;
D & E; co-ed; ent. req. HS dipl; schol; 4 SC, 2 LC. Tui. 6 wk. season
$100.

Aesthetics	Painting
Ceramics	Sculpture
Drawing	

Summer School: Birney Quick and Byron Bradley, Dirs; tui.
$100 for term of 6 wk. beginning July.

ITASCA COMMUNITY COLLEGE, Highway 169, 55744.
Tel: (218) 326-9451
Tyne T. Mike, Art Instr. Estab. 1925; pub; D & E; ent. req. HS
dipl; 2 yr; degree A.A; schol; 5 SC, 1 LC; enrl. D 12, E 2, maj. 8.
Tui. $360 per yr; no campus res.

Aesthetics	Painting
Ceramics	Theatre Arts
Drawing	

Adult ceramics class, 10 wk, tui. $10, enrl. 16-20.
Summer School: Tyne T. Mike, Dir; Ceramics; tui. $24 for term
of 4 wk, beginning June 10; enrl. 20

MANKATO

BETHANY LUTHERAN COLLEGE, 734 Marsh St, 56001.
Tel: (507) 388-2977
Edna Busekist, Prof; 1 instr. Estab. 1959; pvt; D; ent. req. HS
dipl; 2 yr; degree, A.A; schol; 3 SC, 1 LC; enrl. D 65. Tui. $1180
per yr; campus res. $1092.

Drawing	History of Art
Basic Design	Painting
Fabric Design	Pottery

✣MANKATO STATE UNIVERSITY, Department of Art, 56001.
Tel: (507) 389-6413
John E. Spurgin, Acting Chmn; 18 FT, 1 PT instr. Estab. 1867; pub;
D & E; ent. req. HS dipl, ent. exam; 4 yr; degrees, B.S.(Art Educ),
B.F.A, B.A, M.A, M.S, M.A.T; schol; 41 SC, 22 LC, 40 GC. Tui.
$384 per yr, non-res. $16.25 per cr. hr; room and board, $994.

Advertising Design	Illustration
Art Education	Jewelry
Ceramics	Leather
Commercial Art	Lettering
Display	Museum Staff Training
Drawing	Painting
Fiber Design	Photography
Glassworking	Sculpture
Graphic Arts	Teacher Training
Graphic Design	Textile Design
Handicrafts	Wood
History of Art & Archaeology	

Adult hobby classes, painting; tui. $7.25 per cr. hr; enrl. 40. Chil-
dren's classes, varied experiences; no tui; enrl. 100.
Summer School: John E. Spurgin, Dir; tui. $8 per cr. hr, non-
res. $16.25; 2 terms of 5 wk, beginning June 10 & July 15; 1973 enrl.
800.

MINNEAPOLIS

ART INSTRUCTION SCHOOLS, 500 S. 4th St, 55415.
Tel: (612) 339-8721
Dr. A. Conrad Posz, Dir. of Educ, Dr. Don Jardine, Assoc. Dir. of Educ.
Estab. 1914; pvt. Offers courses in:
Advertising Art & Illustrating
Painting
Cartooning

AUGSBURG COLLEGE, Art Department, 731 21st Ave. W,
55454.
Philip Thompson, Chmn; 2 FT, 5 PT instr. Coll. estab. 1869, Art Dept.
1960; den; D & E; ent. req. HS dipl; 4 yr; degree B.A; schol; 15 SC,
4 LC; enrl. D 200, maj. 42, others 1700. Tui. $2115 per yr, board
& room $1161, partial $1125, 5-day lunch plan $234.

Aesthetics	Museum Staff Training
Art Education	Painting
Ceramics	Photography
Drawing	Sculpture
Graphic Design	Stage Design
Handicrafts	Teacher Training
History of Art & Archaeology	Theatre Arts
Jewelry	Weaving
Lettering	

Summer School: Pat Parker, Dir; tui. $160, $90 audit, $15 gen-
eral fee, for term of six or four wk, beginning last wk. May; enrl.
250

MINNEAPOLIS COLLEGE OF ART AND DESIGN, 133 E. 25th St,
55404. Tel: (612) 874-0300
Dr. Jerome J. Hausman, Pres; 46 FT, 14 PT instr. Estab. 1886;
pvt; D & E; co-ed; ent. req. HS dipl. or GED; 4 yr; degree, B.F.A;
schol; 78 SC, 23 LC; enrl. D 655, E 400, maj. 620. Tui. $2200, part-
time $75 per cr; apartments available, cost varies from $600 to
$900 per year depending on accommodations.

Advertising Design	Film History
Audiovisual Production	Graphic Arts
Aesthetics	Graphic Design
Commercial Art	History of Art
Costume Design & Construction	Illustration
Drawing	Painting
Electronic Art	Photography
Fashion Arts	Printmaking
Film	Sculpture
Film Animation	Theatre History

Adult Classes: Sculpture, fashion design, illustration painting and
graphic design; tui. $75 per cr; enrl. 400 per sem.
Summer School: Roman J. Verostko, Dean.

Calligraphy	Painting
Drawing	Photography

Fashion Design	Printmaking
Graphic Design	Sculpture
Illustration	Video/Cinetography

NORTH HENNEPIN COMMUNITY COLLEGE, Art Department, 7411
85th Ave. N, 55445. Tel: (612) 425-4541 Exten. 152
Frank Schreiber, Art Instr; 2 FT, 4 PT instr. Estab. 1964; pub; D &
E; ent. req. HS dipl, ent. exam; 2 yr; degree A.A; schol; 15 SC, 4 LC;
enrl. D 500, E 100, maj. 200, others 100. Tui. $360 per yr, $8.50 per
cr; non-res.

Advertising Design	Graphic Design
Aesthetics	History of Art & Archaeology
Architecture	Illustration
Audiovisual	Lettering
Commercial Art	Occupational Therapy
Contemporary Arts	Painting
Display	Photography
Drawing	Stage Design
Graphic Arts	Theatre Arts

Adult hobby classes: Painting, video and photography; tui. $8.50 or
free per cr; enrl. 30-100.
Summer School: Don Durand, Dir; Theatre, Costume, Drawing
and Introduction to Arts; tui. $8.50 per cr. for term of 5 wk. begin-
ning June 13; enrl. 700.

UNIVERSITY OF MINNESOTA,* Institute of Technology, School of
Architecture & Landscape Architecture, 110 Architecture Building, 55455. Tel: (612) 373-2198
Ralph E. Rapson, Head; 12 FT, 25 PT instr. Estab. 1912; pub; D &
E; ent. req. completion of recommended first yr. college work and
selective admission; 4, 5, 6 yr; degrees, B.Arch, B.Landscape Arch,
B.Environmental Design, M.Arch, M.Landscape Arch; schol. and
fel; 20 SC, 25 LC, 15 GC. 3 options, Architecture (1 yr), City Design
(1 yr), Hospital Design (2 yr).

Department of Art History, College of Liberal Arts, 108 Jones
Hall, 55455. Tel: (612) 373-3057
Carl D. Sheppard, Chmn; 14 FT instr. Dept. estab. 1947, separate
dept. status, 1966; degrees, B.A, M.A, M.A. in Museology, Ph.D;
fel, American Art and Kress Foundation Fellowships; enrl. maj. 125,
grad. 65.

Department of Studio Art, 208 Art Bldg, West Bank, 55455.
Tel: (612) 373-3663
Curtis C. Hoard, Acting Chmn; 22 FT instr, 15 teaching asst. Pvt;
D & E; ent. req. HS dipl, ent. exam; 4-7 yr; degrees, B.A, B.F.A,
M.F.A; schol. Tui. $182 per quarter; student services $45.50 per
quarter; campus res. $410 per quarter incl. meals and phone.

Ceramics	Painting
Drawing	Photography
Glassblowing	Sculpture
Graphic Arts	

Summer School: Willard L. Thompson, Dir; tui. $12.50 per cr.
plus $22 student services per session, for term of 5 wk. beginning
June 18 and July 23, 1973.

MOORHEAD

CONCORDIA COLLEGE,* Art Department, 56560.
Tel: (218) 299-4623
Paul Allen, Chmn; 4 FT, 1 PT instr. Estab. 1891; den; D; co-ed;
ent. req. HS grad, ent. exam, character references; 4 yr; degrees,
B.A, B.S, B.S. Mus; schol; 10 SC, 5 LC; enrl. 275, total 2475, maj.
54. Tui. $1950, Student Assoc. dues $25; campus res. $825.

Art Education	History of Art & Archaeology
Ceramics	Multi-Media
Drawing	Painting
Graphic Arts	Sculpture

Summer School: Donald Dale, Registrar; tui. $280, for term of
6 wk. beginning May 13 and June 10, 1974; 1973 enrl. art 43, total
199.

Art Education	Sculpture
Art History	Special Studies
Drawing	Travel Seminar
Painting	

MOORHEAD STATE UNIVERSITY, Art Department, 1104 Seventh
Ave. S, 56560. Tel: (218) 236-2151
P. R. Szeitz, Chmn; 10 FT instr. Estab. 1887; pub; D & E; ent. req.
HS grad, ACT; 4 yr; degrees, B.A, B.S, M.A; schol; 59 SC, 19 LC,
23 GC; enrl. D 180, grad. 10. Tui. $8 per cr. hr, non-res. $16.25.

Art Education	Drawing
Art History	Graphics & Graphic Design
Ceramics	Painting
Design	Sculpture

Adult classes: Weaving, ceramics and painting; tui. same as above.

Summer School: Dr. William Jones, Dir; courses in all the above fields; tui. $8 res, $16.25 non-res, grad. res. $10.25, grad. non-res. $20.25.

MORRIS

UNIVERSITY OF MINNESOTA, MORRIS, 56267.
Tel: (612) 589-2211
Fred Peterson, Coordinator Art History, Lois Hodgell, Coordinator Studio Arts; 3 FT, 1 PT instr. Estab. 1960; pub; D & E; ent. req. HS dipl; 4 yr; degrees, B.A.(Art History, Studio Arts); 7 SC, 8 LC; enrl. maj. 45. Tui. $630 per yr, $210 quarterly; campus res. $1098.

Aesthetics	Painting
Art Education	Photography
Ceramics	Sculpture
Drawing	Stage Design
Graphic Arts	Theatre Arts

NORTHFIELD

CARLETON COLLEGE, Department of Art, 55057.
Tel: (507) 645-4431 Exten. 219
D. K. Haworth, R. I. Jacobson, Co-Chmn; 6 FT instr. Estab. 1921; pvt; 4 yr; degree; schol; 14 SC, 15 LC; enrl. maj. 30, others 550. Tui. $4600 all inclusive; campus res.
Art History
General Art

ST. OLAF COLLEGE,* Department of Art, 55057.
Tel: (507) 645-5621
Arnold W. Flaten, Chmn; 4 FT, 2 PT instr. Estab. 1932; den; 4 yr; degree; 9 SC, 1 LC; enrl. 400.

Architecture	Drawing & Painting
Art History	Film
Ceramics	Graphics
Design	Sculpture
Drafting	Teacher Training

ST. CLOUD

ST. CLOUD STATE UNIVERSITY, Department of Art, 56301.
Tel: (612) 255-4283
Dr. James Roy, Chmn; 14 FT, 8 PT instr. Pub; D & E; ent. req. HS dipl; 4 yr; degrees, B.A, B.S, M.S, M.A.(Studio Art); 65 SC, 15 LC, 20 GC; enrl. maj. 400, students 60. Tui. undergrad: $9 per cr. hr. res, $18 per cr. hr. non-res, grad: $11.50 per cr. hr. res, $22.50 per cr. hr. non-res. Summer School.

Advertising Design	Illustration
Aesthetics	Jewelry
Art Education	Lettering
Ceramics	Museum Staff Training
Commercial Art	Painting
Display	Photography
Drawing	Sculpture
Glass Blowing	Teacher Training
Graphic Arts	Textile Design
Graphic Design	Weaving
History of Art & Archaeology	

ST. JOSEPH

✠COLLEGE OF SAINT BENEDICT, Art Department, 56374.
Tel: (612) 363-5777 Exten. 5910
Sister Dennis Frandrup, Chmn; D 6 FT, 3 PT, E 2 PT instr. Estab. 1913, den, D & E, W, ent. req. HS grad. or equivalent; Academic Exchange Program with St. John's Univ, Collegeville, Minn; 4 yr; degree, B.A.(Art Maj); schol. & fel; enrl. 1500, maj. 90, others 400.

Art History (many specialized courses)	Painting
	Photography
Ceramics	Printmaking
Drawing	Sculpture
Graphic Arts	Teacher Training
Lettering	Theatre Arts

Children's Sat. classes; enrl. 40.

ST. PAUL

THE COLLEGE OF ST. CATHERINE, Visual Arts Department, 2004 Randolph, 55105. Tel: (612) 698-5571 Exten. 6635
Robert Clark Nelson, Chmn; 6 FT, 3 PT instr. Pvt; D; W; ent. req. HS dipl; 4 yr; degree, B.A.(Art); schol.

Art Education	History of Art & Archaeology
Arts Core Program	Jewelry
Ceramics	Lettering
Drawing	Painting

Graphic Arts	Photography
Graphic Design	Sculpture

Children's classes: Summer high school workshop.
Summer School: Robert Clark Nelson, Dir.

HAMLINE UNIVERSITY, Department of Art, 55104.
Tel: (612) 641-2230
Dr. Frederick D. Leach, Chmn; 5 FT, 2-3 PT instr. Estab. 1859; pvt; D; 4 yr; degree; 12 SC, 10 LC; enrl. maj. 120, others 350. Tui. $2450 per yr.
Fine Arts

MACALESTER COLLEGE, Department of Art, 1600 Grand Ave, 55105. Tel: (612) 647-6279
Anthony Caponi, Head; 4 FT, 4 PT instr. Estab. 1946; den; D; 4 yr; degrees; 9 SC, 8 LC; schol; av. enrl. per class 20. Tui. $3000; campus res.

Aesthetics	Modern & Oriental Art
American Art	Painting
Ceramics	Primitive Art
Design	Principals
Drawing	Processes & Application
Graphic Arts	Sculpture
History of Art	Senior Seminar

Summer School: Anthony Caponi, Chmn; Tui. 1 course $180, 2 courses $360 for 4 wk. from June 8-July 3; 2nd session July 6-31.

SCHOOL OF THE ASSOCIATED ARTS, 344 Summit Ave, 55102.
Tel: (612) 224-3416
Ronald Swenson, Head Fine Arts Div, Virginia Rahja, Dir, John Lenertz, Head Commercial Div, Dean DuVander, Head Interior Design Div; 10 FT, 9 PT instr. Estab. 1923; pvt; ent. req. HS grad; 3-6 yr; Cert, B.F.A, M.F.A; schol, fels; 63 SC, 27 LC, 14 GC. Tui. $2200 per yr, $1100 per sem.

Advertising	Graphic Art
Advertising Art	History of Architecture
Architectural Design & Rendering	History of Art
	Illustration
Business Practices (for Interior Designers)	Interior Design
	Display & Package Design
Color Psychology	Painting
Commercial Art	Photography
Creative Design	Sculpture
Drafting	Teacher Training
Drawing	Textiles
Environmental Design	Typography

Summer School: Tui. $750 for 12 wk, from May 25 to Aug. 14.

UNIVERSITY OF MINNESOTA, College of Home Economics, Design Department, McNeal Hall, 55108. Tel: (612) 373-1015
Gertrude Esteros, Head; 9 FT, 7 PT instr. Estab. 1912; pub; D; co-ed; ent. req. HS dipl, in upper 60 percentile; 4 yr; degrees, B.S, M.A, M.S, Ph.D; schol; 46 SC, 18 LC and seminars per quarter; enrl. undergrad. maj. interior design 299, design 74, costume design 61, housing 45, grad. 42. Tui. $228 per quarter not incl. incidental fees; campus res. $468 per quarter.

Art History	History of Costume
Costume Design & Construction	History of Decorative Arts
Color	History of European Furniture & Interiors
Drawing	Interior Design
Design	Housing
Fashion Arts	Jewelry
Fashion Illustration	Textile Design
History of American Furniture & Interiors	

Summer School: Offerings varied each year.

ST. PETER

GUSTAVUS ADOLPHUS COLLEGE, Art Department, Schaefer Fine Arts Center, 56082. Tel: (507) 931-4300 Exten. 462
Bruce A. McClain, Chmn; 4 FT, 1 PT instr, 1 artist-in-residence. Estab. 1876; den; D; co-ed; ent. req. HS grad, ent. exam; 4 yr; degree, B.A; schol; 27 SC; enrl. 2000, all school, art 750, maj. 80. Tui. $3800 per yr. (comprehensive fee); part-time $200 per course.

Art Education	Jewelry
Basic Design	Life Drawing
Bronze Casting	Painting
Ceramics	Photography
Costume Design & Construction	Printmaking
	Sculpture
Drawing	Stage Design
Film History	Teacher Training
Film Making	Textile Design
Graphic Design	Theatre Arts
History of Art	Weaving

Summer School: Dean Ellis J. Jones, Dir; tui. $200 per course; two 4 wk. terms, June 6-July 3 and July 8-Aug. 2; 1973 enrl. approx. 50.

Ceramics
Painting

Photography
Printmaking

WILLMAR

WILLMAR COMMUNITY COLLEGE, 56201.
  Tel: (612) 235-2131
Robert Mattson, Dept. Head, 1 FT, 1 PT instr. Estab. 1962-63; pub; D & E; ent. req. HS dipl; 2 yr; degrees, A.A, A.S, A.A.A; 8 SC, 3 LC; enrl. D 50, maj. 15. Tui. $8 per hr; no campus res.

Art Education
Ceramics
Display
Drawing
Graphic Arts
Graphic Design

History of Art & Archaeology
Introduction to Studio Practices
Painting
Structure
Teacher Training

Adult hobby classes: Painting, etching, design and history of art.

WINONA

✣WINONA STATE COLLEGE,* Division of Fine & Applied Arts, Department of Art, 55987. Tel: (612) 334-3012
Floretta Murray, Dir; 2 FT, 1 PT instr. Estab. 1858; pub; 5 yr; degrees, B.S, B.A, M.S.Educ; schol; 14 SC, 5 LC.

Art Structure
Commercial Art
Design & Crafts
History of Art
Interior Design
Introduction to Art

Lettering
Painting
Pottery
Teacher Training
Weaving

Summer School: Two 5 wk. sessions.

MISSISSIPPI

BOONEVILLE

NORTHEAST MISSISSIPPI JUNIOR COLLEGE, Art Department, 38829.
Barbara B. Curlee, Chmn. Dept; 2 FT instr. Estab. 1948; pub; D & E; ent. req. HS dipl, ent. exam; 2 yr; no degrees; schol; 5 SC, 3 LC; enrl. D 1800, maj. 30. Tui. $91 per yr; campus res. $221.

Aesthetics
Art Education
Art History
Ceramics
Drafting

Drawing
Painting
Teacher Training
Theatre Arts

CLEVELAND

✣DELTA STATE COLLEGE, Art Department, 38732.
  Tel: (601) 843-2151
Malcolm Mark Norwood, Head; 9 FT instr. Estab. 1924; pub; D & E; ent. req. HS grad. or ent. exam; 4 yr; degrees, B.A, B.F.A, B.S, B.S.E; 33 SC, 9 LC; enrl. D 1165, E 85, maj. 115. Tui. $440; campus res. $592.

Advertising Design
Art Education
Ceramics
Commercial Art
Drawing
Graphic Arts
Graphic Design
Handicrafts
History of Art & Archaeology

Industrial Design
Lettering
Painting
Paper Mache
Sculpture
Stage Design
Stitchery
Teacher Training
Weaving

Summer School: Malcolm M. Norwood, Head; tui. $120 for term of 4 wk. beginning May 31; 1975 enrl. 242.

Art for Elementary Grades
Art History
Ceramics
Commercial Design

Drawing
General Art & Design
Interior Decoration

CLINTON

MISSISSIPPI COLLEGE, Art Department, 39056.
  Tel: (601) 924-5131
Dr. Samuel M. Gore, Head; D 3 FT, 2 PT, E 2 PT instr. Estab. coll, 1825, art dept. 1950; den; ent. req. HS grad; degrees, B.A, B.Educ.(Art), M.Educ.(Art); Freshman Art Merit, schol. and student assistantships offered; 22 SC, 3 LC; enrl. maj. 80, others 300. Tui. $500 per sem; campus res. $250 per sem.

Art Education
Art History

Drawing & Painting
Foundry Casting

Ceramics
Commercial Art

Interior Design
Sculpture

Summer School: Samuel M. Gore, Dir; tui. $25 per sem. hr.

Art Appreciation
Art Education
Basic Design

Ceramics
Painting

COLUMBUS

MISSISSIPPI UNIVERSITY FOR WOMEN, Department of Art, Fine Arts Building, Room 104, 39701. Tel: (601) 328-4881
Charles E. Ambrose, Head; 10 FT, 1 PT instr. Estab. 1885; pub; D & E; W; ent. req. HS grad; 4 yr; degrees, B.A, B.S, B.F.A; schol; 38 SC, 8 LC, 5 GC; enrl. maj. 200, others 800. Tui. $237 per sem, non-res. $537 per sem; total expenses for res.(incl fees and room and board) $717 per sem.

Advertising Art
Art Education
Art History
Ceramics
Commercial Design
Costume Design
Design
Drafting
Drawing and Painting

Fabric Design
Fashion Drawing
General Art
Glassblowing
Interior Design
Jewelry
Printmaking
Sculpture
Weaving

Children's classes, Sat; $10 for 8 wk.
      Summer School: Charles E. Ambrose, Dir.

Art Education
Ceramics
Crafts
Drawing & Painting

Graduate Research & Studio
Interior Design
Printmaking

ELLISVILLE

JONES COUNTY JUNIOR COLLEGE,* Art Department, 39437.
  Tel: (601) 477-3141
James E. Davis, Instr; 2 FT instr. Estab. 1927; pub; D; co-ed; ent. req. HS dipl; 2 yr; degree, A.A; schol; 12 SC, 4 LC; enrl. D 100, E 12, maj. 15, others 12. Tui. $120; campus res. $405.

Advertising Design
Architecture
Art Education
Ceramics
Commercial Art
Display

Drafting
Drawing
Graphic Arts
History of Art & Archaeology
Lettering
Painting

Adult hobby classes in painting; tui. $5 per quarter hr; enrl. 20.
      Summer School: B.F. Ogletree, Dir; courses offered same as above; tui. $40 for term of 4 wk. beginning June; 1969 enrl. 768.

HATTIESBURG

UNIVERSITY OF SOUTHERN MISSISSIPPI, School of Fine Arts, Department of Art, 39401.
Jeff R. Bowman, Chmn. Estab. 1910, present name 1962; ent. req. HS grad, ACT; degrees; schol. and fel.

WILLIAM CAREY COLLEGE, Art Department, Tuscan Ave, 39401.
  Tel: (601) 582-5051 Exten. 237.
Lucile Parker, Chmn; 2 FT, 1 PT instr. Estab. coll. 1908, dept. 1973; den; D & E; ent. req. 15 HS cr; 4 yr; degrees, B.A, B.S, B.M, B.S.N, M.M; 7 SC, 3 LC; enrl. art D 120, E 25, minors 14. Tui. $620 per sem, PT $180, plus $30 per sem. hr; campus res. $395 per sem.

Aesthetics
Art Education
Basic Design
Ceramics
Copper Enameling
Costume Design & Construction

Drawing
History of Art & Archaeology
Mosaics
Painting
Teacher Training
Theatre Arts

Adult hobby classes, ceramics, painting; tui. $25 per sem; enrl. 48.
      Summer School: Dr. Joseph M. Ernest, Acad. V.Pres; tui. $180 for term of 5 wk. beginning June 1.

Art for Elementary Teachers
Drawing

Painting
Principles of Education

JACKSON

JACKSON STATE COLLEGE,* Department of Art, Lynch at Dalton St, 39207. Tel: (601) 948-8533
Lawrence A. Jones, Head; 8 FT instr. Estab. 1949; pub; D; co-ed; enr. req. HS dipl; 4 yr; degree, B.S.(Maj. in Art); schol; 16 SC, 7 LC, 1 GC; enrl. D 486, maj. 112. Tui. $350; part-time $13 per quarter hr; grad. $16 per quarter hr; campus res. $74, 28 day period.

Advertising Design
Art Education
Ceramics
Costume Design & Construction

Jewelry
Leather
Painting
Stage Design

Drawing
Graphic Arts
History of Art & Archaeology
Adult hobby classes, Athenian Art Club activities; enrl. 80.
Teacher Training
Weaving

Summer School: Dr. Wilbert Greenfield, Dir; courses and tui. same as above.

LORMAN

ALCORN STATE UNIVERSITY,* Department of Fine Arts, 39096.
Tel: (601) 877-3711
Joyce J. Bolden, Chmn; 2 FT instr. Estab. 1871; pub; D & E; ent. req. HS dipl; 4 yr; degree, B.A; 6 SC, 2 LC; enrl. D 200, E 30. Tui. $800 per yr.
Art Education
Ceramics
Drawing
Graphic Arts
History of Art & Archaeology
Painting
Stage Design
Teacher Training
Theatre Arts

Summer School: Mel Hardin, Chmn.

MERIDIAN

MERIDIAN JUNIOR COLLEGE,* Art Department, 39301.
Tel: (601) 483-8241
Charles R. Shoults, Head; D 1 FT, E 1 FT instr. Estab. 1938; pub; 2 yr; degree, A.A; 3 SC, 1 LC; normal enrl. 150. Tui. $70, non-res. $100.
Ceramics
Design
Drawing & Painting
Independent Study
Printmaking
Sculpture

Summer School: Dr. William Scaggs, Dir; $5 per hr; Ceramics, Painting, enrl. 15.

MOORHEAD

MISSISSIPPI DELTA JUNIOR COLLEGE, Department of Fine Arts, 38761.
Joe Abrams, Chmn; Jean Abrams, Art Coordinator; 2 FT, 1 PT instr. Estab. 1926; pub; D & E; ent. req. HS dipl, ent. exam; 2 yr; degrees, A.A, A.S.(Commercial Art); 11 SC, 2 LC; enrl. D 68, E 29, maj. 28. Tui. $106 per yr; campus res. $309.
Advertising Design
Art Appreciation
Ceramics
Commercial Art
Drawing
Graphic Arts
Painting

Adult hobby classes, ceramics, painting; tui. $45 per class; enrl. 29.

RAYMOND

HINDS JUNIOR COLLEGE, Department of Art, 39154.
Tel: (601) 857-5261 Exten. 302
Bob A. Dunaway, Chmn; 4 FT instr. Estab. 1918; pub; D & E; ent. exam; 2 yrs; degree, A.A; 5 SC, 2 LC; enrl. D 400, E 75, maj. 60. Tui. $185 per yr; campus res. $700.
Advertising Design
Ceramics
Commercial Art
Display
Drawing
Lettering
Painting

Summer School: Bob A. Dunaway, Dir; tui. $42 for term of 5 wk. beginning June; 1973 enrl. 40.
Art Appreciation
Ceramics
Drawing
Introduction to Watercolors

SCOOBA

EAST MISSISSIPPI JUNIOR COLLEGE, Art and Photography Department, 39358. Tel: (601) 476-5669
Terry Cherry, Chmn; 1 FT instr Estab. 1927; pub; D & E; ent. req. HS dipl, ent. exam; 2 yr; degree, A.A; schol; 12 SC, 2 LC; enrl. D 35, maj. 20. Tui. non-res. $400 per yr; campus res. $1000.
Advertising Design
Art Appreciation
Ceramics
Commercial Art
Design
Display
Drafting
Drawing
Fashion Arts
Graphic Arts
History of Art Crafts
Illustration
Inventive Crafts
Painting
Photography
Sculpture

TOUGALOO

✠TOUGALOO COLLEGE,* Department of Art, 39174.
Tel: (601) 982-4242
Ronald Schnell, Asst. Prof.

UNIVERSITY

UNIVERSITY OF MISSISSIPPI, Department of Art, 38677.
Tel: (601) 232-7211
Robert L. Tettleton, Chmn; 8 FT, 6 PT instr. Estab. 1949; pub; 4 yr; degrees, M.A.(Art History, Art Education), M.F.A.(Painting, Printmaking, Ceramics, Design, Sculpture); enrl. maj. 150, grad. 20, others. 350. Tui. $276.50, non-res. $576 50, no SC fees; campus res.
Art Education
Art History
Ceramics
Design
Drawing
Painting
Printmaking
Sculpture
Teacher Training (with Dept. of Educ)

Summer School: Two 6 wk. sessions.

MISSOURI

CANTON

CULVER-STOCKTON COLLEGE,* Division of Fine Arts, 63435.
Tel: (314) 288-5221 Exten. 60
Dr. A. Wesley Tower, Head; 2 FT instr. Estab. 1853; pvt; D; co-ed; ent. req. HS grad, ACT or coll. board ent. exam; 4 yr; degrees, B.A.(Visual Arts), B.S.(Art Educ), B.S.(Arts Management); schol; 16 SC, 6 LC; enrl. 844, maj. 30. Tui. $1410; campus res. $950.
Aesthetics
Art Education
Ceramics
Costume Design & Construction
Drawing
Graphic Arts
History of Art & Archaeology
Illustration
Jewelry
Museum Staff Training
Painting
Photography
Sculpture
Stage Design
Teacher Training
Theatre Arts

A special pre-teacher training course called SITE (situations for initial teaching experiences). Arts Management program is a double maj. in arts and business.

Summer School: Olga Bays, Reg; Art Appreciation, Art Education, Ceramics; tui. $260 for two 5 wk. terms beginning June 8 and Aug. 14.

CAPE GIRARDEAU

SOUTHEAST MISSOURI STATE UNIVERSITY, Department of Art, Normal Ave, 63701. Tel: (314) 334-8211 Exten. 214
Jake Wells, Head; 10 FT, 2 PT instr. Univ. estab. 1873, dept. art, 1920; pub; D (limited E offerings); ent. req. HS grad; 4 yr; degrees, B.S, B.S.Educ, B.A, M.A.T; 26 SC, 8 LC, 18 GC, also independent study; enrl. dept. 1200. Tui. $110 per sem, non-res. $310; campus res $838-$898.
Art Appreciation
Art Education
Art History
Ceramics
Commercial Art
Crafts
Design
Drawing
Graphics
Jewelry & Metal
Oil Painting
Printmaking
Sculpture
Teacher Training
Watercolor
Weaving

Summer School: Jake Wells, Head; courses same as above, more grad. offerings in summer; two short sessions or full summer session; tui. $70, non-res. $160; enrl. dept. undergrad 200, grad. 50.

COLUMBIA

COLUMBIA COLLEGE, Art Department, Christian College Ave, 65201. Tel: (314) 449-0531
Sidney Larson, Chmn. Dept; 6 FT, 3 PT instr. Estab. 1851; pvt. den; D; ent. req. HS dipl. or equivalent, ACT or SAT requested, also accept transfer students; degrees, A.A, B.A, B.F.A; schol; 30 SC, 4 LC; enrl. maj. 125. Tui. $2150; campus res. $1340
Advertising Design
Architecture
Art Education
Ceramics
Commercial Art
Costume Design & Construction
Display
Drawing
Fashion Arts
Graphic Design
History of Art & Archaeology
Illustration
Jewelry
Lettering
Painting
Photography
Sculpture
Stage Design
Teacher Training
Textile Design
Theatre Arts

STEPHENS COLLEGE, Art Department, 65201.
Tel: (314) 442-2211 Exten. 302
Gardiner McCauley, Head; 9 FT, 3 PT instr. Estab. 1833; pvt; W; ent. req. SAT or ACT plus interview, advanced placement on appli-

cation to dept. head; 3-4 yr; degrees, B.A, B.F.A; schol, student assistantships for jr. and sr; off-campus and overseas study programs, 97 SC, 13 LC, enrl. maj. 150, dept. 1500 per yr. Tui. incl. room and board $4175.

Ceramics	Painting
Drawing	Photography & Film
Environmental Design	Printmaking
Graphic Design	Sculpture
History of Art	Stained Glass
Interior Design	Teacher Training

⚓UNIVERSITY OF MISSOURI, Art Department, A 126 Fine Arts, 65201   Tel: (314) 882-3555
Lawrence Rugolo, Chmn; 18 FT instr, 10 grad. teaching asst. Estab. 1901; pub; D & E; ent. req. contact Admis. Office; 4-6 yr; degrees, B.A. in Art (Coll. Arts & Sciences), B.S. in Art Educ.(Coll. Educ), M.A. in Art, M.Ed, D.Ed.(Coll Educ); 76 SC, 1 LC, 53 GC; enrl. maj. 285, gen. sem. 1600. Tui. free to Mo. res. and grad. students, Univ. fees vary; campus res. Art History courses are offered by the Department of Art History and Archaeology.

Art Appreciation	Jewelry
Art Education	Painting
Ceramics	Photography
Crafts	Printmaking
Design	Sculpture
Drawing	Serigraphy
Graphic Design	Weaving

Summer School: Tui. as above; enrl. 175.

Art Education	Painting
Ceramics	Photography
Design	Printmaking
Drawing	Sculpture
Graphic Design	Weaving

FAYETTE

CENTRAL METHODIST COLLEGE, Art Department, 65248.
   Tel: (816) 248-3391 Exten 238
Pat Stapleton, Head; 1 FT instr. Estab. 1855; pvt; D; 4 yr; 13 SC, 4 LC. Tui. incl. room and board $2550. Summer School.

Art History	Painting
Ceramics	Printmaking
Design	Sculpture
Drawing	Teacher Education

FERGUSON

FLORISSANT VALLEY COMMUNITY COLLEGE, Art Department, 3400 Pershall Rd, 63135. Tel: (314) 524-2020 Exten 221
Charles J. Jones, Chmn; 9 FT, 20 PT instr. Estab. 1963; pub; D & E; ent. req. HS dipl; 2 yrs; degrees, A.A, A.S; schol; 33 SC, 3 LC; enrl. D 250, E 100. Tui. $15 and $42 per cr. hr; out of state and foreign, $54.

Advertising Design	History of Art & Archaeology
Ceramics	Illustration
Commercial Art	Lettering
Drawing	Painting
Figure Drawing	Photography
Graphic Arts	Sculpture

Summer School: Tui. $15 cr. hr for term of 9 wk. beginning June 12; 1975 enrl. 150.

FULTON

WILLIAM WOODS/WESTMINSTER COLLEGES, Department of Art, 65251. Tel: (314) 642-2251 Exten. 314
George E. Tutt, Chmn; 6 FT, 1 PT instr. Estab. 1870; pvt; D; William Woods W, Westminster M; cooperative program; ent. req. HS dipl, SAT; 4 yr; degrees, B.S, B.A, B.F.A; 44 SC, 13 LC; enrl. maj. 90-100- Tui. incl. room and board and fees $3875 (paid in installments).

Aesthetics	Jewelry
Art Education	Painting
Ceramics	Sculpture
Drawing	Stage Design
Fashion Arts	Teacher Training
Graphic Arts	Theatre Arts
History of Art & Archaeology	Weaving

JEFFERSON CITY

LINCOLN UNIVERSITY,* Art Department, Lafayette at Dunklin St, 65102.
James Dallas Parks, Head; 3 FT instr. Estab. 1927; pub; 4 yr; degrees, B.S.Art, B.S.Art Educ; enrl. maj. 69, others 365. Tui. $250, campus res. room and board $550.
Teacher Training

JOPLIN

MISSOURI SOUTHERN STATE COLLEGE, Art Department, Newman & Duquesne Rds, 64801. Tel: (417) 624-8100 Exten. 263
Darral A. Dishman, Head; 4 FT instr. Estab. 1965; pub; D & E; ent. req. HS dipl; 4 yrs; degrees, B.A, B.S.(Educ); schol; 19 SC, 5 LC; enrl. E 23, maj. 106. Tui. res. of Juco-Dist, $95 juco div. per sem, $150 senior div. per sem, res. Mo. outside dist, $150 per sem, non-res. $345 per sem; campus res. $880 fall-spring sem. only, $210 per summer school.

Art Appreciation	History of Art & Archaeology
Art Education	Jewelry
Ceramics	Painting
Commercial Art	Sculpture
Drawing	Teacher Training
Graphic Arts	Two & Three dimensional Design

Children's classes, sponsored by Spiva Art Center, taught by coll. students; tui. $20 for 10 sessions; enrl. 56.

KANSAS CITY

AVILA COLLEGE, Fine Arts Department, 11901 Wornall, 64145.
   Tel: (816) 942-8400 Exten. 259
Sister Margaret Reinhart, Art Coordinator; 3 FT, 5 PT instr. Estab. 1916; den; D & E; ent. req. HS dipl, SAT or ACT; 4 yr; degree, B.A; schol; 35 SC, 5 LC; enrl. D 300, E 50, maj. 40. Tui. incl. campus res. $2850 per yr, PT $53 per cr. hr, E PT $35.

Art Education	Jewelry
Batik	Lettering
Ceramics	Painting
Drawing	Photography
Enameling	Sculpture
Field Study	Stage Design
Gallery Design	Teacher Training
Graphic Arts	Textile Design
History of Art & Archaeology	Theatre Arts
Illustration	Visual Communication

Summer School: Sister Margaret Reinhart, Dir; tui. D $45 per cr. hr, E $30; campus res. $42-$52 per wk; term of 6 wk. begins June 11, 1976; enrl. 100.

Art Education	Graphics
Batik	Jewelry
Ceramics	Painting
Drawing	Textiles

KANSAS CITY ART INSTITUTE, 4415 Warwick Blvd, 64111.
   Tel: (816) 561-4852
John W. Lottes, Pres; Jerome L. Grove, Dean. Estab. 1885; pvt; D, E and Sat; ent. req. HS grad, art portfolio, personal interview, and ent. exam; 4 yr; degree, B.F.A; schol. and student loans; accredited by North Central Association of Coll. and Nat. Assoc. of Schools of Art; enrl. 550. Tui. $1275 per sem, three 15 wk. sem. offered.

Ceramics	Industrial Design
Environmental Design	Painting & Printmaking
Fibers	Photography & Cinematography
Graphic Design	Sculpture

UNIVERSITY OF MISSOURI-KANSAS CITY, Department of Art & Art History, 5100 Rockhill Rd, 64110. Tel: (816) 276-1501
James C. Olson, Chancellor; Lee Anne Miller, Chmn; 12 FT, 1 PT instr. Estab. 1933; pub; D & E; ent. req. contact Admis. Office; enrl. maj. 210. Tui. $305 per sem, non-res. $845 for 1975-76

Art History	Painting
Drawing	Printmaking
Graphic Design	Sculpture

Summer School: 1 term. For information contact Admis. Office.

KIRKSVILLE

NORTHEAST MISSOURI STATE UNIVERSITY, Division of Fine Arts, 63501.
Dale A. Jorgenson, Head; 9 FT, 2 PT instr. Estab. 1867; D & E; degrees, 4 yr. plus M.A.(Art Educ); 27 SC, 7 LC, 8 GC; enrl. maj. 175, total 5700. Tui. $140 per sem, non-res. $380. Summer Session.

LIBERTY

WILLIAM JEWELL COLLEGE,* Art Department, 64068.
   Tel: (816) 781-3806
David Busch, Head. Estab. 1950; ent. req HS grad; 4 SC, 1 LC.
Drawing
Painting
Sculpture

MARYVILLE

NORTHWEST MISSOURI STATE UNIVERSITY, Department of Art,
    64468. Tel: (816) 582-3591, 2145
James Broderick, Chmn; 9 FT instr. Estab. 1905; pub; D & E;
ent. req. HS dipl; 4 yr; degrees, A.B, B.S.(Educ), B.F.A; schol. and
loans; 45 SC, 20 LC; enrl. maj. 200, others 750, total 5100. Tui.
$165, non-res $360; campus res. $490.

Art Education	Jewelry
Ceramics	Photography
Design	Printmaking
Drawing & Painting	Sculpture
History of Art	

Summer School: 10 wk. (two 5 wk. sessions plus full 10 wk.)
incl. grad. study.

NEOSHO

CROWDER COLLEGE, Department of Art, 64850.
    Tel: (417) 451-3223
Richard Boyt, Instr; 1 FT, 5 PT instr. Estab. 1964; pub; D & E.
ent. req. HS grad. or equivalent; 2 yr; degrees, A.A, A.A.S; schol;
enrl. D 1000, E 300, maj. 15, others 100. Tui. $80 per sem, PT
$8-$10 per sem. hr, out-of-district $145, out-of-state $225;
campus res. $405.

Ceramics	Introduction to Visual Arts
Commercial Art	Painting
Drawing	Photography
History of Art	Weaving

Summer School: J. Cavanough, Dean of the Coll; varied academic
courses; tui. $8-$10 per sem. hr. for term of 8 wk. beginning in June.

NEVADA

COTTEY COLLEGE, Fine Arts Division, 64772.
    Tel: (417) 667-5547
Evelyn Milam, Pres; Harry Chew, Chmn; 3 FT instr. Estab. 1884;
pvt; D; W; ent. req. HS grad, AC Board; 2 yr; degree, A.A; 15 SC,
4 LC; enrl. maj. 12-15, total 369. Tui. incl. room and board $2750.

Art Appreciation	Fabric
Art History	Metal Craft
Ceramics	Mosaics
Design	Painting
Drawing	Printmaking
Enameling	Wood

ST. CHARLES

THE LINDENWOOD COLLEGES, Art Department, 63301.
    Tel: (314) 723-7152 Exten. 241
W. Dean Eckert, Chmn; 5 FT, 4 PT instr. Estab. 1827; pvt; D & E;
ent. req. HS dipl, ent. exam; 4 yr; degrees, B.A, B.S, B.F.A, M.A;
schol; 42 SC, 24 LC; enrl D 200, E 100, maj. 45, continuing educ.
25. Tui. $2250 per yr.

Art Education	Painting
Ceramics	Photography
Drawing	Printmaking
History of Art & Archaeology	Sculpture
Museum Staff Training	Teacher Training

ST. JOSEPH

MISSOURI WESTERN STATE COLLEGE, Department of Fine Arts,
    4525 Downs Dr, 64507. Tel: (816) 233-7192 Exten. 420, 422
James Estes, Chmn; 5 FT instr. Estab. 1968; pub; D & E; ent. req.
HS dipl; 4 yr; degrees, B.A.(Art); B.S.(Art Educ); schol; 17 SC,
8 LC; enrl. D 3600, E 400, maj. 65. Tui. $270, non-res. $720;
campus res. $850.

Aesthetics	History of Art & Archaeology
Art Education	Painting
Ceramics	Photography
Costume Design & Construction	Sculpture
Drawing	Stage Design
Graphic Arts	Teacher Training
Graphic Design	Theatre Arts

Summer School: Acad. V.Pres; tui. $67.50-$180 for term of 8
wk. beginning June; 1975 enrl. 1500.

Art Appreciation	Ceramics
Art Education	Drawing
Art History	Painting

ST. LOUIS

ART-MART STUDIO, 9983 Manchester Rd, 63122.
    Tel: (314) 822-3900
Jim W. Harmon, Dir; D 11 PT, E 6 PT instr. Estab. 1955; pvt;
17 SC.

Graphics	Portrait Painting
Painting	Sculpture

Children's classes Sat. AM.

MARYVILLE COLLEGE 13550 Conway Rd,
    63141.
Kent Addison, Fine Arts Coordinator; 4 FT, 7 PT instr. Estab.
1872; pvt; D & E; ent. req. HS dipl; 4 yr; degrees, Cert. Interior
Design, B.A.(Studio), B.F.A.(Studio, Interior Design); schol;
75 SC, 10 LC; enrl. D 178, maj. 71, others 101. Tui. $2150 per
yr; campus res. $1400.

Ceramics	Jewelry
Drafting	Lettering
Drawing	Painting
Graphic Arts	Photography
History of Art & Archaeology	Sculpture

NOTRE DAME COLLEGE, Art Department, 320 E. Ripa Ave, 63125.
    Tel: (314) 544-0455 Exten. 36
Sister Angelee Fuchs, Dir; 2 FT, 2 PT instr. Estab. 1954; pvt;
D & E; ent. req. HS dipl, ACT; 3-4 yr; degrees, Teacher Cert, B.A;
schol; 23 SC, 6 LC; enrl. D 25, maj. 25. Tui. $1050 per yr.
Adult hobby classes, ceramics, crafts, fabric design.

Summer School: Sister Angelee Fuchs, Dir; courses offered,
Crafts, Painting; tui. $35 per cr. hr.

WASHINGTON UNIVERSITY, 63130.
    Tel: (314) 863-0100

School of Architecture, Givens Hall, Box 1079.
C. Michaelides, Dean; 19 FT, 19 PT instr. Estab. 1910; pvt; D;
4 yr; degrees, B.A.(Architecture), M.Arch, M.Arch. & Urban
Design; enrl. undergrad. 200, grad. 115. Tui. $3350; campus
res. Combined degree programs at the grad. level with Grad. Sch.
Business Admin. and Grad. Sch. Social Work.
Courses in ‡Architecture.

School of Fine Arts. Tel: (314) 863-0100 Exten. 4257
Lucian Krukowski, Dean; 25 FT, 12 PT instr. Estab. 1879; pvt; D;
ent. req. HS grad. with appropriate distribution of subjects, SAT or
ACT, portfolio; 4 yr; degrees, B.F.A, M.F.A; enrl. 430. Tui.
$3350; campus res. $1650.

Ceramics	Painting
Fashion Design	Photography
Graphic Communication	Printmaking
Metalsmithing	Sculpture
Multi-Media	

Summer workshop for HS students.

WEBSTER COLLEGE,* Art Department, 470 E. Lockwood St,
    63119. Tel: (314) 968-0500.
Gabriel M. Hoare, Chmn; 7 FT, 3 PT instr. Estab. 1915; pvt; D; ent.
req. HS dipl, 2 average; 4 yr; degree, B.A.(art maj. 41-55 studio
hrs, 9 hrs. art history); schol, fel, work-study grants; 34 SC, 10
LC; 4 art teacher cert; enrl. maj. 85; others approx. 1000. Tui.
$70 per cr. hr, campus res, room and board $1000.

Color Workshop	Graphic Workshop
Communication Workshop	History of American Landscape
Drawing V & VI	Photography
Elementary Art Practicum	Materials Workshop
Etching	Photographic Interpretation of
Film Workshop	Modern Poetry

Summer School: Dr. Fred Stopsky, Dir; design, painting, graphics; tui. $70 per cr. hr. for 6 wk. term beginning June 19; enrl. art
classes approx. 30, M.A.T. approx. 200.

SPRINGFIELD

DRURY COLLEGE,* Art and Art History Department, 65802.
    Tel: (417) 869-0511
John H. Simmons, Chmn; 2 FT, 1 PT instr. Estab. 1873; pvt; den;
4 yr; degree; schol; 12 SC, 5 LC; enrl. 200.
General Art
Teacher Training

SOUTHWEST MISSOURI STATE UNIVERSITY, Department of Art,
    901 S. National, 65802. Tel: (417) 831-1561 Exten. 204
James L. Richardson, Head; 24 FT, 9 PT instr. Estab. 1901; D & E;
ent. req. HS grad, ent. exam; 4 yr; degrees, B.F.A, B.S.(Educ, Educ.
Comprehensive), B.A; schol; 31 SC, 14 LC; enrl. maj. 450, others
2000, total 12,000. Tui. $180, non-res. $270; campus res. $405 per
sem.

Art Appreciation	Jewelry & Silversmithing
Art Education	Painting
Art History	Photography & Cinematography
Ceramics	Printmaking & Lithography

Drawing	Sculpture & Bronze Casting
Fibers	Teacher Training (with Dept.
Graphic Design	of Educ)

Summer School: Dean Russell Keeling, Dir; courses selected from the above curriculum; tui. $20 per cr. hr; 4, 5 and 8 wk. sessions; enrl. total 3500; special workshops available during summer session.

UNION

✠EAST CENTRAL JUNIOR COLLEGE, Art Department, P.O Box 529, 63084. Tel: (314) 583-5193
Larry Pogue, Head; 1 FT, 6 PT instr. Estab. 1968; pub; D & E; ent. req. HS dipl, ent. exam; 2 yr; degrees, A.A, A.A.S; schol; 8 SC, 8 LC; enrl. D 370, E 120, maj. 37. Tui. $110 per sem. Summer School.

Art Appreciation	History of Art & Archaeology
Art Education	Introduction to Art
Commercial Art	Painting
Drawing	Printmaking
Graphic Design	Sculpture
Handicrafts	

WARRENSBURG

CENTRAL MISSOURI STATE UNIVERSITY, Department of Art, 64093. Tel: (816) 429-4480
Edwin C. Ellis, Head; 12 FT instr. Estab. 1871; pub; ent. req. HS grad; 4 yr; degrees, B.S, B.S.Educ, B.A, B.F.A, M.S.Educ; schol; LC, Lab.C; normal enrl. 9000-10,000, 20-30 per art class. Tui. $100. Summer School.

Advertising Art	Drawing
Advertising Design	Environmental Design
Art & Architecture	Interior Decoration & Design
Art Appreciation	Lithography
Art Education	Painting
Art History	Printmaking
Calligraphy	Product Design
Commercial Design	Sculpture & Ceramics
Designing for Television	

MONTANA

BILLINGS

EASTERN MONTANA COLLEGE, 1500 N. 30th St, 59101. Tel: (406) 657-2011
Ben C. Steele, Head; D 3 FT, E 3 FT instr. Estab. 1927; pub; ent. req. HS grad; 4 yr; degrees, B.S. in Educ, B.A. in Liberal Arts; affiliated with Univ. of Montana; 19 SC, 1 LC.

Ceramics	History of Art
Commercial Illustration	Lettering and Layout
Crafts	Metalwork & Jewelry
Design	Painting
Drawing	Sculpture
Graphics	

Summer School: Usually 6 courses with emphasis on courses for teachers.

ROCKY MOUNTAIN COLLEGE, 1511 Poly Drive, 59102. Tel: (406) 245-6151
Robert Morrison, Assoc Prof; 1 FT, 1 PT instr. Estab. 1947; pvt; D; ent. req. HS dipl; 4 yr; degree B.F.A; schol; 13 SC, 6 LC; enrl. D 72, maj. 13, others 2. Tui. $1650 per yr; campus res. $1100.

Art Education	History of Art & Archaeology
Ceramics	Lettering
Commercial Art	Painting
Drawing	Photography
Graphic Arts	Sculpture
Graphic Design	Stage Design

BOZEMAN

MONTANA STATE UNIVERSITY, School of Art, 59715. Tel: (406) 994-4501
John Bashor, Dir; 13 FT, 7 PT instr. College estab. 1893; pub; ent. req. non-res. upper half of grad. class or exam; 4 yr; degrees, B.A. Art, M.A, M.A.A; 10 LC, 25 Lab.C, 3 GC; enrl. maj. 250, others 417. Tui. $500 for 3 quarters, non-res. $1371; campus res. room and board about $1110 for 3 quarters.

| Applied Arts | Art History |
| Art Education | Professional Design |

Summer School: 5 FT instr; two 4½ wk. sessions or full 9 wk. quarter.

School of Architecture, Creative Arts Complex. Tel: (406) 994-4255
Ilmar Reinvald, Dir; 14 FT, 1 PT instr. Pub; 5 yr; degree, B.Arch; 15 Lab.C, 14 LC; enrl. maj. 300. Tui. $500 for 3 quarters, non-res. $1371; campus res. room and board about $1100 for 3 quarters.
Architecture

DILLON

WESTERN MONTANA COLLEGE, Art Department, 710 S. Atlantic, 59725. Tel: (406) 683-7312
Don Walters, Chmn; 3 FT instr. Estab. 1897; pub; D & E; ent. req. HS dipl; 4 yrs; degrees, B.S, M.A, Assoc; schol; 15 SC, 6 LC, 21 GC. Tui. $144.50 per quarter; campus res. $780.

Advertising Design	Illustration
Aesthetics	Industrial Design
Art Education	Jewelry
Ceramics	Lettering
Commercial Art	Painting
Drafting	Photography
Drawing	Sculpture
Graphic Arts	Stage Design
Graphic Design	Teacher Training
Handicrafts	Theatre Arts
History of Art & Archaeology	

Summer School: Don Walters, Chmn; courses offered same as regular yr; tui. $134.50 for term of 4½ and 9 wk. beginning June 18.

GREAT FALLS

COLLEGE OF GREAT FALLS, Depart of Art, 1301 20th St. S, 59405. Tel: (406) 452-9584
Francis W. Dirocco, Dean of Studies; Jack N. Franjevic, Head; 2 FT, 2 PT instr. Estab. 1933; den; D & E; 4 yr; degrees; SC, Lab.C, LC; enrl. varies 1200-1300. Tui. $50 per sem. cr.

Art Education	Photography
Ceramics	Printmaking
Crafts	Sculpture
Design	Silversmithing
Drawing & Painting	Textile Design
Jewelry	

Summer School: Richard Gretch, Dir; 6 wk.

HAVRE

NORTHERN MONTANA COLLEGE, Department of Art, 611 16th St, 59501. Tel: (406) 265-7821 Exten. 231
E. James Brownson, Assoc Prof; 2 FT instr. Estab. 1929; pub; D & E; ent. req. HS dipl; 4 yr; degrees A.A, B.S.(Educ), B.A, M.Sc. (Educ); schol; 15 SC, 5 LC, 9 grad; enrl. D 425, grad. 7. Tui. $450 per yr, $50 per mo, part-time $23.67; campus res. $950.50.

Art Education	Graphic Arts
Ceramics	Painting
Commercial Art	Sculpture
Drafting	Teacher Training
Drawing	

Children's classes, drawing, painting, sculpture, ceramics; tui. $1 enrl. fee; enrl. 60.

Summer School: Dr. Lee Spuhler, Dir; courses offered, Ceramics, Sculpture, Art Appreciation, Art Education; tui. $146.50 for term of 8 wk; enrl. 700 coll, 47 art classes.

MILES CITY

MILES COMMUNITY COLLEGE, Art Department, 2715 Dickinson St, 59301. Tel: (406) 232-3031
Sydney R. Sonneborn, Head; 1 FT, 2 PT instr. Estab. 1939; pub; D & E; co-ed; ent. req. HS grad, ent. exam; 2 yr; degrees, A.A, Junior Coll. Diploma; schol; 11 SC, 4 LC; enrl. D 72, E 85, maj. 5. Tui. $180, $8 per cr. hr. per quarter; no campus res.

Aesthetics	Drawing
Art Education	Humanities
Ceramics	Jewelry
Crafts	Painting
Drafting	Teacher Training

Adult hobby classes, painting, drawing, design, water color; tui. $8 per cr. hr; enrl. 85.
Youth program in summer for children 7 to 12; enrl. (1975) 40.
Summer School: Vernon R. Kailey, Pres; art courses depending on demand; tui. $8 for term of 7 wk. beginning June; enrl. 34.

MISSOULA

UNIVERSITY OF MONTANA, Art Department, 59801. Tel: (406) 243-4181
Prof. James Dew, Acting Chmn; 12 FT instr. Estab. 1909; pub; 4 yr; degrees, B.A, B.F.A, M.A, M.F.A; 28 SC, 18 LC, 26 GC; enrl. maj.

235, grad. 29, others 250. Tui. $162.60 per quarter (12-18 cr. hrs), non-res. $462.60 per quarter (12-18 cr. hrs).

Ceramics	Painting
Crafts	Printmaking
Design	Sculpture
Drawing	Teacher Training
History of Art	

Summer School: Prof. James Dew, Acting Chmn; 4th quarter full program.

NEBRASKA

CHADRON

CHADRON STATE COLLEGE, Division of Fine Arts, 69337.
Tel: (308) 432-4451 Exten. 317
Dr. Harry E. Holmberg, Chmn; 3 FT instr Estab. 1911; pub; D & E; co-ed; ent. req. HS grad; 125 sem. hr (usually 4 yr); degrees B.A, B.S.(Educ); 23 SC, 5 LC; enrl. maj. 75. Tui. $15.50 per hr, $27.50 per hr non-res; campus res. $950.

Aesthetics	History of Art
Art Education	Jewelry
Ceramics	Lettering
Commercial Art	Painting
Drafting	Sculpture
Drawing	Teacher Training
Glass Blowing	Theatre Arts
Graphic Arts	Weaving

Summer School: Dr. Harry E. Holmberg, Chmn; tui. $15.50 per hr. res; $27.50 per hr. non-res. for 2 five-wk. terms, first one starts June 7, 1976.

Advanced Art Studio	Elementary Art
Ceramics	Freehand Drawing
Creative Crafts	Oil Painting & Acrylics
Design & Color	

CRETE

DOANE COLLEGE,* Division of Fine Arts, 68333.
Tel: (402) 826-2161
Hubert Brown, Jr, Chmn. School estab. 1872; den; ent. req. coll. ent. exam. board schores; degree, B.A.
Summer School: Dr. A. J. Nebelsick, Dir.

HASTINGS

HASTINGS COLLEGE, Art Department, 68901.
Tel: (402) 463-2402
Prof. Gary E. Coulter, Chmn; 3 FT instr. Estab. 1925; den; ent. req. HS grad; 4 yr; degree, B.A; schol; 16 SC, 5 LC; enrl. maj. 50, others 350. Tui. $2050, room and board $1090; campus res.

Art Education	Drawing & Painting
Art History	Printmaking
Ceramics	Sculpture
Composition	

Summer School: Dr. A. L. Langvardt, Academic Dean; tui. $175 per unit for 6 wk. beginning June; enrl. 25.

KEARNEY

KEARNEY STATE COLLEGE,* School of Fine Arts and Humanities, Art Department, 68847. Tel: (308) 236-4449
Jack Karraker, Head; 40 FT instr. Estab. 1905; pub; 4 yr; degree, A.B; enrl. maj. 125, others 5000. Tui. res. $15.50 sem hr, non-res. $27.50 sem. hr.

Ceramics	Photography
Foundry	Sculpture
General Arts	Teacher Training
Glass Blowing	Textiles
Painting	

LINCOLN

UNIVERSITY OF NEBRASKA, LINCOLN, Department of Art, 203 Nelle Cochrane Woods Bldg, 68508. Tel: (402) 472-2631
Dan F. Howard, Chmn; D 17 FT, 20 PT, E 7 PT instr. Estab. 1912; pub; 4 & 6 yr; degrees, B.A, B.F.A, B.F.A.(Educ), M.F.A; schol. & fel; 74 SC, 30 LC, 44 GC; enrl. maj. 450, grad. 25, others 600. Tui. $18 per cr. hr, $270 per sem, $579 non-res; campus res.

Ceramics	Painting
Design	Photography
Drawing	Printmaking
Graphic Design	Sculpture
History & Criticism of Art	Teacher Training

Summer School: Alan Seagren, Dir; tui. $18 per cr. hr. for two 5-wk. sessions, June-Aug; enrl. 250.

NORFOLK

NORTHEAST TECHNICAL COMMUNITY COLLEGE, 801 E Benjamin, 68701. Tel: (402) 371-2020 Exten. 245
Patrick Keating, Instr; 1 FT instr. Estab. 1972; pub; D & E; ent. req. HS dipl; 2 yr; degree A.A; schol; 3 SC, 1 LC; enrl. D 50, E 25. Tui. $151 per sem; campus res. $900.

Advertising Design	Painting
Drawing	Photography
History of Art & Archaeology	Teacher Training

Adult hobby classes: Basic drawing, folk art, tole painting, macrame, crewel embroidery, oil & acrylic painting and metal sculpture; tui. $12.
Summer School: Patrick Keating, Dir; Photography, Art History; tui. $12.50 per hr. for term of 8 wk, beginning June 1

OMAHA

COLLEGE OF SAINT MARY, Art Department, 72nd & Mercy Rd, 68124. Tel: (402) 393-8800 Exten. 53
Tom Schlosser, Chmn; 2 FT instr. Estab. 1923; pvt; D & E; W; ent. req. HS dipl; 4 yr; degrees, B.A, B.S; schol; 11 SC, 5 LC; enrl. D 278 in Art, maj. 18, special 2. Tui. full-time $55 per cr. hr; campus res. tui, fees, board & room, etc. approx. $2800 per yr.

Aesthetics	Jewelry
Art Education	Lettering
Ceramics	Painting
Design	Photography
Drawing	Printmaking
Graphic Arts	Sculpture
History of Art & Archaeology	Teacher Training

CREIGHTON UNIVERSITY, Fine Arts Department, 2500 California St, 68178. Tel: (402) 536-3035
Frances Kraft, Chmn; 7 FT, 6 PT instr. Estab. 1966; den; D & E; co-ed; ent. req. regular coll. admis; 4 yr; degrees, B.A.(Maj. in Art), B.F.A; 29 SC, 12 LC; enrl. D 600, maj. 40. Tui. $2300 per yr, $72 per cr. hr; campus res. $1200.

Advertising Design	Intaglio
Aesthetics	Lithography
Art Education	Painting
Ceramics	Photography
Design	Pottery
Drawing	Sculpture
Foundry	Studio Fundamentals
History (Theory)	Teacher Training
History of Art & Archaeology	

Summer School: Father Don Doll, Dir; Ceramics, Art Workshop (for non-art majors); tui. $53 per cr. hr; one term of 5 wk, beginning June 7; enrl. 40.

UNIVERSITY OF NEBRASKA AT OMAHA,* Art Department, 60th & Dodge Sts, 68101; also Box 688, Downtown Station, 68101.
Peter Hill, Chmn; 9 FT, 4 PT instr. Estab. 1908 at Omaha Municipal Univ, merged with Univ. Nebraska 1968; pub; 4 yr; degrees, B.A, B.F.A; schol; 30 SC, 10 LC; enrl. maj. 140. Tui. $18 per cr. hr, non-res. $48.25 per cr. hr.

Art Education
Art History
Studio Art

College of Adult Education and Summer Sessions: William Utley, Dean; Tui. same as day school.

SEWARD

CONCORDIA TEACHERS COLLEGE, Art Department, 800 North Columbia, 68434.
William R. Wolfram, Assoc. Prof; 4 FT instr. Den; D & E; co-ed; ent. req. HS dipl, ent. exam; 4 yr; degrees, B.S, B.A; 12 SC, 4 LC, 2 GC; enrl. c. 60, maj. 36. Tui. $865; campus res. $252 sem.

Art Education	History of Art & Archaeology
Ceramics	Painting
Drawing	Sculpture
Graphic Arts	Teacher Training
Handicrafts	

Summer School: Larry Grothaus Dir; Art Education, Fundamentals of Art.

WAYNE

WAYNE STATE COLLEGE, Art Department, 68787.
Tel: (402) 375-2200 Exten. 235
Richard D. Lesh, Chmn; 3 FT instr. Estab. 1910; pub; ent. req. HS grad; 3-2/3 yr. (tri-mester); degrees, B.A, B.F.A; schol; 21 SC, 8 LC; enrl. maj. 65, others 700, total 2200. Tui. $27.50 per cr. hr.

Art History	Graphic Arts
Ceramics	Handicrafts

Design
Drafting (architectural &
　mechanical)
Drawing & Painting

Jewelry
Sculpture
Teacher Training
Watercolor

　Summer School: Lyle Seymour, Pres; two sessions, Apr. 28-
June 15, June 16-Aug. 4; tui. $180, $265 non-res.

NEVADA

RENO

UNIVERSITY OF NEVADA, RENO, Art Department, 89507.
　Tel: (702) 784-6682
William V. Howard, Chmn; 7 FT instr. Estab. 1940; pub; ent. req.
HS grad. and 16 units; 4 yr; degree, B.A; schol; 20 SC, 6 LC, 5 GC;
enrl. maj. 120, others 800. Summer school.

Art Education
Ceramics
Drawing
History of Art
Painting

Photography
Printmaking
Sculpture
Stitchery
Textile Design

NEW HAMPSHIRE

CONCORD

⚲ST. PAUL'S SCHOOL, Art Department, Art Center in Hargate,
　325 Pleasant St, 03301. Tel: (603) 225-3341 Exten. 58
Thomas R. Barrett, Head; 3 FT, 3 PT instr. Estab. 1967; pvt; D;
independent secondary boarding school, HS dipl; 8 SC, 1 LC; all
students boarding (496, 227 registrations). Tui. $3700.

Aesthetics
Architecture
Ceramics
Drawing
Graphic Arts

History of Art & Archaeology
Painting
Photography
Sculpture
Woodworking

　Summer School: Philip C. Bell, Dir. Advanced Studies Program; Introduction to Creative Arts; tui. $900 for term of 6 wk.
beginning June 22; 1975 enrl. 21.

DURHAM

UNIVERSITY OF NEW HAMPSHIRE, College of Liberal Arts,
　Department of the Arts, 03824.
Arthur Balderacchi, Chmn; 19 FT instr. Estab. 1941; pub; ent. req.
portfolio; 4 yr; degrees, B.A, B.F.A; schol; 33 SC, 20 LC; enrl. maj.
260, others 1000. Tui. $900. non-res. $2150; campus res.

Art History
Ceramics
Drawing
Graphics

Painting
Photography
Sculpture

　Summer School: Dr. Edward Durnall, Dir; tui. $25 per cr. and
reg. fee for 4, 6, 8 wk. sessions beginning June 26; enrl. 1200.

HANOVER

DARTMOUTH COLLEGE, Department of Art, 03755.
　Tel: (603) 646-2306
John G. Kemeny, Pres, Robert L. McGrath, Chmn; 11 FT, 3 PT
instr. Estab. 1906; pvt; co-ed; 4 yr; degree, A.B.(may complete in
11 terms); schol. & fel; 16 SC, 26 LC; enrl. 1500. Tui.(incl. campus
res. fee) $1090 per term; operating 4 terms on year-round basis.

African & Afro-American Arts
African Art & The Festival
Arts of Traditional West Africa
Color Theory

History of Architecture
Photography
3-Dimensional Design

MANCHESTER

MANCHESTER INSTITUTE OF ARTS AND SCIENCES, 148 Concord
　St, 03104. Tel: (603) 623-0313
James K. Boatner, Exec. Dir; 30 PT instr. Estab. 1898; pvt; D & E;
ent. req. none; 16 studios; enrl. 1800. Tui. average $50 per audit
course or per cr. hr, three 10 wk. terms, one 5 wk. summer term,
music.

Ballet
Creative Fibres
Design
Drawing
Early American Decorating
Jewelry & Silversmithing
Languages
Modern Dance
Painting

Photography
Pottery
Printmaking
Sculpture
Sewing
Theatre
Watercolor
Weaving

ST. ANSELM'S COLLEGE,* Department of Fine Arts, 03102.
　Tel: (603) 669-1030 Exten. 328
Joseph E. Scannell, Chmn; 2 FT instr. Estab. 1889; pvt; D & E;
co-ed; ent. req. HS dipl, relative standing, SAT score, interview;
4 yr; degree, B.A; 2 SC, 9 LC, 1 art history seminar; enrl. approx.
1500. Tui. $800 per sem, part-time $35 per hr; campus res. $450
per sem.

Art History
Photography
Studio

　Summer School: Vincent Capowski, Asst. Dean; History of American Art seminar, still photography; tui. same as above; enrl. approx.
10 students per course.

NASHUA

THE ARTS AND SCIENCE CENTER, 14 Court St, 03060.
　Tel: (603) 883-1506
Eleanor Fleming, Administrative Assistant; 35-40 PT instr. Estab.
1958; pub; D & E; no ent. req; no degrees, non-credited; SC, LC.
Tui; no campus res.

Ceramics
Drawing
Enameling
Jewelry
Macrame

Painting
Photography
Sculpture
Theatre Arts
Weaving

Adult hobby classes, hand-built pottery, stained glass; tui. varied.
Children's classes, drawing, painting, jewelry, pottery, puppet
making, pre-school art, sculpture; tui. varied.

　Summer School: Eleanor Fleming, Dir; tui. varied for ten 5 wk.
terms from June to July.

RIVIER COLLEGE,* Art Department,
　03060.
Sister Marie Couture, Chmn; 4 FT instr. Estab. 1933; pvt; D & E;
W (limited number of M accepted); ent. req. HS dipl; 2-4 yr; degrees,
A.A, B.A, B.F.A; schol; 26 SC, 6 LC, 3 L-SC; enrl. D 98, E 24, maj.
30, others 92. Tui. $1500 per yr; campus res. $1200.

Advertising Design
Aesthetics
Art and Religion
Art Education
Art for Special Education
Ceramics
Copper Enameling
Drawing
Graphic Arts
History of American Art

Interior Design
Leather
Painting
Photography
Sculpture
Silver Jewelry
Stitchery
Teacher Training
Textile Design
Weaving

　Summer School: Sister Eunice Fluet, Dir; courses offered,
Design & Color, Drawing & Painting, Weaving & Stitchery.

NEW LONDON

COLBY-SAWYER COLLEGE, Art Department, 03257.
　Tel: (603) 526-2010 Exten. 229
Donald L. Campbell, Head; 5 FT instr. Estab. 1928; pvt; D; W;
2-4 yr; degrees, A.A. (2 yr), A.B. (4 yr); schol; 9 SC, 5 LC in
History of Art; enrl. 250.

Ceramics
Composition
Drawing
Painting
Photography

Printmaking
Sculpture
Three-Dimensional Design
Visual Studies

PETERBOROUGH

SHARON ARTS CENTER, RFD 2, Box 361, 03458.
　Tel: (603) 924-3582
Carl Jackson, Dir; 10 PT instr. Estab. 1947; pvt; D & E; ent. req.
none; schol; 20 SC. Tui. $40 per course, plus $7 mem. fee. Classes
yr. round.

Ceramics
Drawing
Fashion Arts
Graphic Arts
Jewelry

Lettering
Painting
Patchwork & Applique
Textile Design
Weaving

Children's classes, pottery; tui. $30 plus $10 lab fee.

PLYMOUTH

PLYMOUTH STATE COLLEGE, Art Department, 03264.
　Tel: (603) 536-1550 Exten. 201
Mary C. Taylor, Head; 8 FT instr. Estab. 1871; pub; D & E; ent.
req. HS grad, references, health record, transcript, SAT, CEEB,

ACT; 4 yr; degrees, B.S, B.A; schol; 17 SC, 8 LC; enrl. D 2900, maj. 170. Tui. $617, $1550 non-res; campus res. $1050 double, $1150 single

Art Education	History of Art
Ceramics	Painting
Children's Workshop	Screen Painting
Drawing	Sculpture
Graphic Arts	Teacher Training

Summer School: Dr. Julian Schlager, Dir; varied courses; tui. $30 per cr. hr. for term of 6 wk.

RINDGE

FRANKLIN PIERCE COLLEGE, Art Department, 03461.
David Brandis, Chmn; 4 FT, 2 PT instr. Estab. 1962; pvt; D & E; ent. req. HS dipl; 4 yr; degree, B.A.(Creative and Performing Arts); schol; 20 SC, 2 LC. Tui. approx. $3500; campus res. approx. $1000.

Ceramics	Painting
Drawing	Photography
Glassblowing	Primitive Woodworking
Graphics	Sculpture
History of Art	Stage Design
Jewelry & Metalcraft	Stained Glass

Summer School: Anthony Trembley, Dir.

NEW JERSEY

CALDWELL

CALDWELL COLLEGE, Art Department, 07006.
Tel: (201) 228-4424
Sister M. Gerardine, Chmn; 4 FT, 5 PT instr. Estab. art maj. 1964; pvt; D; W; ent. req. HS grad, ent. exam, art portfolio; 3-4 yr; degree, B.A; schol; 24 SC, 12 LC; enrl. maj. 70, dept. 90. Tui. $1900, PT $60 per cr, SC fee $10; campus res. $1250.

Advertising Design	Jewelry
Aesthetics	Lettering
Art Education	Metal Workshop
Ceramics	Painting
Commercial Art	Photography
Drawing	Sculpture
Graphic Arts	Teacher Training
History of Art & Archaeology	

General Crafts Workshop includes leather carving, weaving, chip carving, batik, enameling.

Summer School: Sister M. Regina, Dir; courses offered, Drawing, Printmaking; tui. $60 per cr. for term of 3 wk. beginning June 28.

CAMDEN

RUTGERS UNIVERSITY, Camden College of Arts and Sciences, Art Department, 311 N. Fifth St, 08102. Tel: (609) 757-6242
William M. Hoffman Jr, Chmn; 4 FT, 2 PT instr. Pub; D; ent. req. HS dipl, must qualify for regular coll. admis; 4 yr; degree, B.A.(Art); 13 SC, 5 LC; art enrl. D 250, maj. 30. Tui. $628, non-res. $1213.

Aesthetics	History of Art & Archaeology
Ceramics	Painting
Drawing	Photography
Graphic Arts	Sculpture
Graphic Design	

CONVENT

COLLEGE OF SAINT ELIZABETH, Art Department, Convent Station, 07961. Tel: (201) 539-1600
Sister Marie Imelda Hagan, Chmn; 3 FT instr. Estab. 1899, art dept, 1956; den; D & E; W only; ent. req. HS dipl, ent. exam; 4 yrs; degree, B.A; schol; 17 SC, 4 LC; art dept. enrl. D 250, maj. 27. Tui. $2150 per yr; campus res. $1450.

Art Education	Jewelry
Ceramics	Leather work
Color & Design	Lettering
Drafting	Painting
Drawing	Sand Casting
Graphic Arts	Sculpture
Handicrafts	Stitchery
History of Art & Archaeology	Teacher Training
Interior Design	

Summer School: Sister Mary Kathleen, Dir; courses offered, Art Education, Painting; tui. $67 per cr. for PT students.

DOVER

COUNTY COLLEGE OF MORRIS, Art Department, Rte 10, Center Grove Rd, 07801. Tel: (201) 361-5000 Exten. 361
Dr. Joyce R. Dorr, Head. Estab. 1970; pub; D & E; ent. req. HS dipl; 2 yr; degree, A.A.(Humanities/Art); 15 SC, 3 LC; enrl. maj. 263. Tui. $400 per yr. for Morris County res.

Advertising Design	Painting
Ceramics	Photography
Drawing	Sculpture
History of Art & Archaeology	

GLASSBORO

GLASSBORO STATE COLLEGE,* Department of Art, Route 322, 08028. Tel: (609) 445-7081
Dr. Seymour Blinderman, Chairperson; 22 FT, 5 PT instr. Estab. 1925; pub; D & E; ent. req. HS dipl, ent. exam, portfolio and SAT; 4 yrs; degrees, B.A. & M.A; enrl. D 6100, E 5000, maj. 300, grad. students 100. Tui. $267 per sem.

Aesthetics	Jewelry
Art Education	Lettering
Batik	Painting
Ceramics	Photography
Drawing	Sculpture
Enameling	Stage Design
Graphic Arts	Teacher Training
Handicrafts	Textile Design
History of Art & Archaeology	Theatre Arts

Summer School: Dr. Seymour Blinderman, chairperson.

HACKETTSTOWN

CENTENARY COLLEGE FOR WOMEN,* Fine Arts Division, Art Department, 07840. Tel: (201) 852-1400
Elly J. Havez, Chmn; 2 FT, 2 PT instr. Estab. 1874; pvt; D; W; 2 yr; degree, A.A; Fine and Applied Arts; 11 SC, 2 LC; enrl. maj. 50, others 365, total 678. Tui. $3800; campus res.

JERSEY CITY

JERSEY CITY STATE COLLEGE, Art Department, 2039 Kennedy Blvd, 07305. Tel: (201) 547-3214
Dr. Elaine Foster, Chmn; 22 FT, 8 PT instr. Estab. 1952; pub; D & E; ent. req. HS dipl; 4 yrs; degrees, B.A, M.A; schol; 40 SC, 15 LC, 31 GC; enrl. D & E approx. 500, maj. approx. 500, grad. students approx. 80. Tui. $636 per yr; campus res. $1200.
Internships in museums, public schools and commercial firms and businesses.

Advertising Design	Lettering
Aesthetics	Painting
Art Education	Photography
Ceramics	Sculpture
Commercial Art	Stage Design
Drawing	Teacher Training
Graphic Arts	Textile Design
History of Art	Theatre Arts
Illustration	Weaving
Jewelry	

Summer School: Tui. $20 per sem. hr, non-res. $40 for term of 6 wk. beginning June 25; 1973 enrl. approx. 40.

Art & Society	Relief Printing/Intaglio Printing
Aesthetics of the Visual Arts	Special Problems
Cultural Resources of the Metropolitan Area	Weaving/Lettering Design
Figure Sculpture/Sculpture Studio	

SAINT PETER'S COLLEGE, Fine Arts Department, Kennedy Blvd, 07306. Tel: (201) 333-4400 Exten. 276
Dr. Daniel Serra-Badue, Chmn; 4 FT, 12 PT instr. Estab. 1963; den; D & E; co-ed; ent. req. HS grad; 4 yr; degrees, B.A, B.A. in Cursu Classico, B.S; schol; 4 SC, 13 LC; enrl. D 650, E 250, maj. 20. Tui. $55 per cr. hr; no campus res.

Art History	Music
Drawing & Painting	Sculpture
Film	

Summer School: Dr. Daniel Serra-Badue, Chmn; tui. $48 per cr. hr. for term of 5 wk. beginning June 11; 1975 enrl. 150.

Film History	Primitive Art
Introduction to Music	Visual Arts in America
Introduction to Visual Arts	

WARD MOUNT ART CLASSES, 74 Sherman Pl, 07307.
  Tel: (201) 653-2629
Ward Mount, Dir. Estab. 1939; pvt; D & E; no ent. req; group and
pvt. instruction; spring and fall terms.
Art Appreciation
Drawing & Painting
Sculpture

LAKEWOOD

GEORGIAN COURT COLLEGE, Art Department, Lakewood Ave,
  08701. Tel: (201) 364-2200 Exten. 48
Sister M. Christina Geis, Chmn; 3 FT, 5 PT instr. Estab. 1925; den;
D; W; ent. req. HS grad, B average, SAT scores, portfolio; 4 yr; degree, B.A.(Art, Art Educ, Art History); schol; 14 SC, 9 LC; enrl.
total 760 maj. 60. Tui. $1800, $100 general fees; $45 health fee; cam-
pus res. $1250.

Advertising Design	Handicrafts
Architectural Drafting	History of Art & Archaeology
Art Education	Painting
Basic Design	Photography
Ceramics	Sculpture
Drawing	Stagecraft
Figure Drawing	Teacher Training
Graphic Arts	Textile Design

  Summer School: Courses vary, Ceramics, 19th Century Art
History, Sculpture in 1975; tui. $51 per cr. hr. for term of 6 wk.
beginning June 29; 1975 enrl. 180.

RALYN ART CENTER, 316 Main St, 08701.
  Tel: (201) 363-7500
Ralph F. Salisbury, Dir; 4 PT instr. Estab. 1964; pub; D & E;
no ent. req; no degree; enrl. approx. 50. Tui. $40 for eight
2-hr. classes

Drawing	Sculpture
Oils	Watercolors

Children's classes, drawing, painting; tui. $35 for eight 2-hr.
classes; enrl. approx. 30.

LAWRENCEVILLE

RIDER COLLEGE, Department of Fine Arts, 08648.
  Tel: (609) 896-0800 Exten. 385
Larry Capo, Chmn; 3 FT instr. Estab. 1966; pvt; D & E; co-ed;
ent. req. HS dipl; 4 yr; degree, B.A.(Fine Arts); 9 SC, 4 LC; enrl.
D 3500, E 5169 (fall, spring and summer), maj. 100. Tui. $2300
per 36 sem. hr; campus res. $615 (average).

Ceramics	History of Art & Archaeology
Costume Design & Construction	Painting
Drawing	Sculpture
Graphic Arts	Stage Design
Graphic Design	

  Summer School: Dominick A. Iorio, Dir; tui. $185 per 3 sem. hr.

LAYTON

PETERS VALLEY CRAFTSMEN, INC, Star Rte, 07851
  Tel: (201) 948-5200
Margot K. Raab, Administrator; 7 FT, 30 PT instr. Estab. 1970;
pvt; D; ent. req. craft experience for some courses; no degree;
5 SC; enrl. D 250, E 10. Tui. $60 per wk. of 2 and 3 wk. sessions.
Summer school only.

Blacksmithing	Textile Design
Ceramics	Weaving
Jewelry	Woodworking

MADISON

DREW UNIVERSITY, Art Department,
  07940.
Peter Chapin, Chmn; 3 FT, 5 PT instr. Estab. 1866; pvt; D; ent.
req. HS dipl, ent. exam; 4 yr; degree, B.A; schol; 12 SC, 14 LC;
dept. enrl. D 230, E 40.

Aesthetics	Lithography & Silk Screen
Ceramics	Painting
Drawing	Photography
History of Art & Archaeology	Sculpture
Intaglio & Relief	

New York Semester on Art.
Evening Printmaking Workshops in cooperation with The Print-
making Council of N.J; non-credit.
  Summer School: Dean John McCall, Dir; courses offered, Art
Appreciation, Studios.

MONTCLAIR

✠MONTCLAIR ART MUSEUM, Museum Art School, 3 S. Mountain
  Ave, 07042. Tel: (201) 746-5555
Kathryn E. Gamble, Dir; Patricia P. Barnes, School Registrar;
11 instr. Classes for adults in drawing, painting, portraiture and
weaving; tui. $54 for 12 sessions. Classes for children in clay
modeling and painting; tui. $36-$48 for 12 sessions.

MONTCLAIR STATE COLLEGE, Fine Arts Department, 07043.
  Tel: (201) 893-4308
Dr. Donald Mintz, Dean; Dr. Charles Martens, Chmn; 26 FT, 8 PT
instr. Estab. 1908; pub; ent. req. HS grad and exam, interview,
portfolio; 4 yr; degrees, B.A, M.A; state schol. and other schol. to
res; 35 SC, 18 LC; enrl. maj. 300, grad. maj. 175. Tui. undergrad.
$535.

Art Education	Photography
Art History	Printmaking
Ceramics	Sculpture
Drawing	Textiles
Filmmaking	Theatre Arts
Metalwork, Jewelry	TV as Art
Painting	Urban Cultural Design

NEW BRUNSWICK

RUTGERS, THE STATE UNIVERSITY OF NEW JERSEY, Federated
  College Departments, 08903. Tel: (201) 932-1766
Dr. Bille Pickard-Pritchard, Chmn.

  Cook College, Department of Landscape Architecture, Blake
  Hall. Tel: (201) 932-9317
Roy H. DeBoer, Chmn.
Film & Video
Landscape Architecture

  Douglass College, Walters Hall. Tel: (201) 932-9856, 9857
Virginia L. Bush, Acting Chmn; 15 FT, 12 PT instr. Estab. 1918;
W; 4 yr; degrees, B.S.(Studio, Educ, Art History); schol; 28 SC,
27 LC; enrl. 1000, maj. 150. Tui. $300 per term, non-res. $600.

Art Education	Graphics
Ceramics	History of Art
Design	Mixed Media
Drawing	Painting
Environmental Art	Photography
Film & Video	

  Livingston College, Lucy Stone Hall. Tel: (201) 932-4160, 4161
Robert Cook, Acting Chmn; 15 FT, 8 PT instr. Estab. 1969; co-ed;
4 yr; degrees, B.A.(Studio, Educ, Art History); schol; 37 SC, 16 LC;
enrl. 1000, maj 190. Tui. $300 per term, non-res. $600.

Art Education	Film & Video
Ceramics	Glassblowing
Commercial Art	Graphics
Crafts	History of Art
Design	Performance
Drawing	Photography
Environmental Art	Weaving

  Rutgers College, Voorhees Hall. Tel: (201) 932-7041, 7839
Matthew Baigell, Chmn; 12 FT, 15 PT instr. Estab. 1766; co-ed;
4 yr; B.A.(Studio, Educ, Art History); schol; 32 SC, 33 LC; enrl.
1000, maj. 125. Tui. $300 per term, non-res. $600.

Art and the Computer	History of Art
Art Education	New Materials & Techniques
Drawing	Design
Film & Video	Painting
Foundry/Metal	Photography
Graphic Arts	

  University College, Humanities Department, New Jersey Hall.
  Tel: (201) 932-7239
William Walling, Chmn.
Art History

  Graduate Program in Art History, Voorhees Hall.
  Tel: (201) 932-7041
Olga Berendsen, Dir; 9 FT, 45 PT instr. Co-ed; degrees, M.A.
and Ph.D.(Western Art); enrl. 64. Tui. $35 per cr, non-res. $50.

  Graduate Program in Studio Art, Walters Hall.
  Tel: (201) 932-9699
John Goodyear, Acting Chmn; 12 instr. Co-ed; degrees, M.F.A,
M.A; 10 SC; enrl. 35. Tui. $35 per cr, non-res. $50.

Ceramics	Media
Drawing	Painting
Graphics	Sculpture
Intermedia	

  Summer School; E Classes.

NEWARK

NEWARK SCHOOL OF FINE AND INDUSTRIAL ART,* 550 High St, 07102.
Edward John Stevens, Dir; D 42 PT, E 28 PT instr. Estab. 1882; pub; 3-4 yr; enrl. D 300, E 300. Tui. to res. of Newark $76 plus $10 reg. fee, non-res. $590 plus $10 reg. fee; E free to Newark res. under 20 yr. of age, over 20 yr. $24 to $36, non-res. $115 to $195; Children Sat. AM, 28 sessions free to Newark res. and $50 to non-res.

Advertising Design	Interior Design
Ceramics	Painting
Fashion Illustration	Pictorial Illustration
Fine Arts	Sculpture
Industrial Design	Textile Design

RUTGERS UNIVERSITY, NEWARK Newark College of Arts & Sciences, Art Department, Bradley Hall, 392 High St, 07104.
Prof. Vivian E. Browne, Chmn; 6 FT, 3 PT instr. Pub; D; ent. req. HS dipl, or as specified by the college and the university; 4 yrs; degree, B.A; schol; sem. enrl. D 486, maj. 102.

Aesthetics	History of Art & Archaeology
Art Education	Painting
Ceramics	Photography
Drawing	Sculpture
Environmental Design	Teacher Training
Graphic Arts	

Summer School: Courses offered varies from year to year.

OCEAN CITY

OCEAN CITY CULTURAL ARTS CENTER,* 409 Wesley Ave, 08226.
Tel: (609) 399-7628
Frances J. Taylor, Dir; 26 PT instr. Estab. 1966; pub; D & E; no ent. req; no degrees; 37 SC, 3 LC; enrl. 40. Tui. $35-$50 per 8 wk. trimester.

Classical Ballet	Graphics
Creative Writing	Painting
Drawing	Photography
Drawing for Young People	Sculpture
Figure Study	Yoga

Summer Session: Term of 6 wk. with 3 hr. sessions beginning in July.

OCEAN CITY SCHOOL OF ART,* 409 Wesley Ave, 08826.
Tel: (609) 399-7628
Frances J. Taylor Dir; 15 PT instr. Estab. 1974; pub; D & E; no ent. req; no degrees; 3 yr. cert; 22 SC, 3 LC. Tui. $325-$350.

Color & Design	Journalism
Drawing	Oil Painting
Figure Drawing	Photography
Graphics	Sculpture
History of Art	Watercolor

Summer School: Tui. $35-$50 for 6 wk. term of 3 hr. sessions beginning July.

PRINCETON

PRINCETON UNIVERSITY, 08540.
Tel: (609) 452-3000
Pvt; co-ed; 4 yr; degrees; schol. and fel. Tui. $4000, campus res. $1900.

Department of Art & Archaeology, McCormick Hall.
John R. Martin, Chmn; 23 FT instr. Estab. 1883; 41 LC, 30 GC; enrl. undergrad. 50, grad. 55.
History of Art & Archaeology
Museum Problems

Program in Chinese & Japanese Art & Archaeology
Wen Fong, Chmn. Ph.D. Program.

Program in Classical Archaeology
T. Leslie Shear, Jr, Chmn. Ph.D. Program.

Program in Visual Arts, Room 07, 185 Nassau St.
Tel: (212) 452-5457
James Seanright, Dir; 5 FT, 13 PT instr. Estab. 1971; pvt; D & E; ent. req. univ. admis. 4 yr; degree, B.A; enrl. undergrad. 400, grad. 20.

Ceramics	Painting
Drawing	Photography
Graphic Arts	Sculpture
Graphic Design	

School of Architecture & Urban Planning, Architecture Building
Robert L. Geddes, Dean; 20 FT instr. Estab. 1919; pvt; D; high ent. req. 4 yr; degrees, A.B, M.Arch, M.Arch. & Urban Planning,
Ph.D.(Arch), Ph.D.(Urban Planning); schol. and fel; 6 SC, 13 LC, 6 GC, 17 seminars; new degrees in urban planning; enrl. undergrad. 120, grad. 50.

RIDGEWOOD

RIDGEWOOD SCHOOL OF ART, 83 Chestnut St, 07450.
Tel: (201) 444-7100
Robert Crawford, Dir; 5 FT, 10 PT instr. Estab. 1961; pvt; D; ent. req. HS grad ent. exam; 3 yr; dipl; 28 SC enrl. 250, 4 LC enrl. 80. Tui. $1300 per yr, matriculation and other expenses $200.

Advertising Design	Lettering
Animated Film	19th Century Painting
Ceramics	Packaging Design
Contemporary Art Seminar	Painting
Drawing	Photography
Filmmaking	Product Photography
Graphic Arts	Sculpture
Graphic Design	Technical Drawing
Illustration	

Children's classes.
Summer School: Robert Crawford, Dir; tui. $3 per hr.

Ceramics	Photography
Drawing	Sculpture
Painting	

SOUTH ORANGE

SETON HALL UNIVERSITY, Department of Art and Music, South Orange Ave, 07079. Tel: (201) 762-9000
Louis de Foix-Crenascol, Chmn; 9 FT, 6 PT instr. Dept. estab. 1968; pvt; D & E; 4 yr; degree, B.A; 14 SC, 24 LC, 5 GC. Tui. $67 per cr.

Chinese Brush Painting	Painting
Drawing	Prints
History of Art	Urban Design
Illustration	Watercolor
Indian & Tantric Art	

Summer School: Miriam O'Donnell, Dir; Art Materials & Techniques, Landscape Drawing and Painting; two 4 wk. sessions June and July-Aug.

TRENTON

MERCER COUNTY COMMUNITY COLLEGE,* Art and Design/Communications Media Department, 1200 Old Trenton Rd, 08690.
Tel: (609) 586-4800 Exten. 330
Prof. Samuel Willig, Chmn; 13 FT, 7 PT instr. Coll. estab. 1966; pub; D & E; co-ed; ent. req. HS grad, proof of art subjects taken in HS, or portfolio; 2 yr; degree, A.A; 36 SC and LC; enrl. D 85, E 65, maj. 300, part time and non-art maj. 300. Tui. $350, out-of-state res. $1500; no campus res.

Advertising Design	Instrumental Drawing
Advertising Production	Lettering
Architecture	Life Drawing
Art Appreciation	Motion Picture Techniques
Cinema	Painting
Commercial Art	Photography
Communications Media	Printmaking
Creative Workshop	Radio & Sound Duplication
Design & Color	Sculpture
Design Workshop	Television Production
Drafting	Typography
Drawing	Theatre Arts
Graphic Arts	Visual Communications
Graphic Design	Watercolor & Tempera
History of Art & Archaeology	

Adult hobby classes, painting, sculpture; tui. $15 per cr.(county res); enrl. 50. Children's Sat. classes (ages 6-15); tui. $7.50 per sem; enrl. 240 per sem.
Summer School: Prof. Samuel Willig, Chmn; tui. $15 per cr. (county res.) for term of 8 wk. beginning 25 June; 1973 enrl. 180.

Advanced Painting	History of Art
Art Appreciation	Life Drawing
Basic Drawing	Photography
Drawing & Painting	Sculpture

TRENTON STATE COLLEGE, Department of Art, Pennington Rd, 08625. Tel: (609) 771-1855
Dr. Norval C Kern, Chmn; 15 FT, 5 PT instr, 5 co-adjutant faculty. Estab. 1855; pub; D & E; ent. req. interview, exam, portfolio; 4 yr; degree, B.A; schol; 28 SC, 12 LC, 6 GC; enrl. D 5600, E 3000, maj. 200. Tui. $535, non-res. $1070; campus res. $1250.

Advertising Design	Jewelry
Art Education	Lettering
Art Therapy	Painting
Ceramics	Printmaking

Design
Drawing
Foundations of Art
History of Art
Interior Design
Puppetry
Sculpture
Textile Design
Weaving
Children's classes Sat. AM; no tui; enrl. limited to immediate community (320).
Summer School: Dr. Norval C. Kern, Dir; courses listed above; tui. $20 per cr, non-res. $40 per cr; enrl. approx. 250.

UNION

KEAN COLLEGE OF NEW JERSEY, Fine Arts Department, Morris Ave, 07083. Tel: (201) 527-2307, 2308, 2309
Dr. Robert B. Coon, Chmn; 32 FT, 22 PT instr. Estab. 1855; pub; D & E; ent. req. HS dipl, coll. ent. exam. boards; 4 yr; degree, B.A; 43 SC 23 LC, 24 GC; enrl. D 5000, E 10,000, maj. 400, grad. 75. Tui. $535, plus $100 in fees not incl. books; campus res. $1070.

Advertising Design
Aesthetics
Art Education
Ceramics
Color Theory
Commercial Art
Drawing
Filmmaking
Furniture Making
Graphic Arts
History of Art & Archaeology
Illustration
Jewelry
Interior Design
Jewelry
Lettering
Museum Training
Painting
Photography
Printmaking
Sculpture
Stage Design
Teacher Training
Textile Design
Visual Communications

Summer School: Office of Summer Session and Special Programs; tui. res $20, non-res $40 per cr; 3 wk. Intersession, May 21-June 14; 6 wk. Summer Session, June 25 to Aug. 3.
Art Education
Art History
Interior Design
Studio
Visual Communications

WAYNE

WILLIAM PATERSON COLLEGE,* Division of Fine & Performing Arts, Art Department, 300 Pompton Rd, 07470.
Tel: (201) 881-2402
Dr. Richard L. Reed, Assoc. Dean, Fine and Performing Arts; 20 FT, 2 PT instr. Dept. estab. 1958; pub; 4 yr; degree, B.A; 9 SC, 9 LC; enrl. maj. undergrad. 160; grad. 65, E non-maj. 150. Tui. $267.50, other expenses and materials $100.
Ceramics
Drawing
Enameling
Graphic Arts
Jewelry
Lapidary
Mechanical Drawing
Metal
Painting
Photography
Sculpture
Teacher Training
Textile Design
Theater Arts
Summer School: Dr. Donald Duclos, Dir; tui. $20 per cr. for term of 6 wk. from June 20.

WEST LONG BRANCH

MONMOUTH COLLEGE, Department of Art, Cedar & Norwood Aves, 07764. Tel: (201) 222-6600 Exten. 346
Arie van Everdingen, Chmn; 7 FT, 4 PT instr. Estab. 1933; pvt; D & E; ent. req. HS dipl; 4 yr; degrees, B.A.(Art, Art Education); schol; 20 SC, 8 LC, 3 GC; enrl. D 145, E 5, maj. 150. Tui. $2530 per yr; campus res. approx. $1500.
Architecture
Art Education
Ceramics
Drawing
Graphic Arts
History of Art & Archaeology
Jewelry
Painting
Photography
Sculpture
Teacher Training
Textile Crafts
Summer School: Kenneth Streibig, Dir; tui. $76 per cr. for term of 7 wk. beginning June, 1976.
Appreciation of Art
Art for Children
Ceramics
History of Art
Painting
Sculpture
Watercolor

NEW MEXICO

ALBUQUERQUE

THE AMERICAN CLASSICAL COLLEGE, 614 Indian School Rd. N.W. 87102. Tel: (505) 843-7749
Dr. C. M. Flumiani Dir; 2 FT instr. Estab. 1970; pvt; D; ent. req. ent. exam; 3 yr; no degrees; schol. Tui. FT $100 mo.

Advertising Design
Aesthetics
Art Education
Commercial Art
Drawing
History of Art & Archaeology
Painting
Sculpture

THE CLASSICAL SCHOOL MUSEUM & GALLERY, Art School, 614 Indian School Rd. N.W, 87102. Tel: (505) 843-7749
Dr. C. M. Flumiani, Dir; 2 FT, 2 PT instr. Estab. 1967 in Springfield, Mass, since Jan, 1970, in Albuquerque; pvt; D & E; ent. req. ent. exam; 2 yr; degree, A.A; schol; 10 SC, 3 LC. Tui. full-time $425.
Aesthetics
Art Education
Commercial Art
Drawing
History of Art & Archaeology
Industrial Design
Painting
Teacher Training

UNIVERSITY OF NEW MEXICO, College of Fine Arts, 87131.
Tel: (505) 277-2111
Clinton Adams, Dean. Estab. 1935; pub; 4, 5 & 6 yr; degrees, B.F.A, B.A, M.A, M.Arch, M.F.A, Ph.D; schol. and fel. Tui: $456, non-res. $1284.

School of Architecture. Tel: (505) 277-2903
Morton Hoppenfeld, Dean; 10 FT, 3 PT instr; 4 & 6 yr; 23 SC, 10 LC, 6 GC; enrl. 400.

Department of Art. Tel: (505) 277-4003
Nicolai Cikovsky, Jr, Chmn; 25 FT, 23 PT instr; 4, 5 & 7 yr; 37 SC, 37 LC, 35 GC; enrl. maj. 550, grad. 80.
Art Education (with College of Education)
Ceramics
History of Art
Jewelry
Lithography
Painting
Photography
Sculpture

Tamarind Institute. Tel: (505) 277-3901
Clinton Adams, Dir, Judith Booth, Asst. Dir.

Summer School: 8 wk. from approx. June 1; tui. $19 per cr. hr; non-res. $53.50 per cr. hr.

LAS CRUCES

NEW MEXICO STATE UNIVERSITY, College of Arts and Sciences, Department of Art, 88003. Tel: (505) 646-1705
Dr. Christiane L. Joost-Gaugier, Head; 7 FT instr. Estab. as independent dept. 1975; pub; D & E; co-ed; ent. req. HS grad; 4 yr; degrees, B.A, B.F.A, M.A; schol. for grad. students; 34 SC, 12 LC, 24 GC; enrl. D 740, E 60, maj. 110, grad. 14. Tui. $444, non-res. $1074; campus res. $700.
Aesthetics
Art Education
Ceramics
Drawing
Fashion Arts
Graphic Arts
Graphic Design
History of Art & Archaeology
Jewelry
Leather
Painting
Photography
Sculpture
Teacher Training
Weaving
Adult evening classes, graphics and painting; tui. $16 per cr. hr; open enrl. Children's classes, arts and crafts; weekly meetings; tui. $20 per sem; enrl. 25.
Summer School: Dr. D. Roush, Dir; courses offered in all areas; tui. $80 for term of 6 wks. beginning June 8.

LAS VEGAS

NEW MEXICO HIGHLANDS UNIVERSITY, Department of Arts & Crafts, 87701. Tel: (505) 425-7511 Exten. 361, 362
Prof. H. M. Leippe, Chmn; 6 FT instr. Estab. 1893; pub; D; co-ed; ent. req. HS dipl; 4 yr; degrees, B.A, M.A; schol; 20 SC, 11 LC, 8 GC; enrl. D 150, maj. 100. Tui. per quarter $113, non-res. $302, $1.50 Art Studio charge per cr. hr; campus res. $320-$342.
Art Education
Ceramics
Drawing
Graphic Arts
History of Art & Archaeology
Jewelry
Lettering
Painting
Photography
Sculpture
Teacher Training
Weaving
Summer School: John S. Johnson, Dir; Tui. $105, non-res. $205 for term of 10 wk.
Ceramics
Jewelry
Painting
Prints
Sculpture
Watercolor
Weaving

PORTALES

EASTERN NEW MEXICO UNIVERSITY,* Department of Art and Art Education, 88130. Tel: (505) 562-2652
Chris Gikas, Head; 4 FT instr. Estab. 1934; pub; D & E; ent. req. HS grad. with C average, or G.E.D, ACT scores; 4 yr; degrees, B.A, B.S, B.Univ.Studies; schol; 52 SC and LC, 19 GC; enrl. full-time 4000. Fees (12 or more hrs) res. $234.50 per sem, non-res. $518 per sem; room and board per sem. $445.

Art Education	Painting
Commercial Art	Sculpture
Fine Arts	

Summer School: Chris Gikas, Dir; 8 wk.

RUIDOSO

CARRIZO ART AND CRAFT WORKSHOPS, P.O. Drawer A, 88345. Tel: (505) 257-2375
Mrs. Hilma Greggerson Collier, Mgr; 12 to 16 FT instr. Estab. 1956; pvt; D & E. Tui. $85 to $125 for 2 wk, pvt. room with meals $250, bunkhouse $125. Summer School.

Drawing	Sculpture
Jewelry	Wood Carving & Sculpture
Painting	

SANTA FE

BARNA POTTERY, P.O. Box 226, 87574. Tel: (505) 982-8232
Iris Barna, Dir; 2 FT, 4 PT instr. Estab. 1960; pvt; D & E; ent. req. HS dipl; 3 SC. Tui. PT $75; no campus res.

Aesthetics	History of Art & Archaeology
Ceramics	Needle Work
Display	Sculpture

Apprenticeship in European Style Pottery, 1 yr, room & part board.

INSTITUTE OF AMERICAN INDIAN ARTS, Cerrillos Rd, 87501. Tel: (505) 988-3261
Henry Gobin, Arts Dir; 12 FT instr. Estab. 1962; pvt; D; ent. req. HS dipl; 2 yr; degree A.A.(Fine Arts); 18 SC, 11 LC; enrl. D 263.

Advertising Design	Jewelry
Ceramics	Lettering
Commercial Art	Museum Staff Training
Costume Design & Construction	Painting
Drawing	Sculpture
Fashion Arts	Traditional Indian Techniques
Graphic Arts	
Graphic Design	Two-Dimensional & Three-Dimensional Design
Handicrafts	
History of Art & Archaeology	

NEW YORK

ALBANY

COLLEGE OF SAINT ROSE, Fine Arts Division, 432 Western Ave, 12203. Tel: (518) 471-5111
Patricia Clahassey, Head; 6 FT, 6 PT instr. Estab. 1970; pvt; D & E; ent. req. HS dipl, scores on at least one of three standard tests, SAT, ACT, or Regents Schol. exam; 4 yr; degree, B.S; 33 SC, 16 LC; enrl. D 93, maj. 93. Tui. $1900 per yr; campus res. $1225.

Advertising Design	Graphic Design
Art Education	Handicrafts
Ceramics	History of Art
Drafting	Jewelry
Drawing	Painting
Enameling	Photography
Fashion Arts	Sculpture
Fibers	Teacher Training
Graphic Arts	Weaving

STATE UNIVERSITY OF NEW YORK AT ALBANY, Department of Art, 1400 Washington Ave, 12222. Tel: (518) 457-8487
Richard Callner, Chmn; 12 FT, 4 PT instr. Estab. 1844; pub; 4 yr; degrees, B.A, M.A.(Studio); schol; 37 SC, 19 LC. Tui. plus incidental and service fee per sem; campus res. Summer School.

Architectural Design	Introduction to Cinema
Art as Environment	Introductory Film Production
Art Criticism	Lithography
Baroque & Rococo	Painting
Ceramics	Photography
Cinema	Plastics
Contemporary Art Design	Sculpture
Drawing	Silk Screen
Etching	Stained Glass
Independent Study (Studio)	Techniques of Painting

ALFRED

NEW YORK STATE COLLEGE OF CERAMICS AT ALFRED UNIVERSITY, 14802. Tel: (607) 871-2442
Robert C. Turner, Head, Div. of Art and Design; 20 FT faculty. Estab. 1900; 4 yr; degrees, B.F.A, M.F.A; grad. teaching assistantships; enrl. maj. undergrad. 250, grad. 25, others 250. Two yr. of foundation study and two yr. of upper level studio.

Art Education	Painting
Ceramics	Photography
Design	Printmaking
Glass	Sculpture

Summer School and Grad. School: Lewis Butler, Dean.

ANNANDALE-ON-HUDSON

BARD COLLEGE,* Division of Art, Music, Drama & Dance, 12504. Tel: (914) 758-6072
William Driver, Chmn. & Dir. Drama; Matt Phillips, Dir. Art; Anna Itelman, Dir. Dance; William Sleeper, Dir. Music; 8 FT, 12 PT instr. Estab. 1865; pvt; 4 yr; degree, B.A; schol; enrl. student body 600.

Criticism & History of Art	Sculpture
Drawing	Stage Design
Painting	Woodcut
Printmaking	

AURORA

WELLS COLLEGE, Division of Performing and Creative Arts, Department of Art, 13026. Tel: (315) 364-3011
Crawford R. Thoburn, Div. Chmn; 4 FT instr. Estab. 1868; pvt; W; 4 yr; degree, B.A; ent. schol; 12 SC, 16 LC.

Ceramics	Photography
History & Criticism of Art	Sculpture
Painting	

BAYSIDE

QUEENSBOROUGH COMMUNITY COLLEGE, Department of Art and Design, 11364.
Prof. John Hawkins, Chmn; 9 FT, 17 PT instr. Estab. 1958; pub; D & E; ent. req. HS dipl, ent. exam; degree, A.A, 64 cr; 12 SC 7 LC; enrl. D 1800, E 600.

Advertising Design	Jewelry
Art Education	Painting
Ceramics	Photography
Drawing	Sculpture
History of Art & Archaeology	

Adult hobby classes, art workshop, batik, ceramics, creative needlework, photography, plastics, woodcut and printmaking; tui. $35 for 8 wk.
Children's classes, art for children; tui. $35 for 8 wk.
Summer School: Prof. Norman Berman, Dir.

Ceramics	Painting
Modern Art	Survey of the History of Art

BINGHAMTON

✠ROBERSON CENTER FOR THE ARTS AND SCIENCES, 30 Front St, 13905. Tel: (607) 772-0660
Laura B. Martin, Asst. Dir; 26 FT instr. D & E; no degrees. Fees vary per instruction. Young People's Art Center; Roberson School of Ballet.

Art Experience	Pottery
Crafts	Sculpture
Jewelry	Silk Screen
Mixed Media	Theatre Arts
Painting & Drawing	Weaving
Photography	

Children's classes, craft workshops, jewelry, painting & drawing, pottery, sculpture; tui. varies per class.

STATE UNIVERSITY OF NEW YORK AT BINGHAMTON, Department of Art and Art History, 13901. Tel: (607) 798-2111, 2112
Vincent Bruno, Chmn; 19 FT instr. Estab. 1950; pub; D; 4 yr; degrees, B.A, M.A, Ph.D; grad. assistantships; 16 SC, 8 LC, 11 GC; enrl. maj. 132, grad. 41.

Art History	Graphics
Design	Painting
Drawing	Sculpture

Summer School: Office of Vice President for Academic Affairs.

BRIARCLIFF MANOR

BRIARCLIFF COLLEGE, Art Department, 10510. Tel: (914) 941-6400
Dr. Harold C. Simmons, Chmn: 5 FT, 1 PT instr. Estab. 1903; pvt;

D; W; ent. req. 16 academic subjects incl. 4 English, SAT and English Composition; 2-4 yr; degrees, A.A, B.A, B.S; schol; 46 SC, 22 LC; enrl. 400. Tui. $2975, with campus res. $4775.

Archaeology	Film Making
Art History	Painting
Ceramics	Photography
Design	Printmaking
Drawing	Sculpture

Summer School: Bruce LaRose, Dir; 3 SC; tui. $150 per course.

BROCKPORT

✤STATE UNIVERSITY OF NEW YORK COLLEGE AT BROCKPORT, Department of Art, 204 Fine Arts Bldg, 14220.
Tel: (716) 395-2209
Richard R. Arnold, Chmn; 15 FT instr. Pub; D; ent. req. HS dipl, ent. exam; 4 yr; degrees, B.A, B.S; schol; 23 SC, 29 LC (Art History); enrl. 8188, maj. 200, grad. 2000. Tui. res. $550, non-res. $900; campus res. $650.

Ceramics	Painting
Drawing	Photography
History of Art	Printmaking
Jewelry	Sculpture

BRONX

HERBERT H. LEHMAN COLLEGE,* Art Department, 2 Van Cortlandt Ave. E, 10468. Tel: (212) 960-8256
Roger H. Bolomey, Chmn; 16 FT, 17 PT instr. Pub; D & E; ent. req. HS dipl; 4 yrs; degrees, B.A, B.F.A; 24 SC, 26 LC, 24 GC; enrl. maj. 200, grad. students 60. Tui. N.Y.C. Res. Matriculant, none, non-matriculant, $18 per cr. hr.

Ceramics	History of Art & Archaeology
Drafting	Painting
Drawing	Photography
Graphic Arts	Sculpture
Graphic Design	

Summer School: Lymann Kipp, Chmn.

Art History	Painting & Life Drawing
Design	Photography & Advanced Photography
Drawing & Advanced Drawing	phy
Graphic Arts Workshop & Advanced Graphics	

MANHATTAN COLLEGE, School of Arts and Sciences, Fine Arts Department, Manhattan College Parkway, 10471.
Tel: (212) 548-1400
George L. McGeary, Chmn. Dept; 2 FT, 2 PT instr. Estab. 1853; den; D & E; ent. req. HS dipl; 4 yr; degree, B.A; schol; 21 SC, 26 LC; enrl. D 3600, E 500, maj. 6, grad. students 870. Tui. $2500 per yr; campus res. $1500.

Advertising Design	Jewelry
Aesthetics	Lettering
Art Education	Museum Staff Training
Ceramics	Painting
Drawing	Photography
Graphic Arts	Sculpture
Graphic Design	Stage Design
History of Art & Archaeology	Teacher Training

BRONXVILLE

SARAH LAWRENCE COLLEGE, 10708.
Tel: (914) 337-0700 Exten. 301
A. Uchima, Head, Art Dept; 1 FT, 7 PT instr. Estab. 1928; pvt; D; ent. req. HS dipl; 4 yr; degree, A.B; schol; 10 SC; enrl. 170. Tui. $4150 per yr; campus res. approx. $1000.

Architecture	Painting
Ceramics	Photography
Drawing	Sculpture
Graphic Arts	Stage Design
History of Art & Archaeology	Theatre Arts

Summer School: Mr. Wentworth and Mr. Cogan, Dirs; courses offered in process of being formulated.

BROOKLYN

THE BROOKLYN MUSEUM ART SCHOOL, 188 Eastern Pkwy, 11238.
Tel: (212) 638-4486
George McClancy, Dir; David O'Lenick, Asst. Dir; Marge Stevens, Registrar; 5 FT, 66 PT instr. Estab. 1898; pvt; D & E, FT and PT classes; Max Beckmann Memorial Schols. and foreign and work schols. for advanced painting and ceramics; enrl. approx. 900, HS program 175. Tui. $275 FT, $90-$100 PT per 15 wk sem.

Ceramics	Printmaking
Drawing	Sculpture
Etching	Stained Glass

Lithography	Weaving
Jewelry	Welding
Museum & Galley Tours	Woodworking
Painting	

Summer School: Courses offered, same as above; tui. $150 FT, $60-$70 PT per 8 wk. session.

LONG ISLAND UNIVERSITY, Brooklyn Center, Art Department, 385 Flatbush Ave. Exten, 11201. Tel: (212) 834-6060
Nathan Resnick, Chmn; 3 FT, 3-4 PT instr. Pvt; D & E; ent. req. HS dipl, ent. exam; 4 yr; degrees, B.A, B.S; schol; 5 SC, 3 LC. Tui. $80 per cr.

Art Workshops	Introduction to Media Art
Drawing	Painting
History of Art	Photography
History of the Motion Picture	Visual Experience

Summer School: Nathan Resnick, Dir; courses offered, Drawing, Painting, Photography; tui. $80 per cr. for term of 6 wk. two sessions beginning June 14 and July 26.

BROOKVILLE

C. W. POST CENTER OF LONG ISLAND UNIVERSITY, Art Department, School of the Arts, (P.O. Greenvale, N.Y. 11548).
Tel: (516) 299-2464
Prof. Arnold Simonoff, Chmn; 16 FT, 10 PT, E 5 PT instr. Estab. 1954; pvt; ent. req. portfolio and interviews; 4 yr; degrees, B.A. with maj. in Art, B.A. in Art Educ, B.F.A, M.A. in Art, M.S. in Art Educ; 23 SC, 15 LC, 11 GC; enrl. maj. 300, E 300, non-matriculate 1000. Tui. $2560, $80 per cr. part-time; campus res. room and board $1600.

Ceramics	Painting
Design	Photography
Drawing	Sculpture
Graphics	Teacher Training

Summer School: Prof. Arnold Simonoff, Dir; $80 per cr. for term of 5 wk; two 5 wk. terms July-Aug, Aug.-Sept; enrl. 500.

BUFFALO

ROSARY HILL COLLEGE, Art Concentration, 4380 Main St, 14226.
Tel: (716) 839-3600
James A. Allen, Chmn; 8 FT, 2 PT instr. Estab. 1948; pvt; D & E; ent. req. HS grad, portfolio; 4 yr; degrees, B.F.A, B.S; schol; 38 SC, 7 LC; enrl. art concentration 150, coll. 1300. Tui. $2250; campus res. $1250.

Aesthetics	Painting
Art Education	Photography
Calligraphy	Printmaking
Ceramics	Sculpture
Drawing	Teacher Training
History of Art	Theatre Arts
Jewelry	Weaving
Off-Loom Fibers	

Summer School: Dr. Edward McMahon, Dir.

STATE UNIVERSITY OF NEW YORK COLLEGE AT BUFFALO, Faculty of the Arts, 1300 Elmwood Ave, 14222.
Tel: (716) 862-6326, 6327
Harry Ausprich, Dean; Art Educ. 17 FT, 1 PT, Design 25 FT, Fine Arts 19 FT, 2 PT instr. Estab. 1930; pub; ent. req. HS grad; ent. exam, interview, portfolio; 4-5 yr; degrees, B.S.(Art Educ, Design), B.A.(Art, Art History), B.F.A.(Painting, Printmaking, Photography, Sculpture), M.S.(Art Educ); schol; 73 SC, 53 LC; enrl. Art Educ. 916, Design 1601, Fine Arts 1714. Tui. $650 per yr. plus $250 fees.

Advertising Design	Jewelry
Art Therapy	Lithography
Ceramics	Metalsmithing
Crafts	Modeling
Drawing	Painting
Environmental Design	Photography
Etching	Research in Art
Fibers & Textiles	Research in Art Education
Film	Research in Art History
Graphic Design	Sculpture
History of Art	Serigraphy
Illustration	Teacher Education
Independent Study	Theater Design
Industrial Design	Video & VTR
Interdisciplinary Arts Study	Wood Design
Interior Design	

Summer Workshops and Sessions: Harry Ausprich, Dean. Tui. undergrad. $23 per cr. hr.

STATE UNIVERSITY OF NEW YORK, UNIVERSITY CENTER AT
   BUFFALO, Department of Art and Art History, Bethune Hall,
   2917 Main St, 14214. Tel: (716) 831-5251
Donald C. Robertson, Chmn; 21 FT, 14 PT instr. Estab. 1894; pub;
D & E; ent. req. HS dipl, portfolio, acceptance by Univ; degrees,
B.F.A, B.A.(4 yr), M.F.A.(2 yr), M.A.H.(1 yr); schol, grad. fel;
SC, LC, GC; enrl. D 260, E 150, grad. 60. Tui. D underclass $650,
upperclass $800, res. fee $1500, E underclass $21.50, upperclass
$26.75 per cr, grad. res. $600, non-res. $750.

Art Education	Painting
Art History	Photography
Design	Sculpture
Drawing	Serigraphy
Intaglio	Visual Communications
Lithography	

   Summer School: Theodore B. Fitzwater, Dir; tui. undergrad.
underclass $21.50, upperclass $26.75 per cr, grad. res. $40, out-
of-state $50; enrl. 150.

Design Workshops	Photo/Film Workshops
Drawing	Printmaking Workshops
Painting	Sculpture

VILLA MARIA COLLEGE, Art Department, 240 Pine Ridge Rd,
   14225. Tel: (716) 896-0700 Exten. 37
Katherine G. Verney, Chmn; 2 FT, 1 PT instr. Estab. 1961; pvt;
D & E; ent. req. HS dipl, portfolio; 2 yr; degrees, A.S.(Interior Design), A.A.(Fine Arts and Communications), cert.(Interior Design,
1 yr); schol; 14 SC, 6 LC; enrl. D 155, E 30, maj. 89, non-credit 15.
Tui. $1500 per yr, $50 per cr. hr; off campus res. by arrangement.

Advertising Design	History of Interiors
Art Education	Interior Design
Arts & Crafts for Children	Lettering
Ceramics	Painting
Commercial Art	Photography
Display	Sculpture
Drawing	Window Treatment & Installation
History of Art & Archaeology	

CANTON

ST. LAWRENCE UNIVERSITY, Department of Fine Arts, 13617.
   Tel: (315) 379-5192
J. M. Lowe, Head; 6 FT, 1 PT instr. Estab. Univ. 1856, Dept. 1966;
pvt; ent. req. HS grad, ent. exam; 4 yr; degree, B.A; schol; 10 SC,
14 LC; enrl. 400, maj. 50. Tui. $3170 per yr; campus res. $1465 per
yr.

Aesthetics	Painting
Art Education	Photography
Ceramics	Printmaking
Drawing	Sculpture
History of Art	Teacher Training

   Summer School: J. Van Ness, Dir; tui. $250 for course for term
of 5 wk. beginning June 1.

Ceramics	Introduction to Studio
Drawing	Painting
European Art of the	Sculpture
19th Century	Survey of Art

CAZENOVIA

CAZENOVIA COLLEGE, Department of Fine Arts, 13035.
   Tel: (315) 655-3466
Dr. Stephen M. Schneewelss, Pres; John Alrstars, Dir, Art Program;
1 FT, 4 PT instr. Estab. 1824; pvt; D & E; W; ent. req. HS grad,
interview; 2 yr; degree, A.A.S; 15 SC, 2 LC; enrl. maj. 20.

CHAUTAUQUA

CHAUTAUQUA ART CENTER, Summer School, Wythe Ave, 14722.
   Tel: (716) 357-2771
Oscar E. Remick, Pres; Robert V. Woodside, Asst. to Pres. for
Educ. Estab. 1874; pvt; open ent; schol. Tui. minimum $15 per wk.
State University of New York College at Fredonia credit courses and
workshops for grad. and undergrad. also offered.

Art Appreciation	Metals
Art Criticism	Painting
Ceramics	Pottery
Drawing	Sculpture
Handicrafts	Weaving
Jewelry	

Children's classes, drawing, painting, graphics, textiles, ceramics,
crafts.

CORNING

CORNING COMMUNITY COLLEGE, Humanities Division,
   14830.
John M. Runyon, Chmn, Div; 2 FT, 1 PT instr. Estab. 1958; pub;
D & E; ent. req. HS dipl, ent. exam, HS equivalency exam; 2 yr;
degrees, A.A, A.S; 13 SC, 5 LC; enrl. D 350, E 50, maj. 40. Tui.
$600 per yr; no campus res.

Ceramics	History of Art & Archaeology
Crafts-Design	Painting
Drafting	Sculpture
Drawing	Two & Three Dimensional Design

Adult hobby classes, ceramics, two & three dimensional design,
drawing; tui. $75; enrl. 20.
   Summer and Evening School: Gary A. Yoggy, Dir; courses offered, Ceramics, Drawing; tui. $75 per term of 5 wk. beginning June
1976; enrl. 20.

ELMIRA

ELMIRA COLLEGE, 14901.
   Tel: (607) 734-3911
4 FT, 1 PT instr. Estab. 1855; pvt; D & E; 4 yr; degrees; schol;
2 LC, 12 Lab.C; enrl. 155. Tui. $3100, room and board, $1275
campus res.

Advanced Design	Jewelry & Metalwork
Art Education	Printmaking
Design Techniques	Sculpture, Welding, Casting
Drawing & Painting	Theory & History of Art
Fine Arts	

FREDONIA

STATE UNIVERSITY OF NEW YORK COLLEGE AT FREDONIA,
   Department of Art, 14063. Tel: (716) 673-3537
Emitt Christian, Chmn; 10 FT, 2 PT instr. Estab. 1867; pub; D & E;
ent. req. HS grad, ent. exam, portfolio; 4 yr; degree, B.A; schol; 30
SC, 20 LC, 11 GC; enrl. 700, maj. 150. Tui. $800, non-res. $1300;
campus res. $2500 per yr.

Aesthetics	History of Art
Ceramics	Painting
Drawing	Photography
Graphic Arts	Sculpture

   Summer School: Emmitt Christian, Chmn; courses as above; tui.
$21.50 per cr. hr. for term of 6 wks.

GARDEN CITY

✠ADELPHI UNIVERSITY, Department of Art, 11530.
   Tel: (516) 294-8700 Exten. 387, 388
Grace R. Cantone, Chmn; 8 FT, 5 PT instr. Estab. 1896; pvt; 4 yr;
degrees; 40 SC, 10 LC; enrl. maj. 90, others 600.

Advertising Design	Interior Design
Color Media, Materials	Painting & Drawing
Crafts	Photography
Fashion Design	Sculpture & Ceramics
Graphics	Teaching Methods & Training
History of Art	Two-Dimensional Design

   Summer School: Grace R. Cantone, Dir; 5 wk. 2 sessions D & E,
creative crafts workshops.

NASSAU COMMUNITY COLLEGE, Art Department, Stewart Ave,
   11530. Tel: (516) 742-0600 Exten. 258
Dr. Leon Frankston, Chmn; 13 FT, 23 PT instr. Affiliated with
State Univ. of New York; Dept-School estab. 1962; pub; D & E; 2 yr;
degrees, A.A, A.A.S; enrl. maj. 350.

Advertising Design	Graphics
Ceramics	Handcrafts
Costume Design	Interior Design
Drawing	Painting
Fashion Illustration	Photography
Gallery Survey	Sculpture
General Crafts	

   Summer School: Dr. Leon Frankston, E Supvr; tui. $23 per cr.
for county res, $46 per cr. for non-county res. for two 5 wk. terms.

GENESEO

STATE UNIVERSITY OF NEW YORK COLLEGE AT GENESEO,*
   College of Arts & Science, Department of Art, 14454.
   Tel: (716) 245-5414
Paul H. Hepler, Chmn; 10 FT, 4 PT instr. Estab. 1871; pub; D & E;
ent. req. HS dipl, ent. exam; 3-4 yrs; degree, B.A. in Art; 35 SC,
7 LC; enrl. D 1000, E 1150, maj. approx. 100. Tui. $650 lower div,
$800 upper div, $22.35 per cr. hr; campus res. $1225.

Art Appreciation	Jewelry
Art Education	Modern Architecture

Ceramics	Modern Painting
Drawing	Painting
Fashion Arts	Photography
Graphic Arts	Sculpture
Handicrafts	Textile Design
History of Art	Wood Design

Summer School: Paul H. Hepler, Chmn; courses offered vary.

GENEVA

HOBART & WILLIAM SMITH COLLEGES, Art Department, 14456.
Tel: (315) 789-5500
Prof. Alvin I. Sher, Chmn; 5 FT instr. Estab. approx. 1800; pvt; D;
ent. req. HS dipl, ent. exam; 4 yr; degrees, B.A, B.S; schol; 15 SC,
8 LC; enrl. D 1600. Tui. approx. $300 per yr; campus res. approx.
$1500

Aesthetics	Painting
Architecture	Photography
Drawing	Sculpture
Graphic Arts	Theatre Arts
History of Art & Archaeology	

HAMILTON

COLGATE UNIVERSITY,* Department of Fine Arts, Charles A.
Dana Creative Arts Center, 13346. Tel: (315) 824-1000
Exten. 248
Brooks W. Stoddard, Chmn; 7 FT, 1 PT instr. Estab. 1905; pvt; co-
ed; ent. req. HS grad. plus ent. exam; 4 yr; degree, B.A; schol; loan
funds; 16 SC, 20 LC; enrl. maj. 35, others 650. Tui. $2975, room
$600, board $730, student fees $55; campus res.

Architectural History	Drawing & Painting
Art History	Graphics
Basic Photography	Projects in Scene Design
Ceramics	Sculpture
Creative Design	2 & 3 Dimensional Design
Design in Theatre	

HEMPSTEAD

✠HOFSTRA UNIVERSITY, Department of Fine Arts, 11550.
Tel: (516) 560-3231
Prof. John Hopkins, Chmn; Dr. R. Myron, Chmn. Art History and
Humanities Dept; 14 FT, 3 PT instr. Estab. 1935; pvt; D & E; ent.
req. good secondary school record, coll. ent. board exam; 4 yr; degrees, B.A, B.S.Art Educ; schol; 32 SC, 1 LC, 3 GC. Tui. undergrad. $92 per sem. hr, grad. $95 per sem. hr. (res/fees $780 sem).

Color & Design	Metalsmithing
Current Gallery Develop-	Painting
ments (lecture)	Photography
Etching	Pottery
Fundamentals of Applied	Sculpture
Design, 2 & 3-D	Serigraphy
Fundamentals of Graphic	3-D Design
Expression	2-D Representation
General Crafts	Woodcut
Lithography	

Summer School: H. Lichtenstein, Dean, University College.

HOUGHTON

HOUGHTON COLLEGE, Art Department, 14744.
Tel: (716) 567-2211 Exten. 136
Marjorie O. Stockin, Dept. Head; 2 FT, 1 PT instr. Estab. 1883;
den; D; Ent. req. HS dipl, SAT scores; 4 yr; no art maj; enrl. 122
Studio Courses, 50 Art Survey. Tui. $2500 per yr; campus res.
$1200.

Art Education	History of Art & Archaeology
Ceramics	Painting
Drawing	Sculpture
Graphic Arts	Teacher Training
Graphic Design	

ITHACA

CORNELL UNIVERSITY, College of Architecture, Art and Planning,
14850. Tel: (607) 256-4912
Kermit C. Parsons, Dean; 60 FT, 24 PT instr. Estab. 1871; pvt; 4-5
yr; degrees; 71 SC, 108 LC, 8 Lab.C; schol; normal enrl. 650. Tui.
and fees $3775 in College of Architecture, undergrad. and grad; cam-
pus res.

Department of Art, College of Architecture Art and Planning
Kenneth Evett, Chmn; 14 FT, 6 PT instr. Estab. 1921; degrees;
B.F.A, M.F.A; enrl. 100 maj.

Graphics	Photography
Painting	Sculpture

Department of the History of Art, College of Arts and Sciences,
14850. Tel: (607) 256-4905
Stanley O'Connor, Chmn; 12 FT instr. Estab. 1939; 64 LC, 12 GC.

Archaeology	History of Art
Architecture	Techniques & Materials
Art Criticism	

Department of Design and Environmental Analysis, New York
State College of Human Ecology. Tel: (607) 256-2168
Prof. Rose Steidl, Chmn; 23 FT instr. Estab. 1969 (originally Dept.
of Housing and Design estab. 1940); pub; D; 4 yr; degrees, B.S, M.A,
M.S; enrl. 250-300.

Apparel Design	Interior Design
Design	Product Design
Housing Technology	Textiles
Human Factors	

JAMAICA

CATAN-ROSE INSTITUTE OF ART,* 86-19 150th St, 11435.
Tel: (212) 291-1033; 72-72 112th St, Forest Hills, N.Y, 11375.
Tel: (212) 263-1962
Richard Catan-Rose, Pres. & Dir; 5 FT, 9 PT instr. Estab. 1943;
pvt; ent. req. HS grad, no ent. req. for adult or children's classes;
2 yr. Assoc. Cert. & 4 yr; cert, schol; D & E. Tui. $880 for scho-
lastic year of two sem, $499 for sem. of 16 wk; Adults, $75 per sem,
children's Sat. classes: Jr. group, 10 - 12 AM $65 per sem. of 16
wk; HS students Sat. 10 AM - 1 PM, $70 per sem. Approved for
veterans and Foreign students.

Advertising Design	Illustration
Fashion Illustration	Interior Design
Fine Arts & Design	

Summer School: 7 and 11 wk; foundation courses, Indoor and
Outdoor, Fine Arts, Advertising, Interiors, and Graphic Arts.

ST. JOHN'S UNIVERSITY, Department of Fine Arts, Grand Central
& Utopia Pkwys, 11439. Tel: 969-8000 Exten. 249
Edward J. Manetta, Chmn; 9 FT, 6 PT instr. Pvt; D; ent. req. HS
dipl, ent. exam, portfolio review; 4 yrs; degrees, B.F.A, B.S; schol;
24 SC, 9 LC; enrl. D 1300, maj. 100. Tui. $2200 per yr; no campus
res.

Advertising Design	Handicrafts
Ceramics	Jewelry
Display (Internship)	Museum Staff Training (Internship)
Drawing	Photography
Graphic Arts	Sculpture
Graphic Design	Teacher Training
Saturday scholarship program, art, music.	

Summer School: Dr. Mahdesian, Dir.

LAKE PLACID

✠LAKE PLACID SCHOOL OF ART (formerly Lake Placid Workshop),
Saranac Ave. Center for Music, Drama and Art, 12946.
Tel: (518) 523-2115, 2512
Daniel Claude Patchett, Dir; 7 FT, 5 PT instr. Estab. 1963; pub;
D & E; ent. req. HS dipl, portfolio for placement only; 2 yr; dipl.
program; schol; 18 SC, 2 LC; enrl. D 60, E 60, maj. 30. Tui. $1200
per yr; campus res. room $400.

Ceramics	History of Art & Archaeology
Drawing	Painting
Graphic Arts	Photography

Children's classes, crafts, design, drawing, painting; tui. $25 per
sem; enrl. 25.

Summer School: Daniel Claude Patchett, Dir; tui. $400 for term
of 8 wk. beginning June 23, summer housing $150; enrl. 100.

Ceramics	Lithography
Drawing	Painting
Etching	Photography
Kiln Construction	Screenprinting

LARCHMONT

ADAMY'S PLASTICS AND MOLD-MAKING WORKSHOPS, 19 Elkan
Rd, 10538. Tel: (914) 834-0270
George E. Adamy, Dir; 1 FT instr. Estab. 1968; pvt; D & E; no ent.
req; no degree; 6 SC, 1 LC; enrl. total 70. Tui. from $25 for 2 hr.
open-ended sessions to $225 for 10 sessions advanced course.
Summer School.

Plastics:	Mold-Making
Epoxies	Alginate Moulage
Fiber Glass	Latex
Foams	Plaster
Films	RTV Silcone Rubber
Polyesters	

LOCH SHELDRAKE

SULLIVAN COUNTY COMMUNITY COLLEGE, Art Department, 12759. Tel: (914) 434-5750 Exten. 215
Joseph Hopkins, Chmn; 3 FT instr. Estab. 1968; pub; D & E; ent. req. HS dipl. or equivalent; 2 yr; degree, A.A.S; schol; 53 hr. SC, 44 hr. LC; enrl. 95.
   Summer School: W. F. Schneider, Dr.

MILLBROOK

BENNETT COLLEGE, Fine Arts Department, 12545.
   Tel: (914) 677-3441
Ralph Della-Volpe, Chmn; 3 FT, 1 PT instr. Estab. approx. 1908; pvt; D; W; ent. req. HS dipl, self evaluation, portfolio for maj; 2 yr; degree, A.A.S; schol; 13 SC, 3 LC, electives 246; enrl. total 240. Tui. $3280 (not including art supplies); campus res. $1800.

Drawing	Painting
History of Art	Sculpture

NEW PALTZ

STATE UNIVERSITY OF NEW YORK COLLEGE AT NEW PALTZ, 12561.

   Studio Art Department
Maurice Brown, Chmn; approx. 26 faculty mem. Pub; 4 yr; degrees, B.F.A, M.F.A; enrl. total 8000.

Ceramics	Photography
Gold & Silversmithing	Printmaking
Painting	Sculpture

   Art Education Department
Susan Wisherd, Chmn; approx 5 faculty mem. Degrees, B.S.(Art Educ, M.S.(Art Educ).

   Summer School: Robert Davidson, Dir; 8 wk. sem.

NEW ROCHELLE

THE COLLEGE OF NEW ROCHELLE, Art Department, 10801.
   Tel: (914) 632-5300
Mary Jane Robertshaw, Chmn. Undergrad; Herbert Morris, Chmn. Grad; 7 FT, 12 PT instr. Estab. 1929; pvt; D & E; under-grad. W, grad. co-ed; ent. req. HS dipl; 4 yr; degrees, undergrad. B.A, B.F.A.(with concentrations in Studio Art, Art History, Art Education, Fine Arts, Applied Design, Art/Psychology), grad. M.A.(Art Educ); schol; undergrad. 39 SC, 11 LC, 3 seminars, grad. 34 SC, 8 LC, 2 seminars; enrl. undergrad. 148, grad. 105. Tui. undergrad. $2250, room and board $1600, grad. $75 per cr. hr; campus res.

Advanced Ceramics	Filmmaking
Advanced Drawing	History of Black Art
Advanced Photography	History of Art (Ancient, European,
Advanced Sculpture	American, Oriental, North
American Art	American)
Art Education	History of Italian Renaissance Art
Art Therapy	Humanities in Contemporary Society
Ceramics	Introduction to History of Art
Creative Watercolor	Jewelry
Contemporary Issues in Art	Modern Art
Education	Painting
Coordinating Seminar	Photography
Design	Printmaking
Design, Layout & Printing	Reading Seminar
Designing for Educational	Screen Painting
Media	Sculpture
Drawing	Teacher Training
Enameling	Technical Drawing
Etching	Therapeutic Art
Fabric Design	Watercolor
Figure & Portrait	Weaving

Adult non-credit program; drawing and painting, fabric design, figure drawing, history of modern art, mosaics, sculpture, stained glass, weaving (loomless, tapestry), watercolor, woodcut printmaking; tui. $70 for 12 E sessions; enrl. 15.
Children's classes, Sat. AM; arts and crafts, drawing and painting; tui. $50 for 10 classes; enrl. 30.
   Summer School (M.A. program): Dr. William Scanlon; two 5 wk. sessions, June and July.

Ceramics	Jewelry
Contemporary Issues in Art	Painting
Education	Photography
Creative Arts Workshop	Sculpture
Design Media	Silk Screen Techniques
Drawing	Weaving
History of Contemporary Art	

HARRIET FeBLAND'S ADVANCED PAINTERS WORKSHOP, Premium Point, 10801. Tel: (914) 235-7322
Harriet FeBland, Dir; 4 FT, 2 PT instr. Estab. 1962; pvt; D & E; ent. req. exam. of students previous art work; tui. schol. students of the workshop offered during ann. exhibit as an award; 10 SC, 3 LC; enrl. D 180-200. Tui. $270 each studio class.

Art Education	Drawing
Color Dynamics	Figure Painting
Construction	Graphic Arts
Contemporary Painting (E)	Painting
Creative Painting	Woodcarving (E)
Critiques	

   Summer School: Harriet FeBland, Dir; courses offered, Color Dynamics I, Painting.

NEW YORK CITY

ABBE INSTITUTE,* School of Fine Arts, 100 Fifth Ave, 10011.
   Tel: (212) 924-4364
Leonard S. Friedman, Dir; D 3 FT, 5 PT instr. Estab. 1938, re-opened 1947; pvt; 4 yr; enrl. D 60, E 60. Tui. $900.

Display	Illustration
Drawing & Painting	Interior Decoration
Fashion Illustration	

ABINGDON SQUARE PAINTERS, INC, 242 W. 14th St, 10011.
   Tel: (212) 243-7343
Harriet Fitzgerald, Dir; Edith P. Nolan, Pres; 2 instr. Estab. 1948; pvt; D; ent. req. must show serious intentions; no academic accreditation; a cooperative of professional artists and students offering instruction to beginning and advanced students; studio facilities available 24 hrs. per day; enrl. limited to 15. Mem. $25 per month.

ALBERT PELS SCHOOL OF ART, INC, 2109 Broadway, 10023.
   Tel: (212) 873-4823
Albert Pels, Dir; 4 FT, 5 PT instr. Estab. 1946; pvt; D & E; ent. req. 2 yr. HS educ. or equivalency plus interview with Dir, portfolio exam; 2-3 yr; state-approved cert. of completion; schol; enrl. all students commercial (advertising) art majors. Tui. per yr. $1500, Sept. 1973: full-time $150 mo, part-time $80 mo; reg. fee $10, supply kit $40; no campus res.

Advertising Design	Graphic Design
Architectural Rendering	Illustration (book, ad)
Art Education	Industrial Design
Cartooning	Interior Design and Rendering
Commercial Art	Landscape Architecture
Drawing	Lettering
Fashion Illustration	Packaging
Graphic Arts	Painting

Adult hobby classes, drawing, painting; tui. $25. mo, 1 per wk. Children's classes; tui. $16. mo, 1 per wk.
   Summer School: Albert Pels, Dir, 3 FT instr; tui. $100. for term of 2 months beginning July 9, 1973; courses offered in Commercial Art.

Advertising Design	Lettering
Graphic Arts	Mechanicals
Illustration	Pasteups
Layouts	

ART CENTER OF THE 92nd STREET Y.M.-Y.W.H.A, Lexington Ave. and 92nd St, 10028. Tel: (212) 427-6000 Exten. 722
Elaine Breiger, Art Dir; 16 PT instr. Estab. 1935; pvt; D & E; enrl. 500. Tui. $80-$125 per sem. of 4 mo; children's classes $50-$110 per sem. of 4 mo.

Art Lectures	Glass
Art Tours	Jewelry & Metalcraft
Calligraphy (English &	Multi-Media
Hebrew)	Painting
Crafts	Pottery
Drawing	Sculpture
Etching	Textiles

   Summer School: Same classes as above, June and July.

✠ART STUDENTS LEAGUE OF NEW YORK, 215 W. 57th St, 10019.
   Tel: (212) 347-4510
Stewart Klonis, Exec. Dir; 53 FT and PT instr. Estab. 1875; pvt; no ent. req; schol; LC; enrl. D 1200, E 600, Sat. (adults and children) 450. Tui. $64 mo. for 5 D classes per wk, $58 for 5 E; children and adults Sat. ½ day $28 mo, full day $44; part-time classes D & E

Anatomy	Painting
Fine Arts Calligraphy	Sculpture
Fine Arts Illustration	Textile Design
Graphics	

   Summer School: In New York City $64 mo. beginning June 1; enrl 750; in Woodstock $77 mo. beginning July 1; enrl. 80.

BALLARD SCHOOL,* Young Women's Christian Association, 610
    Lexington Ave, 10022. Tel: (212) 755-4500
Madeleine J. Douet, Dir; 7 PT instr. Estab. 1870; pvt; D & E. Tui.
$60 for 12 lessons for 12 wk.

Chinese Brush Work	Oil Painting
Drawing & Sketching	Portrait Painting
Landscape Painting	Sculpture
Life	Watercolor

Summer School.

CLAYWORKS COOPERATIVE, 332 E. Ninth St, 10003.
    Tel: (212) 677-8311
3 PT instr. Estab. 1971-1972; pvt; D children, E adult; 3 SC. Tui.
$65 adult 3 mo. course.
Ceramics
Children's classes, ceramics: tui. $27.50 for 10 classes; enrl. 3-5
yr. old, approx. 6-8 per class, 5-9 yr. old, approx. 6-8 per class.
    Summer School: Courses offered, 4 wk. intensive beginners
pottery course; tui. $36 for term of 4 wk. beginning July-Aug, Aug-
Sept; enrl. 6-8.

COLUMBIA UNIVERSITY, W. 114th to 121st Sts, 10027.
    Tel: (212) 280-1754

    School of Architecture, Avery Hall.
James Stewart Polshek, Dean; 29 FT, 50 PT instr. Estab. 1881; pvt;
degrees, M.Arch.(3 yr, minimum ent. req. B.A. or B.S), M.S.Arch.
& Urban Design (1 yr, minimum ent. req. B.Arch), M.S.Planning (2
yr, minimum ent. req. B.A, B.S, B.Arch or B.C.E), M.S.Arch.Tech.
(1 yr, minimum ent. req. B.Arch. or B.C.E), M.S.Historic Preservation (1½ yr, minimum ent. req. B.A, B.S. or B.Arch), M.S.Health
Services Planning & Design (1 yr, minimum ent. req. B.Arch);
schol. and fel; normal enrl. 350. Tui. $125 per point; campus res.

Architectural Technology	Health Services Planning & Design
Architecture	Historic Preservation
Architecture & Urban Design	Urban Planning

    Department of Art History and Archaeology,* 811 Schermerhorn
    Building.
Alfred Frazer, Chmn; 24 FT, 28 PT instr. Pvt.

    Columbia College*
George R. Collins, Dept. Rep. Pvt; M; 4 yr; degree, B.A; courses
offered in Western Art, lectures, discussions and seminars. Tui.
$3180 per yr. See subject area listing under Graduate Dept.

    School of General Studies*
Allen Staley, Dept. Rep. Pvt. 4 yr; degree, B.S; courses, lectures
and seminars. See subject area lising under Graduate Dept.

    Graduate Department*
Alfred Frazer, Chmn. Pvt; degrees, M.A.(2 yr), M.Phil.(4 yr),
Ph.D.(7 yr); schol. and fel; courses, lectures and seminars. Tui. FT
$1540 per term, PT $925.

Art & Archaeology of South	History of Western Art
Eastern Asia	Near Eastern Art & Archaeology
Asian Art & Archaeology	Primitive & Pre-Columbian Art &
Classical Art & Archaeology	Archaeology

    School of the Arts,* 617 Dodge, 10027.
Bernard Beckerman, Dean; 17 FT, 40 PT instr. Estab. 1965; pvt;
co-ed; ent. req. Bachelor's degree or equivalent, work submitted;
2 of more yr; degrees, M.F.A.(Painting & Sculpture, Writing, Film),
D.M.A.(Music Composition); schol; enrl. 1220. Tui. $3080, special
students $103 per point; campus res.

Drawing	Painting
Film	Sculpture
Graphic Arts	Writing
Musical Composition	

    Summer School: Frederick M. Keener, Dean; two 6 wk. sessions
beginning early July; tui. $86 per point.

Architecture	Painting
Art History	Sculpture
Film	Urban Planning

    Barnard College, Department of Art History,* 606 W. 120th St,
    10027. Tel: (212) 280-2118
Barbara Novak, Chmn; 4 FT, 4 PT instr. Estab. 1923; pvt; W; 4 yr;
degree; schol; enrl. maj. 29, total 1930. Tui. $2730; campus res.
Courses in History of Art and Painting.

    Teachers College, Department of Art and Education,* 525 W.
    120th St, 10027. Tel: (212) 865-6000
William J. Mahoney, Chmn; 6 FT, 6 PT instr. Estab. 1888; pvt; ent.
req. Bachelor's degree; degrees, M.A, M.Educ, Ph.D; schol. and fel;
grad. courses in Teacher Educ; enrl. 225. Tui. $96 per point, unless
otherwise stated.

Appreciation	Painting

Crafts	Sculpture
Design	Teacher Education
Graphics	

    Summer School: Two 6 wk. sessions beginning early June; tui.
$96 per point.

COOPER UNION SCHOOL OF ART, Cooper Square, Fourth Ave. at
    Seventh St, 10003. Tel: (212) 254-6300
Prof. George Sadek, Dean; 12 FT, 66 PT instr. Estab. 1859; pvt,
endowed; D & E; ent. req. HS grad, 16 yr. and exam; 4 yr; degrees,
cert, B.F.A; 31 SC, 19 LC; enrl. D 329, E 265. Tui. free.
Architecture
Fine Arts

CRAFT STUDENTS LEAGUE OF THE YWCA, 610 Lexington Ave,
    10022. Tel: (212) 755-4500
Madeleine J. Douet, Dir; 42 instr. Estab. 1932; pvt; D & E; enrl.
D & E 1600. Tui. $50-$95.

Appliqué	Needlepoint, Canvas Stitchery
Basketry	& Embroidery
Batik	Oil Painting
Bookbinding	Picture Framing
Calligraphy & Lettering	Printmaking
Candlemaking	Puppetry
Ceramics	Quilting
Cloisonné	Sculpture
Creative Leather	Silk Screening
Crochet	Silversmithing
Decoupage	Spinning & Dyeing
Drawing	Tapestry
Guitar Construction	Watercolor & Drawing
Jewelry & Enameling	Weaving
Lapidary	Wood & Stone Sculpture
Lost Wax Process	Woodworking
Macramé	

DONALD PIERCE SCHOOL OF PAINTING, 463 West St, 10014.
    Tel: (212) 242-5089
Donald Pierce, Dir; 1 FT instr. Estab. 1948; pvt; D; ent. req. over
16 yr. of age; winter session Sept-May. Tui. monthly, part-time
$40, winter session ½ day per wk.

Acrylic	Oil Painting
Drawing	Watercolor

EMANU-EL MIDTOWN YM-YWHA, 344 E. 14th St, 10003.
    Tel: (212) 674-7200
Charles Eanet, Art Dir; 12 PT instr. Estab. 1906; pvt; D & E; no
ent. req; no degrees; 30 SC; enrl. D 250 part time students. Tui.
$30 per 12 sessions Y mem, $45 non-mem.

Ceramics	Painting
Drawing	Photography

FASHION INSTITUTE OF TECHNOLOGY, 227 W. 27th St, 10001.
    Tel: (212) 760-7700
Marvin Feldman, Pres; Richard Streiter, Dean of Students; Robert
Gutman, Assoc. Dean, Art and Design Div; 155 FT, 80 PT instr.
Estab. 1944 sponsored by Board of Educ, became part of State Univ.
program 1951; pub; ent. req. HS grad, ent. exam; 2 yr; degree, A.A.S;
tui. schol; enrl. D 2600, Exten. 4000 (per semester). Tui. per yr.
$462, non-res. $1012; dorm. per yr. $1910. Summer Session.
Winterim (three-week mini-semester in January).
Advertising Curriculum: maj. in Display & Exhibit Design, Illustra-
    tion (Fashion), Advertising Design, Photography
Fine Arts Curriculum: maj. in Fine Arts
Business Curriculum: maj. in Advertising & Communications, Fash-
    ion Buying & Merchandising, Textile & Apparel Marketing
Design Curriculum: maj. in Fashion, Interior, Jewelry and Textile
    Design
Industrial Technology Curriculum: maj. in Management Engineering,
    Textile Technology and Patternmaking Technology.

FORDHAM UNIVERSITY,* Liberal Arts College at Lincoln Center,
    Division of Arts, 60th St & Columbus Ave, 10023.
    Tel: (212) 956-4774, 4775, 4776
Dr. Andree Hayum, Chmn; 7 FT, 8 PT instr. Estab. 1968; pvt; D & E;
ent. req. HS dipl, SAT, applicants considered on individual merit;
4 yr; degree, B.A; schol; 18 SC, 25 LC; enrl. D 900, E 1750, maj. 56.
Tui. $1100 per sem, $55 per cr. in E prog; no campus res. 4-1-4
sem. system.

Aesthetics	Painting
Costume Design & Construction	Photography
Drawing	Sculpture
Graphic Arts	Stage Design
History of Art & Archaeology	Teacher Training
New Media & Concepts	Theatre Arts

    Summer School: Dr. Ruth Naun, Dir; 4 terms per summer for
5 wk. each.

GERMAIN SCHOOL OF PHOTOGRAPHY,* 225 Broadway, 10007.
    Tel: (212) 964-4550
10 FT, 30 PT instr. Estab. 1947; pvt; D & E; ent. req. HS dipl; 1 yr;
cert; schol. Tui. varies.
    Summer School: Dr. Milton W. Willenson, Dir; variety of short
courses at our main school in New York City and branch school in
Kingston, Jamaica, W.I.

GREENWICH HOUSE POTTERY, Ceramic School, 16 Jones St, 10014.
    Tel: (212) 242-4106
Jane Hartsook, Dir; 16 PT instr. Estab. 1902; pvt; D & E; no ent.
req; schol; enrl. 250 (14 students per class). Tui. $90 to $105 per
sem, incl. summer.
Ceramic Art
Pottery
Sculpture
Children's classes, painting, ceramics; tui. $45 to $55 per sem; enrl.
125.

HENRY STREET SETTLEMENT SCHOOL OF ART AND POTTERY,
    265 Henry St, 10002. Tel: (212) 962-1100 Exten. 31
Bess Schuyler, Adminr; 4 FT, 2 PT instr. Estab. 1895; pvt; D & E;
co-ed; no ent. req; schol; 10 SC; enrl. D 40, E 60. Tui. $55-$65 per
course.

Banner Making	Jewelry
Batik	Painting
Ceramics	Photography
Drawing	Silk Screening
Graphic Arts	Stitchery
Handicrafts	Tie Die

Children's classes, pottery, arts & crafts, painting, tie dye; tui. $30
per sem. (free to neighborhood); enrl. 200.
    Summer School: Tui. $40 for term of 8 wk. beginning July 6,
1970; 1969 enrl. 40.

MAYER SCHOOL OF FASHION DESIGN, Art Department, 64 W.
    36th St, 10018.
Herbert Mayer, Dir; 4 FT, 13 PT instr. Estab. 1931; pvt; D & E;
ent. req. ent. exam; 9 mo; cert. in Designing, Patternmaking, Drap-
ing, Fashion Drawing, Dressmaking, Grading; 11 SC; enrl. D 110,
E 350. Tui. $1710 per yr, FT $190 per mo, PT varies; campus res.
no dorms, about $50 per wk, room & board. N.A.T.T.S. accredited.
Summer Session.

Drawing	Fashion Design
Dressmaking	Fashion Draping
Fashion Arts	Patternmaking

MECHANICS INSTITUTE,* 20 W. 44th St, 10036.
    Tel: (212) 687-4279
John I. McCormick, Dir; John Bellevier, Jewelry Design; 3 FT instr.
Estab. 1820; pvt; E; co-ed; 3 yr; enrl. 2042. Free tui, in subjects
related to work of those employed during day.
Architectural Drafting
Jewelry Design

NATIONAL ACADEMY SCHOOL OF FINE ARTS, 5 E. 89th St, 10028.
    Tel: (212) 369-4880
Alice G. Melrose, Dir; D 12 FT, E 3 FT instr. Estab. 1826; pvt; no
ent. req; schol; 12 SC; enrl. 170; reg. by month. Tui. D $64, E $50.

Composition—Portraiture	Life Sketch Class
Drawing	Painting—Oil & Watercolor
Graphic Arts Workshop	Sculpture

    Summer School: June, July and Aug.

NEW YORK INSTITUTE OF PHOTOGRAPHY,* 112 W. 31st St, 10001.
    Tel: (212) 244-3460
Lawrence Esmond, Dir. Estab. 1910; individualized instruction; D &
E; 12 mo; admission any Monday; normal enrl. 500. Approved by
New York State; approved for Veterans. Tui. $425 per course; defer-
red payment; student loans. Home study course.

Airbrush Technique	Oil Coloring
Commercial	Portrait
Motion Picture Production	Retouching
Natural Color Photography	

NEW YORK SCHOOL OF INTERIOR DESIGN, 155 E. 56th St, 10022.
    Tel: (212) 753-5365
Arthur Satz, Dir; 40 instr. Estab. 1916; pvt; D, E & Home; 3 yr. in
4 mo. sections; schol; enrl. D 400, E 200. Tui. $100-850 for 4 mo.
Interior Design & Decoration.
    Summer Session: Arthur Satz, Dir; courses offered, Interior De-
sign and Decoration; tui. $125-$285 for 6 wk. session; enrl. 200.

NEW YORK STUDIO SCHOOL OF DRAWING, PAINTING AND
    SCULPTURE, 8 W. 8th St, 10011. Tel: (212) 673-6466
Mercedes Matter, Dean; 17 FT, 4 PT instr. Estab. 1964 by art
students; pvt; D; ent. req. application, portfolio, interview, selec-

tion by faculty and students; full-time studio course req. 40 hr.
per week, session of 32 wk; no degrees granted; studio cr. given by
art schools and art dept. of accredited coll. for time spent; program
is part of U.I.C.A. student mobility program; 8 SC, 2 LC; schol;
enrl. limited. Tui. $2100 per yr.

Artists on Art (LC)	Painting
Drawing	Sculpture
History of Art	

    New York and Paris Summer Sessions: Tui. $800 each, 8 wk. each.

NEW YORK UNIVERSITY, Institute of Fine Arts, 1 E. 78th St, 10021.
    Tel: (212) 988-5550
Jonathan M. Brown, Chmn. Pvt; D & E; degrees; schol. and fel; enrl.
400 grad. (plus those maintaining matriculation). Tui. $100 per point
cr.

Conservation & Technology of Works of Art	History of Art & Archaeology Museum Training

    School of Education, Department of Art Education & Division of
Creative Arts, 80 Washington Sq. E, 10003. Tel: (212) 598-3478
Howard Conant, Chmn. Dept. of Art and Art Educ; 10 FT, 15 PT instr.
Pvt; D & E; ent. req. coll board ent. exam, 85% HS average, portfolio,
interview; degrees, B.S, M.A, Ed.D, Ph.D; schol, fel, and assistantships; undergrad. 26 SC, 13 LC, grad. 11 SC, 15 LC; enrl. undergrad.
maj. 115, grad. 130. Tui. $100 per point.

Aesthetic Foundations of the Arts	Modern Art & Modern Design Seminars
Art Teacher Training	Philosophy of Art
Art Therapy	Sculpture
Design & Graphics	Technological Experiments in
Drawing & Painting	the Arts
History of Art	

PACE UNIVERSITY, Dyson School of Liberal Arts, Art and Music
    Department, Pace Plaza, 10038. Tel: (212) 285-3000
Peter Fingesten, Chmn; 4 FT, 5 PT instr. Estab. 1950; pvt; D & E;
ent. req. HS dipl, ent. exam; 4 yr; no art major; 4 SC, 20 LC; enrl.
D c. 200, E 150 per sem, art only, 700-800 per yr. Tui. $75 per pt.
cr; campus res.

Architecture	Leather
Ceramics	Macrame
Drawing	Painting
Graphic Design	Sculpture
History of Art & Archaeology	Silver

    Summer School: Dr. Harold Lurier, Dir; courses offered, Art
and Architecture Design; three summer sessions.

✤PARSONS SCHOOL OF DESIGN (affiliated with the New School),
    66 Fifth Ave, 10011. Tel: (212) 741-8900
David C. Levy, Dean; 150 faculty. Estab. 1896; pvt; ent. req. HS
dipl, portfolio; 3-4 yr; degree, B.F.A, cert; schol; enrl. 900. Tui.
$2800 per yr. Pre-Coll. summer session, regular summer session,
E programs, summer and winter.

Art Education	Fashion Illustration
Communication Design	Fine Arts
Crafts	General Illustration
Environmental Design	Photography
Fashion Design	

PRATT-NEW YORK-PHOENIX SCHOOLS OF DESIGN, 160 Lexington
    Ave, 10016. Tel: (212) 685-2973
Robert Riger, Dir; Roz Goldfarb, Assoc. Dir; 30 instr. Estab. 1892;
pvt; ent. req. HS grad; 3 yr; cert; schol. and financial aid; SC, LC;
enrl. 150. Tui. $60 per cr. for 15 wk. sem.

Advertising Design & Photography	Illustration & Fine Arts Textile Design
Fashion Illustration	

    Individual evening courses, Art & Design; curriculum, write
for announcements.
    Individual summer classes, credit and non-credit, 6 wk. be-
ginning mid-June. Write for catalogue.

SCHOOL FOR CREATIVE MOVEMENT IN THE ARTS, 265 W. 87th
    St, 10024. Tel: (212) 724-3102
Jack & Hattie Wiener, Dir; 6 PT instr. Estab. 1963; pvt; D & E; no
ent. req; no degrees granted; enrl. D 40, E 28, grad. 68. No campus
res.

Drawing	Mixed-Media
Graphic Arts	Photography

Adult hobby classes, life-drawing, photography; tui. $90 for 12 wk.
term; enrl. 8 students per 2 hr. class.
Children's classes, pre-school art, mixed-media, movie-making/
animation, graphics; tui. $75-$100 for 17 wk. term.

SCHOOL OF BATIK PAINTING, 29 W. 84th St. 10024.
   Tel: (212) 595-1126
Jyotirindra Roy, Founder-Dir. Estab. in India 1961, in New York 1970; pvt; open to all; ent. req. only a trend in arts, age not below 16 unless exceptionally good in drawing and painting; cert. awarded with cr. after taking prescribed exam, additional special cr. awarded for thesis, eligibility for appearing in exam. is ascertained on the merit of specimen of work submitted by student; three E classes, one Sat. afternoon class, students eligible to attend any number of classes in a week; enrl. 20 students, min. of 6 students in a class.
Basic Technical Course
Junior Certificate Course for Textile Graphics
Senior Certificate Course for Fine Arts

THE SCHOOL OF VISUAL ARTS, 209-213 E. 23rd St, 10010.
   Tel: (212) 679-7350
Silas H. Rhodes, Dir; 300 instr. Estab. 1947; pvt; 4 yr; degree, B.F.A; enrl. 3000. Tui. FT, Fine Arts $900 per sem, Media Arts $900 per sem, Photography $900 per sem, Film $1000 per sem; PT E session per school yr. $100 for 2 cr. to $400 for 8 cr.

Advertising Design	Layout—Lettering
Airbrush	Magazine Illustration
Audio Visual Art	Paste-ups & Mechanicals
Children's Book Illustration	Photography
Decorative Illustration	Photo Retouching
Drawing & Painting	Production
Fashion Illustration	Sculpture
Film Art & Editing	Technical Illustration
Graphics	Textile Design
Journalistic Art	Typographic Design

Note: This school is a professional art school in higher educ. Qualified graduates may complete their studies for a degree at several colleges and universities in New York and out-of-state.

SCULPTURE CENTER,* 167 E. 69th St, 10021.
   Tel: (212) 737-9870
James Savage, Educ. Dir; 10 PT instr. Estab. 1933; pvt; D & E; co-ed; no ent. req; no degree; schol. Tui. $50 per mo. Sculpture courses.
Adult hobby classes, sculpture; tui. $25 per mo, one session per wk.

STUDIO WORKSHOP, 10 W. 18th St, 10011.
   Tel: (212) 242-9615
Richard Rapaport, Pres; 3 FT, 2 PT instr. Estab. 1968; pub; D & E; ent. req. none; schol; 4 SC. Tui. 2½ mo. $80, 3½ mo. $90. Summer School, adult and children's classes.

Ceramics	Sculpture
Drawing	Watercolor
Pottery	

TOBE-COBURN SCHOOL FOR FASHION CAREERS, LTD, 851 Madison Ave, 10021. Tel: (212) 879-4644
Avon Lees Jr, Pres. and Dir; 9 FT, 15 PT instr. Estab. 1937; pvt; D; W; 2 yr. course for HS grad, 1 yr. course for those with 2 or more yr. coll; classroom study alternates with periods of work in stores or projects in fashion field; partial schol; degree, A.A.(Occupational Studies); enrl. 200. Tui. $2200 per yr.

Display	Fashion Retailing
Fabrics	Merchandising
Fashion History	Salesmanship
Fashion Promotion	

TRAPHAGEN SCHOOL OF FASHION, 257 Park Ave. S, 10010.
   Tel: (212) 673-0300
Wanda Wdowka, Dir. Estab. 1923; pvt; non-profit co-ed; D; ent. req. HS dipl. or equivalency; 2-3 yr; cert; transfer cr. for B.F.A. honored at New York Inst. Technol. Tui. $1850 per yr. E, Sat. & 6 wk. summer sessions available.

Clothing Construction	Fashion Sketching
Draping	Interior Design & Decoration
Dressmaking	Layout—Methods & Paste-up
Fashion Design	Life Drawing
Fashion Illustration	Patternmaking & Grading

UMBERTO ROMANO SCHOOL OF CREATIVE ART, 162 E. 83rd St, 10028. Tel: (212) 288-9621
Umberto Romano, Dir. & Instr. Estab. 1933; pvt; D; co-ed. Tui. $480 per yr, $60 per mo.

Drawing	Painting
Graphic Arts	Sculpture

VISUAL ARTS CENTER, Lower West Side Center of The Children's Aid Society, 209 Sullivan St, 10012.
Allen M. Hart, Dir; 14 PT instr. Estab. 1968; D & E; schol; 35 SC; enrl. D 200, E 200. Tui. adults $55 per sem, children $32 per sem.

Batik	Painting

Cabinet Making	Photography
Drawing	Puppet Making
Enameling	

Adult and Children's classes Oct. 6 - Jan. 16, Feb. 2 - May 21.

OAKDALE

DOWLING COLLEGE, Department of Art, Idle Hour Blvd, 11769.
   Tel: (516) 589-6100 Exten. 246
Niel Peper, Arts Div. Coordinator; 7 FT, 17 PT instr; pvt; D & E; ent. req. HS dipl; 4 yrs; degrees, B.A. (Visual Art & Speech, Drama), B.S, B.B.A; schol; enrl. D 1100, E 500. Tui. approx. $2300 per yr; campus res. $800 yr. room, approx. $500 yr. board.

Advertising Design	Graphic Design
Aesthetics	Handicrafts
Architecture	History of Art & Archaeology
Art Education	Painting
Ceramics	Photography
Commercial Art	Sculpture
Drafting—Architectural	Silversmithing
Drawing	Stage Design
Enameling	Teacher Training
Graphic Arts	Theatre Arts

Adult hobby classes, drawing, painting, composition.
   Summer School: Dr. John McConkey, Dean.

OLD WESTBURY

NEW YORK INSTITUTE OF TECHNOLOGY, Fine Arts Department, Wheatley Rd, 11568. Tel: (516) 626-3400 Exten. 231
Dr. Frances Lassiter, Chmn; 11 Ft, 6 PT instr. Estab. 1957; pvt; D & E; ent. req. HS dipl, portfolio; 4 yr; degree, B.F.A; schol; 77 SC, 82 LC; enrl. D 350, maj. 250. Tui. $2100 per yr.

Advertising Design	Interior Design
Aesthetics	Lettering
Art Education	Painting
Commercial Art	Photography
Drawing	Sculpture
Graphic Arts	Stage Design
Graphic Design	Teacher Training
History of Art & Archaeology	Textile Design
Illustration	

ONEONTA

STATE UNIVERSITY OF NEW YORK COLLEGE AT ONEONTA, Department of Art, 13820. Tel: (607) 431-3718
George E. Zimmerman, Chmn; 11 FT instr. Estab. 1889; pub; D & E; ent. req. HS dipl, regents schol. exam. SAT and ACT; 4 yr; degrees, B.A.(Studio Art, Art History), Coll. at Oneonta offers prog. leading to M.A.(Museum History, Folk Art, Conservation & Restoration of Works of Art) in conjunction with the New York State Historical Association at Cooperstown, N.Y. 13326 (Dr. Bruce R. Buckley, SUNY Dir); 31 SC, 22 LC; enrl. D 660, E 35, maj. 123, approx. 25-30 at Cooperstown Center. Tui. lower division $650, $21.50 per hr, upper division $800, $26.75 per hr, tui. higher for non-res; campus res. $1231.

Ceramics	Photography
Drawing	Sculpture
Graphic Arts	Stage Design (Dept. of Speech
History of Art & Archaeology	& Theatre)
Jewelry	Textile Design
Museum Staff Training	Theatre Arts (Dept. of Speech
(Cooperstown Programs)	& Theatre)
Painting	

Adult hobby classes offered only on a subscription basis at normal tui. rates through the Office of Continuing Education.
Children's classes offered only through the Upper Catskill Study Council, Sat. Able and Ambitious Prog; Dr. Robert Porter, Dir. Dept. of Educ; enrl. varies between 20-40 per yr.
   Summer School: Dr. Robert B. Nichols, Dir. Continuing Educ; approx. 6 courses offered depending on demand, Art Criticism, Art History and Studio Courses; tui. same as in regular session; two 6 wk. terms beginning June 2 and July 7, 1975.

OSWEGO

✠STATE UNIVERSITY COLLEGE,* Art Department, 13126.
   Tel: (315) 341-2111
Allen R. Bremmer, Chmn; 22 FT instr. Estab. 1861; pub; 4-5 yr; degrees, B.A, M.A; 45 SC, 11 LC; normal enrl. 7200. Tui. $400, non-res. $600.

Art History	Studio Art
Museum Studies	Teacher Training

   Summer School: Lewis Pophan, Dean; $20 per grad. hr, $13.50 per undergrad. hr. for 6 wk. session; enrl. 2300.

POTSDAM

STATE UNIVERSITY OF NEW YORK COLLEGE AT POTSDAM,
Department of Fine Arts, 13676. Tel: (315) 268-2905
Roger W. Lipsey, Chmn; 11 FT instr. Pub; ent. req. HS grad, ent.
exam; 4 yr; degree, B.A; 23 SC, 16 LC; enrl. maj. 150. Tui. $400-
$600; campus res. room and board $950.

Ceramics	Photography
Drawing	Printmaking
Painting	Sculpture

Summer School: Roger W. Lipsey, Dir; courses offered, Ceramics, History of Art, Painting; tui. $13.50 per cr. for 6 wk; inquire for
current schedule; enrl. 50.

POUGHKEEPSIE

DUTCHESS COMMUNITY COLLEGE, Department of Visual Arts,
1 Pendell Rd, 12601. Tel: (914) 471-4500 Exten. 339
William M. Brown, Head; 10 FT, 3 PT instr. Estab. 1957; pub;
D & E; ent. req. HS dipl; 2 yr; degree, A.A.S.(Commercial Art);
schol; 24 SC, 22 LC; enrl. D 660, E 340, maj. 100. Tui. $22 per cr.
hr.

Ceramics	Lettering
Commercial Art	Metal
Drawing	Painting
Glass	Photography
Graphic Arts	Plastic
History of Art & Archaeology	Sculpture
Illustration	Textile Design
Jewelry	Weaving
Leather	Wood

VASSAR COLLEGE, Art Department, 12601.
Tel: (914) 452-7000 Exten. 2642
Richard Pommer, Chmn; 12 FT, 5 PT instr. Estab. 1861; pvt; D;
ent. req. HS grad, ent. exam; 4 yr; degree, B.A.(major in Art
History only, no major in Studio Art); schol; 8 SC, LC; enrl. maj.
90, others 2400. Tui. $3275; campus res. $1500.

Architecture	History of Art
Drafting	Painting
Drawing	Sculpture

PURCHASE

MANHATTANVILLE COLLEGE, Art Department, 10577.
Tel: (914) 946-9600
Barbara Debs, Pres; Mathew Broner, Chmn; 3 FT, 7 PT instr.
Estab. 1841; pvt; D & E; 4 yr; degrees, B.A, B.F.A; financial aid
available.
Summer School: R. J. Langley, Dir.

STATE UNIVERSITY OF NEW YORK COLLEGE AT PURCHASE,*
Division of Visual Arts, 10577. Tel: (914) 253-5000
Gibson A. Danes, Dean. Estab. 1966, opened fall 1972; pub; the
campus provides facilities for a large Museum of Visual Arts
and some 150,000 gross square feet along with instruction in film,
theatre, dance, music and the various fields in the visual arts.
Courses to be offered:

Aesthetics	Industrial Design
Architecture	Landscape Architecture
Art Education	Painting
Drafting	Photography
Drawing	Sculpture
Graphic Arts	Stage Design
Graphic Design	Theatre Arts
History of Art & Archaeology	

RIVERDALE

COLLEGE OF MT. ST. VINCENT,* Fine Arts Department, West
263rd St. and Riverdale Ave, 10471. Tel: (212) 549-8000
Sister Christine Marie, Chmn; 6 FT, 2 PT instr. Estab. 1847; pvt;
D & E; co-ed 1974 plus cooperation with Manhattan College; ent. req.
HS grad, coll. boards, 4 yr; HS record; 4 yr; degrees, B.A, B.S, B.S.
in Art Education; schol; 25 SC, 8 LC; enrl. D 950, E 50. Tui. $700,
board $800.

Advertising Design	Lettering
Art Education	Painting (oil and water)
Ceramics	Photography
Drawing	Sculpture
Graphic Arts	Design
History of Art	Teacher Training
Jewelry	

Summer School: Mrs. Margaret Higgins, Dir; Photography, Ceramics, Watercolor (course offerings vary in summer); tui. $40 per
cr. $5 reg. fee, for term of 6 wks. beginning June 3.

RIVERSIDE

RIVERSIDE CHURCH ARTS AND CRAFTS, Riverside Dr. at 122nd St,
10027. Tel: (212) 749-8140
Lois Porter, Chairperson, Arts and Crafts Comt; 33 PT instr. Estab.
1930; den; ent. req. must be 16 yr. or older; 30 SC. Tui.
approx. $50 per sem. per course for 3 hr. classes per week, lab and
reg. fees added.

Drawing	Painting
Handicrafts	Photography
Jewelry	Textile Design

ROCHESTER

NAZARETH COLLEGE OF ROCHESTER, Art Department, 4245 E.
Ave, 14610. Tel: (716) 586-2525 Exten. 258
Sister Magdalen LaRow, Chmn; 7 FT, 4 PT instr. Estab. 1924; pvt;
D & E; ent. req. HS dipl; 4 yr; degrees, B.S.(Art Educ), B.S.(Studio),
B.A.(Art History); schol; 30 SC, 7 LC; enrl. D 260, E 51, maj. 211.
Tui. $2340 per yr; campus res. $1414.

Art Education	Museum Staff Training
Ceramics	Painting
Drawing	Photography
Graphic Arts	Sculpture
Graphic Design	Teacher Training
History of Art & Archaeology	Textile Design
Jewelry	Weaving
Lettering	

Summer School: Mrs. Elaine Hayden, Dir; courses offered
varies; tui. $60 per cr. hr. for term of 6 wk. beginning June.

ROCHESTER INSTITUTE OF TECHNOLOGY, College of Fine and
Applied Arts, One Lomb Memorial Dr, 14623.
Tel: (716) 464-2646
Dr. Robert H. Johnston, Dean.

School of Art and Design
31 FT, 5 PT faculty. Estab. 1829; pvt; ent. req. HS grad, ent. exam,
portfolio; 4-5 yr; degrees, A.A.S, B.F.A, M.F.A, M.S.T; enrl. 500.
Tui. undergrad. $2649, grad. $2814; campus res.

Art Education (grad. only)	Painting
Communication Design	Printmaking

School of American Craftsmen
10 FT faculty. Estab. 1946; pvt; ent. req. HS grad, ent. exam: portfolio, Jr. yr. abroad with above academic record; 4-5 yr; degrees,
A.A.S, B.F.A, M.F.A, M.S.T; enrl. 140. Tui. undergrad. $2649,
grad. $2814; campus res.

Ceramics	Weaving & Textile Design
Glassblowing	Woodworking & Furniture Design
Metalcrafts & Jewelry	

Summer School: College of Continuing Education, two 5 wk. terms.

UNIVERSITY OF ROCHESTER, Department of Fine Arts, Morey
Hall, 424, 14627. Tel: (716) 275-4284
Archibald M. Miller, Chmn; D 13 FT, 8 PT, E 3 PT instr. Estab.
1902; 4 yr; degrees; schol; 25 SC, 25 LC; enrl. maj. 45, others 900.
Tui. $3525.

Dance	Photography
History & Criticism of Art	Sculpture
Painting	

SANBORN

NIAGARA COUNTY COMMUNITY COLLEGE, Fine Arts Division,
3111 Saunders Settlement Rd, 14132.
Tel: (716) 731-3271 Exten. 158
Donald R. Harter, Chmn; 0 FT, 6 PT instr. Estab. 1965; pub; D & E;
ent. req. HS dipl; 2 yr; degree, A.S.(Fine Arts); 12 SC, 4 LC; enrl.
D 400, E 120, maj. 140. Tui. res. N.Y. state $650, $1300 out-of-
state.

Aesthetics	Painting
Ceramics	Photography
Design	Printmaking
Drawing	Sculpture
History of Art & Archaeology	Serigraphy
Lettering & Typography	Visual Communications
Life Drawing	

Summer School: Judith Shipengrover, Dr; courses offered same
as regular yr; tui. $27 cr. res, $54 out-of-state for term of 6-7 wk.
beginning June 14, 1976; enrl. 30 art students

SARATOGA SPRINGS

SKIDMORE COLLEGE,* Department of Art, 12866.
Tel: (518) 584-5000
Earl B. Pardon, Chmn; 21 FT, 1 PT instr. Estab. 1911; pvt; co-ed;
ent. req. HS grad, 16 cr, ent. exam, portfolio; 4 yr; degrees, B.S,

B.A; schol; 32 SC, 18 LC; enrl. maj. 255, total course 2000. Tui. $2310, comprehensive fee $3975; campus res.

Art Education	Lettering
Art History	Painting
Design	Photography
Drawing	Pottery
Enameling	Printmaking
Film Making	Screen Printing
Graphic Design	Sculpture
Jewelry	Weaving

Summer School: Richard Upton, Dir; tui. $370, room and board $294; 6 wk; enrl. 60.

Ceramics	Painting
Drawing	Photography
Film Making	

SCHENECTADY

UNION COLLEGE, Department of the Arts, Union St, 12308. Tel: (518) 370-6201
Prof. Hugh Allen Wilson, Chmn; 8 FT instr. Estab. 1795; pvt; D; ent. req. HS dipl, ent. exam; 4 yr; degree, B.A. with emphasis in music, art or drama; schol; 14 SC, 4 LC; enrl. maj. 52. Tui. $3300 per yr; campus res. $750 per yr.

Drawing	Photography
Graphic Arts	Sculpture
Graphic Design	Stage Design
Painting	Theatre Arts

SOUTHAMPTON

SOUTHAMPTON COLLEGE OF LONG ISLAND UNIVERSITY, Art Department, 11968. Tel: (516) 283-4000 Exten. 241, 243
Dr. Donald Kurka, Dir. Div. of Fine Arts; 4 FT, 20 PT instr. Estab. 1963; pvt; D & E; ent. req. HS dipl; 4 yr; degrees, B.A. (Art Educ), B.F.A.(Studio Art); schol; 40 SC, 10 LC, 16 GC; enrl. D 1400, maj. 150. Tui. $2650 per yr; campus res. $1700.

Advertising Design	History of Art & Archaeology
Aesthetics	Jewelry
Art Education	Painting
Ceramics	Photography
Commercial Art	Sculpture
Drafting	Stage Design
Drawing	Teacher Training
Graphic Arts	Theatre Arts

Summer School: Ms. Elizabeth Skinner, Dir; courses offered, Studio/Crafts.

SPARKHILL

ST. THOMAS AQUINAS COLLEGE, Art Department, Rte, 340, 10976. Tel: (914) 359-6400 Exten. 273
Adele Myers, Chmn; 4 FT, 6 PT instr. Pvt; D & E; ent. req. HS dipl, results of SAT, scores of CEEB, Art Program, 3rd sem. portfolio; 4 yr; degree, B.A.(Art, with concentrations in Fine Arts, Art Therapy, Art Educ); schol; 30 SC, 12 LC; enrl. maj. 70. Tui. $1600 per yr; campus res. $1150.

Advertising Design	Jewelry
Art Education	Occupational Therapy
Ceramics (Pottery)	Painting
Drawing	Photography
Fibers	Sculpture
Graphic Arts	Teacher Training
Handicrafts	Theatre Arts
History of Art & Archaeology	

Adult hobby classes, painting; tui. $55 per cr; enrl. 25.
Summer School; Dr. Joseph Keane, Dir; courses offered variable; three summer sessions, D & E, January intersession program; tui. $55 per cr.

STATEN ISLAND

STATEN ISLAND INSTITUTE OF ARTS AND SCIENCES, Staten Island Museum, 75 Stuyvesant Pl, 10301. Tel: (212) 727-1135
Mrs. Freda Esterly, Cur. Educ. 1 FT, 2 PT instr. Estab. 1881; pvt; with added support from New York City; children's classes during the day and adult educ. courses in the late afternoon and evening; no degrees.

Drawing (Life Class)	History of Art & Archaeology
Handicrafts	Painting

WAGNER COLLEGE,* Department of Art, Grymes Hill, 10301. Tel: (212) 390-3192
Mr. Paul Pollaro, Chmn; 5 FT, 6 PT instr. Estab. 1948; den; D & E; ent. req. HS grad; 4 yr; degree, B.A. with a maj. in Art or Art and

Art Educ; schol; 20 SC, 6 LC; enrl. maj. 130, others 2500. Tui. $1950 per yr.(based on 16 cr. per sem), room and board $1200 per yr; campus res.

Art Education	Mixed Media
Art History	Painting
Black Art History	Photography
Ceramics	Printmaking
Crafts Design	Sculpture
Drawing	Three-Dimensional Design
Experiments	Two-Dimensional Design
Film Making	

Summer School: Mr. Paul Pollaro, Dir; tui. $60 per cr. hr; two sessions of 4 wk; special 2 wk. course, 3 cr, Exploring Art in New York.

STONE RIDGE

ULSTER COUNTY COMMUNITY COLLEGE, Department of Visual Arts, 12484. Tel: (914) 687-7621 Exten. 76
Allan Cohen, Chmn; 2 FT, 3 PT instr. Estab. 1963; pub; D & E; ent. req. HS dipl; 2 yr; degree, A.A; schol; 16 SC, 6 LC; enrl. D 250, E 300, maj. 50, PT 100. Tui. $600 per yr, $22 per cr.

Advertising Design	Introduction to the Visual Arts
Aesthetics	Landscape Architecture
Drafting	Life Drawing & Anatomy
Drawing	Painting
Fashion Arts	Photography
Graphic Design	Theatre Arts
History of Art & Archaeology	Three-Dimensional Design
Illustration	Two-Dimensional Design

Adult hobby classes, handweaving, marionettes, pottery, quilting, rug braiding; tui. $22 per cr.
Children's classes, lettering, leathercraft, painting, dance, pantomime; tui. $22 per cr.
Summer School: Allan Cohen, Dir; courses offered, Drawing, History of Art, Painting; tui. $22 per cr. for term of 6-8 wk. beginning June; 1976; enrl. 150.

STONY BROOK

STATE UNIVERSITY OF NEW YORK AT STONY BROOK, Art Department, 11794. Tel: (516) 246-7070
Prof. Jacques Guilmain, Chmn; Prof. Melvin Pekarsky, Studio Dir; 13 FT, 5 PT instr. Dept. estab. 1966; pub; D; ent. req. HS grad, ent. exam; 4 yr; degree, B.A; schol, fel, state and federal loan prog; 13 SC, 21 LC; enrl. maj. 185. Tui. res. freshman and sophomore $650, junior and senior $800, non-res. freshman and sophomore $1075, junior and senior $1300; campus res. $1015 per yr; misc. fees approx. $200.

Art History & Criticism	Graphic Arts
Ceramics	Painting
Drawing	Photography
Experimental Arts	Sculpture

Adult hobby and craft courses given at Stony Brook Union Craft Shop, Tel. (516) 246-3657; jewelry and enamel, patchwork quilting, pottery, ceramic sculpture, silversmithing, photography.
Evening art courses (non-credit) given through Informal Studies, Tel. (516) 246-5939
Summer School: Dr. Samuel Berr, Dir, Tel. (516) 246-6559; courses differ each yr; tui. res. freshman and sophomore $21.50 per cr. hr, junior and senior $26.75, non-res. freshman and sophomore $35.75, junior and senior $43.50; campus res. $14-$21 wk. if available, board a la carte.

Department of Continuing Education. Tel: (516) 246-5936
D 28 undergrad. LC, 31 undergrad. SC, E 8 grad. LC.

Theatre Arts Department. Tel: (516) 246-5670
Costume & Stage Design
Film

SUFFERN

ROCKLAND COMMUNITY COLLEGE, Art Department, 145 College Rd, 10901. Tel: (914) 356-4650 Exten. 285
J. P. Murphy, Chmn; 6 FT, 18 PT instr. Estab. 1965; pub; D & E; ent. req. open admissions; 2 yr; degree, A.A.S; SC plus apprenticeships; enrl. D 900, E 300, maj. 200. Tui. $23 per cr, $472 per yr. plus various fees, double amounts for non-res; no campus res, commuting college.

Advertising Design	Graphic Design
Art Appreciation	History of Art
Art Therapy	Lettering
Color Production	Painting

Drawing
Electric Art
Graphic Arts
Photography
Sculpture

Adult hobby classes, many varied courses; tui. depends on enrl.
Children's classes, many varied courses, overseas programs.
Summer School: J. P. Murphy, Chmn; $23 per cr.

Art History
Drawing
Graphic Techniques
Painting
Sculpture

SYRACUSE

SYRACUSE UNIVERSITY,* College of Visual and Performing Arts,
School of Art, 309 University Place, 13210. Tel: (315) 476-2611
August L. Freundlich, Dean; 55 FT, 35 PT instr. Estab. 1873; pvt;
4-5 yr; degrees; schol. and fel; SC, LC, GC; enrl, 950. Tui. $1440,
campus res. Selected study program.

Advertising Design
Art Education
Art History
Costume Design
Crafts
Design
Fabric Design
Fashion Illustration
Film
Illustration
Industrial Design
Interior Design
Museology
Painting
Printmaking
Sculpture

Summer School: 10 FT instr; $120 per cr. hr. for 6 wk. July-Aug;
enrl. 150.

TARRYTOWN

MARYMOUNT COLLEGE, Art Department, 10591.
Tel: (914) 631-3200
John F. Lochtefeld, Chmn; 6 FT, 4 PT instr. Estab. 1922; pvt; D &
E; W; ent. req. HS dipl; 4 yr; degrees, B.A, B.S; schol; 30 SC, 10
LC; enrl. D 450, maj. 35, special students (art only) 10. Tui. and
room and board $4550, other fees $125.

Ceramics
Design
Drawing
Graphic Arts
History of Art
Image Concepts
Interior Design
Painting
Photography
Scandinavian Crafts
Sculpture
Stitchery
Watercolor
Weaving

TROY

✠THE EMMA WILLARD SCHOOL,* Pawling Ave, 12181.
Tel: (518) 270-3000
Dennis Collins, Prin.

RENSSELAER POLYTECHNIC INSTITUTE, School of Architecture,
12181. Tel: (518) 270-6460
Patrick J. Quinn, Dean; 17 FT, 7 PT instr. Estab. 1929; pvt; D;
4-5 yr; degrees, B.S, M.S, B.Arch, M.Arch; schol; enrl. 230. Tui.
$3400; campus res.
‡Architecture
‡Building Science

✠RUSSELL SAGE COLLEGE, Art Department, 203 Second St, 12180.
Tel: (518) 270-2000
Ross Coates, Chmn; 6 FT, 5 PT instr. Pvt; W; ent. req. HS grad; 4
yr; degree, fine arts and divisional maj. in Music, Art and Drama;
enrl. 20-10 each class.

UTICA

✠MUNSON-WILLIAMS-PROCTOR INSTITUTE, School of Art, 310
Genesse St, 13502. Tel: (315) 797-0000
John R. Manning, Dir; William C. Palmer, Dir. Emer; 12 FT, 10 PT
instr. Estab. 1941; pvt; enrl. adults 650, HS students 75, children
(winter) 350, (summer) 350. Adult tui. $40 per sem. for 1 class per
wk. D & E, children's classes Sat. AM $20-$30 per yr. School yr.
Oct. through May. Also Utica College Fine Arts courses and FT
program in Fine Arts.

Ceramics
Dance
Drawing
Enameling
Graphic Arts
Introduction to Visual Arts
Metal Arts
Painting
Photography
Pottery
Sculpture

Summer School: Children, tui. $10-$15 for 4 AM classes per
wk. for 4 wk, dance $25; adults, tui. $25 for classes on Tues. &
Thurs. afternoon or E for 4 wk.

WATERTOWN

JEFFERSON COMMUNITY COLLEGE, Art Department, P.O. Box
255, 13601. Tel: (315) 782-5250
James E. McVean, Pres; Klaus Ebeling, Prof. of Art; 1 FT instr.
Estab. 1963; pub; D & E; 2 yr; 2 SC, 1 LC; enrl. total 850. Tui.
$325 per sem.

Art Appreciation
Art History
Sculpture Studio
Two-Dimensional Studio

WHITE PLAINS

THE COLLEGE OF WHITE PLAINS OF PACE UNIVERSITY, Division
of Arts and Letters, 10603. Tel: (914) 949-9494
Carol B. Gartner, Chmn; 2 PT instr. Pvt; D & E; ent. req. HS dipl;
4 yr; no art major; 4 SC, 4 LC. Tui. $65 per cr.

Art Education
Drawing
Graphic Arts
History of Art & Archaeology
Painting
Photography
Stage Design
Theatre Arts

Summer School: Sister M. Berchmanns Coyle, Dir; course offered, Painting.

WESTCHESTER ART WORKSHOP, County Center, 10606.
Tel: (914) 949-1300
John Ruddley, Dir. and County Supv. of Art; 40 faculty. Estab. 1925,
administered by Westchester County Dept. of Parks, Recreation &
Conservation; D & E classes for adults, teen-agers and children;
fall, spring, summer terms; annual enrl. adults and teens 4000,
children 600. Tui. adults $28-$42, juniors $28.

Acrylic Painting
Anatomy
Ceramics
Design
Drawing
Dressmaking
Flower Arrangement
Interior Decoration
Jewelry, Silversmithing &
Enameling
Oil Painting
Photography
Printmaking & Graphics
Recreational Crafts
Sculpture
Watercolor
Weaving

YONKERS

ELIZABETH SETON COLLEGE, Art Department, 1061 N. Broadway,
10701. Tel: (914) 969-4000
Sister Margaret Beaudette, Chmn; 3 FT, 1 PT instr. Estab. 1960;
independent; D & E; ent. req. HS dipl. or equivalent, interview, letters
of recommendation; 2 yr; degrees, A.A, A.A.S; schol; 12 SC, 3 LC;
enrl. D 198, E 30, maj. 41. Tui. $1900 per yr, PT $50 per cr. community educ; campus res. $1500.

Advertising Design
Ceramics
Design
Drawing
Fashion Illustration
Graphic Arts
History of Art
Interior Design
Jewelry & Enameling
Lettering
Painting
Sculpture

Children's classes, arts and crafts; tui. $40, 4 wk. summer; enrl. 11.
Office of Continuing Education: Ann Congers Healey, Dir; directs
E, Summer, Jan. Intersession and Weekend Coll. classes; courses
offered same as above; tui. $50 per cr, $40 non-cr. courses.

NORTH CAROLINA

ASHEVILLE

UNIVERSITY OF NORTH CAROLINA AT ASHEVILLE, Department
of Art and Music, University Heights, 28801.
Tel: (704) 254-7415 Exten. 328
S. Tucker Cooke, Head; 3 FT, 1 PT instr. Estab. 1927; pub; D & E;
co-ed; ent. req. HS grad, ent. exam; 4 yr; degree, B.A; 19 SC, 5 LC;
enrl. D 150, E 45, maj.38. Tui. $108.25 per term, $433 for full yr.
(4 sem); campus res. $368 for 4 terms.

Art Education
Ceramics
Drawing
Graphic Arts
History of Art
Jewelry
Painting
Sculpture
Teacher Training

Summer School: S. Tucker Cooke, Head; tui. $11 per sem. hr.
for two 5½ wk. terms beginning June 7 and July 20; 1969 enrl. 40.

BELMONT

SACRED HEART COLLEGE, Department of Art, 28012.
Tel: (919) 825-8543
Sister M. Theophane Field, Chmn; 2 FT, 1 PT instr. Estab. 1968;

pvt, den; D; ent. req. HS dipl; 4 yrs; degrees, B.A, B.S; schol; 12 SC, 3 LC; enrl. D 32, maj. 8. Tui. $1180 per yr; campus res. $1150 per yr.

Art Education	Painting
Ceramics	Photography
Drawing	Teacher Training
Graphic Arts	Textile Design
Graphic Design	Three-Dimensional Design
History of Art & Archaeology	Two-Dimensional Design
Jewelry	

BOONE

APPALACHIAN STATE UNIVERSITY, Department of Art, 28608.
Tel: (704) 262-2220
L. F. Edwards, Chmn; 12 FT, 2 PT instr. Estab. 1960; pub; D; ent. req. HS dipl, ent. exam; 4 yr; degrees B.A, B.S.(Commercial Design, Art Educ, Studio Art); schol; 38 SC, 10 LC, 12 GC; enrl. D 1000, maj. 236, grad. 5. Tui. $534 per yr, $267 per sem, $15 per yr, out-of-state tui. per yr. $2094; campus res. M $1028, W $945.

Art Appreciation	Handicrafts
Art Education	History of Art & Archaeology
Ceramics	Jewelry
Commercial Art	Lettering
Drawing	Painting
Fabric Design	Photography
Graphic Arts	Sculpture
Graphic Design	Teacher Training

Summer School: L. F. Edwards, Dir; courses as above; tui. approx. $20 per hr. for term of 2, 4 & 6 wks, beginning May 31-Aug. 13, enrl. 300.

BREVARD

BREVARD COLLEGE, Coltrane Art Center, 28712.
Tel: (703) 883-8292 Exten. 45
Tim Murray, Dir; 2 FT, 1 PT instr. Den; D & E; ent. req. HS dipl; 2 yr; degree, A.A; schol; 13 SC, 2 LC; total enrl. 520, maj. 40. Tui. $1200 per yr; in state students $1000; campus res. $810.

Ceramics	Painting
Drafting	Photography
Drawing	Printmaking
Graphic Design	Sculpture
History of Art & Archaeology	Theatre Arts

Summer School: Dean Coll; courses offered same as regular yr, no lecture; tui. $35 per sem. hr. for term of 4 wk, beginning June 1 or 2.

CHAPEL HILL

✠ UNIVERSITY OF NORTH CAROLINA AT CHAPEL HILL, Art Department, 27514. Tel: (919) 933-2015
J. Richard Judson, Chmn; 19 FT, 2 PT instr. Estab. 1936; pub; ent. req; cert. from accredited HS & coll. ent. board exam; 4 yr; degrees, B.A, B.F.A, M.A, M.F.A, Ph.D; schol; 34 SC, 39 LC, 24 GC; enrl. maj. 206, others 2586. Tui. & fees per sem. $234-$1056.

Ceramics	Painting
Graphic Arts	Sculpture
History of Art	

Summer School: First term May 24 to June 25, second, July 6 to Aug. 6; 12 SC, 6 LC; enrl. 327.

CHARLOTTE

QUEENS COLLEGE, Art Department, 28207.
Tel: (704) 332-7121
John D. McClanahan, Head; 3 FT, 1 PT instr. Estab. 1857; den; W; degrees; ent. schol; 19 SC, 7 LC.

Ceramics	Fine Arts
Commercial Art	History of Art

UNIVERSITY OF NORTH CAROLINA,* Creative Arts Department, UNCC Station, 28213.
Luca DiCecco, Chmn; 10 FT, 4 PT instr. Estab. 1972; pub; ent. req. HS dipl; 4 yrs; degree, Bachelor of Creative Arts; enrl. D 250.

Aesthetics	Jewelry
Art Education	Painting
Ceramics	Photography
Drawing	Sculpture
Graphic Arts	Teacher Training
Graphic Design	Theatre Arts
Handicrafts	

CULLOWHEE

WESTERN CAROLINA UNIVERSITY, Department of Art, 28723.
Tel: (704) 293-7210
Dr. Perry Kelly, Head; 13 FT instr. Pub; D & E; ent. req. HS dipl, SAT; 4 yr; degrees, B.F.A, B.A, B.S.(Educ); schol; total enrl. D 6000, maj. 200. Tui. NC res. $475, others $997; campus res.

Advertising Design	Handicrafts
Aesthetics	History of Art
Art Education	Illustration
Ceramics	Jewelry
Commercial Art	Lettering
Drafting	Painting
Drawing	Photography
Graphic Arts	Sculpture
Handicrafts	Stage Design
History of Art	Textile Design

Children's classes, gen. studies for HS on Sat; enrl. 20.
Summer School: Dr. Jerry Rice, Dir; gen. program and special workshop courses.

DALLAS

GASTON COLLEGE, Art Department, New Dallas Highway, 28034.
Tel: (704) 922-3136 Exten. 205
Franklin U. Creech, Head; 3 FT, 2 PT instr. Estab. 1965; pub; D & E; ent. req. HS dipl; 2 yr; degrees A.A, A.F.A; 22 SC, 3 LC; enrl. D 140, E 50, maj. 50. Tui. $132 per yr, $44 per mo, $2.75 per hr; no campus res.

Art Education	Jewelry
Ceramics	Painting
Drawing	Sculpture
Graphic Arts	Stage Design
Handicrafts	Theatre Arts
History of Art & Archaeology	

Adult hobby classes: Ceramics, jewelry, macrame and weaving.
Summer School: Franklin U. Creech, Dir; tui. $132 for term of 11 wks, beginning June 10; enrl. 20.

Design	Pottery
Drawing	Sculpture
Painting	

DURHAM

✠ DUKE UNIVERSITY, Department of Art, E. Duke Bldg, 27708.
Tel: (919) 684-2224
Sidney D. Markman, Acting Chmn; 11 FT, 5 PT instr. Estab 1931; pvt; 4 yr; degrees; schol. & fel; 52 LC, 16 Lab.C; enrl. 468. Tui. $3030 per yr. for full B.A. schedule; campus res.
Design—Studio
History of Art

NORTH CAROLINA CENTRAL UNIVERSITY, Department of Art, 27707. Tel: (919) 683-6000-6391
Phillip Lindsay Mason, Chmn; 6 FT instr. School estab. 1910; Dept. 1944; pub; D; co-ed; ent. req. HS grad. and SAT scores; 4 yr; degree, A.B. Art Educ, Fine Arts or Visual Communications; 27 SC, 9 LC; enrl. maj. 70, others 3030. Tui. $421.50 per yr, non-res $1800; campus res. incl. tui, room and board $2021.50, non-res. $2854.50.

Art Appreciation	Painting
Art Education	Sculpture
Art History	Visual Communications
Drawing	

Summer School: C. W. Orr, Dir; Art History, Painting and Art Education; tui. $255, non-res. $340.

ELIZABETH CITY

ELIZABETH CITY STATE UNIVERSITY, Art Department, 27909. Tel: (919) 335-0551 Exten 358
Dr. Vincent J. de Gregorio, Chmn; 4 FT instr. Estab. 1960; pub; D & E; ent. req. HS dipl; 4 yr; degree B.S.(Art Educ); schol; 15 SC, 11 LC; enrl. D 600, E 200, maj. 60. Summer School.

Art Education	History of Art & Archaeology
Ceramics	Lettering
Commercial Art	Painting
Drawing	Sculpture
Graphic Arts	Teacher Training
Graphic Design	Textile Design
Handicrafts	

FAYETTEVILLE

FAYETTEVILLE STATE UNIVERSITY, Murchison Rd, 28391.
Harvey C. Jenkins, Chmn; 4 FT instr. Estab. 1877; pub; D & E; ent.

req. HS dipl, ent. exam; 4 yr; no art majors; enrl. D 60, E 20. Tui. $1413 per yr.

Advertising Design
Aesthetics
Art Education
Arts & Crafts
Ceramics
Drawing
Graphic Arts
Handicrafts

History of Art & Archaeology
Leather Craft
Lettering
Painting
Photography
Sculpture
Weaving

Summer School: Dr. Ronald Smith, Dir.

Art in Childhood Education
Arts & Crafts
Basic Photography

Drawing
Survey of Art

METHODIST COLLEGE, Art Department, Raleigh Rd, 28301.
Tel: (919) 488-7110 Exten. 257
Donald L. Green, Head; 2 FT instr. Estab. 1960; den; D & E; ent. req. HS dipl, ent. exam, SAT; 4 yrs; degrees, B.A, B.S; schol; 6 SC, 4 LC; enrl. D 650, maj. 12. Tui. $700 per yr; campus res. $500.

Art Education
Drawing
Enameling
Graphic Arts
Handicrafts

History of Art & Archaeology
Painting
Paper Work
Sculpture
Weaving

Summer School: Dr. Fred C. McDavid, Dir; courses offered, Art Appreciation, Painting, Sculpture, others as needed, 3 terms, 3 wk. early session, 5 wk. main session, 6 wk. directed study, 1973 enrl. 300.

GREENSBORO

NORTH CAROLINA AGRICULTURAL AND TECHNICAL STATE UNIVERSITY, Art Department, 27411.
Tel: (919) 379-7993/7645
LeRoy F. Holmes, Jr, Chmn; 4 FT, 1 PT instr. Estab. 1930; pub; 4 yr; degree; 29 SC, 7 LC; enrl. maj. 150. Campus res. incl. tui, room and board $656.25; non-res. $1422.75.

Art Design
Art Education
Art History
Arts & Crafts
Ceramics

Commercial Art
Graphic Arts
Painting & Drawing
Three-Dimensional Design
Two-Dimensional Design

Summer School: 6 wk. session and a 2 wk. session.

UNIVERSITY OF NORTH CAROLINA AT GREENSBORO, Art Department, 27412. Tel: (919) 379-5248
Dr. Joan Gregory, Head; 22 FT, 4 PT instr. Dept. estab. 1935; pub; ent. req. HS grad, ent. exam; 4 yr; degrees, B.A, B.F.A, M.Ed, M.F.A; 22 SC, 6 LC, 8 GC; enrl. maj. 500, others 4500. Tui. in-state res. $330, out-of-state res. $1882; campus res. room & board $990.

Advertising Design
Ceramics
Drawing
Fibers
Graphic Arts

Lettering
Painting
Photography
Sculpture
Teacher Training

Summer School: Dr. Jean Eason, Dir; tui. $45 plus $21.50 fees, out-of-state res. $360 plus $21.50 fees, beginning May 22-June 30, July 6-Aug. 13; enrl. 225.

Ceramics
Drawing & Picture Composition
Life Drawing
Mechanical Drawing

Moldmaking-Metal Casting
Sculpture
Watercolor

GREENVILLE

EAST CAROLINA UNIVERSITY, School of Art, 27834.
Tel: (919) 758-6665
Dr. Wellington B. Gray, Dean; 33 FT, 12 PT instr. Estab. 1946; pub; ent. req. HS grad, 15 units, Coll. Board Exam; 4 yr; degrees, A.B, B.S, B.F.A, M.A, M.A.(Educ), M.F.A; 131 SC, 29 LC, 112 GC; enrl. maj. 736. Tui. $834, non-res. $2391; campus res.

Art Education
Art History
Ceramics
Communication Arts
Design

Interior Design
Painting
Printmaking
Sculpture

Summer School: Dr. Susan McDaniel, Dir, Dr. Wellington B. Gray, Art Dir; tui. & fees $276 for 10 wk, beginning June, non-res. $792; enrl. 8183.

HIGH POINT

HIGH POINT COLLEGE, Fine Arts Department, Montlieu Ave, 27262. Tel: (919) 885-5101
Raiford M. Porter, Assoc. Prof; 5 FT, 2 PT instr. Estab. 1925; pvt; D; ent. req. HS dipl, SAT; 4 yr; degree A.B.(Art, Art Educ, Theatre

& Theatre Arts); schol; 10 SC, 20 LC; enrl. D 415, maj. 60. Tui. $1675 per yr; campus res $870.

Aesthetics
Art Education
Ceramics
Drawing
Graphic Arts
Handicrafts
History of Art & Archaeology
Jewelry

Museum Staff Training
Painting
Photography
Sculpture
Stage Design
Teacher Training
Theatre Arts

Summer School: Dr. David Cole, Dir; general college courses.

LAURINBURG

ST. ANDREWS PRESBYTERIAN COLLEGE,* Art Program, 28352.
Tel: (919) 276-3652 Exten. 313
Mark L. Smith, Chmn; 2 FT instr. Estab. 1960; den; D; ent. req. HS dipl, SAT, 2.6 grade point average, 12 academic units; 4 yrs or 37 courses; degrees, B.A, B.S, B.M; schol; 14 SC, 2 LC; enrl. D 852, maj. 15-20. Tui. $2100 per yr; campus res. $995.

Aesthetics
Art Education
Drawing
Graphic Arts
Graphic Design

History of Art & Archaeology
Painting
Sculpture
Stage Design

Summer School: John Daughtrey, Dir, studio courses offered.

MARS HILL

MARS HILL COLLEGE, Department of Art, 28754.
Tel: (704) 689-1200
Prof. Joe Chris Robertson, Head; 3 FT, 1 PT instr. Estab. 1856; den; D; co-ed; ent. req. HS grad, CEEB 800; 4 yr; degrees, B.A, B.S, B.M, B.M.E; schol; 10 SC, 6 LC; enrl. 1600, maj. 50, 13 special students. Tui. $1750; campus res. $800.

Aesthetics
Art Education
Ceramics
Drawing
Graphic Arts
Graphic Design
Handicrafts
History of Art & Archaeology
Jewelry

Metal Enameling
Painting
Sculpture
Stage Design
Stitchery
Teacher Training
Textile Printing
Theatre Arts
Weaving

Summer School: Dr. John Hough, Dir; Art Education, Ceramics, Painting; tui. $50 per cr. hr. for two 5 wk. terms beginning June 7 and July 12; 1975 enrl. 440.

MISENHEIMER

PFEIFFER COLLEGE, Art Program, 28109.
Tel: (704) 463-3111
James Haymaker, Dir; 1 FT, 1 PT instr. Estab. 1965; den; D; ent. req. HS dipl; 3-4 yr; no art major; schol; 4 SC, 4 LC; enrl. D 125. Tui. $1500 per yr, other fees $300; campus res $900.

Art Education
Ceramics
Drawing
History of Art & Archaeology

Painting
Sculpture
Teacher Training

PEMBROKE

PEMBROKE STATE UNIVERSITY,* Art Department, P.O. Box 66, 28372. Tel: (919) 521-4214 Exten. 216
Paul Van Zandt, Head; 5 FT instr. Estab. 1941; pub; ent. req. CEEB scores, HS record, scholastic standing in HS grad. class, recommendation of HS guidance counselor and principal; 4 yr; degrees, B.A, B.S; 30 SC, 12 LC; enrl. maj. 80. Tui. res. $194.50 per sem, non-res. $865.

Art Education
Art History
Ceramics
Commercial Art
Design

Drawing & Painting
Graphic Arts
Photography & Crafts
Sculpture

Summer School.

PENLAND

PENLAND SCHOOL OF CRAFTS,* 28765.
Tel: (704) 765-2359
Concentrated Program and Summer Session; two 8 wk. sessions per fall and spring sessions; undergrad. and grad. coll. cr. for this prog. through East Tennessee State University; ent. req. 18 yr. old, resume and slides or photographs of most recent work; enrl. limited to 10-15 per class. Tui. $55 per wk. for 8 wk, room and board $75

per wk. for 8 wk, lab fee $10 per wk. for 8 wk, glassblowing fee $20 per wk for 8 wk, firing charge and materials are extra.

Ceramics	Photography
Glassblowing	Textile Weaving
Jewelry-Metalsmithing	

RALEIGH

MEREDITH COLLEGE, Department of Art, 27611.
Tel: (919) 833-6461 Exten. 257
Leonard White, Chmn; 3 FT, 4 PT instr. Estab. 1898; den; D & E; W; ent. req. HS dipl; 4 yr; degree, A.B; schol; 15 SC, 5 LC; enrl. D 250, E 40, maj. 50, others 10. Tui. $1800 per yr; room & board $1000 per yr.

Art Education	Graphic Design
Ceramics	History of Art
Commercial Art	Painting
Costume Design & Construction	Photography
Drawing	Sculpture
Graphic Arts	

Adult hobby classes, painting, sculpture & art history; tui. $40-$60 non-cr or $60 per sem. for cr.
Summer School: John Hiott, Dir; courses variable; tui. $60 per sem. hr.

NORTH CAROLINA STATE UNIVERSITY AT RALEIGH, School of Design, 27607. Tel: (919) 737-2201
Claude E. McKinney, Dean; Basil Honikman, Asst. Dean; Richard R. Wilkinson, Dir, Landscape Architecture Program; John Loss, Dir, Architecture Program; Vincent M. Foote, Dir, Product Design Program; 34 FT, 3 PT instr. Estab. 1948; pub; ent. req. coll. board, ent. exam; 4-6 yr; degrees, B.Env.Design (in Architecture, Landscape Architecture, Product Design & Product Design, Visual Design Option), M.Arch, M.Landscape Arch, M.Urb.Design, M.Product Design; enrl. Architecture 354, Landscape Architecture 77, Product Design 105, special students 10. Tui. & fees (not including living expenses) res. approx. $524.30, non-res. approx. $2170.30.

ST. MARY'S COLLEGE, 900 Hillsborough St, 27601.
Tel: (919) 828-2521
Margaret Click-Williams, Chmn; 2 FT instr. Estab. 1842; pvt; D; W; ent. req. HS dipl, SAT; 2 yr; degrees HS dipl & A.A; schol; 5 SC, 2 LC; enrl. D 148. Tui, room & board $3800 annually.

Art Education	History of Art
Ceramics	Painting
Drawing	Stage Design
Graphic Arts	Theatre Arts

Summer School: Dr. Frank Pisani, Dir; courses varied; term of 4 wks, beginning June; enrl. c. 40.

WILMINGTON

UNIVERSITY OF NORTH CAROLINA AT WILMINGTON, Art Department, 28401. Tel: (919) 791-4330
Claude Howell, Assoc. Prof. of Art; 4 FT instr. Estab. 1947; pub; D & E; co-ed; ent. req. HS dipl, ent. exam; 4 yr; degrees; schol; enrl. approx. 175 art students.

Art Education	Painting
Design & Color	Sculpture
Drawing	Stage Design
Graphic Arts	Teacher Training
History of Art & Archaeology	Theatre Arts
Jewelry	Three-Dimensional Design

Adult hobby classes, painting, sculpture.
Summer School: Same courses offered.

WILSON

ATLANTIC CHRISTIAN COLLEGE, Art Department, 27893.
Tel: (919) 237-3161
Edward C. Brown, Chmn; 4 PT instr. Art dept. estab. 1953; den; D & E; ent. req. HS grad, ent. exam. and interview; 4 yr; degrees, A.B, B.S, B.F.A; schol; 9 SC, 5 LC; enrl. maj. 65-70, others 35-40, total enrl. 1775. Tui. $1050 per yr, room and board $820 per yr; campus res.

Advertising Design	Graphics
Art Education	Hand Crafts
Art History	Painting
Ceramics	Sculpture
Drawing	

Summer School: G. Harry Swain, Dir; Two 5-6 wk. terms beginning June 8; tui. $280 per term; enrl. approx. 500 per term.

WINGATE

WINGATE COLLEGE, Art Department, 28174.
Tel: (704) 233-4241
Louise S. Napier, Chmn; 3 FT instr. Coll. estab. 1896, Art Dept. 1958; den; D, E on demand; co-ed; ent. req. HS grad; 2 yr; degrees, A.A, A.S; schol; enrl. D 608, E 50. Tui. $1000; campus res. $1070.

Art Appreciation	Gallery Tours
Arts & Crafts	History of Art
Ceramics	Introduction to Fine Arts
Cinema	Painting
Composition	Photography
Drafting (Engineering Dept)	Sketching
Children's classes in art.	

Summer School: Dr. Thomas E. Corts, Pres; all regular class work available if demand warrants; tui. $100 for term of 5 wk, beginning 1st wk. June; 1974 enrl. 350.

WINSTON-SALEM

ARTS AND CRAFTS ASSOCIATION, INC, 610 Coliseum Dr, 27106.
Tel: (919) 723-7395
S. O. McSwain, Pres; Frances H. Malcolm, Mgr. Inc. 1953; offers classes on all levels of skill in art and craft areas to both adults and children; classes offered in four sessions; children's classes on Sat. mornings; workshops with outstanding artists and craftsmen. Invitational Summer Art Honors Program for junior-senior high students. Student shows in Hanes Gallery.

SALEM COLLEGE, Art Department, 27108.
Tel: (919) 723-7961 Exten. 349
William Mangum, Assoc. Prof; 3 FT, 3 PT instr. Den; D; W; ent. req. HS dipl; 4 yr; degree, B.A; schol; enrl. D 642, maj. 44. Tui. $3900 per yr; campus res.

Art Education	History of Art
Ceramics	Painting
Drawing	Sculpture
Graphic Arts	

WAKE FOREST UNIVERSITY, Department of Art, Box 7232, 27109.
Tel: (919) 725-9711 Exten. 439
Sterling M. Boyd, Chmn; 4 FT instr. Estab. 1968; den; D; ent. req. HS dipl, ent. exam; 4 yr; degree, B.A; 3 SC. Tui. approx. $2300 per yr.
History of Art & Archaeology
Painting

NORTH DAKOTA

DICKINSON

DICKINSON STATE COLLEGE, Division of Art, 58601.
Tel: (701) 227-2312
Dennis Navrat, Chmn; 3 FT instr. Estab. 1918, Dept. 1963; pub; D & E; co-ed; ent. req. HS grad, ACT; 4 yr; degrees, B.A, B.S; schol; 25 SC, 8 LC; enrl. per quarter 180, maj. 30. Tui. res. $135; campus res. $120 per quarter.

Art Education	Leather
Ceramics	Lettering
Color	Painting
Drawing	Plastics
Graphic Arts	Sculpture
History of Art	Teacher Training
Jewelry	

Summer School: Dennis Navrat, Dir; Art, Art Education, Art History; tui. $315 non-res. for term of 8 wks, beginning June 7; 1975 enrl. 50.

GRAND FORKS

UNIVERSITY OF NORTH DAKOTA, College of Fine Art, Visual Arts Department, 58202. Tel: (701) 777-2257
Ronald Schaefer, Chmn; D 10 FT, 4 GTA. Estab. 1883; pub; 4 yr; 30 SC, 4 LC, 14 GC; enrl. maj. 120, others 1000. Campus res. with room and board.

Art History	Graphic Arts
Ceramics	Lab. School
Commercial Art	Painting
Design	Sculpture
Drawing	Teacher Training
Elementary Art	Welding
Figure Drawing	

Summer School: Ronald Schaefer, Chmn.

JAMESTOWN

JAMESTOWN COLLEGE, Art Department, 58401.
  Tel: (701) 252-4331 Exten. 256
Robert Carter, Chmn; 1 FT, 1 PT instr. Pvt; D; ent. req. HS dipl;
4 yr; degrees B.A, B.S; schol; 13 SC, 4 LC; enrl. 146, maj. 8. Tui.
$1700; campus res. & board $1225. Directed study and individual
study in advanced studio areas, private studios for junior and senior
majors.

Art Education	Painting
Art History	Printmaking
Drawing	Two-Dimensional Design
Figure Drawing	

  Summer School: Dr. Andresen, Dir; Silkscreen; tui. $125 for 6
wk. term beginning June 15.

MAYVILLE

MAYVILLE STATE COLLEGE,* Art Department, 58257.
  Tel: (701) 786-2301
William J. Lee, Dir; 1 FT instr. Estab. 1890; pub; 4 yr; degree;
20 SC, 4 LC. Summer School.
Teacher & Professional Training

MINOT

MINOT ART ASSOCIATION, Highway 83 N,
  58701.
Mrs. Trish Noeven, Pres. Estab. 1970; pub; D & E.

Art Education	Macrame
Drawing	Painting
Handicrafts	Weaving

MINOT STATE COLLEGE, Division of Fine Arts, 58701.
  Tel: (701) 838-6101 Exten. 363
C. R. Schwieger, Chmn; 3 FT, 2 PT instr. Estab. 1913; pub; 4 yr;
degrees, B.A, B.S; 30 SC; enrl. per quarter 300, maj. 75. Tui. in-
state $149.50, out-of-state $328.50; campus res.

Advanced Ceramics	Graphics
Advanced Graphics	Jewelry
Advertising	Painting
Art History	Photography
Ceramics	Sculpture
Crafts	Silk Screen
Design	Weaving
Drawing	

VALLEY CITY

VALLEY CITY STATE COLLEGE, Art Department, 58072.
  Tel: (701) 845-7561
Floyd D. Martin, Head; D 2 FT instr. Estab. 1921; pub; 4 yr; degrees, A.A, B.A, B.S; 11 SC, 3 LC; enrl. maj. 28, others 100. Tui.
$105 per quarter res, $284 per quarter non-res; campus res. $390
per quarter room and board. Summer School.
Teacher Training

WAHPETON

NORTH DAKOTA STATE SCHOOL OF SCIENCE, Sixth St,
  58075.
Mary Sand, Dir; 1 PT instr. Estab. 1970; pub; D & E; ent. req. open;
enrl. D varied, E 15.

Art Education	Handicrafts
Drawing	Lettering
General Craft	Occupational Therapy
Graphic Design	Painting

Adult painting classes; tui. $30; enrl. 15.
  Summer School: Mary Sand, Dir; teacher's art workshop; 2 wk.
term, 3 hr. per day.

OHIO

ADA

OHIO NORTHERN UNIVERSITY, Department of Art, 45810.
  Tel: (419) 634-9921 Exten. 222
Thomas L. Gordon, Chmn; 4 FT instr. Pvt; D; ent. req. HS dipl,
ent. exam; 4 yr; degrees B.A, B.F.A; schol; 30 SC, 8 LC; enrl. maj.
30. Tui. $2361 per yr, part-time $66 per quarter hr; campus res.
$1140.

Aesthetics	Jewelry
Art Education	Lettering
Ceramics	Painting
Costume Design & Construction	Sculpture

Drawing	Stage Design
Graphic Arts	Teacher Training
History of Art & Archaeology	Theatre Arts

  Summer School: Dr. Bernard Linger, Dir.

AKRON

UNIVERSITY OF AKRON, Department of Art, 44325.
  Tel: (216) 375-7010
Stephen Bayless, Head; 17 FT, 16 PT instr. Dept. estab. 1926; pub;
D & E; 4 yr; degrees, B.A, B.F.A, B.S.(Educ).

Art Education	Metalsmithing
Art History	Painting
Ceramics	Photography
Drawing	Printmaking
Graphic Design	Sculpture
Illustration	Weaving

  Summer School: Dean Caesar Carrino, Dir.

ASHLAND

ASHLAND COLLEGE, Art Department, College Ave, 44805.
  Tel: (419) 289-4005
Leon F. Schenker, Chmn; 7 FT, 1 assoc. instr. Estab. 1878; den;
D & E; ent. req. HS dipl, portfolio for B.F.A. program; 4 yr; de-
grees, B.A, B.S.(Art Educ) & B.F.A; schol; enrl. D 2000, maj. 50,
minors 40. Tui. $2652 per yr; campus res. $1260.

Art Education	Painting
Ceramics	Photography
Drawing	Sculpture
Graphic Arts	Stage Design
Graphic Design	Teacher Training
Crafts	Theater Arts
History of Art	

ATHENS

✤OHIO UNIVERSITY, College of Fine Arts, School of Art, 45701.
  Tel: (614) 594-5667/5668
J. L. Barrio-Garay, Dir; 27 FT, 24 PT instr. Estab. 1936; pub; D &
E; secondary school dipl-portfolio; 4-5 yr; degrees B.F.A, M.A,
M.F.A; schol & fel; 88 SC, 30 LC, 29 LGC, 50 SGC; enrl. maj. 573,
others 1718.

Art Education	Graphic Design
Art History	Illustration
Ceramics	Painting
Drawing	Photography
Fibers	Printmaking
Glass	Sculpture

  Summer School: Dr. J. L. Barrio-Garay, Dir; two 5 wk. sessions: June 21-July 24, July 26-Aug. 28; 18 quarter hr. maximum
per session; SC, LC, GC; tui. $260, non-res. $660.

BEREA

✤BALDWIN-WALLACE COLLEGE, Department of Art, 44017.
  Tel: (216) 826-2900 Exten. 2152
Prof. Harold D. Cole, Chmn; 5 FT, 1 PT instr. Estab. 1845; den;
D & E; co-ed; 4 yr; degree, A.B; 23 SC, 12 LC; enrl. total 1900,
maj. 65. Tui. $2529 per yr; campus res. $1215.

Art Education	Painting
Ceramics & Crafts	Photography
Design & Color	Printmaking
Drawing	Sculpture
History of Art	

BOWLING GREEN

✤BOWLING GREEN STATE UNIVERSITY, School of Art, 43403.
  Tel: (419) 372-2786
Dr. Joseph R. Spence, Dir; 26 FT, 2 PT instr. Estab. 1946; pub;
D & E; ent. req. upper half for state res, upper quarter for out-
of-state; degrees, 4 yr. req. for B.A, B.S, B.F.A; 1 yr. for M.A;
2 yrs. for M.F.A; 16 grad. assistantships, 18 art talent schol. for
undergrad; 54 SC, 14 LC; enrl. 15,000. Tui. $780 per yr, $1143
non-res. Campus res.

Art History Survey	Jewelry Design
Ceramics	Painting
Design	Photography
Drawing	Printmaking
Glass Blowing (grad.)	Sculpture
Graphic Arts	Teacher Training
History of Art	Weaving

  Summer School: Special workshops; two 5 wk. sessions, one 5 wk.
session $260, $381 non-res.

CANTON

MALONE COLLEGE, 515 25th St. NW, 44709.
  Tel: (210) 454-3011
Mary Louise Robson, Head; 1 FT, 3 PT instr. Estab. 1956; den; D &
E; ent. req. HS dipl, ent. exam; 4 yr; degrees B.A, B.S.(Educ), B.S.
(Music); schol; 20 SC, 2 LC; enrl. D 75, maj. 30. Tui. $63 per cr.
hr; campus res. approx. $1000.

Advertising Design	Leather
Art Education	Lettering
Ceramics	Painting
Drawing	Photography
Graphic Arts	Sculpture
Graphic Design	Teacher Training
History of Art & Archaeology	Textile Design
Jewelry	

  Summer School: Art Education, Music and Art in the Western
World; tui. $63 cr. for term of 5 wks, beginning June 15 & July 15;
enrl. 850.

CINCINNATI

ART ACADEMY OF CINCINNATI, Eden Park, 45202.
  Tel: (513) 721-5205
Gerald L. McDowell, Dir; 18 instr. Estab. 1887; pvt; D & E; ent.
req. HS grad; 4-5 yr; cert, B.S. collaboration with Univ. of Cincin-
nati, B.F.A, with Northern Kentucky State Coll; schol; enrl. 165.
Tui. $600 per sem.

Art History	Illustration
Communication Design	Painting
Drawing	Photography
Graphic Arts	Sculpture

  Summer School: Anne Miotke, Supvr; tui. $225 for 8 cr. hrs,
term of 8 wks; enrl. 64.

Life Drawing	Photography
Painting	Printmaking

CENTRAL ACADEMY OF COMMERCIAL ART, INC, 2326 Upland
  Place, 45206. Tel: (513) 961-2484
Jackson Grey Storey, Owner; 2 FT, 2 PT instr. Estab. 1931; pvt;
D; ent. req. HS dipl, interview, presentation of portfolio; 2 yr; cert;
enrl. D 78. Tui. $1400 per yr.
Commercial Art
  Summer School: Michael C. McGuire, Dir; courses same; tui.
$350 for term of 9 wks, beginning June; enrl. approx. 25.

CINCINNATI ART MUSEUM,* Education Department, Eden Park,
  45202. Tel: (513) 721-5204 Exten. 70, 71
Roslynne V. Wilson, Curator of Education; 20-25 PT instr. Museum
estab. 1881; pvt; D & E; ent. req. must be museum member or child
of member; no degree; schol; enrl. D 190 children, E 150 adults.
Tui. $25 family or individual membership, plus $30 per child per
session or $10 per adult per session.

Drawing	Photography
Handweaving	Textile Design
Painting	

  Summer School: Roslynne V. Wilson, Dir; adult courses offered,
Landscape Drawing & Painting; children's classes; tui. membership
fee plus $2 for children or $5 for adults for term of 6 wk. beginning
June 21, 1976; enrl. 300 children, 45 adults.

EDGECLIFF COLLEGE, Art Department, 2220 Victory Parkway,
  45206. Tel: (513) 961-3770
Sister Mary Rosine Allgeyer, Chmn; 5 FT, 2 PT instr. Estab. 1935;
den; D & E; ent. req. HS grad, portfolio for acceptance as an art maj.
by end of soph. yr; 4 yr; degree, B.A; schol; 20 SC, 6 LC; enrl. D
190, E 25, maj. 120. Tui. approx. $1600, $53 per cr. hr; campus
res. $1400.

Aesthetics	Jewelry
Art Education	Lettering
Batik	Painting
Ceramics	Printmaking
Drawing	Sculpture
Graphic Arts	Teacher Training
Handicrafts	Textile Design
History of Art	Weaving

  Summer School: Sister Mary Rosine, Dir; History of Art; tui.
$53 per cr. hr. for term of 5 wks, beginning June 21; enrl. 40.

GEBHARDT ART SCHOOL, 124 E. Seventh St,
  45202.
James E. Price, Dir; 2 FT, 10 PT instr. Estab. 1947; pvt; D & E;
ent. req. HS dipl; 2 yr; dipl. courses in: Commercial Art (24
months), tui. $3400, plus supplies $1200, Professional Photography
(24 months), tui. $3400 plus supplies $1200, lab fees $400, equip-
ment up to $900, Fine Art (24 months), tui. $3400 plus supplies,
Interior Design (9 months), tui. $675 plus $100 supplies; total enrl.
115.

✤UNIVERSITY OF CINCINNATI, College of Design, Architecture and
  Art, 45221.
Bertram Berenson, Dean; 77 FT, 30 PT instr. Estab. 1922; pub;
full-time programs; also cooperative programs whereby student
spends alternate periods in classroom and in establishments in his
chosen profession; degrees, B.Arch, B.Community Planning, B.S.
(Design) (with maj. in Fashion Design, Graphic Design, Industrial
Design and Interior Design), B.F.A, B.F.A.(Art Educ), B.A.(Art
History), M.F.A. (2 yr), M.F.A.(Art Educ) (1 yr), M.A.(Art History)
(1 yr), M.S.(Arch) (1 yr), Ed.D; enrl. full-time 1800. Tui. full-time
Cincinnati res. $580, full-time State res. $750, full-time non-res.
$1270. Sat. children's art classes available.

CLEVELAND

CASE WESTERN RESERVE UNIVERSITY, Department of Art, 5290
  Crawford Hall, 44106.
Walter S. Gibson, Chmn; 5 FT, 23 PT instr. Estab. 1885; pvt; D & E;
co-ed; ent. req. HS transcript; degrees, B.S.& M.A. in Art Educ,
B.A, M.A. & Ph.D. in Art History; approx. 30 SC, 48 LC Art History.
Tui. undergrad. $3000, room $825 to $975, board undergrad. $750;
grad. tui. $125 per cr. hr. Cooperates with Cleveland Institute of
Art and Cleveland Museum of Art. Special programs: Museum
Studies for B.A, M.A, Ph.D, Double Master's in Art History and Li-
brary Science.

CLEVELAND INSTITUTE OF ART, 11141 East Blvd, 44106.
  Tel: (216) 421-4322
Joseph McCullough, Pres; Dr. Ann Roulet, Dean of Students; 34 FT,
45 PT instr. Estab. 1882; pvt; D & E; ent. req. application, HS
transcript, art portfolio; 4 yr. B.S.(Educ) degree with Case Western
Reserve Univ, 5 yr. for B.F.A; schol; 40 SC; enrl. D 500. Tui.
$1975, E $164 for 32 wks, one E a wk; children Sat. 24 wk. $60.
Summer School.

Ceramics	Painting
Enameling	Photography
Graphic Design	Printmaking
Industrial Design	Sculpture
Jewelry & Silversmithing	Teacher Training
Medical Illustration	Weaving & Textile Design

THE CLEVELAND STATE UNIVERSITY,* Department of Art, Euclid
  at E. 24th, 44115.
David Evett, Acting Chmn; 12 FT instr. Estab. 1965; pub; D & E;
ent. req. HS dipl; 4 yrs; degree, B.A; schol; 24 SC, 22 LC. Tui.
$230 per quarter, $460 out of state students; campus res. $435
room only.

Aesthetics	Graphic Design
Art Education	Handicrafts
Ceramics	History of Art & Archaeology
Drawing	Painting
Glass	Sculpture
Graphic Arts	

COOPER SCHOOL OF ART,* 2341 Carnegie Ave, 44115.
  Tel: (216) 241-1486
Nicholas Livaich, Dir; Joseph Hruby, Dean; 32 FT & PT instr.
Estab. 1936; pvt; co-ed; ent. req. HS grad, art portfolio and personal
interview; 3 yr. program, schol, 9 quarter to complete; dipl; SC;
enrl. 500. Tui. $390 per quarter; full-time, $3780 total cost. Evening School, 25 courses, $45 per course; Sat. and Summer classes
for HS students; Sat. adult workshops, $65 per course.

Advertising	Illustration
Art History	Painting
Design	Photography
Drawing	Portrait
Fashion	Printmaking
Film	Watercolor
Graphic Design	

  Summer School: 3 sessions, starting in June.

CUYAHOGA COMMUNITY COLLEGE, 700 Carnegie Ave, 44115.
  Tel: (216) 241-5966 Exten. 462
Curtis Jefferson, Dean, Metro Campus, Dr. Martin L. Krauss, Dean,
Western Campus, Dr. William R. Williams, Dean, Eastern Campus;
9 FT, 17 PT instr. Estab. 1964; pub; D & E; ent. req. HS dipl, ent.
exam; 2 yr; degree A.A; schol; 28 SC, 8 LC. Tui. $330 per yr, $7.70
per cr. hr; no campus res. Summer School.

Art Education	Illustration
Ceramics	Occupational Therapy
Commercial Art	Painting
Drafting	Photography
Drawing	Sculpture
Graphic Arts	Textile Design
Graphic Design	Theatre Arts
History of Art & Archaeology	

COLUMBUS

COLUMBUS COLLEGE OF ART AND DESIGN* (of the Columbus Gallery of Fine Arts), 486 Hutton Place, 43215. Tel: (614) 224-9101
Joseph V. Canzani, Dean; Mary T. Kinney, Registrar; 48 instr.
Estab. 1879; pvt; D & E; ent. req. HS grad, art portfolio; 4 yr; degree, B.F.A; schol; approved for Veterans.

Advertising Design	Interior Design
Advertising-Merchandising	Magazine Illustration
Fashion Illustration	Packaging Design
Fine Arts	Painting
Graphics	Photography
Industrial Design	Sculpture

OHIO DOMINICAN COLLEGE,* 1216 Sunbury Rd, 43219.
    Tel: (614) 253-2741
Sister Mary Eugene, Assoc. Prof; 2 FT, 1 PT, E 1 FT instr. Den; 4 yr; degree, B.A; 8 SC, 5 LC. Summer School.

Advertising Design	Painting
Ceramics	Sculpture
Drawing	Teacher Training
Graphic Arts	Weaving
Jewelry	Woodworking
Lettering	

OHIO STATE UNIVERSITY,* School of Architecture, 190 W. 17th Ave, 43210.
Laurence C. Gerckens, Dir; 32 FT, 19 PT instr. Estab. 1899; pub; 4-6 yr; degrees, B.S.Arch, B.S.Land. Arch, M.Arch, M.C.P; enrl, Architecture 396, Lanscape Architecture 131, City & Regional Planning 145. Tui. per quarter $250, non-res. $560.
Architecture
City & Regional Planning
Landscape Architecture

College of The Arts, Mershon Auditorium, 30 W. 15th Ave, 43210. Tel: (614) 422-5171
Lee Rigsby, Dean. College estab. 1968, classes since 1906; pub; 4 yr; degrees; fel. Tui. quarter fee $210, non-res. $350; campus res. Summer School.

Division of Art
Francis A. Ruzicka, Chmn; 36 FT, 34 PT instr. Degrees, B.A, B.F.A, M.A, M.F.A; 56 SC, 6 LC, 30 GC.

Ceramic Art	General Fine Arts
Drawing, Painting, Graphics	Sculpture

Division of Art Education
Kenneth Marantz, Chmn; 10 FT, 11 PT instr. Degrees, B.A.Educ, M.A, Ph.D; 4 SC, 9 LC, 9 GC. Courses in Art Education.

Department of Industrial Design
Charles A. Wallschlaeger, Chmn; 11 FT, 4 PT instr. Degrees, B.S. in Industrial Design, M.A; 29 SC, 1 LC, 15 GC.

Product Design	Visual Communication Design
Space and Enclosure Design	

Division of the History of Art
Franklin M. Ludden, Chmn; 15 FT, 20 PT instr. Degrees, B.A, B.F.A, M.A, Ph.D; 37 LC, 52 GC. Courses in History of Art.

CUYAHOGA FALLS

STUDIOS OF JACK RICHARD CREATIVE SCHOOL OF DESIGN, 2250 Front St, 44221. Tel: (216) 929-1575
Jack Richard, Dir; 1 FT instr. and guest demonstrators. Estab. 1960; pvt; D & E; no ent. req; no degree; schol; 4 SC, 10 LC; enrl. D 50-60, E 50-60. Tui. $80-$200.

Aesthetics	Occupational Therapy
Art Education	Painting
Ceramics	Photography
Drawing	Sculpture
Illustration	

Adult hobby classes, drawing and painting; tui. $7 per class; enrl. 100-120 per session.
    Summer School: Jack Richard, Dir; courses offered, design, drawing, painting; tui. $68.75 for term of 8 wk. beginning June 15; 1975 enrl. 60.

DAYTON

COLLEGE OF THE DAYTON ART INSTITUTE,* 456 Belmonte Park N, 45495. Tel: (513) 223-1242
Sherwin Silverman, Dir; William T. Matthias, Dean; Martin Hunger, Registrar; 10 FT, 8 PT instr. Estab. 1919; pvt; D & E; ent. req. HS dipl, ACT; 4 yr; degree, B.F.A, dipl, additional academics required

at another institution (affiliated with Miami Valley Consortium); schol; enrl. D 130, E 100, Sat. 173. Tui. D $1200, E $60; Sat. (children's classes) $50, special studio (HS students) $80.

Advertising Design	Illustration
Art History	Painting
Ceramics	Photography
Design	Printmaking
Drawing	Sculpture

Summer School: Adult classes, $50 per cr. hr, enrl. 50; children's classes, $40, enrl. 50; pre-college classes (HS) $100, enrl. 40.

Ceramics	Photography
Drawing	Printmaking
Illustration	Sculpture
Painting	

✠MT. ST. JOHN NORMAL SCHOOL,* 4370 Patterson Rd, 45430
Rev. Wm. Ferrer, Dir.

SINCLAIR COMMUNITY COLLEGE, Department of Art, 444 W. Third St, 45402. Tel: (513) 226-2500
John Polston, Chmn; 3 FT, 14 PT instr. Estab. 1973; pub; D & E; ent. req. HS dipl, ent. exam; 2 yr; degree, A.A. Tui. $10 per cr. hr; no campus res.

Advertising Design	Painting
Ceramics	Sculpture
Commercial Art	Theatre Arts
Drawing	

WRIGHT STATE UNIVERSITY, Art Department, Col. Glenn Highway, 45431. Tel: (513) 426-6650 Exten. 246
Prof. Edward Levine, Chmn; 8 FT, 2 PT instr. Estab. 1964 as a campus of the state univ. system, 1967 independent status; pub; D & E; ent. req. HS dipl, ent. exam; 4 yr; degrees, B.A, B.F.A; 45 SC, 13 LC; enrl. D 1170, maj. 82. Tui. $650 per yr, $250 per mo, $22 per cr. hr; campus res. $1380 per yr.

Aesthetics	Multi-Media
Drawing	Painting
Film	Photography
Graphic Arts	Sculpture
History of Art	

DELAWARE

OHIO WESLEYAN UNIVERSITY, Department of Fine Art, 43015
    Tel: (614) 369- 4431
Justin Kronewetter, Head; 7 FT instr. Estab. 1864; den; 4 yr; degrees, B.A, B.F.A; fel; 21 SC, 13 LC.
General Art
Teacher Training with
    Department of Education

FINDLAY

FINDLAY COLLEGE, Art Department, 1000 North Main St, 45840.
    Tel: (419) 422-8313 Exten. 236
Dr. Roland Anfinson, Chmn. Div. Fine Arts; 2 FT, 2 PT instr. Estab. 1889; pvt; D & E; ent. req. HS dipl, ent. exam; 4 yrs; degrees, B.A, B.S; schol; 17 SC, 3 LC; enrl. D approx. 1000, maj. 25. Tui. $2085 for 3 terms of 10 wks; campus res. $990.

Aesthetics	Drawing
Art Education	Graphic Arts
Arts & Crafts	Handicrafts
Ceramics	History of Art & Archaeology
Commercial Art	Painting
Design	Sculpture

Adult classes, painting, ceramics; tui. $50 1 1/5 term cr; enrl. 10-30 per term.
    Summer School: Dr. Jack Lizotte, Dir; courses offered, Arts & Crafts, Independent Study.

GAMBIER

KENYON COLLEGE, Art Department, 43022.
    Tel: (614) 427-2244 Exten. 465
Martin Garhart, Chmn; 7 FT instr. Estab. 1824; pvt; D; co-ed; ent. req. HS grad, coll. boards, recommendation, others; 4 yr; degrees B.A, B.F.A; schol; 18 SC, 20 LC; enrl. 1500, maj. 65. Tui. $3200, $1854 (fees, room, board).

Aesthetics	Painting
Design	Photography
Drawing	Printmaking
Film	Sculpture
History of Art & Archaeology	

GRANVILLE

✣DENISON UNIVERSITY, Department of Art, P O Box M, 43023.
Tel: (614) 587-0810 Exten. 596
George Bogdanovitch, Chmn; 7 FT, 1 PT instr. Estab. 1831; pvt;
D; ent. req. HS grad; 4 yr; degrees, B.A, B.F.A; schol; 28 SC, 19
LC Art History; enrl. 2100. Tui. $1500 per sem, room & board
$1300.

Art History	Life Drawing
Ceramics	Museology
Design	Painting
Drawing	Photography
European Study	Sculpture
Graphics	University Gallery
Independent Study	

HIRAM

HIRAM COLLEGE, Art Department, 44234.
Tel: (216) 569-3211 Exten. 243/244
Paul A. Rochford, Chmn; 4 FT, 2 PT instr. Estab. 1850; pvt; D;
ent. req. HS dipl; 4 yr; degree, A.B; schol; 19 SC, 12 LC; enrl. D
1300, maj. 65. Tui. $2455 per yr; campus res. $915 per yr.

Aesthetics	History of Art & Archaeology
Art Education	Lettering
Ceramics	Painting
Drawing	Photography
Fabrics	Sculpture
Film Making	Teacher Training
Graphic Arts	Theatre Arts
Graphic Design	

Summer School: Paul A. Rochford, Dir; courses vary; enrl. 180.

KENT

✣KENT STATE UNIVERSITY, College of Fine and Professional Arts,
School of Art, 44242. Tel: (216) 672-2193
Dr. Stuart Schar, Dir; 43 FT, 10 PT instr. Estab. 1913; pub; 4 yr;
degrees, B.A, B.F.A, B.S, M.A, M.F.A, M.Educ; schol. normal enrl.
maj. 900. Tui. undergrad. per quarter $270, non-res $670, grad.
$345, non-res. $745.

Art Education	Graphic Design
Art History	Industrial Design
Cinematography	Jewelry
Ceramics	Painting
Drawing	Printmaking
Enameling	Sculpture
Glass	Weaving

Summer school includes special Blossom-Kent Art Program.

MARIETTA

MARIETTA COLLEGE, Art Department, 45750.
Tel: (614) 373-4643
William Gerhold, Chmn; 4 FT, 1 PT instr. Estab. 1835; pvt; 4 yr;
degree A.B; grants in aid and student loans; 20 SC, 7 LC; enrl. maj.
75, total coll. enrl. approx. 1600.

Ceramics	Painting
Costume Design	Sculpture
Drafting	Teacher Training
Drawing	Television
Graphic Arts	Theatre Arts
Lettering	

MOUNT ST. JOSEPH

COLLEGE OF MOUNT ST. JOSEPH ON THE OHIO, Art Department,
45051.
Sister Ann Austin, Chmn; 5 FT, 3 PT instr. Estab. 1920; pvt; D & E;
W (some men in E classes); ent. req. ent. exam, portfolio (slides are
accepted); 4 yr; degrees, B.A, B.F.A; schol; 22 SC, 6 LC; enrl. D 850
(all courses), E 53, maj. 78, others 30. Tui. $60 per cr. hr. plus
fees; campus res. $1320 per yr.

Art Education	Interior Design
Basic Design	Jewelry
Ceramics	Painting
Drafting	Photography
Drawing	Sculpture
Experiments in Art Education	Teacher Training
Graphic Arts	Visual Communication
History of Art	Weaving

Adult classes, ceramics and weaving, metalcraft, interior design;
tui. $60 per cr; enrl. 50.
Summer School: Sister Ann Austin, Chmn; Workshop Studio
Courses.

NEW CONCORD

MUSKINGUM COLLEGE,* Art Department, 43762.
Tel: (614) 826-8101
James P. Anderson, Chmn; 3 FT instr. Estab. 1837; pvt; D; ent.
req. HS dipl, ent. exam, specific school standards; 4 yrs; degrees,
B.A, B.S, B.Music; schol; 13 SC, 6 LC; enrl. D 300, maj. 14. Tui.
$2550 per yr; campus res. $1100 per yr.

Aesthetics	Jewelry
Art Education	Museum Staff Training
Ceramics	Painting
Commercial Art	Sculpture
Drawing	Teacher Training
Graphic Arts	Theatre Arts
History of Art & Archaeology	

Summer School: Larry Nelson, Dir.

OBERLIN

OBERLIN COLLEGE, College of Arts and Sciences, Department of
Art, 44074. Tel: (216) 775-8665
Paul B. Arnold, Chmn; 10 FT instr. Estab. 1833; pvt; D & E; co-ed;
ent. req. any undergrad. may register for courses, maj. admitted
after satisfactory work in introductory courses and conference with
maj. advisor, grad. credentials, recommendations submitted to faculty; undergrad. 4 yr, B.A, grad. 2 yr, M.A.(Art Hist); undergrad.
schol, grad. schol. and fel; 17 SC, 33 LC, 9 GC; enrl. maj. 90, grad.
16, total 1500. Tui. $3300, fees $225, room $660, board $800.

Art Conservation	Museum Training
Classical Archaeology	Painting
Drawing	Printmaking
History of Art	Sculpture

Children's classes, general class by museum on Sat. mornings to
children of museum mem; enrl. approx. 25.

OXFORD

MIAMI UNIVERSITY, School of Fine Arts, 45056.
Tel: (513) 529-6010
Charles Spohn, Dean. Estab. 1928; pub; D; 4 yr; degrees, B.Environ.
Design, B.S.(Art), B.F.A, M.Arch, M.F.A, M.A.(Art). Tui. $870 per
yr, non-res. $2070; campus res.

Department of Architecture
Harold A. Truax, Acting Chmn; 12 FT instr. 4 yr; 12 SC, 15 LC.
Courses in Architecture.

Department of Art
Robert B. Butler, Chmn; 23 FT instr. 4 yr; degrees, B.S.(Art),
B.F.A; 35 SC, 10 LC.

Advertising Arts	Metals
Ceramics	Painting
Design	Printmaking
Fabrics	Sculpture

Summer School: Two 5 wk. terms; $145 per term, non-res. $345.

PAINESVILLE

LAKE ERIE COLLEGE/GARFIELD SENIOR COLLEGE,* Art Depart-
ment, 44077. Tel: (216) 352-3361 Exten. 248, 305
Roger Williams, Head; 3 FT, 4 PT instr. Estab. 1856; pvt; Lake Erie,
W. Garfield, co-ed; ent. req. coll. board exam; 4 yr; degrees, B.A,
B.F.A; 20 SC, 7 LC; total enrl. 800. Tui. comprehensive $3400.

Art Education	Introductory Art
Ceramics	Painting
Design	Sculpture
History & Appreciation of Art	

SPRINGFIELD

SPRINGFIELD ART CENTER, 107 Cliff Park Rd, 45501.
Tel: (513) 325-4673
Patricia D'Arcy Catron, Dir; 20 PT instr. Estab. 1951; pvt; D & E;
schol; all SC; enrl. approx. 600 per yr. total. Tui. $40 per quarter.

Ceramics	Painting
Commercial Art	Photography
Drawing	Pottery
Jewelry	Sculpture

Adult hobby classes; tui. $40 per quarter.
Children's classes: Drawing, painting, pottery and sculpture; tui.
$25 per quarter.

WITTENBERG UNIVERSITY, Department of Art, 45501.
Tel: (513) 327-6311
John O. Schlump, Head; 6 FT, 2 PT instr. Estab. 1894; den; ent.
req. HS grad; 4 yr; degrees A.B, B.F.A; schol; 32 SC, 19 LC; enrl.
maj. 105. Tui. $2787 per yr. (3 terms).

Ceramics	Printmaking

Commercial Art
Drawing
Painting

Sculpture
Teacher Preparation

    Summer School: Dr. Richard Ortquist, Dir; tui. first course $190, second course $170, third course $150, $90 per workshop; enrl. 300.

Art Workshops
Ceramics
Crafts

Drawing
Painting
Printmaking

TIFFIN

HEIDELBERG COLLEGE,* 44883.
    Tel: (419) 448-2000
Prof. George Keester, Head; 3 FT instr. Estab. 1850; pvt; D; ent. req. HS dipl, each applicant's qualifications are considered individually; 4 yr; degree, A.B; schol; 22 SC, 9 LC; enrl. 200; maj. 24. Tui. (1973-1974) $2365 full time, $90 per sem. hr; campus res. $945.

Advertising Design
Aesthetics
Art Education
Ceramics
Chip Carving
Commercial Art
Copper Enameling
Display
Drawing
Graphic Arts
Graphic Design
History of Art & Archaeology

Illustration
Jewelry
Lettering
Metal Tooling
Mosaic
Museum Staff Training
Painting
Sculpture
Stage Design (Speech Dept.)
Teacher Training
Theatre Arts (Speech Dept.)

Independent study; honors work available.
    Summer School: Dr. Roy Bacon, Dir; Practical Arts, Materials and Methods in Teaching Art; tui. (1973) $78 per cr. hr. for term of 6 wk. beginning June 18; 1973 enrl. 10.

TOLEDO

✠TOLEDO MUSEUM SCHOOL OF DESIGN, Box 1013, 43697.
    Tel: (419) 255-8000
Charles F. Gunther, Asst. Dir. (Educ); 13 FT, 5 PT instr. Estab. 1919; pvt; D & E; 4 yr; degree in cooperation with Univ. of Toledo; schol; adult classes meet PM and E; enrl. adults 1200 per quarter, children 2000. Tui. $30 per cr. hr; free classes for children on Sat. in art and music.

Ceramics
Design
Drawing
Glass Craftsmanship
History of Art & Appreciation

Interior Design
Metalsmithing
Painting
Printmaking
Sculpture

WESTERVILLE

OTTERBEIN COLLEGE,* Department of Visual Arts, 43081.
    Tel: (614) 882-3000
Earl Hassenpflug, Chmn. Dept; 3 FT instr. Pvt; ent. req. HS dipl; 4 yrs; degree, B.A; schol; 11 SC, 4 LC; enrl. D 1400, maj. 32. Tui. $3500 comprehensive fee.

Architecture
Art Education
Art Psychotherapy
Bronze Casting
Ceramics
Drawing
Graphic Design
Handicrafts

History of Art & Archaeology
Macrame
Painting
Photography
Sculpture
Stage Design
Teacher Training
Theatre Arts

WILBERFORCE

CENTRAL STATE UNIVERSITY, Department of Art, 45384.
    Tel: (513) 376-6610
Hayward R. Dinsmore, Chmn; 3 FT instr. Estab. 1856; D; ent. req. HS dipl; 4 yr; degrees, B.A, B.S.(Educ); 20 SC, 8 LC; enrl. D 175, maj. 45, others 130. Tui. $75, out-of-state $200; campus res. $1131.

Advertising Design
Art Education
Ceramics
Drawing
Graphic Arts

History of Art & Archaeology
Lettering
Painting
Sculpture
Teacher Training

    Summer School: H. R. Dinsmore, Chmn; tui. $12.50 plus $98 fees for 12 wks, beginning June 16, two sessions; enrl. maj. 20, others 100.

Art for the Elementary Teacher
Art History
Black Artists

Introduction to Art
Painting
Sculpture

WILLOUGHBY

AKA-THE SCHOOL OF FINE ARTS, 38660 Mentor Ave, 44094.
    Tel: (216) 951-7500
Doris Foster, Art Coordinator; 8 PT instr. Estab. 1960; pvt; D & E; no ent. req. unless enrl. through Lakeland Coll; 2 yr. prog. in co-operation with Lakeland Coll; schol; 7 SC; enrl. D 30, E 150. Tui. approx. $25 per class hr; no campus res. Summer School.

Ceramics
Drawing
Life Drawing

Painting
Photography

Adult hobby classes, same as offered above; tui. approx. $25 per class hr; enrl. 40.
Children's classes, ceramics, drawing; tui. approx. $25 per class hr; enrl. 100.

WOOSTER

COLLEGE OF WOOSTER, Department of Art, 44691.
    Tel: (216) 264-1234 Exten. 388
Dr. Thalia Gouma-Peterson, Chmn; 4 FT, 2 PT instr. Estab. 1866; den; 4 yr; degree; schol; 15 SC, 13 LC; enrl. 800, total 1850. Tui. $3300; campus res.

American Art
Art Education
Ceramics
City Through History
Design
Drawing
Greek Art & Archaeology

Graphics
History of Art
Independent Study
Painting
Photography
Sculpture

Community-college art center program (just starting), drawing, filmmaking, photography, sculpture, watercolor, weaving for adults, creative dance, geology, mixed media and preschool art for children; fees $10-25 for 3 sessions; from 2 hr. per wk. for children to 12 hr. per wk. for adults, depending on classes.
    Summer School: Dr. William E. Hoffman, Dir; tui. $325 per course.

Ceramics I & II
Experiments in Sculpture

Printmaking I & II
3-Dimension Design & Multi-Media

YELLOW SPRINGS

✠ANTIOCH COLLEGE,* Department of Art, 45387.
    Tel: (513) 767-7331
James Jordan, Chmn; 7 FT, 2 PT instr. Estab. 1853; pvt; cooperative plan of alternating work and study inaugurated 1921; students work in positions applicable to their fields; art apprenticeships and interim study at branch campuses, cooperating institutions, or with individual artists in this country and abroad; degrees, B.A. in area of concentration, B.A. or B.S. in interdisciplinary or experimental art areas (incl. architecture and design); enrl. approx. 1000 per quarter. Tui. may vary according to sequence of study, generally around $3900 per yr, incl. tui, community government fee, health fee and insurance, room and board.

Aesthetics
Architecture
Art History
Ceramics
Communications
Crafts
Environmental Design
Film History & Aesthetics

Film Production
Interdisciplinary Studies
Life Drawing
Painting
Photography
Printmaking
Sculpture
Stained Glass

    Summer School: Regular quarter.

YOUNGSTOWN

YOUNGSTOWN STATE UNIVERSITY, Art Department, 410 Wick Ave, 44555. Tel: (216) 746-1851 Exten. 451
Prof. Jon Naberezny, Chmn; 12 FT, 14 PT instr. Estab. Univ. 1908, Dept. 1941; pub; D & E; ent. req. HS dipl; 4 yr; degrees, A.A, A.B, B.F.A, B.S.(Educ); 37 SC, 24 LC, 9 GC; quarterly enrl. D 800, E 300, maj. 300, grad. students 15. Tui. $650 per yr; non-res. additional $160 per quarter; campus res. $925 per yr.

Advertising Design
Aesthetics
Art Education
Ceramics
Commercial Art
Crafts
Drawing
Graphic Arts
History of Art & Archaeology
Illustration

Jewelry
Lettering
Museum Staff Training
Painting
Photography
Puppetry
Sculpture
Stage Design
Teacher Training
Weaving

Adult hobby classes, continuing educ. dept. offers a good number of studio arts and art history classes for no cr.
    Summer School: Studio arts, art history.

ZANESVILLE

ZANESVILLE ART CENTER, 1145 Maple Ave, 43701.
Tel: (614) 452-0741
Dr. Charles Dietz, Dir; 8 PT instr. Estab. 1936; pvt; D & E; ent.
req. conference; schol; 12 SC; enrl. D 135, E 70. Tui. quarterly
$20 adults, $6 children.

Ceramics	Needlepoint
Drawing	Painting
Handicrafts	Sculpture
Macrame	

Adult hobby classes: Macrame & needlepoint.
Children's classes: Drawing & painting; tui. $6 per quarter, enrl. 60.

OKLAHOMA

ADA

EAST CENTRAL UNIVERSITY, Art Department, 74820.
Tel: (405) 332-8000
Dee J. Lafon, Chmn; 4 FT instr. Estab. 1909; pub; ent. req. HS grad;
4-5 yr; degrees, B.S, B.A, M.T; schol; 21 SC, 8 LC; enrl. maj. 90,
others 3300 (440 enrl. in all art classes). Tui. general fees $10.50
per sem. hr, non-res. $25. Summer school.

Animated Film	Metal Design
Art History	Metal Foundry
Ceramics	Painting
Design	Sculpture
Drawing	Teacher Education
Graphics	Wood Design

ALVA

NORTHWESTERN OKLAHOMA STATE UNIVERSITY, Art Department, 73717. Tel: (405) 327-1700
Don Bellah, Head; 1 FT instr. Estab. 1897; pub; D & E; co-ed; ent.
req. HS grad, ACT, C average in HS, application; degrees, B.A.(art),
B.A.(Educ); schol; 26 SC, 4 LC, 3 GC. Tui. $11 per hr, non-res.
$27.50; campus res. $880 for 9 mo.

Art Education	History of Art & Archaeology
Ceramics	Illustration
Commercial Art	Lettering
Crafts (Elementary &	Metalwork & Jewelry
Indian)	Painting
Drafting	Sculpture
Drawing	Teacher Training
Graphic Arts	Textile Design

Summer School: Don Bellah, Head; tui. $11 per hr. for term of
10 wks, beginning May 30.

CHICKASHA

OKLAHOMA COLLEGE OF LIBERAL ARTS,* Art Department,
73018. Tel: (405) 224-3140 Exten. 311
Derald T. Swineford, Head; 2 FT, 1 PT instr. Estab. 1909; pub; D;
co-ed; 124 hr. req. for grad; degree; 26 SC, 3 LC; enrl. maj. 57,
others 180. Tui. $512, non-res. $715.

Commercial Art	Painting & Drawing
Design	Pottery & Modeling
History of Art	Sculpture & Ceramic Sculpture
Jewelry & Crafts	Teacher Training

Summer School: Derald T. Swineford, Head; tui. $10.50 per cr.
hr, non-res. $25.

CLAREMORE

CLAREMORE JUNIOR COLLEGE, Art Department, College Hill,
74017. Tel: (918) 341-7510 Exten. 231/313
Fred R. Warford, Dir; 1 FT, 3 PT instr. Estab. 1971; pub; D & E;
ent. req. HS dipl; 2 yr; degree A.A; schol; 17 SC, 3 LC; enrl. D 150,
E 150, maj. 50. Tui. $7.75 per sem. hr; campus res. $990.

Art Appreciation	Illustration
Art Education	Lettering
Ceramics	Painting
Drawing	Sculpture
Graphic Design	Serigraphy
History of Art & Archaeology	Teacher Training

Children's art classes; tui. $30 for 6 wks; enrl. 30.

Summer School: Fred R. Warford, Dir; tui. $7.75 per hr. for
term of 8 wks, beginning May 15; enrl. 100

Art Appreciation	Drawing
Ceramics	Painting
Design	Watercolor

DURANT

SOUTHEASTERN STATE COLLEGE,* Art Department, 74701.
Tel: (405) 924-0121 Exten. 2411
Dr. Allen A. Platter, Head; 4 FT instr. Estab. 1909; pub; ent. req.
HS grad, coll. exam; 4-5 yr; degrees, B.A, B.S, M.Educ; enrl. art
dept. 330. Tui. $176.

Applied Design	Modeling—clay
Ceramics	Painting—oil & watercolor
Crafts	Perspective Drawing
Design	Pictorial Composition
History of Art	

EDMOND

CENTRAL STATE UNIVERSITY, Art Department Bldg, 73034.
Tel: (405) 341-2980 Exten. 201/202
Kathryn Alcorn, Chmn; 10 FT, 4 PT instr. Estab. 1890; state; D & E;
co-ed; ent. req. HS dipl, health exams, IQ test, schol. tests; 3-4 yr;
degrees, B.A, B.S, M.Educ; schol; enrl. maj. 280, grad. 20, dept.
1168, school 10,000. Tui. available at Office of Admissions.

Advertising Design	Jewelry & Metal Design
Art Appreciation	Modeling
Art Education	Painting
Art in America	Perspective & Composition
Arts & Crafts	Puppetry & Related Arts
Ceramics	Sculpture
Commercial Art	Studio Art
Design	Teacher Training
Etching & Lithography	Watercolor
Figure Drawing	Weaving
History of Art	

ENID

PHILLIPS UNIVERSITY, Department of Art, 73701.
Tel: (405) 237-4433
John W. Randolph, Head; 4 FT, 2 PT instr. Estab. 1907; den; D & E;
co-ed; ent. req. HS grad. or exam; 4 yr; degree, B.F.A; schol; 30 SC,
12 LC; enrl. 1500. Tui. $45 per cr. hr. Summer School.
Adult hobby classes, ceramics, jewelry; tui. $60.

LANGSTON

LANGSTON UNIVERSITY, General Delivery, 73050.
Tel: (405) 446-2281 Exten. 227
Wallace Owens, Chmn; 3 FT instr. Pub; D & E; ent. req. HS dipl;
4 yr; degrees B.A.(Art Educ), B.A.(Art, Science); 15 SC, 6 LC; enrl.
D 92, E 30, maj. 42. Tui. $170; campus res. $900.

Art Education	Jewelry
Ceramics	Lettering
Commercial Art	Painting
Drawing	Sculpture
Graphic Arts	Teacher Training
History of Art & Archaeology	Theatre Arts

Summer School: Wallace Owens, Dir; Drawing, Painting, Elementary School Art; tui. $90 for term of 8 wks, beginning first
wk. June.

LAWTON

CAMERON UNIVERSITY, Art Department, 2800 Gore Blvd, 73501.
Tel: (405) 248-2200 Exten. 66
Jack Bryan, Chairperson; 5 FT, 2 PT instr. Estab. 1970; pub; D &
E; ent. req. HS dipl; 4 yr; degree B.A; schol; 22 SC, 5 LC; enrl. D
417, E 90, maj. 60. Tui. $10.50 per hr. sem; campus res. $531 per
sem.

Art Education	History of Art & Archaeology
Ceramics	Jewelry
Drawing	Painting
Graphic Arts	Sculpture
Graphic Design	

Summer School: Jack Bryan, Dir.

Art Education	Jewelry
Ceramics	Painting
Graphics	

NORMAN

UNIVERSITY OF OKLAHOMA,* School of Art, 73069.
Tel: (405) 536-0900
Joe F. Hobbs, Dir; 15 FT, 1 PT instr. Estab. 1911; pub; 4 yr; degrees, B.F.A, M.F.A, M.Art Educ; schol; 27 SC, 22 LC, 12 GC;
enrl. maj. 350, others 1200. Tui. $14 per cr. hr. per sem, non-res.
$36.

Advertising Design	History of Art
Art Education	Metal Design

Ceramic Design
Drawing
Film
Graphics

Painting
Product Design
Sculpture

OKLAHOMA CITY

GOETZ ART SCHOOL, 800 N.E. 21st St, 73105.
   Tel: (405) 524-9211, 525-2484
Richard V. Goetz, Dir; 2 FT, 2 PT. Estab. 1946; pvt; D & E; 6 SC;
enrl. D 75, E 70. Tui. $240, PT $25.
Drawing
Painting

OKLAHOMA CITY UNIVERSITY, Art Department, 73106.
   Tel: (405) 525-5461
Brunel D. Faris, Chmn, Art Dept; 2 FT, 3 PT instr. Estab. 1904;
den; D & E; 4 yr; degrees; schol; 2 LC; enrl. maj. 50. Tui. men
$2727, women $2767 per yr, includes books, lab fee estimates, tui,
meals and dorm room.

Advertising Art
Ceramics
Design
Figure Drawing
Graphics
History of Art

Jewelry
Painting
Sculpture
Teacher Training
Watercolor

   Summer School: Brunel D. Faris, Dir; $55 per cr. hr. for two 6
wk. sessions, June 1-July 10 and July 13-Aug. 21; enrl. 300.

SHAWNEE

OKLAHOMA BAPTIST UNIVERSITY, College of Liberal Art, Art
   Department, 74801.
Leroy Bond, Head; 2 FT, 1 PT instr. Estab. 1926; den; 4 yr; degree
B.A; schol; 10 SC, 1 LC; enrl. maj. 29, others 22. Tui. $1050 per yr;
campus res.
Teacher Training

STILLWATER

OKLAHOMA STATE UNIVERSITY, Art Department, 74074.
   Tel: (405) 372-6211 Exten. 332
J. Jay McVicker, Head; 12 FT, 4 PT instr. Estab. 1890; pub; D;
4 yr; degrees, B.A, B.A.E, B.F.A; 22 SC, 6 LC; enrl. maj. 160,
others 800. Tui. $448, campus res, room and board $800; non-
res. additional fee $832 per yr.

Art History
Ceramics
Color
Design

Drawing
Graphics
Painting
Sculpture

   Summer School: J. Jay McVicker, Head; tui. $14 per cr. hr,
non-res. $40.

TAHLEQUAH

NORTHEASTERN OKLAHOMA STATE UNIVERSITY, Division of Arts
   and Letters, 74464. Tel: (918) 456-5511 Exten. 2503
Dr. Theo M. Nix, Chmn; 3 FT, 1 PT instr. Estab. 1885; pub; D;
co-ed; ent. req. HS dipl, 4 yr; degrees, B.A, B.A.Educ, M.Educ; 16
SC, 5 LC, 6 GC; enrl. 150(all courses) maj. 40, grad. 3, others 110.
Tui. $11.50 per sem. hr; campus res. $855.

Art Education
Ceramics
Display
Drawing
Graphic Arts
History of Art & Archaeology

Lettering
Painting
Sculpture
Teacher Training
Textile Design

   Summer School: Dr. Theo M. Nix, Chmn; Art Education, Painting; tui. $11.50 per sem. hr. for term of 8 wk. beginning June 3.

TULSA

GREENWICH VILLAGE ART INSTITUTE,* 1316 E. Sixth St, 74120.
   Tel: (918) 583-6075 932-1766
Ruth Davis, Owner-Pres; 1 FT, 2 PT instr. Estab. 1955; pvt;
D & E; no ent. req; degrees, commercial & fine arts; 2 SC, 2 GC.
Tui. $1200 per yr, $100 mo, PT $25 mo; campus res. $2400.

Advertising Design
Art Education
Ceramics
Commercial Art
Display
Drawing
Fashion Arts

History of Art & Archaeology
Illustration
Jewelry
Lettering
Painting
Sculpture

Adult hobby classes, painting, sculpture; tui. $25 mo; Children's
classes, painting, sculpture; tui. $25 mo.

   Summer School: Ruth Davis, Dir; courses offered, painting,
sculpture; tui. $175 for term of 6 wk. beginning June 10.

UNIVERSITY OF TULSA, Department of Art, 600 S. College Ave,
   74104. Tel: (918) 939-6351 Exten. 202
Bradley E. Place, Head; D 8 FT, E 6 PT instr, 3 grad. teaching asst.
Estab. 1898; pvt; 4 yr; degrees B.F.A, B.A, B.S, M.A, M.T.A, M.F.A;
schol; 20 SC, 13 LC, 22 GC; enrl. maj. 160, others 400. Tui. $700
per sem; campus res.

Advertising Design
Ceramics
Drawing & Painting
Graphic Arts
Handicrafts

Industrial Design
Sculpture
Teacher Training
Technical Illustration
Television (Speech Department)

   Summer School: Bradley E. Place, Dir; $55 per lecture cr. hr,
$55 per lab. cr. hr; two sessions, one in June, one in July; enrl. 150.

WARNER

CONNORS STATE COLLEGE, Art Department, 74469.
   Tel: (918) 463-2931
Jack Best, Head; 1 FT, 1 PT instr. Estab. 1908; pub; D; ent. req.
HS dipl; 2 yr; degree, A.A; 8 SC, 1 LC; enrl. 120. Tui. $8 per hr,
non-res. $20.05; campus res. $410 per sem.

Advertising Design
Drafting
Drawing
Graphic Arts

Graphic Design
History of Art & Archaeology
Painting

OREGON

ALBANY

LINN BENTON COMMUNITY COLLEGE, Art Department, 6500 S.W.
   Pacific Blvd, 97321. Tel: (503) 928-2361
Kenneth D. Cheney, Chmn. Humanities Div; 5 FT, 1 PT instr. Estab.
1968; pub; D & E; ent. req. open entry; 2 yr; degrees, A.A, A.S,
A.G.S; 14 SC, 2 LC; enrl. D 2000, E 4000. Tui. in-state, in dist. $105
per term, PT $8.75 per cr.

Advertising Design
Aesthetics
Ceramics
Commercial Art
Display
Drafting
Drawing
Graphic Arts
Graphic Design
Handicrafts
History of Art & Archaeology

Illustration
Jewelry
Lettering
Painting
Photography in Motion Pictures
Sculpture & Architecture
Stitchery
Textile Design
Theatre Arts
Weaving

Adult hobby classes: tole painting, watercolor and painting.

ASHLAND

OREGON COLLEGE OF ART, 30 S. First St, 97520.
   Tel: (503) 482-0113
Dr. Richard K. Walsh, Pres; 2 FT, 5 PT instr. Estab. 1971; pvt; D;
ent. req. HS dipl, portfolio; 4 yr; degrees: Bachelor of Professional
Arts or cr. transfer for A.A. or B.A. at adjacent Southern Oregon
State Coll; schol; 24 SC, 5 LC; enrl. D 40. Tui. $1125 per yr, $125
mo; supplies approx. $45 per 3 month term; campus res. approx.
$1000.

Advertising Design
Art Education
Ceramics
Commercial Art
Costume Design & Construction
Drawing
Fashion Arts
Graphic Arts
Graphic Design

History of Art & Archaeology
Illustration
Jewelry
Lettering
Painting
Sculpture
Teacher Training
Textile Design
Theatre Arts

SOUTHERN OREGON STATE COLLEGE, Art Department, 97520.
   Tel: (503) 482-6386
Clifford Sowell, Chmn; 11 FT instr. Estab. 1926; pub; D & E;
ent. req. HS grad; degrees, B.A, or B.S.Art Educ, B.A. or B.S.
Art; enrl. 4500. Tui. $136 per term, $408 per yr; non-res $359
per term, $1077 per yr.

Art Education
Art History
Calligraphy
Ceramics
Crafts (special class)
Design
Drawing
Enameling

Jewelry
Lettering
Metalsmithing
Painting
Photography
Sculpture
Watercolor
Weaving

BEND

CENTRAL OREGON COMMUNITY COLLEGE, Art Department, 97701.
Tom Temple, Head; 2 FT, 4 PT instr. Estab. 1949; pub; D & E; no ent. req; 2 yrs; degrees, A.A, A.S; schol; 8 SC, 8 LC; enrl. D 300, E 100, maj. 60. Tui. $105 per yr.

Basic Design	Jewelry
Ceramics	Lettering
Drawing	Painting
Graphic Arts	Watercolor
History of Art & Archaeology	

Adult hobby classes, glass, textiles; tui. $18 per term; enrl. 60.
    Summer School: Dave Hubura, Dir; tui. $105 for term of 8 wk. beginning June; 1973 enrl. 60.

Ceramics	Painting
Drawing	Printmaking
Jewelry	Weaving

COOS BAY

COOS ART MUSEUM, 515 Market Ave, 97420.
    Tel: (503) 267-3901
Jo Reid, Educ. Dir; 7 PT instr. Estab. 1966; pvt; D & E; 7 SC; enrl. D 15, E 100.

Calligraphy	Lettering
Children's Dance	Painting
Children's Craft & Stitchery	Sculpture
Display	Spinning
Drawing	Stitchery
Jewelry	Weaving

Adult hobby classes; tui. for 10 wks. non-mem. $18, mem. $15; enrl. 100.
Children's classes same as above; enrl. 40.
    Summer School: Jo Reid, Dir; Children's Craft, Drawing & Painting; tui. same as above.

CORVALLIS

OREGON STATE UNIVERSITY, College of Liberal Arts, 97331.
    Tel: (503) 754-2511
Gordon W. Gilkey, Dean

    Department of Art, Fairbanks Hall. Tel: (503) 754-1745
John H. Rock, Chmn; 20 FT instr. Estab. 1908; pub; D & E; ent. req. HS grad; 4 yr; degrees, B.A, B.S.(Art), B.F.A; schol; 40 SC, 15 LC; enrl. 1400. Tui. res. $213 per quarter term, non-res. $700 per quarter term.

Advertising Design	Illustration
Ceramics	Jewelry & Metal Design
Design	Painting
Drawing	Photography
Elementary Art Education	Printmaking
Fabric Design	Sculpture
History of Art	Secondary Art Education

    Summer School: An 8-11 week term is conducted with similar offerings to those listed above. The equivalent to one quarter term of work may be accomplished. Tui. undergrad. $191, grad. $286 (res. & non-res).

    Department of Architecture and Landscape Architecture, Peavy Hall. Tel: (503) 754-2606
Russel E. Ellis, Chmn; 9 FT instr. Architecture estab. 1947, Landscape Architecture, 1908, combined department 1971; 4 yr; liberal studies degrees, B.S. or B.A. with maj. emphasis in each area, professional degree at Univ. of Oregon; 36 SC, 12 LC, 3 field classes; enrl. 800.

Architectural Design & Drawing	Influence of Man on His Physical
Architectural Design Studios	Environs
Construction & Materials	Interior Design
Graphics & Delineation	Landscape Design Studios
History & Theory	Landscape Design & Theory
Housing & Architectural	Maintenance & Construction
Philosophy	Plant Materials & Composition

EUGENE

LANE COMMUNITY COLLEGE, Art and Applied Design Department, 4000 E. 30th Ave, 97405. Tel: (503) 747-4501 Exten. 306
Roger Cornell McAlister, Chmn; 8 FT, 4 PT instr. Estab. 1965; pub; D & E; no ent. req; 2 yr; degrees A.A, A.S; schol; 44 SC, 7 LC; enrl. maj. 75, 200 F.T.E. students per yr. or 3000 total. Tui. $10 per cr. hr. or $100 per quarter full-time.

Ceramics	Metalsmithing
Drafting	Painting
Drawing	Photography
Graphic Arts	Sculpture

Handicrafts	Theatre Arts
History of Art & Archaeology	Weaving
Jewelry	

Adult hobby classes varied; tui. approx. $20-$30 per term; enrl. approx. 1000.
    Summer School: Roger Cornell McAlister, Chmn; tui. $10 per cr. hr. for term of 8 wks. beginning late June.

Ceramics	Painting
Design	Sculpture
Drawing	

MAUDE KERNS ART CENTER, 1910 E. 15th Ave, 97403.
John F. Connor, Dir; 40 PT instr. Estab. 1940; pvt; D & E; co-ed; schol; 45 SC; enrl. D & E 450. Tui. $22-$40 per class per quarter. Summer School.

Calligraphy	Painting
Ceramics	Photography
Graphic Arts	Stitchery
Handicrafts	Theatre Arts (Children)
Jewelry	Weaving

Adult hobby classes: see above; tui. $22-$48; enrl. 420.
Children's classes: ceramics and drawing; tui. $13; enrl. 30.

UNIVERSITY OF OREGON, School of Architecture and Allied Arts, 97403. Tel: (503) 686-3631
Robert S. Harris, Dean; 60 FT, 21 PT instr. Estab. 1914; pub; 4-5 yr yr; degrees; schol. and grad. teaching fel; 68 SC, 150 LC, 104 GC; normal enrl. Arch. 750, Allied Arts 900. Tui. $215.50 per quarter, non-res. $702.50.

Architecture	Landscape Architecture
Art Education	Painting
Ceramics	Printmaking
Graphic Design	Sculpture
History of Art & Architecture	Urban Planning (masters program
Interior Architecture	only)
Jewelry & Metalwork	Weaving

    Summer School: $215.50 (res. & non-res) for 8 wk. term.

LA GRANDE

EASTERN OREGON STATE COLLEGE,* Art Department, 97850.
H. Paul Bruncke, Head Dept; 6 FT, 1 PT instr. Estab. 1929; pub; D & E; ent. req. GPA 2.00 or above; 4 yrs; degrees, B.A, B.S; schol; 55 SC, 3 LC, 5 GC; enrl. D 800, E 250, maj. 50, grad. students 100. Tui. res. $173 per quarter, non res. $413; campus res. $983.

Advertising Design	Jewelry
Art Education	Leather
Ceramics	Lettering
Commercial Art	Painting
Display	Photography
Drawing	Sculpture
Glass Blowing	Stage Design
Graphic Arts	Teacher Training
Handicrafts	Textile Design
History of Art & Archaeology	

    Summer School: Dr. Carlos Easley, Dir; tui. $173 for term of 8 wk. beginning June 20; 1973 enrl. 100.

Art Education	Glass Blowing
Ceramics	Painting
Drawing	

McMINNVILLE

LINFIELD COLLEGE, Art Department, 97128.
    Tel: (503) 472-4121
Randall Jelinek, Chmn; 1 FT, 3 PT instr. Pvt; D; ent. req. HS dipl, ent. exam; 4 yr; degree, B.A; schol. Tui. $2440 per yr; campus res. $1350.

Advertising Design	Jewelry
Aesthetics	Multi-Media Workshop
Art Education	Painting
Ceramics	Photography
Commercial Art	Sculpture
Costume Design & Construction	Stage Design
Drawing	Teacher Training
Graphic Arts	Textile Design
Graphic Design	Theatre Arts
History of Art	

MONMOUTH

OREGON COLLEGE OF EDUCATION, Art Department, 97361.
    Tel: (503) 838-1220 Exten. 340
Daniel G. Cannon, Chmn; 11 FT instr. Estab. 1856; pub; D & E; 4

yr; degrees, B.A, B.S; 63 SC, 17 LC, 6 GC; enrl. total 3500. Tui. (all 3 terms) res. undergrad. $573, non-res. undergrad. $1494, grad. $849.

Art Education	Light Image (Photography)
Art History	Mixed Media
Contemporary Problems	Oil & Acrylic Painting
Crafts	Printmaking
Design	Sculpture
Drawing & Composition	Textile Design
Environmental Design	The Art Idea: Visual Thinking
Individual Studies	Visual Learning & Communication
Lettering	Watercolor
Life Drawing	

Summer School: Daniel G. Cannon, Chmn; courses as above; tui. undergrad. $171 for 12-21 hrs, grad. $253 for 9-16 hrs.

PORTLAND

LEWIS AND CLARK COLLEGE, Art Department, 97219.
    Tel: (503) 244-6161 Exten. 528
Ken Shores, Chmn; 4 FT instr. Estab. 1946; pvt; D; ent. req. HS grad. plus College Board exam; degrees, A.B, B.S; 12 SC, 6 LC; enrl. maj. 40, coll. enrl. 2200. Tui. $2820; campus res. $4160.

Advertising Layout	History of Art
Calligraphy	Painting
Ceramics	Print Making
Drawing	Sculpture

Summer School: Dr. John Richards, Dir.

MUSEUM ART SCHOOL,* Portland Art Museum, West Park & Madison, 97205. Tel: (503) 226-4391
Warren A. Wolf, Dean; 12 FT, 20 PT instr. Estab. 1909; pvt; D & E; B.F.A. program, cooperative program with Reed College for B.A. or HS Teachers cert; enrl. D 165, E 300, children 150. Tui. D $1200, E $60 for 16 wk.

Art History	Lithography
Bronze Casting	Painting
Ceramics	Screen Printing
Composition	Sculpture
Drawing	Woodcut
Etching	

Summer Workshops (6 wk): Children $50, adults $60.

PORTLAND STATE UNIVERSITY,* Art Department, P.O. Box 751, 97207. Tel: (503) 229-3515
Frederick H. Heidel, Prof. Art; 18 FT, 15 PT instr. Estab. 1955, affiliated with Oregon State System of Higher Educ; pub; ent. req. HS grad; 4 yr; degrees, B.S, B.A, M.S.T, M.A.T, M.F.A; schol; 36 SC, 8 LC; enrl. maj. 500. Tui. $516, non-res. $1575. Acad. yr. of 3 terms.

Art Education	Lettering
Art History	Painting
Ceramics	Pre-Architecture
Design	Sculpture
Drawing	Watercolor
Graphic Design	Weaving
Jewelry & Metalsmithing	

Summer School: Dr. Charles White, Dir; tui. $24.50 per cr. hr, (min. $49), $172 full-time; 8 wk. sessions; reg. from June 12, classes begin June 17; enrl. 300.

REED COLLEGE, Department of Art, 97202.
    Tel: (503) 771-1112
Charles S. Rhyne, Chmn; 4 FT, 1 PT instr. Estab. 1911; pvt; D; 3 5 yrs; degree, B.A; schol; 7 SC, 5 LC; enrl. D 1150, E 15. Tui. $3070 per yr, campus res. $1500 per yr.

Aesthetics	History of Art & Archaeology
Calligraphy & Paleography	Painting
Drawing	Sculpture

SCHOOL OF THE ARTS AND CRAFTS SOCIETY, 616 N.W. 18th Ave, 97209. Tel: (503) 228-4741
Bridget Beattie McCarthy, Dir; 40 PT instr. Estab. 1906; pvt; D & E; no ent. req; no degrees; 55 SC; enrl. D 350, E 250. Tui. average $45 per course per quarter.

Batik	Lettering
Calligraphy	Metalsmithing
Ceramics	Natural Dyes
Clothing as Art	Painting
Cooking	Paper (Handmade, Oil Float)
Costume Design & Construction	Patchwork & Quilting
Design & Composition	Photo Silkscreen
Drawing	Photography
Enameling	Sculpture
Fabric Collage	Silversmithing
Glass Blowing	Stitchery
Graphic Arts	Textile Design

Graphic Design	Weaving
Jewelry	Wood Block Printing
Leathersmithing	

18 children's classes, calligraphy, leathersmithing, metal arts, metal sculpture, painting, pinhole photography and pottery; tui. approx. $25 per quarter; enrl. 35 per term.
    Summer School: Bridget Beattie McCarthy, Dir; courses offered are similar to regular year.

PENNSYLVANIA

ALLENTOWN

CEDAR CREST COLLEGE, Art Department, 18104.
    Tel: (215) 437-4471
Ryland W. Greene, Chmn; 3 FT, 2 PT instr. Estab. 1867; pvt; D & E; co-ed; ent. req. HS dipl, CEEB; 4 yr; degrees, B.A, B.S, Interdisciplinary Fine Arts Maj. (art, theatre, music, dance, creative writing); schol; 11 SC, 4 Art History courses; enrl. 750. Tui. D student $2715, with campus res. $3940.

Aesthetics	Jewelry
Art Education	Metal Forming
Ceramics	Painting
Comparative Study of Art	Sculpture
Drawing	Theatre Arts
History of Art	

Cooperative summer school with Muhlenberg College; courses offered, Ceramics, Jewelry-Metalsmithing.

BETHLEHEM

LEHIGH UNIVERSITY, Department of Fine Arts, Coppee Hall, Bldg. 33, 18015 Tel: (215) 619-7000 Exten. 525
Prof. Richard J. Redd, Chmn; 5 FT, 1 PT instr. Estab. 1925; pub; D; ent. req. HS dipl, SAT, CEEB; 4 yr; degree, B.A; schol; 19 SC, 12 LC; enrl. 565, maj. 40. Tui. $3300 per yr, $138 per cr. hr; campus res. $580-$775 for res. only.

Architecture	Painting
Basic Design	Photography
Ceramics	Printmaking
Drawing	Urban Design
History of Art & Archaeology	

Summer School: Dr. Norman Sam, Dir; courses offered, Teacher Training.

BLOOMSBURG

BLOOMSBURG STATE COLLEGE, Department of Art, Bakeless Center for the Humanities, 17815.
Dr. Percival R. Roberts, III, Chmn; Robert Bunge, Registrar; 9 FT instr. Estab. 1839, Pvt. Academy, today one of the 13 state colls; pub; D & E; ent. req. HS dipl, ent. exam; 4 yr; degree, A.B; State and Federal work study grants available; 20 plus SC, 20 plus LC; enrl. D 1000, E 60, maj. 60, coll. 5000, grad. 1200.

Aesthetics	Painting
Art Education	Philosophy and Psychology of Art
Ceramics	Sculpture
Design	Stage Design
Drawing	Teacher Training (elem. educ)
General Crafts	Textile Design
Graphics	Theatre Arts
History of Architecture	Visual
History of Art & Archaeology	Weaving
Jewelry, Media	

Summer School: Dr. Richard O. Wolfe, Dean Extended Programs; tui. $31 per cr. hr, non-res. $46 for term from July 14 - Aug. 22, 1975.

Ceramics	Independent Study in Art History
Children's Art	Introduction to Art
Design	Painting
Drawing	Sculpture
Graphics	Special Problems

BRYN MAWR

BRYN MAWR COLLEGE, Department of the History of Art, 19010.
    Tel: (215) 525-1000 Exten. 249, 250
Charles Dempsey, Chmn; 6 FT, 1 PT instr. Estab. 1913; pvt; W. (men in grad. school); 4 yr; degrees, B.A, M.A, Ph.D; schol. and fel; 10 LC, 8 GC; enrl. maj. 20, grad. 30, others 150. Tui. $3725, grad. $3050; campus res.
History of Art

HARCUM JUNIOR COLLEGE, Department of Fine Arts, 19010.
Tel: (215) 525-4100 Exten. 215
Martin Zipin, Chmn; 1 FT, 5 PT instr. Estab. 1915; pvt; D & E;
W; ent. req. HS dipl; 2 yr; degree, A.A; schol; 7 SC, 1 LC; enrl.
D 40, E 8, maj. 10. Tui. $1700; campus res. $1650.

Commercial Art	History of Art & Archaeology
Drawing	Lettering
Fashion Arts	Painting
Graphic Design	Sculpture

CARLISLE

✠DICKINSON COLLEGE,* Department of Fine Arts, 17013.
Tel: (717) 243-5121 Exten. 344
Dennis Askin, Chmn; 4 FT instr. Estab. 1773; pvt; D; 4 yr; SC, LC;
enrl. 1500.

CHAMBERSBURG

WILSON COLLEGE, Department of Fine Arts, 17201.
Tel: (717) 264-4141 Exten. 353
Josephine M. Harris, Chmn; 3 FT, 2 PT instr. Pvt; W; ent. exam;
4 yr; degrees, B.A.(Studio, Art History, Dance, Drama); 16 SC, 19
LC, seminars in studio, art history, dance, drama; enrl. maj. 18.
Tui. $2700, with campus res. $4200.

Dance Composition & Performance	Graphic Arts
Drawing & Painting	Independent Study
Elements of Staging	Problems in Acting
	Sculpture

CHELTENHAM

CHELTENHAM ART CENTRE, School of Fine Arts, 439 Ashbourne
Rd, 19012.
Gersley Kieserman, Pres; Gladys Wagner, Dir. Educ. Prog; 39 instr.
Estab. 1940; pvt; D & E; ent. req. mem. art centre. Tui. $25-$70
plus mem. dues $8, non-res. Cheltenham Township $9.

Art Education	Painting
Ceramics	Photography
Drawing	Sculpture
Graphic Arts	Stage Design
Jewelry	Theatre Arts

Children's classes, clay, painting, sculpture; tui. $35-40 plus mem.
fee. Teenage classes, jewelry, pottery, printmaking, sculpture;
tui. $35-$50 plus mem. fee.

CHEYNEY

CHEYNEY STATE COLLEGE, Department of Art,
19319.
Samuel L. Curtis, Chmn; 7 FT instr. Estab. 1837; pub; D & E;
ent. req. HS dipl, ent. exam; 4 yr; degree, B.A; schol; 16 SC, 4 LC.
Tui. res. $830, non-res. $1552; campus res. $918.

Aesthetics	Handicrafts
Art Therapy	History of Art & Archaeology
Ceramics	Painting
Drawing	Sculpture
Graphic Arts	

CLARION

✠CLARION STATE COLLEGE, Department of Art, 16214.
Tel: (814) 226-6000
Dr. Robert D. Hobbs, Chmn; 9 FT instr. Estab. 1867; pub; D & E;
ent. req. HS dipl; 4 yr; degree, B.A.(Art); 10 SC, 8 LC; enrl. maj.
16, total approx. 950. Tui. $400 per yr, PT $31 per cr. hr, non-res.
$46 per cr; campus res. $882 per yr.

Art Education	Jewelry
Arts & Crafts	Painting
Ceramics	Sculpture
Drawing	Teacher Training
Graphic Arts	Theatre Scene Painting
History of Art	

Summer School: Dr. Robert D. Hobbs, Dir; tui. $31 per cr. for
two 6 wk. sessions beginning June 2 and July 14; enrl. total 197.

Art Media	Elementary Art
Arts & Crafts	Painting
Ceramics	Three-Dimensional Design
Drawing & Composition	Visual Arts

CRESSON

MOUNT ALOYSIUS JUNIOR COLLEGE, Art Department, 16630.
Tel: (814) 886-4131 Exten. 40.
Hettie Jane Osborne, Assoc. Prof; 4 FT instr. Estab. 1939; den;
D & E; ent. req. HS dipl, SAT, ACT, health record, art portfolio
and interview; 2 yr; degree, A.A; schol; 10 SC, 12 LC; enrl. D 153,
E 8, maj. 23. Tui $60 per cr; campus res. $650 per sem.

Art Appreciation	Graphic Design
Art Therapy	History of Art & Archaeology
Color & Design	Occupational Therapy
Design	Painting
Drawing	Sculpture
Fabrics	Weaving
Fashion & Textile Design	Woodworking

DALLAS

COLLEGE MISERICORDIA, Art Department, 18612.
Tel: (717) 675-2181 Exten 234
Ralph G. Kaleshefski, Chmn; 4 FT, 4 PT instr. Estab. 1924; pvt;
D & E; ent. req. HS dipl; 4 yr; degrees, B.A.(Art Educ, Art); schol;
32 SC, 8 LC, 5 GC; enrl. D 52, maj. 52, grad. 14. Tui. $750 per yr,
$60 per cr; campus res. $1100.

Art Education	Metal Craft
Ceramics	Painting
Drafting	Photography
Drawing	Printmaking
Enameling	Sculpture
Graphic Arts	Stage Design
Handicrafts	Teacher Training
History of Art & Archaeology	Weaving
Illustration	

Summer School: Registrar; various courses and workshops depending on available faculty; tui. depends on course or workshop.
1973 art enrl. 64.

EASTON

LAFAYETTE COLLEGE, Department of Art, 18042.
Tel: (215) 253-6281 Exten. 328
Dr Joseph W. Gluhman, Head; 3 FT, 2 PT instr. Estab. 1827; pvt;
D & E; ent. req. HS dipl, ent. exam, selective admis; 4 yr; degrees,
B.S, A.B; schol; 8 SC, 12 LC; enrl. D 300, E 250, maj. 4. Tui.
$3300; campus res. $1370.

Art History	Printmaking
Drawing	Sculpture
History of Architecture	Three-Dimensional Design
Painting	Two-Dimensional Design

Summer School: Earl G. Peace, Dir.

EDINBORO

EDINBORO STATE COLLEGE, Department of Art, 16412.
Tel: (814) 732-2406 Exten. 2705, 2731
Dr. Richard H. Laing, Head; 48 FT instr. Estab. 1857; pub; D & E;
4 yr; degrees, B.S.(Art Educ), B.A.(Humanities/Art History); schol;
SC, LC; enrl. maj. 950, total 7200. Tui. res. basic fee $820 per yr,
res. undergrad. $33 per cr, grad. $43, non-res. undergrad. $60 per
cr, grad. $80.

Art Education	Painting
Ceramics	Photography
Cinema	Printmaking
Communication Graphics	Sculpture
Drawing	Teacher Training
Furniture	Textile Design
Jewelry-Metal	Weaving
Multi-Media	

Summer School: 12 wk.(3-6-3); tui. $26 per cr.

ERIE

MERCYHURST COLLEGE, Art Department, 501 E. 38th St, 16501.
Tel: (814) 864-0681 Exten. 257
Ernest Mauthe, Dir; 6 FT, 2 PT instr. Coll. estab. 1926, dept.
approved 1950; pvt; D & E; co-ed; ent. req. coll. boards; 4 yr;
degree, B.A; schol; 45 SC, 12 LC; enrl. D 100, E 30, maj. 100, total
1400. Tui. $1990; campus res. $1150.

Art Appreciation	History of Architecture
Art Education	Independent Study
Art Foundations	Individualized Studio
Art History & Criticism	Introduction to Art Studio
Ceramics	Jewelry
Child Art	Painting
Contemporary Art Theories	Photography, Cinematography
Creative Arts for Adolescents	Printmaking
Creative Arts for Children	Senior Seminar
Creativity	Sculpture
Drawing	Teaching Internship

Fibers/Fabrics   Television Internship
Gallery Internship   Visual Communication
The art program offerings are also open to the College of Older
Americans at Mercyhurst and cooperates with the Mercy Center
of the Arts for Children, Gannon College and Villa Maria College.
    Summer School: Ernest Mauthe, Dir; various courses from the
above list; tui. $160 per course.

GETTYSBURG

✠GETTYSBURG COLLEGE,* Art Department, 17325.
   Tel: (717) 334-3131
Ingolf J. Qually, Head.

GLENSIDE

BEAVER COLLEGE, Department of Fine Arts, 19038.
   Tel: (215) 884-3500 Exten. 367
Jack Davis, Chmn; 4 FT, 4 PT instr. Estab. 1853; pvt; D; co-ed;
ent. req. HS dipl; 4 yr; degrees, B.A, B.F.A; schol; 26 SC, 7 LC;
enrl. total 900, maj. 75.

Advertising Design	History of Art
Ceramics	Interior Design
Commercial Art	Jewelry & Metals
Drawing	Painting
Graphic Arts	Printmaking
Graphic Design	

    Summer School: Courses offered, Metals & Jewelry, Painting,
Printmaking; enrl. 25.

GREENSBURG

SETON HILL COLLEGE, Department of Art, 15601.
   Tel: (412) 834-2200
Sister Mary Janice Grindle, Chmn; 5 FT instr. Estab. art maj.
1950; pvt; D & E; W; ent. req. HS dipl, ent. exam, review portfolio;
4 yr; degree, B.A; schol; 30 SC, 9 LC; enrl. D 300, E 40, maj. 70.
Tui. $2150, studio and materials fees $15 to $50 for each course in
studio; campus res. $1150.

Aesthetics	Lettering
Art Education	Painting
Ceramics	Photography
Drawing	Printmaking
Filmmaking	Sculpture
Graphic Design (Layout &	Teacher Training
Calligraphy)	Textile Design
History of Art	Weaving
Jewelry	

Advertising Design and Museum Staff Training as part of apprenticeship program only.
Adult hobby classes, photography, spring 1970; tui. $50 for 12 E;
enrl. 15.
HS students, 6 wk. period in summer or 10 Sat. during fall and spring
terms; tui. $60 plus materials; enrl. 10-20.
    Summer School: Sister Mary Janice Grindle, Chmn; courses
vary each summer-summer 1970, Painting and Design; tui. $42 per cr.
for term of 8 wk. beginning June 17; 1969 enrl. 10.

GREENVILLE

THIEL COLLEGE, Art Department, College Ave, 16125.
   Tel: (412) 500-7700
Ronald A. Pivovar, Chmn; 4 FT instr. School estab. 1866, dept.
1965; den; D; ent. req. HS dipl, interviews; 4 yr; degree, B.A;
schol; 18 SC, 12 LC; coll. enrl. 1100, maj. 75. Tui. $2080 per
yr; campus res. $1000 per yr.

Art Education	History of Art & Archaeology
Ceramics	Jewelry
Crafts	Painting
Drawing	Sculpture
Graphic Arts	Teacher Training

Co-operative Programs with Drew University (1 sem.) and Art
Institute of Pittsburgh (1 sem. or yr).

HAVERFORD

HAVERFORD COLLEGE, Fine Arts Department, 19041.
   Tel: (215) 649-9600 Exten. 266
Christopher Cairns, Chmn; 3 FT Haverford, 1 FT Bryn Mawr instr.
Coll. estab. 1833, dept. art. 1969; pvt; D; M; ent. req. HS dipl;
4 yr; programs in cooperation with the Bryn Mawr College Fine Arts
Department; degree, B.A; schol; 10 Haverford, 5 Bryn Mawr SC,
1 Haverford, 12 Bryn Mawr LC, GC in History of Art at Bryn Mawr;

enrl. 15 maj. Tui. $2975 per yr, special students $450 per course per
sem; campus res. $1700.

Drawing	Painting
Graphic Arts	Photography
History of Art & Archaeology	Sculpture

HUNTINGDON

JUNIATA COLLEGE, Department of Art, Moore St, 16652.
   Tel: (814) 643-4310
Alex McBride, Chmn; 1 FT, 1 PT instr. Estab. 1876; pvt; D; ent.
req. HS dipl; 4 yr; degree, B.A; schol; 12 SC, 3 LC; enrl. 300, maj.
10. Tui. $3990 inclusive; campus res.

Aesthetics	History of Art & Archaeology
Art Education	Painting
Ceramics	Photography
Drawing	Teacher Training
Graphic Arts	Theatre Arts

    Summer School: Dr. Hartman, Dir; courses offered, Art History,
Ceramics, Studio Art.

INDIANA

✠INDIANA UNIVERSITY OF PENNSYLVANIA, Department of Art and
   Art Education, 15701. Tel: (412) 357-2530
Benjamin T. Miller, Chmn; 22 FT instr. Univ. estab. 1875, art dept.
1906; pub; D & E; ent. req. HS grad. and coll. ent. board exam; 4 yr;
degrees, B.S.(Art Educ), B.A.(Humanities with Art Concentration),
M.Ed, M.A; enrl. undergrad. 400, grad. 70, total school 10,500. Tui.
$400 per sem, PT $33 per sem. hr, non-res. $66, activity fee $10.50
main session, $5.25 pre-post basic fee.

Art Education	Professional Art
General Art	Teacher Training

Children's Visual Imagery, evenings; fee $3. Adult evening classes.
    Summer School: Tui. $33 per sem. hr.(minimum), contingent fee
each session $87.

KUTZTOWN

KUTZTOWN STATE COLLEGE, School of Art, 19530.
   Tel: (215) 683-3511 Exten. 309
Dr. Evan J. Kern, Dean; 35 instr. Estab. 1866; pub; ent. req. Coll.
Board ent. exam, HS record; 4 yr; degrees, B.S. and M.Ed.(Art
Educ), B.F.A.(Advertising, Painting, Sculpture); enrl. art 850, total
5000. Tui. undergrad. $800 for 36 wk, non-res. $50 per sem. hr,
grad. $42 per sem. hr, non-res. $46 per sem. hr.
Teacher Education
    Summer School: Dr. Evan J. Kern, Dean; tui. undergrad. $50 per
sem. hr, grad. $46.

LANCASTER

FRANKLIN AND MARSHALL COLLEGE, Art Department, 17604.
   Tel: (717) 393-3612 Exten. 320
Folke T. Kihlstedt, Chmn; 4 FT, 1 PT instr. Estab. 1966; pvt; D & E;
ent. req. HS dipl, ent. exam; 4 yr; degrees, B.A, B.S; schol. for
students with pronounced talent; 4 SC, 8 LC; enrl. D 600, E 120, maj.
8, Independent Study Program 24. Tui. $3100, PT (fewer than 3
courses) $450 per course; campus res. $1020.

Art Education	Painting
Basic Design	Printmaking
Drawing	Sculpture
History of Art & Archaeology	Theatre Arts

LEWISBURG

BUCKNELL UNIVERSITY, Department of Art, 17837.
   Tel: (717) 524-1307
Gerald Eager, Chmn; 6 FT instr. Estab. 1846; pvt; D; 4 yr; degree,
B.A; schol. and fel; 17 SC, 22 LC; enrl. maj. 40, others approx. 500.
Tui. $3325; campus res.

Arts of China	Japanese Art
Art of Indian & Southeast Asia	Pre-Columbian Art

    Summer School: Hugh McKeegan, Dir; 3 SC, 3 LC; tui. $200 per
course; enrl. 50.

MANSFIELD

MANSFIELD STATE COLLEGE, Art Department, 16933.
   Tel: (717) 662-4092
Jay D. Kain, Chmn; 10 FT instr. Pub; D; ent. req. portfolio evaluation and personal interview; 4 yr; degree, B.S.(Art Educ). Tui. res.
$400 per sem, res. $33 per cr. hr. for over 18 cr, non-res. $750 per
sem, non-res. $60 per cr. hr. for over 18 cr.

Aesthetics	History of Art
Art Education	Jewelry

Ceramics
Color & Design
Crafts
Drawing
Graphic Arts

Painting
Sculpture
Teacher Training
Textile Design

Children's art classes; Sat; tui. $5.
Graduate courses offered.
Summer School.

Ceramics
Crafts
Drawing
Jewelry

Painting
Sculpture
Weaving

MEADVILLE

ALLEGHENY COLLEGE, Division of Humanities, Department of
Art, 16335. Tel: (814) 724-3371
Carl F. Heeschen, Head; 4 FT instr. Estab. 1815; pvt; ent. req. ent.
exam; 4 yr; degree, B.A; 12 SC, 9 LC; enrl. art 600. Tui. $2850;
campus res.

MERCERSBURG

MERCERSBURG ACADEMY, Department of Fine Arts, 17236.
Tel: (717) 328-2151
Bouldin G. Burbank, Chmn; 2 FT, 5 PT instr. Dept. estab. 1972;
pvt; D; ent. exam req; secondary school, granting HS dipl;
schol; 4 SC, 3 LC; enrl. 100. Tui. $4200 per yr.

Ceramics
Drawing
Graphic Arts
Graphic Design
Handicrafts
History of Art & Archaeology
Painting

Photography
Pottery
Sculpture
Stage Design
Textile Design
Theatre Arts
Weaving

MILLERSVILLE

✤MILLERSVILLE STATE COLLEGE, Art Department, 17551.
Tel: (717) 872-5411 Exten. 253
R. Gordon Wise, Dir; 14 FT, 1 PT instr. Estab. 1855; pub; D & E;
ent. req. HS dipl, ent. exam; 4 yr; degrees, B.A, B.S; schol; 56 SC,
15 LC, 1 GC; enrl. D 1300, E 60, maj. 260. Tui. $350; campus res.
$720.

Aesthetics
Art Education
Ceramics
Cinematography
Design
Drawing
Graphic Arts
History of Art

Illustration
Jewelry
Lettering
Painting
Photography
Sculpture
Teacher Training
Visual Communications

Summer School: Courses offered, Art Education, Art History &
Studio courses as indicated above; tui. $180 for two 5 wk. terms
beginning June 7 and July 19.

MOUNTAINHOME

DREISBACH ART GALLERY, Rte 191,
18342.
C. I. Dreisbach, Owner. Estab. 1958; pvt; D; no ent. req; enrl. 200.
Tui. $7 per day. Summer school only.
Painting

NEW KINSINGTON

PENNSYLVANIA STATE UNIVERSITY AT NEW KENSINGTON,*
3550 Seventh St, 15068.
Grant Dinsmore, Head; 1 FT instr. Estab. 1968; pub; D; ent. req.
coll. boards; 2 yr.(option for 4 yr. at Main Campus at University
Park); schol; 3-4 SC, 1 LC per sem. No campus res.

Art Education
Design
Drawing
History of Art

Painting
Theatre Arts
Watercolor

NEW WILMINGTON

✤WESTMINSTER COLLEGE, Art Department, 16142.
Tel: (412) 946-8761 Exten. 366
Nelson E. Oestreich, Head; 3 instr. Estab. 1852; den; D; co-ed;
ent. req; 4 yr; degrees, B.S, B.A.(Fine Arts, Educ); enrl. maj. 50,
total 1500. Tui. incl. campus res. $3374.

NEWTOWN

BUCKS COUNTY COMMUNITY COLLEGE, Department of Applied
Fine Arts, Swamp Rd, 18940. Tel: (215) 968-5861 Exten. 236
Bruce Katsiff, Chmn; 15 FT, 17 PT instr. Estab. 1964; pub; D & E;
ent. req. HS dipl; 2 yr; degree, A.A; 39 SC, 4 LC; enrl. D 175, E 57,
maj. 232. Tui. $400 per yr.

Advertising Design
Ceramics
Commercial Art
Drawing
Glassblowing
Graphic Arts
Graphic Design
History of Art & Archaeology

Illustration
Jewelry
Painting
Photography
Sculpture
Stained Glass Windows
Woodworking

PHILADELPHIA

ANTONELLI SCHOOL OF PHOTOGRAPHY, INC, 1210 Race St,
19107. Tel: (215) 563-8558
Robert M. Opfer, Dir; 8 FT, 3 PT instr. Estab. 1938; pvt; D & E;
ent. req. HS dipl; 2-3 yr; degree, dipl. in commercial and portrait
photography; 8 SC. Tui. FT $2175 per yr, PT $1250, lab and chemical fee $150 per yr; no campus res.
Offers Photography Courses.

ART INSTITUTE OF PHILADELPHIA, 1818 Cherry St, 19103.
Tel: (215) 567-7080
Philip Trachtman, Dir; 2 FT, 24 PT instr. Estab. 1966; pvt; D; ent.
req. HS dipl, portfolio; 3 yr; degree, dipl; 15 SC, 3 LC; enrl. 170.
Tui. $1600 per yr. Summer School.

Advertising Design
Commercial Art
Drafting
Drawing
Fashion Arts

Graphic Design
History of Art & Archaeology
Illustration
Lettering
Painting

DREXEL UNIVERSITY, Nesbitt College, Department of Design,
Nesbitt Hall, 33rd & Market Sts, 19104. Tel: 895-2390
Marjorie E. Rankin, Dean; Mary Epstein, Head Design Dept; 10 FT,
10 PT instr. Estab. 1891; pvt; ent. req. coll. board exam; 4 yr;
degrees, B.S, M.S, and cooperative plan; schol; 39 SC, 9 LC; enrl.
maj. 300, others 414. Tui. $3071 plus $217 univ. fee; campus res.
for M and W.
Design and Merchandising
Fashion Design
Interior Design
Summer School: Marjorie E. Rankin, Dean; tui. undergrad. $72
per cr. hr, grad. $86 per cr. hr. for 6 or 12 wk; enrl. 159.

HUSSIAN SCHOOL OF ART, INC, 1300 Arch St, 19107.
Tel: (215) 563-5726
Ronald Dove, Pres; 3 FT, 15 PT instr. Estab. 1946; pvt; D; ent. req.
HS dipl, portfolio interview; 4 yr; no degree; enrl. 148. Tui. $1350
per yr; no campus res.

Advertising Design
Commercial Art
Drawing
Graphic Arts
Graphic Design

History of Art & Archaeology
Illustration
Lettering
Painting
Photography

LA SALLE COLLEGE, Department of Fine Arts, 20th St. and Olney
Ave, 19141. Tel: (215) 848-8300 Exten. 397
George Diehl, Chmn; 4 FT, 4 PT instr. Dept. estab. 1970; den;
D & E; co-ed; ent. req. ent. exam; 4 yr; degrees, B.A.(Art History);
2 SC, 4 LC; enrl. D 330, E 3200. Tui. $2270, PT $70 per cr.

History of Art
History of Graphic Art

Painting & Graphic Art
Photography (Chestnut Hill College)

Summer School: Dr. Thomas Coffee, Dir; our basic general art
course is offered; tui. $47 per cr. for term of 6 wk; enrl. approx. 15.

MOORE COLLEGE OF ART,* 20th & Race Sts, 19103.
Tel: (215) 568-4515
Dr. Mayro Bryce, Pres; 50 FT, 30 PT instr. Estab. 1844; pvt; W;
ent. req. SAT score, art portfolio, HS grad; 4 yr; degrees, B.F.A
in 12 fields, B.A. in Art History, B.S in Art Educ; schol. and fel;
enrl. D 600, Sat. 207. Tui. $2500, $50 and $5 general fee for Sat.
classes.

Advertising Art
Art Education
Art History
Ceramics
Fashion Design
Fashion Illustration
Illustration

Interior Design
Jewelry & Metalsmithing
Painting
Photography
Printmaking
Sculpture
Textile Design

Summer Session: 4-6 wk. for HS and coll. level.

✠PENNSYLVANIA ACADEMY OF THE FINE ARTS, Broad & Cherry
  Sts, 19102. Tel: (215) 299-5086
Henry Hotz, Dean; 24 FT, 7 PT instr. Estab. 1806; pvt; 4 yr; cert,
B.F.A. degree opportunity in cooperation with the Philadelphia Coll.
of Art; enrl. D 385, E 175. Tui. D $1100, E $240.
Graphics
Painting
Sculpture
    Summer School: 4 wk. $117, 6 wk. $175, June and July; European
travel schol. and awards.

✠PHILADELPHIA COLLEGE OF ART, Broad and Pine Sts, 19102.
  Tel: (215) 546-0545
Thomas F. Schutte, Pres; Richard H. Reinhardt, Dean of Faculty;
86 FT, 79 PT instr. Pvt; 4 yr; degrees, A.A, B.S, B.F.A, M.A.(Art
Educ, Community Design); schol; enrl. D 1100, E 800, Sat. 287.
Tui. $92 per cr. for 9 mo, Sat. $150; campus res. available, fee
varies.

Advertising	Graphic Design
Art Education	Illustration
Art Therapy	Industrial
Community Design Program	Painting
Crafts	Photography & Filmmaking
Environmental Design	Printmaking
Fibres	Sculpture
Foundation Program	

PHILADELPHIA COLLEGE OF TEXTILES & SCIENCE, School of
    Textiles, School House Lane & Henry Ave, 19144.
    Tel: (215) 843-9700
Lawson A. Pendleton, Pres; Fred Fortess, Dir. Sch; Peter Mills,
Dir. Evening and Summer School. Estab. 1884; pvt; no ent. req;
4 yr; degree, B.S; schol; enrl. D 1065, E 784. Tui. $1400.

Apparel Design	Fashion Textile Retailing
Apparel Management	Knitted Design
Basic Design	Life Science
Business Administration	Management & Marketing
Chemistry	Print Design
Chemistry & Dyeing	Textile Engineering
Drawing	Textile Quality Control & Testing
Fabric Design	Weaving Design

SAMUEL S. FLEISHER ART MEMORIAL, 715-721 Catharine St,
    19147. Tel: (215) 922-3452
Louis P. Hirshman, Dir. Instruction: 41 PT instr. Estab. 1898;
pvt; E; no ent. req; no degree; 14 SC, 1 LC.
Ceramics
History of Art & Archaeology
Children's classes, graphics, painting, sculpture; enrl. 200 wk.
    Summer School: Louis P. Hirshman, Dir.

Ceramics	Photography
Drawing	Printmaking
Painting	Sculpture

TYLER SCHOOL OF ART OF TEMPLE UNIVERSITY, Beech and
    Penrose Aves, 19126. Tel: (215) 224-7575
Dr. Jack Wasserman, Dean; 58 FT, 6 PT instr. Estab. 1935; pub;
ent. req. HS grad, SAT, portfolio; 4 yr.(2 yr. work in all arts
required before specializing); degrees, B.F.A, M.F.A, M.Ed; grad.
asst. and schol; enrl. D 650, E 250. Tui. $1200, non-res. $2400.
Rome Branch, Jr. yr. or grad. study. Summer and Evening School.

Animated Film	Painting
Art Education	Photography
Art History	Printmaking
Ceramics	Sculpture
Drawing	Silkscreen Printing
Graphic Design	Typography
Metalsmithing	Weaving

    Summer School: Don Lantzy, Associate Dean.

Ceramics	Printmaking
Drawing	Sculpture
Metalsmithing	Watercolor
Painting	Weaving
Photography	

UNIVERSITY OF PENNSYLVANIA, Graduate School of Fine Arts,
    19174. Tel: (215) 243-8321
Peter Shepheard, Dean. Estab. 1874; pvt; ent. req. ent. exam;
degrees; schol. and fel; GC. Tui. grad. $3940; campus res.

    Department of Architecture
Peter McCleary, Chmn; 7 FT, 25 PT instr. Degrees, M.Arch, Ph.D;
10 LC, 9 GC in Design; normal enrl. 160.
Courses in Architectural Design & Construction.

    Department of City and Regional Planning
William Grigsby, Chmn; 11 FT, 8 PT instr. Degrees, M.C.P, Ph.D;
21 LC, 4 GC in Design; normal enrl. 100.

    Department of Landscape Architecture and Regional Planning
Ian L. McHarg, Chmn; 8 FT, 5 PT instr. Degrees, M.L.A, M.R.P;
7 LC, 4 Design Courses; grad; normal enrl. 60.

    Department of Fine Arts
Robert Engman, Neil G. Welliver, Co-Chmn; 7 FT, 4 PT instr. De-
grees, B.F.A, M.F.A; 21 SC, 5 LC; GC; normal enrl. 60.
Graphics
Painting
Sculpture

PITTSBURGH

ART INSTITUTE OF PITTSBURGH, 526 Penn Ave, 15222.
    Tel: (412) 471-5651
John A. Johns, Pres; D 53 FT, 16 PT, E 6 FT, 3 PT instr. Estab.
1921; pvt; ent. req. HS grad; 2 yr; D-A.A, E-dipl; enrl. D 1500,
E 150. Tui. D $510 per quarter (Photography $625), E $60 per
mo.(Photography $72).

Airbrush Technique (E)	Photography—Audio Visual—
Fashion Illustration	Multi-Media
Interior Design	Visual Communications
Photography (E)	

    Commercial Art Prep School; 6 wk. summer FT; tui. $150.
Teenage summer classes, 6 wk. ½ day; tui. $90; Sat. teenage
classes, $12 per mo. Free 2 wk. art instructors workshop.

CARLOW COLLEGE, Art Department, 3333 Fifth Ave,
    15213.
Richard Devlin, Chmn; 2 FT, 3 PT instr. Estab. 1945; den; D & E;
ent. req. HS dipl, coll. boards, HS record; 4 yr; degrees in Art,
Art Educ, Art Therapy Preparation; schol; 17 SC, 6 LC; enrl. 200,
maj. 42. Tui. $2200 per yr, $75 per cr; campus res. $1200.

Aesthetics	Jewelry
Art & Psychology	Lettering
Art Education	Metalcraft
Art Therapy	Painting
Batik	Photography
Ceramics	Sculpture
Drawing	Teacher Training
Graphic Arts	Theatre Arts
History of Art & Archaeology	Weaving

    Summer School: Sister Elizabeth McMillan, Academic Dean;
courses offered, Art Fundamentals, Ceramics; tui. $250 for term
of 6 wk. beginning June 20; enrl. approx. 40.

✠CARNEGIE-MELLON UNIVERSITY,✲ College of Fine Arts,
    Schenley Park, 15213. Tel: (412) 621-2600.
Akram Midani, Dean. Estab. 1905; pvt; ent. req. coll. board ent.
exam plus auditions or portfolio; 4-5 yr; degrees; schol. and fel.
Tui. $2900; campus res. Summer School incl. some pre-coll.
courses, 6 wks.

    Department of Architecture
Delbert Highlands, Head; 23 FT, 5 PT instr. GC, M.Arch, 1st and
2nd degree, Ph.D. in conjunction with School of Urban and Public
Affairs; enrl. 206. Courses in Architecture.

    Department of Design
Joseph Ballay, Head; 11 FT, 6 PT instr. GC, M.F.A. Design, enrl.
162.

Design Theory	Industrial Design
Graphic Design	Interior Environments
Illustration	

    Department of Painting and Sculpture
Orville Winsand, Head; 22 FT, 3 PT instr. GC, M.F.A, D.A; enrl.
235.

Art Education	Printmaking
Crafts	Sculpture
Painting	

    Department of Drama
Earle R. Gister, Head; 24 FT, 1 PT instr. GC, M.F.A, Ph.D;
enrl. 223.

Acting	Stage Design
Directing	Technical Practice
Lighting	Theatre Dance
Production	Theatrical Costume Design
Stagecraft	

CHATHAM COLLEGE, Department of Art, Woodland Rd, 15232.
    Tel: (412) 441-8200
William Sterling, Chmn; 3 FT, 2 PT instr. Estab. 1869; pvt; W; ent.
req. HS grad; 4 yr; degree, B.A; 17 SC, 7 LC. Tui. and res. fees
$4550.

Basic Photography	History of Art
Ceramics	Painting
Drawing	Sculpture
Graphic Arts	

IVY SCHOOL OF PROFESSIONAL ART, University Ave, 15214.
Tel· (412) 323-8800
Morris B. Kirshenbaum, Dir. and Pres; 6 FT, over 100 PT instr.
Estab. 1960; pvt; D; ent. req. HS dipl, portfolio, test score mini-
mums, letters of reference and recommendations; 2 yr.(incl. summers); dipl; schol; all SC; enrl. 300. Tui. $500 per quarter; campus
res. $185 per mo.(at Duquesne Univ. dorms).

Advertising Design	History of Art
Animation	Illustration
Art in Therapy	Interior Design
Commercial Art	Lettering & Typography
Drawing	Painting
Exposition & Trade Show Design	Photography
Fashion Arts	Printmaking
Filmmaking	Sculpture
Fine Arts	Weaving
Graphic Design	

Saturday teen classes, drawing, design, photography, graphics,
prints; tui. $50 per sem; enrl. 25.
Ivy Art Workshop for Adults, no credit, PT, no professional classes;
tui. $100 for 1 session a wk. for 12 wk, $500 for 5 sessions a wk.

UNIVERSITY OF PITTSBURGH, Henry Clay Frick Fine Arts
Building, 15260.

Department of Fine Arts. Tel: (412) 624-4121
Millard F. Hearn, Chmn; 12 FT instr. Estab. 1927; pvt; D; degrees,
undergrad maj. in Art History, grad. prog. M.A. and Ph.D. in
Western and Oriental Art History; schol. and fel; 34 LC, 5 GC; enrl.
1200. Tui. $40 per cr. hr, grad. $51 per cr. hr, non-res. undergrad.
$80 per cr. hr, grad. $105 per cr. hr.

Department of Studio Arts. Tel: (412) 624-4118
Virgil D. Cantini, Chmn; 8 FT instr. Estab. 1968; pvt; D; undergrad.
maj. in Studio Arts; 34 LC; enrl. 1500. Tui. $40 per cr. hr, non-res.
$80.
Painting
Graphics
Sculpture

See Museum Section for Henry Clay Frick Fine Arts Library and
University Art Gallery.

RADNOR

CABRINI COLLEGE, Department of Fine Arts, Eagle and King of
Prussia Rds, 19087. Tel: (215) 687-2100 Exten. 53
Sister Salesia LeDieu, Chmn; 1 FT, 1 PT instr. Estab. 1957; den;
D & E; ent. req. HS dipl, satisfactory average and rank in secondary
school class, SAT, recommendations; 4 yr; degrees, B.A, B.S,
B.S.Ed, no art major; schol; 11 SC, 4 LC, 4 courses available through
Eastern College; enrl. D 74, E 20. Tui. $2000 per yr, PT D $65 per
cr, E $45 per cr; campus res. $1500 per yr.

Art Education	History of Art & Archaeology
Ceramics	Painting
Design & Composition	Teacher Training
Drawing	

Summer School: Sister Julia Toto, Dir; courses offered vary
according to demand; tui. $45 per cr. for term of 6 wk. beginning
May 20 and July 1; enrl. 350.

ROSEMONT

ROSEMONT COLLEGE, Division of the Arts, 19010.
Tel: (215) 527-0200
Patricia M. Nugent, Chmn; 4 FT, 10 PT instr. Estab. 1925; pvt; D;
W (exchange with Villanova Univ); ent. req. HS dipl, ent. exam; 4 yr;
degrees, B.A.(Studio Art, Art History), B.F.A.(Studio Art); schol;
6 hr. Studio Art, 3 hr. Art History; enrl. total coll. 705, art 300,
grad. approx. 15. Tui. $1600; campus res. $1600.

Aesthetics	Lettering
Art Education	Music
Ceramics	Painting
Dance	Photography
Design	Sculpture
Drawing	Teacher Training
Graphic Arts	Theatre
History of Art & Architecture	

SCRANTON

MARYWOOD COLLEGE,* Art Department, 2300 Adams Ave, 18509.
Tel: (717) 343-6521 Exten. 252
Sister Ave Maria Foley, I.H.M, Acting Chmn; 5 FT, 4 PT instr.
Estab. 1926; pvt; D & E; co-ed; ent. req. HS dipl, portfolio and
interview; 4 yr; degrees, A.B, B.S.Art Educ; schol; 28 SC, 7 LC,

12 GC; enrl. maj. 98, grad. 17. Tui. $46 per cr. plus fees, grad.
$53 per cr. plus fees; campus res. $1300.

Advertising Design	Illustration & Fashion
Aesthetics	Jewelry
Art Education	Lettering
Art Seminar	Metalcraft
Ceramics	Painting
Design I & II	Philosophy of Art
Drawing I & II	Photography
Enameling	Sculpture I & II
Graphic Arts	Teacher Training
Handicrafts	Theatre Arts
History of Art (I, II,	Weaving & Textile Designs
Contemporary)	

Summer School: Sister Ave Maria Foley, I.H.M, Acting Chmn;
tui. undergrad. $46 per cr. plus fees, grad. $53 per cr. plus fees;
6 wk. term beginning June 25; 1973 enrl. 59.

Art for the Elementary	Graduate Figure Drawing
Teacher	History of Art
Ceramics	Painting
Chinese Brush Painting	Printmaking
Design Research	Sculpture
Directed Readings	Special Class Arts & Crafts

SCHOOL OF INTERIOR DESIGN AND ART, International Correspon-
dence Schools, 18515. Tel: (717) 342-7701 Exten. 260
Robert G. Donovan, V.Pres. of Educ; Elaine G. Thomas, Dir. Estab.
1900; pvt; no ent. req; enrl. 3000.
Commercial Art
Interior Decoration & Design

SELINSGROVE

SUSQUEHANNA UNIVERSITY,* Department of Art, 17870.
Tel: (717) 374-2345
George R. Bucher, Assoc. Prof. Art; 1 FT, 1 PT instr. Estab.
1858; den; D & E; ent. req. Coll. Ent. Exam. Board tests, HS
class standing, personal interview; 4 yr; degrees, B.A, B.S,
B.Mus; enrl. 1400. Tui. and fees $2240; campus res. $1050.

Art History & Appreciation	Painting
Graphic Design	Theatre Arts

SHIPPENSBURG

SHIPPENSBURG STATE COLLEGE, Art Department, 17257.
Tel: (717) 532-9121 Exten. 533
Dr. Harry D. Bentz, Chmn. Dept; 5 FT instr. Estab. 1871; pub; D;
ent. req. HS dipl, ent. exam; 4 yrs; degrees, B.A, B.S; 10 SC, 4 LC,
3 GC; enrl. D 3937, grad. 1324, continuing educ. 46. Tui. $700,
$26 per cr. hr; campus res. $720.

Art Education	Graphic Arts
Ceramics	History of Art
Drawing	Painting
Elementary Education Arts	Sculpture
& Crafts	Teacher Training

Summer School: Dr. Harry Bentz, Dir; courses offered are
same as regular yr; tui. $26 per cr. hr. for term of 12 wk. beginning
in June.

SLIPPERY ROCK

SLIPPERY ROCK STATE COLLEGE, Department of Art, 16057.
Tel: (412) 794-7271
Jon D. Wink, Chmn; 9 FT instr. Pub; D & E; ent. req. HS dipl; 4 yr;
degree, B.A.(Art); 27 SC, 3 LC; enrl. maj. 55. Tui. $750 per yr;
campus res. $826. Summer School.

Art Education	Jewelry
Ceramics	Painting
Drawing	Photography
Graphic Arts	Sculpture
History of Art & Archaeology	Textile Design

SWARTHMORE

SWARTHMORE COLLEGE, Art Department, 19081.
Tel: (215) 544-7900 Exten. 315
T. Kaori Kitao, Chmn; 6 FT, 1 PT instr. Estab. 1925; pvt; D; ent.
req. HS grad; 4 yr; degree, B.A; schol; 8 SC, 27 LC, 9 seminars in
Art History; enrl. maj. 25, others 300. Tui. $3170, total charges
$5020.

Ceramics	Painting
Graphics	Sculpture

UNIONTOWN

PENNSYLVANIA STATE UNIVERSITY, FAYETTE CAMPUS, College of Arts and Architecture, Department of Art, Hwy. 119 S, 15401. Tel: (412) 437-2801 Exten. 29.
Zeljko Kujundzic, Assoc. Prof; 3 FT, 1-2 PT instr. Estab. 1968; pub; D & E; ent. req. HS dipl; 2-4 yr; degrees, B.F.A.(Art Educ, Architecture); schol; 8 SC, 3 LC; enrl. D 85, E 25. Tui. $1005 per yr, PT $35 per cr; no campus res.

Aesthetics	Drawing
Architecture (2 yr. only)	History of Art
Art Education	Landscape Architecture (2 yr. only)
Ceramics	Teacher Training
Drafting	Three-Dimensional Design

UNIVERSITY PARK

PENNSYLVANIA STATE UNIVERSITY, College of Arts and Architecture, 16802.
Walter H. Walters, Dean. Pub; 4-5 yr; degrees; schol. and fel; extension courses. Tui. $365 per term, non-res. $765.

Department of Architecture
Raniero Corbelletti, Head; 17 FT instr. Estab. 1912; 27 SC, 5 LC, 7 GC; enrl. maj. 278, others 150.
Courses in Architecture.

Department of Art
Robert H. Gray, Head; 26 FT, 2 PT instr. Estab. 1910; 37 SC, 1 LC, 6 GC; enrl. maj. 390, others 1000.

Ceramics	Painting
Design	Photography
Drawing	Sculpture
Graphics	

Department of Art History
Helmut Hager, Head; 10 FT, 1 PT instr. 45 LC, 11 GC; enrl. maj. 75, others 650.
Courses in Art History.

WASHINGTON

WASHINGTON AND JEFFERSON COLLEGE, Art Department, Lincoln St, 15301. Tel: (412) 222-4400 Exten. 309
Paul B. Edwards, Chmn; 3 FT instr. Coll. estab. 1787, dept. 1959, art maj. 1973; pvt; co-ed; ent. req. HS grad. ent. exam; 4 yr; degrees, B.A, B.S; schol. and fel; 10 SC, 8 LC; enrl. 160. Tui. $2950 per yr; campus res. $1300

Art of the Americas	Sculpture Studio
Ceramics	Watercolor
The Renaissance, Technique & Media	

Summer School: Dr. W. Leake, Dir; $55 per cr. hr. from June 12 for 4 wk, 6 wk. or 8 wk; enrl. 150.

WAYNE

WAYNE ART CENTER, 413 Maplewood Ave, 19087. Tel: (215) 688-3553
Virginia B. Clark, Pres; 8 PT instr. Estab. 1930; pvt; D & E; no ent. req; 12 SC. Tui. $60 per painting class per sem, $85 per sculpture class per sem.

Drawing	Painting
Graphic Arts	Sculpture

Children's art classes.
Summer School: Virginia Clark, Dir; courses offered, Drawing, Painting; term of 6 wk.

WILKES BARRE

WILKES COLLEGE, Department of Fine Arts, S. Franklin St, 18702. Tel: (717) 824-4651 Exten. 480, 486, 368
H. R. Caselli, Chmn; 6 FT, 2 PT instr. Estab. 1947; pvt; D & E; ent. req. HS dipl, SAT; 4 yr; degree, B.A; schol; 15 SC, 4 LC; enrl. D 100, E 75, maj. 100, special 20. Tui. $2300 per yr; campus res. $1300.

Aesthetics	History of Art
Art Education	Industrial Design
Batik & Fabric Design	Jewelry
Ceramics	Life Drawing & Painting
Drawing	Photography
Exhibition Techniques	Sculpture
Graphic Arts	Teacher Training
Graphic Design	Theatre Arts
Handicrafts	Weaving

HS Student Enrichment Program, ceramic sculpture, drawing, painting, printmaking; on Sat, regular session and during intersession (January).

Evening and Summer School: H. R. Caselli, Dir; write to Directory of Evening and Summer School for course offerings and dates; tui. $65 per cr. hr. for term of 5 wk.

WILLIAMSPORT

LYCOMING COLLEGE, Art Department, 17701. Tel: (717) 326-1951 Exten. 260
Roger D. Shipley, Chmn; 3 FT, 3 PT instr. Estab. 1812; D & E; ent. req. HS dipl, ent. exam, early admis. for accelerated students; 4 yr; degree, B.A; schol; 20 SC, 8 LC; enrl. D 365, maj. 45. Tui. $3800 per yr; campus res. $1275.

Drawing	Painting
Fabric Design & Weaving	Photography
Graphic Arts	Pottery
Jewelry	Sculpture

Adult hobby classes, drawing; tui. $10-$15; enrl. 15-20.
Summer School: Robert Glunk, Registrar; tui. $150 for term beginning June 1.

Color Theory	Photography
Crafts	Stained Glass

YORK

YORK ACADEMY OF ARTS, 625 E. Philadelphia St, 17403. Tel: (717) 848-1447
William A. Falkler, Dir; 6 FT, 11 PT instr. Estab. 1952; pvt; D & E; ent. req. HS dipl, presentation of portfolio of art work; 3 yr; no degree; schol; 34 SC, 4 LC; enrl. D 223. Tui. $1188 per yr; no campus res.

Advertising Design	Jewelry
Commercial Art	Lettering
Display	Painting
Graphic Arts	Photography
Graphic Design	Silk Screening
Illustration	

Adult hobby classes, painting, figure drawing, photography, art for beginners; tui. $28. Children's classes, beginners, intermediate, advanced; tui. $22.
Summer School: William A. Falkler, Dir; courses offered, Art for Beginners, Painting; tui. $100 for term of 4 wk. beginning in June; 1975 enrl. 50.

RHODE ISLAND

BRISTOL

ROGER WILLIAMS COLLEGE, Department of Art, 02809. Tel: (401) 255-1000
James Cathers, Coordinator of Art; 3 FT instr. Estab. 1969; pvt; D & E; ent. req. HS dipl. or HS equivalency exam; 4 yr; degrees A.A, B.A; schol; 15 SC, 7 LC; enrl. D 200, E 30, maj. 50. Tui. $2096; campus res. $1500.

Aesthetics	Industrial Design
Architecture	Macrame
Ceramics	Painting
Costume Design & Construction	Photography
Design	Sculpture
Drafting	Stage Design
Drawing	Teacher Training
Handicrafts	Theatre Arts
History of Art & Archaeology	Weaving

Summer School: Harold Payson, Dir; tui. $30 per cr.

Art History	Painting
Ceramics	Sculpture
Design	Weaving
Drawing	

KINGSTON

UNIVERSITY OF RHODE ISLAND, Department of Art, Fine Arts Center, 02881. Tel: (401) 792-2131/5821
Prof. Richard Fraenkel, Chmn; 14 FT, 3 PT instr. Estab. 1892; pub; D (exten. E & D); co-ed; ent. req. same as required for College of Arts & Sciences; 4 yr; degrees, B.A, B.F.A; schol; 21 undergrad. SC (3 cr. each), 24 grad. studio seminars (no grad. prog. offered), 23 LC; enrl. maj. 165, others approx. 900. Tui. free to res, non-res. $800, general and other fees $436.

Art History	Painting
Drawing	Photography
Filmmaking	Printmaking
Graphic Design	Sculpture

Summer School: Dr. Frank Woods, Dean; two terms; tui. $25 per cr. hr; enrl. approx. 200.

Art History
Design
Painting

Photography
Printmaking
Sculpture

NEWPORT

SCHOOL OF THE ART ASSOCIATION OF NEWPORT, 76 Bellevue Ave, 02840. Tel: (401) 847-0179
James Cathers, Dir. Art Educ; Mrs. Caroline Cathers, Exec. Dir; 7 faculty instr. Estab. 1913; pvt; D & E; ent. req. mem. of Art Asn. of Newport; enrl. 180. Tui. $32 per course per term (3 terms and summer), plus studio fee.

Art History
Classical Ballet
Creative Writing

Gallery Management
Printmaking
Sculpture

Children's classes, ceramics, collage, drawing, painting, sculpture and weaving; tui. $20 per term (3 terms and summer), classes limited to 15 students each of two classes ages 7 through 12; tui. includes all materials and mem. in Art Asn. of Newport; enrl. 30.
Summer School: July and Aug, same as above.

PROVIDENCE

BROWN UNIVERSITY, Art Department, 02912.
Tel: (401) 863-2421
Kermit S. Champa, Chmn; 18 FT instr. Estab. 1925; pvt; D; co-ed; 4 yr; degrees, B.A, M.A, Ph.D; academic courses at Univ, technical courses at Univ. and at Rhode Island School of Design; normal enrl. 5000. Tui. $3250; campus res.

PROVIDENCE COLLEGE, Department of Fine Arts, River Ave. and Eaton St, 02918. Tel: (401) 865-1000
Prof. Lawrence M. Hunt, Chmn; 8 FT, 4 PT instr. Estab. 1969; den; D & E; ent. req. HS dipl, interview and portfolio required of transfer students; 4 yr; degree A.B.(Fine Arts); 7 SC, 11 LC; enrl. D 200, E 90, maj. 47. Tui. $2366; campus res. $1450.

Art Education
Ceramics
Drawing
Graphic Arts
Handicrafts

History of Art & Archaeology
Painting
Photography
Sculpture
Weaving

Adult hobby classes same as above; tui. $23 per cr. hr; enrl. 175.
Summer School: Michael Murphy, Dir; tui. $33 per cr. hr. for term of 6 wks, beginning June 21; enrl. 75. Summer Session held in Pietrasanta, Italy; Art History, Drawing, History, Italian Language, Literature, Painting and Sculpture.

Art History & Analysis
Ceramics
Drawing

Painting
Photography

RHODE ISLAND COLLEGE, Department of Art, 600 Mt. Pleasant Ave, 02908. Tel: (401) 831-6600
Angelo V. Rosati, Chmn; 15 FT, 1 PT instr. Estab. 1854; pub; D & E; ent. req. HS dipl, score of 500 on SAT; 4 yr; degrees, B.A.(Art History), B.A.(Medical Illustration), B.S.(Art Educ), B.A.(Art Studio), M.A.T.(Art Educ); schol; 27 SC, 15 LC, 36 GC; enrl. D 350, E 50, maj. 350. Tui. $504 in-state per yr, $28 per cr. hr; campus res. $1500.

Aesthetics
Art Education
Ceramics
Drawing
Fiber
Filmmaking
Graphic Arts
Graphic Design

Handicrafts
History of Art & Archaeology
Jewelry
Metal
Painting
Photography
Sculpture
Teacher Training

Children's Sat. morning prog, Donald Gray, Dir.
Summer School: Dr. William Small, Dir; tui. $23 per cr. hr. for term of 6-8 wks, beginning June 20; 1973 enrl. approx. 200.

Art History
Ceramics
Drawing
Fiber

Filmmaking
Painting
Photography
Printmaking

✦RHODE ISLAND SCHOOL OF DESIGN, 2 College St, 02903.
Tel: (401) 331-3507
Lee Hall, Pres; 97 FT, 55 PT instr. Estab. 1877; pvt; endowed; ent. req. HS grad; 4-5 yr; degrees, B.Arch, B.Landscape Arch, B.I.D, M.I.D, M.A.T, M.A.(Art Educ), B.F.A, M.F.A; schol; grants-in-aid to res, student loans, fel; enrl. D 1353, E 650. Tui. D $3300, room $750, board $750; E $65 per course, children 20 wk. of Sat. classes $110; campus res. and approved housing. Museum of Art is an integral part of the corporation; Library of 52,229 vols, 75,098 slides,

29,631 mounted photographs, 843 color reproductions, 149,563 clippings and 828 records.

Apparel Design
‡Architecture
Ceramics
Film Studies
Graphic Design
Illustration
Industrial Design
Interior Architecture
Jewelry & Metalsmithing

‡Landscape Architecture
Painting & Printmaking
Photography
Sculpture (Glass)
Teacher Education (graduate level only)
Television Studies
Textile Design
Wood & Furniture Design

Summer School: Bruce Helander, Dir; Pre-Coll. Foundation Program; Summer Program in Provincetown, Massachusetts; Transfer Session; Workshops in several fine arts and design area; tui. $400 average; enrl. 800.

WARWICK

RHODE ISLAND JUNIOR COLLEGE, Department of Art, 400 East Ave, 02886. Tel: (401) 825-2267; Providence Campus, 235 Promenade St. Tel (401) 331-5500 will transfer to new Blackstone Valley Campus, Route 146, Lincoln, fall 1976. Art courses will be taught at both campuses.
Rita C. Lepper, Chmn; 10 FT, 2 PT instr. Estab. 1964; pub; D & E; ent. req. HS dipl, ent. exam, equivalency exam; 2 yr; degrees A.A, A.S, A.A.S; schol; 16 SC, 3 LC, 1 seminar; enrl. D 4600. Tui. $420 per yr; no campus res.

Ceramics
Commercial Art
Crafts
Drafting (Vocational-Technical Div)
Drawing

Graphic Arts
Graphic Design
History of Art & Archaeology
Painting
Photography
Sculpture

Continuing Education School: Dean John G. Marmaras, Beginning and Advanced Studio, Ceramics, Life Drawing, Commercial Art and Photography; tui. $15 per cr. for 6 wks, $10 registration fee; 1975 enrl. 2800.

SOUTH CAROLINA

CHARLESTON

BAPTIST COLLEGE AT CHARLESTON, Department of Art, Hwy. 78 at I-26, 29411. Tel: (803) 997-4177
Joseph Ward, Chmn; 2 FT instr. Estab. 1960; den; D & E; ent. req. GED or HS dipl; 4 yr; degrees, B.A, B.S; schol; 14 SC, 2 LC; enrl. D 80, E 71, maj. 15. Tui. $1750 per yr, PT (9 hr) $225 per sem; campus res. $3300 per yr.

Art Education
Batik
Ceramics
Drawing
Graphic Arts
History of Art & Archaeology

Painting
Paper Mache
Sculpture
Teacher Training
Theatre Arts (Drama Dept)
Weaving

Summer School: Courses offered same as above; tui. $150 for two 5 wk. sessions beginning June 1; enrl. 1500.

COLLEGE OF CHARLESTON, Department of Fine Arts, 66 George St, 29401. Tel: (803) 722-0181
Dr. Diane Chalmers Johnson, Chmn; 14 FT, 5 PT instr. Estab. 1966; pub; D & E; ent. req. HS dipl; 4 yr; degree, B.A.(Fine Arts); 36 SC, 24 LC. Tui. $500 per yr.

Aesthetics
Architecture
Costume Design & Construction
Drawing
Graphic Arts

History of Art & Archaeology
Painting
Sculpture
Stage Design
Theatre Arts

CLEMSON

✠CLEMSON UNIVERSITY, College of Architecture, Department of History and Visual Studies, Lee Hall, 29631. Tel: (803) 656-3081
Thomas E. McPeak, Head; 10 FT, 2 PT instr. Estab. 1967; pub; D; ent. req. available on request; degree, M.F.A.(60 hr); 24 grad. courses, 40 undergrad SC, 29 LC (undergrad. courses for service to pre-architecture and other Univ. requirements); enrl. approx. 1500 annually, grad. maj. 10. Tui. res. and non-res. $320 per sem.
Service courses in Art and Architectural History.

Ceramics
Drawing
Graphic Design
Painting

Photography
Printmaking
Sculpture

COLUMBIA

BENEDICT COLLEGE,* Visual Art Studies, Taylor and Harden Sts,
29204. Tel: (803) 779-4930 Exten. 354
David I. Johnson Sr, Visual Art Studies Dir; 2 FT instr. Estab.
1870; pvt; D; ent. req. HS dipl; 4 yrs; degree, B.A. in Teaching of
Art and general art major; schol; 11 SC, 6 LC. Tui. $1400 per yr,
FT $117, PT $50 per sem hr, art supplies approx. $250 per yr,
insurance $16.50 per yr; campus res. $800.

Art Education	History of Art & Archaeology
Arts & Crafts	Lettering
Ceramics	Painting
Drawing	Photography
Graphic Arts	Sculpture
Graphic Design	Teacher Training

Summer School: Bobby L. Brisbon, Dir; courses offered, art
appreciation plus selected four others; tui. $225 for term of 5 wk.
beginning June 5; 1973 enrl. 57.

✣RICHLAND ART SCHOOL, 1112 Bull St, 29201.
Tel: (803) 799-2810
Dr. J. R. Craft, Dir; 3 FT, 5 PT instr. Estab. 1950; operates as
service of the Columbia Museum of Art; D & E; no ent. req. Tui.
$60 plus materials fees per sem. of 4 mo. Studio courses for youths
and adults in all branches of:

Ceramics	Jewelry
Crafts	Painting
Figure Drawing	Photography
Graphics	Sculpture

UNIVERSITY OF SOUTH CAROLINA, Department of Art, 29208.
Tel: (803) 777-4236
John O'Neil, Head; 24 FT, 15 PT instr. Estab. 1925; pub; D & E;
ent. req. CEEB; 4 yr; degrees, B.A, B.S, B.F.A, M.A, M.A.T, M.F.A;
assistantships available; 72 SC, 44 LC, 58 GC; enrl. maj. 650, others
2000. Tui. $327 per sem, non-res. $707 per sem; campus res. $450.

Advertising Design	Metalsmithing
Art Education	Museology
Art History	Painting
Ceramics	Photography
Crafts	Printmaking
Drawing	Sculpture
Filmmaking	Video as Art
Interior Design	

Children's classes; Sat. AM; tui. $15; enrl. 40 per sem.
Summer School: On campus classes in Art Education, Art
History, and Art Studio; 2 sessions.

DUE WEST

ERSKINE COLLEGE, Department of Art, 29639.
Tel: (803) 379-2131
Felix Bauer, Head. Estab. 1839; den; D; co-ed; ent. req; 4 yr; de-
gree; 3 SC, 1 LC; enrl. approx. 80 per sem.
Summer School: F. Bauer, Head; courses offered, Art Apprecia-
tion, Art for Teachers, K-6.

GAFFNEY

LIMESTONE COLLEGE, Art Department, 29340.
Tel: (803) 489-7698 Exten. 164
James A. Cox, Head; 2 FT instr. Estab. 1845; pvt; D & E; ent. req.
HS dipl, ent. exam; 4 yr; degrees, B.S.(Educ, Studio); schol; 19 SC,
9 LC; enrl. D 112, maj. 42, others 3. Tui. $1825 per yr; campus res.
$1175.

Aesthetics	Painting
Art Education	Printmaking (Wood-Block &
Ceramics	Silk-Screen)
Drawing	Sculpture
History of Art & Archaeology	Teacher Training
Jewelry	Theatre Arts

Summer School: Dr. Nelson, Dir; courses offered, Art Appreciation, Ceramics, Drawing & Painting; tui. $45 per hr. for term of 6 wk.
beginning June.

GREENVILLE

BOB JONES UNIVERSITY, School of Fine Arts, 29614.
Tel: (803) 242-5100
Dwight Gustafson, Dean; Emery Bopp, Chmn, Art Dept; 5 FT, 1 PT
instr. Estab. 1927; pvt; D; ent. req. HS grad; 4 yr; degrees, B.A, B.S,
M.F.A, M.A; work schol, grad. assistantships; enrl. 5048. Tui.
$450 per sem; campus res.

Art Appreciation	Drawing & Painting
Art Education	History of Art
Ceramics	Lettering

Commercial Art	Printmaking
Crafts	Scenic Design
Design	Sculpture

FURMAN UNIVERSITY, Department of Art, 29613.
Tel: (803) 294-2074, 2000
Thomas E. Flowers, Chmn; 3 FT instr. Estab. 1821; pvt; ent. req.
HS grad. and ent. exam; 4 yr; degrees, B.A, B.S, B.M, M.A; schol;
14 SC enrl. average 10, 6 LC enrl. average 20; total enrl. 2300.
Tui. and fees $2224, campus res. $1416.

Ceramics	History of Art
Design	Painting
Drawing	Sculpture
Graphic Arts	Teacher Training
Handicrafts	

MUSEUM SCHOOL OF ART, Greenville County Museum of Art, 420
College St, 29601. Tel: (803) 271-7570
Sharon H. Whitley, Dir; 1 FT, 18 PT instr. Estab. 1960; pub; D & E;
no ent. req; 2-3 yr; degrees, A.A.A, A.F.A; schol; 12 SC, 2 LC, 6 GC;
enrl. D 200, E 100. Tui. $60 per sem. course, PT $50, lab and
materials fees $10-$15 extra.

Advertising Design	Photography
Crafts	Pottery
Drawing	Printmaking
History of Art	Sculpture
Painting	Video
Philosophy of Art	Weaving

Youth classes, ages 6-12, mixed-media; tui. $30 per course per sem;
enrl. approx. 15 per course.
Summer School: Sharon Whitley, Dir; courses offered are same
as regular sem; tui. $50 for 4 wk. term; enrl. approx. 300 per sem.

GREENWOOD

LANDER COLLEGE, Department of Visual Studies, 29646.
Tel: (803) 229-5521 Exten. 231
Robert Harold Poe, Coordinator of Visual Studies; 3 FT, 2 PT instr.
Coll. estab. 1872; pub; D & E; ent. req. HS dipl; 4 yr; degree, B.A.
(Art); schol; 25 SC, 5 LC; enrl. D 235, E 60, maj. 35. Tui. $250 per
sem; campus res. $2400.

Advertising Design	Graphic Design
Aesthetics	History of Art & Archaeology
Art Education	Illustration
Ceramics	Painting
Commercial Art	Sculpture
Drawing	Teacher Training
Graphic Arts	

HARTSVILLE

COKER COLLEGE, Art Department, 29550.
Tel: (803) 332-1381 Exten. 417
R. Nickey Brumbaugh, Head; 2 FT, 1 PT instr. Estab. 1908; pvt;
D & E; ent. req. HS dipl, ent. exam; 4 yr; degrees, A.B, B.S; schol;
29 SC, 8 LC; enrl. D 545, maj. 29. Tui. $1880 per yr; campus
res. $1245.

Art Education	Handicrafts
Ceramics	History of Art
Commercial Art	Painting
Crafts	Photography
Drawing	Sculpture
Graphic Arts	

Summer School: Write to Academic Dean; courses offered, Art
Appreciation and Education; tui. $360 for term of 5 wk.

NEWBERRY

NEWBERRY COLLEGE, Art Department,
29108.
K. David Brown, Program Coordinator; 1 FT, 1 PT instr. Coll. estab.
1856, dept. 1972; den; D & E; ent. req. HS dipl, coll. ent. exam, no
specific req. for special art classes; no major in Art; 5 SC; enrl.
D 42, E 38. Tui. $2100 per yr, special students pay $75 per sem. hr;
campus res. $3200.

Advertising Design	Lettering
Art Education	Painting
Commercial Art	Teacher Training
Drawing	Theatre Arts
Industrial Design	

ORANGEBURG

SOUTH CAROLINA STATE COLLEGE, Department of Music and
Fine Arts, 29115.
Leo F. Twiggs, Dir. Art Prog; 3 FT instr. Estab. 1972; pub; D;

ent. req. ent. exam; 4 yr; degree, B.A; enrl. art. 50. Tui. $1520 per yr.

Art Education	Mosaics
Batik	Painting
Ceramics	Sculpture
Drawing	Textile Printing

Summer School: Dr. Algenon S. Belcher, Dir; courses offered, Art Appreciation, Arts & Crafts for Children.

ROCK HILL

WINTHROP COLLEGE, Department of Art, 29733.
Tel: (803) 323-2126
Edmund Lewandowski, Chmn; 8 FT instr. Estab. 1886; pub; degree, B.V.A.

Art Education	Painting
Ceramics	Photography
Crafts	Printmaking
Graphic-Advertising Design	Sculpture

Summer School: Edmund Lewandowski, Dir; two 5 wk. terms beginning June 3, 1976.

SPARTANBURG

CONVERSE COLLEGE, Division of the Fine Arts, Department of Art, 29301. Tel: (803) 585-6421 Exten. 251
Mayo MacBoggs, Chmn; 4 FT, 2 PT instr. Estab. 1889; pvt; D & E; W (men accepted in Arts & Music); ent. req. 16 units or equivalent; 4 yr; degrees, B.A, B.F.A; schol; 25 SC, 12 LC.

Ceramics	Interior Design
Drawing	Painting
Graphic Arts	Photography
History of Art	Sculpture

SOUTH DAKOTA

ABERDEEN

NORTHERN STATE COLLEGE, Art Department, 57401.
Tel: (605) 622-2514
James Gibson, Dir; 6 FT instr. Estab. 1901; pub; D; co-ed; ent. req. HS dipl, ent. exam, ACT; 2-4 yr; degrees, A.A, B.A, B.S.Educ; schol; 35 SC, 18 LC, 10 GC; enrl. 150, maj. 119, grad. 3. Tui. $11.50 per cr; campus res. $700.

Advertising Design	Jewelry
Art Education	Painting
Ceramics	Printmaking
Commercial Art	Sculpture
Drawing	Teacher Training
History of Art & Archaeology	Weaving

Summer School: Jim Gibson, Dir; courses same as above; tui. $15.75 per cr. for term of 5 wk. beginning June; 1974 enrl. c. 70.

BROOKINGS

SOUTH DAKOTA STATE UNIVERSITY, Department of Art, 57006.
Tel: (605) 688-4223
Fredrick W. Bunce, Chmn; 8 FT, 2 PT instr. Pub; D; ent. req. HS dipl; 4 yr; degrees, B.A, B.S; schol; 23 SC, 7 LC; enrl. D 755, maj. 89. Tui. $16.75 per cr. hr; non-res. $38.50 per cr. hr; campus res. $707.

Art Education	Lettering
Ceramics	Painting
Drawing	Printmaking
Graphic Arts	Sculpture
Graphic Design	Textile Design
History of Art & Archaeology	Weaving

Summer School: Dr. Fredrick Bunce, Dir; course offered, Design; tui. $34.50 for term of 8 wk. beginning June 6; 1973 enrl. 10.

HURON

HURON COLLEGE,* Art Department, 57350.
Tel: (605) 352-8721 Exten. 272
Mirle E. Freel, Jr, Head; 2 FT instr. Pub; D; ent. req. HS dipl, ent. exam; 4 yrs; degrees, B.A, B.S; schol; 9 SC, 2 LC; enrl. D 580. Tui. $2410 per yr, $200 per unit; campus res. $975.

Art Education	Painting
Drawing	Photography
Graphic Arts	Sculpture
Graphic Design	Teacher Training
History of Art & Archaeology	

Summer School: Dr. Phillip H. Mergler, Dir; courses offered Drawing Techniques, Three Dimensional Design.

MADISON

DAKOTA STATE COLLEGE,* Division of Fine and Applied Art, 57042. Tel: (605) 256-3551 Exten. 219
Larry D. Ferguson, Art Coordinator; 2 FT instr. Estab. 1881; pub; D; ent. req. HS dipl, ACT; 4 yrs; degree, B.S; schol; 16 SC, 5 LC; enrl. D 120, maj. 20. Tui. $424 per yr, non-res. $992; campus res. $860.

Art Education	Jewelry
Ceramics	Painting
Drawing	Sculpture
History of Art & Archaeology	Teacher Training

Summer School: Dr. Dale Hanke, Dean; tui. $13.25 per cr. hr, non-res. $31, plus $37 fees for term of 8 wk. beginning June 10; 1973 enrl. 30.

MITCHELL

DAKOTA WESLEYAN UNIVERSITY,* Department of Art, University Blvd, 57301. Tel: (605) 996-5685
Milton Kudlacek, Head; 1 FT instr. Estab. 1885; den; ent. req. upper half of HS class; 4 yr; degree; schol; SC, LC; enrl. 200.
General Art
Summer School.

SIOUX FALLS

AUGUSTANA COLLEGE,* Art Department, 57102.
Tel: (605) 336-5426
John Carlander, Head; 4 FT instr. Estab. 1860; den; D & E; co-ed; ent. req. HS dipl, ent. exam; 4 yr; degrees, B.A; M.A.E; schol; 14 SC, 3 LC; enrl. total 1861. Tui. $1900; campus res. $700.

Art Education	History of Art
Ceramics	Lithography
Drawing	Painting
Etching	Sculpture

Summer School: Dr. Arthur Olsen, Dir; Arts and Crafts, Drawing; tui. $167 per course for term of 8 wk. beginning June 8.

SIOUX FALLS COLLEGE,* Division of Fine Arts, Department of Art, 1501 S. Prairie St, 57101.
Jay Olson, Chmn; 1 FT instr. Estab. 1883; pub; 4 yr; degrees, B.A with maj. in Art or Art Educ; schol; SC, LC; enrl. 1000. Tui. $1200 per yr; campus res.

Art Education	Design & Illustration
Art History	Drawing
Crafts	Painting

Summer School: Courses in crafts, design, drawing and education.

SPEARFISH

BLACK HILLS STATE COLLEGE, Art Department, 57783.
Tel: (605) 642-6272
Dr. Victor Weidensee, Chmn. Fine Arts Division; 4 FT instr. Estab. 1883; pub; D; ent. req. HS dipl, transcripts, ACT, physical exam; 4 yr; degree, B.A; schol; 15 SC, 4 LC; enrl. maj. 50. Tui. $15.75 per cr. hr, non-res. $33.50; campus res. $835 per yr.

Art Education	Lettering
Ceramics	Painting
Commercial Art	Photography
Drafting	Sculpture
Drawing	

Summer School: Dr. Victor Weidensee, Dir; tui. $15.75 per cr. hr.

Art in Our Lives	Painting
Drawing	School Arts & Crafts

SPRINGFIELD

UNIVERSITY OF SOUTH DAKOTA, SPRINGFIELD, 57062.
Tel: (605) 369-2264
Ed Gettinger, Head; 1 FT instr. Estab. 1881; pub; D; ent. req. HS dipl; 2 yr; degrees, A.A, A.S, A.A.S; schol; 12 SC, 2 LC; enrl. D 70, maj. 14, grad. 70. Tui. $16.50 per sem. hr, non-res. $31; campus res. $445 per sem.

Ceramics	Painting
Drawing	Sculpture
Graphic Design	Technical Illustration
Lettering	

Adult hobby classes, painting, ceramics; tui. $10; enrl. 15.
Summer School: Tui. $16.50 per sem. hr. for term of 5 wk. beginning June 2; enrl. 20.

Art Appreciation	Independent Study
Design	Painting
Drawing	

VERMILLION

UNIVERSITY OF SOUTH DAKOTA, College of Fine Arts, Department of Art, 57069.
Dr. Aidron Duckworth, Chmn; 10 FT, 1 PT instr. Estab. 1968; pub; D & E; ent. req; 4 yr; degrees, B.F.A, B.Sc.(Art Educ); enrl. approx. 100 art maj. Tui. $720-$815 per sem, $14.25 per cr. hr, non-res. $1100-$1200, $36 per cr. hr. Summer School.

Aesthetics	Graphic Design
Art Education	Mural Painting
Art History	Painting
Ceramics	Photography
Design	Printmaking
Drawing	Sculpture

YANKTON

MOUNT MARTY COLLEGE,* Art Department, 1100 W. 5th, 57078.
Tel: (605) 668-1523
John A. Day, Head; 3 FT instr. Estab. 1936; den; D & E; co-ed; ent. req. HS dipl; 4 yr; degrees, B.A, B.S; schol; 20 SC, 3 LC; enrl. D 150, E 20, maj. 20, others 10. Tui. $900, part-time $35 per cr. hr; campus res. $800.

Advertising Design	Painting
Art Education	Photography
Ceramics	Sculpture
Drawing	Teacher Training
Graphic Arts	Textile Design
History of Art & Archaeology	Theatre Arts
Lettering	

Adult hobby classes, crafts, photography, calligraphy; regular tui. or non-cr. plan of $45 per course; enrl. 30. Children's classes, basic art; materials fee $20; enrl. 20 per sem.
Summer School: Dr. Bruce Weier, Dir; tui. $150 for term of 4 wk. beginning June 4; 1969 enrl. 26.

Arts & Crafts of the Plains	Crafts
Indian	Photography
Ceramics	

YANKTON COLLEGE,* Department of Art, 57078.
Tel: (605) 665-3661
Jerome Gallagher, Head; 3 PT instr. Estab. 1881; pvt; den; ent. req. HS grad; 4 yr; degree; schol; SC, LC.

Art Education Foundations	Inter-Disciplinary Courses w/other
Ceramics	depts.
Drawing	Painting (Oil & Acrylic)
Foundations	Sculpture
History of Art	Weaving

TENNESSEE

ATHENS

TENNESSEE WESLEYAN COLLEGE, Department of Art, P.O. Box 40, 37303. Tel: (615) 745-5906
Robert Jolly, Chmn; 1 FT instr. Coll. estab. 1857, dept. 1966; den; D & E; ent. req. HS dipl; 4 yr; degrees, B.A, B.S; schol; 7 SC, 5 LC; enrl. total 500, maj. 10. Tui. $990, campus res. $1800.

Art Education	History of Art
Design	Painting
Drawing	Sculpture

Summer School: Dr. Robert Evans, Acad. Dean; public school art courses; tui. $155 per course for term of 5 wk. beginning June 10; enrl. 360.

CHATTANOOGA

UNIVERSITY OF TENNESSEE AT CHATTANOOGA, Department of Art, 37401. Tel: (615) 755-4177
George Cress, Head; 6 FT, 3 PT instr. Estab. 1945; pub; 4 yr; degrees; 13 SC, 7 LC; enrl. maj. 130, others 600. Tui. 12 hr. $228, 18 hr. $432, non-res. 12 hr. $728, 18 hr. $1242.

Art History	Graphic Design
Ceramics	Sculpture
Commercial Design	Teacher Training
Drawing & Painting	

Summer School: George Cress, Dir; three 5 wk. terms.

CLARKSVILLE

AUSTIN PEAY STATE UNIVERSITY, Department of Fine Arts, 37040. Tel: (615) 648-7333
Dr. Charles T. Young, Chmn; D 6 FT, 1 PT, E 1 FT instr. Estab. 1927; pub; D & E; ent. req. HS grad. 15 units cert. by HS; 4 yr;

degrees, B.S, B.F.A, B.A; schol; 30 SC enrl. 105, 9 LC enrl. 217; enrl. maj. 125, others 850. Tui. $1170 per yr.

Advertising Design	Lettering
Ceramics	Painting
Drawing	Photography
Graphic Arts	Sculpture
Handcrafts	Teacher Training
Illustration	

Summer School: Charles T. Young, Dir; tui. $90 for 12 wk. beginning June; enrl. 200.

Art Appreciation	Painting
Art Education	Teacher Art Workshops
Drawing	

COLLEGEDALE

SOUTHERN MISSIONARY COLLEGE,* Art Department, 37315.
Eleanor Jackson, Dept. Head; 3 FT, 1 PT instr. Estab. 1969; den; D & E; ent. req. HS dipl, ent. exam; 4 yrs; degrees, B.A. in Art, B.A. in Art Educ; 3 LC; enrl. maj. 34. Tui. $1776 per yr; FT $222 mo; PT $65 per hr.

Advertising Design	Industrial Design
Art Education	Landscape Architecture
Ceramics	Painting
Drawing	Photography
Graphic Arts	Sculpture
Graphic Design	Teacher Training
Handicrafts	Textile Design
History of Art & Archaeology	

FRANKLIN

THE HARRIS SCHOOL OF ADVERTISING ART, INC,* Route 8, Battlewood Estates, Hillsboro Rd, 37064. Tel: (615) 794-8544
Isaac Harris, Pres. and Dir; Elizabeth Ions Harris, V.Pres. and Dir; 3 FT instr. Estab. 1932; pvt; D; ent. req. HS dipl; 2, 3 and 4 yr; cert; SC, LC; enrl. 75. Tui. $1100. A small personal school with professional standards offering a practical curriculum, personalized to each student's individuality. Two, three and four yr. cert. courses in advertising art.

Airbrush Rendering	Lithography
Artistic Anatomy	Mechanical Art & Paste-up
Composition & Design	Perspective Drawing
Figure Drawing & Painting	Photo-Engraving
Head Drawing & Painting	Printing Processes
Lettering & Typography	Still Life Painting

GREENVILLE

TUSCULUM COLLEGE, Division of Creative Arts & Humanities, 37743. Tel: (615) 639-2861
J. Clement Allison, Asst. Prof; 2 FT instr. Coll. estab. 1794; den; D; ent. req. HS dipl; 4 yr; degrees, B.A, B.S; schol; 25 SC, 3 LC; enrl. D 445, maj. 18. Tui. $1800 per yr; campus res. $1410.

Art Education	Painting
Ceramics	Printmaking
Drawing	Sculpture
Glassblowing	Three-Dimensional Design
History of Art & Archaeology	Two-Dimensional Design
Life Drawing	

Adult continuing education classes, painting; tui. $68; enrl. 14.

JACKSON

LANE COLLEGE, Art Department, 38301.
Tel: (901) 424-4600
Phyllis Carol Shieber, Assoc. Prof; 1 FT instr. Den; D; ent. req. HS dipl; 4 yr; no art major; schol; 8 SC, 3 LC; enrl. 165. Tui. $1182 per yr; campus res. $1060.

Art Education	History of Art & Archaeology
Ceramics	Painting
Drawing	

UNION UNIVERSITY, Department of Art, 38301.
Tel: (901) 422-2576
Grove Robinson, Chmn; 2 FT, 1 PT instr. Estab. 1825; den; D & E; ent. req. HS dipl, ent. exam; 4 yr; degree, B.A; schol; 18 SC, 4 LC. Tui. $1360; campus res. $710.

Art Education	History of Art & Archaeology
Ceramics	Lettering
Crafts	Painting
Drawing	Sculpture
Graphic Design	

JEFFERSON CITY

CARSON-NEWMAN COLLEGE, Art Department, 37760.
Tel: (615) 475-9061 Exten. 242
R. Earl Cleveland, Chmn; 2-3 FT instr. Coll. estab. 1851, art maj.
1963; den; D & E; ent. req. HS dipl; 4 yr; degree, B.A.(Art); schol;
26 SC, 7 LC; enrl. maj. 36. Tui. $1300 per yr, studio fees $5-$25;
campus res. $1000; total minimum cost per sem. $1157 not incl.
books.

Aesthetics	Painting
Art Education	School & Recreation Crafts
Ceramics	Sculpture
Drawing	Stage Design
Graphic Arts	Teacher Training
History of Art & Archaeology	Theatre Arts
Lettering	

Summer School: R. Earl Cleveland, Chmn; courses offered
usually Art Appreciation, Teacher Workshops, and Travel Study in
Europe.

JOHNSON CITY

EAST TENNESSEE STATE UNIVERSITY, Art Department, 37601.
Tel: (615) 929-4247
Radford Thomas, Chmn; 13 FT, 3 PT, E 1 PT instr. Estab. 1911;
pub; D & E; 4 yr; degrees, B.S, B.A, B.F.A, M.A, M.F.A; schol. and
fel; 91 SC, 31 LC, 38 GC; enrl. maj. 300. Tui. undergrad. $12 per
quarter hr, grad. $15, non-res. undergrad. $20 per quarter hr,
grad. $20.

Art Education	Jewelry
Art History	Metal Work
Ceramics	Painting
Cinemaphotography	Photography
Drawing	Printmaking
Enameling	Sculpture
Graphic Design	Weaving

Summer School: Two terms of approx. 5 wk. each.

KNOXVILLE

UNIVERSITY OF TENNESSEE, Department of Art, 927 Volunteer
Blvd, 37916. Tel: (615) 974-3408
C. Kermit Ewing, Head; 25 FT, 14 PT instr. Estab. 1948; pub; D;
ent. req. HS dipl; 4 yr; degrees, B.A, B.F.A, M.A.(1 yr), M.F.A.(2
yr); schol; 81 SC, 22 LC, 43 GC; enrl. 2000, maj. 500, grad. 15.
Tui. non-res. $284 per quarter, $47 per quarter hr, maintenance
fee $134 per quarter; campus res. $1095.

Advertising Design	History of Art
Commercial Art	Illustration
Communication Design	Lettering
Drawing	Painting
Graphic Arts	Printmaking
Graphic Design	

Summer School: C. Kermit Ewing, Head; tui. non-res. undergrad.
$27 per quarter hr, grad. $35 per quarter hr; two 6 wk. sessions.

Art History	Painting
Communication Design	Printmaking
Drawing	Sculpture

Department of Related Art, Crafts, and Interior Design,* 37916.
Tel: (615) 974-2360
Dr. Robbie G. Blakemore, Chmn; 9 FT, 1 PT instr. Estab. 1794;
pub; D (occasional E); ent. req. as set forth by Univ; 4 yr; degrees,
B.S, M.S; schol. and 3 grad. assistantships; 34 SC, 4 LC, 14 GC;
enrl. undergrad. 228, grad. 25. Tui. $120 per quarter, non-res.
$220 per quarter

Art Applied to Daily Living	Teacher Training (with College
Crafts	of Education)
Interior Design	

Summer School: Two 6 wk. terms from June 15; fee assessed at
regular quarter rate. Arrowment School for Arts and Crafts at
Gatlinburg, Tennessee, in cooperation with Pi Beta Phi School.

MARYVILLE

MARYVILLE COLLEGE, Division of Fine Arts, Art Section, 37801.
Tel: (615) 982-9132
Thelma Roper Bianco, Head; 2 FT, 1 PT instr. Estab. 1937; den;
4 yr; degrees; schol; 10 SC, 5 LC.

Art Education	Jewelry
American Art History	Painting
Ancient & Medieval Art History	Printmaking & Fabric Design
Ceramic Sculpture	Renaissance Art History
Contemporary Art History	17th-19th Century Art History
Drawing & Composition	Visual Theory & Design
Enameling	Weaving

Children's art classes, art education, crafts.

MEMPHIS

✠MEMPHIS ACADEMY OF ARTS, Overton Park, 38112.
Tel: (901) 726-4085
Jameson M. Jones, Dir; 18 FT, 13 PT instr. Estab. 1936; pvt; D & E;
4 yr; degree, B.F.A. and cert; schol; enrl. FT 240, PT 300.
Tui. FT $525 per sem, non-res. $575, PT $50 per cr hr.

Advertising Design	Lettering
Architectural Rendering	Lithography
Art History	Metalsmithing
Design	Painting
Drawing	Photography
Enameling	Pottery
Etching	Sculpture
Fashion Illustration	Silk Screening
Intaglio	Typography
Interior Design	Weaving
Jewelry	Woodcut

Children's classes, drawing, jewelry, painting, pottery, sculpture;
tui. $60 for school yr. of 25 wk; enrl. 200.

Summer School: 6 wk. from early June for adults and children;
enrl. 500.

Drawing	Photography
Enameling	Pottery
Jewelry	Sculpture
Metalsmithing	Watercolor
Painting	Weaving

MEMPHIS STATE UNIVERSITY, Art Department, 38152.
Tel: (901) 454-2216
Dr. Dana D. Johnson, Chmn; 28 FT, 5 PT instr. Estab. 1912; pub;
D & E; ent. req. HS dipl, ent. exam; 4 yr; degrees, B.A, B.F.A,
M.F.A, M.A, M.A.T; schol; 80 SC, 20 LC; enrl. D 5000, E 200, maj.
200.

Advertising Design	Interior Design
Art Education	Jewelry
Ceramics	Museum Staff Training
Commercial Art	Painting
Display	Photography
Drawing	Sculpture
Graphic Arts	Teacher Training
Graphic Design	Textile Design
History of Art & Archaeology	Weaving
Illustration	

Some adult hobby classes; children's classes in summer.

Summer School: Dr. Dana D. Johnson, Dir; two 5 wk. terms; 1976
enrl. 400.

Art Education	Drawing
Art History	Introduction to Art
Design	

SOUTHWESTERN AT MEMPHIS,* Art Department, 2000 N. Parkway,
38112. Tel: (901) 274-1800 Exten. 321
Lawrence K. Anthony, Chmn; 2 FT, 4 PT instr. Estab. 1848; den;
D; ent. req. ent. exam, 16 ent. cr.(13 academic, 4 yr. Eng, 2 yr.
algebra, 1 yr. geometry, 2 yr. foreign language); 2 yr. res; degrees,
B.A, B.S, B.M; schol; 30 SC, 10 LC; enrl. D 300. Tui. $2000 per yr;
campus res. $980.

Aesthetics	Painting
Drawing	Photography
Graphic Arts	Sculpture
History of Art & Archaeology	Theatre Arts
Museum Staff Training	Weaving

MURFREESBORO

✠MIDDLE TENNESSEE STATE UNIVERSITY, Art Department, 37132.
Tel: (615) 898-2455
Dr. C. M. Brandon, Head; 12 instr. Estab. 1911; pub; ent. req. HS
grad; 4 yr; degrees, B.S.(Art Educ), B.A, B.F.A; SC, LC, GC; enrl.
maj. 190, others 700. Tui. $203 per sem, non-res. $629.

Art Education
Art History
General Art

Children's classes, Creative Art in Education Clinic, grades 1-12;
fee $5 per sem.

NASHVILLE

FISK UNIVERSITY, Department of Art, 37203.
Tel: (615) 244-3580 Exten. 258
David C. Driskell, Chmn; 5 FT, 3 PT instr. Estab. 1935; pvt; ent.
req. coll. board exam; 4 yr; degree, B.S; 25 SC, 7 LC; enrl. maj.
30. Tui. $1500, lab. fee $10; campus res. $900.

Ceramics	Museum Science Training
Cinematography	Painting
Drawing & Design	Photography
Graphic Arts	Sculpture

GEORGE PEABODY COLLEGE FOR TEACHERS, Art Faculty,
37203. Tel: (615) 327-8178
Dr. Walter E. Rutkowski, Chmn; 8 FT instr. Estab. 1914; pub;
D & E; ent. req. B average; 4 yr; degrees, B.S, M.S; for schol. or
financial aid contact Financial Aid Office. Tui. undergrad. $60 per
sem. hr, grad. $80 per sem. hr.

Aesthetics & Art Criticism	Glassworking
Art & the Humanities	Jewelry & Silversmithing
Art History Survey	Painting
Ceramics	Photography
Crafts	Printmaking
Design	Sculpture
Drawing	Teacher Education

Summer School: Dr. Walter E. Rutkowski, Chmn; 10 wk.
regular session.

✵TENNESSEE FINE ARTS CENTER, Cheek Road, Cheekwood,
37205. Tel: (615) 352-5310 Exten. 23
John Henry Nozynski, Dir; Linda Thompson, Cur. Educ; 12 PT
instr. Chartered 1957; pvt; D & E; pre-school to senior citizens;
no ent req. or degree.

Art (4-8)	Mixed Media (9-13)
Ballet (4-8, Adult Beginners,	Painting (Adults)
Adult Advanced)	Period Furniture
Drama (8-13, 12-14, Adult)	Photography (Adults)
Drama Workshop (HS & College)	Teen Workshop (13-18)
Landscape Painting (Adults)	

VANDERBILT UNIVERSITY, Department of Fine Arts, 37235.
Tel: (615) 322-2831
F. Hamilton Hazlehurst, Chmn; 9 FT, 1 PT instr. Estab. 1944; pvt;
ent. req. HS grad. and ent. exam; 4 yr; degrees, B.A, M.A.(Art
History); schol; 6 SC, 28 LC, 28 GC; enrl. maj. 70. Tui. $2600 per
yr; campus res. $1400.
Summer School: Parker L. Coddington, Dir; LC; term of 10 wk.
beginning June 7.

WATKINS INSTITUTE,* Sixth and Church,
37219.
C. H. Sargent, Dir; 7 PT instr. Estab. 1913; pvt; D & E; non-cr.
adult educ. program, must be 17 yr. of age or older; no degree;
4 SC, 1 LC; enrl. D 125, E 200. Tui. $18 per quarter.

Art Education	Painting
Commercial Art	Photography
Drawing	

SEWANEE

THE UNIVERSITY OF THE SOUTH, Department of Fine Arts,
37375. Tel: (615) 598-5780
Thomas Frasier, Chmn; 3 FT, 1 PT instr. Pvt; D; ent. req. ent.
exam; 4 yr; degree, B.A; schol; 25 SC, 20 LC; enrl. 450, maj. 25.
Tui. information contact Dir. of Admis.

Art History	Photography
Drawing	Printmaking
Painting	Sculpture

TEXAS

ABILENE

ABILENE CHRISTIAN COLLEGE,* Art Department, 79601.
Tel: (915) 677-1911 Exten. 674
Norman W. Whitefield, Head; 5 FT, 2 PT instr. Estab. 1906; den;
D & E; ent. req. upper three-fourth HS grad. class, or at 15 stan-
dard score ACT composite; 4 yr; degrees, B.F.A, B.A, B.S.Educ;
24 SC, 8 LC; enrl. maj. 54. Tui. 16 hr. $704.

Commercial Art	Painting
Design	Pottery
Drawing	Sculpture
History of Art	Teacher Training

Summer School: Dr. Ed Enzor, Dir; $39 per cr. hr. for 5½ wk.
beginning June 2.

HARDIN-SIMMONS UNIVERSITY, Department of Art, 79601.
Tel: (915) 677-7281 Exten. 220
Ira M. Taylor, Head; D 2 FT, E 3 PT instr. School estab. 1891;
den; ent. req. HS grad; 4 yr; degrees, B.A, B.S; schol; 17 SC, 10
LC, 4 GC; enrl. maj. 50. Tui. $39 per sem. hr; campus res. with
room and board $397-$465 per sem.

Art History	Drawing & Painting
Ceramics	Printmaking
Crafts	Sculpture
Design	Teacher Training

Summer School: $35 per sem. hr. 12 wk. (2 terms) beginning
June 5; enrl. 60.

McMURRY COLLEGE, Art Department, 79605.
Tel: (915) 692-4130 Exten. 280
Sherwood Suter, Head; 3 FT instr. Estab. 1923; pvt; ent. req. HS
grad; 4 yr; degree; 8 SC, 2 LC; enrl. maj. 38, others 1400 (incl.
Dyess Air Base classes). Tui. $660 per sem. with room and
board $1160; campus res.

Ceramics	Landscape Painting
Design	Life Drawing
Drawing & Painting	Portrait Painting
Fine Arts (Lecture)	Sculpture
History of Art (Lecture)	Teacher Training—Art Education
Jewelry	

Summer School: Dr. Allen Cordts, Dir; tui. $44 per sem. hr. for
term of 6 wk. beginning June 2; one wk. workshop in Art Education
for Elementary Teachers in June. No graduate courses.

ALPINE

SUL ROSS STATE UNIVERSITY, Art Department, 79830.
Tel: (915) 837-3461
Dr. Roy E. Dodson, Chmn; 3 FT instr. Estab. 1920; pub; D & E;
ent. req. HS dipl, ent. exam; 4 yr; degrees, B.S, B.F.A, M.Ed.(Art);
52 SC, 4 LC, 20 GC; enrl. D 240, maj. 37, grad. students 15. Tui.
19 cr. hr. res. $138, non-res. and foreign students $822, exempt foreign students $328; campus res. $490 per sem. Summer School.

Advertising Design	History of Art
Art Education	Jewelry
Ceramics	Painting
Drawing	Sculpture
Graphic Arts	Teacher Training

Adult hobby classes, oil painting; enrl. 12

AMARILLO

AMARILLO COLLEGE, Department of Art, P.O. Box 447, 79178.
Tel: (806) 376-5111
Denny T. Fraze, Chmn; 3 PT instr. Estab. 1926; pub; D & E;
ent. req. ACT, CEEB, SAT; 2 yrs; degrees, A.A, A.S; schol; 10 SC,
2 LC. Tui. $125 per yr; no campus res.

Ceramics	Jewelry
Drawing	Painting
Graphic Arts	Sculpture
History of Art & Archaeology	

ARLINGTON

UNIVERSITY OF TEXAS AT ARLINGTON, Department of Art, 76019.
Tel: (817) 275-3211
Ronald M. Bernier, Chmn; 19 FT, 2 PT instr. Estab. 1937; pub;
D; ent. req. college boards; 4 yr; degree, B.F.A; 54 SC, 7 LC; enrl.
total 15,000. Tui. $175 per sem; campus res.

Advertising Design	Film Production
Art Education	Metals/Jewelry
Art History	Painting
Ceramics	Printmaking
Fashion Art	Sculpture

Summer School: Two 6 wk. terms; D; tui. $45.50 per term; enrl.
7000.

AUSTIN

CONCORDIA LUTHERAN COLLEGE, Department of Art, 3400
Interregional, 78705.
Virginia Erickson, Head; 1 PT instr. Estab. 1925; den; D; ent. req.
HS dipl; 2 yr; degree, A.A; schol; 1 SC, 1 LC; enrl. D 350. Tui.
$660 per yr; campus res. $1010.

Art Fundamentals
Drawing
Painting

UNIVERSITY OF TEXAS,* School of Architecture, P.O. Box 7908,
University Station, 78712. Tel: (512) 471-1922
Alan Y. Taniguchi, Dir; 20 FT, 10 PT instr. Estab. 1910; pub; ent.
req. 16 cr. incl. 3½ Math, 1 Science; 5-6 yr; degree; enrl. 387. Tui.
$50 per sem, non-res. $200 per sem.
‡Architecture

Department of Art, College of Fine Arts
Ralph White, Acting Chmn; 49 FT, 4 PT instr. Estab. 1938; 4 yr;
degree; 78 SC, 21 LC; enrl. maj. 1000; others 1162. Tui. res. $50,
non-res. $200, plus $9.50 or $13.25 for each SC.

Ceramics	History & Criticism of Art
Commercial Art & Illustration	Painting
Crafts	Pictorial Composition
Design	Sculpture

Drawing
Graphic Arts

Teacher Education with College
of Education

Summer School: Two 6 wk. terms.

BEAUMONT

LAMAR UNIVERSITY, Department of Art, Bos 10027, 77710.
Tel: (713) 838-7427
Robert C. Rogan, Head; 9 FT, 2 PT instr. Estab. 1951; pub; D & E;
ent. req. HS dipl; 4 yr; degrees, B.S, B.F.A; schol; 44 SC, 9 LC;
enrl. D 12,000, E 500, maj. 220. Tui. $120, student fees $30, building fees $26, student center $10; campus res. $1160 per yr.

Advertising Design
Art Education
Ceramics
Commercial Art
Drawing
Graphic Arts

Graphic Design
History of Art & Archaeology
Painting
Photography
Sculpture
Teacher Training

Summer School: Robert C. Rogan, Head; tui. $69 for term of 6
wk. beginning June.

Art Education
Ceramics
Commercial Art

History
Painting
Photography

BELTON

MARY HARDIN-BAYLOR COLLEGE, Art Department, 76513.
Tel: (817) 939-5811 Exten. 44
Ted L. Austin, Chmn; 2 FT instr. Estab. 1845; den; D & E; co-ed;
ent. req. upper half of HS grad. class; 4 yr; degrees, B.A, B.F.A,
B.S; schol; 6 SC, 1 LC and 1 independent learning course per sem.
Tui. $35 per sem. hr, room, board and tui. 15 hr. $985 per sem. D
classes studio, E classes Art History

Art Education
Art History
Ceramics
Design

Drawing
Graphics
Jewelry
Painting

Summer School: Ted L. Austin, Dir; Crafts and Independent
Learning, from 1 to 4 hr. cr; tui. room and board for sem. of 5 wk,
$375.

BIG SPRING

HOWARD COLLEGE, Department of Art, Birdwell Lane, 79720.
Tel: (915) 267-6311
Mrs. Kathleen Rathert, Chmn; 2 FT, 1 PT instr. Estab. 1972; pub;
D & E; ent. req. ent. exam, SAT, ACT; 2 yr; degree, A.A; schol;
6 SC, 2 LC; enrl. D 100, E 20, maj. 40. Tui. $150 per yr; campus
res. $400.

Advertising Design
Art Education
Ceramics
Commercial Art
Drawing
Graphic Arts

History of Art & Archaeology
Jewelry
Painting
Theatre Arts
Weaving

Adult hobby classes, macrame, oil, pottery, watercolor; tui. $12
for 6 wk; enrl 10.
Children's classes, general art; tui. $12 for 6 wk; enrl. 12.
Summer School: Mrs. Kathleen Rathert, Dir; courses offered,
Introduction to Visual Arts, Art History; tui. $40 for term of 6 wk;
enrl. 12.

BROWNSVILLE

TEXAS SOUTHMOST COLLEGE, Fine Arts Department, 83 Fort
Brown, 78520.
Jean Serafy, Chmn; 2 FT, 1 PT instr. Estab. 1973; pub; D & E; ent.
req. HS dipl; 2-3 yr; degree, A.A.(Fine Arts); schol; 10 SC, 10 LC; enrl.
D 300, E 100.

Art Education
Ceramics
Design I and II
Drawing

Graphic Design
History of Art & Archaeology
Painting
Sculpture

Adult hobby classes, ceramics and drawing.
Summer School: Courses offered in Art Appreciation; tui. $40
per cr. hr. for term of 16 wk.

BROWNWOOD

HOWARD PAYNE UNIVERSITY, School of Fine and Applied Arts,
Department of Art, Howard Payne Station, 76801.
Tel: (915) 646-2502 Exten. 245
Charles A. Stewart, Dean; 4 FT instr. Estab. 1889; den; D & E;
ent. req. HS dipl, ent. exam; 4-5 yr; degrees, B.F.A.(Studio or Art

Educ), B.A, B.S; 18 SC, 12 LC; enrl. D 200, E 69, maj. 30. Tui.
$1140 per yr; campus res. $2100-$2200.

Advertising Design
Aesthetics
Art Education
Ceramics
Commercial Art
Drawing

History of Art & Archaeology
Metalcrafts
Painting
Photography
Sculpture
Teacher Training

Adult hobby classes, metalcrafts, painting, weaving; tui. $35 per
course; enrl. 30.
Summer School: Charles A. Stewart, Dir; courses offered, Art
Education, Crafts, Painting; tui. $228 for term of 6 wk. beginning
June 1; enrl. 75.

CANYON

WEST TEXAS STATE UNIVERSITY,* Department of Art, 79015.
Tel: (806) 655-7141 Exten. 2223
Dr. Emilio Caballero, Head; D 7 FT, E 3 PT instr. Estab. 1910; pub;
ent. req. HS grad; 5 yr; degrees, B.A, B.S, M.A; 25 SC, 5 LC; enrl.
maj. 175, others 400, total 8000. Tui. $89, non-res. $239 per sem;
campus res.

General Art
Teacher Training with Dept.
of Educ.

Summer School: Dr. Emilio Caballero, Dir; 12 wk. beginning June.

COLLEGE STATION

TEXAS A & M UNIVERSITY, College of Architecture and Environmental Design, 77843.
Raymond D. Reed, Dean; 55 FT instr. Estab. 1905; pub; D; ent. req.
SAT, CEEB, Achievement, HS average; 4 yr; degrees, B.Environ.
Design, B.S.(Landscape Arch), M.Arch, M.Land, M.Planning, D.En-
viron.Design; enrl. maj. Architecture 820, total 1500. Tui. res. $4
per sem. cr. hr, non-res. $40 per sem. cr. hr; fees approx. $652.

COMMERCE

EAST TEXAS STATE UNIVERSITY, Art Department, 75428.
Tel: (214) 468-2216
Charles E. McGough, Head; 11 FT, 6 PT instr. Estab. 1917; pub;
D & E; ent. req. HS dipl; 4 yr; Advertising Art cert. 3 yr; degrees,
B.A, B.S, B.F.A, M.A, M.S, M.F.A; schol. and fel; 64 SC, 12 LC,
19 GC; enrl. 400 plus. Tui. $156 per sem, non-res. varies; campus
res.

Glass
Plastics

Teacher Training (with Dept.
of Educ)

Summer School: Charles E. McGough, Dir; 20 courses; tui.
$96 for 6 wk, non-res. $384; enrl. 200.

CORPUS CHRISTI

DEL MAR COLLEGE, Department of Art, 101 Baldwin Blvd, 78404.
Tel: (512) 882-6231
Prof. Joseph A. Cain, Chmn; 4 FT, 2 PT instr. Estab. 1938; pub;
D & E; ent. req. HS dipl, ent. exam, SAT or CEEB; 2 yrs; degree,
A.A; schol; 14 SC, 3 LC; enrl. D 420, E 120, maj. 114. Tui. $4 per
sem. hr, non-res. $17, plus $10 maximum bldg. and matriculation
fee; no campus res.

Art Education
Design
Drawing
Graphic Arts
History of Art & Archaeology

Introduction to the Visual Arts
Life Drawing
Painting
Sculpture
Survey of Mexican Art

Adult hobby classes, painting, drawing; tui. $18 per short term.
Summer School: Joseph A. Cain, Dir; same as regular schedule;
tui. $50 incl. fees for 6 hr. cr. for term of 6 wk, beginning July 16.

CORSICANA

NAVARRO COLLEGE, Art Department, Box 1170, 75110.
Tel: (214) 874-6501
Margaret Hicks, Dir; 1 FT, 1 PT instr. College estab. 1946; pub;
D & E; ent. req. HS dipl, ent. exam, special permission; 60 sem. hr;
degrees, A.A, A.S, A.Gen.Educ, A.Appl.Sci; schol; 11 SC, 1 LC; enrl.
D 50, maj. 15. Tui. $200 per yr; campus res. $820.

Advertising Design
Commercial Art
Drawing
Illustration

Lettering
Painting
Photography

Adult hobby classes, painting; tui. $1 per class hr; enrl. 20.

DALLAS

DALLAS ART INSTITUTE,* 2523 McKinney Ave, 75201.
   Tel: (214) 742-8353
Eugene Boswell, Pres; 13 FT, 3 PT instr. Estab. 1926; pvt; D & E;
ent. req. HS dipl; 3 yrs; degrees, B.F.A. and bachelors degree in
visual communication; 90 SC, 10 LC; enrl. D approx. 50, E approx.
20. Tui. $960 per yr; FT $80 mo. PT $60 mo, $20 application fee;
no campus res.

Advertising Design	Graphic Design
Aesthetics	History of Art & Archaeology
Ceramics	Lettering
Commercial Art	Painting
Drawing	Sculpture
Graphic Arts	

Adult hobby classes, painting; tui. $20 mo; enrl. 5-10.
Children's classes, painting; tui. $20; enrl. 5-10.
   Summer School: Eugene Boswell, Pres; courses offered are the
same as regular yr; same fees as during regular yr.

SOUTHERN METHODIST UNIVERSITY, Meadows School of the Arts,
   Division of Fine Arts, 75275. Tel: (214) 692-2489
Dr. Eleanor Tufts, Chairperson; 21 FT, 6 PT instr. Estab. 1917; pvt;
D; selective admission, non-degree students accepted; degrees, B.F.A.
(4 yr), M.F.A.Art (2 yr), M.A. (1½ yr); 28 SC, 38 art history courses,
70 GC; enrl. maj. 240, grad. 20. Tui. $1255 per sem. plus fees;
campus res. $675 per sem.

Art Education	Jewelry
Ceramics	Painting
Drawing	Printmaking
Graphic Design	Sculpture
History of Art	Weaving

   Summer School: Tui. $80 per cr. hr. plus fees, campus res.
$200 per sem.

DENTON

NORTH TEXAS STATE UNIVERSITY, Art Department, 76203.
   Tel: (817) 788-2071
Edward L. Mattil, Chmn; 27 FT, 12 PT instr. Estab. 1890; pub;
5 yr; degrees, B.F.A, M.A, M.F.A, Ph.D; ent. schol. to Texas res;
44 SC, 14 LC, 19 GC; enrl. maj. 1000. Tui. $40 per sem. hr, non-
res. varies; campus res.

Advertising Art	Interior Design
Art Education	Pre-Architecture
Art History	Printmaking
Crafts	Photography
Drawing & Painting	Sculpture
Fashion Design	

   Summer School: Tui. $40 per sem. hr. for 6 wk; two 6 wk.
terms.

TEXAS WOMAN'S UNIVERSITY, College of Fine Arts, Department
   of Art, Box 23548, TWU Station, 76204. Tel: (817) 382-8923
Dr. Wilgus Eberly, Dean; Dr. Donald E. Smith, Chmn; 8 FT, 1 PT
instr. Estab. 1903; pub; W; 4 yr; degrees, B.A, B.S, M.A; ent. schol;
37 SC, 7 LC, 15 GC; enrl. maj. 150, others 340. Tui. long term $4
per sem. hr, non-res. $40 per sem. hr, foreign students $14 per sem.
hr; campus res.

Advertising Design	Interior Design
Art Education	Jewelry & Metal Work
Ceramics	Medical Art
Costume Design & Fashion	Painting
Illustration	Photography
Fibers	Sculpure

   Summer School: Two terms of 6 wk. from June 4; tui. $57 per
term plus fee, non-res. $277 plus fee.

EDINBURG

PAN AMERICAN UNIVERSITY, Art Department, 78539.
   Tel: (512) 381-3141
Dr. Nancy Prince, Head; 7 FT, 1 PT instr. Estab. 1928; pub; D & E;
ent. exam; 4 yr; degrees, B.A, B.F.A; schol; 37 SC, 10 LC, 2 GC;
enrl. D 600, E 100, maj. 160. Tui. $160 per yr, non-res. $1600;
campus res. $930.

Advertising Design	History of Art & Archaeology
Art Education	Jewelry
Ceramics	Painting
Drawing	Sculpture
Graphic Arts	Teacher Training

   Summer School: Dr. Nancy Prince, Dir; tui. $85 for 2 terms of 4
wk. beginning June 3 & July 12; 1973 enrl. 400.

Art Education	Design
Art History	Drawing
Ceramics, Jewelry	Painting

EL PASO

UNIVERSITY OF TEXAS AT EL PASO, Department of Art, 79968.
   Tel: (915) 747-5181
Dr. Clarke H. Garnsey, Head; 9 FT, 1 PT instr. Estab. 1939; pub;
D & E; 4-5 yr; degrees, B.A.(4 yr), B.F.A.(5 yr); schol; 24 SC,
7 LC, 7 GC; enrl. 750. Tui. $187.50 per term, non-res. $774.

Art Education	Graphics
Art History	Jewelry
Ceramics	Painting
Design	Sculpture & Modeling
Drawing	Silversmithing

Adult hobby classes through Extension Div; fees vary from class to
class.
   Summer School: Dr. Clarke H. Garnsey, Head; two terms June 1-
July 7 and July 9 - Aug. 14; tui. $150 per term, non-res $270.

FORT WORTH

FORT WORTH ART MUSEUM SCHOOL,* 1309 Montgomery St, 76107.
   Tel: (817) 738-9215
Henry T. Hopkins, Dir; C. Dean Lee, Asst. to Dir. D & E classes
during summer sem. for adults, regular sem. for adults; no ent. req.
except where specified in brochure; non-accredited. School is being
reorganized at the present time to reopen late spring or summer
1974.

Ceramics	Jewelry
Drawing	Painting
Figure	Watercolor

TEXAS CHRISTIAN UNIVERSITY, Art Department, 76129.
   Tel: (817) 926-2461 Exten. 240, 241, 591
Prof. Anthony Jones, Chmn; 9 FT, 9 PT instr. Estab. 1909; pvt;
4 yr; undergrad, 2 yr. minimum grad; degrees, B.A, B.F.A, B.S,
Ed, M.F.A, M.A.(American Studies & Museum Training); schol.
and grad. fel. and assistantships; 35 SC, 10 LC, GC; enrl. maj.
150, others 450. Tui. $70 per sem. hr; campus res. Summer
School.

Art Education	Drawing, Design & Painting
Art History & Criticism	Graphics
Ceramics	Metals
Commercial Art	Sculpture

TEXAS WESLEYAN COLLEGE,* Department of Art, P.O. Box 3277,
   76105. Tel: (817) 534-0251 Exten. 289
Mary McConnell, Chmn; 1 FT, 2 PT instr. Den; D & E; ent. req. HS
dipl; 4 yr; degree, B.A; schol; SC, LC. Tui. $35 per hr; campus res.
$915.

Art Education	Painting
Ceramics	Printmaking
Drawing	Teacher Training
History of Art & Archaeology	

   Summer School: Course offered, Basic Art; tui. $175 for term of
5 wk. beginning in June.

HOUSTON

HOUSTON BAPTIST COLLEGE, Department of Fine Arts, 7502
   Fondren Rd, 77036. Tel: (713) 774-7661 Exten. 253
Dr. R. Paul Green, Chmn; 2 FT instr. Estab. 1963; Pvt. den;
D & E; ent. req. HS dipl, ent. exam; degrees, B.S, B.A; schol;
7 SC, 9 LC; enrl. D 1300, maj. 35. Tui. $1500 per yr.

Art Education	History of Art & Archaeology
Ceramics	Painting
Drawing	Sculpture
Graphic Arts	Teacher Training

✸RICE UNIVERSITY, Department of Fine Arts, 77001.
   Tel: (713) 528-4141 Exten. 357
Philip Oliver-Smith, Chmn; 13 FT, 2 PT instr. Estab. 1912; pvt; D;
ent. req. HS dipl, Coll. Board ent. exam, interview; 4 yr; degree,
B.A; fel; 19 SC, 25 LC; enrl. maj. 38, total 3255. Tui. $2300; campus
res. room and board $1697.

Design	Painting
Drawing	Photography
Experimental Media	Sculpture
Filmmaking	Theatre
History of Art	

✸SCHOOL OF ART, The Museum of Fine Arts, P.O. Box 6826, 77005.
   Tel: (713) 529-7659
Kenneth R. Jewesson, Dir; 24 faculty mem. Estab. 1927; pvt; D & E;
3 yr. dipl. plan; schol; 47 SC, 5 LC (Art History); enrl. 398 (spring
sem. 1975). Tui. full-time: first yr. 4 studio, 1 art history $433;

second yr. 4 studio, 1 art history $433; third yr. 5 studio $473; tui. part-time: $105 per studio course, $50 per art history course. Lab fee for some.

Art History	Painting
Ceramics	Printmaking
Color Design	Sculpture
Drawing	Three-Dimensional Design
Jewelry	Two-Dimensional Design
Life Drawing	Watercolor

Children's classes, ages 4-6 yr. through 15-18 yr, drawing, painting design, color, shape and form, clay work at particular age level; tui. ages 4-14 $50 per class, 1 1/4 hr. class per wk, ages 15-18 $75 per class, 2 hr. class per wk.

Summer Classes: 6 wk. adult session; regular curriculum; tui. full-time $230 for 3 studio courses, part-time $85 per studio course plus lab fees for some.

TEXAS SOUTHERN UNIVERSITY, Department of Art, 3201
Wheeler Ave, 77004. Tel: (713) 527-7011 Exten. 7326
Dr. John T. Biggers, Head; 6 FT, 1 PT instr. Estab. 1949; pub; D & E; ent. req. HS dipl; 5 yr; degrees, B.F.A, B.Art Educ; schol; 31 SC, 12 LC, 4 GC; enrl. maj. 85, other 100. Tui. $358 per yr, $40 per mo, $20 PT; campus res. $1200.

Advertising Design	History of Art & Archaeology
Aesthetics	Lettering
Art Education	Painting
Ceramics	Sculpture
Commercial Art	Teacher Training
Drawing	Textile Design
Graphic Arts	Weaving
Graphic Design	

Summer School: Dr. John T. Biggers, Head; tui. $60 for term of 6 wk. beginning June; enrl. average 100.

Art Appreciation in Educational Program	Mural Painting in School Problems in Art Education
Advanced Crafts for Teachers	Problems in Secondary Art Education
Basic Art for Elementary Teachers	Research Projects
Ehibition	

UNIVERSITY OF HOUSTON, Department of Art, 3801 Cullen Blvd, 77004. Tel: (713) 749-2601
Prof. George R. Bunker, Chmn; 25 FT, 8 PT instr. Pub; ent. req. HS grad, with required minimum units; 4 yr; degrees, B.A, B.F.A, M.F.A; approx. 98 classes each semester; enrl. maj. 780, others 125. Tui. $50 for 12 or more cr. hr, non-res. higher fee. Complete gallery facilities.

Art History	Painting
Ceramics	Printmaking
Environmental Design	Sculpture
Graphic Communications	Teacher Training with College of Educ.
Jewelry & Metalsmithing	

Summer School: Two 5 wk. terms.

HUNTSVILLE

SAM HOUSTON STATE UNIVERSITY, Art Department, 77340.
Tel: (713) 295-6221 Exten. 2181
Gene M. Eastman, Dir; 12 FT instr. Estab. 1879; pub; D; ent. req. HS dipl, ent. exam; 4 yr; degrees, B.F.A, B.A, B.A.Teaching, M.F.A; two fels; 31 SC, 7 LC, 14 GC; enrl. 836 per sem, maj. 200, minors 128. Tui. $60, fees $80; campus res. $500.

Advertising Design	History of Art
Art Education	Painting
Ceramics	Printmaking
Drawing	Sculpture
Fabric Crafts	

Adult classes in drawing and painting.

Summer School: Gene M. Eastman, Dir; tui. $25 for term of 6 wk; enrl. 200.

INGRAM

HILL COUNTRY ARTS FOUNDATION, Box 176, 78025.
Tel: (512) 367-5121
Ro Dillard and Eleanore Collier, Co-Chmn; 20 PT instr. Estab. 1959; pub. foundation; D; no ent. req; no degrees; schol; 20 SC; cnrl. 440. Tui. $40 for one wk. workshop; $70 for two wk. workshops. Summer School.

Ceramics	Photography
Costume Design & Construction	Sculpture
Drawing	Stage Design
Macrame	Stitchery
Needle Weaving	Theatre Arts
Painting	Writer's Workshop

Children's classes, creative arts & crafts; tui. $40 for 4 wk. session, $12 for 1 wk; enrl. 39.

KINGSVILLE

TEXAS A&I UNIVERSITY, Art Department, 78363.
Tel: (512) 595-2619
Dr. Richard Scherpereel, Chmn; 7 FT, 4 PT instr. Estab. 1930; pub; D & E; ent. req. HS dipl; 4 yr; degrees, B.A, B.S, B.F.A, M.A, M.S; schol; 22 SC, 5 LC, 4 GC; enrl. D 700, E 100, maj. 150, grad. 20. Tui. $300; campus res. $800.

Aesthetics	Graphic Design
Advertising Art	History of Art & Archaeology
Art Education	Painting
Drawing	Sculpture
Graphic Arts	Teacher Training

Summer School: R. Scherpereel, Chmn; regular curriculum; tui. $15 per cr. hr; 1973 enrl. 300.

LEVELLAND

SOUTH PLAINS COLLEGE, Art Department, College Ave, 79336.
Tel: (806) 894-4921 Exten. 242
Don Stroud, Chmn; 3 FT instr. Estab. 1958; pub; D & E; ent. req. HS dipl; 2 yr; degree, A.A; schol; 10 SC, 5 LC; enrl. D 186, E 51, maj. 154. Tui. in-dist. $64 per sem, out-of-dist. $80, out-of-state $200; campus res, $455.

Advertising Design	History of Art
Ceramics	Lettering
Commercial Art	Painting
Drafting	Photography
Drawing	Sculpture
Graphic Arts	Teacher Training
Graphic Design	

Adult hobby classes, oil painting, photography, china painting, flower arranging, gift wrapping, tole painting; tui. $40; enrl. varies.

LUBBOCK

TEXAS TECH UNIVERSITY, Department of Art, P.O. Box 4720, 79409. Tel: (806) 742-1146, 1147
Dr. Bill Lockhart, Chmn; 2 FT, 3 PT instr. Pub; D & E; ent. req. HS dipl; 4-5 yr; degrees, B.A, B.F.A, B.S.Educ, M.A.E, M.F.A, Ph.D.(Fine Arts); schol; 65 SC, 23 LC, 43 GC; enrl. maj. 750, grad. students 50. Tui. $120 per yr; campus res. $435-$625.

Advertising Design	Illustration
Aesthetics	Interior Design
Art Education	Jewelry
Ceramics	Lettering
Commercial Art	Painting
Drawing	Photography
Enameling	Printmaking
Graphic Arts	Sculpture
Graphic Design	Teacher Training
History of Art & Archaeology	Textile Design

MARSHALL

WILEY COLLEGE, Department of Fine Arts, Roseborough Springs Rd, 75680. Tel: (214) 938-8341
Cherry Lou Violette, Head; f FT, 2 PT instr. Estab. 1873; den; D & E; ent. req. HS dipl; 4 yr; no art major; schol; 16 SC, 2 LC; enrl. D 56. Tui. $40 per hr, plus special fees; campus res. $1050.

Advertising Design	Graphic Arts
Art Education	Graphic Design
Ceramics	History of Art & Archaeology
Commercial Art	Painting
Decoupage	Teacher Training
Drawing	Theatre Arts
Enameling	Weaving
Fashion Arts	

Summer School: Dr. David R. Houston, Dir; courses offered as required; tui. $40 per hr. for term of 8 wk. beginning June 2.

NACOGDOCHES

STEPHEN F. AUSTIN STATE UNIVERSITY, Department of Art, 75961. Tel: (713) 569-4804
Dr. Creighton H. Delaney, Head; 20 FT instr. Estab. 1927; pub; ent. req. HS grad; 3-4 yr; degrees, B.F.A, M.A; M.F.A; schol; 35 SC, 10 LC; enrl. approx. 1575.

Advertising Design	Drawing & Painting
Art Appreciation	Graphic Arts
Art Education	Handicrafts
Art History	Lettering
Ceramics	Photography
Crafts	Sculpture
Design & Color	Teacher Training

Summer School: Dr. Creighton H. Delaney, Dir; 12 wk. from June 1; enrl. approx. 600.

ODESSA

✠UNIVERSITY OF TEXAS OF THE PERMIAN BASIN, Faculty of
Art, 79762. Tel: (915) 367-2133
Prof. William A. King, Chmn; 3 FT, 4 PT instr. Estab. 1969; pub;
D & E; ent. req. completion of two yr. of coll; degrees, B.A, M.A;
schol; 10 SC, 5 LC, 15 GC; enrl. maj. 60, grad. students 12. Tui.
$100 per yr; no campus res.

Aesthetics	History of Art & Archaeology
Art Education	Jewelry
Ceramics	Painting
Concepts of Art	Photography
Drawing	Sculpture
Graphic Arts	Teacher Training

Summer School: William A. King, Dir; courses offered, Aboriginal American Art, study in Mexico and New Mexico.

PASADENA

SAN JACINTO COLLEGE, Department of Art, 8060 Spencer Highway,
77505. Tel: (713) 479-1501 Exten. 230
Charles R. Brown, Chmn. Div. Fine Arts; 5 FT, 1 PT instr. Estab.
1961; pub; D & E; ent. req. HS dipl, GED; 2 yrs; degree, A.A, 2 yr.
terminal degree in advertising; schol; 6 SC; enrl. D 4000, E 3000,
maj. 165. Tui. $5 per sem. hr. in dist, $10 per hr. out of dist, plus
$200 out-of-state; no campus res.

Aesthetics	Lettering
Commercial Art	Painting
Design	Sculpture
Drawing	

Summer School: Charles R. Brown, Dir; 2 wk. summer art workshop; tui. $40 for term of 2 wk. beginning June 10; 1973 enrl. 35.

PLAINVIEW

WAYLAND BAPTIST COLLEGE, Department of Art, Box 54, 1900
W. Seventh, 79072. Tel: (806) 296-5521 Exten. 46
J. D. Whitnker, Chairperson; 1 FT instr. Den; D & E; ent. req. HS
dipl, ent. exam; 4 yr; degrees, B.A, B.S; schol; 15 SC, 2 LC; enrl.
D 81, E 24, maj. 10. Tui. $30 per cr. hr.

Aesthetics	Jewelry
Art Education	Lettering
Ceramics	Museum Staff Training
Drawing	Painting
Graphic Arts	Photography
Graphic Design	Sculpture
History of Art & Archaeology	Teacher Training
Illustration	

Summer School: J. D. Whitnker, Dir; courses offered vary each
micro term.

ROCKPORT

SIMON MICHAEL SCHOOL OF FINE ARTS, P.O. Box 1283, 510 E.
King St, 78382. Tel: (512) 729-6233
Simon Michael, Owner. Estab. 1947; pvt; D & E; no ent. req; no
degrees.

Architecture	Painting
Drawing	Sculpture
Landscape Architecture	

Summer School: Simon Michael, Dir; courses offered, Painting.

SAN ANTONIO

INCARNATE WORD COLLEGE,* Division of Art, 4301 Broadway,
78209. Tel: (512) 826-3292 Exten. 56
Bill Reily, Head; 2 FT, 2 PT instr. Estab. 1881; den; D & E; co-ed;
ent. req. HS dipl, ent. exam; 4 yr; degree, B.A; schol; 18 SC, 5 LC;
enrl. D 183, E 28, maj. 27. Tui. $32 per sem. hr; campus res. $938.

Art Education	History of Art & Archaeology
Ceramics	Painting
Drawing	Teacher Training
Graphic Arts	

OUR LADY OF THE LAKE COLLEGE, Department of Art, 411 S.W.
24th St, 78285. Tel: (512) 434-6711
Sister M. Tharsilla Fuchs, Chmn; 1 FT, 2 PT instr. Den; D & E;
ent. req. HS dipl; 4 yr; degree, B.A.(with art maj); schol; 11 SC,
3 LC, GC 9 sem. hr. by arrangement; enrl. maj. 34, grad. and undergrad. 1800. Tui. $53 per sem. hr. undergrad. cr, art lab. fee $5
per three sem. hr. cr; campus res. $535-$635 per sem.

Art Appreciation	History of Modern Art
Art History Survey	Houseplanning & Interior
Art In Education	Decoration
Art Study Tour	Painting I and II
Costume Design	Practicum in Creative Art

Design I and II	Problems
Drawing	Sculpture
Figure Drawing	

ST. MARY'S UNIVERSITY OF SAN ANTONIO, Department of
Fine Arts, 2700 Cincinnati Ave, 78284. Tel: (512) 433-2311
Louis Reile, S.M, Dir; 6 FT, 3 PT instr. Estab. 1852; den; D & E;
ent. req. HS dipl, ent. exam; 4-5 yrs; degree, B.A; schol; 10 SC,
20 LC; enrl. D 60, maj. 58. Tui. $46 per sem. hr, $10 lab fee per
course; campus res. $165-250.

Aesthetics	History of Art & Archaeology
Art Education	Lettering
Ceramics	Painting
Cinema-Arts	Photography
Drafting	Sculpture
Drawing	Teacher Training
Graphic Design	Theatre Arts

Adult hobby classes vary from sem; tui. $25; enrl. 75-100.
Summer School: Louis Reile, S.M. Dir; courses offered vary.

SAN ANTONIO ART INSTITUTE, P.O. Box 6092, 78209.
Tel: (512) 822-1212; Ceramic Studio 826-9791
Alden H. Waitt, Pres. and Chmn; 5 FT instr. Estab. 1939; pub;
D & E; no ent. req; non-credit; schol; 17 SC, 2 LC. No campus res.

Art Appreciation	Life Drawing
Art History	Painting
Ceramics	Sculpture
Design	Sketching
Graphics	
Children's Summer Workshop.	

SAN ANTONIO COLLEGE, Art Department, 1300 San Pedro Ave,
78284. Tel: (512) 734-7311 Exten. 226
Prof. James Wogstad, Chmn; 11 FT, 3 PT instr. Estab. 1955;
pub; D & E; ent. req. HS dipl, ent. exam; 2 yr; degrees, A.A, A.S;
schol; 32 SC, 3 LC; enrl. D 1000-1300, E 250-450. Tui. $92 per
sem, Tex. res; no campus res.

Advertising Design	Industrial Design
Architecture	Jewelry
Art Education	Lettering
Display	Painting
Drawing	Photography
History of Art & Archaeology	Sculpture
Illustration	

TRINITY UNIVERSITY, Art Department, 715 Stadium Dr, 78284.
Tel: (512) 736-7216
William A. Bristow, Chmn; 7 FT, 5 PT instr. Estab. 1869; pvt;
D & E; ent. req. HS dipl, ent. exam, CEEB, SAT; 4 yrs; degree,
B.A. in Art; schol; 38 SC, 13 LC; total enrl. D & E 1358, maj. approx.
75. Tui. $2250 per yr, $90 per cr. hr; campus res. $1290.

Advertising Design	Graphic Design
Art Education	History of Art & Archaeology
Ceramics	Illustration
Commercial Art	Painting
Drawing	Sculpture
Fashion Arts	Teacher Training
Graphic Arts	

Summer School: William A. Bristow, Dir; regular courses,
reduced schedule; tui. $90 per sem. hr. for term of 5 wk. beginning
June 2 & July 10; 1973 enrl. approx. 145.

SAN MARCOS

SOUTHWEST TEXAS STATE UNIVERSITY, Department of Art,
78666. Tel: (512) 245-2184
C. J. Suckle, Chmn; 17 FT instr. Estab. 1903; pub; D & E; ent. req.
HS dipl, ACT; 4 yrs; degrees, B.S. in Educ, B.S. in Commercial Art,
B.A. in Art; schol; 34 SC, 4 LC, 4 GC; enrl. E 80, maj. 400, total art
2100. Tui. $284 per yr; campus res. $506.

Advertising Design	History of Art & Archaeology
Art Education	Illustration
Ceramics	Jewelry
Commercial Art	Lettering
Drafting	Painting
Drawing	Sculpture
Graphic Arts	Teacher Training
Graphic Design	Textile Design

Summer School: C. J. Suckle, Chmn; tui. $118 for term of 5½ wk.
beginning June & July; 1974 enrl. 355.

Drawing	Painting
Design	Watercolor

SEQUIN

TEXAS LUTHERAN COLLEGE, Department of Art, 78155.
  Tel: (512) 379-4161 Exten. 58
Elmer P. Petersen, Chmn; 2 FT instr. Estab. 1961; den; D; ent.
req. HS dipl; 4 yr; degree, B.A.(Art); 18 SC, 3 LC; enrl. 1000, maj.
23. Tui, room, board and fees, $2750, $980 per sem, $780 Jan.
Interim; campus res.

Art Education	Painting
Ceramics	Sculpture
Drawing	Teacher Training
History of Art	

Workshops on photography, stained glass, metal jewelry, welding,
etc. offered for ½ cr.
  Summer School: Courses offered are changed each summer; tui.
$56 per cr. hr.

SHERMAN

AUSTIN COLLEGE, Department of Art, 75090.
  Tel: (214) 892-9101 Exten. 218
Dr. Carl R. Neidhardt, Chmn; 3 FT, 1 PT instr. Estab. coll. 1849;
pvt; D; co-ed; ent. req. ent. exam, top 50% of grad. class; 4 yr; degree, B.A.; schol; 12 SC, 3 LC, many independent and directed study
courses; enrl. D 1200, maj. 75. Tui. $3600 incl. campus res. $1200.

Advertising Design	History of Art
Art Education	Jewelry
Ceramics	Painting
Drawing	Photography
Graphic Arts	Sculpture
Graphic Design	Teacher Training

Summer School: Dr. Carl R. Neidhardt, Chmn; courses variable,
Summer 1970 Art Fundamentals and Art History; tui. $170 per
course for term of 6 wk. beginning June 4; 1969 enrl. 140.

TEXARKANA

TEXARKANA COLLEGE, Art Department, 75501.
  Tel: (214) 838-4541
William R. Caver, Chmn; 2 FT, 2 PT instr. Estab. 1927; pub;
D & E; ent. req. HS dipl, ent. exam; 2 yr; degree, A.A; schol; 8 SC,
7 LC; enrl. D 260, E 100, maj. 55. Tui. $230 per yr, $115 per sem;
no campus res.

Art Education	History of Art
Ceramics	Painting
Drafting	Sculpture
Drawing	Teacher Training
Elementary Design	Weaving

Adult hobby class, ceramics; tui. $35; enrl. 30.
  Summer School: William R. Caver, Chmn; tui. $50 for term of
6 wk. beginning May 31.

Art Education	Drawing
Ceramics	Painting
Design	

WACO

BAYLOR UNIVERSITY, Department of Art, 76703.
  Tel: (817) 772-1867
J. B. Smith, Chmn; 6 FT, 2 PT instr. Estab. 1845; den; ent. req.
HS grad, upper half of grad. class; 4-5 yr; degrees, A.B, B.F.A;
schol; 32 SC, 7 LC; enrl. maj. 150. Tui. $1200 per yr, room and
board $900.

Advertising Design	History of Art
Ceramics	Printmaking
Crafts	Teacher Education
Drawing & Painting	

Summer School: J. B. Smith, Chmn; tui. $40 per sem. hr. for
6 or 12 wk. beginning June 3; enrl. 75.

WHARTON

WHARTON COUNTY JUNIOR COLLEGE, Department of Art, 911
  Boling Highway, 77488. Tel: (713) 532-4560
Phil Blue, Chmn; 2 FT, 1 PT instr. Estab. 1948; pub; D & E; ent.
req. HS dipl; 60 hr; degrees, A.A, A.A.S; schol; 11 SC; enrl.
D 720, E 25, maj. 30. Tui. in- and out-of-district $4 per sem. hr;
out-of-state $40 per sem. hr, foreign students $14 per sem. hr.

Art Appreciation	Ceramics
Art History	Painting
Beginning & Advanced Design	Sculpture
Beginning & Advanced Drawing	

Summer School: Dr. Ora E. Roades, Dir.

UTAH

CEDAR CITY

SOUTHERN UTAH STATE COLLEGE, Department of Art, 84720.
  Tel: (801) 586-9481
Thomas A. Leek, Chmn; 4 FT, 2 PT instr. Estab. 1897; pub; D & E;
co-ed; ent. req. HS dipl, ent. exam; 4 yr; degrees, B.A, B.S; schol;
29 SC, 6 LC; enrl. D 300, E 80, maj. 60, minors 45. Tui. $276; cam-
pus res. $800.

Advertising Design	History of Art & Archaeology
Art Education	Illustration
Ceramics	Lettering
Commercial Art	Painting
Drawing	Sculpture
Graphic Arts	Teacher Training
Graphic Design	

Summer School (Special Programs): Tui. $90 for term of 8 wk.
beginning June 15.

Art History	Drawing
Ceramics	Painting

LOGAN

UTAH STATE UNIVERSITY, College of Humanities and Arts, 84322.
  Tel: (801) 752-4100
Estab. 1889; pub; 4 yr; degrees; schol. Tui. & reg. $161.50, non-res.
$392.50.

  Department of Landscape Architecture, Exten. 7346
Richard Toth, Head; 6 FT, 4 PT instr. Enrl. 155.

  Department of Art, Exten. 7538
Ray W. Hellberg, Head; 12 FT, 2 PT instr. Degrees, B.A, B.F.A,
M.A, M.F.A; enrl. 280.

Advertising Design	Painting
Art Education	Photography
Art History	Printmaking
Ceramics	Sculpture & Metalsmithing
Drawing	Textile Design
Illustration	

OGDEN

WEBER STATE COLLEGE, Art Department, 3750 Harrison Blvd,
  84403. Tel: (801) 399-5941 Exten. 462
Peter L. Koenig, Chmn; 8 FT instr. Estab. 1889; pub; D & E; ent.
req. HS dipl, ent. exam, ACT; 2-4 yr; degrees, A.A, A.S, B.A, M.A;
schol; 38 SC, 5 LC; enrl. D 2953, E 451, maj. 200. Tui. res. $465,
non-res. $951; res. $155, non-res. $317 per quarter; PT $39 per cr.
hr; campus res. $155 per quarter.

Advertising Design	Illustration
Art Appreciation	Jewelry
Art Education	Lettering
Ceramics	Painting (Oil & Watercolor)
Commercial Art	Perspective
Design & Color	Photography
Drawing (incl. Anatomy)	Sculpture
Graphic Arts	Teacher Training
Graphic Design	2 & 3-D Design
History of Art & Archaeology	

Adult hobby classes, ceramics, jewelry design; tui. $15-$35 plus lab
fees; enrl. approx. 480.
  Summer School: Dr. Richard O. Ulibarri, Dir; tui. $39 per cr.
hr. for term of 8 wks, beginning June; 1975 enrl. 3890.

PROVO

BRIGHAM YOUNG UNIVERSITY, College of Fine Arts, Department
  of Art and Design, 84602. Tel: (801) 374-1211 Exten. 4266
Lael J. Woodbury, Dean; W. Douglas Stout, Chmn; 25 FT, 16 PT
instr. Estab. 1875; pvt; D & E; ent. req. HS grad; 4-5 yr; degrees
B.A, B.F.A, M.A, M.F.A; schol, fel, assistantships; enrl. maj. 530,
others 2790. Tui. $350-$400 per sem.

Art Education	Graphic Design
Art History	Industrial Design
Ceramics C	Painting
Commercial Art	Printmaking
Crafts	Sculpture

Spring and Summer Terms: 6 weeks each.

ST. GEORGE

DIXIE COLLEGE, Art Department, 255 S. 700 E, 84770.
  Tel: (801) 673-4811 Exten. 297
Gerald Olson, Coordinator; 2 FT, 1 PT instr. Pub; D & E; 2 yr;

A.S, A.A; school; 27 SC, 3 LC; enrl. D 525, E 50, maj. 25. Tui. res. $365 per yr, $127 per quarter full-time, non-res. $725 per yr, $247 per quarter.

Advertising Design	Handicrafts
Architecture	History of Art & Archaeology
Art Education	Illustration
Ceramics	Jewelry
Commercial Art	Painting
Costume Design & Construction	Photography
Drafting	Sculpture
Drawing	Stage Design
Fashion Arts	Teacher Training
Graphic Arts	Textile Design
Graphic Design	Theatre Arts

Summer School: Dr. George Rampton, Dir; Basic Drawing & Design; tui. $10 per cr. hr. for term of 6 wks, beginning June 8; enrl. 200.

SALT LAKE CITY

UNIVERSITY OF UTAH, College of Fine Arts, Department of Art, 84112. Tel: (801) 581-8678
Edward D. Maryon, Dean; Robert S. Olpin, Acting Chmn; 20 FT, 8 PT instr. Estab. 1882; State Univ; D & E; ent. req. portfolio, portfolio and references for grad. students; 4 yr; degrees, B.A, B.F.A, M.A, M.F.A; 83 SC, 40 LC, grad. maj. SC 19, grad. maj. LC 10; enrl. D 20,000, maj. 450. Tui. $175 per quarter, non-res. $445.

Art	Film Making
Art History	

WESTMINSTER COLLEGE, Department of Art, 1840 S. 13th E, 84105. Tel: (801) 484-7651 Exten. 66
Don Doxey, Head; 2 FT, 5 PT instr. Estab. 1875; pvt; D; ent. req. HS dipl, ent. exam, acceptable HS grade point average; 4 yr; degrees, B.S, B.A; school; 25 SC, 2 LC; enrl. D 900-1000, maj. 25. Tui. $1300 per yr; campus res. approx. $550.

Art Education	Photography
Ceramics	Printmaking
Drawing	Sculpture
History of Art & Archaeology	Teacher Training
Jewelry	Weaving
Painting	

VERMONT

BENNINGTON

BENNINGTON COLLEGE, 05201. Tel: (802) 442-5401
Gail Thain Parker, Pres; 70 FT instr. Estab. 1932; pvt; co-ed; 4 yr; degrees, A.B, M.A; school. Tui. $6280 incl. campus res.

Architecture	History of Art
Ceramics	Painting
Drawing	Photography
Graphic Arts	Sculpture

BURLINGTON

UNIVERSITY OF VERMONT, College of Arts & Sciences, Department of Art, 05401. Tel: (802) 655-2014
Richard Janson, Chmn; 16 instr. Pub; D & E; 4 yr; degrees, B.A, B.S; enrl. 650. Tui. $1100, non-res. $2930.

Art Education	Fine Metal Crafts
Art History	Painting
Ceramics	Photography
Design	Printmaking
Drawing	Sculpture

Summer School: John Bushey, Dir; 8 wks, beginning May 30-Aug. 13; tui. $35 per cr. hr, non-res. $48; incl. University of Vermont-Shelburne Museum program in American Art, Design & History.

CASTLETON

CASTLETON STATE COLLEGE, Art Department, 05735. Tel: (802) 468-5611
Robert D. Robinson, Chmn; 4 FT instr. Estab. 1787; pub; D & E; ent. req. HS dipl, ent. exam, ACT or SAT; 4 yr; degrees, B.S, B.A; 12 SC, 3 LC, 1 GC; enrl. D 1300, E 300, maj. 25, grad. 10. Tui. res. $620, non-res. $1950; campus res. $1320.

Advertising Design	History of Art
Art Education	Lettering
Ceramics	Photography
Costume Design & Construction	Sculpture
Drawing	Stage Design

Graphic Arts	Teacher Training
Graphic Design	Theatre Arts
Handicrafts	

Summer School: Dr. Walter Reuling, Dir; courses offered: crafts, printmaking.

JOHNSON

JOHNSON STATE COLLEGE, Division of Humanities, 05656. Tel: (802) 635-2356 Exten. 221
John Duffy, Chmn. Div. Humanities; 5 FT, 2 PT instr. Pub; D & E; ent. req. HS dipl; 4 yr; degree B.A; school, Vermont res. only; 19 SC, 4 LC; enrl. D 400. Tui. $962; campus res. $1200.

Aesthetics	History of Art & Archaeology
Art Education	Painting
Ceramics	Photography
Drawing	Sculpture
Graphic Arts	Teacher Training

MIDDLEBURY

✣MIDDLEBURY COLLEGE, Department of Art, Johnson Building, 05753. Tel: (802) 388-2762
Robert F. Reiff, Chmn; 6 FT, 1 PT instr. Estab. 1942; pvt; D; ent. req. exam and cert; degree, A.B; 8 SC, 14 LC; enrl. maj. 15, others 350. Tui. incl. campus res. $4250.

Art History	Printmaking
Design	Sculpture
Drawing & Painting	

POULTNEY

GREEN MOUNTAIN COLLEGE,* Department of Art, 05764. Tel: (802) 287-9305
Raymond A. Withey, Pres; 2 FT instr. Estab. 1834; pvt; W; 2 yr; degree, A.A; 8 SC, 3 LC; enrl. maj. 63.

Advertising Design	Lettering
Display	Painting
Drawing	

STOWE

WRIGHT SCHOOL OF ART, 05672. Tel: (802) 253-4305
Stanley Marc Wright, Dir; 2 FT instr. Estab. 1949; 5 SC, 4 LC; enrl. 50. Tui. $40 per wk, Children's classes 4 Sat. AM $5 per lesson, June 15 to Sept. 15.
Drawing & Painting

VIRGINIA

BLACKSBURG

VIRGINIA POLYTECHNIC INSTITUTE AND STATE UNIVERSITY, College of Arts and Sciences, 24061. Tel: (703) 951-5421
William C. Havard, Dean; Dean Carter, Head Dept. Art; 8 FT, 2 PT instr. Estab. 1969; pub; 4 yr; degree, B.A; 17 SC, 7 LC. Tui. $657, non-res. $1287.

BRISTOL

SULLINS COLLEGE, Art Department, 24201. Tel: (703) 669-6112
Guy H. Benson, Chmn; 1 FT, 4 PT instr. Estab. 1870; pvt; D; W; ent. req. HS grad; 2 yr; degree, A.F.A; school; 12 SC, 1 LC; enrl. maj. 30, others 15. Tui. $3650 over-all incl. room and board.

Advanced Painting	Interior Design
Beginning Design	Jewelry
Beginning Drawing & Painting	Photography
Ceramics	Sculpture
History of Art	Set Design
Independent Studio Study	Weaving

VIRGINIA INTERMONT COLLEGE, Department of Art, 24201. Tel: (703) 669-6101
Tedd Blevins, Coordinator Dept. Art; 3 FT instr. Estab. 1884; den; D; ent. req. HS dipl; 4 yr; degrees B.A.(Art), B.A.(Art Educ); school; 24 SC, 5 LC; enrl. D 195, maj. 31. Tui. $1850, $45 per hr. for less than full-time; campus res. $1350.

Art Education	History of Art & Archaeology
Ceramics	Lettering
Commercial Art	Painting
Costume Design & Construction	Photography
Drawing	Sculpture
Graphic Arts	Teacher Training

BUENA VISTA

SOUTHERN SEMINARY JUNIOR COLLEGE,* 24416.
Tel. (703) 261-6181
Roscoe L. Strickland, Jr, Pres; LeRoy U. Rudasill, Jr, Head; 2 FT instr. Estab. 1867; pvt; D; W; ent. req. SAT and HS grad, evidence of ability to do the work; 2 yr; degrees, A.A, A.S; 7 SC, 1 LC; enrl. 300. Tui. and campus res. $3230.

Costume	Illustration
Design	Interior Decoration
Drawing & Painting	Sculpture
Fashion Illustration	Teacher Training (kindergarten
Graphics	art only)
Handicrafts	

CHARLOTTESVILLE

UNIVERSITY OF VIRGINIA, Department of Art, Fayerweather Hall, 22903. Tel: (703) 924-3057
Frederick Hartt, Chmn; 18 FT instr. Estab. 1951; pub; co-ed; ent. req. HS grad; 4 yr; degrees, B.A, M.A, Ph.D. in Art History; grad. fel; 13 SC, 58 LC; enrl. 1500. Tui. $622, non-res. $1447.

Design	History of Art
Drawing	Painting
Experimental Art	Sculpture
Graphics	Stained Glass

Summer School: Frederick Hartt, Chmn.

FARMVILLE

LONGWOOD COLLEGE, Art Department, 23901.
Tel: (804) 392-9359
Barbara L. Bishop, Chmn; 9 FT, 1 PT instr. Estab. 1839; pub; D; co-ed; ent. req. HS grad; 4 yr; degrees B.S, B.A; schol; 32 SC, 10 LC, 1 GC; enrl. art courses 700 per sem, coll. enrl. 2200. Tui. D $705, with room and board $2085, non-res. $2535.

Art Education	Jewelry & Metals
Art History & Appreciation	Painting
Ceramics	Photography
General Crafts	Printmaking & Graphic Design
Drawing & Composition	Sculpture
Enamels	Weaving
Filmmaking	

Children's classes, one per sem; tui. fee $10; enrl. 20.
Summer School: Workshops and studio.

FREDERICKSBURG

MARY WASHINGTON COLLEGE,* Art Department, Melchers Hall, 22401. Tel: (703) 373-7250 Exten. 368
Pauline G. King, Chmn; 10 FT, 1 PT instr. Estab. 1911; pub; D & E; co-ed; ent. req. HS grad, coll. board ent. exam; 4 yr; degrees, B.A, B.S, art history and studio art maj; enrl. 600 per sem, 14 SC maj, 26 LC maj. (art history).

History & Theory of Art

American Art	Oriental Art
Classical & Near Eastern	Renaissance
Connoisseurship (Use of Sur-	17th & 18th Century Art
rounding Museums)	Special Studies (Early Christian,
Independent Study	Byzantine, Decorative Arts,
Medieval	Graphics, Specific Artists, etc)
19th & 20th Century Art	

Studio Art

Basic Design	Painting
Ceramics	Printmaking
Drawing	Sculpture
Independent Study	Special Studies

HAMPTON

HAMPTON INSTITUTE,* Art Department, 23368.
Tel: (703) 723-6581 Exten. 406
Douglas Reynolds, Chmn; 7 FT, 2 PT instr. Estab. 1869; pvt; D; co-ed; ent. req. HS grad; 4 yr; degrees B.A, B.S, M.A. in Art Educ. and Fine Arts, B.F.A; schol; 22 SC, 7 LC, 9 GC; enrl. maj. 53, others 300, 5 grad. Tui. $2500; campus res.

Advanced Commercial Art	Motalwork & Jewelry
Ceramics	Painting (incl. fresco)
Design	Photography
Egg Tempora	Teacher Training
History of Art	

Summer School: Dr. Edward Kollman, Dir; tui. $25 per sem. hr. plus $22 fees.

Advanced Workshop in	Commercial Art
Ceramics	Design
Art Education Methods	Drawing and Composition

Art Methods for the Elem-	Graphics
entary School	Motalwork & Jewelry
Basic Design	Painting
Ceramics	Understanding the Arts

HARRISONBURG

MADISON COLLEGE, Art Department, Main at Grace St, 22801.
Tel: (703) 433-6216
Dr. Joh David Diller, Head; 16 FT instr. Estab. 1908; pub; D & E; enr. req. HS dipl, class standing and test scores; 4 yr; degrees, B.A, B.S, B.F.A, M.A; schol. to grad. asst; 30 SC, 12 LC, 17 GC; enrl. D 2400, E 75, maj. 210, grad. 22. Tui. $672 per yr, non-res. $1172, PT $16 per cr. hr; campus res. $1265.

Advertising Design	Illustration
Aesthetics	Interior Design
Art Education	Jewelry
Ceramics	Painting
Drawing	Photography
Graphic Arts	Sculpture
Graphic Design	Teacher Training
Handicrafts	Textile Design
History of Art & Archaeology	

Adult hobby classes, painting, audit or cr; tui. $48.
Summer School: John David Diller, Chmn; res. tui. $16 per cr. hr. undergrad, $25 grad. for term of 8 wks, beginning June 14; one three wk. session offered in May.

Art Appreciation	Painting
Art Criticism	Printmaking
Art Education	Sculpture
Art History	Weaving & Textile Design
Ceramics	

HOLLINS

HOLLINS COLLEGE, Division of Fine Arts, Department of Art, 24020. Tel: (703) 362-6000
Prof. W. L. Whitwell, Chmn; 5 FT, 2 PT instr. Dept. estab. 1936; pvt; W; 4 yr; degree B.A; schol; 12 SC, 16 LC (history); enrl. maj. 50, others 200. Tui. incl. room and board $4600; campus res.

Design	History of Art
Drawing	Painting
Graphics	Photography

LEXINGTON

WASHINGTON AND LEE UNIVERSITY, Department of Art, 24450.
Dr. Gérard Maurice Doyon, Chmn; 4 FT, 2 PT instr. Estab. 1742; pvt; D; M; ent. req. HS dipl, ent. exam, SAT; 4 yrs; degree, B.A; schol; 9 SC, 14 LC; enrl. D 31, maj. 31. Tui. $2300 per yr; campus res. $2000.

Aesthetics	Museum Staff Training
Architecture	Painting
Drafting	Sculpture
Drawing	Stage Design
Graphic Arts	Theatre Arts
History of Art & Archaeology	

Art in Mexico, 6 wk. at the Instituto Allende, Mexico, Art in Taiwan, 6 wk. in China; Art of the Classical World, 6 wk. in Europe.

LYNCHBURG

LYNCHBURG COLLEGE, Division of Fine Arts, Department of Art, 24501. Tel: (804) 845-9071 Exten. 295
Dr. Robert C. Hailey, Chmn. Div. Fine Arts; W. Donald Evans, Chmn. Dept Art; 4 FT instr. Estab. 1903; den; ent. req. HS grad, coll. board exam, English achievement test and others; degrees, B.A, B.S, M.S, M.Educ; 8 SC, 5 LC.

Art Appreciation	Drawing
Art for Communications	History of Art
Art for Elementary &	Painting
Secondary Teachers	Photography
Art Fundamentals	Printmaking
Ceramics	Sculpture
Crafts	

RANDOLPH-MACON WOMAN'S COLLEGE, Department of Art, 24503. Tel: (804) 846-7392 Exten. 366
Elliott R. Twery, Chmn; 3-4 FT instr. Estab. 1891; pvt; D; W; 4 yr; degree B.A; schol; 18 SC, 15 LC; enrl. maj. 35, others 305. Tui. and campus res. $3950.

American Painting	Printmaking I & II
Filmmaking	Sculpture & Ceramics

NORFOLK

NORFOLK STATE COLLEGE, Department of Fine Arts, 2401
    Corprew Ave, 23504. Tel: (804) 623-8844
Dr. James F. Wise, Chmn; 9 FT, 2 PT instr. Estab. 1950; state; D;
co-ed; ent. req. HS dipl; 4 yr; degree B.A; schol; 27 SC, 5 LC; enrl.
D 150, maj. 150. Tui. $464; campus res. room $530 per yr.(food not
included) plus fees.

Advertising Design	Handicrafts
Art Education	History of Art
Ceramics	Lettering
Commercial Art	Painting
Drawing	Photography
Graphic Arts	Sculpture
Graphic Design	Teacher Training

Classes consist of laboratory and lecture.
    Summer School: Dr. Roy A. Woods, Dean Academic Affairs;
workshops and courses vary from summer to summer; tui. $18 per
sem. hr. for term of 6 wks, beginning June 17.

OLD DOMINION UNIVERSITY, Art Department, Hampton Blvd, 23508.
    Tel: (804) 489-6213
Evelyn Gay Dreyer, Chairperson; 13 FT, 7 PT instr. Pub; D & E;
ent. req. exam; 4 yr; degrees B.A, B.A.(Art History), B.F.A; schol;
38 SC, 10 LC, 4 GC; enrl. D 204, E 52, maj. 156, students 3. Tui.
$576.

Art Education	Museum Staff Training
Ceramics	Painting
Drawing	Photography
Graphic Arts	Sculpture
Graphic Design	Teacher Training
Handicrafts	Textile Design
History of Art & Archaeology	Weaving
Jewelry	

VIRGINIA WESLEYAN COLLEGE, Art Department, Wesleyan Dr,
    23502. Tel: (703) 464-6291
Barclay Sheaks, Head; 1 FT, 3 PT instr. Estab. 1966; pvt; D & E;
ent. req. HS dipl, college boards; 4 yr; degree, B.A; schol; 6 SC,
1LC; enrl. total 650. Tui. $1500; campus res. $1000.

Art Education	Painting
Ceramics	Sculpture
Crafts	Teacher Training
Drawing	

PETERSBURG

VIRGINIA STATE COLLEGE, Department of Fine Arts, 23803.
    Tel: (804) 526-5111
Dr. A. D. Macklin, Chmn; 5 FT instr. Estab. 1883; Art Dept. 1935;
pub; D & E; ent. req. HS grad; 4 yr; degrees. Tui. $738, non-res.
$1198; board & room $764-$809. Summer School.

Art Education	History of Art
Ceramics	Jewelry
Crafts	Painting
Design	Printmaking
Drawing	Sculpture

Adult evening classes (no cr), batik, printmaking, macramé, painting,
jewelry, ceramics.

RADFORD

RADFORD COLLEGE, Art Department, Powell Hall, 24142.
    Tel: (703) 731-5475
Dr. G. Lynn Gordon, Chmn; 8 FT instr. Estab. 1913; pub; D & E;
W; ent. req. HS dipl, SAT; 4 yr; degrees, B.S.(Art Educ), B.A.(Art),
M.S.(Art), M.A; schol; 43 SC, 13 LC, 15 GC; enrl. 5200. Tui. $1971,
out-of-state $2421, $20 per sem. hr; campus res. included in tui.

Advertising	Lettering
Art Education	Painting
Art Supervision	Printmaking
Ceramics	Raku
Drawing	Sculpture
Enameling	Stitchery
Fiber Techniques	Teacher Training
Graphic Arts	Textile Design
History of Art	Watercolor
Jewelry	Weaving

    Summer School: Dr. G. Lynn Gordon, Chmn; full curriculum
offered.

RICHMOND

UNIVERSITY OF RICHMOND, Art Department, Modlin Fine Arts
    Bldg, 23173. Tel: (804) 285-6246
Dr. Charles W. Johnson, Jr, Chmn; 3 FT, 2 PT instr. Pvt; D & E;
co-ed; ent. req. HS dipl, coll. board; 4 yr; degrees B.A, B.S; 31 SC,

13 LC, 1 GC; enrl. D 300, E 20 (grad). Tui. $2200; campus res.
$3200 for res. (exclusive of special charges).

Aesthetics	Graphic Design
Art Education	History of Art & Archaeology
Ceramics	Painting
Costume Design & Construction	Sculpture
Design	Stage Design
Drawing	Teacher Training
Graphic Arts	Theatre Arts

Painting and drawing class for adults.
    Summer School: Dr. Max Graeber, Dean.

VIRGINIA COMMONWEALTH UNIVERSITY, School of the Arts,
    325 N. Harrison St, 23284. Tel: (804) 770-7261
Dr. Herbert J. Burgart, Dean; 139 FT, 53 PT instr. Estab. 1838;
pub; D & E; co-ed; ent. req. portfolio; degrees B.F.A, B.M.(4 yr),
M.F.A, M.A, MM, M.A.E, M.M.E.(2 yr); schol, grad. assistantships, fel; enrl. Arts School FT 2130, Univ. 17,500. Tui. undergrad. $650, grad. $650; non-res. $1300, grad. $930; art fees approx.
$100 per yr. per sem. cr.

Applied Music	Jewelry
Art Education	Music Education
Art History	Music History & Theory
Ceramics	Painting & Printmaking
Communication Arts & Design	Photography
Fabric Design	Sacred Music
Fashion Design	Sculpture
Furniture Design	Speech
Interior Design	Theatre

Children's art classes, full summer school offerings.

STAUNTON

MARY BALDWIN COLLEGE,* Art Department, 24401.
    Tel: (703) 885-0811
Ulysse Desportes, Chmn; 3 FT instr. Estab. 1872; den; D & E;
W (predominantly); ent. req. HS cert; 3-4 yr.(124 academic credits);
degree, A.B; schol; 10 SC, 18 LC; enrl. D 130, E 50. Tui. $3900
comprehensive, day students $2175.

SWEET BRIAR

SWEET BRIAR COLLEGE, Art History Department, 24595.
    Tel: (703) 381-5451
Aileen H. Laing, Chmn; 3 FT instr. Estab. 1906; pvt; W; 4 yr;
degree A.B; schol; 13 SC, 15 LC; enrl. maj. 26, others 265. Tui.
$4300 comprehensive fee; campus res.
History & Criticism of Art

    Art Studio Department.
Loren Oliver, Chmn.

WILLIAMSBURG

✠COLLEGE OF WILLIAM AND MARY, Department of Fine Arts,
    23185. Tel: (804) 229-3000 Exten. 385
Richard K. Newman, Chmn; 8 FT, 2 PT instr. Estab. 1937; pub; 4
yr; degree, B.A; schol; 15 SC, 21 LC; enrl. maj. 75. Tui. $378 per
sem, out-of-state $963.

Architecture	History of Art
Basic Design	Painting
Ceramics	Sculpture
Drawing	Watercolor
Graphics	

    Summer School: Paul Clem, Dir; two 5 wk. sessions beginning
June 15.

WASHINGTON

BELLEVUE

BELLEVUE COMMUNITY COLLEGE, Art Department, 98007.
    Tel: (206) 641-2358
Robert Purser, Chmn; 2 FT, 2-3 PT instr. Estab. 1966; pub; D & E;
no ent. req; 2 yr; degree, A.A; 15 SC, 5 LC; total enrl. 3400, art
enrl. 300, maj. 60. Tui. $83 quarterly; no campus res.

Drawing	Photography
Graphic Design	Sculpture
History of Art & Archaeology	Textile Design
Painting	

Adult hobby classes, ceramics, design, drawing, jewelry, painting,
photography, sculpture; tui. $8.30 per contact hr. wk; enrl. 600.

BELLINGHAM

WESTERN WASHINGTON STATE COLLEGE, Art Department, 00005.
Tel: (206) 676-3660
Dr. Thomas Schlotterback, Chmn; 15 FT instr. Estab. 1899; pub;
4 yr; degrees, B.A, B.A.Educ, M.Educ; schol; 50 SC, 20 LC; enrl.
art 1500, coll. 8800. Tui. $165 per quarter, non-res. $453; campus
res.
Arts & Science
Graduate Teacher Education
Teacher Education
Summer School: Two terms of 9 wk. or 3 and 6 wk.

BREMERTON

OLYMPIC COMMUNITY COLLEGE, Division of Languages and Arts,
16th and Chester, 98310. Tel: (206) 478-4866
Dr. Robert J. Dietz, Chmn; 4 FT, 4 PT art instr. Estab. 1946; pub;
D & E; ent. req. HS dipl; 2 yr; degree, A.A; schol; 33 SC, 3 LC;
enrl. D 300, E 150, maj. 50. Tui. $249 per yr, $83 per quarter; no
campus res.

Ceramics	Lettering
Drawing	Painting
History of Art & Archaeology	Photography
Jewelry	Sculpture

Adult hobby classes, recreational painting, ceramics, jewelry.

CHENEY

EASTERN WASHINGTON STATE COLLEGE, Department of Art,
99004. Tel: (509) 359-2493
Gregory W. Hawkins, Chmn; 12 FT, 3 PT instr. Estab. 1890; pub;
D & E; ent. req. HS dipl, ent. exam; 4 yr; degrees, B.A, B.A.(Educ),
M.Ed, M.A.(Community Coll. Teaching); schol; 11 SC, 13 LC, 8 GC;
enrl. D 700, maj. 132, grad. students 10. Tui. $495 per yr, non-res.
$1359; campus res. $876.

Applied Design	Jewelry
Art Education	Museum Staff Training
Ceramics	Painting
Drawing	Photography
Graphic Arts	Sculpture
Graphic Design	Teacher Training
History of Art & Archaeology	Textile Design

Summer School: Gregory W. Hawkins, Chmn; same courses as
regular yr; tui. $165 for term of 8 wk. beginning June 13; 1973
enrl. 265.

ELLENSBURG

CENTRAL WASHINGTON STATE COLLEGE, Department of Art,
98926. Tel: (509) 963-2665
George Stillman, Chmn; 17 FT instr. Estab. 1891; pub; D; ent.
req. GPA 2; 4-5 yr; degrees, B.A, M.A, M.Ed; five grad. assistantships; enrl. maj. 300, others 4500. Tui. $17 per quarter hr;
campus res.

Art Education	Jewelry
Commercial Art	Painting
Crafts	Photography
Design	Pottery
Drawing	Print
History of Art	Sculpture

Summer School: Dean Dave Dillard, Dir; 9 wk. session.

MOSES LAKE

BIG BEND COMMUNITY COLLEGE, Art Department, Hwy. 17 &
Nelson Rd, 98837. Tel: (509) 765-7821
Stephen Tse, Head; 1 FT, 2 PT instr. Estab. 1961; pub; D & E; ent.
req. HS dipl; 2 yr; degree, A.A; 18 SC, 1 LC. Tui. $249 per yr, FT
mo. $83, PT $22.70 per cr. hr; campus res. $980. Summer School.

Ceramics	History of Art & Archaeology
Drawing	Lettering
Graphic Design	Painting

MOUNT VERNON

SKAGIT VALLEY COLLEGE, Department of Art, 2405 College Way,
98273. Tel: (206) 424-1031
Orville K. Chatt, Chmn; 2 FT, 6 PT instr. Estab. 1926; pub; D & E;
open door ent; 2 yr; degree, A.A; schol; 32 SC, 1 LC; enrl. D 1300,
E 3200, maj. 50. Tui. $83 per quarter, non-res. $227 per quarter;
no campus res.

Art Appreciation	Painting
Ceramics	Photography
Crafts	Printmaking

Design	Sculpture
Drawing	Stained Glass
Jewelry	

PULLMAN

WASHINGTON STATE UNIVERSITY, Fine Arts Department, 99163.
Tel: (509) 335-8686
Richard Thornton, Chmn; 13 FT, 3 PT instr. Estab. 1892; pub;
D & E; degrees, B.A, M.F.A; schol. and fel; 45 SC, 12 LC, 26 GC;
enrl. maj. 250, others 2100, E 60. Tui. $282, non-res. $790.50.

Fine Arts	Photography
Glass	Teacher Training (with School
Graphic Design	of Education)
Jewelry	

Summer School: Richard Thornton, Dir; $20 per cr. hr. for 2
wk. workshops beginning June 17; enrl. 200.

SEATTLE

BURNLEY SCHOOL OF PROFESSIONAL ART, 905 E. Pine St, 98122.
Tel: (206) 322-0596
Jess Cauthorn, Dir; 5 FT, 9 PT instr. Estab. 1946; pvt; ent. req. HS
grad. and portfolio; 3 yr; prof. dipl. issued; schol; enrl. 150. Tui.
$950 per yr.

Advertising Design	Lettering & Type
Advertising Illustration	Package & Display
Art Direction	Production Procedures (all media)
Dimensional Design	Retail Art
Layout	

CORNISH SCHOOL OF ALLIED ARTS, 710 E. Roy, 98102.
Tel: (206) 323-1400
Melvin Strauss, Pres; Francis Murphy, Chmn. Fine Arts; Dallas
Zeiger, Chmn. Design; 4 FT, 20 PT instr. Estab. 1914; pvt; D & E;
ent. req. HS dipl, portfolio, personal interview for applicant for FT
courses only; 4 yr; degrees, B.F.A, dipl; schol. and financial aide
available; 44 SC, 7 LC; enrl. PT 84, maj. 102. Tui. $650 per sem,
PT $55 per cr. hr; no campus res.

Allied Arts	Jewelry
Ceramics	Metalwork
Color Theory	Packaging (Design)
Design	Painting
Drafting	Paste Up & Production (Design)
Drawing	Photography
Fibre Art/Weaving (Design)	Printmaking
Furniture Design	Rendering (Design)
Graphic Arts (Design)	Sculpture
History of Art & Archaeology	Structural Systems (Design)
History of Design	Video
Illustration	Watercolor
Interior Design	

Adult continuing education, drawing, metalwork, jewelry, woodcut,
sculpture, painting, raku, ceramics, photography, tempera, video,
clay sculpture, papermaking, brushmaking; tui. $55 per cr. hr;
enrl. 84. Children's classes, painting, drawing, block printing,
collage, mobiles, sculpture, illustration; tui. $44-$64; enrl. 22.
Summer School: Tui. $55 per cr. hr, children's classes
$48-$75; enrl. 87.

Acrylics	Metalwork
Children's Art	Model Building (Design)
Clay	Painting (Mixed Media)
Design Theory	Rendering (Design)
Drawing	Sculpture
Jewelry	

SEATTLE CENTRAL COMMUNITY COLLEGE, 1718 Broadway,
98122.
Estab. 1970; pub; D & E; ent. req. HS dipl, ent. exam; 2 yr; schol.
Tui. $250 per yr, FT $29, PT varies; no campus res.

Division of Humanities. Tel: (206) 587-3877
John Doty, Chmn; 3 FT, 2 PT instr. 15 SC, 5 LC; enrl. D 70, E 50;
degree, A.A. Courses in Art History, Fine Arts (Painting), Sculpture.
5 FT, 9 PT instr. 50 SC, 22 LC; enrl. D 200, E 50; degree, A.S.
Courses in Advertising Art, Photography.

SHORELINE COMMUNITY COLLEGE, Humanities Division, 16101
Greenwood Ave. N, 98133. Tel: (206) 546-4741
A. W. McGuire, Chmn; 4 FT, 4-6 PT instr. Estab. 1964; pub; D & E;
ent. req. HS dipl, ent. exam; 2 yr; degree, A.A; 20 SC, 2 LC; approx.
enrl. D 300, E 100, maj. 60, total school 7500, E 5000. Tui. $83
quarterly, non-res. $227 quarterly, PT $8.30 quarter hr; local housing
available.

Advertising Design	Lettering & Poster Design
Basic Design	Painting
Ceramics	Photography

Commercial Art	Sculpture
Drafting	Stage Design
Drawing	Theatre Arts
History of Art & Archaeology	Visual Communications
Illustration	Technology

Summer School: term of 8 wk. beginning June 24.

Ceramics	Painting
Design	Sculpture
Drawing	

UNIVERSITY OF WASHINGTON, School of Art, 98195.
Tel: (206) 543-0970
Spencer Moseley, Dir; John W. Erickson, Assoc. Dir; 58 FT, 11 PT
instr. Estab. 1915; pub; D & E; 1-5 yr; degrees, B.A, B.F.A, M.A,
M.F.A, M.A.T, Ph.D; schol. and fel; 102 SC, 65 LC, 33 GC; enrl.
maj. 1086. Tui. res. $564, non-res. $1581.

Art Education	Interior Design
Art History	Metal Design
Ceramic Art	Painting & Drawing
General Art	Printmaking
Graphic Design	Sculpture
Industrial Design	

Summer School: Marion E. Marts, Dir; tui. $188 for 9 wk, June
18-Aug. 17.

SPOKANE

FORT WRIGHT COLLEGE, Department of Art, W. 4000 Randolph Rd,
99204.
Sister Paula Turnbull, Chmn; 7 FT instr. Den; D & E; ent. req. HS
dipl. or ent. exam; 4 yr; degrees, B.S.(Art), B.F.A; schol; 25 SC,
4 LC; enrl. D 54, E 18, maj. 36. Tui. $810 per sem, $55 per sem.
hr; campus res. $1000.

Art Education	Metalsmithing
Design	Painting
Drawing	Photography
Exhibition	Sculpture
Graphic Arts	Teacher Training
Jewelry Making	Theatre Arts
History of Art & Archaeology	

Summer School: Sister Paula Turnbull, Chmn; tui. $35 per sem.
hr. for term of 6 wk. beginning June 18.

Drawing	Painting
Graphics	Sculpture

GONZAGA UNIVERSITY, School of Arts and Sciences, Department of
Art, Boone Ave, 99258.
Robert Gilmore, Chmn; 3 FT, 3 PT instr. Estab. 1962; pvt; D & E;
ent. req. HS dipl; 4 yr; degrees, B.A, grad. cert. in art; 20 SC,
5 LC, 12 GC; enrl. D 250 incl. maj. 50, grad. 8, others 80. Tui.
$2000; campus res. $700.

Art Education	Painting
Ceramics	Printmaking
Commercial Art	Sculpture
Drawing	Teacher Training
History of Art & Archaeology	

Summer School: Bud Hazel, Dir; tui. $40 per cr. hr. for term of
6 wk. beginning June 16, 1976.

Ceramics	Printmaking
Drawing	20th Century Art History
Painting	

SPOKANE FALLS COMMUNITY COLLEGE, Creative Art Department, W. 3410 Fort George Wright Dr, 99204.
Donald N. Nepean, Chmn; 23 FT, 8 PT instr. Estab. 1959; pub;
D & E; ent. req. ent. exam; 2 yr; degrees, A.A, A.S; schol; SC;
enrl. D 600, E 200. Tui. $270 per yr, FT mo. $90, PT $8.30 per
cr; no campus res.

Advertising Design	Illustration
Architecture	Interior Design
Art Education	Jewelry
Ceramics	Lettering
Commercial Art	Painting
Display Design	Photography
Drafting	Sculpture
Drawing	Textile Design
Fashion Arts	Visual Media Technician
Graphic Arts	

Adult hobby classes, batik, weaving, leaded glass, lapidary.
Summer School: Lowell Jacobs, Dir; course offered, Photography; tui. $83 for term of 11 wk. beginning June 11.

WHITWORTH COLLEGE, Art Department, 99251.
Tel: (509) 489-3550 Exten. 331
J. R. Larson, Chmn; 3 FT, 3 PT instr. Estab. 1890; den; D & E;
ent. req. HS dipl, SAT scores; 4 yr; degrees, B.A, M.A; schol. and

teaching assistantships; 27 SC, 4 LC, 10 GC; enrl. D 300 each term,
E 60, maj. 35, grad. 10. Tui. $2475 per yr; campus res. $684-713
Fall Term, $516-$537 Spring Term.

Aesthetics	Lettering
Art Education	Museum Staff Training
Ceramics	Painting
Drawing	Sculpture
Graphic Arts	Teacher Training
History of Art & Archaeology	Textile Design
Jewelry	

Summer School: Dr. Alvin Quall, Dir; tui. $110-$120 per course
for 2, 4 or 6 wk. beginning May 20 - Aug. 15; enrl. 80.

Ceramics	Painting
Crafts	Textiles
Elementary Art Methods	

TACOMA

PACIFIC LUTHERAN UNIVERSITY, Art Department, 98447.
Tel: (206) 531-6900 Exten. 392
David T. Keyes, Chmn; 8 FT, 2 PT instr. Estab. 1890; pvt; D; ent.
req. HS dipl, coll. board exam, ACT, or Washington Pre-Coll. Test;
4 yr; degrees, B.A, B.F.A: B.A.Ed; schol; 20 SC, 12 LC; enrl. 1000.
Tui. $226 per course, $66.50 per sem. cr. hr; campus res. $1035.

Art Education	Graphic Design
Ceramics	History of Art & Archaeology
Cinematography	Illustration
Commercial Art	Painting
Drawing	Photography
Film Animation	Sculpture
Glassblowing	Teacher Training
Graphic Arts	Textile Design

Summer School: Dr. Richard Moe, Dir; tui. $54 per sem. hr.
for 2 terms of 4 wk. beginning mid-June and mid-July; enrl. 100.

Bronze Casting Workshop	Raku Workshop
Film Arts	Textiles

UNIVERSITY OF PUGET SOUND,* Art Department, 1500 N. Warner
St, 98416. Tel: (206) 759-3521
Dr. Ronald Fields, Chmn, 11 FT, 5 PT instr. Estab. 1935; don; D & E;
co-ed; ent. req. HS grad; 4 yr; degrees, B.A, M.A, M.F.A; 41 SC, 11
LC, 23 GC, 177 undergrad. Tui. $1025 per sem, $2050 per yr; $1000
room and board, $110 other fees.

Art History	Jewelry
Ceramics	Lettering
Composition & Design	Painting
Drawing	Sculpture
Graphic Arts	Teacher Training

Summer School: Dean Gibbs, Dir; 9 wk. beginning June 15.

WALLA WALLA

WALLA WALLA COMMUNITY COLLEGE, 500 Tausick Way, 99362.
Tel: (509) 527-4295
L. T. Renz, Dir. Acad. Div; 3 PT instr. Estab. 1967; pub; D & E;
ent. req. HS dipl; 2 yr; degrees, A.A; 3 SC, 1 LC. Tui. $250 per yr;
no campus res.

Art Education	Drawing
Ceramics	Painting

Adult hobby classes, tole painting; tui. $25.

WHITMAN COLLEGE,* Art Department, Boyer Ave, 99362.
Tel: (509) 529-5100
Richard J. Rasmussen, Chmn; 3 FT, 1 PT instr. Pvt; D; ent. req.
HS dipl, ent. exam; 4 yrs; degree, B.A; 15 SC, 8 LC; enrl. D 225,
maj. 10.

Aesthetics	History of Art & Archaeology
Art Education	Painting
Ceramics	Sculpture
Drawing	Stage Design

WENATCHEE

WENATCHEE VALLEY COLLEGE,* Department of Art, 5th St,
98801. Tel: (509) 663-5126
Robert Graves, Instr; 3 FT, 4 PT instr. Estab. 1939; pub; D & E;
co-ed; no ent. req; 2 yr; schol; enrl. D 1100, E 500. Tui. $210.

Ceramics	Jewelry
Commercial Art	Lettering
Drafting	Painting
Drawing	Photography
Graphic Arts	Sculpture
History of Art & Archaeology	Stage Design

Children's classes, art and painting; tui. $9 per cr. hr; enrl. 50.
Summer School: Ed Hill, Dir; basic courses offered; tui. $9 per
cr. hr. for term of 6 wk. beginning June; 1969 enrl. 200.

WEST VIRGINIA

ATHENS

CONCORD COLLEGE, Art Department, 24712.
Tel: (304) 384-3115 Exten. 348
M. R. Coiner, Chmn; 4 FT instr. Coll. estab. 1872, dept. 1921; pub; D & E; ent. req. HS dipl, GED; 4 yr; degrees, A.B, B.S.Educ; 30 SC, 5 LC; enrl. maj. 198. Tui. $153, non-res. $603, PT $22 per sem. hr; campus res. room $327, board $323.

Advertising Design	History of Art & Archaeology
Aesthetics	Illustration
Art Education	Jewelry
Ceramics	Lettering
Commercial Art	Painting
Drawing	Sculpture
Graphic Arts	Teacher Training
Graphic Design	Theatre Arts

Drawing and painting offered for organized groups.
Summer School: J. Arthur Butcher, Chmn.

BETHANY

BETHANY COLLEGE, Art Department, 26032.
Tel: (304) 829-7541
Walter L. Kornowski, Chmn; 2 FT, 1 PT instr. Estab. 1840; pvt; D (some arranged E classes); ent. req. SAT or ACT, transcript, personal profile, 15 or more units of coll-preparatory work; 4 yr; degree, B.A; schol; 15 SC, 16 LC; enrl. D 275, maj. 35. Tui. $2875 plus fees; campus res. room $495, board $700.

Advertising Design	Illustration
Aesthetics	Jewelry
Art Education	Lettering
Ceramics	Painting
Commercial Art	Photography
Drawing	Sculpture
Graphic Arts	Stage Design
Graphic Design	Teacher Training
History of Art & Archaeology	Theatre Arts

BUCKHANNON

WEST VIRGINIA WESLEYAN COLLEGE, Department of Fine Arts, 26201. Tel: (304) 473-8181
William B. Oldaker, Head; 4 FT instr. Estab. 1890; den; ent. req. HS grad; 4 yr; degree, B.A; schol; enrl. maj. 40, others 650.

Art Appreciation	Drawing & Painting
Art History	Printmaking
Ceramics	Sculpture
Crafts	Teacher Training
Design	Watercolor

Summer School: Regular summer sessions and Art Institute for teachers. For information apply to Registrar.

CHARLESTON

MORRIS HARVEY COLLEGE, Art Department, 2500 MacCorkle Ave, 25304. Tel: (304) 346-9471
Henry C. Keeling, Head; 3 FT instr. Estab. 1888; pvt; D & E; ent. req. usual coll. res; 4 yr; degree; 16 SC, 3 LC; enrl. maj. 58, others 600. Tui. $30 per cr. hr, non-res. fee $300.

Advanced Studio	Design
Art Appreciation	Painting
Art Education	Printmaking
Art History	Sculpture
Ceramics	

Summer School: Henry C. Keeling, Head; tui. $30 per cr. hr, 10 wk. in 2 terms; 1st term June 12, 2nd term July 17; enrl. 100 each term.

ELKINS

DAVIS AND ELKINS COLLEGE, Department of Art, 26241.
Tel: (304) 636-3439 Exten. 51
Jesse F. Reed, Chmn; 1 FT, 2 PT instr. Den; D; ent. req. HS dipl; 4 yr; degree, B.A; schol; 15 SC, 5 LC; enrl. maj. 12. Tui. $2850 per yr; campus res. $1300.

Art Education	History of Art
Ceramics	Painting
Drawing	Sculpture
Graphic Arts	Teacher Training

Special summer workshop in mountain crafts.
Adult hobby classes; enrl. 90.
Summer School: Dr. Margaret Goddin, Dir; 2, 4 and 6 wk. terms beginning July; 1975 enrl. 200.

Basketry	Pottery
Caning	Weaving

GLENVILLE

GLENVILLE STATE COLLEGE, Department of Art, 26351.
Tel: (304) 462-7361 Exten. 243, 244
Charles C. Scott, Head; 3 FT, 1 PT instr. Estab. 1872; pub; D & E; no ent. req. 2-4 yr; degrees, A.A, A.B; total enrl. 1350, art D 168, E 50. Tui. $137 per sem, non-res. $587; campus res. Two-Yr. Craft Prog.

Ceramics	Heritage Crafts
Design	Lapidary
Drawing	Painting

Summer School: William K. Simmons, Dean; courses offered, Art Education, Drawing, Painting; tui. $29 per 3 hr.

HUNTINGTON

MARSHALL UNIVERSITY, Department of Art, 16th St. and Third Ave, 25701. Tel: (304) 696-6760
June Q. Kilgore, Chmn; 9 FT instr. Estab. 1903; pub; ent. req. HS grad; 4 yr; degrees, A.B, M.A, M.S.(Art Educ, Studio); enrl. maj. incl. grad. 275. Total reg. fee $165.50 per sem, non-res. $640.50; campus res.

Art Education	Graphic Processes
Ceramics	History of Art
Design	Painting
Drawing	Sculpture

Summer School: Two 5 wk. terms; tui. $67.10 for 6 sem. hr, non-res. $304.70.

INSTITUTE

WEST VIRGINIA STATE COLLEGE, Art Department, 25112.
Tel: (304) 766-3196
Della Brown Taylor, Acting Chmn; 5 FT instr. D & E; ent. req. HS dipl; 4 yr; degrees, B.S.Ed.(Art), B.A.(Art); schol; 26 SC, 11 LC. Tui. $50 per yr, non-res. $350; campus res. $1050.52.

Art Education	Painting
Ceramics	Photography
Commercial Art	Sculpture
Drawing	Stage Design
Graphic Arts	Teacher Training
History of Art	Textile Design
Jewelry	Theatre Arts

Children's college, tui. $10 per 10 wk. course.
Summer School: Provost Acad. Affairs, Dir; courses offered are flexible; tui. non-res. $58; two 5 wk. terms; enrl. approx. 50.

MONTGOMERY

WEST VIRGINIA INSTITUTE OF TECHNOLOGY, Fine and Applied Arts Department, 25136. Tel: (304) 442-9581
Arthur Ray Pierce, Head. Estab. 1896; pub; ent. req. HS grad; 2-4 yr; degrees, A.S, B.A, B.S; schol; total enrl. 2750. Tui. $50 per yr, non-res. $300.

Art Appreciation	Design
Ceramics	Painting

MORGANTOWN

WEST VIRGINIA UNIVERSITY, Division of Art, Creative Arts Center, 26506. Tel: (304) 293-3140
Urban Couch, Chmn; 11 FT, 1 PT instr. Estab. 1939; pub; ent. req. HS grad; 4 yr; degrees, B.A, B.F.A, M.A, M.F.A; schol. and assistantships; 27 SC, 7 LC, 16 GC; enrl. maj. 250, others 1000. Tui. $186 per sem, non-res. $676; campus res. Summer School.

Art Appreciation	History of Art
Basic Design	Painting
Ceramics	Sculpture
Drawing	Teacher Training
Graphic Design	

SHEPHERDSTOWN

SHEPHERD COLLEGE, Art Department, 25443.
Tel: (304) 876-2511 Exten. 294
Dr. R. L. Jones, Jr, Chmn; 4 FT, 2 PT instr. Estab. 1872; pub; D; ent. req. HS dipl; 4 yr; degrees, B.S, B.A, B.A.Educ; 16 SC, 7 LC; enrl. maj. 80. Tui. $234; campus res. $780.

Aesthetic Criticism	Graphic Arts & Printmaking
Applied Design	History of Art
Art Education	Jewelry
Ceramics	Lettering
Commercial Art	Painting
Design	Sculpture
Drawing	Teacher Training
General Crafts	

Summer School: Dr. H. Schlossberg, Dir; courses offered on demand; tui. $60 for two 5 wk. sessions beginning June 1.

WEST LIBERTY

WEST LIBERTY STATE COLLEGE, Art Department, 26074.
   Tel: (304) 336-8019
Bernie K. Peace, Chmn; 5 FT, 2 PT instr. Estab. 1837; pub; D & E;
ent. req. ACT test; 4 yr; degrees, A.B, B.S; schol. and fel; SC, LC;
enrl. total 3000. Tui. $250 per yr, non-res. $1000.

Art Education	Filmmaking
Art History	Painting
Ceramics	Photography
Commercial Art	Printmaking
Crafts	Sculpture
Drawing	

   Summer School: Two 5 wk. sessions, June-Aug; tui. $50 per
term, non-res. $208.50; enrl. 1600.

Art Education	Painting
Crafts	Special Education
Drawing	

WISCONSIN

APPLETON

LAWRENCE UNIVERSITY, Department of Art, 54911.
   Tel: (414) 739-3681
E. Dane Purdo, Chmn; 6 FT instr. Estab. 1847; ent. req. HS performance, CEEB scores, recommendation; 4 yr; degree, B.A; 8 SC,
17 LC. Tui. incl. room and board $4440 per 3 term yr.

Art Education	Metalwork
Art History	Painting
Ceramics	Photography
Design	Printmaking
Drawing & Composition	Sculpture

BELOIT

BELOIT COLLEGE, Department of Art, 53511.
   Tel: (608) 365-3391 Exten. 677, 678
Richard W. Olson, Head; 7 FT instr. Estab. 1847; pvt; D & E; ent.
req. top third of class, 3 yr. foreign language, 4 yr. English, 3 yr.
math, 2 yr. lab sciences, SAT or ACT score encouraged but not required; 4 yr. (8 terms modified tri-sem); degrees, B.A, B.S, M.A.T;
14 SC, 10 LC; enrl. maj. 85, gen. coll. enrl. 1525. Tui. $3300 plus
$1280 room and board for two terms.

American Art	Independent Studies
Baroque	Modern Architecture
Ceramics	Modern Art
Design	Painting
Drawing	Photography
Far Eastern Art	Renaissance
Filmmaking	Sculpture
Graphics	Seminar in Art
History of Art I & II	

Children's classes, tui. fall terms only, $5-$10; enrl. 20.
   Summer Session: Part of normal tri-sem. program.

DE PERE

ST. NORBERT COLLEGE, Art Department,
54115.
X. G. Colevechio, Head Division Humanities and Fine Arts; 4 FT
instr. Estab. 1898; pvt den; D; ent. req. HS dipl, ent. exam; 4
yrs; degree, B.A; schol; 19 SC, 5 LC; enrl. D 60, maj. 60. Tui.
$2300 per yr; campus res. $1100.

Art Education	History of Environmental
Ceramics	Aesthetics
Drawing	Jewelry
Filmmaking	Painting
Graphic Arts	Photography
Graphic Design	Sculpture
History of Art	Teacher Training

   Summer School: John Giovannini, Dir; tui. $100 per course for
term of 6 wk. beginning July; 1973 enrl. 85.

Art Education	History of Art
Ceramics	Painting
Drawing	Sculpture

EAU CLAIRE

UNIVERSITY OF WISCONSIN-EAU CLAIRE, Department of Art,
   Park and Garfield Aves, 54701. Tel: (715) 836-3278
Charles Campbell, Acting Chmn; 16 FT, 1 PT instr. Estab. 1916;
pub; D & E; ent. req. HS dipl, ent. exam; 4 yr; degrees, B.A, B.F.A;
schol; 31 SC, 12 LC; enrl. maj. 250. Tui. per yr. $1774, monthly,
full-time $287; campus res. $858.50.

Advertising Design	Metalsmithing
Art Education	Painting
Ceramics	Sculpture
Drawing	Teacher Training
Graphic Arts	Textile Design
Graphic Design	Theatre Arts
History of Art & Archaeology	Weaving

Adult hobby classes, pottery, ceramics
   Summer School: Term of 8 wk. beginning June 11.

Art Appreciation	Painting
Art Education	Pottery
Art History	Weaving
Drawing	

FOND DU LAC

MARIAN COLLEGE OF FOND DU LAC, Department of Art, 45 S.
   National Ave, 54935. Tel: (414) 921-3900
Sister Pascal Lowes, Coordinator of Art Prog; 3 FT instr. Estab.
1935; pvt; D & E; ent. req. HS dipl; 4 yr; degrees, B.A.(Art, Art
Educ), B.S.(Art, Art Educ); 19 SC, 10 LC; enrl. D 327. Tui. $1400
plus fees per yr, $40 per cr; campus res. $1050 per yr.

Aesthetics	Jewelry
Art Education	Lettering
Ceramics	Painting
Drawing	Sculpture
Graphic Arts	Teacher Training
Handicrafts	Textile Design

   Summer School: Workshop of 6 wk. course in 1 or 2 of the above
areas as requested; tui. $40 per cr. for term of 6 wk. beginning
end of June and end of Aug.

GREEN BAY

UNIVERSITY OF WISCONSIN-GREEN BAY, Visual Arts Option,
   College of Creative Communication, 54302.
Thomas J. Tasch, Head; 5 FT, 2 PT instr. Estab. 1970; pub; D & E;
ent. req. HS dipl, ent. exam; 4 yr; degrees, B.S. or B.A; 29 SC, 3
LC; enrl. D 5500.

Aesthetics	Painting
Art Education	Photography
Ceramics	Sculpture
Drawing	Stage Design
Graphic Arts	Teacher Training
Jewelry	Theatre Arts

   Summer School: Various courses offered.

KENOSHA

UNIVERSITY OF WISCONSIN-PARKSIDE, Division of Humanistic
   Studies-Art Discipline, Wood Rd, 53140. Tel: (414) 553-2380
John Murphy, Discipline Coordinator; 5 FT, 1 PT instr. Estab.
1969; pub; D & E; ent. req. HS dipl; degrees, B.A, B.S; schol; 25
SC, 7 LC. Res. tui. $308 per sem, $33 per cr. hr; no campus
res. Summer School.

Aesthetics	History of Art & Archaeology
Art Education	Painting
Ceramics	Photography
Drawing	Sculpture
Graphic Arts	Teacher Training

LA CROSSE

UNIVERSITY OF WISCONSIN-LA CROSSE, Art Department, 1725
State St, 54601. Tel: (608) 784-6050 Exten. 257
Dr. Leslie F. Crocker, Chmn; 9 FT instr. Estab. 1905; pub; D & E;
ent. req. HS dipl; 4 yr; degrees, B.A, B.S; schol; 25 SC, 5 LC; total
fall sem. enrl. 7600. Tui. $332.50, non-res. $1045.50; campus res.
$245, meal plan $293.50 and $252. Summer School.

Art Education	Jewelry
Ceramics	Painting
Drawing	Sculpture
Graphic Arts	Theatre Arts
History of Art & Archaeology	

VITERBO COLLEGE, Department of Art, 815 S. 9th St, 54601.
Tel: (608) 785-3450
Sister Carlene Unser, Chmn. Dept; 4 FT instr. Estab. 1939; pvt;
D; ent. req. ent. exam; 4 yrs; degrees, B.A, B.A. in Art Educ;
26 SC, 14 LC; enrl. maj. 50. Tui. $1690 per yr; PT students, 1-6
sem. hrs. $50 per hr; 7-11 sem. hrs. $65 per hr; campus res.
approx. $1000.

Art Education	Painting
Ceramics	Sculpture
Commercial Art	Stage Design
Costume Design & Construction	Teacher Training
Drawing	Theatre Arts
Graphic Arts	Weaving
History of Art	

MADISON

EDGEWOOD COLLEGE, Art Department, 855 Woodrow St, 53711.
Tel: (608) 257-4861 Exten. 207
John C. Barsness, Chmn; 4 FT instr. Estab. 1941; den; D & E; ent.
req. HS dipl, ent. exam; 4 yr; degrees, B.A, B.S; schol; 10 SC, 3 LC;
enrl. 600, maj. 15. Tui. $1100; campus res. $1000.

Aesthetics	History of Art & Archaeology
Art Education	Painting
Ceramics	Photography
Drawing	Sculpture
Graphic Arts	Teacher Training
Handicrafts	Theatre Arts

Summer School: Course offered, Art Education.

MADISON AREA TECHNICAL COLLEGE, Art Department, 211 N.
Carroll St, 53703.
Charles M. Haycock, Chmn; 12 FT, 31 PT instr. Estab. 1930; pub;
D & E; ent. req. HS dipl. or GED; 2 yr; degree, A.S.(Art); 234 SC,
1100 LC; enrl. D 310, E 900. Tui. $180 per yr; no campus res.

Advertising Design	History of Art
Aesthetics	Illustration
Architecture	Interior Design
Batik	Jewelry
Ceramics	Landscape Architecture
Chair Carving	Leather
Commercial Art	Lettering
Costume Design & Construction	Occupational Therapy
Display	Off-Loom Weaving
Drafting	Painting
Drawing	Photography
Fashion Arts	Rosemaling
Graphic Arts	Textile Design
Graphic Design	

Adult hobby classes, full program above; tui. $35 an hr; enrl. 900.

UNIVERSITY OF WISCONSIN, School of Education, Department of
Art, 6241 Humanities Building, 455 North Park, 53706.
Tel: (608) 262-1660
L. E. Moll, Chmn; 40 FT, 18 PT instr. Estab. 1911; pub; 4 yr;
degrees, B.S.(Art, Art Educ), M.A.(Art, Art Educ), M.F.A.(Art),
Ph.D.(Art Educ); undergrad. schol, grad. schol. and fel; 47 SC,
2 LC, 19 GC; enrl. maj. 850. Tui. res. undergrad. $315 per sem,
grad. $450, non-res. undergrad. $1103, grad. $1428.

Art Education	Photography
Art Metal	Photo-Offset
Ceramics	Relief Printing
Design	Sculpture
Drawing	Serigraphy
Etching	Stage Design & Lighting
Glassblowing	Typography
Lithography	Watercolor
Painting	Woodworking

✤College of Letters and Science, Department of Art History,
Elvehjem Art Center, 800 University Ave, 53706.
Tel: (608) 263-2340
Frank R. Horlbeck, Chmn; 8 FT, 2 PT instr. Univ. estab. 1849,
dept, 1925; pub; D; ent. req. HS dipl; 4 yr; degrees, B.A, M.A,
Ph.D; schol; enrl. 2011, maj. 42, grad. 31. Tui. res. undergrad.
$630, grad. $900, non-res. undergrad. $2206, grad. $2856, PT res.
$56.50 per cr, non-res. $170 per cr.
Architecture
History of Art
Museum Staff Training
Summer Session: Six courses offered; tui. res. undergrad. $26
per cr, grad. $50, non-res. undergrad. $85, grad. $165; term of 8 wk.

School of Family Resources and Consumer Sciences, Environment
and Design Program Area, 234 Home Economics Building, 53706.
Tel: (608) 262-3190, 3191, 2651, 2652
Prof. Emma Jordre, Coordinator; 15 FT, 3 PT instr. Dept. estab.
1903 as part of Dept. of Home Economics; pub; D; ent. req. HS dipl,

ent. exam; 4 yr; degrees, B.S, M.S, Ph.D; schol. and fel; 18 SC, 3 LC,
2 GC; enrl. 850-000 per sem, maj.(Jr. and Sr) 100, grad. 44. Tui.
res. undergrad. $315, grad. $450, non-res. undergrad. $1103, grad.
$1428, PT res. undergrad. $26.50 per cr, grad. $56.50, non-res.
undergrad. $92.50, grad. $179.

Apparel Design	Museum Decorative Arts
Crafts	Textile Design
Costume Design	Textile Science
Interior Design	Textiles & Clothing Retailing
General Textiles & Clothing	

MENOMINIE

✤UNIVERSITY OF WISCONSIN-STOUT, School of Liberal Studies,
Art Department, 54751. Tel: (715) 235-1141
Dr. Orazio Fumagalli, Chmn; 19 FT instr. Estab. 1964; pub; D & E;
co-ed; ent. req. HS dipl; 4 yr; degrees, B.S.Art, B.S.Art Educ; 20 SC,
22 LC; enrl. D 600, maj. 300. Tui. $528 per yr; campus res. $1036.

Aesthetics	History of Art & Archaeology
Art Education	Interior Design
Art Metal	Painting
Ceramics	Sculpture
Drawing	Teacher Training
Graphic Arts	

Children's classes, art, dance and drama; tui. $10; enrl. 70.
Summer School: Dr. Orazio Fumagalli, Dir; tui. $198 for term of
8 wk. beginning June.

Art History	Drawing
Art Metal	Painting
Ceramics	Printmaking
Design	Sculpture

MILWAUKEE

ALVERNO COLLEGE,* Art Department, 3401 S. 39 St, 53215.
Tel: (414) 671-5400, Exten. 255
George Brownlee, Chairperson; 4 FT, 3 PT instr. Estab. 1948; pvt;
D & E; W only in degree program; ent. req. GPA, class rank and
ACT or SAT; 4 yr. (or 128 cr); degree, B.A; schol; 20 SC, 5 LC;
enrl. D 200, E 50, maj. 35. Tui. $1400; campus res. $900.

Art Education	Metal working
Ceramics	Painting
Drawing	Printmaking
Enameling (Cloisonne)	Sculpture
General Crafts	Stage Design
History of Art	Teacher Training
Introduction to Visual Art	Weaving

Summer School: Sister Bernarda Handrup, Dir; Art Education,
Studio Art; tui. $35 per cr, June 18 to August 14.

CARDINAL STRITCH COLLEGE, Department of Art, 6801 N. Yates
Rd, 53217. Tel: (414) 352-5400
Sister Thomasita, Chmn; 4 FT, 8 PT instr. Estab. 1947; den; W; 2
yr; degrees, B.A, B.F.A; schol; accredited by North Central Association of Colleges & Secondary Schools, The University of Wisconsin,
American Association for Colleges of Teacher Education; 31 SC,
7 LC; enrl. art dept. 125. Tui. approx. $775 per sem; campus res,
tui, room and board $1120. Summer School.

Aesthetics	History of Art
Applied Design	Industrial Design
Art Education	Interior Design
Ceramics	Materials Workshop
Chinese Brush Painting	Painting
Commercial Art	Photography
Creative Fibers	Sculpture
Design & Lettering	Stage Design
Drawing & Composition	Textile Design
Graphic Arts	Weaving

Adult hobby classes, ceramics, fibers, graphics, painting.
Children's classes, art; fee $35; enrl. 60.

CONCORDIA COLLEGE, Art Department, 3201 W. Highland, 53209.
Tel: (414) 344-3400
William L. Chander, Chmn; 1 FT instr. Den; D & E; ent. req. HS
dipl; 2 yr; degree, A.A; 7 SC, 1 LC; enrl. D 75, E 25, maj. 10. Tui.
$700 per sem, $45 per cr.

Aesthetics	Painting
Drawing	Sculpture
Handicrafts	Survey of Art
Independent Study	Two-Dimensional Design

Adult hobby classes and continuing education program; tui. $25-$50;
enrl. 10.

LAYTON SCHOOL OF ART AND DESIGN,* 4650 N. Port Washington
Rd, 53212. Tel: (414) 962-0215
Neil Lieberman, Pres; 27 FT, 18 PT instr. Estab. 1920; pvt; D & E;

ent. req. HS dipl. and portfolio presentation; 4 yr; degree, B.F.A; schol; all SC; enrl. 450. Tui. $1300 per yr.

Ceramics	Painting
Glassblowing	Printmaking
Graphic Design	Sculpture
Illustration	Silversmithing
Industrial Design	Weaving
Interior Design	

Summer School: Ralph R. Thomas, Dir; tui. $50; enrl. 50.

Ceramics & Sculpture	Painting
Drawing	Printmaking

MILWAUKEE AREA TECHNICAL COLLEGE, Division of Graphic and Applied Arts, 1015 N. Sixth St, 53203. Tel: (414) 278-6433
A. V. Karpowtiz, Dean; A. J. Gradian, Instructional Chmn. Photography; H. A. Milbrath, Instructional Chmn. Commercial Art; 28 FT, 2 PT instr. Division estab. 1958; pub; D & E; ent. req. HS dipl; 2 yr; degree, A.A; SC, LC; enrl. D 260-340, E 160-170. Tui. (incl. materials and fees) Commercial Art $290 (1st yr), $290 (2nd yr), Photography $335 (1st yr), $550 (2nd yr), Printing and Publishing $285 (1st yr), $225 (2nd yr), Visual Communications $260 (1st yr), $180 (2nd yr), non-res. $37 per cr.

Advertising Design	Illustration
Display Design	Photography
Drawing	Printing & Publishing
Graphic Design	Visual Communications

Adult vocational classes, crafts, commercial art, photography, printing; D & E; tui. $15-$25 per course.

Summer School: Basic courses offered; enrl. limited to 22 per course.

MOUNT MARY COLLEGE, Art Department, 53222.
Tel: (414) 258-4810
Sister Mary Nora Barber, Pres; Sister M. Regine Collins, Head; 5 FT, 7 PT instr. Estab. 1913; den; ent. req. HS grad; W; 4 yr; degree, B.A; 22 SC, 12 LC; enrl. maj. 160. Tui. $1600; campus res. $1150-$1300.

Art Metal	History of Art
Art Therapy	Interior Design
Ceramics	Jewelry
Design	Lettering
Drawing	Living Arts
Fashion Advertising	Materials & Enameling
Fashion Design	Painting
Fashion Drawing	Sculpture
Fiber-Fabric Design	Teacher Training
Film	Textile Design
Graphic Arts	Weaving

Summer School: Sister Patricia Ann, Dir; $50 per cr. hr. for 6 wk. beginning June 15.

UNIVERSITY OF WISCONSIN-MILWAUKEE, School of Fine Arts, Department of Art, 53201. Tel: (414) 963-4200
Howard Schroedter, Chmn; 35 FT, 3 PT instr. Degrees, B.S.(Art), B.S.(Art Educ), B.F.A.(Art), B.F.A.(with Teacher Cert), M.S.(Art), M.S.(Art Educ), M.F.A.(Art), M.F.A.(with Teacher Cert); enrl. approx. 860 art maj. Tui. $250, non-res. $1000.

Art Education	Graphics
Art Metal	Photography
Ceramics	Sculpture
Design	Visual Communication
Drawing & Painting	Weaving

OSHKOSH

UNIVERSITY OF WISCONSIN-OSHKOSH, Department of Art, 54901. Tel: (414) 424-2222
Michael Brandt, Chmn; 25 FT instr. Estab. 1871; pub; D & E; ent. req. HS dipl; 4 yr; degrees, B.A.E, B.S.(Art), B.A; schol. to grad. students; 56 SC, 14 LC, 31 GC; enrl. D 10,500, E 2500, maj. 300, grad. 15, minors 50. Tui. $644 per yr, PT $21.25 per sem. cr, non-res. $1021 per sem; campus res. $440.

Advertising Design	Lettering
Art Education	Museology
Ceramics	Painting
Commercial Art	Photography
Drawing	Sculpture
Graphic Arts	Teacher Training
History of Art & Archaeology	Textile Design
Jewelry	Woodcraft

PLATTEVILLE

UNIVERSITY OF WISCONSIN-PLATTEVILLE, Department of Art, 53818. Tel: (608) 342-1781
Thomas C. Hendrickson, Head; 7 FT instr. Estab. 1866; pub; D &

ent. req. HS dipl, ent. exam; 4 yr; degrees, B.A, B.S; 30 SC, 5 LC, 3 GC; enrl. maj. 105. Tui. $300; campus res. $1200.

Aesthetics	Industrial Design
Architecture	Jewelry
Art Education	Painting
Ceramics	Photography
Drafting	Sculpture
Drawing	Stage Design
Graphic Arts	Teacher Training
History of Art & Archaeology	Theatre Arts

Summer School: Harold Hutchison, Dir; courses total dept. offering; tui. $100 for term of 8 wk. beginning June 15; 1969 enrl. 2200.

RIPON

RIPON COLLEGE, Art Department, 54971.
Tel: (414) 748-8110
Dr. Erwin Breithaupt, Chmn; 3 FT instr. Estab. 1851; pvt; D; ent. req. grad. from accredited secondary school, SAT or ACT is recommended, but not required; 4 yr; degree, A.B; schol. and financial aid; 13 SC, 8 LC; enrl. maj. 20. Tui. $4150 comprehensive fee.

Art History	Multi-Media
Design	Painting
Drawing	Printmaking

RIVER FALLS

UNIVERSITY OF WISCONSIN-RIVER FALLS,* Art Department, 54022. Tel: (715) 425-3266
Patricia Clark, Chairwoman; 11 FT instr. Estab. 1874; pub; D; 4 yr; degree; enrl. maj. 200, others 3800; Tui. $179.08 per quarter, non-res. $560.74. Summer School, same as regular school yr.

Art Education	History of Art
Ceramics	Introduction to Visual Arts
Crafts	Jewelry & Metalcraft
Design	Painting
Drawing	Printmaking
Fibers	Sculpture
Glass Blowing	

STEVENS POINT

UNIVERSITY OF WISCONSIN-STEVENS POINT,* Department of Art, Fine Arts College, 54481. Tel: (715) 346-2669
Henry M. Runke, Chmn; 13 FT, 1 PT instr. Estab. 1894; pub; D & E; ent. req. HS dipl; 4 yrs; degree, B.S; 23 SC, 10 LC, 1 GC; enrl. D 900, E 100, maj. 200. Tui. $259 per sem; campus res. Room $268 per sem, board $255 per sem. plus 4% sales tax.

American Indian	Jewelry
Architecture	Lettering
Art Education	Painting
Ceramics	Printed Textiles
Drawing	Sculpture
Graphic Arts	Teacher Training
Handicrafts	Textile Design
History of Art & Archaeology	Weaving

Summer School: Winthrop Difford, Dir.

SUPERIOR

UNIVERSITY OF WISCONSIN-SUPERIOR, Art Department, 54880. Tel: (715) 392-8101
Dr. Arthur Kruk, Chmn; 10 FT, 1 PT instr. Estab. 1896; pub; D & E; ent. req. HS dipl; 4 yr; degrees, B.S, D.A, D.F.A, M.S, M.A; schol; 60 SC, 14 LC, 30 GC; enrl. total 3100, maj. 178, grad. 32. Tui. undergrad. $337 per sem, grad. $391, non-res. undergrad. $1050, grad. $1090; campus res. room $285-$390, board $355. Summer School.

Advertising Design	Handicrafts
Aesthetics	History of Art & Archaeology
Art Education	Jewelry
Batik	Painting
Ceramics	Photography
Commercial Art	Sculpture
Display	Stage Design
Drawing	Teacher Training
Graphic Arts	Theatre Arts
Graphic Design	Weaving

WHITEWATER

UNIVERSITY OF WISCONSIN-WHITEWATER, 53190.
Tel: (414) 472-1324
Dr. Jack Schoof, Chmn; 18 FT instr. Estab. 1868; pub; D & E; ent. req. HS dipl; 4 yr; degrees, B.A, B.S.(Art, Art Educ, Art History);

41 SC, 18 LC; enrl. D 270, maj. 270. Tui. $675 per yr; campus res. ₵1100.

Advertising Design	History of Art & Archaeology
Aesthetics	Illustration
Art Education	Jewelry
Ceramics	Lettering
Commercial Art	Painting
Drawing	Sculpture
Graphic Arts	Teacher Training
Graphic Design	Textile Design
Handicrafts	Weaving

Summer School: Tui. $50 per cr. for term of 8 wk. beginning June 18.

WYOMING

CASPER

CASPER COLLEGE,* Department of Art, 125 Community Dr, 82601.
W. Ossa, Head; 5 FT, 1 PT instr. Estab. 1945; pub; D; ent. req. HS dipl, ACT; 2 yr; degrees, A.A, A.S, A.A.S; schol; 32 SC, 2 LC; enrl. D 2000, E 1000. Tui. $220 per yr; campus res. $880.

Advertising Design	Graphic Design
Art Education	History of Art & Archaeology
Ceramics	Illustration
Commercial Art	Lettering
Display	Painting
Drafting	Sculpture
Drawing	Textile Design
Graphic Arts	Weaving

CHEYENNE

LARAMIE COUNTY COMMUNITY COLLEGE, Art Department, 1400 E. College Dr, 82001. Tel: (307) 634-5853, Exten. 132
Thomas Neal, Chmn. Div Humanities; 2 FT, 5 PT instr. Estab. 1969; pub; D & E; ent. req. HS dipl, ACT if going for a degree; 2 yr; degrees A.A, A.S, A.A.S; 14 SC, 4 LC; enrl. D 109, E 79. Tui. res. $127.50 per sem, out-of-state $300 per sem; no campus res.

Advertising Design	Jewelry
Art History	Painting
Ceramics	Sculpture
Design Fundamentals	Watercolor
Drawing	

Summer School: Daniel H. Ackermann, Dir; tui. $11 per cr. hr. for term of 8 wks, beginning May 27.

Ceramics	Painting
Drawing	Sculpture
Jewelry	Watercolor

LARAMIE

✤UNIVERSITY OF WYOMING, Department of Art, 82071.
Tel: (307) 766-3269
Herbert W. Gottfried, Acting Head; 8 FT instr. Estab. 1946; pub; 4 yr; degrees B.A, B.S, B.F.A, M.A, M.A.T, M.F.A; 28 SC, 12 LC, 11 GC; enrl. maj. 120. Tui. $205.25, non-res. $688.25

Advertising Design	Sculpture
Art History & Theory	Teacher Training (with College
Painting	of Education)
Printmaking	

Summer School: 4 FT, 2 PT instr; 8 wk. June 7-July 30.

POWELL

NORTHWEST COMMUNITY COLLEGE, Art Department, 82435.
Tel: (307) 754-5151 Exten. 34
John Banks, Asst. Prof; 3 FT, 7 PT instr. Estab. 1946; pub; D & E; 2 yr; degrees A.A, A.T; schol; 18 SC, 1 LC; enrl. D 100, E 175, maj. 22. Tui. res. $260, non-res. $700; campus res. $990.

Advertising Design	Jewelry
Art Education	Lettering
Ceramics	Occupational Therapy
Commercial Art	Painting
Drafting	Photography
Drawing	Sculpture
Graphic Design	Teacher Training
Introduction to General Crafts	Weaving

Adult hobby classes; tui. $33 per sem. hr; enrl. 175.

RIVERTON

CENTRAL WYOMING COLLEGE, Art Center, 82501.
Tel: (307) 856-9291
Willis Patterson, Chmn. Humanities, Head Dept; 1 FT, 3 PT instr.

Estab. 1966; pub; D & E; ent. req. open door policy, grad. req. HS dipl. GED; 2 yr; degrees A.A, A.S; schol; 15 SC, 1 LC; enrl. D 400, E 800, maj. 15, others 20. Tui. $240 per yr.

Advertising Design	Lapidary
Art Appreciation	Painting
Basic Sculpture	Photography
Crafts	Pottery
Design	Printmaking
Drafting	Silversmithing
Drawing	Weaving
Jewelry	

Adult classes: pottery, tole painting, sculpture, acrylic and oil painting, landscape painting, Western sculpture, weaving, silversmithing; tui. $15-$45; enrl. 100.

ROCK SPRINGS

WESTERN WYOMING COLLEGE, Art Department, 82901.
Tel: (307) 382-2121 Exten. 152
Gary Grubb, Head; 2 FT, 4 PT instr. Estab. 1959; pub; D & E; ent. req. HS dipl; 2 yr; degree A.A; schol; 12 SC, 1 LC; enrl. D 125, E 40, maj. 20. Tui. $135; campus res. approx. $700.

Ceramics	Painting
Drawing	Photography
Handicrafts	Sculpture
History of Art & Archaeology	Theatre Arts

Adult hobby classes: Drawing, painting, pottery and crafts; tui. $12; enrl. 100.

SHERIDAN

SHERIDAN COLLEGE, Art Department, 82801.
Tel: (307) 674-4421
Prof. Richard Martinsen, Chmn; 4 FT instr. Estab. 1951; pub; D & E; ent. req. HS grad; 2 yr; degree, A.S, A.A, A.A.S; enrl. maj. 10.

Ceramics	Life Drawing
Design	Painting
Drawing	Sculpture

Adult hobby classes, non-credit.

TORRINGTON

EASTERN WYOMING COLLEGE, Art Department, 3200 West C St, 82240. Tel: (307) 532-4191 Exten. 31
Mrs. Sue Milner, Head; 1 FT, 2 PT instr. Estab. 1948; pub; D & E; ent. req. varied; 2 yr; degrees A.A, A.A.S; schol; 3 SC, 1 LC; enrl. D 40, E 15, maj. 2. Tui. $260, out-of-state $430 per yr; campus res. $1025.

Ceramics	Painting
Drawing	Photography
Graphic Arts	Sculpture
History of Art & Archaeology	

Children's classes: General subjects; 4 wk. in summer; tui. $10; enrl. 25.

AMERICAN SAMOA

PAGO PAGO

AMERICAN SAMOA COMMUNITY COLLEGE, P.O. Box 2609, 96799.
One PT instr. Estab. 1970; pub; D; ent. req. HS dipl, 18 yrs; 2 yr; degrees A.A, A.S; enrl. D 10.
Ceramics

PUERTO RICO

MAYAGUEZ

UNIVERSITY OF PUERTO RICO, MAYAGUEZ, Department of Humanities, 00708. Tel: (809) 832-4040 Exten. 3156/3160
Dr. Luis E. Baco, Assoc. Dir; 7 FT instr. Estab. 1970; pub; D; ent. req. HS dipl; 4 yr; degrees, B.A.(Art Theory), B.A.(Plastic Arts); 67 SC, 8 LC; enrl. 345, maj. 86.
Seminar in Romanesque Art

PONCE

CATHOLIC UNIVERSITY OF PUERTO RICO, Fine Arts Department, 00731. Tel: (809) 844-4150 Exten. 316
Julio Micheli, Head; 4 FT instr. Estab. 1964; den; D; ent. req. HS dipl, ent. exam; 4 yr; degree B.A; schol; 18 SC, 4 LC, 3 GC; enrl.

maj. 30. Tui. $1200 average per yr; $35 per cr. hr. plus fees; campus res. $400.

Advertising Design
Art Education
Ceramics
Drawing
Graphic Design

History of Art & Archaeology
Painting
Printmaking
Teacher Training

Summer School: Julio Rivera, Dir; program varies each yr, two art courses in summer.

SAN GERMAN

INTER-AMERICAN UNIVERSITY OF PUERTO RICO, SAN GERMAN, Art Department, 00753.
Noemi Ruiz, Dir; 5 FT, 5 PT instr. Estab. 1912; pvt; D & E; ent. req. HS dipl, ent. exam; 3 yrs; degree, B.A; schol; 25 SC, 8 LC. Tui. $1010 per yr; campus res. $920.

Art Education
Ceramics
Design in Metals
Drawing
Experimental Design in Native Media
Graphic Arts

Handicrafts
History of Art & Archaeology
Painting
Photography
Sculpture
Teacher Training

Adult hobby classes, pottery.
Summer School: Noemi Ruiz, Dir.

SAN JUAN

ESCUELA DE ARTES PLASTICAS,* Instituto de Cultura Puertorriqueña, Box 4184, 500 Ave. Ponce de León Pda 8, 00905. Tel: (809) 725-1522
Dr. José R. Oliver, Dir; 20 PT instr. Estab. 1966; pub; D; ent. req.

HS dipl, ent. exam; 4 yrs; degree, Bachiller; schol.

Aesthetics
Anatomy
Art Education
Ceramics
Drawing
Graphic Arts
Graphic Design
History of Art & Archaeology
Lettering
Lithography

Mosaic
Mural Painting
Painting
Photography
Sculpture
Stage Design
Teacher Training
Theatre Arts
Vitrales

Summer School: Dr. José R. Oliver, Dir.

Drawing
Escenographic
Painting

Pedagogist
Photography

VIRGIN ISLANDS

ST. CROIX

ST. CROIX SCHOOL OF THE ARTS, INC, P.O. Box 1086, 00820.
Tel: (809) 772-3767
Dorothy F. Raedler, Dir; 12 PT instr. Estab. 1970; pvt; D; ent. req. recommendation; schol; 27 SC; enrl. D 203. Tui. $45 per hr. for a 15 wk. sem, Sat.

Batik
Ceramics
Dance
Drawing
Fashion Arts
Jewelry

Macrame
Needle Crafts
Painting
Sculpture
Silk Screen
Theatre Arts

Canadian Art Schools

ALBERTA

BANFF

BANFF CENTRE SCHOOL OF FINE ARTS, T0L 0C0.
  Tel: (403) 762-3391
Takao Tanabe, Head, Art Div; David Leighton, Dir; 20 PT instr.
Estab. 1933; summer school and winter studio program; ent. req.
Senior matriculation and art school for cr. courses; schol; enrl. Art
Div. 200, others 1200. Tui. $250 for 6 wk, $200 per 12 wk. term
studio program. All media, studio and location in scenic Canadian
Rockies.

CALGARY

ALBERTA COLLEGE OF ART, Division of The Southern Alberta
  Institute of Technology, 1301 16th Ave. N.W, T2M 0L4.
  Tel: (403) 289-6641
K. G. Sturdy, Head; D 47 FT, 9 PT instr. Estab. 1926; pub; ent. req.
Grade 11; 4 yr; dipl; schol; enrl. 600. Tui. $74.

Ceramics	Printmaking
Fabric	Sculpture
Metal	Visual Communications
Painting	Weaving

Art classes for children; fee $25.
Continuing Education Classes:

Applied Design	Life Drawing
Batik	Painting
Ceramics	Painting Workshop
Composition & Painting	Printmaking
Fabric Printing	Puppetry
General Drawing	Sculpture
Jewelry	Weaving
Lettering	

MOUNT ROYAL COLLEGE, 4825 Richard Rd, S.W,
  T3E 6K6.
Richard V. Peterson, Chmn; 6 FT, 8 PT instr. Estab. 1910; pub;
D & E; ent. req. HS dipl; 1-2 yr; dipl; schol; 12 SC, 17 LC. Tui.
$12 per cr. hr.

Architecture	History of Art & Archaeology
Ceramics	Lettering
Display	Painting
Drafting	Photography
Drawing	Sculpture
Graphic Arts	Stage Design
Graphic Design	

UNIVERSITY OF CALGARY, Department of Art, 2920 24th Ave. N.W,
  T2N 1N4. Tel: (403) 284-5252
V. R. Brosz, Head; 28 FT, 7 PT instr. Estab. 1965; pub; D & E; ent.
req. HS dipl; 4 yr; degree B.F.A; schol; 25 SC, 10 LC, 12 GC; enrl. D
167, E 58, all maj. Tui. $225 half-yr, $450 full-yr; campus res.
$1000 per yr.

Art Education	History of Art
Ceramics	Painting
Graphic Arts	Photography
Graphic Design	Sculpture

  Summer School: V. R. Brosz, Dir; tui. $170 per course for 2
terms of 6 wk, May 15-June 4 & July 2-Aug. 16; 1975 enrl. 400.

Art History	Drawing
Ceramics	Graphics
Design	Painting

EDMONTON

UNIVERSITY OF ALBERTA, Department of Art and Design, T6G 2C9.
  Tel: (403) 432-3261
R. A. Davey, Chmn; 26 FT, approx. 10 PT instr. Estab. 1946; pub;
D & E; ent. req. Senior matriculation; 3-4 yr; degrees, B.A. (3 yr),
B.F.A. (4 yr), B.A. (Hons), Art History (4 yr), M.V.A. (2 yr); some
grad. teaching and grad. service assistantships; enrl. all classes
1600. Tui. $459, gen. fees approx. $275.

Drawing & Painting	Printmaking
History of Art	Sculpture
Industrial Design	Topography
Photography	Visual Communications

  Summer School: J. C. T. Clarke, Dir; spring and summer.

LETHBRIDGE

UNIVERSITY OF LETHBRIDGE,* Department of Art.
  Tel: (403) 327-2171
Charles Crane, Chmn; 6 FT, 2 PT instr. Estab. 1967; pub; D & E;
ent. req. HS grad; 4 yr; degree, B.A. in Art; schol; 19 SC, 8 LC;
enrl. D 287, maj. 30. Tui. $200.

Art Education	History of Art & Archaeology
Ceramics	Painting
Drawing	Photography
Graphic Arts	Sculpture

Children's classes, ceramics and painting (Sat. AM).
  Summer School: Larry Weaver, Chmn; tui. $65 per course
for two terms of 3 wk. beginning July 2 and July 27; 1969 enrl. 50
(art).

Art History	Painting
Drawing	Sculpture

RED DEER

RED DEER COLLEGE,* Department of Art and
  Design.
Ian Cook, Chmn. Fine and Performing Art; 4 FT, 4 PT instr.
Estab. 1973; pub; D & E; ent. req. HS dipl, portfolio; 2 yr; dipl. in
art & design; 13 SC, 1 LC; enrl. D FT 40, E PT 60. Tui. $260 per
yr. plus cost of materials; campus res. $1100.

Ceramics	Painting
Commercial Art	Photography
Drawing	Sculpture
Graphic Arts	Stage Design
Graphic Design	Theatre Arts
History of Art & Archaeology	

Adult hobby classes, batik, painting, weaving; tui. $30 per course;
enrl. 80. Children's classes, ceramics, painting; $20 per course;
enrl. 40.
  Summer School: Ian Cook, Dir; courses offered, Introductory
Ceramics, Outdoor Landscape Painting; tui. $30 per course.

BRITISH COLUMBIA

NELSON

SELKIRK COLLEGE, Kootenay School of Art Division, Box 480,
  V1L 5R3. Tel: (604) 352-6601
D. O. MacGregor, Dir; 8 FT instr. Estab. 1960; pub; D & E; ent. req.
HS dipl, ent. exam; 3-4 yr; dipl. B.F.A. & B.Ed. with Concentration
granted through Notre Dame Univ; 23 SC, 6 LC, 5 GC; enrl. D 150, E
40, maj. 2. Tui. $135 per yr, $15 mo.

Advertising Design	History of Art & Archaeology
Applied Design	Illustration
Art Education	Jewelry
Batik	Lettering
Ceramics	Museum Staff Training
Commercial Art	Painting
Display	Photography
Drawing	Sculpture

Enameling	Spinning
Graphic Arts	Teacher Training
Graphic Design	Textile Design
Handicrafts	Weaving

VANCOUVER

UNIVERSITY OF BRITISH COLUMBIA, School of Architecture.
Tel: (604) 228-2779
Robert Macleod, Dir; FT, PT instr. Estab. 1946; pub; 3 yr;
degrees, B.Arch, M.Arch; enrl. 227. Tui. $560.
Architecture

Department of Fine Arts.* Tel: (604) 228-5650
George Knox, Head; 21 FT, 3 PT instr. Estab. 1958; pub; D & E;
4 yr; degrees, B.A, B.F.A, M.A; 7 SC, 40 undergrad. LC, 12 grad.
LC; enrl. 50 in B.F.A. prog, total course 2000. Summer School
courses offered at Vancouver and in Florence.

VANCOUVER CITY COLLEGE, LANGARA, 100 W. 49th St, V5Y 2Z6.
Tel: (604) 324-5511
C. E. Broderick, Chmn; 6 FT, 4 PT instr. Estab. 1970; pub; D & E;
ent. req. HS dipl, portfolio of art work; 2 yr; dipl. in art; schol;
studio & lecture classes; enrl. D 300. Tui. $150 per sem; no campus
res. Summer courses.

Advertising Design	Graphic Design
Ceramics	History of Art & Archaeology
Design	Painting
Display/Interior Design	Photography
Drawing	Printmaking
Fabric Arts	Sculpture

VANCOUVER SCHOOL OF ART,* 249 Dunsmuir St, 3.
Tel: (604) 681-9525
Robin C. Mayor, Prin. Estab. 1925; 4 yr; 2 yr. cert, 4 yr. dipl,
grad studies in variety of disciplines.

Ceramics	Painting
Design Research & Design	Photography
Drawing	Printmaking
Film Animation	Sculpture
Graphic Design (Commercial Art)	

VICTORIA

UNIVERSITY OF VICTORIA, Department of Visual Arts, Box 1700,
V8W 2Y2. Tel: (604) 477-6911
John Dobereiner, Chmn; 8 FT instr. Estab. 1966; pub; D; ent. req.
HS dipl, univ. exam; 4 yr; degree, B.F.A; schol; 16 SC; enrl. D 47,
maj. 47; service courses for faculty of educ. Tui. $428 per yr;
campus res. $1098 for double room; $1195 for single.

Drawing	Photography
Graphic Arts	Sculpture
Painting	

MANITOBA

WINNIPEG

UNIVERSITY OF MANITOBA,* School of Art.
Tel: (204) 474-9303
Donald K. Reichert, Acting Dir; 20 FT, 3 PT instr. Estab. 1950;
pub; D & E; ent. req. dipl. none, degree senior matriculation; degrees, B.F.A.(hons), 4 yr, B.F.A.(gen), 3 yr, dipl. 4 yr; 7 SC, 11
LC; enrl. degree students 220, dipl. students 50. Tui. degree
course $445 per yr, dipl. $345.

Art History	Painting
Ceramics	Printmaking
Drawing	Sculpture
Graphic Design	

Summer School: University Credit Courses.

Faculty of Architecture.* Tel: (204) 474-9286
Roy Sellors, Dean; Peter W. Forster, Asst. to Dean; Carl R. Nelson,
Jr, Head, Dept. Environmental Studies; Kum-Chew Lye, Head, Dept.
Arch; Alexander Rattray, Head, Dept. Landscape Arch; Joan M.
Harland, Head, Dept. Interior Design; V. J. Kostka, Head, Dept.
City Planning; 47 FT, 6 PT, E 2 PT instr. Estab. 1913; pub; ent.
req. for Environmental Studies Senior Matriculation with 60% aver-
age; for Arch. degree of Bach. of Environmental Studies or equiva-
lent; for Interior Design Senior Matriculation or Bach. of Environmental Studies; for Landscape Arch. Bach. of Environmental Studies
or equivalent; Arch. 6 yr; Lands.Arch. (as of 1971) 5 yr; Int. Des. 4
yr; City Planning GC 2 yr; degrees; schol; enrl. Env. Studies 243;
Arch. 127, Int. Des. 268; C.P. GC 44. Tui. $540 (Arch. & Env.
Studies); $440 (Int. Des); $375 (City Planning); campus res.

Environmental Studies (3yr)	Interior Design (4 yr)
Architecture (3 yr. after Env. Studies)	City Planning GC (2 yr)
Landscape Architecture (2 yr. after Env. Studies)	

NEW BRUNSWICK

EDMUNDSTON

COLLEGE SAINT-LOUIS-MAILLET, E3V 2S8.
Tel: (506) 735-8808
Bertille Beaulieu, Head Dept. Arts & Language; 2 FT, 2 PT instr.
Estab. 1968; pvt; D & E; ent. req. HS dipl; 4 yr; degrees B.A.(Fine
Arts); schol; 8 SC, 3 LC; enrl. D 50, E 40, maj. 15. Tui. $550;
campus res. $800.

Ceramics	Macrame
Copper Enamels	Painting
Drawing	Sculpture
History of Art & Archaeology	

Adult hobby classes: Copper enamels & macrame; tui. $25; enrl. 40.
Children's classes: Introduction to fine arts; tui. $25; enrl. 40.
Summer School: Roger Beaulieu, Dir; Ceramics, Drawing,
Sculpture, Painting; tui. $120 for term of 6 wks, beginning July; enrl.
30.

FREDERICTON

NEW BRUNSWICK CRAFT SCHOOL, Hut 3, Woodstock Rd.
Tel: (506) 453-2305, 2331
John Archibald, Dir. Handicrafts; 7 FT instr. Estab. 1946; pub;
D & E; ent. req. residents who have completed Grade 12 or Jr.
matriculation will be given preference; 2 yr.(approx. 35 wk. per
yr); dipl; enrl. 4000 summer school, 10-15 winter season. Studio
fee $200 to res, others $400; approx. $200 for materials first year
students. Extension courses.

Ceramics	Macrame & Guild Loom Weaving
Design	Spinning & Dyeing
Floor Loom Weaving	Textiles
Jewellery	Wood

UNIVERSITY OF NEW BRUNSWICK,* Faculty of Education, Art
Education Section. Tel: (506) 455-8901 Exten. 251
Thomas R. Smith, Head. Univ. enrl. 5000, educ. 200.
Art & Child Development
Art Education for Elementary Teachers
Pottery & Clay Sculpture
Evening Pottery Course.
Children's Sat. AM classes.
Summer School: Course offered, Art for Children.

MONCTON

UNIVERSITE DE MONCTON,* Department of Visual Arts.
Tel: (506) 855-2070
Claude Roussel, Head; 3 FT instr. Estab 1967; pub; D & E; co-ed;
ent. req. HS dipl; 4 yr; degree, B.A.Fine Arts; 7 SC, 3 LC; enrl. D
80, E 40, grad. 10. Tui. $600; campus res. $700.

Aesthetics	Painting
Art Education	Photography
Ceramics	Sculpture
Drawing	Teacher Training
History of Art & Archaeology	

SACKVILLE

MOUNT ALLISON UNIVERSITY, Department of Fine Arts, E0A 3C0.
Tel: (506) 536-2040 Exten. 492
Virgil Hammock, Head; 6 instr. Estab. 1894; 4 yr; degree B.F.A;
SC, LC; enrl. B.F.A. students 60. Tui. $665; campus res. $1205.

Art History	Painting
Design	Photography
Drawing	Printmaking

Adult classes locally and out-of-town under Univ. Exten. Dept.

NOVA SCOTIA

HALIFAX

NOVA SCOTIA COLLEGE OF ART AND DESIGN, 5163 Duke St,
B3J 3J6. Tel: (902) 422-7381
Garry N. Kennedy, Pres; 34 FT, 8 PT instr. Estab. 1887; pvt; ent.
req. Jr. matriculation; 4-5 yr; degrees, B.F.A. (fine art or fine art

and educ), B.Des.(environmental design or communication design), 2 yr. degree, M.F.A. dipl. (fine arts or graphic design); CC, SC, LC, E; enrl. 385 full-time. Summer School.

NOVA SCOTIA TECHNICAL COLLEGE, School of Architecture, P.O. Box 1000, B3J 2X4.
Dr. Peter Manning, Dir; 17 FT, 20 PT instr. Estab. 1961; pvt. with substantial support from Provincial Govt; D; ent. req. satisfactory completion of 2 yrs. at another univ, incl. one yr. univ. math; 4 yr; degrees, B.Arch, M.Arch; schol; 1 SC per term, many LC, 1 GC; enrl. approx. 200, maj. 25. Tui. $325 per term; campus res.

Architecture
Drafting
Drawing
Industrial Design
Lettering
Photography
Adult exten. classes; tui. $65 per course.

ONTARIO

DOWNSVIEW

YORK UNIVERSITY,* Department of Visual Arts, Fine Arts Bldg, 4700 Keele St.
Edward Fort Fry, Chmn; 22 FT, 6 PT instr. Estab. 1969; pub; D & E; ent. req. HS dipl, interview and portfolio evaluation; 4 yrs; degree, Honours B.A.; 26 SC, 17 LC; enrl. D over 400, maj. 400; others approx. 120. Tui. $660 per yr.

Drawing
Graphic Arts
Graphic Design
History of Art & Archaeology
Painting
Photography
Sculpture

GUELPH

UNIVERSITY OF GUELPH, Department of Fine Art, N1G 2W1. Tel: (519) 824-4120 Exten. 2413
Dr. Thomas Tritschler, Chmn. Dept; 13 FT instr. Estab. 1966; pub; D & E; ent. req. HS dipl; 3-4 yr; degree B.A.; schol; 22 SC, 25 LC; enrl. D 2900, maj. 269.

Drawing
Graphic Arts
History of Art & Archaeology
Painting
Sculpture

HAMILTON

McMASTER UNIVERSITY, Department of Art and Art History, L8S 4L8. Tel: (416) 522-9140
P. H. Walton, Chmn; 9 FT, 2 PT instr. Estab. 1934; 3-4 yr; degrees, pass B.A. in studio and in art history, Honours B.A. in studio and in art history; 12 SC, 29 LC; enrl. 85. Tui. $637.50; campus res.

Studio Art Program.
History of Art

KINGSTON

QUEEN'S UNIVERSITY, Department of Art. Tel: (613) 547-6172
Joseph Polzer, Head; 17 FT, 5 PT instr. Estab. 1932; pub; D & E; ent. req. Grade XIII; degrees, B.A. (3 yr), B.A. Hons. (4 yr), B.A.E. (Bachelor of Art Education) (4 yr), M.A. Conservation; 16 SC, 25 LC. University admission and fees apply; campus res. Summer School.

Design
Drawing
History of Art
History of Technique
Painting
Printmaking
Sculpture

LONDON

UNIVERSITY OF WESTERN ONTARIO, Department of Visual Arts, N6A 3K7. Tel: (519) 679-2440
D. deKergommeaux, Acting Chmn; 10 FT, 1 PT instr. Estab. 1967; pub; D & E; co-ed; ent. req. HS dipl, ent. exam, portfolio and interview; 3-4 yr; Honours B.A. in Visual Arts; 11 SC, 15 LC; enrl. maj. 160. Tui. $662; campus res. $1505.

Drawing
History of Art & Archaeology
Museum Staff Training
Painting
Photography
Printmaking
Sculpture
Summer School: Miss A. M. Armitt, Dir; Visual Arts courses; tui. $139.80 for term of 6 wk, beginning July 1; enrl. limited.

OTTAWA

CARLETON UNIVERSITY, Department of Art History, Colonel By Dr. Tel: (613) 231-2700
Dr. D. G. Burnett, Chmn; 5 FT, 3 PT instr. Estab. 1964; D & E; ent. req. HS dipl; 3-4 yr; degrees, B.A. & Honors; schol; 2 SC, 25 LC, 3 GC; enrl. D over 700, maj. 135. Tui. $650 for res; campus res. $1000.

Architecture
History of Art & Archaeology
Museum Staff Training
Adult hobby classes: Ceramics, drawing and painting.
Summer School: Dr. D. G. Burnett, Chmn; 3 Art History courses.

REXDALE

HUMBER COLLEGE OF APPLIED ARTS AND TECHNOLOGY, Creative and Communication Arts Division, Humber College Blvd, M9W 5L7. Tel: (416) 676-1200
Jack Ross, Dean; 53 FT, 24 PT instr. Estab. 1967; pub; D & E; ent. req. HS dipl, mature student status, one year of employment plus 19 yrs. of age; 2 & 3 yr. dipl. courses; no degrees; 300 SC, 75 LC, 6 grad. programs; enrl. grad. students 50, PT students 25. Tui. $285, PT $30-$50 per cr. course; no campus res.

Advertising Design
Architecture
Batik
Ceramics
Commercial Art
Display
Drafting
Drawing
Film/TV Production
Furniture Design
Graphic Arts
Graphic Design
Handicrafts
History of Art & Archaeology
Illustration
Industrial Design
Interior Design
Jewelry
Journalism
Landscape Architecture
Leathercraft
Lettering & Typography
Macrame
Music
Packaging Design
Painting
Photography
Printing Processes
Professional Writing
Radio Broadcasting
Sculpture
Social Dance
Stage Design
Studio Methods
Theatre Arts
Weaving
Wood Crafts
Adult hobby classes: Crochet and batik, with beginning classes in most of the regular courses; tui. $15-$20; enrl. 210.
Children's classes: Beginning arts and crafts, painting, music; tui. $10-$15, enrl. 87.
Summer School: Jack Ross, Dean of Creative Arts; beginning and advanced classes in most of regular courses; tui. $30-$50 for term of 10-16 wks, beginning May and June; 1975 enrl. 540.

SOUTHAMPTON

SOUTHAMPTON ART SCHOOL Southampton, Ont.
Edna Johnson, Dir; 4 PT instr. Estab. 1957; pvt; D, July & Aug; no ent. req; no degrees. Tui. $60 per wk; no campus res.

Art Education
Drawing
Painting

TORONTO

THE GEORGE BROWN COLLEGE OF APPLIED ARTS AND TECHNOLOGY, Box 1015, Station B, M5T 2T9. Tel: (416) 967-1212
H. Greville, Subject Supvr; 9 FT, 10 PT instr. Estab. 1970; pub; D & E part-time only; ent. req. HS dipl, ent. exam; 2-3 yr; dipl. and specialist cert; 20 SC, 4 LC, 5 GC; enrl. D 145, E 90. Tui. $295.

Advertising Design
Commercial Art
Graphic Design
History of Art & Archaeology
Lettering

ONTARIO COLLEGE OF ART,* 100 McCaul St, M5T 1W1. Tel: (416) 366-4977
Clifford C. Pitt, Pres; 87 instr. Estab. 1876; ent req. HS grad; 4 yr. undergrad, 1 yr. grad; enrl. D 750, E 400, grad. 25. Tui $469.

Advertising & Graphic Design
Animation
Art History & Criticism
Ceramics
Communication Design
Corporate Design
Environmental Design
Film & Video
Furniture Design
Illustration
Industrial Design
Interior Design, Space Planning
Jewelry
Packaging
Painting
Photography
Plastics
Print
Product & System Design
Sculpture
Television Art
Textiles
Wood

THREE SCHOOLS, 296 Brunswick Ave, M5S 2M7.
 Tel: (416) 920-8370
John Sime, Pres.

 New School of Art (full-time day school)
Gordon Rayner, Dir; 20 PT instr. Estab. 1962; pvt; D; ent. interview;
1-4 yr. in contemporary visual arts; no degree; enrl. 100. Tui.
$500 1st yr.

 Artists' Workshop (part-time school)
Barbara Wood, Dir; 70 PT instr. Estab. 1951; D & E; enrl. 2000.
Tui. approx. $47.50 per course of 11 wks; children's art classes tui.
$60 for 25 wk. program. Visual and performing arts, crafts, writing.

Acting & Directing	Music
Ceramics	Painting
Dance/Movement/Yoga	Photography
Drawing	Printmaking
Filmmaking	Sculpture
Graphic Design	Textile Arts
Hand Bookbinding	Writing
Illustration	

 New School of Theatre (full-time day school)
James H. Burt, Dir; 7 PT instr. Estab. 1974; D; ent. interview and
audition; enrl. 30. Tui. $685 for the 26 wk. academic yr.

 Hockley Valley School (summer school)
John Sime, Dir; visual and performing arts and crafts, children's art
classes and nursery; tui. approx. $40 per wk. Month of July in the
country. Enrl. 100 per wk. Estab. 1962.

 Other Place (part-time E school)
Barbara Wood, Dir; lecture courses in the arts and allied subjects;
E; 20 PT instr. Estab. 1973. Tui. approx. $37 per course of 10 wk.

TORONTO SCHOOL OF ART, 225 Brunswick Ave, M5S 2M6.
 Tel: (416) 921-3986
Barbara Barrett, Dir-Prin; 13 PT instr. Estab. 1967; pvt; D & E;
no ent. req; 4 yr; no degree; schol; 14 SC, 1 LC; enrl. D 167, E 12,
maj. or special 10, grad. students 12, others 3. Tui. $450 per yr;
no campus res.

Art Composition	Handicrafts
Art Education	History of Art
Batik	Life Drawing & Portraiture
Drawing	Painting
Environmental Design	Sculpture
Graphic Arts	Silk Screen Printing

Children's classes, batik, collage, drawing, painting, screen printing,
weaving; tui. $40 for 12 wk; enrl. 20.

UNIVERSITY OF TORONTO,* Department of Fine Art, Sidney Smith
 Hall, M5S 1A1. Tel: (416) 928-6272
F. E. Winter, Chmn; 17 FT, 1 PT instr. Estab. 1934; pub; 3-4 yr;
degrees; LC, GC. Campus res.
History of Art

 Faculty of Architecture, Urban and Regional Planning and Landscape Architecture, 230 College St. Tel: (416) 928-2573
Thomas Howarth, Dean; 30 FT, 25 PT instr. Estab. 1890; faculty
1967.

 Department of Architecture
Peter Prangnell, Chmn; 20 FT, 12 PT instr. 5 yr; degree; GC; enrl.
250. Tui. $822.

 Department of Urban and Regional Planning
Dr. Alan Waterhouse, Chmn; 6 FT, 8 PT instr. 2 yr; degree GC, 1
yr. dipl GC; enrl 38. Tui. $605.

 Department of Landscape Architecture
Richard A. Strong, Chmn; 4 FT, 5 PT instr. 4 yr; degree; enrl. 72.
Tui. $822.

WINDSOR

UNIVERSITY OF WINDSOR, Fine Arts Department, Huron Church
 Rd. at College. Tel: (519) 253-4232 Exten. 359
Antonio P. Doctor, Chmn; 9 FT, 7 PT instr. Estab. 1960; pub; D & E;
ent. req. HS dipl, grade 13, adult; 3-4 yr; degrees, B.A, Honours B.A,
B.F.A; schol; 22 SC, 18 LC; enrl. D 137, E approx. 110, maj. 192,
others 10. Tui. $650 per yr; campus res. $600 double, $700 single.

Drawing	Printmaking
History of Art & Archaeology	Sculpture
Painting	

 Summer School: Antonio P. Doctor, Head; tui. $125 for studio
courses, $125 for art history for term of 6 wk. beginning July 2; 1973
enrl. 118.

Art Fundamentals	Ceramics
Art History Survey	Intermediate Drawing

Basic Drawing	Printmaking
Beginning Painting	Sculpture

 European Summer Program: Antonio P. Doctor, Head; Intermediate Drawing, Printmaking & Independent Studio Work in Drawing &
Printmaking; tui. $125 per course ($250 for 2), students must take 2
courses, 6 wk. beginning July 7-Aug. 15; enrl. 10.

PRINCE EDWARD ISLAND

CHARLOTTETOWN

HOLLAND COLLEGE, Commercial Design Department, P.O. Box 878,
 Charlottetown, Prince Edward Island, Canada.
 Tel: (902) 892-4191 Exten. 226
Mr. Henry Purdy, Chmn; 2 FT, 2 PT instr. Estab. Sept. 1969; pub;
D & E; co-ed; ent. req. HS dipl, interview; 3 yr; degree, dipl. Com-
mercial Art; schol; enrl. D 40, E 70. Tui. $200 per yr, monthly,
part-time $10.

Advertising Design	Industrial Design
Art Education	Lettering
Commercial Art	Painting
Display	Photography
Drawing	Sculpture
Graphic Arts	Stage Design
Graphic Design	Textile Design
Illustration	

Adult hobby classes, tui. $45 for 60 hr; enrl. 70.

QUEBEC

MONTREAL

McGILL UNIVERSITY,* Department of Fine Arts, 805 Sherbrooke,
 West (2)
W. O. Judkins, Head; 3 FT instr. Estab. 1947; admis. University
School cert, exam or equivalent; 4 yr; B.A. One introductory Studio
Course in Drawing and Painting.
History of Art

 School of Architecture,* 3484 University St.
John Bland, Dir; 2 FT, 8 PT instr. Estab. 1896; ent. exam; 6 yr;
degrees; fel; 12 SC, 7 LC.
Architectural Design
Drawing
History of Art & Architecture

SCHOOL OF ART AND DESIGN, Montreal Museum of Fine Arts,
 3430 Ave. du Musée, H3G 2C7.
Richard S. Halliday, Dean; 28 FT and PT instrs. Estab. 1940; pvt;
D & E; co-ed; ent. req. HS grad, portfolio; 3 yr; dipl. in Visual Arts,
Animation Design and Interior Design.
Continuing Education Evening Courses. Children's Sat. Art Classes.
Enrl. 450.

SIR GEORGE WILLIAMS UNIVERSITY,* Department of Fine Arts,
 1435 Drummond St, 108. Tel: (514) 879-4132
Prof. E. F. Cooke, Chmn; 29 FT and PT instr. D & E; degrees, B.F.A,
B.A, post-B.F.A. dipl. in Art Educ, 1 yr. full-time leading to teaching
cert, M.A. in Art Educ, 1 yr. full-time, M.F.A. in studio or art history,
2 yr. full-time; 5 yr. res. req. for full and part-time students. Non-cr.
E courses in Life Drawing, Painting and Portrait Sculpture, experimental children's art classes (4-16 yr. of age).

Art Education	Graphics
Art History	Music
Crafts	Painting
Design	Photography
Film	Sculpture
Graphic Design	Theatre Arts

UNIVERSITE DU QUEBEC A MONTREAL, FAMILLE DES ARTS,
 Pavillon des Arts, 125 Sherbrooke St. W, 129.
 Tel: (514) 282-7001
Vice-dean. Estab. 1969; 3 yr; ent. req. 2 yr. after HS; degree, Bac-
calauréat spécialisé. Tui. $500 per yr. Programs offered:

Dramatic Arts	Musicotherapy
Environmental Design	Plastic Art (Engraving, Sculpture,
Graphic Design	Painting)
History of Art	Plastic Art Teaching
Music Teaching	

Those programs include courses on:

Aesthetics	Graphic Techniques
Anatomy	Modeling

Architectural Drafting
Ceramic Sculpture
Composition
Design
Drawing
Etching & Engraving
Fresco

Mural Painting
Painting
Perspective
Publicity
Stone & Wood Carving
Teacher Training

QUEBEC

ECOLE DES ARTS VISUELS (School of Visual Arts), Faculté des Arts, Université Laval Cité Universitaire, G1K 7P4. Tel: (418) 656-7631.

Pierre Larochelle, Dir; 27 FT, 16 PT instr. Estab. 1970; pub.(under Université Laval, Québec, PQ); D; co-ed; ent. req. 2 yr. Coll; 3 yr. for Baccalauréat en Arts plastiques or Baccalauréat en Communication graphique plus 1 yr. for cert. in art teaching; enrl. 300. Tui. $510 per yr.

Drawing
Engraving
Film Animation
Graphic Design
Graphics
Illustration
Lithography

Movement
Painting
Photography
Sculpture
Silk Screen
Stained Glass
Tapestry

TROIS RIVIERES

UNIVERSITY OF QUEBEC, TROIS RIVIERES, Fine Arts Section, P.O. Box 500, G9A 5H7. Tel: (819) 376-5330

J. Jacques Besner, Head; 9 FT, 9 PT instr. Estab. 1969; pub; D & E; ent. req, ent. exam. or D.E.C; 3 yr; degree, specialized baccalaureat in fine arts; 12 SC, 8 LC, 28 GC; enrl. D 150, E 100. Tui. $50 per course plus $12.50 for inscription; no campus res.

Aesthetics
Art Administration
Art Education
Basic Design
Ceramics
Drafting
Drawing

Glass
Graphic Arts
History of Art & Archaeology
Painting
Sculpture
Weaving

Adult hobby classes, painting, weaving; enrl. 100.

Summer School: Henri-Georges St-Louis, Dir; tui. $50 per course of 3 wk.

SASKATCHEWAN

REGINA

UNIVERSITY OF SASKATCHEWAN, Regina Campus, Department of Visual Arts, S4S 0A2. Tel: (306) 584-4872

J. C. Nugent, Head; 11 FT instr. Pub; ent. req. HS grad; degrees, 3 yr. B.A.(maj. in Art), 4 yr. B.F.A, 2 yr. M.F.A, 2 yr. Cert; enrl. 200. Tui. $410.

Drawing
Film
Graphics
History of Art

Painting
Pottery
Sculpture

Department of Art Education, Faculty of Education
Tel: (306) 584-4546

Dr. Les Groome, Chmn; 3 FT, 1 PT instr. Estab. 1965; pub; D & E; ent. req. HS dipl, matriculation or degree for maj. in art; 5 yr; degrees, B.Ed, B.A, M.Ed; schol; 6 LC; enrl. D 160, E 20, maj. 10, night teachers in field. Tui. $500, campus res. approx. $800.

Aesthetics
Art Education

Children's classes, Sat; Tui. $10.

Summer School: H. Kindred, Exten. Courses; Dr. Toombs, Dean Educ; tui. $80 for term of 3 to 6 wk, beginning May 1; 1973 enrl. 500-1000.

SASKATOON

UNIVERSITY OF SASKATCHEWAN, Saskatoon Campus, Department of Art, S7N 0W0.

Prof. Don Rogers, Head; 14 FT, 4 PT instr. Estab. 1936; pub; D; co-ed; ent. req. HS grad; 3-6 yr; degrees, B.A.(maj. in Art) 3 yr-15 classes, B.A.Honors, Art History 4 yr-20 classes, B.F.A. 4 yr-20 classes, M.A. in Studio Art 2 yr. grad. program, B.Ed.(maj. in Art) available from Coll. Educ; schol; SC, LC, GC; open studio program; enrl. approx. 850, B.F.A. program 130, grad. 5. Tui. $110 per class, 5 classes per academic yr, 1 class during Intersession and 1 class during summer school.

Art Education
Drawing
History of Western Art
Painting
Photography

Pottery
Printmaking
Sculpture
Survey Studio-Art History
Seminars

Summer School: Emma Lake Campus and Saskatoon Campus; courses change each yr.

Art Schools Abroad

ARGENTINA

BUENOS AIRES

ESCUELA NACIONAL DE BELLAS ARTES 'MANUEL BELGRANO'*
(National School of Fine Arts 'Manuel Belgrano'), Cerrito 1350.
Marta L. De Sagesse, Dir; 120 PT instr. Estab. 1799; pub; D & E;
co-ed; ent. req. ent. exam, 3 yr. secondary school; 4 yr; degree,
Maestro Nacional de Artes Visuales; 13 SC; enrl. D 476, E 276.

Art Education	Engraving
Composition System & Analysis of Works	History of Art
	Painting
Drawing	Sculpture

ESCUELA SUPERIOR DE BELLAS ARTES DE LA NACION ERNESTO
DE LA CARCOVA,* (National Superior School of Fine Arts
Ernesto De La Carcova), Tristan Achaval Rodriguez 1701
Avenida Costanera Sur esquina Brasil). Tel: 31-5144, 31-4419
Jorge E. Lezama, Rector Prof; Ines B. Meseguer, Secy; 24 PT
instr. Estab. 1923; pub; D; ent. exam, 1st and 2nd fine arts
schools dipl; 4 yrs; degree, Superior Professor granted in the
chosen subject; 4 SC, 2 LC; enrl. D 85. No tui.

Aesthetics	Lettering
Ceramics	Movie Design
Costume Design & Construction	Mural Painting
Drawing	Painting
Graphic Arts	Sculpture
Graphic Design	Stage Design
History of Art & Archaeology	TV Design
Illustration	Teacher Training

AUSTRALIA

MELBOURNE

THE VICTORIAN COLLEGE OF THE ARTS, School of Art,
234 St. Kilda Rd, 3004. Tel: 62-5061
William Kelly, Dean School of Art; 6 FT, 1 PT Lecturers. Estab.
1973 (previously National Gallery of Victoria Art School, estab.
1868); pub; D; co-ed; ent. req. for dipl. matriculation or equivalent, for grad. dipl. dipl. or equivalent; degrees, 3 yr. dipl. arts,
2 yr. grad. dipl. Fine Art; enrl. dipl. 68, grad. dipl. 12. Tui.
free.
Painting
Printmaking
Sculpture

SYDNEY

NATIONAL ART SCHOOL,* Department of Technical Education,
NSW, Forbes St, Darlinghurst, 2010. Tel: 310266
H. Abbott, Head. Estab. first classes 1918; pub; D & E; co-ed; ent.
req. ent. exam, higher school certificate; 5 yr; degree, ASTC (Associateship of Sydney Technical College); schol; enrl. 939 full-time,
3064 part-time, day and evening. Tui. 78 £A; no campus res.

Ceramics	Industrial Design
Commercial Art	Interior Design
Costume Design & Construction	Painting
Graphic Design	Sculpture
Illustration	

Adult hobby classes, ceramics, drawing, painting, sculpture; tui.
13.50 £A for 3 hr.
Children's classes, various subjects; tui. 6£A,

AUSTRIA

VIENNA

HOCHSCHULE FÜR ANGEWANDTE KUNST IN WIEN (Academy of
Applied Art in Vienna), Stubenring 3, A-1011. Tel: 0222-72 21 91
Johannes Spalt, Rector; 106 FT, 28 PT instr. Founded 1868; pub; D;
4-5 yr; dipl.(M.A); enrl. 650.

Architecture	History of Interiors
Art Appreciation	Illustration
Art History	Jewelry/Enameling
Art Teacher Education	Lettering
Bookbinding	Metalcraft
Calligraphy	Mosaics
Cartooning	Painting
Ceramics	Pictorial Composition
Design	Pottery
Drawing	Printmaking
Fashion Illustration	Sculpture
History of Culture & Civilization	Weaving

BELGIUM

ANTWERP

NATIONAAL HOGER INSTITUUT VOOR BOUWKUNST EN
STEDEBOUW,* (National Higher Institute of Architecture and
Town Planning), Mutsaertstreet 31, 2000. Tel: 32.41.61
F. DeGroodt, Dir; 17 instr. Estab. 1663; pub; ent. req. complete
high school; 5 yr; Architectural Degree.

NATIONAAL HOGER INSTITUUT VOOR SCHONE KUNSTEN-
ANTWERPEN,* (National Higher Institute of Fine Arts),
Mutsaertstraat 31. Tel: 335619
M. Macken, Dir; 49 instr. Estab. 1663; pub; ent. req. practical
exam & general formation of HS (16 yr); 5 & 6 yr. For National
Higher Institute of Fine Arts, knowledge of Dutch, French, Eng-
lish or German languages is required.

BRUSSELS

ACADEMIE ROYALE DES BEAUX-ARTS, ECOLE SUPERIEURE DES
ARTS DECORATIFS ET ECOLE SUPÉRIEURE D'ARCHITEC-
TURE DE BRUXELLES,* (Royal Academy of Fine Arts, Brussels)
144 rue du Midi.
Richard Vandendaele, Dir; 54 prof, 6 asst. Founded 1711; D & E;
3, 4 & 6 yr. degrees; advanced courses; schol. and awards. Representative courses:

Advertising	Graphic Arts
Aesthetics	History of Architecture
Architecture	History of Art
Decorative Arts	History of Costume
Design	Painting
Drawing	Plastic Arts
Engraving	Sculpture

ECOLE DES ARTS ET METIERS D'ETTERBEEK, 78, Rue General
Tombeur, B-1040. Tel: 02.733.75.99
J. Ado Baltus, Dir; 22 FT instr. Estab. 1919; pub; E; no ent. req. for
first yr, then exam req. to go on; cert. after 4 yr, dipl. after 2 more
yr; classes in French; 25 SC, 1 LC. Tui. free; no campus res.

Advertising Design	Illustration
Cabinet Construction	Jewelry
Ceramics	Lettering
Display	Painting
Drafting	Photography

Drawing	Pottery
Enamel	Sculpture
Graphic Arts	Tapestry & Weaving
History of Art & Archaeology	Wrought Iron

ECOLE NATIONALE SUPERIEURE D'ARCHITECTURE ET DES
ARTS VISUELS (National School of Architecture and Decorative
Arts), 21 abbaye de la Cambre
Robert L. Delevoy, Dir; 24 FT instr. Estab. 1926; 4 & 5 yr; schol;
enrl. 300. Tui. $6 for Belgian and Benelux students, $100 for foreign
students.

Architecture	Experimental Animation
Cinematography	Industrial Design
Decorative Arts	

BULGARIA

SOFIA

INSTITUT FÜR BILDENDE KUNST NIKOLAJ PAWLOWITSCH,*
(Institute of Fine Arts Nicolai Pavlovich), rue Sipka 1.
Dr. S. Krumov, Rector; Dr. B. Grigorov, V.Rector; Prof. P. Pana-
jotov, Dean Faculty of Fine Arts; Dr. V. Joncev, Dean Faculty of
Applied Arts; 65 teachers. First founded 1896; reorganized as an
Institute 1954. 427 students.

BURMA

MANDALAY

STATE SCHOOL OF FINE ARTS,* East Moat Rd.
Tel: 176
U Win Pe, Prin; 18 FT instr. Estab. 1953; pub; D & E; co-ed; ent.
req. Middle School dipl, ent. exam; 3 yr; dipl; schol. K50 per
mo, for 3 yr, open to Durmese nationality; SC, LC, GC; enrl. 1969-
70 D 179, E 50. Tui. free D, E K10 per mo; campus res, room and
board approx. K400 per academic yr.

Drawing	Painting
Commercial Art	Sculpture

REPUBLIC OF CHINA (TAIWAN)

TAIPEI

NATIONAL TAIWAN ACADEMY OF ARTS,* Pan-chiao Park.
Tel: 220
Chu Tsun-I, Pres; 82 FT, 168 PT instr. Estab. 1955; pub; D & E;
co-ed; ent. req. ent. exam. with HS dipl, Music Dept. with jr. HS
dipl; D 3 yr, Music 5 yr, E 4 yr; degree; schol. open to Chinese
student only. Tui. $1700-$2100 N.T; campus res. $350 N.T.

Chinese Music	Industrial Arts—Ceramics,
Cinema & Drama	Commercial Art, Indus-
Fine Arts—Arts Education,	trial Design
Chinese Arts, Drawing,	Music (incl. Dancing)
Western Arts	Radio & Television
Graphic Arts—Photography,	
Printing	

COLOMBIA

BOGOTA

UNIVERSIDAD JAVERIANA FACULTAD DE ARQUITECTURA Y
DISENO (Javeriana University School of Architecture and Design),
Carrera 7, Calle 41. Tel: 458983, 455102
Pedro P. Polo, Dean Studies; 2 FT, 68 PT instr. Estab. 1952; pvt;
D; ent. req. HS dipl, ent. exam, interviews; 3-5 yr; degrees, B.Arch,
Technician in Advertising Art or Architectural Drawing; ent. req.
B.Arch, interview; 2 yr; degree, M.A; 10 SC, 40 LC; enrl. D 750.
Tui. approx. $250 per sem, grad. $400; no campus res.

Advertising Design	Graphic Arts
Architecture	History of Art & Archaeology
Commercial Art	Lettering
Construction	Photography
Drafting	Restoration of Monuments
Drawing	Town Planning

CZECHOSLOVAKIA

PRAGUE

AKADEMIE VYTVARNYCH UMENI,* (Academy of Fine Arts),
U Adademie 172, 7.
Prof. K. Souček, Rector; 16 members, Founded 1799.

VYSOKA SKOLA UMELECKOPRUMYSLOVA,* (Academy of Applied
Arts), nam. Krasnoarmejcu 80, 1.
Prof. Jan Kavan, Rector. Founded 1885; enrl. 310.

DENMARK

COPENHAGEN

DEN GRAFISKI HØJSKOLE (Graphic College of Denmark),
Julius Thomsengade 3 B.
Leif Monies, Dir.

Drafting	Layout
Graphics	Reproduction Techniques

DET KONGELIGE DANSKE KUNSTAKADEMI (The Royal Danish
Academy of Fine Arts), Kongens Nytorv 1, 1050 K.
Tobias Faber, Dir; School of Architecture; Ole Schwalbe, Dir. School
of Painting & Sculpture. Estab. 1754; under supervision of Ministry
of Cultural Affairs; 5 yr; cert. Foreigners may be admitted to the
Academy as temporary students. They are not admitted as beginners
in the different subjects, but may take part in voluntary instruction at
the School of Painting & Sculpture and may also join Advanced Classes at the School of Architecture, e.g, the special subjects such as
furniture designing, town-planning, garden-planning, etc. Must produce independent work for approval for entrance.
Architecture
Painting
Sculpture
No Summer School.

FRANCE

AIX-EN-PROVENCE

INSTITUTE FOR AMERICAN UNIVERSITIES, 27 Place de
l'Universite, 13625. Tel: (91) 26.63.68
Norma Benney, Dir. Art in Provence Summer Program; 1 FT instr.
Estab. 1964; pvt; D; schol; enrl. 10. Tui, field trips and room $589
for 6 wk. in summer, July 16 - Aug. 30.

Drafting	Handicrafts
Drawing	Painting

FOUNTAINEBLEAU

FONTAINEBLEAU SCHOOL OF FINE ARTS, Palais de Fontainebleau
77305. (American Office: Fontainebleau Fine Arts and Music
Schools Association, Inc, 1083 Fifth Ave, New York, N.Y. 10028.
Tel: (201) 348-2297)
Marion Tournon-Branly, Dir. Estab. 1923; pvt; D; ent. req. scholastic transcript and two letters of reference from present or former
teachers or employers in chosen field, detailed resume of background;
enrl. 60. Tui. $1200 for term of 8 wk. in July and August, school
flight $320.40, fine arts field trips $95. Summer school only.

Architecture	Landscape Architecture
History of Art & Archaeology	Painting

PARIS

ECOLE DU LOUVRE, (School of the Louvre), 34 quai du Louvre,
Ier.
J. Chatelain, Prin; 41 instr. Estab. 1881; 3 yr; degrees for post-
grads; LC. Tui. 25 francs per yr.
Summer School: 100 francs for 4 wk. from July 1.

ECOLE NATIONALE SUPERIEURE DES ARTS DECORATIFS,*
(National College of Decorative Arts), 31 rue d'Ulm, 5e.
Tel: DAN 76-79
M. Tourliere, Dir. Estab. 1766 as the Royal School of Design;
ent. req. ent. exam, entrants must be between 17 (min.) and 25 (max.)
yr. old and must have previous training; 4 yr; dipl.

Advertising & Graphic Arts	Metalwork
Decorative Art	Mural Painting
Design for Modern Industry	Sculpture
Interior Decoration	Stage Design
Jewelry	Textiles

ECOLE NATIONALE SUPERIEURE DES BEAUX-ARTS (National
College of Fine Arts), 17, Quai Malaquais, 6e.
M. Bertin, Dir; 200 instr. Founded 1648; enrl. 5000.

Architecture	Painting
Drawing	Sculpture
Engraving	

PARIS AMERICAN ACADEMY, 9 Rue Des
Ursulines.
Richard Roy, Dir; 4 FT, 4 PT instr. Estab. 1966; pvt; D & E; no
ent. req; 4 SC; 4 LC; enrl. D 100, E 60, maj. 58. Tui. $3000 per
yr, includes lodgings plus various excursion and vacations.

Ceramics	Photography
Drawing	Sculpture
History of Art & Archaeology	Theatre Arts
Painting	

Summer School: Richard Roy, Dir; courses offered same as
during yr; tui. $685 for term of 6 wk. beginning July 1; 1973 enrl.
100.

UNIVERSITE DE PARIS I A LA SORBONNE, INSTITUT D'ART ET
D'ARCHEOLOGIE* (University of Paris I at the Sorbonne, Institute of Art and Archaeology), 3 rue Michelet, 75006.
R. Martin, Dir. Ent. req. exam, B.A, B.S, dipl. Classical Literature. 2 yr; degrees, B.A. or dipl. Doctorates in Archaeology; enrl.
300.

GERMANY

BERLIN

STAATLICHE HOCHSCHULE FÜR BILDENDE KÜNSTE BERLIN*
(State College of Fine Arts), Hardenbergstrasse 33, 12.
Tel: 31 03 31
Prof. Konrad Sage, Dir; 182 instr. Estab. 1696; pub; D & E;
ent. req. HS dipl, ent. exam; degree, Dipl, Ing, architecture only;
enrl. 1973-1974, 1.6.73. Fee DM 775.55 for term of 26 wk. beginning
Jan. 10, 1973.

Advertising Design	Graphic Design
Architecture	Illustration
Art Education	Industrial Design
Ceramics	Landscape Architecture
Commercial Art	Lettering
Costume Design & Construction	Painting
Drawing	Sculpture
Fashion Arts	Stage Design
Graphic Arts	Textile Design

DUSSELDORF

STAATLICHE KUNSTAKADEMIE, DUSSELDORF,*
(State Academy of Art)
Eiskellerstrasse 1, D-4000. Tel: 1.09.91
Prof. Norbert Kricke, Dir; 37 FT, 8 PT instr. Estab. 1773; pub;
ent. req. exam, submission of portfolio; 4 yr; degrees; cert; schol.
& fel; enrl. (summer terms) c. 650.

Applied Graphic Arts	Fine Graphic Arts
Architecture	Painting
Art Education	Sculpture
Film	Stage Design

HAMBURG

HOCHSCHULE FÜR BILDENDE KÜNSTE (College of Fine Arts),
D 2000 Hamburg 76, Lerchenfeld 2. Tel: 22811
Dr. Freiherr von Buttlar, Pres.

Architecture	Metalwork
Art Education	Painting
Art History	Photography
Ceramics	Sculpture
Drawing	Textile Design
Film	Typography
Furniture Design	Video
Graphic Arts	Weaving
Industrial Design	

HEIDELBERG

SCHILLER COLLEGE-EUROPE, Fine Arts Department, Central
Administration, Friedrich-Ebert-Anlage 4, 69. Tel:
Tel: (06221) 12046.
J. G. Eggert, Academic Dean; 144 instr. Estab. 1964; pvt; D & E;
instruction in English; ent. req. HS dipl; degrees, A.A, B.A, M.A,
B.F.A, M.F.A, B.M, M.M, A.B.A, B.B.A; enrl. 650 (student body

composed of students from 45 various countries). Tui. $2250.
Study Centers in Heidelberg, London, Madrid, Paris and Strasbourg.

Ceramics	Printmaking
Drawing	Sculpture
European Art History	Stage Design
Painting	Theatre Arts

Academic-Yr-Abroad and Interim Programs.
Summer School: Tui. incl. room $780 for 6 wk. prog. beginning
end of June; enrl. 160.

KARLSRUHE

STAATLICHE AKADEMIE DER BILDENDEN KUNSTE,* (State Academy of Fine Arts), Reinhold-Frank-Strasse 81-83, 75.
Prof. Harry Kögler, Rector; 15 instr. Founded 1854.

MUNICH

AKADEMIE DER BILDENDEN KUNSTE,* (Academy of Fine Arts),
Akademiestrasse 2. Tel: 33 85 21
Dr. Aloys Goergen, Man. Pres; Prof. Gerhard Berger, Co.Pres;
16 FT, 4 PT instr. Estab. 1770, re-estab. 1808, merged with
Academy of Fine Arts 1946. Studies limited to 10 sem; degrees;
dipl; schol. for foreigners; schol. of German Academy's Exchange
Program and the Bavarian State Department of Education. Tui.
winter sem. 115 German marks, spring sem. 95 German marks.

Architecture	Jewelry Design
City Planning	Painting
Furniture Design	Sculpture
Graphic Arts	Stagecraft
Interior Decoration	Textile Design

NUREMBERG

AKADEMIE DER BILDENDEN KUNSTE IN NÜRNBERG* (Academy of
Fine Arts in Nüremberg), Bingstrasse 60, 8500 Nürnberg 36.
Tel: 40.50.61
Prof. Clemens Fischer, Pres; 11 FT, 1 PT instr. Estab. 1662; ent.
req. exam; 4-6 yr; enrl. 236. No student fee, social contribution,
DM 21. per sem; no campus res. but meals available, DM 1,50.

Anatomy	Metalcraft
Architecture	Painting
Art History	Sculpture
Graphic Design	Textile Design
Jewelry Design	

STUTTGART

STAATLICHE AKADEMIE DER BILDENDEN KUNSTE* (State
Academy of Fine Arts), Am Weissenhof 1, 7000.
Tel: 0711 221161
Prof. Dr. Wolfgang Kermer, Rektor; Prof. Hans Gottfried von
Stockhausen, Stellvertretender Rektor; 70 instr. Estab. 1869;
pub; D; ent. req. Abitur for Art Educ, practical experience in
applied arts, ent. exam for all calsses; dipl. in art educ; SC,
LC, GC; enrl. approx. 900.

Art Education	Painting
Art History	Product Design
Ceramics	Sculpture
Furniture Design	Stage Design
Graphic Arts	Textile Design
Interior Decoration	

GREAT BRITAIN

BIRMINGHAM

CITY OF BIRMINGHAM POLYTECHNIC,* Art and Design Centre,
New Corporation St, B4 7DX. Tel: 021-359 6721
Malcolm Ford, Dean Art and Design. Pub; ent. req. vary according
to course; grad. 4-5 yr.

Architecture	Pre-Diploma & Foundation Studies
Art Education	Three-Dimensional Design—
Fashion & Textiles—	Ceramics, Furniture, Indus-
Embroidery, Fashion,	trial Design, Interior Design,
Printed Textiles, Woven	Jewellery & Silversmithing,
Textiles	Painting & Decorating, Theatre
Fine Art—Painting, Printmak-	Design
ing, Sculpture	Town Planning
History of Art & Comple-	Visual Communication—Graphic
mentary Studies	Design, Photography

BRIGHTON

BRIGHTON POLYTECHNIC, Faculty of Art and Design, Grand
  Parade, BN2 2YJ. Tel: 01144 273 64141
Robin J. Plummer, Asst. Dir; 80 FT, 80 PT instr. Estab. 1965;
pub; D & E; co-ed; minimum qualifications for certain courses;
4 yr; degree, CNAA; total of 40 courses; enrl. D 392, E 257, also
FT, short FT and sandwich 507. Tui. non-advanced £240 per
session, advanced £330.

Advertising Design	Illustration
Art Education	Jewelry
Ceramics	Metal
Crafts	Painting
Drawing	Photography
Furniture	Sculpture
Graphic Design	Textile Design

Adult recreation classes in most of the subjects listed above.

LEICESTER

LEICESTER POLYTECHNIC (Incorporating the Former Leicester
  College of Art and Design), P.O. Box 143, LE1 9BH.
  Tel: 0533-50181
David Bethel, Dir; Albert Pountney, Head School Fine Art; Grace
Best, Head School Fashion and Textile Design; G. B. Karo, Head
School Graphics; B. Former, Head School Architecture; 3000 FT,
2500 PT instr. Estab. 1870 designated as a Polytechnic 1969; pub;
D & E; co-ed; ent. req. HS dipl. or equivalent and selection proce-
dure; 3 yr. (following 1 yr. Foundation Course); B.A.(Hons), M.A. in
Art and Design (2nd degree equivalent). Tui. £165 average per yr,
overseas students £340; campus res. approx. £1200 per yr.

Architecture	Graphics
Art Education	History of Art & Archaeology
Art Teacher Training	Illustration
Ceramics	Industrial Design
Commercial Art	Interior Design
Contour Fashion (Foundation	Jewelry
Garment, Leisurewear and	Lettering
Lingerie Design)	Painting
Costume Design & Construction	Photography
Drawing	Sculpture
Fashion	Silver
Fashion Art	Textile Design
Furniture	Textile Technology
Glass	Three-Dimensional Design

LONDON

CENTRAL SCHOOL OF ART AND DESIGN, Southampton Row,
  WC1B 4AP. Tel: 01-405-1825
Michael Pattrick, Principal; 44 FT, 156 PT instr. Estab. 1896;
controlled by Inner London Education Authority; ent. req. sub-
mission of work; Foundation Course (1 yr), B.A.(3 yr, Art & Design),
M.A.(2 yr, Industrial Design), M.A.(1 yr, Textile Design & Graphic
Design), Central School Dipl; enrl. 470. Tui. Foundation £200,
others £320; no campus res.

Ceramics	Painting
Enameling	Printmaking
Etching	Sculpture
Graphic Design	Stained Glass
Industrial Design	Textile Design
Jewelry Design	Theatre Design

CHELSEA SCHOOL OF ART,* Manresa Road, SW3 6LS.
  Tel: 01-352-4846
Frederick Brill, Prin; D 20 FT, 50 PT, E 10 PT instr. Estab. 1895,
ent. req. academic qualifications, ent. exam, submission of work,
interview; 3-4 yr; dipl, cert; enrl. 250. Tui. £50 per yr: £150 and
£250 per yr. for overseas students.

Graphics	Printed Surface Design
Painting	Sculpture

CITY & GUILDS OF LONDON ART SCHOOL,* 122-4 Kennington Park
  Rd, S.E. 11.
Sir Edward Chadwycke-Healey, Bt, MC; 17 instr. Estab. 1879; full
and part-time courses; D, E. & Sun. classes.

Engraving	Painting
Lettering	Sculpture
Lithography	Woodcarving

HEATHERLEY SCHOOL OF FINE ART, 33 Warwick Square,
  SW1V 2AH.
John Walton, Principal. Estab. 1845; all aspects of art study, including Printing and Sculpture; pre-diploma work, vocational and non-
vocational courses; non-selective; studio space available; special
courses arranged by negotiation; educational advice supplied.

ROYAL ACADEMY OF ARTS, Burlington House, Piccadilly,
  W1V-0DS.
Peter Greenham, Keeper. Founded 1768.
Painting
Sculpture

ROYAL COLLEGE OF ART, Kensington Gore, SW7 2EU.
  Tel: 01-584 5020
Lord Esher, Rector; 38 FT, 79 PT instr. Estab. 1837; pub; D; ent.
exam; 2-3 yr postgrad. degrees, M.A.(RCA), M.Des.(RCA), Ph.D.
(RCA); enrl. 600. Fees £338pa.

Automotive Design	Illustration
Ceramics & Glass	Industrial Design
Design Methodology	Jewelry Design
Environmental Design	Painting
Fashion Design	Photography
Film & Television	Printmaking
Furniture Design	Sculpture
General Studies	Silversmithing
Graphic Design	Textile Design: Knitted, Printed,
Graphic Information	Woven & Tapestry

SAINT MARTIN'S SCHOOL OF ART, 107/111 Charing Cross Rd,
  WC2H 0DU. Tel: 01-437-0058
Ian Simpson, Principal; 35 FT, 180 PT instr. Estab. 1854; pub;
D & E; ent. req. HS dipl, ent. exam, portfolio; 4 yr; degrees, B.S.
(Hons) in Fine Art, Graphic Design, Fashion; all SC, with 15% con-
tent History of Art; enrl. D 600, E 400, maj. 520, grad. 80. Tui.
$656 per yr; campus res. $1435.

Advertising Design	History of Art
Commercial Art	Illustration
Costume Design & Construction	Lettering
Drawing	Painting
Fashion Arts	Photography
Graphic Arts	Sculpture
Graphic Design	Textile Design

SLADE SCHOOL OF FINE ART, University College London, Gower
  St, WC1E 6BT.
Prof. Lawrence Gowing, Dir; 4 yr; course leads to Univ. of London
B.A.(Fine Arts), 2 yr. postgrad course leads to Univ. of London
higher dipl. in Fine Arts, 2 yr. postgrad course also leads to dipl. in
Film Studies and research facilities lead to Univ. of London M.Phil.
or Ph.D.(Fine Art or Film Studies); enrl. 180.

Drawing	Sculpture
Engraving	Silk-Screen Printing
Etching	Study of the Film
Lithography	Theatre Design
Painting	

MANCHESTER

MANCHESTER POLYTECHNIC (Formerly Manchester College of
  Art and Design), Faculty of Art and Design, Cavendish St, All
  Saints, M15 6BR.
Sir Alex Smith, Dir; B.C.C. Hirst, Dean of Faculty. Estab. 1838;
degrees, B.A.(Hons) in Art and Design (3 yr), Foundation Course
(1 yr. recommended for first degrees in Art and Design), B.A.(Hons)
in Architecture, Associateship of the Institute of Landscape Architects (4 yr), Theatre (3 yr), Printing Technology (3 yr), post grad.
cert. in Educ. (1 yr), M.A. in Art and Design (1-2 yr).

Architecture	Interior Design
Art Education	Landscape Architecture
Embroidery	Printing Technology
Fashion	Textiles (Printed & Woven)
Fine Art (Painting,	Theatre (Speech & Drama)
Sculpture, Fine Prints)	Three-Dimensional Design
Graphic Design	Wood, Metal, Ceramics)
Industrial Design	Urban Design

NOTTINGHAM

TRENT POLYTECHNIC SCHOOL OF ART AND DESIGN,* Burton St.
  Tel: 061-48248
R. Hedley, Dir; 72 FT, 60 PT instr. Estab. 1843 (Govt. School of
Design); pvt; ent. req. exam. G.C.E. on O and A levels, or equivalent;
4 yr; dipl; enrl. 500 FT. Tui. £89, overseas students £250.

Architectural Ceramics	Graphics
Creative Photography	Interior Design
Fashion/Textiles	Textiles Technology
Fine Art	Theatre Design
Furniture Design	

OXFORD

RUSKIN SCHOOL OF DRAWING & FINE ART, University of Oxford,
74 High St, OX1 4BG.
Philip Morsberger, Dir. Estab. 1871; ent. req. B.F.A; 2-3 yr. cert.
in fine art; enrl. 80.

Anatomy	Painting
Drawing	Printmaking
History of Art	

SCOTLAND

EDINBURGH

EDINBURGH COLLEGE OF ART,*
Lauriston Place EH3 9DF.
J. T. Hunter, Prin. Estab. 1907.

Architecture	Painting
Crafts	Planning
Design	Sculpture
Drawing	

GUATEMALA

GUATEMALA CITY

INSTITUTO NACIONAL DE BELLAS ARTES, ESCUELA DE ARTES
PLASTICAS,* (School of Plastic Arts), 8a. Avenida 12-44 zona 1.
Tel: 25667
Max Saravia Gual, Escultor; 15 PT instr. Estab. 1920; pub; E; ent.
req. Primary School dipl. (to have a degree 3 yr. of HS); 3 yr; de-
grees, Bachiller of Maestro en pintura, escultura, grabado, etc; 13
SC, 2 LC; enrl. E 150. Tui. free.

Advertising Design	Graphic Arts
Architecture	History of Art & Archaeology
Artistic Naked	Mural Painting-Laboratory
Ceramics	Painting
Commercial Art	Painting Restoration
Drafting	Sculpture
Drawing	

Children's classes in painting, tui. free; enrl. 20.

INDIA

BARODA

THE MAHARAJA SAYAJIRAO UNIVERSITY OF BARODA,* University
Road, Pushpa-Baug, 2.
Prof. R. N. Mehta, Dean, Faculty of Arts; K. G. Subramanyam, Dean,
Faculty of Fine Arts. Estab. 1949.

Advertising Art	Photography
Art History	Sculpture
Lithography	Woodcrafts
Painting	

VARANASI

BANARAS HINDU UNIVERSITY,* College of Music and Fine Arts,
Uttar Pradesh, Varanasi 5
Prof. S. Bhattachara, Dean, Faculty of Arts; Dr. L. M. Misra, Fac-
ulty of Music and Fine Arts; 5 FT instr. Estab. 1950; a Constituent
Coll. of Banaras Hindu Univ; ent. req. aptitude test in Dipl; 3 yr;
dipl in Fine Arts, degrees in Painting (B.F.A), Sculpture (B.F.A.),
Applied Arts (B.A.A.).

IRAQ

BAGHDAD

ACADEMY OF FINE ARTS, Department of Plastic Arts,
Waziriya.
Prof. Ismail Al-Sheikhli, Chmn; 25 FT, 10 PT instr. Estab. 1968;
pub; D; ent. req. HS dipl, ent. exam, grad. Inst. Fine Arts, Baghdad;
4 yr; degree, B.A; schol. paid by Univ. Baghdad for Arab students
only; enrl. 150. Tui. free; campus res.

Advertising Design	Illustration
Aesthetics	Industrial Design
Art Education	Lettering
Ceramics	Painting
Commercial Art	Photography
Drawing	Sculpture
Graphic Arts	Teacher Training
Graphic Design	Textile Design
History of Art & Archaeology	

IRELAND

DUBLIN

NATIONAL COLLEGE OF ART AND DESIGN, Kildare St, 2.
Tel: 682911
Jonah Jones, Dir; 42 FT, 18 PT instr. Estab. 1746; pub; D & E;
ent. req. HS dipl, ent. exam; 4 yr; degree, Associate of National
Coll. Art; schol. to Irish citizens; 3 SC; enrl. D 250, E 600.
Tui. $200 per yr, foreign students $600; no campus res.

Advertising Design	History of Art & Archaeology
Aesthetics	Illustration
Art Education	Industrial Design
Ceramics	Jewelry
Costume Design & Construction	Lettering
Display	Painting
Drafting	Photography
Drawing	Sculpture
Fashion Arts	Stage Design
Graphic Arts	Teacher Training
Graphic Design	Textile Design

Adult hobby classes, offers the above subjects; tui. $15 per class;
enrl. 300.

ITALY

BOLOGNA

ACCADEMIA DI BELLE ARTI E LICEO ARTISTICO (Academy of
Fine Arts), via Belle Arti 54.
Prof. Pasqualini Enzo, Dir.

FLORENCE

ACCADEMIA DI BELLE ARTI,* (Academy of Fine Arts), via
Ricasoli 66.
Founded 1801.

ROSARY COLLEGE, Graduate School of Fine Arts at Schifanoia
Villa, via Boccaccio, 123, 50133. Tel: 055.576.195
Sister Jean Richter, Dean; 18 PT instr. Estab. 1948; pvt; affiliated
with Rosary College, River Forest, Ill; D; ent. req. B.F.A.(Art) or
B.A.(Art); 1-3 yr; degrees, M.A, M.F.A; schol; GC in music also;
enrl. 40. Tui. $3600 annually.

Art History	Printmaking
Art Restoration (3 yr)	Sculpture
Painting	

Summer School: Course offered, Italian Romanesque Art &
Architecture (field trip); tui. $600, plus cost of travel.

MILAN

ACCADEMIA DI BELLE ARTI DI BRERA,* (Academy of Fine Arts
of Brera), Palazzo di Brera, via Brera 28.
Dr. A. de Micheli, Pres; 13 FT instr. Estab. 1776; ent. req. submission of work; 4 yr; dipl; enrl. approx. 255.

Decoration
Painting
Sculpture

NAPLES

ACCADEMIE DI BELLE ARTI E LICEO ARTISTICO,* (Academy of
Fine Arts), via Bellini 36.
Prof. Constanza Lorenzetti, Dir. Founded 1838.

PERUGIA

ACCADEMIA DI BELLE ARTI (Academy of Fine Arts),* Piazza San
Francesco al Prato
Avv. V. Parlavecchio, Pres; Prof. P. Frenguelli, Dir; Prof. G.F.
Bissietta, Coordinator. D & E; cert. Tui. $13,000 Lire per yr.
normal courses, 20,000 Lire per yr. free courses.

Architecture	Painting
Decoration	Sculpture
History of Modern & Ancient	Theory of Art
Art	Stage Craft
History of the Theatre	

Summer Courses: 25,000 Lire for one month for foreign students.

Art	Fresco
Art History	Landscape
Art Tours	Marble & Stone Work
Bronze Casting	Painting
Ceramics	Restoration
Engraving	Sculpture

RAVENNA

ACCADEMIA DI BELLE ARTI RAVENNA ITALIA (Academy of Fine Arts), Loggetta Lombardesca, Via Roma, 48100.
Tel: 23935 30178
Prof. Raffaele De Grada, Dir; Rag. Gianfranco Bustacchini, Gen. Secy; 8 FT, 3 PT instr. Pub; D; ent. req. ent. exam; 4 yr; degree, specializzazione mosaico; 4 SC, 4 LC. Tui. free for foreigners; no campus res.
Mosaics

ROME

ACCADEMIA DE BELLE ARTIE LICEO ARTISTICO (Academy of Fine Arts), via Ripetta 218 - 222, 00186. Tel: 688.834, 688.861
Prof. Luigi Montanarini, Dir; 42 FT, 26 PT instr. Founded 1470, licensed 1873 and 1924; no ent. req. except with degree, 21 yr. of age; 4 yr; dipl; SC, LC; enrl. 1975.

Architecture	Ornamental Modeling
Art of Engraving	Painting
Artistic Anatomy	Scene Painting
Decoration	Scenery Technique
History of Art	School of Modeling
History of Costumes	School of the Nude in Art
(Popular & Folk)	Sculpture
History of Movies & Theatre	Techniques of Art with Marble
Interior Decorating	
Adult hobby classes.	

AMERICAN ACADEMY IN ROME, Via Angelo Masina 5, 00153.
Henry A. Millon, Dir; Frank E. Brown, Prof. in Charge Classical Studies. Estab. 1894; ent. req. Rome Prize Competition; fels.
Note: The American Academy in Rome is not a school; it offers no courses of instruction and maintains no teaching staff; it is simply a place where the Rome Prize Fellows (in architecture, landscape architecture, painting, sculpture, music composition, classics, post classical studies, art history) work and live. Information about these fellowships must be obtained from, Secretary, American Academy in Rome, 41 E. 65th St, New York, N.Y. 10021.

BRITISH SCHOOL AT ROME, via A. Gramsci 61.
D. B. Whitehouse, Dir. Founded 1901, inc. by Royal Charter 1912; schol. for 1 or 2 yr; enrl. varies, maximum c. 15.

INSTITUTO CENTRALE DEL RESTAURO,* (Central Institute for the Restoration of Works of Art), Piazza San Francesco di Paola 9, 00186. Tel: 960161
Dr. Giovanni Urbani, Dir; 15 FT instr. Estab. 1939; pub; D & E; co-ed; ent. req. secondary school dipl. (license) or equivalent; 3 yr; dipl. to conduct or practice restoration; 7 SC; enrl. 24 students, 24 brokers. Tui. free.

Art Education	Natural Science
Chemistry	Physics
History of Antique, Medieval	Techniques of Restoration
& Modern Art	
Law Governing Antique & Fine	
Arts	

VENICE

ACCADEMIA DI BELLE ARTI E LICEO ARTISTICO,* (Academy of Fine Arts), Dorsoduro 1050.
Conte Ing. Alessandro Passi, Pres. Founded 1750.

JAPAN

KANAZAWA CITY

KANAZAWA BIJUTSU KOGEI DAIGAKU* (Kanazawa College of Art), 11-1, Kodachino 5-chome, 920. Tel: 0762-62-3531.
Mamoru Osawa, Pres; 47 FT, 55 PT instr. Estab. 1950; pub; D; ent. req. HS dipl, ent. exam; 4 yrs; degree, M.F.A; schol; 40 SC, 86 LC; enrl. D 530, maj. 20, grad. students 530, others 20. Tui. ¥36,000 per yr, mo. FT ¥3000, billet rate ¥17,000 mo; no campus res.

Advertising Design	History of Art & Archaeology
Aesthetics	Illustration
Art Education	Industrial Design
Ceramics	Lettering
Commercial Art	Museum Staff Training
Drafting	Painting
Drawing	Photography
Graphic Arts	Sculpture
Graphic Design	Teacher Training
Handicrafts	Textile Design

Adult hobby classes, series of Sat. lectures for citizens on various topics of arts and crafts; no tui; enrl. 150.
Summer School: Prof. Kenji Fujimori.

KYOTO

KYOTO CITY UNIVERSITY OF FINE ARTS, School of Art, 50, Hiyoshi-cho, Imagumano, Higashiyama-ku.
Takeshi Umehara, Dir; 60 FT, 41 PT instr. Estab. 1880; ent. req. exam. for HS grad; 2 yr.(post-grad); 4 yr; degrees; enrl. 125.

Design	Pottery
Japanese Painting	Sculpture
Lacquer	Textile Design
Oil Painting	

MEXICO

CHOLULA

UNIVERSITY OF THE AMERICAS, Art Department, Ex-Hacienda de Sta. Catarina. Tel: 47-06-55 Exten. 128
Jorge Duron, Chmn; 8 FT, 3 PT instr. Estab. 1947; pvt; D & E; ent. req. HS dipl, for advanced standing presentation of portfolio and/or transparencies; 3 yr; degrees, B.A.(Fine Arts, Art History), B.F.A.(Painting, Sculpture, Graphics, Photography), M.F.A.(Painting, Sculpture); grad. schol; 32 SC, 25 LC, 10 GC; enrl. approx. 200 per quarter. Tui. $325 per quarter, $27 per cr. hr; campus res. room $130-$230.

Aesthetics	History of Art & Archaeology
Conservation &	Mexican Crafts
Restoration Techniques	Painting
Design	Photography
Drawing	Sculpture
Graphic Arts	

GUADALAJARA

UNIVERSIDAD DE GUADALAJARA, Cursos de Verano/Cursos de Invierno, Apdo. Postal 1-2543, Belen 120.
Jorge Martinez Lopez, Dir; 13 FT instr. Cursos de Verano estab. 1947, Cursos de Invierno estab. 1972; pub; D; ent. req. HS dipl; no degree; 10 SC, 3 LC, 8 GC. Tui. $120 per school term.

Ceramics	Painting
Drawing	Sculpture
History of Art & Archaeology	

MEXICO CITY

ESCUELA NACIONAL DE ARTES PLASTICAS,* (National School of Plastic Arts), Academia 22.
Prof. Antonio Trejo Osorio, Dir; 109 prof. Founded 1781; enrl. 750.

Commercial Art	Painting
Drawing	Sculpture
Engraving	

SAN MIGUEL

INSTITUTO ALLENDE
(Allende Institute)
Stirling Dickinson, Pres. and Dir; Nell Fernandez, Adminr; James Pinto, Dean of Faculty; William Parker, Dean Students; Fred Samuelson, Head. Grad. Studies; Robert Somerlott, Head Writing Center; 25 FT, 15 PT instr. Estab. 1938; pvt, inc. with the Univ. Guanajuato; ent. req. HS grad; 3-4 yr; degrees, B.A, B.F.A, M.A, M.F.A; schols. plus assistantships and working schols; enrl. approx. 1500 per yr. Tui. $200 per three month term, plus applicable lab. fees, $125 per mo. for Intensive Spanish Study. Pergola and Del Conde Art Galleries.

Archaeology	Lost Wax
Art History	Non-Fiction
Botany	Photography
Drawing & Painting	Poetry
Enameling	Psychology
Fiction	Sculpture
Graphic Arts	Silverwork
History of Mexico	Sociology
Intensive Spanish	Textile Design
Leather Work	Weaving

Adult hobby classes (non-cr), courses as above, all seasons.
Summer School: Stirling Dickinson, Dir; 10 wk. term starting nearest Mon. to June 15.

NETHERLANDS

AMSTERDAM

RIJKSAKADEMIE VAN BEELDENDE KUNSTEN,* (State Academy of
  Fine Arts), Stadhouderskade 86. Tel: 79.78.11

Fine Arts	Scenography
History of Art	Visual Communication

THE HAGUE

KONINKLIJKE ACADEMIE VAN BEELDENDE KUNSTEN (Royal
Academy of Fine and Applied Arts), 4 Prinsessegracht 4.
J. J. Beljon, Dir; 120 FT instr. Estab. 1684; pub; ent. req. HS
dipl; 28 D classes, 20 E classes. Tui. f.200 per yr.

Graphic Design	Painting
Industrial Design	Sculpture
Interior Decoration	Textile Design

STICHTING DE VRIJE ACADEMIE PSYCHOPOLIS VOOR
  BEELDENDE KUNSTEN (Foundation The Free Academy
  Psychopolis for Audio-Visual Arts—International Art
  Laboratory) De Gheijnstraat 129, P.O. Box 6390.
  Tel: 070-638968
George Lampe, Dir; approx. 40 PT instr. Estab. 1947, ressorting
under the Ministry of Culture and The Residence The Hague, Fine
Arts; no ent. req, must be at least 17 yr. of age; no dipl. Tui.
fl.300, fl.400, or fl.600 per yr. for complete prog, fl.50 per sem.
for separate units; campus res. fl.600 per mo. 33 localities,
dark rooms and studios.

Art in Architecture	Illustration
Ceramics	Jewelry
Costume Design & Construction	Painting
Drawing	Photography
Fashion Arts	Sculpture
Glass	Textile Design
Graphic Arts	Theatre Arts
Graphic Design	Wood Work

ROTTERDAM

ACADEMIE VAN BEELDENDE KUNSTEN (Academy of Fine Arts),
  G.J. de Jonghweg 4. Tel: 010366244, no. 31
Klaas de Jong, Dir; 80 PT instr. Estab. 1773; pub; 24 classes; 5 yr.

Audio-Visual	Graphic Design
Fashion	Interior-Architecture
Fine Arts	Sculpture

NEW ZEALAND

AUCKLAND

UNIVERSITY OF AUCKLAND, School of Fine Arts, Private
  Bag.
Prof. Paul J. Beadle, Dean Faculty & School Fine Arts; 12 FT, 6 PT
instr. Estab. 1885 as Elam School of Art & Design, transferred to
the University of Auckland 1950, since 1967 named the School of
Fine Arts; pub; D; ent. req. univ. ent. and fine arts preliminary or
higher; 4-6 yr; degrees, B.F.A, M.F.A; schol; 4 SC, 4 LC, 1 GC;
enrl. D 150, grad. 18. Tui. $NZ160; no campus res.

Art Education	Industrial Design
Costume Design & Construction	Jewelry
Drawing	Lettering
Graphic Arts	Painting
Graphic Design	Photography
History of Art & Archaeology	Sculpture
Illustration	

NORWAY

OSLO

STATENS KUNSTAKADEMI,* (State Art Academy), Uranienborgvien
  2.
Prof. Alf-Jorgen Aas, Rector; Conrad Løwø, Adminr; 5 FT, 6 PT
instr. Estab. 1909; ent. req. exam; 4 yr. No tui.
Drawing
Modeling
Painting
  No Summer School.

PHILIPPINES

MANILA

PHILIPPINE COLLEGE OF ARTS AND TRADES, Ayala Blvd. corner
  San Marcelino St, Ermita P.O. Box 3171.
Prof. Diosado, Jr, Head Graphics Div. & Art School; 190 FT, 7 PT
instr. Estab. 1901; pub; D & E; ent. req. HS dipl, ent. exam; 2-4 yr;
degrees, B.S.(Industrial Educ), M.A.(Industrial Educ); schol; enrl.
D 2261, E 2428, grad. 266. Tui. undergrad. $50, grad. $60.

Art Education	Flower Making
Bamboo Craft	Graphic Arts
Basketry	Handicrafts
Ceramics	Illustration
Coconut Shell Craft	Industrial Design
Drafting	Seashell Craft
Drawing	Teacher Training
Ethnic Art	Wire Craft
Fiber Craft	Wood Craft

  Summer School: Jose R. Vergara, Pres; all regular courses in
the day program are offered and opened if there are enough students;
term of 5 wk. beginning April; 1973 enrl. 1179.

POLAND

CRACOW

AKADEMIA SZTUK PIEKNYCH,* (Academy of Fine Arts), Plac
  Matekji, 13.
Prof. Marian Konieczny, Rector.

Advertising	Posters
Conservation of Works of Art	Scenography
Graphic Arts	Sculpture
Interior Decoration	Textile Design
Painting	Town Planning

LODZ

PAŃSTWOWA WYZSZA SZKOŁA SZTUK PLASTYCZNYCH*
(The Higher State School of Applied Arts), Fundamental Education Dept, Graphic Art Dept, Textile and Fashion Art Design
Dept, ul. Narutowicza 77 90-138. Tel: 87583.
Prof. Roman Artymowski, Rector; 52 FT, 28 PT instr. Estab. 1945;
pub; D; co-ed; ent. req. HS dipl, ent. exam, competitive exam; 5 yr;
degree, M.A; schol; 23 SC, 13 LC, 16 GC; enrl. 356, grad. 48. Tui,
room and board for foreign students c.$1500 per yr.

Advertising Design	Illustration
Carpet & Gobelin Design	Jewelry
Costume Design & Construction	Lettering
Drawing	Packing Design
Fashion Arts	Painting
Graphic Arts	Photography
Graphic Design	Sculpture
History of Art & Archaeology	Textile Design

WARSAW

AKADEMIA SZTUK PIEKNYCH,* (Academy of Fine Arts), Krakowskie
  Przedmiescie 5.
Prof. Kazimier Nita, Rector.

Conservation of Works of Art	Pedagogical
Graphic Arts	Sculpture
Interior Architecture	Textiles
Painting	Theatre Set Design

PORTUGAL

LISBON

ESCOLA SUPERIOR DE BELAS ARTES,* (School of Fine Arts),
  Largo da Biblioteca Publica.
Joaquim Correia, Dir. Estab. 1836.

OPORTO

ESCOLA SUPERIOR DE BELAS ARTES,* (Higher School of Fine
  Arts), Av. Rodriques de Freitas.
Carlos Ramos, Dir. Estab. 1836.

ROMANIA

CLUJ-NAPOCA

INSTITUTUL DE ARTE PLASTICE ION ANDREESCU (Institute of
Plastic Arts Ion Andreescu), Piata Libertatii 31, 3400.
Tel: 951-11577
Mircea Balau, Assoc. Prof; 61 FT, 6 PT instr. Estab. 1949; pub;
D; ent. req. HS dipl, ent. exam; 4 yr; licensed for fine art with the
mention of the specialty; schol; 24 SC, 21 LC, 6 GC; enrl. D 252,
maj. 5. Tui. free.

Advertising Design	History of Art & Archaeology
Aesthetics	Industrial Design
Art Education	Lettering
Ceramics	Painting
Commercial Art	Photography
Costume Design & Construction	Sculpture
Drawing	Teacher Training
Graphic Arts	Textile Design
Graphic Design	

REPUBLIC OF SOUTH AFRICA

PORT ELIZABETH

PORT ELIZABETH SCHOOL OF ART OF THE COLLEGE FOR
ADVANCED TECHNICAL EDUCATION, Private Bag 6011, 6000.
G. H. H. Nesbit, Head School Art; 18 FT, 7 PT instr. Estab. 1882;
pub; D; ent. req. HS dipl; 3 yr; National Dipl.(Art, Design, Photog-
raphy), Higher National Dipl; enrl. 140. Tui; campus res.
R.240,00 p a.

Advertising Design	History of Art & Archaeology
Art Education	Illustration
Ceramics	Lettering
Commercial Art	Painting
Costume Design & Construction	Photography
Drawing	Sculpture
Fashion Arts	Teacher Training (with Univ. of
Graphic Arts	Port Elizabeth)
Graphic Design	Textile Design

SPAIN

BARCELONA

ESCUELA SUPERIOR DE BELLAS ARTES DE SAN JORGE,*
(Barcelona School of Fine Arts), Plaza Veronica 2.
Prof. Frederico Mares Deulovol, Dir.

MADRID

ESCUELA NACIONAL DE ARTES GRAFICAS,* (Madrid School of
Graphic Arts), Calle Jesus Maestro, 3.
Luis Gimeno Soldevilla, Dir. 32 FT instr. Estab. 1911; 3 yr; enrl.
223.
Graphic Arts

SEVILLE

ESCUELA SUPERIOR DE BELLAS ARTES DE SEVILLE,* (Seville
School of Fine Arts), Gonzaldo Bilbao 7-9.
Jose Hernandez Diaz, Dir. Founded 1940; 106 students. Fine Arts.

VALENCIA

ESCUELA SUPERIOR DE BELLAS ARTES DE SAN CARLOS,*
(Valencia School of Fine Arts), Calle del museo 2.
Daniel de Neuda Llisiona, Dir; 26 instr. Estab. 1765; affiliated
with the Univ. of Valencia; 5 yr; schol; enrl. 300.
Summer School: 8 wk. from July 1 to Sept. 1.

SWEDEN

GOTHENBURG

GOTEBORGS UNIVERSITET,* (Gothenburg University), Vasaparken,
41124.
Prof. P. G. Hamberg, Dean, Faculty of Arts. Estab. 1891; pub; ent.
req. HS exam; 3-4 yr; enrl. 8000.

KONSTINDUSTRISKOLAN I GÖTEBORG (Gothenburg School of
Design), Kristinelundsgatan 6-8, 411 37. Tel: 160517 or 208765
Gösta Andren, Prinicpal; D 20 FT, 32 PT, E 33 PT instr. Estab.
1848; pub; ent. req. ent. exam and artistic talent; 4 yr; enrl. 500.
Tui. approx. $40 per yr; the school does not assume room, board,
and other expenses.

STOCKHOLM

KONSTFACKSKOLAN (Swedish State School of Art and Design),
Valhallavagen 191, 115 27.
Ake H. Huldt, Principal & Dir; 105 teachers. Estab. 1844; D & E;
all instruction in Swedish; accepts foreign students for 1 yr. of
advanced study only; ent. req. curriculum vitae, copies of dipl. or
records; cert. from professional practice; recommendations,
15-20 slides of work, also applicant must indicate which of the
departments below he is interested in; cert.(does not give specified
univ. cr); enrl. 1100. No tui. but fees for costs of materials;
no campus res.

Ceramics & Glass	Painting
Furniture & Interior Design	Sculpture
Graphic Design	Textiles
Metalwork	

KUNGL. KONSTHOGSKOLAN (Royal Academy Art School),
Fredsgatan 12, Box 16 317, 103 26.
Sven Ljungberg, Dir; 19 FT instr. Estab. 1735; affiliated with
the Royal Swedign Academy of Fine Arts. 5 yr; no fees. Foreign
students can be accepted as guest students for one year at a time
and generally not more than two years in all, or as special students
following parts of the instruction, all in very limited numbers, on
presentation of testimonials to prove they have been enrolled as
regular students of some foreign Art Institute of the same status
(University). Applicants are required to submit specimens of their
work. The Academy cannot secure accomodations for its students.

Architecture	Painting
Drawing	Restoration
Graphic Art	Sculpture

SWITZERLAND

GENEVA

ECOLES D'ART DE GENEVE (Geneva Schools of Art), 9, Bd.
Helvetique, 1205.
M. Michel Rappo, Dir. Estab. 1748.

Ecole des Beaux-Arts (School of Fine Arts). Tel: 29.05.10
M. Jean-Luc Daval, Head. Founded 1748; ent. req. HS grad, ent.
exam; dipl.

Audio-Visual Expression	Painting
Design	Perspective
Engraving	Sculpture
Modeling	

Ecole des Arts Decoratifs (School of Decorative Arts),
15, Bd. James-Fazy. Tel: 31.37.57
M. Claude Malinjod, Head. Founded 1876; ent. req. HS grad, ent.
exam; cert.

Ceramics	Industrial Art
Enameling	Interior Design
Graphics	Jewelry

LAUSANNE

ECOLE CANTONALE DES BEAUX-ARTS ET D'ART APPLIQUE,*
(School of Fine & Applied Art), 4, avenue de l'Elysée, 1006.
Jacques Monnier, directeur; 1 FT, 24 PT instr. Estab. 1821; pub; D;
co-ed; ent. req. ent. exam; 5 yr; certificats Beaux-Arts, Etudes
artistiques générales, arts graphiques diplome industrial design;
enrl. grad. 105. Tui. $120.

Advertising Design	Illustration
Aesthetics	Industrial Design
Art Education	Lettering
Drawing	Painting
Graphic Arts	Photography
Graphic Design	Sculpture
History of Art & Archaeology	Teacher Training

U.S.S.R.

TALLINN, ESTONIAN S.S.R.

EESTI NSV RIIKLIK KUNSTIINSTITUUT* (State Art Institute of the
Estonian S.S.R), Tallinn, Tartu mnt. 1.
J. Vares, Rector; P. Tarvas, Asst. Rector; L. Habicht, Dean; H.
Parmas, Dean; 95 FT, 14 PT instr. Estab. 1914; pub; ent. req.
secondary educ, preliminary training in art; 5-6 yr; degrees;
schol; SC, LC. Children's classes.

Architecture	Leather
Ceramics	Metalwork
Design	Painting
Fashion	Scene Decoration
Glass	Sculpture
Graphics	Textiles
Interior Decoration	

State Arts Councils

This Directory of State Arts Councils was compiled by the Associated Councils of the Arts, 1564 Broadway, New York, N.Y. 10036. Permission to include the listing in the American Art Directory is gratefully acknowledged by the Editors.

NATIONAL ENDOWMENT FOR THE ARTS

Regional Coordinators

Dale Kobler
Pacific Area
P.O. Box 245
Sausalito, CA 94965
(415) 332-0526

Mrs. Frances Poteet
Lower Plains Area
601 East Austin, No. 1410
Alama, TX 78516
(512) 787-6756

Mrs. Lara Mulholland
Mid-Atlantic States
11511 Links Drive
Reston, VA 22090
(703) 437-4019

Mr. Rudolph Nashan
Northeastern States
30 Savoy Street
Providence, RI 02906

Charles Springman
Southeastern States
630 North Blount Street, Apt. 4
Raleigh, NC 27604

Terry Melton
3404 Liberty Road South, Apt. 7
Salem, OR 97302
(503) 581-5264

Mrs. Bertha Masor
4200 Marine Drive
Chicago, IL 60513
(312) 525-6748

UNITED STATES

Alabama State Council on the Arts and Humanities

Mr. Aubrey D. Green, Chairman
P.O. Drawer G
York, AL 36952
Home: (205) 392-5211

M. J. Zakrezewski, Executive Director
449 South MacDonough Street
Montgomery, AL 36130
Home: (205) 834-2667
Office: (205) 832-6757

Alaska State Council on the Arts

Mrs. Jean Mackin, Chairman
1114 Nenana
Fairbanks, AK 99701
Home: (907) 452-2094

Roy H. Helms, Executive Director
360 K Street
Anchorage, AK 99501
Office: (907) 279-3824

Arizona Commission on the Arts and Humanities

Lewis J. Ruskin, Chairman
5800 Foothills Drive
Scottsdale, AZ 85253
Home: (602) 948-6080
Office: (602) 271-5884

Mrs. Floyd J. Tester, Executive Director
6330 North 7th Street
Phoenix, AZ 85014
Office: (602) 271-5884

Arkansas State Council on the Arts and Humanities

Mrs. M. M. Llewellyn, Chairman
1174 South 74th Street
Fort Smith, AR 72901
Home: (501) 452-1586

Dr. Sandra Perry, Executive Director
Old State House
300 West Markham
Little Rock, AR 72201
Home: (501) 565-4991
Office: (501) 372-4000

California Arts Council

Chairman
808 O Street
Sacramento, CA 95814
Office: (916) 445-1530

Eloise Smith, Executive Director
808 O Street
Sacramento, CA 95814
Office: (916) 445-1530

The Colorado Council on the Arts and Humanities

Dean Robert B. Yegge, Chairman
College of Law, University of Denver
200 West 14th Avenue
Denver, CO 80204
Offices: (303) 753-2896; 297-1545

Robert N. Sheets, Executive Director
1550 Lincoln Street
Room 205
Denver, CO 80203
Home: (303) 333-3974
Office: (303) 892-2617

Connecticut Commission on the Arts

Marcia P. Alcorn, Chairperson
Russell Avenue
Suffield, CT 06078
Home: (203) 668-7306
Office: (203) 566-4770

Anthony S. Keller, Executive Director
340 Capitol Avenue
Hartford, CT 06106
Home: (203) 523-0330
Office: (203) 566-4770

Delaware State Arts Council

Mr. Gene Derrickson, Chairman
Wilmington Tower
1105 Market Street
Wilmington, DE 19801
Home: (302) 798-6228
Office, (302) 571-3540

Mrs. Sophie Consagra, Executive Director
Wilmington Tower
1105 Market Street
Wilmington, DE 19801
Home: (302) 654-3475
Office: (302) 571-3540

District of Columbia Commission on the Arts

Ms. ViCurtis Hinton, Chairman
1310 Farragut Street, Northwest
Washington, D.C. 20011
Home: (202) 882-5757

Leroy A. Washington, Acting Executive Director
Munsey Building, Room 1023
1329 E Street, Northwest
Washington, D.C. 20004
Office: (202) 347-5905

Fine Arts Council of Florida

Ira Mc Koger, Chairman
P.O. Box 4520
Jacksonville, FL 32210
Home: (904) 389-8173

Executive Director
Fine Arts Council of Florida
Department of State, The Capitol
Tallahassee, FL 32304
Office: (904) 488-2416

Georgia Council for the Arts

Mrs. Isabelle Watkins, Chairman
3920 Club Drive, Northeast
Atlanta, GA 30319
Home: (404) 233-6589

John Bitterman, Executive Director
225 Peachtree Street, Northeast
Atlanta, GA 30303
Office: (404) 656-3990

Hawaii—The State Foundation on Culture and the Arts

Masaru Yokouchi, Chairman
2180 Main Street, Suite 616
Wailuku, Maui, HI 96793
Home: (808) 244-4662
Office: (808) 244-7991

Alfred Preis, Executive Director
250 South King Street, Room 310
Honolulu, HI 96813
Home: (808) 988-3155
Office: (808) 548-4145

Idaho State Commission on the Arts and Humanities

Arthur L. Troutner, Chairman
Prus Jois Corporation
9777 Chinden Boulevard
Boise, ID 83701
Office: (208) 375-4450

Suzanne D. Taylor, Executive Director
506 North 5th Street, Annex 3
Boise, ID 83720
Home: (208) 343-3155
Office: (208) 384-2119

Illinois Arts Council

Bruce Sagan, Chairman
Southtown Economist
5959 South Harlem Avenue
Chicago, IL 60638
Home: (312) 924-1530
Office: (312) 586-8800

Michele Brustin, Executive Director
111 North Wabash Avenue, Room 1610
Chicago, IL 60602
Home: (312) 871-1865
Office: (312) 793-3520

Indiana Arts Commission

Mrs. J. Irwin Miller, Chairman
2760 Highland Way
Columbus, IN 47201
Home: (812) 376-8567

Janet I. Harris, Executive Director
155 East Market, Suite 614
Indianapolis, IN 46204
Office: (317) 633-5649

Iowa State Arts Council

Wayne A. Norman, Sr., Chairman
1525 Douglas
Dubuque, IA 52201
Home: (319) 582-6655

Jack E. Olds, Executive Director
State Capitol Building
Des Moines, IA 50319
Home: (515) 279-9572
Office: (515) 281-5297

Kansas Arts Commission

Mrs. Ellis Cave, Chairman
2010 La Mesa Drive
Dodge City, KS 67801
Home: (316) 225-1444

Jonathan Katz, Executive Director
117 West Tenth, Suite 100
Topeka, KS 66612
Office: (913) 296-3335

The Kentucky Arts Commission

B. Hudson Milner, Chairman
Louisville Gas & Electric Co.
311 West Chestnut Street
Louisville, KY 40202
Office: (502) 582-3511

Ms. Nash Cox, Executive Director
Main & High Street
Frankfort, KY 40601
Home: (502) 223-5211
Office: (502) 564-3757

Louisiana Council for Music and Performing Arts, Inc.

Mrs. Earl K. Long, Chairman of the Board of Directors
7449 Boyce Drive
Baton Rouge, LA 70804
Home: (504) 926-4161
Office: (504) 731-5363

Mrs. Edwin H. Blum, President and Acting Director
611 Gravier Street, Suite 804
New Orleans, LA 70130
Home: (504) 527-5070
Office: Same

Maine State Commission on the Arts and Humanities

Phillip Isaacoson, Chairman
2 Renson Street
Lewiston, ME 04240
Home: (207) 783-2207

Denny Wilson, Director
State House
Augusta, ME 04330
Office: (207) 289-2724

Maryland Arts Council

Dr. Carl Bode, Chairman
7008 Partridge Place
Hyattsville, MD 20780
(301) 864-6134

Executive Director
15 West Mulberry Street
Baltimore, MD 21201
(301) 685-7470

Massachusetts Council on the Arts and Humanities

Vernon R. Alden, Chairman
The Boston Company
1 Boston Place
Boston, MA 02109
(617) 722-7030

Louise G. Tate, Director
One Ashburton Place
Boston, MA 02108
(617) 727-3668

Michigan Council for the Arts

Walter R. Boris, Chairman
Vice President, Consumers Power Co.
212 West Michigan Ave.
Jackson, MI 49201
Home: (517) 783-5691
Office: (517) 788-0550

E. Ray Scott, Executive Director
1200 6th Avenue
Executive Plaza Room P160
Detroit, MI 48226
Home: (313) 961-1314
Office: (313) 256-3731

Minnesota Arts Board

Dr. Walther Prausnitz, Chairman
2614 South 11th Street, Apt. 19
Moorhead, MN 56560
Home: (218) 236-5370
Office: (218) 299-4321

Stephen Sell, Executive Director
314 Clifton Avenue
Minneapolis, MN 55403
Office: (612) 874-1335

Mississippi Arts Commission

Dr. W. D. McCain, Chairman
Southern Station
Box 5164
Hattiesburg, MS 39401

Mrs. Lida Rogers, Executive Director
Box 1341
Jackson, MS 39205
Office: (601) 354-7336
Home: (601) 584-6870

Missouri State Council on the Arts

Mr. Stanley Goodman, Chairman
The May Department Stores
601 Olive Street
St. Louis, MO 63101
Office: (314) 436-3300

Emily Rice, Executive Director
111 South Bemiston, Suite 410
St. Louis, MO 63105
Office: (314) 721-1672

Montana Arts Council

Ms. Maxine M. Blackmer, Chairman
635 Hastings Avenue
Missoula, MT 59801
Home: (406) 549-0457

David E. Nelson, Executive Director
235 East Pine Street
Missoula, MT 59801
Office: (406) 543-8286

Nebraska Arts Council

Leo A. Daly, Chairman
8600 Indian Hills Drive
Omaha, NE 68114
Home: (402) 391-9508
Office: (402) 391-8111

Gerry Ness, Executive Director
Oak Park, 7367 Pacific Street
Omaha, NE 68114
Home: (402) 393-3978
Office: (402) 554-2122

Nevada State Council on the Arts

Merle I. Snider, Chairman
560 Mill Street
Reno, NV 89502
Home: (702) 322-5660
Office: (702) 784-6231

James D. Deere, Executive Director
560 Mill Street
Reno, NV 89502
Home: (702) 323-5207
Office: (702) 784-6231

New Hampshire Commission on the Arts

Alden Burt, Chairman
Box 8911
Lebanon, NH 03766
Home: (603) 448-2062

John G. Coe, Executive Director
Phenix Hall
40 North Main Street
Concord, NH 03301
(603) 271-2789

New Jersey State Council on the Arts

Alvin E. Gershen, Chairman
126 West State Street
Trenton, NJ 08618
Office: (609) 989-8500

Brann J. Wry, Executive Director
27 West State Street
Trenton, NJ 08625
Office: (609) 292-6130

New Mexico Arts Commission

Mrs. Consuelo Thompson, Chairman
P.O. Drawer JJ
Espanola, NM 87532
Home: (505) 753-3076

Bernard B. Lopez, Executive Director
Lew Wallace Building
Capitol Complex
Santa Fe, NM 87501
Office: (505) 827-2061

New York State Council on the Arts

Mrs. Joan Davidson, Chairman
250 West 57 Street
New York, NY 10019
(212) 397-1700

Kent Barwick, Director
250 West 57th Street
New York, NY 10019
Office: (212) 397-1700

North Carolina Arts Council

Thad G. Stem, Jr., Chairman
P.O. Box 6
Oxford, NC 27565
Home: (919) 693-8169
Office: (919) 693-6518

Halsey M. North, Executive Director
Cambridge House
407 North Person St.
Raleigh, NC 27611
Home: (919) 829-7897

North Dakota Council on the Arts and Humanities

John Hove, Chairman
North Dakota State University
Department of English
Fargo, ND 58102
Home: (701) 237-5477
Office: (701) 237-7143

Glenn Scott, Director
Project 1202 North 2
Fargo, ND 58102
Home: (701) 237-4917
Office: (701) 237-7143

Ohio Arts Council

John Henle, Chairman
Chamber of Commerce
50 West Broad Street
Columbus, OH 43215
Home: (614) 885-7810
Office: (614) 221-1321

James Edgy, Executive Director
50 West Broad Street, Suite 2840
Columbus, OH 43215
Office: (614) 466-2613

Oklahoma Arts and Humanities Council

Howard Mc Gee, Chairman
905 Maxwell
Ardmore, OK 73401
Home: (405) 223-3263
Office: (405) 226-1300

William Jamison, Executive Director
P.O. Box 53553
Oklahoma City, OK 73105
Home: (405) 528-1558
Office: (405) 521-2931

Oregon Arts Commission

Hope Pressman, Chairman
Susan Campbell Hall
University of Oregon
Eugene, OR 97403

Peter de C. Hero, Executive Director
316 Oregon Building
494 State Street
Salem, OR 97301
Office: (503) 378-3625

Commonwealth of Pennsylvania Council on the Arts

Hiram Hershey, Chairman
P.O. Box 64
RD 1
Harleysville, PA 19438

Otis B. Morse, Executive Director
2001 North Front Street
Harrisburg, PA 17102
Office: (717) 787-6883

Rhode Island Council on the Arts

Vincent J. Buonanno, Chairman
4365 Post Road
East Greenwich, RI 02818
Office: (401) 884-6410

Ann Vermel, Executive Director
4365 Post Road
East Greenwich, RI 02818
Home: (401) 421-1784
Office: (401) 884-6410

South Carolina Arts Commission

Mr. Douglas A. Smith, Chairman
South Carolina Arts Commission
WFBC-TV
P.O. Box 788
Greenville, SC 29602

Rick George, Executive Director
Boylston House
829 Richland Street
Columbia, SC 29201
Home: (803) 799-0527
Office: (803) 758-3442

South Dakota State Fine Arts Council

Dr. Wayne Knutson, Chairman
College of Fine Arts
University of South Dakota
Vermillion, SD 57069
Home: (605) 624-3293
Office: (605) 677-5481

Mrs. Charlotte Carver, Executive Director
108 West 11 Street
Sioux Falls, SD 57102
Home: (605) 332-7257
Office: (605) 334-7651

Tennessee Arts Commission

Mrs. Richard Austin, Chairman
6227 Meadowgrove
Memphis, TN 38138
Home: (901) 683-5901
Office: (615) 741-1701

Norman Worrell, Executive Director
222 Capitol Hill Building
Nashville, TN 37219
Home: (615) 298-2592
Office: (615) 741-1701

Texas Commission on the Arts and Humanities

Edward R. Hudson, Jr., Chairman
Hudson & Hudson
First National Bank Building
Fort Worth, TX 76102
Home: (817) 732-4595
Office: same

Maurice D. Coats, Executive Director
P.O. Box 13406, Capitol Station
202 West 13th Street
Austin, TX 78711
Home: (512) 451-2570
Office: (512) 475-6593

Utah State Institute of Fine Arts

Dr. Keith M. Engar, Chairman
Pioneer Memorial Theatre
University of Utah
Salt Lake City, UT 84112
Home: (801) 581-9418
Office: (801) 581-6178

Ruth R. Draper, Executive Director
609 East South Temple Street
Salt Lake City, UT 84102
Home: (801) 582-4144
Office: (801) 328-5895

Vermont Council on the Arts

Michael Boylen, Chairman
RD 2
West Burke, VT 05871
Home: (802) 467-3335

Ellen McCulloch-Lovell, Executive Director
Administrative Building
Montpelier, VT 05602
Office: (802) 828-3291

Virginia Commission of the Arts and Humanities

Mr. Peter A. G. Brown, Chairman
Colonial Williamsburg Foundation
Williamsburg, VA 23185
Office: (804) 229-1000

Frank R. Dunham, Executive Director
1215 State Office Building
Richmond, VA 23219
Home: (804) 272-2645
Office: (804) 770-4492

Washington State Arts Commission

Mrs. Robert (Peggy) Goldberg, Chairperson
11001 Southeast Lake Road
Bellevue, WA 98004
Home and Office: (206) 454-3419

James L. Haseltine, Executive Director
1151 Black Lake Blvd.
Olympia, WA 98504
Home: (206) 866-4157
Office: (206) 753-3860

West Virginia Arts and Humanities Council

William M. Davis, Chairman
Bank of West Virginia
Tennessee Avenue & Roane Street
Charleston, WV 25302
Home: (304) 343-2955
Office: (304) 344-1621

Norman L. Fagan, Executive Director
Room B-531, State Office Building No. 6
1900 Washington Street, East
Charleston, WV 25305
Home: (304) 586-3777
Office: (304) 348-3711

Wisconsin Arts Board

Ruth Kohler, Chairman
John Michael Kohler Art Center
608 New York Avenue
Sheboygan, WI 53081
Office: (414) 458-6144

Jerrold B. Rouby, Executive Director
Loraine Hotel
1 West Wilson Street
Madison, WI 53702
Home: (608) 233-6105
Office: (608) 266-8106

Wyoming Council on the Arts

Adrian, Malone, Chairman
23 North Main Street
Sheridan, WY 82801
Home: (307) 672-2314
Office: (307) 674-4476

Michael F. Haug, Executive Director
Cheyenne, WY 82002
Home: (307) 634-9950
Office, (307) 777-7742

UNITED STATES TERRITORIES

American Samoa Arts Council

Mr. Palauni M. Tuiasosopo
Office of the Governor
GAS American Samoa
Pago Pago 96799
Home: (overseas) 633-4060
Office: (overseas) 633-4116

Mr. Misiuaita A. Maga, Arts Administrator
Office of the Governor
GAS American Samoa
Pago Pago 96799
Home: (overseas) 622-7417
Office: (overseas) 633-4116

Guam—Insular Arts Council

Pete C. Sanchez, President
University of Guam
P.O. Box EK
Agana, Guam 96910

Louis Hotaling, Director
University of Guam
Box EK
Agana, Guam 96910
Office: 729-2466

A. B. Won Pat, Local Representative
200 Maryland Avenue, Northeast
Suite 301
Washington, DC 20242
Office: (202) 963-4655

Institute of Puerto Rican Culture (Instituto del Cultura Puertorriquena)

Enrique Laguerre, Chairman
Apartado Postal 4184
San Juan, Puerto Rico 00905
Office: (809) 723-2115

Luis M. Rodrigues Morales, Executive Director
Apartado Postal 4184
Puerto Rico, 00905
Office: (809) 723-2115

Virgin Islands Council on the Arts

Evan A. Francois, Chairman
P.O. Box 276
Charlotte Amalie
St. Thomas, USVI 00801
Office: (809) 774-1450

Stephen J. Bostic, Executive Director
Caravelle Arcade
Christiansted, St. Croix, USVI 00820
Office: (809) 773-3075
Home: (809) 773-1869

CANADA
Provincial Arts Councils

Alberta

Walter H. Kassa, Assistant Deputy Minister for Cultural
Development
Department of Culture, Youth and Recreation
Government of Alberta
11th Floor, CN Tower
10004 104th Avenue
Edmonton, Alberta T5J OK5

British Columbia

T. G. Fielding, Chairman
British Columbia Cultural Programme
Department of Provincial Secretary
466 Superior Street
Victoria, BC

The Secretary
First Citizens' Fund
Parliament Buildings
Victoria, BC

Manitoba

Dr. Jack Thiessen, Chairman
200-185 Carlton Street
Winnipeg, Manitoba R3C IP3
University of Winnipeg: (204) 786-7811 Local 394
Home: (204) 453-5598

Mrs. Marlene Neustaedter, Executive Secretary
200-185 Carlton Street
Winnipeg, Manitoba R3C IP3
Office: (204) 943-6325
Home: (204) 489-5237

New Brunswick

Walter Learning
The Playhouse
Fredericton, NB

Newfoundland

John C. Perlen, Director of Cultural Affairs
Governments of Newfoundland & Labrador
Newfoundland Arts and Culture Center
P.O. Box 1854
St. John's, Newfoundland

Nova Scotia

Mr. J. L. Martin, Director
Cultural Resources Program
1747 Summer Street
Halifax, NS

Ontario

Mr. Frank F. McEachren, Chairman
Province of Ontario Council for the Arts
151 Bloor Street West, 5th Floor
Ministry of Colleges & Universities
Toronto, Ont. M5S LT6
Office: (416) 961-1660

Louis Applebaum, Executive Director
Province of Ontario Council for the Arts
151 Bloor Street West, 5th Floor
Naomi G. Lightbourn, Executive Director
Ministry of Colleges & Universities
Toronto, Ont. M5S LT6
Office: (416) 961-1660
Home: (416) 449-7307

Prince Edward Island

Honorable T. Earle Hickey, Minister
Duncan MacAdams, Deputy Minister
Department of the Environment and Tourism
P.O. Box 2000
Charlottetown, PEI

Quebec

Guy Fregault, Sous Ministre
Ministres des Affaires Culturelles
Hotel de Gouvernment
Quebec 4, Quebec

Saskatchewan

Vern E. Bell, Executive Director
Saskatchewan Arts Board
200 Lakeshore Drive
Regina, Saskatchewan S4S 0A4

Yukon

John C. Thoresen, Director of Recreation
Department of Education
Recreation Branch
P.O. Box 2703
Whitehorse, YT

Directors and Supervisors of Art Education in School Systems

Compiled from a survey made by the National Art
Education Association under the direction of
Dr. John J. Mahlmann, Executive Secretary.

ALABAMA

Mrs. Jessie Butler Jones
Art Consultant, Division of Secondary Education
State Department of Education
State Office Building
Montgomery, Alabama 36104

Sarah H. Johnson
Art Consultant, Division of Elementary Education
State Department of Education
State Office Building
Room 607
Montgomery, Alabama 36104

ALASKA

Marilou Madden
Educational Program Support
Alaska Department of Education
Pouch F
Juneau, Alaska 99811

ARIZONA

Raymond G. Van Diest
Director, Arts and Humanities
State Department of Education
Phoenix, Arizona 85007

ARKANSAS

Jerry C. Swope
Supervisor of Art Education
Arch Ford Education Building
Capitol Mall
Little Rock, Arkansas 72201

CALIFORNIA

Louis P. Nash
Consultant Arts and Humanities Education
California State Department of Education
721 Capitol Mall
Sacramento, California 95814

COLORADO

No position

CONNECTICUT

Robert J. Saunders
Art Education Consultant
State Department of Education
P.O. Box 2219
Hartford, Connecticut 06115

DELAWARE

Mr. James R. Gervan
Supervisor of Art and Music Education
Department of Public Instruction
Townsend Building
Dover, Delaware 19901

DISTRICT OF COLUMBIA

Director (position open)

Mrs. Marie B. Williams
Supervisory Director of Art
Public Schools of D.C.
14th & Jackson Streets, N.E.
Room 117
Washington, D.C. 20017

FLORIDA

Neil Mooney
Art Consultant
State Department of Education
Suite 10, Miles Johnson Building
Tallahassee, Florida 32304

GEORGIA

Ruth Gassett
Consultant, Art Education
Education Annex
156 Trinity Street, S.W.
Atlanta, Georgia 30303

HAWAII

Stanley I. Yamamoto
Program Specialist, Art Education
Room 1201
1270 Queen Emma Street
Honolulu, Hawaii 96804

IDAHO

Bert A. Burda
Fine Arts Representative
State Department of Education
Boise, Idaho 83707

ILLINOIS

Larry L. Emmons
Art Education Specialist
Illinois Office of Education
100 North First Street
Springfield, Illinois 62777

INDIANA

Ann Timberman
Art Consultant
State Department of Public Instruction
Division of Curriculum
120 West Market
Indianapolis, Indiana 46204

IOWA

Dr. A. John Martin
Director, Division of Curriculum
Department of Public Instruction
Grimes State Office Building
Des Moines, Iowa 50319

KANSAS

Gary L. Kroeger
Art Consultant
Department of Education
State of Kansas
120 East 10th Street
Topeka, Kansas 66612

KENTUCKY

Mrs. Ruth West
Consultant, Art Education
State Department of Education
Frankfort, Kentucky 40601

LOUISIANA

Mrs. Myrtle Kerr
State Supervisor of Art
P.O. Box 44064
Baton Rouge, Louisiana 70804

MAINE

Virgilio Mori
Art Coordinator
State of Maine Department of Education
Augusta, Maine 04330

MARYLAND

Harold H. Lott
Consultant of Art
State Department of Education
International Towers Building
P.O. Box 8717, BWI Airport
Baltimore, Maryland 21240

MASSACHUSETTS

William E. Farrington
Senior Supervisor of Art Education
State Department of Education
182 Tremont Street
Boston, Massachusetts 02111

MICHIGAN

Dorothy I. Brooks
Fine Arts Specialist
Michigan Department of Education
P.O. Box 420
Lansing, Michigan 48902

MINNESOTA

Robert M. Paul
Art Coordinator
State Department of Education
Division of Instruction
Room 639, Capitol Square
St. Paul, Minnesota 55101

MISSISSIPPI

Miss Sandra Nichola
State Department of Education
P.O. Box 771
Jackson, Mississippi 39205

MISSOURI

Richard L. Stokes
Supervisor of Art
State Department of Education
Division of Instruction
Section of Fine Arts
Jefferson City, Missouri 65101

MONTANA

Elsom Eldridge, Jr.
Arts and Humanities Coordinator
Office of the Superintendent of Public Instruction
State Capitol Building
Helena, Montana 59601

NEBRASKA

Steven Lahr
State Art Consultant
Nebraska Department of Education
233 South 10th Street
Lincoln, Nebraska 68508

NEVADA

Tom Summers
Consultant in Humanities
Nevada Department of Education
Capitol Complex
Carson City, Nevada 89710

NEW HAMPSHIRE

John Michael Gray
Consultant, Art Education
Department of Education
64 North Main Street
Concord, New Hampshire 03301

NEW JERSEY

Al Kochka
President, NASDAE
Department of Education
County of Sussex
County Service Building
Newton, New Jersey 07860

NEW MEXICO

Rollie V. Heltman
Director of Fine Arts
State Department of Education
State Capitol Building
Santa Fe, New Mexico 87501

NEW YORK

Vincent J. Popolizio
Supervisor of Art Education
Bureau of Art Education
State Education Department
Albany, New York 12224

NORTH CAROLINA

Doc McCulloch
State Art Supervisor
Jefferson Plaza, Suite 900
1411 Jefferson Davis
Raleigh, North Carolina 27602

NORTH DAKOTA

Harold Michelson
Director of Secondary Education
North Dakota Public Instruction
Capitol Building
Bismarck, North Dakota 58501

OHIO

Jerry Tollifson
Supervisor, Art Education
Department of Education
Ohio Department Building
Room 815
65 South Front Street
Columbus, Ohio 43215

OKLAHOMA

Ms. Peggy Long
Curriculum Specialist
Department of Fine Arts
State Department of Education
Oklahoma City, Oklahoma 73105

OREGON

Verne A. Duncan
Department of Public Instruction
State Arts Education
Salem, Oregon 97310

PENNSYLVANIA

Clyde M. McGeary
Fine Arts Education Advisor
Department of Education
Bureau of General and Academic Education
Division of Fine Arts
Harrisburg, Pennsylvania 17126

RHODE ISLAND

Arlene I. Wilson
Art Consultant
Department of Education
Roger Williams Building
Hayes Street
Providence, Rhode Island 02908

SOUTH CAROLINA

    Thomas A. Hatfield
    Supervisor of Art
    South Carolina Department of Education
    801 Rutledge Building
    Columbia, South Carolina 29201

SOUTH DAKOTA

    Mr. Philvik
    Art Director
    N.E. Field Service Center
    Box 853-NSC
    Aberdeen, South Dakota 57401

TENNESSEE

    Robert Daniel
    Supervisor of Instruction in Arts
    Building 307
    11th Avenue
    Smyrna, Tennessee 37167

TEXAS

    Ida Nell Williams
    Art Consultant
    Texas Education Agency
    201 East 11th Street
    Austin, Texas 78711

UTAH

    Charles B. Stubbs
    State Specialist in Fine Arts
    1500 University Club Building
    136 East South Temple
    Salt Lake City, Utah 84111

VERMONT

    Miss M. Rita Pfeifer
    Arts Consultant
    Department of Education
    Montpelier, Vermont 05602

VIRGINIA

    Mrs. Shirlee C. Loomer
    Assistant Supervisor of Art
    State Department of Education
    Richmond, Virginia 23216

WASHINGTON

    William Radcliffe, Jr.
    Supervisor of Art Programs
    State Office of Public Instruction
    P.O. Box 527
    Olympia, Washington 98501

WEST VIRGINIA

    Virginia Walker
    Supervisor of Art Education
    Department of Education
    Capitol Building
    Charleston, West Virginia 25305

WISCONSIN

    Earl Collins
    State Supervisor of Art Education
    126 Langdon Street
    Madison, Wisconsin 53702

WYOMING

    Candace Noble
    Coordinator, Foreign Language, Bilingual Education and Fine Arts
    State Office Building West
    Cheyenne, Wyoming 82002

PUERTO RICO

    Carmen Tuya
    Director, Visual Arts Program
    Commonwealth of Puerto Rico
    Department of Education
    Hato Rey, Puerto Rico

VIRGIN ISLANDS

    Douglas Covey
    Supervisor of Art
    Department of Education
    P.O. Box 1
    Christiansted, St. Croix, Virgin Islands 00820

SCHOOL SYSTEMS OF 500,000 & OVER IN POPULATION

Birmingham Public Schools

    Mrs. Lila J. Wells
    Supervisor of Art
    P.O. Box 114
    Birmingham, Alabama 35201

Phoenix Union High School District

    Mrs. Dorothy Johnson Bergamo
    Chairman, Department of Performing Arts
    Trevor G. Browne High School
    7402 W. Catalina Drive
    Phoenix, Arizona 85033

Long Beach Unified School District

    Sherry E. Swan
    Resource Teacher, Fine Arts Education
    701 Locust Avenue
    Long Beach, California 90814

Los Angeles Unified School District

    Mrs. Winifred Hall
    Instructional Specialist, Art
    Instructional Planning Division A-311
    P.O. Box 3307
    Los Angeles, California 90054

San Diego Unified School District

    Dr. Leven C. Leatherbury
    Specialist in Art Education
    4100 Normal Street
    San Diego, California 92103

San Francisco Unified School District

    Herbert R. Simon
    Director of Art
    135 Van Ness Avenue
    San Francisco, California 94102

Dade County Public Schools

    Charles M. King
    Art Supervisor
    1410 Northeast Second Avenue
    Miami, Florida 33132

Lee County Public Schools

    Mrs. Margaret A. Bare
    Art Consultant
    School Annex, First Street
    Fort Myers, Florida 33901

De Kalb County Schools

    Mrs. Sara Jo Sirmans
    Supervisor of Art
    1144 Hancock Drive, N.E.
    Atlanta, Georgia 30306

Chicago Public Schools

    Mrs. Mary Cole Emerson
    Director, Division of Art
    228 North LaSalle Street
    Chicago, Illinois 60601

Indianapolis Public Schools

    Ted A. Moore
    Supervisor of Art
    120 East Walnut Street
    Indianapolis, Indiana 46204

Davenport Community School District

Lars H. Souder
Coordinator of Art Education
1001 Harrison
Davenport, Iowa 50307

Des Moines Independent Community School District

Ruth Mobberly
Art Education Supervisor
1800 Grand Avenue
Des Moines, Iowa 50307

Baltimore City Public Schools

Richard L. Micherdzinski
Director of Art
Oliver and Eden Streets
Baltimore, Maryland 21213

Prince George's County Public Schools

Mary Beth Wackwitz
Supervisor of Art, K-12
Supervisors
Board of Education of Prince George's County
Upper Marlboro, Maryland 20870

Boston Public Schools

Miss Elizabeth H. Gilligan
Director of Fine Arts
15 Beacon Street
Boston, Massachusetts 02108

Chicopee Public Schools

Miss Margaret L. Mannix
Supervisor of Art
244 Oak Street
Holyoke, Massachusetts 01040

Benton Harbor Public Schools

Mr. Charles Murray
Art Department Chairman
870 Colfax Avenue
Benton Harbor, Michigan 49022

Detroit Public Schools

Mr. Jules Trattner
Director, Art Education
Board of Education
5057 Woodward Avenue
Detroit, Michigan 48202

Flint Board of Education

Maurice D. Frost
Coordinator of Fine Arts
902 East Sixth Street
Flint, Michigan 48503

Wayne Community School District

Miss Suan Price
Coordinator of Visual Arts
3712 Williams Street
Wayne, Michigan 48184

Osseo Senior High School District

Eugene Waldowski
Art Teacher
317 Second Avenue, N.W.
Osseo, Minnesota 55369

Kansas City Public Schools

Leonard Pryor
District Coordinator of Art Education
Room 808
1211 McGee Street
Kansas, Missouri 64106

Raytown Consolidated School District 2

Miss Jean Harrison
Art Supervisor
10500 East 60th Terrace
Raytown, Missouri 64133

St. Louis Public Schools

Dr. Marie L. Larkin
Supervisor of Art
5329 Columbia Avenue
St. Louis, Missouri 63139

Buffalo Public Schools

John M. Gaylord
Director of Art Education
Room 709 C City Hall
Buffalo, New York 14202

Rochester City School District

Burt A. Towne
Director of Art
13 Fitzhugh Street S.
Rochester, New York 14614

Cincinnati Public Schools

Donald P. Sowell
Instructional Consultant, Art Education
230 East Ninth Street
Cincinnati, Ohio 45202

Columbus Public Schools

Miss Helen Sandfort
Director of Fine and Performing Arts
270 East State Street
Columbus, Ohio 43215

Toledo Board of Education

Mary Ryan
Director of Art
Toledo Board of Education
Manhattan & Elm
Toledo, Ohio 43608

Willoughby-Eastlake City Schools

Mrs. Uarda Overbaugh
Art Consultant
Willoughby-Eastlake City Schools
Royalview Elementary School
31500 Royalview Drive
Willowick, Ohio 44094

The School District of Philadelphia

Jack Bookbinder
Director of Art Education
Board of Education
21 & Parkway
Philadelphia, Pennsylvania 19103

Austin Independent School District

Sherilyn Howze
Art Coordinator
6100 Guadalupe
Austin, Texas 78752

Houston Independent School District

Mrs. Mary Pearl Temple
Director of Art Education
Supervisor, Art Education
3830 Richmond Avenue
Houston, Texas 77027

Federal Way School District 210

Scott Pepper
Art Consultant
31455 28th Avenue South
Federal Way, Washington 98002

Seattle School District 1

Mr. Henry W. Petterson
Art Specialist
815 Fourth Avenue N.
Seattle, Washington 98107

Milwaukee Public Schools

    Gordon Borchardt
    Director of Art Education
    P.O. Drawer 10K
    Milwaukee, Wisconsin 53201

SCHOOL SYSTEMS OF 100,000 TO 499,999

Bessemer Public Schools

    Margaret K. Elm
    Art Consultant
    417 South 18th
    Bessemer, Alabama 35020

Jefferson County Board of Education

    Mr. DeLeon Fancher
    1810 25th Court South
    Birmingham, Alabama 35209

Gadsden City Schools

    Mrs. Ma Lou Smith
    Art Specialist
    P.O. Box 184
    Gadsden, Alabama 35902

Opelika Public Schools

    Roslyn B. Stern
    Art Consultant
    P.O. Box 311
    Opelika, Alabama 36801

Tuscaloosa City Schools

    Mrs. Ronna Lasser
    Art Teacher - Coordinator, Elementary
    1100 21st Street E.
    Tuscaloosa, Alabama 35401

Anchorage Borough School District

    Dr. Ruth Keitz
    Art Coordinator
    670 Fireweed Lane
    Anchorage, Alaska 99503

Mesa Public Schools

    Dr. Edna Gilbert
    Art Director
    Mesa Public Schools
    14 West Second Avenue
    Mesa, Arizona 85202

Phoenix Elementary District 1

    Miss Betty Lou Richards
    Art Director
    125 East Lincoln
    Phoenix, Arizona 85004

Prescott Elementary Schools

    Ella F. Fisher
    Supervisor of Art Education
    Prescott Elementary Schools
    146 South Granite Street
    Prescott, Arizona 86301

Tucson Elementary Schools

Sunnyside School District 12
    Rubina F. Gallo
    Los Ninos Elementary School
    Elementary Art Consultant
    470 West Valencia Road
    Tucson, Arizona 85704

Tucson Public Schools District 1

    Nik Krevitsky
    Director of Art and Educational Materials Center
    1010 East Tenth Street
    Box 4040
    Tucson, Arizona 85717

Alum Rock Union Elementary School District

    Mrs. Arline L. Cox
    Program Coordinator of Cultural Arts
    2930 Gay Avenue
    San Jose, California 95127

Alameda Unified School District

    Miss Olivia Krause
    Supervisor of Art Education
    400 Grand Street
    Alameda, California 94501

Alhambra City Schools

    Mrs. Ann Wollen
    Art Consultant
    15 West Alhambra Road
    Alhambra, California 91801

Bakersfield City School District

    Mrs. Mary K. Mueller
    Consultant, Art Education
    Education Center
    1300 Baker Street
    Bakersfield, California 93305

Baldwin Park Unified School District

    Kathryn McIlreath
    Art Specialist
    Baldwin Park USD
    3699 North Holly Avenue
    Baldwin Park, California 91706

Berkeley Unified School District

    Philip St. Martin
    Chairman, Art, Industry and Design
    Berkeley High School
    Berkeley, California 94709

Burbank Unified School District

    Miss Marjorie Simpson
    Supervisor, Department of Art
    245 East Magnolia Boulevard
    Burbank, California 91504

Campbell Elementary School District

    Mrs. Marcia Wells
    Art Consultant
    155 North Third Street
    Campbell, California 95008

Campbell Union High School District

    Ross C. Deniston
    Art Supervisor
    Camden High School
    2075 Camden Avenue
    San Jose, California 95124

Chula Vista City School District

    Mrs. Leona Wulff
    Art Consultant
    84 East "J" Street
    P.O. Box 907
    Chula Vista, California 92012

Compton City School District

    Kenneth Gregg
    Staff Teacher Art
    Mrs. Billie Jackson
    Staff Teacher Art
    Compton Unified School District
    604 South Tamarind Avenue
    Compton, California 90220

    Kenneth R. Gregg
    Staff Teacher, Art
    Area I Instructional Services
    1623 E. 118th Street
    Los Angeles, California 90059

Compton Union High School District

Leonard F. Fisher
District Curriculum Assistant, Art
417 West Alondra Boulevard
Compton, California 90220

Danville Unified School District

Jeanne P. Rinaldi
Art Consultant
599 Old Orchard Drive
Danville, California 94526

Escondido Union School District

Rex Hamilton
Fine Arts Specialist
Fifth & Maple
Escondido, California 92025

Fresno City Unified School District

Mr. Ralph E. Gomas
Art Coordinator
Curriculum Services Center
3132 East Fairmont
Fresno, California 93726

Fullerton Elementary School District

Mrs. Gelsomina Barton
Fine Arts Coordinator
1401 West Valencia Drive
Fullerton, California 92633

Garden Grove Unified School District

Bernard M. Jones, Jr.
Art Specialist
10331 Stanford Avenue
Garden Grove, California 92640

Glendale Unified School District

Mrs. Audrey A. Welch
Arts Supervisor
411 East Wilson Avenue
Glendale, California 91206

Hudson School District

Mrs. Lona Hoffman
Consultant
15959 East Gale Avenue
La Puente, California 91745

La Mesa-Spring Valley School District

Pauline N. Ritter
Art Coordinator
4750 Date Avenue
La Mesa, California 92041

Montebello Unified School District

Mrs. Jewel Bishop
Consultant, Art
123 South Montebello Boulevard
Montebello, California 90640

Monterey Peninsula Unified School District

Miss Mildred Koch
Art Consultant
Walter Colton Junior High School
Box 1031
Monterey, California 93940

Mt. Diablo Unified School District

Mr. James E. Snowden
Art Consultant
1936 Carlotta Drive
Concord, California 94519

Monroe Valley Unified School District

Dr. Robert Banister
District Art Supervisor
13911 Perris Boulevard
Sunnymead, California 92388

Newport-Mesa Unified School District

Jenean Romberg
Newport-Mesa School District
1601 Sixteenth Street
Newport Beach, California 92660

Novato Unified School District

Lee Hilton
Curriculum Specialist, Art
1015 Seventh Street
Novato, California 94947

Oakland Unified School District

Stanley H. Cohen
Art Consultant/Staff Development
1025 Second Avenue
Oakland, California 94606

Ocean View School District

Mrs. Rose Clark
Resource Teacher, Art
7871 Warner Avenue
Huntington Beach, California 92647

Palo Alto Unified School District

Mrs. Kathryn M. Alexander
Art Consultant
25 Churchill Avenue
Palo Alto, California 94306

Pasadena City Unified School District

Norman E. Schmidt
Art Education Consultant
351 South Hudson
Pasadena, California 91109

Pasadena Secondary School District

Sr. Mary Bendorf
St. Andrew High School
42 Chestnut Street
Pasadena, California 91103

Pomona Unified School District

Dr. Jean Henschel
Coordinator of Art Education
800 South Garey Avenue
P.O. Box 2900
Pomona, California 91766

San Jose Unified School District

Mr. William Shelley
Supvervisor of Art Education
1605 Park Avenue
San Jose, California 95126

San Lorenzo Unified School District

James Brown
Supervisor of Music & Fine Arts
15510 Usher Street
San Lorenzo, California 94580

San Mateo City School District

Richard Sperisen
Art Consultant & Director
School Design
P.O. Box K
San Mateo, California 94402

Santa Barbara High School District

Janice Y. Lorber
Art Department
700 E. Anapamu Street
Santa Barbara, California 93103

Santa Clara Unified School District

Miss Janet E. Tellefsen
Art Consultant
P.O. Box 397
Santa Clara, California 95052

Santa Monica Unified School District

Richard Wagnon
Supervisor of Music and Art
Joan F. Vaupen
Art Teacher, Curriculum Assistant
Art Office, Santa Monica Bd. of Education
1723 Fourth Street
Santa Monica, California 90401

San Mateo Union High School District

Gregg MacGibbon
Art Curriculum Council Chairman
Crestmoor High School
300 Piedmont Avenue
San Bruno, California 94066

Sweetwater Union High School District

Mr. Frank Buzga
District Art Committee Chairman
Sweetwater Union High School District
1130 Fifth Avenue
Chula Vista, California 92011

Ventura Unified School District

Howard Quam
Art Coordinator
120 East Santa Clara
Ventura, California 93001

School District 12, Adams County

Gregory D. Wolfe
Coordinator of Art
10280 North Huron Street
Denver, Colorado 80221

Adams-Arapahoe Joint School District 28

Richard D. Schafer
Coordinator of Art
1085 Peoria Street
Aurora, Colorado 80011

Arapahoe County School District 6

Mrs. Augusta Schreiber
Consultant in Art Education, K-12
6558 South Acoma Street
Littleton, Colorado 80120

Boulder Valley Public School District

Helen B. Davis
Coordinator of Art, K-12
P.O. Box 11
Boulder, Colorado 80302

Colorado Springs Public Schools, District 11

Robert Simpich
Director, Art Education
1115 North El Paso Street
Colorado Springs, Colorado 80903

Jefferson County School District R-1

Larry T. Schultz
Coordinator of Art
809 Quail Street
Lakewood, Colorado 80215

Poudre School District R-1

Miss Sylvia B. Maxey
Art Coordinator
2407 La Porte Street
Fort Collins, Colorado 80521

Bridgeport Public Schools

John C. Nerreau
Supervisor of Art
Board of Education
Room 302, City Hall
45 Lyon Terrace
Bridgeport, Connecticut 06604

Bristol Public Schools

Mrs. Carol Bloomquist
Department Head
Box 1601
Bristol, Connecticut 06010

East Hartford Board of Education

Mrs. Ruby Towle
Art Supervisor
50 Chapman Street
East Hartford, Connecticut 06108

Fairfield School System

Mr. Peter Clarke
Art Coordinator
c/o Andrew Warde High School
Fairfield, Connecticut 06430

Greenwich School System

Harold L. Krevolin
Art Curriculum Coordinator K-12
Art Department
P.O. Box 292
Greenwich, Connecticut 06830

Hartford Public Schools

Paul J. Dilworth
Supervisor, Department of the Arts
249 High School
Hartford, Connecticut 06103

Meriden Public Schools

Thomas F. Potter
Supervisor of Art
Board of Education
City Hall
Meriden, Connecticut 06450

Milford Public Schools

Frank J. Vespi
Department Head
Elementary Art Department
91 Stowe Avenue
Milford, Connecticut 06460

New Canaan Public Schools

Alois Fabry, Jr.
Director of Art
New Canaan, Connecticut 06849

New Haven public Schools

Margaret F. Ring
Supervisor of Art
765 Elm Street
New Haven, Connecticut 06511

Norwalk Public Schools

Dr. Donald Rogers
Art Department Head
Board of Education Offices
105 Main Street
Norwalk, Connecticut 06852

Stamford Public Schools

Mayo Sorgman
Supervisor of Arts
60 Washington Avenue
Stamford, Connecticut 06902

Newark School District

Harley S. Hastings
Supervisor of Music and Art
Newark School District
83 East Main Street
Newark, Delaware 19711

Wilmington Public Schools

Joseph A. Corbi
Supervisor of Art and Unified Arts
Wilmington Public Schools
1400 Washington Street
Wilmington, Delaware 19801

District of Columbia Public Schools

Mrs. Marie B. Williams
Supervising Director
Room 1010
415 12th Street, N.W.
Washington, D.C. 20004

Broward County School System

Mrs. Jeanette McArthur
Director of Art Education
1320 S.W. Fourth Street
P.O. Box 8369
Fort Lauderdale, Florida 33312

Duval County School Board

William H. Dodd
Supervisor of Art Education
1701 Davis Street
Jacksonville, Florida 32209

Escambia County School Board

Miss Mary Jo Burgess
Supervisor of Art
P.O. Box 1470
Pensacola, Florida 32502

Hillsborough County Board of Public Instruction

Flo Bottari
Supervisor of Art
Instructional Services Center
707 East Columbus Drive
Tampa, Florida 33602

Lee County Public Schools

Mrs. Margaret A. Bare
Coordinator of Fine Arts
School Annex
First Street
Fort Myers, Florida 33902

Leon County School System

Maribelle L. Custer
Supervisor of Art
725 North Macomb Street
Tallahassee, Florida 32304

Manatee County School System

Mrs. Eleanor H. Paul
Acting Art Supervisor
5886 17th Street, West
Bradenton, Florida 33505

School Board of Okaloosa County

Collis V. Porter
Art Supervisor
201 Marilyn Street
Fort Walton Beach, Florida 32548

Palm Beach County Public Schools

Mrs. Jo D. Kowalchuk
Supervisor
School Board of Palm Beach County
South Administrative Offices
505 South Congress Avenue
Boynton Beach, Florida 33435

Panama City Public Schools

Mrs. Nelyne Allan
Supervisor Art Education
Bay County Schools
1855 Liddon Road
Panama City, Florida 32401

School Board of Pinellas County, Florida

Phyllis M. Thurston
Art Supervisor
100 North Greenwood
Clearwater, Florida 33515

Polk County School Board

Joe P. Mitchell
Coordinator of Art Instruction
P.O. Box 391
Bartow, Florida 33830

St. Lucie County School Board

Mr. Harold Supank
2909 Delaware Avenue
Fort Pierce, Florida 33450

Sarasota County School Board

Mary Francis MacDonald
Supervisor of Art Education
2418 Hatton Street
Sarasota, Florida 33577

Volusia County Board of Public Instruction

Mrs. Dorothy Johnson
Art Supervisor
P.O. Box 1910
Daytona Beach, Florida 32015

Atlanta Public Schools

Mrs. Lucia G. Dubro
Coordinator, Arts and Humanities Center
1280 Peachtree Street, N.E.
Atlanta, Georgia 30309

Callaway Educational Association

Carolyn Ann Page
Art Director
Dallis Street
La Grange, Georgia 30240

Clark County School District

Mrs. Mary Jane Root
Art Supervisor
Box 1708
Athens, Georgia 30601

Clayton County Board of Education

Mrs. Martha Ellen Stilwell
Curriculum Coordinator, Art, Music
120 Smith Street
Jonesboro, Georgia 30236

Eastman Public Schools

Earl W. Woodward
Art Supervisor, Title III
Cultural Enrichment Project
Eastman, Georgia 31023

Fulton County School District

Miss Emory Rose Wood
Director of Art Education
786 Cleveland Avenue, S.W.
Atlanta, Georgia 30315

Macon Public Schools

Miss J. Elizabeth McElroy
Art Supervisor, Area 4
Hunt School
990 Shurling Drive
Macon, Georgia 31201

Peach City Schools

Mrs. Jean D. Pervis
Art Consultant
Fort Valley High School
Knox Valley, Georgia 31031

Walton County Public Schools

Mrs. Perry Nelle Darby
Art Consultant
Walton City Board of Education
Monroe, Georgia 30655

Kamehameha Schools

Mrs. Frances Pickens
Art Instructor, Senior High School Division
Bernice Pauahi Bishop Estate
Kapalama Heights
Honolulu, Hawaii 96817

Independent School District of Boise City

Robert Wand
Supervisor of Art
1207 Fort Street
Boise, Idaho 83702

Arlington Township High School District 214

Edward Fischer
District Coordinator of Fine Arts
High School District 214 Administration Center
799 West Kensington Road
Mount Prospect, Illinois 60056

Cicero Elementary District 99

Emil R. Proska
Art Consultant
5110 West 24th
Cicero, Illinois 60650

Champaign County Schools

Kenneth B. Cottingham
Visual Arts Coordinator
202 West Columbia
Champaign, Illinois 61820

Mrs. Josephine W. Payne
Elementary Art Consultant
2035 South New Street
Champaign, Illinois 61820

Danville Community Consolidated School District 118

Mrs. Iris Gillis
Coordinator of Art
516 North Jackson Street
Danville, Illinois 61832

Elgin Public Schools, District U-46

Mrs. Corinne Loeh
Director of Art Education
4 South Gifford Street
Elgin, Illinois 60120

District 65 Schools, Evanston

Stanley C. Drabinowicz
Director of Art
1314 Ridge Avenue
Evanston, Illinois 60201

Granite City Community Unit 9

Eugene L. Aiassi
Administrative Consultant of Art Education
2545 Westmoreland Drive
Granite City, Illinois 62040

Moline Public Schools

Marie Ringquist
Coordinator of Art
1619 Eleventh Avenue
Moline, Illinois 61265

Oak Park Elementary Schools

Floyd Freerksen
970 Madison
Oak Park, Illinois 60302

District 15 Schools, Palatine

Mrs. Josephine L. Heyden
Art Chairman
789 North Inverway
Palatine, Illinois 60067

Rockford Public Schools

Paul Pullin
Supervisor of Art
201 South Madison Street
Rockford, Illinois 61101

Rock Island Public Schools

Richard T. Klatt
Director of Art
1400 25th Avenue
Rock Island, Illinois 61201

Springfield Public Schools, District 186

Martha L. Wasylik
Director of Art Education K-8
Unit School District 60
574 McAlister Avenue
Waukegan, Illinois 60085

Western Springs Public Schools

Wesley R. Buchwald
Supervisor of Art
Area B
4815 South Karlov Avenue
Western Springs, Illinois 60632

Anderson Public Schools

Doris Noel
Supervisor of Art
528 West 11th Street
Anderson, Indiana 46016

Bartholomew Consolidated School Corporation

Karl McCan
Supervisor of Art Education
Senior High School
Columbus, Indiana 47201

Bedford Public Schools

Miss Marie M. McCord
Art Supervisor
N.L.C. School
2222 West Eighth Street
Bedford, Indiana 47421

Evansville-Vanderburgh School Corporation

Harry C. Friley
Supervisor of Art Education
1 South East Ninth Street
Evansville, Indiana 47708

Fort Wayne Community Schools

Mr. Gene P. Porter
Consultant for Art
1230 South Clinton Street
Fort Wayne, Indiana 46802

Gary Public Schools

Mrs. John A. Mohamed
Supervisor of Art K-12
620 East 10th Place
Gary, Indiana 46408

Hammond Public Schools

Robert Lee Fischer
Curriculum Consultant
524 173rd Street
Hammond, Indiana 46320

Kokomo-Center Township Consolidated School Corporation

James Osborne
Coordinator of Art Education
100 West Lincoln Road
Kokomo, Indiana 46901

Marion Community Schools

George Kind
Art Coordinator
Marion High School
716 West 26th Street
Marion, Indiana 46952

Michigan City Area Schools

Mrs. Kay Behrndt
Director of Art
609 Lafayette Street
Michigan City, Indiana 46360

Muncie Community Schools

Miss Beulah Book
Supervisor of Art
328 East Washington Street
Muncie, Indiana 47305

New Castle Schools

Mrs. Shirley A. Liby
Art Supervisor
New Castle Schools Administration Building
522 Elliott Avenue
New Castle, Indiana 47362

Richmond Community Schools

Edward L. Loar
Supervisor of Art
Administration Building
300 Whitewater Boulevard
Richmond, Indiana 47374

South Bend Community School Corporation

Kenneth Geoffroy
Coordinator of Fine Arts
635 South Main Street
South Bend, Indiana 46623

Vigo County School Corporation

Mrs. Harriet McCullough
Elementary School Art Chairman
Washington School
13th and College
Terre Haute, Indiana 47802

Metropolitan School District of Washington Township

Max I. Briggs
Chairman, Art Department
North Central High School
1801 East 86th Street
Indianapolis, Indiana 46240

Cedar Rapids Community School District
Archie E. Bauman
Coordinator of Art Education
346 Second Avenue, S.W.
Cedar Rapids, Iowa 52404

Sioux City Community School District

Margaret Pedersen
Division Head
Art Department
1221 Pierce Street
Sioux City, Iowa 55101

Unified School District 500, Kansas City

E. Eileen Hughes
Supervisor of Art
2019 Tauromee
Kansas City, Kansas 66102

Shawnee Mission Public School District 512

Peter Perdaris
Coordinator of Art
7200 Belinder
Shawnee Mission, Kansas 66208

Unified School District 501, Shawnee County

Mrs. Edwin L. Smith
Supervisor of Art
1601 Van Buren
Topeka, Kansas 66612

Unified School District Wichita, 529

William W. King
Director of Art Education
640 North Emporia
Wichita, Kansas 67214

Jefferson County Public Schools

Norma E. Brown
Art Supervisor
3332 Newburg Road
Louisville, Kentucky 40218

Louisville Independent Public Schools

Martha Christensen
Supervisor of Art Education
Louisville Public Schools
506 West Hill Street
Louisville, Kentucky 40208

Caddo Parish School System

Mrs. Zelphia B. Layton
Supervisor of Related Arts Education
1961 Midway
P.O. Box 3700
Shreveport, Louisiana 71108

Calcasieu Parish School System

Brad Daigle
Supervisor, Music and Art
1732 Kirkman Street
Lake Charles, Louisiana 70601

New Orleans Public Schools

Mrs. Dagny K. Andreassen
Supervisor of Art
731 St. Charles Avenue
New Orleans, Louisiana 70130

Ouachita Parish School System

Henry Camp
Fine Arts Coordinator
P.O. Box 1642
Monroe, Louisiana 71201

Allegany County Public Schools

Harry R. Mandel
Supervisor of Art Education
108 Washington Street
Cumberland, Maryland 21502

Anne Arundel County Public Schools

Mary E. Wellham
Coordinator of Art
Anne Arundel County Board of Education
27 Chinquapin Round Road
Annapolis, Maryland 21401

Baltimore County Public Schools

James B. Laubheimer
Coordinator of Art
John L. Crossin
Supervisor of Art
Patricia A. Agee
Art Specialist
Board of Education of Baltimore County
Towson, Maryland 21204

Carroll County Public School System

Dr. Robert E. Kersey
Supervisor of Art and Music
Carroll County Board of Education
Box 500
Westminster, Maryland 21157

Charles County Board of Education

Ann S. Richardson
Supervisor of Art
I.M.C. Board of Education of Charles County
La Plata, Maryland 20646

Frederick County Public Schools

Carroll H. Kehne, Jr.
Supervisor of Art
115 East Church Street
Frederick, Maryland 21701

Howard County Public Schools

H. Eugene Miller
Supervisor, Art and Music
Howard County Board of Education
Clarksville, Maryland 21029

Montgomery County Public Schools

Marjorie B. St. Clair
Emil Hrebenach
Supervisor of Art
850 North Washington Street
Rockville, Maryland 20850

Washington County Public Schools

Mr. Clyde H. Roberts
Supervisor of Art
Box 730
Hagerstown, Maryland 21740

Bourue Public Schools

Jeremiah M. Lyon
Art Director
Bourue High School
Bourue, Massachusetts 02532

Brockton Public Schools

Pasquale F. Morano
Director of Art Education
50 Summer Street
Brockton, Massachusetts 02402

Cambridge School Department

Joseph L. C. Santoro
Director of Art
1700 Cambridge Street
Cambridge, Massachusetts 02138

Fall River Public Schools

Edmond St. Laurent
Director of Fine Arts
417 Rock Street
Fall River, Massachusetts 02720

Framingham Public Schools

Neal Cotton
Director of Art
49 Lexington Street
Framingham, Massachusetts 01701

Braintree Public Schools

Margaret D. Puffer
Director of Art
Braintree Public Schools
Ten Tremont Street
South Braintree, Massachusetts 02185

Greenfield Public Schools

Mrs. Shirley A. Crowell
Art Coordinator
197 Federal Street
Greenfield, Massachusetts 01301

Lexington Public Schools

Paul A. Ciano
Director of Art Education K-12
Lexington Public Schools
Lexington, Massachusetts 02173

Lowell Public Schools

Thomas McGuire
Director of Art
Lowell, Massachusetts

Lynn Public Schools

Lucy A. Towne
Supervisor of Art
School Administration Building
42 Franklin Street
Lynn, Massachusetts 01902

Medford Public Schools

Frances Fanning
Coordinator of Art
25 Hall Avenue
Medford, Massachusetts 02155

New Bedford Public Schools

Raymond Bisaillon
Art Education Director
County Street Administration Building
New Bedford, Massachusetts 02740

Newton Public Schools

Albert Hurwitz
Coordinator of Art
88 Chestnut Street
West Newton, Massachusetts 02165

Pittsfield Public Schools

Mrs. Winifred Bell
Art Coordinator, K-12
Pittsfield Public Schools
Central Annex, Second Street
Pittsfield, Massachusetts 01201

Osterville Public Schools

Deborah A. Barrows
Elementary Art Supervisor
Box 424
Centerville, Massachusetts 02632

Quincy Public Schools

Mr. Walter E. Lunsman
Director of Art
Quincy Public Schools
Coddington Street
Quincy, Massachusetts 02169

Somerville Public Schools

Charles Khirallah
Director of Art
Burns School
58 Cherry Street
Somerville, Massachusetts 02144

Springfield Public Schools

Robert L. Drummond
Director of Fine and Industrial Arts
195 State Street
Springfield, Massachusetts 01103

Weymouth Public Schools

Philip S. Dolan
Lead Teacher
Weymouth South High School
360 Pleasant Street
South Weymouth, Massachusetts 02190

Waltham School Department

Paul D. Shea
Art Director
Waltham Public Schools
Waltham, Massachusetts 02154

Worcester Public Schools

Ora J. Gatti
Director of Art
20 Irving Street
Worcester, Massachusetts 01609

Ann Arbor Public Schools

Mrs. Ruth L. Beatty
Coordinator of Art
Public School Administration Building
1220 Wells Street
Ann Arbor, Michigan 48104

Battle Creek Public Schools

Max D. Misner
Art Consultant
Willard Library Building
Battle Creek, Michigan 49106

Bay City Public Schools

Jane D. Miller
Director of Art Education
1800 Columbus Avenue
Bay City, Michigan 48706

Benton Harbor Public Schools

Charles Murray
Art Department Chairman
870 Colfax Avenue
Benton Harbor, Michigan 49022

Dearborn Public Schools

Eleanor Heth
Donald Boughner
Art Resource Teacher
4824 Lois Avenue
Dearborn, Michigan 48126

East Detroit Public Schools

Donald Olesklewicz
Chairman, Art Department
15550 Couzens
East Detroit, Michigan 48021

Farmington Public Schools

Mrs. Beverly L. Ellis
Elementary Art Consultant
32500 Shiawassee
Farmington, Michigan 48024

Garden City Public Schools

Donald L. Beatty
Asstistant Superintendent, Curriculum
1333 Radcliff Street
Garden City, Michigan 48135

Grand Rapids Public Schools

Mrs. Vee Matusko
Supervisor of Art
143 Bostwick, N.E.
Grand Rapids, Michigan 49502

Kalamazoo Public Schools

Marian Andros
Coordinator/Specialist, Art
1220 Howard Street
Kalamazoo, Michigan 49001

Lansing School District

Sara Jane Venable
Director of Art Instruction
3426 South Cedar Street
Lansing, Michigan 48910

Midland City School District

James Hopfensperger
Coordinator of Art
600 E. Carpenter Street
Midland, Michigan 48640

City of Pontiac School District

Otha Whitcomb
Art Specialist
Franklin Elementary School
661 Franklin Road
Pontiac, Michigan 48513

Portage Public Schools

Mary Gave
Chairman, Art Department
Portage Public Schools
Portage, Michigan 49081

Port Huron Area School District

Vincent S. McPharlin
Director, Art Education
509 Stanton Street
Port Huron, Michigan 48060

Roseville Public Schools

Curt Winnega
Chairman, Art Department, Secondary Schools
Brablec High School
Roseville, Michigan 48066

Saginaw City School District

Eleanor Bangham
Director of Art Education
550 Millard Street
Saginaw, Michigan 48607

Anoka-Hennepin Independent School District 11

Bert Dahlman
Art Coordinator
Anoka, Minnesota 55303

Independent School District 709, Duluth

Sheldon Johnson
Supervisor of Art
Board of Education Building
226 North First Avenue, E.
Duluth, Minnesota 55802

Minneapolis Public Schools

Dr. Eugenia M. Oole
Consultant in Art
807 North East Broadway
Minneapolis, Minnesota 55413

Independent School District 281, Robbinsdale Area

Pearl Halverson
Ivy Raben
Elementary Art Consultants
4148 Winnetka Avenue, North
Minneapolis, Minnesota 55427

Osseo Senior High School District

Eugene Waldowski
Art Teacher
317 Second Avenue, N.W.
Osseo, Minnesota 55369

Rochester, District 535

Kenneth Bauman
Elementary Art Consultant
463 Northern Heights Drive, N.E.
Rochester, Minnesota 55901

St. Louis Park Public Schools

Robert Anderson
Department Chairman
Art Education
6425 West 33rd Street
St. Louis Park, Minnesota 55426

Independent School District 621, Mounds View

Ellsworth E. Erickson
District Art Coordinator
Art Research, Resource Center
3555 North Victoria
St. Paul, Minnesota 55172

Independent School District 625, St. Paul

Stephen Conger
Supervisor of Art
Independent School District 625
Saint Paul Public Schools
360 Colborne
St. Paul, Minnesota 55102

Independent School District 624, White Bear Lake

Franklin J. Zeller
Art Coordinator
Lincoln Elementary School
1413 Sixth Street
White Bear Lake, Minnesota 55110

Jackson Public Schools

Mary Dell Burford
Supervisor of Art
Elementary Schools
1593 West Capital Street
Jackson, Mississippi 39203

Berkeley Public Schools

Arthur B. Kennon
Elementary Art Coordinator
6001 Berkeley Drive
Berkeley, Missouri 63134

Ferguson-Florissant School District

Mrs. Alice P. Ulbright
Coordinator of Art Education
655 January Avenue
Ferguson, Missouri 63135

Independence School District

Louis H. Braley
Art Consultant
1231 South Windsor
Independence, Missouri 64055

Parkway School District

Jerrel L. Swingle
Art Coordinator
Parkway School District
455 North Woods Mill Road
Chesterfield, Missouri 63017

Kirkwood Public Schools

Mrs. Carroll H. Loren
Art Coordinator K-6
230 Quau Avenue
Kirkwood, Missouri 63122

North Kansas City

Katherine Smith
Elementary Art Supervisor
2000 North East 46th Street
Kansas City, Missouri 64116

The School District of St. Joseph

Marie Corcoran
Art Consultant
School District of St. Joseph
Tenth and Felix Streets
St. Joseph, Missouri 64501

Ritenour Consolidated School District

Mrs. Verneta Sevier
District Art Coordinator
Ritenour Consolidated School District
2420 Woodson Road
St. Louis County, Missouri 63114

School District of Springfield R12

Bill Stockstill
Coordinator of Art
Secondary Schools
Parkview High School
516 West Meadows
Springfield, Missouri 65804

School District 2, Billings

Archie Elliot
Director of Art Education
101-Tenth Street West
Billings, Montana 59102

School District 1, Great Falls

James D. Poor
Supervisor of Art
1100 Fourth Street South
Great Falls, Montana 59401

Lincoln Public Schools

Roger Dean Von Deventer
Art Consultant K-12
Public School Administration Building
P.O. Box 200
Lincoln, Nebraska 68501

Omaha Public Schools

Gerald Pabst
Supervisor
3902 Davenport Street
Omaha, Nebraska 68131

Ralston Public Schools

Mrs. Judith C. Pittack
Elementary Art Supervisor
79th and Seymour
Ralston, Nebraska 68127

Las Vegas City Schools

Mrs. Marjorie A. Phillips
Phil Leger
Robertson High School
Las Vegas, New Mexico 87701

Manchester School Union 37

Leonard R. Armstrong
Director of Art
88 Lowell Street
Manchester, New Hampshire 03104

Cherry Hill Public Schools

Yvonne L. Bieberbach
Art Coordinator
1155 Marklress Road
Cherry Hill, New Jersey 08034

Clifton Public Schools

Richard Ebert
Director of Music and Art
Clifton Public Schools
School No. 4
Clifton, New Jersey 07011

East Orange Public School System

Bernice E. Magnie
Director of Art
21 Winans Street
East Orange, New Jersey 07017

Elizabeth Public Schools

Mrs. Marion Quin Dix
Director of Art Education
330 West Jersey Street
Elizabeth, New Jersey 07202

Jersey City Public Schools

Paul F. X. Hearns
Supervisor of Art
100 Newkirk Street
Jersey City, New Jersey 07306

Middletown Township Public Schools

Wayne Ehlers
Middletown Township Public Schools
59 Tindall Road
Middletown, New Jersey 07748

Newark Public Schools

Dr. Ruth K. Assarsson
Director of Art Education
Department of Art Education
15 State Street
Newark, New Jersey 07102

Paterson Board of Education

Edward B. Epstein
Supervisor of Fine Arts
Board of Education
33 Church Street, B-4
Paterson, New Jersey 07505

Summit Public Schools

Arthur E. DeBrito
Chairman, Art Department K-12
Summit Public Schools
Summit, New Jersey 07901

Trenton Public Schools

John T. Cunningham
Director of Fine Arts
Board of Education
Nine South Stockton Street
Trenton, New Jersey 08611

Wayne Public Schools

Gayle Reed
Art Coordinator
50 Nellis Drive
Wayne, New Jersey 07470

Albany Public Schools

Margaret M. Smith
Director of Art Education
Albany Board of Education
Academy Park
Albany, New York 12207

Binghamton City School District

Anne Greiner
Chairman Art Department
31 Main Street
Binghamton, New York 13905

Brentwood Public Schools

Manuel R. Vega
Coordinator of Art and Administrative Assistant
Brentwood Public Schools
Administration Building
Third Avenue and Fourth Street
Brentwood, New York 11717

Buffalo Public Schools

John M. Gaylord
Thomas A. Jambro
Supervisor of Art
Room 709 C
City Hall
Buffalo, New York 14202

Union Free School District 10

Mr. Sidney Cumins
District Art Consultant
80 Hauppauge Road
Commack, New York 11725

Connetquot City School District 7

Eugene Lissandrello
Director of Art
Connetquot Central School District of Islip
District Central Office
780 Ocean Avenue
Bohemia, New York 11716

East Meadow Public Schools

Phyllis B. Nelson
Director of Art Education
Curriculum Center
Meadowbrook Elementary School
East Meadow, New York 11554

City School District of Elmira

Elbert Ryerson
Director of Art
Administration Building
951 Hoffman Street
Elmira, New York 14905

Farmingdale Public Schools

Frank Cole
Roger Hartford
Department Chairman
Farmingdale Senior High School
Lincoln Street
Farmingdale, New York 11735

Kenmore-Town of Tonawanda Public Schools

Robert Freeland
Area Consultant in Art (K-12)
1500 Colvin Boulevard
Kenmore, New York 14223

Levittown Union Free School District

Casimir Cetnarowski
Supervisor of Art
Board of Education Offices
North Village Green
Levittown, New York 11756

Lindenhurst Public Schools

Mrs. Barbara Payne
Elementary Art Coordinator K-6
E. W. Bower School
Montauk Highway

Raphael P. Knopf
Art Department Chairman, Grades 7-12
Lindenhurst Senior High School
300 Charles Street
Lindenhurst, New York 11757

Massapequa Public Schools

Morris Brewer
Coordinating Chairman, Art
Administrative Wing, Massapequa High School
4925 Merrick Road
Massapequa, New York 11758

Middle Country Central School District 11

Henry Lechowicz
Art Coordinator
Seldon, New York 11784

Mount Vernon Public Schools

C. Andrew Randall
Coordinator of Music & Art
Education Center
165 North Columbus Avenue
Mt. Vernon, New York 10550

Community School District New Rochelle

Mortimer H. Slotnick
Supervisor of Art and Humanities
515 North Avenue
New Rochelle, New York 10801

New York City Public Schools

George Kaye
Acting Director of Art
Board of Education
131 Livingston Street
Brooklyn, New York 11201

North Syracuse Central Schools

Roger E. Hyndman
Coordinator of Art Education
Lawrence Road Curriculum Center
North Syracuse, New York 13212

School District of Niagara Falls

Donald Banks
Supervisor of Art
607 Walnut Avenue
Niagara Falls, New York 14301

Oceanside Union Free School District

    Paul C. Olivia
    Director of Art Education
    145 Merle Avenue
    Oceanside, New York 11572

Central School District 4, Plainview-Old Bethpage

    Charles Burge
    District Art Coordinator
    Central School District 4
    Plainview, New York 11803

Rome City School District

    Guy Nasci
    Director of Art
    108 E. Garden Street
    Rome, New York 13440

Rochester City School District

    Burt Towne
    Director, Arts and Humanities
    13 Fitzhugh Street South
    Rochester, New York 14614

Schenectady Public Schools

    Edwin G. Weinheimer
    Supervisor of Art
    108 Union Street
    Schenectady, New York 12305

Sewanhaka Central District 2

    Ruth Backiel
    Art Coordinator
    Sewanahaka Art Department
    500 Tulip Avenue
    Floral Park
    Long Island, New York 11001

Smithtown Public Schools

    Richard Mello
    Art Coordinator
    Smithtown Central School District 1
    St. James
    Long Island, New York 11780

South Huntington, Union Free School District 13

    Mrs. Maree Galvin
    Coordinator of Art, K-6
    31 Walt Whitman Road
    Huntington Station, New York 11746

Syracuse City School District

    Robert J. Pfister, Jr.
    Associate in Elementary and Secondary Education
    Department of The Visual & Performing Arts
    Central Offices
    409 West Genesee Street
    Syracuse, New York 13202

Three Village Central School District 1

    Edward T. Goebel
    Director of Art
    Three Village Central School District 1
    Nicoll Road
    Setauket, New York 11733

Wappingers Central School District

    Anthony J. Caccamo
    Director of Art Education
    Wappingers Central School District
    John Jay High School
    Route 52
    Hopewell Junction, New York 12533

White Plains Public Schools

    John Ruddley
    Westchester County Supervisor of Art
    Department of Parks, Recreation and Conservation
    County Center
    White Plains, New York 10606

Yonkers Public Schools

    Mrs. Ellen Kruger
    Supervisor of Art
    Board of Education
    Yonkers, New York 10701

Charlotte-Mecklenburg Schools

    Mrs. Elizabeth Mack
    Director, Visual Arts
    P.O. Box 149
    Charlotte, North Carolina 28201

Durham City Schools

    Director of Art
    P.O. Box 2246
    Durham, North Carolina 27702

Greensboro Public Schools

    Mrs. E. Frances Crimm
    Art Supervisors
    712 North Eugene Street
    Greensboro, North Carolina 27402

Fort Bragg Dependents Schools

    Miss Claudia J. Sailor
    Art Coordinator
    Fort Bragg Dependents Schools
    Drawer A
    Fort Bragg, North Carolina 28307

High Point City Schools

    Gwendolyn Doggett
    Supervisor
    Post Office, Box 789
    High Point, North Carolina 27261

Raleigh City Schools

    Rose Melvin
    Director of Art Education
    1600 Fayetteville Road
    Raleigh, North Carolina 27605

Wayne County Schools

    Thomas L. Evans
    Supervisor of Art Education
    P.O. Drawer 27
    Goldsboro, North Carolina 27530

Winston-Salem/Forsyth County Schools

    Antony Swider
    Coordinator of Art Education
    P.O. Box 2513
    Winston-Salem, North Carolina 27102

Fargo Public Schools

    Bruce McGhie
    Art Consultant
    1104 Second Avenue South
    Fargo, North Dakota 58102

Akron Public Schools

    Brian B. Heard
    Director of Art Education
    70 North Broadway
    Akron, Ohio 44308

Berea City Schools

    Charles Armstrong
    Art Supervisor
    390 Fair Street
    Berea, Ohio 44017

Canton City Schools

    Mari Niarchos
    Art Consultant (K-12)
    618 High Avenue, N.W.
    Canton, Ohio 44703

Cleveland Public Schools

Ronald N. Day
Directing Supervisor of Art
1380 East Sixth Street
Cleveland, Ohio 44114

Cuyahoga Falls City Schools

Ronald Simon
Head, Art Department
c/o Falls High School
2300 Fourth Street
Cuyahoga Falls, Ohio 44221

Dayton Public Schools

Armand Martino
Supervisor of Art
Dayton Board of Education
Service Building
4280 North Western Avenue
Dayton, Ohio 45427

Elyria City Schools

Charles R. Rose
Supervisor of Art Education
520 Clark Street
Elyria, Ohio 44035

Findlay Public Schools

Alexander Baluch
Art Supervisor
1001 Blanchard Avenue
Findlay, Ohio 45840

Kettering City School District

Robert Thygerson
Supervisor, Music and Fine Arts
Kettering City School District
3490 Far Hills Avenue
Kettering, Ohio 45429

Lima City School District

Richard E. Clark
Art Supervisor
515 South Calumet Avenue
Lima, Ohio 45804

Mansfield City Schools

Lois Beveridge
Art Resource Teacher
145 West Park Boulevard
Mansfield, Ohio 44902

Mentor Public Schools

Ted Keller
Supervisor of Art
Mentor High School
6477 Center Street
Mentor, Ohio 44060

Parma City Schools

Joseph Charnigo
Director of Art Education
6726 Ridge Road
Parma, Ohio 44129

Springfield City Schools

John Grube
Supervisor of Art
49 East College Avenue, Box 89
Springfield, Ohio 45501

Warren City Schools

James G. Friend
Supervising Teacher of Art
1360 Autumn Drive, N.W.
Warren, Ohio 44458

Washington Local Schools

Mrs. Donna Johnston
Art Coordinator
5201 Douglas Road
Toledo, Ohio 43613

Youngstown City Schools

Andrew Nadzam
Supervisor of Art
20 West Wood Street
Youngstown, Ohio 44503

Enid Public Schools, Independent 57

Eldon Ames
Art Supervisor
111 South Taylor
Enid, Oklahoma 73701

Oklahoma City Public Schools

Pat Merchant
Consultant, Art
900 North Klein
Oklahoma City, Oklahoma 73106

Tulsa Public Schools

Mrs. Bobbie Jean Brophy
Supervisor of Art
3027 South New Haven
Tulsa, Oklahoma 74145

Beaverton School District 48

Omer Gosnell
Productions Specialist
Curriculum Specialist
P.O. Box 200
Beaverton, Oregon 97005

Bend Public School District 1

Richard G. Dedlow
Art Director
School District 1
Administration Building
Bend, Oregon 97701

Eugene Public Schools, District 4J

Mrs. Freda Young
Art Education Coordinator
200 North Monroe
Eugene, Oregon 97402

David Douglas School District

Joseph B. Kleven
Supervisor of Art
2900 South East 122nd Avenue
Portland, Oregon 97236

Area IV Portland Public Schools

Austin O. Myers
Consultant
Area IV Curriculum Center
Barlow School
3700 South East 92nd
Portland, Oregon 97226

Portland Public Schools

Roberta J. Caughlan
Project Manager
Eco-Aesthetics Continuum
Portland Public Schools
7700 S.E. Reed College Place
c/o Dunway School
Portland, Oregon 97202

Salem Public Schools, District 24J

Don Walton
Consultant
P.O. Box 87
Salem, Oregon 97308

Abington School District

Louis S. Mohollen
Supervisor of Art
Abington School District
1841 Susquehanna
Abington, Pennsylvania 19001

Allentown Public Schools

David T. Lehman
Supervisor of Art
31 South Penn Street
Allentown, Pennsylvania 18105

Altoona Area School District

Calvin E. Folk
Supervisor of Art
1415 Seventh Avenue
Altoona, Pennsylvania 16603

Armstrong School District

Charles Milton Hanna
Department Chairman
Fourth and Tenth
Ford City, Pennsylvania 16226

Bethlehem Area School District

Dr. Frederick G. Gilmartin
Art Coordinator
Bethlehem Schools
2307 Rodgers Street
Bethlehem, Pennsylvania 18018

Bristol Township Public Schools

Joseph Pavone
Administrative Teacher, Art
Lafayette Elementary School
Fayette Drive
Bristol, Pennsylvania 19007

Chambersburg Area School District

Mrs. Joyce S. Wyatt
Elementary Art Department Chairman
511 South Sixth Street
Chambersburg, Pennsylvania 17201

Chester Public Schools

Robert E. Vaughan
Director of Fine Arts
Chester Upland School District
18th and Melrose
Chester, Pennsylvania 19013

Erie School District

Paul Grack
Coordinator of Art
224 French Street
Erie, Pennsylvania 16507

Harrisburg City School District

Ray P. Firestone
Associate Director, Art Education
1201 North Sixth Street
Harrisburg, Pennsylvania 17102

Hazelton Area School District

Albert Sarkas
Supervisor of Art
950 Peace Street
Hazelton, Pennsylvania 18201

Greater Johnstown School District

M. Josephine Paul
Supervisor of Art
Chestnut Building
501-509 Chestnut Street
Johnstown, Pennsylvania 15906

Lancaster Public Schools

Albert B. Mimich
Director of Art
225 West Orange Street
Lancaster, Pennsylvania 17604

New Castle Public Schools

Jesse W. Badger
Art Supervisor
421 Fern Street
New Castle, Pennsylvania 16101

Pennsbury School District

Karl C. Schantz
Art Teacher, Quarry Hill School
Pennsbury School District
Fallsington, Pennsylvania 19054

Pittsburgh Public Schools

Ruth M. Ebken
Director of Art
Board of Public Education
341 South Bellefield Avenue
Pittsburgh, Pennsylvania 15213

Reading School District

Dr. Harry Bentz
Art Supervisor
Administration Building
Eighth & Washington Streets
Reading, Pennsylvania 19601

Scranton Public Schools

Terrence Gallagher
Supervisor of Art
425 North Washington Avenue
Scranton, Pennsylvania 18503

Upper Darby School District

H. Janice Guiesinger
District Art Supervisor
Upper Darby, Pennsylvania 19084

Warren County School District

James Hill
Elementary Art Supervisor
Market Street Elementary School
Market and Second Streets
Warren, Pennsylvania 16365

West Chester Area School District

Mrs. Betty L. Wright
Head, Art Department
Henderson Senior High School
Lincoln & Montgomery Avenue
West Chester, Pennsylvania 19380

West Shore School District

Mrs. Eleanor P. Stanton
Coordinator of Art
1833 Bridge Street
New Cumberland, Pennsylvania 17070

Williamsport Area School District

Dr. June E. Baskin
Supervisor of Art
605 West Fourth Street
Williamsport, Pennsylvania 17701

Pawtucket School Department

Mrs. Veronica M. Farrell
Art Director
Administration Building
Park Place
Pawtucket, Rhode Island 02860

Providence School System

Mrs. Catherine W. Hill
Supervisor of Art
150 Washington Street
Providence, Rhode Island 02903

Warwick School Department

Dorothy Desmond
Department Head, Elementary Art
Box 507 Conimicut Station
34 Warwick Lake Avenue
Warwick, Rhode Island 02889

Charleston County School District

Dr. Maxie E. Beaver
Director of Fine Arts
Charleston County School District
3 Chisolm Street
Charleston, South Carolina 29401

Darlington County

Mrs. W. H. Bristow, Jr.
Art Supervisor
St. John's High School
Darlington, South Carolina 29532

Florence School District 1

James H. Rash
Art Supervisor
109 West Pine Street
Florence, South Carolina 29501

Greenville County School District

Mrs. Margaret L. Gilliam
Art Consultant
P.O. Box 5575, Station B
Greenville, South Carolina 29606

Greenwood School District 50

Mrs. Ray Young
Art Supervisor
P.O. Box 248
Greenwood, South Carolina 29646

Spartanburg County School District 7

Betty Jane Bramlett
Art Director
Spartanburg City Schools
P.O. Box 970
Spartanburg, South Carolina 29301

Rapid City Public Schools

Diana M. Tollefson
Bureau of Indian Affairs
Cheyenne-Eagle Butte High School
Eagle Butte, South Dakota 57625

Sioux Falls Instructional School District 1

A. J. Cerny
Art Supervisor K-12
Instructional Planning Center
201 East 38th
Sioux Falls, South Dakota 57102

Chattanooga Public Schools

Fred Arnold
Supervisor of Art
Box 2013
1161 West 40th Street
Chattanooga, Tennessee 37409

Knoxville City Schools

Mrs. Billie Connatser
Supervisor of Art
101 East Fifth Avenue
Knoxville, Tennessee 37917

Knox County Board of Education

Mrs. VaLera Lewis
Supervisor of Art
400 West Hill Avenue
Knoxville, Tennessee 37902

Metropolitan Nashville Davidson County Public Schools

James D. Hughes
Supervisor, Art Education
2601 Bransford Avenue
Nashville, Tennessee 37204

Abilene Public Schools

Scott Darr
Art Supervisor
P.O. Box 981
Abilene, Texas 79604

Corpus Christi Independent School District

Neva G. Christian
Art Coordinator
1045 Hamlin
Corpus Christi, Texas 78411

El Paso Independent School District

Jane Walshe
Art Consultant
P.O. Box 1710
El Paso, Texas 79999

Edgewood Independent School District

Mrs. Isabel DeLaGarza
Art Supervisor
6458 West Commerce
San Antonio, Texas 78237

Fort Worth Independent School District

Ted C. Couch
Consultant in Art Education
3210 West Lancaster
Fort Worth, Texas 76107

Galveston Independent School District

Mignon Weisinger
Art Supervisor
Secondary Schools
Ball High Schools
4115 Avenue O
Galveston, Texas 77558

Goose Creek Consolidated Independent School District

Tommy F. Seale
Director of Music, Art and Crafts
P.O. Box 30
Baytown, Texas 77520

Killeen Independent School District

H. F. Groth
Asstistant Superintendent for Instruction
P.O. Box 967
Killeen, Texas 76541

Midland Independent School District

Bill R. Cormack
Coordinator of Fine Arts
702 North "N"
Midland, Texas 79701

North East Independent School District

Mrs. Margaret Ivy
Consultant, Art Education
10214 Sommers Drive
San Antonio, Texas 78217

Pasadena Independent School District
M. Virginia Wallace
Supervisor of Art
3010 Bayshore Drive
Pasadena, Texas 77502

Amarillo Independent School District

Marjorie Gudgen
Director of Art Education
910 West Eighth Avenue
Amarillo, Texas 79101

Richardson Independent School District

Mrs. Madge D. Darnett
Secondary Art Supervisor
1233 Ottawa Drive
Richardson, Texas 75080

San Angelo Independent School District

Mrs. Velma Jo Whitfield
Art Supervisor
100 North Magdalen Street
San Angelo, Texas 76901

Spring Branch Independent School District

Mrs. Janetta Smith
Art Consultant
955 Campbell Road
Houston, Texas 77024

Wichita Falls Independent School District

Walter Ehlert
Art Coordinator
San Jacinto School
Fifth and Bluff
Wichita Falls, Texas 76301

Davis County School District

Ivan Cornia
Art Supervisor
Davis County School District
Farmington, Utah 84025

Granite School District

Delbert W. Smedley
Supervisor, Art Education
340 East 3545 South
Salt Lake City, Utah 84115

Jordan School District

David R. Roberts
Art Consultant
Jordan School District
9361 South 400 East
Sandy, Utah 84070

Ogden City School District

Norman L. Skanchy
Principal, Horace Mann School
1300 Ninth Street
Ogden, Utah 84404

Salt Lake City Board of Education

Russell E. Bjorklund
Specialist in Art
440 East First South
Salt Lake City, Utah 84111

Barre City Schools

Helen D. Cate
Art Supervisor
Barre City Schools
Barre City, Vermont 15641

Alexandria City Public Schools

Joseph J. Adgate
Coordinator, Art, K-12
418 South Washington Street
Alexandria, Virginia 22313

Chesapeake Public Schools

Mrs. Edith G. Franklin
Supervisor of Art Education
School Administration Building
P.O. Box 15204
Chesapeake, Virginia 23320

Chesterfield County Public Schools

William Troxell
Supervisor of Fine Arts
School Board Administration Building
Chesterfield, Virginia 23832

Fairfax County Public Schools

Dr. Beverly A. Heinle
Art Curriculum Specialist
10700 Page Avenue
Fairfax, Virginia 22030

Hampton City Schools

Leroy Hubbard
Supervisor of Art
Thomas Street School Board Annex
1306 Thomas Street
Hampton, Virginia 23369

Arlington County Public Schools

Dr. Richard G. Wiggin
Supervisor of Art
1426 North Quincy Street
Arlington, Virginia 22207

Henrico County Public Schools

W. Randolph Cheatham
Coordinator of Art
P.O. Box 40
Highland Springs, Virginia 23075

Newport News Public Schools

Virginia Mitchell
Supervisor of Art
12465 Warwick Boulevard
Newport News, Virginia 23606

Norfolk City Schools

Kay White Baker
Supervisor
School Administration Building
800 East City Hall Avenue
Norfolk, Virginia 23510

Pittsylvania County Schools

Jeffrey R. Guenther
Supervisor of Art
Pittsylvania County Schools
Chatham, Virginia 24531

Portsmouth Public Schools

Mr. John Backley
Supervisor Fine Arts
Portsmouth Public Schools
253 Constitution Avenue
Portsmouth, Virginia 23704

Prince William County Public Schools

Gerald DiVecchia
Supervisor of Art
P.O. Box 389
Manassas, Virginia 22110

Richmond City Public Schools

Helen Cynthia Rose
Supervisor of Art
Richmond Public Schools
301 North Ninth Street
Richmond, Virginia 23219

Roanoke City Public Schools

Dr. Betty Tisinger
Art Supervisor
P.O. Box 2129
Roanoke, Virginia 24009

Bellevue Public Schools

Lewis G. McCord
Coordinator of Art Education
310 102nd, N.E.
Bellevue, Washington 98004

Clover Park School District 400

James D. Blanchard
Supervisor of Art
5214 Steilacoom Boulevard, S.W.
Lakewood Center, Washington 98499

Edmonds School District 15

Jerry Conrad
Consultant Teacher in Art
3800 196th Street S.W.
Lynnwood, Washington 98036

Everett School District 2

    Patrick Maher
    Supervisor of Secondary Art

    Mrs. Maryalice Salget
    Supervisor of Elementary Art
    P.O. Box 2098
    4730 Colby
    Everett, Washington 98201

Highline School District 401

    Marie Dunstan
    Art Coordinator
    Highline School District 401
    15675 Ambaum Boulevard, S.W.
    Seattle, Washington 98166

Kent School District 415

    Mrs. Frances Monson
    Coordinator of Art
    508 North Central Avenue
    Kent, Washington 98031

Lake Washington School District 414

    Chester Potuzak
    Coordinator of Fine/Performing Arts
    410 First Street
    Kirkland, Washington 98033

Renton School District 403

    Hal Chambers, Art Resource Teacher
    1525 North Fourth Street
    Renton, Washington 98055

Spokane Public Schools

    Mrs. Shirley A. Cross
    Coordinator of General Programs
    West 825 Trent Avenue
    Spokane, Washington 99201

Tacoma Public Schools

    Jack D. Motteler
    Assistant in Curriculum, Art
    Tacoma Public Schools
    P.O. Box 1357
    Tacoma, Washington 98401

Vancouver School District 37

    William Murray
    Supervisor of Art
    605 North Devine Road
    Vancouver, Washington 98661

Yakima School District 7

    Richard Williams
    Director of Art Education
    Yakima Public Schools
    104 North Fourth Avenue
    Yakima, Washington 98902

Cabell County Public Schools

    Libby K. Caligan
    Director of Art
    620 20th Street
    Huntington, West Virginia 25709

Kanawha County Schools

    Mrs. Rita Peak
    Consultant of Art K-12
    200 Elizabeth Street
    Charleston, West Virginia 25311

Marion County Board of Education

    Mrs. Sara Adams
    Supervisor of Art
    200 Gaston Avenue
    Fairmont, West Virginia 26554

Monongalia County Schools

    Wilbur V. Bauer
    Coordinator of Art Education
    48 Edgewood Street
    Morgantown, West Virginia 26505

Appleton Public Schools

    Monica Cooney
    Elementary Art Coordinator

    Harold Carlson
    Secondary Art Coordinator
    120 East Harris Street
    Appleton, Wisconsin 54911

Kenosha Unified School District 1

    Sam P. Christy
    Coordinator of Art
    4001 60th Street
    Kenosha, Wisconsin 53140

Madison Public Schools

    Frank C. Lindl
    Coordinator, Art Education
    545 West Dayton Street
    Madison, Wisconsin 53703

Milwaukee Public Schools

    Mr. Kent Anderson
    Curriculum Specialist, Art
    P.O. Drawer 10K
    Milwaukee, Wisconsin 53201

Unified School District 1

    Dr. Helen F. Patton
    Consultant in Art
    2230 Northwestern Avenue
    Racine, Wisconsin 53404

Sheboygan Public Schools

    Allen Hanson
    Art Supervisor
    830 Virginia Avenue
    Sheboygan, Wisconsin 53081

Waukesha City Schools Joint District 1

    Roland Schrupp
    K-12, Art Learning Specialist
    627 West College Avenue
    Waukesha, Wisconsin 53186

Joint City School District 1, West Allis-West Milwaukee

    Kenneth B. Cottingham, Supervisor
    9333 West Lincoln Avenue
    West Allis, Wisconsin 53227

Laramie County School District 1

    Irene White, Coordinator of Art
    308 West Fifth Avenue
    Cheyenne, Wyoming 82001

Guam Department of Education

    Adriano B. Pangelinan, Art Consultant
    Department of Education
    Agana, Guam 96910

Art Magazines

Note — A for Annuals; M for Monthlies; W for Weeklies; Q for Quarterlies.

A C C Outlook (Bi-M)—Lois Moran, Ed; American Crafts Council, 44 W. 53 St, New York, NY 10019
Yearly 18.50

African Arts/Arts D'Afrique (Q)—John Povey, Ed; African Studies Center, University of California, 405 Hilgard Ave, Los Angeles, CA 90024
Yearly 14.00

American Art Journal (Bi-A)—John D. Morse & Lawrence Fleischman, Ed; 40 W. 57th St, 5th Floor, New York, NY 10019
Yearly 10.00

American Art Review (Bi-M)—Thomas R. Kellaway, Ed. & Publ; Box 65007, Los Angeles, CA 90065
Yearly 18.00

American Artist (M)—Susan E. Meyer, Ed; 1515 Broadway, New York, NY 10036
Yearly 15.00

American Graphic Artists of the Twentieth Century (Irreg)—Brooklyn Museum, Eastern Parkway, Brooklyn, NY 11238
4.00

American Journal of Archaeology (Q)—Jerome J. Pollitt, Ed; Archaeological Institute of America, 260 W. Broadway, New York, NY 10013
Yearly 15.00

Antiques (M)—Wendell Garrett, Ed; 551 Fifth Ave, New York, NY 10017
Yearly 18.00

Appollo Magazine (M)—Denys Sutton, Ed; 22 Davies St, London, W. 1, England
Yearly 32.00

Archaeology (Q)—Phyllis Pollak Katz, Ed; Archaeological Institute of America, 260 W. Broadway, New York, NY 10013
Yearly 8.50

Architectural Record (M)—Walter F. Wagner, Jr, Ed; 1220 Ave. of the Americas, New York, NY 10020
Yearly 12.00

Art Bulletin (Q)—Howard Hibbard, Ed; 16 E. 52nd St, New York, NY 10022
Yearly 15.00

Art Direction (M)—Elaine Lovie, Ed; 19 W. 44th St, New York, NY 10036
Yearly 11.00

Artforum (M)—John Coplans, Ed; 667 Madison Ave, New York, NY 10021
Yearly 22.50

The Art Gallery Magazine (M except Aug. & Sept)—William C. Bendig & Jay Jacobs, Ed; Ivoryton, CT 06442
Single 1.50 Yearly 13.00

Art in America (Bi-M)—Elizabeth C. Baker, Ed; 150 E. 58th St, New York, NY 10022
Yearly 16.50

Art in Focus (M Oct-June)—Dorothy Grafly, Ed. & Publ; 131 N. 20th St, Philadelphia, PA 19103
Single 1.00 Yearly 6.00

Art Index (Q)—David J. Patten, Ed; The H. W. Wilson Co, 950 University Ave, New York, NY 10452
Subscription on service basis. Write for rates.

Art International (10/yr)—James Fitzsimmons, Ed. & Publ; Via Maraini 17-A, Lugono, Switzerland
Yearly 36.00

Art Journal (Q)—Diane Kelder, Ed; 16 E. 52nd St, New York, NY 10022
Yearly 8.00

Art Magazine (Q)—Pat Fleisher, Ed; 2498 Yonge St, Suite 18, Toronto, Ont. M4P 2H8
Yearly 7.00

Art Material Trade News (M)—C. Edwin Shade, Ed; (National Art Material Trade Asn), Syndicate Magazines Inc, 25 W. 45th St, New York, NY 10036
Yearly 18.00

Art News (M Sept-May, Q June-Aug)—Milton Esterow, Ed; 750 Third Ave, New York, NY 10017
Yearly 15.00

Art Quarterly (Q)—Jerrold Lanes, Ed; Founders Society, Detroit Institute of Arts, 5200 Woodward Ave, Detroit, MI 48202
Yearly 16.00

Artist (M)—Peter Garrard, Ed; 155 W. 15th St, New York, NY 10011
Yearly 8.00

Artist's Proof (A)—Fritz Eichenberg, Ed; Pratt Center for Contemporary Printmaking, 831 Broadway, New York, NY 10003
Membership price 12.50

Artscanada (Bi-M)—Anne Brodgley, Ed; 3 Church St, Toronto M5E, Ontario, Canada
Yearly 17.00

Arts in America (Bi-M)—Elizabeth C. Baker, Ed; Whitney Communication Corp, 150 E. 58th St, New York, NY 10022
Yearly 16.50

Arts Magazine (M Nov-June, Bi-M Sept-Oct-Dec-Jan)—Richard Martin, Ed; 23 E. 26th St, New York, NY 10010
Yearly 20.00

Artweek (Weekly Sept-May, Bi-M June-Aug)—Cecile N. McCann, Ed; 1305 Franklin St, Oakland, CA 94612
Yearly 8.00

Avalanche (Q)—Liza Bear, Ed; Center for New Art Activities, 93 Grand St, New York, NY 10013
Yearly 10.00

CA Magazine (Bi-M)—Richard S. Coyne, Ed; 410 Sherman Ave (P.O. Box 10300), Palo Alto, CA 94303
Single 3.00 Annual 18.00

California Design (Triennial)—E. M. Moore, Ed; California Design Program, Pasadena Art Museum, 411 W. Colorado Blvd, Pasadena, CA 91101
Yearly 7.50

Ceramics Monthly (M)—Spencer Davis, Ed; Professional Publications, Inc, Box 4548, Columbus, OH 43212.
Yearly 8.00

Cimaise (Bi-M)—Jean Robert Arnaud, Ed; Wittenborn & Co, 1018 Madison Ave, New York, NY 10021
Yearly 36.00

Connoisseur, The (M)—Bevis Hillier, Ed; National Magazine Co, Ltd, Chestergate House, Vauxhall Bridge Rd, London, SW1V 1HF, England
Yearly 30.00

Contemporary American Painting and Sculpture (Bi-A)—University of Illinois Press, Urbana, IL 61801

Craft Horizons (Bi-M)—Mrs. Rose Slivka, Ed; 44 W 53rd St, New York, NY 10022
Yearly 10.00

Design Quarterly (Q)—Mildred Friedman, Ed; Walker Art Center, Vineland Place, Minneapolis, MN 55403
Yearly 5.00

Feminist Art Journal (Q)—Ann Calderwood, Ed; 41 Montgomery Place, Brooklyn, NY 11215
Yearly Individual 5.00 Institution 10.00

Gazette des Beaux-Arts (10 issues)—Daniel Wildenstein, Dir; Imprimeries Runies, 33, Ave. de la Gare, CH-1001
Yearly 24.00

Graphic Design (Q)—Masura Katzumie, Ed; Wittenborn & Co, 1018 Madison Ave, New York, NY 10021
Single 7.25 Yearly 24.50

Graphis Annual (A)—Walter Herdeg, Ed; Dufourstrasse 107, CH-8008 Zurich, Switzerland
Single 19.50

Graphis Magazine (Bi-M)—Walter Herdeg, Ed; Dufourstrasse 107, CH-8008 Zurich, Switzerland
Yearly 39.00

Handweaver & Craftsman (Q)—Eileen McCarthy, Ed; 220 Fifth Ave, New York, NY 10001
Yearly 5.00

House & Garden (M)—Mary Jane Pool, Ed; 350 Madison Ave, New York, NY 10017
Yearly 10.00

House & Home (M)—John F. Goldsmith, Ed; 1221 Ave. of the Americas, New York, NY 10020
Yearly 12.00

House Beautiful (M)—Wallace Guenther, Ed; 717 Fifth Ave, New York, NY 10022
Yearly 10.00

Illustrator Magazine (Q)—Don L. Jardine, Ed; 500 S. Fourth St, Minneapolis, MN 55415
Single 1.00 Yearly 3.00

Illustrators Annual: The Annual of American Illustration (A-Fall)—Published for Society of Illustrators by Hastings House, Publishers, 10 E. 40th St, New York, NY 10016
Yearly 19.50

Industrial Design (10 issues)—Roger Guilfoyle, Ed; 130 E. 59th St, New York, NY 10022
Single 1.50 Yearly 10.00

Interior Design (M)—Sherman Emery, Ed; 150 E. 58th St, New York, NY 10022
Yearly 14.00

Interiors (M)—C. Ray Smith, Ed; One Astor Plaza, New York, NY 10022
Yearly 15.00

International Poster Annual (Bi-A)—Arthur Niggli, Ed; Texts in English, French and German; Hastings House, Publishers, 10 E. 40th St, New York, NY 10016
Yearly 16.00

Journal of Aesthetics & Art Criticism (Q)—John Fisher, Ed; Temple University, Department of Philosophy, Philadelphia, PA 19122
Membership 10.00 (Non-members 15.00)

Journal of the Society of Architectural Historians (Q)—James F. O'Gorman, Ed; 1700 Walnut St, Room 716, Philadelphia, PA 19103
Yearly 20.00 (membership)

Kunst und das schoene Heim (M)—Guenter Thiemig, Ed; Wittenborn & Co, 1018 Madison Ave, New York, NY 10021
Single 2.00 Yearly 20.00

Kunstwerk (Bi-M)—Klaus Juergen-Fischer, Ed; Wittenborn & Co, 1018 Madison Ave, New York, NY 10021
Yearly 12.50

Landscape Architecture (Q)—Grady Clay, Ed; 1190 E. Broadway, Louisville, KY 40204
Yearly 10.00

Leonardo: Art Science and Technology (Q)—Frank J. Malina, Ed; Pergamon Press, Inc, Journals Dept, Maxwell House, Fairview Park, Elmsford, NY 10523 (and Headington Hill Hall, Oxford 0X3 OBW, England)
Yearly 50.00

Marsyas (Irreg)—Editor varies; Institute of Fine Arts, New York University, 1 E. 78th St, New York, NY 10021
Single 8.00

Metropolitan Museum of Art Bulletin (Q)—Katharine H. B. Stoddert, Ed; Fifth Ave. at 82nd St, New York, NY 10028
Yearly 10.00

Mobilia (M)—Mette Bratvold, Ed; Wittenborn & Co, 1018 Madison Ave, New York, NY 10021
Single 3.00 Yearly 27.50

Modern Publicity: International Advertising Art (A)—Ella Moody, Ed; The Viking Press, 625 Madison Ave, New York, NY 10022
Issue 12.50

Museum News (M)—Roberta H. Paul, Ed; American Association of Museums, 2233 Wisconsin Ave, N.W, Washington, DC 20007 (incl. membership in Am. Assn. of Museums)
Yearly 15.00

National Endowment for the Arts. Guide to Programs (1-2/yr)—National Endowment for the Arts, Superintendent of Documents, U.S. Government Printing Office, Washington, DC 20402
1.00

National Sculpture Review (Q)—Adolph Block, Ed; 75 Rockefeller Plaza, New York, NY 10019
Single .85 Yearly 3.00 Foreign 3.50 (U.S. Funds) Membership (non-members 4.00)

New Jersey Music and Arts Magazine (M Sept-June)—Ruthann Williams, Ed; P.O. Box 567 (572 Main St), Chatham, NJ 07928
Yearly 6.00

Old-Time New England (Q)—Abbott Lowell Cummings, Ed; The Society for the Preservation of New England Antiquities, 141 Cambridge St, Boston, MA 02114
Single .75 Yearly 5.00

Opus International (Bi-M)—Editions Georges Fall, 15 Rue Paul Fort, Paris (14e) France
Yearly 15 F.

Pantheon (Q)—Dr. Erich Steingraeber, Ed; Wittenborn & Co, 1018 Madison Ave, New York, NY 10021
Yearly 25.00

Penrose Annual (A)—Herbert Spencer, Ed; 10 E. 40th St, New York, NY 10016
Price varies

Photographis: International Annual of Advertising Photography (A)—Walter Herdeg, Ed; Dufourstrasse 107, CH-8008 Zurich, Switzerland
Single 27.50

Pictures on Exhibit (M Oct-May)—Charles Z. Offin, Ed; 30 E. 60th St, New York, NY 10022
Yearly 5.00

Praxis (3/yr)—Ronald Reimers, Ed; 2125 Hearst Ave, Berkeley, CA 94709
Yearly 8.00 Individual; 14.00 Institutions

Print, American Graphic Design Magazine (Bi-M)—Martin Fox, Ed; 19 W. 44th St, New York, NY 10036
Yearly 14.00

Pro: The Voice of the Cartooning World (M)—Arnold L. Wagner, Ed. & Publ; 1130 N. Cottage, Salem, OR 97301
Yearly 10.00

Progressive Architecture (M)—John Morris Dixon, Ed; 600 Summer St, Stamford, CT 06904
Yearly 7.00

Royal Society of Arts Journal (M)—J. S. Skidmore, Ed; 6 John Adam St, Adelphi, London W.C.2, England
Yearly 11.55

School Arts Magazine (M Sept-June)—George F. Horn, Ed; Davis Publications Inc, Printers Bldg, Worcester, MA 01608
Yearly 8.00

Sculpture International (Bi-A)—Pergamon Press, Maxwell House, Fairview Park, Elmsford, NY 10523
Yearly 10.00

Southwest Art Magazine (M except July)—Vicki Baucum, Ed; P.O. Box 13037, Houston, TX 77019
Yearly 15.00

Southwestern Art (Q)—John H. Jenkins, Ed; Box 1763, Austin, TX 78767
Yearly 8.50

Stained Glass (Q)—Dr. Norman L. Temme, Ed; 1125 Wilmington Ave, St. Louis, MO 63111
Yearly 8.00

Structure (Irreg)—Joost Baljeu, Ed; Wittenborn & Co, 1018 Madison Ave, New York, NY 10021
Single 1.75 Yearly 2.75

Structurist (A)—Eli Bornstein, Ed; Wittenborn & Co, 1018 Madison Ave, New York, NY 10021
Per Issue 4.50

Studio International (6/yr)—Peter Townsend, Ed; Studio International Publications Ltd, 14 W. Central St, London WC1A 1JH, England
Yearly 29.00 Individuals; 24.00 Institutions

Vingtieme Siecle (XX e Siecle) (Bi-A)—Gino di San Lazzaro, Ed; Wittenborn & Co, 1018 Madison Ave, New York, NY 10021
Single 18.50 Yearly 35.00

Washington International Arts Letter (10 issues except July & Dec)—Daniel Millsaps, Ed. & Publ; 1321 Fourth St, S.W, Washington, DC 20024
Yearly 6.00 Individual; 32.00 Institutions

Werk (M)—Lucius Burckhardt & Diego Peverelli, Ed; Association of Swiss Architects; Wittenborn & Co, 1018 Madison Ave, New York, NY 10021
Yearly 6.00 Individual; 32.00 Institutions

Zodiac (A)—Renzo Zorzi, Ed; Wittenborn & Co, 1018 Madison Ave, New York, NY 10021
Single 17.00

Newspapers Carrying Art Notes

With name of art editor or critic.

ALABAMA

   *Alabama Journal, Montgomery—Bill Myrick
   *Birmingham News—Oliver Roosevelt
   Fayette County Broadcaster, Fayette—Jack Black
   *The Mobile Press Register—Gordon Tatum, Jr.
   Tuscaloosa News—Dr. J. Fred Goossen

ALASKA

   Anchorage Times—Connie Godwin
   *Daily News, Anchorage—Molly B. Jones

ARIZONA

   Arizona Daily Star, Tucson—Adina Wingate
   Arizona Living, Phoenix—Ann Dutton
   *Arizona Republic, Phoenix—Thomas Goldthwaite
   Mesa Tribune—Ruth Wiley
   *The Phoenix Gazette—Jim Newton
   Scottsdale Progress—Harry Wood
   *Tempe Daily News—Jan Young
   *Tucson Citizen—Sheldon Reich & Robert M. Quinn
   Verde Independent, Cottonwood—Eugene N. Marten

ARKANSAS

   *The Arkansas Democrat, Little Rock—Ray White
   Arkansas Gazette, Little Rock—Bill Lewis
   Paragould Daily Press—Kathy Craft
   *Stuttgart Daily Leader—Clavin Mannen

CALIFORNIA

   The Anaheim Bulletin—Angele Haddad
   The Claremont Courier (Montclair Courier, Upland Courier, The
      Newspaper), Claremont—Thelma O'Brien
   Contra Costa Times, Walnut Creek—Margaret Crum
   Daily Pilot, Costa Mesa—Jackie Hyman
   *Escondido Daily Times-Advocate—Kathlyn Russell
   Fresno Bee—David Hale
   *Fullerton News Tribune—Sue Campbell
   The Hanford Sentinel—Ruth J. Gomes
   Independent-Journal, San Rafael—Ada Garfinkel
   *Independent, Press-Telegram, Long Beach—Elise Emery
   Los Angeles Herald-Examiner—Betje Howell
   Los Angeles Times—Henry Seldis
   Los Gatos Times-Observer—George R. Kane
   Monterey Peninsula Herald—Irene Lagorio
   The Oakland Tribune—Charles Shere
   Pacific Sun, Mill Valley—Tom Cervenak
   Palo Alto Times—Paul Emerson
   Palos Verdes Peninsula News—Reid L. Bundy
   Pasadena Star News—Larry Palmer
   *Redlands Daily Facts—Josephine Reay
   *The Richmond Independent—Paul Allman
   *Riverside Press—John F. Muncie
   Sacramento Bee—Charles Johnson
   Sacramento Union—Richard Simon
   *Salinas Californian—Helen Manning
   San Bernardino Sun-Telegram—Rosemary Hite
   San Diego Evening Tribune—Jan Jennings
   San Diego Union—Dick Reilly
   San Francisco Chronicle—Alfred Frankenstein
   San Francisco Examiner—Alexander Fried & Arthur Bloomfield

   San Jose Mercury-News—Marta Morgan
   *San Mateo Times—Vera Graham
   Santa Ana Register—Ann Terrill
   *Santa Barbara News-Press—Richard Ames
   Santa Monica Evening Outlook—Barry Brennan
   Turlock Daily Journal—Carl Baggese

COLORADO

   Boulder Daily Camera—Barbralu Fried
   *Colorado Springs Gazette Telegraph—John Fetler
   *Colorado Springs Sun—Kay Woestendiek
   Denver Post—James Mills
   Pueblo Chieftain—Bob Thomas
   Pueblo Star Journal—Bob Thomas
   *Rocky Mountain News, Denver—Duncan Pollock

CONNECTICUT

   *The Bridgeport Post & Sunday Post—Betty Tyler
   *The Darien Review—Ray Yates
   Gazette, East Hartford—Phyllis M. Charest
   The Greenwich Time—Dorothy Friedman
   The Hartford Courant—Jolene Goldenthal
   *The Hartford Times—Florence Berkman
   *Meriden Journal—Tom Potter
   *The New Britain Herald—Judith W. Brown
   New Canaan Advertiser—Dean Hadley
   *New Haven Register—Shirley Gonzales
   New London Day—Raymond K. Bordner
   The News-Times, Danbury—Jean R. Buoy
   *The Stamford Advocate—Bella O'Hara
   *Waterbury American—Katherine Davidson
   *The West Hartford News—Shirlee Westbrook
   *Westport News—Shelley List

DELAWARE

   *Wilmington News—Otto Dekom
   Wilmington Journal—Philip F. Crosland

DISTRICT OF COLUMBIA

   The Washington Post—Paul Richard
   The Washington Star—Benjamin Forgey

FLORIDA

   Boca Raton News—Mary Crowe Dorst
   Clearwater Sun—Carol Gautier
   Florida Times-Union, Jacksonville—Tracy Conners
   Fort Lauderdale News—Shubert Jonas
   Gainesville Sun—Diane Chun
   *Jacksonville Journal—Elihu Edelson
   The Ledger, Lakeland—Jeff Kline
   *The Miami Beach Sun-Reporter—Josephine A. Bruun
   The Miami Herald—Griffin Smith
   *Miami News—Bill Von Maurer
   Orlando Sentinel Star—Mary Joyce
   Palm Beach Daily News, West Palm Beach—Millie Wolff
   Palm Beach Post—Georgia Dupuis
   The St. Augustine Record—Fred Whitley
   *St. Petersburg Independent—Jeannette Crane
   *St. Petersburg Times—Charles Benbow
   Sarasota Herald-Tribune—Pat Buck

*Sarasota Journal—R. N. Robertson
*Tallahassee Democrat—Mary Ann Lindley
The Tampa Times—Robert L. Martin
Tampa Tribune—Gordon Deats
Venice Gondolier—Dorothy E. Lippstreuer
Winter Park Sun Herald—Nancy Long

GEORGIA

Athens Banner-Herald—Masie Underwood
*Athens Daily News—Douglas Matyka
The Atlanta Constitution—Helen C. Smith
The Atlanta Journal—Clyde Burnett
*Columbus Enquirer—Harry E. Franklin
*Columbus Ledger—Edge R. Reid
Savannah New Press—Marshall L. Reed

HAWAII

*The Honolulu Advertiser—Web Anderson
*The Star Bulletin, Honolulu—Jean Charlot

IDAHO

The Idaho State Journal, Pocatello—J. B. Brugger
The Idaho Statesman, Boise—Julie T. Monroe
Lewiston Morning Tribune—Mary Joan O'Connell
*Times-News, Twin Falls—Richard G. High

ILLINOIS

*Chicago Daily News—Franz Schulze
The Chicago Sun-Times—Harold Haydon
Chicago Tribune—Alan Artner
*Clinton Journal-Public—Donald C. Kemp
*The Courier, Champaign—Mrs. Stephen Tager
Daily Courier-News—Peter Powell & Howard Elliott
Decatur Herald & Review—William Ward
*Galesburg Register-Mail—Isabelle Buncher
The Herald Whig, Quincy—Betty Moritz
*Joliet Herald-News—Lorrie Gawla
The Lake Forester, Highland Park—Dorothy Andries
*Marion Daily Republican—Oldham Paisley
Monmouth Daily Review Atlas—Martha Hamilton
*Pantagraph, Bloomington—Tony Holloway
Peoria Journal Star—Gerald (Jerry) Klein
The Pioneer Press, Wilmette—Dorothy Andries
*Rockford Morning Star—David Zimmerman
*Rockford Register-Republic—David Zimmerman
The Sunday Register-Star, Rockford—David Zimmerman

INDIANA

Anderson Herald—Holly Miller
The Brown County Democrat, Nashville—Bruce Gregory Temple
Evansville Courier—Jeanne Suhrheinrich
*Evansville Press—Gail McLeod
Gary Post-Tribune—John Forwalter
Indianapolis News—Marion Simon Garmel
*The Indianapolis Star—Corbin Patrick
Journal-Gazette, Fort Wayne—Laura Pipino
Lafayette Journal & Courier—Chris Huber
Lafayette Leader—Rebecca Sawyer
LaPorte Herald-Argus—Maxine Ford
Muncie Evening Press—Robert Loy
The Muncie Star—David Stearns
*New Albany Tribune—Patricia Cornwell
*News-Sentinel, Fort Wayne—Gene Porter
South Bend Tribune—Johnathon J. White
*The Terre Haute Tribune-Star—Beatrice Biggs

IOWA

The Ames Daily Tribune—Pam Witmer
The Anamosa Eureka—James Andrew Mayer
The Anamosa Journal—James Andrew Mayer
Cedar Rapids Gazette—Mary Burke
The Charles City Press—Dividicus Noman
*Cherokee Daily Times—Tom Miller
Des Moines Register—Nicholas G. Baldwin
Fairfield Daily Ledger—Olive Schanfeldt

*The Fort Dodge Messenger—Lois Johnson
Mason City Globe-Gazette—Thomas Thoma
*The Sioux City Journal—Julie Goodson
*The Times-Democrat, Davenport—Julie Jensen
Waterloo Daily Courier—Phyllis Singer

KANSAS

Atchison Daily Globe—Margaret Schwein
*Clay Center Dispatch—H. E. Valentine
The Daily Reporter, Independence—Georgia High
*The Hutchinson News—Kathy Brown
Lexington Herald Leader—John Alexander
Russell Daily News—Harold L. "Prince" Elmquist
*Topeka Capital-Journal—Peggy Greene
*The Wichita Eagle-Beacon—Dorothy Wood

KENTUCKY

Berea Citizen—Barbara H. Bordelon
*The Louisville Courier-Journal & Times—Sarah Lansdell

LOUISIANA

*Alexandria Town Talk—Verdis Dowdy
The Courier, New Orleans—S. Joslyn Fosberg
East Bank Guide, Metairie—Mrs. Byron J. E. Hoover
*Monroe News Star World—Ms. J. C. Huntley
The Morning Advocate, Baton Rouge—Anne K. Price
*The Shreveport Journal—Larry Shor
*The Shreveport Times—Jim Montgomery
*The State Times, Baton Rouge—Cara Lu Salam
The Times Picayune, New Orleans—Alberta Collier

MAINE

Bangor Daily News—Robert H. Newall
*The Camden Herald—Mary Sullivan
The Courier-Gazette, Rockland—Ivy W. Dodd
*Lewiston Daily Sun—A. Kent Foster
*Maine Sunday Telegram, Portland—Edwin Fitzpatrick
*Rockland Courier-Gazette, Inc—Flora G. Cullen
*Waterville Morning Sentinel—Tony Betts

MARYLAND

*The Annapolis Evening Capital—Marie Bailey
*Baltimore News-American—R. P. Harriss
Baltimore Sun—Lincoln F. Johnson
*Hagerstown Daily Mail—Harry Warner
*Hagerstown Morning Herald—Harry Warner, Jr.

MASSACHUSETTS

Amherst Record—Frances Chastain
The Berkshire Eagle, Pittsfield—Winifred Bell
The Boston Globe—Robert Taylor
The Boston Phoenix—Kenneth Baker
Brockton Enterprise-Times—Dorothy Dale
*Cambridge Chronicle—Ann Philips
*Daily Hampshire Gazette, Northampton—Martha Beaver
The Daily Sentinel-Enterprise, Fitchburg—Kay Tobin
Falmouth Enterprise—William J. Adelman
Gloucester Daily Times—Barbara H. Erkkila
*Greenfield Recorder—Daniel Weck
*The Inquirer & Mirror, Nantucket—Mary Kennedy Wright
*The Lowell Sun—Ann Schecter
Malden Evening News—Joan T. Wheeler
*The Marblehead Messenger—David Ramsay
Quincy Patriot Ledger—Jon Lehman
The Real Paper, Cambridge—Carol Eron
*Salem Evening News—James M. Shea
*The Southbridge Evening News—Linda Megathlin
Springfield Daily News—Tom Hart
Springfield Sunday Republican—Normand E. Henchey
*Springfield Union—Daniel Weck
*Standard Times, New Bedford—Earl J. Dias
*Wellesley Townsman—Herbert S. Austin
Westfield Evening News—Deborah Baker
*The Worcester Gazette—David D. Oswell
*The Worcester Telegram—Marilyn W. Spear

MICHIGAN

Alpena News—Betty Werth
*The Ann Arbor News—Jean Paul Slusser
Cheboygan Tribune—Alta L. Riggs
Detroit Free Press—Marsha Miro
Detroit News—Joy Hakanson (Mrs. Raymond L. Colby)
*The Eccentric, Birmingham—Rodney G. Landsman
Enquirer and News, Battle Creek—James A. Dean
The Flint Journal—James E. Harvey
*Kalamazoo Gazette—Victor W. Rauch
Grand Rapids Press—Bernice Winslow Mancewicz
*Jackson Citizen Patriot—Ray Dennis
*Lansing State Journal—Paul Palmer
Macomb Daily, Mount Clemens—George Hagan
*Muskegon Chronicle—Christine Valmassei
The Oakland Press—Sue Hegenbarth
The Saginaw News—James W. Henderson
Towne Courier, East Lansing—Phyllis Thomas

MINNESOTA

Duluth Herald—James F. Hefferman
Mankato Free Press—Robert L. Girouard
*Minneapolis Star—Peter Altman
Minneapolis Tribune—Mike Steele
News Tribune, Duluth—James F. Hefferman
Owatonna People's Press—Bruce Benidt
*Rochester Post-Bulletin—Pauline Walle
*St. Paul Dispatch—John H. Harvey
St. Paul Pioneer Press—Robert L. Protzman
Winona Daily News—Carolyn Kosidowski

MISSISSIPPI

*Clarion Ledger, Jackson—Louis Dollarhide
Columbus Commercial Dispatch—Patrick K. Lynn
Greenwood Commonwealth—Pamela Tims
Jackson Daily News—O. C. McDavid
*Laurel Leader-Call—J. W. West
Meridian Star—Nancy Duvergne Smith

MISSOURI

The Kansas City Star—Donald Hoffman
*Maryville Daily Forum—Muriel M. Alcott
The National Catholic Reporter, Kansas City—Harry J. Cargas
St. Joseph News-Press—Don E. Thornton
St. Louis Globe-Democrat—John Brod Peters
St. Louis Post-Dispatch—E. F. Porter, Jr.
Southeast Missourian, Cape Girardeau—Judith Ann Crow
*Springfield Daily News—Ed Albin
*Times, Kansas City—Donald Hoffmann

MONTANA

Anaconda Leader—Sally Campbell
*Billings Gazette—Kathryn Wright
Bozeman Chronicle—Florence Trout
The Daily Inter Lake, Katispell—Marlin Hanson
The Montana Standard, Butte—Kathleen Cook

NEBRASKA

Lincoln Journal—Helen J. Haggie
*Omaha World-Herald—Judy Van Wagner

NEVADA

*Henderson Home News—Barbara Lauer
Las Vegas Review-Journal—A. Wilber Stevens
Las Vegas Sun—Steve Lesnick

NEW HAMPSHIRE

*Keene Sentinel—Ernest Hebert
*Manchester Union Leader—George Woodbury
The Nashua Telegraph—Deborah Ladd
The New Hampshire Times, Corcord—Steve Sherman

NEW JERSEY

Courier News, Bridgewater—Donald Rublneam
*Courier-Post, Camden—Edith De Shazo
The Daily Register, Red Bank—Carol Jacobson
Homes News, New Brunswick—Doris E. Brown
Hunterdon Review, White House Station—Rachel Mullen
Newark Star-Ledger—Eileen Watkins
*Paterson Evening News—Abe J. Greene
*Princeton Packet—Elaine P. Heinemann & Susan Santangelo
The Record, Hackensack—David Spengler
Summit Herald—Betty McAndrews
Town Topics, Princeton—Helen Schwartz
Verona-Cedar Grove Times, Verona—Brian Donadio

NEW MEXICO

The Albuquerque Journal—Leroy Perkins & Jennie Lusk
The Albuquerque Tribune—Lynn B. Villella
The New Mexican, Santa Fe—John Hamilton
The Taos News—Billie Blair

NEW YORK

Albany Times-Union—Valerie Restivo
Buffalo Courier-Express—Nancy Tobin Willig
The Buffalo Evening News—Hal Crowther
Clinton Courier—William Boynton
*The Daily Freeman, Kingston—Tobie Geertsema
East Hampton Star—Phyllis Braff
*Elmira Star-Gazette—Salle Richards
*Elmira Sunday Telegram—Salle Richards
Evening News, Newburgh—Al Rhoades
Hamilton County News, Speculator—George List, Jr.
*The Ithaca Journal—Jack Sherman
*Jamestown Post-Journal—William M. Flynn
The Knickerbocker News-Union-Star, Albany—C. Robie Booth
The Long Island Press, Jamaica—Jeanne Paris
Nassau Star, Long Beach—Dr. Irwin S. Grodner
*New York Post—Emily Genauer
*The New York Times—Hilton Krames
*News, New York—Al Paladini
Niagara Gazette, Niagara Falls—Susan Greenwood
Oneonta Star—Jessie Nichols
Potsdam Courier Freeman—Michael Billington
Poughkeepsie Journal—Jeffrey Borak
*The Press, Binghamton—Gerald Handte
Red Hook Rhinebeck, Hyde Park—Jean C. McGregor
Rochester Democrat & Chronicle—Sally Walsh
*Saratogian, Saratoga Springs—Shelley Riley
*Schenectady Union-Star—Marjorie Feiner
*The Skaneateles Press—Mrs. J. Lee Wood
Staten Island Advance—Elaine Boies
Syracuse Herald Journal—Richard Case
*Tarrytown Daily News—Thomas Flynn
Times Record, Troy—Cynthia C. Davidson
*The Times-Union, Rochester—Rosemary Teres
*The Village Voice, New York—John Perreault
The Villager, New York—different contributors

NORTH CAROLINA

Asheville Citizen-Times—Richard VanKleeck
The Chapel Hill Newspaper—Charles Horton
Charlotte Observer—Alan Oren
The Daily Reflector, Greenville—Jerry S. Raynor
The Durham Herald—Mrs. Blue Greenberg
*Greensboro Daily News—Mrs. Patricia Krebs
*The Greensboro Record—Candy Johnson
The Hickory Daily Record—Marjorie Lee Millholland
The News and Observer, Raleigh—Ernie Wood
The Sun-Journal, New Bern—Jonathan Segal
*Wilmington Star News—Bill Stover
*Winston-Salem Journal & Sentinel—Beverly Wolter

NORTH DAKOTA

The Forum, Fargo—Carol Knapp
*Grand Forks Herald—Ken Retallic
Times Record, Valley City—Mark E. Bowden

OHIO

*Akron Beacon Journal—Carolyn Carr
*Cincinnati Enquirer—Elmer Wetenkamp
Cincinnati Post—Ellen Brown
Cleveland Plain Dealer—Helen B. Cullinan
*Cleveland Press—Dick Wootten
*Columbus Dispatch—Frances Piper
Dayton Daily News—Betty Dietz Krebs
Dayton Journal Herald—Walt McCaslin
*Mansfield News Journal—Ellen McClarran
News-Herald, Willoughby—W. C. Miller, III
*North Canton Sun—Thomas V. Sell
Painesville Telegraph—Peggy Samartini
*Springfield News-Sun—James Hays
*The Times Recorder, Zanesville—Dr. Charles Dietz
The Toledo Blade—Louise Bruner
*The Toldeo Times—Joseph V. Knack
Youngstown Vindicator—Clyde Singer

OKLAHOMA

Bartlesville Examiner Enterprise—Jim Wood
The Daily Oklahoman, Oklahoma City—Jon Denton
Lawton Constitution—Bill Crawford
Morning Press, Lawton—Bill Crawford
*Muskogee Daily Phoenix & Times Democrat—Joan Morrison
*Norman Transcript—Jack Craddock
Oklahoma City Times—Jon Denton
The Oklahoma Journal, Oklahoma City—Nancy Gilson
*Stillwater News-Press—James C. Stratton
The Tulsa World—Maurice de Vinna

OREGON

*Corvallis Gazette-Times—Saundra Donaldson
The Oregon Journal, Portland—Andy Rocchia
The Oregonian,
*Portland Scribe—Paul Sutinen
World, Coos Bay—J. Paul Baron

PENNSYLVANIA

Centre Daily Times, State College—Joan A. Kurilla
*Chestnut Hill Local—Marguerite Stork
The Daily Intelligencer, Doylestown—Donald P. Davis
*The Daily Pennsylvanian, Philadelphia—Erika Wallace
*The Daily Republican, Phoenixville—Joseph P. Ujobai
*Erie Times-News—Fred Livingston
*The Evening Chronicle, Allentown—Albert Hofammann
The Globe Times, Bethlehem—Paul Willistein
Harrisburg Patriot-News—Robert J. Evans
*Intelligencer Journal, Lancaster—James L. Kinter
Kutztown Patriot—Ade-Rolfe Floreen
*Lock Haven Express—Sarah Loria
The News, Aliquippa—R. A. Palket
News-Tribune, Beaver Falls—Nadine Huff
Philadelphia Bulletin—Nessa Forman
Philadelphia Inquirer—Victoria Donahoe
The Pittsburgh Post-Gazette—Donald Miller
The Pittsburgh Press—Margaret Carlin
*The Reading Eagle—LeRoy A. Gensler
*The Scranton Times—Daniel L. Cusick
*The Scranton Tribune—Mrs. Gene Brislin
Times-Leader, Wilkes Barre—Roy Morgan
York Daily Record—Walt Partymiller
*York Dispatch—Jean Farlow

RHODE ISLAND

The Evening Bulletin, Providence—Bradford F. Swan
Narragansett Times, Wakefield—Arline M. Aissis
Newport Daily News—William Kutik
Providence Journal—Bradford F. Swan
*Warwick Beacon—Joan Christian & Tom Izzo
The Westerly Sun—George H. Utter

SOUTH CAROLINA

Columbia Record—Richard Smurthwaite
Georgetown Times—Cathy McConnell
*Greenville News—Lucille B. Green

The Greenville Piedmont—Miriam Goodspeed
*Index-Journal, Greenwood—Ann M. Tuck
*The News and Courier, Charleston—Barbara S. Williams
Rock Hill Evening Herald—Bud Newcomb
*The State, Columbia—Adger Brown
The Sumter Daily Item—Bob Williams

SOUTH DAKOTA

*Rapid City Journal—Ruth Brennan
*Sioux Falls Argus-Leader—Ralph Green
Vermillion Plain Talk—Mary Arnold
Yankton Press & Dakotan—James Lyle Van Osdel

TENNESSEE

The Chattanooga News-Free Press—Jim Hazard
Chattanooga Times—Wes Hasden
*The Commercial Appeal, Memphis—Guy Northrop
Johnson City Press Chronicle—Walter Miller
*Kingsport Times-News—Margy Clark
*Knoxville Journal—Stephen Horne
*Knoxville News-Sentinel—Frank Weirich
Nashville Banner—Julie Pursell
*The Nashville Tennessean—Clara Hieronymus
The Oak Ridger, Oak Ridge—Dorothy Senn
*Press Scimitar, Memphis—Jane Sanderson
*Winchester Herald-Chronicle—Dorothy C. Drewry

TEXAS

Abilene Reporter-News—Alice Miller
Amarillo Daily News—Dorothy Nordyke
Amarillo Globe-Times—Dorothy Nordyke
*The Austin American Statesman—Margaret Taylor Dry
Avalanche-Journal, Lubbock—Pat Henry
*Beaumont Enterprise—Bonnie Oglethorpe
Beaumont Journal—Lela Davis
Caller-Times, Corpus Christi—Maurice Schmidt
*Canyon News—Ann Melin
Dallas Morning News—Janet Kutner
Dallas Times Herald—Lorraine Haacke
*El Paso Herald Post—Betty Pierce
El Paso Times—Bernice Schwartz
*Fort Worth Press—Drenda Williams
*Fort Worth Star-Telegram—Diane Bonelli
The Houston Chronicle—Ann Holmes & Charlotte Moser
*The Houston Post—George Christian
Kerrville Daily Times—Kit West
The Odessa American—Jerry Ashley
Orange Leader—Andrea Wheaton & Gayle Standridge
*Plainview Herald—Myrna Smith
San Angelo Standard-Times—Cheryl Vannoy
*San Antonio Express & News—Ron White
The San Antonio Light—Glenn Tucker
Waco Tribune Herald—Henry L. Beckham

UTAH

*Box Elder News and Journal, Brigham City—Sara Yates
*The Deseret News, Salt Lake City—Charles Nickerson
The Provo Daily Herald—Charlene Winters
Salt Lake Tribune, Salt Lake City—George S. Dibble
*Springville Herald—Pat Conover

VERMONT

Addison County Independent, Middlebury—Celine Slator
*The Bennington Banner—Geoffrey Chapman
*The Rutland Daily Herald—Thomas K. Slayton

VIRGINIA

*Charlottesville Daily Progress—Ruth Latter
The Gazette, Alexandria—Kat Bergeron
The Ledger-Star, Norfolk—John Levin & Cornelia Justice
Lynchburg News—Cecil Mullan
*Richmond Times-Dispatch—F. D. Cossitt
*The Roanoke Times—Mrs. Peyton Klein
The Times-Herald, Newport News—H. Reid
Virginia Gazette, Williamsburg—Jim Spencer
The Virginian-Pilot, Norfolk—F. D. Cossitt

WASHINGTON

*The Daily Olympian, Olympia—Robert Lee Eskridge
*Longview Daily News—Bob Peterson
*Pierce County Herald, Puyallup—Lori Price
Seattle Post-Intelligencer—R. M. Campbell
The Seattle Times—Deloris Tarzan
*Spokesman-Review, Spokane—Gladys E. Guilbert
Tacoma News Tribune—Eve Reynolds
Walla Walla Union-Bulletin—Marianna Jones
Yakima Herald-Republic—Patricia Wren

WEST VIRGINIA

*The Advertiser, Huntington—Angela Green
Bluefield Daily Telegraph—David Lee Williams
*The Charleston Daily Mail—Mel Verost
*The Charleston Gazette—Della Brown Taylor
The Herald Dispatch, Huntington—Estelle Belanger

WISCONSIN

*Beloit Daily News—Minnie Mills Enking
Capital Times, Madison—David Wagner
*Green Bay Press-Gazette—Daphne Tobit
Milwaukee Journal—James M. Auer
Milwaukee Sentinel—Dean Jensen
*Northwestern, Oshkosh—Polly Zimmerman
*The Post Crescent, Appleton—David Wagner
*Sheboygan Press—Shirley Jarvis
*Wisconsin State Journal, Madison—Donald K. Davies

WYOMING

Laramie Boomerang—Robert A. Wilson
*Northern Wyoming News, Worland—Helen Turner
Wyoming Eagle, Cheyenne—Rosalind Routt

PUERTO RICO

*El Mundo, San Juan—Antonio J. Molina

CANADA

ALBERTA

Calgary Herald—Carol Hogg
*The Edmonton Journal—Bob Harvey

BRITISH COLUMBIA

*Columbian, New Westminster—Margherita Leech
Vancouver Province—Art Perry
Vancouver Sun—Joan Lowndes
*Victoria Colonist—Erith Smith
*Victoria Daily Times—Gordon Rice

MANITOBA

Winnipeg Free Press—John W. Graham
*Winnipeg Tribune—Jan Kamienski

NEWFOUNDLAND

*The Evening Telegram, St. John's—Peter Bell

NOVA SCOTIA

*Dartmouth Free Press—John H. Colville
*Halifax Mail-Star—Gretchen Pierce

ONTARIO

The Globe & Mail, Toronto—James Purdie
Kitchener-Waterloo Record—Carol Jankowski
*The London Free Press—Lenore Crawford
Ottawa Citizen—Kathleen Walker
The Ottawa Journal—W. Q. Ketchum
St. Catharines Standard—Linda Turner
*Sarnia Observer—Geoffrey H. Lane
The Spectator, Hamilton—Jenny Sheppard
Toronto Daily Star—Gary Michael Dault
The Windsor Star—Nora-Jean Perkins

QUEBEC

The Gazette, Montreal—Virginia Nixon
*Mediart, Montreal—Normand Theriault
*Montreal Le Devoir—Christian Allegre
Montreal Photo-Journal—Marcel Huguet
The Montreal Star—Henry Lehmann & Georges Bogardi
La Presse, Montreal—Gilles Toupin
Quebec City Le Soleil—Paul Roux
*Sherbrooke La Tribune—Rene Berthiaume

Scholarships and Fellowships

OFFERED BY	AMOUNT	OPENED TO	DURATION	WHEN OFFERED
Academy of Art College 625 Sutter St, San Francisco, CA 94102	$1875	Full-time B average 2nd year student	One year	Annually
Academy of the Arts*, Harrison & South Sts, Easton, MD 21601	$100 per year	High school students going to art school	One year	Annually
Adirondack Lakes Center for the Arts, Blue Mountain Lake, NY 12812	Up to $30	7th to 12th grade students	Summer session	
Alabama Art League, Montgomery Museum of Fine Arts, 440 S. Mc- Donough St, Montgomery, AL 36104	$100	Any student	One year	Annually
Alaska Association for the Arts, P.O. Box 2786, Fairbanks, AK 99707	$200 minimum	High school or college students	One year	Annually
Alberta Association of Architects 217 Revillon Bldg, Edmonton AB T5J 1B2, Canada	$250	Architectural technology students at Northern and Southern Alberta Institutes of Technology	One year	Annually
Alberta College of Art, Southern Alberta Institute of Technology, 1301 16th Ave. N.W, Calgary, AB T2M 0L4, Canada	$15,000 (total)	Students	One year	Annually
Alberta Culture, Visual Arts, Gov- ernment of the Province of Alberta, Edmonton, AB, Canada	$100 - $750, (total) $15,000	Residents of Alberta	One year	Annually
Alice Lloyd College, Pippa Passes, KY 41844	Variable	Anyone - Appalachian preferred	One or two years	Annually
Allied Artists of America, Inc, 1083 Fifth Ave, New York, NY 10028	$200	Any student attending National Academy School of Fine Arts	One year	Annually
Amarillo Art Center, Box 447, Amarillo, TX 79178	Variable	Primarily to disabled or deprived children and young adults	Each semester	
American Academy, 41 E. 65th St, New York, NY 10021	$6000, plus residency	Citizens of the U.S.	One year	Annually
American Antiquarian Society, 185 Salisbury St, Worcester, MA 01609	$1200 - $1600 per month	Qualified scholars	Six months - one year	Annually
American Association of University Women, 240 Virginia Ave. N.W, Washington, DC 20037	$14,000	Women	One year	Annually
American Numismatic Society Broadway at 155th St, New York, NY 10032	$3500 Fellowship (10) $750 grants	Graduate student Graduate students and junior mem- bers of faculty	One year June 8 - August 7	Annually Annually
American Oriental Society*, Secre- tary, 329 Sterling Memorial Li- brary, Yale Station, New Haven, CT 06520	$5000 for the study of the history of Chinese painting	Students who have completed 3 years of Chinese language study at a recognized university, or the equivalent, and all requirements for a Ph.D. in Chinese painting studies, except for travel, the written dissertation and its de- fense		
American-Scandinavian Founda- tion*, 127 E. 73rd St, New York, NY 10021	$500 - $4000	Applicants with B.A. degree (Un- restricted fields) for Denmark, Finland, Iceland, Norway and Sweden	Up to one year	Annually
American Society of Interior De- signers Educational Foundation, 730 Fifth Ave, New York, NY 10019	Variable	Interior design students and teachers	One year	Annually
American Watercolor Society*, 1083 Fifth Ave, New York, NY 10028	Variable	Art schools and colleges for further award to outstanding stu- dents of watercolor painting	One year	Annually
Anchorage Community College*, 2533 Providence Ave, Anchorage, AK 99504	$250 plus state aid	All art students		Annually
Anderson Fine Arts Center*, 226 W. Eighth St, Anderson, IN 46016	Membership or class fee	Students	One year	Annually

OFFERED BY	AMOUNT	OPENED TO	DURATION	WHEN OFFERED
Archaeological Institute of America 260 W. Broadway, New York, NY 10013	Variable - $7000 and up	Students of Aegean, Italian, or Mesopotamian archaeology	One year	Annually
Arkansas Arts Center, MacArthur Park, Little Rock, AR 72203	Varies as to class	Qualified applicant	By semesters	
Arkansas State University, Fine Arts Center, State University, AR 72467	$400, full tuition scholarship, 6 awarded annually	1st and 2nd semester freshmen	One year	Annually
Armstrong Museum of Art and Archaeology, Olivet College, Olivet, MI 49076	Variable	Prospective college students and college students	One - two years	Annually
Art Association of Richmond, Indiana, McGuire Memorial Hall, Whitewater Blvd, Richmond, IN 47374	$350	High school senior studying art	One year	Annually
The Art Barn, 143 Lower Cross Rd, Greenwich, CT 06830	$200	Children		Semi-annually
Art Center Association*, 100 Park Rd, Anchorage, KY 40223	$7500 (total)	Students	One year	Semi-annually
Art Gallery of Ontario, Grange Park, Toronto, ON M5T 1G4, Canada	Varied subsidized grants, Gallery pays 85%	Secondary school students	One year - 25 week course	Annually
Art in Architecture, Joseph Young, 1434 S. Spaulding Ave, Los Angeles, CA 90019	$200 - $500	Graduate students	One year	Annually
Art Institute of Chicago*, Michigan Ave. at Adams St, Chicago, IL 60603	$3000	Full-time degree students in need	One year	Annually
Art Institute of Ft. Lauderdale*, 3000 E. Las Olas Blvd, Ft. Lauderdale, FL 33316	Variable	Graduating high school seniors	Two years	Annually
Art Institute of Pittsburgh, 536 Penn Ave, Pittsburgh, PA 15222	Variable	High school seniors, in-school students, etc.	Varies	Quarterly
Art Patrons League of Mobile, Inc, Box 8055, Mobile, AL 36608	$1000	Student attending Mobile area college	One year	Annually
Art Students League of New York*, 215 W. 57th St, New York, NY 10019	Tuition $4000 Traveling Scholarships (2)	League students League students	One year One year	Annually Annually
Artists' Guild, c/o Art Museum of the Palm Beaches, Inc, P.O. Box 2300, West Palm Beach, FL 33402	$300	High school graduate art student of South Florida		
Arts and Crafts Center of Pittsburgh, Mellon Park, Pittsburgh, PA 15232	Nominal	Underprivileged qualified students, Pittsburgh residents only	One term	Each term
The Arts and Crafts Society of Portland, 616 N.W. 18th Ave, Portland, OR 97209	Work exchange scholarships for school tuition	Students in financial need	Per term	Per term
Arts Club of Washington, 2017 Eye St. N.W, Washington, DC 20006	$600	Students at local universities or colleges only	One year	Annually
The Arts and Science Center, 14 Court St, Nashua, NH 03060	For education classes at the Center (4 semesters)	Qualified applicants	Ten weeks	Quarterly
Asheville Art Museum, Civic Center, Asheville, NC 28801	Variable	All persons upon need	One year	Per semester
Association of Medical Illustrators, 6650 Northwest Hwy, Chicago, IL 60631	$100	2nd year medical illustration students	One year	Annually
Ball State University, 1500 University Ave, Muncie, IN 47306	$2800 graduate assistantship ($385 summer term)	Degree candidate in Art Department	One year (renewable)	Annually
	$3225 fellowship ($440 summer term)	Doctoral candidate in Art Department	One year (renewable)	Annually
Bassist Institute, 923 S.W. Taylor St, Portland, OR 97205	$2000	Students	One and two years	Annually
Battle Creek Civic Art Center, 265 Emmett St, Battle Creek, MI 49017	$15 - $25 per person each term	Public school students in the greater Battle Creek area only	Per term	Each Semester
Baylor University Department of Art, Waco, TX 76703	$400	Anyone qualifying for admission to Baylor	Semester	Semi-annually
Beloit College, Beloit, WI 53511	Variable	Qualified students	One year (renewable)	Annually
Berkshire Art Association, P.O. Box 385, Pittsfield, MA 01201	$1000	Art major		Annually
Birmingham-Bloomfield Art Association, 1516 S. Cranbrook Rd, Birmingham, MI 48009	Full, dependent upon course cost	All	Per term	
Boston Architectural Center*, 320 Newbury St, Boston, MA 02115	Variable	Qualified attending students		Annually
Bradley University, School of Art, Peoria, IL 61625	Undergraduate $2600; 8 graduate assistantships of $1200 each	Any student in or entering the art program	One year (renewable)	Annually
Archie Bray Foundation, 2915 Country Club Ave, Helena, MT 59601	$151 work scholarships (8)	Students only	Three weeks	Annually

OFFERED BY	AMOUNT	OPENED TO	DURATION	WHEN OFFERED
Briarcliff College, Elm Rd, Briarcliff Manor, NY 10510	$500 per year	Entering freshmen and transfer students	Four years	Annually
Brigham Young University, Harris Fine Arts Center, Provo, UT 84601	Tuition	Qualified freshman applicants, transfer and continuing students	One year	Annually
British Government, Marshall Scholarships. Apply: British Consulate-General in Atlanta, Boston, Chicago, Philadelphia or San Francisco. Closing date for applications Oct. 22	(30) in the order of £1750 a year. In certain circumstances a marriage allowance is also payable	U.S. citizens. Available to college or university graduates under 26 years of age for study of any subject leading to the award of a British University degree. Candidates may apply either in region in which they live or where they received at least two years of college training.	Two years (with possibility of extension for a third year)	Annually
Brockton Art Center - Art Workshops, Oak St, Brockton, MA 02401	$40	Needy children	Per term	Semi-annually
Bucknell University, Department of Art, Lewisburg, PA 17837	$2000 plus tuition	Registered graduate students	One year (renewable)	Annually
Caldwell College Art Department, Caldwell, NJ 07006	$500 - $2100	Academically qualified	One year	Renewable annually
	Grants: $100 and up	Economically qualified	One year	Renewable annually
California College of Arts and Crafts, 5212 Broadway, Oakland, CA 94618	Variable. Scholarships, loans, grants	Grants, loans, employment open to all students. Scholarships open to continuing students who have attended for two or more consecutive semesters and are currently enrolled	One year	Annually
California Institute of the Arts, 24700 McBean Pkwy, Valencia, CA 91355	$600,000 total per year	Needy and/or merit students	Four years (with satisfactory educational advancement)	Annually
California State University, Chico, Taylor Hall Art Gallery, First St. & Normal Ave, Chico, CA 95926	$1000	Art students	One year	Annually
California State University, Hayward, Art Dept, 25800 Hillary St, Hayward, CA 94542	Variable ($100 - $300 annually from	Any art student	One year	
California State University, San Diego, 5402 College Ave, San Diego, CA 92182	$500 - $1000	Upper division students	One year	Annually
Campbellsville College*, Department of Fine Arts, Campbellsville, KY 42718	$100 per semester	All applicants who can show proficiency	Four years (renewable)	Semi-annually
Canadian Society for Education Through Art, Faculty of Education, University of Regina, Regina, SK, Canada	$300 (4)	High school graduates	One year	Annually
Catholic University of America, 620 Michigan Ave. N.E, Washington, DC 20017	(2) half-tuition scholarships	B.A. and M.F.A. students	Usually the length of the program	Annually
Catholic University of Puerto Rico, Fine Arts Department, Ponce, PR 00731	(1) Full tuition	Low income freshmen with art talent	Four years	Biennially or every four years
Centenary College of Louisiana,* Department of Art, Centenary Blvd, Shreveport, LA 71104	Varied from full tuition to nominal amounts	Outstanding students	One year	Annually
Center for Creative Studies, College of Art and Design, 245 E. Kirby St, Detroit, MI 48202	$1950 scholarship (1)	High school seniors	One year	Annually through Scholastic Art Awards
	Scholarships to freshmen (5)	High school seniors	One year	Annually, judged at the school
Central Wyoming College*, Art Center, Riverton, WY 82501	Tuition	Anyone with artistic potential regardless of age, race, or sex	One year	Annually
Chabot College*, 25555 Hesperin Blvd, Hayward, CA 94545	$100 annually from California Art Society	Fine arts majors	One year	Annually
Charles River Creative Arts Program, Centre St, Dover, MA 02030	$2000	Those needing financial aid	One year	Annually
The Charleston Art Gallery of Sunrise, 755 Myrtle Rd, Charleston, WV 25314	Tuition	Underprivileged and competition winners	One year	Annually
Cherokee National Historical Society, Inc, P.O. Box 515, Tahlequah, OH 74464	Variable	Graduate level students of Cherokee descent studying for the museum and archival professions		
Cheyenne Artists Guild, Inc, 1010 E. 16th St, Cheyenne, WY 82001	$200	Senior high school students of Cheyenne only	One year	Annually
Chicago Public School Art Society, Art Institute of Chicago, Michigan Ave at Adams St, Chicago, IL 60603	$130	Children who are involved in Society's Art Form program	Per semester	Semi-annually
The Children's Aid Society, Lower West Side Center, 209 Sullivan St, New York, NY 10012	Variable	Depending on economic situation	One year	Semi-annually
Cleveland Institute of Art, 11141 East Boulevard, Cleveland, OH 44106	$65,000 (total)	Qualified students	One year	Annually

OFFERED BY	AMOUNT	OPENED TO	DURATION	WHEN OFFERED
Colby Community College, Art Department, 1255 S. Range, Colby, KS 67701	Full tuition and fees	Any applicant, juried portfolio	Two years	Annually
Colby-Sawyer College, New London, NH 03257	Approximately $350	Entering and upperclass students	One year	Annually
College of Mount St. Joseph on the Ohio, Art Department, Mount St. Joseph, OH 45051	One year $1920	High school graduates. Special scholastic scholarship	One year	Annually
College of New Rochelle, Castle Pl, New Rochelle, NY 10801	Variable, depending on need	Incoming freshmen with portfolio	Four years	Annually in March
The College of St. Catherine*, Visual Arts Department, 2004 Randolph, St. Paul, MN 55105	Variable	Art majors	One year	Annually
College of the Ozarks, Art Department, 610 Johnson St, Clarksville, AR 72830	$200	Art majors	One year	Annually
Colorado Women's College, Montview at Quebec, Denver, CO 80220	Variable	Art students	One year	Annually
Columbia College, Eighth and Rogers, Columbia, MO 65201	Up to $1000 plus work study	Students showing talent and/or need	One year	Annually
Columbia University*, School of the Arts, 617 Dodge, New York, NY 10027	Variable	All registered students in competition		Annually
Community Arts Council of Chilliwack, Box 53, Chilliwack, BC, Canada	$300	Those seeking higher education in the fine arts	One year	Annually
Compton Community College*, Art Department, 1111 E. Artesia Blvd, Compton, CA 90224	$200 - $300	Art majors	One year	Annually
Concordia College, Moorhead, MN 56560	Up to $1500	Entering freshmen and upper classmen	One year	Annually
Contemporary Arts Museum, 5216 Montrose, Houston, TX 77006	$120 - $125	Underprivileged	Semester basis	
Cooper School of Art, 2341 Carnegie Ave. S.W, Cleveland, OH 44115	Full and partial tuition, total $12,000	High school seniors	One year (renewable)	Annually
Coppini Academy of Fine Arts, 115 Melrose Pl, San Antonio, TX 78212	Senior $400 Junior $100 - $250	Ages 21 - 30 Ages 16 - 20		Annually Annually
Corcoran School of Art*, 17th & New York Ave. N.W, Washington, DC 20006	William Wilson Corcoran Scholarship	Students from area high schools	Summer course	Annually in April
	Rohsheim Memorial Award	Outstanding first year students	One semester	Annually in May
	Kenneth Stubbs Memorial Award	Outstanding drawing students	One semester	Annually in May
	Mary Lay Thom Sculpture Prize	Outstanding sculpture students	One semester	Annually in May
	Eugene Weisz Memorial Scholarship	Outstanding painting students	One semester	Annually in May
	Sarah Pickens Roberts Memorial Award	Student whose work is judged most promising	One semester	Annually in May
	Cash prizes in Final Annual Graduation Exhibition	Prize-winning students		Annually in May
Cornell College, Mt. Vernon, IA 52314	$3700	Selected on recommendation of Art Dept. Also based on need		Annually
Cornish School of Allied Arts, 710 E. Roy, Seattle, WA 98102	Variable amounts, tuition scholarships	Registered full-time students	One year	Annually
Craft Center, 25 Sagamore Rd, Worcester, MA 01605	$60	People in need	Ten week semester	Annually
Cranbrook Academy of Art, Bloomfield Hills, MI 48013	$50,000 annually	Qualified first and second year students in Architecture, Ceramics, Design, Fabric Design, Metalsmithing, Painting, Photography, Printmaking, Sculpture	One year	Annually
	Ford Foundation scholarships	First-year qualified students		
	Additional grants provided and awarded by Studio Council	Second-year students	One semester	Annually
Dayton Art Institute, Forest & Riverview Ave, Dayton, OH 45405	$2000 - $3000 (total)	Qualified students		Semi-annually
Dean Junior College Visual and Performing Arts, 99 Main St, Franklin, MA 02038	Variable	Full-time students	One year	Annually
Delaware Art Museum, 2301 Kentmere Pkwy, Wilmington, DE 19806	Variable	Public school pupils	One year	Semi-annually
Detroit Artists' Market, 1452 Randolph St, Detroit, MI 48226	$1000	Any qualified student who is attending the specific school whose turn it is to receive the scholarship; given on rotating basis to Center for Creative Studies, Wayne State University and Cranbrook Academy of Art	One year	Annually

OFFERED BY	AMOUNT	OPENED TO	DURATION	WHEN OFFERED
Dickinson State College, Dickinson, ND 58601	$500 TMI Systems Design Corporation Scholarship	Any art or business student	One year	Annually
	$100 Tom Niemitalo Memorial Art Scholarship	Any art major or minor	One year	Annually
	$100 DSC Alumni Foundation Scholarships	Freshmen	One year	Annually
Drake University*, Des Moines, IA 50311	$50 - $300 (total of $9500)	Art majors	One year (renewable)	Annually
Dumbarton Oaks Research Library and Collection*, 1703 32nd St. N.W, Washington, DC 20007	Variable	Graduate students of Byzantine studies and Pre-Columbian studies	One year	Annually
Dutchess Community College, Department of Visual Arts, 1 Pendell Rd, Poughkeepsie, NY 12601	$250	Second-year students	One year	Annually
East Central Junior College, P.O. Box 529, Union, MO 63084	$110	Students	One year	Annually
East Mississippi Junior College, Art and Photography Department, Scooba, MS 39358	Determined on merit basis	All students in art major curriculum	One year	Annually
East Tennessee State University, Carroll Reece Museum, Johnson City, TN 37601	$3000	High school seniors and college students	One year	Annually
Edgecliff College, 2220 Victory Pkwy, Cincinnati, OH 45206	$1760 per year	Graduating high school seniors	Four years	Annually
El Camino College, 16007 Crenshaw Blvd, Via Torrance, CA 90506	$300 per year	Junior standing and transfer to an accredited school for more art training	One year	Annually
El Paso Museum of Art, 1211 Montana Ave, El Paso, TX 79902	$500	Junior and senior high school students of El Paso	Per year	
Eleutherian Mills-Hagley Foundation, Greenville, Wilmington, DE 19807	Variable	Graduate of accredited college for study toward M.A. or Ph.D. degrees in history at the University of Delaware	Two - four years	Deadline for applications February 15
Erie Art Center, 338 W. Sixth St, Erie, PA 16507	Generally for amount of tuition	Anyone demonstrating financial need	One term	Semi-annually
Essex Institute, 132 Essex St, Salem, MA 01970	Fellowships arranged through Boston University American Studies program	Graduate students in American Studies	One year	Annually
Fine Arts Center of Clinton, 119 W. Macon St, Clinton, IL 61727	Tuition only	Qualified students		Annually
Flint Institute of Arts, DeWaters Art Center, 1120 E. Kearsley St, Flint, MI 48503	Partial	Gifted children	One semester	
Florida Gulf Coast Art Center, Inc, 222 Ponce de Leon Blvd, Clearwater, FL 33516	Variable	Junior and senior high school students	Summer	Annually
Florida State University*, Tallahassee, FL 32306	Assistantships $1600 - $1800	Graduate students in art	One year	Annually
	Fellowships $3000	Graduate students	One year	Annually
Folger Shakespeare Library, 201 E. Capitol St. S.E, Washington, DC 20003	$600 - $10,000	Qualified advanced scholars	One month - one year	Semi-annually
Fort Hays Kansas State College, Hays, KS 67601	$9000	Graduate students and art students	One year	Annually
Franklin and Marshall College*, Lancaster, PA 17604	Variable	Students with pronounced talent		Annually
Freer Gallery of Art*, 12th & Jefferson Dr. S.W, Washington, DC 20560	Variable	Ph.D. candidate from University of Michigan in Oriental art field; Ph.D. candidate in field of Chinese art	Variable	No set formula
Fresno Arts Center, 3033 E. Yale Ave, Fresno, CA 93703	$900	School students	Each class session (3)	
Grand Canyon College Art Department, 3300 W. Camelback Rd, P.O. Box 11097, Phoenix, AZ 85061	Up to 50%	Majors accepted into degree program	One year (renewable)	Annually
Grants for Graduate Study Abroad. Write: Sales and Correspondence Unit, Institute of International Education, 809 United Nations Plaza, New York, NY 10017	Note: People in the arts may apply for any of these awards (Fulbright-Hays and Foreign Governments), but they must be affiliated with an educational institute abroad while pursuing their studies.		One academic year	
Greater Fall River Art Association*, 80 Belmont St, Fall River, MA 02720	$100	Students entering Art Department of Southeastern Massachusetts University	One year	Annually
Green Country Art Center, 1825 E. 15th St, Tulsa, OK 74104	$750	Students enrolled in university fine art department	One year	Annually
Elizabeth Greenshields Memorial Foundation, 1814 Sherbrooke St. W, Montreal, PQ, H3H 1E4, Canada	various (30)	Nationals of any country for study in any country in painting and sculpture	One year	No closing date

OFFERED BY	AMOUNT	OPENED TO	DURATION	WHEN OFFERED
John Simon Guggenheim Memorial Foundation*, 90 Park Ave, New York, NY 10016	Adjusted to needs of fellows	Citizens or permanent residents of U.S, Canada, other American states, Caribbean, Philippines, and French, Dutch, and British possessions in Western Hemisphere, normally 30 to 45 years of age	One year	Annually
Harford Community College, 401 Thomas Run Rd, Bel Air, MD 21014	$50	Student matriculating in an art program	One year	Annually
Hastings College Art Department, Hastings, NE 68901	$200 - $500	All art majors	Four years	Annually
The Havre Art Association Tuition Award, Northern Montana College, Havre, MT 59501	$50	An art major or minor who has demonstrated high art ability and who is in need of financial aid	No limit established	Annually
Haystack Mountain School of Crafts, Deer Isle, ME 04627	$600 (16)	Candidates with one year or more graduate specialization in crafts	Six weeks	Annually
Henry E. Huntington Library and Art Gallery, San Marino, CA 91108	$600 per month	Scholars (not to candidates for advanced degrees)	One to twelve months	Annually. Applications received Oct. 1 - Dec. 31 for awards beginning the following June
The Henry Francis du Pont Winterthur Museum, Winterthur, DE 19735	Base stipend $3000	College graduates for fellows in Winterthur Program in Early American Culture and Winterthur Program in the Conservation of Artistic and Historic Objects only	Two years	Annually
Herron School of Art*, Indiana University-Purdue University at Indianapolis, 1701 N. Pennsylvania St, Indianapolis, IN 46202	Scholarships, total per year $10,000. Also various financial aid available through Indiana University	Any student	One year	Annually
Historical Society of Delaware*, Market St, Wilmington, DE 19801	Summer internship program	College juniors interested in museum and historical society work	Summer	Annually
Historical Society of York County, 250 E. Market St, York, PA 17403	$100 - $200	Summer interns	Six weeks	Annually
Honolulu Academy of Arts, 900 S. Beretania St, Honolulu, HI 96814	$880 (year's tuition)	Students who successfully completed first year study	One year	Annually
Howard University Gallery of Art, College of Fine Arts, Sixth & Fairmont Sts. N.W, Washington, DC 20001	Up to $2000	Students	One year	Annually
Hudson River Museum, 511 Warburton Ave, Yonkers, NY 10701	Based on financial need of applicant	All who apply	Depending on type of school	Each semester (4 per year)
Hutchinson Art Association, 321 E. First St, Hutchinson, KS 67501	$250	Junior college art students	One year	Annually
Incorporated E. A. Abbey Scholarships for Mural Painting in the U.S.A*, 1083 Fifth Ave, New York, NY 10028	$6000 scholarship for study in mural painting in U.S. and abroad	U.S. citizens not more than 35 years of age	One year	Biennially
Industrial Designers Society of America, 1750 Old Meadow Rd, McLean, VA 22101	Walter Dorwin Teague Research Fund; depends on amount required for research projects	Practicing designers	One year	Annually
Institute of American Indian Arts, Cerrillos Rd, Santa Fe, NM 87501	Full - board, room, all materials plus two years high school	Any native American	Two years	Annually
Institute of Contemporary Art, University of Pennsylvania, 34th & Walnut Sts, Philadelphia, PA 19174	Cost of lecture series	Applicants	One year	Annually
Instituto Allende*, San Miguel de Allende, Guanajuato, Mexico	From full tuition of $200 per quarter, renewable, to $2500 for tuition and cash grant per year	Anyone; apply to Dean of Admissions at address shown		Quarterly from Jan. 1st
Instituto de Cultura Puertorriquena, Apartado 4184, San Juan, PR 00905	Variable	Artists, writers, and scholars	One year	Annually
Interamerican University, San German, PR 00753	Variable	All with talent		Annually, semi-annually
International Museum of Photography at George Eastman House, 900 East Ave, Rochester, NY 14607	$7200 (3)	Post-masters degree	One year	Annually
Ivy School of Professional Art, University Ave, Pittsburgh, PA 15214	Tuition	Teens - Saturday classes	One year	Annually
Jackson Art Association*, Jackson, TN 38301	$75	Talented, handicapped, elementary school children for summer art lessons	Three months	Annually
Junior Arts Center, 4814 Hollywood Blvd, Los Angeles, CA 90027	Tailored to students' needs	Promising artists	To fulfill project	As requested
Kansas City Art Institute, Kansas City, MO 64111	$100 to full tuition	High school and college transfers based on need	Two semesters (renewable)	Each semester
Kansas State University, Department of Art, Manhattan, KS 66506	$2300 - $3000 Teaching Assistantships	Students working for Master's degree	Nine months	Annually
	$200 - $900 Work Assistantships	Undergraduate or graduate students	Nine months	Annually
	Variable scholarship awards	Sophomore - senior undergraduates	One year	Annually

OFFERED BY	AMOUNT	OPENED TO	DURATION	WHEN OFFERED
Kappa Pi International Honorary Art Fraternity, Box 7843, Midfield, Birmingham, AL 35228	$500	Student members	One year	Annually
Maude Kerns Art Center, 1910 E. 15th Ave, Eugene, OR 97403	$600 per year Work scholarship for adults Scholarship for children	Qualified applicant	One quarter	All year
Kimbell Art Museum, Will Rogers Rd. W, Ft. Worth, TX 76107	Variable	Those in curatorial, conservation programs	One year	Annually
Kootenay School of Art Division, Selkirk College, 2001 Silver King Rd, Nelson, BC, V1L 1C8, Canada	Variable	Students of Kootenay School of Art	One year	Annually
Lafayette Art Center, 101 S. Ninth St, Lafayette, IN 47901	Up to $500	Eligible students, low income and merit	One semester (24 sessions)	Semi-annually
Lahaina Arts Society, 649 Wharf St, Lahaina, HI 96761	$1000 per year	High school seniors	One year	Annually
Lake Placid School of Art, Center for Music, Drama and Art, Saranac Ave, Lake Placid, NY 12946	$5000	Students who show financial need. (Annual scholarships offered to Union of Independent Colleges of Art students)	One year	Annually
Las Vegas Art Museum, Sponsored by Las Vegas Art League, 3333 W. Washington, Las Vegas, NV 89107	Membership and tuition to any class	Graduating high school seniors, each high school in area	One year	Annually
Le Musee Regional de Rimouski, 35 ouest Saint-Germain, Rimouski, PQ, Canada	$500	Artists - groups	One year	Annually
The Lindenwood Colleges*, Art Department, St. Charles, MO 63301	$500 - $2000	Art majors	One year	Annually
Little Gallery of Arts, 155 E. Main, Vernal, UT 84078	$100	High school seniors	One year	Annually
Loch Haven Art Center, Inc, 2416 N. Mills Ave, Orlando, FL 32803	Varies (class tuition)	Qualified applicants	Ten-week class	Each quarter
Los Angeles County Museum of Art*, 5905 Wilshire Blvd, Los Angeles, CA 90036	Contemporary Art Councils $1200 Award	Young local artists	One year	Annually
The Louisville School of Art*, 100 Park Rd, Anchorage, KY 40223	$5250 (annual total)	Those demonstrating need	One semester	Semi-annually
Loyola Marymount University, Malone Art Gallery, 7101 W. 80th St, Los Angeles, CA 90045	Related to financial status	Financially deprived	One semester	Semi-annually
Lyman Allyn Museum, 100 Mohegan Ave, New London, CT 06320	$45 for childrens' art classes	Needy children	One year	Annually
The MacDowell Colony, Inc, Peterborough, NH 03458 (applications obtainable: The MacDowell Colony, Inc, 145 W. 58th St, New York, NY 10019. Attn: Shirley Blanchard	Resident fellowships to professional writers, painters, sculptors, filmmakers, printmakers, and composers provide board, room, use of studio for maximum of three months. A token charge of $49 per week is waived in cases of need	Nationals of any country	One to two months (summer) One to three months (winter)	
Eliot McMurrough School of Art, 306 Fifth Ave, Indialantic, FL 32703	Work scholarships	Those in need who are already enrolled	One term	Semi-annually
McMurry College, Art Department, Sayles Blvd. & S. 14th St, Abilene, TX 79605	Variable	Art students who show special ability	One year	Annually
McNeese State University, Department of the Visual Arts, 4000 Ryan St, Lake Charles, LA 70601	$250	Majors	One year	Annually
Madison College, Duke Fine Arts Center, Main at Grace St, Harrisonburg, VA 22801	$1000 - $3000	Graduate students in the Department of Art	One year	
Madonna College, 36600 Schoolcraft Rd, Livonia, MI 48150	Robert Svoboda Scholarship $2500	Student interested in art or journalism	One year	Annually
Maitland Art Center, Research Studio, 231 W. Packwood Ave, Maitland, FL 32751	$500 each	Applicants	One year	Annually
Manatee Junior College, 26th St. W, Bradenton, FL 33505	Full tuition	Students majoring in art; preference given to Fla. residents		Semi-annually
Manitoba Association of Architects, Winnipeg 2, MB, Canada	$300	Architecture students enrolled at the University of Manitoba only	One year	Annually
Marion Art Center, Main St, Marion, MA 02739	$250	High school seniors	One year	Annually
Maryland School of Art, 640 University Blvd. E, Silver Spring, MD 20901	Variable	Incoming students and current students	One year	Semi-annually
The Memphis Academy of Arts, Overton Park, Memphis, TN 38112	$50,000 (total)	High school graduates and college transfers	One year	Annually

OFFERED BY	AMOUNT	OPENED TO	DURATION	WHEN OFFERED
Mercyhurst College, 501 E. 38th St, Erie, PA 16501	Open	All art or art education applicants	One year (renewable)	Annually
Mesa College, Grand Junction, CO 81501	Tuition scholarships (4)	One each class - freshman, sophomore, junior, senior	Continuous with annual review	Annually
Mesa Community College, 1833 W. Southern Ave, Mesa, AZ 85201	Six at $100 cash	Area students	One year	Annually
Metropolitan Museum and Art Center, 7867 N. Kendall Dr, Miami, FL 33156	Approximately $1200 per year	Children		
Metropolitan Museum of Art, The Main Bldg, Fifth Ave. at 82nd St, New York, NY 10028	Variable	Scholars researching art historical fields relating to Metropolitan Museum of Art collections	One year	
Midway Studios, University of Chicago, 6016 S. Ingleside, Chicago, IL 60637	Full tuition and stipend	Outstanding entering graduate students		Deadline: Jan. 15
Millikin University Art Department, 1184 W. Main, Decatur, IL 62522	$500	Qualified students	Four years	Annually
Mississippi University for Women, Columbus, MS 39701	$100 - $300	Undergraduates	One year	Annually
Missouri Southern State College, Art Department, Newman & Duquesne Rds, Joplin, MO 64801	$250 (2) and $200 (2)	Top quality students with art skills	One year	Annually
Missouri Western State College*, Department of Fine Arts, 4525 Downs Dr, St. Joseph, MO 64507	$125 - $240	Any qualifying student majoring in art	One year	Annually
Mobile Art Association, Inc, c/o Vasco Geer, Jr, 30 Alverson Rd, Mobile, AL 36608	$500	Second year art students	One year	Annually
Monroe City-County Fine Arts Council, 1555 S. Raisinville Rd, Monroe, MI 48161	$300	County residents	One year	Annually
Montana State University, School of Art, Bozeman, MT 59715	$2700	Graduate students	One year	Annually - May 1
Montclair State College, School of Fine and Performing Arts, Upper Montclair, NJ 07043	$2500	Qualified graduate students	One year	Annually
Monterey Peninsula Museum of Art, 559 Pacific St, Monterey, CA 93940	$500 per semester (2)	Local college students	One year	Semi-annually
Moore College of Art, Philadelphia, PA 19103	Partial and full tuition scholarships	Undergraduates and entering freshmen	One year	Annually
C. S. Mott Community College Fine Arts Division, 1401 E. Court St, Flint, MI 48503	Up to $450	Current art students		Annually
Mount Aloysius Junior College*, Cresson, PA 16630	$1000	Anyone eligible for entry with art portfolio and interview	Two years	Semi-annually
Mount Holyoke College, New Art Building, South Hadley, MA 01075	$300 - $1000	Alumnae	One year	Annually
Mount Marty College, 1100 W. Fifth, Yankton, SD 57078	Up to $1000	Especially talented students		Annually
Mount Saint Clare College, 400 N. Bluff, Clinton, IA 52732	$150; other financial aid available	Incoming freshmen and students already enrolled	Renewable if work merits it	
Mount Wachusett Community College, Art Department, Gardner, MA 01440	Approximately $100	Art majors in transfer	One year	Annually
Mulvane Art Center, Washburn University, Topeka, KS 66621	$3000	Qualified students	One year plus	Annually
Muncie Art Association*, Bertha Crosley Ball Art Center, 600 Court, 600 S. Tillotson, Muncie, IN 47303	$300	Ball State University art students	One year	Annually
Municipal Art Society of Baltimore City, c/o Mr. Beverley C. Compton, Jr, Alex Brown & Sons, 135 E. Baltimore St, Baltimore, MD 21202	Traveling scholarship	Senior students of the Graduate School, Maryland Institute, Baltimore	One year	Annually
The Museum of Fine Arts, Houston, 1001 Bissonnet St, Houston, Tex 77005	Variable	Students, on basis of portfolio	One year	Annually
Museum Without Walls, RCEDA Inc, P.O. Box 45, Morris Ave, Friendsville, MD 21531	$400,000 (total)	Community college students in areas where program circulates	Two years	Semi-annually
Mystic Seaport, Inc, Mystic, CT 06355 (In cooperation with University of Connecticut)	$1.35 per course in 1976	Graduate students and teachers or other professionals who wish to broaden their backgrounds	June 28 - August 6, 1976	Annually

OFFERED BY	AMOUNT	OPENED TO	DURATION	WHEN OFFERED
National Collection of Fine Arts, Smithsonian Institution, Washington, DC 20560	$9000	Ph.D.s and doctoral candidates in art history	September 1 - July 31	Deadline: February 15
	Limited stipend	College seniors and graduate students in art history and studio art	Nine weeks, commencing in June	Deadline: February 15
National Endowment for the Arts, Washington, DC 20506	$3000 - $10,000 (nonacademic fellowships)	Professional artists, critics, craftsmen, choreographers, designers, museum professionals, jazz, folk and ethnic musicians, composers and librettists, creative writers	One year	
National Gallery of Art, Constitution Ave. at Sixth St. N.W, Washington, DC 20565 (Note: Applications for the following fellowships are accepted only in the form of recommendations from the chairman of a graduate department of art history)	David E. Finley Fellowship	Ph.D. candidates	Two years, plus eight months at the National Gallery	Annually (deadline Jan. 31)
	Samuel H. Kress Fellowships	Ph.D. candidates	One year	Annually (deadline Jan. 31)
	Chester Dale Fellowships	Ph.D. candidates	One year	Annually (deadline Jan. 31)
	Robert H. and Clarice Smith Fellowship	Ph.D. candidates or holders	One year	Annually (deadline Jan. 31)
National Institute of Arts and Letters and American Academy of Arts and Letters, 633 W. 155th St, New York, NY 10032	$3000 awards	Painters, sculptors, graphic artists (cannot be applied for)		Annually
Nazareth College of Rochester, 4245 East Ave, Rochester, NY 14610	Variable	Qualified high school graduates, i.e, B+ average, total score of 1200 CEEB, and/or impressive art portfolio	One year (renewable)	Annually
New Mexico State University, Art Department, Box 3572, Las Cruces, NM 88003	$100 - $2800	Graduate students	One - two years	Annually
New School of Art, 296 Brunswick Ave, Toronto 179, ON, Canada	Up to $200	Students who have completed one year or more	One year	Annually
New York School of Interior Design, 155 E. 56th St, New York, NY 10022	$850	Design students; preference given to second and third year students	One semester (renewable)	Annually (deadline May 1)
North Park College, Fine Arts Division, 5125 N. Spaulding, Chicago, IL 60625	$800	Sophomore and junior art majors	One year	Annually
North Shore Arts Association, Rear 197 E. Main St, Gloucester, MA 01930	$100	Local students	One year	Annually
North Shore Art League, Winnetka Community House, 620 Lincoln, Winnetka, IL 60093	$1500	Art Institute of Chicago students	One year	Annually
Northeast Louisiana University, Department of Art, Monroe, LA 71201	$2400 lab assistantship; $3000 teaching assistantship	Graduate students	Two years	Annually
Northeastern Illinois University, Art Department, St. Louis at Bryn Mawr Ave, Chicago, IL 60625	$476 (2 terms)	Board of Governors Talent Scholarships available to gifted art students	Two terms	Annually
Northern Michigan University, c/o Prof. Cappuccio, Marquette, MI 49855	$500	Sophomore art and design majors who have been majors in NMU art dept. at least one semester	One year	Annually
Northwest Nazarene College, Holly at Dewey, Boise, ID 83651	Variable	Fine arts majors	One year	Annually
Northwestern College Art Department, Orange City, IA 51041	$100 - $250	Art majors	One year	Annually
Oak Ridge Community Art Center, P.O. Box 105, Oak Ridge, TN 37830	Varies according to class	Anyone	One quarter	Quarterly
Oakland City College, Oakland City, IN 47660	Variable	Outstanding ability shown in art (competitive)	One year (renewable)	Annually
The Oakland Museum*, 1000 Oak St, Oakland, CA 94607	$1000	California artists	One year	Annually
Oberlin College, Oberlin, OH 44074	$3000 (3 graduate assistantships)	Graduates with B.A. degree who qualify	One year (renewable)	Annually
Occidental College, 1600 Campus Rd, Los Angeles, CA 90041	Open	Art majors who can demonstrate financial need	Renewable for four years	Annually
Ohio University School of Art, Athens, OH 45701	Tuition scholarship Assistantships	Undergraduate students Graduates	One year (renewable)	Annually
Oklahoma Art Center, 3113 Pershing Blvd, Oklahoma City, OK 73107	$150	Young Talent in Oklahoma winners	One year	Annually
Old Dominion University, Hampton Blvd, Norfolk, VA 23508	$500	All art students	One year	Annually
Old Sturbridge Village (through National Endowment for the Humanities grant), Sturbridge, MA 01566	Variable	Persons interested in careers in historical, preservation and conservation agencies	Twelve months	Annually
Ontario Arts Council, Kitchener Waterloo Art Gallery, 43 Benton St, Kitchener, ON N2G 3H1, Canada	Up to $1500	Young Ontario artists	One year	Annually

OFFERED BY	AMOUNT	OPENED TO	DURATION	WHEN OFFERED
Ontario College of Art*, 100 McCaul St, Toronto, ON M5T 1W1, Canada	Variable	Students only	One year	Annually
Otero Junior College, 18th & Colorado, La Junta, CO 81050	$300	Colorado residents with artist promise	One year	Annually
Otis Art Institute of Los Angeles County, 2401 Wilshire Blvd, Los Angeles, CA 90057	Variable	Students enrolled at Otis in the BFA or MFA degree programs	Academic year	Annually
Ottumwa Heights College, Ottumwa, IA 52501	$300	Full-time students in art, drama, and/or music	One year, renewable second year	Annually
Our Lady of the Lake University, 411 S.W. 24th St, San Antonio, TX 78285	Variable	Majors in art		Annually
Palomar College, San Marcos, CA 92069	$75 Lake San Marcos Art League Award	Returning sophomore majoring in art		
	$50 Catherine Ann (Tim) Sawday Memorial Scholarship	Deserving student majoring in art or science		
	$100 San Dieguito Art Guild Scholarship	Graduate planning to pursue a career in painting		
	$300 Fallbrook Art Association	Art major continuing on to a 4-year accredited art school		
	$50 Showcase of the Arts	Returning sophomore majoring in art		
	$150 Showcase of the Arts - Evelyn Surface Memorial	Two awards - one for art student returning to Palomar and one for a graduating art student going on to a 4-year institution		
Palos Verdes Art Center and Museum, 5504 W. Crestridge Rd, Rancho Palos Verdes, CA 90274	Class fees	High school students	One semester	
Albert Pels School of Art, Inc,* 2109 Broadway, New York, NY 10023	$1500 per year	High school seniors	One year (renewable)	Annually
	$1500 per year	Enrolled student working scholarship	One year	Annually
Pennsylvania Academy of the Fine Arts, Broad & Cherry Sts, Philadelphia, PA 19102	Scholastic Magazine Art Award (1) 1 year tuition	High school seniors	One year	Annually
	$1300 tuition scholarships	2nd, 3rd & 4th year Academy students	One year	Annually
	Cresson European Travel Scholarship and tuition - $3300	3rd, 4th year Academy students	Three months	Annually
	Schiedt & Ware Travel Scholarship - $2000	3rd, 4th year Academy students	Three months	Annually
Peoria Art Guild*, 1831 N. Knoxville Ave, Peoria, IL 61603	$500	Students who would benefit from artistic instructions, but who would be otherwise unable to afford art classes	One year	Annually
Pitzer College, Claremont, CA 91711	Variable	Qualified students		Annually
Place des Arts, 166 King Edward St, Coquitlam, BC, Canada	Up to $400 through the Coquitlam Fine Arts Council	Any artist living within the area	One year	Annually
The Ponca City Art Association, Box 1394, Ponca City, OK 74601	$50 (2)	Outstanding art student, one boy and one girl	One year	Annually
Pontiac Creative Arts Center, 47 Williams St, Pontiac, MI 48053	$20 and $50 (children and adults' tuitions)		Ten-week terms	
Portland School of Art of the Portland Society of Art, 97 Spring St, Portland, ME 04101	$200	Greater Portland resident (entering)	One year	Annually
	$200	State of Maine outside of Greater Portland (entering)	One year	Annually
	$200 (2)	Qualified students	One year	Annually
Pratt Graphics Center, extension of Pratt Institute, 831 Broadway, New York, NY 10003	Tuition up to a period of one year	Talented artists	Up to one year	
Prince Rupert Art Club, c/o Ms. Johan C. Woodland, Corresp. Secy, Court House, Prince Rupert, BC, Canada	$100	Any deserving amateur or student	Summer course	Annually
Providence Art Club, 11 Thomas St, Providence, RI 02903	Tuition and fees (3)	Rhode Island School of Design students	One year	Annually
The Provincetown Workshop, A School of Painting and Drawing, 492 Commercial St, Provincetown, MA 02657	$285 (20)	Students of art schools	One season	Annually, summers
Quincy Art Center*, 1515 Jersey St, Quincy, IL 62301	Approximately $250 annually	Underprivileged children	One year	Semi-annually
Quincy College, Art Department, 1831 College Ave, Quincy, IL 62301	Variable	Art student majors	One year	Annually
Rensselaer County Historical Society, 59 Second St, Troy, NY 12180	$1000 funded by NYSCA summer museum intern program	Senior Russell Sage students		Annually, if funded
Rio Hondo College, 3600 Workman Mill Rd, Whittier, CA 90608	$100	Second year art students	One year	Annually

OFFERED BY	AMOUNT	OPENED TO	DURATION	WHEN OFFERED
Riverside Art Center and Museum, 3425 Seventh, Riverside, CA 92501	$200 per year	Based on need and talent	$50 per quarter	Quarterly
Roberson Center for the Arts and Sciences, 30 Front St, Binghamton, NY 13905	Variable, covering the class fee only	Talented and interested students in art, music, dance	One year	
Rocky Mountain School of Art*, 1441 Ogden St, Denver, CO 80218	$270 quarterly (job scholarship only)	Five students every two years	Two years	
Rogue Valley Art Association*, P.O. Box 763, Medford, OR 97501	$200	Students	Summer classes	Annually
Rosary College, Director of Foreign Studies, River Forest, IL 60305	(10 - 12) of $500 - $1000 each	Nationals of U.S. for study in Florence, Italy for study in painting, sculpture, printmaking, art history and art restoration at Rosary College Graduate School of Fine Arts, Villa Schifanoia, to men and women qualified for graduate study in fine arts who hold B.A. or equivalent and have knowledge of Italian	One - two years	
Roswell Museum and Art Center, 11th & Main Sts, Roswell, NM 88201	Grant provides home, studio, maintenance, materials, and stipend. Stipend varies according to family size	Painters, sculptors, printmakers, weavers, and ceramicists	Grant period can vary—usually six - twelve months	Information supplied upon request
The Royal Architectural Institute of Canada, Suite 1104, 151 Slater St, Ottawa, ON K1P 5H3, Canada	Andre Francou Scholarship $2000	Graduate students of the School of Architecture at the University of Montreal		Annually
	Ernest Wilby Memorial Scholarship $500	A student entering the year before the final year of the main architectural course at a Canadian School of Architecture who shows definite promise and talent in his work and who requires financial assistance		Annually
Royal Canadian Academy of Arts, 40 University Ave, Toronto, ON M5J 1T1, Canada	Varying amounts through RCA Trust Fund	Applicants	One year	Annually
Saginaw Art Museum*, 1126 N. Michigan Ave, Saginaw, MI 48602	Tuition for art classes	All students	One year	Annually
St. Thomas Aquinas College, Art Department, Rte. 340, Sparkill, NY 10976	Variable	All eligible applicants	One year	Semi-annually
Salem Art Association, Bush Barn Art Center, 600 Mission St, Salem, OR 97301	Amount of a class tuition	Any person of any age	Ten-week term	Quarterly
Salmagundi Club, 47 Fifth Ave, New York, NY 10003	Scholarship Membership pro-rated over four-year period	Qualified applicants, artist under 30 years of age, three examples of work to be submitted for approval by committee	Four years	
San Bernardino Art Association, P.O. Box 2272, 1640 E. Highland, San Bernardino, CA 92406	$400	High school art seniors		Annually
San Francisco Art Institute*, 800 Chestnut St, San Francisco, CA 91433	$1800 Hector Escobosa Painting Scholarship	Full tuition for upper division continuing student in painting	Academic year	March for coming academic year
	$1800 Ellen Hart Bransten Scholarship	Full tuition for upper division continuing student in painting		
	Partial tuition scholarships	Continuing students		
Santa Cruz Art League, 526 Broadway, Santa Cruz, CA 95060	$200	Between ages 15 and 19	One year	Annually
Saskatchewan Arts Board*, 200 Lakeshore Dr, Regina, SK S4S 0A4, Canada	$1000 grants	Saskatchewan artists		Semi-annually
School Art League of New York City, 1 Times Square, New York, NY 10036	$100,000 annually	High school students	One year (to be continued at the discretion of the granting institutions	Annually
School of American Research, P.O. Box 2188, Santa Fe, NM 87501	$500 per month, plus apartment	Southwestern anthropologists	One year	Annually
School of the Associated Arts, 344 Summit Ave, St. Paul, MN 55102	Variable	Students	One year	Annually
School of the Worcester Art Museum, 55 Salisbury St, Worcester, MA 01608	Up to full tuition depending on financial need	Matriculating students at the School of the Worcester Art Museum only; accepted applicants will be considered upon receipt of tuition deposit	One academic year	Annually (deadline Apr. 1)
Scottsdale Artists' League, P.O. Box 1071, Scottsdale, AZ 85252	Variable	Various schools, colleges and universities in Arizona	One year	Annually
Ella Sharp Museum*, 3225 Fourth St, Jackson, MI 49203	Amount of classes	General public	One year	Annually
Shasta College*, Art Department, Old Oregon Trail, Redding, CA 96001	Various	Art students		
Sheldon Memorial Art Gallery, Lincoln, NE 68508	$3450	University of Nebraska graduate students	One year	Annually

OFFERED BY	AMOUNT	OPENED TO	DURATION	WHEN OFFERED
Skowhegan School of Painting and Sculpture, Skowhegan, ME 04976	(15) $1750 full scholarships	Qualified U.S. art students 18 years years of age and over	Nine weeks July & Aug.	Annually
	(25) Less than full scholarships	Qualified U.S. art students 18 years of age and over	Nine weeks July & Aug.	Annually
	Cash purchase prizes in Final Exhibition, scholarships to winter art schools	Current Skowhegan students		
Smithsonian Institution, Office of Academic Studies, Washington, DC 20560	$10,000	Post-doctoral scholars in American art, Oriental art, 20th century art	September 1 - August 31	Deadline: Jan. 15
	$5000	Doctoral candidates in American art, Oriental art, 20th century art	September 1 - August 31	Deadline: Jan. 15
South Bend Art Center*, 121 N. Lafayette Blvd, South Bend, IN 46601	$300	Qualified applicants		Semi-annually
South Carolina Arts Commission, Brown Bldg, 1205 Pendleton St, Columbia, SC 29201	$130,000 annually	Arts organizations and artists	One year	Quarterly
South County Art Association, 1319 Kingstown Rd, Kingston, RI 02881	$500	High school seniors majoring in art	One year	Annually
South Plains College*, Art Department, College Ave, Levelland, TX 79336	Variable	Talented, needy students	One year	Annually
Southampton College of Long Island University, Art Department, Southampton, NY 11968	One-half tuition	Students	Four years	Annually
Southern Baptist College, Walnut Ridge, AR 72476	Variable	Most outstanding art student annually		Annually
Southern Utah State College, Cedar City, UT 84720	Tuition and supplies	Residents of Utah and nonresidents	One year	Annually and quarterly
	$256	Sophomores, juniors and seniors	Two years	Annually
Southwest Craft Center, 300 Augusta St, San Antonio, TX 78205	Class tuition and supplies	Deserving students	Two - sixteen weeks	Quarterly
Southwest Missouri State University, 901 S. National, Springfield, MO 65802	$240	Art majors and graduating seniors of Southwest Missouri State University	One year	Annually
Spiva Art Center, Inc, Newman & Duquesne Rds, Joplin, MO 64801	Variable	Prospective college art students	One year (renewable)	
Springfield Art and Historical Society, 9 Elm Hill, Springfield, VT 05156	$300	Any student in music and/or art	One year	Annually
Springfield Art Center, 107 Cliff Park Rd, Springfield, OH 45501	$25 - $100	Children, some adults, by semester		
Springfield College, 263 Alden St, Springfield, MA 01109	Variable	Qualified students	One year	Annually
Springville Museum of Art, 126 E. 400 South, Springville, UT 84663	Arrange for scholarships to nine Utah universities and colleges as awards to Exhibit participants	Participants in annual all Utah High School Art Exhibit	One year	Annually
State University Center, Department of Art and Art History, Binghamton, NY 13901	Variable graduate assistantships and teaching assistantships	Incoming and resident graduate students	Two years (renewable each year)	Annually, Feb.
Stephens College, Columbia, MO 65201	$2000 per year; (2) available in studio art or art history	Honors students by competitive application	Renewable up to four years	Annually
Studio Workshop, 3 W. 18th St, New York, NY 10011	To be determined	Qualified students	One year	Annually, semi-annually
Summit Art Center, 68 Elm St, Summit, NJ 07901	$35 - $55 per session	Students in need	Fifteen-week session	Per session
Sunbury Shores Arts and Nature Centre, Inc*, 139 Water St, (P.O. Box 100), St. Andrews, NB, Canada	Approximately $1000	High school students	Summers	Annually
Swain School of Design, 19 Hawthorn St, New Bedford, MA 02740	Approximately $8000	Swain students with need	Up to four years	Annually
Margaret Fort Tahern Gallery, Austin Peay State University Art Department, Clarksville, TN 37040	$300 (total)	High school art seniors in central Tennessee	One year	Annually
Tampa Bay Art Center, 320 N Blvd, Tampa, FL 33606		Low socio-economically handicapped; elementary age, high school age, retired citizens		Quarterly
Texarkana College, Art Department, Texarkana, TX 75501	$100	Art majors	One year	Annually
Texas Southern University, Department of Art, 3201 Wheeler Ave, Houston, TX 77004	$2000	All art students with completion of one year's course work in art at T.S.U. may apply	Four years	Annually
Texas Tech University, Department of Art, Box 4720, Lubbock, TX 79409	Variable	Upper level art students		
The Gallery/Stratford, 54 Romeo St, North Stratford, ON N5A 3C7, Canada	$200	Graduating high school students for further art education	One year	Annually

OFFERED BY	AMOUNT	OPENED TO	DURATION	WHEN OFFERED
Louis Comfort Tiffany Foundation, 1083 Fifth Ave, New York, NY 10028	$2000 (maximum)	U.S. citizens of demonstrated talent	One year	Annually
The Toledo Museum of Art, Monroe St at Scottwood Ave, Toledo, OH 43609	Variable	Graduate students	One year	Annually
Toronto School of Art, 225 Brunswick Ave, Toronto, ON M5S 2M6, Canada	Variable	Students chosen by staff	One year	
Traphagen School of Fashion, 257 Park Ave. S, New York, NY 10010	$1850 Famous Alumni Scholarship	Second year students	One year	Annually
	$1850 School Art League, New York City Scholarship	First year students		Annually
	$1850 National Scholastic Magazine Scholarship	First year students		Annually
	$1850	First year students (two years) Flemington Fur Co. Competition (open to high school juniors and seniors in NY, NJ, CT, DE, MD, and PA)		Annually
	Above scholarships are renewable upon performance each year			
Truro Center for the Arts at Castle Hill, Inc, Castle Rd, Box 756, Truro, MA 02666	5 working scholarships in exchange for tuition; no housing	Any qualified person, preferably 20 years and older	June 21 - September 7	Annually
Tucson Museum of Art, 235 Walameda, Tucson, AZ 85701	Tuition and part tuition	Disadvantaged youth who show artistic talent	One term	Variable
Tufts University in Affiliation with The Boston Museum of Fine Arts School*, Cohen Arts Center, Medford, MA 02155	Variable	According to need and ability		Annually
Tusculum College*, Department of Art, Greeneville, TN 37743	$400 - $800	Students in upper 40% of their class who show leadership talent, art talent	One year	Annually
Union University*, Jackson, TN 38301	Variable	Those demonstrating talent and promise	One year (renewable)	
U.S. Government Grants for Graduate Study Abroad under the Fulbright-Hays Act. Write: Sales and Correspondence Unit, Institute of International Education, 809 United Nations Plaza, New York, NY 10017	Variable	Graduate students who are U.S. citizens with B.A. degree or in the creative and performing arts, 4 years of professional study and/or experience, and who have a knowledge of the language of the country for which application is made	One year	Annually
University of Alaska, Fine Arts Complex, Main Campus, Fairbanks, AK 99701	In or out of state tuition	Art students, incoming and continuing	One year	Annually
University of Arkansas*, Fayetteville, AR 72701	$1500 Assistantships	Graduate students	Two years or more	Annually
	$400 scholarship	Sophomore, junior or senior art students enrolled in the Art Department at the University of Arkansas	One year	Annually
University of California, Art Department, Santa Barbara, CA 93106	Variable	Graduate students approved by the Art Department chairman	Academic year	Annually
University of Colorado, Fine Arts Department, Boulder, CO 80302	In-state tuition	Undergraduates	One year	Annually
	$2500 plus tuition waiver	Graduate students	One year	Annually
University of Delaware, Newark, DE 19711 (in cooperation with Winterthur Museum)	Five to ten fellowships of $3000 each for graduate study	College graduates in one of the humanities, social sciences, or American studies	Two years	Annually
University of Denver School of Art, University Park, Denver, CO 80210	Variable, modest	Graduate students, eligible when accepted for admission; undergraduate, one through the National Scholastic Competition, others on modest scale	Varying	Usually quarterly
University of Illinois at Urbana-Champaign, Graduate College, Urbana, IL 61801	$2500	Graduate students and applicants with B.A. degree	Nine months	Annually
	$3000	Graduate students and applicants with B.A. degree	Eleven months	Annually
University of Iowa, School of Art and Art History, Iowa City, IA 52242	Graduate College Scholarships up to $1700	All scholarships listed available to graduate students and some undergraduate students	One year (renewable)	Annually
	Ford Foundation B.F.A. and M.F.A. Scholarships up to $1800			
	Paula P. Grahame Scholarship up to $1500			
	Kress Foundation Fellowship in Art History $3500, Travel Grants to $1200			
	Assistantships $3600 - $4000			
University of Lethbridge, Lethbridge, AB, Canada	Variable	Qualified students		Annually
University of Louisville, Allen R Hite Art Institute, Louisville, KY 40208	Variable	Art and art history students	One year (renewable)	Annually

OFFERED BY	AMOUNT	OPENED TO	DURATION	WHEN OFFERED
University of Maryland, Art-Sociology Bldg, College Park, MD 20742	$100 - $3100	Students with excellent scholarship and teaching promises	One year	Annually
		Graduate students in the Museum Training Program	One year	Annually
University of Massachusetts Fine Arts Center, Amherst, MA 01002	$1200 - $2000 assistantships	Graduate students	One - two years	Annually
	$2800 University Fellowship	Graduate students with a 3.5 Q.P.A. or better	One - two years	Annually
University of Michigan, History of Art Department, Ann Arbor, MI 48104	Charles L. Freer Scholarship in Oriental Art. Amounts vary up to $2400 plus fees	Graduate student beginning advanced work in Oriental art	One year	Annually
	Charles L. Freer Fellowships in Oriental Art. $400 per month	Advanced graduate students in Oriental art—residence at Freer Gallery, Washington, DC	One year	Annually
	Samuel H. Kress Foundation Scholarship and Fellowship. Amounts vary up to $2400 plus fees	Advanced graduate students	One year	Annually
	Graduate Fellowships offered by Horace H. Rackham School of Graduate Studies. Amounts vary up to $2400 plus fees	Graduate students	One year	Annually
	Teaching Fellowships approx. $4000 per academic year	Graduate students of the second year and beyond	Maximum of three years	Annually
	Regional Museum Internships. Stipend approx. $2500 plus fees	Advanced graduate students	One year	Annually
University of Minnesota, Duluth, School of Fine Arts, Duluth, MN 55812	$500 scholarships (7)	Undergraduates	One year	Annually
	Assistantships (9)	Graduate students	One year	Annually
University of Minnesota*, Department of Studio Art, St. Paul, MN 55101	Variable	Competitive	One year	
University of Mississippi Fine Arts Center, University, MS 38677	$1300	Graduate students in art	Nine months	Annually
University of Nebraska-Lincoln, Department of Art, Woods Hall, Lincoln, NE 68588	Thomas Coleman Memorial Scholarship in Printmaking, $150 each	Outstanding graduate and undergraduate student in prints		Annually
	Francis Vreeland Award in Art, 3 awards of $500 each	Outstanding graduate and undergraduate students in studio art		Annually
	Woods Graduate Fellowships, 1 or 2 awards of $3000 each	Graduate students pursuing M.F.A. program in department, usually for third year of study		Annually
University of New Mexico, Albuquerque, NM 87131	$2500 and $2700 $3100 and $3300	Graduate students	One academic year	Annually
University of North Carolina at Greensboro, Greensboro, NC 27412	Variable	University art students	Up to four years	Annually
	$900 graduate assistantships in Weatherspoon Art Gallery	Graduates	Semester	Semi-annually
University of Oregon, Eugene, OR 97403	$100 - $300 (20 units)	Students with one year residence	One year	Annually
	$2500 - $2800 (14 units) graduate assistantships	Qualified students at graduate level; nonresident must submit photographic exhibit of recent work (most reserved for 2nd year of residence)	One year	Annually
University of Pittsburgh, Schenley Plaza, Pittsburgh, PA 15260	$3140-TA, $3350-TF, $3500-Mellon Tuition scholarships	Fine arts graduate students (art history)	One year (renewable)	Annually
University of San Diego, Alcala Park, San Diego, CA 92170	$1500	Art students at University of San Diego	One year	Annually
University of Southern California, Idyllwild School of Music and the Arts, P.O. Box 38, Idyllwild, CA 92349	$33,000 (total)	Students with proven ability and need	Ten-week summer program	Annually
University of Southern California, University Park, Los Angeles, CA 90007	Graduate teaching assistantships Contact Department of Fine Arts	Fine art students, graduate and undergraduate	One year	Annually
	Graduate fellowships. Contact The Graduate School			
	Financial assistance in general. Contact Director of Student Aid			
The University of Texas of the Permian Basin, Faculty of Art, Odessa, TX 79762	$800	Qualified students	One year	Annually
University of Windsor, Fine Arts Department, Huron Church Rd. at College, Windsor, ON, Canada	Variable	Fine arts students, other university students	One year	Annually
University of Wisconsin-Eau Claire, Financial Aids Office, Eau Claire, WI 54701	Variable	Qualified students	One year	Annually
The University of Wyoming, University Station, Box 3138, Laramie, WY 82071	$3150	Both in-state and out-of-state students	One year (renewable)	Annually
Vancouver City College*, Langara, 100 W. 49th St, Vancouver, BC, Canada	$15 - $300	Any art student taking any academic and studio courses	One year	Annually

OFFERED BY	AMOUNT	OPENED TO	DURATION	WHEN OFFERED
Ventura College, Fine Arts Department, 4667 Telegraph Rd, Ventura, CA 93003	Various amounts	All art students	One year	Annually
Villa Montalvo Center for the Arts*, P.O. Box 158, Saratoga, CA 95070	Resident artists may apply for free or half resident-scholarship	Qualified artists	Three - six months	
Virginia Museum of Fine Arts, Richmond, VA 23221	$100 - $250 per month	Virginians who were born in the State, or who have resided in it for a period of at least five years	One year	Annually
Virginia Polytechnic Institute and State University, Blacksburg, VA 24061	$150	Art majors who are rising seniors	One year	Annually
Wadsworth Atheneum, 600 Main St, Hartford, CT 06103	Art classes scholarships	Deserving students	Two months	
Waldorf College, Forest City, IA 50436	Variable with need	Art majors	One year	Annually
Washington and Lee University, Lexington, VA 24450	Varies according to need	Art majors, college men only	One year (renewable up to four years)	Annually
Washington University, St. Louis, MO 63130	$200 - $3650	Full-time students in the School of Fine Arts	One year (usually renewable)	Annually
Wayland Baptist College Department of Art, Box 54, 1900 W. Seventh, Plainview, TX 79072	Various amounts	Everyone majoring in art	Semester	Semi-annually
Wenatchee Valley College Department of Applied and Fine Arts, Fifth St, Wenatchee, WA 98801	$252 (6)	Best qualified applicants		
West Georgia College Art Department, Carrollton, GA 30117	Various	Art majors	One year	Annually
Western College Center for the Arts Inc, 1803 N. Seventh St, Grand Junction, CO 81501	As needed for children's classes	Applicants	Ten weeks	Term
Western Wyoming College Art Department, Rock Springs, WY 82901	Tuition	High school graduates with strong interest in the arts	One year	Annually
Westmar College*, Le Mars, IA 51031	Variable	Those of outstanding artistic ability and those who can demonstrate financial need		Annually
Wichita Art Association, 9112 E. Central, Wichita, KS 67206. Awarded through public school system and various service organizations	$2000	Art students of the Wichita area	One year	Annually
Williams College*, Williamstown, MA 01267	$3000 Hubbard Hutchinson Memorial Scholarship	Williams senior for two years of graduate work	Two years at $3000 a year	Annually
	Cadwallader Evans III Memorial Scholarship	Williams student beginning junior year and majoring in English or art	One year (may be extended second year)	Annually
	Edith Weston Andrews Scholarship	Williams student majoring in art or music	One year (may be extended second year)	Annually
	Beatrice Stone Scholarship	Williams student majoring in art or music	One year (may be extended second year)	Annually
Windward Artists Guild, Box 851, Kailua, HI 96734	$100	High school students		Annually
Catharine Lorillard Wolfe Art Club, 802 Broadway, New York, NY 10003	$200	Art Students League and National School of Design students	One year	Annually
Charles A. Wustum Museum of Fine Arts, 2519 Northwestern Ave, Racine, WI 53404	$500 to other institutions, $400 to our own classes	Residents of Racine		Annually
Young Harris College*, Department of Art, Young Harris, GA 30582	$400	Art majors	One year	Annually
York Academy of Arts*, 625 E. Philadelphia St, York, PA 17403	$4293	Open to students who have successfully completed one year of study, based on financial need and academic standing	One year	Annually

Open Exhibitions
National, Regional and State-Wide

ALABAMA

DIXIE ANNUAL, Montgomery. Annual, Mar or Apr. All two-dimensional works on paper except photographs. Open to artists of 13 states—Ala, Ark, Fla, Ga, Ky, La, Miss, Mo, NC, SC, Tenn, Tex & Va. Jury, prizes awarded in the form of museum purchases. Fee $5, three works per artist; maximum 5 ft by 5 ft. Entries & entry cards due six weeks prior to the opening of the exhibition. For further information write Registrar, Montgomery Museum of Fine Arts, 440 S McDonough St, Montgomery, AL 36104.

WATERCOLOR SOCIETY OF ALABAMA JURIED COMPETITION, Birmingham. Annual, Sept. All aqueous media applied to paper. Open to all US artists. Jury, cash awards, purchase awards. Fee $5 per entry, limit two entry cards. Due date Sept 2, deadline Sept 8. For further information write Thelma H. Pritchell, 552 Benbow Rd, Birmingham, AL 35226.

ALASKA

ALL ALASKA JURIED EXHIBITION, Anchorage. Annual, Feb, Anchorage; Mar, Fairbanks; Apr, Juneau. Paintings, prints, drawings, wall hangings, sculpture, pottery, jewelry & photography. Open to Alaska residents only. Jury, cash awards. Fee $2 per item, two items per category. Entries due Jan 23. For further information write Alaska Artists' Guild Ltd, PO Box 1888, Anchorage, AK 99501.

ARIZONA

DOUGLAS ART ASSOCIATION TWO FLAGS ART FESTIVAL. Annual, Oct. Open to all artists of US & Mex. Cash awards, prizes & purchase awards. Entry fee $3, limit two, 20% comn. For further information write Douglas Art Association, Box 256, 300 11th St, Douglas, AZ 85607.

HEARD MUSEUM GUILD, Phoenix. Annual, Nov-Dec. All original arts & crafts. Open to Indians of NAm, Indian students & those of Indian descent. Cash awards & ribbons. Fee 20% comn. Entry forms & work due Oct 9-Nov 6. For further information write Florence Knight, Chmn, Heard Museum Guild Indian Arts & Crafts Exhibition, 22 E Monte Vista Rd, Phoenix, AZ 85004.

PHOENIX ART MUSEUM CRAFTS EXHIBITION. Biennial, April. Crafts. Open to craftsmen of Ariz, Colo, NMex & Utah. Jury, awards. Fee. Entries due as announced. For further information write Registrar, Phoenix Art Museum, 1625 N Central Ave, Phoenix, AZ 85004.

PHOENIX ART MUSEUM PHOTOGRAPHY EXHIBITION. Biennial, July. Open to Ariz photographers. Jury, awards. Fee. Entries due as announced. For further information write Registrar, Phoenix Art Museum, 1625 N Central Ave, Phoenix, AZ 85004.

TUCSON FESTIVAL EXHIBITION. Biennial, Apr-May. All craft media. Open to all residents of Ariz. Juror, $2000 awards. Fee $4 per work. Entries due Mar 1-3. For further information write Tucson Museum of Art, 235 W Alameda, Tucson, AZ 85701.

TUCSON MUSEUM OF ART/ARIZONA'S OUTLOOK '76. Biennial, Mar-Apr. Paintings, sculpture, graphics & drawings. Open to Ariz residents. Jury, purchase & cash awards totaling $2000. Fee $4 per entry. Entries due Feb 5-7. For further information write Gerrit Cone, Assistant Museum Director, Tucson Museum of Art, 235 W Alameda, Tucson, AZ 85701.

ARKANSAS

ARKANSAS ARTS CENTER DELTA ART EXHIBITION, Little Rock. Annual, Oct-Nov. All paintings & sculpture (not over 500 pounds). Open to artists born in or residing in Ark, La, Miss, Mo, Okla, Tenn & Tex. Jury, $1000 Grand Award, $3000 purchase awards. Fee $5, limit two. Entries & work due Sept 24. For further information write Townsend Wolfe, The Arkansas Arts Center, MacArthur Park, PO Box 2137, Little Rock, AR 72203.

ARKANSAS ARTS CENTER PRINTS: DRAWINGS & CRAFTS EXHIBITION, Little Rock. Annual, May-June. Prints in all media; drawings in all media (except watercolors); photographs in color and/or monochrome; crafts in metal, clay, textile, glass, wood, plastics & combined media. Open to artists born in or residing in Ark, La, Miss, Mo, Okla, Tenn & Tex. Jury, awards & $2000 purchase prizes. Fee $5, limit three. Entry cards & work due Apr 23. For further information write Townsend Wolfe, Director, The Arkansas Arts Center, MacArthur Park, PO Box 2137, Little Rock, AR 72203.

ARKANSAS ARTS CENTER TOYS DESIGNED BY ARTISTS EXHIBITION, Little Rock. Annual, Dec-Jan. Toys in all media. Open to all artists. $1000 in purchase awards. Fee $5. Entries & work due Nov 14. For further information write Townsend Wolfe, Director, The Arkansas Arts Center, MacArthur Park, PO Box 2137, Little Rock, AR 72203.

FORT SMITH ART CENTER. Annual, Mar. Painting, watercolor, drawing. Open to artists of Ark, Kans, La, Mo, Okla, Miss, Tenn & Tex. Jury, prizes & purchase awards. Fee $5. Entry cards & work due Feb. For further information write Registrar, Fort Smith Art Center, 423 N Sixth St, Fort Smith, AR 72901.

CALIFORNIA

ALL-CALIFORNIA PRINT EXHIBITION, Los Angeles. Annual, Jan. All prints. Open to living Calif artists. Jury, over $1500 awards. Fee, limit on entries. Fees, forms & work due Jan. For further information write Betty Anderson, Los Angeles Printmaking Society, 1028 Mission St, South Pasadena, CA 91030.

CALIFORNIA SMALL IMAGES EXHIBITION, Los Angeles. Biennial, Jan. Painting, prints, drawing, any media, sculpture (maximum size 18 inches). Open to residents of Calif. Jury, purchase awards. Fee $2 plus $2 handling per work, payable to Cart & Crate. Entries due around Nov 24-Dec 9. For further information write Josine Ianco, Gallery Dir, Art Dept, California State University at Los Angeles, 5151 State College Dr, Los Angeles, CA 90032.

LAGUNA BEACH ALL CALIFORNIA SHOW. Annual, July-Aug. All media. Open to members & residents of Calif. Jury, $1500 cash awards. Fee $4. Entry cards & work due July 3. For further information write Laguna Beach Museum of Art, 307 Cliff Dr, Laguna Beach, CA 92651.

LOS ANGELES PRINTMAKING SOCIETY NATIONAL PRINT EXHI-
BITION. Annual, Nov. Prints excluding mono or photographs.
Open to all US citizens residing in US. Cash awards, purchase
awards. Fee $5 for 2 slides, 20% comn. Entry cards & slides
due July 1, work due Oct 30. For further information write J.
Bockman, 18330 Black Hawk, Northridge, CA 91324.

MANY MEDIA MINI EXHIBITION, Redlands. Annual, Oct. All media,
original work, total size not to exceed 15 inches in any direction
(no photog). Open to all Calif artists. Fee $3 per entry, limit
three. For further information write Redlands Art Association,
12 E Vine St, Redlands, CA 92373.

NATIONAL WATERCOLOR SOCIETY, Los Angeles. Annual, Oct.
All water-based media. Open to all US artists. Jury, purchase
awards & cash awards. Work due Sept 18. For further information write Ruth Rossman, President, 401 Cascada Way, Los
Angeles, CA 90049.

RICHMOND ART CENTER. Biennial, Dec-May (dates change).
Painting, alternating with sculpture. Open to all artists. Jury,
awards. Fee. Work to be hand delivered. For further information write Richmond Art Center, Civic Center Plaza, Richmond,
CA 94804.

RICHMOND ART CENTER DESIGNER-CRAFTSMAN EXHIBITION.
Annual, Sept-Nov (dates change). All craft media. Open to all
artists. Jury, awards. Fee. Work to be hand delivered by artist
or agent. For further information write Richmond Art Center,
Civic Center Plaza, Richmond, CA 94804.

SAN BERNARDINO ART ASSOCIATION INLAND EXHIBITION. Annual, Oct. Oil, acrylic, watercolor, mixed, collage, graphics (no
sculpture or photog). Open to all Calif artists. Cash awards &
purchase awards. Fee $3 per entry, limit two, 30% comn. Entry
cards & work due Sept 30. For further information write San
Bernardino Art Association, PO Box 2272, San Bernardino, CA
92406.

SANTA CRUZ ART LEAGUE. Annual, Apr. Oil, watercolor & mixed
media, representational art only. Open to all Calif residents.
Jury. Fee $4 per entry, limit three in each medium. For further
information write Santa Cruz Art League, 526 Broadway, Santa
Cruz, CA 95060.

COLORADO

ROCKY MOUNTAIN NATIONAL WATERMEDIA EXHIBITION, Golden.
Annual, Aug-Sept. Watermedia on paper, unvarnished; no pastels. Open to all artists residing in the US. Jury, cash awards
of $9000. Fee $5 per slide, limit 2, 25% comn. Entry slides
due June 14, accepted work due July 14. For further information
write The Foothills Art Center, 809 15th St, Golden, CO 80401.

WESTERN COLORADO CENTER FOR THE ARTS, Grand Junction.
Biennial (74-76-78-80), July. All painting & graphics. Open to
artists of Ariz, Colo, Kans, Nebr, NMex, Okla, Tex, Utah & Wyo.
Slide prejuried, cash awards. Fee $5 per slide, limit 3, 25%
comn. For further information write 8 West Biennial, Western
Colorado Center for the Arts, 1803 N Seventh St, Grand Junction,
CO 81501.

CONNECTICUT

CONNECTICUT ACADEMY OF FINE ARTS, Hartford. Annual, May.
All media except watercolor. Open to all artists. Prizes. Fee
20% comn. For further information write Secy, Connecticut
Academy of Fine Arts, 31 Winding Lane, Avon, CT 06001.

CONNECTICUT SOCIETY OF WOMEN PAINTERS, West Hartford.
Annual, May. All original work. Open to women who reside in
Conn. Cash awards. Fee $5 mem, $8 non-mem, per entry, limit
two. Entry cards & work due Apr 27 & 28, St Joseph College,
West Hartford. For further information write Vincenza Uccello,
Chmn, 207 Branford St, Hartford, CT 06112.

CONNECTICUT WATERCOLOR SOCIETY EXHIBITION. Annual,
June-July. All water media framed under glass. Open to all
Conn resident artists. Cash awards, prizes. Fee $10 for one
entry or $15 for 2, 20% comn. Entry cards & work due June 14.
For further information write Eileen Welsh, Exec Secy, Mountain
Spring Rd, RFD, Rockville, CT 06066.

NEW HAVEN PAINT AND CLAY CLUB. Annual, Mar-Apr. Oil,
watercolor, acrylic, graphics & sculpture. Open to artists from
the New Eng states & NY. Prizes & purchase awards. Fee $6
for first entry, $4 for second, 15% comn. Entry cards & work
due Feb 27. For further information write Shirley Price, Secy,
26 Fern Dr, Northford, CT 06472.

SILVERMINE GUILD OF ARTISTS NATIONAL PRINT EXHIBITION,
New Canaan. Biennial, Mar (next show, 78). All print media
except monotypes. Open to all artists. Jury, purchase prizes.
Fee; three works per artist allowed. For further information
write Exhib Secy, Silvermine Guild of Artists, Inc, 1037 Silvermine Rd, New Canaan, CT 06840.

SILVERMINE GUILD OF ARTISTS NEW ENGLAND EXHIBITION OF
PAINTING AND SCULPTURE, New Canaan. Annual, June. All
painting & sculpture. Open to artists of the six New Eng States
& NY, NJ & Pa. Jury; more than $6000 in cash awards. Fee.
For further information write Exhib Secy, Silvermine Guild of
Artists, Inc, 1037 Silvermine Rd, New Canaan, CT 06840.

SLATER MEMORIAL MUSEUM, Norwich. Annual, Apr. All media.
Open to all resident Conn artists. Jury, prizes. Fee $4 per
piece, limit two; sculpture limited to 200 pounds. Entry cards &
work due Mar 14. For further information write The Slater
Memorial Museum, 108 Crescent St, Norwich, CT 06360.

WASHINGTON, DC

LIBRARY OF CONGRESS, PRINTS AND PHOTOGRAPHS DIVISION,
NATIONAL EXHIBITION OF PRINTS, Washington, DC. Biennial,
date varies. All fine print media, original prints, black & white
or color, exclusive of monotypes, drawings, photographs or
prints colored after printing. Open to printmakers of US. Jury,
purchases for the J & E R Pennell Collection. No fee. For further information write Prints & Photographs Div, Library of
Congress, Washington, DC 20540.

MINITURE PAINTERS, SCULPTORS & GRAVERS SOCIETY, Washington, DC. Annual, Oct. All media, size limited to 8 by 10,
heads not more than $1\frac{1}{2}$ inches. Open to all prof artists. Prizes.
Fee, out-of-town entries $9, local entries $6; 30% comn. Entry
cards due Sept 12; work due Sept 20. For further information
write Evelyn A Gladstone, 4825 Quebec St, NW, Washington, DC
20016

FLORIDA

ART GUILD OF BOCA RATON. Annual, Feb. Original painting &
sculpture. Open to all artists. Jury. Entries due Feb to be delivered by hand only. For further information write Art Guild of
Boca Raton, 801 W Palmetto Park Rd, Boca Raton, FL 33432.

CAPE CORAL NATIONAL. Annual, Jan. All paintings (maximum
size 50 by 50 inches). Open to all US artists. Jury, cash awards.
Details not yet firmed for 1977. For further information write
Cape Coral Art League, Box 425, Cape Coral, FL 33904.

LATIN QUARTER ART GALLERY, Tampa. Annual, Feb. All media.
Open to all artists. Jury, prizes. Fee $5 one entry, $8 two entries. Entry cards & work due Jan, all work must be hand delivered. For further information write Oscar Aguayo, PO Box
5287, Tampa, FL 33675.

SOCIETY OF THE FOUR ARTS EXHIBITION OF CONTEMPORARY
AMERICAN PAINTINGS, Palm Beach. Annual, Dec. Oils, watercolor, drawings, mixed, & flat collages completed since Jan, 75.
Open to artists residing in the US. Cash awards. Fee $3, limit
2 entries (fee refunded if entry accepted); comn 10%. Specific
dates on which entry cards & work are due are announced in
prospectus available upon request in Sept. For further information write The Society of the Four Arts, Four Arts Plaza, Palm
Beach, FL 33480.

HAWAII

ART HAWAII ONE, Honolulu. Annual, May-June. Paintings drawings, prints, photographs, sculpture & mixed media. Open to all artists residing in Hawaii. Juror. Fee $2 per entry, limited to three. Entries due early Apr. For further information write Selden Washington, Asst Dir, Honolulu Academy of Arts, 900 S Beretania St, Honolulu, HI 96814.

ART HAWAII TWO, Honolulu. Annual, June-July. Functional & non-functional objects of craft-arts. Open to all artists residing in Hawaii. Juror. Fee $2 per entry, limited to five. Entries due early May. For further information write Selden Washington, Asst Dir, Honolulu Academy of Arts, 900 S Beretania St, Honolulu, HI 96814.

HAWAII NATIONAL PRINT EXHIBITION, Honolulu. Biennial, Nov-Dec, 77. All media except monoprints. Open to all artists living in the US. Jury. Fee $3 per artist, three entries per artist. Entries due no later than Sept 1. For further information write Joseph Feher, Honolulu Academy of Arts, 900 S Beretania St, Honolulu, HI 96814.

IDAHO

BOISE GALLERY OF ART. Annual, Mar or Apr. All media (two-dimensional, three-dimensional). Open to current residents of Idaho only. Jury, cash awards, special mention. Fee $4 per object. Entries due mid-Feb or mid-Mar. For further information write Dir, Boise Gallery of Art, PO Box 1505, Boise, ID 83701.

ILLINOIS

ART INSTITUTE OF CHICAGO. Biennial, Mar-May. All media, not over 7 by 10 by 5 feet or weigh over 1000 pounds. Open to artists, 18 or over, legal residents of 100-mile radius of Chicago. Jury, awards. Fee none. Entries due Feb. For further information write Painting & Sculpture Dept, The Art Institute of Chicago, Michigan & Adams, Chicago, IL 60603.

NORTH SHORE ART LEAGUE NEW HORIZONS IN ART, Chicago. Annual, May. Painting, sculpture, graphics, photog. Open to Ill artists. Cash awards, purchase awards & ribbons. Fee 15% comn. Entry cards & work due early May. For further information write North Shore Art League, 620 Lincoln Ave, Winnetka, IL 60093.

ROCKFORD ART ASSOCIATION. Annual, Mar. Oil, watercolor, sculpture, graphic arts. Open to artists within 200 miles of Rockford. Fee $10 per entry, $5 for mem. Entries due Feb 21 & 22. For further information write Rockford Art Association, 737 N Main St, Rockford, IL 61103.

INDIANA

BALL STATE UNIVERSITY DRAWING & SMALL SCULPTURE SHOW, Muncie. Annual, May-June. Drawings & small sculpture. Open to all artists. Jury, awards. Sculpture slides for pre-judging due Jan 31, work due Mar 31. For further information & prospectus write Art Gallery, Ball State University, Muncie, IN 47306.

EVANSVILLE MUSEUM OF ARTS & SCIENCE MID-STATES ART EXHIBITION. Annual, Nov. Painting, sculpture, watercolor, graphic arts, collage & mobiles (no photographs). Open to artists within a radius of 200 miles from Evansville or any resident of the State of Indiana. Jury, awards. Fee $10 for one or limit of two works in any combination of categories. Entries due in Oct. For further information write Art Comt, Evansville Museum of Arts & Science, 411 SE Riverside Dr, Evansville, IN 47713.

EVANSVILLE MUSEUM OF ARTS & SCIENCE MID-STATES CRAFT EXHIBITION. Annual, Feb. Ceramics, textiles, silver & metal work, wood, enamel, glass & others. Open to artists within a radius of 200 miles from Evansville or any resident of the State of Indiana. Jury, awards. Fee $5 for three objects or less. Entries due Jan. For further information write Craft Comt, Evansville Museum of Arts & Science, 411 SE Riverside Dr, Evansville, IN 47713.

HOOSIER SALON, Indianapolis. Annual, Jan-Feb. All media & sculpture. Open to Indiana artists, native or by residence in the state for one yr minimum. Jury, awards $4000-$5000. Fee $7.50. Entry due early Jan. For further information write Hoosier Salon, 951 N Delaware, Indianapolis, IN 46202.

INDIANAPOLIS MUSEUM OF ART INDIANA ARTISTS EXHIBITION. Biennial, Mar, 77. Painting & sculpture. Open to artists who reside or have resided in Indiana. Jury, awards. Fee $5 per entry, limit two per artist. Entries due early or mid-Feb. For further information write Miss Jill Aszling, Indianapolis Museum of Art, 1200 W 38th St, Indianapolis, IN 46208.

INDIANAPOLIS MUSEUM OF ART OBJECTS & CRAFTS EXHIBITION. Biennial, Mar-Apr, 77. Hand-crafted articles. Open to past or present Indiana residents. Jury, awards. Fee $5 per artist, limit two. Entries due early or mid-Feb. For further information write Miss Jill Aszling, Indianapolis Museum of Art, 1200 W 38th St, Indianapolis, IN 46208.

INDIANAPOLIS MUSEUM OF ART WORKS ON PAPER EXHIBITION. Biennial, Nov, 76. Open to past or present residents of Indiana. Jury, awards. Fee $5 per artist, limit two. Entries due mid-Sept. For further information write Miss Jill Aszling, Indianapolis Museum of Art, 1200 W 38th St, Indianapolis, IN 46208.

MICHIANA REGIONAL ART EXHIBITION, South Bend. Biennial, Apr-May, 76. Painting, sculpture, graphics & crafts. Open to artists in Mich & Ind, or former residents. Jury, awards. Fee $7, limited to two entries. Entries due one mo in advance (Mar). For further information write South Bend Art Center, South Bend, IN 46601.

WABASH VALLEY EXHIBITION, Terre Haute. Annual, Mar. All media. Open to artists within a 160 mile radius of Terre Haute. Jury, awards. Fee $4 for first entry, $3 for second and third, limit to three. Entries due Feb. For further information write Curator, The Sheldon Swope Art Gallery, 25 S Seventh St, Terre Haute, IN 47807.

IOWA

NORWEGIAN-AMERICAN MUSEUM NATIONAL ROSEMALING EXHIBITION, Decorah. Annual, July. Rose painting on wood. Open to anyone who has been resident of the US for last five years. Jury, $25 blue ribbon, $15 red ribbon, $10 white ribbon. Fee $1.50 per entry. Entries due July 15. For further information write Norwegian-American Museum, 502 W Water St, Decorah, IA 52101.

SIOUX CITY ART CENTER. Annual, Fall. Prints, drawings, even years; sculpture, odd years. Open to residents of Iowa, Nebr, Minn & SDak. One-man jury, up to $1200 in purchase & cash awards. Entries due Sept-Oct. For further information write Dir, Sioux City Art Center, 513 Nebraska St, Sioux City, IA 51101.

KANSAS

KANSAS WATERCOLOR SOCIETY EXHIBITION, Wichita. Annual, Dec. Transparent aqueous on paper. Open to all artists living in Kans. Cash awards, prizes & purchase awards. Fee $5; comn 20%. Entry cards due before Oct 1 & work due Oct 1. For further information write Lucinda Foster, Pres, Kansas Watercolor Society, 600 Longford Lane, Wichita, KS 67206.

WICHITA ART ASSOCIATION NATIONAL GRAPHIC ARTS & DRAWING EXHIBITION. Biennial, Apr & May. Print media & original drawings done within previous two yrs. Open to all living American artists. Fee $4, limit two entries. For further information write Wichita Art Association, 9112 E Central, Wichita, KS 67206.

LOUISIANA

LOUISIANA WATERCOLOR SOCIETY INTERNATIONAL, Baton Rouge. Annual, Nov-Dec. Water based, recent original paintings on paper. Open to all artists. Cash awards & purchase prizes. Fee $3 per entry, no limit to number of entries. Work due Oct 9-Nov 6. For further information write Mrs Martha Guthrie, 3917 Jurgens St, Metairie, LA 70002.

NEW ORLEANS MUSEUM OF ART. Biennial, Spring. Focus on contemporary art by prof artists from thirteen-state region of Southeastern US. Single juror, purchase awards. No fee. For further information write Artists' Biennial, New Orleans Museum of Art, PO Box 19123, Lelong Ave, City Park, New Orleans, LA 70179.

MAINE

OGUNQUIT ART CENTER NATIONAL PAINTING EXHIBITION. Annual, June-Sept. Oil, watercolor, mixed (originals only). Open to all US artists. Cash awards. Fee $10, 25% comn. Entry cards due June 1 & work due June 5. For further information write Mrs F Nims, The Ogunquit Art Center, Hoyt's Lane, Ogunquit, ME 03907.

MARYLAND

ACADEMY OF THE ARTS MARYLAND ART EXHIBITION, Easton. Annual, Apr-May. All painting, collages, graphics, sculpture. Open to artists born or residing in Md, students at Md art schs & members of Acad. Jury, cash prizes & purchase awards. No fee. Entry cards due Mar 29 & work due Mar 31. For further information write The Academy of the Arts, PO Box 605, Easton, MD 21601.

BALTIMORE MUSEUM OF ART BIENNIAL EXHIBITION. Biennial, during the even year. All media (slides or photographs of work not acceptable). Open to artists born or currently residing in Md. Jury, prizes & awards. No fee. Entries due as announced, usually a mo before exhib. For further information write Mrs Alice C Steinbach, Dir Pub Info, Baltimore Museum of Art, Art Museum Dr, Baltimore, MD 21218.

CUMBERLAND VALLEY ANNUAL PHOTOGRAPHIC SALON, Hagerstown. Annual, Feb. Photographs. Open to residents & former residents of the Cumberland Valley region. Jury, prizes & awards. Fee $3. Entries due Jan 15. For further information write Washington County Museum of Fine Arts, PO Box 423, Hagerstown, MD 21740.

CUMBERLAND VALLEY ARTISTS ANNUAL EXHIBITION, Hagerstown. Annual, June. Open media. Open to residents & former residents of the Cumberland Valley region. Jury, prizes & awards. Fee $5. Entries due May 15. For further information write Washington County Museum of Fine Arts, PO Box 423, Hagerstown, MD 21740.

MASSACHUSETTS

ARTS ATLANTIC NATIONAL, Gloucester. Annual, Sept-Oct. Oil, watercolor, sculpture & graphics. Open internationally to all artists. Cash awards & medals. Fee $10 first entry, $5 each addn entry, 25% comn. Entry cards and work due by mid-Sept. For further information write to Arts Atlantic, Box 281, Rockport, MA 01966.

BERKSHIRE ART ASSOCIATION, Pittsfield. Annual, Oct. All painting, pastels, graphics, collages, sculpture. Open to artists of New Eng & NY only. Cash awards, prizes & purchase awards. Fee $6. Entry cards & work due on published date in Sept. For further information write Mrs Glenn L Jorn, Pres, 101 Patricia Ave, Dalton, MA 01226.

BOSTON PRINTMAKERS. Annual, location & dates change yearly. All print media except monotypes. Open to all printmakers. Jury, awards. Fee $5, limit two. For further information write Mrs S M Rantz, Secy, 299 High Rock St, Needham, MA 02192.

CULTURAL AFFAIRS COMMISSION NATIONAL PRINT EXHIBITION, Springfield. Annual, May. All print, no monotypes. Open to all US artists. Jury, purchase prizes and one-man show award. Fee $4, limit two. Entry cards and work due Apr 19. For further information write Prof Josephine L Cecco, Springfield College, 263 Alden St, Springfield, MA 01109.

GREATER FALL RIVER ART ASSOCIATION NATIONAL. Annual, May. Painting, graphics, sculpture, pottery, glass, textiles. Open to all artists in the US & Can. Jury, prizes & purchase awards. Fee $5 per entry. Entry cards & slides due Mar 1. For further information write John Gagnon, 80 Belmont St, Fall River, MA 02720.

MARION ART CENTER BISTATE SHOW. Annual, Aug-Sept. Painting, print, sculpture, photog. Open to artists of Mass & RI. Jury, prizes. Fee $5 for two entries. Entry cards & fee due Aug 15 & work due Aug 23. For further information write Marion Art Center, Front St, Marion, MA 02738.

NEW ENGLAND ARTISTS TRADITIONAL OPEN SHOW, Fall River. Annual. Paintings, graphics. Jury, cash awards. Fee $3. Entries due Nov. For further information write Mrs Edward A Doyle, Dir, 80 Belmont St, Fall River, MA 02720.

SPRINGFIELD ART LEAGUE NON-JURIED EXHIBITION. Annual, Nov-Dec. Oil, watercolor, mixed, graphics, sculpture. Open to all artists, hand-delivered work only. Non-juried. Fee $7. Entry cards & work due Oct. For further information write Joan Tivnan, 33 Carew Terrace, Springfield, MA 01104.

SPRINGFIELD ART LEAGUE NATIONAL EXHIBITION. Annual, Mar-Apr. Oil, watercolor, mixed, graphics, sculpture. Open to all artists residing in US. Jury, cash awards. Fee $7. Entry cards & work due Mar 23. For further information write Joan Tivnan, 33 Carew Terrace, Springfield, MA 01104.

MICHIGAN

HARTLAND ART COUNCIL ART SHOW. Annual, June. Open to all Mich artists. Jury, prizes & purchase awards. Fee. For further information write William Nelson, Pres, Hartland Art Council, Box 126, Hartland, MI 48029.

MICHIGAN ARTIST-CRAFTSMEN EXHIBITION, Detroit. Biennial, Nov (next 77). Ceramics, metal, wood, textiles & plastics. Open to all Mich craftsmen. Jury, awards. Fee $3 per artist, maximum of five works per artist. Entries & cards due Oct. For further information write Dept of Contemporary Art, Detroit Institute of Arts, 5200 Woodward Ave, Detroit, MI 48202.

MICHIGAN ARTISTS EXHIBITION, Detroit. Biennial, Nov (next 76). Painting (any media), sculpture, prints, drawings & photogs. Open to all Mich artists. Jury, awards. Fee $3 per artist, maximum two entries per artist. Entries & cards due Oct. For further information write Dept of Contemporary Art, Detroit Institute of Arts, 5200 Woodward Ave, Detroit, MI 48202.

MICHIGAN PAINTERS-PRINTMAKERS EXHIBITION, Grand Rapids. Biennial (with craftsmen show in off yrs), Sept-Oct. Paintings & prints (No competition 76, to resume in 78). Open to Mich residents. Jury, prizes to $3000. Fee $2 per work, limit of three works. Entries due Aug 14-24 (except Aug 20). For further information write Miss Idamarie Holmer, Grand Rapids Art Museum, 230 E Fulton, Grand Rapids, MI 49502.

MID-MICHIGAN ANNUAL EXHIBITION, Midland. Annual, Feb. All media & mixed media (painting, drawing, prints, sculpture, plastics, ceramics, textiles, jewelry, enameling, metalwork, woodwork, photography). Open to Mich artists 18 yrs and over, only original work completed within the past 2 yrs. Jury, prizes & awards. Fee $5 per artist, limit three entries; no fee for MAC members. Entries due Jan. For further information write The Midland Art Council of Midland Center for the Arts, Inc, 1801 W St Andrews, Midland, MI 48640.

MISSOURI

MID-AMERICA EXHIBITION, St Louis. Biennial. Oil, tempera, painting, sculpture & others. Open to residents of Mo & the states bordering Mo. Jury, prizes. Fee $4. For further information write The St Louis Art Museum, Curator's Office, Forest Park, St Louis, MO 63110.

WATERCOLOR U S A, Springfield. Annual, Apr-June. Watercolor only. Open to artists from all fifty states. Jury, $10,000 in purchase & cash awards. Fee $5. Entries due Apr 10. For further information write Kenneth M Shuck, Dir, Springfield Art Museum, 1111 E Brookside Dr, Springfield, MO 65804.

MONTANA

FLATHEAD VALLEY ART ASSOCIATION HOCKADAY ART COMPETITION, Kalispell. Annual, Sept. All media. Open to all artists. Jury, cash awards. Fee $5, 25% comn. Entry cards & work due Sept 12. For further information write Hockaday Center for the Arts, Box 83, Kalispell, MT 59901.

MONTANA INSTITUTE OF THE ARTS 10 STATE BI-CENTENNIAL JURIED ART SHOW, Great Falls. Annual, Apr. Painting, ceramics, graphics, sculpture, crafts, mixed. Open to all artists in Idaho, Iowa, Kans, Mo, Mont, Nebr, NDak, SDak, Ore, Wash. Jury, $3000 minimum prize. Fee $5 each entry, limit one per category; 30% comn. Slides due Jan 5 for pre-jury, work due Mar 19. For further information write C M Russell Museum, 1201 Fourth Ave N, Great Falls, MT 99401.

NEBRASKA

JOSLYN ART MUSEUM MIDWEST BIENNIAL, Omaha. Biennial, held in even-numbered yrs, late winter or spring. Painting, sculpture, graphics. Open to artists in Ark, Colo, Ill, Iowa, Kans, La, Minn, Mo, Mont, Nebr, NMex, NDak, Okla, SDak, Tex & Wyo. Jury, awards. Fee $5. Entries due Feb, or as announced. For further information write Midwest Biennial, Joslyn Art Museum, 2200 Dodge St, Omaha, NE 68102.

NORTH PLATTE VALLEY ARTISTS' GUILD, Scottsbluff. Annual, Apr. All media. Open to residents of Mont, Nebr, NDak, SDak & Wyo. Prizes, purchase awards & ribbons. Fee $5 per entry for adults & $1.50 for youths. Entry cards due Apr 2, work due Apr 9. For further information write Steve Settles, North Platte Valley Artists' Guild, PO Box 1041, Scottsbluff, NE 69361.

NEVADA

LAS VEGAS ART LEAGUE NATIONAL ART ROUND-UP. Annual, Apr. All painting, graphics, textiles, sculpture, ceramics, jewelry. Open to all artists. $2000 in cash awards, purchase awards & ribbons. Fee $8 for one or two entries, 20% comn. Entry cards & color slides (2 x 2 in) due Feb 1, work due Mar 18. For further information write Las Vegas Art League, 3333-6 W Washington, Las Vegas, NV 89107.

NEW JERSEY

ART CENTRE OF THE ORANGES, East Orange. Annual, Mar-Apr. Oil, watercolor, graphics, sculpture. Open to artists of Conn, NJ, NY & Pa. Jury, prizes. Fee $6 for one, $10 for two entries; 25% comn. Entry cards due Mar 1, work due Mar 10-11. For further information write Art Centre of the Oranges, 16 Washington St, East Orange, NJ 07017.

ART FROM NEW JERSEY, Trenton. Annual, Mar-May. Painting, graphics, sculpture. Open to all artists living or working in NJ. Jury, purchase prizes. No fee. For further information write Al Hilborn, Publ Ed, New Jersey State Museum, W State St, Trenton, NJ 08625.

THE HUDSON ARTISTS STATEWIDE EXHIBITION, Jersey City. Annual, Oct. Oil, watercolor, graphics, sculpture. Open to all professional artists. Jury, cash awards, prizes. Fee. Work due Oct 4. For further information write Gary T Erbe, Pres, 16 Oak St, Weehawken, NJ 07087.

HUNTERDON ART CENTER NATIONAL PRINT EXHIBITION, Clinton. Annual, Mar-Apr. All print media except monotype. Open to all artists in the US. Jury, purchase awards. Fee $9 for 1 or 2 prints includes insurance & return of work, mem $7. For further information write A S Marsh, Hunterdon Art Center, 7 Center St, Clinton, NJ 08809.

MINIATURE ART SOCIETY OF NEW JERSEY, Nutley. Annual, May. Original miniature art work (no crafts). Open to all artists. Jury, prizes & purchase awards. Fee $8, limit three (mem seven). Entry cards & fee due Feb 23, work due Mar 3. For further information write Mrs H Wietsma, 451 Lookout Ave, Hackensack, NJ 07601.

NEW JERSEY CHAPTER AMERICAN ARTISTS PROFESSIONAL LEAGUE, West Orange. Annual, Nov. Oil, watercolor, mixed, graphics. Open to all realistic artists. Cash awards. Fee members $3 for one entry, $5 for two, non-members $5 for one, $7 for two. Entry cards due Sept & work due Oct 21. For further information write Mrs Patricia Sprouls, 188 Kaywin Dr, Paramus, NJ 07652.

NEW JERSEY WATERCOLOR SOCIETY, alternate yrs Morris Museum, Morristown & Monmouth Museum, Lincroft. Annual, Nov-Dec. Watercolor, casein, tempera. Open to all present or former residents of NJ. Jury, awards. Fee subject to yearly decision of board. For further information write Mrs Nat Lewis, 51 Overlook Rd, Caldwell, NJ 07006.

PAINTERS & SCULPTOR SOCIETY OF NEW JERSEY. Annual. Oil, watercolor, casein, acrylic, graphics, sculpture. Open to all artists in US & Can. Fee $7. Entries due May 8. For further information write Suzan Sanford, 267 Parker Ave, Clifton, NJ 07011.

WESTFIELD ART ASSOCIATION, Cranford. Annual, Mar-Apr. All painting, original work only. Open to all NJ residents. Jury, prizes & cash awards. Fee $5 per entry. Work due Mar 18. For further information write Mrs Elven Sheahan, 721 Clark St, Westfield, NJ 07090.

NEW MEXICO

MUSEUM OF NEW MEXICO, Santa Fe. Biennial (New Mexico Biennial & Southwestern Biennial held alternate yrs), Apr-May. All painting & sculpture media. Open to artists of South-Southwest. Jury, awards. For further information write Don Strel, Div Dir, Museum of Fine Arts, Museum of New Mexico, PO Box 2087, Santa Fe, NM 87501.

NEW MEXICO ART LEAGUE SMALL PAINTING SHOW, Albuquerque. Annual, Feb. All media. Open to all artists. Jury, prizes. Fee $6 per entry, limit two. Entry cards due Jan 10, work due Jan 15. For further information write New Mexico Art League, Old Town Gallery, 400 Romero St NW, Albuquerque, NM 87104.

NEW MEXICO ARTS AND CRAFTS FAIR, Albuquerque. Annual, last weekend in June. All media except home arts or crafts. Open to all artists & craftsmen residing in NMex. Jury. Fee $45 each exhibitor & booth. Entry cards & 3 samples of work due Feb 19 & 20. For further information write Mrs Jean Gallegos, PO Box 8801, Albuquerque, NM 87108.

NEW YORK

ALLIED ARTISTS OF AMERICA, New York. Annual, Oct-Nov. Oil, watermedia, sculpture. Open to American artists. Jury, awards. Fee $8. Entry cards & work due Oct. For further information write Allied Artists of America, 1083 Fifth Ave, New York, NY 10028.

THE AMERICAN WATERCOLOR SOCIETY, New York. Annual, Apr. Watercolor, watermedia. Jury, cash awards with medals. Fee $8. Submission can be by slides. For further information write The American Watercolor Society, 1083 Fifth Ave, New York, NY 10028.

ART DIRECTORS CLUB, New York. Annual Exhibition of Advertising & Editorial Art & Design, Spring. Open to advertising or editorial materials, promotion, posters, packaging & others. Jury, medals & certificates. Fee $2 per proof; $7.50 each TV film. Entries due Dec. For further information write The Art Directors Club, 488 Madison Ave, New York, NY 10022.

AUDUBON ARTISTS, New York. Annual, Jan-Feb. Oil, watercolor, graphics, sculpture, casein, polymer. Open to all artists. Jury, awards. Fee $8, one entry per artist. Entry due Jan. For further information write Secy, Audubon Artists, 1083 Fifth Ave, New York, NY 10028.

CATHARINE LORILLARD WOLFE ART CLUB, New York. Annual, Nov. Oil, watercolor, graphics, sculpture. Open to all prof women artists working in realistic manner. Jury, prizes. Fee. Entry cards due Oct 23 & work due Oct 30. For further information and a prospectus next year, write Mrs Helen De Cozen, 118 E 60th St, New York, NY 10022.

CHAUTAUQUA EXHIBITION OF AMERICAN ART. Annual, July. Oil, polymer, watercolor, tempera, casein, mixed. Open to all artists residents of US & territories. Jury, cash prizes. Fee $6. Entry cards & slides due Apr 10 & work due June 1. For further information write Chautauqua Art Association, Chautauqua, NY 14722.

COOPERSTOWN ART ASSOCIATION NATIONAL EXHIBITION. Annual, July-Aug. Painting, graphics, sculpture & crafts (no photog). Open to any adult in the US. $3000 in prizes. Fee $7.50 each entry, 20% comn. Entry cards & work due June 1-16 by mail, June 23-26 if hand delivered. For further information write Cooperstown Art Association, 22 Main St, Cooperstown, NY 13326.

EVERSON MUSEUM OF ART NATIONAL CERAMIC EXHIBITION, Syracuse. Biennial, Nov-Dec. Ceramics. Open to potters & enamelists in the US & Can. Jury, purchase prizes. Fee. For further information write Everson Museum of Art, 401 Harrison St, Syracuse, NY 13202.

HUDSON VALLEY ART ASSOCIATION, White Plains. Annual, May. All media including sculpture. Open to all artists in traditional works. Jury, awards. Fee for non-mem, $10, limit one. Entry due Apr. For further information write Rayma Spaulding, Pres, 15 Minivale Rd, Stamford, CT 06907.

KNICKERBOCKER ARTISTS EXHIBITION, New York. Annual, Oct. Oil, watercolor, acrylic, casein, graphics, sculpture. Open to all artists. Jury, prizes. Fee $8. Work due Oct 3. For further information write Ann Kovach, 100-36 Bellaire Pl, Bellaire, NY 11429.

LONG BEACH ART ASSOCIATION. Annual, May. All media. Open to all adults. July, prizes. Fee. Entry cards & work due Apr 21. For further information write Mrs Carol Merzer, 111 McKinley Ave, Island Park, NY 11558.

NATIONAL ACADEMY OF DESIGN, New York. Annual, Feb-Mar. Oil, sculpture, watercolors, graphics. Open to all artists. Jury, awards. No fee. Entry due Feb. For further information write National Academy of Design, 1083 Fifth Ave, New York, NY 10028.

NATIONAL ART LEAGUE SPRING EXHIBITION, Douglaston. Annual, May. Oil, watercolor, casein, black/whites & small sculpture. Open to all artists & sculptors. Cash awards, prizes, ribbons. Fee $6. Entry cards & work due May 3. For further information write Harriet Buchabaum, Chmn, 64-15 192nd St, Flushing, NY 11365.

NATIONAL SCULPTURE SOCIETY, New York. Annual, Mar. Sculpture only. Open to all American sculptors on a juried basis. Jury prizes & awards. No fee. Write for prospectus approx Jan 1. For further information write National Sculpture Society, 75 Rockefeller Plaza, New York, NY 10019.

NATIONAL SOCIETY OF PAINTERS IN CASEIN & ACRYLIC, New York. Annual, Feb. Casein & acrylic. Open to all artists. Jury, cash awards & medals. Fee $6. Entries due Feb. For further information write Lily Shuff, 155 W 68th St, New York, NY 10023.

PASTEL SOCIETY OF AMERICA NATIONAL JURIED ALL PASTEL SHOW, New York. Annual, Sept. Pastel media. Open to all artists. Jury, cash awards, prizes. Mem fee $5 for 1 or 2 entries, $3 each additional; non-mem, $10 for 1 or 2, $5 each additional. Entry cards & work due Sept 3, slides accepted from out of town until Aug 4. For further information write Ms Flora B Giffuni, 180-16 Dalny Rd, Jamaica, NY 11432.

PRINT CLUB OF ALBANY NATIONAL PRINT EXHIBITION. Biennial, Nov. All print media except monotypes. Open to all printmakers residing in the US. Jury, awards. Fee $4 each, limit of four. Entries due Sept. For further information write Alice Pauline Schafer, 33 Hawthorne Ave, Albany, NY 12203.

PRINT CLUB OF ALBANY SMALL PRINT EXHIBITION. Biennial, Dec. All print media except monotypes. Open to all printmakers residing in the US. Jury, awards. Fee $4 each, limit of four. Entries due Nov. For further information write Alice Pauline Schafer, 33 Hawthorne Ave, Albany, NY 12203.

SOCIETY OF AMERICAN GRAPHIC ARTISTS, New York. Annual. All prints except monotype. Open to all printmakers. Jury, awards. Fee $5, limit one (30 inches maximum). For further information write Society of American Graphic Artists, 1083 Fifth Ave, New York, NY 10028.

SUFFOLK COUNTY ARTISTS LEAGUE, Babylon. Annual, Mar. Oils, watercolor, acrylic, sculpture. Open to all artists. Jury, cash awards. Fee $4 per entry, limit two. For further information write Mario Grimaldi, Dir, Suffolk County Artists League, 39 E Main St, Babylon, NY 11702.

SUMI-E SOCIETY OF AMERICA EXHIBITION, New York. Annual, May. Oriental brush painting only; subjects must be original. Open to all artists. Jury, prizes. Fee $10 for non-mem, limit 2. Receiving date Apr 12. For further information write Mrs Ann O'Connell, 1341 Woodside Dr, McLean, VA 22101.

NORTH CAROLINA

DAVIDSON NATIONAL PRINT & DRAWING COMPETITION. Annual, Mar-Apr. All prints & drawings. Open to all US artists. Jury, prizes & purchase awards of at least $8000. Fee $6, limit one. Entry cards & work due Feb. For further information write Herb Jackson, Box 2495, Davidson College, Davidson, NC 28036.

NORTH CAROLINA ARTISTS EXHIBITION, Raleigh. Annual, Dec-Jan. Painting, graphics, sculpture. Open to natives & residents of NC. Cash awards, prizes & purchase awards. Fee $5 per artist, limit three works. Entry cards & work due Oct 23. For further information write Cur of Art, North Carolina Museum of Art, 107 E Morgan St, Raleigh, NC 27601.

SOUTHEASTERN CENTER FOR CONTEMPORARY ART, Winston-Salem. Semi-annual, Apr & Nov. Prints, drawings & photography in Apr; painting & sculpture in Nov. Open to all artists, 18 years & older, residing in the ten southeastern states. Jury, purchase awards. Fee $5. For further information write Southeastern Center for Contemporary Art (SECCA), 500 S Main St, Winston-Salem, NC 27101.

NORTH DAKOTA

MINOT STATE COLLEGE NATIONAL PRINT & DRAWING EXHIBITION. Annual, Feb. All prints, drawings. Open to all US artists. Purchase awards. Fee $5 for 3 slide entries. Slides due Dec 12. For further information write National Print & Drawing Exhibition, Art Department, Minot State College, Minot, ND 58701.

NORTH DAKOTA PRINT & DRAWING EXHIBITION, Grand Forks. Annual, Apr. All print & drawing. Open to all US artists. Jury, prizes. Fee $5. Work due Mar 1. For further information write North Dakota Annual, Art Dept, University of North Dakota, Grand Forks, ND 58201.

OHIO

ALL-OHIO GRAPHICS, PHOTOGRAPHY & FILM MAKING EXHIBITION, Dayton. Annual, Nov-Dec. Prints, drawings, photographs, films. Jury, awards. Entry due Nov. For further information write Mark A. Clark, Registrar, Dayton Art Institute, 405 Riverview Ave, Dayton, OH 45401.

ALL-OHIO PAINTING & SCULPTURE EXHIBITION, Dayton. Biennial, Feb-Mar. Painting & sculpture. Open to artists residing in Ohio. Jury, awards. Fee $5, limit two; 10% comn. Work due Jan 12-17. For further information write The Dayton Art Institute, 405 Riverview Ave, PO Box 941, Dayton, OH 45401.

BUTLER INSTITUTE OF AMERICAN ART MIDYEAR SHOW, Youngstown. Annual, July-Sept. Oil, watercolor, acrylic, casein. Open to artists of the US. Jury, awards. Fee $8. Entry cards & work due June. For further information write Secy, Butler Institute of American Art, 524 Wick Ave, Youngstown, OH 44502.

MAINSTREAMS, MARIETTA COLLEGE INTERNATIONAL COMPETITION. Annual, April-May. Open to all painters & sculptors. Jury, prizes & purchase awards. Fee $10, limit five. Entry cards due Feb 2. For further information write William Gerhold, Dir, Mainstreams, Marietta College, Marietta, OH 45750.

MARIETTA COLLEGE CRAFTS NATIONAL. Annual. Crafts & sculpture. Open to craftspeople in the US. Jury, $5000 in awards & prizes. Fee $10. Slides due Sept 11. For further information write Arthur Howard Winer, Dir, MCCN, Marietta College, Marietta, OH 45750.

MASSILLON MUSEUM REGIONAL PAINTING EXHIBITION. Biennial, Mar (next 78). Oil, watercolor, collage, polymer, acrylic & mixed media. Open to residents of Ohio & former residents. Jury, prizes & purchase awards. Fee $2. Work due Feb 11. For further information write Miss Mary Merwin, The Massillon Museum, 212 Lincoln Way E, Massillon, OH 44646.

OHIO ARTISTS & CRAFTSMEN SHOW, Massillon. Biennial, July-Aug (next 77). Print, drawing, photog, all crafts & sculpture. Open to all present & former residents of Ohio. Prizes & purchase awards. Fee $2, 10% comn. Work due June 11. For further information write Miss Mary Merwin, The Massillon Museum, 212 Lincoln Way E, Massillon, OH 44646.

OHIO CERAMIC & SCULPTURE SHOW, Youngstown. Annual, Jan-Feb. Ceramic, enamel, sculpture. Open to present & former Ohio residents. Jury, purchase awards. Fee $3 per class plus $3 per shipping container. Entries due Nov 2-Dec 12. For further information write Secy, Butler Institute of American Art, 524 Wick Ave, Youngstown, OH 44502.

OKLAHOMA

GREEN COUNTRY ART ASSOCIATION DOGWOOD ART FESTIVAL, Poteau. Annual, Easter-Mothers Day. Paintings & sculpture only. Open to artists of Ark, Kans, Mo, Okla & Tex. Jury. Fee. Entry cards due Apr 2, work due Apr 14. For further information write Eloise J Schellstede, Pres, Green Country Art Association, 1825 E 15th St, Tulsa, OK 74119.

GREEN COUNTRY ART ASSOCIATION PLUS 65 ART SHOW, Tulsa. Annual, Mar. Paintings & sculpture only. Open to artists of Ark, Kans, Mo, Okla & Tex. No fee to artists 65 yrs & older or mem, others $10; 10% comn. Entries due Mar 5-17. For further information write Eloise J Schellstede, Pres, Green Country Art Association, 1825 E 15th St, Tulsa, OK 74119.

LAWTON-FORT SILL ART COUNCIL INTERNATIONAL. Annual, Sept. All media. Open to all adult artists. Jury, awards, prizes, purchase awards & ribbons. Fee $2 per entry, limit three. Entry cards due Sept 10 & work due Sept 13. For further information write Sue Burgess, 210 Mimosa Lane, Lawton, OK 73501.

LAWTON JUNIOR SERVICE LEAGUE EXHIBITION OF PAINTING & SCULPTURE. Annual, Feb. All painting & sculpture. Open to all artists. Jury, cash prizes & purchase awards. Fee $4 per entry, 20% comn. Entry cards & work due Feb 5. For further information write Mrs Robert T Steel, 3404 Baltimore, Lawton, OK 73501.

NATIONAL COMPETITION FOR AMERICAN INDIAN ARTISTS, Tulsa. Annual, May. Painting, sculpture & graphics. Open to artists of American Indian descent living in the US. Jury, prizes. No fee. Entries due first Sat in Apr. For further information write Dr Donald G Humphrey, Dir, Philbrook Art Center, 2727 S Rockford Rd, Tulsa, OK 74114.

OKLAHOMA ART CENTER EIGHT STATE EXHIBITION OF PAINTING & SCULPTURE, Oklahoma City. Biennial, Sept-Oct. Painting & sculpture. Open to residents of Ark, Colo, Kans, La, Mo, NMex, Okla & Tex. Jury, purchase awards. Fee $5. Entries due by Aug. For further information write, Oklahoma Art Center, 3113 Pershing Blvd, Oklahoma City, OK 73107.

OKLAHOMA ART CENTER NATIONAL PRINT & DRAWING EXHIBITION, Oklahoma City. Annual, Apr. Prints & drawings. Open to any resident of the US. Jury, awards. Fee $5. For further information write Oklahoma Art Center, 3113 Pershing Blvd, Oklahoma City, OK 73107.

OKLAHOMA MUSEUM OF ART ARTISTS' SALON, Oklahoma City. Annual, May. Oil, watercolor, graphics, sculpture. Open to artists of Okla & surrounding states. Jury, cash prizes. Fee $2 per entry. Entry cards due Apr 5 & work due Apr 12. For further information write James K Reeve, Dir, 7316 Nichols Rd, Oklahoma City, OK 73120.

PHILBROOK ART CENTER OKLAHOMA ANNUAL, Tulsa. Annual, Apr. Painting, sculpture & graphics. Open to residents of Okla or former residents who have lived in the state at least one year. Jury, prizes. Fee $1 per entry. Entries due first Sat in Mar. For further information write Dr Donald G Humphrey, Dir, Philbrook Art Center, 2727 S Rockford Rd, Tulsa, OK 74114.

PENNSYLVANIA

AMERICAN COLOR PRINT SOCIETY, Philadelphia. Annual, Mar. All print media in color. Open to all printmakers working in color. Jury, awards. Fee $2.75. Entry due Feb. For further information write American Color Print Society, 2022 Walnut St, Philadelphia, PA 19103.

CARNEGIE INSTITUTE THREE RIVERS ARTS FESTIVAL, Pittsburgh. Annual, May. Painting, sculpture, crafts, photographs, banners & prints. Open to all artists within the Tri-State area—Ohio, Pa, WVa. Fee, 20% comn. Entry cards & work due Apr 19. For further information write Barbara L Widdoes, Exec Dir, Three Rivers Arts Festival, 4400 Forbes Ave, Pittsburgh, PA 15213.

PENNSYLVANIA PRINTMAKERS, Bethlehem. Annual, Mar. Contemporary prints. Open to all printmakers statewide. Submit 3 slides including name, size & media of any print media including hand-colored & photographics with self-stamped envelope no later than Oct 31. For further information write Pennsylvania Printmakers, Lehigh University, Dept of Fine Arts, Coppes Hall, Building 33, Bethlehem, PA 18015.

WASHINGTON & JEFFERSON COLLEGE NATIONAL PAINTING SHOW, Washington. Annual, Mar-Apr. All painting. Open to any US artist, 18 yrs old. Prizes & purchase awards. Fee $3 for one or two slide entries. Entry cards & slides due Jan, work due Mar. For further information write Paul B Edwards, Art Dept, Washington & Jefferson College, Washington, PA 15301.

RHODE ISLAND

ART ASSOCIATION OF NEWPORT. Annual, July. Oil, watercolor, prints, drawings, photographs (alternate with small sculpture). Open to all American artists. Jury, awards. Fee $7 ($7 for 2 photographs). Entry due early June. For further information write Art Association of Newport, 76 Bellevue Ave, Newport, RI 02840.

PROVIDENCE ART CLUB. Three open shows every year, scheduled at different times & varied from season to season; for instance, an open small sculpture show, an open drawing or print show, or perhaps a painting or craft show. For further information write Mrs Tore Dalenius, Providence Art Club, 11 Thomas St, Providence, RI 02903.

PROVIDENCE WATERCOLOR CLUB. Annual, Oct-Nov. Watercolor. Open to New Eng artists. Cash awards, prizes & ribbons. Fee $8. Work due Oct 14. For further information write Barbara Besson, 6 Thomas St, Providence, RI 02906.

SOUTH COUNTY ART ASSOCIATION ANNUAL OPEN SHOW, Kingston. Annual, Apr. All media. Open to all professional artists. Jury, cash awards. Fee $3 per entry, limit 3 per artist. Entries due first Fri & Sat in Apr. For further information write South County Art Association, Helme House, 1319 Kingstown Rd, Kingston, RI 02881.

TENNESSEE

BROOKS MEMORIAL ART GALLERY MID-SOUTH EXHIBITION, Memphis. Biennial, date for next exhibition not set. Paintings, drawings, sculpture, prints. Open to artists residing within 250 air miles of Memphis. Jury, awards. For further information write Mid-South Exhibition, Brooks Memorial Art Gallery, Overton Park, Memphis, TN 38112.

DULIN NATIONAL PRINT & DRAWING COMPETITION, Knoxville. Annual, May. Prints & drawings. Open to all artists living & working in the US. Prizes. Fee $5. Entry cards due mid-Mar, work due late Mar. For further information write Dulin Gallery of Art, 3100 Kingston Pike, Knoxville, TN 37919.

HUNTER ANNUAL EXHIBITION, Chattanooga. Annual, usually Apr. All media. Open to artists in Ala, Ark, Fla, Ga, Ky, La, Miss, NC, SC, Tenn, Va. Jury, $4000 in museum purchases. Fee $5. Entries due 2 to 3 weeks before opening date. For further information write Hunter Museum of Art, Bluff View, Chattanooga, TN 37403.

MISSISSIPPI RIVER CRAFT SHOW, Memphis. Biennial, date for next exhibition not set. Open to craftsmen residing within the ten mid-continent states bordering the Mississippi River. For further information write Mississippi River Craft Show, Brooks Memorial Art Gallery, Overton Park, Memphis, TN 38112.

TENNESSEE ALL-STATE ARTISTS EXHIBITION, Nashville. Annual, Nov. Oil, mixed, pastel, watercolor, graphics & sculpture. Open to all artists residing in Tenn. Purchase awards. Fee $3 per entry; 10% comn. Entry cards & work due Sept 25-Oct 13. For further information write Watkins Institute, Sixth & Church, Nashville, TN 37219.

TENNESSEE ART LEAGUE & PARTHENON OF NASHVILLE CENTRAL STATES ART EXHIBITION. Annual, May. Painting, graphics, sculpture. Open to artists of Ala, Ark, Ga, Ky, Miss, NC, SC, Tenn, Va & other areas within 300 miles of Nashville. Jury, purchase awards & prizes. Fee $3 per entry, limit three. Work due Mar 25-Apr 2. For further information write Central States Art Exhibition, The Parthenon, Nashville, TN 37203.

TEXAS

DEL MAR COLLEGE DRAWING & SMALL SCULPTURE SHOW, Corpus Christi. Annual, May. Any drawing or sculpture. Open to all US artists. Jury, prizes & purchase awards. Fee $5 per entry, no limit. Entry cards due Mar 1, work due Apr 1. For further information write Joseph A Cain, Chmn, Dept of Art, Del Mar College, Corpus Christi, TX 78404.

EL PASO MUSEUM OF ART NATIONAL SUN CARNIVAL. Annual, Dec. All painting. Open to any US citizen residing in the US and its territories. Jury, purchase awards. For further information write Secy to Cur of Collections, El Paso Museum of Art, 1211 Montana, El Paso, TX 79902.

RIO GRANDE VALLEY ARTS & CRAFTS EXPOSITION, Brownsville. Annual, Nov. All media. Open to all artists & craftsmen. Fee $25, no comn. Entry cards due Oct & work due Nov. For further information write Mrs Tencha Sloss, Gen Chmn, Brownsville Art League, PO Box 3404, Brownsville, TX 78520.

TEXAS FINE ARTS ASSOCIATION ANNUAL EXHIBITION, Austin. Annual, May-June. Oil, acrylic, watercolor, drawing, sculpture & mixed media. Open to all artists residing in US. Jury, prizes, cash awards & purchase awards of approximately $5000. Fee $5 (no fee for member's first slide). Slides due Feb 1, work due Apr. For further information write Mrs John D Haltom, Exec Dir, PO Box 5023, Austin, TX 78763.

TEXAS WATERCOLOR SOCIETY EXHIBITION, San Antonio. Annual, Feb. Transparent or opaque watercolor on paper. Open to present & former residents of Tex. Cash awards, purchase awards. Fee $7.50 per painting for non-mem, 10% comn. Entry cards & work due Jan 10. For further information write Joyce Ward, Exhib Chmn, 5652 Lookhill Rd, San Antonio, TX 78240.

WEST TEXAS NATIONAL WATERCOLOR SHOW, Lubbock. Annual, Dec-Jan. Watercolor. Open to all artists in US. Over $2500 in purchase prizes & awards. Fee $5 per entry, no limit. All will be by slides only; deadline for slides Oct 22. For further information write The Museum, Texas Tech University, Lubbock, TX 79409.

UTAH

SALT LAKE ART CENTER, Salt Lake City. Utah Biennial of Painting & Sculpture, odd numbered years. Intermountain Biennial of Painting & Drawing, even numbered years. Utah Biennial open to all Utah artists. Intermountain Biennial open to all artists from Colo, Mont, Nev, Utah & Wyo. Jury, awards & purchases. Fee $3. Entries due mid-Feb. For further information write Wayne F Gledhill, Dir, Salt Lake Art Center, 54 Finch Lane, Salt Lake City, UT 84102.

UTAH DESIGNER CRAFTSMEN EXHIBITION, Salt Lake City. Annual. All crafts. Open to all Utah craftsmen. Jury, awards. Fee $2. Entries due mid-Nov. For further information write Utah Designer Craftsmen, c/o Salt Lake Art Center, 54 Finch Lane, Salt Lake City, UT 84102.

UTAH STATEWIDE COMPETITION AND EXHIBIT, Salt Lake City. Annual, June through Labor Day. Painting, drawing, watercolor. Open to residents of Utah. Jury, $1000 purchase award, other awards as merited. Fee $2. Entries due approx May 15 (varies each yr). For further information write Utah State Division of Fine Arts, 609 E South Temple St, Salt Lake City, UT 94108.

VIRGINIA

AMERICAN DRAWING EXHIBITION, Norfolk. Biennial, Jan-Feb (odd years). Drawing. Open to all adult artists residing in the US. Jury, awards. Entries due Nov. For further information write American Drawing Biennial, Chrysler Museum at Norfolk, Olney Rd & Mowbray Arch, Norfolk, VA 23510.

IRENE LEACHE MEMORIAL EXHIBITION, Norfolk. Biennial, Mar-Apr (even years). All painting & drawing media (pastels not acceptable). Open to artists residing in Del, Md, NC, Va, Washington, DC & WVa & natives of those states. Jury, cash awards. Limit three. Entry & cards due Jan. For further information write Irene Leache Memorial Exhibition, Chrysler Museum of Norfolk, Olney Rd & Mowbray Arch, Norfolk, VA 23510.

NATIONAL SEAWALL ART SHOW, Portsmouth. Annual, May. All original oil, acrylic, watercolor, graphics, photog, sculpture & crafts. Open to all artists. Over $4500 in cash awards, prizes, purchase awards & ribbons. Fee $12.50. Entries due May 15 & work due first day of show; artist must be present. For further information write Wendy Harder, Portsmouth Parks & Recreation Dept, 1 High St, Portsmouth, VA 23704.

VIRGINIA ARTISTS, Richmond. Biennial, May-June (odd years). Original paintings, drawings, watercolor, collages & sculpture. Jury, awards. Limit three works. Entries due Jan 1. For further information write Virginia Museum of Fine Arts, Boulevard & Grove Aves, Richmond, VA 23221.

VIRGINIA CRAFTSMEN, Richmond. Biennial, Mar-Apr. Personally designed crafts in metal, textile, wood, ceramics & leather. Open to natives & residents of Va & those former residents who lived in Va for three years. Jury, awards. Limit of three works. Entries due by Jan. For further information write Virginia Museum of Fine Arts, Boulevard & Grove Aves, Richmond, VA 23221.

VIRGINIA DESIGNERS, Richmond. Biennial, Jan-Feb. Magazine & newspaper advertisements, brochures, folders, catalogues, programs, posters & others. Open to natives & residents of Va & those former residents who lived in Va for three years. Jury, awards. Fee $5, limit of ten panels. Entries due by Nov. For further information write Virginia Museum of Fine Arts, Boulevard & Grove Aves, Richmond, VA 23221.

VIRGINIA PHOTOGRAPHERS, Richmond. Biennial, Oct-Nov. Monochrome & color photographic prints & color transparencies. Open to natives & residents of Va & those former residents who lived in Va for three years. Jury, awards. Fee $5 for non-mem (mem free); limit five prints & five transparencies. Entries by Aug. For further information write Virginia Museum of Fine Arts, Boulevard & Grove Aves, Richmond, VA 23221.

WASHINGTON

NORTHWEST WATERCOLOR SOCIETY EXHIBITION, Seattle. Annual, exact date for 1976 exhib not yet set. Water based painting on paper. Open to all artists living in Alaska, Idaho, Mont, Ore, Wash & BC. Cash awards, purchase prizes. Fee $5, 20% comn. For further information or prospectus write Flora Correa, 8253 SE 29th St, Mercer Island, WA 98040 or Victoria Savage, 20309 8th NW, Seattle, WA 98177.

WEST VIRGINIA

HUNTINGTON GALLERIES PHOTOGRAPHY & CINEMATOGRAPHY 280. Biennial, Nov (77). Open to photographers above high school age, living within 280 miles of Huntington. Jury, awards. Fee. Entry due Oct. For further information write Photography & Cinematography 280, Huntington Galleries, Huntington, WV 25701.

HUNTINGTON GALLERIES REGIONAL EXHIBITION 280. Biennial, Oct (76). Paintings, graphics, sculpture, crafts. Open to artists above high school age, living within 280 miles of Huntington. Jury, awards. Fee. Entry due Sept. For further information write Exhibition 280, Huntington Galleries, Huntington, WV 25701.

WISCONSIN

STEVENS POINT FINE ARTS EXHIBITION. Annual, Oct. Painting, drawing, graphics. Open to all artists residing in Wis. Jury, $500 top award, other cash & purchase awards. Fee $5. Entry cards & work due Oct 6-8. For further information write Mrs James Delzell, 1124 Ridge Rd, Stevens Point, WI 54481.

WYOMING

SHOW IN MINIATURE, Laramie. Annual, Sept. All media excluding painting & sculpture 9 x 12 inch frame. Open to all artists residing in Colo, Mont, Nebr, SDak, Wyo. Cash awards. Fee $3 each entry, 20% comn. Entries & fee due Aug 10. For further information write Linda Budge, 1054 Alta Vista, Laramie, WY 82070.

WESTERN STATES ART EXHIBITION, Cody. Annual, June-July. Oil, watercolor, graphics, pastels, sculpture, ceramics & other (all work must be suitable for hanging). Open to all artists. Cash awards & ribbons. Fee $5 prof, $3.50 amateur for each work, limit three. For further information write Cody County Art League, PO Box 1524, Cody, WY 82414.

CANADA

ONTARIO

WESTERN ONTARIO EXHIBITION, London. Annual, May. All painting media, sculpture, prints, drawings, wall hangings (batik or woven). Open to all residents of Southwestern Ont. Jury, prizes & awards. No fee. Entries due early Apr. For further information write Secy, Annual Western Ontario Exhibition, London Art Gallery, 305 Queen's Ave, London, ON, Can N6B 1X2.

SOUTHWEST 36, Windsor. Annual, May. All media. Open to artists of the Southwestern Ont Region. Jury, prizes. Fee $3. Entries due April 20. For further information write The Art Gallery of Windsor, 445 Riverside Dr W, Windsor, ON, Can N9A 6T8.

Traveling Exhibitions Booking Agencies

Many of the State Arts Councils (see pp. 439-444) have traveling exhibitions. Consult your State Arts Council for information.

Alabama Art League
Montgomery Museum of Fine Arts, 440 S. McDonough St, Montgomery, Ala. 36104
A. Phillip Coley, Pres.
Exhibit—approx. 25-30 drawings, prints and small paintings selected from the annual juried exhibit by juror. No rental fee; in-state, pulled via trailer by Art League member; out-of-state, arrangements can be made. Catalog available.

American Abstract Artists
218 W. 20th St, New York, N.Y. 10011
Leo Rabkin, Pres.
Traveling shows available. No set rental fees.

The American Federation of Arts
41 E. 65th St, New York, N.Y. 10021
Wilder Green, Dir.
Approximately 30 exhibitions circulated in the U.S. and abroad—Painting, sculpture, graphic arts, photography, design and crafts. Exhibitions and catalogues organized by AFA with guest curators for museums, colleges, schools and art centers. AFA Chapter Members are entitled to reduced participation fees. (See page 4 for current program)

The American Institute of Graphic Arts
1059 Third Ave, New York, N.Y. 10021
Flora Gross, Exec. Dir.
Annual exhibitions in two or more sets—Fifty Books of the Year; Communication Graphics (Printing for Commerce); and bi-annually Children's Books, Textbooks and Learning Materials, Covers and Insides, Packaging, Illustration. Show list and conditions of rental from Bonnie Doughty, Exhibition Schedule Secretary.

Anchorage Historical and Fine Arts Museum
121 W. Seventh Ave, Anchorage, Alaska 99501
R. L. Shalkop, Dir.
Circulation of exhibitions in Alaska only. No rental fee; transportation variable. No catalogs available.

Arkansas Arts Center, State Services
MacArthur Park, P.O. Box 2137, Little Rock, Ark. 72203
June Freeman, State Services Dir.
14 exhibits—DisFarmer Prints; Shape; Texture; The Kent Bicentennial Portfolio - Spirit of Independence; Ten West Coast Artists; Ten Delta Award Winners; Ten Intaglio Prints; County Clare Suite; Works by Robert Andrew Parker; Young Arkansas Artists; Inez Whitfield Watercolors; Leonard Baskin Exhibition; Crafts Exhibition; How To Kill Series. 6 exhibits developed by the Metropolitan Museum—Rembrandt: Love and Compassion; Art of Black Africa; The Art of Discovery; Abstract Painting; Tutankhamen's Treasures; Protest and Hope. Rental fees: free, $25 or $50 plus transportation. Catalogs available.

Associated American Artists
663 Fifth Ave, New York, N.Y. 10022
Sylvan Cole, Jr, Pres.
Estelle L. Yanco, V.Pres.
Original prints in all media by artists of many countries. Etchings, lithographs, woodcuts, serigraphs, intaglios, stencils, in black and white and color.

Group Exhibitions: American Master Prints, New Talent in Printmaking, American Prints of the Sixties, Projections 1976, Robert Malone and James Butler.

One-Man Shows: Milton Avery, Thomas Hart Benton, Lyonel Feininger, Jacob Landau, Raphael Soyer, Paul Wunderlich, Will Barnet, Armin Landeck, John Taylor Arms, John Steuart Curry.

Private and public organizations and institutions having facilities for the care of fine prints eligible. Rental fees from $100 to $250. For additional traveling exhibition information, contact Robert Koo.

Charles Burchfield Center
State University of New York College at Buffalo, 1300 Elmwood
Buffalo, N.Y. 1422
Dr. Edna M. Lindemann, Dir.
Exhibition—Burchfield Wallpapers, includes approx. 50 framed pieces of the original Burchfield wallpaper produced by the Birge Company, 1921-29, up to 4 original paintings by the artist for wallpaper, 1 of 2 panels of original watercolor for Riviera scenic paper, 2 panels mounted on masonite of the three oringinal Burchfield papers: The Birches, Modernistic Pattern, Stylized Flowers in Diagonal Pattern, and 1 panel mounted on masonite of the 1973 reproduction of the Sunflowers. Rental fee according to total amount of work requested. In New York traveling arrangements are made through the GANYS; others by arrangement. Catalogs available at $5 each.

George W. Carver Museum
Tuskegee Institute, Tuskegee Institute, Ala. 36088
Stefania Jarkowski, Dir. Art Gallery
Exhibits—William H. Johnson, Black artist, 20 works in oil, gouache, watercolor and ink; collection of 35 contemporary Polish posters, all posters are matted and covered with acetate; collection of 48 watercolors by the contemporary leading artists of Poland, all paintings are matted and covered with acetate. All exhibitions' starting dates available Sept, 1976. No catalogs available.

Charleston Art Gallery of Sunrise
755 Myrtle Rd, Charleston, W.Va. 25314
Mary Black, Cur. Fine Arts
Mountain Artisans Exhibition: Mountain Artisans creates contemporary versions of traditional and primitive art in clothing and home furnishings. Their work can be seen in retail stores around the country. Dorothy Weatherford, Coty Award winning designer, designs all products, including the adaptations of traditional patterns. Exhibit includes clothing and home furnishings; totals approx. 80 pieces. Rental fee: $300 for 4 weeks, $250 for colleges, plus in-coming shipping. Small brochure available.

Cherokee National Museum
P.O. Box 515, TSA-LA-GI, Tahlequah, Okla. 74464
M. A. Hagerstrand, Exec. V.Pres.
Temporary exhibitions arranged with small institutions to their needs and desires and our capabilities and schedule. Subjects available are Cherokee history and culture and limited Indian art on the Trail of Tears theme. Rental fees arranged for each exhibit. No catalogs available.

Craftsmen's Guild of Mississippi
P.O. Box 1341, Jackson, Miss. 39205
Dan Overly, Dir.
Exhibit—Cotton Comes Home, international fiber show containing approx. 100 pieces of original work using cotton as the basic material. Rental fee: $500 plus transportation one-way. Catalog available. Tel: (601) 354-7336.

Fort Hays Kansas State College, Department of Art
Hays, Kans. 67601
John C. Thorns, Jr, Chmn.
Varied exhibitions available depending upon the desire of the individual renting the exhibition. Rental fee: $100 plus shipping charges. No catalog available.

French Cultural Services, Exhibitions Department
972 Fifth Ave, New York, N.Y. 10021
J. S. Cartier, Head Exhibition Dept.
Exhibits cover a wide range of subject matter, from a look at the French approach to environmental problems and mass transit, to book exhibits, artifacts and exhibitions of a strictly cultural nature dealing with famous authors, poets, musicians and artists—
Four French Photographers, a black and white and tinted photo collection, in collaboration with the Department of Photography, Bibliotheque Nationale, Paris; The Viva Group Project, a photoessay consisting of 60 black and white prints by 6 photojournalists, each looking at a French family; Saur/Kuligowski, 49 black and white photographs expressing two different ways of looking at reality, in collaboration with the Prints Department, Bibliotheque Nationale, Paris; Cartier-Bresson, black and white 78-frame strip narrated in English; Burgundy, an appreciative look at a French province renowned for her past and her celebrated gastronomy and wines; Criticism - From Where? To Where; Traditional Criticism; Creative Criticism; Criticism; Towards a Revolution; Art; Gastronomy; Sports; Environment; Le Roman Du Roman (French Novelists of Our Time); French Contemporary Novel; Moliere 1622-1673; Original Posters of the 1890's; Transpofrance; French Cheeses and Wines; Women in France, a core for complementary activities.
No rental fees, but one-way shipping costs plus insurance paid by exhibitor. Press kits are available upon request. These exhibits are ready for display and may be borrowed by universities, libraries, clubs and other institutions for 2 or 3 wk. periods. Catalog available.

International Business Machines Corporation
590 Madison Ave, New York, N.Y. 10022
N. A. Costantino, Mgr. Design and Arts Programs
Models of inventions of Leonardo da Vinci. No rental fee. Transportation costs assumed by IBM on loans to museums, galleries, colleges and other qualified non-profit institutions. Catalog on request.

International Exchange Print Exhibitions
Oregon State University, Corvallis, Ore. 97331
Gordon W. Gilkey, Dir.
3 exhibits—Of 100 each contemporary original graphic arts from abroad (Norway, Yugoslavia-two exhibits) with new exhibits imported each year. Prorated expenses plus one-way transportation. Catalogs on request.

International Exhibitions Foundation
1729 H St. N.W, Washington, D.C. 20006
Mrs. John A. Pope, Pres.
Circulates special loan exhibitons throughout the United States and Canada in the fields of painting, sculpture, photography, drawings, prints and the decorative arts. Available to museums and galleries at specified rental fees plus forwarding charges to the next exhibitor. A number of major exhibitions from abroad available.

International Museum of Photography at George Eastman House
900 East Ave, Rochester, N.Y. 14607
Robert Doherty, Dir.
22 exhibits—Eugene Atget; Harry Callahan/City (50 prints); Contemporary Photographers VI; Contemporary Photographers VII; Bruce Davidson; Robert Doisneau; Robert Frank; From the George Eastman House Collection; Lewis Hine II; Eadweard Muybridge; Arnold Newman; Photo/Graphics; W. Eugene Smith; Terminal Landscapes; Tulsa/Larry Clark; Jerry Uelsmann; West of the Rockies; Carl Toth; Josef Sudek; Gary Hallman; Mark Cohen; A Panorama of the American Movie Still Photograph. Rental for one month periods, cost includes insurance and one-way transportation. Slide sets relating to the history of photography are also available. For further information on exhibitions or slides write to the museum's Office of Extension Activities, above address. Tel: (716) 271-3361

Kiah Museum
505 W. 36th St, Savannah, Ga. 30311
Virginia Jackson Kiah, Cur.
Headquarters for National Conference of Artists student traveling shows. These projects have been spearheaded at the Kiah Museum with student NCA members taking part from at least 20 states and 17 foreign countries. Some of the art received in exchange from foreign students, and from each other, has been matted, acetate covered and organized. Exhibits—International Student Artists Show, 52 pieces of acrylics, pencil, pen and inks, lithographs and watercolors from 18 countries; Hawaiian Show, 25 pieces of tree bark, shell and sand designs; African Collection, 35 pieces of watercolors, pen and inks, and crayons from Mawuli School, HoGhana, West Africa; American Collection, 30 pieces of watercolors, lithographs, pencil sketches, pen and inks and mixed media. No rental fees, but exhibitor is responsible for transportation and insurance expenses. Catalogs available.

Rudolph E. Lee Gallery
College of Architecture, Clemson University
Clemson, S.C. 29631
Tom Dimond, Coordinator of Educ. Media & Exhibits
2 exhibits—Foundry Art, wooden patterns of industrial machines from 1900-1970, 50 pieces plus 20 photos; 300 Years of South Carolina Architecture, 50 photographic panels. Rental information available on request. Catalogs on request.

Maurice Spertus Museum of Judaica
618 S. Michigan Ave, Chicago, Ill. 60605
Judith Benjamin, Asst. to Dir.
Exhibition—The Jews of Sandor, 25 photographs, 1 lead photograph, 1 map panel, 1 synagogue floor plan panel and label copy.
This photographic exhibition provides a glimpse into the life of Sandor, a now extinct Jewish village from Iraqi Kurdistan, whose entire population emigrated to Israel. The exhibition reveals life in this agrarian community, which until its assimilation into Israeli society, had changed little since Babylonian times. Highlighting religious practices, economy, dress and the history which caused their emigration, the exhibition is the first to document this unique diaspora community. Rental fee: $350 for 200 catalogues and the rental of the show, including insurance, for 2 months; cost of transportation borne by borrower. Catalogues vend for $1.50 each.

Midtown Galleries
11 E. 57th St, New York, N.Y. 10022
Mrs. Alan D. Gruskin, Dir.
Exhibitions arranged—group or one man shows of drawings, watercolors, oils by contemporary American artists. Available to museums, universities, colleges and art centers. Rental fees plus transportation. Rental fee cancelled upon museum purchase. Inquiries invited.

The Museum of Modern Art
11 W. 53rd St, New York, N.Y. 10019

Exhibition Program
Richard L. Palmer, Coordinator of Exhibitions
Marie Frost, Admin. Asst.
A number of exhibitions directed by members of the Museum's curatorial staff are offered to other qualified museums on a participating basis. These exhibitions are generally either full-scale projects or reduced versions of shows initially presented at The Museum of Modern Art. Although exhibitions are not necessarily available at all times in all media, the traveling program does cover the entire range of the Museum's New York program—painting, sculpture, drawings, prints, photography, architecture and design. Participating fees usually begin at $750 for smaller exhibitions and range up to several thousand dollars for major exhibitions. Tour participants are also asked to cover prorated transport costs.

International Program
Waldo Rasmussen, Dir, International Prog.
The primary function of the program is to encourage cultural exchange in all the visual arts on a broad international level. Exhibitions of painting, sculpture, drawings, prints, photography, architecture, design, and film are circulated by the Museum to foreign countries under the auspices of The International Council of The Museum of Modern Art. Exhibitions representing art of other countries or cultures are also prepared for showing in the U.S. Rental fee plus transportation from preceding exhibitor. Programs with overseas libraries and visiting foreign specialists.

Circulating Film Program
Margareta Akermark, Assoc. Dir, Dept. of Film
Programs drawn from the Museum's international archive of films are available to educational institutions in the U.S. for study purposes. The films exemplify or illustrate the history, development and technique of the motion picture. Rental fee plus transportation. The 1973 Catalogue and Supplements list more than 500 titles ranging from films of the 1890's to recent independent productions.

Museum Without Walls
104 Morris Ave.
P.O. Box 197, Friendsville, Md. 21531
Richard Kibbey, Dir. Museum
A large collection, including photographs from all periods, woodcuts, engravings, etchings, lithographs, silkscreens, monotypes, watercolors, drawings, paintings, and sculpture; access to a great deal more, ranging from folk art to antique maps and toys. Current exhibits—Jacob Riis: Turn-of-the-Century Photographer, Lewis Hine Early Twentieth Century Photographer, The Graven Image, illustrates how an artist conceives of and produces an intaglio print, complete with drawings and numerous states of prints, including the final version; The Human Image, selections from 500 years of printmaking; Contemporary Silkscreen Prints; Artists' Themes from Literature and Theatre; Interpretations of Architecture and Man-Made

Space; Silkscreens from Workshop, Inc; Plain 'n Fancy: The Art of Needlework, 1800 to 1950, The Jolly Corner Suite; Ukiyo-e and The Japanese Print; The Bromoils of Edward Bafford. The Museum has organized exhibitons and lectures for students of art, history and philosophy, and for those who are totally unfamiliar with art. All exhibitions are available in modular exhibition cases, installed and ready to be set up in 10 to 30 minutes. The cases are especially designed to minimize security risks while creating a professional, gallery-like appearance. Rental fees and transportation are variable from one exhibition to another.

National Cowboy Hall of Fame and Western Heritage Center
1700 N.E. 63rd St, Oklahoma City, Okla. 73111
Richard Muno, Art Dir.
Western Art Exhibition—award winning paintings and bronzes worth over $250,000. All works done by today's best contemporary western artists. Exhibit usually contains a combination of at least 25 paintings, watercolors and drawings and 5 bronzes. The Cowboy Hall furnishes free standing 4 x 8 feet panels and pedestals. Staff members of the Hall assemble and disassemble the exhibition. Rental fee: $1 per mile one way from Oklahoma City of a minimum of $1000 for approx. 2-3 wk.

National Sculpture Society
75 Rockefeller Plaza, New York, N.Y. 10019
Claire A. Stein, Exec. Dir.
Enlarged photographs available of Ecclesiastical, Garden, Portrait and Animal Sculpture in various media. Rental fee: one-way transportation to next exhibitor or back to the warehouse mentioned in correspondence.

Newport Harbor Art Museum
2211 W. Balboa Blvd, Newport Beach, Calif. 92663
Betty Turnbull, Cur.
Phyllis Lutjeans, Cur. Assoc.
Current exhibitions: Terry Schoonhoven: The Los Angeles Fine Arts Squad Paints a Mural for the Newport Harbor Art Museum, consists of a 10 x 27 ft. painting (Sons of the Desert), 10 preliminary drawings; 10 dry mount photos of the painting in preparation and 80 slides of other Fine Arts Squad wall paintings. 25 brochures and posters of the mural are included. Rental fee: $850 plus on-going transportation. The Flute and The Brush: Indian Paintings from the Collection of William Theo Brown and Paul Wonner, consists of 50 framed miniatures offering excellent examples of 23 schools and spanning a period from 1600 to late 1800; emphasis is placed on indigenous art of Punjab Hills, Rajasthan and Deccan areas. Rental fee: $850 plus on-going transportation. Catalogues available at $5. Forthcoming exhibit: 3 Compatible Sensibilities, works by Agnes Denes, Channa Horowitz and Joyce Shaw, all concerning themselves with metaphysical inquiry into universal truth through personal hieratic systems of logic. Available after Nov, 1976. Fee will be around $1500. Catalogue will be available.

Old Bergen Art Guild
43 W. 33rd St, Bayonne, N.J. 07002
William D. Gorman, Dir.
Jan Gary, Assoc. Dir.
Over 70 group and one-man traveling exhibits—Oils, watercolors, caseins and graphics in all styles by contemporary American artists. Available to museums, art centers, universities, colleges, and libraries. No fee, except for one-way express charge. Send stamped, addressed envelope for free catalog.

Philadelphia Museum of Art
26th & Parkway
P.O. Box 7646, Philadelphia, Pa. 19101

Slide Department
Mary Anne Dutt Justice, Cur.
23,000 2'' x 2'' color slides available for sale; slide rental to educational institutions in the Philadelphia area. Catalogues available on request from Slide Department.

Film Library
100 16mm, optical sound films available for rent to educational institutions and art organizations. Catalogues available on request from Division of Education.

Pratt Graphics Center
831 Broadway, New York, N.Y. 10003
Andrew Stasik, Dir.
Exhibition of graphic arts—original prints, available to art schools, universities, art associations. Current shows: Contemporary Graphic Protest and the Grand Tradition; Retrospective/3 American Printmakers/Gene Kloss, Armin Landeck, Reynold Weidenaar; A Survey of Intaglio Printmaking; Photography in Printmaking; Fifth International Miniature Print Exhibition; The Presidency: Irreverent & Relevant; Five Contemporary Masters of the Black and White Print;

The Black Experience in Prints; The Figure and Machine in the Print Today; Monotypes; Contemporary Serigraphs; New Directions in Printmaking; The Relief Prints of Manuel Manilla: 19th Century Mexican Printmaker; The Collagraph: A New Print Medium; Contemporary American Fine Arts Posters. Minimum rental fee. Write Andrew Stasik.

Segy Gallery
50 W. 57th St, New York, N.Y. 10019
Ladislas Segy, Dir.
Exhibits—African sculptures, masks, statues, some utensils, in wood, ivory and bronze. 30 African sculptures for 3 weeks period. 5 circuits each season. Rental fee: $300 for 3 weeks, insurance and one way transportation included. Art and Science Museums, art departments and galleries of universities and colleges, college Student Unions, art clubs, libraries and others eligible. Catalog on request. Mr. Segy is available for lectures on African and Modern Art. Conditions upon request.

Smithsonian Institution Traveling Exhibition Service (SITES)
Washington, D.C. 20560
Dennis A. Gould, Dir.
Anne R. Gossett, Sr. Exhibits Coordinator
Eileen Rose, Project Coordinator-International Program.
200 exhibitions—Architecture, cultural history, decorative arts, design, environment, paintings, prints & drawings, photography, science & technology. Available to educational, scientific, cultural and on occasion, commercial institutions. Educational materials and program activities supplement the exhibits. Catalogs, posters and brochures accompany specific exhibits. Annual catalog Update available. See National Museum, p. 51.

Southern Association of Sculptors, Inc.
Art Department, University of Alabama, Huntsville, Ala. 35801
Jeff Bayer, Pres.
Annual regional and national competitive traveling sculpture exhibitions of 15 to 30 pieces of sculpture. Fee: $400 plus shipping for one direction with each institution receiving 200 illustrated catalogs. Exhibition booked a year in advance and tours for one year.

State Capitol Museum
211 W. 21st Ave, Olympia, Wash. 98504
Christy Nicandri, Admin. Asst.
Exhibitions, which change yearly, contain works done by Washington artists. There are 2 historical exhibits also, one on small towns in Washington and the other woodcuts by Winslow Homer. No rental fee or insurance fee. Exhibitor must pay the prepaid shipping fee to the next exhibitor; if the organization borrowing the exhibit is out of the state, they must pay the shipping fee both ways. Catalogs available for some shows.

State University of New York College at Potsdam
Pierrepont Ave, Potsdam, N.Y. 13676
Benedict Goldsmith, Dir. Art Gallery
Dr. Roland Gibson, Cur.
Exhibits—Roland Gibson Collection of Contemporary Japanese Art, 25-30 paintings, sculpture objects and prints; College Collection of Contemporary Prints, 15-25 prints. Available for use by neighboring institutions, within 100 mile radius.

Texas Fine Arts Association
3809 W. 35th St, Austin, Tex. 78703
Mrs. John D. Haltom, Exec. Dir.
Approx. 7 exhibitions containing 19-20 paintings each. Travel throughout Texas only. Rental fee: $50 plus $15 prorated insurance and out-going freight. Catalogs and biographic material available.

The University Museums
Illinois State University, Normal, Ill. 61761
Dr. Barry E. Moore, Cur.
2 exhibits—Development of the Figure Concept in Graphic Art Work by Children from Different Countries, 65 originals, requiring display space of 180-240 running feet, insurance $650; The Development of Spatial Relations in the Graphic Art Work by Children from Different Countries, 59 originals requiring display space of 180-240 running feet, insurance $590. Rental fee: $100 plus return transportation. Explanatory text includes script, a list notating age, sex, size, country, title and accession number.

University of Arizona Museum of Art
Olive & Speedway Sts, Tucson, Ariz. 85721
William E. Steadman, Dir.
3 exhibits—The C. Leonard Pfeiffer Collection, American paintings and drawings; The Samuel H. Kress Collection, paintings of the 13th century to 19th century European art; The Edward Joseph Gallagher Memorial Collection, contemporary paintings and sculpture of the 20th century. Catalogs available for a fee.

Virginia Polytechnic Institute and State University
Owens Hall, Department of Art, Blacksburg, Va. 24061
Prof. Dean Carter, Head. Dept.
Faculty exhibition. No rental fee, but borrower must pay freight both ways and insurance. No catalog.

Western Association of Art Museums
Mills College, Box 9989, Oakland, Calif. 94613
Kerry Marshall, Exhibitions Coordinator
Approx. 30-50 exhibits—Varied media, exhibition themes. Rental fee: $75 to $2000. Catalog on request. Tel: (415) 568-2775

Western Montana College
Dillon, Mont. 59725
Jim Corr, Asst. Prof. Art
2 exhibits, 30 pieces of work each, matted and covered with acetate—Drawings, prints, watercolors and some photographs. One crate of approx. 30 pounds. Geared to the small schools who often have difficulty obtaining art shows. No rental fee. May be shipped by bus or mailed parcel post. No catalogs.

Westminster College Art Gallery
New Wilmington, Pa. 16142
Robert Godfrey, Gallery Dir.
Exhibits—The Figure in Recent American Painting, 24 large to medium size paintings; In Praise of Space - The Landscape in American Art, 58 large to small size paintings, drawings, watercolors by contemporary painters; The Figure in Recent American Drawings, 50 framed drawings by 25 contemporary artists; Recent American Narrative Painting; The Portrait in Recent American Painting. Rental fee: approx. $700 within 500 mile radius and includes transportation, insurance, installation (if requested) and 100 catalogs.

Index

No effort has been made to check the extent of information beyond that which was given on the questionnaires. The resulting index to collections may therefore lack certain information. Main headings such as <u>ART CRITICS</u>, are underlined in capital letters. COLLECTIONS appear in Capital Letters.